BREWER'S DICTIONARY
OF PHRASE & FABLE

BREWER'S
DICTIONARY OF
PHRASE & FABLE

REVISED & ENLARGED

NEW YORK
HARPER & BROTHERS PUBLISHERS

KEY TO PRONUNCIATION

VOWELS

a   as in far (far)
ă   ,,   fat (făt).
ā   ,,   fate (fāt)
aw ,,   fall (fawl)
ä   ,,   fair (fär)

e   ,,   bell (bel)
ĕ   ,,   her (hĕr)
ē   ,,   beef (bēf)

i   ,,   bit (bit).
ī   ,,   bite (bit)

o   as in not (not).
ō   ,,   no (nō).
ô   ,,   north (nôrth)
oo ,,   food (food).

u   ,,   bull (bul).
ŭ   ,,   sun (sŭn)
û   ,,   muse (mūz).

ou ,,   bout (bout).
oi ,,   join (join).

A dot placed over a, e, o, or u (ȧ, ė, ȯ, u̇,) signifies that the vowel has an obscure, indeterminate, or slurred sound, as in —
advice (ȧd-vīs'), current (kûr'ent), notion (nō'shon).

CONSONANTS

"s" is used only for the sibilant "s" (as in "toast," tōst,) the sonant "s" (as in "toes" is printed "z" (tōz)
"c" (except in the combinations "ch" and "ch"), "q," and "x" are not used
b, d, f, h (see the combinations below), k, l, m, n (see *n* below), p, r, t, v, z, and w and y when used as consonants, have their usual values

ch   as in church (chĕrch)
c͟h   ,,   loch (loc͟h)

g   ,,   get (get)
j   ,,   join (join).

hw   ,,   white (hwīt)

n   as in cabochon (ka-bō-cho*n*).

sh   ,,   shawl (shawl)
zh   ,,   measure (mezh'ur).

th   ,,   thin (thin).
th ,,   thine (*th*īn).

The accent (') follows the syllable to be stressed

A

A. The form of this letter is modified from the Egyptian hieroglyph which represents the eagle   The Phœnician (Hebrew) symbol was א (*aleph*=an ox), which has been thought, probably erroneously, to represent an ox-head in outline   The Greek A (*alpha*) was the symbol of a bad augury in the sacrifices   *See also* SCARLET LETTER

A in logic denotes a universal affirmative. A asserts, E denies Thus, syllogisms in *bArbArA* (*q v*) contain three universal affirmative propositions

A1 means first-rate—the very best. In Lloyd's Register of British and Foreign Shipping, the character of the ship's hull is designated by *letters*, and that of the anchors, cables, and stores by *figures*   A1 means hull first-rate, and also anchors, cables, and stores, A2, hull first-rate, but fittings second-rate   Vessels of an inferior character are classified under the letters Æ, E, and I

Aaron (âr on)   The name of the patriarch of the Jewish priesthood, possibly connected with haaron, " the ark "

   Aaron's Beard. The popular name of many wild plants, including Great St. John's Wort (Rose of Sharon), the Ivy-leaved Toadflax, Meadowsweet, Saxifrage Sarmentosa, etc

   Aaron's Rod. The name given (with reference to *Num* xvii, 8) to various flowering plants, including Golden Rod, Great Mullein, and others.

   Aaron's serpent. Something so powerful as to eliminate minor powers.

> And hence one master passion in the breast,
> Like Aaron's serpent swallows up the rest
> POPE   *Essay on Man*, ii, 131

The allusion is to *Exod* vii, 10-12

A B. *See* ABLE-BODIED

Aback   This was originally a nautical term used when a gust of wind forced the sails back against the mast and suddenly stayed the ship's progress   From this comes the phrase "I was taken aback," meaning "I was astounded, taken by surprise "

Abacus (ăb' a kus)   A primitive calculating machine, consisting of a small frame with wires stretched across it in one direction, each wire having threaded on it ten balls which can be shifted backwards or forwards   It is used to teach children addition and subtraction and was employed by the Greeks and Romans for calculations, as a modification of it was used to a much later date by the Chinese. The word is derived from the Greek, ἄβαξ, a cyphering table (a slab covered with sand).

The multiplication table invented by Pythagoras is called *Abacus Pythagoricus*

In architecture the *abacus* is the topmost member of a capital

Abaddon (a băd' on)   The angel of the bottomless pit (*Rev* ix, 11), from Heb *abad*, he perished

Milton uses the name for the bottomless pit itself —

> In all her gates Abaddon rues
> Thy bold attempt
>   *Paradise Regained*, iv, 624

Abaris (ăb' a ris)   A mythical Greek sage of the 6th century B.C (surnamed "the Hyperborean") mentioned by Herodotus, Pindar, etc   Apollo gave him a magic arrow which rendered him invisible, cured diseases, gave oracles, and on which he could ride through the air   Abaris gave it to Pythagoras, who, in return, taught him philosophy Hence *the dart of Abaris*

Abatement (O.Fr *batre*, to beat down).   In heraldry, a mark of depreciation annexed to coat armour, whereby the honour of it is abated

Abaton (ăb' a ton) (Gr *a*, not; βαίνω, I go) *As inaccessible as Abaton*   A name given to various places of antiquity difficult of access.

Abbassides (ăb' a sīdz)   A dynasty of thirty-seven caliphs who reigned over the Mohammedan Empire from 750 to 1258   They were descended from Abbas, uncle of Mohammed   Haroun al-Raschid (born 765, reigned 786-808), of the *Arabian Nights*, was one of their number

Abbot of Misrule. *See* KING OF MISRULE

Abbotsford. The name given by Sir Walter Scott to Clarty Hole, on the south bank of the Tweed, after it became his residence in 1812. Sir Walter devised it from the fancy that the *abbots* of Melrose Abbey used to pass over the *ford* of the Tweed near by.

A B C. An abbreviation having a number of meanings that can be decided only by the context   Thus, "So-and-so doesn't know his A B C" means that he is intensely ignorant· "he doesn't understand the A B C of engineering" means that he has not mastered its rudiments   So, an *A B C Book*, or *Absey Book*, is a primer which used to be used as a child's first lesson book and contained merely the alphabet and a few rudimentary lessons often set in catechism form. as is evident from Shakespeare's lines —

> That is question now,
> And then comes answer like an Absey book
>   *King John*, i, 1

Abd in Arabic=slave or servant, as Abdiel (*q v*.) and Abd-Allah (*servant of God*), Abd-el-Kader (*servant of the Mighty One*), Abd-ul-Latif (*servant of the Gracious One*), etc

Abdallah (ăb däl' à)   The father of Mohammed   He died shortly before his famous son

1

was born, and is said to have been so beautiful that when he married Amina, 200 virgins broke their hearts from disappointed love — *See* Washington Irving's *Life of Mahomet*

Abdals (ăb' dalz). The name given by Mohammedans to certain mysterious persons whose identity is known only to God, and through whom the world is able to continue in existence When one of them dies another is secretly appointed by God to fill the vacant place.

Abdera (ăb dēr' a) A maritime town of Thrace (said to have been founded by Abdera, sister of Diomede), so overrun with rats that it was abandoned, and the inhabitants migrated to Macedonia The *Abderites*, or *Abderitans*, were proverbial for stupidity, yet the city gave birth to some of the wisest men of Greece, among them being Democritus (the laughing philosopher, from whom we get the phrases *Abderian laughter*, meaning "scoffing laughter," and an *Abderite*, or "scoffer"), Protagoras (the great sophist), Anaxarchos (the philosopher and friend of Alexander), and Hecatæus (the historian)

Abdiel (ăb' dēl) (Arab , *the servant of God*; *cf* ABD). In Milton's *Paradise Lost* (v. 805, 896, etc) the faithful seraph who withstood Satan when he urged the angels to revolt.

Abecedarian (ă be si dâr' i an) Usually, one who teaches or is learning his A B C, but also the name of a 16th-century sect of Anabaptists who regarded the teaching of the Holy Spirit (as extracted by them from the Bible) as sufficient for every purpose in life, and hence despised all learning of every kind, except so much of the A B C as was necessary to enable them to read The sect was founded in 1520 by Nicholas Stork, a weaver of Zwickau, hence they are also spoken of as "the *Zwickau prophets* "

Abecedarian Hymns Hymns the lines or other divisions of which are arranged in alphabetical order. In Hebrew the 119th Psalm is abecedarian. *See* ACROSTIC POETRY

Abelites (ăb' e lītz), **Abelians**, or **Abelonians** A Christian sect of the 4th century mentioned by St Augustine as living in North Africa They married but remained virgin, as they affirmed Abel did—on the assumption that because no children of his are mentioned in Scripture he had none The sect was maintained by adopting the children of others

Abhorrers *See* PETITIONERS

Abidhamma (ăb id a' ma) The third pitaka of the three Pali texts (Tripitaka) which together form the sacred canon of the Buddhists The *Abidhamma* contains "the analytical exercises in the psychological system on which the doctrine is based," in seven treatises *See* TRIPITAKA.

Abif *See* HIRAM ABIF.

Abigail (ăb' i gāl) A lady's maid Abigail, wife of Nabal and afterwards of David, is a well-known Scripture heroine (1 *Sam*. xxv, 3) Marlowe called the daughter of Barrabas, his *Jew of Malta*, by this name, and it was given by Beaumont and Fletcher to the "waiting

gentlewoman" in *The Scornful Lady* Swift, Fielding, and other novelists of the period employ it in their novels, and it was further popularized by the notoriety of Abigail Hill, better known as Mrs Masham, Queen Anne's Lady in Waiting and personal friend

Abimelech (a bim' e lek) A Canaanitish regal title probably meaning "Melech, the divine king, is father" Besides the two of this name in the Bible (*Gen* xxvi and *Judges* ix) it occurs as that of a prince of Arvad in the Annals of Assurbanipal, and in the Amarna tables as that of an Egyptian governor of Tyre

Abingdon Law. *See* CUPAR JUSTICE

Able-bodied Seaman, An, or, *an able seaman,* is a skilled seaman, a sailor of the first class A crew is divided into three classes (1) skilled seamen, termed A B (Able-Bodied), (2) ordinary seamen, and (3) boys, which include "green hands," or inexperienced men, without regard to age or size

Aboard. A ship is said to fall aboard another when it runs against it

Aboard main tack is an old sea-term meaning to draw one of the lower corners of the mainsail down to the chess-tree

Abolitionists. In U S A the term applied to those who advocated and agitated for the abolition of Negro slavery In Australia the name was given to those who between 1820 and 1867 sought to obtain by law the abolition of the transportation of convicts to Australia.

Abolla (a bol' a) An ancient military garment worn by the Greeks and Romans, opposed to the *toga* or robe of peace The abolla being worn by the lower orders, was affected by philosophers in the vanity of humility

Abomination of Desolation, The, mentioned in *Dan* (chs ix, xi, and xii), and in *Matt* xxiv,15, probably refers to some statue set up in the Temple by either the heathens or the Romans The subject is very obscure, the best Hebrew and Greek scholarship leaving the actual thing intended unidentified, Dr. Cheyne concluding that "the 'abomination' which thrusts itself into the 'holy place' has for its nature 'desolation'—*i e* finds its pleasure in undoing the divine work of a holy Creator "

Abonde (a bond') Dame Abonde is the French equivalent of Santa Claus, a good fairy who brings children presents while they are asleep on New Year's Eve

Abou-Bekr (ă boo bekr) (571-634), called *Father of the Virgin*, i e Mohammed's favourite wife He was the first caliph, or successor of Mohammed, of the Sunni Moslems, and reigned for only two years

Abou Hassan (ă boo hăs' ăn) A rich merchant (in *The Arabian Nights*), transferred during sleep to the bed and palace of the Caliph Haroun al-Raschid. Next morning he was treated as the caliph, and every effort was made to make him forget his identity (*The Sleeper Awakened*) The same story, localized to Shakespeare's own Warwickshire, forms the

Induction to *The Taming of the Shrew*, where a tinker, Christopher Sly, takes the place of Abou Hassan The incident is said by Burton (*Anatomy of Melancholy*, II, iv) actually to have occurred during the wedding festivities of Philip the Good of Burgundy (about 1440) *The Ballad of the Frolicsome Duke, or the Tinker's Good Fortune* in the *Percy Reliques*, and another version in Calderon's play, *Life's a Dream* (c 1633), go to show how popular and widely spread was this Oriental fable

Abou ibn Sina, commonly called *Avicenna* from his birthplace, Afshena, near Bokhara A great Persian physician whose canons of medicine were founded on those of Galen, Hippocrates, and Aristotle, and whose teaching had great influence on western mediæval medicine He died in 1037

Above-board. Honest and open According to Johnson, this is a figurative expression ' borrowed from gamesters, who, when they put their hands under the table, are changing their cards "

Above par. A commercial term meaning that the article referred to is at more than its nominal value *See* PAR

Above your hook. *See* HOOK

Ab ovo. From the very beginning Stasinus, in his *Cypria*, a poem in 11 books belonging to the Homeric cycle and forming an introduction to the *Iliad*, does not rush (as does the *Iliad* itself) *in medias res*, but begins with the eggs of Leda, from one of which Helen was born If Leda had not laid this egg, Helen would never have been born, therefore Paris could not have eloped with her, therefore there would have been no Trojan War, etc The English use of the phrase probably derives from the line in Horace's *De Arte Poetica*'—

Nec gemino bellum Troianum orditur ab ovo

Abracadabra. A cabalistic charm, said to be made up from the initials of the Hebrew words Ab (Father), Ben (Son), and Ruach ACadsch (Holy Spirit), and formerly used as a powerful antidote against ague, flux, toothache, etc The word was written on parchment, and suspended from the neck by a linen thread, in the following form —

```
ABRACADABRA
ABRACADABR
ABRACADAB
ABRACADA
ABRACAD
ABRACA
ABRAC
ABRA
ABR
AB
A
```

Abracax *See* ABRAXAS.

Abraham Mohammedan mythology adds the following legends to those told us in the Bible concerning the patriarch His parents were Prince Azar and his wife, Adna As King Nimrod had been told that one shortly to be born would dethrone him, he proclaimed a "massacre of the innocents," and Adna retired to a cave where Abraham was born. He was nourished by sucking two of her

1*

fingers, one of which supplied milk and the other honey At the age of fifteen months Abraham was equal in size to a lad of fifteen, and was so wise that his father introduced him to the court of King Nimrod

Other Mohammedan traditions relate that Abraham and his son "Ismail" rebuilt for the fourth time the Kaaba over the sacred stone at Mecca that Abraham destroyed the idols manufactured and worshipped by his father, Terah, and that the mountain (called in the Bible "Mount Moriah") on which he offered up his son was "Arfaday "

The Ghebers say that the infant Abraham was thrown into the fire by Nimrod's order, but the flame turned into a bed of roses, on which he went to sleep Hence Moore's allusion in *Lalla Rookh*:—

Sweet and welcome as the bed
For their own infant prophet spread,
When pitying Heaven to roses turned
The death-flames that beneath him burned.
Fire Worshippers

To sham Abraham. *See* ABRAM-MAN

Abrahamic covenant. The covenant made by God with Abraham (*Gen* xii, 2, 3, and xvii), interpreted to mean that the Messiah should spring from his seed This promise was given to Abraham, because he left his father's house to live in a strange land, as God told him

Abraham Newland, An. A bank-note So called from the name of the chief cashier at the Bank of England from 1782 to 1807, without whose signature no Bank of England notes were genuine

Abraham's bosom. The repose of the happy in death—

The sons of Edward sleep in Abraham's bosom.
Richard III, iv, 3

The allusion is to *Luke* xvi, 22, and refers to the ancient custom of allowing a dear friend to recline on one's bosom, as did John on the bosom of Jesus

There is no leaping from Delilah's lap into Abraham's bosom—*i e* those who live and die in notorious sin must not expect to go to heaven at death

Abram-colour. "Abram" here is a corruption of *auburn* In *Coriolanus*, ii, 3, the word is so printed in the first three Folios—

Our heads are some brown, some black, some Abram, some bald

But in the fourth Folio (1685) and in later editions *auburn* is given Kyd's tragedy, *Soliman and Perseda* (1588) has —

Where is the eldest son of Priam, the Abram-coloured Trojan?

And Middleton, in *Blurt, Master Constable* (1601), mentions —

A goodly, long, thick Abram-coloured beard

Abram-man, or **Abraham cove.** A pretended maniac who, in Tudor and early Stuart times, wandered about the country as a begging impostor, a Tom o' Bedlam (*q v*), hence the phrase, *to sham Abraham*, meaning to pretend illness or distress, in order to get off work

Inmates of Bedlam (*q v*) who were not dangerously mad were kept in the "Abraham

Ward," and allowed out from time to time in a distinctive dress They were permitted to supplement their scanty rations by begging This gave an opportunity to impostors, and large numbers availed themselves of it Says *The Canting Academy* (Richd Head, 1674), they

"used to array themselves with party-coloured ribbons, tape in their hats, a fox-tail hanging down, a long stick with streamers," and beg alms, but "for all their seeming madness, they had wit enough to steal as they went along "

There is a good picture of them in *King Lear*, ii, 3, and see also Beaumont and Fletcher's *Beggar's Bush*, ii, 1.—

Come, princes of the ragged regiment
And these, what name or title e'er they bear,
Jarkman or *Patrico, Cranke* or *Clapper-dudgeon,*
Frater or *Abram-man,* I speak to all
That stand in fair election for the title
Of King of Beggars

Abraxas (ă braks' as) A cabalistic word used by the Gnostics to denote the Supreme Being, the source of 365 emanations, the sum of the numbers represented by the Greek letters of the word totalling 365 It was frequently engraved on gems (hence known as *abraxas stones*), that were used as amulets or talismans *See* BASILIDIANS By some authorities the name is given as that of one of the horses of Aurora

Absalom and Achitophel (a kit' ŏ fel). A political satire published in 1681, the first part by Dryden and the second by Nahum Tate and revised by Dryden. Of the principal characters, *David* stands for Charles II, *Absalom* for his natural son James, Duke of Monmouth (handsome and rebellious); *Achitophel* for Lord Shaftesbury, *Zimri* for the Duke of Buckingham; and *Abdael* for Monk The accommodation of the biblical narrative to contemporary history is so skilfully made that the story of David seems to repeat itself.

Absent. "Out of mind as soon as out of sight " This is the form in which the proverb is given by Fulke Greville, Lord Brooke (d. 1628) in his *56th Sonnet*, but it appears with its more usual wording—"Out of sight, out of mind," as the title of one of Barnabe Googe's *Eclogs* (1563).

The absent are always wrong. The translation of the French proverb, *Les absents ont toujours tort,* which implies that it is always easy to lay the blame on someone who is not present to stand up for himself

Absence makes the heart grow fonder. A tag of doubtful truth, that comes from a song, *The Isle of Beauty* by T Haynes Bayly (1797-1839).

Absent flag A small blue signal flown by a yacht to indicate that the owner is not aboard.

Absolute. A Captain Absolute, a bold, despotic man, determined to have his own way, so called from the character in Sheridan's *Rivals*

Absolute weight. The weight of a body in vacuum

Absolute zero. The temperature at which a theoretically perfect gas, kept at constant volume, would exert no pressure. In practice this is—273 1° C

Absquatulate (ăb skwot' ū lāt) To run away or abscond An artificial American word, possibly from Lat *ab,* from and *squat,* a squatting being a tenement taken in some unclaimed part, without purchase or permission It seems to have been first used in 1833, in *The Kentuckian,* a play by W. B Bernard

Abstinence is the voluntary total forbearance from taking alcohol, certain foods, etc ; it differs from *temperance,* for this admits of their being taken habitually in moderation. In ecclesiastical parlance Days of Abstinence are those when the eating of meat is not permitted; Fasting Days are when only one full meal is allowed in the twenty-four hours

Abstract Numbers are numbers considered without reference to anything else 1, 2, 3; if we say 1 year, 2 feet, 3 men, etc , the numbers are no longer abstract, but *concrete.*

Things are said to be taken **in the abstract** when they are considered absolutely, that is, without reference to other matters or persons. Thus, in the abstract, one man may be as good as another, but is yet not so socially and politically

An abstract of title is a legal expression, meaning an epitome of the evidences of ownership

Abstraction. Alexander Bain, in *The Senses and the Intellect* (1855), defines abstraction as "the generalizing of some property, so as to present it to the mind, apart from the other properties that usually go along with it in nature", or it is, as Locke put it· "Nothing more than leaving out of a number of resembling ideas what is peculiar to each " This process is apt to result in what we call *an empty abstraction,* a mere ideality, of no practical use, and sooner or later we turn away from such unsatisfying ideas, as did Wordsworth —

Give us, for our abstractions, solid facts;
For our disputes, plain pictures
Excursion v, 636

Gladstone furnished an excellent illustration of the meaning of the term when he said, "Laws are abstractions until they are put into execution "

Absurd meant originally "quite deaf," (Lat. *ab,* intensive, and *surdus,* deaf), but the Lat. compound, *absurdus,* had the meaning, "out of time," "discordant," hence "harsh" or "rough," and hence the figurative (and now common) meaning "irrational," ' silly" or "senseless "

Reductio ad absurdum. *See* REDUCTIO

Abudah (a bū' da) Thackeray's allusion —

Like Abudah, he is always looking out for the Fury, and knows that the night will come with the inevitable hag with it.

is to a story in Ridley's *Tales of the Genii* of a merchant of Bagdad who is haunted every night by an old hag

Abundant Number, An. A number the sum of whose aliquot parts is greater than itself Thus 12 is an abundant number, because its divisors, 1, 2, 3, 4, 6=16, which is greater than 12 *Cp.* DEFICIENT NUMBER, PERFECT NUMBER

Abus (ăb' us) An old name of the river Humber. *See* Spenser's *Faerie Queene*, II, x, 16 —

> He [Locrine] then encountred, a confused rout,
> Forbye the River that whylome was hight
> The ancient Abus

See Geoffrey of Monmouth's *Chronicles*, Bk ii, 2.

Abyla *See* Calpe

Abyssinian Christians. A branch of the Coptic Church *See* Copts

Academy. Originally the proper name of a garden near Athens (from *Academos*, the reputed founder) where Plato taught; hence, the philosophical school or system of Plato, and, later, a place where the arts and sciences, etc , are taught, and a society or institution for their cultivation

Plato's Academy was divided into the *Old*, his own philosophic teaching, and that of his immediate followers Xenocrates, Crates, and others; the *Middle*, a modified Platonic system, founded by Arcesilaus about 244 b c ; and the *New*, the half-sceptical school of Carneades, founded about 160 b c Plato's followers were known as Academics In addition to its usage in reference to an academy or university, the adjective *academic* has since been employed to signify "theoretical, scholarly, abstract, unpractical, merely logical ' *See* Platonism

The principal modern Academies are —

In Italy, the *Academia de Lincei* founded in 1603, with Galileo among its earliest members; it became the National Academy in 1870.

The **French Academy** (*Académie française*), formally established in 1635 by Cardinal Richelieu, with 40 members, its principal function being.—

> To labour with all the care and diligence possible, to give exact rules to our language, to render it capable of treating the arts and sciences

The **Royal Academy of Arts**, founded in 1768 by George III for the establishment of an art school and the holding of annual exhibitions of works by living artists The following is a list of the Presidents of the Royal Academy.—

1768 Sir Joshua Reynolds	1878 Lord Leighton
1792 Benjamin West	1896 Sir John Millais
1805 James Wyatt (temp)	1896 Sir Edward Poynter
1806 Benjamin West	1919 Sir Aston Webb
1820 Sir Thos Lawrence	1924 Sir F, Dicksee
1830 Sir Martin Archer	1928 Sir W Llewellyn
Shee	1938 Sir E Lutyens
1850 Sir Charles Eastlake	1944 Sir A L Munnings
1866 Sir Francis Grant	1950 Sir G F Kelly

The **Royal Military Academy, Woolwich,** was founded in 1741 for the training of artillery and engineer officers, the Royal Military Academy, Sandhurst, was founded in 1799 for the training of candidates for commissions in the infantry, cavalry, and other arms These two were amalgamated in 1946 as the Royal Military Academy, at Sandhurst.

The **Royal Spanish Academy** was founded at Madrid in 1713 for purposes similar to those of the French Academy There is also a **Royal Academy** of Science at Berlin (founded 1700), at Stockholm (the **Royal Swedish** Academy, founded 1739), and at Copenhagen (founded 1742). The **Imperial Academy of Sciences** at St Petersburg (Leningrad) was established by Catherine I in 1725

Academy figures. Drawings in black and white chalk, on tinted paper, usually about half life-size and from the nude

Acadia (à kā' diá) The early name of Nova Scotia, introduced to Europe by the Florentine explorer, Verazzani, who reported in 1524 that it was known by that name to the inhabitants. In 1621 Sir Wm Alexander obtained a grant of the land, and its name was changed to Nova Scotia The old French inhabitants refused to take the oath of allegiance to the British crown and were in a state of constant rebellion, so in 1755 they were forcibly evacuated, Longfellow's *Evangeline* tells of the resulting sufferings

Acadine (ăk' a dīn) A Sicilian fountain mentioned by Diodorus Siculus as having magic properties. Writings were thrown into it for the purpose of being tested, if genuine they floated, if spurious they sank to the bottom

Acanthus (a kăn' thus) The conventionalized representation of the leaf of *Acanthus mollis* used as a decoration in the capitals of Corinthian and composite columns The story is that an acanthus sprang up around a basket of flowers that Callimachus had placed on his daughter's grave, and that this so struck the fancy of the architect that he introduced the design into his buildings

Accents. *See* Typographical Signs

Accessory. Accessory before the fact is one who is aware that another intends to commit an offence, but is himself absent when the offence is perpetrated.

Accessory after the fact is one who screens a felon, aids him in eluding justice, or helps him in any way to profit by his crime. Thus, the receiver of stolen goods, knowing or even suspecting them to be stolen, is an accessory *ex post facto*

Accident. A logical accident is some property of quality which a substance possesses, the removal or change of which would not necessarily affect the substance itself, as the height of our bodies, the redness of a brick, the whiteness of paper, etc Theologians explain the doctrine of transubstantiation by maintaining that the *substance* of the bread and wine is changed into that of the body and blood of Christ, but their *accidents* (flavour, appearance, and so on) remain the same as before

Accidental colours. *See* Colours

Accidentals in music are signs indicating sharps, flats, naturals, and double sharps and flats, other than those sharps and flats prescribed by the key-signature

Accius Nævius (ăk' si us nē' vi ûs) A legendary Roman augur in the reign of Tarquin the Elder. When he forbade the king to increase the number of centuries (*i.e* divisions of the army) instituted by Romulus, without consulting the augurs, Tarquin asked him if, according to the augurs, the thought then in his, Tarquin's, mind was feasible of accomplishment "Undoubtedly," said Accius, after consultation "Then cut through this whetstone with the razor in your hand " The priest gave a bold cut, and the block fell in two (Livy, 1, 36)

Accolade (ăk ō lād') The touch of a sword on the shoulder in the ceremony of conferring knighthood, originally an embrace or touch by the hand on the neck (Lat *ad collum* on the neck) In music the brace ({) that connects two or more staves in the score is called an accolade.

Accommodation In commercial use, a loan of money

Accommodation note or bill. A bill of exchange for which value has not been received, used for the purpose of raising money on credit.

Accommodation ladder. A flight of steps hung over the side of a ship at the gangway

Accord means "heart to heart" (Lat *ad corda*) If two persons like and dislike the same things, they are heart to heart with each other

Similarly, "concord" means heart with heart; "discord," heart divided from heart, "record"—*i e. re-cordāre*—properly means to bring again to the mind or heart, and secondarily to set this down in writing

Account, To open an. To enter a customer's name on your ledger for the first time (Lat *accomputāre*, to calculate)

To keep open account Merchants are said to keep open account when they agree to honour each other's bills of exchange

A current account or "account current," a/c A commercial term, meaning the account of a customer who does not pay for goods received at time of purchase

On account. A commercial phrase implying "in part payment for "

On the account was an old pirates' phrase for sailing a-pirating.

To cast accounts To give the results of the debits and credits entered, balancing the two, and carrying over the surplus

The account on the Stock Exchange means' the credit allowed on dealings for the fortnightly settlement, or the fortnightly settlement itself, which is also called *account-day*, or *settling-day.*

To be sent to one's account. To have final judgment passed on one The Ghost in Hamlet uses the phrase as a synonym for death.—

Sent to my account
With all my imperfections on my head
Hamlet, 1, 5

Accusative. Calvin was so called by his college companions. An "accusative age" is an obsolete expression denoting an age that is *searching*, one that eliminates error by *accusing* it

This hath been a very accusative age —Sir E Dering (16th century)

Ace The unit of cards or dice, from *as,* which was the Latin unit of weight. In World War I the French term *as,* applied to an airman who had brought down ten enemy aeroplanes, was imported in its English equivalent *ace* This sense of the word has since been extended to include any more than usually expert flier, bridge-player, golfer, etc

Within an ace. Within a hair's breadth of, he who wins within an ace wins within a single mark *See* Ambsas

To bate an ace is to make an abatement, or to give a competitor some start or other advantage, in order to render the combatants more equal *See* Bolton Taylor, the water poet (1580-1654), speaking of certain women, says—
Though bad they be, they will not bate an ace
To be call'd Prudence, Temp'rance, Faith, and Grace.

Aceldama (a sel' da ma) The 'field of blood" near Jerusalem, mentioned in *Matt* xxvii, 8, and *Acts* 1, 19 It was appropriated as a cemetery for strangers, and was used as a burial-place by Christians during the Crusades and even as late as the 17th century The name, which is Aramaic and means " the field of blood," is figuratively used for any place of great slaughter

Acephalites (à sef' a litz) (Gr *akephale*, without a head) The name given to various rebellious and discontented groups of early Christians, principally to (1) a faction among the Monophysites who seceded from the authority of Peter, (2) certain bishops of the Eastern Church exempt from the jurisdiction and discipline of their patriarch; (3) a party of English levellers in the reign of Henry I, who acknowledged no leader

The name is also given to the monsters described in various legends and mediæval books of travel as having no head, the eyes and mouth being placed elsewhere

Acestes (a ses' těz) The arrow of Acestes. In a trial of skill Acestes, the Sicilian, discharged his arrow with such force that it took fire (*Æneid*, V, 525)
Acestes . shooting upward, sends his shaft
to show
An archer's art, and boast his twanging bow,
The feathered arrow gave a dire portent—
And latter augurs judge from this event—
Chafed by the speed, it fired, and as it flew
A trail of following flames ascending drew
DRYDEN *Æn* , V, 687

Achæan League (à kē' an) The first Achæan League was a religious confederation of the twelve towns of Achæa, lasting from very early times till it was broken up by Alexander the Great. The second was a powerful political federation of the Achæan and many other Greek cities, formed to resist Macedonian domination in 280 b c , and dissolved by the Romans in 147 b c

Achates (à kā' těz) A fidus Achates is a faithful companion, a bosom friend Achates in Virgil's *Æneid* is the chosen companion of the hero in adventures of all kinds

Achemon (a ke' mon) According to Greek fable Achemon and his brother Basalas were

two Cercopes forever quarrelling One day they saw Hercules asleep under a tree and insulted him, but Hercules tied them by their feet to his club and walked off with them, heads downwards, like a brace of hare Everyone laughed at the sight, and it became a proverb among the Greeks, when two men were seen quarrelling—"Look out for Melampygos¹" (i e. Hercules).—
Nē insidas in Melampygum

Acheron (ăk' er on) A Greek word meaning "the River of Sorrows", the river of the infernal regions into which Phlegethon and Cocytus flow also the lower world (Hades) itself
They pass the bitter waves of Acheron
Where many souls sit wailing woefully
SPENSER *Faerie Queene*, I, v, 33

Acherontian Books. *See* TAGES

Acherusia (ăk er ooz' i a) A cavern on the borders of Pontus, through which Hercules dragged Cerberus to earth from the infernal regions

Acheulian (à sher' li an) The name given to the paleolithic period identified by the remains found in the cave of St Acheul, France

Achillea (ăk il ē' à). A genus of herbaceous plants of the aster family, including the common yarrow (*Achillea millefolium*), so called from Achilles The tale is, that when the Greeks invaded Troy, Telephus, son-in-law of Priam, attempted to stop their landing, but, Bacchus causing him to stumble, Achilles wounded him with his spear The young Trojan was told by an oracle that "Achilles (meaning milfoil or yarrow) would cure the wound", instead of seeking the plant he applied to the Grecian chief, and promised to conduct the host to Troy if he would cure the wound Achilles consented to do so, scraped some rust from his spear, and from the filings rose the plant milfoil, which being applied to the wound, had the desired effect It is called by the French the *herbe aux charpentiers*—i e carpenters' wort, because it was supposed to heal wounds made by carpenters' tools.

Achilles (a kil' ēz) In Greek legend, the son of Peleus and Thetis and grandson of Eacus, king of the Myrmidons (in Thessaly), and hero of the *Iliad* (q v). He is represented as being brave and relentless, but, at the opening of the poem, in consequence of a quarrel between him and Agamemnon, commander-in-chief of the allied Greeks, he refused to fight. The Trojans prevailed, and Achilles sent Patroclus to oppose them. Patroclus fell, and Achilles, rushing into the battle, killed Hector (q v) He himself, according to later poems, was slain at the Scaean gate, before Troy was taken, by an arrow in his heel. *See* ACHILLES TENDON

Death of Achilles It was Paris who wounded Achilles in the heel with an arrow (a post-Homeric story)

Achilles's horses. Balios and Xanthos (*see* HORSE).

Achilles's mistress in Troy. Hippodamia, surnamed Briseis (q v.)

Achilles's tomb. In Sigœum, over which no bird ever flies —*Pliny*, x, 29

Achilles's tutors. First, Phœnix, who taught him the elements: then Chiron the centaur, who taught him the uses and virtues of plants

Achilles's wife. Deidamia (q v.)

The English Achilles. John Talbot, first Earl of Shrewsbury (1388?-1453)

Achilles of England. The Duke of Wellington (1769-1852)

Achilles of Germany. Albert Elector of Brandenburg (1414-1486).

Achilles of Lombardy. In Tasso's *Jerusalem Delivered*, the brother of Sforza and Palamedes, brothers in the allied army of Godfrey Achilles of Lombardy was slain by Corinna

Achilles of Rome Lucius Sicinius Dentatus, tribune of the Roman plebs, 454 B C, put to death 450 B C ; also called the *Second Achilles*

Achilles of the West Roland the Paladin, also called "The Christian Theseus"

Achilles and the tortoise The allusion is to the following paradox proposed by Zeno In a race Achilles, who can run ten times as fast as a tortoise, gives the latter 100 yards start; but it is impossible for him to overtake the tortoise and win the race, for, while he is running the first hundred yards the tortoise runs ten, while Achilles runs that ten the tortoise is running one, while Achilles is running one the tortoise runs one-tenth of a yard, and so on *ad infinitum*

Achilles's spear. Shakespeare's lines —
That gold must round engirt these brows of mine
Whose smile and frown, like to Achilles' spear,
Is able with the change to kill and cure
2 *Henry VI*, v, 1
is an allusion from the story told above (s v. ACHILLEA) of the healing of Telephus It is also referred to by Chaucer —
speche of Thelophus the king,
And of Achilles with his queynte spere,
For he coude with it both hele and dere (*harm*)
Squire's Tale, 238.

Achilles tendon. A strong sinew running along the heel to the calf of the leg, frequently strained by athletes. The tale is that Thetis took her son Achilles by the heel, and dipped him in the river Styx to make him invulnerable The water washed every part, except the heel in his mother's hand It was on this vulnerable point the hero was slain, and the sinew of the heel is called, in consequence, *tendo Achillis* A post-Homeric story.

The heel of Achilles. The vulnerable or weak point in a man's character or of a nation.

Aching Void, An. That desolation of heart which arises from the recollection of some cherished endearment no longer possessed.
What peaceful hours I once enjoy'd,
How sweet their memory still,
But they have left an aching void
The world can never fill
COWPER *Walking with God.*

Achitophel (à kit' ō fel). Ahithophel was David's traitorous counsellor, who deserted to Absalom, but his advice being disregarded, he hanged himself (2 *Sam.* xvii, 23) The Achitophel of Dryden's satire (*see* ABSALOM AND ACHITOPHEL) was the Earl of Shaftesbury

Achor (ā' kôr). Said by Pliny to be the name of the deity prayed to by the Cyreneans for the averting of insect pests *See* FLIES, GOD OF

Acid Test. The application of acid is a certain test of gold Hence the phrase is used of a test or trial which will conclusively decide the value. worth, or reliability of anything

Acis (ā' sis) In Greek mythology, the son of Faunus, in love with Galatea. His rival, Polyphemus, the Cyclop, crushed him to death beneath a huge rock

Ack emma. *See* PIP EMMA

Acme (ăk' mi) (Gr a point) The highest pitch of perfection, the term used by old medical writers for the crisis of a disease They divided the progress of a disease into four periods: the *arche*, or beginning, the *anabasis*, or increase, the *acme*, or term of its utmost violence, and the *paracme*, or decline

Aconite (ăk' o nīt) The herb Monkshood or Wolfsbane Classic fabulists ascribe its poisonous qualities to the foam which dropped from the mouths of the three-headed Cerberus, when Hercules, at the command of Eurystheus, dragged the monster from the infernal regions (Gr. ἀκόνιτον, Lat *aconitum*)

Lurida terribiles miscent Aconita novercæ
OVID· *Metamorphoses*, 1, 147

Acrasia (a krā' zi ā) In Spenser's *Faerie Queene* (Bk. II, ca 12), an enchantress, mistress of the "Bower of Bliss." She transformed her lovers into monstrous shapes, and kept them captives. Sir Guyon captures her, frees her victims, destroys the bower, and sends her in chains of adamant to the Faerie Queene She is the personification of Intemperance, the name signifying "lack of self-control."

Acre O.E. *æcer*, is akin to the Lat *ager* and Ger. *acker* (a field). God's Acre, a cemetery or churchyard Longfellow calls this an "ancient Saxon phrase," but as a matter of fact it is a modern borrowing from Germany

Acre-shot. An obsolete name for a land tax "Shot" is *scot. See* SCOT AND LOT.

Acres, Bob. A coward by character in Sheridan's *The Rivals*, whose courage always "oozed out at his fingers' ends." Hence, a man of this kind is sometimes called "a regular Bob Acres."

Acropolis (à krop' ō lis) (Gr *akros*, point, height, *polis*, city) An elevated citadel, especially of ancient Athens, where was built in the 15th century B.C the Parthenon, the Erechtheum, and the Propylæa or monumental gate

Acrostic (Gr *akros*, extremity; *stichos*, row, line of verse) A piece of verse in which the initial letters of each line read downwards consecutively form a word, if the final letters

read in the same way also form a word it is a *double acrostic*; if the middle letters as well it is a *triple acrostic* The term was first applied to the excessively obscure prophecies of the Erythræan sibyl, they were written on loose leaves, and the initial letters made a word when the leaves were sorted and laid in order. (*Dionys* iv, 62.)

Acrostic Poetry among the Hebrews consisted of twenty-two lines or stanzas beginning with the letters of the alphabet in succession (*cp* ABECEDARIAN HYMNS)

Act and Opponency. An "Act," in our University language, consists of a thesis publicly maintained by a candidate for a degree, with the "disputation" thereon The person "disputing" with the "keeper of the Act" is called the "opponent," and his function is called an "opponency". In some degrees the student is required to keep his Act, and then to be the opponent of another disputant. This custom has long been given up at Oxford, but at Cambridge the thesis and examination for the doctor's degree in Divinity, Law, and Medicine is still called an 'Act."

Act of Faith. *See* AUTO DA FE

Act of God Loss arising from the action of forces uncontrollable by man, such as a hurricane, lightning, etc , is said to be due to an "act of God," and hence has no legal redress A Devonshire jury once found—"That deceased died by the act of God, brought about by the flooded condition of the river."

Act of Man. The sacrificing of cargo, spars, or furnishings, by the master of a vessel for the preservation of his ship All persons with an interest in the ship and cargo stand a fair share of the loss.

Act of Parliament. This is the official name for a measure which has become the law of the land. The word Bill is applied to a measure on its introduction, and for it to become an Act it has to be read three times in each House of Parliament (during which time it is debated) and receive the royal assent. The Acts of each session are arranged in chapters and officially quoted according to the year of the reign in which they are passed *See* REGNAL YEAR. The Acts of the English Parliament go back to 1235

Actæon (ăk tē' on) In Greek mythology a huntsman who, having surprised Diana bathing, was changed by her into a stag and torn to pieces by his own hounds A stag being a horned animal, he became a representative of men whose wives are unfaithful *See* HORN.

Like Sir Actæon he, with Ringwood at thy heel.
SHAKESPEARE *Merry Wives*, ii, I

The Emperors themselves did wear Actæon's badge
BURTON: *Anatomy of Melancholy* (1621)

Actian Games (ăk' ti an) The games celebrated at Actium in honour of Apollo They were reinstituted by Augustus to celebrate his naval victory over Antony, 31 B.C , and were held every five years

Action Sermon. A sermon (in the Scots Presbyterian Church) preached before the celebration of Communion.

Acton. A taffeta, or leather-quilted dress, worn under the habergeon to keep the body from being chafed or bruised (Fr *hoqueton*, cotton-wool, padding.)

Actresses. Coryat, in his *Crudities* (1611), says "When I went to a theatre (in Venice) I observed certain things that I never saw before, for I saw women acte. . . I have heard that it hath sometimes been used in London," but the first public appearance of a woman on the stage in England was on 8 Dec., 1660, when Margaret Hughes, Prince Rupert's mistress, played Desdemona in *Othello* at a new theatre in Clare Market, London. Previous to that female parts had always been taken by boys, Edward Kynaston (d 1706) seems to have been the last male actor to play a woman on the English stage, in serious drama.

Whereas, women's parts in plays have hitherto been acted by men in the habits of women . . we do permit and give leave for the time to come that all women's parts be acted by women

Charles II's licence of 1662

Acu tetigisti. *See* REM ACU

Ad inquirendum (ăd in kwi ren′ dum) (Lat.). A judicial writ commanding an inquiry to be made into some complaint.

Ad Kalendas Græcas (ăd ka len′ dăs grē′ kăs) (Lat.) (Deferred) to the Greek Calends— *i e* for ever (It shall be done) on the Greek Calends—*i e* never—for the Greeks had no Calends (*q v.*). Suetonius tells us that this used to be the reply of Augustus to the question when he was going to pay his creditors.

Ad libitum (ăd lib′ i tum) (Lat.). To choice, at pleasure, without restraint

Ad rem (ăd rem′) (Lat.). To the point in hand; to the purpose.

Ad valorem (ăd văl ôr′ em) (Lat.). According to the price charged. A commercial term used in imposing customs duties according to the value of the goods imported. Thus, if teas pay duty *ad valorem*, the high-priced tea will pay more duty per pound than the lower-priced tea

Ad vitam aut culpam (ăd vī′ tam awt kŭl′ păm) (Lat.) A phrase, meaning literally "to life-time or fault," used in Scottish law of the permanency of an appointment, unless forfeited by misconduct

Adam. The Talmudists say that Adam lived in Paradise only twelve hours, and account for the time thus·—

I. God collected the dust and animated it
II. Adam stood on his feet
IV. He named the animals
VI. He slept and Eve was created.
VII. He married the woman
X. He fell
XII. He was thrust out of Paradise.

Mohammedan legends add to the Bible story the tradition that—

God sent Gabriel, Michael, and Israfel one after the other to fetch seven handfuls of earth from different depths and of different colours for the creation of Adam (thereby accounting for the varying colours of mankind), but that they returned empty-handed because Earth foresaw that the creature to be made from her would rebel against God and draw down His curse on her, whereupon Azrael was sent. He executed the commission, and for that reason was appointed to separate the souls from the bodies and hence became the Angel of Death. The earth he had taken was carried into Arabia to a place between Mecca and Tayef, where it was kneaded by the angels, fashioned into human form by God, and left to dry for either forty days or forty years. It is also said that while the clay was being endowed with life and a soul, when the breath breathed by God into the nostrils had reached as far as the navel, the only half-living Adam tried to rise up and got an ugly fall for his pains. Mohammedan tradition holds that he was buried on Aboucais, a mountain of Arabia

In Greek the word *Adam* is made up of the four initial letters of the cardinal quarters.—

Arktos, north; *Dusis*, west,
Anatole, east; *Mesembria*, south.

The Hebrew word (without vowels) forms an anagram with the initials. A[dam], D[avid], M[essiah]

According to Moslem writers. After the Fall Adam and Eve were separated, Adam being placed on Mt. Vassem, in the east, Eve at Jeddah, on the Red Sea coast of Arabia. The Serpent was exiled to the coast of Ebleh. After a hundred years had been thus spent, Adam and Eve were reunited at Arafat, in the vicinity of Mecca. Adam died on Friday, April 7, at the age of 930 years. His body was wrapped in cerements by the Archangel Michael; Gabriel performed the last rites. The body was buried in the grotto of Ghar′ ul Kenz, near Mecca. When Noah went into the Ark he took Adam's coffin with him, after the Flood restoring it to its original burial place

The old Adam. The offending Adam, etc.

Consideration, like an angel, came
And whipped the offending Adam out of him.
SHAKESPEARE· *Henry V*, i, 1

Adam, as the head of unredeemed man, stands for "original sin," or "man without regenerating grace."

The second Adam. The new Adam, etc. Jesus Christ is so called

The Tempter set
Our second Adam, in the wilderness,
To show him all earth's kingdoms and their glory
Paradise Lost, xi, 383

Milton probably derived the idea from *Rom.* vi, 6, or 1 *Cor* xv, 22:—

For as in Adam all die, even so in Christ shall all be made alive

Compare the address of God to the Saviour in *Paradise Lost*, iii:—

Be thou in Adam's room
The head of all mankind, though Adam's son
As in him perish all men, so in thee,
As from a second root, shall be restored
As many as are restored

In the same way Milton calls Mary our "second Eve" (*Paradise Lost*, v, 387, and x, 183)

When Adam delved:—

When Adam delved and Eve span,
Who was then the gentleman

This, according to the *Historia Anglicana* of Thos Walsingham (d 1422), was the text of

John Ball's speech at Blackheath to the rebels in Wat Tyler's insurrection (1381). It seems to be an adaptation of some lines by Richard Rolle of Hampole (d *c* 1349):—

When Adam dalfe and Eve spanne
To spire of thou may spede,
Where was then the pride of man,
That now marres his meed?

Cp *Jack's as good as his master*, under JACK (*phrases*)

Adam Bell. *See* CLYM OF THE CLOUGH

Adam Cupid—*i e* Archer Cupid, probably alluding to Adam Bell In all the early editions the line in *Romeo and Juliet* (II, 1, 13). "Young Adam Cupid, he that shot so trim," reads "Young *Abraham* Cupid, ' etc. The emendation was suggested by Steevens

Adam's ale. Water, because the first man had nothing else to drink. In Scotland sometimes called *Adam's Wine*

Adam's apple. The protuberance in the forepart of the throat, the anterior extremity of the thyroid cartilage of the larynx; so called from the superstition that a piece of the forbidden fruit stuck in Adam's throat.

Adam's needle. *Gen* iii, 7, tells us that Adam and Eve "sewed fig leaves together," needles were (presumably) not then obtainable, but certain plants furnish needle-like spines, and to some of these the name has been given The chief is the Yucca, a native of Mexico and Central America

Adams, Parson. The type of a benevolent, simple-minded, eccentric country clergyman, ignorant of the world, bold as a lion for the truth, and modest as a girl Henry Fielding's *Joseph Andrews* (1742)

Adam's Peak. A mountain in Ceylon where, according to Mohammedan legend, Adam bewailed his expulsion from Paradise, standing on one foot for 200 years to expiate his crime, then Gabriel took him to Mount Arafat, where he found Eve

In the granite is a curious impression resembling a human foot, above 5 feet long by 2½ broad, the Hindus, however, assert that it was made by Buddha when he ascended into heaven.

Adam's profession. Gardening or agriculture is sometimes so called—for obvious reasons

There is no ancient gentlemen but gardeners, ditchers, and grave-makers, they hold up Adam's profession.

SHAKESPEARE *Hamlet*, v, 1.

Adamites (ăd' a mīts) The name given to various heretical sects who supposed themselves to attain to primitive innocence by rejecting marriage and clothing There was such a sect in North Africa in the 2nd century, the *Abelites* (*q v*) were similar, the heresy reappeared in Savoy in the 14th century, and spread over Bohemia and Moravia in the 15th and 16th. One Picard, of Bohemia, was the leader in 1400, and styled himself " Adam, son of God." There are references to the sect in James Shirley's comedy *Hyde Park* (II, iv) (1632), and in *The Guardian*, No 134 (1713)

Adamant (from Gr *a*, not, *damao*, I tame) A word used for any stone or mineral of excessive hardness (especially the diamond, which is really the same word), also for the magnet or loadstone; and, by poets, for hardness or firmness in the abstract.

In *Midsummer Night's Dream*, ii, 1
You draw me, you hard-hearted adamant,
But yet you draw not iron, for my heart
Is true as steel
we have an instance of the use of the word in both senses *Adamant* as a name for the loadstone, or magnet, seems to have arisen through an erroneous derivation of the word by early mediæval Latin writers from Late Lat , *adamare*, to take a liking for, to have an attraction for. Thus Shakespeare —
As true as steel, as plantage to the moon,
As sun to day, as turtle to her mate,
As iron to adamant
                    Troilus and Cressida, iii, 2.

Adamastor (ăd à măs' tôr) The spirit of the stormy Cape (Good Hope), described by Camoens in the *Lusiad* as a hideous phantom that appears to Vasco da Gama and prophesies disaster to all seeking to make the voyage to India

Addison of the North. A sobriquet of Henry Mackenzie (1745-1831), author of the *Man of Feeling*

Addison's disease. A state of anæmia, languor, irritable stomach, etc , associated with disease of the suprarenal glands so named from Dr. Thos Addison, of Guy's Hospital (1793-1860), who first described it.

Addisonian termination. The name given by Bishop Hurd to the construction which closes a sentence with a preposition, such as— ' which the prophet took a distinct view of " Named from Joseph Addison, who frequently employed it

Addle is the Old English *adela*, mire, or liquid filth, hence rotten, putrid, worthless

Addle egg. An egg which has no germ, also one in which the chick has died Hence, fig , *addle-headed*, *addle-pate*, empty-headed As an addle-egg produces no living bird so an addle-pate lacks brains.

The Addled Parliament. The second Parliament of James I, 5th April to 7th June, 1614 It refused to grant supplies until grievances had been redressed, and is so called because it did not pass a single measure

Adelantado (ä de län ta'dō) Spanish for "his excellency" (from *adelantar*, to promote), and given to the governor of a province Hence, a figure of importance

Open no door If the adelantado of Spain were here he should not enter —BEN JONSON. *Every Man out of his Humour*, v, 4

Middleton, in *Blurt, Master Constable* (IV, iii), uses *lantedo* as an Elizabethan abbreviation of this word

Adelphi, The A block of residential buildings, off the Strand in London, designed by Robert Adam in 1768—now largely demolished Adam himself, Garrick, and in later times Hardy, Barrie, and the Savage Club had accommodation in the main building

Adept means one who has attained (Lat *adeptus*, participle of *adipisci*) The alchemists applied the term *vere adeptus* to those persons who professed to have "attained to the knowledge of" the elixir of life or of the philosopher's stone.

Alchemists tell us there are always 11 adepts, neither more nor less Like the sacred chickens of Compostella, of which there are only 2 and always 2—a cock and a hen

In Rosicrucian lore as learn'd
As he that *vere adeptus* earn'd
BUTLER *Hudibras*, I, i, 546

Adeste Fideles (a des' ti fī dē' lēz) ("O come, all ye faithful"). A Christmas hymn the familiar tune of which was composed by John Reading (1677-1764), organist at Winchester and author of "Dulce Domum "

Adiaphorists (ăd ī ăf' or ists) (Gr indifferent) Followers of Melanchthon, moderate Lutherans, who held that some of the dogmas of Luther are matters of indifference They accepted the Interim of Augsburg (*q.v*)

Adieu (Fr to God) An elliptical form for *I commend you to God* (*cp* GOOD-BYE)

Adjective Colours are those which require a mordant before they can be used as dyes.

Admirable, The Abraham ben Meir ibn Ezra, a celebrated Spanish Jew (1092-1167), was so called He was noted as a mathematician, philologist, poet, astronomer, and commentator on the Bible.

The Admirable Crichton James Crichton (1560-1585?), Scottish traveller, scholar, and swordsman So called by Sir Thomas Urquhart.

Admirable Doctor (*Doctor mirabilis*). Roger Bacon (1214?-1294), the English mediæval philosopher

Admiral, corruption of Arabic *Amir* (lord or commander), with the article *al*, as in *Amir-al-ma* (commander of the water), *Amir-al-Oma* (commander of the forces), *Amir-al-Mumimm* (commander of the faithful).

Milton uses the old form for the ship itself, speaking of Satan, he says'—

His spear—to equal which the tallest pine
Hewn on Norwegian hills, to be the mast
Of some great ammiral, were but a wand—
He walked with
Paradise Lost, i, 292

In the Royal Navy there are now four grades of Admiral, viz *Admiral of the Fleet*, *Admiral*, *Vice-Admiral*, and *Rear-Admiral* There used to be three classes, named from the colour of their flag—*Admiral of the Red*, *Admiral of the White*, and *Admiral of the Blue*, who, in engagements, held the centre, van, and rear respectively The distinction was abolished in 1864

Admiral of the Blue (*see above*), used facetiously for a butcher who dresses in blue, or a tapster, from his blue apron.

As soon as customers begin to stir
The Admiral of the Blue cries, "Coming, Sir!"
Poor Robin (1731)

Admiral of the Red (*see above*), facetiously applied to a winebibber whose face and nose are red.

Admittance. This word is not synonymous with *admission* From permission to enter, and thence the right or power to enter, it extends to the physical act of entrance, as "he gained admittance to the church " You may have *admission* to the director's room, but there is no *admittance* except through his secretary's office An old meaning of the word indicates the privilege of being admitted into good society —

Sir John you are a gentleman of excellent breeding of great admittance
Merry Wives of Windsor, ii, 2

Admonitionists, or **Admonitioners.** Certain Protestants who in 1571 sent an *admonition* to the Parliament condemning everything in the Church of England which was not in accordance with the doctrines and practices of Geneva

Adonai (â dō' nī) (Heb pl of *adon*, lord). A name given to the Deity by the Hebrews, and used by them in place of Yahweh (Jehovah), the "ineffable name," wherever this occurs. In the Vulgate, and hence in the Wyclif, Coverdale, and Douai versions, it is given for Jehovah in *Exod.* vi, 3, where the A V reads —

And I appeared unto Abraham, and unto Isaac, and unto Jacob, by the name of God Almighty, but by my name JEHOVAH was I not known to them

Thus James Howell says of the Jews.—

they sing many tunes, and *Adonai* they make the ordinary name of God. Jehovah is pronounced at high Festivals
Letters, Bk i, sec vi, 14 (3 June, 1633)

Adonists. Those Jews who maintain that the vowels of the word Adonai (*q v*) are not the vowels necessary to make the tetragrammaton (*q v*), JHVH, into the name of the Deity. *See also* JEHOVAH.

Adonais (ad ō na' is) The poetical name given by Shelley to Keats in his elegy on the death of the latter (1821), probably in allusion to the mourning for Adonis

Adonia (â dō' ni a) The feast of Adonis, celebrated in Assyria, Alexandria, Egypt, Judæa, Persia, Cyprus, and Greece, for eight days. Lucian gives a long description of these feasts, which were generally held at midsummer and at which the women first lamented the death and afterwards rejoiced at the resurrection of Adonis—a custom referred to in the Bible (*Ezek.* viii, 14), where Adonis appears under his Phœnician name, Tammuz (*q v*).

Adonis (â dō' nis) In classical mythology a beautiful youth who was beloved by Venus, and was killed by a boar while hunting. Hence, usually ironically, any beautiful young man, as in Massinger's *Parliament of Love*, II, 2 '—

Of all men
I ever saw yet, in my settled judgment
Thou art the ugliest creature, and when trimm'd up
To the height, as thou imagin'st, in mine eyes,
A leper with a clap-dish (to give notice
He is infectious), in respect of thee
Appears a young Adonis.

And Leigh Hunt was sent to prison for libelling George IV when Regent, by calling him "a corpulent Adonis of fifty" (*Examiner*, 1813).

Adonis Flower, according to Bion, the rose, Pliny (i, 23) says it is the anemone, others, the field poppy, but now generally used for the pheasant's eye, called in French *goute-de-sang*, because in fable it sprang from the blood of the gored hunter

Adonis garden. A worthless toy, very perishable goods.

Thy promises are like Adonis' gardens
That one day bloom'd and fruitful were the next.
       SHAKESPEARE. 1 *Henry VI*, i, vi.

The allusion is to the baskets or pots of earth used at the Adonia (*q.v*), in which quick-growing plants were sown, tended for eight days, allowed to wither, and then thrown into the sea or river with images of the dead Adonis In Spenser's *Faerie Queene* (Bk. III, ca vi) the Garden of Adonis is where—

All the goodly flowres,
Wherewith dame Nature doth her beautifie
And decks the girlonds of her paramoures,
Are fetcht there is the first seminarie
Of all things that are borne to live and die,
According to their kindes

It is to these gardens that Milton also refers in *Paradise Lost* (ix, 440)'—

Spot more delicious than those gardens feigned
Or of revived Adonis, or renowned
Alcinous, host of old Laertes' son.

Adonis River. A stream which flows from Lebanon to the sea near Byblos which runs red at the season of the year when the feast of Adonis was held

Thammuz came next behind,
Whose annual wound in Lebanon allured
The Syrian damsels to lament his fate
In amorous ditties all a summer's day,
While smooth Adonis from his native rock
Ran purple to the sea, supposed with blood
Of Thammuz yearly wounded
      MILTON *Paradise Lost*, i, 446

Adoption. Adoption by arms. An ancient custom of giving arms to a person of merit, which laid him under the obligation of being your champion and defender

Adoption by baptism Being godfather or godmother to a child The child by baptism is your godchild

Adoption by hair. Boson, King of Provence (879-889), is said to have cut off his hair and to have given it to Pope John VIII as a sign that the latter had adopted him

Adoption Controversy. Elipand, Archbishop of Toledo, and Felix, Bishop of Urgel (in the 8th century), maintained that Christ in his *human* nature was the son of God by adoption only (*Rom* viii, 29), though in his pre-existing state he was the "begotten Son of God" in the ordinary catholic acceptation Duns Scotus, Durandus, and Calixtus were among the Adoptionists who supported this view, which was condemned by the Council of Frankfort in 794

Adoptive Emperors In Roman history, the five Emperors—Nerva, Trajan, Hadrian, Antoninus Pius, and Marcus Aurelius—each of whom (except Nerva, who was elected by the Senate) was the adopted son of his predecessor Their period (96-180) is said to have been the happiest in the whole history of Rome

Adoration of the Cross *See* ANDREW, ST.

Adrammelech (a drăm' e lek) A Babylonian deity to whom, apparently, infants were burnt in sacrifice (2 *Kings* xvii, 31) Possibly the sun god worshipped at Sippar (*i e* Sephar-vaim).

Adrastus (à drăs' tus). (i) A mythical Greek king of Argos, leader of the expedition of the " Seven Against Thebes " (*see under* SEVEN). (ii) In Tasso's *Jerusalem Delivered* (Bk xx), an Indian prince who aided the King of Egypt against the crusaders He was slain by Rinaldo.

Adriatic. *See* BRIDE OF THE SEA

Adullamites (à dŭl' a mits) The adherents of R. Lowe and E Horsman, seceders in 1866 from the Reform Party John Bright said of these members that they retired to the cave of Adullam, and tried to gather round them all the discontented. The allusion is to David, who, in his flight from Saul—

Escaped to the cave Adullam, and every one that was in distress, and every one that was in debt, and every one that was discontented, gathered themselves unto him.
      1 *Sam* xxii, 1, 2

Adulterous Bible. *See* BIBLE, SPECIALLY NAMED.

Advancer. In venery this is the name given to the second branch of a buck's horns.

Advent (Lat *adventus*, the coming to). The four weeks immediately preceding Christmas, commemorating the first and second coming of Christ, the first to redeem, and the second to judge the world. The season begins on St. Andrew's Day (30th Nov), or the Sunday nearest to it

Adversary, The. A name frequently given in English literature to the Devil (from 1 *Pet* v, 8)

Advocate (Lat. *ad*, to; *vocare*, to call). One called to assist pleaders in a court of law.

The Devil's Advocate A carping or adverse critic From the *Advocatus diaboli*, the person appointed to contest the claims of a candidate for canonization before a papal court He advances all he can against the candidate, and is opposed by the *Advocatus dei* (God's Advocate), who says all he can in support of the proposal

Advocates' Library, in Edinburgh, was founded in 1682, by Sir George Mackenzie of Rosehaugh, Dean of the Faculty of Advocates, *i e.* the body of members of the Scottish bar It is one of the libraries to which books must be sent for purposes of copyright (*q v*).

Advowson (Lat. *advocatio*, a calling to, a summons· *cp* ADVOCATE). Originally the obligation to be the *advocate* of a benefice or living and to defend its rights, the word now means the right of appointing the incumbent of a church or ecclesiastical benefice.
The different advowsons are —

Advowson appendant. A right of presentation which belongs to and passes with the manor This usually had its origin in the ownership of the advowson by the person who built or endowed the church

Advowson collative. In which the bishop himself is patron and, as he cannot "present" to himself, does by the act of "collation" or conferring the benefice all that is done in other cases by presentation and institution

Advowson donative In which a secular patron (usually the Crown) has the right of disposing of the benefice to any legally qualified person without institution or induction or examination by the bishop or ordinary

Advowson in gross An advowson which has become legally separated from the manor to which it was appendant   *See* Gross

Advowson presentative. In which the patron (who may be a layman) presents to the bishop who, unless he is satisfied that there is sufficient legal or ecclesiastical disability, must "institute" the clerk

Adytum (Gr *aduton*, not to be entered, *duo*, to go) The Holy of Holies in the Greek and Roman temples, into which the general public were not admitted, hence, a sanctum

Ædiles. Those who, in ancient Rome, had charge of the public buildings (*ædes*), such as the temples, theatres, baths, aqueducts, sewers, including roads and streets also.

Ægeus. A fabulous king of Athens who gave the name to the Ægean Sea His son, Theseus, went to Crete to deliver Athens from the tribute exacted by Minos Theseus said, if he succeeded he would hoist a white sail on his home-voyage, as a signal of his safety. This he neglected to do; and Ægeus who watched the ship from a rock, thinking his son had perished, threw himself into the sea

This incident is repeated in the tale of Tristram and Isolde. *See* Tristram.

Æginetan Sculptures. Sculptures discovered in 1811 at the temple of Pallas Athene, in the little island of Ægina. They consist of two groups of five and ten figures representing exploits of Greek heroes at Troy, and probably date from about 500 B C, i e. a little before Phidias They were restored by Thorwaldsen, and were long the most remarkable ornaments of the Glyptothek, at Munich

Ægir (ě' jir, ě' gir) In Norse mythology the god of the ocean, husband of Ran They had nine daughters (the billows), who wore white robes and veils

Ægis (ē' jis) (Gr goat skin). The shield of Jupiter made by Vulcan and covered with the skin of the goat Amalthæa, who had suckled the infant Zeus. It was sometimes lent to Athena, daughter of Zeus, and when in her possession carried the head of the Gorgon By the shaking of his ægis Zeus produced storms and thunder, in art it is usually represented as a kind of cloak fringed with serpents, and it is symbolical of divine protection—hence the modern use of the word in such phrases as *I throw my ægis over you*, I give you my protection.

Ægrotat (ē grō' tăt) (Lat he is ill). In university parlance, a medical certificate of indisposition to exempt the bearer from sitting examinations

'A E I', a common motto on jewellery, is Greek, and stands for "for ever and for aye."

A. E. I. O. U. The device adopted by Frederick V, Archduke of Austria, on becoming the Emperor Frederick III in 1440 The letters had been used by his predecessor, Albert II, and then stood for—

Albertus Electus Imperator Optimus Vivat

The meaning that Frederick gave them was—
Archidux Electus Imperator Optime Vivat.

Many other versions are known, including—
Austriæ Est Imperare Orbi Universo
Alles Erdreich Ist Oesterreich Unterthan.
Austria's Empire Is Overall Universal

To which wags added after the war of 1866—
Austria's Empire Is Ousted Utterly.

Frederick the Great is said to have translated the motto thus —
Austria Erit In Orbe Ultima (*Austria will be lowest in the world*)

Aemilian Law (ē mil' i an) A law made by the prætor Aemilius Mamercus empowering the eldest prætor to drive a nail in the Capitol on the ides of September This was a ceremony by which the Romans supposed that a pestilence could be stopped or a calamity averted

Æneas (ē nē' às) The hero of Virgil's epic, son of Anchises, king of Dardanus, and Aphrodite. According to Homer he fought against the Greeks in the Trojan War and after the sack of Troy reigned in the Troad Later legends tell how he carried his father Anchises on his shoulders from the flames of Troy, and after roaming about for many years, came to Italy, where he founded a colony which the Romans claim as their origin. The epithet applied to him is *pius*, meaning "dutiful."

Æneid The epic poem of Virgil (in twelve books) So called from *Æneas* and the suffix *-is*, plur *ides* (belonging to)

The story of Sinon (says Macrobius) and the taking of Troy is borrowed from Pisander.

The loves of Dido and Æneas are taken from those of Medea and Jason, in Apollonius of Rhodes

The story of the Wooden Horse and burning of Troy is from Arctinus of Miletus.

Æolian Harp (ē ō' li an) The wind harp A box on which strings are stretched Being placed where a draught gets to the strings, they utter musical sounds

Awake, Æolian lyre, awake,
And give to rapture all thy trembling strings.
      Gray *Progress of Poesy*

Æolian Mode, in Music, the ninth of the church modes, also called the Hypodorian, the range being from A to A, the dominant F or E, and the mediant E or C It is characterized as "grand and pompous though sometimes soothing "

Æolian Rocks. A geological term for those rocks the formation and distribution of which has been due more to the agency of wind than to that of water Most of the New Red Sandstones, and many of the Old Red, are of Æolian origin

Æolic Digamma (ē ol' ik di' găm a) The sixth letter of the early Greek alphabet (F), sounded like our w Thus *oinos* with the digamma was sounded *woinos*, whence the Latin *vinum*, our *wine* Gamma, or *g*, was shaped thus Γ, hence digamma = double *g*, it was early disused as a letter, but was retained as the symbol for the numeral 6 True Æolic was the dialect of Lesbos

Æolus (ē' ō lùs), in Roman mythology, was ' god of the winds "

Æon (ē'on) (Gr. *aion*) An age of the universe, an immeasurable length of time, hence the personification of an age, a god, any being that is eternal Basilides reckons there have been 365 such Æons, or gods, but Valentinius restricts the number to 30

Aerated Waters (ā' ĕr ā ted). Effervescent waters charged (either artificially or naturally) with carbon dioxide

Æschylus (ēs' ki lus) (525-456 B C), the father of the Greek tragic drama Titles of seventy-two of his plays are known, but only seven are now extant Fable has it that he was killed by a tortoise dropped by an eagle (to break the shell) on his bald head, which the bird mistook for a stone.

Æschylus of France. Prosper Jolyot de Crebillon (1674-1762).

Æsculapius (ēs kū lā' pi us) The Latin form of the Greek Asklepios, god of medicine and of healing Now used for "a medical practitioner " The usual offering to him was a cock, hence the phrase "to sacrifice a cock to Æsculapius"—to return thanks (or pay the doctor's bill) after recovery from an illness

When men a dangerous disease did scape,
Of old, they gave a cock to Æsculape
BEN JONSON *Epigram*

Legend has it that he assumed the form of a serpent (*q v*) when he appeared at Rome during a pestilence; hence it is that the goddess of Health bears in her hand a serpent

Æsir (ē' zer). The collective name of the celestial gods of Scandinavia, who lived in Asgard (*q v*). (1) Odin, the chief; (2) Thor (his eldest son, god of thunder); (3) Tiu (another son, god of wisdom); (4) Balder (another son, Scandinavian Apollo), (5) Bragi (god of poetry); (6) Vidar (god of silence), (7) Hoder the blind (slayer of Balder), (8) Hermoder (Odin's son and messenger); (9) Hœnir (a minor god), (10) Odnir (husband of Freyja, the Scandinavian Venus), (11) Loki (the god of mischief), (12) Vali (Odin's youngest son).

Æson's Bath (ē' son)

I perceive a man may be twice a child before the days of dotage, and stands in need of *Æson's* Bath before three score —Sir THOMAS BROWNE *Religio Medici, Section* 42

The reference is to Medea rejuvenating Æson, father of Jason, with the juices of a concoction made of sundry articles After Æson had imbibed these juices, Ovid says —

Barba comæque,
Canitie posita, nigrum rapuere, colorem
Metamorphoses, vii, 288

Æsop's Fables (ē' sop) are traditionally ascribed to Æsop, a deformed Phrygian slave of the 6th century B C , but many of them are far older, some having been discovered on Egyptian papyri of 800 or 1,000 years earlier.

Babirus, probably an Italian, compiled a collection of 137 of the fables in choliambic verse about A D 230, and this version was for long used in the mediæval schools

Pilpay (*q v*) has been called the Æsop of India.

Aetion (ē' ti òn) in Spenser's *Colin Clout's Come Home Again* typifies Michael Drayton, the poet

Aetites (ā ē ti' tēz) (Gr *aetos*, an eagle) Eagle-stones hollow stones composed of several crusts, having a loose stone within, which were supposed at one time to be found in eagles' nests, to which medicinal virtues were attributed, and which were supposed to have the property of detecting theft *See* Pliny x 4, and xxx, 44, also Lyly's *Euphues* (1578)—

The precious stone Aetites which is found in the filthy nests of the eagle

Ætolian Hero, The (ē tō' li an) Diomede, who was king of Ætolia *Ovid*

Afreet, Afrit (āf' rēt) In Mohammedan mythology the most powerful but one (Marids) of the five classes of Jinn, or devils They are of gigantic stature, very malicious, and inspire great dread Solomon, we are told, once tamed an Afreet, and made it submissive to his will

Africa. *Teneo te, Africa.* When Cæsar landed at Adrumetum, in Africa, he tripped and fell—a bad omen, but, with wonderful presence of mind, he pretended that he had done so intentionally, and kissing the soil, exclaimed, "Thus do I take possession of thee, O Africa" The story is told also of Scipio, and of Cæsar again at his landing in Britain, and of others in similar circumstances

Africa semper aliquid novi affert "Africa is always producing some novelty " A Greek proverb quoted (in Latin) by Pliny, in allusion to the ancient belief that Africa abounded in strange monsters

African Sisters, The. The Hesperides (*q v*), who lived in Africa

Afridi (ā frē' di) A Pathan tribe of the Indo-Afghan frontier against whom the British sent several punitive expeditions in the late 19th century

After-cast An obsolete expression for something done too late, literally, a throw of the dice after the game is ended

Ever he playeth an after-cast
Of all that he shall say or do.
GOWER

After-clap. A catastrophe or misfortune after an affair is supposed to be over, as in thunderstorms one may sometimes hear a "clap" after the rain subsides, and the clouds break

What plaguy mischief and mishaps
Do dog him still with after-claps
BUTLER *Hudibras*, Pt i, 3

After-guard. The men whose duty is to tend the gear at the after part of a ship The expression is also used for the officers, who have their quarters aft

After me the deluge. *See* APRÈS MOI LE DELUGE

Aft-meal. An extra meal; a meal taken after and in addition to the ordinary meals
> At aft-meals who shall pay for the wine?
> THYNNE *Debate* (c 1608)

Agag (ā' găg), in Dryden's *Absalom and Achitophel*, is Sir Edmondbury Godfrey, the magistrate before whom Titus Oates made his declaration, and who was afterwards found barbarously murdered in a ditch near Primrose Hill. Agag was hewed to pieces by Samuel.
> And Corah [Titus Oates] might for Agag's murder call
> In terms as coarse as Samuel used to Saul
> I, 675-6

The name is usually associated with the Biblical phrase, "And Agag came to him [Samuel] delicately" (1 *Sam* xv, 32).

Agamemnon (ăg a mem' non) In Greek legend, the King of Mycenæ, son of Atreus, and leader of the Greeks at the siege of Troy.
> Goodly Agamemnon
> The glorie of the stock of Tantalus,
> And famous light of all the Greekish hosts,
> Under whose conduct most victorious,
> The *Dorick* flames consumed the *Iliack* posts
> SPENSER· *Virgil's Gnat.*

His *brother* was Menelaos
His *daughters* were Iphigenia, Electra, Iphianassa, and Chrysothemis (*Sophocles*)
He was *grandson* of Pelops
He was *killed* in a bath by his wife Clytemnestra, after his return from Troy
His *son* was Orestes, who slew his mother for murdering his father, and was called Agamemnonides
His *wife* was Clytemnestra, who lived in adultery with Egistheus At Troy he fell in love with Cassandra, a daughter of King Priam

Vixere fortes ante Agamemnona, a quotation from Horace (*Od* IV, ix), paraphrased by Byron in *Don Juan* (I, v).
> Brave men were living before Agamemnon
> And since, exceeding valorous and sage,
> A good deal like him too, though quite the same none,
> But then they shone not on the poet's page,
> And so have been forgotten

Aganippe (ăg a nip' i) In Greek legend a fountain of Bœotia at the foot of Mount Helicon, dedicated to the Muses, because it had the virtue of imparting poetic inspiration From this fountain the Muses are sometimes called Aganippides

Agape (ăg' á pi). A love-feast (Gr *agape*, love) The early Christians held a love-feast before or after communion when contributions were made for the poor. In course of time they became a scandal, and were condemned at the Council of Carthage, 397. The name is also given by Spenser to the fairy mother of Priamond, Diamond, Triamond, and Cambina (*Faerie Queene*, IV, ii, 41 ff)

Agapemone (ăg a pem' ō ni) An association of men and women followers of Henry James Prince (1811-1899), who founded a sect in the 60s of last century, holding the theory that the time of prayer was past and the time of grace come They lived on a common fund at an Agapemone, or Abode of Love, at Spaxton, Somersetshire, and were constantly in trouble with the authorities In the early years of the present century the "Agapemonites" again attracted attention by the claims of one Smyth Piggott to be Christ

Agapetæ (ăg a pē' tē) (Gr beloved) A group of 3rd-century ascetic women who, under vows of virginity, contracted spiritual marriage with the monks and attended to their wants Owing to the scandals occasioned the custom was condemned by St Jerome and suppressed by various Councils

Agate (ăg' at) So called, says Pliny (xxxvii, 10), from Achates or Gagates, a river in Sicily, near which it is found in abundance
> These, these are they, if we consider well,
> That saphirs and the diamonds doe excell,
> The pearle, the emerauld, and the turkesse bleu,
> The sanguine corrall, amber's golden hiew,
> The christall, jacinth, *achate*, ruby red
> TAYLOR *The Waterspout* (1630)

Agate is supposed to render a person invisible, and to turn the sword of foes against themselves
A very small person has been called an agate, from the old custom of carving the stone with diminutive figures for use as seals Shakespeare speaks of Queen Mab as no bigger than an agate-stone on the forefinger of an alderman
> I was never manned with an agate till now
> SHAKESPEARE. 2 *Henry IV*, i, 2

For the same reason the very small type between nonpareil and pearl, known in England as "ruby," was called agate in America

Agatha, St. (ăg' a tha), was tortured and martyred at Catania, in Sicily, during the Decian persecution of 251 She is sometimes represented in art with a pair of shears or pincers, and holding a salver on which are her breasts, these having been cut off Her feast day is 5 February

Agave (a gā' vi), named from Agave, daughter of Cadmus (*q v*), or "American aloe," a Mexican plant, naturalized in many parts of Europe, and fabled by English gardeners to bloom only once in a hundred years It was introduced into Spain in 1561, and is used in Mexico, Switzerland, Italy, and elsewhere for fences The Mohammedans of Egypt regard it as a charm and religious symbol, and pilgrims to Mecca hang a leaf of it over their door as a sign of their pilgrimage and as a charm against evil spirits

Agdistes (ăg dis' tēz) The name is that of a Phrygian deity connected with the symbolic worship of the powers of Nature and by some identified with Cybele He was hermaphrodite, and sprang from the stone Agdus, parts of which were taken by Deucalion and Pyrrha to cast over their shoulders for repeopling the world after the flood

Age. A word used of a long but more or less indefinite period of history, human and pre-human, distinguished by certain real or mythical characteristics and usually named from these characteristics or from persons connected with them, as the *Golden Age* (*q v*), the *Middle Ages*, the *Dark Ages* (*qq v.*), the *Age of the Antonines* (from Antoninus Pius, 138, to Marcus Aurelius, 180), the *Prehistoric Age*, etc   Thus, Hallam calls the 9th century the *Age of the Bishops*, and the 12th, the *Age of the Popes*

Varro (*Fragments*, p 219, Scaliger's edition, 1623) recognizes three ages   From the beginning of mankind to the Deluge, a time wholly unknown.   From the Deluge to the First Olympiad, called the mythical period   From the first Olympiad to the present time, called the historic period

Shakespeare's passage on the seven ages of man (*As You Like It*, ii, 7) is well known, and Titian symbolized the three ages of man thus An infant in a cradle   A shepherd playing a flute   An old man meditating on two skulls

According to Lucretius also there are three ages, distinguished by the materials employed in implements (v. 1282), viz   *The age of stone*, when celts or implements of stone were employed   *The age of bronze*, when implements were made of copper or brass   *The age of iron*, when implements were made of iron, as at present.

The term *Stone Age* as now used includes the *Eolithic*, *Palæolithic*, and *Neolithic Ages* (*qq v*)

Hesiod names five ages, viz.   The *Golden* or patriarchal, under the care of Saturn   The *Silver* or voluptuous, under the care of Jupiter   The *Brazen* or warlike, under the care of Neptune   The *Heroic* or renaissant, under the care of Mars.   The *Iron* or present, under the care of Pluto.

Age of Animals.   An old Celtic rhyme, put into modern English, says —

> Thrice the age of a dog is that of a horse,
> Thrice the age of a horse is that of a man,
> Thrice the age of a man is that of a deer,
> Thrice the age of a deer is that of an eagle

Age of Consent.   This is the age at which a girl's consent is valid; beneath that age to have carnal knowledge of her is a criminal offence   In English and Scottish law the age of consent is 16.

Age of Discretion.   In English law a subject is deemed capable of using his discretion at the age of 14.

Canonical Age.   Ecclesiastical law enjoins that the obligation of fasting begins at the age of 21, profession of religious vows after the age of 16, a bishop must have completed his 30th year.

Age hoc (a' je hok)   "Attend to this"   In sacrifice the Roman crier perpetually repeated these words to arouse attention   In the Common Prayer Book the attention of the congregation is frequently aroused by the exhortation, "Let us pray," though nearly the whole service is that of prayer

Agelasta (ăj e lǎs' tà) (Gr. joyless).   The stone on which Ceres rested when worn down by fatigue in searching for her daughter, Persephone.

Agenor (ă jen' or).   A son of Neptune. and founder of a nation in Phœnicia   His descendants, Cadmus, Perseus, Europa, etc , are known as the Agenorides.

Agent.   Is man a free agent?   This is a question of theology, which has long been mooted.   The point is this.   If God foreordains all our actions, they must take place as he foreordains them, and man acts as a watch or clock, but if, on the other hand, man is responsible for his actions, he must be free to act as his inclination leads him.   Those who hold the former view are called *necessitarians*, those who hold the latter, *libertarians*

Aggie Westons, Aggies.   The Royal Sailors' Rest Homes in Portsmouth, Devonport, and Chatham, founded by Dame Agnes E. Weston (1840-1918)

Agglutinate Language.   A language the chief characteristic of which is that its words are simple or root words combined into compounds, without loss of original meaning. Thus, *inkstand* and *comeatable* are agglutinate words   Agglutination is a feature of most Turanian languages   it implies that the root words are *glued* together to form other words, and may be "unglued" so as to leave the roots distinct

Agio (a' jō) (Ital ease, convenience)   A commercial term denoting the percentage of charge made for the exchange of paper money into cash

Agis (ā' jis)   King of Sparta (338-330 B C). He tried to deliver Greece from the Macedonian yoke and was slain in the attempt

> The generous victim to that vain attempt
> To save a rotten state—Agis, who saw
> Even Sparta's self to servile avarice sink
>   THOMSON   *Winter*, 488-9

Agist (a jist')   To take in cattle to graze at a certain sum   The pasturage of these beasts is called *agistment*.   The words are from the French *agister* (to lie down).

Aglaia (a glī' a).   One of the three Graces (*see* GRACES)

Aglaonice (ăg lă ō nī' si), the Thessalian, being able to calculate eclipses, pretended to have the moon under her command, and to be able when she chose to draw it from heaven Her secret being found out, her vaunting became a laughing-stock, and gave birth to the Greek proverb cast at braggarts, "Yes, as the Moon obeys Aglaonice"

Agnes.   A sort of female "Verdant Green" (*q v*), who is so unsophisticated that she does not even know what love means· from a character in Molière's *L'Ecole des Femmes*

Agnes, St., was martyred in the Diocletian persecution (about 303) at the age of 13   She was tied to a stake, but the fire went out, and Aspasius, set to watch the martyrdom, drew his sword, and cut off her head   St Agnes is the patron of young virgins   She is commemorated on January 21st.   Upon St Agnes's night, says Aubrey in his *Miscellany*, though he should have said St Agnes' Eve, you take a row of pins, and pull out every one, one after another   Saying a paternoster, stick a pin in your sleeve, and you will dream of him or her you shall marry; and in Keats's *The Eve of St Agnes*, we are told—

> how, upon St Agnes' Eve,
> Young virgins might have visions of delight,
> And soft adorings from their loves receive
> Upon the honey'd middle of the night,
> If ceremonies due they did aright,
> As, supperless to bed they must retire

Agnoïtes (ăg' nŏ ïtz) (Gr. *a*, not, *gignoskein*, to know)

(1) Certain heretics in the 4th century who maintained that God had no certain knowledge of the future God did *not know* everything

(2) Another sect, in the 6th century, who maintained that Christ did not know the time of the day of judgment.

Agnostic (Gr *a*, not; *gignoskein*, to know) A term coined by Prof. Huxley in 1869 (with allusion to St Paul's mention of an altar to "the Unknown God") to indicate the mental attitude of those who withhold their assent from whatever is incapable of proof, such as an unseen world, a First Cause, etc. Agnostics neither dogmatically accept nor reject such matters, but simply say *Agnosco*—I do not know—they are not capable of proof. *Cp.* THEIST

Agnus Bell. *See* AGNUS DEI.

Agnus-castus. *See* VITEX.

Agnus Dei (ăg'n us dē' ĭ, dā' ē). A cake of wax or dough stamped with the figure of a lamb supporting the banner of the Cross, and distributed by the Pope on the Sunday after Easter. This is a relic of the ancient custom of collecting and distributing to the worshippers the wax of the Paschal candle, which was stamped with the lamb The part of the Mass and English communion service beginning with the words *Agnus Dei, qui tolles peccata mundi* (O Lamb of God, that takest away the sins of the world), is also known as the *Agnus Dei* In Catholic services it is introduced by the ringing of the *Agnus bell*

Agog (à gog'). **He is all agog,** in nervous anxiety, on the *qui vive* The word is connected with the Old French phrase *en gogues*, meaning "in mirth" the origin of O F *gogue* and Norman *goguer*, to be mirthful, is unknown

Agonistes (ă gon is' tēz) This word in *Samson Agonistes* (the title of Milton's drama) is Greek for "champion," so the title means simply "Samson the Champion" *Cp* AGONY

Agonistics (ă gon is' tiks) A fanatical sect of peripatetic ascetics, adherents to the Donatist schismatics of the early 4th century. They gave themselves this name (meaning "Champions," or "Soldiers," of the Cross), the Catholics called them the *Circumcelliones*, from their wandering about among the houses of the peasants (*circum cellas*)

Agony, meaning great pain or anguish, is derived through French from the Greek word *agonia*, from *agon*, which meant first "an assembly," then "an arena for contests," and hence the "contest" itself, so *agonia*, meaning first a struggle for mastery in the games, came to be used for any struggle, and hence for mental struggle or anguish

Agony column. A column in a newspaper containing advertisements of missing relatives and friends

Agrarian Law (a grâr' i án) (Lat *ager*, land) In Roman history, a law regulating landed property or the division of conquered territory, hence, a law for making land the common property of a nation, and not the particular property of individuals. In a modified form, a redistribution of land, giving to each citizen a portion

Ague, from Lat *acuta*, sharp, is really an adjective, as in French *fièvre aigue*. English folklore gives a number of curious charms for curing ague, and there was an old superstition that if the fourth book of the *Iliad* was laid under the head of a patient it would cure him at once This book tells how Pandarus wounds Menelaus, and contains the cure of Menelaus by Machaon, "a son of Æsculapius "

Aguecheek Sir Andrew Aguecheek, a straight-haired country squire, stupid even to silliness, self-conceited, living to eat, and wholly unacquainted with the world of fashion The character is in Shakespeare's *Twelfth Night.*

Agur's Wish (ā' gerz) (*Prov* xxx, 8) "Give me neither poverty nor riches "

Ahasuerus (a hăz ū ēr' us) Under this name the Emperor Xerxes (486-465 B C) appears in the biblical books of Ezra and Esther The Ahasuerus of Daniel has not been identified. This is also the name given to the Wandering Jew (*q v.*).

Ahithophel (a hith' ŏ fel) A treacherous friend and adviser. Ahithophel was David's counsellor, but joined Absalom in revolt, and advised him ' like the oracle of God" (2 *Sam* xvi, 20-23) *See* ACHITOPHEL

Ahmed, **Prince** (a' med), in the *Arabian Nights*, is noted for the tent given him by the fairy Paribanou, which would cover a whole army, but might be carried in one's pocket; and for the apple of Samarcand, which would cure all diseases. The qualities ascribed to the magic tent are the common property of many legends and romances. *See* CARPET, and SKIDHBLADHNIR

Aholah and **Aholibah** (a hō' la, a hō lī' ba) [*Ezek* xxiii]. Personifications of prostitution. Used by the prophet to signify religious adultery or running after false faiths. These Hebrew names signify "she in whom are tents," and have reference to the worship at the high places.

Ahriman (a' ri man) In the dual system of Zoroaster, the spiritual enemy of mankind, also called *Angra Mainyu*, and *Druj* (deceit) He has existed since the beginning of the world, and is in eternal conflict with Ahura Mazda, or Ormuzd (*q v*)

Their evil principle, the demon Ahriman, might be represented as the rival or as the creature of The God of Light.

GIBBON. *Decline and Fall*, ch. li.

Ahura Mazda. *See* ORMUZD

Aide toi et le Ciel t'aidera (ād twä ā lě sě el tā de ra'). A line from La Fontaine (vi, 18), meaning "God will help those who help themselves," taken as the motto of a French political society, established in 1824 The society intended to induce the middle classes to resist the Government, it aided in bringing about the Revolution of 1830, and was dissolved in 1832. Guizot was at one time its president, and *Le Globe* and *Le National* its organs

Aigrette (ā' gret) French for the Egret, or Lesser White Heron, the beautiful crest of which has been worn as a hat decoration, as a tuft for military helmets, etc The French call any jewelled or feathery head-ornament an *aigrette.*

Aim, to give. A term in archery, meaning to *give* the archers information how near their arrows fall to the mark *aimed at,* hence, to give anybody inside information

> But, gentle people, give me aim awhile,
> For nature puts me to a heavy task
> SHAKESPEARE· *Titus Andronicus,* v, 3

To cry aim. To applaud, encourage In archery it was customary to appoint certain persons to cry *"Aim !"* for the sake of encouraging those who were about to shoot

> All my neighbours shall cry aim
> SHAKESPEARE *Merry Wives of Windsor,* iii, 2

Aim-crier. An abettor, one who encourages In archery, the person employed to "cry aim"

> Thou smiling aim-crier at princess' fall
> GERVAIS MARKHAM *English Arcadia* (1638)

Air. Held by Anaxagoras to be the primary form of matter, and given by Aristotle as one of the four elements *See* ELEMENT.

The air of the court, the air of gentility · a good air (manner, deportment) means the pervading habit, hence, *to give oneself airs*—to assume in manner, appearance, and tone, a superiority to which one has no claim.
The plural is essential in this case, air, in the singular is generally complimentary, but in the plural conveys censure In Italian, we find the phrase, *Si da delle arie*

Air (in music) is that melody which predominates and gives its character to the piece.

Hot air *See* HOT

To air one's opinion. To state opinions openly, to give air to one's opinions

Air-brained. A mis-spelling of hare-brained (*q v*)

Air-line. A direct line, taken—as a crow flies—through the air *Cp* BEE-LINE

Airship. Formerly an epithet applied to any kind of balloon, but now restricted to a large aerial vehicle, depending for flotation upon gases contained in a balloon or in a series of enclosed ballonets, and, instead of being at the mercy of the winds, capable of being driven along and steered by mechanical means.

Aisle. The north and south wings of a church, from the Lat , *ala* (*axilla, ascella*), through the French, *aile,* a wing The intrusive "s" did not take root till the middle of the 18th century, and is probably due to a confusion with "isle." In some church documents the aisles are called *alleys* (walks), the choir of Lincoln Cathedral used to be called the "Chanters' alley", and Olden tells us that when he came to be churchwarden, in 1638, he made the Puritans "come up the middle alley on their knees to the raile "

Aitch-bone. Corruption of "naitch-bone," *i e* the haunch-bone (Lat *nates,* a haunch or buttock) For other instances of the coalescence of the "n" of "an" with an initial vowel (or the coalescence of the "n" with the article), *see* APRON NEWT

Ajax (ā jāks) (1) *The Greater* The most famous hero of the Trojan War after Achilles, king of Salamis, a man of giant stature, daring, and self-confident, son of Telamon When the armour of Hector was awarded to Ulysses instead of to himself, he turned mad from vexation and stabbed himself —Homer and later poets
(2) *The Less* Son of Oileus, King of Locris, in Greece The night Troy was taken, he offered violence to Cassandra, the prophetic daughter of Priam, in consequence of which his ship was driven on a rock, and he perished at sea —Homer and later poets

Akbar (āk' bar) An Arabic title, meaning ' Very Great " Akbar Khan, the "very great Khan," is applied especially to the great Mogul emperor in India who reigned 1556-1605 His tomb at Secundra, a few miles from Agra, is one of the wonders of the East.

Alabama (ā la ba' ma) The name of this state of the U S A is the Indian name of a river in the state, the meaning of which is "here we rest "

Alabama claims were made by the U S A. against Great Britain for losses caused during the Civil War by Confederate vessels—the chief being the *Alabama*—fitted out in or supplied from British ports The matter was referred to an international tribunal which, in 1871, awarded the U S A $15,500,000

Alabaster. A stone of great purity and whiteness, used for ornaments The name is said by Pliny (*Nat Hist ,* xxxvi, 8) to be from an Egyptian town, Alabastron, but nothing is known of this town, nor of the ultimate origin of the Greek word

Aladdin, (a lăd' in) in the *Arabian Nights,* obtains a magic lamp, and has a splendid palace built by the genie of the lamp. He marries the daughter of the sultan of China, loses his lamp, and his palace is transported to Africa.

Aladdin's lamp. The source of wealth and good fortune After Aladdin came to his wealth and was married, he suffered his lamp to hang up and get rusty

Aladdin's ring, given him by the African magician, was a "preservative against every evil "

To finish Aladdin's window—*i e* to attempt to complete something begun by a great genius, but left imperfect The palace built by the genie of the lamp had twenty-four windows, all but one being set in frames of precious stones, the last was left for the sultan to finish, but after exhausting his treasures, the sultan was obliged to abandon the task as hopeless

Alamo (al' ăm o) American cottonwood tree In 1718 Franciscan monks founded the Mission of San Antonio de Valero at San Antonio, Texas It was commonly called the Alamo Mission since it stood in a grove of cottonwood trees By 1793 it was no longer a mission but the buildings were sometimes used as a fort In 1806 a Texan garrison of 180 was besieged overpowered and slaughtered by 4000 Mexicans under Santa Anna In the subsequent campaign in which the Texans, under Sam Houston, defeated the Mexicans and captured Santa Anna, "remember the Alamo" became the Texan war cry. The buildings are now a National Monument.

Alans. Large dogs, of various species, used for hunting They were introduced to Britain from Spain, whither they are said to have been brought by the Alani, a Caucasian tribe which invaded Western Europe in the 4th century They were used in war as well as for hunting, and Chaucer, in his *Knight's Tale*, describes Lycurgus on his throne, guarded by white "alauntes, twenty or mo, as grete as any steer," wearing muzzles and golden collars Scott, in the *Talisman* (ch vi), speaks of three—

Skins of animals slain in the chase were stretched on the ground and upon a heap of these lay three *alans*, as they were called, *i e* wolf greyhounds of the largest size

Al Araf (al ä' räf) (Arab the partition, from *'arafa*, to divide) A region, according to the Koran, between Paradise and Jahannam (hell), for those who are neither morally good nor bad, such as infants, lunatics, and idiots Others regard it as a place where those whose good and evil deeds were about equally balanced can await their ultimate admission to heaven, a kind of "limbo" (*q v*).

Alarum Bell. "Alarum" is a variant of "alarm," produced by rolling the "r" in prolonging the final syllable In feudal times a 'larum bell was rung in the castle in times of danger to summon the retainers to arms

Awake! awake!
Ring the alarum bell! Murder and treason!
SHAKESPEARE: *Macbeth*, ii, 3

The word is now used only (except sometimes in poetry) for the peal or chime of a warning bell or clock, or the mechanism producing it.

Alasnam (a läs' năm) In the *Arabian Nights* Alasnam had eight diamond statues, but was required to find a ninth more precious still, to fill the vacant pedestal The prize was found in the woman who became his wife, at once the most beautiful and the most perfect of her race.

Alasnam's mirror. The "touchstone of virtue," given to Alasnam by one of the Genii. If he looked in this mirror and it

remained unsullied so would the maiden he had in mind, if it clouded, she would prove faithless

Alastor (a läs' tor). The evil genius of a house; a Nemesis Cicero says "Who meditated killing himself that he might become the *Alastor* of Augustus, whom he hated" Shelley has a poem entitled *Alastor, or The Spirit of Solitude* The word is Greek (*alastor*, the avenging god, a title applied to Zeus), the Romans had their Jupiter Vindex, and we read in the Bible, "Vengeance is mine, I will repay, saith the Lord" (*Rom* xii, 19)

Alauda. A Roman legion raised by Julius Cæsar in Gaul, and so called because they carried a *lark's tuft* on the top of their helmets

Alawy (a la' wi) The Nile is so called by the Abyssinians The word means "the giant"

Alb (älb) (Lat *albus*, white) A long white vestment worn by priests under the chasuble and over the cassock when saying Mass. It is emblematical of purity and continence

Alban, St. (ôl' ban), like St Denis and many other saints, is sometimes represented as carrying his head in his hands. His attributes are a sword and a crown.

SS Aphroditus, Aventine, Desiderius, Chrysolius, Hilarian, Leo, Lucanus, Lucian, Proba, Solangia, and several other martyrs, are represented in the same way it is the conventional symbol adopted by the artist to show that the martyr met death by beheading

Albano Stone or Peperino, used by the Romans in building, a volcanic tufa quarried at Monte Albano

Albany, Albainn, or **Albin.** An ancient name applied to the northern part of Scotland, called by the Romans "Caledonia," and inhabited by the Picts From Celtic *alp* or *ailpe*, a rock or cliff The name Albany survives in Breadalbane, the hilly country of Albainn, *i e* western Perthshire

In Spenser's *Faerie Queene* (II, x, 14, etc) northern Britain is called *Albania*

Also the name of a block of residential chambers running between Piccadilly and Burlington Gardens in London, designed by Sir William Chambers about 1770 with additions by Henry Holland, 1804. Many famous men of letters have resided there, including Byron

Albatross. The largest of web-footed birds, called by sailors the *Cape Sheep*, from its frequenting the Cape of Good Hope. Many fables are told of the albatross, it is said to sleep in the air, because its flight is a gliding without any apparent motion of its long wings, and sailors say that it is fatal to shoot one. *See also* ANCIENT MARINER

Alberich. The all-powerful king of the dwarfs in Scandinavian mythology In Wagner's version of the *Nibelungenlied* he appears as a hideous gnome and steals the magic gold (*Das Rheingold*) guarded by the Rhine Maidens Later he is captured by the gods, and is forced to give up all he has in return for his freedom.

Albert, An. A watch chain across the waistcoat from one pocket to another or to a buttonhole So called from Albert, Prince Consort. When he went to Birmingham, in 1849, he was presented by the jewellers of the town with such a chain, and the fashion took the public fancy

Albigenses (ăl bı jen´ sēs). A common name for a number of anti-sacerdotal sects in southern France during the 13th century, so called from the Albigeois, inhabitants of the district which now is the department of the Tarn, the capital of which was Albi, Languedoc, where their persecution began, under Innocent III in 1208.

Albin. *See* ALBANY.

Albino (al bē nō) (Lat *albus*, white). A term originally applied by the Portuguese to those Negroes who were mottled with white spots; but now to persons who, owing to the congenital absence of colouring pigment, are born with red eyes and white hair and skin. The term is also applied to beasts and plants, and even, occasionally, in a purely figurative way: thus, Oliver Wendell Holmes, in the *Autocrat of the Breakfast Table* (ch vıiı), speaks of Kirke White as one of the "sweet Albino poets," whose "plaintive song" he admires; apparently implying some deficiency of virility, and possibly playing upon the name.

Albion. An ancient and poetical name for Great Britain: probably from the white (Lat *albus*) that face Gaul, but possibly from the Celtic *alp*, *ailp* (*see* ALBANY), a rock, cliff, mountain "Albion" or "Albany" may have been the Celtic name of all Great Britain, but was subsequently restricted to Scotland, and then to the Highlands of Scotland

Legend gives various origins for the name One derivation is from a giant son of Neptune, named Albion, who discovered the country and ruled over it for forty-four years According to another story the fifty daughters of the king of Syria, the eldest of whom was named Albia, were all married on the same day and all murdered their husbands on the wedding-night. As punishment they were packed into a ship and set adrift, eventually reaching this western isle where they went ashore and duly married natives, "a lawless crew of devils."

In *Polyolbion* Michael Drayton says that Albion came from Rome and was the first Christian martyr in Britain

Although the phrase **Perfide Albion** is attributed to Napoleon, the sentiment is much older, for Bossuet (1627-1704) wrote, "L'Angleterre, ah¹ la perfide Angleterre "

Al Borak. *See* BORAK.

Album. A blank book for photographs, stamps, autographs, miscellaneous jottings, scraps, and so on. The Romans applied the word to certain tables overlaid with gypsum, on which were inscribed the annals of the chief priests, the edicts of the prætors, and rules relating to civil matters. In the Middle Ages, "album" was the general name of a register or list; so called from being kept

either on a white (*albus*) board with black letters, or on a black board with white letters.

Alcaic Verse (ăl kā´ ik) or *Alcaics*. A Greek lyrical metre, so called from *Alcæos*, a lyric poet, who is said to have invented it Alcaic measure is little more than a curiosity in English poetry, probably the best example is Tennyson's —

O migh | ty-mouthed | in | ventor of | harmonies,
O skilled | to sing | of | Time or E | ternitv
   God-gift | ed or | gan-voice | of Eng | land,
    Milton, a | name to re | sound for | ages

Alcantara, Order of (ăl kăn´ ta rä) A military and religious order instituted in 1213 (on the foundation of the earlier order of San Juan del Pereyro, which had been created about 1155 to fight the Moors) by Alfonso IX, King of Castile, to commemorate the taking of Alcantara from the Moors In 1835 the Order, which had been under the Benedictine rule, ceased to exist as a religious body, but it remained as a civil and military order under the Crown

Alceste (ăl sest´). The hero of Molière's *Misanthrope* He is not unlike Shakespeare's character of Timon, and was taken by Wycherley for the model of his Manly (*q* ν).

Alchemilla (ăl ke mil´ a) A genus of plants of the rose family; so called because alchemists collected the dew of its leaves for their operations Also called "Lady's Mantle," from the Virgin Mary, to whom the plant was dedicated

Alchemy (ăl´ ke mı) The derivation of this word is obscure the *al* is the Arabic article, *the*, and *kimia* the Arabic form of Greek *chemeia*, which seems to have meant Egyptian art, hence "the art of the Egyptians." Its main objects were the transmutation of baser metals into gold, the universal solvent (alkahest, *q.v.*), the panacea (*q* ν), and the elixir of life.

Alcimedon (ăl sim´ ė don) A generic name for a first-rate carver in wood

         Pocula ponam
Fagina, cœlatum divini opus Alcimedontis
            VIRGIL *Eclogue*, iii, 36.

Alcina (ăl sē´ na) The personification of carnal pleasure in *Orlando Furioso*, the *Circe* of fable.

Alcinoo poma dare (ăl sın´ ō ō pō´ ma da´ re (to give apples to Alcinous) To carry coals to Newcastle The gardens of Alcinous, the legendary king of the Phæacians on the island of Scheria, by whom Odysseus was entertained, were famous for their fruits. Thus, Milton speaks of Eden as a

Spot more delicious than those gardens feigned
Or of revived Adonis, or renowned
Alcinous, host of old Laertes' son
             Paradise Lost, ix, 4, 9

Alcion. *See* GIANTS OF MYTHOLOGY

Alcmena (ălk mē´ na) In Greek mythology, daughter of Electryon, king of Mycenæ, wife of Amphitryon, and mother (by Zeus) of Hercules The legend is that at the conception of Hercules Zeus, for additional pleasure with Alcmena, made the night the length of three ordinary nights.

Alcofribas Nasier (ăl ko' fre băs nă' syer). The anagrammatic pseudonym of François Rabelais, adopted as the name of the author of his first two books, *Gargantua* and *Pantagruel*.

Alcuith, a place mentioned by the Venerable Bede, now Dumbarton

Aldebaran (ăl deb' a răn) (Arab *al*, the, *davaran*, the follower, because its rising follows that of the Pleiades) A red star of the first magnitude, α Tauri, one of the brightest in the heavens It forms the bull's eye in the constellation Taurus

Alderman. A senior or elder· now applied to certain magistrates in corporate towns In the City of London aldermen were first appointed by a charter of Henry III in 1242; there are 25 (or, counting the Lord Mayor, or chief magistrate, 26), and they are elected for life, one for each ward Of the larger cities of England: Birmingham has 34 aldermen; Liverpool, 39; Manchester, 36, Sheffield, 25, Leeds, 26, and Bristol, 28

Aldgate Pump, a draught on. A worthless cheque or bill The pun is on the word draught, which may mean either an order on a bank or a sup of liquor.

Aldiborontephoscophornio (ăl' di bō ron' ti fos' ko fōr 'ni ō) A courtier in Henry Carey's burlesque, *Chrononhotonthologos* (1734)

Aldine Editions. Editions of the Greek and Latin classics, published and printed under the superintendence of Aldo Manuzio, his father-in-law Andrea of Asolo, and his son Paolo, from 1490 to 1597, most of them are in small octavo, and all are noted for their accuracy. The father invented the type called *italics*, once called *Aldine*, and first used in printing *Virgil*, 1501.

Ale is the Anglo-Saxon *ealu*, connected with the Scandinavian *ol*, and Lithuanian *alus* Beer is the Anglo-Saxon *beor* (M E , *bere*), connected with the German *bier* and Icelandic *bjorr* A beverage made from barley is mentioned by Tacitus and even Herodotus Hops were introduced from Holland and used for brewing about 1524, but their use was prohibited by Act of Parliament in 1528—a prohibition which soon fell into disuse Ale is made from pale malt, whence its light colour, porter and stout from malt more highly dried The word *beer* is of general application, and in many parts of England it includes ale, porter, and stout In some parts *ale* is used for the stronger malt liquors and *beer* for the weaker, while in others the terms are reversed Called ale among men · but by the gods called beer
The Alvismal (10th-cent *Scandinavian poem*)
See also CHURCH-ALE.

Aleberry. A corruption of ale-bree A drink made of hot ale, spice, sugar, and toast Burns speaks of the barley-bree (A S *briw*, broth)
Cause an aleberry to be made for her, and put into it powder of camphor —*The Pathway to Health*

Ale-dagger. A dagger used in self-defence in alehouse brawls
He that drinkes with cutters must not be without his ale-dagger —*Pappe with a Hatchet* (1589)

Ale-draper. The keeper of an ale-house *Ale-drapery*, the selling of ale, etc
No other occupation have I but to be an ale-draper —CHETTLE *Kind-harts' Dreame* (1592)

Ale-knight. A tippler, a sot

Ale-silver. Formerly, the annual fee paid to the Lord Mayor for the privilege of selling ale within the City of London.

Ale-stake. The pole set up before alehouses by way of sign, often surmounted by a bush or garland Thus, Chaucer says of the Somnour —
A garland had he set upon his head
As great as it were for an ale-stake
Cant Tales, Prol , 666

Ale-wife. The landlady of an alehouse In America a fish of the herring kind, only rather larger, is known as the *ale-wife* Some think it is a corruption of a North American Indian name, *aloofe*, and some of the French *alose*, a shad

Alecto (a lek' tō) In classical mythology, one of the three Furies (*q v*), her head was covered with snakes
Then like Alecto, terrible to view,
Or like Medusa, the Circassian grew
HOOLE. *Jerusalem Delivered*, Bk. vi

Alectorian Stone (å lek tō' i an) (Gr *alector*, a cock) A stone, fabled to be of talismanic power, found in the stomach of cocks Those who possess it are strong, brave, and wealthy Milo of Crotona owed his strength to this talisman As a philtre it has the power of preventing thirst or of assuaging it.

Alectryomancy (å lek tri ō măn' si) Divination by a cock Draw a circle, and write in succession round it the letters of the alphabet, on each of which lay a grain of corn. Then put a cock in the centre of the circle, and watch what grains he eats The letters will prognosticate the answer Libanus and Jamblicus thus discovered who was to succeed the emperor Valens. The cock ate the grains over the letters t, h, e, o, d = Theod[orus]

Alexander and the Robber. The story is that the pirate Diomedes, having been captured and brought before Alexander, was asked how he dared to molest the seas "How darest *thou* molest the earth?'' was the reply. "Because I am the master only of a single galley I am termed a robber, but you who oppress the world with huge squadrons are called a king." Alexander was so struck by this reasoning that he made Diomedes rich, a prince, and a dispenser of justice See the *Gesta Romanorum*, cxlvi

You are thinking of Parmenio and I of Alexander—*i e*, you are thinking of what you ought to receive, and I what I ought to give; you are thinking of those castigated or rewarded, but I of my position, and what reward is consistent with my rank. The allusion is to the tale that Alexander said to Parmenio, "I consider not what Parmenio should receive, but what Alexander should give "

Only two Alexanders Alexander said, " There are but two Alexanders—the invincible son of Philip, and the inimitable painting of the hero by Apelles ''

The continence of Alexander. Having gained the battle of Issus (333 B C) the family of Darius III fell into his hand, but he treated the women with the greatest decorum A eunuch, having escaped, reported this to Darius, and the king could not but admire such nobility in a rival   *See* CONTINENCE

Alexander. So Paris, son of Priam, was called by the shepherds who brought him up

Alexander of the North. Charles XII of Sweden (1682-1718), so called from his military achievements He was conquered at Pultowa (1709), by Peter the Great
Repressing here
The frantic Alexander of the North
THOMSON *Winter*

Alexander the Corrector   The self-assumed nickname of Alexander Cruden (1701-1770), compiler of the *Concordance of the Bible* After being, on more than one occasion, confined in a lunatic asylum he became a reader for the Press, and later developed a mania for going about constantly with a sponge to wipe out the licentious, coarse, and profane chalk scrawls which met his eye

Alexander's beard. A smooth chin, no beard at all   An Amazonian chin (*q v*)
I like this trustie glasse of Steele . .
Wherein I see a Sampson's grim regarde
Disgraced yet with Alexander's bearde
GASCOIGNE *The Steele Glas*

Alexandra Day. To celebrate the fiftieth year of her residence in England, Queen Alexandra (1844-1925) inaugurated a fund for the assistance of hospitals, convalescent homes, etc , to be raised by the sale of artificial wild roses made by the blind and cripples   On a day in June these are sold in the streets, the buyers wearing the roses as a sign of having contributed to the fund

Alexandra limp. In the 60s of last century Queen Alexandra (then Princess of Wales) had a slight accident which for a time caused her to walk with an almost imperceptible limp   In a spirit of servile imitation many of the women about the court adopted this method of walking, which hence became known as the "Alexandra limp."

Alexandrian. Anything from the East was so called by the old chroniclers and romancers, because Alexandria was the depot from which Eastern stores reached Europe
Reclined on Alexandrian carpets [*i e* Persian]
ROSE *Orlando Furioso*, x, 37

Alexandrian Codex   A Greek MS of the Scriptures written (probably in the 5th century) in uncials on parchment, which is supposed to have originated at Alexandria   In 1628 it was presented to Charles I by Cyril Sucar, patriarch of Constantinople, and in 1753 was placed in the British Museum   It contains the Septuagint version (except portions of the Psalms), a part of the New Testament, and the Epistles of Clemens Romanus

Alexandrian Library.   Founded by Ptolemy Soter, in Alexandria, in Egypt   The tale is that it was burnt and partly consumed in 391, but when the city fell into the hands of the calif Omar, in 642, the Arabs found books sufficient to "heat the baths of the city for six months "   It is said that it contained 700,000 volumes, and the reason given by the Mohammedan destroyer for the destruction of the library was that the books were unnecessary in any case, for all knowledge that was necessary to man was contained in the Koran, and that any knowledge contained in the library that was not in the Koran must be pernicious

Alexandrian School   An academy of learning founded about 310 B C by Ptolemy Soter, son of Lagus, and Demetrius of Phaleron, especially famous for its grammarians and mathematicians   Of the former the most noted are Aristarchus (*c* 220-145 B C), Eratosthenes (*c* 275-195 B.C), and Harpocration (A D 2nd century), and of its mathematicians, Claudius Ptolemæus (A D 2nd century) and Euclid (*c* 300 B C.), the former an astronomer, and the latter the geometer whose *Elements* were once very generally used in schools and colleges

Alexandrine. In *prosody*, an iambic or trochaic line of twelve syllables or six feet with, usually, a cæsura (break) at the sixth syllable   So called either from the 12th-century French metrical romance, *Alexander the Great* (commenced by Lambert-li-Cort and continued by Alexandre de Bernay), or from the old Castilian verse chronicle, *Poema de Alexandro Magno*, both of which are written in this metre   The final line of the Spenserian stanza is an Alexandrine
A needless Alexandrine ends the song,
Which, like a wounded snake,—drags its slow length along
POPE *Essay on Criticism*, ii, 356

Alexandrine Age. From about A D 323 to 640, when Alexandria, in Egypt, was the centre of science, philosophy, and literature.

Alexandrine Philosophy. A system of philosophy which flourished at Alexandria in the early centuries of the Christian era, characterized by its attempt to combine Christianity and Greek philosophy. It gave rise to Gnosticism and Neoplatonism

Alexandrite   A variety of chrysoberyl found in the mica-slate of the Urals   So named from Alexander II of Russia, on whose birthday it was discovered   The stone is green by natural and red by artificial light.

Alexis, St.   Patron saint of hermits and beggars   The story goes that he lived on his father's estate as a hermit till death, but was never recognized   It is given at length in the *Gesta Romanorum* (Tale xv)   His feast day is July 17th. He is represented in art with a pilgrim's habit and staff.   Sometimes he is drawn as if extended on a mat, with a letter in his hand, dying

Alfadir (al fa' der) (father of all)   In Scandinavian mythology, one of the epithets of Odin (*q v*)

Alfana.   *See* HORSE

Alfonsin, Alfonsine Fables   *See* ALPHONSIN, etc

Alfred the Great   (848?-900).   King of Wessex, father of the British Navy and leader of the opposition to the invading Danish armies In January 878 he was surprised and defeated at Chippenham, with the remains of his forces he withdrew to Athelney and continued his resistance. A legend having no basis in fact says that he fled from Chippenham to Athelney and took refuge in a peasant's hut, where the housewife, not recognizing him in his rags, put him to watching cakes baking by the fire He was so absorbed in his meditations that he allowed the cakes to burn and was scolded as an idle and useless wretch After his final victory he built a monastery at Athelney in celebration of and in thanksgiving for his resistance there In 1693, the beautiful Saxon ornament, bearing his name and known as *Alfred's Jewel*, was found at Athelney It is now in the Ashmolean Museum, Oxford

Alfred's scholars. When Alfred the Great set about the restoration of letters in England he founded a school and gathered around him learned men from all parts; these became known as "Alfred's scholars", the chief among them are Werfrith, Bishop of Worcester, Ethelstan and Werwulf, two Mercian priests, Plegmund (a Mercian), afterwards Archbishop of Canterbury, Asser, a Welshman, Grimbald, a French scholar from St. Omer, and John the Old Saxon

Algarsife (ăl′ gar sif). In Chaucer's unfinished *Squire's Tale*, son of Cambuscan, and brother of Camballo, who "won Theodora to wife "

> This noble king, this Tartre Cambuscan,
> Had two sones by Elfeta his wife,
> Of which the eldest sone highte Algarsife,
> That other was ycleped Camballo
> A doghter had this worthy king also
> That youngest was and highte Canace.

Hence the reference in Milton's *Il Penseroso* —

> Call him up that left half told
> The story of Cambuscan bold,
> Of Camball, and of Algarsife,
> And who had Canace to wife

Algebra is the Arabic *al jebr* (the equalization), "the supplementing and equalizing (process)", so called because the problems are solved by equations, and the equations are made by supplementary terms Fancifully identified with the Arabian chemist Gebir *See also* WHETSTONE OF WITTE

Alhambra (ăl hăm′ brà) The citadel and palace built at Granada by the Moorish kings in the 13th century The word is the Arabic *al-hamra*, or at full length *kal′-at al hamra* (the red castle)

Ali (a′ lē). Cousin and son-in-law of Mohammed, the beauty of whose eyes is with the Persians proverbial, in so much that the highest term they employ to express beauty is *Ayn Hali* (eyes of Ali)

Alias (ā′ li as) "You have as many aliases as Robin of Bagshot," said to one who passes under many names The phrase is from Gay's *Beggar's Opera·* Robin of Bagshot, one of Macheath's gang, was *alias* Gordon, *alias* Bluff Bob, *alias* Carbuncle, *alias* Bob Booty

Ali Baba (ă′ lē ba′ ba) The hero of a story in the *Arabian Nights Entertainments*, who sees a band of robbers enter a cavern by means of the magic password "Open Sesame " When they have gone away he enters the cave, loads his ass with treasure and returns home. The Forty Thieves discover that Ali Baba has learned their secret and resolve to kill him, but they are finally outwitted by the slave-girl Morgiana.

Alibi (Lat elsewhere). A plea of having been at another place at the time that an offence is alleged to have been committed A clock which strikes an hour, while the hands point to a different time, the real time being neither one nor the other, has been humorously called an *alibi clock*.

> Never mind the character, and stick to the alley bi Nothing like an alley bi, Sammy, nothing —DICKENS *Pickwick Papers*

A modern and incorrect usage of this word makes it mean an excuse, a pretext.

Aliboron. The name of a jackass in La Fontaine's *Fables*, hence Maitre Aliboron = Mr. Jackass   *See* GONIN

Alice in Wonderland and its companion *Through the Looking-glass* are probably the most famous and widely read of children's books. Their author was C L Dodgson, an Oxford mathematician who wrote under the pseudonym of Lewis Carroll *Alice* appeared in 1865 and *Looking-glass* in 1871, both books being illustrated by Sir John Tenniel The original of Alice was Alice Liddell, daughter of Dean Liddell, himself famous as part-author of Liddell & Scott's Greek Lexicon

Alien (ā′ li ĕn) This term is legally applied to a person living in a different country from that of his birth, and not having acquired citizenship in the land of his residence Later usage has given the word a pejorative implication An *alienist* is a physician or scientist who specializes in the study and treatment of insanity

Alien priory. A priory which is dependent upon and owes allegiance to another priory in a foreign country A sub-priory, such as Rufford Abbey, Notts, which was under the prior of Rievaulx in Yorkshire, has sometimes been erroneously called an alien priory

Alifanfaron (ăl i făn′ fa ron) Don Quixote attacked a flock of sheep, and declared them to be the army of the giant Alifanfaron Similarly Ajax, in a fit of madness, fell upon a flock of sheep, which he mistook for Grecian princes

Al Kadr (ăl kădr) (the divine decree). A particular night in the month Ramadan, when Mohammedans say that angels descend to earth, and Gabriel reveals to man the decrees of God —*Al Koran*, ch xcvii.

Alkahest (ăl′ ká hest) The hypothetical universal solvent of the alchemists The word was invented, on Arabic models, by Paracelsus

All and Some An old English expression meaning "one and all," confused sometimes with "all and *sum*," meaning the whole total It appears in the early 14th-century romance, *Cœur de Lion* —

> They that wolde nought Crystene become,
> Richard lect sleen hem alle and some.

All Fool's Day (April 1st). *See* APRIL FOOL.

All Fours. A game of cards; so called from the four points that are at stake, viz High, Low, Jack, and Game.

To go on all fours is to crawl about on all four limbs, like a quadruped or an infant. The phrase used to be (more correctly) *all four*, as in *Lev* xi, 42, ' whatsoever goeth upon all four."

It does not *go on all fours* means it does not suit in every particular, it limps as a quadruped which does not go on all its four legs. Thus, the Latin saying, *Omnis comparatio claudicat* (All similes limp) was translated by Macaulay as "No simile can go on all fours"

All-Hallows Summer. Another name for St. Martin's Summer (*see* SUMMER), because it sets in about All Hallows; also called St. Luke's Summer (St. Luke's Day is Oct 18th), and the Indian summer (*q v*). Shakespeare uses the term—

"Farewell, thou latter spring; farewell, All-hallows Summer!"

1 *Henry IV*, i, 2.

All-Hallows' Day. All Saints' Day (Nov. 1st), "hallows" being the Old English *halig*, a holy (man), hence, a saint. The French call it *Toussaint*. Between 603 and 610 the Pope (Boniface IV) changed the heathen Pantheon into a Christian church and dedicated it to the honour of all the martyrs The festival of All Saints was first held on May 1st, but in the year 834 it was changed to November 1st

All-Hallows' Eve. Many old folklore customs are connected with All-Hallows' Eve (October 31st), such as bobbing for apples, cracking nuts (mentioned in the *Vicar o Wakefield*), finding by various "tests" whether one's lover is true, etc Burns's *Hallowe'en* gives a good picture of Scottish customs; and there is a tradition in Scotland that those born on All-Hallows' Eve have the gift of double sight, and commanding powers over spirits. Thus, Mary Avenel, in Scott's *The Monastery*, is made to see the White Lady, invisible to less gifted visions

All is lost that is put in a riven dish In Latin, *Pertusum quicquid infunditur in dolium perit.* (It is no use helping the insolvent)

All my eye and Betty Martin. All nonsense, bosh, rubbish The origin of this curious phrase cannot now be discovered The Betty Martin is a later addition; "All my eye" is the old saying, as Goldsmith makes the Bailiff say in the *Good-natured Man* (iii) "That's all my eye, the king only can pardon, as the law says " In his *Classical Dictionary of the Vulgar Tongue* (1785), Grose gives "That's my eye, Betty Martin." Southey says in *The Doctor* (1837) "Who was Betty Martin, and wherefore should she be so often mentioned in connection with my precious eye or yours?"

Joe Miller, the 18th-century joke-monger exhibited a typical piece of his wit when he gave the following origin for the phrase A Jack Tar went into a foreign church, where he heard someone uttering these words—*Ah! mihi, beate Martine* (Ah' grant'] me, Blessed Martin) On giving an account of his adventure, Jack said he could not make much out of it, but it seemed to him very like "All my eye and Betty Martin."

All-overish. A colloquial expression meaning a feeling of general discomfort, not exactly ill but far from well

All Saints. *See* ALL HALLOWS.

All serene (Sp *seréna*) In Cuba the word was used as a countersign by sentinels, and is about equivalent to our "All right," or "All's well " In the late 19th century it was a colloquial catch-word.

All Sir Garnet. During the 80s of the last century, when Sir Garnet Wolseley was winning his victories in Egypt, the Army phrase "All Sir Garnet" came into common usage, indicating that all was going well, everything was as it should be

All Souls College, Oxford. This was founded in 1437 by Henry Chichele, Archbishop of Canterbury, as a chantry where masses should be said for the souls of those killed in the wars of Henry V and Henry VI. It has a Warden and fifty fellows, few of whom are in residence, but is unique in having no undergraduates.

All Souls' Day. November 2nd, so called because Catholics on that day seek by prayer and almsgiving to alleviate the sufferings of souls in purgatory. It was instituted in the monastery of Cluny in 993.

According to tradition, a pilgrim, returning from the Holy Land, was compelled by a storm to land on a rocky island, where he found a hermit, who told him that among the cliffs was an opening into the infernal regions through which huge flames ascended, and where the groans of the tormented were distinctly audible. The pilgrim told Odilo, abbot of Cluny, of this, and the abbot appointed the day following, which was November 2nd, to be set apart for the benefit of those souls in purgatory.

All standing. A nautical expression meaning to be completely equipped

To turn in all standing is to retire while still fully dressed

All the Talents. This is the name given to the administration formed by Lord Grenville in 1806 on the death of William Pitt. It was an attempt at a coalition of Tories, moderate Whigs and extreme Whigs, and included Charles James Fox as Foreign Secretary. It accomplished nothing spectacular, however, though one great measure will always stand to its credit—the abolition of the slave trade. The Government was dissolved in 1807.

All this for a song! Said to be Burleigh's remark when Queen Elizabeth ordered him to give £100 to Spenser as a royal gratuity.

All to break (*Judges* ix, 53) "A certain woman cast a piece of millstone upon Abimelech's head, and all to brake his skull" does not mean for the sake of breaking his skull, but that she wholly smashed his skull The *to* belongs to the verb, being an intensifying prefix (as is *zu* in German), and the *all* coming in as a natural addition   It is common among our early writers, as witness Chaucer's—

> Al is to-broken thilke regioun
>
>   *Knight's Tale*, 2759

Allah (äl′ ä)   The Arabic name of the Supreme Being, from *al*, the, *illah*, god *Allah il Allah*, the Mohammedan war-cry, and also the first clause of their confession of faith, is a corruption of *la illah illa allah*, meaning "there is no God, but the God" Another Mohammedan war-cry is *Allah akbar*, "God is most mighty."

Allan-a-Dale   A minstrel in the Robin Hood ballads, who appears also in Scott's *Ivanhoe* He was assisted by Robin Hood in carrying off his bride when on the point of being married against her will to a rich old knight.

Alleluiah.   *See* HALLELUJAH.

Alley or Ally   A choice, large playing-marble made of stone or alabaster, from which it takes its name   The alley tor (more correctly taw) beloved of Master Bardell (*Pickwick Papers*, 34) was a special ally that had won many taws or games.

Alley, The.   An old name for Change Alley in the City of London, where dealings in the public funds, etc., used to take place.

> Why did 'Change Alley waste thy precious hours
> Among the fools who gap'd for golden show'rs?
> No wonder if we found some poets there,
> Who live on fancy and can feed on air,
> No wonder they were caught by South-Sea schemes,
> Who ne'er enjoy'd a guinea but in dreams.
>
>   THOMAS GAY, to Mr T SNOW,
>   goldsmith.

Alhensis, Dies (dī′ ēz äl ı en′ sıs)   June 16th, 390 B.C., when the Romans were cut to pieces by the Gauls near the banks of the river Allia. It was ever after held to be a *dies nefastus*, or unlucky day.

Alligator.   When the Spaniards first saw this reptile in the New World, they called it *el lagarto* (the lizard)   Sir Walter Raleigh called these creatures *lagartos*, in the 1st Quarto of *Romeo and Juliet* (v, 1) the animal is called an *aligarta*, and in Ben Jonson's *Bartholomew Fair* an *alligarta*

Alligator Pear.   The name given to the fruit of the West Indian tree, *Persea gratissima*. It is a corruption either of the Carib *aouacate*, called by the Spanish discoverers *avocado* or *avigato*, or of the Aztec *abuacath*, which was transmitted through the Fr. *avocat* and Sp. *aguacate*   In any case the fruit has nothing to do with the reptile.

Alliteration   The rhetorical device of commencing adjacent accented syllables with the same letter or sound, as in Quince's ridicule of it in *Midsummer Night's Dream* (v 1) —

> With blade, with bloody blameful blade,
> He bravely broached his boiling bloody breast

Alliteration was a *sine qua non* in Anglo-Saxon and early English poetry, and in modern poetry it is frequently used with great effect, as in Coleridge's —

> The fair breeze blew, the white foam flew
>   The furrow followed free.
>
>   *Ancient Mariner*.

And Tennyson's·—

> The moan of doves in *immemorial* elms,
> And *murmuring* of *innumerable* bees
>
>   *Princess*, vii

Many fantastic examples of excessive alliteration are extant, and a good example from a parody by Swinburne will be found under the heading AMPHIGOURI.   Hugbald composed an alliterative poem on Charles the Bald, every word of which begins with *c*, and Henry Harder a poem of 100 lines, in Latin hexameters, on cats, each word beginning with *c*, called *Canum cum Catis certamen carmine compositum currente calamo C Catulli Caninii*   The first line is—

> Cattorum canimus certamina clara canumque

Tusser, who died 1580, has a rhyming poem of twelve lines, every word of which begins with *t*; and in the 1890s there was published a *Serenade* of twenty-eight lines, "sung in M flat by Major Marmaduke Muttinhead to Mademoiselle Madeline Mendoza Marriott," which contained only one word—in the line, "Meet me *by* moonlight, marry me"—not beginning with M

The alliterative alphabetic poem beginning—

> An Austrian army awfully arrayed
> Boldly by battery besieged Belgrade.
> Cossack commanders, cannonading come
> Dealing destruction's devastating doom, .

is well known   It was published in *The Trifler*, May 7th, 1817, ascribed to Rev. B Poulter, later revised by Alaric A Watts, though claimed for others.
Another attempt of the same kind begins thus —

> About an age ago, as all agree,
> Beauteous Belinda, brewing best Bohea
> Carelessly chattered, controverting clean,
> Dublin's derisive, disputatious dean . .

Allodials (Med. Lat from Old Frankish *al*, all; *od*, estate)   Lands held by absolute right, without even the burden of homage or fidelity, opposed to feudal

Allopathy (a lop′ a thi) is in opposition to Homœopathy (*q.v*)   It is from the Greek, *allo pathos*, a different disease   In homœopathy the principle is that "like is to cure like", in allopathy the disease is to be cured by its "antidote"

Alma (äl′ mä) (Ital soul, spirit, essence), in Prior's poem of this name typifies the mind or guiding principles of man   Alma is queen of "Body Castle," and is beset by a rabble rout of evil desires, foul imaginations, and silly conceits for seven years (*the Seven Ages*). In Spenser's *Faerie Queene* (II, ix-xi) Alma typifies the soul   She is mistress of the House of Temperance, and there entertains Prince Arthur and Sir Guyon

Alma Mater.   A collegian so calls the university of which he is a member   The words are Latin for "fostering mother," and in ancient Rome the title was given to several goddesses, especially Ceres and Cybele
They are also used for other "fostering mothers," as in—

> You might divert yourself, too, with Alma Mater, he Church
>
>   HORACE WALPOLE *Letters* (1778)

Almack's. A suite of assembly rooms in King Street, St James's (London), built in 1765 by William Almack, an ex-valet, who a short time previously had founded the club now known as Brooks's, and who died in 1781 Balls, presided over by a committee of ladies of the highest rank, used to be given here, and to be admitted was almost as great a distinction as to be presented at Court After 1840 they became known as Willis's Rooms, from the name of the then proprietor, and were used chiefly for large dinners The rooms were closed in 1890, and destroyed in an air raid in 1941

Almagest (ăl' ma jest). The English form of the Arabic name given to Ptolemy's *Mathematike syntaxis*, the great astronomical treatise composed during the 2nd century A D. of which an Arabic translation was made about 820. It is in the third book of this work (which contains thirteen books in all) that the length of the year was first fixed at 365¼ days

Almanac. A mediæval Latin word for a table of days and months with astronomical data, etc

The derivation of the word is obscure, though it clearly comes from the Sp Arabic *al*, the, *manakh*, a sun-dial This is not, however, a true Arabic word, but is probably of Greek origin

Some early almanacs are —
Before invention of printing
By Solomon Jarchi	in and after 1150
,, Peter de Dacia	about 1307
,, Walter de Elvendene	1327
,, John Somers, Oxford	1380
,, Nicholas de Lynna	1386
,, Purbach	1150-1461

After invention of printing
First printed by Gutenberg at Mainz	1457
By Regiomontanus, at Nuremberg	1474
,, Zainer, at Ulm	1478
,, Richard Pynson (*Sheapeherd's Kalendar*)	1497
,, Stoffler, in Venice	1499
Poor Robin's Almanack	1652
Francis Moore's Almanack between 1698 and 1713	
Almanach de Gotha,	first published 1764
Whitaker's Almanack	first published 1869

The man i' the almanac stuck with pins (Nat Lee), is a man marked with points referring to signs of the zodiac, and intended to indicate the favourable and unfavourable times of letting blood

Almanzor (ăl măn' zòr). The word means "the invincible" and was adopted as a title by several Mussulman potentates, notably the second Abbasside Caliph Abu Jafar Abdullah It was a royal title given to the kings of Fez, Morocco, and Algiers —
> The kingdoms of Almansor, Fez, and Sus, Marocco and Algiers
> *Paradise Lost*, xi, 403

The Caliph Almanzor founded the city of Bagdad, which he named after a beggar who had prophesied that he would do so

One of the characters in Dryden's *Conquest of Granada* (1672) is an Almanzor; the name figures also as one of the lackeys in Molière's *Précieuses Ridicules*

Almesbury. It was in a sanctuary at Almesbury that Queen Guenever, according to

Malory, took refuge, after her adulterous passion for Lancelot was revealed to the king (Arthur) Here she died, but her body was buried at Glastonbury

Almeyda. *See* BENBOW.

Almighty Dollar. Washington Irving seems to have been the first to use this expression —
> The almighty dollar, that great object of universal devotion throughout our land
> W. IRVING *Wolfert's Roost Creole Village* (1837)

Ben Jonson in his *Epistle to Elizabeth, Countess of Rutland*, speaks of " almighty gold '

Almonry. The place where the almoner resides, or where alms are distributed An almoner is a person whose duty it is to distribute alms, which, in ancient times, consisted of one-tenth of the entire income of a monastery

The word has become confused with Ambry (*q v*), and the Close in Westminster now known as "Ambry Close" used to be called "Almonry Close "

Almonry is from the Latin *eleemosynarium*, a place for alms
> The place wherein this Chapel or Almshouse stands was called the "Elemosinary" or Almonry, now corrupted into Ambrey, for that the alms of the Abbey are there distributed to the poor —STOW *Survey*

Alms (amz) (O E. *ælmysse*, ultimately from Lat *elemosina* from Gr *eleemosyne*, compassion), gifts to the poor

Dr Johnson says the word has no *singular*, the O E D. says it has no *plural* It is a singular word which, like *riches* (from Fr *richesse*), has in modern usage become plural In the Bible we have "he asked *an* alms" (*Acts* iii, 3), but Dryden gives us "alms *are* but the vehicles of prayer" (*Hind and the Panther*, iii, 106)

Alms Basket (in *Love's Labour's Lost*, v, 1) To live on the alms basket. To live on charity

Alms-drink Leavings, the liquor which a drinker finds too much, and therefore hands to another, also, liquor left over from a feast and sent to the alms-people *See Antony and Cleopatra*, ii, 7

Alms-fee. Peter's pence (*q v*)

Almshouse A house for the use of the poor, usually supported by the endowment of some wealthy patron who built the houses. Almshouses are generally a number of small dwellings built together, often in a row, and are devoted to housing and supporting persons who find themselves poor or destitute in old age

Alms-man. One who lives on alms

Alnaschar's Dream. Counting your chickens before they are hatched Alnaschar the barber's fifth brother (in the *Arabian Nights* story), invested all his money in a basket of glassware, on which he was to make a profit which, being invested, was to make more, and this was to go on till he grew rich enough to marry the vizier's daughter Being angry with his imaginary wife he gave a kick, overturned his basket, and broke all his wares.

A.L.O.E. These initials represent A Lady Of England, the pseudonym of Charlotte Maria Tucker (1821-1893), an author of children's allegories and tales that enjoyed great popularity

Aloe (Gr *aloe*) A very bitter plant, hence the line in Juvenal's sixth satire (181), *Plus aloes quam mellis habet,* "He has in him more bitters than sweets," said of a writer with a sarcastic pen The French say, *"Le côte d'Adam contient plus d'aloes que de miel,"* where *côte d'Adam,* of course, means woman or one's wife

Alombrados. *See* ILLUMINATI

Alonzo of Aguilar When Fernando, King of Aragon, was laying siege to Granada in 1501, he asked who would undertake to plant his banner on the heights Alonzo, "the lowmost of the dons," undertook the task but was cut down by the Moors His body was exposed in the wood of Oxijera, and the Moorish damsels, struck with its beauty, buried it near the brook of Alpuxarra The incident is the subject of a number of ballads

Aloof. A sea term, *to stand aloof,* meaning originally to bear to windward, or *luff* The *a* is the same prefix as in *afoot* or *asleep,* and means *on, loof* is the Dutch *loef,* windward *To hold aloof* thus means literally "to keep to the windward," and as one cannot do that except by keeping the head of the ship *away,* it came to mean "to keep away from ' as opposed to ' to approach "

A l'outrance (a loo' trons) An incorrect English version of the French *a outrance* To the uttermost

Alpha (ăl' fa) *"I am Alpha and Omega, the first and the last"* (*Rev* 1, 8) "Alpha" is the first, and "Omega" (Ω) the last letter of the Greek alphabet *Cp* TAU

Alphabet. This is the only word of more than one syllable compounded solely of the names of letters The Greek *alpha* (a) *beta* (b), our A B C (book), etc
Some curiosities of the alphabet are these—
Ezra vii, 21, contains all the letters of the English alphabet, presuming *I* and *J* to be identical
Even the Italian alphabet is capable of more than seventeen trillion combinations, that is, 17 followed by eighteen other figures, as—
17,000,000,000,000,000,000,000,
while the English alphabet will combine into more than twenty-nine thousand quatrillion combinations, that is, 29 followed by twenty-seven other figures, as—
29,000,000,000,000,000,000,000,000,000
Yet we have no means of differentiating our vowelsounds, take *a,* we have *fate, fat, Thames, war, orange, ware, abide, calm, swan,* etc So with *e,* we have *era, the, there prey* (a), *met, England, sew, herb, clerk,* etc The other vowels are equally indefinite

See LETTER.

Alpheus and Arethusa (ăl fē' us, ăr e thū' za) The Greek legend is that a youthful hunter named Alpheus was in love with the nymph Arethusa, she fled from him to the island of Ortygia on the Sicilian coast and he was turned into a river of Arcadia in the Peloponnesus Alpheus pursued her under the sea,
B D.—2

and, rising in Ortygia, he and she became one in the fountain hereafter called Arethusa The myth seems to be designed for the purpose of accounting for the fact that the course of the Alpheus is for some considerable distance underground

Alphonsin (ăl fon' sin) An old surgical instrument for extracting bullets from wounds So called from Alphonse Ferri, a surgeon of Naples, who invented it (1552)

Alphonsine Tables A revision of the Ptolemaic planetary tables made at the command of Alphonsus X of Castile—himself a noted astronomer—by a body of 50 or more of the most learned astronomers of the time. They were completed in 1252

Alpieu (Ital *al piu,* for the most) In the game of Basset, doubling the stake on a winning card
> What pity 'tis those conquering eyes,
> Which all the world subdue,
> Should, while the lover gazing dies,
> Be only on alpieu
>   ETHEREGE *Basset*

Alpine Race. This is another name for the large Celtic Race and is applied to the thickset men, with broad faces, hazel eyes, and light chestnut hair who inhabited the northwest extremity of France, Savoy, Switzerland, the Ardennes, Vosges, and the Biscayan coasts They were a midway race between the Scandinavian Nordics and the dark Mediterranean folk, the zenith of their culture was the so-called La Tene period (500 B C. to A D 1).

Al Rakim (ăl ra' kim) The dog in the legend of the Seven Sleepers of Ephesus

Alruna-wife, An (ăl roo' na) The Alrunes were the *lares* or *penates* of the ancient Germans, and an Alruna-wife, the household goddess

Alsatia (ăl să' sha) The Whitefriars district of London, which from early times till the abolition of all privileges in 1697 was a sanctuary for debtors and law-breakers It was bounded on the north and south by Fleet Street and the Thames, on the east and west by the Fleet River (now New Bridge Street) and the Temple, and was so called from the old Latin name of Alsace, which was for centuries a debatable frontier ground and a refuge of the disaffected The life and state of this rookery is described in *The Squire of Alsatia* (1688), a comedy by Shadwell, who was the first to use the name in literature

Al-Sirat (Arab the path) In Mohammedan mythology, the bridge leading to paradise, a bridge over mid-hell, no wider than the edge of a sword, across which all who enter heaven must pass

Alsvidur. *See* HORSE.

Altar (Lat *altus,* high, a high place) The oblong block or table, made of wood, marble, or other stone, consecrated and used for religious sacrifice. In Christian churches the term is applied to the communion table According to the rubric laid down in the Book of Common Prayer the celebrant at Holy Communion shall stand at the north side of the table, thus sideways to the communicants who can in this way observe his motions in the act of consecration. This was enacted in order to do away with the alleged mystery of the Mass, but it is not always observed to-day

Led to the altar. Married Said of a woman who, as a bride, is led up the aisle to the altar-rail where marriages are solemnized

The north side of the altar. The side on which the Gospel is read The north is the dark part of the earth, and the Gospel is the light of the world which shineth in darkness—"*illuminare his qui in tenebris et in umbra mortis sedent*"

Privileged altar. In R.C churches this is an altar with certain indulgences attached to all Masses for the dead said at it

Alter ego (ăl' ter eg' ō) (Lat other I, other self) One's double, one's intimate and thoroughly trusted friend, one who has full powers to act for another *Cf* "One's second self" *under* SECOND

Althea. The divine Althea of Richard Lovelace was Lucy Sacheverell, also called by the poet, "Lucasta"

> When Love with unconfined wings
> Hovers within my gates,
> And my divine Althea brings
> To whisper at the grates.

Lovelace was thrown into prison by the Long Parliament for his petition in favour of the king, hence the grates referred to.

Althæa's Brand (ăl' thē â), a fatal contingency Althæa's son, Meleager, was to live just so long as a log of wood, then on the fire, remained unconsumed. With her care it lasted for many years, but being angry one day with Meleager, she pushed it into the midst of the fire, it was consumed in a few minutes and Meleager died in great agony at the same time —Ovid. *Metamorphoses*, viii, 4.

> The fatal brand Althæa burned
>   SHAKESPEARE 2 *Henry VI*, i, 1

Altis. The sacred precinct of Zeus at Olympia, containing the great temple and oval altar of Zeus, the Pelopium (grave of Pelops), the Heræum, with many other buildings and statues It was connected by an arched passage with the Stadium, where the Olympian games were held

Alto relievo. Italian for "high relief" A term used in sculpture for figures in wood, stone, marble, etc, so cut as to project at least one-half from the tablet

Alumbrado, a perfectionist, so called from a Spanish sect which arose in 1575, and claimed special illumination. (Spanish, meaning "illuminated," "enlightened")

Alvina weeps, or "Hark! Alvina weeps," i e. the wind howls loudly, a Flemish saying. Alvina was the daughter of a king, who was cursed by her parents because she married unsuitably From that day she roamed about the air invisible to the eye of man, but her moans are audible

Alzire (ăl' zēr) A daughter of Montezuma invented by Voltaire and made the central character of one of his greatest plays of the same name (1736). The scene is shifted from Mexico to Peru .

A.M. or M.A. When the Latin form is intended the A comes first, as *Artium Magister*, but where the English form is meant the M precedes, as *Master of Arts*

The abbreviation "A M" also stands for *ante meridiem* (Lat), before noon, and *anno mundi*, in the year of the world

Amadis of Gaul (a ma' dis). The hero of a prose romance of the same title, supposed to have been written by the Portuguese, Vasco de Lobeira (d 1403), with additions by the Spaniard Montalvo, and by many subsequent romancers, who added exploits and adventures of other knights and thus swelled the romance to fourteen books The romance was referred to as early as 1350 (in Egidis Colonna's *De Regimine Principium*), it was first printed in 1508, became immensely popular, and exerted a wide influence on literature far into the 17th century

Amadis, called the "Lion Knight," from the device on his shield, and "Beltenebros" (darkly beautiful), from his personal appearance, was a love-child of Perion, King of Gaula (Wales), and Elizena, Princess of Brittany He was cast away at birth and became known as the Child of the Sun, and after many adventures including wars with the race of Giants, a war for the hand of his lady-love Oriana, daughter of Lisuarte, King of Greece, the Ordeal of the Forbidden Chamber, etc , he and Oriana are married He is represented as a poet and a musician, a linguist and a gallant, a knight-errant and a king, the very model of chivalry

Other names by which Amadis was called were the *Lovely Obscure*, the *Knight of the Green Sword*, the *Knight of the Dwarf*, etc

Amadis of Greece. A Spanish continuation of the seventh book of Amadis of Gaul (*q v*), supposed to be by Feliciano de Silva. It tells the story of Lisuarte of Greece, a grandson of Amadis

Amaimon (a mī' â mon) One of the chief devils in mediæval demonology, king of the eastern portion of hell Asmodeus is his chief officer He might be bound or restrained from doing hurt from the third hour till noon, and from the ninth hour till evening

> Amaimon sounds well, Lucifer well
>   SHAKESPEARE *Merry Wives of Windsor*, ii, 2.

Amalfitan Code (a mäl' fi tan) The oldest existing collection of maritime laws, compiled in the eleventh century at Amalfi, then an important commercial centre

Amalthæa (ăm al thē' a) In Greek mythology, the nurse of Zeus In Roman legend Amalthea is the name of the Sibyl who sold the Sibylline Books (*q v*) to Tarquin.

Amalthea's horn. The cornucopia or "horn of plenty" (*q v*) The infant Zeus was fed with goats' milk by Amalthea, one of the daughters of Melisseus, King of Crete Zeus, in gratitude, broke off one of the goat's horns, and gave it to Amalthea, promising that the possessor should always have in abundance everything desired. See ÆGIS.

When Amalthea's horn
O'er hill and dale the rose-crowned Flora pours,
And scatters corn and wine, and fruits and flowers
CAMOENS *Lusiad*, Bk ii

Amaranth (ăm' a rănth) (Gr. *amarantos*, everlasting) The name given by Pliny to some real or imaginary fadeless flower Clement of Alexandria says—*Amarantus flos, symbolum est immortalitatis* Among the ancients it was the symbol of immortality, because its flowers retain to the last much of their deep blood-red colour

The best-known species are "Love lies bleeding" (*Amarantus caudatus*), and 'Prince's feather" (*Amarantus hypochondriacus*)

Immortal amarant, a flower which once
In Paradise, fast by the Tree of Life,
Began to bloom, but, soon for man's offence
To heaven removed where first it grew, there grows
And flowers aloft, shading the Fount of Life . .
With these, that never fade, the Spirits elect
Bind their resplendent locks
MILTON *Paradise Lost*, iii, 353

Spenser mentions "sad Amaranthus" as one of the flowers "to which sad lovers were transformed of yore" (*Faerie Queene*, III, vi, 45), but there is no known legend to this effect

In 1653 Christina, Queen of Sweden, instituted the order of the *Knights of the Amaranth*, but it ceased to exist at the death of the Queen

Amaryllis (ăm a ril'is) A rustic sweetheart The name is borrowed from a shepherdess in the pastorals of Theocritus and Virgil

To sport with Amaryllis in the shade
MILTON *Lycidas*, 68

In Spenser's *Colin Clout's Come Home Again*, Amaryllis is intended for Alice Spenser, Countess of Derby

Amasis, Ring of (a mā' sis). Herodotus tells us (iii, 4) that Polycrates, tyrant of Samos, was so fortunate in everything that Amasis, king of Egypt, fearing such unprecedented luck boded ill, advised him to part with something which he highly prized Polycrates accordingly threw into the sea a ring of great value A few days afterwards, a fish was presented to the tyrant, in which the ring was found Amasis now renounced friendship with Polycrates, as a man doomed by the gods; and not long afterwards, a satrap put the too fortunate despot to death by crucifixion

Amati (a ma' ti) A family famous for making stringed instruments at Cremona (*q v*) in the 16th and 17th centuries Either Andrea Amati or Gaspar da Salo produced the first violin similar to those in use to-day, the earliest surviving Amati instrument being dated 1564

Amaurote (ăm ô rō' te) (Gr. the shadowy or unknown place), the chief city of Utopia (*q v*.) in the political romance of that name by Sir Thomas More Rabelais, in his *Pantagruel*, introduces Utopia and "the great city

of the Amaurots" (Bk II, ch xxiii) He had evidently read Sir Thomas More's book

To add to the verisimilitude of the romance, More says he could not recollect whether Hythloday had told him it was 500 or 300 paces long, and he requested his friend Peter Giles, of Antwerp, to put the question to the adventurer Swift, in *Gulliver's Travels*, uses very similar means of throwing dust in his reader's eyes He says —

I cannot recollect whether the reception room of the Spaniard's Castle in the Air is 200 or 300 feet long I will get the next aeronaut who journeys to the moon to take the exact dimensions for me, and will memorialise the learned society of Laputa

Amazement. Not afraid with any amazement (I *Pet* iii, 6), introduced at the close of the marriage service in the Book of Common Prayer. The meaning is, you will be God's children so long as you do his bidding, and are not drawn aside by any sort of bewilderment or distraction Shakespeare uses the word in the same sense —

Behold, distraction, frenzy and amazement,
Like witless antics one another meet
Troilus and Cressida, v, 3

Amazon (ăm' a zon) A Greek word meaning *without breast*, or rather, 'deprived of a pap " According to Herodotus there was a race of female warriors, or Amazons, living in Scythia, and other Greek stories speak of a nation of women in Africa of a very warlike character There were no men in the nation, and if a boy was born, it was either killed or sent to its father, who lived in some neighbouring state The girls had their right breasts burnt off, that they might the better draw the bow The term is now applied to any strong, brawny woman of masculine habits

She towered, fit person for a Queen
To lead those ancient Amazonian files;
Or ruling Bandit's wife among the Grecian isles
WORDSWORTH *Poems of the Imagination*, xviii.

Amazonia (ăm a zō' ni a) An old name for the regions about the river Amazon in South America, which was so called because the early Spanish explorers (1541), under Orellana, thought they saw female warriors on its banks

Amazonian chin A beardless chin, like that of a woman warrior

When with his Amazonian chin he drove
The bristled lips before him
SHAKESPEARE *Coriolanus*, II, ii.

Amber A yellow, translucent, fossilized vegetable resin, the name of which originally belonged to ambergris (*q v*). Beaumont and Fletcher use it as a verb meaning to perfume with ambergris.—

Be sure
The wines be lusty, high, and full of spirit,
And amber'd all
Custom of the Country, III, ii.

Legend has it that amber is a concretion, the tears of birds who were the sisters of Meleager and who never ceased weeping for the death of their brother.—OVID: *Metamorphoses*, viii, 270

Around thee shall glisten the loveliest amber
That ever the sorrowing sea-bird hath wept
T MOORE *Fire Worshippers*.

Insects, small leaves, etc., are often preserved in amber, hence such phrases as "preserved for all time in the imperishable amber of his genius "

Pretty! in amber, to observe the forms
Of hairs, or straws, or dirt, or grubs or worms,
The things, we know, are neither rich nor rare,
But wonder how the devil they got there
POPE *Ep to Arbuthnot*, 169-72

Amber, meaning a repository, is an obsolete spelling of *ambry* (*q v*)

Ambergris. A waxy, aromatic substance found floating on tropical seas and in the intestines of the cachalot. It is a marbled ashy grey in colour and is used in perfumery Its original name was simply *amber* (*see* AMBER) from Fr *ambre*, which denoted only this substance, when it came to be applied to the fossil resin (Fr *ambre jaune*, yellow amber), this grey substance became known as *amber gris* (grey amber).

Ambidexter properly means both hands right hands, and so one who can use his left hand as deftly as his right, in slang use, a double-dealer

Ambree, Mary. An English heroine, immortalized by her valour at the siege of Ghent in 1584. See the ballad in Percy's *Reliques* —
When captains couragious, whom death cold not
daunte,
Did march to the siege of the citty of Gaunt,
They mustred their souldiers by two and by three,
And the formost in battle was Mary Ambree.

Her name is proverbial for a woman of heroic spirit
My daughter will be valiant,
And prove a very Mary Ambry i' the bushes
BEN JONSON *Tale of a Tub*, i, 4

Ambrose, St., Bishop of Milan (b *c.* 340) In 384 he instituted reforms in Church music and introduced from the Eastern Church the Ambrosian Chant, which was used until Pope Gregory the Great introduced Gregorian Chant two centuries later His feast day is December 7th. His emblems are (1) a beehive, in allusion to the legend that a swarm of bees settled on his mouth when lying in his cradle, (2) a scourge, by which he expelled the Arians from Italy

Ambrosian Library. Library in Milan founded by Count Federigo Borromeo (1564-1631), Cardinal Archbishop of Milan, in 1609, so called in compliment to St Ambrose, the patron saint It is famous for its collection of illuminated MSS., including the earliest known—a 4th-century codex of Homer

Ambrosia (ăm brō′ zi ă) (Gr. *a*, privative, *brotos*, mortal) The food of the gods, so called because it made them immortal Anything delicious to the taste or fragrant in perfume is so called from the notion that whatever is used by the celestials must be excellent.

So fortunate
Whom the Pierian sacred sisters love
That　　with the Gods, for former vertues meede
On nectar and Ambrosia do feede
SPENSER *Ruines of Time*, 393.

Ambrosian Nights. At Ambrose's Hotel, Edinburgh, John Wilson (Christopher North), James Hogg, and other literary figures of the time forgathered of an evening with conviviality and brilliant conversation, recorded (with embellishments) by North in his *Noctes Ambrosianæ*, 1822).

Ambrosius Aurelianus. A semi-mythical champion of the British race The story is that he was a descendant of the Emperor Constantine, that he lived in the 5th century, and that he led the Romanized Britons against the Saxon invaders under Hengist He is mentioned by Gildas as "the last of the Romans," and he may have been a Count of the Saxon Shore

Ambry (am′ bri) (Old Fr *armarie*, from Lat *armaria*, chest or cupboard, from *arma*, tools, gear) A cupboard, locker, or recess The ambry in a church is a closed recess in the wall which is used for keeping books, vestments, the sacramental plate, consecrated oil, and so on (*cp* ALMONRY)
Avarice hath almaries,
And yren-bounden cofres
Piers Plowman, xiv, 494

Ambs-as or **Ambes-ace** (ămz ās) (Lat *amboasses*, both or two aces) Two aces, the lowest throw in dice; figuratively, bad luck
I had rather be in this choice than throw ames-ace
for my life —*All's Well*, ii, 3

It was also the name of a card game, and was sometimes spelt **aumo-ace.**

Ame damnée (Fr), literally, a damned, or lost, soul, hence one's familiar or tool, one blindly devoted to another's wishes, and, sometimes, a scapegoat

Amelia. A model of conjugal affection, in Fielding's novel of that name It is said that the character is intended for his own wife
The name is also associated with Amelia Sedley, one of the heroines of *Vanity Fair*

Amen Corner, at the west end of Paternoster Row, London, was where the monks used to finish the *Pater Noster* as they went in procession to St Paul's Cathedral on Corpus Christi Day They began in *Paternoster* Row with the Lord's Prayer in Latin, which was continued to the end of the street, then said *Amen*, at the corner or bottom of the Row, then turning down *Ave Maria* Lane, commenced chanting the "Hail, Mary!" then crossing Ludgate, entered *Creed* Lane chanting the *Credo*
Paternoster Row, Amen Corner, and much of Ave Maria Lane were completely destroyed in an air raid on December 28th, 1940

Amen-Ra. The supreme King of the Gods among the ancient Egyptians, usually figured as a great man with two long plumes rising straight above his head, but sometimes with a ram's head, the ram being sacred to him He was the patron of Thebes, his oracle was at the oasis of Jupiter Ammon, and he was identified by the Greeks with Zeus

Amende honorable An anglicized French phrase signifying a full and frank apology In mediæval France the term was applied to a degrading punishment inflicted on traitors, parricides, and sacrilegious persons, who were brought into court with a rope round their neck, stripped to the shirt, and made to beg pardon of God, the king, and the court.

A mensa et thoro. *See* A VINCULO

Amenthes (a men' thēz) The Egyptian Hades, the abode of the spirits of the dead who were not yet fully purified

America. *See* UNITED STATES OF AMERICA.

Amerindian (ăm er in' di an) This is a "portmanteau" word combining *American* and *Indian* and is applied descriptively to the native Red Indian races and Eskimos of the North American continent

Ames-ace. *See* AMBS-AS

Amethea. *See* HORSE

Amethyst (ăm' e thist) (Gr *a-*, not, *methuein*, to be drunken) A violet-blue variety of crystalline quartz supposed by the ancients to prevent intoxication

Drinking-cups made of amethyst were a charm against inebriety, and it was the most cherished of all precious stones by Roman matrons, from the superstition that it would preserve inviolate the affection of their husbands

Amiable or **Amicable Numbers.** Any two numbers either of which is the sum of the aliquots of the other thus, the aliquots of 220 are 1, 2, 4, 5, 10, 11, 20, 22, 44, 55, 110 the sum of which is 284, and the aliquots o 284 are 1, 2, 4, 71, 142, the sum of which is 220, so 220 and 284 are amicable numbers

Amicus curiæ (a mī' kus kū' ri ē) (Lat a friend to the court) One in court who is not engaged in the trial or action, but who is invited or allowed to assist with advice or information The term is now used to describe a disinterested adviser

Amiel (am' i el) In Dryden's *Absalom and Achitophel*, this is meant for Edward Seymour, Speaker of the House of Commons

The name is an anagram of Eliam (= God is kinsman). Eliam in 2 *Sam* xxiii, 34, is son of Ahithophel the Gilonite, and one of David's heroes, in 2 *Sam* xi, 3, it is given as the name of Bathsheba's father, which, in 1 *Chron* iii, 5, appears as "Ammiel "

Aminadab (a min' a dāb) A Quaker The Scripture name has a double *m*, but in old comedies, where the character represents a Quaker, the name has generally only one Obadiah is used, also, to signify a Quaker, and Rachel a Quakeress

Amiral or **Ammiral.** An early form of the word "admiral" (*q v*)

Amis and Amile. *See* AMYS

Ammon (ăm' on) The Libyan Jupiter, the Greek form of the name of the Egyptian god, Amun (*q v*).

Son of Ammon. Alexander the Great, who, on his expedition to Egypt, was thus saluted by the priests of the Libyan temple

Ammon's great son one shoulder had too high
POPE *Epistle to Dr Arbuthnot* 117

His father, Philip, claimed to be a descendant of Hercules, and therefore of Jupiter

Ammonites (ăm' ŏn ītz) Fossil molluscs allied to the nautilus and cuttlefish So called because they resemble the horn upon the ancient statues of Jupiter Ammon They were set in brooches or as earrings in the mid-19th century

Also the people of Ammon that is, the descendants of Lot by the son of his younger daughter, Ben-ammi (*Gen* XIX, 38), who are frequently mentioned in the Old Testament

Amok. *See* AMUCK

Amoret (ăm' ŏr et), in Spenser's *Faerie Queene*, is the type of female loveliness—young, handsome, gay, witty, and good, soft as a rose, sweet as a violet, chaste as a lily, gentle as a dove, loving everybody and by all beloved Hence it became a term for a sweetheart, love-song, love-knot, or love personified

He will be in his amorets, and his canzonets, his pastorals, and his madrigals —HEYWOOD *Love's Mistress*

For not icladde in silke was he,
But all in flouris and flourettes,
I-paintid all with amorettes
Romance of the Rose, 892

Amorous, The Philip I of France (1060-1108), so called because he divorced his wife Berthe to espouse Bertrade, who was already married to Foulques, count of Anjou.

Amour propre (a' moor propr) (Fr) One's self-love, vanity, or opinion of what is due to self *To wound his amour propre*, is to gall his good •opinion of himself—to wound his vanity.

Ampersand (ăm' per sănd) The character "&" for *and* In the old horn books, after giving the twenty-six letters, the character & was added (X, Y, Z, &), and was called "Ampersand," a corruption of "and per-se &" (and by itself, and) The symbol is an adaptation of the written *et* (Lat *and*), the transformation of which can be traced if we look at the italic ampersand—*&*—where the "e" and the cross of the "t" are clearly recognizable *See* TIRONIAN

Amphialus (ăm fī' á lus) In Sidney's *Arcadia* the valiant and virtuous son of the wicked Cecropia, in love with Philoclea, he ultimately married Queen Helen of Corinth

Amphictyonic Council (ăm fik ti on' ik) (Gr *amphictiones*, dwellers round about). In Greek history, the council of the Amphictyonic League, a confederation of twelve tribes, the deputies of which met twice a year, alternately at Delphi and Thermopylæ. Throughout the whole of ancient Greek history it exercised paramount authority over the oracles of the Pythian Apollo and conducted the Pythian games.

Amphigouri (ăm fi goor' i). A verse composition which, while sounding well, contains no sense or meaning A good example is Swinburne's well-known parody of his own style, *Nephelidia*, the opening lines of which are —

From the depth of the dreamy decline of the dawn through a notable nimbus of nebulous noonshine,
Pallid and pink as the palm of the flag-flower that flickers with fear of the flies as they float,
Are they looks of our lovers that lustrously lean from a marvel of mystic miraculous moonshine,
These that we feel in the blood of our blushes that thicken and threaten with throbs through the throat?

Here there is everything that goes to the making of poetry—except sense; and that is absolutely (and, of course, purposely) lacking

Amphion (ăm fi′ on). The son of Zeus and Antiope who, according to Greek legend, built Thebes by the music of his lute, which was so melodious that the stones danced into walls and houses of their own accord.

> The gift to king Amphion
> That walled a city with its melody
> Was for belief no dream
> WORDSWORTH *Poems of the Imagination,*
> *On the Power of Sound*

Amphisbæna (ăm fis bē′ nă)   A fabulous venomous serpent supposed to have a head at each end and to be able to move in either direction·

> Complicated monsters head and tail,
> Scorpion, and asp, and amphisbæna dire,
> Cerastes horn'd, hydrus and elops drear,
> And dipas . .
> *Paradise Lost,* x, 524

The name is applied to a genus of S. American lizards

Amphitrite (ăm fi trī′ ti) In classic mythology, the goddess of the sea, wife of Poseidon, daughter of Nereus and Doris   (Gr *amphitrio* for *tribo,* rubbing or wearing away [the shore] on all sides)

> His weary chariot sought the bowers
> Of Amphitrite and her tending nymphs
> THOMSON *Summer* (l 1625)

Amphitryon (ăm fit′ ri on)   *Le véritable Amphitryon est l'Amphitryon ou l'on dine* (Molière). That is, the person who *provides the feast* (whether master of the house or not) is the real host. The tale is that Jupiter assumed the likeness of Amphitryon for the purpose of visiting the latter's wife, Alcmena (*q v*), and gave a banquet at his house, but Amphitryon came home and claimed the honour of being the master of the house. As far as the servants and the guests were concerned, the dispute was soon decided—"he who gave the feast was to them the host "

Amphrysian Prophetess (ăm fri′ zi an) (*Amphrysia Vates*)   The Cumæan sibyl, so called from Amphrysus, a river of Thessaly, on the banks of which Apollo fed the herds of Admetus

Ampoulle, La Sainte (la sănt am pool′)   The vessel containing oil used in anointing the kings of France, and said to have been brought from heaven by a dove for the coronation service of St Louis   It was preserved at Rheims till the first Revolution, when it was destroyed

Amram's Son Moses (*Exod.* vi, 20).

> As when the potent rod
> Of Amram's son, in Egypt's evil day,
> Waved round the coast
> MILTON *Paradise Lost,* i, 338.

Amri (ăm′ ri) In Dryden's *Absalom and Achitophel* is designed for Heneage Finch, Earl of Nottingham and Lord Chancellor

Amrita (ăm rē′ ta) (Sanskrit).   In Hindu mythology, the elixir of immortality, the soma-juice, corresponding to the ambrosia (*q.v*) of classical mythology.

> Lo, Krishna ! lo, the one that thirsts for thee !
> Give him the drink of amrit from thy lips
> Sir EDWIN ARNOLD *Indian Song of Songs*

Amuck. A Malay adjective, *amog,* meaning to be in a state of frenzy. To run amuck is to indulge in physical violence while in a state of frenzy

> Satire's my weapon, but I'm too discreet
> To run amuck and tilt at all I meet
> POPE *Satires,* i, 69-70

Amulet Something worn, generally round the neck, as a charm   The word was formerly connected with the Arabic *himalah,* the name given to the cord that secured the Koran to the person and was sometimes regarded as a charm, but it has nothing to do with this, and is from the Latin *amuletum,* a preservative against sickness, through French *amulette*

The early Christians used to wear amulets called *Ichthus* (*q v*)   *See also* NOTARIKON.

Amun (ăm′ un)   An Egyptian deity, usually represented with a ram's head with large curved horns, and a human body, or as a human figure with two long upright plumes springing from the head and holding a sceptre and the symbol of life   An immense number of temples were dedicated to him and he was, identified by the Greeks with Zeus   His oracle was in the oasis of Jupiter Ammon. *See* AMMON

Amyclæan Silence (ăm i klē′ an)   Amyclæ was a Laconian town in the south of Sparta, ruled by the mythical Tyndareus   The inhabitants had so often been alarmed by false rumours of the approach of the Spartans, that they made a decree forbidding mention of the subject   When the Spartans actually came no one dare give warning, and the town was taken   Hence the proverb, *more silent than Amyclæ*

Castor and Pollux were born at Amyclæ, and are hence sometimes referred to as the **Amyclæan Brothers.**

Amyris plays the Fool (a mī′ ris). An expression used of one who assumes a false character with an ulterior object, like Junius Brutus   Amyris was a Sybarite sent to Delphi to consult the Oracle, who informed him of the approaching destruction of his nation· he fled to Peloponnesus and his countrymen called him a fool, but, like the madness of David, his "folly" was true wisdom, for thereby he saved his life

Amys and Amylion (ă′ mis, a mil′ i on) A French romance of the 13th century telling the story of the friendship between two heroes of the Carlovingian wars   The story culminates in Amylon's sacrifice of his children to save his friend

Anabaptists. Originally, a Christian sect which arose in Germany about 1521, the members of which did not believe in infant baptism and hence were baptized *over again* (Gr *ana*=over again) on coming to years of discretion

Applied in England as a nickname, and more or less opprobriously, to the Baptists, a body of Dissenters holding similar views

Anacharsis (ăn à kar′ sis) A princely Scythian named Anacharsis left his native country to travel in pursuit of knowledge. He reached Athens about 594 B C and became acquainted with Solon

In 1788 the Abbé Barthélemy published *Le voyage du Jeune Anacharsis*, a description of Greece in the time of Pericles and Philip He worked thirty years on preparing this book and at one time it was extremely popular and had great influence on the young. Baron Jean Baptiste Clootz (1755-1794), a Prussian brought up in France, assumed the name of Anacharsis after travelling about Greece and other countries in search of knowledge He was caught up in the Revolution, when he took to himself the title of The Orator of the Human Race He was guillotined by Robespierre in 1794

Anaclethra. Another name for the *agelasta* (q v)

Anacreon (ă năk' rı on) A Greek lyric poet, who wrote chiefly in praise of love and wine (about 563-478 B C)

Anacreon Moore Thomas Moore (1779-1852), who not only translated Anacreon into English, but also wrote original poems in the same style

Anacreon of Painters. Francesco Albano, a painter of beautiful women (1578-1660)

Anacreon of the Guillotine. Bertrand Barère de Vieuzac (1755-1841), president of the National Convention, so called from the flowery language and convivial jests used by him towards his miserable victims

Anacreon of the Temple. Guillaume Amfrye (1639-1720), abbé de Chaulieu, French man of letters and man of the world, called by Voltaire (whom he encouraged) " the greatest of neglected poets "

Anacreon of the Twelfth Century. Walter Mapes (about 1140-1210), also called "The Jovial Toper." His best-known piece is the famous drinking-song, "Meum est propositum in taberna mori "

The French Anacreon Pontus de Thiard, one of the Pleiad poets (1521-1605); also P. Laujon (1727-1811)

The Persian Anacreon. Hafiz (b. Shiraz, d c. 1389), greatest of Persian poets, his collected odes are known as *The Duan*

The Scottish Anacreon Alexander Scot, who flourished about 1550.

The Sicilian Anacreon. Giovanni Meli (1740-1815)

Anachronism (Gr *ana chronos*, out of time) An event placed at a wrong date

Shakespeare has several more or less glaring examples In 1 *Henry IV*, ii, 5, the carrier complains that the turkeys in his pannier are quite starved, whereas turkeys were introduced from America, which was not discovered until a century after Henry's time Again, in *Julius Cæsar*, ii, 1, the clock strikes and Cassius says, "The clock has stricken three " But striking clocks were not invented until some 1400 years after the days of Cæsar The great mine of literary anachronisms is to be found in the mediæval romances of chivalry, where Charlemagne, Edward III, Saracens and Romans all appear as living persons

Anagram (Gr *ana graphein*, to write over again) A word or phrase formed by transposing and writing over again the letters of some other word or phrase Among the many famous examples are —

Dame Eleanor Davies (prophetess in the reign of Charles I) = *Never so mad a lady*
Gustavus = *Augustus.*
Horatio Nelson = *Honor est a Nilo*
Queen Victoria's Jubilee Year = *I require love in a subject.*
Quid est Veritas (*John* xviii, 38)? = *Vir est qui adest*
Marie Touchet (mistress of Charles IX, of France) = *Je charme tout* (made by Henry IV)
Voltaire is an anagram of *Arouet l(a)j(eune).*

These are interchangeable words —
Alcuinus and Calvinus, Amor and Roma; Eros and Rose, Evil and Live, and many more.

Ananas [Peruvian *nanas*]. The pineapple Through the final "s" having been mistaken for the sign of the plural, an erroneous singular, *anana*, is sometimes used —

Witness thou, best Anana' thou the pride
Of vegetable life
　　　　　　　THOMSON· *Summer*, 685

Anastasia, St. (ăn as tă' zı a) A saint martyred in the reign of Nero, and commemorated on April 15 Her emblems are a stake and faggots, with a palm branch in her hand.

Anathema (ă năth' i ma). A denunciation or curse The word is Greek and means "a thing devoted"—originally, a thing devoted to any purpose, *e.g* to the gods, but later only a thing devoted to evil, hence, an accursed thing It has allusion to the custom of hanging in the temple of a patron god something devoted to him. Thus Gordius hung up his yoke and beam, the shipwrecked hung up their wet clothes, retired workmen hung up their tools, cured cripples their crutches, etc

Anatomy. He was like an anatomy—*i e* a mere skeleton, very thin, like one whose flesh had been anatomized or cut off Shakespeare uses *atomy* as a synonym Thus in 2 *Henry IV*, v, 4, Quickly says to the Beadle " Thou atomy, thou' " and Doll Tearsheet caps the phrase with, " Come, you thin thing, come you rascal "

Ancæus (ăn sē' ŭs) Helmsman of the ship Argo, after the death of Tiphys He was told by a slave that he would never live to taste the wine of his vineyards. When wine from his own grapes was set before him on his return, he sent for the slave to laugh at his prognostications; but the slave made answer "There's many a slip 'twixt the cup and the lip." At this instant a messenger came in, and told Ancæus that the Calydonian boar was laying his vineyard waste, whereupon he set down his cup, went out against the boar, and was killed in the encounter

Anchor. In Christian symbolism the anchor is the sign of hope, in allusion to *Heb.* vi, 19, "Hope we have as an anchor of the soul " In art it is an attribute of Clement of Rome and Nicholas of Bari Pope Clement, in A D. 80, was bound to an anchor and cast into the sea; Nicholas of Bari is the patron saint of sailors

The anchor is apeak. That is, the cable of the anchor is so tight that the ship is drawn completely over it

The anchor comes home. The anchor has been dragged from its hold Figuratively, the enterprise has failed, notwithstanding the precautions employed

To weigh anchor To haul in the anchor, that the ship may sail away from its mooring Figuratively, to begin an enterprise which has hung on hand

Anchor light A white light shown from the forward part of an anchored vessel and visible all round the horizon

Anchor watch. A watch of one or two men, while the vessel rides at anchor, in port
See BOWER ANCHOR SHEET ANCHOR

Anchorite (ăng' kor ĭt) This is from a Greek word meaning "recluse," and it was applied to those who retired to the desert or solitary places for a life of contemplation and religious exercises The classes of such ascetics are: *monks*, who adopt a secluded form of life but live in community; *hermits*, who withdraw to desert places but live in caves and occupy themselves manually, *anchorites*, who choose the greatest solitudes and deny themselves shelter and all but a minimum of food

Ancien Régime (Fr) The old order of things, a phrase used during the French Revolution for the old Bourbon monarchy, or the system of government, with all its evils, which existed prior to that great change

Ancient. A corruption of *ensign*—a flag and the officer who bore it. Pistol was Falstaff's "ancient"
> Ten times more dishonourable ragged than an old-faced ancient—SHAKESPEARE 1 *Henry IV*, IV, 2
> My whole charge consists of ancients, corporals, lieutenants, gentlemen of companies .
>   1 *Henry IV*, IV, 2

Ancient Mariner. The story in Coleridge's *Rime of the Ancient Mariner* (first published in the *Lyrical Ballads*, 1798) is founded partly on a dream told by the author's friend, Cruickshank, and partly on passages in various books that he had read Wordsworth told him the story of the privateer George Shelvocke who, while rounding Cape Horn in the *Speedwell*, in 1720, shot a black albatross. For many weeks following the vessel encountered bad weather, being driven hither and thither before making the coast of Chile, and this ill luck was attributed to the shooting of the bird Thomas James's *Strange and Dangerous Voyage* (1683) is thought to have suggested some of the more eerie episodes, while the *Letter of St. Paulinus to Macarius*, in which he relates astounding wonders concerning the shipwreck of an old man (1618), giving a story of how there is only one survivor of a crew and how the ship was navigated by angels and steered by "the Pilot of the World," may have furnished the basis of part of the *Rime*

Ancient of Days. A scriptural name given to God (*Dan* vii, 9)

Ancile (ăn' sĭl) The Palladium of Rome, the sacred buckler said to have fallen from heaven in the time of Numa To prevent its being stolen, he caused eleven others to be made precisely like it, and confided them to the twelve Salii, dancing priests of Mars (*see* SALIENS), who bore them in procession through the city every year at the beginning of March

And, "&" *See* AMPERSAND

Andiron (ănd' ĭr on). A fire-dog, that is, a contrivance consisting of a short horizontal bar projecting from an upright stand or rod, the whole usually of iron, for the purpose of holding up the ends of logs in a wood fire Though the contrivance is made of iron the word originally had nothing to do with the metal, but is from the Old French *andier*, after the late Latin *andedus*, *andena*, or *anderius* The English form of the word—like the Latin—has, even in modern times, had many variations, such as *end-iron* and *hand-iron* Andirons are also known as *dogs*, or *fire-dogs*

Andrea Ferrara (ăn drā' à fĕ ra' ra) A sword, also called, from the same cause, an *Andrew* and a *Ferrara*. All these expressions are common in Elizabethan literature So called from a famous 16th-century sword-maker of the name
> Here's old tough Andrew .
>   JOHN FLETCHER *The Chances* (1618)

Andrew, a name used in old plays for a valet or manservant *See* MERRY ANDREW

Andrew, St, depicted in Christian art as an old man with long white hair and beard, holding the Gospel in his right hand, and leaning on a St Andrew's cross His day is November 30th It is said that he suffered martyrdom in Patræ (A D 70) *See* RULE, ST

Andrew Macs, The. A slang name for the crew of H M S *Andromache* Similarly, the *Bellerophon* was called by English sailors "Billy ruffian," and the *Achilles* the "Ash heels" These corruptions are similar to some of those given under BEEFEATER (*q v*)

Androcles and the Lion (ăn drŏ' klēz) An Oriental apologue on the benefits to be expected as a result of gratitude, told in Æsop, and by Aulus Gellius, in the *Gesta Romanorum*, etc , but of unknown antiquity

Androcles was a runaway slave who took refuge in a cavern A lion entered, and instead of tearing him to pieces, lifted up his fore paw that Androcles might extract from it a thorn The slave being subsequently captured, was doomed to fight with a lion in the Roman arena. It so happened that the same lion was let out against him, and recognizing his benefactor, showed towards him every demonstration of love and gratitude

Android. An old name for an automaton figure resembling a human being (Gr. *androseidos*, a man's likeness)

Andromache (ăn drom' a ki) In Greek legend she was the wife of Hector, subsequently of Neoptolemus, and finally of Helenus, Hector's brother It is also the title of a play of Euripides.

Andromeda (ăn drom' e da) Daughter of Cepheus and Cassiopeia. Her mother boasted that the beauty of Andromeda surpassed that of the Nereids, so the Nereids induced Neptune to send a sea-monster to the country, and an oracle declared that Andromeda must be given up to it She was accordingly chained to a rock, but was delivered by Perseus, who married her and, at the wedding, slew Phineus, to whom she had been previously promised, with all his companions After death she was placed among the stars

Angary, Right of. The right of a belligerent, under stress of necessity, to confiscate or destroy neutral property, especially shipping, subject to claim for compensation

Angel. In post-canonical and apocalyptic literature angels are grouped in varying orders, and the hierarchy thus constructed was adapted to Church uses by the early Christian Fathers In his *De Hierarchia Celesti* the pseudo-Dionysius (early 5th century) gives the names of the nine orders; they are taken from the Old Testament, *Eph*, i, 21, and *Col* i, 16, and are as follows —

Seraphim and Cherubim, in the first circle
Thrones and Dominions, in the second,
Virtues, Powers, Principalities,
Archangels and Angels in the third.

Botticelli's great picture, *The Assumption of the Virgin*, in the National Gallery, London, well illustrates the mediæval conception of the " triple circles "

The seven holy angels are—Michael, Gabriel, Raphael, Uriel, Chamuel, Jophiel, and Zadkiel Michael and Gabriel are mentioned in the Bible, Raphael in the Apocrypha, and all in the apocryphal book of *Enoch* (viii, 2)

Milton (*Paradise Lost*, Bk i, 392) gives a list of the fallen angels

Mohammedans say that angels were created from pure, bright *gems*, the genii, of *fire*, and man, of *clay*

Angel. An obsolete English coin, current from the time of Edward IV to that of Charles I, its full name being the Angel-noble, as it was originally a reissue of the noble (*q.v*), bearing the figure of the archangel Michael slaying the dragon Its value varied from 6s 8d in 1465 (when first coined) to 10s under Edward VI. It was the coin presented to persons touched for the King's Evil (*q v.*)

Angel. In modern theatrical parlance the word is used to denote the financial backer to a play

Angel. *See* PUBLIC-HOUSE SIGNS

Angel of the Schools. St Thomas Aquinas *See* ANGELIC DOCTOR

On the side of the angels *See* SIDE.

Angels of Mons. The 3rd and 4th Divisions of the Old Contemptibles, under the command of Gen Smith-Dorrien, were sorely pressed in the retreat from Mons, August 26th and 27th, 1914. Their losses were heavy, and that they survived at all was by some attributed to divine interposition Writing from Fleet Street, Arthur Machen, a London journalist, described with great verisimilitude the host of angels who, clad in conventional white and

armed with flaming swords, held back the might of the German First Army What at first had been a "might have been" became with some a "had been"; the Angels of Mons thus grew into a phrase and a fable

Angel-beast A 17th-century card-game Five cards were dealt to each player, and three heaps formed—one for the king, one for play, and the third for Triolet The name of the game was *la bête* (beast), and an angel was a usual stake, hence the full name, much as we speak of "halfpenny nap," or "shilling auction."

This gentleman offers to play at Angel-beast, though he scarce knows the cards —SEDLEY *Mulberry Garden* (1668)

Angel visits Delightful intercourse of short duration and rare occurrence
VISITS

Like those of angels, short and far between
BLAIR *Grave*, ii, 586
Like angel visits, few and far between
CAMPBELL *Pleasures of Hope*, ii, 378

Angel-water An old Spanish cosmetic, made of roses, trefoil, and lavender So called because it was originally made chiefly of angelica

Angel-water was the worst scent about her
Sedley Bellam

Angelic Brothers. A sect of Dutch Pietists founded in the 16th century by George Gichtel Their views on marriage were similar to those held by the Abelites and Adamites (*qq v*).

Angelic Doctor. Thomas Aquinas was so called, because of the purity and excellence of his teaching His exposition of the most recondite problems of theology and philosophy was judged to be the fruit of almost more than human intelligence, and within the present century a Pope has laid it down that from St. Thomas and his *Summa Theologica* all teaching must derive

Angelic Hymn, The The hymn beginning with *Glory be to God in the highest* etc (*Luke* ii, 14), so called because the former part of it was sung by the angel host that appeared to the shepherds of Bethlehem

Angelic Salutation, The. The Ave Maria (*q v*)

Angelical Stone The speculum of Dr Dee He asserted that it was given him by the angels Raphael and Gabriel It passed into the possession of the Earl of Peterborough, thence to Lady Betty Germaine, by whom it was given to the Duke of Argyll, whose son presented it to Horace Walpole It was sold in 1842, at the dispersal of the curiosities of Strawberry Hill

Angelica (ǎn jel' i ka). This beautiful but fickle young woman was the heroine of Boiardo's *Orlando Innamorato* and Ariosto's *Orlando Furioso* Orlando's unrequited love for her drove him mad The name was used also by Congreve for the principal character in *Love for Love* and by Farquhar in *The Constant Couple* and *Sir Harry Wildair*.

Angelus, The (ǎn' je lûs) A Roman Catholic devotion in honour of the Incarnation, consisting of three texts, each said as versicle and response and followed by the Ave Maria, and a prayer So called from the first words, "Angelus Domini" (The Angel of the Lord, etc.).

The prayer is recited three times a day, at 6 a.m., noon, and 6 p.m., at the sound of a bell called the *Angelus*.

Angevin Kings of England (ăn' je vin) The early Plantagenet kings, from Henry II to John. Anjou first became connected with England in 1127, when Matilda, daughter of Henry I, married Geoffrey V, Count of Anjou, their son became Henry II of England (and Count of Anjou), and until 1205 Anjou was united to the English crown *Cp.* PLANTA-GENET.

Angle, A Dead. A term applied in old books on fortification to the ground before an angle in a wall which can neither be seen nor defended from the parapet.

Angle with a silver hook. To buy fish at market, said of an angler who, having been unsuccessful, purchases fish that will enable him to conceal his failure.

The Father of Angling, Izaak Walton (1593-1683). *See* GENTLE CRAFT, THE.

Angles. *Non Angli, sed angeli* (Not Angles, but angels) Pope Gregory the Great (reigned 590-604) who sent St Augustine to convert the English, is said to have made this remark. He saw some fair-haired boys from England in the Roman slave market and inquired about them On being told that they were Angles, he said, "Not Angles, but Angels—had they but the Gospel "

Anglo-Saxon Chronicle This relates the history of England from the birth of Christ to 1154. It is written in Anglo-Saxon, is in prose, and was probably begun in the time of Alfred the Great It is valuable for the information it gives regarding the 8th and 9th centuries

Angra Mainyu. *See* AHRIMAN

Angurvadel. Frithiof's sword, inscribed with runic letters, which blazed in time of war, but gleamed with a dim light in time of peace. *See* SWORD

Anima Mundi (ăn' i mä mŭn' dī) (the soul of the world), with the oldest of the ancient philosophers, meant "the source of life", with Plato, it meant "the animating principle of matter," inferior to pure spirit, with the Stoics, it meant " the whole vital force of the universe "

G E. Stahl (1660-1734) taught that the phenomena of animal life are due to an immortal *anima*, or vital principle distinct from matter.

Animals in Heaven. According to Mohammedan legend the following ten animals have been allowed to enter paradise:—

(1) Jonah's whale, (2) Solomon's ant; (3) the ram caught by Abraham and sacrificed instead of Isaac, (4) the lapwing of Balkis; (5) the camel of the prophet Saleh, (6) Balaam's ass, (7) the ox of Moses; (8) the dog Kratim of the Seven Sleepers, (9) Al Borak, Mohammed's ass; and (10) Noah's dove

Animals in art Some animals are appropriated to certain saints· as the calf or ox to St Luke; the cock to St Peter; the eagle to St John the Divine, the lion to St. Mark and St Jerome, the raven to St Benedict, etc.

Animals sacred to special deities. To Apollo, the wolf, the griffon, and the crow; to Bacchus, the dragon and the panther; to Diana, the stag, to Æsculapius, the serpent, to Hercules, the deer, to Isis, the heifer; to Jupiter, the eagle, to Juno, the peacock and the lamb, to the Lares, the dog; to Mars, the horse and the vulture, to Mercury, the cock, to Minerva, the owl, to Neptune, the bull, to Tethys, the halcyon, to Venus, the dove, the swan, and the sparrow, to Vulcan, the lion, etc.

Animals in symbolism. The lamb, the pelican, and the unicorn, are symbols of Christ.

The dragon, serpent, and swine, symbolize Satan and his crew.

The ant symbolizes frugality and prevision, ape, uncleanness, malice, lust, and cunning, ass, stupidity; bantam cock, pluckiness, priggishness, bat, blindness, bear, ill-temper, uncouthness, bee, industry; beetle, blindness; bull, strength, straightforwardness, bull-dog. pertinacity, butterfly, sportiveness, living in pleasure, camel, submission; cat, deceit; calf, lumpishness, cowardice; cicada, poetry; cock, vigilance, overbearing insolence; crow, longevity; crocodile, hypocrisy, cuckoo, cuckoldom, dog, fidelity, dirty habits, dove, innocence, harmlessness, duck, deceit (French, *canard*, a hoax), eagle, majesty, inspiration, elephant, sagacity, ponderosity, fly, feebleness, insignificance, fox, cunning, artifice; frog and toad, inspiration, goat, lasciviousness, goose, conceit, folly; gull, gullibility; grasshopper, old age, hare, timidity, hawk, rapacity, penetration; hen, maternal care, hog, impurity, horse, speed, grace, jackdaw, vain assumption, empty conceit, jay, senseless chatter, kitten, playfulness, lamb, innocence, sacrifice, lark, cheerfulness, leopard, sin, lion, noble courage, lynx, suspicious vigilance; magpie, garrulity, mole, blindness, obtuseness, monkey, tricks, mule, obstinacy; nightingale, forlornness, ostrich, stupidity, ox, patience, strength, and pride, owl, wisdom; parrot, mocking verbosity, peacock, pride; pigeon, cowardice (pigeon-livered), pig, obstinacy, dirtiness, gluttony, puppy, conceit, rabbit, fecundity, raven, ill luck, robin redbreast, confiding trust, serpent, wisdom, sheep, silliness, timidity; sparrow, lasciviousness, spider, wiliness; stag, cuckoldom, swan, grace, tiger, ferocity, tortoise, chastity; turkeycock, official insolence, turtle-dove, conjugal fidelity, vulture, rapine, wolf, cruelty, ferocity, worm, cringing, etc.

Animals, Cries of. To the cry, call, or voice of many animals a special name is given, to apply these names indiscriminately is always wrong and frequently ludicrous. Thus, we do not speak of the " croak " of a dog or the " bark " of a bee Apes gibber, asses bray; bees hum, beetles drone, bears growl, bitterns boom, blackbirds and thrushes whistle; bulls bellow, cats mew, purr, swear, and caterwaul, calves bleat, chaffinches chirp or pink, chickens peep, cocks crow, cows moo or low; crows caw; cuckoos cry cuckoo; deer bell, dogs bark, bay, howl, and yelp, doves coo; ducks quack, eagles, vultures, and peacocks scream, falcons chant, flies buzz, foxes bark and yelp, frogs croak, geese cackle and hiss; grasshoppers chirp and pitter, guineafowls cry "Come back", and guinea-pigs and hares squeak, hawks scream, hens cackle and cluck, horses neigh and whinny, hyenas laugh, jays and magpies chatter, kittens mew, linnets chuckle in their call, lions and tigers roar and growl, mice squeak and squeal, monkeys chatter and gibber, nightingales pipe and warble—we also speak of its "jug-jug"; owls hoot and screech, oxen low and bellow; parrots talk, peewits cry pee-wit, pigeons coo, pigs grunt, squeak, and squeal, ravens croak. rooks caw, screech-owls screech or shriek; sheep and lambs baa or bleat, snakes hiss; sparrows chirp, stags bellow and call, swallows twitter, swans cry and are said to sing just before death (see SWAN), turkey-cocks gobble; wolves howl Most birds, besides many of those here mentioned, sing, but we speak of the chick-chick of the black-cap, the drumming of the grouse, and the chirr of the whitethroat

Animosity meant originally animation, spirit, as the fire of a horse, called in Latin *equi animositas* Its present exclusive use in a bad sense is an instance of the tendency which words originally neutral have to assume a bad meaning.

Animula, vagula, etc. (an im' ū lā vǎg' ū lā) The opening of a poem to his soul, ascribed by his biographer, Ælius Spartianus, to the dying Emperor Hadrian.—

Animula, vagula, blandula,
Hospes, comesque corporis,
Quae nunc abibis in loca,
Pallidula, rigida, nudula,
Nec ut soles, dabis jocos!

It was Englished by Byron —

Ah! gentle, fleeting, wavering sprite,
Friend and associate of this clay!
To what unknown region borne,
Wilt thou now wing thy distant flight?
No more with wonted humour gay,
But pallid, cheerless, and forlorn

Ann, Mother. Ann Lee (1736-1784), the founder and "spiritual mother" of the American Society of Shakers (*q v*)

Annabel, in Dryden s *Absalom and Achitophel*, is designed for Anne Scott, Duchess of Monmouth and Countess of Buccleuch, the richest heiress in Europe The duke was faithless to her, and, after his death, the widow, still handsome, married again
To all his [Monmouth's] wishes, nothing he [David] denied,
And made the charming Annabel his bride
               I, 33

Annates (ăn' ātz) (Lat *annus*, a year) One entire year's income claimed by the Pope on the appointment of a bishop or other ecclesiastic in the Catholic Church, also called the *first fruits* By the Statute of Recusants (25 Hen. VIII, c 20, and the Confirming Act),

the right to English Annates and Tenths was transferred to the Crown, but, in the reign of Queen Anne, annates were given up to form a fund for the augmentation of poor livings. *See* QUEEN ANNE'S BOUNTY

Anne's Great Captain. The Duke of Marlborough (1650-1722)

Annie Laurie was eldest of the three daughters of Sir Robert Laurie, of Maxwelton, born December 16th, 1682 William Douglas, of Finglad (Kirkcudbright), wrote the popular song, but Annie married, in 1709, James Fergusson, of Craigdarroch, and was the grandmother of Alexander Fergusson, the hero of Burns's song called *The Whistle*

Anno Domini (ăn' ŏ dom' i nī) (Lat) In the Year of our Lord, *i e* in the year since the Nativity; generally abbreviated to "A D " It was Dionysius Exiguus who fixed the date of the Nativity, he lived in the early 6th century, and his computation is probably late by some three to six years
The phrase is sometimes used as a slang synonym for old age, thus, "Anno Domini is his trouble," means that he is suffering from senile decay

Annunciation, The Day of the. March 25th, also called *Lady Day*, on which the angel announced to the Virgin Mary that she would be the mother of the Messiah

Order of the Annunciation. An Italian order of military knights, founded as the Order of the Collar by Amadeus VI of Savoy in 1362, and dating under its present name from 1518 It has on its collar the letters F E R T *Fert* (Lat he bears) is an ancient motto of the House of Savoy, but the letters have also been interpreted as standing for the initials of *Fortitudo Ejus Rhodum Tenuit*, in allusion to the succour rendered to Rhodes by Savoy in 1310; *Fœdere et Religione Tenemur*, on the gold doubloon of Victor Amadeus I (1718-1730), or, *Fortitudo Ejus Rempublicam Tenet*

Sisters of the Annunciation. See FRANCISCANS

Annus Luctus (ăn' us lŭk' tūs) (Lat the year of mourning) The period during which a widow is supposed to remain unmarried If she marries within about nine months from the death of her husband and a child is born, a doubt might arise as to its paternity Such a marriage is not illegal.

Annus Mirabilis (ăn' us mir ăb' i lis) The year of wonders, 1666, memorable for the great fire of London and the successes of English arms over the Dutch Dryden wrote a poem with this title, in which he described both these events

Anodyne Necklace, An. An anodyne is a medicine to relieve pain, and the anodyne necklace was an amulet supposed to be efficacious against various diseases. In Johnson's *Idler*, No 40, we read.—
The true pathos of advertisements must have sunk deep into the heart of every man that remembers the zeal shown by the seller of the *anodyne necklace*, for the ease and safety of poor toothing infants

The term soon came to be applied to the hangman's noose, and we have George Primrose saying:—

> May I die by an anodyne necklace, but I had rather be an under-turnkey than an usher in a boarding-school —GOLDSMITH *Vicar of Wakefield*, ch xx.

Anon. The O E *on ane*, in one (state, mind, course, body, etc), the present meaning—*soon, in a little while*—being a misuse of the earlier meaning—*straightway, at once*—much as *directly* and *immediately* are misused *Mark* 1, 30, gives an instance of the old meaning—

> But Simon's wife's mother lay sick of a fever, and anon they tell him of her

this is the Authorized Version, the Revised Version gives *straightway* Wordsworth s—

> Fast the churchyard fills,—anon
> Look again and they all are gone
> *White Doe of Rylstone*, i, 31

exemplifies the later meaning The word also was used by servants, tapsters, etc , as an interjectory reply meaning ' Coming, sir ' "

Answer is the O E *and-swaru*, verb *and-swarian* or *swerian*, where *and* is the preposition=the Lat. *re* in *re-spond-eo* To *swear* (*q.v.*) means literally ' to affirm something," and to *an-swear* is to ' say something" by way of rejoinder

To answer its purpose To carry out what was expected or what was intended

To answer more Scotico. To divert the direct question by starting another question or subject

Antæus (ăn tē' us), in Greek mythology, a gigantic wrestler (son of Earth and Sea, Ge and Poseidon), whose strength was invincible so long as he touched the earth When he was lifted his strength diminished, but it was renewed by touching the earth again.

Antarctica (ăn tark' tik a) The name given to the great continent that covers the region of the South Pole. Its area is about 5,000,000 sq miles. It contains mountains from 8,000 to 15,000 ft in height, with several volcanoes, of which only one, Mt Erebus, is now active There are no land animals, but it is notable for its penguins There is no international agreement as to territorial rights, which lie largely between Britain, the Commonwealth of Australia and Argentina.

Antediluvian Before the Deluge The word is colloquially used in a disparaging way for anything that is very out of date

Anthology. The Greek anthology is a collection of several thousand short Greek poems by many authors of every period of Greek literature from the Persian war to the decadence of Byzantium The most complete edition was published in 1794-1814

Anthony the Great, St. The patron saint of swineherds; he lived in the 4th century, and was the founder of the fraternity of ascetics who lived in the deserts The story of his temptations by the devil is well known in literature and art His day is 17th January Not to be confused with **St. Anthony of Padua**, who was a Franciscan of the 13th century, and

is commemorated on June 13th. *See also* TANTONY

St. Anthony's fire. Erysipelas is so called from the tradition that those who sought the intercession of St. Anthony recovered from the pestilential erysipelas called the *sacred fire*, which proved so fatal in 1089

St. Anthony's pig A pet pig, the smallest of the litter, also called the "tantony pig ' (*q v*), in allusion to St Anthony being the patron saint of swineherds

The term is also used of a sponger or hanger-on Stow says that the officers of the market used to slit the ears of pigs unfit for food. One day one of the proctors of St Anthony's Hospital tied a bell about a pig whose ear was slit, and no one would ever hurt it . The pig would follow like a dog anyone who fed it

Anthroposophus (ăn thrō pos' ŏ fus) The nickname of Thomas Vaughan (1622-1666), the alchemist, twin-brother of Henry Vaughan, the Silurist He was rector of St Bridget's in Brecknockshire, and was so called from his *Anthroposophia Teomagica* (1650), a book written to show the condition of man after death.

Anthroposophy (ăn thrō pos' ŏ fi) The word comes from the Greek *anthropos*, a man, and *sophia*, knowledge, and is the name given to a system of esoteric philosophy enunciated by Rudolf Steiner (1861-1925) who defined it as "the knowledge of the spiritual human being and of everything which the spirit man can perceive in the spiritual world "

Antic Hay. *See* HAY

Antichrist The many legends connected with Antichrist, or the Man of Sin, expected by some to precede the second coming of Christ, that were so popular in the Middle Ages are chiefly founded on 2 *Thes* ii, 1-12, and *Rev* xiii. In ancient times Antichrist was identified with Caligula, Nero, etc , and there is little doubt that in 2 *Thes* ii, 7, St Paul was referring to the Roman Empire Mohammed was also called Antichrist, and the name has been given to many disturbers of the world's peace, even to Napoleon and to William II of Germany (*see* NUMBER OF THE BEAST) The Mohammedans have a legend that Christ will slay the Antichrist at the gate of the church at Lydda, in Palestine.

Anti-pope. A pope chosen or nominated by temporal authority in opposition to one canonically elected by the cardinals; or one who usurps the papacy. the term is particularly applied to rival claimants to the papal Throne during the Great Schism of the West, 1309-1376 They are —

Nicholas V	1328-1330	Clement XIII	1424-1429
Clement VII	1378-1394	Benedict XIV	1424
Benedict XIII	1394-1424	Felix V	1439-1449

Antigone (ăn tig' ŏ ni). The subject of a tragedy by Sophocles, she was the daughter of Œdipus by his mother, Jocasta. In consequence of disobeying an edict of Creon she was imprisoned in a cave, where she slew herself She was famed for her devotion to her brother, Polynices, hence the Duchess of

Angoulême (1778-1851), sister and prison companion of Louis XVII, was sometimes called *the Modern Antigone*

Antimony (ăn' tĭ mon ĭ)   A word of unknown, but (as it was introduced through alchemy) probably of Arabian, origin   "Popular etymology" has been busy with this word, and Johnson—copying earlier writers—in his *Dictionary* derives it from the Greek *antimon-achos* (bad for monks), telling the story that a prior once gave some of this mineral to his convent pigs, who thrived upon it, and became very fat   He next tried it on the monks, who died from its effects

Antinomian (ăn tĭ nō' mĭ ăn) (Gr *anti-nomos*, exempt from the law)   One who believes that Christians are not bound to observe the "law of God, ' but "may continue in sin that grace may abound "   The term was first applied to John Agricola by Martin Luther, and was given to a sect that arose in Germany about 1535

Antinous (ăn tin' ŏ ŭs)   A model of manly beauty   He was the page of Hadrian, the Roman Emperor

Antiquarian.   A standard size of drawing paper measuring 53 in   by 31 in

Antisthenes (ăn tis' the nēz)   Founder of the Cynic School in Athens, born about 444 B C , died about 370   He wore a ragged cloak, and carried a wallet and staff like a beggar   Socrates, whose pupil he was, wittily said he could "see rank pride peering through the holes of Antisthenes' rags "

Antoninus (ăn tō nī' nus)   *The Wall of Anto-ninus*   A wall of regularly laid sods resting on a stone pavement, built by the Romans about 100 miles north of Hadrian's Wall, from Dumbarton on the Clyde to Carriden on the Forth, under the direction of Lollius Urbicus, governor of the province under Antoninus Pius, about A D 140   It was probably some 14 ft thick at the base and about the same height; it was fortified at frequent intervals, and was fronted by a deep ditch

Antrustions (ăn trŭs' tĭ onz) (O Fr , from O H Ger *trost*, trust, fidelity).   The chief followers of the Frankish kings, who were specially trusty to them

> None but the king could have antrustions
>   STUBBS *Constitutional History*, I, ix

Anubis (a nū' bis)   In Egyptian mythology similar to the Hermes of Greece, whose office it was to take the souls of the dead before the judge of the infernal regions   Anubis was the son of Osiris the judge, and is represented with a human body and jackal's head

Anvil.   It is on the anvil, under deliberation, the project is in hand

Anzac.   Word coined in 1915 from the initials of Australian and New Zealand Army Corps.   It was then applied to the area in Gallipoli where those troops landed   The word was used again in World War II.

Anzac Day, April 25th, commemorating the landing of the Corps in Gallipoli in 1915

Anzac Pact.   The agreement between Australia and New Zealand in 1944.

Aonian (ā ō' nĭ an)   Poetical, pertaining to the Muses.   The Muses, according to Greek mythology, dwelt in Aonia, that part of Bœotia which contains Mount Helicon and the Muses' Fountain   Milton speaks of "the Aonian mount" (*Paradise Lost*, i, 15), and Thomson calls the fraternity of poets

> The Aonian hive
> Who praised are, and starve right merrily
>   *Castle of Indolence*, ii, 2.

À outrance   *See* À L'OUTRANCE

Apache (a păch' ĭ)   The name of a tribe of North American Indians, given to—or adopted by—the hooligans and roughs of Paris about the opening of the present century (in this case pronounced a păsh')   The use of the name for this purpose has a curious parallel in the Mohocks (*q v*) of the 17th century

Ape.   To copy, to imitate

The buffoon ape, in Dryden's *The Hind and the Panther*, means the Freethinkers

> Next her [*the bear*] the buffoon ape, as atheists use,
> Mimicked all sects, and had his own to choose
>   Part i, 39

He keeps them, like an ape, in the corner of his jaw; first mouthed, to be last swallowed (*Hamlet* iv, 2)   Most of the Old World monkeys have cheek pouches, which they use as receptacles for food

To lead apes in hell   It is an old saying (frequent in the Elizabethan dramatists) that this is the fate of old maids   Hence, *ape-leader*, an old maid.

> I will even take sixpence in earnest of the bear-ward, and lead his apes into hell
>   SHAKESPEARE *Much Ado about Nothing*, ii, 1
> Women, dying maids, lead apes in hell
>   *The London Prodigal*, i, 2
> I will rather hazard my being one of the Devil's
> Ape-leaders, than to marry while he is melancholy
>   BROME *The Jovial Crew*, ii.

To play the ape, to play practical jokes   to play silly tricks, to make facial imitations, like an ape

To put an ape into your hood (or cap)—*i e.* to make a fool of you   Apes were formerly carried on the shoulders of fools and simpletons

To say an ape's paternoster, is to chatter with fright or cold, like an ape   One of the books in Rabelais' "Library of St. Victor" is called "The Ape's Paternoster "

Apelles (a pel' ēz)   A famous Grecian painter, contemporary with Alexander the Great   He was born at Colophon, on the coast of Asia Minor, and is known as the *Chian painter*—

> The Chian painter, when he was required
> To portrait Venus in her perfect hue,
> To make his work more absolute, desired
> Of all the fairest maids to have the view
>   SPENSER. *Dedicatory Sonnets*, xvii

Apemantus (ăp e măn 'tus)   A churlish philosopher, in *Timon of Athens*

A-per-se (ā pěr sē)   An A 1, a person or thing of unusual merit   'A" all alone, with no one who can follow, *nemo proximus aut secundus*

Chaucer calls Cresseide "the floure and A-per-se of Troi and Greek "

> London, thou art of townes *A-per-se*
>   DUNBAR (1501)

Apex. The topmost height, summit, or tiptop; originally the pointed olive-wood spike on the top of the cap of a Roman flamen; also the crest or spike of a helmet

Aphrodite (ăf′ rō dī tı) (Gr *aphros*, foam) The Greek Venus; so called because she sprang from the foam of the sea

Aphrodite's girdle. The cestus (*q v.*)

Apicius (a pıs′ı us) A gourmand Marcus Gabius Apicius was a Roman gourmand of the time of Augustus and Tiberius, whose income being reduced by his luxurious living to only ten million sesterces (about £80,000), put an end to his life, to avoid the misery of being obliged to live on plain diet

A-pigga-back. *See* PICK-A-BACK

Apis (ā′ pıs) In Egyptian mythology, the bull of Memphis, sacred to Osiris of whose soul it was supposed to be the image The sacred bull had to have natural spots on the forehead forming a triangle, and a half-moon on the breast. It was not suffered to live more than twenty-five years, when it was sacrificed and buried with great pomp Cambyses, King of Persia (529-522 B.C), and conqueror of Egypt, slew the sacred bull of Memphis with his own hands, and is said to have become mad in consequence

Apocalyptic Number 666 *See* NUMBER OF THE BEAST

Apocrypha (a pok′ rı fa) (Gr *apokrupto*, hidden), hence, of unknown authorship the explanation given in the Preface to the Apocrypha in the 1539 Bible that the books are so called ' because they were wont to be read not openly . . but, as it were, in secret and apart" is not tenable Those books included in the Septuagint and Vulgate versions of the Old Testament, but which, at the Reformation, were excluded from the Sacred Canon by the Protestants, mainly on the grounds that they were not originally written in Hebrew, and were not looked upon as genuine by the Jews. They are not printed in Protestant Bibles in ordinary circulation, but in the Authorized Version, as printed in 1611, they are given immediately after the Old Testament The books are as follows:—

1 and 2 Esdras	Baruch, with the Epistle of Jeremiah
Tobit	
Judith	The Song of the Three Children.
The rest of Esther	The Story of Susanna
Wisdom	The Idol Bel and the Dragon
Ecclesiasticus	1 and 2 Maccabees

The New Testament also has a large number of apocryphal books more or less attached to it · these consist of later gospels and epistles, apocalypses, etc., as well as such recently discovered fragments as the *Logia* (sayings of Jesus) of the Oxyrhynchus papyrus The best-known books of the New Testament apocrypha are:—

Protevangelium, or the Book of James
Gospel of Nicodemus, or the Acts of Pilate.
The Ascent of James.
The Acts of Paul and Thecla
Letters of Abgarus to Christ
Epistles of Paul to the Laodiceans, and to the Alexandrines, and the Third Epistle to the Corinthians.
The Teaching of the Apostles (Didache)
The three Books of the Shepherd of Hermas

Apollinarians (a pol ın âr′ ı anz) An heretical sect founded in the middle of the 4th century by Apollinaris, a presbyter of Laodicea. They denied that Christ had a human soul, and asserted that the *Logos* supplied its place The heresy was condemned at the Council of Chalcedon, the fourth General Council, 451

Apollo (a pol′ ō) In Greek and Roman mythology, son of Zeus and Leto (Latona), one of the great gods of Olympus, typifying the sun in its light- and life-giving as well as in its destroying power, often identified with Helios, the sun-god He was god of music, poetry, and the healing art, the latter of which he bestowed on his son, Æsculapius He is represented in art as the perfection of youthful manhood

　　　　The fire-robed god,
Golden Apollo
　　　　SHAKESPEARE· *Winter's Tale*, ıv, 4
Apollo with the plectrum strook
The chords, and from beneath his hands a crash
Of mighty sounds rushed forth, whose music shook
The soul with sweetness, and like an adept
His sweeter voice a just accordance kept,
　　　　SHELLEY *Homer's Hymn to Mercury*, lxxxv

A perfect Apollo is a model of manly beauty, referring to the Apollo Belvedere (*q v*).

Apollo of Portugal. Luis Camoens (c 1524-1580), author of the *Lusiad*, the great Portuguese poet, who ended his days in poverty

Apollo Belvedere. An ancient marble statue, supposed to be a Roman-Greek copy of a bronze votive statue set up at Delphi in commemoration of the repulse of an attack by the Gauls on the shrine of Apollo in 279 B C It represents the god holding the remains of a bow, or (according to some conjectures) an ægis, in his left hand, and is called Belvedere from the Belvedere Gallery of the Vatican, where it stands It was discovered in 1495, amidst the ruins of Antium and was purchased by Pope Julius II

Apollodoros (a pol′ ō dôr′ us) Plato says· "Who would not rather be a man of sorrows than Apollodoros, envied by all for his enormous wealth, yet nourishing in his heart the scorpions of a guilty conscience?" (*The Republic*) This Apollodorus was the tyrant of Cassandrea. He obtained the supreme power 379 B C, exercised it with the utmost cruelty, and was put to death by Antigonos Gonatas

Apollonius of Tyre. *See* PERICLES.

Apollonius of Tyana (fl *c.* 4 B C) A Pythagorean philosopher He professed to have powers of magic and it was he who discovered that the young Phoenician woman whom Menippus Lycius intended to wed was in fact a serpent, or *lamia* This story was noted by Robert Burton in his *Anatomy of Melancholy*, and it forms the subject of Keats's *Lamia*

Apollyon (â pol′ yon) The Greek name of Abaddon (*q v.*), king of hell and angel of the bottomless pit. (*Rev* ıx, 11) His introduction by Bunyan into the *Pilgrim's Progress* has made his name familiar.

Aposiopesis. *See* QUOS EGO.

Apostate, The Julian, the Roman emperor (331-363) He was brought up as a Christian, but on his accession to the throne (361) he announced his conversion to paganism and proclaimed the free toleration of all religions.

A posteriori (ā pos tē′ rı ŏr′ ī) (Lat from the latter) An *a posteriori* argument is proving the cause from the effect Thus, if we see a watch we conclude there was a watchmaker. Robinson Crusoe inferred there was another human being on the desert island, because he saw a human footprint in the wet sand. It is thus the existence and character of God are inferred from His works *See* A PRIORI

Apostles In the preamble of the statutes instituting the Order of St. Michael, founded in 1469 by Louis XI, the archangel is styled "my lord," and is created a knight The apostles had been already ennobled and knighted We read of "the Earl Peter," "Count Paul,' "the Baron Stephen," and so on. Thus, in the introduction of a sermon upon St. Stephen's Day, we have these lines'—

Contes vous vueille la patron
De St Estreul le baron
The Apostles were gentlemen of bloude . . and Christ . . might, if He had esteemed of the vayne glorye of this world, have borne coat armour
The Blazon of Gentrie

The badges or symbols of the fourteen apostles (i e the twelve original apostles-with Matthias and Paul)

Andrew, *an X-shaped cross,* because he was crucified on one

Bartholomew, *a knife,* because he was flayed with a knife.

James the Great, *a scallop shell, a pilgrim's staff,* or *a gourd bottle,* because he is the patron saint of pilgrims *See* SCALLOP SHELL

James the Less, *a fuller's pole,* because he was killed by a blow on the head with a pole, dealt him by Simeon the fuller

John, *a cup with a winged serpent flying out of it,* in allusion to the tradition about Aristodemos, priest of Diana, who challenged John to drink a cup of poison John made the sign of a cross on the cup, Satan like a dragon flew from it, and John then drank the cup which was quite innocuous

Judas Iscariot, *a bag,* because he had the bag and "bare what was put therein" (*John* xii, 6)

Jude, *a club,* because he was martyred with a club

Matthew, *a hatchet* or *halberd,* because he was slain at Nadabar with a halberd

Matthias, *a battleaxe* because he was first stoned, and then beheaded with a battleaxe

Paul, *a sword,* because his head was cut off with a sword The convent of La Lisla, in Spain, boasts of possessing the very instrument

Peter, *a bunch of keys,* because Christ gave him the "keys of the kingdom of heaven " *A cock,* because he went out and wept bitterly when he heard the cock crow (*Matt* xxvi, 75)

Philip, *a long staff surmounted with a cross,* because he suffered death by being suspended by the neck from a tall pillar

Simon, *a saw,* because he was sawn to death, according to tradition

Thomas *a lance,* because he was pierced through the body, at Meliapour, with a lance

According to Catholic legend, seven of the Apostles are buried at Rome.

ANDREW lies buried at Amalfi (Naples).

BARTHOLOMEW, at Rome, in the church of Bartholomew, on the Tiber Island

JAMES THE GREAT was buried at St Jago de Compostella, in Spain.

JAMES THE LESS, at Rome, in the church of SS Philip and James

JOHN, at Ephesus

JUDE, at Rome

MATTHEW, at Salerno (Naples)

MATTHIAS, at Rome, under the altar of the Basilica

PAUL, somewhere in Italy

PETER, at Rome, in the church of St Peter.

PHILIP, at Rome

SIMON or SIMEON, at Rome

THOMAS, at Ortona (Naples) (? Madras)

The supposed remains of MARK THE EVANGELIST were buried at Venice, about 800

LUKE THE EVANGELIST is said to have been buried at Padua

N B—Italy claims thirteen of these apostles or evangelists—Rome seven, Naples three, Mark at Venice, Luke at Padua, and Paul at Rome.

See EVANGELISTS.

Apostles of

Abyssinians, St. Frumentius (Fourth century)

Alps, Felix Neff (1798-1829)

Andalusia, Juan de Avila (1500-1569)

Ardennes, St Hubert (656-727)

Armenians, Gregory of Armenia, "The Illuminator " (256-331)

Brazil, Jose de Anchieta, a Jesuit missionary (1533-1597)

English, St. Augustine (Died 604) St George.

Free Trade, Richard Cobden (1804-1865)

French, St Denis (Third century)

Frisians, St Willibrod (657-738)

Gauls, St Irenæus (130-200), St Martin of Tours (338-401).

Gentiles, St Paul

Germany, St Boniface (680-755)

Highlanders, St Columba (521-597)

Hungary, St Anastatius (954-1044)

Indians (American), Bartolomé de Las Casas (1474-1566), John Eliot (1604-1690).

Indies (East), St Francis Xavier (1506-1552)

Infidelity, Voltaire (1694-1778)

Ireland, St Patrick (373-463)

North, St Ansgar or Anscarius, missionary to Scandinavia (180-864), Bernard Gilpin, Archdeacon of Durham, evangelist on the Scottish border (1517-1583)

Peru, Alonzo de Barcena, a Jesuit missionary (1528-1598)

Picts, St Ninian (Fifth century)

Scottish Reformers, John Knox (1505-1572)

Slavs, St Cyril (c 820-869)

Spain, St James the Great (Died 62)

The Sword, Mohammed (570-632)

Temperance, Father Mathew (1790-1856)

Yorkshire, Paulinus, bishop of York and Rochester (Died 644)

Wales, St David (Died about 601)

Prince of the Apostles. St Peter (*Matt* xvi, 18, 19)

Twelve Apostles. The last twelve names on the poll or list of ordinary degrees were so called, when the list was arranged in order of merit, and not alphabetically, as now, they were also called the *Chosen Twelve* The last of the twelve was designated "St Paul," from a play on the verse 1 *Cor.* xv, 9 The same term was later applied to the last twelve in the Mathematical Tripos

Apostle spoons Spoons having the figure of one of the apostles at the top of the handle, formerly given at christenings Sometimes twelve spoons, representing the twelve apostles; sometimes four, representing the four evangelists, and sometimes only one, was presented Occasionally a set occurs containing in addition the " Master Spoon " and the " Lady Spoon "

Apostles' Creed. A Church creed supposed to be an epitome of doctrine taught by the apostles. It was received into the Latin Church, in its present form, in the 11th century, but a formula somewhat like it existed in the 2nd century Items were added in the 4th and 5th centuries, and verbal alterations much later.

Apostolic Fathers. Christian authors born in the 1st century, when the apostles lived. John is supposed to have died about A D 99, and Polycarp, the last of the Apostolic Fathers, born about 69, was his disciple Clement of Rome (died about 100), Ignatius (died about 115), Polycarp (about 69-155), St Barnabas, to whom an apocryphal epistle (now usually assigned to the 2nd century) was ascribed by Clemens Alexandrinus and Origen (martyred, 61), Hermas (author of *The Shepherd of Hermas*, and possibly identical with the Hermes of *Rom* xvi, 14), and Papias, a bishop of Hierapolis, mentioned by Eusebius

Apostolic Majesty A title borne by the emperors of Austria, as kings of Hungary It was conferred by Pope Sylvester II on the King of Hungary in 1000. *Cp* RELIGIOUS

Apostolic Succession This is the term in use for the doctrine that the mission given to the apostles by Christ (*John* xx, 23 and *Matt* xxviii, 19) must extend to their legitimate successors in an unbroken line This means in practice that only those clergy who have been ordained by bishops who are themselves in the succession can administer the sacraments and perform other sacerdotal functions

Apparel One meaning of this word used to be "ornament" or "embellishment," especially the embroidery on ecclesiastical vestments In the 19th century it was revived, and applied to the ornamental parts of the alb at the lower edge and at the wrists. Pugin says —

The albe should be made with apparels worked in silk or gold, embroidered with ornaments —*Glossary of Ecclesiastical Ornament* (1844)

Appeal to the Country, To. To ask the nation to express their opinion on some moot question In order to obtain such public opinion Parliament must be dissolved and a general election held

Appiades (ăp' i a děz). Five divinities whose temple stood near the fountains of Appius, in Rome. Their names are Venus, Pallas, Concord Peace, and Vesta They were represented on horseback, like Amazons

Appian Way (ăp' i an) The oldest and best known of all the Roman roads, leading from Rome to Brundisium (Brindisi) by way of Capua This "queen of roads" was begun by Appius Claudius, the decemvir, 313 B C

Apple The well-known story of Newton and the Apple originated with Voltaire, who tells us that Mrs Conduit, Newton's niece, told him that Newton was at Woolsthorpe (visiting his mother) in 1666, when, seeing an apple fall, he was led into the train of thought which resulted in his establishment of the law of gravitation (1685)

Apple of Discord. A cause of dispute, something to contend about At the marriage of Thetis and Peleus, where all the gods and goddesses met together, Discord (Eris), who had not been invited, threw on the table a golden apple "for the most beautiful " Juno, Minerva, and Venus put in their separate claims, the point was referred to Paris (*q v*), who gave judgment in favour of Venus This brought upon him the vengeance of Juno and Minerva, to whose spite the fall of Troy is attributed

The apple appears more than once in Greek story; *see* ATALANTA'S RACE, HESPERIDES

There is no mention of an apple in the Bible story of Eve's temptation. We have no further particulars than that it was "the fruit of the tree in the midst of the garden," and the Mohammedans leave the matter equally vague, though their commentators hazard the guess that it may have been an ear of wheat, or the fruit of the vine or the fig The apple is a comparatively late conjecture.

For the story of William Tell and the apple, *see* TELL

Prince Ahmed's apple. In the *Arabian Nights* story of Prince Ahmed, a cure for every disorder The prince purchased it at Samarcand

Apples of Istakhar are "all sweetness on one side, and all bitterness on the other "

Apples of Paradise, according to tradition, had a bite on one side, to commemorate the bite given by Eve

Apples of perpetual youth. In Scandinavian mythology, the golden apples of perpetual youth, in the keeping of Idhunn, daughter of the dwarf Svald, and wife of Bragi It is by tasting them that the gods preserve their youth

Apples of Pyban, says Sir John Mandeville, fed the pigmies with their odour only

Apples of Sodom. Thevenot says—"There are apple-trees on the sides of the Dead Sea which bear lovely fruit, but within are full of ashes " Josephus Strabo, Tacitus, and others speak of these apples, and are probably referring to the gall-nuts produced by the insect *Cynips insana* The phrase is used figuratively for anything disappointing

You see, my lords, what goodly fruit she seems:
Yet like those apples travellers report
To bow where Sodom and Gomorrah stood,
I will but touch her, and straight you will see
She'll fall to soot and ashes
                    WEBSTER *The White Devil*

Apple of the eye The pupil, because it was anciently supposed to be a round solid ball like an apple Figuratively applied to anything extremely dear or extremely sensitive He kept him as the apple of his eye —*Deut* xxxii, 10

Apple-cart. To upset the apple-cart To ruin carefully laid plans To have one's expectations blighted, as a farmer's might be when his load of apples was overturned This phrase is recorded as in use as early as 1796

Apple-jack. An apple-turnover is sometimes so called in East Anglia In the United States the name is given to a drink distilled from fermented apple juice—like French Calvados

Apple-john. An apple so called from its being at maturity about St John's Day (Dec. 27th) We are told that apple-johns will keep for two years, and are best when shrivelled.

> I am withered like an old apple-john.
> SHAKESPEARE 1 *Henry IV*, III, 3.

Sometimes incorrectly called the Apples of King John

Apple-pie bed A bed in which the sheets are so folded that a person cannot get his legs down, perhaps a corruption of "a *nappe-plit* bed," from the Fr *nappe pliee*, a folded sheet Also incorrectly used by schoolboys to describe a bed into which a quantity of strange objects have been piled to discomfit the occupant.

Apple-pie order Prim and precise order. The origin of this phrase is still doubtful. Perhaps the suggestion made above of *nappe-pli* (Fr *nappes pliees*), folded linen, neat as folded linen) is near the mark

Apple-polishing An attempt to win favour by gifts or flattery From the practice of American schoolchildren of bringing shiny apples to their teachers

Apple Tree Gang The name given to John Reid, and his friends, from Scotland, who were responsible for the introduction of Golf into U S A in 1888, at Yonkers, N Y The name was coined in 1892 when Reid and his friends moved to their 3rd "course" at Yonkers—a 34-acre orchard which yielded six holes

Après moi le déluge. After me the deluge—I care not what happens after I am dead and gone It is recorded that Madame de Pompadour (1721-64) mistress of Louis XV said, *Après nous le déluge*, when remonstrated with on account of the extravagances of the Court It is probable that she had heard the phrase on the lips of her royal lover Metternich, the Austrian statesman (1773-1859) also used the expression, but his meaning was that when his guiding hand was removed, things would probably go to rack and ruin.

April The month when trees unfold and the womb of Nature opens with young life (Lat. *aperire*, to open)
The old Dutch name was *Gras-maand* (grass-month), the old Saxon, *Easter-monath* (orient or pascal-month) In the French Republican calendar it was called *Germinal* (the time of budding, March 21st to April 19th)

April fool. Called in France *un poisson d'Avril* (*q v*), and in Scotland a *gowk* (cuckoo) In Hindustan similar tricks are played at the Huli Festival (March 31st) So that it cannot refer to the uncertainty of the weather, nor yet to a mockery of the trial of our Redeemer, the two most popular explanations A better solution is this As March 25th used to be New Year's Day, April 1st was its octave, when its festivities culminated and ended
It may be a relic of the Roman "Cerealia," held at the beginning of April The tale is that Proserpina was sporting in the Elysian meadows, and had just filled her lap with daffodils, when Pluto carried her off to the lower world Her mother, Ceres, heard the echo of her screams and went in search of "the voice", but her search was a fool's errand, it was hunting the gowk, or looking for the ' echo of a scream "

A priori (ā prī ôr ′ı) (Lat. from an antecedent) An *a priori* argument is one in which a fact is deduced from something antecedent, as when we infer certain effects from given causes All mathematical proofs are of the *a priori* kind, whereas judgments in the law courts are usually *a posteriori* (*q.v*), we infer the animus from the act.

Apron (O Fr *napperon*) Originally *napron* in English, this word is representative of a considerable number that have either lost or gained an "n' through coalescence—or the reverse—with the article ' a" or "an" *A napron* became *an apron*. Other examples are *adder* for *a nadder*, *auger* for *a nauger*, and *umpire* for *a numpire* The opposite coalescence may be seen in *newt* for *an ewt*, nickname for *an ekename*, and the old *nuncle* for *mine uncle* Cp NONCE.

A bishop's apron represents the short cassock which, by the 74th canon, all clergymen were enjoined to wear

A kilt-apron is a brown linen washable apron with a pocket in front in lieu of a sporran, worn with the kilt by Scottish troops in battle or when they have dirty work to do

Apron-string tenure. A tenure held in virtue of one's wife Tied to his mother's apron-string Completely under his mother's thumb Applied to a big boy or young man who is still under mother rule

Aqua Regia (āk′ wa rē′ ja) (Lat royal water) A mixture of one part of nitric acid, with from two to four of hydrochloric acid, so called because it dissolves gold, *the king of metals.*

Aqua Tofana (āk′ wà tof′ ä nà). A poisonous liquid containing arsenic, much used in Italy in the 18th century by young wives who wanted to get rid of their husbands. It was invented about 1690 by a Greek woman named Tofana, who called it the *Manna of St Nicholas of Bari*, from the widespread notion that an oil of miraculous efficacy flowed from the tomb of that saint

Aqua vitæ (āk′ wa vī′ tē) (Lat water of life) Bransy, any spirituous liquor, also, formerly, certain ardent spirits used by the alchemists Ben Jonson terms a seller of such an "acquavitæ man" (*Alchemist*, i 1). The "elixir of life " (*q v*) was made from these spirits *See* EAU DE VIE

Aquarius (a kwâr′ ı us) (Lat. the water-bearer). The eleventh of the twelve zodiacal constellations, representing the figure of a man with his left hand raised and with his right pouring from a ewer a stream of water; it is the eleventh division of the ecliptic, which the sun enters on January 21st, though this does not now coincide with the constellation

Aquila non captat muscas (āk′ wı la non cǎp′ tǎt mūs′ kǎs) A Latin phrase, "An eagle does not hawk at flies," a proverbial saying implying that little things are beneath a great man's contempt

Aquiline. Raymond's matchless steed *See* HORSE

Aquinian Sage, The. Juvenal is so called because he was born at Aquinum, a town of the Volscians.

Arabesque. An adjective and noun applied to the Arabian and Moorish style of decoration and architecture. One of its chief features is that no representation of animal forms is admitted. During the Spanish wars in the reign of Louis XIV, arabesque decorations were profusely introduced into France.

Arabia It was Ptolemy who was the author of the threefold division into **Arabia Petræa,** "Stony Arabia", **Arabia Felix** (*Yemen*), "Fertile Arabia," *i e* the south-west coast; and **Arabia Deserta,** "Desert Arabia "

Arabian Bird, The. The phœnix; hence, figuratively, a marvellous or unique person.

> All of her that is out of door most rich!
> If she be furnish'd with a mind so rare,
> She is alone the Arabian bird
>   SHAKESPEARE *Cymbeline,* i, 6.

Arabian Nights Entertainments, The. A collection of ancient Oriental tales, first collected in its present form about 1450, probably in Cairo. The first European translation was the French one by Antoine Galland (12 vols, 1704-8), which is a free rendering of the oldest known MS (1548). There are English translations founded on this by R. Heron (4 vols., 1792), W Beloe (4 vols , 1795), and others. In 1840 E W Lane published an entirely new translation (3 vols) made from the latest Arabic edition (Cairo 1835); John Payne's translation appeared in 4 vols , 1882-4 Sir Richard Burton's literal translation was the first unexpurgated edition, and is enriched by a great number of exhaustive notes on Oriental manners and customs It was issued by the Kamashastra Society of Benares, in 10 vols , 1885-6, followed by 6 vols. of *Supplemental Nights* in 1886-8. The standard French translation is that by J. C. Mardrus, 16 vols., 1899-1904, which has been severely criticized by Arabic scholars.

Arabians. A name given to the early Nestorians and Jacobites in Arabia, also to an heretical Arabian sect of the 3rd century, which maintained that the soul dies with the body; and to a sect which believed that the soul died and rose again with the body

Arabic figures The figures 1, 2, 3, 4, etc So called because they were introduced into Europe (Spain) by the Moors or Arabs (about the end of the 10th century), who brought them from India about 250 years earlier. They were not generally adopted in Europe till after the invention of printing Far more important than the characters, is the decimalism of these figures *1* figure = units, 2 figures = tens, 3 figures = hundreds, and so on *ad infinitum* *Cp.* NUMERALS

The figures i, ii, iii, iv, v, vi, vii, viii, ix, x, etc , are called Roman figures

Street Arabs. Children of the houseless poor; street children So called because, like the Arabs, they are nomads or wanderers with no settled home

Arachne's Labours (a räk' ni) In Greek legend Arachne was so skilful a spinner that she challenged Minerva to a trial of skill, and hanged herself because the goddess beat her Minerva then changed her into a spider Hence **arachnida,** the scientific name for spiders, scorpions, and mites

Aram, Eugene (âr' am) (1704-59) This murderer was a man of considerable learning, who, while a schoolmaster at Knaresborough, became involved with a man named Clark in a series of frauds in 1745 he murdered Clark, but the crime was not discovered until 1758, when Clark's skeleton was found. Aram was arrested while teaching in a school at King's Lynn, tried and executed, 6 August, 1759 He was said to be a proficient scholar in Latin, Greek, Hebrew, Arabic, French, and Welsh. His story forms the theme of Lytton's novel *Eugene Aram*

Aratus (a rā' tūs) A Greek statesman and general (271-213 B C), famous for his patriotism and devotion to freedom He liberated his native Sicyon from the usurper Nicocles, and would not allow even a picture of a king to exist He was poisoned by Philip of Macedon

> Aratus, who awhile relumed the soul
> Of fondly-lingering liberty in Greece
>   THOMSON *Winter*, 491, 492

Arbor Day. A day set apart in Canada and the United States for planting trees It was first inaugurated about 1885 in Nebraska

Arbor Judæ. *See* JUDAS TREE

Arcadia (ar kā' di a). A district of the Peloponnesus which, according to Virgil, was the home of pastoral simplicity and happiness. The name was taken by Sidney as the title of his romance (1590), and it was soon generally adopted in English

Arcadian beasts An old expression, to be found in Plautus, Pliny, etc. *See Persius,* iii, 9 —

> Arcadiæ pecuaria rudere credas

and *Rabelais,* V, vii. So called because the ancient Arcadians were renowned as simpletons. *Juvenal* (vii, 160) has *arcadicus juvenis,* meaning a stupid youth

Arcades ambo (ar' kå dēz ăm' bō) (Lat). From Virgil's seventh Eclogue. "*Ambo florentes ætatibus, Arcades ambo*" (Both in the flower of youth, Arcadians both), meaning " both poets or musicians," now extended to two persons having tastes or habits in common. Byron gave the phrase a whimsical turn —

> Each pulled different ways with many an oath,
> " Arcades ambo "—*id est,* blackguards both.
>   *Don Juan,* IV, xciii.

Arcas. *See* CALISTO

Archangel In Christian legend, the title is usually given to Michael, the chief opponent of Satan and his angels and the champion of the Church of Christ on earth. In the mediæval hierarchy (*see* ANGEL) the Archangels comprise an order of the third division.

According to the Koran, there are four archangels. Gabriel, the angel of revelations, who writes down the divine decrees, Michael, the champion, who fights the battles of faith, Azrael, the angel of death, and Israfel, who is commissioned to sound the trumpet of the resurrection

Archers. The best archers in British history and story are Robin Hood and his two comrades Little John and Will Scarlet.

The famous archers of Henry II were Tepus his bowman of the Guards, Gilbert of the white hind, Hubert of Suffolk, and Clifton of Hampshire

Nearly equal to these were Egbert of Kent and William of Southampton *See also* CLYM OF THE CLOUGH.

Domitian, the Roman emperor, we are told, could shoot four arrows between the spread fingers of a man's hand.

Tell, who shot an apple set on the head of his son, is a replica of the Scandinavian tale of Egil, who, at the command of King Nidung, performed a precisely similar feat

Robin Hood, we are told, could shoot an arrow a mile or more

Arches, Court of. The ecclesiastical court of appeal for the province of Canterbury, which was anciently held in the church of St Mary-le-Bow (*S Maria de Arcubus*), Cheapside, London

Archeus (ar kē' us) The immaterial principle which, according to the Paracelsians, energizes all living substances There were supposed to be numerous *archei*, but the chief one was said to reside in the stomach

Archies. This was the name given in World War I to anti-aircraft guns and batteries —probably from Archibald, the eponymous hero of one of George Robey's songs

Archilochian Bitterness (ar ki lō' ki an) Ill-natured satire, so named from Archilochus, the Greek satirist (fl 690 B C)

Archimago (ar ki mā' gō) The enchanter in Spenser's *Faerie Queene* (Bks. I and II), typifying hypocrisy and false religion.

Archimedean Principle (ar ki mē' di an) The quantity of water displaced by any body immersed therein will equal in bulk the bulk of the body immersed This scientific fact was noted by the philosopher Archimedes of Syracuse (c 287-212 B C) *See* EUREKA

Archimedean screw. An endless screw, used for raising water, etc , invented by Archimedes

Architecture, Orders of These five are the classic orders Tuscan, Doric, Ionic, Corinthian, and Composite

In ancient times the following was the *usual* practice.

CORINTHIAN, for temples of Venus, Flora, Proserpine, and the Water Nymphs

DORIC, for temples of Minerva, Mars, and Hercules

IONIC, for temples of Juno, Diana, and Bacchus

TUSCAN, for grottoes and all rural deities

Archon. In ancient Greece the archon was a chief magistrate, in the 2nd century a sect of the Gnostics, known as Archontics, applied the word as a subordinate power (analogous, perhaps, to the angels), who, at the bidding of God, made the world

Arcite (ar si' ti, ar' sit). A young Theban knight, made captive by Duke Theseus, and imprisoned with Palamon at Athens Both captives fell in love with Emily, the duke's sister, sister-in-law, or daughter (according to different versions), and after they had gained their liberty Emily was promised by the duke to the victor in a tournament Arcite won, but, as he was riding to receive the prize, he was thrown from his horse and killed Emily became the bride of Palamon The story has been told many times and in many versions, notably by Boccaccio, Chaucer (*Knight's Tale*), Dryden, and Fletcher (*Two Noble Kinsmen*).

Arcos Barbs. War steeds of Arcos, in Andalusia, very famous in Spanish ballads *See* BARB

Arctic Region means the region of Arcturos (the Bear stars), from Gr *arktos*, meaning both the animal and the constellation, and *arktikos*, pertaining to the bear, hence, northern Arcturus (the bear-ward) is the name now given to the brightest star in Bootes that can be readily found by following the curve of the Great Bear's tail; but in *Job* xxxviii, 32, it means the Great Bear itself

Arden, The Forest of. This was once a large tract of forest land in Warwickshire, to the north of the Avon Shakespeare was well acquainted with the forest and laid the rural scenes of *As You Like It* among its glades.

Arden, Enoch. The story in Tennyson's poem of this name, first published in 1864 (of a husband who mysteriously and unwillingly disappears, and returns years later to find that his wife—who still loves his memory—is married to another), was, he says—

founded on a theme given me by the sculptor Woolner I believe that his particular story came out of Suffolk, but something like the same story is told in Brittany and elsewhere

It is not uncommon, either in fact or fiction. Tennyson said that several similar true stories had been sent to him since its publication, and four years before it appeared Adelaide Anne Procter's *Homeward Bound*, to which *Enoch Arden* bears a strong resemblance, was published in her *Legends and Lyrics* (1858) Mrs Gaskell's *Manchester Marriage* has a similar plot

Arden of Feversham. This tragedy, first printed in 1592, was at one time attributed to Shakespeare, it is possibly the work of Thomas Kyd (c 1557-c. 1595) The story is of Alice Arden, whose love for her base paramour Mosbie leads her to plan the murder of her husband This is carried out while he and Mosbie are playing a game of draughts; on Mosbie giving the signal by saying, "Now I take you," a couple of hired ruffians dash in and murder Arden.

In 1736 George Lillo wrote a play on this theme, which was not acted until 1759 Thus, again, being altered, the revised play was put on the stage in 1790.

Areopagus (ār e op' a gus) (Gr the hill of Mars, or Ares) The seat of a famous tribunal in Athens, so called from the tradition that the first cause tried there was that of Mars or Ares, accused by Neptune of the death of his son Halirrhothius.

Then Paul stood in the midst of Mars' Hill —*Acts* xvii, 22

Ares (âr' ēz). The god of war in Greek mythology, son of Zeus and Hera   In certain aspects he corresponds with the Roman Mars.

Aretinian Syllables   *Ut, re, mi, fa, sol, la*, used by Guido d'Arezzo in the 11th century for his hexachord, or scale of six notes.   They are the first syllables of some words in the opening stanza of a hymn for St John's Day (*see* DOH). *Si*, the seventh note, was not introduced till the 17th century

Argan (ar'gòn)   The principal character in Molière's *Malade Imaginaire*, a hypochondriac   uncertain whether to think more of his ailments or of his purse

Argand Lamp.   A lamp with a circular wick, through which a current of air flows, to supply oxygen to the flame, and increase its brilliancy. Invented by Aimé Argand, 1789

Argenis (ar' jen is).   A political allegory by John Barclay, written originally in Latin and published in 1621   It is apparently a romance of gallantry and heroism, and it contains double meanings throughout   "Sicily" is France, "Poliarchus" (with whom Argenis is in love), Henry IV, "Hyanisbe," Queen Elizabeth, and so on   It deals with the state of Europe, and more especially of France, during the time of the league

Argentine, Argentina (ar' jen tīn, ar jen tē' nà)   The name of this great S American republic means The Silver Republic and is akin to that of its principal river, Rio de la Plata, turned into English as the River Plate   Buenos Aires, the capital city, was founded in 1535, and direct Spanish rule lasted until 1816, when a republic was declared.   Spanish-American politics do not lend themselves to a concise summary, suffice it to say that Argentina is now one of the richest and most powerful states on the S American continent

Argo (Gr *argos*, swift)   The galley of Jason that went in search of the Golden Fleece.

> The wondred Argo, which in venturous peece,
> First through the Euxine seas bore all the flower of
>   Greece
>   SPENSER *Faerie Queene*, II, xii, 44

The story is told by Apollonius of Rhodes   Hence, a ship sailing on any specially adventurous voyage, and figuratively.

> Such an Argo, when freighted with such a fleece, will unquestionably be held in chase by many a pirate
>   BROOKE *Fool of Quality*

Argonauts.   The sailors of the ship *Argo* who sailed from Greece to Colchis in quest of the Golden Fleece   The name is also given to the paper-nautilus, a cephalopod mollusc

Argosy.   Originally a merchant ship built at, or sailing from, Ragusa in Dalmatia   The word is particularly interesting as an early example of the adaptation of a place-name to ordinary use, it was frequent in the 16th-century English

> He hath an argosy bound to Tripolis, another to the Indies .   a third to Mexico, a fourth to England
>   SHAKESPEARE *Merchant of Venice*, i, 3

Argot (ar' gō)   Slang or flash language   The word is French, and was formerly used only for the canting jargon of thieves, rogues, and vagabonds

Argus-eyed.   Jealously watchful   According to Grecian fable, the fabulous creature, Argus, had 100 eyes, and Juno set him to watch Io, of whom she was jealous   Mercury, however, charmed Argus to sleep and slew him; whereupon Juno changed him into a peacock with the eyes in the tail (*cp* PEACOCK'S FEATHER). Hence the name *Argus* for a genus of Asiatic pheasant

> Return to your charge, be Argus-eyed,
> Awake to the affair you have in hand
>   BEN JONSON *Staple of News*, III, ii
> So praysen babes the Peacocks spotted traine,
> And wondren at bright Argus blazing eye
>   SPENSER *Shepherd's Calendar*, October

Argyle (ar gīl'), of whom Thomson says, in his *Autumn* (928-30)—

> On thee, Argyle,
> Her hope, her stay, her darling, and her boast,
> Thy fond, imploring country turns her eye——

was John, the *great duke*, who lived only two years after he succeeded to the dukedom   Pope (*Ep Sat* ii, 86, 87) says—

> Argyle the state's whole thunder born to wield,
> And shake alike the senate and the field

"God bless the Duke of Argyle" is a phrase, supposed to be ejaculated by Highlanders when they scratched themselves   The story is that a Duke of Argyle caused posts to be erected in a treeless portion of his estates so that his cattle might have the opportunity of rubbing themselves against them and so easing themselves of the "torment of flies"   It was not long before the herdsmen discovered the efficacy of the practice, and as they rubbed their itching backs against the posts they thankfully muttered the above words.

Ariadne (ă ri ăd' ni)   In Greek mythology, daughter of the Cretan king, Minos   She helped Theseus to escape from the labyrinth, and later went with him to Naxos, where he deserted her and she became the wife of Bacchus (*q v*)

Arians (âr' i anz).   The followers of Arius, a presbyter of the Church of Alexandria, in the 4th century.   He maintained (1) that the Father and Son are distinct beings, (2) that the Son, though divine, is not equal to the Father, (3) that the Son had a state of existence previous to His appearance on earth, but not from eternity, and (4) that the Messiah was not real man, but a divine being in a case of flesh   Their tenets varied from time to time and also among their different sections   The heresy was formally anathematized at the Council of Nicæa (325), but the sect was not, and never has been, wholly extinguished

Ariel (âr'iel)   The name of a spirit   Used in cabalistic angelology, and in Heywood's *Hierarchie of the Blessed Angels* (1635) for one of the seven angelic "princes" who rule the waters, by Milton for one of the rebel angels (*Paradise Lost*, vi, 371), by Pope (*Rape of the Lock*) for a sylph, the guardian of Belinda, but especially by Shakespeare, in the *Tempest*, for "an ayrie spirit"

He was enslaved to the witch Sycorax, who overtasked him, and in punishment for not doing what was beyond his power, shut him up in a pine-rift for twelve years   On the death of Sycorax, Ariel became the slave of

Caliban, who tortured him most cruelly. Prospero liberated him from the pine-rift, and the grateful fairy served him for sixteen years, when he was set free.

Aries (âr´ ēz) The Ram The sign of the Zodiac in which the sun is from March 21st to April 20th; the first portion of the ecliptic, between 0° and 30° longitude.

> At last from Aries rolls the bounteous sun
> THOMSON *Spring*, 20.

The first point of Aries is the spot in the celestial equator occupied by the sun at the spring equinox It is in celestial mensuration what the meridian of Greenwich is in terrestrial.

Arimanes (a ri ma´ nēz) The same as Ahriman (*q v*) In *Manfred* Byron introduces him under this name, seated " on a Globe of Fire, surrounded by the Spirits "

Arimaspians (ăr im ăs´ pi ånz) A one-eyed people of Scythia (spoken of in Lucan's *Pharsalia*, iii, 280, by Pliny, Herodotus, and others), who adorned their hair with gold They were constantly at war with the gryphons who guarded the gold mines

> As when a gryphon, through the wilderness . . .
> Pursues the Arimaspian, who by stealth
> Had from his wakeful custody purloined
> The guarded gold
> MILTON *Paradise Lost*, ii, 943.

Rabelais (IV, lvi, and V, xxix) uses the name for the peoples of Northern Europe who had accepted the Reformation, the suggestion being that they had lost one eye—that of faith

Arioch (ăr´ i ok) In *Paradise Lost* (vi, 371) one of the fallen angels The word means *a fierce lion*, Milton took it from *Dan* ii, 14, where it is the name of a man.

Arion (á rī´ on) A Greek poet and musician who flourished about 700 B C, and who, according to legend, was cast into the sea by mariners, but carried to Tænaros on the back of a dolphin

Ariosto of the North (ăr i os´ tō) So Byron called Sir Walter Scott (*Childe Harold*, iv, 40)

Aristides (a ris´ ti dēz) An Athenian statesman and general, who died about 468 B C., and was surnamed "The Just" He was present at the battles of Marathon and Salamis, and was in command at Platæa

> Then Aristides lifts his honest front,
> Spotless of heart, to whom the unflattering voice
> Of Freedom gave the noblest name of " Just "
> THOMSON *Winter*, 459

"The British Aristides" was Andrew Marvell, the poet and satirist (1621-78) "The French Aristides" was François Paul Jules Grévy, president of the Third Republic from 1879 till he was compelled to resign in 1887 in consequence of a scandal connected with the sale of offices and honours

Aristippus (ă ris tip´ pus) A Greek philosopher (fl 375 B C), pupil of Socrates, and founder of the Cyrenaic school of hedonists *See* HEDONISM.

Aristocracy (Gr *aristo-cratia*, rule of the best born) Originally, the government of a state by its best citizens. Carlyle uses the term in this sense in his *Latter-day Pamphlets* (iii, 41): "The attainment of a truer and truer Aristocracy, or Government again by the Best " The word is to-day generally applied to the patrician order, or to a class that is, or claims to be, specially privileged by reason of birth or wealth

Aristophanes (ăr is tof´ a nēz) The greatest of the Greek comic dramatists He was born about 450 B C. and died about 380 B.C , and is specially notable as a satirist

The English or modern Aristophanes Samuel Foote (1720-77)

The French Aristophanes Molière (1622-73)

Aristotle (ăr´ is totl) One of the greatest of the Greek philosophers, pupil of Plato, and founder of the Peripatetic School *See* PERIPATETICS.

Aristotelian philosophy (ăr is tot ē´ li ån) Aristotle maintained that four separate causes are necessary before anything exists: the material cause, the formal, the final, and the moving cause The first is the antecedents from which the thing comes into existence, the second, that which gives it its individuality; the moving or efficient cause is that which causes matter to assume its individual forms, and the final cause is that for which the thing exists According to Aristotle, matter is eternal

Aristotelian Unities. *See* DRAMATIC UNITIES

Arm, Arms. This word, with the meaning of the limb, has given rise to a good many common phrases, such as —

Arm in arm Walking in a friendly way with arms linked

Arm of the sea. A narrow inlet

Secular arm. Civil, in contra-distinction to ecclesiastical jurisdiction

> The relapsed are delivered to the secular arm.
> PRIESTLEY: *Corruptions of Christianity*.

To chance your arm. *See* CHANCE.

At arm's length. At a good distance, hence, with avoidance of familiarity

Infant in arms One that cannot yet walk and so has to be carried, but a nation in arms is one in which all the people are prepared for war

With open arms. Cordially; as persons receive a dear friend when they open their arms for an embrace

The word "arm" is almost always plural nowadays when denoting implements or accoutrements for fighting, etc , and also in heraldic usage Among common phrases are.—

A passage of arms. A literary controversy, a battle of words.

An assault at arms (or of arms) A hand-to-hand military exercise.

Small arms. Those which do not, like artillery, require carriages

To appeal to arms. To determine to decide a litigation by war

To arms. Make ready for battle.

> "To arms!" cried Mortimer,
> And couched his quivering lance
> GRAY <i>The Bard</i>

To lay down arms. To cease from armed hostility, to surrender.

Under arms. Prepared for battle, in battle array.

Up in arms. In open rebellion, figuratively, roused to anger

King of Arms. *See* HERALDS

The right to bear arms. The right to use an heraldic device, which can be obtained only by direct grant from the College of Heralds (and the payment of certain fees), or by patrimony, *i e* direct descent from one on whom the grant has been conferred. In either case a small annual licence must be paid if the coat of arms is used in any way, such as on one's carriage, silver, or stationery. A person having such right is said to be *armigerous*

The Royal Arms of England. The three lions passant gardant were introduced by Richard Cœur de Lion after his return from the third Crusade, the lion rampant in the second quarter is from the arms of Scotland, it having first been used in the reign of Alexander II (1214-49); and the harp in the fourth quarter represents Ireland; it was assigned to Ireland in the time of Henry VIII, before that time her device was three crowns The lion supporter is English, and the unicorn Scottish; they were introduced by James I. The crest, a lion statant gardant first appears on the Great Seal of Edward III

The correct emblazoning of the arms of the United Kingdom of Great Britain and Ireland is:—

Quarterly, first and fourth gules, three lions passant gardant in pale, or, for England, second or, a lion rampant with a double tressure flory-counterflory gules, for Scotland, third azure, a harp or, stringed argent, for Ireland, all surrounded by the Garter. *Crest*—Upon the royal helmet, the imperial crown proper, thereon a lion statant gardant or, imperial crowned proper. *Supporters.*—A lion rampant gardant, or, crowned as the crest. Sinister, a unicorn argent, armed, crined, and unguled proper, gorged with a coronet composed of crosses patee and fleur de lis, a chain affixed thereto passing between the forelegs, and reflexed over the back, also or. *Motto*—"Dieu et mon Droit" in the compartment below, the shield, with the Union rose, shamrock, and thistle engrafted on the same stem

From the time of Edward III (1340) until the Union of Great Britain and Ireland (1800) the reigning sovereigns styled themselves "of Great Britain, France and Ireland, King," (Elizabeth said that if the Salic Law forbade her to be Queen of France she would e'en be King) and the fleur de lys of France was quartered with the arms of England and Scotland. The empty title was abandoned as from 1 January, 1801 and from that date and for that reason all diplomatic correspondence thenceforward was carried on in English instead of French.

Nor has this been the only change in the Royal Arms. On the accession of George I (1714) the White Horse of Hanover was borne in pretence (*i e* superimposed in the centre of the royal coat of arms) On the death of William IV (1837) the Salic Law prohibited the accession of Victoria to the throne of Hanover, and on her uncle the Duke of Cumberland succeeding to that throne, the Hanoverian arms were dropped from the British royal arms

Armada (ar mä' da) Originally Spanish for 'army," the word is now used, from the Spanish Armada, for any fleet of large size or strength Formerly spelt *armado*

> At length resolv d t'assert the wat ry ball,
> He [Charles II] in himself did whole Armadoes bring;
> Him aged seamen might their master call,
> And choose for general were he not their king.
> DRYDEN <i>Annus Mirabilis</i>, XIV.

The Spanish Armada. The fleet assembled by Philip II of Spain, in 1588, for the conquest of England It consisted of 129 vessels, carried 8,000 sailors, 19,000 soldiers, 2,000 guns and provisions to feed 40,000 men for six months After battle and storm no more than 54 vessels got back to Spain, carrying a few sick and exhausted men

Armageddon (ar mä ged' on) The name given in the Apocalypse (*Rev* xvi, 16) to the site of the last great battle that is to be between the nations before the Day of Judgment, hence, any great battle or scene of slaughter

The place where the author of the Apocalypse had in mind was probably the mountainous district near Megiddo, generally identified with the modern Lejjun, about 54 miles due north of Jerusalem

Arme Blanche (arm blonsh) (Fr white arm) Steel weapons—the sword, sabre, bayonet, or spear—in contradistinction to firearms

Armenian Church, The. Said to have been founded in Armenia by St Bartholomew. Its members are to be found in Armenia, Persia, Syria, Poland, Asia Minor, etc., they attribute only one nature to Christ and hold that the Spirit proceeds from the Father only, enjoin the adoration of saints, have some peculiar ways of administering baptism and the Lord's Supper, and communicate infants, they do not maintain the doctrine of purgatory.

Armida (ar mē' da) In Tasso's *Jerusalem Delivered* a beautiful sorceress, with whom Rinaldo fell in love, and wasted his time in voluptuous pleasure After his escape from her, Armida followed him, but not being able to allure him back, set fire to her palace, rushed into a combat, and was slain

In 1806, Frederick William of Prussia declared war against Napoleon, and his young queen rode about in military costume to arouse the enthusiasm of the people When Napoleon was told of it, he said, "She is Armida, in her distraction setting fire to her own palace"

Arminians. Followers of Jacobus Harmensen, or Arminius (1560-1609), a Protestant divine in Leyden They were an offshoot of Calvinism, and formulated their creed (called the *Remonstrance*) in 1610, in five points. They asserted that God bestows forgiveness and eternal life on all who repent and believe, that He wills all men to be saved, and that His predestination is founded on His foreknowledge

Armistice Day. Hostilities in World War I ended at 11 o'clock on November 11th, 1918, when an armistice was signed In subsequent years November 11th was kept as Armistice Day, marked by a two-minute silence and cessation of work at 11 a m, followed in various places by ceremonies In 1946 the old name was changed to Remembrance Day, to include a memorial of the close of the 1939-45 war and it is kept on the Sunday nearest 11th November

Armoury. Heraldry is so called, because it first found its special use in direct connexion with military equipments, knightly exercises, and the *mêlée* of actual battle

> Armory is an Art rightly prescribing the true knowledge and use of Armes
> *Gutllim's Display of Heraldrie* (1610)

Armour, Coat, or a **Coat of Arms,** was originally a drapery of silk or other rich stuff worn by a knight over his armour and embroidered in colours with his distinguishing device This practice was adopted by the Crusaders, who found it necessary to cover their steel armour from the rays of the sun.

Armoury. The place where armour and arms are kept.

> The sword
> Of Michael from the armoury of God
> Was given him
>   MILTON *Paradise Lost,* vi, 320

The word may also mean armour collectively, as in *Paradise Lost,* IV, 553 —

> nigh at hand
> Celestial armoury, shields, helms, and spears,
> Hung high, with diamond flaming and with gold.

Arnauts (ar' nauts) (Turk. brave men). Albanian mountaineers

> Stained with the best of Arnaut's blood
>   BYRON *The Giaour*

Arod. In Dryden's *Absalom and Achitophel* is designed for Sir William Waller.

> But in the sacred annals of our plot
> Industrious Arod never be forgot,
> The labours of this midnight magistrate
> May vie with Corah's [Titus Oates] to preserve
> the state.
>   Part II.

Aroint thee A phrase that first appears in Shakespeare's *Macbeth* (I, iii, 6) and *King Lear* (III, iv, 129), on both occasions in connexion with witches It signifies "get ye gone," "be off "; and its origin is unknown The Brownings made a verb of it, Mrs Browning in her *To Flush*—"Whiskered cats arointed flee," and Browning in *The Two Poets of Croisic,* and elsewhere.

Arondight (ar' on dit) The sword of Sir Launcelot of the Lake *See* SWORD

Arras (ar' as) Tapestry, the cloth of Arras, in Artois, formerly famed for its manufacture When rooms were hung with tapestry it was easy for persons to hide behind it, thus Hubert hid the two villains who were to put out Arthur's eyes, Polonius was slain by Hamlet while concealed behind the arras, Falstaff proposed to hide behind it at Windsor, etc

Arria (ar' i a). The wife of Cæcina Pætus, who, being accused of conspiring against the Emperor Claudius, was condemned to death by suicide. As he hesitated to carry out the sentence Arria stabbed herself, then presenting the dagger to her husband, said, "Pætus, it gives no pain" (*non dolet*) (A D. 42) *See* PLINY, vii

Arrière ban. *See* BAN

Arrière pensée (Fr "behind-thought"). A hidden or reserved motive, not apparent on the surface.

Arrow. *See* BROAD ARROW: JONATHAN'S ARROWS

Artaxerxes (ár táks erks' ēz), called by the Persians Artakhshathra, and surnamed the long-handed (*Longimanus*), because his right hand was longer than his left, was the first Persian king of that name, and reigned from 465 to 425 B C He was the son of Xerxes, and is mentioned in the Bible in connexion with the part he played in the restoration of Jerusalem after the Captivity *See Ezra* iv, vi, and vii, and *Neh* ii, v, and xiii

Artegal, or **Arthegal, Sir** (ar' te gál). The hero of Bk v of Spenser's *Faerie Queene,* lover of Britomart, to whom he is made known by means of a magic mirror He is emblematic of Justice, and in many of his deeds, such as the rescue of Irena (Ireland) from Grantorto, is typical of Arthur, Lord Grey of Wilton, who went to Ireland as Lord Lieutenant in 1580 with Spenser as his secretary. *See* ELIDURE.

Artemis. *See* DIANA

Artemus Ward. This was the pseudonym of Charles Farrar Browne (1834-67), the American humourist He began as a lecturer in 1861 and visited England in 1866, dying in Southampton before he could get back to America The famous character he created was that of a Yankee showman

Artesian Wells So called from *Artois,* the Old French name for Artois, in France, where they were first bored They are sunk with a boring or drilling apparatus into water or oil-bearing strata from which the liquid rises by its own pressure to the top of the bore

Artful Dodger. A young thief in Dickens s *Oliver Twist,* pupil of Fagin His name was Jack Dawkins, and he became a most perfect adept in villainy.

Arthegal. *See* ARTEGAL.

Arthur. A shadowy British chieftain of the 6th century, first mentioned by Nennius, a Breton monk of the 10th century He fought many battles and is said to have been a king of the Silures, a tribe of ancient Britons, to have been mortally wounded in the battle of Camlan (537), in Cornwall, during the revolt of his nephew, Modred (who was also slain), and to have been taken to Glastonbury, where he died.

His wife was Guinevere, who committed adultery with Sir Launcelot of the Lake, one of the Knights of the Round Table

Arthur was the natural son of Uther and Igerna (wife of Gorlois, duke of Cornwall), and was brought up by Sir Ector

He was born at Tintagel Castle, in Cornwall

His chief home and the seat of his court was Caerleon, in Wales, and he was buried at Avalon (*q v*)

His sword was called Excalibur, his spear, Rone, and his shield, Pridwin His dog was named Cavall See ROUND TABLE, KNIGHTS OF THE

Arthur's Seat. A hill overlooking Edinburgh from the east The name is not connected with King Arthur, it is a corruption of the Gaelic *Ard-na-said*, the height of the arrows, hence, a convenient ground to shoot from.

Arthurian Romances. The stories which have King Arthur as their central figure appear as early as the 12th century in the *Historia Regum Britanniæ* of Geoffrey of Monmouth (d 1154), which drew partly from the work of Nennius (*see* ARTHUR), partly—according to the author—from an ancient British or Breton book (lost, if ever existing) lent him by Walter, Archdeacon of Oxford, and partly from sources which are untraced, but the originals of which are probably embedded in Welsh or Celtic legends, most of them being now non-extant The original Arthur was a very shadowy warrior, Geoffrey of Monmouth, probably at the instigation of Henry I and for the purpose of providing the new nation with a national hero, made many additions, the story was taken up in France and further expanded, Wace, a French poet (who is the first to mention the Round Table, *q v*), turned it into a metrical chronicle of some 14,000 lines (*Brut d'Angleterre, c* 1155), Celtic and other legends, including those of the Grail (*q v*) and Sir Tristram, were superadded, and in about 1205 Layamon, the Worcestershire priest, completed his *Brut* (about 30,000 lines), which included Wace's work and amplifications such as the story of the fairies at Arthur's birth, who, at his death, wafted him to Avalon, as well as Sir Gawain and Sir Bedivere In France the legends were worked upon by Robert de Borron (fl 1215), who first attached the story of the Grail (*q v*) to the Arthurian Cycle and brought the legend of Merlin into prominence, and Chrestien de Troyes (*c.* 1140-90), who is responsible for the presence in the Cycle of the tale of Enid and Geraint, the tragic loves of Launcelot and Guinevere, the story of Perceval, and other additions for many of which he was indebted to the Welsh *Mabinogion* Many other legends in the form of ballads, romances, and Welsh and Breton songs and lays were popular, and in the 15th century the whole *corpus* was collected, edited, and more or less worked into a state of homogeneity by Sir Thomas Malory (d 1471), his *Le Morte d'Arthur* being printed by Caxton in 1485 For the different heroes, sections, etc , of this great Cycle of Romance, *see* the various names throughout this Dictionary

Articles of Roup. The conditions of sale at a roup (*q v*), as announced by a crier

Artists, The Prince of. Albrecht Durer (1471-1528) was so called by his countrymen.

Arts Degrees in Arts. In the mediæval ages the full course consisted of the three subjects which constituted the *Trivium*, and the four subjects which constituted the *Quadrivium* — The *Trivium* was grammar, logic, and rhetoric

The *Quadrivium* was music, arithmetic, geometry, and astronomy.

The *Master of Arts* was the person qualified to teach or be the master of students in arts, as the *Doctor* was the person qualified to teach theology, law, or medicine

Arundel See HORSE

Arundelian Marbles. A collection of ancient sculptures made at great expense by Thomas Howard, Earl of Arundel, and presented to the University of Oxford in 1667 by his grandson, Henry Howard, afterwards Duke of Norfolk They contain tables of ancient chronology, especially that of Athens, from 1582 to 264 B C, engraved in old Greek capitals, and the famous " Parian Chronicle," said to have been executed in the island of Paros about 263 B C

Arvakur. See HORSE

Arval Brothers. An ancient Roman college of priests, revived by Augustus It consisted of 12 priests (including the Emperor), whose sole duty was to preside at the festival of Dea Dia in May, they worshipped in the groves of that goddess on the Via Campana, 5 miles from Rome

Aryans. The parent stock of what is called the Indo-European family of nations Their original home is quite unknown, authorities differing so widely as between a locality enclosed by the river Oxus and the Hindu-kush mountains, and the shores of the Baltic, or Central Europe The Aryan family of languages includes Sanskrit, Zend, Latin, Greek, Celtic, Persian and Hindu, with all the European, except Basque, Turkish, Hungarian, and Finnish. Sometimes called the Indo-European, sometimes the Indo-Germanic, and sometimes the Japhetic

Under the Nazi regime in Germany the word was prostituted by being applied to any race, person or thing that was not Semitic, even the Japanese being classified as Aryans

Arzina A river that flows into the North Sea, near Wardhus, where Sir Hugh Willoughby's three ships were ice-bound, and the whole crew perished of starvation

> In these fell regions, in Arzina caught,
> And to the stony deep his idle ship
> Immediate sealed, he with his hapless crew . . .
> Froze into statues
> THOMSON *Winter*, 930

Asaph. In the Bible, a famous musician in David's time (1 *Chron* xxv, 1, 2) There was probably no such person, but in post-exilic times there were two hereditary choirs that superintended the musical services of the Temple, one of which was *b'ne Asaph*, and the other *b'ne Korah* The Asaph mentioned in *Chronicles* is the supposed founder of the first named

Tate, who wrote the second part of *Absalom and Achitophel*, lauds Dryden under this name
> While Judah's throne and Sion's rock stand fast
> The song of Asaph and the fame shall last
> *Absalom and Achitophel*, Pt ii, 1063.

Ascalaphus. In Greek mythology, an inhabitant of the underworld who, when Pluto gave Proserpine permission to return to the upper world if she had eaten nothing, said that she had partaken of a pomegranate. In revenge Proserpine turned him into an owl by sprinkling him with the water of Phlegethon.

Ascendant. An astrological term. In casting a horoscope the point of the ecliptic or degree of the zodiac which is just rising at the moment of birth is called the *ascendant*, and the easternmost star represents the house of life (*see* HOUSE), because it is in the act of ascending. This is a man's strongest star, and when his outlook is bright, we say *his star is in the ascendant*.

The house of the Ascendant, includes five degrees of the zodiac above the point just rising, and twenty-five below it. Usually, the point of birth is referred to.

The lord of the Ascendant is any planet within the 'house of the Ascendant.' The house and lord of the Ascendant at birth were said by astrologers to exercise great influence on the future life of the child. Deborah referred to the influence of the stars when she said ' the stars in their courses fought against Sisera'' (*Judges* v. 20)

Ascension Day, or **Holy Thursday** (*q v*). The day set apart by the Christian Churches to commemorate the ascent of our Lord from earth to heaven. It is the fortieth day after Easter. *See* BOUNDS, BEATING THE

Asclepiads, or **Asclepiadic Metre** (ăs kle pǐ' ădz) A term in Greek and Latin prosody denoting a verse (invented by Asclepiades) which consists of a spondee, two (or three) choriambi, and an iambus, usually with a central cæsura, thus —

$$— | — \smile — \| — \smile — |$$

The first ode of Horace is Asclepiadic. The first and last two lines may be translated in the same metre, thus —

Dear friend, patron of song, sprung from the race of kings,
Thy name ever a grace and a protection brings.
My name, if to the lyre haply you chance to wed,
Pride would high as the stars lift my exalted head.

Ascot Races A very fashionable meeting, run early in June on Ascot Heath (6 miles from Windsor). These races were instituted early in the 18th century.

Ascræan Poet, or **Sage** (ăs krē' an) Hesiod, the Greek didactic poet, born at Ascra in Bœotia. Virgil (*Eclogues*, vii, 70) calls him the " Old Ascræon."

Asgard (ăs' gard) (*As*, a god, *gard* or *gardh*, an enclosure, garth, yard) The realm of the *Æsir* or the Northern gods, the Olympus of Scandinavian mythology. It is said to be situated in the centre of the universe, and accessible only by the rainbow-bridge (*Bifrost*) It contained many regions and mansions, such as Gladsheim and Valhalla.

Ash Tree, or **Tree of the Universe.** *See* YGGDRASIL.

Ash Wednesday. The first Wednesday in Lent, so called from an ancient Roman Catholic custom of sprinkling on the heads of penitents who had confessed that day the ashes of the palms that were consecrated on the previous Palm Sunday which themselves had been consecrated at the altar. The custom, it is said, was introduced by Gregory the Great.

Ashes. **Ashes to ashes, dust to dust.** A phrase from the English Burial Service, used sometimes to signify total finality. It is founded on various scriptural texts, such as "Dust thou art, and unto dust thou shalt return" (*Gen* iii, 19), and "I will bring thee to ashes upon the earth in the sight of all them that behold thee" (*Ezek* xxviii, 18)

Ashes to ashes and dust to dust,
If God won't have him the Devil must.

According to Sir Walter Scott (*see* his edition of Swift's *Journal to Stella* March 25th, 1710-11), this was the form of burial service given by the sexton to the body of Guiscard, the French refugee who, in 1711, attempted the life of Harley.

To recover the ashes A cricket term applied to the England-Australia cricket seasons played alternately in the two countries, the "ashes" being the mythical prize contended for. When England was beaten in 1882 a humorous epitaph on English cricket appeared in a sporting journal, and it wound up with the remark that " the body will be cremated and the ashes taken to Australia." There are several more or less fabulous embroideries of this story.

Ashmolean Museum (ăsh mō' li an) The first public museum of curiosities in England. It was presented to the University of Oxford in 1677 by Elias Ashmole (1617-92), the antiquarian, who had inherited the greater part of the contents from his friend John Tradescant. Ashmole later gave his library to the University. The museum building was the work of Sir Christopher Wren.

Ashtoreth (ăsh' to reth) The goddess of fertility and reproduction among the Canaanites and Phœnicians, called by the Babylonians *Ishtar* (Venus), and by the Greeks *Astarte* (*q v*) She may possibly be the " queen of heaven " mentioned by Jeremiah (vii, 18, xliv, 17, 25) Formerly she was supposed to be a moon-goddess, hence Milton's reference in his *Ode on the Nativity*

Mooned Ashtaroth,
Heaven's queen and mother both.

Ashur *See* ASSHUR.

Asinego (ăs i nē' gō) (Port) A young ass, a simpleton.

Thou hast no more brain than I have in mine elbows, an asinego may tutor thee—
SHAKESPEARE *Troilus and Cressida*, ii, 1

Asir. *See* ÆSIR

Ask The dialectal *ax* was the common literary form down to about the end of the 16th century. The word comes from the O E *ascian*, which, by metathesis, became *acsian*, and so *axian*. Chaucer has —

How sholde I axen mercy of Tisbe
Whan I am he that have yow slain, allas!
Legend of Good Women, 835

and the Wyclif version of *Matt* vii, 7-10, reads —

Axe ye and it schal be gyven to you, seke yee, and yee schulen fynde, knocke ye and it schal be openid to you. For ech that axith, takith, and he that sekith, fundith and it schal be opened to him that knockith. What man of you is, that if his sone axe him breed whether he wole take him a stoon? Or if he axe fish, whether he wole give him an Eddre?

Aslo. *See* HORSE

Asmodeus (ăs mō dē'us, ăs mō'dĭ ŭs) The "evil demon" who appears in the Apocryphal book of *Tobit*, borrowed (and to some extent transformed) from Aeshma, one of the seven archangels of Persian mythology The name is probably the Zend *Aeshmo daeva* (the demon Aeshma), and is not connected with the Heb. *samad*, to destroy The character of Asmodeus is explained in the following passage from *The Testament of Solomon*—

> I am called *Asmodeus* among mortals and my business is to plot against the newly-wedded, so that they may not know one another And I sever them utterly by many calamities, and I waste away the beauty of virgins, and estrange their hearts

In *Tobit* Asmodeus falls in love with Sara, daughter of Raguel, and causes the death of seven husbands in succession, each on his bridal night After her marriage to Tobias, he was driven into Egypt by a charm, made by Tobias of the heart and liver of a fish burnt on perfumed ashes, and being pursued was taken prisoner and bound.

> Better pleased
> Than Asmodeus with the fishy fume
> That drove him, though enamoured, from the spouse
> Of Tobit's son, and with a vengeance sent
> From Media post to Egypt, there fast bound
>   MILTON *Paradise Lost*, iv, 167

Le Sage gave the name to the companion of Don Cleofas in his *Devil on Two Sticks.*

Asmodeus flight. Don Cleofas catching hold of his companion's cloak, is perched on the steeple of St. Salvador Here the foul fiend stretches out his hand, and the roofs of all the houses open in a moment, to show the Don what is going on privately in each respective dwelling.

Asoka (ăs' ō kå). An Indian king of the Maurya dynasty of Magadha, 263-226 B C, who was converted to Buddhism by a miracle and became its "nursing father," as Constantine was of Christianity He is called " the king beloved of the gods."

Aspasia (a spā' zi a). A Milesian woman (fl 440 B.C.), celebrated for her beauty and talents, who lived at Athens as mistress of Pericles, and whose house became the centre of literary and philosophical society She was the most celebrated of the Greek Hetæræ, and on the death of Pericles (429 B c.) lived with the democratic leader, Lysicles

Aspatia (a spā' shà), in the *Maid's Tragedy*, of Beaumont and Fletcher, is noted for her deep sorrows, her great resignation, and the pathos of her speeches Amyntor deserts her, women point at her with scorn, she is the jest and byword of everyone, but she bears it all with patience

Aspen. The aspen leaf is said to tremble, from shame and horror, because our Lord's cross was made of this wood In fact, owing to the shape of the leaf and its long, flexible leaf-stalk, it is peculiarly liable to be acted on by the least breath of air

Asphaltic Lake. The Dead Sea, where asphalt abounds both on the surface of the water and on the banks. Asphalt is a bitumen.

> There was an asphaltic and Bituminous nature in that Lake before the fire of Gomorrah
>   SIR THOS BROWNE *Religio Medici*, i, 19

There is a bituminous, or asphalt, lake in Trinidad

Asphodel (ăs' fō del) Old-fashioned garden flowers of the natural order Liliaceæ The name daffodil is a corruption of asphodel In the language of flowers it means "regret " It was said that the spirits of the dead sustained themselves on the roots of this flower, and the ancients planted them on graves Pliny and others said that the ghosts beyond Acheron roamed through the meadows of asphodel, in order to reach the waters of Lethe or Oblivion.

Ass The dark stripe running down the back of an ass, crossed by another at the shoulders, is, according to tradition, the cross that was communicated to the creature when our Lord rode on the back of an ass in His triumphant entry into Jerusalem

Till the ass ascends the ladder—*i e* never A rabbinical expression The Romans had a similar one, *Cum asinus in tegulis ascenderit* (When the ass climbs to the tiles).

That which thou knowest not perchance thine ass can tell thee. An allusion to Balaam's ass

Ass, deaf to music This tradition arose from the hideous noise made by "Sir Balaam" in braying *See* ASS-EARED

An ass in a lion's skin. A coward who hectors, a fool that apes the wise man The allusion is to the fable of an ass that put on a lion's hide, but was betrayed when he began to bray.

To make an ass of oneself. To do something very foolish To expose oneself to ridicule.

Sell your ass. Get rid of your foolish ways

The ass waggeth his ears. This proverb is applied to those who lack learning, and yet talk as if they were very wise, men wise in their own conceit The ass, proverbial for having no "taste for music," will nevertheless wag its ears at a "concord of sweet sounds," just as if it could well appreciate it

An ass with two panniers. Said of a man walking the streets with a lady on each arm. The Italian equivalent is a *pitcher with two handles*, and formerly it was called in London walking *bodkin* (*q v*) Our expression is from the French *faire le panier à deux anses*, a colloquialism for walking with a lady on each arm

Ass's bridge. *See* PONS ASINORUM

Well, well! honey is not for the ass's mouth. Persuasion will not persuade fools The gentlest words will not divert the anger of the unreasonable

Wrangle for an ass's shadow. To contend about trifles. The tale told by Demosthenes is, that a man hired an ass to take him to Megara· and at noon, the sun being very hot, the traveller dismounted, and sat himself down in the shadow of the ass Just then the owner came up and claimed the right of sitting in this shady spot, saying that he let out the ass for hire, but there was no bargain made about the ass's shade. The two men then fell to blows to settle the point in dispute While they were wrangling the ass took to its heels and ran away, leaving them both in the glare of the sun

Asses as well as pitchers have ears. Children, and even the densest minds, hear and understand many a word and hint which the speaker supposed would pass unheeded

Feast of Asses *See* FOOLS

Asses that carry the mysteries (*asini portant mysteria*). A classical knock at the Roman clergy. The allusion is to the custom of employing asses to carry the *cista* which contained the sacred symbols, when processions were made through the streets (Warburton. *Divine Legation*, ii, 4)

Golden Ass *See* GOLDEN

Ass-eared Midas had the ears of an ass The tale says Apollo and Pan had a contest, and chose Midas to decide which was the better musician Midas gave sentence in favour of Pan, and Apollo, in disgust, changed his ears into those of an ass

Avarice is as deaf to the voice of virtue, as the ass to the voice of Apollo —*Orlando Furioso*, xvii

Assassins (a säs'inz). A sect of Oriental fanatics of a military and religious character, founded in Persia in 1090 by Hassan ben Sabbah, better known as the *Old Man* (or *Sheikh*) *of the Mountains* (*see under* MOUNTAIN), because the sect migrated to Mount Lebanon and made it its stronghold. This band was the terror of the world for two centuries, and, to the number of 50,000 strong, offered formidable opposition to the Crusaders Their religion was a compound of Magianism, Judaism, Christianity, and Mohammedanism, and their name is derived from *haschisch* (bang), an intoxicating drink, with which they are said to have "doped" themselves before perpetrating their orgies of massacre They were finally put down by the Sultan Bibars, about 1272

Assay (a sā), or *Essay* (through O.Fr. from Lat. *exagium*, to weigh) To try or test, to determine the amount of different metals in an ore, etc , and, formerly, to taste food or drink before it is offered to a sovereign; hence, *to take the assay* is to taste wine to prove it is not poisoned

The aphetic form of the word, "say," was common down to the 17th century, and Edmund, in *King Lear* (v, 5), says to Edgar, "Thy tongue, some *say* of breeding breathes", *i e*. thy speech gives indication of good breeding—it savours of it

Assay, as a noun, means a test or trial, as in—

[He] makes vow before his uncle never more
To give the assay of arms against your majesty
　　　　　　　SHAKESPEARE· *Hamlet*, ii, 2

But for the last three hundred years the spelling *essay* has been adopted (from French) for the noun, in all uses except those connected with the assaying of metals

Assaye Regiment. *See* REGIMENTAL NICKNAMES

Assemblage, Nouns of Long custom and technical usage have ascribed certain words to assemblages of animals, things, or persons Some of the principal are given here:

Animals, birds, etc.

antelopes a herd
asses a pace or herd
badgers a cete
bears· a sleuth
bees a swarm, a grist
birds a flock, flight, congregation, volery
bitterns a sedge or siege.
boars a sounder
bucks a brace or leash
buffaloes a herd
cattle a drove or herd
chickens· a brood
choughs a chattering.
coots a covert
cranes a herd, sedge or siege
cubs a litter
curlews a herd
deer a herd
ducks (in flight) a team
elk a gang
ferrets a fesnyng
fishes a shoal, draught, haul, run, or catch
flies a swarm
foxes a skulk
geese (in flight) a skein, (on the ground), a gaggle
gnats a swarm or cloud
goats a herd or tribe
goldfinches a charm
grouse (a single brood), a covey, (several broods) a
　　pack
hares a down or husk
hawks a cast
hens a brood
herons a sedge or siege.
herrings a shoal
hounds a pack or mute
kangaroos a troop
kine a drove.
kittens a kindle
larks an exaltation.
leopards a leap
lions a pride
mares a stud
monkeys a troop
nightingales a watch
oxen a yoke, drove, team, or herd.
partridges a covey
peacocks. a muster
pheasants a nye or nide
pigeons a flock or flight
pilchards a shoal
plovers a wing or congregation
porpoises· a school.
pups a litter
quails a bevy.
rooks a building or clamour
seals a herd or pod
sheep a flock
swans a herd or bevy
swifts a flock
swine a sounder or drift
whales a school, gam, or pod.
wolves a pack, rout, or herd
woodcock a fall

Things

aeroplanes a flight, squadron
arrows a sheaf
bells a peal
boats a flotilla
bowls a set
bread a batch
cards a pack, a deck (Am)
cars a fleet
eggs a clutch
flowers a bouquet or nosegay
golf-clubs a set

guns (sporting), a pair
grapes a cluster or bunch
onions a rope
pearls a rope or string
rags a bundle
sails· an outfit
ships a fleet or squadron.
stars a cluster or constellation
steps a flight
trees a clump

Persons

actors a company, cast or troupe
angels a host
baseball team a nine
beaters a squad
bishops a bench
cricket team an eleven
dancers a troupe
football (Association), an eleven, (Rugby), a fifteen.
girls a bevy
labourers a gang
lacrosse team a twelve
magistrates a bench.
minstrels a troupe
musicians, a band, an orchestra
players a side or team.
police a posse
polo team. a four
rowing an eight, a four, a pair
runners a field
sailors: a crew.
savages a horde
servants a staff
slaves a gang
worshippers a congregation

Asshur. The chief god of the Assyrian pantheon, perhaps derived from the Babylonian god of heaven, Anu His symbol was the winged circle in which was frequently enclosed a draped male figure carrying three horns on the head and with one hand stretched forth, sometimes with a bow in the hand His wife was Belit (*i e* the Lady, *par excellence*), who has been identified with the Ishtar (*see* ASHTORETH) of Nineveh

Out of that land went forth Asshur, and builded Nineveh.—*Gen* x, 11

Assiento Treaties (Sp *asiénto*, agreement) Contracts entered into by Spain with Portugal, France, and England to supply her South American colonies with Negro slaves England joined in 1713, after the peace of Utrecht, and kept the disgraceful monopoly (with a few breaks) till 1750

Association Cup This is the trophy competed for annually by football clubs playing the Association game The first final was played at Kennington Oval, 16th March, 1872, when Bolton Wanderers beat the Royal Engineers, 1—0 Since then the cup has been contested year by year except for the war years 1939-45 Since 1930 the winners have been —

1931	West Bromwich Albion
1932	Newcastle United
1933	Everton
1934	Manchester City
1935	Sheffield Wednesday.
1936	Arsenal
1937	Sunderland
1938	Preston North End
1939	Portsmouth
1946	Derby County
1947	Charlton Athletic
1948	Manchester United
1949	Wolverhampton Wanderers
1950	Arsenal
1951	Newcastle United.

Assumption, Feast of the. In the R C Church the principal feast day of the Virgin Mary, observed on August 15th. On November 1st, 1950, Pope Pius XII declared *ex cathedra* that thenceforth it would be a dogma of the Church that at the death of the Virgin her body was preserved from corruption, and that shortly afterwards it was assumed (Lat *assumere*, to take to) into heaven and reunited to her soul.

Assurance. Audacity, brazen self-confidence "His assurance is quite unbearable "

Assurance provides for the contingence of a certainty, *e g* life assurance is a financial provision for the certain fact of death Insurance provides against what may or may not happen. *e g* burglary, fire

To make assurance doubly sure. To make security doubly secure

But yet I'll make assurance double sure,
And take a bound of fate
SHAKESPEARE *Macbeth*., iv, 1

Astarte (a star' ti) The Greek name for Ashtoreth (*q.v*), sometimes thought to have been a moon-goddess Hence Milton's allusion —

With these in troop
Came Astoreth, whom the Phœnicians called
Astarte, queen of heaven, with crescent horns.
Paradise Lost, i, 437

Byron gave the name to the lady beloved by Manfred in his drama, *Manfred* It has been suggested that Astarte was drawn from the poet's sister, Augusta (Mrs Leigh)

Astolat (ǎs' tō lǎt) This town, mentioned in the Arthurian legends, is generally identified with Guildford, in Surrey, though there can be no certainty.

The Lily Maid of Astolat. Elaine (*q v*)

Astoreth. *See* ASHTORETH

Astræa (ǎs trē' á) Equity, innocence During the Golden Age this goddess dwelt on earth, but when sin began to prevail, she reluctantly left it, and was metamorphosed into the constellation *Virgo*

When hard-hearted interest first began
To poison earth, Astræa left the plain
THOMSON *Castle of Indolence*, I, x

Pope gave the name to Mrs Aphra Behn (1640-89), playwright and novelist, author of the once-popular novel *Oroonoko*

Sir John Davies (1569-1626) wrote a series of twenty-six acrostics, entitled *Hymns to Astraea*, in honour of Queen Elizabeth

Astrakhan. Takes its name from the province of Astrakhan in Russia and is the fur, or wool, of a karakul lamb

Astral Body. In theosophical parlance, the phantasmal or spiritual appearance of the physical human form, that is existent both before and after the death of the material body, though during life it is not usually separated from it, also the "kamarupa' or body of desires, which retains a finite life in the astral world after bodily death

Astral spirits. The spirits of the dead that occupy the stars and the stellar regions, or astral world According to the occultists, each star has its special spirit; and Paracelsus maintained that every man had his attendant star, which received him at death, and took charge of him till the great resurrection.

Astrology. The ancient and mediæval so-called "science" that professed to foretell events by studying the position of the stars and discovering their occult influence on human affairs It is one of the most ancient superstitions, it prevailed from earliest times among the Chaldeans, Egyptians, Etruscans, Hindus, Chinese, etc , and had a powerful influence in the Europe of the Middle Ages *Natural Astrology*—i e the branch that dealt with meteorological phenomena and with time, tides, eclipses, the fixing of Easter, etc—was the forerunner of the science of Astronomy, what is now known as "astrology" was formerly differentiated from this as *Judicial Astrology*, and dealt with star-divination and the occult planetary and sidereal influences upon human affairs *See* HOUSES, ASTROLOGICAL, HOROSCOPE, MICROCOSM

Astronomers Royal. (1) Flamsteed, 1675, (2) Halley, 1719, (3) Bradley, 1742; (4) Bliss, 1762, (5) Maskelyne, who originated the Nautical Almanack, 1765, (6) Pond, 1811, (7) Airy, 1835, (8) Christie, 1881, (9) Sir F. W Dyson, 1910, (10) Sir H S Jones, 1933

Astrophel (ăs' trō fel). Sir Philip Sidney (1554-86) "Phil Sid " being a contraction of *Philos Sidus*, and the Latin *sidus* being changed to the Greek *astron*, we get *astron-philos* (star-lover) The "star" that he loved was Penelope Devereux, whom he called *Stella* (star), and to whom he was betrothed Spenser wrote a pastoral called *Astrophel*, to the memory of his friend and patron, who fell at the battle of Zutphen

Asur (ăs' ûr) The national god of the ancient Assyrians, the supreme god over all the gods. *See* ASSHUR

Asurbanipal *See* SARDANAPALUS

Asylum means, literally, a place where pillage is forbidden (Gr *a*, not, *sulon*, right of pillage) The ancients set apart certain places of refuge, where the vilest criminals were protected, from both private and public assaults

Asynja (ăs ın' ya) The goddesses of Asgard, the feminine counterparts of the Æsir

At Home *See* HOME

Atalanta's Race (ăt a lăn' ta) Atalanta, in Greek legend, was a daughter of Iasus and Clymene She took part in the Calydonian hunt and, being very swift of foot, refused to marry the suitor should first defeat her in a race Milanion overcame her at last by dropping, one after another, during the race, three golden apples that had been given him for the purpose by Venus Atalanta was not proof against the temptation to pick them up, and so lost the race and became a wife. In the Bœotian form of the legend Hippomenes takes the place of Milanion

Atargatis (ăt ar găt' is). A fish-goddess of the Phœnicians. Her temple at Carnaim is mentioned in the Apocryphal book of 2 *Maccabees* (xii, 26), and she had another at Ascalon.

Ate (ā' tē) In Greek mythology, the goddess of vengeance and mischief, she was driven out of heaven, and took refuge among the sons of men

With Ate by his side come hot from hell
Cry " Havoc " and let slip the dogs of war.
SHAKESPEARE *Julius Cæsar*, iii, 1

In Spenser's *Faerie Queene* (IV, 1, iv, ix, etc), the name is given to a lying and slanderous hag, the companion of Duessa

Atellanæ, or **Atellan Farces** (a tē la' nē) Licentious interludes in the Roman theatres, introduced from Atella, in Campania. The characters of Macchus and Bucco are the fore-runners of our Punch and Clown.

Athanasian Creed (ăth a nā' shan) One of the three creeds accepted by the Roman and Anglican Churches, so called because it embodies the opinions of Athanasius respecting the Trinity It was compiled in the 5th century by Hilary, Bishop of Arles.
In the Episcopal Prayer Book of America this creed is omitted

Atheists. During World War II Father W. T Cummings, an American army chaplain at Bataan, in one of his sermons used the phrase, "there are no atheists in foxholes," meaning that no one can deny the existence of God in the face of imminent death.

Athenæum (ăth e nē' um) A famous academy or university situated on the Capitoline Hill at Rome, and founded by Hadrian about A.D 133. So called in honour of Athene As now used the name usually denotes a literary or scientific institution.
The Athenæum Club in London was established in 1824, the review of this name (now merged in the *Spectator*) was founded by James Silk Buckingham in 1828.

Athene (a thē' ne) The goddess of wisdom and of the arts and sciences in Greek mythology: the counterpart of the Roman Minerva (*q.v*).

Athens. When the goddess of wisdom disputed with the sea-god which of them should give name to Athens, the gods decided that it should be called by the name of that deity which bestowed on man the most useful boon. Athene (the goddess of wisdom) created the olive tree, Poseidon created the horse The vote was given in favour of the olive tree, and the city was called Athens An olive branch was the symbol of *peace*, and was also the highest prize of the victor in the Olympic games The horse, on the other hand, was the symbol of *war*.

Athens of Ireland. Belfast

Athens of the New World. Boston.

Athens of the West. Cordoba in Spain, was so called in the Middle Ages

The Modern Athens Edinburgh

Athenian Bee. Plato (429-327 B C), a native of Athens, was so called because, according to tradition, when in his cradle a swarm of bees alighted on his mouth, and in consequence his words flowed with the sweetness of honey The same tale is told of St.

Ambrose, and others *See* BEE Xenophon (444-359 B C.) is also called "the Bee of Athens," or "the Athenian Bee"

Athole Brose (Scots) A compound of oatmeal, honey, and whisky

Atkins. *See* TOMMY ATKINS

Atlantean Shoulders. Shoulders able to bear a great weight, like those of Atlas (*q v.*)

> Sage he stood,
> With Atlantean shoulders, fit to bear
> The weight of mightiest monarchies
> MILTON *Paradise Lost*, ii, 305

Atlantes (ăt lăn' tēz) Figures of men, used in architecture as pillars So called from Atlas (*q v*) Female figures are called Caryatides (*q v*). *See also* TELAMONES

Atlantic Charter. President Roosevelt and Winston Churchill after meeting at sea during the 1939-45 War made a declaration of their common principles, August 14th 1941, known as the Atlantic Charter They declared, among other things, that the U S and Great Britain desired no aggrandizement, that they wished all peoples to live under their chosen form of Government and to have access to those raw materials necessary to their economic prosperity, that they hoped for improved labour standards and social security for all, and that when peace came they wished all men to live free from fear and from want. Finally, they urged general disarmament at the end of hostilities

Atlantic Ocean. The ocean is so called either from the Atlas mountains, the great range in north-west Africa which, to the ancients, seemed to overlook the whole ocean, or from Atlantis (*q.v.*).

Atlantic Wall. The name given by the Germans in World War II to their defences built up around the west coast of France to resist the expected Allied landings

Atlantis. A mythical island of great extent which was anciently supposed to have existed in the Atlantic Ocean. It is first mentioned by Plato (in the *Timæus* and *Critias*), and Solon was told of it by an Egyptian priest, who said that it had been overwhelmed by an earthquake and sunk beneath the sea 9,000 years before his time. *Cp.* LEMURIA, LYONESSE.

The New Atlantis. An allegorical romance by Bacon (written between 1614 and 1618) in which he describes an imaginary island where was established a philosophical commonwealth bent on the cultivation of the natural sciences *See* UTOPIA, CITY OF THE SUN.

Mrs Manley, in 1709, published under the same title a scandalous chronicle, in which the names of contemporaries are so thinly disguised as to be readily recognized

Atlas (ăt' las) In Greek mythology, one of the Titans condemned by Zeus for his share in the War of the Titans to uphold the heavens on his shoulders He was stationed on the Atlas mountains in Africa, and the tale is merely a poetical way of saying that they prop up the heavens, because they are so lofty

> Bid Atlas, propping heaven, as poets feign,
> His subterranean wonders spread!
> THOMSON: *Autumn*, 797.

A book of maps is so called because the figure of Atlas with the world on his back was employed by Mercator on the title-page of his collection of maps in the 16th century. In the paper trade *Atlas* is a standard size of drawing-paper measuring 26 × 34 in.

Atli. *See* ETZEL.

Atman (ăt' man) in Buddhist philosophy, is the noumenon of one's own self Not the Ego, but the ego divested of all that is objective, the "spark of heavenly flame" In the Upanishads the Atman is regarded as the sole reality.

The unseen and unperceivable, which was formerly called the soul, was now called the self, Atman. Nothing could be predicated of it except that it was, that it perceived and thought, and that it must be blessed MAX MULLER

Atomic Energy and the Atomic Bomb. All matter consists of atoms, and science asserts that each atom is composed of three types of particle, the proton, the electron and the neutron, the first possesses a positive electric charge, the second a negative charge of equal value, the neutron has no such charge. The protons, neutrons and some of the electrons form a nucleus around which the remainder of the electrons revolve The binding force of the nucleus is not the same for every element When the nucleus of one atom of Uranium 235 is split up energy is released, due to the formation of an element with a lower binding force In addition neutrons are emitted which, in their turn, split up other atoms If the whole process expands in this way it is called a chain reaction, and if sufficient material is available a terrific explosion results.

Atomic philosophy. The hypothesis of Leucippus, Democritus, and Epicurus, that the world is composed of a concourse of atoms, or particles of matter so minute as to be incapable of further diminution *Cp* CORPUSCULAR PHILOSOPHY

Atomic theory. The doctrine that all elemental bodies consist of aggregations of *atoms* (i e. the smallest indivisible particles of the element in question), not united fortuitously, but according to fixed proportions. The four laws of Dalton are—constant proportion, reciprocal proportion, multiple proportion, and compound proportion

Atomic volume. The space occupied by a quantity of an element compared with, or in proportion to, atomic weight

Atomic weight. The weight of an atom of an element, compared with an atom of hydrogen, the standard of unity

Atomy. *See* ANATOMY.

Atossa (atos' a). Sarah, Duchess of Marlborough (1660-1744), so called by Pope (*Moral Essays*, ii), was the friend of Lady Mary Wortley Montagu, whom he calls *Sappho*. Herodotus says that Atossa, the mother of Xerxes, was a follower of Sappho.

A-trip The anchor is *a-trip* when it has just been drawn from the ground in a perpendicular direction. A sail is *a-trip* when it has been hoisted from the cap, and is ready for trimming

Atropos (ăt′ rō pos). In Greek mythology the eldest of the Three Fates, and the one who severs the thread of human life.

Attaint (etymologically the same word as *attain*, through Fr from Lat *ad*, to, *tangere*, to touch) An old term in chivalry, meaning to strike the helmet and shield of an antagonist so firmly with the lance, held in a direct line, as either to break the lance or overthrow the person struck Hence, to convict, condemn, hence, to condemn one convicted of treason to loss of honours and death The later development of the word was affected by its fanciful association with *taint*.

Attic. The Attic Bee, Sophocles (495-405 B C), the tragic poet, a native of Athens, so called from the great sweetness of his compositions *See also* ATHENIAN BEE

The **Attic Bird.** The nightingale; so called either because Philomel was the daughter of the King of Athens, or because of the great abundance of nightingales in Attica.
> Where the Attic bird
> Trills her thick-warbled notes the summer long
>   MILTON: *Paradise Regained*, IV, 245.

The **Attic Boy.** Cephalos, beloved by Aurora or Morn, passionately fond of hunting.
> Till civil-suited Morn appear,
> Not tricked and frounced, as she was wont
> With the Attic boy to hunt,
> But kerchiefed in a comely cloud
>   MILTON *Il Penseroso*

Attic faith. Inviolable faith, the very opposite of Punic faith *See* PUNICA FIDES

The **Attic Muse.** Xenophon (444-356 B C), the historian, a native of Athens, so called because the style of his composition is a model of elegance

Attic salt. Elegant and delicate wit Salt, both in Latin and Greek, was a common term for wit, or sparkling thought well expressed; thus Cicero says, *Scipio omnes sale superabat* (Scipio surpassed all in wit). The Athenians were noted for their wit and elegant turns of thought.

Atticus (ăt′ i kus). The most elegant and finished scholar of the Romans, and a bookseller (109-32 B C) His admirable taste and sound judgment were so highly thought of that even Cicero submitted several of his treatises to him

The **Christian Atticus.** Reginald Heber (1783-1826), Bishop of Calcutta, a great bookcollector

The **English Atticus.** Joseph Addison (1672-1719), so called by Pope (*Prologue to Satires*), on account of his refined taste and philosophical mind

The **Irish Atticus.** George Faulkner (1700-75), bookseller, publisher, and friend of Swift; so called by Lord Chesterfield when Viceroy of Ireland

Attila. *See* ETZEL.

Attis. *See* ATYS

Attorney (a ter′ ni) (Fr *atourner*, to attorn, or turn over to another) One who acts as agent for another, especially in legal matters The work of an attorney is now undertaken by a solicitor, and the term is only used in "Power of Attorney" described below. A solicitor is one who solicits or petitions in Courts of Equity through counsel. At one time solicitors belonged to Courts of Equity, and attorneys to the other courts.

From and after Act 36, 37 Vict lxvi, 87, " all persons admitted as solicitors, attorneys, or proctors   empowered to practise in any court, the jurisdiction of which is hereby transferred to the High Court of Justice, or the Court of Appeal, shall be called Solicitors of the Supreme Court ' (1873)

Power of Attorney. Legal authority given to another to collect rents, pay wages, invest money, or to act in matters stated in the instrument, according to his own judgment In such cases *quod aliquis facit per aliquem, facit per se.*

Warrant of Attorney The legal instrument which confers on another the "Power of Attorney"

The **Attorney-General** is the chief law officer of the Government and head of the Bar. He conducts cases on behalf of the Crown, advises the various departments of State on legal matters, and, if necessary, justifies such advice and action in Parliament

Atys (ā′ tis) The Phrygian counterpart of the Greek Adonis and Phœnician Tammuz. He was beloved by Cybele, the mother of the gods, who changed him into a pine-tree as he was about to commit suicide A three-days' festival was held in his honour every spring; great grief and mourning was expressed, he was sought for on the mountains, and on the third day brought back to the shrine of Cybele amid great rejoicing

A U.C. Abbreviation of the Lat *Anno Urbis Conditæ*, "from the foundation of the city" (Rome) It is the starting point of the Roman system of dating events, and corresponds with 753 B.C.

Au courant (ō koo′ ron) (Fr.), "acquainted with" (literally, in the current [of events]) To keep one *au courant* of everything that passes, is to keep one familiar with, or informed of, passing events

Au fait (Fr) Skilful, thorough master of; as, He is quite *au fait* in those matters, i e quite master of them or conversant with them.

Au pied de la lettre (Fr.) *Literatim et verbatim*, according to the strict letter of the text
> Arthur is but a boy, and a wild, enthusiastic young fellow whose opinions one must not take *au pied de la lettre*.
>   THACKERAY: *Pendennis*, i, 11

Au revoir (Fr) "Good-bye for the present " Literally, *till seeing you again*

Aubaine. *See* DROIT D'AUBAINE.

Aubry's Dog. *See* DOG.

Auburn (aw′ bern) It is supposed that this hamlet described by Goldsmith in *The Deserted Village* was Lissoy, County Westmeath, Ireland.

Audley. We will John Audley it. A theatrical phrase meaning to abridge, or bring to a conclusion, a play in progress. It is said that in the 18th century a travelling showman named Shuter used to lengthen out his performance till a goodly number of newcomers were waiting for admission to the next house An assistant would then call out, "Is John Audley here?" and the play was brought to an end as soon as possible

Audrey. In Shakespeare's *As You Like It*, an awkward country wench, who jilted William for Touchstone *See also* TAWDRY

Augean Stables (aw jē' an) The stables of Augeas, the mythological king of Elis, in Greece. In these stables he had kept 3,000 oxen, and they had not been cleansed for thirty years. One of the labours of Hercules (*q v*) was to cleanse them, and he did so by causing two rivers to run through them Hence the phrase, to cleanse the Augean stables, means to clear away an accumulated mass of corruption, moral, religious, physical, or legal

Augsburg Confession The chief standard of faith in the Lutheran Church, drawn up by Melancthon and Luther in 1530, and presented to Charles V and the Diet of the German Empire, which was sitting at Augsburg

The **Interim of Augsburg** A Concordat drawn up by Charles V in 1548 to allay the religious turmoil of Germany It was a provisional arrangement, based on the Augsburg Confession, and was to be in force till some definite decision could be pronounced by the General Council to be held at Trent The **Interim of Ratisbon** was a similar temporary arrangement, resulting from the Diet of Ratisbon (1541)

Augury (aw' gū ri) (probably from Lat *avis*, a bird, and *garrire*, to talk), means properly the function of an augur, *i e* a religious official among the Romans who professed to foretell future events from omens derived chiefly from the actions of birds The augur, having taken his stand on the Capitoline Hill, marked out with his wand the space of the heavens to be the field of observation, and divided it from top to bottom If the birds appeared on the left of the division the augury was unlucky, but if on the right it was favourable

This form of divination may have been due to the earliest sailors, who, if they got out of sight of land, would watch the flight of birds for indications of the shore. *Cp* INAUGURATE, SINISTER.

August This month was once called *sextilis*, as it was the sixth from March, with which the year used to open, but it was changed to *Augustus* in compliment to Augustus (63 B C - A D 14), the first Roman Emperor, whose "lucky month" it was *Cp.* JULY It was the month in which he entered upon his first consulship, celebrated three triumphs, received the oath of allegiance from the legions which occupied the Janiculum, reduced Egypt, and put an end to the civil wars

The old Dutch name for August was *Oostmaand* (harvest-month), the old Saxon *Weodmonath* (weed-month), where weed signifies vegetation in general In the French Republican calendar it was called *Thermidor* (hot-month, July 19th to August 17th).

Augustus. A title conferred in 27 B C. upon Caius Julius Cæsar Octavianus, the first Roman Emperor, meaning *reverend*, or *venerable*, and probably in origin *consecrated by augury*. In the reign of Diocletian (284-313) the two emperors each bore the title, and the two viceroys that of *Cæsar* Prior to that time Hadrian limited the latter to the heir presumptive

Augustus was the name given to Philippe II of France (1165-1223) and to Sigismund II of Poland (1520-72) both of whom were born in the month of August

Augusta. The Roman name for the town that occupied the site of the City of London

Augustan Age. The most fruitful and splendid time of Latin literature, so called from the Emperor Augustus Horace, Ovid, Propertius, Tibullus, Virgil, etc , flourished in his reign, from 27 B C to A D 14

Augustan Age of English Literature. The period of the classical writers of the time of Queen Anne and George I.

Augustan History. A series of histories of the Roman Empire from Hadrian to Numerianus (117-285), of unknown authorship and date, but ascribed to Ælius Spartianus, Julius Capitolinus, Ælius Lampridius, Vulcatius Gallicanus, Trebellius Pollio, and Flavius Vopiscus

Augustine, The Second Thomas Aquinas, the *Angelic Doctor* (*q v*)

Augustinian Canons. An order of monks founded in the 11th century by Ivo, Bishop of Chartres. and following the traditionary rule of Augustine, Bishop of Hippo (d 430) They came to England in the reign of Henry I, and had houses at Oxford, Bristol, Carlisle, Walsingham, Newstead, etc

Augustinian, or Austin, Friars A mendicant order founded by Innocent IV in 1250, they came to England two years later *See* BEGGING FRIARS

Auld Brig and New Brig. Robert Burns thus refers to the bridges over the river Ayr

Auld Hornie. After the establishment of Christianity, the heathen deities were degraded by the Church into fallen angels, and Pan, with his horns, crooked nose, goat's beard, pointed ears, and goat's feet, was transformed to his Satanic majesty, and called Old Horney.

> O thou, whatever title suit thee,
> Auld Hornie, Satan, Nick, or Clootie
> BURNS

Auld Reekie. Edinburgh old town, so called because it generally appeared to be capped by a cloud of "reek" or smoke

Aulic Council (Lat *aula*, a court). The council of the Kaiser in the Holy Roman Empire, from which there was no appeal It was instituted in 1501, and came to an end with the extinction of the Empire in 1806, though the name was afterwards given to the Emperor of Austria's Council of State

Aulis (aw' lis) A harbour in Bœotia where the Greek fleet is said to have assembled before sailing against Troy. The goddess Artemis becalmed the vessels because Agamemnon had once killed a stag in the grove sacred to her, and it was declared that she could be propitiated only by the sacrifice of Agamemnon's daughter Iphigenia The story is the subject of an opera (1774) by Gluck.

Aums-ace. *See* AMBSAS

Aunt Sally. A game in which sticks or cudgels are thrown at a wooden head mounted on a pole, the object being to hit the nose of the figure, or break the pipe stuck in its mouth The word *aunt* was anciently applied to any old woman, thus, in Shakespeare, Puck speaks of

> The wisest aunt telling the saddest tale
> *Midsummer Night's Dream,* ii, 1

Aureole Strictly speaking the same as the *vesica piscis* (*q v*), *i e* an elliptical halo of light or colour surrounding the whole figure in early paintings of the Saviour and sometimes of the saints Now, however, frequently used as though synonymous with *nimbus* (*q v*) Du Cange informs us that the aureole of nuns is *white*, of martyrs *red*, and of doctors *green*.

Aurignacian (aw rig nā′ shun). An early palæolithic period in which the graphic arts were developed, as evidenced in the grotto at Aurignac, Haute Garonne, France Flint and bone instruments and ornaments belong to this period

Auri sacra fames (aw′ ri sāk′ ra fā′ mēz) A Latin ' tag" from the *Æneid* (III, 57), meaning, the cursed hunger for wealth. It is applied to that restless craving for money which is almost a monomania

Aurora (aw rôr′ a) Early morning According to Grecian mythology, the goddess Aurora, called by Homer "rosy-fingered," sets out before the sun, and is the pioneer of his rising.

> The Orator hath yoked
> The Hours, like young Aurora, to his car
> WORDSWORTH: *Prelude,* vii, 501.

Aurora's tears. The morning dew

Aurora borealis. The electrical lights occasionally seen in the northern part of the sky, also called "Northern Lights," and "Merry Dancers" *See* DERWENTWATER The similar phenomenon that occurs in the south and round the South Pole is known as the *Aurora Australis*

Ausone, Chateau (aw sōn). A very fine claret, so called because the vineyard is reputed to be on the site of a villa built by the poet Ausonius (4th century A D) at Lucaniacum (St Emilion).

Ausonia (aw sō′ ni a) An ancient name of Italy, so called from Auson, son of Ulysses, and father of the Ausones.

> England, with all thy faults I love thee still .
> I would not yet exchange thy sullen skies,
> And fields without a flower for warmer France
> With all her vines, nor for Ausonia's groves
> Of golden fruitage, and her myrtle bowers
> COWPER *The Task,* ii, 206-15

Auspices (aw′ spi sēz) In ancient Rome the *auspex* (pl *auspices,* from *avis,* a bird and *specere,* to observe) was one who observed the flight of birds and interpreted the omens. *Cp* AUGURY

Only the chief in command was allowed to take the auspices of war, and if a subordinate

B D —3

gained a victory, he was said to win it "under the good auspices" of his superior Hence our modern use of the term

Aussie (aw′ si, os′ i) This was a familiar name given to the Australian troops during and after World War I Among themselves a common colloquial epithet was "digger"

Auster (Gr *austeros,* hot, dry) A wind pernicious to flowers and health In Italy one of the South winds was so called, its modern name is the *Sirocco* In England it is a damp wind, generally bringing wet weather

> Whan the wode wexeth rody of rosene floures, in the first somer sesoun, thorugh the brethe of the winde Zephirus that wexeth warm, yif the cloudy wind Auster blowe felliche, than goth away the fairnesse of thornes
> CHAUCER *Boethius,* II, in

Austin Friars *See* AUGUSTINIAN FRIARS The narrow lane in the City of London of this name is so called because it is on part of the site of an Augustinian priory, the church of which remained until 1941 when it was destroyed by an aerial bomb

Australia The States of Australia have their own familiar names —

> South Australia, the Wheat State
> Queensland, Bananaland
> Victoria, the Cabbage Patch.
> New South Wales, Ma State
> Northern Territory, Land of the White Ant

Among the cities, Perth is called The Swan City, Adelaide, The City of the Churches; Melbourne, City of the Cabbage Garden

Austrian Lip No one who has seen portraits of the Spanish royal family of Hapsburgs can have failed to notice the curiously protruded lower jaw and lip that marked them all This is one of the most famous cases of inherited physical deformities It is said to have been derived originally through marriage with a daughter of the Polish princely family of Jagellon Describing the Emperor Charles V, at the age of fifty-five, Motley says "the lower jaw protruded so far beyond the upper that it was impossible for him to bring together the few fragments of teeth which still remained, or to speak a whole sentence in an intelligible voice " Of Charles II of Spain, his descendant in the fourth generation, and the last of the Hapsburgs, Macaulay says, "the malformation of the jaw, characteristic of his family, was so serious that he could not masticate his food."

Autarchy and Autarky (aw′ tar ki) These homonyms have widely different meanings *Autarchy* is despotism, self-government, absolute dictatorship, *autarky* means self-sufficiency, independence, especially in the economic sphere.

Aut Cæsar aut nullus (awt sē′ sar awt nūl′ us) Everything or nothing, all or not at all Cæsar used to say, "he would sooner be first in a village than second at Rome." The phrase was used as a motto by Cæsar Borgia (1478-1507), the natural son of Pope Alexander VI.

Authentic Doctor. A title bestowed on the scholastic philosopher, Gregory of Rimini (d 1358).

Authorized Version, The. *See* BIBLE, THE ENGLISH

Autocrat of the Breakfast Table. A name given to Oliver Wendell Holmes, who wrote a series of essays under this title for the first twelve numbers of the *Atlantic Monthly* in 1857 They were published in volume form the following year

Auto da Fe (aw' tō da fā) (Port an act of faith). An assembly of the Spanish Inquisition for the examination of heretics, or for the carrying into execution of the sentences imposed by it Those who persisted in their heresy were delivered to the secular arm and usually burnt The reason why inquisitors *burnt* their victims was, because they were forbidden to "shed blood", a tergiversation based on the axiom of the Roman Catholic Church, *Ecclesia non novit sanguinem* (The Church is untainted with blood)

Autolycus (aw tol' i kus) In Greek mythology, son of Mercury, and the craftiest of thieves. He stole the flocks of his neighbours, and changed their marks, but Sisyphus outwitted him by marking his sheep under their feet Autolycus, delighted with this device, became friends with Sisyphus Shakespeare uses his name for the rascally pedlar in *The Winter's Tale*, and says —

My father named me Autolycus, who being, as I am, littered [*i e.* born] under Mercury, was likewise a snapper-up of unconsidered trifles
Winter's Tale, iv, 2

Automedon (aw tom' ē don) A coachman He was, according to Homer, the companion and the charioteer of Achilles, but according to Virgil the brother-in-arms of Achilles's son, Pyrrhus.

Autumn. The third season of the year, *astronomically*, from September 21st to December 21st, but *popularly* comprising (in England) August, September, and October.

Figuratively the word may mean the fruits of autumn, as in Milton's —

Raised of grassy turf
Their table was, and mossy seats had round,
And on her ample square, from side to side,
All autumn piled.
Paradise Lost, v, 391.

or, a season of maturity or decay, as in Shelley's —

His limbs were lean, his scattered hair,
Sered by the autumn of strange suffering,
Sung dirges in the wind
Alastor, 248

He is come to his autumn. A colloquialism, which may mean that he has entered on his period of (natural or induced) decay.

Ava (a' và) A ruined city in Burma, situated on the Irawaddy, some 10 miles south-west of Mandalay It was the capital of the Burman empire until 1782 and again from 1823 to 1837. On being raised to the marquisate in 1888, the Earl of Dufferin, who had negotiated the annexation of Upper Burma, added the name of Ava to his title, becoming 1st Marquis of Dufferin and Ava

Avalon (ăv' a lon) A Celtic word meaning "the island of apples," and in Celtic mythology applied to the Island of Blessed Souls, an earthly paradise set in the western seas In the Arthurian legends it is the abode and burial-place of Arthur, who was carried hither by Morgan le Fay. Its identification with Glastonbury (*q v*) rests on etymological confusion Ogier le Dane and Overon also held their courts at Avalon

Avant-courier (ă' von kur' yer) An Anglicized form of Fr *avant-coureur*, a messenger sent before, one who is to get things ready for a party of travellers, soldiers, etc, or to announce their approach Figuratively, anything said or done to prepare the way for something more important, a feeler, a harbinger

Avant-garde (ă' von gard) (Fr) The advanced guard of an army, usually nowadays cut down to *vanguard* The term is also applied to ulta-modern and experimental young artists and writers.

Avars. *See* BANAT

Avatar (Sans *avatara*, descent; hence, incarnation of a god) In Hindu mythology, the advent to earth of a deity in a visible form The ten avataras of Vishnu are by far the most celebrated The 1st advent (the Matsya), in the form of a fish, 2nd, (the Kurma), in that of a tortoise, 3rd (the Varaha), of a boar, 4th (the Narasinha), of a monster, half man and half lion; 5th (the Vamana), in the form of a dwarf, 6th (Parashurama), in human form, as Rama with the axe, 7th (Ramachandra), again as Rama; 8th, as Krishna (*q v*), 9th, as Buddha These are all past The 10th advent will occur at the end of four ages, and will be in the form of a white horse (Kalki) with wings, to destroy the earth.

The word is used metaphorically to denote a manifestation or embodiment of some idea or phase —

I would take the last years of Queen Anne's reign as the zenith, or palmy state, of Whiggism, in its divinest avatar of common sense
COLERIDGE *Table-talk*

Ave (a' vi, a' vä) Latin for ' Hail!"

Ave atque vale. *See* VALE.

Ave Maria (Lat Hail, Mary!) The first two words of the angel's salutation to the Virgin Mary (*Luke* i, 28) In the Roman Catholic Church the phrase is applied to an invocation to the Virgin beginning with those words, and also to the smaller beads of a rosary, the larger ones being termed *paternosters*

Avenger of Blood, The The man who, in the Jewish polity, had the right of taking vengeance on him who had slain one of his kinsmen (*Josh* xx, 5, etc). The Avenger in Hebrew is called *goel*

Cities of refuge were appointed for the protection of homicides, and of those who had caused another's death by accident (*Num* xxxv, 12). The Koran sanctions the Jewish custom

Aver. *See* AVOIRDUPOIS

Avernus (a věr' nus) (Gr. *a-ornis*, "without a bird"). A lake in Campania, so called from the belief that its sulphurous and mephitic vapours caused any bird that attempted to fly over it to fall into its waters. Latin mythology placed the entrance to the infernal regions near it; hence Virgil's lines —

Facilis decensus Averno
Noctes atque dies patet atri janua Ditis,
Sed revocare gradum, superasque evadere ad auras,
Hoc opus, hic labor est

Æneid, vi, 126

Englished by Dryden as follows:—
Smooth the descent and easy is the way
(The Gates of Hell stand open night and day),
But to return, and view the cheerful skies,
In this the task and mighty labour lies.

Bad habits are easily acquired, but very hard to give up

Avesta (a ves' ta)   The Zoroastrian and Parsee Bible, dating in its present form from the last quarter of the 4th century, A D, collected from the ancient writings, sermons, etc , of Zoroaster (fl before 800 B c), oral traditions, etc   It is only a fragment, and consists of (1) the Yasna, the chief liturgical portion, which includes *Gathas*, or hymns, (2) the Vispered, another liturgical work, (3) the Vendidad, which, like our Pentateuch, contains the laws, (4) the Yashts, dealing with stories of the different gods; together with prayers and other fragments

The books are sometimes erroneously called the Zend-Avesta, this is a topsy-turvy misunderstanding of the term "Avesta-Zend," which means simply "text and commentary"

Avianus (ăv i ā' nus)   A writer of imitations of Æsop's fables in the decline of the Roman Empire   In the Middle Ages they were used as a first lesson book in schools

Avicenna.   *See* ABOU IBN SINA

Avignon Popes (à vē' nyon)   In 1309 Pope Clement V left Rome and transferred the papal court to Avignon, where the popes remained for seventy years of strife and confusion   The Avignon popes were

Clement V	1305-1314	Innocent VI	1352-1362
John XXII	1316-1334	Urban V	1362-1370
Benedict XII	1334-1342	Gregory XI	1370-1378
Clement VI	1342-1352		

A vinculo matrimonii (ā ving' kū lō măt ri mō ni i) (Lat).   A total divorce from marriage ties   A divorce *a mensa et thoro* (i e from table and bed—from bed and board) is partial, because the parties may, if they choose, come together again; but a divorce *a vinculo matrimonii* is granted in cases in which the "marriage" was never legal owing to a precontract (bigamy), consanguinity, or affinity

Avoid Extremes   A traditional saying of Pittacus of Mitylene (652-569 B c), one of the seven Wise Men of Greece   It is echoed in many writers and literatures   Compare the advice given by Phœbus to Phaethon when he was preparing to drive the chariot of the sun —

Medio tutissimus ibis (You will go more safely in the middle) —OVID *Met*, ii, 137

Avoirdupois (ăv' ĕr dū poiz)   Fr. *avoir, aver* or *avier*, goods in general, and *poise = poids* (weight)   Not the verb, but the noun *avoir*. Properly *avoir de poids* (goods having weight), goods sold by weight   There is an obsolete English word *aver*, meaning goods in general, hence also cattle, whence such compounds as *aver-corn, aver-penny, aver-silver* and *aver-land*

Awar.   One of the sons of Eblis (*q v*)

A-weather.   A sailor's term, towards the weather, or the side on which the wind strikes, the reverse of *a-lee*, which is in the *lee* or shelter, and therefore opposite to the wind side

Awkward Squad   Military recruits not yet fitted to take their place in the ranks
A "squad" is a contraction of "squadron "

Awl   "I'll pack up my awls and be gone," i e all my goods   The play is on *awl* and *all*

Axe   To hang up one's axe.   To retire from business, to give over a useless project   The allusion is to the battle-axe, formerly devoted to the gods and hung up when fighting was over   *See* ASK.

To put the axe on the helve   To solve a difficulty   To hit the right nail on the head.

To send the axe after the helve.   To spend money in the hope of recovering bad debts

He has an axe to grind.   Some selfish motive in the background, some personal interest to answer   Franklin tells of a man who wanted to grind his axe, but had no time to turn the grindstone   Going to the yard where he saw young Franklin, he asked the boy to show him how the machine worked, kept praising him till his axe was ground, and then laughed at him for his pains.

Axinomancy (ăks' in ō măn' si)   A method of divination practised by the ancient Greeks with a view to discovering crime   An agate, or piece of jet, was placed on a red-hot axe, and indicated the guilty person by its motion (Gr *axine manteia*)

Axis.   The term used by the Fascist states of Central Europe, in the sense of an alliance
It was first used by Mussolini, in 1936 in a speech in which he declared the German-Italian agreement to be "an axis round which all European states animated by the will to collaboration and peace can also assemble "

Axis of advance   A military term for the road or track running through an area to be attacked and used by the attackers to maintain direction

Ayah (ī' ya).   Now an Anglo-Indian word, but originally Portuguese.   A native Hindu nurse or lady's maid.

Ayeshah (ī yesh' a)   Mohammed's second and favourite wife   He married her when she was only nine years old, and died in her arms She was born about 611 and died about 678

Aymon, The Four Sons of (ā' mon)   Aymon is a semi-mythical hero, and was father of Reynaud (or Rinaldo, *q v*), Guiscard, Alard, and Richard, all of whom were knighted by Charlemagne   The earliest version was probably compiled by Huon de Villeneuve from earlier chansons in the 13th century.   The brothers, and their famous horse Bayard (*q v*), appear in many poems and romances, including Tasso's *Jerusalem Delivered*, Pulci's *Morgante Maggiore*, Boiardo's *Orlando Innamorato*, Ariosto's *Orlando Furioso*, etc , and the story formed the basis of a number of French chap-books

Ayrshire Poet   Robert Burns (1759-96), who was born at Alloway near the town of Ayr

Azazel (a zăz' el)   In *Lev* xvi we read that among other ceremonies the high priest, on the Day of Atonement, cast lots on two goats, one lot was *for the Lord*, and the other lot *for Azazel*   Milton uses the name for the standard-bearer of the rebel angels (*Paradise Lost*, i, 534).   In Mohammedan legend, Azazel is a jinn of the desert, when God commanded the angels to worship Adam, Azazel replied, "Why should the son of fire fall down before a son of clay?" and God cast him out of heaven   His name was then changed to *Eblis* (*q.v.*), which means ' despair "

Azaziel (a zăz' i el).   In Byron s *Heaven and Earth*, a seraph who fell in love with Anah, a granddaughter of Cain   When the flood came, he carried her under his wing to another planet

Azilian (a zil' i an)   The main period of the Mesolithic Age, of which many harpoons made from stag bones have been found in the Pyrennean cave at Mas Azil

Azoth (ăz'oth) (Arab)   The alchemists' name for mercury, also the panacea or universal remedy of Paracelsus   Browning, in his poem *Paracelsus* (Bk v), gives the name to Paracelsus's sword.

> Last, my good sword ah, trusty, Azoth, leapest
> Beneath thy master's grasp for the last time'

Azrael (ăz' rāl)   In Mohammedan legend, the angel that watches over the dying, and takes the soul from the body, the angel of death He will be the last to die, but will do so at the second trump of the archangel   *See* ADAM

   The Wings of Azrael   The approach of death, the signs of death coming on the dying

Azrafil   *See* ISRAFIL.

Aztecs (ăz' teks)   A branch of the Nahuatl Indians who came (probably) from the north-west and settled in the valley of Mexico about the 11th or 12th century, and ultimately subjugated the aborigines   A wealthy and highly civilized people renowned for their building Their power was brought to an end by the Spaniards under Cortes between 1519 and 1530

Azure (ăzh' ŭr, ā' zŭr)   Heraldic term for the colour blue.   Represented in royal arms by the planet Jupiter, in noblemen's by the sapphire   The ground of the old shield of France was azure   Emblem of fidelity and truth   Represented in heraldic devices by horizontal lines   Ultimately Arabic or Persian, and connected with "lapis *lazuli*," for which the word "azure' used to stand   Also used as a synonym for the clear, blue sky

Azuriel.   *See* KENSINGTON GARDENS.

B

B.   The form of the Roman capital "B" can be traced through early Greek to Phœnician and Egyptian hieratic; the small "b" is derived from the cursive form of the capital   The letter is called in Hebrew *beth* (a house), in Egyptian hieroglyphics it was represented by the crane.

B in *Roman notation* stands for 300; with a *line above*, it denotes 3,000.

   Marked with a B.   In the Middle Ages, and as late as the 17th century (especially in America), this letter was branded on the forehead of convicted blasphemers   In France *être marqué au 'b"* means to be either one-eyed, hump-backed, or lame (*borgne*, *bossu*, *boiteux*), hence, a poor, miserable sort of creature

   Not to know B from a battledore, or from a bull's foot   To be quite illiterate, not to know even one's letters   Conversely, *I know B from a bull's foot*, means ' I'm a sharp, knowing person; you can't catch *me*'"   *Cp* HAWK and HANDSAW

B. and S.   Brandy and soda

B C.   In dates an abbreviation for "Before Christ," before the Christian era.

   Marked with B C.   When a soldier disgraced himself by insubordination he was formerly marked with "B C " (bad character) before he was drummed out of the regiment.

B Flats.   Bugs, which obnoxious insects are characterized by their flatness

B of B. K.   Some mysterious initials applied to himself in his diary by Arthur Orton, ' the Tichborne Claimant "   Supposed to denote "Baronet of British Kingdom "   For some time it was a phrase applied popularly to anyone who put on airs

Baal.   A Semitic word meaning *proprietor* or *possessor*, primarily the title of a god as lord of a place (*e g   Baal-peor*, lord of Peor), or as possessor of some distinctive characteristic or attribute (*e g. Baal-zebub*, or *Beelzebub*, *q v.*). The worship of the Baals—for each village community had its own—was firmly established in Canaan at the time of the Israelites' incursion, the latter adopted many of the Canaanitish rites, and grafted them on to their own worship of Jahwe (Jehovah), Jahwe becoming—especially when worshipped at the "high places"—merely the national Baal   It was this form of worship that Hosea and other prophets denounced as heathenism.   Bel (*q v*) is the Assyrian form of the name.   *See also* BELPHEGOR

Baalbec.   *See* CHILMINAR

Babau (ba bō)   A French bogeyman, once used to terrify unruly children.

Babbitt (băb' it)   The leading character in Sinclair Lewis's novel of this name   He is a prosperous "realtor" or estate agent in the Western city of Zenith, a simple, likeable fellow, with faint aspirations to culture that are forever smothered in the froth and futile "hustle" of American business life   Drive (which takes him nowhere), hustle (by which he saves no time) and efficiency (which does not enable him to do anything) are the keynotes of his life.   Babbitt has been accepted as the type of an American business man

Babel.   A perfect Babel.   A thorough confusion   "A Babel of sounds "   A confused uproar, in which nothing can be heard but hubbub   The allusion is to the confusion of tongues at Babel (*Gen.* xi).

Babes in the Wood. *See* CHILDREN The phrase has been humorously applied to (1) simple trustful folks, never suspicious, and easily gulled, (2) insurrectionary hordes that infested the mountains of Wicklow and the woods of Enniscorthy towards the close of the 18th century, and (3) men in the stocks or in the pillory

Babes, Protecting deities of According to Varro, Roman infants were looked after by Vagitanus, the god who caused them to utter their first *cry*, Fabulinus, who presided over their *speech*, Cuba, the goddess who protected them in their cots, and Domiduca, who brought young children safe home, and kept guard over them when out of their parents' sight In the Christian Church St Nicholas is the patron saint of children

Babies in the Eyes. Love in the expression of the eyes Love is the little babe Cupid, and hence the conceit, originating from the miniature image of oneself in the pupil of another's eyes

> In each of her two crystal eyes
> Smileth a naked boy [Cupid]
> LORD SURREY

> She clung about his neck, gave him ten kisses,
> Toyed with his locks, looked babies in his eyes
> HEYWOOD: <i>Love's Mistress</i>

Babylon (băb′ ĭ lŏn) The Modern Babylon. So London is sometimes called, on account of its wealth, luxury, and dissipation; also (with allusion to Babel) because of the many nationalities that meet, and languages that are spoken there

The hanging gardens of Babylon. *See* HANGING

The whore of Babylon An epithet bestowed on the Roman Catholic Church by the early Puritans and some of their descendants The allusion is to *Rev* xvii–xix (*Cp.* SCARLET WOMAN.) In the book of the *Revelation* Babylon stands for Rome, the capital of the world, the embodiment of luxury, vice, splendour, tyranny, and all that the early Church knew was against the spirit of Christ

Babylonian Captivity. The seventy years that the Jews were captives in Babylon. They were made captives by Nebuchadnezzar, and released by Cyrus (536 B C)

Babylonian numbers. *Nec Babylonios temptaris numeros* (Horace *Odes*, Bk 1, xi, 2) Do not pry into futurity by astrological calculations and horoscopes Do not consult fortune-tellers The Chaldeans were the most noted of astrologers

Babylonish garment, A. *Babylonica vestis,* a garment woven with divers colours. *Pliny,* viii, 74.

> I saw among the spoils a goodly Babylonish garment
> <i>Josh</i>, vii, 21

Baca, The Valley of (ba′ ka) An unidentified place mentioned in *Ps* lxxxiv, 6, meaning the Valley of Weeping, and so translated in the Revised Version Baca trees were either mulberry trees or balsams

Bacbuc (băk′ bŭc) A Chaldean or Assyrian word for an earthenware pitcher, cruse, or bottle, taken by Rabelais as the name of the

Oracle of the Holy Bottle (and of its priestess), to which Pantagruel and his companions made a famous voyage The question to be proposed was whether or not Panurge ought to marry The Holy Bottle answered with a click like the noise made by a glass snapping. Bacbuc told Panurge the noise meant *trinc* (drink), and that was the response, the most direct and positive ever given by the oracle. Panurge might interpret it as he liked, the obscurity would always save the oracle. *See* ORACLE

Bacchus (băk′ ŭs) In Roman mythology, the god of wine, the Dionysus of the Greeks, son of Zeus and Semele He is represented in early art as a bearded man and completely clad, but after the time of Praxiteles as a beautiful youth with black eyes, golden locks, flowing with curls about his shoulders, and filleted with ivy In peace his robe was purple, in war he was covered with a panther's skin His chariot was drawn by panthers

In the famous statue in Rome he has a bunch of grapes in his hand and a panther at his feet. Pliny tells us that, after his conquest of India, Bacchus entered Thebes in a chariot drawn by elephants, and, according to some accounts, he married Ariadne after Theseus had deserted her in Naxos

The name "Bacchus" is a corruption of Gr *Iacchus* (from *Iache*, a shout), and was originally merely an epithet of Dionysus as the noisy or rowdy god.

> As jolly Bacchus, god of pleasure,
> Charmed the wide world with drink and dances,
> And all his thousand airy fancies
> PARNELL.

Bacchus sprang from the thigh of Zeus. The tale is that Semele, at the suggestion of Juno, asked Zeus to appear before her in all his glory, but the foolish request proved her death. Zeus saved the child which was prematurely born by sewing it up in his thigh till it came to maturity

What has that to do with Bacchus? *i e* what has that to do with the matter in hand? When Thespis introduced recitations in the vintage songs, the innovation was suffered to pass, so long as the subject of recitation bore on the exploits of Bacchus, but when, for variety's sake, he wandered to other subjects, the Greeks pulled him up with the exclamation, "What has that to do with Bacchus?"

Bacchus a noyé plus d'hommes que Neptune. The ale-house wrecks more men than the ocean

A priest, or son, of Bacchus. A toper.

Bacchus, in the *Lusiad,* is the evil demon or antagonist of Jupiter, the lord of destiny As Mars is the guardian power of Christianity, Bacchus is the guardian power of Mohammedanism

Bacchanalia. The triennial festivals held at night in Rome in honour of Bacchus, called in Greece *Dionysia,* Dionysus being the Greek equivalent of Bacchus. In Rome, and in later times in Greece, they were characterized by drunkenness, debauchery, and licentiousness of all kinds; but originally they were very different and were of greater importance than any other ancient festival on account of their connexion with the origin and development of the drama, for in Attica, at the Dionysia choragic literary contests were held, and from these both tragedy and comedy originated Hence *bacchanalian*, drunken The terms are now applied to any drunken and convivial orgy on the grand scale

Bacchanals (băk' à nalz) (*see also* BAG O' NAILS), *Bacchants, Bacchantes* Priests and priestesses, or male and female votaries, of Bacchus, hence, a drunken roysterer

Bacchante (ba kăn' ti) A female winebibber, so called from the "bacchantes," or female priestesses of Bacchus They wore fillets of ivy

Bacharach (băk' à răk) A brand of Rhine wine made in this small Rhenish town some 23 miles south of Coblentz It once enjoyed great popularity in England and the name appears in many forms in Elizabethan and later literature—*backrack, backrag, baccharic,* etc

> I'm for no tongues but dry'd ones, such as will
> Give a fine relish to my backrag
> MAYNE. *The City Match* (1629)
> Good backrack . to drink down in healths
> FLETCHER. *Beggar's Bush*

Bachelor. A man who has not been married. This is a word whose ultimate etymology is unknown, it is from O.Fr. *bacheler*, which is from a late Latin word *baccalaris* This last may be merely a translation of the French word, as it is only of rare and very late occurrence, but it may be allied to *baccalarius*, a late Latin adjective applied to farm labourers, the history of which is very doubtful.
In the Prologue to the *Canterbury Tales* (1, 80), Chaucer uses the word in its old sense of a knight not old enough to display his own banner, and so following that of another

> With him ther was his sone, a young Squyer,
> A lovyere, and a lusty bacheler

Taxes on bachelors. By an Act of 1694 a tax was imposed on unmarried male persons above the age of twenty-five, varying in amount from £12 10s. to 1s. according to the taxpayer's status. It was repealed in 1706. In 1785 bachelors' servants were subjected to a higher tax than those of other persons In the graduated Income Tax designed by Pitt in 1799 the rate for bachelors was higher than for married men In the existing Income Tax system a bachelor pays at a higher rate than a married man by having no allowances for wife, children, etc

Bachelor of Arts. A student who has taken the university degree below that of Master

Bachelor of Salamanca. The last novel of Le Sage (published in 1736), the hero is a bachelor of arts, Don Cherubin de la Ronda, he is placed in different situations of life, and associates with all classes of society

Bachelor's buttons Several flowers are so called Red batchelor's buttons, the double red campion, yellow the upright crowfoot, white, the white ranunculus, or white campion

> The similitude these flowers have to the jagged cloath buttons anciently worne gave occasion . . to call them Bachelor's Buttons
> GERARD *Herbal*

Or the phrase may come from a custom sometimes observed by countrymen of carrying the flower in their pockets to know how they stand with their sweethearts If the flower dies, it is a bad omen, but if it does not fade, they may hope for the best

Bachelor's fare. Bread and cheese and kisses

Bachelor's porch. An old name for the north door of a church Menservants and poor men used to sit on benches down the north aisle, and maidservants and poor women on the south side After service the men formed one line and the women another, down which the clergy and gentry passed

Bachelor's wife. A hypothetical ideal or perfect wife

> Bachelors' wives and maids' children be well taught.
> HEYWOOD *Proverbs*

Back, To. To support with money, influence, or encouragement, as to "back a friend"; to lay money on a horse in a race, "backing" it to win or for a place
A commercial term, meaning to *endorse* When a merchant backs or endorses a bill, he guarantees its value.
Falstaff says to the Prince:—

> You care not who sees your back. Call you that backing of your friends? A plague upon such backing!
> 1 *Henry IV*, ii, 4

Back-of-beyond. A phrase originating in Australia to describe the wide inland spaces, the *great Outback*. The phrase backblock is found in 1850, referring to those vast territories divided up by the government into blocks for settlement.

Back the oars, or **back water,** is to row backwards, that the boat may move the reverse of its ordinary direction

Back and edge. Entirely, heartily, tooth and nail, with might and main The reference is, perhaps, to a wedge driven home to split wood

> They were working back and edge for me
> BOLDREWOOD *Robbery under Arms*, ch ii.

Laid on one's back. Laid up with chronic ill-health, helpless.

Thrown on his back. Completely beaten A figure taken from wrestling

To back and fill. A nautical phrase, denoting a mode of tacking when the tide is with the vessel and the wind against it Metaphorically, to be irresolute.

To back out. To withdraw from an engagement, bargain, etc , to retreat from a difficult position

To back the field. To bet on all the horses bar one

To back the sails. So to arrange them that the ship's way may be checked

To back up. To uphold, to support As one who stands at your back to support you An advance by the batsman not taking strike at cricket in order to be ready to take a quick run if the striker makes an opportunity

To break the back of. To finish the hardest part of one's work.

To get one's back up. To be irritated. The allusion is to a cat, which sets its back up when attacked by a dog or other animal

To go back on one's word. To withdraw what one has said, to refuse to perform what one has promised To go back on a person is to betray him

To have one's back to the wall. To act on the defensive against odds One beset with foes tries to get his back against a wall that he may not be attacked by foes behind.

To see his back ; to see the back of anything. To get rid of a person or thing, to see it leave

To take a back seat. To withdraw from a position one has occupied or attempted to occupy, to retire into obscurity, usually as a confession of failure

To the back To the backbone, entirely

To turn one's back on another. To leave, forsake, or neglect one. To leave him by going away.

Backbite, To. To slander behind one's back

To be prynces in pryde and pouerte to despise
To backbite, and to bosten and bere fals witnesse
        Piers Plowman
He that backbiteth not with his tongue
        Psalm xv, 3

Backgammon The A S *bac gamen* (back game), so called because the pieces (in certain circumstances) are taken up and obliged to go back to enter at the table again

Back-hander A blow with the back of the hand Also one who takes *back* the decanter in order to *hand* himself another glass before the decanter is passed on
I'll take a back-hander, as Clive don't seem to drink
   THACKERAY *The Newcomes*, ch xliii
A back-handed compliment a compliment which is so phrased as to imply an insult

Backroom boys A name given familiarly to the scientists and others who, unknown to the general public, devised and developed in their studies and laboratories methods of scientific warfare The name has since been applied generally to such unknown workers in all branches of technology

Back-slang. A species of slang which consists in pronouncing the word as though spelt backwards Thus *police* becomes *ecilop* (hence the term *slop* for a policeman), *parsnips*, *spinsrap*, and so on. It was formerly much used by "flash" Cockneys, thieves, etc

Back-speir, To. To cross-examine (Scots)
He has the wit to lay the scene in such a remote
. . country that nobody should be able to back-speir him
      SCOTT *The Betrothed*

Backstairs influence Private or unrecognized influence, especially at Court Royal palaces have more than one staircase, and those who sought the sovereign upon private matters would use one in an unobtrusive position, it was, therefore, highly desirable to conciliate the servants or underlings in charge of the "back stairs "
Hence, *backstairs gossip*, tittle-tattle obtained from servants, *backstairs plots*, or *politics*, underground or clandestine intrigue

Backward blessing A curse To say the Lord's Prayer backwards was to invoke the devil.

Backwardation. A Stock Exchange term denoting the sum paid by a speculator on a "bear account" (i e a speculation on a *fall* in the price of certain stock), in order to postpone the completion of the transaction till the next settling day *Cp* CONTANGO

Backwater. This means properly a pool or creek of still water fed indirectly by a river or stream. It has come to mean figuratively any state in which one is isolated from the active flow of life

Bacon. To baste your bacon To strike or scourge one Bacon is the outside portion of the sides of pork, and may be considered generally as the part which would receive a blow
Falstaff's remark to the travellers at Gadshill, "On, bacons, on!" (1 *Henry IV*, ii, 2) is an allusion to the fact that formerly swine's flesh formed the staple food of English rustics, hence such terms as *bacon-brains* and *chawbacon* for a clownish blockhead

To bring home the bacon. To bring back the prize, to succeed This phrase may have originated in reference to the contest for the Dunmow flitch, or to the sport of catching a greased pig at country fairs.

To save one's bacon. To save oneself from injury, to escape loss. The allusion may be to the care taken by our forefathers to save from the numerous dogs that frequented their houses the bacon which was laid up for winter
But here I say the Turks were much mistaken,
Who, hating hogs, yet wished to save their bacon
    BYRON. *Don Juan*, vii, 42

He may fetch a flitch of bacon from Dunmow. He is so amiable and good-tempered he will never quarrel with his wife The allusion is to the Dunmow Flitch. *See* DUNMOW

Baconian Philosophy A system of philosophy based on principles laid down by Francis Bacon, Lord Verulam, in the 2nd book of his *Novum Organum* It is also called inductive philosophy

Baconian Theory. The theory that Lord Bacon wrote the plays attributed to Shakespeare

Bacon's Brazen Head. *See* BRAZEN HEAD.

Bactrian Sage. Zoroaster, or Zarathrusthra, the founder of the Perso-Iranian religion, who is supposed to have flourished in Bactria (the modern Balkh) before 800 B C

Bad. Among rulers surnamed "The Bad" are William I, King of Sicily from 1154 to 1166, Albert, Landgrave of Thuringia and Margrave of Meisen (d 1314), and Charles II, King of Navarre (1332-87)

Bad blood. Vindictiveness, ill-feeling: hence, *to make bad blood*, or *to stir up bad blood*, to create or renew ill-feeling and a vindictive spirit.

You are in my bad books. *See* BLACK BOOKS

Bad debts. Debts not likely to be paid.

Bad egg. A disreputable character, a thoroughly bad fellow

A bad excuse is better than none An adage that first appeared in Nicolas Udall's *Ralph Roister Doister* (1541), the first comedy written for the English stage

Bad form. Not in good taste

The Bad Lands. In America, the *Mauvaises Terres* of the early French settlers west of Missouri, extensive tracts of sterile, alkali hills, rocky, desolate, and almost destitute of vegetation, in South Dakota.

A bad lot. A person of bad moral character, or one commercially unsound Also a commercial project or stock of worthless value Perhaps from auctioneering slang, meaning a lot which no one will bid for

A bad shot. A wrong guess A sporting phrase; a bad shot is one which does not bring down the bird shot at, one that misses the mark

He is gone to the bad. Has become a ruined man, or a depraved character He is mixing with bad companions, has acquired bad habits, or is (usually implying "through his own fault") in bad circumstances

To the bad. On the wrong side of the account, in arrears

Badge-men Licensed beggars, or almshouse men, so called because they wore some special dress, or other badge, to indicate that they belonged to a particular foundation

> He quits the gay and rich, the young and free,
> Among the badge-men with a badge to be
> CRABBE *Borough*

In former times those who received parish relief also had to wear a badge It was the letter P, with the initial of the parish to which they belonged, in red or blue cloth, on the shoulder of the right sleeve *See* DYVOUR

Badger, A. A hawker, huckster, or itinerant dealer, especially in corn, but also in butter, eggs, fish, etc The word is still in use in some dialects its derivation is not certainly known, but it is not in any way connected with a badge worn. Fuller derived it from Lat. *bajulare*, to carry, but there is no substantiation for this The modern hawker's licence dates from the licences that badgers had to obtain from a Justice under Act 5 and 6 Edw VI, c. 14, §7.

> Under Dec 17, 1565, we read of "Certain persons upon Humber side who . buy great quantities of corn, two of whom were authorised badgers "
> *State Papers* (Domestic Series)

To badger. To tease, annoy, or persistently importune, in allusion to badger-baiting A badger was kennelled in a tub, where dogs were set upon him to worry him out When dragged from his tub the poor beast was allowed to retire to it till he recovered from the attack. This process was repeated several times

It is a vulgar error that the legs of a badger are shorter on one side than on the other

> I think that Titus Oates was as uneven as a badger.
> MACAULAY.

Drawing a badger, is drawing him out of his tub by means of dogs.

In the U S A badger is the slang name of an inhabitant of Wisconsin.

Badinguet (ba' din gä) A nickname given to Napoleon III It is said to be the name of the workman whose clothes he wore when he contrived to escape from the fortress of Ham, in 1846

> If Badinguet and Bismarck have a row together let them settle it between them with their fists, instead of troubling hundreds of thousands of men who . have no wish to fight
> ZOLA *The Downfall*, ch ii.

Napoleon's adherents were known as *Badingueux*

Badminton (băd' min ton) The country seat of the Dukes of Beaufort in Gloucestershire. It has given its name to a drink and a game. The drink is a claret-cup made of claret, sugar, spices, soda-water, and ice In pugilistic parlance blood, which is sometimes called "claret" (*q v*), is also sometimes called "badminton," from the colour.

The game badminton is a predecessor of, and is similar to, lawn tennis; it is played with shuttlecocks instead of balls

Badoura (ba doo' ra). "The most beautiful woman ever seen upon earth," heroine of the story of Camaralzaman and Badoura in the *Arabian Nights*

Baedeker (bä' dē ker) Starred in Baedeker. For many years tourists the world over have flocked to places of interest, red guide-book in hand Karl Baedeker (1801-59) brought out his first guide-book (to Holland, Belgium and the Rhine) by arrangement with Mr John Murray in 1839 In subsequent years he and his agents wrote exhaustive guide-works of almost every part of the world Baedeker inaugurated the somewhat invidious and not always reliable system of marking with one or more stars objects and places of interest according to their historic or aesthetic importance.

Baedeker Raids A phrase first used in Britain April 29th, 1942, to describe German air raids which, in reprisal for damage done to Cologne and Lubeck, were deliberately directed on historic monuments (*e.g* Bath, Canterbury, Norwich) listed as such in Baedeker's guide

Baffle Originally a punishment meted out to a recreant or traitorous knight by which he was degraded and thoroughly disgraced, part of which seems to have consisted in hanging him or his effigy by the heels from a tree and loudly proclaiming his misdeeds *See* Spenser's *Faerie Queene*, VI, vii, 26 —

> Letting him arise like abject thrall
> He gan to him object his haynous crime,
> And to revile, and rate, and recreant call,
> And lastly to despoyle of knightly bannerall
> And after all, for greater infamie,
> He by the heeles he hung upon a tree
> And baffuld so, that all which passed by,
> The picture of his punishment might see,
> And by the like ensample warned bee
> How ever they through treason doe trespasse

Bag and Baggage, as "Get away with you, bag and baggage," *i e* get away, and carry with you all your belongings   Originally a military phrase signifying the whole property and stores of an army and of the soldiers composing it.   Hence the bag and baggage policy   In 1876 Gladstone, speaking on the Eastern question, said, "Let the Turks now carry away their abuses in the only possible manner, namely, by carrying away themselves. .   One and all, *bag and baggage*, shall, I hope, clear out from the province they have desolated and profaned "   *See also* BAGGAGE

A bag of bones   Very emaciated, generally "A mere bag of bones "

Bag o' Nails.   Corruption of *Bacchanals* A not uncommon inn-sign, *The Devil and the Bag o' Nails*, represents Pan, with his cloven hoofs and his horns, accompanied by satyrs

A bag of tricks, or the whole bag of tricks. The whole lot, the entire collection   This is an allusion to the conjuror's bag in which he carries the various properties and impedimenta for performing his tricks

The bottom of the bag.   The last expedient, having emptied every other one out of one's bag, a trump card held in reserve

In the bag.   As good as certain

To be left holding the bag.   To have one's comrades decamp or withdraw leaving one with the entire onus of what was originally a group responsibility.

To empty the bag.   To tell the whole matter and conceal nothing (Fr *vider le sac*, to expose all to view)

To give the bag, now means the same as **to give the sack** (*see* SACK), but it seems originally to have had the reverse meaning; a servant or employee leaving without having given notice was said to have given his master "the bag "

To let the cat out of the bag.   *See* under CAT.

To bag   Secure for oneself, probably an extension of the sporting use of the word, meaning, to put into one's bag what one has shot, caught, or trapped   Hence, a good bag, a large catch of game, fish, or other animals sought after by sportsmen

Bag-man, A.   A commercial traveller, who carries a bag with samples to show to those whose custom he solicits   In former times commercial travellers used to ride a horse with saddle-bags sometimes so large as almost to conceal the rider

Bags I   *See* FAINS

Bags   Slang for "trousers," which may be taken as the bags of the body   When the pattern was very staring and "loud," they once were called *howling-bags*

Oxford bags are wide-bottomed flannel trousers.

Bags of mystery   Slang for sausages or saveloys, the allusion is obvious

Baga de Secretis.   Records in the Record Office of trials for high treason and other State offences from the reign of Edward IV to the close of the reign of George III   These records contain the proceedings in the trials of

Anne Boleyn, Sir Walter Raleigh, Guy Fawkes, the regicides, and of the risings of 1715 and 1745.

Baggage, as applied to a worthless or a flirtatious woman, dates from the days when soldiers' wives taken on foreign service with the regiment travelled with the regimental stores and baggage.

Bagstock, Major.   A blustering old toady figuring in Dickens's *Dombey and Son*   He always alludes to himself in the third person as "Joey B.," "Old Josh B ," and so forth.

Bahram (ba' răm)   Governor of Media, and a famous Persian general in the 6th century A D.   He was "Bahram the Great Hunter" of Omar Khayyam   The Aga Khan's horse of this name won the Derby in 1935

Bail (Fr *bailler*, to deliver up)   Security given for the temporary release of an accused person pending his trial or the completion of his trial, also the person or persons giving such security.   *See also* LEG-BAIL

Common bail, or bail below.   A bail given to the sheriff to guarantee the appearance of the defendant in court at any day and time the court demands

Special bail, or bail above.   A bail which includes, besides the guarantee of the defendant's appearance, an undertaking to satisfy all claims made on him.

Bail up!   The Australian bushranger's equivalent for the highwayman's "Stand and deliver!"

Bailey (probably in ultimate origin from O Fr. *bailler*, to enclose)   The external wall of a mediæval castle, forming the first line of defence; also the outer court of the castle, the space immediately within the outer wall   The entrance was over a drawbridge, and through the embattled gate   When there were two courts they were distinguished as the outer and inner bailey   Subsequently the word included the court and all its buildings, and when the court was abolished, the term was attached to the castle, as the Old Bailey (London) and the Bailey (Oxford).

Bailey bridge   The name given in World War II to a metal bridge made of easily portable sections of amazing strength which could be speedily erected   A major factor in the rapidity of Allied advances, particularly in N W Europe, was the employment of these bridges   They were invented by the British engineer, D C Bailey

Bailiff.   *See* BUM-BAILIFF

Bailiwick (bā' li wik)   The county in which a sheriff, as bailiff of the King, exercises jurisdiction; or the liberty of some lord "who has an exclusive authority within its limits to act as the sheriff does in the county "

The sheriff of the shire, whose peculiar office it is to walke continuallye up and downe his balywick as ye would have a marshall,
SPENSER *State of Ireland*, 1597

Out of one's bailiwick, far from home, on strange ground.

3*

Baily's Beads. *See* BEAD.

Bain Marie (băn ma rē) The French name for a double saucepan like a glue-pot The term is sometimes used in English kitchens. It appears earlier (as in Mrs Glasse's *Cookery Book*, 1796) under its Latin name, *Balneum Mariæ*, hence the "St Mary's bath" of Ben Jonson's *Alchemist*, II, iii The name is supposed to be due to the gentleness of this method of heating

Bairam (bī' răm) The name given to two great Mohammedan feasts The Lesser begins on the new moon of the month Shawwal, at the termination of the fast of Ramadan, and lasts three days The Greater ('Idul'-Kabir) is celebrated on the tenth day of the twelfth month (Dhul Hijja), lasts for four days, and forms the concluding ceremony of the pilgrimage to Mecca. It comes seventy days after the Lesser Bairam.

Bajadere. *See* BAYADERE

Bajan, Bajanella *See* BEJAN.

Bajazet (băj' a zet) Sultan of the Turks from 1389 to 1403, he was a great warrior, among his other victories being that of Nicopolis in 1396 when he defeated the allied armies of the Hungarians, Poles, and French But he was himself beaten by Timur at Ankara (1402) and held prisoner by him until his death There is no warrant whatsoever for the story that Timur carried him about in an iron cage, but the story inspired both Marlowe and Rowe to some of their finest writing

Baked Meats, or **Bake-meats** Meat pies ' The funeral baked meats did coldly furnish forth the marriage tables " (*Hamlet*, i, 2), *i e.* the hot meat pies served at the funeral and not eaten, were served cold at the marriage banquet

Baker, The. Louis XVI was called 'the Baker," the queen was called "the baker's wife" (or *La Boulangère*), and the dauphin the "shop boy ', because they gave bread to the mob of starving men and women who came to Versailles on October 6th, 1789

The return of the baker, his wife, and the shop-boy to Paris [after the king was brought from Versailles] had not had the expected effect Flour and bread were still scarce.—A DUMAS *The Countess de Charny*, ch ix

Baker's dozen. Thirteen for twelve When a heavy penalty was inflicted for short weight, bakers used to give a surplus number of loaves, called the *inbread*, to avoid all risk of incurring the fine The 13th was the "vantage loaf"

To give one a baker's dozen, in slang phraseology, is to give him a sound drubbing —*i e* all he deserves and one stroke more

Baker's knee. Knock-knee Bakers were said to be particularly liable to this deformity owing to the constrained position in which they have to stand when kneading bread

Bakha The sacred bull of Hermonthis in Egypt He changed colour every hour of the day, and is supposed to have been an incarnation of Menthu, the Egyptian personification of the heat of the sun

Baksheesh (băk' shĕsh). A Persian word for a gratuity These gifts are insolently and persistently demanded throughout the Near East by beggars, camel-men, servants and all sorts of officials more as a claim than a gratuity

I was to give the men, too, a *"baksheish,"* that is a present of money, which is usually made upon the conclusion of any sort of treaty —KINGLAKE *Eothen.*

Balaam (bā' lăm) (1) In Dryden's *Absalom and Achitophel*, the Earl of Huntingdon, one of the rebels in Monmouth's army

(2) The "citizen of sober fame," who lived hard by the Monument, in Pope's *Moral Essays, Ep.* iii, was drawn, in part, from Thomas Pitt ("Diamond Pitt," *see* PITT DIAMOND), grandfather of the Earl of Chatham He "was a plain, good man, religious, punctual, and frugal", he grew rich; got knighted, seldom went to church, became a courtier, "took a bribe from France", was hanged for treason, and all his goods were confiscated to the State

This word was also used for matter kept in type for filling up odd spaces in periodicals Lockhart, in his *Life of Scott* (ch lxx) tells us —

Balaam is the cant name for asinine paragraphs about monstrous productions of nature and the like, kept standing in type to be used whenever the real news of the day leaves an awkward space that must be filled up somehow

Hence **Balaam** basket or box, the printer's slang term for the receptacle for such matter, and also (in America) for the place where stereotyped "fill-ups" are kept

Balafré, Le (băl' a frä) (Fr the gashed) Henri, second Duke of Guise (1550-88) In the Battle of Dormans he received a sword-cut which left a frightful scar on his face Henri's son, François, third Duke of Guise, also earned—and was awarded—the same title, and it was given by Scott (in *Quentin Durward*) to Ludovic Lesly, an archer of the Scottish Guard

Balan (bā' lan) The name of a strong and courageous giant in many old romances In *Fierabras* (*q v*) the "Sowdan of Babylon", father of Fierabras, ultimately conquered by Charlemagne In the Arthurian cycle, brother of Balin (*q v*)

Balance, The. "Libra," an ancient zodiacal constellation between Scorpio and Virgo, also the 7th sign of the zodiac, which now contains the constellation Virgo, and which the sun enters a few days before the autumnal equinox

According to Persian mythology, at the Last Day a huge balance, as big as the vault of heaven, will be displayed, one scale pan will be called that of light, and the other that of darkness In the former all good will be placed, in the latter all evil, and everyone will receive his award according to the verdict of the balance

In commercial parlance one's *balance* is the total money remaining over after all assets are realized and all liabilities discharged Hence the phrases —

He has a good balance at his banker's. His credit side shows a large balance in his favour

To strike a balance. To calculate the exact difference, if any, between the debit and credit side of an account

Balance of trade. The money-value difference between the exports and imports of a nation

Balance of power. Such an adjustment of power among sovereign States as results in no one nation having such a preponderance as could enable it to endanger the independence of the rest.

Balclutha (băl cloo' tha) A fortified town on the banks of the Clutha (*i e.* the Clyde) mentioned in *Carthon*, one of the Ossian poems It was captured and burnt by Fingal's father, Comhal, in one of his forays against the Britons

Bald Charles le Chauve. Charles I of France (823, 840-77), son of Louis le Debonnaire, was surnamed "the Bald" (*le Chauve*)

Baldheaded To go for someone baldheaded, that is without restraint or compunction, probably dates from the days when men wore wigs, and any energetic action required that the wig should be thrown aside and the owner go into the fray unencumbered

Baldachin (bol' da kın) The dais or canopy under which, in Roman Catholic processions, the Holy Sacrament is carried also the canopy above an altar It is the Ital *baldacchino*, so called from Baldacco (Ital for Bagdad), where the cloth was originally made

Balder (bol' der). Son of Odin and Frigga, the Scandinavian god of light, who dwelt at Breidhablik, one of the mansions of Asgard. He is the central figure of many myths, the chief being connected with his death He is said to have been slain by his rival Hodhr while fighting for possession of the beautiful Nanna Another legend tells that Frigga bound all things by oath not to harm him, but accidentally omitted the mistletoe, with a twig of which Balder was slain His death was the prelude to the final overthrow of the gods

Balderdash A word of uncertain origin, formerly meaning froth, also a mixture of incongruous liquors (such as wine and beer or beer and milk), but now denoting nonsensical talk, ridiculous poetry, jumbled ideas, etc It may be connected with the Dan *balder*, noise, clatter, but in view of the earlier senses of the word this is, at least, doubtful

Baldwin. (1) In the Charlemagne romances, nephew of Roland and the youngest and comeliest of Charlemagne's paladins
(2) Brother of Godfrey of Bouillon, whom he succeeded (1100) as King of Jerusalem. He figures in Tasso's *Jerusalem Delivered* as the restless and ambitious Duke of Bologna, leader of 1,200 horse in the allied Christian army He died in Egypt, 1118.

Bale. When bale is highest, boot is nighest. An old Icelandic proverb that appears in Heywood and many other English writers It means, when things have come to the worst they must needs mend *Bale* means "evil," and is common to most Teutonic languages, *boot* (*q v*) is the M E *bote*, relief remedy

Bale out The literal meaning of this phrase is to ladle out with buckets, as when one empties the water out of a small boat. Among flying men "to bale out" means to descend from an aeroplane by parachute when some emergency necessitating this arises, and in the army to get out of a tank in a hurry when it is hit

Balfour of Burley, John. Leader of the Covenanters in Scott's *Old Mortality* His prototype in real life was John Balfour of Kinloch Scott seems to have confused him with John, Lord Balfour of Burleigh, who died in 1688 and was not a Covenanter

Balin (băl' ın) Brother to Balan in the Arthurian romances They were devoted to each other, but they accidentally met in single combat and slew one another, neither knowing until just before death who was his opponent At their request they were buried in one grave by Merlin The story is told in Malory, Bk ii Tennyson gives a much altered version in the *Idylls of the King*

Balios. *See* HORSE

Balisarda. *See* SWORD.

Balistraria (băl ıs trâr' ı ă) (mediæval Lat) Narrow apertures in the form of a cross in the walls of ancient castles, through which cross-bow-men discharged their arrows

Balk (bawk) Originally a ridge or mound on the ground (O E. *balca*), then the ridge between two furrows left in ploughing, the word came to be figuratively applied to any obstacle, stumbling-block, or check on one's actions; as in billiards, the balk (or *baulk*) is the part of the table behind the *baulk-line* from which one has to play when, in certain circumstances, one's freedom is checked So, also, *to balk* is to place obstacles in the way of

A balk of timber is a large beam of timber, often in the rough

To make a balk. To miss a part of the field in ploughing Hence, to disappoint, to withhold deceitfully

Balker One who from an eminence on shore directs fishermen where shoals of herrings have gathered together Probably from the Dutch *balken*, to shout, and connected with the O E *bælcan*, with the same meaning

Balkis (bol' kıs) The Mohammedan name for the Queen of Sheba, who visited Solomon

Ball "Ball," the spherical body, is a Middle English and Old Teutonic word, "ball," the dancing assembly, is from O.Fr *balei*, to dance, from late Lat *ballare*. The two are in no way connected

To keep the ball a-rolling To continue without intermission To keep the fun, or the conversation, etc , alive, to keep the matter going A metaphor taken from several games played with balls

To have the ball at your feet. To have a great opportunity. A metaphor from football

To take the ball before the bound. To anticipate an opportunity, to be over-hasty A metaphor from cricket

The ball is with you. It is your turn now.

A ball of fortune. One tossed like a ball, from pillar to post; one who has experienced many vicissitudes of fortune.

To open the ball. To lead off the first dance at a ball.

To strike the ball under the line. To fail in one's object The allusion is to tennis, in which a line is stretched in the middle of the court, and the players standing on each side have to send the ball *over* the line

Ball-game. The game of baseball

"Play ball". Phrase used by the umpire in baseball to indicate that the game may begin

Balls, The three golden. The well-known sign of the pawnbroker, it was originally the sign hung up over their places of business in London by the Lombard merchants who were the first recognized moneylenders in England

Also the emblem of St Nicholas of Bari, who is said to have given three purses of gold to three virgin sisters to enable them to marry.

Ballad. Originally a song to dance-music, or a song sung while dancing It is from late Lat *ballare*, to dance (as "ball," the dance), through Provençal *balada*, and O Fr *balade*

Let me make the ballads, and who will may make the laws. Andrew Fletcher of Saltoun, in Scotland, wrote to the Marquis of Montrose, "I knew a very wise man of Sir Christopher Musgrave's sentiment. He believed, if a man were permitted to make all the ballads, he need not care who should make the laws" (1703)

Ballade (băl ad′). This is an artificial verse-form originating with the Provençal troubadours In its normal type it consists of three stanzas of eight lines, followed by a verse of four lines known as the Envoi The principal rules for the ballade are The same set of rhymes in the same order they occupy in the first stanza must repeat throughout the whole of the verses No word used as a rhyme must be used again for that purpose throughout the ballade Each stanza and the Envoi must close with the refrain, the Envoi always taking the same rhymes as the last half of the preceding verse Only three rhymes are permissible The sequence of the rhymes is usually — a, b, a, b, b, c, b, c, for each verse and b, c, b, c, for the Envoi

Ballet A theatrical representation of some adventure, intrigue, or emotional phase by pantomime and dancing. Baltazarini, director of music to Catherine de Medici, is said to have been the inventor of ballets as presented in modern times for long they were an integral part of Italian opera

Balliol College, Oxford, founded in 1263, by Sir John de Baliol (father of Baliol, King of Scotland) and his wife, Devorguilla.

Balloon. The balloon was invented by Jacques Etienne Montgolfier (1745-1799) The first ascent was made in 1783, the balloon being caused to rise by hot air In 1825 Charles Green went up in the first gas-filled balloon During the siege of Paris, in 1871, fifty-four balloons were dispatched carrying 2,500,000 letters In World War I captive balloons were largely used by both sides to observe the enemy's movements and dispositions A barrage of captive balloons was used in both World Wars as a defence of cities against enemy aircraft

Ballot This method of voting is so called because it was originally by the use of small balls secretly put into a box, as is still done in clubs, etc Voting for Parliamentary elections was first carried out by ballot in 1870 (the Ballot Act was two years later) and the method then introduced has since obtained The names of candidates are printed in alphabetical order on a voting paper, the elector marks a cross against his choice, and the folded paper is then slipped into a sealed box

Ballyhoo (băl i hoo′) The word is said to come from Ballyhooly, a village in Co Cork, but in its present sense its origin is in the U.S A Ballyhoo means noisy demonstration to attract attention, exaggerated publicity, or extravagant advertisement.

Balm (Fr *baume*, a contraction of *balsam*). An aromatic, resinous gum exuding from certain trees, and used in perfumery and medicine, hence, a soothing remedy or alleviating agency.

Is there no balm in Gilead? (*Jer* viii, 22). Is there no remedy, no consolation? 'Balm' in this passage is the Geneva Bible's translation of the Heb *sori*, which probably means mastic, the resin yielded by the mastic tree, *Pistacia Lentiscus*, which was formerly an ingredient used in many medicines In Wyclif's Bible the word is translated 'gumme," and in Coverdale's "triacle " *See* TREACLE

The gold-coloured resin now known as "Balm of Gilead" is that from the *Balsomodendron Gileadense*, an entirely different tree

Balmerino (băl mer′ i nō) The story was long current that when Lord Balmerino was executed for his part in the Jacobite rebellion of 1745, the executioner bungled and only half cut off his head, whereupon his lordship turned round and grinned at him

Balmy. "I am going to the balmy"—*i e*. to "Balmy sleep", one of Dick Swiveller's pet phrases (Dickens *Old Curiosity Shop*)

For *balmy* in the sense of silly, or mildly idiotic, *see* BARMY.

Balniharbi (băl ni bar′ bi) A land occupied by projectors (Swift *Gulliver's Travels*)

Balthazar (băl thăz′ ār) One of the kings of Cologne *See* MAGI.

Baltic Sea Scandinavia used to be known as *Baltia* There is a Lithuanian word, *baltas*, meaning "white," from which the name may be derived, but it may also be from Scand *balta*, a strait or *belt*, and the Baltic would then be the sea of the " belts "

Baltic, The, in commercial parlance is the familiar name of the *Baltic Mercantile and Shipping Exchange*, which was founded in the 17th century It deals with chartering of ships, freights, marine insurance, etc , all over the world.

Bamberg Bible, The *See* BIBLE, SPECIALLY NAMED

Bambino (băm bē' nō) An image of the infant Jesus, swaddled The word is Italian, meaning an infant

Bambocciades (băm boch' ı ădz) Pictures of scenes in low life, such as country wakes, penny weddings, and so on, so called from the Ital *bamboccio*, a cripple, a nickname given to Pieter van Laar (*c* 1613–*c* 1674), a noted Dutch painter of such scenes. *See* MICHAEL-ANGELO DES BAMBOCHES

Bamboozle. To cheat by cunning, or daze with tricks It is a slang term of uncertain origin which came into use about the end of the 17th century

All the people upon earth, excepting those two or three worthy gentlemen, are imposed upon, cheated, bubbled, abused, bamboozled
ADDISON. *The Drummer.*

Bampton Lectures. Founded by the Rev John Bampton, canon of Salisbury, who, in 1751, left £120 per annum to the university of Oxford, to pay for eight divinity lectures on given subjects to be preached yearly at Great St Mary's, and printed afterwards M A s of Oxford or Cambridge are eligible as lecturers, but the same person may never be chosen twice *Cp* HULSEAN LECTURES

Ban (A S. *bannan*, to summon, O Teut to proclaim). Originally meaning to summon, the verb came to mean to imprecate, to anathematize, to pronounce a curse upon; and the noun from being a general proclamation was applied specifically to an ecclesiastical curse or denunciation, a formal prohibition, a sentence of outlawry, etc. Banish and BANNS (*q v*), are from tne same root

Lever le ban et l'arrière ban (Fr). To levy the *ban* was to call the king's vassals to active service, to levy the *arrière ban* was to levy the vassals of a suzerain or under-lord

Ban, King. In the Arthurian legends, father of Sir Launcelot du Lac He died of grief when his castle was taken and burnt through the treachery of his seneschal

Banagher, That beats (băn 'a her). Wonderfully inconsistent and absurd—exceedingly ridiculous Banagher is a town in Ireland, on the Shannon, in Offaly It formerly sent two members to Parliament, and was a famous pocket borough When a member spoke of a family borough where every voter was a man employed by the lord, it was not unusual to reply, "Well, that beats Banagher"

Grose, however, gives another explanation According to him Banagher (or Banaghan) was an Irish minstrel famous for telling wonderful stories of the Munchausen kind

"Well," says he, ' to gratify them I will So just a morsel But, Jack, this beats Bannagher "—W B YEATS: *Fairy Tales of the Irish Peasantry,* p 196

Banat (băn' at) A territory under a *ban* (Persian for lord, master), particularly certain districts of Hungary and Croatia The word was brought into Europe by the Avars, a Ural-Altaic people allied to the Huns, who appeared on the Danube and settled in Dacia in the latter half of the 6th century.

Banbury A town in Oxfordshire, proverbially famous for its Puritans, its " cheese-paring," its cakes, and its cross Hence a *Banbury man* is a Puritan or bigot The term is common in Elizabethan literature· Zeal-of-the-land-busy, in Jonson's *Bartholomew Fair*, is described as a " Banbury man " and Braithwaite's lines in *Drunken Barnabee's Journal* (1638) are well known·

In my progresse travelling Northward,
Taking my farewell o'th Southward,
To *Banbery* came I, O prophane one!
Where I saw a Puritane one,
Hanging of his Cat on Monday,
For killing of a Mouse on Sonday

As thin as Banbury cheese In Marston's *Jack Drum's Entertainment* (1600) we read, "You are like a Banbury cheese, nothing but paring ", and Bardolph compares Slender to Banbury cheese (*Merry Wives*, I, 1) The Banbury cheese is a rich milk cheese about an inch in thickness

Banbury cake is a sort of spiced, pastry turnover, once made exclusively at Banbury

Banbury Cross was removed by the Puritans as a heathenish memorial in 1646, but the present one was placed on the site in its stead in 1858

Banco (băng' kō) A commercial term denoting bank money of account as distinguished from currency, it is used principally in exchange business and in cases where there is an appreciable difference between the actual and the nominal value of money

In banco A late Latin legal phrase, meaning "on the bench", it is applied to sittings of the Superior Court of Common Law in its own bench or court, and not on circuit, or at *Nisi Prius* (*q v*)

Mark Banco. The mark of fixed value employed as an invariable standard in the old Bank at Hamburg, and used by the Hanseatic League Deposits in gold and silver were credited in *Mark Banco*, and all banking accounts were carried on in *Mark Banco*, so that it was a matter of no moment how exchange varied

Bancus Regius (băng' kus) The King's or Queen's Bench. **Bancus Communis,** the bench of Common Pleas

Bandana or **Bandanna** (băn dăn' a) An Indian word (*bandhnu*, a mode of dyeing) now usually restricted to handkerchiefs of either silk or cotton having a dark ground of Turkey red or blue, with white or yellow spots

Bandbox, He looks as if he were just out of a. He is so neat and precise, so carefully got up in his dress and person, that he looks like some company dress, carefully kept in a bandbox, a cardboard box for millinery formerly used by parsons for keeping their clerical bands (*q.v.*) in.

Neat as a bandbox. Neat as clothes folded and put by in a bandbox

The Bandbox Plot. Rapin (*History of England*, iv, 297) tells us that a bandbox was sent to the lord-treasurer, in Queen Anne's reign, with three pistols charged and cocked, the triggers being tied to a pack-thread fastened to the lid When the lid was lifted, the pistols would go off and shoot the person who opened the lid He adds that Dean Swift happened to be by at the time the box arrived, and seeing the pack-thread, cut it, thereby saving the life of the lord-treasurer.

> Two ink-horn tops your Whigs did fill
> With gunpowder and lead;
> Which with two serpents made of quill,
> You in a bandbox laid,
> A tinder-box there was beside,
> Which had a trigger to it
> To which the very string was ty'd
> That was designed to do it.
> *Plot upon Plot* (about 1713)

Bandicoot To bandicoot is an Australian phrase meaning to steal vegetables—often by removing the roots—as with potatoes and carrots—and leaving the tops standing in the ground so that the theft is not noticed

Bands. Clerical bands are a relic of the ancient *amice*, a square linen tippet tied about the neck of priests during the saying of Mass They are rarely worn in England nowadays, but are still used by Presbyterian ministers and clerics on the Continent

Legal bands are a relic of the wide falling collars which formed a part of the ordinary dress in the reign of Henry VIII, and which were especially conspicuous in the reign of the Stuarts In the showy days of Charles II the plain bands were changed for lace ends

> The eighth Henry, as I understand,
> Was the first prince that ever wore a band.
> JOHN TAYLOR, *the Water Poet* (1580-1654).

Bandwagon. On the bandwagon To get on the bandwagon is to show strong and open support for some popular movement or cause It was formerly the custom in American elections for a wagon carrying a band to parade through the streets, in order to arouse enthusiasm for a particular candidate. Local political leaders who supported that candidate would then jump on to the wagon and ride with the band.

Bandy. I am not going to bandy words with you—*i e* to wrangle The metaphor is from the Irish game bandy (the precursor of hockey), in which each player has a stick with a crook at the end to strike a wooden or other hard ball. The ball is bandied from side to side, each party trying to beat it home to the opposite goal The derivation of the word is quite uncertain It was earlier a term in tennis, as is shown by the passage in Webster's *Vittoria Corombona* (iv, 4), where the conspirators regret that the handle of the racket of the man to be murdered had not been poisoned—

> That while he had been bandying at tennis,
> He might have sworn himself to hell, and strook
> His soul into the hazard

Bane really means ruin, death, or destruction (A.S. *bana*, a murderer), and "I will be his bane" means I will ruin or murder him Bane is, therefore, a mortal injury

> My bane and antidote are both before it
> This [sword] in a moment brings me to an end.
> But this [Plato] assures me I shall never die
> ADDISON *Cato*

Bangers (băng′ erz) One of the many slang terms for sausages

Bangorian Controversy. A theological paper-war stirred up by a sermon preached March 31st, 1717, before George I, by Dr. Hoadly, Bishop of Bangor, on the text, " My kingdom is not of this world," the argument being that Christ had not delegated His power or authority to either king or clergy The sermon was printed by royal command, it led to such discord in Convocation that this body was prorogued, and from that time till 1852 was allowed to meet only as a matter of form

Banian, Banyan (băn′ yăn) (Sanskrit *vaniy*, a merchant) This was the name applied to a caste of Hindu traders, who wore a particular dress, were strict in their observance of fasts, and abstained from eating any kind of flesh It is from this circumstance that sailors speak of **Banyan Days** (*q v*)

The word is also used to describe a sort of loose house-coat worn by Anglo-Indians

Bank. The original meaning was "bench" or "shelf"; in Italy the word (*banco*) was applied specially to a tradesman's counter, and hence to a money-changer's bench or table, which gives the modern meaning of an establishment which deals in money, investments, etc

Bank of a river. Stand with your back to the source, and face to the sea or outlet, the *left* bank is on your left, and *right* bank on your right hand

Bankside. Part of the borough of Southwark on the right bank of the Thames, between Blackfriars and Waterloo Bridges In Shakespeare's time it was noted for its theatres, its prison, and its brothels Hence, *Sisters of the Bank*, an old term for prostitutes

> Come I will send for a whole coach or two of
> Bankside ladies, and we will be jovial —RANDOLPH
> *The Muses' Looking Glass*, II, iv

Bankrupt. In Italy, when a moneylender was unable to continue business, his bench or counter (*see* BANK) was broken up, and he himself was spoken of as a *bancorotto—i e* a bankrupt This is said to be the origin of our term

Banks's Horse. A horse trained to do all manner of tricks, called Marocco, and belonging to one Banks about the end of the reign of Queen Elizabeth One of his exploits is said to have been the ascent of St Paul's steeple A favourite story of the time is of an apprentice who called his master to see the spectacle ' Away, you fool," said the shopkeeper, "what need I go to see a horse on the top when I can see so many asses at the bottom!" When Banks went to Paris in 1601 he was packed off to prison, as the city authorities and the Church suspected that Marocco's tricks were performed by black magic.

Bannatyne Club. A literary club, named after George Bannatyne (d about 1608), to whose industry we owe the preservation of much early Scottish poetry It was instituted in 1823 by Sir Walter Scott, and had for its object the publication of rare works illustrative of Scottish history, poetry, and general literature. The club was dissolved in 1859

Banner of the Prophet, The. What purports to be the actual standard of Mohammed is preserved in the Eyab mosque of Constantinople It is called *Sin'aqu'sh-sharif* and is 12 feet in length It is made of four layers of silk, the topmost being green, embroidered with gold In times of peace the banner is guarded in the hall of the "noble vestment," as the dress worn by the Prophet is styled In the same hall are preserved many other relics including the stirrup, the sabre, and the bow of Mohammed

Banner of France, The sacred, was the *Oriflamme* (*q v*).

Banners in churches. These are suspended as thank offerings to God Those in St George's Chapel, Windsor, Henry VII's Chapel, Westminster, etc , are to indicate that the knight whose banner is hung up avows himself devoted to God's service

Banneret. One who leads his vassals to battle under his own banner Also an order of knighthood formerly conferred on the field of battle for deeds of valour The first knight-banneret to be made seems to have been John de Copeland, who, in 1346, captured King David Bruce at Neville's Cross The order was allowed to become extinct soon after the first creation of baronets, in 1611.

Banns of Marriage. The publication in the parish church for three successive Sundays of an intended marriage It is made after the Second Lesson of the Morning Service To announce the intention is called "Publishing the banns," from the words "I publish the banns of marriage between . " The word is from the same root as BAN (*q v*)

To forbid the banns To object formally to the proposed marriage
And a better fate did poor Maria deserve than to have a banns forbidden by the curate of the parish who published them —STERNE *Sentimental Journey*

Banquet used at one time to have, besides its present meaning, the meaning of dessert Thus, in the *Pennyless Pilgrimage* (1618) John Taylor, the Water Poet, says "Our first and second course being three-score dishes at one boord, and after that, always a banquet " The word is from Ital *banco* (*see* BANK), a bench or table, at which one sits for a meal, hence "bad manners at table "

Banshee. The domestic spirit of certain Irish or Highland Scottish families, supposed to take an interest in its welfare, and to wail at the death of one of the family The word is the Old Irish *ben side*, a woman of the elves or fairies

Bantam. A little bantam cock. A plucky little fellow that will not be bullied by a person bigger than himself The bantam cock will encounter a dunghill cock five times his own weight, and is therefore said to "have a great soul in a little body." The bantam originally came from Bantam, in Java

Banting. Reducing superfluous fat by living on meat diet, and abstaining from beer, farinaceous food, and vegetables, according to the method adopted by William Banting (1797-1878), a London cabinet-maker, once a very fat man The word was introduced about 1864.

A greater benefactor to mankind was Sir Frederick Grant Banting (1890-1941) who discovered insulin in 1922

Bantling. A child, a brat, usually with a depreciatory sense, or meaning an illegitimate child It is from Ger. *bankling*, a bastard, from *bank*, a bench, hence, a child begotten casually, as on a bench, instead of in the marriage-bed The word has been confused with *bandling*, taken to mean a little one in swaddling clothes

Banyan Day. An old English nautical phrase to describe a day in which no meat came in the rations In Australia it found its way to outstations where the hands were likely to have eaten all their meat before the last day of the ration period, thus becoming involuntary vegetarians In Australia it is found in official documents in the later 18th century.

Banzai. The Japanese victory cry, meaning " Ten thousand years "

Baphomet. An imaginary idol or symbol, which the Templars were said to worship in their mysterious rites The word is a corruption of Mahomet (Fr *Baphomet*, O Sp. *Matomat*)

Baptes. Priests of the goddess Cotytto, the Thracian goddess of lewdness, whose midnight orgies were so obscene that they disgusted even the goddess herself They received their name from the Greek verb *bapto*, to wash, because of the so-called ceremonies of purification connected with her rites. (*Juvenal*, ii, 91)

Baptism. This sacrament of the Christian Church dates back in one form or another to pre-apostolic times

Baptism for the dead was the baptism of a living person instead of and for the sake of one who had died unbaptized.

Baptism of blood was martyrdom for the sake of Christ and supplied the place of the sacrament if the martyr was unbaptized

Baptism of desire is the virtue or grace of baptism acquired by one who dies earnestly desiring baptism before he can receive it

Baptism of fire is really martyrdom, but the phrase was misapplied by Napoleon III to one who went under fire in battle for the first time

Bar. The whole body of barristers; as *bench* means the whole body of judges. The bar is the partition separating the seats of the benchers from the rest of the hall, and, like the rood-screen of a church, which separates the chancel from the rest of the building, is due to the old idea that the laity form an inferior order of beings

To be called to the bar To be admitted a barrister. Students having attained a certain status used to be called from the body of the hall within the bar, to take part in the proceedings of the court. To disbar means to expel a barrister from his profession

To be called within the bar. To be appointed King's Counsel

Trial at Bar. By full court of judges in the King's Bench division These trials are for very difficult causes, before special juries, and occupy the attention of the four judges in the superior court, instead of at *Nisi Prius*

At the bar. The prisoner at the bar, the prisoner in the dock before the judge.

Bar, excepting In racing phrase a man will bet "Two to one, bar one," that is, two to one against any horse in the field with one exception. The word means "barring out," shutting out, debarring, as in Shakespeare's —
> Nay, but I bar to-night you shall not gage me by what we do to-night.—*Merchant of Venice*, ii, 2

Bar. An honourable ordinary, in heraldry, consisting of two parallel horizontal lines drawn across the shield and containing a fifth part of the field
> A barre . is drawne overthwart the escochon
> . . it containeth the fifth part of the Field
> GWILLIM *Heraldry*

Bar sinister. A phrase popularly used to imply bastardy, though the heraldic sign intended is a *bend sinister* (*q.v.*).

Barring out. In the brave days when schoolboys played pranks on their masters, they occasionally vented their humour—and sometimes their spleen—on one by barricading windows and doors to prevent his entering the school Miss Edgeworth has a story thus entitled.
> Revolts, republics, revolutions, most
> No graver than a schoolboys' barring out
> TENNYSON *The Princess*

Baralipton. *See* SYLLOGISM.

Barataria. Sancho Panza's island-city, in *Don Quixote*, over which he was appointed governor. The table was presided over by Doctor Pedro Rezio de Aguero, who caused every dish set upon the board to be removed without being tasted—some because they heated the blood, and others because they chilled it, some for one ill effect, and some for another, so that Sancho was allowed to eat nothing The word is from Span. *baruto*, cheap

Barataria is also the setting of Act II of *The Gondoliers*

Barathron, or **Barathrum.** A deep ditch behind the Acropolis of Athens into which malefactors were thrown, somewhat in the same way as criminals at Rome were cast from the Tarpeian Rock Sometimes used figuratively, as in Massinger's *New Way to Pay Old Debts*, where Sir Giles Overreach calls Greedy a "barathrum of the shambles" (iii, 2), meaning that he was a sink into which any kind of food or offal could be thrown
> *Mercury* Why, Jupiter will put you all into a sack together, and toss you into Berathrum, terrible Barathrum
> *Carion.* Barathrum? What's Barathrum?
> *Mer.* Why, Barathrum is Pluto's boggards [privy]. you must be all thrown into Barathrum
> RANDOLPH: *Hey for Honesty*, v, 1 (*c* 1630)

Barb (Lat. *barba*, a beard). Used in early times in England for the beard of a man, and so for similar appendages such as the feathers under the beak of a hawk; but its first English use was for a curved-back instrument such as a fish-hook (which has one backward curve, or

barb), or an arrow (which has two) The *barb* of an arrow is, then, the metal point having two iron "feathers," which stick out so as to hinder extraction, and does not denote the feather on the upper part of the shaft.

Barb A Barbary steed, noted for docility, speed, endurance, and spirit, formerly also called a Barbary, as in Ben Jonson's —
> You must be seen on your barbary often, or leaping over stools for the credit of your back
> *Silent Women*, IV, 1

Cp also BARBARY ROAN.

Barbara. *See* SYLLOGISM

Barbara, St. The patron saint of arsenals and powder magazines Her father delivered her up to Martian, governor of Nicomedia, for being a Christian. After she had been subjected to the most cruel tortures, her unnatural father was about to strike off her head, when a lightning flash laid him dead at her feet Hence, St. Barbara is invoked against lightning Her feast day is December 4th

Barbari (bar' ber ē). **Quod non fecerunt barbari, fecerunt Barberini,** *i.e* What the barbarians left standing, the Barberini contrived to destroy. A saying current in Rome at the time when Pope Urban VIII (Barberini) converted the bronze fittings of the Pantheon—which had remained in splendid condition since 27 B C—into cannon (1635)

Barbarian. The Greeks and Romans called all foreigners *barbarians* (babblers, men who spoke a language not understood by them), the word was probably not merely imitative of unintelligible speech, but may have been an actual word in some outlandish tongue.
> If then I know not the meaning of the voice [words], I shall be to him that speaketh a barbarian, and he that speaketh will be a barbarian unto me
> 1 *Cor* xiv, 11.

Barbarossa (bar bá ros' a) (*Red-beard*, similar to *Rufus*) The surname of Frederick I of Germany (1121-90) *Khaireddin Barbarossa*, the famous corsair, became Dey of Algiers in 1518, and in 1537 was appointed high admiral of the Turkish fleet With Francis I he captured Nice in 1543, he died at Constantinople three years later

Barbary Roan, the favourite horse of Richard II *See* HORSE
> O, how it yearned my heart when I beheld
> In London streets that coronation day,
> When Bolingbroke rode on roan Barbary!
> That horse that thou [Rich. II] so often hast bestrid,
> That horse that I so carefully have dressed
> SHAKESPEARE· *Richard II*, v, 5.

Cp BARBED STEED

Barbason (bar' bá son). A fiend mentioned by Shakespeare in the *Merry Wives of Windsor*, ii, 2, and in *Henry V*, ii, 1.
> Amaimon sounds well, Lucifer well, Barbason well, yet they are . the names of fiends —*Merry Wives*

The name seems to have been obtained from Scot's *Discoverie of Witchcraft* (1584), where we are told of "Marbas, alias Barbas," who—is a great president, and appeareth in the forme of a mightie lion, but at the commandment of a conjuror cummeth up in a likenes of a man, and answereth fullie as touching anie thing which is hidden or secret.

Barbecue (bar' be kū) (Sp *barbacoa*, a wooden framework set on posts) A term used in America formerly for a wooden bedstead, and also for a kind of large gridiron upon which an animal could be roasted whole Hence, an animal, such as a hog, so roasted, also the feast at which it is eaten, and the process of roasting it.

Oldfield, with more than harpy throat subdued,
Cries, " Send me, ye gods, a whole hog barbecued!"
POPE *Satires*, ii, 25

Barbed Steed A horse in armour *Barbed* should properly be *barded*, it is from the Fr *barde*, horse-armour Horses' " bards " were the metal coverings for the breast and flanks

And now, instead of mounting barbed steeds
To fright the souls of fearful adversaries,
He capers nimbly in a lady's chamber,
To the lascivious pleasing of a lute
SHAKESPEARE *Richard III*, i., 1.

Barber. Every barber knows that.
Omnibus notum tonsoribus.
HORACE 1 *Satires*, vii, 3

In ancient Rome, as in modern England, the barber's shop was a centre for the dissemination of scandal, and the talk of the town.

Barber Poet Jacques Jasmin (1798-1864), a Provençal poet, who was also known as " the last of the Troubadours," was so called He was a barber

Barber's pole. This pole, painted spirally with two stripes of red and white, and displayed outside barber's shops as a sign, is a relic of the days when the callings of barber and surgeon were combined; it is symbolical of the winding of a bandage round the arm previous to blood-letting. The gilt knob at its end represents the brass basin which is sometimes actually suspended on the pole. The basin has a curved gap cut in it to fit the throat, and was used for lathering customers before shaving them The Barber-Surgeons' Company was founded in 1461 and was re-incorporated in 1540. In 1745 it was decided that the business or trades of barber and surgeon were really independent of each other and the two branches were separated, but the ancient company, or guild, was allowed to retain its charter The last barber-surgeon in London is said to have been one Middleditch, of Great Suffolk Street in the Borough, who died in 1821.

To this year (1541), (says Wornum) belongs the Barber-Surgeons' picture of Henry (VIII) granting a charter to the Corporation. The barbers and surgeons of London, originally constituting one company, had been separated, but were again, in the 32 Henry VIII, combined into a single society, and it was the ceremony of presenting them with a new charter which is commemorated by Holbein's picture, now in their hall in Monkwell Street

Barber of Seville. The comedy by this name (*Le Barbier de Seville*) was written by Beaumarchais and produced in Paris in 1775 In it appeared for the first time the famous character of Figaro In 1780 Paisiello produced an opera bouffe on the same lines, but this was eclipsed in 1816 by the appearance of Rossini's *Barbiere di Siviglia*, with words by Sterbini On its first appearance it was hissed but it has since maintained its place as one of the most popular operas ever written

Barbican. The outwork intended to defend the drawbridge in a fortified town or castle

(Fr *barbacane*). Also an opening or loophole in the wall of a fortress, through which guns may be fired The street of this name in London is built partly on the site of a barbican that was in front of Aldersgate

Barcarole (bar ka rōl). Properly, a song sung by Venetian boatmen as they row their gondolas (It *barcaiuolo*, a boatman).

Barcelona (bar se lō' nå) A fichu, piece of velvet for the neck, or small necktie, made at Barcelona, and common in England in the early 19th century Also a neckcloth of some bright colour, as red with yellow spots

Now on this handkerchief so starch and white
She pinned a Barcelona black and tight
PETER PINDAR *Portfolio (Dinah)*

Barchester. An imaginary cathedral town (said to be Salisbury), in the county of Barsetshire, the setting of the Barchester Novels by Anthony Trollope (1815-82) These are: *The Warden*, 1855, *Barchester Towers*, 1857, *Doctor Thorne*, 1858, *Framley Parsonage*, 1861, *The Small House at Allington* (1864), and *Last Chronicle of Barset*, 1867

Barcochebah or **Barcochebas** (Shimeon) (bar koch' e ba) An heroic leader of the Jews against the Romans A D 132 He took Jerusalem in 132, and was proclaimed king, many of the Jews believing him to be the Messiah. but in 135 he was overthrown with great slaughter Jerusalem was laid in ruins, and he himself slain It is said that he gave himself out to be the " Star out of Jacob " mentioned in *Numb* xxiv, 17 (Bar Cochba in *Hebrew* means " Son of a star.")

Bard. The minstrel of the ancient Celtic peoples, the Gauls, British, Welsh, Irish, and Scots, they celebrated the deeds of gods and heroes, incited to battle. sang at royal and other festivities, and frequently acted as heralds The oldest bardic compositions that have been preserved are of the 5th century

Bard of Avon. William Shakespeare (1564-1616), who was born and buried at Stratford-upon-Avon

Bard of Ayrshire. Robert Burns (1759-96), a native of Ayrshire

Bard of Hope. Thomas Campbell (1777-1844), author of *The Pleasures of Hope*

Bard of the Imagination. Mark Akenside (1721-70), author of *Pleasures of the Imagination*

Bard of Memory. Samuel Rogers (1763-1855), author of *The Pleasures of Memory.*

Bard of Olney. William Cowper (1731-1800), who resided at Olney, in Bucks, for many years.

Bard of Prose. Boccaccio (1313-75), author of the *Decameron*

The Bard of Prose, creative spirit! he
Of the Hundred Tales of Love
BYRON: *Childe Harold*, IV, lvi

Bard of Rydal Mount. William Wordsworth (1770-1850), so called because Rydal Mount was his mountain home.

Bard of Twickenham. Alexander Pope (1688-1744), who resided at Twickenham.

Bardolph (bar' dolf) One of Falstaff's inferior officers Falstaff calls him " the knight of the burning lamp," because his nose was so red, and his face so " full of meteors " He is a low-bred, drunken swaggerer, without principle, and poor as a church mouse. (*Merry Wives*, *Henry IV*, 1, 2)

Barebones Parliament, The. The Parliament convened by Cromwell in 1653, so called from Praise-God Barebones, a fanatical leader, who was a prominent member Also called the *Little Parliament*, because it comprised fewer than 150 members and lasted only five months

Barefaced. The present meaning, *audacious*, *shameless*, *impudent*, is a depreciation of its earlier sense, which was merely *open* or *unconcealed* A ' bare face " is, of course, one that is beardless, one the features of which are in no way hidden. The French equivalent is *à visage découvert*, with uncovered face

Barefooted. Certain friars and nuns (some of whom use sandals instead of shoes), particularly the reformed section of the Order of Carmelites (White Friars) that was founded by St Theresa in the 16th century These are known as the *Discalced Carmelites* (Lat *calceus*, a shoe). The practice is defended by the command of our Lord to His disciples: ' Carry neither purse, nor scrip, nor shoes " (*Luke* x 4). The Jews and Romans used to put off their shoes in mourning and public calamities, by way of humiliation

Bare Poles, Under. A nautical term, implying that on account of rough weather and high winds the ship carries no sails on the masts. Figuratively applied to a man reduced to the last extremity
> We were scudding before a heavy gale, under bare poles —Capt MARRYAT

Bargain. Into the bargain. In addition thereto, besides what was bargained for

To make the best of a bad bargain To bear bad luck, or bad circumstances with equanimity.

To stand to a bargain. To abide by it, the Lat. *stare conventis*, *corditionibus stare*, *pactis stare*, etc

Barisal Guns. A name given to certain mysterious booming sounds heard in many parts of the world as well as Barisal (Bengal), generally on or near water They resemble the sound of distant cannon, and are probably of subterranean origin. At Seneca Lake, New York, they are known as *Lake guns*, on the coast of Holland and Belgium as *mistpoeffers*, and in Italy as *bombiti*, *baturlio marina*, etc.

Bark. Dogs in their wild state never bark, they howl, whine, and growl, but do not bark Barking is an acquired habit.

Barking dogs seldom bite. Huffing, bouncing, hectoring fellows rarely possess cool courage Similar proverbs are found in Latin, French, Italian, and German

To bark at the moon To rail uselessly, especially at those in high places, as a dog thinks to frighten the moon by baying at it

There is a superstition that when a dog does this it portends death or ill-luck
> I'd rather be a dog, and bay the moon,
> Than such a Roman
> SHAKESPEARE *Julius Cæsar*, iv, 3

His bark is worse than his bite. He scolds and abuses roundly, but does not bear malice, or do mischief

To bark up the wrong tree. To waste energy, to be on the wrong scent The phrase comes from raccoon hunting This sport always takes place in the dark, with dogs which are supposed to mark the tree where the raccoon has taken refuge, and bark until the hunter arrives But even dogs can mistake the tree in the dark, and often bark up the wrong one.

Barker. A pistol, which barks or makes a loud report
The term is also used by circus people, etc , for the man who stands at the entrance to a side-show and shouts out the attraction to be seen within

Barkis is willin'. The message sent by Barkis to Peggotty by David Copperfield, expressing his desire to marry. It has passed into a proverbial expression indicating willingness.

Barlaam and Josaphat (bar' lam, jos' a fat) An Eastern romance telling how Barlaam, an ascetic monk of the desert of Sinai, converted Josaphat, son of a Hindu king, to Christianity Probably written in the first half of the 7th century, it seems to have been put into its final form by St John of Damascus, a Syrian monk of the 8th century, it became immensely popular in the Middle Ages, and includes (among many other stories) the Story of the Three Caskets, which was used by Shakespeare in the *Merchant of Venice* A poetical version was written by von Ems (13th cent).

Barley. To cry barley. To ask for truce (in children's games) Probably a corruption of *parley*, from Fr *parler*, to speak In Scots, to have a barley is to have a break, to pause for a moment's rest

Barley-break. An old country game like the modern " Prisoners' Base," having a " home " which was called " hell " Herrick has a poem, *Barley-break*, or *Last in Hell*

Barley-bree. Ale malt liquor brewed from barley, also called *barley-broth*
> The cock may craw, the day may daw,
> And aye we'll taste the barley-bree
> BURNS *Willie Brew'd a Peck o' Maut*

To wear the barley cap. To be top-heavy or tipsy with barley-bree

John or **Sir John Barleycorn** A personification of malt liquor The term was made popular by Burns
> Inspiring bold John Barleycorn,
> What dangers thou canst make us scorn!
> *Tam o' Shanter*, 105, 106

Barley-mow. A heap or stack of barley. (A.S *muga*, cp Icel *muge*, a swathe) *See* Mow

Barmecide's Feast (bar me sīd) An illusion particularly one containing a great disappointment. The reference is to the Story of the Barber's Sixth Brother in the *Arabian Nights*. A prince of the great Barmecide family in

Bagdad, wishing to have some sport, asked Schacabac, a poor, starving wretch, to dinner, and set before him a series of empty plates "How do you like your soup?" asked the merchant "Excellently well," replied Schacabac. "Did you ever see whiter bread?" "Never, honourable sir," was the civil answer Illusory wine was later offered him, but Schacabac excused himself by pretending to be drunk already, and knocked the Barmecide down The latter saw the humour of the situation, forgave Schacabac, and provided him with food to his heart's content

Barmy. Mad, crazy Sometimes spelled "balmy," but properly as above, as from "barm," froth, ferment Burns has —

> Just now I've taen the fit o' rhyme
> My barmie noddle's working prime.
>
> *To James Smith,* 19

Hence, in prison slang **to put on the barmy stick** is to feign insanity, and the "Barmy Ward" is the infirmary in which the insane, real or feigned, are confined

Barnabas St. **Barnabas' Day,** June 11th. St. Barnabas was a fellow-labourer of St Paul. His symbol is a rake, because June 11th is the time of hay harvest

Barnabites. An Order of regular clerks of St Paul, founded 1533, so called because the church of St Barnabas, in Milan, was given to them to preach in.

Barnaby Bright. An old provincial name for St Barnabas' Day (June 11th) Before the reform of the calendar it was the longest day, hence the jingle in Ray's *Collection of Proverbs*—

> Barnaby bright! Barnaby bright!
> The longest day and the shortest night.

Barnaby Lecturers. Four lecturers in the University of Cambridge, elected annually on St. Barnabas' Day (June 11th), to lecture on mathematics, philosophy, rhetoric, and logic

Barnaby Rudge The principal interest in this book is the picture it gives of the Gordon Riots of 1780. For the general impression he gives and some of the particulars Dickens relied upon the descriptions given to him by those who remembered the event clearly The book came out in parts in 1840. only sixty years after the riots

Barnacle. A species of wild goose allied to the brent goose, also the popular name of the Cirripedes, especially those which are attached by a stalk to floating balks of timber, the bottoms of ships, etc In mediæval times it was thought that the two were different forms of the same animal (much as are the frog and the tadpole), and as late as 1636 Gerard speaks of "broken pieces of old ships on which is found certain spume or froth, which in time breedeth into shells, and the fish which is hatched therefrom is in shape and habit like a bird "

The origin of this extraordinary belief is very obscure, but it is probably due to the accident of the identity of the name coupled with the presence in the shell-fish of the long feathery cirri which protrude from the shells and, when in the water, are very suggestive of plumage. In England the name was first attached to the bird. It is thought to be a diminutive of the M.E *bernake,* a species

of wild goose The name of the shell-fish, on the other hand, may be from a diminutive (*pernacula*) of the Lat *perna,* a mussel or similar shell-fish, though no such diminutive has been traced With an identity of name it was, perhaps, natural to look for an identity of nature in the two creatures.

The name is given figuratively to close and constant companions, hangers on, or sycophants; also to placemen who stick to their offices but do little work, like the barnacles which stick to the bottoms of ships but impede their progress

Barnacles. Spectacles, especially those of a heavy or clumsy make or appearance A slang term, from their supposed resemblance in shape to the twitches or "barnacles" formerly used by farriers to keep under restraint unruly horses during the process of bleeding, shoeing, etc This instrument consisted of two branches joined at one end by a hinge, and was employed to grip the horse's nose The word is probably a diminutive of the O Fr *bernac,* a kind of muzzle for horses

Barnard's Inn. One of the old Inns of Chancery, formerly situated on the south side of Holborn, east of Staple Inn It was once known as "Mackworth's Inn," because Dean Mackworth of Lincoln (d 1454) lived there

Barn-burners. Destroyers, who, like the Dutchman of story, would burn down their barns to rid themselves of the rats.

Barnstormer A slang term for a strolling player, and hence for any second-rate actor, especially one whose style is of an exaggerated declamatory kind. From the custom of itinerant troupes of actors giving their shows in village barns when better accommodation was not forthcoming

Barnwell, George. The chief character in *The London Merchant, or the History of George Barnwell,* a prose tragedy by George Lillo, produced in 1731 It is founded on a popular 17th-century ballad which is given in Percy's *Reliques* Barnwell was a London apprentice who was seduced by Sarah Millwood, a disappointed and repulsive woman of the town, to whom he gave £200 of his master's money He next robbed and murdered his pious uncle, a rich grazier at Ludlow Having spent the money, Sarah turned him out, each informed against the other, and both were hanged The story is mentioned frequently in 19th-century literature

Baron is from late Lat *baro* (through O Fr *barun*), and meant originally "a man," especially opposed to something else, as a freeman to a slave, a husband to a wife, etc , and also in relation to someone else, as "the king's man " From the former comes the legal and heraldic use of the word in the phrase *baron and feme*, husband and wife· from the latter the more common use, the king's "man" or "baron" being his vassal holding tenure of the king by military or other service To-day a baron is a member of the lowest order of nobility, he is addressed as "Lord," and by the Sovereign as "Our right trusty and well beloved " The premier English barony is that of De Ros, dating from 1264

The War of the Barons was the insurrection of the barons, under Simon de Montfort against the arbitrary government of Henry III, 1263-65   Drayton's poem *The Barons' War*, was published in 1603

Baron Bung   Mine host, master of the beer bung

Baron Munchausen.   *See* MUNCHAUSEN

Baron of beef.   Two sirloins left uncut at the backbone   The *baron* is the backpart of the ox, called in Danish, the *rug*   Jocosely, but wrongly, said to be a pun upon *baron* and *sir* loin

Baronet   An hereditary titled order of commoners, ranking next below barons and next above knights, using (like the latter) the title "Sir" before the Christian name, and the contraction "Bt " after the surname   The degree, as it now exists, was instituted by James I, and the title was sold for £1,000 to gentlemen possessing not less than £1,000 per annum, for the plantation of Ulster, in allusion to which the Red Hand of Ulster (*see under* HAND) is the badge of Baronets of England, the United Kingdom, and of Great Britain, also of the old Baronets of Ireland (created prior to the Union in 1800)

The premier baronetcy is that of Bacon of Redgrave. originally conferred in 1611 on Nicholas, half-brother of Sir Francis Bacon, Viscount St. Albans

Barque, barquentine (bark, bar' kèn tēn)   In the old days of sailing these words described two different rigs   A barque was a sailing ship with three masts, having the fore- and mainmasts square rigged and the mizen-mast fore-and-aft rigged.   A barquentine was a three-masted vessel square-rigged on the fore-mast and fore-and-aft rigged on the main- and mizen-mast   *See* SHIP

Barrack.   To barrack, is to jeer or shout rude commentaries at the players of games   The word came into use about 1880 in Australia where barracking is considered a legitimate and natural hazard with which, for instance, first-class cricketers have to contend

Barracks.   Soldiers' quarters of a permanent nature   The word was introduced in the 17th century from Ital *baracca*, a tent, through Fr. *baraque*, a barrack.

Barrage (bă' razh) (Fr.).   The original meaning of this word was an artificial dam or bar across a river to deepen the water on one side of it, as the great barrage on the Nile at Assouan   But from World War I the term is applied to a curtain of projectiles from artillery which is ranged to fall in front of advancing troops, or to keep off raiding aircraft, or to shield offensive operations, etc   *cp.* BALLOON.

Creeping barrage.   A curtain of artillery fire moving forward on a time schedule

Box barrage   A curtain of artillery fire laid down round a locality either to contain or exclude the enemy

Barratry   A legal term denoting (1) the offence of vexatiously exciting or maintaining lawsuits, and (2)—the commoner use—fraud

or criminal negligence on the part of the master or crew of a ship to the detriment of the owners   Like many of our legal terms, it is from Old French

Barrell's Blues.   The 4th Foot, so called from the colour of their facings, and William Barrell, colonel of the regiment (1734-9)   Now called "The King's Own (Royal Lancaster Regiment) "   They were called "Lions" from their badge, the Lion of England

Barricade.   To block up a street, passage, etc   The term rose in France in 1588, when Henri de Guise returned to Paris in defiance of the king's order   The king sent for his Swiss Guards, and the Parisians tore up the pavement, threw chains across the streets, and piled up barrels (Fr. *barriques*) filled with earth and stones, behind which they shot down the Swiss.

The day of the Barricades—
(1) May 12th, 1588, when the people forced Henry III to flee from Paris.
(2) August 5th, 1648, the beginning of the Fronde (*q v*)
(3) July 27th, 1830, the first day of *la grande semaine* which drove Charles X from the throne
(4) February 24th, 1848, which resulted in the abdication of Louis Philippe
(5) June 25th, 1848, when the Archbishop of Paris, was shot in his attempt to quell the insurrection
(6) December 2nd, 1851, the day of the *coup d'état*, when Louis Napoleon made his appeal to the people for re-election to the Presidency for ten years.

Barrier Treaty.   A treaty fixing frontiers, especially that of November 15th, 1715, signed by Austria, Great Britain, and the Netherlands, by which the Low Countries were guaranteed to the House of Austria, and the Dutch were to garrison certain fortresses   The treaty was annulled at Fontainebleau in 1785

Barrister.   One admitted to plead at the bar, one who has been "called to the bar."   *See* BAR.   They are of two degrees, the lower order being called simply "barristers," or formerly "outer" or "utter" barristers; the higher "King's Counsel "   Until 1880 there was a superior order known as "Serjeants-at-Law" (*q.v*)   The King's Counsel (K C.) is a senior, and when raised to this position he is said to "take silk," being privileged to wear a silk gown and, on special occasions, a full-bottomed wig.   The junior counsel, or barristers, wear a plain stuff gown and a short wig

A Revising Barrister.   One appointed to revise the lists of electors for members of parliament

A Vacation Barrister.   Formerly one newly called to the bar, who for three years had to attend in "Long Vacation "   The practice (and consequently the term) is now obsolete

Barristers' Bags.   *See* LAWYERS

Barristers' gowns.   "Utter barristers wear a stuff or bombazine gown, and the puckered material between the shoulders of the gown is all that is now left of the purse into which, in early days, the successful litigant . . dropped his . pecuniary tribute . for services rendered " (*Notes and Queries*, March 11th, 1893, p 124) The fact is that the counsel was supposed to appear merely as a friend of the litigant Even now he cannot recover his fees by legal process

Barry Cornwall, poet The *nom de plume* of Bryan Waller Pioctor (1787-1874) Writer of once-popular songs

Bar-sur-Aube. *See* CASTLE OF BUNGAY.

Bartholomew, St. The symbol of this saint is a knife, in allusion to the knife with which he was flayed alive He is commemorated on August 24th, and is said to have been martyred in Armenia, A D 44

Bartholomew doll. A tawdry, over-dressed woman, like one of the flashy, bespangled dolls offered for sale at Bartholomew Fair.

Bartholomew Fair. A fair held for centuries from its institution in 1133 at Smithfield, London, on St. Bartholomew's Day after the change of the calendar in 1752 it was held on September 3rd While it lasted the Fair was the centre of London life, Elizabethan and Restoration playwrights and story-tellers are full of its amusements and dissipations Besides the refreshment stalls, loaded with roast pork and cakes, there were innumerable sideshows —

Here's that will challenge all the fairs
Come buy my nuts and damsons, and Burgamy pears!
Here's the *Woman of Baylon, the Devil and the Pope,*
And here's the little girl, just going on the rope!
Here's *Dives and Lazarus,* and the *World's Creation,*
Here's the Tall Dutchwoman, the like's not in the nation
Here is the booths where the high Dutch maid is,
Here are the bears that dance like any ladies,
Tat, tat, tat, tat, says little penny trumpet,
Here's Jacob Hall, that does so jump it, jump it;
Sound trumpet, sound, for silver spoon and fork,
Come, here's your dainty pig and pork!
Wit and Drollery (1682)

Not even the Puritans were able to put down the riotings of Bartholomew Fair, and it went on in ever increasing disrepute until 1840, when it was removed to Islington. This was its death, and in 1855 it disappeared from utter neglect and inanition Ben Jonson wrote a comedy satirizing the Puritans under this name

Bartholomew, Massacre of St The slaughter of the French Huguenots in the reign of Charles IX, begun on St Bartholomew's Day, August 24th, 1572, at the instigation of Catherine de' Medici, the mother of the young king It is said that 30,000 persons fell in this dreadful persecution

Bartholomew pig. A very fat person. At Bartholomew Fair one of the chief attractions used to be a pig, roasted whole, and sold piping hot. Falstaff calls himself—
A little tidy Bartholomew boar-pig —2 *Henry IV,* ii, 4

Bartolist. One skilled in law or, specifically, a student of Bartolus Bartolus (1314-57) was an eminent Italian lawyer who wrote extensive commentaries on the Corpus Juris Civilis, and did much to arouse and stimulate interest in the ancient Roman law.

Bas Bleu. *See* BLUE STOCKING

Base Tenure. Originally, tenure not by *military,* but by *base,* service, such as a serf or villein might give later, a tenure in fee-simple that was determinate on the fulfilment of some contingent qualification.

Base of operations. In military parlance, the protected place from which operations are conducted, where magazines of all sorts are formed, and upon which (in case of reverse) the army can fall back.

Bashaw (ba shaw'). An arrogant, domineering man; a corruption of the Turkish *pasha,* a viceroy or provincial governor.

A three-tailed bashaw. A beglerbeg or prince of princes among the Turks, who has a standard of three horse-tails borne before him The next rank is the bashaw with two tails, and then the bey, who has only one horse-tail

Bashi-bazouk (bäsh' i bä zook') A savage and brutal ruffian The word is Turkish and means literally "one whose head is turned"; it is applied in Turkey to non-uniformed irregular soldiers who make up in plunder for what they do not get in pay It came into prominence at the time of the Crimean War, and again in that of the Bulgarian atrocities of 1876.

Basil (băz' il) (Gr *basilikos,* royal). An aromatic plant so called because it was thought to have been used in making royal perfume. The story of Isabella who placed her murdered lover's head in a pot and planted basil on top, which she watered with her tears, was taken by Keats from Boccaccio's *Decameron,* V, 5

Basilian Monks Monks of the Order of St. Basil, who lived in the 4th century It is said that the Order has produced 14 popes, 1,805 bishops, 3,010 abbots, and 11,085 martyrs

Basilica (ba zil' i kà) (Gr *basilikos,* royal) Originally a royal palace, but afterwards (in Rome) a large building with nave, aisles, and an apse at one end, used as a court of justice and for public meetings By the early Christians they were easily adapted for purposes of worship; the church of St John Lateran at Rome was an ancient basilica

Basilics (ba zil' iks) The legal code of the Eastern Empire, being a digest of the laws of Justinian and others prepared by the order of the Byzantine emperor Basilius, and completed by his son Leo towards the end of the 9th century.

Basilisco (bă zil is 'kō) A cowardly, bragging knight in Kyd's tragedy, *Solyman and Perseda* (1588). Shakespeare (*King John,* i, 1) makes the Bastard say to his mother, who asks him why he boasted of his ill-birth, "Knight, knight, good mother, Basilisco-like"—i e my boasting has made me a knight In the earlier play Basilisco, speaking of his name, adds, "Knight, good fellow, knight, knight!" and is answered, "Knave, good fellow, knave, knave!"

Basilisk (băz' i lisk) The king of serpents (Gr *basileus,* a king), a fabulous reptile, also called a *cockatrice* (q v), and alleged to be hatched by a serpent from a cock's egg, supposed to have the power of "looking any-one dead on whom it fixed its eyes."

> The Basiliske
> From powerful eyes close venim doth convay
> Into the lookers hart, and killeth farre away
> SPENSER *Faerie Queene*, IV, vii, 37.

Also the name of a large brass cannon in use in Elizabethan times

> Thou hast talk d
> Of sallies and retires, of trenches, tents,
> Of palisadoes, frontiers, parapets,
> Of basilisks, of cannon
> SHAKESPEARE 1 *Henry IV*, ii, 3

Basinful He's got a basinful, meaning, He's got just as much trouble, etc , as he can stand

Basket. To be left in the basket. Neglected or uncared for At one time foundling hospitals used to place baskets at their doors for the reception of abandoned babies

To give a basket To refuse to marry In Germany it was an old custom to fix a basket to the roof of one who had been jilted.

To go to the basket. Old slang for to go to prison· referring to the dependence of the lowest grade of poor prisoners (those in the "Hole") for their sustenance upon what passers-by put in the basket for them

Basochians (bà sosh' yanz) An old French term for Clerks of the Parlements, hence, lawyers. The chief of the Basochians was called *Le roi de la basoche*, and had his court, com, and grand officers He reviewed his "subjects" every year, and administered justice twice a week The *basoche* was responsible for public amusements, the presentation of farces, *sotties*, and moralities, etc. Henri III suppressed the "king," and transferred all his functions and privileges to the Chancellor

Hence *monnaie de Basoche*, worthless money, from the coins at one time made and circulated by the lawyers of France, which had no currency beyond their own community

Bass (bàs). The inner bark of the limetree, or linden, properly called *bast*, a Teutonic word the ultimate origin of which is unknown. It is used by gardeners for packing, tying up plants, protecting trees, etc , also for making mats, light baskets, hats, and (in Russia) shoes. while in parts of Central Europe a cloth is woven from it

Bast. *See* BUBASTIS

Bastard An illegitimate child, a French word, from the Old French and Provençal *bast*, a pack-saddle The pack-saddles were used by muleteers as beds, hence, as *bantling* (*q v*) is a "bench-begotten" child, so is *bastard*, literally, one begotten on a pack-saddle bed

The name was formerly given to a sweetened Spanish wine (white or brown) made of the bastard muscadine grape

Baste. I'll baste your jacket for you, *i e.* cane you I'll give you a thorough basting, *i.e.* beating (A word of uncertain origin).

Bastille (bàs tēl') means simply a building (O.Fr. *bastir*, now *bâtir*, to build) The famous state prison in Paris was commenced by Charles V as a royal château in 1370, and

it was first used as a prison by Louis XI. It was seized and sacked by the mob in the French Revolution, July 14th, 1789, and on the first anniversary its final demolition was begun and the Place de la Bastille laid out on its site. July 14th is the national holiday in France

Bat Harlequin's lath wand (Fr. *batte*, a wooden sword).

Off his own bat. By his own exertions, on his own account A cricketer's phrase, meaning runs won by a single player

To carry out one's bat (in cricket) Not to be "out" when the time for drawing the stumps has arrived

Parliament of Bats. *See* CLUB PARLIAMENT

To get along at a great bat. Here the word means *beat, pace,* rate of speed

To have bats in the belfry. To be crazy in the head, bats in this case being the nocturnal creatures

Batman A military officer's soldier-servant, but properly a soldier in charge of a *bat-horse* (or pack-horse) and its load. From Fr *bat*, a pack-saddle (O Fr *bast, see* BASTARD)

Batavia (bà tā' vi à). The Netherlands; so called from the Batavi, a German tribe which in Roman times inhabited the modern Holland

Bate me an Ace. *See* BOLTON

Bath. Knights of the Bath. This name is derived from the ceremony of bathing, which used to be practised at the inauguration of a knight, as a symbol of purity The last knights created in this ancient form were at the coronation of Charles II in 1661 The Order was revived by George I, in 1725, and remodelled by the Prince Regent in 1815 G C B stands for *Grand Cross of the Bath* (the first class), K C B *Knight Commander of the Bath* (the second class), C B *Companion of the Bath* (the third class)

Bath brick. Alluvial matter compressed to the form of a brick, and used for cleaning knives, polishing metals, etc It is made at Bridgwater, the material being dredged from the river Parrett, which runs through Bridgwater

Bath chair. A chair mounted on wheels and used for invalids First used at Bath, which for long has been frequented by invalids on account of its hot springs.

There, go to Bath with you! Don't talk nonsense Insane persons used to be sent to Bath for the benefit of its mineral waters. The implied reproof is, what you say is so silly, you ought to go to Bath

Bath, King of. Richard Nash (1674-1762), generally called Beau Nash, a celebrated master of the ceremonies at Bath for fifty-six years

Bath King-of-Arms *See* HERALDRY (*College of Arms*)

Bath metal. An alloy like pinchbeck (*q v*) consisting of about sixteen parts copper and five of zinc

Bath Oliver. A special kind of biscuit invented by Dr William Oliver (1695-1764), physician to the Bath Mineral Water Hospital, and an authority on gout

Bath post. A letter paper with a highly glazed surface, used by the ultra-fashionable visitors of Bath when that watering-place was at its prime   *See* POST-PAPER

Bath shillings. Silver tokens coined at Bath in 1811-12 and issued by various tradespeople, with face values of 4s , 2s , and 1s

Bath stone A limestone used for building, and found in the Lower Oolite, near Bath   It is easily wrought in the quarry but hardens on exposure to the air

Bath, St. Mary's. *See* BAIN MARIE.

Bathia (băth′ ı a)   The name given in the Talmud to the daughter of Pharaoh who found Moses in the ark of bulrushes.

Bath-kol (băth kol′) (daughter of the voice) A sort of divination common among the ancient Jews after the gift of prophecy had ceased   When an appeal was made to Bath-kol, the first words uttered after the appeal were considered oracular   *See* Ray's *Three Physico-Theological Discourses*, iii, 1693.

Bathos (bă′ thos) (Gr *bathos*, depth) A ludicrous descent from grandiloquence to commonplace

The Taste of the Bathos is implanted by Nature itself in the soul of man —POPE *Bathos Art o Sinking*, ii (1727)

A good example is the well-known couplet given by Pope

And, thou, Dalhousie, the great god of war,
Lieutenant-general to the earl of Mar
Ibid , ix

Bathsheba (băth′ she ba).   In Dryden's *Absalom and Achitophel*, intended for the Duchess of Portsmouth, a favourite of Charles II.   The allusion is to the wife of Uriah the Hittite, beloved by David (2 *Sam.* xi).

Bathyllus (băth′ ı lus)   A beautiful boy of Samos, greatly beloved by Polycrates the tyrant, and by the poet Anacreon (Horace: *Epistle* xiv, 9)

Batiste (ba tēst′)   A kind of cambric (*q v*), so called from Baptiste of Cambrai, who first manufactured it in the 13th century

Baton de commandement (băt′ ŏn de kom and′ mon) (Fr literally "commander s truncheon") The name given by archæologists to a kind of rod, usually of reindeer horn, pierced with one or more round holes, and sometimes embellished with carvings   It belongs to the Magdalenian age, but its use or purpose is quite unknown

Batrachomyomachia (bă′ trak ŏ mī′ ŏ mă kya). A storm in a puddle, much ado about nothing The word is the name of a mock heroic Greek epic, supposed to be by Pigres of Caria, but formerly attributed to Homer   It tells, as its name imports, of a *Battle between the Frogs and Mice*

Batta (băt′ a)   An Anglo-Indian term for perquisites   Properly, an extra allowance to troops when in the field or on special service. Sometimes spelt *batty*

He would rather live on half-pay in a garrison that could boast of a fives-court than vegetate on full batta where there was none —G R GLEIG *Thomas Munro*, vol i, ch. iv, p 287

Battels (băt′ elz)   At Oxford University the accounts for board and provisions, etc , provided by the kitchen and also (more loosely) one s total accounts for these together with fees for tuition, membership of clubs, etc., for the term   The word has also been used for the provisions or rations themselves, which is the earlier use has never been decided, and the derivation of the word is still a matter for conjecture

Battersea   You must go to Battersea to get your simples cut   A reproof to a simpleton, or one who makes a very foolish observation. The market gardeners of Battersea used to grow simples (medicinal herbs), and the London apothecaries went there to select or cut such as they wanted

Battle. A pitched battle.   A battle which has been planned, and the ground pitched on or chosen beforehand

Battle royal.   A certain number of cocks, say sixteen, are pitted together, the eight victors are then pitted, then the four, and last of all the two, and the winner is victor of the battle royal   Metaphorically, the term is applied to any contest of wits, etc.

A close battle.   Originally a naval fight at "close quarters," in which opposing ships engage each other side by side

Line of battle.   The formation of the ships in a naval engagement   A *line of battle ship* was a capital ship fit to take part in a main attack   Frigates did not join in a general engagement.

Half the battle.   Half determines the battle Thus, "The first stroke is half the battle," that is, the way in which the battle is begun determines what the end will be.

Trial by battle.   The submission of a legal suit to a combat between the litigants, under the notion that God would defend the right

Wager of battle.   One of the forms of ordeal or appeal to the judgment of God, in the old Norman courts of the kingdom   It consisted of a personal combat between the plaintiff and the defendant, in the presence of the court itself Abolished by 59 Geo III, c 46 (1819).

Battle above the Clouds.   *See* CLOUDS.

Battle bowler.   This was a nickname given in World War I to the steel helmet or "tin hat" worn at the front   Used again 1939-45, when it was also called a "tin topee."

Battle of the Books.   A satire by Swift (written 1697, published 1704), on the literary squabble as to the comparative value of ancient and modern authors   In the battle the ancient books fight against the modern books in St James's Library   *See* BOYLE CONTROVERSY

Battle of Britain.   The prolonged aerial operations over Southern England and the Channel, August-September 1940, in which the

German Luftwaffe endeavoured to seize superiority in the air from the R A F (as a necessary prelude to the invasion of Britain) and was defeated.

Battle of the Frogs and Mice. *See* BATRA-CHOMYOMACHIA

Battle of the Giants. *See* GIANTS

Battle of the Herrings. *See* HERRINGS

Battle of the Nations. *See* NATIONS

Battle of the Poets, The. A satirical poem (1725) by John Sheffield, Duke of Buckingham, in which the versifiers of the time are brought into the field

Battle of the Spurs. *See* SPURS

Battle of the Standard. *See* STANDARD

Battle of the Three Emperors. *See* THREE EMPERORS

Battle-painter, The, or **Delle Battaglie.** Michael Angelo Cerquozzi (1600-1660), a Roman artist noted for his battle-scenes, was so called.

Battle, Sarah. A character in one of Lamb's *Essays of Elia*, who considered that whist "was her life business, her duty, the thing she came into the world to do, and she did it She unbent her mind afterwards over a book."

Battledore. Originally the wooden bat used in washing linen The etymology of the word is not at all certain, but there is an old Provençal *batedor*, meaning a washing-beetle

Battledore book. A name sometimes formerly given to a horn-book (*q v*), because of its shape Hence, perhaps, the phrase "Not to know B from a battledore " *See* B

Battue (bă tū) A French word meaning literally "a beating," used in English as a sporting term to signify a regular butchery of game, the "guns" being collected at a certain spot over which the birds are driven by the beaters who "boat" the bushes, etc , for the purpose Hence, a wholesale slaughter, especially of unarmed people

Batty. *See* BATTA.

Baturlio marina. *See* BARISAL GUNS.

Baubee. *See* BAWBEE

Bauble. A fool should never hold a bauble in his hand. "'Tis a foolish bird that fouls its own nest " The bauble was a short stick, ornamented with ass's ears, carried by licensed fools (O Fr. *babel*, or *baubel*, a child's toy, perhaps confused with the M E *babyll* or *babulle*, a stick with a thong, from *bablyn*, to waver or oscillate)

If every fool held a bauble, fuel would be dear. The proverb indicates that the world contains a vast number of fools

To deserve the bauble. To be so foolish as to be qualified to carry the fool's emblem of office

Baucis. *See* PHILEMON

Bauld Wullie. *See* BELTED WILL.

Baulk. *See* BALK

Baviad, The (băv' ı ăd) A merciless satire by Gifford on the Della Cruscan poetry, published 1794, and republished the following year with a second part called *The Mæviad*. Bavius and Mævius were two minor poets pilloried by Virgil (*Eclogue*, ııı, 9)
> He may with foxes plough, and milk he-goats,
> Who praise Bavius or on Mævius dotes
And their names are still used for inferior versifiers
> May some choice patron bless each grey goose quill,
> May every Bavius have his Bufo still
> POPE *Prologue to Satires*, 249

Bavieca. The Cid's horse

Bavius. *See* BAVIAD

Bawbee A debased silver coin representing six Scots pennies and about equal in value to a halfpenny English, first issued in 1541, in the reign of James V The word is probably derived from the laird of Sillebawby, a contemporary mint-master, as appears from the Treasurer's account, September 7th, 1541, "*In argento receptis a Jacobo Atzinsone, et Alexandro Orok de Sillebawby respective.*"

Jenny's bawbee Her marriage portion.
> Wha'll hire, wha'll hire, wha'll hire me?
> Three plumps and a wallop for ae bawbee
An old rhyme embodying a reflection on the supposed parsimony and poverty of the Scots The tradition is that the people of Kirkmanhoe were so poor, they could not afford meat for their broth A cobbler bought four sheepshanks, and for the payment of one bawbee would "plump" one of them into the boiling water, and give it a "wallop" or whisk round The sheep-shank was called a *gustin bone*, and was supposed to give a rich "gust" to the broth

Bawtry. Like the saddler of Bawtry, who was hanged for leaving his liquor (Yorkshire proverb) It was customary for criminals on their way to execution to stop at a certain tavern in York for a "parting draught " The saddler of Bawtry refused to accept the liquor and was hanged If he had stopped a few minutes at the tavern, his reprieve, which was on the road, would have arrived in time to save his life.

Baxterians Followers of Richard Baxter (1615-91), a noted English Nonconformist. His chief doctrines were—(1) That Christ died in a spiritual sense for the elect, and in a general sense for all , (2) that there is no such thing as reprobation, (3) that even saints may fall from grace He thus tried to effect a compromise between the "heretical" opinions of the Arminians and the Calvinists

Bay The shrub was anciently supposed to be a preservative against lightning, because it was the tree of Apollo Hence, according to Pliny, Tiberius and other Roman emperors wore a wreath of bay as an amulet, especially in thunder-storms
> Reach the bays—
> I'll tie a garland here about his head;
> 'Twill keep my boy from lightning
> WEBSTER *Vittoria Corombona*, v, 1.
The bay being sacred to Apollo is accounted for by the legend that he fell in love with, and was rejected by, the beautiful Daphne, daughter of the river-god Peneos, in Thessaly,

who had resolved to pass her life in perpetual virginity. She fled from him and sought the protection of her father, who changed her into the bay-tree, whereupon Apollo declared that henceforth he would wear bay leaves instead of the oak, and that all who sought his favour should follow his example

The withering of a bay-tree was supposed to be the omen of a death Holinshed refers to this superstition —

In this yeare [1399] in a manner throughout all the realme of England, old bare trees withered, and, afterwards, contrarie to all mens thinking, grew greene againe, a strange sight, and supposed to impart some unknown event —III, 496, 2, 66

Shakespeare makes use of this note in his *Richard II*, ii, 4 —

'Tis thought the king is dead We'll not stay—
The bay-trees in our country are withered

In another sense Bay is a reddish-brown colour, generally used of horses The word is the Fr *bai*, from Lat *badius*, a term used by Varro in his list of colours appropriate to horses Bayard (*q v*) means "bay-coloured."

Crowned with bays. A reward of victory from the custom that obtained in ancient Rome of so crowning a victorious general

The Queen's Bays The 2nd Dragoon Guards, so called because they are mounted on bay horses often known, "for short," as *The Queen's*

Bay at the moon, To. *See* BARK.

Bay salt Coarse-grained salt, formerly obtained by slow evaporation of sea-water and used for curing meat, etc. Perhaps so called because originally imported from the shores of the *Bay* of Biscay. 'Bay," in this case, does not signify the colour

Bay Psalm Book A metrical version of the Psalms published by Stephen Daye at Cambridge, Massachusetts, in 1680 One of the first printed works of the New World, and now highly prized "What the Gutenberg Bible is to Europe, the *Bay Psalm Book* is to the United States"—A E Newton In 1947 a copy changed hands at auction for $151,000 00.

Bay State, The. Massachusetts In Colonial days its full title was "The Colony of Massachusetts Bay" hence the name

Bayadere (bä ya' där) A Hindu dancing girl employed both for religious dances and for private amusement The word is a French corruption of the Portuguese *bailadeira*, a female dancer

Bayard (bä' yard) A horse of incredible swiftness, given by Charlemagne to the four sons of Aymon. *See* AYMON If only one of the sons mounted, the horse was of the ordinary size, but if all four mounted, his body became elongated to the requisite length He is introduced in Boiardo's *Orlando Innamorato*, Ariosto's *Orlando Furioso*, and elsewhere, and legend relates that he is still alive and can be heard neighing in the Ardennes on Midsummer Day The name is used for any valuable or wonderful horse, and means a "high bay-coloured horse "

Bold as Blind Bayard Foolhardy If a blind horse leaps, the chance is he will fall into a ditch Grose mentions the following expression, To ride Bayard of ten toes—"Going by the marrow-bone stage"—*i e* walking

Keep Bayard in the stable. Keep what is of value under lock and key

Bayard, The Chevalier de. Pierre du Terrail (1475-1524), a celebrated French knight and national hero, distinguished in the Italian campaigns of Charles VIII, Louis XII, and François I *Le chevalier sans peur et sans reproche*

The Bayard of the East, or of the Indian Army. Sir James Outram (1803-63)

The British Bayard Sir Philip Sidney (1554-86).

The Polish Bayard Prince Joseph Poniatowski (1762-1813), who served with the greatest distinction under Napoleon.

Bayardo. The famous steed of Rinaldo (*q v*), which once belonged to Amadis of Gaul. *See* HORSE

Bayardo's Leap. Three stones, about thirty yards apart, near Sleaford It is said that Rinaldo was riding on his favourite steed, when the demon of the place sprang up behind him, but Bayardo in terror took three tremendous leaps and unhorsed the fiend

Bayes (bāz) A character in the *Rehearsal*, by the Duke of Buckingham (1671), designed to satirize Dryden The name refers to the laureateship

Dead men may rise again, like Bayes's troops, or the savages in the Fantocini. In the *Rehearsal* a battle is fought between footsoldiers and great hobby-horses. At last Drawcansir kills all on both sides Smith then asks how they are to go off, to which Bayes replies, "As they came on—upon their legs"; upon which they all jump up alive again.

Bayeux Tapestry (bī' yer) A strip of linen 231 ft long and 20 in wide on which is represented in tapestry the mission of Harold to William, Duke of Normandy (William the Conqueror), and all the incidents of his history from then till his death at Hastings in 1066 It is preserved at Bayeux, and is supposed to be the work of Matilda, wife of William the Conqueror

In the tapestry, the Saxons fight on foot with javelin and battle-axe, and bear shields with the British characteristic of a boss in the centre. The men are moustached

The Normans are on horseback, with long shields and pennoned lances The men are not only shaven, but most of them have a complete tonsure on the back of the head, whence the spies said to Harold, "There are more priests in the Norman army than men in Harold's "

Bayonet (bä' ö net). A stabbing weapon fixed to a rifle for shock action by infantry Its name is said to be taken from Bayonne where it was first made The bayonet is mentioned in the memoirs of Puysegur, in 1647, it was introduced into the English army in 1672 In its original form it was a plug bayonet, fitted into the barrel of the musket, and had therefore to be removed before the gun could be fired.

Bayonets. A synonym of "rank and file," that is, privates and corporals of infantry. As, "the number of bayonets was 25,000 "

It is on the bayonets that a Quartermaster-General relies for his working and fatigue parties —HOWITT. *Hist of Eng* (year 1854, p 260)

Bayou State (bī' yoo) The State of Mississippi, so called from its numerous bayous A bayou is a creek, or sluggish and marshy overflow of a river or lake The word may be of native American origin, but is probably a corruption of Fr. *boyau,* gut.

Bazooka. American one-man, short-range anti-tank weapon (1941-45) The name became freely applied to the British and German weapons of the same nature (P I A T —projectile infantry anti-tank—and *Panzerfaust*)

To be bazookaed. To be in a tank struck by such a projectile

Beachcomber. One who, devoid of other means of existence, subsists on what flotsam and jetsam he can find on the seashore The word originated in New Zealand, where it is found in print by 1844; an earlier form (1827) was *beach ranger,* analogous to *Bushranger* (*q v*)

Bead. From A S -*bed* (in *gebed*), a prayer, *biddan,* to pray "Bead," thus originally meant simply ' a prayer"; but as prayers were "told" (*i.e* account kept of them) on a "paternoster," the word came to be transferred to the small globular perforated body a number of which, threaded on a string, composed this paternoster or 'rosary."

To count one's beads. To say one's prayers *See* ROSARY

To draw a bead on. *See* DRAW

To pray without one's beads. To be out of one's reckoning

Baily's beads. When the disc of the moon has (in an eclipse) reduced that of the sun to a thin crescent, the crescent assumes the appearance somewhat resembling a string of beads. This was first described in detail by Francis Baily in 1836, whence the name of the phenomenon, the cause of which is the sun shining through the depressions between the lunar mountains

St. Cuthbert's beads. Single joints of the articulated stems of encrinites They are perforated in the centre, and bear a fanciful resemblance to a cross, hence, they were once used for rosaries (*q v*) St Cuthbert was a Scottish monk of the 6th century, and may be called the St Patrick of the Border Legend relates that he sits at night on a rock in Holy Island and uses the opposite rock as his anvil while he forges the beads

On a rock of Lindisfarn
St Cuthbert sits, and toils to frame
The sea-born beads that bear his name
SCOTT *Marmion*

St. Martin's beads. Flash jewellery. St Martin-le-Grand was at one time a noted place for sham jewellery

Bead-house. An almshouse for beadsmen

Bead-roll. A list of persons to be prayed for, hence, also, any list

Beadsman or **Bedesman.** Properly, one who prays, hence, an inmate of an almshouse, because most charities of this class were instituted so that the inmates might "pray for the soul of the founder " *See* BEAD.

Seated with some grey beadsman
CRABBE *Borough.*

Beadle. A person whose duty it is to *bid* or cite persons to appear to a summons, also a church servant, whose duty it is to *bid* the parishioners to attend the vestry, or to give notice of vestry meetings. It is ultimately a Teutonic word (Old High Ger *bitel,* one who asks, whence the A S *beodan,* to bid, and *bydel,* a herald), but it came to us through the O Fr *badel,* a herald. *See* BEDEL

Beak Slang for a police magistrate, but formerly (16th and 17th cent) for a constable Various fanciful derivations have been suggested, but the etymology of the word is unknown

Beaker A drinking-glass; a rummer, a wide-mouthed glass vessel with a lip, used in scientific experiments A much-travelled word, having come to us by way of the Scandinavian *bikkar,* a cup (Dut *beker,* Ger *becher*), from Greek *bikos,* a wine-jar, which was of Eastern origin Our *pitcher* is really the same word

O for a beaker full of the warm South,
Full of the true, the blushful Hippocrene
KEATS *Ode to a Nightingale.*

Beam. **Thrown on my beam-ends.** Driven to my last shift An old phrase of the days of sail, for a ship was said to be on her beam-ends when she was laid by a heavy gale completely on her side, i e the part where her *beams end* Not infrequently the only means of righting her in such a case was to cut away her masts.

On the starboard beam. A distant point out at sea on the right-hand side, and at right angles to the keel

On the port beam. A similar point on the left-hand side

On the weather beam. On that side of a ship which faces the wind

To kick the beam. *See* KICK

To be on the beam is to be on the right course A modern phrase coming from the directing of aircraft by means of a radio beam

Beam (of a stag) The main trunk of the horn, the part that bears the branches (A S *béam,* a tree)

Bean. **Every bean has its black.** *Nemo sine vitiis nascitur* (Everyone has his faults) The bean has a black eye (*Ogni grano ha la sua semola*)

He has found the bean in the cake. He has got a prize in the lottery, has come to some unexpected good fortune The allusion is to twelfth cakes in which a bean is buried When the cake is cut up and distributed, he who gets the bean is the twelfth-night king *See* BEAN-KING.

Jack and the bean-stalk. *See* JACK

Old bean. A slang expression of good-natured familiarity that became very common early in the 20th century

Bean-feast. Much the same as wayz-goose (*q v*). A feast given by an employer to those he employs. Probably so called because either beans or a bean-goose used to be a favourite dish on such occasions

Bean-goose. A migratory bird which appears in England in the autumn, so named from a mark on its bill like a horse-bean. It is next in size to the greylag-goose.

Bean-king. *Rey de Habas*, the child appointed to play the part of king on twelfth-night. Twelfth-night was sometimes known as *the Bean-king's festival.*

Beans. Slang for property, money, also for a sovereign, and (formerly) a guinea. In this sense it is probably the O Fr cant, *biens*, meaning property, but in such phrases as *not worth a bean*, the allusion is to the bean's small value

Like a beane [alms-money] in a monkeshood
                          COLGRAVE

Blue beans. Bullets or shot, hence, "Three blue beans in a blue bladder," a rattle for children

Fort (Of his purse) Hark' dost rattle?
Strad Yes, like three beans in a blue bladder, rattle bladder, rattle, your purse is like my belly, th' one's without money, th' other without meat
         DEKKER *Old Fortunatus*, I, ii

Three small bullets or large shot in a bladder would make a very good rattle for a child.

Beans are in flower. A catch-phrase said to one by way of accounting for his being so silly. Our forefathers imagined that the perfume of the flowering bean made men silly or light-headed

He knows how many beans make five. He is "up to snuff", he is no fool, he is not to be imposed upon. The reference is to an old trap. Everyone knows that five beans make five, and on this answer being correctly given the questioner goes on, "But you don't know how many blue beans make five white ones" The complete answer to this is 'Five—*if peeled*"

Full of beans. Said of a fresh and spirited horse; hence, in good form, full of health and spirits

I'll give him beans. I'll give him a thrashing There is a similar French proverb, *S'il me donne des pois, je lui donnerai des feves* (i e If he gives me peas I will give him beans), I will give him tit for tat, a Roland for an Oliver.

In ancient times Pythagoras forbade the use of beans to his disciples—not the use of beans as food, but for political elections. Magistrates and other public officers were elected by beans cast by the voters into a helmet, and what Pythagoras advised was that his disciples should not interfere with politics or "love beans"—*i e* office. But according to Aristotle the word *bean* implied venery, and that the prohibition to "abstain from beans" was equivalent to "keeping the body chaste"

Without a bean. Penniless, "broke"

To spill the beans. To give away a secret, to let the cat out of the bag.

Bear. In the phraseology of the Stock Exchange, a speculator for a fall. (*Cp* BULL)

Thus, **to operate for a bear**, or **to bear the market**, is to use every effort to depress prices, so as to buy cheap and make a profit on the rise. Such a transaction is known as a Bear account.

The term is of some antiquity, and was current at least as early as the South Sea Bubble, in the 18th century. Its probable origin will be found in the proverb, 'Selling the skin before you have caught the bear" One who sold stocks in this way was formerly called a *bearskin jobber*

The Bear. Albert, margrave of Brandenburg (1106-70). He was so called from his heraldic device

The bloody bear, in Dryden's *The Hind and the Panther*, means the Independents.

The bloody bear, an independent beast,
Unlicked to form, in groans her hate expressed
                        Pt i, 35, 36

In mediæval times it was popularly supposed that bear-cubs were born as shapeless masses of flesh and fur, and had to be literally "licked into shape" by their mothers. Hence the reference in the above quotation, and the phrase *"to lick into shape"* (*q v*)

The Great Bear, and Little Bear. These constellations were so named by the Greeks, and their word, *arktos*, a bear, is still kept in the names Arcturus (the bear-ward, *ovrcs*, guardian) and Arctic (*q v*). The Sanskrit name for the Great Bear is from the verb *rakh* to be bright, and it has been suggested that the Greeks named it *arktos* as a result of confusion between the two words. *Cp* CHARLES'S WAIN, NORTHERN WAGONER.

The wind-shaked surge, with high and monstrous mane,
Seems to cast water on the burning bear
And quench the guards of th' ever-fixed pole
         SHAKESPEARE *Othello*, ii, i

The *guards* referred to in the above extract are β and γ of Ursa Minor. They are so named, not from any supposed guarding that they do, but from the Sp *guardare*, to behold, because of the great assistance they were to mariners in navigation

The classical fable is that Calisto, a nymph of Diana, had two sons by Jupiter, which Juno changed into bears, and Jupiter converted into constellations

'Twas here we saw Calisto's star retire
Beneath the waves, unawed by Juno's ire.
         CAMOENS *Lusiad*, Bk. v

The Northern Bear. In political cartoons, etc , Russia is depicted as a bear

A bridled bear. A young nobleman under the control of a travelling tutor. See BEAR-LEADER

The bear and ragged staff. A crest of the Nevil es and later Earls of Warwick, often used as a public-house sign. The first earl is said to have been Arth or Arthgal, of the Round Table, whose cognizance was a *bear*, *arth* meaning a bear (Lat *ursa*). Morvid, the second earl, overcame, in single combat, a mighty giant, who came against him with a club consisting of a tree pulled up by the roots, but stripped of its branches. In remembrance of his victory over the giant he added "the ragged staff"

The bear and the tea-kettle. Said of a person who injures himself by foolish rage The story is that one day a bear entered a hut in Kamschatka, where a kettle was on the fire Master Bruin smelt at it and burnt his nose, greatly irritated, he seized it with his paws, and squeezed it against his breast This, of course, made matters worse, for the boiling water scalded him terribly, and he growled in agony till some neighbours put an end to his life with their guns.

A bear sucking his paws It used to be believed that when a bear was deprived of food it sustained life: by sucking its paws The same was said of the badger The phrase is applied to industrious idleness

As savage as a bear with a sore head. Unreasonably ill-tempered

> As a bear has no tail,
> For a lion he'll fail

The same as *Ne sutor supra crepidam* (Let not the cobbler aspire above his last) Robert Dudley, Earl of Leicester, a descendant of the Warwick family is said to have changed his own crest, "a green lion with two tails," for the Warwick "bear and ragged staff " When made governor of the Low Countries, he was suspected of aiming at absolute supremacy, or the desire of being the monarch of his fellows, as the lion is monarch among beasts Some wit wrote under his crest the Latin verse, *Ursa caret cauda non queat esse leo*, i e —

> Your bear for lion needs must fail,
> Because your true bears have no tail

To take the bear by the tooth. To put your head into the lion's mouth, needlessly to run into danger

Bear garden. This place is a perfect bear garden—that is, full of confusion, noise, tumult, and quarrels In Elizabethan and Stuart times the gardens where bears were kept and baited for public amusement were famous for all sorts of riotous disorder.

Bear-leader. A common expression in the 18th century denoting a travelling tutor who escorted a young nobleman, or youth of wealth and fashion, on the "Grand Tour." From the old custom of leading muzzled bears about the streets, and making them show off in order to attract notice and money. This practice was made illegal only in 1925

Bear! (said *Dr Pangloss* to his pupil) Under favour young gentleman, I am the bear-leader, being appointed your tutor —G COLMAN *Heir-at-Law*.

Bear, To. Come, bear a hand! Come and render help. Bring a hand, or bring your hand to bear on the work going on

To bear arms. To do military service; to be entitled to heraldic coat of arms and crest

To bear away (nautical) To keep away from the wind

To bear one company. To be one's companion

> His faithful dog shall bear him company
> POPE *Essay on Man*, epistle 1, 112

To bear down. To overpower.

To bear down upon (nautical) To approach from the weather side

Bear in mind Remember, do not forget. Carry in your recollection.

To bear out. To corroborate, to confirm

To bear up. To support; to keep the spirits up

To bear with. To show forbearance, to endure with complacency

To bear the bell. *See* BELL

Beard Among the Jews, Turks, and Eastern nations generally the beard has long been regarded as a sign of manly dignity To cut it off wilfully was a deadly insult, and the Jews were strictly forbidden to cut it off ceremonially, though shaving it was a sign of mourning No greater insult could be offered a man than to pluck or even touch his beard, hence the phrase **to beard one**, to defy him, to contradict him flatly, to insult him. By touching or swearing by one's own beard one's good faith was assured

The dyeing of beards is mentioned by Strabo, and Bottom the Weaver satirizes the custom when he undertakes to play Pyramus, and asks, "What beard were I best to play it in ? "

I will discharge it in either your straw-colour beard, your orange-tawny beard your purple-in-grain beard, or your French-crown-colour beard (your perfect yellow).

> *Midsummer Night's Dream*, 1, 2.

Beards are encouraged in the Royal Navy, but not permitted in the other Services, though in World War II the Army turned a blind eye to the beards of some individuals performing unusually hazardous duty behind the enemy's lines

To beard the lion in his den To defy personally or face to face

To make one's beard To have one wholly at your mercy, as a barber has when holding a man's beard to dress it, or shaving the chin of a customer, So to be able to do what you like with one, to outwit or delude him

> Though they preye Argus, with his hundred yen,
> To be my warde-cors, as he can best,
> In feith, he shal nat kepe me but me lest;
> Yet coude I make his berd, so moot I thee
> CHAUCER *Wije of Bath's Prologue*, 358.

I told him to his beard. I told him to his face, regardless of consequences; I spoke to him openly and fearlessly.

Maugre his beard. In spite of him

"'Tis merry in hall when beards wag all"— i e when feasting goes on

> Then was the minstrel's harp with rapture heard,
> The song of ancient days gave huge delight;
> With pleasure too did wag the minstrel's beard,
> For Plenty courted him to drink and bite.
> PETER PINDAR *Elegy to Scotland*

To laugh at a man's beard. To attempt to make a fool of him—to deceive by ridiculous exaggeration

"By the prophet! but he laughs at our beards," exclaimed the Pacha angrily "These are foolish lies "—MARRYAT *Pacha of Many Tales*

To laugh in one's beard. To laugh up one's sleeve, that is, surreptitiously.

To lie in one's beard. To accuse someone of so doing is to stress the severity of the accusation (Elizabethan).

To run in one's beard. To offer opposition to a person, to do something obnoxious to a person before his face

With the beard on the shoulder. (Sp) In the attitude of listening to overhear something, with circumspection, looking in all directions for surprises and ambuscades

They rode, as the Spanish proverb expresses it, "with the beard on the shoulder," looking round from time to time, and using every precaution against pursuit —SCOTT *Peveril of the Peak*, ch vii

Tax upon beards Peter the Great imposed a tax upon beards Every one above the lowest class had to pay 100 roubles, and the lowest class had to pay a copeck, for enjoying this "luxury" Clerks were stationed at the gates of every town to collect the beard tax

Bearded Master (*Magister barbatus*) So Persius styled Socrates, under the notion that the beard is the symbol of wisdom

The bearded. A surname or nickname (*Pogonatus*) given to Constantine IV, Emperor of the East, 668-85, also to Baldwin IV, Count of Flanders, 988-1036, Geoffrey the Crusader, Bouchard of the house of Montmorency, and St Paula *See* BEARDED WOMEN

Bearded women. St Paula the Bearded, a Spanish saint of uncertain date of whom it is said that when being pursued by a man she fled to a crucifix and at once a beard and moustache appeared on her face, thus disguising her and saving her from her would-be ravisher. A somewhat similar story is told of St. Wilgefortis, a mythical saint supposed to have been one of seven daughters born at a birth to a king of Portugal, also of the English saint, St. Uncumber

Many bearded women are recorded in history, among them may be mentioned —

Bartel Grætje, of Stuttgart, born 1562

Charles XII had in his army a woman whose beard was a yard and a half long She was taken prisoner at the battle of Pultawa, and presented to the Czar, 1724

Mlle Bois de Chêne, born at Geneva in 1834, and exhibited in London in 1852-3, she had a profuse head of hair, a strong black beard, large whiskers, and thick hair on her arms and back

Julia Pastrana, found among the Digger Indians of Mexico, was exhibited in London in 1857, died, 1862, at Moscow, was embalmed by Professor Suckaloff, and the embalmed body was exhibited in London

Bearings. I'll bring him to his bearings. I'll bring him to his senses, put him on the right track. Bearings is a term in navigation signifying the direction in which an object is seen Thus to keep one's bearings is to keep on the right course, in the right direction

To lose one's bearings. To become bewildered, to get perplexed as to which is the right road.

To take the bearings. To ascertain the relative position of some object.

Béarnais, Le Henry IV of France (1553-1610), so called from *Le Béarn*, his native province.

Beast. The Number of the Beast. *See* NUMBER.

Beast of Belsen. In World War II the name applied to Joseph Kramer, commandant of the notorious Belsen Concentration Camp.

Beasts of heraldry. In English heraldry all manner of creatures have been borne as charges or as crests, the principal being the lion, bear, bull, boar, cat, swallow (called a martlet), pelican, unicorn, stag The attitude or position of the animals is described as follows: *couchant*, squatting, with head erect, *dormant*, lying down asleep, *passant*, walking, with one paw raised, *passant guardant*, walking but looking at the spectator; *rampant*, on its hind legs, *rampant combattant*, two beasts rampant facing one another; *rampant endorsed*, two beasts rampant back to back A beast can be *proper*, which is emblazoned in some colour similar to its natural colour · *naissant*, showing its upper half as though it were emerging from the womb; *erased*, showing its head and shoulders only

Beat (A S *beatan*). The first sense of the word was that of striking, that of overcoming or defeating followed on as a natural extension A track, line, or appointed range A walk often trodden or beaten by the feet, as a policeman's beat The word means a beaten path

Not in my beat Not in my line; not in the range of my talents or inclination

Off his beat Not on duty, not in his appointed walk, not his speciality or line.

Off his own beat his opinions were of no value
EMERSON *English Traits*, ch i

On his beat. In his appointed walk, on duty

Out of his beat. In his wrong walk, out of his proper sphere

Dead beat. So completely beaten or worsted as to have no leg to stand on. Like a dead man with no fight left in him, quite tired out

Dead beat escapement (of a watch). One in which there is no reverse motion of the escape-wheel

That beats Banagher. *See* BANAGHER: TERMAGANT

To beat about. A nautical phrase, meaning to tack against the wind

To beat about the bush To approach a matter cautiously or in a roundabout way, to shilly-shally, perhaps because one goes carefully when beating a bush to find if any game is lurking within.

To beat an alarm. To give notice of danger by beat of drum

To beat a retreat (Fr. *battre en retraite*), *to beat to arms, to beat a charge* Military terms similar to the above

To beat down. To make a seller abate his price

To beat or drum a thing into one. To repeat as a drummer repeats his strokes on a drum

To beat hollow, or to a mummy, a frazzle, to ribbons, a jelly, etc. To beat wholly, utterly, completely

To beat the air. To strike out at nothing, merely to bring one's muscles into play, as pugilists do before they begin to fight, to toil without profit, to work to no purpose

So fight I, not as one that beateth the air.—1 *Cor* ix, 26.

To beat the booby. *See* BOOBY

To beat the bounds. *See* BOUNDS

To beat the bush. To allow another to profit by one's exertions, "one beat the bush and another caught the hare." "Other men laboured, and ye are entered into their labours" (*John* iv, 38) The allusion is to beaters, whose business it is to beat the bushes and start the game for a shooting party

To beat the devil's tattoo. *See* TATTOO

To beat the Dutch. To draw a very long bow, to say something very incredible   To beat the band means the same thing

To beat time. To mark time in music by beating or moving the hands, feet, or a baton

To beat up against the wind. To tack against an adverse wind, to get the better of the wind

To beat up someone's quarters. To hunt out where he lives, to visit without ceremony. A military term, signifying to make an unexpected attack on an enemy in camp

To beat up the quarters of some of our less-known relations —LAMB *Essays of Elia*

To beat up recruits or supporters To hunt them up or call them together, as soldiers are summoned by beat of drum

To beat one with his own staff To confute him by his own words   An *argumentum ad hominem.*

Can High Church bigotry go farther than this? And how well have I since been beaten with mine own staff—J. WESLEY [He refers to his excluding Bolzius from communion because he had not been canonically baptized]

Beati Possidentes (bē a' tī pos i den' tēz) Blessed are those who have (for they shall receive) ' Possession is nine points of the law ''

Beatific Vision. The sight of God, or of the blessed in the realms of heaven, especially that granted to the soul at the instant of death. *See Is* vi, 1-4, and *Acts* vii, 55, 56

Beatification (bē āt i fi kā' shun). In the R C Church this is a solemn act by which a deceased person is formally declared by the Pope to be one of the blessed departed and therefore a proper subject for a mass and office in his honour, generally with some local restriction Beatification is usually, though not necessarily, a step to canonization

Beatitude (bē āt' it tūd) In theology this is the perfect good which completely satisfies all desire

The Beatitudes are the eight blessings pronounced by Our Lord at the opening of the Sermon on the Mount (*Matt* v 3-11)

Beatrice Celebrated by Dante in the *Vita Nuova* and the *Divina Commedia*, this girl was born 1266 and died in 1290, under twenty-four years old. She was a native of Florence, of the Portinari family, and married Simone de' Bardi in 1287. Dante married Gemma Donati about two years after Beatrice's death

Beau (bō)   The French word, which means "fine," or "beautiful," has, in England, often been prefixed to the name of a man of fashion, or a fop as an epithet of distinction   The following are well known —

Beau Brummel   George Bryan Brummel (1778-1840).

Beau D'Orsay. Count D'Orsay (1801-52), called by Byron *Jeune Cupidon*

Beau Feilding. Robert Feilding (d 1712), called "Handsome Feilding" by Charles II He died in Scotland Yard, London. after having been convicted of bigamously marrying the Duchess of Cleveland, a former mistress of Charles II He figures as Orlando in Steele's *Tatler* (Nos 50 and 51)

Beau Hewitt. The model for "Sir Fopling Flutter," hero of Etheredge's *Man of Mode.*

Beau Nash. Richard Nash (1674-1762) Son of a Welsh gentleman, a notorious diner-out He undertook the management of the rooms at Bath, and conducted the public balls with a splendour and decorum never before witnessed

Beau Didapper, in Fielding's *Joseph Andrews* and **Beau Tibbs,** noted for his finery, vanity, and poverty in Goldsmith's *Citizen of the World,* may also be mentioned

In America the word *beau* is applied to a girl's favourite admirer, or lover

Beau ideal Properly, the ideal Beautiful, the abstract idea of beauty, *idéal,* in the French, being the adjective, and *beau,* the substantive. but in English the parts played by the words are usually transposed, and thus have come to mean the ideal type or model of anything in its most consummate perfection

Beau monde The fashionable world, people who make up the coterie of fashion

Beau trap. An old slang expression for a loose paving-stone under which water lodged, and which squirted up filth when trodden on, to the annoyance of the smartly dressed

Beauclerc (bō' klērk) (*good scholar*) Applied to Henry I (1068-1135), who had clerk-like accomplishments, very rare in the times in which he lived

Beaumontague or **Beaumontage.** Material used for filling in accidental holes in wood- or metal-work, repairing cracks, disguising bad joinery, etc Said to be so called from the celebrated French geologist, Elie de Beaumont (1798-1874), who also gave his name to **beaumonlite,** a silicate of copper

Beauseant (bō sā' on) The battle-cry of the Knights Templar *See* TEMPLAR

Beautiful Parricide. Beatrice Cenci, daughter of Francesco Cenci, a dissipated and passionate Roman nobleman With her brothers, she plotted the death of her father because of his unmitigated cruelty to his wife and children. She was executed in 1599, and at the trial her counsel, native of the view of still further gaining popular sympathy for his client, accused the father, probably without foundation, of having attempted to commit incest with her. Her story has been a favourite theme in poetry and art, Shelley's tragedy *The Cenci* is particularly noteworthy

Beauty   Beauty is but skin deep.
> O formose puer, nimium ne crede colori.
> VIRGIL *Eclogues*, ii

(O my pretty boy, trust not too much to your pretty looks)

Beauty and the Beast   The hero and heroine of the well-known fairy tale in which Beauty saved the life of her father by consenting to live with the Beast, and the Beast, being disenchanted by Beauty's love, became a handsome prince, and married her
The story is found in Straparola's *Piacevoli Notti* (1550), and it is from this collection that Mme le Prince de Beaumont probably obtained it when it became popular through her French version (1757)   It is the basis of Grétry's opera *Zemire et Azor* (1771)
The story of a handsome and wealthy prince being compelled by enchantment to assume the appearance and character of a loathsome beast or formidable dragon until released by the pure love of one who does not suspect the disguise, is of great antiquity and takes various forms. Sometimes, as in the story of Lamia, and the old ballads *Kempion* and *The Laidley Worm of Spindlestoneheugh*, it is the woman—the "Loathly Lady" of the romances—who is enchanted into the form of a serpent and is only released by the kiss of a true knight.

Beauty of Buttermere.   Mary Robinson, married in 1802 to John Hatfield (*c* 1758-1802), a heartless impostor, and already a bigamist, who was executed for forgery at Carlisle in 1803   She was the subject of many dramas and stories
> a story drawn
> From our own ground,—The Maid of Buttermere,—
> And how, unfaithful to a virtuous wife
> Deserted and deceived, the Spoiler came
> And wooed the artless daughter of the hills,
> And wedded her, in cruel mockery
> Of love and marriage bonds
> WORDSWORTH *Prelude*, vii, 288

Beauty sleep.   Sleep taken before midnight Those who habitually go to bed, especially during youth, after midnight, are supposed to become pale and more or less haggard.

Beaux Esprits (bō zā sprē) (Fr)   Men of wit or genius (singular, *Un bel esprit*, a wit, a genius)

Beaux yeux (bō zyĕr') (Fr)   Beautiful eyes or attractive looks   'I will do it for your *beaux yeux*" (because you are so pretty, or because your eyes are so attractive)

Beaver   The lower and movable part of a helmet, so called from Fr *bavière*, which meant a child's bib, to which this part had some resemblance   It is not connected with *bever* (*q v*), the afternoon draught in the harvest-field
> *Hamlet*   Then you saw not his face?
> *Horatio*   O yes, my lord, he wore his beaver up.
> SHAKESPEARE *Hamlet*, i, 2

Beaver is also an old name for a man's hat, because they used to be made of beaver fur For some years in the 1920s the word was applied to anyone wearing a beard

Becasse (bā kas).   French for a woodcock and also for a booby or "softy"   The word is sometimes used in the latter sense in English.

Bed   The great bed of Ware.   A bed eleven feet square, and capable of holding twelve persons   It dates from the last quarter of the 16th century   In 1931 it came into the possession of the Victoria and Albert Museum
> Although the sheet were big enough for the bed of Ware in England —SHAKESPEARE *Twelfth Night*, iii, 2

As you make your bed you must lie on it. Everyone must bear the consequences of his own acts   "As you sow, so must you reap " "As you brew, so must you bake "

To bed out. To plant what are called "bedding-out plants" in a flower-bed.   Bedding-out plants are reared in pots, generally in a hothouse, and are transferred into garden-beds early in the summer   Such plants as geraniums, marguerites, fuchsias, pentstemons, petunias, verbenas, lobelias, calceolarias, etc , are meant.

To make the bed   To arrange it and make it fit for use   In America this sense of "make" is more common than it is with us   "Your room is made," arranged in due order

You got out of bed the wrong way, or with the left leg foremost. Said of a person who is patchy and ill-tempered   It was an ancient superstition that it was unlucky to set the left foot on the ground first on getting out of bed The same superstition applies to putting on the left shoe first, a "fancy" not yet wholly exploded   Augustus Cæsar was very superstitious in this respect.

Bed of justice. *See* LIT

A bed of roses. A situation of ease and pleasure.

A bed of thorns. A situation of great anxiety and apprehension

In the twinkling of a bed-post or bed-staff. As quickly as possible   In old bed-frames it is said that posts were placed in brackets at the two sides of the bedstead for keeping the bed-clothes from rolling off, there was also in some cases a staff used to beat the bed and clean it   In the reign of Edward I, Sir John Chichester had a mock skirmish with his servant (Sir John with his rapier and the servant with the bed-staff), in which the servant was accidentally killed.   Wright, in his *Domestic Manners*, shows us a chambermaid of the 17th century using a bed-staff to beat up the bedding   'Twinkling" is from A S. *twinclian*, a frequentative verb connected with *twiccan*, to twitch, and connotes rapid or tremulous movement
> I'll do it instantly, in the twinkling of a bed-staff
> SHADWELL *Virtuoso*, i, 1 (1676)

The phrase is probably due to the older and more readily understandable one, *in the twinkling of an eye*, in the smallest thinkable fraction of time —
> We shall all be changed in a moment, in the twinkling of an eye, at the last trump —1 *Cor* xv, 51, 52

Bedchamber Question.   In May, 1839, Lord Melbourne's Whig ministry resigned, and when Sir Robert Peel formed a government he intimated to Queen Victoria that he would expect the Whig ladies of the bedchamber to be replaced by Tories. The Queen refused to accede to this request, and persisting in her refusal, called Lord Melbourne to her aid A new Whig ministry was formed, which lasted until 1841, by which time the Prince Consort was able to smooth over the difficulty when a Tory government was formed

Bede. *See* VENERABLE BEDE.

Bedel, or **Bedell** (bē' del) Old forms of the word *beadle* (*q v*), still used at Oxford and Cambridge in place of the modern spelling for the officer who carries the mace before the Vice-Chancellor and performs a few other duties At Oxford there are four, called *bedels*, at Cambridge there are two, called *bedells*, or *esquire-bedells*.

Beder (bē' der) A village between Medina and Mecca famous for the first victory gained by Mohammed over the Koreshites (624 A D) In the battle he is said to have been assisted by 3,000 angels, led by Gabriel, mounted on his horse Haizum

Bedesman. *See* BEADSMAN

Bedford Level. The large tract of marshy land about 60 miles in breadth and 40 in length which lies in the counties of Norfolk, Suffolk, Cambridge, Huntingdonshire, Northamptonshire, and Lincolnshire, and includes the Isle of Ely and the whole of the Fen district. So called from Francis, fourth Earl of Bedford, who undertook the draining of the Fens in 1634.

Bedford Book of Hours. An illuminated manuscript of extraordinary beauty made for John, Duke of Bedford, second son of King Henry IV, whose wife presented it to King Henry VI at Christmas, 1430 It is now in the British Museum

Bedivere, or **Bedver.** In the Arthurian romances, a knight of the Round Table, butler and staunch adherent of King Arthur It was he who, at the request of the dying king, threw Excalibur into the Lake, and afterwards bore his body to the ladies in the barge which was to take him to Avalon

Bedlam A lunatic asylum or madhouse; a contraction for *Bethlehem*, the name of a religious house in London, converted into a hospital for lunatics. St Mary of Bethlehem was the first English and the second European lunatic asylum Founded in Bishopsgate, London, in 1247, it became a madhouse in 1403. In 1676 it was transferred to Moorfields, near where Liverpool-St Station now stands, and was one of the sights of London, where, for twopence, anyone might wander in and gaze at the poor distracted wretches behind their bars and bait them with foolish and cruel questions It was a holiday resort and place for assignations, one of the disgraces of 17th-century London

> All that I can say of Bedlam is this, 'tis an almshouse for madmen, a showing room for harlots, a sure market for lechers, a dry walk for loiterers
> WARD'S *London Spy* (1698)

In 1815 Bedlam was moved to St George's Fields, Lambeth, and in 1926 to the country, near Beckenham, Kent

Bedlamite. A madman, a fool, an inhabitant of Bedlam *See* ABRAM-MAN.

Bedlam, Tom o'. *See* TOM

Bednall Green. *See* BEGGAR'S DAUGHTER

Bedouins (bed' ou inz) French (and thence English) form of an Arabic word meaning "a dweller in the desert," given indiscriminately by Europeans to the nomadic tribes of Arabia and Syria, and applied in journalistic jargon to gipsies, or the homeless poor of the streets In this use it is merely a further extension of the term "street Arab," which means the same thing

Bed-rock. American slang for one's last shilling. A miner's term for the hard basis rock which is reached when the mine is exhausted "I'm come down to the bed-rock," *i e* my last dollar

Bedver. *See* BEDIVERE.

Bee. Legend has it that Jupiter was nourished by bees in infancy, and Pindar is said to have been nourished by bees with honey instead of milk

The Greeks consecrated bees to the moon With the Romans a flight of bees was considered a bad omen Appian (*Civil War*, Bk ii) says a swarm of bees lighted on the altar and prognosticated the fatal issue of the battle of Pharsalia

The coins of Ephesus had a bee on the reverse.

When Plato was an infant, bees settled on his lips when he was asleep, indicating that he would become famous for his honeyed words.

> And as when Plato did i' the cradle thrive,
> Bees to his lips brought honey from their hive
> W BROWNE *Britannia's Pastorals*, ii

The same story is told of Sophocles, Pindar, St Chrysostom, and others, including St Ambrose, who is represented with a beehive.

The Bee was the emblem of Napoleon I

The name bee is given, particularly in America, to a social gathering for some useful work, the allusion being to the social and industrious character of bees The name of the object of the gathering generally precedes the word, as a *spelling-bee* (for a competition in spelling), *apple-bees*, *husking-bees*, etc It is an old Devonshire custom, carried across the Atlantic in Stuart times, but the *name* appears to have originated in America.

See also ANIMALS IN SYMBOLISM.

The Athenian Bee. *See* ATHENIAN.

The Bee of Athens. *See* ATHENIAN and ATTIC BEE.

Bee-line. The shortest distance between two given points, such as a bee is supposed to take in making for its hive. *Air-line* is another term for the same thing

To have your head full of bees, or to have a bee in your bonnet. To be cranky; to have an idiosyncrasy, to be full of devices, crotchets, fancies, inventions, and dreamy theories. The connexion between bees and the soul was once generally maintained hence Mohammed admits bees to Paradise. Porphyry says of fountains, "they are adapted to the numphs, or those souls which the ancient called bees." *Cp.* MAGGOT.

Beef. This word, from the O Fr *boef* (mod Fr *bœuf*), an ox, is, like *mutton* (Fr. *mouton*), a reminder of the time when, in the years following the Norman Conquest, the Saxon was the down-trodden servant of the conquerors the Normans had the cooked meat, and when set before them used the word they were accustomed to, the Saxon was the herdsman, and while the beast was under his charge called it by its Saxon name

Beefeaters The popular name of the Yeomen of the Guard in the royal household, appointed, in 1485, by Henry VII, to form part of the royal train at banquets and on other grand occasions, also of the Yeomen Extraordinary of the Guard, who were appointed as Warders of the Tower of London by Edward VI, and wear the same Tudor-period costume as the Yeomen of the Guard themselves

There is no evidence whatever for the old guess that the word is connected with the French *buffet*, and signifies "an attendant at the royal buffet, or sideboard", on the contrary, every indication goes to show that it means exactly what it says, viz "eaters of beef" That "eater" was formerly used as a synonym for "servant" is clear, not only from the fact that the O E *hlaf-æta* (literally, "loaf-eater") meant "a menial servant," but also from the passage in Ben Jonson's *Silent Woman* iii, 2, (1609) where Morose, calling for his servants, shouts,

Bar my doors! bar my doors! Where are all my eaters? My mouths, now? Bar up my doors, you varlets!

Sir S D Scott, in his *The British Army* (1, 513), quotes an early use of the word from a letter of Prince Rupert's dated 1645, and shows (p 517) that the large daily allowance of beef provided for their table makes the words in their literal meaning quite appropriate.

There is plenty of evidence to show that in the 17th century there was little doubt of the meaning of the word e g. Cartwright's *The Ordinary*, ii, 1 (1651) —

Those goodly Juments of the guard would fight
(As they eat beef) after six stone a day

Beef-steak Club. The present Beef-steak Club dates from 1876, but the original club of this name was founded about 1707. Its badge was a gridiron, and it was said to comprise "the chief wits and great men of the nation." In 1735 the "Sublime Society of the Steaks," which has sometimes been confused with this, but which scorned to be called a club, was inaugurated through a chance dinner taken by Lord Peterborough in the scene-room of Rich, over Covent Garden Theatre His lordship was so delighted with the steak provided and cooked by the actor that he proposed to repeat the entertainment every Saturday The "Sublime Society," which was then founded, continued to meet at Covent Garden till the fire of 1808, and, after various vicissitudes, was finally dissolved in 1867. The original gridiron on which Rich broiled the peer's steak is still in existence.

Beelzebub The name should be spelt *Beelzebul* (or, rather, *Baalzebul*, *see* BAAL), and means "lord of the high house", but, as this title was ambiguous and might have been

B.D —4

taken as referring to Solomon's Temple, the late Jews changed it to *Beelzebub*, which has the meaning "lord of flies " Beelzebub was the particular Baal worshipped originally in Ekron and afterwards far and wide in Palestine and the adjacent countries To the Jews he came to be the chief representative of the false gods, and he took an important place in their hierarchy of demons. He is referred to in *Matt* xii, 24, as "the prince of the devils," and hence Milton places him next in rank to Satan

One next himself in power, and next in crime,
Long after known in Palestine, and named
Beelzebub *Paradise Lost*, i, 79

Beer *See* ALE

He does not think small beer of himself. *See* SMALL BEER

Life is not all beer and skittles, i e not all eating, drinking, and play; not all pleasure, not all harmony and love

Sport like life, and life like sport,
Isn't all skittles and beer

Beeswing. The second crust, or film, composed of shining scales of mucilage, which forms in good port and some other wines after long keeping, and which bears some resemblance to the wings of bees. Unlike the "crust" which forms on the bottle, it is not detrimental if it passes into the decanter at decanting

Beetle, To. To overhang, to threaten, to jut over The word seems to have been first used by Shakespeare

Or to the dreadful summit of the din,
That beetles o'er his base into the sea
Hamlet, i, 4

It is formed from the adjective, *beetle-browed*, having prominent or shaggy eyebrows; and it is not the case, as has sometimes been stated, that the adjective was formed from the verb. The derivation of *beetle* in this use is not quite certain, but it probably refers to the tufted antennæ which, in some beetles, stand straight out from the head

Befana (be fa' na). The good fairy of Italian children, who is supposed to fill their stockings with toys when they go to bed on Twelfth Night Someone enters the children's bedroom for the purpose, and the wakeful youngsters cry out, ' *Ecco la Befana* ' According to legend, Befana was too busy with house affairs to look after the Magi when they went to offer their gifts, and said she would wait to see them on their return, but they went another way, and Befana, every Twelfth Night, watches to see them The name is a corruption of *Epiphania*.

Before the Lights. *See* LIGHTS

Before the Mast. *See* MAST

Beg. A Turkish chief or governor. *See* BEY.

Beg the Question, To. To assume a proposition which, in reality, involves the conclusion Thus, to say that parallel lines will never meet because they are parallel, is simply to assume as a fact the very thing you profess to prove. The phrase is the common English equivalent of the Latin term, *petitio principii*

Beggar. A beggar may sing before a pickpocket. *Cantabit vacuus coram latrone viator*

(*Juvenal*, x, 22). A beggar may sing in the presence of thieves because he has nothing in his pocket to lose

Beggar of Bednall Green. *See* BESSEE, THE BEGGAR'S DAUGHTER

Beggars cannot be choosers. Beggars must take what is given them, and not dictate to the giver what they like best. They must accept and be thankful

Beggars' barm. The thick foam which collects on the surface of ponds, brooks, and other pieces of water where the current meets stoppage It looks like barm or yeast, but, being unfit for use, is only beggarly barm at best

Beggars' bullets. Stones

To go by beggar's bush, or Go home by beggar's bush—*i e* to go to ruin Beggar's bush is the name of a tree which once stood on the left hand of the London road from Huntingdon to Caxton, so called because it was a noted rendezvous for beggars These punning phrases and proverbs are very common

Bessee, the beggar's daughter of Bednall Green, the heroine of an old ballad given in Percy's *Reliques*, and introduced by Chettle and Day into their play *The Blind Beggar of Bednal Green* (1600). Sheridan Knowles also has a play on the story (1834) Bessee was very beautiful, and was courted by four suitors at once—a knight, a gentleman of fortune, a London merchant, and the son of the innkeeper at Romford She told them that they must obtain the consent of her father, the poor blind beggar of Bethnal Green When they heard that, they all slunk off except the knight, who went to ask the beggar's leave to wed the "pretty Bessee" The beggar gave her £3,000 for her dower, and £100 to buy her wedding gown. At the wedding feast he explained to the guests that he was Henry, son and heir of Sir Simon de Montfort

Beggar's Opera. Opera produced in London in 1727 with enormous success The words are by Gay and the music, partly traditional ballads and partly contemporary "hits," was arranged by Pepusch The 'hero" is a highwayman, MacHeath, and the originality lay in composing an opera round criminals and Newgate Prison

King of the beggars Bampfylde Moore Carew (1693-1770), a famous English vagabond who was elected King of the Gipsies He fell into the hands of the Law, was transported to Maryland but escaped and got back to England He was one of the Young Pretender's troopers in the '45 and followed him to Derby.

Set a beggar on horseback, and he'll ride to the de'il. There is no one so proud and arrogant as a beggar who has suddenly grown rich

Such is the sad effect of wealth—rank pride—
Mount but a beggar, how the rogue will ride!
PETER PINDAR *Epistle to Lord Lonsdale*
The proverb is common to many languages

Begging Friars. *See* MENDICANT ORDERS

Beghards (be gardz). A monastic fraternity which rose in the Low Countries in the 12th century, so called from Lambert le Begue, a priest of Liege, who also founded a sisterhood They took no vows, and were free to leave the society when they liked In the 17th century, those who survived the persecutions of the Popes and Inquisition joined the Tertiarii of the Franciscans *See* BEGUINES.

Beglerbed *See* BASHAW

Begorra. An Irish form of the English minced oath "begad," for "By God"

Beguine (be gēn'). A popular Martinique and South American dance, or music for this dance, in bolero rhythm. This rhythm inspired Cole Porter's success of the 1930s, "Begin the Beguine"

Beguines (bā gēn) A sisterhood founded in the 12th century by Lambert le Begue (*see* BEGHARDS). The Beguines were at liberty to quit the cloister and to marry, they formerly flourished in the Low Countries, Germany, France, and Italy, and there are still communities with this name in Belgium The cap called a *beguin* was named from this sisterhood

Begum A lady, princess, or woman of high rank in India; the wife of a ruler (fem of *Beg*, *see* BEY).

Behemoth (be hē' moth) The animal described under this name in *Job* xl, 15 *et seq*, is, if an actual animal were intended, almost certainly the hippopotamus, but modern scholarship rather tends to the opinion that the reference is purely mythological The English poet Thomson, apparently took it to be the rhinoceros

Behold! in plaited mail,
Behemoth rears his head
The Seasons Summer, 709

The word is sometimes pronounced Be' hemoth, but Milton, like Thomson, places the accent on the second syllable.

Scarce from his mold
Behemoth, biggest born of earth, upheaved
His vastness
Paradise Lost, vii, 471

Behmenists (bā' men ists) A sect of theosophical mystics, so called from Jacob Behmen, or Bohme (1575-1624), their founder The first Behmenist sect in England was founded under the name of *Philadelphists* by a certain Jane Leade, in 1697.

Behram (bā' răm) The most holy kind of fire, according to Parseeism (*q v.*) *See also* GUEBRES

Bejan (bē' jan). A freshman or greenhorn. This term was introduced into some of the Scottish Universities from the University of Paris, and is a corruption of Fr *bec jaune*, yellow beak, with allusion to a nestling or unfledged bird At Aberdeen a woman student is called a *banjanella* or *bejanella*

In France *bejaune* is still the name for the repast that the freshman is supposed to provide for his new companions

Bel. The name of two Assyrio-Babylonian gods; it is the same word as Baal (*q v*) The story of Bel and the Dragon, in which we are told how Daniel convinced the king that Bel was not an actual living deity but only an image, was formerly part of the *Book of Daniel*, but is now relegated to the Apocrypha

Bel Esprit (bel es prē) (Fr) Literally, fine mind, means, in English, a vivacious wit, one of quick and lively parts, ready at repartee (pl. *beaux esprits*)

Belch, Sir Toby. A reckless, roistering, jolly fellow from the knight of that name in Shakespeare's *Twelfth Night*

Belcher A pocket-handkerchief—properly, one with white spots on a blue ground, so called from Jim Belcher (1781-1811), the pugilist, who adopted it The Belcher ring was a massive gold affair, sometimes set with a precious stone

Beldam An old woman This is not from the French *belle dame*, but from English *dam*, a mother, and *bel-*, a prefix expressing relationship as does *grand-* in *grandmother*, etc *Belfather* is an old term for *grandfather*.

> Old men and beldames in the streets
> Do prophesy upon it dangerously
> SHAKESPEARE King John, iv, 2

Belfast Regiment, The. *See* REGIMENTAL NICKNAMES

Bel-fires *See* BELTANE

Belfry. A military tower, pushed by besiegers against the wall of a besieged city, that missiles may be thrown more easily against the defenders (From O Fr *berfrei*, *berfroi*, Mid High Ger *bercfrit*—*berc*, shelter, *fride*, peace— a protecting tower) A church steeple is called a belfry from its resemblance to these towers, and not because bells are hung in it

Belial (bē'li ăl) (Heb) The worthless or lawless one, *i e* the devil

> What concord hath Christ with Belial?
> 2 Cor vi, 15

Milton, in his pandemonium, makes him a very high and distinguished prince of darkness

> Belial came last—than whom a spirit more lewd
> Fell not from heaven, or more gross to love
> Vice for itself
> *Paradise Lost*, bk 1, 490

Sons of Belial. Lawless, worthless, rebellious people

> Now the sons of Eli were sons of Belial
> 1 Sam ii, 12

Belisarius (bel i sâr' i us) **Belisarius begging for an obolus.** Belisarius (d 565), the greatest of Justinian's generals, being accused of conspiring against the life of the emperor, was deprived of all his property The tale is that his eyes were put out, and that when living as a beggar in Constantinople he fastened a bag to his roadside hut, with the inscription, "Give an obolus to poor old Belisarius " This tradition is of no historic value

Belit. *See* ASSHUR

Bell, Acton, Currer, and Ellis These were the names under which Anne, Charlotte, and Emily Bronte wrote their novels

Bell As the bell clinks, so the fool thinks, or, **As the fool thinks, so the bell clinks** The tale says when Whittington ran away from his master, and had got as far as Highgate Hill,

he was hungry, tired, and wished to return Bow Bells began to ring, and Whittington fancied they said, "Turn, again, Whittington, Lord Mayor of London " The bells clinked in response to the boy's thoughts

At three bells, at five bells, etc. A term on board ship with much the same meaning as our expression *o'clock* Five out of the seven watches last four hours, and each half-hour is marked by a bell, which gives a number of strokes corresponding to the number of half-hours passed Thus, ' three bells" denotes the third half-hour of the watch, "five bells" the fifth half-hour of the watch, and so on The two short watches, which last only two hours each, are from four to six and six to eight in the afternoon "Eight bells" is rung at noon, four, and eight o'clock, and is the signal for the beginning of a new watch *See* WATCH

Bell, book, and candle In the greater excommunication, introduced into the Catholic Church in the 8th century, after reading the sentence a *bell* is rung, a *book* closed, and a *candle* extinguished From that moment the excommunicated person is excluded from the sacraments and even from divine worship The form of excommunication closed with the words "Close the book, quench the candle, ring the bell!"

> Bell, book, and candle shall not drive me back
> SHAKESPEARE King John, iii, 3

Hence, in spite of bell, book, and candle, signifies in spite of all the opposition which even the Christian hierarchy can offer.

Give her the bells and let her fly. Don't throw good money after bad, make the best of the matter, but do not attempt to bolster it up. The metaphor is from falconry, when a hawk was worthless the bird was suffered to escape, even at the expense of the bells attached to her.

I'll not hang all my bells on one horse I'll not leave all my property to one son The allusion is manifest

Like sweet bells jangled, out of tune and harsh (*Hamlet*, iii, 1) A metaphor for a deranged mind, such as that of Ophelia, or of Don Quixote.

Passing bell The hallowed bell which used to be rung when persons were *in extremis*, to scare away evil spirits which were supposed to lurk about the dying ready to pounce on the soul while *passing* from the body It is a very ancient custom, and the Athenians used to beat on brazen kettles at the moment of a decease to scare away the Furies A secondary object was to announce to the neighbourhood the fact that all good Christians might offer up a prayer for the safe *passage* of the soul into Paradise The bell rung at a funeral is sometimes improperly called the "passing bell "

The Koran says that bells hang on the trees of Paradise, and are set in motion by wind from the throne of God, as often as the blessed wish for music

> Bells as musical
> As those that, on the golden-shafted trees
> Of Eden, shook by the eternal breeze
> T MOORE Lalla Rookh, pt 1.

Ringing the hallowed bell. Consecrated bells were believed to be able to disperse storms and pestilence, drive away devils (*see* PASSING BELL, *above*), and extinguish fire In France in quite recent times it was by no means unusual to ring church bells to ward off the effects of lightning, and as lately as 1852 it is said that the Bishop of Malta ordered the church bells to be rung for an hour to "lay a gale of wind."

Funera plango, fulgura frango, sabbata pango,
Excito lentos, dissipo ventos, paco cruentos
A Helpe to Discourse (1668)

(Death's tale I tell, the winds dispel, ill-feeling quell,
The slothful shake, the storm-clouds break, the Sabbath wake)

The legend on the Münster bell, cast at Basle in 1486, known as Schiller's bell because it furnished him with the idea for his *Lied von der Glocke*, reads:

Vivos Voco · Mortuos Plango Fulgura Frango

Ringing the bells backwards, is ringing a muffled peal *Backwards* is often used to denote "in a reverse manner," as. ' I hear you are grown rich——" · Yes, backwards," meaning "quite the reverse " A muffled peal is a peal of sorrow, not of joy, and was formerly sometimes employed as a tocsin, or notice of danger

Sound as a bell. Quite sound A cracked bell is useless

Blinde Fortune did so happily contrive,
That we as sound as bells did safe arive
At Dover
Taylor's Workes, ii, 22 (1630)

Tolling the bell for church. The ' church-going bell," as Cowper called it (*Alexander Selkirk*) was in pre-Reformation days rung, not as an invitation to church, but as an Ave Bell, to invite worshippers to a preparatory prayer to the Virgin

To bear or **carry away the bell.** To be first fiddle; to carry off the palm to be the best The leader of the flock, the "bellwether," bore the bell, hence the phrase, but it has been confused with an old custom of presenting to winners of horse-races, etc , a little gold or silver bell as a prize

Jockey and his horse were by their masters sent
To put in for the bell
They are to run and cannot miss the bell
NORTH *Forest of Varieties*

Warwick shakes his bells. Beware of danger, for Warwick is in the field Trojans beware, Achilles has donned his armour. A metaphor from falconry, the bells being those of a hawk

Neither the king, nor he that loves him best,
Dares stir a wing, if Warwick shakes the bells
SHAKESPEARE 3 *Henry VI*, i, 1.

Who is to bell the cat? Who will risk his own life to save his neighbour's? Anyone who encounters great personal hazard for the sake of others undertakes to "bell the cat "

Bell-the-Cat Archibald Douglas, fifth Earl of Angus (d 1514), was so called. James III made favourites of architects and masons. One mason, named Cochrane, he created Earl of Mar. The Scottish nobles held a council in the church of Lauder for the purpose of putting down these upstarts, when Lord Gray asked,

"Who will bell the cat?" "That will I, ' said Douglas, and he fearlessly put to death, in the king's presence, the obnoxious minions The allusion is to the fable of the cunning old mouse (given in *Piers Plowman* and elsewhere), who suggested that they should hang a bell on the cat's neck to give notice to all mice of her approach "Excellent," said a wise young mouse, "but who is to undertake the job?"

Bellman. A town-crier Before the present police force was established, watchmen or bellmen used to parade the streets at night, and at Easter a copy of verses was left at the chief houses in the hope of obtaining an offering These verses were the relics of the old incantations sung or said by the bellman to keep off elves and hobgoblins

Bell-rope. A humorous name for a curl worn by a man—a "rope" for the "belles" to play with Cp. BOW-CATCHER.

Bell Savage. *See* LA BELLE SAUVAGE

Bell-wavering. Vacillating, swaying from side to side like a bell A man whose mind jangles out of tune from delirium, drunkenness, or temporary insanity, is said to have his wits gone bell-wavering

Bellwether of the flock. A jocose and rather deprecatory term applied to the leader of a party The allusion is to the wether or sheep which leads the flock with a bell fastened to its neck

Belladonna (bel a don' a) The Deadly Nightshade The name is Italian, and means "beautiful lady", it is not certainly known why it should have been given to the plant. One account says that it is from a practice once common among ladies of touching their eyes with it to make the pupils large and lustrous, but another has it that it is from its having been used by an Italian poisoner, named Leucota, to poison beautiful women It is used today by ophthalmic surgeons in order to enlarge the pupil so that they may more easily examine the inside of the eye

Bellarmine (bel' ar min) A large Flemish gotch, or stone beer-jug, originally made in Flanders in ridicule of Cardinal Bellarmine (1542-1621), the great persecutor of the Protestants there. It carried a rude likeness of the cardinal Cp GREYBEARD

Belle (bel) (Fr) A beauty. **The Belle of the ball.** The most beautiful woman in the room

La belle France A common French phrase applied to France, as "Merrie England" is to our own country.

Belles lettres (bel letr) Polite literature, poetry, and standard literary works which are not scientific or technical the study or pursuit of such literature. The term—which is French —has given birth to the very ugly words *bellettrist* and *bellettristic*

Bellerophon (be ler' ō fon) The Joseph of Greek mythology; Antæa, the wife of Prœtus, being the "Potiphar's wife" who tempted him, and afterwards falsely accused him Her husband, Prœtus, sent Bellerophon with a letter to Iobates, the King of Lycia, his wife's father, recounting the charge, and praying that the bearer might be put to death	Iobates, unwilling to slay him himself, gave him many hazardous tasks (including the killing of the Chimæra, *q v*), but as he was successful in all of them Iobates made him his heir	Later Bellerophon is fabled to have attempted to fly to heaven on the winged horse Pegasus, but Zeus sent a gadfly to sting the horse, and the rider was thrown

Bellerophon has frequently been used for the name of a ship in the British Navy	The most famous took part in the Battle of the Nile, Trafalgar, etc , and was the vessel in which Napoleon surrendered himself to the British and which brought him to England	It was corrupted by sailors, etc , to "Billy Ruffian," ' Bully-ruffran," ' Belly-ruffron " etc

Why, she and the Belly-ruffron seem to have pretty well shared and shared alike —Captain MARRYAT *Poor Jack*, ch. xiii

Bellerus (bĕ lē' rus)	The name of a giant invented by Milton by way of accounting for ' Bellerium," the old Roman name for the Land's End district of Cornwall

Sleep'st by the fable of Bellerus old
	MILTON *Lycidas*, 160

Milton had originally written "Corineus" (*q v*), a name already well known in British legend.

Bellona.	In Roman mythology, the goddess of war and wife (or sometimes sister) of Mars She was probably in origin a Sabine deity.

**Belly.	The belly and its members.**	The fable of Menenius Agrippa to the Roman people when they seceded to the *Sacred Mount*. ' Once on a time the members refused to work for the lazy belly, but, as the supply of food was thus stopped, they found there was a necessary and mutual dependence between them "	The fable is given by Æsop and by Plutarch, whence Shakespeare introduces it in his *Coriolanus*, i, 1

The belly has no ears.	A hungry man will not listen to advice or arguments	The Romans had the same proverb, *Venter non habet aures*; and in French, *Ventre affamé n'a point d'oreilles*

Belly-timber.	Food	The term is quite an old one, and was not originally slang	It is used seriously by Massinger and other Elizabethan dramatists, and is given by Cotgrave (1611) as a translation of the French *Carrelure de ventre* (literally, a resoling, or refurnishing, of the stomach)

. through deserts vast
And regions desolate they pass'd
Where belly-timber above ground
Or under, was not to be found.
	BUTLER, *Hudibras*.

Belomancy (bel' ŏ măn si) (Gr)	Divination by arrows	Labels being attached to a given number of arrows, the archers let them fly, and the advice on the label of the arrow which flies farthest is accepted and acted on.	Sir Thomas Browne describes a method of belomancy in *Pseudodoxia Epidemica*, v, 23, and says that it—

hath been in request with Scythians, Alanes, Germans, with the Africans and Turks of Algier.

Beloved Disciple.	St. John (*John* xiii, 23, etc)

Beloved Physician.	St. Luke.	(*Col.* iv, 14)

Belphegor (bel' fe gôr)	The Assyrian form of ' Baal-Peor " (*see* BAAL), the Moabitish god to whom the Israelites became attached in Shittim (*Numb* xxv, 3)

The name was given in a mediæval Latin legend to a demon who was sent into the world from the infernal regions by his fellows to test the truth of certain rumours that had reached them concerning the happiness—and otherwise—of married life on earth	After a thorough trial, the details of which are told with great intimacy, he fled in horror and dismay to the happy regions where female society and companionship was non-existent Hence, the term is applied both to a misanthrope and to a nasty, licentious, obscene fellow.

The story is found in Machiavelli's works, and became very popular	Its first appearance in English is in Barnabe Rich's *Farewell to the Military Profession* (1581), and it either forms the main source of, or furnishes incidents to, many plays including *Grim, the Collier of Croydon* (1600), Jonson's *The Devil is an Ass* (1616), and John Wilson's *Belphegor, or the Marriage of the Devil* (1691).

Belphœbe (bel fē' bi).	The huntress-goddess in Spenser's *Faerie Queene*, daughter of Chrysogone and sister of Amoret, typifies Queen Elizabeth as a model of chastity.	She was of the Diana and Minerva type, cold as an icicle, passionless, immovable, and, like a moonbeam, light without warmth.

**Belt.	To hit below the belt.**	To strike unfairly.	It is prohibited in the Queensberry rules of prize-fighting to hit below the waistbelt

To hold the belt.	To be the champion	In pugilism, a belt usually forms part of the prize in big events, and is typical of the championship

Belted earl, knight.	This refers to the belt and spurs with which knights, etc , were invested when raised to the dignity

Belted Will.	Lord William Howard (1563-1640), a Border chief, son of the fourth Duke of Norfolk, and warden of the western marches	He was so called by Scott.	To his contemporaries he was known as "Bould Wullie "	His wife was called ' Bessie with the braid apron."

Beltane (bel' tăn).	In Scotland, old Mayday, the beginning of summer, also the festival that was held on that day, a survival of the ancient heathen festival inaugurating the summer, at which the Druids lit two "bel-fires" between which the cattle were driven, either preparatory to sacrifice or to protect them against disease	The word is Gaelic, and means literally "the blaze-kindling "

Belvedere (bel' ve dēr)	A sort of pleasure house built on an eminence in a garden, from which one can survey the surrounding prospect, or a look-out on the top of a house. The word is Italian, and means a *fine sight*

Benares (ben âr' ĕz) The holy city of the Hindus, being to them what Mecca is to the Moslems It was founded about 1200 B C. and was for many years a Buddhist centre, being conquered by the Mohammedans in 1193 It is celebrated for its temples and shrines to which pilgrims go from all India

Benbow. A name almost typical of a brave sailor, from John Benbow (1653-1702), a noted English Admiral It is told of him that in an engagement with the French near St Martha, on the Spanish coast, in 1701, his legs and thighs were shivered into splinters by a chain-shot, but, supported in a wooden frame, he remained on the quarter deck till morning, when Du Casse bore away Almeyda, the Portuguese governor of India, in his engagement with the united fleet of Cambaya and Egypt, had his legs and thighs shattered in a similar manner, but, instead of retreating, had himself bound to the ship's mast, where he "waved his sword to cheer on the combatants," till he died from loss of blood

Whirled by the cannon's rage, in shivers torn,
His thighs far shattered o'er the waves are borne,
Bound to the mast the god-like hero stands,
Waves his proud sword and cheers his woeful bands,
Though winds and seas their wonted aid deny,
To yield he knows not but he knows to die
　　　　　　　　　　CAMOËNS Lusiad, Bk v

Somewhat similar stories are told of Cynægiros and Jaafer (qq.)

Bench. Originally the same word as BANK, it means, properly, a long wooden seat, hence the official seat of judges in Court, bishops in the House of Lords, aldermen in the council chamber, etc , hence, by extension judges, bishops, etc , collectively, the court or place where they administer justice or sit officially, the dignity of holding such an official status, etc Hence **Bench of bishops** The whole body of prelates, who sit in the House of Lords

To be raised to the bench. To be made a judge

To be raised to the Episcopal bench. To be made a bishop

King's (or Queen's) Bench See KING'S.

Bench and Bar Judges and barristers See BAR; BARRISTER

Benchers Senior members of the Inns of Court They exercise the functions of calling students to the bar (q v) and have powers of expulsion

Bend. In heraldry, an ordinary formed by two parallel lines drawn across the shield from the dexter chief (i e the top left-hand corner when looking at the shield) to the sinister base point (i e the opposite corner) It is said to represent the sword-belt

Bend sinister A bend running across the shield in the opposite direction, i e from right to left It often is an indication of bastardy (cp BAR SINISTER), hence the phrase "he has a bend sinister," he was not born in lawful wedlock

Beyond my bend, i e my means or power The phrase is probably a corruption of beyond my bent, but it may be in allusion to a bow or spring, which, if strained beyond its bending power, breaks

Bendemeer (ben' de mēr) A river that flows near the ruins of Chilminar or Istachar, in the province of Chusistan, in Persia

There's a bower of roses by Bendemeer's
　　　　　　　　　　　　　　　stream,
And the nightingale sings round it all the day
　　　　　　　　　　　　　　　long
　　　　　　　　MOORE Lalla Rookh, I

Bender. A sixpenny-piece, perhaps because it can be bent without much difficulty Also (in schoolboy slang) a 'licking" with the cane, the culprit being in a bent position In Scotland it is an old term for a hard drinker, and in the United States it is still given to a drinking bout

Bendigo (ben' di gō) The nickname (said to be a corruption of "Abednego") of William Thompson (1811-89), a well-known pugilist. He left his nickname to a township in Victoria, Australia, and also to a rough fur cap The Australian town changed its name to Sandhurst, but subsequently officially reverted to its original appellation

Bendy, Old. One of the numerous euphemistic names of the devil, who is willing to bend to anyone's inclination

Benedicite (ben e dīs' i ti) The 2nd pers pl imperative of the Latin verb, benedicere, meaning "bless you," or "may you be blessed" In the first given sense it is the opening word of many old graces ("Bless ye the Lord," etc), hence, a grace, or a blessing

The second sense accounts for its use as an interjection or expression of astonishment, as in Chaucer's

The god of love, A benedicite,
How myghty and how great a lord is he!
　　　　　　　　Knight's Tale, 927

Benedick. A sworn bachelor caught in the snares of matrimony from Benedick in Shakespeare's Much Ado about Nothing

Let our worthy Cantab be bachelor or Benedick, what concern is it of ours —Mrs EDWARDS A Girton Girl, ch xv

Benedick and **Benedict** are used indiscriminately, but the distinction should be observed

Benedict. A bachelor, not necessarily one pledged to celibacy, but simply a man of marriageable age, not married St Benedict was a most uncompromising stickler for celibacy

Is it not a pun? There is an old saying, "Needles and pins, when a man marries his trouble begins " If so, the unmarried man is benedictus —Life in the West (1843)

Benedictine. A liqueur made at the Benedictine monastery at Fécamp, France

Benedictines. Monks who follow the rule of St Benedict They recite the Divine Office at the canonical hours, and are at other times employed in study, teaching or manual labour They are known as the "Black Monks" (the Dominicans being the Black Friars) The Order was founded by St Benedict at Subiaco and Monte Cassino, Italy, about 530, and its members have from the earliest times been renowned for their learning A similar order for nuns was founded by St Scholastica, sister of St Benedict.

Benefice. Under the Romans certain grants of lands made to veteran soldiers were called *beneficia*, and in feudal times an estate held for life in return for military or other service *ex mero beneficio* of the donor was called "a benefice " When the popes assumed the power of the feudal lords with reference to ecclesiastical patronage the name was retained for a "living "

Benefit of Clergy. Originally, the privilege of exemption from trial by a secular court enjoyed by the clergy if arrested for felony In time it comprehended not only the ordained clergy, but all who, being able to write and read, were capable of entering into holy orders It seems to have been based on the text, "Touch not mine anointed, and do my prophets no harm" (1 *Chron* xvi, 22), and it was finally abolished in the reign of George IV (1827) *Cp* NECK-VERSE.

Benelux. A name for the customs union (1947) of Belgium, Netherlands, and Luxemburg, the first letters of which form this convenient portmanteau word

Benevolence A means of raising money by forced loans and without the instrumentality of Parliament, first resorted to in 1473 by Edward IV It seems to have been used for the last time by James I in 1614, but it was not declared illegal till the passing of the Bill of Rights in 1689

Bengal Tigers The old 17th Foot, whose badge, a royal tiger, was granted them for their services in India (1802-23). Now the Leicester Regiment and known simply as 'The Tigers "

Bengodi (ben gō´ dı). A "land of Cockaigne" mentioned in Boccaccio's *Decameron* (viii, 3), where "they tie the vines with sausages, where you may buy a fat goose for a penny and have a gosling into the bargain, where there is also a mountain of grated Parmesan cheese, and people do nothing but make cheesecakes and macaroons There is also a river which runs Malmsey wine of the very best quality", etc , etc

Benicia Boy (ben is´ ya). John C. Heenan, the American pugilist, who challenged and fought Tom Sayers for "the belt" in 1860; so called from Benicia in California, his birthplace

Benjamin The pet, the youngest, in allusion to Benjamin, the youngest son of Jacob (*Gen* xxxv, 18) Also (in early- and mid-19th cent), an overcoat; so called from a tailor of the name, and rendered popular by its association with Joseph's "coat of many colours "

Benjamin's mess The largest share. The allusion is to the banquet given by Joseph, viceroy of Egypt, to his brethren. "Benjamin's mess was five times so much as any of theirs" (*Gen* xliii, 34)

Benjamin tree. A tree of the Styrax family that yields benzoin, of which the name is a corruption, and so used by Ben Jonson in *Cynthia's Revels* (V, ii), where the Perfumer says —

Taste, smell, I assure you, sir, pure benjamin, the only spirited scent that ever awaked a Neapolitan nostril

Benthos (ben´ thos) This is a new word in English, coming directly from a Greek word meaning the sea-bottom. It is now applied particularly to the bottom of deep oceans and to the minute aquatic organisms that live down there.

Beowulf (bā´ ō wulf) The hero of the ancient Anglo-Saxon epic poem of the same name, of unknown date and authorship, but certainly written before the coming of the Saxons to England, and modified subsequent to the introduction of Christianity

The scene is laid in Denmark or Sweden the hall (Heorot) of King Hrothgar is raided nightly by Grendel (*q v*), whom Beowulf mortally wounds after a fierce fight Grendel's dam comes next night to avenge his death Beowulf pursues her to her lair under the water and ultimately slays her with a magic sword Beowulf in time becomes king, and fifty years later meets his death in combat with a dragon, the guardian of an immense hoard, the faithful Wiglaf being his only follower at the end

The epic as we know it dates from the 8th century, but it probably represents a gradual growth which existed in many successive versions In any case, it is not only the oldest epic in English, but the oldest in the whole Teutonic group of languages

Bereans Followers of John Barclay, of Kincardineshire, who seceded from the Scottish Kirk in 1773 They believed that all we know of God is from revelation, that all the Psalms refer to Christ; that assurance is the proof of faith, and that unbelief is the unpardonable sin They took their name from the Bereans, mentioned in *Acts* xvii, 11, who "received the Word with all readiness of mind, and searched the Scriptures daily "

Berecynthian Hero Midas, the mythological king of Phrygia, so called from Mount Berecyntus, in Phrygia

Berenice. The sister-wife of Ptolemy Euergetes, king of Egypt (247-222 B C). She vowed to sacrifice her hair to the gods, if her husband returned home the vanquisher of Asia She suspended her hair in the temple of Arsinoe at Zephyrium, but it was stolen the first night, and Conon of Samos told the king that the winds had wafted it to heaven, where it still forms the seven stars near the tail of Leo, called *Coma Berenices*. The story has been used as the subject of many great works, particularly Racine's tragedy and an opera by Handel

Bergomask (ber´ gō mask) A rustic dance (*see Midsummer Night's Dream*, v, 1), so called from Bergamo, a Venetian province, the inhabitants of which were noted for their clownishness Also, a clown.

Berkshire (bark´ shĕr) From the A.S *Berrocshyre*, either from its abundance of *berroc* (box-trees), or the *bare-oak-shire*, from a polled oak common in Windsor Forest, where the Britons used to hold meetings

Berlin. An old-fashioned four-wheeled carriage with a hooded seat behind   It was introduced into England by a German officer about 1670

Berlin Decree.   A decree issued at Berlin by Napoleon I in November, 1806, forbidding any of the nations of Europe to trade with Great Britain, proclaiming her to be in a state of blockade, declaring all British property forfeit, and all British subjects on French soil prisoners of war.

Bermoothes (bĕr mō ooth′ ēz).   The name of the island in *The Tempest*, feigned by Shakespeare to be enchanted and inhabited by witches and devils

From the still-vexed Bermoothes, there she's hid
The Tempest, i, 2
Shakespeare almost certainly had the recently discovered Bermudas in his mind

Bermudas (bĕr mū′ daz).   The Bermudas was an old name for a district of London—thought to have been the narrow alleys in the neighbourhood of Covent Garden, St Martin's Lane, and the Strand—which was an Alsatia (*q v*), where the residents had certain privileges against arrest   Hence, to live in the Bermudas, to skulk in some out-of-the-way place for cheapness or safety.

Bernard, St.   Abbot of the monastery of Clairvaux in the 12th century (1091-1153). His fame for wisdom was very great, and few Church matters were undertaken without his being consulted

Bonus Bernardus non videt omnia   We are all apt to forget sometimes, events do not always turn out as they are planned beforehand

Poor Peter was to win honours at Shrewsbury school, and carry them thick to Cambridge; and after that a living awaited him, the gift of his godfather, Sir Peter Arley, but *Bonus Bernardus non videt omnia*, and Poor Peter's lot in life was very different to what his friends had planned —Mrs GASKELL *Cranford*, ch. vi.

St. Bernard Soup.   *See* STONE SOUP

Petit Bernard.   Solomon Bernard, engraver of Lyons (16th century)

Poor Bernard.   Claude Bernard, of Dijon, philanthropist (1588-1641)

Lucullus Bernard.   Samuel Bernard. a famous French capitalist (1651-1739)

Le gentil Bernard   Pierre Joseph Bernard, the French poet (1710-75).

St. Bernard dogs.   *See* ST BERNARD PASSES.

Bernardine.   A monk of the Order of St Bernard of Clairvaux, a Cistercian (*q v*).

Bernardo del Carpio.   A semi-mythical Spanish hero of the 9th century, and a favourite subject of the minstrels, and of Lope de Vega who wrote many plays around his exploits He is credited with having defeated Roland at Roncesvalles

Bernesque Poetry   Serio-comic poetry; so called from Francesco Berni (1498-1535), of Tuscany, who greatly excelled in it   Byron's

Beppo is a good example of English bernesque; and concerning it Byron wrote to John Murray, his publisher —

Whistlecraft is my immediate model, but Berni is the father of that kind of writing

Berserker.   In Scandinavian mythology, a wild, ferocious, warlike being who was at times possessed of supernatural strength and fury   The origin of the name is doubtful, one account says that it was that of the grandson of the eight-handed Starkader and the beautiful Alfhilde, who was called *bær-serce* (bare of mail) because he went into battle unharnessed   Hence, any man with the fighting fever on him

Another disregards this altogether and holds that the name means simply "men who have assumed the form of bears."   It is used in English both as an adjective denoting excessive fury and as a noun denoting one possessed of such

Berth.   He has tumbled into a nice berth. A nice situation or fortune   The place in which a ship is anchored is called its berth, and the sailors call it a *good* or *bad* berth as they think it favourable or otherwise.   The space also allotted to a seaman for his hammock is called his berth

To give a wide berth.   Not to come near a person, to keep a person at a distance; literally, to give a ship plenty of room to swing at anchor.

Bertha, Frau.   A German impersonation of the Epiphany, corresponding to the Italian Befana (*q v*)   She is a white lady, who steals softly into nurseries and rocks infants asleep, but is the terror of all naughty children   Her feet are very large, and she has an iron nose

Berthe au Grand Pied (bert ō gron pē ā) Mother of Charlemagne, and great-granddaughter of Charles Martel, so called because she had a club-foot.   She died at an advanced age in 783.

Bertram, Count of Rousillon, beloved by Helena, the hero of Shakespeare's *All's Well that Ends Well*

I cannot reconcile my heart to Bertram, a man noble without generosity, and young without truth, who marries Helena as a coward, and leaves her as a profligate —Dr JOHNSON

Besaile.   A word formerly used in England for a great-grandfather, it is the French *bisaieul*

Writ of besaile.   An old legal term meaning —

A writ that lies for the heire, where his great grandfather was seized the day that he died, or died seised of Land in fee-simple, and a stranger enters the day of the death of the great grandfather, or abates after his death, the heire shall have writ against such a disseisor or abator —*Termes de la Ley* (1641).

Besant.   *See* BEZANT

Beside the Cushion, an odd phrase first used by Judge Jeffreys in the sense of "beside the question," "not to the point."   Any cogent point raised by some wretch in his own defence was ruthlessly swept away as "beside the cushion."

Besom To hang out the besom. To have a fling when your wife is gone on a visit To be a quasi bachelor once more. *Cp* the French colloquialism, *rôtir le balai*
(Literally, "to roast the besom") which means "to live a fast life" or "to go on the razzle-dazzle "

Jumping the besom Omitting the marriage service after the publication of banns, and living together as man and wife

In Lowland Scots, *besom* is a contemptuous name applied to a prostitute or woman of low character, but it is by no means certain that the word is connected with either of the above usages

Bess, Good Queen Queen Elizabeth (1533-1603)

Bess o' Bedlam. A female lunatic vagrant *See* BEDLAM

Bess of Hardwick Elizabeth Talbot, Countess of Shrewsbury (1518-1608), to whose charge, in 1569, Mary Queen of Scots was committed The countess treated the captive queen with great harshness, being jealous of the earl her husband Bess of Hardwick married four times Robert Barlow (when she was only fourteen) Sir William Cavendish, Sir William St Loe, Captain of Queen Elizabeth's Guard, and lastly, George, sixth Earl of Shrewsbury. She built Hardwick Hall, and founded the wealth and dignity of the Cavendish family

Bessie Bell and Mary Gray. A ballad relating how two young women of Perth, to avoid the plague of 1666, retired to a rural retreat called the Burnbraes, near Lynedock, the residence of Mary Gray A young man, in love with both, carried them provisions, and they all died of the plague and were buried at Dornock Hough

Bessie with the braid apron. *See* BELTED WILL

Bessee of Bednall Green. *See* BEGGAR'S DAUGHTER

Bessemer Process. The conversion of cast iron to steel by oxidizing the carbon by passing currents of air through the molten metal, patented by Sir Henry Bessemer in 1856.

Best. At best or **At the very best.** Looking at the matter in the most favourable light Making every allowance
Man is a short-sighted creature at best—DEFOE *Colonel Jack*

At one's best. At the highest or best point attainable by the person referred to

For the best. With the best of motives, with the view of obtaining the best results

I must make the best of my way home. It is getting late and I must use my utmost diligence to get home as soon as possible

To best somebody. To get the better of him; to outwit him and so have the advantage.

To have the best of it, or, **To have the best of the bargain** To have the advantage or best of a transaction

To make the best of the matter. To submit to ill-luck with the best grace in your power
See also BETTER.
4*

Bestiaries or **Bestials.** Books very popular in the 11th, 12th, and 13th centuries, containing accounts of the supposed habits and peculiarities of animals, which, with the legendary lore connected with them, served as texts for devotional homilies They were founded on the old *Physiologi,* and those in English were, for the most part, translations of Continental originals The *Bestiaires* of Philippe de Thaon, Guillaume le Clerc, and *Le Bestiaire d'Amour,* by Richard de Fournival, were among the most popular

Bête Noire (bāt nwar) (Fr black beast) The thorn in the side, the bitter in the cup, the spoke in the wheel, the black sheep, the object of aversion A black sheep has always been considered an eyesore in a flock, and its wool is really less valuable In times of superstition it was looked on as bearing the devil's mark
The Dutch sale of tin is the *bête noire* of the Cornish miners —*The Times.*

Beth Gelert (Beddgelert), or "the Grave of the Greyhound " A ballad by the Hon William Robert Spencer (1769-1834). The tale is that one day Llewelyn returned from hunting, when his favourite hound, covered with gore, ran to meet him The chieftain ran to see if anything had happened to his infant son, found the cradle overturned, and all around was sprinkled with blood Thinking the hound had eaten the child, he stabbed it to the heart Afterwards he found the babe quite safe, and a huge wolf under the bed, dead, Gelert had killed the wolf and saved the child The story is of very old origin and very widespread with variations it is found in Sanskrit and in most ancient literatures
It is told of Tsai Piras of Russia and in the *Gesta, Romanorum,* of Folliculus a knight, but instead of a wolf the dog is said to have killed a serpent The story occurs again in the *Seven Wise Masters* In the Sanskrit version the dog is called an ichneumon and the wolf a "black snake " In the *Hitopadesa* (iv, 3) the dog is an otter, in the Arabic a weasel, in the Mongolian a polecat, in the Persian a cat, etc

Bethlehemites. An order of reformed Dominicans, the friars of which wore a star upon the breast in memory of the Star of Bethlehem, introduced into England about 1257. Also a branch of the Augustinians, founded in Guatemala in 1653 by Peter Betancus, a native of the Canaries, for spreading the Gospel and serving the sick in Spanish America. Its members wore a shield on the right shoulder, on which was shown the manger of Bethlehem

Bethlemenites. Followers of John Huss, so called because he used to preach in the church called Bethlehem of Prague

Bethnal Green. *See* BEGGAR'S DAUGHTER.

Betrothal. An engagement is nowadays considered a more or less private affair which may or may not be made the occasion of celebrations It was formerly—and still is on the Continent—a ceremony of more public importance. Canon law recognizes betrothal as a formal ceremony consisting of an exchange of rings (hence the English engagement ring), a kiss (not unknown in England either), and the joining of hands in the presence of witnesses. In France all this had to be done in the presence of the parish priest It was also usual for the parties to break a coin and each keep a portion This ceremony was binding, though the engagement could be broken by mutual consent. The Church, however, reserved to itself the right to excommunicate either party who, without cause or agreement with the other, broke it off In England the Civil Law came down in the same sense when, in 1735, an Act was passed enabling an aggrieved party to bring an action at common law for breach of promise

Betrothed, The Curiously enough, this title was chosen independently of one another by two great writers who published historical novels in the same year, 1825. Sir Walter Scott's *Betrothed* is a tale of the Crusaders and Wales, Manzoni's *Betrothed (I Promessi Sposi)* is about Milan in the 17th century

Better. Better off. In easier circumstances

For better for worse For ever From the English marriage service, expressive of an indissoluble union

My better half. A jocose way of saying my wife. As the twain are one, each is half Horace calls his friend *animæ dimidium meæ* (*Odes* 1, iii, 8).

To be better than his word. To do more than he promised

To think better of the matter To give it further consideration, to form a more correct opinion respecting it

Bettina. The name taken by Elizabeth Brentano, Countess von Arnim (1785-1859), in her publication, *Letters to a Child*, in 1835. The letters purported to be her correspondence with Goethe (1807-11), but they are largely spurious

Betubium (be tū' bi ūm) The old poetic name for the Cape of St. Andrew, Scotland.

The north-inflated tempest foams
O'er Orka's and Betubium's highest peak
THOMSON. *Autumn*

Between. Between hay and grass. Neither one thing nor yet another, a hobbledehoy, neither a man nor yet a boy

Between cup and lip. *See* SLIP

Between Scylla and Charybdis. *See* CHARYBDIS.

Between two fires Between two dangers Troops caught between fire from opposite sides.

Between two stools you fall to the ground The allusion is to a practical joke played at sea, in which two stools are set side by side, and it is arranged that the victim shall unexpectedly fall between them Compare —

Like a man to double business bound,
I stand in pause where I shall first begin,
And both neglect
SHAKESPEARE *Hamlet*, iii, 3

He who hunts two hares leaves one and loses the other.
Simul sorbere ac flare non possum

Between you and me. In confidence be it spoken Sometimes, **Between you and me and the gatepost** (or bed-post) These phrases, for the most part, indicate that some illnatured remark or slander is about to be made of a third person, but occasionally they refer to some offer or private affair Between ourselves is another form of the same phrase

Betwixt. Betwixt and between Neither one nor the other, but somewhere between the two Thus, grey is neither white nor black, but betwixt and between the two

Betwixt wind and water. A nautical phrase denoting that part of the hull that is below the water-line except when the ship heels over under pressure of the wind It was a most dangerous place for a man-of-war to be shot in; hence a "knock-out" blow is often said to have caught the victim betwixt wind and water

Beulah. *See* LAND OF BEULAH

Bever (bev' er) A "snack" or light repast (originally a drink) between meals through O Fr. *beivre* (Mod Fr *boire*) from Lat *bibere*, to drink—*beverage* has the same ancestry. At Eton they used to have "Bever days," when extra beer and bread were served during the afternoon in the College Hall to scholars, and any friends whom they might bring in

He is none of these same ordinary eaters, that will devour three breakfasts, and as many dinners without any prejudice to their bevers, drinkings, or suppers
BEAUMONT and FLETCHER *Woman Hater*, i, 3

Chapman, in the *Odyssey*, however, uses the word for ' supper'' —

" So chance it, friend," replied Telemachus,
" Your bever taken, go In first of day
Come and bring sacrifice the best you may "
Bĸ xvii, 794

Bevin Boys Under the Emergency Powers Defence Bill, of 1940, certain lads were directed to work in coal mines Ernest Bevin (1881-1951) was Minister of Labour and National Service, and his name was popularly attached to the boys thus directed

Bevis (bē' vis). Marmion's horse *See* HORSE.

Sir Bevis of Hamtown A mediæval chivalric romance, slightly connected with the Charlemagne cycle, which (in the English version) tells how the father of Bevis was slain by the mother, and how, on Bevis trying to avenge the murder, she sold him into slavery to Eastern merchants After many adventures he converts and carries off Josian, daughter of the Soldan, returns to England gets his revenge, and all ends happily. "Hamtown" is generally taken as meaning "Southampton," but it is really a corruption of *Antona,* for in the original Italian version the hero is called "Beuves d'Antone," which, in the French, became "Beuves d'Hantone " Drayton tells the story in his *Polyolbion*, Song ii, lines 260-384

Bevoriskius (be vôr is' ki us), whose *Commentary on the Generations of Adam* is referred to by Sterne in the *Sentimental Journey*, was Johan van Beverwyck (1594-1647), a Dutch medical writer and author of a large number of books

Bevy. A throng or company of ladies, roe-bucks, quails, or larks. The word is the Italian *beva*, a drink, but it is not known how it acquired its present meaning. It may be because timid, gregarious animals, in self-defence, go down to a river to drink in companies.

> And upon her deck what a bevy of human flowers —young women, how lovely!—young men, how noble'—DE QUINCEY *Dream-fugue*

Bey. A Turkish word for the governor of a town or province, also a title conferred by the Sultan, and a courtesy title given to the sons of Pashas. *See* BASHAW, BEGUM, and *cp* DEY

Bezaliel (be zā′ li el) In Dryden's *Absalom and Achitophel* is meant for Henry Somerset, 3rd Marquis of Worcester and 1st Duke of Beaufort (1629-1700) He was an adherent of Charles II

> Bezaliel with each grace and virtue fraught,
> Serene his looks, serene his life and thought,
> On whom so largely Nature heaped her store,
> There scarce remained for arts to give him more
> Pt ii, 947

Bezant (be zănt′) (from *Byzantium*, the old name of Constantinople) A gold coin of greatly varying value struck at Constantinople by the Byzantine Emperors. It was current in England till the time of Edward III. In *heraldry*, the name is given to a plain gold roundel borne as a charge, and supposed to indicate that the bearer had been a Crusader

Bezoar (bē′ zōr) A stone from the stomach or gall-bladder of an animal, set as a jewel and believed to be an antidote against poison

Bezonian (be zō′ ni an) A new recruit, applied originally in derision to young soldiers sent from Spain to Italy, who landed both ill-accoutred and in want of everything (Ital *besogni*, from *bisogno*, need, Fr *besoin*) "Under which king, bezonian? Speak or die" (2 *Hen IV*, v, 3) Choose your leader or take the consequences.

> Great men oft die by vile bezonians
> SHAKESPEARE 2 *Henry VI*, iv, 1

Bianchi (bē āng′ ki) The political faction in Tuscany to which Dante belonged. It and the Neri, both being branches of the Guelph family, engaged in a feud shortly before 1300 which became very violent in Florence and the neighbouring cities, and eventually the Bianchi joined the Ghibellines, the opponents of the Guelphs. In 1301 the Bianchi, includ-ing Dante, were exiled from Florence

Bias (bī′ as) The weight in bowls which makes them deviate from the straight line, hence any favourite idea or pursuit, or what-ever predisposes the mind in a particular direction
Bowls are not now loaded, but the bias depends on the shape of the bowls. They are flattened on one side, and therefore roll obliquely

> Your stomach makes your fabric roll
> Just as the bias rules the bowl
> PRIOR *Alma*, iii

Bib. Best bib and tucker *See* TUCKER

Biberius Caldius Mero The punning nick-name of Tiberius Claudius Nero (the Roman Emperor, Tiberius, who reigned from A D 14

to 37). Biberius (Tiberius) drink-loving, Caldius Mero (Claudius Nero), by metathesis for *calidus mero*, hot with wine

Bible, The English. The principal versions of the English Bible in chronological order are —

Wyclif's Bible. The name given to two translations of the Vulgate, one completed in 1380 and the other a few years later, in neither of which was Wyclif concerned as a translator. Nicholas of Hereford made the first version as far as *Baruch* iii, 20, who was responsible for the remainder is unknown. The second version has been ascribed to John Purvey, a follower of Wyclif. The Bible of 1380 was the first complete version in English, as a whole it remained unprinted until 1850, when the monumental edition of the two versions by Forshall and Madden appeared, but in 1810 an edition of the New Testament was published by H H Baber, an assistant librarian at the British Museum.

Tyndale's Bible. This consists of the New Testament (printed at Cologne, 1525), the Pentateuch (Marburg, Hesse, 1530 or 1531), *Jonah*, Old Testament lessons appointed to be read in place of the Epistles, and a MS translation of the Old Testament to the end of *Chronicles* which was afterwards used in Matthew's Bible (*q v*). His revisions of the New Testament were issued in 1534 and 1535. Tyndale's principal authority was Erasmus's edition of the Greek Testament, but he also used Erasmus's Latin translation of the same, the Vulgate, and Luther's German version. Tyndale's version fixed the style and tone of the English Bible, and subsequent Protestant versions of the books on which he worked should—with one or two minor exceptions—be looked upon as revisions of his, and not as independent translations

Coverdale's Bible. The first complete English Bible to be printed, published in 1535 as a translation out of Douche (i e. German) and Latin by Myles Coverdale. It consists of Tyndale's translation of the Pentateuch and New Testament, with translations from the Vulgate, a Latin version (1527-8) by the Italian Catholic theologian, Sanctes Pagninus, Luther's German version (1534) and the Swiss-German version of Zwingli and Leo Juda (Zurich, 1527-9). The first edition was printed at Antwerp, but the second (Southwark, 1537) was the first Bible printed in England. Mat-thew's Bible (*q v*) is largely based on Cover-dale's. *See* BUG BIBLE *below*

Matthew's Bible. A pronouncedly Protes-tant version published in 1537 as having been 'truly and purely translated into English by Thomas Matthew," which was a pseudonym, adopted for purposes of safety, of John Rogers, an assistant of Tyndale. It was probably printed at Antwerp, and the text is made up of the Pentateuch from Tyndale's version together with his hitherto unprinted translation of *Joshua* to 2 *Chronicles* inclusive and his revised edition of the New Testament, with Coverdale's version of the rest of the Old Testament and the Apocrypha. It was quickly superseded by the Great Bible (*q.v.*), but it is of importance as it formed the starting-point for the revisions which culminated in the Authorized Version   *See* Bug Bible *below*.

The Great Bible   Coverdale's revision of his own Bible of 1535 (*see* Coverdale's Bible *above*), collated with Tyndale's and Matthew's, printed in Paris by Regnault, and published by Grafton and Whitchurch in 1539 It is a large folio, and a splendid specimen of typography   It is sometimes called "Cromwell's Bible," as it was undertaken at his direction, and it was made compulsory for all parish churches to purchase a copy   The Prayer Book version of the Psalms comes from the November, 1540, edition of the Great Bible   *See also* Cranmer's Bible

Cranmer's Bible   The name given to the Great Bible (*q v*) of 1540   It, and later issues, contained a prologue by Cranmer, and on the wood-cut title-page (by Holbein) Henry VIII is shown seated while Cranmer and Cromwell distribute copies to the people.

Cromwell's Bible.   The Great Bible (*q v.*) of 1539   The title-page (*see* Cranmer's Bible *above*) includes a portrait of Thomas Cromwell

The Bishops' Bible.   A version made at the instigation of Archbishop Parker (hence also called "Matthew Parker's Bible"), to which most of the Anglican bishops were contributors.   It was a revision of the Great Bible (*q v*), first appeared in 1568, and by 1602 had reached its eighteenth edition   It is this edition that forms the basis of our Authorized Version.   *See* Treacle Bible *below*.

The Geneva Bible.   A revision of great importance in the history of the English Bible, undertaken by English exiles at Geneva during the Marian persecutions and first published in 1560   It was the work of William Whittingham, assisted by Anthony Gilby and Thomas Sampson   Whittingham had previously(1557) published a translation of the New Testament   The Genevan version was the first English Bible to be printed in roman type instead of black letter, the first in which the chapters are divided into verses (taken by Whittingham from Robert Stephen's Greek-Latin Testament of 1537), and the first in which italics are used for explanatory and connective words and phrases (taken from Beza's New Testament of 1556).   It was immensely popular; from 1560 to 1616 no year passed without a new edition, and at least two hundred are known   In every edition the word "breeches" occurs in *Gen* iii, 7, hence the Geneva Bible is popularly known as the "Breeches Bible" (*q v*)   *See* Goose Bible, Place-makers' Bible, *below*

The Authorized Version.   This, the version in general use in England, was made by a body of scholars working at the command of King James I (hence sometimes called "King James's Bible ") from 1604 to 1611, and was published in 1611.   The modern "Authorized Version" is, however, by no means an exact reprint of that authorized by King James, a large number of typographical errors which occurred in the first edition have been corrected, the orthography, punctuation, etc., has been modernized, and the use of italics, capital letters, etc, varied   The Bishops'

Bible (*q v*) was used as the basis of the text, but Tyndale s, Matthew's, Coverdale's, and the Geneva translations were also followed when they agreed better with the original

The Revised Version.   A revision of the Authorized Version commenced under a resolution passed by both Houses of Convocation in 1870 by a body of twenty-five English scholars (assisted and advised by an American Committee), the New Testament published in 1881, the complete Bible in 1885, and the Apocrypha in 1895

Rheims-Douai Version.   *See* Douai Bible *below*

Taverner's Bible.   An independent translation by a Greek scholar, Richard Taverner, printed in 1539 (the same year as the first Great Bible) by T Petit for T Berthelet   It had no influence on the Authorized Version, but is remarkable for its vigorous, idiomatic English, and for being the first English Bible to include a third Book of Maccabees in the Apocrypha

The Douai Bible (dou' ā)   A translation of the Vulgate, made by English Catholic scholars in France for the use of English boys designed for the Catholic priesthood   The New Testament was published at Rheims in 1582, and the Old Testament at Douai in 1609, hence sometimes called the Rheims-Douai version   *See* Rosin Bible

King James's Bible.   The Authorized Version (*q v*)

Matthew Parker's Bible.   The Bishops' Bible (*q v.*).

There have been several versions of the scriptures in modern English, of which the following are noteworthy.

The New Testament in Modern Speech, translated from the Greek by R F Weymouth, 1903.

A new translation of the Bible by James Moffat (N T , 1913, O T , 1924)

A new translation from the Vulgate by R A Knox, 1944

Specially named editions of the Bible   The following Bibles are named either from typographical errors or archaic words that they contain, or from some special circumstance in connexion with them.—

Adulterous Bible.   The "Wicked Bible" (*q v*).

Affinity Bible, of 1923, which contains a table of affinity with the error "A man may not marry his grandmother's wife "

The Bear Bible.   The Spanish Protestant version printed at Basle in 1569, so called because the woodcut device on the title-page is a bear.

Bedell's Bible.   A translation of the Authorized Version into Irish carried out under the direction of Bedell (d 1642), Bishop of Kilmore and Ardagh

The Breeches Bible   The Genevan Bible (*see above*) was popularly so called because in it

Gen III, 7, was rendered, "The eyes of them bothe were opened   and they sowed figge-tree leaves together, and made themselves breeches " This reading occurs in every edition of the Genevan Bible, but not in any other version, though it is given in the then unprinted Wyclif MS ("ya swiden ye levis of a fige tre and madin brechis"), and also in the translation of the Pentateuch given in Caxton's edition of Voragine's *Golden Legend* (1483)

The Brother's Bible. The " Kralitz Bible " (*q v*)

The Bug Bible. Coverdale's Bible (*q v*), of 1535, is so called because *Ps* xci, 5, is trans-lated, "Thou shalt not nede to be afrayed for eny bugges by night " The same reading occurs in Matthew's Bible (*q v*.) and its re-prints, the Authorized and Revised Versions both read " terror "

Camels Bible, of 1823   *Genesis* xxiv, 61 reads "And Rebekah arose, and her camels" for " damsels."

Complutensian Polyglot   The great edition, in six folio volumes, containing the Hebrew and Greek texts, the Septuagint, the Vulgate and the Chaldee paraphrase of the Pentateuch with a Latin translation, together with Greek and Hebrew grammars and a Hebrew Diction-ary, prepared and printed at the expense of Cardinal Ximenes, and published at Alcala (the ancient Complutum) near Madrid, 1513-17.

The Denial Bible was printed in Oxford in 1792   In *Luke* XXII, 34 the name Philip is substituted for Peter, as the apostle who should deny Jesus

The Discharge Bible   An edition printed in 1806 containing *discharge* for *charge* in 1 *Tim* v, 21 "I *dis*-charge thee before God, . . . that thou observe these things, etc "

The Ears to Ear Bible.   An edition of 1810, in which *Matt* XIII, 43, reads "Who hath ears to *ear*, let him hear "

The Ferrara Bible   The first Spanish edition of the Old Testament, translated from the Hebrew in 1553 for the use of the Spanish Jews   A second edition was published in the same year for Christians

The Fool Bible.   During the reign of Charles I an edition of the Bible was printed in which the text of Psalm xliv, 1 read "The fool hath said in his heart there is a God " For this mistake the printers were fined £3,000 and all copies were suppressed

Forgotten Sins Bible, of 1638   *Luke* vii, 47 reads "Her sins which are many are for-gotten "

The Forty-two Line Bible.   The " Mazarin Bible " (*q.v*).

The Goose Bible.   The editions of the Genevan Bible (*q v*) printed at Dort, the Dort press had a goose as its device

The Gutenberg Bible.   The " Mazarin Bible " (*q v*)

The He Bible   In the two earliest editions of the Authorized Version (both 1611) in the first (now known as "the He Bible") *Ruth* iii, 15, reads: "and *he* went into the city"; the

other (known as "the She Bible") has the variant *"she"* "He" is the correct trans-lation of the Hebrew, but nearly all modern editions—with the exception of the Revised Version—perpetuate the confusion and print "she "

The Idle Bible.   An edition of 1809, in which "the idole shepherd" (*Zech* xi, 17) is printed " the idle shepherd " In the Revised Version the translation is "the worthless shepherd "

Incunabula Bible.   The date on the title-page reads 1495 instead of 1594

Indian Bible   The first complete Bible printed in America, being translated into the dialect of the Indians of Massachusetts by John Eliot, and published by Samuel Green and Marmaduke Johnson (with the king's permission) in 1663

Judas Bible of 1611   *Matt* xxvi, 36 reads "Judas" instead of "Jesus "

The Kralitz Bible.   The Bible published by the United Brethren of Moravia (hence known also as the *Brother's Bible*) at Kralitz, 1579-93

The "Large Family" Bible.   An Oxford edition of 1820 prints *Isaiah* lxvi, 9 "Shall I bring to the birth and not cease [instead of *cause*] to bring forth."

The Leda Bible.   The third edition (second folio) of the Bishops' Bible (*q.v.*), published in 1572, and so called because the decoration to the initial at the *Epistle to the Hebrews* is a startling and incongruous woodcut of Jupiter visiting Leda in the guise of a swan. This, and several other decorations in the New Testament of this edition, were from an edition of Ovid's *Metamorphoses*, they created such a storm of protest that they were never afterwards used

The Leopolita Bible.   A Polish translation of the Vulgate by John of Lemberg (anc , Leopolis) published in 1561 at Cracow

The Lions Bible   A Bible issued in 1804 contains a great number of printers' errors of which the following are typical· *Numbers* xxxv, 18, "The murderer shall surely be put together" instead of "to death"; 1 *Kings* viii, 19, "but thy son that shall come forth out of thy lions" instead of "loins"; *Galatians* v, 17, "For the flesh lusteth after the Spirit" instead of "against the Spirit"

The Mazarin Bible.   The first printed Bible (an edition of the Vulgate), and the first known book to be printed from movable type.   It contains no date, but was printed probably in 1455, and was certainly on sale by the middle of 1456   It was printed at Mainz, probably by Fust and Schoeffer, but as it was for long credited to Gutenberg—and it is not yet agreed that he was not responsible—it is frequently called the Gutenberg Bible.   By bibliographers it is usually known as the *Forty-two Line Bible* (it having 42 lines to the page), to differentiate it from the Bamberg Bible of 36 lines   Its popular name is due to the fact that the copy discovered in the Mazarin Library, Paris, in 1760, was the first to be known and described   A copy of Vol. I in unusually fine state and contemporary binding fetched a record price of £21,000 at auction in London, in 1947.

"More Sea" Bible, of 1641. *Rev* xxi, 1 reads "and there was more sea" instead of ' no more sea "

The Murderers' Bible An edition of 1801 in which the misprint *murderers* for *murmurers* makes *Jude*, 16, read These are murderers, complainers, walking after their own lusts, etc."

The Old Cracow Bible. The "Leopolita Bible" (*q v*)

The Ostrog Bible. The first complete Slavonic edition, printed at Ostrog, Volhynia, Russia, in 1581

Pfister's Bible The "Thirty-six Line Bible" (*q v*)

The Place-makers' Bible. The second edition of the Geneva Bible (*q v.*), 1562, so called from a printer's error in *Matt* v, 9, "Blessed are the placemakers [peacemakers], for they shall be called the children of God " It has also been called the 'Whig Bible "

The Printers' Bible. An edition of about 1702 which makes David pathetically complain that "printers [princes] have persecuted me without a cause " (*Ps* cxix, 161)

The Proof Bible (Probe-Bibel) The revised version of the first impression of Luther s German Bible A final revised edition appeared in 1892

The Rosin Bible The Douai Bible (*q v*) 1609, is sometimes so called, because it has in *Jer*. viii, 22: "Is there noe rosin in Galaad " The Authorized Version translates the word by 'balm," but gives "rosin" in the margin as an alternative *Cp* TREACLE BIBLE *below*

Sacy's Bible. A French translation, so called from Louis Isaac le Maistre de Sacy, director of Port Royal, 1650-79. He was imprisoned for three years in the Bastille for his Jansenist opinions, and there translated the Bible, 1667, completing it a few years later, after his release

Schelhorn's Bible A name sometimes given to the "Thirty-six Line Bible" (*q v*)

The September Bible. Luther's German translation of the New Testament, published anonymously at Wittenberg in September, 1522

The She Bible. *See* HE BIBLE

"Sin on" Bible. The first Bible printed in Ireland was dated 1716. *John* v, 14 reads "sin on more" instead of ' sin no more " The mistake was not found out until the impression of 8,000 copies had been printed and bound.

The Standing Fishes Bible. An edition of 1806 in which *Ezek* xlvii, 10, reads ' And it shall come to pass that the fishes [instead of *fishers*] shall stand upon it, etc."

Sting Bible, of 1746 *Mark* vii, 35 reads "the sting of his tongue" instead of "string."

The Thirty-six Line Bible. A Latin Bible of 36 lines to the column, probably printed by A Pfister at Bamberg in 1460. It is also known as the Bamberg, and Pfister's, Bible, and sometimes as Schelhorn's, as it was first described by the German bibliographer J. G Schelhorn, in 1760

The To-remain Bible In a Bible printed at Cambridge in 1805 *Gal* iv, 29, reads "Persecuted him that was born after the spirit to remain, even so it is now " The words "to remain" were added in error by the compositor, the editor having answered a proofreader's query as to the comma after 'spirit" with the pencilled reply "to remain" in the margin The mistake was repeated in the first 8vo edition published by the Bible Society (1805), and again in their 12mo edition dated 1819.

The Treacle Bible A popular name for the Bishops' Bible (*q v*), 1568, because in it, *Jer* viii, 22, reads "Is there no tryacle in Gilead, is there no phisition there?" *Cp* ROSIN BIBLE *above* In the same Bible " tryacle " is also given for "balm" in *Jer* xlvi, 11, and *Ezek.* xxvii, 17 Coverdale's Bible (1535) also uses the word "triacle " *See* TREACLE

The Unrighteous Bible. An edition printed at Cambridge in 1653, containing the printer's error,' Know ye not that the unrighteous shall inherit [for *shall not inherit*] the Kingdom of God?" (1 *Cor*. vi, 9) The same edition gave *Rom* vi, 13, as ' Neither yield ye your members as instruments of righteousness unto sin," in place of "*un*righteousness " This is also sometimes known as the "Wicked Bible "

The Vinegar Bible. An edition printed at Oxford in 1717 in which the chapter heading to *Luke* xx is given as "The parable of the Vinegar" (instead of "Vineyard")

The Whig Bible. Another name for the ' Place-makers' Bible" (*q v*)

The Wicked Bible. So called because the word *not* is omitted in the seventh commandment, making it, "Thou shalt commit adultery " Printed at London by Barker and Lucas, 1632. The ' Unrighteous Bible " (*q v*) is also sometimes called by this name

The Wife-hater Bible. An 1810 edition of the Bible gives *Luke* xiv, 26 as "If any man come to me, and hate not his father and mother   yea, and his own wife also" instead of "life "

Wuyck's Bible The Polish Bible authorized by the Roman Catholics and printed at Cracow in 1599 The translation was made by the Jesuit, Jacob Wuyck

The Zurich Bible. A German version of 1530 composed of Luther's translation of the New Testament and portions of the Old, with the remainder and the Apocrypha by other translators.

STATISTICS OF THE BIBLE The following statistics are those given in the *Introduction to the Critical Study and Knowledge of the Bible*, by Thos Hartwell Horne, D D , first published

in 1818. They apply to the English Authorized Version.

	O T.	N T	Total
Books	39	27	66
Chapters	929	260	1,189
Verses	23,214	7,959	31,173
Words	593,493	181,253	774,746
Letters	2,728,100	838,380	3,566,480

Apocrypha Books, 14, chapters, 183, verses,
6,031, words, 125,185, letters, 1,063,876

	O T	N T.
Middle book	Proverbs	2 Thess
Middle chapter	Job xxix	Rom xiii and xiv
Middle verse	2 Chron xx,	Acts xvii, 17
	17 & 18	
Shortest verse	1 Chron i, 25	John xi, 35
Shortest chapter	Psalm cxvii	
Longest chapter	Psalm cxix	

Ezra vii, 21, contains all the letters of the alphabet
except j
2 Kings xix, and Isaiah xxxvi., are exactly alike
The last two verses of 2 Chron and the opening
verses of Ezra are alike
Ezra ii, and Nehemiah vii, are alike
The word *and* occurs in the O T 35,543 times, and
in the N.T 10,684 times
The word *Jehovah* occurs 6,855 times, and *Lord*
1,855 times
About 30 books are mentioned in the Bible, but
not included in the canon

Bible-backed. Round-shouldered, like one
who is always poring over a book

Bible-carrier. A vagrant's term for an
itinerant vendor of ballads who does not sing
them; also a scornful term for an obtrusively
pious person.
Some scoffe at such as carry the scriptures with
them to church, terming them in reproach *Bible-
carriers* —GOUGE *Whole Armour of God*, p. 318
(1616).

Bible Christians. An evangelical sect
founded in 1815 by William O'Bryan, a
Wesleyan, of Cornwall, also called Bryanites

Bible-Clerk. A sizar of certain colleges at
Oxford who formerly got advantages for
reading the Bible at chapel.

Biblia Pauperum (*the poor man's Bible*) A
picture-book, widely used by the illiterate in
the Middle Ages in place of the Bible It was
designed to illustrate the leading events in the
salvation of man, and later MSS as a rule had
a Latin inscription to each picture These
biblia were among the earliest books to be
printed, and they remained popular long after
the invention of movable type See MIRROR
OF HUMAN SALVATION.

Bibliomancy. Divination by means of the
Bible See SORTES BIBLICÆ.

Bibliomania. A love of books pursued to the
point of unreason or madness There is a
legend that Don Vicente, a Spanish scholar,
committed murder to obtain possession of
what he thought was a unique book.

Bibliophilia is a devotion to books and the
collecting of them, that stops short of bibliomania

Bibulus (bib' û lus) Colleague of Julius
Cæsar, a mere cipher in office, whence his
name has become proverbial for one in office
who is a mere *fainéant*

Bickerstaff, Isaac. A name assumed by Dean
Swift in a satirical pamphlet against Partridge,
the almanack-maker This produced a paper

war so diverting that Steele issued the *Tatler*
under the editorial name of "Isaac Bickerstaff,
Esq , Astrologer" (1709) Later there was an
actual Isaac Bickerstaffe, a playwright, born
in Ireland in 1735

Bicorn (bī' kôrn) A mythical beast, fabled by
the early French romancers to grow very fat
and well-favoured through living on good and
enduring husbands It was the antitype to
Chichevache (*q v.*)
Chichevache (or *lean cow*) was said to live on good
women, and a world of sarcasm was conveyed in
always representing Chichevache as very poor,—
all ribs, in fact—her food being so scarce as to keep
her in a wretched state of famine Bycorne, on
the contrary, was a monster who lived on good men,
and he was always bursting with fatness, like a prize
pig —SIDNEY LANIER *Shakespere and his Forerunners*, ch vi
Bi-corn (two-horns) contains an allusion
to the horned cuckold

Bid The modern verb, "to bid," may be
from either of the two Anglo-Saxon verbs,
(1) *beodan*, meaning to stretch out, offer,
present, and hence to inform, proclaim,
command, or (2) *biddan*, meaning to importune, beg, pray, and hence also, command.
The two words have now become very confused, but the four following examples are
from (1), *béodan*.—

To bid fair To seem likely; as "He bids
fair to do well", "It bids fair to be a fine day "

To bid for (votes). To promise to support
in Parliament certain measures, in order to
obtain votes

To bid against one. To offer or promise a
higher price for an article at auction

I bid him defiance. I offer him defiance, I
defy him.

The examples next given are derived from
(2), *biddan*.—

I bid you good night. I wish you good night,
or I pray that you may have a good night
"Bid him welcome"
Neither bid him God speed —2 *John* 10, 11

To bid one's beads To tell off one's prayers
by beads See BEADS

To bid the (marriage) banns. To ask if
anyone objects to the marriage of the persons
named "*Si quis*" (*q.v*)

To bid to the wedding. In the New Testament is to ask to the wedding feast

Bid-ale. An entertainment at which drinking formed the excuse for collecting people
together so that they could subscribe money for
the benefit of some poor man or other charity
Bid-ales frequently developed into orgies.
There was an antient custom called a Bidale or
Bidder-ale . . when any honest man decayed in
his estate was set up again by the liberal benevolence
and contributions of friends at a feast to which those
friends were bid or invited It was most used in
the West of England, and in some counties called
a Help-ale
BRAND'S *Popular Antiquities* (1777)

Bidding-prayer (A S. *biddan*; *see* BID). This
term, now commonly applied to a prayer for
the souls of benefactors said before the sermon,
is due to its having been forgotten after the
Reformation that when the priest was telling

the congregation who or what to remember in "bidding their prayers" he was using the verb in its old sense of "pray," *i e.* "praying their prayers" Hence, in Elizabeth's time the "bidding of prayers" came to signify ' the directing" or " enjoyning " of prayers, and hence the modern meaning

Biddy (*i e.* Bridget) A generic name for an Irish servant-maid, as Mike is for an Irish labourer These generic names were once very common for example, Tom Tug, a waterman, Jack Pudding, a buffoon, Cousin Jonathan, a citizen of the United States, Cousin Michel, a German, John Bull, an Englishman, Colin Tompon, a Swiss, Nic Frog, a Dutchman, Mossoo, a Frenchman, John Chinaman, and many others

In Arbuthnot's *John Bull* Nic Frog is certainly a Dutchman, and Frogs are called "Dutch Nightingales " As the French have the reputation of feeding on frogs the word has been transferred to them, but, properly, Nic Frog is a Dutchman

Red Biddy is a highly intoxicating concoction with a basis of cheap port. It is popular among certain elderly women in the East End of London

Bideford Postman Edward Capern (1819-94), the poet, so called from his former occupation and abode

Bidpai. *See* PILPAY.

Bifrost (Icel *bifa*, tremble, *iost*, path) In Scandinavian mythology, the bridge between heaven and earth, Asgard and Midgard, the rainbow may be considered to be this bridge, and its various colours are the reflections of its precious stones

The keeper of the bridge is Heimdall (*q v*)

Big. To look big To assume a consequential air

To look as big as bull beef. To look stout and hearty, as if fed on bull beef Bull beef was formerly recommended for making men strong and muscular

To talk big. To boast or brag

Big Ben. The name given to the large bell in the Clock Tower (or St Stephen's Tower) at the Houses of Parliament It weighs 13½ tons, and is named after Sir Benjamin Hall, Chief Commissioner of Works in 1856, when it was cast

Big Bertha. A gun of large calibre used by the Germans to shell Paris from a range of 75 miles, during the 1914-18 War It was so named by the French in allusion to Frau Bertha Krupp, of armament fame

To get the big bird (*i e* the goose) To be hissed, to receive one's congé, originally purely a theatrical expression To-day the more usual phrase is "to get the bird "

Big-endians. In Swift's *Gulliver's Travels*, a party in the empire of Lilliput, who made it a matter of conscience to break their eggs at the *big end*, they were looked on as heretics by the orthodox party, who broke theirs at the *little end* The *Big-endians* typify the Catholics, and the *Little-endians* (*q v*) the Protestants

Big Gooseberry Season, The. The "silly season," the dead season, when newspapers are glad of any subject to fill their columns, monster gooseberries will do for such a purpose

Big House, an American slang term for prison

Big-wig. A person in authority, a "nob " Of course, the term arises from the custom of judges, bishops, and so on, wearing large wigs Bishops no longer wear them

Bigamy (big' a mi) Though many plots and stories have been worked up on the theme of supposed bigamous marriages, the Law is very plain and outspoken on the matter If a spouse has not been heard of for seven years or more before a second marriage, the prosecution has to prove that the prisoner had good cause to believe that the real spouse was alive, if he or she is able to convince the Court that there was every reason to believe the missing spouse dead, even though seven years had not elapsed since the last communication, the prisoner is entitled to a verdict of Not Guilty The maximum punishment is seven years' penal servitude

Bigaroon (big a roon'). A white-heart cherry (Fr *bigarreau*, variegated, Lat *bis varellus*, double-varied, red and white mixed)

Bight (bit) To hook the bight—*i e* to get entangled A nautical phrase, the bight is the bend or doubled part of a rope, and when the fluke of one anchor gets into the "bight" of another's cable it is "hooked "

Bilbo (bil' bō) A rapier or sword. So called from Bilbao, in Spain, once famous for its finely tempered blades Falstaff says to Ford

I suffered the pangs of three several deaths, first, an intolerable fright, to be detected   , next, to be compassed, like a good bilbo   , hilt to point, heel to head, and then   . .—*Merry Wives*, iii, 5

Bilboes. A bar of iron with fetters annexed to it, by which mutinous sailors or prisoners were linked together The word is probably derived, as the preceding, from Bilbao, in Spain, where they may have been first made Some of the bilboes taken from the Spanish Armada are still kept in the Tower of London.

Now a man that is marry'd, has as it were, d'ye see, his feet in the bilboes, and mayhap mayn't get 'em out again when he would —CONGREVE. *Love for Love*, iii, 6

Bile. It rouses my bile. It makes me angry or indignant In Latin, *bihosus* (a bilious man) meant a choleric one According to the ancient theory, bile is one of the humours of the body, black bile is indicative of melancholy, and when excited abnormally bile was supposed to produce choler or rage

It raised my bile
To see him so reflect their grief aside,
HOOD *Plea of Midsummer Fairies*, stanza 54.

Bilge-water. Stale dregs, bad beer, any nauseating drink Slang from the sea; the bilge is the lowest part of a ship, and, as the rain or sea-water which trickles down to this part is hard to get at, it is apt to become foul and very offensive

In slang *bilge* is any worthless or sickly sentimental stuff

Bilk. Originally a word used in cribbage, meaning to spoil your adversary's score, to *balk* him; perhaps the two words are mere variants

The usual meaning now is to cheat, to obtain goods and decamp without paying for them, especially to give a cabman less than his fare, and, when remonstrated with, give a false name and address.

Bill. The nose, also called the beak Hence, "Billy" is slang for a pocket-handkerchief

Lastly came Winter, clothed all in frize,
Chattering his teeth for cold that did him chill;
Whilst on his hoary beard his breath did freeze,
And the dull drops that from his purpled bill,
As from a limbeck did adown distill
SPENSER *Faerie Queene*, VII, vii, 31

Bill, A. The draft of an Act of Parliament. When a Bill is passed and has received the royal sanction it becomes an Act

A public bill is the draft of an Act affecting the general public.

A private bill is the draft of an Act for the granting of something to a company, corporation, or certain individuals

A true bill. Under the old judicial system before a case went to the criminal Assizes it was examined by the Grand Jury whose duty it was to decide whether or not there was sufficient evidence to justify a trial If they decided that there *was* they were said "to find a true bill", if, on the other hand, they decided there was *not* sufficient evidence they were said "to ignore the bill " Hence *to find a true bill* is a colloquial way of saying that after proper examination one can assert that such and such a thing is true

Bill of Attainder. A legislative Act, introduced and passed exactly like any other Bill, declaring a person or persons attainted It was originally used only against offenders who fled from justice, but was soon perverted to the destruction of political opponents, etc The last Bill of Attainder in England was that passed in 1697 for the attainting and execution of Sir John Fenwick for participation in the Assassination plot

Bill of exchange. An order transferring a named sum of money at a given date from the debtor ("drawee") to the creditor ("drawer") The drawee having signed the bill becomes the "acceptor," and the document is then negotiable in commercial circles just as is money itself

We discovered, many of us for the first time, that the machinery of commerce was moved by bills of exchange I have some of them—wretched, crinkled, scrawled over, blotched, frowsy—and yet these wretched little scraps of paper moved great ships, laden with thousands of tons of precious cargo, from one end of the world to the other. What was the motive power behind them? The honour of commercial men.—LLOYD GEORGE *Speech to London Welshmen*, Sept 19th, 1914

Bill of fare. A list of the dishes provided, or which may be ordered, at a restaurant, etc.; a menu

Bill of health. A document, duly signed by the proper authorities, to certify that when the ship set sail no infectious disorder existed in the place This is a *clean* bill of health, and the term is frequently used figuratively.

A foul bill of health is a document to show that the place was suffering from some infection when the ship set sail. If a captain cannot show a *clean bill*, he is supposed to have a foul one

Bill of lading. A document signed by the master of a ship in acknowledgment of goods laden in his vessel In this document he binds himself to deliver the articles in good condition to the persons named in the bill, certain exceptions being duly provided for. These bills are generally in triplicate—one for the sender, one for the receiver, and one for the master of the vessel

Bill of Pains and Penalties. A legislative Act imposing punishment (less than capital) upon a person charged with treason or other high crimes It is like a Bill of Attainder (*q.v.*), differing from it in that the punishment is never capital and the children are not affected

Bill of quantities. An abstract of the probable cost of a building, etc

Bill of Rights. The declaration delivered to the Prince of Orange (William III) on his election to the British throne, and accepted by him, confirming the rights and privileges of the people. (Feb 13th, 1689)

Bill of sale. When a person borrows money and delivers goods as security, he gives the lender a " bill of sale," that is, permission to sell the goods if the money is not returned on a stated day

Bills of Mortality. In 1592, when a great pestilence broke out, the Company of Parish Clerks, representing 109 parishes in and around London, began to publish weekly returns of all deaths occurring, these later included births or baptisms, but continued to be known as "bills of mortality " The term is now used for those abstracts from parish registers which show the births, deaths, and baptisms of the district

Within the Bills of Mortality means within the district covered by the 109 parishes mentioned above.

Bills payable Bills of exchange, promissory notes, or other documents promising to pay a sum of money

Bills receivable. Promissory notes, bills of exchange, or other acceptances held by a person to whom the money stated is payable

Billabong (Austr) A dried-up water course, from *billa*, a creek, and *bong*, to die

Billings, Josh. The *nom de plume* of Henry Wheeler Shaw (1818-85), an American humorist For many years he published an annual known as *Josh Billings' Farmers' Allminax.*

Billingsgate. The site of an old passage through that part of the city wall that protected London on the river side · so called from the Billings, who were the royal race of the Varini, an ancient tribe mentioned by Tacitus Billingsgate has been the site of a fish-market for many centuries, and its porters, etc., were famous for their foul and abusive language at least three hundred years ago

> Parnassus spoke the cant of Billingsgate
> DRYDEN *Art of Poetry*, c, 1

To talk Billingsgate. To slang, to use foul, abusive language, to scold in a vulgar, coarse style.

You are no better than a Billingsgate fish-fag You are as rude and ill-mannered as the women of Billingsgate fish-market

Billingsgate pheasant. A red herring, a bloater

Billy. A policeman's staff, which is a little bill or billet

A pocket-handkerchief (*see* BILL) "A blue billy" is a handkerchief with blue ground and white spots

The tin in which originally Australian station-hands made tea and did most of their cooking. The word probably comes from *billa*, a creek—hence water

Billy Barlow. A street droll, a merry-andrew; so called from a half-idiot of the name, who fancied himself some great personage He was well known in the East of London in the early half of last century, and died in Whitechapel workhouse. Some of his sayings were really witty, and some of his attitudes really droll.

Billy and Charlie *See* FORGERIES

Billy boy. A bluff-bowed, North Country coasting vessel of river-barge build.

Billy goat. A male goat From this came the term once common for a tufted beard—a "billy"—or goatee.

Billycock Hat (bil' i kok) A round, low-crowned. soft felt hat with a wide brim One account says that the name is the same as "bully-cocked," that is, cocked in the manner of a bully, or swell, a term which was applied to a hat in the description of an Oxford dandy in Amherst's *Terræ Filius* (1721) Another account says that it was first used by Billy Coke (Mr. William Coke) at the great shooting parties at Holkham about 1850, and old-established hatters in the West End still call them " Coke hats."

Bi-metallism (bI met' a lizm). The employment for coinage of two metals, silver and gold, which would be of fixed relative value

Binary Arithmetic (bI' na ri) Arithmetic in which the base of the notation is 2 instead of 10, a method suggested for certain uses by Leibnitz. The unit followed by a *cipher* signifies two, by another *unit* it signifies three, by *two ciphers* it signifies four, and so on Thus, 10 signifies 2, 100 signifies 4; while 11 signifies 3. etc.

Binary Theory. A theory which supposes that all acids are a compound of hydrogen with a simple or compound radicle, and all salts are similar compounds in which a metal takes the place of hydrogen

Bingham's Dandies. The 17th Lancers, so called from their colonel, the Earl of Lucan, formerly Lord Bingham The uniform was noted for its admirable fit and smartness. Now called "The Duke of Cambridge's Own Lancers "

Binnacle (bin' akl). The case of the mariner's compass, which used to be written *bittacle*, a corruption of the Span *bitacula*, from Lat *habitaculum*, an abode

Birchin Lane I must send you to Birchin Lane, *i e* whip you The play is on *birch* (a rod)

A suit in Birchin Lane Birchin Lane was once famous for all sorts of apparel; references to second-hand clothes in Birchin Lane are common enough in Elizabethan books

> Passing through Birchin Lane amidst a camp-royal of hose and doublets, I took occasion to slip into a captain's suit—a valiant buff doublet stuffed with points and a pair of velvet slops scored thick with lace —MIDDLETON *Black Book.* (1604)

Bird This is the Middle English and Anglo-Saxon *brid* (occasionally *byrde* in M.E), which meant only the *young* of feathered flying animals, *foul, foule,* or *fowel* being the M E corresponding to the modern *bird*

An endearing name for a girl

> And by my word, your bonnie bird
> In danger shall not tarry,
> So, though the waves are raging white,
> I'll row you o'er the ferry
> CAMPBELL *Lord Ullin's Daughter*

This use of the word is connected with *bird* (*q v*), a poetic word for a maiden (*cf.* Bride) which has long been obsolete, except in ballads. In modern slang " bird " has by no means the same significance as it is a rather contemptuous term for a young woman

Bird is also a familiar term for the shuttle-cock used in Badminton

A bird in the hand is worth two in the bush ; a pound in the purse is worth two in the book. Possession is better than expectation

It is found in several languages

Italian E meglio aver oggi un uovo, che domani una gallina.

French Un, Tiens vaut, ce dit-on, mieux que deux Tu l'auras

L'un est sur, l'autre ne l'est pas
> La Fontaine, v, iii

German. Ein vogel in der hand ist besser als zehn uber land

Besser ein spatz in der hand, als ein storch auf dem dache

Latin: Certa amittimus dum incerta petimus (*Plautus*).

On the other side we have "Qui ne s'aventure, n'a ni cheval ni mule " "Nothing venture, nothing gain " "Use a sprat to catch a mackerel " " Chi non s'arrischia non guadagna "

A bird of ill-omen. A person who is regarded as unlucky, one who is in the habit of bringing ill news The phrase dates from the time of augury (*q v*) in Greece and Rome, and even to-day many look upon owls, crows, and ravens as unlucky birds, swallows and storks as lucky ones

Ravens, by their acute sense of smell, can locate dead and decaying bodies at a great distance, hence, perhaps, they indicate death Owls screech when bad weather is at hand, and as foul weather often precedes sickness, so the owl is looked on as a funeral bird

A bird of passage. A person who shifts from place to place; a temporary visitant, like a cuckoo, the swallow, starling, etc

A little bird told me so. From *Eccles* x, 20, "Curse not the king, no not in thy thought, . . for a bird of the air shall carry the voice, and that which hath wings shall tell the matter "

Birds of a feather flock together. Persons associate with those of a similar taste and station as themselves   Hence, *of that feather*, of that sort

> I am not of that feather to shake off
> My friend, when he must need me
>   SHAKESPEARE *Timon of Athens*, 1, 1

Fine feathers make fine birds. *See* FEATHER

Old birds are not to be caught with chaff Experience teaches wisdom

One beats the bush, another takes the bird. The workman does the work, master makes the money   *See* BEAT

The Arabian bird. The phœnix (*q v*).

The bird of Juno. The peacock.   Minerva's bird is either the cock or the owl, that of Venus is the dove.

The bird of Washington. The American or bald-headed eagle
The well-known bald-headed eagle, sometimes called the Bird of Washington —WOOD.

Thou has kept well the bird in thy bosom. Thou hast remained faithful to thy allegiance or faith.   The expression was used of Sir Ralph Percy (slain in the battle of Hedgeley Moor in 1464) to express his having preserved unstained his fidelity to the House of Lancaster

'Tis the early bird that catches the worm. It's the energetic man who never misses an opportunity who succeeds.

To get the bird. To be hissed, to meet with a hostile reception. *See* BIG BIRD.

To kill two birds with one stone. To effect two objects with one outlay of trouble.

Birdie. A hole at golf which the player has completed in one stroke less than par (the official figure)   Two strokes less is an *eagle*.

BIRDS PROTECTED BY SUPERSTITIONS:
Choughs were protected in Cornwall, because the soul of King Arthur was fabled to have migrated into a chough

The Hawk was held sacred by the Egyptians, because it was the form assumed by Ra or Horus, and the Ibis because it was said that the god Thoth escaped from the pursuit of Typhon disguised as an Ibis.

Mother Carey's Chickens, or Storm Petrels, are protected by sailors, from a superstition that they are the living forms of the souls of deceased sailors

The Robin is protected, both on account of Christian tradition and nursery legend   *See* ROBIN REDBREAST.

The Stork is a sacred bird in Sweden, from the legend that it flew round the cross, crying *Styrka, Styrka,* when Jesus was crucified. *See* STORK.

Swans are superstitiously protected in Ireland from the legend of the Fionnuala (daughter of Lir), who was metamorphosed into a swan and condemned to wander in lakes and rivers till Christianity was introduced. Moore wrote a poem on the subject

Birdcage Walk (St James's Park, London): so called from an aviary that used to be there for the amusement of Charles II

Birler. In Cumberland, a *birler* is the master of the revels at a bidden-wedding, who is to see that the guests are well furnished with drink   To *birl* is to carouse or pour out liquor (A.S. *byrelian*)

Birmingham Poet. John Freeth, who died at the age of seventy-eight in 1808   He was wit, poet, and publican, who not only wrote the words and tunes of songs, but sang them also, and sang them well.

Birnam Wood (ber´ nam).   Birnam is a hill in Perthshire, 11 miles north-west of Perth, and formerly part of the royal forest known as Birnam Wood.

Birthday Suit. He was in his birthday suit. Quite nude, as when born

Birthstones. *See* PRECIOUS STONES.

Bis (Lat , twice)   French and Italian audiences at theatres, concerts, etc , use this word as English audiences use " Encore."

Bis dat, qui cito dat (he gives twice who gives promptly)—*i e.* prompt relief will do as much good as twice the sum at a future period (*Publius Syrus Proverbs*).

Biscuit. The French form of the Lat. *bis coctum, i.e.* twice baked.   In English it was formerly spelt as pronounced—*bisket*—the irrational adoption of the foreign spelling without the foreign pronunciation is comparatively modern

In pottery, earthenware or porcelain, after it has been hardened in the fire, but has not yet been glazed, is so called   Porcelain groups so prepared at Sèvres, and neither coloured nor glazed, were made fashionable in the 1750s by Mme de Pompadour, who had a great liking for them.

Bise (bēz)   A keen dry wind from the north, sometimes with a bit of east in it, that is prevalent in Switzerland and the neighbouring parts.

> The Bise blew cold.
>   ROGERS *Italy*, pt 1, div ii, stanza 4.

Bishop (A S *biscop*, from Lat *episcopus*, and Gr *episkopos*, an inspector or overseer).   One of the higher order of the Christian priesthood who presides over a diocese (either actually or formally) and has the power of ordaining and confirming in addition to the rights and duties of the inferior clergy

The name is given to one of the men in chess (formerly called the "archer "), to the lady-bird (*see* BISHOP BARNABEE *below*), and to a drink made by pouring red wine (such as claret or burgundy), either hot or cold, on ripe bitter oranges, the liquor being sugared and spiced to taste   Similar drinks are *Cardinal*, which is made by using *white* wine instead of red, and *Pope*. which is made by using *tokay*.

See also BOY BISHOP

The bishop hath put his foot in it. Said of milk or porridge that is burnt, or of meat over-roasted Tyndale says, 'If the porage be burned to, or the meate ouer rosted we saye the byshope hath put his fote in the potte," and explains it thus, "because the bishopes burn who they lust" Such food is also said to be *bishopped*

To bishop. There are two verbs, "to bishop," both from proper names One is obsolete and meant to murder by drowning it is from a man of this name who, in 1831, drowned a little boy in Bethnal Green and sold his body to the surgeons for dissection The other is slang, and means to conceal a horse's age by "faking" his teeth

Bishop Barker An Australian term used around Sydney for the largest glass of beer available, named from Frederick Barker (1808–82), Bishop of Sydney (consecrated 1854) who was a very tall man

Bishop Barnabee. The May-bug, ladybird, etc.

There is an old Sussex rhyme —

Bishop, Bishop Barnabee,
Tell me when my wedding shall be,
If it be to-morrow day,
Ope your wings and fly away

Bishop in Partibus *See* IN PARTIBUS

The Bishop's Bible. *See* BIBLE, THE ENGLISH

Bissextile (bi seks' til) Leap-year (*q v*). We add a day to February in leap-year, but the Romans counted February 24th twice. Now, February 24th was called by them "*dies bissextus*" (*sexto calendas Martias*), the sexule or sixth day before March 1st, and this day being reckoned twice (*bis*) in leap-year, which was called "*annus bissextus*"

Bisson (bis' ón) Shakespeare (*Hamlet*, ii, 2) speaks of *bisson rheum* (blinding tears), and in *Coriolanus* ii, 1, "What harm can your bisson conspectuities glean out of this character?" This is the M E *bisen* and O E *bisene*, purblind The ultimate origin of the word is unknown, but there was an A S *sten*, power of seeing, and it may be from this with the privative prefix *be-*, as in *behead*

Bistonians (bis tō' ni anz) The Thracians; so called from Biston, son of Mars, who built Bistonia on the Lake Bistonis.

So the Bistonian race, a maddening train,
Exult and revel on the Thracian plain,
With milk their bloody banquets they allay,
Or from the lion rend his panting prey,
On some abandoned savage fiercely fly,
Seize, tear, devour, and think it luxury.
PITT. *Statius*, bk. ii

Bit. A piece, a morsel. Really the same word as *bite* (A S. *bitan*), meaning a piece bitten off, hence a piece generally; it is the substantive of *bite*, as *morsel* (Fr *morceau*) is of *mordre*

Also used for a piece of money, as a "threepenny-bit," a "two-shilling bit," etc

Bit is old thieves' slang for money generally, and a coiner is known as a "bit-maker", but in Spanish North America and the West Indies it was the name of a small silver coin representing a portion, or "bit," of the dollar In U S.A a "bit" is 12½ cents, half a quarter.

In the 1920s *bit* was a contemptuous phrase for someone's girl, short for "bit of fluff"

Bit (*of a horse*) **To take the bit in** (*or* between) **one's teeth** To be obstinately self-willed, to make up one's mind not to yield When a horse has a mind to run away, he catches the bit "between his teeth," and the driver has no longer control over him

Bite A cheat; one who *bites* us "The biter bit" explains the origin We say "a man was bitten" when he 'burns his fingers" meddling with something which promised well but turned out a failure Thus, Pope says, "The rogue was bit," he intended to cheat, but was himself taken in "The biter bit" is the moral of Æsop's fable called *The Viper and the File*, and Goldsmith's mad dog, which, "for some private ends, went mad and bit a man," but the biter was bit, for "The man recovered of the bite, the dog it was that died"

Bites and Bams. Hoaxes and quizzes, humbug

[His] humble efforts at jocularity were chiefly confined to . bites and bams—SCOTT. *Guy Mannering*, ch. 3

To bite one's thumb at another. To insult or defy a man by putting the thumbnail into the mouth and clicking it against the teeth It is difficult to see why this should have such provocative significance

Gregory I will frown as I pass by, and let them take it as they list

Sampson Nay, as they dare I will bite my thumb at them which is a disgrace to them, if they bear it. SHAKESPEARE. *Romeo and Juliet*, i, 1.

To bite the dust, or the ground. To be struck from one's horse, hence to be slain. The phrase "Another Redskin bit the dust" was used in R A F. circles, 1939–45, to indicate that an exploit just recounted was considered a "line" (*q v*), it originates from the fabulous Western Stories of Buffalo Bill and other heroes who slew incredible numbers of Red Indians and always survived.

To bite the lip, indicative of suppressed chagrin, passion, or annoyance

She had to bite her lips till the blood came in order to keep down the angry words that would rise in her heart —Mrs GASKELL *Mary Barton*, ch xi

To bite upon the bridle To champ the bit, like an impatient or restless horse

Bitt. **To bitt the cable** is to fasten it round the "bitt" or frame made for the purpose, and placed in the fore part of the vessel

Bitter End, The. *À outrance*, with relentless hostility; also applied to affliction, as, "she bore it to the bitter end," meaning to the last stroke of adverse fortune "Bitter end" in this phrase is a sea term meaning the end of a rope, or that part of the cable which is "abaft the bitts" When there is no windlass the cables are fastened to bitts, that is, wooden posts fixed in pairs on the deck, and when a rope is payed out until all of it is let out and no more remains, the end at the bitts—hence the *bitter* end, as opposed to the other end—is reached   In Captain Smith's *Seaman's Grammar* (1627) we read —

> A Bitter is but the turne of a Cable about the Bits, and veare it out by little and little And the Bitters end, is that part of the Cable doth stay within boord

However, we read in *Prov* v, 4, "Her end is bitter as wormwood," which may share the origin of the modern use of this phrase

Bittock. A little bit, -ock as a diminutive is preserved in bull-ock, hill-ock, butt-ock. etc "A mile and a bittock" is a mile and a little bit

Black for mourning was a Roman custom (*Juvenal*, x, 245) borrowed from the Egyptians Mutes at funerals who wore black cloaks, were sometimes known as the *blacks*, and sometimes as the Black Guards Cp. BLACK-GUARDS.

> I do pray ye
> To give me leave to live a little longer
> You stand about me like my Blacks.
> BEAUMONT and FLETCHER *Monsieur Thomas*, iii, 1

In several of the Oriental nations it is a badge of servitude, slavery, and low birth Our word *blackguard* (*q v*) seems to point to this meaning, and the Lat. *niger*, black, also meant *bad*, *unpropitious* *See under* COLOURS for its symbolism, etc

Black as a crow, etc. Among the many common similes used in connexion with "black" fare black 'as a crow, a raven, a raven's wing, ink, hell, hades, death, the grave, your hat, a thundercloud, Egypt's night, a Newgate knocker (*q v*), ebony, a wolf's mouth, a coal-pit, coal, pitch, soot, etc Most of these are self-explanatory

Beaten black and blue. So that the skin is black and blue with the marks of the beating

Black in the face. Extremely angry The face is discoloured with passion or distress

Mr Winkle pulled . till he was black in the face.—DICKENS *Pickwick Papers*

He swore himself black in the face —*Peter Pindar* (*Wolcott*)

I must have it in black and white, *i e.* in plain writing, the paper being white and the ink black.

O, he has basted me rarely, sumptuously! but I have it here in black and white [*pulls out the warrant*], for his black and blue shall pay him.

JONSON *Every Man in His Humour*, iv, 2

To say black's his eye, *i e* to vituperate, to blame. The expression, **Black's the white of his eye,** is a modern variation To say the eye is black or evil, is to accuse a person of an evil heart or great ignorance

I can say black's your eye though it be grey I have connived at this —BEAUMONT and FLETCHER· *Love's Cure*, ii, 1

To swear black is white. To swear to any falsehood no matter how patent it is.

Black and Tans. Members of the irregular force enlisted in 1920 for service in Ireland as auxiliaries to the Royal Irish Constabulary So called because their original uniform was the army khaki with the black leather accoutrements of the R.I.C.

Black Act. An Act passed in 1722 (9 Geo I, c. 22) imposing the death penalty for certain offences against the Game Laws, and specially directed against the Waltham deer-stealers, who blackened their faces and, under the name of *Blacks*, committed depredations in Epping Forest This Act was repealed in 1827

Black Art. The art practised by conjurors, wizards, and others who professed to have dealings with the devil, so called from the idea that necromancy (*q v.*) was connected with the Lat *niger*, black

Wi' deils, they say, L——d safe s' colleaguin'
At some black art
BURNS *On Grose's Peregrinations*

Black Assize. July 6th, 1577, when a putrid pestilence broke out at Oxford during the time of assize The chief baron, the sheriff, and a large number of the Oxford gentry (some accounts say 300) died.

Blackamoor. Washing the blackamoor white —*i e.* engaged upon a hopeless and useless task The allusion is to one of Æsop's fables so entitled

Black-balled. Not admitted to a club, or suchlike, the candidate proposed is not accepted as a member In voting by ballot, those who accepted the person proposed used to drop a white or red ball into the box, but those who would exclude the candidate dropped into it a black one.

Blackbeetles *See* MISNOMERS

Blackbirds Slang for Negro slaves or indentured labourers Hence *blackbirding*, capturing or trafficking in slaves. Cp BLACK CATTLE.

Black books. To be in my black books. In bad odour, in disgrace; out of favour. A *black book* is a book recording the names of those who are in disgrace or have merited punishment Amherst, in his *Terræ Filius*. or *the Secret History of the Universities of Oxford* (1726), speaks of the Proctor's black book, and tells us that no one can proceed to a degree whose name is found there

Black Book of the Admiralty. An old navy code, said to have been compiled in the reign of Edward III

Black Book of the Exchequer. An official account of the royal revenues, payments, perquisites, etc, in the reign of Henry II Its cover was black leather There are two of them preserved in the Public Record Office

Black Brunswickers. A corps of 700 volunteer hussars under the command of Frederick William, Duke of Brunswick, who had been forbidden by Napoleon to succeed to his father's dukedom They were called "Black" because they wore mourning for the deceased Duke Frederick William fell at Quatre-Bras, 1815.

Black cap. A small square of black cloth This is worn by a judge when he passes sentence of death on a prisoner; it is part of the judge's full dress, and is also worn on November 9th, when the new Lord Mayor takes the oath at the Law Courts. Covering the head was a sign of mourning among the Israelites, Greeks, Romans, and Anglo-Saxons Cp. *2 Sam.* xv, 30.

Black Cattle Negro slaves. *Cp.* BLACK-BIRDS, and *see* BLACK OX.

Black Country, The. The crowded manufacturing district of the Midlands of which Birmingham is the centre It includes Wolverhampton, Walsall, Redditch, etc , and has been blackened by its many coal and iron mines, and smoking factory shafts

Black Death. A plague which ravaged Europe in 1348-51, it was a putrid typhus, in which the body rapidly turned black It reached England in 1349, and is said to have carried off twenty-five millions (one fourth of the population) in Europe alone, while in Asia and Africa the mortality was even greater

Black Diamonds Coals Coals and diamonds are both forms of carbon

Black Dog. *See* DOG A common name in the early 18th century for counterfeit silver coin It was made of pewter double washed ' Black," as applied to bad money, was even then an old term.

To blush like a black dog. *See* DOG

Black Doll. The sign of a marine store shop The doll was a dummy dressed to indicate that cast-off garments were bought *See* DOLL'S SHOP

Black Douglas. *See* DOUGLAS

Blackfellows. The name given to the aborigines of Australia. Their complexion is not really black, but a dark coffee colour

Black Flag. The pirate's flag; the "Jolly Roger " Pirates of the Chinese Sea who opposed the French in Tonquin were known as "the Black Flags," as also were the troops of the Caliph of Bagdad because his banner—that of the Abbasides—was *black*, while that of the Fatimites was *green* and the Ommiades *white* It is said that the black curtain which hung before the door of Ayeshah, Mohammed's favourite wife, was taken for a national flag, and is still regarded by Mussulmans as the most precious of relics It is never unfolded except as a declaration of war A black flag is run up over a prison immediately after an execution has taken place within its walls.

Blackfoot. A Scottish term for a matchmaker, or an intermediary in love affairs, if he chanced to play the traitor he was called a *white-foot* In the first half of the 19th century the name was given to one of the Irish agrarian secret societies —
And the Blackfoot who courted each foeman's
    approach,
Faith¹ 'tis hot-foot he'd fly from the stout Father
    Roach
                                        LOVER

Blackfeet. The popular name of two North American Indian tribes, one an Algonquin nation calling themselves the *Siksika*, and coming originally from the Upper Missouri district, the other, the *Sihasapa*.

Black Friars. The Dominican friars; so called from their black cloaks The district of

this name in the City of London is the site of a large monastery of Dominicans who used to possess rights of sanctuary, etc

Black Friday. December 6th, 1745, the day on which the news arrived in London that the Pretender had reached Derby; also May 10th, 1886, when widespread panic was caused by Overend, Gurney and Co , the brokers, suspending payment

Black Game. Heath-fowl, in contra-distinction to red game, as grouse The male bird is called a blackcock.

Black Genevan. A black preaching gown, formerly used in many Anglican churches, and still used by Nonconformists So called from Geneva, where Calvin preached in such a robe

Blackguards The origin of this term, which for many years has been applied to low and worthless characters generally, and especially to roughs of the criminal classes, is not certainly known It may be from the link-boys and torch-bearers at funerals, who were called by this name, or from the scullions and kitchen-knaves of the royal household who, during progresses, etc , had charge of the pots and pans and accompanied the wagons containing these, or from an actual body, or guard, of soldiers wearing a black uniform The following extract from a proclamation of May 7th, 1683, in the Lord Steward's office would seem to bear out the second suggestion :—
> Whereas . a sort of vicious, idle, and masterless boyes and rogues, commonly called the Black guard, with divers other lewd and loose fellows . do usually haunt and follow the court . Wee do hereby strictly charge all those so called,— with all other loose, idle men . who have intruded themselves into his Majesty's court and stables . . to depart upon pain of imprisonment

Black Hand. A lawless secret society, formerly active in the U S A ; most of the members were Italians

Black Hole of Calcutta. A dark cell in a prison into which Suraja Dawlah thrust 146 British prisoners on June 20th, 1756 Next morning only twenty-three were found alive The punishment cell or lock-up in barracks is frequently called the "black hole "

Black Horse The 7th Dragoon Guards, or "the Princess Royal's Dragoon Guards " Their "facings" are black Also called "Strawboots," "The Blacks "

Black jack. A large leather gotch, or can, for beer and ale, so called from the outside being tarred
He hath not pledged one cup, but looked most
    wickedly
Upon good Malaga, flies to the black-jack still,
And sticks to small drink like a water-rat
                MIDDLETON. *The Witch,* i, 1
    Fill, fill the goblet full with sack¹
    I mean our tall black-jerkin Jack.
    Whose hide is proof 'gainst rabble Rout
    And will keep all ill weather out
            ROBT HEATH *Song in a Siege* (1650)

In Cornwall the miners call blende or sulphide of zinc "Black Jack," the occurrence of which is considered by them a favourable indication Hence the saying, **Black Jack** rides a good horse, the blende rides upon a lode of good ore

A blackjack is a small club weighted at the end, much used by gangsters for knocking people unconscious

Blacklead. *See* MISNOMERS

Black-leg. An old name for a swindler, especially in cards and races, now used almost solely for a non-union workman, one who works for less than trade-union wages, or one who continues to work during a strike

Black letter. The Gothic or German type which, in the early days of printing, was the type in commonest use The term came into use about 1600, because of its heavy, black appearance in comparison with roman type

Black letter day An unlucky day; one to be recalled with regret The Romans marked their unlucky days with a piece of black charcoal, and their lucky ones with white chalk, but the allusion here is to the old liturgical calendars in which the saints' days and festivals are distinguished by being printed in red.

Black list. A list of persons in disgrace, or who have incurred censure or punishment, a list of bankrupts for the private guidance of the mercantile community. *See* BLACK BOOKS.

Blackmail (blăk′ māl). "Mail" here is the Old English and Scottish word meaning rent, tax, or tribute In Scotland *mails* and *duties* are rents of an estate in money or otherwise Blackmail was originally a tribute paid by the Border farmers to freebooters in return for protection or for immunity from molestation Hence the modern signification—any payment extorted by intimidation or pressure

Black Maria The van which conveys prisoners from the police courts to jail There is an unsupported tradition that the term originated in America Maria Lee, a negress of great size and strength, kept a sailors' boarding house in Boston, and when constables required help it was a common thing to send for "Black Maria," who soon collared the refractory and led them to the lock-up

During World War I *Black Maria* was one of the names given to large enemy shells that emitted dense smoke on bursting

Black market. A phrase that came into use during World War II, to describe illicit dealing in rationed goods

Black Mass. This is the name given to the sacrilegious mass said by diabolists in which the Devil was invoked in place of God and various obscene rites performed in ridicule of the proper ceremony

Black Monday. Easter Monday, April 14th, 1360, was so called Edward III was with his army lying before Paris, and the day was so dark, with mist and hail, so bitterly cold and so windy, that many of his horses and men died Monday after Easter holidays is called "Black Monday," in allusion to this fatal day Launcelot says.

It was not for nothing that my nose fell a-bleeding on Black Monday last, at six o'clock i' the morning
SHAKESPEARE *Merchant of Venice*, ii, 5.

February 27th, 1865, was so called in Melbourne from a terrible sirocco from the NNW., which produced dreadful havoc between Sandhurst and Castlemain. Schoolboys give the name to the first Monday after the holidays are over, when lessons begin again.

Black money. *See* BLACK DOG *above*

Black Monks. The Benedictines (*q v*).

Black-out. From the day war was declared against Germany (Sept 3, 1939) to the day hostilities ceased (May 8, 1945) it was obligatory throughout Great Britain to shield windows at night so that no slightest gleam of light should be visible from without. By this means enemy raiding aircraft were deprived of the help of landmarks and were literally left in the dark as to where there were towns or villages.

Black ox. The black ox has trod on his foot—*i e* misfortune has come to him. Black oxen were sacrificed to Pluto and other infernal deities

Black Parliament. This is the name often given to the Parliament that was opened in Nov, 1529, for the purpose of furthering Henry VIII's seizing and consolidating his thefts of Church property. During the six and a half years of its existence it carried out the king's arbitrary orders with a servility no parliament has shown before or since.

Black Pope. *See* POPE.

Black Prince. Edward, Prince of Wales (1330-76), eldest son of Edward III. Froissart says he was "styled black by terror of his arms" (*c.* 169) Stuitt confirms this saying: "for his martial deeds surnamed Black the Prince" (*Antiquities*) Meyrick says there is not the slightest proof that he ever wore black armour, and, indeed, there is indirect proof against the supposition Thus, there was a picture on the wall of St. Stephen's Chapel, Westminster, in which the prince was clad in *gilt* armour, Stothard says "the effigy is of copper gilt", and in the British Museum is an illumination of Edward III granting to his son the duchy of Aquitaine, in which both figures are represented in silver armour with gilt joints The first mention of the term "Black Prince" occurs in a parliamentary paper of the second year of Richard II; so that Shakespeare has good reason for the use of the word in his tragedy of that king —

Brave Gaunt, thy father and myself
Rescued the Black Prince, that young Mars of men,
From forth the ranks of many thousand French.
Richard II, ii, 3.

That black name, Edward Black Prince of Wales.
Henry V, ii, 4

Black Rod. The short title of a Court official, who is styled fully "Gentleman Usher of the Black Rod," so called from his staff of office—a black wand surmounted by a golden lion He is the Chief Gentleman Usher of the Lord Chamberlain's Department, and also Usher to the House of Lords and the Chapter of the Garter.

Black Rood of Scotland. The "piece of the true cross" or *rood*, set in an ebony crucifix, which St Margaret, the wife of King Malcolm Canmore, left to the Scottish nation at her death in 1093. It fell into the hands of the English at the battle of Neville's Cross (1346), and was deposited in St Cuthbert's shrine at Durham Cathedral, but was lost at the Reformation

Black Russia. A name formerly given to Central and Southern Russia, from its black soil.

Blacks, The. The 7th Dragoon Guards *See* BLACK HORSE

Black Saturday. August 4th, 1621; so called in Scotland, because a violent storm occurred at the very moment the Parliament was sitting to enforce episcopacy on the people

Black Sea, The. Formerly called the Euxine (*q v*), this sea probably was given its present name by the Turks who, accustomed to the Ægean with its many islands and harbours, were terrified by the dangers of this larger stretch of water which was destitute of shelter and was liable to sudden and violent storms and thick fogs

Black sheep. A disgrace to the family or community, a *mauvais sujet* Black sheep are looked on with dislike by some shepherds, and are not so valuable as white ones. *Cp* BÊTE NOIRE

Black Shirts. The black shirt was the distinguishing garment worn by the Italian Fascists and adopted in England by their imitators

Blacksmith. A smith who works in black metal (such as iron), as distinguished from a whitesmith, who works in tin or other white metal. *See* HARMONIOUS, LEARNED

Black strap. Bad port wine. A sailor's name for any bad liquor In North America, 'Black-strap" is a mixture of rum and molasses, sometimes vinegar is added
The teething blackstrap was pronounced ready for use,
PINKERTON *Molly Maguires* (1882)

Black swan. *See* RARA AVIS

Blackthorn winter. The cold weather which frequently occurs when the blackthorn is in blossom. *See* ICE-SAINTS.

Black Thursday. February 6th, 1851, so called in Victoria, Australia, from a terrible bush-fire which then occurred

Black Tom. The Earl of Ormonde, Lord Deputy of Ireland in the reign of Elizabeth, so called from his ungracious ways and "black looks."

Black velvet A drink composed of champagne and Guinness stout in equal parts It was the favourite drink of the Iron Chancellor, Bismarck

Black Watch. Originally companies employed about 1725 by the English government to watch the Islands of Scotland They dressed in a "black" or dark tartan. They were enrolled in the regular army as the 42nd regiment under the Earl of Crawford, in 1737 Their tartan is still called "The Black Watch Tartan." The regiment is now officially called "The Royal Highlanders," but is still called "The Black Watch " They are easily recognized by the small bunch of red feathers, known as the

red hackle, which they wear on their bonnets in lieu of a regimental badge

Blade. A knowing blade, a sharp fellow a regular blade, a buck or fop As applied to a man the word originally carried the sense of a somewhat bullying bravado, a fierce and swaggering man, and he was probably named from the sword that he carried.

Bladud (blā' dŭd) A mythical king of England, father of King Lear He built the city of Bath, and dedicated the medicinal springs to Minerva Bladud studied magic, and, attempting to fly, fell into the temple of Apollo and was dashed to pieces (*Geoffrey of Monmouth*)

Blanch, To A method of testing the quality of money paid in taxes to the King, invented by Roger of Salisbury in the reign of Henry I 44 shillings' worth of silver coin was taken at random from the amount being paid The Master of the Assaye then melted a pound's weight of it and the impurities were skimmed off If the resulting mass was then light, the tax-payer had to throw in enough pennies to balance the scale

Blanchefleur (blonsh' flĕr) The heroine of the Old French metrical romance, *Flore et Blanchefleur*, which was used by Boccaccio as the basis of his prose romance, *Il Filocopo* The old story tells of a young Christian prince who falls in love with the Saracen slave-girl with whom he has been brought up They are parted, but after many adventures he rescues her unharmed from the harem of the Emir of Babylon It is a widespread story, and is substantially the same as that of Dorigen and Aurelius by Chaucer, and that of Dianora and Ansaldo in the *Decameron See* DORIGEN

Blank. To draw blank *See* DRAW.

Blank cartridge. Cartridge with powder only, that is, without shot, bullet, or ball. Used in drill and in saluting Figuratively, empty threats

Blank cheque. A cheque duly signed, but without specifying any sum of money, the amount to be filled in by the payee
To give a blank cheque is, figuratively, to give *carte blanche* (*q v*)

Blank verse. Rhymeless verse in continuous decasyllables with iambic or trochaic rhythm, first used in English by the Earl of Surrey in his version of the *Æneid*, about 1540. There is other unrhymed verse, but it is not usual to extend to such poems as Collins's *Ode to Evening*, Whitman's *Leaves of Grass*, or the *vers libre* of to-day, the name blank verse

Blanket. The wrong side of the blanket. An illegitimate child is said to come of the wrong side of the blanket
A wet blanket A discouragement; a marplot or spoil-sport A person is a wet blanket who discourages a proposed scheme "Treated with a wet blanket," discouraged. "A wet blanket influence," etc A wet blanket is used to smother fire, or to prevent one escaping from a fire from being burnt.

Blanketeers. The name given to a body of some 5,000 working men out of employment who assembled on St. Peter's Field, Manchester, March 10th, 1817, and provided themselves with blankets intending to march to London, to lay before the Prince Regent a petition of grievances Only six got as far as Ashbourne Bridge, when the expedition collapsed.

In more recent times journalists have applied the name to similar bodies of unemployed, both in Great Britain and in America.

Blarney. Soft, wheedling speeches to gain some end, flattery, or lying, with unblushing effrontery Blarney is a village near Cork. Legend has it that Cormack Macarthy held its castle in 1602, and concluded an armistice with Carew, the Lord President, on condition of surrendering the fort to the English garrison. Day after day his lordship looked for the fulfilment of the terms, but received nothing but soft speeches, till he became the laughingstock of Elizabeth's ministers, and the dupe of the Lord of Blarney

To kiss the Blarney Stone. In the wall of the castle at Blarney, about twenty feet from the top and difficult of access, is a triangular stone containing this inscription "Cormac Mac Carthy *fortis me fieit fecit*, A D 1446." Tradition says that to whomsoever can kiss this is given the power of being able to obtain all his desires by cajolery. As it is almost impossible to reach, a substitute has been provided by the custodians of the castle, and it is said that this is in every way as efficacious as the original

Among the criminal classes of America "to blarney" means to pick locks.

Blasphemy (blăs'fē mı) The Greek from which this word comes means "evil speaking" but in English the term is limited to any impious or profane speaking of God or of sacred things In Law blasphemy is constituted by the publication of anything ridiculing or insulting Christianity, or the Bible, or God in the shape of any Person of the Holy Trinity At one time the courts held that unorthodox arguments constituted blasphemy. In 1930 a Bill was introduced to make prosecutions for blasphemy illegal, but it was dropped.

Blasphemous Balfour. Sir James Balfour, the Scottish judge, was so called because of his apostasy He died in 1583 He is said to have served, deserted, and profited by all parties

Blast. To strike by lightning; to cause to wither The "blasted oak" This is the sense in which the word is used as an expletive
If it [the ghost] assume my noble father's person,
I'll cross it, though it blast me
SHAKESPEARE· *Hamlet*, 1, 1

The use of Blast! as an imprecation goes back to at least Stuart times, as an imprecatory adjective—"a blasted rascal"—it is employed even by the elegant Chesterfield.

In full blast. In full swing; "all out " As one might say, "The speakers at Hyde Park on Saturday were in full blast." A metaphor from the blast furnace in full operation.

Blatant Beast. In Spenser's *Faerie Queene* "a dreadful fiend of gods and men, ydrad"; the type of calumny or slander He was begotten of Cerberus and Chimæra, and had a hundred tongues and a sting, with his tongues he speaks things "most shameful, most unrighteous, most untrue"; and with his sting "steeps them in poison." Sir Calidore muzzled the monster, and drew him with a chain to Faërie Land The beast broke his chain and regained his liberty The word "blatant" seems to have been coined by Spenser, and he never uses it except as an epithet for this monster, who is not mentioned till the twelfth canto of the fifth book It is probably derived from the provincial word *blate*, meaning to bellow or roar.

Blayney's Bloodhounds. The old 89th Foot, so called because of their unerring certainty, and untiring perseverance in hunting down the Irish rebels in 1798, when the corps was commanded by Lord Blayney
This regiment was later called "the Second Battalion of the Princess Victoria's Irish Fusiliers." The *first* battalion is the old 87th Foot

Blaze A white mark in the forehead of a horse, and hence a white mark on a tree made by chipping off a piece of bark and used to serve as an indication of a path, etc The word is not connected with the *blaze* of a fire, but is from Icel *blesı*, a white star on the forehead of a horse, and is connected with Ger. *blavz*, pale

To blaze abroad. To noise abroad. ' Blaze" here is the Icel *blasa*, to blow, from O Teut *blæsan*, to blow, and is probably ultimately the same as Lat *flare*. Dutch *blazen* and Ger *blasen* are cognate words. *See* BLAZON
He began to publish it much and to blaze abroad the matter.—*Mark* 1, 45

Blazer. A brightly coloured jacket, used in boating, cricket, and other summer sports Originally applied to those of the Lady Margaret crew (Camb), whose boat jackets are the brightest possible scarlet
A blazer is the red flannel boating jacket worn by the Lady Margaret, St John's College, Cambridge, Boat Club.—*Daily News*, August 22nd, 1889.

Blazon. To blazon is to announce by a blast or blow (*see* BLAZE ABROAD *above*) of a trumpet, hence the Ghost in *Hamlet* says, "But this eternal blazon must not be to ears of flesh and blood," *i e* this talk about eternal things, or things of the other world, must not be made to persons still in the flesh. Knights were announced by the blast of a trumpet on their entrance into the lists, the flourish was answered by the heralds, who described aloud the arms and devices borne by the knight hence, to blazon came to signify to "describe the charges borne", and blazonry is "the science of describing or deciphering arms " *See* HERALDRY

Blé de Mars. *See* BLOODY MARS

Bleed. To make a man bleed is to make him pay dearly for something, to victimize him. Money is the life-blood of commerce

It makes my heart bleed It makes me very sorrowful
Take your own will, my very heart bleeds for thee
FLETCHER: *Queen of Corinth*, 11, 3

Bleeding Heart, Order of the. One of the many semi-religious orders instituted in the Middle Ages in honour of the Virgin Mary, whose "heart was pierced with many sorrows."

Bleeding of a dead body. It was at one time believed that, at the approach of a murderer, the blood of the murdered body gushed out. If in a dead body the slightest change was observable in the eyes, mouth, feet, or hands, the murderer was supposed to be present. The notion still survives in some places.

Bleeding the monkey. The same as *Sucking the Monkey*. See MONKEY.

Blefuscu (ble füs' kū). An island in Swift's *Gulliver's Travels*, (q v). In describing it Swift satirized France.

Blemmyes (blem' iz). An ancient nomadic Ethiopian tribe mentioned by Roman writers as inhabiting Nubia and Upper Egypt. They were fabled to have no head, their eyes and mouth being placed in the breast. *Cp.* ACEPHALITES; CAORA.

Blenheim Palace (blen' im). The mansion near Woodstock, Oxfordshire, given by the nation to the Duke of Marlborough, for his victory over the French at Blenheim, Bavaria, in 1704.

When Europe freed confessed the saving power
Of Marlborough's hand, Britain, who sent him forth,
Chief of confederate hosts, to fight the cause
Of liberty and justice, grateful raised
This palace, sacred to the leader's fame.
LORD GEO LYTTELTON *Blenheim*

The building was completed in 1716, and the architect was Sir John Vanbrugh, for whom the epitaph was written —

Lie heavy on him, Earth, for he
Laid many a heavy load on thee

And of all his buildings Blenheim was probably the heaviest.

The Palace has given its name to a small dog, the *Blenheim Spaniel*, a variety of King Charles's Spaniel, and to a golden-coloured apple, the *Blenheim Orange*.

Blenheim Steps. Going to Blenheim Steps meant going to be dissected, or unearthed from one's grave. There was an anatomical school, over which Sir Astley Cooper presided at Blenheim Steps, Bond Street. Here "re-surrectionists" were sure to find a ready mart for their gruesome wares, for which they received sums of money varying from £3 to £10, and sometimes more.

Bless. He has not a sixpence to bless himself with, *i e* in his possession, wherewith to make himself happy. This expression may perhaps be traced to the time when coins were marked with a deeply indented cross, silver is still used by gipsy fortune-tellers and so on for crossing one's palm for good luck.

Blessing. Among Greek and R.C ecclesiastics the thumb and first two fingers, representing the Trinity, are used in ceremonial blessing in the name of the Father, and of the Son, and of the Holy Ghost. The thumb, being strong, represents the *Father*; the long or second finger, *Jesus Christ*, and the first finger, the *Holy Ghost*, which proceedeth from the Father and the Son.

Blighter. Slightly contemptuous but good-natured slang for a man, a fellow, generally with the implication that he is a bit of a scamp or, at the moment, somewhat obnoxious.

Blighty. Soldiers' slang for England or the homeland—came into popular use during World War I, but was well known to soldiers who had served in India long before. It is the Urdu *Vilayati* or *Bilati*, an adjective meaning provincial, removed at some distance, hence adopted by the military for England.

Blimey. One of the numerous class of mild oaths or expletives whose real meaning is little understood by those who use them. This is a corruption of "blind me'."

Blimp, Colonel. The term "blimp" was originally applied to a captive observation balloon, numbers of which were anchored along the front line in World War I. 'Colonel Blimp" was invented by David Low, the cartoonist, to embody the elderly, dyed-in-the-wool Tory, mouthing stale political cliches and opposing any change in any shape. Colonel Blimp is usually depicted with white walrus moustache and naked save for a towel wrapped round him, as his great ideas occur in the Turkish bath.

Blind. A pretence, something ostensible to conceal a covert design. The metaphor is from window-blinds, which prevent outsiders from seeing into a room.

As an adjective *blind* is one of the many euphemisms for "drunk"—short for "blind drunk," *i e.* so drunk as to be unable to distinguish things clearly.

Landlady, count the lawin,
The day is near the dawin,
Ye're a' blind drunk, boys,
And I'm but jolly fou

In engineering a tube, valve or aperture of which one end which would be expected to be open is in fact closed, either as called for in the design or unintentionally through faulty workmanship, is described as blind.

Blind as a bat. A bat is not blind, but if disturbed and forced into the sunlight it cannot see, and blunders about. It sees best in the dusk.

Blind as a beetle. Beetles are not blind, but the dor-beetle or hedge-chafer, in its rapid flight, will occasionally bump against one as if it could not see.

Blind as a mole. Moles are not blind, but as they work underground, their eyes are very small. There is a mole found in the south of Europe, the eyes of which are covered by membranes, and probably this is the animal to which Aristotle refers when he says, ' the mole is blind."

Blind as an owl. Owls are not blind, but being night birds, they see better in partial darkness than in the full light of day.

Blind leaders of the blind. Those who give advice to others in need of it, but who are, themselves, unfitted to do so. The allusion is to *Matt* xv, 14.

To go it blind. To enter upon some undertaking without sufficient forethought, inquiry, or preparation.

When the devil is blind. A circumlocution for "never." For similar phrases *see* NEVER.

You came on his blind side. His soft or tender-hearted side. Said of persons who wheedle some favour out of another. He yielded because he was not wide awake to his own interest.

Blind alley, A. A *cul de sac*, an alley with no outlet. It is blind because it has no "eye" or passage through it.

Blind Beggar of Bethnal Green. *See* BEGGAR'S DAUGHTER. There is a public-house of this name in the Whitechapel Road.

Blind Department, The. In Post Office parlance, a colloquialism for the "Returned Letter Office" (formerly known also as the "Dead Letter Office"), the department where letters with incoherent, insufficient, or illegible addresses are examined, and, if possible, put upon the proper track for delivery. The clerk in charge was called "The Blind Man."

One of these addresses was "Santlings, Hilewite" (St Helen's, Isle of Wight). Dr Brewer had one from France addressed, "A Mons E Cobham, brasseur, Angleterre," and it reached him. Another address was "Haselfeach in no famtshere" (Hazelbeach, Northamptonshire)

Blind ditch. One which cannot be seen. Here blind means obscure, or concealed, as in Milton's "In the blind mazes of this tangled wood" (*Comus*, 181)

Blind Half-hundred, The An old name for the 50th Regiment of Foot. Many of them suffered from ophthalmia in the Egyptian campaign of 1801

Blind Harper, The. John Parry, who died in 1782. He lived at Ruabon, and published collections of Welsh music.

Blind Harry. A Scottish minstrel of the 15th century. He died about 1492 and left in MS an epic on Sir William Wallace which runs to 11,858 lines

Blind hedge. A ha-ha (*q v*)

Blind Magistrate, The. Sir John Fielding, knighted in 1761, was born blind. Sitting at Bow Street, he was in the commission of the Peace for Middlesex, Surrey, Essex, and the liberties of Westminster

Blind Man. *See* BLIND DEPARTMENT

Blindman's buff. A very old-established name for an old and well-known children's game. "Buff" here is short for 'buffet,' and is an allusion to the three buffs or pats which the "blind man" gets when he has caught a player.

Blindman's holiday. The hour of dusk, when it is too dark to work, and too soon to light candles. The phrase was in common use at least as early as Elizabethan times.

What will not blind Cupid doe in the night, which is his blindman's holiday
T. NASHE *Lenten Stuffe* (1599)

Blindmen's Dinner, The. A dinner unpaid for, the landlord being made the victim. Eulenspiegel (*q v*) being asked for alms by twelve blind men, said, "Go to the inn; eat, drink, and be merry, my men, and here are

twenty florins to pay the bill." The blind men thanked him, each supposing one ot the others had received the money. Reaching the inn, they told the landlord of their luck, and were at once provided with food and drink to the amount of twenty florins. On asking for payment, they all said, "Let him who received the money pay for the dinner", but none had received a penny.

Blindworm. *See* MISNOMERS.

Blind spot. This is a small area not sensitive to light, situated on the retina where the optic nerve enters. The term is used figuratively to describe some area in one's discernment where judgment and understanding are lacking.

Block. **To block a Bill.** In parliamentary language means to postpone or prevent the passage of a Bill by giving notice of opposition, and thus preventing its being taken after half-past twelve at night.

A chip of the old block. *See* CHIP

To cut blocks with a razor. *See* CUT.

Blockhead. A stupid person, one without brains. The allusion is to a wig-maker's dummy or *tête a perruque*, on which he fits his wigs

Your wit will not so soon out as another man's will, 'tis strongly wedged up in a blockhead
SHAKESPEARE *Coriolanus*, ii, 3

Blockhousers. The oldest Negro Regiment in the U S Army, nicknamed from its gallant assault on a blockhouse in the Spanish-American War

Blondin (blon'din) One of the most famous acrobats of all time. He was a Frenchman (b 1824, d 1897), his real name being Jean François Gravelet. He began performing at the age of five and acquired considerable repute by his aerial tricks. His great feat, however, was performed in 1859 when he crossed the Niagara Falls on a tight-rope. This he did several times, embellishing the performance by wheeling a barrow, twirling an umbrella, etc. He made a fortune by this show, and soon after his return settled in England, where he gave performances until too old to do so

Blood. In figurative use, *blood*, being treated as the typical component of the body inherited from parents and ancestors, came to denote members of a family or race as distinguished from other families and races, hence family descent generally, and hence one of noble or gentle birth, which latter degenerated into a buck, or aristocratic rowdy

The gallants of those days pretty much resembled the bloods of ours
GOLDSMITH *Reverie at the Boar's Head Tavern*

A blood horse. A thoroughbred, a horse of good parentage or stock.

A prince of the blood. One of the Royal Family. *See* BLOOD ROYAL

Bad blood. Anger quarrels, as, *It stirs up bad blood.* It provokes to illfeeling and contention

Blood and iron policy—*i e* war policy. No explanation needed

Blood is thicker than water. Relationship has a claim which is generally acknowledged It is better to seek kindness from a kinsman than from a stranger Water soon evaporates and leaves no mark behind, not so blood So the interest we take in a stranger is thinner and more evanescent than that which we take in a blood relation. The proverb occurs in Ray's Collection (1672) and is probably many years older.

Blood money. Money paid to a person for giving such evidence as shall lead to the conviction of another, money paid to the next of kin to induce him to forgo his "right" of seeking blood for blood, or (formerly) as compensation for the murder of his relative, money paid to a person for betraying another, as Judas was paid blood-money for his betrayal of the Saviour

Blood relation. One in direct descent from the same father or mother, one of the same family stock

Blue blood. *See* BLUE.

In cold blood Deliberately, not in the excitement of passion or of battle

It makes one's blood boil. It provokes indignation and anger

It runs in the blood It is inherited or exists in the family or race
   It runs in the blood of our family —SHERIDAN *The Rivals*, iv, 2

Laws written in blood Demades said that the laws of Draco were written in blood, because every offence was punishable by death

My own flesh and blood My own children, brothers, sisters, or other near kindred

The blood of the Grograms. Taffety gentility, make-believe aristocratic blood. Grogram is a coarse silk taffety stiffened with gum (Fr. *gros grain*).
   Our first tragedian was always boasting of his being "an old actor," and was full of the "blood of the Grograms "
                  C THOMSON *Autobiography*, p 200.

Blood, toil, tears and sweat. The words used by Winston Churchill in his speech to the House of Commons, 13 May, 1940, on becoming Prime Minister "I would say to the House as I have said to those who have joined this government, I have nothing to offer but blood, toil, tears and sweat " In his *Anatomie of the World* John Donne says, "Mollifie it with thy teares, or sweat, or blood "

The field of blood. Aceldama (*Acts* i, 19), the piece of ground purchased with the blood-money of our Saviour, and set apart for the burial of strangers.
   The field of the battle of Cannæ, where Hannibal defeated the Romans, 216 B C., is also so called.

Young blood. Fresh members, as, "To bring young blood into the concern " The term with the article, "a young blood," signifies a young rip, a wealthy young aristocrat of convivial habits

Blood Royal The royal family or race, also called simply "the blood," as "a prince of the blood "

Man of blood. Any man of violent temper David was so called in 2 *Sam* xvi, 7 (Rev. Ver), and the Puritans applied the term to Charles I

Man of Blood and Iron. An epithet bestowed on Bismarck (1815-98), for many years Chancellor of Prussia and Germany, on account of his war policy and his indomitable will expressed in his first speech after appointment as Minister-General

Bloodhound Figuratively, one who follows up an enemy with pertinacity Bloodhounds used to be employed for tracking wounded game by the blood spilt, subsequently they were employed for tracking criminals and slaves who had made their escape, and were hunters of blood, not hunters *by* blood The most noted breeds are the African, Cuban, and English.

Bloodstone. *See* HELIOTROPE

Bloodsucker. An animal like the leech, or the fabled vampire which voraciously sucks blood and which, if allowed, will rob a person of all vitality. Hence, a sponger, a parasite, or one intent upon another s material ruin
   See REGIMENTAL NICKNAMES

Bloody. Several fanciful derivations have been found for this expletive, once considered more vulgar than recent usage suggests. The most romantic of these was that the word is a corruption of "By our Lady", another school of thought imagined that it came from an association of ideas with "bloods" or aristocratic rowdies There is little doubt, however, that its original meaning was, as it implies, "covered with blood " Partly owing to its unpleasant, violent, and lurid associations, it easily became applied as an intensive in a general way.
   It was bloody hot walking to-day —SWIFT *Journal to Stella*, letter xxii

As a title the adjective has been bestowed on Otto II, Emperor of the Holy Roman Empire, 973-983, and the English Queen Mary (1553-58), has been called "Bloody Mary" on account of the religious persecutions which took place in her reign.

The Bloody Eleventh. The old 11th Foot "The Devonshire Regiment," was so called from their having been several times nearly annihilated, as at Almanza, Fontenoy, Roucoux, Ostend, and Salamanca (1812), in capturing a French standard

Bloody Assizes. The infamous assizes held by Judge Jeffreys in 1685. Three hundred were executed, more whipped or imprisoned, and a thousand sent to the plantations for taking part in Monmouth's rebellion

Bloody Bill. The 31 Henry VIII, c. 14, which denounced death, by hanging or burning, on all who denied the doctrine of transubstantiation

Bloody-bones. A hobgoblin, generally "Raw-head and Bloody-Bones "

Bloody Eleventh. *See* REGIMENTAL NICKNAMES

Bloody hand. A term in old Forest Law denoting a man whose hand was bloody, and was therefore presumed to be the person guilty of killing the deer shot or otherwise slain In *heraldry*, the "bloody hand" is the badge of a baronet, and the armorial device of Ulster In both uses it is derived from the O'Neils *See* RED HAND, and HAND, THE RED

Bloody Mars. A local English name for a variety of wheat It is a corruption of the French *blé de Mars*, March grain

Bloody-nose. The popular name of the common wayside beetle, *Timarcha lævigata*, which can emit a reddish liquid from its joints when disturbed

Bloody Pots, The. *See* KIRK OF SKULLS

Bloody Thursday. The Thursday in the first week in Lent used to be so called

Bloody Wedding. The massacre of St. Bartholomew in 1572 is so called because it took place during the marriage feast of Henri (afterwards Henri IV) and Marguerite (daughter of Catherine de' Medici).

Bloom, Leopold. *See* ULYSSES.

Bloomers. A female costume consisting of a short skirt and loose trousers gathered closely round the ankles, so called from Mrs Amelia Bloomer, of New York, who tried in 1849 to introduce the fashion Nowadays "bloomers" is usually applied only to the trousers portion of the outfit

Blooming. A meaningless euphemism for the slang epithet "bloody"

Blouse. A short smock-frock of a blue colour worn commonly by French workmen *Bleu* is French argot for *manteau*.

A garment called *bliaut* or *bliaus*, which appears to have been another name for a surcoat . In this *bliaus* we may discover the modern French *blouse*, a . . smock-frock
PLANCHE *British Costume*

The word is more commonly used for a woman's light bodice worn with a skirt

Blow. The English spelling *blow* represents three words of different origin, viz.—

(1) To move as a current of air, to send a current of air from the mouth, etc , from the A.S *blawan*, cognate with the Mod Ger *blähen* and Lat *flare*.

(2) To blossom, to flourish, from A S *blowan*, cognate with *bloom*, Ger *blühen*, and Lat *florera*, and

(3) A stroke with the fist, etc , which is most likely from an old Dutch word, *blau*, to strike

In the following phrases, etc , the numbers refer to the group to which each belongs

A blow out (1). A "tuck in," or feast which swells out the paunch Also applied to the sudden flattening of a pneumatic tyre when the inner tube is punctured

At one blow (3). By one stroke.

Blow me tight (1). A mild oath or expletive

If there's a soul, will give me food, or find me in employ,
By day or night, then blow me tight' (he *was* a vulgar boy)
Ingoldsby Legends: Misadventures at Margate

You be blowed (1). A mild imprecation or expletive

Don't link yourself with vulgar folks, who've got no fixed abode,
Tell lies, use naughty words, and say " they wish they may be blow'd!"
Ingoldsby Legends, ibid

To blow one's top (1) To lose one's temper

Blown (1), in the phrase ' fly-blown," is a legacy from pre-scientific days, when naturalists thought that maggots were actually blown on to the meat by blow-flies.

Blown (1) Phrase applied to an internal combustion engine in which the fuel is forced into the cylinders with the aid of a super-charger, or blower

Blown herrings (1). Herrings bloated, swollen, or cured by smoking, another name for bloaters

Blown upon (1) Made the subject of a scandal. *His reputation has been blown upon*, means that he has been the subject of talk wherein something derogatory was hinted at or asserted. Blown upon by the breath of slander.

Blow-point (1) A game similar to pea-puffing, only instead of peas small wooden skewers or bits of pointed wood were puffed through the tube The game is alluded to by Florio, Strutt, and several other authors

It will soon blow over (1) It will soon be no longer talked about, it will soon come to an end, as a gale or storm blows over or ceases

I will blow him up sky high (1) Give him a good scolding The metaphor is from blasting by gunpowder.

The first blow is half the battle (3) Well begun is half done Pythagoras used to say, "The beginning is half the whole" "*Incipe Dimidium facti est cœposse*" (Ausonius). "*Dimidium facti, qui cœpit, habet*" (Horace) "*Ce n'est que le premier pas qui coûte*"

To blow a cloud (1) To smoke a cigar, pipe, etc This term was in use in Queen Elizabeth's reign.

To blow a trumpet (1) To sound a trumpet

But when the blast of war blows in our ears,
Let us be tigers in our fierce deportment
Henry V, iii, 1

To blow great guns (1) Said of a wind which blows so violently that its noise resembles the roar of artillery

To blow hot and cold (1) To be inconsistent The allusion is to the fable of a traveller who was entertained by a satyr Being cold, the traveller blew his fingers to warm them, and afterwards blew his hot broth to cool it The satyr, in great indignation, turned him out of doors, because he blew both hot and cold with the same breath.

To blow off steam (1) To get rid of super-fluous temper The allusion is to the forcible escape of superfluous steam no longer required

To blow the gaff (1) To let out a secret, to inform against a companion, to "peach." Here *gaff* is a variant of *gab* (*q v*)

To blow up (1). To inflate, as a bladder, to explode, to burst into fragments, to censure severely. *See I will blow him up*, above

Without striking a blow Without coming to a contest.

Blower. A common term in the Army for wireless and telephone apparatus Also term in motor sport used for a supercharger, a supercharged engine is said to be "blown '

Blowzelinda (blou ze lin´ dä) A common 18th-century name applied to a rustic girl *See* Gay's *Shepherd's Week* —

Sweet is my toil when Blowzelind is near,
Of her bereft, 'tis winter all the year .
Come, Blowzelinda, ease thy swain's desire,
My summer's shadow and my winter's fire
Pastoral, i

A *blouze* was a ruddy fat-cheeked wench —
Sweet blowze, you are a beauteous blossom, sure
SHAKESPEARE *Titus Andronicus*, iv, 2

Blowzy. Coarse, red-faced, bloated, applied to women. The word is allied to blush, blaze, etc.

A face made blowzy by cold and damp
GEORGE ELIOT *Silas Marner*

Blubber (M E *bloberen*, probably of imitative origin) To cry like a child, with noise and slavering, *cp slobber*, *slaver*

I play the boy, and blubber in thy bosom
OTWAY *Venice Preserved*, i, 1

The word is also used attributively, as in blubber-lips, blubber-cheeks, fat flabby cheeks, like whale's blubber.

Bluchers (bloo´ kerz) Half boots, so called after Field-Marshal von Blucher (1742-1819)

Bludger (Austr) Originally (19th century) a pimp, but later any scrounger or one taking profit without risk In World War I *to bludge on the flag* meant to slack in the army. The opprobrious adjective *bludging* is now widely used

Blue or *Azure* is the symbol of Divine eternity and human immortality Consequently, it is a mortuary colour—hence its use in covering the coffins of young persons When used for the garment of an angel, it signifies faith and fidelity As the dress of the Virgin, it indicates modesty In *blazonry*, it signifies chastity, loyalty, fidelity, and a spotless reputation, and seems frequently to represent silver, thus we have the *Blue Boar* of Richard III, the *Blue Lion* of the Earl of Mortimer, the *Blue Swan* of Henry IV, the *Blue Dragon*, etc

The *Covenanters* wore blue as their badge, in opposition to the scarlet of royalty They based their choice on *Numb* xv, 38 "Speak unto the children of Israel, and bid them that they make them fringes in the borders of their garments . . and that they put upon the fringe . . a ribband of blue."

See COLOURS for its symbolisms

A blue, or a "staunch blue," descriptive of political opinions, for the most part means a Tory, for in most counties the Conservative colour is blue *See* BLUE-COAT SCHOOL, BLUE STOCKING.

Also, at Oxford and Cambridge, a man who has been chosen to represent his 'Varsity in rowing, cricket, etc Some sports, such as

hockey and lacrosse, come in a lower category, and for these a "half blue" is awarded

A dark blue An Oxford man or Harrow boy

A light blue. A Cambridge man or Eton boy

The Oxford Blues The Royal Horse Guards were so called in 1690, from the Earl of Oxford their commander and the blue facings Wellington, in one of his dispatches, writes —"I have been appointed colonel, of the Blues "

True blue will never stain A really noble heart will never disgrace itself The reference is to blue aprons and blouses worn by butchers, which do not show blood-stains

True as Coventry blue The reference is to a blue cloth and blue thread made at Coventry, noted for its permanent dye.

'Twas Presbyterian true blue (*Hudibras*, i, 1) The allusion is to the blue apron which some of the Presbyterian preachers used to throw over their preaching-tub before they began to address the people In one of the Rump songs we read of a person going to hear a lecture, and the song says—

Where I a tub did view,
Hung with an apron blue,
'Twas the preacher's, I conjecture

To look blue. To be depressed

He was blue in the face. He had made too great an effort, was breathless and exhausted either bodily or with suppressed anger or emotion

A priest of the blue bag. A cant name for a barrister *See* LAWYER'S BAG.

Bluebeard A bogy, a merciless tyrant, in Charles Perrault's *Contes du Temps* (1697) The tale of Bluebeard (Chevalier Raoul) is known to every child, but many have speculated on the original of this despot Some say it was a satire on Henry VIII, of wife-killing notoriety Dr C Taylor thinks it is a type of the castle lords in the days of knight-errantry Holinshed calls Giles de Retz, Marquis de Laval, the original Bluebeard, he lived at Machecoul, in Brittany, was accused of murdering six of his seven wives, and was ultimately strangled and burnt in 1440

Campbell has a Bluebeard story in his *Tales of the Western Highlands*, called *The Widow and her Daughters*; it is found also in Strapola's *Nights*, the *Pentamerone*, and elsewhere *Cp* the *Story of the Third Calender* in the *Arabian Nights*

Bluebeard's key. When the blood stain of this key was rubbed out on one side, it appeared on the opposite side, so prodigality being overcome will appear in the form of meanness, and friends, over-fond, will often become enemies

Blue billy A blue neckcloth with white spots *See* BILLY.

Blue Bird of Happiness This is an idea elaborated from Maeterlinck's play of that name, first produced in London in 1910 It tells the story of a boy and girl seeking ' the blue bird" which typifies happiness. This fancy of Maeterlinck's introduced for a time the phrase into English

Blue blood High or noble birth or descent; it is a Spanish phrase, and refers to the fact that the veins shown in the skin of the pure-blooded Spanish aristocrat, whose race had suffered no Moorish or other admixture, were more blue than those of persons of mixed, and therefore inferior, ancestry.

Blue Boar. A public-house sign; the cognisance of Richard III In Leicester is a lane in the parish of St Nicholas, called the *Blue Boar Lane*, because Richard slept there the night before the battle of Bosworth Field

> The bristly boar, in infant gore,
> Wallows beneath the thorny shade
>   GRAY *The Bard*

Blue Bonnets, or Blue Caps The Highlanders of Scotland, or the Scots generally. So called from the blue woollen cap at one time in very general use in Scotland, and still far from uncommon.

> He is there, too,   and a thousand blue caps more.
>   1 *Henry IV*, ii, 4

Blue Books. In England, parliamentary reports and official publications presented by the Crown to both Houses of Parliament Each volume is in folio, and is covered with a blue wrapper

Short Acts of Parliament, etc , even without a wrapper, come under the same designation.

The official colour of Spain is *red*, of Italy *green*, of France *yellow*, of Germany and Portugal, *white*

In America the "Blue Books" (like our "Red Books") contain lists of those persons who hold government appointments

Blue bottle A constable, a policeman; also, formerly, an almsman, or anyone whose distinctive dress was blue.

> You proud varlets, you need not be ashamed to wear blue when your master is one of your fellows
>   DEKKER *The Honest Whore* (1602)

Shakespeare makes Doll Tearsheet denounce the beadle as a "blue-bottle rogue."

> I ll have you soundly swinged for this, you blue-bottle rogue —SHAKESPEARE 2 *Henry IV*, v, 4

Blue Caps. See BLUE BONNETS

Blue-coat School. Christ's Hospital is so called because the boys there wear a long *blue coat* girded at the loins with a leather belt. Some who attend the mathematical school are termed *King's boys*, and those who constitute the highest class are *Grecians* The school was founded by Edward VI the year of his death It was moved from London to Horsham in 1902

Blue-eyed Maid. Minerva, the goddess of wisdom, is so called by Homer

> Now Prudence gently pulled the poet's ear,
> And thus the daughter of the Blue-eyed Maid,
> In flattery's soothing sounds, divinely said,
> " O Peter, eldest-born of Phœbus, hear "
>   PETER PINDAR *A Falling Minister*

Blue fish, The. The shark, technically called *Carcharias glaucus*, the upper parts of which are blue This should be distinguished from *blue fish*, an edible fish found in American waters

Blue gown. A harlot. Formerly a blue gown was a dress of ignominy for a prostitute who had been arrested and placed in the House of Correction

The bedesmen, to whom the kings of Scotland distributed certain alms, were also known as *blue gowns*, because their dress was a cloak or gown of coarse blue cloth. The number of these bedesmen was equal to that of the king's years, so that an extra one was added at every returning birthday. These paupers were privileged to ask alms through the whole realm of Scotland See GABER-LUNZIE

Blue Guards. So the Oxford Blues, now called the Royal Horse Guards, were called during the campaign in Flanders (1742-5)

Blue Hen's Chickens. The nickname for inhabitants of the State of Delaware It is said that in the Revolutionary War a certain Captain Caldwell commanded, and brought to a high state of efficiency, a Delaware regiment. He used to say that no cock could be truly game whose mother was not a blue hen. Hence the Delaware regiment became known as "Blue Hen's Chickens," and the name was transferred to the inhabitants of the State generally

Bluejackets. Sailors, so called because the colour of their jackets is blue.

Blue John. A blue fluor-spar, found in the Blue John mine near Castleton, Derbyshire, so called to distinguish it from the Black Jack, an ore of zinc Called John from John Kirk, a miner, who first noticed it

Blue laws This is a phrase used in U.S.A. to describe laws which interfere with personal freedom, tastes and habits, such as sumptuary laws and those regulating private morals The name was first given to several laws of this kind said to have been imposed in the colonies of Connecticut and New Haven in the early 18th century.

Blue-light Federalists. A name given to those Americans who were believed to have made friendly ("blue-light") signals to British ships in the war of 1812.

Bluemantle One of the four English Pursuivants (*q v*) attached to the College of Arms, or Heralds' College, so called from his official robe

Blue Monday The Monday before Lent, spent in dissipation It is said that dissipation gives everything a blue tinge. Hence "blue" means tipsy

Blue moon. Once in a blue moon. Very rarely indeed

Blue murder. To shout **blue murder.** Indicative more of terror or alarm than of real danger It appears to be a play on the French exclamation *morbleu*, there may also be an allusion to the common phrase "blue ruin "

Blue-noses The Nova Scotians

> "Pray, sir," said one of my fellow-passengers, "can you tell me the reason why the Nova Scotians are called ' Blue-noses ' ? "
> "It is the name of a potato," said I, "which they produce in the greatest perfection, and boast to be the best in the world The Americans have, in consequence, given them the nickname of *Blue Noses*."
>   HALIBURTON. *Sam Slick.*

Blue Peter. A flag with a blue ground and white square in the centre, hoisted as a signal that the ship is about to sail. It takes its name from a "repeater", a naval flag hoisted to indicate that a signal has not been read and should be repeated, this flag having been used with that meaning originally

To hoist the blue Peter To leave
"When are you going to sail?"
"I cannot justly say. Our ship's bound for America next voyage but I've got to go to the Isle of Man first -. And I may have to hoist the blue Peter any day."
Mrs GASKELL *Mary Barton* ch XIII

Blue Ribbon. The blue ribbon is the Garter, the badge of the highest and most coveted Order of Knighthood in the gift of the British Crown, hence the term is used to denote the highest honour attainable in any profession, walk of life, etc. The blue ribbon of the Church is the Archbishopric of Canterbury, that in law is the office of Lord Chancellor *See* CORDON BLEU

The Blue Ribbon of the Turf. The Derby Lord George Bentinck sold his stud, and found to his vexation that one of the horses sold won the Derby a few months afterwards. Bewailing his ill-luck, he said to Disraeli, "Ah! you don't know what the Derby is" "Yes, I do," replied Disraeli, ' it is the blue ribbon of the turf."
A weal from a blow has had the term "blue ribbon" applied to it, because a bruise turns the skin blue
' Do you want a blue ribbon round those white sides of yours, you monkey?" answered Orestes because, if you do, the hippopotamus hide hangs ready outside "—KINGSLEY *Hypatia*, ch IV

Blue Ribbon Army. The Blue Ribbon Army was a teetotal society founded in the early eighties of the last century by Richard Booth in the U S A., and soon extending to Great Britain. The members were distinguished by wearing a piece of narrow blue ribbon in the buttonhole of the coat. From this symbol the phrase Blue Ribbon Army came in time to be applied to the body of teetotallers generally, whether connected with the original society or not. In 1883 the society took the name of Gospel Temperance Union

Blue Shirts. A force of Irish Volunteers taken to Spain by General O'Duffy to help General Franco in the civil war, 1936-9

Blue Squadron. One of the three divisions of the British Fleet in the 17th century. *See* ADMIRAL OF THE BLUE

Blue stocking A female pedant. In 1400 a society of ladies and gentlemen was formed at Venice, distinguished by the colour of their stockings, and called *della calza* It lasted till 1590, when it appeared in Paris and was the rage among the lady *savants*. From France it came to England in 1780, when Mrs Montague displayed the badge of the Bas-bleu club at her evening assemblies. Mr Benjamin Stillingfleet was a constant attendant of the *souees*. The last of the clique was Miss Monckton, afterwards Countess of Cork, who died 1840, but the name has survived.

Blues. A traditional form of American Negro folk-song, of obscure origin, but expressive of the unhappiness of slaves in the Deep South. Usually consists of 12 bars, made up of three 4-bar phrases in 4/4 time. Both the words and accompaniment (which form an antiphonal) should be improvised, though many famous Blues have been written down, the subject matter is usually love, the troubles which have beset the singer, or a nostalgic longing for home. The best-known Blues singer was Bessie Smith (d 1936)

Bluey The Australian name for blue-coloured blankets in wide use in the 19th century. From this the word became attached to the swag which tramps carried in their blankets. In Tasmania a bluey was a blue shirt-like garment issued to convicts

Bluff, To. In Poker and other card-games, to stake on a bad hand. This is a dodge resorted to by players to lead an adversary to throw up his cards and forfeit his stake rather than risk them against the "bluffer."
So, by extension, to bluff is to deceive by pretence. To call someone's bluff is to unmask his deception

Bluff Harry or Hal. Henry VIII, so called from his bluff and burly manners (1491-1547).

Blunderbore. A nursery-tale giant, brother of Cormoran, who put Jack the Giant Killer to bed and intended to kill him, but Jack thrust a billet of wood into the bed, and crept under the bedstead. Blunderbore came with his club and broke the billet to pieces, but was much amazed at seeing Jack next morning at breakfast-time. When his astonishment was abated he asked Jack how he had slept "Pretty well," said the Cornish hero, "but once or twice I fancied a mouse tickled me with its tail." This increased the giant's surprise. Hasty pudding being provided for breakfast, Jack stowed away such huge stores in a bag concealed within his dress that the giant could not keep pace with him. Jack cut the bag open to relieve "the gorge," and the giant, to affect the same relief, cut his throat and thus killed himself

Blunderbuss. A short gun with a large bore. (Dut. *donderbus*, a thunder-tube.)

Blunt. Ready money, a slang term, the origin of which is unknown
To get a Signora to warble a song,
You must fork out the blunt with a haymaker's prong!
HOOD *A Tale of a Trumpet.*

Blurb. A paragraph printed on the dust-wrapper or in the preliminary leaves of a book purporting to tell what the book is about, written by the publisher and usually of a laudatory nature. The phrase was coined by Gelett Burgess, the American novelist (1866-1951), about the year 1900, when he defined it as "self-praise to make a noise like a publisher."

Blurt Out, To To tell something from impulse which should not have been told. To speak incautiously, or without due reflection. Florio makes the distinction, to "flurt with one's fingers, and blurt with one's mouth "

Blush. At first blush, at first sight, on the first glance The word comes from the Old English *blusch*, a gleam, a glimpse, a momentary view This sense of the word dropped out of use in the 16th century, except in the above phrase

To hide a blisful blusch of the bright sunne
Sir Gawayne and the Green Knight
At the first blush we thought they had been shippes
come from France —*Hakluyt's Voyages*, III

To blush like a blue dog. *See* Dog

To put to the blush. To make one blush with shame, annoyance, or confusion.

Bo. You cannot say Bo ! to a goose—*i.e* you are a coward who dare not say bo! even to a fool It is said that once when Ben Jonson was introduced to a nobleman, the peer was so struck with his homely appearance that he exclaimed, "What! are you Ben Jonson? Why, you look as if you could not say Bo! to a goose " "Bo!" exclaimed the dramatist, turning to the peer and making his bow. (*Cp.* Lat *bo-are*, Gr. *boa-ein* to cry aloud)

Boa. Pliny (*Natural History*, VIII, xiv) says the word is from Lat *bos* (a cow), and arose from the belief that the boa sucked the milk of cows

Boadicea (bō á dis ē' á) Much has been written about this heroic queen of the ancient Britons She was the wife of Prasutagus, king of the Iceni, on whose death the Romans seized the territory, scourged the widow and ill-treated the daughters Enfuriated and crying for vengeance, Boadicea raised a revolt of the Iceni and Trinobantes, burned Camulodunum and Londinium (Colchester and London) but was eventually defeated (A D 62) by Suetonius Paulinus Rather than fall into the hands of the Romans she took poison and died

Boanerges (bō a nēr 'jēz) A name given to James and John, the sons of Zebedee, because they wanted to call down "fire from heaven" to consume the Samaritans for not "receiving" the Lord Jesus It is said in the Bible to signify "sons of thunder," but "sons of tumult ' would probably be nearer its meaning (*Luke* ix, 54, *see Mark* iii, 17).

Boar, The. Richard III *See* BLUE BOAR.
The wretched, bloody, and usurping boar
That spoiled your summer fields and fruitful vines
  This foul swine   lies now
Near to the town of Leicester, as we learn
SHAKESPEARE *Richard III*, v 3.

Buddha and the boar. A Hindu legend relates that Buddha died from eating boar's flesh dried The third avatar of Vishnu was in the form of a boar, and in the legend "dried boar's flesh" probably typifies esoteric knowledge prepared for popular use None but Buddha himself must take the responsibility of giving out occult secrets, and he died while preparing for the general esoteric knowledge.
B.D —5

The bristled Baptist boar. So Dryden denominates the Anabaptists in his *Hind and Panther*
The bristled Baptist boar, impure as he [*the ape*],
But whitened with the foam of sanctity,
With fat pollutions filled the sacred place,
And mountains levelled in his furious race
Pt i, 43

The Calydonian boar In Greek legend, Œneus, king of Calydon, in Ætolia, having neglected to sacrifice to Artemis, was punished by the goddess sending a ferocious boar to ravage his lands. A band of heroes collected to hunt the boar, which was wounded by Atalanta, and killed by Meleager

The wild boar of the Ardennes. Guillaume Comte de la Marck (died 1485), so called because he was fierce as the wild boar, which he delighted to hunt Introduced by Scott in *Quentin Durward*

Boar's Head The Old English custom of serving this as a Christmas dish is said to derive from Scandinavian mythology Freyr, the god of peace and plenty, used to ride on the boar Gullinbursti, his festival was held at Yuletide (*winter solstice*), when a boar was sacrificed to his honour.
The head was carried into the banqueting hall, decked with bays and rosemary on a gold or silver dish, to a flourish of trumpets and the songs of the minstrels Many of these carols are still extant (*see* CAROL), and the following is the first verse of that sung before Prince Henry at St. John's College, Oxford, at Christmas, 1607 —
  The Boar is dead,
  So, here is his head,
    What man could have done more
  Than his head off to strike,
  Meleager like
    And bring it as I do before?

The Boar's Head Tavern. Made immortal by Shakespeare, this used to stand in Eastcheap, on the site of the present statue of William IV. The sign was the cognisance of the Gordons, the progenitor of which clan slew, in the forest of Huntley, a wild boar, the terror of all the Merse (1093)

Board. In all its many senses, this word is ultimately the same as the A S *bord*, a board, plank, or table; but the verb, *to board*, meaning to attack and enter a ship by force, hence to embark on a ship, and figuratively to accost or approach a person, is short for Fr *aborde*, from *aborder*, which itself is from the same word, *bord*, as meaning the side of a ship In *starboard, larboard, on board* and *overboard* the sense ' the side of a ship" is still evident
I'll board her, though she chide as loud
As thunder
Taming of the Shrew, i, 2

A board. A council which sits at a board or table, as "Board of Directors," "Board of Guardians," "School Board," "Board of Trade," etc

The Board of Green Cloth. A Court that used to form part of the English Royal Household, and was presided over by the Lord Steward It was so called because it sat at a table covered with green cloth It existed certainly in the reign of Henry I, and probably earlier. It is now concerned with the royal domestic arrangements, under the authority of the Master of the Household

Board of Green Cloth, June 12th, 1681 Order was this day given that the Maides of Honour should have cherry-tarts instead of gooseberry-tarts, it being observed that cherrys are threepence a pound

In modern slang *the board of green cloth* is the card-table or billiard-table

Board School. An undenominational elementary school managed by a School Board as established by the Elementary Education Act in 1870, and supported by a parliamentary grant collected by a rate When the School Boards were abolished by the Education Act of 1902 and the County Councils were given their duties, the name *Board School* was dropped and the schools became known as County or Council Schools

He is on the boards. He is an actor by profession

To sweep the board. To win and carry off all the stakes in a game of cards, or all the prizes at some meeting

To board. To feed and lodge together, is taken from the custom of the university members, etc , dining together at a common table or board

Boarding school. A school where the pupils are fed and lodged as well as taught. The term is sometimes applied to "prison"
I am going to boarding school, going to prison to be taught good behaviour.

Board wages Wages paid to servants which includes the cost of their food Servants "on board wages" provide their own victuals

Board, in many sea phrases, is all that space of the sea which a ship passes over in tacking

To go by the board. To go for good and all, to be quite finished with, thrown overboard Here *board* means the side of the ship

To make a good board. To make a good or long tack in beating to windward

To make a short board To make a short tack. "To make short boards," to tack frequently

To make a stern board. To sail stern foremost.

To run aboard of To run foul of another ship. *See also* ABOARD

Boast of England, The. A name given to "Tom Thumb" or "Tom-a-lin" by Richard Johnson, who in 1599 published a "history of this ever-renowned soldier, the Red Rose Knight, surnamed The Boast of England, showing his honourable victories in foreign countries, with his strange fortunes in Faery Land, and how he married the fair Angliterra, daughter of Prester John . "

Boatswain. (bō' zan). The officer who has charge of the boats, sails, rigging, anchors, cordage, cables, and colours. Swain is the old Scand *sveinn,* a boy, servant, attendant,

hence the use of the word in poetry for a shepherd and a sweetheart

> The merry Bosun from his side
> His whistle takes
>   DRYDEN *Albion and Albanius.*

Boaz *See* JACHIN

Bob. Slang for a shilling The origin of the word is unknown It dates from about 1800

Bob. A term used in campanology denoting certain changes in the long peals rung on bells A *bob minor* is rung on six bells, a *bob triple* on seven, a *bob major* on eight, a *bob royal* on ten, and a *bob maximus* on twelve

To give the bob to anyone To deceive, to balk Here *bob* is from M E *bobben,* O.Fr *bober,* to befool

> With that, turning his backe, he smiled in his sleeve, to see howe kindely hee had given her the bobbe —GREENE *Menaphon* (1589)

To bob for apples or cherries is to try and catch them in the mouth while they swing backwards and forwards *Bob* here means to move up and down buoyantly, hence, the word also means "to curtsy," as in the Scottish song, **If it isn't weel bobbit we'll bob it again,** signifying, if it is not well done we'll do it again.

To bob for eels is to fish for them with a *bob,* which is a bunch of lobworms like a small mop Fletcher uses the word in this sense:—

> What, dost thou think I fish without a bait, wench?
> I bob for fools he is mine own, I have him
> I told thee what would tickle him like a trout,
> And, as I cast it, so I caught him daintily
>   *Rule a Wife and Have a Wife,* ii, 4.

To bob means also to thump, and a *bob* is a blow

> He that a fool doth very wisely hit,
> Doth very foolishly, although he smart,
> Not to seem senseless of the bob
>   *As You Like It,* ii, 7

Bear a bob. Be brisk The allusion is to bobbing for apples, which requires great agility and quickness

A bob wig. A wig in which the bottom locks are turned up into bobs or short curls

Bobbed hair is hair that has been cut short—docked—like a bobtailed horse's tail.

Bob's your uncle. In other words, "That'll be all right; you needn't bother any more " The origin of the phrase is unknown, it was certainly in use in the 1880s, but no satisfactory explanation of who "Bob" was has been brought forward

Pretty bobbish. Pretty well (in spirits and health), from *bob,* as in the phrase *bear a bob* above

Bobby A policeman, this slang word is derived from Sir *Robert* Peel, and became popular through his having in 1828 remodelled the Metropolitan Police Force *Cp* PEELER

Bobby-sox. Ankle-length socks affected by teen-age girls in the U S A in the early 1940s; hence the noun **Bobby-soxers,** young women who achieved notoriety by unruly demonstrations at the public appearances of fashionable crooners.

Bobadil. A military braggart of the first water Captain Bobadil is a character in Ben Jonson's *Every Man in his Humour* This name was probably suggested by Bobadilla, first governor of Cuba, who sent Columbus home in chains.

Bobbery, as **Kicking up a bobbery,** making a squabble or tumult, kicking up a shindy. It is much used in India, and most probably comes from Hind *bapre,* "Oh, father!" a common exclamation of surprise.

Boccus, King. *See* SIDRAC.

Bockland or *Bookland* Land severed from the *folkland* (i e the common land belonging to the people) and held either communally or in severally, and converted into a private estate of perpetual inheritance by a written *boc* (or *book*) *i.e.* a deed
The place-name *Buckland* is derived from this word.

Boden-See. The German name for the Lake of Constance, so called because it lies in the Boden, or low country at the foot of the Alps

Bodkin. A word of uncertain origin, originally signifying a small dagger. In the early years of Elizabeth's reign it was applied to the stiletto worn by ladies in the hair In the *Seven Champions,* Castria took her silver bodkin from her hair, and stabbed to death first her sister and then herself, and it is probably with this meaning that Shakespeare used the word in the well-known passage from *Hamlet,* "When he himself might his quietus make with a bare bodkin"

To ride bodkin. To ride in a carriage between two others, the accommodation being only for two There is no ground for the suggestion that *bodkin* in this sense is a contraction of *bodykin,* a little body The allusion to something so slender that it can be squeezed in anywhere is obvious

> If you can bodkin the sweet creature into the coach
>   GIBBON
> There is hardly room between Jos and Miss Sharp, who are on the front seat, Mr Osborne sitting bodkin opposite, between Captain Dobbin and Amelia
>   THACKERAY. *Vanity Fair*

Bodle. A Scotch copper coin, worth about the sixth of a penny, said to be so called from Bothwell, a mint-master
> Fair play, he car'd na deils a boddle
>   BURNS *Tam o' Shanter,* 110

To care not a bodle is equivalent to our English phrase, "Not to care a farthing."

Bodleian Library (bod lē′ an) (Oxford). So called because it was restored by Sir Thomas Bodley in 1597. It was originally established in 1455 and formally opened in 1488, but it fell into neglect in the course of the next century. It is now, in size and importance, second only to the library of the British Museum, and is one of the five libraries to which a copy of all copyright books must be sent.

Body (A S *bodig*)

A compound body, in old chemical phraseology, is one which has two or more *simple* bodies or *elements* in its composition, as water

A regular body, in geometry, means one of the five regular solids, called "Platonic" because first suggested by Plato *See* PLATONIC BODIES

The heavenly bodies. The sun, moon, stars, and so on

The seven bodies (of alchemists) The seven metals supposed to correspond with the seven "planets"

Planets			Metals.
1 Apollo, or the Sun			Gold.
2 Diana, or the Moon			Silver
3 Mercury	.	.	Quicksilver.
4 Venus	.	.	Copper
5 Mars	.	.	Iron
6 Jupiter	..	..	Tin
7 Saturn	.	.	Lead.

To body forth To give mental shape to an ideal form

> Imagination bodies forth
> The forms of things unknown
> SHAKESPEARE. *Midsummer Night's Dream,* v, 1.

To keep body and soul together. To sustain life, from the notion that the soul gives life The Latin *anima,* and the Greek *psyche,* mean both soul and life, and, according to Homeric mythology and the common theory of "ghosts," the departed soul retains the shape and semblance of the body *See* ASTRAL BODY

Body colour. Paint containing body or consistency Water-colours are made opaque by mixing with white lead

Body corporate. An aggregate of individuals legally united into a corporation

Body politic. A whole nation considered as a political corporation; the state. In Lat , *totum corpus reipublicæ*

Bodyline. A cricket term for fast bowling at the batsman instead of at the wicket, with the object of forcing him to give a catch while defending his person The accurate but dangerous bowling of Larwood and Voce won the Ashes (*q v*) for England in Australia in 1932-33, but precipitated a crisis which caused a change in the rules of the game

Body-snatcher. One who snatches or purloins bodies, newly buried, to sell them to surgeons for dissection. The first instance on record was in 1777, when the body of Mrs. Jane Sainsbury was "resurrected" from the burial ground near Gray's Inn Lane The "resurrection men" (*q v*) were imprisoned for six months
By a play on the words, a bum-bailiff was so called, because his duty was to snatch or capture the body of a delinquent

Bœotia (bē ō′ sha). The ancient name for a district in central Greece, probably so called because of its abundance of cattle, but according to fable, because Cadmus was conducted by an ox (Gr. *bous*) to the spot where he built Thebes

Bœotian (bē ō′ shan) A rude, unlettered person, a dull blockhead The ancient Bœotians loved agricultural and pastoral pursuits, so the Athenians used to say they were dull and thick as their own atmosphere, yet Hesiod

Pindar, Corinna, Plutarch, Pelopidas, and Epaminondas, were all Bœotians.

Bœotian ears. Ears unable to appreciate music or rhetoric.

Well, friend, I assure thee thou hast not got Bœotian ears [*because you can appreciate the beauties of my sermons*] —LE SAGE *Gil Blas*, vii, 3.

Boethius (bō ē' thi us) Interest in this Roman author (A.D *c* 475-*c* 524) chiefly arises from the fact that his *De Consolatione Philosophiae* was translated by King Alfred and by Chaucer, who mentions him in the *Canterbury Tales*

Boffin. A nickname given in the R A F during World War II to research scientists or "backroom boys" (*q v*)

Bogey. *See* BOGY

Bogomili (bog ō mil' i) An heretical sect which seceded from the Greek Church in the 12th century Their chief seat was Thrace, and they were so called from a Bulgarian priest, Bogomil, a reformer of the 10th century Their founder, Basilius, was burnt by Alexius Comnenus in 1118, they denied the Trinity, the institutions of sacraments and of priests, believed that evil spirits assisted in the creation of the world, etc

Bog-trotters. Irish tramps; so called from their skill in crossing the Irish bogs, from tussock to tussock, either as guides or to escape pursuit.

Bogus. An adjective applied to anything spurious, sham, or fraudulent, as *bogus currency, bogus transactions* The word came from America, and is by some connected with *bogy*, but there are other suggestions. One is that it is from an Italian named *Borghese* who, about 1837, was remarkably successful in amassing a fortune in the Western States by means of forged bills, fictitious cheques, etc., another, that ten years before this the name was given to an apparatus for coining false money, while Lowell (*Biglow Papers*) says, "I more than suspect the word to be a corruption of the French *bagasse* "

Bogy. A hobgoblin; a person or object of terror; a bugbear The word appeared only in the early 19th century, and is probably connected with the Scottish *bogle*, and so with the obsolete *bug*

Colonel Bogy. A name given in golf to an imaginary player whose score for each hole is settled by the committee of the particular club and is supposed to be the lowest that a good average player could do it in *Beating Bogy* or *the Colonel*, is playing the hole in a less number of strokes

During World War I troops on the march were forbidden to sing a catchy song entitled *Colonel Bogy* as the words they substituted for the real ones were not considered edifying.

Bohea (bō hē') A type of tea much favoured in the 18th century The name is a corruption of Wu-i, the hills in China upon whose slopes it is grown.

Bohemia, The Queen of. This old public-house sign is in honour of Elizabeth, daughter of James I, who was married to Frederick, elector palatine, for whom Bohemia was raised into a separate kingdom It is through her that the Hanoverians succeeded to the throne of Great Britain.

Bohemian. A slang term applied to literary men and artists of loose and irregular habits, living by what they can pick up by their wits Originally the name was applied to the gipsies, from the belief that before they appeared in western Europe they had been denizens of Bohemia, or because the first that arrived in France came by way of Bohemia (1427) When they presented themselves before the gates of Paris they were not allowed to enter the city, but were lodged at La Chapelle, St Denis The French nickname for gipsies is *cagoux* (unsociables)

Bohemian Brethren A religious sect formed out of the remnants of the Hussites They arose at Prague in the 15th century, and are the forerunners of the modern Moravians.

Boiling-point. He was at boiling-point. Very angry indeed. Properly the point of heat at which water, under ordinary conditions, boils (212° Fahrenheit, 100° Centigrade, 80° Reaumur).

Bold. Bold as Beauchamp. It is said that Thomas Beauchamp, Earl of Warwick, with one squire and six archers, overthrew 100 armed men at Hogges, in Normandy, in 1346.

This exploit is not more incredible than that attributed to Captal-de-Buch, who, with forty followers, cleared Meux of the insurgents called *La Jacquerie*, 7,000 of whom were slain by this little band, or trampled to death in the narrow streets as they fled panic-struck (1358).

Bold as brass. Downright impudent; without modesty Similarly we say "brazen-faced"

I make bold to say. I take the liberty of saying; I venture to say

Bolerium Promontory (bol ē' ri um) Land's End, the Bellerium (*see* BELLERUS) of the Romans.

Bolero (bo lâr' ō) A Spanish dance, so called from the name of the inventor

Bolingbroke (bōl' ing bruk). Henry IV of England, so called from Bolingbroke, in Lincolnshire, where he was born (1367-1413).

Bollandists. Editors of the *Acta Sanctorum* begun by John Bollandus, Dutch Jesuit martyrologist (1596-1665); the first two volumes were published in 1643, these contain the saints commemorated in January. The work is not yet finished, but the sixty-first folio volume was published in 1875.

Bollen. Swollen The past participle of the obsolete English verb, *bell*, to swell Hence "joints bolne-big" (*Golding*), and "bolne in pride" (*Phaer*). The seed capsule or pod of flax or cotton is called a "boll "

The barley was in the ear and the flax was bolled
Exod ix, 31

Bologna Stone (bo lon' ya) A sulphate of baryta found in masses near Bologna. After being heated, powdered, and exposed to the light it becomes phosphorescent

Bolognese School. There were three periods to the Bolognese School in painting—the Early, the Roman, and the Eclectic The first was founded by Marco Zoppo, in the 15th century, and its best exponent was Francia The second was founded in the 16th century by Bagnacavallo, and its chief exponents were Primaticio, Tibaldi, and Nicolo dell' Abate The third was founded by the Carracci, at the close of the 16th century, and its best masters have been Domenichino, Lanfranco, Guido, Schidone, Guercino, and Albani

Bolorey (bô lō′ ni) Originally meaning a Bologna sausage, the word is now used to describe something pretentious but useless and worthless "Bunk" and "hooey" are employed in this same way

Boishevik (bol′ she vik) or (less correctly) **Bolshevist** Properly, a member of the Russian revolutionary party that seized power under Lenin in 1917, declared war on capitalism and the bourgeoisie in all lands, and aimed at the establishment of supreme rule by the proletariat The Bolshevik government was so called because it professed to act in the name of the majority (*bolshe* is the comparative of the adjective *bolshoi*, big, large, and *bolsheviki* = majority).

Bolt. Originally meaning a short thick arrow with a blunt head, is an Anglo-Saxon word, and must not be confused with the old word *bolt* (O Fr *bulter*, connected with Lat. *burra*, a coarse cloth) meaning a sieve, or to sieve This latter word is almost obsolete, but is used by Browning —

> The curious few
> Who care to sift a business to the bran
> Nor coarsely bolt it like the simpler sort
> *Ring and the Book*, 1, 923

From meaning an arrow *bolt* came to be applied to the door fastening, which is of a similar shape, and these meanings (a missile capable of swift movement, and a fastening) have given rise to combinations and phrases of very separated meaning, as will be seen from the following

Bolted arrow. A blunt arrow for shooting young rooks with a cross-bow, called "bolting rooks " A gun would not do, and an arrow would mangle the little things too much

Bolt upright Straight as an arrow

> Winsinge she was, as is a jolly colt,
> Long as a mast, and upright as a bolt
> CHAUCER *Miller's Tale*, 77

The fool's bolt is soon spent. A foolish archer shoots all his arrows so heedlessly that he leaves himself no resources in case of need

The horse bolted. The horse shot off like a bolt or arrow

To bolt food. To swallow it quickly without waiting to chew it, hence, **to bolt a Bill**, a political phrase used of Bills that are passed whole before proper time or opportunity has been given for their consideration

To bolt out the truth. To blurt it out, also **to bolt out**, to exclude or shut out by bolting the door

A bolt from the blue A sudden and wholly unexpected catastrophe or event, like a

"thunderbolt" from the blue sky, or flash of lightning without warning and wholly unexpected Here "bolt" is used for lightning, though, of course, in strict language, a meteorite, not a flash of lightning, is a thunderbolt

> Namque Diespiter
> Igni corusco nubila dividens,
> Plerumque, per purum tenantes
> Egit equos volucremque currum .
> *Horace* 1 *Ode* xxxiv, 5, etc

Bolt in tun. In heraldry, a bird-bolt, in pale, piercing through a tun, often used as a public-house sign The punning crest of Serjeant Bolton, who died 1787, was "on a wreath a tun erect proper, transpierced by an arrow fesseways or " Another family of the same name has for crest "a tun with a bird-bolt through it proper " A third, harping on the same string, has "a bolt gules in a tun or " The device was adopted as a public-house sign in honour of some family who own it as a coat of arms

Bolton. Bate me an ace, quoth Bolton. Give me some advantage. What you say must be qualified, as it is too strong Ray says that a collection of proverbs was once presented to the Virgin Queen, with the assurance that it contained all the proverbs in the language; but the Queen rebuked the boaster with the proverb, "Bate me an ace, quoth Bolton," a proverb omitted in the compilation John Bolton was one of the courtiers who used to play cards and dice with Henry VIII, and flattered the king by asking him to allow him an *ace* or some advantage in the game.

Bolus Properly, a rather large-sized pill, so called from a Greek word meaning a roundish lump of clay

Bomb. A metal shell filled with an explosive From the Gr *bombos*, any deep, especially humming, noise (ultimately the same word as *boom*)

King Bomba. A nickname given to Ferdinand II, King of Naples, in consequence of his cruel bombardment of Messina in 1848, in which the slaughter and destruction of property was most wanton

Bomba II was the nickname given to his son Francis II for bombarding Palermo in 1860. He was also called *Bombalino* (Little Bomba).

Bombshell A word used figuratively in much the same way as *bolt* in *a bolt from the blue*

Bombast literally means the produce of the bombyx, or silk-worm (Gr. *bombux*), formerly applied to cottonwool used for padding, and hence to inflated language

> We have received your letters full of love
> And in our maiden council rated them
> As bombast and as lining to the time
> SHAKESPEARE *Love's Labour's Lost*, v, 2

Bombastes Furioso (bom băs′ tēz fū ri ō′ zō). One who talks big or in an ultra-bombastic way From the hero of a burlesque opera so called by William Barnes Rhodes, produced in 1813 in parody of *Orlando Furioso*

Bombay Duck. A fish, the bummalo, which is dried and eaten with curries

Bombiti. *See* BARISAL GUNS

Bon Gaultier Ballads (bon gol' tyêr)   Parodies of contemporary poetry by W E Aytoun and Sir Theodore Martin   They first appeared in *Tait's*, *Fraser's*, and *Blackwood's Magazines* in the 'forties, and were published in volume form in 1885

Bon mot (bong mō) (Fr).   A good or witty saying, a pun; a clever repartee

Bon ton (Fr.)   Good manners or manners accredited by good society

Bon vivant (Fr)   A free liver; one who indulges in the "good things of the table " *Bon viveur* means much the same, but is rather stronger, suggesting one who makes a pursuit of other pleasures besides those of the table.

Bona Fide (bō' nà fī' dı) (Lat)   Without subterfuge or deception; really and truly   Literally, *in good faith*   To produce bona fides is to produce credentials, to give proof that someone is what he appears to be or can perform that which he says he can

Bonanza (bon ăn' zà)   This is a Spanish and Portuguese word meaning fair weather at sea, and prosperity generally   It found its way into English through the miners on the Pacific coast of N America who applied it to any very rich body of ore in a mine.   The silver deposits of the Comstock Mine in Nevada were thus called the Bonanza Mines

Bona-roba (bō' nà rō' ba) (from Ital *buona roba*, good stuff, fine gown, fine woman).   A courtesan, so called from the smartness of her robes or dresses

> We knew where the bona-robas were
> 2 *Henry IV*, iii, 2

Bond.   Wines, and spirits and any dutiable article may be imported and left *in bond* in warehouses supervised by H M Customs and Excise without duty being paid   This enables a merchant to re-export without financial complications, or to import in bulk and pay duty on part of the goods at a time as he requires them   Wines and spirits are sometimes described as "bottled in bond"—*i e.* bottled in H M warehouses, before there could be any adulteration

Bonduca (bon dū' ka)   One of the many forms of the name of the British Queen, which in Latin was frequently (and in English is now usually) written *Boadicea* (*q.v*)   Fletcher wrote a fine tragedy with this name (1616), the principal characters being Caractacus and Bonduca

Bone.   Old thieves' slang for "good," "excellent "   From the Fr *bon*   The lozenge-shaped mark chalked by tramps and vagabonds on the walls of houses where they have been well received is known among the fraternity as a ' bone."

Also slang for dice and counters used at cards, and the man who rattles or plays the bones in a negro minstrel show is known as "Uncle Bones "

Bone, To.   To filch, as, *I boned it*   Shakespeare (2 *Henry VI*, i, 3) says, "By these ten bones, my lord . . ." meaning the tenfingers, and (*Hamlet*, iii, 2) calls the fingers "pickers and stealers "   So "to bone" may mean to finger, that is, "to pick and steal."

Other suggested explanations of the origin of the term are that it is in allusion to the way in which a dog makes off with a bone, and that it is a corruption of the slang "bonnet" (*q.v*)

> You thought that I was buried deep
> Quite decent-like and chary,
> But from her grave in Mary-bone,
> They've come and boned your Mary!
>   HOOD: *Mary's Ghost*

A bone of contention.   A disputed point, a point not yet settled   The metaphor is taken from two dogs fighting for a bone

Bred in the bone.   A part of one's nature "What's bred in the bone will come out in the flesh "   A natural propensity cannot be repressed

I have a bone in my throat.   I cannot talk, I cannot answer your question.

I have a bone in my leg   An excuse given to children for not moving from one's seat   Similarly, ' I have a bone in my arm," and must be excused using it for the present

Napier's bones   *See* NAPIER

One end is sure to be bone.   It won't come up to expectation   "All is not gold that glitters."

To give one a bone to pick   To throw a sop to Cerberus, to give a lucrative appointment to a troublesome opponent or a too zealous ally in order to silence him and keep him out of the way   It is a method frequently resorted to in political life, one whose presence is not convenient in the House of Commons is sent to the Lords, given a Colonial appointment, or a judgeship, etc

To have a bone to pick with someone   To have an unpleasant matter to discuss and settle   This is another allusion from the kennel   Two dogs and one bone invariably forms an excellent basis for a fight

To make no bones about the matter.   To do it, say it, etc , without hesitation, to offer no opposition, present no difficulty or scruple   Dice are called "bones," and the Fr *flatter le de* (to mince the matter) is the opposite of our expression   To make no bones of a thing is not to flatter, or "make much of," or humour the dice in order to show favour   Hence, *without more bones*   Without further scruple or objection.

Bone-lace.   Lace woven on bobbins made of trotter-bones

Bone-shaker   An "antediluvian," dilapidated four-wheel cab, also an early type of bicycle in use before rubber tyres, chain drive, spring saddles, etc , were thought of.

Boney (bō' nı).   "If you aren't a good boy Boney will catch you" was an old threat of the short-tempered nurse, Boney being Napoleon Bonaparte, whose threatened invasion of England was a real scare in the early 19th century.

Bonfire.   Originally a *bone-fire*, that is, a fire made of *bones*, see the *Festyvall* of 1493, printed by Wynkyn de Worde in 1515 "In the worship of St. John, the people made three manner of fires· one was of clean bones and no wood, and that is called a bonefire; another of clean wood and no bones, and that is called a wood-fire . . and the third is made of wood and bones, and is called ' St. John's fire'"; and:—

In some parts of Lincolnshire . they make fires in the public streets . with bones of oxen, sheep, etc . . heaped together hence came the origin of bon-fires —LELAND (1552).

Bonhomie (bon' o mē) (Fr). Kindness, good nature, free and easy manners; the quality of being "a good fellow "

The other redeeming qualities of the Meccan are his courage, his bonhomie, his manly suavity of manners.—R F BURTON, *El-Medinah.*

Bonhomme. A French peasant *See* JACQUES BONHOMME.

Boniface. A sleek, good-tempered, jolly landlord From Farquhar's comedy of *The Beaux Stratagem* (1707).

St. Boniface The apostle of Germany, an Anglo-Saxon whose original name was *Winfrid* or *Winfrith* (680-750)

St. Boniface's cup An extra cup of wine, an excuse for an extra glass Pope Boniface, we are told in the *Ebrietatis Encomium,* instituted an indulgence to those who drank his good health after grace, or the health of the Pope of the time being This probably refers to Boniface VI, an abandoned profligate who was elected Pope by the mob in 896 and held the position for only fifteen days. The only *Saint* Boniface to be Pope was Boniface I, who died in 422.

Bonne Bouche (Fr). A delicious morsel, a tit-bit

Bonnet. A player at a gaming-table, or bidder at an auction, to lure others to play or bid, so called because he blinds the eyes of his dupes, just as if he had struck their bonnet over their eyes

Braid bonnet The old Scottish cap, made of milled woollen, without seam or lining

Glengarry bonnet. The Highland bonnet, which rises to a point in front

He has a green bonnet. Has failed in trade In France it used to be customary, even in the 17th century, for bankrupts to wear a green *bonnet* (cloth cap)

He has a bee in his bonnet. *See* BEE

Bonnet lairds. Local magnates or petty squres of Scotland, who wore the braid bonnet, like the common people

Bonnet-piece. A gold coin of James V of Scotland, the king's head on which wears a bonnet

Bonnet Rouge. The red cap of Liberty worn by the leaders of the French revolution It is the emblem of Red Republicanism.

Bonnie Dundee. John Graham, of Claverhouse, Viscount Dundee. Born about 1649, he became a noted soldier in the Stuart cause, and was killed at the Battle of Killiecrankie in 1689

Bonnivard. *See* CHILLON.

Bonny-clabber. Sour buttermilk used as a drink. (Irish, *bainne*, milk; *claba*, thick or thickened)

It is against my freehold, my inheritance,
My Magna Charta, *cor lætificat,*
To drink such balderdash or bonny-clabber!
Give me good wine!
BEN JONSON· *The New Inn,* I, i

Bono Johnny. John Bull is so called in the East Indies.

Bonus. Something "extra"; something over and above what was expected, due, or earned, something "to the good" (Lat *bonus,* good) An extra dividend paid to shareholders out of surplus profits is called a bonus, so is the portion of profits distributed to certain insurance-policy-holders, and also—as was the custom in the case of Civil Servants and others—a payment made to clerks, workmen, etc , over and above that stipulated for to meet some special contingency that had been unprovided for when the rate was fixed

Bonze. The name given by Europeans to the Buddhist clergy of the Far East, particularly of Japan In China the name is given to the priests of the Fohists

Booby. A spiritless fool, who suffers himself to be imposed upon.

Ye bread-and-butter rogues, do ye run from me?
An my side would give me leave, I would so hunt ye,
Ye porridge-gutted slaves, ye veal-broth boobies!
BEAUMONT and FLETCHER
Humorous Lieutenant, III, 7.

The player who comes in last in whistdrives, etc , the lowest boy in the class Also a species of Gannet, whose chief characteristic is that it is so tame that it can often be taken by hand.

A booby will never make a hawk The booby, that allows itself to be fleeced by other birds, will never become a bird of prey itself.

To beat the booby. A sailors' term for warming the hands by striking them under the armpits.

Booby-prize. The prize—often one of a humorous or worthless kind—given to the "booby" at card parties, children's parties, etc , i e. to the player who makes the lowest score

Booby trap. A trap set to discomfit an unsuspecting victim —e g among children, placing a book on top of a door to fall on whoever opens the door, in war, attaching an explosive charge to the door so that whoever opens it will be killed.

Boogie-woogie (boo' gi woo' gi) A style of piano playing of obscure origin, but probably developed among self-taught Negroes in Chicago during the early 1920s Consists in maintaining a heavy repetitive pattern in the bass over which the right hand improvises at will

Boojum. *See* SNARK

Book (A S *boc,* Dan. *beuke,* Ger *buche,* a

beech-tree) Beech-bark was employed for carving names before the invention of printing

Here on my trunk's surviving frame,
Carved many a long-forgotten name. . . .
As love's own altar, honour me
Spare, woodman, spare the beechen tree
                CAMPBELL *Beech Tree's Petition*

In betting the *book* is the record of bets made by the *bookmaker* with different people on different horses

In whist, bridge, etc , the *book* is the first six tricks taken by either side The whole pack of cards is sometimes called a "book"— short for "the Devil's picture-book "

Bell, book and candle. *See* BELL.

Beware of a man of one book. Never attempt to controvert the statement of anyone in his own special subject. A shepherd who cannot read will know more about sheep than the wisest bookworm This caution is given by St Thomas Aquinas

He is in my books, or in my good books The former is the older form, both mean to be in favour The word book was at one time used more widely, a single sheet, or even a list being called a book To be in my books is to be on my list of friends

I was so much in his books, that at his decease he left me his lamp —ADDISON

He is in my black (or bad) books. In disfavour *See* BLACK BOOKS.

On the books. On the list of a club, the list of candidates, the list of voters, or any official list At Cambridge University they say "on the boards "

Out of my books. Not in favour, no longer on my list of friends

The Battle of the Books The Boyle controversy (*q v*)

That does not suit my book. Does not accord with my arrangements The reference is to betting-books, in which the bets are formally entered

The Book of Books. The Bible; also called simply "the Book," or "the good Book "

The Book of Life, or of Fate. In Bible language, a register of the names of those who are to inherit eternal life (*Phil* iv, 3, *Rev.* xx, 12)

To book it To take down an order, to make a memorandum, to enter in a book

To bring him to book. To make him prove his words, to call him to account Make him show that what he says accords with what is written down in the indentures, the written agreement, or the book which treats of the subject

To kiss the book. *See* KISS

To know one's book. To know one's own interest, to know on which side one's bread is buttered Also, to have made up one's mind

To speak by the book. To speak with meticulous exactness To speak *literatim,* according to what is in the book

To speak like a book. To speak with great precision and accuracy, to be full of information Often used of a pedant

To speak without book. To speak without authority, from memory only, without consulting or referring to the book.

To take one's name off the books. To withdraw from a club In the passive voice it means to be excluded, or no longer admissible to enjoy the benefits of the institution *See* ON THE BOOKS, above

Book-binding. A craft practised since the early Middle Ages when books had become made up of leaves instead of being in a long roll. Most styles of binding are known by the names of their practitioners, but there are others which are known either from the type of design or the name of the patron commissioning them, *e g* —

Aldine A simple design including a few graceful arabesques, the style in which the Venetian printer Aldus Manutius (fl 1494-1515) had his wares bound for the general public

Blind-tooled A binding on which the ornament is colourless, *i e* the tools are pressed direct on to the leather without gold

Canevari A style combining gilt arabesques with a cameo, usually of some classical subject, impressed in the centre in blind Generally ascribed to the Italian Demetrio Canevari, first half 16th century.

Cathedrale Bindings executed during the second quarter of the 19th century Under the influence of the Gothic Revival in France and England, the designs resemble the tracery of church windows, hence *reliures a la cathedrale*

Club. Highly ornamental bindings executed at the "Club Bindery," the private workshop organized by the Grolier Club, New York, during the first decade of the 20th century.

Cottage A style peculiar to England in the later 17th century, the frame-work in the gilt design includes at top and bottom a triangle resembling a low gable Associated with the name of Samuel Mearne, a stationer who (though not himself a binder) was binder by appointment to Charles II

Dentelle (Fr) "Lace" style, so called from the fact that the design in gilt was of an intricacy and delicacy which resembled lace Associated particularly with the Padeloup family of binders in France, first half 18th century

Dos à Dos (Fr) Back to back Two books share three boards between them and open on opposite sides Popular in the 17th century for binding books in pairs, such as the Old and New Testaments

Fanfare (Fr , pomp) Very rich bindings with an intricate pattern in gold over the whole, working out to the edges from a small oval in the centre which was either left plain or contained the coat of arms of the owner Particularly brilliant exponent was the French binder Nicolas Eve, late 16th century

Grolier Bindings in the Italian arabesque style done for the French statesman and bibliophile Jean de Grolier (1479-1565) They all bear on the upper cover the lettering *J Grolerii et amicorum*

Harleian. A style of binding used upon the

great collection of Robert Harley, first Earl of Oxford (1661-1724) Usually red leather, with an ornate diamond-shaped pattern in the centre, surrounded by a broad rectangular border

Little Gidding Nicholas Ferrar set up an English Protestant Nunnery at Little Gidding (Huntingdon) in 1625, at which binding was practised by all the inmates Many bindings, particularly embroidered ones, are ascribed to them, but without any certainty.

Lyonese An intricate pattern of strapwork in gold is supplemented and heightened by staining the leather or inlaying it with another colour As these bindings, which date from the second half of the 16th century, are mostly found on books printed at Lyons, they are so called, though it is not certain that they were done there

Macabre Bindings executed for Henry III of France after the death of the Princesse de Clèves, and using tears, skulls and bones tooled in silver to express his grief

Pointillé In this style all gilt lines are broken into a series of little dots to give a shimmering brilliance. The best exponent was the French binder Le Gascon, mid-17th century

Roxburghe. Quarter bound in brown leather with crimson paper sides, the style chosen by the Roxburghe Club, an association of wealthy and noble bibliophiles at the beginning of the 19th century

Sombre Bindings in black leather tooled entirely in blind, a style affected in the 17th century in England for religious works.

Wotton Bindings executed for Thomas Wotton, called the English Grolier because, copying the French collector. he had *Thomae Wottoni et amicorum* stamped on his books Mid-16th century

Full bound Bound fully in leather

Half bound Leather back and corners, with cloth or paper sides

Quarter bound Leather back with cloth or paper sides.

Booking office. In coaching days, when accommodation in the stage coaches was very limited, the traveller had to enter his name in a book kept in the office of the coaching inn, and wait his turn for a place in the coach For the first few years after the introduction of railways all tickets were written out and entered up in their books by the clerks in the booking offices

Book-keeper. Clerk who keeps the accounts in merchant's offices, etc.

Book-keeping is the system of keeping debtor and creditor accounts in books provided for the purpose, either by single or by double entry In the first named each debit or credit is entered only once into the ledger, either as a debit or credit item, under the customer's or salesman's name, in double entry, each item is entered twice into the ledger, once on the debit and once on the credit side

Waste book. A book in which items are not posted under heads, but as each transaction occurred

5*

Day book. A book in which are set down the debits and credits which occur day by day. These are ultimately "posted" in the ledger (*q v*).

Bookmaker. A professional betting man who makes a "book" (*see above*) on horse-races, etc Also called a *bookie*

Bookworm. One always poring over books; so called in allusion to the maggot that eats holes in books, and lives both in and on their leaves.

Boom (boom). A sudden and great demand of a thing, with a corresponding rise in its price. This usage of the word seems to have arisen in America, probably with allusion to the suddenness and rush with which the shares "go off," the same word being used for the rush of a ship under press of sail The word arises from the sound of booming or rushing water, and the sound made by the bittern is known as *booming*

The boom was something wonderful Everybody bought, everybody sold —MARK TWAIN *Life on the Mississippi*, ch. 57

It is also used of a period of rising prices and prosperity, general or particular

Also a spar on board ship, or the chained line of spars, balks of timber, etc , used as a barrier to protect harbours, is the Dutch *boom*, meaning a tree or pole, our *beam*

Boom-passenger. A convict on board a transport ship, who was chained to the boom when made to take his daily exercise

Boomer. The Australian name, in use since the early 19th century, for their national animal, the kangaroo It is possibly of Tasmanian aboriginal derivation.

Boon Companion. A convivial or congenial companion A *bon vivant* is one fond of good living. "Who leads a good life is sure to live well" (Fr *bon*, good)

Boondoggling An expression used in the early 1930s to denote useless spending, usually referring to the spending of money by the U S government to combat the depression

Boot. An instrument of torture made of four pieces of narrow board nailed together, of a length to fit the leg. The leg being placed therein, wedges were inserted till the victim confessed or fainted

All your empirics could never do the like cure upon the gout as the rack in England or your Scotch boots —MARSTON *The Malcontent.*

Boot and saddle. The order to cavalry for mounting It is a corruption of the Fr *boute selle*, put on the saddle, and has nothing to do with boots

I measure five feet ten inches without my boots. The meaning is obvious but there is also an allusion to the chopine (*q v*) or high-heeled boot, worn at one time to increase the stature

Like old boots Slang for vigorously, "like anything " "I was working like old boots" means "I was doing my very utmost "

Seven-leagued boots. The boots worn by

the giant in the fairy tale, called *The Seven-leagued Boots* A pace taken in them measured seven leagues.

The boot is on the other foot. The case is altered, you and I have changed places, and whereas before *I* appeared to be in the wrong *you* are now shown to be

The order of the boot. "The sack"; notice of dismissal from one's employment

To go to bed in his boots. To be very tipsy.

To have one's heart in one's boots. To be utterly despondent, a humorous way of saying to be as *down*-hearted, or *low*-spirited, as possible

I will give you that to boot, *i e.* in addition. The A.S *bōt* (Gothic *bota*) means advantage, good, profit, as in Milton's "Alas, what boots it with uncessant care" (*Lycidas*), Alas, what profit is it . . .?
It also meant compensation paid for injury, reparation. *Cp* HOUSE-BOTE
> As anyone shall be more powerful . . or higher
> in degree, shall he the more deeply make boot
> for sin, and pay for every misdeed
> *Laws of King Ethelred*

Bootless errand. An unprofitable or futile message
> I sent him
> Bootless home and weather-beaten back
> SHAKESPEARE 1 *Henry IV*, iii, 1.

When bale is highest boot is nighest. *See* . BALE

Boot-Jack. *See* JACK

Boots. A servant at inns, etc , whose duty it is to clean the boots Dickens has a Christmas Tale (1855) called *The Boots of the Holly-tree Inn*
The bishop with the shortest period of service in the House of Lords, whose duty it is to read prayers, is colloquially known as the "Boots," perhaps because he walks into the House in a dead man's shoes or boots, *i e* he was not there till some bishop died and left a vacancy

Boötes (bō oo′ tēz) Greek for "the plough-man"; the name of the constellation which contains the bright star, Arcturus *See* ICARIUS. According to ancient mythology, Boötes invented the plough, to which he yoked two oxen, and at death, being taken to heaven with his plough and oxen, was made a constellation Homer calls it "the wagoner," *i e* the wagoner of "Charles's Wain," the Great Bear
> Wide o'er the spacious regions of the north,
> That see Boötes urge his tardy wain
> THOMSON *Winter*, 834

Booty. The spoils of war

Playing booty. A trick of dishonest jockeys —appearing to use every effort to come in first, but really determined to lose the race.
> Mr Kemble [in the *Iron Chest*] gave a slight touch
> of the jockey, and "played booty." He seemed to
> do justice to the play, but really ruined its success
> *George Colman the Younger*

Booze. To drink steadily and continually. Though regarded as slang, this is the M.E *bousen*, to drink deeply, probably connected with Dut *buizen*, and Ger. *bousen*, to drink to excess Spenser uses the word in his description of Gluttony —
> Still as he rode, he somewhat still did eat,
> And in his hand did beare a bouzing can,
> Of which he supt so oft, that on his seat
> His drunken corse he scarse upholden can
> *Faerie Queene*, I, iv, 22

Bor. A familiar term of address in East Anglia to a lad or young man, as, "Well, bor, I saw the mauther you spoke of"—*i.e.* "Well, boy, I saw the lass . ." It is connected with the Dut *boer*, a farmer, and with *-bour* of neighbour.

Borachio (bō ra′ chō) Originally a Spanish wine bottle made of goat-skin, hence a drunkard, one who fills himself with wine
A follower of Don John, in *Much Ado About Nothing*, is called Borachio, he thus plays upon his own name.—
> I will like a true drunkard [*borachio*], utter all to
> thee —Act iii, 5

Borak or Al Borak (bōr′ ak) (the lightning) The animal brought by Gabriel to carry Mohammed to the seventh heaven, and itself received into Paradise It had the face of a man, but the cheeks of a horse, its eyes were like jacinths, but brilliant as the stars, it had the wings of an eagle, spoke with the voice of a man, and glittered all over with radiant light

Bordar. In Anglo-Saxon England, a villein of the lowest rank who did menial service for his lord in return for his cottage, the *bordars*, or *bordarii*, were the labourers, and the word is the Med Lat *bordarius*, a cottager.

Border, The. The frontier of England and Scotland, which, from the 11th to the 15th century, was the field of constant forays, and a most fertile source of ill blood between North and South Britain
> March, march, Ettrick and Teviotdale
> Why the deil dinna ye march forward in order?
> March, march, Eskdale and Liddesdale—
> All the Blue Bonnets are bound for the border.
> SCOTT *The Monastery*

Border Minstrel. Sir Walter Scott (1771-1832) because he sang of the border.

Border States, The The five "slave" states (Delaware, Maryland, Virginia, Kentucky, and Missouri) which lay next to the "free states" were so called in the American Civil War, 1861-65.

Bore. A person who bestows his tediousness on you, one who wearies you with his prate, his company, or his solicitations
The derivation of the word is uncertain; in the 18th century it was used as an equivalent for *ennui*; hence, for one who suffers from *ennui*, and afterwards for that which, or one who, causes *ennui*
In racing terminology *to bore* is to ride so that another horse is thrust or pushed off the course, a sense in which it is also used of boats in rowing, in pugilistic language it is to force one's opponent on to the ropes of the ring by sheer weight

Bore of the Severn. In the Severn and other river estuaries certain winds cause a bore, or great tidal wave that rushes up the channel with violence and noise. In England it is best known in the Severn, Trent, Wye, and Solway Firth, but bores also occur in the Ganges, Indus, and Brahmapootra, in which last the wave rises to some 12 feet

Boreas (bôr' ē ǎs) In Greek mythology, the god of the north wind, and the north wind itself He was the son of Astræus, a Titan, and Eros, the morning, and lived in a cave of Mount Hæmus, in Thrace

Hence *boreal*, of or pertaining to the north

> In radiant streams,
> Bright over Europe, bursts the Boreal morn
> THOMSON. *Autumn,* 98

Borgias (bôr' jăz) A glass of wine with the Borgias was a great and sometimes fatal honour, for Cæsar and Lucretia Borgia, children of Pope Alexander VI, were reputed to be adept in ridding themselves of foes or unwanted friends by inducing them to respond to pledges in poisoned wine

Borley or **bawley** (baw' lı) The local name for a fishing-boat at the mouth of the Thames

Born. **Born in the purple** (a translation of Gr *porphyrogenitus*). The infant of royal parents in opposition to one **born in the gutter**, or the child of beggars. This refers to the chamber lined with porphyry by one of the Byzantine empresses for her accouchement, and has nothing to do with the purple robes of royalty.

Born with a silver spoon in one's mouth. Born to good luck, born with hereditary wealth The reference is to the usual gift of a silver spoon by the godfather or godmother of a child. The lucky child does not need to wait for the gift, for it is born with it in its mouth or inherits it at birth A phrase with a similar meaning is **born under a lucky star,** this, of course, is from astrology

In all my born days. Ever since I was born, in all my experience

Not born yesterday. Not to be taken in, worldly wise

Poets are born, not made. One can never be a poet by mere training or education if one has been born without the "divine afflatus " A translation of the Latin phrase *Poeta nascitur non fit,* of which an extension is *Nascimur poetæ fimus oratores,* we are born poets, we are made orators

Borough (bŭ' ro) There are several kinds of civic government classed under this term

A Municipal Borough is a town with a fully organized municipal government with a mayor and corporation, usually possessing certain privileges granted by royal charter

A Parliamentary Borough is one that sends at least one member to Parliament

A Rotten or Pocket Borough was one of the small boroughs (sometimes consisting of but three or four electors) controlled by a wealthy or influential landowner, who as often as not sold the right of sitting in Parliament as representative of this borough for some thousands of pounds. These men were frequently called Borough-mongers

The Borough, used as a proper name, is applied to Southwark It is also the title of a collection of poetical tales by George Crabbe (1810) about the Suffolk borough of Aldeburgh. One of these tales forms the theme of *Peter Grimes,* an opera by Benjamin Britten

The word is sometimes spelled "burgh" and sometimes "boro" but it is always pronounced as above

Borough English. A custom by which real estate passes to the *youngest* instead of the *eldest* son It is of English, as opposed to French, origin, and was so called to distinguish it from the Norman custom.

If the father has no son, then the youngest daughter is sole heiress. If neither wife, son, nor daughter, the youngest brother inherits; if no brother, the youngest sister, if neither brother nor yet sister, then the youngest next of kin. *See* CRADLE-HOLDING, and *cp.* GAVELKIND

> The custom of Borough English abounds in Kent, Sussex, Surrey, the neighbourhood of London, and Somerset In the Midlands it is rare, and north of the Humber . it does not seem to occur —F POLLOCK. *Macmillan's Magazine,* xlvi (1882)

Borowe. *See* BORROW.

Borrow. Originally a noun (A.S *borg*) meaning a pledge or security, the modern sense of the verb depended on the actual giving in pledge of something as security for the loan; a security is not now essential in a borrowing transaction, but the idea that the loan is the property of the lender and must be returned some day is always present The noun sense is seen in the old oath *St. George to borowe,* which is short for "I take St George as pledge," or "as witness", also in —

> Ye may retain as borrows my two priests —SCOTT: *Ivanhoe,* ch. xxxiii.

Borrowed or **borrowing days.** The last three days of March are said to be "borrowed" from April," as is shown by the proverb in Ray's *Collection*—"March borrows three days of April, and they are ill " The following is an old rhyme on the same topic.—

> March said to Aperill,
> I see 3 hoggs [*hoggets, sheep*] upon a hill
> And if you'll lend me dayes 3
> I'll find a way to make them dee [*die*].
> The first o' them was wind and weet,
> The second o' them was snaw and sleet,
> The third o' them, was sic a freeze
> It froze the birds' nebs to the trees,
> But when the Borrowed Days were gane
> The 3 silly hoggs came hirpling [*limping*] hame.

February also (in Scotland) has its "borrowed" days. They are the 12th, 13th and 14th, which are said to be borrowed from January If these prove stormy the year will be favoured with good weather, but if fine, the year will be foul and unfavourable They are called by the Scots *Faoilteach,* and hence *faoilteach* means execrable weather

Borrowed time, to live on. To continue to live after every reasonable presumption is that one should be dead, *i e* living on time borrowed from Death.

Borstall (A S *beork,* a hill, and *steall,* place, or *stigol,* stile) A narrow roadway up the steep ascent of hills or downs The word has given the name to the village of Borstal, near Rochester (Kent), and hence to the *Borstal*

system, a method of treating youthful offenders against the law by technical instruction and education in order to prevent their drifting into the criminal classes The first reformatory of this kind was instituted at Borstal in 1902.

Bosey (Austr) A cricket term for a googly (*q v*) and so called from the English bowler B J. T. Bosanquet who toured Australia in 1903-04 The term was also applied to a single bomb dropped from a plane, in World War II.

Bosh. A Persian word meaning worthless It was popularized by James Morier in his novel *Ayesha* (1834), and other eastern romances
> I always like to read old Darwin's *Love of the Plants*: bosh as it is in a scientific point of view
> KINGSLEY: *Two Years Ago*, ch x

Bosky. On the verge of drunkenness This is a slang term, and it is possibly connected with the legitimate *bosky* meaning bushy, or covered with thickets, as in Shakespeare's —
> And with each end of the blue bow dost crown
> My bosky acres and my unshrubb'd down
> *Tempest*, iv, 1, 81

As " bosky acres " were overshadowed or obscured, so can a " bosky man " be said to be

Bosom Friend. A very dear friend Nathan says, "It lay in his bosom, and was unto him as a daughter" (2 *Sam* xii, 3). Bosom friend, *ami de cœur*. St John is represented in the New Testament as the "bosom friend" of Jesus

Bosom sermons. Sermons committed to memory and learnt by heart, not extempore ones or those delivered from notes
> The preaching from "bosom sermons," or from writing, being considered a lifeless practice before the Reformation
> BLUNT *Reformation in England*, p. 179.

Bosporus (bos' pôr us) (incorrectly written **Bosphorus**) is a Greek compound meaning "the ford of the ox," or "Oxford." Legend says that Zeus greatly loved Io, he changed her into a white cow or heifer from fear of Hera, to flee from whom Io swam across the strait, which was thence called *bos poros*, the passage of the cow Hera discovered the trick, and sent a gadfly to torment Io, who was made to wander, in a state of frenzy, from land to land The wanderings of Io were a favourite subject of story with the ancients Ultimately, the persecuted Argive princess found rest on the banks of the Nile

Boss, a master, is the Dut *baas*, head of the household. Hence the great man, chief, an overseer
The word was originally more widely used in the United States than in England, it having been attached to political leaders, financial magnates, etc , who—generally by dubious methods—seek to obtain a preponderating influence Hence *boss-rule*, and the verb *to boss*, which has become common in England also

Boss-eyed Slang for having one eye injured, or a bad squint, or for having only one eye in all Hence, **boss one's shot**, to miss one's aim, as a person with a defective eye

might be expected to do, and *a boss*, a bad shot **Boss-backed**, a good old word for "hump-backed," is in no way connected with this *Boss* here is a protuberance or prominence, like the bosses on a bridle or a shield

Boston Tea-party. An incident leading up to the American War of Independence The British Parliament had passed laws which favoured the London East India Company at the expense of American traders Three cargoes of tea which arrived at Boston Harbour in 1773, shortly after the legislation, were thrown overboard as a protest by a party of colonists dressed as Indians This act of defiance is known as the Boston Tea-party

Botanomancy (bot' ăn ō măn' si) Divination by leaves. One method was by writing sentences on leaves which were exposed to the wind, the answer being gathered from those which were left, another was through the crackling made by the leaves of various plants when thrown on the fire or crushed in the hands

Botany Bay. An extensive inlet in New South Wales, discovered by Captain Cook in 1770 It was the first place of his landing upon Australian soil, and Cook himself thus named it on account of the great variety of new plants found there Botany Bay was wrongly applied as a name of the convict settlement established in 1788 at Sydney Cove In contemporary parlance the name was applied not only to New South Wales but even to the whole of Australia

Bothie (both' i) An Irish or Gaelic word for a hut or cottage, The *bothie system* is a custom common in Scotland of housing the unmarried menservants attached to a farm in a large, one-roomed bothie
> The bothie system prevails, more or less, in the eastern and north-eastern districts —J. BEGG, D D

The Bothie of Tober-na-Vuolich (1848) is a long hexameter poem by Arthur Hugh Clough

Botley Assizes. The joke is to ask a Botley man, "When are the assizes coming on?" The reference is to the tradition that the men of Botley once hanged a man because he could not drink so deep as his neighbours.

Bo-tree The pipal tree, or *Ficus religiosa*, of India, allied to the banyan, and so called from Pali *Bodhi*, perfect knowledge, because it is under one of these trees that Gautama attained enlightenment and so became the Buddha At the ruined city of Anuradhapura in Ceylon is a bo-tree that is said to have been grown from a cutting sent by King Asoka in 288 B.C.

Bottle. The accepted commercial size of a wine bottle is one holding 26⅔ fluid ounces per reputed quart Large bottles are named as follows —

Magnum	. holding 2 ordinary bottles		
Double-magnum or Jeroboam	,,	4	,, ,,
Rehoboam	.. ,,	6	,, ,,
Methuselah	.. ,,	8	,, ,,
Salmanazar	,,	12	,, ,,
Balthazar	. ,,	16	,, ,,
Nebuchadnezzar	,,	20	,, ,,

A three-bottle man A toper who can drink three bottles of port at a sitting

Brought up on the bottle. Said of a baby which is artificially fed instead of being nursed at the breast.

Looking for a needle in a bottle of hay, or in a **haystack.** Looking for a very small article amidst a mass of other things. Bottle is a diminutive of the Fr *botte*, a bundle, as *botte de foin*, a bundle of hay

Methinks I have a great desire to a bottle of hay
Midsummer Night's Dream, iv, 1

To bottle up one's feelings, emotions, etc. To suppress them, to hold them well under control

To put new wine into old bottles A saying founded on *Matt* ix, 17, typical of incongruity. New wine expands as it matures If put in a new skin (bottle) the skin expands with it, if in an old skin, when the wine expands the skin bursts

Bottle-chart A chart of ocean surface currents made from the track of sealed bottles thrown from ships into the sea

Bottle-holder. One who gives moral but not material support The allusion is to boxing or prize-fighting, where the attendant on each combatant, whose duty it is to wipe off blood, refresh him with water, and do other services to encourage his man to persevere and win, is called "the bottle-holder"

Lord Palmerston considered himself the bottle-holder of oppressed States He was the steadfast partisan of constitutional liberty in every part of the world —*The Times*

Bottle-washer. Chief agent, the principal man employed by another, a factotum The full phrase—which usually is applied more or less sarcastically—is "chief cook and bottle-washer"

Bottled moonshine. Social and benevolent schemes, such as Utopia, Coleridge's Pantisocracy, the dreams of Owen, Fourier, St Simon, the New Republic, and so on

The idea was probably suggested by Swift's Laputan philosopher, in *Gulliver's Travels*, who

Had been eight years upon a project of extracting sunbeams out of cucumbers, which were to be put into phials hermetically sealed, and let out to warm the air in raw inclement summers

Bottom. In nautical language the keel of a ship, that part of the hull which is below the waves, hence, the hull itself, and hence extended to mean the whole ship, especially in such phrases as *goods imported in British bottoms* or *in foreign bottoms*.

A vessel is said to have a *full bottom* when the lower half of the hull is so disposed as to allow large stowage, and a *sharp bottom* when it is capable of speed.

Never venture all in one bottom—*i e* "do not put all your eggs into one basket," has allusion to the marine use of the word

My ventures are not in one bottom trusted
SHAKESPEARE *Merchant of Venice*, i, 1.

At bottom. Radically, fundamentally as, the young prodigal lived a riotous life, but was good at bottom, or below the surface

Talking of a very respectable author who had married a printer's devil, Dr Johnson told us . "She did not disgrace him, the woman had a bottom of good sense" The word bottom thus introduced was so ludicrous that most of us could not forbear tittering and laughing Looking awful to make us feel how he could impose restraint . he slowly pronounced "I say the woman was fundamentally sensible" We all sat composed as at a funeral
BOSWELL'S *Johnson*

At the bottom. At the base or root .
Pride is at the bottom of all great mistakes
RUSKIN *True and Beautiful*, p 426

From the bottom of my heart. Without reservation

If one of the parties . be content to forgive from the bottom of his heart all that the other hath trespassed against him —*Prayer Book*

He was at the bottom of it. He really instigated it, or prompted it

To have no bottom. To be unfathomable; to be unstable

To get to the bottom of the matter To ascertain the entire truth, to bolt a matter to its bran

To knock the bottom out of anything. *See* KNOCK

To stand on one's own bottom To be independent "Every tub must stand on its own bottom"

To touch bottom To reach the lowest depth

A horse of good bottom means of good stamina, good foundation

Bottom the Weaver A man who fancies he can do everything, and do it better than anyone else Shakespeare has drawn him as profoundly ignorant, brawny, mock heroic, and with an overflow of self-conceit He is in one part of *Midsummer Night's Dream* represented with an ass's head, and Titania, queen of the fairies, under a spell, caresses him as an Adonis

The name is very appropriate, as one meaning of *bottom* is a ball of thread used in weaving, etc Thus in Clark's *Heraldry* we read, "The coat of Badland is *argent*, three bottoms in fess *gules*, the thread or"

Bottomless Pit, The Hell is so called in the book of *Revelation*, xx, 1 The expression had previously been used by Coverdale in *Job* xxxvi, 16

William Pitt was humorously called *the bottomless Pitt*, in allusion to his remarkable thinness

Bottomry. A nautical term implying a contract by which in return for money advanced to the owners a ship, or *bottom* (*q v*), is, in a manner, mortgaged If the vessel is lost the lender is not repaid, but if it completes its voyage he receives both principal and interest

Boudicca. The preferred form of Boadicea (*q v*)

Boudoir. Properly speaking, a room for sulking in (Fr *bouder*, to sulk) When the word was introduced into England in the last quarter of the 18th century it was as often applied to a man's sanctum as to a woman's retiring room, now, however, it is used only for a private apartment where a lady may retire, receive her intimate friends, etc

Bought and Sold, or Bought, Sold, and Done For. Ruined, done for, outwitted

> Jocky of Norfolk, be not too bold,
> For Diccon, thy master, is bought and sold
> *Richard III*, v, 3

It would make a man mad as a buck to be so bought and sold —*Comedy of Errors*, iii, 1.

Bouillabaisse (boo' ya bäs) A soup, for which Marseilles is celebrated, made of fish boiled with herbs in water or white wine.

Boulangism (boo lonj' izm) This was a sort of political frenzy that swept over France in 1886-87. General Boulanger (1837-91) was a smart soldier who, in 1886, was appointed minister of war By genuine reforms in the army, but more by a spectacular display of his handsome person on a fine horse at reviews, he won the hearts and stirred the imagination of the Paris mob, who cried that he was the one man in France to retrieve the glories lost in the disastrous Franco-Prussian war. But Boulanger was really a man of straw, played on by all the reactionary parties in France, and after sweeping the country in a wave of patriotism and xenophobia, the Boulangist movement died out from lack of any man to lead it Boulanger fled to exile, and eventually committed suicide in Brussels

Boulle (bool) A kind of marquetry in which brass, gold, or enamelled metal is inlaid into wood or tortoise-shell, named after André Charles Boulle (1642-1732), the celebrated cabinet-maker who worked for Louis XIV on the decorations and furniture at Versailles

Bounce. Brag, swagger; boastful and mendacious exaggeration

> He speaks plain cannon, fire, and smoke, and bounce
> SHAKESPEARE *King John*, ii, 2

On the bounce. Ostentatiously swaggering Trying to effect some object "on the bounce" is trying to attain one's end through making an impression that is unwarrantable

That's a bouncer. A gross exaggeration, a braggart's lie A *bouncing* lie is a *thumping* lie, and a *bouncer* is a *thumper*

Bounds, Beating the An old custom, still kept up in a few English parishes, of going round the parish boundaries on Holy Thursday, or Ascension Day The school-children, accompanied by the clergymen and parish officers, walked through their parish from end to end, the boys were switched with willow wands all along the lines of boundary, the idea being to teach them to know the bounds of their parish.

Many practical jokes were played even during the first quarter of the nineteenth century, to make the boys remember the delimitations such as "pumping them," pouring water clandestinely on them from house windows, beating them with thin rods, etc

Beating the bounds was called in Scotland *Riding the marches* (bounds), and in England the day is sometimes called *gang-day*

Bounder. To call a man a bounder was to stigmatize him as a vulgar, ill-mannered cad, an outsider, one who did not behave himself, especially where women are concerned

Bounty. *See* QUEEN ANNE'S BOUNTY

Bounty, The Mutiny of the. Much has been written and acted on the theme of this famous tragedy in 1788 Captain William Bligh was sent in command of H M S. *Bounty* to the Society Islands to collect vegetable products with a view to propagating them in the W Indies In April, 1789, his crew mutinied and Bligh, with 18 loyal sailors, was set adrift in an open boat, ultimately landing in Timor, near Java. Meanwhile the crew of the *Bounty* reached Tahiti, whence nine of them, accompanied by some native men and women, sailed to the uninhabited Pitcairn Island where they settled Ten years later only one of the men, John Adams, was alive, but there were several women and children from whom the present inhabitants are descended

Bouquet. French for nosegay, bunch of flowers The word is used in English also for the flavour or aroma of wine, a jewelled spray, and a large flight of rockets or of pheasants which have been driven by the beaters

Bourbon (boor' bon) The Bourbon Kings of France were Henry IV, Louis XIII XIV, XV, and XVI (1589-1793), Louis XVIII and Charles X (1814-30). The family is so named from the seigniory of Bourbon, in the Bourbonnais, in Central France, and is a branch of the Capet stock, through the marriage of Beatrix, heiress of the Bourbons, to Robert, Count of Clermont, sixth son of Louis IX, in 1272. Henry IV was tenth in descent from Louis IX and the twentieth king to succeed him

Bourbons also reigned over Naples and the two Sicilies, and the present royal house of Spain is Bourbon, being descended from Philippe, Duke of Anjou, a grandson of Louis XIV, who became King of Spain in 1700

It was said of the Bourbons that they forgot nothing and learned nothing

In U.S A the term Bourbon is used for whisky made from Indian corn, sometimes with rye or malt added The name comes from Bourbon (*pron* bèr' bùn) County, Kentucky, where the whisky was originally made

Bourgeois (Fr) Our burgess; a member of the class between the "gentlemen" and the peasantry. It includes merchants, shopkeepers, and the so-called "middle class."

In typography, *bourgeois* (pronounced burjois') is the name of a size of type between long primer and brevier

Bourgeoisie (Fr) The merchants, manufacturers, and master-tradesmen considered as a class.

> The Commons of England, the Tiers-Etat of France, the bourgeoisie of the Continent generally, are the descendants of this class [artisans] generally
> MILL. *Political Economy*

In recent years, particularly since the Russian Revolution, when this class was held to be chiefly responsible for the continuance of privilege and for all sorts of abuses during the old regime and the early part of the new, the word *bourgeoisie* has been applied more particularly to the unimaginative, conventional and narrow-minded section of the middle classes

Bouse. *See* BOOZE

Boustrapa. A nickname of Napoleon III; in allusion to his unsuccessful attempts at a *coup d'état* at *Bou*logne (1840) and *Stra*sburg (1836) and the successful one at *Paris* (1851).

Boustrophedon (boo strof' e don). A method of writing found in early Greek inscriptions in which the lines run alternately from right to left and left to right, like the path of oxen in ploughing. (Gr. *boustrepho*, ox-turning)

Bouts-rimés (boo rē' mā) (Fr rhymed-endings). A parlour game which, in the 18th century, had a considerable vogue in literary circles as a test of skill A list of words that rhyme with one another is drawn up, this is handed to the competitors, and they have to make a poem to the rhymes, each rhyme-word being kept in its place on the list

Bovey Coal. A lignite found at Bovey Tracy, in Devonshire

Bow (bō) (A S *boga*, connected with the O Teut *beguan*, to bend)

Draw not your bow till your arrow is fixed. Have everything ready before you begin.

He has a famous bow up at the castle. Said of a braggart or pretender

He has two strings to his bow. Two means of accomplishing his object, if one fails, he can try the other The allusion is to the custom of bowmen carrying a reserve string in case of accident

To be too much of the bow-hand. To fail in a design, not be sufficiently dexterous. The *bow-hand* is the left hand, the hand which holds the bow

To draw a bow at a venture. To attack with a random remark, to make a random remark which may hit the truth.

A certain man drew a bow at a venture and smote the King of Israel —1 *Kings*, xxii, 34

To draw the longbow. To exaggerate The longbow was the famous English weapon till gunpowder was introduced, and it is said that a good archer could hit between the fingers of a man's hand at a considerable distance, and could propel his arrow a mile The tales told about longbow adventures, especially in the Robin Hood stories, fully justify the application of the phrase

To unstring the bow will not heal the wound (Ital) René of Anjou, king of Sicily, on the death of his wife, Isabeau of Lorraine, adopted the emblem of a bow with the string broken, with the words given above for the motto, by which he meant, "Lamentation for the loss of his wife was but poor satisfaction "

Bow (bou) The fore-end of a boat or ship (A S *bog* or *boh*, connected with Dan, *boug*, Icel *bogr*, a shoulder.)

On the bow. Within a range of 45° on one side or the other of the prow.

Up in the bows, To be. To be thoroughly enraged.

Bow Bells (bō). **Born within sound of Bow bells.** Said of a true cockney St Mary-le-Bow long had one of the most celebrated bell-peals in London John Dun, mercer, gave in 1472 two tenements to maintain the ringing of Bow bell every night at nine o'clock, to direct travellers on the road to town, and in 1520 William Copland gave a bigger bell for the purpose of "sounding a retreat from work " Bow Church, in Cheapside, is in the centre of the City The interior of the church was totally destroyed in an air raid in 1941, but the tower remained almost unharmed though the bells were destroyed

Bow-catcher (bō). A corruption of "Beau catcher," a love-curl, termed by the French an *accroche cœur* A love-curl worn by a man is a *Bell-rope*, i e. a rope to pull the *belles* with

Bow-street Runners (bō) Detectives who scoured the country to find criminals, before the introduction of the police force Bow Street, near Covent Garden, is where the principal London police-court stands.

Bow-wow Word (bou wou) A word in imitation of the sound made, as hiss, cackle, murmur, cuckoo, etc Hence *the bow-wow school*, a term applied in ridicule to philologists who sought to derive speech and language from the sounds made by animals The terms were first used by Max Müller

Bowden (bou' den) **Not every man can be vicar of Bowden.** Not everyone can occupy the first place Bowden is one of the best livings in Cheshire

Bowdlerize (bou' dler īz) To expurgate a book. Thomas Bowdler, in 1818, gave to the world an edition of Shakespeare's works "in which nothing is added to the original text; but those words and expressions are omitted which cannot with propriety be read aloud in a family." This was in ten volumes Bowdler subsequently treated Gibbon's *Decline and Fall* in the same way. Hence the words Bowdlerist, Bowdlerizer, Bowdlerism, etc.

Bowels of Mercy Compassion, sympathy The affections were at one time supposed to be the outcome of certain secretions or organs, as the bile, the kidneys, the heart, the head, the liver, the bowels, the spleen, and so on Hence such words and phrases as *melancholy* (black bile), the Psalmist says that his *reins*, or kidneys, instructed him (*Ps.* x, 7), meaning his inward conviction, the *head* is the seat of understanding, the *heart* of affection and memory (hence "learning by heart"), the *bowels* of mercy, the *spleen* of passion or anger, etc

His bowels yearned over, upon, or towards him. He felt a secret affection for him.

Joseph made haste, for his bowels did yearn upon his brother —*Gen* xliii, 30, *see also Kings*, iii, 26

Bower. A lady's private room. (A S *bur*, a chamber)

> But come to my bower, my Glasgerion.
> When all men are at rest
> As I am a ladie true of my promise,
> Thou shalt bee a welcome guest
>   From the ballad *Glasgerion*

Hence, *bower-woman*, a lady's maid and companion.

Bower, the term used in euchre, is an

entirely different word It is *bauer*, a peasant or knave

> But the hands that were played
> By that heathen Chinee,
> And the points that he made,
> Were quite frightful to see—
> Till at last he put down a right bower
> Which the same Nye had dealt unto me
> BRET HARTE *Plain Language from Truthful James*

The *right bower* is the knave of trumps, the *left bower* is the other knave of the same colour

Bower anchor An anchor carried at the bow of a ship There are two: one called the *best bower* and the other the *small bower*

> Starboard being the best bower, and port the small bower —SMYTH *Sailor's Word-book*

Bower of Bliss In Spenser's *Faerie Queene* (Bk II) the beautiful enchanted home of Acrasia

Bowie Knife (bō′ı) A long, stout knife with a horn handle and a curved blade some 15 in. long and 1½ in. wide at the hilt, carried by hunters in the Western States of America. So called from Colonel James Bowie (d 1836), one of the most daring characters in the States

Bowing (bou′ing). We uncover the head when we wish to salute anyone with respect, but the Jews, Turks, Siamese, etc , uncover their feet The reason is this With us the chief act of investure is crowning or placing a cap on the head, but in the East it is putting on the slippers To take off our symbol of honour is to confess we are but "the humble servant" of the person whom we thus salute

Bowler Hat This stiff, felt hat—known in America as a Derby hat—was the invention of a London hatter The *Daily News* for August 8th, 1868, says: "Mr. Bowler, of 15 St. Swithin's Lane has, by a very simple contrivance invented a hat that is completely ventilated whilst, at the same time, the head is relieved of the pressure experienced in wearing hats of the ordinary description " The last words apply to the hot and heavy top hats until then in universal use.

Bowling, Tom (bō ling) The type of a model sailor; from the character of that name in Smollett's *Roderick Random.*

The Tom Bowling referred to in Dibdin's famous sea-song was Captain Thomas Dibdin, brother of Charles Dibdin (1768-1833), who wrote the song and father of Thomas Frognall Dibdin, the bibliomaniac

> Here a sheer hulk lies poor Tom Bowling,
> The darling of the crew

Bowls. They who play bowls must expect to meet with rubbers. Those who touch pitch must expect to defile their fingers. Those who enter upon affairs of chance, adventure, or dangerous hazard must make up their minds to encounter crosses, losses, or difficulties The *rubber* is the final game which decides who is the winner.

Bowral Boy. The name familiarly given to Sir Donald Bradman, the great Australian cricketer, who first played in the Bowral school team

Bowse. *See* BROWSE.

Bowyer God. The "archer god," usually Cupid, but in his translation of the *Iliad* Bryant (I, v, 156) applies the epithet to Apollo.

Box. I've got into the wrong box I am out of my element, or in the wrong place Lord Lyttelton used to say that whenever he went to Vauxhall and heard the mirth of his neighbours, he used to fancy pleasure was in every box but his own Wherever he went for happiness, he somehow always got into the wrong box.

To be in the same box. To be in the same predicament as somebody else, to be equally embarrassed

To box Harry. A phrase in use among commercial travellers, applied to one who avoids the *table d'hôte* and takes something substantial for tea, in order to save expense, also, to cut down one's expenditure after a bout of extravagance To box a tree is to cut the bark to procure the sap and these travellers drain the landlord by having a cheap tea instead of an expensive dinner. To "box the fox" is to rob an orchard

To box the compass. A nautical phrase meaning to name the thirty-two points of the compass in their correct order Hence, a wind is said "to box the compass" when in a short space of time it blows from every quarter in succession, hence, the figurative use of the term—to go right round, in political views, etc., or in direction, and to end at one's starting-place.

Box up. Mixed or muddled up, an Australian expression, originally applied to mixing up sheep Found in Boldrewood, *Robbery Under Arms*

Box and Cox has become a phrase which can only be explained by the story Box and Cox were two lodgers who, unknown to each other, occupied the same room, one being out at work all day, the other all night

Box-cars. In throwing dice, in the U S A , a double six is known as a box-cars, from its resemblance to freight cars, or goods wagons

Box Days In the Scottish Court of Session, two days in spring and autumn, and one at Christmas, during vacation, in which pleadings may be filed This custom was established in 1690, for the purpose of expediting business Each judge has a private box with a slit, into which informations may be placed on box days, and the judge, who alone has the key, examines the papers in private

Boxing-Day. *See* CHRISTMAS BOX

Boxing weights.—

Flyweight,	112 lb	and under
Bantam,	118 lb	,,
Feather,	126 lb	,,
Light,	135 lb	,,
Welter,	147 lb	,,
Middle,	160 lb	,,
Light heavy,	175 lb	,,
Heavy,	all over 175 lb	

Boxers. A secret society in China which took a prominent part in the rising against foreigners in 1900 and was suppressed by joint European action The Chinese name was *Gee Ho Chuan*, signifying "righteousness, harmony, and fists," and implying training as in athletics, for the purpose of developing righteousness and harmony

Boy. In a number of connexions "boy" has no reference to age In India, the colonies, and elsewhere, for instance, a native or negro servant or labourer of whatever age is called a boy, and among sailors the word refers only to experience in seamanship A crew is divided into able seamen, ordinary seamen, and boys or greenhorns A "boy" is not required to know anything about the practical working of the vessel, but an "able seaman" must know all his duties and be able to perform them.

The Boy, meaning champagne, takes its origin from a shooting-party at which a boy with an iced bucket of wine was in attendance When the Prince of Wales (Edward VII), who was one of the shots, needed a drink he shouted "Where's the boy?", and thence the phrase found its way into would-be smart parlance.

He will say that port and sherry his nice palate
always cloy,
He'll nothing drink but " B and S " and big magnums of " the boy "
Punch (1882)

Boy Bishop St Nicholas of Bari was called "the Boy Bishop" because from his cradle he manifested marvellous indications of piety, the custom of choosing a boy from the cathedral choir, etc., on his day (December 6th), as a mock bishop, is very ancient The boy possessed episcopal honour for three weeks, and the rest of the choir were his prebendaries If he died during his time of office he was buried *in pontificalibus* Probably the reference is to Jesus Christ sitting in the Temple among the doctors while He was a boy The custom was abolished in the reign of Henry VIII.

Naked boy. *See* NAKED

Boy Scouts were started in Great Britain by General Baden-Powell in 1908, with the purpose of training lads to be good citizens with high ideals of honour, thoughtfulness for others, cleanliness, obedience and self-reliance The movement spread to other countries and in 1950 had a membership of over five million young people Scouts are graded according to age into three classes, Wolf Cubs, 8 to 11, Scouts, 11 and upwards, Rover Scouts over 17 *See also* GIRL GUIDES

Boycott. To boycott a person is to refuse to deal with him, to take any notice of him, or even to sell to him The term arose in 1881 when Captain Boycott, an Irish landlord, was thus ostracized by the Irish agrarian in-surgents

One word as to the way in which a man should be boycotted When any man has taken a farm from which a tenant has been evicted, or is a grabber, let everyone in the parish turn his back on him, have no communication with him, have no dealings with him You need never say an unkind word to him, but never say anything at all to him If you must meet him in fair, walk away from him silently Do him no violence, but have no dealings with him. Let every man's door be closed against him, and make him feel himself a stranger and a castaway in his own neighbourhood —J DILLON, M P *Speech to the Land League* (February 26th, 1881)

Boyle Controversy. A book-battle between Charles Boyle, fourth Earl of Orrery, and the famous Bentley, respecting the *Epistles of Phalaris,* which were edited by Boyle in 1695 Two years later Bentley published his cele-brated *Dissertation,* showing that the epistles (*see* PHALARIS) were spurious, and in 1699 published another rejoinder, utterly annihilat-ing the Boyle partisans Swift's *Battle of the Books* (*q v*) was one result of the controversy

Boyle's law The volume of a gas is inversely proportional to the pressure if the temperature remains constant If we double the pressure on a gas, its volume is reduced to one-half, if we quadruple the pressure, it will be reduced to one-fourth, and so on, so called from the Hon Robert Boyle (1627-91).

Boyle Lectures. A course of eight sermons on natural and revealed religion delivered annually at St Mary-le-Bow Church, London They were instituted by the Hon Robert Boyle, and began in 1692, the year after his death.

Boz. Charles Dickens (1812-70)
"Boz, my signature in the *Morning Chronicle,*" he tells us, "was the nickname of a pet child, a younger brother, whom I had dubbed Moses, in honour of the *Vicar of Wakefield,* which, being pronounced *Boses,* got shortened into *Boz* "

Bozzy. James Boswell (1740-95), the bio-grapher of Dr Johnson

Bozzaris, Marco. *See* LEONIDES OF MODERN GREECE .

Brabançonne (bra ban son) The national an-them of Belgium, composed by Van Campen-hout in the revolution of 1830, and so named from Brabant, of which Brussels is the chief city.

Braccata. *See* GENS BRACCATA, GALLIA.

Brace of Shakes. *See* SHAKES

Bradamante (bräd´ a mänt) The sister of Rinaldo in *Orlando Furioso* and *Innamorato* She is represented as a wonderful Christian Amazon, possessed of an irresistible spear which unhorsed every knight it struck.

Bradbury. A £1-note, as issued by the Treasury 1914-28, bearing the signature of J S Bradbury (subsequently Baron Bradbury), who was at that time Permanent Secretary to the Treasury

Bradshaw's Guide was started in 1839 by George Bradshaw (1801-53) printer, in Manchester The *Monthly Guide* was first issued in December, 1841, and consisted of thirty-two pages, giving tables of forty-three lines of English railway.

Brag. A game at cards, so called because the players brag of their cards to induce the company to make bets. The principal sport of the game is occasioned by any player *bragging* that he holds a better hand than the rest of the party, which is declared by saying ' I brag," and staking a sum of money on the issue (*Hoyle*)

Brag is a good dog, but Holdfast is a better. Talking is all very well, but doing is far better

Trust none,
For oaths are straws, men's faiths are wafer-cakes
And hold-fast is the only dog, my duck

SHAKESPEARE *Henry V*, ii, 3

Jack Brag. A vulgar, pretentious braggart, who gets into aristocratic society, where his vulgarity stands out in strong relief The character is in Theodore Hook's novel of the same name.

Braggadocio (brăg ȧ dō′ si ō) A braggart, one who is valiant with his tongue but a great coward at heart *Cp.* ERYTHYNUS. The character is from Spenser's *Faerie Queene*, and a type of the "Intemperance of the Tongue" After a time, like the jackdaw in borrowed plumes, Braggadocio is stripped of all his glories. his shield is claimed by Sir Marinell, his lady is proved by the golden girdle to be the false Florimel, his horse is claimed by Sir Guyon, Talus shaves off his beard and scourges his squire; and the pretender sneaks off amidst the jeers of everyone It is thought that the poet had the Duke d'Alençon, a suitor of Queen Elizabeth, in his eye when he drew this character (*Faerie Queene*, ii, 3; iii, 5, 8, 10; iv, 2, 4; v, 3, etc)

Brahma (bra′ ma) In Hinduism Brahma, properly speaking, is the Absolute, or God conceived as entirely impersonal, this theological abstraction was later endowed with personality, and became the Creator of the universe, the first in the divine Triad, of which the other partners were Vishnu, the maintainer, and Siva (or Shiva), the destroyer As such the Brahmins claim Brahma as the founder of their religious system

Whate'er in India, holds the sacred name
Of piety or lore, the Brahmins claim,
In wildest rituals, vain and painful, lost,
Brahma, their founder, as a god they boast
CAMOENS· *Lusiad*, Bk vii

Brahmin. A worshipper of Brahma, the highest caste in the system of Hinduism, and of the priestly order. *See* CASTE

Brahmo Somaj (Sanskrit, "the Society of Believers in the One God"). A monotheistic sect of Brahmins, founded in 1818 in Calcutta by Ramohun Roy (*c.* 1777-1833), a wealthy and well-educated Brahmin who wished to purify his religion and found a National Church which should be free from idolatry and superstition In 1844 the Church was reorganized by Debendro Nath Tagore, and since that time its reforming zeal and influence has gained it many adherents

Brains Trust Originally a name applied by James M Kieran of the *New York Times* to the advisers of Franklin Roosevelt in his election campaign Later applied to the group of college professors who advised him in administering the New Deal In England the name was given to a popular radio programme in which well-known public figures aired their views on questions submitted by listeners

Brain-wave. A sudden inspiration, "a happy thought."

Bran. If not Bran, it is Bran's brother.

' Mar e Bran, is e a brachair" (if it be not Bran, it is Bran's brother) was the proverbial reply of Maccombich —SCOTT *Waverley*, ch xiv

If not the real "Simon Pure," it is just as good A complimentary expression. Bran was Fingal's dog, a mighty favourite *See also* BRENNUS

Bran-new or **Brand-new** (A S *brand*, a torch) Fire new Shakespeare, in *Love's Labour Lost*, i, 1, says, "A man of fire-new words." And again in *Twelfth Night*, iii, 2, "Fire-new from the mint"; and again in *King Lear*, v, 3, "Fire-new fortune", and again in *Richard III*, i, 3, "Your fire-new stamp of honour is scarce current " Originally applied to metals and things manufactured in metal which shine Subsequently applied generally to things quite new

Brand. The merchant's or excise mark branded on the article itself, the vessel which contains the article, the wrapper which covers it, the cork of the bottle, etc , to guarantee its being genuine, etc.

He has the brand of villain in his looks It was once customary to brand convicted persons with a red-hot iron, thus, in the reign of William III convicted criminals were branded with R (rogue) on the shoulders, M (manslayer) on the right hand, and T (thief) on the left, and felons were branded on the cheek with an F The custom was abolished by law in 1822

Ranchers whose herds roamed the Western plains of the U S A branded their cattle with a distinctive iron One enterprising rancher named Maverick made his fortune by declaring that he had no iron, and appropriating any cattle on which no brand was visible Hence a Maverick is a wanderer, knowing no master

Brandan, St., or Brendan A semi-legendary Irish saint, said to have died and been buried at Clonfert (at the age of about 94), in 577, where he was abbot over 3,000 monks

He is best known on account of the very popular mediæval story of his voyage in search of the Earthly Paradise, which was supposed to be situated on an island in mid-Atlantic The voyage lasted for seven years, and the story is crowded with marvellous incidents, the very birds and beasts he encountered being Christians and observing the fasts and festivals of the Church'

And we came to the Isle of a Saint who had sailed with St Brendan of yore,
He had lived ever since on the Isle and his winters were fifteen score.
TENNYSON. *Voyage of Maeldune*

Brandenburg Confession of Brandenburg A formulary or confession of faith drawn up in the city of Brandenburg in 1610, by order of the elector, with the view of reconciling the tenets of Luther with those of Calvin, and to put an end to the disputes occasioned by the Confession of Augsburg

Brandon. An obsolete form of *brand*, a torch *Dominica de brandonibus* (St. Valentine's Day), when boys used to carry about brandons (Cupid's torches).

Brandy is a spirit distilled from the fermented juice of the grape, and may be made wherever wine is made   The most famous are those made in the Cognac and Armagnac districts of France

Brandy Nan.   Queen Anne who was very fond of brandy   On her statue in St Paul's Churchyard a wit once wrote —
Brandy Nan, Brandy Nan, left in the lurch,
Her face to the gin-shop, her back to the church

A "gin palace" used to stand at the south-west corner of St. Paul's Churchyard

Brank.   A Scotch word for a gag for scolds. It consisted of an iron framework fitting round the head, with a piece projecting in-wards which went into the mouth and pre-vented the "tongue-wagging."   One is pre-served in the vestry of the church of Walton-on-Thames   It is dated 1633, and has the inscription:
Chester presents Walton with a bridle
To curb women's tongues that talk too idle

Brant-goose.   *See* BRENT-GOOSE

Brasenose (brāz′ nōz) (Oxford)   Over the gate is a brass nose, the arms of the college, but the word is a corruption of *brasenhuis*, a brasserie or brewhouse, the college having been built on the site of an ancient brewery.   For over 550 years the original nose was at Stam-ford, for in the time of Edward III the students, in search of religious liberty, migrated thither, taking the brazen nose with them.   They were soon recalled, but the nose remained on their Stamford gateway till 1890, when, the property coming into the market, it was acquired by the College

Brass.   Impudence, effrontery   **As bold as brass**, with barefaced effrontery   **Brass** is also a slang term for money
A church **brass** is a funeral effigy made in latten and fastened down to a tombstone forming part of the floor of a church   Such effigies are mostly of the 14th and 15th centuries and are decorative in design   Rub-bings can be made most successfully with cobbler's wax on coarse paper

The Man of Brass.   Talus, the work of Vulcan   He traversed Crete to prevent strangers from setting foot on the island, threw rocks at the Argonauts to prevent their landing, and used to make himself red-hot, and then hug intruders to death

Brass Hat.   A soldier's name for a staff officer, or an officer of high rank.   It dates from the South African War (1899-1902), and refers to the gold oak leaves with which such officers' hats were ornamented on the brim

To get down to brass tacks.   To get down to the essentials, or the tacks which hold the structure together

Brassbounder.   A premium apprentice on a merchant ship.

Brat.   A child, especially in contempt.   The origin of the word is unknown, but it may be from the Welsh *breth*, swaddling clothes, or Gaelic *brat*, an apron
O Israel!   O household of the Lord!
O Abraham's brats!   O brood of blessed seed!
GASCOIGNE *De Profundis*

Brave.   A fighting man, among the American Indians, was so called
Alonso IV, of Portugal (1290-1357) was so called.

Bravest of the Brave (Le Brave des Braves)   Marshal Ney (1769-1815)   So called by the troops of Friedland (1807), on account of his fearless bravery.   Napoleon said of him, "That man is a lion."

Bravery.   Finery is the Fr. *braverie.*   The French for courage is *bravoure*
What woman in the city do I name
When that I say the city woman bears
The cost of princes on unworthy shoulders?
Who can come in and say that I mean her? . .
Or what is he of basest function
That says his bravery is not of my cost?
As You Like It, ii, 7.

Brawn.   The test of the brawn's head.   A little boy one day came to the court of King Arthur, and, drawing his wand over a boar's head, declared, "There's never a cuckold's knife can carve this head of brawn."   No knight in the court except Sir Cradock was able to accom-plish the feat   (Percy's *Reliques*.)

Bray.   *See* VICAR.

Brazen Age.   The age of war and violence   It followed the silver age.
To this next came in course the brazen age,
A warlike offspring, prompt to bloody rage,
Not impious yet   Hard steel succeeded then,
And stubborn as the metal were the men.
DRYDEN *Metamorphoses*, i.

Brazen-faced.   Bold (in a bad sense), without shame
What a brazen-faced varlet art thou!
SHAKESPEARE *King Lear*, ii, 2

Brazen head.   The legend of the wonderful head of brass that could speak and was omniscient is common property to early romances, and is of Eastern origin   In *Valentine and Orson*, for instance, we hear of a gigantic head kept in the castle of the giant Ferragus (*q v*) of Portugal   It told those who consulted it whatever they required to know, past, present, or to come, but the most famous in English legend is that fabled to have been made by the great Roger Bacon
It was said if Bacon heard it speak he would succeed in his projects, if not, he would fail. His familiar, Miles, was set to watch, and while Bacon slept the Head spoke thrice. "Time is", half an hour later it said, "Time was."   In another half-hour it said, "Time's past," fell down, and was broken to atoms   Byron refers to this legend
Like Friar Bacon's brazen head, I've spoken,
"Time is," "Time was," "Time's past."
References to Bacon's Brazen Head are frequent in literature   Most notable is Robert Greene's *Honorable History of Friar Bacon and Friar Bungay*, 1594   Among other allusions may be mentioned:
Bacon trembled for his brazen head.
POPE· *Dunciad*, iii, 104
Quoth he, "My head's not made of brass,
As Friar Bacon's noddle was."
BUTLER *Hudibras*, ii, 2
See also SPEAKING HEADS.

Brazen out, To. To stick to an assertion knowing it to be wrong, to outface in a shameless manner, to disregard public opinion

Breach of Promise. A contract to marry is as binding in English law as any other contract, and if it is broken the party breaking it is liable to pay damages The woman who breaks an engagement is just as liable in law as a man. In actions for breach of promise of marriage the plaintiff is entitled to the recovery of any pecuniary loss, such as the cost of a trousseau, and such sentimental or punitive damages as the jury may consider appropriate *See* BETROTHAL

Breaches, meaning *creeks* or *small bays*, is to be found in *Judges* v, 17 Deborah, complaining of the tribes who refused to assist her in her war with Sisera, says that Asher remained "in his breaches," that is, creeks on the seashore

> Spenser uses the word in the same way —
> The heedful Boateman strongly forth did stretch
> His brawnie armes, and all his body straine,
> That th' utmost sandy breach they shortly fetch.
> *Faerie Queene*, II, xii, 21

In Coverdale's version of the Bible the passage is rendered

> Asser sat in the haven of the see, and taried in his porcions

Bread. Cast thy bread upon the waters: for thou shalt find it after many days (*Eccles* xi, 1) When the Nile overflows its banks the weeds perish and the soil is disintegrated. The riceseed being cast into the water takes root, and is found in due time growing in healthful vigour

Don't quarrel with your bread and butter. Don't foolishly give up the pursuit by which you earn your living.

To break bread. To partake of food Common in Scripture language

> Upon the first day of the week, when the disciples came together to break bread, Paul preached to them —*Acts* xx, 7.

Breaking of bread. The Eucharist.

> They continued . . in breaking of bread, and in prayer —*Acts* ii, 42 and 46

He took bread and salt, *i.e.* he took his oath. In Eastern lands bread and salt were formerly eaten when an oath was taken

To know which side one's bread is buttered. To be mindful of one's own interest

To take the bread out of someone's mouth. To forestall another, to say something which another was on the point of saying, to take away another's livelihood

Bread-basket. The stomach

Bread and cheese. The barest necessities of life

Breadalbane *See* ALBANY

Break, To. To bankrupt (*q v*).

To break a bond. To dishonour it

To break a butterfly on a wheel To employ superabundant effort in the accomplishment of a small matter.

> Satire or sense, alas! can Sporus feel,
> Who breaks a butterfly upon a wheel
> POPE *Epistle to Dr Arbuthnot*, 307-8.

To break a journey To stop before the journey is accomplished, with the intention of completing it later

To break a matter to a person To be the first to impart it, and to do so cautiously and piecemeal

To break bread *See* BREAD

To break cover To start forth from a hiding-place

To break down. To lose all control of one's feelings, to collapse, to become hysterical. A *break-down* is a temporary collapse in health, it is also the name given to a wild kind of negro dance

To break faith. To violate one's word or pledge, to act traitorously

To break ground To commence a new project As a settler does

To break in. To interpose a remark To train a horse to the saddle or to harness, or to train any animal or person to a desired way of life

To break one's fast To take food after long abstinence, to eat one's breakfast after the night's fast

To break one's neck. To dislocate the bones of one's neck

To break on the wheel. To torture on a "wheel" by breaking the long bones with an iron bar *Cf* COUP DE GRACE

To break out of bounds To go beyond the prescribed limits

To break the ice. To prepare the way; to cause the stiffness and reserve of intercourse with a stranger to relax, to impart to another bit by bit distressing news or a delicate subject

To break your back To make you bankrupt, to reduce you to a state of impotence The metaphor is from carrying burdens on the back

To break up. To discontinue classes at the end of term time and go home, to separate. Also, to become rapidly decrepit or infirm "Old So-and-so is breaking up, he's not long for this world."

To break up housekeeping To discontinue keeping a separate house

To break with someone. To cease from intercourse

> If thou dost love fair Hero, cherish it,
> And I will break with her, and with her father,
> And thou shalt have her
> *Much Ado*, i, 1

To get a break. To have an unexpected chance, to have an opportunity of advancing oneself in business, etc

To make a break may mean either to make a complete change, or it may imply the committing of some social error, an unfortunate mistake

To run up a score in billiards or snooker

Break. A short solo improvisation in jazz music

Breakers Ahead. Hidden danger at hand Breakers in the open sea always announce sunken rocks, sand banks, etc

Breaking a Stick. Part of the marriage ceremony of certain North American Indians, as breaking a wineglass is part of the marriage ceremony of the Jews

In one of Raphael's pictures we see an unsuccessful suitor of the Virgin Mary breaking his stick This alludes to the legend that the several suitors were each to bring an almond stick, which was to be laid up in the sanctuary over-night, and the owner of the stick which budded was to be accounted the suitor which God approved of. It was thus that Joseph became the husband of Mary

In Florence is a picture in which the rejected suitors break their sticks on Joseph's back

Breast **To make a clean breast of it.** To make a full confession, concealing nothing

Breath. All in a breath. Without taking breath (Lat *continenti spiritu*)

It takes one's breath away The news is so astounding it causes one to hold one's breath with surprise

Out of breath. Panting from exertion; temporarily short of breath

Save your breath to cool your porridge. Don't talk to me, it is only wasting your breath

You might have saved your breath to cool your porridge —Mrs GASKELL *Libbie Marsh.* (Era 111)

To catch one's breath. To check suddenly the free act of breathing

" I see her," replied I, catching my breath with joy.
Capt MARRYAT *Peter Simple*

To hold one's breath Voluntarily to cease breathing for a time

To take breath. To cease for a little time from some exertion in order to recover from exhaustion of breath

Under one's breath. In a whisper or under-tone of voice.

To breathe one's last. To die

Brèche de Roland. A deep defile in the crest of the Pyrenees, some three hundred feet in width, between two precipitous rocks The legend is that Roland, the paladin, cleft the rock in two with his sword Durandal, when he was set upon by the Gascons at Roncesvalles

Then would I seek the Pyrenean Breach
Which Roland clove with huge two-handed sway.
WORDSWORTH *Aix-la-Chapelle.*

Breeches. To wear the breeches. Said of a woman who usurps the prerogative of her husband Similar to **The grey mare is the better horse.** *See* GREY

Breeches Bible, The. *See* BIBLE, SPECIALLY NAMED

Breeches buoy. A pair of short canvas breeches forming a cradle in which, by means of a pulley and rope, people can be conveyed from ship to ship or ship to shore.

Breeze, meaning a light gale or strongish wind (and, figuratively, a slight quarrel) is from the Fr *brise,* and Span *brisa,* the north-east wind *Breeze,* the small ashes and cinders used in burning bricks, and nowadays worked up into breeze-blocks for building, is the Fr *braise,* older form *brese,* meaning glowing embers, or

burning charcoal, and is connected with Swed. *brasa,* fire, and our *brazier* *Breeze* in *breeze-fly* is A S *briosa* So the three words, *breeze,* are in no way connected

The breeze-fly. The gad-fly, called from its sting (A S. *briosa;* Gothic, *bry,* a sting).

Breezy A breezy person is one who is open, jovial, perhaps inclined to be a little boisterous

Brehon Laws (brē' hon). This is the English name for an ancient legal system which prevailed in Ireland from about the 7th century They cover every phase of Irish life and furnish an interesting picture of the country in those early days

Brendan, St. *See* BRANDAN

Bren-gun The World War II equivalent of a Lewis (*q v*) machine-gun. It was originally made in Brno, Czechoslovakia, and then manufactured in Enfield, England. The word "bren" is a blend of Brno and Enfield

Brennus. The name of the Gaulish chief who overran Italy and captured Rome about 390 B.C. is the Latin form of the Celtic word *Brenhin,* king or war-chief *Bran,* a name of frequent occurrence in Welsh history, is the same word.

Brent. Without a wrinkle Burns says of Jo Anderson, in his prime of life, his "locks were like the raven," and his "bonnie brow was brent "

Brent-hill means the eyebrows *Looking or gazing from under brent-hill,* in Devonshire means "frowning at one", and in West Cornwall *to brend* means to wrinkle the brows

Brent-goose. Formerly in England, and still in America, called properly a *brant-goose,* the *branta bernicla,* a brownish-grey goose of the genus *branta*

For the people of the village
Saw the flock of brant with wonder.
LONGFELLOW *Hiawatha,* pt xvi, stanza 32.

Brentford. Like the two kings of Brentford smelling at one nosegay Said of persons who were once rivals, but have become reconciled. The allusion is to *The Rehearsal* (1672), by the Duke of Buckingham. "The two kings of Brentford enter hand in hand," and the actors, to heighten the absurdity, used to make them enter " smelling at one nosegay " (act ii, sc 2)

Bressummer (bres' um er), or *Breast-summer* (Fr *sommier,* a lintel or bressummer) A beam supporting the whole weight of the building above it, as, the beam over a shop-front, the beam extending over an opening through a wall when a communication between two contiguous rooms is required; but properly applied only to a bearing beam in the face of a building *Summer,* here, is the O.Fr *somier,* for Lat. *sagmarius* (late Lat *saumarius*), a pack-horse, also a beam on which a weight can be laid

Bretwalda (bret' wol' dà) The name given to Egbert and certain other early English kings who exercised a supremacy—often rather shadowy—over the kings of the other English states. *See* HEPTARCHY It means "ruler" or "overlord of the Brets" or "Britons."

The office of Bretwalda, a kind of elective chieftainship, of all Britain, was held by several Northumbrian kings, in succession
EARLE *English Tongue*, p 26

Brevet Rank (brev' ét) Titular rank without the pay that usually goes with it A brevet major had the title of major, but the pay of captain, or whatever his *substantive* rank happened to be (Fr *brevet*, dim of *bref*, a letter, a document)

Breviary (brē' vi år i) A book containing the daily ' Divine Office," which those in orders in the Roman Catholic Church are bound to recite. The Office consists of psalms, collects, readings from Scripture, and the life of some saint or saints

Brew. Brew me a glass of grog, *i.e* mix one for me *Brew me a cup of tea,* i e make one for me *The tea is set to brew,* i e to draw. The general meaning of the word is to boil or mix; the restricted meaning is to make malt liquor

As you brew, so you will bake. As you begin, so you will go on, you must take the consequences of your actions, as you make your bed, so you will lie in it

Nick Boy, have they appointed to fight?
Boy· A;, Nicholas; wilt thou not go see the fray?
Nick No, indeed, even as they brew, so let them bake I will not thrust my hand into the flame, an I need not .. they shall strike with the sword shall be beaten with the scabbard —PORTER· *Two Angry Women of Abington* (1599)

To brew up. To burn. Said of tanks in World War II

Brewer. The Brewer of Ghent, Jakob van Artevelde (d 1345), a popular Flemish leader who, though by birth an aristocrat, was a member of the Guild of Brewers

Brian Boru, or **Boroma** (bri' án ho roo', bo ro' ma) This great Irish chieftain was king of Munster in 978 and became chief king of all Ireland in 1002. On Good Friday, 1014, his forces defeated the Danes at the battle of Clontarf, but Brian, who was too old to fight, being almost eighty, was killed in his tent.

Briareus (brī âr' ē ùs), or Ægeon. A giant with fifty heads and a hundred hands. Homer says the gods called him Briareus, but men called him Ægeon (*Iliad*, i, 403). He was the offspring of Heaven and Earth and was of the race of the Titans, with whom he fought in the war against Zeus

He [Ajax] hath the joints of every thing, but every thing so out of joint that he is a gouty Briareus, many hands and no use, or purblind Argus, all eyes and no sight —
SHAKESPEARE *Troilus and Cressida*, i, 2

The Briareus of languages. Cardinal Mezzofanti (1774-1849), who is said to have spoken fifty-eight different tongues. Byron called him "a walking polyglot, a monster of languages, a Briareus of parts of speech "

Bold Briareus. Handel (1685-1759), so called by Pope —

Strong in new arms, lo' giant Handel stands,
Like bold Briareus, with a hundred hands,
To stir, to rouse, to shake the soul he comes,
And Jove's own thunders follow Mars's drums
POPE *Dunciad*, iv, 65

Briar-root Pipe. A tobacco-pipe made from the root-wood of the large heath (*bruyère*), which grows in the south of France.

Bribery and Corruption is a phrase often used rather loosely in English In English law a bribe is a gift or other material inducement held out to a person to betray a trust or duty Bribing at an election is a very serious offence, of which briber and bribed are held to be equally guilty The payment of secret commissions to induce business is forbidden by the Prevention of Corruption Act of 1906 The servant or agent asking for such a bribe is equally punishable with the briber, the maximum punishment being a fine of £500 with or without imprisonment for a maximum of two years

Briboci (bri bō' si). Inhabitants of part of Berkshire and the adjacent counties referred to by Cæsar in his *Commentaries*

Bric-à-brac. Odds and ends of curiosities In French, a *marchand de bric-à-brac* is a seller of rubbish, as old nails, old screws, old hinges, and other odds and ends of small value, but we employ the phrase for odds and ends of vertu *Bricolei* in archaic French means *Faire toute espèce de métier*, to be Jack of all trades *Brac* is the ricochet of *bric*, as fiddle-faddle and scores of other double words in English Littré says that it is formed on the model of *de bric et de broc*, by hook or by crook.

Brick. A regular brick. A jolly good fellow, perhaps because a brick is solid, four-square, plain, and reliable

A fellow like nobody else, and in fine, a brick —
GEORGE ELIOT *Daniel Deronda*, Bk ii, ch 16

To make bricks without straw To attempt to do something without having the necessary material supplied. The allusion is to the Israelites in Egypt, who were commanded by their taskmasters so to do (*Ex* v, 7).

To drop a brick. To make a highly tactless remark.

Brick-and-mortar franchise. A Chartist phrase for the £10 household system, long since abolished

Brickdusts. *See* REGIMENTAL NICKNAMES

Brickfielder (Austr) A southerly gale experienced at Sydney which used to blow dust into the city from the nearby brickfields.

Brick tea. The inferior leaves of the plant mixed with a glutinous substance (sometimes bullock's or sheep's blood), pressed into cubes, and dried These blocks were frequently used as a medium of exchange in Central Asia.

Bride The bridal wreath is a relic of the *corona nuptialis* used by the Greeks and Romans to indicate triumph

Bride-ale *See* CHURCH-ALE It is from this word that we get the adjective *bridal*

Bride cake. A relic of the Roman *confarreatio*, a mode of marriage practised by the highest class in Rome It was performed before ten witnesses by the Pontifex Maximus, and the contracting parties mutually partook of a cake made of salt, water, and flour (*far*) Only those born in such wedlock were eligible for the high sacred offices

Bride or **wedding favours** represent the true lover's knot, and symbolize union

Bride of the Sea. Venice, so called from the ancient ceremony of the wedding of the sea by the Doge, who threw a ring into the Adriatic, saying, "We wed thee, O sea, in token of perpetual domination." This took place each year on Ascension Day, and was enjoined upon the Venetians in 1177 by Pope Alexander III, who gave the Doge a gold ring from his own finger in token of the victory achieved by the Venetian fleet at Istria over Frederick Barbarossa, in defence of the pope's quarrel At the same time his Holiness desired that the doges should throw a similar one into the sea on each succeeding Ascension Day, in commemoration of the event. *See* BUCENTAUR.

Bridegroom. In O E. this word was *bridegome* (A.S *bryd-guma*), from Gothic *guma*, a man. In M E. times the *-gome* became corrupted into *grome*, and owing to this confusion and the long loss of the archaic *guma*, the word became connected with *grom*, or *grome*, a lad (which gives our *groom*), and hence the modern *bridegroom*

Bridegroom's men. In the Roman marriage by *confarreatio*, the bride was led to the Pontifex Maximus by bachelors, but was conducted home by married men. Polydore Virgil says that a married man preceded the bride on her return, bearing a vessel of gold and silver *See* BRIDE CAKE.

Bridewell. A generic term for a house of correction, or prison, so called from the City Bridewell, in Blackfriars, which was built as a hospital on the site of a former royal palace over a holy well of medical water, called St Bride's (Bridget's) Well After the Reformation, Bridewell was made a penitentiary for unruly apprentices and vagrants It was demolished in 1863

At my first entrance it seemed to me rather a Prince's Palace than a House of Correction, till gazing round me, I saw in a large room a parcel of ill-looking mortals stripped to their shirts like haymakers, pounding hemp From thence we turned to the women's apartment, who we found were shut up as close as nuns. But like so many slaves they were under the care and direction of an overseer who walked about with a very flexible weapon of offence to correct such hempen journeywomen as were unhappily troubled with the spirit of idleness —NED WARD *The London Spy*

Bridge. A variety of whist, said to have originated in Russia, in which one of the hands ("dummy") is exposed. **Auction Bridge** is a modification of bridge, in which there are greater opportunities for gambling.

Contract Bridge is a development of Auction Bridge in which the pair of partners cannot score the tricks they win towards making a game unless they have previously contracted to do so. To win a game one of the pairs must score 100 points for tricks as contracted, the value of the tricks being reckoned in points according to whatever suit is trumps The further ramifications of Contract Bridge call

for a modern "Hoyle" rather than a modern "Brewer."

Bridge of Gold. According to a German tradition, Charlemagne's spirit crosses the Rhine on a golden bridge at Bingen, in seasons of plenty, to bless the vineyards and cornfields.

Thou standest, like imperial Charlemagne,
Upon thy bridge of gold
　　　　　　LONGFELLOW. *Autumn*

Made a bridge of gold for him, *i e* enabled a man to retreat from a false position without loss of dignity

Bridge of Jehennam. Another name for Al-Sirat (*q.v*).

Bridge of Sighs. Over this bridge, which connects the palace of the doge with the state prisons of Venice, prisoners were conveyed from the judgment-hall to the place of execution

I stood in Venice on the Bridge of Sighs,
A palace and a prison on each hand
　　BYRON *Childe Harold's Pilgrimage*, iv, 1

A bridge over the Cam at St John's College, Cambridge, which resembles the Venetian original, is called by the same name

Waterloo Bridge, in London, used, some years ago, when suicides were frequent there, to be called *The Bridge of Sighs*, and Hood gave the name to one of his most moving poems —

One more Unfortunate,
Weary of breath,
Rashly importunate,
Gone to her death!

Bridgehead. In war a small perimeter beyond a bridge seized by assault-troops to keep the enemy at bay while larger forces cross and deploy A **beachhead** is a similar perimeter established on shore for a sea-borne landing, and it is often improperly referred to as a "bridgehead "

Bridgewater Treatises. Instituted by the Rev. Francis Henry Egerton, Earl of Bridgewater, in 1829 He left the interest of £8,000 to be given to the author of the best treatise on "The power, wisdom, and goodness of God, as manifested in the Creation " The money was divided between the following eight authors :— Dr. Chalmers, Dr. John Kidd, Dr Whewell, Sir Charles Bell, Dr. Peter M Roget, Dean Buckland, the Rev. W Kirby, and Dr William Prout.

Bridle. To **bite on the bridle** is to suffer great hardships. Horses bite on the bridle when trying, against odds, to get their own way.

Bridle road or **way.** A way for a riding-horse, but not for a horse and cart.

To bridle up. In Fr *se rengorger*, to draw in the chin and toss the head back in scorn or pride. The metaphor is to a horse pulled up suddenly and sharply.

Bridport. **Stabbed with a Bridport dagger,** *i e*. hanged. Bridport, in Dorsetshire, was once famous for its hempen goods, and monopolized the manufacture of ropes, cables, and tackling for the British navy. The hangman's rope being made at Bridport gave birth to the proverb —Fuller *Worthies.*

Brief. In legal parlance, a summary of the relevant facts and points of law given to a counsel in charge of a case   Hence, a *briefless barrister*, a barrister with no briefs, and therefore no clients.

Brief is also the name given to a papal letter of less serious or important character than a bull (*q v*), and, in the paper trade, to foolscap ruled with a marginal line, and either thirty-six or forty-two transverse lines, also to the size of a foolscap sheet when folded in half

Brig, brigantine (brig, brig' an tēn)   The terms applied to two smaller types of sailing vessel   A brig was a two-masted craft with both masts square-rigged, the brigantine, also two-masted, had the fore-mast square-rigged and the main-mast fore-and-aft rigged.

Brigade of Guards. *See* HOUSEHOLD TROOPS

Brigand. A French word, from the Ital *brigante*, pres part of *brigare*, to quarrel   In England *brigands* were originally light-armed, irregular troops, like the Bashi-Bazouks, and, like them, were addicted to marauding   The *Free Companies* of France were brigands

In course of time the Ital *brigante* came to mean a robber or pirate, hence the use of *brigandine*, later *brigantine*, for a sailing vessel, and also *brig* (*q v*)

Brigandine (brig' an dīn)   The armour of a brigand, consisting of small plates of iron on quilted linen, and covered with leather, hemp, or something of the kind   The word occurs twice in *Jeremiah* (xlvi, 4, li, 3), and in both of these passages the Revised Version reads "coats of mail," while for the first Coverdale gives "breastplates"   In the Geneva Version Goliath's coat of mail is called a "brigandine "

Brilliant. A form of cutting of precious stones introduced by Vincenzo Peruzzi at Venice in the late 17th century   Most diamonds are now brilliant-cut, ard the word "brilliant" commonly means a diamond cut in this way. In a perfect brilliant there are 58 facets

Brilliant Madman, The. Charles XII of Sweden   (1682, 1697-1718)
Macedonia's madman or the Swede.
JOHNSON *Vanity of Human Wishes*

Bring. To bring about. To cause a thing to be done

To bring down the house. To cause rapturous applause in a theatre

To bring into play. To cause to act, to set in motion

To bring round. To restore to consciousness or health; to cause one to recover (from a fit, etc)

To bring to. To restore to consciousness, to resuscitate   There are other meanings
"I'll bring her to," said the driver, with a brutal grin, "I'll give her something better than camphor "
Mrs. STOWE *Uncle Tom's Cabin*

To bring to bear. To cause to happen successfully.

To bring to book. To detect one in a mistake

To bring to pass. To cause to happen

To bring to the hammer. To offer or sell by public auction

To bring under. To bring into subjection

To bring up. To rear from birth or an early age   Also numerous other meanings

Brinvilliers, Marquise de (brin vē' yā), a noted French poisoner   She was born about 1630 and was executed in Paris in 1676   Having ruined her husband, the Marquis, and squandered his fortune, she became the lover of the Seigneur de Sainte Croix, who instructed her in the use of a virulent poison, supposed to have been aqua tofana   With this she poisoned her father and other members of her family in order to obtain possession of the family lands and wealth   Her crimes came to light when she accidentally poisoned Sainte Croix, in 1672.

Briny. I'm on the briny.   The sea, which is salt like brine

Brioche (brē' osh)   A kind of sponge-cake made with flour, butter, and eggs   When Marie Antoinette was talking about the bread riots of Paris during October 5th and 6th, 1789, the Duchesse de Polignac naïvely exclaimed, "How is it that these silly people are so clamorous for *bread*. when they can buy such nice brioches for a few sous?"   It is said that our own Princess Charlotte avowed "that she would for her part *rather eat beef than starve*," and wondered that the people should be so obstinate as to insist upon having bread when it was so scarce

Brisbane Line. In World War II a defensive position running from north of Brisbane to north of Adelaide, to which it was intended to retire if the Japanese invaded Australia in 1942

Briseis (brī' sē is)   The patronymic name of Hippodamia, daughter of Briseu.   She was the cause of the quarrel between Agamemnon and Achilles, and when the former robbed Achilles of her, Achilles refused any longer to go to battle, and the Greeks lost ground daily Ultimately, Achilles sent his friend Patroclus to supply his place; he was slain, and Achilles, towering with rage, rushed to battle, slew Hector, and Troy fell.

Brissotins A nickname given to the advocates of reform in the French Revolution, because they were "led by the nose" by Jean Pierre Brissot   The party was subsequently called the Girondists (*q v*)

Bristol Board. A stiff drawing-paper with a smooth surface, or a fine quality of cardboard composed of two or more sheets pasted together, the substance of board being governed by the number of sheets   Said to have been first made at Bristol.

Bristol Boy, The Thomas Chatterton (1752-70), who was born at Bristol, and there composed his *Rowley Poems   See* ROWLEY
The marvellous boy,
The sleepless soul that perished in his pride.
WORDSWORTH *Resolution and Independence*

Bristol cream is a particularly fine rich brand of sherry.   *See* BRISTOL MILK

Bristol diamonds. Brilliant crystals of colourless quartz found in St Vincent's Rock, Clifton, near Bristol

Spenser refers to them as "adamants" —

> But Avon marched in more stately path,
> Proud of his Adamants, with which he shines
> And glisters wide, as als of wondrous Bath,
> And Bristowe faire
>
> *Faerie Queene*, IV, xi, 31

Bristol fashion, In. Methodical and orderly. More generally **Shipshape and Bristol fashion.** A sailor's phrase, said in Smyth's *Sailor's Word Book* to refer to the time "when Bristol was in its palmy commercial days . and its shipping was all in proper good order "

Bristol milk. Sherry sack, at one time given by the Bristol people to their friends

> This metaphorical milk, whereby Xeres or Sherry-sack is intended —FULLER· *Worthies*

Bristol waters Mineral waters of Clifton, near Bristol, with a temperature not exceeding 74°, formerly celebrated in cases of pulmonary consumption They are very rarely used now.

Britain. The derivation of this word is not certainly known, but its first recorded use is by the Greeks, who probably obtained it through the Greek colony at Massilia (Marseilles) *Itan*, or *etan*, in Basque signifies a district or country; the root appears in many names, e g Aquitania, Lusitania, Mauretania.

Another suggestion is that it is from the Cymric-Celtic root, *brith*, meaning "to paint," with allusion to woad-painting of their bodies by the aborigines

Great Britain consists of "Britannia prima" (England), "Britannia secunda" (Wales), and "North Britain" (Scotland), united under one sway The term first came into use in 1604, when James I was proclaimed "King of Great Britain "

Greater Britain. The whole British Empire, i e Great Britain, the Dominions and Colonies

Britannia. The first known representation of Britannia as a female figure sitting on a globe, leaning with one arm on a shield, and grasping a spear in the other hand, is on a Roman coin of Antoninus Pius, who died A.D. 161 The figure reappeared on our copper coin in the reign of Charles II, 1665, and the model was Frances Stewart, afterwards created Duchess of Richmond The engraver was Philip Roetier, 1665

> The King's new medall, where in little, there is Mrs Stewart's face . and a pretty thing it is, that he should choose her face to represent Britannia by.—*Pepys's Diary.*

British Council. This was established in 1934 for the purpose of encouraging British cultural interests abroad, including the formation of schools, the introduction of foreign students to this country, and the projection of a knowledge of all aspects of British life and thought through the press, films, distribution of literature, exhibitions, lectures, concerts and plays The British Council is financed by Parliament, on a Foreign Office vote.

British Empire, Order of the. This order was instituted in 1917 with two divisions, military and civil. It is conferred for services rendered to the Empire, whether at home or abroad and is given to women equally with men There are five classes: Knight Grand Cross (G B E), Knight Commander (K.B E.); Commander (C.B E), Officer (O B E), and member (M B E) In the case of women D B E (D = dame) takes the place of K B E.

British lion, The. The pugnacity of the British nation, as opposed to the John Bull, which symbolizes the substantiality, solidity, and obstinacy of the people, with all their prejudices and national peculiarities

To twist the tail of the British lion used to be a favourite phrase in America for attempting to annoy the British people and government by abuse and vituperation This was usually resorted to with the object of currying favour with citizens of Irish birth and getting their votes

Britisher, A. An American term for a Briton, a native of the British Isles, often with a derogatory implication.

Britomart (brit' ō mart) In Spenser's *Faerie Queene*, a female knight, daughter of King Ryence of Wales She is the personification of chastity and purity; encounters the "savage, fierce bandit and mountaineer" without injury, and is assailed by "hag and unlaid ghost, goblin, and swart fairy of the mine," but "dashes their brute violence into sudden adoration and blank awe " She finally marries Artegall

Spenser got the name, which means " sweet maiden," from Britomartis, a Cretan nymph of Greek mythology, who was very fond of the chase. King Minos fell in love with her, and persisted in his advances for nine months, when she threw herself into the sea

Briton To fight like a Briton is to fight with indomitable courage.

To work like a Briton is to work hard and perseveringly

Certainly, without the slightest flattery, dogged courage and perseverance are the strong characteristics of John Bull. A similar phrase is "To work like a Trojan "

Brittany, The Damsel of. Eleanor, daughter of Geoffrey, second son of Henry II of England, and Constance, daughter of Conan IV of Brittany At the death of Prince Arthur (1203) she was heiress to the English throne, but John confined her in Bristol castle, where she died in 1241.

Broach. To broach a new subject. To start one in conversation. The allusion is to beer barrels, which are tapped by means of a peg called a *broach* So "to broach a subject" is to introduce it, to bring it to light, as beer is drawn from the cask after the latter has been *broached*

> I did broach this business to your highness
>
> *Henry VIII*, ii, 4.

Broad Arrow. The representation of an arrowhead placed on Government stores, and also upon the uniform of convicts. It was introduced by Henry, Earl of Romney, who was Master General of the Ordnance, 1693-1702 and employed his own cognisance of a pheon, or broad arrow

Broad Bottom Ministry. An administration formed by a coalition of parties in 1744 Pelham retained the lead, Pitt supported the Government, Bubb Doddington was treasurer of the navy It held office till 1754.

Broadcasting. This is the term used to describe the sending out of wireless programmes of news, music, etc, to be received by those who have the necessary apparatus to listen in. The first transmitting station for entertainment and educational purposes began broadcasting in 1920 In May, 1922, the Marconi Co began a programme of speech and music from Marconi House, London (2LO). In October of the same year the British Broadcasting Company came into being, and in 1926 this became the British Broadcasting Corporation (B B C) with a royal charter In 1950 the number of licences issued amounted to nearly twelve million.

Broadcloth. The best cloth for men's clothes. So called from its great breadth. It required two weavers, side by side, to fling the shuttle across it Originally two yards wide, now about fifty-four inches; but the word is now used to signify a fine, plain-wove, black cloth.

> An honest man, close-button'd to the chin,
> Broadcloth without, and a warm heart within
> COWPER *Epistle to Joseph Hill*

Broadside. A large sheet of paper printed on one side only, strictly, the whole should be in one type and one measure, *i e* must not be divided into columns It is also called a *broadsheet* ,

> Van Critters gives the best account of the trial.
> I have seen a broadside which confirms his narrative.
> MACAULAY *History*

In naval language, a *broadside* means the whole side of a ship; and to "open a broadside on the enemy" is to discharge all the guns on one side at the same moment

Brobdingnag. In Swift's *Gulliver's Travels*, the country of giants, to whom Gulliver was a pigmy "not half so big as a round little worm plucked from the lazy finger of a maid " Hence the adjective, *Brobdingnagian*, colossal

Brocken. *See* SPECTRE

Brodie, Steve. He jumped off Brooklyn Bridge 23rd July, 1886 Known as "the man who wouldn't take a dare," he made this leap to win a bet of $200.

Brogue. An Irish word, *brog*, a shoe, connected with A S *broc*, breeches A *brogue* is properly, a stout coarse shoe of rough hide; and secondarily hose, trousers The use of *brogue* for the dialect or manner of speaking may be from this—*i e.* "brogue" is the speech of those who wear "brogues", but it is by no means certain.

Broken Music. In Elizabethan England this term meant (*a*) part, or concerted music, *i.e* music performed on instruments of different classes, such as the] "consorts" given in Morley's *Consort Lessons* (1599), which are written for the treble lute, cithern, pandora, flute, treble viol, and bass viol, and (*b*) music played by a string orchestra, the term in this sense probably originating from harps, lutes, and such other stringed instruments as were played without a bow, not being able to sustain a long note It is in this sense that Bacon uses the term·—

> Dancing to song is a thing of great state and pleasure I understand it that the song be in quire, placed aloft and accompanied with some broken music —*Essays Of Masques and Triumphs.*

Shakespeare two or three times makes verbal play with the term·—

> *Pand* . What music is this?
> *Serv* I do but partly know, sir; it is music in parts .
> *Pand* . . Fair Prince, here is good broken music
> *Paris* You have broke it, cousin, and by my life, you shall make it whole again
> *Troilus and Cressida*, iii, 1

Broken on the Wheel. *See* BREAK

Broker This word meant originally a man who broached wine, and then sold it; hence, one who buys to sell again, a retailer, a second-hand dealer, a middleman The word is formed in the same way as *tapster*, one who *taps* a cask In modern use some restricting word is generally prefixed as bill-broker, cotton-broker, ship-broker, stock-broker, etc

Bromide. A person given to making trite remarks, later, the remark itself It was first used in this sense by the American novelist Gelett Burgess (1866-1951) in his novel *Are You a Bromide?* 1906.

Brontes (bron' tēz). A blacksmith personified; in Greek mythology, one of the Cyclops. The name signifies *Thunder*

> Not with such weight, to frame the forky brand,
> The ponderous hammer falls from Brontes' hand
> HOOLE *Jerusalem Delivered*, Bk. xx.

Broom. The small wild shrub with yellow flowers (Latin *planta genista*) from which the English royal dynasty, the Plantagenets, took their name The founder of the dynasty, Geoffrey of Anjou (father of Henry II) is said to have worn a sprig of it in his hat The name was officially adopted by Richard of York (father of Richard III) about 1460

Broom. A broom is hung at the masthead of ships about to be sold—to be "swept away " The idea is popularly taken from Admiral van Tromp (*see* PENNANT), but probably this allusion is more witty than true The custom of hanging up something special to attract notice is very common, thus an old piece of carpet from a window indicates household furniture for sale, a wisp of straw indicates oysters for sale; a bush means wine for sale, etc , etc.

New brooms sweep clean Those newly appointed to an office are as a rule very zealous and sometimes ruthless in sweeping away old customs

Brosier-my-dame. A phrase used at Eton for eating out of house and home When a dame keeps an unusually bad table, the boys agree together on a day to eat, pocket, or waste everything eatable in the house The censure is well understood, and the hint is generally effective. (Gr *broso*, to eat)

Brother. A fellow-member of a religious order Friar, from Lat *frater*, and Fr *frère*, is really the same word

Also used as the official title of certain members of livery companies, of the members (always known as "Elder Brethren") of Trinity House (*q v*), and the official mode of address of one barrister to another.

Brother used attributively with another substantive denotes a fellow-member of the same calling, order, corporation, etc Thus *brother birch*, a fellow-schoolmaster, *brother-blade*, a fellow-soldier or companion in arms, *brother bung*, a fellow licensed victualler, *brother mason*, a fellow freemason, etc , etc

Brother Jonathan. When Washington was in want of ammunition, he called a council of officers, but no practical suggestion could be offered "We must consult brother Jonathan," said the general, meaning His Excellency Jonathan Trumbull, governor of the State of Connecticut This was done, and the difficulty was remedied "To consult Brother Jonathan" then became a set phrase, and Brother Jonathan became the "John Bull" of the United States

Brougham (brō' âm, brum) In old horse-drawn days this was the name given to a closed four-wheel carriage drawn by one horse, very similar to the old "growler" horse cab. It was named after Lord Brougham (1778-1868), a prominent Regency and Victorian lawyer and politician

Browbeat. To beat or put a man down with sternness, arrogance, insolence, etc , from knitting the brows and frowning on one's opponent

Brown. A copper coin, a penny; so called from its colour Similarly a sovereign is a "yellow boy "

To be done brown. To be deceived, taken in; to be "roasted " This is one of many similar expressions connected with cooking *See* COOKING

Browned off. This is a slang phrase that came into general use during World War II, meaning "fed up," bored or disillusioned Various derivations of the phrase have been suggested, but none of them appears satisfactory

Brown Bess. A familiar name for the old flint-lock musket formerly in use in the British Army In 1808 a process of browning was introduced, but the term was common long before this, and probably referred to the colour of the stock *Bess* is unexplained, but may be a counterpart to *Bill* (*see below*)

Brown Bill. A kind of halbert used by English foot-soldiers before muskets were employed They were staff weapons, with heads like bill-hooks but furnished with spikes at the top and back The *brown* probably refers to the rusty condition in which they were kept; though, on the other hand, it may stand for *burnished* (Dut. *brun*, shining), as in the old phrases "my bonnie brown sword," "brown as glass," etc Keeping the weapons *bright*, however, is a modern fashion; our fore-

fathers preferred the honour of blood stains In the following extract the term denotes the soldiers themselves —

> Lo, with a band of bowmen and of pikes,
> Brown bills and targetiers
> MARLOWE *Edward II*, l, 1324

Brown Bomber Joe Louis (*b*. 1914), undefeated heavyweight champion of the world from 1937 until his retirement in 1949 On his return in 1950 he was defeated by Ezzard Charles He began his professional career in 1934, winning 27 fights, all but four by knockouts He won the heavyweight title from Jim Braddock and successfully defended it more than 22 times before joining up in the U.S army Louis is possibly the greatest heavyweight boxer ever known The phrase applied to him springs from his being a Negro and (presumably) from the lethal power of his punches.

Brown, Jones, and Robinson. The typification of middle-class Englishmen, from the adventures of three Continental tourists of these names which were told and illustrated in *Punch* in the 1870s by Richard Doyle These sketches hold up to ridicule the gaucherie, insular ideas, vulgarity, extravagance, conceit, and snobbism that too often characterize the class, and are in themselves an almost unsurpassed example of Victorian snobbery in their senseless and ill-mannered jeers at uneducated people.

Brown study. Absence of mind, apparent thought, but real vacuity The corresponding French expression explains it—*sombre rêverie* Sombre and *brun* both mean sad, melancholy, gloomy, dull

> Invention flags his brain grows muddy,
> And black despair succeeds brown study
> CONGREVE *An Impossible Thing.*

Brownie. The house spirit in Scottish superstition. He is called in England Robin Goodfellow. At night he is supposed to busy himself in doing little jobs for the family over which he presides Farms are his favourite abode Brownies are brown or tawny spirits, in opposition to fairies, which are fair or elegant ones *See also* GIRL GUIDE

It is not long since every family of considerable substance was haunted by a spirit they called Browny, which did several sorts of work, and this was the reason why they gave him offerings on what they called " Browny's stone "—MARTIN *Scotland.*

Brownists. Followers of Robert Brown, of Rutlandshire, a vigorous Puritan controversialist in the time of Queen Elizabeth The later "Independents" held pretty well the same religious tenets as the Brownists Sir Andrew Aguecheek says'—

> I'd as lief be a Brownist as a politician
> SHAKESPEARE *Twelfth Night*, iii, 2

Browse his Jib, To. A sailors' phrase, meaning to drink till the face is flushed and swollen The *jib* means the face, and to *browse* here means "to fatten " A piece of slang formed on the nautical phrase "to bowse the jib," the metaphor signifies that the man is "tight."

Bruin (broo' in) In Butler's *Hudibras*, one of the leaders arrayed against the hero His prototype in real life was Talgol, a Newgate butcher who obtained a captaincy for valour at Naseby   He marched next to Orsin (Joshua Gosling, landlord of the bear-gardens at Southwark).

Sir Bruin. The bear in the famous German beast-epic, *Reynard the Fox.*

Brumaire (brü'mâr)   The month in the French Republican Calendar from October 23rd to November 21st.   It was named from *brume*, fog (Lat *bruma*, winter)   The celebrated 18th Brumaire (November 9th, 1799) was the day on which the Directory was overthrown and Napoleon established his supremacy

Brumby. An Australian wild horse. The origin of the word is obscure

Brummagem (brŭm'a jem)   Worthless or very inferior metal articles made in imitation of better ones   The word is a local form of the name *Birmingham*, which is the great mart and manufactory of gilt toys, cheap jewellery, imitation gems, and the like.

Brunhild (broon'hild).   Daughter of the King of Issland (*i e* Isalaland, in the Low Countries), beloved by Günther, one of the two great chieftains in the *Nibelungenlied*   She was to be carried off by force, and Günther asked his friend Siegfried to help him   Siegfried contrived the matter by snatching from her the talisman which was her protector, but she never forgave him for his treachery

Brunswicker   *See* BLACK BRUNSWICKERS

Brunt. To bear the brunt.   To bear the worst of the heat, and collision   The "brunt of a battle" is the hottest part of the fight.   *Cp* FIRE-BRAND

Brunt is partly imitative (like *dint*), and is probably influenced by the Icel *bruna*, to advance with the speed of fire, as a standard in the heat of battle

Brush. The tail of a fox or squirrel, which is brush-like and bushy

He brushed by me. He just touched me as he went quickly past   Hence also *brush*, a slight skirmish.

Give it another brush. A little more attention; bestow a little more labour on it, return it to the file for a little more polish.

To brush up. To renovate or revive, to bring again into use what has been neglected as, "I must brush up my French."

Brut (brut)   A rhyming chronicle of British history beginning with the mythical *Brut*, or *Brute* (*q.v.*), and so named from him   Wace's *Le Roman de Brut*, of *Brut d'Angleterre*, written in French about 1150, is a rhythmical version of Geoffrey of Monmouth's *History* with additional legends   It is here that first mention is made of Arthur's Round Table   Wace's work formed the basis of Layamon's *Brut* (early 13th cent), a versified history of England from the fall of Troy to A D 689   Layamon's poem contains 32,250 lines, Wace's rather over 14,000.   *See* ARTHUR

Brute or **Brutus** (broot).   In the mythological history of England, the first king of the

Britons was son of Sylvius (grandson of Ascanius and great-grandson of Æneas)   Having inadvertently killed his father, he first took refuge in Greece and then in Britain   In remembrance of Troy, he called the capital of his kingdom Troy-novant (*q v*), now London

Brutum fulmen (broo'tum fŭl'men) (Lat.)   A noisy but harmless threatening, an innocuous thunderbolt

The phrase is from Pliny's *"Bruta fulmina et vana, ut quæ nulla veniant ratione naturæ"* (II, xliii, 113)—Thunderbolts that strike blindly and harmlessly, being traceable to no natural cause

The Actors do not value themselves upon the Clap, but regard it as a mere *Brutum fulmen*, or empty Noise, when it has not the sound of the Oaken Plant in it—ADDISON   *Spectator* (November 29th, 1711).

Brutus, Junius (broo'tus joo'ni us)   In legend, the first consul of Rome, fabled to have held office about 509 B C   He condemned to death his own two sons for joining a conspiracy to restore to the throne the banished Tarquin   He was—

The public father who the private quelled, And on the dread tribunal sternly sat THOMSON: *Winter*

Brutus, Marcus (85-42 B C.).   Cæsar's friend, who joined the conspirators to murder him because he made himself a king

And thou, unhappy Brutus, kind of heart, Whose steady arm, by awful virtue urged, Lifted the Roman steel against thy friend THOMSON   *Winter*, 324-6

Et tu, Brute. Thou, too, Brutus!   The reference is to the exclamation of Julius Cæsar when he saw that his old friend was one of the conspirators engaged in stabbing him to death.

The Spanish Brutus. Alphonso Perez de Guzman (1258-1320)   While he was governor, Castile was besieged by Don Juan, who had revolted from his brother, Sancho IV   Juan, who held in captivity one of the sons of Guzman, threatened to cut his throat unless Guzman surrendered the city.   Guzman replied, "Sooner than be a traitor, I would myself lend you a sword to slay him," and he threw a sword over the city wall   The son, we are told, was slain by the father's sword before his eyes.

Bryanites   *See* BIBLE CHRISTIANS.

Bub. Drink, particularly strong beer

Drunk with Helicon's waters and double-brewed bub —PRIOR   *To a Person who wrote ill*

Bubastis   Greek name of Bast, or Pasht, the Diana of Egyptian mythology, she was daughter of Isis and sister of Horus, and her sacred animal was the cat   *See* CAT

Bubble, or Bubble Scheme. A project or scheme of no sterling worth and of very ephemeral duration—as worthless and frail as a bubble   The word was in common use in the 18th century to denote a swindle.   *See* MISSISSIPPI; SOUTH SEA.

The Bubble Act. An Act of George I, passed in 1719, its object being to punish the promoters of bubble schemes   It was repealed in 1825.

Bubble and squeak. Cold boiled potatoes and greens fried up together, sometimes with bits of cold meat as well   They first bubbled in water when boiled, and afterwards hissed or squeaked in the frying-pan

Bucca (bŭk′ a)   A goblin of the wind, supposed by the ancient inhabitants of Cornwall to foretell shipwrecks, also a sprite fabled to live in the tin-mines.

Buccaneer (bŭk a nēr′)   Properly, a seller of smoke-dried meat, from the Brazilian word *boucan*, a gridiron or frame on which flesh was barbecued, which was adopted in France, and *boucanier* formed from it   *Boucanier* was first applied to the French settlers in Hayti, whose business it was to hunt animals for their skins and who frequently combined with this business that of a marauder and pirate. *Buccaneer* thus became applied to any desperate, lawless, piratical adventurer.

Bucentaur (bū sen′ tôr)   The name of the Venetian state-galley employed by the Doge when he went on Ascension Day to wed the Adriatic   The word is Gr *bous*, ox, and *centauros*, centaur; and the original galley was probably ornamented with a man-headed ox

> The spouseless Adriatic mourns her lord
> And, annual marriage now no more renew'd,
> The Bucentaur lies rotting unrestored,
> Neglected garment of her widowhood
>   BYRON   *Childe Harold*, iv, 9

The last *Bucentaur*, third of the name, was destroyed by the French in 1798.   *See* BRIDE OF THE SEA

Bucephalos (*bull-headed*)   A horse. Strictly speaking, the favourite charger of Alexander the Great

Buchan's Weather Periods (bū′ kan). Alexander Buchan (1829-1907) was secretary of the Scottish Meteorological Society which, under his influence, built an observatory on Ben Nevis   As a result of many years' observation of weather and temperatures he worked out a curve of recurrent periods, six cold and two warm, in the year   The cold periods are Feb 7-10, April 11-14, May 9-14, June 29-July 4, Aug 6-11, Nov 6-12   The warm periods are July 12-15, Aug 12-15.   It should be remembered that these dates are the mean of many observations and do not predict the probable weather for every year

Buchanites   A sect of fanatics who appeared in the west of Scotland in 1783   They were named after Mrs or Lucky Buchan, their founder, who called herself "Friend Mother in the Lord," claiming to be the woman mentioned in *Rev* xii, and maintaining that the Rev Hugh White, a convert, was the "man-child"

> I never heard of alewife that turned preacher, except Luckie Buchan in the West
>   SCOTT   *St Ronan's Well*, c ii

Buck.   A dandy; a gay and spirited fellow, a fast young man

> A most tremendous buck he was, as he sat there serene, in state, driving his greys
>   THACKERAY   *Vanity Fair*, ch vi

The word is also American slang for a dollar

Buck-basket.   A linen-basket. To buck is to wash clothes in lye   When Cade says

his mother was "descended from the Lacies," two men overhear him, and say, "She was a pedlar's daughter, but not being able to travel with her furred pack, she washes bucks here at home" (2 *Henry VI*, iv, 2)   The word is probably connected with Ger *beuche*, clothes steeped in lye, and Fr. *buer*, to steep in lye, and perhaps with A S *buc*, a pitcher

Buck-bean.   The popular name of *Menyanthes trifoliata*, a water-plant, an Elizabethan translation of the Flemish name *bocks boonen* (Mod. Dut *bocksboon*), goat's beans   The name *bog-bean*, also given to this plant, is considerably later

Bucket, To.   An obsolete slang term for to cheat.

To give the bucket, to get the bucket.   To give (or receive) notice of dismissal from employment   Here *bucket* is synonymous with *sack* (*q v*).

To kick the bucket.   To die   *Bucket* here is a beam or yoke (O Fr. *buquet*, Fr. *trebuchet*, a balance), and in East Anglia the big frame in which a newly slaughtered pig is suspended by the heels is still called a "bucket"   An alternative theory is offered that the bucket was a pail kicked away by a suicide, who stood on it the better to hang himself

Bucket-shop.   A term (probably from the old slang "to bucket," *above*) which originated in America, denoting the office of an "outside" stock-broker, *i e*   one who is not a member of the official Stock Exchange   As these offices are largely used for the sole purpose of *gambling* in stocks and shares as apart from making *investments*, and as many of them have been run by very shady characters, the name is rarely used except with a bad significance

Buckhorn.   *See* STOCKFISH

Buckhorse.   A severe blow or slap on the face. So called from John Smith, a pugilist of about 1740, whose nickname it was   'Buckhorse' was so insensible to pain that, for a small sum, he would allow anyone to strike him on the side of the face with all his force

Buckingham.   Fuller, in his *Worthies*, speaks of the beech-trees as the most characteristic feature of this county, and the name is derived from the *Bocingas*, or dwellers among the beech-trees (A S *boc*), a tribe which anciently inhabited that county.

Off with his head!   So much for Buckingham! A famous line, often searched for in vain in Shakespeare's *Richard III*   It is not to be found there, but is in Act iv, Sc iii, of Colley Cibber's *The Tragical History of Richard III*, altered from Shakespeare (1700)

Buckle   I can't buckle to.   I can't give my mind to work   The allusion is to buckling on one's armour or belt.

To cut the buckle.   To caper about, to heel and toe it in dancing   In jigs the two feet buckle or twist into each other with great rapidity

> Throth, it wouldn't lave a laugh in you to see the parson dancin' down the road on his way home, and the minister and methodist praicher cuttin' the buckle as they went along —W B. YEATS   *Fairy Tales of the Irish Peasantry*, p 98.

To talk buckle.   To talk about marriage.

Buckler. *See* SHIELDS

Bucklersbury (London) was at one time the noted street for druggists and herbalists, hence Falstaff says —

> I cannot cog, and say thou art this and that, like a many of these lisping hawthorn buds, that come like women in men's apparel, and smell like Bucklersbury in simple time
>
> SHAKESPEARE *Merry Wives of Windsor*, iii, 3

Stow tells us that "the Peperers and Grocers" had their shops there

Buckley's Chance (Austr.) An extremely remote chance Two explanations of the phrase's origin exist According to the first it comes from a convict named Buckley who escaped in 1803 and lived over thirty years with Aborigines The second explanation derives it from the well-known Melbourne business house of Buckley and Nunn—hence the pun "There are just two chances, Buckley's or None "

Buckmaster's Light Infantry. *See* REGIMENTAL NICKNAMES.

Buckram. A strong coarse kind of cloth stiffened with gum, perhaps so called (like *Astrakhan*, from the Eastern city) from Bokhara. In the Middle Ages the name was that of a valuable fabric that came from the East

Men in buckram Hypothetical men existing only in the brain of the imaginer. The allusion is to the vaunting tale of Falstaff to Prince Henry (Shakespeare 1 *Henry IV*, ii, 4) Hence, "a buckram army," one the strength of which exists only in the imagination

Buckshee (buk' shē) This word undoubtedly comes from baksheesh (*q v.*) though in its new usage it means something given away free, something thrown in gratis

Buck-tooth. A large projecting front-tooth, formerly also called a *butter-tooth*

Buckwheat. A corruption of *beech-wheat* (A S *boc*, beech, *see* BUCKINGHAM), so called because its seeds are triangular, like beech-mast The botanical name is *Fagopyrum* (beech-wheat).

> The buckwheat
> Whitened broad acres, sweetening with its flowers
> The August wind
>
> BRYANT *The Fountain*, stanza 7

Buddha (bŭd' a) (Sanskrit, "the Enlightened"). The title given to Prince Siddhartha or Gautama (*q v*), also called (from the name of his tribe, the Sakhyas) Sakya muni, the founder of Buddhism, who lived from about 623 B C to 543 B C

Buddhism. The system of religion inaugurated by the Buddha in India in the 6th century B C. The general outline of the system is that the world is a transient reflex of deity, that the soul is a 'vital spark' of deity, and that it will be bound to matter till its "wearer" has, by divine contemplation, so purged and purified it that it is fit to be absorbed into the divine essence.

The four sublime verities of Buddhism are as follows —
(1) Pain exists
(2) The cause of pain is "birth sin" The Buddhist supposes that man has passed through many previous existences, and all of the heaped-up sins accumulated in these previous states constitute man's "birth-sin "
(3) Pain is ended only by Nirvana.
(4) The way that leads to Nirvana is—right faith, right judgment, right language, right purpose, right practice, right obedience, right memory, and right meditation (eight in all)

The abstract nature of the religion, together with the overgrowth of its monastic system and the superior vitality and energy of Brahminism, caused it to decline in India itself, but it spread rapidly in the surrounding countries and took so permanent a hold that it is computed that at the present time it has some 140 million adherents, of whom 10¾ millions are in India, and the rest principally in Ceylon, Tibet, China, and Japan

Esoteric Buddhism. *See* THEOSOPHY

Bude or **Gurney Light.** A very bright light obtained by supplying an argand gas-jet with oxygen, invented by Sir Goldsworthy Gurney (1793-1875) about 1834, and first used in a lighthouse at Bude, Cornwall

Budge Lambskin with the wool dressed outwards, worn on the edge of capes, graduates' hoods, and so on. Hence the word is used attributively and as an adjective to denote pedantry, stiff formality, etc.

> O foolishness of men' that lend their ears
> To those budge-doctors of the stoic fur
>
> MILTON *Comus*, 706

Budge Row, Cannon Street, is so called because it was chiefly occupied by budge-makers

Budge Bachelors. A company of men clothed in long gowns lined with budge or lambs' wool, who used to accompany the Lord Mayor of London at his inauguration

Budgeree (bŭj' ér rē) An Aboriginal Australian word meaning excellent, especially good.

Budget. The statement which the Chancellor of the Exchequer lays annually before the House of Commons, respecting the national income and expenditure, taxes, and salaries The word is the old Fr *bougette*, a wallet, and the present use arose from the custom of bringing to the House the papers pertaining to these matters in a leather bag, and laying them on the table Hence, *to budget*, to prepare a budget or estimate

A budget of news. A bagful of news, a large stock of news

Cry budget. A watchword or shibboleth, short for Mumbudget (*q v*). Slender says to Shallow —

> We have a nay-word how to know one another I come to her in white and cry *mum* she cries *budget* and by that we know one another
>
> SHAKESPEARE. *Merry Wives of Windsor*, v, 2

Buff. Properly, soft, stout leather prepared from the skin of the *buffalo*; hence, any light-coloured leather, and hence the figurative use, the bare skin "To stand in buff" is to stand without clothing in one's bare skin. "To strip to the buff" is to strip to the skin

To stand buff To stand firm, without flinching Here *buff* means a blow or buffet. *Cp* BLINDMAN'S BUFF

> And for the good old cause stood buff,
> 'Gainst many a bitter kick and cuff
> > BUTLER *Hudibras's Epitaph*

I must even stand buff and outface him —FIELDING

The phrase also occurs as to **stand bluff.** Sheridan, in his *School for Scandal,* ii, 3, says.—

> That he should have stood bluff to old bachelor so long, and sink into a husband at last

Here the allusion is probably nautical; a "bluff shore" is one with a bold and almost perpendicular front

Buffs *See* REGIMENTAL NICKNAMES

Buffalo Bill. This was the name made famous by William Frederick Cody (1846-1917), one of the world's greatest showmen He was born in Iowa and when little more than a boy was a rider of the Pony Express (*q v*) In 1861 he became a scout and guide for the U S army, and fought in the Civil War. In 1867 he made a contract to supply the labourers constructing the Kansas Pacific railway with buffalo meat, hence his sobriquet Later on he was fighting once more in the Indian wars and single-handed killed Yellowhand, the Cheyenne chief In 1883 he organized his Wild West show, which he brought to Europe for the first time in 1887. He paid various visits after this and toured the Continent in 1910 He died at Denver. It is no exaggeration to say that his show, with its Indians, cowboys, sharp-shooters and rough-riders has never been surpassed.

Buffer. A chap, a silly old fellow. In M E *buffer* meant a stutterer, and the word is used in *Is* xxii, 4, in Wyclif's version, where the Authorized Version reads, "And the tongue of the stammerers shall be ready to speak plainly"

Buffer of a railway carriage is an apparatus to *rebuff* or deaden the force of collision.

Buffer State A small, self-governing state separating two larger states, and thus tending to prevent hostilities between the two The term seems to have originated on the north-west frontiers of India.

Buffoon. Properly, one who puffs out his cheeks, and makes a ridiculous explosion by causing them suddenly to collapse (Ital *buffone,* from *buffare,* to puff out the cheeks, hence, to jest)

Bug. An old word for goblin, sprite, bogy; probably from Welsh *bwg,* a ghost. The word is used in Coverdale's Bible, which is hence known as the "Bug Bible" (*see* BIBLE, SPECIALLY NAMED), and survives in *bogle, bogy,* and in *bugaboo,* a monster or goblin, introduced into the tales of the old Italian romancers, and *bugbear,* a scarecrow, or sort of hobgoblin in the form of a bear

> For all that here on earth we dreadfull hold,
> Be but as bugs to fearen babes withall
> > SPENSER: *Faerie Queene,* II, vii, 25

> Warwick was a bug that feared us all
> > SHAKESPEARE 3 *Henry IV,* v, 3.

> To the world no bugbear is so great
> As want of figure and a small estate.
> > POPE: *Satyres,* iii, 67-68.

> Making believe
> At desperate doings with a bauble-sword
> And other bugaboo-and-baby-work
> > BROWNING. *Ring and the Book,* v, 949

In common usage the word bug is applied to almost any kind of insect or germ, though more especially to a beetle or an insect that creeps or crawls. Colloquially it can be used to refer to any mental infection, such as "he has the money bug" of one whose sole interest is making money.

A big bug. A person of importance—especially in his own eyes; a swell, a pompous or conceited man There is an old adjective *bug,* meaning pompous, proud

> Dainty sport toward, Dalyall' sit, come sit,
> Sit and be quiet: here are kingly bug-words
> > FORD *Perkin Warbeck,* ii

Buhl. An incorrect form of Boulle (*q.v*)

Bulbul. An Eastern bird of the thrush family, noted for its beautiful singing; hence applied to the nightingale The word is Persian, and was familiarized by Tom Moore

> 'Twas like the notes, half-ecstasy, half pain,
> The bulbul utters.
> > MOORE *Lalla Rookh (Veiled Prophet,* i, 14)

Bull. A blunder, or inadvertent contradiction of terms, for which the Irish are proverbial. *The British Apollo* (No. 22, 1708) says the term is derived from one Obadiah Bull, an Irish lawyer of London, in the reign of Henry VII, whose blundering in this way was notorious, but there is no corroboration of this story, which must be put down as *ben trovato.* There was a M.E verb *bull,* to befool, to cheat, and there is the O.Fr *boule* or *bole,* fraud, trickery; the word may be connected with one of these

Slang for a five-shilling piece. " Half a bull " is half a crown. Possibly from *bulla* (see POPE'S BULL *below*), but, as *bull's eye* was an older slang term for the same thing, this is doubtful Hood, in one of his comic sketches, speaks of a crier who, being apprehended, "swallowed three hogs (shillings) and a bull " It is also short for bull's eye (*q.v*)

In Stock Exchange phraseology, a bull is a speculative purchase for a rise, also a buyer who does this, the reverse of a *bear* (*q v*) A bull-account is a speculation made in the hope that the stock purchased will rise before the day of settlement.

In astronomy, the English name of the northern constellation (Lat *Taurus*) which contains Aldebaran and the Pleiades, also the sign of the zodiac that the sun enters about April 22nd and leaves a month later. It is between Aries and Gemini. The time for ploughing, which in the East was performed by oxen or bulls.

> At last from Aries rolls the bounteous sun,
> And the bright Bull receives him
> > THOMSON: *Spring,* 26.

The Pope's bull. An edict or mandate issued by the Pope, so called from the heavy leaden seal (Lat *bulla*) appended to the document *See* GOLDEN BULL

Bull is also the name given to a drink made from the swillings of empty spirit-casks. *See* BULLING THE BARREL.

A bull in a china shop. A maladroit hand interfering with a delicate business, one who produces reckless destruction

A brazen bull. An instrument of torture. *See* PHALARIS.

He may bear a bull that hath borne a calf (Erasmus' *Proverbs*)—"He that accustometh hym-selfe to lytle thynges, by lytle and lytle shal be able to go a waye with greater thynges" (*Taverner*).

To score a bull. *See* BULL'S-EYE

To take the bull by the horns. To attack or encounter a threatened danger fearlessly, to go forth boldly to meet a difficulty

John Bull. *See* JOHN BULL.

Bull-baiting. Bull- and bear-baiting were popular sports in Tudor and Stuart England. The beasts were tethered and set upon by dogs specially trained for this "sport." In his Diary for June 16th, 1670, John Evelyn describes what he calls "a rude and dirty pastime." Baiting was not prohibited in England until 1835

Bull-ring. In Spain, the arena where bull-fights take place; in England, the place where bulls used to be baited. The name still survives in many English towns, as in Birmingham. *See* MAYOR OF THE BULL-RING

Bull's-eye. The inner disk or centre of a target.

To make a bull's-eye, or **to score a bull.** To gain some signal advantage; a successful *coup* To fire or shoot an arrow right into the centre disk of the target

A black globular sweetmeat with whitish streaks, usually strongly flavoured with peppermint.

Also, a small cloud suddenly appearing, seemingly in violent motion, and expanding till it covers the entire vault of heaven, producing a tumult of wind and rain (1 *Kings* xviii, 44).

Also, a thick disk or boss of glass. Hence, a *bull's-eye lantern*, also called a *bull's-eye*.

Bull sessions. In U S A this phrase is applied to long talks, among men only, about life in general or some particular problem.

Bull and Gate. Bull and Mouth. Public-house signs. A corruption of Boulogne Gate or Mouth, adopted out of compliment to Henry VIII, who took Boulogne in 1544. The public-house sign consisting of a plain (or coloured) bull is usually with reference to the cognizance of the house of Clare. The sign of the famous Bull and Mouth Inn in Aldersgate St, London, bore the words

Milo the Cretonian
An ox slew with his fist,
And ate it up at one meal,
Ye gods, what a glorious twist.

The bull and the boar were signs used by the partisans of Clare, and Richard, Duke of Gloucester (*Richard III*)

Bulldog. A man of relentless, savage disposition is sometimes so called. A "bulldog courage" is one that flinches from no danger. The "bulldog" was the dog formerly used in bull-baiting.

In University slang the "bulldogs" or "bullers" are the two myrmidons (*q v*) of the proctor, who attend his heels like dogs, and are ready to spring on any offending undergraduate

Boys of the bulldog breed. Britons especially with reference to their pugnacity The phrase comes from the song, "Sons of the sea, all British born," that was immensely popular at the close of the 19th century.

Bullet. Every bullet has its billet. Nothing happens by chance, and no act is altogether without some effect

Bulletin. An official report of an officer to his superior, or of medical attendants respecting the health of persons of notoriety. The word is borrowed from the French, who took it from the Ital *bulletino*, a passport or lottery ticket, from *bulla* (*see* POPE'S BULL *above*). because they were authenticated by an official *bulla* or seal

News bulletin is the term used for the periodical broadcasts of news by radio, etc.

Bulling the barrel Pouring water into a rum cask, when it is nearly empty, to prevent its leaking. The water, which gets impregnated with the spirit and is frequently drunk, is called *bull*

Seamen talk of *bulling the teapot* (making a second brew), *bulling the coffee*, etc

Bullion. Gold or silver in the mass as distinguished from manufactured articles or coined money, also, a fringe made of gold or silver wire. The word is from the Fr *bouillon*, boiling, and seems to refer to the 'boiling," or melting, of the metal before it can be utilized

Bully. To overbear with words. *A bully* is a blustering menacer. The original meaning of the noun was "sweetheart," as in—

I kiss his dirty shoe, and from heart-string
I love the lovely bully
SHAKESPEARE Henry V, iv, 1

It is probably to be derived from Dut. *boel*, a lover, and the later meaning may have been influenced by Dut *bul* a bull, also a clown, and *bulderen*, to bluster

Bully-beef. Tinned, compressed beef Probably from Fr *bouilli*, boiled meat

Bully-rag. To intimidate, *bully-ragging* is abusive intimidation According to Halliwell, a *rag* is a scold, and hence a "ragging" means a scolding.

Bully-rook. Shakespeare uses the term (*Merry Wives*, I, iii, 2) for a jolly companion, but it later came to mean a hired ruffian

Bum. An old word, now almost restricted to schoolboy slang, for the buttocks, posterior It is an American term for a vagrant, hence a slang word describing any worthless fellow

Bum-bailiff. The Fr *pousse-cul* seems to favour the notion that *bum*-bailiff is no corruption These officers, who made an arrest for debt by touching the debtor on the back, are frequently referred to as *bums*

Scout me for him at the corner of the orchard, like a bum-bailiff —*Shakespeare Twelfth Night*, iii, 4

Bum-boat. A small wide boat to carry provisions to vessels lying off shore Also called "dirt-boats," being used for removing filth from ships lying in the Thames.

Bumble. A beadle. So called from the officious, overbearing beadle in Dickens's *Oliver Twist*, hence *bumbledom*, fussy officialism, especially on the part of the parish officers; also parochial officials collectively.

Bummaree A class of middlemen or fish-jobbers in Billingsgate Market, whose business is *bummareeing*, i e buying parcels of fish from the salesmen, and then retailing them The etymology of the word is unknown, but it has been suggested that it is a corruption of *bonne marée*, good fresh fish, *marée* being a French term for all kinds of fresh sea-fish.

Bumper. A full glass, generally connected with a "toast " It may be so called because the surface of the wine "bumps up" in the middle, but it is more likely from the notion that it is a "bumping" or "thumping," i e a large glass

Bumpkin. A loutish person Dut *boomken*, a little tree, a small block, hence, a blockhead.

Bumptious. Arrogant, full of mighty airs and graces, apt to take offence at presumed slights A humorous formation from *bump*, probably modelled on *presumptuous*

Bun. A tail *See* BUNNY.

Bun. "Hot cross buns" on Good Friday were supposed to be made of the dough kneaded for the host, and were marked with the cross accordingly As they are said to keep for twelve months without turning mouldy, some persons still hang up one or more in their house as a "charm against evil "

It may be remarked that the Greeks offered to Apollo, Diana, Hecate, and the Moon, cakes with "horns " Such a cake was called a *bous*, and (it is said) never grew mouldy. The round bun represented the full moon, and the "cross" symbolized the four quarters

Good Friday comes this month the old woman runs
With one a penny, two a penny "hot cross buns".
Whose virtue is, if you believe what's said,
They'll not grow mouldy like the common bread.
       Poor Robin's Almanack, 1733

Buna. The German name for synthetic rubber developed during World War II It was made by the polymerization of butadrene

Bunce. A slang term for money, particularly for something extra or unexpected in the way of profit Thought to be a corruption of *bonus* (q v).

Bunch, Mother. A noted London ale-wife of the late Elizabethan period, on whose name have been fathered many jests and anecdotes, and who is mentioned more than once in Elizabethan drama, e g —

Now, now, mother Bunch, how dost thou? What, dost frowne, Queen Gwyniver, dost wrinckle?
       DEKKER *Satiromastix*, iii, 1

In 1604 was published *Pasquil's Jests, mixed with Mother Bunches Merriments*, and in the "Epistle to the Merrie Reader" is given a humorous description of her—

She spent most of her time in telling of tales, and when she laughed, she was heard from Aldgate to the Monuments at Westminster, and all Southwarke stood in amazement, the Lyons in the Tower, and the Bulls and Beares of Parish Garden roar'd louder than the great roaring Megge . She dwelt in Cornhill, neere the Exchange, and sold strong Ale . and lived an hundred, seventy and five yeares, two dayes and a quarter, and halfe a minute.

Other books were named after her, such, for instance, as *Mother Bunch's Closet newly Broke Open*, containing rare secrets of art and nature, tried and experienced by learned philosophers, and recommended to all ingenious young men and maids, teaching them how to get good wives and husbands

Bunch of Fives. Slang for the hand or fist.

Bundle Off Get away *To bundle a person off*, is to send him away unceremoniously. Similar to *pack off* The allusion is obvious.

Bundles for Britain. An organization founded in U.S.A., January 1940, by Mrs. Wales Latham to send comfort parcels to Britain during World War II

Bundle of sticks Æsop, in one of his fables, shows that sticks one by one may be readily broken ; not so when several are bound together in a bundle The lesson taught is that "Union gives strength "

The symbol was adopted by, and gave its name to the political system of Fascism, from Lat *fasces*, a bundle of sticks

Bundling The curious and now obsolete New England custom of engaged couples going to bed together fully dressed and thus spending the night It was a recognized proceeding to which no suggestion of impropriety was attached

Stopping occasionally in the villages to eat pumpkin pies, dance at country frolics, and bundle with the Yankee lasses —WASHINGTON IRVING. *Knickerbocker*.

The same custom existed in Wales

Bung. A cant term for a publican; also for a toper "Away, . . you filthy bung," says Doll to Pistol (2 *Henry IV*, ii, 4)

Bung up Close up, as a bung closes a cask.

Bungalow. Originally, the house of a European in India, generally of one floor only with a verandah all round it, and the roof thatched to keep off the hot rays of the sun A *dak-bungalow* is a caravansary or house built by the Government for the use of travellers (Hindustani, *bangla*, of Bengal)

Bungay. *See* FRIAR BUNGAY.

Go to Bungay with you!—i e get away and don't bother me, or don't talk such stuff Bungay, in Suffolk, used to be famous for the manufacture of leather breeches, once very fashionable Persons who required new ones, or to have their old ones new-seated, went or sent to Bungay for that purpose Hence rose the cant saying, "Go to Bungay, and get your breeches mended," shortened into "Go to Bungay with you!"

My castle of Bungay *See* CASTLE

Bunkum. Claptrap. A representative at Washington being asked why he made such a flowery and angry speech, so wholly uncalled for, made answer, "I was not speaking to the House, but to Buncombe," which he represented (North Carolina)

When a critter talks for talk's sake, just to have a speech in the paper to send to home, and not for any other airthly puppus but electioneering, our folks call it bunkum —HALIBURTON. *Sam Slick*

Bunny. A rabbit So called from the provincial word *bun*, a tail, especially of a hare, which is said to "cock her bun " Bunny, a diminutive of bun, applied to a rabbit, means the animal with the "little tail "

Bunting. In Somersetshire *bunting* means sifting flour Sieves were at one time made of a strong gauzy woollen cloth, which was tough and capable of resisting wear It has been suggested that this material was found suitable for flags, and that the name for the stuff of which they are now made is due to this.
A "bunt-mill" is a machine for sifting corn.

Bunyan, Paul A legendary hero of the lumber camps of the north-western U S A. His feats —such as cutting the Grand Canyon of the Colorado by dragging his pick behind him— are told and retold with embellishments by the lumbermen, some of them were collected in a curious volume titled, *Paul Bunyan Comes West*

Burble (bĕr' bel) To mutter nonsense. In its modern use this is a word invented by Lewis Carroll (*Looking-glass*) with the meaning to make a sound somewhere between a bubble and a gurgle.
> The Jabberwock, with eyes of flame,
> Came whiffling through the tulgy wood
> And burbled as it came

Burd. A poetic word for a young lady (*cp* BIRD), obsolete except in ballads. Burd Helen, who is a heroine of Scottish ballad, is a female personification of the Fr *preux* or *prudhomme*, with this difference, that she is discreet, rather than brave and wise

Burden of a Song. A line repeated at intervals so as to constitute a refrain or chorus. It is the Fr *bourdon*, the big drone of a bagpipe, or double-diapason of an organ, used in forte parts and choruses.

Burden of Isaiah "The burden of Babylon, which Isaiah the son of Amoz did see" *Burden*, here, is a literal translation of the Heb. *massa* (rendered in the Vulgate by *onus*), which means "lifting up" either a burden or the voice, hence "utterance," hence a prophecy announcing a calamity, or a denunciation of hardships on those against whom the burden is uttered

The burden of proof. The obligation to prove something
> The burden of proof is on the party holding the affirmative [because no one can prove a negative, except by *reductio ad absurdum*]
> GREENLEAF On Evidence, vol 1, pt 2, ch. iii.

Bureaucracy. A system of government in which the business is carried on in bureaux or departments. Hence, *bureaucrat*, the head of a department in a bureaucracy The Fr *bureau* means not only the office of a public functionary, but also the whole staff of officers attached to the department
As a word of reproach, bureaucracy means the senseless and soulless application of rules and regulations

Burglary means, in English law, breaking into a house by night with intent to commit a felony In Common Law "night" means between sunset and sunrise, but by the Larceny Act of 1861, it is limited to the hours between 9 p m and 6 a m This Act makes it equally burglary to break out of a house at night after having committed a felony in it When committed by day these offences are known as house-breaking and are viewed somewhat differently by the Law

Burgundian. A Burgundian blow, *i e* decapitation The Duc de Biron, who was put to death for treason by Henri IV, was told in his youth, by a fortune-teller, "to beware of a Burgundian blow." When going to execution, he asked who was to be his executioner, and was told he was a man from Burgundy

Burgundy. A name loosely applied in England to dark red wine of more than usual alcoholic strength, but really wine (both red and white) from the province of Burgundy, grown between Dijon and Chasne, south of Beaune

Burgundy pitch. See MISNOMERS

Burial of an Ass. No burial at all, just thrown on a refuse-heap
> He shall be buried with the burial of an ass, drawn and cast forth beyond the gates of Jerusalem
> *Jer* xxii, 19

Buridan's Ass. A man of indecision, like one "on double business bound, who stands in pause where he should first begin, and both neglects." Buridan was a French scholastic philosopher who died about 1360 He is incorrectly reputed to be the father of the well-known sophism —
> If a hungry ass were placed exactly between two haystacks in every respect equal, it would starve to death, because there would be no motive why it should go to one rather than to the other

Burke. To murder by smothering So called from William Burke, an Irish navvy, who, with his accomplice William Hare, used to suffocate his victims and sell the bodies to surgeons for dissection. Hanged at Edinburgh, 1829.

To burke a question. To smother it in its birth. *The publication was burked*, suppressed before it was circulated

Burlaw See BYRLAW

Burleigh. As significant as the shake of Lord Burleigh's head. In Sheridan's *Critic* is introduced a mock tragedy called *The Spanish Armada*. Lord Burleigh is supposed to be too full of state affairs to utter a word, he shakes his head, and Puff explains what the shake means.

Burler See BIRLER

Burlesque. Father of burlesque poetry. Hipponax of Ephesus (6th cent B C.)

Burma Road, The. This great highway was constructed to open up the western interior of China by communication with the sea. It was made in 1937-39, for a distance of 770 miles from Lashio to Kunming, in Yunnan. During the war it was the chief highway for war supplies to China until the Japanese cut it in 1941 It was recaptured in 1945 Lorries do the entire trip in seven days, and by means of the extension being made and planned, will be able to penetrate far into the country

Burn His money burns a hole in his pocket. He cannot keep it in his pocket, or forbear spending it

The burnt child dreads the fire. Once caught, twice shy "What! wouldst thou have a serpent sting thee twice?"

To burn one's boats. To cut oneself off from all means of hope of retreat The allusion is to Julius Cæsar and other generals, who burned their boats or ships when they invaded a foreign country, in order that their soldiers might feel that they must either conquer the country or die, as retreat would be impossible.

To burn one's fingers To suffer loss by speculation or mischance The allusion is to taking chestnuts from the fire

To burn the Thames. To set the Thames afire. *See* THAMES

You cannot burn the candle at both ends You cannot do two opposite things at one and the same time, you cannot exhaust your energies in one direction, and yet reserve them unimpaired for something else If you go to bed late you cannot get up early

We burn daylight. We waste time in talk instead of action (Shakespeare · *Merry Wives of Windsor*, ii, 1)

Burning crown. A crown of red-hot iron set on the head of a regicide
        He was adjudged
To have his head seared with a burning crown.
                        Tragedy of Hoffmann (1631)

Burnt Candlemas The name given by the Scots to the period around Candlemas Day (*q v*), 1355-6, when Edward III marched through the Lothians with fire and sword He burnt to the ground Edinburgh and Haddington, and then retreated through lack of provisions

Bursa (Gr , a hide). So the citadel of Carthage was called The tale is that when Dido came to Africa she bought of the natives "as much land as could be encompassed by a bull's hide " The agreement was made, and Dido cut the hide into thongs, so as to enclose a space sufficient for a citadel *Cp* DONCASTER

The following is a similar story. The Yakutsks granted to the Russian explorers as much land as they could encompass with a cow's hide; but the Russians, cutting the hide into strips, obtained land enough for the port and town of Yakutsk

The Indians have a somewhat similar tradition. The fifth incarnation of Vishnu was in the form of a dwarf called Vamen Vamen obtained permission to have as much land as he could measure in three paces to build a hut on. The request was laughed at but freely granted, whereupon the dwarf grew so prodigiously that, with three paces, he strode over the whole world

Burst. To inform against an accomplice Slang variety of "split" (turn king's evidence, impeach) The person who does this *splits* or breaks up the whole concern

I'm bursting to tell you so-and-so. I'm all agog to tell you, I can't rest till I've told you.

On the burst. *See* BUST.

Burton Gone for a Burton. It is now difficult to ascertain the origin of this phrase which, starting among flying men in World War II, has now taken its place in the language It probably suggests that the missing airman has gone for a pint of Burton ale or stout Its meaning is always sinister, implying that whoever has gone for a Burton has crashed or come to grief in some way

Bury the Hatchet. Let bygones be bygones The "Great Spirit" commanded the North American Indians, when they smoked their calumet or peace-pipe, to bury their hatchets, scalping-knives, and war-clubs, that all thought of hostility might be put out of sight
        Buried was the bloody hatchet,
        Buried was the dreadful war-club,
        Buried were all warlike weapons,
        And the war-cry was forgotten.
        Then was peace among the nations
                        LONGFELLOW *Hiawatha*, xiii

Burying at cross roads. *See* CROSS-ROADS

Bus. A contraction of *omnibus* (*q.v*) The word is used by airmen and motorists in a humorous, almost affectionate, way for their conveyances

Busman's holiday. There is a story that in old horse-bus days a driver spent his holiday travelling to and on a bus driven by one of his pals From this has arisen the phrase, which means occupying one's spare and free time in carrying on with one's usual work, in other words, a holiday in name only

Busby. A frizzled wig, also the tall cap of a hussar, artilleryman, etc , which hangs from the top over the right shoulder It is not known what the word is derived from: Doctor Busby, master of Westminster School from 1638 to 1695, did not wear a frizzled wig, but a close cap, somewhat like a Welsh wig *See* WIG

Bush. One beats the bush, but another has the hare. *See* BEAT THE BUSH

Good wine needs no bush. A good article will make itself known without being puffed An ivy-bush (anciently sacred to Bacchus) was once the common sign of taverns, and especially of private houses where beer or wine could be obtained by travellers
        Some ale-houses upon the road I saw,
        And some with bushes showing they wine did draw.
                        Poor Robin's Perambulations (1678)
The proverb is Latin, and shows that the Romans introduced the custom into Europe "*Vino vendibili hedera non opus est*" (Columella) It was also common to France "*Au vin qui se vend bien, il ne faut point de lierre.*" If it be true that good wine needs no bush, 'tis true that a good play needs no epilogue.
        SHAKESPEARE *As You Like It* (Epilogue)

To take to the bush. To become bush-rangers, like runaway convicts, who live by plunder *See* BUSH, below

Bush. An Australian term for wild, wooded country, derived from the Dutch *bosch* The word was imported from South Africa before 1820, and gave rise to a whole vocabulary—*bushman, bush telegraph, bush ranger*, etc.

Bushrangers. Originally escaped convicts in Australia who were forced to live in the wilds to escape recapture, in which sense it is found in the Sydney *Gazette* in 1805 The word has a modern sense of those who take advantage of their fellows, by sharp practice or crime

Bushmen (Dut *Boschjesman*). Natives of South Africa who live in the "bush", the aborigines of the Cape, dwellers in the Australian " bush ", bush farmers

Busnmen   are the only nomads in the country They never cultivate the soil, nor rear any domestic animal save wretched dogs
LIVINGSTONE *Travels*, ch ii

Bush-shanty (Austr) A hut selling illegal liquor, often in the gold-rush areas. Hence *to shanty* is to pub-crawl.

Bushwhacker (Austr.) One who lives in the bush. (U S A.) a deserter in the Civil War who looted behind the lines.

Bushed. An Australian word meaning "lost " It has wandered so far from its original connotation of "bush" that we find such a phrase as ' a small ship became bushed in the great Van Dieman Gulf."
BARRATT, *Coast of Adventure*, 1944.

Bush telegraph. In early Australian slang, one who informed the *bushrangers* (*q v*) of police movements, now widespread to indicate any unofficial and mysterious source of information

Bushmaster A large and very poisonous South American snake—*Lachesis mutus*

Bushel To measure other people's corn by **one's own bushel** To make oneself the standard of right and wrong, to appraise everything as it accords or disagrees with one's own habits of thought and preconceived opinions. The bushel was measured in a wooden or earthenware container, hence **under a bushel**, secretly, in order to hide it

Neither do men light a candle and put it under a bushel, but on a candlestick —*Matt* v, 15

Business. A S *bisigness*, from *bisigian*, to occupy, to worry, to fatigue. In theatrical parlance "business" or "biz" means by-play Thus, Hamlet trifling with Ophelia's fan, Lord Dundreary's hop, and so on, are the special "business" of the actor of the part As a rule, the "business" is invented by the actor who creates the part, and it is handed down by tradition.

Business to-morrow. When the Spartans seized upon Thebes they placed Archias over the garrison Pelopidas, with eleven others, banded together to put Archias to the sword A letter containing full details of the plot was given to the Spartan polemarch at the banquet table, but Archias thrust the letter under his cushion, saying, "Business to-morrow " But long ere that sun arose he was numbered with the dead

Mind your own business. Don't get poking your nose into *my* affairs; your advice is not needed

The business end. The end of the tool, etc , with which the work is done. The ' business

end of a tin-tack" is its point, of a revolver, its muzzle, and so on.

To do someone's business for him. To ruin him, to settle him for ever, kill him.

To mean business. To be determined to carry out one's project; to be in earnest.

Busiris (bū sī' ris) A mythical king of Egypt who, in order to avert a famine, used to sacrifice to the gods all strangers who set foot on his shores Hercules was seized by him, and would have fallen a victim, but he broke his chain, and slew the inhospitable king

Milton, following Sir Walter Raleigh who, in his *History of the World*, says he was "the first oppressor of the Israelites," gives the name to the Pharaoh who was drowned in the Red Sea

Vex'd the Red Sea coast, whose waves o'er-threw Busiris and his Memphian chivalry
Paradise Lost, i, 306

Busker. There is an old verb *to busk*, meaning to improvise, and it is from this that the word *busker* is derived, to describe a street or beach singer or performer.

Buskin. Tragedy. The Greek tragic actors used to wear a sandal some two or three inches thick, to elevate their stature. The whole foot-piece made a buskin, and was called *cothurnus* *Cp* SOCK

Or what (though rare) of later age Ennobled hath the buskined stage
MILTON *Il Penseroso*, 79

Buss To kiss The word is obsolete, it is probably onomatopœic in origin, but *cp* Lat. *basium*, Ital *bacio*, Sp *beso*, and Fr *baiser*

Yon towers, whose wanton tops do buss the clouds, Must kiss their own feet.
SHAKESPEARE *Troilus and Cressida*, iv, 5

Bust. A frolic, a drunken debauch. The word is a vulgarization of *burst* (*q v*).

Busted. Done for, exploded

To go on the bust. To go on the spree; to paint the town red

A bust up is a violent quarrel, a row

Buster. Anything of large or unusual size or capacity, a "whacking great lie "

To come a buster To come a cropper; to meet with a serious set-back or fall

In Australia a **Southerly Buster** is a heavy gale from the south, striking the east coast of Australia and New Zealand

Butcher. A title given to many soldiers and others noted for their bloodthirstiness. Achmed Pasha was called *djezzar* (the butcher), and is said to have whipped off the heads of his seven wives He is famous for his defence of Acre against Napoleon I

The Bloody Butcher. The Duke of Cumberland (1721-65), second son of George II So called from his barbarities in suppressing the rebellion of the Young Pretender

The Royalist Butcher. Blaise de Montluc (1502-77), a Marshal of France, distinguished for his cruelties to the Protestants in the reign of Charles IX.

Butter. This word is sometimes used figuratively for flattery, soft soap, "wiping down" with winning words. *Punch* expressively calls it "the milk of human kindness churned into butter." (A S *butere*, Lat *butyrum*, Gr. *boutyron*, i e *bouturos*, cow-cheese, as distinguished from goat- or ewe-butter.)

Buttered ale A beverage made of ale or beer mixed with butter, sugar, and cinnamon.

He knows which side his bread is buttered. He knows his own interest

> I know what's what I know on which side
> My bread is butter'd
>   FORD *The Ladies Triall* (1638)

He looks as if butter would not melt in his mouth. He seems suspiciously amiable He looks quite harmless and expressly made to be played upon Yet beware, and ' touch not a cat but a glove "

> She smiles and languishes, you'd think that butter would not melt in her mouth —THACKERAY *Pendennis, lx*

Soft or **fair words butter no parsnips.** Saying "'Be thou fed,' will not feed a hungry man " Mere words will not find salt to our porridge, or butter to our parsnips

> Fair words butter no cabbage
>   WYCHERLEY *Plain Dealer*, v, 3 (1674)
> Fine words, says our homely old proverb, butter no parsnips —LOWELL

To butter one's bread on both sides To be wastefully extravagant and luxurious, also, to run with the hare and hunt with the hounds, to gain advantages from two sides at once

Buttercups. So called because they were once supposed to increase the butter of milk. No doubt those cows give the best milk that pasture in fields where buttercups abound, not because these flowers produce butter, but because they grow only on sound, dry, old pastures, which afford the best food Miller, in his *Gardener's Dictionary*, says they were so called "under the notion that the yellow colour of butter is owing to these plants "

Butter-fingers. Said of a person who lets things fall out of his hand. His fingers are slippery, and things slip from them as if they were greased with butter Often heard on the cricket field.

> I never was a butter-fingers, though a bad batter.
>   H. KINGSLEY.

Butterfly. A light, flippant, objectless young person who flutters from pleasure to pleasure One who is in good form when all is bright and when every prospect pleases, but is "done for" when the clouds gather.

In the cab-trade the name used to be given to those drivers who took to the occupation only in summer-time, and at the best of the season

> The feeling of the regular drivers against these "butterflies" is very strong
>   *Nineteenth Century* (March, 1893, p 177)

Butterfly kiss. A kiss with one's eyelashes, that is, stroking the cheek with one's eyelashes

Button. The two buttons on the back of a coat, in the fall of the back, are a survival of the buttons on the back of riding-coats and military frocks of the 18th century, occasionally used to button back the coat-tails

A decoy in an auction-room is colloquially known as a *button*, because he "buttons" or ties the unwary to bargains offered for sale The button fastens or fixes what else would slip away

Buttons A page, whose jacket in front is remarkable for a display of small round buttons, as close as they can be inserted, from chin to waist

> The titter of an electric bell brought a large fat buttons, with a stage effect of being dressed to look small —HOWELL *Hazard of New Fortunes*, ch vii

Bachelor's buttons. See BACHELOR.

Dash my buttons Here, "buttons" means lot or destiny, and ' dash" is a euphemistic form of a stronger word

He has not all his buttons. He is half-silly; "not all there", he is "a button short "

The buttons come off the foils. Figuratively, the courtesies of controversy are neglected. The button of a foil is the piece of cork fixed to the end to protect the point and prevent injury in fencing

> Familiarity with controversy . will have accustomed him to the misadventures which arise when, as sometimes will happen in the heat of fence, the buttons come off the foils
>   *Nineteenth Century* (June, 1891, p 925)

The button of the cap. The tip-top. Thus, in *Hamlet*, Guildenstern says "On fortune's cap we are not the very button" (ii, 2), i e. the most highly favoured The button on the cap was a mark of honour Thus, in Imperial China the first grade of literary honour was the privilege of adding a gold button to the cap, a custom adopted in several collegiate schools of England, and the several grades of mandarins are distinguished by a different coloured button on the top of their cap *Cp* PANJANDRUM

'Tis in his buttons. He is destined to obtain the prize; he is the accepted lover. It used to be common to hear boys count their buttons to know what trade they are to follow, whether they are to do a thing or not, and whether some favourite favours them

> 'Tis in his buttons, he will carry 't.
>   *Merry Wives of Windsor*, iii, 2

To have a soul above buttons To be worthy, or, rather, to consider oneself worthy, of better things, to believe that one has abilities too good for one's present employment This is explained by George Colman in *Sylvester Daggerwood* (1795) " My father was an eminent button-maker . but I had a soul above buttons . . . and panted for a liberal profession "

To press the button. To set in motion, literally or figuratively, generally by simple means as the pressing of a button will start electrically-driven machinery or apparatus.

> Mediation was ready to come into operation by any method that Germany thought possible if only Germany would " press the button " in the interests of peace —Sir EDW. GREY to the British Ambassador at Berlin, July 29th, 1914

To take by the button. To buttonhole *See below*

Buttonhole. A flower or nosegay worn in the buttonhole of a coat

To buttonhole a person. To detain him in conversation, to apprehend, as, "to take fortune by the button." The allusion is to a custom, now discontinued, of holding a person by the button or buttonhole in conversation. The French have the same locution. *Serrer le bouton (à quelqu'un)*

> He went about buttonholing and boring everyone
> H. KINGSLEY *Mathilde*

To take one down a buttonhole. To take one down a peg, to lower one's conceit

> Better mind yerselves, or I'll take ye down a buttonhole lower.—Mrs. STOWE *Uncle Tom's Cabin*, iv.

Buy To buy in. To collect stock by purchase, to withhold the sale of something offered at auction, because the bidding has not reached the "reserve price." On the Stock Exchange *buying in* is the term used when, a seller having sold stock that he is unable to deliver, the buyer purchases the stock himself in the market and charges the extra cost, if any, to the original seller

To buy off. To give a person money to drop a claim, put an end to contention, or throw up a partnership.

To buy out To redeem or ransom
> Not being able to buy out his life
> Dies ere the weary sun set.
> SHAKESPEARE *Comedy of Errors*, i, 2

To buy over. To induce one by a bribe to renounce a claim, to gain over by bribery

To buy over a person's head. To outbid him

To buy up To purchase stock to such an amount as to obtain a virtual monopoly, and thus command the market, to make a corner, as "to buy up corn," etc

Buying a pig in a poke. *See* PIG

Buzfuz (būz' fūz) Sergeant Buzfuz was the windy, grandiloquent counsel for Mrs Bardell in the famous breach of promise trial described in *Pickwick Papers* He represented a type of barrister that flourished in the early 19th century, seeking to gain his case by abuse of the other side and a distortion of the true facts

Buzz, To. Either, to empty the bottle to the last drop, or, when there is not enough left in it to allow of a full glass all round the party, to share it out equally Perhaps a corruption of *bouse* *See* BOOZE

Buzz. A rumour, a whispered report.
> Yes, that, on every dream,
> Each buzz, each fancy,
> He may enguard his dotage
> SHAKESPEARE *King Lear*, i, 4

Buzzard. In Dryden's *Hind and Panther* is meant for Dr Burnet, whose figure was lusty

Buzzard called hawk by courtesy. It is a euphemism—a brevet rank—a complimentary title
> The noble Buzzard ever pleased me best,
> Of small renown, 'tis true, for, not to lie
> We call him but a hawk by courtesy
> DRYDEN *Hind and Panther*, iii, 1221

Between hawk and buzzard. Not quite the master or mistress nor quite a servant Applied to "bear-leaders" (*q v*), governesses, and other grown-up persons who used to be allowed to come down to dessert, but not to the dinner-table.

By-and-by now means a little time hence, but when the Bible was translated it meant instantly "When persecution ariseth . . . by-and-by he is offended" (*Matt.* xiii, 12), rendered in *Mark* iv, 17, by the word "immediately" Our *presently* means in a little time or soon, but formerly it meant "at present," "at once," and in this sense it is not uncommonly still used in U S A

By and large. Taking one thing with another, speaking generally This is really a nautical phrase When a vessel was close-hauled, order might be given to sail "by and large," that is, slightly off the wind, or easier for the helmsman and less likely for the vessel to be taken aback under his steering

By-blow. An illegitimate child
> I it is have been cheated all this while,
> Abominably and irreparably,—my name
> Given to a cur-cast mongrel, a drab's brat,
> A beggar's bye-blow
> BROWNING *Ring and the Book*, iv, 612

By-laws. Local laws From *by*, a borough *See* BYRLAW Properly, laws by a town council, and bearing only on the borough or company over which it has jurisdiction

By-line. A journalist's signature When a newspaper reporter progresses from anonymous to signed articles, he is said to have got a by-line

By-the-by. *En passant*, laterally connected with the main subject "By-play" is side or secondary play; "by-roads and streets" are those which branch out of the main thoroughfare The first "by" means *passing from one to another*, as in the phrase "Day by day." Thus "By-the-by" is passing from the main subject to a *by* or secondary one

By-the-way. An introduction to an incidental remark thrown in, and tending the same way as the discourse itself

Bycorne. *See* BICORN.

Bye Plot (bī) This was a plot hatched in 1603 by a Catholic priest, Watson, who worked up a number of Catholic gentry to secure the person of James I and force him to grant toleration to Catholics and Puritans. The plot was muddled and mismanaged from the outset, Watson was beheaded, his fellow conspirators were imprisoned or banished

Byerly Turk. *See* DARLEY ARABIAN

Byrlaw A local law in the rural districts of Scotland The inhabitants of a district used to make certain laws for their own observance, and appoint one of their neighbours, called the *Byrlaw-man*, to carry out the pains and penalties *Byr* = a burgh, common in such names as *Derby*, the burgh on the Derwent, *Grimsby* (*q v*), Grims-town, etc, and is present in *by-law* (*q v*)

Byron. The Polish Byron Adam Mickiewicz (1798-1855)

The Russian Byron. Alexander Sergeivitch Pushkin (1799-1837)

Byrsa. *See* BURSA

Byzantine (bɪ zăn′ tĭn)   Another name for the *bezant* (*q v*)

Byzantine art (from Byzantium, the ancient name of Constantinople).   That symbolical system which was developed by the early Greek or Byzantine artists out of the Christian symbolism   Its chief features are the circle, dome, and round arch, and its chief symbols the lily, cross, vesica, and nimbus   St Sophia, at Constantinople, and St Mark, at Venice, are excellent examples of Byzantine architecture and decoration, and the Roman Catholic Cathedral at Westminster is a development of the same

Byzantine Empire.   The Eastern or Greek Empire, which lasted from the separation of the Eastern and Western Empires on the death of Theodosius in A.D. 395, till the capture of Constantinople by the Turks in 1453.

Byzantine historians.   Certain Greek historians who lived under the Eastern Empire between the 6th and 15th centuries   They may be divided into three groups'—(1) Those whose works form together continuous and complete history of the Byzantine empire; (2) general chroniclers who wrote histories of the world from the oldest period; and (3) writers on Roman antiquities, statistics, and customs

C

C.   The form of the letter is a rounding of the Gr *gamma* (Γ), which was a modification of the Phœnician sign for *gimel*, a camel.   It originally corresponded with Gr. *gamma*, as its place in the alphabet would lead one to suppose.

When the French *c* has a mark under it, thus ç, called a cedilla, it is to be pronounced as an *s*.

There is more than one poem written of which every word begins with C   There is one   by Hamconius, called   "*Certamen catholicum cum Calvinistis,*" and another by Henry Harder.   *See* ALLITERATION

Ca' canny.   A Scots expression meaning "go easily," "don't exert yourself "   It is used in trade-union slang for working to rule, and is the method adopted by workmen for the purpose of bringing pressure on the employers when, in the workmen's opinion, a strike would be hardly justifiable, expedient, or possible. *Ca'* is Scots *caw*, to drive or impel.

Ça ira (it will go).   The name, and refrain, of a popular patriotic song in France which became the *Carillon National* of the French Revolution (1790).   It went to the tune of the *Carillon National*, which Marie Antoinette was for ever strumming on her harpsichord

As a rallying cry it was borrowed from Benjamin Franklin, who used to say, in reference to the American revolution, "*Ah'* *ah′ ça ira, ça ira!*" ('twill be sure to do)

The refrain of the French revolutionary version was.—

> Ah¹ ça ira, ça ira, ça ira,
> Les aristocrates a la lanterne.

Caaba.   *See* KAABA

Cab.   A contraction of *cabriolet*, a small, one-horse carriage, so called from Ital *capriola*, a caper, the leap of a kid, from the lightness of the carriage when compared with the contemporary cumbersome vehicles   Cabs were introduced in London about 1823

Cabal.   A junto (*q v*) or council of intriguers   One of the Ministries of Charles II was called a "cabal" (1670), because the initial letters of its members formed the word   Clifford, Ashley, Buckingham, Arlington, and Lauderdale   This accident may have popularized the word, but it was in use in England many years before this, and is the Hebrew *qabbalah.* *See* CABBALA

These ministers were emphatically called the Cabal, and they soon made the appellation so infamous that it has never since   . been used except as a term of reproach —MACAULAY. *England*, I, ii

Cabala, Cabalist.   *See* CABBALA

Caballero   A Spanish knight or gentleman (literally, one who rides a horse, *caballo*); also a grave and stately dance, so called from the ballad to the music of which it was danced.   The ballad begins—

> Esta noche le mataron al caballero.

Cabbage.   An old slang term for odd bits of cloth, etc , left over after making up suits and so on, appropriated by working tailors as perquisites.   Thus the Tailor in Randolph's *Hey for Honesty* (about 1633) says —

> O iron age¹ that like the ostrich, makes me feed on my own goose.   This   cross-legged infelicity, sharper than my needle, makes me eat my own cabbage —*Act V*, sc 1

Hence, a tailor is sometimes nicknamed "Cabbage," and *to cabbage* means *to* pilfer, to filch.

Cabbala.   The oral traditions of the Jews, said to have been delivered by Moses to the rabbis and from them handed down through the centuries from father to son by word of mouth.   In mediæval times the term included the occult philosophy of the rabbis, and the *cabbala* and its guardians, the *cabbalists*, were feared as possessing secrets of magical power   The word is the Heb *qabbalah*, accepted tradition.

Cabbalist.   In the Middle Ages the cabbalists were chiefly occupied in concocting and deciphering charms, mystical anagrams, etc , by unintelligible combinations of certain letters, words, and numbers, in search for the philosopher's stone, in prognostications, attempted or pretended intercourse with the dead, and suchlike fantasies

Cabinet Ministers.   In British politics, a deliberative committee of the principal members of the Government, who are privileged to consult and advise the sovereign (originally in his private *cabinet*, or chamber), and who lead, and are responsible to, Parliament.   The number of members has varied from a dozen to as many as twenty-two, but it always contains the chief officers of state, viz the

Prime Minister, the First Lord of the Treasury (these offices are often combined), the Lord High Chancellor, Lord President of the Council, Lord Privy Seal, Chancellor of the Exchequer, the First Lord of the Admiralty, the Secretaries for Home Affairs, Foreign Affairs, the Colonies, Dominions, Scotland, War, and Air, the President of the Board of Trade, and the Ministers of Labour, Fuel, Education, Health, and Agriculture Of the other Ministers the following are sometimes included in the Cabinet the Chancellor of the Duchy of Lancaster, the Postmaster-General, Ministers of Supply, Food, Pensions, Works, Town and Country Planning, National Insurance, Civil Aviation, Information

Cabiri (ka bī′ rī) The Phoenician name for the seven planets collectively, also mystic and minor divinities worshipped in Asia Minor, Greece, and the islands (Phœn *kabir*, powerful.)

Cable's Length. 100 fathoms, a tenth of a sea-mile—607 56 feet.

Cabochon (ka bō shong) A term applied to a precious stone, cut in a rounded shape, without facets Garnets, sapphires, and rubies are the stones most commonly cut *en cabochon*.

Caboodle (ka boodl′) **The whole caboodle,** the whole lot The origin of the word is obscure, but it may come from the Dutch *boedel*, possession, household goods, property In this sense it has long been a common term among New England long-shoremen

Caboose (ka boos′) On American railroads, a wagon used for transporting workmen or the train crew

Cachecope Bell (kăsh′ kōp) In some parts of England it was customary to ring a bell at a funeral when the pall was thrown over a coffin. This was called the cachecope bell, from Fr , *cache corps*, conceal the body

Cachet (kăsh′ ă) (Fr.). A seal, hence, a distinguishing mark, a stamp of individuality

Lettres de cachet (letters sealed) Under the old French regime, warrants, sealed with the king's seal, which might be obtained for a consideration, and in which the name was frequently left blank Sometimes the warrant was to set a prisoner at large, but it was more frequently for detention in the Bastille During the administration of Cardinal Fleury (1726-43) 80,000 of these *cachets* are said to have been issued, the larger number being against the Jansenists In the reigns of Louis XV and XVI fifty-nine were obtained against the one family of Mirabeau. This scandal was abolished January 15th, 1790

Cacodæmon (kăk ō dē′ mon). An evil spirit (Gr. *kakos daimon*) Astrologers give this name to the Twelfth House of Heaven, from which only evil prognostics proceed

> Hie thee to hell for shame, and leave the world,
> Thou cacodemon
> SHAKESPEARE *Richard III*, ı, 3

Cacoethes (kăk ō ēth′ ēz) (Gr) A "bad habit "

> As soon as he came to town, the political *Cacoethes* began to break out upon him with greater violence, because it had been suppressed
> SWIFT. *Life of Steele.*

Cacoethes loquendi. A passion for making speeches or for talking.

Cacoethes scribendi The love of rushing into print, a mania for authorship.

> Tenet insanabile multos
> Scribendi cacoethes *Juv VII,* 51.
> The incurable itch for scribbling infects many

Cacus (kă′ kus). In Classical mythology, a famous robber, represented as three-headed, and vomiting flames He lived in Italy, and was strangled by Hercules The curate of La Mancha says of the Lord Rinaldo and his friends, "They are greater thieves than Cacus." (*Don Quixote*)

Cad. A low, vulgar ill-mannered fellow; also, before the term fell into its present disrepute, an omnibus conductor The word is, like the Scots *caddie* (q.v), probably from cadet (q v)

Caddice or Caddis. Worsted yarn or binding, crewel So named from the O Fr *cadaz*, the coarsest part of silk, with which the Ir *cadan*, cotton, may be remotely connected. *See also* CADDY

> He hath ribands of all the colours i' the rainbow,
> caddisses, cambrics, lawns
> SHAKESPEARE *Winter's Tale*, ıv, 3

Caddice-garter. A servant, a man of mean rank When garters were worn in sight, the cheaper variety was worn by small tradesmen, servants, etc Prince Henry calls Poins a "caddice-garter" (1 *Henry IV*, ıı, 4).

> Dost hear,
> My honest caddis-garter?
> GLAPTHORNE *Wit in a Constable* (1639)

Caddie. This means now almost solely the boy or man who carries a golfer's clubs on the links (and, now and then, gives the tyro advice) It is another form of *cadet* (q v), and was formerly in common use in Scotland for errand boys, odd-job men, chairmen, etc.

> All Edinburgh men and boys know that when sedan-chairs were discontinued, the old cadies sank into ruinous poverty, and became synonymous with roughs The word was brought to London by James Hannay, who frequently used it —M PRINGLE.

Caddy. In some English dialects a ghost, a bugbear, from *cad*, a word of uncertain origin which in the 17th century meant a familiar spirit. This has no connexion (as has been suggested) with *caddis*, a grub, which is probably from *caddice* (q v), the allusion being to the similarity of the caddis-worm to the larva of the silk-worm

Caddy in tea-caddy is a Malay word (*kati*), and properly denotes a weight of 1 lb 5 oz. 2 dr , that is used in China and the East Indies

Cadency, Marks of. *See* DIFFERENCE

Cader Idris (kă′ der id′ ris) *Cader* in Welsh is "chair," and *Idris* is the name of one of the old Welsh giants The legend is that anyone who passes the night sitting in this "chair" will be either a poet or a madman

Cadet (ka det′) Younger branches of noble families are called cadets from Fr. *cadet*, formed on Provençal *capdet*, a diminutive of Lat *caput*, a head, hence, little head, little chieftain Their armorial shields bore the *mark of cadency* (Lat *cadere*, to fall) *See* DIFFERENCE

Cadet is a student at the Royal Military College at Sandhurst, with which Woolwich Academy was amalgamated in 1946, or in one of H.M training ships From these places the boys are sent (after passing certain examinations) into the army as ensigns or second lieutenants, and into the navy as midshipmen.

Cadger. A sponger, one who lays himself out to obtain drinks, "unconsidered trifles," and so on, without paying for them or standing his share; a whining beggar Originally an itinerant dealer in butter, eggs, etc., who visited remote farmhouses and made what extra he could by begging and wheedling The word may be connected with *catch*, but this is not certain

Cadi (kā′dı) Arabic for a town magistrate or inferior judge

Cadmus. In Greek mythology, the son of Agenor, king of Phœnicia, and Telephassa; founder of Thebes (Bœotia) and the introducer of the alphabet into Greece. (*Cp.* PALAMEDES) The name is Semitic for "the man of the East " Legend says that, having slain the dragon which guarded the fountain of Dirce, in Bœotia, he sowed its teeth, and a number of armed men sprang up surrounding Cadmus with intent to kill him By the counsel of Athene, he threw a precious stone among them, who, striving for it, killed one another

Cadmean letters. The sixteen simple Greek letters said, in Greek mythology, to have been introduced by Cadmus (*q v*) from Phœnicia. The Cadmeans were those who in pre-Trojan times occupied the country afterwards called Bœotia. Hence the Greek tragedians often called the Thebans Cadmeans

Cadmean victory. A victory purchased with great loss The allusion is to the armed men who sprang out of the ground from the teeth of the dragon sown by Cadmus (*q v*), who fell foul of each other, only five escaping death.

Cadogan (kå dŭg′ an) or Catogan A fashion of dressing the hair, in which the hair is secured at the back by a ribbon. Worn by men in the mid and late 18th century Its name comes from a popular portrait of the first Earl of Cadogan Dashing ladies also affected the fashion, which was introduced at the court of Montbéliard by the Duchesse de Bourbon.

Cadre (kad′ er; kad′ rı). (Fr , frame) In military parlance a skeleton of trained or key men, so arranged that the addition of untrained personnel will yield a full-size efficient unit

Caduceus. A white wand carried by Roman heralds when they went to treat for peace, the wand placed in the hands of Mercury, the herald of the gods, of which poets feign that he could therewith give sleep to whomsoever he chose, wherefore Milton styles it "his opiate rod" in *Paradise Lost*, xı, 133. It is generally pictured with two serpents twined about it (a symbol thought to have originated in Egypt), and—with reference to the serpents of

6*

Æsculapius—it was adopted as the badge of the Royal Army Medical Corps.

So with his dread caduceus Hermes led
From the dark regions of the imprisoned dead,
Or drove in silent shoals the lingering train
To Night's dull shore and Pluto's dreary reign
  DARWIN *Loves of the Plants*, ıı, 291

Caedmon (kăd′ mon) (d 680) Anglo-Saxon poet famed for his *Hymn* Bede tells us that he was an ignorant man who knew nothing of poetry Commanded by an angel in a dream to sing the Creation, Caedmon straightway did so. On waking he remembered his verses and composed more. He was received into the monastery of Whitby, where he spent his life praising God in poetry Except for Caedmon's *Hymn*, preserved in Bede's Latin, all his work is lost

Cærite Franchise, The (sē′ rīt). A form of franchise in a Roman præfecture which gave the right of self-government, but did not confer the privileges of a Roman citizen or entitle the holder to vote This was a privilege first given to the inhabitants of Cære who, during the Gallic War, had assisted the Romans Later, cities and citizens who had merited disfranchisement were degraded to the same position, and consequently the term became one of disgrace

Caerleon (kâr′ lē′ on). The Isca Silurum of the Romans, a town on the Usk, in Wales, about 3 miles N E of Newport It is the traditional residence of King Arthur, where he lived in splendid state, surrounded by hundreds of, knights, twelve of whom he selected as Knights of the Round Table.

Cæsar (sē′ zar). The cognomen of Caius Julius Cæsar was assumed by all the male members of his dynasty as a part of the imperial dignity, and after them by the successive emperors After the death of Hadrian (138) the title was assigned to those who had been nominated by the emperors as their successors and had been associated with them in ruling The titles *Kaiser* and *Tsar* are both forms of *Cæsar.*

Thou art an emperor, Cæsar, keisar, and Pheezar
  SHAKESPEARE· *Merry Wives of Windsor*, ı, 3.
No bending knees shall call thee Cæsar now
  SHAKESPEARE 3 *Henry VI*, ııı, 1.

Cæsar's wife must be above suspicion. The name of Pompeia having been mixed up with an accusation against P Clodius, Cæsar divorced her; not because he believed her guilty, but because the wife of Cæsar must not even be suspected of crime (Suetonius: *Julius Cæsar*, 74)

Cæsarian operation. The extraction of a child from the womb by cutting the abdomen, so called because Julius Cæsar was thus brought into the world

Caf. *See* KAF

Caftan (kåf′ tan). A garment worn in Turkey and other Eastern countries It is a sort of under-tunic or vest tied by a girdle at the waist *Cp* GABERDINE.

Picturesque merchants and their customers, no longer in the big trousers of Egypt, but [in] the long caftans and abas of Syria.
  B TAYLOR· *Lands of the Saracen*, ch. ıx.

Cage. *To whistle or sing in the cage.* The cage is a jail, and to whistle in a cage is to turn king's evidence, or peach against a comrade The lift in which miners descend the pit shaft is termed a cage

Cagliostro (kǎ lyos' trō) Count Alessandro di Cagliostro was the assumed name of the notorious Italian adventurer and impostor, Giuseppe Balsamo (1743-95), of Palermo He played a prominent part in the affair of the Diamond Necklace (*q v*), and among his many frauds was the offer of everlasting youth to all who would pay him for his secret.

Cagmag (kǎg' mǎg) Offal, bad meat, also a tough old goose, food which none can relish

Cagot (ka' gō) A sort of gipsy race living in the Middle Ages in Gascony and Bearn, supposed to be descendants of the Visigoths, and shunned as something loathsome *Cp* CAQUEUX, COLLIBERTS In modern French, a hypocrite or an ultra-devout person is called a *cagot* From this use of the word came *cagoule*, meaning a penitent's hood or cowl, and from this, again, the sinister *cagoulards* took their name—French political plotters hiding their infamy beneath masks and hoods.

Cain-coloured Beard. Yellowish, or sandy red, symbolic of treason In the ancient tapestries Cain and Judas are represented with yellow beards, but it is well to note that in the extract below the word, in some editions, is printed "*cane-coloured*" *See* YELLOW

He hath but a little wee face, with a little yellow beard, a Cain-coloured beard
SHAKESPEARE *Merry Wives of Windsor*, i, 4.

Cainites (kā' nītz) An heretical sect of the 2nd century They renounced the New Testament in favour of *The Gospel of Judas*, which justified the false disciple and the crucifixion of Jesus; and they maintained that heaven and earth were created by the evil principle, and that Cain with his descendants were the persecuted party

Caird (kǎrd) This is a North Country and Scottish name for a tramp, a tinker, a Gipsy or even a jockey. It comes from the Gaelic *ceard*, a smith, brazier

Caius (kēs) **College** (Cambridge). Elevated by Dr John Kay, or Keye (1510-73), of Norwich, into a college, from its previous status of a hall (Gonville), in 1558 It had been originally established by Edmund Gonville in 1348 The full name is now Gonville and Caius

Cake. Obsolete slang for a fool, a poor thing *Cf.* HALF-BAKED

Cakes and ale A good time. Life is not all cakes and ale Life is not all beer and skittles—all pleasure

My cake is dough. All my swans are turned to geese. *Occisa est res mea. Mon affaire est manquée*, my project has failed

The Land of Cakes. Scotland, famous for its oatmeal cakes.
Land o' cakes and brither Scots —*Burns.*

To go like hot cakes. To be a great success, to sell well

To take the cake. To carry off the prize The reference is to the negro *cake walk*, the prize for which was a cake It consists of walking round the prize cake in pairs, while umpires decide which pair walk the most gracefully From this a dance developed which was popular in the early part of the 20th century before the serious introduction of Jazz

In ancient Greece a cake was the award of the toper who held out the longest, and in Ireland the best dancer in a dancing competition was rewarded, at one time, by a cake
A churn-dish stuck into the earth supported on its flat end a cake, which was to become the prize of the best dancer. At length the competitors yielded their claims to a young man who taking the cake, placed it gallantly in the lap of a pretty girl to whom he was about to be married —BARTLETT and COYNE *Scenery and Antiquities of Ireland*, vol ii, p 64.

You cannot eat your cake and have it too. You cannot spend your money and yet keep it You cannot serve God and Mammon.

Calaboose (kǎl' a boos). This is a slang term in USA for a prison. It comes from the Spanish (originally from the Arabic), and is more especially applied to the common jail or lock-up

Calabre (kǎl' a ber). Squirrel fur; perhaps so called because originally imported from Calabria Ducange says 'At Chichester the 'priest vicars' and at St Paul's the 'minor canons' wore a calabre amyce", and Bale, in his *Image of Both Churches*, alludes to the "fair rochets of Raines [Rennes], and costly grey amices of calaber and cats' tails "
The Lord Mayor and those aldermen above the chair ought to have their coats furred with grey amis, and also with changeable taffeta, and those below the chair with calabre and with green taffeta
HUTTON *New View of London*

Calainos (kǎ li' nos) The most ancient of Spanish ballads Calainos the Moor asked a damsel to wife; she consented, on condition that he should bring her the heads of the three paladins of Charlemagne—Rinaldo, Roland, and Oliver Calainos went to Paris and challenged the paladins First Sir Baldwin, the youngest knight, accepted the challenge and was overthrown, then his uncle Roland went against the Moor and smote him

Calamanco (kǎl à mǎng' kō) A Low German word of uncertain origin denoting a glossy woollen fabric, sometimes striped or variegated. The word has been applied attributively to a cat, in which connexion it means striped or tortoiseshell.

Calatrava, Order of (kǎl à tra' va). A Spanish military Order of Knighthood founded by Sancho III of Castile in 1158 to commemorate the capture of the fortress of Calatrava from the Moors in 1147. The first knights were the keepers of the fortress, their badge is a red cross, fleury, and is worn on the left breast of a white mantle

Calceolaria (kǎl sē ō lâr' i a) Little-shoe flowers, so called from their resemblance to fairy slippers (Lat *calceoluo*)

Calculate is from the Lat. *calculi* (pebbles), used by the Romans for counters. In the abacus (*q v*), the round balls were called *calculi*. The Greeks voted by pebbles dropped into an urn—a method adopted both in ancient Egypt and Syria, counting these pebbles was "calculating" the number of voters

I calculate. A peculiarity of expression common in the western states of North America In the southern states the phrase is "I reckon," in the middle states "I expect," and in New England "I guess" All were imported from the Mother Country by early settlers.

Your aunt sets two tables, I calculate, don't she?
         SUSAN WARNER *Queechy*, ch xix

The calculator A number of mathematical geniuses have been awarded this title, among them are —

Alfragan, the Arabian astronomer. Died 830

Jedediah Buxton (1707-72), of Elmton, in Derbyshire; a farm labourer of no education who exhibited in London in 1754

George Bidder and Zerah Colburn (1804-40), who exhibited publicly

Inaudi exhibited "his astounding powers of calculating" at Paris in 1880, his additions and subtractions, contrary to the usual procedure, were left to right

Buxton, being asked "How many cubical eighths-of-an-inch there are in a body whose three sides are 23,145,786 yards, 5,642,732 yards, and 54,965 yards?" replied correctly without setting down a figure

Colburn, being asked the square root of 106,929 and the cube root of 268,336,125, replied before the audience had set the figures down
         PRICE *Parallel History*, vol ii, p 570

Caledonia. Scotland; the ancient Roman name, now used only in poetry and in a few special connexions, such as the Caledonian Railway, the Caledonian Canal, the Caledonian Ball, etc.

Not thus, in ancient days of Caledon,
Was thy voice mute amid the festal crowd
         SCOTT.

O Caledonia, stern and wild,
Meet nurse for a poetic child
         SCOTT *Lay of the Last Minstrel*

Calembour (ka lem boor') (Fr) A pun, a jest From Wigand von Theben, a priest of *Kahlenberg* in Lower Austria, who was introduced in *Eulenspiegel* (*q v*), and other German tales He was noted for his jests, puns, and witticisms, and in the French translations appeared as the Abbé de Calembourg, or Calembour.

Calendar.

The Julian Calendar *See* JULIAN.

The Gregorian Calendar. A modification of the Julian, introduced in 1582 by Pope Gregory XIII, and adopted in Great Britain in 1752 This is called "the New Style " *See* GREGORIAN YEAR

The Mohammedan Calendar, used in Moslem countries, dates from July 16th, 622, the day of the Hegira (*q v*) It consists of 12 lunar months of 29 days 12 hours, 44 minutes each, consequently the Mohammedan year consists of only 354 or 355 days A cycle is 30 years

The French Revolutionary Calendar, adopted on October 5th, 1793, retrospectively as from September 22nd, 1792, and in force in France till January 1st, 1806, consisted of 12 months of 30 days each, with 5 intercalary days, called Sansculotides (*q v*) at the end It was devised by Gilbert Romme (1750-95), the names of the months having been given by the poet, Fabre d'Eglantine (1755-94).

The Newgate Calendar. *See* NEWGATE

Calender The Persian *qalandar*, a member of a begging order of dervishes, founded in the 13th century by Qalandar Yusuf al-Andalusi, a native of Spain, who, being dismissed from another order, founded one of his own, with the obligation on its members of perpetual wandering This feature has made the calenders prominent in Eastern romance, the story of the Three Calenders in the *Arabian Nights* is well known

Calends. The first day of the Roman month. Varro says the term originated in the practice of calling together or assembling the people on the first day of the month, when the pontifex informed them of the time of the new moon, the day of the nones, with the festivals and sacred days to be observed The custom continued till A U C 450, when the *fasti* or *calendar* was posted in public places. *See* GREEK CALENDS.

Calepin, A. (kăl' e pin) A dictionary. (Ital. *calepino*) Ambrosio Calepino, of Calepio, in Italy, was the author of a famous Latin dictionary (1502), so that "my Calepin" was used in earlier days as my Euclid, my Liddell and Scott, according to Cocker, etc, became common later Generally called Calepin, but the subjoined quotation throws the accent on the *le*

Whom do you prefer
For the best linguist? And I sillily
Said that I thought Calepine's Dictionary
         DONNE *Fourth Satire*

Calf. Slang for a dolt, a "mutton-head," a raw, inexperienced, childish fellow. *See also* CALVES.

The golden calf *See* GOLDEN (PHRASES)

There are many ways of dressing a calf's head. Many ways of saying or doing a foolish thing; a simpleton has many ways of showing his folly, or, generally, if one way won't do we must try another The allusion is to the banquets of the Calves' Head Club (*q v*)

To cut the calf in the cow's belly. To be over-ready to anticipate, to count one's chickens before they are hatched

To kill the fatted calf. To welcome with the best of everything. The phrase is taken from the parable of the prodigal son (*Luke* xv, 30)

Calf-love. Youthful fancy, immature love as opposed to a lasting attachment
"It's a girl's fancy just, a kind of calf-love "
         Mrs. GASKELL *Sylvia's Lovers*

Calf-skin. Fools and jesters used to wear a calf-skin coat buttoned down the back In allusion to this custom, Faulconbridge says insolently to the Archduke of Austria, who had acted most basely to Richard Cœur-de-Lion —

Thou wear a lion's hide! Doff it, for shame,
And hang a calf-skin on those recreant limbs
         SHAKESPEARE *King John*, iii, 1.

Caliban (kăl′ ĭ băn). Rude, uncouth, unknown The allusion is to Shakespeare's Caliban (*The Tempest*), the deformed, half-human son of a devil and a witch, slave to Prospero In this character it has been said that Shakespeare had not only invented a *new creation*, but also a *new language*.

Coleridge says, " In him [Caliban], as in some brute animals, this advance to the intellectual faculties, without the moral sense, is marked by the appearance of vice."

Caliburn (kăl′ ĭ bĕrn). Same as *Excalibur*, King Arthur's well-known sword.

Onward Arthur paced, with hand
On Caliburn's resistless brand
SCOTT *Bridal of Triermain*

Calico So called from Calicut, in Malabar, once the great emporium of Hindustan and, next to Goa, the chief port for trade with Europe

Calidore, Sir (kăl′ ĭ dôr) In Spenser's *Faerie Queene* (Bk. vi) the type of *courtesy*, and the lover of "fair Pastorella " He is described as the most courteous of all knights, and is entitled the "all-beloved", he typifies Sir Philip Sidney or the Earl of Essex

Caligula (ka lig′ ū la). Roman emperor (A D 37-41), so called because, when he was with the army as a boy, he wore a military sandal called a *caliga*, which had no upper leather, and was used only by the common soldiers

Caligula was a voluptuous brute whose cruelty and excesses amounted almost to madness Hence Horace Walpole coined the word *Caligulism* Speaking of Frederick, Prince of Wales, he says —

—Alas′ it would be endless to tell you all his Caligulisms —*Letter to France*, November 29th, 1745

Caligula's horse. Incitatus. It was made a priest and consul, had a manger of ivory, and drank wine from a golden goblet.

Calipash and Calipee (kăl ĭ păsh′, kăl ĭ pē′) These are apparently fancy terms (though the former may come from the word Carapace) to describe choice portions of the turtle Calipash is the fatty, dull-greenish substance belonging to the upper shield, calipee is the light-yellow, fatty stuff belonging to the lower shield. Only epicures and aldermen can tell the difference.

Cut off the bottom shell, then cut off the meat that grows to it (which is the callepy or fowl)
Mrs RAFFALD. *English Housekeeping* (1769)

Caliph (kā′ lif) A title given to the successors of Mohammed (Arab. *Khalifah*, a successor; *khalafa*, to succeed) Among the Saracens a caliph is one vested with supreme dignity The caliphate of Bagdad reached its highest splendour under Haroun al-Raschid, in the 9th century For the last 200 years the appellation has been swallowed up in the titles of *Shah*, *Sultan*, *Emir*, etc The last Sultan of Turkey claimed the title in a vain attempt to impose his authority on all Moslem lands, it is still used of rulers of Mohammedan States in their capacity as successors of Mohammed

Calisto and Arcas (ka lis′ tō, ar′ kas) Calisto was an Arcadian nymph metamorphosed into a she-bear by Jupiter Her son Arcas having met her in the chase, would have killed her, but Jupiter converted him into a he-bear, and placed them both in the heavens, where they are recognized as the Great and Little Bear.

Calixtines (ka liks′ tīnz) A religious sect of Bohemians in the 15th century, so called from *Calix* (the chalice), which they insisted should be given to the laity in the sacrament of the Lord's Supper, as well as the bread or wafer. They were also called Utraquists (*q v*)

Call. A "divine" summons or invitation, as "a call to the ministry "

A curtain call. An invitation to an actor to appear before the curtain, and receive the applause of the audience

A call bird. A bird trained as a decoy

A call-boy A boy employed in theatres to "call" or summon actors, when it is time for them to make their appearance on the stage.

A call-box. A public telephone booth

Call day, or **call night.** The name given at the Inns of Court to the dates on which students are called to the Bar

A call of the House. An imperative summons sent to every Member of Parliament to attend. This is done when the sense of the whole House is required

A call on shareholders. A demand to pay the balance of money due for shares allotted in a company, or a part thereof

A call to the Bar. The admission of a law student to the privileges of a barrister. *See* BAR.

A call to the pastorate. An invitation to a minister by the members of a Presbyterian or Nonconformist church to preside over a certain congregation.

Payable at call. To be paid on demand.

The call of Abraham. The invitation or command of God to Abraham, to leave his idolatrous country, under the promise of becoming the father of a great nation.

The call of God. An invitation, exhortation, or warning, by the dispensations of Providence (*Isa* xxii, 12); divine influence on the mind to do or avoid something (*Heb.* iii, 1)

To call. To invite. as, the trumpet calls.

If honour calls, where'er she points the way,
The sons of honour follow and obey
CHURCHILL *The Farewell*

In U S A. to call means somewhat ambiguously "to telephone " "He called me" may mean "he summoned me" or "he telephoned me."

To call (a man) out. To challenge him, to appeal to a man's honour to come forth and fight a duel

To call God to witness. To declare solemnly that what one states is true

To call in question. To doubt the truth of a statement; to challenge the truth of a statement "*In dubium vocare* "

To call over the coals. *See* COALS

To call to account. To demand an explanation, to reprove

To be called (or sent) to one's account. To be removed by death   To be called to the judgment seat of God to give an account of one's deeds, whether they be good, or whether they be evil

> Cut off even in the blossoms of my sin,
> Unhouseled, disappointed, unaneled,
> No reckoning made, but sent to my account
> With all my imperfections on my head,
> O horrible!   O horrible! most horrible
> SHAKESPEARE *Hamlet*, i, 5

To call to arms.   To summon to prepare for battle   "*Ad arma vocare* "

To call to mind.   To recollect, to remember.

Caller Herrings.   Fresh herrings   The adjective is also applied in Scotland to fresh air, water, etc

Calligraphy.   The art of handwriting   The finest calligraphy in western civilization is the *Cancelleresca Corsiva* or Cursive Chancellery hand used by the Apostolic Secretaries in the 15th century, the hand on which italic type is based   To-day it is applied generally to the art of the scribe preparing manuscripts such as rolls of honour or professional presentations   A handwriting which is based on a good model and has any artistic pretentions is called a calligraphic hand

Calliope (ka lī' ō pī)   (Gr, beautiful voice) Chief of the nine Muses (*q v.*), the muse of epic or heroic poetry, and of poetic inspiration and eloquence.   Her emblems are a stylus and wax tablets

The word is also applied to a steam-organ composed of steam-whistles making a raucous blare.

Callippic Period (ka lip' ik)   An intended correction of the Metonic Cycle (*q v.*) by Callippus, the Greek astronomer of the 4th century B C   To remedy the defect in the Metonic Cycle Callippus quadrupled the period of Meton, making his Cycle one of seventy-six years, and deducted a day at the end of it, by which means he calculated that the new and full moons would be brought round to the same day and hour   His calculation, however, is not absolutely accurate, as there is one whole day lost every 553 years

Callirrhoe (kă lir' ō i)   The lover of Chæreas, in Chariton's Greek romance entitled the *Loves of Chæreas and Callirrhoe*, probably written in the 6th century A D

Calomel (kăl' ō mel)   Hooper says — This name, which means " beautiful black," was originally given to the Æthiop's mineral, or black sulphuret of mercury   It was afterwards applied in joke by Sir Theodore Mayerne to the chloride of mercury, in honour of a favourite negro servant whom he employed to prepare it   As calomel is a *white* powder, the name is merely a jocular misnomer

Calotte (ka lot') (Fr)   *Regime de la calotte* Administration of government by ecclesiastics. The *calotte* is the small skull-cap worn over the tonsure

Régiment de la Calotte.   A society of witty and satirical men in the reign of Louis XIV When any public character made himself ridiculous, a calotte was sent to him to "cover the bald or brainless part of his noddle "

Caloyers (kā lō' yẽrz)   Monks in the Greek Church, who follow the rule of St Basil.   They are divided into *cenobites*, who recite the offices from midnight to sunrise, *anchorites*, who live in hermitages; and *recluses*, who shut themselves up in caverns and live on alms.   (Gr. καλός and γέρων, beautiful old man)

Calpe (kăl' pī)   Gibraltar, one of the Pillars of Hercules, the other, the opposite promontory in Africa (mod. Jebel Musa, or Apes' Hill), being anciently called *Abyla*   According to one account, these two were originally one mountain, which Hercules tore asunder, but some say he piled up each mountain separately, and poured the sea between them

The pack of hounds introduced into the Peninsula by Wellington's officers is the Calpe Hunt

Calumet (kăl' u met)   This name for the tobacco-pipe of the North American Indians, used as a symbol of peace and amity, is the Norman form of Fr *chalumeau* (from Lat *calamus*, a reed), and was given by the French-Canadians to certain plants used by the natives as pipe-stems, and hence to the pipe itself

The calumet, or 'pipe of peace," is about two and a half feet long, the bowl is made of highly polished red marble, and the stem is a reed, which is decorated with eagles' quills, women's hair, and so on

To present the calumet to a stranger is a mark of hospitality and goodwill, to refuse the offer is an act of hostile defiance.

> Giche Manito, the mighty,
> Smoked the calumet, the Peace-Pipe
> As a signal to the nations
> LONGFELLOW *Hiawatha*, 1

Calvary.   The Latin translation of the Gr *golgotha* (*q v*), which is a transliteration of the Hebrew word for "a skull "   The name given to the place of our Lord's crucifixion   Legend has it that the skull of Adam was preserved here, but the name is probably due to some real or fancied resemblance in the configuration of the ground to the shape of a skull

The actual site of Calvary has not been determined, though there is strong evidence in favour of the traditional site, which is occupied by the Church of the Holy Sepulchre   Another position which has strong claims is an eminence above the grotto of Jeremiah, outside the present wall and not far from the Damascus Gate on the north side of Jerusalem.

A Calvary   A representation of the successive scenes of the Passion of Christ in a series of pictures, etc, in a church   The shrine containing the representations

A Calvary cross.   A Latin cross mounted on three steps (or grises)

Calvary clover.   A common trefoil, *Medicago echinus*, said to have sprung up in the track made by Pilate when he went to the cross to see his "title affixed" (Jesus of Nazareth, king of the Jews)   Each of the three leaves has a little carmine spot in the centre, in the daytime they form a sort of cross, and in the flowering season the plant bears a little yellow flower, like a "crown of thorns." Julian tells us that each of the three leaves had in his time a white cross in the centre, and that the centre cross lasts visible longer than the others.

Calvert's Entire. The 14th Foot, now called the Prince of Wales's Own (West Yorks Regiment) Called from their colonel, General Sir Harry Calvert (1763-1826) of a well-known family of brewers, and *entire*, because three entire battalions were kept up for the good of Sir Harry, when adjutant-general

Calves The inhabitants of the Isle of Wight were sometimes so called from a tradition that a calf once got its head firmly wedged in a wooden pale, and, instead of breaking up the pale, the farm-man cut off the calf's head

His calves are gone to grass Said of a spindle-legged man And another mocking taunt is, "Veal will be dear, because there are no calves"

Calves' Head Club Instituted in ridicule of Charles I, and apparently first mentioned in a tract (given in the *Harleian Miscellany*) of 1703 by Benjamin Bridgwater, stating that it first met in 1693 It lasted till about 1735 The annual banquet was held on January 30th, and consisted of calves' heads dressed in sundry ways to represent Charles and his courtiers, a cod's head, to represent Charles, independent of his kingly office, a pike with little ones in its mouth, an emblem of tyranny, a boar's head with an apple in its mouth to represent the king preying on his subjects, etc After the banquet, the *Icon Basilike* was burnt, and the parting cup "To those worthy patriots who killed the tyrant," was drunk

Calvinism One of the sternest and most uncompromising sects of Christianity, and a joyless seriousness is often to be found among those who follow its tenets This frequently evinces itself in a rigid sabbatarianism and a suspicion of the theatre and other forms of art
The five chief points of Calvinism are
(1) Predestination, or particular election
(2) Irresistible grace
(3) Original sin, or the total depravity of the natural man, which renders it morally impossible to believe and turn to God of his own free will
(4) Particular redemption
(5) Final perseverance of the saints

Calydon (kăl' i don) In classical geography, a city in Ætolia, Greece, near the forest which was the scene of the legendary hunt of the Calydonian boar (*see* BOAR) Also, in Arthurian legend, the name given to a forest in the northern portion of England.

Calypso (ka lip' sō) In classical mythology, the queen of the island Ogygia on which Ulysses was wrecked She kept him there for seven years, and promised him perpetual youth and immortality if he would remain with her for ever Ogygia is generally identified with Gozo, near Malta

A **calypso** is a type of popular song evolved by the Negroes of the West Indies

Cam and Isis. The universities of Cambridge and Oxford, so called from the rivers on which they stand
> May you, my Cam and Isis, preach it long,
> "The right divine of kings to govern wrong."
> POPE *Dunciad*, IV, 187

Cama. The god of young love in Hindu mythology His wife is Rati (*voluptuousness*), and he is represented as riding on a sparrow, holding in his hand a bow of flowers and five arrows (*i e* the five senses)
> Over hills with peaky tops engrail'd,
> And many a tract of palm and rice
> The throne of Indian Cama slowly sail'd
> A summer fann'd with spice
> TENNYSON *The Palace of Art*

Camacho (kam a' chō) A rich but unfortunate man in one of the stories in *Don Quixote* who is cheated out of his bride just when he has prepared a great feast for the wedding, hence the phrase "Camacho's wedding" to describe useless show and expenditure

Camargo (kä mar' gō) Marie-Anne Cuppi (1710-1770) The greatest dancer of the 18th century, flourished in France, from her the modern Society in London devoted to the Ballet takes its name

Camarilla (kam a ril' a) Spanish for a small chamber or cabinet, hence, a clique, a nest of intriguers, the confidants or private advisers of the sovereign

Camarina. *Ne moveas Camarinam* (Don't meddle with Camarina) Camarina, a lake in Sicily, was a source of malaria to the inhabitants, who, when they consulted Apollo about draining it, received the reply, "Do not disturb it" Nevertheless, they drained it, and ere long the enemy marched over the bed of the lake and plundered the city The proverb is applied to those who remove one evil, but thus give place to a greater—leave well alone

Camber. In British legend, the second son of Brute (*q v*) Wales fell to his portion, which is one way of accounting for its ancient name of Cambria

Cambria (kăm' bri a) The ancient name of Wales, the land of the Cimbri or Cymry
Cambria's fatal day —GRAY *Bard*
> The Cambrian mountains, like far clouds,
> That skirt the blue horizon dusky rise
> THOMSON *Spring*, 961-62

Cambrian Series. The earliest fossiliferous rocks in North Wales, consisting principally of marine sediments which were formed after the close of Archean times and before the Ordovician period So named by Sedgwick (1836)

Cambric A kind of very fine white linen cloth, so named from Cambrai (Flem *Kameryk*), in Flanders, where for long it was the chief manufacture.
> He hath ribands of all the colours i' the rainbow;
> inkles, caddisses, cambricks, and lawns
> SHAKESPEARE *Winter's Tale*, IV, 3

Cambridge Apostles, The A debating society founded at Cambridge by John Sterling in 1826, and remarkable for the talent of its undergraduate members and for the success to which they attained in after life. Among them may be mentioned besides Sterling himself, Frederick Denison Maurice, Richard Chenevix Trench, John Kemble, Spedding, Monckton Milnes, Tennyson, and A H. Hallam

Cambridge colours (*boat crews*). *See* COLOURS

Cambuscan (kăm' bus kăn) In Chaucer's unfinished *Squire's Tale*, the King of Sarra, in Tartary, model of all royal virtues. His wife was Elfeta, his two sons, Algarsife and Cambalo, and his daughter, Canace. Milton refers to the story in *Il Penseroso*—

Him that left half-told
The story of Cambuscan bold

Cambyses (kăm bī' sēz) A pompous, ranting character in Thomas Preston's "lamentable tragedy" of that name (1570)

Give me a cup of sack, to make mine eyes look red, for I must speak in passion, and I will do it in King Cambyses' vein

SHAKESPEARE 1 *Henry IV*, ii, 4

Camden Society. An historical society founded in 1838 for the publication of early historic and literary remains connected with English history, and so named in honour of William Camden (1551-1623), the antiquary In 1897 it amalgamated with the Royal Historical Society, and its long series of publications was transferred to that body

Camel. The name of Mohammed's favourite camel was Al Kaswa The mosque at Koba covers the spot where it knelt when Mohammed fled from Mecca He considered the kneeling of the camel as a sign sent by God, and remained at Koba in safety for four days The swiftest of his camels was Al Adha, who is fabled to have performed the whole journey from Jerusalem to Mecca in four bounds, and, in consequence, to have had a place in heaven allotted him with Al Borak (*q v*), Balaam's ass, Tobit s dog, and the dog of the seven sleepers

To break the camel's back. To pile on one thing after another till at last the limit is reached and a catastrophe or break-down caused. The proverb is "It is the last straw that breaks the camel's back." *See* STRAW

It is easier for a camel to go through the eye of a needle, than for a rich man to enter into the kingdom of God (*see* EYE) In the Koran we find a similar expression "The impious shall find the gates of heaven shut, nor shall he enter till a camel shall pass through the eye of a needle " In the Rabbinical writings is a passage which goes to prove that the word *camel* should not be changed into *cable*, as Theophylact suggests "Perhaps thou art one of the Pampedithians, who can make an elephant pass through the eye of a needle."

It is as hard to come, as for a camel
To thread the postern of a needle's eye
SHAKESPEARE *Richard II*, v, 5

Some think to avoid a difficulty by rendering *Matt* xix, 24, "It is easier for a *cable* to go through the eye of a needle . ", but the word is κάμηλον and the whole force of the passage rests on the "impossibility" of the thing, as it is distinctly stated in *Mark* x, 24 "How hard is it for them that trust in [their] riches, ἐπὶ τοῖς χρήμασιν . ." It is impossible by

the virtue of money or by bribes to enter the kingdom of heaven.

Camelot (kăm' e lot) In British fable, the legendary spot where King Arthur held his court It has been tentatively located at various places—in Somerset, near Winchester (*q v*), in Wales, and even in Scotland

Hanmer, referring to *King Lear*, ii, 2, says Camelot is Queen Camel, Somersetshire, in the vicinity of which "are many large moors where are bred great quantities of geese, so that many other places are from hence supplied with quills and feathers." Kent says to the Duke of Cornwall:—

Goose, if I had you upon Sarum Plain,
I'd drive ye cackling home to Camelot.

It seems, however, far more probable that Kent refers to Camelford, in Cornwall, where the Duke of Cornwall resided, in his castle of Tintagel He says, "If I had you on Salisbury Plain [where geese abound], I would drive you home to Tintagel, on the river Camel " Though the Camelot of Shakespeare is Tintagel or Camelford, yet the Camelot of King Arthur may be Queen Camel, and indeed visitors are still pointed to certain large entrenchments at South Cadbury (Cadbury Castle) called by the inhabitants "King Arthur's Palace "

Cameo (căm' i ŏ) An ornamental carving in relief on a precious or semi-precious stone. It is the opposite of *intaglio*, which is an incised carving Onyx and sardonyx, with their layers of light and dark, were much used by the cameo cutters of Greece and Rome, and have always been the favourite stones for these ornaments However, amethysts, turquoises and most gems have at some time been cut as cameos In the nineteenth century, cameos were cut in shells, coral, and jet *Cameos* (1900) by Cyril Davenport, F S A., gives further information.

Cameron Highlanders. The 79th Regiment of Infantry, raised by Allan Cameron, of Errock, in 1793 Now called "The Queen's Own Cameron Highlanders "

Cameronian Regiment. The 26th Infantry, which had its origin in a body of Cameronians (*q.v.*), in the Revolution of 1688 Now the 1st Battalion of the Scottish Rifles, the 2nd Battalion is the old No 90

Cameronians. The strictest sect of Scottish Presbyterians, organized in 1680, by the Covenanter and field preacher, Richard Cameron, who was slain in battle at Aird's Moss in 1680 He objected to the alliance of Church and State, and seceded from the Kirk, but in 1690 his followers submitted to the General Assembly, and they became merged with the Covenanters

Camilla (kå mil' å) In Roman legend a virgin queen of the Volscians Virgil (*Æneid*, vii, 809) says she was so swift that she could run over a field of corn without bending a single blade, or make her way over the sea without even wetting her feet

Not so when swift Camilla scours the plain,
Flies o er the unbending corn and skims along the main
POPE *Essay on criticism*, 372

Camisarde or **Camisado** (kăm′ ı sard, kăm ı sa′ dō)   A night attack, so called because the attacking party wore a *camise* or camisard over their armour, both to conceal it, and that they might the better recognize each other in the dark.

Camisards.   In French history, the Protestant insurgents of the Cevennes, who resisted the violence of the dragonnades, long after the revocation of the edict of Nantes (1685), and so called from the white shirts (*camisards*) worn by the peasants   Their leader was Jean Cavalier (1681-1740), afterwards Governor of Jersey

Camisole.   A loose jacket worn by women when dressed in *néglige*, an underbodice worn immediately beneath a blouse

Camisole de force   A strait waistcoat Frequently mentioned in accounts of capital punishments in France

Camlan, Battle of.   In Arthurian legend the battle which put an end to the Knights of the Round Table, and at which Arthur received his death wound from the hand of his nephew Modred, who was also slain   It took place about a d. 537, but its site (traditionally placed in Cornwall) is as conjectural as that of Camelot (*q v*)

Camlet, camelot.   There are two different dress materials to which this word is applied.   As far back as the 13th century camlet was a rich stuff originally made of silk and camel's hair —
> After dinner I put on my new camelott suit, the best that I ever wore in my life, the suit costing me above £24 —Pepys *Diary* (June 1st, 1664).

Camlet was later the name of a very durable plain cloth used for cloaks, etc , also for a waterproof material used before the introduction of indiarubber

Cammock.   As crooked as a cammock.   The cammock is a crooked staff, or a stick with a crook at the head, like a hockey stick or shinty club, also, a piece of timber bent for the knee of a ship   The word is probably of Gaulish origin, it is found in Middle English, and there are Gaelic, Welsh, Irish, and Manx variants.
> Though the cammock, the more it is bowed the better it serveth, yet the bow, the more it is bent and occupied the weaker it waxeth —Lyly· *Euphues*

Camorra (ka mor′ a)   A lawless, secret society of Italy organized early in the 19th century It claimed the right of settling disputes, etc , and was so named from the blouse (Ital. *camorra*) worn by its members, the *Camorrists*

Campaign Wig.   This style of wig came from France in the early 18th century   It was made very full, was curled, and was 18 ins in length in the front, with drop locks   Sometimes the back part of the wig was put in a black silk bag   The name refers to Marlborough's campaign in the Netherlands

Campania (kăm pā′ ni ả) (Lat , level country) The ancient geographical name for the district south-east of the Tiber, containing the towns of Cumæ, Capua, Baiæ, Puteoli, Herculaneum, Pompeii, etc.
> Disdainful of Campania's gentle plains
> Thomson *Summer*

Campaspe (kăm păs′ pe).   A beautiful woman, the favourite concubine of Alexander the Great   Apellas, it is said, modelled his Venus Anadyomene from her
> Cupid and my Campaspe play'd
> At Cards for kisses, Cupid paid
> Lyly *Song from "Campaspe"*

Campbells are coming, The.   This stirring song was composed in 1715, when the Earl of Mar raised the standard for the Stuarts against George I.   John Campbell was Commander-in-Chief of his Majesty's forces, and the rebellion was quashed
   It is the Regimental March of the Argyll and Sutherland Highlanders, and at the Relief of Lucknow, in 1857, as troops of this Regiment approached, a Scots woman lying ill on the ground heard the pipes and exclaimed, 'Dinna ye hear it?   Dinna ye hear it?   The pipes o' Havelock sound "

Campbellites.   Followers of John McLeod Campbell (1800-72), who taught the universality of the atonement, for which, in 1830, he was ejected by the General Assembly of the Church of Scotland
   In the United States the name is sometimes given to the *Disciples of Christ*, a body founded by Thomas and Alexander Campbell in Pennsylvania in 1809   They reject creeds, practise immersion and weekly communion, and uphold Christian union on the foundation of the Bible alone.   They are also known as Christians

Campceiling   A ceiling sloping on one side from the vertical wall towards a plane surface in the middle   A corruption of *cam* (twisted or bent)   ceiling   (Halliwell gives *cam*, "awry.")

Campeador.   The Cid (*q v*)

Camp-followers.   The old-time armies, which lived on the country, moved in leisurely fashion and laid up in winter quarters, were accompanied by a number of civilian followers such as washerwomen and sutlers who sold liquors and provisions, etc   These were called camp-followers.
   In the moment of failure (at Bannockburn) the sight of a body of camp-followers whom they mistook for reinforcements to the enemy, spread panic through the English host
> J R Green *Short History*

Canaille (ka nī′) (Fr., a pack of dogs)   The mob, the rabble, a contemptuous name for the populace generally
> To keep the sovereign canaille from intruding on the retirement of the poor king of the French
> Burke

Canard (kăn′ ar) (Fr., a duck)   A hoax, a ridiculously extravagant report   Littré says that the term comes from an old expression, *vendre un canard à moitié*, to half-sell a duck.   As this is no sale at all it came to mean "to take in," "to make a fool of "   Another explanation is that a certain Cornelissen, to try the gullibility of the public, reported in the papers that he had twenty ducks, one of which he cut up and threw to the nineteen, who devoured it greedily   He then cut up another, then a third, and so on till the nineteenth was gobbled up by the survivor—a wonderful proof of duck voracity

Canary. Wine from these islands was very popular in the 16th and 17th centuries

> *Host* Farewell, my hearts, I will to my honest knight Falstaff, and drink canary with him
> *Merry Wives of Windsor*, iii, 2

Cancan. A fast and extremely dexterous dance, sometimes accompanied by extravagant and often indecent postures, and originally performed in the casinos of Paris The most famous example is in Offenbach's opera *Orpheus in the Underworld.*

> They were going through a quadrille with all those supplementary gestures introduced by the great Rigolboche, a notorious *danseuse*, to whom the notorious cancan owes its origin
> A EGMONT HAKE *Paris Originals* (1878)

Cancel. A leaf printed and inserted in a book to replace that which was originally printed, because of last minute corrections or errors detected after printing. In bibliographical terminology the new leaf being inserted is called the *cancellans* and that which it replaces is the *cancellanda*

Cancer. One of the twelve signs of the zodiac (the Crab) It appears when the sun has reached its highest northern limit, and begins to go backward towards the south, but, like a crab, the return is sideways (June 21st to July 23rd)

According to fable, Juno sent Cancer against Hercules when he combated the Hydra of Lerna It bit the hero's foot, but Hercules killed the creature, and Juno took it up to heaven

Candaules (kǎn daw' lēz). King of Lydia about 710 to 668 B C Legend relates that he exposed the charms of his wife to *Gyges* (*q v*).

Candid Camera. An unseen camera which is used to photograph an unsuspecting subject. Candid camera shots, which are often ridiculous, are much used in pictorial journalism

Candidate (Lat *candidatus,* clothed in white). One who seeks or is proposed for some office, appointment, etc Those who solicited the office of consul, quæstor, prætor, etc , among the Romans, arrayed themselves in a loose white robe It was loose that they might show the people their scars, and white in sign of fidelity and humility.

Candide (kan' dēd) The hero of Voltaire's philosophical novel, *Candide, ou l'Optimisme* (1759) All sorts of misfortunes are heaped upon him, and he bears them with unfailing optimism, in the belief that all's for the best in the best of all possible worlds.

Candle. Bell, book, and candle. *See* BELL

Fine (or Gay) as the king's candle. "*Bariolé comme la chandelle des rois,*" in allusion to an ancient custom of presenting on January 6th, a candle of various colours at the shrine of the three kings of Cologne. It is generally applied to a woman overdressed, especially with gay ribbons and flowers. "Fine as fivepence "

He is not fit to hold the candle to him. He is very inferior. The allusion is to link-boys who held candles in theatres and other places of night amusement

> Some say, compared to Buononcini
> That Mynheer Handel's but a ninny;
> Others aver that he to Handel
> Is scarcely fit to hold a candle.
> BYRON· *Feuds between Handel and Buononcini*

The game is not worth the candle. The effort is not worth making the result will not pay for the trouble, even the cost of the candle that lights the players

To burn the candle at both ends. *See* BURN

To hold a candle to the devil. To aid or countenance that which is wrong The allusion is to the Catholic practice of burning candles before the images of saints.

To sell by the candle. A species of sale by auction A pin is thrust through a candle about an inch from the top, and bidding goes on till the candle is burnt down to the pin, when the pin drops into the candlestick the last bidder is declared the purchaser

> The Council thinks it meet to propose the way of selling by "inch of candle," as being the most probable means to procure the true value of the goods
> MILTON. *Letters,* etc

To vow a candle to the devil. To propitiate the devil by a bribe, as some seek to propitiate the saints in glory by a votive candle.

What is the Latin for candle? *See* TACE.

Candle-holder. An abettor. The reference is to the practice in the Catholic Church of holding a candle for the reader. In ordinary parlance it applies to one who assists in some slight degree but is not a real sharer in an action or undertaking.

> I'll be a candle-holder and look on
> SHAKESPEARE· *Romeo and Juliet,* i, 4.

Candlemas Day. February 2nd, the feast of the Purification of the Virgin Mary, when Christ was presented by her in the Temple; one of the quarter days in Scotland In Catholic churches all the candles which will be needed in the church during the year are consecrated on this day, they symbolize Jesus Christ, called "the light of the world," and "a light to lighten the Gentiles " The Romans had a custom of burning candles to scare away evil spirits.

> If Candlemas Day be dry and fair,
> The half o' winter's come and mair,
> If Candlemas Day be wet and foul,
> The half o' winter was gane at You!
> *Scotch Proverb*

> The badger peeps out of his hole on Candlemas Day, and, if he finds snow, walks abroad, but if he sees the sun shining he draws back into his hole.
> *German Proverb*

Candour, Mrs. In *The School for Scandal* Sheridan drew the perfect type of female back-biter, concealing her venom under an affectation of frank amiability.

Canephorus (ka nef' ôr ús) (pl *canephori*) A sculptured figure of a youth or maiden bearing a basket on the head In ancient Greece the canephori bore the sacred things necessary at the feasts of the gods

Canicular Days (Lat. *canicula,* dim of *canis,* a dog) The dog-days (*q.v.*)

Canicular period. The ancient Egyptian cycle of 1461 years or 1460 Julian years, also called a *Sothic period*, (*q v*), during which it was supposed that any given day had passed through all the seasons of the year

Canicular year. The ancient Egyptian year, computed from one heliacal rising of the Dog Star (*Sirius*) to the next

Canister Shot. A projectile, used before the invention of the shell, consisting of a container full of shot which disintegrated and showered its contents on the enemy

Canker. The briar or dog-rose

> Put down Richard, that sweet lovely rose
> And plant this thorn, this canker, Bolingbroke
> SHAKESPEARE 1 *Henry IV*, i, 3.

Also a caterpillar that destroys leaves, buds, etc

> As killing as the canker to the rose
> MILTON *Lycidas*

Canmore. *See* GREAT HEAD

Cannæ The place where Hannibal defeated the Romans under Varro and L Æmilius Paulus with great slaughter in 216 B C, by means of withdrawing his centre and so enveloping the enemy—one of the most difficult manœuvres in war to perform Any fatal battle that is the turning point of a great general's prosperity may be called his Cannæ. Thus Moscow was the Cannæ of Napoleon

Cannel Coal. A corruption of *candle coal*, so called from the bright flame unmixed with smoke, which this highly bituminous coal yields in combustion

Cannibal. A word applied to those who eat human flesh. It is the Sp *Canibales*, a corruption of *Caribes*, *i e* the *Caribs*, inhabitants of the Antilles, some of whom, when discovered by Columbus, were said to be man-eaters

> The natives live in great fear of the canibals [*i e* Caribals, or people of Cariba] —COLUMBUS

Cannon. This term in billiards is a corruption of *carom*, which is short for Fr *carambole*, the red ball (*caramboler*, to touch the red ball). A cannon is a stroke by which the player's ball touches one of the other balls in such a way as to glance off and strike the remaining ball.

Canny *See* CA' CANNY.

Canoe. Like *cannibal*, *canoe* is one of the very few words we get from native West Indian This is a Haitian word, *canoa*, and was brought to Europe by the Spaniards It originally meant a boat hollowed out of a tree-trunk.

Paddle your own canoe. Mind your own business The caution was given by President Lincoln, but it is an older saying and was used by Capt Marryat (*Settlers in Canada*, ch viii) in 1844 Sarah Bolton's poem in *Harper's Magazine* for May, 1854, popularized it:—

> Voyage upon life's sea,
> To yourself be true,
> And, whate'er your lot may be,
> Paddle your own canoe

Canon From Lat and Gr *canon*, a carpenter's rule, a rule, hence a standard (as "the canons of criticism"), a model, an ordinance, as in Shakespeare's:—

> Or that the Everlasting had not fixed
> His canon 'gainst self-slaughter
> *Hamlet*, i, 2

The canon. Canon law (*q v*)

> Self-love which is the most inhibited sin in the canon.
> *All's Well that Ends Well*, i, 1

In music, from the same derivation, a composition written strictly according to rule, for two or three voices which sing exactly the same melody one a few beats after the other, either at the same or a different pitch—as *Three Blind Mice*.

Also, the body of the books in the Bible which are accepted by the Christian Church generally as genuine and inspired, the whole Bible from *Genesis* to *Revelation*, excluding the Apocrypha. Called also the *sacred canon* and the *Canonical Books*.

The Church dignitary known as a *Canon* is a capitular member of a cathedral or collegiate church, usually living in the precincts, and observing the statutable rule or canon of the body to which he is attached The canons, with the dean at their head, constitute the governing body, or *chapter*, of the cathedral.

Canon law. A collection of ecclesiastical laws which serve as the rule of church government The professors or students of canon law are known as *canonists*

> Doubt not, worthy senators! to vindicate the sacred honour and judgment of Moses your predecessor, from the shallow commenting of scholastics and canonists —MILTON *Doctrine of Divorce, Introd*

Canonical dress. The distinctive or appropriate costume worn by the clergy according to the direction of the canon Bishops, deans, and archdeacons, for instance, wear canonical hats This distinctive dress is sometimes called simply "canonicals", Macaulay speaks of "an ecclesiastic in full canonicals" The same name is given also to the special robes of other professions, and to special parts of such robes, such as the *pouch* on the gown of an M D., originally designed for carrying drugs; the *lamb-skin* on a B.A hood, in imitation of the *toga candida* of the Romans; the *tippet* on a barrister's gown, meant for a wallet to carry briefs in, and the proctors' and proproctors' *tippet*, for papers—a sort of sabretache.

Canonical Epistles. The seven catholic epistles, *i e* one of James, two of Peter, three of John, and one of Jude The epistles of Paul were addressed to specific churches or to individuals

Canonical hours. The different parts of the Divine Office which follow and are named after the hours of the day. They are seven—viz matins, prime, tierce, sext, nones, vespers, and compline Prime, tierce, sext, and nones are the first, third, sixth, and ninth hours of the day, counting from six in the morning Compline is a corruption of *completorium* (that which completes the services of the day) The reason why there are seven canonical hours is that David says, "Seven times a day do I praise thee" (*Ps* cxix, 164).

In England the phrase means more especially the time of the day within which persons can be legally married, *i.e.* from eight in the morning to six p m

Canonical obedience. The obedience due by the inferior to the superior clergy Thus bishops owe canonical obedience to the archbishop of the same province

Canopus (ka nō′ pus). A seaport in ancient Egypt, 15 miles N E of Alexandria. Also the name of the bright star in the southern constellation *Argo navis* Except for Sirius this is the brightest star in the heavens

> We drank the Libyan sun to sleep, and lit
> Lamps which out-burn'd Canopus.
> TENNYSON *Dream of Fair Women.*

Canopic vases Vases used by the Egyptian priests for holding the viscera of bodies embalmed, four being provided for each body So called from Canopus, in Egypt, where they were first used

Canopy properly means a *gnat curtain* Herodotus tells us (ii, 95) that the fishermen of the Nile used to lift their nets on a pole, and form thereby a rude sort of tent under which they slept securely, as gnats will not pass through the meshes of a net Subsequently the hangings of a bed were so called, and lastly the canopy borne over kings. (Gr. *konops*, a gnat)

Canossa (ká nos′ a). Canossa, in the duchy of Modena, is where, in January, 1077, the Emperor, Henry IV, went to humble himself before Gregory VII (Hildebrand)

Hence, **to go to Canossa**, to eat humble pie; to submit oneself to a superior after having refused to do so

Cant. A whining manner of speech, class phraseology, especially of a pseudo-religious nature (Lat *canto*, to sing, whence "chant") It seems to have been first used of the whining manner of speech of beggars, who were known as "the canting crew" (*q v*). In Harman's *Caveat, or Warning, for Common Cursetors, vulgarly called Vagabonds* (1567), we read:—

> As far as I can learne or understand by the examination of a number of them, their language—which they terme peddelars Frenche or Canting—began but within these xxx yeeres

And one of the examples of "canting" that he gives begins:—

> Bene Lightmans to thy quarromes, in what tipken hast thou lypped in this darkemans, whether in a lybbege or in the strummel? (Good-morrow to thy body, in what house hast thou lain in all night, whether in a bed or in the straw?)

The term was in familiar use in the time of Ben Jonson, signifying "professional slang," and "to use professional slang."

> The doctor here .
> When he discourses of dissection
> Of *vena cava* and of *vena porta* .
> What does he else but cant? Or if he run
> To his judicial astrology,
> And trowl the *trine*, the *quartile*, and the *sextile* . . .
> Does he not cant?
> BEN JONSON *The Staple of News,* IV, iv (1625)

Cant also means insincerity or conventionality in speech or thought

> Rid your mind of cant
> Dr. JOHNSON.

From this it is extended to include any assumption or affectation of enthusiasm for high thoughts or aims.

Canting crew. Beggars, gipsies, thieves, and vagabonds, who use "cant" (*q v*) In 1696 "E. B Gent," published the first English Slang Dictionary, with the title "A New Dictionary of the Terms, Ancient and Modern, of the Canting Crew in its several Tribes."

Cantabrian Surge. The Bay of Biscay So called from the Cantabri who dwelt about the Biscayan shore Suetonius tells us that a thunderbolt fell in the Cantabrian Lake (Spain) ' in which twelve axes were found " (*Galba,* viii)

> She her thundering army leads
> To Calpé [Gibraltar] . . or the rough
> Cantabrian Surge
> AKENSIDE· *Hymn to the Naiades*

Cantate Sunday (kăn ta′ te) Rogation Sunday, the fourth Sunday after Easter. So called from the first word of the introit of the mass "Sing to the Lord " Similarly "Lætare Sunday " (the fourth after Lent) is so called from the first word of the mass

Canteen means properly a wine-cellar (Ital *cantina*, a cellar) Then a refreshment house in a barrack for the use of the soldiers, whence it has now come to be applied to a communal restaurant for members of a large firm, etc. Then a vessel for holding liquid refreshment, carried by soldiers on the march, and finally a complete outfit of cutlery.

Canter An easy gallop, originally called a *Canterbury pace* or *gallop,* from the ambling gait adopted by mounted pilgrims to the shrine of St Thomas à Becket at Canterbury

A preliminary canter. Something which precedes the real business in hand. The reference is to the "trial trip" of horses before the race begins.

To win in a canter. Easily; well ahead of all competitors

Canterbury Tales. Chaucer set it forth that he was in company with a party of pilgrims going to Canterbury to pay their devotions at the shrine of Thomas à Becket. The party assembled at an inn in Southwark, called the Tabard, and there agreed to tell one tale each, both in going and returning He who told the best tale was to be treated with a supper on the homeward journey The work is incomplete, and we have none of the tales told on the way home.

Canucks (ka nŭks′). The name given in the U S A. to Canadians generally, but in Canada itself to Canadians of French descent The origin is uncertain, but it has been suggested that it is a corruption of *Connaught,* a name originally applied by the French Canadians to Irish immigrants

Canvas means cloth made of hemp (Lat. *cannabis,* hemp). **To canvas a subject** is to strain it through a hemp strainer, to sift it; and **to canvass a borough** is to solicit the votes

Caora (ka ōr′ a) A river described by Elizabethan voyagers (*see* Hakluyt), on the banks of which dwelt a people whose heads grew beneath their shoulders. Their eyes were in their shoulders, and their mouths in the middle of their breasts Raleigh, in his *Description of Guiana,* gives a similar account of a race of men *Cp* BLEMMYES.

Cap. The word is used figuratively by Shakespeare for the top, the summit (of excellence, etc); as in *They wear themselves in the cap of the time* (*All's Well*, II, 1), i e "They are the ornaments of the age"; *a very riband in the cap of youth* (*Hamlet*, IV, 7), *Thou art the cap of all the fools alive* (*Timon*, IV, 3), *on fortune's cap we are not the very button* (*Hamlet*, II, 2), etc

Black cap. *See* BLACK.

Cap acquaintance A bowing acquaintance One just sufficiently known to touch one's cap to.

Cap and bells. The insignia of a professional fool or jester

Cap and feather days. The time of childhood
Here I was got into the scenes of my cap and feather days —COBBETT.

Cap and gown. The full academical costume of a university student, tutor, or master, worn at lectures, examinations, and after "hall" (dinner)
Is it a cap and gown affair?
C BEDE *Verdant Green*

Cap in hand. Submissively To wait on a man cap in hand is to wait on him like a servant, ready to do his bidding

Cap money. Money collected in a cap or hat, hence an improvised collection

Cap of liberty. When a slave was manumitted by the Romans, a small Phrygian cap, usually of red felt, called *pileus*, was placed on his head, he was termed *libertinus* (a freedman), and his name was registered in the city tribes. When Saturninus, in 100 B C, possessed himself of the Capitol, he hoisted a similar cap on the top of his spear, to indicate that all slaves who joined his standard should be free, Marius employed the same symbol against Sulla; and when Cæsar was murdered, the conspirators marched forth in a body, with a cap elevated on a spear, in token of liberty
In the French Revolution the cap of liberty (*bonnet rouge*) was adopted by the revolutionists as an emblem of their freedom from royal authority.

Cap of Maintenance. A cap of dignity anciently belonging to the rank of duke, the fur cap of the Lord Mayor of London, worn on days of state; a cap carried before the British sovereigns at their coronation The significance of *maintenance* here is not known, but the cap was an emblem of very high honour, for it was conferred by the Pope three times on Henry VII and once on Henry VIII By certain old families also it is borne in the coat of arms, either as a charge or in place of the wreath

Cater cap. A square cap or mortar-board. (Fr *quartier*)

College cap. A trencher like the caps worn at the English Universities by students and bachelors of art, doctors of divinity, etc

Fool's cap. A conical cap with feather and bells, such as licensed fools used to wear. For the paper so called, *see* FOOLSCAP

Forked cap. A bishop's mitre.

John Knox cap. An early form of the trencher, mortar-board, or college cap (*q v*), worn at the Scottish Universities

Monmouth cap. *See* MONMOUTH

Phrygian cap. Cap of liberty (*q v*)

Scotch cap. A cloth cap worn in Scotland as part of the national dress

Square cap. A trencher or mortar-board, like the college cap (*q v*)

Statute cap. A woollen cap ordered by a statute of Queen Elizabeth in 1571 to be worn on holidays by all citizens for the benefit of the woollen trade To a similar end, persons were at one time obliged to be buried in woollens
Well, better wits have worn plain statute caps
SHAKESPEARE *Love's Labour's Lost*, v, 2

Trencher cap, or **mortar-board** A cap with a square board, generally covered with black cloth, and a tassel, worn with academical dress; a college cap (*q v*)

A feather in one's cap. An achievement to be proud of, something creditable

I cap to that. I assent to it The allusion is to a custom among French judges Those who assent to the opinion stated by any of the bench signify it by lifting their toque from their heads

I must put on my thinking cap I must think about the matter before I give a final answer The allusion is to the official cap of a judge, formerly donned when passing any sentence, but now only when passing sentence of death

If the cap fits, wear it. If the remark applies to you, apply it yourself. Hats and caps differ very slightly in size and appearance, but everyone knows his own when he puts it on.

Setting her cap at him. Trying to catch him for a sweetheart or a husband In the days when ladies habitually wore caps they would naturally put on the most becoming, to attract the attention and admiration of the favoured gentleman

To cap. To take off, or touch, one's cap to, in token of respect, also to excel
Well, that caps the globe —C BRONTË *Jane Eyre*

To cap a story. To go one better; after a good story has been told to follow it up with a better one of the same kind

To cap verses. Having the metre fixed and the last letter of the previous line given, to add a line beginning with that letter, thus.
The way was long, the wind was cold (D)
Dogs with their tongues their wounds do heal (L).
Like words congealed in northern air (R).
Regions Cæsar never knew (W)
With all a poet's ecstasy (Y)
You may deride my awkward pace, etc , etc.

There are parlour games of capping names, proverbs, etc , in the same way, as · Plato, Otway, Young, Goldsmith, etc , "Rome was not built in a day," "Ye are the salt of the earth," "Hunger is the best sauce," "Example is better than precept," "Time and tide wait for no man," etc.

To cap it all   To surpass what has gone before, to make things even worse

To gain the cap.   To obtain a bow from another out of respect

Such gains the cap of him that makes them fine,
But keeps his book uncrossed
                    SHAKESPEARE *Cymbeline*, iii, 3

To pull caps.   To quarrel like two women, who pull each other's caps   An obsolete phrase, used only of women.   In a description of a rowdy party in 18th-century Bath we read —

At length they fairly proceeded to pulling caps, and everything seemed to presage a general battle they suddenly desisted, and gathered up their caps, ruffles, and handkerchiefs
            SMOLLETT *Humphrey Clinker · Letter* xix

To send the cap round.   To make a collection   This is from the custom of street musicians, acrobats, etc ,of sending a cap round among the onlookers to collect their pennies

Wearing the cap and bells.   Said of a person who is the butt of the company, or one who excites laughter at his own expense.   The reference is to licensed jesters formerly attached to noblemen's establishments   *See* CAP AND BELLS *above*   Their headgear was a cap with bells.

One is bound to speak the truth   .   whether he mounts the cap and bells or a shovel hat [like a bishop] —THACKERAY.

Your cap is all on one side.   Many workmen, when they are bothered, scratch their heads and to do this push the cap on one side of the head, generally over the right ear, because the right hand is occupied

Capful of wind.   Olaus Magnus tells us that Eric, King of Sweden, was so familiar with evil spirits that what way soever he turned his cap the wind would blow, and for this he was called *Windy Cap*.   The Laplanders drove a profitable trade in selling winds, as have many ancient and primitive peoples, and even so late as 1814, Bessie Millie, of Pomona (Orkney), used to sell favourable winds to mariners for the small sum of sixpence

To be capped.   A player who has represented England, Scotland, Ireland, or Wales in an international match at any of the major field sports may wear a cap bearing the national emblem   Hence the phrase: He was capped for England.

Capability Brown.   Lancelot Brown (1715-83) landscape gardener and architect, one of the founders of the modern or English style of landscape gardening   He received this name because he habitually assured prospective employers that their land held "great capabilities."

Cap-à-pie (kăp à pē).   From head to foot; usually with reference to arming or accoutring   From O.Fr. *cap à pie* (Mod Fr *de pied en cap*).

Armed at all points exactly cap-a-pie
                    SHAKESPEARE *Hamlet*, i, 2.
I am courtier, cap-a-pe
            SHAKESPEARE *Winter's Tale*, iv, 3

Cape.   The Cape.   Cape of Good Hope Province

Cape cart.   This is the name given to a two-wheeled, hooded, horse-drawn cart originally used in Cape Colony and S Africa generally.

Cape gooseberry.   Although it takes its name from the Cape, this plant originally came from S America and its botanical name is *Physalis peruviana*.   It is much prized for its decorative bladder-like calyx.

Spirit of the Cape.   *See* ADAMASTOR.

Cape of Storms.   *See* STORMS

Capel Court.   A lane adjacent to the Stock Exchange in London where dealers congregate to do business   hence used sometimes for the Stock Exchange itself.   Hence also *Capel Courtier*, a humorous term for a professional stock-dealer.   So called from Sir William Capel, Lord Mayor in 1504.

Caper.   The weather is so foul not even a Caper would venture out.   A Manx proverb.   A Caper is a fisherman of Cape Clear in Ireland, who will venture out in almost any weather.

To cut capers   To spring upwards in dancing, and rapidly interlace one foot with the other; figuratively, to act in an unusual manner with the object of attracting notice.   Caper here is from Ital *capra*, a she-goat, the allusion being to the erratic way in which goats will jump about

Cut your capers!   Be off with you!

I'll make him cut his capers, *i e* rue his conduct

Caper Merchant.   A dancing-master who cuts "capers"

Capet.   Hugh Capet, the founder of the Capetian dynasty of France, is said to have been so named from the *cappa*, or monk's hood, which he wore as lay abbot of St. Martin de Tours   The Capetians reigned over France till 1328, when they were succeeded by the House of Valois; but *Capet* was considered the family name of the kings, hence, Louis XVI was arraigned before the National Convention under the name of Louis Capet.

Capital.   Money or money's worth available for production

His capital is continually going from him [the merchant] in some shape and returning to him in another
            ADAM SMITH *Wealth of Nations*, Bk. ii, ch 1

Active capital.   Ready money or property readily convertible into it

Circulating capital.   Wages, or raw material.   This sort of capital is not available a second time for the same purpose

Fixed capital.   Land, buildings, and machinery, which are only gradually consumed

To make capital out of.   To turn to account: thus, in politics, one party is always ready to make political capital out of the errors of the other.

Capitano, El Gran (el grän kăp i ta' nō) (*i e.* the Great Captain)   The name given to the famous Spanish general Gonsalvo de Cordova (1453-1515), through whose efforts Granada and Castile were united.

Capitulary (kăp it' ū lär i).   A collection of ordinances or laws, especially those of the

Frankish kings. The laws were known as *capitulars* because they were passed by a chapter (*q v*)

Capon (kā' pon) Properly, a castrated cock; but the name has been given to various fish, perhaps originally in a humorous way by friars who wished to evade the Friday fast and so eased their consciences by changing the name of the fish, and calling a chicken a *fish out of the coop* Thus we have—

A **Crail's capon.** A dried haddock

A **Glasgow capon.** A salt herring.

A **Severn capon.** A sole

A **Yarmouth capon.** A red herring.

Capon is also an obsolete term for a love-letter, after the Fr *poulet*, which means not only a chicken but also a love-letter, or a sheet of fancy notepaper Thus Henri IV, consulting with Sully about his marriage, says: "My niece of Guise would please me best, though report says maliciously that she loves poulets in paper better than in a fricassee."

Boyet . break-up this capon [*i e* open this love-letter]

SHAKESPEARE *Love's Labour's Lost*, iv, 1.

Capricorn (kăp' ri kôrn). Called by Thomson, in his *Winter*, "the centaur archer." Anciently, the winter solstice occurred on the entry of the sun into Capricorn, *i e.* the Goat but the stars, having advanced a whole sign to the east, the winter solstice now falls at the sun's entrance into Sagittarius (the centaur archer), so that the poet is strictly right, though we commonly retain the ancient classical manner of speaking Capricorn is the tenth, or, strictly speaking, the eleventh, sign of the zodiac (December 21-January 20)

According to classical mythology, Capricorn was Pan, who, from fear of the great Typhon, changed himself into a goat, and was made by Jupiter one of the signs of the zodiac

Captain. The Great Captain. *See* CAPITANO, EL GRAN

A led captain. An obsequious person, who dances attendance on the master and mistress of a house, for which service he has a knife and fork at the dinner table

Captain Armstrong. A name for a cheating jockey—one who pulls a horse with a *strong arm*, and so prevents his winning.

Captain Cauf's Tail In Yorkshire, the commander-in-chief of the mummers who used to go round from house to house on Plough Monday (*q v*) He was most fantastically dressed, with a cockade and many coloured ribbons; and he always had a genuine calf's (cauf's) tail affixed behind

Captain Copperthorne's Crew All masters and no men

Capua (kăp' ū a) Capua corrupted Hannibal Luxury and self-indulgence will ruin anyone Hannibal was everywhere victorious over the Romans till he took up his winter quarters at Capua, the most luxurious city of Italy. When he left Capua his star began to wane, and, ere long, Carthage was in ruins and himself an exile Another form of the saying is—

Capua was the **Cannæ** of Hannibal (*see* CANNÆ).

Capuchin (kăp' ū chin) A friar of the Franciscan Order (*q.v*) of the new rule of 1525; so called from the *capuce* or pointed cowl.

Capulet (kăp' ū let) A noble house in Verona, the rival of that of Montague, Juliet is of the former, and Romeo of the latter Lady Capulet is the beau-ideal of a proud Italian matron of the 15th century (Shakespeare *Romeo and Juliet*). The expression so familiar, "the tomb of all the Capulets," is from Burke; he uses it in his reflections on the *Revolution in France* (vol iii, p 349), and again in his *Letter to Matthew Smith*, where he says:—

I would rather sleep in the southern corner of a country churchyard than in the tomb of the Capulets

Caput Mortuum (kăp' ut môr' tū um) (Lat , dead head). An alchemist's term, used to designate the residuum left after exhaustive distillation or sublimation, hence, anything from which all that rendered it valuable has been taken away Thus, a learned scholar paralysed is a mere *caput mortuum* of his former self. The French Directory, towards its close, was a mere *caput mortuum* of a governing body

Caqueux (ka ke). A sort of gipsy race in Brittany, similar to the Cagots of Gascony, and Colliberts of Poitou

Carabas (kär' a ba) He is a Marquis of **Carabas.** An ultra-conservative nobleman, of unbounded pretensions and vanity, who would restore the lavish foolery of the reign of Louis XIV, one with Fortunatus's purse, which was never empty The character is taken from Perrault's tale of *Puss in Boots*, where he is Puss's master

Prêtres que nous vengeons
Levez la dîme et partageons,
Et toi, peuple animal,
Porte encor le bât féodal . .
Chapeau bas' Chapeau bas'
Gloire au marquis de Carabas!

Béranger (1816)

The Marquis of Carabas in Disraeli's *Vivian Grey* is intended for the Marquis of Clanricarde

Carabinier. *See* CARBINEER

Caracalla (kär' a kăl' ä) Aurelius Antoninus, Roman Emperor, 211-17, was so called because he adopted the Gaulish *caracalla* in preference to the Roman toga. It was a large, close-fitting, hooded mantle, reaching to the heels, and slit up before and behind to the waist. *Cp* CURMANTLE

Carack *See* CARRACK

Caradoc (kă răd' ok). A Knight of the Round Table, noted for being the husband of the only lady in the queen s train who could wear "the mantle of matrimonial fidelity " He appears (as Craddocke) in the old ballad *The Boy and the Mantle* (given in Percy's *Reliques*) —

Craddocke called forth his ladye,
And bade her come in,
Saith, Winne this mantle, ladye,
With a little dinne.

Also, in history, the British chief whom the Romans called Caractacus (lived about A D. 50)

Caran d'Ache (kǎ ran dash') This was the pseudonym of Emanuel Poiré (1858-1909), a well-known French caricaturist. He was famous in his time as an illustrator of military subjects, and his biting cartoons and caricatures appeared in various papers and magazines

Carat. A measure of weight, about ⅟₁₄₂ of an ounce, used for precious stones, also a proportional measure of ⅟₂₄th used to describe the fineness of gold, thus, gold of 22 carats has 22 parts pure gold and 2 parts alloy. The Arabic *qirat*, meaning the seed of the locust tree, the weight of which represented the Roman *siliqua*, was ⅟₇₂th of the golden *solidus* of Constantine, which was ⅟₃th of an ounce It is from these fractions that it has come about that a carat is a twenty-fourth part The name may come from the Arabic, or from Greek κεράτιον, seed of the locust-tree. *See* GOLD

Caraway (kǎr' á wä) The flavouring of cakes with caraway seeds was once more common than is now the case. Cakes so flavoured were called caraways, hence Shallow's invitation to Falstaff —

Nay, you shall see my orchard, where in an arbour we will eat a last year's pippin of my own braffing, with a dish of caraways

2 *Henry IV*, v, 3

Carbineer or **Carabineer.** A soldier armed with a short light rifle (called a *carbine*) such as is used by cavalry. The word is from Fr. *carabine*, which is either from *Calabrinus*, a Calabrian (in which case the word would originally mean a skirmisher or light horseman), or from late Lat. *chadabula*, a kind of ballista for hurling projectiles The 6th Dragoon Guards in the British Army are known as the *Carabiniers*.

Carbonado (kar bon ä' dō). Grilled meat or fish Strictly speaking, a carbonado is a piece of meat cut crosswise for the gridiron (Lat *carbo*, a coal).

If he do come in my way, so, if he do not—if I come in his willingly, let him make a carbonado of me.

SHAKESPEARE 1 *Henry IV*, v, 3

Carbonari (kar bo na' rē) (singular, *carbonaro*). This name, assumed by a secret political society in Italy (organized 1808-14), means *charcoal burners* Their place of muster they called a "hut", its inside, the place for selling charcoal"; and the outside, the "forest." Their political opponents they called "wolves" Their object was to convert the kingdom of Naples into a republic The name was later applied to other secret political societies.

Carcanet (kar' kä net) A small chain of jewels for the neck (Fr *carcan*, a collar of gold) The famous collar of Agnes Sorel, favourite of Charles VII of France (1422-50), which she called her *carcanet*, was said to have been composed of rough diamonds

Like captain jewels in a carcanet.
SHAKESPEARE. *Sonnets*

Carcass The shell of a house before the floors are laid and walls plastered, the skeleton of a ship, a wreck, etc. The body of a dead animal, so called from Fr *carcasse*, Lat. *carcosum*.

The Goodwins, I think they call the place; a very dangerous flat and fatal, where the carcases of many a tall ship lie buried

SHAKESPEARE. *Merchant of Venice*, iii, 1.

The name was also given to an obsolete type of incendiary shell projected from a mortar.

Charlestown,   having been fired by a carcass from Copp's Hill, sent up dense columns of smoke
LESSING *United States*

Card. Slang for a queer fellow, an eccentric, a "character"

You're a shaky old card, and you can't be in love with this Lizzie

DICKENS· *Our Mutual Friend*, Bk. iii, ch 1

Perhaps suggested by the phrase, "a sure card" *See below* We thus have such phrases as the following —

A cool card. A person who coolly asks for something preposterous or outrageous. "Cool" in this connexion means coolly impudent Cp. COOLING CARD *below*.

A great card. A bigwig, the boss of the season, a person of note

A knowing card. A sharp fellow, next door to a sharper The allusion is to cardsharpers and their tricks.

Whose great aim it was to be considered a knowing card —DICKENS· *Sketches, etc*

A loose card. A worthless fellow who lives on the loose

A loose card is a card of no value, and consequently the properest to throw away —HOYLE *Games, etc*

A queer card. An eccentric person, "indifferent honest", one who *may* be "all right," but whose proceedings arouse mild suspicion and do not inspire confidence.

A sure card. A person one can fully depend on, a person sure to command success. A project to be certainly depended on As a winning card in one's hand

A clear conscience is a sure card.
LYLY· *Euphues* (1579)

Other phrases are directly from card-games, or from the "card" of a compass, i e the dial on which the points of the compass are displayed. The first-named group gives us, among others, such phrases as —

A cooling card. An obsolete expression for something that cools one's ardour, probably derived from some old game of cards. It is quite common in Elizabethan literature. In *Euphues* (1579) Lyly calls the letter to Philantus "a cooling card for Philantus and all fond lovers," and says—

The sick patient must keep a straight diet, the silly sheep a narrow fold, poor Philantus must believe Euphues, and all lovers (he only excepted) are cooled with a card of ten or rather fooled with a vain toy

A card of ten was evidently an important card; Shakespeare has·—

A vengeance on your crafty wither'd hide!
Yet I have faced it with a card of ten
Taming of the Shrew, i, 2.

which means either to put a bold face on it, or to meet an attack with craft and subtlety.

A leading card. The strongest point in one's argument, etc , a star actor. In card games a person leads from his strongest suit

He played his cards well. He acted judiciously and skilfully, like a whist-player who plays his hand with judgment

On the cards Likely to happen, projected, and talked about as likely to occur This phrase may have allusion to the programme or card of the races, but is more likely to derive from fortune-telling by cards

That's the card. The right thing, probably referring to card games—"that is the right card to play"—but it may refer to tickets of admission, cards of the races, programmes, etc.

10s is about the card
MAYHEW *London Labour, etc*

That was my trump card. My best chance, my last resort

The cards are in my hands I hold the disposal of events which will secure success, I have the upper hand, the whip-end of the stick

To ask for one's card. To resign one's job, derived from the National Health Insurance card kept by the employer while the workman is on the job

To count on one's cards. To anticipate success under the circumstances, to rely on one's advantages.

To go in with good cards. To have good patronage; to have excellent grounds for expecting success

To play one's best card To do that which one hopes is most likely to secure victory.

To throw up the cards. To give up as a bad job, to acknowledge you have no hope of success In some games of cards, as poker, a player has the liberty of saying whether he will play or not, and if his hand is hopelessly bad he throws in his cards and sits out till the next deal.

From the compass card we have the phrase **To speak by the card,** to be careful with one's words, to be as deliberate, and have as much claim to be right, as a compass

Law . . . is the card to guide the world by
HOOKER *Ecc Pol*, Pt ii, sec 5

We must speak by the card, or equivocation will undo us —SHAKESPEARE *Hamlet,* v, i

It is possible that this phrase has reference to written documents, such as agreements made between a merchant and the captain of a vessel To speak by the card may be to speak according to the indentures or written instructions, but when Osric tells Hamlet (v, 2) that Laertes is "the card and calendar of gentry" the card is a card of a compass, containing all its points Laertes is the card of gentry, in whom may be seen all its points

Cards. It is said that there never was a good hand at whist containing four clubs Such a hand is called "The Devil's Four-poster"

In Spain, spades used to be *columbines*; clubs, *rabbits*, diamonds, *pinks*, and hearts, *roses* The present name for spades is *espados* (swords), of clubs, *bastos* (cudgels); of diamonds, *dineros* (square pieces of money used for paying wages); of hearts, *copas* (chalices).

The French for spade is *pique* (pikemen or soldiers), for club, *trefle* (clover, or husbandmen); of diamonds, *carreaux* (building tiles, or flagstones), of hearts, *cœur*

The English spade is the French form of a pike, and the Spanish name, the club is the French trefoil, and the Spanish name

Court cards *See* COURT.

Cardigan (car′ di gan) This is a knitted woollen over-waistcoat, with or without sleeves, and it takes its name from the 7th Earl of Cardigan, who commanded the Light Brigade and led it in the famous charge at Balaclava The garment appears to have been first worn by our men in the bitter cold of the Crimean winter

Cardinal. The Lat *cardo* means a hinge, its adjective, *cardinalis* (from which we get "cardinal"), meant originally "pertaining to a hinge," hence 'that on which something turns or depends," hence "the principal, the chief " Hence, in Rome a "cardinal church" (*ecclesia cardinalis*) was a principal or parish church as distinguished from an oratory attached to such, and the chief priest (*presbyter cardinalis*) was the "cardinal," the body (or "College") of cardinals forming the Council of the Pope, and electing the Pope from their own number. This did not become a stabilized regulation till after the third Lateran Council (1173), since when the College of Cardinals has consisted of six cardinal bishops, fifty cardinal priests, and fourteen cardinal deacons

The cardinal's red hat was made part of the official vestments by Innocent IV (1245) "in token of their being ready to lay down their life for the gospel "

Cardinal humours. An obsolete medical term for the four principal "humours" of the body, viz blood, phlegm, yellow bile, and black bile

Cardinal numbers The natural, primitive numbers, which answer the question "how many? " such as 1, 2, 3, etc. 1st, 2nd, 3rd, etc , are *ordinal* numbers

Cardinal points of the compass. Due north, west, east, and south So called because they are the points on which the intermediate ones, such as NE , NW , NNE , etc , hinge or hang (Lat *cardo*, a hinge)

The poles, being the points upon which the earth turns, were called in Latin *cardines* (*cardo*, a hinge, *see* CARDINAL *above*), and the *cardinal points* are those which lie in the direction of the poles and of sunrise and sunset Thus, also, the winds that blow due east, west, north, and south are known as the *cardinal winds* It is probably from the fact that the cardinal points are *four* in number that the cardinal humours, virtues, etc., are also *four*

Cardinal signs (of the zodiac) The two equinoctial and the two solstitial signs, Aries and Libra, Cancer and Capricorn.

Cardinal virtues Justice, prudence, temperance, and fortitude, on which all other virtues hang or depend A term of the Schoolmen, to distinguish the "natural" virtues from the "theological" virtues (faith, hope, and charity)

Care. **Care killed the cat.** It is said that "a cat has nine lives," yet care would wear them all out.

> Hang sorrow! care'll kill a cat.
> BEN JONSON *Every Man in his Humour*, 1, 3.

Care Sunday. The fifth Sunday in Lent. "Care" here means trouble, suffering, and Care Sunday means Passion Sunday (as in Old High Ger *Kar-fritag* is Good Friday)
Care Sunday is also known as *Carle*, or *Carling Sunday*. It was an old custom, especially in the north, to eat parched peas fried in butter on this day, and they were called *Carlings*

Care-cloth. The fine silk or linen cloth formerly laid over the newly-married in the Catholic Church, or held over them as a canopy

Carême (kâ rām') Lent, a corruption of *quadragesima*.

Caricatures mean sketches "overloaded"; hence, exaggerated drawings (Ital *caricatura*, from *caricare*, to load or burden.)

Carillons (ka ril' yonz), in France, are chimes or tunes played on bells, but in England the suites of bells that play the tunes The word is the O Fr *quarignon*, from late Lat *quatrinto*, a chime played on four bells, carillons were formerly rung on four bells; nowadays the number is usually eight, but the 'bob maximus" (*see* BOB) is rung on twelve

Carle Sunday; Carlings *See* CARE SUNDAY.

Carlists (kar' lists) Don Carlos (1788-1855) was the second son of Charles IV of Spain, and on the death of his brother, Ferdinand VII would have become king of Spain had not the Salic Law been set aside and Ferdinand's daughter Isabella declared Queen He set up his claim to the throne, the Church sided with him, and for years Spain was rent by factious war between the Carlists and the queen's party. The Carlist activities did not really cease until the death of Don Carlos II, in 1909 The last pretender died childless in 1936, and the following year the party was merged by General Franco in his Falange

Carlovingians (kar lo ving' gianz) or *Carolingians* So called from Carolus Magnus, or Charlemagne They were descended from Frankish lords in Austria in the 7th century, and furnished the second royal dynasty in France (751-987), a dynasty of German Emperors (752-911), and of Italian kings (774-961).

Carmagnole (kar ma nyōl) Originally the name of a kind of jacket worn in France in the 18th century, and introduced there from Carmagnola, in Piedmont, where it was the dress of the workmen It was adopted by the Revolutionists, and the name thus came to be applied to them, to the soldiers of the first Republic, and to a song and a wild kind of dance that became immensely popular and was almost invariably used at the executions of

1792 and 1793 The first verse of the song is:—

> Madame Veto avait promis
> De faire égorger tout Paris,
> Madame Veto avait promis
> De faire egorger tout Paris
> Mais son coup a manqué
> Grace a nos canonnie
> Dansons la carmagnole, Vive le son, vive le son,
> Dansons la carmagnole, Vive le son du canon

Madame Veto was the people's name for Queen Marie Antoinette, as she was supposed to have inspired the king's unfortunate use of the veto
The word was subsequently applied to other revolutionary songs, such as *Ça ira*, the *Marseillaise*, the *Chant du depart*, also to the speeches in favour of the execution of Louis XVI, called by Barère, *des Carmagnoles*

Carmelites (kar' me līts) Mendicant friars, the first rule of whose Order is said to have been given by John, patriarch of Jerusalem, A D 400, and to have been formed from the records of the prophet Elijah's life on Mount Carmel Also called White Friars, from their white cloaks. *See* BAREFOOTED.

Carmen Sylva (kar' men sil' va) This was the pen-name of Queen Elizabeth of Rumania (1843-1916) She was a woman of cultivated tastes, a musician, painter, and writer of poems and stories

Carminative (kar min' a tiv). A medicine given to relieve flatulence. The name is a relic of the mediæval theory of humours, it is from Lat *carminare*, to card wool, which, in Italian, also meant "to make gross humours fine and thin " The object of carminatives is to expel wind, and they were supposed to effect this by combing out the gross humours as one combs out (or cards) the knots in wool

Carney To wheedle, to caress, to coax An old dialect word of unknown origin.

Carnival. The season immediately preceding Lent, ending on Shrove Tuesday, and a period in many Roman Catholic countries devoted to amusement, hence, revelry, riotous amusement From the Lat *caro, carnis*, flesh, *levare*, to remove, signifying the abstinence from meat during Lent The earlier word, *carnlevamen*, was altered in Italian to *carnevale*, as though connected with *vale*, farewell—farewell to flesh

Carol (from O Fr *carole*, which is probably from Lat *choraula*, a dance) The earliest meaning of the word in English is a round dance, hence a song that accompanied the dance, hence a light and joyous hymn, a meaning which came to be applied specially to, and latterly almost confined to, such a hymn in honour of the Nativity and sung at Christmas time by wandering minstrels. The earliest extant English Christmas carol dates from the 13th century, and was originally written in Anglo-Saxon, a translation of the first verse is here given. The first printed collection of Christmas carols came from the press of Wynkyn de Worde in 1521, it included the Boar's Head Carol, which is still sung at

Queen's College, Oxford   For another example, *see* BOAR'S HEAD

> Lordlings, listen to our lay—
> We have come from far away
> To seek Christmas,
> In this mansion we are told
> He his yearly feast doth hold,
> 'Tis to-day!
> May joy come from God above.
> To all those who Christmas love

Carolingians. *See* CARLOVINGIANS

Carolus (kä rō' lus)   A gold coin of the reign of Charles I   It was at first worth 20s , but afterwards 23s

Carouse (ka rouz').   To drink deeply, to make merry with drinking; hence a drinking bout. The word is the German *garaus*, meaning literally "right out" or "completely", it was used specially of completely emptying a bumper to someone's health.
 The word *rouse*, a bumper, as in Shakespeare's —

> The king doth wake to-night, and takes his rouse.
> *Hamlet*, 1, 4

probably arose from the similarity of sound between "to drink carouse", and "to drink a rouse"

Carpathian Wizard.   Proteus, who lived in the island of Carpathus (now Scarpanto), between Rhodes and Crete, who could transform himself into any shape he pleased   He is represented as carrying a sort of crook in his hand, because he was an ocean shepherd and had to manage a flock of sea-calves
 By the Carpathian wizard's book
                                    MILTON *Comus*, 872.

Carpe Diem (kar' pā dī' em)   Enjoy yourself while you have the opportunity.   Seize the present day   "*Dum vivimus, vivamus*"
 Carpe diem quam minimum credula postere
                                    HORACE *Odes*, I, xi, 8,
 Seize the present, trust to-morrow e'en as little as you may —CONNINGTON

Carpet.   The magic carpet.   The carpet which, to all appearances, was worthless, but which, if anyone sat thereon, would transport him instantaneously to the place he wished to go, is one of the stock properties of Eastern wonder-tales and romance   It is sometimes termed *Prince Housain's carpet*, because of the popularity of the *Story of Prince Ahmed* in the *Arabian Nights*, where it supplies one of the principal incidents, but the chief magic carpet is that of King Solomon, which, according to the Mohammedan legend related in the Koran, was of green silk   His throne was placed on it when he travelled, and it was large enough for all his forces to stand upon, the men and women on his right hand, and the spirits on his left   When all were arranged in order, Solomon told the wind where he wished to go, and the carpet, with all its contents, rose in the air and alighted at the place indicated   In order to screen the party from the sun, the birds of the air with outspread wings formed a canopy over the whole party

To be on the carpet, or to be carpeted.   To be reprimanded, to be "called over the coals"

To bring a question on the carpet: to bring it up for consideration: a translation of Fr *sur le tapis* (on the tablecloth)—*i e.* before the House, under consideration.   The question has been laid on the table of the House, and is now under debate.

Carpet-bagger.   The name given in the U S A to the Northern political adventurers, who sought a career in the Southern States after the Civil War of 1865   Their only "property qualification" was in the personal baggage they brought with them, and they were looked upon with great suspicion   In U S A. members of Congress and the State legislatures almost invariably reside in the district which they represent

Carpet knight.   One dubbed at Court by favour, not having won his spurs by military service in the field   Perhaps because mayors, lawyers, and civilians generally are knighted as they kneel *on a carpet* before their sovereign in contradistinction to those knighthoods that used to be conferred on the actual field of battle, but more probably with allusion to the preference shown by non-martial knights for the carpeted drawing-room over the tented field.

> You are women
> Or, at the best, loose carpet-knights
> MASSINGER   *Maid of Honour*, ii, 5

Carrack.   A large merchant ship which, in Elizabethan times, carried the valuable cargoes from the Spice Islands and the Far East to Portugal, and could readily be fitted out as a man-of-war
> "And now hath Sathanas," seith he, "a tayl
> Brodder than of a carrik is the sayl "
> CHAUCER · *Somnour's Prologue*, 23

Carriage.   This used to mean, that which is carried, luggage, also the supports or mount of a piece of ordnance
> And after those days we took up our carriages, and went up to Jerusalem —*Acts* xxi, 15

In *Num* iv, 24, where the text gives "burdens," the marginal rendering is "carriage," and the usage is not at all uncommon in the English of that date

Carriage company.   Persons who go visiting in their private carriage
> Seeing a great deal of carriage company —*Thackeray*

Carronade (kär o näd').   A short gun of large calibre like a mortar, having no trunnions and so differing from howitzers, first made in 1779 at the Carron foundry, Scotland. Carronades are fastened to their carriages by a loop underneath, and were chiefly used on ships, to enable heavy shot to be thrown at close quarters.

Carry.   Carry arms !   Carry swords !   Military commands directing that the rifle or drawn sword is to be held in a vertical position in the right hand and against the right shoulder.

Carry coals.   *See* COALS

To carry everything before one   To be beyond competition; to carry off all the prizes; to be a successful competitor in any form of examination or sport

To carry fire in one hand and water in the other.   To say one thing and mean another;

to flatter, to deceive; to lull suspicion in order the better to work mischief

Altera manu fert aquam, altera ignem,
Altera manu fert lapideum, altera panem ostentat
                                                    Plautus

In one hand he carried water, in the other fire, in one hand he bears a stone, in the other he shows a piece of bread

To carry on. (1) To continue an activity from the point already reached, particularly in military parlance (2) To make a scene, lose one's temper—"he carried on something dreadful"

To carry one's point. To succeed in one's aim Candidates in Rome were balloted for, and the votes were marked on a tablet by points Hence, *omne punctum ferre* meant "to be carried *nem. con*," or to gain every vote, and "to carry one's point" is to carry off the points at which one aimed

To carry out or through To continue a project to its completion

To carry one's bat Said of a cricketer who is "not out" at the close of the game Hence, figuratively, to outlast one's opponents, to succeed in one's undertaking

Carry swords ! *See* CARRY ARMS!

To carry the day. To win the contest, to carry off the honours of the day

To carry weight In horse racing, to equalize the weight of two or more riders by adding to the lighter ones till both (or all) the riders are made of uniform weight

He carries weight! he rides a race!
'Tis for a thousand pounds
                        COWPER. *John Gilpin*

Also, to have influence

Cart To put the cart before the horse is to reverse the right order or allocation of things.

This methinkes is playnely to sett the carte before the horse —*The Babees Book* (Early English Tract Society, p xxiii)

The phrase has its counterpart in other languages —

French Mettre la charette avant les bœufs
Latin Currus bovem trahit
                Præpostere
Greek, Hysteron proteron
German Die pferde hinter den wagen spannen
Italian Metter il carro innanzi ai buoi

Carte **Carte blanche** (Fr). A paper with only the signature written on it, so that the person to whom it is given may write his terms knowing that they will be accepted Literally, a blank paper. It was originally a military phrase, referring to unconditional surrender; but it is now used entirely in a figurative sense, conferring absolute freedom of action on one to whom it is given.

Carte de visite (Fr) A visiting card, a photographic likeness on a card, originally intended to be used as a visiting card The idea was started in 1857, but it never "caught on," as such, although the small size of photograph became very popular

Cartel (kar tel'). This is a word with several meanings Originally it was applied only to a written agreement between opponents in a war arranging the exchange of prisoners From

that it was extended to include the ship used for such an exchange It has since come to mean a working arrangement between rival commercial concerns in one or more countries to regulate the price of the commodity they are interested in, invariably at the expense of the community

Cartesian Philosophy (kar tē zhán) The philosophical system of René Descartes (1596-1650), a founder of modern philosophy The basis of his system is *cogito ergo sum See* COGITO Thought must proceed from soul, and therefore man is not wholly material, that soul must be from some Being not material, and that Being is God. As for physical phenomena, they must be the result of motion excited by God, and these motions he termed *vortices.*

Carthage of the North (kar' thaj) This was the name given to Lübeck, when it was the head of the Hanseatic League.

Carthaginem esse delendam. *See* DELENDA EST CARTHAGO

Carthaginian faith. Treachery *See* PUNICA FIDES.

Carthusians. An order of monks, founded about 1086 by St Bruno, of Cologne, who, with six companions, retired to the solitude of La Grande Chartreuse, thirteen miles northeast of Grenoble, and there built his famous monastery In 1902 the monks were evicted by order of the French government, and in the following year their buildings and property were sold, the monks themselves settling at the Certosa (Charterhouse) near Lucca

The first English Charterhouse was established in 1178, the monks of the London Charterhouse were among the staunchest opponents of Henry VIII. In 1833 the Carthusians were re-established in the Charterhouse at Parkminster, Sussex. *See* CHARTREUSE

Cartoon. Originally a design drawn on *cartone* (pasteboard) to serve as a model for a work of art, such as a fresco or tapestry Now applied to a caricature or political sketch.

Cartridge Paper. A stout, rough paper, originally manufactured for cartridges. The word is a corruption of *cartouche*, from *carta* (paper).

Carvel-built. A term in shipbuilding applied to a vessel whose planks are set edge to edge and do not overlap From *Caravella* (Ital) a large sailing ship *See* CLINKER-BUILT.

Carvilia. *See* MORGAN LE FAY.

Caryatides (kăr i ăt' idz) Figures of women in Greek costume, used in architecture to support entablatures Caryæ, in Laconia, sided with the Persians at Thermopylæ, in consequence of which the victorious Greeks destroyed the city, slew the men, and made the women slaves Praxiteles, to perpetuate the disgrace, employed figures of these women, instead of columns *Cp* ATLANTES, CANEPHORUS

Casabianca, Louis (kăs a bi ăng' ka) Captain of the French man-of-war, *L Orient* At the battle of Aboukir, having first secured the safety of his crew, he blew up his ship, to prevent it falling into the hands of the English. His little son, Giacomo Jocante, refusing to leave him, perished with his father. Mrs Hemans made a ballad on the incident, which was also celebrated by the French poets Lebrun and Chenier.

Case. The case is altered. See PLOWDEN

To case. To skin an animal, to deprive it of its "case." See FIRST CATCH YOUR HARE, s v CATCH

Case-hardened. Impenetrable to all sense of honour or shame. The allusion is to steel hardened by carbonizing the surface

Cashier. To dismiss an officer from the army, to discard from society (Dut casveren, Fr casser, to break; Ital. cassai e, to blot out)
> The ruling rogue, who dreads to be cashiered,
> Contrives, as he is hated, to be feared
> SWIFT Epis'le to Mr Gay, 137

Cashmere. See KERSEYMERE.

Casino (ka sē' nŏ) Originally, a little casa or room near a theatre where persons might retire, after the play was over, for dancing or music

Cask. A vessel for the storing of wine in bulk Some local names for casks are as follows '—
Arroba, Spain, basil, Portugal, barile, Italy; barrique, France, Breute, Switzerland, Dreiling, Eimer, or Fuder, Austria, Oxhoft, Hamburg, bochonok, Russia

Casket Homer. See HOMER.

Casket Letters, The. Letters supposed to have been written between Mary Queen of Scots and Bothwell, at least one of which was held to prove the complicity of the Queen in the murder of her husband, Darnley. They were kept in a casket which fell into the hands of the Earl of Morton (1567), they were examined and used as evidence (though denounced as forgeries by the Queen—who was never allowed to see them), and they disappeared after the execution of the Regent, the Earl of Gowrie (1584), in whose custody they had last been. They have never been recovered, and their authenticity is still a matter of dispute

Casper (kăs' pĕr) A huntsman who sells himself to Zimeel, the Black Huntsman in Weber's opera Der Freischutz

Cassandra (ka sǎn' dra) A prophetess. In Greek legend the daughter of Priam and Hecuba, gifted with the power of prophecy, but Apollo, whose advances she had refused, brought it to pass that no one believed her predictions, although they were invariably correct. She appears in Shakespeare's Troilus and Cressida
> A Cassandra of the Crew [gipsies], after having examined my Lines very diligently told me, etc
> Spectator, July 30th, 1711

Cassation. The Court of Cassation, in France, is the highest Court of Appeal, the Court which can casser (quash) the judgment of other Courts

Cassi. Inhabitants of what is now the Cassio hundred, Hertfordshire, referred to by Cæsar, in his Commentaries. The name can still be traced in Cassiobury Park, just outside Watford

Cassibelan (kăs ib' el an) Uncle to Cymbeline, mentioned in Shakespeare's play of that name. He is the historical Cassivellaunus, a British prince who ruled over the Catuvellauni (in Herts, Bucks, and Berks), about 50 B C, and was conquered by Cæsar
Shakespeare drew his particulars from Holinshed, where it is Guiderius, not Cymbeline, who refuses to pay the tribute.

Cassiopeia (kăs i ŏ pē' a). In Greek mythology, the wife of Cepheus, King of Ethiopia, and mother of Andromeda (q v) In consequence of her boasting of her beauty, she was sent to the heavens as the constellation Cassiopeia, the chief stars of which form the outline of a woman seated in a chair and holding up both arms in supplication
> That starred Ethiop queen that strove
> To set her beauty's praise above
> The sea-nymphs and their powers offended
> MILTON Il Penseroso.

Cassiterides (kăs i ter' i dēz) The tin islands, generally supposed to be the Scilly Islands and Cornwall, but possibly the isles in Vigo Bay are meant. It is said that the Veneti procured tin from Cornwall, and carried it to these islands, keeping its source a profound secret The Phœnicians were the chief customers of the Veneti

Cast. A cast of the eye A squint. One meaning of the word cast is to twist or warp. Thus, a fabric is said to "cast" when it warps, the seamen speak of "casting," or turning the head of a ship on the tack it is to sail. We also speak of a "casting vote" (q v)
> My goode bowe clene cast [twisted] on one side
> ASCHAM Toxophilus

Cast down. Dejected. (Lat dejectus)

To cast a sheep's eye at one. See SHEEP.

To cast about. To deliberate, to consider, as, "I am casting about me how I am to meet the expenses." A sporting phrase. Dogs, when they have lost scent, "cast for it," i e spread out and search in different directions to recover it

To cast accounts. To balance or keep accounts. To cast up a line of figures is to add them together and set down the sum they produce. To cast or throw the value of one figure into another till the whole number is totalled

To cast anchor. To throw out the anchor in order to bring the vessel to a standstill. (Lat anchoram jacēre)

To cast aside. To reject as worthless

To cast beyond the moon. To form wild conjectures. One of Heywood's proverbs. At one time the moon was supposed to influence the weather, to affect the ingathering of fruits, to rule the time of sowing, reaping, and slaying cattle, etc
> I talke of things impossible, and cast beyond the moon —HEYWOOD

To cast in one's lot To share the good or bad fortune of another

To cast in one's teeth. To throw reproof at one The allusion is to knocking one's teeth out by stones

> All his faults observed,
> Set in a note book, learned and conned by rote,
> To cast into my teeth.
> SHAKESPEARE *Julius Cæsar*, IV, 3

To cast pearls before swine To give what is precious to those who are unable to understand its value· a biblical phrase (*see Matt* VII, 6) If pearls were cast to swine, the swine would trample them under foot

Casting vote. The vote of the presiding officer when the votes of the assembly are equal This final vote casts, turns, or determines the question

Castaly (kǎs′ ta li). A fountain of Parnassus sacred to the Muses Its waters had the power of inspiring with the gift of poetry those who drank of them

> What was the great Parnassus' self to Thee,
> Mount Skiddaw? In his natural sovereignty
> Our British Hill is nobler far, he shrouds
> His double front among Atlantic clouds,
> And pours forth streams more sweet than Castaly
> WORDSWORTH *Miscellaneous Sonnets*, V

Caste (Port *casta*, race) One of the hereditary classes of society in India, hence any hereditary or exclusive class, or the class system generally The four Hindu castes are *Brahmins* (the priestly order), *Shatriya* (soldiers and rulers), *Vaisya* (husbandmen and merchants), *Sudra* (agricultural labourers and mechanics). The first issued from the mouth of Brahma, the second from his arms, the third from his thighs, and the fourth from his feet. Below these come thirty-six inferior classes, to whom the Vedas are sealed, and who are held cursed in this world and without hope in the next

To lose caste. To lose position in society To get degraded from one caste to an inferior one

Castle. Castle in the air. A visionary project, day-dream, splendid imagining which has no real existence In fairy tales we often have these castles built at a word, and vanishing as soon, like that built for Aladdin by the Genie of the Lamp. Also called *Castles in Spain*; the French call them *Chateaux d'Espagne* or *Chateaux en Asie* See CHATEAU.

Castle of Bungay. In Camden's *Britannia* (1607) the following lines are attributed to Lord Bigod of Bungay on the borders of Suffolk and Norfolk —

> Were I in my Castle of Bungay
> Upon the river of Waveney,
> I would ne care for the King of Cockney

The events referred to belong to the reign of Stephen or Henry II The French have a proverb *Je ne voudrais pas être roi, si j'étais prévot de Bar-sur-Aube*, I should not care to be king if I were Provost of Bar-sur-Aube (the most lucrative and honourable of all the provostships of France). A similar idea is expressed in the words—

> And often to our comfort we shall find,
> The sharded beetle in a safer hold
> Than is the full-winged eagle
> SHAKESPEARE *Cymbeline*, iii, 3.

Almost to the same effect Pope says —

> And more true joy Marcellus exiled feels,
> Than Cæsar with a senate at his heels
> *Essay on Man*, IV, 257

Castle of Indolence. In Thomson's poem of this name (1748) it is situated in the land of Drowsiness, where every sense is steeped in enervating delights The owner was an enchanter, who deprived all who entered his domains of their energy and free will

Castle Terabil (or " Terrible ") in Arthurian legends stood in Launceston. It had a steep keep environed with a triple wall Sometimes called Dunheved Castle.

Castor and Pollux (kas′ tor, pol′ uks) In Roman mythology, the twin sons of Jupiter and Leda. Jupiter is said to have visited Leda in the form of a swan, she produced two eggs, from one of which sprang Castor and Clytemnestra, and from the other Pollux and Helen Castor and Pollux, also known as the Dioscuri (*q v*), had many adventures, were worshipped as gods, and were finally placed among the constellations

Their names used to be given by sailors to the St Elmo's Fire or Corposant (*q*) If only one flame showed itself, the Romans called it *Helen*, and said that it portended that the worst of the storm was yet to come, but two or more luminous flames they called *Castor and Pollux*, and said that they boded the termination of the storm.

Casuist. One who resolves *casus conscientiæ* (cases of conscience); figuratively, a hair-splitter M. le Fèvre called casuistry "the art of quibbling with God "

Casus belli (kā′ sŭs bel′ ī) (Lat.). A ground for war, an occurrence warranting international hostilities.

M Cambon asked me what we should say about the violation of the neutrality of Belgium I said that was a much more important matter, we were considering what statement we should make in Parliament to-morrow—in effect, whether we should declare violation of Belgian neutrality to be a *casus belli* —Sir EDW GREY to the British Ambassador at Paris, August 2nd, 1914

Cat. Called a "familiar," from the mediæval superstition that Satan's favourite form was a black cat Hence witches were said to have a cat as their familiar. The superstition may have arisen from the classical legend of Galinthias who was turned into a cat and became a priestess of Hecate

In ancient Rome the cat was a symbol of liberty The goddess of Liberty was represented as holding a cup in one hand, a broken sceptre in the other, and with a cat lying at her feet No animal is so great an enemy to all constraint as a cat

In Egypt the cat was sacred to Isis, or the moon. It was held in great veneration, and was worshipped with great ceremony as a symbol of the moon, not only because it is more active after sunset, but from the dilatation and contraction of its pupil, symbolical of waxing and waning. The goddess Bast (*see* BUBASTIS), representative of the life-giving solar heat, was portrayed as having the head of a cat, probably because that animal likes to bask in the sun. Diodorus tells us that whoever killed a cat, even by accident, was by the Egyptians punished by death, and according to ancient tradition, Diana assumed the form of a cat, and thus excited the fury of the giants

The male, or Tom, cat was formerly—and in Scotland still is—known as a Gib cat, the female as a Doe cat The word "cat" has other connotations, e g , a spiteful woman, hence a spiteful remark is said to be "catty." In early days "cat" was a slang term for a harlot

CAT PROVERBS AND SAYINGS

A cat has nine lives. A cat is more tenacious of life than many animals It is a careful, sly, and suspicious beast, and—in the wild state—is strong, hardy, and ferocious, also, after a fall, it generally lights upon its feet without injury, the foot and toes being well padded

> *Tyb* What wouldst thou have with me?
> *Mer* Good king of cats, nothing but one of your nine lives
>   SHAKESPEARE· *Romeo and Juliet*, iii, 1

A cat has nine lives, and a woman has nine cats' lives —FULLER· *Gnomologia*

A cat may look at a king. An impertinent remark by an inferior, meaning, "I am as good as you." There was a political pamphlet published with this title in 1652

All cats love fish but fear to wet their paws. An old adage, said of one who is anxious to obtain something of value but does not care to incur the necessary trouble or risk It was to this saying that Shakespeare referred in *Macbeth*, i, 7 —

> Letting "I dare not" wait upon "I would,'
> Like the poor cat i' the adage

Before the cat can lick her ear. Never, before the Greek kalends No cat can lick her ear. *See* NEVER

Care killed the cat. *See* CARE

Cat i' the adage. *See* ALL CATS LOVE FISH *above*

To cat. *See* SICK AS A CAT *below*.

To cat the anchor. To hang the anchor on the cathead, a piece of timber outside the ship to which the anchor is hung to keep it clear of the ship.

> The decks were all life and commotion, the sailors on the forecastle singing "Ho! cheerily, men!'" as they catted the anchor.
>   H MELVILLE *Omoo*, xxxvi p 191

Cheshire cat *See* TO GRIN LIKE A CHESHIRE CAT *below*

Dick Whittington and his cat. *See* WHITTINGTON

Enough to make a cat laugh, incongruously ridiculous.

Enough to make a cat speak. Said of something (usually good liquor) that will loosen one's tongue.

> Come on your ways; open your mouth, there is that which will give language to your cat, open your mouth'—SHAKESPEARE *Tempest*, ii, 2

Hang me in a bottle like a cat (*Much Ado about Nothing*, i, 1) In olden times a cat was for sport enclosed in a bag or leather bottle, and hung to the branch of a tree, as a mark for bowmen to shoot at Percy mentions a variant of this "sport" in his *Reliques of Ancient English Poetry* (1765) —

It is still a diversion in Scotland to hang up a cat in a small cask or firkin, half filled with soot, and then a parcel of clowns on horseback try to beat out the ends of it, in order to show their dexterity in escaping before the contents fall upon them
>   Vol I, p 155 (Edn. of 1794)

It is raining cats and dogs. Very heavily.

> I know Sir John would go, though he was sure it would rain cats and dogs
>   SWIFT *Polite Conversation*, ii

Like a cat on hot bricks. Very uneasy, not at all "at home" in the situation, whatever it may be

Muffled cats catch no mice (Ital *Catta guantata non piglia sorce*) Said of those who work in gloves for fear of soiling their fingers

Not room to swing a cat. Swinging cats as a mark for sportsmen was at one time a favourite amusement There were several varieties of this diversion *See* HANG ME IN A BOTTLE *above*, and To FIGHT LIKE KILKENNY CATS *below* It is probable that the custom of tormenting cats by the ignorant arose from their supposed connexion with witches

> Mrs Crupp had indignantly assured him that there wasn't room to swing a cat there, but as Mr Dick justly observed to me,   "You know, Trotwood, I don't want to swing a cat, I never do swing a cat Therefore what does that signify to me!"
>   DICKENS *David Copperfield*, ch. xxxv

Smollett had previously used the phrase in *Humphrey Clinker, Lett.* xxxvi, and it is quite possible that *cat* was originally *cot*, the phrase being a sailor's expression, and the allusion to a swung hammock or cot

See how the cat jumps. See "which way the wind blows", which of two alternatives is likely to be the successful one before you give any opinion of its merit or adhesion to it, either moral or otherwise The allusion is either to the game called "tip-cat," in which before you strike you must observe which way the "cat" has jumped up, or to the cruel sport mentioned above *See* HANG ME IN A BOTTLE

> He soon saw which way the cat did jump,
> And his company he offered plump
>   *The Dog's-meat Man* (*Universal Songster*, 1825).

Sick as a cat. Cats are very subject to vomiting Hence one is said *to cat*, or *to shoot the cat* in vomiting.

To bell the cat. *See* BELL

To fight like Kilkenny cats. To fight till both sides have lost their all, to fight with the utmost determination and pertinacity The story is that during the Irish rebellion of 1798 Kilkenny was garrisoned by a troop of Hessian soldiers, who amused themselves by tying two cats together by their tails and throwing them across a clothes-line to fight The authorities resolved to put a stop to the "sport," but, on the officer on duty approaching, one of the troopers cut the two tails with a sword, and the cats made off When the officer inquired the meaning of the bleeding tails, he was told that two cats had been fighting and had devoured each other all but the tails.

To grin like a Cheshire cat. An old simile, popularized by Lewis Carroll,—

> "Please would you tell me," said Alice a little timidly,   "why your cat grins like that?"
> "It's a Cheshire cat," said the Duchess, "and that's why"—*Alice in Wonderland* (1865), ch vi

The phrase has never been satisfactorily accounted for, but it has been said that cheese was formerly sold in Cheshire moulded like a cat that looked as though it was grinning. The humorous explanation is that the cats there know that Cheshire is a County Palatine (*q v*), and that the idea is so funny that they are perpetually amused at it!

To let the cat out of the bag. To disclose a secret It was formerly a trick among country folk to substitute a cat for a sucking-pig, and bring it in a bag to market. If any greenhorn chose to buy a "pig in a poke" without examination, all very well, but if he opened the sack, "he let the cat out of the bag," and the trick was disclosed

To lead a cat and dog life. To be always snarling and quarrelling, as a cat and dog, whose aversion to each other is intense

> There will be jealousies, and a cat-and-dog life over yonder worse than ever
>
> CARLYLE *Frederick the Great*, vol ii, bk ix

To turn cat-in-pan. To turn traitor, to be a turncoat. The phrase seems to be the Fr. *tourner côte en peine* (to turn sides in trouble)

> When George in pudding-time came o'er
> And moderate men looked big, sir,
> I turned a cat-in-pan once more,
> And so became a Whig, sir.
> *Vicar of Bray*

> There is a cunning which we in England call the turning of the *cat in the pan*, which is, when that which a man says to another, he lays it as if another had said it to him —BACON *Essays Of Cunning*

The origin of the term is unknown Johnson in his *Dictionary* says —

> Imagined by some to be rightly written *Catipan*, as coming from *Catipania* An unknown correspondent imagines, very naturally, that it is corrupted from *Cate in the pan*

Neither suggestion is accepted by modern philologists

Touch not a cat but a glove. The punning motto of the Mackintosh clan, whose crest is "a cat-a-mountain salient guardant proper," with for supporters "two cats proper." An early meaning of "but" was "without" or "except" for another example of this use, see the Prayer Book Version of *Ps* xix, 3

What can you have of a cat but her skin? Said of something that is useless for any purpose but one In former times the cat's fur was used for trimming cloaks and coats, but the flesh is no good for anything

When the cat's away the mice will play. Advantage will be taken of the absence of the person in authority. An old proverb, found in many languages It is given in Ray's Collection.

CAT NAMES, PHRASES, ETC

Cat and Fiddle. Several fanciful derivations have been found for this inn sign. There can be little doubt that it comes from the nursery rhyme, with a possible reference to the once popular game of tip-cat or trap-ball, and the fiddle for a dance that were provided as attractions for customers It is worth mentioning that the *Dunciad* (i, 224) refers in contempt to Cibber as "the *Bear* and *Fiddle* of the town."

Cat and Kittens. A public-house sign, alluding to the range of pewter-pots of various sizes that were so called. Stealing these pots was termed "cat and kitten sneaking."

Cat and Mouse Act. *To play cat and mouse* with one is "to have him on a string", while he is in your power to pretend constantly to let him go, but not actually to do so During the Suffragette agitation at the beginning of the 20th century an Act was passed in 1912 with the object of rendering nugatory the tactics of imprisoned suffragettes who went on "hunger-strike." Under this Act such "hunger-strikers" could be set at liberty, but were liable to re-arrest as soon as they were sufficiently recovered to undergo the remainder of their sentence This unenlightened Act was not particularly successful

Cat-call. A kind of whistle used at theatres by the audience to express displeasure or impatience. A hideous noise like the *call* or *waul* of a *cat*.

> I was very much surprised with the great consort of cat-calls . . . to see so many persons of quality of both sexes assembled together in a kind of cater-wauling
> *Spectator*, No 361.

Cat-eyed. Able to see in the dark.

Cat ice. Very thin, almost transparent ice from which the water that was underneath has receded; so slight as to be unable to bear a cat

Cat-lap. A contemptuous name for tea, or other "soft" drink such as a cat could swallow; a non-alcoholic liquor.

> A more accomplished old woman never drank cat-lap —SCOTT· *Redgauntlet*, ch xii

Cat o' mountain. The wild-cat; also the leopard, or panther, hence a wild, savage sort of man

Cat-nap. To snatch a few minutes sleep in a chair or in a car, between one's appointments or activities, from the propensity of cats for dozing off wherever they are and in any position.

Cat-o'-nine-tails. A whip with nine lashes, used for punishing offenders, briefly called *a cat*. Popular superstition says that it has *nine* tails because a flogging by a "trinity of trinities" would be both more sacred and more efficacious. Lilburn was scourged, in 1637, with a whip having only three lashes, but there were twenty knots in each tail, and, as he received a lash every three paces between the Fleet and Old Palace Yard, Cook says that 60,000 stripes were inflicted. Titus Oates was scourged, in the reign of James II, with a cat having six lashes, and, between Newgate and Tyburn, received as many as 17,000 lashes Thrashing in the British army and navy is no longer employed, but a modified form of it is still, though rarely, used as a civil punishment for crimes committed with violence.

Cat Stane. The name given to certain monoliths in Scotland (there is one near Kirkliston, Linlithgow), so called from Celtic *cath*, a battle, because they mark the site of some battle They are not Druidical stones

Cat's-brains. This curious name is given to a geological formation of sandstone veined with chalk It is a phrase frequently met with in old agricultural deeds and surveys.

Cat's cradle. A game played with a piece of twine by two children The suggestion that the name is a corruption of *cratch-cradle*, or the manger cradle in which the infant Saviour was laid (cratch is the Fr *crèche*, a rack or manger), is unsupported by any evidence

Cat's eye A gem which possesses chatoyancy, or a changeable lustre The true, or precious, cat's eye is a variety of chrysoberyl The semi-precious cat's eye is a kind of quartz.

To live under the cat's foot To be under petticoat government, to be henpecked A mouse under the paw of a cat lives but by sufferance and at the cat's pleasure

To be made a cat's paw of, i e the tool of another, the medium of doing another's dirty work. The allusion is to the fable of the monkey who wanted to get some roasted chestnuts from the fire, and used the paw of his friend, the cat, for the purpose
I had no intention of becoming a cat's paw to draw European chestnuts out of the fire —Com RODGERS.

At sea, light air during a calm causing a ripple on the water, and indicating a storm, is called by sailors a *cat's paw*, and seamen affirm that the frolics of a cat indicate a gale

Cat's whisker. In the old-fashioned crystal wireless sets this was the name given to the fine wire that made contact with the crystal

Catacomb (kăt' a cōm) A subterranean gallery for the burial of the dead, especially those at Rome. The origin of the name is unknown, but it does not appear to have been used till about the 5th century of our era (though the catacombs themselves were in existence, and used for burial, long before), and then only in connexion with one cemetery, that of St. Sebastian, on the Appian Way. This was called the Cœmeterium Catacumbas, or, shortly, *Catacumbas*, which name in course of time was applied equally to similar cemeteries. *Catacumbas* was probably, therefore, a place-name, denoting the site of this particular cemetery

Cataian (kat ā' yan) A native of Cathay or China, hence, a thief, a liar, or scoundrel, because the Chinese had the reputation of being such
I will not believe such a Cataian, though the priest of the town commended him for a true man
SHAKESPEARE. *Merry Wives*, ii, 1

Catalogue raisonné (rä' zo nā) A catalogue of books, paintings, etc, classed according to their subjects and often with explanatory notes or comments

Catamaran (kăt à mà răn') A scraggy old woman, a vixen, so called by a play on the first syllable It properly means a raft consisting of three logs lashed together with ropes, used on the coasts of Coromandel and Madras.
No, you old catamaran, though you pretend you never read novels .
THACKERAY. *Lovel the Widower*, ch i

Catastrophe (ka tăs' trō fi) (Gr. *kata*, downwards, *strephein*, to turn) A turning upside down. Originally used of the change which produces the *dénouement* of a drama, which is usually a "turning upside down" of the beginning of the plot
All the actors must enter to complete and make up the catastrophe of this great piece
Sir T BROWNE *Religio Medici*
Pat, he comes, like the catastrophe of the old comedy.—*King Lear*, i, 2

Catch. **Catch as catch can.** Get by hook or crook all you can, a phrase from the child's game of this name, or from the method of wrestling so called, in which the wrestlers are allowed to get a grip anyhow or anywhere.
All must catch that catch can
JOHNSON *Rambler*, No 197

Catch me at it. Most certainly I shall never do what you say
"Catch me going to London!" exclaimed Vixen
Miss BRADDON. *Vixen*

Catch weights. A term in racing, wrestling or boxing, meaning without restrictions as to weight

First catch your hare. It is generally believed that Mrs. Glasse, in the *Art of Cookery*, gave this direction, but the exact words are, "Take your hare when it is cased, and make a pudding, . etc." To "case" means to take off the skin, as in *All's Well*, iii, 6, "We'll make you some sport with the fox ere we case him " "First catch your hare," however, is a very old phrase, and in the 13th century Bracton (Bk. iv, tit 1, ch xxi, sec 4) has these words —
Vulgariter dicitur, quod primo oportet cervum capere, et postea, cum captus fuerit, illum excoriare (it is vulgarly said that you must first catch your deer, and then, when it is caught, skin it)

Hannah Glasse, who was the author of *The Art of Cookery made Plain and Easy*, 1747, and various other books of a similar nature, was habit-maker to the Prince of Wales, 1757

To be caught bending. To be caught at a disadvantage If you catch a small boy bending over it is easy to smack him on that portion of his anatomy provided by nature for the purpose. Some time about 1903 one of George Robey's songs declared —
What ho! If I catch you bending!

To be caught napping. To suffer some disadvantage while off one's guard Pheasants, hares, and other animals are sometimes surprised "napping "

To catch a crab. A rowing phrase used when the oarsman fails to catch the water with the oar He is then struck by the handle of the oar as it is caught in the water and rises.

To catch a tartar. To catch a troublesome prisoner, to have dealings with a person who is more than a match for one, to think that one is going to manage a person, only to find it is no easy job
We are like the man who boasted of having caught a Tartar when the fact was that the Tartar had caught him —*Cautions for the Times*

To catch on To make its way; to become popular. As in

One can never tell what sort of song will catch on with the public, but the one that does is a little gold mine

To be caught out. To be unmasked in a lie or subterfuge, from ball games in which to have a catch caught by a fieldsman puts the striker out

To catch the Speaker's eye. To find the eye of the Speaker fixed on you; to be observed by the Speaker. In the House of Commons the member on whom the eye of the Speaker is fixed has the privilege of addressing the House

To lie upon the catch. To lie in wait, to try to catch one tripping

You'll catch it. You'll get severely punished   Here "it" stands for the undefined punishment, such as a whipping, a scolding, or other unpleasant consequence.

Catchpenny A worthless article puffed up to catch the pennies of those who are foolish enough to buy it

Catchpole. A constable, a law officer whose business it was to apprehend criminals This is nothing to do with a *pole* or staff, nor with *poll*, the head, but is mediæval Lat *chassipullus*, one who hunts or chases fowls (*pullus*, a fowl)

Catchword A popular cry, a word or a phrase adopted by any party for political or other purposes   "Three acres and a cow," "Your food will cost you more," are good examples.

In printing, the first word on a page which is printed at the foot of the preceding page is known as the *catchword*,   The first book so printed was a *Tacitus*, by John de Spira, 1469

Printers also use the same name for the main words in a dictionary, *i e* those at the start of each article, printed in bold type so as to catch the eye

In theatrical parlance, the cue, *i e* the last word or so of an actor's speech, is called the *catchword*

Catechumen (kăt e kū' men)   One taught by word of mouth (Gr. *katecheein*, to din into the ears).   Those about to be baptized in the Early Church were first taught by word of mouth, and then catechized on their religious faith and duties.

Caterans, or **Catherans** (kăt' e rănz)   Highland Scottish freebooters, the word occurs in Scottish romances and ballads

Cater-cousin   An intimate friend; a remote kinsman.   The name probably has reference to persons being *catered* for together, or boarded together, who would naturally become   more   or   less   intimate,   "friends   so familiar that they eat together"

His master and he, saving your worship's reverence, are scarce cater-cousins

SHAKESPEARE   *Merchant of Venice*, ii, 2

Caterpillar.   Caterpillar Club.   An unofficial club started by the Irvin Parachute Company, during the 1939-45 war, who presented a small gold caterpillar pin to any R.A F.

B.D —7

airman who had baled out in action, on his supplying the number of the parachute which had saved his life.   A similar organization known as the *Goldfish Club* existed for those who had been forced to use their rubber dinghies

Caterpillar traction   This is a device for moving a heavy load over soft ground where wheels will sink   Round the wheels passes an endless band of linked plates which so forms a track along which the vehicle progresses.   The device is much used for agricultural vehicles and for tanks and other military vehicles.

Catgut.   Cord of various thicknesses, made from the intestines of animals (usually sheep, but never cats), and used for strings of musical instruments and racquets for ball games   Why it should have been called *cat*-gut has never been satisfactorily explained, but it may be a corruption of *kit-gut, kit* being an old word for a small fiddle   In support of this we have the following from Cartwright's *The Ordinary* (1634) —

> *Hearsay*   Do you not hear her guts already squeak
> Like kit-strings?
> *Slicer*   They must come to that within
> This two or three years   by that time
> she'll be
> True perfect cat   Act i, 2

Here's a tune indeed' pish,
I had rather hear one ballad sung i' the nose now
Than all these simpering tunes played upon cat's-guts
And sung by little kitlings

MIDDLETON·   *Women Beware Women*, iii, 2

Shakespeare, however, definitely gives catgut its true origin.—

Now, divine air!   Now is his soul ravished!   Is it not strange that sheep's guts should hale souls out of men's bodies?   Well, a horn for my money when all's done —*Much Ado*, ii, 3

Catgut scraper.   A fiddler

Catharine, St.   St Catharine was a virgin of royal descent in Alexandria, who publicly confessed the Christian faith at a sacrificial feast appointed by the Emperor Maximinus, for which confession she was put to death by torture by means of a wheel like that of a chaff-cutter   Hence

Catharine wheel, a sort of firework, in the form of a wheel which is driven round by the recoil from the explosion of the various squibs of which it is composed

Catharine-wheel window.   A wheel-window, sometimes called a rose-window, with radiating divisions.

The Order of St Catharine.   A Russian order founded for ladies of the nobility by Peter the Great after his naval victory of Åland in 1714, and so named in compliment to his wife, Catharine

To braid St. Catharine's tresses.   To live a virgin

Thou art too fair to be left to braid St Catharine's tresses —LONGFELLOW   *Evangeline*

Catharine Théot (tā' ō)   This French visionary was somewhat like our Joanna Southcott, calling herself The Mother of God and changing her name to Theos (God)   In the height of the Revolution she preached the worship of the Supreme Being and announced that Robespierre was the forerunner of The Word Robespierre himself believed in her, and she called him her well-beloved son and chief prophet She was guillotined in 1795, being just seventy years of age

Cathay (ka thā') Marco Polo's name for a country in Eastern Asia, roughly identical with Northern China, from *Ki-tah*, the name of the ruling race in those parts in the 10th century

> Better fifty years of Europe than a cycle of Cathay.
> TENNYSON *Locksley Hall*

Cathedrals of the Old Foundation. The ancient cathedrals that existed in England before Henry VIII founded and endowed new cathedrals out of the revenues of the dissolved monasteries These latter are known as *Cathedrals of the New Foundation*, they are Chester, Gloucester, Peterborough, Bristol, and Oxford

Catherine. *See* CATHARINE

Catholic. The word (Gr. *katholikos*, general, universal) means general, universal, comprehensive—a sense which is seen in such a sentence as Wordsworth's —

> Creed and test
> Vanish before the unreserved embrace
> Of catholic humanity
> *Ecclesiastical Sonnets*, III, xxxvi

Hence from the Church point of view, it distinguishes first the whole body of Christians as apart from "Jews, heretics, and infidels" secondly, a member of a Church which claims the Apostolic Succession and direct descent from the earliest body of Christians, and thirdly, a member of the Roman Catholic Church, *i.e.* the Western or Latin branch of the ancient Catholic (or *universal*) Church.

Alphonso I, King of Asturias, 739-757, was surnamed *The Catholic* on account of his zeal in erecting and endowing monasteries and churches *See* CATHOLIC KING

A man of catholic tastes is one who is interested in a wide variety of subjects

Catholic Church. The entire body of Christians considered as a whole, as distinguished from the Churches and sects into which it has divided At the Reformation the Western Church was called by the Reformers the Roman Catholic Church, and the Established Church of England was called the ' Protestant Church," or the "Reformed National Church." Many members of the Anglican Church still consider and call themselves Catholics

Catholic and Apostolic Church The name given to the followers of Edward Irving (1792-1834) and to the Church founded by him in 1829 Also called Irvingites

Catholic Epistles. Those Epistles in the New Testament not addressed to any particular church or individual, the *general* epistles, viz those of James, Peter, and Jude, and the first of John; 2 John is addressed to a "lady," and 3 John to Gaius, and these are usually included.

Catholic King, or His Most Catholic Majesty. A title given by the Pope to Ferdinand, King of Aragon (1474-1516), for expelling the Moors from Spain, and thereafter used as the appellation of the kings of Spain. *Cp* RELIGIOUS

Catholic League A confederacy of Catholics formed in 1614 to counter-balance the Evangelic League of Bohemia The two Leagues kept Germany in perpetual disturbance, and ultimately led to the Thirty Years War (1618-48)

Catholic Roll. A document which English Roman Catholics were obliged to sign on taking their seats as Member of Parliament It was abolished, and a single oath prescribed to all members by the 29, 30 Victoria, c. 19 (1866)

Catholicon (kà thol' i kon) A panacea, a universal remedy

> Meanwhile, permit me to recommend,
> As the matter admits of no delay,
> My wonderful catholicon
> LONGFELLOW *The Golden Legend*, i

Catholicos (ka thol' i kôs) The head of the Assyrian Nestorians Now called the Patriarch of Armenia

Catiline's Conspiracy (kăt' i lin) Lucius Sergius Catilina, 64 B C, conspired with a large number of dissolute young nobles to plunder the Roman treasury, extirpate the senate, and fire the capitol Cicero, who was consul, got full information of the plot, and delivered his *first* Oration against Catiline November 8th, 63, whereupon Catiline quitted Rome Next day Cicero delivered his *second* Oration, and several of the conspirators were arrested On December 4th Cicero made his *third* Oration, respecting what punishment should be accorded to the conspirators. And on December 5th, after his *fourth* Oration, sentence of death was passed Catiline tried to escape into Gaul, but, being intercepted, he was slain fighting, 62 B c.

Cato (kā' tō). He is a Cato. A man of simple life, severe morals, self-denying habits, strict justice, brusque manners, blunt of speech, and of undoubted patriotism, like the Roman censor of that name (234-149 B c)

Cato Street Conspiracy. A scheme entertained by Arthur Thistlewood (1770-1820) and other conspirators to overthrow the Government by assassinating the Cabinet Ministers (February 1820) So called from Cato Street (now Horace Street), Edgware Road, where their meetings were held.

Catsup. *See* KETCHUP.

Caucasian (kaw kā' shan) This is the term employed to designate the white or European race of mankind It originated with Blumenfeld (1752-1840) who, in 1775, selected a Georgian skull as the perfect type—a view that has since proved wrong The term is, however, still retained in modern ethnology, though with certain reservations.

Caucus (kaw' kus). An American word, first recorded as having been used in Boston about 1750, introduced into English political slang and popularized by Joseph Chamberlain about 1878. In America it means a meeting of some division, large or small, of a political or legislative body, for the purpose of agreeing upon a united course of action in the main assembly In England it is applied opprobriously to an inner committee or organization which seeks to manage affairs behind the backs of its party. The origin of the word is unknown, but it may be connected with the Algonquin word *cau-cau-as-u*, one who advises

In all these places is a severall commander, which they call *Werowance*, except the *Chickahamanians*, who are governed by the priests and their Assistants, or their Elders called *caw-cawwassoughes* —Capt JOHN SMITH'S " *Travels in Virginia* ", *6th Voyage* (1606)

Caudillo (kaw dil' yō)   The title adopted by Gen Franco, head of the Falangist government in Spain   It was taken in imitation of Mussolini's "Duce" and Hitler's "Fuhrer," like them meaning "Leader"

Caudine Forks (kaw' dīn)   A narrow pass in the mountains near Capua, now called the Valley of Arpaia.   It was here that the Roman army, under the consuls T Veturius Calvinus and Sp Postumius, fell into the hands of the Samnites (321 B C), and were made to pass under the yoke.

Hard as it was to abandon an enterprise so very dear to him .   he did not hesitate to take the more prudent course of passing under (*sic*) the Caudine Forks of the Monroe doctrine, and leave Maximilian and the French bondholders to their fate
Standard, November 17th, 1866

Caudle.   Any sloppy mess, especially that sweet mixture of gruel and wine or spirits given by nurses to recently confined women and their "gossips" who call to see the baby during the first month   The word simply means something warm (Lat *calidus*)

Caudle lecture.   A curtain lecture   The term is derived from a series of papers by Douglas Jerrold, which were published in *Punch* (1846).   These papers represent Job Caudle as a patient sufferer of the lectures of his nagging wife after they had gone to bed and the curtains were drawn

Caught Napping.   *See under* CATCH

Caul.   In the Middle Ages and down to the 17th century this word was used for a net confining a woman's hair, now called a snood —

Her head with ringlets of her hair is crowned, And in a golden caul the curls are bound
DRYDEN   *Aeneid* vii

It was also used to describe any membrane enclosing the viscera, *e g* The caul that is above the liver, Ex XXXIX, 13

The membrane on the head of some new-born infants is called the caul and is supposed to be a charm against death by drowning

To be born with a caul was with the Romans tantamount to our phrase, "To be born with a silver spoon in one's mouth," meaning "born to good luck."

You were born with a caul on your head
BEN JONSON   *Alchemist,* i. 1.

Cauld-lad, The, of Hilton Hall   A housespirit, who moved about the furniture during the night   Being resolved to banish him, the inmates left for him a green cloak and hood, before the kitchen-fire, which so

delighted him that he never troubled the house any more, but sometimes he might be heard singing —

Here's a cloak, and here's a hood, The cauld-lad of Hilton will do no more good

Caurus (kaw' rus)   The Latin name for the west-north-west wind, Anglicized by Chaucer as Chorus

the sonne is hid whan the sterres ben clustred by a swifte winde highte Chorus —BOETHIUS Bk, i, Mett iii

The ground by piercing Caurus seared
THOMSON. *Castle of Indolence,* ii, 78

Causa causans (kaw' za kaw' zănz)   The initiating cause, the primary cause

Causa causata   The cause which owes its existence to the *causa causans*; the secondary cause

Causa vera (*a*) The immediate predecessor of an effect; (*b*) a cause verifiable by independent evidence   (Mill)

In theology God is the *causa causans*, and creation the *causa causata*   The presence of the sun above the horizon is the *causa vera* of daylight, and his withdrawal below the horizon is the *causa vera* of night

Cause, The.   A mission; the object or project.   To make common cause.   To work for the same object   Here "cause" is the legal term, meaning *pro* or *con*, as it may be, the cause or side of the question advocated.

Cause célebre (Fr)   Any famous law case or trial

Aristotelian causes are these four
(1) **The Efficient Cause.**   That which immediately produces the effect
(2) **The Material Cause.**   The matter on which (1) works.
(3) **The Formal Cause.**   The Essence of "Form" (= group of attributes) introduced into the matter by the efficient cause
(4) **The Final** or **Ultimate Cause.**   The purpose or end for which the thing exists or the causal change takes place   But God is called the ultimate Final Cause, since, according to Aristotle, all things tend, so far as they can, to realize some Divine attribute

God is also called **The First Cause,** or the Cause Causeless, beyond which even imagination cannot go

Causerie (kō' zĕr i).   Gossip, small-talk, in journalism a chatty kind of essay or article, a set of gossipy paragraphs   (Fr. *causer*, to chat.)

Caution.   So-and-so's a caution, meaning that he is odd in his ways, likely to do something unexpected, often with a quaint twist to it   The phrase is originally American, and had a somewhat wider application —

The way the icy blast would come down the bleak shore was a caution
C F HOFFMAN   *Winter West* (1835).

His wife was what the Yankees call a Caution
MORTIMER COLLINS   *Vivien* (1870).

Caution money.   A sum deposited before entering college, or an Inn of Court, etc., by way of security for good behaviour

Cavalier   A horseman, whence a knight, a gentleman (Span *caballero*, *b* and *v* being interchangeable in that language)

Personages styled The Cavalier.

Eon de Beaumont (1728-1810), French diplomat and secret agent, *Chevalier d'Eon*.

Charles Breydel (1677-1744), Flemish landscape painter

Francesco Cairo (*Cavaliere del Cairo*) (1598-1674), Italian historical and portrait painter.

Jean le Clerc, *le chevalier* (1587-1633), French painter

Giov Battista Marini (1569-1625), Italian poet. *Il cavalier*

Andrew Michael Ramsay (1686-1734), Scottish-French writer

Cavalier or Chevalier de St. George. James Francis Edward Stuart, called "the Pretender," or "the Old Pretender" (1688-1765)

The Young Cavalier or the Bonnie Chevalier. Charles Edward, the "Young Pretender" (1720-85)

The Laughing Cavalier. Name given to the famous portrait of an unknown gallant, by the Dutch painter Franz Hals, now in the Wallace Collection, London

Cavaliers. Adherents of Charles I Those of the opposing Parliament party were called *Roundheads.*

Cavaliere servente (kăv a lyēr' ı sēr ven' te) (Ital) A cavalier in attendance, especially a man who devotes himself to running about after a married woman, much the same as a *cicisbeo* (*q.v*)

> An English lady asked of an Italian,
> What were the actual and official duties
> Of the strange thing some women set a value on
> Which hovers oft about some married beauties,
> Call'd "cavalier servente"? a Pygmalion
> Whose statues warm (I fear, alas[1] too true 't is)
> Beneath his art The dame, press'd to disclose them
> Said—"Lady, I beseech you to *suppose them* "
> BYRON *Don Juan*, IX, li.

Cave of Adullam. *See* ADULLAMITES

Caveat (kā' vē ăt). Lat , "let him beware", a notice directing the recipient to refrain from some act pending the decision of the Court. Hence, **to enter a caveat.** To give legal notice that the opponent is not to proceed with the suit in hand until the party giving the notice has been heard, to give a warning or admonition.

Caveat emptor Lat , "let the purchaser beware", *i e* the buyer must keep his eyes open, for the bargain he agrees to is binding The full legal maximum is —

> Caveat emptor, quia ignorare non debuit quod jus alienum emit—Let a purchaser beware, for he ought not to be ignorant of the nature of the property which he is buying from another party

Cavel. A parcel or allotment of land; originally, a lot (that is cast) From Dut *kavel*, a lot, whence *kaveln*, to assign by lot

Cavendish (kăv' en dish) It is not now known who was the Cavendish who gave his name to this tobacco, which is sometimes called Negro-head Sweetened with syrup or molasses, it is a softened tobacco pressed into quadrangular cakes It is used for smoking or chewing

Caviare (kăv i âr) The roe of the sturgeon, pickled, salted, and prepared for use as a relish Caviare is an acquired taste and, as a rule, it is not appreciated by people until they have got used to it; hence Shakespeare's *caviare to the general* (*Hamlet*, ii, 2), above the taste or comprehension of ordinary people.

> He [Cobbett] must, I think, be caviare to the Whigs
> HAZLITT *Table-talk*

Cavo-rilievo (ka' vō ril yā' vō)   "Relief," cut below the original surface, the highest parts of the figure being on a level with the surface

Caxon. A worn-out wig, also a big cauliflower wig, worn out or not It has been suggested that the word is from the personal name Caxon

> People scarce could decide on its phiz,
> Which looked wisest—the caxon or jowl
> PETER PINDAR *The Portfolio.*

Caxton, William. Father of English printing, hence his name is widely applied to branded articles in the printing and paper trades Born in the Weald of Kent, he learnt his printing in Cologne and Bruges. He set up shop at the Sign of the Red Pale in the shadow of Westminster Abbey about 1476 and died about 1491, by which time he had printed about a hundred books

Cayuse. An Indian pony The Cayuses were a Red Indian tribe Since about 1880 the word has meant "a horse of little value."

Cean (sē' ȧn). **The Cean poet.** Simonides, of Ceos.

> The Cean and the Teian muse
> BYRON *Don Juan* (*Song The Isles of Greece*)

Cecilia, St. (se sil' i a)   A Roman who underwent martyrdom in the 3rd century   She is the patron saint of the blind, being herself blind, she is also patroness of musicians, and "inventor of the organ."

> At length divine Cecilia came,
> Inventress of the vocal frame.
> DRYDEN. *Alexander's Feast.*

According to tradition an angel fell in love with her for her musical skill   Her husband saw the heavenly visitant, who gave to both a crown of martyrdom which he brought from Paradise

St Cecilia's Day is November 22nd, on which the Worshipful Company of Musicians, a Livery Company of London, meet and go in procession for divine service in St Paul's Cathedral

Cecil's Fast A dinner off fish William Cecil, Lord Burghley, chief minister to Queen Elizabeth for nearly forty years, introduced a Bill to enjoin the eating of fish on certain days in order to restore the fish trade

Ceelict, St. An English name of St Calixtus, who is commemorated on October 14th, the day of the Battle of Hastings

Brown Willis tells us there was a tablet once in Battle parish church with these words —

> This place of war is Battle called, because in battle here
> Quite conquered and o'erthrown the English nation were
> This slaughter happened to them upon St Ceelict's day, etc

Ceiling. This is the term applied to the maximum height to which an aeroplane can climb The phrase has also been extended to mean the highest prices that can be reached for any article Also used in aeronautical circles to denote the height of the cloud base above ground level Ceiling zero means that the clouds or mist are down to the ground itself, or so near it as to make the taking-off or landing of aircraft impracticable except by instruments

Celarent. *See* SYLLOGISM

Celestial City. Heaven is so called by John Bunyan in his *Pilgrim's Progress*

Celestial Empire, China a translation of the Chinese *Tien Chao*, literally 'heavenly dynasty," alluding to the belief that the old Emperors were in direct descent from the gods Hence the Chinese themselves are sometimes spoken of as *Celestials*

Celestines. An order of reformed Benedictine monks, founded about 1254 by Pietro di Murrone who, in 1294, became Pope as Celestine V.

Celt (selt, kelt) A piece of stone, ground artificially into a wedge-like shape, with a cutting edge Used before the employment of bronze and iron, for knives, hatchets, and chisels

Celtic (sel' tik, kel' tik). Applied to the peoples and languages of the great branch of the Aryans which includes the Irish, Manx, Welsh, ancient Cornish, Breton, and Scottish Gaels Anciently the term was applied by the Greeks and Romans to the peoples of Western Europe generally, but when Cæsar wrote of the Celtæ he referred to the people of middle Gaul only The word *Celt* probably means a warrior, fable accounts for it by the story of Celtina, daughter of Britannus, who had a son by Hercules, named Celtus, who became the progenitor of the Celts.

Cemetery properly means a sleeping-place (Gr *koimeterion*, a dormitory) The Persians call their cemeteries "The Cities of the Silent."

Cenci. *See* BEAUTIFUL PARRICIDE

Cenomanni (sen ō ma' ni). The name given to the inhabitants of Norfolk, Suffolk, and Cambridge by Cæsar in his *Commentaries*

Cenotaph (sen' ō tăf) (Gr *kenos*, empty, *taphos* tomb) A sepulchral monument raised to the memory of a person buried elsewhere. By far the most noteworthy to all of British race is that in Whitehall, designed by Sir E Lutyens, which was dedicated on November 11th, 1920, to those who fell in World War I It has since been adapted to commemorate those who fell in the World War II.

Among the noted cenotaphs of the ancients are those of —

ÆNEAS to Deiphobus (*Æneid*, i, 6, v, 505)
ANDROMACHE to Hector (*Æneid*, i, 3, v 302).
ARISTOTLE to Hermias and Eubulus (*Diogenes Laertius*)
The ATHENIANS to the poet Euripides
CALLIMACHUS to Sopolis, son of Dioclides (*Epigram of Collimachus*, 22)
CATULLUS to his brother (*Epigram of Catullus*, 103)
DIDO to Sichæus (*Justin*, XVIII, 6).
The ROMANS to Drusus in Germany, and to Alexander Severus, the emperor, in Gaul (*Suetonius Life of Claudius*, and the *Anthologia*)
STATIUS to his father (*The Sylvæ of Statius*, v Epicedium 3)
XENOCRATES to Lysidices (*Anthologia*).

Centaur. Mythological beast, half horse and half man Centaurs are said to have dwelt in ancient Thessaly, a myth the origin of which is probably to be found in the expert horsemanship of the original inhabitants. *See* IXION. The Thessalian centaurs were invited to a marriage feast, and, being intoxicated, behaved with great rudeness to the women The Lapithæ took the women's part, fell on the centaurs, and drove them out of the country.

Cent Nouvelles Nouvelles (son noo vel' noo vel') This collection of "a hundred new tales" first appeared in a MS dated 1456 It is on much the same lines as the *Decameron* and tells in French some of the stories already made familiar by the Italian novelists Saintsbury calls it the best of all the late mediæval prose works

Cento (Lat, a patchwork) Poetry made up of lines borrowed from established authors It was an art freely practised in the decadent period of Greece and Rome, and Ausonius, who has a nuptial idyll composed from verses selected from Virgil, composed rules governing their manufacture Among well-known examples are the *Homerocentones*, the *Cento Virgilianus* by Proba Falconia (4th cent), and the hymns made by Metellus out of the Odes of Horace Of modern centos the following portion of a Shakespearean cento that appeared in English, November, 1919, may serve as an example —

> Let fame that all hunt after in their lives
> Among the buzzing pleased multitude
> For present comfort and for future good,
> Taint not thy mind· nor let thy soul contrive
> With all the fierce endeavour of your wit
> To woo a maid in way of marriage,
> As it is common for the younger sort,
> The lunatic, the lover, and the poet:
> Thus bad begins, and worse remains behind
> I see a man's life is a tedious one,
> For it appears, by manifest proceeding,
> There's nothing serious in mortality.
> Life's but a walking shadow, a poor player,
> And one man in his time plays many parts,
> As an unperfect actor on the stage.

Centre Party. In politics, the party occupying a place between two extremes. the *left centre* is the more radical wing, and the *right centre* the more conservative In the French Revolution *the Centre* of the Legislative Assembly included the friends of order

In the Fenian rebellion, 1866, the chief movers were called *Head Centres*, and their subordinates *Centres*.

Centurion (sen tū' ri on) (Lat. *centum*, a hundred) A Roman officer who had the command of 100 men There were sixty centurions, of varying ranks, to a legion, the chief being the first centurion of the first maniple of the first cohort, his title was Primus pilus prior, or Primipilus The centurion's emblem of office was a vine-staff

Cephalus and Procris (sef' a lùs, prok' ris) Cephalus was husband of Procris, who, out of jealousy, deserted him. He went in search of her, and rested awhile under a tree. Procris, knowing of his whereabouts, crept through some bushes to ascertain if a rival was with him; and he, hearing the noise and thinking it to be made by some wild beast, hurled his javelin into the bushes and slew her When the unhappy man discovered what he had done, he slew himself in anguish of spirit with the same javelin

> *Pyramus* Not Shafalus to Procrus was so true
> *Thisbe* As Shafalus to Procrus, I to you
>   SHAKESPEARE *Midsummer Night's Dream*, v 1

Cepheus (sē' fūs) A northern constellation, named from Cepheus, King of Ethiopia, husband of Cassiopeia and father of Andromeda

Cepola (sep' ō la). **Devices of Cepola.** Quips of law are so called from Bartholomew Cepola whose law-quirks, teaching how to elude the most express law, and to perpetuate lawsuits *ad infinitum*, have been frequently reprinted—once in 8vo, in black letter, by John Petit, in 1503.

Cerberus (sēr' bē rus) A grim, watchful keeper, house-porter, guardian, etc Cerberus, according to Roman mythology, is the three-headed dog that keeps the entrance of the infernal regions Hercules dragged the monster to earth, and then let him go again Orpheus lulled Cerberus to sleep with his lyre; and the Sibyl who conducted Æneas through the Inferno, also threw the dog into a profound sleep with a cake seasoned with poppies and honey *See under* SOP

The origin of the fable of Cerberus may be found in the custom of the ancient Egyptians of guarding graves with dogs

Ceremonious, The. Pedro IV of Aragon (1336-87) was so surnamed

Ceremony (Lat *cærimonia*) By way of accounting for this word, which is probably connected with Sanskrit *karman*, a religious action, a rite, Livy tells that when the Romans fled before Brennus, one Albinus, who was carrying his wife and children in a cart to a place of safety, overtook at Janiculum the Vestal virgins bending under their load, took them up and conveyed them to Cære, in Etruria Here they remained, and continued to perform their sacred rites, which were consequently called "Cære-monia "

Master of the Ceremonies. A Court official, first appointed by James I, to superintend the reception of ambassadors and strangers of rank, and to prescribe the formalities to be observed in levees and other grand public functions The title is now given to one whose duty it is to see that all goes smoothly at balls and suchlike social gatherings frequently abbreviated to "M C "

Don't stand on ceremony Feel at home, be natural, don't be formal

Ceres (sē' rēs) The Roman name of *Mother Earth*, the protectress of agriculture and of all the fruits of the earth, later identified with the Greek Demeter.

Cess A tax, contracted from assessment ("sess"), as a "church-cess " In Ireland the word is used sometimes as a contraction of success, meaning luck, as "bad cess to you!"

Out of all cess Beyond all estimation or valuation

> The poor jade is wrung in the withers out of all cess.
> —SHAKESPEARE *1 Henry IV*, ii, 1

C'est magnifique *C'est magnifique, mais ce n'est pas la guerre* "It is magnificent, but it

is not war " The criticism on the charge of the Light Brigade at Balaclava (Oct 25th, 1854), made on the field at the time, by the French General Bosquet to A H. Layard

Cestui que vie This and the two following are old Anglo-French legal terms (*cestui* = he, or him) The person for whose life any lands or hereditaments may be held

Cestui que use, the person to whose use anyone is infeoffed of lands or tenements

Cestui que trust, the person for whose benefit a trust has been created

Cestus (ses' tus) The girdle of Venus, made by her husband Vulcan, but when she wantoned with Mars it fell off, and was left on the 'Acidalian Mount " It was of magical power to move to ardent love By a poetical fiction all women of irresistible attraction are supposed to be wearers of Aphrodite's girdle, or the cestus

The word was also applied to the Roman boxing-glove, composed of leather bands wound round the hand and wrist, and often loaded with iron

Chacun a son goût (shăk'ûn a son goo) "Everyone has (*a*) his taste", or, "Everyone to (*à*) his taste " The former is French, the latter is English-French for *à chacun son goût* or *chacum (a) son goût* The phrase is much more common with us than it is in France, where we meet with the phrases—*Chacun a sa chacunerie* (everyone has his idiosyncrasy), and *chacun a sa marotte* (everyone has his hobby) In Latin *sua cuique voluptas*, every man has his own pleasures.

Chad. A small gnome whose bald head and large nose were depicted on public places as appearing over a wall and inquiring, "Wot, no [word filled in to suit the circumstance]?", as a sarcastic protest against an inexplicable shortage or shortcoming Its origin (about 1945) is unknown.

Chadband (chăd' bănd) This synonym for a religious hypocrite is taken from the character in Dickens's *Bleak House*—a gluttonous, unctuous, illiterate rogue, minister of some indeterminate sect.

Chadpennies. Lichfield cathedral is dedicated to St Mary and St Chad, the Whitsuntide offerings used to be devoted to the upkeep of the building and were called Chadpennies

Chaff. An old bird is not to be caught with chaff. An experienced man, or one with his wits about him, is not to be deluded by humbug The reference is to throwing chaff instead of bird-seed to allure birds Hence, perhaps—

You are chaffing me Making fun of me A singular custom used to exist in Notts and Leicestershire some half a century ago When a husband illtreated his wife, the villagers emptied a sack of chaff at his door, to intimate that "thrashing was done within."

Chair, The. The office of chief magistrate in a corporate town, the office of a professor, etc , as "The chair of poetry, in Oxford, is now vacant " The word is furthermore applied to

the president of a committee or public meeting
Hence the chairman himself   When debaters
call out "Chair," they mean that the chairman
is not properly supported, and his words not
obeyed as they ought to be   Another form
of the same expression is, "Pray support the
Chair"

Below the chair. Said of one who has not
yet reached the presidential position, as of an
alderman who has not yet served the mayoralty

Passed the chair. One who has served the
chief office

To take the chair. To become the chairman
or president of a public meeting. The
chairman is placed in some conspicuous place,
like the Speaker of the House of Commons,
and his decision is absolutely final in all points
of doubt   Usually the persons present
nominate and elect their own chairman, but
in some cases there is an *ex officio* chairman.
    As a slang expression, to **be in the chair** may
mean to be host or to be called on to pay for a
round of drinks

Chair of St. Peter. The office of the Pope
of Rome, founded by St Peter, the apostle,
but *St Peter's Chair* means the Catholic
festival held in commemoration of the two
episcopates founded by the apostle, one at
Rome, and the other at Antioch (January 18th
and February 22nd)

Chalk Chalk it up. Put it to his credit.

I'll chalk out your path for you—*i e* lay
it down or plan it out as a carpenter or shipbuilder plans out his work with a piece of
chalk

I can walk a chalk as well as you. I am no
more drunk than you are   The allusion is to
one of the tests given to men suspected of
drunkenness   They are required to walk
along a line chalked on the floor, without
deviating to the right or left.

I cannot make chalk of one and cheese of the
other. I must treat both alike, I must show
no favouritism

**I know the difference between chalk and
cheese.** Between what is worthless and what is
valuable, between a counterfeit and a real
article   Of course, the resemblance of chalk
to cheese has something to do with the saying,
and the alliteration helps to popularize it.

The tapster is undone by chalk, *i e* credit
The allusion is to the old tavern-keeper's
custom of scoring on a door or board the
amounts owed him by his customers   This
was common enough early in the 19th century,
when milk scores, bread scores, as well as beer
scores, were general

I beat him by a long chalk. Thoroughly.
In allusion to the ancient custom of making
merit marks with chalk, before lead pencils
were so common

Walk your chalk. Get you gone   Lodgings
wanted for the royal retinue used to be taken
arbitrarily by the marshal and sergeant-
chamberlain, the inhabitants were sent to the
right about, and the houses selected were
notified by a chalk mark   When Marie de'

Medicis, in 1638 came to England, Sieur de
Labat was employed to mark "all sorts of
houses commodious for her retinue in Colchester"   The phrase is "Walk, you're
chalked," corrupted into *Walk your chalk*
    At one time it was customary for a land-
lord to give the tenant notice to quit by chalk-
ing the door

The prisoner has cut his stick, and walked his chalk,
and is off to London —C KINGSLEY *Two Years Ago,* i

Challenge This meant originally an accusation or charge, and secondarily a claim, a
defiance   It comes through French from the
Lat *calumnia,* a false accusation, and is thus
etymologically the same word as "calumny"

Challenging a jury. This may be to object
to all the jurors from some informality in the
way they have been "arrayed" or empanelled,
or to one or more of the jurors, from some real
or supposed disqualification or bias of judgment.   In the first case it is a **challenge to the
array,** and this must be based on some default
of the sheriff, or his officer who arrayed the
panel
    If any member of the jury is thought not
qualified to serve, or if he is supposed to be
biased, he may be challenged   In capital
cases a prisoner may challenge persons without
assigning any reason, and in cases of treason
as many as thirty-five

Cham (kăm)   The sovereign prince of Tartary,
now written "khan"

Fetch you a hair off the great Cham's beard —
SHAKESPEARE *Much Ado About Nothing,* ii, 1

The great Cham of Literature. An epithet
applied to Dr Johnson (1709-84) by Tobias
Smollett.

Chambré (shom' brā).   From French *chambre,*
a room   Used of wine which has been
warmed to raise it from cellar temperature to
the temperature of the room in which it is to
be served, which for red wine is ideal

Chambre Ardente (shombr ar dont') (Fr.).
In French history, the name given to certain
Courts of Justice held under the *ancien régime,*
for trying exceptional cases, such as charges of
heresy, poisoning, etc   They were usually
held at night, and both then and when held in
the daytime were lighted by torches   These
courts were devised by Cardinal Lorraine
The first was held in the reign of François
I, for trying heretics   Brinvilliers and her
associates were tried in a darkened court in
1680
    The same name is given to the room or hall
in which a lying-in-state takes place, because
it is usually furnished with lighted candles

Chameleon. You are a chameleon, *i e.* very
changeable—shifting according to the opinions
of others, as the chameleon, to a very limited
extent, can change its hue to that of contiguous
objects

As the chameleon, who is known
To have no colours of its own,
But borrows from his neighbour's hue,
His white or black, his green or blue
                                PRIOR

Champ de Mars (shon dĕ mars)   Clovis and
the early Frank kings held meetings in March
when feudal gifts and fees were paid and

homage received. It was this ancient custom
that was seized upon in the French Revolution
when, in the summer of 1790, an enormous
amphitheatre was dug by the Paris citizens, and
the Federation of Freedom sworn at the altar
of the Fatherland

Napoleon I gave the name of **Champ de Mai**
to the assembly he called together on May 1st,
1815, when he proclaimed the result of the
plebiscite ratifying the liberal *Acte additionnel*
on his return from Elba

Champak (chăm' păk)   An Indian magnolia
(*Michelia Champaca*).   The wood is sacred to
Buddha, and the strongly scented golden
flowers are worn in the black hair of Indian
women.

> The Champak odours fail
>   SHELLEY · *Lines to an Indian Air.*

Champerty (chăm' pĕr ti) (Lat. *campi partitio*,
division of the land).   A bargain with some
person who undertakes at his own cost to
recover a property on condition of receiving
a share thereof if he succeeds.

Champerty is treated as a worse offence, for by this
a stranger supplies money to carry on a suit, on
condition of sharing in the land or other property.—
PARSONS *Contracts* (vol ii, pt ii, ch 3, p 264)

Champion of England.   A person whose office
it is to ride up Westminster Hall on a Coronation Day, and challenge anyone who disputes
the right of succession   The office was
established by William the Conqueror, and
was given to Marmion and his male descendants, with the manor of "broad Scrivelsby"
De Ludlow received the office and manor
through the female line, and at the Coronation
of Richard II Sir John Dymoke succeeded
through the female line also.   Since then the
office has continued in the Dymoke family, but
the actual riding and challenge has been
discontinued since the coronation of George
IV   Instead, the Champion bears the king's
standard at the coronation.

Chance.   *See* MAIN CHANCE.

To chance your arm, or **your luck.**   To run
a risk in the hope of "bringing it off" and
obtaining a profit or advantage of some sort.

Chancel means a lattice screen   In the
Roman law courts the lawyers were cut off
from the public by such a screen.   (Lat
cancellus)

Chancel of a church   That part of a church
which contains the altar, and the seats set
apart for the choir   It is generally raised a
step or more above the floor of the nave

Chancellery.   "The chancelleries of Europe"
is a favourite journalistic phrase   The word
chancellery is applied to the office attached
to an embassy or consulate, where dispatches
are drafted and written, incoming dispatches
decoded and considered, and all the embassy
clerical work carried through

Chancellor.   A petty officer (*cancelarius*) in the
Roman law courts stationed at the chancel
(*q v*) as usher of the court   In the Eastern
Empire he was a secretary or notary, subsequently invested with judicial functions   The
office was introduced into England by Edward
the Confessor, and under the Norman kings

the chancellor was made official secretary of all
important legal documents   In France the
chancellor was the royal notary, president of
the councils, and keeper of the Great Seal

Chancellor, Dancing.   *See* DANCING.

The Lord Chancellor, or the **Lord High
Chancellor.**   The highest judicial functionary
of Britain, who ranks above all peers, except
princes of the blood and the Archbishop
of Canterbury.   He is "Keeper of the Great
Seal," is called "Keeper of His (or Her)
Majesty's Conscience," and presides on the
Woolsack in the House of Lords, and in the
Chancery Division of the Supreme Court

Chancellor of the Exchequer.   The minister
of finance in the Cabinet, the highest financial
official of State in the kingdom

Chancery.   One of the three divisions of the
High Court of Justice   It is concerned with
Equity and is presided over by the Lord
Chancellor.   All its work is done in London.

To get a man's head into chancery is to get
it under your arm, where you can pummel
it as long as you like, and he cannot get it free
without great difficulty   The allusion is to the
long and exhausting nature once characteristic
of Chancery suits.   If a man once got his
head there, the lawyers could punish him to
their hearts' content.

When I can perform my mile in eight minutes, or a
little less I feel as if I had old Time's head in chancery.
—HOLMES *Autocrat*, ch vii

A Ward in Chancery is the term applied to
a minor whose guardianship is vested in the
Court of Chancery for any one of various legal
reasons   It is contempt of court to marry a
ward of Chancery without the court's consent.

Change. Ringing the changes.   Repeating
the same thing in different ways   The
allusion is to bell-ringing   For the sharper's
meaning of the term, *see* RINGING.

To know how many changes can be rung
on a peal, multiply the number of bells in the
peal by the number of changes that can be rung
on a peal consisting of one bell less, thus 1
bell no change, 2 bells, 1 by 2 = 2 changes,
3 bells, 2 by 3 = 6 changes; 4 bells, 6 by 4 = 24
changes; 5 bells, 24 by 5 = 120 changes, 6 bells,
720 changes, etc

Changeling.   A peevish, sickly child.   The
notion used to be that the fairies took a healthy
child, and left in its place one of their starveling
elves which never thrived

> The king doth keep his revels here to-night
> Take heed the queen come not within his sight,
> For Oberon is passing fell and wrath,
> Because that she as her attendant hath
> A lovely boy, stolen from an Indian king:
> She never had so sweet a changeling
> SHAKESPEARE *Midsummer Night's Dream*, ii, 1.

Chant du départ (shon dü dä par).   After the
Marseillaise, this was the most celebrated song
of the French Revolution   It was written by
M J. Chenier, for a public festival, 1794, to
commemorate the taking of the Bastille   The
music is by Méhul   A mother, an old man,
a child, a wife, a girl, and three warriors sing
a verse in turn, and the sentiment of each is,

"We give up our claims on the men of France for the good of the Republic." *Cp* CAR-MAGNOLE.

La republique nous appelle,
Sachons vaincre ou sachons perir,
Un Français doit vivre pour elle,
Pour elle un Français doit mourir

Chantage. Blackmail, money accepted by low-class journals to prevent the publication of scandals, etc *Chantage* is the common name in France for this form of subsidy, and the word has been used in the same way in England

Chanticleer. The cock, in the tale of *Reynard the Fox*, and in Chaucer's *Nonne Prestes Tale*; also in Rostand's well-known play of this name produced in Paris in 1910. (Fr *chanter-clair*, to sing *clairment*, i e distinctly)

My lungs began to crow like chanticleer.
SHAKESPEARE: *As You Like It*, ii, 7

Chantrey Bequest When Sir Francis Leggatt Chantrey (1781-1841), the sculptor, died he left a sum yielding about £3,000 a year to the Royal Academy, of which the President was to receive £300, the secretary £50, and the remainder was to be devoted to the purchase for the nation of works of art executed in Great Britain

Chaonian Bird (kā ō' ni an). This is the poetic name for a dove, and takes its origin from the legend that the dove bore the oracles of Chaonia

Chaonian food. Acorns So called from the oak trees of Chaonia or Dodona. Some think *beech-mast* is meant, and tell us that the bells of the oracle were hung on beech-trees, not on oaks

Chap. A man, properly a merchant. A chap-man (O.E. *ceap-mann*) is a merchantman or tradesman "If you want to buy, I'm your chap." A good chap-man or chap became in time a good fellow. Hence, *A good sort of chap, a clever chap*, etc.

An awkward customer is an analogous phrase

Chap-book. A cheap little book containing tales, ballads, lives, etc., sold by chapmen

Chapeau bras (shăp ō bra). A soft three-cornered flat silk hat which could be folded and carried under the arm (Fr *chapeau*, hat, *bras*, arm) It was used in France with the court dress of the 18th century.

Chapeau de Paille (Fr , straw hat). This is the name given to Rubens's portrait of Susanna Fourment, the sister of his second wife It is in the National Gallery, London, and was one of the chief paintings round which the pro- and anti-cleaning controversy raged in London in 1947. The title is of obscure origin since in the painting the girl is not wearing a straw hat

Chapel. Originally, a chest containing relics, or the shrine thereof, so called from the *capella* (little cloak or cope) of St. Martin, which was preserved by the Frankish kings as a sacred relic The place in which it was kept when not in the field was called the *chapelle*, and the keeper thereof the *chapelain* Hence, the name came to be attached to a sanctuary, or a

7*

private place of worship other than a parish or cathedral church, and is also used for a place of worship not connected with the State, as a Methodist Chapel, a Baptist Chapel, etc

In printing-house parlance a *chapel* is an association of journeymen (compositors, machine-men, etc), who meet periodically to discuss matters of common interest connected with their work, to decide upon the course of action to be taken in cases of disputes or differences between themselves and their employers, etc The chairman is known as the "father of the chapel" The origin of the term is obscure, an accepted but far from certain derivation, traces it back to the early days of printing, when presses were set up in the chapels attached to abbeys, as those of Caxton in Westminster Abbey. *Cp* MONK; FRIAR.

Chapel of ease. A place of worship for the use of parishioners residing at a distance from the parish church.

Chaperon (shăp' e rōn) A married or elderly woman who attends a young unmarried girl in public places and acts as her guide, adviser, and, when necessary, protector So called from the Spanish hood worn by duennas in former times

To chaperon. To accompany a young unmarried woman *in loco parentis*, when she appears in public or in society.

Chapter. From Lat. *caput*, a head. The *chapter* of a cathedral, composed of the canons (*see* CANON) and presided over by the dean, is so called from the ancient practice of the canons and monks reading at their meetings a *capitulum* (*cp.* CAPITULARY) or chapter of their Rule or of Scripture *Ire ad capitulum* meant "to go to the (reading of the) chapter," hence, to the meeting, hence to the body which composed the meeting

Chapter of accidents Series of unforeseen events. **To trust to a chapter of accidents** is to trust that something unforeseen may turn up in your favour.

Chapter of possibilities. A may-be in the course of events

To the end of the chapter. To the end of a proceeding The allusion is obvious.

To give chapter and verse. To give the exact authority of a statement, as the name of the author, the title of the book, the date, the chapter referred to, and any other particular which might render the reference easily discoverable

Char (char) This is a common abbreviation for "charwoman," a woman who chars or chares, i e works by the hour or day at house-cleaning The word comes from O.E. *cerr, cerran*, meaning to turn It has come back to England from U S A in the form of "chore," a monotonous but necessary task, household or otherwise.

The Army slang word "char," meaning tea appears to come from the Hind *cha*, with various Indian and Chinese words of similar sound, all meaning tea.

Character An oddity One who has a distinctive peculiarity of manner· Sam Weller is a character, so is Pickwick

In character In harmony with personality or habitual behaviour

Out of character. Not in harmony with a person's actions, writings, profession, age, or status in society.

Chare Thursday. Another form of *Shear* or *Shere Thursday*, the same as *Maundy Thursday* (*q v*)

Charge, To. To make an attack or onset in battle

Curate in charge. A curate placed by a bishop in charge of a parish where there is no incumbent, or where the incumbent is suspended.

To charge oneself with. To take upon oneself the onus of a given task.

To charge a person. To accuse him formally of a crime or misdemeanour It must be answered before the appropriate court or authority

To give charge over. To set one in authority over

I gave my brother Hanani . charge over Jerusalem.—*Neh* vii, 2.

To give in charge. To hand over a person to the charge of a policeman

To have in charge. To have the care of something.

To return to the charge. To renew the attack.

To take in charge. To "take up" a person given in charge; to take upon oneself the responsibility of something, to make an arrest

Charge-sheet. The form setting out in correct language and according to Law the specific charges which an accused person has to answer Evidence cannot be admitted in court which is not relevant to the charge on the charge-sheet, if it becomes apparent that the accused has been guilty of a further—but different—crime than that for which he is on trial, such crime must be made the subject of a fresh charge at another time. But a man found guilty may ask for other crimes *of a similar nature* to that on the charge-sheet to be taken into consideration in assessing his sentence, in this way he can admit to crimes which he is suspected of having committed but for which he cannot be brought to book for want of evidence, thus enabling him when he comes out of prison to make a fresh start in life without fear of his undiscovered crimes being suddenly pinned on him

Chargé d'Affaires. The proxy of an ambassador, or the diplomatic agent where none higher has been appointed

Charing Cross. The original "Charing Cross" was erected in the centre of the ancient village of Charing, which stood midway between the cities of London and Westminster, by Edward I to commemorate his Queen, Eleanor, because it was there that her coffin was halted for the last time on its progress from Harby, Notts, where the Queen died, to Westminster, where she was buried.

The present cross is a copy (made to scale) by E M. Barry, R A , of the original one that was demolished by the Puritans in 1647, and that stood on the south side of Trafalgar Square on the site now occupied by the equestrian statue of Charles I It was erected in 1865 in the courtyard of Charing Cross Station.

Chariot. According to Greek mythology, the chariot was invented by Erichthonius to conceal his feet, which were those of a dragon.

Chariot of the gods. So the Greeks called Sierra Leone, in Africa, a ridge of mountains of great height A sierra means a saw, and is applied to a ridge of peaked mountains

Her palmy forests, mingling with the skies,
Leona's rugged steep behind us flies.
— CAMOENS *Lusiad*, Bk v.

Chariots or **cars** That of
ADMETUS was drawn by lions and wild boars,
BACCHUS by panthers
CERES by winged dragons.
CYBELE by lions
DIANA by stags
JUNO by peacocks
NEPTUNE by sea-horses
PLUTO by black horses
The SUN by seven horses (the seven days of the week).
VENUS by doves

Charity. Charity begins at home. "Let them learn first to show piety at home" (1 *Tim.* v, 4).

Cold as charity. An ironic allusion to unsympathetic benevolence

Charivari (shā ri va′ ri). The clatter made with pots and pans, whistling, bawling, hissing, and so on Our concert of "marrow-bones and cleavers", the German *Katzenmusik*, got up to salute with ridicule unequal marriages The name was taken as that of a satirical journal founded in Paris by Charles Philipon in 1832, and hence in 1841 *Punch* adopted as its sub-title *The London Charivari*.

Charlatan (shar′ là tan) This word comes originally from the Italian *ciarlare*, to prate, to chatter, to babble It is usually applied to one who sells quack remedies and covers his ignorance in a torrent of high-sounding and often meaningless words

Saltimbancoes, Quacksalvers, and Charlatans deceive the people in lower degrees —SIR T. BROWNE, *Vulgar Errors*, 1646

Charlatans and impostors have always thriven on the ignorance and credulity of mankind, and it is to draw a fine distinction in roguery to differentiate between them A charlatan, however, is one who, such as a quack or astrologer, claims to possess special knowledge of medicine or more abstruse matters, the imposter pretends to be something or someone he really is not

It is difficult to make choice among the charlatans of history Nostradamus (1503-66) was an astrologer and physician who, in 1555, brought out a book of prophecies so vague in their terms that whether they were fulfilled or not is mere matter of conjecture.

John Partridge (1644-1715) was a good example of the English breed, rendered forever a laughing-stock by Swift's skit on his astrological achievements   Cagliostro (Joseph Balsamo, 1743-95) was rather an impostor than a charlatan, though he shined in either category   Perhaps the most striking example of modern charlatanry was Sequoa, a white man posing as Red Indian, who toured Britain about 1890, in a coach with attendant Redskins and a brass band, drawing teeth "painlessly " (all squeals drowned by the band) and supplying an "Indian oil" to cure all manner of aches and pains

Charlemagne (sharl' măn) (742-814).   Charles the Great became king of the Franks in 771, and in 800 founded the Holy Roman Empire   He ruled over nearly all western Europe and was noted for his work as a law-giver, administrator, protector of the Church and promoter of education.

Charlemagne and his Paladins are the centre of a great series of chivalric romances   (See PALADINS, LA SOYENSE)   We are told that the great emperor was eight feet in height, and of correspondingly enormous strength, so that with his hands alone he could bend three horseshoes at once   He was buried at Aix la Chapelle (Aachen), but according to legend he waits, crowned and armed, in Oldenburg, Hesse, for the day when Antichrist shall appear, he will then go forth to battle and rescue Christendom.   Another legend says that in years of plenty he crosses the Rhine on a golden bridge, to bless the cornfields and vineyards

Charles.   An ill-omened name for rulers·
England   Charles I was beheaded by his subjects   (*See also below*)
Charles II lived long in exile.   (*See also below*)
Charles Edward, the Young Pretender, died in poverty and disgrace in France
France   Charles II, the Fat, reigned wretchedly, was deposed, and died a beggarly dependant on the stinting bounty of the Archbishop of Metz
Charles III, the Simple, died a prisoner in the castle of Péronne.
Charles IV, the Fair, reigned six years, married thrice, but buried all his children except one daughter, who was forbidden by the Salic law to succeed to the crown.
Charles VI lived and died an idiot or madman.
Charles VII starved himself to death, partly through fear of being poisoned and partly because of a painful and incurable abscess in his mouth
Charles VIII accidentally smashed his head against the lintel of a doorway in the Château Amboise, and died in agony, leaving no issue
Charles IX died at the age of twenty-four, harrowed in conscience for the part he had taken in the " Massacre of St Bartholomew "
Charles X spent a quarter of a century in exile, and less than six years after he succeeded to the throne, fled for his life and died in exile.
Charles le Téméraire, of Burgundy, lost his life at Nancy, where he was utterly defeated by the Swiss

Naples   Charles I saw the French massacred in the "Sicilian Vespers," and experienced only disasters.
Charles II, the Lame, was in captivity at his father's death.
Charles III, his grandson, was assassinated
Charles I of England.   When Bernini's bust of Charles I was brought home, the King was sitting in the garden of Chelsea Palace   He ordered the bust to be uncovered, and at the moment a hawk with a bird in its beak flew by, and a drop of blood fell on the throat of the bust   The bust was ultimately destroyed when the palace was burnt down
The bronze statue of Charles I looking down Whitehall has an interesting history.   It was modelled by Le Soeur and cast in 1639   After the execution of the King his statue was taken down by order of Parliament and sold to a brazier named Rivers, on the express condition that it should be melted down.   But Rivers buried the statue, though he turned a pretty penny by selling bronze knives, forks, etc , which were alleged to be made from the "martyred" king's statue   On the Restoration he dug up the figure, and in 1674 it was placed on a new pedestal on its present site

Charles and the Oak.   When Charles II fled from the Parliamentary army after the battle of Worcester, he took refuge in Boscobel House; but it being unsafe to remain there, he concealed himself in an oak (September 3rd, 1651)   Dr. Stukeley says that this tree "stood just by a horse-track passing through the wood, and the king, with Colonel Carlos, climbed into it by means of the hen-roost ladder   The family reached them victuals with a nut-hook." (*Itinerarium Curiosum*, ii, p 57, 1724)

Charles's Wain.   An old popular name for the Great Bear (*see* BEAR).   The constellation forms the rough outline of a wheelbarrow or rustic wagon, and the "Charles" stands for "Charlemagne," possibly owing to the similarity of the names *Arcturus* (*see* ARCTIC) and *Arturus* (Lat. for *Arthur*), and the confusion in the popular mind between the legendary cycles of romance connected with King Arthur and Charlemagne respectively

Charlie Dunn   To give a Charlie Dunn (Austr.).   To expel for cheating.   The origin of this phrase is obscure

Charley More.   A British naval term for anything honest or reasonable.   It originated in the tavern sign of a publican in Malta, in 1840, which read " Charley More—the Fair Thing "

Charleys, or Charlies.   The old night watch, before the police force was organized in 1829; perhaps from Charles I, under whom the police system in London was reorganized in 1640.

Charleston.   A fox-trot popular c. 1925-27.   It originated among the American Negroes.   It is also the name of a cotton-trading seaport in South Carolina the population of which is half Negro.

Charm.   Deriving from the Latin *carmen*, a song, a charm is an incantation that is alleged to work magic, though the word is usually applied to some object that averts ill luck or brings good Volumes have been written about charms, for since the earliest dawn of intelligence mankind has sought to propitiate the beneficent powers or placate the malevolent ones There are still all kinds of charms in use, often half-ashamedly—touching wood to avert bad luck, avoiding the number 13, first-footing at the New Year, and so forth, these are but a few relics of more credulous days A good selection of charms is to be found described in Brand's *Antiquities*

Charon's Toll. A coin, about equal to a penny, placed in the mouth or hand of the dead by the ancient Greeks to pay Charon (*see* STYX) for ferrying the spirit across the river Styx to the Elysian fields.

Chartism. The political system of the Chartists, a body consisting principally of working men who, in 1838, demanded the **People's Charter**, which included universal suffrage, annual parliaments, stipendiary members, vote by ballot, equal representation, and the abolition of the property qualification for members of Parliament The Chartists disappeared as a party about 1849

Chartreuse. A greenish or yellowish liqueur, made of brandy, and various aromatic herbs

When the monks returned to La Chartreuse after their expulsion during the French Revolution they found the place in ruins and all their property alienated To supply the wants of the community they concocted and sold the liqueur and before long were making a large revenue This has always been spent on the maintenance of Carthusian houses, though the greater proportion of it has been devoted to charity The recipe has now been sold and the production of the liqueur commercialized *See* CARTHUSIANS

Charybdis (kà rib' dis) A whirlpool on the coast of Sicily Scylla and Charybdis are employed to signify two equal dangers. Thus Horace says an author trying to avoid Scylla, drifts into Charybdis, *i e* seeking to avoid one fault, falls into another

The Homeric account says that Charybdis dwelt under an immense fig-tree on the rock, and that thrice every day he swallowed the waters of the sea and thrice threw them up again, but later legends have it that he stole the oxen of Hercules, was killed by lightning, and changed into the gulf.

Thus when I shun Scylla, your father I fall into Charybdis, your mother —SHAKESPEARE *Merchant of Venice*, iii, 5

Chase. A small, unenclosed deer-forest held, for the most part, by a private individual, and protected only by common law Forests are *royal* prerogatives, protected by the "Forest Laws"

An iron frame used by printers for holding sufficient type for one side of a sheet, where it is held tight by quoins, or small wedges of wood, is also called a *chase*. Here the word is the French *chasse*, from Lat *capsa,* a case: the other *chase* given above is O.Fr. *chacier,* from Lat *captiare,* to chase, itself from *capere,* to take.

Chasidim (chās' i dim). After the Babylonish captivity the Jews were divided into two groups—those who accepted and those who rejected the Persian innovation The former were called *chasidim* (pietists), and the latter *zadikim* (the upright ones)

Chastity Girdle. A padded, metal appliance in the shape of a belt that a man could fasten around his wife in such a way as to preclude possibility of unfaithfulness during his prolonged absence. It is said to have come into vogue in the times of the Crusades when men set forth on protracted journeys and campaigns One or two examples only are to be found in museums

Chasuble (chāz' û bêl). This is one of the most richly ornamented ecclesiastical garments, some of the older examples being embroidered with exquisite workmanship The chasuble is the principal vestment worn by the priest when saying Mass It is supposed to represent the seamless coat of Christ, and is a rectangular, sleeveless garment, with a hole for the head in the middle, thus hanging down both back and front to between the hips and knees

And ye, louely ladyes, with youre longe fyngres,
That ye han silke and sendal to sowe, what tyme is,
Chesibles for chapelleynes cherches to honoure
PIERS PLOWMAN

Château (shä tō). French for castle, mansion, country seat, and hence, an estate in the country

The wines of the Bordeaux district of France are all named after the château of the estate on which they are grown A Château-bottled wine is one bottled on the estate by the proprietor, which he only does in years when he is satisfied with the quality.

Château en Espagne, a castle in the air (*q v*).

Chatelaine (shät' e lān) Originally the mistress of a château, a chatelaine now usually signifies a brooch or clasp from which a variety of objects hang on short chains They are the things which the mistress of the castle was likely to use—keys, a watch, scissors, knives and trinkets Chatelaines have been made in gold, silver, enamel, and cut steel, and in imitations of these materials Since 1900 they have been little used, and their use during the century before was a fashionable affectation In 1947 a fashion for so-called chatelaines arose in the U.S.A. These were ornaments formed of two or more brooches, preferably old and valuable, pinned across the corsage and joined by chains

Chatelaine's (shät' e lānz) This was a famous ordinary in Covent Garden, established soon after the Restoration and a favourite resort of wits and men of fashion Mention of the place occurs in many plays, etc , of the period
Met their servant coming to oring me to Chatelin's and there with music and good company mighty merry till ten at night
Pepys's Diary, 22/4/1668.

Sparkish Come, but where do we dine?
Horner Even where you will
Sparkish. At Chatelaine's
WYCHERLEY *The Country Wife.*

Chatterbox. A talkative person. Shakespeare speaks of the clack-dish "His use was to put a ducat in her clack-dish" (*Measure for Measure*, iii, 2)—i e. the box or dish used by beggars for collecting alms, which the holder clatters to attract attention. We find also chatter-basket in old writers, referring to the child's rattle

Chatterpie. A familiar name for the magpie; also used figuratively for a chatterbox (q v).

Chautauqua (sha tawk′ wa). This is the name given in U.S A to an assembly for educational purposes, held largely out of doors, with lectures, entertainments, etc , and modelled on the Chautauqua Assembly. This was started in 1874, at the village and summer resort on Lake Chautauqua, New York State In 1878 the Assembly developed into the Chautauqua Literary and Scientific Circle, for the promotion of home reading and study.

Chauvinism (shō′ vin izm). Blind and pugnacious patriotism of an exaggerated kind; unreasoning jingoism Nicholas Chauvin, a soldier of the French Republic and Empire, was madly devoted to Napoleon and his cause He was introduced as a type of exaggerated bellicose patriotism into quite a number of plays (Scribe's *Le Soldat laboureur*, Cogniard's *La Cocarde tricoleur*, 1831, Bayard and Dumanoir's *Les Aides de camps*. Charet's *Conscrit Chauvin*, are some of them), and his name was quickly adopted on both sides of the Channel.

Chawbacon. A contemptuous name for an uncouth rustic, supposed to eat no meat but bacon.

Che sara, sara (chā sa ra′, sa ra′) What shall be, will be. The motto of the Russells (Bedford).

> What doctrine call ye this, *Che sera, sera*
> What will be, shall be?
> MARLOWE *Dr Faustus*, i, 48.

Cheap as a Sardinian A Roman phrase referring to the great crowds of Sardinian prisoners brought to Rome by Tiberius Gracchus, and offered for sale at almost any price.

Cheap jack. A travelling vendor of small wares, who is usually ready to "cheapen" his goods, i e. take less for them than the price he first named

Cheapside bargain A weak pun, meaning that the article was bought cheap or under its market value Cheapside, is on the south side of the *Cheap* (or *Chepe*), one of the principal market-places of Old London, so called from A.S. *ceapian*, to buy, *cypan*, to sell, *ceap*, a price or sale

Cheater. Originally an *Escheator* or officer of the king's exchequer appointed to receive dues and taxes The present use of the word shows how these officers were wont to fleece the people. *Cp.* CATCHPOLE; also the New Testament word "publicans," or collectors of the Roman tax in Judæa, etc.

Checkmate. A term in chess meaning to place your adversary's king in such a position that, had it been any other piece, it could not escape capture Figuratively, " to checkmate" means to foil or outwit another; 'check-

mated," outmanœuvred The term is from the Arabic *shah mat*, the king is dead, the phrase having been introduced into Old Spanish and Portuguese as *xaque mate*

Checks. To hand in one's checks. *See* HAND.

Cheek. Cheek by jowl. Side by side, close together. Cheek is the A S *ceace*, and jowl is from A S. *ceafl*, jaw, which became in M E. *chowl*, and was confused with M E *cholle*, from A S *ceolur*, throat.

> I'll go with thee, cheek by jowl —SHAKESPEARE: *Midsummer Night's Dream*, iii, 2

To cheek, or to give cheek. To be insolent, to be saucy.

None of your cheek. None of your insolence We say a man is very cheeky, meaning that he is saucy and presumptuous

To have the cheek. To have the face or assurance. "He hadn't the cheek to ask for more "

Cheese. Tusser in his *Five Hundred Points of Good Husbandry* (1573) says that a cheese, to be perfect, should not be like (1) Gehazi, i e dead white, like a leper; (2) not like Lot's wife, all salt, (3) not like Argus, full of eyes; (4) not like Tom Piper, 'hoven and puffed," like the cheeks of a piper, (5) not like Crispin, leathery, (6) not like Lazarus, poor; (7) not like Esau, hairy, (8) not like Mary Magdalene, full of whey or maudlin; (9) not like the Gentiles, full of maggots or gentils, and (10) not like a bishop, made of burnt milk, this last is a reference to the old phrase, *the bishop hath put his foot in it See* BISHOP

A green cheese. An unripe cheese, also a cheese that is eaten fresh (like a cream cheese) and is not kept to mature

Big cheese. (Slang) The boss, or person of importance.

Bread and cheese. Food generally, but of a frugal nature "Come and take your bread and cheese with me this evening"—that is, come and have a light supper, anything that's going

Cheese it! Stop it′ stow it′ Also (in thieves' slang) clear off, make yourself scarce.

Cheesed off. Army slang for disgusted, disgruntled.

Hard cheese. Hard lines; rotten luck

He is quite the cheese or just the cheese—i.e. quite the thing. Here "cheese" is the Persian and Urdu *chiz* (or *cheez*), meaning "thing " The phrase is of Anglo-Indian origin; but it has been popularly treated as being connected with the Eng. *cheese*, and thus we get the slang varieties, *That's prime Stilton*, or *double Gloster—i e*. slap up Hence such phrases as —

It is not the cheese. Not the right thing; said of something of rather dubious propriety or morals.

> Who ever heard of a young lady being married without something to be married in?
> Well, I've heard Nudity is not the cheese on public occasions!
> CHAS READE *Hard Cash*, ii, 186

The moon made of green cheese. *See* MOON

'Tis an old rat that won't eat cheese It must be a wondrously toothless man that is inaccessible to flattery, he must be very old indeed who can abandon his favourite indulgence, only a very cunning rat knows that cheese is a mere bait

Cheesemongers. An old popular name (before the Peninsular War) for the 1st Life-guards, either because up to that time they had never served overseas, or (traditionally) because when the regiment was remodelled in 1788 certain commissions were refused on the ground that the ranks were composed of tradesmen instead of, as formerly, gentlemen It is said that at Waterloo the commanding officer, when leading the regiment to a charge, cried, "Come on, you damned cheesemongers!"' since when the name was accepted as a compliment rather than a reproach

Cheeseparer. A skinflint; one who would pare or shave off very thinly the rind of his cheese so as to waste the smallest possible quantity The tale is told of a man who chose his wife out of three sisters by the way they ate their cheese One pared it—she (he said) was mean, one cut it off extravagantly thick—she was wasteful, the third sliced it off in a medium way, and there his choice fell

Cheese-toaster A sword, also called a "toasting-fork," etc

> Put up thy sword betime,
> Or I'll so maul you and your toasting-iron
> That you shall think the devil is come from hell
>   SHAKESPEARE· *King John*, IV, 3

The sight of the blade, which glistened by moonlight in his face, checked, in some sort, the ardour of his assailant, who desired he would lay aside his toaster, and take a bout with him at equal arms.—SMOLLETT· *Peregrine Pickle*, ch xxiv

Cheesewring, The Devil's. A mass of eight stones, towering to the height of thirty-two feet, in the Valley of Rocks, Lynmouth, Devon, so called because it looks like a gigantic cheesepress The Kilmarth Rocks, and part of Hugh Lloyd's Pulpit present somewhat similar piles of stone

Chef d'Œuvre (Fr , literally, a chief work) A masterpiece

Chemosh (kē' mosh) The national god of the Moabites; very little is known of his cult, but human beings were sacrificed to him in times of crisis

> Next, Chemos, the obscene dread of Moab's sons,
> From Aroer to Nebo, and the wild
> Of southmost Abarim
>   MILTON *Paradise Lost*, i, 406-8.

Chequers (chek' erz) A public-house sign The arms of Fitzwarren, the head of which house, in the days of the Henrys, was invested with the power of licensing vintners and publicans, may have helped to popularize this sign, which indicated that the house was duly licensed, but it has been found on houses in Pompeii, and probably referred to some game, like draughts, which might be indulged in on the premises Gayton, in his *Notes on Don Quixote* (p 340), in speaking of our public-house signs, refers to our notices of ' billiards,

kettle-noddy-boards, tables, truncks, shovel-boards, fox-and-geese, and the like " Also, payment of doles, etc., used to be made at certain public-houses, and a chequer-board was provided for the purpose In such cases the sign indicated the house where the parish authorities met for that and other purposes.

Chequers, the country seat of the Prime Minister of England for the time being, was presented to the nation for this purpose by Sir Arthur and Lady Lee (Lord and Lady Lee of Fareham) in 1917, and was first officially occupied by the then Prime Minister (Mr. David Lloyd George) in January, 1921 It is a Tudor mansion, standing in a large and well-wooded estate in the Chilterns, about three miles from Princes Risborough

Cheronean (kē rō nē' an) The **Cheronean Sage.** Plutarch, who was born at Chæronea, in Bœotia (A.D 46-120)

Cherry. Cherry-breeches or **cherry-pickers.** Familiar names for the 11th Hussars *See* CHERUBIMS.

Cherry fairs. The old counterpart of the modern tea-gardens, cherry-orchards where sales of fruit were held, such gatherings frequently developing into boisterous scenes From their temporary character they came to be used as typifications of the evanescence of life, thus Gower says of this world, "Alle is but a cherye-fayre," a phrase frequently met with

> This life, my son, is but a chery-fayre.—*MS Bodl* 221 (quoted by HALLIWELL)

Cherry trees and the cuckoo. The cherry tree is strangely mixed up with the cuckoo in many cuckoo stories, because of the tradition that the cuckoo must eat three good meals of cherries before he is allowed to cease singing.

> Cuckoo, cuckoo, cherry-tree,
> Good bird, prithee, tell to me
> How many years I am to see

The answer is gathered from the number of times the cuckoo repeats its cry.

The whole tree or not a cherry on it. "*Aut Cæsar aut nullus* " All in all or none at all

To make two bites of a cherry. To divide something too small to be worth dividing, to take two spells over a piece of work that should be done in one.

Cherubims The name once given popularly to the 11th Hussars It seems inevitable that "Cherry bums" should be applied to men with cherry-pink uniform breeches.

Cheshire Cat. To grin like a Cheshire cat. *See* CAT.

Chess. "The game of the kings", the word *chess* being the modern English representative of Persian *shah* (*see* CHECKMATE), a king. This word in Arabic was pronounced *shag*, which gave rise to the late Lat *scaccus*, whence the O Fr *eschec*, Mod Fr *échecs*, and E *chess*. Derivatives in other languages are *scacco* (Ital), *jaque* (Span), *xaque* (Port), *schach* (Ger)

Chestnut. A stale joke The term is said to have been popularized in America by a Boston actor named Warren, who, on a certain apposite occasion, quoted from *The Broken Sword*, a forgotten melodrama by William Dimond, first produced in 1816 at Covent Garden Captain Xavier, a principal character, is for ever repeating the same yarns, with variations He was telling about one of his exploits connected with a cork-tree, when Pablo corrected him, "A chestnut-tree, you mean, captain " "Bah!" replied the captain, "I say a cork-tree " "A chestnut-tree," insisted Pablo "I must know better than you," said the captain, "it was a cork-tree, I say." " A chestnut," persisted Pablo "I have heard you tell the joke twenty-seven times, and I am sure it was a chestnut "

Chestnut Sunday. A Sunday in spring, generally that immediately before or after Ascension Day, is so called in the London district, because about that time the chestnut avenue at Hampton Court bursts into bloom.

Cheval (she văl) (Fr , a horse).

Cheval de bataille (Fr , literally "horse of battle") One's strong argument; one's favourite subject

Cheval de frise. An apparatus consisting of a bar carrying rows of pointed stakes, set up so that the bar can revolve It was used in warfare as a defence against enemy cavalry, and is so called because first employed by the Frisians—who had few or no horses—in the siege of Groningen, Friesland, in 1594 A somewhat similar engine had been used before, but was not called by the same name In German it is "a Spanish horseman" (*ein Spanischer Reiter*).

Cheval glass A large, swinging mirror, long enough to reflect the whole of the figure; so called from the "horse," or framework, which supports it

Chevalier de St. George. *See* CAVALIER

Chevalier d'industrie. A man who lives by his wits and calls himself a gentleman, an adventurer, swindler

Be cautiously upon your guard against the infinite number of fine-dressed and fine-spoken chevaliers d'industrie and avanturiers, which swarm at Paris — CHESTERFIELD *Letters to his Son*, cxc (April 26th, 1750)

Cheveril (chev'er il). He has a cheveril conscience. An accommodating one, one that will easily stretch like cheveril or kid leather

Oh, here's a wit of cheveril, that stretches from an inch narrow to an ell broad!—SHAKESPEARE *Romeo and Juliet*, ii, 4

Your soft cheveril conscience would receive, If you might please to stretch it. SHAKESPEARE *Henry VIII*, ii, 3

Chevy Chase. There had long been a rivalry between the families of Percy and Douglas, which showed itself by incessant raids into each other's territory Percy of Northumberland one day vowed he would hunt for three days in the Scottish border, without condescending to ask leave of Earl Douglas. The Scots warden said in his anger, "Tell this vaunter he shall find one day more than sufficient " The ballad called *Chevy Chase* mixes up this hunt with the battle of Otterburn, which, Dr. Percy justly observes, was "a very different event."

Chian Painter, The. *See* APELLES.

Chiaroscuro (kyar os koo' rō) A style of painting to represent only two colours, now called "black and white", also the production of the effects of light and shade in drawings, paintings, etc.

Chiar-oscuro   is the art of representing light in shadow and shadow in light, so that the parts represented in shadow shall still have the clearness and warmth of those in light; and those in light, the depth and softness of those in shadow —*Chambers's Encyclopædia*, ii, p 171

Chic (shik) A French word of uncertain origin meaning the knack of being able to do anything well In English the word is applied more especially to good taste in dressing, to smartness and style, to being "just right" in appearance

The word may be connected with German *schick*, skill, tact, but this is by no means certain

Chicane (shi kān). A term used in bridge for a hand containing no trumps Its general meaning is the use of mean, petty subterfuge, especially legal dodges and quibbles. It is a French word which, before being used for sharp practice in lawsuits, meant a dispute in games, particularly mall, and originally the game of mall itself It seems to be ultimately from Persian *chaugan*, the crooked stick used in polo

Chichivache (chich' e vash) A fabulous animal that lived only on good women, and was hence all skin and bone, because its food was so extremely scarce, the antitype to Bicorn (*q v*) Chaucer introduced the word into English from French, but in doing so he changed *chichifache* (thin or ugly face) into *chichivache* (lean or meagre-looking cow), and hence the animal was pictured as a kind of bovine monstrosity

O noble wyves, ful of heigh prudence,
    Let noon humilitie your tonges nayle·
Ne lat no clerk have cause or diligence
    To write of you a story of such mervayle
As of Griselde, pacient and kynde,
    Lest Chichivache you swolwe in hir entraile
        CHAUCER· *Envoy to the Clerk's Tale*

Lydgate wrote a poem entitled *Bycorne and Chichevache*

Chicken. Children and chicken must always be pickin'. Are always hungry and ready to eat food

Curses like chickens come home to roost. *See* CURSES

Don't count your chickens before they are hatched. Don't anticipate profits before they come One of Æsop's fables describes a market woman saying she would get so much for her eggs, with the money she would buy a goose, the goose in time would bring her so much, with which she would buy a cow, and so on; but in her excitement she kicked over her basket and all her eggs were broken "Don't crow till you are out of the wood" has a similar meaning *Cp.* ALNASCHAR'S DREAM

Mother Carey's chickens. *See* MOTHER CAREY.

She's no chicken. She's not so young as she used to be

Where the chicken got the axe. See *To get it in the neck*, under NECK.

Chicken of St. Nicholas. So the Piedmontese call our "ladybird," the little red beetle with spots of black The Russians know it as "God's little cow," and the Germans, who say it is sent as a messenger of love, "God's little horse."

Chicken-hearted or **chicken-livered.** Cowardly. Young fowls are remarkably timid, and run to the wing of the hen upon the slightest cause of alarm

Child. At one time this was a provincial term for a female infant, and was the correlative of boy

Mercy on 's! A barne, a very pretty barne A boy or a child, I wonder?—SHAKESPEARE *Winter's Tale*, III, 3

Child of God. In the Anglican and Catholic Church, one who has been baptized, others consider the phrase to mean one converted by special grace and adopted into the holy family of God's Church

In my baptism, wherein I was made a member of Christ, the child of God, and an inheritor of the Kingdom of Heaven.—*Church Catechism*

Childe. In *Childe Harold, Childe Roland, Childe Tristam*, etc, "Childe" is a title of honour, like the Spanish "infante" and "infanta." In the time of chivalry, noble youths who were candidates for knighthood were, during their time of probation, called *infans, valets, damoysels, bacheliers*, and *childe*

Childe Harold Byron's poem depicts a man sated of the world, who roams from place to place to flee from himself The "Childe" is, in fact, Lord Byron himself, who was only twenty-one when he began, and twenty-eight when he finished the poem. In canto I (1809), he visited Portugal and Spain; in canto II (1810), Turkey in Europe, in canto III (1816), Belgium and Switzerland; and in canto IV (1817), Venice, Rome, and Florence.

Childermass. The Old English name for the festival, or mass, of the Holy Innocents (December 28th)

The children or babes in the wood The foundation of this ballad, which is told in Percy's *Reliques*, appears again in a crude melodrama of 1599 by Robert Farrington, entitled *Two Lamentable Tragedies. the one of the Murder of Maister Beech, a chandler in Thames Streete, the other of a young child murthered in a wood by two ruffins with the consent of his unkle* It is not known which is the earlier, the play or the ballad The story is, shortly, as follows —The master of Wayland Hall, Norfolk, left a little son and daughter to the care of his wife's brother, both were to have money, but if the children died first the uncle was to inherit. After twelve months the uncle hired two ruffians to murder the babes, one of the ruffians relented and killed his fellow, leaving the children in a wood, they died during the night, and "Robin Redbreast" covered them over with leaves All things went ill with the wicked uncle, his sons died, his barns were fired, his cattle died, and he himself perished in gaol. After seven years the ruffian was taken up for highway robbery, and confessed the whole affair

Children Three hundred and sixty-five at a birth. It is said that a Countess of Henneberg accused a beggar of adultery because she carried twins, whereupon the beggar prayed that the countess might carry as many children as there are days in the year According to the legend, this happened on Good Friday, 1276 All the males were named John, and all the females Elizabeth The countess was forty-two at the time

Chiliasts (kǐl′ ǐ ǎsts) (Gr *chilias*, a thousand) Those who believe that Christ will return to this earth and reign a thousand years in the midst of His saints Originally a Judaistic theory, it became a heresy in the early Christian Church, and though it was condemned by St Damasus, who was Pope from 366 to 384, it was not extirpated Article xli of the English Church, as published in 1553, further condemned Chiliasm, this Article was omitted in 1562. *Millenarians* is another name for the Chiliasts

Chillingham Cattle. A breed of cattle preserved in the Northumberland park of the Earl of Tankerville, supposed to be the last remnant of the wild oxen of Britain.

Chillon (shē′ yong) **Prisoner of Chillon** François de Bonnivard (d about 1570), a Genevan prelate and politician Byron makes him one of six brothers, all of whom suffered for their opinions The father and two sons died on the battlefield, one was burnt at the stake; three were incarcerated in the dungeon of Chillon, on the edge of the Lake of Geneva —of these, two died, and François, who had been imprisoned for "republican principles" by the Duke-Bishop of Savoy, was set at liberty by "the Béarnais" after four years' imprisonment

Chilminar and Baalbec (kil min ar′, bāl′ bek). Two cities built, according to Eastern legend, by the Genii, acting under the orders of Jan ben Jan, who governed the world long before the time of Adam. Chilminar, or the "Forty Pillars," is Persepolis They were intended as lurking places for the Genii to hide in

Chilo. One of the "Seven Sages of Greece" (*q v*)

Chiltern Hundreds There are three, viz Stoke, Desborough, and Burnham, Bucks At one time the Chilterns, between Bedford and Hertford, etc., were much frequented by robbers, so a steward was appointed by the Crown to put them down The necessity has long since ceased, but the office remains, and, since 1740, when a Member of Parliament wishes to vacate his seat, one way of doing so is by applying for the stewardship of the Chiltern Hundreds, for no member of Parliament may resign his seat, but if he accepts an office of profit under the Crown he is obliged to be re-elected if he wishes to remain a member. The Stewardship of the Manor of Northstead (Yorks) is used in the same way. The gift of both is in the hands of the Chancellor of the Exchequer, it was refused to a member for Reading in 1842

The Stewardships of Old Sarum (Wilts), East Hendred (Berks), Poynings (Sussex), Hempholwic (Yorks), were formerly used for the same purpose, as were (till 1838) the Escheatorships of Munster and Ulster.

Chimæra (kI mē′ rà) (Gr *chimaira*, a she-goat) A fabulous monster of Greek mythology, described by Homer as a monster with a goat's body, a lion's head, and a dragon's tail. It was born in Lycia, and was slain by Bellerophon Hence the term is used in English for an illusory fancy, a wild, incongruous scheme

Chimney Money or Hearth Money. A yearly tax of two shillings on every fireplace in England and Wales. first levied in 1663 and abolished in 1689.

Chimneypot hat. The cylindrical black silk hat, usually known as the top-hat or silk hat

China Clay A mineral, obtained largely from Cornwall, used in the manufacture of porcelain, and by papermakers to obtain finish and consistency, also for coating art and chromo papers

Chinaman. A left-hander's googly, a cricketing term (*see* GOOGLY)

Chinatown A part of any city where the population is Chinese, the most famous being in the United States.

Chindit (chin′ dit) Stylized lions characteristic of Burmese and Malayan sculpture and religious architecture Adopted as the insignia of the troops operating in the Malay jungle behind the Japanese lines under Brigadier Wingate in the 1939-45 war, who hence were familiarly known as *Chindits.*

Chinese Gordon General Gordon (killed at Khartoum in 1885), who in 1863 was placed in command of the Ever-Victorious Army (*q v.*) and in the following year succeeded, after thirty-three engagements, in putting down the Taeping rebellion, which had broken out in 1851 For this service Gordon was rewarded by the Emperor with the yellow jacket and peacock's feather of a mandarin of the first class

When the Mahdi's rebellion broke out in the Sudan, Gordon was sent to assist the Egyptian army, and defended Khartoum for nearly a year. Wolseley was sent to relieve him but arrived at Khartoum two days too late, Gordon having been killed on Jan. 26th, 1885

Chingachgook. The Indian chief in Fenimore Cooper's *Last of the Mohicans, Pathfinder, Deerslayer,* and *Pioneer* Called in French *Le Gros Serpent*

Chink. Money, so called because it chinks, or jingles in the purse It was formerly in good repute as a synonym of coin

Have chinks in thy purse.—TUSSER *Five Hundred Points* (1573)

    I tell you, he that can lay hold of her
    Shall have the chinks
        SHAKESPEARE. *Romeo and Juliet*, i, 5.

Chintz. A plural word that has erroneously become singular The Hindi *chint* (from Sanskrit *chitra*, variegated) was the name given in the 17th century to the painted and stained

calico imported from the East; but as the plural (*chints*) was more common in commercial use than the singular it came to be taken for a singular, and was written *chince* or *chinse* and finally *chintz*.

Chios (kI′ os) **The man of Chios.** Homer, who lived at Chios, near the Ægean Sea. Seven cities claim to be his place of birth—Smyrna, Rhodos, Colophon, Salamis, Chios, Agos, Athenæ

Chip. A carpenter is known by his chips A man is known to be a carpenter by the chips in his workshop, so the profession or taste of other men may be known by their manners or mode of speech

A chip of the old block A son or child of the same stuff as his father The chip is the same wood as the block Burke applied the words to William Pitt.

To have a chip on one's shoulder. To be seeking a quarrel A person who is always ready to take offence is said to go about with a chip on his shoulder.

Brother Chip. Properly a brother carpenter, but in its extended meaning applied to anyone of the same vocation as oneself
The ship's carpenter is, at sea, commonly addressed as " Chips "

Saratoga chips. Potatoes sliced thin while raw, and fried crisp Sometimes called chipped potatoes, but more generally "chips."

Such carpenters, such chips. As the workman, so his work will be.

Chiron (kI′ ron) The centaur who taught Achilles and many other heroes music, medicine, and hunting Jupiter placed him in heaven among the stars as Sagittarius (*the Archer*).
In the *Inferno* Dante gives the name to the keeper of the lake of boiling blood, in the seventh circle of hell

Chirping Cup A merry-making glass or cup of liquor. Wine that maketh glad the heart of man, or makes him sing for joy

  A chirping cup is my matin song,
  And my vesper bell is my bowl, Ding dong!
        A Friar of Orders Grey.

  The chirping and moderate bottle
        BEN JONSON.

He takes his chirping pint, and cracks his jokes.
        POPE *Moral Essays*, iii.

Chisel. **I chiselled him means, I cheated him,** or cut him out of something.

Chivalry (shiv′ al ri). This is a general term for all things pertaining to the romance of the old days of knighthood The word is of similar origin to *cavalry*, coming from Fr. *cheval*, a horse, and *chevalier*, a horseman. Chivalry embodied the Middle Age conception of the ideal life, where valour, courtesy, generosity and dexterity in arms were the summit of any man's attainment

For him behoveth to be of soch chiualrie and so a-venturouse that he com by hymselfe and enquere after the seint Graal that my feire doughter kepeth.
        Merlin (E.E T.S , iii)

A great literature arose out of chivalry—The Roland epics, those of Charlemagne, and

Arthur It was, perhaps, prophetic of the fate of chivalry itself that in every case these great epics end in tragedy:

The paladins of Charlemagne were all scattered by the battle of Roncesvalles

The champions of Dietrich were all assassinated at the instigation of Chriemhild, the bride of Etzel, King of the Huns

The Knights of the Round Table were all extirpated in the fatal battle of Camlan

The flower of chivalry See FLOWER

Chivy To chase or urge someone on, also a chase in the game of "Prisoners' Base" One boy "sets a chivy" by leaving his base, when one of the opposite side chases him, and if he succeeds in touching him before he reaches "home," the boy touched becomes a prisoner The word is a variant spelling of *chevy*, from *Chevy Chase* (*q v*).

Chivy or **chivvy.** Slang for the face An example of rhyming slang (*q v*) Here the full term to rhyme with *face* is *Chevy Chase.*

Chloe (klō' ê) The shepherdess beloved by Daphnis in the pastoral romance of Longus, entitled *Daphnis and Chloe,* and hence a generic name among romance writers and pastoral poets for a rustic maiden—not always of the artless variety

In Pope's *Moral Essays* (ii) Chloe is intended for Lady Suffolk, mistress of George II ' Content to dwell in decencies for ever", and Prior uses the name for Mrs Centlivre

Chock-full. Chock-a-block Absolutely full, no room for any more. It is a very old expression in English, dating back at least to Chaucer's time, though, apparently, not used by him It does not seem to have any etymological connexion with *choke* (as though meaning "full enough to choke one"), but this spelling—as well as *chuck*—has been in common use.

Ayr was holding some grand market, streets and inn had been chokefull during the sunny hours — CARLYLE, in *Froude's June W Carlyle,* vol i, letter lxxxvii

Chocolate. The produce of the cocoa-berry was introduced into England from Central America in the early 16th century as a drink; it was sold in the London coffee-houses from the middle of the 17th century. The *Cocoa Tree* was one of the most famous coffee-houses of the early 18th century

Chocos (Austr). A diminutive of *chocolate soldiers,* applied to militiamen and conscripts in World War II

Choice. Choice spirit. A specially select or excellent person, a leader in some particular capacity. From Antony's speaking of Cæsar and Brutus as—

The choice and master spirit of this age.
SHAKESPEARE *Julius Cæsar,* iii, 1.

Choice spirit of the age. Figuratively used for a gallant of the day, one who delights to exaggerate the whims of fashion

Hobson's choice. *See* HOBSON.

Of two evils choose the less. The proverb is given in John Heywood's collection (1546), but it is a good deal earlier, and occurs in Chaucer's *Troilus and Criseyde* (ii, 470) as—

Of harmes two, the lesse is for to chese

Thomas à Kempis (*Imit Christi,* iii, 12) has—

De duobus malis minus est semper eligendum (Of two evils the less is always to be chosen)

which is an echo of Cicero's

Ex malis eligere minima oportere (Of evil one should select the least) —*De Officiis,* iii, I

Choke. May this piece of bread choke me, f what I say is not true. In ancient times a person accused of robbery had a piece of barley bread, over which Mass had been said, given him He put it in his mouth uttering these words and if he could swallow it without being choked he was pronounced innocent. Tradition ascribes the death of Earl Godwin to choking with a piece of bread after this solemn appeal *See* CORSNED

The narrowing of a shot-gun barrel to effect greater range and concentration of shot is called the *choke* The barrel habitually used second is often choked, as by then a bird missed with the first barrel is farther away.

Choke-pear. A kind of pear with a rough, astringent taste From this the term was applied to anything that stopped speaking, such as an unanswerable argument or a biting sarcasm

He gaue him a choake-peare to stoppe his breath,
LYLY *Euphues*

Pardon me for going so low as to talk of choke-pears RICHARDSON *Clarissa*

Choker. Formerly a broad neck-cloth, worn in full dress, and by waiters and clergymen, now a high, stiff collar or a necklace worn tight round the neck

Chop. The various modern uses of *chop* represent two or three different words To *chop,* meaning to cut a piece off with a sudden blow, is a variant spelling of *chap,* a cleft in the skin, and *to chap,* to open in long slits or cracks From this we get.—

Chops of the Channel The short broken motion of the waves experienced in crossing the English Channel, also the place where such motion occurs In this use, however, the word may be *chops,* the jaw (*see below*), because the Chops of the Channel is an old and well-understood term for the entrance to the Channel from the Atlantic

Chop house. An eating-house where chops and steaks are served

I dine at the *Chop-House* three days a week, where the good company wonders they never see you ot late —STEELE *Spectator,* No 308 (22 Feb , 1712)

In the three following phrases *chop* comes from the same root as *chap* in *chapman* (*q v*), and signifies to barter, exchange, or sell

To chop and change To barter by rule of thumb, to fluctuate, to vary continuously.

To chop an article also means to dispose of it arbitrarily, even at a loss.

To chop logic. To bandy words, to altercate Bacon says, "Let not the council chop with the judge."

How now, how now, chop logic! What is this?
"Proud," and "I thank you," and "I thank you not,"
And yet "not proud "
SHAKESPEARE *Romeo and Juliet,* iii, 5.

The wind chops about. Shifts from point to point suddenly Hence, *choppy,* said of a variable wind, and of the rough sea produced by such, and *to chop round—*

How the House of Lords and House of Commons chopped round —THACKERAY *The Four Georges* (George I)

Chop, the face, and chops, the jaws or mouth, is a variant spelling of *chap* (as in *Bath chap,* the lower part of a pig's face, cured) From this come

Chop-fallen, or chap-fallen Crestfallen; down in the mouth

Down in the chops. Down in the mouth, in a melancholy state; with the mouth drawn down

To lick one's chops. To relish in anticipation

Finally, in the slang phrase first chop, meaning excellent, the word is the Hindi *chhap,* a print or stamp, used in India and China by English residents for an official seal, also for a passport or permit, and a Chinese custom-house is known as a chop-house.

Chopsticks. The two thin sticks of wood or ivory that the Chinese use to eat with. They attain marvellous dexterity in the use of these implements, and the word is a rendering of Chin *k'wai-tsze,* meaning " the quick ones " In pidgin English (*q v.*) *chop* means "quick "

Choragus (kôr a gus) The leader of the chorus in the ancient Athenian drama

At Oxford the title is given to the assistant of the Professor of Music, but formerly to the officer who superintended the practice of music *See* CORYPHÆUS

Choriambic Metre. Horace gives us a great variety, but the main feature in all is the prevalence of the choriambus ($-\smile\smile-$) Specimen translations in two of these metres are subjoined.

(1) Horace, 1 *Odes,* VIII

$-\smile\smile-|\smile--$
$-\smile|--|-\smile\smile-|-\smile\smile-|\smile--$

Lydia, why on Stanley,
By the great gods, tell me, I pray, ruinous love you centre?
Once he was strong and manly,
Never seen now, patient of toil Mars' sunny camp to enter   E C B

(2) The other specimen is 1 *Odes,* XII

$--|-\smile\smile-|\smile-$
$--|-\smile\smile-|-\smile\smile-|\smile-$

When you, with an approving smile,
Praise those delicate arms, Lydy, of Telephus,
Ah me! how you stir up my bile!
Heart-sick that for a boy you should forsake me thus.
                                                            E C B

Chouans (shoo' ong) French insurgents of the Royalist party during the Revolution Jean Cottereau was their leader, nicknamed *Chouan* (a corruption of Fr *chat-huant,* a screech-owl), because he was accustomed to warn his companions of danger by imitating the screech of an owl Cottereau (killed 1794) was followed by George Cadoudal (executed 1804) *See also* COMPANIONS OF JEHU, VENDEE

Choughs Protected. See BIRDS

Chouse (chouz) This is a rather odd word, meaning to cheat or swindle It has an interesting origin, coming from the Turkish *cha'ush,* an interpreter, messenger, etc. The interpreter of the Turkish embassy in England in 1609 defrauded his government of £4,000, and the notoriety of the swindle caused the word *chiaus* or *chouse* to be adopted

Dapper   What do you think of me,
                    That I am a Chiause?
Face   What's that?
Dapper.   The Turk was here—
                    As one would say, do you think
                    I am a Turk
                              BEN JONSON *Alchemist,* 1. 2
You shall chouse him out of horses, clothes, and money, and I'll wink at it —DRYDEN *Wild Gallant,* ii, 1

Chriem-hild   *See* KRIEMHILD

Chrisom or Chrism signifies properly "the white cloth set by the minister at baptism on the head of the newly anointed with chrism" —a composition of oil and balm (Gr *chrisma,* anointing, unction). In the Form of Private Baptism is this direction· "Then the minister shall put the white vesture, commonly called the chrisome, upon the child " The child thus baptized is called a *chrisom* or *chrisom child* If it dies within the month, it is shrouded in the vesture, and hence, in the bills of mortality, even to 1726, infants that died within the month were termed chrisoms

A' made a finer end and went away an it had been any chrisom child.—SHAKESPEARE *Henry V,* ii, 3

Chriss-cross, or Christ-cross, Row. The alphabet in a hornbook, which had a cross like the Maltese cross (✠) at the beginning and end

Sir Ralph I wonder, wench, how I thy name might know
Mall Why, you may find it, sir, in th' Christcross row.
Sir Ralph Be my schoolmistress, teach me how to spell it
Mall No, faith, I care not greatly, if I tell it,
My name is Mary Barnes
PORTER *Two Angry Women of Abington,* v, 1 (1599)

The word appears as *Christ-cross, criss-cross,* etc , and Shakespeare shortened it to *cross-row.—*

He hearkens after prophecies and dreams,
And from the cross-row plucks the letter G,
And says a wizard told him that by G
His issue disinherited should be
                                           Richard III, I, i

As the Maltese cross was also sometimes used in place of XII to mark that hour on clocks the word has occasionally been used for noon —

The feskewe of the Diall is upon the Chriss-crosse of Noone —*The Puritan Widow,* iv, 2 (*Anon,* 1607)

Christendom. All Christian countries generally, formerly it also meant the state or condition of being a Christian Thus, in Shakespeare's *King John,* the young prince says:—

By my christendom!
So I were out of prison and kept sheep,
I should be merry as the day is long
                                           Act iv, sc. 1

Christian. A follower of Christ So called first at Antioch (*Acts* xi, 26) Also, the hero of Bunyan's allegory, *Pilgrim's Progress* He flees from the City of Destruction, and journeys to the Celestial City He starts with a heavy burden on his back, but it falls off when he stands at the foot of the cross

Christian Brothers. A secret society formed in London in the early 16th century to distribute the New Testament in English The name is now better known as that of the teaching congregation of laymen, founded in 1684 by St. John Baptist de la Salle

Most Christian Doctor. John Charlier de Gerson (1363-1429)

Most Christian King. The style of the King of France since 1469, when it was conferred on Louis XI by Pope Paul II Previously to that the title had been given in the 8th century to Pepin le Bref by Pope Stephen III (714-68), and again in the 9th century to Charles le Chauve
Cp. RELIGIOUS

Christiana (kris ti an' ä). The wife of Christian in Pt ii of Bunyan's *Pilgrim's Progress*, who journeyed with her children and Mercy from the City of Destruction some time after her husband.

Christinos. Supporters of the Queen-Regent Christina during the Carlist wars in Spain, 1833-40.

Christmas. December 25th is Christmas Day. In England, from the 7th to as late as the 13th century, the year was reckoned from Christmas Day, but in the 12th century the Anglican Church began the year on March 25th, a practice which was adopted by civilians at the beginning of the 14th century, and which remained in force till the reformation of the calendar in 1752. Thus, the civil, ecclesiastical, and legal year, which was used in all public documents, began on Christmas Day till the end of the 13th century, but the historical year had, for a very long time before then, begun on January 1st

Christmas box. A small gratuity given on Boxing Day (the day after Christmas Day) Boxes placed in churches for casual offerings used to be opened on Christmas Day, and the contents, called the "dole of the Christmas box," or the "box money," were distributed next day by the priests Apprentices used, also, to carry a box round to their masters' customers for small gratuities.

Christmas cards. These are of comparatively recent origin, the earliest having, it is said, been designed in 1844 by W C T Dobson, R A , a painter of pretty works of that nature

Christmas decorations. The great feast of Saturn was held in December, when the people decorated the temples with such green things as they could find The Christian custom is the same transferred to Him who was born in Bethlehem on Christmas Day. The holly or holy-tree is called Christ's-thorn in Germany and Scandinavia, from its use in church decorations and its putting forth its berries about Christmas time The early Christians gave an emblematic turn to the custom, referring to the "righteous branch," and justifying the custom from *Isaiah* lx, 13— "The glory of Lebanon shall come unto thee, the fir-tree, the pine-tree, and the box together, to beautify the place of my sanctuary."

The custom of having a Christmas tree decorated with candles and hung with presents came to England with the craze for German things that followed Queen Victoria's marriage to Prince Albert of Saxe-Coburg-Gotha in 1840 Santa Claus (whose name has not even yet become anglicized) with his reindeer had been unknown until then.

Christopher, St. Legend relates that St Christopher was a giant who one day carried a child over a brook, and said, "Chylde, thou hast put me in grete peryll I might bere no greater burden." To which the child answered, "Marvel thou nothing, for thou hast borne all the world upon thee, and its sins likewise " This is an allegory: Christopher means *Christ-bearer*, the *child* was Christ, and the *river* was the river of death.

Christy Minstrels. For many years the mid-Victorian publics of London and New York were entertained and delighted by the troupe of black-faced minstrels organized by an American, Edwin Christy (1815-62) To the accompaniment of various stage-negro antics they sang plantation songs and cracked innocent jokes with Bones, Sambo, and the rest They were succeeded by the Moore and Burgess, and other troupes of the same genre

Chronicle of Worcester Early in the 12th century a monk of Worcester, named Florence, wrote a chronicle from the creation to the year 1118, when he died The work was carried on until 1141, and it was printed in London in 1592. With all its inevitable defects and errors it serves as a key to the Saxon chronicle.

Chronicle small beer, To. To note down events of no importance whatsoever

> She was a wight, if ever such wight were .
> To suckle fools and chronicle small beer.
> SHAKESPEARE. *Othello*, ii, 1

Chronogram. A sentence or inscription in which certain letters stand for a date or epoch In this double Chronogram upon the year 1642, (one part in Latin and the other in the English of that Latin) the capitals in each produce the total of 1642

JV DeVs IaM propItIVs sIs regI regnoqVe
 hVIC VnIVerso
O goD noVV sheVV faVoVr to the kIng
 anD thIs VVhoLe LanD.

| VDVIMIIVIIVVICVIV | 1642. |
| DVVVVVVIDIVVLLD | 1642. |

Chronon-hoton-thologos (krō' non hŏ' tonthol' ō gos) A burlesque pomposo, King of Queerummania, in Henry Carey's farce of the same name—"the most tragical tragedy ever tragedized"—(1734) The name is used for any bombastic person who delivers an inflated address. *See* ALDIBORONTEPHOSCOPHORNIO.

Chrysippus. *Nisi Chrysippus fuisset, Porticus non esset* Chrysippus of Soli was a disciple of Zeno the Stoic and Cleanthes, his successor He did for the Stoics what St Paul did for Christianity—that is, he explained the system, showed by plausible reasoning its truth, and how it was based on a solid foundation Stoicism was founded by Zeno; but if Chrysippus had not advocated it, it would never have taken root

Chum. A crony, a familiar companion, properly a bedfellow. The word first appeared in the 17th century, its origin has not been ascertained

To chum in with. To be on very intimate and friendly terms with.

Church. This is the A S *circe*, or *clrice*, which comes through W Ger *kirika*, from Gr. *kuriakon*, a church, the neuter of the adjective *kuriakos*, meaning of, or belonging to, the Lord

The Anglican Church. Since the Reformation the English branch of the Protestant Church which, since 1532, has been known as the "Established Church of England," because established by Act of Parliament. It disavows the authority of the Pope, and rejects certain dogmas and rules of the Roman Church

The Catholic Church The Western Church called itself so when it separated from the Eastern Church It is also called the Roman Catholic Church, to distinguish it from the Anglican Church or Anglican Catholic Church, a branch of the Western Church.

The Established Church. The State Church, the Church officially recognized and adopted by any country. In England it is Episcopalian (*see* ANGLICAN CHURCH *above*), in Scotland Presbyterian, but in Wales, since the disestablishment of the Church of England in Wales by Act of Parliament in 1920, there is no Established Church.

Church of North America (Episcopalian) established November 1784, when Bishop Seabury, chosen by the Churches of Connecticut, was consecrated in Scotland The first convention was held at Philadelphia in 1787.

Church of Scotland. *See* PRESBYTERIAN, which became the established religion of Scotland on the abolition of Episcopacy in 1638. The head of the Church is the Moderator, and it is regulated by four Courts: the General Assembly, Synod, Presbytery, and Kirk Sessions

Church-ale. The word "ale" is used in such composite words as *bride-ale, clerk-ale, church-ale, lamb-ale, Midsummer-ale, Scot-ale, Whitsun-ale*, etc , for revel or feast, ale being the chief liquor given.

The multitude call Church-ale Sunday their revelyng day, which day is spent in bulbeatings, bearbeating... dicyng, and drunkenness —W KETHE (1570)

The Church Invisible. Those who are known to God alone as His sons and daughters by adoption and grace *See* CHURCH VISIBLE

There is . a Church visible and a Church invisible the latter consists of those spiritual persons who fulfil the notion of the Ideal Church—the former is the Church as it exists in any particular age, embracing within it all who profess Christianity — F W. ROBERTSON *Sermons* (series IV, 11)

The Church Militant. The Church as consisting of the whole body of believers, who are said to be "waging the war of faith" against "the world, the flesh, and the devil " It is therefore militant, or in warfare.

Church scot. A tribute paid on St Martin's Day (November 11th) in support of the clergy in Anglo-Saxon times It was originally paid in corn, but later other goods in kind, or money, were taken.

The Church Triumphant. Those who are dead and gone to their rest Having fought the fight and triumphed, they belong to the Church triumphant in heaven

The Church Visible. All ostensible Christians; all who profess to be Christians, all who have been baptized and admitted into Church Communion. *Cp* CHURCH INVISIBLE,

The Seven Churches of Asia. *See* SEVEN.

To church a woman To read the appointed service when a woman comes to church after a confinement to return thanks to God for her "safe deliverance" and restored health.

To go into the Church. To take holy orders, or become an "ordained" clergyman

Churchwarden. A long clay pipe, such as churchwardens used to smoke a century or so ago when they met together in the parish tavern, after they had made up their accounts in the vestry, or been elected to office at the Easter meeting

Churchyard cough A deep, chesty cough which sounds like a presage of death

Churrigueresque (chu rig er esk´) Overornate, as applied to architecture The word, frequently used by Richard Ford (1796-1858) in his writings on Spain, derives from Jose Churriguera (1650-1723) a Spanish architect of the baroque school.

Ci-devant (sē de vong) (Fr) Former, of times gone by As *Ci-devant governor*—i e once a governor, but no longer so *Ci-devant philosophers* means philosophers of former days In the time of the first French Republic the word was used as a noun, and meant a nobleman of the *ancien régime*.

Cicero (sis´ er ō). The great Roman orator, philosopher, and statesman (106-43 B C), Marcus Tullius, said by Plutarch to have been called *Cicero* from Lat *cicer* (a wart or vetch), because he had "a flat excrescence on the tip of his nose "

La Bouche de Ciceron. Philippe Pot, prime minister of Louis XI (1428-94).

The Cicero of France Jean Baptiste Massillon (1663-1742), a noted pulpit orator.

The Cicero of Germany. Johann III, elector of Brandenburg. (1455-99)

The Cicero of the British Senate. George Canning (1770-1827)

The British Cicero. William Pitt, Earl of Chatham (1708-78)

The Christian Cicero. Lucius Coelius Lactantius, a Christian father, who died about 330

The German Cicero. Johann Sturm, printer and scholar (1507-89)

Cicerone. A guide to point out objects of interest to strangers So called from the great orator Cicero, in the same way as Paul was called by the men of Lystra "Mercurius, because he was the chief speaker."

Cicisbeo (chich is bä' ō)   A dangler about women, the professed gallant of a married woman   *Cp* CAVALIERE SERVENTE   Also the knot of silk or ribbon which is attached to fans, walking-sticks, umbrellas, etc   *Cicisbeism*, the practice of dangling about women.

Cid (sid)   A corruption of *seyyid*, Arabic for *lord*   The title given to Roderigo or Ruy Diaz de Bivar (born about 1040, died 1099), also called El Campeador, the national hero of Spain and champion of Christianity against the Moors   His exploits, real and legendary, form the basis of many Spanish romances and chronicles, as well as Corneille's tragedy, *Le Cid* (1636)

Cid Hamet Benengeli.   The supposititious author upon whom Cervantes fathered *The Adventures of Don Quixote*
Of the two bad cassocks I am worth . I would have given the latter of them as freely as even Cid Hamet offered his   to have stood by —STERNE

Cigars and Cigarettes.   The word *cigar* comes from *cicada*, the Spanish cigar-shaped beetle   The natives of Cuba were already smoking tobacco in this form when the white men first invaded their country   Cigars as we know them were introduced into U S A by General Putnam, in 1762, on his return from the capture of Havana by the Earl of Albemarle, and this fashion of smoking soon spread to Europe. Cheroots (from the Tamil *shuruttu*, a roll) are made from tobacco grown in S India or the Philippines, and are merely rolled, with the ends cut square.
Cigarettes originated in Spain (Borrow called them paper cigars, and the Spanish call them *cigarillos*, little cigars), and at first were rolled by the smoker as he needed them It was not until the late 19th century that they were sold rolled and in packets   Even ready-made cigarettes in Spain to-day are designed to be untwisted at the ends and re-rolled before smoking.

Cimmerian Darkness (si mēr' i ân)   Homer (possibly from some story as to the Arctic night) supposes the Cimmerians to dwell in a land "beyond the ocean stream," where the sun never shone   (*Odys* , xi, 14)
I carried am into waste wildernesse,
Waste wildernes, amongst Cymerian shades,
Where endles paines and hideous heavinesse,
Is round about me heapt in darksome glades
SPENSER *Virgil s Gnat*
In dark Cimmerian desert ever dwell
MILTON *L'Allegro.*

The Cimmerians were known in post-Homeric times as an historical people on the shores of the Black Sea, whence the name *Crimea*

Cinch (sinch)   This word, which comes from the Spanish, is the term used in western U S A for the strong leather or canvas girth of a saddle or pack.   From that it came to mean a tight grip, and by an easy transition a sure thing, a safe proposition

Cinchona (sin chō' na) or *Quinine*   So named from the wife of the Conte del Chinchon, viceroy of Peru, who was cured of a tertian fever by its use, and who brought it to Europe in 1640   Linnæus erroneously named it

Cinchona for *Chinchona*   *See* PERUVIAN BARK

Cincinnatus (sin si nä 'tus)   A legendary Roman hero of about 500 to 430 B.C , who, after having been consul years before, was taken from his plough to be Dictator.   After he had conquered the Æquians and delivered his country from danger, he laid down his office and returned to his plough
The Cincinnatus of the Americans.   George Washington (1732-99).

The Cincinnati were members of a society of officers of the American Army after the peace of 1783 "to perpetuate friendship, and to raise a fund for relieving the widows and orphans of those who have fallen during the war."   On their badge was a figure of Cincinnatus   The society dissolved itself, as it was regarded with suspicion by the populace
The Ohio city of this name, originally called Losantiville, was rechristened in 1790 in honour of Gen St Clair, governor of the North West Territory, who was president of the society of Cincinnati.

Cinderella (sin der rel' a)   Heroine of a fairy tale of very ancient, probably Eastern, origin, that was mentioned in German literature in the 16th century and was popularized by Perrault s *Contes de ma mère l'oye* (1697) Cinderella is drudge of the house, dirty with housework, while her elder sisters go to fine balls   At length a fairy enables her to go to the prince's ball, the prince falls in love with her, and she is discovered by means of a glass slipper which she drops, and which will fit no foot but her own
The *glass* slipper is a mistranslation of *pantoufle en vair* (a fur, or sable, slipper), not *en verre*   Sable was worn only by kings and princes, so the fairy gave royal slippers to her favourite.

Cinquecento (ching' kwè chen' tō)   The Italian name for the sixteenth century (1501-1600), applied as an epithet to art and literature with much the same significance as Renaissance or Elizabethan   It was the revival of the classical or antique, but is generally understood as a derogatory term, implying debased or inferior art.

Cinque Ports, The.   Originally the five sea-ports, Hastings, Sandwich, Dover, Romney, and Hythe, which were granted special privileges from the 13th to the 17th centuries, and even later, in consideration of their providing ships and men for the defence of the Channel   Subsequently Winchelsea and Rye were added.

Cinter (sin' ter)   This is frequently confused with the word "centre," though it comes from the same original as the French *ceinture*, a girdle   A cinter, or cintre, is the wooden shape on which an arch is built.

Cipher   This word comes from the Arabic *cifr*, meaning zero, naught   Through various ways it has come to be used for a message so set forth on paper as to be comprehensible only to one acquainted with that particular and secret system of writing   The simplest cipher is that once employed by Julius Cæsar, who used certain letters in place of the right ones, *e g d* for *a*, *e* for *b*, and so on through the alphabet Later ciphers used numbers or invented characters to replace letters. In more recent years the most complicated systems of ciphering have come into use by spies, diplomatic observers, etc., but experts claim that no cipher has yet been invented that cannot be "broken down" by close study and the application of certain recognized methods

Circe (sĕr' sı) A sorceress in Greek mythology, who lived in the island of Ææa When Ulysses landed there, Circe turned his companions into swine, but Ulysses resisted this metamorphosis by virtue of a herb called *moly* (*q.v*), given him by Mercury

> Who knows not Circe,
> The daughter of the Sun, whose charmed cup
> Whoever tasted lost his upright shape,
> And downward fell into a grovelling swine?
> MILTON· *Comus*, 50-53

Circle. Great circle. Navigation, whether on the sea or in the air, is principally done with the aid of a great circle This is a line on the earth's surface which lies in a plane through the centre of the earth, or any circle on the earth's surface which divides the world into two equal parts. The shortest line between any two points on the earth's surface is on a great circle, hence the ascertaining of great circles is of the utmost importance in nautical or aerial navigation

Circle of Ulloa. A white rainbow or luminous ring sometimes seen in Alpine regions opposite the sun in foggy weather. Named from Antonio de Ulloa (1716-95), a Spanish naval officer who founded the observatory at Cadiz and initiated many scientific enterprises

Circuit. The journey made through the counties of Great Britain by the judges twice a year There are six circuits in England, two in Wales, and three in Scotland Those in England are called the South-Eastern, Midland, Northern, North-Eastern, Oxford, and Western Circuit, those of Wales, the North Wales and Chester, and the South Wales Division, and those of Scotland, the Southern, Western, and Northern.

Circumlocution Office. A term applied in ridicule by Dickens in *Little Dorrit* to our public offices, because each person tries to shuffle off every act to someone else, and before anything is done it has to pass through so many departments and so much time elapses that it is hardly worth having bothered about it

> Whatever was required to be done, the Circumlocution Office was beforehand with all the public departments in the art of perceiving—How not to do it —DICKENS *Little Dorrit*, ch x

Cist (kıst) (Gr. *kıste*, Lat *cısta*) A chest or box Generally used as a coffer for the remains of the dead The Greek and Roman cist was a deep cylindrical basket made of wickerwork The basket into which voters cast their tablets was called a "cist", but the mystic cist used in the rites of Ceres was latterly made of bronze. *Cp* KIST OF WHISTLES

Cistercians. A monastic order, founded at Cistercium or Citeaux by Robert, abbot of Molême, in Burgundy, in 1098, as a branch of the Benedictines, the monks are known also as *Bernardines*, owing to the patronage of St Bernard of Clairvaux about 1200 In 1664 the order was reformed on an excessively strict basis by Jean le Boutillier de Rance

Citadel (Ital *cıtadella*, a little city) In fortification, a small strong fort, constructed either within the place fortified, or at its most inaccessible spot, to give refuge for the garrison, that it may prolong the defence after the place has fallen, or hold out for the best terms of capitulation Citadels generally command the interior of the place, and are useful, therefore, for overawing a population which might otherwise strive to shorten a siege

Citizen King, The. Louis Philippe of France So called because he was elected King of the French (not king of France) by the citizens of Paris (Born 1773, reigned 1830-48, died 1850)

City. Strictly speaking, a large town with a corporation and cathedral; but any large town is so called in ordinary speech In the Bible it means a town having walls and gates

> The eldest son of the first man [Cain] builded a city (Gen. iv, 17)—not, of course, a Nineveh or a Babylon, but still a city —RAWLINSON *Origin of Nations*, pt. i, ch i

The City of a Hundred Towers. Pavia, in Italy, famous for its towers and steeples

The City College. An old irony. Newgate

The City of Bells. Strasburg

The City of Brotherly Love. A somewhat ironical, but quite etymological, nickname of Philadelphia (Gr *philadelphia* means "brotherly love").

The City of David. Jerusalem. So called in compliment to King David (2 *Sam* v, 7, 9)

The City of Destruction. In Bunyan's *Pilgrim's Progress*, the world of the unconverted

The City of God. The Church, or whole body of believers, the kingdom of Christ, in contradistinction to the City of Destruction (*q v*) The phrase is that of St Augustine, one of his chief works bearing the title, *De Civitate Dei*

The City of Lanterns. A supposititious city in Lucian's *Veræ Historiæ*, situate somewhere beyond the zodiac *Cp*. LANTERN-LAND

The City of Legions. Caerleon-on-Usk, where King Arthur held his court.

The City of Lilies. Florence

The City of Magnificent Distances. Washinton, D C , famous for its wide avenues and splendid vistas

The City of Palaces Agrippa, in the reign of Augustus, converted Rome from "a city of brick huts to one of marble palaces "

> Marmoream se relinquere quam latericiam accepisset —SUETONIUS *Aug* xxix

Calcutta is called the "City of Palaces "

City of Refuge. Moses, at the command of God, set apart three cities on the east of Jordan, and Joshua added three others on the west, whither any person might flee for refuge who had killed a human creature inadvertently The three on the east of Jordan were Bezer, Ramoth, and Golan, the three on the west were Hebron, Shechem, and Kedesh (*Deut.* IV, 43, *Josh* XX, 1-8).

By Mohammedans, Medina, in Arabia, where Mohammed took refuge when driven by conspirators from Mecca, is known as "the City of Refuge" He entered it, not as a fugitive, but in triumph 622 A D Also called the *City of the Prophet.*

The City of St. Michael. Dumfries, of which city St Michael is the patron saint

The City of Saints. Montreal, in Canada, is so named because all the streets are named after saints Salt Lake City, Utah, U S A, also is known as the "City of the Saints," from the Mormons who inhabit it

The Cities of the Plain. Sodom and Gomorrah

Abram dwelled in the land of Canaan, and Lot dwelled in the cities of the plain, and pitched his tent toward Sodom —*Gen* XIII, 12

The City of the Golden Gate. San Francisco. *See* GOLDEN GATE

The City of the Prophet. Medina *See* CITY OF REFUGE

The City of the Seven Hills. Rome, built on seven hills (*Urbs septacollis*) The hills are the Aventine Cælian, Capitoline, Esquiline, Palatine, Quirinal, and Viminal.

The AVENTINE HILL was given to the people It was deemed unlucky, because here Remus was slain It was also called "Collis Dianæ," from the Temple of Diana which stood there

The CÆLIAN HILL was given to Cælius Vibenna, the Tuscan, who came to the help of the Romans in the Sabine war.

The CAPITOLINE HILL or "Mons Tarpeius," also called "Mons Saturni," on which stood the great castle or capitol of Rome It contained the Temple of Jupiter Capitolinus

The ESQUILINE HILL was given by Augustus to Mecænas, who built thereon a magnificent mansion.

The PALATINE HILL was the largest of the seven. Here Romulus held his court, whence the word "palace" (*palatium*)

The QUIRINAL HILL was where the Quirés or Curés settled It was also called "Cabalinus," from two marble statues of a horse, one of which was the work of Phidias, the other of Praxiteles

The VIMINAL HILL was so called from the number of osiers (*vimnes*) which grew there It contained the Temple of Jupiter Viminalis

The City of the Sun Baalbec, Rhodes, and Heliopolis, which had the sun for tutelary deity, were so called. It is also the name of a treatise on the Ideal Republic by the Dominican friar Campanella (1568-1639), similar to the *Republic* of Plato, *Utopia* of Sir Thomas More, and *Atlantis* of Bacon.

The City of the Three Kings Cologne; the reputed burial-place of the Magi (*q v.*).

The City of the Tribes. Galway, because it was anciently the home of the thirteen "tribes" or chief families, who settled there in 1232 with Richard de Burgh.

The City of the Violated Treaty. Limerick; because of the way in which the Pacification of Limerick (1691) was broken by England

The City of the Violet Crown. Athens is so called by Aristophanes (ἰοστέφανοξ)— *Equites*, 1323 and 1329, and *Acharnians*, 637. Macaulay refers to Athens as the "violet-crowned city." Ion (a violet) was a representative king of Athens whose four sons gave names to the four Athenian classes, and Greece, in Asia Minor, was called Ionia Athens was the city of "Ion crowned its king" or "of the Violet crowned."

Civic Crown *See* CROWN.

Civil List. The grant voted annually by Parliament to pay the personal expenses of the Sovereign, the household expenses, and the pensions awarded by Royal bounty, before the reign of William III it embraced all public expenditure, except that on the army and navy.

Civil Service Estimates. The annual Parliamentary grant to cover the expenses of the diplomatic services, the post office and telegraphs, education, the collection of revenue, and other expenses neither pertaining to the Sovereign nor the armed services,

Civil war. War between citizens (*civiles*). In English history the term is applied to the war between Charles I and his Parliament, but the War of the Roses was a civil war also. In America, the War of Secession (1861-65).

Civis Romanus sum (siv' is rō mā' nus sŭm) "I am a Roman citizen," a plea which sufficed to arrest arbitrary condemnation, bonds, and scourging Hence, when the centurion commanded Paul "to be examined by scourging," he asked, "Is it lawful for you to *scourge* a Roman citizen, and *uncondemned*?" (1) No Roman citizen could be condemned unheard, (2) by the Valerian Law he could not be bound, (3) by the Sempronian Law it was forbidden to *scourge* him, or to beat him with rods *See also Acts* XVI, 37, etc.

The phrase later gained an English fame from the peroration of Palmerston's greatest speech, in 1850 "As the Roman, in days of old, held himself free from indignity when he could say *Civis Romanus sum*, so also a British subject, in whatever land he may be, shall feel confident that the watchful eye and the strong arm of England will protect him against injustice and wrong."

Civvie Street (siv' i) In the 1939-45 War this was the term by which men in the Services referred to civilian life

Clabber Napper's Hole. Near Gravesend; said to be named after a freebooter, but more likely the Celtic *Caerber l'arber* (water-town lower camp).

Clack Dish. A dish or basin with a movable lid Some two or three centuries ago beggars used to proclaim their want by clacking the lid of a wooden dish.

Can you think, I get my living by a bell and clack-dish? . . . How's that?
Why, begging, sir
      MIDDLETON *Family of Love* (1608).

Clam. A bivalve mollusc like an oyster, which burrows in sand or mud In America especially clams are esteemed as a delicacy. They are gathered only when the tide is out, hence the saying, "Happy as a clam at high tide " The word is also used as slang for the mouth, and for a close-mouthed person

Close as a clam. Mean, close-fisted, from the difficulty with which a clam is made to open its shell and give up all it has worth having.

Clan The system whereby the head of the family, or clan, had entire jurisdiction over its members is said to have arisen in Scotland in the early 11th century The legal power and hereditary jurisdiction of the head of a clan was abolished in 1747, following the '45 rebellion Nevertheless the heads of certain clans, notably McLeod, still exercise considerable authority over their members and hold punctiliously attended gatherings The phrase **a gathering of the clans** has been taken into slang use to imply any coming together of like-minded persons, usually for convivial purposes.

Clan-na-Gael, The (klän nå gāl') An Irish Fenian organization founded in Philadelphia in 1881, and known in secret as the "United Brotherhood", its avowed object being to secure "the complete and absolute independence of Ireland from Great Britain, and the complete severance of all political connexion between the two countries, to be effected by unceasing preparation for armed insurrection in Ireland."

Clapboard. From Ger. *klappholz* (*holz*, wood), meaning small pieces of split oak used by coopers for cask staves. In the U S A. a roofing board, made thin at one edge and overlapping the next one, a weatherboard.

In England the word was formerly used by coopers in the same way as in Germany, and also for wainscoting

Clapperclaw. To jangle, to claw or scratch; to abuse, revile, originally meaning to claw with a clapper of some sort.

Now they are clapper-clawing one another; I'll go look on —SHAKESPEARE *Troilus and Cressida,* v. 4

Clapper-dudgeons. Abram-men (*q v.*), beggars from birth The *clapper* is the tongue of a bell, and in cant language the human tongue *Dudgeon* is the hilt of a dagger; and perhaps the original meaning is one who knocks his *clap dish* (or CLACK DISH, *q v*) with a dudgeon

Clap-trap. Something introduced to win applause, something really worthless, but sure to take with the groundlings A *trap* to catch applause

Claque (klåk) A body of hired applauders at a theatre, etc.; said to have been originated or first systematized by a M. Sauton, who, in 1820, established in Paris an office to ensure the success of dramatic pieces. The manager ordered the required number of *claqueurs*, who were divided into *commissaires*, those who commit the pieces to memory and are noisy in pointing out its merits, *rieurs*, who laugh at the puns and jokes, *pleureurs*, chiefly women, who are to hold their pocket-handkerchiefs to

their eyes at the moving parts, *chatouilleurs*, who are to keep the audience in good humour, and *bisseurs*, who are to cry ' bis " (encore).

Claque is also the French for an opera-hat, and Thackeray uses it with this sense :—

A gentleman in black with ringlets and a tuft stood gazing fiercely about him, with one hand in the armhole of his waistcoat and the other holding his claque. —*Pendennis,* ch xxv

Clare, Order of St. A religious order of women, the second that St Francis instituted. It was founded in 1212, and took its name from its first abbess, Clara of Assisi The nuns are called Minoresses and Poor Clares, or Nuns of the order of St Francis. *See* FRANCISCANS.

Clarenceux King-of-Arms (klär' en sū) The second in rank of the three English Kings-of-Arms (*q v*) attached to the Heralds' College (*q.v.*) His jurisdiction extends over the counties east, west, and south of the Trent. The name was taken in honour of the Duke of Clarence, third son of Edward III

Clarendon. The Constitutions of Clarendon. Laws made by a general council of nobles and prelates, held at Clarendon, in Wiltshire, in 1164, to check the power of the Church, and restrain the prerogatives of ecclesiastics. These famous ordinances, sixteen in number, define the limits of the patronage and jurisdiction of the Pope in these realms

Clarendon type. A bold-faced, condensed type, such as that used for the "catch-words" which head these articles

Claret. The English name for the red wines of Bordeaux, originally the yellowish or light red wines as distinguished from the white wines. The name—which is not used in France—is the O.Fr. *claret*, diminutive of *clair*, from Lat. *clarus*, clear. The *colour* receives its name from the *wine*, not vice versa.

Claret cup. A drink made of claret, brandy, lemon, borage sugar, ice, and carbonated water

To broach one's claret, or to tap one's claret jug. To give one a bloody nose.

Clarke. Nobby Clarke is the British Army name for every man of the name of Clarke. It originated in the dressy—or "nobby"—turn-out affected by clerks and other black-coat workers in the early 19th century.

Classics. The best authors The Romans were divided by Servius into five classes. Any citizen who belonged to the highest class was called *classicus,* all the rest were said to be *infra classem* (unclassed) From this the best authors were termed *classici auctores* (classic authors), *i e.* authors of the best or first class. The high esteem in which Greek and Latin were held at the revival of letters obtained for these authors the name of classic, emphatically; and when other first-rate works are intended some distinctive name is added, as the English, French, Spanish, etc, classics

Classic Races. The five chief horse-races in England, all for three-year-olds, are The One Thousand Guineas, for fillies only, and the Two Thousand Guineas, for fillies and colts, both run at Newmarket The Oaks, for fillies only, and the Derby, for fillies and colts, both run at Epsom The St. Leger, for fillies and colts, run at Doncaster

Claude Lorraine (i e of Lorraine) This incorrect form is generally used in English for the name of Claude Gelée (1600-82), the French landscape painter, born at Chamagne, in Lorraine

Clause Rolls. See CLOSE ROLLS

Clavie. Burning of the Clavie on New Year's Eve (old style) in the village of Burghead, on the southern shore of the Moray Firth The clavie is a sort of bonfire made of casks split up One of the casks is split into two parts of different sizes, and an important item of the ceremony is to join these parts together with a huge nail made for the purpose Whence the name, from *clavus* (Lat), a nail Chambers, who in his *Book of Days* (vol ii, p. 789) minutely describes the ceremony, suggests that it is a relic of Druid worship The two unequal divisions of the cask probably symbolize the unequal parts of the old and new year.

Claw. The sharp, hooked nail of bird or beast, or the foot of an animal armed with claws. *To claw* is to lay one's hands upon things; to clutch, to tear or scratch as with claws, formerly it also meant to stroke, to tickle, hence to please, flatter, or praise Thus *Claw me I will claw thee*, means, "praise me, and I will praise you," or, "scratch my back, and I'll scratch yours "
> Laugh when I am merry, and claw no man in his humour —SHAKESPEARE *Much Ado*, i, 3

Claw-backs. Flatterers Bishop Jewel speaks of "the Pope's claw-backs "

Clay, Feet of An unexpected flaw in the character of an admired person. The phrase arises from the image in Nebuchadnezzar's dream, (*Daniel* ii, 31, 32) of which the head was of gold, the breast and arms of silver, the belly and thighs of brass, the legs of iron, and the feet of iron and clay

Claymore. The two-edged sword anciently used by Scottish Highlanders, from Gaelic *claidheamh* (a sword), and *mor* (great)
> I've told thee how the Southrons fell
> Beneath the broad claymore.
> AYTOUN *Execution of Montrose*

Clean Free from blame or fault.
> Create in me a clean heart, O God, and renew a right spirit within me —*Psalm* li, 10

Used adverbially, it means entirely, wholly; as, "you have grown clean out of knowledge," i e. wholly beyond recognition
> Contricioun hadde clene forgeten to crye and to wepe
> PIERS PLOWMAN, xx.
> The people . . passed clean over Jordan
> *Joshua* iii, 17

A clean tongue. Not abusive, not profane, not foul.

Cleanliness is next to godliness An old saying, quoted by John Wesley (*Sermon* xcii, *On Dress*), Matthew Henry, and others The origin is said to be found in the writings of Phinehas ben Yair, an ancient Hebrew rabbi

To clean down. To sweep down, to swill down.

To clean out. To purify, to make tidy. Also, to win another's money till his pocket is quite empty; to impoverish him of everything. De Quincey says that Richard Bentley, after his lawsuit with Dr Colbatch, "must have been pretty well cleaned out "

To clean up. To wash up, to put in order, to wash oneself

To have clean hands To be quite clear of some stated evil Hence *to keep the hands clean*, not to be involved in wrong-doing; and "clean-handed",—
> He that hath clean hands and a pure heart
> *Psalm* xxiv, 4

To live a clean life. To live blameless and undefiled

To make a clean breast of it. To make a full and unreserved confession

To show a clean bill of health See BILL

To show a clean pair of heels. To make one's escape by superior speed, to run away Here " clean " means free from obstruction

Clean and unclean animals. Among the ancient Jews (*see Lev* xi) those animals which chew the cud and part the hoof were clean, and might be eaten Hares and rabbits could not be eaten because (although they chew the cud) they do not part the hoof Pigs and camels were unclean, because (although they part the hoof) they do not chew the cud Birds of prey were accounted unclean Fish with fins and scales were accounted fit food for man

According to Pythagoras, who taught the doctrine of the transmigration of the soul, it was lawful for man to eat only those animals into which the human soul never entered, and those into which the human soul did not enter were unclean or not fit for human food This notion existed long before the time of Pythagoras, who learnt it in Egypt

Clear (verb). **To be quite cleared out.** To have spent all one's money, to have not a farthing left *Cleared out* means, my purse or pocket is cleared out of money.

To clear an examination paper To floor it, or answer every question set.

To clear away. To remove, to melt away, to disappear

To clear for action. The same as "to clear the decks " See below

To clear off. To make oneself scarce, to remove oneself or something else

To clear out. To eject, to empty out, to make tidy

To clear out for Guam. A now forgotten shipping phrase, used when a ship is bound for no specific place In the height of the gold fever, ships carried passengers to Australia without making arrangements for return cargoes. They were, therefore, obliged to leave Melbourne in ballast, and to sail in search of homeward freights The Custom House regulations required, however, that, on clearing outwards, some port should be named, and it became the habit of captains to name

"Guam" (a small island of the Ladrone group) as the hypothetical destination Hence, the phrase meant to clear out for just anywhere.

To clear the air To remove the clouds, mists, and impurities, figuratively, to remove the misunderstandings or ambiguities of a situation, argument, etc

To clear the court. To remove all strangers, or persons not officially concerned in the suit.

To clear the decks. To prepare for action by removing everything not required, playfully used of eating everything eatable on the dinner-table, etc.

To clear the dishes. To empty them of their contents

To clear the land. A nautical phrase meaning to have good sea room

To clear the room. To remove from it every thing or person not required

To clear the table. To remove what has been placed on it

To clear up. To become fine after rain or cloudiness, to make manifest, to elucidate what was obscure; to tidy up.

Clear (the adjective). Used adverbially, *clear* has much the same force as the adverb *clean* (*q v*)—wholly, entirely, as, "He is gone clear away," "Clear out of sight."

A clear day. An entire, complete day "The bonds must be left three clear days for examination," means that they must be left for three days not counting the first or the last

A clear head. A mind that is capable of understanding things clearly

A clear statement. A straightforward and intelligible statement.

A clear style (of writing) A lucid method of expressing one's thoughts.

A clear voice A voice of pure intonation, neither husky, mouthy, nor throaty

Clear grit. The right spirit, real pluck; also the genuine article, the real thing Originally a piece of American slang

In Canadian politics the name *Clear-grits* was given in the early 80s of last century to the Radicals

Clearing house The office or house where bankers do their 'clearing," that is, the exchanging of bills and cheques and the payment of balances, etc Also, the house where the business of dividing among the different railway companies the proceeds of traffic passing over several lines for one covering payment was carried through In London, the bankers' clearing house has been in Lombard Street since 1775 Each bank sends to it daily all the bills and cheques not drawn on its own firm, these are sorted and distributed to their respective houses, and the balance is settled by transfer tickets

A "clearing banker" is a banker who has the *entrée* of the clearing house

London has become the clearing-house of the whole world, the place where international debts are exchanged against each other And something like 5,000 million pounds'-worth of checks and bills pass that clearing yearly —A C PERRY *Elements of Political Economy*, p 363.

Cleave Two quite distinct words, the one meaning to *stick to*, and the other to *part from* or to *part asunder* A man "shall cleave to his wife" (*Matt* xix, 5) As one that "cleaveth wood" (*Ps* cxli, 7) The former is the A.S *clifian*, to stick to, and the latter is *cleofan*, to split

Clement, St. Patron saint of tanners, being himself a tanner. His day is November 23rd, and his symbol is an anchor, because he is said to have been martyred by being thrown into the sea tied to an anchor

Clench and Clinch. The latter is a variant of the former, which is the M.E. *clenchen*, from A S (*be-*)*clencan*, to hold fast In many uses the two words are practically synonymous, meaning to grasp firmly, to fasten firmly together, to make firm, but *clench* is used in such phrases as "he clenched his fists," "he clenched his nerves bravely to endure the pain," "to clench one's teeth", while *clinch* is used in the more material senses, such as to turn the point of a nail in order to make it fast, and also in the phrase "to clinch an argument" In business, " to clinch a deal " is to ratify it, to make it certain

That was a clincher. That argument was not to be gainsaid, that remark drove the matter home, and fixed it

Cleopatra (klē ō pät′ rā) (69-30 B C) She was Queen of Egypt, being joint ruler with and wife of her brother Ptolemy Dionysius. In 48 B C she was ousted from the throne but in 47 was reinstated by Julius Cæsar, who was captivated by her charms In 41 Mark Antony fell under her spell and repudiated his wife Octavia for her sake Fighting with Octavian, Mark Antony was defeated at Actium and committed suicide Cleopatra also killed herself by means of the bite of an asp

Cleopatra and her pearl. It is said that Cleopatra made a banquet for Antony, the costliness of which excited his astonishment, and, when Antony expressed his surprise, Cleopatra took a pearl ear-drop, which she dissolved in a strong acid, and drank to the health of the Roman triumvir, saying, "My draught to Antony shall far exceed it " There are two difficulties in this anecdote—the first is, that vinegar would not dissolve a pearl; and the next is, that any stronger acid would be wholly unfit to drink

A similar story has been told of Sir Thomas Gresham It is said that when Queen Elizabeth visited the Royal Exchange he pledged her health in a cup of wine in which a precious stone worth £15,000 had been crushed to atoms Heywood refers to this in his play *If you know not me you know nobody* (1604)—

Here fifteen thousand pounds at one clap goes
Instead of sugar, Gresham drinks the pearl
Unto his queen and mistress

Cleopatra's Needle. The obelisk so called, now in London on the Thames Embankment, was brought there in 1878 from Alexandria, whither it and its fellow (now in Central Park, New York) had been moved from Heliopolis by Augustus about 12 B C It has no connexion with Cleopatra, and it has carved on it hieroglyphics that tell of its erection by Thothmes III, a Pharaoh of the 18th dynasty who lived many centuries before her time.

Cleopatra's nose. It was Blaise Pascal (1623-62) who said, "If the nose of Cleopatra had been shorter, the whole face of the earth would have been changed" (*Pensées* VIII, 29); the allusion, of course, being to the tremendous results brought about by her enslavement through her charm and beauty, first of Julius Cæsar and then of Mark Antony

Clergy. Ultimately from Gr *kleros*, a lot or inheritance, with reference to *Deut* XVIII, 2, and *Acts* I, 17, thus, the men of God's lot or inheritance In St Peter's first epistle (ch v, 3) the Church is called "God's heritage" or lot In the Old Testament the tribe of Levi is called the "lot or heritage of the Lord "

Benefit of Clergy *See* BENEFIT.

Clerical Titles. *Clerk* As in ancient times the clergyman was about the only person who could write and read, the word *clerical*, as used in "clerical error," came to signify an orthographical error As the respondent in church was able to read, he received the name of *clerk*, and the assistants in writing, etc , are so termed in business. (Lat. *clericus*, a clergyman)

Curate One who has the cure of souls As the cure of the parish used to be virtually entrusted to the clerical stipendiary, the word *curate* was appropriated to this assistant

Parson. The same word as *person* As Blackstone says, a parson is *"persona ecclesiæ,* one that hath full rights of the parochial church "

Though we write "parson" differently, yet 'tis but "person", that is the individual person set apart for the service of such a church, and 'tis in Latin *persona*, and *personatus* is a parsonage Indeed with the canon lawyers, *personatus* is any dignity or preferment in the church —SELDEN: *Table-talk*

Rector. One who has the parsonage and great tithes. The man who rules or guides the parish (Lat , a ruler.)

Vicar. One who does the "duty" of a parish for the person who receives the tithes (Lat *vicarius*, a deputy) *Incumbents* and *Perpetual Curates* are now termed Vicars.

The French *cure* equals our vicar, and their *vicaire* our curate.

Clerical vestments. *White.* Emblem of purity, worn on all feasts, saints' days, and sacramental occasions.

Red. The colour of blood and of fire, worn on the days of martyrs and on Whit Sunday, when the Holy Ghost came down like tongues of fire.

Green. Worn only on days which are neither feasts nor fasts.

Purple The colour of mourning, worn on Advent Sundays, in Lent, and on Ember days

Black Worn on Good Friday, and when masses are said for the dead

Clerihew (kler' i hū) The name given to a particular kind of humorous verse invented by E Clerihew Bentley It is usually satirical and often biographical, consisting of four rhymed lines of uneven length. For inclusion in this Dictionary Mr Bentley suggested the following —

> It was a weakness of Voltaire s
> To forget to say his prayers,
> And one which, to his shame
> He never overcame

He also wrote —

> Sir Christopher Wren
> Said, "I'm going to dine with some men
> If anyone calls,
> Say I'm designing St Paul's "

Clerkenwell (klark' en wel) At the holy well in this district the parish clerks of London used to assemble yearly to play some sacred piece

Client. In ancient Rome a *client* was a plebian under the patronage of a patrician, who was therefore his *patron* The client performed certain services, and the patron was obliged to protect his life and interests The word in English means a person who employs the services of a legal adviser to protect his interests

Climacteric (klī māk' ter ik) It was once believed by astrologers that the 7th and 9th years, with their multiples, especially the *odd* multiples (21, 27, 35, 45, 49, 63, and 81), were critical points in life, these were called the *Climacteric Years* and were presided over by Saturn, the malevolent planet 63, which is produced by multiplying 7 and 9 together, was termed the *Grand Climacteric*, which few persons succeeded in out-living.

There are two years, the seventh and the ninth, that commonly bring great changes in a man's life, and great dangers, wherefore 63, that contains both these numbers multiplied together, comes not without heaps of dangers.—*Levinus Lemnius*

Climax means a *ladder* (Gr), and is the rhetorical figure in which the sense rises gradually in a series of images, each exceeding its predecessor in force or dignity Popularly, but erroneously, the word is used to denote the last step in the gradation, the point of highest development.

Clinch, Clincher. *See* CLENCH.

Clinker-built, said of a ship whose planks overlap each other, and are riveted together. The opposite to clinker-built is carvel-built (*q v.*).

Clio (klī' ō) was one of the nine Muses, the inventress of historical and heroic poetry.

Addison adopted the name as a pseudonym, and many of his papers in the *Spectator* are signed by one of the four letters in this word, probably the initial letters where they were written—of Chelsea, London, Islington, Office *Cp.* NOTARIKON.

Clipper. A fast sailing-ship; in Smyth's *Sailor's Word Book* (1867) said to be "formerly applied to the sharp-built raking schooners of America, and latterly to Australian passenger-ships."

The name is now applied almost exclusively to a transatlantic flying-boat.

She's a clipper. Said of a stylish or beautiful woman.

Clippie (klip' i). The name given familiarly to the women bus-conductors during and after World War II

Cliquot (klē' kō) A nickname of Frederick William IV of Prussia (1795-1861), so called from his fondness for champagne

Cloacina (klō a sī' na). Goddess of sewers (Lat. *cloaca*, a sewer)

Then Cloacina, goddess of the tide,
Whose sable streams beneath the city glide,
Indulged the modish flame the town she roved,
A mortal scavenger she saw, she loved
         GAY *Trivia*, ii

Cloak and Sword Plays. Swashbuckling plays, full of fighting and adventure The name comes from the Spanish comedies of the 16th-century dramatists, Lope de Vega and Calderon —the *Commedia de capa y espada*, but whereas with them it signified merely a drama of domestic intrigue and was named from the rank of the chief characters, in France—and, through French influence, in England—it was applied as above.

Knight of the Cloak Sir Walter Raleigh. So called from his throwing his cloak into a puddle for Queen Elizabeth to step on as she was about to enter her barge

Clock So church bells were once called. (Ger *glocke*, Fr. *cloche*, Mediæval Lat *cloca*.)

Clock. The tale about St. Paul's clock striking thirteen is given in Walcott's *Memorials of Westminster*, and refers to John Hatfield, who died 1770, aged 102 He was a soldier in the reign of William III, and was accused before a court-martial of falling asleep on duty upon Windsor Terrace. In proof of his innocence he asserted that he heard St Paul's clock strike thirteen, which statement was confirmed by several witnesses

A strange incident is related concerning the striking of Big Ben On the morning of Thursday, March 14th, 1861, "the inhabitants of Westminster were roused by repeated strokes of the new great bell, and most persons supposed it was for the death of a member of the royal family. It proved, however, to be due to some derangement of the clock, for at four and five o'clock ten and twelve strokes were struck instead of the proper number." It was within twenty-four hours of this that the Duchess of Kent (Queen Victoria's mother) was declared by her physicians to be dying, and early on the 16th she was dead.

Clodhopper. A rustic, a farmer's labourer, who hops or walks amongst the clods Infantry are called "clodhoppers" or "footsloggers," because they have to walk.

Clog Almanac. A primitive almanac or calendar, originally made of a four-square "clog," or log of wood; the sharp edges were divided by notches into three months each, every week being marked by a bigger notch. The faces contained the saints' days, the festivals, the phases of the moon, and so on, sometimes in Runic characters, whence the "clog" was also called a "Runic staff" They are not uncommon, and specimens may be seen in the British Museum, the Bodleian, the Ashmolean, and other places at home and abroad

Clogs are also wooden shoes

"Clogs to clogs is only three generations" is an old Lancashire saying, implying that however a man may prosper and raise himself from poverty, his grandson will be wearing clogs, and back where the family started from

Cloister He retired into a cloister, a monastery Almost all monasteries have a cloister or covered walk, which generally occupies three sides of a quadrangle Hence *cloistered*, confined, withdrawn from the world in the manner of a recluse·—

I cannot praise a fugitive, and cloistered virtue, unexercised and unbreathed, that never sallies out and sees her adversary, but slinks out of the race where that immortal garland is to be run for, not without dust and heat.—MILTON *Areopagitica.*

Clootie.   **Auld Clootie.**   Old Nick   The Scotch call a cloven hoof a *cloot*, so that Auld Clootie is Old Cloven-foot

And maybe, Tam, for a' my cants.
My wicked rhymes an' drucken rants
I'll gie auld Cloven Clootie's haunts
     An unco slip yet,
An' snugly sit, amang the saunts
     At Davie's hip yet!
       BURNS *Reply to a Trimming Epistle*

Close Rolls. Mandates, letters, and writs of a private nature, addressed, in the Sovereign's name, to individuals, and folded or *closed* and sealed on the outside with the Great Seal.

Close Rolls contain all such matters of record as were committed to close writs These Rolls are preserved in the Tower.—JACOB *Law Dictionary*

Patent Rolls (*q v.*) are left *open*, with the seal hanging from the bottom.

Close-time for Game. *See* SPORTING SEASONS.

Cloth, The. This word was formerly applied to the customary garb of any trade, and is akin in usage to the word *livery*. About the 17th century it became restricted to the clergy; the clerical office, thus we say " having respect for the cloth "

Cloth-yard. A measure for cloth, differing slightly from the yard of to-day.

Cloth-yard shaft. An arrow a cloth-yard in length

Clotho. One of the Three Fates in classic mythology. She presided over birth, and drew from her distaff the thread of life; Atropos presided over death and cut the thread of life, and Lachesis spun the fate of life between birth and death. (Gr. *klotho*, to draw thread from a distaff)

Cloud. A dark spot on the forehead of a horse between the eyes. A white spot is called a star, and an elongated star is a blaze. *See* BLAZE.

Agrippa. He [Antony] has a cloud on his face.
Enobarbus He were the worse for that were he a horse
     SHAKESPEARE. *Antony and Cleopatra*, iii, 2.

A clouded cane. A malacca cane clouded or mottled from age and use These canes were very fashionable in the first quarter of last century and earlier.

Sir Plume of amber snuff-box justly vain,
And the nice conduct of a clouded cane
     POPE *Rape of the Lock*, iv, 123.

Every cloud has a silver lining. There is some redeeming brightness in the darkest prospect, "while there is life there is hope "

He is in the clouds. In dreamland; entertaining visionary notions and so having no distinct idea about the matter in question.

He is under a cloud. Under suspicion, in disrepute.

The Battle above the Clouds A name given to the battle of Lookout Mountain, part of the Battle of Chattanooga fought during the American War of Secession on November 24th, 1863. The Federals under Grant defeated the Confederates, and part of the fight took place in a heavy mist on the mountains: hence the name

To blow a cloud. See BLOW.

Cloven Foot. To show the cloven foot, i e. to show a knavish intention a base motive. The allusion is to Satan, represented with the legs and feet of a goat, and, however he might disguise himself, he could never conceal his cloven feet. See BAG O' NAILS, CLOOTIE.

Clover. He's in clover. In luck, in prosperous circumstances, in a good situation The allusion is to cattle feeding in clover fields.

Clown. It is probable that the circus clown, in his baggy costume and whitened face with grotesque red lips and odd little tuft of black hair, is a relic of the devil as he appeared in the medieval miracle plays He has come to us, with his drolleries and antics, through a succession of fools and jesters. Of the many famous clowns that have amused generations of children and grown-ups, two figures are outstanding—Joseph Grimaldi (1779-1837) and, in recent times the Swiss Grock (Charles Adrien Wettach). See HARLEQUIN.

Club. In England the club has played an important part in social life, especially during the 18th century John Aubrey (1626-97) says "we now use the word clubbe for a sodality in a taverne" Clubs came into vogue in the reign of Queen Anne, as we see from the *Tatler* and *Spectator* Some of them were political, such as the "October," the "Saturday," and the "Green Ribbon," at which adherents or opponents of the ministry of the day forgathered. But the social clubs where cultured men could meet and exchange conversation had their parent in Dr Johnson whose Ivy Lane Club (founded in 1749) and Literary Club (1763) gathered many of the leading men of the day and set a standard for the times For many years clubs met in taverns and coffee-houses, and it was not until the Regency that they began to occupy their own premises In the first quarter of the 19th century a great number came into existence, some such as Watiers. being solely gambling centres. The first ladies' club was the Alexandra (1883) to which no man—not even the Prince of Wales—was allowed admittance Among the principal London clubs are the following, with their dates of foundation —

Army and Navy, 1838	Junior Carlton, 1864.
Athenæum, 1824.	Lansdowne, 1935
Bath, 1894	Lyceum, 1904.
Beefsteak, 1876	M C C, 1787
Boodle's, 1763	Marlborough, 1868
Brooks's, 1764	National Liberal, 1882.
Carlton, 1832	Reform, 1832
Cavalry, 1890	Royal Automobile, 1897.
Conservative, 1840	Savage, 1857
Constitutional, 1883.	Savile, 1868
Devonshire, 1875	Thatched House, 1869.
Garrick, 1831.	Travellers, 1819.
Guards, 1813	Turf, 1868
Junior Army & Navy, 1911	United Services, 1815
	White's 1693

In France clubs assumed great political importance at the time of the Revolution They dated from about 1782 The Club des Cordeliers numbered Danton and Desmoulins among its members The most famous was the Club des Jacobins From these two the Mountain party emerged They disappeared with the coming of the Directory in 1799

Club-bearer, The. In Greek mythology, Periphetes, the robber of Argolis, is so called because he murdered his victims with an iron club.

Club-land. The West End of London round St James's, where the principal clubs are situated; the members of such clubs

Club-law. The law of might or compulsion through fear of chastisement, "might is right", "do it or get a hiding."

Club Parliament. The Parliament held at Nottingham in 1426, during the quarrel between the Duke of Gloucester and Cardinal Beaufort, so called because the members, being forbidden to wear swords, came armed with cudgels, or "bats" Also called the Bats Parliament

Clue I have not yet got the clue ; to give a clue, i e a hint. A clue is a ball of thread (A.S *cleowen*) The only mode of finding the way out of the Cretan labyrinth was by a skein of thread, which, being followed, led the right way

Clumsy A Scandinavian word, meaning originally "numbed with cold," and so "awkward," 'unhandy' Piers Plowman has "thou clomsest for cold," and Wyclif has "with clomsid handis " (*Jer* xlvii, 3).

Cluricaune. An elf in Irish folklore. He is of evil disposition and usually appears as a wrinkled old man He has knowledge of hidden treasure and is the fairies' shoemaker. Another name for him is *Leprechaun* or *Lepracaun* (q v.).

Clydesdale Horses. See SHIRE HORSES

Clym of the Clough A noted archer and outlaw, supposed to have lived shortly before Robin Hood, who, with Adam Bell and William of Cloudesly, forms the subject of one of the ballads in Percy's *Reliques*, the three becoming as famous in the north of England as Robin Hood and Little John in the midland counties. Their place of resort was in Englewood Forest, near Carlisle Clym of the Clough means Clement of the Cliff. He is mentioned in Ben Jonson's *Alchemist* (I, ii, 46)

Clytie. In classical mythology, an ocean nymph, in love with Apollo. Meeting with no return, she was changed into the heliotrope, or sunflower, which, traditionally, still turns to the sun, following him through his daily course

Cnidian Venus, The. The exquisite statue of Venus by Praxiteles, formerly in her temple at Cnidus It is known through the antique reproduction now in the Vatican

Coach. When railways replaced the old forms of road travel in the 30s and 40s of the last century, they took over the old coaching terms familiar to all who travelled about the country. Carriage, coach, driver, guard, "Right, away!" are all words reminiscent of old coaching days.

It is from this association that a private tutor, or the trainer of an athletic team is coach, for it is his task to get his pupil or team trained as fast as possible

A slow coach. A dullard, an unprogressive person

What a dull, old-fashioned chap thou be'st   but thou wert always a slow-coach.—MRS GASKELL *Cibbie Marsh* (Era 2)

To dine in the coach. In the captain's private room   The *coach* or *couch* of one of the old, large-sized men-of-war was a small apartment near the stern, the floor being formed of the aftmost part of the quarter-deck, and the roof by the poop

To drive a coach and four through an Act of Parliament. To find a way of infringing it or escaping its provisions without rendering oneself liable at law   It is said that a clever lawyer can always find for his clients some loophole of escape

It is easy to drive a coach-and-four through wills, and settlements, and legal things —H R HAGGARD. [Rice] was often heard to say   that he would drive a coach and six horses through the Act of Settlement —WELWOOD

Coal. To blow the coals. To fan dissensions, to excite smouldering animosity into open hostility, as dull coals are blown into a blaze with a pair of bellows.

To call, or haul, over the coals. To bring to task for shortcomings, to scold   At one time the Jews were "bled" whenever the kings or barons wanted money; and one very common torture, if they resisted, was to haul them over the coals of a slow fire, to give them a "roasting"   In Scott's *Ivanhoe,* Front-de-Bœuf threatens to haul Isaac over the coals

To carry coals. To be put upon. "Gregory, o' my word, we'll not carry coals"—*i e.* submit to be "put upon" (*Romeo and Juliet,* i, 1). So in *Every Man out of his Humour,* "Here comes one that will carry coals, *ergo,* will hold my dog." The allusion is to the dirty, laborious occupation of charcoal carriers

To carry coals to Newcastle. To do what is superfluous; to take something where it is already plentiful   The French say, "*Porter de l'eau a la riviere*" (to carry water to the river).

To heap coals of fire on one's head   To melt down one's animosity by deeds of kindness; to repay bad treatment with good

If thine enemy be hungry, give him bread to eat, and if he be thirsty, give him water to drink, for thou shalt heap coals of fire upon his head.—*Prov* xxv, 21, 22.

To post the coal, or cole   *See* COLE

Coal brandy   Burnt brandy   The ancient way to set brandy on fire was to drop in it a live or red-hot piece of charcoal

Coaling, in theatrical slang, means telling phrases and speeches, as, "My part is full of 'coaling lines.'" Possibly from *cole* (*q v*), money, such a part being a profitable one.

Coalition Government. A government formed by various parties by mutual consent to waive differences of policy and opinion in face of more serious considerations   Examples are those under Fox and North in 1783, of Whigs and Peelites in 1852 of Conservatives and Liberal-Unionists in 1895   In 1915 H H Asquith formed a coalition of Unionists and Liberals to carry through the World War I, and this was re-formed by Lloyd George in 1916, lasting until 1922   In 1931 Ramsay MacDonald formed a National Government to deal with the crisis of the Gold Standard In 1940 Winston Churchill formed a Coalition Government to carry on the World War II, and this lasted until 1945 when, at the General Election, Labour was returned to power with an overwhelming majority.

Coast, To. To free-wheel down a hill on a bicycle, etc , to come down the hill without working the pedals, or—of motor-cycles and cars—with the engine cut off   The term was originally American or Canadian, an ice-covered slope down which one slides on a sledge being called a *coast,* and hence the action of sliding being termed *coasting*

Coasting lead. A sounding lead used in shallow water.

Coasting trade. Trade between ports of the same country carried on by coasting vessels

Coasting waiter. An officer of Customs in the Port of London, whose duty it was to visit and make a return of coasting vessels which (from the nature of their cargo) were not required to report or make entry at the Custom House, but which were liable to the payment of certain small dues   The coasting waiter collected these, and searched the cargo for contraband goods   Like tide waiters, coasting waiters were abolished in the latter half of last century, and their duties have since been performed by the examining officer

The coast is clear. There is no likelihood of interference   It was originally a smuggling term, implying that no coastguards were about.

Coat. Cut your coat according to your cloth. Curtail your expenses to the amount of your income, live within your means   *Si non possis quod velis, velis id quod possis*

To baste someone's coat. To dust his jacket; to beat him

To wear the king's coat   To be a soldier.

Turning one's coat for luck. It was an ancient superstition that this was a charm against evil spirits   *See* TURNCOAT.

William found

A means for our deliverance "Turn your cloaks," Quoth hee, "for Pucke is busy in these oakes." RICHARD CORBETT (1582-1635) *Iter Boreale*

Coat of Arms. Originally, a surcoat worn by knights over their armour, decorated with devices by which the wearer could be described and recognized, hence the heraldic device of a family   The practice of bearing on the armour or its covering some distinguishing mark is of very ancient date   It was introduced into England by the Crusaders who in the Holy Land were forced to cover their armour with cloth to ward off the fierce sun, at that time its rules and customs were codified, and "heraldry" was brought almost to a science.

Cob A short-legged, stout variety of horse, rather larger than a pony, from thirteen to nearly fifteen hands high The word means big, stout It also meant a tuft or head (from *cop*), hence eminent, large, powerful The "*cob of the county*" is the great boss thereof A rich cob is a plutocrat Hence also a male, as a cob-swan

Riding horses run between fifteen and sixteen hands in height, and carriage horses, between sixteen and seventeen hands

Cobalt From the Ger. *Kobold*, a gnome, the demon of mines This metal, from which a deep blue pigment is made, was so called by miners partly because it was thought to be useless and partly because the arsenic and sulphur with which it was found in combination had bad effects both on their health and on the silver ores. Its presence was consequently attributed to the ill offices of the mine demon

Cobber (Austr). A friend or companion, possibly from the old Suffolk *to cob*, to form a friendship

Cobber Kain—Flying Officer E J Kain, D F C , was the first New Zealand air ace; he was killed on active service in June 1940

Cobbler. A drink made of wine (sherry), sugar, lemon, and ice It is sipped up through a straw. *See* COBBLER'S PUNCH

This wonderful invention, sir,   is called cobbler —Sherry cobbler, when you name it long, cobbler when you name it short—DICKENS. *Martin Chuzzlewit*, XVII

A cobbler should stick to his last Let no one presume to interfere in matters of which he is ignorant

Ne supra crepidam sutor judicaret
                          Pliny, xxv, x, 85

The tale goes that a cobbler detected a fault in the shoe-latchet of one of Apelles's paintings, and the artist rectified the fault The cobbler next ventured to criticize the legs; but Apelles answered, "Keep to your trade"— you understand about shoes, but not about anatomy.

The Cobbler Poet Hans Sachs of Nuremberg, prince of the master-singers of Germany (1494-1576)

Cobbler's punch. Gin and water, with a little treacle and vinegar

Cobbler's toast. Schoolboys' bread and butter, toasted on the dry side and eaten hot

Coburg. A corded or ribbed cotton cloth made in Coburg (Saxony), or an imitation thereof Chiefly used for ladies' dresses.

Cobweb. The net spun by a spider to catch its prey. *Cob*, or *cop*, is an old word for a spider, so called from its round, stubby body, it is found in the A S. *attorcoppa*, poisonous spider

Cochineal (koch´ i nēl) A red dye used for colouring materials and also food. It is made from the insect of the same name, which

acquires its colour from feeding on the cactus. Cochineal was brought to Europe by the Spaniards, soon after the conquest of Mexico, in 1518

Cock (noun). In classical mythology the cock was dedicated to Apollo, the sun-god, because it gives notice of the rising of the sun It was dedicated to Mercury, because it summons men to business by its crowing And to Æsculapius, because "early to bed and early to rise, makes a man healthy "

According to Mohammedan legend the Prophet found in the first heaven a cock of such enormous size that its crest touched the second heaven. The crowing of this celestial bird arouses every living creature from sleep except man The Moslem doctors say that Allah lends a willing ear to him who reads the Koran to him who prays for pardon, and to the cock whose chant is divine melody When this cock ceases to crow, the day of judgment will be at hand

Peter Le Neve affirms that a cock was the warlike ensign of the Goths, and therefore used in Gothic churches for ornament

The weathercock is a very old symbol of vigilance From its position at the top of steeple or tower it can be seen far and wide As the cock heralds the coming day, so does the weathercock tell the wise man what the weather will likely be

A cock and bull story. A long, rambling, idle, or incredible yarn, a canard There are various so-called explanations of the origin of the term, but the most likely is that it is connected with the old fables in which cocks, bulls, and other animals discoursed in human language on things in general In Bentley's *Boyle Lecture* (1692) occurs the passage.—

That cocks and bulls might discourse, and hinds and panthers hold conferences about religion

The "hind and panther" allusion is an obvious reference to Dryden's poem (published five years before), and it is possible that the "cocks and bulls" would have had some meaning that was as well known to contemporaries but has been long since forgotten See also the closing chapter of Sterne's *Tristram Shandy*, the last words in the book are.—

L—d! said my mother, what is all this story about? —A COCK and a BULL, said *Yorick*—And one of the best of its kind, I ever heard

The French equivalents are *faire un coq à l'âne* and *un conte de ma mere l'oie* (a mother goose tale), and it is worth noting that in Scotland a satire or lampoon and also a rambling, disconnected story used to be called a *cockalane*, direct from the Fr *coq à l'âne*.

A cock of hay or haycock. A small heap of hay thrown up temporarily (Ger *kocke*, a heap of hay; Norw *kok*, a heap)

By cock and pie. We meet with *cock's bones, cock's wounds, cock's mother, cock's body. cock's passion*, etc , where we can have no doubt that the word is a minced oath, and stands for God The *pie* is the table or rule in the old Catholic office, showing how to find out the service for each day (from Med Lat *pica*).

By cock and pie, sir, you shall not away to-night.— SHAKESPEARE *2 Henry IV*, v, 1

Cock and Pie (as a public-house sign) is probably "The Cock and Magpie."

Cock and Bottle. A public-house sign, probably meaning that draught and bottled ale may be had on the premises If so, the word "cock" would mean the tap

Cock of the North. George, fifth Duke of Gordon (1770-1836), who raised the Gordon Highlanders in 1795, is so called on a monument erected to his honour at Fochabers, in Morayshire.

The brambling, or mountain finch, is also known by this name.

Cock of the walk. The dominant bully or master spirit The place where barndoor fowls are fed is *the walk*, and if there is more than one cock, they will fight for the supremacy of this domain

Every cock crows on its own dunghill, or **Ilka cock crows on its ain midden** It is easy to brag of your deeds in your own castle when safe from danger and not likely to be put to the proof.

Nourish a cock, but offer it not in sacrifice. This is the eighteenth Symbolic Saying in the Protreptics of Iamblichus. The cock was sacred to Minerva, and also to the sun and moon, and it would be impious to offer a sacrilegious offering to the gods What is already consecrated to God cannot be employed in sacrifice

That cock won't fight. *See* COCK-FIGHTING

The red cock will crow in his house. His house will be set on fire
"We'll see if the red cock craw not in his bonnie barnyard ae morning." "What does she mean?" said Mannering . "Fire-raising," answered the . . dom'nie—SCOTT *Guy Mannering*, ch iii

To cry cock. To claim the victory, to assert oneself to be the superior. As a "cock of the walk" (*q v.*) is the chief or ruler of the whole walk, so to cry cock is to claim this cockship.

Cock-boat. A small ship's boat; a very light or frail craft
> That now no more we can the maine-land see,
> Have care, I pray, to guide the cock-bote well
> SPENSER *Faerie Queene*, III, viii, 24

This "cock-bote" had previously (III, vii, 27) been called a "little bote" and a "shallop " *Cokke* or *cocke*, is an obsolete word for a small boat, and is probably connected with *cog*, an early kind of ship, from Scan *kog*, *kogge*, a small vessel without a keel Originally a wicker frame covered with leather or oilcloth The Welsh fishers used to carry them on their backs. *Cock* is here the M E *cog* or *cogge*, and O Fr *coque* or *cogue*, a kind of boat. *Cog* was once used in English for a small boat, as by Chaucer—
> This messalger adoun him gan to hye,
> And fond Jasoun, and Ercules also,
> That in a cogge to londe were y-go,
> Hem to refreshen and to take the eyr
> *Legend of Good Women, l*, 1479

Cock-crow. The Hebrews divided the night into four watches (1) The "beginning of the watches" or "even" (*Lam.* ii, 19), (2) "The middle watch" or "midnight" (*Judges* vii, 19), (3) "The cock-crowing", (4) "The
B D —8

morning watch" or "dawning" (*Exod* xiv, 24)
Ye know not when the master of the house cometh, at even, or at midnight, or at the cock-crowing, or in the morning —*Mark* xiii, 35

The Romans divided the day into sixteen parts, each one hour and a half, beginning at midnight. The third of these divisions (3 a m.) they called *gallicinium*, the time when cocks begin to crow, the next was *conticinium*, when they ceased to crow, and fifth was *diluculum*, dawn

If the Romans sounded the hour on a trumpet three times it would explain the diversity of the Gospels "Before the cock crow" (*John* xiii, 38, *Luke* xxii, 34, and *Matt* xxvi, 34), but "Before the cock crow *twice*" (*Mark* xiv, 30)—that is, before the trumpet has finished sounding

Apparitions vanish at cock crow. This is a Christian superstition, the cock being the watch-bird placed on church spires, and therefore sacred
> The morning cock crew loud,
> And at the sound it [the Ghost] shrunk in haste away,
> And vanished from our sight
> SHAKESPEARE. *Hamlet*, i, 2

Cock-eye. A squint. Cock-eyed, having a squint, cross-eyed There seems to be no connexion between this and the Irish and Gaelic *caog*, a squint, it may mean that such an eye has to be *cocked*, as the trigger of a gun is cocked, before it can do its work effectively, or it may be from the verb *to cock* in the sense of "turning up"—as in *to cock the nose.*

Cock-eyed is also slang for nonsensical

Cock-fighting was introduced into Britain by the Romans It was a favourite sport both with the Greeks and with the Romans

In the 12th century it was the sport of schoolboys on Shrove Tuesday The cockpit at Whitehall was added by Henry VIII, and the "royal diversion," as it was called, was very popular with James I and Charles II. Cock-fighting was made illegal in Britain in 1849; it continued in New York until the 1870s

That beats cock-fighting. That is most improbable and extraordinary. The allusion is to the extravagant tales told of fighting-cocks

That cock won't fight. That dodge won't answer; that tale won't wash The allusion is to a bet being made on a favourite cock, which, when pitted, refuses to fight

To live like fighting-cocks. To live in luxury. Fighting-cocks used to be high fed in order to aggravate their pugnacity and increase their powers of endurance.

Cock-horse To ride a cock-horse. A cock-horse is really a hobby-horse, but the phrase means to sit astride a person's foot or knee while he jogs it up and down.

Cock Lane Ghost A tale of terror without truth, an imaginary tale of horrors In Cock Lane, Smithfield (1762), certain knockings were heard, which Mr. Parsons, the owner, declared proceeded from the ghost of Fanny Kent, who died suddenly, and Parsons wished people to suppose that she had been murdered by her husband. All London was agog with this story Royalty and the nobility made up parties to go to Cock Lane to hear the ghost; Dr. Johnson and other men of learning and repute investigated the alleged phenomena, but in the end it was found that the knockings were produced by Parsons's daughter (a girl twelve years of age) rapping on a board which she took into her bed Parsons was condemned to stand in the pillory *Cp.* STOCKWELL GHOST

Cock Lorell's Bote A pamphlet published by Wynkyn de Worde about 1510, satirizing contemporary lower-middle-class life and introducing all sorts of rogues and vagabonds in the guise of a crew which takes ship and sails through England

Cock-pit The arena in which game-cocks were set to fight, also the name of a 17th-century theatre built about 1618 on the site of a cock-pit in Drury Lane, and of that of the after part of the orlop deck of an old man-of-war, formerly used as quarters for the junior officers and as a sick-bay in time of war

Captain Hardy, some fifty minutes after he had left the cock-pit, returned, and, again taking the hand of his dying friend and commander, congratulated him on having gained a complete victory —SOUTHEY. *Life of Nelson*, ch ix

In aeroplanes the space where the pilot sits is called the cockpit

The judicial committee of the Privy Council was also so called, because the council-room is built on the old cock-pit of Whitehall palace

Great consultations at the cockpit about battles, duels, victories, and what not —*Poor Robin's Almanack*, 1730

Cock-pit of Europe. Belgium is so called because it has been the site of more European battles than any other country; among them, Oudenarde (1708), Ramillies (1706), Fontenoy (1745), Fleurus (1794), Jemmapes (1792), Ligny, Quatre Bras and Waterloo (1815); Mons, Ypres and the continuous battles of the World War I; the invasion of the country by the Germans, 1940-45

Cockshut, or **Cockshut time.** Twilight, the time when the *cockshut, i e* a large net employed to catch woodcocks, used to be spread The net was so called from being used in a glade through which the woodcocks might *shoot* or *dart.*

Let me never draw a sword again,
Nor prosper in the twilight, cockshut light
When I would fleece the wealthy passenger ..
If I, the next time that I meet the slave,
Cut not the nose from off the coward's face
Arden of Feversham, iii, 2 (1592).

See also Shakespeare's *Richard III*, v 3

Cockshy A free fling or "shy" at something The allusion is to the once popular Shrove-Tuesday sport of shying or casting stones or sticks at cocks

The phrase became popular in military circles during the World War II to imply an ill-considered, ill-prepared attempt at something

Cock sure. As sure as a cock: meaning either "with all the assurance (brazen-faced impudence) of a game-cock," or "as sure as the

cock is to crow in the morning," or even "with the security and certainty of the action of a cock, or tap, in preventing the waste of liquor "

Shakespeare employs the phrase in the sense of "sure as the cock of a firelock "

We steal as in a castle, cock-sure —1 *Henry IV*, ii, 1

And the phrase 'Sure as a gun" seems to favour the latter explanation.

Cock (verb) In the following phrases, all of which connote assertiveness, obtrusiveness, or aggressiveness in some degree, the allusion is to game-cocks, whose strutting about, swaggering, and ostentatious pugnacity is proverbial

To cock the ears To prick up the ears, or turn them as a horse does when he listens to a strange sound

To cock the nose or **cock up the nose.** To turn up the nose in contempt *See* COCK YOUR EYE

To cock up your head, foot, etc Lift up, turn up your head or foot

To cock your eye. To shut one eye and look with the other in a somewhat impertinent manner, to glance at questioningly *Cp.* COCK-EYE

To cock your hat To set your hat more on one side of the head than on the other, to look knowing and pert

To cock a snook. To make a long nose; to put the thumb to the nose and spread wide the fingers This is a very ancient gesture of disrespect, contempt, or defiance

Cock-a-hoop. Variously explained as being referable (*a*) to an old custom of taking the *cock* (*i e* the spigot) out of the barrel and setting it on the *hoop* thereof before commencing a regular drinking bout, and (*b*) to the Fr *huppe*, a tufted crest, hence a specially feathered, and so specially lively or valuable, game-cock

And having routed a whole troop
With victory was cock-a-hoop
BUTLER *Hudibras*, i, 3

To sit cock-a-hoop. Boastful, defiant, like a game-cock with his houpe or crest erect, eagerly expectant

Cocked hat. A hat with the brim turned, like that of a bishop, dean, etc It is also applied to the *chapeau bras* (*q v*) and the military full-dress hat, pointed before and behind, and rising to a point at the crown, the *chapeau à cornes* "Cock" in this phrase means to turn, *cocked,* turned up.

Knocked into a cocked hat. In the game of ninepins, three pins were set up in the form of a triangle, and when all the pins except these three were knocked down, the set was technically said to be "knocked into a cocked hat." In modern colloquial usage, to knock someone into a cocked hat is to beat him in a contest of skill, etc

Cockade. A badge worn on the head-dress of menservants of Royalty and of those holding His Majesty's commission, such as naval and military officers, diplomatists, lord-lieutenants, high sheriffs, etc. The English cockade is black and circular in shape with a projecting fan at the top, except for naval officers, for whom the shape is oval without the fan   This form of cockade was introduced from Hanover by George I, under Charles I the cockade had been scarlet, but Charles II changed it to white, and thus the *white cockade* became the badge of the Pretenders, William III adopting an orange cockade (as Prince of Orange). From Fr *cocarde*, a plume, rosette, or bunch of ribbons, originally worn by Croatian soldiers serving in the French army, and used to fix the flaps of the hat in a cocked position

To mount the cockade. To become a soldier

Cockaigne, Land of (kok ān´)   An imaginary land of idleness and luxury, famous in mediæval story, and the subject of more than one poem, one of which, an early translation of a 13th-century French work, is given in Ellis's *Specimens of Early English Poets*   In this "the houses were made of barley sugar and cakes, the streets were paved with pastry, and the shops supplied goods for nothing "

London has been so called (*see* COCKNEY), but Boileau applies the name to Paris

Allied to the Ger *kuchen*, a cake   Scotland is called the "land of cakes."

Cockatoo. Old Australian slang for a convict serving his sentence on Cockatoo Island, Sydney, which began to be used for that purpose in 1839   Also used of small farmers in Australia who were described as "just picking up the grains of a livelihood like cockatoos do maize."

Cockatrice. A fabulous and heraldic monster with the wings of a fowl, tail of a dragon, and head of a cock.   So called because it was said to be produced from a cock's egg hatched by a serpent   According to legend, the very look of this monster would cause instant death   In consequence of the *crest* with which the head is crowned, the creature is called a basilisk (*q v*)   Isaiah says, "The weaned child shall put his hand on the cockatrice' den" (xi, 8), to signify that the most obnoxious animal should not hurt the most feeble of God's creatures

Figuratively, it means an insidious, treacherous person bent on mischief
> They will kill one another by the look, like cockatrices —SHAKESPEARE   *Twelfth Night*, iii, 4

Cocker. According to Cocker. All right, according to Cocker. According to established rules, according to what is correct   Edward Cocker (1631-75) published an arithmetic which ran through sixty editions   The phrase, "According to Cocker," was popularized by Murphy in his farce, *The Apprentice* (1756)   *Cp* GUNTER.

Cockle. A bivalve mollusc, the shell of which was worn by pilgrims in their hats (*see* COCKLE HAT)   The polished side of the shell was scratched with some crude drawing of the Virgin, the Crucifixion, or some other subject connected with the pilgrimage.   Being blessed by the priest, the shells were considered amulets

against spiritual foes, and might be used as drinking vessels.

Cockle-boat   *See* COCK-BOAT

Cockle hat   A pilgrim's hat, especially the hat of a pilgrim to the shrine of St. James of Compostella, in Spain; his symbol was really a scallop-shell, but the word *cockle* was more usually applied to it
> And how shall I your true love know
>   From many another one?
> Oh, by his cockle hat and staff
>   And by his sandal shoon.
> *Old Ballad   The Friar of Orders Grey.*

Hot cockles.   *See* HOT.

The Order of the Cockle. An order of knighthood created by St Louis in 1269, in memory of a disastrous expedition made by sea for the succour of Christians   Perrot says it scarcely survived its foundation

To cry cockles. To be hanged, from the gurgling noise made in strangulation.

To warm the cockles of one's heart. Said of anything that pleases one immensely and gives one a gratifying sensation, such as does a glass of really good port   (Lat *cochleæ cordis*, the ventricles of the heart)

Cockney. This is the M E *cokeney*, meaning "a cock's egg " (*-ey* = A S *æg*, an egg)   i e a small egg with no yolk that is occasionally laid by hens, hence applied originally to a foolish, spoilt, cockered child —
> I made thee a wanton and thou hast made me a fool, I brought thee up like a cockney and thou hast handled me like a cock's-comb, I made more of thee than became a father and thou less of me than beseemed a child
> LYLY: *Euphues* (1578)

From this the word came to signify a foolish or effeminate person, hence, by the country-dwellers—the majority of the population— it was applied to townsmen generally, and finally became restricted to its present meaning, one born within sound of Bow Bells, London, one possessing London peculiarities of speech, etc , one who, hence, is—or is supposed to be —wholly ignorant of country sports, country life, farm animals, plants, and so on.
> As Frenchmen love to be bold, Flemings to be drunk   Welchmen to be called Britons, and Irishmen to be costermongers, so cockneys, especially she cockneys, love not aqua-vitæ when 'tis good for them.
> —DEKKER and WEBSTER   *Westward Hoe*, ii, 2, (1607).

Shakespeare uses the word for a squeamish woman —
> Cry to it, nuncle, as the cockney did to the eels, when she put them into the paste alive —*King Lear*, ii, 4

The Cockney School. A nickname given by Lockhart (*see* quotation below) to a group of writers including Leigh Hunt, Hazlitt, Shelley, and Keats   It was a term of opprobrium, on account of the kind of rhymes they used in their verse, which smacked too much of every-day life instead of the classic purity preferred by the critics
> If I may be permitted to have the honour of christening it, it may be henceforth referred to by the designation of the "Cockney School "—LOCKHART. *Blackwood's Magazine*, Oct., 1817.

The king of cockneys. A master of the revels chosen by students of Lincoln's Inn on Childermas Day (December 28th).

Cocktail. An aperitif, or short drink taken before a meal, concocted of spirits (usually gin), bitters, flavouring, etc. There are many varieties of cocktail, most of them of U S.A. origin   Champagne cocktail is champagne flavoured with Angostura bitters and brandy, soda cocktail is soda-water, sugar, and bitters.

Did ye iver try a brandy cocktail, Cornel?—
THACKERAY: *The Newcomes*, XIII

Cocky. Bumptious. overbearing, conceited, and dogmatic; like a little bantam cock.

Coconut. Milk in the coconut. *See* MILK.

Cocqcigrues. At the coming of the Cocqcigrues. More correctly Coquecigrues (kok' sĕ groo). These are fabulous animals of French legend, and they have now become labels for an idle story. In French the above phrase—*à la venue des coquecigrues* is equivalent to saying Never

"That is one of the seven things," said the fairy Bedonebyasyoudid, "I am forbidden to tell till the coming of the Cocqcigrues."—C KINGSLEY *The Water Babies*, ch vi.

Cocvtus (ko sī' tŭs). One of the five rivers of hell   The word means the "river of lamentation "   The unburied were doomed to wander about its banks for 100 years   It flows into the river Acheron

Cocytus, named of lamentation loud
Heard on the rueful stream.
MILTON *Paradise Lost*, ii, 579.

Cod. You can't cod me. You can't deceive me, or take a rise out of me

Codger. A familiar and somewhat disrespectful term applied to an elderly man, generally one with some minor eccentricities Originally a mean, stingy old chap probably a variant of *cadger* (*q v*)

Codille (kō dil')   Triumph   A term in the game of ombre   When one of the two opponents of ombre has more tricks than ombre, he is said to have won codille, and takes all the stake that ombre played for Thus Belinda is said, in the *Rape of the Lock*, to have been "between the jaws of ruin and Codille."   She wins with the "king of hearts," and *she wins codille.*

Coehorn (kō' hôrn)   Small howitzer of about 4½ inches calibre, so called from Baron van Coehorn, of Holland   These guns were in use in the early 18th century.

Cœnobites or **Cenobites** (sen' ō bīt)   Monks who live in common, in contradistinction to hermits or anchorites   (Gr *koinosbios*)

Cœur de Lion (kĕr de lā' on)   Richard I of England, called the lion-hearted from the prodigies of personal valour performed by him in the Holy Land   (1157, 1189-99)

The traditional stage pronunciation of this is kôr de lī' on.

Coffee. The Turkish word is *qahwah*, which is pronounced *kahveh* and is applied to the infusion only, not to the plant or its berries

Coffee was introduced into England in 1641; the first coffee-house in this country was opened at Oxford in 1650, and the first in London dates from the following year.

It was an old custom in the Ardennes to take ten cups of coffee after dinner, and each cup had its special name   (1) Cafe, (2) Gloria, (3) Pousse Cafe, (4) Goutte, (5) Regoutte, (6) Surgoutte, (7) Rincette, (8) Re-rincette, (9) Sur-rincette, and (10) Coup de l'etrier.

Gloria is coffee with a small glass of brandy in lieu of milk, those following it have an ever-increasing quantity of alcohol; and the last is the "stirrup cup "

Poussé café is now a common term for a liqueur after coffee

Coffin. A raised crust, like the lid of a basket Hence Shakespeare speaks of a `custard coffin" (*Taming of the Shrew*, IV, 3). (Gr. *kophinos*, a basket)

Oj the paste a coffin will I rear
SHAKESPEARE *Titus Andronicus*, v 2

To drive a nail into one's coffin. To do anything that would tend to cut short one's life, to put a spoke in one's wheel

Care to our coffin adds a nail, no doubt;
But every grin so merry draws one out
PETER PINDAR *Expostulatory Odes*, XV

Cog   A boat.   *See* COCK-BOAT

Coggeshall (kog' shăl)   **A Coggeshall job.** The saying is, that the Coggeshall (Essex) folk wanted to divert the current of a stream, and fixed hurdles in the bed of it for the purpose. Another tale is that a mad dog bit a wheelbarrow, and the people, fearing it would go mad, chained it up in a shed   *Cp* GOTHAM.

Cogito, ergo sum. The axiom formulated by Descartes (1596-1650) as the starting-place of his system of philosophy   it means   I think, therefore I am "   Descartes, at the beginning, provisionally doubted everything, but he could not doubt the existence of the *ego*, for the mere fact that *I* doubt presupposes the existence of the *I*, in other words   the *doubt* could not exist without the *I* to doubt

He [Descartes] stopped at the famous formula, "I think, therefore I am " Yet a little consideration will show this formula to be full of snares and verbal entanglements In the first place, the "therefore ' has no business there The "I am" is assumed in the "I think," which is simply another way of saying "I am thinking." And, in the second place, "I think" is not one simple proposition, but three distinct assertions rolled into one The first of these is "something called I exists", the second is, "something called thought exists", and the third is, "the thought is the result of the action of the I."

Now, it will be obvious to you, that the only one of these three propositions which can stand the Cartesian test of certainty is the second —HUXLEY. *Descartes' Discourse on Method*

Cohort (kō' hôrt)   The sixth part of a legion in the Roman army, numbering 420 infantry and 300 cavalry, the word is used, however, to describe any large armed force

The Assyrian came down like a wolf on the fold
And his cohorts were gleaming in purple and gold
BYRON *Destruction of Sennacherib*

Coif   Originally, a close-fitting mail cap worn under his helmet by a knight, afterwards, the special head-dress of serjeants-at-law—hence sometimes called *Serjeants of the Coif* It seems to have been a white hood, and its final representative was the white border to the wigs worn by serjeants the patch of black silk in the centre of the crown representing the cornered cap that was worn above it.

It was also, in the 13th century, a cap worn to hide the tonsure, by any renegade priest who chose to remain illegally as an advocate in the secular courts

Coin. **Paid in his own coin.** Tit for tat

To coin money. To make money with rapidity and ease

See ANGEL, BAWBEE, CAROLUS, CROSS AND PILE, CROWN, DOLLAR, FARTHING FLORIN, GROAT, GUINEA, MANCUS, PENNY, PIECES OF EIGHT, SHILLING, SOVEREIGN, etc

Coke. **Coke upon Littleton.** Eighteenth-century slang for a mixture of tent and brandy Tent was a deep-red Spanish wine *Coke upon Littleton* is the lawyers' name for the reprint and translation of Littleton's *Tenures* (about 1465), published in 1628 with a commentary by Sir Edward Coke (1552-1634)

Go and eat coke. A vulgar exclamation of contempt or impatience

To cry coke. To cry peccavi; to ask for mercy.

Colbronde or **Colbrand.** The Danish giant slain by Guy of Warwick By his death the land was delivered from Danish tribute

> I am not Samson, nor Sir Guy, nor Colbrand
> To mow 'em down before me
> SHAKESPEARE *Henry VIII*, v, 4

Colcannon (kŏl kăn' ŏn) Potatoes and cabbage pounded together and then fried in butter (Irish) "Col" is cole or cale, *i e.* cabbage.

About 1774 Isaac Sparks, the Irish comedian, founded in Long Acre a Colcannon Club —*The Athenæum*, January 20th, 1875

Cold. **Done in cold blood.** (Fr. *sang froid*) Not in the heat of temper; deliberately, and with premeditation The allusion is to the ancient notion that the blood grew hot and cold, and this difference of temperature ruled the temper

Cold-blooded animals. As a rule, all invertebrate animals, and all fishes and reptiles are cold-blooded, the temperature of their blood being about equal to the medium in which they live

Cold chisel. A steel chisel made in one piece and so tempered that it will cut cold metal when struck with a hammer

Cold-drawn oil. Oil that is extracted or expressed without the use of heat

To have cold feet is to be timorous or cowardly An expression originating in the U.S A. in the 1890s

To show or **give one the cold shoulder** is to assume a distant manner towards a person, to indicate that you wish to cut him

The persuasion of cold steel is persuasion enforced at the point of the sword or bayonet.

Cold-water ordeal. An ancient method of testing guilt or innocence The accused, being tied under the arms, was thrown into a river. If he sank to the bottom he was held to be guiltless, and drawn up by the cord; but if he floated the water rejected him, because of his guilt.

Cold without An elliptical expression, meaning spirits mixed with cold water *without* sugar

Cold-Bath Fields. A district of Clerkenwell, London, so called from the baths established there, in 1697, for the cure of rheumatism, convulsions, and other nervous disorders.

The Fields were famous for the prison which was established there in the time of James I and not finally closed till 1886

> As he went through Cold-Bath Fields he saw
> A solitary cell,
> And the Devil was pleased, for it gave him a hint
> For improving his prisons in Hell
> COLERIDGE *The Devil's Thoughts*

Coldbrand *See* COLBRONDE

Coldstream Guards. The second of the five regiments of Foot Guards It was raised by General Monk in 1659-60 and, in January, 1660, marched under him from Coldstream in Berwickshire with the object of bringing back Charles II to the throne In 1661 the regiment was constituted as the 2nd Regiment of Footguards The name Coldstream has no plural.

Cole. An old canting term for money. *Cp* COALING

> My lusty rustic, learn and be instructed Cole is, in the language of the witty, money, the *ready*, the *rhino*
> —SHADWELL *Squire of Alsatia*, IV, xvi (1688)

To post or **tip the cole.** To pay or put down the cash.

> If he don't tip the cole without more ado, give him a taste of the pump, that's all.—HARRISON AINSWORTH: *Jack Sheppard.*

Cole, King. A legendary British king, described in the nursery rhyme as "a merry old soul" fond of his pipe, fond of his glass, and fond of his "fiddlers three." Robert of Gloucester says he was father of St. Helena (and consequently grandfather of the Emperor Constantine), and Colchester has been said to have been named after him, though it is more probable that the town is named from Lat *colonia*

Colettines *See* FRANCISCANS

Colin Clout. A name which Spenser assumes in *The Shepherd's Calendar*, and in the pastoral entitled *Colin Clout s Come Home Again*, which represents his return from a visit to Sir Walter Raleigh, "the Shepherd of the Ocean" Skelton had previously (about 1520) used the name as the title of a satire directed against the abuses of the Church, he says —

> And if ye stande in doute
> Who brought this ryme aboute,
> My name is Colyn Cloute

Colin Tampon. The old nickname of a Swiss, as John Bull is of an Englishman, Brother Jonathan of a North American, and Monsieur Crapaud of a Frenchman

Coliseum. *See* COLOSSEUM.

Collar. **Against the collar.** Somewhat fatiguing. When a horse travels uphill the collar distresses his neck, so foot travellers often find the last mile or so 'against the collar," or distressing

In collar In harness The allusion is to a horse's collar, which is put on when about to go to work

Out of collar. Out of work, out of a place.

To collar. To seize (a person) by the collar; to steal, to appropriate without leave, to acquire (of possessions).

To collar the bowling. In cricket, to hit the bowlers all over the field so that they become more easy to score off through losing their length

To collar the cole. To steal the money *See* COLE.

To slip the collar. To escape from restraint; to draw back from a task begun

To work up to the collar. To work tooth and nail, not to shirk the work in hand A horse that lets his collar lie loose on his neck without bearing on it does not draw the vehicle at all, but leaves another to do the real work

Collar-day. A day on which the knights of the different orders when present at levees or other Court functions wear all their insignia and decorations, including the collar There are about thirty-five collar-days in the year.

Collar of SS. A decoration restricted to the Lord Chief Justice, the Lord Mayor of London, the Kings-of-Arms, the Heralds, the Sergeant-at-Arms, and the Sergeant Trumpeter It is composed of a series of golden S's joined together, and was originally the badge of the adherents of the House of Lancaster

Collectivism. The opposite of Individualism. A system in which the government would be the sole employer, the sole landlord, and the sole paymaster Private property would be abolished, the land, mines, railways, etc , would be nationalized, everyone would be obliged to work for his living, and the State obliged to find the work.

College The Lat *collegium*, meaning colleagueship or partnership, hence a body of colleagues, a fraternity In English the word has a very wide range, as, College of the Apostles, College of Physicians, College of Surgeons, Heralds' College, College of Justice, etc , and on the Continent we have College of Foreign Affairs, College of War, College of Cardinals, etc.

In old slang a prison was known as a *college*, and the prisoners as *collegiates* Newgate was "New College," and *to take one's final at New College* was to be hanged The King's Bench Prison was "King's College," and so on

College port. The vintage port laid down in university college cellars for the special use of the senior Common Room The excellence of this is often a source of college pride.

Colliberts A sort of gipsy race, similar to the *Cagots* of Gascony and the *Caqueux* of Brittany, who lived on boats on the rivers, chiefly in Poitou, now nearly extinct In feudal times a collibert was a serf partly free, but bound to certain services (Lat *collibertus*, a fellow freedman)

Collins (kol′ inz) A word sometimes applied to the "bread-and-butter letter" one writes after staying at another person's house. In *Pride and Prejudice* Mr Collins appears as a bore and snob of the first water, after a protracted and unwanted visit at the Bennetts' his parting words are· "Depend upon it, you will speedily receive from me a letter of thanks for this as well as for every other mark of your regard during my stay in Hertfordshire "

Tom Collins. *See* TOM

Colly, my Cow. *Colly* is an old term of endearment for a cow, and properly refers only to a polled cow, one deprived of its horns It is from Scan *kolla*, a beast without horns (Icel *kollr*, a shaven crown)

Collywobbles The gripes, or stomach-ache, usually accompanied with sundry rumblings in the stomach.

Cologne (ko lōn) **The three kings of Cologne.** The three Wise Men of the East, the Magi (*q v*), Caspar, Melchior, and Balthazar, whose bones, according to mediæval legend, were deposited in Cologne Cathedral

Eau de Cologne. *See* EAU DE COLOGNE.

Colombier A standard size of drawing and plate papers measuring 23¼ by 34½ inches The name is derived from an ancient watermark of a dove (Fr *colombe*), the emblem of the Holy Ghost.

Colonel. Regiments in the British Army have two Colonels (i) Honorary Colonel, a courtesy title accepted by a member of the Royal Family, elder statesman or member of the peerage associated with the territory from which the regiment is raised, (ii) Colonel, a senior officer, usually of General rank, who has served in the Regiment, and who becomes its titular head and its spokesman *vis-à-vis* the War Office The commanding officer of a battalion is a lieutenant-colonel

Colonnade, The. *See* CYNIC TUB.

Colophon. The statement containing information about the date, place, printer, and edition which, in the early days of printing, was given at the end of the book but which now appears on the title page From Gr *kolophon*, the top or summit, a word which, according to Strabo, is from Colophon, a city of Ionia, the inhabitants of which were such excellent horsemen that they would turn the scale of battle to the side on which they fought, hence *To add a colophon* means "to supply the finishing stroke "

The volume was uninjured from title-page to colophon —SCOTT *The Antiquary*

The term is now loosely applied to a printer's or publisher's house device, such as the Belle Sauvage appearing on the title-page of this volume.

Coloquintida, St. (col ō kwin′ ti da) Charles I was so called by the Levellers (*q v*), to whom he was as bitter as gall, or coloquintida (colocynth), the bitter-apple

Colorado (U S A) The river (and hence the State) was so named by the Spanish explorers from its *coloured* (i.e reddish) appearance.

Colorado beetle. This beetle, which is the terror of the potato-grower, for it will devastate whole fields, was first observed in the Rocky Mountain regions in 1859 It has since spread over large areas of America and has made its way at times into Europe, despite the most stringent precautions taken by the governments of the countries threatened

Colosseum (kol o sē' ûm) The great Flavian amphitheatre of ancient Rome, said to be so named from the colossal statue of Nero that stood close by in the Via Sacra It was begun by Vespasian in A D 72, and for 400 years was the scene of the gladiatorial contests The ruins remaining are still colossal and extensive, but quite two-thirds of the original building have been taken away at different times and used for building material

Byron, adapting the exclamation of the 8th-century pilgrims (and adopting a bad spelling), says—

> While stands the Coliseum, Rome shall stand
> When falls the Coliseum, Rome shall fall,
> And when Rome falls—the world
>   *Childe Harold*, IV, cxlv

The name has since been applied to other amphitheatres and places of amusement *Cp.* PALLADIUM

Colossus or **Colossos** (ko los' us) (Lat and Gr for a gigantic statue) The Colossus of Rhodes, completed probably about 280 B C, was a representation of the sun-god, Helios, and commemorated the successful defence of Rhodes against Demetrius Poliorcetes in 304 B C It was one of the Seven Wonders of the World, it stood 105 ft high, and is said to have been made by the Rhodian sculptor Chares, a pupil of Lysippus from the warlike engines abandoned by Demetrius. The story that it was built striding across the harbour and that ships could pass full sail, between its legs, rose in the 16th century, and has nothing to support it, neither Strabo nor Pliny makes mention of it, though both describe the statue minutely Tickell out-Herods Herod in the following lines —

> So, near proud Rhodes, across the raging flood,
> Stupendous form! the vast Colossus stood,
> While at one foot the thronging galleys ride,
> A whole hour's sail scarce reached the further side,
> Betwixt his brazen thighs, in loose array,
> Ten thousand streamers on the billows play
>   *On the Prospect of Peace*
> He doth bestride the narrow world
> Like a Colossus
>   SHAKESPEARE *Julius Cæsar*, i, 2

Colour. PHRASES

A man of colour. An old-fashioned term for a Negro, or, more strictly speaking, one with Negro blood

His coward lips did from their colour fly (Shakespeare *Julius Cæsar*, i, 2) He was unable to speak As cowards run away from their regimental colour, so Cæsar's lips, when he was ill, ran away from their colour and turned pale

I should like to see the colour of your money. I should like to have some proof that you have any, I should like to receive payment.

Off colour. Not up to the mark, run down, seedy, tainted.

To change colour To blush, especially to look awkward and perplexed when found out in some deceit or meanness

To colour up. To turn red in the face, to blush

To come off with flying colours. To be completely triumphant, to win "hands down " The allusion is to a victorious fleet sailing into port with all the flags flying at the mastheads

To come out in one's true colours. To reveal one's proper character, divested of all that is meretricious

To describe (a matter) in very black colours. To see it with a jaundiced eye, and describe it accordingly, to describe it under the bias of strong prejudice

To desert one's colours. To become a turncoat, to turn tail. The allusion is to the military flag

To get one's colours To be rewarded for athletic achievement by the privilege of wearing some special garment, (as cap and blazer in cricket) decorated with or composed of one's school or college colours *See* CAPPED, FLANNELS.

To give colour or some plausible colour to the matter. To render it more plausible, to give it a more specious appearance

To paint in bright or lively colours. To see or describe things in *couleur de rose*

To put a false colour on a matter. To misinterpret it, or put a false construction on it.

To sail under false colours. To act hypocritically, to try to attain your object by appearing to be other than you are. The term is a nautical one, and refers to the practice of pirates approaching their unsuspecting prey with false colours at the mast.

To see things in their true colours. To see them as they really are.

Under colour of. Under pretence of; under the alleged authority of

Wearing his colours. Taking his part; being strongly attached to him. The idea is from livery

With colours nailed to the mast. Holding out to the bitter end If the colours are nailed to the mast they cannot be lowered in sign of defeat or submission

With the colours. Said of a soldier who is on the active strength of a regiment, as opposed to one in the reserve

Colours. TECHNICAL TERMS

Accidental colours. Those colours seen on a white ground after looking for some time at a bright object, such as the sun The accidental colour of *red* is bluish green, of *orange* dark blue, of *violet* yellow, and the converse

Complementary colours. Colours which, in combination, produce white light The colour transmitted is always complementary to the one reflected

Fast colours. Colours which do not wash out in water.

Fundamental colours The seven colours of the spectrum violet, indigo, blue, green, yellow, orange, and red

Primary, or simple colours. Colours which cannot be produced by mixing other colours Those generally accepted as primary are red, yellow, and blue, but violet is sometimes substituted for the last named

Secondary colours. Those which result from the mixture of two or more primary colours, such as orange, green, and purple.

Colours of university boats.—Cambridge—light blue Oxford—dark blue.

National colours *See* FLAGS

Regimental colours. The flags peculiar to Regiments, once carried into battle, on which they are entitled to embroider their battle-honours—the names of actions in which they distinguished themselves, and associated with the unit by permission of the King These flags are now laid up on the outbreak of war in the Cathedral or great church of the territory from which the Regiment is raised The Royal Regiment of Artillery has no colours, regarding its guns with special veneration instead (to allow one's guns to be captured by the enemy being the same disgrace as having one's colours captured) The Regimental colours of Napoleon's Army were the famous eagle standards, copied from the eagles of the Roman legions, the capture of a Napoleonic eagle was such an unusual feat that Regiments which did so (such as the Scots Greys) usually incorporated the eagle into their Regimental device.

Colours. IN SYMBOLISM, ECCLESIASTICAL USE, etc

Black
In blazonry, sable, signifying prudence, wisdom, and constancy, it is engraved by perpendicular and horizontal lines crossing each other at right angles
In art, signifying evil, falsehood, and error
In Church decoration it is used for Good Friday.
As a mortuary colour, signifying grief, despair, death (In the Catholic Church violet may be substituted for black)
In metals it is represented by lead.
In precious stones it is represented by the diamond.
In planets it stands for Saturn

Blue:
Hope, love of divine works (in dresses) divine contemplation, piety, sincerity
In blazonry, azure, signifying chastity, loyalty, fidelity, it is engraved by horizontal lines
In art (as an angel's robe) it signifies fidelity and faith, (as the robe of the Virgin Mary), modesty and (in the Catholic Church) humility and expiation.
In Church decoration, blue and green are used indifferently for ordinary Sundays, and blue for all weekdays after Trinity Sunday
As a mortuary colour it signifies eternity (applied to Deity), immortality (applied to man).
In metals it is represented by tin.
In precious stones it is represented by sapphire.
In planets it stands for Jupiter

Pale Blue
Peace, Christian prudence, love of good works, a serene conscience

Green
Faith, gladness, immortality, the resurrection of the just, (in dresses) the gladness of the faithful
In blazonry, vert, signifying love, joy, abundance, it is engraved from left to right
In art, signifying hope, joy, youth, spring (among the Greeks and Moors it signifies victory).
In Church decoration it signifies God's bounty, mirth, gladness, the resurrection, and is used indifferently with blue for ordinary Sundays
In metals it is represented by copper
In precious stones it is represented by the emerald
In planets it stands for Venus.

Pale Green:
Baptism.

Purple·
Justice, royalty
In blazonry, purpure, signifying temperance, it is engraved by lines slanting from right to left
In art, signifying royalty
In metals it is represented by quicksilver
In precious stones it is represented by amethyst
In planets it stands for Mercury

Red
Martyrdom for faith, charity, (in dresses) divine love Innocent III says of martyrs and apostles, "*Hi et illi sunt flores rosarum et lilia convallium.*" (*De Sacr alto Myst* , i, 64)
In blazonry, gules, blood-red is called sanguine The former signifies magnanimity, and the latter, fortitude, it is engraved by perpendicular lines
In Church decoration it is used for martyrs, for Ash Wednesday, for the last three days of Holy Week, and for Whit Sunday
In metals it is represented by iron (the metal of war)
In precious stones it is represented by the ruby.
In planets it stands for Mars

White
In blazonry, argent; signifying purity, truth, innocence, in engravings *argent* is left blank
In art, priests, Magi, and Druids are arrayed in white Jesus after the resurrection should be draped in white
In Church decoration it is used for festivals of Our Lord, for Easter, and for all Saints except Martyrs
As a mortuary colour it indicates hope
In metals it is represented by silver
In precious stones it is represented by the pearl.
In planets it stands for Diana or the Moon

Yellow
In blazonry, or, signifying faith, constancy, wisdom, glory, in engravings it is shown by dots
In modern art, signifying jealousy, inconstancy, incontinence In France the doors of traitors used to be daubed with yellow, and in some countries Jews were obliged to dress in yellow In Spain the executioner is dressed in red and yellow
In Christian art Judas is arrayed in yellow, but St Peter is also arrayed in golden yellow
In metals it is represented by gold
In precious stones it is represented by the topaz.
In planets it stands for Apollo or the Sun

Violet Brown, or Grey
are used *in Church decoration* for Advent and Lent, and in other symbolism *violet* usually stands for penitence, and *grey* for tribulation

Colour-blindness. Incapacity of discerning one colour from another The term was introduced by Sir David Brewster; formerly it was known as *Daltonism,* because it was first described by John Dalton (1766-1844), the scientist (who himself suffered from it), in 1794 It is of three sorts (1) inability to discern any colours, so that everything is either black or white, shade or light, (2) inability to distinguish between primary colours, as red, blue, and yellow, or secondary colours, as green, purple, and orange, and (3) inability to distinguish between such composite colours as browns, greys, and neutral tints Except in this one respect, the colour-blind may have excellent vision

Colour sergeant. Originally the senior non-commissioned officer of a military unit, who had charge of the regimental colours in the field It is now a rank, bearing a sergeant's chevrons but carrying with it extra pay, and is awarded for special responsibilities greater than those of a sergeant but not sufficient to deserve warrant officer's rank The equivalent in the Royal Regiment of Artillery, which does not bear colours, is staff sergeant

Colporteur. A hawker or pedlar, so called because he carries his basket or pack round his neck (Fr *col*, neck, *porter*, to carry). The term is more especially applied to hawkers of religious books

Colt. A person new to office, an awkward young fellow who needs "breaking in", specifically, in legal use, a barrister who attended a sergeant-at-law at his induction

I accompanied the newly made Chief Baron as his colt —POLLOCK

In cricket a Colt team is made up of a club's most promising young players.

The word is used as an abbreviation for "Colt s Revolver," patented by Col Sam Colt (U S.A) in 1835, and it is also an old nautical term for a piece of knotted rope 18 inches long for the special benefit of ship boys, a cat-o'-nine-tails

To colt. Obsolete slang for to befool, gull, cheat

Harebrain We are fools, tame fools!
Bellamore Come, let's go seek him
      He shall be hanged before he colt us so basely
BEAUMONT and FLETCHER *Wit Without Money*, iii, 2

The verb is still used in provincial dialects for making a newcomer pay his footing

Colt-pixy. A pixy, puck, or mischievous fairy To colt-pixy is to take what belongs to the pixies, and is specially applied to the gleaning of apples after the crop has been gathered in.

Colt's-tooth The love of youthful pleasure Chaucer uses the word "coltish" for skittish, and his Wife of Bath says:—

He was I trowe, a twenty winter old,
And I was fourty, if I shal seye sooth,
But yet I hadde alwey a coltes tooth
                              Prologue 602

Horses have colt's teeth at three years old, a period of their life when their passions are strongest

      Well, said, Lord Sands,
Your colt's-tooth is not cast yet
      SHAKESPEARE *Henry VIII*, 1, 3
Her merry dancing-days are done,
She has a colt's-tooth still, I warrant
                        KING *Orpheus and Eurydice*

Columbine A stock character in old Italian comedy, where she first appeared about 1560, and thence transplanted to English pantomime She was the daughter of Pantaloon (*q v*), and the sweetheart of Harlequin (*q v*), and, like him, was supposed to be invisible to mortal
8*

eyes. Columbina in Italian is a pet name for a lady-love, and means dove-like

Columbus of the Skies, The Sir William Herschel (1738-1822), discoverer of Uranus, was so called. The name has also been applied to Galileo (1564-1642), Tycho Brahe (1546-1601), and Sir Isaac Newton (1642-1727).

Column The Column of Marcus Aurelius Erected at Rome in memory of the Emperor Marcus Aurelius Antoninus Like that of Trajan (*q v*), this column is covered externally with spiral bas-reliefs representing the wars carried on by the emperor It is a Roman Doric column of marble on a square pedestal, and (omitting the statue) is 95 ft. in height

Sixtus V caused the original statue of this column to be replaced, in 1589 by a figure of St Paul.

The Column at Boulogne, or The Column of the Grand Army, a marble Doric column, 176 ft high, surmounted by a bronze statue of Napoleon I, to commemorate the camp of Boulogne, formed 1804-5 with the intention of invading England

The Duke of York's Column, in London, at the top of the Waterloo Steps leading from Waterloo Place into the Mall Erected in 1830-3 in memory of Frederick, Duke of York, second son of George III, who died in 1827. It is of the Tuscan order, was designed by R. Wyatt, and is made of Aberdeen granite It is 124 ft. in height, it contains a winding staircase to the platform, and on the summit is a statue of the duke by Sir R Westmacott.

Columns, or Pillars, of Hercules. See PILLAR

The Column of July. Erected in Paris in 1840, on the spot where the Bastille stood, to commemorate the revolution of July, 1830, when Charles X abdicated It is a bronze Corinthian column, 13 ft in diameter, and 154 ft in height and is surmounted by a gilded statue of Liberty

London's Column. See MONUMENT

The Nelson Column. In Trafalgar Square, London, was erected in 1843 The four lions, by Landseer, were added in 1867. It is a Corinthian column of Devonshire granite on a square base, copied from a column in the temple of Mars Ultor (the avenging god of war) at Rome, it stands 145 ft high, the statue surmounting it (by E H Baily, R A) being 17 ft high The following reliefs in bronze are on the sides of the pedestal —(*North*) the battle of the Nile, where Nelson was wounded, (*south*) Nelson's death at the battle of Trafalgar; (*east*) the bombardment of Copenhagen, and (*west*) the battle of St. Vincent

Column of the Place Vendôme. Paris, 1806-10, made of marble encased with bronze, and erected in honour of Napoleon I The spiral outside represents in bas-relief the battles of Napoleon I, ending with Austerlitz in 1805. It is 142 ft in height and is an imitation of Trajan's Column. In 1871 the statue of Napoleon, which surmounted it, was hurled to the ground by the Communards, but in 1874 a statue of Liberty was substituted.

Trajan's Column. At Rome; made of marble A D 114, by Apollodorus It is a Roman Doric column of marble, 127½ ft in height, on a square pedestal, and has inside a spiral staircase of 185 steps lighted by 40 windows It was surmounted by a statue of the Emperor Trajan, but Sixtus V supplanted the original statue by that of St Peter The spiral outside represents in bas-relief the battles of the emperor

Coma Berenices. *See* BERENICE.

Comazant (kom´ a zănt) Another name for Corposant (*q v*).

Comb A crabtree comb. Slang for a cudgel To smooth your hair with a crabtree comb, is to give the head a knock with a stick

Reynard's wonderful comb. This comb existed only in the brain of Master Fox He said it was made of the Panthera's bone, the perfume of which was so fragrant that no one could resist following it, and the wearer of the comb was always cheerful and merry (*Reynard the Fox*)

To comb out. To disentangle the hair, or remove foreign bodies from it, with a comb During World War I the term was given a slang use in connexion with the English recruiting campaigns under the Military Service Acts A comb-out was a thorough clearing out or clean sweep of men of military age in offices, works, etc , and getting them into the Army

To comb the cat. An old military and naval phrase for untangling the cords of a cat-o'-nine-tails by drawing it through the fingers

To comb your noddle with a three-legged stool (*Taming of the Shrew*, i, I) is to beat you about the head with a stool Many stools, such as those used by milkmaids, are still made with three legs, and these handy weapons seem to have been used at one time pretty freely, especially by angry women

To cut someone's comb. To take down a person's conceit In allusion to the practice of cutting the combs of capons

To set up one's comb To be cockish and vainglorious.

Come. A come down. Loss of prestige or position

Can you come that? Can you equal it? Here, ' come" means to arrive at, to accomplish

Come February, Michaelmas, etc. A colloquialism for ' next February," etc
Come Lammas-eve at night shall she be fourteen
  SHAKESPEARE *Romeo and Juliet*, i, 3.

Come home Return to your house, to touch one's feelings or interest
I doe now publish my Essayes which, of all my other workes, have been most currant for that, as it seems, they come home to men's businesse and bosomes —BACON *Epistle Dedicatory to the Essays*, 1625

Come inside. A humorously scornful remark at one time made to one who was talking nonsense or behaving in a foolish manner. The allusion is to a picture in *Punch* showing a lunatic looking over the wall of an asylum at an angler fishing, and, when he hears that the latter has been there all day without getting a bite and proposes still to remain, the lunatic feelingly invites him to 'come inside" to the asylum

Come out Said of a young woman after she has been presented at Court, or has entered into society as a "grown up" person. She "comes out into society.'

Don't try to come it over me. Don't try to boss me or order me about, don't set yourself in a position above me

Has he come it? Has he lent the money? Has he hearkened to your request? Has he come over to your side?

If the worst comes to the worst. *See* WORST.

Marry come up. *See* MARRY

To come a cropper. *See* CROPPER.

To come down a peg. *See* PEG

To come down handsome. To pay a good price, reward, subscription, etc

To come down upon one. To reproach, to punish severely, to make a peremptory demand

To come it strong. To lay it on thick, to exaggerate or overdo *See* DRAW IT MILD

To come off. To occur, to take place, as "my holiday didn't come off after all "

To come off with honours. To proceed to the end successfully

To come over one. To wheedle one to do or give something, to cheat or overreach one, to conquer or get one's own way

To come round. *See* COMING

To come short. Not to be sufficient. ' To come short of" means to miss or fail of attaining

To come the old soldier over one. To attempt to intimidate or bully one by an assumption of authority

To come to. To amount to, to obtain possession "It will not come to much " To regain consciousness after a fainting-fit, etc

To come to blows. To start fighting

To come to grief, to hand *See* GRIEF, HAND

To come to pass To happen, to befall, to come about
It came to pass in those days that there went out a decree —*Luke* ii, 1
What thou hast spoken is come to pass —*Jer* xxxii, 24

To come to stay. An expression used of something which possesses permanent qualities

To come to the hammer, the point, the scratch. *See* HAMMER; POINT; SCRATCH

To come under. To fall under, to be classed under.

To come up smiling To laugh at discomfiture or punishment, to emerge from disaster unruffled.

To come up to. To equal, to obtain the same number of marks, to amount to the same quantity

To come upon the parish. To live in the workhouse, to be supported by the parish

What's to come of it? What's to come of him? A contracted form of *become*

To come of a good stock is to be descended from a good family.

He is coming round Recovering from sickness, recovering from a fit of the sulks, returning to friendship, **he is coming round to my way of thinking,** he is beginning to think as I do

Comedy means a village song (Gr. *komĕ-ōdĕ*), referring to the village merry-makings, in which songs still take a conspicuous place. The Greeks had certain festal processions of great licentiousness, held in honour of Dionysus, in the suburbs of their cities, and termed *komoi* or village revels On these occasions an ode was generally sung, and this ode was the foundation of Greek comedy. *Cp.* TRAGEDY.

The Father of Comedy. Aristophanes (about 450-380 B.C), the Athenian dramatist

Comet Wine. A term denoting wine of superior quality A notion prevailed that the grapes of "comet years," *i e* years 'in which remarkable comets appear, are better in flavour than those of other years
The old gentleman yet nurses some few bottles of the famous comet year (*i e* 1811), emphatically called comet wine —*The Times*

Command Night. In theatrical parlance, a night on which a certain play is performed by Royal command

Commandment. The ten commandments. A common piece of slang in Elizabethan days for the ten fingers or nails
Could I come near your beauty with my nails
I'd set my ten commandments in your face
SHAKESPEARE 2 *Henry VI*, i, 3

The eleventh commandment An ironical expression, signifying "Thou shalt not be found out "

Commando (ko man' dō) This word was originally used in the South African War, being the term used by the Boers to designate a mobile body of armed men In World War II it was used as the name of the volunteer body of special troops trained for hazardous assault tasks The word has since been again extended to mean a member of such a body, one of a commando.

Comme il faut (kom ēl fō) (Fr) As it should be, quite proper, quite according to etiquette or rule
It never can have been *comme il faut* in any age or nation for a man of note to be continually asking for money —MACAULAY in Trevelyan's *Life*, vol ii, ch. xiv.

Commendam (kom en' dăm). A **living in commendam** is a living temporarily held by someone until an incumbent is appointed The term was specially applied to a bishop who, when accepting the bishopric, had to give up all his preferments, but to whom such preferments were *commended* by the Crown till they could be properly transferred This practice was abolished by Act of Parliament in 1836

Commendation Ninepence. This was a bent silver ninepenny piece, commonly used in the 17th century as a love-token, giver and receiver saying, "To my love, from my love " Sometimes the coin was broken, each keeping a part
Like commendation ninepence, crooked,
With "To and from my love" it looked.
Hudibras

Commissar (kom' i sar). An official in the U S S R who has charge of a separate branch of government administration The Council of People's Commissars is composed of the chairman, his deputy, and people's commissars for Foreign Affairs, Armed Forces, Foreign Trade, Posts, Finance, etc They are responsible to the Supreme Council of the U S.S R

Committee. A committee of the whole house, in Parliamentary language, is when the Speaker leaves the chair and all the members form a committee, where anyone may speak once or more than once. In such cases the chair is occupied by the Chairman of Committees, elected with each new Parliament

A joint committee is a committee nominated partly by the House of Lords and partly by the House of Commons

A standing committee is a committee which continues to the end of the current session. To this committee are referred all questions which fall within the scope of its appointment

Commodore. A corruption of "commander" (Fr *commandeur*, Dut *kommandeur*) A naval officer ranking above a captain and below a rear-admiral, ranking with brigadier in the army By courtesy the title is given to the senior captain when two or more ships are in company, also to the president of a yacht club.
In the United States Navy the office has been abolished since 1899, but the title was retained as a retiring rank for captains

Common Short for common land, which is public property A common cannot be enclosed and denied to the use of the public without an Act of Parliament. Until the late 18th and early 19th centuries every village in England had its common lands, divided into strips of which each villager had the use of one or more to cultivate for his own use. When the crops had been taken in from these, the whole area was thrown open for the common grazing of cattle, etc By various Acts of Parliament these common lands were taken from the villagers and enclosed by larger farmers, etc , only the less fertile portions being left uncultivated and given over to the common grazing purposes of the community. In Scotland an Act of 1695 gave power to divide the common land among the persons who had rights thereon.

Common Pleas. Civil actions at law brought by one subject against another—not by the Crown against a subject　The *Court of Common Pleas* was for the trial of civil (not capital) offences, in 1875 it was abolished, and in 1880 it was represented by the Common Pleas Division and merged in the King's Bench Division

Common Prayer. The Book of Common Prayer. The book used by the Established Church of England in "divine service" Common, in this case, means *united*, or *general*

The first complete English Book of Common Prayer (known as the First Prayer-book of Edward VI) appeared in 1549, this was revised in 1552 and 1559, slight alterations were made at the Hampton Court Conference (1604), and it received its final form, except for some very minor changes after the Savoy Conference of 1662

In 1927 a revised Prayer Book was accepted by the Houses of Convocation and the Church Assembly　It was, however, rejected by the House of Commons on the grounds that the proposed changes weakened the Protestant character of the book.

Common sense. Natural intelligence, good, sound, practical sense, general sagacity Formerly the expression denoted a supposed internal sense held to be common to all five senses, or one that acted as a bond or connecting medium for them

Commoner. The Great Commoner. The elder William Pitt (1708-78), afterwards Earl of Chatham

Commons　To put someone on short commons To stint him, to give him scanty meals　In the University of Cambridge the food provided for each student at breakfast was called his *commons*, hence food in general or meals

To come into commons　To enter a society in which the members have a common or general dinner table　To be removed from the society is to be *discommonsed*.—

He [Dryden] was in trouble [at Cambridge] on July 19th, 1652, when he was discommonsed and gated for a fortnight for disobedience and contumacy—SAINTSBURY *Dryden*, ch 1

Commonwealths, Ideal. The most famous ideal, or imaginary, Commonwealths are those sketched by Plato in the *Republic* (from which all the others derive), by Cicero in his *De Republica*, by St Augustine in his *De Civitate Dei* (*The City of God*), by Dante in his *De Monarchia*, by Sir Thomas More in *Utopia* (1516), by Bacon in the *New Atlantis* (a fragment, 1616), by Campanella, a Dominican friar (about 1630), and by Samuel Butler in *Erewhon* (1872)

To these some would add Johnson's *Rasselas* (1759), Lytton's *Coming Race* (1871), Bellamy's *Looking Backward* (1888), Wm Morris's *News from Nowhere* (1891), H G Wells's *In the Days of the Comet* (1906) and *The World Set Free* (1914).

Communist　An adherent of communism

Communism means a self-supporting society distinguished by common labour, common property, and common means of intelligence and recreation—G J HOLYOAKE, in "*The Labour World,*" No 11, 1890

Companion Ladder. The ladder leading from the poop to the main deck, also the staircase from the deck to a cabin

Companions of Jehu. The *Chouans* (*q v*) were so called, from a fanciful analogy between their self-imposed task and that appointed to Jehu, on being set over the kingdom of Israel Jehu was to cut off Ahab and Jezebel, with all their house, and all the priests of Baal　The Chouans were to cut off all who assassinated Louis XVI, and see that his brother (*Jehu*) was placed on the throne

Comparisons are Odorous　So says Dogberry (*Much Ado About Nothing*, iii, 5)

　　We own your verses are melodious,
　　But then comparisons are odious
　　　　SWIFT *Answer to Sheridan's "Simile."*

Compass, Mariner's.　*See* MARINER'S COMPASS

Complementary Colours.　*See* COLOURS.

Complex. A combination of memories and wishes which exercise an influence on the personality

Inferiority complex. A term applied to a supposed feeling of inferiority in persons who appear over-conscious of their own shortcomings

To have a complex about something　To have a strong feeling either for or against something, to be over-concerned about it

Compline (kom' plin)　The last of the seven R C canonical hours, said about 8 or 9 p m, and so called because it *completes* the series of the daily prayers or hours.　From M E and O Fr. *complie*, Lat *completa* (hora)

In ecclesiastical Lat *vesperinus*, from *vesper*, means evening service, and *completinus* seems to be formed on the same model.

Complutensian Polyglot.　*See* BIBLE, SPECIALLY NAMED.

Compos mentis.　*See* NON COMPOS MENTIS.

Compostella (kom pos tel' a).　The city in Spain where are preserved the relics of St. James the Great, a corruption of *Giacomopostolo* (James the Apostle)　Its full name is Santiago (*i e.* St James) de Compostella　*See* JAMES, ST.

Compostella, Sacred chickens of.　*See* ADEPT

Comrades. Literally, those who sleep in the same *chamber* (*camera*)　It is a Spanish military term derived from the custom of dividing soldiers into chambers, and the early form of the word in English is *camerade*

Comus (kō' mus).　In Milton's masque of this name, the god of sensual pleasure, son of Bacchus and Circe　The name is from the Gr *komos*, carousal

In the masque the elder brother is meant for Viscount Brackley, the younger brother is Thomas Egerton, and the lady is Lady Alice

Egerton, children of the Earl of Bridgewater, at whose castle in Ludlow it was first presented in 1634.

Con amore (kon a môr' i) (Ital.) With heart and soul, as, "He did it *con amore*"—*i. e.* lovingly, with delight, and therefore in good earnest

Con spirito (Ital.). With quickness and vivacity. A musical term.

Conan (kō' nan) The Thersites of *Fingal* (in Macpherson's *Ossian*), brave even to rashness

Blow for blow or claw for claw, as Conan said. Conan made a vow never to take a blow without returning it, when he descended into the infernal regions, the arch fiend gave him a cuff, which Conan instantly returned, saying "Claw for claw"

Conceptionists. *See* FRANCISCANS.

Concert Pitch The degree of sharpness or flatness adopted by musicians acting in concert, that all the instruments may be in accord In England "concert pitch" is usually slightly higher than the pitch at which instruments are generally tuned

Hence the figurative use of the term to **screw oneself up to concert pitch** is to make oneself absolutely ready, prepared for any emergency or anything one may have to do

Conchy. *See* CONSCIENTIOUS OBJECTOR

Concierge (kon' se ârj) (Fr) The door-porter of a public building, an hotel, or a house divided into flats, etc.

Conciergerie (Fr) The office or room of a concierge, a porter's lodge; a state prison. During the Revolution it was the prison where the chief victims were confined prior to execution.

Conclamatio. Amongst the ancient Romans, the loud cry raised by those standing round a death-bed at the moment of death It probably had its origin in the idea of calling back the departed spirit, and was similar to the Irish howl over the dead "One not howled over" (*corpus nondum conclamatum*) meant one at the point of death; and "one howled for" was one given up for dead or really deceased Hence the phrase *conclamatum est*, he is dead past all hope, he has been called and gives no sign Virgil makes the palace ring with howls when Dido burnt herself to death

> Lamentis, gemituque, et fœmineo ululato,
> Texta fremunt   *Æneid*, iv, 667.

Conclave. Literally, a set of rooms, all of which can be opened by one key (Lat. *con clavis*) The word is applied to the little cells erected for the cardinals who meet to choose a new Pope; hence, the assembly of cardinals for this purpose; hence, any private assembly for discussion. The conclave of cardinals dates back to 1271 Some days after the death of a Pope the cardinals assembled in Rome enter the conclave apartments of the Vatican and are there locked in in such stringent seclusion that no contact whatsoever occurs between them and the outside world Votes are taken morning and evening until one candidate has secured a two-thirds majority of the votes He is then acclaimed Pope.

Shakespeare used the word for the body of cardinals itself —

> And once more in my arms I bid him [Cardinal Campeius] welcome,
> And thank the holy conclave for their loves
>   *Henry VIII*, ii, 2

To meet in solemn conclave is a phrase used to describe any gathering to decide matters which are important to them.

Concordat (kon kôr' dăt) An agreement made between a ruler and the Pope, as the Concordat of 1801 between Napoleon and Pius VII, the Concordat of 1516 between François I and Leo X to abolish the "pragmatic sanction", and the Germanic Concordat of 1448 between Frederick III and Nicholas V In 1929 a concordat between the Papacy and the Italian government established the Vatican State

Concrete Numbers. *See* ABSTRACT

Condominium (con dŏ min' i um) This is a political phrase to describe the joint government or sovereignty of two or more powers over a region or country An example of this is the condominium of the New Hebrides shared by Britain and France

Condottieri. Leaders of mercenaries and military adventurers, particularly from about the 14th to 16th centuries The most noted of these brigand chiefs in Italy were Guarnieri, Lando, Francesco of Carmagnola, and Francesco Sforza. The singular is Condottiere

Confederate States The eleven States which seceded from the Union in the American Civil War (1861-66)—viz Georgia, North and South Carolina, Virginia, Tennessee, Alabama, Louisiana, Arkansas, Mississippi, Florida, Texas They were all readmitted into the Union between 1866 and 1870

Confederation of the Rhine. Sixteen German provinces in 1806 dissolved their connexion with Germany, and allied themselves with France It was dissolved in 1813.

Confession, Seal of. Confession is a collective term for the whole administration of the R.C. sacrament of penance. The priest who bears the penitent's confession is bound under the most binding vows not to divulge anything he hears in the confessional, nor can he be forced to reveal in the witness-box of a court of law any information he may have thus obtained.

Confusion Worse Confounded. Disorder made worse than before

> With ruin upon ruin, rout on rout,
> Confusion worse confounded
>   MILTON *Paradise Lost*, ii, line 996

Congé (kon jā') (Fr , leave) "To give a person his congé" is to dismiss him from your service. "To take one's congé" is to give notice to friends of your departure This is done by leaving a card at the friend's house with the letters P P C (*pour prendre conge*, to take leave) inscribed on the left-hand corner.

Congé d'elire (Fr , leave to elect) A royal warrant given to the dean and chapter of a diocese to elect the person nominated by the Crown to their vacant see

Congleton Bears Men of Congleton The tradition is that a Congleton parish clerk sold the church Bible to buy a bear, so that the townsmen could have some fun at bearbaiting

Congregationalists. Those Protestant Dissenters who maintain that each congregation is an independent community, and has a right to make its own laws and choose its own minister They derive from the Puritans and Independents of the time of Queen Elizabeth

Congress (kon' gres) In its particular sense this word is applied to the supreme legislative body of the U.S.A., composed of the Senate and the House of Representatives (96 senators and 435 representatives). Senators are elected for 6 years, representatives for 2 years The President can veto any legislation passed by Congress, but if it be passed again by a two-thirds majority it becomes law

The Indian National Congress was founded in 1885, but after various vicissitudes was reformed by Gandhi in 1920 for the purpose of winning the independence of India This was gained in 1947 with the formation of the Republic of India, and Dominion of Pakistan

Congreve Rockets. A special kind of rocket invented in 1808 for use in war by Sir William Congreve (1772-1828) He was Controller of the Royal Laboratory at Woolwich.

Congreves. Predecessors of Lucifer matches, also invented by Sir Wm. Congreve The splints were first dipped in sulphur, and then tipped with chlorate of potash paste, in which gum was substituted for sugar, and there was added a small quantity of sulphide of antimony The match was ignited by being drawn through a fold of sandpaper with pressure *Cp* PROMETHEANS, LUCIFERS

Conjuring Cap. I must put on my conjuring cap—*i e* your question requires deliberate thought, and I must reflect on it Tradition says that Eric XIV, King of Sweden (1560-77), was a great believer in magic, and had an "enchanted cap" by means of which he pretended to exercise power over the elements. When a storm arose, his subjects used to say "The king has got on his conjuring cap."

Conker (cong' kĕr) This is a children's name for a horse-chestnut, and is possibly derived from the French *conque*, a shell Schoolboys thread the chestnuts on a string and then play conkers by each taking his turn at striking his opponent's conker with his own until one or other is destroyed

Another curious slang use of this word is *conk*, meaning a nose, hence *conky* a big- or beak-nosed person

The phrase to conk out, meaning to break down, to cease to fire (of a motor) is probably onomatopoeic.

Connecticut (kŏ net' i kut), is the Mohegan dialect word *Quonaughicut*, meaning "long tidal river"

Conqueror. The title was applied to the following —

Alexander the Great *The conqueror of the world* (356-323 B C)

Alfonso I, of Portugal (About 1109-1185.)

Aurungzebe the Great The most powerful of the Moguls (1619, 1659-1707)

James I of Aragon (1206, 1213-76.)

Mohammed II, Sultan of Turkey. (1430-81)

Othman or Osman I Founder of the Turkish power (1259, 1299-1326.)

Francisco Pizarro *Conquistador.* So called because he conquered Peru (1475-1541)

William, Duke of Normandy. So called because he obtained England by conquest. (1027, 1066-87)

Conqueror's nose. A prominent straight nose, rising at the bridge Charlemagne had such a nose, so had Henry the Fowler (Heinrich I of Germany), Rudolf I of Germany, Friedrich I of Hohenzollern, famous for reducing to order his unruly barons by blowing up their castles (1382-1440), our own "Iron Duke", Bismarck, the Iron Chancellor of Prussia, etc

Conquest, The. The accession of William I to the crown of England (1066)

Conscience Conscience clause. A clause in an Act of Parliament to relieve persons with conscientious scruples from certain requirements in it It generally has reference to religious matters, but it came into wider prominence in connexion with the Compulsory Vaccination Act of 1898

Conscience money. Money paid anonymously to Government by persons who have defrauded the revenue, or who have understated their income to the income-tax assessors The sum is advertised in the *Gazette*

Court of Conscience. Established for the recovery of small debts in London and other trading places in the reign of Henry VIII They were also called Courts of Requests, and are now superseded by county courts

Why should not Conscience have vacation,
As well as other courts o' the nation?
BUTLER *Hudibras*, ii, 2.

Have you the conscience to [demand such a price]? Can your conscience allow you to [demand such a price]?

In all conscience. As, "And enough too, in all conscience" Meaning that the demand made is as much as conscience would tolerate without accusing the person of actual dishonesty to the verge of that fine line which separates honesty from dishonesty

My conscience! An oath. I swear by my conscience.

To make a matter of conscience of it. To treat it according to the dictates of conscience, to deal with it conscientiously

To speak one's conscience To speak one's own mind, give one's own private thoughts or opinions

By my troth, I will speak my conscience of the king
—SHAKESPEARE· *Henry V*, 1, 4.

Conscientious objector. One who takes advantage of a *conscience clause* (*q v*), and so does not have to comply with some particular requirement of the law in question. The name used to be applied specially to those who would swear legally that they had a conscientious objection to vaccination

In the two World Wars the term was applied to those who obtained exemption from military service on grounds of conscience. These were also known as *Conchies* and *C O s*.

Conscript Fathers In Lat *Patres Conscripti* The Roman senate Romulus instituted a senate consisting of a hundred elders, called *Patres* (Fathers) After the Sabines joined the State, another hundred were added Tarquinius Priscus, the fifth king, added a third hundred, called *Patres Minorum Gentium* When Tarquinius Superbus, the seventh and last king of Rome, was banished, several of the senate followed him, and the vacancies were filled up by Junius Brutus, the first consul The new members were enrolled in the senatorial register and called *Conscripti*, the entire body was then addressed as *Patres* [*et*] *Conscripti* or *Patres, Conscripti*

Consentes Dii. The twelve chief Roman deities—
Jupiter, Apollo, Mars, Neptune, Mercury, and Vulcan
Juno, Vesta, Minerva, Ceres, Diana, and Venus
Ennius puts them into two hexameter verses —
Juno, Vesta, Minerva, Ceres, Diana, Venus, Mars, Mercurius, Jovi', Neptunus, Vulcanus, Apollo.

Called " *consentes*," says Varro,
Quia in consilium Jovis adhibebantur —*De Lingua Latina*, vii, 28

Consenting Stars Stars forming configurations for good or evil In *Judges* v, 20, we read that "the stars in their courses fought against Sisera," *i e* formed unlucky or malignant configurations
. . . Scourge the bad revolting stars
That have consented unto Henry's death
SHAKESPEARE 1 *Henry VI*, 1, 1

Conservative. One who wishes to preserve the union of Church and State, and not radically to alter the constitution The word was first used in this sense in January, 1830, by J Wilson Croker in the *Quarterly Review*—"We have always been conscientiously attached to what is called the Tory, and which might with more propriety be called the Conservative, party" (p 276)
Canning, ten years previously, had used the word in much the same way in a speech delivered at Liverpool in March, 1820

Conservators of the Public Liberties. Officers chosen in England to inspect the treasury and correct abuses in administration, under an enactment of 1244 Conservators were also appointed in ports to take action in the event of breaches of the peace at sea The word is found to-day only in such phrases as *The Thames Conservancy Board* which is concerned with the maintenance of amenities on that river

Consistory. An ecclesiastical court In the Church of Rome it is the assembly in council of the Pope and cardinals, in England it is a diocesan court, presided over by the chancellor of the diocese

Consolidated Fund. In 1751 an Act was passed for consolidating the nine loans bearing different interests, into one common loan bearing an interest of three per cent In 1889 this interest was reduced to two and three-quarter per cent , and in 1903 to two and a half per cent The fund is pledged for the payment of the interest of the national debt, the civil list, the salaries of the judges, ambassadors, and other high officials, etc

Consols. A contraction of Consolidated Fund *See above*

Constable (Lat *comes-stabuli*) means "Master of the Horse" (with which office, however, it now has no connexion in Britain) *Cp* MARSHAL The *Constable of France* was the title of the principal officer of the household of the early Frankish kings, and from being the head groom of the stable he ultimately became commander-in-chief of the army, supreme judge of all military matters and matters pertaining to chivalry, etc The office was abolished in 1627
Constable is also a term for the governor of a fortress, as the Constable of the Tower of London.

The Constable of England, or Lord High Constable, was a similar official in existence before 1066, but since 1521 the title has been granted only temporarily, for the purposes of Coronations

The Lord High Constable of Scotland was an office instituted about 1147 by David I. Conferred by Robert Bruce in 1321 on Sir Gilbert Hay, created Earl of Erroll, heritably, in which family the office still remains

Drink the constable. *See* MOROCCO

To overrun or outrun the constable. To get into debt; to spend more than one's income; to talk about what you do not understand
Quoth Hudibras, Friend Ralph, thou hast
Outrun the constable at last,
For thou hast fallen on a new
Dispute, as senseless as untrue
BUTLER *Hudibras*, i, 3

Who's to pay the constable? Who is to pay the score?

Constantine, Donation of. *See* DECRETALS.

Constantine's Cross. *See* CROSS

Constituent Assembly. The first of the national assemblies of the French Revolution, so called because its chief work was the drawing up of a new constitution for France It sat from 1788 to 1791
After the chaos resultant on the World War II a National Constituent Assembly of 522 deputies was elected in France, according to the constitution promulgated in October, 1945

Constitution. The fundamental laws of a state, the way in which a state is organized or constituted—despotic, aristocratic, democratic, monarchic, oligarchic etc.

To give a nation a constitution. To give it fixed laws, and to limit the powers of the nominal ruler or head of the state, so that the people are not subject to arbitrary government or caprice A despotism or autocracy is solely under the unrestricted will of the despot or autocrat

Constitutions of Clarendon. *See* CLARENDON

Apostolic Constitutions. A doctrinal code relating to the Church, the duties of Christians, etc, contained in eight books of doubtful date, possibly as early as the 3rd century, but certainly later than the time of the Apostles, to whom at one time they were attributed

Consummatum est (kon sŭm' ā tum est) (Lat). It is finished the last words of our Lord on the cross (*John* xix, 30)

> *Meph* O, what will I not do to obtain his soul?
> *Faust* Consummatum est, this pill is ended,
> And Faustus hath bequeathed his soul to Lucifer
> MARLOWE *Doctor Faustus*, v, 74

Contango (kon tăng' gō) In Stock Exchange parlance, the sum paid by the purchaser of stock to the seller for the privilege of deferring the completion of the bargain till the next, or some future, settling day *Cp* BACKWARDATION

Contemplate. To meditate or reflect upon, to consider attentively The word takes us back to the ancient Roman augurs, for the *templum* (whence our *temple*) was that part of the heavens which he wished to consult Having mentally divided it into two parts from top to bottom, he watched to see what would occur, and this watching of the *templum* was called *contemplating*

Contempt of Court. Refusing to conform to the rules of the law courts *Consequential* contempt is that which tends to obstruct the business or lower the dignity of the court by indirection *Direct* contempt is an open insult or resistance to the judge or others officially employed in the court

Contemptibles, The Old. The original Expeditionary Force of 160,000 men that left England in August, 1914, to join the French and Belgians against Germany. The soldiers gave themselves this name as a compliment, from an army order that was said to have been given at Aix on August 19th by the Kaiser to his generals

> It is my royal and imperial command that you exterminate the treacherous English, and walk over General French's contemptible little army

It is only fair to add that this 'order'' is almost certainly apocryphal

Contenement (kon ten' e ment) A word used in Magna Charta, the exact meaning of which is not ascertainable, but which probably denotes the lands and chattels connected with a tenement, whatever befits the social position of a person, as the arms of a gentleman, the merchandise of a trader, the ploughs and wagons of a peasant, etc

> In every case the contenement (a word expressive of chattels necessary to each man's station) was exempted from seizure —HALLAM *Middle Ages*, Pt. 11, ch viii

Contests of Wartburg. Sometimes called The Battles of the Minstrels, these were annual contests held at the Wartburg, a castle in Saxe-Weimar, for a prize given for the best poem Some 150 of these poems are still extant, the best being by Walter von der Vogelweid (1168-1230). The most famous representation

of these contests is in Wagner's opera the *Meistersingers* It was in this same castle that Luther translated the Bible into German

Continence of a Scipio. It is said that a beautiful princess fell into the hands of Scipio Africanus, and he refused to see her, "lest he should be tempted to forget his principles '' Similar stories, whether fable or not, are told of many historical characters, including Cyrus and Alexander

Continental. Not worth a Continental Worthless. No more valuable than the bank-notes issued by the American Continental Congress during the War of Independence and until the adoption of the Constitution, which were backed by no reserves whatever

Continental System. A name given to Napoleon's plan for shutting out Great Britain from all commerce with the continent of Europe He forbade under pain of war any nation of Europe to receive British exports, or to send imports to any of the British dominions. It began November 21st, 1806

Contingent The quota of troops furnished by each of several contracting powers, according to agreement The word properly means something happening by chance, hence we call a fortuitous event a contingency

Continuity Man, Girl. The technique of cinematography allows of a play, etc , being photographed in scenes and incidents not necessarily in sequence Each scene, etc , is, moreover, "shot" many times It is therefore essential that the greatest care be taken to see that every detail of costume, scenery, etc,, is correct when one scene or incident is ' shot' several times With poor continuity an actress may be wearing a ring when she sits down to dinner, and later in the same meal be found without one It is the task of the continuity man or girl to see that such a mistake is averted

Contra (l at) Against, generally in the phrase *pro and contra* or *pro* and *con* (*q v*) In bookkeeping a *contra* is an entry on the right-hand, or credit side, of the ledger. *See* PER CONTRA

A **contra-account** is one kept by a firm which both buys from and sells to the same client, so that the transactions cancel out as paper entries

Contra bonos mores (Lat) Not in accordance with good manners, not *comme il faut* (*q v*)

Contra jus gentium (Lat) Against the law of nations, specially applied to usages in war which are contrary to the laws or customs of civilized peoples

Contra mundum (Lat). Against the world at large Used of an innovator or reformer who sets his opinion against that of everyone else, and specially connected with Athanasius in his vehement opposition to the Arians

Contretemps (Fr.). A mischance, something inopportune. Literally, "out of time ''

Conventicle. The word was applied originally by the early Christians to their meeting-places, but it was soon used contemptuously by their opponents, and it thus acquired a bad or derisive sense, such as a clandestine meeting with a sinister intention, a private meeting of monks to protest against the election of a proposed abbot, for instance, was called a conventicle   It now means a religious meeting, or meeting-place, of Dissenters, a chapel (*q v.*)

Conventicle Act. An Act passed in 1664 declaring that a meeting of more than five persons held for religious worship and not in accordance with the Book of Common Prayer was a seditious assembly.   It was repealed by the Toleration Act (1689)

Convention, The. Two Parliaments were so called· one in 1660, because it was not held by the order of the king, but was convened by General Monk, and that convened on January 22nd, 1689, to confer the crown on William and Mary

In the U S A a convention is a meeting of a number of persons, as delegates, for any common purpose   The meeting held by a political party for the purpose of selecting a candidate for the presidential election is called a National Convention.   In the French Revolution the National Convention was the sovereign assembly convened by the Constituent Assembly   It governed France from Sept , 1792, to Oct , 1795

Convey. A polite term for *steal.*   Thieves are, by a similar euphemism, called *conveyers* (Lat *con-veho*, to carry away)

> Convey, the wise it call, Steal! foh' a fico for the phrase.—SHAKESPEARE *Merry Wives of Windsor*, 1, 3
> Bolingbroke . Go, some of you, convey him to the Tower.
> Rich II O, good' "Convey" Conveyers are ye all, That rise thus nimbly by a true king's fall
> *Richard II*, iv, **4.**

Cooing and Billing, like Philip and Mary on a shilling   The reference is to coins struck in 1555, in which Mary and her consort are placed face to face, and not cheek by jowl, the usual way

> Still amorous, and fond, and billing,
> Like Philip and Mary on a shilling
> *Hudibras*, Pt iii, 1

Cook, Cooking. Terms belonging to cuisine applied to man under different circumstances. Sometimes he is well *basted*, he *boils* with rage, is *baked* with heat, and *burns* with love or jealousy   Sometimes he is *buttered* and well buttered, he is often *cut up*, *devoured* with a flame, and *done brown*   We *dress his jacket* for him, sometimes he is *eaten up* with care; sometimes he is *fried*   We *cook his goose* for him, and sometimes he makes a goose of himself   We make a *hash* of him, and at times he makes a hash of something else   He gets into *hot water*, and sometimes into a *mess* Is made into *mincemeat*, makes mincemeat of his money, and is often in a *pickle*   We are often asked to *toast* him, sometimes he gets well *roasted*, is sometimes *set on fire*, put into a *stew*, or is in a *stew* no one knows why.

A "soft' is *half-baked*, one severely handled is well *peppered*, to falsify accounts is to *cook* or *salt* them, wit is *Attic salt*, and an exaggerated statement must be taken *cum grano salis*

A pert young person is a *sauce box*, a shy lover is a *spoon*, a rich father has to *fork out*, and is sometimes *dished* of his money

A conceited man does not think small *beer* (or small potatoes) of himself, and one's mouth is called a *potato-trap*   A simpleton is ,a *cake*, a *gudgeon*, and a *pigeon*   Some are *cool as a cucumber*, others *hot as a quail*   A chubby child is a little *dumpling*   A woman may be a *duck*, a courtesan was called a *mutton* or *laced mutton*, and a large, coarse hand is a *mutton fist*   A greedy person is a *pig*, a fat one is a *sausage*, and a shy one, if not a sheep, is certainly *sheepish*, while a Lubin casts *sheep's eyes* at his lady-love   A coward is *chicken*-hearted, a fat person is *crummy*, and a cross one is *crusty*, while an aristocrat belongs to the *upper crust* of society   A Yeoman of the Guard is a *beef-eater*, a soldier a *red herring*, or a *lobster*, and a stingy, ill-tempered old man is a *crab*   A walking advertiser between two boards is a *sandwichman*   An alderman in his chain is a *turkey hung with sausages.*   Two persons resembling each other are like as *two peas*   A chit is a mere *sprat*, a delicate maiden a *tit-bit*, and a colourless countenance is is called a *whey-face*   Anything unexpectedly easy is a *piece of cake*

What's cooking? What is in hand   what's doing.

Cook your goose. *See* GOOSE.

Cooked. *The books have been cooked*   The ledger and other trade books have been tampered with, in order to show a false balance.

Cookie-pusher (U S A).   A young and junior diplomat whose most onerous duties appear to consist in handing round plates at official receptions.

Cool. *Cool card; cooling card. See* CARD.

Cool hundred, thousand (or any other sum). The whole of the sum named   Cool, in this case, is merely an emphatic; it may have originally had reference to the calmness and deliberation with which the sum was counted out and the total made up

> He had lost a cool hundred, and would no longer play —FIELDING   *Tom Jones*, VIII, xii

Cool tankard or cool cup.   A drink made of wine and water, with lemon, sugar, and borage; sometimes also slices of cucumber

Coon, A. Short for raccoon, a small North American animal, about the size of a fox, valued for its fur   The animal was adopted as a badge by the old Whig party in the United States about 1840   In the 19th century the word was slang for a Negro

A coon's age. Quite a long time, a "month of Sundays" (U S slang).

A gone coon. A person in a terrible fix; one on the verge of ruin   The coon being hunted for its fur is a "gone coon" when it is treed and so has no escape from its pursuers

To go the whole coon. An American equivalent of the English "to go the whole hog"   *See* HOG.

Coop. U S slang for prison

To fly the coop is to escape from prison.

Cooper. Half stout and half porter The term arose from the old practice at breweries of allowing the coopers a daily portion of stout and porter As they did not like to drink porter after stout, they mixed the two together

Coot. A silly coot. Stupid as a coot. The coot is a small waterfowl

Bald as a coot The coot has a strong, straight, and somewhat conical bill, the base of which tends to push up the forehead, and there dilates, so as to form a remarkable bare patch.

Cop. To catch, lay hold of, capture. To "get copped" is to get caught by the police, whence *cop* and *copper* (*q v*), a policeman Perhaps connected with Lat *capere*, to take, etc

A fair cop is applied to the case of a criminal caught *in flagrante delicto*

The word is used for catching almost anything, as punishment at school, or even an illness, fever, or cold —

> They thought I was sleepin', ye know,
> And they sed as I'd copped it o' Jim,
> Well, it come like a bit of a blow,
> For I watched by the deathbed of him
> SIMS *Dagonet Ballads* (*The Last Letter*)

The East Anglian word to *cop* meaning to throw or toss (whence *cop-halfpenny*, a name for chuck-farthing) is not connected with this

Copenhagen (kō pen hā′ gĕn) This was the name of the horse ridden by the Duke of Wellington at Waterloo "from four in the morning till twelve at night " He was a rich chestnut, 15 hands high Pensioned off in the paddocks of Stratfieldsaye, Copenhagen lived to the age of twenty-seven, his skeleton is in the United Services Museum, Whitehall

Copernicanism. The doctrine that the earth moves round the sun, in opposition to the doctrine that the sun moves round the earth; so called after Nicolas Copernicus (1473-1543), the Prussian astronomer. *Cp.* PTOLEMAIC SYSTEM

> Whereas it has come to the knowledge of the Holy Congregation that that false Pythagorean doctrine altogether opposed to Holy Scripture, on the mobility of the earth and the immobility of the sun, taught by Nicholas Copernicus This congregation has decreed that the said book of Copernicus be suspended until it be corrected —*Decree of the Holy Congregation of the Index*, 1616

Cophetua (ko fet′ ū a) An imaginary king of Africa, of great wealth, who ' disdained all womankind," and concerning whom a ballad is given in Percy's *Reliques* One day he saw a beggar-girl from his window, and fell in love with her He asked her name, it was Penelophon, called by Shakespeare Zenelophon (*Love s Labour's Lost*, iv, 1) They lived together long and happily, and at death were universally lamented

> King Cophetua loved the beggar-maid
> SHAKESPEARE *Romeo and Juliet*, ii, 1

Copper. Among the old alchemists copper was the symbol of Venus

The name is given to the large vessel used for laundry purposes, cooking, etc , which was formerly made of copper but is now more usually of iron, also to pence, halfpence, farthings, cents, etc , although nowadays they are made of bronze, true copper coinage has not been minted in England since 1860

In slang a **copper** is a policeman, *i e.* one who "cops," or catches, offenders.

Copper captain. A "Brummagem," or sham, captain, a man who "swanks about" with the title but has no right to it Michael Perez is so called in *Rule a Wife and have a Wife*, by Beaumont and Fletcher

> To this copper-captain was confided the command of the troops —W. IRVING *Knickerbocker*

Copper Nose. Oliver Cromwell, also called "Ruby Nose," "Nosey," and "Nose Almighty," no doubt from some scorbutic tendency which showed itself in a big red nose

Copper-nose Harry. Henry VIII When Henry VIII had spent all the money left him by his miserly father, he minted an inferior silver coin, in which the copper alloy soon showed itself on the more prominent parts, especially the nose of the face, and hence the people soon called the king "Old Coppernose "

Copperheads. Secret foes Copperheads are poisonous snakes of North America (*Trigonocephalus contortrix*), which, unlike the rattlesnakes, give no warning of their attack The name was applied by the early colonists to the Indians, then to the Dutch (*see* Washington Irving's *History of New York*), and, finally, in the Civil War to the pro-Southerners among the Northerners, the covert friends of the Confederates

Copts. The Jacobite Christians of Egypt, who have been since the Council of Chalcedon in 451 in possession of the patriarchal chair of Alexandria The word is probably derived from Coptos, the metropolis of the Thebaid These Christians conduct their worship in a dead language called "Coptic" which is descended from ancient Egyptian.

> The Copts [or Egyptians] circumcise, confess to their priests, and abstain from swine's flesh They are Jacobites in their creed —S OLIN *Travels in Egypt*, vol i, ch viii.

Copus (kō′ pus) University slang for a drink made of beer, wine, and spice heated together, and served in a "loving-cup " Variously accounted for as being dog-Latin for *cupellon Hippocratis* (a cup of hippocras), or short for *episcopus*, in which case it would be the same as the drink "bishop " (*q v*)

Copy A printer's term for original MS, typescript, or printed matter that is to be set up in type

That's a mere copy of your countenance. Not your real wish or meaning, but merely one you choose to present to me

Copyhold estate. Land held by a tenant by virtue of a copy of the roll made by the steward of the manor from the court-roll kept in the manor-house It was ended by legislation in 1925

Copyright. The exclusive right of multiplying for sale copies of works of literature, art, etc , or substantial parts thereof, allowed to the author or his assignees The first copyright Act in England is that of 1709, modifications and additions to it were made at various times, and in 1842 a new Act was passed granting copyright for forty-two years after publication or until the expiration of seven years from the death of the author, whichever should be the longer

The question of international copyright was settled by the Berne Convention of 1908, to which all countries subscribed except U S A, Russia, and China   To carry out the articles of the convention so far as Great Britain was concerned the Copyright Act of 1911 was passed, by which protection was granted for 50 years from the death of the author or the publication of the work, whichever date was the later.   In U.S.A protection of copyright can be secured only by the complete production of the work in U S.A   It lasts for 28 years, with right to renew for another similar period.

The Act of 1911 deals also with the copyright in photographs, engravings, architectural designs, musical compositions, gramophone records, etc

A copy of every copyright book has to be presented to the British Museum and, on application being made, to the Bodleian, the Cambridge University Library, the Advocates' Library at Edinburgh, Trinity College, Dublin, and the National Library of Wales at Aberystwyth   Before the Act of 1842 Sion College, Glasgow, Aberdeen, and St Andrews Universities, and King's Inns, Dublin, also had compulsory presentation copies

Coq à l'âne.   See COCK, A COCK AND BULL STORY.

Corah (kôr' a), in Dryden's *Absalom and Achitophel* (*q v*), is meant for Titus Oates. *See Numb* XVI

Sunk were his eyes, his voice was harsh and loud,
Sure signs he neither choleric was, nor proud,
His long chin proved his wit, his saint-like grace
A church vermilion, and a Moses' face
His memory, miraculously great,
Could plots, exceeding man's belief, repeat.
    DRYDEN: *Absalom and Achittophel*, 1, 646.

Coral.   The Romans used to hang beads of red coral on the cradles and round the necks of infants, to "preserve and fasten their teeth," and save them from "the falling sickness."   It was considered by soothsayers as a charm against lightning, whirlwind, shipwreck, and fire   Paracelsus says it should be worn round the neck of children as a preservative "against fits, sorcery, charms, and poison," and Norse legend says that it is fashioned beneath the waves by Marmendill   The *bells* on an infant's coral are a Roman Catholic addition, the object being to frighten away evil spirits by their jingle

Coral is good to be hanged about the neck of children   to preserve them from the falling sickness It has also some special sympathy with nature, for the best coral   . will turn pale and wan if the party that wears it be sick, and it comes to its former colour again as they recover —SIR HUGH PLATT *Jewel-House of Art and Nature* (1594)

Coram judice (kôr' am joo' di si) (Lat)   Under consideration, still before the judge.

Cordelia (kôr dē' li à)   The youngest of Lear's three daughters, and the only one that loved him   She appears in Holinshed's *Chronicle* (whence Shakespeare drew most of his facts) as "Cordeilla," as "Cordell" in the *Mirour for Magistrates* (1555) and as "Cordella" in

the older play of *Leir* (1594)   The form "Cordelia" seems to appear for the first time in Spenser's *Faerie Queene* (ii, 10)   See LEAR, KING.

Cordelia's gift.   A "voice ever soft, gentle, and low, an excellent thing in woman " Shakespeare. *King Lear*, v, 3

It is her voice that he hears prevailing over the those [*sic*] of the rest of the company,   for she has not Cordelia's gift —MISS BROUGHTON   *Dr Cupid.*

Cordelier (kôr dē' lya, kôr de lēr'), i e "cord-wearer "   A Franciscan friar of the strict rule, an Observantin   See FRANCISCANS   In the Middle Ages they distinguished themselves in philosophy and theology.   Duns Scotus was one of their most distinguished members. The tale is that in the reign of St Louis these Minorites repulsed an army of infidels, and the king asked who those *gens de cordelies* (corded people) were   From this they received their appellation.

In the French Revolution the name *Club des Cordeliers* was given to a political club, because it held its meetings in an old convent of Cordeliers   The Cordeliers were the rivals of the Jacobins, and numbered among their members Pare (the president), Danton, Marat, Camille Desmoulins, Hébert, Chaumette, Dufournoy de Villiers, Fabre d'Eglantine, and others   They were far in advance of the Jacobins, and were the first to demand the abolition of the monarchy and the establishment of a commonwealth   The leaders were put to death between March 24th and April 5th, 1794.

This club was nicknamed "The Pandemonium," and Danton was called the "Archfiend " When Bailly, the mayor, locked them out of their hall in 1791, they met in the Tennis Court (Paris), and changed their name into the "Society of the Rights of Man", but they are best known by their original appellation

Il ne faut pas parler Latin devant les Cordeliers.   Don't talk Latin before the Cordeliers, i e   the Franciscans.   A common French proverb, meaning that one should be careful what one says on a subject before those who are masters of it.

Cordon (Fr.).   A ribbon or cord: especially the ribbon of an order of chivalry, also, a line of sentries or military posts enclosing some position, hence, an encircling line

Cordon bleu   A knight of the ancient order of the *St Esprit* (Holy Ghost), so called because the decoration is suspended on a blue ribbon   It was at one time the highest order in the kingdom of France

The title is also given, as a compliment, to a good cook.

Cordon noir.   A knight of the Order of St Michael, distinguished by a black ribbon

Cordon rouge.   A chevalier of the Order of *St Louis*, the decoration being suspended on a red ribbon.

Cordon sanitaire.   A line of watchers posted round an infectious district to keep it isolated and prevent the spread of the disease, a sanitary cordon

Un grand cordon.   A member of the French *Légion d'Honneur*   The cross is attached to a *grand* (broad) ribbon.

Un repas de cordon bleu. A well-cooked and well-appointed dinner The commandeur de Souve, Comte d'Olonne, and some others, who were *cordons bleus* (*i e* knights of St. Esprit), met together as a sort of club, and were noted for their excellent dinners. Hence, when anyone has dined well he said, "*Bien. c'est un vrai repas de cordon bleu.*"

Corduroy. A corded fabric, originally made of silk and worn by the kings of France in the chase (Fr. *corde du roy*) It is also a coarse, thick, ribbed cotton stuff, capable of standing hard wear

Corduroys Trousers made of corduroy. Brown corduroy trousers were worn by officers of the British 8th Army in the Western Desert, 1940-2, not, as many have thought, as an affectation, but because this material stood up to wear in the sand better than battle-dress serge, and was less chafing in the heat

Corduroy road A term applied to roads formed of tree trunks sawn in two longitudinally, and laid transversely. Such a road presents a ribbed appearance, like corduroy

Cordwainer. Not a twister of cord, but a worker in leather Our word is the Fr *cordouannier* (a maker or worker of *cordouan*), the former a corruption of *Cordovanier* (a worker in Cordovan leather)
The Cordwainers are one of the smaller though wealthier Livery Companies of the City of London

Corineus. A mythical hero in the suite of Brute, who conquered the giant Goemagot (Gogmagog), for which achievement the whole western horn of England was allotted him He called it Corinea, and the people Corineans, from his own name. *See* BELLERUS
> In meed of these great conquests by them got,
> Corineus had that province utmost west
> To him assigned for his worthy lot,
> Which of his name and memorable gest,
> He called Cornwall
> SPENSER. *Faerie Queene*, ii, 10

Corinth. Non cuivis homini contingit adire Corinthum. A tag from Horace (Ep I xvii), quoted of some difficult attainment that can be achieved only by good fortune or great wealth Professor Conington translates it:—
> You know the proverb, "Corinth town is fair,
> But 'tis not every man that can get there"

Gellius in his *Noctes Atticæ*, i, 8, says that Horace refers to Lais (*q v*), who sold her favours at so high a price that not everyone could afford to purchase them, but Horace says, "To please princes is no little praise, for it falls not to every man's lot to go to Corinth " That is it is as hard to please princes as it is to get to Corinth, perhaps because of the expense, and perhaps because it is situated between two seas, and hence called Bimâris Corinthus

There is but one road that leads to Corinth There is only one right way of doing anything

Corinthian. A licentious libertine The loose-living of Corinth was proverbial both in Greece and in Rome
In the Regency the term was applied to a hard-living group of sportsmen whose time was largely spent in practising pugilism and horse-racing The sporting rake in Pierce

Egan's *Life in London* (1821) was known as "Corinthian Tom", in Shakespeare's day a "Corinthian" was the "fast man" of the period *Cp* EPHESIAN.
> I am no proud Jack, like Falstaff, but a Corinthian, a lad of mettle, a good boy —1 *Henry IV*, ii, 4.

The only survival of the term to-day is in the Corinthian amateur football club.

Corinthian Order The most richly decorated of the five orders of Greek architecture The shaft is fluted, and the capital is bell-shaped and adorned with acanthus leaves. *See* ACANTHUS

Corinthian brass. An alloy made of a variety of metals (said to be gold, silver, and copper) melted at the conflagration of Corinth in 146 B C, when the city was burnt to the ground by the consul Mummius Vases and other ornaments, made by the Romans of this metal, were of greater value than if they had been silver or gold.
> I think it may be of Corinthian brass,
> Which was a mixture of all metals, but
> The brazen uppermost
> BYRON *Don Juan*, vi, 56.

Corked. Properly used of a bottle of wine which has not been opened, generally used in place of "corky"—*i e.* the wine itself has become tainted through the cork being a bad one

Corker That's a corker. That's a tremendous example of whatever is in question—a story, a ball in cricket or anything you wish. Perhaps the allusion is to something that quite closes the discussion, settles the matter, ' corks" it up.

Corking-pins. Pins of the largest size, at one time used by ladies to keep curls on the forehead fixed and in trim They used to be called *calkin* (pronounced *cawkin*) pins, but it is not known why

Cormoran. The Cornish giant, who in the nursery tale, fell into a pit dug by Jack the Giant killer. For this doughty achievement Jack received a belt from King Arthur, with this inscription—
> This is the valiant Cornish man
> That slew the giant Cormoran
> *Jack the Giant-killer.*

Corn. There's corn in Egypt. There is abundance, there is a plentiful supply The reference is to the Bible story of Joseph in Egypt (*Ex.* xlii, 2)

To tread on his corns To irritate his prejudices, to annoy another by disregard to his pet opinions or habits.

Up corn, down horn. An old saying suggesting that when corn is high or dear, beef is down or cheap, because people have less money to spend on meat

Corn Laws. In 1815 a law was passed forbidding the importation of foreign corn when the price of native corn was under 80s a quarter In 1828 a sliding scale was introduced whereby the duty was increased as the price fell until corn at 64s a quarter meant a duty of 23s These high prices raised the cost of living to such an extent that the poor were faced with starvation. In 1838 an Anti-Corn

Law League was founded, and in 1846 Sir Robert Peel passed a law repealing the duties

The Corn-Law Rhymer, Ebenezer Elliott (1781-1849) denounced the Corn Laws in scathing verse that appealed to the public for which he wrote The Corn-Law Rhymes appeared in 1831.

Cornage. A rent in feudal times fixed with relation to the number of horned cattle in the tenant's possession. In Littleton's *Tenures* (1574) it was mistakenly said to be "a kind of tenure in grand serjeanty," the service being to blow a horn when an invasion of the Scots was imminent   Until the true meaning of the term was given in the Oxford Dictionary this was the explanation always given

Corner. The condition of the market with respect to a commodity which has been largely bought up, in order to create a virtual monopoly and enhance its market price, as a corner in pork, etc   The idea is that the goods are piled and hidden in a corner out of sight
    The price of bread rose like a rocket, and speculators wished to corner what little wheat there was.— *New York Weekly Times* (June 13 1894)

To make a corner. To combine in order to control the price of a given article, and thus secure enormous profits

Corner-stone. A large stone laid at the base of a building to strengthen the two walls forming a right angle, in ancient buildings they were sometimes as much as 20 feet long and 8 feet thick. In figurative use, Christ is called (*Eph* ii, 20) the chief corner-stone because He united the Jews and Gentiles into one family; and daughters are called cornerstones (*Ps.* cxliv. 12) because, as wives and mothers, they unite together two families
    Why should we make an ambiguous word the corner stone of moral philosophy?—JOWETT *Plato*, iv, 30

Cornet. The terrible cornet of horse A nickname of the elder Pitt (1708-78) He obtained a cornetcy in Cobham's Horse in 1731.

Cornish. Cornish hug. A hug to overthrow you. The Cornish men were famous wrestlers, and tried to throttle their antagonist with a particular grip or embrace called the Cornish hug.
    The Cornish are Masters of the Art of Wrestling
.   Their Hugg is a cunning close with their fellow-combatant, the fruits whereof is his fair fall, or foil at the least It is figuratively appliable to the deceitful dealing of such who secretly design their overthrow, whom they openly embrace —FULLER· *Worthies* (1661)

Cornish language. This member of the Brythonic branch of the Celtic languages became virtually extinct nearly 200 years ago. It is supposed that Dolly Pentreath (Dorothy Jeffery, 1685-1777) was the last to speak Cornish as a native language. It is still spoken as an acquired language by a few cultured Cornishmen and there is a certain literature available.

Cornish names.
    By Tre, Pol, and Pen
    You shall know the Cornishmen.
Thus, *Tre* (a town) gives Trefry, Tregengon, Tregony, Tregothnan, Trelawy, Tremayne, Trevannion, Treveddoe, Trewithen, etc

Pol (a head) gives Polkerris Point, Polperro, Polwheel, etc
Pen (a top) gives Penkevil, Penrice, Penrose, Pentire, etc

The Cornish Wonder. John Opie (1761-1807), of Cornwall, the painter It was "Peter Pindar" (John Wolcot) who gave him this name

Cornstalks. In Australia, especially in New South Wales, youths of colonial birth are so called, perhaps because they are often taller and more slender than their parents.

Cornubian Shore Cornwall, famous for its tin mines.
    . . from the bleak Cornubian shore
    Dispense the mineral treasure, which of old
    Sidonian pilots sought
                        AKENSIDE *Hymn to the Naiads.*

Cornucopia   See AMALTHÆA'S HORN.

Cornwall. The county is probably named from Celtic *corn, cornu,* a horn, with reference to the configuration of the promontory. For the legendary explanation of the name, *see* CORINEUS.

Corny. U S slang for anything, such as music, which is affectedly and spuriously sweet It is also used of anything of poor quality or hackneyed.

Coronach (kor' ō nach) Lamentation for the dead, as anciently practised in Ireland and Celtic Scotland (Gael *comh ranach,* crying together) Pennant says it was called by the Irish *hululoo.*

Coronation Chair. *See* SCONE

Coroner. Properly, the crown officer (Lat. *corona,* crown). In Saxon times it was his duty to collect the Crown revenues, next, to take charge of Crown pleas; but at present his duties are almost entirely confined to searching into cases of sudden or suspicious death The coroner also holds inquiries, or inquests, on treasure trove *Crowner* was formerly a correct way of pronouncing the word, hence Shakespeare's—
    But is this law?
    Ay, marry, is't, crowner's quest law.
                        Hamlet, v, 1

Coronet. A crown inferior to the royal crown A *duke's* coronet is adorned with strawberry leaves above the band, that of a *marquis* with strawberry leaves alternating with pearls, that of an *earl* has pearls elevated on stalks, alternating with leaves above the band; that of a *viscount* has a string of pearls above the band, but no leaves; that of a *baron* has only six pearls.

Coronis (kōr ō' nis) Daughter of a King of Phocis, changed by Athene into a crow to enable her to escape from Neptune There was another Coronis, mother of Æsculapius by Apollo, who slew her for infidelity.

Corporal Violet. *See* VIOLET

Corporation. A *municipal corporation* is a body of men elected for the local government of a city or town, consisting of the mayor, aldermen, and councillors. The word is facetiously applied to a large paunch, from the tendency of civic magnates to indulge in well-provided feasts and thus acquire generous figures

Corposant. The St Elmo's Fire (*q v*) or "Castor and Pollux" of the Romans; the ball of fire which is sometimes seen playing round the masts of ships in a storm So called from Span. *corpo santo*, holy body Sometimes known as *comazant*

Corps legislatif (kôr' lej is la tēf'). At various periods of modern French history this phrase has been used for the lower house of the legislature In 1799 Napoleon substituted a *Corps legislatif* and a tribunal for the two councils of the Directory In 1807 there was a *c l* and a *conseil d'etat*, in 1849 a *c.l.* was formed with 750 deputies, and under Napoleon III the legislative power was vested in the Emperor, the Senate and the *Corps legislatif*

Corps Diplomatique (Fr) A diplomatic body, the foreign representatives at a Court collectively

Corpse Candle The *ignis fatuus* is so called by the Welsh because it was supposed to forebode death and to show the road that the corpse would take. The large candle used at lich wakes—*i e* at the watching of a corpse before interment—had the same name

Corpus (kôr' pus) (Lat , a body) The whole body or substance. especially the complete collection of writings on one subject or by one person. as the *Corpus poetarum Latinorum*, the *Corpus historicum medii ævi*, etc

Also, short for Corpus Christi College.

Corpus Christi. A festival of the Church, kept on the Thursday after Trinity Sunday, in honour of the Blessed Sacrament It was instituted by Urban IV in 1264, and was the regular time for the performance of religious dramas by the trade guilds In England many of the Corpus Christi plays of York, Coventry, and Chester are extant

Corpus Christi College at Cambridge was founded in 1352, and the College of the same name at Oxford in 1516

Corpus delicti (Lat) The material thing in respect to which a crime has been committed; thus a murdered body or a portion of the stolen property would be a "corpus delicti "

Corpuscular Philosophy. The theory promulgated by Robert Boyle which sought to account for all natural phenomena by the position and motion of corpuscles. *Cp.* ATOMIC PHILOSOPHY

Corrector. *See* ALEXANDER THE CORRECTOR.

Corroboree. The name of a dance indulged in by Australian aborigines on festal or warlike occasions, hence any hilarious or slightly riotous assembly. The word belongs to the language of the natives of Port Jackson, (Sydney), New South Wales

Corruption of Blood. Loss of title and entailed estates in consequence of treason, by which a man's *blood* is *attainted* and his issue suffers

Corsair (kôr' sâr) means properly "one who gives chase " Applied to the pirates of the northern coast of Africa (Ital. *corso*, a chase; Fr *corsaire*; Lat *cursus*)

Byron's poem in heroic couplets, *The Corsair*, was written in 1813

Corsican (kôr' si kan) For many years this was the derogatory epithet applied to Napoleon, as Consul and Emperor, in allusion to his place of birth It was often expanded to "the Corsican upstart" by the Colonel Blimps of the day.

Corsned (kôrs' ned) The piece of bread "consecrated for exorcism," formerly given (in one form of the Old English "ordeal") to a person to swallow as a test of his guilt (A S *cor*, choice, trial, *snæd*, piece) The words of ' consecration" were "May this morsel cause convulsions and find no passage if the accused is guilty, but turn to wholesome nourishment if he is innocent " *See* CHOKE

Cortes (kôr' tez) The Spanish or Portuguese parliament. The word means "court officers "

Cortina (kôr' tĭ na) (Lat , cauldron) The tripod of Apollo, which was in the form of a cauldron, hence, any tripod used for religious purposes in the worship of the ancient Romans

Corvinus (kôr vī' nus). Matthias I, King of Hungary, 1458-90, younger son of Janos Hunyady, was so called from the raven (Lat. *corvus*) on his shield He was one of the greatest of all book collectors, and for his superb library some of the earliest gilt-tooled bindings were executed They may be recognized by the raven introduced into the design, and are among the highest prizes of bibliophily.

Marcus Valerius is also said to have been so called because, in a single combat with a gigantic Gaul during the Gallic war, a raven flew into the Gaul's face and so harassed him that he could neither defend himself nor attack his adversary.

Corybantes (kor i bän' tēz) The Phrygian priests of Cybele, whose worship was celebrated with orgiastic dances and loud, wild music. Hence, a wild, unrestrained dancer is sometimes called a *corybant*, and Prof Huxley (1890) even referred to the members of the Salvation Army as being "militant missionaries of a somewhat corybantic Christianity "

Corycian Cave (kor is' i an). A cave on Mount Parnassus, so called from the nymph Corycia The Muses are sometimes in poetry called Corycides or the Corycian Nymphs.

> The immortal Muse
> To your calm habitations, to the cave
> Corycian . . will guide his footsteps.
>   AKENSIDE *Hymn to the Naiads*

Corydon (kor' i don) A conventional name for a rustic, a shepherd; a brainless, love-sick fellow; from the shepherd in Virgil's *Eclogue* VII, and in Theocritus

Coryphæus (kôr i fē' us) The leader and speaker of the chorus in Greek dramas; hence, figuratively, the leader generally, the most active member of a board, company, expedition, etc At Oxford University the assistant of the Choragus (*q v.*) is called the Coryphæus.

In the year 1626, Dr William Heather, desirous to ensure the study and practice of music at Oxford in future ages, established the offices of Professor, Choragus, and Coryphæus, and endowed them with modest stipends —*Grove's Dictionary of Music.*

The **Coryphæus of German literature.** Goethe, "prince of German poets" (1749-1832).

The **Coryphæus of Grammarians** Aristarchus of Samothrace (2nd century B C), a prince of grammarians and critics

The **Coryphæus of Learning.** Richard Porson (1759-1808), the great English classical scholar

Coryphée. A ballet-dancer; strictly speaking, the leader of the ballet.

Cosmopolite (kos mop' ō līt) (Gr *cosmospolites*) A citizen of the world One who has no partiality to any one country as his abiding place, one who looks on the whole world with "an equal eye "

Coss, Rule of An old name for algebra (also called the *Cossic Art*), from Ital *regola di cosa*, *cosa* being an unknown quantity, or a "thing " *See* WHETSTONE OF WITTE

Cosset. A pet; especially a pet lamb brought up in the house Hence, *to cosset*, to make a pet of, to fondle, caress Probably from A S. *cot-sæta*, a dweller in a cottage

Costa Brava (kos' ta bra' va) The precipitous coast of Spain lying on the Mediterranean between Port Bou and San Feliu de Guixols.

Costard. A large, ribbed apple, and, metaphorically, a man's head *Cp* COSTER-MONGER
Take him over the costard with the hilts of thy sword —SHAKESPEARE *Richard III*, 1, 4

Shakespeare gives the name to a clown in *Love's Labour's Lost*, who apes the court wit of the period, but misapplies and miscalls like Mrs Malaprop or Dogberry

Costermonger. A seller of eatables about the streets, properly an apple-seller from *costard* (*q v*), and *monger*, a trader, A S *mangian*, to trade; a word still retained in iron-monger, cheese-monger, fish-monger, etc It is usually abbreviated to *coster* and is often applied generically to a Cockney of the East End.

Côte (kōt) (Fr , coast)

Côte d'Azur. The Mediterranean coast of France between Menton and Cannes, so named in 1887 by the poet Stephen Liegeard.

Côte d'Or. The department of France of which Dijon is the chief town It is famous for its vineyards, for within its boundaries the whole of the best Burgundy is produced The area extends south from Dijon, embracing Gevrey, Chambolle, Vougeot, Vosne, Nuits, Aloxe-Corton, Beaune, Pommard, Volnay, Meursault, Santenay, and ends at Chasne

Côtes-du-Rhône. The name given collectively to the wines grown in the Rhône valley, below Lyons, of which the most famous are Chateauneuf-du-Pape, and Hermitage

Cote-hardi (kōt ar dē). A tight-fitting tunic buttoned down the front.
He was clothed in a cote-hardi upon the gyse of Almayne [i e in the German fashion] —*Geoffroi de la Tour Landry.*

Coterie (kōt' e rē) A French word originally signifying something like our "guild," a

society where each paid his *quota*, but now applied to an exclusive set or clique, especially one composed of persons of similar tastes, aims, prejudices, etc

Cotillon (ko til' yon) Originally a brisk dance by four or eight persons, in which the ladies held up their gowns and showed their underpetticoats (Fr *cotillon*, a petticoat) Later the dance became a very elaborate one with many added figures, but it is very rarely seen in modern ball-rooms

Cotset (kot' set) This is a word that is met with frequently in Domesday Book, where it describes one of the lowest types of feudal bondsmen, a cottage-dweller (A.S. *cot-sæta*) who was bound to work most of his time for the lord

Cotswold. **You are as long a-coming as Cotswold barley** The Cotswold Hills, in Gloucestershire, are very cold and bleak, exposed to the winds, and very backward in vegetation, but they yield a good late supply of barley.

Cotswold lion. An ironical name for a sheep, for which Cotswold hills are famous.
Then will he look as fierce as a Cotswold lion
UDALL· *Roister Doister*, IV, vi (c 1566)

Cottage. This word, now applied to any small dwelling in the country, is found in law in the 13th century as signifying a small house without land

Cottage Countess, The. Sarah Hoggins, of Shropshire, daughter of a small farmer, who, in 1791, married Henry Cecil, nephew and heir presumptive of the 9th Earl of Exeter At the time he had no courtesy title and was a plain "Mr " He was living under the name of John Jones, and was separated from his wife, from whom he subsequently obtained a divorce and an Act of Parliament to legitimatize the children of his second wife Sarah Hoggins was seventeen at the time of her marriage, and "John Jones" was thirty They were married by licence in the parish church of Bolas Magna, Salop and lived there for two years until his succession to the peerage made her a Countess She died in 1797, four years before her husband's elevation to the Marquessate Tennyson's poem, *The Lord of Burleigh*, is founded on this episode

Cottage loaf. A loaf of bread in two round lumps, a smaller on top of a larger, and baked with a good crust

Cottage piano. A small upright pianoforte

Cotton **A cotton king.** A rich Manchester cotton manufacturer, a king in wealth, style of living, equipage, number of employees, etc. Many county families had this origin

To cotton to a person. To cling to or take a fancy to a person To stick to a person as cotton sticks to our clothes

To cotton on. To catch on, to grasp a line of thought

Cottonopolis. Manchester, the great centre of cotton manufactures in Great Britain during the 19th century

Cottonian Library. The remarkable library founded by the noted antiquary Sir Robert

Bruce Cotton (1571-1631), It was augmented by his son and grandson, and having been secured for the nation by statute in 1700, was eventually deposited in the British Museum on the foundation of that institution in 1753 It is particularly rich in early MSS

Cottys (kot' is)   One of the three hundred-handed giants, son of Uranus (Heaven) and Gaea (Earth)   His two brothers were Briareus and Gyges   *See* HUNDRED-HANDED

Cotytto (ko tï' tō)   The Thracian goddess of immodesty, worshipped at Athens with licentious rites   *See* BAPTES

> Hail¹ goddess of nocturnal sport,
> Dark-veiled Cotytto
> > MILTON· *Comus* 129,130.
> Where are they, Cotytto or Venus,
> Astarte or Ashtaroth, where?
> > SWINBURNE *Dolores*

Couleur de rose (koo lĕr de rōs) (Fr., rose-coloured).   Highly coloured, too favourably considered; overdrawn with romantic embellishments, like objects viewed through glass tinted with rose pink.

Council, Privy, Œcumenical, etc.   *See these words.*

Count. A title of honour, used on the Continent and equivalent to English *earl* (A S. *eorl*, a warrior), of which *countess* is still the feminine and the title of the wife or widow of an earl   *Count* is from Lat. *comitem*, accusative of *comes*, a companion, which was a military title, as *Comes Littoris Saxonici*, Count of the Saxon Shore, the Roman general responsible for the south-eastern coasts of Britain

Count, To. From O.Fr *conter*, Lat *computare* (*putare*, to think), to compute, to reckon

To count kin with someone. A Scots expression meaning to compare one's pedigree with that of another

To count out the House. To declare the House of Commons adjourned because there are not forty members present   The Speaker has his attention called to the fact, and if he finds that this is so, he declares the sitting over

To be counted out is said of a boxer who, after being knocked down, fails to regain his feet during the ten seconds counted out loud by the referee.   **Count me out.** Do not reckon me in on this.

To count upon. To rely with confidence on someone or something, to reckon on

To count without your host   *See* RECKON

Countenance, To. To sanction, to support Approval or disapproval is shown by the countenance   The Scripture speaks of "the light of God's countenance," i e the smile of approbation; and to "hide His face" (or countenance) is to manifest displeasure

To keep in countenance. To encourage, or prevent someone losing his countenance or feeling dismayed.

To keep one's countenance   To refrain from smiling or expressing one's thoughts by the face.

Out of countenance. Ashamed, confounded With the countenance fallen or cast down

To put one out of countenance is to make one ashamed or disconcerted   To "discountenance" is to set your face against something done or propounded

Counter. Under the counter is a phrase that came into use during World War II in connection with dishonest tradesmen who, when commodities were in short supply, kept out of sight under the counter sufficient quantities to sell to favoured customers, often at enhanced prices

Counter-caster. One who keeps accounts, or casts up accounts by counters.   Thus, at the opening of *Othello*, Iago in contempt calls Cassio "a great arithmetician," and "this counter-caster", and in *The Winter's Tale*, the Clown says. "Fifteen hundred shorn, what comes the wool to? I cannot do 't without counters" (IV, 3)

Countercheck Quarrelsome. Sir, how dare you utter such a falsehood? Sir, you know that it is not true This, in Touchstone's classification (Shakespeare's *As You Like It*, V, 4), is the third remove from the lie direct, or rather, the lie direct in the third degree

The Reproof Valiant, the Countercheck Quarrelsome, the Lie Circumstantial, and the Lie Direct, are not clearly defined by Touchstone *That* is not true, how *dare* you utter such a falsehood, *if* you say so, you are a liar, you lie, or are a liar, seem to fit the four degrees

Counter-jumper   A contemptuous epithet applied by the ignorant to a shop assistant, who may be supposed to have to jump over the counter to go from one part of the shop to another

Counterpane. A corruption of *counter-point*, from the Lat. *culcita puncta*, a stitched quilt   This, in French, became *courte-pointe*, corrupted into *contre-pointe*, *counterpoint*, where point is pronounced "poyn," corrupted into "pane "

Countess. *See* COUNT, COTTAGE COUNTESS

Country. **Black Country.** *See* BLACK

Country dance. A corruption of the Fr. *contre danse*, i e. a dance where the partners face each other, as in Sir Roger de Coverley.

Father of his country. *See* FATHER

To appeal, or go, to the country. To dissolve Parliament in order to ascertain the wish of the country by a new election of representatives

County. A shire, originally the district ruled by a count   The name is also officially applied to *county boroughs*, i e towns with more than 50 000 inhabitants which, under the Local Government Act of 1888, rank as administrative counties   For various names of divisions of counties, *see* HUNDRED

County family. A family belonging to the nobility or gentry with an ancestral seat in the county.

County palatine   Properly, the dominion of an earl palatine (*see* PALATINATE), a county over which the count had royal privileges. Cheshire and Lancashire are the only Counties

Palatine in England now, but formerly Durham, Pembroke, Hexhamshire, and the Isle of Ely had this rank

Coup (koo) (Fr) Properly a blow or stroke, but used both in French and English in a large number of ways, as for a clap of thunder, a draught of liquids, a piece of play in a game (a move in chess, etc), a stroke of policy or of luck, a trick, etc

A good coup. A good hit or haul

Coup d'essai. A trial-piece, a piece of work serving for practice

Coup d'état. A state stroke, and the term is applied to one of those bold measures taken by Government to prevent a supposed or actual danger, as when a large body of men are arrested suddenly for fear they should overturn the Government

The famous *coup d'état*, by which Louis Napoleon became possessed of absolute power, took place on December 2nd, 1851.

Coup de grâce. The finishing stroke, the stroke of mercy When a criminal was tortured by the wheel or otherwise, the executioner gave him a *coup de grâce*, or blow on the head or breast, to put him out of his misery.

Coup de main. A sudden stroke, a stratagem whereby something is effected suddenly, a *coup*

It appears more like a line of march than a body intended for a *coup de main*, as there are with it bullocks and baggage of different kinds —WELLINGTON· *Dispatches*, vol i, p 25

Coup d'œil. A view, glance, prospect, the effect of things at the first glance; literally "a stroke of the eye."

Coup de pied de l'âne. Literally, a kick from the ass's hoof. figuratively, a blow given to a vanquished or fallen man, a cowardly blow; an insult offered to one who has not the power of returning or avenging it The allusion is to the fable of the sick lion kicked by the ass

Coup de soleil. A sunstroke, any malady produced by exposure to the sun

Coup de théâtre. An unforeseen or unexpected turn in a drama producing a sensational effect, a piece of clap-trap, something planned for effect Burke throwing down the dagger in the House of Commons (*see* DAGGER SCENE) intended a *coup de théâtre*.

Coup manqué. A false stroke, a miss, a failure

Shoot dead, or don't aim at all but never make a *coup manqué* —OUIDA *Under Two Flags*, ch xx

Coupon. In commercial phraseology, a coupon is a certificate of interest which is to be cut off (Fr. *couper*) from a bond and presented for payment It bears on its face the date and amount of interest to be paid

In times when rationing has been necessary the word has been employed for the detachable portions of a ration-book required to buy clothing, etc

In political phraseology *the coupon* was the official recognition given by Lloyd George and Bonar Law to parliamentary candidates who proclaimed their allegiance to the coalition

programme at the General Election of December, 1918 Hence, *couponeer*, a politician who accepted the "coupon."

Course. Another course would have done it. A little more would have effected our purpose It is said that the peasants of a Yorkshire village tried to wall in a cuckoo in order to enjoy an eternal spring They built a wall round the bird, and the cuckoo just skimmed over it "Ah!" said one of the peasants, "another carse would 'a' done it "

There is a school of moralists who, connecting sundry short-comings with changes in manners, endeavour to persuade us that only "another carse" is wanted to wall in the cuckoo —*Nineteenth Century*, December, 1892, p 920

In course ; in the course of nature. In the due and proper time or order, etc in the ordinary procedure of nature.

Of course. Naturally, as would be expected A **matter of course** is something that belongs to ordinary procedure, or that is customary

To hold, or **keep on the course.** To go straight, to do one's duty in that course [path] of life in which we are placed The allusion is to navigation.

Court. From Lat *cohors, cohortem*, originally a coop or sheepfold. It was on the Latium hills that the ancient Latins raised their *cors* or *cohors*, small enclosures with hurdles for sheep, etc Subsequently, as many men as could be cooped or folded together were called a *cohort*. The cattle-yard, being the nucleus of the farm, became the centre of a lot of farm cottages, then of a hamlet, town, fortified place, and lastly of a royal residence

Court cards. A corruption of coat card, so called because these cards bear the representation of a clothed or *coated* figure, and not because the king, queen, and knave may be considered to belong to a Court

The king of clubs may originally have represented the arms of the Pope; of spades, the king of France, of diamonds, the King of Spain; and of hearts, the King of England. The French kings in cards are called David (spades), Alexander (clubs), Cæsar (diamonds), and Charles (hearts)—representing the Jewish, Greek, Roman, and Frankish empires The queens or dames are Argine—*i e* Juno (hearts), Judith (clubs), Rachel (diamonds), and Pallas (spades)—representing royalty, fortitude, piety, and wisdom They were likenesses of Marie d'Anjou, the queen of Charles VII, Isabeau, the queen-mother; Agnes Sorel, the king's mistress, and Jeanne d'Arc, the dame of spades, or war.

Court Circular. The information concerning the movements and doings of Royalty and the Court generally, supplied to the newspapers by the Court Newsman He gives reports of levees, drawing-rooms, state balls, royal concerts, meetings to ministers, and so on George III, in 1803, introduced the custom to prevent misstatements on these subjects

Court cupboard. A movable buffet to hold flagons, cans, cups, and beakers

Away with the joint-stools, remove the court-cupboard, look to the plate —SHAKESPEARE *Romeo and Juliet*, i, 5

Court fools. *See* FOOLS.

Court holy water. An obsolete Elizabethan term for fair speeches, which look like promises of favour, but end in nothing

O nuncle, court holy-water in a dry house is better than this rain-water out o' door.—SHAKESPEARE *King Lear*, iii, 2

In Florio s Italian Dictionary (1598) *Mantellizzare* is translated by ' to flatter or fawne upon, to court one with faire words or give court holywater "

Court-leet. *See* LEET.

Court martial A court convened as circumstances may require to try a person subject to military law In Great Britain such courts were instituted in consequence of the Mutiny Act of 1690

Court plaster. The plaster of which the court ladies made their patches These patches worn on the face, were cut into all sorts of fanciful shapes, some even patching their faces with a coach and four, a ship in full sail, a chateau, etc This ridiculous fashion was in vogue in the reign of Charles I; and in Queen Anne's time was employed as a political badge

Your black patches you wear variously,
Some cut like stars, some in half-moons, some lozenges
BEAUMONT AND FLETCHER *Elder Brother*, iii, 2

Court of Arches. *See* ARCHES

Court of love. A judicial court for deciding affairs of the heart, established in Provence during the days of the Troubadours The following is a case submitted to their judgment A lady listened to one admirer, squeezed the hand of another, and touched with her toe the foot of a third Query Which of these three was the favoured suitor ?

Court of Pie-powder. *See* PIE-POWDER.

Court of Session. The supreme civil tribunal in Scotland. It dates from 1532, and represents the united powers of the Session of James I of Scotland, the Daily Council of James IV and the Lords Auditors of Parliament Since 1830 it has consisted of an Inner and an Outer House, the total number of judges is thirteen, including the Lord President (or Lord Justice General) and the Lord Justice Clerk.

They are but in the Court of the Gentiles. They are not wholly God's people, they are not the elect, but have only a smattering of the truth. The "Court of the Israelites" in the Jewish temple was for Jewish men; the "Court of the Women" was for Jewish women; the "Court of the Gentiles" was for those who were not Jews

Out of court. Not admissible evidence within the terms of reference of the trial being conducted by the Court in question.

To settle out of court. A case, almost invariably involving damages, which is settled by the respective litigants' solicitors, before it is called to court, agreeing on a sum to be paid by the litigant who admits himself to be in the wrong

Courtepy. *See* PEA-JACKET.

Courtesy (kĕr' te si) Civility, politeness It was at the courts of princes and great feudatories that all in attendance practised the refinements of the age in which they lived The word originally meant the manners of the court

Courtesy titles. Titles assumed or granted by social custom, but not of any legal value The courtesy title of the eldest son of a duke is *marquis*, of a marquis is *earl*, of an earl is *viscount* Younger sons of peers are by courtesy called *lord* or *honourable*, and the daughters are *lady* or *honourable* These titles do not give the holders the right to sit in the House of Lords

Cousin. Blackstone says that Henry IV, being related or allied to every earl in the kingdom. artfully and constantly acknowledged the connexion in all public acts The usage has descended to his successors, and in British royal writs and commissions an *earl* is still styled "Our right trusty and well-beloved cousin," a *marquis* "Our right trusty and entirely-beloved cousin," and a *duke* "Our right trusty and right-entirely-beloved cousin "

The word is also used by sovereigns in addressing one another formally, and in Italy it was a very high honour to be nominated by the king a "Cousin of the King "

Cousin Betsy, or Betty. A half-witted person, a "Bess of Bedlam" (*q v*)

[None] can say Foster's wronged him of a penny, or gave short measure to a child or a cousin Betsy.— MRS GASKELL

Cousin-german. The children of brothers and sisters, first cousins, kinsfolk (Lat *germanus*, a brother, one of the same stock)

There is three cozen-germans that has cozened all the hosts of Reading, of Maidenhead, of Colebrook, of horses and money—SHAKESPEARE *Merry Wives of Windsor*, iv, 5

Cousin Jack. So Cornishmen are called in the western counties, and in places where they are working as miners.

Cousin Michael. The Germans are so called *Michel*, in Old German, means "gross", Cousin Michael is meant to indicate a slow, heavy, unrefined, coarse-feeding people

To call cousins. This formerly meant to claim relationship—

He is half-brother to this Witword by a former wife, who was sister to my Lady Wishfort, my wife's mother, if you marry Millamant you must call cousins too.—CONGREVE *Way of the World*, i, 5

I wouldn't call the king my cousin. I am perfectly satisfied with things as they are, they couldn't be bettered even if I were cousin to the king

Couvade. The name given by anthropologists to the custom prevalent among some primitive races by which the father of a newly born infant makes a pretence of going through the same experiences as the mother, lies up for a time, abstains from certain foods, etc , as though he, too, were physically affected by the birth (from Fr *couver*, to hatch) The custom has been observed by travellers in Guiana and other parts of South America, among some African tribes, in parts of China, Borneo, etc , and it was noted by the ancients as occurring in Corsica and among the Celtiberians

Cove. An individual; as a *flash cove* (a swell), a *rum cove* (a man whose position and character are not quite obvious), a *gentry cove* (a gentleman), a *downy cove* (a very knowing individual), etc The word is old thieves' cant, it appears (as *cofe*) in Harman's *Caveat* (1567).

> There's a gentry cove here.
>   *Wits' Recreations* (1654)
> A ben cove, a brave cove, a gentry coffin
> MIDDLETON AND DEKKER *The Roaring Girl*, v, 1

Covenanters. A term applied, during the civil wars, to the Scottish Presbyterians, who, in 1643, united by "solemn league and covenant" (*see under* SOLEMN) to resist the encroachments of Charles I on religious liberty On the Restoration (1660) all toleration of Presbyterians ceased and for twenty-five years the Covenanters were harried and proscribed, their sad history being lightened by many acts of devotion and heroism under cruel persecution

Covent Garden. A corruption of *Convent* Garden, the garden and burial ground attached to the convent of Westminster, and turned into a fruit and flower market in the reign of Charles II. At the dissolution of the monasteries the site was granted to the Duke of Somerset; on his attainder in 1552 it passed to the Earl of Bedford, to whose descendants it belonged till 1914, when it was sold by the 11th Duke

Covent Garden has various claims to fame. During the 17th and 18th centuries it was the centre of the rowdier element of London's social life, the stamping-ground of the Mohocks and other semi-fashionable ruffians. Its coffee-houses and taverns were favourite resorts of such men of parts as Dryden, Otway, Steele, Fielding, Foote, Garrick, etc The vegetable market was opened in the early 17th century, but was not properly organized until 1828

Covent Garden Theatre was opened by Rich, the harlequin, in 1732 with Congreve's *Way of the World* After Rich's death it was sold to George Colman the elder, who, in 1777, brought out *She Stoops to Conquer* The house has been twice burned down (1808 and 1856), in 1847 it started a famous career as The Royal Italian Opera House, and in the years that have followed it has become one of the greatest opera-houses in Europe.

Coventry. Coventry Mysteries. Miracle plays supposed to have been acted at Corpus Christi (*q v*) at Coventry till 1591 They were published in 1841 for the Shakespeare Society, but, though called *Ludus Coventriæ* by Sir Robert Bruce Cotton's librarian in the time of James I, it is doubtful whether they had any special connexion with the town.

Parliaments held at Coventry. Two parliaments have been held in this city, one in 1404, styled *Parliamentum Indoctorum*, and the other in 1459, called *Parliamentum Diabolicum*.

To send one to Coventry. To take no notice of him, to make him feel that he is in disgrace by having no dealings with him. *Cp* BOYCOTT It is said that the citizens of Coventry had at one time so great a dislike to soldiers

that a woman seen speaking to one was instantly tabooed, hence, when a soldier was sent to Coventry he was cut off from all social intercourse

Hutton, in his *History of Birmingham*, gives a different version He says that Coventry was a stronghold of the Parliamentary party in the Civil Wars, and that troublesome and refractory Royalist prisoners were sent there for safe custody

Cover. To break cover. To start from the covert or temporary lair The usual earthholes of a fox being blocked the night before a hunt, the creature makes some gorse-bush or other cover its temporary resting-place, and as soon as it quits it the hunt begins

Coverdale's Bible. *See* BIBLE, THE ENGLISH

Coverley. Sir Roger de Coverley A member of an hypothetical club in the *Spectator*, "who lived in Soho Square when he was in town " Sir Roger is the type of an English squire in the reign of Queen Anne, He figures in thirty papers of the *Spectator*

Who can be insensible to his unpretending virtues and amiable weaknesses, his modesty, generosity, hospitality, and eccentric whims; the respect for his neighbours, and the affection of his domestics?—HAZLITT

The well-known country dance was known by this name (or, rather, as *Roger of Coverly*) many years before Addison's time

Cow. The cow that nourished Ymir with four streams of milk was called Audhumla

Always behind, like a cow's tail. A proverbial saying of ancient date. *Cp Tanquam coda vituli* (Petronius)

Curst cows have curt horns. Angry men cannot do all the mischief they wish Curst means "angry" or "fierce," and curt is "short," as curt-mantle, curt-hose The Latin proverb is, *Dat Deus immiti cornua curta bovi*

> You are called plain Kate,
> And bonny Kate, and sometimes Kate the curst
>   *Taming of the Shrew*, ii, 1.

The cow knows not the worth of her tail till she loses it, and is troubled with flies, which her tail brushed off

The tune the old cow died of *See* TUNE

The whiter the cow, the surer is it to go to the altar. The richer the prey, the more likely is it to be seized.

The system of impropriations grew so rapidly that, in the course of three centuries, more than a third part of all the benefices in England became such, and those the richest, for the whiter the cow, the surer was it to go to the altar —BLUNT *Reformation in England*, p 63

Cow-lick. A tuft of hair on the forehead that cannot be made to lie in the same direction as the rest of the hair

This term must have been adopted from a comparison with that part of a cow's hide where the hairs, having different directions, meet and form a projecting ridge, supposed to be occasioned by the animals licking themselves.—BROCKETT *Glossary of North Country Words*

Coward. Ultimately from Lat *cauda*, a tail, the allusion seems to be either from an animal "turning tail" when frightened, or from its cowering with its tail between its legs In the French version of *Reynard the Fox* the

Hare is called *Coart*, which may refer either to his timidity or to the conspicuousness of his tail (O Fr *coe*) as it runs away

A beast *cowarded*, in *heraldry*, is one drawn with its tail between its legs

Cowper Justice Cupar Justice (*q v*).

Cowper-Temple Clause. Clause 14 of the Education Act of 1870 (so called from its author, W Cowper-Temple (1811-88), which regulated religious teaching in public elementary schools It enacted that "in any school provided by a School Board, no religious catechism or religious formulary which is distinctive of any particular denomination, shall be taught "

Coxcomb An empty-headed, vain person The ancient licensed jesters were so called because they wore a cock's comb in their caps.

> Coxcombs, an ever empty race
> Are trumpets of their own disgrace
>   GAY *Fables*, xix

Coxswain (cok' son) The helmsman, originally the *swain* or *servant* of a *cock* (see COCK-BOAT). The old spelling of the word was *Cockswain*

Coyne and Livery. An old Irish term for food and entertainment for soldiers, and forage for their horses, formerly exacted from private persons by Irish chiefs when on the march *Coyne* is Irish *coinnemh*, billeting, or one billeted.

Coystril. A term of reproach, meaning a low fellow, a knave, a varlet

> He's a coward and a coystril that will not drink to my niece —SHAKESPEARE *Twelfth Night*, i, 3

It is a variant of obsolete *custrel*, an attendant on a knight, which seems to be connected with O Fr *coustillier*, a soldier armed with a *coustille*, i e a two-edged dagger Every soldier in the life-guards of Henry VIII was attended by a man called a *coystrel* or *coystril*

Cozen To cheat This is the same word as *cousin*, the Fr. *cousiner* means "to sponge on" as well as " to call cousin ", and in England a person who *cozened* another was one who went and stayed at his house and lived on him just because they were "cousins " *See* Shakespeare's *Merry Wives*, iv, 2, and v, 5

Crab. A walking-stick made of crab-apple wood, a crabstick

> Our bolts her husband upon me with a fine taper crab in his hand —GARRICK *Lying Valet*, i, 2

To catch a crab. *See* CATCH

Crack. First-rate, excellent quite at the top of its class; something that is "cracked up" (*see below*), as a crack regiment a crack hand of cards, a crack shot, etc Formerly the word was used substantively for a lively young fellow, a wag —

> Indeed, la ! 'tis a noble child, a crack, madam
>   SHAKESPEARE *Coriolanus*, i, 3

A gude crack In Scottish dialect, a good chat or conversation, also a good talker.

> Wi' merry sangs, an' friendly cracks,
> I wat they did na weary,
> And unco tales, an' funnie jokes—
> Their sports were cheap an' cheery.
>   BURNS. *Halloween*

To be a gude crack was essential to the trade of a "puir body" of the more esteemed class —SCOTT. *Antiquary* (Introduction)

Crack-brained. Eccentric, slightly mad

Cracked pipkins are discovered by their sound. Ignorance is betrayed by speech

> They bid you talk—my honest song
> Bids you for ever hold your tongue,
> Silence with some is wisdom most profound—
> Cracked pipkins are discovered by the sound
>   PETER PINDAR *Lord B and his Motions*

In a crack. Instantly In a snap of the fingers, in the time taken by a crack or shot

> Do pray undo the bolt a little faster—
> They re on the stair just now, and in a crack
> Will all be here
>   BYRON *Don Juan*, I, cxxxvii

To crack a bottle. In this phrase the word means to open and drink —

> They went to a tavern and there they dined,
> And bottles cracked most merrilie
>   *Bold Pedlar and Robin Hood*

> You'll crack a quart together Ha, will you not,
> Master Bardolph —2 *Henry IV*, v 3

> Dear Tom, this brown jug that now foams with mild ale,
> From which I now drink to sweet Nan of the Vale,
> Was once Toby Filpot's, a thirsty old soul
> As e'er cracked a bottle, or fathomed a bowl
>   O'KEEFE *Poor Soldier*

To crack a crib. To break into a house as a thief *See* CRIB Hence, *cracksman*, a burglar

To crack up. To praise highly, to eulogize.

> We find them cracking up the country they belong to, no matter how absurd may be the boast —JAS PAYN *By Proxy*, ch i

It also means to break down in health or mind, or to crash an aeroplane or motor car.

Cracker A word used in several senses

A small firework (U S A . fire-cracker)

A bon-bon containing sweets or toys with an appropriate motto, in use at Christmas

A flaky, unsweetened water biscuit, in the U S A the word is applied to any kind of biscuit

Poor white folk in the Southern U S A , and back-country folk generally This is an early 19th-century term, arising from the long whips they cracked at their horse teams

Crackers. 20th-century slang phrase for mentally unbalanced

Cracksman. A burglar. *See* To CRACK A CRIB *above*.

Cradle-holding. A name given to land held by Borough English (*q v*)

Craft. Skill, ability, trade (A S *cræft*) A craftsman is a mechanic A handicraft is manual skill, i e mechanical skill, *leechcraft* is skill in medicine (A S , *læce*, a physician), and before *crafty* adopted its bad sense it meant merely skilful, ingenious

Small craft. Such vessels as schooners, sloops, cutters, and so on

The Craft is the word usually employed by Freemasons to describe their fraternity

Cram. To tell what is not true. **A crammer,** an untruth The allusion is to stuffing a person with useless rubbish. It is, perhaps, in this connexion that working at high pressure for an examination is termed to cram.

Crambo A game which consists in someone setting a line which another is to rhyme to, but no one word of the first line must occur in the second The word is of uncertain origin, but possibly it comes from the billiards term *carambole*

Get the maids to crambo of an evening and learn the knack of rhyming —CONGREVE *Love for Love*, i, 1.

Dumb crambo is a somewhat similar game, but there the words are expressed in pantomime or dumb show.

Cramp-ring A ring that was consecrated by the king on Good Friday and was supposed to protect the wearer against cramp, "falling sickness," etc

Because Coshawk goes in a shag-ruff band, with a face sticking up in't which shows like an agate set in a cramp-ring, he thinks I'm in love with him — MIDDLETON *The Roaring Girl*, IV, ii (1611)

The superstitious use of cramp-rings, as a preservative against fits, is not entirely abandoned, instances occur where nine young men of a parish each subscribe a crooked sixpence, to be moulded into a ring for a young woman afflicted with this malady — ROKEWODE *The Hundred of Thingoe (Suffolk), Introd.* (1838).

To scour the cramp-ring. To be put into fetters. to be imprisoned The allusion is obvious

There's no muckle hazard o' scouring the cramp-ring —SCOTT *Guy Mannering*, ch xxiii

Crank In Elizabethan thieves' slang, an Abram-man (*q v*); so called from Ger. *krank* (sickly) It was formerly used of a leaky ship, and is still employed in the U S.A. in the sense of weak or sickly Nowadays a **crank** is a person with a mental twist, an eccentric person, and the name is obviously an extension of the mechanical crank, which is a bent axle or handle designed to convert lineal into rotary motion, or to impart motion to a wheel

Cranmer's Bible. *See* BIBLE, THE ENGLISH

Crannock. An Irish measure which, in the days of Edward II, contained either eight or sixteen pecks *Curnock* is another form of the word this was a dry measure of varying capacity, but usually 3 bushels for wheat, 4 bushels for corn, and from 10 to 15 bushels for coal, lime, etc

Crapaud or Johnny Crapaud. A Frenchman, according to Guillim's *Display of Heraldry* (1611), so called from a device of the ancient kings of France, "three toads [Fr *crapauds*] erect, saltant " *See* FLEUR-DE-LIS

Les anciens crapauds prenderont Sara. One of the cryptic "prophecies" of Nostradamus (1503-66) Sara is *Aras* reversed, and when the French under Louis XIV took Arras from the Spaniards, this verse was remembered

Crape. A saint in crape is twice a saint in lawn. (Pope *Ep to Cobham*, 136) Crape (a sort of bombazine, or alpaca) is the stuff of which cheap clerical gowns used to be made, "lawn" refers to the lawn sleeves of a bishop Crape was also the material used for mourning dresses, etc It is said to have been first made by St. Badorn, Queen of France. c 680

Cratur. A drop of the cratur *See* CREATURE

Cravat (kra văt') This neckcloth was introduced into France in the 17th century by Croatian soldiers, or, as they called themselves, Cravates (O.Slav *khruvat*) The Croats guarded the Turkish frontiers of Austria, and when France organized a regiment on the model of the Croats, their linen neckcloths were imitated, and the regiment was called 'The Royal Cravat "

The Bonny Cravat. An old public-house sign at Woodchurch, Kent, a corruption of *La bonne corvette* Woodchurch was noted for smuggling, and the "Bonnie Cravat" was a smuggler's hostelry

To wear a hempen cravat. To be hanged

Craven. In M E *crauant*, the word is the O Fr *cravant*, pres part of *craver* or *crever*, to burst or break, hence to be overcome The '-en" is a mistake for "-ant", it makes the word look like a past participle instead of what it really is, a present.

When controversies were decided by an appeal to battle, the combatants fought with batons, and if the accused could either kill his adversary or maintain the fight till sundown he was acquitted If he wished to call off, he cried out "Craven!" and was held infamous

Crawler (Austr) A convict who escaped with the connivance of the overseer, allowing himself to be re-captured in order that the overseer might collect the reward In this sense it is found in *The Adventures of Philip Rashleigh* (1825) and it thus considerably antedates the modern use as a sycophant.

Crawlers. *See* GROWLERS

Crawley. Crooked as Crawley or Crawley brook, a river in Bedfordshire That part called the brook, which runs into the Ouse, is so crooked that a boat would have to go eighty miles in order to make a direct progress of eighteen (Fuller *Worthies*)

Creaking Doors Hang the Longest. Delicate persons often outlive the more robust

Creature. Wine, whisky or other spirits The use of the word is a facetious adaptation of the passage "Every creature of God is good," 1 *Tim* iv, 4, used in the defence of wine as a legitimate drink

I find my master took too much of the creature last night, and now is angling for a quarrel.— DRYDEN. *Amphitryon*, iii, i.

A drop of the creature. A little whisky The Irish call it "a drop of the cratur "

Creature-comforts. Food and other things necessary for the comfort of the body. Man being supposed to consist of body and soul, the body is the creature, but the soul is the " vital spark of heavenly flame "

Mr. Squeers had been seeking in creature-comforts [brandy and water] temporary forgetfulness of his unpleasant situation —DICKENS *Nicholas Nickleby*

Credence Table (krē' dēns) The table near the altar on which the bread and wine are deposited before they are consecrated. In former times food was placed on a credence-table to be tasted previously to its being set before the guests This was done to assure the guests that the meat was not poisoned. (Ital *credenza*, a shelf or buffet)

Crédit Foncier (krā' dē fong' si ā) Loans to landowners, first introduced by Frederick the Great in 1763 to alleviate distress caused by the prolonged wars

Crédit Mobilier (krā' dě mō bil' yǎ) A joint-stock company, founded Paris 1852, licensed to indulge in any form of trading for profits

Credo (krē' dō). A statement of belief *Credo quia impossibile* (Lat), I believe it because it is impossible A paradox ascribed to St Augustine, but founded on a passage in Tertullian's *De Carne Christi*, IV.—

Credibile est, quia ineptum est   certum est quia impossibile

Crème de la Crème (krǎm de la krǎm) (Fr) Literally, 'cream of the cream', used figuratively for the very choicest part of something which itself is very choice

Cremona (kre mō' nả) A town in Lombardy famous for a school of violin-makers, 1550-1750 The most famous makers were Nicolo Amati (1596-1684), teacher of Andrea Guarneri (fl 1650-95) and Antonio Stradivari (1649/50-1737) The term is loosely applied to any good instrument.

The organ-stop known as the *cremona* has no connexion with the above but the term is a corruption of the German *krummhorn*, crooked horn It is a reed stop of 8-foot tone

Cremorne Gardens (kre môrn') These pleasure gardens were in Chelsea, on the site now largely occupied by the Lots Road Power Station The Gardens were opened in 1845 and for some years furnished the gayer side of London with much the same fare that Vauxhall had previously supplied Spectacular balloon ascents were made from there, a mediæval tournament was got up, and every night there was dancing to be had, with all the other attractions of shady paths, flickering lamps, and attractive girls Eventually the Gardens became such a centre of rowdiness that the neighbourhood revolted, and they were closed for good in 1877 Their memory is preserved in some of Whistler's Nocturnes.

Creole (krē' ōl) A person of European parentage born in the West Indies or central America—a term of 16th-century Spanish origin (from *criollo* W Indian corruption of Sp *Criadillo*, from *criado* = bred, brought up). Used by the French of white residents (whether Fr. or Sp) in Louisiana The Empress Josephine was a Creole from Martinique

Crêpe Rubber (krǎp) is a term employed to describe raw, unvulcanized sheet rubber that has not been chemically treated in any way It is crinkly (hence its name, *crêpe*, Fr wavy) and is largely used for shoe soles, etc

Crescelle (kre sel'). A wooden rattle used in R C. churches in Holy Week in place of the bell rung at the elevation, etc , during mass

Crescent. Tradition says that "Philip, the father of Alexander, meeting with great difficulties in the siege of Byzantium, set the workmen to undermine the walls, but a crescent moon discovered the design, which miscarried, consequently the Byzantines erected a statue to Diana, and the crescent became the symbol of the state."

Another legend is that Othman, the Sultan, saw in a vision a crescent moon, which kept increasing till its horns extended from east to west, and he adopted the crescent of his dream for his standard, adding the motto, "*Donec repleat orbem*"

Crescent City. The descriptive name in the U S A for New Orleans

Cresset A beacon light The original cresset was an open metal cup at the top of a pole, the cup being filled with burning grease or oil Hence the name, from O Fr *craisse* (Mod. Fr *graisse*), grease

Cressida (kres' i da), Cressid Daughter of Calchas, a priest, beloved by Troilus (*q v*) They vowed eternal fidelity to each other, and as pledges of their vow Troilus gave the maiden a sleeve, and Cressid gave the Trojan prince a glove Scarce had the vow been made when an exchange of prisoners was agreed to Diomed gave up three Trojan princes, and was to receive Cressid in lieu thereof Cressid vowed to remain constant, and Troilus swore to rescue her She was led off to the Grecian's tent, and soon gave all her affections to Diomed —nay, even bade him wear the sleeve that Troilus had given her in token of his love

As false
As air, as water, wind, or sandy earth,
As fox to lamb, as wolf to heifer's calf,
Pard to the hind, or step-dame to her son,
"Yea," let them say, to stick the heart of falsehood,
"As false as Cressid "
Troilus and Cressida, III, 2

Cresswell, Madam A notorious bawd who kept a house of ill-fame in London between 1670 and 1684 In her old age she became a religious devotee and bequeathed £10 for a funeral sermon, in which nothing ill should be said of her The Earl of Rochester is said to have written the sermon, which was as follows
"All I shall say of her is this—she was born *well*, she married *well*, lived *well*, and died *well*, for she was born at Shad-well, married to Cress-well, lived at Clerken-well, and died in Bride-well "

Crestfallen. Dispirited The allusion is to fighting cocks, whose crest falls in defeat and rises rigid and of a deep-red colour in victory.
Shall I seem crest-fallen in my father's sight?
SHAKESPEARE *Richard II*, I, 1

Crete (krēt) **Hound of Crete.** A bloodhound
Coupe le gorge, that's the word I thee defy again,
O hound of Crete SHAKESPEARE *Henry V*, II, 1.

The Infamy of Crete. The Minotaur (*q v.*)
There lay stretched
The infamy of Crete, detested brood
Of the feigned heifer
DANTE *Hell*, XII (Cary's translation)

Cretinism (kret' in izm) Mental imbecility accompanied by goitre. So called from the Crétins of the Alps The word is a corruption of Christian (*Chretien*), because, being baptized, and only idiots, they were "washed from original sin," and incapable of actual sin Similarly, idiots are called *innocents* (Fr. *crétin*)

Crewel Garters. Garters made of worsted or yarn
Ha ! ha ! look, he wears cruel garters
SHAKESPEARE *King Lear*, II, 4
The resemblance in sound between *crewel*

(the derivation of which is unknown) and *cruel* formerly gave rise to many puns, *e g* —
Wearing of silk, why art thou so cruel?
Woman's a Weathercock (1612).

Crib. Thieves' slang for a house or dwelling, as "Stocking Crib" (a hosier's shop), "Thimble Crib" (a silversmith's); also slang for a petty theft, and for a translation from Latin, Greek, etc., surreptitiously used by schoolboys in doing their lessons. To crib is to pilfer or purloin, and to copy someone else's work without acknowledging it, to plagiarize

The word originally denoted a manger with bars, hence its application to a child's cot

To crack a crib. *See* CRACK

Cricket. The earliest mention of the game appears to be the reference in the Guild Merchant Book of Guildford, dated 1598, when John Denwick of Guldeford, being then about fifty-nine years of age, deposed that he had known a certain parcel of land "for the space of Fyfty years and more," and that "hee and several of his fellowes did runne and play there at Creckett and other plaies" when he was a scholar at the Guildford Free School This would take the game back to the end of Henry VIII's reign, and it was certainly a Wykehamist game in the days of Elizabeth

In 1700 two stumps were used 24 inches apart and 12 inches high, with long bails atop. A middle stump was added by the Hambledon Club in 1775. The height of the stumps was raised to 28 inches in 1929. The length of run is 22 yards.

The first cricket club was the Hambledon, which practically came to an end in 1791, but existed in name till 1825

The Marylebone Cricket Club (M.C C), which is regarded as the governing body of the game, was founded in 1787. Its ground was originally on the site now occupied by Dorset Square, in 1811 the groundsman, Thomas Lord, moved it to Regent's Park, and in 1814 to its present position in St John's Wood, known after him as Lord's Cricket Ground

The word *cricket* is probably from A S *cric, cryec*, a staff, and is thus connected with *crutch*

It's not cricket. It's not done in a fair and sportsmanlike way.

Merry as a cricket. *See* GRIG

Crikey (krī′ kı) An exclamation, a mild oath, originally a euphemistic modification of *Christ*.

Crillon (krē′ yon) **Where wert thou, Crillon?** Crillon, surnamed *the Brave*, in his old age went to church, and listened intently to the story of the Crucifixion In the middle of the narrative he grew excited, and, unable to contain himself, cried out, " *Où étais-tu, Crillon?* " One of the finest hotels in Paris, in the Place de la Concorde, is named from this hero, it was the German Headquarters during the occupation, 1940-44

Crillon (1541-1615) was one of the greatest captains of the 16th century. He fought at the battle of Ivry (1590), and was entitled by Henri IV *"le brave des braves"*

Henri IV, after the battle of Argives (1589), wrote to Crillon *"Prend-toi, brave Crillon nous avons vaincu a Arques, et tu n'y etais pas "* This letter has become proverbial

Crimen læsæ majestatis (krī′ men lē′ ze mäj es tā′ tis) (Lat) High treason *See* LÈSE-MAJESTE

Crimp. A decoy, especially one of those riverside pests who purport to supply ships with sailors, but who are in league with public-houses and low-class lodging-houses, into which they decoy the sailors and relieve them of their money under one pretence or another.

Crinoline (krın′ ō lēn) The word comes from Latin *crinis*, hair, and *linum*, linen, and originally meant the stiff horsehair and linen material used to swell out the skirts of women's dresses When enormous skirts became fashionable, about 1856, cages of steel or whalebone were worn to keep them spread to their full extent, and these also were called crinolines The crinoline reached its largest spread about 1866, and then quickly subsided, to be replaced by the bustle

Cripplegate. This district in the City of London was so called before the Conquest from the number of cripples who resorted thither to beg, because of the parish church of St. Giles (*q v.*), the patron of cripples (*Stow*) Churches dedicated to this saint are common in the suburbs of large towns, as St. Giles of Norwich, Cambridge, Salisbury, etc

Crishna. *See* KRISHNA

Crisis properly means the "ability to judge " Hippocrates said that all diseases had their periods, when the humours of the body ebbed and flowed like the tide of the sea. These tidal days he called *critical days*, and the tide itself a *crisis*, because it was on these days the physician could determine whether the disorder was taking a good or a bad turn. The seventh and all its multiples were critical days of a favourable character (Gr *krinein*, to decide or determine)

Crispin. A shoemaker St Crispin was a shoemaker, and was therefore chosen for the patron saint of the craft. It is said that two brothers, Crispin and Crispian, born in Rome, went to Soissons, in France (A D 303), to propagate the Christian religion, and maintained themselves wholly by making and mending shoes Probably the tale is fabulous, for *crepis* is Greek for a shoe, Latin *crepid-a*, and St Crepis or Crepid became Crepin and Crispin

St Crispin's Day. October 25th, the day of the battle of Agincourt Shakespeare makes Crispin Crispian one person, and not two brothers Hence Henry V says to his soldiers—

And Crispin Crispian shall ne'er go by .
But we in it shall be remembered
Henry V, iv, 3

St. Crispin's holiday. Every Monday, with those who begin the working week on Tuesday, a no-work day with shoemakers

St. Crispin's lance. A shoemaker's awl.

Criss-cross Row. *See* CHRISS-CROSS

Critic A judge, an arbiter (Gr *krinein*, to judge, to determine)

A captious, malignant critic is called a Zoilus (*q v*).

"And what of this new book the whole world makes such a rout about?" "Oh, it is out of all plumb, my lord, quite an irregular thing' not one of the angles at the four corners is a right angle I had my rule and compasses in my pocket " "Excellent critic!"

"And for the epic poem your lordship bade me look at upon taking the length, breadth, height, and depth of it, and trying them at home upon an exact scale of Bossu's [Bossut's], 'tis out, my lord, in every one of its dimensions " "Admirable connoisseur!"—STERNE' *Tristram Shandy*, vol iii, ch xii

The abbé Charles Bossut (1730-1814) was a noted mathematician and geometer.

Prince of critics. Aristarchus, of Byzantium, who compiled the rhapsodies of Homer (2nd cent B C)

Stop-watch critics.

"And how did Garrick speak the soliloquy last night?" "Oh, against all rule, my lord, most ungrammatically. Betwixt the substantive and the adjective, which should agree together in number, case, and gender, he made a breach thus—stopping as if the point wanted settling, and betwixt the nominative case, which, your lordship knows, should govern the verb, he suspended his voice in the epilogue a dozen times, three seconds and three-fifths by a stop-watch, my lord each time " "Admirable grammarian' But in suspending his voice was the sense suspended likewise? Did no expression of attitude or countenance fill up the chasm? Was the eye silent? Did you narrowly look?' ' 'I looked only at the stop-watch, my lord " "Excellent observer!"—STERNE *Tristram Shandy*, vol iii, ch xii

Croak, To. In slang this means to die, the term probably coming from the hoarse death rattle or croak of the expiring breath A hedge doctor, or wandering quack is known as a *Crocus*, or one who makes his patients croak

Croaker. A raven, so called from its croak, one who takes a desponding view of things. Goldsmith, in his *Good-natured Man*, has a character so named

Croakumshire. Northumberland is so called from the peculiar croaking of the natives in speaking. This is especially observable in Newcastle and Morpeth, where the people are said to be born with a burr in their throats, which prevents their giving effect to the letter *r*

Crocodile. A symbol of deity among the Egyptians, because. says Plutarch, it is the only aquatic animal which has its eyes covered with a thin transparent membrane, by reason of which it sees and is not seen, as God sees all, Himself not being seen To this he subsequently adds another reason, saying, "The Egyptians worship God symbolically in the crocodile, that being the only animal without a tongue, like the Divine Logos, which standeth not in need of speech " (*De Iside et Osiride*, vol ii, p. 381)

Achilles Tatius says, "The number of its teeth equals the number of days in a year." Another tradition is that, during the seven days held sacred to Apis, the crocodile will harm no one.

Crocodile tears. Hypocritical tears. The tale is, that crocodiles moan and sigh like a person in deep distress, to allure travellers to the spot, and even shed tears over their prey while in the act of devouring it.

As the mournful crocodile
With sorrow snares relenting passengers
SHAKESPEARE 2 *Henry VI*, iii, 1

Crœsus (krē' sus) **Rich as Crœsus** Crœsus, King of Lydia (560-546 B C), was so rich and powerful that all the wise men of Greece were drawn to his court, and his name became proverbial for wealth

Crofters. Small holders in the Highlands of Scotland, also Cottars (*cf* Burns, *Cottar's Saturday Night*)

Cromlech (krom' lek) A megalithic monument of prehistoric times, consisting of a large flat stone resting on two or more others, like a table (Welsh *crom*, bent, *llech*, a flat stone) They are probably the uncovered remains of sepulchral chambers or cairns

Weyland Smith's cave (Berkshire), Trevethy Stone (Cornwall), Kit's Coty House (Kent), are examples, and there are others at Plâs Newydd (Anglesey) and in Cornwall, not a few are found in Ireland, as the "killing-stone" in Louth In Brittany, where they are known as *dolmens* (*q v*), Denmark, Germany, and some other parts of Europe, cromlechs are to be found

Cromwell's Bible. *See* BIBLE, THE ENGLISH.

Crone. From Old North Fr *carone*, a worn-out horse, which gives in Mod. Fr *carogne*, a contemptuous word for an old woman It is from Lat *caro*, flesh, and is so connected with *carrion* Crone was also applied to an old ewe, and in this case is direct from Mid. Dutch, *kronie, karonie*, an old sheep, which has the same origin as *carone*

Take up the bastard, take 't up, I say, give 't to thy crone —SHAKESPEARE *Winter's Tale*, ii, 3

Cronian Sea The north polar sea, so called from Cronos. Pliny says "*A Thule unius diei navigatione mare concretum, a nonnullis* cronium *appellatur* " (*Nat Hist*, iv, 16)

As when two polar winds blowing adverse
Upon the Cronian sea
MILTON *Paradise Lost*, x, 290

Cronos or Cronus (krō' nos) *See* KRONOS

Crony. A familiar friend *An old crony* is an intimate of times gone by The word was originally (17th cent) University slang, and seems to have no connexion with *crone* (*q.v*), it may be from Gr. *kronios*, long-lasting (*kronos*, time), meaning a long-lasting friend

Crook. By hook or crook. *See* HOOK.

There is a crook in the lot of every one. There is vexation bound up in every person's life When lots were drawn by bits of stick, it was desirable to get sticks which were smooth and straight, but one without a crook, knot, or some other defect is rare Thomas Boston (1677-1732) published a sermon entitled *The Crook in the Lot*

The term *Crook* as applied to a criminal or sharper came into use in the second half of the 19th century.

To crook the elbow, or finger. The American equivalent to the English elbow-lifting, *i e.* having a drink, especially drinking as a habit

Crooked as Crawley. *See* CRAWLEY

Crooning. A competent musical critic describes crooning thus "A reprehensible form of singing that established itself in light entertainment music about the 1930s
The principle of crooning is to use as little voice as possible and instead to make a sentimental appeal by prolonged moaning somewhere near the written notes, but preferably never actually on those notes The smallest vocal equipment is sufficient for the purpose of crooning, one of its admirers' delusions being that it does not become wholly satisfactory until it is amplified by a microphone " (Eric Blom)

Crop Up or Out. To rise out of, to appear at the surface. A mining term. Strata which rise to the surface are said to *crop out* We also say, such and such a subject *crops up* from time to time—*i e.* rises to the surface, such and such a thing *crops out* of what you were saying —*i e.* is *apropos* thereof

Share-cropper (U S A) Under-privileged classes in the Southern States who work on the cotton plantations and take a share of the crops in lieu of wages.

He came a cropper. He fell head over heels.

To come a cropper. To get a bad fall "Neck and crop ' means altogether, and to "come a cropper" is to come to the ground neck and crop.

Croquemitaine. A hobgoblin, an evil sprite or ugly monster, used by French nurses to frighten their charges into good behaviour. In 1863 M L'Epine published a romance with this title, telling the story of a god-daughter of Charlemagne whom he called "Mitaine " It was translated by Tom Hood (the Younger)

Croquet (krō′ kı) This once popular garden game takes its name from the French *croc*, a hook, as the early croquet mallets were shaped like hockey-sticks It came into fashion in Britain about 1856

Crore In India, a hundred lacs of rupees

Crosier (from late Lat *crocia*, connected with our *crook*, confused with Fr *croisier* from *crois*, Lat. *crux*, *crucis*, a cross) The pastoral staff of an abbot or bishop, and sometimes (but incorrectly) applied to an archbishop's staff, which terminates in a floriated cross, while a bishop's crosier has a curved, bracken-like head
A bishop turns his staff *outwards*, to denote his wider authority; an abbot (whose staff is the same as a bishop's) carries it turned *inwards* to show that his jurisdiction is limited to his own inmates When walking with a bishop an abbot covers his staff with a veil hanging from the knob, to show that his authority is veiled in the presence of his superior

Cross. The cross is not solely a Christian symbol, originating with the crucifixion of the Redeemer In Carthage it was used for ornamental purposes, runic crosses were set up

by the Scandinavians as boundary marks, and were erected over the graves of kings and heroes, Cicero tells us (*De Divinatione*, ii, 27, and 80, 81) that the augur's staff with which they marked out the heaven was a cross, the Egyptians employed the same as a sacred symbol, and two buns marked with the cross were discovered at Herculaneum It was a sacred symbol among the Aztecs long before the landing of Cortes, in Cozumel it was an object of worship, in Tabasco it symbolized the god of rain, and in Palinque it is sculptured on the walls with a child held up adoring it. It was one of the emblems of Quetzalcoatl, as lord of the four cardinal points, and the four winds that blow therefrom

The cross of the crucifixion is legendarily said to have been made of four sorts of wood (palm, cedar, olive, and cypress), to signify the four quarters of the globe

Ligna crucis palma, cedrus, cupressus, oliva

In his *Monasteries of the Levant* (1848) Curzon gives the legend that Solomon cut down a cedar and buried it on the spot where the pool of Bethesda stood later A few days before the crucifixion, this cedar floated to the surface of the pool, and was employed as the upright of the Saviour's cross

It is said that Constantine, on his march to Rome, saw a luminous cross in the sky, in the shape and with the motto *In hoc vinces*, by this [sign] conquer In the night before the battle of Saxa Rubra (312) a vision appeared to the Emperor in his sleep, commanding him to inscribe the cross and the motto on the shields of his soldiers He obeyed the voice of the vision, and prevailed The monogram is XPιστος (Christ) *See* Gibbon's *Decline and Fall*, ch xx

This may be called a standing legend, for, besides St Andrew's cross, and the Dannebrog (*q v*), there is the story concerning Don Alonzo before the battle of Ourique in 1139 when the figure of a cross appeared in the eastern sky, Christ suspended on it, promised the Christian king a complete victory, and the Moors were totally routed This legend is commemorated by Alonzo's device, in a field argent five escutcheons azure, in the form of a cross, each escutcheon being charged with five bezants in memory of the five wounds of Christ *See* LABARUM

In heraldry, as many as 285 varieties of cross have been recognized, but the twelve in ordinary use, and from which the others are derived, are —(1) The ordinary cross, (2) the cross humetté, or couped, (3) the cross urde, or pointed, (4) the cross potent, (5) the cross crosslet, (6) the cross botonné, or treflé, (7) the cross moline, (8) the cross potence; (9) the cross fleury, (10) the cross patte, (11) the Maltese cross (or eight-pointed cross), (12) the cross cleché and fitche

As a mystic symbol the number of crosses may be reduced to four,

The Greek cross found on Assyrian tablets, Egyptian and Persian monuments, and on Etruscan pottery

The crux decussata generally called St. Andrew's cross Quite common in ancient sculpture.

The Latin cross or *crux immissa* This symbol is found on coins, monuments, and medals long before the Christian era

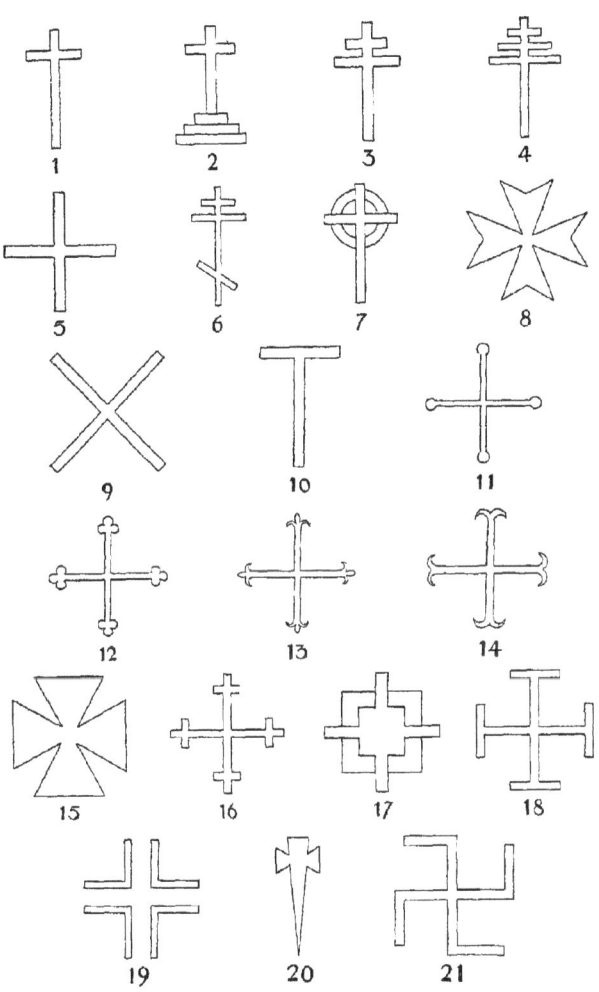

Crosses —1 Latin 2 Calvary 3. Patriarchal, Archiepiscopal, Lorraine 4 Papal. 5 Greek 6 Russian 7. Celtic. 8. Maltese. 9 St Andrew's 10. Tau 11 Pommé 12 Botonne 13. Fleury 14 Moline. 15 Patte 16. Crosslet 17 Quadrate 18 Potent. 19 Voided and couped 20. Patte fiché 21 Fylfot, Swastika.

The tau cross or *crux commissa* Very ancient indeed, and supposed to be a phallic emblem

The tau cross with a handle, or *crux ansata*, is common to several Egyptian deities, as Isis Osiris, etc., and is the emblem of immortality and life generally The circle signifies the eternal preserver of the world, and the T is the monogram of Thoth, the Egyptian Mercury, meaning wisdom *See* Cross.

The Invention of the Cross. A church festival held on May 3rd, in commemoration of the discovery (Lat *invenire*, to discover) of the Cross (326) by St Helena (*q v*) At her direction, after a long and difficult search in the neighbourhood of the Holy Sepulchre (which had been over-built with heathen temples), tne remains of the three buried crosses were found. These were applied to a sick woman, and that which effected her cure was declared to be the True Cross The Empress had this enclosed in a silver shrine (after having carried a large piece to Rome), and deposited in a church that was built on the spot for the purpose

The Cross of Lorraine, with two bars, was adopted as the emblem of the Free French during World War II

The Red Cross on a white ground, sometimes called the Cross of Geneva, is the Swiss flag reversed, and indicates the neutrality of hospitals and ambulances

Everyone must bear his own cross. His own burden or troubles The allusion is to the law that the person condemned to be crucified was to carry his cross to the place of execution.

Hot cross buns. *See* Bun

On the cross. Not "on the square," not straightforward To get anything "on the cross" is to get it unfairly or dishonestly

The judgment of the cross. An ordeal instituted in the reign of Charlemagne The plaintiff and defendant were required to cross their arms upon their breast, and he who could hold out the longest gained the suit

To cross it off or out. To cancel it by running your pen across it

To cross swords. To fight a duel, metaphorically, to meet someone in argument or debate

To cross the hand Gypsy fortune-tellers always bid their dupe to "cross their hand with a bit of silver ' This, they say, is for luck The silver remained with the owner of the crossed hand The sign of the cross warded off witches and all other evil spirits, and, as fortune-telling belongs to the black arts, the palm is signed with a cross to keep off the wiles of the devil "You need fear no evil, though I am a fortune-teller, if by the sign of the cross you exorcise the evil spirit "

To cross the line—*i e.* the equator To pass to the other side of the equator. It is still the custom on board ship to indulge in horseplay when crossing the line, and those who are doing so for the first time are usually subjected to humorous indignities.

Cross and Ball. The orb of royalty is a sphere or ball surmounted by a cross, an emblem of empire introduced in representations of our Saviour The cross stands *above* the ball, to signify that the spiritual power is above the temporal

Cross and Pile. The obverse and reverse sides of a coin, head and tail; hence, money generally, pitch and toss, etc *Pile* is French for the reverse of a coin, and the other side for centuries was marked with a cross

A man may now justifiably throw up cross and pile for his opinions —Locke *Human Understanding*

Marriage is worse than cross I win, pile you lose
                                Shadwell *Epsom Wells*

I have neither cross nor pile Not a penny in the world The French phrase is, "*N'avoir ni croix ni pile* "

Whacum had neither cross nor pile
                                Butler *Hudibras*, pt ii, 3

Cross-belts The 8th King's Royal Irish Hussars, raised by William III, in 1693 The unit fought in Spain in 1710, during one fight practically destroying a Spanish cavalry regiment, whose cross-belts they removed and wore themselves.

Cross-bench. Seats set at right angles to the rest of the seats in the House of Commons and the House of Lords, and intended for those members who are independent of any recognized party Hence, *cross-bencher*, an independent, and the *cross-bench mind*, an unbiased or neutral mind.

Crossbill. The red plumage and the curious bill (the horny sheaths of which cross each other obliquely) of this bird are accounted for by a mediæval fable which says that these distinctive marks were bestowed on the bird by the Saviour at the Crucifixion, as a reward for its having attempted to pull the nails from the Cross with its beak Schwenckfeld in 1603 (*Theriotropheum Silesiæ*) gave the fable in the Latin verses of Johannes Major; but it would be better known to English readers through Longfellow's "Legend of the Crossbill" from the German of Julius Mosen

Cross-biting Cheating, properly, cheating one who has been trying to cheat you—biting in return. Hence, *cross-biter*, a swindler *Laurence Crossbiter* is the name given to one of the rogues in *Cock Lorell's Bote* (*q v*)

Cross-bones. *See* Skull and Cross-bones.

Cross-legged Knights. Crusaders were generally represented on their tombs with crossed legs

To dine with cross-legged knights. *See* Dine.

Cross questions and crooked answers. A parlour game which consists in giving ludicrous or irrelevant answers to simple questions Hence. the phrase is used of one who is "hedging," or trying by his answers to conceal the truth when he is being questioned

Cross-roads All (except suicides) who were excluded from holy rites were piously buried at the foot of the cross erected on the public road, as the place next in sanctity to consecrated ground Suicides were ignominiously

buried on the highway, generally at a crossing with a stake driven through their body.
Our orthodox coroner doubtless will find it a felo-de-se,

And the stake and the cross-road, fool, if you will,
    does it matter to me?   TENNYSON, *Despair*

Cross-row   Short for CHRISS-CROSS ROW

Crossword puzzle   A puzzle in which words must be discovered to fill in, letter by letter, the squares into which a rectangular diagram is divided   Clues are furnished and most of the letters form parts of two words, one reading across and the other down the rectangle   There have long been simple puzzles of this nature, but the more ingenious crossword was invented in U S A , about 1923, and immediately welcomed in Britain

Cross, meaning irritable, bad tempered.

As cross as a bear with a sore head, as the tongs, as two sticks.   Common phrases used of one who is very vexed, peevish, or cross The allusions are obvious

Cross-grained.   Patchy, ill-tempered, self-willed   Wood must be worked with the grain, when the grain crosses we get a knot or curling, which is hard to work uniform

Cross-patch.   A disagreeable, ill-tempered person   male or female   Patch (q v) is an old name for a fool, and with the meaning "fellow" it is common enough in Shakespeare, as a "scurvy patch," a 'soldier's patch," "What patch is made our porter?" "a crew of patches," etc

Cross-patch, draw the latch,
Sit by the fire and spin,
Take a cup, and drink it up,
Then call your neighbours in
       Old Nursery Rhyme

Crotona's Sage (kro tō′ na)   Pythagoras So called because at Crotona he established his chief school of philosophy (about 530 B C) Such success followed his teaching that the whole aspect of the town became more moral and decorous in a marvellously short time.

Crouchmas.   An old name for the festival of the Invention of the Cross (May 3rd), also for Rogation Sunday and Rogation week "Crouch" is an old word for cross, especially in its religious signification, from Lat *crux.*

From bull-cow fast,
Till Crouchmas be past
       TUSSER *May Remembrances.*

Croud.   *See* CROWD

Crow   A crow symbolizes contention, discord, strife

As the crow flies.   The shortest route between two given places   The crow flies straight to its destination   *Cp* BEE-LINE.

Jim Crow   *See* JIM.

I must pluck a crow with you, I have a crow to pick with you.   I am displeased with you, and must call you to account   I have a small complaint to make against you   In Howell's proverbs (1659) we find the following 'I have a *goose* to pluck with you," used in the same sense

If a crow help us in sirrah, we ll pluck a crow together —SHAKESPEARE *Comedy of Errors,* III, 1.
If not, resolve before we go,
That you and I must pull a crow
       BUTLER *Hudibras,* pt II, 2

To crow over one.   To exult over a vanquished or abased person   The allusion is to cocks, who always crow when they have gained a victory

To eat crow.   To be forced to do something extremely disagreeable   The expression arose from an incident during an armistice in the war between Britain and the U S A in 1812 A New Englander having crossed the British lines by mistake, while out hunting, brought down a crow A British officer, who heard the shot, determined to punish him. He was himself unarmed, but gained possession of the American's gun by praising his marksmanship and asking to see his weapon Covering the huntsman with his own gun, the soldier declared that he was guilty of trespass and ordered him to take a bite out of the crow The American was forced to obey However, when the soldier returned the gun and told him to go, the American in his turn covered the soldier and compelled him to eat the remainder of the crow

Crow's Nest.   The ' look out"—originally a barrel fixed to the masthead of an old-fashioned whaling-ship

Crowd, Croud, or Crouth.   An ancient Celtic species of fiddle with from three to six strings (Welsh *crwth*)   Hence *crowder,* a player on a *crowd*   The last noted player on this instrument was John Morgan, who died in 1720

Harke how the minstrels gin to shrill aloud
  Their merry musick that resounds from far
The pipe, the tabor, and the trembling croud,
That well agree withouten breach or jar
       SPENSER *Epithalamion*

I never heard the olde song of *Percy and Duglas,* that I found not my heart mooved more then with a trumpet and yet is it sung but by some blinde Crouder, with no rougher voyce, then rude stile — SIDNEY *Apologie for Poetrie*

Crown.   In heraldry, nine crowns are recognized: The oriental, the triumphal or imperial, the diadem, the obsidional crown, the civic, the crown vallery, the mural crown, the naval, and the crown celestial

Among the Romans of the Republic and Empire crowns of various patterns formed marks of distinction for different services, the principal ones were —

The blockade crown (*corona obsidionalis*), presented to the general who liberated a beleaguered army. This was made of grass and wild flowers gathered from the spot

A camp crown (*corona castrenses*) was given to him who first forced his way into the enemy's camp It was made of gold and decorated with palisades

A civic crown to one who saved a *civis* or Roman citizen in battle It was of oak leaves, and bore the inscription, H O C S —*i e hostem occidit, civem servavit* (*a foe he slew, a citizen saved*)

A mural crown was given to that man who first scaled the wall of a besieged town It was made of gold and decorated with battlements

A naval crown, of gold, decorated with the beaks of ships, was given to him who won a naval victory

An olive crown was given to those who distinguished themselves in battle in some way not specially mentioned

An ovation crown (*corona ovatio*) was by the Romans given to a general in the case of a lesser victory It was made of myrtle

A triumphal crown was by the Romans given to the general who obtained a triumph It was made of laurel or bay leaves Sometimes a massive gold crown was given to a victorious general *See* LAUREL

The iron crown of Lombardy is the crown of the ancient Longobardic kings It was used at the coronation of Agilulph, King of Lombardy, in 591, and among others that have since been crowned with it are Charlemagne as King of Italy (774), Henry of Luxemburg (the Emperor Henry VII), as King of Lombardy (1311), Frederick IV (1452), Charles V (1530), and in 1805 Napoleon put it on his head with his own hands

In 1866, at the conclusion of peace, it was restored by Austria to Italy and was replaced in the cathedral at Monza, where Charlemagne had been crowned and whence it had been taken in 1859. The crown is so called from a narrow band of iron about three-eighths of an inch broad, and one-tenth of an inch in thickness, within it, said to be beaten out of one of the nails used at the Crucifixion According to tradition, the nail was given to Constantine by his mother, St. Helena, who discovered the cross The outer circlet is of beaten gold, and set with precious stones.

Crowns of Egypt *See* EGYPT

The crown, in English coinage, is a five-shilling piece, and is so named from the French *denier à la couronne*, a gold coin issued by Philip of Valois (1339) bearing a large crown on the obverse The English crown was a gold coin of about 43½ grs. till the end of Elizabeth's reign, except for a silver crown which was issued in the last coinage of Henry VIII and one other of Edward VI

In the paper trade, crown is a standard size of printing paper measuring 15 by 20 inches, so called from an ancient watermark

Crown Office, The A department of the Central Office of the Supreme Court. It consists of the King's Coroner and Attorney, who is also Master, two Assistant Masters, a Chief Clerk, and some minor officials

Crown of the East. Antioch, capital of Syria, which consisted of four walled cities, encompassed by a common rampart, that "enrounded them like a coronet "

Crowner. An old pronunciation of "coroner" (*q v*), perhaps with the suggestion that he is an officer of the Crown.
The crowner hath sat on her, and finds it Christian burial —*Hamlet*, v 1

Crowquill, Alfred. This was the name used by Alfred Henry Forrester (1805-72), the black-and-white artist of *Punch* and the *Illustrated London News* He was famous in his day as the illustrator of *Dr Syntax*, the *Bon Gaultier Ballads*, *Baron Munchausen* and other popular works

Crozier. *See* CROSIER

Crucial (kroo' shǎl) **A crucial test.** A very severe and undeniable one The allusion is to a fancy of Lord Bacon, who said that two different diseases or sciences might run parallel for a time, but would ultimately cross each other thus, the plague might for a time resemble other diseases, but when the *bubo* or boil appeared, the plague would assume its specific character Hence the phrases *instantia crucis* (a crucial or unmistakable symptom), a crucial experiment, example, question, etc *Cp.* CRUX

Cruel, The. Pedro, King of Castile (1334, 1350-69)

Cruel garters. *See* CREWEL

Cruet In common parlance this word is used in the plural to mean the salt, pepper, and mustard usually placed on the table for meals A cruet is really a small bottle and is used specifically for each of the small bottles in which the water and wine for the eucharist and the ablutions of the Mass are served upon the altar

Cruiser. Cruiser weight is the same as light-heavy weight *See* BOXING

Cruller In the U S A a sweet cake or biscuit in the form of strips or twists or rings, which has been fried in deep fat

Crummy. In obsolete slang, expressive of something desirable, as *that's crummy*, that's good, also meaning plump, well developed, as *she's a crummy woman*, a' fine, handsome woman. Among soldiers, however, the word has always meant lousy, infested with lice, and this is now the only meaning attached to the word

Crumpet. *See* MUFFINS

Crusade (kroo sǎd). A war undertaken in late mediæval times by Christians against the Turks and Saracens for the recovery of the Holy Land and, nominally at least, for the honour of the Cross Each nation had its special colour, which, says Matthew Paris (i, 446), was *red* for France; *white* for England; *green* for Flanders; for Italy it was *blue* or *azure*, for Spain, *gules*; for Scotland, *a St. Andrew's cross*, for the Knights Templars, *red on white*

There were eight principal crusades:—

1 A crusade proclaimed by Urban II, in 1095. Two columns led by Peter the Hermit and Walter the Pennyless, set out in 1096 and were destroyed A second expedition under Hugh the Great (father of Hugh Capet, later king of France), Raymond Count of Toulouse, Robert Duke of Normandy, and Godfrey de Bouillon, was successful and ended by achieving the proclamation of Godfrey as King of Jerusalem, 1099

2 An unsuccessful expedition, promoted by St. Bernard, under the leadership of the Emperor Conrad III and Louis VII of France, 1147-49

3 Jerusalem and Ascalon having been lost in 1187, a crusade for their recovery was preached by Gregory VIII, and Frederick Barbarossa set out in 1189; Philip II Augustus, King of France and Richard I of England started the following year. A stalemate was reached and the crusade abandoned in 1192.

4 A crusade was preached by Fulke of Neuilly in 1198 It was led by Baldwin of Flanders and the Doge of Venice Constantinople was captured and Baldwin was elected Emperor in 1202

5 In 1217 an unsuccessful expedition set out under Andrew, King of Hungary, to return in 1221

6 The Emperor Frederick II set out in 1228, and the following year was crowned King of Jerusalem.

7. Following the loss of the Holy Land in 1244, St Louis (Louis IX of France) set out in 1248 He was captured by the Saracens in 1250, a ten years' truce was declared and Louis returned to France

8. Louis and Prince Edward (afterwards Edward I) of England set out in 1270 St Louis died on August 25, and the crusade ended with a twenty years' truce in 1272

The Children's Crusade, consisting of a body of 30 000 boys and girls between the ages of ten and sixteen, led by a shepherd boy, Stephen, set out from Vendôme to capture Jerusalem in 1212. The King of France, parents and priests had all forbidden their departure, but they got to Marseilles where they were embarked for Palestine Some perished at sea and the rest were sold through the treachery of the ship-owners as slaves to Barbary There were two other contingents, from the Germanies, one of which lost half its numbers while crossing the Mont Cenis the remainder being kidnapped or dying of want and weariness, the other crossed the St Gothard, reached Brindisi, and were sold as slaves to the Moors

Crush. To crush a bottle—_i e._ drink one Milton has _crush the sweet poison_ (_Comus_, 47) The idea is that of crushing the grapes Shakespeare has also _burst_ a bottle in the same sense (Induction of _Taming of the Shrew_) _See_ CRACK.

> Come and crush a cup of wine
> SHAKESPEARE _Romeo and Juliet_, 1, 2

To crush a fly on a wheel. Another form of "to break a butterfly on a wheel" _See under_ BREAK.

To have a crush on someone, meaning to have a very passing infatuation for someone—a schoolgirl's phrase and emotion

Crush-room. An old term for a room in a theatre or opera house, etc , where the audience can collect and talk during intervals, wait for their carriages, and so on.

Crust. The upper crust (of society) The aristocracy, the upper ten-thousand The phrase was first used in _Sam Slick_. The upper crust was at one time the part of the loaf placed before the most honoured guests. Thus, in Wynkyn de Worde's _Boke of Kervinge_ (carving) we have these directions. "Then take a lofe in your lyfte hande, and pare ye lofe rounde about; then cut the ouer-cruste to your souerayne . ."

Crusted port When port is first bottled its fermentation is not complete, in time it precipitates argol on the sides of the bottle, where it forms a crust Crusted port, therefore, is port which has completed its fermentation. A splash of whitewash is usually dabbed on the bottle so that it will be kept the right way up, for careless movement would cause the crust to slip and spoil the wine

Crusting An American hunting term for taking big game in winter when the ice of ponds, rivers and lakes will bear the weight of a man but not that of a moose or deer

Crusty. Ill-tempered, apt to take offence, cross, peevish In Shakespeare's play Achilles addresses the bitter Thersites with :—

> How now, thou core of envy!
> Thou crusty batch of nature, what's the news?
> _Troilus and Cressida_, v, 1

Crutched Friars (krūch ed fri' ars) is the Lat _cruciati_ (crossed)—_i e_ having a cross embroidered on their dress They were a minor order of friars, the Canons Regular of the Holy Cross, founded at Bologna about 1169, who first appeared in England in 1244

Crux A knotty point, a difficulty _Instantia crucis_ means a crucial test (_q v_), or the point where two similar diseases _crossed_ and showed a special feature It does not refer to the cross, an instrument of punishment, but to the crossing of two lines, called also a _node_ or knot, hence a trouble or difficulty _Quæ te mala crux agitat?_ (Plautus); What evil cross distresses you ?—_i e_ what difficulty, what trouble are you under?

Crux pectoralis. The cross which bishops of the Church of Rome suspend over their breast
See also CROSS.

Cry. For names of the distinctive cries of animals, _see_ ANIMALS.

A far cry. A long way, a very considerable distance, used both of space and of time, as, ".it is a far cry from David to Disraeli," but they both were Jews, 'it's a far cry from Clapham to Kamschatka " Sir Walter Scott several times uses the phrase, "It's a far cry to Lochow (Lochawe)," and he tells us that this was a proverbial expression among the Campbells, meaning that their ancient hereditary dominions lay beyond the reach of an invading enemy —_Legend of Montrose_ ch xii

Great cry and little wool. A proverbial saying expressive of contempt or derision for one who promises great things but never fulfils the promises
Originally the proverb ran, "Great cry and little wool, as the Devil said when he sheared the hogs", and it appears in this form in the ancient mystery of _David and Abigail_, in which Nabal is represented as shearing his sheep, and the Devil imitates the act by "shearing a hog "

> Thou wilt at best but suck a bull,
> Or shear swine, all cry and no wool
> BUTLER _Hudibras_, I, 1, 851

Hue and cry. _See_ HUE

In full cry. In full pursuit A phrase from hunting, with allusion to a yelping pack of hounds in chase

It's no good crying over spilt milk. It's useless bewailing the past

To cry aim. _See_ AIM

To cry cave (kā' vi) To give warning (Lat. _cave_, beware), used by schoolboys when a master comes in sight.

To cry havoc _See_ HAVOCK

To cry off. To get out of a bargain; to refuse to carry out one's promise

To cry quits. _See_ QUIT.

To cry stinking fish. To belittle one's own endeavours, offerings, etc "To cry" here is to offer for sale by shouting one's wares in the street

To cry up To praise loudly and publicly

To cry wolf *See* WOLF.

Crypto-Catholic. A person who is secretly a Catholic but for some ulterior motive conceals the fact and poses as a Protestant The term is also applied (Crypto-Communist, -Fascist, etc) to one who secretly works for the cause of his party though outwardly appearing to have no connection with it.

Crystal Gazing, or, as it is somet.mes termed, Scrying, is a very ancient form of divination. It is alleged that certain people can, by gazing fixedly and deeply into a polished crystal ball, see what is about to happen or what is actually happening at some distant place It is said that scenes are enacted and places are recognizable as clearly as in the view-finder of a camera Crystal gazing has been, and, indeed, still is, a practice that lends itself to the skill of impostors, and from a psychic standard it is not to be encouraged

Crystal Palace. This was one of the glories of the Victorian era The original Crystal Palace, built entirely of glass and iron, was erected in Hyde Park to house the 1851 Great Exhibition When the exhibition closed the building was moved (1854) to Sydenham where it was re-erected with some alterations and the addition of two towers which for many years were visible for many miles around Exhibitions, concerts, and other events took place in the Palace, which became national property in 1911. The whole building was entirely destroyed by fire in November, 1936.

The crystalline sphere. According to Ptolemy, the ninth orb, identified by some with "the waters which were above the firmament" (*Gen* 1, 7), it was placed between the "primum mobile" and the firmament or sphere of the fixed stars and was held to have a shivering movement that interfered with the regular motion of the stars

They pass the planets seven, and pass the fixed
And that crystalline sphere, whose balance weighs
The trepidation talked
                    MILTON: *Paradise Lost*, iii, 481.

Cub. An ill-mannered lout The cub of a bear is said to have no shape until its dam has licked it into form.

A bear's a savage beast, of all
Most ugly and unnatural,
Whelped without form until the dam
Has licked it into shape and frame.
                    BUTLER *Hudibras*, i, 3

Cubbing, or **Cub-hunting.** This is the term employed to describe the preliminary training given to young foxhounds before regular hunting begins. Fox cubs have not the craftiness nor staying power of the older beast, and thus furnish better sport for young hounds and young riders

Cuba The Roman deity who kept guard over infants in their cribs and sent them to sleep. Lat *cubo*, to lie down in bed.

Cubism (kū′ bizm) The doctrine of an early-20th-century school of painters who depict surfaces, figures, tints, light and shade, etc., on canvas by means of a multiplicity of cubes The name was given to this school, somewhat disparagingly, by Henri Matisse, in 1908. It was a form of art wholly devoid of representation and divorced from realism, excluding any attempt to depict actual appearances and spurning all the accepted canons of art Picasso was its great exponent; Braque, Leger, and Derain explored its possibilities in many of their works

Cubit (kū′ bit). An ancient measure of length, the word coming from the Latin *cubitum*, the elbow Approximately it applied to the length from the elbow to the tip of the longest finger The Hebrews had two cubits, the ordinary cubit as above measuring about 22 in and a longer one used by Ezekiel for measuring the Temple The most ancient cubit was the Egyptian, which measured 20 64 in and was divided into seven palms It was employed in the design and building of the Pyramids, and measuring sticks have been found proving the use of this measure for at least three centuries before Christ The Roman cubit measured 17 4 in

Cucking-stool. A kind of chair formerly used for ducking scolds, disorderly women, dishonest apprentices, etc , in a pond "Cucking" is from the old verb *cuck*, to void excrement, and the stool used was often a close-stool.

Now, if one cucking-stool was for each scold,
Some towns, I fear, would not their numbers hold.
                    Poor Robin (1746)

Cuckold. The husband of an adulterous wife; so called from *cuckoo*, the chief characteristic of this bird being to deposit its eggs in other birds' nests Johnson says "it was usual to alarm a husband at the approach of an adulterer by calling out 'Cuckoo,' which by mistake was applied in time to the person warned." Greene calls the cuckoo "the cuckold's quirister" (*Quip for an Upstart Courtier*, 1592), and the Romans used to call an adulterer a "cuckoo," as "*Te cuculum uxor ex lustris rapit*" (Plautus· *Asinaria*, v, 3). Cp. ACTÆON, HORN, *and see quotation under* LADY'S SMOCK.

Cuckold's Point. A spot on the riverside near Deptford So called from a tradition that King John there made love successfully to a labourer's wife.

Cuckoo. There are many old folk rhymes about this bird, one says.—

In April the cuckoo shows his bill,
In May he sings all day;
In June he alters his tune,
In July away he'll fly,
In August go he must.

Other sayings are —

Turn your money when you hear the cuckoo, and you'll have money in your purse till he come again

And—

The cuckoo sings from St Tiburtius' Day (April 14th) to St. John's Day (June 24th)

Cuckoo oats and woodcock hay make a farmer run away. If the spring is so backward that oats cannot be sown till the cuckoo is heard (*i.e.* April), or if the autumn is so wet that the aftermath of hay cannot be got in till woodcock shooting (middle of November), the farmer must be a great sufferer

Cuckoo-spit. A frothy exudation deposited on plants by certain insects, especially the frog-hopper (*Aphrophora spumaris*), for the purpose of protecting the larvæ So called from an erroneous popular notion that the froth was spat out by cuckoos.

It must be likewise understood with some restriction what hath been affirmed by *Isidore*, and yet delivered by many, that Cicades are bred out of Cuccow spittle or Woodsear, that is, that spumous, frothy dew or exudation, or both, found upon Plants, especially about the joints of Lavender and Rosemary, observable with us about the latter end of May —SIR THOMAS BROWNE. *Pseud Epidemica*, v, 3.

Don't be a cuckoo! Don't be a silly ass; don't go and make a fool of yourself

To wall in the cuckoo. *See* COURSE.

Cuddy, an abbreviation of Cuthbert, is the North Country and Scottish familiar name for a donkey, as elsewhere he is called Neddy or Jack.

Cudgel. To cudgel one's brains. To make a painful effort to remember or understand something The idea is from taking a stick to beat a dull boy under the notion that dullness is the result of temper or inattention

Cudgel thy brains no more about it, for your dull ass will not mend his pace with beating —SHAKE-SPEARE *Hamlet*, v, 1.

To take up the cudgels. To maintain an argument or position To fight, as with a cudgel, for one's own way

Cue (kū) The tail of a sentence (Fr. *queue*), the catchword which indicates when another actor is to speak, a hint

When my cue comes, call me, and I will answer.— *A Midsummer Night's Dream*, IV, 1.

To give the cue. To give the hint In another sense *cue* means a person's frame of mind—in a good or bad skin

My uncle was in thoroughly good cue DICKENS *Pickwick Papers*

Cuerp *See* QUERPO

Cuffy. A Negro, both a generic word and proper name, possibly from the English slang term "cove" (*q v*).

Sambo and Cuffey expand under every sky —MRS. BEECHER STOWE: *Uncle Tom's Cabin*

Cui bono? (kwī bō' nō) Who is benefited thereby? To whom is it a gain? A common, but quite erroneous, meaning attached to the words is, What good will it do? For what good purpose? It was the question of the Roman judge L Cassius Pedanius *See* Cicero, *Rosc Am.*, xxx, 84

Cato, that great and grave philosopher, did commonly demand, when any new project was propounded unto him, *cui bono*, what good will ensue in case the same is effected?—FULLER: *Worthies* (The Design, 1)

Cul de Sac (kul de säk) (Fr) A blind alley, or road blocked up at one end like a sack Figuratively, an argument, etc , that leads to nothing

Culdees (kūl dēz') An ancient religious order in Ireland and Scotland from about the 8th to the 13th centuries. So called from the Old Irish *céle dé*, servant of God The culdees were originally hermits or anchorites, but were later gathered into communities and were, finally, little more than secular canons

Cullinan Diamond (ku lin' an) The largest diamond ever known It was discovered in 1905 at the Premier Mine in South Africa, and when found weighed 3,025¼ carats (about 1 lb 6 oz), as against the 186$\frac{1}{16}$ carats of the famous Koh-i-Nor (*q v*) in its uncut state. It was purchased by the South African Government for £150,000 and presented to Edward VII, and now forms part of the Crown Jewels, its estimated value being over £1,000,000 It was cut into a number of stones, of which the two largest weigh over 516 and 309 carats respectively It was named from the manager of the mine at the time of its discovery.

Cully. A fop, a fool, a dupe Perhaps a contracted form of *cullion*, a despicable creature (Ital *coglione*) Shakespeare uses the word two or three times, as "Away, base cullions'" (2 *Henry VI*, 1, 3), and again in *Taming of the Shrew*, IV, 2—"And makes a god of such a cullion " *Cp* GULL.

You base cullion, you. BEN JONSON *Every Man in his Humour*, III, 2

Culross Girdles. The thin plate of iron in Scotland, on which oat cakes, scones, etc are cooked, is called a "girdle," for which Culross was long celebrated

Locks and bars, plough-graith and harrow-teeth! and why not grates and fireprongs, and Culross girdles?—SCOTT· *Fair Maid of Perth*, ch II

Cultus (kūl' tūs) In usual parlance this means a cult, or system of religious belief, but in the Far Western States of the U S A the word, taken from the Indian, was used as signifying worthless

Culver (kūl'ver). A dove or pigeon, from A S *culfre*, which is probably an English word and unconnected with Lat *columba* Hence culver-house, a dovecote.

On liquid wing,
The sounding culver shoots
THOMSON· *Spring* 452

Culverin (kūl' vĕr in). A long, slender piece of artillery employed in the 16th century It was 5¼ in bore and fired a projectile of 18 lb Queen Elizabeth's "Pocket Pistol" in Dover Castle is a culverin So called from Lat *colubrinus* (Fr *coulevrine*), snake-like

Culverkeys (kūl' vĕr kēz) An old popular name for various plants, such as the bluebell, columbine, squill, etc , the flowers of which have some resemblance to a bunch of keys (O E *culfre*, a dove).

Cumberland Poets, or Lake Poets One or other of these terms used often to be applied to the poets Wordsworth (1770-1850), Southey (1774-1843), and Coleridge (1772-1834) who lived about the the lakes of Cumberland According to Jeffrey, of the *Edinburgh Review*, they combined the sentimentality of Rousseau with the simplicity of Kotzebue and the homeliness of Cowper

Cumberland Presbyterians. A sect found in Kentucky and Tennessee which was opposed to college-trained ministers

Cum grano salis (kŭm grā′ nō sā′ lis) (Lat.) With a grain of salt, there is some truth in the statement, but we must use great caution in accepting it

Cummer. A gudewife, old woman   A variety of *gammer* which is a corruption of *grandmother*, as *gaffer* is of *grandfather*   It occurs scores of times in Scott's novels

Cumshaw (kŭm′ shaw)   This is a pidjin English word meaning a tip, a douceur, palm-oil   It may be a corruption of the English word "commission," or it may derive from the Chinese *kan′ hiseh*, grateful thanks

Cunctator (kŭngk tā tôr) (Lat , *the delayer*) Quintus Fabius Maximus (d 203 B C) the Roman general who baffled Hannibal by avoiding direct engagements, and wearing him out by marches, countermarches, and skirmishes from a distance   This was the policy by which Duguesclin forced the English to abandon their French possessions in the reign of Charles V   *Cp* FABIAN

Cuneiform Letters (kū nē′ i fôrm)   Letters like wedges (Lat *cuneus*, a wedge)   They form the writing of ancient Persia, Babylonia, Assyria, etc , and, dating from about 3800 B C to the early years of the Christian era, are the most ancient specimens of writing known to us   Cuneiform inscriptions first attracted interest in Europe in the early 17th century, but no deciphering was successful until 1802 (by Grotefend, of Hanover).

Cunning. This is a word to which various meanings are attached and on which several phrases depend   It originally comes from the same word as does "ken," to know, and was applied to someone who *knew* things   As Wyclif's bible translates *Genesis* ii, 9

> A tree of kunnynge of good and euil

By an extension of this came the meaning of skill —

> If I forget thee, O Jerusalem, let my right hand forget her cunning —*Psalm* cxxxvii

The word had, however, already begun to infer a knowledge of occult and evil matters —

> We take cunning for a sinister and crooked wisdom
> —BACON   *Cunning*

and a Cunning Man, or Woman, was merely another name for a wizard, or witch.   Hence it grew to mean sly and crafty, the sense in which it is commonly used now

The American usage, in the sense of charming, or pretty or engaging, was customary there by the mid-19th century

Cunobelin (kū′ nō bel′ in)   Cunobelinus, King of the Catuvellauni (A D. 5-40), and the father of Caractacus   His name is preserved, in modified form, in Cymbeline, and in "Cunobelin's gold-mines," the local name for the dene-holes in the chalk beds of Little Thurrock, Essex, which were traditionally used by Cunobelin for hiding

Cup   A mixture of strong ale with sugar, spice, and a lemon, properly served up hot in a silver cup   Sometimes a roasted orange takes the place of a lemon.   If wine is added, the cup is

called *bishop* (*q.v*), if brandy is added, the beverage is called *cardinal*

Cider cup, claret cup, etc , are drinks made of cider, claret, etc , with sugar, fruit, and herbs

Cup Final. *See* ASSOCIATION FOOTBALL CUP

He was in his cups. Intoxicated.   *Inter pocula, inter vina.* (Horace · 3 *Odes*, vi, 20)

Let this cup pass from me   Let this trouble or affliction be taken away, that I may not be compelled to undergo it, this cup is "full of the wine of God's fury," let me not be compelled to drink it   The reference is to Christ's agony in the garden (*Matt* xxvi, 39)

My cup runs over.   My blessings overflow   Here cup signifies portion or blessing

> My cup runneth over   goodness and mercy shall follow me all the days of my life.—*Ps* xxiii, 5, 6

The cup of vows.   In Scandinavia it was anciently customary at feasts to drink from cups of mead, and vow to perform some great deed worthy of the song of a skald   There were four cups. one to Odin, for victory, one to Freyja, for a good year, one to Niord, for peace, and one to Bragi, for celebration of the dead in poetry

There's many a slip 'twixt the cup and the lip. *See* ANCÆUS

We must drink the cup.   We must bear the burden awarded to us, the sorrow which falls to our lot

Not my cup of tea.   A phrase meaning, it does not suit me, this is not the sort of thing I want

Cupper. A comfortable colloquial abbreviation of "a cup of tea."   "Come in and have a nice cupper," i e ' Come in and have a nice cup of tea "

Cups as sports trophies.   An engraved (usually silver) cup is a common form of trophy.   One of the oldest is the Waterloo Cup for coursing, which originated in 1836 and owes its name to the fact that its leading promoter was landlord of the Waterloo Hotel, Liverpool

The **Davis Cup** for an international lawn tennis championship was presented by Dwight Davis in 1900   Another tennis trophy is the **Wightman Cup,** given by Mrs George Wightman, in 1923, for competition between teams of women players from U S A. and Great Britain

The **America Cup,** for an international yacht race, was originally named the Queen's Cup, and was offered by the Royal Yacht Squadron in 1851   In 1857 it was won by an American yacht and has since been called the America Cup.   For many years Sir Thomas Lipton built yachts in an endeavour to win back the Cup but it has remained in American hands

The **Ryder Cup** for international golf matches was presented by Samuel Ryder in 1927, though up to the present only the British and American professional teams have competed for it—no other country being able to produce a team of sufficiently high standard   The **Walker Cup** was given in 1922 by an American, George H Walker, for a golf match

9*

to be played twice a year between teams of amateurs of Great Britain and U.S A The Curtis Cup, given in 1923 by two American lady champions, the Misses Margaret and Harriot Curtis, is for a golf match between teams of ladies of Great Britain and the U S A.
See also ASSOCIATION FOOTBALL CUP

Cupar (koo′ par) He that will to Cupar maun to Cupar A Scottish proverbial saying, meaning, he that will have his own way, must have it even to his injury The reference is to the Cistercian monastery, founded there by Malcolm IV

Cupar justice Same as "Jedburgh justice" hang first and try afterwards It is sometimes called "Cowper law," and it had its rise from a baron-baile in Coupar-Angus, before heritable jurisdictions were abolished. Abingdon Law is a similar phrase It is said that Major-General Browne, of Abingdon, in the Commonwealth, first hanged his prisoners and then tried them. *See* JEDWOOD JUSTICE LYDFORD LAW

Cupboard Love. Love from interested motives The allusion is to the love of children to some indulgent person who gives them something nice from her cupboard
Cupboard love is seldom true —*Poor Robin*

Cupid. The god of love in Roman mythology (Lat *cupido*, desire, passion), identified with the Greek Eros, son of Mercury and Venus. He is usually represented as a beautiful winged boy, blindfolded, and carrying a bow and arrows, and one legend says that he whets with blood the grindstone on which he sharpens his arrows
Ferus et Cupido,
Semper ardentes acuens sagittas
HORACE *2 Odes*, viii, 14, 15.

Cupid and Psyche (sī′ ki) An episode in the *Golden Ass* (*q v*) of Apuleius It is an allegory representing the progress of the soul to perfection William Morris retells the story in his *Earthly Paradise* (*May*), as also does Walter Pater in *Marius the Epicurean See* PSYCHE.

Cupid's golden arrow Virtuous love
Cupid's leaden arrow, sensual passion
Deque sagittifera promisit duo tela pharetra
Diversorum operum, fugat hoc, facit illud amorem
Quod facit auratum est et cuspide fulget acuta —
Quod fugat obtusum est, et habet sub arundine
plumbum.   OVID *Apollo and Daphne*
I swear to thee by Cupid's strongest bow,
By his best arrow with the golden head . .
By that which knitteth souls and prospers love.
A Midsummer Night's Dream.

Cupidon, Le Jeune (le zhĕrn kū′ pē dong) Count D'Orsay (1801-52) was so styled by Lord Byron

Cur. A mongrel or worthless dog; hence, a fawning, mean-spirited fellow The word is from Scandinavian *kurra*, to snarl, to grumble, and is first used in England with "dog"— *kur-dogge*, a growling or snarling dog
Like a wylde Bull, that being at a bay
Is bayted of a mastiffe, and a hound,
And a curre-dog
SPENSER *Faerie Queene*, VI, v, 19.
What would you have, you curs,
That like nor peace nor war?
SHAKESPEARE. *Coriolanus*, i, 1.

Curate *See* CLERICAL TITLES

Curate's egg. Among the catch-phrases that *Punch* has introduced into the English language, "Good in parts, like the curate's egg" is, perhaps, the most commonly used The illustrated joke showed a nervous young curate, at his bishop's breakfast table He has been asked by his lordship whether his egg is to his liking, terrified to say that it is bad, he stammers out that " it's good in parts "

Curé de Meudon (kū′ rä de mĕ don)—*i e* Rabelais (*c* 1495-1553), who was first a monk, then a leech, then prebend of St Maur, and lastly cure of Meudon

Curfew (kĕr′ fū) The custom of ringing a bell every evening as a signal to put out fires and go to bed The word comes from the Fr *couvre feu*, and shows its Norman origin William the Conqueror instituted the curfew in England in 1068, fixing the hour at eight in the evening The word is now extended to mean the period commonly ordered by all occupying armies in time of war or civil commotion when civilians must stay within doors
The curfew tolls the knell of parting day
GRAY'S *Elegy*

Curmudgeon (kĕr mŭj′ on) A grasping, miserly churl Concerning this word Johnson says in his dictionary "It is a vitious manner of pronouncing *cœur méchant*, Fr., an unknown correspondent," meaning that this suggestion was supplied by some correspondent unknown. By a ridiculous blunder, Ash (1775) copied it into his dictionary as "from Fr *cœur*, unknown, *méchant*, correspondent"! The actual etymology of the word has not been traced

Curnock. *See* CRANNOCK

Currant. A corruption of *Corinth*, whence currants were imported probably in the 16th century. Originally called "raisins of Corauntz," *Corauntz* being Anglo-French for Corinth

Currency. A word applied in early Australia to the wide variety of coins then in circulation, as apart from English gold coins, which were called sterling The word assumed the connotation of "Australian," and in novels of the mid-19th century the word "uncurrency" is found in the sense of "unAustralian"

Current. The drift of the current is the rate per hour at which the current runs
The setting of the current is that point of the compass towards which the waters of the current run

Curry Favour. A corruption of the M E *to curry favel*, to rub down Favel· *Favel* (or *Fauvel*) being the name of the horse in the 14th-century French satire *Roman de Fauvel*, which was a kind of counterpart to the more famous romance, *Reynard the Fox* Fauvel, the fallow-coloured horse, takes the place of Reynard, and symbolizes cunning or duplicity, hence, to curry, or stroke down, Favel was to enlist the services of duplicity, and so, to seek to obtain by insincere flattery or officious courtesy.

Curse. Curses, like chickens, come home to roost. Curses fall on the head of the curser, as chickens which stray during the day return to their roost at night

Cursing by bell, book, and candle *See* BELL

Not worth a curse. I don't care a curse (or cuss) Here "curse" is the O E *cresse* or *cerse* Mod E *cress*, *i e* something quite valueless. Similarly, the Lat *nihil* (*nihilum*) is *ne hilum*, not (worth) the black eye of a bean. Other phrases are "not a straw," "not a pin," "not a rap," "not a bit," "not a jot," "not a pin's point," "not a button"

> Wisdom and witt nowe is not worthe a kerse.
> LANGLAND *Piers Plowman*

The curse of Cain One who is always on the move and has no abiding place is said to be "cursed with the curse of Cain" The allusion is to God's judgment on Cain after he had slain his brother Abel—

> And now art thou cursed from the earth, . a fugitive and a vagabond shalt thou be in the earth.—
> *Gen* iv, 11-12

The curse of Scotland. The nine of diamonds It may refer to the arms of Dalrymple, Earl of Stair—viz or, on a saltire argent, nine lozenges of the first The earl was justly held in abhorrence for the massacre of Glencoe, and he was also detested in Scotland for his share in bringing about the Union with England in 1707. The phrase seems to be first recorded in the early 18th century, for in Houston's *Memoirs* (1715-47) we are told that Lord Justice Clerk Ormistone became universally hated in Scotland, where they called him the Curse of Scotland, and when the ladies were at cards playing the Nine of Diamonds (commonly called the Curse of Scotland) they called it the Justice Clerk

Other attempts at accounting for the nickname are (1) The nine of diamonds in the game of *Pope Joan* is called the Pope, the Antichrist of the Scottish reformers (2) In the game of *comette*, introduced by Queen Mary, it is the great winning card, and the game was the curse of Scotland because it was the ruin of many families (3) The word "curse" is a corruption of *cross*, and the nine of diamonds is so arranged as to form a St Andrew's Cross, but as there is no evidence that the St Andrew's Cross was ever looked upon in Scotland as a curse, and as also the nine of hearts would do as well, this explanation must be abandoned (4) Some say it was the card on which the "Butcher Duke" wrote his cruel order after the Battle of Culloden, but this took place in 1746, which would seem to make it too late for the reference given above.

> Grose says of the nine of diamonds "Diamonds imply royalty and every ninth King of Scotland has been observed for many ages to be a tyrant and a curse to the country."—*Tour Thro' Scotland*, 1789

Curst cows have curt horns. *See* COW

Cursitor (kĕrs′ i tor) In the procedure of the old Courts of Chancery, which was revised in the mid-19th century, the issue of writs by the court was done by 24 cursitors, who between them covered all the counties in England and Wales. The word comes from the Latin *cursor*, a runner, and refers to the long journeys they had to perform when issuing the writs Cursitor Street, Chancery Lane, takes its name from the office of the cursitors. built by Sir Nicholas Bacon (1509-79), father of the great chancellor

Curtain. Curtain lecture The nagging of a wife after she and her husband are in bed *See* CAUDLE LECTURE

> Besides what endless brawls by wives are bred,
> The curtain lecture makes a mournful bed
> DRYDEN

Curtain raiser. *See* LEVER DE RIDEAU

To ring down the curtain. To bring a matter to an end A theatrical term When the play is over, the bell rings and the curtain comes down

The last words of Rabelais are said to have been, "Ring down the curtain, the farce is played out"

Curtal Friar (kĕr′ tal). *Curtal* was originally applied to horses—a "curtal horse" was one with its tail docked, hence the adjective came to be used for things in general that were cut down or shortened, and a "curtal friar" was one who wore a short cloak. In later use (especially by Scott) it acquired a vaguely derisory or belittling significance

Curtana (kĕr tā′ na) The sword of mercy borne before the English kings at their coronation, it has no point and is hence *shortened* (O Fr *curt*, Lat *curtus*). It is called the sword of Edward the Confessor, which, having no point, was the emblem of mercy The royal sword of England was so called to the reign of Henry III.

> But when Curtana will not do the deed
> You lay the pointless clergy-weapon by,
> And to the laws, your sword of justice fly.
> DRYDEN *Hind and Panther*, Pt ii, 419

Curthose (kĕrt′ hōz) Robert II, Duke of Normandy (1087-1134), eldest son of William the Conqueror He was also called "Short thigh," as in Drayton's *The Tragicall Legend of Robert, Duke of Normandy, surnamed Short-thigh* (1596).

Curtmantle (kĕrt′ măn tel) Henry II. He introduced the Anjou mantle, which was shorter than the robe worn by his predecessors. (1133, 1154-89) *Cp* CARACALLA.

Curule Chair (kū′ rul) The chair of state among the ancient Romans, an elaborate kind of camp-stool inlaid with ivory, etc. As dictators, consuls, prætors, censors, and the chief ediles occupied such a chair, they were termed *curule* magistrates or *curules*. The word is connected either with *currus*, a chariot—perhaps because the chair was originally intended for use in a chariot—or with *curvus*, through the shape of its legs

Cushcow Lady. A Yorkshire name for the ladybird (*q.v.*)

Cushion. Cushion dance. A lively dance in which kissing while kneeling on a cushion was a prominent feature, popular in early Stuart times

> In our time in Queen Elizabeth's time, gravity and state was kept up, in King James's time things were pretty well, but in King Charles's time there has been nothing but Trench-more and the cushion dance, *omnium gatherum*, tolly polly, *hoyte cum toyte*—
> SELDEN's *"Table Talk" (King of England).*

The dance survived in rural districts until comparatively recent times, and is probably still practised   John Clare (1793-1864), the peasant poet of Northamptonshire, mentions it in his *May-Day Ballad* —

And then comes the *cushion*, the girls they all shriek,
And fly to the door from the old fiddler's squeak,
But the doors they are fastened, so all must kneel
   down,
And take the rude kiss from th' unmannerly clown

To miss the cushion. To make a mistake, to miss the mark

Cuspidor. Name coined for a spitoon, brought into prominence by the habit of chewing tobacco, dominantly, but not entirely, of American usage   The word is found used in print before 1780

Cuss A fellow, usually used with an epithet as in the case of "customer" (*q v*)   Presumably from "curse" which in 19th-century U S was found used in the same way

Cussedness. Perversity; malice prepense, an evil temper. In this sense the word seems to have been originally an Americanism, the M E word *cursydnesse* meant sheer wickedness

Custard Coffin. *See* COFFIN

Customer. Slang for a man or a fellow in a general way, usually with some qualification, as, *an ugly customer, a rum customer*, a person better left alone, as he is likely to show fight if interfered with. *Cp* CARD.

Custos Rotulorum (*keeper of the rolls*) The chief civil officer or principal justice of the peace of a county, to whose custody are committed the records or rolls of the sessions.

Cut. Cut and come again. Take a cut from the joint, and come for another if you like, a colloquial expression for "there's plenty of it, have as much as you like "   It is used by Swift in *Polite Conversation*, ii

Cut and dried. Already prepared. "He had a speech all cut and dried "   The allusion is to timber, cut, dried, and fit for use

Sets of phrases, cut and dry,
Evermore thy tongue supply
        SWIFT *Betty the Grizette*

Cut and run Be off as quickly as possible   A sea phrase, meaning cut your cable and run before the wind

Cut neither nails nor hair at sea. Petronius says —

Non licere cuiquam mortalium in nave neque unges neque capillos deponere nisi cum pelago ventus irascitur

The cuttings of the nails and hair were votive offerings to Proserpine, and it would excite the jealousy of Neptune to make offerings to another in his own special kingdom

Cut no ice. Be of no account, make no impression, presumably borrowed from figure skating

To cut a swath To make an impression   An American colloquialism usually used in the negative. A swath is the amount of grass or crop cut down with one sweep of a scythe

Cut out of whole cloth Entirely false   Suggested probably by the mendacious claims of tailors' advertisements

The cut of his jib The contour or expression of his face   A sailor's phrase   The cut of a jib or foresail of a ship indicates her character, hence a sailor says of a suspicious vessel, he ' does not like the cut of her jib "

Cut off with a shilling. Disinherited   Blackstone tells us that the Romans set aside those testaments which passed by the natural heirs unnoticed, but if any legacy was left, no matter how small, it proved the testator's intention   English law has no such provision, but the notion at one time prevailed that the name of the heir should appear in the will, and if he was bequeathed "a shilling," that the testator had not forgotten him, but disinherited him intentionally

Cut your coat according to your cloth. *See* COAT

Cut your wisdom teeth. *See* WISDOM TOOTH

Diamond cut diamond. *See* DIAMOND

He has cut his eye teeth. *See* TEETH

He'll cut up well. He is rich, and his property will cut into good slices

His life was cut short. He died prematurely.   The allusion is to Atropos, one of the three Parcæ, cutting the thread of life spun by her sister Clotho

I must cut my stick.—*i e* leave   The Irish usually cut a shillelah before they start on an expedition   *Punch* gives the following derivation —"Pilgrims on leaving the Holy Land used to cut a palm-stick, to prove that they had really been to the Holy Sepulchre   So brother Francis would say to brother Paul.   ' Where is brother Benedict ? '   'Oh (says Paul), he has cut his stick ' '—*i e* he is on his way home "

To cut. To renounce acquaintance   There are four sorts of cut—

(1) The *cut direct* is to stare an acquaintance in the face and pretend not to know him

(2) The *cut indirect*, to look another way, and pretend not to see him

(3) The *cut sublime*, to admire the top of some tall edifice or the clouds of heaven till the person cut has passed by

(4) The *cut infernal*, to stoop and adjust your boots till he has gone past.

To cut a dash. To make a show, to get oneself looked at and talked about for a showy or striking appearance   "Dashing" means *striking*—*i e* showy, as a "dashing fellow," a " dashing equipage "

To cut blocks with a razor To do something astounding by insignificant means, to do something more eccentric than expedient, to "make pin-cushions of sunbeams" (Swift)   The tale is that Accius Nævius, a Roman augur, opposed king Tarquin the Elder, who wished to double the number of senators   Tarquin sneered at his pretensions of augury, and asked if he could do what was then in his thoughts   "Undoubtedly," replied Nævius, and Tarquin with a laugh said, "Why, I was thinking whether I could cut through this whetstone with a razor" "Cut boldly," cried Nævius, and the whetstone was cleft in two This story forms the subject of the *Bon Gaultier Ballads*, and Goldsmith refers to it in his *Retaliation*—

In short, 'twas his [Burke's] fate, unemployed or in place, sir,
To eat mutton cold, and cut blocks with a razor

To cut capers *See* CAPERS

To cut one's comb. *See* COMB

To cut short is to shorten   "Cut short all intermission" (*Macbeth*, IV, 3)

To cut it short (cp AUDLEY) means to bring to an end what you are doing or saying.

To cut the ground from under one, or from under his feet. To leave an adversary no ground to stand on, by disproving all his arguments

To cut the knot. To break through an obstacle   The reference is to the Gordian knot (*q v*) shown to Alexander, with the assurance that whoever loosed it would be made ruler of all Asia, whereupon the Macedonian cut it in two with his sword, and claimed to have fulfilled the prophecy.

To cut the painter. *See* PAINTER.

To cut up rough. To be disagreeable or quarrelsome about anything

Cut-off. The American equivalent of the English short cut

Cut out. Left in the lurch, superseded.   In cards, when there are too many for a game (say whist), it is customary for the players to cut out after a rubber, in order that another player may have a turn   This is done by the players cutting the cards on the table, when the lowest turn-up gives place to the new hand

He is cut out for a sailor. His natural propensities are suited for the vocation   The allusion is to cutting out cloth, etc., for specific purposes

Cute. An American colloquialism for smart, pretty, attractive   It is a contraction of "acute," and is found in Nathan Bailey's dictionary of 1721.

Cuthbert   A name given during World War I to fit and healthy men of military age who, particularly in Government offices, were not "combed out" to go into the Army, also, of course, to one who actually avoided military service   It was coined by " Poy," the · cartoonist of the *Evening News*, who represented these civilians as frightened-looking rabbits

St. Cuthbert's beads. See BEAD

St. Cuthbert's duck   The eider duck, so called because it breeds in the Farne Islands, St Cuthbert's headquarters, and figures in the legends of the saint

St. Cuthbert's Stone, and Well   A granite rock in Cumberland, and a spring of water close by

Cuthbert Bede was the pen-name of the Rev Edward Bradley (1827-89), author of *Verdant Green* (*q v*) and other pieces of Victorian humour

Cutler's Poetry   Mere jingles or rhymes   Knives had, at one time, a distich inscribed on the blade by means of aqua fortis.

Whose posy was
For all the world like cutler's poetry
Upon a knife
SHAKESPEARE   *Merchant of Venice*, v, 1

Cutpurse. Now called "pickpocket"   The two words are of historical value   When purses were worn suspended from a girdle, thieves cut the string by which the purse was attached, but when pockets were adopted, and purses were no longer hung on the girdle, the thief was no longer a cutpurse, but became a pickpocket

To have an open ear, a quick eye, and a nimble hand, is necessary for a cutpurse —SHAKESPEARE *Winter's Tale*, IV, 3

Moll Cutpurse.   The familiar name of Mary Frith (about 1585-1660), a woman of masculine vigour, who not infrequently assumed man's attire.   She was a notorious thief and once attacked General Fairfax on Hounslow Heath, for which she was sent to Newgate   She escaped by bribery, and died at last of dropsy. Middleton and Dekker's play, *The Roaring Girl* (1611) is founded on her doings

Cutteau, Cuttoe, Culto.   A knife, from the Fr *couteau*.   It was in use in England and America from the 17th century until about 1850.

Cutter.   A single-masted, deep-keeled and fore-and-aft rigged sailing vessel   The term is also applied to a light-armed naval vessel—a revenue cutter—used to prevent smuggling, etc.

Cutter's law.   Not to see a fellow want while we have cash in our purse.   Cutter's law means the law of purse-cutters, robbers, brigands, and highwaymen

I must put you in cash with some of your old uncle's broad-pieces   This is cutter's law; we must not see a pretty fellow want, if we have cash ourselves —SCOTT *Old Mortality*, ch IX

Cuttle   Captain Cuttle.   An eccentric, kind-hearted sailor in Dickens's *Dombey and Son*   simple as a child, credulous of every tale, and generous as the sun   He is immortalized by his saying, "When found make a note of." This phrase was adopted by *Notes and Queries*.

Cutty   Scots for short, as *cutty pipe*, a short clay pipe, *cutty spoons*, *cutty sark*, a short-tailed shirt, a *cutty*, a stumpy girl or woman, *cutty gun*, a popgun

Cutty stool.   A small stool on which offenders were placed in the Scottish church when they were about to receive a public rebuke.   Cp STOOL OF REPENTANCE

Cwt. is C. *centum*, wt. *weight*, meaning hundredweight.   Cp. DWT

Cyanean Rocks, The (sī ǎn' i an)   The Symplegades, two movable rocks at the entrance of the Euxine, *i.e* where the Bosphorus and Black Sea meet   They were said to close together when a vessel attempted to sail between them, and thus crush it to pieces Cyanean means *blue-coloured*, and Symplegades means *dashers together*.

Cycle A period or series of events or numbers which recur everlastingly in precisely the same order

Cycle of the moon, called " Meton's Cycle," from Meton, who discovered it, is a period of nineteen years, at the expiration of which time the phases of the moon repeat themselves on the same days as they did nineteen years previously *See* CALLIPPIC PERIOD

Cycle of the sun. A period of twenty-eight years, at the expiration of which time the Sunday letters recur and proceed in the same order as they did twenty-eight years previously In other words, the days of the month fall again on the same days of the week

The Platonic cycle or great year. That space of time which, according to ancient astronomers, elapses before all the stars and constellations return to their former positions in respect to the equinoxes Tycho Brahe calculated this period at 25,816 years, and Riccioli at 25,920

> Cut out more work than can be done
> In Plato's year, but finish none
>   BUTLER *Hudibras,* iii, 1

Cyclic Poets (sī′klĭk) Epic poets who, on the death of Homer, caught the contagion of his poems, and wrote continuations, illustrations, or additions thereto These poets wrote between 800 and 550 B C , and were called *cyclic* because they confined themselves to the cycle of the Trojan war. The chief were Agias, Arctinos, Eugamon, Lesches and Strasinos

Cyclops (sī′klops) (Gr , circular-eye) One of a group of giants that, according to legend, inhabited Thrace They had only one eye each, and that in the centre of their forehead, and their work was to forge iron for Vulcan They were probably Pelasgians, who worked in quarries, and attached a lantern to their forehead to give them light underground *Cp.* ARIMASPIANS

Cyclopean Masonry (sī klō′plan) The old Pelasgic ruins of Greece, Asia Minor, and Italy. such as the Gallery of Tiryns, the Gate of Lions at Mycenæ, the Treasury of Athens, and the Tombs of Phoroneus and Danaos They are composed of huge blocks fitted together without mortar, with marvellous nicety, and are fabled to be the work of the Cyclops (*q.v*) The term is also applied to similar structures in many parts of the world.

Cygnus. *See* PHAETON'S BIRD

Cyllenius (sī lē′ nĭ us) Mercury So called from Mount Cyllenē, in Peloponnesus, where he was born

Cymbeline. *See* CASSIBELAN, CUNOBELIN.

Cymodoce (sī mod′ ō si) A sea nymph and companion of Venus in Virgil's *Georgics* (iv, 338) and *Æneid* (v, 826) In Spenser's *Faerie Queene* (III, iv and IV, xii), she is a daughter of Nereus and mother of Marinell by Dumarin She frees Florimel from the power of Proteus. The word means "wave-receiving "

The Garden of Cymodoce. Sark, one of the Channel Islands It is the title of a poem by Swinburne in his *Songs of the Springtides.*

Cynic (sĭn′ ĭk) The ancient school of Greek philosophers known as the *Cynics* was founded by Antisthenes, a pupil of Socrates, and made famous by his pupil, Diogenes. They were ostentatiously contemptuous of ease, luxury, or wealth, and were given their name because Antisthenes held his school in the Gymnasium, *Cynosarges* (white dog), so called because a white dog once carried away part of a victim which was there being offered to Hercules The effigy over Diogenes's pillar was a dog, with this inscription —

> "Say, dog, I pray, what guard you in that tomb?"'
> "A dog ª"—' His name?"—"Diogenes "—"From far '"
> "Sinope "—'"What' who made a tub his home?"'
> " The same, now dead, amongst the stars a star "

Cynic Tub, The. The tub from which Diogenes lectured Similarly we speak of the "Porch" (*q v*), meaning Stoic philosophy, the "Garden" (*q v*), Epicurean philosophy; the ' Academy" (*q.v*), Platonic philosophy, and the "Colonade," meaning Aristotelian philosophy.

> [They] fetch their doctrines from the Cynic tub
>   MILTON *Comus,* line 708

Cynosure (sĭn′ ō shur) The Pole star, hence. the observed of all observers Greek for *dog's tail,* and applied to the constellation called *Ursa Minor* As seamen guide their ships by the north star and observe it well, the word "cynosure" is used for whatever attracts attention, as "The cynosure of neighbouring eyes" (*Milton*), especially for guidance in some doubtful matter

Cynthia (sĭn′ thĭ á) The moon, a surname of Artemis or Diana The Roman Diana, who represented the moon, was called Cynthia from Mount Cynthus in Delos, where she was born

> And from embattled clouds emerging slow,
> Cynthia came riding on her silver car
>   BEATTIE *Minstrel*

Pope, speaking of the inconstant character of woman, "matter too soft a lasting mark to bear," says—

> Come, then, the colours and the ground prepare'
> Dip in the rainbow, trick her off in air,
> Choose a firm cloud, before it fall, and in it
> Catch, ere she change, the Cynthia of the minute
>   *Epistle,* ii, 17-20

By Elizabethan poets—Spenser, Phineas Fletcher, Raleigh, Ben Jonson, and others— the name was one of the many that was applied to Queen Elizabeth

Cypress. A funeral tree, dedicated by the Romans to Pluto, because when once cut it never grows again It is said that its wood was formerly employed for making coffins, hence Shakespeare's "In sad cypress let me be laid" (*Twelfth Night,* ii, 4)

> Cypresse garlands are of great account at funeralls amongst the gentiler sort but rosemary and bayes are used by the commons both at funeralls and weddings They are plants which fade not a good while after they are gathered and intimate that the remembrance of the present solemnity might not dye presently.—
> COLES *Introduction to the Knowledge of Plants*

Cyprian (sĭp′ rĭ an) Cyprus was formerly famous for the worship of Venus, hence the adjective has been applied to lewd or profligate persons and prostitutes.

A Night Charge at Bow Street Office, with other matters worth knowing, respecting the unfortunate CYPRIAN, the feeling COACHMAN, and the generous MAGISTRATE —PIERCE EGAN. *Life in London*, Bk ii, ch ii

Cyprian brass, or *æs Cyprium*, copper Pliny (Bk. xxxiv, c, ii) says, "*in Cypro enim prima æris inventio fuit*"

Cyrano de Bergerac (sē ra´ nŏ de bâr zhèr ak). Cyrano is mostly known as the eponymous hero of Rostand's play, which appeared in 1897 with Coquelin in the title-role The real Cyrano de Bergerac (1619-55) was a novelist and dramatist, as well as a soldier and duelist—the latter largely on account of his great nose His best-known book was *Comic Histories of the States and Empires of the Moon*, 1656

Czechoslovakia (che´ kŏ slŏ văk´ ya) The name of the republic formed after World War I by the union of Bohemia, Moravia, Silesia, Slovakia, and part of Ruthenia, under the presidency of Thomas Masaryk (1850-1937) The capital city is Prague. After appealing in vain to the Western powers for help, it was overrun by Nazi Germany in 1938 regained its freedom in 1945 but fell into Communist hands in 1948

D

D This letter is the outline of a rude archway or door It is called in Phœnician and Hebrew *daleth* (a door) and in Gr. *delta* (*q v.*). In Egyptian hieroglyphics it is a man's hand.

D. or d indicating a penny or pence, is the initial of the Lat *denarius* (*q v*)

As a Roman numeral **D** stands for 500, and represents the second half of CIↃ, the ancient Tuscan sign for one thousand D with a dash over it (D̄) is 5,000.

D O. (Letter) Demi-official A British War Office term for a letter on official business but addressed personally from one officer to another.

D O.M An abbreviation of the Lat *Deo Optimo Maximo* (to God the best, the greatest), or *Datur omnibus mori* (it is allotted to all to die)

D T.s. A contraction of *delirium tremens*

Da Capo (D.C.). (Ital) A musical term meaning, from the beginning—that is, finish with a repetition of the first strain

Dab. Clever, skilled, as "a dab-hand at it " The origin is unknown, but it has been suggested that it is a contraction of the Lat. *adeptus*, an adept "Dabster" is another form

An Eton stripling, training for the law,
A dunce at learning, but a dab at taw [marbles]
ANON *Logic, or, The Biter Bit*

Dab, Din, etc
Hab Dab and David Din
Ding the deil o'er Dabson's Linn.

"Hab Dab ' (Halbert Dobson) and "David Din" (David Dun) were Cameronians who

lived in a cave near "Dabson's Linn," a waterfall near the head of Moffat Water.

Here, legend relates, they encountered the devil in the form of a pack of dried hides, and after fighting him for some time, they "dinged" him unto the waterfall

Dabbat (*Dabbatu 'l-arz*). In Mohammedan mythology the monster (literally "reptile of the earth") that shall arise at the last day and cry that mankind has not believed in the Divine revelations

By some it is identified with the Beast of the Apocalypse (*Rev.* xix, 19, xx, 10)

Dacia (dā´ si ä) A Roman province in part of what is now Hungary

Dacoit (dä koit´) This is an Urdu word meaning a robber It is applied to the bands of robbers and pirates who infest the forests and rivers of Burma, and to organized bands of robbers in India In Indian law dacoity means robbery with violence by not less than five men

Dactyls. Mythical beings connected with the worship of Cybele, in Crete, to whom is ascribed the discovery of iron Their number was originally three—the Smelter, the Hammer, and the Anvil, but was afterwards increased to five males and five females, whence their name Dactyls or Fingers

In prosody a dactyl is a foot of three syllables, the first long and the others short (-``)—again from the similarity to the joints of a finger

Dad or Daddy. A child's word (common to many languages) for "father", for example Gaelic, *daidein*; Welsh, *tad*, Cornish, *tat*; Latin, *tata, tatula* (papa); Greek, *tata, tetta*, used by youths to an elder; Sanskrit, *tata*, Lap *dadda*.

Dad and Dave Two figures rapidly becoming traditional in Australian humour They first appeared in A H Davis's *On Our Selection*, 1899, but they have since been used extensively in radio serials

Daddy Long-legs. A crane-fly, applied also to the long-legged spiders called "harvest-men."

Dadaism (da´ da izm). A school of art, painting, and writing that had its beginning in New York and Zurich in 1916, arising from indignation and despair at the catastrophe of World War I and increasing with the ensuing peace The artists endeavoured to free themselves from *all* previous artistic conventions in an iconoclastic attack on what they considered cultural shams. The movement died about 1922 and was succeeded by Surrealism (*q v*) The name Dadaism was derived from the French phrase *aller à dada*, ride a cock-horse, and was chosen at random from a dictionary. Its principal exponents were Tristan Tzara, Max Ernst, Picabia.

Dædalus (dē´ dà lus). A Greek who formed the Cretan labyrinth, and made for himse'f wings, by means of which he flew from Crete across the Archipelago He is said to have invented the saw, the axe, the gimlet, etc , and his name is perpetuated in our *dædal*, skilful, fertile of invention, *dædalian*, labyrinthine or ingenious, etc. *Cp.* ICARUS.

Daffodil. Legend says that the daffodil, or "Lent Lily," was once white, but Persephone, who had wreathed her head with them and fallen asleep, was captured by Pluto, at whose touch the white flowers turned to a golden yellow Ever since the flower has been planted on graves Theophilus and Pliny tell us that they grow on the banks of Acheron and that the spirits of the dead delight in the flower, called by them the Asphodel In England it used to be called the Affodil (French, *asphodile*, Lat , *asphodelus*, Gr *asphodelos*)

An attempt was made in the 20th century in Britain to introduce it as the national emblem of Wales because the leek was considered vulgar

Flour of daffodil is a cure for madness —*Med MS Lincoln Cathedral*, f 282

Dagger or **Long Cross** (†), used for reference to a note after the asterisk (*), is a Roman Catholic character, originally employed in church books, prayers of exorcism, at benedictions, and so on, to remind the priest where to make the sign of the cross. This sign is sometimes called an obelisk—that is, "a spit " (Gr , *obelos*, a spit)

In the arms of the City of London, the dagger commemorates Sir William Walworth's dagger, with which he slew Wat Tyler in 1381 Before this time the cognizance of the City was the sword of St. Paul

Brave Walworth, knight, lord mayor, that slew
Rebellious Tyler in his alarmes,
The king, therefore, did give him in lieu
The dagger to the city armes
Fourth year of Richard II (1381), *Fishmongers' Hall*

Dagger ale. The ale of the *Dagger*, a low-class gambling-house in Holborn, famous in Elizabethan times for its strong drink, furmety, and meat-pies There was another tavern of the same name in Cheapside The exact site of neither is known

My lawyer's clerk I lighted on last night
In Holborn, at the *Dagger*.
BEN JONSON *The Alchemist*, i, 1

Dagger-scene in the House of Commons Edmund Burke, during the French Revolution, threw down a dagger on the floor of the House, exclaiming as he did so. "There's French fraternity for you' Such is the weapon which French Jacobins would plunge into the heart of our beloved king " Sheridan spoilt the dramatic effect, and set the House in a roar by his remark "The gentleman, I see, has brought his knife with him, but where is his fork?" *Cf* COUP DE THÉÂTRE

Daggle-tail or **Draggle-tail** A slovenly woman, the bottom of whose dress trails in the dirt. *Dag* (of uncertain origin) means loose ends, mire or dirt, whence *dag-locks*, the soiled locks of a sheep's fleece, and *dag-wool*, refuse wool

Dago (dā' gō) A disparaging epithet applied to a Spaniard, Portuguese, or Italian generally The word originated in Louisiana where a man of Spanish parentage was popularly called Diego

Dagobert (dăg' ŏ bert) **King Dagobert and St. Eloi.** There is a popular French song with this title. St. Eloi tells the king his coat has a hole in it, and the king replies, "*C'est vrai, le tien est bon: prête-le moi*" After many such complaints and answers St Eloi says, "My lord, death is at hand!" "Why can't you die instead of me?" says the king From the Revolution onwards many adaptations of this song have been made suited to the political events of the times In 1814 it became very popular on account of verses against Napoleon and the Russian campaign and was forbidden by the police The return of the Bourbons produced other topical verses

Dagon. A god of the Philistines, supposed—from very uncertain etymological and mythological indications—to have been symbolized as half woman and half fish

Dagon his name, sea-monster, upward man
And downward fish, yet had his temple high
Rear'd in Azotus d eaded through the coast
Of Palestine, in Gath and Ascalon,
And Accaron and Gaza s frontier bounds
MILTON *Paradise Lost*, i, 462

Dagonet, Sir. The fool of King Arthur in the Arthurian legends, he was knighted by the king himself

I remember at Mile End Green, when I lay at Clement's Inn, I was then Sir Dagonet in Arthur's show —*2 Henry IV*, iii, 2 (Justice Shallow)

"Dagonet" was the name under which G R Sims (1847-1922) wrote weekly articles in the *Referee* which were very popular in their day

Daguerreotype (da gâr' ŏ tīp) A photographic process invented by L J M Daguerre (1789-1851) and J N Niepce (d 1833) The process, which was introduced in 1839. consisted in exposing in a camera a plate of silvered copper on which a film of silvered iodide had been formed by iodine vapour It was the first photographic process to yield a technically good result

Dahlia (dā' lyà) This plant, bearing strikingly beautiful flowers, was discovered in Mexico by Humboldt in 1789, he sent specimens to Europe, and in 1791 it was named in honour of Andrew Dahl, the Swedish botanist and pupil of Linnæus It was cultivated in France in 1802, and two years later in England

Daibutsu (dī but' soo) The great bronze Buddha at Kamakura, formerly the capital of Nippon (Japan) It is in a sitting posture, and is 50 ft high and 97 ft in circumference, the face is 8 ft. long and the thumbs a yard round

Above the old songs turned to ashes and pain,
Under which Death enshrouds the idols and trees with mist of sigh,
(Where are Kamakura's rising days and life of old?)
With heart heightened to hush, the Daibutsu for ever sits *Yone Noguchi.*

Daikoku (da ē' kŏ ku) One of the seven gods of Good Fortune in the Japanese pantheon, he is invoked specially by artisans

Dais The raised floor at the head of a dining-room, designed for the high, or principal, table, but originally the high table itself, from late lat *discus*, a table The word was also used (as it still is in French) for a canopy, especially the canopy over the high table Hence, *Sous le dais*, in the midst of grandeur.

Daisy. Ophelia gives the queen a daisy to signify "that her light and fickle love ought not to expect constancy in her husband " So the daisy is explained by Greene to mean a *Quip for an upstart courtier*

The word is *Day's eye* (A.S *dæges eage*), and the flower is so called because it closes its pinky lashes and goes to sleep when the sun sets, but in the morning expands its petals to the light. *Cp* VIOLET

> That well by reason men calle it maie,
> The daisie, or else the eie of daie
> CHAUCER *Legend of Good Women* (*Prol*),

Daisy-roots. Legend says that these, like dwarf-elder berries stunt the growth, a superstition which probably arose from the notion that everything had the property of bestowing its own speciality on others *Cp* FERN SEED.

> She robbed dwarf-elders of their fragrant fruit
> And fed him early with the daisy root,
> Whence through his veins the powerful juices ran,
> And formed the beauteous *miniature* of man
> TICKELL *Kensington Gardens*

Dak-bungalow. *See* BUNGALOW.

Dalai-Lama. *See* LAMA

Dalkey, King of. A burlesque officer, like the Mayor of Garratt (*q v*) Dalkey is a small island in St George's Channel, near Kingstown, to the south of Dublin Bay

Dalmatica or **Dalmatic** (dăl măt′ ı ka). A vestment open in front, reaching to the knees, worn by Catholic bishops and deacons over the *alb* or *stole* It is in imitation of the regal vest of Dalmatia, and was imported into Rome by the Emperor Commodus

A similar robe is worn by kings at coronations and other great solemnities

Daltonism. *See* COLOUR-BLINDNESS

Dam. The female parent of animals such as the horse, sheep, etc ; the counterpart of "sire", when used of human beings the word is always a very opprobious significance It is another form of *dame* *See* THE DEVIL AND HIS DAM

Damascening (dăm à sēn′ ıng) 'Producing upon steel a blue tinge and ornamental figures, sometimes inlaid with gold and silver, as in Damascus blades, so called from Damascus, which was celebrated in the Middle Ages for this class of ornamental art

Damask. Linens and silks first made at Damascus, imitated by the French and Flemish Introduced into England by refugee Flemish weavers about 1570 The *damask rose* was brought to England from Southern Europe by Dr Linacre, physician to Henry VIII, about 1540.

Damiens' Bed of Steel (dăm′ ı enz) Robert François Damiens, in 1757, attempted the life of Louis XV As a punishment, and to strike terror into the hearts of all regicides, he was chained to an iron bed that was heated, his right hand was burned in a slow fire, his flesh was torn with pincers and the wounds dressed with molten lead, boiling wax, oil, and resin, and he was ultimately torn to pieces by wild horses

> The uplifted axe, the agonizing wheel,
> Luke's iron crown, and Damiens' bed of steel
> GOLDSMITH: *The Traveller* (1768)

Damn. Not worth a damn. Worthless; not even worth cursing The derivation of the phrase from the Indian coin, a *dam* (96 to the penny) has no foundation in fact. Goldsmith, in his *Citizen of the World*, uses the expression, "Not that I care three damns " Another vague imprecation, said to have been commonly used by the great Duke of Wellington, is *Not a twopenny damn*

To damn with faint praise. To praise in such measured terms as to deprive the praise of any real value

> Damn with faint praise, assent with civil leer,
> And, without sneering, teach the rest to sneer.
> POPE *Epistle to Arbuthnot*

Damocles's Sword. Impending evil or danger Damocles, a sycophant of Dionysius the Elder, of Syracuse, was invited by the tyrant to try the felicity he so much envied. Accepting, he was set down to a sumptuous banquet, but overhead was a sword suspended by a hair Damocles was afraid to stir, and the banquet was a tantalizing torment to him.

Damon (dā′ mon) The name of a goatherd in Virgil's *Eclogues*, and hence used by pastoral poets for rustic swains.

Damon and Pythias. A type of inseparable friends They were Syracusans of the first half of the 4th century B C. Pythias being condemned to death by Dionysius the tyrant, obtained leave to go home to arrange his affairs after Damon had agreed to take his place and be executed should Pythias not return. Pythias being delayed, Damon was led to execution, but his friend arrived just in time to save him Dionysius was so struck with this honourable friendship that he pardoned both of them

Damper An Australian term for bread baked in the ashes of a fire It was in use in the 1820s Small dampers are called "beggars-on-the-coals", of a somewhat similar nature are the Australian "johnny-cakes".

Damsel. Its usual meaning is a virgin, a maiden, often a waiting-maid From the old French *damoisele*, the feminine form of *damoisel*, a squire, this is from Med. Lat. *domicellus*, a contracted form of *dominicellus*, the diminutive of *dominus* lord (*Cp* DONZEL) In mediæval France the *domicellus* or *damoiseau* was the son of a king, prince, knight, or lord before he entered the order of knighthood, the king's bodyguards were called his *damoiseaux* or *damsels* Froissart styles Richard II *le jeune damoisel Richart*, and Louis VII (*Le Jeune*) was called the *royal damsel*

Damson Originally called the *Damascene plum*, from *Damascus*, it having been imported from Syria

Dan A title of honour meaning *Sir* or *Master* (Lat *dominus*, *cp* Span *don*), common with the old poets, as Dan Phœbus, Dan Cupid, Dan Neptune, Dan Chaucer, etc. (*Cp*. DOM)

> Dan Chaucer, well of English undefiled,
> On Fame's eternal beadroll worthy to be filed.
> SPENSER *Faerie Queene*, IV, ıı, 32

From Dan to Beersheba. From one end of the kingdom to the other, all over the world, everywhere The phrase is Scriptural, Dan being the most northern and Beersheba the most southern cities of the Holy Land. We have a similar expression, "From Land's End to John o' Groats "

Danace (dăn′ ăs) An ancient Persian coin, worth rather more than the Greek *obolus* (*q v*), and sometimes, among the Greeks, placed in the mouth of the dead to pay their passage across the ferry of the Lower World

Danaë (dăn′ a ĕ) An Argive princess, daughter of Acrisius, King of Argos He, told that his daughter's son would put him to death, resolved that Danae should never marry, and accordingly locked her up in an inaccessible tower Zeus foiled the king by changing himself into a shower of gold, under which guise he readily found access to the fair prisoner, and she thus became the mother of Perseus

Danaides (dăn ā′ i dēz) The fifty daughters of Danaus, King of Argos They married the fifty sons of Ægyptus, and all but Hypermnestra, wife of Lynceus, at the command of their father murdered their husbands on their wedding night. They were punished in Hades by having to draw water everlastingly in sieves from a deep well

Dance. I'll lead you a pretty dance. I'll bother or put you to trouble The French say, *Donner le bal à quelqu'un* The reference is to the complicated dances of former times, when all followed the leader

St. Vitus's dance. *See* VITUS

To dance and pay the piper. To work hard to amuse and to have to bear all the expense and take all the trouble oneself as well The allusion is to *Matt.* xi, 17 —' We have piped unto you, and ye have not danced "

To dance attendance. To wait obsequiously, to be at the beck and call of another. It was an ancient custom at weddings for the bride, no matter how tired she was, to dance with every guest.

Then must the poore bryde kepe foote with a dauncer, and refuse none, how scabbed, foule, droncken, rude, and shameless soever he be —CHRISTEN *State of Matrimony*, 1543
>
> I had thought
> They had parted so much honesty among them
> (At least, good manners) as not thus to suffer
> A man of his place, and so near our favour,
> To dance attendance on their lordships' pleasures.
> SHAKESPEARE *Henry VIII*, v, 2.

To dance upon nothing To be hanged

Dance of Death. An allegorical representation of Death leading all sorts and conditions of men in a dance to the grave, originating in Germany in the 14th century as a kind of morality play, quickly becoming popular in France and England, and surviving later principally by means of pictorial art There is a series of woodcuts, said to be by Hans Holbein (1538), representing Death dancing after all sorts of persons, beginning with Adam and Eve. He is beside the judge on his bench, the priest in the pulpit, the nun in her cell, the doctor in his study, the bride, and the beggar, the king and the infant, but he is "swallowed up at last "

On the north side of Old St Paul's was a cloister, on the walls of which was painted, at the cost of John Carpenter, town clerk of London (15th century), a "Dance of Death," or "Death leading all the estate, with speeches of Death, and answers," by John Lydgate The Death-Dance in the Dominican Convent of Basle was retouched by Holbein.

Dances, National. When Handel was asked to point out the peculiar taste of the different nations of Europe in dancing, he ascribed the *minuet* to the French, the *saraband* to the Spaniard, the *arietta* to the Italian, and the *hornpipe* and the *morris-dance* to the English To these might be added the *reel* to the Scots, and the *jig* to the Irish

Astronomical dances, invented by the Egyptians, designed to represent the movements of the heavenly bodies

The Bacchic dances were of three sorts grave (like our minuet), gay (like our gavotte), and mixed (like our minuet and gavotte combined)

The dance Champêtre, invented by Pan, quick and lively The dancers (in the open air) wore wreaths of oak and garlands of flowers

Children's dances, in Lacedemonia, in honour of Diana. The children were nude, and their movements were grave, modest, and graceful

Corybantic dances, in honour of Bacchus, accompanied with timbrels, fifes, flutes, and a tumultuous noise produced by the clashing of swords and spears against brazen bucklers

Funereal dances, in Athens, slow, solemn dances in which the priests took part The performers wore long white robes, and carried cypress slips in their hands

Hymeneal dances were lively and joyous The dancers were crowned with flowers

Jewish dances David danced in certain religious processions (2 *Sam* vi, 14) The people sang and danced before the golden calf (*Exod* xxxii, 19) And in the book of *Psalms* (cl, 4) we read, "Praise Him with the timbrel and dance " Miriam, the sister of Moses, after the passage of the Red Sea, was followed by all the women with timbrels and dances (*Exod* xv, 20).

Of the Lapithæ, invented by Pirithous These were exhibited after some famous victory, and were designed to imitate the combats of the Centaurs and Lapithœ These dances were both difficult and dangerous

May-day dances at Rome. At daybreak lads and lasses went out to gather "May" and other flowers for themselves and their elders, and the day was spent in dances and festivities.

Military dances The oldest of all dances executed with swords, javelins, and bucklers Said to be invented by Minerva to celebrate the victory of the gods over the Titans

Nuptial dances A Roman pantomimic performance resembling the dances of our Harlequin and Columbine

Pyrrhic dance. See PYRRHIC

Salic dances, instituted by Numa Pompilius in honour of Mars. They were executed by twelve priests selected from the highest of the nobility, and the dances were performed in the temple while sacrifices were being made and hymns sung to the god

The **Dancing Dervishes** celebrate their religious rites with dances, which consist chiefly of spinning round and round a little allotted space, not in couples, but each one alone

In ancient times the Gauls, the Germans, the Spaniards, and the English had their sacred dances In fact, in all religious ceremonies the dance was, and in many religions still is, an essential part of divine worship.

Dancing Chancellor, The. Sir Christopher Hatton (1540-91) was so called, because he 'first attracted Queen Elizabeth's notice by his graceful dancing in a masque at Court He was Lord High Chancellor from 1587 till his death

His bushy beard, and shoestrings green,
His high-crowned hat and satin doublet,
Moved the stout heart of England's queen,
Though Pope and Spaniard could not trouble it.
GRAY *A Long Story*

Dancing-water. A magic elixir, common to many fairy-tales, which beautifies ladies, makes them young again, and enriches them In the Countess d'Aulnoy's *Contes des Fées* it fell in a cascade in the Burning Forest, and could only be reached by an underground passage Prince Chery fetched a bottle of it for his beloved Fair-star, but was aided by a dove

Dandelion (dăn' de lī on) The leaves of the plant have jagged, tooth-like edges; hence its name, which is a form of the M E. *dent de lyoun*, from Fr. *dent de lion*, lion tooth. Its Lat name is *Taraxacum dens leonis*

Dander. Is your dander up or riz? Is your anger excited? Are you in a rage? This is generally considered to be an Americanism, but it is of uncertain origin, and as a synonym for *anger* has been a common dialect word in several English counties. In the present sense it is more likely that it is one of the words (like *waffle*, and *hook* for a point of land) imported into America by the early Dutch colonists, from *donder*, thunder, the Dutch *op donderen* is to burst into a sudden rage.

He was as spunky as thunder, and when a Quaker gets his dander up, it's like a Northwester.
SEBAR SMITH *Letters of Major Jack Downing* (1830)

Dandie Dinmont. A jovial, true-hearted store-farmer, in Scott's *Guy Mannering* Also a hardy, hairy short-legged terrier

From this dog descended Davidson of Hyndlee's breed, the original Dandie-Dinmont —T BROWN *Our Dogs*

Dandiprat (dăn' di prăt) A small coin issued in the reign of Henry VII, value three half-pence The term was also applied to a dwarf and to a page—perhaps much as we now speak of a "little twopenny-ha'penny fellow", and in his translation of Virgil's *Æneid*, Bk i (1582) Stanyhurst calls Cupid a "dandiprat."

Dando (dăn' dō) One who frequents hotels, restaurants and such places, satisfies his appetite, and decamps without payment. From Dando, hero of many popular songs in the early 19th century, who was famous for this

Dandy. A coxcomb, a fop The term seems to have originated in Scotland in the late 18th century, and may be merely the name *Andrew*, or a corruption of *dandiprat* (*q v.*) or of the earlier *Jack-a-dandy*

In paper-making the *dandy*, or *dauby-roller*, is the cylinder of wire gauze which comes into contact with paper while on the machine in a wet and elementary stage. It impresses the watermark, and also the ribs in "laid" papers.

Dane-geld. A tribute paid by the English to stop the ravages of the Danes in the late 10th and early 11th centuries

Daniel Lambert, *see* LAMBERT

Dannebrog or **Danebrog** (dăn' e brog) The national flag of Denmark (*brog* is Old Danish for cloth) The tradition is that Waldemar II of Denmark saw in the heavens a fiery cross which betokened his victory over the Esthonians (1219) This story is very similar to that of Constantine (*see* under CROSS) and of St. Andrew's Cross

The order of Danebrog The second of the Danish orders of knighthood, instituted in 1219 by Waldemar II restored by Christian V in 1671, and several times modified since.

Dannocks. Hedging-gloves The word is said to be a corruption of *Doornick*, the Flemish name of Tournay, where they may have been originally manufactured *Cp.* DORNICK

Dansker (dăn' sker) A Dane Denmark used to be called Danske Hence Polonius says to Reynaldo, 'Inquire me first what Danskers are in Paris " (*Hamlet*, ii, 1)

Dante and Beatrice (dăn' te, bē' à tris, bā a trē' chi) Beatrice Portinari was only eight years old when the poet first saw her. His abiding love for her was pure as it was tender. Beatrice married a nobleman, named Simone de Bardi, and died young, in 1290 Dante married Gemma, of the powerful house of Donati In the *Divina Commedia* the poet is conducted first by Virgil (who represents human reason) through hell and purgatory, then by the spirit of Beatrice (who represents the wisdom of faith), and finally by St. Bernard (who represents the wisdom from on high)

Dantesque (dăn' tesk) Dante-like—that is, a minute lifelike representation of horrors, whether by words, as in the poet, or in visible form, as in Dore's illustrations of the *Inferno*.

Daphne (dăf' ni) Daughter of a river-god, loved by Apollo She fled from the amorous god, and escaped by being changed into a laurel, thenceforth the favourite tree of the sun-god

Nay, lady, sit If I but wave this wand
Your nerves are all chain'd up in alabaster,
And you a statue, or, as Daphne was,
Root-bound, that fled Apollo
MILTON *Comus*, 678

Daphnis (dăf' nis) In Greek mythology, a Sicilian shepherd who invented pastoral poetry He was a son of Mercury and a Sicilian nymph, was protected by Diana, and was taught by Pan and the Muses.

The lover of Chloe (*q v*) in the Greek pastoral romance of Longus, in the 4th century. Daphnis was the model of Allan Ramsay's *Gentle Shepherd*, and the tale is the basis of St Pierre's *Paul and Virginia*.

Dapple The name given in Smollett's translation of *Don Quixote* to Sancho Panza's donkey (in the original it has no name) The word is probably connected with Icel *depill*, a spot, and means blotched, speckled in patches. A *dapple-grey* horse is one of a light grey shaded with a deeper hue, a *dapple-bay* is a light bay spotted with bay of a deeper colour.

Darbies. Handcuffs. Probably so-called from a personal name, the phrase "father Derbies bands" for handcuffs is found in George Gascoigne's *Steele Glas*, 1576.

Hark ye! Jem Clink will fetch you the darbies — SCOTT *Peveril of the Peak.*

Johnny Darbies, policemen, is a perversion of the French *gendarmes*, in conjunction with the above

Darby and Joan The type of loving, old-fashioned, virtuous couples The names belong to a ballad written by Henry Woodfall, and the characters are said to be John Darby, of Bartholomew Close, who died 1730, and his wife, "As chaste as a picture cut in alabaster. You might sooner move a Scythian rock than shoot fire into her bosom." Woodfall served his apprenticeship to John Darby; but another account localizes the couple in the West Riding of Yorkshire.

The French equivalent is *C'est St Roch et son chien*

Darbyites (dar' bi Itz) A name sometimes given to the Plymouth Brethren (*q v*), from John Nelson Darby (1800-82), the founder.

Dardanelles (dar da nelz) The entrance to the Straits of Gallipoli, commanded by the two forts of Sestos and Abydos, built by the Sultan Mahomet IV in 1659, and taking their name from the adjacent town of Dardanus The British fleet passed through the Straits in 1807 and 1853, but the campaign to force the Straits in 1915 was unsuccessful

Daric. An ancient Persian gold coin, probably so called from *dara*, a king (*see* DARIUS), much in the same way as our *sovereign*, but perhaps from Assyrian *dariku*, weight. Its value is put at about 23s There was also a silver daric, worth one twentieth of the gold.

Darien, Isthmus of (dâr' i ên). Central America, discovered by Columbus. 1494 Balboa crossed the isthmus and first saw the Pacific, 1513 "Silent, upon a peak in Darien"— Keats, *On First looking into Chapman's Homer* (where the poet erroneously refers to Cortez).

Darius (da ri' us) A Greek form of Persian *dara*, a king, or of Sanskrit *darj*, the maintainer Gushtasp, or Kishtasp assumed the title on ascending the throne in 521 B.C., and is generally known as Darius the Great

Legend relates that seven Persian princes agreed that he should be king whose horse neighed first; and the horse of Darius was the first to neigh

It is said that Darius III (Codomanus), the last king of Persia, who was conquered by Alexander the Great (331 B C), when Alexander succeeded to the throne, sent to him for the tribute of golden eggs, but the Macedonian answered, "The bird which laid them is flown to the other world, where Darius must seek them." The Persian king then sent him a bat and ball, in ridicule of his youth; but Alexander told the messengers, with the bat he would beat the ball of power from their master's hand Lastly, Darius sent him a bitter melon as emblem of the grief in store for him, but the Macedonian declared that he would make the Shah eat his own fruit.

Dark. A dark horse. A racing term for a horse of good pretensions, but of which nothing is positively known by the general public The epithet is applied to a person whose abilities are untried or whose probable course of action is unknown

A leap in the dark. A step the consequences of which cannot be foreseen Thomas Hobbes is reported to have said on his death-bed, "Now am I about to take my last voyage—a great leap in the dark" Hallam considered this term to apply to the period lasting from A D 475 to about the middle of the 12th century; in 1868 Lord Derby applied the words to the Reform Bill

The Dark Ages. The earlier centuries of the Middle Ages (*q v*), so called because of the intellectual darkness thought to be characteristic of the period

Dark and bloody ground Kentucky So called by the Indians because of the fierce wars waged in the forests, and later so known by the whites for the same reason in their struggle against the red man

The dark Continent. Africa, concerning which the world was so long "in the dark," and which, also, is the land of dark races

The darkest hour is that before the dawn. When things have come to their worst, they must mend In Lat , *Post nubila Phœbus.*

To keep dark. To lie perdu, to lurk in concealment

To keep it dark. To keep it a dead secret, to refuse to enlighten anyone about the matter

To darken one's door To cross one's threshold almost entirely used only in a threatening way, as "Don't you dare to darken my door again!"

Darkie. A former colloquial name for an American Negro, found as early as 1775

Darley Arabian. In 1704 Thomas Darley sent from Aleppo to his father Richard Darley, of Aldby Park, Yorks, an Arab horse of the best Maneghi breed From this thoroughbred stallion came a famous breed of race-horses, including Eclipse (*q.v*) who was Darley Arabian's great-grandson

It is interesting to note that the entire thoroughbred race throughout the world is descended from three Arabs, of which Darley Arabian was one The others were Byerley Turk, the charger of Capt Byerley at the Battle of the Boyne, and Godolphin Arabian, brought to England in 1730 by Edward Coke, from whose hands he passed into the possession of the Earl of Godolphin

Darn and dern are minced forms of *damn* and date from the late 18th and early 19th centuries

Darnex. *See* DORNICK.

Dart. *See* ABARIS

D'Artagnan (dar ta nyón) The hero of Dumas's novels *The Three Musketeers, Twenty Years After,* etc , was a real man— Charles de Baatz, Seigneur d'Artagnan, a Gascon gentleman who was born at Lupiac in 1611   He rose to be captain in Louis XIV's Mousquetaires and eventually became general of brigade   He was killed at the siege of Maestricht, in 1673   Dumas and his collaborator Maquet worked up the story from the *Memoires de M. D'Artagnan*, written by Courtilz de Sandras and published in Cologne, 1701-02

Darwinian Theory   Charles Darwin (1809-82) published in 1859 *Origin of Species*, to prove that the numerous species now existing on the earth sprang originally from one or at most a few primal forms; and that the present diversity is due to special development and natural selection   In recent times the Darwinian theory has undergone very considerable modification but it is still the basis of scientific research   *See* EVOLUTION.

Dash.   *One* dash under a word in MS means that the part so marked must be printed in italics, *two* dashes means small capitals, *three* dashes, large capitals

Cut a dash. *See* CUT.

Dash my wig, buttons, etc   Dash is a euphemism for "damn," and the words *wig, buttons* etc , are relics of a fashion at one time adopted in comedies and by "mashers" of swearing without using profane language

Date   Not up to date.   Not in the latest fashion, behind the times

To have a date.   To have an appointment, more particularly with someone of the opposite sex

Datum Line (dā' tŭm).   A term used in surveying and engineering to describe a line from which all heights and depths are measured. The datum line upon which the Ordnance Survey maps of Great Britain are based was, until 1921, the mean sea-level at Liverpool, since that date it has been the mean sea-level at Newlyn, Cornwall

Daughter   The daughter of Peneus.   The bay-tree was so called because it grew in greatest perfection on the banks of the River Peneus

The daughter of the horseleech.   One very exigeant, one for ever sponging on another. *Prov* xxx, 15
> The horseleech hath two daughters, crying,
> Give, Give

The scavenger's daughter.   *See* SCAVENGER.

Dauphin (daw' fin)   The heir of the French crown under the Valois and Bourbon dynasties   Guy VIII, Count of Vienne, was the first so styled, because he wore *a dolphin* as his cognizance   The title descended in the family till 1349, when Humbert III ceded his seigneurie, the Dauphiné, to Philippe VI (de Valois), one condition being that the heir of France assumed the title of *le dauphin*   The first French prince so called was Jean, who succeeded Philippe, and the last was the Duc d'Angoulême, son of Charles X, who renounced the title in 1830

Grand Dauphin.   Louis, Duc de Bourgogne (1661-1711), eldest son of Louis XIV, for whose use was published the Delphin Classics (*q v.*)

Second or Little Dauphin.   Louis, son of the Grand Dauphin (1682-1712)

Davenport (dav' en pôrt)   This word, which owes its origin to the name of some now-forgotten craftsman, is applied to two different articles of furniture; one kind of davenport is a small desk with drawers on each side; the other is a large upholstered sofa or settee that can also be made up into a bed

Davenport Brothers, The.   Two impostors from America whose alleged spiritualistic manifestations caused a great sensation in the early 1860s   Their imposture was exposed in 1865

David.   In Dryden's *Absalom and Achitophel* (*q v*), represents Charles II
> Once more the godlike David was restored
> And willing nations knew their lawful lord

St. David   The patron saint of Wales (d 544)   legend relates that he was son of Xantus, Prince of Cereticu, now called Cardiganshire; he was brought up a priest, became an ascetic in the Isle of Wight, preached to the Britons, confuted Pelagius, and was preferred to the see of Caerleon or Menevia.   Here the saint had received his early education, and when Dyvrig, the archbishop, resigned his see to him, St David removed the archiepiscopal residence to Menevia, which was henceforth called St David's   *Cp* TAFFY

David and Jonathan.   A type of inseparable friends   Similar examples of friendship were Pylades and Orestes (*q.v*), Damon and Pythias (*q.v*); etc
> I am distressed for thee, my brother Jonathan   Very pleasant hast thou been to me   Thy love to me was wonderful, passing the love of women —2 *Sam* i, 26

Davidians, Davists   *See* FAMILISTS

Davis Cup   A silver trophy for an international Lawn Tennis team championship, presented by the American politician, Dwight F Davis (1875-1945) in 1900   Its holders have been —

1903-06,	Great Britain
1907-11,	Australasia
1912	Great Britain
1913	U S A
1914-19,	Australasia
1920-26,	U S A
1927-32,	France
1933-36,	Great Britain
1937-38,	U.S.A.
1939-45,	Australia
1946-49,	U S A
1950	Australia

Davy   I'll take my davy of it.   I'll take my "affidavit" it is true.

Davy Jones.   A sailor's name for the supposed evil spirit of the sea

He's gone to Davy Jones's locker.   The nautical way of saying that a messmate is dead and has been buried at sea   It has been conjectured that Jones is a corruption of Jonah the prophet who was thrown into the sea
> This same Davy Jones, according to the mythology of sailors, is the fiend that presides over all the evil spirits of the deep, and is seen in various shapes warning the devoted wretch of death and woe —
> SMOLLETT *Peregrine Pickle*, xiii

Davy Lamp. A miner's safety-lamp invented by Sir Humphry Davy (1778-1829) and brought into use in the mines in 1816.

Dawson, Bully. A noted London sharper, who swaggered and led a most abandoned life about Blackfriars, in the reign of Charles II

Bully Dawson k..cked by half the town and half the town kicked by Bully Dawson —CHARLES LAMB

Jemmy Dawson. The hero of a pathetic ballad by Shenstone, given in Percy's *Reliques* Captain James Dawson (*c* 1717-46) joined the "Young Chevalier," and was one of the Manchester rebels who was hanged, drawn and quartered on Kennington Common in 1746 A lady of gentle blood was in love with the gallant young rebel, and died of a broken heart after witnessing his execution

Young Dawson was a gallant youth,
A brighter never trod the plain,
And well he lov'd one charming maid,
And dearly was he lov'd again

Day. When it begins (1) With *sunset* The Jews in their "sacred year," and the Church—hence the eve of feast-days; the ancient Britons *"non dierum numerum, ut nos, sed noctium computant,"* says Tacitus—hence "se'n-night" and "fort'night", the 'Athenians, Chinese, Mohammedans, etc, (2) With *sunrise* The Babylonians, Syrians, Persians, and modern Greeks (3) With *noon* The ancient Egyptians and modern astronomers (4) With *midnight* The English, French, Dutch, Germans, Spanish, Portuguese, Americans, etc

A day after the fair. Too late, the fair you came to see is over

Day in, day out All day long and every day

Every dog has its day. *See* DOG

I have had my day. My prime of life is over;
Old Joe, sir was a bit of a favourite once, but he has had his day —DICKENS *Dombey and Son*

I have lost a day. The exclamation (*Perdidi diem*) of Titus, the Roman emperor, when on one occasion he could call to mind nothing done during the past day for the benefit of his subjects.

To-day a man, to-morrow a mouse. In Fr, *"Aujourd'hui roi, demain rien"* Fortune is so fickle that one day we may be at the top of the wheel, and the next day at the bottom.

To lose the day. To lose the battle, to be defeated. **To win** (or gain) **the day** is to be victorious

Day of the Barricades, Dupes. *See these words*

Daylight. Toast-masters used to cry out, "Gentlemen, no daylights nor heeltaps." This meant that the wineglass was to be full to the brim so that light could not be seen between the edge of the glass and the top of the wine, and that every drop of it must be drunk *See* HEELTAP

Daylight Saving. A system of advancing the clock by an hour on some specified day in the Spring, and putting back the hands one hour on a specified day in autumn By this device greater advantage can be taken of the longer evenings of summertime The originator was

William Willett (1856-1915) a London builder who advocated the scheme for some years but died before it was adopted (as a war measure) in 1916 By an Act of 1925 Daylight Saving started the third week in April and ended the first week in October, but since the outbreak of World War II the dates have varied from year to year

In 1941 a system of Double Summer Time was introduced, the clock being set back yet another hour (i e two hours in advance of G M T) during the height of summer, approx. April to August

Daylights. Pugilists' slang for the eyes

To beat the living daylights out of him, to heavily chastise To let daylight into him, to pierce a man with sword or bullet

Daysman. An umpire, judge, or intercessor. The obsolete verb *to day* meant to appoint a day for the hearing of a suit, hence to judge between, and the man who *dayed* was the *daysman* The word is used in *Job* IX, 33, also by Spenser and others.

If neighbours were at variance, they ran not straight to law,
Daysmen took up the matter, and cost them not a straw
ANON *New Custom, I, II (Morality Play · temp Edw VI)*

Dayspring. The dawn

The dayspring from on high hath visited us — *Luke* I, 78

Daystar. The morning star Hence the emblem of hope or better prospects

Again o'er the vine-covered regions of France,
See the day-star of Liberty rise —WILSON *Noctes*

De die in diem (dē dī' ē in dī' em) (Lat) From day to day continuously, till the business is completed

The Ministry have elected to go on *de die in diem.—Newspaper paragraph*

De facto (Lat) Actually, in reality, in opposition to **de jure**, lawfully or rightfully. Thus John was *de facto* king, but Arthur was so *de jure* A legal axiom says· *"De jure Judices, de facto Juratores, respondent"*, Judges look to the law, juries to the facts

De jure. *See* DE FACTO, *above*.

De mortuis nil nisi bonum (dē môr' tū is nil nī' si bō' num) (Lat) Of the dead speak kindly or not at all "Speak not evil of the dead" was one of the maxims of Chilo (*q v*)

De novo (dē nō' vō) (Lat) Afresh, over again from the beginning.

De profundis (dē prō fŭn' dis) (Lat) Out of the deep, hence, a bitter cry of wretchedness *Ps.* cxxx is so called from the first two words in the Latin version It forms part of the Roman Catholic burial service

These words were chosen as the title of Oscar Wilde's apologia, published posthumously in 1905.

De rigueur (dē rigēr') (Fr) According to strict etiquette, quite *comme il faut*, in the height of fashion

De trop (dē trō) (Fr) One too many, when a person's presence is not wished for, that person is *de trop*

Deacon. To deacon apples, etc , is an American phrase arising out of the thrifty habits ascribed to the rural New England deacons who are said to have put the best or largest specimens of fruit, etc , on the top of the baskets in which they were being sold, the inferior goods being concealed beneath them.

Dead. Dead as a door-nail. The door-nail is either one of the heavy-headed nails with which large outer doors used to be studded, or the knob on which the knocker strikes As this is frequently knocked on the head, it cannot be supposed to have much life left in it The expression is found in *Piers Plowman*

Come thou and thy five men, and if I do not leave you all as dead as a door-nail, I pray God I may never eat grass more —SHAKESPEARE 2 *Henry VI*, iv, 10

Other well-known similes are "Dead as a shotten herring," "as the nail in a coffin," "as mutton," and Chaucer's "as stoon [stone] "

Let the dead bury the dead. (*Matt.* viii, 22). Let bygones be bygones Don't rake up old and dead grievances

Let me entreat you to let the dead bury the dead, to cast behind you every recollection of bygone evils, and to cherish, to love, to sustain one another through all the vicissitudes of human affairs in the times that are to come —GLADSTONE *Home Rule Bill* (February 13th, 1893)

The wind is dead against us. Directly opposed to our direction Instead of making the ship more lively, its tendency is quite the contrary

Dead beat. Exhausted. In the U S A. the word is used as a noun, a worthless fellow.

Dead drunk. So intoxicated as to be wholly powerless.

Pythagoras has finely observed that a man is not to be considered dead drunk till he lies on the floor and stretches out his arms and legs to prevent his going lower —S WARREN

Dead-eye. A block of wood with three holes through it, for the lanyards of rigging to reeve through, without sheaves, and with a groove round it for an iron strap An old name for them is "dead men's eyes "

Dead hand. One who is a " dead hand " at anything can do it every time without fail *See also* HAND, DEAD MAN'S, MORTMAIN.

First-rate work it was, too, he was always a dead hand at splitting —BOLDREWOOD *Robbery Under Arms*, xv

Dead-heads. Those admitted to theatres, etc., without payment, they are "dead" so far as the box-office receipts are concerned The term is also applied to persons who receive something of value for which the taxpayer has to pay.

In nautical language, an obstruction floating so low in the water that only a small part of it is visible

Dead heat. A race in which two (or more) leading competitors reach the goal at the same time, thus making it necessary to run the race over again *See* HEAT

Flogging the dead horse. *See* HORSE.

To work a dead horse. To perform work already paid for; to pay off a debt

Dead languages. Languages no longer spoken; such as Latin and Sanskrit.

Dead letter. A law no longer acted upon Also a letter which cannot be delivered by the postal authorities because the address is incorrect, or the person addressed cannot be found

Dead-letter Office *See* BLIND DEPARTMENT, *and* DEAD LETTER *above*

I am at a dead lift. In a strait or difficulty where I greatly need help, a hopeless exigency A dead lift is the lifting of a dead or inactive body, which must be done by sheer force

Dead lights. Strong wooden shutters to close the cabin windows of a ship

To ship the dead lights. To fasten the shutter over the cabin window to keep out the sea when a gale is expected

Dead lock. A lock which has no spring catch Metaphorically, a state of things so entangled that there seems to be no practical solution

Dead men Empty bottles.

Down among the dead men let me lie. Let me get so intoxicated as to slip from my chair, and lie under the table with the empty bottles

Dead men's shoes. *See* SHOE

Dead reckoning A calculation of the ship's place without any observation of the heavenly bodies An approximation made by consulting the log, compass, chronometer, the direction, wind, and so on.

Dead right. Entirely right

Dead ropes. Those which are fixed or do not run on blocks.

Dead Sea. The salt lake in Palestine, in the ancient Vale of Siddim, so called by the Romans (*Mare Mortuum*), also *Lacus Asphaltites* The water is limpid, and of a bluish-green colour, it supports no life other than microbes and a few very low organisms It is about 46 miles long by 10 miles broad, its surface is about 1,300 ft below sea-level, and it attains a depth of nearly 1,300 ft. The percentage of salt in the ocean generally is about three or four, but of the Dead Sea it is twenty-six or more

Dead Sea fruit. *See* APPLES OF SODOM

To be at a dead set To be set fast, so as not to be able to move The allusion is to machinery.

To make a dead set upon someone. To make a steady and unwavering concentration of activity upon someone's attention or notice, to concentrate one's endeavours to gaining a person's affection The allusion being to dogs, bulls, etc , set on each other to fight

Dead weight. The weight of something without life, a burden that does nothing towards easing its own weight, a person who encumbers us and renders no assistance. *Cp* DEAD LIFT

Dead works. A theologian's term (from *Heb* ix, 14) denoting such works as do not earn salvation, or even assist in obtaining it

Dead water, the eddy-water which closes in with a ship's stern as she passes through the water.

Deaf   **Deaf as an adder.** "They are like the deaf adder that stoppeth her ear; which will not hearken to the voice of charmers, charming never so wisely." (*Ps* lviii, 4, 5)   In the East, if a viper entered the house, the charmer was sent for, who enticed the serpent and put it into a bag   According to tradition, the viper tried to stop its ears when the charmer uttered his incantation, by applying one ear to the ground and twisting its tail into the other

In the United States deaf adder is one of the names of the copperhead (*q v*)

Deaf as a beetle   It is not the insect that is here alluded to, but the heavy wooden mallet used to level paving-stones or drive in stakes

Deaf as a post. Quite deaf, or so inattentive as not to hear what is said   One might as well speak to a gatepost or log of wood

Deaf as a white cat. It is said that white cats are deaf and stupid.

None so deaf as those who won't hear. The French have the same locution

Il n'y a de pire sourd que celui qui ne veut pas entendre

Deal   This is a word to which several meanings are attached   It can mean a business transaction, the distribution of a pack of cards, pinewood or fir wood, a plank of this wood measuring not less than 6 ft long, 7 in. across, and 3 in thick, a lot, a quantity, a share.

To deal in is to trade in.

To deal with is to be concerned with, or to handle, or to do business with

To deal out is to hand out in shares, esp cards in a game.

Dean (Lat *decanus*, one set over ten) The ecclesiastical dignitary who presides over the chapter (*q v*) of a cathedral or collegiate church, this having formerly consisted of *ten* canons (*q.v*)   In ecclesiastical use there are also deans not having chapters (such as the Deans of Westminster and Windsor, and the Bishop of London is *ex officio* Dean of the Province of Canterbury   **Rural deans** are subsidiary officers of archdeacons

The title "Dean" is also borne by certain resident Fellows at English Universities who have special functions, by the head of Christ Church, Oxford, and, in Scotland by the President of the Faculty of Advocates (*Dean of Faculty*), and certain magistrates (*Dean of Guild*)   In the U.S A , a dean is an administrative officer of a college or university, who supervises a school, a faculty, or a body of Students, *e g*. Dean of Women, Dean of the Graduate School.

The chief or senior of any group of men may be called a dean, as dean of the diplomatic corps.

Dean of the Arches. The judge presiding over the Court of Arches. *See* ARCHES

Dear   **Dear bought and far brought,** or felt. A gentle reproof for some extravagant purchase of luxury.

My dearest foe. As "my dearest friend" is one with whom I am on the greatest terms of friendship, so "my dearest foe" is one with whom I am on the greatest terms of enmity

Would I had met my dearest foe in heaven,
Or ever I had seen that day, Horatio
          SHAKESPEARE *Hamlet*, 1, 2

Oh, dear me! A very common exclamation; there is no foundation for the suggestion that it is a corruption of the Ital *O Dio mio!* (Oh, my God!), it is more likely to have originated as a euphemism for the English "*Oh, damn me!*"

Death. Milton makes Death keeper, with Sin, of Hell-gate

The other shape
(If shape it might be called that shape had none
Distinguishable in member, joint or limb,
Or substance might be called that shadow seemed,)
The likeness of a kingly crown had on
          MILTON *Paradise Lost* ii, 666-673

Angel of Death. *See* AZRAEL.

At death's door   On the point of death, very dangerously ill

Black death   *See* BLACK

In at the death   Present when the fox was caught and killed, hence, present at the climax, or the final act, of an exciting event

Till death us do part   *See* DEPART.

Death or Glory Boys, the 17th Lancers (Duke of Cambridge's Own) whose regimental badge is a Death's Head and Crossbones, with the words "Or Glory "

Death from Strange Causes.

Æschylus was killed by the fall of a tortoise on his bald head from the claws of an eagle in the air   Valerius Maximus, ix, 12, and Pliny, *History*, vii, 7

Agathocles, tyrant of Sicily, was killed by a toothpick at the age of ninety-five.

Anacreon was choked by a grape-stone. Pliny, *History*, vii, 7

Bacon died of a cold contracted when stuffing a fowl with snow to see whether by this means it would "keep "

Robert Burton (of the *Anatomy of Melancholy*) died on the very day that he himself had astrologically predicted

Chalchas, the soothsayer, died of laughter at the thought of having outlived the predicted hour of his death

Charles VIII, of France, conducting his queen into a tennis-court, struck his head against the lintel, and it caused his death

Fabius, the Roman prætor, was choked by a single goat-hair in the milk which he was drinking   Pliny, *History*, vii, 7.

Frederick Lewis, Prince of Wales, son of George II, died from the blow of a cricket-ball.

Gabrielle (*La belle*), the mistress of Henri IV, died from eating an orange

Lepidus (*Quintus Æmilius*), going out of his house, struck his great toe against the threshold and expired

Louis VI met with his death from a pig running under his horse and causing it to stumble

Otway, the poet, in a starving condition, had a guinea given him, with which he bought a loaf of bread, and died while swallowing the first mouthful

Philomenes died of laughter at seeing an ass eating the figs provided for his own dessert Valerius Maximus

George, Duke of Clarence, brother of Edward IV, was drowned in a butt of malmsey *See* MALMSEY.

Saufeius (*Appius*) was choked to death supping up the white of an under-boiled egg Pliny, *History*, vii, 33

Death in the pot   During a dearth in Gilgal, there was made for the sons of the prophets a pottage of wild herbs, some of which were poisonous When the sons of the prophets tasted the pottage, they cried out, "There is death in the pot" Then Elisha put into it some meal, and its poisonous qualities were counteracted (2 *Kings* iv, 40)

Death under shield   Death in battle Her imagination had been familiarised with wild and bloody events   and had been trained up to consider an honourable "death under shield" (as that in a field of battle was termed) a desirable termination to the life of a warrior —SCOTT *The Betrothed*, ch vi.

Death-bell. A tinkling in the ears, supposed by the Scottish peasantry to announce the death of a friend.

O lay, 'tis dark, an' I heard the death-bell,
An' I darena gae yonder for gowd nor fee
JAMES HOGG *Mountain Bard*

Death-watch Any species of *Anobium*, a genus of wood-boring beetles, that make a clicking sound, once supposed to presage death

Death's head. Bawds and procuresses used to wear a ring bearing the impression of a death's head in the time of Queen Elizabeth. Allusions are not uncommon in plays of the period
Sell some of the cloaths to buy thee a death's head, and put upon thy middle finger your least considering bawd does so much —MASSINGER *The Old Law*, iv, 1

Death's-head Moth *Acherontia atropos*, is so called from the markings on the back of the thorax, which closely resemble a skull It is also called the Hawk Moth

Death's-man An executioner, a person who kills another brutally but lawfully.
He's dead, I'm only sorry
He had no other death's-man
King Lear, iv, 6.

Debatable Land. A tract of land between the Esk and Sark, claimed by both England and Scotland, and for a long time the subject of dispute It was the haunt of thieves and vagabonds

Debon *See* DEVONSHIRE

Debonair (de bon âr') (*Le Débonnaire*) Louis I of France (778, 814-40), also called *The Pious*, son and successor of Charlemagne, a man of courteous manners, cheerful temper, but effeminate and deficient in moral energy

Debt of Nature. To pay the debt of Nature. To die Life is a loan, not a gift, and the debt is paid off by death
The slender debt to Nature's quickly paid
QUARLES *Emblems*

Decameron (de kăm'ě ron) The collection of 100 tales by Boccaccio (1353) represented as having been told in ten days (Gr *deka*, ten, *hemera*, day) during the plague at Florence in 1348 The storytellers were also ten (seven ladies and three gentlemen), and they each told a tale on each day.

Decathlon. An athletic contest in the modern Olympic games, consisting of ten events 100 metres race, long jump, putting the shot, high jump, 400 metres race, 110 metres hurdles, discus, pole vault, throwing the javelin, and 1,500 metres race.

December (Lat , *the tenth month*) So it was when the year began in March with the vernal equinox, but since January and February have been inserted before it, the term is etymologically incorrect
The old Dutch name was *Winter-maand* (winter-month), the old Saxon, *Mid-winter-monath* (mid-winter-month), whereas June was *Mid-sumor-monath.* Christian Saxons called December *Se ura geola* (the anti-yule) In the French Republican calendar it was called *Frimaire* (hoar-frost month, from November 22nd to December 20th)

The Man of December. Napoleon III (1808-73) He was made President of the French Republic December 11th, 1848, made his *coup d'état* December 2nd, 1851, and became Emperor December 2nd, 1852

Decimo-sexto An obsolete expression for a little, insignificant person The term comes from the book-trade *sexto-decimo* (16 mo) is a book in which each sheet is folded to a sixteenth of its size, giving 32 pages, hence it is a small book. *Cp* DUODECIMO
How now' my dancing braggart in decimo-sexto'
Charm your skipping tongue
BEN JONSON *Cynthia's Revels*, I, 1

Deck. A pack of cards, or that part of the pack which is left after the hands have been dealt The term was used in England until the 19th century it is now in use in the U S A
But whilst he thought to steal the single ten,
The king was slyly fingered from the deck
3 *Henry VI*, v, 1

Clear the decks. Get everything out of the way that is not essential get ready to set to work A sea term Decks are cleared before action.

To sweep the deck To clear off all the stakes. *See above*

To deck is to decorate or adorn. (Dut *dekken*, to cover, perhaps connected with A S *theccan*, to thatch)
I thought thy bride-bed to have decked, sweet maid,
And not have strewed thy grave
SHAKESPEARE *Hamlet*, v, 1

Deckle Edge The feathery edge occurring round the borders of a sheet of handmade or mould-made paper, due to the *deckle* or frame of the mould It can be imitated in machine-made papers

Décolleté (dā kol' e tā) The French for a "dress cut low about the bosom "

Decoration Day or Memorial Day. May 30th; set apart in the United States for decorating the graves of those who fell in the Civil War (1861-5).

Decoy Duck. A bait or lure, a duck taught to allure others into a net, and employed for this purpose

Decree nisi. *See* NISI

Decretals. The name given by ecclesiastical historians to the second part of the canon law, which contains the decrees and decisions of the early popes on disputed points

The False or Forged Decretals were designed to support the claim of the popes to temporal as well as spiritual authority, and purport to be the decisions of some thirty popes of the first three centuries. They comprise nearly a hundred letters written in the names of the early popes, as Clement and Anacletus, as well as letters from their supposed correspondents and acts of fictitious councils

The 9th-century forgery known as the *Donation of Constantine* is also among the False Decretals This purports to relate how Constantine the Great, when he retired to the Bosporus in 330, conferred all his rights, honours, and property as Emperor of the West on the Pope of Rome and his successors It is said, also, to have been confirmed by Charlemagne

The Isidorian Decretals were genuinely compiled in the 9th century, and assigned to Isidore of Seville, who died in 636.

Decuman Gate. A Roman military term The principal entrance to a camp, situated on the side farthest from the enemy, and so called because it was guarded by the 10th cohort of each legion (*decimus*, tenth)

Dedaliab *See* DÆDALUS

Dedalus, Stephen (dĕd' a lùs). The young man whose literary and moral development is described in James Joyce's *Portrait of the Artist as a Young Man* He also appears as a character in *Ulysses*

Dee, Dr. John Dee (1527-1608) was a famous astrologer, he was patronized by Queen Elizabeth, and was a man of vast knowledge, whose library, museum, and mathematical instruments were valued at £2,000 On one occasion the populace broke into his house and destroyed the greater part of his valuable collection, under the notion that Dee held intercourse with the devil He ultimately died a pauper, at the advanced age of eighty-one and was buried at Mortlake He professed to be able to raise the dead, and had a magic mirror, a piece of solid pink-tinted glass about the size of an orange, in which persons were told they could see their friends in distant lands and how they were occupied It was afterwards in Horace Walpole's collection at Strawberry Hill, and is now in the British Museum

Deed Poll (dĕd pōl) A deed drawn by one party, and so called because such deeds were formerly written on parchment with a polled or straight edge, in distinction to the indentures, which had an indented or wavy edge It is by deed poll that one changes one's name or executes any deed that does not concern another party

Deer. Supposed by poets to shed tears The drops, however, which fall from their eyes are not tears, but an oily secretion from the so-called tear-pits

> A poor sequestered stag
> Did come to languish   and the big round tears
> Coursed one another down his innocent nose
> In piteous chase.   *As You Like It*, ii, 2

Small deer. Any small animal, and used metaphorically for any collection of trifles or trifling matters

> But mice and rats, and such small deer
> Have been Tom's food for seven long year
>   *Lear*, iii, 4

Deerslayer The first of the Leatherstocking Novels (*q v*) by Fenimore Cooper, and one of the names given to the hero Natty Bumpo

Default. Judgment by default is when the defendant does not appear in court on the day appointed. The judge gives sentence in favour of the plaintiff, not because the plaintiff is right, but from the default of the defendant

Defeat. "What though the field be lost? all is not lost." (Milton. *Paradise Lost*, i, lines 105-6)

"All is lost but honour" (*Tout est perdu fors l'honneur*). A saying founded on a letter written by François I to his mother after the Battle of Pavia in 1525

Defender of the Faith. A title (Lat *fidei defensor*) given by Pope Leo X to Henry VIII of England, in 1521, for a Latin treatise *On the Seven Sacraments* Many previous kings, and even subjects, had been termed "defenders of the Catholic faith," "defenders of the Church," and so on, but no one had borne it as a title

> God bless the king! I mean the "faith's defender!"
> God bless—no harm in blessing—the Pretender
> But who Pretender is, or who is king—
> God bless us all! that's quite another thing
>   JOHN BYRON (1692-1763).

Richard II, in a writ to the sheriffs, uses these words '*Ecclesia cujus nos defensor sumus*," and Henry VII, in the Black Book, was styled ' Defender of the Faith "

Defenestration of Prague A phrase used to describe an incident during the religious struggles which rent Central Europe in the 17th century In March, 1618, the two leading Catholic members of the Bohemian National Council were thrown out of a window of the castle of Prague by the Protestant members They landed in the moat and sustained only minor injuries.

Deficient. A *deficient* number is one of which the sum of all its divisors is less than itself, as 10, the divisors of which are 1, 2, 5 = 8, which is less than 10

Deficit, Madame. Marie Antoinette, so called because she was always demanding money of her ministers, and never had any According to the Revolutionary song —

> La Boulangère a des écus,
> Qui ne lui content guère

See BAKER.

Degrees, Songs of Another name for the Gradual Psalms (*q v.*)

Dei Gratia (dē ī grä' sha) (Lat.). By the grace of God Introduced into English charters in

1106 It appears as "D G " on English coins *Cp* GRACELESS FLORIN

From the time of Offa, King of Mercia (A D 780), we find occasionally the same or some similar assumption as, *Dei dono, Christo donante*, etc

From about 676 to 1170 the Archbishop of Canterbury and some other ecclesiastical dignitaries used the same style, the Archbishop is now *divina providentia*

Dei Judicium (dē ĭ joo dish' ĭ um) (Lat) The judgment of God, so the judgment by ordeals was called, because it was taken as certain that God would deal rightly with the appellants

Deidamia (dē ĭ dā' mia) When Achilles (*q v*) was concealed in the island of Scyrus dressed as a woman he met this daughter of Lycomedes, and she became by him the mother of Pyrrhus or Neoptolemus.

Deist. *See* THEIST.

Deities. The more important deities of classical, Teutonic, and Scandinavian mythology are given as entries in this work, the present list is only intended to include collective names and the gods of a few special localities, functions, etc.
Air Ariel; Elves *See* ELF
Caves or Caverns. Hill-people, Pixies
Corn Ceres (Gr , Demĕter)
Domestic Life Vesta
Eloquence· Mercury (Gr., Hermes)
Evening Vesper
Fairies (*q v*)
Fates, The Three in number (Gr , Parcæ, Moiræ, Keres; Scand , Norns)
Fire Vulcan (Gr , Hephaistŏs), Vesta, Mulciber.
Furies, The Three in number (Gr , Eumenides, Erinnyes)
Gardens Priāpus, Vertumnus with his wife Pomōna.
Graces, The Three in number (Gr , Charltes)
Hades Pluto, with his wife Proserpine (Gr , Aidēs and Persephōna)
Hills Pixies; Trolls There are also Wood Trolls and Water Trolls.
Home Spirits (*q v*) Penātes, Lares.
Hunting Diana (Gr , Artemis)
Justice Themis, Astræa, Nemesis
Love Cupid (Gr , Eros)
Marriage Hymen
Medicine Æsculāpius
Morning Aurora (Gr , Eōs)
Mountains Orēads, from the Gr , ὄρος, a mountain, Trolls
Ocean Oceanides *See* SEA, below
Poetry and Music· Apollo, the nine Muses (*q v*)
Rainbow Iris
Riches Plutus
Rivers and Streams Fluviāles (Gr , Potamĕides, Naiads, Nymphs)
Sea, The Neptune (Gr , Poseidon), his son Triton, Nixies, Mermaids, Nereids
Shepherds and their Flocks Pan, the Satyrs
Springs, Lakes, Brooks, etc. Nĕreides or Naiads. *See* RIVERS, above.
Time. Saturn (Gr , Chrŏnos)
Trees See WOODS, below
War Mars (Gr , Arēs), Bellōna, Thor.
Water-nymphs. Naiads, Undine.
Winds. Æŏlus
Wine Bacchus (Gr , Dionysus)
Wisdom Minerva (Gr , Pallas, Athēnē, or Pallas-Athēnē)
Woods Dryads (A Hamadryad presides over some particular tree), Wood-Trolls
Youth. Hēbē.

Déjeuner à la Fourchette (Fr) A fork lunch, a cold collation with meat and wine

The two gentlemen were consulting as to the best means of being useful to Mrs Becky, while she was finishing her interrupted *déjeuner à la fourchette* — THACKERAY *Vanity Fair*, ch. lxv

Delaware (del' a wâr) The name of a State river, and bay in the United States, so called from Thomas West, Baron De la Warr (1577-1618), first Governor of Virginia, in 1611

Delectable Mountains. In Bunyan's *Pilgrim's Progress*, a range of mountains from which the "Celestial City" may be seen They are in Immanuel's land, and are covered with sheep, for which Immanuel had died

Delenda est Carthago (dĕ len' dà est kar' tha gō), Lat "Carthage must be destroyed ' The words with which Cato the Elder concluded every speech in the Senate when Carthage was such a menace to the power of Rome They are now proverbial, and mean, ' That which stands in the way of our greatness must be removed at all hazards "

Delft, or more correctly *Delf* A common sort of pottery made at Delft in Holland, a town noted from the 16th to the 18th centuries for its very excellent pottery

Delight. The delight of mankind. So Titus, the Roman emperor, was entitled (40, 79-81) on account of his benevolence and munificence

Delirium. From the Lat *lira* (the ridge left by the plough), hence the verb *de-lirare*, to make an irregular ridge in ploughing *Delirus* was one who couldn't plough a straight furrow, hence a crazy, doting person, one whose mind wandered from the subject in hand; and *delirium* is the state of such a person *Cp* PREVARICATION

Della Cruscans (del' a krūs' kanz) or *Della Cruscan School* A school of poetry started by some young Englishmen at Florence in the latter part of the 18th century. Their silly, sentimental affectations, which appeared in the *World* and the *Oracle*, created for a time quite a furore, but were mercilessly gibbeted in the *Baviad* and *Mæviad* of Gifford (1794 and 1795) The clique took its name from the famous Accademia della Crusca (literally, Academy of Chaff) which was founded in Florence in 1582 with the object of purifying the Italian language—sifting away its "chaff" —and which in 1611 published an important dictionary.

Delos. A floating island, according to Greek legend, ultimately made fast to the bottom of the sea by Poseidon. Apollo having become possessor of it by exchange, made it his favourite retreat It is the smallest of the Cyclades.

Delphi or **Delphos.** A town of Phocis, at the foot of Mount Parnassus (the modern Kastri), famous for a temple of Apollo and for an oracle which was silenced only in the 4th century A D by Theodosius, and was celebrated in every age and country

Delphi was looked upon by the ancients as the "navel of the earth," and in the temple was kept a white stone bound with a red ribbon, to represent the navel and umbilical cord.

In the *Winter's Tale* (the same play in which he gives Bohemia a seacoast) Shakespeare makes Delphos an island

Delphin Classics. A set of Latin classics edited in France by thirty-nine scholars, under the superintendence of Montausier, Bossuet, and Huet, for the use of the Dauphin (Lat *in usum Delphini*), *i e* the son of Louis XIV, called the *Grand Dauphin.* They were first published in 1674, and their chief value consists in their verbal indexes or concordances

Delta. A tract of alluvial land enclosed by the mouth of a river. The name, from the Greek letter △, *delta* was originally given to the area of the mouths of the Nile, which was of triangular shape it has since been applied to similar formations, such as the deltas of the Danube, Rhine, Ganges, Indus, Mississippi, etc

Deluge The Bible story of Noah's Flood has its counterpart in several mythologies and folk lores In Babylonia it appears in the 11th tablet of the Gilgamesh Epic but on a higher level of civilization, for Utnapishtim (Noah) takes into the ark with him craftsmen and treasure.

Apollodorus tells the story of Deucalion and Pyrrha (*q v.*) Of this story there are several versions, in one of which Deucalion is replaced by Ogyges.

One of the Indian deluge stories tells how Manu was warned by a fish, which towed the boat he made and brought it to safety.

In all these stories it is observable that, as in the case of Noah, the survivors' first act was to render thanks to the god who had preserved their lives.

Somewhat similar deluge stories are found in China, Burma, New Guinea, Polynesia and both the American continents

See also AFTER ME THE DELUGE.

Demerit (dĕ mer' it) has reversed its original meaning (Lat *dēmērere*, to merit, to deserve). The *de-* was originally intensive, as in "demand," "de-scribe," "de-claim," etc , but in mediæval Latin it came to be regarded as privative, and in English the word hence had both a good and a bad sense, of which the latter is now the only one remaining.

My demerits [deserts]
May speak unbonneted
Othello, 1, 2

Demesne. *See* MANOR.

Demeter (de mē' ter) One of the great Olympian deities of ancient Greece, identified with the Roman Ceres (*q.v*) She was the goddess of fruits, crops, and vegetation generally, and the protectress of marriage Persephone (Proserpine) was her daughter.

Demijohn (dem' i jon). A glass vessel with a large body and small neck, enclosed in wickerwork like a Florence flask, and containing more than a bottle The word is from the Fr *dame-jeanne*, "Madame Jane," which has been thought to be a corruption of *Damaghan*, a town in Persia There is, however, no support for this, it is more likely that the word is simply a popular name—"Dame Jane"—

like " Bellarmine " (*q* 1), but it is possible that it is from the Lat. *de mediana*, of middle size, or even *dimidium*, half

Demi-monde (dem' i mond) Female society only half acknowledged, as *le beau monde* is Society. The term was first used by Dumas *fils*, and has been sometimes incorrectly applied to fashionable courtesans

[Dumas'] *demi-monde* is the link between good and bad society . the world of compromised women a social limbo, the inmates of which are perpetually struggling to emerge into the paradise of honourable and respectable ladies —*Fraser's Magazine,* 1885

Demi-rep (dem' i rep) A woman whose character has been blown upon, one "whom everybody knows to be what nobody calls her" (*Fielding*) A contraction of *demi-reputation*

Demi-urge (dem'i ĕrj) In the language of the Platonists, that mysterious agent which made the world and all that it contains The Logos or Word spoken of by St John, in the first chapter of his gospel, is the Demiurgus of Platonizing Christians In the Gnostic systems, Jehovah (as an eon or emanation of the Supreme Being) is the Demi-urge *See* MARCIONITES

In some of the ancient Greek states the chief magistrate was called the *demiurgus*

Democracy. A form of Government in which the sovereign power is in the hands of the people, and exercised by them directly or indirectly: also, a State so governed, and the body of the people, especially the non-privileged classes (Gr *demos-kratia*, the rule of the people)

Democrats. Advocates of government by the people. A term adopted by the French revolutionists to distinguish themselves from the *aristocrats* Adopted by the pro-slavery Southern States in the U S A , now a political party more of the left than the Republicans

Democritus (de mok' ri tus). The laughing philosopher of Abdera (lived about 460-357 B C) He should rather be termed the *deriding* philosopher, because he derided or laughed at people's folly or vanity It is said that he put out his eyes that he might think more deeply.

Democritus, dear droll, revisit earth,
And with our follies glut thy heightened mirth
PRIOR

Democritus Junior. Robert Burton (1577-1640), author of *The Anatomy of Melancholy.*

Demogorgon (dem ŏ gor' gon) A terrible deity, whose very name was capable of producing the most horrible effects. He is first mentioned by the 4th-century Christian writer, Lactantius who, in so doing is believed to have broken the spell of a mystery, for *Demogorgon* is supposed to be identical with the infernal Power of the ancients, the very mention of whose name brought death and disaster, to whom reference is made by Lucan and others.—

Must I call your master to my aid,
At whose dread name the trembling furies quake,
Hell stands abashed, and earth's foundations shake?
ROWE *Lucan's Pharsalia,* vi

Hence Milton speaks of "the dreaded name of Demogorgon" (*Paradise Lost*, ii , 956) According to Ariosto Demogorgon was a king of the elves and fays who lived on the Himalayas, and once in five years summoned all his subjects before him to give an account of their stewardship Spensei (*Faerie Queene*, iv, ii, 47) says that he dwells in the deep abyss with the three fatal sisters

Demon (Austr) A convict serving his sentence of transportation in Van Diemen's Land (Tasmania)

Demons, Prince of. Asmodeus (*q v.*), also called "The Demon of Matrimonial Unhappiness "

Demos, King (dē' mos) A facetious term for the electorate, the proletariat Those who choose and elect our senators, and are therefore the virtual rulers of the nation

Demurrage (de mûr' ij) An allowance made to the master or owners of a ship by the freighters for detaining her in port longer than the time agreed upon (Lat , *demorari*, to delay)
The extra days beyond the lay days are called days of demurrage —KENT *Commentaries*, vol. iii, pt v, lecture xlvii, p 159   •

Demy (de mī') A size of paper between royal and crown, measuring 17¼ by 22½ in in printing papers, and 15½ by 20 in in writing papers It is from Fr *demi* (half), probably meaning "half imperial "

A **Demy** of Magdalen College, Oxford, is a foundation scholar, whose allowance or "commons" was originally *half* that of a Fellow

Den. God ye good den ' An abbreviated form of the old salutation "God give you *good even*(ing) "
Nurse   God ye good morrow, gentlemen
Mer   God ye good den, fair gentlewoman
SHAKESPEARE *Romeo and Juliet*, ii, 4

Denarius (den âr' i ûs). A Roman silver coin equal in value to ten ases (*deni-ases*), or about 8¼d The word was used in France and England for the inferior coins, whether silver or copper, and for ready money generally The initial "d " for penny (£ s d) is from *denarius*
The denarius shown to our Lord . . was the tribute-money payable by the Jews to the Roman emperor, and must not be confounded with the tribute paid to the Temple —MADDEN *Jewish Coinage*, ch. xi

Denarius Dei (Lat , God's penny). An earnest of a bargain, which was given to the church or poor

Denarii St Petri. Peter's pence (*q v*)

Denizen. A person who lives in a country as opposed to foreigners who live *outside* (Lat *de-intus*, from within, through O.Fr. *deinzein*) In English law the word means a made citizen —*i e* an alien who has been naturalized by letters patent
A denizen is a kind of middle state, between an alien and a natural-born subject, and partakes of both — BLACKSTONE *Commentaries*, Bk 1, ch x

Denmark. According to the *Roman de Rose*, Denmark means the country of Danaos, who settled here with a colony after the siege of Troy, as Brutus is said by the same sort of name-legend to have settled in Britain. Saxo-Germanicus, with equal absurdity, makes Dan, the son of Humble, the first king, to account for the name of the country.
The true origin of the word is from the march, or boundary of the Danes

Denys, St (de nē') The apostle to the Gauls and patron saint of France He is said to have been beheaded at Paris in 272, and, according to tradition, carried his head, after martyrdom, for six miles in his hands and laid it on the spot where stands the cathedral bearing his name The tale may have taken its rise from an ancient painting of the incident, in which the artist placed the head between the martyr's hands so that the trunk might be recognized

Montjoie Saint Denys ' *See* MONTJOIE

Deo gratias (dē' ō grā shās) (Lat.). Thanks to God *Cp* DEI GRATIA

Deo juvante (dē' ō joo văn' te) (Lat) With God's help; God willing

Deo volente (dē' ō vō len' te) (Lat) God being willing, by God's will; usually contracted into D V

Deoch-an-doruis. *See* DOCH-AN-DOROCH

Deodand (dē' ō dănd) Literally, something "given to God" (Lat *deo-dandum*) In English law, a personal chattel which had been the cause of the death of a person which (till the custom was abolished in 1846) was forfeited and sold for some pious use For instance, when a man met with his death through injuries inflicted by the fall of a ladder, the ross of a bull, or the kick of a horse, the cause of death was sold, and the proceeds given to the Church The custom originated in the idea that as the person was sent to his account without the sacrament of extreme unction, the money could serve to pay for masses for his repose

Depart. Literally, to part thoroughly, to separate effectually The marriage service in the old prayer-books had "till death us depart," which has been corrupted into "till death us do part "
"Depart" is sound English for "part asunder," which was altered to "do part" in 1661, at the pressing request of the Puritans, who knew as little of the history of their national language as they did of that of their national Church —J H BLUNT *Annotated Book of Common Prayer.*

Department. France is divided into departments, as Great Britain and Ireland are divided into counties or shires. From 1768 it was divided into *governments*, of which thirty-two were *grand* and eight *petit* In 1790, by a decree of the Constituent Assembly, it was mapped out *de novo* into eighty-three departments In 1804 the number of departments was increased to 107, and in 1812 to 130. In 1815 the territory was reduced to eighty-six departments, and continued so till 1860, when Savoy and Nice were added. The present number is ninety, including Corsica and the provinces of Alsace and Lorraine

Depot. The American term for a railway station, in use since the first introduction of railways into that country

Derby (dër' bi) The American term for the hat known as the Bowler (*q v*) in England The Brown Derby is a well-known restaurant in Hollywood, shaped like a hat, frequented by the film colony

Derby Scheme (dar' bi). As a compromise with conscription the Government introduced a scheme in 1915 (when the Earl of Derby was at the War Office) of voluntary enlistment for men between 18 and 41, who would be called to the colours in age groups It did not succeed, and conscription was introduced in January, 1916

Derby Day is the day when the Derby stakes are run for, during the great Epsom Summer Meeting; it is usually during the week before or after Whit Sunday The Derby, known as the ' Blue Ribbon of the Turf," is for colts and fillies of three years old only, consequently, no horse can win it twice *See* CLASSIC RACES

Derby Stakes (dar' bi). Started by Edward Stanley, the twelfth Earl of Derby, in 1780, the year after his establishment of the Oaks stakes (*q v.*)

Derrick. A temporary crane to remove goods from the hold of a vessel, etc , so called from Derrick, the Tyburn hangman early in the 17th century. The name was first given to the gibbet, hence, from the similarity in shape, to the crane

> He rides circuit with the devil, and Derrick must be his host, and Tyborne the inn at which he will light —
> DEKKER *Bellman of London* (1608)

Derwentwater. Lord Derwentwater's lights A local name for the Aurora Borealis, James, Earl of Derwentwater, was beheaded for rebellion February 24th 1716, and it is said that the northern lights were unusually brilliant that night

Desert Rats. Sobriquet of the 7th Armoured Division which, already in the Western Desert before the outbreak of war in 1939, served in the Eighth Army throughout the North African campaigns Afterwards served in N W Europe Its divisional sign was a red desert rat on a black ground The 4th Armoured Brigade, also of long standing in the desert, used a black rat on a white ground The name was given contemptuously by Mussolini but adopted with pride and pleasure

Desmas. *See* DYSMAS

Despair. Giant Despair, in Bunyan's *Pilgrim's Progress,* lived in "Doubting Castle" He caught unwary pilgrims and shut them up in his grim castle, from which Christian and Hopeful escaped by using the key called Promise

Dessert means simply the cloth removed (Fr *desservir,* to clear the table), and dessert is that which comes after the cloth is removed

Destruction Prince of Destruction. Tamerlane or Timour the Tartar (1333-1405), the terror of the East He was conqueror of Persia and a great part of India, and was threatening China when he died

Desultory. Those who rode two or more horses in the circus of Rome, and used to leap from one to the other, were called *desultores* (*de,* and *saltire,* to leap); hence *desultor* came in Latin to mean one inconstant, or who went from one thing to another, and desultory means the manner of a desultor

Deucalion's Flood The Deluge, of Greek legend Deucalion was son of Prometheus and Clymene, and was king of Phthia, in Thessaly When Zeus sent the deluge Deucalion built a ship, and he and his wife, Pyrrha, were the only mortals saved The ship at last rested on Mount Parnassus, and Deucalion was told by the oracle at Themis that to restore the human race he must cast the bones of his mother behind him His interpretation of this was the stones of his mother Earth, so the two cast these as directed and those thrown by Deucalion became men, and those thrown by his wife became women

Deuce. The two, in games with cards, dice, etc (Fr *deux*) The three is called "Tray" (Fr *trois,* Lat *tres*)

Deuce-ace. A throw of two dice, one showing *one* spot and the other showing *two,* hence, exceptionally bad luck

There are various origins ascribed to the word *deuce* used as a euphemism for *devil* It may derive in reverse meaning from the Latin expletive *Deus!,* My god! Or it may come from the Celtic *dus, teuz,* a phantom, spectre Or, again, there is the Old German *durse, turse,* meaning a giant. Finally, there is a suggestion that it comes from the two at dice being an unlucky throw

Deuce take you Get away! you annoy me

It played the deuce with me. It made me very ill, it disagreed with me, it almost ruined me

The deuce is in you. You are a very demon

What the deuce is the matter ? What in the world is amiss ?

Deus Deus ex machina. The intervention of some unlikely event, in order to extricate one from difficulties Literally, it means "a god (let down upon the stage) from the machine," the 'machine" being part of the furniture of the stage in an ancient Greek theatre

Deva. Chester, or the Dee
> Nor yet where Deva spreads her wizard stream
>   MILTON *Lycidas*

Devil. Represented with a cloven foot, because by the Rabbinical writers he is called *seirizzim* (a goat). As the goat is a type of uncleanness, the prince of unclean spirits is aptly represented under this emblem

In his *Divina Commedia* Dante gives the following names to the various devils.—

Alichino, the allurer, *Barbariccia,* the malicious, *Calcobrina,* the grace-scorner, *Caynazzo,* the snarler, *Ciriato Sannuto,* the tusked boar, *Dragnignazzo,* the fell dragon, *Farfarello,* the scandalmonger, *Grafficane,* the doggish, *Libicocco,* the ill-tempered, *Rubicante,* the red with rage, *Scarmiglione,* the baneful

In legal parlance a *devil* is a leader's assistant (also a barrister) who gets up the facts of a brief, with the laws bearing on it, and summarizes the case for the pleader

The Attorney-General's devils are the Counsel of the Treasury, who not unfrequently get promoted to the bench

A printer's devil. A printer's message boy, formerly, the boy who took the printed sheets from the tympan of the press Moxon says (1683) "They do commonly so black and bedaub themselves that the workmen do jocosely call them devils "

As the devil loves holy water. That is, not at all, holy water drives away the devil The Latin proverb is, "*Sicut sus amaricinum amat*" (as swine love marjoram) Lucretius, vi, 974, says, "*amaricinum fugitat sus* "

Beating the devil's tattoo. Tapping on the table with one's finger a wearisome number of times, or on the floor with one's foot, repeating any rhythmical mechanical sound with annoying pertinacity

Between the devil and the deep sea. Between Scylla and Charybdis, between two evils, each equally hazardous. The allusion seems to be to the herd of swine and the devils called Legion (*Luke*, viii, 26 ff)

Cheating the devil. Mincing an oath, doing evil for gain, and giving part of the profits to the Church, etc In a literal sense, cheating the devil is by no means unusual in monkish traditions Thus the "Devils' Bridge," over the Fall of the Reuss, in the canton of the Uri, Switzerland, is a single arch over a cataract It is said that Satan knocked down several bridges, but promised the abbot, Giraldus of Einsiedeln, to let this one stand, provided he would give him the first living thing that crossed it The abbot agreed, and threw across it a loaf of bread, which a hungry dog ran after, and "the rocks re-echoed with peals of laughter to see the devil thus defeated " (Longfellow *Golden Legend*, v)

Rabelais says that a farmer once bargained with the devil for each to have on alternate years what grew under and over the soil The canny farmer sowed carrots and turnips when it was his turn to have the under-soil share, and wheat and barley the year following (*Pantagruel*, Bk iv, ch xlvi)

Give the devil his due Give even a bad man or one hated like the devil the credit he deserves

Poins Jack, how agrees the devil and thee about thy soul, that thou soldest him on Good Friday last, for a cup of Madeira, and a cold capon s leg?
Prince Sir John stands to his word, the devil shall have his bargain, for he was never yet a breaker of proverbs, he will give the devil his due
                                        1 *Henry IV*, i, 2.

Go to the devil. The obvious meaning of this phrase is, to go to ruin In the 17th century, however, wits used to make a play on the applicability of the phrase to the Devil Tavern, Temple Bar, one of the most famous taverns in the City, and a haunt of lawyers from the neighbouring Temple The sign of the tavern was the Devil pulling St Dunstan's nose The Devil was a favourite resort of Ben Jonson, and numerous references to it appear in Elizabethan and Stuart literature

Bloodhound As you come by Temple Bar make a step to th' Devil
Tim. To the Devil, father?
Sim: My master means the sign of the Devil, and he cannot hurt you, fool, there's a saint holds him by the nose
                W ROWLEY *A Match at Midnight*, 1633

He needs a long spoon who sups with the devil. *See* SPOON

Here's the very devil to pay. Here's a pretty kettle of fish I'm in a pretty mess, this is confusion worse confounded *Cp.* THE DEVIL TO PAY *below*

Needs must when the devil drives. If I must, I must The French say "*Il faut marcher quand le diable est aux trousses*", and the Italians "*Bisogna andare, quando il diavolo è nella coda.*"

He must needs go that the Devil drives
SHAKESPEARE *All's Well that Ends Well*, i, 3.

Pull devil, pull baker. Lie, cheat, and wrangle away, for one is as bad as the other Sometimes "parson" is substituted for "baker," but the origin of neither is known

Like Punch and the Deevil rugging about the Baker at the fair —SCOTT. *Old Mortality*, ch xxxviii

Talk of the devil and he's sure to appear. Said of a person who has been the subject of conversation, and who unexpectedly makes his appearance An older proverb still is: "Talk of the Dule and he'll put out his horns"; but the modern euphemism is "Talk of an angel and you'll hear the fluttering of its wings."

Forthwith the devil did appear,
For name him, and he's always near
                        PRIOR. *Hans Carvel.*

Tell the truth and shame the devil. A very old saying, of obvious meaning.

Glendower I can teach you, cousin, to command the devil
Hotspur And I can teach thee, coz, to shame the devil
By telling truth tell truth and shame the devil
            SHAKESPEARE 1 *Henry IV*, iii, 1

The devil among the tailors. Said when a good slanging match is in progress, it is also the name of a game in which a top (the "devil") is spun among a number of wooden men ("tailors") and knocks down as many as possible.

The first-mentioned use of the phrase is said to have originated through a row at a benefit performance about 1830 for the well-known actor William Dowton (1764-1851) The piece was a burlesque called *The Tailors a Tragedy for Warm Weather*, and a large number of tailors caused a riot outside the theatre (the Haymarket) as they considered it insulting to the trade

The devil and all. Everything, especially everything bad

The devil and his dam. The devil and something even worse. Dam (*q.v*) here may mean either *mother* (the usual meaning), or *wife*. Quotations may be adduced in support of either of these interpretations, and it is to be noted that frequently (*cp Paradise Lost*, ii) there is no differentiation Also, Rabbinical tradition relates that Lilith was the wife of Adam, but was such a vixen that Adam could not live with her, and she became the devil's dam We also read that Belphegor "came to earth to seek him out a dam "

In many mythologies the devil is typified by an animal, the Irish and others call him a *black cat*, the Jews speak of him as a *dragon* (which idea is carried out in our George and the Dragon); the Japanese call him a species of *fox*, others say he is a *goat*, a *camel*, etc , and Dante associates him with *dragons*, *swine*, and *dogs*. In all which cases dam for mother is not inappropriate

The devil catch the hindmost A phrase from late mediæval magic; it was said that the devil had a school at Toledo, or at Salamanca, where the students, when they had made a certain progress in their studies, were obliged to run through a subterranean hall, and the last man was seized by the devil and became his imp

The devil in Dublin City. The Scandinavian form of Dublin was *Divelin[a]*, and the Latin *Dublinia* "Dublin" is the Gael. *dhu linn*, the black pool Devlin, in Co Mayo, is the same word and preserves the Scandinavian form.

> Is just as true's when the deil's in hell
> Or Dublin city
> Burns *Death and Dr Hornbrook.*

The devil is not so black as he is painted. Said in extenuation or mitigation, especially when it seems that exaggerated censure has been given

The devil looking over Lincoln Said of a vitriolic critic or a backbiter. Fuller, in his *Worthies* (under *Oxford*), says the phrase may allude either to the "stone picture of the Devil which doth [1661] or lately did overlook Lincoln Colledge," or to a grotesque sculpture at Lincoln Cathedral The phrase occurs as early as 1562 (John Heywood's *Proverbs*).

> Than wolde ye looke ouer me with stomoke swolne
> Like as the diuell lookt ouer Lincolne

The devil rides on a fiddlestick. Much ado about nothing Beaumont and Fletcher, Shakespeare, and others, use the phrase "Fiddlesticks!" as an exclamation, meaning rubbish! nonsense! When the prince and his merry companions are at the *Boar's Head*, first Bardolph rushes in to warn them that the sheriff's officers are at hand, and anon enters the hostess to put her guests on their guard But the prince says —

> Heigh, heigh' the devil rides upon a fiddlestick;
> what's the matter?—1 *Henry IV*, ii, 4

The following is perhaps a reminiscence of the old phrase —

> The Devil, that old stager　. who leads
> Downward, perhaps, but fiddles all the way
> Browning. *Red Cotton Night-cap Country*, ii

The devil's advocate See Advocate

The devil's daughter's portion.The saying is —

> Deal, Dover, and Harwich,
> The devil gave with his daughter in marriage,

because of the scandalous impositions practised in these seaports on sailors and occasional visitors.

The devil's door. A small door in the north wall of some old churches, which used to be opened at baptisms and communions to "let the devil out " The north used to be known as "the devil's side " where Satan and his legion lurked to catch the unwary

The devil sick would be a monk.

> When the Devil was sick, the devil a monk would be,
> When the Devil got well, the devil a monk was he

Said of those persons who in times of sickness or danger make pious resolutions, but forget them when danger is past and health recovered The lines are found as an interpolation in Urquhart and Motteux's translation of Rabelais (Bk. iv, ch xxiv) A correct translation of what Rabelais actually wrote is —

> "There's a rare rogue for you," said Eusthenes, "there's a rogue, a rogue and a half This makes good the Lombard's proverb, 'Passato el Pericolo, gabbato el Santo' " [when the danger is passed, the Saint is mocked]

The devil to pay and no pitch hot. The ' devil" is a seam between the garboard-strake and the keel, and to "pay" is to cover with pitch (O Fr *payer*, to pitch, whence Fr *poix, see* Pay) In former times, when vessels were often careened for repairs, it was difficult to calk and pay this seam before the tide turned Hence the locution, the ship is careened, the devil is exposed, but there is no hot pitch ready, and the tide will turn before the work can be done

To hold a candle to the devil See Candle

To kindle a fire for the devil. To offer sacrifice, to do what is really sinful, under the delusion that you are doing God's service

To lead one the devil's own dance. To give him endless trouble, to lead him right astray

To play the very devil with something. To muddle and mar it in such a way as to spoil it utterly

To pull the devil by the tail. To struggle constantly against adversity

To say the devil's paternoster. To grumble, to rail at providence.

To whip the devil round the stump. An American phrase meaning to enjoy the fruits of evil-doing without having to suffer the penalty, to dodge a difficulty dishonestly but successfully

When the devil is blind. Never

Why should the devil have all the good tunes? A saying originating with Charles Wesley about 1740, when he utilized the music of the popular songs of the day to get his hymns sung and known.

Devil In Topographical Nomenclature.

Devil's Arrows Three remarkable "Druid" stones near Boroughbridge, Yorks, like *Harold's Stones*

Devil's Bridge. There is a village in Cardiganshire of this name, so called because of its double bridge across a gorge of the river Mynach The lower bridge dates from the 11th century, and is locally known as the Monks' Bridge, because it was built by, and for the use of, the monasteries in the neighbourhood; the upper bridge dates from 1735 *See also Cheating the Devil, in* Phrases *above*

The Devil's Cheesewring. See Cheesewring.

Devil's Coits. *See* Hackell's Coit

The Devil's Current Part of the current of the Bosporus is so called, from its great rapidity

Devil's Den. A cromlech in a valley, near Marlborough It now consists of two large uprights and an impost The third upright has fallen.

The Devil's Dyke. A ravine in the South Downs, Brighton The legend is, that St.

Cuthman, walking on the downs, prided himself on having Christianized the surrounding country, and having built a nunnery where the dyke-house now stands Presently the devil appeared and told him all his labour was vain, for he would swamp the whole country before morning St Cuthman went to the nunnery and told the abbess to keep the sisters in prayer till after midnight, and then illuminate the windows The devil came at sunset with mattock and spade, and began cutting a dyke into the sea, but was seized with rheumatic pains all over his body He flung down his mattock and spade, and the cocks, mistaking the illuminated windows for sunrise, began to crow, whereupon the devil fled in alarm, leaving his work not half done

The same name is given to a prehistoric earthwork in Cambridgeshire, stretching across Newmarket Heath from Rech to Cowledge

The Devil's Frying-pan. A Cornish tin-mine worked by the Romans

The Devil's Hole. A name of the Peak Cavern, in Derbyshire

The Devil's Nostrils Two vast caverns separated by a huge pillar of natural rock in the mainland of the Zetland Islands

The Devil's Punch Bowl. A deep combe on the S W. side of Hindhead Hill, two miles N of Haslemere, in Surrey A similar dell in Mangerton Mountain near Killarney, has the same name.

The Devil's Throat. Cromer Bay So called from its danger to navigation

The Devil's Tower. A great rectangular granite obelisk, over 600 feet in height, in the Black Hills, Dakota, U S A.

IN PERSONAL NOMENCLATURE

Devil Dick. A nickname of Richard Porson (1759-1808), the great English Greek scholar

Robert the Devil. *See* ROBERT LE DIABLE

The French Devil. Jean Bart (1651-1702), an intrepid French sailor, born at Dunkirk

The Devil's missionary. A nickname given to Voltaire (1694-1778), and very likely to others.

Son of the Devil. Ezzelino (1194-1259), the noted Ghibelline leader and Governor of Vicenza; so called for his infamous cruelties.

The White Devil was the name given to Vittoria Corombona, an Italian murderess whose story was dramatized by John Webster under that name, 1608

The White Devil of Wallachia Scanderbeg, or George Castriota (1403-68), was so called by the Turks

IN COMMON TERMS AND NAMES

Devil and bag o' nails. *See* BAG O' NAILS

Devil dodger. A sly hypocrite, a ranting preacher

Devil may care. Wildly reckless, also a reckless fellow.

Devil on two sticks. The English name of Le Sage's novel *Le diable boiteux* (1707), in which

D D —10

Asmodeus (*q v*) plays an important part It was dramatized by Foote in 1768 *See also* DIABOLO

Devil's apple. The mandrake, also the thorn apple.

Devil's bedpost In card games, the four of clubs *Cp.* DEVIL'S FOUR-POSTER *below*

Devil's Bible. *See* DEVIL'S BOOKS *below*

Devil's bird. A Scots name for the yellow bunting; from its note, *deil*

Devil's bones Dice, which are made of bones and lead to ruin

Devil's books, or **Devil's picture-book.** Playing cards A Presbyterian phrase, used in reproof of the term King's Books, applied to a pack of cards, from the Fr *livre des quatre rois* (the book of the four kings) Also called the *Devil's Bible.*

Devil's candle So the Arabs call the mandrake, from its shining appearance at night.

Devil's candlestick. The common stinkhorn fungus, *Phallus impudicus*; also called the *devil's horn* and the *devil's stinkpot*

Devil's coach-horse. A large rove-beetle, *Goerius olens.*

Devil's coach-wheel. The corn crowfoot.

Devil's daughter. A shrew. *Cp.* DEVIL'S DAUGHTER'S PORTION *in* PHRASES *above*

Devil's dozen Thirteen, twelve, and one over for the devil *Cp* BAKER'S DOZEN

Devil's dust. The flock made from old rags torn up by a machine called the "devil"; also the shoddy made from this
Does it beseem thee to weave cloth of devil's dust instead of pure wool? —CARLYLE (1840)

Devil's fingers. The starfish, also belemnites.

Devil's four-poster A hand at whist with four clubs It is said that such a hand is never a winning one. *Cp* DEVIL'S BEDPOST *above.*

Devil's horn. *See* DEVIL'S CANDLESTICK *above*

Devil's livery. Black and yellow Black for death, yellow for quarantine.

Devil's luck. Astounding good luck. Persons always lucky were thought at one time to have compounded with the devil

Devil's mass. Swearing at everybody and everything

The Devil's Own The 88th Foot, the Connaught Rangers So called by General Picton from their bravery in the Peninsular War, 1809-14 Also the Inns of Court Regiment, which was at one time chiefly recruited from among lawyers.

The Devil's Parliament. The parliament which met at Coventry in 1459 and impeached the Yorkist leaders

The Devil's Paternoster. *See in* PHRASES *above*

Devil's snuff-box. A puff-ball; a fungus full of dust, one of the genus *Lycoperdon.*

Devonshire English legend accounts for the name (which is really from that of the ancient

Celtic inhabitants, the Damnonii) by saying that it is from Debon, one of the heroes who came with Brutus from Troy. When Brutus allotted out the island, this portion became *Debon's share.*

> In mede of these great conquests by them got
> Corineus had that province utmost west .
> And Debon's share was that is Devonshire
> SPENSER *Faerie Queene*, II, x, 12

The Devonshire Poet. O Jones, a journeyman wool-comber, who lived at the close of the 18th century Other Devonshire poets are John Gay (1685-1732) of Barnstaple and Edward Capern (1819-94), called "The rural Postman of Bideford."

Dew Ponds. On the heights of the chalk downs and in other places where there is no visible means of replenishment there are ponds which remain full in the heat of summer when ponds at lower levels dry up These dew ponds are often of prehistoric origin, dating back to the Stone Age and beyond They are cunningly made, with a lower layer of straw or reeds, and an upper layer of clay, and are kept filled mostly by mist and dew. The presence of a dew pond is a sure sign that ancient man dwelt in the neighbourhood.

Dexter (deks' tẽr) A Latin word meaning "to the right, on the right-hand side", hence *dextrous* originally signified "right-handed " In Heraldry the term *dexter* is applied to that side of the shield which is to the right of the person bearing it upon the arm, hence it indicates the *left* side of the shield as seen by the spectator, either when viewed as an actual shield or when seen depicted

Dey. The title of the Mohammedan governors of Algiers, Tripoli, and Tunis, originally applied to the commander of Janissaries at Algiers who (1710) became ruler From Turk *dai*, maternal uncle

Diable, Le. Olivier Le Dain, the tool of Louis XI, and once the king's barber So called because he was as much feared as the devil himself and even more disliked. He was hanged in 1484, after the death of the king.

Diabolo An old game that was revived about 1907, in which the players have each two sticks connected with a cord on which they spin, and pass from one to the other, a reel-shaped top It used to be called the "devil on two sticks," the top being the "devil "

Diadem (di' a dem) In ancient times the headband or fillet worn by kings as a badge of royalty was called a diadem; it was made of silk or linen and was tied at the back, with the ends falling on the neck The diadem of Bacchus was a broad band which might be unfolded to make a veil. The Emperor Constantine was the first to wear a diadem of jewels, and from his time rows of pearls and precious stones have made up the royal and imperial diadems.

> To him who wears the regal diadem
> *Paradise Lost*
> Mont Blanc is the monarch of mountains
> They crown'd him long ago
> On a throne of rocks, in a robe of clouds,
> With a diadem of snow
> BYRON *Manfred*, i, 1.

Dialectics. Logic in general, the art of disputation, the investigation of truth by analysis, that strictly logical discussion which leads to reliable results. Gr *dialegein*, to speak thoroughly

Kant used the word to signify the critical analysis of knowledge based on science, and Hegel for the philosophic process of reconciling the contradictions of experience in a higher synthesis

The following questions from John of Salisbury are fair specimens of the dialectics of the Schoolmen (*q v*) —

> When a person buys a whole cloak, does the cowl belong to his purchase?
> When a hog is driven to market with a rope round its neck, does the man or the rope take him

Diamond. A corruption of *adamant* (*q v*) So called because the diamond, which cuts other substances, can be cut or polished with no substance but itself (Gr *a damao*, what cannot be subdued)

In Spenser s *Faerie Queene* (Bk iv), Diamond is one of the three sons of Agapē He was slain by Cambalo

Diamond is the playing area in the game of Baseball

A diamond of the first water. A specially fine diamond, one of the greatest value for its size The colour or lustre of a diamond is called its "water "

A rough diamond An uncultivated genius; a person of excellent parts, but without society manners.

> As for Warrington, that rough diamond had not had the polish of a dancing-master, and he did not know how to waltz —THACKERAY

Black diamonds. *See* BLACK

Diamond cut diamond. Cunning outwitting cunning, a hard bargain over-reached A diamond is so hard that it can only be ground by diamond dust, or by rubbing one against another

Diamond hammer. A pick for "whetting" millstones. It is provided with several sharp-pointed teeth to give a uniform roughness to the surface of the stone Also a steel pick with diamond-shaped point at each extremity to recut grooves in stone

Diamond Jim. Jim Brady, an American railway magnate who liked to cover his person with diamonds of great size in the form of rings, buttons, tie pins, etc.

The diamond jousts. Jousts instituted by King Arthur, "who by that name had named them, since a diamond was the prize." The story, as embroidered by Tennyson in his *Lancelot and Elaine* from Malory (Bk xviii, ch 9-20) is that Arthur found nine diamonds from the crown of a slain knight and offered them as the prize of nine jousts in successive years

The Diamond Necklace. The famous "Diamond Necklace Affair" of French history (1783-5) centres round Marie Antoinette, Cardinal de Rohan, a profligate and ambitious churchman, and an adventuress, the Countess de Lamotte Partly by means of the queen's signatures, which were almost certainly forged, Rohan was induced to purchase for the queen, for about £85,000, a diamond necklace originally made for Mme Dubarry He handed the necklace to the countess who was to pass it on to the queen, but she sold it to an English jeweller and kept the money When the time of payment arrived Boehmer, the jeweller, sent his bill in to the queen, who denied all knowledge of the matter A nine months' trial ensued which created immense scandal The necklace is still in existence

Diamond Pitt. Thomas Pitt (1653-1726), owner of the famous Pitt Diamond (*q v*), and grandfather of the Earl of Chatham, was so known

The Diamond Sculls. An annual race for amateur single-scullers taking place at the Henley Royal Regatta, and first rowed in 1844. The prize is a pair of crossed silver sculls not quite a foot in length, surmounted by an imitation wreath of laurel, and having a pendant of diamonds. It passes from winner to winner; but each winner receives a silver cup as a souvenir

Diana (dĭ ăn' a) An ancient Italian and Roman divinity, later identified with the Olympian goddess Artemis, who was daughter of Zeus and Leto, and twin-sister of Apollo She was the goddess of the moon and of hunting, protectress of women, and—in earlier times at least—the great mother goddess or Nature goddess. *Cp* SELENE The temple of Diana at Ephesus, one of the Seven Wonders of the World (*q v*), built by Dinochares, was set on fire by Herostratos, for the sake of perpetuating his name. The Ionians decreed that anyone who mentioned his name should be put to death, but this very decree gave it immortality The temple was discovered in 1872.

Diana of Ephesus This statue, a cone surmounted by a bust covered with breasts, we are told, fell from heaven If so, it was an aerolite, but Minucius (2nd cent A D), who says he saw it, describes it as a wooden statue, and Pliny, a contemporary, tells us it was made of ebony. Probably the real "image" was a meteorite, and in the course of time a wooden one was substituted

The palladium of Troy, the most ancient image of Athena at Athens, the statues of Artemis at Tauris and Cybele at Pessinus, the sacred shield of the Romans, and the shrine of our Lady of Loretto, are examples of objects of religious veneration which were said to have been sent from heaven.

Great is Diana of the Ephesians A phrase sometimes used to signify that self-interest blinds the eyes, from the story in *Acts* xix, 24-8 of Demetrius, the Ephesian silversmith who made shrines for the temple of Diana

The Tree of Diana. *See* PHILOSOPHER S TREE

Diana's Worshippers. Midnight revellers So called because they return home by moonlight, and so, figuratively, put themselves under the protection of Diana (*q v*)

Diapason (dĭ a pā' son) The word is Greek (short for *dia pason chordon* through all the chords) and means an harmonious combina-

tion of notes, hence harmony itself Dryden says —

> From harmony, from heavenly harmony
>   The universal frame began,
> From harmony to harmony
> Thro' all the compass of the notes it ran,
> The diapason closing full in man
>   *Song for St Cecilia's Day*

According to the Pythagorean system, the world is a piece of harmony and man the full chord *Cp* MICROCOSM

Draper (drā' ă pēr) A sort of variegated white cloth, so called from Gr *dia*, through, *aspros*, white, white in places. The name is not connected with *Ypres*, nor with *jasper*

It is usually a repeated pattern of squares or lozenges, and in this sense is used in heraldry for a pattern on the field or an ordinary of other than heraldic bearings A more homely usage of the word applies it to a baby's "nappy"

Diavolo, Fra Michele Pozza, an insurgent of Calabria (1760-1806), round whom Scribe wrote a libretto for Auber's comic opera (1830).

Dibs. Money *Cp* Tips, gifts to schoolboys

The knuckle-bones of sheep used for gambling purposes are called dibbs, and Locke speaks of stones used for the same game, which he calls *dibstones*

Dicers' Oaths False as dicers' oaths. Worthless or untrustworthy, as when a gambler swears never to touch dice again (*Hamlet*, iii, 4)

Dichotomy (dĭk ot' ō mĭ) This comes from a Greek word meaning a cutting in two, and it is applied in biology and logic to a continuous division into pairs usually of opposite characteristics A good example of dichotomy in all its senses is the mistletoe, the main stem of which divides into two, each part of which divides again into two, and so on to the little berries which appear in twos.

Dick Richard, from *Ric,* short for the Anglo-Norman *Ricard*, the diminutive "Dicky" is also common

> Jockey of Norfolk [Lord Howard], be not too bold,
> For Dickon [or Dicky], thy master, is bought and sold,
>   *Richard III*, v, 3

(Dickon is Richard III)

That happened in the reign of Queen Dick— i e. never, there never was a Queen Richard

Richard Cromwell (1626-1712), son of the Protector whom, for a few months, he succeeded, was sometimes scornfully referred to as King Dick", and there were many popular sayings introducing the Crown as "Dick's hatband". Among them are —

Dick's hatband was made of sand His regal honours were "a rope of sand "

As queer as Dick's hatband Few things have been more ridiculous than the exaltation and abdication of the Protector's son

As tight as Dick's hatband The crown was too tight for him to wear with safety.

Dickens. *Dickens,* in **What the dickens,** is probably a euphemism for the devil, or Old *Nick,* and is nothing to do with Charles Dickens. In Low German we find its equivalent, *De duks !* Mrs Page says —

> I cannot tell what the dickens his name is —*Merry Wives of Windsor,* iii, 2

Dickey. In George III's time, a flannel petticoat

> A hundred instances I soon could pick ye—
> Without a cap we view the fair,
> The bosom heaving alto bare,
> The hips ashamed, forsooth, to wear a dicky.
>
> PETER PINDAR *Lord Auckland's Triumph*

It was afterwards applied to what were called false shirts—i e a starched shirt front worn over a flannel shirt, also to any other article of dress pretending to be what it isn't; and to leather aprons, children's bibs, the rumble behind a carriage, etc

Dicky. A donkey, especially in East Anglia, where it was anciently called a Dick-ass or Dicky-ass It is a term of endearment, as we call a pet bird a *dicky-bird* The ass is called Dicky (little Richard), Cuddy (little Cuthbert), Neddy (little Edward), Jack-ass, Moke or Mike, etc

Dicky Sam A native-born inhabitant of Liverpool, as Tim Bobbin is a native of Lancashire.

Didactic Poetry Poetry which uses the beauties of expression, imagination, sentiment, etc , for teaching some moral lesson, as Pope's *Essay on Man*, or the principle of some art or science, as Virgil's *Georgics*, Garth's *Dispensary*, or Darwin's *Botanic Garden* (Gr *didasko*, I teach)

Diddle. To cheat in a small way, as "I diddled him out of   " Edgar Allan Poe wrote an essay on "Diddling Considered as one of the Exact Sciences "

> A certain portion of the human race
> Has certainly a taste for being diddled.
>
> HOOD *A Black Job*

Jeremy Diddler An adept at raising money on false pretences From Kenny's farce called *Raising the Wind*

Diderick *See* DIETRICH.

Dido. The name given by Virgil to Elissa, founder and queen of Carthage She fell in love with Æneas, driven by a storm to her shores, who, after abiding awhile at Carthage, was compelled by Mercury to leave the hospitable queen Elissa, in grief, burnt herself to death on a funeral pile (*Æneid*, i, 494-iii, 650) Dido is really the Phœnician name of Astarte (Artemis), goddess of the moon and protectress of the citadel of Carthage.

It was Porson who said he could rhyme on any subject, and being asked to rhyme upon the three Latin gerunds, which, in the old Eton Latin grammar, are called *-di, -do, -dum*, gave this couplet —

> When Dido found Æneas would not come,
> She mourned in silence, and was Di-do dum(b).

Didoes, To cut up. (U S A 19th-century slang), to make merry, rag about

Didymus (did' i mus) This being the Greek word for a twin it was applied to St Thomas (*q v*) as the name Thomas means, in Aramaic, a twin

Die. The die is cast. The step is taken, and I cannot draw back So said Julius Cæsar when he crossed the Rubicon—*jacta alea esto*, let the die be cast!

> I have set my life upon the cast,
> And I will stand the hazard of the die
>
> *Richard III*, v, 4

Never say die. Never despair, never give up

Whom the gods love die young. This is from Menander—*Hon hoi theoi philousin apothneskei neos* Demosthenes has a similar apophthegm Plautus has the line, *Quem di diligunt adolescens moritur* (*Bacch* IV, vii, 18)

Die-hards In political phraseology *Die-hards* are the crusted members of any party who stick to their long-held theories through thick and thin, regardless of the changes that time or a newly awakened conscience may bring, those who would rather "die in the last ditch" than admit the possibility of their having been short-sighted

The **Die Hards** The Middlesex Regiment, the 57th Foot, which was raised in 1755 At the Battle of Albuera, May 16th, 1811, the regiment was hard pressed, Colonel Inglis (later General Sir William) who was badly wounded, refused to be taken to the rear, but lay where he fell, crying, "Die hard, men, die hard!"

Diego, San (săn dI ē' gō, dē ā' gō) A modification of Santiago (St James), champion of the red cross, and patron saint of Spain

Dies (dī' ēz) **Dies Alliensis.** *See* ALLIENSIS

Dies Iræ (Lat , Day of Wrath) A famous mediæval hymn on the last judgment, probably the composition of Thomas of Celano, a native of Abruzzi, who died in 1255 It is derived from the Vulgate version of *Joel* ii, 31, and is used by Catholics in the Mass for the Dead and on All Souls' Day Scott has introduced the opening into his *Lay of the Last Minstrel*

> Dies iræ, dies illa
> Solvet sæclum in favilla,
> Teste David cum Sibylla
>
> On that day, that wrathful day,
> David and the Sibyl say,
> Heaven and earth shall melt away

Dies non (Lat , a "not" day) A non-business day A law phrase, meaning a day when the courts do not sit and legal business is not transacted, as Sundays, the Purification, in Hilary term, the Ascension, in Easter term, St John the Baptist, in Trinity term, and All Saints', with All Souls', in Michaelmas term A contracted form of "*Dies non juridicus*," a non-judicial day

Dietrich of Bern (dē' trik) The name given by the German minnesingers to Theodoric the Great (454-526), king of the Ostrogoths (Bern=Verona) He appears in many Middle High German poems, especially the *Nibelungenlied*, where he is one of the liegemen of King Etzel

Dieu (dyē) **Dieu et mon droit** (God and my right) The parole of Richard I at the battle of Gisors (1198), meaning that he was no vassal of France, but owed his royalty to God alone The French were signally beaten, but the battle-word does not seem to have been adopted as the royal motto of England till the time of Henry VI

Dieu-donné. Name given to Louis XIV in his infancy

Difference. When Ophelia is distributing flowers (*Hamlet*, iv, 5) and says· "You must wear your rue with a difference," she is using the word in the heraldic sense and means "you must wear it as though it were marked in such a way as will slightly change the usual meaning of the plant," which was a symbol of repentance ("herb of grace"), or, on the assumption that she was offering the flower to the queen, Ophelia may have implied that they were both to wear rue the one as the affianced of Hamlet, eldest son of the late king, the other as the wife of Claudius his brother, and the cadet branch.

In heraldry, *Differences* or *marks of cadency* indicate the various branches of a family

The eldest son, during the lifetime of his father, bears a *label*, i e a bar or fillet, having three pendants broader at the bottom than at the top The second son bears a *crescent* The third, a *mullet* (i e. a star with five points) The fourth, a *martlet* The fifth, an *annulet* The sixth, a *fleur-de-lis* The seventh, a *rose*. The eighth, a *cross-moline* The ninth, a *double quatre foil.*

To **difference** is to make different by the superimposition of a further symbol

Digest (dī' jest) A compendium or summary arranged under convenient headings and titles, especially (and originally) the extracts from the body of Roman law compiled by Tribonian and sixteen assistants by order of Justinian, and arranged in 50 books (A D 533) *Cp* PANDECTS

Digger. An Australian The phrase was in use in that country before 1850, having come into prominence when gold was discovered In World War I the name was applied to Anzac troops fighting in Flanders and was revived in World War II *Digger* was the name given to the 17th-century Levellers (1649) who followed Winstanley and Everard in applying communistic principles to land ownership

Diggings. Lodgings, rooms, apartments A word imported from California and its gold diggings

My friend here wants to take diggings, and as you were complaining that you would get someone to go halves with you, I thought I had better bring you together.—SIR ARTHUR CONAN DOYLE: *A Study in Scarlet*, ch 1

Digits The first nine numerals, so called from the habit of counting as far as ten on the fingers. (Lat *digitus*, a finger) In astronomy, the word signifies the twelfth part of the diameter of the sun or moon; it is used principally in expressing the magnitude of an eclipse

Dii Penates (dī' i pe nā' tēz) (Lat). Household gods; now used colloquially for articles about the house that are specially prized *Cp.* LARES

Dilemma The horns of a dilemma A difficulty of such a nature that whatever way you attack it you encounter an equal amount of disagreeables Macbeth, after the murder of Duncan, was "on the horns of a dilemma " If he allowed Banquo to live, he had reason to believe that Banquo would supplant him, if, on the other hand, he resolved to keep the crown for which "he had 'filed his hands," he must "step further in blood," and cut Banquo off

"Lemma" means an assumption, a thing taken for granted (Gr *lambanein*, to take). "Dilemma" is a double lemma, a two edged sword, or a bull which will toss you whichever horn you lay hold of, called by the Schoolmen *argumentum cornutum*

A young rhetorician said to an old sophist, "Teach me to plead, and I will pay you when I gain a cause " He never had a cause till his old tutor master sued for payment, and he argued, "If I gain the cause I shall not pay you, because the judge will say I am not to pay, and if I lose my cause I shall not be required to pay, according to the terms of our agreement ' To this the master replied, "Not so, if you gain your cause you must pay me according to the terms of our agreement, and if you lose your cause the judge will condemn you to pay me "

Dilettante (di le tăn' ti) (Ital , pl *dilettanti*) An amateur of the fine arts, a would-be connoisseur, frequently applied to a trifling pretender to knowledge of some art or science.

Diligence. A four-wheeled stage-coach, drawn by four or more horses, common in France before the introduction of railroads The word is the same as the noun from *diligent*, which formerly meant speed, dispatch, as in Shakespeare's "If your diligence be not speedy I shall be there before you" (*King Lear*, i, 5)

Dilly. A stage-coach, as in the *Derby Dilly*. The word is, of course, an abbreviation of the above.

Dime (U S A.). A ten-cent piece.

Dime novel (U S A). Cheap publication of a lurid nature, originally costing a dime.

Dimensions. *See* FOURTH DIMENSION.

Dimetæ (dim' e tē) The ancient inhabitants of Carmarthenshire, Pembrokeshire, and Cardiganshire.

Dimissory (dim' i sôr i) **A letter dimissory** is a letter from the bishop of one diocese to some other bishop, giving leave for the bearer to be ordained by him Lat *di-mittere*, to send away

Dimity (dim' i ti) Stout cotton cloth woven with raised patterns It has been said to be so called from Damietta, in Egypt, but is really from the Gr *di-mitos* (double-thread). *Cp* SAMITE

Dine. To dine with Democritus To be cheated out of one's dinner Democritus was the derider, or philosopher, who laughed at men's folly.

To dine with Duke Humphrey; to dine with Sir Thomas Gresham. To go dinnerless. *See* HUMPHREY

To dine with Mohammed To die, and dine in paradise.

To dine with the cross-legged knights. That is, to have no dinner at all *Cp.* "to dine with Duke Humphrey " The knights referred to are the stone effigies of the Temple Church, where, at one time, lawyers met their clients

Dingbats. An Australian colloquial term for delirium tremens

Ding-dong. A ding-dong battle. A fight in good earnest. *Ding-dong* is an onomatopœic word, reproducing the sound of a bell, and here the suggestion is that the blows fell regularly and unfalteringly, like the hammer-strokes of a bell.

Dinkum (ding' kum) (Austr) Generally something genuine or honest. **Hard dinkum,** meaning hard work, was first used in Australia by Rolf Boldrewood in *Robbery Under Arms,* 1881 In World War I the Australian troops were called Dinks or Dinkums The adjective **dinky,** with the sense of pretty or nice, is probably from the Scottish *to dink,* or dress up

Dinmont. *See* SHEEP

Dandie Dinmont. *See* DANDIE

Dinnyhayser (Austr) A knock-out blow, as delivered by the fighter Dinny Hayes

Dinos *See* HORSE.

Dint. By dint of war : by dint of argument ; by dint of hard work Dint means a blow or striking (A S *dynt*), whence perseverance, power exerted, force; it also means the indentation made by a blow

Diogenes (dī oj' e nēz) A noted Greek cynic philosopher (about 412-323 B.C.), who, according to Seneca, lived in a tub Alexander the Great so admired him that he said, "If I were not Alexander I would wish to be Diogenes "

> The whole world was not half so wide
> To Alexander, when he cried
> Because he had but one to subdue,
> As was a paltry narrow tub to
> Diogenes   BUTLER *Hudibras,* i, 3

Diogenes was also the surname of Romanus IV, Emperor of the East, 1067-71

Diomedes (dī ō mē' dēz) or **Diomed.** In Greek legend, a hero of the siege of Troy, among the Greeks second only to Achilles in bravery With Odysseus he removed the Palladium from the citadel of Troy He appears as the lover of Cressida in Boccaccio's *Filostrato* and in later works

Diomedean exchange, in which all the benefit is on one side. The expression is founded on an incident related by Homer in the *Iliad* Glaucus recognizes Diomed on the battlefield, and the friends change armour.—

> For Diomed's brass arms, of mean device,
> For which nine oxen paid (a vulgar price),
> He gave his own, of gold divinely wrought,
> An hundred beeves the shining purchase bought
>   POPE *Iliad,* vi.

Dione (dī ō' nī) A Titaness, daughter of Oceanus and Tethys, and mother by Jupiter of Venus The name has been applied to Venus herself, and Julius Cæsar, who claimed descent from her, was hence sometimes called *Dionæus Cæsar*

> So young Dione, nursed beneath the waves,
> And rocked by Nereids in their coral caves
> Lisped her sweet tones, and tried her tender smiles
>   DARWIN *Economy of Vegetation,* ii

Dionysia. *See* BACCHANALIA

Dionysus (dī ō nī' sus). The Greek name of Bacchus (*q v*)

Diophantine Analysis (dī ō făn' tin). Finding commensurate values of squares, cubes, triangles, etc ; or the sum of a given number of squares which is itself a square, or a certain number of squares, etc , which are in arithmetical progression, so named from Diophantus, a celebrated Alexandrian mathematician of the 4th century A D

The following examples will give some idea of the theory —
1 To find two whole numbers, the *sum* of whose squares is a square,
2 To find three square numbers which are in arithmetical progression,
3 To find a number from which two given squares being severally subtracted, each of the remainders is a square

Dioscuri Castor and Pollux (*q v*). Gr *Dios kouros,* sons of Zeus

The horses of the Dioscuri. Cyllaros and Harpagos *See* HORSE

Dip The **dip of the horizon** is the apparent slope of the horizon as seen by an observer standing above sea level This slope is due to the convexity of the earth

Dip of the needle is the inclination of a compass needle vertically At the magnetic poles this is 90° and at the magnetic equator 0°.

To dip the flag is to lower it for a moment and then hoist again, as a form of salute

To dip the headlights of a car is to lower them and turn them on again

To go for a dip. To go bathing This is a very old English phrase

Dip. A cheap and common kind of candle, made by dipping into melted tallow the cotton which forms the wick

A farthing dip, like *a rush,* is a synonym for something that is almost valueless.

Dipping (U S A) The name given in Virginia and N. Carolina to the habit, there once prevalent, of chewing snuff

Diphthera (dif' thē ra) (Gr) A piece of prepared hide or leather, specifically, the skin of the goat Amalthea, on which Jove wrote the destiny of man. **Diphtheria** is an infectious disease of the throat, so called from its tendency to form a false membrane

Diploma (dip lō' má) (Gr) Literally, something folded. Diplomas used to be written on parchment, folded, and sealed The word is applied to licences given to graduates to assume a degree, to clergymen, to physicians, etc , and also to the credentials of an ambassador. etc , authorizing him to represent his Government, whence *diplomacy,* the negotiations, privileges, tact, etc , of a *diplomatist.*

Diplomatics. The name formerly (and sometimes still) given to the science of palæography —that is, deciphering and investigating old charters, diplomas, titles, etc Papebroch, the Bollandist, originated the study in 1675, but Mabillon, another Bollandist, reduced it to a science in his *De re Diplomatica,* 1681 Toustain and Tassin further developed it in their treatise entitled *Nouveau Traité de Diplomatique,* 1750-60.

Diptych (Gr *diptuchos,* folded in two) A register folded into two leaves, opening like a book The Romans kept in a book of this sort the names of their magistrates, and Catholics employed the word for the registers in which were written the names of those who were to be specially commemorated when oblations were made for the dead The name is also given to altar pieces and other paintings that fold together in the middle on a hinge.

Dircæan Swan. Pindar, so called from Dirce, a fountain in the neighbourhood of Thebes, the poet's birthplace (518-442 B C) The fountain is named from Dirce, who was put to death by the sons of Antiope for her brutal treatment of their mother, and was changed into the spring by Bacchus.

Direct Action. A method of attaining, or attempting to attain, political ends by non-political means (such as striking or with-drawing labour)

Direct tax. One collected *directly* from the owner of property subject to the tax, as the income-tax *Indirect taxes* are taxes upon marketable commodities, such as tea and sugar, the tax on which is added to the article, and is thus paid by the purchaser indirectly

Direction of Labour is a phrase that came into being in World War II to describe the administrative action taken by the British Government to ensure a supply of labour for essential munition and other works All persons between certain ages, if not in the Forces, were obliged to register, they were then allocated to essential work in the neigh-bourhood of their homes, and were unable to change this except through a Labour Exchange. This was revoked in 1945, but in 1947 a similar order was issued by the Minister of Labour, though only controlling the *re-employment* of men and women, without compulsory registra-tion

Directory, The. In French history, the con-stitution of 1795, when the executive was vested in five "Directors," one of whom retired every year After a sickly existence of four years, it came to an end at Napoleon's *coup d'état* of 18 Brumaire (November 9th), 1799.

Dirleton. Doubting with Dirleton, and resolving those doubts with Stewart. Doubting and answering those doubts, but doubting still It is a Scottish phrase; and the allusion is to the *Doubts and Questions in the Law* (1698), by Sir John Nisbet of Dirleton, the Lord President, and Sir James Stewart's *Dirleton's Doubts and Questions . Resolved and Answered* (1715) Of the former work Lord Chancellor Hard-wicke remarked, "His *Doubts* are better than most people's *certainties* "

Dirt. The origin of this word is Teutonic and we find its equivalent in the Icelandic *drit,* meaning excrement In modern usage the sense has been extended to include loose or packed soil, alluvial earth, gravel, etc., and, figuratively, obscenity of any kind, especially in language

Pay dirt. Soil containing gold or diamonds, whichever is being sought

Dirt cheap. Very low-priced

Throw plenty of dirt and some will be sure to stick. Scandal always leaves a trail behind, find plenty of fault, and some of it will be believed. In Lat , *Fortiter calumniari, aliquid adhærēbit*

To eat dirt. To put up with insults and mortification

Dirt-track racing is a form of motor-cycle racing on a track of cinders or similar sub-stance Features of the sport are the shortness of the laps (about 440 yards) and the sharpness of the turns It was introduced into England from Australia in 1928

The Dirty Half-Hundred. The 50th Foot (The Queen's Own), so called because during a Peninsular War battle the men wiped their sweaty faces with their black cuffs.

The Dirty Shirts The 101st Foot (2nd Mun-ster Fusiliers), which fought at Delhi in their shirt-sleeves (1857)

Dis The Roman name of the Greek Pluto (*q.v*)

> Proserpine gathering flowers,
> Herself a fairer flower, by gloomy Dis
> Was gathered
>   MILTON· *Paradise Lost,* iv, 270

Disastrous Peace, The (*La Paix Malheureuse*) A name given to the Treaty of Câteau Cam-bresis (1559), which followed the battle of Gravelines It was signed by France, Spain, and England, and by it France ceded the Low Countries to Spain, and Savoy, Corsica, and 200 forts to Italy But she retained Calais

Discalced. *See* BAREFOOTED

Discharge Bible, The *See* BIBLE, SPECIALLY NAMED

Disciples of Christ. *See* CAMPBELLITES

Discipline, A. A scourge used for penitential purposes
> Before the cross and altar a lamp was still burning, and on the floor lay a small discipline or penitential scourge of small cord and wire, the lashes of which were stained with recent blood —SCOTT *The Talis-man,* ch iv

This is a transferred sense of one of the ecclesiastical uses of the word—the morti-fication of the flesh by penance.

Discord. Literally, severance of hearts (Lat. *discorda*) It is the opposite of *concord,* the coming together of hearts In music, it means disagreement of sounds, as when a note is followed by or played with another which is disagreeable to a musical ear

The apple of discord. *See* APPLE

Discount. At a discount. Not in demand, little valued, less esteemed than formerly; below par (Lat *dis-computare,* to depreciate)

Dished. I was dished out of it. Cheated out of it; or rather, someone else contrived to obtain it When one is *dished* he is completely done for, and the allusion is to food which, when it is quite *done,* is *dished.* Hence, "dishing the Whigs "
> Where's Brummel? Dished!
>   BYRON *Don Juan*

Dismal Science, The. *See* SCIENCE.

Dismas, St. *See* DYSMAS.

Disney Professor. The Professor of Archæology at Cambridge. This chair was founded in 1851

by John Disney (1779-1857), who also bequeathed his collection of marble to the University.

Dispensation (Lat *dispensatio*, from *dis-* and *pendere*, to weigh). The system which God chooses to *dispense* or establish between Himself and man The dispensation of *Adam* was that between Adam and God, the dispensation of *Abraham*, and that of *Moses*, were those imparted to these holy men, the *Gospel* dispensation is that explained in the Gospels

A **dispensation from the Pope**. Permission to *dispense* with something enjoined, a licence to do what is forbidden, or to omit what is commanded by the law of the Church, as distinct from the moral law

Displaced Persons, a phrase that arose in World War II when it was applied to the millions of homeless and uprooted people in Germany who had either been imported there by the German government as slaves when their homes were overrun and destroyed or who had lost their homes in the ravages caused by the Russian invasion Colloquially known as "Displaced persons" since their rehabilitation presented such appalling problems to the soldiers first charged with the task

Distaff. The staff from which the flax was drawn in spinning, hence, figuratively, woman's work, and a woman herself, the allusion being to the old custom of women, who spun from morning to night. *Cp* SPINSTER.

> I blush that we should owe our lives to such
> A king of distaffs! BYRON· *Sardanapalus*, II, 1

St Distaff's Day. January 7th So called because the Christmas festival terminated on Twelfth Day, and on the day following the women returned to their distaffs or daily occupations It is also called *Rock Day*, "rock" being an old name for the distaff

> Give St Distaff all the right,
> Then give Christmas sport good night,
> And next morrow every one
> To his own vocation   (1657.)
> What! shall a woman with a rock drive thee away?
> Fye on thee, traitor!   *Digby Mysteries*

The distaff side The female side of a family; a branch descended from the female side

To have tow on the distaff. To have work in hand

> He hadde more tow on his distaf
> Than Gerveys knew
>   CHAUCER· *Miller's Tale*, 588

Distemper An undue mixture (Lat *distemperare*, to mix amiss). In medicine a distemper arises from the redundancy of certain secretions or morbid humours The distemper in dogs is an undue quantity of secretions manifested by a running from the eyes and nose

Distemper, the paint, is so called because, instead of being mixed with oil, it is mixed with a vehicle (as size or glue) that is soluble in water

Ditch. To ditch an aeroplane is to make a forced landing on the sea, to throw away

Dithyrambic (dith i ram' bik) (Gr *dithyrambo*, a choric hymn) Dithyrambic poetry was originally a wild, impetuous kind of Dorian lyric in honour of Bacchus, traditionally ascribed to the invention of Arion of Lesbos (about 620 B C), who has hence been called the father of dithyrambic poetry

Dittany (dit' a ni) This plant (*Origanum dictamnus*), so named from Dicte in Crete, where it grew in profusion, was anciently credited with many medicinal virtues, especially in enabling arrows to be drawn from wounds and curing such wounds In Tasso's *Jerusalem Delivered* (Bk ix) Godfrey is healed in this way

> Stags and hinds, when deeply wounded with darts, arrows, and bolts, if they do but meet the herb called dittany, which is common in Candia, and eat a little of it, presently the shafts come out, and all is well again, even as kind Venus cured her beloved by-blow Æneas —*Rabelais (Urquhart and Motteux)* Bk iv, ch lxii

Ditto (dit' ō) (Ital *detto*, said, from Lat *dictum*) That which has been said before, the same or a similar thing The word is often, in writing, contracted to *do*

A **suit of dittoes** Coat, waistcoat, and trousers all alike, or all ditto (the same).

To say ditto. To endorse somebody else's expressed opinion

Divan (Tur and Pers) Primarily, a collection of sheets, hence, a collection of poems, a register (and the registrar) of accounts, the office where accounts are kept, a council or tribunal, a long seat or bench covered with cushions, a court of justice, and a custom house (whence *douane*) The word, in its ramifications and extensions, is somewhat like our *board* (*q v*); in England its chief meanings are (1) a comfortable sofa, (2) a bed without head-board or foot-board, and formerly (3) a public smoking-saloon.

Dive. A low resort The phrase, of 19th-century U.S A origin, spread to common use in England in the 20th century

Dives (dī' vēz) The name popularly given to the rich man (Lat *dives*) in the parable of the Rich Man and Lazarus (*Luke* xvi, 19). it is taken direct from the Vulgate

> Lazar and Dives liveden diversely,
> And diverse guerdon hadden they ther-by,
>   CHAUCER *Somnour's Tale*, 169

Divide. When the members in the House of Commons interrupt a speaker by crying out *divide*, they mean, bring the debate to an end and put the motion to the vote—*i e* let the ayes divide from the noes, one going into one lobby, and the others into the other

Divide and govern (Lat *divide et impera*) A maxim of Machiavelli (1469-1527) meaning that if you divide a nation into parties, or set your enemies at loggerheads, you can have your own way Coke, in his *Institutes* (pt. iv, cap i) speaks of the maxim as "that exploded adage "

> Every city or house divided against itself shall not stand —*Matt* xii, 25

Divination (div i nā' shun) There are numerous species of divination referred to in the Bible The following are the most notable, and to most of these there are many other allusions in the Bible beside those indicated

> JUDICIAL ASTROLOGY (*Dan* ii, 2)
> WITCHCRAFT (1 *Sam* xxviii)
> ENCHANTMENT (2 *Kings* xxi, 6)

CASTING LOTS (*Josh* xviii, 6)
By NECROMANCY (1 *Sam* xxviii, 12)
By RHABDOMANCY or rods (*Hos.* iv, 12)
By TERAPHIM or household idols (*Gen* xxxi, 1 *Sam* xv, 23, R V.)
By HEPATOSCOPY or inspecting the liver of animals (*Ezek* xxi, 21, 26)
By DREAMS and their interpretations (*Gen* xxxvii, 10)
Divination by fire, air, and water, thunder, lightning, and meteors, etc
The *Urim and Thummim* was a prophetic breastplate worn by the High Priest
(Consult *Gen* xxxvii, 5-11, xl, xli, 1 *Sam.* xxviii. 12, 2 *Chron* xxxiii, 6, *Prov.* xvi, 33; *Ezek* xxi, 21; *Hos* iii, 4, 5, etc)

Divine, The. Theophrastus, the name of the Greek philosopher (390-287 B C), means "the Divine Speaker," an epithet bestowed on him by Aristotle, on account of which he changed his name from Tyrtamus

Hypatia (*c* 370-415), who presided over the Neoplatonic School at Alexandria, was known as "the Divine Pagan."

Jean de Ruysbroek (*see* ECSTATIC DOCTOR) was also called "the Divine Doctor "

A name given to Michael Angelo (1475-1564) was "the Divine Madman "

Ariosto (1474-1533), Italian poet, Raphael (1483-1520) the painter, Luis de Morales (1509-86), a Spanish religious painter, and Ferdinand de Herrera (1534-67), the Spanish lyric poet, were all known as "the Divine "

The Divine Plant Vervain *See* HERBA SACRA.

The divine right of kings The notion that kings reign by direct ordinance of God, quite apart from the will of the people This phrase was much used in the 17th century on account of the pretensions of the Stuart kings, and the idea arose from the Old Testament, where kings are called "God's anointed," because they were God's vicars on earth, when the Jews changed their theocracy for a monarchy.

The right divine of kings to govern wrong.
POPE *Dunciad*, iv, 188

Divining rod. A forked branch of hazel, one prong of which is held in either hand The inclination of the rod, when controlled by a qualified person, called a *diviner*, is said to indicate by its movements the presence of water-springs, precious metal, oil, etc

Divining, or *dowsing* (*see* DOWSE), as it is also called, has been the subject of numerous scientific investigations, and while these have shown that the claims of diviners can in many cases be substantiated, there is still no satisfactory scientific explanation of the phenomenon. This method of discovering hidden treasure naturally lends itself to the exploitation of the fraudulent and the "gulling" of the credulous

Division. The sign — for division was brought into use by John Pell (1611-85), the noted Cambridge mathematician who became Professor of Mathematics at Amsterdam in 1643

In its *military* sense a *division* is the largest formation in an army which has a constant establishment, so designed as to be self-contained with its own services. Invented by Napoleon In the British army it totals 15,000 men

Divisionism. A school of painting in late-19th-century France which applied complementary colours in separate dabs side by side,
10*

relying on the eye of the beholder to blend them into the desired effect. The protagonist of Divisionism was Georges Seurat (1859-91).

Divorcement A bill of divorcement is a phrase going back to the days of the old divorce procedure Before the Divorce Act of 1857 divorce could be granted only by the ecclesiastical courts of the various dioceses Even then remarriage by either of the parties was prohibited, except a special Bill was taken to Parliament and passed after debate—a procedure so expensive that few could afford it

Divus (dī' vūs) (Lat , a god, godlike). After the Augustan period this was conferred as an epithet on deceased Roman emperors, more with the idea of canonizing them, of proclaiming them to be "of blessed memory," than with that of enrolling them among the divinities Thus, *Divus Augustus* means "Augustus of blessed memory," not "Divine Augustus "

The new cult of the "divi imperatores" spread throughout the Empire, and became a force which helped to weld together the populations and to secure their loyalty to the ruling power The cult gave a new semblance of dignity to the Senate At the end of every reign it sat in judgment and decided whether the dead emperor was to be enrolled among the "divi" or whether his memory was to be reckoned accursed ('damnatio memoriæ") —J S REID (in *A Companion to Latin Studies*, 1910, ch vi).

Dixie Land. The Southern States of the U S A. The name, according to one story, originated in the "dix," or ten-dollar bank-note of Louisiana When times were prosperous, these bills circulated so freely that Louisiana was called the "land of dixies " It has also been said to have got its name from "Mason and *Dixon's* Line" (*q v*), which formed the boundary between the slave-holding and the "free" States The explanation given below is the most likely to be correct —

When slavery existed in New York, one DIXIE owned a large tract of land on Manhattan Island, and a large number of slaves The increase of the slaves and of the abolition sentiment caused an emigration of the slaves to more thorough and secure slave sections, and the negroes who were thus sent off (many being born there) naturally looked back to their old houses, where they had lived in clover, with feelings of regret, as they could not imagine any place like DIXIE'S Hence it became synonymous with an ideal locality combining ease, comfort, and material happiness of every description.—*Charlestown Courier* June 11th, 1885

A song of this name, by Albert Pike, was adopted as the marching song of the Southern armies —

Advance the flag of Dixie!
Hurrah! Hurrah!
For Dixie's land we'll take our stand
To live and die for Dixie

Dixie, the soldier's name for a large cooking kettle, is the Hindi *degshi*, a pot, vessel

Dizzy. A nickname of Benjamin Disraeli (Lord Beaconsfield) (1805-81).

Djinn. *See* JINN

Djinnestan. The realm of the jinns or genii of Oriental mythology

Do (in *Music*) *See* DOH

Do. A contraction of *ditto* (*q v*).

Do. A verb, and auxiliary, that forms part of countless phrases and lends itself to almost countless uses. Its chief modern significations are —

(Transitive) To put, as in *To do to death*; to bestow, cause to befall, etc , as *It did him no harm, To do a good turn*, to perform, perpetrate, execute, etc , as *To do one's work, Thou shalt do no murder, What will he do with it? All is done and finished*

(Intransitive) To exert actively, to act in some way, as *Let us do or die, I have done with you, How do you do? I'm doing very well, thank you, That will do*

(Causal and Auxiliary) Used instead of a verb just used, as *He plays as well as you do* Periphrastically as an auxiliary of the Pres and Past Indicative and the Imperative, used for the sake of emphasis, euphony, or clarity, also in negative and interrogative sentences *I DO wish you would let me alone, Not a word did he say, Billiards and drinking do make the money fly, Do you like jazz? I do not care for it Do tell me where you've been! Don't stop!*

A do. A regular swindle a fraud, a party.

Do as you would be done by. Behave to others as you would have them behave to you

To do away with. To abolish, put an end to, destroy entirely

To do for. To act for or manage for *A man ought to do well for his children*, a landlady *does for* her lodgers Also, to ruin destroy, wear out. *I'll do for him.* I'll ruin him utterly, or even, I'll kill him; *taken in and done for*, cheated and fleeced, *this watch is about done for*, it's nearly worn out

To do it on one's head. Said of doing something with consummate ease, a rather scornful expression. "I bet you couldn't walk a mile in seven minutes"; "Pooh! I could do it on my head!"

To do on. *See* DON

To do one, to do one down, or brown, to do one out of something To cheat him, or trick him out of something, to get the better of him

To do one proud. To flatter him; to treat him in an exceptionally lavish and hospitable way

To do oneself proud, or **well.** To give oneself a treat

To do the grand, amiable, etc To act (usually with some ostentation) in the manner indicated by the adjective.

To do up To repair, put in order "This chair wants doing up," *i e* renovating Also, to make tidy, to put up or fasten a parcel, and to wear out, tire "I'm quite done up," I'm worn out, exhausted *Cp* DUP

To do up brown (U S A) To do thoroughly, in a good sense, or bad—as beating someone up *badly*.

To do without so-and-so. To deny oneself it, to manage without it

To have to do with. To have dealings or intercourse with, to have relation to "That has nothing to do with the case "

Well to do. In good circumstances, well off, well provided for

Dobbin A steady old horse, a child's horse **Dobby,** a silly old man, also a house-elf similar to a brownie All these are one and the same word, an adaptation of *Robin*, diminutive of *Robert*

> Sober Dobbin lifts his clumsy heel
> BLOOMFIELD *Farmer's Boy* (Winter).

The dobbie elves lived in the house, were very thin and shaggy, very kind to servants and children, and did many a little service when people had their hands full

> The Dobby's walk was within the inhabited domains of the Hall.—SCOTT: *Peveril of the Peak*, ch x

Docetes An early Gnostic heretical sect, which maintained that Jesus Christ was divine only, and that His visible form, the crucifixion, the resurrection, etc , were merely illusions (The word is Greek, and means *phantomists*)

Doch-an-doris (Gaelic). A Scottish term made familiar by one of Sir Harry Lauder's songs, for a stirrup-cup, a final drink before saying "Good-night" and going home. Variants are *doch-an-doroch, deoch-an-dorus*, etc

Dock Brief In English law anyone accused of an offence and brought to trial is entitled to defend himself or be defended by counsel When a prisoner in the dock pleads inability to employ counsel, the presiding judge can instruct a barrister present in court to undertake the defence, a small fee for this being paid by the court.

Doctor. A name given to various adulterated or falsified articles because they are "doctored," *i e* treated in some way that strengthens them or otherwise makes them capable of being passed off as something better than they actually are Thus a mixture of milk, water, nutmeg, and rum is called *Doctor*, the two former ingredients being "doctored" by the two latter.

Brown sherry is so called by licensed victuallers because it is concocted from a thin wine with the addition of unfermented juice and some spirituous liquor

In nautical slang the ship's cook is known as "the doctor," because he is supposed to "doctor" the food, and a seventh son used to be so dubbed from the popular superstition that he was endowed with power to cure agues, the king's evil, and other diseases

Doctored dice. Loaded dice, dice which are so "doctored" as to make them turn up winning numbers, also called simply *doctors*

> "The whole antechamber is full, my lord—knights and squires, doctors and dicers "
> "The dicers with their doctors in their pockets, I presume."—SCOTT *Peveril of the Peak*, ch xxviii.

Doctor Fell.

> I do not like thee, Dr Fell,
> The reason why I cannot tell,
> But this I know, I know full well,
> I do not like thee, Dr. Fell.

These well-known lines are by the "facetious" Tom Brown (1663-1704), and the person referred to was Dr. John Fell, Dean of Christ Church (1625-86), who expelled him, but said he would remit the sentence if Brown translated the thirty-third Epigram of Martial

> Non amo te, Zabidi, nec possum dicere quare
> Hoc tantum possum dicere non amo te

The above is the translation, which is said to have been given impromptu

It was this Dr Fell who in 1667 presented to the University of Oxford a complete type-foundry containing punches and matrices of a large number of founts—Arabic, Syriac, Coptic and other learned alphabets, as well as the celebrated 'Fell" Roman

The three best doctors are Dr Quiet, Dr. Diet, and Dr. Merryman.

Si tibi deficiant medici, medici tibi fiant
Hæc tria, Mens-læta, Requies, Moderam-Diæta

To doctor the accounts. To falsify them The allusion is to drugging wine, beer, etc, and to adulteration generally

To doctor the wine. To drug it, or strengthen it with brandy, to make weak wine stronger, and "sick" wine more palatable The fermentation of cheap wines is increased by fermentable sugar As such wines fail in aroma, connoisseurs smell at their wine.

To have a cat doctored. A colloquialism for having a young tom-cat "cut," or castrated

To put the doctor on a man. To cheat him The allusion to "doctored dice" is obvious.

Who shall decide when doctors disagree? When authorities differ, the question *sub judice* must be left undecided (POPE: *Moral Essays*, ep iii, line 1)

Doctors of the Church. Certain early Christian Fathers, especially four in the Greek (or Eastern) Church and four in the Latin (or Western) Church

(a) *Eastern Church* St. Athanasius of Alexandria (331), who defended the divinity of Christ against the Arians; St. Basil the Great of Cæsarea (379) and his co-worker St. Gregory of Nazianzen (376), and the eloquent St John Chrysostom (398), Archbishop of Constantinople

(b) *Western Church* St Jerome (420), translator of the Vulgate, St. Ambrose (397), Bishop of Milan, St Augustine (430), Bishop of Hippo, and St Gregory the Great (604), the pope who sent Augustine, the missionary, to England

Dr. Faustus. *See* FAUST

Dr. Fell. *See above.*

Doctor Mirabilis. Roger Bacon (1214-92).

Dr Sangrado.⎫
Dr. Slop ⎬*See under their names.*
Dr. Syntax. ⎭

Doctors of Learning, Piety, etc.
Admirable Doctor Roger Bacon (1214-92).
Angelic Doctor St. Thomas Aquinas (1224-74).
Divine Doctor John Ruysbroek (1294-1381)
Invincible Doctor: William Occam (1276-1347)
Irrefragable Doctor. Alexander of Hales (d 1245)
Mellifluous Doctor. St Bernard of Clairvaux (1091-1153)
Seraphic Doctor St Bonaventura (1221-74).
Subtle Doctor Duns Scotus (1265-1308)
Wonderful Doctor: Roger Bacon (1214-92).

Doctors' Commons A locality near St Paul's, where the ecclesiastical courts were formerly held, wills preserved. and marriage licences granted, and where was held the common table of the Association of Doctors of Civil Law in London (dissolved 1858) To "common ' (q v) means to dine together; and the doctors had to dine there four days in each term The actual building was demolished in 1867

Documentary film. A film devised and produced for the sole purpose of giving a realistic and accurate picture of some aspect of everyday life or work

Doddypoll. A blockhead, a silly ass. *Poll*, of course, is the head, and *doddy* is the modern *dotty*, silly, from the verb *to dote*, to be foolish or silly. There is an Elizabethan romantic comedy (about 1595) called *The Wisdom of Doctor Doddypoll*, thought by some to be by George Peele

As wise as Dr Doddypoll. Not wise at all; a dunce

Dodger. A "knowing fellow" One who knows all the tricks and ways of London life, and profits by such knowledge

(U S A) A hard cake, or biscuit

The Artful Dodger. The sobriquet of John Dawkins, a young thief in Dickens's *Oliver Twist*

Dodman. A snail; the word is still in use in Norfolk Fairfax, in his *Bulk and Selvedge* (1674), speaks of "a snayl or dodman "

Doddiman, doddiman, put out your horn,
Here comes a thief to steal your corn
Norfolk rhyme.

Hodmandod is another variation of the same word

Dodona (do dō' nà) A famous oracle in the village of Dodona in Epiros, and the most ancient of Greece It was dedicated to Zeus, and the oracles were delivered from the tops of oak and other trees, the rustling of the wind in the branches being interpreted by the priests. Also, brazen vessels and plates were suspended from the branches, and these, being struck together when the wind blew, gave various sounds from which responses were concocted Hence the Greek phrase *Kalkos Dodones* (brass of Dodona), meaning a babbler, or one who talks an infinite deal of nothing

The black pigeons of Dodona *See under* PIGEON

Dodson and Fogg. The lawyers, employed by the plaintiff in the famous case of "Bardell v. Pickwick" (*Pickwick Papers*), typical of the unscrupulous solicitors who battened on the public before the law reforms of the mid-19th century.

Doe. John Doe and Richard Roe. Any plaintiff and defendant in an action of ejectment They were sham names used at one time to save certain "niceties of law"; but the clumsy device was abolished in 1852 Any mere imaginary persons, or men of straw. The names "John o' Noakes" and "Tom Styles" are similarly used

Doeg (dō′eg) In Dryden's *Absalom and Achitophel* (*q v*), is meant for Elkanah Settle, a poet who wrote satires upon Dryden, but was no match for his great rival

Doff is do-off, as "Doff your hat." So *Don* is do-on, as "Don your clothes." *Dup* is do-up, as "Dup the door" (*q v*)

> Doff thy harness, youth
> And tempt not yet the brushes of the war
> *Troilus and Cressida*, v, 3

Dog. This article is subdivided into five parts ·
  1 Dogs in Phrases and Colloquialisms
  2. Dogs of note in the Classics and in legend
  3 Dogs famous in History, Literature, Fiction, etc
  4 Dogs in Symbolism and Metaphor
  5 Dog—or dog's—in combination

(1) IN PHRASES AND COLLOQUIALISMS

A black dog has walked over him. Said of a sullen person Horace tells us that the sight of a black dog with its pups was an unlucky omen, and the devil has been frequently symbolized by a black dog.

A cat and dog life. *See* CAT (To live a, etc)

A dead dog Something utterly worthless. A Biblical phrase (*see* 1 *Sam* xxiv, 14, "After whom is the king of Israel come out? After a dead dog?") *Cp also* Is THY SERVANT, etc , *below*.

A dirty dog. One morally filthy, one who talks and acts nastily In the East the dog is still held in abhorrence, as the scavenger of the streets. "Him that dieth in the city shall the dogs eat" (1 *Kings* xiv, 11)

A dog in a doublet A bold, resolute fellow In Germany and Flanders the strong dogs employed for hunting the wild boar were dressed in a kind of buff doublet buttoned to their bodies Rubens and Sneyders have represented several in their pictures A false friend is called *a dog in one's doublet*

A dog in the manger. A churlish fellow, who will not use what is wanted by another, nor yet let the other have it to use. The allusion is to the well-known fable of a dog that fixed his place in a manger, would not allow an ox to come near the hay and would not eat it himself

A living dog is better than a dead lion. The meanest thing with life in it is better than the noblest without The saying is from *Eccles* ix, 4. The Italians say "A live ass is worth more than a dead doctor."

A dog's age. A very long time

A surly dog. A human being of a surly temper *Dog* is often used for 'chap" or "fellow" thus we have *a gay dog*, a man who is always out and about on pleasure, and a *sad dog*, which means much the same, but carries with it a touch of reproof

A well-bred dog hunts by nature Breeding "tells." The French proverb is "*Bon chien chasse de race*"

Barking dogs seldom bite. *See* BARK

Brag's a good dog, etc *See* BRAG.

Dog don't eat dog. A similar phrase to "There's honour among thieves."

Dogs howl at death. A widespread superstition

> In the rabbinical book it saith
> The dogs howl when, with icy breath,
> Great Sammael, the angel of death,
> Takes thro the town his flight
> LONGFELLOW *Golden Legend* iii

Every dog has his day. You may crow over me to-day, but my turn will come by and by. In Latin *Hodie mihi, cras tibi* "To-day to me, tomorrow to thee." "*Nunc mihi, nunc tibi, benigna*" (*fortuna*), fortune visits every man once, she favours me now, but she will favour you in your turn

> Thus every dog at last will have his day—
> He who this morning smiled, at night may sorrow,
> The grub to-day's a butterfly to-morrow.
> PETER PINDAR *Odes of Condolence*

Give a dog a bad name and hang him. If you want to do anyone a wrong, throw dirt on him or rail against him When once a person's reputation has been besmirched he might as well be hanged as try to rehabilitate himself

He who has a mind to beat his dog will easily find a stick. If you want to abuse a person, you will easily find something to blame. Dean Swift says, "If you want to throw a stone, every lane will furnish one."

Hungry dogs will eat dirty pudding Those really hungry are not particular about what they eat and are by no means dainty The Proverb is given by Heywood (1546) "To the hungry soul every bitter thing is sweet" (*Prov* xxvii, 7) "When bread is wanting oaten cakes are excellent."

When Darius in his flight from Greece drank from a ditch defiled with dead carcasses, he declared he had never drunk so pleasantly before

I am his Highness' dog at Kew, Pray tell me, sir, whose dog are you? Frederick Prince of Wales had a dog given him by Alexander Pope, and these words are said to have been engraved on his collar They are still sometimes quoted with reference to an overbearing, bumptious person.

Is thy servant a dog, that he should do this thing? Said in contempt when one is asked to do something derogatory or beneath him. The phrase is (slightly altered) from 2 *Kings* viii, 13

> Sydney Smith, when asked if it was true that he was about to sit to Landseer, the animal painter, for his portrait, replied, "What' is thy servant *a dog* that he should do this thing?"

It was the story of the dog and the shadow. A case of one who gives up the substance for its shadow The allusion is to the well-known fable of the dog who dropped his bone into the stream because he opened his mouth to seize the reflection of it.

Lazy as Lawrence's, or Ludlam's dog *See* LAZY

Let sleeping dogs lie, don't wake a sleeping dog Let well alone, if some contemplated course of action is likely to cause trouble or land you in difficulties you had better avoid it.

> It is nought good a sleping hound to wake,
> Nor yeve a wight a cause to devyne.
> CHAUCER *Troilus and Criseyde*, iii, 764

Love me love my dog. If you love me you must put up with my defects

Not to have a word to throw at a dog. Said of one who is sullen or sulky.

Cel Why, cousin! why, Rosalind! Cupid have mercy! Not a word?
Ros. Not one to throw at a dog
As You Like It, i, 3

Old dogs will not learn new tricks People in old age do not readily conform to new ways.

St. Roch and his dog. Emblematic of inseparable companions, like "a man and his shadow " One is never seen without the other *See* ROCH, ST.

Sick as a dog. Very sick We also say "Sick as a cat " *See* CAT The Bible speaks of dogs returning to their vomit (*Prov* xxvi, 11, 2 *Pet* ii, 22)

The dogs of war. The horrors of war, especially famine, sword, and fire.

And Cæsar's spirit, ranging for revenge,
With Até by his side, come hot from hell.
Shall in these confines, with a monarch's voice,
Cry "Havoc," and let slip the dogs of war
Julius Cæsar, iii, 1

The hair of the dog that bit you. It used to be considered that the best cure for a "thick head" was another drink, it is, perhaps, a matter for trial and error The allusion is to an ancient notion that the burnt hair of a dog is an antidote to its bite *Similia similibus curantur.*

The more I see of men the more I love dogs A misanthropic saying, the meaning of which is obvious It is probably French in origin— *Plus je vois les hommes, plus j'admire les chiens*

There are more ways of killing a dog than by hanging There is more than one way of achieving your object. The proverb is found in Ray's *Collection* (1742)

Throw it to the dogs. Throw it away, it is useless and worthless

Throw physic to the dogs! I'll none of it.
Macbeth, v, 3

To blush like a dog, or like a blue or black dog. Not to blush at all.

To call off the dogs To desist from some pursuit or inquiry; to break up a disagreeable conversation In the chase, if the dogs are on the wrong track, the huntsman calls them off

To die like a dog. To have a shameful, or a miserable, end

To go to the dogs. To go to utter ruin, morally or materially, to become impoverished

To help a lame dog over a stile. To give assistance to one in distress, to hold out a helping hand, to encourage

Do the work that's nearest,
Though it's dull at whiles,
Helping, when we meet them,
Lame dogs over stiles
CHARLES KINGSLEY: *The Invitation*

To lead a dog's life. To be bothered and harried from pillar to post, never to be left in peace

To put on the dog. To behave in a conceited or bumptious manner.

To rain cats and dogs *See* CAT (*It is raining*, etc)

To wake a sleeping dog. *See* LET SLEEPING DOGS LIE, *above*

Try it on the dog! A jocular phrase used o medicine that is expected to be unpalatable, or of food that is suspected of being not quite fit for human consumption

What! keep a dog and bark myself! Must I keep servants and myself do their work?

You can never scare a dog away from a greasy hide It is difficult to free oneself from bad habits The line is from Horace s *Satires* (ii, v, 83) *Canis a corio nunquam absterrebitur uncto*

(2) DOGS OF NOTE IN THE CLASSICS AND IN LEGEND

Geryon's dogs Gargittios and Orthos The latter was the brother of Cerberus, but had one head less Hercules killed both these monsters.

Icarius's dog. Mæra (*the glistener*) *See* ICARIUS

Orion's dogs. Arctophonos (*bear-killer*), and Ptoophagos (the *glutton of Ptoon*, in Bœotia)

Procris's dog. Lælaps *See* PROCRIS

Ulysses's dog. Argos, he recognized his master after his return from Troy, and died of joy.

Aubry's dog, or the dog of Montargis. Aubry of Montdidier was murdered, in 1371, in the forest of Bondy His dog, Dragon, excited suspicion of Richard of Macaire, by always snarling and flying at his throat whenever he appeared Richard was condemned to a judicial combat with the dog, was killed, and, in his dying moments, confessed the crime

Cuchullain's hound Luath (*q v*).

Fingal's dog. Bran (*q.v*)

King Arthur's favourite hound Cavall.

Llewelyn's greyhound. Beth Gelert (*q.v*)

Mauthe dog (*See* MAUTHE)

Montargis, Dog of. Aubry's dog (*See above.*)

Roderick the Goth's dog. Theron

Seven Sleepers, Dog of the. Katmir who, according to Mohammedan tradition, was admitted to heaven He accompanied the seven noble youths who fell asleep for 309 years to the cavern in which they were walled up and remained standing for the whole time, neither moving, eating, drinking, nor sleeping

Tristran's dog. Hodain, or Leon

(3) DOGS FAMOUS IN HISTORY, LITERATURE, FICTION, ETC

Boatswain. Byron's favourite dog, the poet wrote an epitaph on him and he was buried in the garden of Newstead Abbey
Bounce Alexander Pope's dog
Boy. Prince Rupert's dog, he was killed at the battle of Marston Moor
Brutus Landseer's greyhound, jocularly called ' The Invader of the Larder."

Dash. Charles Lamb's dog

Diamond The little dog belonging to Sir Isaac Newton One winter's morning he upset a candle on his master's desk, by which papers containing minutes of many years' experiments were destroyed On perceiving this terrible catastrophe Newton exclaimed "Oh, Diamond, Diamond, thou little knowest the mischief thou hast done!" and at once set to work to repair the loss

Flush Elizabeth Barrett Browning's dog

Geist One of Matthew Arnold's dachshunds He wrote the poem *Geist's Grave* in memory of him

Giallo Walter Savage Landor's dog

Hamlet. A black greyhound belonging to Sir Walter Scott

Kaiser Another of Matthew Arnold's dachshunds (*See* GEIST *above*) In his poem, *Kaiser Dead*, the poet mentions also Toss, Rover, and Max

Lufra. The hound of Douglas, in Scott's *Lady of the Lake.*

Maida Sir Walter Scott's favourite deerhound

Mathe Richard II's greyhound It deserted the king and attached itself to Bolingbroke

Toby. Punch's famous dog, named after the dog that followed Tobit in his journeys, a favourite in mediæval biblical stories and plays

(4) IN SYMBOLISM AND METAPHOR.

Dogs, in mediæval art, symbolize fidelity A dog is represented as lying at the feet of St. Bernard, St Benignus, and St Wendelin, as licking the wounds of St Roch, as carrying a lighted torch in representations of St Dominic.

Dogs in effigy In funeral monuments a dog is often sculptured at the foot of the central effigy, this has no symbolical significance, it is usually a memento of the dead person's pet

Lovell the Dog. *See* RAT

The dog. Diogenes (412-323 B C) When Alexander went to see him the young King of Macedonia introduced himself with these words. "I am Alexander, surnamed the Great," to which the philosopher replied: "And I am Diogenes, surnamed the Dog" The Athenians raised to his memory a pillar of Parian marble, surmounted by a dog (*See* CYNIC)

The Dog of God So the Laplanders call the bear which "has the strength of ten men and the wit of twelve"

The Thracian dog. Zoilus (4th cent. B.C.), the carping critic of ancient Greece

Like curs, our critics haunt the poet's feast,
And feed on scraps refused by every guest;
From the old Thracian dog they learned the way
To snarl in want, and grumble o'er their prey
　　　　　　　　　PITT· *To Mr Spence*

(5) IN COMBINATION

Dog-, or dog's-, in combinations is used (besides in its literal sense as in dog-biscuit, dog-collar) for

(*a*) denoting the male of certain animals, as dog-ape, dog-fox, dog-otter

(*b*) denoting inferior plants, or those which are worthless as food for man, as dog-brier, dog-cabbage, dog-leek, dog-lichen, dog-mercury, dog-parsley, dog-violets (which have no

perfume), dog-wheat *Cp* DOG-GRASS, DOG-ROSE *below.*

(*c*) expressing spuriousness or some mongrel quality, as dog's-logic, dog-Latin (*q v*)

Dogsbody An undistinguished and unskilled individual, required for menial tasks

Dog-cheap. Extremely cheap, "dirt-cheap "

Dog-days. Days of great heat. The term comes from the Romans, who called the six or eight hottest weeks of the summer *caniculares dies* According to their theory, the dog-star Sirius, rising with the sun, added to its heat, and the dog-days (about July 3rd to August 11th) bore the combined heat of the dog-star and the sun *See* DOG-STAR

Dogs'-ears. The corners of pages crumpled and folded down

Dogs'-eared. Pages so crumpled and turned down. The ears of many dogs turn down and seem quite limp

Dogface. American infantryman (World War II)

Dog-fall A fall in wrestling, when the two combatants touch the ground together

Dog fight, a skirmish between fighter planes

Dog-grass. Couch grass (*Triticum repens*), which is eaten by dogs when they have lost their appetite; it acts as an emetic and purgative

Dog-head The part of a gun which bites or holds the flint.

Dog house. **In the dog house.** In disgrace, as a dog confined to his kennel Usually applied to a husband who has been misbehaving and whose wife treats him with disdain

Dog-Latin. Pretended or mongrel Latin An excellent example is Stevens's definition of a kitchen.

As the law classically expresses it, a kitchen is "camera necessaria pro usus cookare, cum saucepannis, stewpannis, scullero, dressero, coalholo stovis, smoak-jacko, pro roastandum boilandum fryandum et plum-pudding-mixandum　　"—*A law Report (Daniel v Dishclout)*

Dog-rose. The common wild rose (*Rosa canina,* Pliny's *cynorrodon*), so called because it was supposed by the ancient Greeks to cure the bite of mad dogs

Dogs, Isle of. *See* ISLE

Dog's-nose Gin and beer

"Dog's-nose, which is, I believe, a mixture of gin and beer "

"So it is," said an old lady.—*Pickwick Papers.*

Dog-sleep A pretended sleep, also a light, easily broken sleep Dogs seem to sleep with "one eye open "

Dog-star. Sirius, the brightest star in the firmament, whose influence was anciently supposed to cause great heat pestilence, etc. *See* DOG-DAYS.

Dog-vane A nautical term for a small vane placed on the weather gunwale to show the direction of the wind Sailors also apply it to a cockade.

Dog-watch. The two short watches on board ship, one from four to six, and the other from six to eight in the evening, introduced to prevent the same men always keeping watch at the same time *See* WATCH

Dog-whipper. A beadle who used to keep dogs from the precincts of a church Even so late as 1856 Mr John Pickard was appointed "dog-whipper" in Exeter Cathedral, "in the room of Mr Charles Reynolds, deceased "

Dog-whipping Day October 18th (St Luke's Day) It is said that a dog once swallowed the consecrated wafer in York Minster on this day

Doggo. To lie doggo. To get into hiding and remain there, to keep oneself secluded

Dog-goned. An American euphemism for the oath 'God-damned "

> But when that choir got up to sing,
> I couldn't catch a word,
> They sung the most doggonedest thing
> A body ever heard!
> WILL CARLETON *Farm Ballad.*

See also DOGS, DOG'S, *below*

Dog Tags. American identity discs (World War II)

Dog-tired. Exhausted, usually after exercise, and wanting only to curl up like a dog and go to sleep.

Dogaressa. The wife of a doge (*q.v*).

Dogberry. An ignorant · self-satisfied, over-bearing, but good-natured night-constable in Shakespeare's *Much Ado About Nothing*, hence, an officious and ignorant Jack in office.

Doge (dōj) (Lat *dux*, a duke or leader) The chief magistrate in Venice while it was a Republic The first doge was Paolo Anafesto (Paoluccio), 697, and the last, Luigi Manin (1789) *See* BRIDE OF THE SEA
> For six hundred years her [Venice's] government was an elective monarchy, her . doge possessing, in early times at least, as much independent authority as any other European sovereign —RUSKIN' *Stones of Venice*, vol I, ch 1

The chief magistrate of Genoa was called a doge from 1339 (Simon Boccanegra) down to 1797, when the government was abolished by the French

Doggerel (dog' er el) This is an old word, with no obvious connexion with *dog* It was originally applied to a loose, irregular measure in burlesque poetry, such as that of Butler's *Hudibras*, and it is in this sense that Chaucer uses the word —
> "Now such a rym the devel I beteche!
> This may wel be rym dogerel," quod he
> *Prol. to Tale of Melibeus*

The word is now applied only to verse of a mean and paltry nature, lacking both sense and rhythm.

Dogget Dogget's coat and badge The prize given in a rowing match for Thames watermen, which takes place, under the auspices of the Fishmongers' Company, on or about August 1st every year. So called from Thomas Dogget (d 1721), an actor of Drury Lane, who signalized the accession of George I by instituting the race. It is from the Swan Steps at London Bridge to the Swan at Chelsea The average time taken is 30 mins The coat is an orange-coloured livery jacket.

Dogmatic School. *See* EMPIRICS

Doh, or **Do** (dō) The first or tonic note of the solfeggio system of music
Do, re, mi, fa, sol, la (Ital), *ut, re, mi, fa. sol, la* (Fr.) The latter are borrowed from a hymn by Paulus Piaconus, addressed to St John, which Guido of Arezzo, in the 11th century, used in teaching singing
> *Ut* queant laxis, *Re*-sonare fibris,
> *Mi*-ra gestorum *Fa*-muli tuorum,
> *Sol*-ve polluti *La*-bits reatum
> *Sancte Joannes.*
> *Ut*-tered be thy wondrous story,
> *Re*-prehensive though I be,
> *Me* make mindful of thy glory,
> *Fa*-mous son of Zacharee,
> *Sol*-ace to my spirit bring,
> *La*-bouring they praise to sing   E C. B.

See ARETINIAN SYLLABLES.

Doily. A small cloth used to cover dessert plates, or a mat or napkin on which to stand plates, glasses, bottles, etc In the 17th century the word was an adjective denoting a cheap woollen material, thus Dryden speaks of "doyley petticoats," and Steele in No 102 of the *Tatler*, speaks of his 'doiley suit " The Doyleys, from which the stuff was named, were linen-drapers in the Strand, from the late 17th century to 1850

Doit. An old Dutch coin, worth about half a farthing, hence, any coin of very small value. In England the doit was prohibited by 3 Henry V c. 1.
> When they will not give a doit to relieve a lame beggar, they will lay out ten to see a dead Indian —
> *The Tempest*, ii, 2

Dolce far niente (dol' chi far ni en' ti) (Ital). Delightful idleness Pliny has '*Jucundum tamen nihil agere*" (*Ep.* viii, 9)

Dolcinists. *See* DULCINISTS

Doldrums, The A condition of depression. slackness, or inactivity, hence applied by sailors to a region where ships are likely to be becalmed, especially that part of the ocean near the equator noted for calms, squalls, and baffling winds, between the NE and SE trade winds
> But from the bluff-head, where I watched to-day,
> I saw her in the doldrums
> BYRON. *The Island*, canto ii, stanza 21

In the doldrums. In the dumps

Dole (Lat. *dolor*, grief, sorrow) Lamentation.
> What if .
> He now be dealing dole among his foes,
> And over heaps of slaughtered walk his way?
> MILTON *Samson Agonistes*, 1529

To make dole. To lament, to mourn
> Yonder they lie, the poor old man, their father, making such pitiful dole over them that all the beholders take his part with weeping.—*As You Like It*, i, 2

Dole (A S *dal*, a portion, *dæl*, deal) A portion allotted a charitable gift, alms The word was later usually applied to the weekly paymen. made for a limited period to certain classes of unemployed from funds contributed by workers, employers, and the State

Happy man be his dole. May his share or lot be that of a happy or fortunate man

Your father and my uncle have made motions if it be my luck, so, if not, happy man be his dole!—*Merry Wives*, iii, 4

Dollar. The sign $, is probably a modification of the figure 8 as it appeared on the old Spanish "pieces of eight," which were of the same value as the dollar

The word is a variant of *thaler* (Low Ger *dahler*; Dan *daler*), and means "a valley", (our *dale*), The counts of Schlick, at the close of the 15th century, extracted from the mines at *Joachim's thal* (Joachim's valley) silver which they coined into ounce-pieces These pieces, called *Joachim's thalers*, gained such high repute that they became a standard coin Other coins being made like them were called *thalers* only The American dollar equals 100 cents, in English money about 7s 2d It was adopted as the monetary unit of the U S A in 1785 but was not coined until 1792

Dolly Shop. A marine store where rags and refuse are bought and sold, so called from the black doll suspended over it as a sign to denote the sale of Indian silks and muslins

Dolmen (dol' men) The name given in France to cromlechs (*q v*), particularly those of Brittany (Breton *tol*, a table, *men*, stone) They are often called by the rural population devils' tables, fairies' tables, and so on

The **Constantine Dolmen**, Cornwall, is 33 ft long, 14½ deep, and 18½ across It is calculated to weigh 750 tons, and is poised on the points of two natural rocks

Dolphin. *Cp* DAUPHIN The dolphin is noted for its changes of colour when taken out of the water.

Parting day

Dies like the dolphin, whom each pang imbues

With a new colour as it gasps away

The last still loveliest

BYRON *Childe Harold*, iv, 29.

D.O.M., inscribed on bottles of Benedictine liqueur, among other places, stands for *Deo optimo maximo*, To God the best and greatest

Dom (Lat *dominus*) A title applied in the Middle Ages to the Pope, and at a somewhat later period to other Church dignitaries It is now restricted to priests and choir monks of the Benedictine Order, and to some few other monastic orders The Sp *don*, Port *dom*, and M.E *dan* (as in *Dan Chaucer*) are the same word

Domdaniel (dom dän' yel) A fabled abode of evil spirits, gnomes, and enchanters, "under the roots of the ocean" off Tunis, or elsewhere It first appears in Chaves and Cazotte's *Continuation of the Arabian Nights* (1788-93), was introduced by Southey into his *Thalaba*, and used by Carlyle as synonymous with a den of iniquity The word is Lat *domus*, house or home, *Danielis*, of Daniel, the latter being taken as a magician.

Domesday Book. The book containing a record of the census or survey of England, giving the ownership, extent, value, etc , of all the different holdings, undertaken by order of William the Conqueror in 1086 It is in Latin, is written on vellum, and consists of two volumes, one a large folio of 382 pages, and the other a quarto of 450 pages It was formerly kept in the Exchequer, under three different locks and keys, but is now in the Public Record Office Northumberland, Cumberland, Westmorland, and Durham are not included, though parts of Westmorland and Cumberland are taken.

The value of all estates is given, firstly, as in the time of the Confessor, secondly, when bestowed by the Conqueror, and, thirdly, at the time of the survey It is also called *The King's Book*, and *The Winchester Roll* because it was kept there Printed in facsimile in 1783 and 1816

The book was so called from A S *dom*, judgment, because every case of dispute was decided by an appeal to these registers *Cp* EXON DOMESDAY

Domiciliary Visit (dom i sil' ya ri) An official visit paid by the police or other authorities to a private dwelling in order to search for incriminating papers, etc In Britain a magistrate s warrant must be obtained before a domiciliary visit can be made

Dominations. *See* DOMINIONS.

Dominic, St. (1170-1221), who preached with great vehemence against the Albigenses, was called by the Pope "Inquisitor-General," and was canonized by Gregory IX He is represented with a sparrow at his side, and a dog carrying in its mouth a burning torch The devil, it is said, appeared to the saint in the form of a sparrow, and the dog refers to the story that his mother, during her pregnancy, dreamt that she had given birth to a dog, spotted with black and white spots, which lighted the world with a burning torch

Dominical Letters. The letters which denote the Sunday of *dies dominica* The first seven letters of the alphabet are employed, if January 1st is a Sunday the dominical letter for the year will be A, if the 2nd is a Sunday it will be B, if the 3rd, C, and so on In Leap years there are two dominical letters, one for the period up to February 29th, and the other for the rest of the year

Dominicans An order of preaching friars, instituted by St Dominic in 1215, and introduced into England (at Oxford) in 1221 They were formerly called in England *Black Friars*, from their black dress, and in France *Jacobins*, because their mother-establishment in Paris was in the Rue St Jacques They have always been one of the intellectual pillars of the Church, largely on account of their most distinguished member, St Thomas Aquinas. They were also called "Hounds of the Lord," *Domini canes*.

Dominions. The sixth of the nine orders in the mediæval hierarchy of the angels *See* ANGEL They are symbolized in art by an ensign, and are also known as 'Dominations''

The word is also applied to the self-governing possessions of the British Crown The word was first given in this sense to the Dominion of Canada, which was formed by the federation of the Canadian provinces in 1867.

The other British Dominions are· The Commonwealth of Australia, 1900, The Dominion of New Zealand, 1907, The Union of South Africa, 1909, the Republic of India, 1947, the Dominion of Pakistan, 1947, the Dominion of Ceylon, 1948 In 1925 a Secretary-ship of State for Dominion Affairs was created, to deal with business connected with the Dominions, as well as the affairs of Southern Rhodesia and the S. African territories of Basutoland, Bechuanaland, and Swaziland The Dominions are represented in London by High Commissioners

Domino (dom' i nō) (Ital) Originally a hooded cloak worn by canons, hence a disguise worn at masquerades consisting of a hooded garment, then the hood only, and finally the half mask covering an inch or two above and below the eyes, worn as a disguise

The name came to be applied to the game probably through a custom of calling *faire domino* when winning with the last piece—much as the French still say *faire capot* (*capot* also means ' hood''); in the Navy and Army the last lash of a flogging was known as *the domino*

Don is do-on, as "Don your bonnet " *See* Doff, Dup

> Then up he rose, and donned his clothes,
> And dupp'd the chamber door
>   *Hamlet,* iv, 5

Don A man of mark, an aristocrat At the universities the masters and fellows are termed *dons*. The word is the Spanish form of Lat *dominus Cp* Dan, Dom

Don Juan (don joo' an) Don Juan Tenorio, the hero of a large number of plays and poems, as well as of Mozart's opera, *Don Giovanni*, round whom numerous legends have collected, was the son of a leading family of Seville in the 14th century, and killed the commandant of Ulloa after seducing his daughter. To put an end to his debaucheries the Franciscan monks enticed him to their monastery and killed him, telling the people that he had been carried off to hell by the statue of the commandant, which was in the grounds

His name has passed into a synonym for a rake, roue, or aristocratic libertine, and in Mozart's opera (1787) Don Giovanni's valet, Leporello, says his master had "in Italy 700 mistresses, in Germany 800 in Turkey and France 91, in Spain 1,003 " His dissolute life was dramatized by Gabriel Tellez in the 17th century, by Molière, Corneille, Shadwell, Grabbe (German), Dumas, and others, and in the 20th century by Bataille, and Rostand

In Byron's well-known poem (1819-24), when Juan was sixteen years old he got into trouble with Donna Julia, and was sent by his mother, then a widow, on his travels. His adventures in the Isles of Greece, at the Russian Court, in England, etc , form the story of the poem, which, though it extends to sixteen cantos, is incomplete

Don Quixote (don kwik' zot). The hero of the great romance of that name by Miguel de Cervantes Saavedra (1547-1616). It was published at Madrid, Part I in 1605, Part II in 1615 Don Quixote is a gaunt country gentleman of La Mancha, gentle and dignified, affectionate and simple-minded, but so crazed by reading books of knight-errantry that he believes himself called upon to redress the wrongs of the whole world, and actually goes forth to avenge the oppressed and run atilt with their oppressors Hence, a **quixotic** man is a dreamy, unpractical, but essentially good, man—one with a "bee in his bonnet "

Donation of Constantine. *See* Decretals

Donation of Pepin, The When Pepin conquered Ataulf (755) the exarchate of Ravenna fell into his hands Pepin gave it, with the surrounding country and the Republic of Rome, to the Pope (Stephen II), and thus founded the Papal States and the whole fabric of the temporal power of the Popes.

With the exception of the city of Rome the Papal States were incorporated in the kingdom of Italy in 1860, and Rome itself became Italian in 1870, the Pope declaring himself a "prisoner" in the Vatican In 1929 a concordat was settled with the Italian government whereby a small area on the right bank of the Tiber was declared the Vatican City, together with the estate of Castel Gandolfo in the Alban mountains.

Donatists. Followers of Donatus, a Numidian bishop of the 4th century who, on puritanical grounds, opposed Cecilianus. Their chief dogma is that the outward Church is nothing, "for the letter killeth, it is the spirit that giveth life " St Augustine of Hippo vigorously combated their heresies

Doncaster. The "City on the river Don " Celt. *Don*, that which spreads. Sigebert, monk of Gemblours, in 1100, derived the name from *Thong-ceaster*, the "castle of the thong," and says that Hengist and Horsa purchased of the British king as much land as they could encompass with a leather thong, which they cut into strips, and so encompassed the land occupied by the city.

Donkey. An ass The word is of comparatively recent origin, being first recorded about 1785 (*Hickey's Memoirs*, ii, 276), and seems at first to have rhymed with "monkey " It is a diminutive, and may be connected with *dun*, in reference to its tint "Dun," in "Dun in the mire" was a familiar name for a horse, and the "donkey" is a smaller, or more diminutive beast of burden For the tradition concerning the "cross" on the donkey's back, *see* Ass

Not for donkey's years. Not for a long time. The allusion is to the old tradition that one never sees a dead donkey

The donkey means one thing and the driver another. Different people see from different standpoints, their own interest in every case directing their judgment The allusion is to a fable in Phædrus, where a donkey-driver exhorts his donkey to flee, as the enemy is at hand The donkey asks if the enemy will load him with double pack-saddles "No," says the man "Then", replies the donkey, "what care I whether you are my master or someone else?"

To ride the black donkey To be pig-headed, obstinate like a donkey Black is added, not so much to designate the colour, as to express what is bad

Two more, and up goes the donkey. An old cry at fairs, the showman having promised the credulous rustics that as soon as enough pennies are collected his donkey will balance himself on the top of the pole or ladder, as the case may be. Needless to say, it is always a matter of "two more pennies," and the trick is never performed

Who stole the donkey? An old gibe against policemen When the force was first established a donkey was stolen, but the police failed to discover the thief, and this gave rise to the laugh against them The correct answer is "The man with the white hat,' because white hats were made of the skins of donkeys, many of which were stolen and sold to hatters

Donkey engine, pump, etc Small auxiliary engines or machines for doing subsidiary work.

Donnybrook Fair. This fair, held in August from the time of King John, till 1855, was noted for its bacchanalian orgies and light-hearted rioting Hence it is proverbial for a disorderly gathering or a regular rumpus The village was a mile and a half south-east of Dublin, and is now one of its suburbs.

Donzel. A squire or young man of good birth not yet knighted This is an anglicized form of Ital. *doncello*, from late Lat *domicellus See* DAMSEL.
He is esquire to a knight-errant, donzel to the damsels.—BUTLER: *Characters*

Doodle. To draw designs, patterns, sketches, etc., aimlessly and absent-mindedly while occupied in conversation, listening, and the like Psychologists profess to find considerable significance in the drawings thus made
Though the habit has existed for many centuries the word was brought into prominence as a result of the film *Mr. Deeds goes to Town*, 1936.

Doodle-bug. This was a name popularly given to the pilotless aeroplane bombs, also known as V1 and "Flying Bombs," showered on the southern portions of Britain by the Germans in 1944

Doom (A S *dom*). The original meaning was law, or judgment, that which is set up as a statute: hence, the crack of doom, the signal for the final judgment. The book of judgments compiled by King Alfred was known as the *dom-boc.* This word is sometimes used to designate the frescoes, etc, found in old churches depicting the Day of Judgment, e g the Wenhaston Doom

Doomsday Book. *See* DOMESDAY.

Doomsday Sedgwick. William Sedgwick (*c.* 1610-69), a fanatical prophet and preacher during the Commonwealth. He pretended to have it revealed to him in a vision that doomsday was at hand; and, going to the house of

Sir Francis Russell, in Cambridgeshire, he called upon a party of gentlemen playing at bowls to leave off and prepare for the approaching dissolution

Door. The Anglo-Saxon *dor* (fem *duru*) The word in many other languages is similar, thus, Dan *dor*, Icel. *dyrr*, Gr *thura*, Lat *fores*, Ger *thure*

Dead as a door-nail. *See* DEAD.

Door-money. Payment taken at the doors for admission to an entertainment, etc

He laid the charge at my door. He accused me of doing it

Indoors. Inside the house also used attributively, as, *an indoor servant*

Next door to it. Within an ace of it (*see* ACE), very like it, next-door neighbour to it

Out of doors. Outside the house in the open air

Sin lieth at the door (*Gen* iv, 7) The blame of sin attaches to the wrongdoer, and he must take the consequences

The door must be either shut or open. It must be one way or the other; there is no alternative. From De Brueys and de Palaprat's comedy, *Le Grondeur* (produced 1691) the master scolds his servant for leaving the door open. The servant says that he was scolded the last time for shutting it, and adds "Do you wish it shut?"—"No "—"Do you wish it open?"—"No '—"Why," says the man, 'it must be either shut or open "

To make the door. To make it fast by shutting and bolting it
Why at this time the doors are made against you — *Comedy of Errors*, iii, 1
Make the door upon a woman's wit, and it will out at the casement —*As You Like It*, iv. 1

Dope. Properly, some thick or semi-fluid liquid used for food or as a lubricant (Dut *doopen*, to dip) The name was applied to a varnish used for aeroplane wings, the odour of which in some cases had a stupefying effect upon the workers. Hence it came to be used for noxious drugs such as cocaine, and confirmed drug-takers have since been called *dope-fiends* Dope is also used, figuratively, for flattery, or words that are intended to lead one into a false sense of security, power, etc., also for information

Dora. The popular name of D O R A, the Defence of the Realm Act, 1914-21, under which many hundreds of regulations temporarily curbing the liberty of the subject were made. It passed into common speech in 1914 after having been used in the Law Courts by Mr Justice Scrutton.

Dorado, El. *See* EL DORADO

Dorcas Society. A woman's circle for making clothing for the poor. So called from Dorcas, in *Acts* ix, 39, who made "coats and garments" for widows

Dorian, Doric. Pertaining to Doris, one of the divisions of ancient Greece, or to its inhabitants, a simple, pastoral people

Dorian mode. The scale represented by the white keys on a pianoforte, beginning with D A simple, solemn form of music, the first of the authentic Church modes.

Doric dialect. The dialect spoken by the natives of Doris, in Greece It was broad and hard Hence, any broad dialect such as that of rustics Robert Burns's verses are an example of British Doric

Doric Order. The oldest, strongest and simplest of the Grecian orders of architecture The Greek Doric is simpler than the Roman imitation The former stands on the pavement without fillet or other ornament, and the flutes are not scalloped The Roman column is placed on a plinth, has fillets, and the flutings, both top and bottom, are scalloped.

The Doric Land. Greece, Doris being a part of Greece

> Through all the bounds
> Of Doric land
> > MILTON *Paradise Lost,* Bk 1, 519

The Doric reed. Pastoral poetry. Everything Doric was very plain, but cheerful, chaste, and solid.

> The Doric reed once more
> Well pleased, I tune
> > THOMSON. *Autumn,* 3.

Dorigen (dôr´i jen) The heroine of Chaucer's *Franklin's Tale,* which was taken from Boccaccio's *Decameron* (X, v), the original being in the Hindu *Vetala Panchavinsati.*

Dorinda, in the verses of the Earl of Dorset, is Catherine Sedley, Countess of Dorchester, mistress of James II.

Doris. *See* NEREIDS.

Dormer Window. The window of an attic standing out from the slope of the roof, properly, the window of a bedroom (O Fr *dormeor,* a dormitory)

Dormy. A golfing term of uncertain origin (perhaps connected with Fr. *dormir,* to sleep), which is applied to a player who is as many holes ahead of his opponent as there are holes left to play in the round. Thus, if when there are still three holes left A is three ahead of B , A is said to be "dormy three "

Dormy House. Sleeping quarters at a golf club.

Dornick. Stout figured linen for tablecloths, etc , so called from Doornick, the Flemish name of Tournay, where it was originally made *Cp* DANNOCKS. The word is spelt in many ways, *e.g* Dornock, Darnex

> I have got a fair Darnex carpet of my own
> Laid cross for the more state
> > FLETCHER. *The Noble Gentleman,* v, 1.

Dorothea, St. (dor ŏ thē´ a) A martyr under Diocletian about 303 She is represented with a rose-branch in her hand, a wreath of roses on her head, and roses with fruit by her side, The legend is that Theophilus, the judge's secretary, scoffingly said to her, as she was going to execution, "Send me some fruit and roses, Dorothea, when you get to Paradise " Immediately after her execution, a young angel brought him a basket of apples and roses, saying, "From Dorothea in Paradise,"

and vanished The story forms the basis of Massinger's tragedy, *The Virgin Martyr* (1620)

Dorset. Once the seat of a British tribe, calling themselves *Dwr-trigs* (dwellers by the water) The Romans colonized the settlement, and Latinized *Dwr-trigs* into *Duro-triges* Lastly came the Saxons, who translated the original words into their own tongue, *dor-sætta, sætta* being a seat or settlement

Doss. Slang for a sleep, also for a bed or a place where one sleeps—a *doss-house, dossing-ken* The word dates from the 18th century, and is probably connected with the old *dorse,* a back (Lat *dorsum,* Fr *dos).* Hence also *dosser,* one who sleeps in a common lodging-house

Dotheboys Hall (doo *the* boiz) A school in Dickens's *Nicholas Nickleby* where boys were taken in and done for by Mr Wackford Squeers, a brutish, ignorant, overbearing knave, who starved them and taught them nothing. The ruthless exposure of this kind of "school" led to the closing or reformation of many of them

Dot. *See* I.

Dot and carry one. An infant just beginning to toddle, one who limps in walking, a person who has one leg longer than the other.

Dotterel. A doting old fool, an old man easily cajoled So called from the bird, a species of plover, which is easily approached and caught.

To dor the dotterel. Dor is an obsolete word meaning to trick or cheat Whence the phrase means to cheat the simpleton

Douai Bible. *See* BIBLE, THE ENGLISH The English college at Douai was founded by William Allen (afterwards cardinal) in 1568 The Douai Bible translates such words as *repentance* by the word *penance,* etc , and the whole contains notes by Roman Catholic divines.

Double (Lat. *duplus,* twofold) One's double is one's *alter ego (q v)* The word is applied to such pairs as the Corsican brothers, the Dromio brothers, and the brothers Antipholus.

Double-bank. A phrase used in Britain in reference to two or more cars or cyclists abreast on a road, in Australia it is applied to two people riding one horse

To double-cross. To betray or cheat an associate, more especially an associate in an already shady undertaking

A double first. In the first class both of the classical and mathematical final examinations, Oxford; or of the classical and mathematical triposes, Cambridge. Now, a first class in any two final examinations.

Double dealing. Professing one thing and doing another inconsistent with that promise

Double Dutch. Gibberish, jargon, of a foreign tongue not understood by the hearer Dutch is a synonym for foreign, and double implies something excessive, in a twofold degree

Double-edged. Able to cut either way, used metaphorically of an argument which makes both for and against the person employing it, or which has a double meaning

"Your Delphic sword," the panther then replied,
"Is double-edged and cuts on either side"
      DRYDEN *Hind and Panther*, pt III, 191

Double entendre An incorrect English version of the French *double entente*, a word which secretly expresses a rude or coarse covert meaning, generally of an indelicate character. *Entendre* is the infinitive mood of the French verb, and is never used as a noun

Double or quits The winner stakes his stake, and the loser promises to pay twice the stake if he loses again, but if he wins the second throw his loss is cancelled and no money passes

Double time. A military phrase, applied to orderly running on the march, etc It is quick march, the rate of progress (officially 165 steps of 33 in , *i e.* 453½ ft , to the minute) being *double* that of the ordinary walking pace *See* To DOUBLE UP *below.*

Double-tongued. Making contrary declarations on the same subject at different times, deceitful, insincere.

Be grave, not double-tongued —1 *Tim* III 8.

Double X. *See* X

Double-headed Eagle. *See* EAGLE

To double a cape. Said of a ship that sails round or to the other side of a cape, its course is, as it were, bent back on itself

What capes he doubled, and what continent,
The gulfs and straits that strangely he had past
      DRYDEN · *Ideas*, stanza 1

To double a part. Said of an actor playing two parts in the same piece

To double and twist To prevaricate, act evasively, try by tortuous means to extricate oneself from a dilemma or difficulty The phrase is taken from coursing—a hare "doubles and twists" in the endeavour to escape from the hounds. In weaving, "to double and twist" is to add one thread to another and twist them together

To double back. To turn back on one's course.

To double up. To fold together ' To double up the fist" is to fold the fingers together so as to make the hand into a fist "To double a person up" is to strike him in the wind, so as to make him double up with pain

In military phraseology, "Double up there!" is an order to hurry, to "get a move on, ' run Also to put two people in the space normally allocated to one if accommodation is temporarily short *See* DOUBLE TIME *above.*

Double summer time *See* DAYLIGHT SAVING

Double take. An acting trick. It consists in looking away from the person who has addressed a remark to you, and then looking back at him quickly when the purport of the remark sinks in

To work double tides. To work extra hard, with all one's might

Doubting Castle The castle of the giant Despair, in which Christian and Hopeful were incarcerated, but from which they escaped by means of the key called "Promise " (BUNYAN. *Pilgrim's Progress*)

Doubting Thomas. *See* THOMAS, ST.

Douceur (Fr) A gratuity for service rendered or promised , a tip.

Doughboy (U S A.) First. doughcake baked for sailors, then the buttons on their coats, then buttons on infantry uniforms (civil war), thence infantry man

Doughface (U S A). Inhabitant of the Northern States who was in favour of maintaining slavery in the South

Douglas. The Scottish family name is from the river Douglas in Lanarkshire, which is the Celtic *dhu glaise*, black stream, a name in use also in Ireland, the Isle of Man, etc , and in Lancashire corrupted to *Diggles*. Legend explains it by inventing an unknown knight who came to the assistance of some Scottish king After the battle the king asked who was the "Du-glass" chieftain, his deliverer, and received for answer *Sholto Du-glass*, which is said to be good Gaelic for "Behold the dark-grey man you inquired for."

'I will not yield him an inch of way, had he in his body the soul of every Douglas that has lived since the time of the Dark Gray Man "—SCOTT *The Abbot*, ch xxvii

Black Douglas Sir William Douglas lord of Nithsdale, who died about 1392 It was of this Douglas that Scott said —

The name of this indefatigable chief has become so formidable, that women used, in the northern counties, to still their froward children by threatening them with the Black Douglas —*History of Scotland*, ch xi.

The "Black Douglas" introduced by Scott in *Castle Dangerous* is James, eighth Lord Douglas, who lived about 100 years earlier, and twice took Douglas Castle from the English by stratagem

The Douglas Tragedy. A ballad in Scott's *Border Minstrelsy*, telling how Lord William steals away Lady Margaret Douglas and is pursued by her father and two brothers A fight ensues, the father and his two sons are sore wounded, Lord William, also wounded, creeps to his mother's house and there dies, and the lady dies next morning

Douse the Glim. Put out the candle, also, by extension, to blind a man Among sailors "to douse a sail" means to lower it in haste

A douse in the chops. A heavy blow in the face.

My fellow-servant Umphry Klinker bid him be siwil, and he gave the young man a douse in the chops, but I'fachins, Mr Klinker wa'n't long in his debt—with a good oaken sapling he dusted his doublet — SMOLLETT *Humphrey Clinker Lett* xxxiv

Dout. A contraction of *do-out*, as don is of *do-on*, doff of *do-off*, and dup of *do-up* In some southern counties they still say *dout* the candle and *dout the fire*, and call extinguishers *douters*

The dram of eale
Doth all the noble substance dout
         Hamlet, 1, 4

Dove. The name means "the diver-bird"; perhaps from its habit of ducking the head So also Lat *columba* is the Gr *kolumbis* (a diver).

In Christian art the dove symbolizes the Holy Ghost, and the seven rays proceeding from it the seven gifts of the Holy Ghost It also symbolizes the soul, and as such is sometimes represented coming out of the mouth of saints at death

A dove bearing a ring is an attribute of St Agnes, St David is shown with a dove on his shoulder, St Dunstan and St Gregory the Great with one at the ear, St Enurchus with one on his head, and St Remigius with the dove bringing him holy chrism

The clergy of the Church of England are allegorized as doves in Dryden's *Hind and Panther*, part iii, 947, 998-1002.

Dove's dung. In *2 Kings* vi, 25, we are told that during the siege of Samaria "there was a great famine . and . an ass's head was sold for fourscore pieces of silver and the fourth part of a cab of dove's dung for five pieces of silver ' "Ass's head" and "dove's dung" are both undoubtedly incorrect, the true rendering probably being "a homer of lentils" and ' pods of the carob (or locust) tree," the Hebrew for which expressions could easily be misread for the Hebrew of the others. Locust pods are still commonly sold in the East for food, and it is thought that they are the "husks" referred to in the parable of the Prodigal Son.

Dover. In the professional slang of English cooks a *resurrection pie* or any *rechauffe* is called a *dover* (do over again)

A Jack of Dover. *See* JACK

When Dover and Calais meet. Never.

Merry Dun of Dover. *See* MERRY.

Dovercourt (dō' ver côrt) A confused gabble; a babel According to legend, Dovercourt church, in Essex, once possessed a cross that spoke, and Foxe says the crowd to the church was so great "that no man could shut the door " But Dovercourt also seems to have been noted for its scolds and chattering women

> And now the rood of Dovercourt did speak,
> Confirming his opinions to be true
>   *Grim, the Collier of Croydon* (1600)
> When bells ring round and in their order be,
> They do denote how neighbours should agree;
> But when they clam, the harsh sound spoils the sport
> And 'tis like women keeping Dovercourt.
>   *Lines in the Belfry of St Peter's, Shaftesbury.*

Dovetail. Metaphorically, to fit on or fit in nicely, to correspond In carpentry it means the fitting one board into another by a tenon in the shape of a dove's tail, or wedge reversed

Dower. Gifts by a husband to his wife before marriage That portion of a man's estate which the wife enjoys for life after her husband's death Most large estates have a Dower house to which the widow retires, leaving the big house to the heir who has inherited the estate.

Dowlas, Mr. (dou' lás) A generic name for a linendraper, who sells dowlas, a coarse linen cloth, so called from Daoulas, in Brittany, where it was manufactured

Mrs Quickly I bought you a dozen of shirts to your back

Falstaff Dowlas, filthy dowlas I have given them away to bakers' wives, and they have made bolsters of them.

Mrs. Quickly Now, as I am true woman, holland of eight shillings an ell   *1 Henry IV*, iii, 3.

Down. Down and out. Said of one who has not only come right down in the world but has, apparently, not the slightest chance of getting up again.

Down at heel *See* HEEL.

Down in the dumps. *See* DUMPS

Down in the mouth. Out of spirits, disheartened When persons are very sad and low spirited, the corners of the mouth are drawn down. Down in the jib is a nautical phrase of the same meaning

Down on his luck. In ill luck, short of cash and credit

Down on the nail. *See* NAIL

Down with (so-and-so)! Away with! A cry of rage and exasperation, like the Fr *à bas*

He is very much run down Very out of sorts, in need of a thorough rest and overhauling, like a clock that has *run down*.

I was down on him in a minute. I pounced on him directly, I detected his trick immediately. The allusion is to birds of prey

That suits me down to the ground *See* GROUND

The down train. The train away from London or the local centre, in contradistinction to *the up train*, which goes to it We also have *the down platform*, etc

To down tools To lay one's tools aside and come out on strike.

To have a down on. To have a grudge or spite against

To run a man down *See* RUN

Ups and downs. The twists and turns of fortune, one's successes and reverses

Fraudulent transactions have their downs as well as their ups.—DICKENS *Martin Chuzzlewit*, ch xvi

Down-easter. An American from New England

Down-town. Business district of an American city, so called from New York where financial houses are concentrated in the southern tip of Manhattan Island.

Downing College. A college at Cambridge, founded by the will of Sir George Downing (c 1684-1749) (a grandson of the Sir George of Downing Street, *q v.*) The college was chartered in 1800, after much litigation He also founded the chair occupied by the *Downing Professor*, the Professor of the Laws of England at Cambridge.

Downing Street. A name often given to the heads of the British Government collectively No 10 was given in 1735 by George II to Sir Robert Walpole as the official residence of the Prime Minister, and it is there that the meetings of the Cabinet are usually held The house retains its old façade but has been altered inside from time to time No 11 is the official residence of the Chancellor of the Exchequer, No 12 is the Government Whips' office The street was named in honour of Sir George Downing (c. 1623-84), a noted Parliamentarian and ambassador, who served under both Cromwell and Charles II.

Downright. Thoroughly, from top to bottom, throughout; "downright honest," "downright mad", outspoken; fixed in opinions; utter, as a "downright shame "

Downright Dunstable. *See* DUNSTABLE.

Downy. An old slang word long since in disuse

Gone to the downy, gone to bed, bed being stuffed with down

A downy cove. A knowing fellow, *up to,* or, as formerly, *down to* every dodge

Downy here means wideawake, knowing; and in Vaux.'s *Flash Dictionary* (1812) *down* is given as a synonym for "awake" —

> When the party you are about to rob sees or suspects your intention, it is then said that *the cove is down*

Dowsabell. A common name for a sweetheart, especially an unsophisticated country girl, in poems of Elizabethan times. It is the Fr *douce et belle*, sweet and beautiful.

> It were not good . to cast away as pretty a dowsabell as any could chance to see in a summer's day —*The London Prodigal,* IV, 1 (1605)

Drayton has a poem, *The Ballad of Dowsabell.*

Dowse (*see also* DOUSE) To search for water, etc., with a divining-rod (*q.v*), which is also called a *dowsing-rod,* and the practitioners of the art *dowsers* The origin of the term is disputed, but as the art was introduced from Germany (in the 16th cent) it may be connected with Ger *deuten,* to declare or interpret

Doxology (doks ol' ō ji). This comes from a Greek word meaning a hymn of praise to God. The Greater Doxology is the hymn *Gloria in Excelsis Deo* at the Eucharist The Lesser Doxology is the *Gloria Patri* (Glory be to the Father, etc) sung at the end of each psalm in the liturgy The hymn "Praise God from whom all blessings flow" is also known as the Doxology.

Doxy. This is an old word, though it has always been slang, for a paramour, more especially the wench of a tramp or tinker. The common—and inoffensive—habit of calling a girl "ducky" or "ducks" has precisely the same origin

Doyley. *See* DOILY

Dozen. Twelve: the word is all that is left (in English) of the Latin *duodecim,* twelve, the -*en* representing the Latin suffix -*ena* A *long dozen* is thirteen *See* BAKER'S DOZEN.

To talk nineteen to the dozen. To talk at a tremendous rate, or with excessive vehemence.

D P. The House of Lords (Lat. *Domus Procerum*) Also Displaced Persons (*q v*)

Drachenfels (drak' en felz) (Ger , Dragonrock). So called from the legend that it was the home of the dragon slain by Siegfried, the hero of the *Nibelungenlied.*

> The castled crag of Drachenfels
> Frowns o'er the wide and winding Rhine,
> Whose breast of waters broadly swells
> Between the banks which bear the vine
>   BYRON. *Childe Harold,* III, 55.

Draconian Code (drá kō' ni an) One very severe. Draco was an Athenian law-maker of

the 7th cent B C, and the first to produce a written code of laws for Athens As nearly every violation of his laws was a capital offence, Demades the orator said that "Draco's code was written in blood "

Draft. A draft on Aldgate pump. *See* ALDGATE.

(Military) A body of men of any size sent to a unit or formation for service, presumably having the same origin as a draft or cheque, since it fully or partially fills the requirement for which the unit has indented

Draggle-tail. *See* DAGGLE-TAIL

Dragoman (drăg' ō măn) (pl dragomans). A cicerone, a guide or interpreter to foreigners. (Arab *targuman,* an interpreter, whence *targum*)

> My dragoman had me completely in his power, and I resolved to become independent of all interpreters —
> BAKER *Albert Nyanza,* ch 1, p 3

Dragon The Greek word *drakon* comes from a verb meaning "to see," to "look at," and more remotely "to watch" and 'to flash "

A dragon is a fabulous winged crocodile, usually represented as of large size, with a serpent's tail; whence the words serpent and dragon are sometimes interchangeable The word was used in the Middle Ages as the symbol of sin in general and paganism in particular, the metaphor being derived from *Rev* xii 9, where Satan is termed "the great dragon" and *Ps* xci 13, where it is said that the saints "shall trample the dragon under their feet " Hence, in Christian art the dragon symbolizes Satan or sin, as when represented at the feet of Christ and the Virgin Mary, and St John the Evangelist is sometimes represented holding a chalice, from which a dragon is issuing

Among the many saints who are usually pictured with dragons may be mentioned St Michael, St George, St Margaret, Pope Sylvester, St. Samson (Archbishop of Dol), St. Donatus, St Clement of Metz, St Romain of Rouen, who destroyed the huge dragon, La Gargouille, which ravaged the Seine, St Philip the Apostle, who killed another at Hierapolis, in Phrygia, St. Martha, who slew the terrible dragon, Tarasque, at Aix-la-Chapelle, St Florent, who killed a dragon which haunted the Loire, St Cado, St Maudet, and St Pol who did similar feats in Brittany, and St Keyne of Cornwall

In classical legend the idea of *watching* is retained in the story of the dragon who guards the golden apples in the garden of the Hesperides.

Among the ancient Britons and Welsh the dragon was the national symbol on the war standard; hence the term, Pendragon (*q v*) for the *dux bellorum,* or leader in war (*pen*=head or chief)

A duenna is poetically called a dragon —

> In England the garden of beauty is kept
> By a Dragon of prudery placed within call
>   T MOORE *Irish Melodies*

Dragon's Blood A picturesque name given to no more awesome substance than the red resinous exudation from the fruits of a number of palms It was formerly used as an astringent in medicine, and is still employed as a colouring matter for varnishes.

A flying dragon. A meteor.

The Chinese dragon In China, a five-clawed dragon is introduced into pictures and embroidered on state dresses as an amulet

The Dragon of Wantley *See* WANTLEY.

To sow dragons' teeth. To foment contentions, to stir up strife or war, especially to do something that is intended to put an end to strife but which brings it about later The Philistines "sowed dragons' teeth" when they took Samson, bound him, and put out his eyes; the ancient Britons did the same when they massacred the Danes on St Bryce's Day, as also did the Germans when they robbed France of Alsace Lorraine.

The reference is to the classical story of Cadmus, who slew the dragon that guarded the well of Ares and sowed some of its teeth, from which sprang up the men called Sparti, or the Sown-men, who all killed each other except five, who became the ancestors of the Thebans Those teeth which Cadmus did not sow came to the possession of Æetes, King of Colchis; one of the tasks he enjoined on Jason was to sow them and slay the armed warriors that rose therefrom

Dragon's Hill. A site in Berkshire where one legend has it that St. George killed the dragon A bare place is shown on the hill, where nothing will grow, for there the blood of the dragon ran out

In Saxon annals we are told that Cerdic, founder of the West Saxon kingdom, slew there Naud (or Natanleod, the people's refuge), the pen-dragon, with 5,000 men.

Dragonades. A series of religious persecutions by Louis XIV, prior to the revocation of the Edict of Nantes, which drove many thousand Protestants out of France Their object was to root out "heresy", if the heretics would not recant, they had *dragoons* (hence the name) billeted on them, who were given a free hand to treat them in any way they liked The origin of this name for a type of mounted soldier is obscure In 1554 Marshal Brissac armed some of his horsemen with short carbines on the muzzles of which were engraved dragons spouting fire, and some ascribe the term to these More likely, however, is the theory that the word comes from the *dragon*, or standard, borne by a mounted regiment formed in the French army in 1585.

Drama. Father of Danish drama. Ludwig von Holberg (1684-1754).

Father of French drama. Etienne Jodelle (1532-73)

Father of Greek drama. Thespis (6th cent B C.)

Father of Modern German drama. Andreas Gryphius (1616-64).

Father of Spanish drama. Lope de Vega (1562-1635).

Dramatic unities. The three dramatic unities, viz the rules governing the so-called "classical" dramas, are founded on Renaissance misconceptions of passages in Aristotle's *Poetics*, and are hence sometimes, though very incorrectly, styled the *Aristotelean Unities* They

are, that in dramas there should be (1) Unity of Action, (2) Unity of Time, and (3) Unity of Place Aristotle lays stress on (1), meaning that an organic unity, or a logical connexion between the successive incidents, is necessary, but (2) was deduced by Castelvetro (1505-71), the 16th-century Italian scholar and critic, from the passage in the *Poetics* where Aristotle, in comparing Epic Poetry and Tragedy, says that the former has no limits in time but the latter

endeavours, as far as possible, to confine itself to a single revolution of the sun, or but slightly to exceed this limit

—a passage which was merely an incidental reference to a contemporary custom and was never intended as the enunciation of an inviolable law of the drama Having thus arrived at the Unity of Time, (3) the Unity of Place followed almost perforce, though there is not even a hint of it in Aristotle.

The theory of the Three Unities was formulated in Italy nearly a century before it was taken up in France (Cintio, Robortelli, Maggi, and Scaliger being the principal exponents), where it became, after much argument, the corner-stone of the literary drama The principle had little success in England—despite the later championship of Dryden (see his *Essay on Dramatic Poesy*), Addison (as exemplified in his *Cato*), and others It was not till Corneille's triumph with *Le Cid* (1636) that the convention of the Three Unities can be said to have been finally adopted. It is almost unnecessary to add that Shakespeare, and every great dramatist not bound by a self-imposed tradition, was with Aristotle in holding that so long as the Unity of Action is observed the others do not matter Ben Jonson's *The Alchemist* (1610) is, perhaps, the best example of the small class of English plays in which the Unities of Place and Time have been purposely adhered to

Dramatis Personæ (drăm' a tĭs pĕr sō' nē). The characters of a drama, novel, or (by extension), of an actual transaction

Drapier's Letters (drā' pēr) A series of letters written by Dean Swift to the people of Ireland and published in 1724, advising them not to take the copper money coined by William Wood The patent had been granted to him by George I through the influence of the Duchess of Kendal, the king's mistress, and Wood and the Duchess were to share the profits (40 per cent) These letters, which were signed "M. B Drapier," crushed the infamous job and the patent was cancelled

Drat. A variant of *Od rot!* "Od" (*q v*) being a minced form of "God," and the vowel showing the same modification as in "Gad!" or "Gadzooks!"

Draupnir (drawp' nēr) Odin's magic ring, from which every ninth night dropped eight rings equal in size and beauty to itself It was fashioned by the dwarfs

Draw. A drawn game, battle, etc One in which the result is in doubt, neither side having achieved success. perhaps so called from a battle in which the troops on both sides are *drawn off*, neither side claiming the victory.

A good draw. A first-rate attraction—"Performing elephants are always 'a good draw' at circuses." The noun also may mean a drawn game, or the result of drawing lots, etc

Draw it mild! Don't exaggerate! don't make your remarks (or actions, as the case may be) stronger than necessary. The allusion is to the drawing of beer

Hanged, drawn, and quartered Strictly speaking, the phrase should read *Drawn, hanged, and quartered*, for the allusion is to the sentence formerly passed on those convicted of high treason, which was that they should be *drawn* to the place of execution on a hurdle or at a horse's tail instead of being carried or allowed to walk, then hanged, and then quartered

Later, drawing, or disembowelling, the criminal was added to the punishment after the hanging and before the quartering, and it was sometimes supposed that the "drawn" in the phrase referred to this process instead of to the earlier one Thus the sentence on Sir William Wallace was that he should be drawn (*detrahatur*) from the Palace of Westminster to the Tower, then hanged (*suspendatur*), then disembowelled or drawn (*devaletur*), then beheaded and quartered (*decolletur et decapitetur*)

Lord Ellenborough used to say to those condemned, "You are drawn on hurdles to the place of execution, where you are to be hanged, but *not* till you are dead, for, while still living, your body is to be taken down, your bowels torn out and burnt before your face, your head is then cut off, and your body divided into four quarters—*Gentleman's Magazine*, 1803.

To draw a bead on somebody. To take aim at him with a rifle or revolver The "bead" referred to is the foresight

To draw a badger. *See* BADGER

To draw a furrow To plough or draw a plough through a field so as to make a furrow

To draw a person out. To entice a person to speak on any subject, to obtain information, to encourage one too shy to talk.

To draw amiss. To take the wrong direction A hunting term, *to draw* meaning to follow scent

To draw blank. To meet with failure in one's pursuit The allusion is to sportsmen "drawing" a covert and finding no game *To draw a blank* refers to having no luck in a lottery, sweepstake, etc To fail in a search

To draw the cork. To give one a bloody nose *Cp* CLARET

To draw the King's (or Queen's) picture To coin false money

To draw the nail. To release oneself from a vow It was a custom in Cheshire to register a vow by driving a nail into a tree, swearing to keep your vow as long as it remained there If you wished to retract, the nail was withdrawn and the vow thereby cancelled

To draw rations, stores, etc. A military phrase, to go to the appointed place of issue and receive same

To draw rein. To pull up short, to check one's course

To draw stumps. To mark the final close of

a game of cricket the stumps are drawn from the ground and taken away

To draw the line To set a definite limit beyond which one refuses to go, to impose a restriction on one's behaviour from fear of going too far "He was utterly unprincipled, but he drew the line at blackmail," *i e* he would stop short at blackmail

To draw a bow at a venture; to draw the long bow. *See* BOW

Drawback Something to set against the profits or advantages of a concern. In commerce, it is duty charged on goods paid back again when the goods are exported

It is only on goods into which dutiable commodities have entered in large proportion and obvious ways that drawbacks are allowed —H GEORGE *Protection or Free Trade?* ch ix

In common parlance a *drawback* is an inconvenience in something otherwise desirable

Drawcansir A burlesque tyrant in Buckingham's *Rehearsal* (1671); hence, a blustering braggart The character was a caricature of Dryden's Almanzor (*Conquest of Granada*) Drawcansir's opening speech (he has only three) is —

He that dares drink, and for that drink dares die,
And, knowing this, dares yet drink on, am I.
          Rehearsal, iv, 1

which parodies Almanzor's:—

He who dares love, and for that love must die,
And, knowing this, dares yet love on, am I.
         Conquest of Granada, IV, iii

Cp BAYES, BOBADIL.

Drawing-room. This was originally a room into which the women withdrew after dinner, leaving the men to remain at table drinking When this custom fell into desuetude the drawing-room became a room for entertainment and conversation as distinct from the dining-room reserved for meals In the Victorian suburban villa the drawing-room was a sort of state apartment, rarely entered and yet more rarely used The word is also applied to a levee where ladies are presented to the sovereign

Drawlatch. An old name for a robber, a housebreaker, *i e* one who entered by drawing up the latch with the string provided for the purpose and stole all he could carry away with him

Dreadnought. The name given to a large battleship (17,900 tons) in the British Navy, built in 1906, and hence to the class of which it was the earliest The name was in use in Queen Elizabeth's time.

The Seamen's Hospital at Greenwich (founded in 1821) is often spoken of as the Dreadnought Hospital, because it was originally housed in the Thames on an old man-of-war of this name It was drawn ashore in 1870

Dreams, The Gates of. There are two, viz. that of ivory and that of horn Dreams which delude pass through the Ivory Gate, those which come true pass through the Gate of Horn.

That children dream not the first half-year, that men dream not in some countries, with many more, are unto me sick men's dreams, dreams out of the ivory gate, and visions before midnight —SIR THOMAS BROWNE *On Dreams*

This fancy depends upon two puns ivory in Greek is *elephas*, and the verb *elephairo* means "to cheat with empty hopes", the Greek for horn is *keras*, and the verb *karanoo* means "to accomplish "

The Immortal Dreamer. John Bunyan (1628-88)

Dreng. An ancient Northumbrian term (from Danish) for a free tenant who held his land by a tenure dating from before the Conquest. It occurs in Domesday Book

Dresser In theatrical parlance this is the person who looks after dresses, and prepares for the stage an actor or actress In furniture a dresser is a large stand with shelves for holding dishes, plates, etc, and drawers for cutlery and silver

Dreyfusard, Dreyfusite. An advocate of the innocence of Capt. Alfred Dreyfus (1859-1935), a French artillery officer of Jewish descent, who was convicted in 1894 on a charge of having betrayed military secrets, degraded and sent to Devil's Island. In 1899 the first trial was annulled. He was brought back to France, retried, and again condemned, but shortly afterwards pardoned, though it was not until 1914 that he was finally and completely rehabilitated.

Drink. Drink-money. A "tip", a small gratuity to be spent on drinking the health of the giver; a *pourboire* (Fr, for drink)

Drinking horns. In the East drinking cups made of rhinoceros horn used to be specially valued, as they were supposed to sweat if they contained any poison In the North those made of narwhal tusk were considered the best, for they were held to counteract any poisonous effects.

Drinking of healths. *See* GABBARA; HEALTH.

In the drink In the sea, in the water, a service colloquial term of World War II.

The big drink. An American expression for any large stretch of water, such as the Atlantic (*cp* HERRING-POND) or Lake Superior
In airman's slang to be ditched in the drink is to make a forced landing on water, esp the sea

It is meat and drink to me. It is something that is almost essential to my well-being or happiness, something very much to be desired
> It is meat and drink to me to see a clown.
> *As You Like It*, v, 1.

One must drink as one brews. One must take the consequences of his actions, "as one makes his bed so must he lie in it "
> I am grieved it should be said he is my brother, and take these courses well, as he brews, so shall he drink
> —JONSON· *Every Man in his Humour*, ii, 1

Those who drink beer will think beer A saying attributed to Warburton, Bishop of Gloucester (1698-1779). Some non-teetotaller parodied it with "And those that drink water will think water " Neither suggestion calls for explanation

To drink at Freeman's Quay. To get one's drink at someone else's expense It is said that at one time all porters and carmen calling at Freeman's Quay, near London Bridge, had a pot of beer given them gratis, but the explanation is scarcely necessary and probably untrue

To drink deep. To drink heavily, to excess, or habitually Shakespeare uses the expression metaphorically:—
> *Cant* If it pass against us,
> We lose the better half of our possession;
> And to the coffers of the king beside,
> A thousand pounds by the year Thus runs the bill
> *Ely.* This would drink deep
> *Cant*. 'Twould drink the cup and all
> *Henry V*, 1, 1

To drink like a fish. To drink abundantly or excessively Many fish swim with their mouths open, thus appearing to be continually drinking The expression is found in Beaumont and Fletcher

To drink the cup of sorrow, etc *See* CUP.

To drink the waters. To take medicinal waters, especially at a spa

Drive. He is driving pigs, or **driving pigs to market.** Said of one who is snoring, because the grunt of a pig resembles the snore of a sleeper

To drive a good bargain. To exact more than is quite equitable
> Heaven would no bargain for its blessings drive —
> DRYDEN *Astraa Redux*, i, 137

To drive a quill. *See* QUILLDRIVERS

To drive a roaring trade. To do a brisk business

To drive the swine through the hanks of yarn. To spoil what has been painfully done, to squander thrift In Scotland, the yarn wrought in the winter (called *the gude-wife's thrift*) is laid down by the burn-side to bleach, and is thus exposed to damage from passing animals, such as a herd of pigs, which may stray over it and do a vast amount of harm

To let drive. To attack, to fall foul of.
> Thou knowest my old ward; here I [Falstaff] lay, and thus I bore my point Four rogues in buckram let drive at me —SHAKESPEARE 1 *Henry IV*, ii, 4.

What are you driving at? What do you want to prove? What do you want me to infer?

Who drives fat oxen should himself be fat Henry Brooke, in his *Gustavus Vasa* (1739), says "Who rules o'er free-men should himself be free", Dr Johnson parodied the line—and the sentiment, with which he did not agree (Boswell.)

Droit d'Aubaine (drwa' dō bān) *Aubain* (Fr) means "alien," and *droit d'aubaine* the "right over an alien's property " In France the king was entitled, at the death of foreign residents (except Swiss and Scots), to all their movable estates, a right that was not finally abolished till 1819
> Had I died that night of an indigestion, the whole world could not have suspended the effects of the *droits d'aubaine* My shirts and black pair of breeches, portmanteau and all must have gone to the king of France —STERNE: *Sentimental Journey* (Intro).

Dromio (drō' mi ō) **The brothers Dromio.** Two brothers exactly alike, who served two brothers exactly alike, and the mistakes of masters and men form the fun of Shakespeare's

Comedy of Errors, based on the *Menæchmi* of Plautus

Drone. The male of the bee, which does no work but lives on the labours of the worker-bees, hence a sluggard; an idle person who lives on the work or means of another

The three lower pipes of a bagpipe are called the drones, because they produce an unchanging, monotonous bass humming like that of a bee

Drop. A drop in one's eye. Not exactly intoxicated, but having had quite enough

We are na fou, we're nae that fou,
But just a drappie in our e'e!
BURNS *Willie Brew'd a Peck o' Maut*

A drop in the ocean. An infinitesimal quantity, something that scarcely counts or matters in comparison with the whole

A drop of the cratur. *See* CREATURE

A dropping fire An irregular fusillade from small-arms, machine guns, etc

Drop serene. An old name for amaurosis, a disease of the optic nerve, causing blindness, without affecting the appearance of the eye It was at one time thought that it was caused by a transparent, watery humour distilling on the nerve The name is the English form of the Lat *gutta serena.*

So thick a drop serene hath quenched these orbs
MILTON *Paradise Lost*, iii, 25

Prince Rupert's drops. *See* RUPERT

To drop across. To encounter accidentally or casually.

To drop an acquaintance To allow acquaintanceship to lapse

To drop in. To make a casual call, not invited, to pay an informal visit

To get the drop on someone. To have him in your power, probably from the early method of pistol shooting whereby the weapon was raised high and then lowered, or dropped, towards its target.

To drop off. "Friends drop off," fall away gradually. "To drop off to sleep," to fall asleep (especially in weariness or sickness)

To take a drop A euphemism for taking what the drinker chooses to call by that term It may be anything from a sip to a Dutchman's draught

To take one's drops. To drink spirits in private

Drown Drowning men catch at straws. Persons in desperate circumstances cling in hope to trifles wholly inadequate to rescue or even help them

To drown the miller *See* MILLER

Drows. *See* TROWS

Drug *See* DOPE A drug in the market. Something *not* called for, which no one will buy

Druid (droo'id) A member of the ancient Gaulish and British order of priests, teachers of religion, magicians, or sorcerers The word is the Lat *druidæ* or *druides* (always plural), which was borrowed from the Old Irish *drui*

and Gaelic *draoi* The druidic cult presents many difficulties, and practically our only literary sources of knowledge of it are Pliny and the Commentaries of Cæsar, whence we learn that the rites of the Druids were conducted in oak-groves and that they regarded the oak and the mistletoe with peculiar veneration, that they studied the stars and nature generally, that they believed in the transmigration of souls, and dealt in "magic" Their distinguishing badge was a serpent's egg (*see below*), to which very powerful properties were credited. The order seems to have been highly organized, and according to Strabo every chief had his druid, and every chief druid was allowed a guard of thirty men

In Butler's *Hudibras* (III, i) there is an allusion to the

Money by the Druids borrowed,
In t'other world to be restored

This refers to a legend recorded by one Patricius (? St Patrick) to the effect that the Druids were wont to borrow money to be repaid in the life to come His words are "*Druidæ pecuniam mutuo accipiebant in posteriore vita reddituri*"

On account of the inferred connexion between the Druids and the bards the name is still kept in use by the Welsh Eisteddfods, and it is with this sense that Collins employed it in his eulogy on Thomson —

In yonder grave a Druid lies

United Ancient Order of Druids. A secret benefit society founded in London in 1781 and introduced to U S A in 1883. It now has lodges, or "groves" as they are called, in many parts of the world

The Druids' egg. This wonderful egg was hatched by the joint labour of several serpents, and was buoyed into the air by their hissing. The person who caught it had to ride off at full speed, to avoid being stung to death, but the possessor was sure to prevail in every contest, and to be courted by those in power. Pliny says he had seen one of them, and that it was about as large as a moderate-sized apple.

Druj. *See* AHRIMAN

Drum. A popular name in the 18th century—and later—for a crowded evening party, so called from its resemblance in noise to the drumming up of recruits The more riotous of these parties were called *drum-majors*

This is a riotous assembly of fashionable people, of both sexes, at a private house, consisting of some hundreds, not unaptly styled a drum, from the noise and emptiness of the entertainment —SMOLLETT *Advice, a Satire* (1746)

To drum up To get together unexpectedly or in an emergency, as "to drum up a meal"

John (or Jack) Drum's entertainment. Turning an unwelcome guest out of doors

O' for the love of laughter, let him fetch his drum; he says he has a stratagem for 't When your lordship sees the bottom of his success in 't, and to what metal this counterfeit lump of ore will be melted, if you give him not John Drum's entertainment, your inclining cannot be removed —*All's Well*, iii, 6

John Marston wrote a comedy with the title *Jack Drum's Entertainment* (1600), in which he is supposed to have satirized Ben Jonson.

Drum ecclesiastic The pulpit cushion, often vigorously thumped by what are termed "rousing preachers"

> When Gospel trumpeter, surrounded
> With long-eared rout, to battle sounded;
> And pulpit, drum ecclesiastic,
> Was beat with fist instead of a stick
> BUTLER *Hudibras*, I, i

Drum-head court-martial. One held in haste, a court-martial summoned on the field round the drum to deal summarily with an offender

Drumsticks. Legs, especially very thin ones, or the legs of a cooked fowl

Drummers. An Americanism for commercial travellers, their vocation being to collect customers as a recruiting officer "drums up" recruits

Drummond Light. The limelight So named from the inventor, Thomas Drummond (1797-1840), about 1825.

Drunk Drunk as a fiddler The reference is to the fiddler at wakes, fairs, and on board ship, who used to be paid in liquor for playing to the dancers

Drunk as a lord. In the late 18th century and early 19th the habit of gross drinking was at its height and a man of fashion was judged —or prided himself—on the number of bottles of port he could drink at a sitting Few dinners ended without placing the guests under the table in a hopeless state of intoxication, hence the expression

Drunk as Chloe Chloe was the cobbler's wife of Linden Grove, to whom Prior, the poet, was attached. She was notorious for her drinking habits

Drunk as David's sow. *See* DAVY'S SOW Chaucer has *drunk as a mouse*, Wilson (1553) *drunk as a rat*, Massinger *drunk as a beggar*, other common similes are *drunk as a tinker*, and *drunk as a boiled owl*, or "as an owl"

Drunkard's cloak. A tub with holes for the arms to pass through, used in the 17th century for drunkards and scolds by way of punishment.

Drunken Parliament, The. The Parliament assembled at Edinburgh, January 1st, 1661, of which Burnet says the members "were almost perpetually drunk."

Drury Lane. This famous London street (and, consequently, the theatre) is named from Drury House, built in the time of Henry VIII by Sir William Drury. It stood on a site about in the middle of the present Aldwych

The first Drury Lane Theatre was opened on April 8, 1663, and nine years later was burned down Its successor was designed by Wren, and this was replaced in 1794 by a third theatre, which was destroyed by fire in 1809 The present building was designed by Wyatt and opened in 1812 It was on its boards that Edmund Kean achieved his first great triumph, as Shylock, in 1814

Druses. A people and sect of Syria, living about the mountains of Lebanon and Anti-Libanus Their faith is a mixture of the Pentateuch, the Gospel, the Koran, and Sufism They offer up their devotions in both mosques and churches, worship the images of saints, and yet observe the fast of Ramadan Their name is probably from that of their first apostle, Ismail Darazi, or Durzi (11th century A D)

Dry. Thirsty Hence to drink is to "wet your whistle" (*i e*. throat); and malt liquor is called "heavy wet "

Dry bob. A boy at Eton College who plays cricket and football instead of going in for rowing.

Dry goods. Merchandise such as cloth, stuffs, silks, laces, and drapery in general, as opposed to groceries

Dry lodgings. An old expression for sleeping accommodation without board Gentlemen who took their meals at clubs lived in "dry lodgings "

Dry rot is a diseased condition of timber due to the ravages of certain species of fungi The affected parts crumble away to a brownish powder upon exposure to a dry atmosphere. Dry rot cannot develop in wood to which air currents have free access, hence the necessity of having air-bricks in an outside wall beneath the floor level.

Dry shave. A shave without soaping the face, to scrape the face with a piece of iron hoop, to scratch the face, to box it and bruise it

> The fellow will get a dry shave.
> PETER PINDAR *Great Cry and Little Wool*, Ep. 1
> I'll shave her, like a punished soldier, dry
> PETER PINDAR *The Lousiad*, canto ii

Dry wine. Opposed to sweet or fruity wine. In sweet wine some of the sugar is not yet decomposed, in *dry* wine all the sugar has been converted into alcohol. In the same way we speak of a *dry biscuit* as opposed to a sweet biscuit

Not dry behind the ears. As innocent as a new-born child When young animals are born, the last place to become dry after birth is the small depression behind each ear.

Dryad (drī' ăd) In classical mythology, a tree-nymph (Gr *drus*, a tree) Who was supposed to live in the trees and die when the trees died Eurydice, the wife of Orpheus the poet, was a dryad. Also called *hamadryads* (Gr. *hama*, with)

Dryasdust (drī' az dŭst) The name given by Scott to the fictitious "reverend Doctor," a learned pundit, to whom he addressed the prefaces, etc , of many of his novels, hence, a heavy, plodding author, very prosy, very dull, and very learned; an antiquary.

> The Prussian Dryasdust, otherwise an honest fellow, and not afraid of labour, excels all other Dryasdusts yet known . . He writes big books wanting in almost every quality, and does not even give an *Index* to them —CARLYLE

Dualism (dū' a lizm) A system of philosophy which refers all things that exist to two ultimate principles, such as Descartes' Thought (*res cogitans*) and Extension (*res extensa*), or—in the theological sense—good and evil In modern philosophy it is opposed to monism (*q v*), and insists that the creator and creation, mind and body, are distinct entities

Dub. To make a knight by striking him on the shoulder with a sword; to give the accolade. The word probably comes from the Old French *aduber*, to equip with arms, to invest with armour, though it has undoubtedly got mixed with the other Old French word *dober*, to strike

Dub up. Pay down the money, "fork out!" Another form of *dup* (*q v*), do up

Dubglas. According to the *Historia Brittonum* by Nennius (about A D. 800), the second, third, fourth, and fifth of King Arthur's twelve great battles were fought on this river Nennius places it in Linnuis (*i e* Lindsey, Lincolnshire), but, as is the case in all Arthurian topography, its probable site is matter for conjecture

Ducat (dŭk' at) A piece of money first coined in 1140 by Roger II of Sicily as Duke of the duchy (*ducato*) of Apulia This was a silver coin In 1284 the Venetians struck a gold coin with the legend *Sit tibi, Christe, datus, quem tu regis, iste ducatus* (may this duchy which you rule be devoted to you, O Christ), and through this the name, already in use, gained wider currency. The ducat mentioned by Shakespeare in *The Merchant of Venice* is the Spanish coin, valued at about 6s. 8d

Duce (doo' chā) This title, meaning in Italian a leader, was adopted by the Fascist dictator Benito Mussolini (1883-1945) On his assumption of power in 1922 "Duce! Duce!" was the cry of the crowds stirred almost to frenzy by his impassioned oratory

Duchess. The wife or widow of a duke, in slang use contracted to *dutch*, and applied to the wife of a coster, as in the song "My old dutch "

Duck A contraction of duck's egg (*see below*)

A lame duck A stock-jobber or dealer who will not, or cannot, pay his losses He has to "waddle out of the alley like a lame duck "

"I don't like the looks of Mr Sedley's affairs He's been dabbling on his own account I fear   and unless I see Amelia's ten thousand down you don't marry her I'll have no lame duck's daughter in my family"—THACKERAY *Vanity Fair*, ch xiii

Duck Lane. Duck Lane (now Duke Street, leading from Little Britain to Long Lane, in the City of London), in Queen Anne's time was famous for its second-hand bookstalls

Scotists and Thomists now in peace remain
Amidst their kindred cobwebs in Duck Lane
POPE *Essay on Criticism*

Duck's egg. In cricket a score of 0—*i e* no score at all, the cipher on the sheet resembling an egg *To break one's duck's egg*, or *one's duck*, is, of course, to make one run or more

Ducks and drakes The ricocheting or rebounding of a stone thrown from the hand to skim along the surface of a pond or river To **play ducks and drakes** with one's money is to throw it away carelessly and just on amusement, or for the sake of watching it go and making a splash

What figured slates are best to make
On watery surface duck and drake
BUTLER *Hudibras*, ii, 3

Like a dying duck in a thunderstorm. Quite chop-fallen, very woebegone

Dud. Something or somebody that is useless or a failure The word became very common in World War I, when it was applied to shells that did not explode, inefficient officers, unworkable pieces of mechanism, etc Its origin is not known Dut *dood* means dead, but no connexion between this and *dud* has been traced

A dudder or dudsman is a scarecrow, or man of straw dressed in cast-off garments to frighten birds, also a pedlar who deals in articles of clothing and materials

Dude (dūd). A masher One who renders himself conspicuous by affectation of dress, manners, and speech The word was invented in America about 1883, and soon became popular in London

I should just as soon expect to see Mercutio smoke a cigarette, as to find him ambling about the stage with the mincing manners of a dude —JEFFERSON *Century Magazine*, January, 1890

Dude Ranch. Ranch in the Western States of America especially organized as a holiday camp for inexperienced horsemen

Dudgeon (dŭj' on) The handle of a dagger, at one time made of boxwood root, called "dudgeon-wood"; a dagger with such a handle Shakespeare says,

I see thee still,
And on thy blade and dudgeon gouts of blood,
Which was not so before.
SHAKESPEARE *Macbeth*, ii, 1

As indicating resentment or sulkiness, the word *dudgeon* comes from an old Welsh word, *dygen*, meaning malice

Dudman and Ramhead. When Dudman and Ramhead meet Never Dudman and Ramhead (now spelt Ramehead) are two forelands on the Cornish coast, about twenty miles apart. *See* NEVER

Duds A word in use for five hundred years at least, signifying clothes of some sort, formerly coarse cloaks, but in modern use slang for any clothes, usually with a disparaging implication. Its origin is unknown.

Duenna (dū en 'à) The female of the Spanish *don* (*q v*), strictly, the chief lady in waiting on the Queen of Spain, but, in common parlance, a woman who is half companion and half governess, in charge of the younger female members of a Spanish or Portuguese family; hence, in England a chaperon—especially one who takes her duties very seriously

There is no duenna so rigidly prudent and inexorably decorous as a superannuated coquette.—W IRVING *Sketch-book* (*Spectre Bridegroom*).

Duessa (dū es' a) (*Double-mind* or *Falsehood*). In Spenser's *Faerie Queene* (Bk I) the "scarlet woman,' typifying the Roman Catholic Church, and (Bk V) Mary Queen of Scots She was the daughter of Deceit and Shame, and assumed divers disguises to beguile the Red Cross Knight

Duffer. A stupid, foolish, incompetent person, one of slow wit, the origin of the word is not clear, but *duff* is old thieves' slang for "to fake," and as a counterfeit coin was called a *duffer* the name may have been transferred to persons who, similarly, were "no good "

Dug-out. (1) a canoe cut out of a solid tree trunk (2) An artificial cave in war or peace (3) A retired officer brought back into service

Duke (Lat *dux*, leader) The title belonging to the highest rank of nobility in England The first English dukedom to be created was that bestowed by Edward III on his eldest son, the Black Prince, in 1338, when he was raised from Earl of Cornwall to Duke of Cornwall The title is very rarely conferred, and except for royal dukes, since 1874 (Duke of Westminster) it has been conferred only on the Earl of Fife, who was created Duke of Fife on his marriage with Princess Louise (1889) On his death in 1912 his daughter, Princess Arthur of Connaught, became Duchess of Fife in her own right, by special remainder There are four royal and twenty-six noble dukedoms

Duke Combe William Combe (1741-1820), author of *The Tours of Dr Syntax*, etc , was so called, because of the splendour of his dress, the profusion of his table, and the magnificence of his deportment, in the days of his prosperity Having spent all his money he turned author, but passed the last fifteen years of his life in the King's Bench Prison.

Duke Humphrey. *See* HUMPHREY

The Duke of Exeter's daughter. A rack in the Tower of London, so called from a minister of Henry VI, who sought to introduce its use into England (1447)

The Great Duke The Duke of Wellington (1769-1852) also called "the Iron Duke," a name later given to a famous battleship (1913).

To meet one in the Duke's Walk. To fight a duel Duke's Walk, near Holyrood Palace, was the favourite promenade of the Duke of York, afterwards James II, during his residence in Scotland; and it became the common rendezvous for settling "affairs of honour," as the fields behind the present British Museum were in England

Dukeries. A district in Nottinghamshire, so called from the number of noble residences in the vicinity, including Welbeck Abbey (Duke of Portland), Clumber (Duke of Newcastle), Thoresby (Earl Manvers), etc

Dulcarnon (dūl kar' non) The horns of a dilemma (or *Syllogismum cornutum*), at my wits' end, a puzzling question From an Arabic word meaning "the possessor of two horns " The 47th proposition of the First Book of Euclid is called the Dulcarnon, as the 5th is the Pons Asinorum, because the two squares which contain the right angle roughly represent horns Chaucer uses the words in *Troilus and Criseyde*, Bk. iii, 931, 933

To be in Dulcarnon To be in a quandary, or on the horns of a dilemma

To send me to Dulcarnon To daze with puzzles

Dulce Domum (dūl' si dō' mum) A school holiday song the words mean—*not*, as often supposed, "sweet home," but—"the sweet (sound of the word) 'home'." The song originated at Winchester, and is said to have been written by a boy who was confined for misconduct during the Whitsun holidays, "as report says, tied to a pillar " On the evening preceding the Whitsun holidays, the master, scholars, and choristers still walk in procession round the pillar, chanting the six stanzas of the song The music is by John Reading (d 1692), organist of Winchester Cathedral, who also composed the Adeste Fideles (*q v*)
Dulce domum resonemus
Let us make the sweet song of home to resound

Dulce est desipere in loco (dūl' si est de sip' e ri in lō' kō) It is delightful to play the fool occasionally, it is nice to throw aside one's dignity and relax at the proper time (Horace 4 *Odes*, xii, 28)

Dulce et decorum est pro patria mori (dūl si et de kôr' um est prō pat' ri a mōr' i). It is sweet and becoming to die on our country's behalf, or to die for one's country (Horace 3 *Odes*, ii, 13)

Dulcimer (dūl' si mer) In *Dan* iii, 5, etc , this word is used to translate a Hebrew word rendered in Greek by *symphonia*, which was applied to a kind of bagpipe In modern use a dulcimer is a hollow triangular box strung with wires of varying lengths, which are struck with a little rod held in each hand

Dulcinea (dūl sin' ē a) A lady-love. Taken from the name of the lady to whom Don Quixote paid his knightly homage Her real name was Aldonza Lorenzo, but the knight dubbed her Dulcinea del Toboso
Sancho Panza says she was "a stout-built sturdy wench, who could pitch the bar as well as any young fellow in the parish."

Dulcinists (dūl' si nists). Heretics who followed the teaching of Dulcin or Dolcinus, who taught that God reigned from the beginning to the coming of Messiah; and that Christ reigned from His ascension to the 14th century, when He gave up His dominion to the Holy Ghost Dulcin was burnt by order of Clement IV (1307) There is a reference to Dulcin in Dante's *Inferno* (xxviii, 55)

Dulia. *See* LATRIA.

Dullness King of dullness. So Pope calls Colley Cibber (1671-1757), appointed poet laureate in 1730
"God save king Cibber!" mounts in every note . .
So when Jove's block descended from on high
Loud thunder to the bottom shook the bog,
And the hoarse nation croaked, "God save king Log "
POPE· *Dunciad*, Bk. i

Dum-dum. A half-covered steel-cased bullet which expands on impact and so produces a very terrible wound So called from Dum-dum, near Calcutta, the former headquarters of the Bengal artillery and of the ammunition factory where they were first made A similar effect is produced by filing flat the steel cap of an ordinary bullet. The use of dum-dum bullets is prohibited in warfare by practically every civilized nation.

Dum sola (Law Lat). While single or unmarried

Dum vivimus vivamus (dŭm vi vī' mus vi vā' mūs) (Lat). While we live, let us enjoy life The motto adopted by Dr. Doddridge (1702-

51), who translated and expanded it into the subjoined epigram —

"Live, while you live," the epicure would say
"And seize the pleasures of the present, day,"
"Live, while you live," the sacred preacher cries,
"And give to God each moment as it flies,"
Lord, in *my* views let each united be,
I live in pleasure, when I live to thee

Dumb-bell. Originally, an apparatus for developing the muscles, similar to that which sets church bells in motion. It consisted of a flywheel with a weight attached, which the gymnast had to raise The present dumb-bell, which answers a similar purpose, has been given the same name

The **dumb-bell Nebula.** Nebula in the constellation Vulpecula, so called from its apparent shape

Dumb barge. The name given to a barge without sails, generally used as a pier or wharf

Dumb crambo. *See* CRAMBO

Dumb Ox, The. St Thomas Aquinas (1224-74), known afterwards as "the Angelic Doctor" or "Angel of the Schools ' Albertus Magnus, his tutor, said of him "The dumb ox will one day fill the world with his lowing "

Dumb waiter. A piece of dining-room furniture, fitted with shelves, to hold glasses, dishes, and plate So called because it answers all the purposes of a waiter, and is not possessed of a tongue

Dummy. In bridge or in three-handed whist the exposed hand is called dummy. Double-dummy bridge is bridge played by only two players but with the usual four hands.

Dump Although this is a fairly modern colloquialism it is really an old word, coming from the Middle English *dumpen*, to cast down
The modern usage of the word is, to unload roughly, to toss on to a refuse heap, to throw quantities of goods on to a foreign market. usually at a loss
The noun, a *dump*, besides meaning a refuse heap, is more generally applied to a military or other deposit of supplies for storage, or waiting for future use
The word is also used for various "dumpy" objects of little value, such as leaden disks, and small coins such as one that was current in Australia in the early 19th century and was made by cutting a portion out of a Spanish dollar. Hence, *not worth a dump* The word is probably a back formation from *dumpy*, short and thick

Death saw two players playing cards,
But the game was not worth a dump
HOOD *Death's Ramble*, stanza 14

Dumps. To be in or **down in the dumps.** Out of spirits; Gay's Third Pastoral is *Wednesday, or the Dumps.*

Why, how now, daughter Katharine? In your dumps?—*Taming of the Shrew*, ii, 1

In Elizabethan times the name was given to any plaintive tune, and also to a slow and mournful sort of dance

They would have handled me a new way;
The devil's dump had been danced then.
BEAUMONT AND FLETCHER. *The Pilgrim*, v, 4

Dun. One who importunes for payment of a bill The tradition is that it refers to Joe Dun,

a bailiff of Lincoln in the reign of Henry VII. The *British Apollo* (1708) said he was so active and dexterous in collecting bad debts that when anyone became "slow to pay" the neighbours used to say to the creditors, "Dun him" (send Dun after him)

An Universitie dunne   . is an inferior creditor of some ten shillings or downewards, contracted for horse hire, or perchance drinke, too weake to be put in suite.—EARLE *Microcosmographia* (1628).

Squire Dun. The hangman between Richard Brandin and Jack Ketch

And presently a halter got,
Made of the best strong hempen teer;
And, ere a cat could lick his ear,
Had tied him up with as much art
As Dunn himself could do for 's heart
COTTON *Virgil Travestied*, Bk. iv

Dun Cow. The savage beast slain by Guy of Warwick (*q v*) A huge tusk, probably that of an elephant, is still shown at Harwich Castle as one of the horns of the dun cow
The fable is that it belonged to a giant, and was kept on Mitchell (Middle) Fold, Shropshire Its milk was inexhaustible, but one day an old woman who had filled her pail, wanted to fill her sieve also This so enraged the cow that she broke loose from the fold and wandered to Dunsmore heath, where she was slain

The Book of the Dun Cow. A twelfth-century Irish manuscript, *Lebor na h-uidre*, compiled in part by Moelmuire Mac Celechair, who was slain in 1106 It derives its name from a legend that Ciarán of Clonmacnoise took down the story of the *Tain Bó Cualnge* on a parchment made from the hide of his favourite cow Ciarán died in 544, but in the 15th century the name was given to the 12th-century manuscript, though the contents were entirely different.

To draw Dun out of the mire. To lend a helping hand to one in distress, to assist when things are at a standstill The allusion is to an Old English game, in which a log of wood, called Dun (a name formerly given to a cart-horse), is supposed to have fallen into the mire, and the players are to pull it out Each does all he can to obstruct the others, and as often as possible the log is made to fall on someone's toes. Constant allusion is made to this game

Sires, what? Dun is in the mire.—CHAUCER *Prologue to Maunciples Tale*

If thou art dun, we'll draw thee from the mire.
Romeo and Juliet, i, 4

Well done, my masters lend s your hands,
Draw Dun out of the ditch
Draw, pull, helpe all So, so, well done.
THOMAS DRUE *Duchesse of Suffolke* (1624)

Dunce A dolt, a stupid person The word is taken from *Duns* Scotus (about 1265-1308), so called from his birthplace, Dunse, in Scotland the learned schoolman His followers were called Dunsers or Scotists (*q v*) Tyndal says, when they saw that their hair-splitting divinity was giving way to modern theology, "the old barking curs raged in every pulpit" against the classics and new notions, so that the name indicated an opponent to progress, to learning, and hence a dunce

He knew what's what, and that's as high
As metaphysic wit can fly
A second Thomas, or at once
To name them all, another Dunse
BUTLER *Hudibras*, i, 1

Duns Scotus was buried at Cologne, his epitaph reads:—

Scotia me genuit, Anglia me suscepit,
Gallia me docuit, Colonia me tenet.

The Parliament of Dunces. Convened by Henry IV at Coventry, in 1404, and so called because all lawyers were excluded from it Also known as the Lawless, and Unlearned, Parliament

Dunciad. The dunce-epic, a satire by Alexander Pope first published in 1728 with Theobald figuring as the Poet Laureate of the realm of Dullness, but republished with an added fourth part in 1741 with Colley Cibber in that rôle. Pope makes use of his mock epic to pillory many of the writers of his time—writers who would now be forgotten were it not for his scathing gibes and denunciations

Dunderhead. A blockhead, or, rather, a muddle-headed person The history of the word is obscure *dunder* may be connected with the Scottish *donnered*, or merely be modelled on *blunder* It appears in early-17th-century works

Dundreary, Lord The impersonation of a good-natured, indolent, blundering, empty-headed swell, from the chief character in Tom Taylor's *Our American Cousin* (1858) E A Sothern created the character by the genius of his acting and the large additions he made to the original text The theatrical make-up for the part included a pair of long, silky whiskers, which set a fashion among the young men about Town

Dunedin. *See* EDINBURGH.

Dungarees (dŭng′ gà rēz). This comes from a Hindustani word, *dungri*, meaning a kind of coarse cotton cloth It is applied to an overall suit of coarse (usually blue) cloth

Dunghill! Coward! Villain! This is a cockpit phrase, all cocks, except gamecocks, being called dunghills.

Out, dunghill! dar'st thou brave a nobleman?
King John, IV, 3

That is, Dare you, a dunghill cock, brave a thoroughbred gamecock?

Every cock crows on its own dunghill. *See* COCK.

Dunheved Castle. *See* CASTLE TERABIL

Dunk, To. (U S A) To dip bread, toast, or doughnuts in one's coffee

Dunkers. *See* TUNKERS

Dunmow (dŭn′ mō) **To eat Dunmow bacon.** To live in conjugal amity, without even wishing the marriage knot to be less firmly tied. The allusion is to a custom said to have been instituted by Juga, a noble lady, in 1111, and restored by Robert de Fitzwalter in 1244; which was, that

any person from any part of England going to Dunmow, in Essex, and humbly kneeling on two stones at the church door, may claim a gammon of bacon, if he can swear that for twelve months and a day he has never had a household brawl or wished himself unmarried

Between 1244 and 1772 eight claimants were

admitted to eat the flitch Their names merit immortality

1445 Richard Wright, labourer, Bauburgh, near Norwich
1467 Steven Samuel, of Little Ayston, Essex.
1510 Thomas Ley fuller, Coggeshall, Essex.
1701 William and Jane Parsley, butcher, Much-Easton, Essex Same year, John and Ann Reynolds, Hatfield Regis
1751 Thomas Shakeshaft, woolcomber, Weathersfield, Essex.
1763 *Names not recorded*
1772 John and Susan Gilder, Tarling, Essex

Allusions to the custom are very frequent in 17th- and 18th-century literature, and in the last years of the 19th century it was revived A travesty of the old ceremony

Dunscore. The saut lairds o' Dunscore. Gentlefolk who have a name but no money. The tale is that the "puir wee lairds of Dunscore" (a parish near Dumfries) clubbed together to buy a stone of salt, which was doled out to the subscribers in small spoonfuls, that no one should get more than his due quota.

Duns Scotus. *See* DUNCE.

Dunstable (dŭn′ stăbl). Bailey, as if he actually believed it, gives the etymology of this word *Duns′ stable*, adding Duns or "Dunus was a robber in the reign of Henry I, who made it dangerous for travellers to pass that way." It is Celtic *dun*, a hill-fortress, and *staple*, an emporium or market (from late Lat or O Fr)

Downright Dunstable. Very blunt, plain speaking, straightforward, like the Dunstable road (a part of the Roman Watling Street), which runs very evenly from London and has many long, straight stretches Hence also the phrase **Plain as the road to Dunstable.** As Shakespeare says, "Plain as way to parish church."

Dunstan, St. (d 988) Archbishop of Canterbury (961), and patron saint of goldsmiths, being himself a noted worker in gold. He is represented in pontifical robes, and carrying a pair of pincers in his right hand, the latter referring to the legend that on one occasion at Glastonbury (his birthplace) he seized the devil by the nose with a pair of red-hot tongs and refused to release him till he promised never to tempt him again *See also* HORSE-SHOES

The name St. Dunstan's is now intimately associated with work for the blind, on account of the institution founded during World War I, and for many years run by Sir Arthur Pearson (himself blind) at St. Dunstan's House, Regent's Park, for the welfare and training of blinded soldiers and later of blind civilians

Dunsterforce. The name given to the men sent to Baku in 1918 under the command of Maj.-Gen L. C Dunsterville (1865-1946), who had been a schoolfellow of Rudyard Kipling and the hero of *Stalky & Co* The purpose of this expedition was to prevent the Turks and Germans reaching Baku and its oil wells. Dunsterforce held the town successfully and prevented the enemy from reaching the Caspian Sea, the whole affair making a very gallant adventure

Duodecimo (dū ō des' ı mō) A book whose sheets are folded into twelve leaves each (Lat. *duodecim*, twelve), often called "twelvemo," from the contraction 12mo. The book is naturally a small one, hence the expression is sometimes applied to other things of small size, such as a dwarf Cp DECIMO-SEXTO

Dup is *do up* Thus Ophelia says in one of her snatches, he "dupped the chamber door", *i e* did up or pushed up the latch, in order to open the door, that he might "let in the maid" (*Hamlet*, ıv, 1)

Iche weene the porters are drunk Will they not dup the gate to-day—EDWARDS *Damon and Pythias* (1571)

Dupes, Day of the In French history, November 11th, 1630, when Marie de Medicis and Gaston, Duc d'Orleans extorted from Louis XIII a promise that he would dismiss his Minister, the Cardinal Richelieu The cardinal went in all speed to Versailles, the king repented, and Richelieu became more powerful than ever. Marie de' Medicis and Gaston, the 'dupes," had to pay dearly for their short triumph

Duration. In World Wars I and II the engagement of men called to the colours in Britain was "for the duration of the emergency," which meant that their services could be retained until the King signed an Order declaring the state of emergency to be at an end Hence the phrase became synonymous with "a long time," or a time in the far distant future

Durbar (dĕr' bar) The word comes from the Persian *der*, a door, and *bar*, admittance, and is properly used in India for the court, council, or council-chamber of a native ruler. It is also used for an official reception on a large scale, or for a state ceremony such as the magnificent durbar for the proclamation of George V as Emperor of India, in 1911

Durden, Dame. A generic term for a good, old-fashioned housewife In the old song she kept five serving girls to carry the milking pails, and five serving men to use the spade and flail, and of course the five men loved the five maids

'Twas Moll and Bet, and Doll and Kate, and Dorothy Draggletail,
And John and Dick, and Joe and Jack, and Humphrey with his flail ANON

Dust. Slang for money, probably in allusion to the moralist's contention that money is worthless

Down with the dust! Out with the money; dub up! The expression is at least three hundred years old, and it is said that Swift once took for the text of a charity sermon, "He who giveth to the poor, lendeth to the Lord." Having thrice repeated his text, he added "Now, brethren, if you like the security, *down with your dust*" That ended his sermon!

I'll dust your jacket for you. Give you a good beating; also used with *doublet*, *trousers*, etc , in place of jacket. *See* quotation from Smollett, *under* DOUSE IN THE CHOPS.

To bite the dust *See* BITE.

To kiss or lick the dust. *See* KISS

To raise a dust, to kick up a dust. To make a commotion or disturbance

To shake the dust from one's feet. To show extreme dislike of a place, and to leave it with the firm intention of never returning The allusion is to the Eastern custom

And whosoever shall not receive you or hear your words, when ye depart out of that house or city, shake off the dust of your feet —*Matt* x, 14
But the Jews raised persecution against Paul and Barnabas, and expelled them out of their coasts But they shook off the dust of their feet against them, and came unto Iconium —*Acts* xiii, 50, 51

To throw dust in one's eyes To mislead The allusion is to "the swiftest runner in a sandy race, who to make his fellowes follow aloofe, casteth dust with his heeles into their envious eyes" (*Cotgrave*, 1611)

The Mohammedans had a practice of casting dust into the air for the sake of confounding the enemies of the faith This was done by the Prophet on two or three occasions, as in the battle of Honein, and the Koran refers to it when it says, "Neither didst thou, O Mahomet, cast dust into their eyes, but it was God who confounded them"

The dustman has arrived. or "The sandman is about " It is bedtime, for the children rub their eyes, as if dust or sand was in them

Well, it is none so dusty, or **Not so dusty.** I don't call it bad, rather smart Here *dusty* means mean, soiled, worthless

Dustyfoot. *See* PIEPOWDER COURT

Dutch. The word, properly meaning "Hollandish," is the M Dut *Dutsch* or Ger *Deutsch*, and formerly denoted the people of Germany or Teutons generally The Pennsylvania Dutch, for example, were originally German immigrants In colloquial English use the adjective has a belittling or derisive application, sometimes meaning little more than "foreign" or "un-English," and sometimes with reference to the drinking habits of the 17th-century Dutchman *See* DUTCH COURAGE, CONCERT, GOLD, etc , *below*

Dutch auction. An auction in which the auctioneer offers the goods at gradually decreasing prices, the first bidder to accept being the purchaser, the reverse process to that of an ordinary auction Anyone can sell by Dutch auction, whereas an ordinary auction can be conducted only by a duly licensed auctioneer

Dutch comfort. 'Tis a comfort it was no worse The comfort derivable from the consideration that how bad soever the evil which has befallen you, a worse is at least conceivable

Dutch concert A great noise and uproar, like that made by a party of intoxicated Dutchmen, some singing, others quarrelling, speechifying, wrangling, and so on

Dutch courage. The courage excited by drink, pot valour

The Dutch their wine, and all their brandy lose,
Disarmed of that from which their courage grows,
While the glad English, to relieve their toil,
In healths to their great leader drink the spoil
WALLER *Instructions to a Painter for a Picture of the Victory over the Dutch, June 3, 1665*

Dutch gleek. Tippling. Gleek (*q v.*) is a game, and the phrase implies that the game loved by Dutchmen is drinking

> Nor could be partaker of any of the good cheer except it were the liquid part of it, which they call "Dutch Gleek"—GAYTON *Pleasant Notes upon Don Quixote* (1654)

Dutch gold. Deutsche or German gold. An alloy of copper and zinc, invented by Prince Rupert of Bavaria

Dutch nightingales. Frogs Similarly, Cambridgeshire nightingales; Liège nightingales, etc.

I will talk to you like a Dutch uncle. Will reprove you smartly. For "uncle" cp Horace, 3 *Od.* xii, 3, "*Metuentes patruæ verbera linguæ*" (dreading the castigations of an uncle's tongue), and 2 *Sat* iii, 88, "*Ne sis patruus mihi*" ("don't come the uncle over me")

Dutch treat A meal, amusement, etc, at which each person pays for himself

My old Dutch. Here the word is a contraction of *duchess* (*q v*), and is nothing to do with Holland or Germany.

The Dutch have taken Holland. A quiz when anyone tells what is well known as a piece of wonderful news Similar to *Queen Bess* (or *Queen Anne*) *is dead*

In Dutch. In prison.

I'm a Dutchman if I do. A strong refusal During the rivalry between England and Holland in the 17th century, the word Dutch was synonymous with all that was false and hateful, and when a man said, "I would rather be a Dutchman than do what you ask me," he used the strongest terms of refusal that words could express

If not, I'm a Dutchman, means, I will do it, or I will call myself a Dutchman

The Flying Dutchman *See* FLYING

Well, I'm a Dutchman! An exclamation of strong incredulity

Duty means what is due or owing, a debt which should be paid In this sense it is applied to the tax or impost charged by government on certain goods when imported from foreign countries. Obedience is the debt of citizens to rulers for protection, and service is the debt of persons employed for wages received

> Strictly considered, all duty is owed originally to God only, but . . duties to God may be distributed into duties towards self, towards manhood, and towards God —GREGORY *Christian Ethics*, I, i.

England expects that every man will do his duty. Nelson's signal to his fleet just before the battle of Trafalgar (1805).

Duumvirs (dū' um vẽrz) (Lat. *duumvir*, one of the two men) Certain Roman officials who were appointed in pairs, like our London sheriffs; originally, those who had charge of the Sibylline books Later, *duumviri* were appointed as magistrates, as naval directors, directors of public works, etc.

Dwarf. Dwarfs have figured in the legends and mythology of nearly every race, and Pliny gives particulars of whole races of them,

B D —11

possibly following travellers' reports of African pigmies Among the Teutonic and Scandinavian peoples dwarfs held an important place in mythology They generally dwelt in rocks, caves, and recesses of the earth, were the guardians of its mineral wealth and precious stones, and were very skilful in the working of these They had their own king, as a rule were not inimical to man, but could on occasion be intensely vindictive and mischievous

In England diminutive persons—dwarfs— were popular down to the 18th century as court favourites or household pets; and in later times they have frequently been exhibited as curiosities at circuses, etc

Among those recorded in legend or history (with their reputed heights) the following are, perhaps, the most famous :—

ALBERICH (*q v*), the dwarf of the *Nibelungenlied*

ANDROMEDA and CONOPAS, each 2 ft. 4 in Dwarfs of Julia, niece of Augustus

BEBE, or Nicholas Ferry, 2 ft 9 in A native of France (1714-37) He had a brother and sister, both dwarfs

BORUWLASKI (*Count Joseph*), 3 ft 3 in at the age of thirty (d 1837)

BUCKINGER (*Matthew*), a German, born 1674 He was born without hands, legs, or feet Facsimiles of his writing are amongst the Harleian MSS.

CHE-MAH (a Chinaman), 2 ft 1 in , weight 52 lb. Exhibited in London in 1880

COLOBRI (*Prince*) of Sleswig, 2 ft 1 in., weight 25 lb. at the age of 25 (1851).

CONOPAS *See* ANDROMEDA *above*

COPPERNIN, the dwarf of the Princess of Wales, mother of George III The last court dwarf in England

CRACHAMI (*Caroline*) Born at Palermo; 1 ft. 8 in at death. (1814-24) Exhibited in Bond Street, London, 1824

DECKER or DUCKER (*John*), 2 ft 6 in. An Englishman (1610).

FAIRY QUEEN (*The*), 1 ft 4 in , weight 4 lb. Exhibited in Regent Street, London, 1850. Her feet were less than two inches

GIBSON (*Richard*), a good portrait painter (1615-90). His wife's maiden name was Anne Shepherd Each measured 3 ft 10 in Waller sang their praises:—

> Design or chance makes others wive,
> But Nature did this match contrive

HUDSON (*Sir Jeffrey*) Born at Oakham, Rutlandshire; 3 ft 9 in at the age of thirty (1619-78), he figures in Scott's *Peveril of the Peak*

JARVIS (*John*), 2 ft Page of honour to Queen Mary (1508-56).

LOLKES (*Wybrand*), 2 ft 3 in , weight 57 lb. Exhibited at Astley's in 1790

LUCIUS, 2 ft , weight 17 lb The dwarf of the Emperor Augustus.

MAGRI, COUNT PRIMO *See* WARREN *below*

MARINE (*Lizzie*), 2 ft 9 in , weight 45 lb.

MIDGETS, THE Lucia Zarate, the elder sister, 1 ft. 8 in , weight 4½ lb at the age of eighteen. Her sister was a little taller Exhibited in London, 1881

MILLER (*Miss*), of Virginia, 2 ft 2 in.

MITE (*General*), 1 ft 9 in (weight 9 lb.) at the age of seventeen Exhibited in London, 1881

NUTT, COMMODORE *See* TOM THUMB *below*

PAAP (*Simon*) A Dutch dwarf, 2 ft 4 in , weight 27 lb

SAWYER (*A L*), 2 ft. 6½ in., weight 39 lb Editor in 1883, etc , of the *Democrat*, a paper of considerable repute in Florida

STOBERIN (*C H*), of Nuremberg, 2 ft. 11 in. at the age of twenty

STOCKER (*Nannette*), 2 ft. 9 in Exhibited in London in 1815

STRASSE DAVIT Family Man 1 ft 8 in., woman, 1 ft 6 in ; child, at age of seventeen, only 6 in. Embalmed in the chemical library of Rastadt

TERESIA (*Madame*) A Corsican, 2 ft 10 in , weight 27 lb. Exhibited in London 1773

TOM THUMB (*General*), whose name was Charles S Stratton, born at Bridgeport in Connecticut, U S , (1838-83) Exhibited first in London in 1844. In 1863 he married Lavinia Warren, and was then 31 in. in height, she being 32 in , and 21 years old They visited England in the following year with their dwarf son, Commodore Nutt

WANMER (*Lucy*), 2 ft 6 in , weight 45 lb Exhibited in London, 1801, at the age of forty-five

WARREN (*Lavinia*) *See* TOM THUMB *above* In 1885 she married another dwarf, Count Primo Magri, who was 2 ft 8 in

WORMBERG (*John*), 2 ft 7 in at the age of thirty-eight (Hanoverian period)

XIT was the dwarf of Edward VI.

ZARATE *See* MIDGETS *above*

The Black Dwarf. A gnome of the most malignant character, once held by the dalesmen of the border as the author of all the mischief that befell their flocks and herds Scott has a novel so called (1816), in which the name is given to Sir Edward Mauley, *alias* Elshander, the recluse, Cannie Elshie, and the Wise Wight of Mucklestane Moor

Dwarf Alberich. *See* ALBERICH

Dwt. D-wt , *i e* *denarius-weight* (pennyweight). *Cp* Cwt

Dyed in the Wool Thorough-going, 100 per cent (16th-century origin)

Dying Sayings (real or traditional)

ADAMS (*President*) "Independence for ever "

ADAMS (*John Q*). "It is the last of earth I am content "

ADDISON "See in what peace a Christian can die "

ALBERT (*Prince Consort*) "I have such sweet thoughts " *or* "I have had wealth, rank, and power, but, if these were all I had, how wretched I should be!"

ALEXANDER I (of Russia) "Que vous devez être fatiguee" (to his wife Elizabeth)

ALEXANDER II (of Russia) "I am sweeping through the gates, washed in the blood of the Lamb "

ALFIERI "Clasp my hand, dear friend, I am dying "

ANAXAGORAS (the philosopher, who kept a school, being asked if he wished for anything, replied) "Give the boys a holiday "

ANGELO (*Michael*) "My soul I resign to God, my body to the earth, my worldly goods to my next of kin "

ANTOINETTE (*See* MARIE)

ANTONY (of Padua) "I see my God He calls me to Him "

ARCHIMEDES (being ordered by a Roman soldier to follow him, replied) "Wait till I have finished my problem."

AUGUSTUS (to his friends) "Do you think I have played my part pretty well through the farce of life?"

BACON (*Francis*) "My name and memory I leave to men's charitable speeches, to foreign nations and to the next age "

BAILLY "Yes! But it is with cold." (This he said on his way to the guillotine, when one said to him, "Why, how you tremble ")

BEARD (Dr G M , 1883) "I should like to record the thoughts of a dying man for the benefit of science, but it is impossible "

BEAUMONT (*Cardinal*) "What! is there no escaping death?"

BECKET (*Thomas a*) "I confide my soul and the cause of the Church to God, to the Virgin Mary, to the patron saints of the Church, and to St Dennis " (As he went to the altar in Canterbury Cathedral, where he was assassinated)

BEDE (*The Venerable*) (Having dictated the last sentence of his translation of St John's Gospel, and being told by the Scribe that the sentence was now written) "It is well; you have said the truth it is indeed "

BEECHER (*Henry Ward*)· "Now comes the mystery "

BEETHOVEN (who was deaf) "I shall hear in heaven."

BERRY (*Madame de*) "Is not this dying with courage and true greatness?"

BLOOD (*Colonel*) "I do not fear death "

BOILEAU "It is a great consolation to a poet on the point of death that he has never written a line injurious to good morals "

BOLEYN (*Anne*) "The executioner is, I believe, very expert, and my neck is very slender "

BROUGHTON (*Bishop*) "Let the earth be filled with His glory "

BURKE "God bless you "

BURNS "Don't let the awkward squad fire over my grave "

BYRON "I must sleep now "

CÆSAR "Et tu, Brute ?" (To Brutus, his most intimate friend, when he stabbed him)

CAMERON (*Colonel James*) "Scots, follow me'" (He was killed at Bull Run, July 21st, 1861)

CASTLEREAGH "Bankhead, let me fall into your arms It is all over " (Said to his doctor)

CATESBY (one of the conspirators in the Gunpowder Plot) "Stand by me, Tom, and we will die together "

CATO THE YOUNGER (on seeing that the sword's point was sharp and before thrusting it into his body), "Now I am master of myself "

CHARLEMAGNE "Lord, into Thy hands I commend my spirit " *Cp* COLUMBUS, LADY JANE GREY, and TASSO

CHARLES I (just before he laid his head on the block, to Juxon, Archbishop of Canterbury) "Remember "

CHARLES II "I have been a most unconscionable time a-dying, but I hope you will excuse it." (To James) "Do not, do not let poor Nelly starve "

CHARLES VIII (*of France*) "I hope never again to commit a mortal sin, nor even a venial one, if I can help it "

CHARLES IX (of France, in whose reign occurred the Massacre of St Bartholomew) "Nurse, nurse, what murder! what blood! O! I have done wrong God pardon me "

CHESTERFIELD (*Lord*) "Give Dayrolles a chair "

CHRYSOSTOM "Glory to God for all things Amen "

CICERO (to his assassins) "Strike!"

COKE (*Sir Edward*) "Thy kingdom come, Thy will be done "

COLIGNY "Honour these grey hairs, young man " (To the German who assassinated him)

COLUMBUS "Lord, into Thy hands I commend my spirit " *Cp* CHARLEMAGNE and TASSO

COPERNICUS "Now, O Lord, set Thy servant free " (*See* Luke ii, 29)

CRANMER "That unworthy hand! That unworthy hand'" (As he held in the flames his right hand which had signed his apostasy)

CROME (*John*) "O Hobbema, Hobbema, how I have loved you "

CROMWELL "My design is to make what haste I can to be gone "

CUVIER (to the nurse who was applying leeches) "Nurse, it was I who discovered that leeches have red blood "

DANTON (to the executioner) "Be sure you show the mob my head It will be a long time ere they see its like "

DARWIN "I am not in the least afraid to die "

DEMONAX (the philosopher) "You may go home, the show is over" (*Lucian*) *Cp* RABELAIS

DERBY (*Earl of*) "Douglas, I would give all my lands to save thee "

DIDEROT "The first step towards philosophy is incredulity "

DOUGLAS (*Earl*) "Fight on, my merry men "

EDWARD I "Carry my bones before you on your march, for the rebels will not be able to endure the sight of me, alive or dead "

EDWARDS (*Jonathan*) "Trust in God, and you need not fear "

ELDON (*Lord*) "It matters not where I am going whether the weather be cold or hot "

ELIZABETH (*Queen*) "All my possessions for a moment of time "

ELLIOTT (*Ebenezer*). "A strange sight, sir, an old man unwilling to die."

ELPHEGE (*Archbishop of Canterbury*) "You urge me in vain I am not the man to provide Christian flesh for Pagan teeth, by robbing my flock to enrich their enemy."

ENGHIEN (*Duc d'*) "I die for my king and for France." (Shot by order of Napoleon I in 1804)

EPAMINONDAS (wounded, on being told that the Thebans were victorious) "Then I die happy." *Cp.* WOLFE

ETTY "Wonderful! Wonderful this death!'"

FONTENELLE "I suffer nothing, but I feel a sort of difficulty in living longer."

FOX (*C J*) "It don't signify, my dearest, dearest Liz." (To his wife)

FOX (*George, the Quaker*) "Never heed' the Lord's power is over all weakness and death."

FREDERICK V (of Denmark) "There is not a drop of blood on my hands." *Cp* PERICLES

GAINSBOROUGH "We are all going to heaven and Van Dyck is of the company." *Cp* CROME

GARTH (*Sir Samuel*) "Dear gentlemen, let me die a natural death." (to his physicians, Garth was a doctor himself)

GASTON DE FOIX "I am a dead man! Lord, have mercy upon me!'"

GEORGE IV "Wally, what is this? It is death, my boy. They have deceived me." (Said to his page, Sir Walthen Waller.)

GOETHE "Light! more light!'"

GRANT (*General*) "I want nobody distressed on my account."

GRATTON ' I am perfectly resigned. I am surrounded by my family. I have served my country. I have reliance upon God and I am not afraid of the Devil."

GREELEY (*Horace*). "It is done."

GREGORY VII "I have loved justice and hated iniquity, therefore I die in exile." (He had retired to Salerno after his disputes with the Emperor, Henry IV.)

GREY (*Lady Jane*) "Lord, into Thy hands I commend my spirit." *Cp* CHARLEMAGNE

GUSTAVUS ADOLPHUS "I am sped, brother. Save thyself."

HALE (*Capt Nathan*, hanged by the British Army in America for espionage) "I regret that I have but one life to give for my country."

HANNIBAL "Let us now relieve the Romans of their fears by the death of a feeble old man."

HAVELOCK (*Sir Henry*) "Come, my son, and see how a Christian can die."

HAYDN died singing "God preserve the emperor!'"

HAZLITT. "I have led a happy life."

HENRY II "Now let the world go as it will, I care for nothing more." (When told that his favourite son John was one of those who were conspiring against him.)

HENRY VIII "All is lost! Monks, monks, monks!'"

HERBERT (*George*) "Now, Lord, receive my soul."

HOBBES. "I am taking a fearful leap in the dark."

HOFER (*Andreas*) "I will not kneel. Fire!" (Spoken to the soldiers commissioned to shoot him.)

HOLLAND (*Lord*) "If Mr. Selwyn calls, let him in. if I am alive I shall be very glad to see him, and if I am dead he will be very glad to see me."

HUMBOLDT. "How grand these rays! They seem to beckon earth to heaven."

HUNTER (*Dr William*). "If I had strength to hold a pen, I would write down how easy and pleasant a thing it is to die."

HUSS (*John*) (to an old woman thrusting another faggot on the pile to burn him) ' Sancta simplicitas!'"

JACKSON ("*Stonewall*") "Let us pass over the river, and rest under the shade of the trees."

JAMES V (of Scotland) "It [the crown of Scotland] came with a lass and will go with a lass." (This he said when told that the queen had given birth to a daughter—the future Mary Queen of Scots.)

JEFFERSON (of America). "I resign my spirit to God, my daughter to my country."

JEROME (of Prague) "Thou knowest, Lord, that I have loved the truth."

JOAN OF ARC "Jesus! Jesus! Jesus! Blessed be God."

JOHNSON (*Dr*) "God bless you, my dear." (To Miss Morris).

JULIAN (called the "Apostate") "Vicisti, O Galilee" ("Thou hast conquered, O Galilæan").

KEATS "Severn—I—lift me up—I am dying—I shall die easy, don't be frightened—be firm, and thank God it has come."

KEN (*John*) (*Bishop*). "God's will be done."

KNOX (*John*) "Now it is come."

LAMB (*Charles*) "My bed-fellows are cramp and cough—we three all in one bed."

LAMBERT (the Martyr) "None but Christ' None but Christ!" (As he was pitched into the flames.)

LATIMER. "Be of good cheer, Master Ridley, we shall this day kindle such a candle in England, as, I trust in God, shall never be extinguished" (to Ridley, at the stake)

LAUD (*Archbishop*) "No one can be more willing to send me out of life than I am desirous to go."

LAWRENCE (*Sir Henry*) "Let there be no fuss about me, let me be buried with the men."

LEICESTER (*Earl of*) "By the arm of St James, it is time to die."

LEOPOLD I (*Kaiser*) ' Let me die to the sound of sweet music." *Cp* MIRABEAU

LOCKE (*John*) "Oh! the depth of the riches of the goodness and knowledge of God. Cease now" (To Lady Masham who was reading to him some of the Psalms.)

LOUIS IX "I will enter now into the house of the Lord."

LOUIS XIV "Why weep you? Did you think I should live for ever? I thought dying had been harder."

LOUIS XVI (on the scaffold) ' Frenchmen, I die guiltless of the crimes imputed to me. Pray God my blood fall not on France!'"

MACAULAY "I shall retire early, I am very tired."

MACHIAVELLI "I love my country more than my soul."

MALESHERBES (to the priest) "Hold your tongue' your wretched chatter disgusts me."

MARGARET (of Scotland, wife of Louis XI of France) "Fie de la vie' qu'on ne m'en parle plus."

MARIE ANTOINETTE "Farewell, my children, for ever. I am going to your father."

MARTINEAU (*Harriet*) "I see no reason why the existence of Harriet Martineau should be perpetuated."

MARY (*Queen of England*) "You will find the word Calais written on my heart."

MARY II (to Archbishop Tillotson, who had paused in reading a prayer) "My Lord, why do you not go on? I am not afraid to die."

MELANCTHON (in reply to the question, "Do you want anything?") "Nothing but heaven."

MIRABEAU "Let me fall asleep to the sound of delicious music." *Cp* LEOPOLD.

MOHAMMED "O Allah' Pardon my sins Yes I come."

MONICA (*St*). "In peace I will sleep with Him and take my rest." (*St Augustine Confessions*)

MONMOUTH (*Duke of*) 'There are six guineas for you and do not hack me as you did my Lord Russell."

MONTAGU (*Lady Mary Wortley*) "It has all been very interesting."

MOODY (*the evangelist*) "I see earth receding Heaven is opening, God is calling me."

MOORE (*Sir John*) "I hope my country will do me justice."

MORE (*Sir Thomas*) "See me safe up [i e on ascending the scaffold], for my coming down, let me shift for myself."

MOZART "You spoke of a refreshment, Emile, take my last notes, and let me hear once more my solace and delight."

MURAT (*King of Naples*) "Soldiers, save my face, aim at my heart. Farewell." (Said to the men detailed to shoot him.)

NAPOLEON I "Mon Dieu' La Nation Française Tête d'armee."

NAPOLEON III "Were you at Sedan?" (To Dr. Conneau.)

NELSON "I thank God I have done my duty Kiss me, Hardy."

NERO "Qualis artifex pereo " ("What an artist the world is losing in me!")

NEWTON "I don't know what I may seem to the world But as to myself I seem to have been only like a boy playing on the seashore and diverting myself in now and then finding a smoother pebble or prettier shell than ordinary, whilst the great ocean of truth lay all undiscovered before me "

PALMER (*John, the actor*) "There is another and a better world " (Said on the stage It is a line in the part he was playing—*The Stranger*)

PALMERSTON: ' Die, my dear doctor! that's the *last* thing I shall do "

PASCAL· "My God forsake me not "

PERICLES ' I have never caused any citizen to put on mourning on my account " *Cp* FREDERICK V

PETERS (*Hugh the regicide*) "Friend, you do not well to trample on a dying man." (To his executioner)

PITT (*William the Younger*) "Alas, my country! How I leave my country!"

PLATO "I thank the guiding providence and fortune of my life, first, that I was born a man and a Greek, not a barbarian nor a brute, and next, that I happened to live in the age of Socrates "

POE (*Eagar Allan*) "Lord, help my soul!"

POMPADOUR (*Mme de*) "Stay a little longer, M le Cure, and we will go together "

PONIATOWSKI (after the bridge over the Pliesse was blown up) "Gentlemen, it behoves us now to die with honour "

POPE "Friendship itself is but a part of virtue "

QUIN (*the actor*) "I could wish this tragic scene were over, but I hope to go through it with becoming dignity "

RABELAIS "Let down the curtain, the farce is over " *Cp* DEMONAX Also, 'I am going to seek the great perhaps "

RALEIGH "It matters little how the head lies " (Said on the scaffold when he was to be beheaded)

RENAN "We perish, we disappear, but the march of time goes on for ever "

REYNOLDS (*Sir Joshua*) "I know that all things on earth must have an end and now I am come to mine "

RHODES (*C J*) "So little done, so much to do "

RICHARD I "Youth, I forgive thee" (Said to Bertrand de Gourdon, who shot him with an arrow at Chalus) Then to his attendants he added, "Take off his chains, give him 100 shillings, and let him go "

RICHARD III "Treason! treason!" (At Bosworth, where his best men deserted him and joined Richmond, afterwards Henry VII)

ROCHEJAQUELEIN (the Vendean hero) "We go to meet the foe If I advance, follow me, if I retreat, slay me if I fail, avenge me "

ROLAND (*Madame,* on her way to the guillotine) ' O liberty! What crimes are committed in thy name!"

ROSCOMMON (*Earl of*)·
" My, God, my Father, and my Friend, Do not forsake me at my end "
(Quoting from his own translation of the *Dies Iræ*)

RUSSELL (*Lord;* executed 1683) "The bitterness of death is now past "

SALADIN· "When I am buried, carry my winding-sheet on the point of a spear, and say these words Behold the spoils which Saladin carries with him! Of all his victories, realms, and riches, nothing remains to him but this " *Cp* SEVERUS

SCARRON "Ah, my children, you cannot cry for me so much as I have made you laugh "

SCHILLER "Many things are growing plain and clear to my understanding "

SCOTT (*Sir Walter*) "God bless you all, I feel myself again " (To his family.)

SERVETUS (at the stake) "Christ, Son of the eternal God, have mercy upon me " (Calvin insisted on his saying, "the eternal Son of God " but he would not, and was burnt to death)

SEVERUS "I have been everything, and everything is nothing A little urn will contain all that remains of one for whom the whole world was too little " *Cp.* SALADIN

SHERIDAN "I am absolutely undone "

SIDNEY (*Sir Philip*) (To his brother Robert) "Govern your will and affections by the will and word of your Creator in me beholding the end of this world with all her vanities "

SIWARD (the Dane) "Lift me up that I may die standing, not lying down like a cow " *Cp* VESPASIAN

SOCRATES "Crito, we owe a cock to Æsculapius "

STAEL (*Madame de*) "I have loved God, my father, and liberty "

STEPHEN (the first Christian martyr) "Lord, lay not this sin to their charge "

TALMA "The worst is, I cannot see " (But his last word was) "Voltaire '

TASSO 'Lord, into Thy hands I commend my spirit " Also recorded of CHARLEMAGNE, LADY JANE GREY, COLUMBUS, and others

TAYLOR (*General Zachary*) "I have tried to do my duty, and am not afraid to die I am ready "

TAYLOR (*the "Water-Poet"*) "How sweet it is to rest!"

TENTERDEN (*Lord Chief Justice*) "Gentlemen of the jury, you may retire "

THERAMENES (the Athenian condemned by Critias to drink hemlock, said as he drank the poison)· 'To the health of the fair Critias "

THISTLEWOOD (*executed for high treason,* 1820)· "I shall soon know the grand secret "

THOREAU "I leave this world without a regret "

THURLOW (*Lord*) "I'll be shot if I don't believe I'm dying "

TYNDALE "Lord, open the eyes of the King of England" (*i e* Henry VIII)

VANE (*Sir Harry*) "It is a bad cause which cannot bear the words of a dying man "

VESPASIAN "A king should die standing" (*See* SIWARD); but his last words were, "Ut puto, deus fio" *i e* "I suppose I am now becoming a god," referring to the apotheosization of Cæsars after death

VICTORIA (*Queen*) "Oh, that peace may come" (referring to the war in South Africa then in progress)

VOLTAIRE "Do let me die in peace."

WASHINGTON "It is well I die hard, but am not afraid to go "

WEBSTER (*Daniel*) "Life, life! Death, death' How curious it is!"

WESLEY (*Charles*) "I shall be satisfied with Thy likeness—satisfied "

WESLEY (*John*) "The best of all is, God is with us "

WILBERFORCE (His father said to him, "So He giveth His beloved sleep", to which Wilberforce replied) "Yes, and sweet indeed is the rest which Christ giveth " (Saying this, he never spoke again)

WILLIAM (of Nassau) "O God, have mercy upon me, and upon this poor nation " (This was just before he was shot by Balthasar Gerard)

WILSON (the ornithologist) "Bury me where the birds will sing over my grave "

WISHART "I fear not this fire" (at the stake)

WOLCOT ("*Peter Pindar*") "Give me back my youth!"

WOLFE (*General*) "What! do they run already? Then I die happy " *Cp* EPAMINONDAS

WOLSEY (*Cardinal*)· "Had I but served my God with half the zeal that I have served my king, He would not have left me in my grey hairs "

WORDSWORTH "God bless you! Is that you, Dora?"

ZISKA (*John*) "Make my skin into drum-heads for the Bohemian cause "

Many of these sayings, like all other history, belong to the region of Phrase and Fable

Dymphna (dimf' na) The tutelar saint of the insane She is said to have been the daughter of an Irish prince of the 7th century, and was murdered at Gheel, in Belgium, by her own father, because she resisted his incestuous passion Gheel has long been a centre for the treatment of the mentally afflicted.

Dysmas (dis' mäs) The traditional name of the Penitent Thief, who suffered with Christ at the Crucifixion His relics are claimed by

Bologna, and in some calendars he is commemorated on March 25th In the apocryphal Gospel of Nicodemus he is called *Dimas* (and elsewhere *Titus*), and the Impenitent Thief *Gestas*

Dyvour (dī'vôr). The old name in Scotland for a bankrupt From the 17th century till 1836 *dyvours* were by law compelled to wear an upper garment, half yellow and half brown, with parti-coloured cap and hose.

Dyzemas Day (dız'măs) Tithe day (Por *dızimas*, tithes, Law Lat *decimæ*.)

E

E. This letter is the representative of the hieroglyphic fretwork, ⊓, and of the Phœnician and Hebrew sign for a window, called in Hebrew *he*

In *Logic*, E denotes a universal negative proposition, and is thus the opposite of A (*q v*)

The following legend is sometimes seen engraved under the two tables of the Ten Commandments in churches —

PRSVR Y PRFCT MN
VR KP THS PRCPTS TN
The vowel E
Supplies the key.

E.G., *e g* (Lat. *exempli gratia*). By way of example, for instance

E pluribus unum (ē ploo' ri bus ū' nŭm) (Lat) One unity composed of many parts. The motto of the United States of America, taken from *Moretum* (line 103), a Latin poem attributed to Virgil

Eager Beaver. American expression, in World War II, for a recruit so over-zealous that he would volunteer for jobs on every possible occasion Subsequently passed into civilian use

Eagle. Thy youth is renewed like the eagle's (*Ps* ciii, 5). This refers to the ancient superstition that every ten years the eagle soars into the ' fiery region," and plunges thence into the sea, where, moulting its feathers, it acquires new life *Cp* PHŒNIX

She saw where he upstarted brave
Out of the well .
As eagle fresh out of the ocean wave,
Where he hath lefte his plumes all hory gray,
And decks himself with fethers youthly gay.
SPENSER. *Faerie Queene*, I, xi, 34

In Christian art the eagle is emblematic of St. John the Evangelist, St Augustine, St Gregory the Great and St Prisca Emblematically or in heraldry the eagle is a charge of great honour It was called the Bird of Jove by the Romans, and borne on their army standards France (under the Empires), Austria, Prussia and Russia adopted it as a royal or imperial emblem.

The American Eagle, with outspread wings—spread-eagle—is specifically the emblem of the U S A It is sometimes erroneously called the Bald Eagle, though it is really the white-headed eagle of N America, *Haliaetus leucocephalus* The U.S coin called an eagle is a gold coin of the value of 10 dollars An

earlier coin known as an eagle was found in Ireland in the first years of Edward I, about 1272—again because of the bird impressed upon it.

The Golden Eagle and the **Spread Eagle** are commemorative of the 'Crusades, they were the devices of the emperors of the East, and formerly figured as the ensigns of the ancient kings of Babylon and Persia, of the Ptolemies and Seleucides

The Romans used to let an eagle fly from the funeral pile of a deceased emperor Dryden alludes to this custom in his stanzas on Oliver Cromwell after his funeral, when he says, "Officious haste did let too soon the sacred eagle fly "

Grand eagle. Paper, 28¾ by 42 in : so called from a watermark first met with in 1314

The two-headed eagle. The German eagle has its head turned to our left hand, and the Roman eagle to our right hand When Charlemagne was made "Kaiser of the Holy Roman Empire," he joined the two heads together, one looking east and the other west, consequently, the late Austrian Empire, as the direct successor of the Holy Roman Empire, included the *Double-headed Eagle* in its coat of arms

In Russia it was Ivan Vasilievitch who first assumed the two-headed eagle, when, in 1472, he married Sophia, daughter of Thomas Palæologus, and niece of Constantine XIV, the last Emperor of Byzantium The two heads symbolize the Eastern or Byzantine Empire and the Western or Roman Empire

The eagle doesn't hawk at flies. See AQUILA

The Eagle. Gaudenzio Ferrari (1481-1549), the Milanese painter

The Eagle of the doctors of France. Pierre d'Ailly (1350-1420), French cardinal and astrologer, who calculated the horoscope of Our Lord. and maintained that the stars foretold the deluge

The Eagle of Brittany. Bertrand Duguesclin (1320-80), Constable of France

The Eagle of Divines St Thomas Aquinas (1225-74)

The Eagle of Meaux. Jacques Benigne Bossuet (1627-1704), Bishop of Meaux, the grandest and most sublime of the pulpit orators of France

The Eagle of the North. Count Axel Oxenstierna (1583-1654), the Swedish statesman

Eagle-stones. See AETITES

Ear (A S *eare*) If your ears burn someone is talking about you This is a very old superstition, Pliny says, "When our ears do glow and tingle, some do talk of us in our absence ' In *Much Ado About Nothing* (iii, 1), Beatrice says when Ursula and Hero had been talking of her, "What fire is in mine ears?" Sir Thomas Browne ascribes the conceit to guardian angels, who touch the right ear if the talk is favourable and the left if otherwise This is done to cheer or warn

One ear tingles, some there be
That are snarling now at me
HERRICK *Hesperides*

About one's ears. Causing trouble The allusion is to a hornet's nest buzzing about one's head, thus, to bring the house about one's ears is to set the whole family against him

Bow down thine ear. Condescend to hear or listen (*Ps.* xxxi, 2).

By ear. To sing or play *by ear* means to sing or play without reading the musical notes, depending on the ear only.

Dionysius's Ear. A bell-shaped chamber connected by an underground passage with the king's palace. Its object was to enable the tyrant of Syracuse to overhear what was passing in the prison

A similar remarkable whispering gallery is to be found cut from the solid rock beneath Hastings Castle, where pre-Roman gaolers could listen to prisoners talking—the listening post is again shaped like an ear

Give ear to. Listen to, give attention to

I am all ear. All attention
I was all ear,
And took in strains that might create a soul
Under the ribs of death
MILTON *Comus*, 574

I'll send you off with a flea in your ear. *See* FLEA

In at one ear, and out of the other Forgotten as soon as heard
the sermon　of Dame Resoun ..
It toke no sojour in myn hede
For alle yede out at oon er
That in at that other she did lere
Romaunt of the Rose, 5148 (*c.* 1400).

Lend me your ears. Pay attention to what I am about to say
Friends, Romans, countrymen, lend me your ears,
I come to bury Cæsar, not to praise him
Julius Cæsar, iii, 2

Little pitchers have large ears. *See* PITCHER.

Mine ears hast thou bored. Thou hast accepted me as thy bond-slave for life If a Hebrew servant declined to go free after six years' service, the master was to bore his ear with an awl, in token of his voluntary servitude for life (*Exod* xxi, 6).

No ear A bad ear for music, "ear-blind" or "sound-blind"

Over head and ears. Wholly, desperately, said of being in love, debt trouble, etc

To be willing to give one's ears To be prepared to make a considerable sacrifice The allusion is to the old practice of cutting off the ears of those who refused to disown offensive opinions

To come to the ears of To come to someone's knowledge, especially by hearsay

To get the wrong sow by the ear *See* SOW

To fall together by the ears *See* FALL

To have itching ears To enjoy scandalmongering, hearing news or current gossip (2 *Tim* iv, 3)

To prick up one's ears. To listen attentively to something not expected, as horses prick up their ears at a sudden sound
Like unbacked colts, they pricked their ears,
SHAKESPEARE *Tempest*, iv, 1

To set people together by the ears. To create ill-will among them, to set them quarrelling and, metaphorically, pulling each other's ears, as dogs do when fighting
When civil dudgeon first grew high,
And men fell out, they knew not why,
When hard words, jealousies, and fears,
Set folks together by the ears
BUTLER *Hudibras* (opening lines)

To tickle the ears To gratify the ear either by pleasing sounds or flattering words.

To turn a deaf ear. To refuse to listen; to refuse to accede to a request

Walls have ears. *See* WALL.

Within earshot. Within hearing

You cannot make a silk purse out of a sow's ear. *See* SILK

Ear-finger. The little finger, which is thrust into the ear if anything tickles it

Ear-marked. Marked so as to be recognized, figuratively, marked or set aside for some special purpose The allusion is to setting owner's marks on the ears of cattle and sheep
The late president [Balmaceda] took on board a large quantity of silver, which had been ear-marked for a particular purpose —*Newspaper paragraph*, Sept 4, 1891

Ears to Ear Bible, The. *See* BIBLE. SPECIALLY NAMED

Earing. Ploughing (A S *erian*, to plough, *cp* Lat *aro*)
And yet there are five years, in the which there shall neither be earing nor harvest —*Gen* xlv, 6
If the first heir of my invention prove deformed, I shall be sorry it had so noble a godfather, and never after ear so barren a land, for fear it yield me still so bad a harvest —SHAKESPEARE *Dedication to "Venus and Adonis"*

Earl (A S *eorl*, a man of position, in opposition to *ceorl*, a churl or freeman of the lowest rank, *cp* Dan *jarl*) The third in dignity in the British peerage, ranking next below Marquess (*q v*) In Anglo-Saxon times, it was a title of the highest dignity and eminence, and was even applied to sovereign princes Earl Godwin was a ruler of enormous power, as also were the earls created by the Norman kings *Cp* VISCOUNT William the Conqueror, tried to introduce the word Count, but did not succeed, although the wife of an earl is still called a *countess*

An earl's coronet has eight silver balls mounted on gold rays which reach to the top of the cap, with small strawberry leaves alternating between them
The sheriff is called in Latin vice-comes, as being the deputy of the earl or comes, to whom the custody of the shire is said to have been committed —BLACKSTONE *Commentaries*, I, ix

Earl Marshal. A high officer of state who presides over the College of Arms, grants armorial bearings, and is responsible for the arrangement of State ceremonials, processions, etc Since 1483 the office has been hereditary in the line of the Dukes of Norfolk

Earl of Mar's Grey Breeks. The 21st Foot (the Royal Scots Fusiliers) are so called because they wore *grey breeches* when the Earl of Mar was their colonel (1678-86)

Earthquakes. According to Indian mythology, the world rests on the head of a great elephant, "Muha-pudma," and when, for the sake of rest, the huge monster refreshes itself by moving its head, an earthquake is produced

The lamas say that the earth is placed on the back of a gigantic frog, and when the frog stretches its limbs or moves its head, 't shakes the earth Other Eastern mythologists place the earth on the back of a tortoise

Greek and Roman mythologists ascribe earthquakes to the restlessness of the giants which Jupiter buried under high mountains. Thus Virgil (*Æneid*, iii, 578) ascribes the eruption of Etna to the giant Enceladus

Earwig. A S. *ear-wicga*, ear-beetle, so called from the erroneous notion that these insects are apt to get into our ears, and so penetrate the brain

Metaphorically, one who whispers all the news and scandal going, in order to curry favour, a flatterer

> Court earwigs banish from your ears.
> *Political Ballads* (1688)

Ease From O Fr *eise*, Mod Fr *aise*

At ease. Without pain or anxiety

Chapel of ease *See* CHAPEL.

Ease her! An order given on a small steamer to reduce speed The next order, is generally "Back her!" and then "Stop her!"

Ill at ease. Uneasy, not comfortable, anxious.

Stand at ease! An infantry drill command for a position less rigid than *attention*, with the feet apart and hands joined behind the back. It is intermediate between *attention* and *stand easy!* in which complete freedom (short of moving away) is allowable

To ease one of his money or purse. To steal it

East. The custom of **turning to the east** when the creed is repeated is to express the belief that Christ is the Dayspring and Sun of Righteousness. The altar is placed at the east end of the church to remind us of Christ, the Dayspring and Resurrection, and persons are buried with their feet to the East to signify that they died in the hope of the Resurrection

The ancient Greeks always buried their dead with the face *upwards*, looking towards heaven; and the feet turned to the east or the rising sun, to indicate that the deceased was on his way to Elysium, and not to the region of night (Diogenes Laertius *Life of Solon*, in Greek)

East is East and West is West. A phrase from Rudyard Kipling emphasizing the divergence of views on ethics and life in general between the Oriental and Western races—a dichotomy that appears to admit of no compromise

> Oh, East is East, and West is West and never the
>   twain shall meet,
> Till Earth and Sky stand presently at God's great
>   Judgment Seat
> But there is neither East nor West, Border, nor Breed
>   nor Birth,
> When two strong men stand face to face, though they
>   come from the ends of the Earth
>   *The Ballad of East and West*

Far East, China, Japan, etc

Middle East, Iran, Irak, etc

Near East, Turkey, Syria, Palestine, Asia Minor, etc

East-ender. *See under* END

He came safe from the East Indies, and was drowned in the Thames. He encountered many dangers of great magnitude, but was at last killed where he thought himself secure.

To send to the East Indies for Kentish pippins. To go round about to accomplish a very simple thing To crush a fly on a wheel

Eastern Shore, The. Maryland between the Atlantic Ocean and Delaware Bay

Easter The name was adopted for the Christian Paschal festival from A S *eastre*, a heathen festival held at the vernal equinox in honour of the Teutonic goddess of dawn, called by Bede *Eostre* (cognate with Lat *aurora* and Sanskrit *ushas*, dawn) On the introduction of Christianity it was natural for the name of the heathen festival to be transferred to the Christian, the two falling about the same time

Easter Sunday is the first Sunday after the Paschal full moon, i e the full moon that occurs on the day of the vernal equinox (March 21st) or on any of the next 28 days Consequently, Easter Sunday cannot be earlier than March 22nd or later than April 25th. This was fixed by the Council of Nicæa, A.D 325

It was formerly a common belief that the sun danced on Easter Day.

> But oh, she dances such a way,
> No sun upon an Easter day
>   Is half so fine a sight
> SIR JOHN SUCKLING *Ballad upon a Wedding*

Sir Thomas Browne combats the superstition:—

> We shall not, I hope, disparage the Resurrection of our Redeemer, if we say the Sun doth not dance on Easter day And though we would willingly assent unto any sympathetical evultation, yet cannot conceive therein any more than a Tropical expression — *Pseudodoxia Epidemica*, V, xxii

Easter eggs, or **Pasch eggs,** are symbolical of creation, or the re-creation of spring The practice of presenting them at Easter came into England from Germany in the 19th century It probably derives from the old ecclesiastical prohibition of eating eggs during Lent, but allowing them again at Easter In modern times the Germans have favoured the rabbit as an Easter symbol

> Bless, Lord we beseech thee, this Thy creature of eggs, that it may become a wholesome sustenance to Thy faithful servants, eating it in thankfulness to Thee, on account of the resurrection of our Lord —POPE PAUL V *Ritual*

Easterlings An old name (first used in the 16th century) for any foreigner coming to England from the East, but specially applied to the merchants from the Hanse towns of northern Germany.

Eat To eat together was, in the East, a sure pledge of protection A man once prostrated himself before a Persian grandee and implored protection from the rabble The nobleman gave him the remainder of a peach which he was eating, and when the incensed multitude arrived, and declared that the man had slain the only son of the nobleman, the heart-broken father replied, "We have eaten together, go in peace," and would not allow the murderer to be punished

Let us eat and drink, for to-morrow we die. *Is* xxii, 13 A traditional saying of the Egyptians who, at their banquets, exhibited a skeleton to the guests to remind them of the brevity of human life

To eat a man's salt *See* SALT

To eat coke, humble pie, the leek. *See these words*

To eat dog. An Indian custom at councils of importance Later when white men took exception, they were permitted to avoid offence by placing a silver dollar on the dish and passing it the next man took the dollar and ate the dog Hence the expression in American politics *to eat dog for another*

To eat its head off. Said of an animal (usually a horse) that eats more than he is worth, or whose work does not pay for the cost of keeping

To eat one out of house and home. To eat so much that one will have to part with house and home in order to pay for it It is the complaint of hostess Quickly to the Lord Chief Justice when he asks for "what sum" she had arrested Sir John Falstaff She explains the phrase by "he hath put all my substance into that fat belly of his" (2 *Henry IV*, ii, 1)

To eat one's heart out. To fret or worry unreasonably, to allow grief or vexation to predominate over the mind, tincture all one's ideas, and absorb all other emotions

To eat one's terms. To be studying for the bar Students are required to dine in the Hall of an Inn of Court at least three times in each of the twelve terms before they are "called" to the bar.

To eat one's words. To retract in a humiliating manner, to unsay what you have said

To eat well To have a good appetite. But "It eats well" means that what is eaten is agreeable or flavorous. To ' eat badly" is to eat without appetite or too little

Eau de Cologne. A perfumed spirit, originally prepared at Cologne. It was invented by an Italian chemist, Johann Maria Farina, who settled in Cologne in 1709 The usual recipe prescribes twelve drops of each of the essential oils, Bergamot, citron, neroli, orange, and rosemary, with one dram of Malabar cardomoms and a gallon of rectified spirits, which are distilled together.

Eau de vie (ō de vē) (Fr , water of life) Brandy. A translation of the Latin *aqua vitæ* (*q v*) This is a curious perversion of the Spanish *acqua di vite* (water or juice of the vine), rendered by the monks into *aqua vitæ* instead of *aqua vitis*, and confounding the juice of the grape with the alchemists' elixir of life. The same error is perpetuated in the Italian *acqua vite.*

Eavesdropper. One who listens stealthily to conversation The eavesdrop or eavesdrip was the space of ground liable to receive the water dripping from the eaves of a house An eavesdropper is one who places himself in the eaves-drip to overhear what is said in the house

> Under our tents I'll play the eavesdropper,
> To hear if any mean to shrink from me
> *Richard III*, v, 3

Ebionites (eb' i on ītz) An heretical sect of the 1st and 2nd centuries, who denied the Divinity of Jesus Christ and his birth of a Virgin, and held that he was merely an inspired messenger The name is from Heb *ebyon*, poor, probably in allusion to some claim that they were "the poor in spirit "

Eblis (eb' lis) A jinn of Arabian mythology, the ruler of the evil genii, or fallen angels Before his fall he was called Azazel (*q v*) When Adam was created, God commanded all the angels to worship him, but Eblis replied, "Me thou hast created of smokeless fire, and shall I reverence a creature made of dust?" God turned the disobedient angel into a Sheytân (devil), and he became the father of devils.

> When he said unto the angels, 'Worship Adam,' all worshipped him except Eblis —*Al Koran*, ii

Ebony. God's image done in ebony. Negroes Thomas Fuller gave birth to this expression

Ecce homo (ek' si hō' mō) (Lat , Behold the man) The name given to many paintings of Our Lord crowned with thorns and bound with ropes, as He was shown to the people by Pilate who said to them, "*Ecce homo!*" (*John* xix, 5), notably those by Correggio, Titian, Guido Reni, Van Dyck, Rembrandt, Poussin, and Albrecht Dürer. In 1865 Sir John Seeley published a survey of the life and work of Christ with the title "Ecce Homo "

Ecce signum (ek' si sig' num) See it, in proof Behold the proof
> I am eight times thrust through the doublet, four through the hose; my buckler cut through and through; my sword hacked like a handsaw—ecce signum!—I *Henry IV*, ii, 4.

Eccentric. Deviating from the centre (Lat. *ex centrum*), hence irregular, not according to rule. Originally applied to those planets which apparently wander round the earth, like comets, the earth not being in the centre of their orbit

In geometry the term is applied to two circles, one within the other, with different centres in mechanics it is a wheel with its axle not coaxial with the exact centre of the wheel In general speech eccentric means out of the ordinary, odd, unconventional, abnormal, and an eccentric is a person with these characteristics

Ecclesiastes (e klē' si ăs' tēz) One of the books in the Old Testament arranged next to Proverbs, formerly ascribed to Solomon, because it says (verse 1), "The words of the Preacher, the son of David, king in Jerusalem," but now generally assigned to an unnamed author of the 3rd century B C , writing after Malachi but before the time of the Maccabees The Hebrew name is *Koheleth*, which means "the Preacher"

Ecclesiastical The father of ecclesiastical history. Eusebius of Cæsarea (about 264-340).

Ecclesiasticus. One of the books of the Old Testament Apocrypha, traditionally (and probably correctly) ascribed to a Palestinian sage named Ben Sirah, or Jesus, the Son of Sirach. In the Talmud it is quoted as *Ben Sira*, and in the Septuagint its name is *The Wisdom of Jesus, the Son of Sirach* It was probably written early in the 2nd century B C It was given its present name by early Greek Christians because, in their opinion it was the chief of the apocryphal books, designated by them *Ecclesiastici Libri* (books to be read in churches), to distinguish them from the canonical Scriptures

Echidna (e kid' na) A monster of classical mythology, half woman, half serpent. She was mother of the Chimæra, the many-headed dog Orthos, the hundred-headed dragon of the Hesperides, the Colchian dragon, the Sphinx, Cerberos, Scylla, the Gorgons, the Lernæan hydra, the vulture that gnawed away the liver of Prometheus, and the Nemean lion

Spenser makes her the mother of the Blatant Beast (*q v.*) —

> Echidna is a Monster direfull dred,
> Whom Gods doe hate, and heavens abhor to see;
> So hideous is her shape, so huge her hed,
> That even the hellish fiends affrighted bee
> At sight thereof, and from her presence flee·
> Yet did her face and former parts professe
> A faire young Mayden full of comely glee;
> But all her hinder parts did plaine expresse
> A monstrous Dragon, full of fearefull ugliness
>   *Faerie Queene, VI,* vi, 10.

In zoology an echidna is a porcupine anteater found in Australia and New Guinea, allied to the platypus.

Echo (ek' ō) The Romans say that Echo was a nymph in love with Narcissus, but her love not being returned, she pined away till only her voice remained

> Sweet Echo, sweetest nymph, that liv'st unseen
>   Within thy airy shell,
> By slow Meander's margent green .
> Canst thou not tell me of a gentle pair
> That likest thy Narcissus are?
>   MILTON *Comus,* 230

To applaud to the echo. To applaud vigorously—so loudly as to produce an echo.

Eckhardt (ek' hart) A faithful Eckhardt, who warneth everyone. Eckhardt, in German legends, appears on the evening of Maundy Thursday to warn all persons to go home, that they may not be injured by the headless bodies and two-legged horses which traverse the streets on that night.

Eclectics (ek lek' tiks) The name given to those who do not attach themselves to any special school (especially philosophers and painters), but pick and choose from various systems, selecting and harmonizing those doctrines, methods, etc , which suit them (Gr. *ek-legein*, to choose, select) Certain Greek philosophers of the 1st and 2nd centuries B.C. were styled Eclectics, and there is the Eclectic school of painters, i e. the Italians of the 17th century who followed the great masters

Eclipse, one of the most famous of English race-horses The great-grandson of Darley Arabian (*q.v.*) he was foaled April 1st, 1764, ran his first race May 3rd, 1769, and from then until October, 1770, ran in eighteen races, never being beaten. His skeleton is preserved in the Royal Veterinary College, London **The Eclipse Stakes** is a race for horses of three years and upwards, run at Sandown Park. It was inaugurated in 1884.

Eclipses were considered by the ancient Greeks and Romans as bad omens Nicias, the Athenian general, was so terrified by an eclipse of the moon, that he durst not defend himself from the Syracusans; in consequence of which his whole army was cut to pieces, and he himself was put to death

The Romans would never hold a public assembly during an eclipse. Some of their poets feign that an eclipse of the moon is because she is on a visit to Endymion.

A very general notion was and still is common among backward races that the sun or moon has been devoured by some monster and hence the custom of beating drums and kettles to scare away the monster The Chinese, Laps, Persians, and some others call the evil beast a dragon The East Indians say it is a black griffin

The notion of the ancient Mexicans was that eclipses were caused by sun and moon quarrels.

Ecliptic (e klip' tik) The track in the heavens along which the sun appears to perform its annual march It lies in the middle of the Zodiac (*q.v.*) and is, of course, a purely imaginary line produced by the earth's motion about the sun.

Eclogue (Gr., a selection). The word was originally used for Virgil's *Bucolics,* because they were selected poems; as they were all pastoral dialogues it came to denote such poems, and hence an *Eclogue* is now a pastoral or rustic dialogue in verse

Economy Literally, "household management" (Lat. *œconomia,* from Gr. *oikos,* house *nemein,* to deal out).

There are many British proverbs and sayings teaching the value of economy·—

"No alchemy like frugality", "ever save, ever have", "a pin a day is a great a year"; "take care of the pence, and the pounds will take care of themselves"; "many a mickle makes a muckle"; "frae saving, comes having"; "a penny saved is a penny gained"; "little and often fills the purse", and there is Mr Micawber's wise saying:—

> Annual income twenty pounds, annual expenditure nineteen nineteen six, result happiness Annual income twenty pounds, annual expenditure twenty pounds ought and six, result misery —DICKENS: *David Copperfield,* ch xii

The Christian economy. The religious system based on the teachings of Jesus Christ as recorded in the New Testament.

The economy of nature. The laws of nature, whereby the greatest amount of good is obtained; or the laws by which the affairs of nature are regulated and disposed; the system and interior management of the animal and vegetable kingdoms, etc.

> Animal   economy, according to which animal affairs are regulated and disposed —SHAFTESBURY: *Characteristics.*

11*

The Mosaic economy. The religious system revealed by God to Moses and set forth in the Old Testament

Political economy. Science of the production, distribution, and management of wealth, especially as dealing with the principles whereby the revenues and resources of a nation are made the most of

Ecstasy (Gr. *ek*, out, *stasis*, a standing) Literally, a condition in which one stands out of one's mind, loses one's wits, or is "beside oneself " St Paul refers to this when he says he was caught up to the third heaven and heard unutterable words, "whether in the body, or out of the body, I cannot tell" (2 *Cor* xii 2-4). St John also says he was "in the spirit"—*i.e* in an ecstasy—when he saw the apocalyptic vision (*Rev* i, 10). The belief that the soul left the body at times was very general in former ages, and there was a class of diviners among the ancient Greeks called Ecstatici, who used to lie in trances, and when they came to themselves gave strange accounts of what they had seen while they were "out of the body."

Ecstatic Doctor, The. Jean de Ruysbroek, the mystic (1294-1381).

Ectoplasm (ek' tō plăsm) (Gr *ectos*, outside, *plasma*, form) In biology this is an external modified layer of protoplasm, but it has acquired a wider sense in its spiritualistic meaning of the tangible emanation from a medium employed in materialization

Ector, Sir. The foster-father of King Arthur

Edda. This name—which may be from *Edda*, the great-grandmother in the Old Norse poem *Rigsthul*, or from the old Norse *odhr*, poetry, is given to two separate works or collections, viz *The Elder* or *Poetic Edda*, and *The Younger Edda*, or *Prose Edda* of Snorri. The first-named was discovered in 1643 by an Icelandic bishop, and consists of mythological poems dating from the 9th century, and supposed to have been collected in the 13th century. They are of unknown authorship, but were erroneously attributed to Sæmund Sigfusson (d 1133), and this has hence sometimes been called *Sæmund's Edda* The *Younger Edda* is a work in prose and verse by Snorri Sturluson (d 1242), and forms a guide to poets and poetry It consists of the *Gylfaginning* (an epitome of Scandinavian mythology), the *Skaldskaparmal* (a glossary of poetical expressions, etc), the *Hattatal* (a list of metres, with examples of all known forms of verse, with a preface, history of the origin of poetry, lists of poets, etc)

Eden. Paradise, the country and garden in which Adam and Eve were placed by God (*Gen* ii, 15) but lost by their disobedience. The word means *delight, pleasure*

Eden Hall The luck of Eden Hall. An enamelled drinking-glass, made probably in Venice in the 10th century, in the possession of the Musgrave family at Eden Hall, Cumberland, and traditionally supposed to be endowed with fortune-bringing properties The tale is that it was taken from St Cuthbert's Well in the

garden, when the fairies left this glass by the well while they danced, The superstition is—

If that glass shall break or fall,
Farewell the luck of Eden Hall

With the break-up of the estate in 1920 the cup was sold

Edge (A S *ecg*). It is dangerous to play with edged tools. It is dangerous to tamper with mischief or anything that may bring you into trouble

Not to put too fine an edge on it. Not to mince the matter, to speak plainly

To be on edge. To be very eager or impatient.

To edge away. To move away very gradually, as a ship moves from the edge of the shore

To edge on. *See* EGG ON.

To fall by the edge of the sword. By a cut from the sword, to be slain in battle

To have the edge on someone. To have an advantage

To set one's teeth on edge. To give one the horrors, to induce a tingling or grating sensation in one's teeth, as from acids or harsh noises

In those days they shall say no more, the fathers have eaten a sour grape, and the children's teeth are set on edge.—*Jer* , xxxi, 29

I had rather hear a brazen canstick turned,
Or a dry wheel grate on the axle-tree,
And that would set my teeth nothing on edge,
Nothing so much as mincing poetry.
1 *Henry IV*, iii, 1

Edge-bone *See* AITCH-BONE.

Ediles. *See* ÆDILES

Edinburgh. Edwin's burgh, the fort built by Edwin, king of Northumbria (616-33). Dunedin (Gaelic *dun*, a fortress) and Edina are poetical forms

Eel. A salt eel. A rope's end, used for scourging At one time eelskins were used for whips

With my salt eele, went down in the parler, and there got my boy and did beat him —*Pepys' Diary*

Eel-skins Old-fashioned slang for extra tight trousers, or tightly fitting frocks

Holding the eel of science by the tail. To have a smattering of the subject, the kind which slips from the memory as an eel would wriggle out of one's fingers if held by the tail.

To get used to it, as a skinned eel. It may be unpleasant at first, but habit will get the better of such annoyance; arising from the strange old notion that eels feel little more than a slight discomfort when skinned alive

To skin an eel by the tail To do things the wrong way

Effendi (e fen' di) A Turkish title, equivalent to the English "Mr " or "Esq " but always following the name It is given to emirs, men of learning, the imams of mosques, etc

Effigy. To burn or hang one in effigy. To burn or hang the representation of a person, instead of the person himself, in order to show popular hatred, dislike, or contempt From earliest times and in all countries magic has been worked by treating an effigy as one would fain treat the original In France the public executioner used to hang the effigy of the criminal when the criminal himself could not be found

Égalité (ā gàl' ıtā) Philippe, Duc d'Orleans (b 1747, guillotined 1793), father of Louis-Philippe, King of the French, assumed the name when he renounced his title and voted for the death of Louis XVI The motto of the revolutionary party, with which he sided, was "Liberty, fraternity, and equality (*égalité*)"

Egeria (e jēr' ı ȧ) The nymph who instructed Numa in his wise legislation, hence, a counsellor, adviser

It is these moments that we gaze upon the moon It is in these moments that Nature becomes our Egeria —LORD BEACONSFIELD *Vivian Grey, III,* vi

Egg. *See also* SHELL

A bad egg. A bad speculation, a "bad-lot"; a person or thing that does not come up to expectations

Curate's egg. *See* CURATE

A duck's egg. *See* DUCK.

Don't put all your eggs in one basket. Don't venture all you have in one speculation, don't put all your property in one bank. The allusion is obvious

Easter eggs *See* EASTER, EGG FEAST

Golden eggs Great profits. *See* GOOSE

I got eggs for my money. I gave valuable money, and received such worthless things as eggs When Wolsey accused the Earl of Kildare for not taking Desmond prisoner, the Earl replied, "He is no more to blame than his brother Ossory, who (notwithstanding his high promises) is glad to take eggs for his money," *i e.* is willing to be imposed on. (CAMPION: *History of Ireland*, 1633.)

I have eggs on the spit. I am very busy, and cannot attend to anything else The reference is to roasting eggs on a spit. They were first boiled, then the yolk was taken out, braided up with spices, and put back again; the eggs were then drawn on a spit, and roasted As this required both dispatch and constant attention, the person in charge could not leave them

I forgot to tell you, I write short journals now, I have eggs on the spit —SWIFT

Like as two eggs Exactly alike

They say we are almost as like as eggs —*Winter's Tale,* i, 2

Show him an egg, and instantly the whole air is full of feathers. Said of a very sanguine man, because he is "counting his chickens before they are hatched."

Sure as eggs is eggs. Professor de Morgan suggested that this is a corruption of the logician's formula, "*x* is *x*"

Teach your grandmother to suck eggs. *Attempt to teach your elders*

The mundane egg. The Phœnicians, Egyptians, Hindus, Japanese, and many other ancient nations maintained that the world was egg-shaped, and was hatched from an egg made by the Creator, and in some mythologies a bird is represented as laying the mundane egg on the primordial waters.

Anciently this idea was attributed to Orpheus, hence the "mundane egg" is also called the *Orphic egg*

The opinion of the oval figure of the earth is ascrib'd to Orpheus and his disciples, and the doctrine of the mundane egg is so peculiarly his, that 'tis called by Proclus the Orphick egg —BURNET *The Sacred Theory of the Earth* (1684)

There is reason in roasting eggs Even the most trivial thing has a reason for being done in one way rather than in some other When wood fires were usual, it was more common to roast eggs than to boil them, and some care was required to prevent their being "ill-roasted, all on one side," as Touchstone says (*As You Like It,* iii, 2)

One likes the pheasant's wing, and one the leg,
The vulgar boil the learned roast an egg
POPE *Epistles,* ii

To crush in the egg To nip in the bud, to ruin some scheme before it has been fairly started

To egg on. To incite, to urge on Here *egg* is simply another form of *edge*—to edge on, *r e* to drive one nearer and nearer to the edge until the plunge is taken

To tread upon eggs. To walk gingerly, as if walking over eggs, which are easily broken

Will you take eggs for your money? "Will you allow yourself to be imposed upon? Will you take kicks for halfpence?" This saying was in vogue when eggs were plentiful as blackberries

My honest friend, will you take eggs for money?— *Winter's Tale,* i, 2

Egg Feast or Egg Saturday. In Oxford the Saturday preceding Shrove Tuesday used to be so called because, as the eating of eggs was forbidden during Lent, the scholars took leave of them on that day They were allowed again at Easter, hence the coloured 'Easter egg"

Egg-trot, or Egg-wife's trot. A cautious, jog-trot pace, like that of a housewife riding to market with eggs in her panniers.

Egil. Brother of Weland, the Vulcan of Northern mythology Egil was a great archer, and in the Saga of Thidrik there is a tale told of him the exact counterpart of the famous story about William Tell and the apple *See* TELL.

Eglantine. In the romance of Valentine and Orson, daughter of King Pepin, and bride of her cousin Valentine She soon died

Madame Eglantine. The prioress in Chaucer s *Canterbury Tales* Good-natured, wholly ignorant of the world, vain of her courtly manners, and noted for her partiality to lapdogs, her delicate oath, "by seint Eloy," her "entuning the service swetely in her nose," and her speaking French "after the scole of Stratford atte Bowe"

Ego (Lat, 'I'). In various philosophical systems *ego* is used of the conscious thinking subject and *non-ego* of the object. The term *ego* was introduced into philosophy by Descartes, who employed it to denote the

whole man, body and mind Fichte later used
the term *the absolute ego*, meaning thereby
the non-individual being, neither subject nor object,
which posits the world of individual egos and non-
egos

In psycho-analysis the *ego* is that part of
the mind that perceives and takes cognisance
of external reality and adjusts responses to it.
See ID

Egoism The theory in Ethics which places
man's *summum bonum* in self. The correlative
of altruism, or the theory which places our
own greatest happiness in making others
happy *Egoism* is selfishness pure, altruism is
selfish benevolence. Hence *egoist*, one who
upholds and practises this theory
To say that each individual shall reap the benefits
brought to him by his own powers   is to enunciate
egoism as an ultimate principle of conduct —
SPENCER *Data of Ethics*, p 189

Egotism The too frequent use of the word
I, the habit of talking about oneself, or of
parading one's own doings **Egotist**, one
addicted to egotism.

Egypt, in Dryden's satire of *Absalom and
Achitophel*, means France
Egypt and Tyrus [Holland] intercept your trade,
And Jebusites [Papists] your sacred rites invade
Pt 1, 705-6

Crowns of Egypt Ancient Egypt was divided
into two parts, Upper Egypt, or the South
Land, and Lower Egypt, or the Northern
Land, the kings styling themselves *suten bat*,
kings of the north and south As ruler of the
two countries each king wore the crown made
up of the White Crown of the South and the
Red Crown of the North, and it is from this
crown, named Pschent, that they can be distinguished in hieroglyphics or on monuments

Egyptian days Unlucky days, days on
which no business should be undertaken The
Egyptian astrologers named two in each
month, but the last Monday in April, the
second Monday of August, and the third
Monday of December seem to have been
specially baneful
For there ben xxiiii Egypcyan dayes it folowyth that
god sente mo wreches upon the Egypcyens than ten
—TREVISA *Trans of "De Proprietatibus Rerum" by
Bartholomæus Anglicus* (1398)

Eight Behind the eight ball In a dangerous
position, from which it is impossible to escape.
The phrase comes from the game of Kelly
pool, in one variety of which all the balls must
be pocketed in a certain order, except the
black ball, numbered eight If another ball
touches the eight ball, the player is penalized
Therefore, if the eight ball is in front of the
one which he intends to pocket, he is in a
hazardous position.

One over the eight, a euphemism for slightly
drunk

Eikon Basilike (i' kon băz il' i ki) (Gr., royal
likeness) *EIKΩN BAΣIΛIKH; the Pourtraic-
ture of His Sacred Majestie in His Solitudes and
Sufferings*, was published in 1649 and purported
to set forth the private meditations, prayers,
and thoughts of Charles I on the political
situation during and before his imprisonment
Its authorship was at first attributed by Royal-

ists to the king himself, and so late as 1824
this theory was supported by Christopher
Wordsworth, Master of Trinity College,
Cambridge At the time of the Restoration
John Gauden (1605-62) claimed authorship of
it when putting up for the bishopric of Worcester, but who actually wrote it is still an open
question

Eisell (i' sel) An old name for vinegar (acetic
acid), through old Fr from late Lat *acetillum*,
diminutive of *acetum*. Hamlet asks Laertes,
Wouldst drink up eisell—to show your love to
the dead Ophelia ? In the *Troy Book* of Lydgate
we have the line 'Of bitter eysell and of eager
(sour) wine " And in Shakespeare s sonnets —
I will drink
Potions of eysell, 'gainst my strong infection,
No bitterness that I will bitter think,
Nor double penance to correct correction

Eisenhower Platz Nickname of Grosvenor
Square, London during World War II, when
all the buildings surrounding the square were
occupied by American Military Headquarters

Eisteddfod (I steth' vod). The meetings of the
Welsh bards and others now held annually
for the encouragement of Welsh literature and
music (Welsh, "a sessions," from *eistedd*, to
sit)

El Dorado (el dôr a' dō) (Sp , the gilded).
Originally, the name given to the supposed
king of Manoa, the fabulous city of enormous
wealth as located by the early explorers on the
Amazon He was said to be covered with oil
and then powdered with gold-dust, an operation performed from time to time so that he
was permanently, and literally, gilded Many
expeditions, both from Spain and England
(two of which were led by Sir Walter Raleigh)
tried to discover this king, and the name was
later transferred to his supposed territory
Hence any extraordinarily rich region, or vast
accumulation of gold, precious stones, or
similar wealth

Elagabalus (el à găb' à lus) A Syro-Phœnician
sun-god, worshipped in Rome and represented
under the form of a huge conical stone The
Roman emperor, originally Varius Avitus
Bassanius (A D 205-22), son of a cousin of
Caracalla but put forward as a son of Caracalla himself, was so called because in childhood he had been a priest of Elagabalus (or
Heliogabalus) Of all the Roman emperors
none exceeded him in debauchery His cruelties
were so hideous and his personal habits so
loathsome that there can be no doubt of his
insanity He reigned about four years (A D 218-
22), and was put to death by the prætorians.

Elaine The "lily maid of Astolat" (*q.v*), who
in Tennyson's *Lancelot and Elaine* (*Idylls o,
the King*), in which he follows Malory (Bk
xviii, ch 9-20), loved Sir Lancelot "with that
love which was her doom " *See* DIAMOND
JOUSTS.

Elbow. *See* ELL.

A knight of the elbow. A gambler.

At one's elbow. Close at hand

Elbow grease. Hard manual labour, especially rubbing and scrubbing A humorous

expression that was in use at least three hundred years ago We say "*Elbow grease* is the best furniture oil "

Elbow room. Sufficient space for the work in hand

More power to your elbow. A jocular toast implying that a stronger elbow will lift more glasses to the mouth

Out at elbows. Shabbily dressed, "down at heel "

To elbow one's way in To push one's way through a crowd, to get a place by hook or crook

To elbow out; to be elbowed out. To supersede: to be ousted by a rival.

To lift the elbow To drink, usually said of an habitual drinker

Up to one's elbow. Very busy, full of work Work piled up to one's elbows

Elden Hole. Elden Hole needs filling A reproof given to great braggarts Elden Hole is a deep chasm in the Derbyshire Peak, long reputed to be bottomless. *See* Scott's *Peveril of the Peak*, ch. iii

Elder Brethren. *See* TRINITY HOUSE

Elder-tree. A tree of evil associations in popular legend, and, according to mediæval fable, that on which Judas Iscariot hanged himself, the mushroom-like excrescences on the bark still being known as *Judas's* (or *Jew's) ears*

Sir John Maundeville, speaking (1364) of the Pool of Siloe, says, "Fast by is the elder-tree on which Judas hanged himself when he sold and betrayed our Lord " Shakespeare, in *Love's Labour's Lost*, v 2, says, "Judas was hanged on an elder. '

> Judas he japed
> With Jewen silver,
> And sithen on an eller
> Hanged hymselve
> *Vision of Piers Plowman, Passus* I

See also FIG-TREE; JUDAS TREE

A pleasant, old-fashioned country wine is made from elderberries

Eleanor Crosses. The crosses erected by Edward I to commemorate his queen, Eleanor, whose body was brought from Nottinghamshire to Westminster for burial At each of the following places, where the body rested, a cross was set up Lincoln, Grantham, Stamford, Geddington, Northampton, Stony Stratford, Waltham, West Cheap (Cheapside) Of these only the crosses at Geddington, Northampton and Waltham now exist

See CHARING CROSS

Eleatic Philosophy Founded by Xenophanes of Elea (about 530 B C), who, in opposition to the current Greek system founded on polytheism and anthropomorphism, taught the unity and unchangeableness of the Divine Through Parmenides and Zeno in the 5th century the school exercised great influence on Plato

Elecampane. A composite plant (*Inula helenium*) the candied roots of which (like ginger) are used as a sweetmeat, and which was formerly fabled to have magical properties,

such as curing wounds, conferring immortality, etc Pliny tells us it sprang from Helen's tears

> Here, take this essence of elecampane,
> Rise up, Sir George, and fight again
> *Miracle Play of St. George.*

Elector. A prince who had a vote in the election of the Emperor of the Holy Roman Empire As established by the Golden Bull of 1356 these were the spiritual rulers of Mayence, Treves and Cologne, the temporal rulers of the Rhine Palatinate, Saxony, Brandenburg and Bohemia, and from time to time other German princes such as the rulers of Bavaria (1648), Hanover (1692), etc In 1806 Napoleon broke up the old Empire, and the College of Electors was dissolved.

The Great Elector Frederick William of Brandenburg (1620-88)

Electra. One of the Pleiades (*q v*), mother of Dardanus, the mythical ancestor of the Trojans. She is known as "the Lost Pleiad," for it is said that she disappeared a little before the Trojan war, that she might be saved the mortification of seeing the ruin of her beloved city. She showed herself occasionally to mortal eye, but always in the guise of a comet *See Od ,* v, and *Il* , xviii.

Electra, the sister of Orestes, figures in the *Oresteia* of Aeschylus and two other dramas, both entitled *Electra*, by Sophocles and Euripedes The daughter of Agamemnon and Clytemnestra, she incited Orestes to kill their mother in revenge for the latter's murder of Agamemnon on his return from Troy In modern psychology an Electra complex is a girl's attraction towards her father accompanied with hostility towards her mother.

Electricity (Gr *elektron*, amber) Thales (600 B C.) observed that amber when rubbed attracted light substances, and this observation followed out has led to the present science of electricity

Electronic Brain. An inaccurate term invented by newspaper journalists to describe a calculating machine in which the ordinary mechanical processes of reckoning are performed by the employment of thermionic valves

Electuary (e lek' tū ar i) Coming from a Greek word meaning to lick up, this term is applied in pharmacy to medicines sweetened with honey or syrup, and originally meant to be licked off the spoon by the patient.

Elegant Extracts. The 85th Foot, remodelled in 1813 after the numerous courts-martial which then occurred The officers of the regiment were removed, and officers drafted from other regiments were substituted in their places. The 85th is now called the 'Second Battalion of the Shropshire Light Infantry " The first battalion is the old 23rd.

At Cambridge, in the good old times, men who were too good to be plucked and not good enough for the poll, but who were yet allowed to pass, were nicknamed the *Elegant Extracts*. There was a similar limbo in the honour list, called the Gulf (*q.v*), in allusion to the "great gulf fixed " Both nicknames come from the late-18th-century liking for anthologies called "Elegant Extracts "

Elegiacs. Verse consisting of alternate hexameters (*q v*) and pentameters (*q v*), so called because it was the metre in which the elegies of the Greeks and Romans were usually written In Latin it was commonly used by Ovid, Catullus, Tibullus, and others, the following is a good specimen of English elegiacs.—

> Man with inviolate caverns, impregnable holds in his nature,
> Depths no storm can pierce, pierced with a shaft of the sun
> Man that is galled with his confines, and burdened yet more with his vastness,
> Born too great for his ends, never at peace with his goal
>
>   SIR WM WATSON *Hymn to the Sea* (1899)

Element. In modern scientific parlance an *element* is a substance which resists analysis or splitting up into different substances There are 96 of these But in ancient and mediæval philosophy an *element* was one of the simple substances of which all things were held to be composed Aristotle, following Empedocles of Sicily (*c.* 450 B C), taught that there were four, viz fire, air, water, and earth; but later a fifth, the *quinta essentia,* or *quintessence,* which was supposed to be common to the four and to unify them, was added

> Does not our life consist of the four elements?
>   *Twelfth Night,* ii, 3

The word is often applied loosely and figuratively, and is used to describe the resistance wire and former of a resistance type of electric heater, also to denote one of the electrodes of a primary or secondary cell In *military* parlance it is used to describe portions of a unit or formation detached from their parent unit

In one's element. In one's usual surroundings, within one's ordinary range of activity, enjoying oneself thoroughly. The allusion is to the natural abode of any animals, as the air to birds, water to fish.

> Ferguson was in his element . with the malevolent activity and dexterity of an evil spirit, he ran from outlaw to outlaw, chattered in every ear, and stirred up in every bosom savage animosities and wild desires —MACAULAY *History of England,* ch v

The elements. Atmospheric powers; the winds, storms, etc

> Rumble they bellyful! Spit, fire! spout, rain!
> Nor rain, wind, thunder, fire, are my daughters:
> I tax not you, you elements, with unkindness,
> I never gave you kingdom, call'd you children,
> You owe me no subscription then, let fall
> Your horrible pleasure
>   *King Lear,* iii, 2.

Elephant. Elephants have been used by oriental potentates for state ceremonies or as engines of war from time immemorial When the Romans first saw elephants, in the army of Pyrrhus, they called them "Leuconian oxen"; their horses refused to face the great beasts and galloped back, causing panic among the infantry In 250 B c. Caecilius Metellus vanquished Hasdrubal at Panormus and captured 120 elephants which were taken in strong rafts across the sea to adorn the proconsul's triumph.

A white elephant. Some possession the expense or responsibility of which is more than it is worth. The allusion is to the story of a King of Siam who used to make a present of a white elephant to courtiers whom he wished to ruin

The Order of the White Elephant is a Danish military order of knighthood, traditionally said to have been founded in 1189 in memory of a Danish soldier who slew one Historically it dates from 1462, it was reconstituted in 1693, and is limited to princes of the blood and thirty knights The badge is a white elephant carrying a tower and with a Hindu driver seated on its neck

King of the White Elephant. The proudest title borne by the old kings of Ava and Siam In Ava the white elephant bore the title of "lord," and had a minister of high rank to superintend his household

Only an elephant can bear an elephant's load An Indian proverb: Only a great man can do the work of a great man, also, the burden is more than I can bear, it is a load fit for an elephant

Elephant paper A large-sized drawing-paper measuring 23 inches by 28 *Double Elephant* is a standard size of printing paper 27 by 40 inches *Long Elephant* is a term employed for paper hangings, 12 yards long, usually 22 inches wide The name is probably from an ancient watermark

To see the elephant. (U S.A) To see all there is to see

Elephant and Castle. A public-house sign at Newington that has given its name to a railway station and to a district in South London The sign is the crest of the Cutlers' Company, who owned the site and into whose trade the use of ivory entered largely In ancient times war elephants bore fortified "castles" on their backs from which bowmen and armed knights penetrated into the enemy's ranks

Elephanta (el e fän' ta) A small island in Bombay harbour, 6 miles east of the city It is about 4½ miles in circumference, and is famous for its rock temples and caves with Hindu sculpture It should not be confused with **Elephantine Island,** in the Nile, off Assouan, from which sprang the kings of the Vth dynasty There are royal tombs on the island and the famous Nilometer, dating from Ptolemaic days.

Eleusinian Mysteries. The religious rites in honour of Demeter or Ceres, performed originally at Eleusis, Attica, but later at Athens as part of the state religion There were Greater and Lesser Eleusinia, the former being celebrated between harvest and seedtime and the latter in early spring Little is known about the details, but the rites included sea bathing, processions, religious dramas, etc, and the initiated attained thereby a happy life beyond the grave

Elevation of the Host. This is the term used for the raising of the Host and the Chalice after consecration in the Mass, for the adoration of the faithful

Eleven. This is the A S. *endlesfon,* from a Teutonic *ainlif,* the *ain-* representing "one," and the suffix being cognate with the Lithuanian -*lika* (and probably with Lat. *linquere*, to leave, *liqui*, left) in *wenolika*, eleven, the meaning being that there is still one left to be counted after counting ten (the fingers of the two hands)

At the eleventh hour. Just in time, from the parable in *Matt.* xx, 1-16.

The Eleven Thousand Virgins *See* URSULA

Elf. Originally a dwarfish being of Teutonic mythology, possessed of magical powers which it used either for the benefit or to the detriment of mankind Later the name was restricted to a malignant kind of imp, and later still to those airy creatures that dance on the grass in the full moon, have fair golden hair, sweet musical voices, magic harps, etc

> Spenser relates (*Faerie Queene*, II, x, 70) —
> How first Prometheus did create
> A man, of many partes from beasts derived
> That man so made he called Elfe, to weet
> Quick, the first authour of all Elfin kind

Spenser's remark that *elf* means "quick" is, of course, an invention, as also is the amusing one (mentioned with disapproval by Johnson, *s v* GOBLIN) that *Elf* and *Goblin* are derived from "Guelf and Ghibelline"; the word is A S *ælf*, from Icel *âlfr*, and Teut *alp*, a nightmare

Elf-arrows. Arrow-heads of the neolithic period so called At one time they were supposed to be shot by elves at people and cattle out of malice or revenge

Elf-fire. The ignis-fatuus, also popularly called Will o' the Wisp, Jack o' lanthorn, Peg-a-lantern, or Kit o' the canstick (candlestick)

Elf-locks. Tangled hair It used to be said that one of the favourite amusements of Queen Mab was to tie people's hair in knots. When Edgar impersonates a madman, ' he elfs all his hair in knots " (*Lear*, ii 3)

> This is that very Mab
> That plaits the manes of horses in the night,
> And bakes the elf-locks in foul sluttish hairs.
> *Romeo and Juliet*, i, 4

Elf-marked Those born with a natural defect, according to the ancient Scottish superstition, are marked by the elves for mischief. Queen Margaret called Richard III

> Thou elvish-marked, abortive, rooting hog!
> *Richard III*, i, 3

Elf-shot. Afflicted with some unknown disease which was supposed to have been caused by an elf-arrow.

Elgin Marbles (el' gin). The 7th Earl of Elgin (1766-1841) was envoy to the Sublime Porte (Turkey) from 1799 to 1803, and on visits to Greece—at that time a Turkish possession—he observed that from neglect and depredations many Classical sculptures, etc , were in danger of destruction At his own expense he made a collection of statuary and sculpture (including several works of Phidias) from the Parthenon and the Erechtheion and brought them to England In 1812 he sold them to the British Government for £35,000, which was half what he had paid for their removal He also brought casts of various objects left *in situ*, and a comparison of these casts with the originals as preserved to-day reveals con-siderable damage in the century that has elapsed, and justifies Elgin's removal of what was brought to England

Elia (ē' lya). A *nom de plume* adopted by Charles Lamb (1775-1834)

> The adoption of this signature was purely accidental Lamb's first contribution to the *London Magazine* was a description of the old South-Sea House, where he had passed a few months' novitiate as a clerk, and remembering the name of a gay light-hearted foreigner, who fluttered there at the time, substituted his name for his own.—TALFOURD

Elidure (el' i dūr) A legendary king of Britain, who, according to some accounts, was advanced to the throne in place of his elder brother, Arthgallo (or Artegal), supposed by him to be dead Arthgallo, after a long exile, returned to his country, and Elidure resigned to him the throne Wordsworth has a poem on the subject (*Artegal and Elidure*), and Milton (*History of Britain*, Bk i) says that Elidure had "a mind so noble, and so moderate, as is almost incredible to have been ever found."

Eligius, St. *See* ELOI, ST.

Elijah's Melons. Certain stones on Mount Carmel are so called

> The story is that the owner of the land refused to supply the wants of the prophet, and consequently his melons were transformed into stones—STANLEY *Sinai and Palestine.*

Eliot, George. The pseudonym of Mary Ann Evans (1819-80) Her first novel appearing under this name was *Scenes of Clerical Life*, 1858.

Eliott's Tailors. The 15th (King's) Hussars In 1759 Lieutenant-Colonel Eliott (later Lord Heathfield, hero of Gibraltar) enlisted a large number of tailors into a cavalry regiment modelled after the Prussian hussars This regiment so highly distinguished themselves, that George III granted them the honour of being called "the King's."

Elissa (el is' a) Step-sister of Medina and Perissa, and mistress of Hudibras in Spenser's *Faerie Queene* (II, ii)

By Virgil, Ovid, etc , Dido, Queen of Carthage, was sometimes called "Elissa "

Elixir of Life. The supposed potion of the alchemists that would prolong life indefinitely It was imagined sometimes as a dry drug, sometimes as a fluid *Elixir* (Arabic, a powder for sprinkling on wounds) also meant among alchemists the philosopher's stone, the tincture for transmuting metals, etc , and the name is now given to any sovereign remedy for disease —especially one of a "quack" character.

Elizabeth. The name is originally Hebrew and means "the oath of God," *i e* the oath in memory of the covenant made with Abraham Among its large number of variants are. Eliza, Elsie, Elsabin (Scandinavian), Elspeth, Lizzy, Elisabet, Elisabetta, Elisavetta, Elise, Isabel, Isabeau, Isa, Lescinska (Russian), Betty, Betsy, Bettina, Bess, Bessy, Beth, etc

St. Elizabeth of Hungary Patron saint of queens, being herself a queen. She died in 1231 at the age of 24, and her day is November 19th For the story of the conversion of flowers into bread, *see* MELON

Elizabethan. Belonging to, or having the characteristics of the period of Queen Elizabeth (1558-1603), used especially of literature, architecture, costume and the like The period was one of great vitality, which resulted in a high level of accomplishment in all the arts, especially in poetry and the drama

Ell. An old measure of length which, like *foot*, was taken from a part of the body, viz the forearm The word (A.S *eln*) is from a Teutonic word *alina*, the forearm to the tip of the middle finger, which also gives *elbow* (*q v*) and is cognate with Lat. *uina* The ell was of various lengths The English ell was 45 inches, the Scots ell only 37 inches, while the Flemish ell was three-quarters of a yard, and a French ell a yard and a half

Give him an inch, and he'll take an ell. Give him a little licence, and he will take great liberties, or make great encroachments

The King's Ell-wand. The group of stars called "Orion's Belt."

Ellyllon. The name given by the ancient Welsh bards to the souls of the Druids, which, being too good for hell, and not good enough for heaven, wander upon earth till the Judgment Day, when they will be admitted to a higher state of being

Elmo. *See* St. Elmo

Elohim. The plural form of the Heb *eloah*, God, sometimes used to denote heathen gods collectively (Chemosh, Dagon, Baal etc.), but more frequently used as a singular denoting one god, or God Himself In 1 *Sam* xxviii, 13, where the witch of Endor tells Saul "I saw gods [Heb. *elohim*] ascending out of the earth," this is an exceptional use of the word, and would seem to imply spirits of the departed, rather than gods *See next article*

Elohistic and Jehovistic Scriptures. Elohim and Jehovah (*Jahveh* or *Yahve*) are two of the most usual of the many names given by the ancient Hebrews to the Deity, and the fact that they are both used with interchangeable senses in the Pentateuch gave rise to the theory, widely held by Hebraists and biblical critics, that these books were written at two widely different periods; the Elohistic paragraphs, being more simple, more primitive, more narrative, and more pastoral, being held to be the older, while the later Jehovistic paragraphs, which indicate a knowledge of geography and history, seem to exalt the priestly office, and are altogether of a more elaborate character, were subsequently enwoven with these *See* Jehovah

Eloi, St., or **St. Eligius** (el' oi, el ij' i us) Patron saint of artists and, smiths He was a famous worker in gold and silver, and was made Bishop of Noyon in the reign of Dagobert (6th century) His day is December 1st

Eloquent. The old man eloquent Isocrates (436-338 B.C), the Greek orator When he heard that Grecian liberty was extinguished by the battle of Chæronea, he died of grief
> That dishonest victory
> At Chæronea, fatal to liberty,
> Killed with report that old man eloquent
> Milton *Sonnets* (*To Lady Margaret Ley*).

The eloquent doctor Peter Aureolus (14th century), Archbishop of Aix, a schoolman

Elsinore. The castle at which the action of Shakespeare's *Hamlet* takes place It is actually the Castle Kronstadt, north of Copenhagen The modern Danish name is Helsingor

Elysium (e liz' i ùm) The abode of the blessed in Greek mythology, hence the Elysian Fields, the Paradise or Happy Land of the Greek poets *Elysian* means happy, delightful
> O'er which were shadowy cast Elysian gleams
> Thomson *Castle of Indolence*, i, 44
> Would take the prisoned soul,
> And lap it in Elysium
> Milton *Comus*, 261-2

Elzevir (el' ze vēr) An edition of a classic author, published and printed by the family of Elzevir over the period from 1583 to about 1710 Louis, founder of the family, settled in Leyden about 1580, in 1583 he printed *J Drusii Ebraicum quaestionum*, and in 1592 published at his own risk a Eutropius, by P Merula Louis and his descendants carried on the press at Leyden until 1654, when it was moved to Amsterdam After some years it was split up, a few Elzevir volumes being published in Utrecht (1667-72), and Abraham, the last of the family, being university printer at Leyden, 1681-1712 Many Elzevir editions bear no other typographical mark than the words *Apud Elzeverios*, or *Ex Officina Elzeveriona* The total number of works bearing the name of Elzevir is 1213, of which 968 are in Latin, 44 in Greek, 126 in French and 75 in other languages

Em. The unit of measure in printing. The square of the body of any size of type For standard purposes the pica em is taken, measuring 12 points or one-sixth of an inch The depth and width of a printed page is measured in ems An *en* is half an em, and is the average width of the letters in a fount, it is thus used as a basis for casting-off or estimating a quantity of typed matter

Embargo (em bar' gō) To lay an embargo on To prohibit, to forbid The word comes from the Spanish *embargar*, to detain, and is especially applied to the prohibition of foreign ships to enter or leave a port, or undertake any commercial transaction, also to the seizure of a ship, goods, etc , for the use of the State

Embarras de Richesse (om ba ra' de rē shes') (Fr) A perplexing amount of wealth, or too great an abundance of anything, more matter than can conveniently be employed The phrase was used as the title of a play by the Abbe d'Allainval (1753)

Ember Days. The Wednesday, Friday, and Saturday of the four *Ember Weeks*, which were fixed by the Council of Placentia (1095), as those containing the first Sunday in Lent, Whit Sunday, Holy Cross Day (September 14th), and St Lucia's Day (December 13th) The name is the M E *ymber*, from A S *ymbren* (i e *ymb*, about, *ryne*, running), a period or revolution

Ember goose. The northern diver or loon, called in Norway *imbre*, because it appears on the coast about the time of the Ember days in

Advent. The German name of the bird is *Adventsvogel*

Emblem. A symbolical figure; a picture with a hidden meaning which is "cast into" (Gr *em*, in, *ballein*, to cast) the visible device Thus, a *balance* is an emblem of justice, *white* of purity, a *sceptre* of sovereignty.

Some of the most common and simple emblems of the Christian Church are —

A chalice The eucharist.

The circle inscribed in an equilateral triangle. or *the triangle in a circle* To denote the co-equality and co-eternity of the Trinity

A cross The Christian's life and conflict, the death of Christ for man's redemption.

A crown The reward of the perseverance of the saints

A dove The Holy Ghost

A hand from the clouds To denote God the Father

A lamb, fish, pelican, etc The Lord Jesus Christ

A phœnix The resurrection

Emblematical poems Poems consisting of lines of different lengths so that when printed or written the outline of the poem on the page can be made to represent the object of the verse Thus, George Herbert in the *Temple* prints a poem on the *Altar* that is shaped like an altar, and one on *Easter Wings* like wings George Puttenham in his *Arte of English Poesie* (1589) gives a chapter on this form of word-torture (which he calls "Proportion in Figure"), giving examples of eggs, crosses, pillars, pyramids, etc., and it was gibbeted by Ben Jonson, Dryden, Addison, and others.

As for altars and pyramids in poetry, he has outdone all men that way, for he has made a gridiron and a frying-pan in verse, that besides the likeness in shape, the very tone and sound of the words did perfectly represent the noise that is made by these utensils —SAMUEL BUTLER *Character of a Small Poet*

Emelye (em' e li) The sister-in-law of "Duke Theseus," beloved by the two knights, Palamon and Arcyte, the former of whom had her to wife.

Emerald. According to Eastern tradition, if a serpent fixes its eyes upon an emerald it becomes blind (Ahmed ben Abdalaziz, *Treatise on Jewels*) Other properties were also given to it, and in *The Lover's Complaint* (usually printed as though by Shakespeare) the author speaks of —

The deep-green emerald, in whose fresh regard
Weak sights their sickly radiance do amend.

The Emerald Isle. Ireland This term was first used by Dr. Drennan (1754-1820), in the poem called *Erin* Of course, it refers to the bright-green verdure of the island

Nor one feeling of vengeance presume to defile
The cause or the men of the Emerald Isle.
E. J DRENNAN *Erin.*

Emeritus (e mer' i tus) Deriving from the Latin *emereri*, to serve but one's time, the word is now used of a professor, minister, etc., who is retired from his office by reason of age or illness but retained on the rolls with full honour

Emeute (e mūt') (Fr) A seditious rising or small riot Literally, a moving-out (Lat. *e-moveo*)

Emilie (em' i lē) The "divine Emilie," to whom Voltaire wrote verses, was the Marquise du Châtelet, with whom he lived at Cirey for some ten years, between 1735 and 1749.

Empanel and empannel. These similar words have very different meanings To *empanel* is to form a list of jurors, or to enrol them; to *empannel* (a rarely used word, it is true) is to saddle a horse or ass, or more particularly to put the pack-saddle on a beast of burden.

Empedocles (em ped' ō klēz). A Greek philosopher, poet, and statesman (about 500-430 B C), a disciple of Pythagoras. According to Lucian, he cast himself into the crater of Etna, that persons might suppose he was returned to the gods, but Etna threw out his sandal, and destroyed the illusion (Horace: *Ars Poetica*, 404)

He who, to be deemed
A god, leaped fondly into Ætna flames,
Empedocles   MILTON *Paradise Lost*, iii, 471

Matthew Arnold published (1853) a classical drama with the title *Empedocles on Etna*

Emperor. A title applied to sovereigns of the highest class It was first used in this sense by Julius Cæsar in 58 B C and was assumed by all his successors, the last Roman Emperor of the West was Augustulus, A D 475, the last emperor of the East was Constantine, A D 1453 In 800 Charlemagne revived the Empire and as the Holy Roman Empire it lasted until 1806, the Emperors of Austria retaining the title until the fall of Austria in 1918

In 1804 Napoleon crowned himself Emperor of the French; the First Empire fell in 1815, and the Second Empire under Napoleon III lasted from 1853 until 1870.

In 1870 William I, King of Prussia, was declared Emperor of Germany (Kaiser) and that empire lasted until the abdication of William II, in 1918

Ivan the Terrible was called Tsar, or Emperor of Moscow in 1533, but it was Peter the Great who established the Tsardom of Russia in 1689 The Russian Empire as an autocracy lasted until 1917

Victor Emanuel III, King of Italy, was declared Emperor of Abyssinia in 1936; eight years later he and his family were deposed and exiled from Italy.

The British sovereigns were Emperors of India from 1876 until the partition of the continent into the Republic of India and Dominion of Pakistan, in 1947.

Outside Europe · Brazil was an empire 1821-89; Mexico, 1822-3 and 1864-7; Haiti, 1804-6 The term Emperor has also been applied loosely to the sovereigns of China, Japan, Mongolia, Ethiopia and Manchuria

Emperor. A standard size of drawing paper measuring 48 by 72 inches This is the largest sheet made by hand

Emperor, not for myself, but for my people The maxim of Hadrian, the Roman Emperor (117-138)

The Emperor of Believers. Omar I (581-644), father-in-law of Mohammed, and second caliph of the Mussulmans

Empire City, The New York, the great commercial city of the United States New

York State, on account of its leading position in wealth, population, etc, is called the **Empire State** Hence the name of the tallest skyscraper in the city

Empire Style. The style of furniture, costume, etc, that came into vogue during the Consulate and Empire of Napoleon, lasting approximately from 1800 until 1820 The Empire style followed on after the pseudo-classical fervour of the Revolution, but was itself largely inspired by Napoleon's wish to embellish his court with something of the splendour of imperial Rome The campaign in Egypt added certain Egyptian touches, such as the introduction of the sphinx, into its style of ornamentation In architecture the Empire style was largely an imitation of the Roman, in furniture there was a certain massiveness and angularity, and a great use of metal (chiefly bronze) applique ornament Though Napoleon himself observed the utmost simplicity the court costume was rich and ornate, especially in the military and civil uniforms Women's fashions changed constantly, but the high-waisted Grecian style remained a constant motif

Empirics An ancient Greek school of medicine founded by Serapion of Alexandria, who contended that it is not necessary to obtain a knowledge of the nature and functions of the body in order to treat diseases, but that experience is the surest and best guide (Gr *empeiros*, experienced, from *peira*, trial) They were opposed to the Dogmatic School founded by Hippocrates, which made certain dogmas or theoretical principles the basis of practice Hence any quack or pretender to medical skill is called an *empiric*

> We must not
> So stain our judgment, or corrupt our hope,
> To prostitute our past-cure malady
> To empirics.
>
> *All's Well That Ends Well*, ii, 1

Empyrean (em pi rē′ an) According to Ptolemy, there are five heavens, the last of which is pure elemental fire and the seat of deity; this fifth heaven is called the empyrean (Gr *empuros*, fiery), hence, in Christian angelology, the abode of God and the angels *See* HEAVEN.

> Now had the Almighty Father from above,
> From the pure empyrean where He sits
> High throned above all height, bent down his eye
>
> MILTON. *Paradise Lost*, iii, 56

En bloc (ong blok) (Fr) The whole lot together, *en masse*

En garçon (ong gar′ song) (Fr.) As a bachelor. "To take me *en garçon*," without ceremony, as a bachelor fares in ordinary life

En grande toilette, en grande tenue (ong gron twa let) (Fr) In full dress, dressed for a great occasion

En masse (ong mǎs) (Fr). The whole lot just as it stands; the whole.

En papillotes (Fr) In a state of undress, literally, in curl-papers. Cutlets with frills on them are *en papillotes*.

En famille (ong fa mē) (Fr.). In the privacy of one's own home

En passant (ong pǎs′ ong) (Fr). By the way. A remark made *en passant* is one dropped in, almost an aside

En pension (ong pon′ si on) (Fr) *Pension* is payment for board and lodging, hence, a boarding-house "To live *en pension*" is to live at a boarding-house or at an hotel, etc, for a charge that includes board and lodging

En rapport (ong ra pôr) (Fr) In harmony with, in sympathetic lines with.

En route (ong root) On the way, on the road or journey

Encænia (en sē′ ni å) The annual Commemoration of founders and benefactors at Oxford University, held in June. The word comes from the Greek, meaning a dedication, commemoration

Enceladus (en sel′ a dus) The most powerful of the hundred-armed giants, sons of Tartarus and Ge, who conspired against Zeus (Jupiter) The king of gods and men cast him down at Phlegra, in Macedonia, and threw Mount Etna over him The poets say that the flames of the volcano arise from the breath of this giant

Encomium (en kō′ mi um) From a Greek word meaning a eulogy or panegyric in honour of a victor in the Bacchic games, hence, praise, eulogy, especially of a formal nature The encomium was sung in the procession which marched from *kome* to *kome*, i e. village to village.

Encore (ong kôr) A good example of "English French" (*q.v*), our use of this word is unknown to the French, who say *bis* (twice) if they wish a thing to be repeated. *Encore une tasse* is "another cup," *encore une fois* "once again "

Encratites (en krǎt′ i tēz) A Gnostic and ascetical sect of the 2nd century, which condemned marriage, forbade eating flesh or drinking wine, and rejected all the luxuries and comforts of life. The name is Greek, and signifies "the self-disciplined" or "continent "

Encyclopedia (en sī klō pē′ di a) A book giving clear information on all branches of knowledge or on some particular art or science. One of the earliest known is that of Pliny the Elder (A D 23-79) entitled *Naturalis historia* in 37 books, dealing mainly with geography, medicine and art For many generations this served as a compendium of all that could be or needed to be known In 1360 Bartholomew de Granville wrote *De proprietatibus rerum*, in 19 books, starting with an article on God and ending with a list of birds' eggs In 1704 John Harris (c 1667-1719) produced a *Lexicon technicum or an Universal Dictionary of Arts and Sciences*, but this was soon overshadowed by the work of Ephraim Chambers (d 1740) who, in 1728, brought out his *Cyclopedia a Universal Dictionary of Arts and Sciences*, in two volumes With additions and supplements this was reprinted throughout the 18th century. The *Encyclopædia Britannica* was first published in Edinburgh, in three volumes, 1768-71, and went through many editions, each much larger than its predecessor, until the 11th (1908) which was issued, but not owned by Cambridge University. In 1920 the *Britannica* passed into American hands, and subsequent editions have been issued by them

The French *Encyclopédie ou Dictionnaire raisonné des sciences*, etc., appeared in 28 folio volumes (11 of which were of plates) between 1751 and 1765, with supplements, and an index which was published in 1780 It was edited by Diderot, assisted by d'Alembert, and many of the leading men of letters (hence called Encyclopedists) contributed to it Its frank and objective attitude towards the problems of the times, towards science and religion, made it a potent weapon in the service of the philosophic doctrines that were influential causes of the Revolution

End. A rope's end A short length of rope bound at the end with thread, and used for punishing the refractory

A shoemaker's end A length of thread pointed with a bristle, and used by shoemakers

At a loose end *See* LOOSE

At my wits' end. At a standstill how to proceed farther, nonplussed

East End. *See* WEST END *below*

End it or mend it. Said when an *impasse* or a crisis is reached when things are unbearable and something simply must be done.

He is no end of a fellow A capital chap; a most agreeable companion

Odds and ends. Fragments, remnants, odd ends of miscellaneous articles, bits and pieces of trifling value.

On end Erect, also, in succession, without a break, as "he'll go on talking for days on end "

One's latter end. The close of one's life
So the Lord blessed the latter end of Job more than his beginning —*Job* xlii, 12

The end justifies the means. A false doctrine, frequently condemned by various popes, which teaches that evil means may be employed to produce a good effect The true doctrine is that an act is vitiated by any defect in the act itself, not even the smallest sin may be committed that good may come
The End must justifie the means:
He only Sins who Ill intends
Since therefore 'tis to Combat Evil,
'Tis lawful to employ the Devil.
        PRIOR *Hans Carvel.*

The ends of the earth. The remotest parts of the earth, the regions farthest from civilization

To be one's end. The cause or agent of his death
This apoplexie will be his end.
        2 *Henry IV*, iv, 4

To begin at the wrong end. To attempt to do something unmethodically

To burn the candle at both ends. *See* BURN

To come to the end of one's tether. *See* TETHER.

To go off the deep end. To get unnecessarily excited

To have it at my finger's end. *See* FINGER

To make ends meet. To make one's income cover expenses, to keep out of debt.

To put an end to. To terminate or cause to terminate.

To the bitter end. *See* BITTER.

West end, East end. The quarter or part of a town west or east of the central part In London, and many other large towns, the West End is the fashionable quarter and the East End the part where the population lives that do the work.

End of the world, The According to rabbinical legend, the world is to last six thousand years The reasons assigned are (1) because the name *Yahweh* contains six letters, (2) because the Hebrew letter *m* occurs six times in the book of *Genesis*, (3) because the patriarch Enoch, who was taken to heaven without dying, was the sixth generation from Adam (Seth, Enos. Cainan, Mahalaleel, Jared, Enoch), (4) because God created the world in six days; (5) because six contains three binaries —the first 2000 years were for the law of nature, the next 2000 years the written law, and the last 2000 the law of grace

End-irons Two movable iron cheeks or plates, used in cooking-stoves to enlarge or contract the grate at pleasure The term explains itself, but must not be mistaken for *andirons* or "dogs".

End papers The two leaves front and back of a book, one of which is pasted down on to the inside of the cover and the other is a fly-leaf; they may be coloured or marbled

End-stopped. A term used in prosody denoting that the sense of the line to which it is applied is completed with the line and does not run over to the next, the opposite of *enjambment*. In the following lines the first is an example of enjambment, and the second is end-stopped:—
Awake, my St John, leave all meaner things
To low ambition, and the pride of kings
        POPE *Essay on Man*, i, 1

Endymion (en dim' i on) In Greek mythology, a beautiful youth, sometimes said to be a king and sometimes a shepherd, who, as he slept on Mount Latmus, so moved the cold heart of Selene, the Moon goddess, that she came down and kissed him and lay at his side. He woke to find her gone, but the dreams which she gave him were such that he begged Zeus to give him immortality and allow him to sleep perpetually on Mount Latmus Other accounts say that Selene herself bound him by enchantment so that she might come and kiss him whenever she liked Keats used the story as the framework of his long allegory, *Endymion* (1817), and it forms the basis of Lyly's comedy, *Endimion, the Man in the Moone* (1585)
The moon sleeps with Endymion,
And would not be awaked
        Merchant of Venice, v, 1.

Enemy. How goes the enemy? or **What says the enemy?** What o'clock is it? Time is the enemy of man, especially of those who are behind hand

Enfant terrible (ong fong te rēbl) (Fr.) Literally, a terrible child An embarrassing person, one who says or does awkward things at inconvenient times.

Enfilade (en fi lād) (Fr). means literally to spin out, to put thread in (a needle), as *enfiler une*

aiguille; to string beads by putting them on a thread, as *enfiler des perles* Bullets being compared to thread, we get the meaning to fire them through opposing ranks as thread through a needle, hence, to scour or rake with shot from the flank

England. The name comes from the *Angles* (land of the Angles), who migrated from the east of the Elbe to Schleswig (between the Jutes and the Saxons), and passed over in great numbers to Britain during the 5th century, but Verstegan (1605) has a story that Egbert was "chiefly moved" to call his kingdom England "in respect of Pope Gregory's changing the name of *Engelisce* into *Angellyke* " And this "may have moved our kings upon their best gold coins to set the image of an angel "

England's Darling. A name given to Hereward the Wake (fl. 1070) the patriot who held the Isle of Ely against William the Conqueror After a blockade of three months, Hereward and some of his followers escaped

Little Englander. One who would rather see England small, contented, and as self-contained as possible than have her the head of a world-wide Empire, the possession of which might be a source of trouble and danger to her, the opposite to an Imperialist The term was in use at the time of the South African War of 1899-1902

English. The language of the people of England, also the people themselves *Middle English* is the language as used from about 1150 to 1500; *Old English,* also called somewhat incorrectly *Anglo-Saxon,* is that in use before 1150

In typography, *English* was the name given to a large size of type, two points (*i e* one-thirty-sixth of an inch) larger than pica and four points smaller than great primer

Borough English. See BOROUGH.

English French. A kind of perversity seems to pervade many of the words which we have borrowed from the French. Thus, our *curate* is the Fr. *vicaire,* and our *vicar* the Fr *curé Encore* (Fr. *bis). Epergne* (Fr *surtout), Surtout* (Fr *pardessus) Screw* (Fr *vis),* whereas the French *écrou* we call a *nut,* and our *vice* is *étau* in French Some still say *à l'outrance* (Fr *à outrance).* We say *double entendre,* the French *à deux ententes*

Plain English. Plain, unmistakable terms To tell a person *in plain English* what you think of him is to give your very candid opinion without any beating about the bush

The King's (or Queen's) English. English as it should be spoken The term is found in Shakespeare (*Merry Wives,* i, 4), but it is older, and was evidently common **Queene's English** occurs in Nash's *Strange Newes of the Intercepting Certaine Letters* (1593), and "thou clipst the Kinge's English" in Dekker's *Satiromastix* (1602).

These fine English clerkes will saih thei speake in their mother tongue, if a manne should charge them for counterfeityng the Kinges Englishe—WILSON *Arte of Rhetoricke* (1553)

To put on English (U S A) In billiards, to apply spin to the ball.

Englishman. The national nickname of an Englishman is "John Bull" (*q v*) The old French nickname for him was "Goddam "

An Englishman's house is his castle. Because so long as a man shuts himself up in his own house, no bailiff can break through the door to arrest him or seize his goods In the third of his *Institutes* Sir Edward Coke (d. 1634) says —

A man's house is his castle, *et domus sua cuique tutissimum refugium*

And, again, in his report on Semayne's case·—

The house of everyone is to him as his castle and fortress, as well for his defence against injury and violence as for his repose

Enjambment. See END-STOPPED

Enlightened Doctor, The Raymond Lully of Palma (about 1234-1315), a Spaniard, and one of the most distinguished of the 13th-century scholastic philosophers

Enniskillen See INNISKILLING

Ennius (en' i us) The earliest of the great epic poets of Rome (about 239-169 B C), and chief founder of Latin literature

The English Ennius. Layamon (fl *c* 1200), who made a late Anglo-Saxon paraphrase of Wace's *Roman de Brut,* has been so called, but the title is usually given to Chaucer.

The French Ennius. Guillaume de Lorris (about 1235-65), author of the *Romance of the Rose* Sometimes Jehen de Meung (about 1260-1318), who wrote a continuation of the romance, is so called

The Spanish Ennius Juan de Mena (d 1456), born at Cordova

Enow. The representative of the inflexional plural of the A S adjective *genogh* (mod. *enough),* and still called by Johnson in his Dictionary (1755) "the plural of enough " It was used for numbers reckoned by tale, as There are chairs enow, nails enow, men enow, etc ; but now *enough* does duty for both words, and *enow* is archaic

Ensign (en' sen).

The British Navy The Union Jack (*q v*) The *white* ensign (Royal Navy) is the banner of St. George with the Jack cantoned in the first quarter, the *red* ensign is that of the merchant navy, the *blue,* that of the Navy reserve See FLAG

U S A The Stars and Stripes.

In the British Army an ensign was formerly an officer to whom was entrusted the bearing of the regimental colours It was the lowest commissioned rank, and in 1871 it was abolished, that of second lieutenant being substituted though the rank is still retained in the Footguards. In Shakespearean times the word was twisted into "ancient" or "auncient " In the U S Navy ensign is the lowest commissioned rank, it was instituted in 1862 when the rank of passed midshipman was abolished

Entail (en' tāl) An estate in which the rights of the owner are *cut down* (Fr *tailler,* to cut) by his being deprived of the power of alienating them and so barring the rights of his issue.

To cut off the entail is to put an end to the limitation of an inheritance to a particular line or class of heirs

Entelechy (en tel' e kı) (Gr *telos*, perfection). Aristotle's term for the complete realization or full expression of a function or potentiality, the result of the union of Matter (*potentiality*) and Form (*reality*), e g the soul considered as an end that is attained, is the Entelechy of the body.

You can never get at the final entelechy which differentiates Shelley and Shakespeare from the average versifier, Clu ierus and myself from Pater or from Browne —SAINTSBURY *Hist of English Prose Rhythm, Preface*, (1912)

In Rabelais s *Pantagruel* (Bk. V, ch xix), *entelechy* is the name given to the kingdom of the Lady Quintessence The argument on the name, whether it is *entelechy* (perfecting and coming into actuality) or *endelechy* (duration) reflects the fierce disputes that took place among the mediæval schoolmen on these two words

Entente cordiale (on tont' kôr dı al') (Fr) A cordial understanding between nations, not amounting to an alliance, but something more than a *rapprochement* The term is not new, but is now usually applied to the *entente* between England and France that was arranged largely by the personal endeavours of Edward VII in 1906.

If Guizot remains in office Normanby must be recalled, as the only chance of a renewal of the *entente cordiale* —*Greville's Diary*, p 189 (1847)

Enthusiast Literally, one who is possessed or inspired by a God (Gr *en theos*) Inspired is very similar, being the Lat *in spirare*, to breathe in (the god-like essence). In the 17th and 18th centuries the word *enthusiasm* was applied disparagingly to emotional religion It is, according to Locke, "founded neither on reason nor divine revelation, but rises from the conceits of a warmed or over-weening brain."

Entire. A term rarely used now in connexion with beer but still seen on inn signs, etc Before the introduction of porter in the early 18th century the chief malt liquors were ale, beer, and twopenny (a superior kind of ale sold at 2d a pint) The constant demand for a mixture induced the brewers to combine the flavours of these three in a liquor drawn from one cask This was called Entire or, being much drunk by porters and their like, Porter

Entire is also used of stallions and other uncastrated animals

Entrée (on' trã) In full-course dinners a made dish served between the fish and the joint; from this it has come to mean almost any made dish of meat or poultry.

To have entrée. To have the right or privilege of admission

Entremets (on' trè mã) are served between the roast and the dessert, in other words they are the sweet course, which in the U S A. is known as dessert

Entre nous (Fr) Between you and me, in confidence

Eolian Harp. *See* ÆOLIAN.

Eolithic Age, The (ē ō lith' ık) The name given by palæontologists to the earliest part of the Stone Age (Gr. *eos*, dawn, *lithos*, a stone), which is characterized by the rudest stone implements.

Eolus. *See* ÆOLUS

Eon. *See* ÆON

Epact (ē' pȧkt) (Gr *epagein* to intercalate). The excess of the solar over the lunar year, the former consisting of 365 days, and the latter of 354, or eleven days fewer. The epact of any year is the number of days from the last new moon of the old year to the 1st of the following January. It was formerly used in determining the date of Easter. *See* Tables at beginning of Prayer Book

Epaulette (ep' aw let). A shoulder ornament worn by officers of the Royal Navy above the rank of sub-lieutenant, when in full dress. Epaulettes ceased to be worn in the Army in 1855 Officers of the U S Navy above the rank of ensign wear epaulettes, but since 1872 in the army they are worn by generals only.

Ephebi (e fē' bı) Youths between the age of eighteen and twenty were so called at Athens During this period they were trained to military duties, were maintained at the public cost, and wore a uniform In later times entrance into this class became voluntary and by the 2nd century B c. courses in literature, rhetoric and philosophy had replaced the military duties and instruction

Ephesian A jolly companion, a roysterer The origin of the term is unknown *Cp* CORINTHIAN, which Shakespeare used in much the same way,

It is thine host, thine Ephesian, calls
Merry Wives of Windsor, IV, 5

Diana of the Ephesians. *See* DIANA

The Ephesian poet Hipponax, born at Ephesus in the 6th century B C

Ephialtes. A giant, brother of Otus (*q v*), who was deprived of his left eye by Apollo, and of his right eye by Hercules.

Ephors. Spartan magistrates, five in number, annually elected from the ruling caste. They exercised control even over the kings and senate

Epic. A poem of dramatic character dealing by means of narration with the history, real or fictitious, of some notable action or series of actions carried out under heroic or super-natural guidance Epic poetry may be divided into two main classes (*a*) the popular or national epic, including such works as the Greek *Iliad* and *Odyssey*, the Sanskrit *Mahabharata*, and the Teutonic *Niebelungenlied*; and (*b*) the literary or artificial epic, of which the *Æneid*, Ariosto's *Orlando Furioso*, Tasso's *Gerusalemme Liberata*, and Milton's *Paradise Lost* are examples

Father of Epic Poetry. Homer.

Epicurus (ep ı kū' rus). The Greek philosopher (*c*. 340-270 B C) who founded the Epicurean school. His axiom was that "happiness or enjoyment is the *summum bonum* of life" His disciples corrupted his doctrine into "Good living is the object we should all seek "

Hence, *epicure*, one devoted to the pleasures of the table, *epicurean*, pertaining to good eating and drinking, etc

Epicurean cooks
Sharpen with cloyless sauce his appetite
Antony and Cleopatra, II, 1.

Epigoni. *See* THEBES (*The Seven against Thebes*).

Epigram (ep' ı grăm). This was originally a simple inscription attached to religious offerings, etc., but even in Classic times it came to mean any short piece of verse conveying a single idea with neatness and grace, though usually with a sting in its tail

Treason doth never prosper, what's the reason?
For if it prosper, none dare call it treason
                          SIR JOHN HARINGTON, 1618.
You beat your pate, and fancy wit will come
Knock as you please, there's nobody at home
                          ALEXANDER POPE
The Devil having nothing else to do
Went off to tempt My Lady Poltagrue
My Lady, tempted by a private whim,
To his extreme annoyance, tempted him.
                          HILAIRE BELLOC
Sir, I admit your general rule,
That every poet is a fool
But you yourself may serve to show it,
That every fool is not a poet
                          MATTHEW PRIOR

Epimenides (e pı men' ı dēz) A Cretan poet and philosopher of the 7th century B C who, according to Pliny (*Natural History*), fell asleep in a cave when a boy, and did not wake for fifty-seven years, when he found himself endowed with miraculous wisdom *Cp* RIP VAN WINKLE

Epiphany (e pıf' å nı) (Gr. *epiphaneia*, an appearance, manifestation) The time of appearance, meaning the period when the star appeared to the wise men of the East January 6th is the Feast of the Epiphany in commemoration of this

Episcopal Signatures It is the custom of bishops of the Church of England to sign themselves with their Christian name and name of their see. In some of the older dioceses the Latin form is used, sometimes abbreviated —

Cantuar.	Canterbury	*Roffen.*	Rochester
Winton	Winchester.	*Sarum*	Salisbury
Cicestr:	Chichester	*Truron.*	Truro
Exon	Exeter	*Ebor*	York.
Gloucestr:	Gloucester.	*Dunelm.*	Durham
Norvic	Norwich.	*Carliol.*	Carlisle
Oxon·	Oxford	*Cestr·*	Chester
Petriburg:	Peterborough		

Episode (Gr, coming in besides—ı e adventitious). Originally, the parts in dialogue which were interpolated between the choric songs in Greek tragedy, hence, an adventitious tale introduced into the main story that can be naturally connected with the framework but which has not necessarily anything to do with it

In music, an intermediate passage in a fugue, whereby the subject is for a time suspended.

Epistle (e pıs' él) This word, akin in origin to *apostle*, comes from a Greek verb meaning to send to, and is properly applied to a letter sent to a person at a distance In modern usage a long and somewhat wordy letter is facetiously called an epistle The word is more generally applied to the letters sent by the apostles to the various churches in which they were interested There are thirteen from St Paul, one from St James, two from St Peter, three from St John, one from St Jude and the epistle to the Hebrews of unknown authorship.

The **epistle side** of an altar is to the celebrant's right as he faces it.

Epitaph (ep' ı taf) In its strict meaning this is an inscription on a tomb, but it is frequently extended to include any brief and strikingly apt commemoration of a dead person

Si monumentum requiris circumspice
Sir Christopher Wren's epitaph in St Paul's
Fuller's Earth
Thomas Fuller's epitaph on himself, 1661
Life is a jest, and all things show it
I thought so once, and now I know it
John Gay's epitaph on himself, 1732
Here a pretty baby lies
Sung asleep with lullabies,
Pray be silent, and not stir
Th' easy earth that covers her
Robert Herrick, upon a child
His foe was folly and his weapon wit
Epitaph on W S Gilbert by "Anthony Hope 'Hawkins.

Epoch (ē' pok) (Gr, a stoppage, pause) A definite point of time, also the period that dates from such, the sequence of events that spring from it The word is used with much the same sense as "era", we speak of both the "Epoch" and the "Era" of the Reformation, for instance.

Epode (Gr *epodos*, from *adein*, to sing) In ancient Greek lyric poetry, the part after the strophe and anti-strophe, in the epode the chorus returned to their places and remained stationary

Father of Choral Epode. Stesichoros of Sicily (632-552 B C)

Eppur si muove' (e poor sē mu ō' vı) (Ital , and yet it [*ı e* the earth] does move) The phrase said by a fable that dates only from 1757 to have been uttered in an undertone by Galileo immediately after his recantation of belief in the Copernican theory of the earth, which was made before the Inquisition in 1633 It is certainly apocryphal

Epsom Races. Horse races instituted in the early 17th century and held on Epsom Downs for four days in May The second day (Wednesday) is "Derby day" (*q v*), and on the fourth the "Oaks" (*q v*) is run

There are other races held at Epsom besides the great four-day races—for instance, the City and Suburban and the Great Metropolitan (both handicap races)

Epsom salts. Magnesium sulphate, used medicinally as a purgative, etc , and so called because it was originally (from 1618) obtained by the evaporation of the water of a mineral spring in the vicinity of Epsom, Surrey.

Equality. The sign of equality in mathematics, two parallel lines (=), was invented by Robert Recorde, who died 1558

As he said, nothing is more equal than parallel lines

Equation of Time. The difference between mean and apparent time—ı e the difference between the time as shown by a perfect clock and that indicated by a sundial The greatest difference is at the beginning of November, when the sun is somewhat more than sixteen minutes slow There are days in December, April, June, and September when the sun and the clocks agree

Equipage (ek' wı paj) To *equip* means to arm or furnish, and *equipage* is the furniture of a military man or body of troops Hence *camp equipage* (all things necessary for an encampment), *field equipage* (all things necessary for the field of battle), *tea equipage* (a complete tea-service), a *prince's equipage*, and so on The word was often used for carriage and horses

Era. A series of years beginning from some epoch or starting-point as:—

		B.C
The Era of the Greek Olympiads		776
,,	the Foundation of Rome	753
,,	Nabonassar	747
,,	Alexander the Great .	324
,,	the Seleucidæ .	312
,,	Julian .	45
,,	Abraham starts from Oct 1, 2016 B.C	
,,	Actium starts from Jan. 1, 30 B C	
,,	American Independence, July 4, A.D. 1776	
,,	Armenia, July 9, A D 552	
,,	Augustus, 27 B C	
,,	Diocletian, Aug 29, A D 284	
,,	Tyre, Oct 19, 125 B C	
,,	the Chinese, 2697 B C	
,,	the French Republic, Sept 22, A D 1792	
,,	the Hegira, July 16, A D 622 (The flight of Mohammed from Mecca)	
,,	the Maccabees, 166 B C	
,,	Yezdegird (Persian), June 16, A D 632	

The Christian Era begins theoretically from the birth of Christ, though the actual Nativity was probably in 4 B C

Erastians. The followers of Thomas Lieber (1524-83), a German heretic who wrote a work on excommunication in which he advocated the imposition of restrictions on ecclesiastical jurisdiction. His name was Grecized into *Erastus* (*i e.* the lovely, or beloved) *Erastian- ism*, *i e.* state supremacy or interference in ecclesiastical affairs, is named from him. The Church of England is sometimes called "Erastian," because the State controls its ritual and temporalities, and the sovereign, as the "head" of it, appoints bishops and other dignitaries

Erato One of the nine Muses (*q v.*), the muse of erotic poetry, usually represented holding or playing a lyre

Erebus In Greek mythology, the son of Chaos and brother of Night, hence darkness personi- fied. His name was given to the gloomy cavern underground through which the Shades had to walk in their passage to Hades.

> Not Erebus itself were dim enough
> To hide thee   *Julius Cæsar*, ii, 1

Eretrian The Eretrian bull Menedemos of Eretria, in Eubœa, a Greek philosopher of about 350-270 B C , who founded the Eretrian school, a branch of the Socratic

Erewhon (ĕr' won, âr' e won). The name of the ideal commonwealth in Samuel Butler's philosophical novel of the same name (1872) It is an anagram of "Nowhere." *Cp* COMMON- WEALTH, IDEAL

Erigena. John Scotus, called "Scotus the Wise," who died about 890 He must not be con- fused with Duns Scotus (*see* DUNCE), who lived some four centuries later.

Erigone *See* ICARIUS

Erin. Ireland (*q v.*)

Erin go bragh! Ireland for ever. *See* MAVOUR- NIN.

Erinyes (e rin' yĕz). In Greek mythology, daughters of Ge (Earth), avengers of wrong, the Furies *See* EUMENIDES; FURIES

Erix. A giant mentioned by Rabelais.

Erk. As "airk" (abbreviation of aircraftsman) this nickname was given by the R A F in World War I to aircraftsmen and mechanics It was later transformed into "erk" and, in World War II, the Christian name of Joe was frequently added to it. By an extension of meaning any beginner at a new job was called an erk

Erlking. In German legend, a malevolent goblin who haunts forests and lures people, especially children, to destruction. Goethe has a poem on him, set to music by Schubert

Ermine (ĕr' min) This is another name for the stoat, *Putorius erminea*, which has a brown coat in summer and a white one in winter, with a black tip to the tail The word ermine is applied chiefly to the fur, which in its white state is used for the robes of judges and peers, and women's cloaks It is one of the furs in heraldry, being represented by a number of small arrowheads beneath three dots, all black and symmetrically arranged on a white field There are two other furs, variations of this *ermines* (ĕr' minz) which is the reverse of ermine, being white spots on a black field, and *erminois* (ĕr' min ois), black spots on a gold (or) field. It is unheraldic to wear fur on a fur

Ermine Street. One of the most ancient roads in Britain, originally running from Colchester by way of Godmanchester and Lincoln to York, but later connected by the Romans with London, in the south, and the Wall of Hadrian in the north. The origin of the name is obscure, but it is not Roman It may be connected with Old Teutonic *irmin*, mighty, large. The most important of the other so-called "Roman roads" in Britain are *Watling Street*, *Ickmeld Street*, and the *Fosse Way* (*qq.v*)

Eros. The Greek god of love, the youngest of all the gods, equivalent to the Roman Cupid (*q v*) The name is also given to the bronze winged archer surmounting the memorial to the 7th Earl of Shaftesbury, in the centre of Piccadilly Circus, London The memorial was designed and the figure executed by Sir Alfred Gilbert (1854-1934) and unveiled in 1893.

Erra-Pater. The supposititious author of an almanack published about 1535 as *The Pronostycacion for ever of Erra Pater a Jewe born in Jewery, a Doctour in Astronomye and Physycke*. It is a collection of astrological tables, rules of health, etc , and is arranged for use in any year.

[He] had got him a suit of durance, that would last longer than one of Erra Pater's almanacks, or a cunstable's browne bill —NASH *Nashe's Lenten Stuffe* (1599)

The almanacks were frequently reprinted, and nearly a hundred years later Butler says of William Lilly, the almanack-maker and astrologer —

> In mathematics he was greater
> Than Tycho Brahe or Erra Pater.
>   *Hudibras*, i, 1

Ersatz (âr' zats). A German word meaning artificial, something substituted for a natural

Erse. The native language of the West Highlanders of Scotland. The word, which is now nearly obsolete, is a variant of *Irish*, and was applied by the Lowlanders to the Highland Gaelic In the 18th century Scots was often called Erse, without distinction of Highland and Lowland, and Irish was spoken of as Irish Gaelic

Erudite Most erudite of the Romans. Marcus Terentius Varro (116-27 B.C.), a man of vast and varied erudition in almost every department of literature

Erythynus (e rith' i nûs) **Have no doings with the Erythynus,** *i e.* "don't trust a braggart " The Erythynus is mentioned by Pliny (ix, 77) as a red fish with a white belly, and Pythagoras used it as a symbol of a braggadocio, who fable says is white-livered

Escapist (es kăp' ist). The term applied by psycho-analysts to one who shirks unpleasant realities by withdrawing into a world of fantasy, or by concentrating on other and pleasanter activities or subjects for thought

Escorial, or **Escurial** (es kôr' i al) The ancient palace of the Spanish sovereigns, containing also a monastery, church, and mausoleum, about twenty-seven miles north-west of Madrid. It is one of the most superb structures in Europe, and is built among rocks. It was erected in 1563-84 as the result of a vow to St Laurence (hence the "gridiron" shape of its plan) made by Philip II at the battle of St. Quentin, 1557.

Escuage (es kū' âj) (O Fr. *escu,* Lat *scutum,* a shield). A feudal term meaning "shield service," *i e* the obligation which bound a vassal to serve his lord in the field for forty days in the year at his own private charge

Esculapius. *See* ÆSCULAPIUS.

Escutcheon of Pretence In heraldry, the small shield of a wife, either heiress or co-heiress, placed in the centre of her husband's shield.

Esop. *See* ÆSOP.

Esoteric (Gr). Those within, as opposed to *exoteric,* those without The term originated with Pythagoras, who stood behind a curtain when he gave his lectures Those who were allowed to attend the lectures, but not to see his face, he called his *exoteric disciples,* but those who were allowed to enter the veil, his *esoteric.*

Aristotle adopted the same terms, those who attended his evening lectures, which were of a popular character, he called his *exoterics,* and those who attended his more abstruse morning lectures, his *esoterics*

Esoteric Buddhism. *See* THEOSOPHY.

Esprit de corps (es' prē de kôr) (Fr) The spirit of pride in the society with which you are associated, and regard for its traditions and institutions.

Esquire (Lat. *scutiger,* a shield-bearer). One who carried the *escu* or shield of a knight.

According to a dictum of the College of Heralds —

The following persons are legally "Esquires"'—The sons of peers, the sons of baronets, the sons of knights, the eldest sons of the younger sons of peers, and their eldest sons in perpetuity, the eldest son of the eldest son of a knight, and his eldest son in perpetuity, the kings of arms, the heralds of arms, officers of the Army or Navy of the rank of captain and upwards, sheriffs of Counties for life, J P 's of counties whilst in commission, serjeants-at-law, Queen's [King's] counsel, serjeants-at-arms, Companions of the Orders of Knighthood, certain principal officers in the Royal household, deputy lieutenants, commissioners of the Court of Bankruptcy, masters of the Supreme Court, those whom the Sovereign, in any commission or warrant, styles esquire, and any person who, in virtue of his office, takes precedence of esquires "

To these, doctors of law, barristers, physicians and graduates of the universities not in holy orders are often added, but the general use of the suffix has robbed it of all distinction It is never used in America, and rarely in the overseas parts of the Empire

Essays. Lord Bacon's essays were the first in English that bore the name

To write just treatises requireth leisure in the writer and leisure in the reader . which is the cause which hath made me choose to write certain brief notes . which I have called essays The word is late, but the thing is ancient —*Suppressed Dedication to Prince Henry*

Essenes. A puritanical and mystical sect of Jews, originating about the 2nd century B C , whose doctrines are supposed by some to have influenced those of our Saviour They were communists who abjured every sort of fleshly indulgence, ate no animal food, drank only water, and whose only sacrifices to God were the fruits of the earth They kept the Sabbath extremely strictly, always dressed in white, devoted themselves to contemplative studies, and held the Scriptures in great reverence, but interpreted them allegorically.

Essex Lions. Calves, for which the county is famous

Valiant as an Essex lion. Said ironically of a timid person *Cp.* COTSWOLD.

Estate (O.Fr *estat,* Lat *status* from *stare,* to stand) **Estates of the realm.** The powers that have the administration of affairs in their hands, that on which the realm stands The three estates of Britain are the Lords Spiritual, the Lords Temporal, and the Commons, popularly speaking, the public press is termed the "fourth estate" (*q v*) It is a mistake to call the three estates of England the Sovereign, the Lords, and the Commons

The king and the three estates of the realm assembled in parliament —*Collect for Nov 5*

Est-il-possible (ā tēl pos ēbl) A nickname of Prince George of Denmark (1653-1708), the consort of Queen Anne The story goes that when he was told of the abdication of his father-in-law, James II, all he did was to exclaim, "Est-il possible?" and when told, further, of the several noblemen who had fallen away from him, "Est-il possible?" exhausted his indignation.

Estotiland (es tŏt' i land) An imaginary tract of land near the Arctic Circle in North America, said to have been discovered by John

Scalve, a Pole It is mentioned and shown, in Peter Heylin's *Microcosmos* (1622).

> The snow
> From cold Estotiland.
> MILTON *Paradise Lost*, x, 685.

Estramaçon (es tre mâ son) (Fr) A blow or cut with a sword, hence also "estramaçonner".

Estrich. The old name for the ostrich (*q v*).

Eternal, The. God

The Eternal City. Rome. The epithet occurs in Ovid, Tibullus, etc , and in many official documents of the Empire; also Virgil (*Æneid*. i, 79) makes Jupiter tell Venus he would give to the Romans *imperium sine fine* (an eternal empire)

The eternal fitness of things The congruity between an action and the agent

> Can any man have a higher notion of the rule of right, and the eternal fitness of things?—FIELDING. *Tom Jones*, Bk iv, ch. iv

The eternal tables. In Mohammedan legend, a white pearl extending from east to west, and from heaven to earth, on which God has recorded every event, past, present, and to come.

Etesian Wind (e tē' zhân) A Mediterranean wind which rises annually (Gr. *etos*, a year) about the dog-days, and blows forty days together in the same direction It is gentle and mild

> Deem not, good Porteus, that in this my song
> I mean to harrow up thy humble mind,
> And stay that voice in London known so long,
> For balm and softness, an Etesian wind
> PETER PINDAR *Nil Admirare*.

Ethiopia (ē thi ō' pya) This very ancient name has been revived in modern times as the official designation of Abyssinia From the 11th century B C until the 4th century A D Ethiopia was an independent state, often of considerable power, as when in the 8th century B C it conquered Egypt and for two hundred years imposed its rulers upon her In the 4th century A D Ethiopia was ravaged by Abyssinia, and in the 6th century its place was taken by the Christian state of Nubia Tradition has it that the Queen of Sheba was an Ethiopian, and from her Menelik and the sovereigns of Abyssinia claim descent Candace was the hereditary title of the Queens of Meroe, in Upper Nubia. The monarch of Ethiopia styles himself Emperor, King of Kings Conquering Lion of the Tribe of Judah, Elect of God The country was conquered and overrun by the Italians in 1936, but liberated in 1945 The ancient Ethiopian language of the Church and literature is Geeze (gēz), of the Semitic group.

From earliest times the Ethiopians have been proverbial for their blackness

> Can the Ethiopian change his skin, or the leopard his spots?—*Jer* xiii, 23

> Her beauty hangs upon the cheek of night
> As a rich jewel in an Ethiop's ear.
> *Romeo and Juliet*, i, 5

Ethnophrones (Gr *ethnos-phren*, heathen-minded) A sect of heretics of the 7th century, who combined such pagan practices as divination, augury, astrology, etc , with Christianity

Ethon The eagle or vulture that gnawed the liver of Prometheus

Etiquette. The usages of polite society. The word means a ticket or card, and refers to the ancient custom of delivering a card of directions and regulations to be observed by all those who attended court In French the word originally meant a soldier's billet.

> Etiquette . had its original application to those ceremonial and formal observances practised at Court . The term came afterwards . . to signify certain formal methods used in the transactions between Sovereign States —BURKE: *Works*, vol viii, p 329

Etna (et' nä). The highest active volcano in Europe It stands over the Straits of Messina, 10,750 ft. high, covering an area of 460 sq miles, and is ever active from some of its 200 minor cones. Serious eruptions occurred in 1923 and 1928, yet many towns and villages live within its continual menace In Sicily Etna is known as Monte Gibello. Virgil (*Æneid*, iii, 578, etc) ascribes its eruption to the restlessness of Enceladus, a hundred-headed giant, who lies buried under the mountain, where also the Greek and Latin poets placed the forges of Vulcan and the smithy of the Cyclops.

Etrenne *See* STRENIA.

Etruria is a district in Stoke-upon-Trent founded and so named by Josiah Wedgwood when he established his pottery works there in 1769

Etruscans (e trŭs' kánz) These ancient and mysterious people lived in the region of Italy now corresponding more or less to Tuscany. The many monuments in their old lands have never been deciphered, and very little is known of their language Their art is of high quality, and they have never been excelled in the making of gold jewellery Of recent years it has been discovered that the Etruscans were Orientals, coming from Asia Minor originally, perhaps from Lydia but certainly from between the Hellespont and Syria.

Ettrick Shepherd. The name given to James Hogg (1770-1835), the Scottish poet who was born at Ettrick, Selkirkshire. the son of a shepherd, and himself a shepherd at Willanslee. He obtained his first success in 1807 with a volume of verse entitled *The Mountain Bard*; his principal work is, however, *The Queen's Wake*, 1813. Hogg figures largely in Wilson's *Noctes Ambrosianae*

Etzel. The name given in German heroic legend to Attila (d. A D. 453), King of the Huns, a monarch ruling over three kingdoms and more than thirty principalities

Eucharist. The consecrated Elements in Holy Communion. (Gr. *eucharistos*, grateful). Literally, a thank-offering. Our Lord said, "Do this in remembrance of me"—*i e.* out of gratitude to me. *Cp.* IMPANATION

Euclid (û' klid) Many generations of schoolboys knew geometry only as "Euclid," for the teaching of that branch of mathematics was based on the *Elements* of Euclides, a Greek geometer who lived in Alexandria about 300 B C. Of his 15 books some have been lost and others mutilated by commentators and transcribers. Euclid's methods have been discarded in modern teaching mainly because they ignore measurement and constructive movement

Eucrates (ū krā' tēz) More shifts than Eucrates. Eucrates, the miller, was one of the archons of Athens, noted for his shifts and excuses for neglecting the duties of the office

Eudoxians (ū doks' ι anz) Heretics, whose founder was Eudoxius, patriarch of Antioch in the 4th century They maintained that the Son had a will independent of the Father, and that sometimes their wills were at variance.

Eugenius (ū jē' nι us) The friend and counsellor of Yorick in Sterne's *Tristram Shandy* is intended for John Hall Stevenson (1718-85), the disreputable author of *Crazy Tales*, and a relative of Sterne's

Eulalie, St. (ū' la lē) Eulalon (ι e "the sweetly-spoken") is one of the names of Apollo, but there is a virgin martyr called Eulalie, born at Barcelona When she was only twelve the persecution of Diocletian broke out, and she, in the presence of the Roman judge, cast down the idols he had set up. She was martyred on February 12th, 304, and is the patron saint of Barcelona and of sailors

Eulenspiegel (oi len spē' gel) (ι e "Owl-glass"), **Tyll.** A 14th-century villager of Brunswick round whom clustered a large number of popular tales of all sorts of mischievous pranks, first printed in 1515 The work has been attributed (probably erroneously) to Thomas Murner (1475-1530), it was translated into many languages and rapidly achieved wide popularity The tone poem on the subject by Richard Strauss was first performed in 1895.

Eumæus (ū mē' us) The slave and swineherd of Ulysses, hence, a swineherd

This second Eumæus strode hastily down the forest glade, driving before him   the whole herd of his inharmonious charges —SCOTT

Eumenides (ū men' ι dēz) (Gr , the goodtempered ones) A name given by the Greeks to the Furies, as it would have been ominous and bad policy to call them by their right name, *Erinyes* (*q v*).

Eupatridæ (ū păt' ri dē) The land-owning aristocracy of ancient Attica. These lords of creation were set aside by the time of Pericles, and a democratic form of government established

Euphemism (ū' fe mizm) Word or phrase substituted, to soften an offensive expression. Pope refers to the use of euphemisms in his lines

To rest, the cushion and soft dean invite,
Who never mentions hell to ears polite
Moral Essays, epist ιv, 149.

"His Satanic majesty", "light-fingered gentry", "a gentleman on his travels" (*one transported*), "an obliquity of vision" (*a squint*) are common examples

Eureka (ū rē' ka) (Gr , more correctly *Heureka*, I have found it) An exclamation of delight at having made a discovery, originally that of Archimedes, the Syracusan philosopher, when he discovered how to test the purity of Hiero's crown The tale is, that Hiero delivered a certain weight of gold to a smith to be made into a votive crown, but, suspecting that the gold had been alloyed with an inferior metal, asked Archimedes to test it The philosopher did not know how to proceed, but in stepping into his bath, which was quite full, observed that some of the water ran over It immediately struck him that a body must remove its own bulk of water when it is immersed, silver is lighter than gold, therefore a pound-weight of silver will be more bulky than a pound-weight of gold, and would consequently remove more water In this way he found that the crown was deficient in gold, and Vitruvius says

When the idea flashed across his mind, the philosopher jumped out of the bath exclaiming, "Heureka! heureka!" and, without waiting to dress himself, ran home to try the experiment

"Eureka!" is the motto of California, in allusion to the gold discovered there.

Eurus (ū' rus) The east wind; connected with Gr *eos* and Lat *aurora*, the dawn

While southern gales or western oceans roll,
And Eurus steals his ice-winds from the pole
DARWIN. *Economy of Vegetation*, canto vi

Eurydice (ū rid' i si) In Greek mythology the wife of Orpheus, killed by a serpent on her wedding night. Orpheus went down to the infernal regions to seek her, and was promised she would return on condition that he looked not back till she had reached the upper world When the poet got to the confines of his journey, he turned his head to see if Eurydice were following, and she was instantly caught back again into Hades

Restore, restore Eurydice to life,
Oh, take the husband or return the wife
POPE *Ode on St Cecilia's Day*

Eustathians (ū stā thι anz) The followers of Eustathius, Bishop of Sebaste, in Armenia, who was deposed by the council of Gangra in 380.

Euterpe (ū tĕr' pi) One of the nine Muses (*q v*), the inventor of the double flute, the muse of Dionysiac music; patroness of joy and pleasure, and of flute-players

Eutychians (ū tik' yanz) Heretics of the 5th century, violently opposed to the Nestorians They maintained that Jesus Christ was entirely God previous to the incarnation, and entirely man during His sojourn on earth, and were thus the forerunners of the Monophysites (*q v.*). The founder was Eutyches, an abbot of Constantinople, excommunicated in 448

Euxine Sea (ūks' In) The Greek name for the Black Sea (*q v*), meaning the "hospitable." It was originally called by that people *Axeinos*, inhospitable, on account of its stormy character and rocky shores, but this name was changed euphemistically, as it was never thought wise to give a derogatory (even though true) name to any force of nature *Cp* ERINYES and EUMENIDES.

Evangelic Doctor, The. John Wyclif (1320-84), "the morning star of the Reformation"

Evangelists The four Evangelists, Matthew, Mark, Luke, and John, are usually represented in art as follows:—

Matthew With a pen in his hand, and a

scroll before him, looking over his left shoulder at an angel

Mark Seated writing, and by his side a couchant winged lion

Luke With a pen, looking in deep thought over a scroll, and near him a cow or ox chewing the cud. He is also frequently shown as painting a picture, from the tradition that he painted a portrait of the Virgin

John A young man of great delicacy, with an eagle in the background to denote sublimity

The more ancient symbols were—for Matthew, *a man's face*, for Mark, *a lion*, for Luke, *an ox*, and for John, *a flying eagle*, in allusion to the four living creatures before the throne of God, described in the Book of Revelation "The first was like a lion, and the second .. like a calf, and the third .. had a face as a man, and the fourth was like a flying eagle" (iv, 7)

Another explanation is that Matthew is symbolized by a *man*, because he begins his gospel with the humanity of Jesus, as a descendant of David, Mark by a *lion*, because he begins his gospel with the scenes of John the Baptist and Jesus in the Wilderness; Luke by a *calf*, because he begins his gospel with the priest sacrificing in the temple, and John by an *eagle*, because he soars high, and begins his gospel with the divinity of the Logos The four symbols are those of Ezekiel's cherubim

Irenæus says "The lion signifies the royalty of Christ; the calf His sacerdotal office; the man's face His incarnation, and the eagle the grace of the Holy Ghost."

Evans's Supper Rooms. In the early 19th century this was one of the best-known resorts of London night life. The house, at the northwest corner of Covent Garden, was on the site later occupied by the National Sporting Club In its heyday Evans's was a supper room with entertainment provided solely by male artists Women were not admitted except on giving their names and addresses, and even then were forced to enjoy the privilege of watching from behind a screen. Evans's and the Cyder Cellar, described so graphically in *Pendennis* were the forebears—though far removed—of the music hall and variety show

Even-christian An old term for a fellow-Christian, a neighbour in the Gospel sense

He that hath desdayn of his neighebour, that is to seyn, of his evencristen —CHAUCER *Parson's Tale*

The more pity that great folk should have countenance in this world to drown or hang themselves, more than their even Christian —*Hamlet*, v 1

Events At all events. In any case, be the issue what it may, *utcumque ceciderit*

In the event. "In the event of his being elected," means *in case*, or provided he is elected, if the result is that he is elected

Ever and Anon. From time to time. *See* ANON.

Ever-Victorious Army, The. A force of Chinese, officered by Europeans and Americans, raised in 1861, and placed under the command of Gordon. *See* CHINESE GORDON. By 1864 it had stamped out the Taeping rebellion, which had broken out in 1851.

Everyman The central character in the most famous 15th-century English morality play (*q v*) of the same name, which is considered by some to be a translation from a Dutch original (*c* 1495), by others to have been the original. Everyman is summoned by Death and invites all his acquaintances (such as Kindred, Good Deeds, Goods, Knowledge, Beauty, Strength, etc) to accompany him on his journey, but of them all only Good Deeds will go with him The play in a German translation became world famous between the two world wars on account of Max Reinhardt's lavish production of it upon the steps of the cathedral at successive Salzburg festivals

The Everyman Library was started by Dents, London, in 1906 with 50 titles of which the first was Boswell's Johnson By the end of 1951 the library included 990 titles

Evidence, In. Before the eyes of the people; to the front, actually present (Lat) Evidence, meaning testimony in proof of something, has a large number of varieties, as —

Circumstantial evidence That based on corroborative incidents

Demonstrative evidence That which can be proved without leaving a doubt

Direct evidence That of an eye-witness

External evidence That derived from history or tradition

Internal evidence That derived from conformity with what is known

Material evidence That which is essential in order to carry proof

Moral evidence That which accords with general experience

Presumptive evidence That which is highly probable.

Prima facie evidence That which seems likely, unless it can be explained away

King's evidence That of an accessory against his accomplices, under the promise of pardon

Self evidence That derived from the senses manifest and indubitable

Evil. Evil communications corrupt good manners The words are usually attributed to St Paul (1 *Cor* xv, 33); but he was evidently quoting Menander's saying, ' It must be that evil communications corrupt good dispositions " Similar proverbs are, "he who touches pitch must expect to be defiled" (from *Ecclus* xiii, 1); "one scabbed sheep will infect a whole flock "

Evil Eye. The alleged faculty of causing material harm by means of a glance, in rural England it is called "overlooking " From its Latin name, *fascinum*, comes the word "fascination " The evil eye is a form of witchcraft, owing its origin to the presumption that the human eye is capable of operating at a distance In southern European countries the baleful effect of the evil eye is counteracted by closing the fist except for the forefinger and little finger which are extended This is a gesture of primeval antiquity Virgil speaks of an evil eye making cattle lean

Nescio quis teneros oculus mihi fascinat agnos
Ecl iii, 103.

Evil May Day. The name given to the serious rioting made on May 1st, 1517, by the London apprentices, who fell on the French residents. The insurrection forms the basis of the anonymous Elizabethan play, *Sir Thomas More*

The Evil One. The Devil

Evil Principle *See* AHRIMAN

Of two evils, choose the least. *See* CHOICE.

Ewe-lamb. A single possession greatly prized; in allusion to the story told in 2 *Sam* xii, 1-14

Ex (Lat). From, out of, after, or by reason of, it forms part of many adverbial phrases, of which those in common use in English are given below. As a prefix *ex*, when joined to the name of some office or dignity denotes a former holder of that office, or the holder immediately before the present holder. *An ex-president* is some former holder of the office, *the ex-president* is tne same as "the late president," the one just before the present one.

Ex cathedra. With authority The Pope, speaking *ex cathedra*, is said to speak with an infallible voice—to speak as the successor and representative of St Peter, and in his pontifical character The words mean 'from the chair '— *i e* tne throne of the pontiff—and are applied to all dicta uttered by authority, and ironically to self-sufficient, dogmatic assertions

Ex hypothesi. According to what is supposed or assumed, in consequence of assumption made.

Ex libris. Literally, "from the (collection of) books " The phrase is written in the books or printed on the bookplate, and is followed by the name of the owner in the genitive Hence, a bookplate is often called an *ex libris*

Ex luce lucellum. A gain or small profit out of light It was originally said of the old window-tax, and when Lowe in 1871, proposed to tax lucifer matches, he suggested that the boxes should be labelled *Ex luce lucellum*

Ex officio By virtue of office As, the Lord Mayor for the time being shall be *ex officio* one of the trustees.

Ex parte. Proceeding only from one of the parties, hence, prejudiced An ex-parte statement is a one-sided or partial statement, a statement made by one side without modification from the other

Ex pede Herculem. From this sample you can judge of the whole Plutarch says that Pythagoras calculated the height of Hercules by comparing the length of various stadia in Greece A stadium was 600 feet in length, but Hercules' stadium at Olympia was much longer, therefore, said the philosopher, the foot of Hercules was proportionately longer than an ordinary foot, and as the foot bears a certain ratio to the height, so the height of Hercules can be easily ascertained **Ex ungue leonem,** a lion (may be drawn) from its claw, is a similar phrase

Ex post facto. From what is done afterwards; retrospective. An *ex post facto* law is a law made to meet and punish a crime after the offence has been committed

Ex professo. Avowedly, expressly
I have never written *ex professo* on the subject —
GLADSTONE· *Nineteenth Century*, Nov , 1885

Ex proprio motu. Of his (or its) own accord; voluntarily

Ex uno omnes. From the instance deduced you may infer the nature of the rest. A general inference from a particular example, if one oak bears acorns, all oaks will

Exaltation. In astrology. a planet was said to be in its "exaltation" when it was in that sign of the zodiac in which it was supposed to exercise its strongest influence Thus the exaltation of Venus is in Pisces, and her "dejection" in Virgo
And thus, god woot, Mercurie is desolate
In Pisces, wher Venus is exaltat
  CHAUCER *Wife of Bath's Prologue*, 703

Exaltation of the Cross. A feast held in the Roman Catholic Church on September 14th (Holy Cross Day), in commemoration of the victory over the Persians in 627, when Heraclius recovered and restored to Calvary the cross that had been carried away by Khosroes the Persian

Excalibur (eks kăl' i běr) The name of Arthur's sword (O Fr *Escalibor*), called by Geoffrey of Monmouth *Caliburn*, and in the *Mabinogion Caledvwlch* There was a sword called *Caladbolg*, famous in Irish legend, which is thought to have meant "hard-belly," *i e* capable of consuming anything, this and the name *Excalibur* are probably connected
By virtue of being the one knight who could pull Excalibur from a stone in which it had been magically fixed Arthur was acclaimed as "the right born king of all England " After his last battle, when the king lay sore wounded, it was returned at his command by Sir Bedivere to the Lady of the Lake *See* Malory, Bk. xxi, ch v, and Tennyson's *Passing of Arthur* (*Idylls of the King*)

Excelsior (Lat , higher) Aim at higher things still It is the motto of the United States, and has been made popular by Longfellow's poem so named

Exception. The exception proves the rule Without a rule, there could be no exception, the very fact of an exception proves there must be a rule

To take exception To feel offended, to find fault with

Exchequer Court of Exchequer. In the subdivision of the court in the reign of Edward I, the Exchequer acquired a separate and independent position Its special duty was to order the revenues of the Crown and recover the king's debts It was called the *Scaccarium*, from Lat *scaccum*, a chess-board, because a chequered cloth was used on the table of the court Foss, in his *Lives of the Judges* (1848-57), says —
All round the table was a standing ledge four fingers broad, covered with a cloth bought in the Easter Term, and this cloth was "black rowed with strekes about a span," like a chess-board On tne spaces of this cloth counters were arranged, marked for checking computations.

The Chancellor of the Exchequer is an office that originated under Henry III Now a leading member of the Cabinet, he presents the Budget to the House of Commons and is responsible for the collecting and spending of the national revenue

Excise Literally, a piece cut off (Lat. *excido*) It is a toll or duty levied on articles of home consumption

Taxes on commodities are either on production within the country, or on importation into it, or on conveyance or sale within it, and are classed respectively as excise, customs, or tolls —MILL *Political Economy* Bk v ch iii, p 562

In his Dictionary Dr Johnson defined excise as "A hateful tax levied upon commodities "

Excommunication An ecclesiastical censure by which a person is deprived of the communion of the Church Excommunicants lose the right of attending divine service and receiving the sacraments, they have no share in indulgences or in public prayers or Masses If clerics they are forbidden to administer the sacraments Formal sentence is ordinarily required, but in certain cases excommunication is incurred at once by the commission of a forbidden act, *ipso facto*.

The practice of excommunication was no doubt derived from the Jewish practice at the time of Christ, which entailed exclusion from religious and social intercourse (cp *Luke* vi, 22); cp INTERDICT; BELL, BOOK AND CANDLE.

From the same word-origin, a prisoner could be held *ex communicado, i e* no one whatsoever could talk to him.

Exeat (Lat , he may go out). Permission granted by a bishop to a priest to leave his diocese. In the universities, permission to a student to be out of College for one or more nights, as opposed to an *absit* permitting his absence during the inside of a day

Execrate. This is the direct opposite to *consecrate*, and means to curse, to imprecate evil upon, to detest utterly, abhor, abominate.

They gaze upon the links that hold them fast,
With eyes of anguish, execrate their lot,
Then shake them in despair and dance again.
COWPER: *The Task*, ii.

Exempli gratia (Lat.) For the sake of example: abbreviated to "*e g*" when used as the introduction to an example

Exequatur An official recognition of a person in authorizing him to exercise his power, formerly, the authoritative recognition of a papal bull by a bishop, sovereign, etc The word is Latin, and means, "he may exercise" (the function to which he has been appointed).

Exeter *See also* EXETER.

The Duke of Exeter's daughter. *See* DUKE

The Exeter Book. A MS collection of Anglo-Saxon poetry presented about 1060 by Bishop Leofric to Exeter Cathedral, and still preserved in the library there. It includes poems and "riddles" by Cynewulf (8th century), the legends of St Guthlac and St Juliana, "Widsith," "The Wanderer," "The Complaint of Deor," etc.

The **Exon** or **Exeter Domesday** (*q v*) is also sometimes called the "Exeter Book."

Exhibition. A scholarship, *i e* a fixed sum spread over a definite period given by a school or university, etc , as a result of an examination, for the purpose of assisting in defraying the cost of education The word was formerly used for maintenance generally, pecuniary support, an allowance of meat and drink

They have founded six exhibitions of £15 each per annum, to continue for two years and a half — TAYLOR *The University of Dublin*, ch v

Exhibitions Trade "fairs" for the display of manufactured goods to interested parties date from the Middle Ages, but the idea of attracting the general public was first brought forward by the Paris Exhibition of 1798 Several more were held in France during the first half of the 19th century, and the great success of the Paris exhibition of 1849 inspired the Prince Consort to promote the Great Exhibition of 1851, held in the Crystal Palace which was erected in Hyde Park, London Since that date major exhibitions have been —

Paris, 1855, 1867, 1878, 1889, 1900, 1937.
London, 1862, 1886, 1908, [Wembley] 1924, and the centenary exhibition throughout Great Britain of 1951.
Philadelphia, 1876
Melbourne, 1880, 1888
Chicago, 1893, 1933.
St Louis, 1904
San Francisco, 1915, 1939
New York, 1939

Exhibitionism. In psycho-pathology this is an act of sexual gratification obtained by publicly exhibiting some part of the body normally clothed In a less marked form exhibitionism takes the shape of performing acts likely to attract attention, in a yet milder form, to mere showing-off

Existentialism (eks is ten' shal izm). A philosophical theory originating with Soren Kierkegaard (1815-55) and current for a time in France after World War II, largely owing to the teaching of Jean-Paul Sartre. Man, say the Existentialists can be free only through the full consciousness of his illogical position in a universe that has little relation to himself and is in itself meaningless.

Exit (Lat., he goes out). A stage direction showing when an actor is to leave the stage, hence, the departure of an actor from the stage and departure generally, especially from life; also a door, passage, or way out

All the world's a stage,
And all the men and women merely players:
They have their exits and their entrances.
As You Like It, ii, 7.

Exodus (Gr *ex odos*, a journey out) The second book of the Old Testament, which relates the departure of the Israelites from Egypt under the guidance of Moses; hence, a going out generally, especially a transference of population on a considerable scale, as *the exodus from Ireland*, meaning the departure of the Irish in large numbers for America; and the expulsion of colonists from Nova Scotia in 1755

Exon. One of the four officers in command of the Yeomen of the Guard, the acting officer who resides at the court; an exempt. The word is an Anglicized pronunciation of the Fr. *exempt*, this having been the title of a junior officer (next below an ensign) in the Life Guards

Exon (short for Lat. *Exoniensis*, of *Exonia, i e*. Exeter) is the signature of the Bishop of Exeter *See* EPISCOPAL SIGNATURES

Exon Domesday. A magnificent MS on 532 folio vellum leaves, long preserved among the muniments at Exeter Cathedral, containing the survey of Wilts, Dorset, Somerset, Devon, and Cornwall In 1816 it was published by Sir Henry Ellis as a Supplement to Domesday Book (*q v*)

Exoteric *See* ESOTERIC

Expectation Week. Between the Ascension and Whit Sunday, when the apostles continued praying "in earnest expectation of the Comforter"

Experimental Philosophy. Science founded on experiments or data in contradistinction to moral and mathematical sciences, also called *natural philosophy*

Experto crede (Lat.). Believe one who has had experience in the matter The phrase is used to add significance or weight to a warning

Exposé (Fr). A formal exposition; also, an exposure of something discreditable

Exter. That's Exter, as the old woman said when she saw Kerton. A Devonshire saying, meaning, I thought my work was done, but I find much still remains before it is completed "Exter" is the popular pronunciation of Exeter, and "Kerton" is Crediton The tradition is that the woman in question was going for the first time to Exeter, and seeing the grand old church of Kerton (Crediton) supposed it to be Exeter Cathedral "That's Exter," she said, "and my journey is over"; but alas' she had still eight miles to walk.

Extradition. The return of a criminal to stand trial, on request of the country in which his crimes are committed to the country to which he has fled The first extradition treaty was signed between England and France in 1843

Extreme Unction One of the seven sacraments of the Catholic Church, founded on *James* v, 14, 'Is any sick among you? let him call for the elders of the Church, and let them pray over him, anointing him with oil in the name of the Lord"

Eye A sheet in the wind's eye. An early stage of intoxication.

A sight for sore eyes A proverbial expression used of something that is very welcome, pleasant, and unexpected

Do you see any green in my eye? Do I look credulous and easy to be bamboozled? Do I look like a greenhorn?

Eyes to the blind. A staff, perhaps in allusion to that given to Tiresias (*q v*) by Athene, to serve him for the eyes of which she had deprived him.

In my mind's eye In my perceptive thought.

In the wind's eye. Directly opposed to the wind

In the twinkling of an eye. Immediately, very soon.

Mind your eye. Be careful or vigilant; keep a sharp look out, keep your eyes open to guard against mischief.

My eye! or **Oh, my eye'** an exclamation of astonishment *See* ALL MY EYE.

One-eyed. An expression of contempt, as, "I've never been in such a one-eyed town," *i e* such a poverty-stricken, mean, or unpleasing town

One-eyed peoples *See* ARIMASPIANS, CYCLOPS

One might see that with half an eye. Easily, at a mere glance

The eye of a needle. The words of Christ in *Matt* xix, 24 —
It is easier for a camel to go through the eye of a needle, than for a rich man to enter into the kingdom of God

enshrine a proverbial saying, and there is no need to suppose that by "the eye of a needle" was intended the small arched entrance through the wall of a city, nor is there any evidence that such a gateway had any such name in Biblical times *See* CAMEL A similar Eastern proverb occurs at *Matt* xxiii, 24 —
Ye blind guides, which strain at a gnat and swallow a camel,

and "In Media a camel can dance on a bushel," meaning that there all things are possible, is another ancient Eastern saying

The Eye of Greece. Athens
Athens, the eye of Greece, mother of arts
       MILTON *Paradise Regained*, iv, 240

The Eye of the Baltic. Gottland, in the Baltic.

The eye of the storm. An opening between the storm clouds *Cp* BULL'S EYE

To cast sheep's eyes at one. *See* SHEEP

To cry one's eyes out. To cry immoderately or excessively

To get one's eye in. To adjust one's sight at cricket, billiards, golf, bowls, etc

To give the glad eye to. To cast inviting glances at.

To have, or keep, an eye on To keep strict watch on the person or thing referred to

To have an eye to. To keep constantly in view; to act from motives of policy *See* MAIN CHANCE

To keep one's eyes skinned. To be particularly watchful

To make eyes at. To look amorously or lovingly at

To make someone open his eyes. To surprise him very much, and make him stare with wonder or admiration

To pipe your eye *See* PIPE.

To see eye to eye To be of precisely the same opinion, to think both alike

Up to the eyes. Wholly, completely, as *up to the eyes in work*, very fully occupied, *mortgaged up to the eyes*, to the last penny obtainable.

To hang on by one's eyelashes. To be just able to maintain one's position, hence, to be in difficulties

Eye-opener. Something that furnishes enlightenment, also, a strong, mixed drink, especially a morning pick-me-up.

Eye-service. Unwilling service; the kind that is only done when under the eye of one's master

Servants, be obedient to them that are your masters   not with eye service, as men pleasers, but as the servants of Christ —*Eph* vi, 5, 6

Eye-picking. The phrase used in Australia during the settling days for the practice of buying up here and there the choice lots of land, leaving the waste parts in between to settlers of smaller means, it was called "picking the eyes out of the country." Those who pursued this practice were known as *pea-cockers*

Eye-teeth The canine teeth; so called because their roots extend upwards nearly to the orbits of the eyes

He has cut his eye-teeth See TOOTH

To draw one's eye-teeth. To take the conceit out of a person, to fleece one without mercy,

Eye-wash. Flattery, soft sawder; fulsome adulation given for the purpose of blinding one to the real state of affairs

Eyre (âr). **Justices in Eyre.** The ancient itinerant judges who, from about 1100 to 1285, used to ride on circuit from county to county holding courts *Eyre* is from late Lat *iterare*, to journey, Lat *iter*, a journey

F

F. The first letter in the Runic futhorc (*q.v*), but the sixth in the Phœnician and Latin alphabets and their derivatives The Egyptian hieroglyph represented a horned asp, and the Phœnician and Semitic character a peg

Double F (Ff or **ff)** as an initial in a few personal names, as *Ffoulkes*, *ffrench*, etc., is a mistaken use in *print* of the mediæval or Old English capital F (*ﬀ*) as it appears *written* in engrossed leases, etc In script the old capital *F* looked very much like two small f's entwined, and it so appears in all old documents, and in many modern legal ones, not only in the case of personal names but of all words beginning with a capital *F*. Its modern use is an affectation

F is written on his face. The letter F used to be branded near the nose, on the left cheek of *felons, on their being admitted to* "*benefit of clergy.*" The same was used for brawling in church. The custom was abolished by law in 1822.

F.A.N.Y. (British) First Aid Nursing Yeomanry. founded 1909 The first women to serve with the British Army besides regular nurses In 1916 they began to drive ambulance convoys, and transport duties replaced their previous medical duties. Retained after 1918. Called out during the General Strike 1926. Active again on transport work, 1939-45.

F. E. R T. *See* ANNUNCIATION, ORDER OF THE.

F.F.V. First Families of Virginia, a snobbish term used in the 19th century by descendants of the first settlers

F.O.B. Free on board, meaning that the shipper, from the time of shipment, is free from all risk. Also prices are quoted as, for instance, "F.O B Detroit" where the goods have to make a long and expensive journey from the place of manufacture to their purchaser

Fabius (fā' bi ŭs). *See* CUNCTATOR, *and* FABIAN SOCIETY, *below*.

The American Fabius. George Washington (1732-99), whose military policy was similar to that of Fabius. He wearied out the English troops by harassing them without coming to a pitched battle

Fabian Society (fā' bi an) An association of socialists founded in January, 1884, by a small group of "intellectuals," which included George Bernard Shaw (1856-1950) and Sidney Webb (1859-1947) among others. As announced in its prospectus, it

aims at "the reorganization of society by the emancipation of land and industrial capital from individual and class ownership and the vesting of them in the community for the general benefit"   . and at "the transfer to the community of the administration of such industrial capital as can conveniently be managed socially "

The name is derived from Quintus Fabius (275-203 B C.), surnamed "Cunctator" (*q v*), the Roman general, who won his way against Hannibal by wariness not by violence, by caution, not by defiance

Fables *See* ÆSOP, PILPAY La Fontaine (1621-95) has been called the French Æsop, and John Gay (1685-1732) the English

Fabliaux (fab' lē ō) Metrical tales, for the most part comic and satirical, and intended primarily for recitation by the Trouveres, or early poets north of the Loire, in the twelfth and thirteenth centuries The word is used very widely, for it includes not only such tales as *Revnard the Fox*, but all sorts of familiar incidents of knavery and intrigue, legends, family traditions, and caricatures, especially of women.

Fabricius (fā brish' ŭs) A Roman hero (died *c* 270 B C), representative of incorruptibility and honesty. The ancient writers tell of the frugal way in which he lived on his farm, how he refused the rich presents offered him by the Samnite ambassadors, and how at death he left no portion for his daughters, whom the senate provided for

Fabulinus. The god, mentioned by Varro, who taught Roman children to utter their first word (*fabulor*, to speak). It was Vagitanus who taught them to utter their first cry

Face. A colloquialism for cheek, impudence, self-confidence, etc, as "He has face enough for anything," *i.e.* cheek or assurance enough The use is quite an old one

I admire thy impudence; I could never have had the face to have wheedled the poor knight so — ETHEREGE *She Would If She Could*, I, i (1668)

A brazen face. A bold, defiant look. *See* BRAZEN-FACED, *and cp.* BRASS.

A wry face. The features drawn awry, expressive of distaste.

Face to face. In the immediate presence of each other; two or more persons facing each other.

On the face of it. To all appearance, in the literal sense of the words

That puts a new face on the matter Said when fresh evidence has been produced, or something has happened which sets the case in a new light and makes it look different

To draw a long face. To look dissatisfied or sorrowful, in which case the mouth is drawn down at the corners, the eyes are dejected, and the face has an elongated appearance

To face down. To withstand with boldness and effrontery

To face it out To persist in an assertion which is not true To maintain without changing colour or hanging the head

To face the music. To stand up boldly and meet a crisis without faltering

To fly in the face of. To oppose violently and unreasonably to set at defiance rashly.

To have two faces, or to keep two faces under one hood. To be double-faced, to pretend to be very religious, and yet live an evil life

To look a person in the face, or full in the face. To meet with a steady gaze, implying lack of fear, or sometimes, a spirit of defiance.

To lose face. To be lowered in the esteem of others through an affront to one's dignity—a matter of the utmost importance in the Far East

To make faces. To make grimaces with the face

To put a bold, or a good, face on the matter To make the best of a bad matter, to bear up under something disagreeable

To save one's face. Narrowly to avoid almost inevitable disgrace, disaster, or discomfiture

To set one's face against something. To oppose it; to resist its being done.

To shut the door in one's face. To put an end to the negotiations, or whatever is in hand.

Face-lifting. A method of enhancing beauty or concealing the marks of age by an operation in which the skin of the face is tightened and wrinkles removed.

Faced. With a facing, lining of the cuffs, etc , used of an inferior article bearing the surface of a superior one, as when cotton-velvet has a silk surface.

Bare-faced. *See* BAREFACED

Shame-faced. Having shame expressed in the face. *Cp.* SHAMEFAST

Facer A blow in the face, a sudden check, a dilemma

Face-card or Faced-card. A court card, a card with a face on it.

Facile princeps. By far the best, admittedly first

Facilis descensus Averno. *See* AVERNUS.

Facings. To put someone through his facings To examine; to ascertain if what appears on the surface is superficial only. The term is also used for the lapels and cuffs on regimental uniforms, which used to differ in colour from the body of the coat, *e g* The Buffs (*q v*), so

called from wearing buff facings to their red coats.

Façon de parler. Idiomatic or usual form of speech

Faction. The Romans divided the combatants in the circus into classes, called *factions*, each class being distinguished by its special colour, like the crews of a boat-race The four original factions were the leek-green (*prasina*), the sea-blue (*veneta*), the white (*alba*), and the rose-red (*rosea*). Two other factions were added by Domitian, the colours being golden yellow (*aurata*) and purple As these combatants strove against each other, and entertained a strong *esprit de corps*, the word was easily applied to political partisans

Factor An agent, a substitute in mercantile matters, a commission merchant.

> Asleep and naked as an Indian lay
> An honest factor stole a gem away
> POPE *Moral Essays*, Ep iii

This refers to Thomas Pitt, Governor of Fort St George, who obtained the famous Pitt Diamond (*q v*)

Factory King. The name given to Richard Oastler (1789-1861), of Bradford, who devoted his life to the betterment of factory conditions, especially to the prohibition of child-labour and to the promotion of a Ten Hours Bill.

Factotum (Lat *facere totum*, to do everything required) One who does for his employer all sorts of services Sometimes called a *Johannes Factotum* Formerly the term meant a "Jack-of-all-trades," and it is in this sense that Greene used it in his famous reference to Shakespeare —

> There is an upstart Crow, beautified with our feathers, that with his *Tygers heart wrapt in a Players hide,* supposes he is as well able to bombast out a blanke verse as the best of you but being an absolute *Johannes fac totum,* is in his owne conceit the onely Shake-scene in a countrie.—*Green's Groatsworth of Wit* (1592)

Fad. A hobby, a temporary fancy, a whim Perhaps a contraction of faddle in "fiddle-faddle "

Fade **To fade in, to fade out.** Phrases applied in cinematography to the operation of causing a picture to appear or disappear gradually, and similarly in broadcasting, it describes the fading of sound into silence

In golf, a ball so struck that towards the end of its flight it drifts towards the right is said to have a bit of fade

Fadge Probably a Scandinavian word, connected with *faga*, to suit. To suit or fit together, as, *It won't fadge, we cannot fadge together, he does not fadge with me*

> How will this fadge?
> SHAKESPEARE · *Twelfth Night*, ii, 2

The word is also old slang for a farthing.

Faerie (fā´ ër ı) The land of the fays or faeries The chief fay realms are Avalon, an island somewhere in the ocean; Oberon's dominions, situate "in wilderness among the holtis hairy", and a realm somewhere in the middle of the earth, where was Pari Banou's palace.

> For learned Colin [Spenser] lays his pipes to gage,
> And is to Faery gone a pilgrimage
> DRAYTON *Eclogue*, iii

Faerie Queene, The (fâr ı kwĕn). An allegorical romance of chivalry by Edmund Spenser, originally intended to have been in 12 books, each of which was to have portrayed one of the 12 moral virtues. Only six books of twelve cantos each, and part of a seventh, were written (I to III published in 1590, IV to VI in 1596, and the remaining fragments in 1611). It details the adventures of various knights, who personify different virtues, and belong to the court of Gloriana, the Faerie Queene, who sometimes typifies Queen Elizabeth

Fag. Slang for a cigarette The origin of the word is not known **Fag-end.** The stub of a cigarette

In public schools a fag is a small boy who waits upon a bigger one The system was already established at Eton and Winchester in the 16th century. Dr. Arnold (1795-1842) the famous headmaster of Rugby, described it as "the power given by the supreme authorities of the School to the Sixth Form to be exercised by them over the lower boys for the sake of securing a regular government among the boys themselves and avoiding the evil of anarchy." *Tom Brown's School Days* and many volumes of reminiscences reveal the system at its best and worst.

It's too much fag Too much trouble, too much needless exertion

Quite fagged out. Wearied with hard work; tired out

Fag-end Originally the coarse end of a piece of cloth; hence the remaining part of anything, as "the fag-end of a leg of mutton," "the fag-end of a conversation," or "the fag-end of a session," which means the last few days before dissolution.

I never yet saw a great House so neatly kept . . . The Kitchen and Gutters and other Offices of noise and drudgery are at the fag-end; there's a Back-gate for the Beggars and the meaner sort of Swains to come in at —*Howell's Familiar Letters* (20 May, 1619)

Faggot. A bundle of sticks

In mediæval times heretics were often burned at the stake with faggots, hence an embroidered representation of a faggot was worn on the arm by those who had recanted their "heretical" opinions It was designed to show what they merited but had narrowly escaped

Faggot votes. Votes obtained by the nominal transfer of property to a person whose income was not otherwise sufficient to qualify him for being a voter

The "faggot" was a bundle of property divided into small lots for the purpose stated above

Lord Lonsdale had conveyed to him a certain property, on which he was to vote in that borough, as, what was familiarly called a faggot vote.—Sir F Burdett *Parl Debates*, 1817

The culinary *faggot*, deriving from the Latin *ficatum*, the liver of a pig fattened on figs, is a dish of liver chopped and seasoned with herbs before baking

Fagin (fā' gin) The rascally Jew who taught boys and girls how to pick pockets. This figure from Dickens's *Oliver Twist* was for many years proverbial.

Faience. Majolica So called from Faenza, where, in 1299, it was first manufactured. It is

B D —12

termed majolica because the first specimens the Italians saw came from Majorca.

Fainéant. *Les Rois Fainéants* (the "nonchalant" or "do-nothing" kings) Clovis II (d 656) and his ten Merovingian successors on the French throne The line came to an end in 751, when Pepin the Short usurped the crown Louis V (last of the Carlovingian dynasty, d 987) received the same name.

Fains (fānz). A schoolchildren's formula of unknown origin. When there is some undesirable task to be done, whoever says "Fains I" first is exempted from performing it; *e.g* "Fains I carry the bag!"

Faint. Faint heart ne'er won fair lady. An old proverb, with obvious meaning It occurs in Phineas Fletcher's *Britain's Ida* (ca v, st. 1), 1628, but is probably a good deal older.

Fair. AS PERSONAL EPITHETS
Edwy, or Eadwig, King of Wessex (938-58).
Charles IV, King of France, *le Bel* (1294, 1322-8)
Philippe IV of France, *le Bel* (1268, 1285-1314).

Fair Geraldine. *See* GERALDINE.

The Fair-haired. Harold I, King of Norway (reigned 872-930).

Fair Maid of Anjou. Lady Edith Plantagenet (fl 1200), who married David, Prince Royal of Scotland

Fair Maid of Brittany. Eleanor (d. 1241), granddaughter of Henry II, and, after the death of Arthur (1203), the rightful sovereign of England Her uncle, the usurper King John, imprisoned her in Bristol Castle, which she left to enter a nunnery at Amesbury Her father, Geoffrey, John's elder brother, was Count of Brittany.

Fair Maid of Kent. Joan (1328-85), Countess of Salisbury, wife of the Black Prince, and only daughter of Edmund Plantagenet, Earl of Kent. She had been twice married ere she gave her hand to the prince.

Fair Maid of Norway. Margaret (1283-90), daughter of Eric II of Norway, and granddaughter of Alexander III of Scotland On his death she was recognized by the states of Scotland as successor to the throne She set out for her kingdom, but died at sea from seasickness

Fair Maid of Perth. Katie Glover, heroine of Scott's novel of the same name, is supposed to have lived in the early 15th century, but is not a definite historical character, though her house is still shown at Perth

Fair Rosamond. *See* ROSAMOND.

A day after the fair. Too late for the fun, wise after the event Here *fair* is (through French) from Lat. *feria*, a holiday, and is quite unconnected with the adjective *fair*, which is the A S. *fæger*

A fair field and no favour. Every opportunity being given.

By fair means. Straightforwardly; without deception or compulsion.

Fair and soft goes far in a day. Courtesy and moderation will help one to effect a good deal of his purpose.

Fair and square. Honestly, justly, with straightforwardness

Fair fall you. Good befall you.

Fair game. A worthy subject of banter, one who exposes himself to ridicule and may be fairly made a butt of.

Fair Trade. An old euphemism for smuggling

In politics the phrase signifies reciprocity of protection or free trade, that is, free trade to those nations that grant free trade to us

Fair words butter no parsnips. *See* BUTTER

In a fair way. On the right tack

Fairway. The clear run from hole to hole on a golf-course, etc

The fair sex. Women generally; the phrase was modelled on the French *le beau sexe.*

To bid fair. To give good promise; to indicate future success or excellence as "he bids fair to be a good. ."

Fair Isle One of the Shetlands where a special pattern of knitting is done.

Fairlop Oak. A huge tree in the forest of Hainault, Essex, blown down in 1820. Prior to that a fair was held annually in July beneath its spreading branches.

Fairy. The names of the principal fairies and of groups of similar sprites known to fable and legend are given throughout the DICTIONARY

Fairies of nursery mythology wear a red conical cap, a mantle of green cloth, inlaid with wild flowers, green pantaloons, buttoned with bobs of silk; and silver shoon Some accounts add that they carry quivers of adderslough, and bows made of the ribs of a man buried where "three lairds' lands meet", that their arrows are made of bog-reed, tipped with white flints, and dipped in the dew of hemlock, and that they ride on steeds whose hoofs would not "dash the dew from the cup of a harebell."

> Fairies small Two foot tall,
> With caps red On their head
> Dance a round On the ground
> JASPER FISHER· *Song from Fuimus Troes* (1633).

Fairy darts. Flint arrow-heads. *See* ELF ARROWS

Fairy loaves or stones Fossil sea-urchins, said to be made by the fairies

Fairy money. Found money Said to be placed by some good fairy at the spot where it was picked up "Fairy money" is apt to be transformed into leaves

Fairy of the mine. A malevolent gnome (*q v*) supposed to live in mines, busying itself with cutting ore, turning the windlass, etc , but effecting nothing

> No goblin, or swart fairy of the mine,
> Hath hurtful power o'er true virginity.
> MILTON *Comus*, 447.

Fairy rings. Circles of rank or withered grass, often seen in lawns, meadows, and grass-plots,

and popularly supposed to be produced by fairies dancing on the spot In sober truth, these rings are simply an agaric or fungus below the surface, which has seeded circularly, as many plants do Where the ring is brown and almost bare, the "spawn" has enveloped the roots and thus prevented their absorbing moisture, but where the grass is rank the "spawn" itself has died, and served as manure to the young grass

> You demi-puppets, that
> By moonshine do the green-sour ringlets make,
> Whereof the ewe not bites
> SHAKESPEARE. *Tempest*, v, 1

Fairy sparks. The phosphoric light from decaying wood, fish, and other substances Thought at one time to be lights prepared for the fairies at their revels.

Fait accompli (fā ta kom′ plē) (Fr) An accomplished fact, something already done, a scheme which has been already carried out, often used in the sense of stealing a march on some other party

I pointed out to Herr von Jagow that this *fait accompli* of the violation of the Belgian frontier rendered, as he would readily understand, the situation exceedingly grave —*Sir Edward Goschen, Ambassador in Berlin, to Sir Edward Grey,* 8 Aug , 1914

Faith. Act of faith. *See* AUTO DA FE

Defender of the Faith. *See* DEFENDER.

In good faith "*Bona fide*", "*de bonne foi*", with no ulterior motive.

To pin one's faith to. *See* PIN

Faithful, in Bunyan's *Pilgrim's Progress,* is seized at Vanity Fair, burnt to death, and taken to heaven in a chariot of fire A Puritan used to be called *Brother Faithful* The active disciples of any cult are called *the faithful*

Commander of the Faithful. The Caliph is so called by Mohammedans

Father of the faithful. Abraham (*Rom* iv, *Gal.* iii, 6-9).

Most Faithful King, The. The appellation by which the kings of Portugal used to be addressed by the Vatican Cp RELIGIOUS

Fake. A fraud or swindle, also verb, as "to fake antiques," "to fake the accounts," *i e* to "cook" them, falsify them. The word is old thieves' slang from Dutch or German, and was originally *feague* a horse was making it look younger or stronger for purposes of sale. Cp. TO BISHOP

Fakir (fā′ kēr) Properly, a Mohammedan religious beggar or mendicant Fakirs wear coarse black or brown dresses, and a black turban over which a red handkerchief is tied, and perform menial offices connected with burials, the cleaning of mosques, and so on The use of the word has been extended to include both Moslem and Hindu holy men, often distinguished by their asceticism and indifference to pain or discomfort.

Falbalas. Flounces on petticoats and sleeves, introduced by Madame de Maintenon in the late seventeenth century.

Falcon and Falconet. Pieces of light artillery of the 16th century, the names of which are borrowed from hawks *Cp* SAKER.

Falcon gentle A goshawk.

Falcon peregrine. *See* PEREGRINE

Fald-stool (Old High Ger *faldan*, to fold) A portable folding chair used by a bishop in a church other than his own cathedral, a small desk at which the Litany is sung or said, also the place at the south side of the altar at which sovereigns kneel at their coronations.

Falernian (fa lẽr' nǐ an) A choice Italian wine, much esteemed by the ancient Romans, and so called because it was made of grapes from Falernus There were three sorts—the rough, the sweet, and the dry.

Fall. In music, a sinking of tone, a cadence.

> That strain again! it had a dying fall
> O! it came o'er my ear like the sweet sound
> That breathes upon a bank of violets,
> Stealing and giving odour
> SHAKESPEARE *Twelfth Night*, 1, 1.
> The strains decay,
> And melt away,
> In a dying, dying fall.
> POPE *St. Cecilia's Day*

In the fall. In the autumn, at the fall of the leaf Though now commonly classed as an Americanism the term was formerly in good use in England, and is found in the works of Drayton, Middleton, Raleigh, and other Elizabethans

> What crowds of patients the town doctor kills,
> Or how, last fall, he raised the weekly bills
> DRYDEN. *Juvenal.*

The Fall of man. The degeneracy of the human race in consequence of the disobedience of Adam

The fall of the drop, in theatrical parlance, means the fall of the drop-curtain at the end of the act or play.

Fall line. The point at which rivers begin to fall on their way to the sea It is a term of American geology, but its implications are largely sociological, the fall line determining the location of cities and influencing the lives of those inhabiting the area, who are known as Fall Liners For example, in the Southern States of U S A. the fall line runs through Virginia, down to Georgia and turns across to the Mississippi, producing circumstances and problems of national importance

To ride for a fall. *See* RIDE

To try a fall. To wrestle, when each tries to "fall" or throw the other

> I am given, sir   to understand that your younger brother, Orlando, hath a disposition to come in disguised against me to try a fall.—*As You Like It,* 1, 1.

See also FALLING-BANDS

To fall away. To lose flesh, to degenerate; to quit a party, as "his adherents fell away one by one"

To fall back upon. To have recourse to.

To fall between two stools. To fail, through hesitating between two choices. The French say, *Être assis entre deux chaises*

To fall flat To lie prostrate or procumbent, to fail to interest, as "the last act fell flat."

To fall foul of one To make an assault on someone, to quarrel with, or run up against someone A sea term A rope is said to be *foul* when it is entangled, and one ship *falls foul* of another when it runs against her and prevents her free progress.

To fall from. To violate, as "to fall from his word", to tumble or slip off, as "to fall from a horse", to abandon or go away from, as "to fall from grace," to relapse into sin

To fall in. To take one's place with others, to concur with, as "he fell in with my views"—that is, his views or ideas fell into line with my views or ideas *Cp* FALL OUT.

To fall in love with. To become enamoured of.

To fall in with. To meet accidentally, to come across This is a Latin phrase, *in aliquam casu incidere.*

To fall into a snare. To stumble accidentally into a snare This is a Latin phrase, *insidias incidere* Similarly, to fall into disgrace is the Latin *in offensionem cadere*

To fall out. To quarrel, also, to happen *Cp.* FALL IN

> Three children sliding on the ice
> Upon a summer's day.
> As it fell out they all fell in
> The rest they ran away
> PORSON *Mother Goose.*
> See ye fall not out by the way —*Gen.* xlv, 24

To leave the ranks, hence, to take one's departure, to desert some cause.

To fall short of. To be deficient of a supply. To fall short of the mark is a figure taken from archery, quoits, etc , where the missile falls to the ground before reaching the mark.

To fall sick. To be unwell. A Latin phrase *In morbum incidere Cp* FALLING SICKNESS.

To fall through. To fail of being carried out or accomplished.

To fall to. To begin (eating, fighting, etc)

> Come, Sir, fall to, then, you see my little supper is always ready when I come home, and I'll make no stranger of you.—Cotton, in WALTON'S *Compleat Angler*

To fall to the ground. To fail from lack of support, to become of no account. "In view of what has happened my proposals fall to the ground," *i e* are rendered useless.

To fall together by the ears. To fight and scratch each other; to contend in strife *See* EAR

To fall under. To incur, as, "to fall under the reproach of carelessness", to be submitted to, as, "to fall under consideration "

To fall upon. To attack, as "to fall upon the rear", to throw oneself on, as, "he fell on his sword,"; to happen on, as, "On what day does Easter fall?"

To fall upon one's feet. To find oneself unexpectedly lucky, to find oneself in a situation where everything seems to go right Evidently from the old theory that a cat always falls on its feet and is able to get away unhurt.

Fall-back chaise. A chaise with an adjustable hood.

Falling-bands. Neck-bands which fall on the breast. They were common in the 17th century, when they were also called falls

> Under that fayre ruffe so sprucely set
> Appeares a fall, a falling-band forsooth!
> MARSTON *Scourge of Villanie*, III (1599).

Falling sickness. Epilepsy, in which the patient falls suddenly to the ground. Shakespeare plays on the term —

> And honest Casca, we have the falling-sickness
> *Brutus* He hath the falling-sickness
> *Cassius* No, Cæsar hath it not but you, and I,
>   *Julius Cæsar*, 1, 2.

Falling stars. Meteors Mohammedans believe them to be firebrands flung by good angels against evil spirits when they approach too near the gates of heaven A wish wished as a star falls is supposed to come true.

Fal-lals. Knick-knacks, trifling fripperies, ornaments of small value.

> His dress, his bows and fine fal-lals
>   *Evelyn's Diary.*

Fallow. Fallow land is land ploughed and harrowed but left unsown The word is A S *fælging*, connected with *fælga*, harrows for breaking crops, and is nothing to do with the *fallow* of *fallow deer* Fallow in this sense means "reddish yellow," and is the A S *fealu*, which is related to Dut. *vaal*, Ger. *fahl*, and Lat. *palidus*, pale

False. False colours. *See* COLOUR.

False quantity. A term used in prosody to denote the incorrect use of a long for a short vowel or syllable, or vice versa.

To play false, to act treacherously, to be faithless.

Falstaff (fawl' staf) A fat, sensual, boastful, and mendacious knight; full of wit and humour, he was the boon companion of Henry, Prince of Wales (1 and 2 *Henry IV*, and *Merry Wives of Windsor*.) Hence, *Falstaffian*, possessing Falstaff's characteristics

Falutin' *See* HIGH FALUTIN'

Fame. Temple of Fame. A Pantheon (*q v*.) where monuments to the famous dead of a nation are erected and their memories honoured. Hence, *he will have a niche in the Temple of Fame*, he has done something that will cause his people to honour him and keep his memory green.

> The temple of fame is the shortest passage to riches and preferment —*Letters of Junius: Letter* lix.

Familiar, or **Familiar spirit** (Lat. *famulus*, a servant) A spirit slave, sometimes in human form, sometimes appearing as a cat, dog, raven, or other dumb creature, petted by a "witch," and supposed to be her demon in disguise.

> Away with him! he has a familiar under his tongue.
> —*2 Henry VI*, IV, 7

Familiarity. Familiarity breeds contempt. The proverb appears in English at least as early as the mid-16th century (Udall), and was well known in Latin.

Familists (făm' i lists) Members of the "Family of Love," a fanatical sect founded by David George, or Joriszoon, of Delft, who separated from the Anabaptists about 1535 They were also known as Davists, or Davidians They maintained that all folk are of one family, and should love each other as brothers and sisters, and that complete obedience was due to all rulers, however tyrannical they might be.

Fan. I could brain him with his lady's fan (1 *Henry IV*, ii, 3)—*i e* knock his brains out with something whose weight and strength is very trifling

> Wer't not better
> Your head were broken with the handle of a fan,
> Or your nose bored with a silver bodkin?
>   FLETCHER *Wit at Several Weapons*, v, 1

Fan. Used from about 1900 as an abbreviation of *fanatic* (*q v*), an ardent admirer or devotee Admiring letters written to the object of such devotion are known as fan mail.

Fanatic. Literally one who is possessed of the enthusiasm or madness of the temple, *i e*. engendered by over-indulgence in religious observances (Lat *fanum*, a temple—the Eng *fane*) Among the Romans there were certain persons who attended the temples and fell into strange fits, in which they were credited with being able to see the spirits of the past and to foretell the events of the future.

> Earth's fanatics make
> Too frequently heaven's saints
>   MRS. BROWNING *Aurora Leigh*, ii, 448.

Fancy. Love—*i e*. the passion of the *fantasy* or imagination

> Tell me where is fancy bred
> Or in the heart or in the head
>   *Merchant of Venice*, iii, 2.

The fancy. In early 19th-century sporting parlance a collective name for prize-fighters.

> The patrons of the Fancy are proud
> of their champion's condition
>   GEORGE ELIOT, *Janet's Repentance*

Fancy-man. Originally a *cavaliere servente* (*q v*) or *cicisbeo* (*q v*), one selected by a married woman to escort her to theatres, etc , to ride about with her, and to amuse her. It is now more usually applied to a harlot's *souteneur*.

Fancy-sick. Love-sick

> All fancy-sick she is, and pale of cheer.
>   *Midsummer Night's Dream*, iii, 9.

Fanfaron (făn' făr on) A swaggering bully; a cowardly boaster who blows his own trumpet Scott uses the word for finery, especially for the gold lace worn by military men Fr *fanfare*, a flourish of trumpets Hence, **fanfaronade**, swaggering; vain boasting, ostentatious display

> The bishop copied this proceeding from the fanfaronade of M Boufflers.—SWIFT

Fanny, Lord. A nickname given by Pope to Lord Hervey (1696-1743) for his effeminate and foppish manners He painted his face, and was as pretty in his ways as a boarding-school miss *See* SPORUS.

> The lines are weak, another's pleased to say,
> Lord Fanny spins a thousand such a day
>   POPE *Satires of Horace*, 1.

Fanny Adams. *Sweet Fanny Adams*, meaning "nothing at all," though (especially by its initials alone) with a somewhat ambiguous connotation, is a phrase with a tragic origin. In 1810 a girl Fanny Adams was murdered at Alton, Hants, and her body cut up and thrown into the river Wey With gruesome humour the Navy took up her name as a synonym for tinned mutton, and *Sweet Fanny Adams* became a phrase for anything worthless or, in fact, for nothing at all.

Fantigue (făn tēg'). A fussy anxiety; that restless, nervous commotion which persons have who are over-wrought To get in a fantigue over something, is to get thoroughly excited, hysterical, or out of humour about it.

Fantoccini (făn to chē' ni). A dramatic performance by puppets. (Ital *fantoccio*, a puppet.)

Fantom An old spelling of PHANTOM (*q v*).

Far. A far cry. *See* CRY.

Far and away. Beyond comparison; as, "far and away the best," some person or thing beyond all rivalry.

Far and wide. To a good distance in every direction. "To spread the news far and wide," to blazon it everywhere.

Far-fetched. Not closely connected, strained, as, "a far-fetched simile," a "far-fetched allusion "

The passion for long, involved sentences . . . and far-fetched conceits . . . passed away, and a clearer and less ornate style became popular —LECKY· *England in the Eighteenth Century*, vol. 1, ch 1

Far from it. Not in the least; by no means, quite the contrary If the answer to" Was he sober at the time?" is "Far from it," the implication is that he was in a considerably advanced state of intoxication.

Far gone. Deeply affected as, "far gone in love."

Farce. A grotesque and exaggerated kind of comedy, full of ludicrous incidents and expressions The word is the Old French *farce*, stuffing (from Lat *farcire*, to stuff), hence an interlude stuffed into or inserted in the main piece, such interludes always being of a racy, exaggerated comic character

Farce is that in poetry which grotesque is in a picture The persons and action of a farce are all unnatural, and the manners false, that is inconsisting with the characters of mankind —DRYDEN: *Parallel of Poetry and Painting*

The following couplet was written by Garrick on the self-knighted Sir John Hill (d 1775) a quack whose adventures would make a book in themselves He had written a farce in which Garrick played, and which was a failure:—

For physic and farces his equal there scarce is,
His farces are physic, his physic a farce is

Farcy or Farcin A disease in horses, which consists of a swelling of the ganglions and lymphatic vessels and shows itself in little knots, very like glanders. The name is, like *farce* (above) from Lat. *farcire*, to stuff

Fardle or Fardel. A variant of obsolete *furdle* (from which comes *furl*, to furl a sail), meaning to roll up, hence, that which is rolled up, i e. a bundle or package

Who would fardels bear,
To grunt and sweat under a weary life?
    Hamlet, iii, 1
Like a pedlar she went up and down
For she had got a pretty handsome pack,
Which she had fardled neatly at her back
    DRAYTON *The Muse's Elysium*, vii

Fare. (A.S *faran*, to go, to travel, connected with Lat *portare*, to carry) The noun formerly denoted a journey for which a sum was paid, but now the sum itself, and, by extension, the person who pays it In certain English dialects, *e g* Suffolk, the verb *fare* is used in its original sense of "to go," also as an auxiliary with much the same sense as "to do "

Farewell. Good-bye; adieu It was originally addressed to one about to start on a journey, expressing the wish that the *fare* would be a good one

He cannot fare well but he must cry out roast meat. Said of one who blazons his good fortune on the house-top.

Farmer George. George III, so called from his farmer-like manners, tastes, dress, and amusements

A better farmer ne er brushed dew from lawn.
    BYRON *Vision of Judgment*

Farnese (far nā' zi) A noted Italian family, celebrated in the 16th and 17th centuries as soldiers and patrons of the arts. Its fortunes were laid by Alessandro Farnese, who was Pope as Paul III (1534-49), and who created the Duchy of Parma for his son, Pietro Luigi (1545)

The Farnese Bull. A colossal group attributed to Apollonius and Tauriscus of Tralles, in Asia Minor. They belonged to the Rhodian school, and lived about 300 B.C The group represents Dirce bound to the horns of a bull by Zethus and Amphion, for ill-using their mother It was discovered in the Baths of Caracalla in 1546, and placed in the Farnese palace, in Rome It is now at the Museo Nazionale, Naples.

The Farnese Hercules. Glykon's copy of the famous statue of Lysippus, the Greek sculptor in the time of Alexander the Great It represents the hero leaning on his club, with one hand on his back, as if he had just got possession of the apple of the Hesperides. It is now at the Museo Nazionale, Naples

Farrago (fa ra' gō) A farrago of nonsense A confused heap of nonsense *Farrago* (Lat) is properly a mixture of *far* (meal) with other ingredients for the use of cattle.

A farrago
Or a made dish in Court: a thing of nothing
    BEN JONSON *Magnetick Lady*, 1, 1.
Yet do I carry everywhere with me such a confounded farrago of doubts, fears, hopes, wishes —
SHERIDAN. *Rivals*, 11, 1.

Farthing. A fourth part Silver penny pieces used to be divided into four parts thus, ⊖ One of these quarters was a *feorthing* or fourth part.

I don't care for it a brass farthing. James II debased all the coinage, and issued, amongst other worthless coins, brass pence, halfpence, and farthings.

Farthingale (far' *thing* găl). The hooped understructure of the large protruding skirt fashionable in the reigns of Elizabeth and James I The word is the O Fr *verdugale*, which is a corruption of Span *verdugado*, green rods, referring to the twigs or switches of which the framework was made before whalebone was used for the purpose

Fascinate. Literally, to cast a spell by means of the eye (Lat *fascinum*, a spell). The allusion is to the ancient notion of bewitching by the power of the eye. *Cp* EVIL EYE.

> None of the affections have been noted to fascinate and bewitch, but love and envy —BACON *Essays, Of Envy*

Fascinator. An opera cloak was thus termed in the 18th century, an evening-wear head veil

Fascines (făs' ēnz). Bundles of faggots used to build up defences, or to fill ditches impeding an attack For the latter they were revived in World War II and carried forward by tanks which dumped them mechanically in ditches and small streams From Roman *fasces*

Fascism (făsh' izm, făs' izm) A political movement, originating in Italy, that takes its name from the old Roman *fasces*, a bundle of sticks borne by lictors as an emblem of office Its leader was Benito Mussolini (1883-1945), who took advantage of the discontent felt in Italy after World War I to form a quasi-military party, to combat communism In 1922 the Fascists "marched on Rome," overthrew the existing government and replaced it by a government under Mussolini, with the king as a figurehead Thenceforward Italy was a Fascist country until her defeat in 1943.

Fascism is strictly authoritarian and as such has its followers and imitators in other countries and societies As evolved by Mussolini it was a technique for obtaining power, for exacting a ruthless militarism and rejecting all appeal to ethics Struggles between races are beneficial, said Mussolini: "War is to the man what maternity is to the woman . I find peace depressing and the negation of the fundamental values of man " Fascism denies democracy; the liberty of the individual is abolished in favour of the state, the inequality of men and races is proclaimed as immutable and even beneficial "Credere, obbedire, combattere" (To have faith, to obey, to fight) is the final slogan

Fash. Dinna fash yoursel'! Don't get excited; don't get into a fantigue about it. The word is looked on as Scots, but it is the O Fr *fascher* (Mod Fr *fâcher*)

Fashion. In a fashion or **after a fashion**. "In a sort of a way", as, "he spoke French after a fashion."

Fast. The adjective was used figuratively of a person of either sex who is addicted to pleasure and dissipation, of a young man or woman who "goes the pace "

To play fast and loose. To run with the hare and hunt with the hounds; to blow both hot and cold; to say one thing and do another The allusion is probably to an old cheating game that used to be practised at fairs A belt was folded, and the player was asked to prick it with a skewer, so as to pin it *fast* to the table, having so done, the adversary took the two ends, and *loosed* it or drew it away, showing that it had not been pierced at all.

> He forced his neck into a noose,
> To show his play at fast and loose,
> And when he chanced t'escape, mistook,
> For art and subtlety, his luck
> BUTLER *Hudibras*, iii, 2

Fasti (făs' tī) Working days, when, in Rome, the law-courts were open Holy days (*dies non*), when the law-courts were not open, were, by the Romans, called *ne-fasti.*

The *Fasti* were listed in calendars, and the registers of events occurring during the year of office of a pair of consuls was called *fasti consulares*, hence, any chronological list of events or office-holders became known as *fasti*, and hence such titles as *Fasti Academæi Mariscallanæ Aberdonenses*, selections from the records of the Marischal College, Aberdeen

Fasting. In its literal meaning this is a complete abstention from food and drink, but the word is more usually applied to an extreme limitation of diet In this sense its therapeutical value has been proved in various forms of disease. Fasting has, however, been adopted more as a religious exercise from the earliest times Celts, Mexicans, Peruvians, Assyrians, Egyptians, Hebrews, and Mohammedans have alike used it as a means of penance or purification Contemplatives and men of the stature of Mahatma Gandhi have found it helpful. Fasting plays an important part in Christian Church discipline, with more or less strictness the 40 days of Lenten fasting are observed throughout the Christian world

In more recent times fasting (under the epithet of hunger-striking) has been practised by political and other prisoners as a method of calling attention to alleged injustices

Fat. In printer's slang is composition that does not entail a lot of setting, and hence can be done quickly **A bit of fat.** An unexpected stroke of luck, also, the best part of anything, especially, among actors, a good part in a play.

Fat-head. A silly fool, a dolt

The fat is in the fire. Something has been let out inadvertently which will cause a "regular flare up", it's all over, all's up with it The allusion is to frying, if the grease is spilt into the fire, the coals smoke and blaze so as to spoil the food

The Fat:—
Alfonzo II of Portugal (1212-23)
Charles II of France, *le Gros* (832, 884-8)
Louis VI of France, *le Gros* (1078, 1108-37)

Fata (fä' ta) (Ital , a fairy) Female supernatural beings introduced in Italian mediæval romance, usually under the sway of Demogorgon (*q v*)

Fata Morgana. A sort of mirage in which objects are reflected in the sea, and sometimes on a kind of aerial screen high above it, occasionally seen in the neighbourhood of the Straits of Messina, so named from Morgan le Fay (*q v*) who was fabled by the Norman settlers in England to dwell in Calabria

Fatal Gifts.
See CADMUS, HARMONIA, NECKLACE, NESSUS, NIBELUNGEN HOARD, OPAL, TOLOSA, etc

Fate. The cruel fates. The Greeks and Romans supposed there were three Parcæ or Fates, who arbitrarily controlled the birth, life, and death of every man They were Clotho (who held the distaff), Lachesis (who spun the thread of life), and Atropos (who cut it off when life was ended), called "cruel" because they paid no regard to the wishes of anyone

Father. The name is given as a title to Catholic priests, also to the senior member of a body or profession, as the *Father of the House of Commons*, the *Father of the Bench*, and to the originator or first leader of some movement, school, etc , as the *Father of Comedy* (Aristophanes), the *Father of English Song* (Cædmon) In ancient Rome the title was given to the senators (*cp* PATRICIAN, CONSCRIPT FATHERS), and in ecclesiastical history to the early Church writers and doctors

To father a thing on one. To impute it to him; to assert that he was the originator of it

Father Matthew, Neptune, Prout, etc. *See these names*

Father of Courtesy Richard Beauchamp, Earl of Warwick (d 1439)

Father of English Botany. William Turner (*c* 1520-1568), author of a herbal published in 1568

Father of English History The Venerable Bede (*q v*).

Father of his Country.
Cicero was so entitled by the Roman senate They offered the same title to Marius, but he refused to accept it.
Several of the Cæsars were so called— Julius, after quelling the insurrection of Spain, Augustus, etc
Cosimo de' Medici (1389-1464).
George Washington, the first President of the United States (1732-99).
Andrea Doria (1468-1560) Inscribed on the base of his statue by his countrymen of Genoa
Andronicus Palæologus II assumed the title (about 1260-1332)
Victor Emmaruel II (1820-78) first king of Italy, was popularly called Father of his Country in allusion to his unnumbered progeny of bastard children

Father of the Chapel *See* CHAPEL.

Father of Letters. François I of France (1494, 1515-47).
Lorenzo de' Medici, the Magnificent (1448-92)

Father of Lies Satan.

Father of the People.
Louis XII of France (1462, 1498-1515) Henri IV was also termed "the father and friend of the people" (1553, 1589-1610)
Christian III of Denmark (1502, 1534-59).

Father of Waters. The Irrawaddy, in Burma, and the Mississippi, in North America The Nile is so called by Dr. Johnson in his *Rasselas.*

The epithet *Father* is not uncommonly applied to rivers, especially those on which cities are built
Say, Father Thames, for thou hast seen
Full many a sprightly race
Disporting on thy margent green,
The paths of pleasure trace.
GRAY· *Distant Prospect of Eton College.*
O Tiber, Father Tiber,
To whom the Romans pray
MACAULAY *Lay of Horatius*

Father Thoughtful Nicholas Catinat (1637-1712), a marshal of France, so called by his soldiers for his cautious and thoughtful policy.

Fathers of the Church. All those writers of the first twelve centuries whose works on Christian doctrine are considered of weight and worthy of respect But the term is more strictly applied to those teachers of the first twelve, and especially of the first six centuries who added notable holiness and complete orthodoxy to their learning The chief are.—
1st century, Clement of Rome, *2nd cent* , Cyril of Jerusalem, Ignatius of Antioch, Justin, Irenaeus, Polycarp, *3rd cent* , Cyprian, Dionysius, *4th cent* , Hilary, Ephraem the Syrian, Optatus, Epiphanius, *5th cent.*, Peter Chrysologus, Pope Leo the Great, Cyril of Alexandria, Vincent of Lerins, *6th cent* , Caesarius of Arles, *7th cent* , Isidore, *8th cent* John the Damascene, Venerable Bede, *11th cent* , Peter Damian, *12th cent* , Anselm, Bernard

Fathers of the Desert. The monks and hermits of the Egyptian deserts in the 4th century from whom all Christian monasticism derives. The most famous were St Anthony, who ruled 5,000 monks, Pachomius, the hermit; and Hilarion. There is a good description of their mode of life in Kingsley's *Hypatia.*

Fatima (făt' i mä) The last of Bluebeard's wives *See* BLUEBEARD She was saved from death by the timely arrival of her brother with a party of friends. Mohammed's daughter was called Fatima

Fatted Calf. *See* CALF

Fault. In geology, the break or displacement of a stratum of rock.

At fault. Not on the right track Hounds are at fault when the fox has jumped upon a wall, crossed a river, cut through a flock of sheep, or doubled like a hare, because the scent, *i e.* the track, is broken

For fault of a better (*Merry Wives*, 1, 4) In default of a better; no one (or nothing) better being available
I am the youngest of that name, for fault of a worse.
—*Romeo and Juliet*, ii, 4.

In fault, at fault To blame
Is Antony or we in fault for this?
Antony and Cleopatra, iii, 13

No one is without his faults. No one is perfect.

To a fault. In excess, as, kind to a fault. Excess of every good is more or less evil.

To find fault. To blame, to express disapprobation.

Fauna (faw' nä). The animals of a country at any given period. The term was first used by Linnæus in the title of his *Fauna Suecica* (1746), a companion volume to his *Flora Suecica* of the preceding year, and is the name of a Roman rural goddess, sister of Faunus.

Nor less the place of curious plant he knows—
He both his Flora and his Fauna shows
CRABBE *Borough*

Faust (foust). The hero of Marlowe's *Tragical History of Dr Faustus* (about 1589) and Goethe's *Faust* (1790-1833) is founded on Dr Johann Faust, or Faustus, a magician and astrologer, who was born in Wurtemberg and died about 1538

The idea of making a pact with the devil for worldly reasons is of Jewish origin and dates back to the time of Christ. All subsequent legends of necromancers became crystallized round the person of Faustus In 1587 he appeared for the first time as the central figure in *The History of Dr Faustus, the Notorious Magician and Master of the Black Art* (published at Frankfort-on-Main), which immediately became popular and was soon translated into English, French, and other languages.

The basis of the legend is that, in return for twenty-four years of further life during which he is to have every pleasure and all knowledge at his command, Faust sells his soul to the devil, and the climax is reached when, at the close of the period, the devil claims him for his own.

The story of Faust has struck the fancy of composers Spohr's opera *Faust*, 1816, Wagner's Overture *Faust*, 1839; Berlioz's *Damnation de Faust*, 1846, Gounod's opera, 1859, Boïto's *Mefistophele*, 1868, Zöllner's opera *Faust*, 1887 In addition to these are numerous musical compositions, ballets, etc.

There was another Faust of whom stories used to be told in the 16th century This was Johann Fust or Faust (d *c.* 1466), a German money-lender, who formed a partnership with the printer Gutenberg in 1450. On the termination of this in 1455 Fust demanded the repayment of the capital he had put into the business, and in default of this seized all Gutenberg's types and plant. With this Fust started business on his own account, with his son-in-law Peter Schoffer as manager. Gutenberg was obliged to carry on his business with inferior types and presses

Fauvist (fō' vist). A phrase, meaning "wild beast," applied to an important school of painters, beginning 1904-5, under the leadership of Matisse, and including Derain, Othon Friesz, Marquet, Vlaminck, and Rouault All the group were concerned primarily with the importance of pattern in their work, and prepared to subordinate all else.

Faux pas (fō pä) (Fr). A "false step", a breach of manners or moral conduct

The fact is, his Lordship, who hadn't it seems,
Form'd the slightest idea, not ev'n in his dreams,
That the pair had been wedded according to law,
Conceived that his daughter had made a *faux pas*
BARHAM (INGOLDSBY). *Some account of a New Play*

Favonius (fa vō' ni ùs) The Latin name for the zephyr or west wind It means the wind *favourable* to vegetation

If to the torrid Zone her way she bend,
Her the coole breathing of Favonius lend,
Thither command the birds to bring their quires,
That Zone is temp'rate
HABBINGTON *Castara · To the Spring* (1634)

Favour Ribbons made into a bow are called *favours* from being bestowed by ladies on the successful champions of tournaments (*Cp.* TRUE-LOVERS' KNOT)

Here, Fluellen, wear thou this favour for me, and stick it in thy cap —SHAKESPEARE *Henry V*, iv, 7

To curry favour. *See* CURRY

Favourites. False curls on the temples; a curl of hair on the temples plastered with some cosmetic, whiskers made to meet the mouth

Yet tell me, sire, don't you as nice appear
With your false calves, bardash, and fro'rites here?
MRS CENTLIVRE *The Platonic Lady, Epilogue* (1721)

Fay. *See* FAIRY.

Morgan le Fay. *See* MORGAN.

Fearless (Fr . *Sans peur*) Jean, Duke of Burgundy (1371-1419) *Cp.* BAYARD.

Feast. A day set apart for the commemoration of some event or mystery in the life of Our Lord, His mother, or some event of religious importance Feasts are either immovable or movable.

The chief **immovable feasts** in the Christian calendar are the four quarter-days—viz. the Annunciation or Lady Day (March 25th), the Nativity of John the Baptist (June 24th), Michaelmas Day (September 29th), and Christmas Day (December 25th) Others are the Circumcision (January 1st), Epiphany (January 6th), All Saints' (November 1st), and the several Apostles' days

The **movable feasts** depend upon Easter Sunday They are—

Palm Sunday The Sunday next before Easter Sunday

Good Friday The Friday next before Easter Sunday

Ash Wednesday The first day of Lent, 40 days before Easter.

Sexagesima Sunday. Sixty days before Easter Sunday.

Ascension Day or Holy Thursday Fortieth day after Easter Sunday.

Pentecost or Whit Sunday The seventh Sunday after Easter Sunday

Trinity Sunday The Sunday next after Pentecost

Feast of Reason. Conversation on and discussion of learned and congenial subjects.

There St John mingles with my friendly bowl
The feast of reason and the flow of soul.
POPE *Imitations of Horace*, ii, 1

Feasts of Reason. *See* REASON, GODDESS OF.

Feather. **A broken feather in one's wing.** A scandal connected with one.

A feather in your cap. An honour to you. The allusion is to the very general custom in Asia and among the American Indians of adding a feather to the headgear for every enemy slain. The ancient Lycians, and many others had a similar custom, and it is still usual for the sportsman who kills the first woodcock to pluck out a feather and stick it in his cap.

The custom, in one form or another, seems to be almost universal; in Hungary, at one time, none might wear a feather but he who had slain a Turk, and it will be remembered

that when Gordon quelled the Taiping rebellion he was honoured by the Chinese
Government with the "yellow jacket and
peacock's feather"

Birds of a feather flock together *See* BIRD

Fine feathers make fine birds. Said sarcastically of an overdressed person who does not
live up to his (or her) clothes.

In full feather. Flush of money. In allusion
to birds not on the moult

In grand feather Dressed "to the nines",
also, in perfect health, thoroughly fit.

In high feather. In exuberant spirits, joyous

Of that feather *See* BIRDS OF A FEATHER

Prince of Wales's feathers. *See* PRINCE OF
WALES.

Tarred and feathered. *See* TAR.

Tickled with a feather. Easily moved to
laughter "Pleased with a rattle, tickled with a
straw" (POPE *Essay on Man*), is more usual

To cut a feather. A ship going fast is said to
cut a feather, in allusion to the ripple which
she throws off from her bows Metaphorically,
"to cut a dash"

To feather an oar. To turn the blade parallel
with the surface of the water as the hands are
moved forward for a fresh stroke. The oar
throws off the water in a feathery spray
He feathered his oars with such skill and dexterity.
—*Jolly Young Waterman.*

To feather one's nest well. To provide for one's
own interests; to secure one's own financial
well-being The phrase is commonly used with
a somewhat disapproving implication

To show the white feather. *See* WHITE.

To smooth one's ruffled feathers. To recover
one's equanimity after an insult.

Featherweight. Something of extreme lightness in comparison with others of its kind The
term is applied to a jockey weighing not more
than 4 st 7 lb or to a boxer weighing not more
than 9 st. In the paper trade the name is given
to very light antique, laid, or wove book
papers They are manufactured mainly from
esparto, and are very loosely woven

Feature (Lat. *facere*, to make) formerly meant
the "make" or general appearance of anything. Spenser speaks of God's "secret
understanding of our feature"—*i e* make or
structure It now means principally that part
which is most conspicuous or important Thus
we speak of the chief feature of a painting, a
garden, a book, etc , a moving picture is said
to feature such and such a popular favourite or
incident.

February. The month of purification amongst
the ancient Romans. (Lat *februo*, to purify by
sacrifice.)

Candlemas Day (*q v*), February 2nd, is the
feast of the Purification of the Virgin Mary.
It is said, if the weather is fine and frosty at
the close of January and beginning of February, we may look for more winter to come
than we have seen up to that time
Si sol splendescat Maria Purificante,
Major erit glacies post festum quam fuit ante
SIR T. BROWNE. *Vulgar Errors.*

12*

The Dutch used to term the month *Spokkel-
maand* (vegetation-month); the ancient Saxons, *Sprote-cal* (from the sprouting of pot-
wort or kele), they changed it subsequently to
Sol-monath (from the returning sun) In the
French Republican calendar it was called
Pluviose (rain-month, January 20th to February 20th) *See also* FILL-DYKE

Fecit (Lat , he did it) A word inscribed after
the name of an artist, sculptor, etc , as David
fecit, Goujon *fecit*, *i e* David painted it,
Goujon sculptured it, etc

Federal. The modern usage of this term in the
U.S A. relates to the central government of the
country as distinct from the governments of
the various component States. In this sense
the Federal Bureau of Investigation (F B I)
is an organization of the Department of Justice
of the U S Government which investigates
offences against the laws of the U S A,
especially such crimes as bank robberies,
espionage, blackmail, etc. Its agents are known
familiarly as G-men (Government men) and
are all specially selected for intrepidity as
criminal-hunters.

Federalist The party in America which in
1787 was in favour of adopting the constitution
of that year Besides Washington, it was led by
Alexander Hamilton and John Adams, who
later became enemies. The party controlled the
government until 1801 It was also the name of
a newspaper during this period which provided
a model of good prose.

Federal States. The name given in the
American War of Secession (1861-65) to those
northern states which combined against the
eleven southern or Confederate states (*q.v.*)

Fee. This is an Anglo-French word, from Old
High Ger *fehu*, wages, money, property,
cattle, and is connected with the A S *feoh*,
cattle, goods, money So in Lat *pecunia*,
money, from *pecus*, cattle Capital is *capita*,
heads (of cattle), and chattels is a mere variant.

At a pin's fee. *See* PIN

Fee-farm. A tenure by which an estate is
held in fee-simple without any other services
from the tenant beyond a perpetual fixed rent
Fee-farm-rent is rent paid on lands let to farm,
and not let in recompense of service at a
greatly reduced value

Fee-penny. A fine for money overdue; an
earnest or pledge for a bargain Sir Thomas
Gresham often wrote for money "in order to
save the fee-penny"

Fee simple. An estate held by a person in
his own right, free from condition or limitation,
such as that of inheritance by any particular
class of heirs If restricted by conditions, it is
called a "Conditional Fee"

Fee-tail, A. An estate limited to a person and
his lawful heirs, an entailed estate.

To hold in fee. To hold as one's lawful and
absolute possession.
Once did she hold the gorgeous east in fee
And was the safeguard of the west.
WORDSWORTH *The Venetian Republic*

Feeble. Most forcible Feeble. Feeble is a "woman's tailor," brought to Sir John Falstaff as a recruit (2 *Henry IV*, iii, 2). He tells Sir John "he will do his good will," and the knight replies, "Well said, courageous Feeble! Thou wilt be as valiant as the wrathful dove, or most magnanimous mouse . . . most forcible Feeble."

Feed of Corn. A quartern of oats, the quantity given to a horse on a journey when the ostler is told to give him a feed.

Feet. *See* FOOT

Fehmgericht. *See* VEHMGERICHT

Felix the Cat, hero of early animated cartoons, appeared in 1921, in a production by Pat Sullivan. Throughout his many adventures Felix the black cat kept on walking, and thus originated a once-familiar catch-phrase.

Fell, Dr *See* DOCTOR FELL

Fell's Pointer. U S A. 18th century A resident of the dockside area of Baltimore

Fellow Commoner. An undergraduate of Cambridge, who was formerly privileged to "common" (i e dine) at the fellows' table In Oxford, these demi-dons are termed *Gentlemen Commoners.*

In 'varsity slang these names were given to empty bottles, the suggestion being that such students are, as a class, empty-headed

Fellow-traveller. A person in sympathy with a political party but not a member of that party, used most often of Communist sympathizers

"He is but one of a reputed short list of seven fellow-travellers under threat of expulsion"—Comment in *Time and Tide*, May 1st, 1948, on the Labour Party's expulsion of one of its members

Felo de se (fē'lō dē sē) The act of a suicide when he commits self-murder, also, the self-murderer himself Murder is felony, and a man who murders himself commits this felony—*felo de se.*

Feme-covert (fem kŭv' ert) A married woman, i e. a woman who is under the *cover*, authority, or protection of her husband The word is the Anglo-French and Old French form of Mod Fr *femme couverte*, and *couverte* is still used in fortification, etc , with the sense "protected."

Feme-sole (fem sōl) A single woman Feme-sole merchant, a woman, married or single, who carries on a trade on her own account.

Feminine ending. An extra unaccented syllable at the end of a line of verse, e g in lines 1 and 3 of the following —

> With rue my heart is laden
> For golden friends I had,
> For many a rose-lipt maiden
> And many a light-foot lad
>   A. E HOUSMAN

Femynye (fem' i ni) A mediæval designation for the kingdom of the Amazons Gower terms Penthesilea "queen of Feminee"

> He [Theseus] conquered al the regne of Femynye,
> That whylom was y-claped Scithia,
> And weddede the quene Ipolita
>   CHAUCER *Knightes Tale*, 8

Fence Slang term for a receiver of stolen goods.

Fence month, or season. The fawning time of deer, i e from about fifteen days before Midsummer to fifteen days after it. Also the close season for fishing, etc

To sit on the fence. To take care not to commit oneself, to hedge The characteristic attitude of "Mr Facing-Both-Ways "

Fencibles. Regiments of horse and foot militia raised for home service in 1759, again in 1778-9, and again in 1794, when a force of 15,000 was raised It was disbanded in 1802 The word is short for *defensible.*

Fenians. An Anti-British secret association of Irishmen, formed simultaneously in Ireland by James Stephens and in New York by John O'Mahony in 1857, with the object of overthrowing the domination of England in Ireland, and making Ireland a republic The word is from the Old Irish *Fene*, a name of the ancient Irish, confused with *Fianna*, the semi-mythological warriors who defended Ireland in the time of Finn

The Fenian Brotherhood quickly spread in the United States, and invasions of Canada were attempted The Association made many insurrectionary attempts (including dynamite outrages at Clerkenwell, 1865, and at the Tower of London and Houses of Parliament, 1885), but did nothing that could further their aims. Their leaders were termed "head centres," and their subordinates "centres." *Cp.* CLANNA-GAEL, SINN FEIN.

Fennel. Fennel was anciently supposed to be an aphrodisiac, thus 'to eat conger and fennel" (two hot things together) was provocative of sexual licence Hence Falstaff's remark about Poins —

He plays at quoits well, and eats conger and fennel, and drinks off candles' ends for flap-dragons, and rides the wild mare with the boys —2 *Henry IV*, ii, 4

It was also emblematical of flattery, and may have been included among the herbs distributed by Ophelia (*Hamlet* iv, 5) for this reason

> Fenel is for flaterers,
> An evil thing it is sure
> But I have alwa'es meant truely,
> With constant heart most pure.
> *A Nosegay alwaies Sweet* (in "A Handful of Pleasant Delights," 1584)

Uppon a banke, bordring by, grew women's weedes Feneil I meane for flatterers, fit generally for that sexe.
GREENE. *A Quip for an Upstart Courtier* (1592)

The herb was also credited with being able to clear the sight, and was said to be the favourite food of serpents, with the juice of which they restore their sight when dim

Fen Nightingale A frog, which sings at night in the fens, as nightingales sing in the groves.

Fenrir or **Fenris** (fen' rēr) In Scandinavian mythology the wolf of Loki (*q v*) He was the brother of Hel (*q v*), and when he gaped one jaw touched earth and the other heaven. In the *Ragnarok* he swallows the sun and conquers Odin, but being conquered by Vidar, he was cast into Niflheim, where Loki was confined.

Feræ Naturæ (fer' ē nä tū' rē) (Lat , of savage nature). The legal term for animals living in a wild state, as distinguished from those which are domesticated

Women are not comprised in our Laws of Friendship they are *Feræ Naturæ* —DRYDEN *The Mock Astrologer*, iv.

Ferdinand the Bull, whose adventures were related in a Walt Disney film of 1939, first appeared in a book by Munro Leaf His delight in the smell of flowers became for a time proverbial

Ferguson. It's all very well, Mr. Ferguson, but you can't do that, you mustn't go there, etc. This was a popular catch-phrase in the early and middle 19th century It originated with the bright young men about town who, when brought before the "beak" for knocking down watchmen, wrenching off knockers, etc , gave the name of "Ferguson" in place of their proper name The equivalent of the phrase in more modern days was, "You can't do that there 'ere "

Fermiers Généraux. Those who in France in the 18th century farmed the state taxes They guaranteed an agreed sum to the crown and retained any surplus which they could gather for themselves They grew rich and amongst their activities was the production of a group of extremely rich illustrated books—notably the *La Fontaine* (1762) and the *Boccaccio* (1757-61)

Fern Seed. We have the receipt of fern seed, we walk invisible (1 *Henry IV*, iv, 4) The seed of certain species of fern is so small as to be invisible to the naked eye, and hence the plant was believed to confer invisibility on those who carried it about their person It was at one time believed that plants have the power of imparting their own speciality to their wearer. Thus, the yellow celandine was said to cure jaundice, wood-sorrel, which has a heart-shaped leaf, to cheer the heart; liverwort to be good for the liver, and so on

> Why did you think that you had Gygës' ring,
> Or the herb that gives invisibility?
> BEAUMONT AND FLETCHER *Fair Maid of the Inn*, i, 1
> The seeds of fern, which, by prolific heat
> Cheered and unfolded, form a plant so great,
> Are less a thousand times than what the eye
> Can unassisted by the tube descry
> BLACKMORE· *Creation.*

Ferney. The Patriarch or Philosopher of Ferney. Voltaire (1694-1778), so called because for the last twenty years of his life he lived at Ferney, a small sequestered village near Geneva, from which obscure retreat he poured forth his invectives against the French Government, the Church, nobles, nuns, priests, and indeed all classes

Ferragus. The giant of Portugal in *Valentine and Orson* (q v) The great "Brazen Head" (q.v), that told those who consulted it whatever they required to know, was kept in his castle

Ferrara. See ANDREA FERRARA

Ferrara Bible, The. See BIBLE, SPECIALLY NAMED

Ferrex and Porrex. Two sons of Gorboduc, a mythical British king, who divided his kingdom between them Porrex drove his brother from Britain, and when Ferrex returned with an army he was slain, but Porrex was shortly after put to death by his mother The story is told in Geoffrey of Monmouth's *Historia Regum Britanniæ*, and it forms the basis of the first regular English tragedy, *Gorboduc*, or

Ferrex and Porrex, written by Thomas Norton and Thomas Sackville, Lord Buckhurst, and acted in 1561

Fescennine Verses. Lampoons, so called from Fescennia in Tuscany, where performers at merry-makings used to extemporize scurrilous jests of a personal nature to amuse the audience

Fesse. See HERALDRY.

Fetch A wraith—the disembodied ghost of a living person, hence *fetch-light*, or *fetch-candle*, a light appearing at night and supposed to foretell the death of someone Fetches most commonly appear to distant friends and relations, at the very instant preceding the death of those they represent

Fetches. Excuses, tricks, artifices.

> Deny to speak with me? They are sick? they are weary?
> They have travelled all the night? Mere fetches
> *King Lear*, ii, 4

Fetish (fet' ish) The name given by the early Portuguese travellers to amulets and other objects supposed to have supernatural powers, used by the natives on the Guinea Coast, from Port *feitço*, sorcery, charm (Lat *factitius*, artificial). Hence, an idol, and object of devotion. Fetishism is found in all primitive nations, taking the form of a belief that the services of a spirit may be appropriated by the possession of its material emblem. In psychopathology the word is used to designate a condition or perversion in which sexual gratification is obtained from other than the genital areas of the body, or from some object that has become thus emotionally charged

Fettle, as a verb, means to repair, to smooth, as a noun it means condition, state of health, as in good fettle It is probably from the A S. *fetch*, a girdle, with allusion to girding oneself up.

Fettled ale. Ale warmed and spiced, mulled It is a dialectal use, principally North Country

Feu de joie (Fr) A running fire of guns on an occasion of rejoicing

Feud (fūd) A word of two very different meanings In its more usual sense a feud is a continuous, bitter quarrel between individuals, families, or parties Feuds have never played much part in the English manner of life *See* VENDETTA In its other sense a feud is a fief, or land held in fee (q v)

Feudal System, The. A system founded on the tenure of feuds or fiefs, given in compensation for military service to the lord of the tenants It was introduced into England by William the Conqueror, who made himself owner of the whole country and allowed the nobles to hold it from him by payment of homage and military and other service The nobles in turn had vassals bound to them by similar obligations

Feuillants (fěr' yong). A reformed Cistercian order instituted by Jean de la Barrière in 1586. So called from the convent of Feuillants, in Languedoc, where they were established in 1577

The club of the **Feuillants**, in the French Revolution, was composed of moderate

Jacobins. So called because the convent of the Feuillants, near the Tuileries, was their original club-room (1791-2)

Feuilleton (fě yě tong) (Fr , from *feuille*, a leaf) The part of French newspapers devoted to tales, light literature, etc., hence, in England a serial story in a newspaper, or the "magazine page"

Fey (fā). Epithet applied when a person suddenly breaks into a state of light-heartedness. This was formerly supposed to be an indication of an early approaching death. The word is the A S *fǣge* (on the point of death, or doomed to die)

FFI. *Forces Françaises de l'Interieure* Frenchmen within France who continued the struggle against Germany after the fall of their country in 1940 They were first armed by Britain and their co-operation with British parachute agents was co-ordinated and directed by an organization at the War Office Later the United States also co-operated through their OSS (*q v*). These Frenchmen were familiarly known as *Maquis* (*q v*) As soon as the allied invasion landed in June 1944 they came into the open as a civilian army

Fiacre (fě akr'). A French cab or hackney coach So called from the hotel de St. Fiacre, Paris, where the first station of these coaches was established by M Sauvage, about 1650
   Legend has it that St Fiacre was the son of an Irish king, born in 600, who settled in France and built a monastery at Breuil His day is August 30th

Fiars (fī' ars) Striking the fiars Taking the average price of corn Fiars are the legal prices of grain as fixed by the sheriff of a county for the current year. It is a Scottish term, from M E. and O.Fr. *feor*, Lar. *forum*, a market.

Fiasco. A failure In Italy they cry *Ola, ola, fiasco!* to an unpopular singer
   In Italian *fiasco* means a flask, and it is uncertain how it became, in Venetian slang, to mean a failure, an attempt that comes to nothing

Fiat (fī' ǎt) (Lat., let it be done). **I give my fiat** to that proposal I consent to it A fiat in law is an order of the court directing that something stated be done

Fiat experimentum in corpore vili. *See* CORPUS VILE.

Fiat justitia ruat cœlum. *See* PISO's JUSTICE.

Fib. An attendant on Queen Mab in Drayton's *Nymphidia* Fib, meaning a falsehood, is the Latin *fabula*, a fable

Fico (fī kō) *See* FIG
   Fico for the phrase.
         Merry Wives of Windsor, 1, 3
   I see contempt marching forth, giving me the fico with his thombe in his mouth.—*Wit's Miserie* (1596)

Fiddle (A S. *fithele*, perhaps connected with mediæval Lat *vitula* or *vidula*, whence *violin*). A violin or stringed instrument of that nature In Stock Exchange slang a *fiddle* is one-sixteenth of a pound—1s 3d

Fit as a fiddle. In fine condition, perfect trim or order

He was first fiddle Chief man the most distinguished of the company The allusion is to the leader of concerts, who leads with a fiddle.

To play second fiddle. To take a subordinate part.

To fiddle about. To trifle, fritter away one's time, mess about, play at doing things instead of doing them To fiddle with one's fingers is to move them about as a fiddler moves his fingers up and down the fiddle-strings.

To fiddle To manipulate accounts, etc , to one's own advantage, or to the advantage of the parties concerned "He fiddled it," might indicate that he covered up a deficiency in the accounts

Fiddle-de-dee! An exclamation signifying what you say is nonsense
   All the return he ever had   was a word, too common, I regret to say, in female lips, viz , fiddle-de-dee.—DE QUINCEY *Secret Societies.*

Fiddle-faddle To busy oneself with nothing, to dawdle, to talk nonsense
      Ye may as easily
   Outrun a cloud, driven by a northern blast,
   As fiddle-faddle so
         JOHN FORD *The Broken Heart*, 1, 3. (1633)

Fiddler. Slang for a sixpence; also for a farthing

Drunk as a fiddler. *See* DRUNK

Fiddler's fare or pay. Meat, drink, and money.

Fiddler's Green. The land of sailors where there is perpetual mirth, a fiddle that never ceases playing to untiring dancers, plenty of grog, and unlimited tobacco

Fiddler's money. A silver penny The fee given to a fiddler at a wake by each dancer

Fiddler's news. Stale news carried about by wandering fiddlers

Oliver's fiddler. Sir Roger L'Estrange (1616-1704). So called because he, at one time, was playing a fiddle or viol with others in the house of John Hingston, the composer, when Cromwell was one of the guests

Fiddlesticks! An exclamation signifying what you say is not worth attention, much the same as *fiddle-de-dee* (*q v*)

The devil rides on a fiddlestick. *See* DEVIL (PHRASES)

Fidei Defensor. *See* DEFENDER OF THE FAITH

FIDO. Fog Investigation and Dispersal Operation. A method of dispersing fog on airfields by ejecting burning petrol from jets along the runways, developed in Britain during World War II.

Fie! An exclamation indicating that what is reproved is indelicate or undesirable It is an old word, and is found in many languages; it seems to be an instinctive sound uttered on experiencing something disagreeable
      No word ne wryteth he
   Of thilke wikke ensample of Canacee,
   That lovede hir owne brother sinfully,
   Of swiche cursed stories I sey "fy"
         CHAUCER *Man of Lawes Prologue*, 77.

Field.

In huntsman's language, the field means all the riders.

In heraldry, the entire surface of the shield

In military language, the place where a battle is fought, or is about to be fought, the battle itself, or the campaign.

In sportsmen's language it means all the horses of any one race.

To back the field, means to bet against all the horses except one.

To keep back the field, is to keep back the riders.

In the field. A competitor for a prize. A term in horse-racing, as, "So-and-so was in the field." Also in war, as, "the French were in the field already."

Master of the field. The winner, the conqueror in a battle

To take the field. To make the opening moves in a campaign, to move the army preparatory to battle.

To win the field. To win the battle

Field-day. A day of particular excitement or importance. A military term, meaning a day when troops have manœuvres or field practice.

Field-Marshal. A general officer of the highest rank in the British Army. The title was first used in 1736, and is conferred on generals who have rendered conspicuous services, and on members of royal families

Field Officer. In the British Army any officer between the rank of captain and that of general, i e. major, lieutenant-colonel, colonel, brigadier

Field piece. A piece of field artillery, a field gun

Field works. Works thrown up by an army besieging or defending a fortress, or in strengthening its position

Field of Blood. Aceldama (q.v.).

Field of fire. (Mil) That part of the terrain before infantry or machine guns which their weapons can cover—i e. which is not interrupted by woods, buildings, or the contours of the ground.

Field of force. A term used in physics to denote the range within which a force, such as magnetism, is effective

Field of the Cloth of Gold. The plain, near Guisnes, where Henry VIII met François I in 1520 to discuss the succession to the Empire on the death of Maximilian It was so called from the splendour and magnificence displayed Accompanied by Cardinal Wolsey in an immense panoply of state, Henry met the French king and his nobles who were overawed by this magnificence Many of the imposing ceremonies were spoiled by the rain and wind that swept the countryside.

Field of vision or **view.** The space in a telescope, microscope, etc , within which the object is visible

Field of the Forty Footsteps, or **The Brother's Steps.** At the back of the British Museum, once called Southampton Fields, near the extreme north-east of the present Upper Montagu Street. The tradition is that at the time of the Duke of Monmouth's rebellion two brothers fought each other here till both were killed, and for many years forty impressions of their feet remained on the field, and no grass would grow there, or upon the spot upon a bank where the young woman they were fighting for sat watching the duel The site was built upon about 1800

Fierabras, Sir (fi' er a bràs) One of Charlemagne's paladins, and a leading figure in many of the romances He was the son of Balan (q v), King of Spain, and for height of stature, breadth of shoulder, and hardness of muscle he never had an equal His pride was laid low by Olivier, he became a Christian, was accepted by Charlemagne as a paladin, and ended his days in the odour of sanctity. *See* BALAN

Fiere facias (fi' ĕr i fās' i as) (Lat , cause it to be done) A judicial writ for one who has recovered damages in the courts, commanding the sheriff to see the judgment of the court duly carried out It is often abbreviated to *fi fa.* The term was punningly used in Elizabethan times in connexion with red noses and men with "fiery faces" through drink

Fiery Cross, The. A signal anciently sent round the Scottish clans in the Highlands summoning them to assemble for battle It was symbolical of fire and sword, and consisted of a cross the ends of which had been burnt and then dipped in the blood of some animal slain for the purpose—a relic of Gaelic rites See Scott's *Lady of the Lake,* canto iii, for an account of it.

The Ku Klux Klan adopted this symbol when it arose after the American Civil War

Fifteen, The. The Jacobite rebellion of 1715, when James Edward Stuart, "the Old Pretender," with the Earl of Mar, made a half-hearted and unsuccessful attempt to gain the throne.

Fifth. Fifth column. Persons in a country who, whether as individuals or as members of an organization, are ready to give help to an enemy The origin of the phrase is attributed to General Mola who, in the Spanish Civil War (1936-39), said that he had four columns encircling Madrid and a fifth column working for him in the city.

Fifth-Monarchy Men. A sect of English fanatics of about 1654 to 1660, who maintained that Jesus Christ was about to come a second time to the earth, and establish the fifth universal monarchy The four preceding monarchies were the Assyrian, the Persian, the Macedonian, and the Roman. In politics, the Fifth-Monarchy Men were zealous reformers and levellers

Fifty-four Forty or Fight. A slogan used in the U.S.A. presidential election of 1846. For some years there had been a dispute with Britain as to the northern boundary of the U.S.A. in the far west The U.S.A. claimed that their territory should extend as far north as the southern border of Russian Alaska, which was 54° 40' N , Great Britain rejected this, and in 1818 it was agreed that the disputed territory should be jointly administered for ten years, which was later extended indefinitely In 1846 the question was brought forward again in the U S A as an issue in the election Shortly afterwards, the new President Polk came to an amicable agreement that U S territorial claims should end on the 49th parallel

Fig. Most phrases that include the word *fig* have reference to the fruit as being an object of trifling value, but in

In full **fig,** meaning "in full dress," *figged out,* "dressed up," etc., the word is a variant of *feague (see* FAKE)

To **fig up a horse** is to make it lively and spirited by artificial means

To **fig oneself out,** is to dress oneself up "regardless"
The speaker sits at one end in full fig, with a clerk at the table below —TROLLOPE *West Indies,* ch ix

I **don't care a fig for you;** not worth a fig. Nothing at all Here fig is either an example of something comparatively worthless or the Spanish *fico (q v)*—adopted as English by the Elizabethans—a gesture of contempt made by thrusting the thumb between the first and second fingers, much as we say, "I don't care that for you," snapping the fingers at the same time *See* THUMB (*To bite one's thumb).*
A fig for Peter
2 Henry VI, ii, 9.
The figo for thy friendship
Henry V, iii, 6

I **shan't buy my Attic figs in future, but grow them.** Said by way of warning to one who is building castles in the air—"don't count your chickens before they are hatched." Xerxes boasted that he was going to conquer Attica, where the figs grew, and add it to his own empire, but he met defeat at Salamis, and "never loosed his sandal till he reached Abdera"

In the name of the Prophet, Figs! A burlesque of the solemn language employed in eastern countries in the common business of life The line occurs in the imitation of Dr Johnson's pompous style, in *Rejected Addresses,* by James and Horace Smith

Mercury fig. *See* MERCURY

Fig leaf. The leaf of the fig tree or the banyan, according to the Bible story (*Gen* iii, 7) used by Adam and Eve to cover their nakedness after the Fall In the days of Victorian prudery tin fig leaves were fitted to statuary in the museums, Crystal Palace, etc

Fig Sunday. An old provincial name for Palm Sunday Figs used to be eaten on that day in commemoration of the blasting of the barren fig-tree by Our Lord (*Mark* xi) which took place on the day following the triumphant entry into Jerusalem
Many festivals still have their special foods, as, the goose for Michaelmas, pancakes for Shrove Tuesday, salt cod for Ash Wednesday, etc

Fig-tree. It is said that Judas hanged himself on a fig-tree. *See* ELDER-TREE

Figaro (fig' a rō) A type of cunning dexterity, and intrigue The character is in the *Barbier de Seville* (1775) and *Mariage de Figaro* (1784), by Beaumarchais. In the former he is a barber, and in the latter a valet, but in both he outwits everyone There are several operas founded on these dramas, as Mozart's *Nozze di Figaro,* Paisiello's *Il Barbiere di Siviglia,* and Rossini's *Il Barbiere di Siviglia*

Fight. He that fights and runs away May live to fight another day. An old saw found in many languages Demosthenes, being reproached for fleeing from Philip of Macedon at Chæronea, replied, "A man that runs away may fight again"
He that fights and runs away
May turn and fight another day,
But he that is in battle slain
Can never rise to right again
These lines occur in James Ray's *Complete History of the Rebellion,* 1749 A similar sentiment is expressed in *Hudibras,* iii, 3.
For those that fly may fight again,
Which he can never do that's slain

The Fighting Fifth *See* REGIMENTAL NICK-NAMES

The Fighting Prelate. Henry Spencer, Bishop of Norwich, who greatly distinguished himself in the rebellion of Wat Tyler He met the rebels in the field, with the temporal sword, then absolved them, and sent them to the gibbet

To fight for one's own hand. To uphold one's own cause, to struggle for one's own interest

To fight shy of. To avoid, to resist being brought into contest or conflict

To fight the tiger To play against the bank at faro

To fight with gloves on. To spar without showing animosity, like boxers, with boxing gloves Disputants fight with gloves on so long as they preserve all the outward amenities of debate, and conceal their hostility to each other by courtesy and forbearance

To live like fighting cocks *See* COCK.

Fighting French, or La France Combattante, included all Frenchmen at home and abroad who joined together to collaborate with the Allied Nations in their war against Germany After the fall of France, in 1940, General de Gaulle gathered round him such French troops, etc , as had escaped from France and formed them into a body called the Free French, with the cross of Lorraine for their emblem On July 14th, 1942, this name was changed to The Fighting French Not only did French troops fight side by side with the Allies in Africa, Italy, and wherever else there was fighting to be done, but in France itself they worked and fought behind the lines, organizing resistance and making themselves an annoyance and terror to the German occupying authorities
One of the greatest deeds of this body was the march of General Le Clerc with his column from Lake Chad across the Sahara to join the British 8th Army in Libya Strengthened and made into an armoured division Le Clerc's men fought thenceforward throughout the war

Figure 361 Fingal

and were given the honour of being the first formation to enter Paris, 23rd August, 1944.

Figure. From Lat *fingere*, to shape or fashion, not etymologically connected with Eng *finger*, though the primitive method of calculating was doubtless by means of the fingers. For Roman figures, etc , *see* NUMERALS

A figure of fun. Of droll appearance, whether from untidiness, quaintness, or other peculiarity ' A pretty figure" is a rather stronger expression

Figure-head A figure on the head or projecting cutwater of a sailing ship, which has ornamental value but is of no practical use, hence a nominal leader who has no real authority but whose social or other position inspires confidence

To cut a figure. To make an imposing appearance through dress, equipage, and bearing

To cut a sorry or a pretty figure is the reverse.

To make a figure. To make a name or reputation, to be a notability, as "he makes no figure at court "

What's the figure? How much am I to pay? What "figure" or sum does my debt amount to ?

Filch. To steal or purloin A piece of 16th-century thieves' slang of uncertain origin *File* (*q v*) was used in much the same sense, but there is no evidence of etymological connexion
> With cunning hast thou filched my daughter's heart
> *Midsummer Night's Dream*, i, 2

A *filch* or *filchman* was a staff with a hook at the end, for plucking clothes from hedges, articles from shop windows, etc.

File. Old slang for a rapscallion or worthless person; also for a pick-pocket It comes from the same original as the word *vile*, though in the sense in which it is sometimes used, as meaning a hard-headed, heartless person, it seems to have been connected with the hard, rasping tool, a file.

In single file. Single line; one behind another. (Fr. *file*, a row.).

Rank and file. Soldiers and non-commissioned officers as apart from commissioned officers, hence, the followers in or private members of a movement as apart from its leaders *Rank* refers to men standing abreast, *file* to men standing behind each other.

Filibuster (fil' i būs ter) A piratical adventurer, a buccaneer (*q v*) The word is through Span. *filibustero* from Dut. *vrybuiter*, a free-booter

To filibuster. In U S.A politics, to manœuvre to frustrate the passing of a bill. It is based on the right of a member of Congress not to be interrupted so long as he holds the floor of the House The member may recite or talk about any subject under the sun until the time available for passing the bill is exhausted.

Filioque Controversy (fil i ō' kwe) An argument that long disturbed the Eastern and Western Churches, and the difference of opinion concerning which still forms one of the principal barriers to their fusion. The point was. Did the Holy Ghost proceed from the Father *and* the Son (*Filio-que*), or from the Father only ? The Western Church maintains the former, and the Eastern the latter dogma The *filio-que* was recognized by the Council of Toledo, 589

The gist of the argument is this · If the Son is one with the Father, whatever proceeds from the Father must proceed from the Son also This is technically called "The Procession of the Holy Ghost "

Fill-dyke. The month of February, when the rain and melted snow fills the ditches to over-flowing
> February fill-dyke, be it black or be it white [wet or snowy],
> But if it be white it's better to like   *Old Proverb*

Filter (Lat *feltrum*, felt, *filtrum*, a strainer) Literally, to run through felt, as jelly is strained through flannel The Romans strained the juice of their grapes through felt into the wine-vat, after which it was put into the casks.

Fin de siècle (Fr , end of the century). It has come to mean decadent with particular reference to the 19th century

Finality John. Earl Russell, who maintained that the Reform Bill of 1832 was a *finality*, yet in 1854, 1860, and 1866 brought forth other Reform Bills

Finance. By devious routes this word comes from the late Latin *finis*, a settlement of a debt, or the winding up of a dispute by the payment of ransom Hence, revenue derived from fines or subsidies and, in the plural, available money resources. Thus we say, "My finances are exhausted," meaning I have no more funds or available money.

Financial year. The annual period for which accounts are made up The Finance Act is the name given to the annual Act of Parliament that legalizes the proposals contained in the Budget The financial year of the British Government ends on the 31st of March.

Find. Findings keepings' An exclamation made when one has accidentally found something that does not belong to him. and implying that it is now the finder's property. This old saying is very faulty law

Findon Haddock *See* FINNAN.

Fine. Fine as fivepence. An old alliterative saying meaning splendidly dressed or turned out

Fine feathers make fine birds. *See* FEATHER.

In fine. To sum up, to come to a conclusion, in short

One of these fine days. Some time or other, at some indefinite (and often problematical) date in the future.

The fine arts. Those arts which chiefly depend on a delicate or fine imagination, as music, painting, poetry, and sculpture, as opposed to the *useful arts*, *i.e* those which are practised for their utility and not for their own sake, as the arts of weaving, metal-working, and so on

Fingal (fing' gal). The great Gaelic semi-mythological hero, father of Ossian (*q v.*), who was purported by Macpherson to have been the original author of the long epic poem *Fingal* (1762), which narrates the hero's adventures

Fingal's cave. The basaltic cavern on Staffa, said to have been a home of Fingal. This is the name given to Mendelsohn's Hebridean Overture

Finger (A S *finger*). The old names for the fingers are —

A.S *thuma*, the thumb.

Towcher (the finger that touches), *foreman*, or *pointer*. This was called by the Anglo-Saxons the *scite-finger*, i e the shooting finger, and is now commonly known as the index finger, because it is the one used in pointing

Long-man or *long finger*

Lech-man or *ring-finger* The former means "medical finger," and the latter is a Roman expression, "*digitus annularis*" Called by the Anglo-Saxons the *gold-finger*. This finger between the long and little finger was used by the Romans as a ring-finger, from the belief that a nerve ran through it to the heart Hence the Greeks and Romans used to call it the *medical* finger, and used it for stirring mixtures, under the notion that nothing noxious could touch it without its giving instant warning to the heart It is still a general notion in parts of England that it is bad to rub salve or scratch the skin with any but the ring finger

At last he put on her medical finger a pretty, handsome gold ring, whereinto was enchased a precious toadstone of Beausse —RABELAIS. *Pantagruel*, III, 17

Little-man or *little finger*. Called by the Anglo-Saxons the *ear-finger*, because it can, from its diminutive size, be most easily introduced into the orifice of the ear.

The fingers each had their special significance in alchemy, and Ben Jonson says—

The thumb, in chiromancy, we give to Venus;
The fore-finger to Jove; the midst to Saturn,
The ring to Sol, the least to Mercury.
Alchemist, I, 2.

Blessing with the fingers. *See* BLESSING

Cry, baby, cry; put your finger in your eye, etc This nursery rhyme seems to be referred to in *Comedy of Errors*, II, 2 —

No longer will I be fool,
To put the finger in the eye and weep

Fingers and toes. The farmer's name for anbury, or ambury, i e a spongy wart on horses and oxen

Fingers were made before forks. The saying is used (especially at mealtimes) when one wants to convey that ceremony is unnecessary It makes an interesting commentary on this self-evident statement that forks were not introduced into England until about 1620, before which period fingers were used

Finished to the finger-nail. Complete and perfect in every detail, to all the extremities The allusion is obvious.

His fingers are all thumbs. Said of a person awkward in the use of his hands.

To keep one's fingers crossed. To hope for success, to try to ensure against disaster From the superstition that making the sign of the cross will avert bad luck

Lifting the little finger. Tippling. In holding a tankard or glass, many persons stick out or lift up the little finger

Light-fingered gentry. Pickpockets, thieves

My little finger told me that. The same as "A little bird told me that" (*see* BIRD), meaning, I know it, though you did not expect it The expression is in Molière's *Malade Imaginaire*

By the pricking of my thumbs,
Something wicked this way comes.
Macbeth, IV, 1

The popular belief was that an itching or tingling foretold some change or other

To be finger and glove with another. To be most intimate The more usual expression is *to be hand in glove with*

To burn one's fingers. *See* BURN

To have a finger in the pie. To assist or mix oneself officiously in any matter Said usually in contempt, or censoriously

To have it at one's fingers' ends. To be quite familiar with it and able to do it readily. The Latin proverb is *Scire tanquam ungues digitosque suos*, to know it as well as one's fingers and nails. The allusion is obvious, the Latin tag is referred to by Shakespeare in *Love's Labour's Lost*, v, 1.—

Costard Go to; thou hast it ad dunghill, at the fingers' ends, as they say
Holofernes O, I smell false Latin dunghill for unguem

To lay, or put, one's finger upon. To point out precisely the meaning, cause, etc., to detect with complete accuracy

To twist someone round one's little finger. To do just what one likes with him, to be master of his actions

With a wet finger. Easily, directly. The allusion is to spinning, in which the spinner constantly wetted the fore-finger with the mouth

Flores· Canst thou bring me thither?
Peasant With a wet finger
Wisdom of Dr Dodipoll (about 1596)

Sailors find the wind by holding up a wet finger for the breeze to cool that side whence it comes

Finger-print. An impression taken in ink of the whorls of lines on the finger In no two persons are they alike, and they never change through the entire life of any individual, hence, they are of very great value as a means of identifying criminals

Though the individuality of finger-prints had long been known, the publication of Sir Francis Galton's *Finger Prints* (1893) and *Finger Print Directory* (1895) drew attention to the facts. The full value of finger-prints was developed by Sir Edward Henry who devised a numerical formula for classifying the impressions The Henry system has been widely adopted by the police organizations of the world

Fingle-fangle. A ricochet word from *fangle* (*see* NEW FANGLED) meaning a fanciful trifle It was fairly common in the 17th century, but is not heard nowadays, except as an archaism.

Finnan Haddocks. Haddocks smoked with green wood; so called from a place-name, either Findhorn in Elgin, or Findon in Kincardineshire, both fishing villages where haddocks are cured.

Fionnuala. The daughter of Lir in old Irish legend, who was transformed into a swan, and condemned to wander over the lakes and rivers of Ireland till the introduction of Christianity into that island. Moore has a poem on the subject in his *Irish Melodies*.

Firbolgs. *See* MILESIANS.

Fir-tree. Atys was metamorphosed into a fir-tree by Cybele, as he was about to lay violent hands on himself (OVID: *Metamorphoses*, x, 2.)

Fir-cone. This forms the tip of the thyrsus (*q v*) of Bacchus because the juice of the fir-tree (*turpentine*) used to be mixed by the Greeks with new wine to make it keep

Fire. (A S *fyr*, Gr. *pur*.)

A burnt child dreads the fire. *See* BURN

Between two fires. Subjected to attack, criticism, etc , from both sides at once.

Coals of fire. *See* COALS

Fire away! Say on, say what you have to say The allusion is to firing a gun, as, You are primed up to the muzzle with something you want to say, fire away and discharge your thoughts

Greek fire *See* GREEK.

I have myself passed through the fire; I have smelt the smell of fire. I have had experience in trouble, and am all the better for it. The allusion is to the refining of gold, which is passed through the fire and so purged of all its dross

I will go through fire and water to serve you; *i e* through any difficulties or any test. The reference may be to the ordeals of fire and water which were common methods of trial in Anglo-Saxon times

If you will enjoy the fire you must put up with the smoke. You must take the sour with the sweet, every convenience has its inconvenience.

Letters of fire and sword. Formerly in Scotland if a criminal refused to answer his citation, it was accounted treason, and "letters of fire and sword" were sent to the sheriff, authorizing him to use either or both these instruments to apprehend the contumacious party

More fire in the bed-straw. More mischief brewing A relic of the times when straw was used for beds

No smoke without fire. To every scandal there is some foundation. Every effect is the result of some cause.

St. Anthony's Fire, St. Elmo's Fire, St. Helen's Fire, etc. See these names.

The fat is in the fire. *See* FAT

The Great Fire of London (1666) broke out at Master Farryner's, the king's baker, in Pudding Lane (the Monument now marks the spot) and after three days and nights was arrested at Pie Corner, Smithfield, and at the Temple, Fleet Street. St Paul's Cathedral, eighty-nine other churches, 13,200 houses were burnt down, and 373 acres within the walls and 64 acres without were devastated. In the City itself only 75 acres 3 roods remained unconsumed.

To fire, or to fire out. To discharge from employment suddenly and unexpectedly This use was originally an Americanism

To fire up To become indignantly angry; to flare up, get unduly and suddenly excited.

To set the Thames on fire. *See* THAMES.

We do not fire first, gentlemen. According to tradition this very chivalrous reply was made to Lord Charles Hay (in command of the Guards) at the opening of the battle of Fontenoy (1745) by the French Marquis d'Auteroche after the former had advanced from the British lines and invited the French commander to order his men to fire The story is told by the historian Espagnac as well as by Voltaire, but it is almost certainly *ben trovato*, and is not borne out by the description of the battle written a few days after the encounter by Lord Charles to his father, the Marquis of Tweeddale

Fire-brand. An incendiary, one who incites to rebellion, like a blazing brand which sets on fire all it touches
> Our fire-brand brother, Paris, burns us all.
> *Troilus and Cressida*, ii, 2

Fire-bug. An habitual committer of arson (usually a psychiatric case); a fire-raiser (*see below*) The term is also applied to a glow-worm.

Fire-cross. *See* FIERY CROSS

Fire-drake or **Fire-dragon.** A fiery serpent, an ignis-fatuus of large proportions, superstitiously believed to be a flying dragon keeping guard over hid treasures.
> There is a fellow somewhat near the door, he should be a brazier by his face, for, o' my conscience, twenty of the dog-days now reign in 's nose.   That fire-drake did I hit three times on the head —*King Henry VIII*, v, 3.

Fire-eaters. Persons ready to quarrel for anything. The allusion is to the jugglers who "eat" flaming tow, pour molten lead down their throats, and hold red-hot metal between their teeth Richardson, in the 17th century, Signora Josephine Girardelli (the original Salamander), in the early part of the 19th century; and Chaubert, a Frenchman, of the present century, were the most noted of these exhibitors.

Fire hunting. An American term for hunting at night with the aid of fire-pans, or links.

Fire-new. Spick and span new (*q.v.*).
> You should have accosted her; and with some excellent jests fire-new from the mint.—*Twelfth Night*, iii, 2.

Fire raiser. One guilty of arson for profit, usually to collect insurance money.

Fire-ship. A ship filled with combustibles sent against enemy vessels in order to set them on fire

Fire-worship. Said to have been introduced into Persia by Phœdima, widow of Smerdis, and wife of Hystaspes (521-485 B C) It is not the sun that is worshipped, but God, who is supposed to reside in it, at the same time the Fire Worshippers reverence the sun as the throne of deity. *Cp* PARSEES

First. A diamond of the first water. *See* DIAMOND.

At first hand. By one's own knowledge or personal observation.

First-chop. *See* CHOP.

First Fleet. The first convoy of ships taking convicts to Australia in 1788 The second fleet arrived in 1790 To have been a *first fleeter* became a matter of some pride, and the expression was in use as late as 1848

First floor. In England the first floor is the story next above the ground-floor, or entrance floor, but in America it is the ground floor itself.

First foot, or first footer. The first visitor at a house after midnight on New Year's Eve In Scotland and the North of England the custom of "first-footing" is still very popular

First-fruits. The first profitable results of labour In husbandry, the first corn that is cut at harvest, which, by the ancient Hebrews, was offered to Jehovah We also use the word figuratively, as, the first-fruits of sin, the first-fruits of repentance

First light. Roughly, dawn Used in World War II to signify the earliest time at which infantry can see to make their way forward, *first tank light*, about half an hour later, is the earliest time that a tank, closed down for battle, can see to move The phrases *last light* and *last tank light* are used at the end of the day.

First nighter. One who makes a practice of attending the opening performance of plays

The First Gentleman of Europe. A nickname given to George IV, who certainly was first in rank

He the first gentleman of Europe! There is no stronger satire on the proud English society of that day than that they admired George No, thank God, we can tell of better gentlemen —THACKERAY, *The Four Georges George IV*

The First Grenadier of the Republic A title given by Napoleon to Latour d'Auvergne (1743-1800), a man of extraordinary courage and self-effacement He refused all promotion beyond that of captain

The first stroke is half the battle "Well begun is half done." "A good lather is half the shave "

Fish. The fish was used as a symbol of Christ by the early Christians because the letters of its Greek name—Ichthus (*q v*)—formed a monogram of the words Jesus Christ, Son of God, Saviour.

Ivory and mother-o'-pearl counters used in card games, some of which are more or less fish-shaped, are so called, not from their shape, but from Fr. *fiche*, a peg, a card-counter *La fiche de consolation* (a little piece of comfort or consolation) is the name given in some games to the points allowed for the rubber.

Fish-flake. An 18th-century American term for a frame on which fish were dried

Fish day (Fr *jour maigre*) A day when persons in the Roman Catholic Church are forbidden to eat meat without ecclesiastical permission, viz all Fridays and ember days, Ash Wednesday, the Wednesdays of Lent, the vigils of Pentecost, Assumption, All Saints, and Christmas

Fish-wife A woman who hawks fish about the streets

Fish-wives are renowned for their powers of vituperation, hence the term is applied to any blatant, scolding woman

A fish out of water. Said of a person who is out of his usual environment and so feels awkward and in the way, also of one who is without his usual occupation and is restless in consequence

A loose fish. A man of loose or dissolute habits *Fish* as applied to a human being usually carries with it a mildly derogatory implication

A pretty kettle of fish. *See* KETTLE

A queer fish. An eccentric person

All is fish that comes to my net. I turn everything to some use, I am willing to deal in anything out of which I can make a profit

He eats no fish. An Elizabethan way of saying that he is an honest man and one to be trusted, because he is not a papist Roman Catholics were naturally opposed to the Government, and Protestants, to show their loyalty, refused to adopt their ritual custom of eating only fish on Fridays

I do profess . . to serve him truly . and to eat no fish —*King Lear*, i, 4

I have other fish to fry. I am busy and cannot attend to anything else just now

Neither fish, flesh, nor fowl, or **neither fish, flesh, nor good red herring** Suitable to no class of people, neither one thing nor another Not fish (food for the monk), not flesh (food for the people generally), nor yet red herring (food for paupers).

The best fish swim near the bottom. What is most valuable commercially is not to be found on the surface of the earth, nor is anything else really worth having to be obtained without trouble

There's as good fish in the sea as ever came out of it. Don't be disheartened if you've lost the chance of something good, you'll get another

Fisherman, King. In the legends of the Holy Grail (*q v*) the uncle of Perceval, and dweller in the Castle of the Grail, where the holy vessel is enshrined

Fisherman's Ring A seal-ring with which the Pope is invested at his election, bearing the device of St Peter fishing from a boat It is used for sealing legal briefs, and is officially broken up at his death by the Chamberlain of the Roman Church

To cry stinking fish. *See* CRY

To drink like a fish. *See* DRINK

To feed the fishes. To be drowned; to be sea-sick.

To fish for compliments. To try to obtain praise usually by putting leading questions

To fish in troubled waters. To scramble for personal advantage in times of rebellion, war, etc , to try to make a calamity a means to personal profit

To fish the anchor. A nautical term meaning to draw up the flukes to the bulwarks after the anchor has been "catted."

You must not make fish of one and flesh of the other. You must treat both alike The alliteration has much to do with the phrase.

Fitz The Norman form of the modern French *fils*, son of, as Fitz-Herbert, Fitz-William, Fitz-Peter, etc. It is sometimes assumed by illegitimate or morganatic children of royalties, as Fitz-Clarence, Fitz-roy, etc.

Fitzroy Cocktail (Austr) One of the many concoctions drunk by strong men "out back." The recipe is methylated spirits, ginger beer, and one teaspoonful of boot polish.

Fitzwilliam Museum (Cambridge) So called from the 7th and last Viscount Fitzwilliam, who, in 1816, left £100,000, with books, paintings, etc , to form the nucleus of a museum for the benefit of the university. The present building was begun in 1837. It was considerably extended in 1930-31.

Five. The pentad, one of the mystic numbers, being the sum of 2 + 3, the first *even* and first *odd* compound Unity is God alone, *i e* without creation Two is diversity, and three (being 1+2) is the compound of unity and diversity, or the two principles in operation since creation, and representing all the powers of nature.

Bunch of fives Pugilistic slang for the fist

The Five Boroughs. In English history, the Danish confederation of Derby, Lincoln, Leicester, Stamford, and Nottingham in the 9th and 10th centuries

Five fingers. A fisherman's name for the star-fish

The Five Members. Pym, Hampden, Haselrig, Strode, and Holles, the five members of the Long Parliament whom Charles I attempted to arrest in 1642

The Five-mile Act. An Act passed in 1665 (repealed in 1689) prohibiting ministers who had refused to subscribe to the Act of Uniformity from coming within five miles of any corporate town or within that distance of the scene of their old ministry

The Five Nations. A description applied by Kipling to the British Empire—the Old Country, with Canada, Australia, South Africa, and India

In American history the term refers to the five confederated Indian tribes inhabiting the present State of New York, viz. the Mohawks, Oneidas, Onondagas, Cayugas, and Senecas. Known also as the Iroquois Confederacy

The Five Points. *See* CALVINISM

Five senses. The five senses are feeling, hearing, seeing, smelling, tasting

The Five Towns. Towns in the Potteries in which Arnold Bennett (1867-1931) laid the scene of many of his novels and stories They are Tunstall, Burslem, Hanley, Stoke-upon-Trent, Longton

The five wits. Common *sense, imagination, fantasy, estimation,* and *memory.* Common sense is the outcome of the five senses; imagination is the "wit" of the mind, fantasy is imagination united with judgment, estimation estimates the absolute, such as time, space, locality, and so on, and memory is the "wit" of recalling past events.

> Four of his five wits went halting off
> 　　　　　　　　　　　　　*Much Ado*, i, 1.

These are the five witts removyng inwardly
First, "Common witte," and then "Ymagination," "Fantasy," and "Estimation" truely,
And "Memory "
STEPHEN HAWES. *The Passe-tyme of Plesure* (1515)

Also used to mean the five senses
> Alone and warming her five wits
> The white owl in the belfry sits —TENNYSON.

Fiver. A five-pound note. A ' tenner' is a ten-pound note.

Fix. In a fix. In an awkward predicament

Fixed air. An old name of carbonic acid gas, given to it by Dr Joseph Black (1728-99) because it existed in carbonate of magnesia in a fixed state

Fixed oils. The true oils, *i e.* those which are not changed by heating or distillation, and which harden on exposure to the air, thus differing from *essential oils* The glycarides, such as linseed and walnut oils, are examples

Fixed stars. Stars whose relative position to other stars is always the same, as distinguished from planets, which shift their relative positions.

Flaccus (flak' us) Horace (65-8 B C), the Roman poet, whose full name was Quintus Horatius Flaccus

Flags. The following national flags are described as though flying from a mast on the reader's left-hand side
Argentine 3 horizontal stripes, blue, white, blue
Austria 3 horizontal stripes, red, white, red.
Belgium: 3 vertical stripes, black, yellow, red.
Brazil Green, with yellow lozenge in centre bearing a blue sphere with white band and stars
British Empire *See* UNION JACK.
Chile 2 horizontal bands, white and red, in top left corner a white star on a blue square.
China: Red with blue square in left corner bearing a white sun.
Czechoslovakia 2 horizontal stripes, red and white, with blue triangle in top left corner.
Denmark Red with white cross from edge to edge
Egypt Green with white crescent and 3 5-pointed stars.
Eire 3 vertical stripes, green, white, orange
Ethiopia: 3 horizontal stripes, green yellow, red.
Finland: White field with a blue cross.
France. 3 vertical stripes, blue, white, red.
Germany: 3 horizontal stripes, black, red, gold.
Greece: 9 horizontal stripes, blue and white, with white cross on a blue ground in top left corner.

Hungary 3 horizontal stripes, red, white, green

Iceland Blue, with a white-bordered cross from edge to edge.

India, Republic of: 3 horizontal stripes, saffron, white, green

Iran White bordered with green at top and red at bottom with arms of lion and sun in centre

Iraq 3 horizontal bars, black, white, green, with a red triangle bearing 2 white stars, in left corner.

Italy 3 vertical stripes, green, white, red

Japan. White, charged with red rising sun and 16 rays reaching to the edge

Mexico 3 vertical stripes, green, white, red

Netherlands 3 horizontal stripes, red, white, blue

Norway. Red with a white-bordered blue cross to edges

Pakistan Green with white border, charged with white crescent and star

Peru 3 vertical stripes, red, white, red

Poland Flag divided horizontally, white and red

Portugal Flag divided vertically green and red

Rumania 3 vertical stripes, blue, yellow, red.

Siam·5 horizontal stripes, red, white, blue, white, red.

Spain 3 horizontal stripes, red, yellow, red

Sweden Blue with yellow cross to edges

Switzerland Red field with white cross charged on it.

Turkey· Red with white crescent with star in its centre.

U.S.A See STARS AND STRIPES

U.S.S.R Red with yellow hammer and sickle sur-surmounted by a 5-pointed star, all in the top left corner.

Yugoslavia 3 horizontal stripes blue, white, red

On railways and elsewhere a **red flag** is used for signalling Danger, a **green flag** for Go ahead, or Proceed with Caution.

A **black flag** is the emblem of piracy or of no quarter. *See* BLACK

The **Red Flag** is the symbol of international Socialism, red having been traditionally recognized as the colour of social revolutionary movements ever since the French Revolution. *The Red Flag* is a Socialist anthem written by Jim Connell and set to several tunes.

A **white flag** is the flag of truce or surrender, hence **to hang out the white flag** is to sue for quarter, to give in.

A **yellow flag** signals contagious disease on board ship, and all vessels in quarantine or having contagious disease aboard are obliged to fly it.

To flag down. To stop someone; from motor racing, in which the stewards wave a flag at the winner or at any driver they require to stop or to warn to proceed with caution.

The flag's down. Indicative of distress When the face is pale the "flag is down." Alluding to the ancient custom of taking down the flag of theatres during Lent, when the theatres were closed.

'Tis Lent in your cheeks, the flag's down.—*Dodsley's Old Plays*, vol v, p 314 (*Mad World*)

The flag of distress. A flag hoisted at the masthead in reverse position to signal that trouble of some sort is on board.

To get one's flag. To become an admiral *Cp* FLAG-OFFICER.

I do not believe that the bullet is cast that is to deprive you of life, Jack, you'll get your flag as I hope to get mine.—KINGSTON *The Three Admirals*, xiii

To hang the flag half-mast high is in token of mourning or distress.

To lower one's flag. To eat humble pie, to confess onself in the wrong, to eat one's own words

To strike the flag. To lower it The phrase is used of an admiral relinquishing his command afloat; the action is also a token of respect, submission, or surrender

Trade follows the flag. *See* FOLLOW.

Flag-ship. A ship carrying a flag-officer (*q.v.*)

Flag Captain. The captain commanding a vessel in which an admiral is flying his flag

Flag Lieutenant. An admiral's aide-de-camp.

Flag-officer. An admiral (*q v*), vice-admiral, or rear-admiral These officers alone are privileged to carry a flag denoting rank An admiral of the fleet flies a Union Jack, an admiral a plain St George's Cross, while vice-admirals and rear-admirals have respectively one and two red balls on the cross.

Flagellants (flä jel′ ants) The Latin *flagellum* means a scourge, and this name is given to groups of fanatical persons who performed and administered exaggerated physical penances in public They appeared in several places and times during the Middle Ages, particularly in Italy in 1260, and again in 1348 when the movement spread further afield in Europe Although individuals such as St Vincent Ferrer made use of the flagellant movements for legitimate religious purposes, the Church has never encouraged the practice of public flagellation and has definitely condemned any excesses in this direction

Flagellum Dei (Lat , the scourge of God) Attila was so called *See* SCOURGE OF GOD

Flak. The German abbreviation, adopted into English, of *Flugabwehrkanone*, meaning anti-aircraft gun or gunfire

Flam Flattery For an object, blarney; humbug

They told me what a fine thing it was to be an Englishman, and about liberty and property . I find it was a flam —GODWIN: *Caleb Williams*, vol ii, ch v

Flamboyant Architecture. A florid style which prevailed in France in the 15th and 16th centuries So called from its flame-like tracery. The flamboyant architects of the decline, says Ruskin, were

"nothing but skilful masons, with more or less love of the picturesque, and redundance of undisciplined imagination, flaming itself away in wild and rich traceries, and crowded bosses of grotesque figure sculpture "

Flame. A sweetheart. "An old flame," a quondam sweetheart

Flaming. Superb, captivating, ostentatious. The Fr. *flambant*, originally applied to those persons who dressed themselves in rich dresses "flaming" with gold and silver thread

Flaming swords. Swords with a wavy or *flamboyant* edge, used now only for state purposes The Dukes of Burgundy carried swords of this sort, and they were worn in our country till the accession of William III

The Flaming Tinman, or Black Jack Bosville, is one of the startling characters in George Borrow's *Lavengro*, and the fight in the dingle one of the great scenes of English literature.

Flaminian Way. The great northern road of ancient Italy, constructed by C Flaminius in 220 B C It led from the Flaminian gate of Rome to Ariminium (Rimini).

Flanders. Flanders' Babies. Cheap wooden jointed dolls common in the early 19th century.

Flanders Mare, The. So Henry VIII called Anne of Cleves, his fourth wife whom he married in January, 1540, and divorced in July of the same year She died at Chelsea in 1557.

Flanders Poppies. The name given to the red artificial poppies sold in the streets on Remembrance Day for the benefit of ex-service men The connexion with poppies comes from a poem by John McCrae, which appeared in *Punch*, December 8th, 1915 —

> If ye break faith with us who die
> We shall not sleep, though poppies grow
> In Flanders fields.

Flaneur (Fr) A lounger, gossiper. From *flaner*, to saunter about.

Flannels. To be awarded one's flannels. To gain one's cricket colours at Eton

Flap-dragons. An old name for our "snap-dragon," i e. raisins soaked in spirit, lighted, and floating in a bowl of spirituous liquor. Gallants used to drink flap-dragons to the health of their mistresses, and would frequently have lighted candle-ends floating in the liquor to heighten the effect. Hence —

> He drinks off candles' ends for flap-dragons —2 *Henry IV*, ii, 4

Flap-jack. A cake baked on a griddle or in a shallow pan, and so called from the practice of tossing it into the air when it was done on one side, and catching it flat with the brown side uppermost.

> We'll have flesh for holidays, fish for fasting-days, and more o'er puddings and flap-jacks —*Pericles*, ii, 1

In the 20th century the word has been applied to a woman's flat powder compact

Flapper In the early years of this century a familiar term for a young girl in her teens. The hair was worn long and plaited in a pigtail, tied with a large bow, which may have suggested a flapper.

Flash. Showy, smart, "swagger", as a *flash wedding*, a *flash hotel* In Australia the term *flash* or *flashy* is applied "to anyone who is proud and has nothing to be proud of," J KIRBY: *Old Times in the Bush of Australia*, 1895

Also counterfeit, sham, fraudulent. **Flash notes** are forged notes, a **flash man** is a thief or the companion of thieves

A mere flash in the pan. All sound and fury, signifying nothing; like the attempt to discharge an old flint-lock gun that ends with a flash in the lock-pan, the gun itself "hanging fire."

Flat. One who is not sharp.

Flat-foot. U S A slang for a policeman. In English slang he is a flattie.

To be caught flat-footed. To be caught unprepared, as a football player who is tackled by an opponent before he has been able to advance

To come out flat-footed. To state one's beliefs positively, as though firmly planted on one's feet

Flat top. British and American name for aircraft-carrier (World War II)

Flat as a flounder. I knocked him down flat as a flounder. A flounder is one of the flat-fish.

Flat as a pancake. Quite flat.

Flat race. A race on the "flat" or level ground without obstacles, as opposed to a steeplechase, or "over the sticks."

He is a regular flat-fish. A dull, stupid fellow. The play is upon *flat* (stupid), and such fish as plaice, dabs, and soles

Flatterer. Vitellius (A.D. 15-69), Roman Emperor for a short while in 69. He was a sycophant of Nero's, and his name became a synonym for a flatterer (Tacitus, *Ann.*, vi, 32)

When flatterers meet, the devil goes to dinner. Flattery is so pernicious, so fills the heart with pride and conceit, so perverts the judgment and disturbs the balance of the mind, that Satan himself could do no greater mischief, so he goes to dinner and leaves the leaven of wickedness to operate its own mischief

> Porteus, there is a proverb thou shouldst read:
> "When flatterers meet, the devil goes to dinner"
> PETER PINDAR *Nil Admirari*.

Flea. A flea's jump. It has been estimated that if a man, in proportion to his weight, could jump as high as a flea, he could clear St Paul's Cathedral with ease

Aristophanes, in the *Clouds*, says that Socrates and Chærephon tried to measure how many times its own length a flea jumped. They took in wax the size of a flea's foot; then, on the principle of *ex pede Herculem*, calculated the length of its body. Having found this, and measured the distance of the flea's jump from the hand of Socrates to Chærephon, the knotty problem was resolved by simple multiplication.

A mere flea-bite. A thing of no moment.

Great fleas have lesser fleas. No matter what our station in life, we all have some ' hangers on."

> Hobbes clearly proves that every creature
> Lives in a state of war by nature;
> So naturalists observe a flea
> Has smaller fleas that on him prey,
> And these have smaller still to bite 'em,
> And so proceed *ad infinitum*
> SWIFT. *Poetry, a Rhapsody*.

Sent off with a flea in his ear. Peremptorily A dog which has a flea in the ear is very restless, and runs off in terror and distress.

The phrase is quite an old one, and dates from at least the 15th century in English, and earlier in French. It is found in Heywood's *Proverbs*, Nash's *Pierce Penilesse*, Skoggin's *Jests*, etc.

> Ferardo . whispering Philantus in the ear (who stood as though he had a flea in his ear), desired him to keep silence —LYLY· *Euphues* (1578)

Here the phrase implies that vexatious news has been heard, and in Deloney's *Gentle Craft* (1597) we have a similar instance, where a servant goes away shaking his head "like one that hath a flea in his eare."

Flecknoe, Richard. An Irish priest who printed a host of poems, letters, and travels, and died about 1678. He is now only remembered through Dryden's satire, *MacFlecknoe*, where it is said he

> Reigned without dispute
> Through all the realms of nonsense absolute

Fleeced. Cheated of one's money, sheared like a sheep

Fleet, The. Fleet Marriages. Clandestine marriages, at one time performed without banns or licence by needy chaplains, in the Fleet Prison, London As many as thirty marriages a day were sometimes celebrated in this disgraceful manner, and Malcolm tells us that 2,954 were registered in the four months ending with February 12th, 1705 The practice was suppressed and declared null and void in 1774

Fleet Book Evidence. No evidence at all The books of the Old Fleet prison are not admissible as evidence to prove a marriage

Fleet Prison. The most notorious of the old debtors' prisons, the Fleet Prison stood on the site now occupied by the Memorial Hall, Farringdon Street. Its history was as dismal as the building itself Originally used for prisoners committed by the Star Chamber, on the abolition of that court it became a prison for debtors, bankrupts, and persons charged with contempt of court. It was in charge of a warden, who bought the job and reimbursed himself from the exorbitant fees he charged prisoners for board, lodging, and innumerable privileges they never received. Every day a prisoner took it in turns to beg from passers-by standing in a barred cage opening on the street The prison was burned down in the Great Fire (1666) and again by the Gordon Rioters in 1780. It was rebuilt again but in 1844 the prisoners were removed to the Queen's Bench Prison, and in 1864 the place was pulled down *See* LIBERTIES OF THE FLEET, *under* LIBERTY.

Fleet Street. Now synonymous with journalism and newspaperdom, Fleet Street in London was a famous thoroughfare centuries before the first newspaper was published there at the close of the 18th century. It takes its name from the old Fleet River, which ran from Hampstead through Hockley-in-the-Hole to Saffron Hill, near where it joined the Hole Bourne (whence *Holborn*), flowing on with it under what is now Farringdon Street and New Bridge Street to fall into the Thames at Blackfriars It was navigable for coal-boats, etc, as far as Holborn Bridge (near the present Viaduct), but latterly became so foul that in 1764 it was arched over, and it is now used as a sewer. From earliest days there was a bridge (the Fleet Bridge) across the river at the modern Ludgate Circus

Flemish Account. A sum less than that expected. In Antwerp accounts were kept in *livres*, *sols*, and *pence*, but the *livre* or pound was only 12s , hence, an account of 100 livres Flemish was worth £60 only, instead of £100, to the English creditor

Flemish School. A school of painting established by the brothers Van Eyck, in the 15th century The chief *early* masters were Memling, Weyden, Matsys, and Mabuse. Of the *second* period, Rubens and Van Dyck, Snyders, and the younger Teniers.

Flesh. Sighing for the flesh-pots of Egypt. Hankering for good things no longer at your command The children of Israel said they wished they had died "when they sat by the flesh-pots of Egypt" (*Exod* xvi, 3) rather than embark on their long sojourn in the wilderness

He fleshed his sword. Used it for the first time *Men fleshed in cruelty*—i e initiated or used to it A sportsman's expression A sportsman allows a young dog or hawk to have the first game it catches for its own eating, thus at the same time rewarding it and encouraging its taste for blood This "flesh" is the first it has tasted, and fleshing its tooth thus gives the creature a craving for similar food.

> The wild dog
> Shall flesh his tooth on every innocent
> *2 Henry IV*, iv, 5.

Fleshly School, The In the *Contemporary Review* for October, 1871, Robert Buchanan published a violent attack on the poetry and literary methods of Swinburne, Rossetti, Morris, O'Shaughnessy, John Payne, and one or two others under the heading *The Fleshly School of Poetry*, over the signature "Thomas Maitland" The incident created a literary sensation, Buchanan at first denied the authorship but was soon obliged to admit it, and some years later was reconciled to Rossetti, his chief victim Swinburne's very trenchant reply is to be found in his *Under the Microscope* (1872)

Fleur-de-lis, -lys, or **-luce** (flĕr de lē, loos) (Fr , lily-flower) The name of several varieties of iris, and also of the heraldic lily, which is here shown and which was borne as a charge on the old French royal coat-of-arms.

In the reign of Louis VII (1137-80) the national standard was thickly charged with flowers In 1365 the number was reduced by Charles VI to *three* (the mystical number) Guillim, in his *Display of Heraldrie*, 1611, says the device is "Three toads erect, saltant"; in allusion to which Nostradamus, in the 16th century, calls Frenchmen *crapauds*. The *fleur-de-lis* was chosen by Flavio Gioja to mark the north point of the compass, out of compliment to the King of Naples, who was of French descent Gioja was an early-14th-century Italian navigator to whom has been (incorrectly) ascribed the invention of the mariner's compass (*q v*)

Flibbertigibbet. One of the five fiends that possessed "poor Tom" in *King Lear* Shakespeare got the name from Harsnet's *Declaration of Egregious Popish Impostures* (1603), where we are told of forty fiends which the Jesuits cast out, and among the number was "Fliberdigibet," a name which had previously been used by Latimer and others for a mischievous gossip Elsewhere the name is apparently a synonym for Puck.

Flick. A cinematograph film, **to go to the flicks,** to go to the pictures.

Flimsy (flim' zi). A newspaper journalist's term for newspaper copy, or a telegram It arises from the thin paper (often used with a sheet of carbon paper to take a copy) on which the reporters and others write up their matter for the press *Flimsy* is also used for a £5 bank note

Fling. I must have a fling at . . . Throw a stone at something. To attack with words, especially sarcastically To make a haphazard venture. Allusion is to hurling stones from slings

To have his fling. To sow his wild oats The Scots have a proverb —

Let him tak' his fling and find oot his ain wecht (weight)

meaning, give him a free hand and he'll soon find his level.

Flint. To skin a flint. *See* SKIN

Flirt. A coquette The word is from the verb flirt, as, "to flirt a fan," *i e* to open it, or wave it, with a sharp, sudden motion The fan being used for coquetting, those who coquetted were called "flirts" In Dr. Johnson's day a *flirt*, according to his *Dictionary*, was "a pert hussey", and he gives an account of one in No 84 of *The Rambler*, which, in some few particulars, resembles the modern article.

Flittermouse. A bat (*cp* Ger. *Fledermaus*) An earlier name was *flinder mouse*

Then came . . the flyndermows and the wezel and ther cam moo than xx whiche wolde not have comen yf the foxe had loste the feeld —CAXTON: *Reynard the Fox,* xli

Floating Academy. The hulks (*q.v.*); a convict ship.

Flogging a dead horse. *See* HORSE.

Floor. I floored him. Knocked him down on the floor, hence figuratively, to overcome, beat, or surpass

Flora's Dial. A fanciful or imaginary dial supposed to be formed by flowers which open or close at stated hours.

Florentine Diamond. One of the large and famous diamonds in the world, weighing 133 carats. It formed part of the Austrian crown jewels, and previously belonged to Charles, Duke of Burgundy. Tradition relates that it was picked up by a peasant and sold for half a crown

Florian, St. Patron saint of Poland, he was martyred by being drowned in the Enns, near Lorch, about 230. He is also the patron of mercers, having been himself of that craft His cult was introduced into Poland in 1183; his day is May 4th.

Florid Architecture. The later stages of the pointed style in England (about 1480-1537), often called the Tudor, remarkable for its florid character, or profusion of ornament .

Florida. In 1512 Ponce de Leon sailed from France to the West in search of ' the Fountain of Youth." He first saw land on Easter Day, which was then popularly called in Spain *pascua florida*, flowery Easter, and on that account called the new possession "Florida."

Florimel (flor' i mel) A character in Spenser's *Faerie Queene* typifying the complete charm of womanhood

Florin An English silver coin representing 2s, first issued in 1849 as a tentative introduction of a decimal coinage, being one-tenth of a

pound Camden informs us that Edward III issued gold florins worth 6s., in 1337 The word is generally supposed to be derived from Florence; but as the coin had a lily on one side, probably it is connected with the Lat *flos*, a flower *Cp*. GRACELESS FLORIN.

Florizel (flor' i zel) George IV, when Prince of Wales, corresponded under this name with Mrs Robinson, the actress, generally known as Perdita, that being the character in which she first attracted the prince's attention The names come from Shakespeare's *Winter's Tale*

In Lord Beaconsfield's *Endymion* (1880) *Prince Florizel* is meant for Napoleon III.

Flotsam and Jetsam. Wreckage found in the sea or on the shore "Flotsam," goods found *floating* on the sea, ' jetsam," things thrown out of a ship to lighten it. (O.Fr *floter*, to float, Fr *jeter*, to throw out) *Cp* LAGAN

Flowers and Trees.

(1) Dedicated to heathen gods:
The Cornel cherry-tree to Apollo

„	Cypress	„	Pluto
„	Dittany	„	The Moon
„	Laurel	„	Apollo
„	Lily	„	Juno
„	Maidenhair	„	Pluto
„	Myrtle	„	Venus.
„	Narcissus	„	Ceres.
„	Oak	„	Jupiter
„	Olive	„	Minerva.
„	Poppy	„	Ceres.
„	Vine	„	Bacchus

(2) Dedicated to saints.

Canterbury Bells	to St. Augustine of England
Crocus	„ St Valentine.
Crown Imperial	„ Edward the Confessor.
Daisy	„ St. Margaret.
Herb Christophe	„ St Christopher
Lady's-smock	„ The Virgin Mary
Rose	„ Mary Magdalene
St. John's-wort	„ St John
St Barnaby's Thistle	„ St Barnabas.

(3) National emblems

Leek	emblem of Wales	
Lily (*Fleur-de-lys*)	„	Bourbon France.
„ (*Giglio bianco*)	„	Florence
„ white	„	the Ghibelline badge
„ red	„	badge of the Guelphs.
Linden	„	Prussia
Mignonette	„	Saxony.
Pomegranate	„	Spain
Rose	„	England
„ red, Lancastrians, white, Yorkists		
Shamrock	emblem of Ireland	
Thistle	„	Scotland
Violet	„	Athens
Sugar Maple	„	Canada

(4) Symbols.

Box	a symbol of the resurrection
Cedars	„ the faithful
Corn-ears	„ the Holy Communion
Dates	„ the faithful
Grapes	„ this is my blood.
Holly	„ the resurrection
Ivy	„ the resurrection.
Lily	„ purity
Olive	„ peace
Orange-blossom	„ virginity
Palm	„ victory
Rose	„ incorruption.
Vine	„ Christ our Life
Yew	„ death

N B.—The laurel, oak, olive, myrtle, rosemary, cypress, and amaranth are all funereal plants.

Flowers in Christian Traditions. Many plants and flowers, such as the aspen, elder, passion-flower, etc., play their part in Christian tradition.

The following are said to owe their stained blossoms to the blood which trickled from the cross:—

The *red anemone*, the *arum*, the *purple orchis*; the crimson-spotted leaves of the *roodvelken* (a French tradition), the spotted *persicaria*, snake-weed.

Flowery Kingdom, The. China, a translation of the Chinese *Hwa-kwo*

Flower of Chivalry. A name given to several knights of spotless reputation, *e g* —

Sir William Douglas, Knight of Liddesdale (slain 1353).

Bayard (*le chevalier sans peur et sans reproche*) (1475?-1524)

Sir Philip Sidney (1554–86),

Flower of Kings (Lat. *Flos regum*) King Arthur was so called by John of Exeter, who was Bishop of Winchester and died 1268

Fluellen (floo el' en). A Welsh captain and great pedant in Shakespeare's *Henry V*, who, amongst other learned quiddities, attempted to draw a parallel between Henry V and Alexander the Great, but when he had said that one was born at Monmouth and the other at Macedon, both beginning with the same letter, and that there was a river in both cities, had exhausted his parallelisms

Fluff. To bungle, to foozle, to do something carelessly and unskilfully In theatrical parlance an actor fluffs a part when he loses or has not learned his words.

A little bit of fluff. Edwardian slang for a girl, especially a lively one of the fluffy variety

Fluke. A lucky chance, a stroke or action that accidentally meets with success, as in billiards when one plays for one thing and gets another. Hence an advantage gained by luck more than by skill or judgment

Flummery. Flattering nonsense, palaver In Wales it is a food made of oatmeal steeped in water and kept till it has become sour In Cheshire and Lancashire it is the prepared skin of oatmeal mixed with honey, ale, or milk, pap, blanc-mange. (Welsh, *llymry*, wash-brew, from *llym*, sour or sharp)

Flummux, To. To bamboozle, to deceive; to be in a quandary. "I am regularly flummuxed" —*i e* perplexed It is probably the Old English provincial word *flummocks*, to maul or mangle, or *flummock*, bewilderment, also untidiness or an untidy person.

Flunk. To fail in examinations or a test completely; found in U S A. by mid-19th century

Flunkey. A male livery servant, a footman, lackey. The word usually has a contemptuous implication and suggests snobbery and toady-ism, hence *flunkeydom*, *flunkeyish*, etc , pertaining to toadies Probably a Scottish form of *flanker*, *i e.* one who runs at the side (of carriages, etc). *Cp* Fr. *flanquer*, to run at the side of.

Flurry. The death-struggle of a whale after harpooning

Flush In cards, a whole hand of one suit

Flush of money Full of money Similarly *a flush of water* means a sudden and full flow of water (Lat. *flux-us*)

To flush game. A gun dog is said to flush game when he disturbs them and they take to the air.

Flute The Magic Flute. an opera by Mozart (*Die Zauberflöte*) The "flute" was bestowed by the powers of darkness, and had the power of inspiring love Tamino and Pamina are guided by it through all worldly dangers to the knowledge of Divine Truth

Flutter. Colloquial term for a small gamble

Flutter the Dovecotes, To. To disturb the equanimity of a society The phrase occurs in *Coriolanus* (v, 6).

Fly (plural *flys*) A hackney coach, a cab A contraction of *Fly-by-night*, as sedan chairs on wheels used to be called in the Regency. These ' Fly-by-nights,'' patronized greatly by the Regent and his boon companions during their wild night pranks at Brighton, were invented in 1809 by a carpenter, John Butcher

Fly. An insect (plural *flies*) For the theatrical use, *see* FLYMAN

It is said that no fly was ever seen in Solomon's temple, and according to Mohammedan legend, all flies shall perish except one, and that is the bee-fly

The god or lord of flies. In the temple of Actium the Greeks used annually to sacrifice an ox to Zeus, who, in this capacity, was surnamed Apomyios, the averter of flies. Pliny tells us that at Rome sacrifice was offered to flies in the temple of Hercules Victor, and the Syrians offered sacrifice to the same insects *See* ACHOR, BEELZEBUB

Flies in amber. *See* AMBER

Fly. Perspicacious in an unpleasant way, unlikely to be caught.

No flying without wings Nothing can be done without the proper means

The eagle doesn't hawk at flies. *See* AQUILA

The fly in the ointment. The trifling cause that spoils everything, a biblical phrase.

Dead flies cause the ointment of the apothecary to send forth a stinking savour, so doth a little folly him that is in reputation for wisdom and honour —*Eccles* x, 1.

The fly on the coach-wheel. One who fancies himself of mighty importance, but who is in reality of none at all. The allusion is to Æsop's fable of a fly sitting on a chariot-wheel and saying, "See what a dust I make!"

There are no flies on him. *He's* all right, he's very alert; you won't catch him napping.

To crush a fly on a wheel. An allusion to the absurdity of taking a wheel used for torturing criminals and heretics for killing a fly.

To fly a kite. *See* KITE

To fly in one's face. To get into a passion with a person; to insult, as a hawk, when irritated flies in the face of its master

To fly in the face of danger. To run in a fool-hardy manner into danger, as a hen flies in the face of a dog or cat.

To fly in the face of providence. To act rashly, and throw away good opportunities; to court danger.

To fly out at. To burst or break into a passion

To rise to the fly. To be taken in by a hoax, as a fish rises to the angler's fly and is caught.

Fly-boy. The boy in a printing-office who lifts the printed sheets off the press, so called because he catches the sheets as they fly from the tympan immediately the frisket is opened

Fly-by-night. One who defrauds his creditors by decamping at night-time, also the early name of a sedan-chair, and later of a horsed vehicle (hence FLY, a cab)

Fly-flat A racing man's term for a punter who thinks he knows all the ins and outs of the turf, but doesn't

Flyman. In theatrical language, the scene-shifter or the man in the "flies," i.e. the gallery over the proscenium where the curtains, scenery, etc., are controlled

The flyman's plot. The list of all the articles required by the flyman in the play produced

To come off with flying colours is to succeed triumphantly, as a ship coming out of action with all her colours flying

Flying Dutchman. In the superstitions of seamen a spectral ship that is supposed to haunt the southern seas round the Cape of Good Hope. She is only to be seen in stormy weather and bodes no good to those who pass her There are various stories to account for this mysterious and ghostly craft, that worked out by Wagner in his opera *Der Fliegende Hollander* (1843) was partly suggested by Heinrich Heine Captain Marryat's novel *The Phantom Ship* (1839) tells of Philip Vander-decken's successful but disastrous search for his father, the captain of the *Flying Dutchman.*

Fo'c'sle. *See* FORECASTLE.

Fogy or Fogey. An old fogy. A man of ad-vanced years and somewhat antiquated ideas A disrespectful but good-humoured descrip-tion Several fanciful derivations have been found for this word, but its origin is unknown

Foil. That which sets off something to ad-vantage The allusion is to the metallic leaf used by jewellers to set off precious stones (Fr *feuille*, Lat. *folium*, Gr. *phullon*, a leaf)

Ill be your foil, Laertes In mine ignorance
Your skill shall, like a star i' the darkest night,
Stick fiery off indeed.   *Hamlet*, v, 2

To run a foil. To puzzle; to lead astray. The track of game is called its *foil*, and an animal hunted will sometimes run back over the same foil in order to mislead its pursuers In another sense the word means "to baffle, frustrate, parry." It comes from the O.Fr. *fouler*, to trample upon (we have the same word in the phrase "to full cloth"). *His schemes were foiled,* he was prevented in what he had in mind

Folio. Properly, a ream or sheet in its standard size. but when used of books it denotes a book whose sheets have been folded once only, so that each sheet makes two leaves; hence, a book of large size Demy folio = $11\frac{1}{4} \times 17\frac{1}{2}$ in , crown folio = 10×15 in , and so forth. It is from the Ital *un libro in foglio*, through the Fr. *in-folio.*

Folio so-and-so, in mercantile books, means page so-and-so, and sometimes the two pages which lie exposed at the same time, one containing the credit and the other the debit of one and the same account So called because ledgers, etc , are made in folio

Printers call a page of MS or printed matter a *folio* regardless of size

In conveyances, MSS , typewritten docu-ments, etc , seventy-two words, and in Parlia-mentary proceedings ninety words, make a folio.

Folkland. *See* BOCKLAND.

Folk-lore. The study or knowledge of the superstitions, mythology, legends, customs, traditions, sayings, etc , of a people The word was coined in 1846 by W J Thoms (1803-85), editor of the *Athenæum*

Folk-mote (*folk meeting*) A word used in England before the Conquest for what we now call a county or even a parish meeting.

Follow. Follow-my-leader. A parlour game in which each player must exactly imitate the actions of the leader, or pay a forfeit.

Follow your nose, go straight on.

He who follows truth too closely will have dirt kicked in his face. Be not too strict to pry into abuse.

To follow suit. To do as the person before you has done A phrase from card-playing

Follower. In addition to its proper meaning of one who follows a leader, the word was used in Victorian days to designate a maid-servant's young man

Mrs Marker .   . offers eighteen guineas .
Five servants kept .. No followers.
            DICKENS *Nicholas Nickleby.*

Folly. A fantastic or foolishly extravagant country seat, built for amusement or vainglory. *Fisher's Folly*, a large and beautiful house in Bishopsgate, with pleasure-gardens, bowling-green, and hothouses, built by Jasper Fisher, one of the six clerks of Chancery and a Justice of the Peace, is an historical example. Queen Elizabeth lodged there, in 1620 it was acquired by the Earl of Devonshire, and its site is now occupied by Devonshire Square.

Kirby's castle, and Fisher's folly,
Spinola's pleasure, and Megse's glory.
            STOW· *Survey* (1603)

Fond. A foolish, fond parent. Here fond does not mean affectionate, but silly, from the obsolete *fon*, to act the fool, to become foolish (connected with our *fun*) Chaucer uses the word *fonne* for a simpleton (*Reeve's Tale* 169), Shakespeare has "fond desire," "fond wretch," "fond madwoman," etc , also the well known:—

            Pray, do not mock me:
I am a very foolish fond old man,
Fourscore and upward, not an hour more or less,
And, to deal plainly,
I fear I am not in my perfect mind.
            King Lear, iv, 7.

Font or Fount. A complete set of type of the same body and face, with all the points accents, figures, fractions, signs, etc, that ordinarily occur in printed books and papers A complete fount (which, of course, includes *italics*) comprises 275 separate pieces of type, not including the special characters needed in almanacs, astronomical and medical works, etc The word is French, *fonte*, from *fondre* (to melt or cast) *Cp.* TYPE, LETTER

Fontange An extravagant head-dress or top-knot introduced in France in 1680 by Mlle Fontange (d 1681) In England it was called a *Tower* or *Commode* Pieces of gummed linen, rolled into circular bands, served as a foundation to keep in place various feathers, bows and jewelled ornaments. This head-dress, sometimes rising to a height of 2 feet, was abolished by Louis XIV in 1699.

Fontarabia (font a rā′ bi a) Now called Fuenterrabia (in Lat , *Fons rapidus*), near the Gulf of Gascony Here, according to legend, Charlemagne and all his chivalry fell by the sword of the Saracens The French romancers say that the rear of the king's army being cut to pieces, Charlemagne returned and revenged their death by a complete victory

> When Charlemagne with all his peerage fell
> By Fontarabia.   MILTON *Paradise Lost*, i, 587.

Food Food for powder Soldiers, especially raw recruits levied in times of war, cannon fodder

> *Prince* Tell me, Jack, whose fellows are these that come after?
> *Fal* Mine, Hal, mine
> *Prince* I did never see such pitiful rascals
> *Fal* Tut, tut, good enough to toss, food for powder, food for powder, they'll fill a pit as well as better tush, man mortal men, mortal men   *Henry IV*, iv, 2

The food of the gods *See* AMBROSIA, NECTAR

To become food for the worms, or for the fishes To be dead and buried, or to be drowned

Fool We have many old phrases in which this word plays the chief part; among those which need no explanation are. A fool and his money are soon parted ; Fortune favours fools , There's no fool like an old fool ; etc Others that may be mentioned are.—

A fool's bolt is soon shot (*Henry V*, iii, 7) Simpletons cannot wait for the fit and proper time, but waste their resources in random endeavours. The allusion is to bowmen in battle, the good soldier shot with a purpose, but the foolish soldier at random *Cp. Prov.* xxix, 11

A fool's paradise. To be in a fool's paradise is to be in a state of contentment or happiness that rests only on unreal, fanciful foundations.

As the fool thinks, so the bell clinks. A foolish person believes what he desires.

Every man hath a fool in his sleeve. No one is always wise, there is something of the fool about everyone

At forty every man is a fool or his own physician Said by Plutarch (*Treatise on the Preservation of Health*) to have been a saying of Tiberius It implies that by the age of 40 a man ought to have learnt enough about his own constitution to be able to keep himself in health.

The Feast of Fools A kind of Saturnalia, popular in the Middle Ages Its chief object was to honour the ass on which Our Lord made His triumphant entry into Jerusalem This mummery was held on the Feast of the Circumcision (Jan 1). The office of the day was chanted in travesty, then a procession was formed and all sorts of foolery was indulged in. An ass was an essential feature, and from time to time the whole procession imitated braying, especially in the place of "Amen." It was put down only in the 15th century

The wisest fool in Christendom. James I was so called by Henry IV of France, who learnt the phrase of Sully

To be a fool for one's pains To have worked ineffectively, to have had no reward for one's labours.

To be a fool to. Not to come up to, to be very inferior to, as, "bagatelle is a fool to billiards "

To fool about or around To play the fool; to hang around in an aimless way

To fool away one's time, money, etc To squander it, fritter it away

To make a fool of someone To mislead him

Young men think old men fools, old men know young men are. An old saying quoted by Camden in his *Remains* (1605, p 228) as by a certain Dr Metcalfe It occurs also in Chapman's *All Fools*, v, 2 (acted 1599).

Court fools From mediæval times till the 17th century licensed fools or jesters were commonly kept at court, and frequently in the retinue of wealthy nobles Thus we are told that the regent Morton had a fool, Patrick Bonny, Holbein painted Sir Thomas More's jester, Patison, in his picture of the chancellor, and as late as 1728 Swift wrote an epitaph on Dickie Pearce, the fool of the Earl of Suffolk, who died at the age of 63 and is buried in Berkeley Churchyard, Gloucestershire Dagonet, the fool of King Arthur, is also remembered

Among the most celebrated court fools are —

Rayère, of Henry I, Scogan, of Edward IV; Thomas Killigrew, called "King Charles's jester" (1611-82), Archie Armstrong (d 1672), and Thomas Derrie, jesters in the court of James I

James Geddes, to Mary Queen of Scots, his predecessor was Jenny Colquhoun

Patch, the court fool of Elizabeth, wife of Henry VII

Will Somers (d 1560), Henry VIII's jester, and Patch, presented to that monarch by Cardinal Wolsey, and Robert Grene, jester in the court of Queen Elizabeth

The fools of Charles V of France were Mitton and Thevenin de St Léger, Haincelin Coq belonged to Charles VI, and Guillaume Louel to Charles VII Triboulet was the jester of Louis XII and François I (1487-1536), Brusquet, of whom Brantôme says "he never had his equal in repartee," of Henri II, Sibilot and Chicot, of Henri III and IV, and l'Angély, of Louis XIII

In *chess* the French name for the "bishop" is *fou* (*i. e.* fool), and they used to represent it in a fool's dress, hence, Regnier says· *Les fous sont aux echecs les plus proches des Rois* (14 *Sat*) *Fou* is said to be a corruption of an eastern word for an elephant (*see* Thomas Hyde's *De Ludis Orientalium*, i, 4, 1689), and on old boards the places occupied by our "bishops" were occupied by elephants

Foolscap. A standard size of printing paper measuring $13\frac{1}{2} \times 17$ in and of writing paper measuring $13\frac{1}{4} \times 16\frac{1}{2}$ in The name is derived from an ancient watermark, of which the first known specimen occurs in 1540

Foot. The foot as a measure of length (= 12 in, $\frac{1}{3}$ of a yard, or ·3047075 of a metre) is common to practically all nations and periods, and has never varied much more than does the length of men's feet, from which the name was taken.

In prosody, the term denotes a division in verse which consists of a certain number of syllables (or pauses) one of which is stressed. Here the term, which comes from Greece, refers to beating time with the foot

At one's feet. "To cast oneself at someone's feet" is to be entirely submissive to him, to throw oneself on his mercy.

Best foot foremost Use all possible dispatch. To "set on foot" is to set going If you have various powers of motion, set your best foremost

> Nay, but make haste; the better foot before
> *King John*, iv, 2

Enter a house right foot foremost (*Petronius*). It is unlucky to enter a house or to leave one's chamber left foot foremost Augustus was very superstitious on this point. Pythagoras taught that it is necessary to put the shoe on the right foot first. Iamblichus tells us this symbolized that man's first duty is reverence to the gods.

First foot. *See* FIRST

How are your poor feet? An old street-cry said to have originated at the Great Exhibition of London in 1851 Tramping about the galleries broke down all but trained athletes.

I have not yet got my foot in. I am not yet familiar and easy with the work. The allusion is to the preliminary exercises in Roman foot-races. While the signal was waited for, the candidates made essays of jumping, running, and posturing, to excite a suitable warmth and make their limbs supple This was "getting their foot in" for the race *Cp.* HAND

To foot it. To walk the distance instead of riding it, also to dance.

> Lo how finely the graces can it foote to the Instrument
> They dauncen deftly, and singen soote in their meriment SPENSER *Shepherd's Calendar*, April

To foot the bill. To pay it, to promise to pay the account by signing one's name at the foot of the bill

To have one's foot on another's neck. To have him at your mercy, to tyrannize over, or domineer over him completely *See Josh* x, 24

To measure another's foot by your own last. To apply your personal standards to the conduct or actions of another; to judge people by yourself

To put one's foot down. To make a firm stand, to refuse or insist upon a thing firmly and finally.

To set a man on his feet. To start him off in business, etc, especially after he has "come a cropper."

To show the cloven foot. To betray an evil intention. The devil is represented with a cloven hoof.

To trample under foot. To oppress, or outrage, to treat with the greatest contempt and discourtesy.

With one foot in the grave. In a dying state.

You have put your foot in it nicely. You have got yourself into a pretty mess As the famous Irish bull has it, 'Every time I open my mouth I put my foot in it "

Footloose. Unfettered, a 17th-century expression. It survives to-day in the phrase 'footloose and fancy free "

He is on good footing with the world He stands well with the world

To pay your footing. To give money for drink when you first enter on a trade Entry money for being allowed to put your foot in the premises occupied by fellow-craftsmen *Cp.* GARNISH

Footmen. *See* RUNNING FOOTMEN

Footnotes. Notes placed at the bottom of a page.

Foot-pound. The unit of result in estimating work done by machinery Thus, if we take 1 lb as the unit of weight and 1 ft as the unit of distance, a foot-pound would be 1 lb weight raised 1 ft.

Football Association Cup *See* ASSOCIATION.

Footlights. To appear before the footlights. To appear on the stage, where a row of lights is placed in front along the floor to lighten it up.

Fop's Alley. An old name for a promenade in a theatre, especially the central passage between the stalls, right and left in the opera-house.

Forbidden Fruit, The. Figuratively, unlawful sexual indulgence According to Mohammedan tradition the forbidden fruit partaken of by Eve and Adam was the banyan or Indian fig *See* FIG LEAF.

Forcible Feeble. *See* FEEBLE.

Fore. A cry of warning used by golfers before driving.

To the fore. In the front rank, eminent.

To come to the fore To stand out prominently, to distinguish oneself, to stand forth.

Fore-and-aft. All over the ship, lengthwise, in opposition to "athwartships" or across the line of the keel.

Forecastle (usually printed—and pronounced —fo'c'sle) So called because anciently this part of a vessel was raised and protected like a castle, so that it could command the enemy's deck. Dana's *Seaman's Manual* defines it as.—

That part of the upper deck forward of the foremast. In merchant ships, the forward part of the vessel under the deck, where the sailors live.

Foreclose. To put an end to. A legal term, meaning to close before the time specified

When a mortgager has failed to pay a debt the mortgagee may bring an action to foreclose, and the court will then hold that if the mortgager does not redeem within a certain time the mortgagee shall become owner of the property

Forefather's Day. *See* PILGRIM FATHERS

Forehand In the 17th century forehanded meant provident, thrifty To-day it survives only in games, denoting a stroke in which the player takes a ball on his natural side—*i e* right side for a right-handed player, as opposed to *backhand*

Foreshortening This is a technical term in perspective drawing In a portrait, for example, an arm represented as pointing at full length towards the observer occupies less space than if it were shown as pointing to one side, yet the perspective must clearly indicate that the full length of the arm is the same.

He forbids the fore-shortenings, because they make the parts appear little —DRYDEN

Forestick. The faggot laid in the front of a log fire, which holds all the others in, its opposite is *backlog*

Foreign correspondent. A newspaper correspondent living in foreign parts, not a correspondent who is a foreigner Until *The Times* newspaper originated the system of sending specially equipped men to reside abroad and send news regularly, all foreign news was sent by casual and amateur correspondents whose own political views gave a distinctive colour to the news—or the presentation of it—they transmitted

Foreign Office. The department presided over by the Secretary of State for Foreign Affairs It was instituted in 1782, in place of the old Secretaryship for the Northern Department of Europe, as it had been called since 1688 The Foreign Secretary appoints, sends out, and supervises ambassadors, consuls and other diplomatic agents and keeps himself acquainted with affairs abroad; he represents the British government to foreign ambassadors, etc , who represent their governments in this country, and represents his Government abroad at important international conferences, etc The Foreign Secretary is assisted by a minister of state and three under-secretaries one of whom is the permanent under-secretary and executive of the Foreign Office

Forest City. Cleveland, Ohio

Forgeries. Broadly speaking, a forgery is an attempt to pass off as genuine some piece of spurious work or writing It is not always easy to distinguish a forgery and an imposture; strictly, perhaps, the Rowley poems are impostures rather than forgeries.

Billy and Charley Antiques. In 1857 two men known as Billy and Charley, living in Rosemary Lane, Tower Hill, began to make mediæval "antiquities" on a large scale These were mostly plaques and other objects of no

apparent use, cast in lead or an alloy of lead and copper known as cock-metal, and artificially aged by pitting with acids These objects bore strange and enigmatic devices, usually surrounded by a scroll bearing characters resembling letters, though wholly unintelligible A great number of simple folk and naive collectors were taken in, though the nature of these forgeries was so obvious, and they were full of such anachronisms that but little knowledge was needful to discern their nature The whole business was exposed at a meeting of the British Archæological Association in 1858.

The Ireland Forgeries One of the most famous of literary forgers was William Henry Ireland (1777-1835), the son of a bookseller and amateur antiquarian When only 17 young Ireland produced a number of seemingly ancient leases and other documents purporting to be in the handwriting of William Shakespeare, among them being a love-letter to Ann Hathaway, enclosing a lock of hair. Emboldened by the credulity with which his impostures were accepted, he next came out with two new "Shakespeare" plays—*Vortigern* and *Henry II* Ignoring the protests of Kemble, who was suspicious from the outset, Sheridan produced *Vortigern* at Drury Lane in 1796 During the rehearsals Mrs Siddons and Mrs Palmer resigned their roles and refused to be associated with so palpable a fraud On the opening night the theatre was packed with an audience that grew increasingly critical as the play went on, and when Kemble spoke in his part, "When this solemn mockery is o'er," the house yelled and hissed until the curtain fell—on the first and last performance of *Vortigern.* Meanwhile Malone and other critics had studied the *Miscellaneous Papers* said to be Shakespeare's and had declared them forgeries—eventually extorting a confession from Ireland late in that same year, 1796

The Rowley Poems. Certain poems written by Thomas Chatterton (1752-70), and said by him to have been the work of a 15th-century priest of Bristol named Thomas Rowley, who, in fact, was purely fictitious. Chatterton began to write them before he was 15, and after having been refused by Dodsley, they were published in 1769 Many prominent connoisseurs and litterateurs, including Horace Walpole, were hoaxed by them.

Fork. Old thieves' slang for a finger, hence to fork out, to produce and hand over, to pay up.

A forked cap. A bishop's mitre, so called by John Skelton (early 16th cent) It is cleft or forked

Fingers were made before forks. *See* FINGERS.

The forks. The gallows (Lat. *furca*). The word also meant a kind of yoke, with two arms stretching over the shoulders, to which the criminal's hands were tied. The punishment was of three degrees of severity (1) The *furca ignominiosa*, (2) the *furca pœnālis*, and (3) the *furca capitālis.* The first was for slight offences, and consisted in carrying the *furca* on the shoulders, more or less weighted. The second consisted in carrying the *furca* and being scourged The third was being scourged to death. The word *furcifer* meant what we call a gallows-bird or vile fellow

The Caudine Forks. *See* CAUDINE.

Forlorn Hope. This phrase is the Dutch *verloren hoop*, the lost squad or troop, and is due to a misunderstanding, as the words are not connected with our *forlorn* or *hope*. The French equivalent is *enfants perdus*, the lost ones. The *forlorn hope* was originally a picked body of men sent in front to begin an attack, thus Cromwell says, "Our *forlorn* of horse marched within a mile of the enemy," *i.e* our horse picket sent forward to reconnoitre approached within a mile of the enemy's camp It is now usually applied to a body of men specially selected for some desperate or very dangerous enterprise.

Form. Good or bad form is conformity—or otherwise—with the unwritten laws and conventionalities of society

We'll eat the dinner and have a dance together or we shall transgress all form —STEELE· *Tender Husband*, v. 1.

Forma pauperis (fŏr′ ma paw′ per is) (Lat , plea of poverty) *To sue in forma pauperis*. When a person has just cause of a suit, but is so poor that he cannot raise the money necessary to enter it, the judge will assign him lawyers and counsel without the usual fees.

Fortiter in re (fôrt′ i tĕr in rē) (Lat.) Firmness in doing what is to be done; an unflinching resolution to persevere to the end. *See* SUAVITER IN MODO.

Fortunatus (fôr tū nă′ tŭs) A hero of mediæval legend (from Eastern sources) who possessed an inexhaustible purse, a wishing cap, etc. He appears in a German *Volksbuch* of 1509, Hans Sachs dramatized the story in 1553, and at Christmas, 1599, Dekker's *Pleasant Comedy of Old Fortunatus* was played before Queen Elizabeth.

You have found Fortunatus's purse. Are in luck's way.

Fortune. Fortune favours the brave. The expression is found in Terence—*Fortes fortuna adjuvat* (*Phormio*, i, 4), also in Virgil—*Audentes fortuna juvat* (*Æn.* x, 284), and many other classic writers

Fortunate Islands. An ancient name for the Canary Islands; also, for any imaginary lands set in distant seas, like the "Islands of the Blest."

Their place of birth alone is mute
To sounds that echo farther west
Than your sire's Islands of the Blest
BYRON *The Isles of Greece* (*Don Juan*, iii).

Forty. A number of frequent occurrence in Scripture, and hence formerly treated as, in a manner, sacrosanct. Moses was forty days in the mount, Elijah was forty days fed by ravens, the rain of the flood fell forty days, and another forty days expired before Noah opened the window of the ark; forty days was the period of embalming; Nineveh had forty days to repent; Our Lord fasted forty days; He was seen forty days after His resurrection, etc.

St. Swithin betokens forty days' rain or dry weather; a quarantine extends to forty days, forty days, in the Old English law, was the limit for the payment of the fine for manslaughter, the privilege of sanctuary was for forty days; the widow was allowed to remain in her husband's house for forty days after his decease, a knight enjoined forty days' service of his tenant; a stranger, at the expiration of forty days, was compelled to be enrolled in some tithing; Members of Parliament were protected from arrest forty days after the prorogation of the House, and forty days before the House was convened, a new-made burgess had to forfeit forty pence unless he built a house within forty days, etc. etc.

Fool or physician at forty. *See* FOOL.

Forty stripes save one. The Jews were forbidden by the Mosaic law to inflict more than forty stripes on an offender, and for fear of breaking the law they stopped short of the number If the scourge contained three lashes, thirteen strokes would equal "forty save one."

The Thirty-nine Articles of the Anglican Church used sometimes to be called "the forty stripes save one" by theological students.

Forty winks. A short nap.

The Forty Immortals (or simply the Forty). The members of the French Academy, who number forty

The Hungry Forties. *See* HUNGRY.

The roaring forties. The Atlantic Ocean between 40° and 50° north latitude, well known for its rough and stormy character.

Forty-five, The. The name given to the rebellion of 1745 led by Charles Edward Stuart, the Young Pretender. On July 25th, accompanied by seven followers, he landed in Scotland and raised the banner of his father, "James III," the Old Pretender. A large army of clansmen gathered round him, he defeated Sir John Cope at Preston Pans (Sept 20th) and began his march down into England. On December 4th the Young Pretender reached Derby, but the massing forces of Wade and Cumberland obliged him to retreat to Scotland where, on April 16th, he was utterly defeated on Culloden Moor by the Duke of Cumberland.

"Number 45" is the celebrated number of Wilkes's *North Briton* (April 23rd, 1763), in which Cabinet Ministers were accused of putting a lie into the king's mouth.

Forty-niners. Prospectors for gold, who rushed to California following the discovery of gold there in 1848 Best remembered to-day, perhaps, in the song *Clementine*.

Forty-two Line Bible, The. *See* BIBLE, SPECIALLY NAMED.

Forwards, Marshal. Blücher (1742-1819) was called *Marschall Vorwärts*, from his constant exhortation to his soldiers in the campaigns preceding Waterloo. *Vorwärts!* always *Vorwärts!*

Fosse, The, or **Fosse-way.** One of the four principal highways made by the Romans in England. It leads from Axminster through Bath, Cirencester, Leicester, and Lincoln, and had a fosse or ditch on each side of it *Cp* ERMINE STREET.

Fossick. An old English verb used in Australia in the sense of "to search " In World War II it came widely into use in the British forces in an unfavourable sense—*to fossick around* was to move about aimlessly

Fou. Scots expression for drunk. It is a variant of *full*

> The clachan yill had made me canty
> I was na fou, but just had plenty
> BURNS *Death and Dr Hornbook.*

Foul-weather Jack Admiral John Byron (1723-86), said to have been as notorious for foul weather as Queen Victoria was for fine

Fount of type. *See* FONT; LETTER, TYPE

Fountain pen. This apparently modern invention is really of considerable antiquity In the anonymous "Diary of a Journey to Paris in 1657-58" under date July 11th, 1657 there is reference to a man who "makes pens of silver in which he puts ink, which does not get dry, and without having to take any, one can write a half-quire of paper at a sitting " In 1721 there is an advertisement in a Welsh almanac, ' Inkhorns. Fountain pens, the best sort of Holman's ink powder, and red and black led pencils "

Fountain of Youth. In popular folk-tales, a fountain supposed to possess the power of restoring youth Expeditions were fitted out in search of it, and at one time it was supposed to be in one of the Bahama Islands.

Four. Four Freedoms. Franklin Roosevelt, during World War II, declared as one of the aims of the democratic nations that when the war was over all the peoples of earth might live in freedom from fear, and from want, and with freedom of speech and of worship

The History of the Four Kings (Livre des Quatre Rois). A pack of cards In a French pack the four kings are Charlemagne, David, Alexander, and Cæsar.

Four Letters, The *See* TETRAGRAMMATON.

The Annals of the Four Masters is the name usually given to a collection of old Irish chronicles published in 1632-36 as Annals of the Kingdom of Ireland. The Four Masters (authors or compilers) were Michael O'Clery (1575-1643), Conaire his brother, his cousin Cucoigcriche O'Clery (d 1664), with Fearfeasa O'Mulconry

Four Sons of Aymon. *See* AYMON.

Fourth dimension. The three dimensions of space universally recognized are length, breadth, and height, three in number because we can draw three lines, but no more, all at right angles to one another A piece of line has only one dimension—length, a region of a surface has two—length and breadth, a solid body in space has three After the mathematician has applied Algebra to Geometry he can increase the number of his variables without altering the character of his equations, and retaining for convenience his geometrical vocabulary he constructs what he calls an algebraic geometry of as many dimensions as

he pleases A four-dimensional body may be thought of as bearing the same relation to one in the three-dimensional space which we perceive as volume does to area, or area to length The measurement of time introduces a fourth variable into everyday life; but to say that for that reason time *is* the fourth dimension of space, and is somehow at right angles to every line that we can draw is a confusion of language It is safe to say that in mathematical operations time is sometimes found to be behaving very like a fourth spatial dimension

Fourth Estate of the Realm. The daily Press The most powerful of all, the others (*see* ESTATES) being the Lords Spiritual, the Lords Temporal, and the Commons Burke, referring to the Reporters' Gallery, is credited with having said, "Yonder sits the Fourth Estate, more important than them all," but it does not appear in his published works

Fourth of July. *See* INDEPENDENCE DAY

Fourierism. A communistic system, so called from François Marie Charles Fourier (1772-1837), of Besançon Population was to be grouped into "phalansteries," consisting each of 400 families or 1,800 individuals, who were to live in a common edifice, furnished with workshops, studios, and all sources of amusement The several groups were at the same time to be associated together under a unitary government like the cantons of Switzerland or the United States Only one language was to be admitted, all profits were to go to the common purse, talent and industry were to be rewarded, and no one was to be suffered to remain indigent, or without the enjoyment of certain luxuries and public amusement

Fourteen, in its connexion with Henri IV and Louis XIV, The following are curious and strange coincidences —

HENRI IV·

14 letters in the name Henri-de-Bourbon He was the 14th king of France and Navarre on the extinction of the family of Navarre He was born on Dec 14, 1553, the sum of which year amounts to 14, he was assassinated on May 14, 1610, and lived 4 times 14 years, 14 weeks, and 4 times 14 days

14 May, 1552, was born Marguerite de Valois his first wife

14 May, 1588, the Parisians rose in revolt against him because he was a "heretic "

14 March, 1590, he won the great battle of Ivry

14 May, 1590, was organized a grand ecclesiastical and military demonstration against him, which drove him from the faubourgs of Paris

14 Nov , 1590, the Sixteen took an oath to die rather than submit to a "heretic" king

It was Gregory XIV who issued a Bull excluding Henri from the throne

14 Nov , 1592, the Paris parlement registered the papal Bull

14 Dec , 1599, the Duke of Savoy was reconciled to Henri IV

14 Sept , 1606, was baptized the dauphin (afterwards Louis XIII) son of Henri IV

14 May, 1610, Henry was assassinated by Ravaillac

LOUIS XIV

14th of the name He mounted the throne 1643, the sum of which figures equals 14 He died 1715, the sum of which figures also equals 14 He reigned 77 years, the sum of which two figures equals 14 He was born 1638, died 1715, which added together equals 3353, the sum of which figure comes to 14.

Fourteen Hundred. The cry raised on the Stock Exchange to give notice that a stranger has entered the "House " The term is said to have been in use in Defoe's time, and to have originated at a time when for a considerable period the number of members had remained stationary at 1399

Fourteen Points Conditions laid down by President Woodrow Wilson (1856-1924) as those on which the Allies were prepared to make peace with Germany He outlined them in a speech to Congress on January 11th, 1918, and at the end of the war they were accepted as the basis for the peace. They included the evacuation by Germany of all allied territory, the restoration of Poland, freedom of the seas, reduction of armaments, and open diplomacy.

Fowler, The. Henry I (876-936), son of Otto, Duke of Saxony, and King of Germany from 919 to 936, was, according to an 11th century tradition, so called because when the deputies announced to him his election to the throne, they found him fowling with a hawk on his fist.

Fox. As a name for the Old English broadsword *fox* probably refers to a maker's mark of a dog, wolf, or fox The swords were manufactured by Julian del Rei of Toledo, whose trade-mark was a little dog, mistaken for a fox.

> O signieur Dew, thou diest on point of fox,
> Except, O signieur, thou do give to me
> Egregious ransom —*Henry V*, iv, 4

> I had a sword, ay, the flower of Smithfield for a sword, a right fox i' faith —PORTER *Two Angry Women of Abington* (1599)

To fox. To steal or cheat; keep an eye on somebody without seeming so to do. A dog, a fox, and a weasel sleep, as they say, "with one eye open "

Foxed A print or page of a book stained with reddish brown marks is said to be "foxed," because of its colour

Foxed was also an expression widely used in military parlance during World War II for "bewildered "

Fox-hole A small slit trench for one or more men

A fox's sleep A sleep with one eye Assumed indifference to what is going on *See above*

A wise fox will never rob his neighbour's hen-roost It would soon be found out, so he goes farther from home where he is not known

Every fox must pay his skin to the furrier. The crafty shall be taken in their own wiliness.

I gave him a flap with a fox-tail I cajoled him, made a fool of him The fox-tail was one of the badges of the motley, and to flap with a fox-tail is to treat one like a fool.

Reynard the Fox. *See* REYNARD

The fox and the grapes. "It's a case of the fox and the grapes" is said of one who wants something badly but cannot obtain it, and so tries to create the impression that he doesn't want it at all The allusion is to one of Æsop's fables. *See* GRAPES.

The Old Fox. Marshal Soult (1769-1851) was so nicknamed, from his strategic talents and fertility of resources

To set a fox to keep the geese (Lat *Ovem lupo committere*). Said of one who entrusts his money to sharpers

Fox-fire. The phosphoric light, without heat, which plays round decaying matter. It is the Fr. *faux*, or "false fire," and was first found in 1485.

Foxglove. The flower is named from the animal and the glove The reason for the second half is obvious from the finger-stall appearance of the flower, but it is not known how the fox came to be associated with it It belongs to the botanical genus *Digitalis*, or finger-shaped The leaves of this genus contain several powerful principles which are highly valuable in the treatment of heart disease

Fox-trot. A modern ball-room dance It was introduced from America in the first half of the 20th century A horse's *fox-trot* is the short steps it takes when changing from a trot to a walk

Fra Diavolo (fra dē av' ō lō) Auber's opera of this name (1830) is founded on the exploits of Michele Pozza (1760-1806), a celebrated brigand and renegade monk, who evaded pursuit for many years amidst the mountains of Calabria.

France. *See* FRANK

Francesca da Rimini (från ches' kä da rim' i ni). Daughter of Guido da Polenta, Lord of Ravenna Her story is told in Dante's *Inferno* (canto v). She was married to Giovanni Malatesta, Lord of Rimini, but her guilty love for his younger brother, Paolo, was discovered, and both were put to death by him about 1289 Stephen Phillips has a play (1900), and Silvio Pellico a tragedy, on the subject.

Franche Comté. Territory in upper Burgundy, which was made a county in 915 by Hugh the Black. It got its name of the *free county* by being taken from Reynaud III (1127-48) and later restored to him

Franciscans (från sis' känz) The friars minor founded by St. Francis of Assisi in 1209 They form one Order of Friars Minor, divided into three distinct and independent branches, of which one is known simply as Friars Minor, another as Friars Minor Conventual and the third as Friars Minor Capuchin. The Order had 64 houses in England at the time of the Reformation, being known as Grey Friars, from the indeterminate colour of their habit, which is now brown The Friars Minor observe the unmitigated rule of St Francis, with its insistence on poverty, abstinence, and preaching, Friars Minor Conventual have a modified rule with regard to the holding of property, and wear a black tunic with a white cord The Capuchins, initiated in 1525, have the strictest rules of any, subsisting largely on the begging of the lay brothers The Recollects, or Cordeliers, and Observants were formerly divisions of the Order, and were amalgamated with the Friars Minor by Leo XIII in 1897

The *Order of Franciscan Nuns* was founded in 1212 by St Clare, they are hence known as the *Clares* or *Poor Clares*, also *Minoresses* Various reformations have taken place in the

Order, giving rise to the *Colettines, Grey Sisters, Capuchin Nuns, Sisters of the Annunciation, Conceptionists,* and the *Urbanists,* the last named observing a modified rule and being permitted to hold property.

Frangipane, frangipani (frăn' ji păn, frăn ji pa' nĭ) The name is supposed to come from the Marquis Frangipani, a soldier under Louis XIV. It is applied to a kind of pastry cake filled with cream, almonds, and sugar, also to a perfume made from, or imitating the smell of, the flower of a West Indian tree *Plumeria rubra,* or red jasmine.

Frangipani pudding. Pudding made of broken bread (Lat. *frangere,* to break, *panis,* bread)

Frank. One belonging to the Teutonic nations that conquered Gaul in the 6th century (whence the name *France*) By the Turks, Arabs, etc , of the Levant the name is given to any of the inhabitants of the western parts of Europe, as the English, Germans, Spaniards, French, etc.

Frankalmoin, frankalmoigne (frăngk' al moin) is an old legal term composed of *frank,* free, and *almoin,* an alms-chest, or alms The term was applied to land held by religious bodies in perpetuity free of all encumbrances or dues on condition that the religious and their successors prayed for the soul of the donor

Frankelin's Tale (*Chaucer*) *See* DORIGEN.

Frankenstein (frăng kĕn stīn). The young student in Mary Wollstonecraft Shelley's romance of that name (1818) He made a soulless monster out of corpses from churchyards and dissecting-rooms, and endued it with life by galvanism The tale shows how the creature longed for sympathy, but was shunned by everyone and became the instrument of dreadful retribution on the student who usurped the prerogative of the Creator.

Frankfurter. A small smoked sausage of beef and pork, somewhat akin to the saveloy

Frankincense (frăngk' in sens) The literal meaning of this is pure, or true incense It is a fragrant gum exuded from several trees of the genus *Boswellia,* abundant on the Somali coast and in South Arabia. The ceremonial use of frankincense was practised by the Egyptians, Persians, Babylonians, Hebrews, Greeks, and Romans, and the gum is an ingredient of modern incense used liturgically

Frank-pledge. The system by which, in Anglo-Saxon times, the freemen in a tithing were pledged for each other's good behaviour Hallam says every ten men in a village were answerable for each other, and if one of them committed an offence the other nine were bound to make reparation, or to see that it was made

Frater (frā' ter) The refectory or dining-room of a monastery, where the brothers (Lat *fratres*) met together for meals Also called the *fratry.*

In old vagabonds' slang a *frater* was much the same as an Abram-man (*q v*).

A Frater goeth wyth a Licence to beg for some Spittlehouse or Hospital Their pray is comonly upon poore women as they go and come to the markets — AWDELEY: *Fraternity of Vacabondes* (1575).

Frateretto (frăt' ĕr et' ō) A fiend mentioned by Edgar in *King Lear,* this is another of the names that Shakespeare obtained from Harsnet's *Declaration See* FLIBBERTIGIBBET

Frateretto calls me, and tells me Nero is an angler in the lake of darkness Pray, innocent, and beware of the foul fiend.—*King Lear* iii, 6

Fraternization in war-time parlance means soldiers occupying an enemy country holding communication with the civil inhabitants

Fraticelli (frăt i chel' ē) (*Little Brethren*) A sect of renegade and licentious monks which appeared about the close of the 13th century and threw off all subjection to the Pope, whom they denounced as an apostate They had wholly disappeared by the 15th century

Frazzle (U S A) A frayed edge, hence worn to a frazzle, reduced to a state of nerviness.

Frea *See* FREYJA

Free **A free and easy.** A social gathering where persons meet together without formality to chat and smoke In a free and easy way, with an entire absence of ceremony

A free fight. A fight in which all engage, rules being disregarded

Free on board. Said of goods delivered on board ship, or into the conveyance, at the seller's expense, generally contracted to F O B

I'm free to confess. There's nothing to prevent me admitting . .

To have a free hand *See* HAND

To make free with. To take liberties with, to treat whatever it is as one's own.

Free Bench (*francus bancus*). A legal term denoting a widow's right to a copyhold in certain English manors It is not a dower or gift but a free right independent of the will of the husband Called *bench* because, upon acceding to the estate, she becomes a tenant of the manor, and entitled to sit on the *bench* at manorial courts

Free coup (in Scotland) means a piece of waste land where rubbish may be deposited free of charge, also the right of doing so

Free French. *See* FIGHTING FRENCH.

Free lance. *See* LANCE

Free Trade. The system by which goods are allowed to enter one country from another country without paying customs duty for the protection of home producers For many years it was held that the prosperity of Britain depended upon leaving the ports open to the shipping and goods of all the world In 1932 Great Britain abandoned Free Trade by imposing a general tariff on imported goods.

The Apostle of Free Trade Richard Cobden (1804-65), who established the Anti-Corn Law League in 1838

Freebooter. A pirate, an adventurer who makes his living by plundering, literally, one who obtains his booty free (Dut. *vrij,* free, *buit,* booty).

Freehold. An estate held in fee-simple or fee-tail, one on which no duty or service is owing to any lord but the sovereign. *Cp* COPYHOLD.

Freeman, Mrs. The name assumed by the Duchess of Marlborough in her correspondence with Queen Anne The queen called herself Mrs Morley.

Freeman of Bucks. A cuckold. The allusion is to the buck's horn *See* Horns.

Freemasonry. In its curious and characteristic ritual Freemasonry traces its origins to the building of Solomon's Temple Without accepting or rejecting this theory, however, it can be taken as a fact that it has existed for many centuries as a secret society In mediæval days operative, *i e* actual stone-masons, banded together with secret pass-words, signs and tests, and Masonic students find material for research in the marks engraved on fashioned stones in cathedrals and certain ancient buildings Freemasonry as we know it was already flourishing in the 17th century, and although Sir Christopher Wren's association with the Craft has not been established, it is likely Elias Ashmole describes his own initiation in 1682 The mother Grand Lodge of England was founded in London in 1717 and took under its aegis the many small lodges that were working up and down the country Even the extremely ancient York lodge, which has given its name to most of the Masonic rites of the Continent and U S A , acknowledged its authority. From this first Grand Lodge of England derive all Masonic lodges of whatever kind throughout the world.

In Britain Masonry has three degrees, the first is called Entered Apprentice, the second, Fellow Craft the third, Master Mason. Royal Arch masonry is an adjunct to these, and is peculiar to Britain Mark Masonry is a comparatively modern addition to the fraternity In the U S A the first regular lodge was founded at Boston in 1733, though there are minutes extant of a lodge in Philadelphia in 1730 The ritual side of Freemasonry has appealed to American more than it has to British masons, and many degrees are worked in U S A with elaborate ritual and mysteries In addition to the three degrees of British masonry there are the Cryptic Degrees of Royal and Select Masters, the Chivalric Rite, with three degrees of Knights Red Cross, Temple and of Malta; and the 33 degrees of the Ancient and Accepted Scottish Rite. The various Grand Orients of the Continent (all disowned by the Grand Lodge of England on account of their political activities) were founded at different times and work modifications of the Scottish Rite The part played by masonic lodges in the French Revolution is still obscure; Philippe Egalite was head of the Grand Orient but repudiated it during the Terror Napoleon was reported to have been initiated at Malta in 1798, he certainly favoured masonry and during the Empire Cambacerès, Murat, and Joseph Bonaparte were successive Grand Masters Freemasonry has been condemned by the Holy See not only for being a secret society but for its alleged subversive aims—aims that may be cherished by Continental Masons but which are quite unknown to their British and American brethren.

The Lady Freemason. Women are not admitted into freemasonry, but the story goes
B.D —13

that a lady was initiated in the early 18th century She was the Hon Elizabeth St Leger, daughter of Lord Doneraile, who hid herself in an empty clock-case when the lodge was held in her father's house, and witnessed the proceedings She was discovered, and compelled to submit to initiation as a member of the craft

Freezing-point. The temperature at which a liquid becomes solid if mentioned without qualification, 32° Fahrenheit (0° Centigrade), the freezing-point of water is meant For other liquids the name is added as the freezing-point of milk, sulphuric ether, quicksilver, and so on. In Centigrade and Réaumur's instruments zero marks the freezing-point The zero of Fahrenheit's thermometer is 32° below the freezing-point of water, being the lowest temperature observed by him in the winter of 1709

Freischutz (frī' shutz) (the free-shooter). A legendary German archer in league with the devil, who gave him seven balls, six of which were to hit infallibly whatever the marksman aimed at, and the seventh was to be directed as the devil wished F Kind wrote the libretto, and Weber set to music, the opera based on the legend, called *Der Freischutz* (1820).

French French Cream Brandy, from the custom (which came from France) of taking a cup of coffee with brandy in it instead of cream after dinner

To take French leave To take without asking leave or giving any equivalent, also, to leave a party, house, or neighbourhood without bidding good-bye to anyone; to slip away unnoticed. This kind of backhanded compliment to our neighbours used to be very common (*cp.* "French gout" for venereal disease), and many objectionable things or practices have been called "French."

It is only fair to say that the French have returned the compliment in many ways. The equivalent of "to take French leave" is *S'en aller* (or *filer*) *à l'anglaise*, in the 16th century a creditor used to be called *un Anglais*, a term used by Clement Marot.

French of Stratford at Bow. This has been taken to mean French as spoken by an Englishman, and a Cockney at that, but it has no such ironical connotation. Stratford and Bromley were fashionable suburbs in those days, and at Bromley was the convent of St Leonard's where the daughters of well-to-do citizens and others were taught French by the nuns French was a common acquirement of the time and freely used at Court and in society; but it was a somewhat archaic French, descending from Norman days, and not such as was current in Paris.

> And French, she [the nun] spak ful faire and fetisly,
> After the scole of Stratford atte Bowe,
> For Frensh of Paris was to hir unknowe.
> Chaucer *Canterbury Tales, Prologue,* 124

Frenchman. Nicknames of a Frenchman are "Crapaud" (*q v*), "Jean," "Mossoo," "Robert Macaire" (*q v.*); but of a Parisian "Grenouille" (*frog*).

French Canadian, "Jean Baptiste "

French peasantry, "Jacques Bonhomme."

Done like a Frenchman, turn and turn again (1 *Henry VI*, iii, 4) The French were frequently ridiculed as a fickle, wavering nation Dr Johnson says he once read a treatise the object of which was to show that a weathercock is a satire on the word *Gallus* (a Gaul or cock)

Fresco (fres' kō) A method of painting upon fresh mortar The plaster must be fresh to absorb the colour, and since it dries rapidly, the artist must work with great dexterity and speed The wall must be free of saltpetre, and only such colours can be used as are not affected by lime—many brilliant greens, reds and yellow being thus ruled out. Frescoes should not be confused with wall paintings such as Leonardo's famous Last Supper at Santa Maria delle Grazie, Milan

Freshman An undergraduate of a university in his first term

Freyja (frā' ya). In Scandinavian mythology the sister of Freyr and wife of Odin, who deserted her because she loved finery better than her husband She is the fairest of the goddesses, goddess of love and also of the dead She presides over marriages, and, besides being the Venus, may be called the Juno of Asgard She is also known as *Frea, Frya, Frigg, Frige*, etc , and it is from her that our *Friday* is named.

Friar (Lat *frater*, a brother) A religious, especially one belonging to one of the four great orders, i e Franciscans, Dominicans, Augustinians, and Carmelites *See these names*

In printer's slang a *friar* is a part of the sheet which has failed to receive the ink properly, and is therefore paler than the rest As Caxton set up his press in Westminster Abbey, it is but natural that monks and friars should give foundation to some of the printer's slang. *Cp.* MONK.

Curtal Friar. *See* CURTAL

Friar Bungay (bŭng' gā) A famous necromancer of the 15th century, whose story is much overlaid with legend It is said that he "raised mists and vapours which befriended Edward IV at the battle of Barnet " In the old prose romance *The Famous History of Friar Bacon*, and in Greene's *Honourable History of Friar Bacon and Friar Bungay* (acted 1591), he appears as the assistant to Roger Bacon (d 1292).

Friar John. A prominent character in Rabelais's *Gargantua and Pantagruel*, a tall, lean, wide-mouthed, long-nosed friar of Seville

In the original he is called "Friar John *des Entommeures*": Urquhart mistakenly translated this as "of the Funnels"; "of the Trenchermen" is the best equivalent (*entamer*, to broach, to carve, with reference to a hearty appetite) *Entonnoirs* are "funnels", and as this word has been used as slang for the throat perhaps that accounts for the mistake.

Friar Rush. A legendary house-spirit who originated as a kind of ultra-mischievous and evil-dispositioned Robin Goodfellow in mediæval German folk-tales. A prose *History of Friar Rush* appeared in English as early as

1568, and in 1601 Henslowe records a comedy (now lost), *Friar Rush and the Proud Woman of Antwerp*, by Day and Houghton

Friar Tuck. Chaplain and steward of Robin Hood

In this our spacious isle I think there is not one
But he hath heard some talk of Hood and Little John,
Of Tuck, the merry friar, which many a sermon made
In praise of Robin Hood, his outlaws, and their trade
  DRAYTON *Polyolbion*, xxvi, 311-16.

Friar's Heel. The outstanding upright stone at Stonehenge, formerly supposed by some to stand in the central axis of the avenue, is so called Geoffrey of Monmouth says the devil bought the stones of an old woman in Ireland, wrapped them up in a wyth, and brought them to Salisbury Plain Just before he got to Mount Ambre the wyth broke, and one of the stones fell into the Avon, the rest were carried to the plain After the fiend had fixed them in the ground, he cried out, "No man will ever find out how these stones came here." A friar replied, "That's more than thou canst tell," whereupon the foul fiend threw one of the stones at him and struck him on the heel The stone stuck in the ground and remains so to the present hour

Friar's Lanthorn. One of the many names given to the Will o' the Wisp,

Friars Major (*Fratres majores*). The Dominicans

Friars Minor (*Fratres minores*) The Franciscans

Friar's Tale In the *Canterbury Tales* a tale throwing discredit on Summoners Chaucer obtained it from the Latin collection, *Promptuarium Exemplorum.*

Friday The sixth day of the week was the *dies Veneris* in ancient Rome, i e the day dedicated to Venus. The northern nations adopted the Roman system of nomenclature, and the sixth day was dedicated to their nearest equivalent to Venus, who was Frigg or Freyja (*q v*), hence the name *Friday* (A S *frige-dæg*) In France the Latin name was kept, and Friday is *Vendredi*.

Friday was regarded by the Norsemen as the luckiest day of the week among Christians generally it has been regarded as the unluckiest, because it was the day of Our Lord's crucifixion, and is a fast-day in the Catholic Church Mohammedans (among whom Friday is the Sabbath) say that Adam was created on a Friday, and legend has it that it was on a Friday that Adam and Eve ate the forbidden fruit, and on a Friday that they died Among the Buddhists and Brahmins it is also held to be unlucky, and the old Romans called it *nefastus* from the utter overthrow of their army at Gallia Narbonensis. In England the proverb is that "a Friday moon brings foul weather," but it is not, apparently, unlucky to be born on this day, for, according to the old rhyme, "Friday's child is loving and giving "

Black Friday. *See* BLACK.

Good Friday. *See* GOOD.

He who laughs on Friday will weep on Sunday. Sorrow follows in the wake of joy The line is taken from Racine's comedy, *Les Plaideurs.*

Long Friday. Good Friday was so called by the Saxons, probably because of the long fasts and offices used on that day.

Man Friday. The young savage found by Robinson Crusoe on a Friday, and kept as his servant and companion on the desert island, hence, a faithful and willing attendant, ready to turn his hand to anything

Never cut your nails on a Friday. "Cut them on Friday you cut them for sorrow" *See* NAIL-PARING.

Friend. A Quaker (*q v*), *i e* a member of the Society of Friends, also, one's second in a duel, as "Captain B acted as his friend." In the law courts counsel refer to each other as "my learned friend," though they may be entire strangers, just as in the House of Commons one member speaks of another as "my honourable friend."

A friend at court. Properly, a friend in a court of law who watches the trial and tells the judge if he can discover an error (*see* AMICUS CURIÆ) The term is generally applied to a friend who is in a position to help one by influencing those in power

A friend in need is a friend indeed. The Latin saying (from Ennius) is, *Amicus certus in re incerta cernitur*, a sure friend is made known when (one is) in difficulty.

A friendly suit, or action. An action at law brought, not with the object of obtaining a conviction or damages, but to discover the law on some debatable point, to get a legal and authoritative decision putting some fact on record

Better kinde frend than fremd kinde. This is the motto of the Waterton family, and it means "better kind friend (*i e* neighbour) than a kinsman who dwells in foreign parts" (*cp Prov* xxvii, 10, "Better is a neighbour that is near, than a brother far off") *Fremd* is an Old English word (from Old Teutonic) meaning foreign, strange, outlandish.

The Friend of Man. The name given to the Marquis de Mirabeau (1715-89), father of Mirabeau, the French revolutionary orator. His great work was *L'Ami des Hommes*, hence the nickname.

The soldier's friend. An official appointed by the authorities at the various pension boards to assist soldiers in making out and presenting their claims to pensions, etc.

Friendship. The classical examples of lasting friendship between man and man are Achilles and Patroclus, Pylades and Orestes, Damon and Pythias, and Nisus and Euryalus *See these names* To these should be added David and Jonathan

Frigg, or **Frigga.** *See* FREYJA

Frills. "Airs and graces"; as, **to put on frills,** to give oneself airs.

Fringe. The fringes on the garments of the Jewish priests were accounted sacred, and were touched by the common people as a charm Hence the desire of the woman who had the issue of blood to touch the fringe of Our Lord's garment (*Matt.* ix, 20-22)

Frippery. Rubbish of a tawdry character; worthless finery, foolish levity A *friperer* or *fripperer* was one who dealt in old clothes (*cp.* Fr. *friperie*, old clothes, cast-off furniture, etc.).

> Old clothes, cast dresses, tattered rags,
> Whose works are e'en the frippery of wit
> BEN JONSON *Epig* I, lvi

Also, a shop where odds and ends, old clothes, and so on are dealt in. Hence Shakespeare's —

> We know what belongs to a frippery
> *Tempest*, iv, 1

Frith. By frith and fell. By wold and wild, wood and common. *Frith* means ground covered with scrub or underwood, *fell* is a common

Frithiof (frit' yof) A hero of Icelandic myth who married Ingeborg, daughter of a petty king of Norway, and widow of Hring, to whose dominions he succeeded His adventures are recorded in the saga which bears his name. and which was written about the close of the 13th century The name signifies "the peace-maker."

Fritz Frederick the Great of Prussia (1712, 1740-86) was known as *Old Fritz.* In World War I the men in the trenches commonly hailed any prisoner or German in the enemy lines as *Fritz*

Froebel (frer' bël) The name given to a system of teaching young children devised by F W A. Froebel (1782-1852), a German schoolmaster The main part of his system has been put into practice in kindergartens where children's senses are developed by means of clay-modelling, work with colour-brushes, mat-plaiting, etc , as well as the care of animals, flowers, and suchlike

Frog A frog and mouse agreed to settle by single combat their claims to a marsh, but, while they fought, a kite carried them both off (*Æsop: Fables*, clxvii)

> Old Æsop's fable, where he told
> What fate unto the mouse and frog befel
> CARY *Dante*, cxxiii.

In Ovid's *Metamorphoses* (vi, 4) we are told that the Lycian shepherds were changed into frogs for mocking Latona.

> As when those hinds that were transformed to frogs
> Railed at Latona's twin-born progeny.
> MILTON *Sonnet*, vii.

Frenchmen, properly *Parisians*, have been nicknamed Frogs or Froggies (*grenouilles*) from their ancient heraldic device (*see* FLEUR-DE-LIS), which was three frogs or three toads. *Qu'en disent les grenouilles?*—What do the frogs (people of Paris) say?—was in 1791 a common court phrase at Versailles There was a point in the pleasantry when Paris was a quagmire, called *Lutetia* (mud-land) *See* CRAPAUD Further point is given to the nickname by the fact that the back legs of the edible frog (*Rana esculanta*) form a delicacy in French cuisine that awakened much contemptuous humour in the less exquisite English.

Frogmen. In World War II strong swimmers dressed in rubber suits with paddles on their feet resembling frogs legs, who entered enemy harbours by night and attached explosives to shipping and installations Since the war they have sometimes been used in salvage operations.

Frog's march. Carrying an obstreperous prisoner, face downwards, by his four limbs

It may be fun to you, but it is death to the frogs. A caution, telling one that one's sport should not be at the expense of other people's happiness. The allusion is to Æsop's fable of a boy stoning frogs for his amusement.

Nic Frog The Dutchman in Arbuthnot's *History of John Bull* (1712) Frogs are called "Dutch nightingales"

A frog in the throat. A temporary loss of voice

Fronde (frond) A political party during the ministry of Cardinal Mazarin, in the minority of Louis XIV (1648-53). Its members, who were opposed to the court party, were called *Frondeurs* from *fronde*, a sling, they being likened to boys who sling stones about the streets and scamper away the moment anyone in authority approaches

Frost Saints. *See* ICE SAINTS.

Frozen Words. Everyone knows the incident of the "frozen horn" related by Munchausen, also how Pantagruel and his friends, on the confines of the Frozen Sea, heard the uproar of a battle, which had been frozen the preceding winter, released by a thaw (Rabelais Bk. IV, ch 56) The joke appears to have been well known to the ancient Greeks, for Antiphanes applies it to the discourses of Plato "As the cold of certain cities is so intense that it freezes the very words we utter, which remain congealed till the heat of summer thaws them, so the mind of youth is so thoughtless that the wisdom of Plato lies there frozen, as it were, till it is thawed by the ripened judgment of mature age" (Plutarch's *Morals*)

> Truth in person doth appear
> Like words congealed in northern air
>   BUTLER   *Hudibras*, Pt 1, 1, lines 147-8.

Frying-pan. Out of the frying-pan into the fire. In trying to extricate yourself from one evil, you fall into a greater The Greeks used to say, "Out of the smoke into the flame", and the French say, *"Tomber de la poêle dans la braise."*

Frying-pan brand. An Australian term of the mid-19th century to describe the large brand superimposed by cattle thieves to blot out the rightful owner's brand

Fub. To hoax, impose upon, swindle "You are trying to fub me off with a cock-and-bull story" Connected with Ger *foppen*, to hoax. *Fob* is another form of the same word.

Fuchsia (fū' shä) A genus of highly ornamental shrubs coming from Mexico and the Andes, though two species are found in New Zealand They were so named in 1703, in honour of the German botanist Leonhard Fuchs (1501-66) The best-known varieties in this country are derived from the Chilian species *Fuchsia macrostemma*.

Fudge. A word of contempt bestowed on one who says what is absurd or untrue A favourite expression of Mr. Burchell in the *Vicar of Wakefield*

A sort of soft candy is known as *fudge*.

Fudge-box. An attachment on newspaper printing machines to allow of late news being added on the machine while running This news appears in the "Stop-press" column, which is, consequently, called the *fudge-box* In this sense the word is another form of *fadge* (*q v*)

Fuel. Adding fuel to fire. Saying or doing something to increase the anger of a person already angry.

Fugger (fug' er) A noted family of German merchant-bankers, famous in the 15th and 16th centuries and proverbial for their great wealth, their news-letter, and fine library "Rich as a Fugger" is common in Elizabethan dramatists Charles V introduced some of the family into Spain, where they superintended the mines

I am neither an Indian merchant, nor yet a Fugger, but a poor boy like yourself —*Guzman de Alfarache* (1599)

Fugleman. Originally a leader of a wing (Ger. *flugel*, wing) or file, now applied to a soldier who stands in front of men at drill to show them what to do.

Fuhrer (fū' rer) The title, meaning in German "leader," assumed by Adolf Hitler when he acceded to the supreme power in Germany on the death of Hindenburg in 1934

Fulhams, or Fullams. An Elizabethan name for loaded dice. Dice made with a cavity were called gourds, those made to throw the high numbers were high fullams or gourds, and those made to throw the low numbers were low fullams or gourds

> For gourd and fullam holds
> And "high" and "low" beguile the rich and poor
>   *Merry Wives of Windsor*, 1, 3
> Have their fulhams at command,
> Brought up to do their feats at hand
>   BUTLER   *Upon Gaming*

The name was probably from Fulham, which was notorious as the resort of crooks and rogues of every description

Full. Full dress. The dress worn on occasions of ceremony; court dress, uniform, academicals, evening dress, etc , as the case may be A full-dress debate is one for which preparation and arrangements have been made, as opposed to one arising casually

Full house. A term in the game of poker for a hand holding three of one kind and two of another, *e g* 3 tens and 2 sixes

Full moon, or the full of the moon. The period when the whole disk of the moon is illuminated and it presents a perfect orb to the earth

Full of beans. *See* BEAN

Full up. Quite full, occupied to its utmost capacity Said also of one who is drunk. *Cp* FOU.

In full cry. Said of hounds that have caught the scent, and give tongue in chorus, hence, hurrying in full pursuit.

In full fig. *See* FIG

In full swing Fully at work; very busy, in full operation

Fum, or Fung-hwang. The phœnix (*q v*) of Chinese legend, one of the four symbolical animals presiding over the destinies of China

It originated from fire, was born in the Hill of the Sun's Halo, and has its body inscribed with the five cardinal virtues. It is this curious creature that is embroidered on the dresses of certain mandarins

Fum. *See* GEORGE, ST

Fumage. Another name for Hearth-money or Chimney-money (*q v*) (Lat. *fumus*, smoke)

Fume In a fume. In ill temper, especially from impatience.

Fun. To make fun of. To make a butt of, to ridicule, to play pranks on one

Like fun. Thoroughly, energetically, with delight

On'y look at the dimmercrats, see what they've done, Jest simply by stickin' together like fun
LOWELL *Biglow Papers* (First series, iv, st 5)

Fund. The Funds, or The Public Funds. Money lent at interest to Government on Government security.

The sinking fund. Money set aside by the Government for paying off a part of the national debt This money is "sunk," or withdrawn from circulation, for the bonds purchased by it are destroyed

To be out of funds, out of money

Fundamentalism. A religious movement that arose in U S A about 1919. It opposed all theories of evolution and anthropology, teaching that God transcends all the laws of nature, and that He manifests Himself by exceptional and extraordinary activities Belief in the literal meaning of the Scriptures is an essential tenet In 1925 a professor of science was convicted of violating the State laws of Tennessee by teaching evolution, and this incident aroused interest and controversy far beyond the religious circles of U S A The Fundamentalist attitude was largely set forth by William Jennings Bryan, who insisted that the theory of evolution was a denial of Bible teaching and hence a doctrine inimical to Christianity

Funeral (Late Lat *funeralis*, adj from *funus*, a burial) *Funus* is connected with *fumus* (Sanskrit *dhu-mas*), smoke, and the word seems to have referred to the ancient practice of disposing of the dead by cremation. Funerals among the Romans took place at night by torchlight, that magistrates and priests might not be made ceremonially unclean by seeing a corpse, and so be prevented from performing their sacred duties

Most of our funeral customs are derived from the Romans, as dressing in black, walking in procession, carrying insignia on the bier, raising a mound over the grave, called *tumulus* (whence our *tomb*), etc. In Roman funerals, too, the undertaker, attended by lictors dressed in black, marched with the corpse, and, as master of the ceremonies, assigned to each follower his proper place in the procession The Greeks crowned the dead body with flowers, and placed flowers on the tomb also, and the Romans decked the funeral couch with leaves and flowers, and spread flowers, wreaths, and fillets on the tomb of friends In England the *Passing Bell* or the

Soul Bell used to be tolled from the parish church when a parishioner was dying, and there are many references to it in literature At the funeral the bell would be tolled at intervals as many times as the dead person's age in years

Public games were held both in Greece and Rome in honour of departed heroes. Examples of this custom are numerous, as the games instituted by Hercules at the death of Pelops, those held by Achilles in honour of Patroclus (*Iliad*, Bk xxiii), those held by Æneas in honour of his father Anchises (*Æneid*, Bk. v), etc ; and the custom of giving a feast at funerals came to us from the Romans, who not only feasted the friends of the deceased, but also distributed meat to the persons employed

Thrift thrift, Horatio! the funeral baked meats
Did coldly furnish forth the marriage tables
Hamlet, i, 2

Fung-hwang. *See* FUM

Funk. To be in a funk, or a blue funk, may be the Walloon "*In de fonk zijn*," literally to "be in the smoke " Colloquially to be in a state of trepidation from uncertainty or apprehension of evil It first appeared in England at Oxford in the first half of the 18th century

Funny Bone. A pun on the word *humerus*, the Latin (and hence scientific) name for the upper bone of the arm It is the inner condyle of this, or, to speak untechnically, the knob, or *enlarged end* of the bone terminating where the ulnar nerve is exposed at the elbow. A knock on this bone at the elbow produces a painful sensation.

Furbelow. A corruption of *falbalas* (q.v.).

Furcam et Flagellum (fĕr′ kăm et flå jel′ ŭm) (Lat , gallows and whip) The meanest of all servile tenures, the bondman being at the lord's mercy, both life and limb Cp FORKS

Furies, The. The Roman name (*Furiæ*) for the Greek Erinyes (*q v*), said by Hesiod to have been the daughters of Ge (the earth) and to have sprung from the blood of Uranus, and by other accounts to be daughters of night and darkness They were three in number, Tisiphone (the Avenger of blood), Alecto (Implacable), and Megæra (Disputatious)

The Furies of the Guillotine. Another name for the *tricoteuses* (q.v)

Furphy. In World War I latrine buckets were supplied to the Australian forces by the firm of Furphy & Co , whose name appeared on all their products Hence a "furphy" was a latrine rumour.

Furry Dance (fŭ′ ri) An ancient ceremony of Helston and other Cornish towns, held on May 8th, locally known as Flora's Day. Couples dance through the streets and houses to a tune of immemorial antiquity, probably coeval with the dance, which may be of Druidic origin.

Fusiliers. Foot-soldiers that used to be armed with fusils or light muskets

The Royal English Fusiliers, the first regiment using the name, was raised in 1685.

Fustian (fŭs′ chan) A coarse twilled cotton

cloth with a velvety pile, probably so called from Fustat, a suburb of Cairo

It is chiefly used now in its figurative sense meaning inflated or pompous talk, claptrap, bombast (*q v*), pretentious words.

> Discourse fustian with one's own shadow — *Othello*, ii, 3
>
> Some scurvy quaint collection of fustian phrases, and uplandish words —HEYWOOD *Faire Maide of the Exchange*, ii, 2

Futhorc (fu' thôrk). The ancient Runic alphabet of the Anglo-Saxons and other Teutons, so called, on the same principle as the A B C, from its first six letters, viz , *f, u, th, o, r, k.*

Futurism. An art movement which originated in Turin in 1910 under the influence of F T Marinetti Its adherents sought to introduce into painting a "poetry of motion" whereby, for example, the painted gesture should become actually "a dynamic condition." The Futurists tried to indicate not only the state of mind of the painter but also that of the figures in the picture The original Futurists included Marinetti, Boccioni, Carra, Russolo, and Severini Their first exhibitions were held in Paris, 1911, and London, 1912

Fylfot. A mystic sign or emblem, known also as the *swastika* and *gammadion*, and in heraldry as the *cross cramponee*, used (especially in Byzantine architecture and among the North American Indians) as an ornament, and as of religious import It has been found at Hissarlık, on ancient Etruscan tombs, Celtic monuments, Buddhist inscriptions, Greek coins, etc , and has been thought to have represented the power of the sun, of the four winds, of lightning, and so on. Its shape is that of a right-angled cross, the arms of which are of equal length, with an additional piece at the extremity of each, fixed at a right-angle, each addition being of the same length and in the same direction It is used nowadays in jewellery as an emblem of luck

The name *fylfot* was adopted by antiquaries from a MS. of the 15th century, and is probably *fill foot*, signifying a device to fill the foot of a stained window. *See* SWASTIKA.

G

G. This letter is a modification of the Latin C (which was a rounding of the Greek *gamma*, Γ); until the 3rd century B.C the *g* and *k* sounds were represented by the same letter, C. In the Hebrew and old Phœnician alphabets G is the outline of a camel's head and neck Heb. *gimel*, a camel

G.C.B. *See* BATH.

G.I. In World War II, American enlisted men called themselves G.I s It is actually an abbreviation of Government Issue, a term attached to all their clothing, equipment, etc. After speaking for some time of G I. shirts, G I blankets, and G I haircuts, the soldiers began to apply the term to themselves.

G-man, short for Government Man, an agent of the U.S Federal Bureau of Investigation *See* FEDERAL.

G O M. The initial letters of 'Grand Old Man," a nickname of honour given to W. E. Gladstone (1809-98) in his later years, Lord Rosebery first used the expression in 1882.

Gab. The gift of the gab or gob. Fluency of speech, also the gift of boasting, connected with *gabble*, and perhaps with *gab*, the mouth.

> There was a man named Job
> Lived in the land of Uz,
> He had a good gift of the gob,
> The same thing happen us
> *Book of Job ascribed to Zachary Boyd* (d 1653)

Gabbara. The giant who, according to Rabelais, was "the first inventor of the drinking of healths "

Gabble Ratchet. *See* GABRIEL'S HOUNDS.

Gabelle (gà bel') A tax on salt. All the salt made in France had to be brought to the royal warehouses, and was there sold at a price fixed by the Government. The iniquity was that some provinces had to pay twice as much as others. It was abolished in 1789, together with the *corvee* (forced labour on the roads)

Gaberdine (gǎb' er dēn) A long, coarse cloak or gown, especially as worn in the Middle Ages by Jews and almsmen The word is the Spanish *gabardina*, a frock worn by pilgrims.

> You call me misbeliever, cut-throat dog,
> And spit upon my Jewish gabardine
> *Merchant of Venice,* i, 3.

Gaberlunzie (gǎb' er lŭnzi, gǎb' er lŭn yi) A mendicant, or one of the king's bedesmen, who were licensed beggars The name has also been given to the wallet carried by a *gaberlunzie-man*. Its derivation is unknown.

Gabriel (gā' bri el) (i e man of God). One of the archangels of Hebrew mythology, sometimes regarded as the angel of death, the prince of fire and thunder, but more frequently as one of God's chief messengers, and traditionally said to be the only angel that can speak Syriac and Chaldee The Mohammedans call him the chief of the four favoured angels, and the spirit of truth Milton makes him chief of the angelic guards placed over Paradise

> Betwixt these rocky pillars Gabriel sat,
> Chief of the angelic guards
> *Paradise Lost,* iv, 549

In the *Talmud* Gabriel appears as the destroyer of the hosts of Sennacherib, as the man who showed Joseph the way (*Gen* xxxvii, 15), and as one of the angels who buried Moses (*Deut* xxxiv, 6).

It was Gabriel who (we are told in the Koran) took Mohammed to heaven on Alborak and revealed to him his "prophetic lore " In the Old Testament Gabriel is said to have explained to Daniel certain visions, in the New Testament he announced to Zacharias the future birth of John the Baptist, and appeared to Mary, the mother of Jesus (*Luke* i, 26, etc)

Gabriel's horse. Haizum

Gabriel's hounds, called also *Gabble Ratchet* Wild geese The noise of geese in flight is like that of a pack of hounds in full cry The legend is that they are the souls of unbaptized children wandering through the air till the Day of Judgment.

Gabrielle. La Belle Gabrielle (1571-1599). Daughter of Antoine d'Estrees, grand-master of artillery, and governor of the Ile de France. Towards the close of 1590, Henri IV happened to sojourn for a night at the Château de Cœuvres, and fell in love with her. He married her to Liancourt-Damerval, created her Duchess de Beaufort, and took her to live with him at court

> Charmante Gabrielle,
> Perce de mille dards,
> Quand la gloire m'appelle
> A la suite de Mars   *Henri IV.*

Gad. By gad. A minced form of *God*, occurring also in such forms as Gadzooks, Begad, Egad
> How he still cries "Gad!" and talks of popery coming on, as all the fanatiques do.—PEPYS *Diary*, Nov. 24, 1662

Gad-fly. Not the *roving* but the *goading* fly (A S. *gad*, a goad).

Gadget (gǎj' et) An expressive word introduced into general use during World War I, popularized, apparently, by the R A F where it was used for almost any little tool or appliance

Gadshill (gǎdz hil) About 3 miles N W. of Rochester Famous for the attack of Sir John Falstaff and three of his knavish companions on a party of four travellers, whom they robbed of their purses (1 *Henry IV*, ii, 4), and also as the home of Charles Dickens, who died there in 1870
Gadshill is also the name of one of the thievish companions of Sir John Falstaff.

Gad-steel Flemish steel So called because it is wrought in *gads*, or small bars (A.S. *gad*, a small bar, Icel. *gaddr*, a spike)
> I will go get a leaf of brass,
> And with a gad of steel will write these words
>   *Titus Andronicus*, iv, 1

Gaelic (gǎ' lik). The language of the Gaelic branch of the Celtic race which, in Greek and Roman times, occupied much of Central Europe The name is now applied only to the Celtic language spoken in the Scottish Highlands. In the 18th century this was called Erse.

Gaff. Slang for humbug, also for a cheap public entertainment or a low-class music-hall.

Crooked as a gaff Here *gaff* is an iron hook at the end of a short pole, used for landing salmon, etc, or the metal spur of fighting-cocks (Span. and Port *gafa*, a boat-hook.)

To blow the gaff. *See* BLOW

To stand the gaff. To bear punishment or raillery, with calmness

Gaffer. An old country fellow; a boss or foreman; a corruption of "grandfather." *Cp.* GAMMER
> If I had but a thousand a year, Gaffer Green,
> If I had but a thousand a year.
>   *Gaffer Green and Robin Rough.*

Gag. In theatrical parlance, an interpolation. When Hamlet directs the players to say no more "than is set down" (iii, 2) he cautions them against gagging; also a joke.

Gag-man. One who is employed to supply jokes for films or radio programmes.

To apply the gag Said of applying the closure in the House of Commons. Here *gag* is something forced into the mouth to prevent speech.

Gaiety. Gaiety of Nations. This phrase, now often used in an ironic sense, such as "that won't add much to the gaiety of nations," springs from the words uttered by Dr. Johnson on hearing of the death of David Garrick—' I am disappointed by that stroke of death which has eclipsed the gaiety of nations and impoverished the public stock of harmless pleasure."

Gaiety Girl. One of the beauty chorus for which the old Gaiety Theatre in the Strand was famous in the '90s and Edwardian days Several of them married into the peerage

Gala Day (gā' lǎ) A festive day; a day when people put on their best attire (Ital. *gala*, finery)

Galahad, Sir (gǎl' a hǎd). In the Arthurian legends the purest and noblest knight of the Round Table He is a late addition and was invented by Walter Map in his *Quest of the San Graal* He was the son of Lancelot and Elaine· at the institution of the Round Table one seat (the *Siege Perilous*) was left unoccupied, and could be occupied only by the knight who could succeed in the Quest When Sir Galahad sat there it was discovered that it had been left for him *Vide* Malory's *Morte d'Arthur*, Tennyson's *The Holy Grail*, etc.

Galatea (gǎl a tē' a). A sea-nymph, beloved by Polypheme, but herself in love with Acis Acis was crushed under a huge rock by the jealous giant, and Galatea threw herself into the sea, where she joined her sister nymphs. Handel has an opera entitled *Acis and Galatea* (1732) The Galatea beloved by Pygmalion (*q v*) was a different person

Galaxy, The (gǎl' ǎk si). The "Milky Way " A long white luminous track of stars which seems to encompass the heavens like a girdle According to modern astronomical theory the Galaxy is a vast collection of stars set in a curiously flattened shape something like a double convex lens It is because our Sun—and we ourselves in the planetary system with it—is in the midst of this Galaxy that the mass of stars appears so dense when we are looking lengthwise through it, whereas when we look out sideways, so to speak, we see the constellations of the heavens separately It is supposed that the whole vast Galactic system revolves round a centre somewhere in the constellation of Sagittarius, 30,000 light years (a light year is six million million miles) from the Sun.
According to classic fable, it is the path to the palace of Zeus or Jupiter. (Gr. *gala*, *galaktos*, milk.)
> Through all her courts
> The vacant city slept; the busy winds,
> That keep no certain intervals of rest,
> Moved not, meanwhile the galaxy displayed
> Her fires, that like mysterious pulses beat,
> Aloft,—momentous but uneasy bliss!
> WORDSWORTH· *Vandracour and Julia*, 94

Galen (gā len) A Greek physician and philosopher of the 2nd century A.D. For centuries he was the supreme authority in medicine Hence, *Galenist*, a follower of Galen's medical theories; *Galenical*, a simple, vegetable medicine.

Galen says "Nay" and Hippocrates "Yea." The doctors disagree, and who is to decide? Hippocrates—a native of Cos, born 460 B C — was the most celebrated physician of antiquity

Galère (ga lâr') Que diable allait-il faire dans cette galère? What business had he to be in that galley? This is from Molière's comedy of *Les Fourberies de Scapin* Scapin wants to bamboozle Géronte out of his money, and tells him that his master (Géronte s son) is detained prisoner on a Turkish galley, where he went out of curiosity Géronte replies "What business had he to go on board the galley?" The phrase is applied to a person who finds himself in difficulties through being where he ought not to be, or in some unexpected predicament

Vogue la galère. *See* VOGUE.

Galimatias (găl i mă' shas) Nonsense, unmeaning gibberish. The word first appeared in France in the 16th century, but its origin is unknown; perhaps it is connected with *gallimaufry (q v)* In his translation of Rabelais Urquhart heads ch ii of Bk I a "Galimatias of Extravagant Conceits found in an Ancient Monument."

Gall (gawl) Bile; the very bitter fluid secreted by the liver, hence used figuratively as a symbol for anything of extreme bitterness, colloquially, impudence

Gall and wormwood. Extremely disagreeable and annoying
> And I said, My strength and my hope is perished from the Lord Remembering my affliction and my misery, the wormwood and the gall —*Lam* iii, 18, 19

The gall of bitterness. The bitterest grief, extreme affliction The ancients taught that grief and joy were subject to the gall as affection was to the heart, knowledge to the kidneys, and the gall of bitterness means the bitter centre of bitterness, as the heart of heart means the innermost recesses of the heart or affections In the *Acts* it is used to signify "the sinfulness of sin," which leads to the bitterest grief
> I perceive thou art in the gall of bitterness, and in the bond of iniquity —*Acts* viii, 23

The gall of pigeons. The story goes that pigeons have no gall, because the dove sent from the ark by Noah burst its gall out of grief, and none of the pigeon family has had a gall ever since.
> For sin' the Flood of Noah
> The dow she has nae ga'
> JAMIESON *Popular Ballads (Lord of Rorlin's Daughter)*

Gallant. The meaning of this word varies with its pronunciation. As găl' ănt it is an adjective meaning brave, grand, fine, chivalrous, as gal ănt' it describes the cavalier or admirer of women, a flirt, or the adjective and verb implying this.

Gallery. To play to the gallery. To work for popularity. As an actor who sacrifices his author for popular applause
> The instant we begin to think about success and the effect of our work—to play with one eye on the gallery—we lose power, and touch, and everything else —KIPLING: *The Light that Failed.*

Galley Halfpence. Silver coin brought over by merchants ("galley-men") from Genoa, who used the Galley Wharf, Thames Street These halfpence were larger than our own, and their use was forbidden in England early in the 15th century.

Gallia (găl' i å) France, the Latin name for Gaul

Gallia Braccata (*trousered Gaul*) Gallia Narbonensis—South-western Gaul, from the Pyrenees to the Alps—was so called from the "braccæ," or trousers, which the natives wore in common with the Scythians and Persians

Gallia Comata. That part of Gaul which belonged to the Roman emperor, and was governed by legates (*legati*), was so called from the long hair (*coma*) worn by the inhabitants flowing over their shoulders

Gallicism (găl' i sizm) A phrase or sentence constructed after the French idiom, as, "when you *shall have returned* home you will find a letter on your table." In *Matt* xv, 32, is a Gallicism. "I have compassion on the multitude, because *they continue* with me now three days, and have nothing to eat" Cp *Mark* viii, 2

Galligaskins (găl i găs' kinz) A loose, wide kind of breeches worn by men in the 16th and 17th centuries
> My galligaskins, that have long withstood
> The winter's fury and encroaching frosts
> A horrid chasm disclos'd, with orifice
> Wide, discontinuous
>   J PHILIPS *The Splendid Shilling* (1703)

> The taylor of Bister, he has but one eye,
> He cannot cut a pair of green galagaskins, if he were to try —*Aubrey MS*

The word is a corruption of Fr. *garguesque*, which was the Ital *grechesca*. Greekish, referring to a Greek article of clothing

Gallimaufry (găl i maw' fri). A medley, any confused jumble of things, but strictly speaking, a hotch-potch made up of all the scraps of the larder (Fr *galimafree*, the origin of which is unknown, though it is probably related to *galimatias*)
> He woos both high and low, both rich and poor,
> Both young and old, one with another, Ford;
> He loves the galimaufry [all sorts]
>   *Merry Wives*, ii, 1

Gallo-Belgicus (găl ō bel' ji kus) An annual register in Latin for European circulation, first published in 1598
> It is believed,
> And told for news with as much diligence
> As if 'twere writ in Gallo-Belgicus.
>   THOMAS MAY *The Heir*, 1615.

Galloglass (găl' ō glas) An armed servitor (or foot-soldier) of an ancient Irish chief O.Ir and Gael *gall*, a stranger, *oglach*, a warrior
> The Galloglass are pycked and scelected men of great and mightie bodies, crewel without compassion —JOHN DYMMOK. *Treatice of Ireland* (1600)

Galloway (găl' ō wä) A horse less than fifteen hands high, of the breed which originally came from Galloway in Scotland
> Thrust him downstairs! Know we not Galloway nags?—2 *Henry IV*, ii, 4

Gallup Poll (găl' ûp pōl) A method devised by Dr George Gallup for ascertaining the trend of public opinion by interrogating a cross-section of the population. Trained interviewers question a very small sample of the public, which is carefully chosen with regard to its composition of men or women, geographical distribution, age groups and social position For the British Parliamentary election of 1945 the interviewers spoke to 1,809 persons out of the 25,000,000 voters These were so scientifically selected that the Gallup Poll forecast was less than 1 per cent wrong when the actual voting figures were made known On the other hand, their forecast was as wrong as that of everyone else at the American Presidential election of 1948.

Galore (ga lôr') One of our words from Old Irish *go leor*, to a sufficiency, hence, in abundance, and abundance itself
> For his Poll he had trinkets and gold galore,
> Besides of prize-money quite a store
> *Jack Robinson (A Sailor's Song)*

Galosh (ga losh') The word comes to us from the Span *galocha* (wooden shoes), Ger *galosche*, Fr *galoche*, which is probably from Gr *kalopous*, a shoe-maker's last
The word was originally applied to a kind of clog or patten worn as a protection against wet in days when silk or cloth shoes were common It is in this sense that writers so remote as Langland use the word —
> the kynde of a knyght that cometh to be doubed,
> To geten hus gilte spores and galoches y-couped.
> *Piers Plowman*, xxi, 12

The modern galoshes are rubber overshoes, and are sometimes spelled *goloshes*.

Galway Jury (gawl' wā) An enlightened, independent jury The expression has its birth in certain trials held in Ireland in 1635 upon the right of the king to the counties of Ireland. Leitrim, Roscommon, Sligo, and Mayo gave judgment in favour of the Crown, but Galway opposed it, whereupon the sheriff was fined £1,000, and each of the jurors £4,000.

Gama, Vasco da (văs' kŏ da ga' ma) One of the greatest of the early Portuguese navigators (d 1524), and the first European to double the Cape of Good Hope He is the hero of Camoens's *Lusiad* (1572),
> Gama, captain of the venturous band,
> Of bold emprise, and born for high command,
> Whose martial fires, with prudence close allied,
> Ensured the smiles of fortune on his side.

Gamboge (găm bōzh) So called from Cambodia or Camboja, whence it was first brought. It is a gum resin made from various species of a laurel-like tree of Siam, Cambodia, and Cochin China. When powdered it becomes a brilliant yellow which forms a pigment in water-colour paints

Gambrel A bent piece of wood used by butchers, from which they suspend carcases.

Game. Certain wild animals and birds, legally protected, preserved, and pursued for sport, such as hares, pheasants, partridges, grouse, heath-game, etc *See* SPORTING SEASON.

The game is not worth the candle. *See* CANDLE

The game is up. The scheme, endeavour, etc., has come to nothing, everything has failed.
13*

The game's afoot. The hare has started, the enterprise has begun
> I see you stand like greyhounds in the slips,
> Straining upon the start The game's afoot!
> Follow your spirit!—SHAKESPEARE *Henry V*, iii, I

He's a game 'un! He's got some pluck, he's "a plucked 'un." Another allusion to gamecocks

He's at his little games again, or at the same old game. He's at his old tricks, he's gone back to his old habits or practices

To die game. To maintain a resolute attitude to the last A phrase from cock-fighting

To have the game in one's hands To have such an advantage that success is assured, to hold the winning cards

To play a waiting game To bide one's time, knowing that that is the best way of winning, to adopt Fabian tactics (*q v.*)

To play the game. To act in a straightforward, honourable manner, to keep to the rules.
> This they all with a joyful mind
> Bear through life like a torch in flame,
> And falling, fling to the host behind—
> "Play up! Play up! and play the game!"
> SIR H NEWBOLT *Vitae Lampada*

You are making game of me. You are bamboozling me, "pulling my leg," holding me up to ridicule

Game Chicken. The sobriquet of the pugilist, Hen Pearce Beginning as a pupil of James Belcher, he eventually defeated his teacher in a terrible battle on Barnty Moor near Doncaster, 6th December, 1805

Game Laws. A survival of the forest laws imposed by William the Conqueror. Game licences were first issued in 1784. The seasons during which certain game might be shot were set out in the Game Act of William IV, 1831

Game leg. A lame leg. In this instance *game* is a dialect form of the Celtic *cam*, meaning crooked It is of comparatively modern usage Gammy is also used in this sense.

Gamelyn, The Tale of (găm' lin) A Middle-English metrical romance, found among the Chaucer MSS. and supposed to have been intended by him to form the basis of one of the un-written *Canterbury Tales*. Gamelyn is a younger son to whom a large share of property had been bequeathed by the father. He is kept in servitude and tyrannically used by his elder brother until he is old enough effectually to rebel After many adventures, during which he becomes a leader of outlaws in the woods, he comes to his own again with the help of the king, and justice is meted out to the elder brother and those who aided him Thomas Lodge made the story into a novel—*Rosalynde, or Euphues' Golden Legacie* (1590)—and from this Shakespeare drew a large part of *As You Like It.* The authorship is, however, still in doubt.

Gammadion (ga mā' di ŏn). The *fylfot* (*q v.*), or swastika, so called because it resembles four Greek capital gammas (*Γ*) set at right angles.

Gammer. A rustic term for an old woman, a corruption of *grandmother*, with an intermediate form "granmer" Cp. GAFFER

Gammer Gurton's Needle The earliest English comedy with the exception of *Ralph Roister Doister*; acted at Christ's College, Cambridge, in 1552, and printed in 1575 It was published as "By Mr S Mr of Art," who remained unidentified until Isaac Reed in 1782 announced that it was Bishop Still The comedy is vigorous and it closes with the discovery of Gammer Gurton's missing needle in the seat of Hodge's breeches.

Gammon. This word comes from the same original as *game* and *gamble*, but in Victorian slang it meant to impose upon, delude, cheat; and sometimes, to play a game upon As an exclamation it meant "Nonsense, you're pulling my leg!"

A landsman said, "I twig the chap—he's been upon the Mill,
And 'cause he gammons so the flats, ve calls him Veeping Bill"
Ingoldsby Legends

Gammon, the buttock or thigh of a hog salted and cured, is the Fr. *jambon*, O.Fr. *gambon*, from *gambe*, the leg.

Gamp. Sarah Gamp is a disreputable monthly nurse in Dickens's *Martin Chuzzlewit* famous for her bulky umbrella and perpetual reference to Mrs Harris, a purely imaginary person, whose opinions always confirmed her own. Hence a gamp is a common term for an umbrella

Gamut (găm' ŭt) Originally, the first or lowest note in Guido of Arezzo's scale, corresponding to G on the lowest line of the modern bass stave, later, the whole series of notes recognized by musicians, hence, the whole range or compass.

It is *gamma ut*, *gamma* (the third letter of the Greek alphabet) was used by Guido to mark the first or lowest note in the mediæval scale, and *ut* is the first word in the mnemonic stanza, *Ut queant laxis resonare fibris.* etc (*see* DOH), containing the names of the hexachord *Gamma ut*, or *G ut*, was added to the scale in the 11th century.

Ganelon. A type of black-hearted treachery, figuring in Dante's *Inferno* and grouped by Chaucer (*Nun's Priest's Tale*, 407) with Judas Iscariot and "Greek Sinon, that broghtest Troye al outrely to sorwe " He was Count of Mayence, one of Charlemagne's paladins. Jealousy of Roland made him a traitor; and in order to destroy his rival, he planned with Marsillus, the Moorish king, the attack of Roncesvalles.

Ganesha (găn' esh à). The god of wisdom in Hindu mythology, lord of the Ganas, or lesser deities. He was the son of Siva, is propitiated at the commencement of important work, at the beginning of sacred writings, etc

Gang. A gang of saws. A number of circular power-driven saws mounted together so that they can reduce a tree trunk to planks at a single operation

Gang agley, To (Scot.). To go wrong. The verb *to glee*, or *gley*, means to look asquint, sideways.

The best-laid schemes of mice and men
Gang aft agley. BURNS *To a Mouse.*

Gang-day. The day when boys *gang* round the parish to beat its bounds *See* BOUNDS

Ganges, The (găn' jēz) So named from *ganga* or *gunga*, a river, as in *Kishenganga*, the black river, *Neelganga*, the blue river; *Narainguṇga*, the river of Naranyana or Vishnu etc The Ganges is the *Borra Ganga*, or great river

Those who through the curse, have fallen from heaven, having performed ablution in this stream, become free from sin, cleansed from sin by this water, and restored to happiness, they shall enter heaven and return again to the gods.—*The Ramayana* (section XXXV)

Gangway. Originally, the boarded way (hence sometimes called the *gang-board*, gang, an alley) in the old galleys made for the rowers to pass from stem to stern, and where the mast was laid when it was unshipped, now, the board with a railing at each side by which passengers walk into or out of a ship

As we were putting off the boat they laid hold of the gangboard and unhooked it off the boat's stern —
COOK *Second Voyage,* Bk iii, ch. iv.

Below the gangway. In the House of Commons, on the farther side of the passage-way between the seats which separate the Ministry from the rest of the House. To sit "below the gangway" is to sit amongst the general members, and not among the Ministers or ex-Ministers and leaders of the Opposition

Ganymede (găn' i mēd) In Greek mythology, the cup-bearer of Zeus, successor to Hebe, and the type of youthful male beauty. Originally a Trojan youth, he was taken up to Olympus and made immortal Hence, a cup-bearer generally

Nature waits upon thee still,
And thy verdant cup does fill;
'Tis fill'd wherever thou dost tread
Nature's self's thy Ganymede
COWLEY: *The Grasshopper* (*Anacreontics*)

Gaora (gā ôr' a) According to Hakluyt this was a tract of land inhabited by people without heads, with eyes in their shoulders and their mouths in their breasts *See* BLEMMYES

Gape. Looking for gape-seed. Gaping about and doing nothing A corruption of "Looking agapesing", *gapesing* (still used in Norfolk) is staring about with one's mouth open.

Seeking a gape's nest (Devon) A *gape's nest* is a sight which one stares at with wide-open mouth. *Cp* MARE'S NEST

Garcia (gar' si a) To take a message to Garcia is to be resourceful and courageous, to be able to accept responsibility and carry one's task through to the end The phrase originated in the exploit of Lieut. Andrew Rowan who, in the Spanish-American War of 1898, made his way through the Spanish blockade into Cuba, made contact with General Calixto Garcia, chief of the Cuban insurgent forces, and carried news from him back to Washington.

Garcias. The soul of Pedro Garcias Money. The story is that two scholars of Salamanca discovered a tombstone with this inscription. "Here lies the soul of the licentiate Pedro Garcias", and on searching found a purse with a hundred golden ducats (*Gil Blas*, Preface)

Garden. Garden City A name given alike to Norwich and to Chicago; also, as a general name, to model suburbs and townships that have been planned with a special view to the provision of open spaces, and wide roads.

The Garden or **Garden Sect.** The disciples of Epicurus, who taught in his own private garden.

The Garden of Eden. *See* EDEN The name as applied to Mesopotamia, with its vast sandy deserts, is nowadays somewhat ironical, but it is traditionally supposed to be its "original site "

In many countries the name is applied to the more fertile districts as—

Garden of England. Kent and Worcestershire are both so called

Garden of Europe Italy

Garden of France Amboise, in the department of Indre-et-Loire, also Touraine.

Garden of India. Oude

Garden of Ireland. Carlow.

Garden of Italy. The island of Sicily.

Garden of South Wales. The southern division of Glamorganshire.

Garden of Spain Andalusia.

Garden of Switzerland. Thurgau.

Garden of the Hesperides. *See* HESPERIDES

Garden of the Sun. The East Indian (or Malayan) Archipelago

Garden of the West. Illinois, Kansas ("the Garden State") is also so called.

Garden of the World. The region of the Mississippi.

Gardy loo The cry of warning formerly given by Edinburgh housewives when about to throw the contents of the slop-pail out of the window into the street below. It is a corruption of Fr *garde l'eau,* beware of the water.

At ten o'clock at night the whole cargo is flung out of a back window that looks into some street or lane, and the maid calls "Gardy loo" to the passengers —SMOLLETT *Humphrey Clinker.*

Gargamelle (gar′ ga mel) In Rabelais's satire, daughter of the king of the Parpaillons (*butterflies*), wife of Grangousier, and mother of Gargantua (*q.v*) On the day that she gave birth to him she ate sixteen quarters, two bushels, three pecks, and a pipkin of *dirt,* the mere remains left in the tripe which she had for supper.

She is said to be meant either for Anne of Brittany, or Catherine de Foix, Queen of Navarre

Gargantua (gar găn′ tū a). A giant of mediæval (perhaps Celtic) legend famous for his enormous appetite (Sp *garganta,* gullet), adopted by Rabelais in his great satire (1532), and made the father of Pantagruel. One of his exploits was to swallow five pilgrims with their staves and all in a salad. He is the subject of a number of chap-books, and became proverbial as a voracious and insatiable guzzler

You must borrow me Gargantua's mouth first [before I can utter so long a word], 'tis a word too great for any mouth of this age's size —*As You Like It,* iii, 2.

Gargouille (gar goo ël′). The great dragon that lived in the Seine, ravaged Rouen, and was slain by St. Romanus, Bishop of Rouen, in the 7th century

Gargoyle (gar′ goil) A spout for rain-water in Gothic architecture, projecting from the wall so that the water falls clear, and usually carved into some fantastic shape, such as a dragon's head, through which the water flows So named from Fr *gargouille,* the throat, gullet

Garibaldi (gär i bol′ di). The red shirt made famous by Garibaldi and his men in their deliverance of Italy in 1860 had a very simple origin It was in Montevideo, in 1843, where Garibaldi was raising an Italian legion, that a number of red woollen shirts came on the market owing to the difficulty of export due to the war with Argentina. The Uruguay government bought them up cheaply and handed them over to Garibaldi for his men. When the Italian Legion came over to Europe in 1848 they brought their red shirts with them, thus furnishing Italy with her long-treasured symbol of freedom

The Garibaldi biscuit, in which currants are mixed in the pastry, was a form of food much favoured by the General on his farm in Caprera.

Garland. The primary use of this word, meaning a wreath of flowers either worn or festooned around some object, has been extended to include a collection of pieces in prose or verse, a sort of choice anthology

What I now offer to your Lordship is a collection of Poetry, a kind of Garland of Good Will.—PRIOR'S dedication to his *Poems*

Garlic. The old superstition that garlic can destroy the magnetic power of the loadstone has the sanction of Pliny, Solinus, Ptolemy, Plutarch, Albertus, Matholus, Rueus, Rulandus, Renodæus, Langius, and others Sir Thomas Browne places it among *Vulgar Errors* (Bk ii, ch 3).

Martin Rulandus saith that Onions and Garlick . . hinder the attractive power [of the magnet] and rob it of its virtue of drawing iron, to which Renodæus agrees, but this is all lies —W SALMON. *The Complete English Physician,* ch xxv (1693)

Garnish In old prison slang, the entrance-money, to be spent in drink, demanded by jailbirds of new-comers *Garnish* means embellishment, extra decoration to dress, etc., hence, it was applied by prisoners to fetters, and the garnish-money was money given for the "honour" of wearing them The custom became obsolete with the reform of prisons.

In its original meaning to *garnish* was to *warn,* and it is in this sense that the word is now used legally John X (called the garnishee) is garnished or warned not to pay a sum he owes to Henry Y as Henry Y owes money to George Z but is disputing the debt

Garratt The Mayor of Garratt. Garratt is near Earlsfield, Wimbledon; the first "mayor" was elected in 1778 He was really merely the chairman of an association of villagers formed to put a stop to encroachments on the common, and as his election coincided with a general election, the society made it a law that a new "mayor" should be chosen at every general election This tickled the public fancy, crowds assembled to see the fun (on one occasion there were 80,000 persons present) and the most fantastic candidates came forward under assumed names to contest the "mayoralty" on the most outrageous platforms. The addresses of these mayors, written by Garrick, Wilkes, and others, are satires on the corruption of electors and political squibs The first recorded mayor was "Squire Blowmedown"; the last was "Sir" Harry Dimsdale (1796) a muffin-seller and dealer in tinware

Foote has a farce entitled *The Mayor of Garratt* All that remains of Garratt is a lane so named.

Garraway's. A noted coffee-house in Change Alley, Cornhill, which existed for over 200 years and was founded by Thomas Garway, a tobacconist and coffee merchant in the 16th century Here the promoters of the South Sea Bubble met. Sales were held periodically, and tea was introduced to England in 1657, selling at from 16s to 50s. a pound Garraway's was closed and the house demolished in 1874.

Garrotte (Span *garrote*, a stick) A Spanish method of execution by fastening a cord round the neck of the criminal and twisting it with a *stick* till strangulation ensued In 1851 General Lopez was garrotted for attempting to gain possession of Cuba, and about that time the term was first applied to the practice of London thieves and roughs who strangled their victim while an accomplice rifled his pockets

Garter. The Most Noble Order of the Garter. The highest order of knighthood in Great Britain and in the world, traditionally instituted by King Edward III about 1348, re-constituted in 1805 and 1831 The popular legend is that Joan, Countess of Salisbury, accidentally slipped her garter at a court ball It was picked up by the king, who gallantly diverted the attention of the guests from the lady by binding the blue band round his own knee, saying as he did so, "*Honi soit qui mal y pense*" (Evil—or shame—be to him who thinks evil of it) (*q v*). The order is limited to the Sovereign, and other members of the Royal Family, with twenty-five Knights, and such foreign royalties as may be admitted by statute The only Ladies of the Garter are the Sovereign's Queen and his eldest daughter when she is heir apparent to the throne, and until, in 1912, Viscount Grey (then Sir Edward Grey) was admitted to the order, no commoner for centuries had been able to put "K G" after his name

Each knight is allotted a stall in St George's Chapel, Windsor The habits and insignia are the garter, mantle, surcoat, hood, star, collar, and George—a jewelled figure representing St. George and the Dragon

Wearing the garters of a pretty girl either on the hat or knee was a common custom with our forefathers. Brides usually wore on their legs a host of gay ribbons, to be distributed after the marriage ceremony amongst the bridegroom's friends, and the piper at the wedding dance never failed to tie a piece of the bride's garter round his pipe

Magic garters. In the old romances, etc, garters made of the strips of a young hare's skin saturated with motherwort Those who wore them excelled in speed

Prick the garter. An old swindling game, better known as "Fast and loose" *See under* FAST

Garvies. Sprats, perhaps so called from Inchgarvie, the island in the Firth of Forth that supports the central pier of the Forth Bridge

Gasconade. Absurd boasting, vainglorious braggadocio It is said that a Gascon being asked what he thought of the Louvre in Paris, replied, "Pretty well, it reminds me of the back part of my father's stables." The vainglory of this answer is the more palpable when it is borne in mind that the Gascons were proverbially poor The Dictionary of the French Academy gives the following specimen "A Gascon, in proof of his ancient nobility, asserted that they used in his father's house no other fuel than the bâtons of the family marshals"

Gas mask A popular name for any contrivance designed to preserve the wearer from inhaling poison gas In World War I (when gas was first used) the gas mask went through various forms from a sort of greasy felt domino to a box respirator strapped on the chest In World War II there were several kinds of respirator—for infants, for small children, civilians, civilians on national duty, and for the Services, all of which differed only in the period for which they were effective

Gat-tooth. Chaucer's "Wife of Bath" was *gat-toothed* (*see Prol to Cant. Tales*, 468, and *Wife of Bath's Prol.* 603), this probably means that her teeth were set wide apart, with *gats*, i e openings or gaps between them, but some editors have thought it is *goat-toothed* (A.S *gat*), i e lascivious, like a goat

Gate. Gate money. Money paid at the door or gate for admission to an enclosure where some entertainment or contest, etc, is to take place

Gate of Italy A narrow gorge between two mountain ridges in the valley of the Adige, in the vicinity of Trent and Roveredo

Gate of Tears The passage into the Red Sea So called by the Arabs (*Bub-el-Mandeb*) from the number of shipwrecks that took place there

Gates of Dreams. *See* DREAMS.

Gate-posts. The post on which a gate hangs is called the hanging-post, that against which it shuts is called the banging-post

Gath (găth). In Dryden's *Absalom and Achitophel* (*q v*), this means Brussels, where Charles II long resided while in exile

Tell it not in Gath. Don't let your enemies hear it Gath was famous as being the birthplace of the giant Goliath

Tell it not in Gath, publish it not in the streets of Askelon lest the daughters of the Philistines rejoice, lest the daughters of the uncircumcised triumph —2 *Sam* 1, 20

Gather. He is gathered to his fathers. He is dead A phrase from the Bible "All that generation were gathered unto their fathers" (*Judges* ii, 10)

Gathering is a common phrase among Dissenters to describe any sort of religious or social assembly

Bibliographically, it is any number of leaves which may be put together and joined into a section of the book by being sewn through

Gatling Gun. An early form of automatic weapon invented in the U.S.A in 1867 It had a large number of barrels, the projectiles in which could be discharged in rapid succession. It preceded all types of weapons constructed on the principle of discharging numerous projectiles rapidly through the same barrel, as a machine gun.

Gauche (gōsh) (Fr , the left hand) Awkward

Gaucherie Behaviour not according to the received forms of society; awkward and untoward ways.

Gaucho (gou' chō). A cowboy of the S. American pampas, of mixed Indian and Spanish descent The word is also applied to an itinerant minstrel of the Argentine pampas, who goes from village to village with horse and guitar

Gaudy-day (gaw' di) (Lat *gaudium*, joy) A holiday, a feast-day; especially an annual celebration of some event, such as the foundation of a college

Gaul (gawl) In classical geography, the country inhabited by the Gauls, hence, in modern use, France. *Cisalpine Gaul* lay south and east of the Alps, in what is now northern Italy. *Transalpine Gaul* was north and north-west of the Alps, and included Narbonensis, Aquitania, Lugdunensis, and Belgica It was inhabited by Franks, Germans, Burgundians, Celts and others, as well as Gauls

> Insulting Gaul has roused the world to war.
> THOMSON *Autumn.*
> Shall haughty Gaul invasion threat?—BURNS.

Gaunt. John of Gaunt (1340-99), third son of Edward III; so called from Ghent, in Flanders, the place of his birth

Gauntlet To run the gauntlet. To be attacked on all sides, to be severely criticized The word came into English at the time of the Thirty Years' War as *gantlope*, meaning the passage between two files of soldiers, and is the Swedish *gata*, a way, passage (*cp.* GAT-TOOTH *above*), and *lopp* (connected with our *leap*), a course The reference is to a punishment formerly common among soldiers and sailors; the company or crew, provided with rope ends, were drawn up in two rows facing each other, and the delinquent had to run between them, while every man dealt him as severe a chastisement as he could.

To throw down the gauntlet. To challenge. The custom in the Middle Ages, when one knight challenged another, was for the challenger to throw his gauntlet on the ground, and if the challenge was accepted the person to whom it was thrown picked it up.

Gautama (gaw ta' ma). The family name of Buddha (*q v*). His personal name was Siddhattha, his father's name Suddhodana, and his mother's Maya. *Buddha* means "The Enlightened," "The One Who Knows," and he assumed this title at about the age of 36, when, after seven years of seclusion and spiritual struggle, he believed himself to have attained to perfect truth.

Gauvaine. Gawain (*q v*.).

Gavelkind (găv' el kind). A tenure of Saxon origin, still in force in some parts of Kent and formerly in Wales, Northumberland, and elsewhere, whereby land and property of persons dying intestate descended from the father to all his sons in equal proportions, or to the daughters in the absence of sons. The youngest had the homestead, and the eldest the horse and arms. The word is the A S. *gafol*, tribute, tax (*cp* GABELLE). and *kind*, nature, species. Coke (1 *Institutes*, 140 a) says the word is *gif eal cyn* (give all the kin).

Gawain (ga wān) One of the most famous of the Arthurian knights, nephew of King Arthur, and probably the original hero of the Grail quest He appears in the Welsh *Triads* and the *Mabinogion* as Gwalchmei, and in the Arthurian cycle is the centre of many episodes and poems The Middle English poem (about 1360), *Sir Gawain and the Green Knight*, is a romance telling how Gawain beheads the Green Knight in single combat.

Gay. A gay deceiver. A Lothario (*q v*), a libertine

The Gay Science. A translation of *gai saber*, the old Provençal name for the art of poetry

A guild formed at Toulouse in 1323 with the object of keeping in existence the dying Provençal language and culture was called the *Gai Saber* Its full title was "The Very Gay Company of the Seven Troubadours of Toulouse."

Gaze. To stand at gaze. To stand in doubt what to do. A term in forestry When a stag first hears the hounds it stands dazed, looking all round, and in doubt what to do Heralds call a stag which is represented full-faced, a "stag at gaze"

> As the poor frightened deer, that stands at gaze,
> Wildly determining which way to fly
> *Rape of Lucrece*, 1149

Gaze-hound. *See* LYME-HOUND.

Gazebo (ga zē' bō). A humorous Latin future tense applied to the English *gaze*, to describe a summer-house with an extensive prospect. The word is also used for a balcony, window, or any other vantage spot whence a good view can be obtained.

Gazette. A newspaper The first newspapers were issued in Venice by the Government, and came out in manuscript once a month, during the war of 1563 between the Venetians and Turks The intelligence was read publicly in certain places, and the fee for hearing it read was one *gazetta* (a Venetian coin, somewhat less than a farthing in value).

The first official English newspaper, called *The Oxford Gazette*, was published in 1642, at Oxford, where the Court was held. On the removal of the Court to London, the name was changed to *The London Gazette* This name was revived in 1665, during the Great Fire Now the official *Gazette*, published every Tuesday and Friday, contains announcements of pensions, promotions, bankruptcies, dissolutions of partnerships, etc.

Gazetted. Posted in *The London Gazette* as having received some official appointment, service promotion, etc , or on being declared bankrupt, etc

Gazetteer. A geographical and topographical index or dictionary; so called because the name of one of the earliest in English (L. Eachard's, 1693) was *The Gazetteer's or News-man's Interpreter*, i e. it was intended for the use of journalists, those who wrote for the Gazettes.

Gear In machinery, the wheels, chains, belts, etc., that communicate motion to the working parts are called the gear or *gearing* (Sax. *gearwa*, clothing) The term is more particularly applied to a toothed wheel or a series of toothed wheels for the transmission of motion from one machine to another, or from one part of a machine to another. *High gear* is said of an arrangement of wheels, etc., whereby the driving part moves slowly in relation to the driven part, *Low gear* is the reverse of this, the driving part moving relatively more quickly than the driven, *Differential gear* is a combination of toothed gear wheels connecting two axles but allowing them to revolve at different speeds. *Gear* is also applied to all forms of equipment, as, for example, *sports gear*.

In good gear. To be in good working order

Out of gear. Not in working condition, when the "gearing" does not act properly; out of health.

Gee-up! and Gee-whoa' Interjections addressed to horses meaning respectively "Go ahead!" and "Stop!" From them came the childish "gee-gee," a horse, a term adopted by sporting men and others, as in "Backing the gee-gees."

Geese. *See* GOOSE.

Gehenna (ge hen' a) (Heb.). The place of eternal torment Strictly speaking, it means simply the Valley of Hinnom (*Ge-Hinnom*), where sacrifices to Baal and Moloch were offered (*Jer* xix, 6, etc), and where refuse of all sorts was subsequently cast, for the consumption of which fires were kept constantly burning.

And made his grove
The pleasant valley of Hinnom, Tophet thence
And black Gehenna called, the type of hell
MILTON. *Paradise Lost*, Bk i, 403

Gelert (gel' ert). Llewelyn's dog. *See* BETH GELERT.

Gemara (ge ma' ra) (Aramaic, complement) The second part of the Talmud (*q v*), consisting of annotations, discussions, and amplifications of the *Mishna*, which is the first part. The *Mishna* is the interpretation of the written law, the *Gemara* the interpretation of the *Mishna*. There is the Babylonian *Gemara* and the Jerusalem *Gemara*. The former, which is the more complete, is by the academies of Babylon, and was completed about A D 500, the latter by those of Palestine, completed towards the close of the 4th or during the 5th century A D.

Gemini (jem' i ni). A zodiacal sign. *See* THE TWINS.

Gen (jen), an R.A.F slang word meaning information, full details. It comes from either "General Information" or from "Genuine," and it is sometimes used as a verb, i e. To gen it up, to swot it up.

Gendarmes (zhon' darm) "Men at arms," the armed police of France The term was first applied to those who marched in the train of knights, subsequently to the cavalry, in the time of Louis XIV to a body of horse charged with the preservation of order; after the Revolution to a military police chosen from old soldiers of good character, and now to the ordinary police.

Gender Words. These are words which, prefixed to the noun, indicate an animal's sex —
Bull, cow · Elephant, rhinoceros, seal, whale
Dog, bitch ape, fox (the bitch is usually called a vixen), otter, wolf.
Buck, doe hare, rabbit, deer.
He, she general gender words for quadrupeds.
Cock, hen gender words for most birds
In many cases a different word is used for each of the sexes, *e.g.*:—
Boar, sow; cockerel, pullet, colt, filly, drake, duck, drone, bee, gander, goose, hart, roe; ram, ewe; stag, hind, stallion, mare; steer, heifer, ram, wether, tup, dam.

Generalissimo. The supreme commander, especially of a force drawn from two or more nations, or of a combined military and naval force The title is said to have been coined by Cardinal Richelieu on taking supreme command of the French armies in Italy, in 1629 Called *Tagus* among the ancient Thessalians, *Brennus* among the ancient Gauls, *Pendragon* among the ancient Welsh or Celts
In modern times the title has been applied to Marshal Foch (1851-1929) who was appointed generalissimo of the Allied forces in France in 1918, to Joseph Stalin (b. 1879) who was made marshal and generalissimo of the Soviet forces in 1943, to General Franco (b. 1882) who proclaimed himself generalissimo of the Spanish army in 1939, to Marshal Chiang Kai-Shek, President of the Nationalist Republic of China, and leader of the Chinese armies against the Japanese and internal foes

General Issue. The plea of "Not guilty" to a criminal charge, "Never indebted" to a charge of debt, the issue formed by a general denial of the plaintiff's charge.

Generic Names. *See* BIDDY.

Generous. Generous as Hatim. An Arabian expression Hatim was a Bedouin chief famous for his warlike deeds and boundless generosity. His son was contemporary with Mohammed.
Let Zal and Rustum bluster as they will,
Or Hatim call to Supper—heed not you
FITZGERALD: *Rubaiyat of Omar Khayyam*, x.

Geneva (je ne' va). *See* GIN.

The Geneva Bible. *See* BIBLE, THE ENGLISH

The Geneva Bull. A nickname given to Stephen Marshall (c. 1594-1655), a Presbyterian divine, and one of the authors of *Smectymnuus* (q v.), because he was a disciple of John Calvin, of Geneva, and when preaching he roared like a "bull of Bashan."

Geneva Convention. Henri Dunant, a Swiss, published an account of the sufferings of the wounded at the battle of Solferino in 1859 From this sprang (1) the International Red Cross, and (2) an international convention,

1864, governing the treatment of wounded. At a conference in London in 1872 Dunant suggested a code for the treatment of prisoners of war which was adopted by all civilized nations

Geneva courage Pot valour, the braggadocio which is the effect of having drunk too much gin (*q v*), or *geneva*. Cp DUTCH COURAGE

Geneva Cross *See* RED CROSS.

Geneva doctrines Calvinism Calvin, in 1541, was invited to take up his residence in Geneva as the public teacher of theology From this period Geneva was for many years the centre of education for the Protestant youths of Europe.

Geneviève, St. (je nâ věv) (422-512). Patroness of the city of Paris Her day is January 3rd, and she is represented in art with the keys of Paris at her girdle, a devil blowing out her candle, and an angel relighting it, or as restoring sight to her blind mother, or guarding her father's sheep She was born at Nanterre, and was influential in averting a threatened attack on Paris by Attila, the Hun.

Genius (pl. **Genii**) In Roman mythology the tutelary spirit that attended one from his cradle to his grave, governed his fortunes, determined his character, and so on. The Eastern genii (sing genie) were entirely different from the Roman, not attendant spirits, but fallen angels, dwelling in Djinnistan, under the dominion of Eblis, the Roman were very similar to the guardian angels spoken of in *Matt* xviii, 10, and in this sense Mephistopheles is spoken of as the *evil genius* (the "familiar") of Faust. The Romans maintained that two genii attended every man from birth to death—one good and the other evil. Good luck was brought about by the agency of "his good genius," and ill luck by that of his "evil genius."

The *genius loci* was the tutelary deity of a place

The word is from the Lat *gignere*, to beget (Gr. *gignesthai*, to be born), from the notion that birth and life were due to these *dii genitales* Hence it is used for birth-wit or innate talent; hence propensity, nature, inner man

Genocide (jen' ō sid) A word invented by Prof Raphael Lemkin, of Duke University, U S A, and used in the drafting of the official indictment of war criminals in 1945 It comes from the Greek *genos*, race, and Latin *caedere*, to kill It is defined as acts intended to destroy, in whole or in part, national, ethnical, racial, or religious groups. On 9th December, 1948, it was declared by the United Nations General Assembly to be a crime in international law

Genre Painter (zhon' re). A painter of domestic, rural, or village scenes, such as *A Village Wedding*, *The Young Recruit*, *Blind Man's Buff*, *The Village Politician*, etc. In the drama, Victor Hugo introduced the genre system in lieu of the stilted, unnatural style of Louis XIV's era.

We call those "genre" canvases, whereon are painted idylls of the fireside, the roadside, and the farm; pictures of real life —E. C. STEDMAN; *Poets of America*, ch iv

Gens (jenz) (Lat pl *gentes*) A clan or sept in ancient Rome; a number of families deriving from a common ancestor, having the same name, religion, etc

Gens braccata (Lat) Trousered people The Romans wore no trousers ("breeches") like the Gauls, Scythians, and Persians. *Cp.* GALLIA BRACCATA

Gens togata. *See* TOGA.

Gentle. Belonging to a family of position, well born, having the manners of genteel persons.

We must be gentle, now we are gentlemen.— *Winter's Tale*, v, 2

The word is from Lat. *gentilis*, of the same family or *gens*, through O Fr *gentil*, high-born

The gentle craft. Shoe-making, so called from St. Crispin, who is said to have been a Roman citizen of high birth who was converted to Christianity, left his native city on account of persecution, became a shoemaker at Soissons, and was martyred about 285

As I am a true shoemaker and a gentleman of the gentle craft, buy spurs yourselves, and I'll find ye boots these seven years —DEKKER *The Shoemaker's Holiday, or a Pleasant Comedy of the Gentle Craft*, I, i (1599)

Angling is also known as "the gentle craft" —perhaps because there is nothing that can be called rough about its practice.

The Gentle Shepherd. A nickname given by Pitt to George Grenville (1712-70) In the course of a speech on the cider tax (1763) Grenville addressed the House somewhat plaintively "Tell me where? tell me where?" Pitt hummed a line of a song then very popular, "Gentle shepherd, tell me where?" The House burst into laughter; and the name stuck to Grenville The line is from a song by Samuel Howard (1710-82), a writer of many popular lyrics.

Gentleman (formed on the model of Fr. *gentilhomme*). Properly, a man entitled to bear arms but not of the nobility; hence, one of gentle birth, of some position in society, and with the manners, bearing, and behaviour appropriate to one in such a position

Be it spoken (with all reverent reservation of duty) the King who hath power to make Esquires, Knights, Baronets, Barons, Viscounts, Earls, Marquesses, and Dukes, *cannot make a Gentleman*, for Gentilitie is a matter of race, and of blood, and of descent, from Gentle and noble parents and ancestors, which no Kings can give to any, but to such as they beget — EDMOND HOWES.

Juliana Berners, in her *Boke of St Albans* (1486), in the treatise "Blasyng of Armys," has a curious use of the word —

Of the offspring of the gentilman Jafeth came Habraham, Moyses, Aron, and the profettys and also the kyng of the right lyne of Mary, of whom that gentilman Jhesus was borne very god and man. after his manhode kyng of the londe of Judea of Jues, gentilman by is modre Mary prynce of Cote armure

In the *York Mysteries* also (about 1440) we read, "Ther schall a gentilman, Jesu, unjustely be judged "

A gentleman at large. A man of means, who does not have to work for his living, and is free to come and go as he pleases Formerly the term denoted a gentleman attached to the court but having no special duties.

A gentleman of fortune. A pirate, an adventurer (a euphemistic phrase)

A gentleman of the four outs. A vulgar upstart, with-*out* manners, with-*out* wit, with-*out* money, and with-*out* credit There are variants of the phrase, and sometimes the *outs* are increased to five —

> Out of money, and out of clothes,
> Out at the heels, and out at the toes,
> Out of credit—but, don't forget,
> Never *out of* but aye *in* debt!

A gentleman's gentleman. A manservant, especially a valet.

Fag My master shall know this—and if *he* don't call him out *I* will
Lucy Ha! ha! ha! You gentlemen's gentlemen are so hasty! SHERIDAN. *The Rivals*, II, 11

A nation of gentlemen. So George IV called the Scots when, in 1822, he visited their country and was received with great expressions of loyalty

Gentleman Commoner. *See* FELLOW COMMONER.

Gentleman Pensioner. *See* GENTLEMEN AT ARMS, *below.*

Gentleman-ranker. In the days of the small regular army before World War I this term was applied to a well-born or educated man who enlisted as a private soldier It was considered a last resort of one who had made a mess of things

> We're poor little lambs who've lost our way,
> Baa! Baa! Baa!
> We're little black sheep who've gone astray,
> Baa—aa—aa!
> Gentlemen-rankers out on the spree,
> Damned from here to Eternity,
> God ha' mercy on such as we
> Baa! Yah! Bah!
> KIPLING *Gentlemen Rankers*

Gentleman Usher. A court official belonging to one of four classes, viz : (1) *Gentlemen Ushers of the Privy Chamber*, these are in closest association with the Sovereign, wait on him at chapel, and conduct him in the absence of the Lord Chamberlain (2) *Gentlemen Ushers Daily Waiters*, who are headed by Black Rod (*q v.*) and officiate monthly by turns in the Presence Chamber (3) *Gentlemen Ushers Quarterly Waiters*, who act as deputies for the preceding in their absence (4) The *Gentleman Usher to the Robes*, who replaces the Groom of the Stole (*q v*), an office which was allowed to lapse at the accession of Queen Victoria, the *Mistress of the Robes* taking his place.

Gentlemen at Arms, The Honourable Corps of. The Bodyguard of the Sovereign (formerly called *Gentlemen Pensioners*), acting in conjunction with the Yeomen of the Guard (*q v*) It consists of 40 retired officers of ranks from general to major of the Regular Army and Marines, and has a Captain, Lieutenant, Standard Bearer, Clerk of the Cheque & Adjutant, and a Harbinger

The gentleman in black velvet. It was in these words that the 18th-century Jacobites used to toast the mole that made the molehill that caused William III's horse to stumble and so brought about his death

The Old Gentleman. The Devil; Old Nick. Also a special card in a prepared pack, used for tricks or cheating.

To put a churl upon a gentleman. To drink beer just after drinking wine.

Geomancy (jē' ō măn si) (Gr *ge*, the earth, *manteia*, prophecy) Divining by the earth. Diviners in the 16th century made deductions from the patterns made by earth thrown into the air and allowed to fall on some flat surface, and drew on the earth their magic circles, figures, lines, etc.

Geopolitics (jē ō pol' i tiks). Theories relating to a nation's political dependence on physical environment and its geographical position The chief developers of these theories were Sir Halford Mackinder, Father Walsh (U.S A), and Karl Haushofer in Germany The Nazis seized on the teachings of the last-named and distorted them to support their demand for *lebensraum.*

George. St. George. The patron saint of England since about the time of the institution of the Order of the Garter (*c* 1348), when he was "adopted" by Edward III He is commemorated on April 23rd

St George had been popular in England from the time of the early Crusades, for he was said to have come to the assistance of the Crusaders at Antioch (1089), and many of the Normans (under Robert, son of William the Conqueror) then took him as their patron.

St George suffered martyrdom near Lydda before the 4th century There are various versions of his *Acta*, one saying that he was a tribune and that he was asked to come and subdue a dragon that infested a pond at Silene, Libya, and fed on the dwellers in the neighbourhood St George came, rescued a princess (Sabra) whom the dragon was about to make its prey, and slew the monster.

That St. George is an historical character is beyond all reasonable doubt, but no connexion whatever can be established between this martyr and the Arian bishop George of Cappadocia, as Gibbon and others have suggested.

The legend of St George and the dragon is simply an allegorical expression of the triumph of the Christian hero over evil, which St John the Divine beheld under the image of a dragon Similarly, St. Michael, St Margaret, St Silvester, and St. Martha are all depicted as slaying dragons, the Saviour and the Virgin as treading them under their feet, St. John the Evangelist as charming a winged dragon from a poisoned chalice given him to drink, and Bunyan avails himself of the same figure when he makes Christian prevail against Apollyon

The legend forms the subject of an old ballad given in Percy's *Reliques*, in which St. George was the son of Lord Albert of Coventry.

St. George he was for England, St. Denis was for France. This refers to the war-cries of the two nations—that of England was "St George!" that of France, "Montjoye St. Denis!"

> Our ancient word of courage, fair "St George",
> Inspire us with the spleen of fiery dragons
> *Richard III*, v, 3

St. George's Cross. Red on a white background

When St. George goes on horseback St. Yves goes on foot. In times of war it was supposed that lawyers have nothing to do. St. George is the patron of soldiers, and St. Yves, or Yvo, an early French judge and lawyer noted for his incorruptibility and just decrees (d 1303, canonized 1347), patron of lawyers

George IV was the only English king whose manner of life dubbed him with nicknames. As Prince Regent he was known as "Prinny." "Prince Florizel" (the name under which he corresponded with Mrs Robinson), "The First Gentleman of Europe," "The Adonis of fifty" (for writing this Leigh Hunt was sent to prison in 1813) As king he was called, among less offensive titles, "Fum the Fourth" Byron writes (*Don Juan*, xi. 78) :—

And where is Fum the Fourth, our royal bird?

George Cross and Medal The George Cross is second only to the Victoria Cross It consists of a plain silver cross, with a medallion showing St George and the Dragon in the centre. The words "For Gallantry" appear round the medallion, and in the angle of each limb of the cross is the royal cipher It hangs from a dark blue ribbon. The George Cross was founded in 1940, primarily for civilians, and is awarded only for acts of the greatest heroism or the most conspicuous courage in circumstances of extreme danger. The George Medal (red ribbon with five narrow blue stripes) is awarded in similar circumstances to the Cross where services are not so outstanding as to merit the higher award

As good as George-a-Green. Resolute-minded; one who will do his duty come what may. George-a-green was the mythical *Pinder* (Pinner or Pindar) or pound-keeper of Wakefield, who resisted Robin Hood, Will Scarlett, and Little John single-handed when they attempted to commit a trespass in Wakefield

Were ye bold as George-a-Green,
I shall make bold to turn again
BUTLER *Hudibras*.

Robert Greene wrote a comedy (published 1599) called *George-a-Greene, or the Pinner of Wakefield*

Geraint (ge rānt' ge rīnt') In Arthurian legend, a tributary prince of Devon, and one of the knights of the Round Table In the *Mabinogion* story he is the son of Erbin, as he is in the French original, Chrestien de Troyes' *Eric et Enide*, from which Tennyson drew his *Geraint and Enid* in the *Idylls of the King*

Geraldine (je' rāl dēn) **The Fair Geraldine.** Lady Elizabeth Fitzgerald (d 1589) is so called in the Earl of Surrey's poems. She was the youngest daughter of the Earl of Kildare

Geranium. The Turks say this was a common mallow changed by the touch of Mohammed's garment.

The word is Gr. *geranos*, a crane; and the wild plant is called "Crane's Bill," from the resemblance of the fruit to the bill of a crane

Gerda, or **Gerdhr** (gĕr' da). In Scandinavian mythology (the *Skirnismal*), a young giantess, wife of Frey, and daughter of the frost giant Gymer She is so beautiful that the brightness of her naked arms illumines both air and sea.

Geriatrics (jĕ rī ăt' riks) The study of old age, medically and socially. The word comes from the Greek *geron*, an old man

German or **germane.** Pertaining to, nearly related to, as *cousins-german* (first cousins), *germane to the subject* (bearing on or pertinent to the subject). This word has no connexion with the German nation, but is Lat, *germanus*, of the same germ or stock

Those that are germane to him, though removed fifty times, shall all come under the hangman — *Winter's Tale*, iv, 3

Germany. The English name for the German *Deutschland* (Fr *Allemagne*) is the Lat. *Germania*, the source of which is not certain; it is thought to be the form given by the Romans to the Celtic or Gaulish name for the Teutons, in which case it may be connected either with Celt *gair*, neighbour, *gavim*, war-cry, or *ger*, spear.

Geoffrey of Monmouth, recording popular eponymic legends, says that Ebrancus, a mythological descendant of Brute (*q v*) and founder of York (*Eboracum*), had twenty sons and thirty daughters All the sons, except the eldest, settled in Germany, which was therefore called the land of the *germans* or brothers Spenser, speaking of "Ebranck," says —

An happy man in his first days he was,
And happy father of fair progeny,
For all so many weeks as the year has
So many children he did multiply?
Of which were twenty sons, which did apply
Their minds to praise and chivalrous desire
Those germans did subdue all Germany,
Of whom it hight.   *Faerie Queene*, II, x, 22.

German comb. The four fingers and thumb The Germans were the last nation to adopt periwigs, and while the French were never seen without a comb in one hand, the Germans adjusted their hair by running their fingers through it

He apparelled himself according to the season, and afterwards combed his head with an Alman comb — RABELAIS Bk. 1, 21.

German silver. A silvery-looking alloy of copper, zinc, and nickel. It was first made in Europe at Hildburghausen, in Germany, in the early 19th century, but had been used by the Chinese time out of mind

Geronimo (je ron' i mō) The name taken by Goyathlay (One who Yawns), an Apache chieftain who led a sensational Indian campaign against the Whites in 1885-6 He was captured by General Cook, escaped, was recaptured, and imprisoned for some time. He later became a member of the Dutch Reformed Church, and wrote his memoirs, 1906

Gerrymander (jer i măn' dẽr) So to divide a county or nation into representative districts as to give one special political party undue advantage over others. The word is derived from Elbridge Gerry (1744-1814), who adopted the scheme in Massachusetts in 1812 when he was governor. Gilbert Stuart, the artist, looking at the map of the new distribution, with a little invention converted it into a salamander "No, no!" said Russell, when shown it, "not a Sala-mander, Stuart, call it a Gerry-mander"

Hence, to hocus-pocus statistics, election results, etc., so as to make them appear to give other than their true result, or so as to affect the balance

Gertrude, St. An abbess (d 664), aunt of Charles Martel's father, Pepin She founded hospices for pilgrims, and so is a patron saint of travellers, and is said to harbour souls on the first night of their three days' journey to heaven She is also the protectress against rats and mice, and is sometimes represented as surrounded by them, or with them running about her distaff as she spins

Geryon (ger' i on) In Greek mythology, a monster with three bodies and three heads, whose oxen ate human flesh, and were guarded by Orthros, a two-headed dog Hercules slew both Geryon and the dog

Gessler, Hermann (ges' ler) The tyrannical Austrian governor of the three Forest Cantons of Switzerland who figures in the Tell legend *See* TELL, WILLIAM

Gesta Romanorum (jes' ta rō ma nôr' um) A pseudo-devotional compilation of popular tales in Latin (many from Oriental sources), each with an arbitrary "moral" attached for the use of preachers, assigned—in its collected form—to about the end of the 14th century The name, meaning "The Acts of the Romans," is merely fanciful. It was first printed at Utrecht about 1472, and the earliest English edition is that of Wynkyn de Worde about 1510, but long before this the people had, through the pulpit, come to know it, and many English poets, from Chaucer to William Morris, have laid it under contribution Shakespeare drew the plot of *Pericles* from the *Gesta Romanorum*, as well as the incident of the three caskets in the *Merchant of Venice*

Gestapo (ge sta' pō). A word made up from the German *Geheime Staatspolizei*, the political police who acquired such sinister fame in Nazi Germany. It was organized by Heinrich Himmler as an independent supreme Reich authority, beyond all judicial or administrative control, and to it was committed the execution of all punitive or repressive measures of the government.

Gestas (jes' tăs) The traditional name of the impenitent thief *See* DYSMAS

Get. With its past and past participle *got*, one of the hardest-worked words in the English language; the following example from a mid-Victorian writer shows some of its uses—and abuses —

I got on horseback within ten minutes after I got your letter When I got to Canterbury I got a chaise for town, but I got wet through, and have got such a cold that I shall not get rid of in a hurry. I got to the Treasury about noon, but first of all got shaved and dressed I soon got into the secret of getting a memorial before the Board, but I could not get an answer then, however, I got intelligence from a messenger that I should get one next morning As soon as I got back to my inn, I got my supper, and then got to bed. When I got up next morning, I got my breakfast, and, having got dressed, I got out in time to get an answer to my memorial As soon as I got it, I got into a chaise, and got back to Canterbury by three, and got home for tea I have got nothing for you, and so adieu

For phrases such as To get out of bed the **wrong side**, To get the mitten, To get the wind **up**, etc , see the main word in the phrase

How are you getting on? How do things fare with you? How are you prospering?

To get at. To tamper with, bribe, influence to a wrong end, especially used in horse-racing

To get by. To get along all right, just satisfactorily

To get down to it To set about your work or whatever it is you have in hand in down-right earnest

To get it in the neck. To receive a thorough dressing down, beating, punishment, etc

To get off. To escape, also (of a girl) to become engaged to be married, or to make acquaintanceship with a man.

To get there. To succeed, to "arrive", attain one's object

To get up To rise from one's bed To learn, as "I must get up my history " To organize and arrange, as "We will get up a bazaar."

To get well on, or well oiled. To become intoxicated

Who are you getting at? Who are you trying to take a rise out of? Whose leg are you trying to pull? A question usually asked sarcastically by the intended butt.

Your get-up was excellent. Your style of dress exactly suited the part you professed to enact In the same way, *She was got up regardless*, her dress was splendid, money was no object when obtaining it—it was bought "regardless of expense "

Gethsemane (geth sem' á ni). The *Orchis maculata*, supposed in legendary story to be spotted by the blood of Christ.

Gewgaw. A showy trifle The word may be an imitation of Fr. *jou-jou*, a baby word for a toy (*jouer*, to play), or it may be from *givegove*, a M E reduplication of *give*.

Ghebers, *See* GUEBRES

Ghibelline (gib' e lēn). The imperial and aristocratic faction in Italy in the Middle Ages, opposed to the Guelphs (*see* GUELPHS AND GHIBELLINES) The name was the war-cry of the followers of the Emperor Conrad at the battle of Weinsberg (1140), and is the Italian form of Ger *Waiblingen*, an estate in Wurtemberg, then belonging to the Emperor's family, the House of Hohenstaufen *See* GOBLIN

Ghost. To give up the ghost. To die The idea is that life is independent of the body, and is due to the habitation of the ghost or spirit in the material body.

Man dieth, and wasteth away yea, man giveth up the ghost, and where is he?—*Job* xiv, 10

The ghost of a chance. The least likelihood. "He has not the ghost of a chance of being elected," not the shadow of a probability.

The ghost walks. Theatrical slang for salaries are about to be paid, when there's no money in the treasury actors say "the ghost won't walk this time." The allusion is to *Hamlet* i, 1, where Horatio asks the ghost if it ' walks' because—

Thou hast uphoarded in thy life
Extorted treasure in the womb of earth

Ghost-word. A term invented by Skeat (*Philol Soc Transactions*, 1886) to denote words that have no real existence but are due to the blunders of scribes, printers, or editors, etc Like ghosts we may seem to see them, or may fancy that they exist, but they have no real entity. We cannot grasp them When we would do so, they disappear. *Acre-fight* and *slughorn* (*q v.*) are examples

Intrusive letters that have no etymological right in a word but have been inserted through false analogy with words similarly pronounced (like the *gh* in *sprightly* or the *h* in *aghast*) are sometimes called **ghost-letters**

Ghost writer. The anonymous author who writes speeches, articles, or even books—especially autobiographies—for which another and better-known person gets the credit

Giants, *i e* persons well above the average height and size, are by no means uncommon as "sports" or "freaks of nature", but the widespread belief in pre-existing races or individual instances of giants among primitive peoples is due partly to the ingrained idea that the present generation is invariably a degeneration—"There were giants in the earth in those days" (*Gen.* vi, 4)—and partly to the existence from remote antiquity of cyclopæan buildings, gigantic sarcophagi, etc , and to the discovery from time to time in pre-scientific days of the bones of extinct monsters which were taken to be those of men Among instances of the latter may be mentioned the following —

A skeleton discovered at Lucerne in 1577 19 ft. in height. Dr. Plater is our authority for this measurement

"Teutobochus," whose remains were discovered near the Rhone in 1613 They occupied a tomb 30 ft long The bones of another gigantic skeleton were exposed by the action of the Rhone in 1456 If this was a human skeleton, the height of the living man must have been 30 ft

Pliny records that an earthquake in Crete exposed the bones of a giant 46 cubits (*i.e* roughly 75 ft.) in height, he called this the skeleton of Orion, others held it to be that of Otus.

Antæus is said by Plutarch to have been 60 cubits (about 90 ft.) in height He furthermore adds that the grave of the giant was opened by Serbonius

The "monster Polypheme " It is said that his skeleton was discovered at Trapani, in Sicily, in the 14th century If this skeleton was that of a man, he must have been 300 ft in height.

Giants of the Bible.

ANAK The eponymous progenitor of the Anakim (*see below*) The Hebrew spies said they were mere grasshoppers in comparison with these giants. (*Josh.* xv, 14, *Judges* i, 20, and *Numb.* xiii, 33).

GOLIATH of Gath (*I Sam* xvii, etc) His height is given as 6 cubits and a span. the cubit varied and might be anything from about 18 in to 21 in , and a span was about 9 in , this would give Goliath a height of between 9 ft 9 in and 11 ft 3 in

OG, King of Bashan (*Josh*, xii, 4, *Deut* iii, 8, iv, 47, etc), was "of the remnant of the Rephaim " According to tradition, he lived 3,000 years and walked beside the Ark during the Flood One of his bones formed a bridge over a river. His bed (*Deut* iii, 11) was 9 cubits by 4 cubits.

The ANAKIM and REPHAIM were tribes of reputed giants inhabiting the territory on both sides of the Jordan before the coming of the Israelites. The NEPHILIM, the offspring of the sons of God and the daughters of men (*Gen.* vi, 4), a mythological race of semi-divine heroes, were also giants

The giants of Greek mythology were, for the most part, sons of Tartarus and Ge. When they attempted to storm heaven, they were hurled to earth by the aid of Hercules, and buried under Mount Etna. Those of Scandinavian mythology were evil genii, dwelling in Jotunheim (*giant-land*), who had terrible and superhuman powers, could appear and disappear, reduce and extend their stature at will, etc

Many names of ancient giants will be found in their appropriate places in this Dictionary.

Giants of Later Tradition.

ANDRONICUS II was 10 ft in height. He was grandson of Alexius Comnenus Nicetas asserts that he had seen him

CHARLEMAGNE was nearly 8 ft in height, and was so strong he could squeeze together three horseshoes with his hands

ELEAZER was 7 cubits (nearly 11 ft.) Vitellus sent this giant to Rome, he is mentioned by Josephus Goliath was 6 cubits and a span

GABARA, the Arabian giant, was 9 ft 9 in This Arabian giant is mentioned by Pliny, who says he was the tallest men seen in the days of Claudius

HARDRADA (*Harold*) was nearly 8 ft in height ("5 ells of Norway"), and was called "the Norway giant "

MAXIMINUS I was 8 ft 6 in in height. Roman emperor from about 235 to 238

OSEN (*Heinrich*) was 7 ft 6 in in height at the age of 27, and weighed above 37 st He was born in Norway

PORUS was 5 cubits in height (about 7½ ft) He was an Indian king who fought against Alexander the Great near the Hydaspes (*Quintus Curtius De rebus gestis Alexandri Magni*)

Josephus speaks of a Jew 10 ft 2 in

Becanus asserts that he had seen a man nearly 10 ft. high, and a woman fully 10 ft

Gasper Bauhin speaks of a Swiss 8 ft in height.

Del Rio tells us he himself saw a Piedmontese in 1572 more than 9 ft. in height

A Mr Warren (in *Notes and Queries*, August 14th, 1875) said that his father knew a woman 9 ft in height, and adds "her head touched the ceiling of a good-sized room "

Vanderbrook says he saw in the Congo a black man 9 ft high.

A giant was exhibited at Rouen in the early part of the 18th century 17 ft 10 in (!) in height

Gorapus, the surgeon, tells us of a Swedish giantess, who, at the age of 9, was over 10 ft in height.

Turner, the naturalist, tells us he *saw* in Brazil a giant 12 ft in height

M Thevet published, in 1575, an account of a South American giant, the skeleton of which he measured It was 11 ft 5 in.

Giants of Modern Times.

BAMPORD (*Edward*) was 7 ft. 4 in He died in 1768, and was buried in St Dunstan's churchyard.

BATES (*Captain*) was 7 ft. 11½ in He was a native of Kentucky, and was exhibited in London in 1871 His wife, Anne Hannen Swan, a native of Nova Scotia, was the same height

BLACKER (*Henry*) was 7 ft. 4 in and most symmetrical He was born at Cuckfield, in Sussex, in 1724, and was called "The British Giant."

BRADLEY (*William*) was 7 ft 9 in. in height He was born in 1787, and died 1820 His birth is duly registered in the parish church of Market Weighton, in Yorkshire, and his right hand is preserved in the museum of the College of Surgeons

BRICE (*M J.*) exhibited under the name of Anak, was 7 ft. 8 in in height at the age of 26. He was born in 1840 at Ramonchamp, in the Vosges, and visited England 1862-5 His arms had a stretch of 95½ in.

BRUSTED (*Von*) was 8 ft. in height This Norwegian giant was exhibited in London in 1880.

BUSBY (*John*) was 7 ft. 9 in. in height, and his brother was about the same. They were natives of Darfield, in Yorkshire.

CHANG, the Chinese giant, was 8 ft 2 in in height He was exhibited in London in 1865-6, and again in 1880

COTTER (*Patrick*) was 8 ft 7½ in in height This Irish giant died at Clifton, Bristol, in 1802 A cast of his hand is preserved in the museum of the College of Surgeons

DANIEL, the porter of Oliver Cromwell, was a man of gigantic stature

ELEIZEGUE (*Joachim*) was 7 ft 10 in in height He was a Spaniard, and exhibited in the Cosmorama Regent Street, London, in the mid-19th century

EVANS (*William*) was 8 ft at death He was a porter of Charles I, and died in 1632

FRANK (*Big*) was 7 ft 8 in in height He was Francis Sheridan, an Irishman, and died in 1870

FRENZ (*Louis*) was 7 ft 4 in, in height He was called "the French giant," and his left hand is preserved in the museum of the College of Surgeons

GILLY was 8 ft This Swedish giant was exhibited in the early part of the 10th century

GORDON (*Alice*) was 7 ft in height She was a native of Essex, and died in 1737, in the age of 19

HALE (*Robert*) was 7 ft 6 in in height He was born at Somerton, in Norfolk, and was called "the Norfolk giant" (1820-62)

HOLMES (*Benjamin*) was 7 ft 6 in in height He was a Northumberland man, and was made sword-bearer to the Corporation of Worcester. He died in 1892

LOUISHKIN A Russian giant of 8 ft. 5 in , drum-major of the Imperial Guards

MCDONALD (*James*) was 7 ft 6 in in height Born in Cork, Ireland, and died in 1760

MCDONALD (*Samuel*) was 6 ft 10 in in height This Scot was usually called "Big Sam " He was the Prince of Wales's footman, and died in 1802.

MAGRATH (*Cornelius*) was 7 ft 10 in in height at the age of 16 He was an orphan reared by Bishop Berkeley, and died at the age of 20 (1740-60)

MELLON (*Edmund*) was 7 ft 6 in in height at the age of 19 He was born at Port Leicester, in Ireland (1665-84)

MIDDLETON (*John*) was 9 ft 3 in in height. (*Cp* GABARA, *above*) "His hand was 17 inches long and 8½ broad " He was born at Hale, Lancashire, in the reign of James I (*Dr. Plott· Natural History of Staffordshire*, p 295)

MILLER (*Maximilian Christopher*) was 8 ft in height. His hand measured 12 in , and his forefinger was 9 in long This Saxon giant died in London at the age of 60 (1674-1734)

MURPHY was 8 ft 10 in in height An Irish giant of the late 18th century He died at Marseilles

O'BRIEN, or CHARLES BYRNE, was 8 ft 4 in in height The skeleton of this Irish giant is preserved in the College of Surgeons He died in Cockspur Street, London (1761-83)

O'BRIEN (*Patrick*), was 8 ft 7 in in height. He died August 3, 1804, aged 39

RIECHART (*J N*) was 8 ft. 4 in in height. He was a native of Friedberg, and both his father and mother were of gigantic stature

SALMERON (*Martin*) was 7 ft 4 in. in height He was called 'The Mexican Giant "

SAM (*Big*) See McDONALD

SHERIDAN See FRANK.

SWAN (*Anne Hannen*) See BATES

TOLLER (*James*) was 8 ft at the age of 24 He died in February, 1819

In the museum of Trinity College, Dublin, is a human skeleton 8 ft 6 in. in height.

Thomas Hall, of Willingham, was 3 ft. 9 in. at the age of 3.

Giants, Battle of the. Melagnano or Marignano, situated on the Lambro, 9 miles south-east of Milan. On September 13-14th, 1515 the French under Francis I defeated the Swiss mercenaries defending the city of Milan The same battlefield was the scene of the French victory over the Austrians, June 8th, 1859

Giant's Causeway. A formation of prismatic

basaltic columns, projecting into the sea about 8 miles E N E of Portrush, Co. Antrim, on the north coast of Ireland It is fabled to be the beginning of a road to be constructed by the giants across the channel, reaching from Ireland to Scotland

Giants' Dance, The. Stonehenge, which Geoffrey of Monmouth says was removed from Killaraus, a mountain in Ireland, by the magical skill of Merlin

Giant's Leap, The. A name popularly given in many mountainous districts to two prominent rocks separated from each other by a wide chasm or open stretch of country across which some giant is fabled to have leapt while being pursued and so to have baffled his followers

Giants' Ring, The A prehistoric circular mound near Milltown, Co Down, Ireland It is 580 ft in diameter, and has a cromlech in the centre

Giants' War with Zeus, The. The War of the Giants and the War of the Titans should be kept distinct The latter was *after* Zeus became god of heaven and earth, the former was *before* that time Kronos, a Titan, had been exalted by his brothers to the supremacy, but Zeus dethroned him, after ten years' contest, and hurled the Titans into hell The other war was a revolt by the giants against Zeus, which was readily put down by the help of the other gods and the aid of Hercules

Giaour (jou' er) Among Mohammedans, one who is not an adherent of their faith, especially a Christian; generally used with a contemptuous or insulting implication. The word is a variant of Guebre (*q v*).

The city won for Allah from the Giaour,
The Giaour from Othman's race again may wrest
BYRON *Childe Harold*, c 11, st 77

Gib Cat (jib kăt) A tom-cat. The male cat used to be called Gilbert Tibert or Tybalt (*q v*) is the French form of Gilbert, and hence Chaucer, or whoever it was that translated that part of the *Romance of the Rose*, renders "Thibert le Cas" by "Gibbe, our Cat" (line 6204) Generally used of a castrated cat.

I am as melancholy as a gib cat or a lugged bear —
1 *Henry IV*, i, 2.

Gibberish (jib' er ish) Unmeaning talk; words without meaning, formerly, the lingo of rogues and gipsies. Johnson says in his *Dictionary*—

As it was anciently written *gebrish* it is probably derived from the chymical cant [i e the mystical language of the alchemists], and originally implied the jargon of *Gebir* and his tribe

Geber, the Arabian, was by far the greatest alchemist of the 11th century, and wrote several treatises in mystical jargon Friar Bacon, in 1282, furnishes a specimen of this gibberish He is giving the prescription for making gunpowder, and says —

Sed tamen salis-petræ
LURU MONE CAP URBE
Et sulphuris.

The second line is merely an anagram of *Carbonum pulvere* (pulverized charcoal).

Gibeonite (gib' i on it). A slave's slave, a workman's labourer, a farmer's under-strapper, or Jack-of-all-work The Gibeonites were made "hewers of wood and drawers of water" to the Israelites (*Josh* ix, 27)

Gibraltar (jib rol' taɾ) The "Calpe" and 'Pillars of Hercules'' of the ancients. The modern name is a corruption of *Gebel-al-Tarik*, the Hill of Tarik, Tarik being a Saracen leader who, under the orders of Mousa, landed at Calpe in 710, utterly defeated Roderick, the Gothic King of Spain, and built a castle on the rock It was taken from the Moors in 1462, in 1704 a combined force of English and Dutch took the place, since when it has remained in British hands The Spaniards and French besieged it in 1704-5, the Spaniards in 1727, and the Spaniards and French in 1779-83, when it was held by Lord Heathfield.

Gibson Girl. A type of feminine beauty characteristic of its period depicted by Charles Dana Gibson (1867-1944) in several popular series of black-and-white drawings, dating from 1896. His delineations of the American girl enjoyed an enormous vogue, culminating in the series entitled *The Education of Mr Pipp* which appeared in *Colliers Weekly* (1899) and formed the basis of a play of that name The Gibson girl, who was depicted in various poses and occupations, was tall, bending forward somewhat from the waist, her individuality accentuated by the period costume of sweeping skirts and large hats.

Gibus (jɪ' bus). An opera-hat named after its inventor, a Parisian hat-maker in the early 19th century. It is a cloth top-hat with a collapsible crown that enables the wearer to fold it up when not in use

Giff Gaff. Give and take; good turn for good turn.

Gifford Lectureships founded in the universities of Edinburgh, Glasgow, Aberdeen, and St Andrews in 1885 by a bequest of Adam Lord Gifford Their subject is Natural Theology, without reference to creed or sect.

Gift-horse. Don't look a gift-horse in the mouth. When a present is made, do not inquire too minutely into its intrinsic value The proverb has its counterpart in many languages

Giggle. Have you found a giggle's nest? A question asked in Norfolk when anyone laughs immoderately and senselessly The meaning is obvious—have you found the place where giggles are made? *Cp* GAPE'S NEST.

Gig-lamps. Slang for spectacles, especially large round ones, the reason is obvious

Giglet. Formerly a light, wanton woman, the word is still in common use in the West of England for a giddy, romping, tomboy girl, and in Salop a flighty person is called a "giggle"

> If this be
> The recompense of striving to preserve
> A wanton gigglet honest, very shortly
> 'Twill make all mankind panders.
> MASSINGER. *The Fatal Dowry*, III, i (1619).

Gigman. A quite respectable person (in contempt), hence *gigmanity*, smug respectability, a word invented by Carlyle. A witness in the trial for murder of John Thurtell (1823) said, "I always thought him [Thurtell] a respectable man." And being asked by the judge why he thought so, replied, "He kept a gig"

Gigolo (jig' ō lō). A French slang term for a prostitute's bully, but more commonly applied to a lounge lizard, a fellow who hires himself out as a dancing-partner or male escort to wealthy women

Gilbertian (gil bêr' ti an). A term applied to anything humorously topsy-turvy, any situation such as those W S Gilbert (1836-1911) depicted in the Gilbert and Sullivan operas Of these perhaps the *Mikado* (1885) furnishes the best examples

Gilbertines (gil' bêr tīnz) An English religious order founded in the 12th century by St Gilbert of Sempringham, Lincolnshire The monks observed the rule of the Augustinians and the nuns that of the Benedictines

Gild. To gild the pill. It was the custom of old-time doctors—quacks and genuine—to make their nauseous pills more attractive, at least to the sight, by gilding them over a thin coating of sugar Hence the phrase means to make an unattractive thing at least appear desirable

Gilded Chamber, The. A familiar name for the House of Lords.

Gilderoy. A famous cattle-stealer and highwayman of Perthshire, who is said to have robbed Cardinal Richelieu in the presence of the king, and hanged a judge He was hanged in 1636, he was noted for his handsome person, and his real name was Patrick Macgregor. There are ballads on him in Percy's *Reliques*, Ritson's collection, etc, and a modern one by Campbell.

To be hung higher than Gilderoy's kite is to be punished more severely than the very worst criminal. The greater the crime, the higher the gallows, was at one time a practical legal axiom The gallows of Montrose was 30 feet high. The ballad says.—

> Of Gilderoy sae fraid they were
> They bound him mickle strong,
> Till Edenburrow they led him thair
> And on a gallows hong,
> They hong him high aboon the rest,
> He was so trim a boy . .

Giles. A mildly humorous generic name for a farmer; the "farmer's boy" in Bloomfield's poem was so called.

Giles, St. Patron saint of cripples. The tradition is that Childeric, king of France, accidentally wounded the hermit in the knee when hunting, and the hermit, that he might the better mortify the flesh, refusing to be cured remained a cripple for life.

His day is September 1st, and his symbol a hind, in allusion to the "heaven directed hind" which went daily to his cave near the mouth of the Rhone to give him milk He is sometimes represented as an old man with an arrow in his knee and a hind by his side.

Churches dedicated to St Giles were usually situated in the outskirts of a city, and originally without the walls, cripples and beggars not being permitted to pass the gates. *See* CRIPPLEGATE

Giles of Antwerp. Giles Coignet, the Flemish painter (1530-1600).

Gills. Humorous slang for the mouth

Blue about the gills Down in the mouth; depressed looking

Rosy, or red about the gills. Flushed with liquor

White in the gills. Showing unmistakable signs of fear or terror—sometimes of sickness

Gillie. A Gaelic word for a Highland manservant or attendant, especially one who waits on a sportsman fishing or hunting

Gillies' Hill In the battle of Bannockburn (1314) King Robert Bruce ordered all the gillies, drivers of carts, and camp followers to go behind a height These, when the battle seemed to favour the Scots, desirous of sharing in the plunder, rushed from their concealment with such arms as they could lay hands on, and the English, thinking them to be a new army, fled in panic The height was ever after called The Gillies' Hill

Gillie-wet-foot. A barefooted Highland lad

Gillites. (U S A). Calvinistic followers of Dr Gill in the District of Columbia.

Gillyflower (jil i flou' ĕr) Not the *July-flower*, but Fr *giroflée*, from *girofle* (a clove), called by Chaucer "gylofre." The common stock, the wallflower, the rocket, the clove pink, and several other plants are so called. (Gr *karuophullon*, Lat *caryophyllum*)

> The fairest flowers o' the season
> Are our carnations and streaked gillyflowers
> *Winter's Tale*, iv, 2.

Gilpin, John (gil' pin), of Cowper's famous ballad (1782) is a caricature of a Mr Beyer, an eminent linendraper at the end of Paternoster Row, where it joins Cheapside. He died in 1791, at the age of 98 It was Lady Austin who told the adventure to our domestic poet, to divert him from his melancholy. The marriage adventure of Commodore Trunnion in *Peregrine Pickle* is very similar to the weddingday adventure of John Gilpin

> John Gilpin was a citizen
> Of credit and renown,
> A trainband captain eke was he
> Of famous London town

Gilt-edge Investments. A phrase introduced in the last quarter of the 19th century to denote securities of the most reliable character, such as Consols and other Government and Colonial stock, first mortgages, debentures, and shares in first-rate companies, etc.

Gimlet-eyed (gim' let), keen-eyed, very sharpsighted, given to watching or peering into things. A *gimlet-eye* is occasionally applied to a squint

Gimmer. A jointed hinge, in Somersetshire, *gimmace* These words, as also *gimmal*, are variants of *gemel*, a ring formed of two interlaced rings, from Lat *gemellus*, the diminutive of *geminus*, a twin.

> Their poor jades
> Lob down their heads, dropping the hides and hips .
> And in their pale dull mouths the gimmal bit
> Lies foul with chew'd grass, still and motionless
> *Henry V*, iv, 2.

Gin. A contraction of *Geneva*, the older name of the spirit, from Fr. *genievre* (O.Fr *genèvre*), juniper, the berries of which were at one time used to flavour the extract of malt in the manufacture of gin.

Gin-sling. A long drink composed mainly of gin and lemon It has been attributed to John Collins, famous bar-tender of Limmer's Hotel in London, but it undoubtedly dates from before his time and is found in the U S A. by 1800.

Ginevra (jin ev' ra) A young Italian bride who hid in a trunk with a spring-lock The lid fell upon her, and she was not discovered till the body had become a skeleton (ROGERS. *Italy*)

Gingerbread Tawdry wares, showy but worthless The allusion is to the gingerbread cakes fashioned like men, animals, etc , and profusely decorated with gold leaf or Dutch leaf, which looked like gold, commonly sold at fairs up to the middle of the 19th century

To take the gilt off the gingerbread To destroy the illusion, to appropriate all the fun or profit and leave the dull base behind

Gingerly Cautiously, with hesitating, mincing, or faltering steps The word is over 400 years old in English, it has nothing to do with ginger, but is probably from O Fr *gensour*, comparative of *gent*, delicate, dainty.

> They spend their goods upon their dansing minions, that mins it fel gingerlie, God wot, tripping like gotes, that an egge would not brek under their feet.—STUBBES *Anatomy of Abuses*, II, i, (1583)

Gingham (ging' am). A playful equivalent of umbrella, properly, a cotton or linen fabric dyed usually in stripes or checks, so called from a Malay word *ginggang* (that came to us through Dutch), meaning striped Littre's derivation of *gingham* from *Guingamp*, in Brittany, has nothing to support it.

Ginnunga Gap (gi nung' ga) The abyss between Niflheim (the region of fog) and Muspelheim (the region of heat) It existed before either land or sea, heaven or earth as a chaotic whirlpool (Scandinavian mythology)

Giotto's O (jot' ō) The old story goes that the Pope wishing to employ artists from all over Italy sent a messenger to collect specimens of their work When the man visited Giotto di Bondone (1276-1337) the artist paused for a moment from the picture he was working on and with his paintbrush drew a perfect circle on a piece of paper In some surprise the man returned to the Pope, who, appreciating the perfection of Giotto's artistry and skill by this unerring circle, required no further proof but employed Giotto forthwith Thus the story—ancient but unauthenticated

> I saw . that the practical teaching of the masters of Art was summed up by the O of Giotto —RUSKIN. *Queen of the Air*, iii

Giovanni, Don. *See* DON JUAN.

Gipsy A member of a dark-skinned nomadic race which first appeared in England about the beginning of the 16th century, and, as they were thought to have come from Egypt, were named *Egyptians*, which soon became corrupted to *Gypcians*, and so to its present form They call themselves *Romany* (from Gipsy *rom*, a man, husband), which is also the name of their language—a debased Hindi dialect with large additions of words from Persian, Armenian, and many European languages.

The name of the largest group of European gipsies is *Atzigan*, this, in Turkey and Greece, became *Tshingian*, in the Balkans and Roumania *Tsigan*, in Hungary *Czigany*, in Germany *Zigeuner*, in Italy *Zingari*, in Portugal *Cigano*, and in Spain *Gitano*. The original name is said to mean "dark man." *See also* BOHEMIAN

Serious study of the Gipsies, their origin, history, language, etc , has been carried out by George Borrow, R Hindes-Groome, B Vesey-Fitzgerald, and others

Giralda. The name given to the great square tower of the cathedral at Seville (formerly a Moorish minaret), which is surmounted by a statue of Faith, so pivoted as to turn with the wind *Giralda* is a Spanish word, and means a weather-vane.

Gird To gird up the loins. To prepare for hard work or a journey. The Jews wore a girdle only when at work or on a journey. Even to the present day, Eastern people who wear loose dresses gird them about the loins

To gird with the sword. To raise to a peerage. It was the Saxon method of investiture to an earldom, continued after the Conquest. Thus, Richard I "girded with the sword" Hugh de Pudsey, the aged Bishop of Durham, making (as he said) "a young earl of an old prelate."

Girdle. A good name is better than a golden girdle. A good reputation is better than money. It used to be customary to carry money in the belt, or in a purse suspended from it, and a girdle of gold meant a "purse of gold."

Children under the girdle. Not yet born.

He has a large mouth but small girdle. Great expenses but small means

He has undone her girdle. Taken her for his wife. The Roman bride wore a chaplet of flowers on her head, and a girdle of sheep's wool about her waist. A part of the marriage ceremony was for the bridegroom to loose this

If he be angry, he knows how to turn his girdle (*Much Ado About Nothing*, v, 1) He knows how to prepare himself to fight Before wrestlers engaged in combat, they turned the buckle of their girdle behind them. Thus, Sir Ralph Winwood writes to Mr Secretary Cecil:

I said, "What I spake was not to make him angry " He replied, "If I were angry, I might turn the buckle of my girdle behind me "—Dec 17, 1602.

The girdle of Venus. *See* CESTUS

To put a girdle round the earth To travel or go round it Puck says, "I'll put a girdle round about the earth in forty minutes." (*Midsummer Night's Dream*, ii, 2.)

Girl. This word is not present in Anglo-Saxon, but appears in Middle English (13th cent), and its etymology has given rise to a host of guesses It was formerly applicable to a child of either sex (a boy was sometimes distinguished as a "knave-girl"), and is nowadays applied to an unmarried woman of almost any age It is probably a diminutive of some lost word cognate with Pomeranian *goer* and Old Low German *gor*, a child. It appears nearly 70 times in Shakespeare, but only twice in the Authorized Version (*Joel* iii, 3; *Zech.* viii, 5)

Girl Guides. The opposite number to the Boy Scouts and organized in 1910 by General Baden-Powell and his sister, Miss Agnes Baden-Powell The training is essentially the same as that of the Scouts and is based on similar promises and laws There are three sections Brownies, aged 8 to 11; Guides, 11 to 16, and Rangers for girls over 16 years of age.

In U.S.A , where they were organized in 1921, they are called Girl Scouts

Girondists, or The Gironde. The moderate republicans in the French Revolution (1791-93). So called from the department of Gironde, which chose for the Legislative Assembly men who greatly distinguished themselves for their oratory, and formed a political party They were subsequently joined by Brissot (and were hence sometimes called the *Brissotins*), Condorcet, and the adherents of Roland.

They were the ruling party in 1792 but were overthrown in the Convention by the Mountain in 1793 and many of their leaders were executed, including Brissot, Vergniaud, Gensonne, Ducos and Sillery.

Gis. A corruption of Jesus or J H S Ophelia says, "By Gis and by St. Charity" (*Hamlet*, iv, 5).

Gitano. *See* GIPSY.

Give. For phrases such as **Give the devil his due, Give a dog a bad name and hang him, To give one beans, etc ,** see the principal noun

A given name. In American usage a given name is a first, or Christian name

A give-away is a revealing or betraying circumstance

To give and take. To be fair, in intercourse with others to practise forbearance and consideration. In horse-racing a **give and take** plate is a prize for a race in which the runners which exceed a standard height carry more, and those that come short of it less, than the standard weight.

To give away. To hand the bride in marriage to the bridegroom, to act the part of the bride's father. Also, to let out a secret, inadvertently or on purpose, to betray an accomplice

To give in. To confess oneself beaten, to yield.

To give it anyone, to give it him hot. To scold or thrash a person As "I gave it him right and left." "I'll give it you when I catch you."

To give oneself away. To betray oneself by some thoughtless action or remark; to damage one's own cause by carelessly letting something out

To give out. To make public Also, to come to an end, to become exhausted; as "My money has quite given out "

To give what for. To administer a sound thrashing

To give way. To break down, to yield.

Gizzard. The strong, muscular second stomach of birds, where the food is ground, attributed humorously to man in some phrases.

That stuck in his gizzard. Annoyed him, was more than he could stomach, or digest

Glacis The sloping bank on the outer edge of the covered way in old fortifications

Glad. To give the glad eye. *See* EYE

Glad rags. A demoded slang term for evening dress

Gladiators. Those who fought in the ring in Rome, originally criminals who thus had the choice of death or liberty They first appeared at the funeral ceremonies of the Romans in 263 B C , they were introduced into festivals about 215 B C Such combats were suppressed in the Eastern Empire by Constantine in A D. 325 and in the West by Theodoric in A D 500

Gladstone A leather bag of various sizes, all convenient to be carried, is so called from the famous statesman William Ewart Gladstone (1809-98) His name was also given to cheap claret, because, in 1860. when Chancellor of the Exchequer, he reduced the duty on French wines

Glæsting's Sow *See* GLASTONBURY

Glamorgan (gla mór' gàn). Geoffrey of Monmouth says that Cundah and Morgan, the sons of Gonorill and Regan, usurped the crown at the death of Cordelia The former resolved to reign alone, chased Morgan into Wales and slew him at the foot of a hill, hence called Gla-Morgan or Glyn-Morgan, valley of Morgan (*See* Spenser *Faerie Queene* II, x, 33) The name is really Welsh for "the district by the side of the sea" (*gwlad*, district, *mor*, the sea, *gant* side).

Glasgow. Arms of. *See* KENTIGERN, ST.

Glasgow magistrate. A salt herring, so called because when George IV visited Glasgow some wag placed a salt herring on the iron guard of the carriage of a well-known magistrate who formed one of the deputation to receive him

Glass, Glass breaker. A wine-bibber. In the early part of the 19th century it was by no means unusual with topers to break off the stand of their wineglass, so that they might not be able to set it down, but were compelled to drink it clean off, without heel-taps

Glass House. Army slang for a military prison It was originally applied to the military prison at North Camp, Aldershot, which had a glass roof

Those who live in glass houses should not throw stones. Those who are open to criticism should be very careful how they criticize others An old proverb found in varying forms from the time of Chaucer at least (*Troylus and Cresseide*, Bk II) Cp also *Matt* VII, 1-4

Glass slipper (of Cinderella). *See* CINDER-ELLA

Glasse, Mrs. Hannah A name immortalized by the reputed saying in a cookery book, "First catch your hare" (*which see under* CATCH)

Glassite. A Sandemanian (*q v*)

Glastonbury. An ancient town in Somerset, dating from Roman times, and famous in the Arthurian and Grail cycles as the place to which Joseph of Arimathea came, and as the burial place of King Arthur (*see* AVALON) It was here that Joseph planted his staff—the famous *Glastonbury Thorn*—which took root and burst into leaf every Christmas Eve This name is now given to a variety of Cratægus, or hawthorn, which flowers about old Christmas Day, and is fabled to have sprung from Joseph's staff

The name, A S *Glæstingaburh*, means "the city of Glæstings " Its origin, says Professor Freeman,

lurks in a grotesque shape in that legend of Glæsting and his sow, a manifestly English legend, which either William of Malmesbury himself or some interpolator at Glastonbury has strangely thrust into the midst of the British legends Glæsting s lost sow leads him by a long journey to an apple-tree by the old church, pleased with the land, he takes his family, the Glæstingas, to dwell there —*English Towns*, p 95.

Glauber Salts (glou' ber) A strong purgative, so called from Johann Rudolph Glauber (1604-68), a German alchemist who discovered it in 1658 in his search for the philosopher's stone It is sodium sulphate, crystallized below 34° C

Glaucus (glaw' kùs) The name of a number of heroes in classical legend, including

(1) A fisherman of Bœotia, who became a sea-god endowed with the gift of prophecy and instructed Apollo in the art of soothsaying Milton alludes to him in *Comus* (l 895), and Spenser mentions him in the *Faerie Queene* (IV, xi, 13)

And Glaucus, that wise soothsayer understood

and Keats gives his name to the old magician whom Endymion met in Neptune's hall beneath the sea (*Endymion*, Bk III) *See also* SCYLLA

(2) A son of Sisyphus who would not allow his horses to breed, the goddess of Love so infuriated them that they killed him Hence, the name is given to one who is so overfond of horses that he is ruined by them

(3) A commander of the Lycians in the War of Troy (*Iliad*, Bk VI,) who was connected by ties of ancient family friendship with his enemy, Diomed When they met in battle they not only refrained from fighting but exchanged arms in token of amity. As the armour of the Lycian was of gold, and that of the Greek of brass, it was like bartering precious stones for French paste Hence the phrase **A Glaucus swap.**

Gleek (Ger *gleich*, like) An old card-game, the object being to get three cards all alike, as three aces, three kings, etc *Four* cards all alike, as four aces, four kings, etc , is known as *mournival*

A mournival of aces, gleek of knaves,
Just nine a-piece   *Albumazar*, III, 5.

Poole in his *English Parnassus* (about 1650) called the four elements *Nature's first mournival*

Gleek is played by three persons. The twos and threes are thrown out of the pack, twelve cards are then dealt to each player, and eight are left for stock, which is offered in rotation to the players for purchase The trumps are called Tiddy, Tumbler, Tib, Tom, and Towser Mention of it is of frequent occurrence in 16th-and early-17th-century literature

Gleipnir (glip' nèr) (Old Norse, the fetter). In Scandinavian legend, the chain by which the wolf Fenrır was bound It was extremely light, and made of the noise made by the footfalls of a cat, the roots of the mountains, the sinews of bears, the breath of fishes, the beards of women, and the spittle of birds When the chain breaks, the wolf will be free and the end of the world will be at hand

Glencoe. The massacre of **Glencoe** The treacherous massacre of the Macdonalds of Glencoe on February 13th, 1692. Pardon had been offered to all Jacobites who submitted on or before December 31st, 1691. Mac-Ian, chief of the Macdonalds of Glencoe, delayed till the last minute, and, on account of the state of the roads, did not make his submission before January 6th. The Master of Stair (Sır John Dalrymple) obtained the king's permission "to extirpate the set of thieves." Accordingly, on February 1st, 120 soldiers, led by a Captain Campbell, marched to Glencoe, told the clan they were come as friends, and lived peaceably among them for twelve days; but on the morning of the 13th, the glenmen, to the number of thirty-eight, were scandalously murdered, their huts set on fire, and their flocks and herds driven off as plunder Thomas Campbell and Scott have written poems, and Talfourd a play on the subject

Glendoveer (glen dō vēr′) The name given by Southey in his *Curse of Kehama* to a kind of sylph, the most lovely of the good spirits The name is Sanskrit *ganharva* through the Fr. *grandouver*.

> I am a blessed Glendoveer,
> 'Tis mine to speak and yours to hear
> *Rejected Addresses* (Imitation of Southey).

Glengarry. A narrow valley in Inverness-shire after which the Glengarry bonnet, or cap, is named.

Glim *See* DOUSE THE GLIM

Global (glō′ bal) A word that came into use in World War II, meaning world-wide, extending to every part of the globe.

Gloria (glôr′ i a). A cup of coffee with brandy in it instead of milk, also, a mixture of silk and wool used for covering umbrellas, etc

Gloria in Excelsis (glôr i a ın ek sel′ sis). The doxology, "Glory be to the Father," etc , so called because it begins with the words sung by the angels at Bethlehem. The first verse is said to be by St Basil, and the latter portion is ascribed to Telesphorus, 139 A.D During the Arian controversy it ran thus "Glory be *to* the Father *by* the Son, and *in* the Holy Ghost "

Gloriana (glôr i an′ ả). Spenser's name in his *Faerie Queene* for the typification of Queen Elizabeth. She held an annual feast for twelve days, during which time adventurers appeared before her to undertake whatever task she chose to impose upon them. On one occasion twelve knights presented themselves before her, and their exploits form the scheme of Spenser's allegory of which only six and a half books remain.

Glory, glorious. Hand of Glory. In folk lore, a dead man's hand, preferably one cut from the body of a man who has been hanged, soaked in oil and used as a magic torch by thieves. Robert Graves points out that Hand of Glory

is a translation of the French *main de gloire*, a corruption of *mandragore*, the plant mandragora, whose roots had a similar magic value to thieves *See* HAND

Glory-hole. A small room, cupboard, etc , where all sorts of rubbish and odds and ends are heaped.

Glory be to the Father. *See* GLORIA IN EXCELSIS.

Glorious John. John Dryden, the poet (1631-1701) George Borrow gave this name to the publisher John Murray (1778-1843).

Glorious First of June. June 1st, 1794, when Lord Howe, who commanded the Channel fleet, gained a decisive victory over the French off Cape Ushant.

Glorious Uncertainty of the Law, The The toast at a dinner given to the judges and counsel in Serjeant's Hall. The occasion was the elevation of Lord Mansfield to the peerage and to the Lord Chief Justiceship (1756), and was somewhat prophetic of the legal decisions and innovations that were to follow.

Gloucester (glos′ tēr) The Celtic name of the town was *Caer Glou* (bright city), the Romans Latinized this to *Glevum colonia*, the Saxons restored the old *Glou*, and added *ceaster*, to signify it had been a Roman camp.

Glove In the days of chivalry it was customary for knights to wear a lady's glove in their helmets, and to defend it with their life.

> One ware on his headpiece his ladies sleve, and another bare on hys helme the glove of his dearlynge
> —HALL *Chronicle, Henry IV*

On ceremonial occasions gloves are not worn in the presence of royalty, because one is to stand unarmed, with the helmet off the head and gauntlets off the hands, to show that there is no hostile intention.

Gloves used to be worn by the clergy to indicate that their hands are clean and not open to bribes, and in an assize without a criminal, the sheriff presents the judge with a pair of white gloves Anciently, judges were not allowed to wear gloves on the bench, so to give a judge a pair of gloves symbolized that he need not take his seat. But, on the contrary, bishops were sometimes given gloves as a symbol of accession to their See The Glovers Company of London was founded in 1556

A round with gloves. A friendly contest, a fight with gloves

Glove money. A bribe, a perquisite: so called from the ancient custom of a client presenting a pair of gloves to a counsel who undertook a cause. Mrs. Croaker presented Sir Thomas More, the Lord Chancellor, with a pair of gloves lined with forty pounds in "angels," as a "token." Sir Thomas kept the gloves, but returned the lining. Relics of this ancient custom still survive here and there in the presentation of gloves to those attending weddings and funerals.

There also existed at one time the claim of a pair of gloves by a lady who chose to salute a gentleman caught napping in her company.

Hand in glove. Sworn friends; on most intimate terms; close companions, like glove and hand

He bit his glove. He resolved on mortal revenge On the Border, to bite the glove was considered a pledge of deadly vengeance

> Stern Rutherford right little said,
> But bit his glove and shook his head
> 　　　　SCOTT· *Lay of the Last Minstrel.*

Here I throw down my glove I challenge you In allusion to an ancient custom of a challenger throwing his glove or gauntlet at the feet of the person challenged, and bidding him to pick it up *To take up the glove* means to accept the challenge

> I will throw my glove to Death itself, that there's no maculation in thy heart —*Troilus and Cressida*, iv, 4

Glubdubdrib (glūb dūb' drib) The land of sorcerers and magicians visited by Gulliver in his *Travels.* (SWIFT)

Gluckists (gluk ists). A foolish rivalry excited Paris from 1774 until 1780 between the admirers of Gluck and those of Piccinni. Marie Antoinette favoured Gluck, and many in Young France leant towards the rival claimant In the streets, coffee-houses, private houses, and even schools, the merits of Gluck and Piccinni were canvassed, and all Paris was ranged on one side or the other.

Glumdalclitch (glŭm dăl' klitch). A girl, nine years old, and forty feet high, who had charge of Gulliver in Brobdingnag. (SWIFT. *Gulliver's Travels*)

Glutton, The. Vitellius, the Roman emperor (15-69), reigned from January 4th to December 22nd, A D. 69, was so called *See* APICIUS

Gnome (nōm) According to the Rosicrucian system, a misshapen elemental spirit, dwelling in the bowels of the earth, and guarding the mines and quarries The word seems to have been first used (perhaps invented) by Paracelsus, and to be Gr. *ge-nomos*, earth-dweller. *Cp.* SALAMANDER.

> The four elements are inhabited by spirits called sylphs, gnomes, nymphs, and salamanders The gnomes or demons of the earth, delight in mischief — POPE *Pref Letter to the Rape of the Lock*

Gnostics (nos' tiks) The *knowers*, opposed to *believers*, various sects in the first six centuries of the Christian era, which tried to accommodate Christianity to the speculations of Pythagoras, Plato, and other Greek and Oriental philosophers They taught that knowledge, rather than mere faith, is the true key of salvation In the Gnostic creed Christ is esteemed merely as an eon or divine attribute personified, like Mind, Truth, Logos, Church, etc., the whole of which eons made up this divine pleroma or fullness

Go. A go. A fix, a scrape, as in here's a go or here's a pretty go—here's a mess or awkward state of affairs. Also a share, portion, or tot, as a go of gin.

A go-between. One who acts as an intermediary, one who interposes between two parties

All the go. All the fashion, quite in vogue.

> Her *carte* is hung in the West-end shops,
> With her name in full on the white below,
> And all day long there's a big crowd stops
> To look at the lady who's "all the go".
> SIMS· *Ballads of Babylon* ("Beauty and the Beast)".

A regular goer. One who goes the pace

Go as you please. Not bound by any rules, do as you like; unceremonious

Go it! An exclamation of encouragement, sometimes ironical

Go it alone. From the game of euchre, to play single-handed.

Go to! A curtailed oath "Go to the devil!" or "go to hell!"

> *Cassius* I [am] abler than yourself
> 　　　　To make conditions
> *Brutus.* Go to! You are not, Cassius
> 　　　　　　　　*Julius Cæsar*, iv, 3

Go-to-meeting clothes, behaviour, etc One's best

I'll go through fire and water to serve you. *See* FIRE

I've gone and done it! or **I've been and gone and done it!** There! I've done the very thing I oughtn't to have done!

It is no go. It is not workable.

That goes for nothing. It doesn't count, it doesn't matter one way or the other.

That goes without saying The French say *Cela va sans dire* That is a self-evident fact, well understood or indisputable.

To give one the go-by. To pass without notice

To go ahead. To prosper, make rapid progress towards success, to start.

To go back on one's word. To fail to keep one's promise.

To go bald-headed for a thing. To go for it as hard as possible At the Battle of Warburg, 1760, the Life Guards were commanded by Lord Cranby As he galloped at their head his hat and wig blew off, disclosing a completely bald head Hence the expression, to go at a thing regardless of consequences.

To go by the board, the whole hog, to the wall, with the stream, etc In these and many similar phrases see under the principal word

To go for a man. To attack him, either physically or in argument, etc

To go farther and fare worse. To take more pains and trouble and yet find oneself in a worse position.

To go hard with one. To prove a troublesome matter. "It will go hard with me before I give up the attempt," *i e* I won't give it up until I have tried every means to success, no matter how difficult, dangerous, or painful it may be

To go in for. To follow as a pursuit or occupation.

To go the whole hog. *See* HOG.

To go it. To be fast, extravagant, headstrong in one's behaviour and habits To go it blind is to act without stopping to deliberate In poker, if a player chooses to "go it blind," he doubles the *ante* before looking at his cards

To go off one's head, nut, onion, rocker, etc. Completely to lose control of oneself, to go mad, either temporarily or permanently, to go out of one's mind

To go on all fours. *See* ALL FOURS.

To go to grass. To succumb, give in. From the putting out of race-horses or hunters to grass when they are too old for racing or hunting.

To go to the wall. *See* WALL

To go under. To become ruined; to fail utterly, lose caste

Also to pass as, to be known as, as "He goes under the name of 'Mr. Taylor,' but we all know he is really 'Herr Schneider.' "

Go-backs. Would-be settlers in the Far West who returned East discouraged and spread gloomy rumours about the difficulties they had encountered

Go-getter. An enterprising, ambitious person.

Goat. From very early times the *goat* has been connected with the idea of sin (*cp.* SCAPEGOAT) and associated with devil-lore It is an old superstition in England and Scotland that a goat is never seen during the whole of a twenty-four hours, because once every day it pays a visit to the devil to have its beard combed Formerly the devil himself was frequently depicted as a goat; and the animal is also a type of lust and lechery.

Don't play the giddy goat! Don't make a ridiculous fool of yourself; keep yourself within bounds A goat frolicking about is a very absurd sight

The Goat and Compasses There have been several more or less ingenious derivations found for this inn sign; none of them has yet been endowed with authority A once favourite theory is that the words are a corruption of the old Commonwealth tavern sign "God encompasses us," though there is no ground for supposing that any such inn existed in Puritan days. It is almost certainly of some now-forgotten armorial origin.

To get one's goat An old Americanism for annoying one, making him wild.

To separate the sheep from the goats. To divide the worthy from the unworthy, the good from the evil. A Biblical phrase, the allusion being to *Matt* xxv, 32 —

And before him shall be gathered all nations, and he shall separate them one from another, as a shepherd divideth his sheep from the goats.

Goatsucker or **goat-owl.** A name popularly given to the nightjar, from the ancient and very widespread belief that this bird sucks the udders of goats In Greek, Latin, French, German, Spanish, and some other languages its name has the same signification.

Gobbler. A turkey-cock is so called from its cry

Gobelin Tapestry (go' be lin) So called from the Gobelins, a French family of dyers founded by Jean Gobelin (d. 1476); their tapestry works were taken over by Louis XIV as a royal establishment about 1670, and are still in the Faubourg St. Marcel, Paris. Part of the buildings were burned down by the Communards in 1871.

Goblin. A familiar demon, dwelling, according to popular belief, in private houses and chinks of trees; and in many parts miners attribute those strange noises heard in mines to them The word is the Fr *gobelin*, probably a diminutive of the surname *Gobel*, but perhaps connected with Gr *kobalos*, an impudent rogue, a mischievous sprite, or with the Ger. *kobold* (*q v*)

God. A word common, in slightly varying forms, to all Teutonic languages, probably from a Sanskrit root, *ghu*—to worship, it is in no way connected with *good.*

It was Voltaire who said, "*Si Dieu n'existait pas, il faudrait l'inventer.*"

Greek and Roman gods were divided into *Dii Majores* and *Dii Minores*, the greater and the lesser. The Dii Majores were twelve in number :—

LATIN.	GREEK.
JUPITER (*King*)	ZEUS
Apollo (*the sun*)	Apollōn
Mars (*war*)	Arēs
Mercury (*messenger*)	Hermēs
Neptune (*ocean*)	Poseidon
Vulcan (*smith*)	Hephaistos
JUNO (*Queen*)	HERA.
Cerēs (*tillage*)	Demēter
Diana (*moon, hunting*)	Artēmis.
Minerva (*wisdom*)	Athēne
Venus (*love and beauty*)	Aphrodirē
Vesta (*home-life*)	Hestia.

Their blood was *ichor*, their food was *ambrosia*, their drink *nectar*

Four other deities are often referred to :—

Bacchus (*wine*)	Dionysos
Cupid (*love*)	Eros
Pluto (*the underworld*)	Plutōn.
Saturn (*time*)	Kronos.

Of these Proserpine (Latin) and Persephone (*Greek*) was the wife of Pluto, Cybele was the wife of Saturn, and Rhea of Kronos

In Hesiod's time the number of gods was thirty thousand, and that none might be omitted the Greeks observed a Feast of the Unknown Gods.

Some thirty thousand gods on earth we find
Subjects of Zeus, and guardians of mankind
Hesiod, i, 250.

A god from the machine. *See* DEUS EX MACHINA

Among the gods. In the uppermost gallery of a theatre, just below the ceiling, which was frequently embellished with a representation of a mythological heaven The French call this *paradis*.

God bless the Duke of Argyle. *See* ARGYLE.

God helps those who help themselves. In French, *Aide-toi, le ciel t'aidera*. (*La Fontaine*, vi, 18.), and among the *Fragments* of Euripides is .—

Bestir yourself, and then call on the gods,
For heaven assists the man that laboureth
No 435.

God made the country, and man made the town. Cowper in *The Task* (The Sofa 749) *Cp.* Cowley's "God the first garden made, and the first city Cain" (*On Gardens*). Varro says in *De Re Rustica Divina Natura dedit agros, ars humana ædificavit urbes*

God save the Queen. *See* NATIONAL ANTHEM

God sides with the strongest. Fortune favours the strong. Napoleon I said, *Le bon Dieu est toujours du côté des gros bataillons*, God is always on the side of the big battalions, but the phrase is far older than his day Tacitus (*Hist.* iv, 17) has *Deos fortioribus adesse*, the gods are on the side of the strongest, the Comte de Bussy, writing to the Count of Limoges, used it in 1677, as also did Voltaire in his *Epistle a M le Riche*, February 6th. 1770

God tempers the wind to the shorn lamb The phrase comes from Sterne's *Sentimental Journey* (1782), but it was not original with Sterne, for *Dieu mesure le froid a la brebis tondue* appears in Henri Éstienne's *Les Premices* (1594), and ' To a close-shorn sheep God gives wind by measure" in Herbert's *Jacula Prudentum* (1640) It may be noticed that though Sterne's version is more poetical, he did not improve the sense in substituting *lamb* for *sheep*, for lambs are never shorn !

Man proposes, God disposes. An old proverb found in Hebrew, Greek, Latin, etc In *Prov.* xvi, 9, it is rendered.—
A man's heart deviseth his way, but the Lord directeth his steps,
and Publius Syrus (No 216) has —
Homo semper aliud, Fortuna aliud cogitat
(Man has one thing in view, Fate has another)

Whom God would destroy He first makes mad. A translation of the Latin version (*Quos Deus vult perdere, prius dementat*) of one of the *Fragments* of Euripides. *Cp. also Stultum facit fortuna quem vult perdere* (Publius Syrus, No. 612) He whom Fortune would ruin she roos of his wits

Whom the gods love die young. The Lat. *Quem Di diligunt. adolescens moritur* (Plautus: *Bacchides*, IV. vii, 18) Byron says —
Heaven gives its favourites early death
Childe Harold, iv, 102.

God's Acre. A churchyard or cemetery

Godless Florin *See* GRACELESS FLORIN.

Goddam or Godon (gò dàm', gò don') A name given by the French to the English at least as early as the 15th century, on account of the favourite oath of the English soldiers which was looked upon almost as a shibboleth. Joan of Arc is reported to have used the word on a number of occasions in contemptuous reference to her enemies.

Godfather. To stand godfather. To pay the reckoning, godfathers being often chosen for the sake of the present they are expected to make to the child at christening or in their wills

Godchild. One for whom a person stands sponsor in baptism A godson or a goddaughter

Godiva, Lady (go di' va) Patroness of Coventry In 1040, Leofric, Earl of Mercia and Lord of Coventry, imposed certain exactions on his tenants, which his lady besought him to remove, he said he would do so if she would ride naked through the town Lady Godiva took him at his word, and the Earl faithfully kept his promise.
The legend is recorded by Roger of Wendover (d 1236), in *Flores Historiarum*, and this was adapted by Rapin in his *History of England*, 1732 into the story as commonly known. An addition of the time of Charles II asserts that everyone kept indoors at the time, but a

certain tailor peeped through his window to see the lady pass and was struck blind in consequence He has ever since been called "Peeping Tom of Coventry " Since 1678 the incident of Lady Godiva's ride has been annually commemorated at Coventry by a procession in which ' Lady Godiva" plays a leading part

Godolphin Barb. *See* DARLEY ARABIAN

Goel (gō' el) The name among the ancient Jews for one who redeemed back to the family property that a member of it had sold, as this was usually done by the next of kin, on whom also devolved the duty of the avenger of blood, the name was later applied specially to the avenger of blood

Goemot or Goemagot (gō' mot, gō em' a got). Names given in Geoffrey of Monmouth's *Chronicles* (I, xvi), Spenser's *Faerie Queene* (II, x, 10), etc , to Gog Magog (*q v*).

Gog and Magog In English legend, the sole survivors of a monstrous brood, the offspring of the thirty-three infamous daughters of the Emperor Diocletian, who murdered their husbands. Being set adrift in a ship they reached Albion, where they fell in with a number of demons Their descendants, a race of giants, were extirpated by Brute and his companions, with the exception of Gog and Magog, who were brought in chains to London and were made to do duty as porters at the royal palace, on the site of the Guildhall, where their effigies were placed at least since the reign of Henry V The old giants were destroyed in the Great Fire, and were replaced by figures fourteen feet high, carved in 1708 by Richard Saunders and were subsequently destroyed in the wreck of Guildhall in an air raid in 1940. Formerly wickerwork models were carried in the Lord Mayors' Shows
In the Bible Magog is spoken of as a son of Japhet (*Gen* x, 2), in the *Revelation* Gog and Magog symbolize all future enemies of the kingdom of God, and in *Ezekiel* Gog is a prince of Magog, a terrible ruler of a country in the north, probably Scythia or Armenia By rabbinical writers of the 7th century A D. Gog was identified with Antichrist

Gogmagog Hill. The higher of two hills, some three miles south-east of Cambridge The legend is that Gogmagog fell in love with the nymph Granta, but she would have nothing to say to the huge giant, and he was metamorphosed into the hill (DRAYTON *Polyolbion*, xxi)

Goggles A very ancient word coming, through the old English *gogelen*, to look asquint, from the Celtic *gog*, a nod, a shaking of the head. The word is now applied to spectacles, but until Victorian days it was used to describe any rolling of the eyes or squinting
Such sight have they that see with goggling eyes
SIR P SIDNEY *Arcadia.*
He goggled his eyes and groped in his money-pocket —HORACE WALPOLE *Letters*

Golconda (gol kon' dä). An ancient kingdom and city in India (west of Hyderabad), famous and powerful up to the early 17th century. The name is emblematic of great wealth, particularly of diamonds, but there never were diamond mines in Golconda, the stones were only cut and polished there.

Gold. By the ancient alchemists, gold represented the sun, and silver the moon In heraldry gold (called "or") is depicted by dots.

In Great Britain every article in gold is compared with a given standard of pure gold, which is supposed to be divided into twenty-four parts called *carats* (*q v*), gold equal to the standard is said to be twenty-four carats fine Manufactured articles are never made of pure gold, but the quality of alloy used has to be stated Sovereigns (and most wedding rings) contain two parts of alloy to every twenty-two of gold, and are said to be twenty-two carats fine Thus, 20 lb. troy of standard gold were coined into 934 sovereigns and 1 half-sovereign, 1 oz troy was therefore worth £3 17s 10½d (£46 14s. 6d per lb), and 1 oz of pure gold, on the same basis, £4 4s. 11½d Since 1915 the market price of gold has, however, exceeded these figures The best gold watch-cases contain six parts of silver or copper to eighteen of gold, and are therefore eighteen carats fine, cheaper gold articles may contain nine, twelve, or even fifteen parts of alloy.

A gold brick. An American phrase descriptive of any form of swindling It originated in the gold-rush days when a cheat would sell his dupe an alleged—or even a real—gold brick, in the latter case substituting a sham one before making his get-away In World War II, gold-bricking was synonymous with idling, shirking, or getting a comrade to do one's job.

All he touches turns to gold. All his ventures succeed, he is invariably fortunate The allusion is to the legend of Midas (*q v*).

All that glisters is not gold (Shakespeare *Merchant of Venice*, ii, 7) Do not be deceived by appearances

> All thing which that shineth as the gold
> Nis not gold as that I have heard it told.
> CHAUCER *Canon's Yeoman's Tale*, 243
> Not all that tempts your wand'ring eyes
> And heedless hearts, is lawful prize,
> Nor all that glisters gold
> GRAY *Ode on Death of a Favourite Cat.*

Healing gold. Gold given to a king for "healing" the king's evil, which was done by a touch.

He has got the gold of Tolosa. His ill gains will never prosper Cæpio, the Roman consul, in his march to Gallia Narbonensis, desecrated the temple of the Celtic Apollo at Tolosa (Toulouse), and stole from it all the gold and silver vessels and treasure belonging to the Cimbrian Druids. This, in turn, was stolen from him while it was being taken to Massilia (Marseilles); and when he encountered the Cimbrians both he and Maximus, his brother-consul, were defeated, and 112,000 of their men were left upon the field (106 B C)

Mannheim gold. A sort of pinchbeck, made of copper, zinc, and tin, used for cheap jewellery and invented at Mannheim, Germany.

The gold of the Nibelungen. *See* NIBELUNGEN HOARD.

The Gold Purse of Spain Andalusia is so called because it is the most fertile portion of Spain

Golden. Jean Dorat (1510-88), one of the Pleiad poets of France, was so called ("Auratus") by a pun on his name.

Golden Ball. Edward Hughes Ball, a dandy in the days of the Regency (fl. 1820-30) He married a Spanish dancer

The Golden-mouthed St. Chrysostom (d 407), a father of the Greek Church, was so called for his great eloquence.

The Golden Stream St John Damascene (d. 756), author of *Dogmatic Theology*

The Golden-tongued (Gr *Chrysologos*) St Peter, Bishop of Ravenna (d. about 449), was so called

Golden Age. An age in the history of peoples when everything was as it should be, or when the nation was at its summit of power, glory, and reputation, the best age, as the golden age of innocence, the golden age of literature Ancient chronologers divided the time between Creation and the birth of Christ into ages, Hesiod describes five *See* AGE

The "Golden Ages" of the various nations are usually given as follows —

ASSYRIA From the reign of Esarhaddon, third son of Sennacherib, to the fall of Nineveh (about 700 to 600 B.C.).

CHALDÆO-BABYLONIAN EMPIRE. From the reign of Nabopolassar to that of Belshazzar (about 606-538 B C.)

CHINA The reign of Tae-tsong (618-26), and the era of the Tâng dynasty (626-84)

EGYPT. The reigns of Sethos I and Rameses II (about 1350-1273 B C.), the XIXth Dynasty.

MEDIA. The reign of Cyaxares (about 634-594 B.C.).

PERSIA From the reign of Khosru, or Chosroes, I, to that of Khosru II (about A D. 531-628).

ENGLAND The reign of Elizabeth (1558-1603)

FRANCE Part of the reigns of Louis XIV and XV (1640-1740)

GERMANY. The reign of Charles V (1519-58)

PORTUGAL From John I to the close of Sebastian's reign (1383-1578).

PRUSSIA The reign of Frederick the Great (1740-86).

RUSSIA The reign of Peter the Great (1672-1725).

SPAIN The reign of Ferdinand and Isabella, when the crowns of Castile and Aragon were united (1474-1516)

SWEDEN From Gustavus Vasa to the close of the reign of Gustavus Adolphus (1523-1632)

Golden Apples. *See* APPLE OF DISCORD; ATALANTA'S RACE, HESPERIDES.

Golden Ass, The. A satirical romance by Apuleius, written in the 2nd century, and called the *golden* because of its excellency. It tells the adventures of Lucian, a young man who, being accidentally metamorphosed into an ass while sojourning in Thessaly, fell into the hands of robbers, eunuchs, magistrates, and so on, by whom he was ill-treated; but ultimately he recovered his human form It contains the story of Cupid and Psyche—the latest born of the myths.

Golden Bull, The. An edict by the Emperor Charles IV, issued at the Diet of Nuremberg in 1356, for the purpose of fixing how the German emperors were to be elected. It was sealed with a golden *bulla* See BULL.

To worship the golden calf. To bow down to money, to abandon one's principles for the sake of gain The reference is to the golden calf made by Aaron when Moses was absent on Mt Sinai For their sin in worshipping the calf the Israelites paid dearly (*Exodus*, xxxii).

Golden Fleece, The. The old Greek story is that Ino persuaded her husband, Athamas, that his son Phryxus was the cause of a famine which desolated the land Phryxus was thereupon ordered to be sacrificed, but, being apprised of this, he made his escape over sea on the winged ram, Chrysomallus, which had a golden fleece When he arrived at Colchis, he sacrificed the ram to Zeus, and gave the fleece to King Æetes who hung it on a sacred oak It later formed the quest of Jason's celebrated Argonautic expedition, and was stolen by him. *See* ARGO, JASON

Australia has been called "The Land of the Golden Fleece," because of the quantity of wool produced there

Golden Fleece, The Order of the (Fr *l'ordre de la toison d or*). An order of knighthood common to Spain and Austria, instituted in 1429, for the protection of the Church, by Philip the Good, Duke of Burgundy, on his marriage with the Infanta Isabella of Portugal. Its badge is a golden sheepskin with head and feet attached, and its motto *Pretium laborum non vile* The selection of the fleece as a badge is perhaps best explained by the fact that the manufacture of wool had long been the staple industry of the Netherlands.

Golden Gate, The. The name given by Sir Francis Drake to the strait connecting San Francisco Bay with the Pacific San Francisco is hence called *The City of the Golden Gate.*

Golden Horn, The. The inlet of the Bosporus on which Istanbul is situated So called from its curved shape and great beauty.

Golden Horde. The Mongolian Tartars who in the 13th century established an empire in S E Russia under Bator, grandson of Genghis Khan They invaded Russia and made the great hero Alexander Nevsky Grand Duke in 1252 They were later defeated in 1481

Golden Legend, The. (Lat. *Legenda aurea*) A collection of so-called lives of the saints made by Jacques de Voragine in the 13th century, valuable for the picture it gives of mediæval manners, customs, and thought Jortin says that the "lives" were written by young students of religious houses to exercise their talents by accommodating the narratives of heathen writers to Christian saints

Longfellow's *The Golden Legend* (1851) is based on a story by Hartmann von der Aue, a German minnesinger of the 12th century

Golden number. The number of the year in the Metonic Cycle (*q.v.*) As this consists of

nineteen years it may be any number from 1 to 19, and in the ancient Roman and Alexandrian calendars this number was marked in gold, hence the name. The rule for finding the golden number is :—

Add one to the number of years and divide by nineteen, the quotient gives the number of cycles since 1 B C and the remainder the golden number, 19 being the golden number when there is no remainder

It is used in determining the Epact and the date of Easter.

Golden ointment. Eye salve In allusion to the ancient practice of rubbing "stynas of the eye" with a gold ring to cure them.

"I have a sty here, Chilax."
"I have no gold to cure it "
　　BEAUMONT AND FLETCHER *Mad Lover*, v, i

Golden Roses. An ornament made of gold in imitation of a spray of roses, one rose containing a receptacle into which is poured balsam and musk The rose is solemnly blessed by the Pope on Laetare Sunday, and is conferred from time to time on sovereigns and others, churches and cities distinguished for their services to the Church The last to receive it was Queen Elizabeth of the Belgians in 1925 That presented by Pius IX to the Empress Eugenie in 1856 is preserved in Farnborough Abbey.

Golden Rule, The. "Do as you would be done by "

Whatsoever ye would that men should do to you, do ye even so to them for this is the law and the prophets —*Matt* vii, 12

Golden shower or Shower of gold. A bribe, money. The allusion is to the classical tale of Zeus and Danae *See* DANAE

Golden State, The. California, so called from the gold fever of 1849

Golden Town, The So Mainz or Mayence was called in Carlovingian times

Golden Valley, The. The eastern portion of Limerick is so called, from its great natural fertility. The name is also given to the valley in mid-Wales from Pentrilas to Hay.

Golden Verses. Greek verses containing the moral rules of Pythagoras, usually thought to have been composed by some of his scholars He enjoins, among other things, obedience to God and one's rulers, deliberation before action, fortitude, and temperance in exercise and diet. He also suggests making a critical review each night of the actions of that day

Golden Wedding. The fiftieth anniversary of wedding, husband and wife being both alive

A good name is better than a golden girdle. *See* GIRDLE.

The golden bowl is broken. Death. A biblical allusion:—

Or ever the silver cord be loosed, or the golden bowl be broken, or the pitcher be broken at the fountain, or the wheel broken at the cistern, then shall the dust return to the earth as it was, and the spirit shall return unto God who gave it —*Eccles* xii, 6 7

The golden section of a line. Its division into two such parts that the area of the rectangle contained by the smaller segment and the whole line equals that of the square on the larger segment. (*Euclid*, ii 11)

The three golden balls *See* BALLS

To keep the golden mean To practise moderation in all things The wise saw of Cleobulos, King of Rhodes (about 630-559 B C).

Goldfish Club. World War II It is similar to the Caterpillar Club (*q v*) and is for those who had ditched their aeroplanes and taken to the rubber dinghy A cloth insignia was presented

Golgotha (gol' goth a). The place outside Jerusalem where Christ was crucified The word is Aramaic and means "a skull " and according to Jerome and others the place was so called from a tradition that Adam's skull had been found there The more likely reason is that it designated a bare hill or rising ground, having some fancied resemblance to a bald skull

Golgotha seems not entirely unconnected with the hill of Gareb, and the locality of Goath, mentioned in *Jer* xxxi, 39, on the north-west of the city I am inclined to fix the place where Jesus was crucified . . . on the mounds which command the valley of Hinnom, above Birket-Mamila —RENAN *Life of Jesus*, ch xxv

Golgotha, at the University church, Cambridge, was the gallery in which the "heads of the houses" sat; so called because it was the place of skulls or heads. It has been more wittily than truly said that Golgotha was the place of empty skulls

Goliath (gō li' áth) The Philistine giant, slain by the stripling David with a small stone hurled from a sling (1 *Sam.* xvii, 23-54.)

Golosh. *See* GALOSH

Gombeen Man. A village usurer, a moneylender The word is of Irish extraction

They suppose that the tenants can have no other supply of capital than from the gombeen man.— EGMONT HAKE *Free Trade in Capital*

Gombo. Pidgin French, or French as it is spoken by the coloured population of Louisiana, the French West Indies, Bourbon, and Mauritius

Creole is almost pure French, not much more mispronounced than in some parts of France, but Gombo is a mere phonetic burlesque of French, interlarded with African words, and other words which are neither African nor French, but probably belong to the aboriginal language of the various countries to which the slaves were brought from Africa —E WAKEFIELD, in *The Nineteenth Century*, October, 1891.

Gomerell (gom' êr el), a Scottish word for a stupid senseless person, a blockhead

Gondola (gon' dō là). A long, narrow Venetian boat Also the carriage attached to an airship in which the passengers are carried.

Goneril (gon' er il). One of Lear's three daughters. Having received her moiety of Lear's kingdom, the unnatural daughter first abridged the old man's retinue, then gave him to understand that his company was troublesome. In Holinshed she appears as "Gonorilla." *Cp.* CORDELIA

Gonfalon or **Gonfanon** (gon' fà lon). An ensign or standard A *gonfalonier* was a magistrate in certain of the old Italian republics that had a gonfalon

Ten thousand thousand ensigns high advanced, Standards and gonfalons, 'twixt van and rear Stream in the air, and for distinction serve Of hierarchies, of orders, and degrees. MILTON: *Paradise Lost*, v. 589.

Gonnella's Horse (go nel' a). Gonnella, the domestic jester of the Duke of Ferrara, rode on a horse all skin and bone The jests of Gonnella are in print

His horse was as lean as Gonnella's, which (as the Duke said) "Osso atque pellis totus erat" (Plautus).— CERVANTES *Don Quixote*

Gonsalez (gon sa' lez) Fernan Gonsalez, the hero of many Spanish ballads, lived in the 10th century His life was twice saved by his wife Sancha, daughter of Garcias, King of Navarre.

Gonville and Caius. *See* CAIUS

Good. The Good. Among the many who earned—or were given—this appellation are —
Alfonso VIII (or IX) of Leon, "The Noble and Good" (1158-1214)
Haco I, King of Norway (about 920-960)
Jean II of France, *le Bon* (1319, 1350-64)
Jean III, Duke of Brittany (1286, 1312-41)
Philip the Good, Duke of Burgundy (1396, 1419-67).
René, called *The Good King René*, Duke of Anjou, Count of Provence, Duke of Lorraine, and King of Sicily (1409-80).
The Prince Consort, *Albert the Good* (1819-61), husband of Queen Victoria

Good Duke Humphrey. Humphrey, Duke of Gloucester (1391-1447), youngest son of Henry IV, said to have been murdered by Suffolk and Cardinal Beaufort (Shakespeare 2 *Henry VI*, iii, 2), so called because of his devotion to the Church. **To Dine with Duke Humphrey.** *See* HUMPHREY

Good Friday. The Friday preceding Easter Day, held as the anniversary of the Crucifixion "Good" here means *holy*, Christmas, as well as Shrove Tuesday, used to be called "the good tide "

Born on Good Friday. According to old superstition, those born on Christmas Day or Good Friday have the power of seeing and commanding spirits

Good Parliament, The. Edward III's Parliament of 1376; so called because of the severity with which it pursued the unpopular party of the Duke of Lancaster

Good Regent. James Stewart, Earl of Moray (d 1570), a natural son of James V and half-brother of Mary Queen of Scots. He was appointed Regent of Scotland after the imprisonment of Queen Mary

Good Samaritan. *See* SAMARITAN

There is a good time coming. This has been for a long time a familiar saying in Scotland, and it is introduced by Scott in his *Rob Roy* In 1846 Charles Mackay wrote a once-popular song so called —

There's a good time coming, boys,
A good time coming.
We may not live to see the day,
But earth shall glisten in the ray
Of the good time coming
Cannon-balls may aid the truth,
But thought's a weapon stronger,
We'll win our battle by its aid.—
Wait a little longer

Good and all, For Not tentatively, not in pretence, nor yet temporarily, but *bona fide*, and altogether

The good woman never died after this, till she came to die for good and all.—L'ESTRANGE. *Fables.*

Good-bye. A contraction of *God be with you.* Similar to the French adieu, which is *à Dieu* (I commend you to God)

Goodfellow. *See* ROBIN GOODFELLOW

Goodman. A husband or master In *Matt* xxiv, 43, "If the goodman of the house had known in what watch the thief would come, he would have watched

> There's nae luck about the house
> When our gudeman's awa —*Mickle*

Goodman of Ballengeich. The assumed name of James V of Scotland when he made his disguised visits through the country districts around Edinburgh and Stirling, after the fashion of Haroun-al-Raschid, Louis XI, etc

Goodman's Croft. The name given in Scotland to a strip of ground or corner of a field left untilled, in the belief that unless some such place were left, the spirit of evil would damage the crop Here *Goodman* is a propitiatory euphemism for the devil.

Goods. I carry all my goods with me (*Omnia mea mecum porto*) Said by Bias, one of the seven sages, when Priene was besieged and the inhabitants were preparing for flight.

That fellow's the goods. He's all right, just the man for the job

"He's got the goods on you!" He's got evidence against you

To deliver the goods. Said of one who fulfills his promises or who comes up to expectations.

Goodwin Sands. It is said that these dangerous sandbanks, stretching about 10 miles NE and SW. some 5½ miles off the Kentish coast, consisted at one time of about 4,000 acres of low land (Lomea, the *Infera Insula* of the Romans) fenced from the sea by a wall, and belonging to Earl Godwin William the Conqueror bestowed them on the abbey of St. Augustine, Canterbury, but the abbot allowed the seawall to fall into a dilapidated state, so that the sea broke through in 1100 and inundated the whole. *See* TENTERDEN STEEPLE

Goodwood Races. So called from the park in which they are held They begin the last Tuesday of July, and last four days, the chief being Thursday, called the "Cup Day " These races are held in a private park, the property of the Duke of Richmond The racecourse is one of the oddest shaped in the world, with a curious loop at the end of the 5-furlong gallop The course of the Goodwood Cup is 2 miles 5 furlongs The Cup was first run in 1812, the Goodwood Stakes in 1823, the Stewards Cup in 1840.

Goody. A depreciative, meaning weakly, moral and religious In French, *bon homme* is used in a similar way
The word is also a rustic variant of *goodwife*, the mistress of a household (*cp.* GOODMAN), and is sometimes used as a title, like "Gammer" (*q.v.*), as "Goody Blake," "Goody Dobson "
A **goody** is something especially nice to eat, a sweet, jam tart, or currant bun

Goody-goody. Affectedly, or even hypocritically, pious, but with no strength of mind or independence of spirit.

Goody Two-shoes. This nursery tale first appeared in 1765. It was written for John Newbery (1713-67), the originator of children's books, probably by Oliver Goldsmith.

Googly. A cricket term for a ball bowled so as to break a different way from the way it swerves

Goose. A foolish or ignorant person is called a *goose* because of the alleged stupidity of this bird, a tailor's smoothing-iron is so called because its handle resembles the neck of a goose Note that the plural of the iron is *gooses,* not *geese*

> Come in, tailor, here you may roast your goose —
> *Macbeth*, ii, 3

Geese save the Capitol. The tradition is that when the Gauls invaded Rome a detachment in single file clambered up the hill of the Capitol so silently that the foremost man reached the top without being challenged, but while he was striding over the rampart, some sacred geese, disturbed by the noise, began to cackle, and awoke the garrison Marcus Manlius rushed to the wall and hurled the fellow over the precipice To commemorate this event, the Romans carried a golden goose in procession to the Capitol every year (390 B C)

> Those consecrated geese in orders,
> That to the capitol were warders,
> And being then upon patrol,
> With noise alone beat off the Gaul
> BUTLER *Hudibras*, ii, 3.

The Goose Bible. *See* BIBLE, SPECIALLY NAMED

Goose fair. A fair formerly held in many English towns about the time of Michaelmas (*q v*), when geese were plentiful That still held at Nottingham was the most important

Goose month. The lying-in month for women

His geese are swans. He sees things in too rosy a light, is too pleased with his own doings and his own possessions

Goose step. A form of military marching in which the legs are moved only from the hips, the knees being kept rigid, each leg being swung as high as possible It was never popular in the British army, where it was introduced as a form of recruit drill in the late 18th century. In a modified form it still exists in the slow march The goose step (*Stechschritt*) in its most exaggerated form has been a full-dress and processional march in the German army since the days of Frederick the Great When the Axis flourished it was introduced into the Italian army (*il passo di oca*) but it was soon ridiculed into desuetude

Goose-trap A late-18th-century American colloquialism for a swindle

He can't say Bo! to a goose. *See* BO.

He killed the goose that laid the golden eggs. He grasped at what was more than his due, and lost what he had The Greek fable says a countryman had a goose that laid golden eggs, thinking to make himself rich, he killed the goose to get the whole stock of eggs at once, but lost everything.

He steals a goose, and gives the giblets in **alms** He amasses wealth by over-reaching, and salves his conscience by giving small sums in charity

He's cooked his goose He's done for himself, he's made a fatal mistake, ruined his chances, "dished" himself. The phrase is of 19th-century origin, though how it arose cannot now be traced

> If they come here we'll cook their goose,
> The Pope and Cardinal Wiseman.

Street ballad of 1851, the time of the "Papal Aggression."

Michaelmas goose See MICHAELMAS

Mother Goose Famous as giving the name to *Mother Goose's Nursery Rhymes*, which first seems to have been used in *Songs for the Nursery*: or *Mother Goose's Melodies for Children*, published by T. Fleet in Boston, Mass , in 1719 The rhymes were free adaptations of Perrault's *Contes de ma mère l'oye* ("Tales of my Mother Goose") which appeared in 1697.

The Goose and Gridiron. A public-house sign, properly the coat of arms of the Company of Musicians—viz a *swan* with expanded wings, within a *double tressure* [the gridiron], counter, flory, argent Perverted into a goose striking the bars of a gridiron with its foot, also called "The Swan and Harp."
In the United States the name is humorously applied to the national coat-of-arms—the American eagle with a gridiron-like shield on its breast.

The old woman is plucking her goose. A children's way of saying "it is snowing "

The royal game of goose. The game referred to by Goldsmith (*Deserted Village*, 232) as being present in the ale-house—

> The pictures placed for ornament and use,
> The twelve good rules, the royal game of goose—

was a game of compartments through which the player progressed according to the cast of the dice At certain divisions a goose was depicted, and if the player fell into one of these he doubled the number of his last throw and moved forward accordingly
The "twelve good rules" was a broadside showing a rough cut of the execution of Charles I with the following "rules" printed below — 1 Urge no healths; 2 Profane no divine ordinances, 3 Touch no state matters; 4 Reveal no secrets; 5. Pick no quarrels, 6 Make no comparisons, 7. Maintain no ill opinions, 8 Keep no bad company, 9 Encourage no vice; 10. Make no long meals, 11. Repeat no grievances, 12 Lay no wagers
These were said to have been "found in the study of King Charles the First, of Blessed Memory," and in the 18th century were frequently framed and displayed in taverns

To shoe the goose. To fritter away one's time on unnecessary work, to play about, trifle.

Tuning goose. The entertainment given in Yorkshire when the corn at harvest was all safely stacked

Wayz Goose. See WAYZ

Gooseberry. Gooseberry fool. A dish made of gooseberries scalded and pounded with cream

B.D.—14

The word *fool* is from the French *fouler*, to press or crush.

> Let anything come in the shape of fodder or eatinge stuffe, it is wellcome, whether it be Sawsedge, or Custard, or Flawne, or Foole —JOHN TAYLOR *The Great Eater*, 1610

He played old gooseberry with me. He took great liberties with my property, and greatly abused it, in fact, he played the very deuce with me and my belongings

The big gooseberry season A mid-Victorian phrase applied to the dull time in journalism when Parliament was not sitting, the Law Courts were up, and nobody was in Town, when the old-fashioned editor published accounts of giant gooseberries, sea-serpents, vegetable marrows, sweet peas, just to fill up his paper

To play, or be gooseberry. To act as chaperon; to be an unwanted third when lovers are together. The origin of the phrase is obscure, but it has been suggested that it arose from the charity of the chaperon occupying herself in picking gooseberries while the lovers were more romantically occupied

Goosebridge. Go to Goosebridge "Rule a wife and have a wife " Boccaccio (ix, 9) tells us that a man who had married a shrew asked Solomon what he should do to make her more submissive, and the wise king answered, "Go to Goosebridge " Returning home, deeply perplexed, he came to a bridge which a muleteer was trying to induce a mule to cross The beast resisted, but the stronger will of his master at length prevailed The man asked the name of the bridge, and was told it was "Goosebridge "

Gopher (gō' fer) A native of Minnesota, U S A The word probably comes from the prairie rodent of that name

Gopher wood, the wood of which Noah made his ark (*Gen* vi, 14) There has been much discussion as to what wood is really meant, but it is now considered that it is that of the cypress

Gordian Knot (gôr' di an) A great difficulty. Gordius, a peasant, being chosen king of Phrygia, dedicated his wagon to Jupiter, and fastened the yoke to a beam with a rope of bark so ingeniously that no one could untie it Alexander was told that "whoever undid the knot would reign over the whole East." "Well then," said the conqueror, "it is thus I perform the task," and so saying, he cut the knot in twain with his sword Thus **To cut the Gordian knot** is to get out of a difficult or awkward position by one decisive step, to solve a problem by a single brilliant stroke

> Such praise the Macedonian got
> For having rudely cut the Gordian knot
> WALLER: *To the King.*

> Turn him to any cause of policy,
> The Gordian knot of it he will unloose,
> Familiar as his garter
> *Henry V*, i, 1.

Gordon Riots. Riots in 1780, headed by Lord George Gordon, to compel the House of Commons to repeal the bill passed in 1778 for the relief of Roman Catholics Gordon was of unsound mind, and died in 1793, a proselyte to Judaism. Dickens has given a very vivid description of the Gordon Riots in *Barnaby Rudge*

Gore. A triangular piece of material, or of land, from the low Latin *gora Cp* Kensington Gore, and the Gore, New York (late 18th century)

Gorgon (gôr' gon). Anything unusually hideous, particularly a hideous or terrifying woman In classical mythology there were three Gorgons, with serpents on their heads instead of hair, Medusa was the chief, and the only one that was mortal, but so hideous was her face that whoever set eyes on it was instantly turned into stone. She was slain by Perseus, and her head placed on the shield of Minerva

> What was that snaky-headed Gorgon shield
> That wise Minerva wore, unconquered virgin,
> Wherewith she freezed her foes to congealed stone?
> But rigid looks of chaste austerity,
> And noble grace, that dashed brute violence
> With sudden adoration and blank awe
>   MILTON *Comus*, 458.

Gorgonzola (gôr gon zō' la). A town in Italy some 12 miles north-east of Milan and chiefly famous for the cheese once made there This is of a Stilton nature, made from the whole milk of cows and mottled or veined with a penicillium which is the principal ripening agent It is usually exported with a thin, clay-like coat made of gypsum and lard or tallow.

Gorham Controversy (gôr' ăm) This arose out of the refusal (1848) of the bishop of Exeter to institute the Rev Cornelius Gornam to the vicarage of Brampford Speke, "because he held unsound views on the doctrine of baptism " After two years' controversy, the Privy Council decided in favour of Mr. Gorham

It was a major sensation of its decade and at one time seemed likely to split the Church of England in twain

Gospel. This is an Anglo-Saxon compound word, "god spell," good news It is employed to describe collectively the lives of Christ as narrated by the evangelists in the New Testament, it signifies the message of redemption set forth in those books, it is used as a term for the entire Christian system of religion; and it is applied to any doctrine or teaching set forth for some specific purpose.

The first four books of the New Testament, known as the Gospels, are ascribed to Matthew, Mark, Luke, and John. The first three of these are called "synoptic," as they follow the same lines and have, broadly speaking, the same point of view. The fourth Gospel was written some thirty years later than the others. Critics are still uncertain as to the real authorship of the Gospels.

Gospel according to . . . The chief teaching of [so-and-so]. *The Gospel according to Mammon* is the making and collecting of money

The Gospel of Nicodemus, or "The Acts of Pilate" is an apocryphal book compiled about the 5th century. It gives an elaborate and fanciful description of the trial, death and resurrection of Our Lord; names the two thieves (Dismas and Gestas), Pilate's wife (Procla); the centurion (Longinus), etc , and

ends with the conversion of Annas, Caiaphas, and the Sanhedrin

The Gospel of Peter is an apocryphal book first mentioned in the year 191 Only a fragment remains, and it departs from the canonical gospels in several particulars.

The Gospel of Thomas is a Gnostic apocryphal book full of stories of crude prodigies and puerile fancies.

The gospel of wealth. The hypothesis that wealth is the great end and aim of man, the one thing needful

The Gospel side of the altar is to the left of the celebrant facing the altar

Gospeller. The priest who reads the Gospel in the Communion Service, also a follower of Wyclif, called the "Gospel Doctor", anyone who believes that the New Testament has in part, at least, superseded the Old

Hot Gospellers was an old nickname for the Puritans; it is now frequently applied to the more energetic and vociferous evangelists who conduct revival meetings

Gossamer. According to legend, this delicate thread is the ravelling of the Virgin Mary's winding-sheet, which fell to earth on her ascension to heaven It is said to be *God's seam, i e* God's thread Actually, the name is from M E *gossomer,* literally *goose-summer,* or St. Martin's summer (early November), when geese are eaten and gossamer is prevalent

Gossip A tattler, a sponsor at baptism, a corruption of *God-sibb,* a kinsman in the Lord (A S *sibb,* relationship, whence *sibman,* kinsman, *he is our sib,* is still used)

> 'Tis not a maid, for she hath had gossips [sponsors for her child], yet 'tis a maid, for she is her master's servant, and serves for wages —*Two Gentlemen of Verona,* III, 1

Gotch. In East Anglian dialect a large stone jug with a handle *Fetch the gotch, mor—i.e.* fetch the great water-jug, my girl.

> A gotch of milk I've been to fill.
>   R. BLOOMFIELD *Richard and Kate*

Goth. One of an ancient tribe of Teutons which swept down upon and devastated large portions of southern Europe in the 3rd to 5th centuries, establishing kingdoms in Italy, southern France, and Spain. They were looked on by the civilized Romans as merely destroying barbarians, hence the name came to be applied to any rude, uncultured, destructive people

The last of the Goths. *See* RODERICK

Gotham (gō' thăm) **Wise Men of Gotham—** fools, wiseacres The village of Gotham, in Nottinghamshire, was for centuries proverbial for the folly of its inhabitants, and many tales have been fathered on them, one of which is their joining hands round a thornbush to shut in a cuckoo *Cp* COGGESHALL

It is said that King John intended to make a progress through this town with the view of purchasing a castle and grounds The townsmen had no desire to be saddled with this expense, and therefore when the royal messengers appeared, wherever they went they saw the people occupied in some idiotic pursuit The king being told of it, abandoned his intention, and the "wise men" of the village cunningly remarked, ' More fools pass through Gotham than remain in it "

A collection of popular tales of stupidity was published in the reign of Henry VIII as *Merie Tales of the Mad Men of Gotam, gathered together by A. B of Phisike, Doctour.* This "A. B" has been supposed to be Andrew Boorde (c. 1490-1549), physician and traveller.

Most nations have fixed upon some locality as their limbus of fools, thus we have Phrygia as the fools' home of Asia Minor, Abdera of the Thracians, Bœotia of the Greeks, Nazareth of the ancient Jews, Swabia of the modern Germans, and so on

Gothamites. Inhabitants of New York The term was in use by 1800 The name of Gotham was given to New York by Washington Irving in his *Salmagundi*, 1807

Gothic Architecture. A style prevalent in Western Europe from the 12th to the 16th centuries, characterized by the pointed arch, clustered columns, etc. The name has nothing to do with the Goths, but was bestowed in contempt by the architects of the Renaissance period on mediæval architecture, which they termed clumsy, fit only for barbarians or Goths.
St. Louis built the Ste Chapelle of Paris, the most precious piece of Gothic in Northern Europe
—RUSKIN: *Fors Clavigera*, vol 1.

A revival in England of Gothic architecture and ornament, was started by wealthy *dilettanti* such as Horace Walpole in the 18th century. It was further popularized by Ruskin and Sir Walter Scott, and took a concrete form in the architecture of the Catholic A. W. Pugin (1812-52).

Gouk or **Gowk.** The cuckoo (from Icel. *gaukr*), hence, a fool, a simpleton

Hunting the gowk is making one an April fool. *See* APRIL

A **gowk storm** is a storm consisting of several days of tempestuous weather, believed by the peasantry to take place periodically about the beginning of April, at the time that the gowk or cuckoo visits this country; it is also, curiously enough, a storm that is short and sharp, a "storm in a tea-cup."
That being done, he hoped that this was but a gowk-storm —SIR G. MACKENZIE. *Memoirs*, p 70

Gourd. "Doctored" dice with a secret cavity were called *gourds. See* FULHAMS

Jonah's gourd. This plant (*see Jonah* iv, 6-10), the Heb. *kikayon*, was probably the Palma Christi, called in Egypt *kiki* Niebuhr speaks of a specimen which he himself saw near a rivulet, which in October "rose eight feet in five months' time." And Volney says, "Wherever plants have water the rapidity of their growth is prodigious. In Cairo," he adds, "there is a species of gourd which in twenty-four hours will send out shoots four inches long " (*Travels*, vol. 1, p 71.)

Gourmand and **Gourmet** (goor' mond, goor' mā) (Fr) The *gourmand* is one whose chief pleasure is eating, but a *gourmet* is a connoisseur of food and wines. The *gourmand* regards

quantity more than quality, the *gourmet* quality more than quantity *See* APICIUS

In former times [in France] *gourmand* meant a judge of eating, and *gourmet* a judge of wine . Gourmet is now universally understood to refer to eating, and not to drinking.—HAMERTON. *French and English*, Pt v, ch iv

The gourmand's prayer. "O Philoxenos, Philoxenos, why were you not Prometheus?" Prometheus was the mythological creator of man, and Philoxenos was a great epicure, whose great and constant wish was to have the neck of a crane, that he might enjoy the taste of his food longer before it was swallowed into his stomach. (Aristotle· *Ethics*, iii, 10.)

Gout. The disease is so called from the Fr *goutte*, a drop, because it was once thought to proceed from a "drop of acrid matter in the joints "

Goven St. Goven's Bell. *See* INCHCAPE.

Government Stroke. Early Australian slang for taking a long time over very little work, still a common expression in that country

Gowan (gou' ân) A Scotch word for various field flowers, especially the common daisy, sometimes called the *ewe-gowan*, apparently from the ewe, as being frequent in pastures fed on by sheep.

Gowk. *See* GOUK.

Gown. Gown and town row. In university towns, a scrimmage between the students of different colleges and the townsmen. These feuds go back at least to the reign of King John, when 3,000 students left Oxford for Reading, owing to a quarrel with the men of the town

Gownsman. A student at one of the universities, so called because he wears an academical gown

Graal *See* GRAIL

Grab. To clutch or seize. *He grabbed him, i e* he caught him

Land grabber. A common expression in Ireland during the last two decades of the 19th century, to signify one who takes the farm or land of an evicted tenant. The corresponding phrase in the 18th century was *Land Pirate.*

Grace. A courtesy title used in addressing or speaking of dukes, duchesses, and archbishops "His Grace the Duke of Devonshire," "My Lord Archbishop, may it please Your Grace," etc.

Act of grace. A pardon; a general pardon granted by Act of Parliament, especially that of 1690, when William III pardoned political offenders, and that of 1784, when the estates forfeited for high treason in connexion with "the '45" were restored

Grace before (or after) meat. A short prayer asking a blessing on, or giving thanks for, one's food Here the word (which used to be plural) is a relic of the old phrase *to do graces* or *to give graces*, meaning to render thanks (Fr. *rendre graces*, Lat *gratias agere*), as in Chaucer's
They weren right glad and joyeful, and answereden ful mekely and benignely, yeldinge graces and thankinges to hir lord Melibee —*Tale of Melibeus*, §71.

Grace card or **Grace's card**. The six of hearts is so called in Kilkenny. One of the family of Grace, of Courtstown, in Ireland, equipped at his own expense a regiment of foot and troop of horse, in the service of James II William III promised him high honours if he would join the new party, but the indignant baron wrote on a card, "Tell your master I despise his offer." The card was the six of hearts, and hence the name

Grace cup or **Loving cup**. This is a large tankard or goblet from which the last draught at a banquet is drunk, the cup being passed from guest to guest The name is also applied to a strong brew, as at Oxford, of beer flavoured with lemon-peel, nutmeg and sugar, and very brown toast.

Grace days, or **Days of grace**. The three days over and above the time stated in a commercial bill Thus, if a bill is drawn on June 20th, and is payable in one month, it is due on July 20th, but three "days of grace" are added, bringing the date to July 23rd.

Grace, Herb of. *See* HERB OF GRACE.

Grace notes are musical embellishments, vocal or instrumental, not essential to the harmony or melody of a piece. They used to be much more common in music for the viol and harpsichord than they are for modern instruments, and it was not unusual for a virtuoso to introduce them at his own discretion.

The three Graces. In classical mythology, the goddesses who bestowed beauty and charm and were themselves the embodiment of both. They were the sisters Aglaia, Thalia, and Euphrosyne.

> They are the daughters of sky-ruling Jove,
> By him begot of faire Eurynome,	-
> The first of them hight mylde Euphrosyne,
> Next faire Aglaia, last Thalia merry;
> Sweete Goddesses all three, which me in mirth do
> cherry	SPENSER *Faerie Queene*, VI, x, 22

Andrea Appiani (1754-1817), the Italian fresco artist, was known as *the Painter of the Graces.*

Time of grace. *See* SPORTING SEASONS.

To get into one's good graces To insinuate oneself into the favour of

To fall from grace Apart from a theological implication, this means to relapse from a moral position one has attained.

To take heart of grace. To take courage because of favour or indulgence shown

With a good or **bad grace.** Gracefully or ungracefully, willingly or unwillingly *With a good grace* has an air of rather forced acquiescence.

Year of Grace. The year of Our Lord, Anno Domini. In University language it is the year allowed to a Fellow who has been given a College living, at the end of which he must resign either his fellowship or the living

Graceless or **Godless florin.** The first issue of the English florin (1849), called ' Graceless" because the letters D G ("by God's grace") were omitted, and "Godless" because of the omission of F.D ("Defender of the Faith").

It happened that Richard Lalor Sheil (1791-1851), master of the Mint at the time, was a Catholic, and the suspicion was aroused that the omission was made on religious grounds The florins were called in and re-cast, and Mr Sheil left the Mint the following year on his appointment as minister to Florence

Grade. In American usage this word is used for the more common English *gradient* for the rate of ascent or descent of a road or railway track, also for the hill itself A *grade-crossing* is usually known in Britain as a *level crossing*

To make the grade, to rise to the occasion, to have it in one to do what has to be done; from the analogy of a locomotive succeeding in drawing its load up a steep gradient.

Gradely. A north of England term meaning thoroughly, regularly, as *A gradely fine day* The word is from Scand. *graith*, ready, prompt

Gradgrind, Thomas. A character in Dickens's *Hard Times*, typical of a man who allows nothing for the weakness of human nature, and deals with men and women as a mathematician with his figures.

Gradual An antiphon sung between the Epistle and the Gospel, as the deacon ascends the *steps* (late Lat. *graduales*) of the altar Also, a book containing the musical portions of the service at mass—the *graduals, introits, kyries, gloria in excelsis, credo*, etc.

The Gradual Psalms *Ps* cxx to cxxxiv inclusive, probably so called because they were sung when the ascent to the inner court was made by the priests. In the Authorized Version they are called *Songs of Degrees*, and in the Revised Version *Songs of Ascents. Cp* HALLEL

Græmes, The (grămz) A clan of freebooters who inhabited the Debatable Land (*q v*), and were transported to Ireland at the beginning of the 17th century

Graft. Illicit profit or commission Of U S.A origin, the word is now world wide It seems to have come into use in the 1890s

Grahame's Dyke A popular name for the remains of the old Roman wall between the firths of Clyde and Forth, the Wall of Antoninus

Grail, The Holy. The cup or chalice traditionally used by Christ at the Last Supper, and the centre round which a huge *corpus* of mediæval legend, romance, and allegory revolves

According to one account, Joseph of Arimathæa preserved the Grail, and received into it some of the blood of the Saviour at the Crucifixion He brought it to England, but it disappeared. According to others, it was brought by angels from heaven and entrusted to a body of knights who guarded it on top of a mountain When approached by anyone of not perfect purity it disappeared from sight, and its quest became the source of most of the adventures of the Knights of the Round Table. *But see also* PERCEFOREST

The mass of literature concerning the Grail cycle, both ancient and modern, is enormous, the chief sources of the principal groups of legends are—the *Peredur* (Welsh, given in the

Mabinogion), which is the most archaic form of the Quest story, Wolfram's *Parzifal* (about 1210), the best example of the story as transformed by ecclesiastical influence, the 13th-century French *Perceval le Gallois* (founded on earlier English and Celtic legends which had no connexion with the Grail), showing Perceval in his later rôle as an ascetic hero (translated by Dr Sebastian Evans, 1893, as *The High History of the Holy Grail*), and the *Quête du St Graal*, which, in its English dress, forms Bks 13-18 of Malory's *Morte d'Arthur See* FISHERMAN, KING; GALAHAD, PERCIVAL

It was the French poet Robert le Boron (fl. about 1215), who, in his *Joseph d'Arimathie* or *Le Saint Graal*, first definitely attached the history of the Grail to the Arthurian cycle

The framework of Tennyson's *Holy Grail* (1869, *Idylls of the King*), in which the poet expressed his "strong feeling as to the Reality of the Unseen," is taken from Malory

Grain. A knave in grain. A thoroughgoing knave, a knave all through An old phrase which comes from dyeing The brilliant crimson dye obtained from the kermes and cochineal insects used to be thought to come from some seed, or grain, it was of a very durable and lasting nature, dyed the thing completely and finally, through and through. Hence also the word *ingrained*, as in "an ingrained [i e. ineradicable] habit "

> How the red roses flush up in her cheeks,
> And the pure snow with goodly vermeil stain
> Like crimson dyed in grain!
> SPENSER. *Epithalamion*, 226.

'Tis ingrain, sir, 'twill endure wind and weather — SHAKESPEARE *Twelfth Night*, i, 5.

To go against the grain. Against one's inclination The allusion is to wood, which cannot be easily planed the wrong way of the grain

> Your minds,
> Pre-occupied with what you rather must do
> Than what you should, made you against the grain
> To voice him consul —*Coriolanus*, ii, 3

With a grain of salt. *See* SALT

Gramercy. Thank you very much, from O Fr *grant*, great, *merci*, reward, the full meaning of the exclamation being "May God reward you greatly." When Gobbo says to Bassanio, "God bless your worship!" he replies, "Gramercy Wouldst thou aught with me?" (*Merchant of Venice*, ii, 2)

Grammar. Cæsar is not above the grammarians. Suetonius tells us (*De Grammaticis*, 22) that Tiberius was rebuked by a grammarian for some verbal slip, and upon a courtier remarking that if the word was not good Latin it would be in future, now that it had received imperial recognition, he was rebuked with the words *Tu enim Cæsar civitatem dare potes hominibus, verbis non potes* (Cæsar, you can grant citizenship to men, but not to words) Hence the saying, *Cæsar non supra grammaticos.*

But when a later Emperor, the German Sigismund I, stumbled into a wrong gender at the Council of Constance (1414), no such limitation would be admitted, he replied, *Ego sum Imperator Romanorum, et supra grammaticam* (I am the Roman Emperor, and am above grammar!).

The Scourge of Grammar So Pope, in the *Dunciad* (iii, 149), called Giles Jacob (1686-1744), a very minor poet, who, in his *Register of the Poets*, made an unprovoked attack on Pope's friend, Gay

Prince of Grammarians. Apollonius of Alexandria (2nd cent B.C), so called by Priscian

Grammont (gra' mong) **The Count de Grammont's short memory,** is a phrase arising from a story told of the Count's marriage to Lady Elizabeth Hamilton—La Belle Hamilton—of the Restoration court When he was leaving England after a visit in which this young lady's name had been compromised by him, he was followed by her brothers with drawn swords, who asked him if he had not forgotten something "True, true," said the Count pleasantly; "I promised to marry your sister." With which he returned to London and married Elizabeth, 1663

Granby, The Marquess of. At one time this was a popular inn sign, there being in London alone over twenty public-houses of this name John Manners, Marquess of Granby (1721-70) commanded the Leicester Blues against the Pretender in the '45, was a lieutenant-general at Minden (1759) and commander-in-chief of the British army in 1766 He was a very bald man, and most of the inn-signs exaggerated this defect in his appearance. *See* TO GO BALD-HEADED.

Grand, Le. (Fr , the Great)

Le Grand Batârd Antoine de Bourgogne (d 1504), a natural son of Philip the Good, famous for his deeds of prowess

Le Grand Condé. Louis II of Bourbon, Prince de Condé, one of France's greatest military commanders (1621-86). The funeral oration pronounced at his death was Bossuet's finest composition.

Le Grand Corneille Pierre Corneille, the French dramatist (1606-84).

Le Grand Dauphin. Louis, son of Louis XIV (1661-1711)

La Grande Mademoiselle. The Duchesse de Montpensier (1627-93), daughter of Gaston, Duc d'Orléans, and cousin of Louis XIV

Le Grand Monarque. Louis XIV, King of France (1638-1715)

Le Grand Pan. Voltaire (1694-1778)

Monsieur le Grand. The Grand Equerry of France in the reign of Louis XIV, etc.

Grand.

Grand Alliance. Signed May 12th, 1689, between Germany and the States General, subsequently also by England, Spain, and Savoy, to prevent the union of France and Spain

Grand Guignol. *See* GUIGNOL.

Grand Lama. *See* LAMA.

Grandee In Spain, a nobleman of the highest rank, who has the privilege of remaining covered in the king's presence.

Grandison, Sir Charles, the hero of Samuel Richardson's *History of Sir Charles Grandison,* published in 1753 Sir Charles is the beau-ideal of a perfect hero, the union of a good Christian and a proper English gentleman, aptly described by Sir Walter Scott as "a faultless monster that the world ne'er saw." It has been suggested that Richardson's model for this character was the worthy Robert Nelson (1665-1715), a religious writer and eminent non-juror

Grandison Cromwell. The nickname given by Mirabeau to Lafayette (1757-1834), implying that he had all the ambition of a Cromwell, but wanted to appear before men as a Sir Charles Grandison.

Grandmontines. An order of Benedictine hermits founded by St Stephen of Muret about 1100, with its mother house at Grandmont, Normandy They came to England soon after the foundation and established three houses, one of which, at Craswall, Herefordshire (fl *c.* 1222-1464) is one of the loneliest and most interesting monastic ruins in England.

Grange. Properly the *granum* (granary) or farm of a monastery, where the corn was kept in store In Lincolnshire and the northern counties the name is applied to any lone farm; houses attached to monasteries where rent was paid in grain were also called granges.

> Till thou return, the Court I will exchange
> For some poor cottage, or some country grange
>   DRAYTON· *Lady Geraldine to Earl of Surrey*

Tennyson's poem, *Mariana,* was suggested by the line in Shakespeare's *Measure for Measure* (iii, 1).—

> There, at the moated grange resides this dejected Mariana

The word came into more common use in Victorian times when new and largish houses were being built in the country and often magniloquently called The Grange
In U S A **The Grange** is a nation-wide association for promoting the interests of agriculture.

Grangerize (grān′jĕr īz). To "extra-illustrate" a book, to supplement it by the addition of illustrations, portraits, autograph letters, caricatures, prints, broadsheets, biographical sketches, anecdotes, scandals, press notices, parallel passages, and any other sort of matter directly or indirectly bearing on the subject So called from James Granger (1723-76), vicar of Shiplake, Oxon, who collected some 14,000 engraved portraits and in 1769 published his *Biographical History of England from Egbert the Great to the Revolution* . "with a preface showing the utility of a collection of engraved portraits " The book went through several editions with additional matter, and in 1806 was edited by Mark Noble Collectors made this book a sort of core around which they assembled great collections of portraits, etc, and in 1856 two copies of the book were sold by London booksellers, one in 27 volumes with 1,300 portraits, the other in 19 volumes containing 3,000 portraits There was for many years a fashion of Grangerizing books, with the result that many excellent editions of biographies, etc., were ruined by having the plates torn out, for pasting into some dilettante's collection.

Grangousier. In Rabelais's satire, *Gargantua and Pantagruel,* a king of Utopia, who married in "the vigour of his old age," Gargamelle, daughter of the king of the Parpaillons, and became the father of Gargantua (*q v*) Some say he is meant for Louis XII, but Motteux thinks the "academy figure" of this old Priam was John d'Albret, King of Navarre.

Granite. Granite City, The. Aberdeen

Granite Redoubt. The grenadiers of the Consular Guard were so called at the battle of Marengo in 1800, because when the French had given way they formed into a square, stood like stone against the Austrians, and stopped all further advance

Granite State, The. New Hampshire is so called, because the mountainous parts are chiefly granite

Granny-knot. An ill-tied reef knot which breaks down when any strain is placed upon it

Grape. The grapes are sour. You disparage it because it is beyond your reach The allusion is to Æsop's well-known fable of the fox which tried in vain to get at some grapes, but when he found they were beyond his reach went away saying, "I see they are sour."

Grape shot. A form of projectile at one time much used with smooth-bore guns. It consisted of a large number of cast-iron bullets packed in layers between thin iron plates and then arranged in tiers (usually three), the whole being held together by an iron bolt passing through the centre of the plates When fired the shot broke up and distributed the bullets in showers The well-known phrase "A whiff of grape shot" occurs in Carlyle's *French Revolution* (III, vii, 7)

Grape-sugar. Another name for glucose (dextrose), a fermentable sugar, less sweet than cane-sugar, and obtained from dried grapes and other fruits as well as being made chemically. It is used in the manufacture of jams, beer, etc.

Grapevine telegraph. The intangible and untraceable means whereby rumours—as often as not false—are conveyed around by whisperings, etc

Grass Not to let the grass grow under one's feet. To be very active and energetic

A grass hand is a compositor who fills a temporary vacancy, hence *to grass,* to take only temporary jobs as a compositor

Grass widow. Formerly, an unmarried woman who has had a child, but now, a wife temporarily parted from her husband, also, by extension, a divorced woman The word has nothing to do with *grace* widow (a widow by courtesy). The phrase *grass widower* is used in the same sense.

Grasshopper. Considered as the sign of a grocer because it was the crest of Sir Thomas Gresham, merchant grocer The Royal Exchange, founded by him, used to be profusely decorated with grasshoppers, and the brass one on the eastern part of the present building escaped the fires of 1666 and 1838

Grattan's Parliament. The free Irish Parliament established in Dublin in 1782, when Henry Grattan (1746-1820) obtained the repeal of Poynings' Law (*q v*). It lasted till the coming into force of the Act of Union, January 1st, 1801.

Grave Solemn, sedate, and serious in look and manner. This is Lat *gravis*, heavy, grave, but "grave," a place of interment, is A S. *græf*, a pit, *graf-an*, to dig.

Close as the grave. Very secret indeed.

It's enough to make him turn in his grave. Said when something happens to which the deceased person would have strongly objected

Someone is walking over my grave. An exclamation made when one is seized with an involuntary convulsive shuddering

To carry away the meat from the grave *See* MEAT.

With one foot in the grave. At the very verge of death. The expression was used by Julian, who said he would "learn something even if he had one foot in the grave" The parallel Greek phrase is, "With one foot in the ferry-boat,' meaning Charon's

Gravelled. I'm regularly gravelled Nonplussed, like a ship run aground and unable to move.
When you were gravelled for lack of matter.—*As You Like It*, iv, 1.

Gray. *See* GREY

Gray-back. Confederate soldier in the American Civil War So called from the colour of the Confederate army uniform

Gray's Inn (London) was the inn or mansion of the Lords de Grey, and the property belonged to them from at least as early as 1307 to 1505. It was let to students of law in the 14th century, and is still one of the four Inns of Court (*q v.*) In the Hall, erected 1555-60, Shakespeare's *Comedy of Errors* was first acted, 1594 The walks and gardens were laid out by Sir Francis Bacon, Lord Verulam The library contained some 30,000 volumes and MSS but, together with the Hall, it was destroyed in the air-raids of 1940-41 The Hall was rebuilt and opened in 1951.

Grease. Slang for money, especially that given as a bribe, "palm-oil."

Like greased lightning. Very quick indeed.

To grease one's palm or fist. To give a bribe
Grease my fist with a tester or two, and ye shall find it in your pennyworth —QUARLES: *The Virgin Widow,* iv, 1, p 40

S   You must oyl it first.
C   I understand you—
    Greaze him i' the fist
        CARTWRIGHT *Ordinary* (1651)

To grease the wheels To make things run smoothly, pass off without a hitch; usually by the application of a little money

Greaser. The American name for a Mexican or Spanish American, generally used in contempt.

Great, The. The term is usually applied to the following —
ABBAS I, Shah of Persia (1557, 1585-1628)
ALBERTUS MAGNUS, the schoolman (d 1280)
ALEXANDER, of Macedon. (356, 340-323 B C)
ALFONSO III, King of Asturias and Leon (884, 866-912)
ALFRED, of England (849, 871-901)
ST BASIL, Bishop of Cæsarea. (4th cent)
CANUTE, of England and Denmark (995, 1014-1035)
CASIMIR III, of Poland (1309, 1333-1370)
CHARLES, King of the Franks and Emperor of the Romans, called *Charlemagne* (764-814)
CHARLES III, Duke of Lorraine (1543-1608)
CHARLES EMMANUEL I, Duke of Savoy (1562-1630.)
CLOVIS, King of the Franks (466-511)
CONDÉ *See* LOUIS II, *below.*
CONSTANTINE I, Emperor of Rome (272, 306-337)
CYRUS, founder of the Persian Empire (d. 529 B C)
DARIUS, King of Persia (d 485 B C)
DOUGLAS (*Archibald, the great Earl of Angus,* also called *Bell-the-Cat* [*q v*])
FERDINAND I, of Castile and Leon (Reigned 1034-1065.)
FREDERICK WILLIAM, Elector of Brandenburg, surnamed *The Great Elector* (1620-1688)
FREDERICK II, of Prussia. (1712, 1740-1786)
GREGORY I, Pope (544, 590-604)
GUSTAVUS ADOLPHUS, of Sweden (1594, 1611-1632)
HENRY IV, of France (1553, 1589-1610)
HEROD I, King of Judea (73-3 B C)
JOHN I, of Portugal (1357, 1385-1433)
JUSTINIAN I, Emperor of the East (483, 527-565)
LEO I, Pope (440-461)
LEO I, Emperor of the East (457-474)
LEOPOLD I, of Germany. (1640-1705)
LEWIS I, of Hungary (1326, 1342-1383)
LOUIS II, DE BOURBON, Prince of Conde, Duc d'Enghien (1621-1686), always known as *The Great Conde*
LOUIS XIV, called *Le Grand Monarque* (1638, 1643-1714.)
MAXIMILIAN, Duke of Bavaria, victor of Prague (1573-1651.)
COSMO DE' MEDICI, first Grand Duke of Tuscany (1519, 1537-1574)
GONZALES PEDRO DE MENDOZA, *great Cardinal of Spain,* statesman and scholar (1428-1495.)
MOHAMMED II, Sultan of the Turks (1430, 1451-1481.)
NICHOLAS I, Pope (from 858-867)
OTHO I, Emperor of the Romans (912, 936-973)
PETER I, of Russia. (1672, 1689-1725)
PIERRE III, of Aragon (1239, 1276-1285)
SANCHO III, King of Navarre (About 965-1035.)
SAPOR III, King of Persia (d 380)
SFORZA (*Giacomo*), the Italian general. (1369-1424)
SIGISMUND II, King of Poland (1467, 1506-1548)
THEODORIC, King of the Ostrogoths (454, 475-526)
THEODOSIUS I, Emperor (346, 378-395)
MATTEO VISCONTI, Lord of Milan (1252, 1295-1323)
VLADIMIR, Grand Duke of Russia (973-1015)
WALDEMAR I, of Denmark (1131, 1157-1182)

Great Bear, The. *See* BEAR.

Great Bible, The. *See* BIBLE, THE ENGLISH

Great Bullet-head, George Cadoudal (1771-1804), leader of the *Chouans,* born at Brech, in Morbihan

Great Captain. *See* CAPITANO, EL GRAN

Great Cham of Literature. So Smollett calls Dr Johnson (1709-84)

Great Commoner. William Pitt, Earl of Chatham (1708-78).

Great Dauphin, The *See* GRAND.

Great Divide. The Rocky Mountains

Great Elector, The Frederick William, Elector of Brandenburg (1620-88)

Great Go. At the universities, a familiar term for the final examinations for the B A degree, at Oxford usually shortened to *Greats.* Cp LITTLE GO

Great Harry. The name popularly given to the *Henry Grace de Dieu,* the first double-decked warship in the English navy Built in 1512, and named after Henry VIII, she was a three-master of about 1,000 tons, carried 72 guns and sailed with a crew of 700 men She was burned accidentally at Woolwich, in 1533.

Great Head. Malcolm III, of Scotland, also called *Canmore,* which means the same thing. (Reigned 1057-1093.)

Great Lakes The five American inland seas —Lakes Erie, Huron, Michigan, Ontario, and Superior

Great Mogul. The title of the chief of the Mogul Empire (*q v.*)

Great Scott or **Scot!** An exclamation of surprise, wonder, admiration, indignation, etc. It seems to have originated in America about the late 60s of last century, perhaps in memory of General Winfield Scott (1786-1866) a popular figure in the mid-19th century after his victorious campaign in Mexico in 1847

In England the expression is sometimes humorously extended to "Great Scotland Yard!"

Great Unknown, The. Sir Walter Scott, who published *Waverley* (1814), and the subsequent novels as "by the author of Waverley," anonymously. It was not till 1827 that he admitted the authorship, though it was already pretty well known

The Great White Way. The name formerly applied to Broadway, the theatrical district of New York City.

Greatheart, Mr. The guide of Christiana and her family to the Celestial City in Bunyan's *Pilgrim's Progress,* part II

Grecian. See BLUE-COAT SCHOOL

Grecian bend. An affectation in walking with the body stooped slightly forward, assumed by English women in 1868

Grecian Coffee-house, in Devereux Court, the oldest in London, was originally opened by Pasqua, a Greek slave, brought to England in 1652 by Daniel Edwards, a Turkey merchant This Greek was the first to teach the method of roasting coffee and to introduce that beverage into England

A Grecian nose or **profile** is one where the line of the nose continues that of the forehead without a dip

Greco, El (grek' ō), or **The Greek.** A Cretan named Domenico Theotocopuli, who studied under Titian and Michelangelo, and moved to Spain about 1570 He was the foremost painter of the Castilian school in the 16th century

Greegrees. The name given on the West Coast of Africa to amulets, charms, fetishes, etc

A greegree man. One who sells these

Greek. A merry Greek. In *Troilus and Cressida* (i, 2) Shakespeare makes Pandarus, bantering Helen for her love to Troilus, say, "I think Helen loves him better than Paris", to which Cressida, whose wit is to parry and pervert, replies, "Then she's a merry Greek indeed," insinuating that she was a "woman of pleasure." *See* GRIG.

All Greek to me. Quite unintelligible, an unknown tongue or language Casca says, "For mine own part, it was all Greek to me." (*Julius Cæsar,* 1, 2)

Last of the Greeks. Philopœmen, of Megalopolis, whose great object was to infuse into the Achæans a military spirit, and establish their independence (252-183 B C.).

To play the Greek. To indulge in one's cups The Greeks have always been considered a luxurious race, fond of creature comforts The rule in Greek banquets was *E pithi e apithi* (Quaff, or be off!)

When Greek meets Greek, then is the tug of war. When two men or armies of undoubted courage fight, the contest will be very severe The line is slightly altered from a 17th-century play, and the reference is to the obstinate resistance of the Greek cities to Philip and Alexander, the Macedonian kings.

When Greeks joined Greeks, then was the tug of war.
NATHANIEL LEE *The Rival Queens,* IV, 2

Greek Calends. Never To defer anything to the Greek Calends is to defer it *sine die* There were no calends in the Greek months See NEVER.

Greek Church A name often given inaccurately to the Eastern or Orthodox Church (*q v*) of which the Greek Church is only an autocephalous unit, recognized as independent by the Patriarch of Constantinople in 1850. It is governed by a synod under the presidency of the Archbishop of Athens, and does not differ in any point of doctrine from its parent the Orthodox Church.

Greek Cross *See* CROSS

Greek fire. A combustible composition used for setting fire to an enemy's ships, fortifications, etc, of nitre, sulphur, and naphtha. Tow steeped in the mixture was hurled in a blazing state through tubes, or tied to arrows The invention is ascribed to Callinicos, of Heliopolis, A D 668, and it was used by the Greeks at Constantinople

Greek gift. A treacherous gift The reference is to the Wooden Horse of Troy (*q.v*), or to Virgil's *Timeo Danaos et dona ferentes* (*Æneid,* ii, 49), "I fear the Greeks, even when they offer gifts."

Greek trust. No trust at all "*Græcà fides*" was with the Romans no faith at all

Green. Young, fresh, as *green cheese,* cream cheese, which is eaten fresh, *a green old age,* an old age in which the faculties are not impaired and the spirits are still youthful; *green goose,* a young or mid-summer goose

If you would fat green geese, shut them up when they are about a month old —MORTIMER *Husbandry.*

Immature in age or judgment, inexperienced, young

> My salad days
> When I was green in judgment!
>   *Antony and Cleopatra*, i, 5
> The text is old, the orator too green
>   *Venus and Adonis*, 806.

Simple, raw, easily imposed upon, the characteristic greenhorn (*q v*)

> "He is so jolly green," said Charley —DICKENS
> *Oliver Twist*, ch ix

For its symbolism, etc., see COLOURS

Do you see any green in my eye? See EYE.

If they do these things in the green tree, what shall be done in the dry? (*Luke* xxiii, 31) If they start like this, how will they finish? Or, as Pope says (*Moral Essays, Ep I*) "Just as the twig is bent, the tree's inclined."

To give a girl a green gown. A 16th-century descriptive phrase for romping with a girl in the fields and roiling her on the grass so that her dress is stained green.

> There's not a budding Boye, or Girle, this day,
> But is got up, and gone to bring in May ..
> Many a green-gown has been given,
> Many a kisse, both odd and even
>   HERRICK *Corinna's Going a-Maying*

To look through green glasses To feel jealous of one; to be envious of another's success Cp GREEN-EYED MONSTER *below*

The Board of Green Cloth. See BOARD.

The moon made of green cheese. See MOON

The wearing of the green. An Irish patriotic and revolutionary song, dating from 1798. Green (cp. EMERALD ISLE) was the emblematic colour adopted by Irish Nationalists.

> They're hanging men and women for the wearing of the green

Gentlemen of the Green Baize Road. Whist players "Gentlemen of the Green Cloth Road," billiard players. (*See Bleak House*, ch xxvi, par 1.) Probably the idea of sharpers is included, as "Gentlemen of the Road" means highwaymen

Green belt. A stretch of country around a city or large town that has been set aside to be kept open and free from all building except within certain limits.

Green Dragoons. The old 13th Dragoons (whose regimental facings were green) Later called the 13th Hussars, whose regimental facings have been white since 1861

Green-eyed monster, The. So Shakespeare called jealousy —

> *Iago* · O! beware, my lord, of jealousy,
> It is the green-ey'd monster which doth mock
> The meat it feeds on   *Othello*, iii, 3.

A greenish complexion was formerly held to be indicative of jealousy, and as cats, lions, tigers, and all the green-eyed tribe "mock the meat they feed on," so jealousy mocks its victim by loving and loathing it at the same time

Green fingers, said of a successful gardener whose fingers are supposed to have a sort of magic touch that makes whatever he plants grow and flourish.

Green hands. A nautical phrase for inferior sailors See ABLE-BODIED SEAMAN, *and cp* GREENHORN *below*.

14*

The Green Howards. The official name, since 1920, of the Yorkshire Regiment, the 19th of the line, named after Sir Charles Howard, colonel from 1738 to 1748 Green was the colour of the regimental facings

The Green Isle. Ireland *See* EMERALD ISLE.

The Green Knight In the old romance, *Valentine and Orson*, a Pagan who demanded Fezon in marriage but, overcome by Orson, resigned his claim.

Green Linnets. The 39th Foot, so called from the colour of their facings Now the Dorsetshire, and the facings are white

Green Man. This common public-house sign probably represents either a Jack-in-the-Green (*q.v.*), or a game-keeper, who used at one time to be dressed in green

> But the "Green Man" shall I pass by unsung,
> Which mine own James upon his sign-post hung?
> His sign, his image—for he once was seen
> A squire's attendant, clad in keeper's green
>   CRABBE *Borough*

The public-house sign, *The Green Man and Still*, is probably from the arms of the Distillers' Company, the supporters of which were two Indians, which, by the sign-painters, were depicted as clad in green boughs like a "green man" or Jack-in-the-Green

On a golf course the green-man is the club servant who is responsible for the putting greens

Green Mountain Boys. Men of Vermont, U S A —a term in use since 1775 Vermont, or Vert Mont, so called from its forest-covered mountains, was formed from the states of New Hampshire and New York in 1777, largely through the action of its farmers who agitated for an independent state of their own, and were called the Green Mountain Boys

Green Ribbon Day in Ireland is March 17th, St. Patrick's Day, when the shamrock and green ribbon are worn as the national badge.

Green room. The common waiting-room beyond the stage at a theatre for the performers; so called because at one time the walls were coloured green to relieve the eyes affected by the glare of the stage lights

Green sickness, the old name for chlorosis, a form of anaemia now very rare but once common in adolescent girls. It was characterized by a greenish pallor.

Green wax In old legal practice an estreat (certified extract from an official record) formerly delivered to the sheriff for levy It was under the seal of the court, which was impressed upon green wax

Greenbacks. A legal tender note in the United States, first issued in 1862, during the Civil War, as a war-revenue measure, so called because the back is printed in green

Greengage. A variety of plum introduced into England from France (with others) by Sir William Gage of Hengrave, Suffolk, about 1725, and named in honour of him Called by the French "Reine Claude," out of compliment to the daughter of Anne de Bretagne and

Louis XII, generally called *la bonne reine* (1499-1524).

Greenhorn. A novice at any trade, profession, sport, etc, a simpleton, a youngster *Cp.* GREEN HAND; GREENER

Greensleeves. A very popular ballad in Elizabethan days, first published in 1581, given *in extenso* in Clement Robinson's *Handefull of Pleasant Delites* (1584), and twice mentioned by Shakespeare (*Merry Wives*, ii, 1, and v, 5) The air goes back to Elizabethan times, and was used for many ballads During the Civil Wars it was a party tune to which the Cavaliers sang political ballads Pepys (April 23rd, 1660) mentions it under the title of *The Blacksmith*, by which it was sometimes known.

Greenlander. A native of Greenland, which was originally so called (*Gronland*) by the Norsemen in the 10th century with the idea that if only they gave the country a good name it would induce settlers to go there! Facetiously applied to a greenhorn.

Greenwich. So named by Danish settlers, it means "the green place on the bay" (*wich*, *wig*), or place situated on the coast or near the mouth of a river; as Sandwich, Lerwick, Schleswig.

Greenwich barbers. Retailers of sand; so called because the inhabitants of Greenwich used to "shave the pits" in the neighbourhood to supply London with sand

Greenwich stars. The stars used by astronomers for the lunar computations in the nautical ephemeris.

Greenwich time. Mean time for the meridian of Greenwich, *i e.* the system of time in which noon occurs at the moment of passage of the mean sun over the meridian of Greenwich. It is the standard time adopted by astronomers, Greenwich noon is in legal use throughout Great Britain, Ireland, France, Belgium, Spain, Portugal, the Faroe Islands, Gibraltar, Algeria, St. Thomas and Princes Isles, the Ivory Coast, Dahomey, and Morocco

Since 1883 the system of Standard Time by zones has been accepted by all civilized nations Standard Time differs from Greenwich Mean Time by an integral number of hours, either slow or fast Mid-European Time, is, for example, one hour fast of Greenwich Time; Pacific Time is 9 hours slow, *i e* noon at Greenwich is 3 a.m of the same day in British Columbia

Gregorian. Gregorian Calendar. *See* CALENDAR.

Gregorian chant. Plain-song; a mediæval system of church music, so called because it was introduced into the service by Gregory the Great (600).

Gregorian Epoch. The epoch or day on which the Gregorian calendar commenced in October, 1582.

Gregorian telescope. The first form of the reflecting telescope, invented by James Gregory (1638-75), professor of mathematics at St. Andrews (1663).

Gregorian tree. The gallows; so named from Gregory Brandon and his son, Robert (who

was popularly known as "Young Gregory"), hangmen from the time of James I to 1649 Sir William Segar, Garter Knight of Arms, granted a coat of arms to Gregory Brandon. *See* HANGMEN

> This trembles under the black rod, and he
> Doth fear his fate from the Gregorian tree
> *Mercurius Pragmaticus* (1641).

Gregorian Year. The civil year, according to the correction introduced by Pope Gregory XIII in 1582 *See* CALENDAR. The equinox which occurred on March 25th in the time of Julius Cæsar, fell on March 11th in the year 1582 This was because the Julian calculation of 365¼ days to a year was 11 min 10 sec. too much. Gregory suppressed ten days in October, so as to make the equinox fall on March 21, 1583, as it did at the Council of Nice, and, by some simple arrangements, prevented the recurrence in future of a similar error.

The New Style, as it was called was adopted in England in 1752, when Wednesday, September 2nd, was followed by Thursday, September 14th.

This has given rise to a double computation, as Lady Day, March 25th, Old Lady Day, April 6th; Midsummer Day, June 24th, Old Midsummer Day, July 6th; Michaelmas Day, September 29th, Old Michaelmas Day, October 11th, Christmas Day, December 25th, Old Christmas Day, January 6th

Until 1752 the legal new year in Britain began on March 25th, though New Year's Day was popularly reckoned as January 1st. It was, therefore, customary to put for all dates between January 1st and March 25th the two years involved *e g* January 31st, 1721 in popular reckoning would be written or printed as January 31st, 1720/21, that is, 1720 legally but popularly and actually 1721.

Gregories. Hangmen. *See* GREGORIAN TREE.

Gregory. A feast held on St Gregory's Day (March 12th), especially in Ireland but formerly common to all Europe.

Gremlin (grem' lin) One of a tribe of imaginary elves, whom the R A F in World War II blamed for all inexplicable failures, mechanical or otherwise, in aeroplanes.

Grenadier. Originally a soldier whose duty in battle was to throw grenades, *i e* explosive shells, weighing from two to six pounds. There were some four or five tall, picked men, chosen for this purpose from each company; later each regiment had a special company of them; and when, in the 18th century, the use of grenades was discontinued (not to be revived until World War I), the name was retained for the company composed of the tallest and finest men. In the British Army it now survives only in the Grenadier Guards, the First regiment of Foot Guards (3 battalions), noted for their height, fine physique, traditions, and discipline.

Grendel. The mythical, half-human monster in *Beowulf* (*q.v*), who nightly raided the king's hall and slew the sleepers, he was slain by Beowulf

Gresham, Sir Thomas. *See* CLEOPATRA AND HER PEARL; GRASSHOPPER.

To dine with Sir Thomas Gresham. *See* DINE.

Greta Hall. The poet of Greta Hall. Southey, who lived at Greta Hall, in the Vale of Keswick (1774-1843)

Gretna Green Marriages. Runaway matches In Scotland, all that is required of contracting parties is a mutual declaration before witnesses of their willingness to marry, so that elopers reaching Gretna, a hamlet near the village of Springfield, Dumfriesshire, 8 miles N W. of Carlisle, and just across the border, could (up to 1856) get legally married without either licence, banns, or priest. The declaration was generally made to a blacksmith

By an Act of 1856 the residence in Scotland for at least 21 days of one of the parties is essential before a marriage can be performed.

Grève (grāv). **Place de Grève.** The Tyburn of old Paris, where for centuries public executions took place The present Hôtel de Ville occupies part of the site, and what is left of the *Place* is now called the *Place de l'Hôtel de Ville* The word *greve* means the strand of a river or the shore of the sea, and the *Place* is on the bank of the Seine

Who has e'er been to Paris must needs know the Grève,
The fatal retreat of th' unfortunate brave,
Where honour and justice most oddly contribute
To ease Hero's pains by a halter or gibbet.
        PRIOR *The Thief and the Cordelier.*

Grey. Greys, The. The Royal Scots Greys (2nd Dragoons) were raised in 1678 It is now uncertain whether their name comes from their grey horses or their uniform, which was also grey. The horses survived the uniform, but both have now gone, as the regiment is mechanized.

Greybeard. An old man—generally a doddering old fellow, also an earthen pot for holding spirits, a large stone jar. *Cp* BELLARMINE

Grey Cloak. A City of London alderman who has passed the chair, so called because his official robe is furred with grey amis.

Grey Eminence. The name given to François Leclerc du Tremolay (1577-1638), or Pere Joseph, as he was called, the Capuchin agent and trusty counsellor of Cardinal Richelieu. He owed his sobriquet to the fact that his influence and his policy inspired the Cardinal's actions, and that he was, as it were, a shadowy cardinal in the background.

Grey Friars. Franciscans (*q v*) Black Friars are Dominicans, and White Friars Carmelites.

Grey goose feather, or **wing.** "The grey goose wing was the death of him," the arrow which is winged with grey goose feathers

Grey mare. *See* MARE.

Grey matter, a pseudo-scientific euphemism for the brain, for common sense. The active part of the brain is composed of a greyish tissue which contains the nerve-endings

Grey Sisters *See* FRANCISCANS.

Grey Washer by the Ford, The. An Irish wraith which seems to be washing clothes in a river; but when the "doomed man" approaches she holds up what she seemed to be washing, and it is the phantom of himself with his death wounds from which he is about to suffer.

Greyhound Juliana Berners, in the *Boke of St. Albans* (1486) gives the following as ' the propretels of a goode Grehound":—

A greyhounde shoulde be heded like a snake, And necked like a Drake, Foted like a Kat, Tayled like a Rat, Syded like a Teme, Chyned like a Beme

"Syded like a teme" probably means both sides alike, a plough-team being meant.

Greyhound. The Greyhound as a public-house sign is in honour of Henry VII, whose badge it was; it is still the badge (in silver) of the King's Messengers.

Gridiron. This is emblematic of St. Lawrence whose feast is celebrated on August 10 One unsubstantiated legend says that he was roasted on a gridiron; another that he was bound to an iron chair and thus roasted alive All that is certainly known of him is that he was martyred in the year 258 and is buried in the church dedicated to him outside the walls of Rome. The church of St Lawrence Jewry in the City of London has a gilt gridiron for a vane

Gridironer. An Australian settler who bought land in strips like the bars of a gridiron, so that the land lying between was rendered worthless and could be acquired later at a bargain price

Grief. To come to grief To meet with disaster; to be ruined, to fail in business.

Griffin. A mythical monster, also called *Griffon, Gryphon,* etc , fabled to be the offspring of the lion and eagle. Its legs and all from the shoulder to the head are like an eagle, the rest of the body is that of a lion This creature was sacred to the sun, and kept guard over hidden treasures See ARIMASPIANS

[The Griffin is] an Emblem of valour and magnanimity, as being compounded of the Eagle and Lion, the noblest Animals in their kinds, and so is it applicable unto Princes, Presidents, Generals, and all heroick Commanders, and so is it also born in the Coat-arms of many noble Families of *Europe* — SIR THOMAS BROWNE *Pseudodoxia Epidemica,* III, xi

The Londoners' familiar name for the figure on the monument placed on the site of Temple Bar is *The Griffin*

Among Anglo-Indians a newcomer, a greenhorn (*q.v*) is called a *griffin,* and the residue of a contract feast, taken away by the contractor, half the buyer's and half the seller's, is known in the trade as *griffins*

A griffon is a small, rough-haired terrier used in France for hunting.

Grig. Merry as a grig. A grig is a cricket, or grasshopper; but it is by no means certain that the animal is referred to in this phrase (which is at least as old as the mid-sixteenth century), for *grig* here may be a corruption of *Greek,* "merry as a Greek," which dates from about the same time Shakespeare has: "Then she's a merry Greek", and again, "Cressid 'mongst the merry Greeks" (*Troilus and Cressida,* 1, 2, iv, 4); and among the Romans *Græcari* signified "to play the reveller."

Grim The giant in Bunyan's *Pilgrim's Progress* (pt. ii), who tried to stop pilgrims on their way to the Celestial City, but was slain by Mr Greatheart *See also* GRIMSBY: GRIM'S DYKE.

Grimalkin. An old she-cat, especially a wicked-or eerie-looking one from *grey* and *Malkin* (*q v*) Shakespeare makes the Witch in *Macbeth* say, "I come, Graymalkin " The cat was supposed to be a witch and was the companion of witches.

Grimes Graves is the name given to prehistoric —probably Neolithic—flint mines near Brandon in Suffolk The shaft is some forty feet deep and from it radiate passages in all directions The old flint-miners worked with picks made of deer antlers, some of which have been found at the flint face as left by those ancient toilers

Grimm's Law. The law of the permutation of consonants in the principal Aryan languages, first formulated by Jacob L Grimm, the German philologist, in 1822 Thus, what is *p* in Greek, Latin, or Sanskrit, becomes *f* in Gothic, and *b* or *f* in the Old High German, what is *t* in Greek, Latin, or Sanskrit becomes *th* in Gothic, and *d* in Old High German; etc Thus changing *p* into *f*, and *t* into *th*, "pater" becomes "father." Grimm's Law has, naturally, much greater philological importance than this example shows.

Grimsby (Lincolnshire) Founded, according to the old legend, by Grim, the fisherman who saved the life of Havelok (*q v.*), son of the king of Denmark Grim was laden with gifts by the royal parent, and returned to Lincolnshire, where he built the town whose ancient seal still contains the names of "Gryme" and "Habloc "

Grim's Dyke or Ditch. The name given to the great fortified fosse which was probably built in prehistoric times by the first invaders from the Continent as a protection against the aborigines It can still be traced along most of its length through the Chilterns

Grin. To grin like a Cheshire cat. *See* CAT.

You must grin and bear it. Resistance is hopeless; you may make a face, if you like, but you cannot help yourself.

Grind. To work up for an examination.

To grind one down. To reduce the price asked; to lower wages

To take a grind To take a constitutional, to cram into the smallest space the greatest amount of physical exercise. This is the physical grind The literary grind is a turn at hard study.

Grinders. The double teeth which grind the food put into the mouth. The preacher speaks of old age as the time when "the grinders cease because they are few" (*Eccles* xii, 3)

To take a grinder. An obsolete gesture of obloquy and insult, performed by applying the left thumb to the nose and revolving the right hand round it, as if working a hand-organ or coffee-mill, done when someone had tried to practise on your credulity, or to impose upon your good faith

Griselda or Griselda (gri zil' da, gri zel' dâ) The model of enduring patience and obedience, often spoken of as "Patient Grisel " She was the heroine of the last tale in Boccaccio's *Decameron*, obtained by him from an old French story, *Parement des Femmes*, it was translated from Boccaccio by Petrarch, and thence used by Chaucer for his *Clerk's Tale* in the *Canterbury Tales*.

The synopsis of the story is —

The Marquis of Saluzzo, having been prevailed upon by his subjects to marry, in order to please himself in the affair, made a choice of a countryman's daughter [viz , Griselda], by whom he had two children which he pretended to put to death Afterwards, feigning that he was weary of his wife, and had taken another, he had his own daughter brought home, as if he had espoused her, whilst his wife was sent away destitute At length, being convinced of her patience, he brought her home again, presenting her children, now grown up, and ever afterwards loved and honoured her as his lady

The trials to which the flinty-hearted marquis subjected his innocent wife are almost as unbelievable as the fortitude with which she is credited to have borne them, and perhaps it is just as well that, as Chaucer says in his own "Envoy" to the *Clerk's Tale* —

Grisilde is dead, and eke her pacience,
And both at once buried in Italie

Grist. All's grist that comes to my mill. All is appropriated that comes to me, I can make advantage out of anything; all is made use of that comes in my way Grist is that quantity of corn which is to be ground at one time.

To bring grist to the mill To bring profitable business or gain; to furnish supplies

Grit. *See* CLEAR GRIT, *s v.* CLEAR

Grizel (griz' el) A variant—like *Grissel*—of *Griselda* (*q v*) Octavia, wife of Mark Antony and sister of Augustus Cæsar, is called the "patient Grizel" of Roman story

For patience she will prove a second Grissel.
    Taming of the Shrew, ii, 1

Groaning Chair. A rustic name for a chair in which a woman sits after her confinement to receive congratulations Similarly "groaning cake" and "groaning cheese" (called in some dialects *kenno*, because its making was kept a secret) are the cake and cheese which used to be provided in "Goose month" (*q v*), and "groaning malt" was a strong ale brewed for the occasion.

For a nurse, the child to dandle,
Sugar, soap, spiced pots and candle,
A groaning chair and eke a cradle
    Poor Robin's Almanack, 1676.

Groat. A silver fourpence The Dutch had a coin called a *groot* (*i e. great*, with reference to its thickness), hence the fourpenny-piece of Edward III was the *groat* or *great* silver penny. The modern fourpenny-piece—never officially, but often popularly, called a *groat*—was issued from 1836 to 1856, the issue of the true groat having ceased in 1662

He that spends a groat a day idly, spends idly above six pounds a year —FRANKLIN' *Necessary Hints*

You half-faced groat. A 16th-century colloquialism for "You worthless fellow." The debased groats issued in the reign of Henry VIII had the king's head in profile, but those in the reign of Henry VII had the king's head with the full face *See King John*, i, 1

Thou half-faced groat' You thick-cheeked chitty-face'
MUNDAY· *The Downfall of Robert, Earle of Huntingdon*, (1598)

Groats. Husked oat or wheat, fragments rather larger than grits (A.S *grut*, coarse meal)

Blood without groats is nothing. Family without fortune is worthless The allusion is perhaps to black pudding, which consists chiefly of blood and groats formed into a sausage

Grog. Any spirits, but especially rum, diluted with water Admiral Vernon, who was nicknamed Old Grog by his sailors because he walked the deck in rough weather in a *grogram cloak*, was the first to dilute the rum on board ship, hence the name. Six-water grog is one part rum to six parts of water.

Grog-blossoms. Blotches or pimples on the face produced by over-indulgence in drink

Grogram (grog' răm) A coarse kind of taffeta made of silk and mohair or silk and wool, stiffened with gum A corruption of the Fr. *gros-grain*

> Gossips in grief and grograms clad.
> PRAED · *The Troubadour*, c. 1, st. 5.

The blood of the Grograms. *See* BLOOD.

Grommet. *See* GRUMMET

Grongar Hill, on the right bank of the Towy in Carmarthenshire, was rendered famous by the poem of that name by John Dyer (c 1700-58) Although a native of a nearby village, Llangathen, most of his life was spent in Lincolnshire where he held various livings. His descriptions of Grongar Hill and its neighbourhood have a peculiar fascination

Groom of the Stole. *See* STOLE

Groove. To get into a groove. To get into a narrow, undeviating course of life or habit, to become restricted in outlook and ways

To be in the groove. To be in the right mood, to be doing something successfully. A phrase originating from the accurate reproduction of music by a needle set in the grooves of a gramophone record.

Gross. The French word *gros*, big, bulky, corpulent, coarse, which in English has developed many meanings not present in French Thus, a *gross* is twelve dozen; a *great gross*, twelve gross, *gross weight* is the entire weight without deductions, *gross average* is the general average A *villein in gross* was a villein the entire property of his master, and not attached to the land; a *common in gross* is one which is entirely personal property, and does not belong to the manor. *Cp.* ADVOWSON IN GROSS.

Grotesque. Literally, in "Grotto style" The chambers of ancient buildings revealed in mediæval times in Rome were called *grottoes*, and as the walls of these were frequently decorated with fanciful ornaments and *outré* designs, the word *grotesque* (*grotesco*) came to be applied to similar ornamentation

Grotto. Pray remember the grotto. This cry is still occasionally raised by small children in the streets who collect old shells, bits of coloured stone or pottery, with leaves, flowers, and so on, build a little "grotto," and kneel beside it with their caps ready for pennies The custom should be restricted to July 25th (St James's Day), for it is a relic of the old shell grottoes which were erected with an image of the saint for the behoof of those who could not afford the pilgrimage necessary to pay a visit on that day to the shrine of St. James of Compostella

The scallop shell was the badge worn in the hats or cloaks of pilgrims to the shrine of St James the Greater, probably because it made a useful begging-spoon or bowl

> And how should I know your true love
>   From many another one?
> Oh by his scallop shell and hat
> And by his sandal shoon.
>   *Friar of Orders Grey.*

Ground. Ground floor. The story level with the ground outside, or, in a basement-house, the floor above the basement. In U S A. known as the first floor

Ground swell. A long, deep rolling or swell of the sea, caused by a recent or distant storm, or by an earthquake

It would suit me down to the ground. Wholly and entirely

To break ground. To be the first to commence a project, etc , to take the first step in an undertaking

To gain ground. To make progress, to be improving one's position.

To have the ground cut from under one's feet. To see what one has relied on for support suddenly removed.

To hold one's ground. To maintain one's authority, popularity, etc ; not to budge from one's position.

To lose ground. To become less popular or less successful, to drift away from the object aimed at

To shift one's ground. To try a different plan, to change one's argument or the basis of one's reasoning

To stand one's ground Not to yield or give way; to stick to one's colours, to have the courage of one's opinion

Ground and lofty tumbling. An 18th-century phrase for an acrobatic performance on the ground and upon a tight-rope, or swing

Ground hog. The wood-chuck or N American marmot.

Ground-hog Day. Candlemas (February 2nd), from the saying that the ground hog first appears from his hibernation on that day.

Groundlings. Those who occupied the cheapest portion of an Elizabethan theatre, *i e.* the pit, which was the bare ground in front of the stage, without any seats The actor who to-day "plays to the gallery" in Elizabethan times

> Split the ears of the groundlings
>   *Hamlet*, iii, 2

Growlers. The old four-wheeled cabs were called "growlers" from the surly and discontented manners of their drivers, and "crawlers" from their slow pace

Grub Stake, To. A miner's term for equipping a gold prospector with what he needs in exchange for a share of his finds.

Grub Street. The former name of a London street in the ward of Cripplegate Without, which, says Johnson, was

> Much inhabited by writers of small histories, dictionaries, and temporary poems, whence any mean production is called *grubstreet.*

The word is used allusively for needy authors, literary hacks, and their work.

In 1830 the name was changed to Milton Street—*not* from the poet, though he lived in the neighbourhood for years and was buried at St Giles's, Cripplegate—but in honour of the carpenter and builder who was ground landlord at the time. The street leads north out of Fore Street, Moorfields, to Chiswell Street.

Gruel (groo' el) To take one's gruel, to accept one's punishment, to take what's coming to one.

He had a **gruelling**, he was punished severely (in boxing, etc.)

A **gruelling time,** gruelling heat, etc. Exhausting, over-powering.

Grummet. The cabin-boy on board ship; the youth whose duty it was to take in the topsails or top the yard for furling the sails or slinging the yards The name is also given to a ring of rope made by laying a single strand, and to a powder-wad

Grundy. What will Mrs. Grundy say? What will our strait-laced neighbours say? The phrase is from Tom Morton's *Speed the Plough* (1798) In the first scene Mrs. Ashfield is very jealous of neighbour Grundy, and farmer Ashfield says to her · "Be quiet, wull ye? Always sing, dinging Dame Grundy into my ears. What will Mrs Grundy zay? What will Mrs Grundy think? . . ."

Gruyère Cheese (groo' yâr) A kind of cheese made in the Jura district of Switzerland and France, taking its name from the district of Gruyere in Canton Fribourg The curd is pressed in large, shallow cylindrical moulds, and while still in the mould is well salted for at least a month. The cheese is of a pale yellow colour and is characterized by an abundance of large air-bubbles

Gryll. Let Gryll be Gryll, and have his hoggish mind (Spenser: *Faerie Queene,* II, xii, 87) Don't attempt to wash a blackamoor white, the leopard will never change his spots Gryll is the Gr. *grullos,* a hog When Sir Guyon disenchanted the forms in the Bower of Bliss (*q.v.*) some were exceedingly angry, and Gryll, who had been metamorphosed by Acrasia into a hog, abused him most roundly

Gryphon. *See* GRIFFIN.

Guadiana. According to the old legend the Spanish river was so called from the Squire of Durandarte of this name Mourning the fall of his master at Roncesvalles, he was turned into the river See Don Quixote, ii, 23. Actually, it is Arabic *wadi,* a river, and *Anas,* its classical name (*Strabo*)

Guano (gwa' nō). A fertilizing substance found on many small islands off the western coast of South America and other places It is composed of the droppings of the immense flocks of sea-birds that resort to these rocky islets, and is found in beds as much as 60 ft in depth It is valuable as containing much ammonium oxalate with urates, and phosphates

Guard. To be off one's guard. To be careless or heedless.

To put one on his guard. To "give him the tip," show him where the danger lies.

A **guardroom** is the place where military offenders are detained, and a **guardship** is a ship stationed in a port or harbour for its defence.

Guards, The. *See* HOUSEHOLD TROOPS.

Guards of the Pole. *See* BEAR, THE GREAT.

Gubbings. The wild and savage inhabitants in the neighbourhood of Brent Tor, Devon, who, according to Fuller in his *Worthies* (1661)—

> lived in holes, like swine, had all things in common, and multiplied without marriage. Their language was vulgar Devonian   They lived by pilfering sheep, were fleet as horses, held together like bees, and revenged every wrong One of the society was always elected chief, and called *King of the Gubbings.*

Gudgeon. Gaping for gudgeons. Looking out for things extremely improbable. As a gudgeon is a bait for fish, it means a *lie,* a *deception.*

To swallow a gudgeon. To be bamboozled with a most palpable lie, as silly fish are caught by gudgeons (Fr. *goujon,* whence the phrase *avaler le goujon,* to swallow the bait, to die)

> Make tools believe in their foreseeing
> Of things before they are in being,
> To swallow gudgeons ere they're catched
> And count their chickens ere they're hatched
>   BUTLER *Hudibras,* ii, 3

Gudrun (gud' run) The heroine of the great popular German epic poem, *Gudrun,* or *Kudrun,* written about 1210, and founded on a passage in the prose Edda (*q.v.*).

Gudule or Gudila, St. (gu dūl') Patron saint of Brussels, daughter of Count Witger, died 712 She is represented with a lantern, from a tradition that she was one day going to the church of St Morgelle with a lantern, which went out, but the holy virgin lighted it again with her prayers Her feast day is January 8th.

Guebres or Ghebers (gā' bērz). Followers of the ancient Persian religion, reformed by Zoroaster; fire-worshippers, Parsees The name, which was bestowed upon them by their Arabian conquerors, is now applied to fire-worshippers generally

Guelphs and Ghibellines (gwelfs, gib' e lēnz) Two great parties whose conflicts made so much of the history of Italy and Germany in the 12th, 13th, and 14th centuries The Guelphs were the papal and popular party in Italy, their name is the Italian form of *Welfe,* as "Ghibelline" is that of *Waiblingen,* and the origin of these two words is this At the battle of Weinsberg, in Suabia (1140), Conrad, Duke of Franconia, rallied his followers with the war-cry *Waiblingen* (his family estate), while Henry the Lion, Duke of Saxony, used the cry of *Welfe* (the family name). The Ghibellines supported in Italy the side of the German emperors; the Guelphs opposed it, and supported the cause of the Pope

The reigning dynasty in Great Britain, the royal House of Windsor, is, through the ducal House of Brunswick, descended from the Guelphs

Guenever *See* GUINEVER.

Guerilla War (ge ril′ á). A petty war carried on by bodies of irregular troops acting independently of each other. From Span *guerilla*, diminutive of *guerra*, war The word is applied to the armed bands of peasants, and to individuals, who carry on irregular war on their own account, especially at such time as their government is contending with invading armies.

Guerinists (ger′ i nists) An early 17th-century sect of French Illuminati (*q v*), founded by Peter Guérin. They were Antinomians and claimed a special revelation of the Way to Perfection

Guerino Meschino [*the Wretched*] An Italian romance, half chivalric and half allegorical, first printed in Padua in 1473. Guerino was the son of Millon, King of Albania. On the day of his birth his father was dethroned, and the child was rescued by a Greek slave, and called Meschino When he grew up he fell in love with the Princess Elizena, sister of the Greek Emperor, at Constantinople

Guernsey Lily. *See* MISNOMERS

Guess. The modern American use of the verb, meaning to think, to suppose, to be pretty sure, was good colloquial English before America was colonized. Shakespeare has:—

> Bed.· Ascend, brave Talbot; we will follow thee
> *Tal* Not all together better far, I guess,
> That we do make our entrance several ways
> *1 Henry VI*, ii, 1.

and Spenser.—

> But now is time, I gesse, homeward to go.
> *Shepherd's Calendar:* June, 117.

Gueux, Les (lä gër). The league of Flemish nobles organized in 1565 to resist the introduction of the Spanish Inquisition into the Netherlands by Philip II of Spain The word means "ragamuffins" or "beggars", and the origin of its application is said to be that when the Duchess of Parma made inquiry about them of Count Berlaymont, he told her they were "the scum and offscouring of the people" (*les gueux*) The party took the name in defiance, and dressed like beggars, substituting a fox's tail for a feather, etc

Guides. The military name for men formed into companies for reconnoitring purposes; especially a regiment of cavalry and infantry in the Punjab Frontier Force of the Anglo-Indian army, originally raised by Sir Henry Lawrence in 1846.

Among the incidents in the history of the Guides are the march to Delhi during the Mutiny (1857), the massacre at Kabul (1879) and the relief of Chitral (1895). *See also* GIRL GUIDES

In the French army the Guides were created in 1744 as a small company, but the number was gradually increased, and they relinquished their special duties, till in Napoleon's time they formed a personal bodyguard of 10,000 strong.

Napoleon III made the corps a part of the Imperial Guard

Guignol (gē′ nyol) The principal character in a popular French puppet-show (very like our "Punch and Judy") dating from the 18th century As the performance comprised *macabre* and gruesome incidents the name came to be attached to short plays of this nature, hence *Grand Guignol*, a series of such plays, or the theatre in which they are performed

Guildhall Properly, the meeting-place of a trade guild, i e. an association of persons exercising the same trade or craft, formed for the protection and promotion of their common interests In London the guilds became of importance in the 14th century, and as it came about that the Corporation was formed almost entirely from among their members their Hall was used as the Town Hall or headquarters of the Corporation, as it still is to-day Here are the Court of Common Council, the Court of Aldermen, the Chamberlain's Court, the police court presided over by an alderman, the Corporation Art Gallery, Museum, etc

Portions of the London Guildhall were badly damaged in the air-raids of 1940-41, the Council Chamber and the roof of the great hall being entirely destroyed

The ancient guilds are to-day represented by the Livery Companies (*q v.*)

Guillemites. *See* WILLIAM OF MALEVAL, ST

Guillotine (gil′ ō tēn) So named from Joseph Ignace Guillotin (1738-1814), a French physician, who proposed its adoption to prevent unnecessary pain.

It was introduced April 25th, 1792, and is still used in France A previous instrument invented by Antoine Louis (1723-92), a French surgeon, was called a Louisette The Maiden (*q v*) was a similar instrument.

In English Parliamentary phraseology the terms "guillotine," "to guillotine," "to apply the guillotine," signify the curtailment of a debate by fixing beforehand when the vote on the various parts of a Bill must be taken

Guinea A gold coin current in England from 1663 to 1817, originally made of gold from Guinea in West Africa and intended for use in the Guinea trade The earliest issues bore a small elephant beneath the head of the king The nominal value was originally 20s., from 1717 it was legal tender for 21s., but its actual value varied, and in 1695, owing to the bad condition of silver coin, was as high as 30s.

It is still the custom for professional fees, subscriptions, the price of race-horses, pictures, and other luxuries, to be paid in guineas, though there is no such coin current *See* SPADE GUINEA

Guinea-dropper. A cheat The term is about equal to thimble-rig, and alludes to an ancient cheating dodge of dropping counterfeit guineas

> Who now the guinea-dropper's bait regards,
> Tricked by the sharper's dice or juggler's cards?
> GAY *Trivia*, iii, 249

Guinea fowl. So called because it was brought to us from the coast of Guinea, where it is very common.

Guinea-hen An Elizabethan synonym for a prostitute.

Ere .   I would drown myself for the love of a Guinea-hen, I would change my humanity with a baboon.—*Othello*, i, 3

Guineapig. A term used in financial circles for a purely "ornamental" director of a public company, generally a man of title or social position who allows his name to be used in return for his fees—which formerly amounted to a guinea and a lunch each time he attended a board meeting.

It was also an old name for a midshipman

He had a letter from the captain of the *Indiaman* offering you a berth on board as guineapig, or midshipman —CAPTAIN MARRYAT *Poor Jack*, ch xxxi.

A special juryman who is paid a guinea a case, as is also a clergyman without cure, who takes occasional duty for a guinea a sermon It is now applied to one used as a test case for a medical or psychological experiment

Guineapig Club. A club founded in World War II for severely wounded R A F personnel who had to undergo plastic surgery, or volunteered for experimental operations

Guinever (gwin ´e vēr) (Geoffrey of Monmouth's *Guanhumara*, the Welsh *Gwenhwyvar*, meaning "the white ghost") In the Arthurian legends, the wife of King Arthur According to Malory she was the daughter of Leodegrance, king of the land of Cameliard. She entertained a guilty passion for Sir Launcelot of the Lake, one of the knights of the Round Table, but during the absence of King Arthur in his expedition against Leo, king of the Romans, she was seduced by Modred, her husband's nephew, who had usurped the kingdom Arthur hastened back, Guinever fled, and a desperate battle was fought, in which Modred was slain and Arthur mortally wounded Guinever took the veil at Almesbury, where later she died She was buried at Glastonbury, and has left her name as a synonym for a beautiful, faithless, but repentant wife

Gule (gūl). **The Gule of August.** August 1st, Lammas Day, a quarter day in Scotland, and half quarter day in England The word is probably the Welsh *gwyl* (Lat. *vigilia*), a festival

Gules (gūlz) The heraldic term for red In engraving it is shown by perpendicular parallel lines From mediæval Latin *gulæ*, ermine dyed red

With man's blood paint the ground, gules, gules.
                 Timon of Athens, iv, 3
And threw warm gules on Madeline's fair breast
                 KEATS *Eve of St Agnes*

Gulf. A man that goes in for honours at the Universities who is not good enough to be classed and yet has shown sufficient merit to pass When the list is made out a line is drawn after the classes, and the few names put below are in the "gulf," and those so honoured are "gulfed." In the good old times these men were not qualified to stand for the classical tripos.

The ranks of our curatehood are supplied by youths whom, at the very best, merciful examiners have raised from the very gates of "pluck" to the comparative paradise of the 'Gulf' —*Saturday Review*

A great gulf fixed. An impassable separation The allusion is to the parable of Dives and Lazarus (*Luke* xvi, 26).

Gulf Stream. The great, warm ocean current which flows out of the Gulf of Mexico (whence its name) and, passing by the eastern coast of the United States, is, near the banks of Newfoundland, deflected across the Atlantic to modify the climate of Western Europe as far north as Spitzbergen and Nova Zembla. It washes the shores of the British Isles

Gulistan (Pers , the garden of roses) The famous collection of moral sentences by Sadi (about 1190-1291), the most celebrated of Persian poets, except, perhaps, Omar Khayyam It consists of sections on kings, dervishes, contentment, love, youth, old age, social duties, etc , with many stories and philosophical sayings

Gull. A well-known Elizabethan synonym for one who is easily duped, especially a highborn gentleman (*cp* BEJAN) Dekker wrote his *Gull's Hornbook* (1609) as a kind of guide to the behaviour of contemporary gallants.

The most notorious geck and gull
      That e'er invention played on.
            SHAKESPEARE *Twelfth Night*, v, 1.

Gulliver's Travels (gūl´i ver) This, the best known of the works of Jonathan Swift (1667-1745) was published in 1726. It consists of four travels of Captain Lemuel Gulliver The first is to Lilliput, a country of tiny men and women some six inches high, the second is to Brobdingnag, a land of giants as big in comparison to Gulliver as he was to the Lilliputians His third voyage took him to Laputa, the flying island inhabited by scientific quacks Lastly Gulliver found himself in the country of the Houyhnhnms (pronounced whin´imz), a race of horses endowed with human reason and bearing rule over the race of men called Yahoos. Frequently looked upon as a mere children's book, it is in reality a biting social and political satire.

Whether we read it, as children do, for the story, or as historians, for the political allusions, or as men of the world, for the satire and philosophy, we have to acknowledge that it is one of the wonderful and unique books of the world's literature —EDMUND GOSSE *History of English Literature*

Gully-raker. In early Australian slang, one who combs wild country and appropriates any unbranded cattle he finds there.

Gumbo. A thick vegetable soup eaten in the U.S.A.

Gummed He frets like gummed velvet or gummed taffety. Velvet and taffeta were sometimes stiffened with gum to make them "sit better," but, being very stiff, they fretted out quickly.

Gumption. Common sense, the wit to turn things to account, capability The derivation and origin of the word are unknown.

Gum-shoes. The American name for the English galoshes

Gun. This word was formerly used for some large, stone-throwing engine of war besides the firearm, but it is not certain that the first-mentioned use was the earlier In *The House of*

Fame (III, 553) Chaucer speaks of the trumpet sounding —

As swifte as pelet out of gonne
Whan fire is in the poudre ronne.

and in the *Legend of Good Women* (*Cleopatra*, 58) he seems to use the word in reference to the ballista —

With grisly soune out gooth the grete gonne,
And hertely they hurtelen al attones,
And fro the toppe down cometh the grete stones.

The word is a shortened form of the old Scandinavian female name, *Gunnildr* (*gunnr* is Icelandic for war, and *hildr* for battle), and it may have been given first to the ballista and then, when cannon came into use, transferred to the firearm The bestowing of female names on arms is not uncommon; there are the famous "Mons Meg," "Queen Elizabeth's pocket-pistol," as well as the "Big Bertha" of World War I—the long-range gun that bombarded Paris, so called in honour of Bertha Krupp, wife of the head of the great armament factory at Essen.

Barisal guns, or lake guns. *See* BARISAL.

Evening or **sunset gun.** A gun fired at sunset, or about 9 o'clock p m

He's a great gun. A man of note or consequence.

Minute gun. The firing of a gun once a minute, generally as a salute at a royal or state funeral.

Sure as a gun. Quite certain It is as certain to happen as a gun to go off if the trigger is pressed

To blow great guns. To be very boisterous and windy Noisy and boisterous as the reports of great guns.

To lay a gun. To aim it (used only of artillery).

To run away from one's own guns. To eat one's words, desert what is laid down as a principle The allusion is obvious

To stick to one's guns. To maintain one's position, argument, etc , in spite of opposition.

To gun for someone To set out deliberately to get a person and do him a mischief.

To give it the gun. In R A F. parlance during World War II, to open the throttle of an aeroplane suddenly and hard

Gun cotton. A highly explosive compound. prepared by saturating cotton or other cellulose material with nitric and sulphuric acids

Gun-man. A desperado armed with a revolver and prepared to use it in the most reckless manner A term of American origin.

Gun money. Base money issued in Ireland by James II, made from old brass cannon, with a small admixture of silver.

Gun room. A room in the afterpart of a lower gun-deck for the accommodation of junior officers.

Gun-runner. One who unlawfully smuggles guns into a country for belligerent purposes. The word is formed on the model of *blockade-runner*.

Gunnar. The Norse form of *Gunther* (*q.v*)

Gunner. Kissing the gunner's daughter. Being flogged on board ship At one time sailors in the Royal Navy who were to be flogged were tied to the breech of a cannon.

Gunpowder Plot. The project of a few Roman Catholics to destroy James I with the Lords and Commons when he opened Parliament, on November 5th, 1605

It was to be done by exploding barrels of gunpowder placed in cellars adjacent to the chamber, and Guy Fawkes, a convert to Catholicism, was deputed to fire the train Had the plot succeeded, and king and Parliament been destroyed, Prince Charles and his sister were to have been made captive, and a Catholic rising attempted in the Midlands. One of the Catholic peers was, however, warned to keep away from Parliament that day; he communicated his news to the authorities; the cellars were searched and Guy Fawkes taken, the night of November 4th

The ceremony of searching the vaults of the Houses before the annual opening of Parliament is a legacy of the Gunpowder Plot

Gunter's Chain, for land surveying, is so named from Edmund Gunter (1581-1626), the great mathematician and professor of Astronomy at Gresham College, 1619-26 It is sixty-six feet long, and divided into one hundred links As ten square chains make an acre, it follows that an acre contains 100,000 square links.

Gunter's scale is a two-foot rule having scales of chords, tangents, etc , and logarithmic lines, engraved on it, it is used in surveying and navigation for the mechanical solving of problems.

According to Gunter. Carefully and correctly done, with no possibility of mistake, the American counterpart of "according to Cocker" (*see* COCKER), which is more common in England

Gunther (gun' ter) In the Nibelungen saga, a Burgundian king, brother of Kriemhild (= Gudrun), the wife of Sigurd (= Siegfried) He resolved to wed the martial queen Brunhild (*q v*), who had made a vow to marry only the man who could ride through the flames that encircled her castle. Gunther failed (*see* GRANI), but Siegfried did so in his likeness and remained with the Queen for three nights, his sword being between them all the time Gunther then married Brunhild, but later Kriemhild told Brunhild that it was Siegfried who had ridden through the fire, jealousy sprang up between the families, Siegfried was slain at Brunhild's desire, and she killed herself, her dying wish being to be burnt on a pile with Siegfried at her side, his sword between them. Gunther was slain by Atli because he refused to reveal where he had hidden the hoard of the Nibelungs. Gundicarius, a Burgundian king who, with his whole tribe, perished by the sword of the Huns in 437, is supposed to be the historical character round whom these legends collected.

Gurgoyle. *See* GARGOYLE.

Gurney Light. *See* BUDE.

Guru (goo' roo) A Sanskrit word meaning venerable; it is now applied to a Hindu spiritual teacher and leader.

Gustin Bone. *See* BAWBEE

Gutenberg's Bible. *See* BIBLE, SPECIALLY NAMED

Guthlac, St., (gŭth' lăk) of Crowland, Lincolnshire, is represented in Christian art as a hermit punishing demons with a scourge, or consoled by angels while demons torment him He was a member of the royal family of Mercia in the 7th century.

Guthrum (gŭth' rŭm) **Silver of Guthrum's Lane** Fine silver was at one time so called, because the chief gold and silver smiths of London resided there in the 13th and 14th centuries The street, which is now called *Gutter Lane*, and runs from Cheapside into Gresham Street, was originally *Gudrun's* or *Goderun's Lane* The hall of the Goldsmiths' Company is still in this locality.

Guy. An effigy of a man, stuffed with combustibles and supposed to represent Guy Fawkes, carried round in procession and finally burnt on November 5th, in memory of Gunpowder Plot (*q v*); hence, any dowdy, fantastic figure, a "fright" In American usage the word, as applied to a person, has a much wider significance, and can mean almost anyone

To guy a person, is to chaff him, to make fun of him

To do a guy. To decamp.

Guy of Warwick. An English hero of legend and romance, whose exploits were first written down by an Anglo-Norman poet of the 12th century and were, by the 14th century, accepted as authentic history.

To obtain Phelis (Felice) as his wife he undertook many knightly deeds He rescued the daughter of the Emperor of Germany, and went to fight against the Saracens, slaying the doughty Coldran, Elmaye King of Tyre, and the soldan himself. Then he returned and wedded Phelis; but in forty days went back to the Holy Land, where he slew the giant Amarant, and many others. He again returned to England, and slew at Winchester Colbrand, the Danish giant, in single combat, thus redeeming England from Danish tribute At Windsor he destroyed a boar of "passing might and strength"; on Dunsmore Heath he slew the "Dun-cow of Dunsmore, a monstrous wyld and cruell beast", and in Northumberland a dragon "black as any cole" Having achieved all this, he became a hermit near Warwick Daily he went in rags to his own castle and begged bread of his wife Phelis; but on his death-bed he sent her a ring, by which she recognized her lord, and went to close his dying eyes

I am not Sampson, nor Sir Guy, nor Colbrand, to mow them down before me —*Henry VIII*, v, 3

Guy's Hospital. Founded in 1722 by Thomas Guy (*c.* 1645-1724), bookseller, and philanthropist He amassed an immense fortune in 1720 by speculations in the South Sea Stock and gave £238,292 to found and endow the hospital which is situated in Southwark.

Gwynn, Eleanor or **Nell** (1650-87) was a popular London actress, She first became known when selling oranges at the Theatre Royal, Drury Lane, and in 1665 she appeared as Cydaria in Dryden's *Indian Emperor* She was an illiterate girl but excellent company and soon won the favour of Charles II by whom she had a son, Charles Beauclerk (1670-1726) who was created Duke of St Albans in 1684 Nell Gwynn left the stage in 1682, but she never lost the king's favour, and one of his dying wishes was that she should be looked after

Gyges (gī' jēz) A king of Lydia of the 7th century B C , who founded a new dynasty warred against Asurbanipal of Assyria, and is memorable in legend for his ring and his prodigious wealth.

According to Plato, Gyges descended into a chasm of the earth, where he found a brazen horse, opening the sides of the animal, he found the carcass of a man, from whose finger he drew a brazen ring which rendered him invisible

Why, did you think that you had Gyges ring,
Or the herb that gives invisibility [fern-seed]?
BEAUMONT AND FLETCHER. *Fair Maid of the Inn*, i, 1

It was by the aid of the ring that Gyges obtained possession of the wife of Candaules (*q v*) and, through her, of his kingdom.

Gymnosophists (jim nos' o fists). A sect of ancient Hindu philosophers who went about with naked feet and almost without clothing They lived in woods, subsisted on roots, and never married They believed in the transmigration of souls Strabo divides them into Brahmins and Samans (Gr *gumnos*, naked, *sophistes*, sages)

Gyp (jip) The name at Cambridge (and at Durham) for a college servant, who acts as valet to two or more undergraduates, the counterpart of the Oxford *scout* He differs from a bedmaker, inasmuch as he does not make beds, but he runs on errands, waits at table, wakes men for morning chapel, brushes their clothes, and so on The word is probably from *gippo*, a 17th-century term for a scullion

Gypsy. *See* GIPSY

Gyromancy. A kind of divination performed by walking round in a circle or ring until one fell from dizziness, the direction of the fall being of significance

Gytrash. A north-of-England spirit, which, in the form of horse, mule, or large dog, haunts solitary ways, and sometimes comes upon the belated travellers

I remembered certain of Bessie's tales, wherein figured a   , spirit called a Gytrash —CHARLOTTE BRONTË· *Jane Eyre*, xii.

H

H. The form of our capital H is through the Roman and Greek directly from the Phœnician (Semitic) letter *Heth* or *Kheth*, which, having two cross-bars instead of one, represented a fence. The corresponding Egyptian hieroglyph was a sieve, and the Anglo-Saxon rune is called *hægel*, hail

H.M.S. His *or* Her Majesty's service *or* ship, as H M S *Wellington.*

Habeas Corpus (hä' bē as kôr' pŭs). The Habeas Corpus Act was passed in 1679, and defined a provision of similar character in Magna Charta, to which also it added certain details Its chief purpose was to prohibit any judge, under severe penalties, from refusing to issue to a prisoner a Writ of Habeas Corpus by which the jailer was obliged to produce the prisoner in court in person and to certify the cause of imprisonment, thus preventing people being imprisoned on mere suspicion, and making it illegal for one to be left in prison an indefinite time without trial.

It further provides that every accused person shall have the question of his guilt decided by a jury of twelve, and not by a Government agent or nominee; that no prisoner can be tried a second time on the same charge, that every prisoner may insist on being examined within twenty days of his arrest, and tried at the next session, and that no one may be sent to prison beyond the seas, either within or without the British Dominions

Habeas Corpus means "[I hear] that you have the body"; these being the opening words of the writ

The Habeas Corpus Act has been suspended in times of political and social disturbance, and its provisions have been more than once amended and extended.

A Habeas Corpus Act was passed in Ireland in 1782, and in Scotland its place is taken by the *Wrongous Imprisonment Act* of 1701

Haberdasher. The word is probably connected with O Fr *hapertas*, a word of unknown origin denoting some kind of fabric, but Prof Weekley makes what he calls the "dubious" conjecture that it is from O Fr *avoir (aveir)*, goods, property (as in *avoirdupois*), and Fr and Provençal *ais*, a shop-board

> To match this saint there was another,
> As busy and perverse a brother,
> An haberdasher of small wares
> In politics and state affairs
>   BUTLER *Hudibras*, iii, 2

The Haberdashers is one of the twelve great London livery companies, It was founded in the 15th century as the Merchant Haberdashers' Company. The Hall, destroyed by enemy action in 1940, was built by Christopher Wren.

Habit is Second Nature. The wise saw of Diogenes, the cynic (412-323 B C.)

Shakespeare· "Use almost can change the stamp of nature" (*Hamlet*, iii, 4).

French *L'habitude est une seconde nature.*

Latin. *Usus est optimus magister.*

Habsburg or **Hapsburg** (häbz' bĕrg) is a contraction of *Habichts-burg* (Hawk's Tower), so called from the castle on the right bank of the Aar, built in the 11th century by Werner, Bishop of Strasburg, whose nephew (Werner II) was the first to assume the title of "Count of Habsburg." His great-grandson, Albrecht II, assumed the title of "Landgraf of Sundgau" His grandson, Albrecht IV, in the 13th

century, laid the foundation of the greatness of the House, the original male line of which became extinct on the death of Charles VI in 1740 The late imperial family of Austria were the Habsburg-Lorraines, springing from the marriage of Maria Theresa, daughter of Charles VI, with Francis I, Duke of Lorraine, in 1736.

Habsburg Lip. *See* AUSTRIAN LIP.

Hack. Short for *hackney* (*q v*), a horse let out for hire, hence, one whose services are for hire, especially a literary drudge, compiler, furbisher-up of better men's work. Goldsmith, who well knew from his own experience what the life was, wrote an "Epitaph" on one —

> Here lies poor Ned Purdon, from misery freed,
>   Who long was a bookseller's hack;
> He led such a damnable life in this world,
>   I don't think he'll wish to come back.

Hackell's Coit A vast stone said to weigh about 30 tons, near Stanton Drew, Somerset; so called from a tradition that it was a quo't or coit thrown by Sir John Hautville In Wiltshire three huge stones near Kennet are called the *Devil's coits.*

Hackney. Originally (14th cent) the name given to a class of medium-sized horses, distinguishing them from war-horses They were used for ordinary riding, and later the name was applied to a horse let out for hire— whence hackney carriage and hackney writer or hack (*q v*).

> The knights are well horsed, and the common people and others on litell *hakeneys* and geldynges. —*Froissart.*

The name of the London borough of Hackney has no connection whatever with the foregoing. There is some doubt as to its actual derivation; the earliest mention of the place is in a patent of Edward IV

Had it, To have. An expression which came into wide use during World War II It may have sprung from North Australia where it was used prior to the War in the sense of anything which was past or done with, *i.e.* a book which one had read and finished with had "had it " During the war it came to be synonymous with "done for," *i e* of a man killed or seriously wounded—"he's had it." In both these senses it may be short for "had his time," as the full expression was also found during the war, *i.e.* one who had been caught by shell fire with no cover available and expected to be killed would say afterwards "I thought I'd had my time " Since then the expression has strayed farther from the original sense and is now applied sarcastically to something one has *not* had, *i e.* to one who has missed his train an onlooker will say "you've had it."

Haddock. According to tradition, it was a haddock in whose mouth St. Peter found the piece of money, the *stater* or shekel (*Matt.* xvii, 27), and the two marks on the fish's neck are said to be impressions of the finger and thumb of the apostle. It is a pretty story, but haddocks cannot live in the fresh water of the Lake of Gennesaret Cp JOHN DORY

> O superstitious dainty, Peter's fish,
> How com'st thou here to make so goodly dish?
>   METELLUS *Dialogues* (1693)

Hades (hā′ dēz) In Homer, the name of the god (Pluto) who reigns over the dead, but in later classical mythology the abode of the departed spirits, a place of gloom but not necessarily a place of punishment and torture As the state or abode of the dead it corresponds to the Hebrew *Sheol*, a word which, in the Authorized Version, has frequently been translated by the misleading *Hell* Hence *Hades* is sometimes vulgarly used as a euphemism for *Hell*

The word is usually derived from Gr *a*, privative, and *idein*, to see, *i e* the unseen but this derivation is not at all certain. *Cp* INFERNO.

Hadith (hā′ dith) (Ar., *a saying* or *tradition*). The traditions about the prophet Mohammed's sayings and doings This compilation, which was made in the 10th century by the Moslem jurists Moslin and Bokhari, forms a supplement to the Koran as the Talmud to the Jewish Scriptures The Hadith was not allowed originally to be committed to writing, but the danger of the traditions being perverted or forgotten led to their being placed on record.

Hadj (haj). The pilgrimage to the Kaaba (shrine at the great mosque of Mecca), which every Mohammedan feels bound to make once at least before death. Those who neglect to do so "might as well die Jews or Christians" These pilgrimages take place in the twelfth month of each year, Zu 'll Hajjia, roughly corresponding to our August

Until comparatively recent years none but a Moslem could make this pilgrimage except at risk of his life, and the Hadj was only performed by Burckhardt, Burton and a few other intrepid travellers in the disguise of zealous Mohammedans

Hadji (ha′ jē). A Mohammedan who has made the *Hadj* or pilgrimage to the Prophet's tomb at Mecca Every Hadji is entitled to wear a green turban.

Hadrian's Wall, a Roman rampart that runs for 73½ miles between Wallsend-on-Tyne and Bowness on the Solway Firth It was erected about A D. 122 by the Emperor Hadrian to keep back the Pictish tribes of North Britain, and was repaired by Severus in 208. The wall was 20 ft. high and 8 ft. thick, with strong points every mile or so, and towers between To the south of the wall is a parallel *vallum* or ditch with three ramparts, all of earthworks Excavations and research have been made at various points, notably at the ancient Borcovicus, near the present Housesteads.

Hæmony (hē′ mò ni) The name invented by Milton (*Comus*, 638) for a mythical plant which is of "sovereign use gainst all enchantments, mildew, blasar, or damp, or ghastly Furies' apparition " The reference is probably to *Hæmonia*, an old name for Thessaly, a country specially endowed with mystical associations by the ancient Greeks, but Coleridge rather fancifully says the word is *hæma-oinos* (blood-wine), and refers to the blood of Jesus Christ, which destroys all evil. The leaf, says Milton, "had prickles on it," but "it bore a bright golden flower " With this explanation the *prickles* become the crown of thorns, the *flower* the fruits of salvation.

Hafiz (ha′ fiz) A Persian poet (fl 14th cent), and one of the greatest poets of the world His *ghazels* (*i e* songs, odes) tell of love and wine, nightingales, flowers, the instability of all things human, of Allah and the Prophet, etc ; and his tomb at Shiraz is still the resort of pilgrims The name *Hafiz* is Arabic for "one who knows the Koran and Hadith (*q v.*) by heart."

Hag. A witch or sorceress, originally, an evil spirit, demon, harpy. (A S. *hægtesse*, a witch or hag)

> How now, you secret, black, and midnight hags?
> *Macbeth*, iv, 1

Hag-knots. Tangles in the manes of horses, etc , supposed to be used by witches for stirrups. The term is common in the New Forest. Seamen use the word **hag's-teeth** to express those parts of a matting, etc , which spoil its general uniformity.

Hagarenes (hăg a rēnz). An old name for the Saracens, Arabs, or Moors, who were supposed to be descendants of Hagar, Abraham's bondwoman

> San Diego . . . hath often been seen conquering . . the Hagarene squadrons —CERVANTES: *Don Quixote*, Pt ii, Bk. iv, 6

Hagen (ha′ gen) In the *Nibelungenlied* and the old Norse sagas (where he is called Hogni), a Burgundian knight, liegeman to the king, Gunther (*q v*), in some accounts his brother and in others a distant kinsman

Haggadah (haga′ da) The portion of the Midrash (*q v.*) which contains rabbinical interpretations of the historical and legendary, ethical, parabolic, and speculative parts of the Hebrew Scriptures: the portion devoted to law, practice, and doctrine is called the *Halachah* They were commenced in the 2nd century A D and completed by the 11th.

Hugganah (hăg a na′), the Jewish defence force raised in Palestine during the British mandate (1923-48), for defensive and aggressive action towards establishing the country as a Jewish commonwealth.

Hague, The (hāg), is the English form of the Dutch *'s Gravenhage* or *Den Haag*, the capital of the Netherlands. The Hague Tribunal is an international court of Justice established at the suggestion of Tsar Nicholas II in 1899, when 16 powers signed the agreement by which each power nominates four members to serve for six years Many international cases have been referred to the Court, including one about the sovereignty of Greenland, in 1932, which was adjudicated to Denmark

Ha-ha. A ditch or sunk fence serving the purpose of a hedge without breaking the prospect.

Haidee (hī′ dē). A beautiful Greek girl in Byron's *Don Juan* who died of love when parted from him.

Hail. Health, an exclamation of welcome, like the Lat. *salve* It is from the Icel *heill*, hale, healthy, and represents the A S. greeting *wes hal* (may you) be in whole (or good) health. *Hail*, the frozen rain, is A.S. *hagol!*

> All hail, Macbeth! Hail to thee, thane of Glamis.
> *Macbeth*, i, 3

Hail fellow well met. One on easy, familiar terms; an intimate acquaintance.

> Hail fellow well met, all dirty and wet,
> Find out, if you can, who's master, who's man.
> SWIFT *My Lady's Lamentation.*

To hail a ship. To call to those on board

To hail an omnibus or a cab is to accost the driver in order to stop or hire the vehicle

Hainault (hā´nolt) A province in Belgium Also a forest in Essex which ceased to exist in the 19th century, though the name survives. The Fairlop oak (*q.v*) was here.

Hair. One single tuft is left on the shaven crown of a Mussulman, for Mohammed to grasp hold of when drawing the deceased to Paradise.

> And each scalp had a single long tuft of hair
> BYRON *Siege of Corinth*

The scalp-lock of the North American Indians, left on the otherwise bald head, is for a conquering enemy to seize when he tears off the scalp.

The ancients believed that till a lock of hair is devoted to Proserpine, she refuses to release the soul from the dying body When Dido mounted the funeral pile, she lingered in suffering till Juno sent Iris to cut off a lock of her hair; Thanatos did the same for Alcestis, when she gave her life for her husband, and in all sacrifices a forelock was first cut off from the head of the victim as an offering to the black queen

It was an old idea that a person with red hair could not be trusted, from the tradition that Judas had red hair.

> *Rosalind* His very hair is of the dissembling colour.
> *Celia* Somewhat browner than Judas's —*As You Like It*, iii, 4

A man with black hair but a red beard was the worst of all. The old rhyme says.—

> A red beard and a black head
> Catch him with a good trick and take him dead.

See also RED-HAIRED PERSONS

Byron says, in *The Prisoner of Chillon* —

> My hair is grey, but not with years,
> Nor grew it white
> In a single night,
> As men's have grown from sudden fears.

and it is a well-authenticated fact that this can take, and has taken, place. It is told that Ludovico Sforza became grey in a single night; Charles I, also, while he was on his trial; and Marie Antoinette grew grey from grief during her imprisonment.

Hair shirt, a garment of coarse haircloth (made from horsehair and wool or cotton) worn next the skin by ascetics and penitents.

Hair-spring is a fine, spiral spring in a clock or watch for regulating the movement of the balance

Hair trigger, a trigger that allows the firing mechanism of a rifle or revolver to be operated by a very slight pressure. Invented in the 16th century

Against the hair. Against the grain, contrary to its nature

> If you should fight, you go against the hair of your professions —*Merry Wives of Windsor*, ii, 3

Both of a hair. As like as two peas, or hairs, also, similar in disposition, taste, or trade, etc.

Hair by hair you will pull out the horse's tail Slow and sure wins the race

Plutarch says that Sertorius, in order to teach his soldiers that perserverance and wit are better than brute force, had two horses brought before them, and set two men to pull out their tails One of the men, a burly Hercules, tugged and tugged, but all to no purpose, the other was a sharp, weazen-faced tailor, who plucked one hair at a time, amidst roars of laughter, and soon left the stump quite bare

Keep your hair on! Obsolete slang for Don't lose your temper, don't get excited! *Wool* is sometimes substituted for *hair* in this phrase

The hair of the dog that bit you *See* DOG.

To a hair or **To the turn of a hair.** To a nicety

To comb his hair the wrong way. To cross or vex him by running counter to his prejudices, opinions, or habits

To make one's hair stand on end To terrify Dr Andrews, of Beresford Chapel, Walworth, who attended an execution says· "When the executioner put the cords on the criminal's wrists, his hair, though long and lanky, of a weak iron-grey, rose gradually and stood perfectly upright, and so remained for some time, and then fell gradually down again "

> Fear came upon me and trembling, [and] the hair of my flesh stood up.—*Job* iv, 14, 15.

To split hairs. To argue over petty points, make fine, cavilling distinctions, quibble over trifles

To tear one's hair. To show signs of extreme anguish, grief, or vexation.

Without turning a hair Without indicating any sign of distress or agitation. The phrase is from the stable, for when horses sweat they show it by a roughening of the hair.

Hair-brained. *See* HARE-BRAINED

Hair-breadth 'scape. A very narrow escape from some danger or evil In measurement the forty-eighth part of an inch is called a "hair-breadth"

> Wherein I spake of most disastrous chances
> Of moving accidents by flood and field
> Of hair-breadth 'scapes i' th' imminent deadly breach. *Othello*, i, 3.

Hair Stane. A hoar-stone (*q v*) is so called in Scotland.

Hajar al-Aswad (ha´jar al ăs´wåd). The famous black stone in the north-east corner of the Kaaba, it is an irregular oval, about 7 in in breadth, and is surrounded with a circle of gold. The legend is that when Abraham wished to build the Kaaba, the stones came to him of their own accord, and the patriarch commanded all the faithful to kiss this one.

The stone is probably an aerolite, and it was

worshipped long before Mohammed's day, for in the 2nd century A D. Maximus Tyrius spoke of the Arabians paying homage to it, and Persian legend states that it was an emblem of Saturn.

Hajji Baba (hăj' i ba' ba), the title of the strange story told by J. J. Morier (c. 1780-1849) which has become a classic of its kind Morier was born in Syria and spent much of his life in the East In 1824 he published this remarkable romance of Persia in which Hajji Baba, a barber and a delightful rogue of the Gil Blas genus, narrated his adventures shady and amusing So true to life was the story that the Persian government took pains to prove that it was not an authentic account of a real person but the work of a devil-inspired Ferangi

Hake. We lose in hake, but gain in herring. Lose one way, but gain in another Herring are persecuted by the hake, which are therefore driven away from a herring fishery

Halcyon Days (hăl' si on) A time of happiness and prosperity. Halcyon is the Greek for a kingfisher, compounded of *hals* (the sea) and *kuo* (to brood on) The ancient Sicilians believed that the kingfisher laid its eggs and incubated for fourteen days, before the winter solstice, on the surface of the sea, during which time the waves of the sea were always unruffled

> Amidst our arms as quiet you snall be
> As halcyon brooding on a winter's sea DRYDEN.
> The peaceful king fishers are met togetcer
> About the deck and prophesie calm weather
> WILD *Iter Boreale.*

Half. Half and half A mixture of two liquors, especially porter and ale, in equal quantities

Half done, as Elgin was burnt. In the wars between James II of Scotland and the Douglases in 1452, the Earl of Huntly burnt one-half of the town of Elgin, being the side which belonged to the Douglases, but left the other side standing because it belonged to his own family. (Scott: *Tales of a Grandfather*, xxi)

Half is more than the whole. This is what Hesiod said to his brother Perseus, when he wished him to settle a dispute without going to law He meant "half of the estate without the expense of law will be better than the whole after the lawyers have had their pickings " The remark, however, has a very wide signification

> Unhappy they to whom God has not revealed,
> By a strong light which must their sense control,
> That half a great estate's more than the whole.
> ¶COWLEY *Essays in Verse and Prose*, iv.

Half-seas over. Midway between one condition and another: now usually applied to a person slightly drunk

> I am half-seas o'er to death —DRYDEN
> I have just left the Right Worshipful and his Myrmidons about a Sneaker of Five Gallons The whole Magistracy was pretty well disguised before I gave 'em the Slip Our Friend the Alderman was half Seas over —*Spectator*, No 616 (Nov 5th, 1714)

Half Joe. A Portuguese coin (worth about $4), current on the Atlantic coast of the U S.A in the 18th century

Half the battle. *See* BATTLE.

He is only half-baked. He is soft, a noodle. *See* BAKED

My better half. *See* BETTER

Not half. Not half bad means "not at all bad", pretty good, indeed; better than I had expected, but Not half! has a more ironical meaning, and means something like *"Rather ! I should think so !"*

To do a thing by halves To do it in a slapdash manner, very imperfectly

To go halves. To share something equally with another.

Half-deck. An old sailing-ship term. the quarters of the second mate, carpenters, coopers, boatswain, and all secondary officers *Quarter-deck*, the quarters of the captain and superior officers. In a gun-decked ship *half-deck* is below the *spar-deck*, and extends from the main-mast to the cabin bulkheads

Half-mast high. The position of a flag flying from the middle of the flagstaff in token of respect to a dead person

Half-timer. One engaged in some occupation for only half the usual time, the term was formerly applied to a child attending school for half time and working the rest of the day Half-timers were done away with by the Education Act of 1918.

Half-tone block. A typographic printing-block for illustrations, produced by photographing on to a prepared plate through a screen or grating which breaks up the picture of the object to be reproduced into small dots of varying intensity, thus giving the lights and shades, or *tones*

Half-world. *See* DEMI-MONDE.

Halgaver (hăl' ga vĕr). Summoned before the mayor of Halgaver. The mayor of Halgaver is an imaginary person, and the threat is given to those who have committed no offence against the laws, but are simply untidy and slovenly. Halgaver is a moor in Cornwall, near Bodmin, famous for an annual carnival held there in the middle of July Charles II was so pleased with the diversions when he passed through the place on his way to Scilly that he became a member of the "self-constituted" corporation The mayor of Garratt (*q v.*) is a similar "magnate "

Halifax. Halifax Law. By this (law), whoever committed theft in the liberty of Halifax, Yorkshire, was to be executed on the Halifax gibbet, a kind of guillotine.

> At Hallifax the law so sharpe doth deale,
> That whoso more than thirteen pence doth steale,
> They have a jyn that wondrous quick and well
> Sends thieves all headless into heaven or hell
> TAYLOR (the Water Poet). *Works* ii, (1630).

Hull, Hell, and Halifax. *See* HULL.

Halifax, Nova Scotia, was so called by the Hon. Edward Cornwallis, the governor, in compliment to his patron, the Earl of Halifax (1749).

Hall Mark. The official mark stamped on gold and silver articles after they have been assayed, so called because the assaying or testing and the stamping was done at the Goldsmiths' Hall The hall mark includes (1) the standard mark, (2) the assay office, or ' hall" mark.

(3) the date letter, and sometimes (4) the duty mark With it is found (5) the maker's mark

(1) The standard mark For gold, a *crown* in England and a *thistle* in Scotland, for 22- and 18-carat gold. In Ireland, a *crowned harp* for 22-carat, *three feathers* for 20-carat and a *unicorn's head* for 18-carat Lower standards of gold have the number of carats in figures, without the device

For silver, a *lion passant* in England, a *thistle* in Edinburgh, a *thistle* plus a *lion rampant* in Glasgow, a *crowned harp* in Dublin

(2) The Assay Office mark
London—a leopard's head (*q v*).
Sheffield—a York Rose for gold, a crown for silver
Chester—three sheaves and a sword.
Edinburgh—a castle
Glasgow—the city arms· a tree, a bird, a bell, and a salmon with a ring in its mouth.
Dublin—Hibernia
Marks of Assay Offices now closed, and dates of closing —
Exeter, 1882—a castle.
Newcastle, 1883—three castles
Norwich, 1701—castle over lion.
York, 1856—five lions on a cross.

(3) The date letter. A letter of the alphabet indicates the date of an article. The London Assay Office uses 20 letters of the alphabet, Glasgow 26 and most of the others 25. The letter is changed each year, and at the beginning of each new cycle a new type-face is adopted and the shape of the letters' frame is changed Given the date letter and the Assay Office mark, the date of manufacture of an article may be easily discovered on referring to a table.

(4) The duty mark Articles on which duty has been paid are stamped with the head of the reigning sovereign

(5) The maker's mark. A device or set of initials which the maker has registered at the Assay Office, and which he stamps on goods which he intends to send for hall marking

Hallel (häl' el) A Jewish hymn of praise sung at the four great festivals, consisting of *Ps* cxiii to cxviii both included. *Ps.* cxxxvi was called the Great Hallel. And sometimes the Songs of Degrees (*see* GRADUAL PSALMS) sung standing on the fifteen steps of the inner court seem to be so called (*i e.* cxx to cxxxvii both included)

Hallelujah is the Heb *halelu-Jah*, "Praise ye Jehovah"

Hallelujah Lass. A name given to female members of the Salvation Army in the early days of that movement.

Hallelujah Victory. A victory said to have been gained by some newly baptized Britons over the Picts and Scots near Mold, Flintshire in 429. They were led by Germanus, Bishop of Auxerre, and commenced the battle with loud shouts of "Hallelujah!"

Halloween (häl ō ēn'). October 31st, which in the old Celtic calendar was the last day of the year, its night being the time when all the witches and warlocks were abroad and held their wicked revels On the introduction of Christianity it was taken over as the Eve of

All Hallows, or All Saints, and—especially in Scotland and the north of England—it is still devoted to all sorts of games in which the old superstitions can be traced. *See* Burns's poem *Hallowe'en*

Hall Sunday. The Sunday preceding Shrove Tuesday, the next day is called Hall Monday or Hall Night Shrove Tuesday is also called Pancake Day, and the day preceding it, Callop Monday, from the special foods popularly prepared for those days. All three were days of merrymaking. Hall is a contraction of *Hallow*, meaning holy or festal.

Halo. In Christian art the same as a nimbus (*q.v*). The luminous circle round the sun or moon caused by the refraction of light through a mist is also called a halo The word is from Gr. *halos*, originally a circular threshing-floor.

Ham Actor. A bad actor, especially one who over-acts or performs his part in a stiff and stilted fashion The origin of the term is uncertain, it may arise from the delusion such bad actors often entertain that they can perform that most difficult of parts—Hamlet

Hamadryads *See* DRYAD.

Hambletonian (hăm b ĕl tō' ni ĕn), the name given to a superior strain of horse bred in U S A. for trotting, and descended from a stallion called Hambletonian (1849-76).

Hamet. *See* CID HAMET.

Hamiltonian System. A method of teaching foreign languages by inter-linear translations, suggested by James Hamilton (1769-1831).

Hamlet. It's Hamlet without the Prince. Said when the person who was to have taken the principal place at some function is absent The allusion, of course, is to Shakespeare's *Tragedie of Hamlet, Prince of Denmark*, which would lose all its meaning if the part of the Prince were omitted

The play is based on a crude story told by the 13th-century Saxo Grammaticus (a Danish chronicler) in his *Historia Danica* (first printed 1514), which found a place in Pierre de Belleforest's *Histoires Tragiques* (1570), a French miscellany of translated legend and romance. This formed the groundwork of the lost pre-Shakespearean play—the so-called *Ur-Hamlet* (Ger *Ur*, original)—which Shakespeare transformed into a great dramatic masterpiece

Hammer. In personal appellatives·—
Pierre d'Ailly (1350-1425), *Le Marteau* (hammer) *des Hérétiques*, president of the council that condemned John Huss.

St Augustine (354-430) is called by Hakewell "that renowned pillar of truth and hammer of heresies"

John Faber (1478-1541), the German controversialist, was surnamed *Malleus Hereticorum*, from the title of one of his works.

St. Hilary, Bishop of Poitiers (d 368), was known as "The Hammer of the Arians"

Charles Martel (*q.v*).

Edward I (1239-1307), "Longshanks," was called "The Hammer of the Scots" On his tomb in Westminster Abbey is the inscription *"Edwardus longus Scotorum Malleus hic est"*

The second name of Judas *Maccabeus*, the son of Mattathias the Hasmonean, is thought by some to denote that he was a "Hammer" or "Hammerer," because *Makkebeth* is Hebrew for a certain kind of hammer

Hammer and Sickle. Since 1923, the emblems of the U S S R , symbolic of productive work in the factory and on the land

Gone to the hammer Applied to goods sent to a sale by auction, the auctioneer giving a rap with a small hammer when a lot is sold, to intimate that there is an end to the bidding, hence *to sell under the hammer*

They live hammer and tongs Are always quarrelling

Both parties went at it hammer and tongs, and hit one another anywhere and with anything.—*James Payn.*

To be hammered. A Stock Exchange term, used of one who is in the "House" officially declared a defaulter This is done by the "Head Waiter," who goes into the rostrum and, before making the announcement, attracts the attention of the members present by striking the desk with a hammer

To hammer away at anything. To go at it doggedly, to persevere

Hammercloth The cloth that covers the driver's seat, or "box," in an old-fashioned coach. It may be connected with Dan *hammel*, a swingle-bar, or with *hamnock*, the seat which the cloth covers being formed of straps or webbing stretched between two crutches like a sailor's hammock.

Hammock or Hummock. A small round hill, usually wooded

Hampton Court Conference A conference held at Hampton Court in January, 1604, to settle the disputes between the Church party and the Puritans. It lasted three days. Its chief results were a few slight alterations in the Book of Common Prayer, but it was here that the first suggestion was made for the official retranslation of the Bible which resulted in the Authorized Version of 1611.

Hanaper (hän′ ả për) *Hanap* was the mediæval name for a goblet or wine-cup, and the *hanaper* (connected with *hamper*) was the wickerwork case that surrounded it Hence the name was given to any round wicker basket and especially to one in which documents that had passed the Great Seal were kept in the Court of Chancery The office where the Chancellor carried on his business—the Exchequer, or a branch thereof—thus came to be known as the *Hanaper*, and its officials as Comptrollers, Clerks, etc , of the Hanaper In England these were abolished in 1842, but for many years in Ireland the official title of the Permanent Secretary to the Chancery Division and to the Lord Chancellor remained "Clerk of the Crown and Hanaper."

Hancock. John Hancock (1737-93) was an American statesman and the first to sign the Declaration of Independence, beneath which document his signature stands out boldly *To put your John Hancock* to a deed, etc , was an old American phrase for signing it

Hand. A symbol of fortitude in Egypt, of fidelity in Rome. Two hands symbolize concord, by a closed hand Zeno represented dialectics, and by an open hand eloquence

In early art the Deity was frequently represented by a hand extended from the clouds; sometimes the hand was open, with rays issuing from the fingers, but generally it was in the act of benediction, i e with two fingers raised

In card-games the word is used for the game itself, for an individual player (as "a good *hand* at whist") or the cards held by him

A saint in heaven would grieve to see such "hand"
Cut up by one who will not understand.
           CRABBE *Borough*

Also for style of workmanship, handwriting, etc. ("he writes a good *hand*")

Operatives at a factory are called *hands* As a measure of length *a hand* = four inches. Horses are measured up the fore leg to the shoulder, and are called 14, 15, 16 (as it may be), hands high

Dead man's hand It is said that carrying a dead man's hand will produce a dead sleep Another superstition is that a lighted candle placed in the hand of a dead man gives no light to anyone but him who carries the hand. *Cp* DEAD HAND

The red hand, or bloody hand, in coat armour is the device of Ulster (*see* ULSTER), and is carried as a charge on the coats of arms of English and Irish baronets (*not* on those of Scotland or Nova Scotia). The privilege arose thus.—James I in 1611 created two hundred baronets on payment of £1,000 each to provide means for the settlement of Ulster, and from this connexion with Ulster they were awarded the badge of the "open red hand," up to that time borne by the O'Neills

The "bloody hand" is also borne privately by a few families, its presence is generally connected with some traditional tale of blood

In all instances, however, it is nothing but a heraldic charge or a badge with no personal significance whatever *Cp* BLOODY HAND

Hand gallop. A slow and easy gallop, in which the horse is kept well in hand.

Hand paper. A particular sort of paper well known in the Record Office, and so called from its water-mark, which goes back to the 15th century.

A bird in hand. *See* BIRD

An empty hand is no lure for a hawk. You must not expect to receive anything without giving a return

A note of hand. A promise to pay made in writing and duly signed

An old hand at it. One who is experienced at it.

A poor hand. An unskilful one "He is but a poor hand at it," i e he is not skilful at the work.

All hands. The nautical term for the whole of the crew.

It is believed on all hands. It is generally (or universally) believed

At first or second hand. As the original (*first*) purchaser, owner, hearer, etc, or (*second*) as one deriving, learning, etc., through another party.

At hand. Conveniently near. "Near at hand," quite close by

By hand. Without the aid of machinery or an intermediate agent A letter "sent by hand" is one delivered by a personal messenger, not sent through the post. But a child "brought up by hand" is one reared on the bottle instead of being breast-fed

By the hand of God. *See* ACT OF GOD.

Cap in hand. Suppliantly, humbly, as, "To come cap in hand." *See* CAP.

From hand to hand. From one person to another

Hand in hand In friendly fashion; unitedly

Hand over hand To go or to come up hand over hand, is to travel with great rapidity, as climbing a rope or a ladder, or as one vessel overtakes another Sailors in hauling a rope put one hand over the other alternately as fast as they can. In French, *Main sur main.*

Hands up! The order given by captors when taking prisoners The hands are to be held stretched high above the head to preclude any possibility of resistance or the use of revolvers, etc

He is my right hand My principal assistant, my best and most trustworthy man.

In hand. Under control, in possession, also, under progress.

In one's own hands. In one's sole control, ownership, management, responsibility, etc

Kings have long hands. *See* KING.

Laying on of hands. *See* TO LAY HANDS ON, *below.*

Many hands make light work. An old proverb (given in Ray's *Collection*, 1742) enshrining the wisdom of a fair division of labour The Romans had a similar saying, *Multorum manibus magnum levatur onus*, by the hands of many a great work is lightened

Offhand. In a casual, unceremonious fashion, curt, rude; extempore

Off one's hands. No longer under one's responsibilities. If something—or somebody —is left on one's hands one has to take entire responsibility.

On the other hand. A phrase used in the presentation of a case meaning "from *that* point of view," as opposed to the point of view already mentioned.

Out of hand. At once, done with, over.
> We will proclaim you out of hand.
> > *3 Henry VI*, iv, 7
> And, were these inward wars once out of hand,
> We would, dear lords, unto the Holy Land
> > *2 Henry IV*, iii, 1.

Also with the meaning "beyond control", as, "these children are quite out of hand "

The hand that rocks the cradle rules the world. The line is from the poem "What Rules the World?" by the American poet, William Ross Wallace (1819-81) —
> They say that man is mighty,
> He governs land and sea,
> He wields a mighty sceptre
> O'er lesser powers that be;
> But a mightier power and stronger
> Man from his throne has hurled,
> And the hand that rocks the cradle
> Is the hand that rules the world.

They are hand in glove. Inseparable companions, of like tastes and like affections. They fit each other like hand and glove.

To ask or give the hand of so-and-so To ask or give her hand in marriage

To bear a hand. To come and help.

To change hands. To pass from a possessor to someone else

To come to hand. To be received; to come under one's notice

To come to one's hand. It is easy to do.

To get one's hand in. To become familiar with the work in hand.

To get the upper hand. To obtain the mastery.

To give one's hand upon something To take one's oath on it; to pledge one's honour to keep the promise

To hand down to posterity. To leave for future generations.

To hand in one's checks. To die. An American phrase derived from poker and such games, where *checks* is American for counters. When one handed them in one had finished, was "cleaned out " Also, *to pass in*, or *cash*, *one's checks*

To hand round To pass from one person to another in a regular series

To hand a sail. To take it in, to furl it.

To have a free hand. To be able to do as one thinks best without referring the matter to one's superiors; to be quite uncontrolled by outside influences

To have a hand in the matter. To have a finger in the pie.

My hands are full. I am fully occupied, I have as much work to do as I can manage.

To kiss hands. *See* KISS

To lay hands on To apprehend; to lay hold of.
> Lay hands on the villain.
> > *Taming of the Shrew*, v, 1

In ecclesiastical use the **laying on of hands**, or *imposition of hands*, is the laying on, or the touch, as in signing the cross, of a bishop's hands in ordination or confirmation.

Among the Romans a hand laid on the head of a person indicated the right of property Thus if a person laid claim to a slave, he laid his hand upon him in the presence of the prætor

To lend a hand. To help; to give assistance

To live from hand to mouth. To live without any provision for the morrow.

To play one's own hand. To look after Number One, to act entirely for one's own advantage.

To play into someone's hands. Unwittingly or carelessly to act so that the other party gets the best of it, to do just what will help him and not advance your own cause.

To serve someone hand and foot. To be at his beck and call, to be his slave

To shake hands. To salute by giving a hand received into your own a shake, to bid adieu

> Fortune and Antony part here; even here
> Do we shake hands
> *Antony and Cleopatra*, iv, 10

The custom of shaking hands in confirmation of a bargain has been common to all nations and all ages. In feudal times the vassal put his hands in the hands of his overlord on taking the oath of fidelity and homage.

To strike hands. To make a contract, to become surety for another. *See P*rov xvii, 18, and xxii, 26.

To take a hand. To play a part, especially in a game of cards, etc.

To take in hand. To undertake to do something; to take the charge of

To take something off one's hands. To relieve one of something troublesome.

To wash one's hands of a thing. To have nothing to do with it after having been concerned in the matter: to abandon it entirely The allusion is to Pilate's washing his hands at the trial of Jesus

> When Pilate saw that he could prevail nothing, but that rather a tumult was made, he took water, and washed his hands before the multitude, saying, I am innocent of the blood of this just person, see ye to it. —*Matt.* xxvii, 24

To win hands down. To be victor without the slightest difficulty. The allusion is to horseracing, if the jockey wins with his hands down it shows that he has not had to worry himself —he has had a "walk-over."

With a heavy hand. Oppressively; without sparing

> It is a damned and a bloody work,
> The graceless action of a heavy hand,
> If that it be the work of any hand
> *King John*, iv, 3.

With a high hand. *See* Hɪɢʜ.

With clean hands. *See* Cʟᴇᴀɴ.

Handfasting. A "marriage on approval," formerly in vogue on the Border A fair was at one time held in Dumfriesshire, at which a young man was allowed to pick out a female companion to live with him. They lived together for twelve months, and if they both liked the arrangement were man and wife This was called *hand-fasting* or *hand-fastening*

This sort of contract was common among the Romans and Jews, and is not unusual in the East even now.

Handicap. A game at cards not unlike loo, but with this difference—the winner of one trick has to put in a double stake, the winner of two tricks a triple stake, and so on Thus if six persons are playing, and the general stake is 1s., and A gains three tricks, he gains 6s, and has to "hand i' the cap" or pool 3s for the next deal Suppose A gains two tricks and B one, then A gains 4s. and B 2s , and A has to stake 3s and B 2s. for the next deal

In common parlance a handicap is a difficulty—physical or otherwise—under which a person labours; a short-sighted man is handicapped without his spectacles

Handicap, in racing, is the adjudging of various weights to horses differing in age, power, or speed, in order to place them all, as far as possible, on an equality In golf it is a certain number of strokes allowed to a player to allow him a reasonable chance of scoring par at any game. If two unequal players challenge each other at chess, the superior gives up a piece, and this is his handicap. So called from the custom of drawing lots out of a hat or cap

The Winner's Handicap The winning horses of previous races being pitted together are first handicapped according to their respective merits the horse that has won three races has to carry a greater weight than the horse that has won only two, and this latter more than its competitor who is winner of a single race only

Handirons. *See* Aɴᴅɪʀᴏɴs

Handkerchief. To throw the handkerchief. In some children's games to throw or drop the handkerchief to a child is to signify that he or she is to run after the one who does it

With handkerchief in one hand and sword in the other. Pretending to be sorry at a calamity, but prepared to make capital out of it

> Maria Theresa stands with the handkerchief in one hand, weeping for the woes of Poland, but with the sword in the other hand, ready to cut Poland in sections, and take her share —Cᴀʀʟʏʟᴇ *The Diamond Necklace*, ch iv

Handle. A handle to one's name. Some title, as "lord," "sir," "doctor."

To give a handle to To give grounds for suspicion, as, ' He certainly gave a handle to the rumour '

To fly off the handle. To fly into a rage, or lose one's head, as the head of an axe might fly dangerously off its shaft.

Dead man's handle. A handle on the controller of an electric vehicle so designed that it cuts off the current and applies the brakes if the driver releases his pressure from illness or some other cause.

Handsel (A S. *handselen*, delivery into the hand) A gift for luck, earnest-money; the first money received in a day Hence *Handsel Monday*, the first Monday of the year, when little gifts used to be given before our Boxing Day (*q v*) took its place To "handsel a sword" is to use it for the first time, to "handsel a coat," to wear it for the first time, etc.

Handsome. Handsome is as handsome does. It is one's *actions* that count, not merely one's appearance. The proverb is in Ray's *Collection* (1742), and is also given by Goldsmith in *The Vicar of Wakefield* (ch i).

To do the handsome towards one, to act handsomely. To be liberal, generous.

Handwriting on the Wall. An announcement of some coming calamity, or the imminent fulfilment of some doom The allusion is to the handwriting on Belshazzar's palace wall announcing the loss of his kingdom (*Dan.* v).

Hang. Hang it all! I'll be hanged! Exclamations of astonishment or annoyance, mild imprecations, a mincing form of "damned."

Hanged, drawn, and quartered. *See* DRAWN.

Hanging and wiving go by destiny. "If a man is doomed to be hanged, he will never be drowned" And "marriages are made in heaven," we are told The proverb is given in Heywood's *Collection* (1546) as "Wedding's destiny and hanging likewise", and Shakespeare has —

> The ancient saying is no heresy—
> Hanging and wiving goes by destiny
> *Merchant of Venice*, 11, 9
> If matrimony and hanging go
> By dest'ny, why not whipping too?
> BUTLER *Hudibras*, Pt 11, canto 1, 839-44

To get the hang of a thing. To understand the drift or connexion, *to* acquire the knack

To hang about. To loaf, loiter. In America *to hang around* is more usual

To hang back. To hesitate to proceed

To hang by a thread. To be in a very precarious position The allusion is to the sword of Damocles (*q v*).

To hang fire. To fail in an expected result. The allusion is to a gun or pistol which fails to go off.

To hang a jury. To reduce them to disagreement so that they cannot bring in a verdict

To hang in the bell ropes To have one's marriage postponed after the banns have been published at church

To hang on. To cling to, to persevere, to be dependent on.

To hang on by the eyelids is to maintain one's position only with the greatest difficulty or by the slightest of holds

Where do you hang out? Where are you living or lodging? The phrase may arise from the old custom of shopkeepers and others hanging a sign outside their residence and places of business Inn signs and barbers' poles are among the few survivals of this custom
"I say, old boy, where do you hang out?" Mr Pickwick replied that he was at present suspended at the George and Vulture.—DICKENS · *Pickwick Papers*, ch xxx

Hangdog look. A guilty, shame-faced look

Hanging Gardens of Babylon. A square garden (according to Diodorus Siculus), 400 ft each way, rising in a series of terraces from the river in the northern part of Babylon, and provided with earth to a sufficient depth to accommodate trees of a great size. These famous gardens were one of the Seven Wonders of the World, and according to tradition were constructed by Nebuchadnezzar, to gratify his wife Amytis, who felt weary of the flat plains of Babylon, and longed for something to remind her of her native Median hills

Hangmen and Executioners.
The best known to history are.—
BULL, the earliest hangman whose name survives (about 1593)
JOCK SUTHERLAND
DERRICK, who cut off the head of Essex in 1601.
GREGORY BRANDON (about 1648), and ROBERT BRANDON, his son, who executed Charles I These were known as "the two Gregories" (*see* GREGORIAN TREE).
SQUIRE DUN, mentioned in *Hudibras* (Pt 111, c 2)
JACK KETCH (1678) executed Lord Russell and the Duke of Monmouth His name became a general term to denote a hangman
ROSE, the butcher (1686)
EDWARD DENNIS (1780) introduced in Dickens's *Barnaby Rudge*
THOMAS CHESHIRE, nicknamed "Old Cheese."
WILLIAM CALCRAFT (1800-79) was appointed official hangman in 1829 and was pensioned off in 1874
WILLIAM MARWOOD (1820-83) is known in the profession for having invented the "long drop."
Of French executioners, the most celebrated are Capeluche, headsman of Paris during the terrible days of the Armagnacs and Burgundians; and the two brothers Sanson, who worked the guillotine during the first French Revolution.
The fee given to the executioner at Tyburn used to be 13½d , with 1½d for the rope

> For half of thirteen-pence ha'penny wages
> I would have cleared all the town cages,
> And you should have been rid of all the stages
> I and my gallows groan
> *The Hangman's Last Will and Testament (Rump Songe)*

Noblemen who were to be beheaded were expected to give the executioner from £7 to £10 for cutting off their head; and it is still the case that any peer who comes to the halter can claim the privilege of being suspended by a silken rope.

Hanger. A short sword or dagger that hung from the girdle, also the girdle itself
Men's swords in hangers hang fast by their side —
J. TAYLOR (1630)

Hankey Pankey. Jugglery, fraud The word is probably a variation of Hocus Pocus

Hansard. The printed official report of the proceedings and debates in the British Houses of Parliament, so called from Luke Hansard (1752-1828), who commenced the *Journal of the House of Commons* in 1774 In 1889 Hansard became a public company, and later the work was done by contract, the reports from 1895 to 1908 being supplied by *The Times* Since then the debates have been reported by a government staff, the name Hansard being reintroduced in 1943

Hanse Towns (hǎn′sē) The maritime cities of Germany, which belonged to the Hanseatic League (*q v*)
The Hanse towns of Lübeck, Bremen, and Hamburg are commonwealths even now (1877) —FREEMAN. *General Sketch*, ch. x, p 174.

Hanseatic League (hǎnz ɪ̆ ǎt′ ɪk). The confederacy, first established in 1239, between certain cities of Northern Germany for their mutual prosperity and protection. The diet which used to be held every three years was called the *Hansa* (Old High German for *Association*), and the members of it *Hansards*. The league in its prosperity comprised eighty-five towns, it declined rapidly in the Thirty Years War, in 1669 only six cities were represented, and the last three members of the league (Hamburg,

Lubeck, and Bremen) joined the German Customs Union in 1889

Hansel; Hansel Monday. See HANDSEL

Hansom. A light two-wheeled cab, very popular in London before the introduction of taxi-cabs early in this century It was invented in 1834 by J. Aloysius Hansom (1803-82), the architect of Birmingham Town Hall The original vehicle had two very large wheels with sunk axle-trees and a seat for the driver by the side of the passenger Subsequent improvements reduced the size of the wheels, placed the driver in a dickey at the back, and provided a pair of double doors in front of the passenger with sliding glass folding panels lowered from the roof by the driver

Happy. Happy as a clam See CLAM.

Happy dispatch. See HARA-KIRI.

Happy family. The name given in travelling menageries to a collection of all sorts of animals of different and antagonistic habits living together peaceably It is now more generally associated with a children's card game

Happy-go-lucky. Thoughtless, indifferent, care-free.

Happy is the nation that has no history. The old proverb says in other words what Gibbon remarked in the *Decline and Fall*, ch iii'—
History is, indeed, little more than the register of the crimes, follies, and misfortunes of mankind.
Montesquieu said much the same :—
Heureux les peuples dont l'histoire est ennuyeux.

The Happy Valley. The home of the Prince of Abyssinia in Johnson's tale of *Rasselas* (1759) It was a Garden of Peace, completely isolated from the world, and replete with every luxury, but life there was so monotonous that the philosopher Imlac and the Prince Rasselas were glad to escape.

Bomb-happy. A phrase used in World War II to describe one in a state bordering on hysteria induced by bombing, the term arose from the fact that this hysteria often took the form of wild elation of spirits.

Hapsburg. See HABSBURG.

Hara-kiri (ha ra ki'ri) (Jap. *hara*, the belly, *kiri* to cut) A method of suicide by disembowelling practised by Japanese military officials, daimios, etc , when in serious disgrace or liable to be sentenced to death, or when their honour is irretrievably impugned The first recorded instance of hara-kiri, or *Happy Dispatch*, as it is also called, is that of Tametomo, brother of Sutoku, an ex-Emperor in the 12th century, after a defeat at which most of his followers were slain.

Harbinger. One who looks out for lodgings, etc., a courier; hence, a forerunner, a messenger. (O H.Ger. *hari*, an army, *bergan*, to lodge.)
I'll be myself the harbinger, and make joyful
The hearing of my wife with your approach.
Macbeth, i, 4.

Hard. Hard and fast Strict, unalterable A "hard and fast rule" is one that must be rigidly

adhered to and cannot be relaxed for anyone. Originally a nautical phrase, used of a ship run aground

Hard-boiled, an expressive term for one who is toughened by experience, a person with no illusions or sentimentalities

Hard by Near *Hard* here means close, pressed close together, hence firm or solid, in close proximity to
Hard by a sheltering wood
DAVID MALLET *Edwin and Emma.*

Hard cash. Money, especially actual money —as opposed to cheques or promises—"down on the nail", formerly coin as distinguished from bank-notes.

Hard hit. Seriously damaged by monetary losses; as "He was hard hit in the slump after the war", also, badly smitten with love

Hard labour. Enforced labour added to the punishment of criminals receiving a sentence of six months or over It used to consist largely of working the treadmill, stone-breaking, oakum picking, etc.

Hard lines. Hard terms, "rather rough treatment", exacting *Lines* here means "one's lot in life," as, "The lines are fallen unto me in pleasant places, yea, I have a goodly heritage" (*Ps.* xvi, 6), i e. my lot is excellent

Hard-shell Baptists Baptists in Georgia (U S A.) who stuck to their principles and were impervious to any mellowing influence

Hard tack, ship's biscuit, coarse, hard bread

Hard of hearing. Unable to hear properly, rather deaf.

Hard up. Short of money Originally a nautical phrase, when a vessel was hard put to it by stress of weather the order *Hard up the helm !* was given, and the tiller was put up as far as possible to windward so as to turn the ship's head away from the wind So, when a man is "hard up" he has to weather the storm as best he may.

To go hard with. To fare ill with; usually followed by *but*, implying "unless so-and-so happens "
Speed Nay, that I can deny by a circumstance
Pro. It shall go hard but I'll prove it by another
Two Gentlemen of Verona, i, 1

Hards and Softs. Two schools of finance in the U S.A. in the 19th century. The Hards followed Senator T H Benton (1782-1858) in favouring a currency of metal, the Softs favoured a paper currency

Hardshell. A term used in American politics for an "out-and-outer," one prepared, and anxious, to "go the whole hog." In 1853 a *hardshell* in the Southern States was for the Execution of the Fugitive Slave law, while *soft-shells* were for the maintenance of national harmony at all costs.

Hardy. Brave or daring, hence the phrase, *hardi comme un lion.*
Among those who have been surnamed "The Hardy" are —
William Douglas, defender of Berwick (d. 1302),

Philippe III of France (1245, 1270-85), and Philippe II, Duke of Burgundy (1342, 1363-82)

Hare. It is unlucky for a hare to cross your path, because witches were said to transform themselves into hares.

> A witch is a kind of hare
> And marks the weather
> As the hare doth.
> BEN JONSON *Sad Shepherd*, ii, 2.

In the North, until comparatively recently, if a fisherman on his way to the boats chanced to meet a woman, parson, or hare, he turned back, being convinced that he would have no luck that day

> The superstitious is fond in observation, servile in feare .. This man dares not stirre forth till his breast be crossed, and his face sprinkled if but an hare crosse him the way, he returnes —BP. HALL *Characters* (1608).

According to mediæval "science," the hare was a most melancholy beast, and ate wild succory in the hope of curing itself, its flesh, of course, was supposed to generate melancholy in any who partook of it.

> *Fal.* 'Sblood, I am as melancholy as a gib cat, or a lugged bear
> *Prince* Or an old lion, or a lover's lute.
> *Fal.* Yea, or the drone of a Lincolnshire bagpipe.
> *Prince* What sayest thou to a hare, or the melancholy of Moor-ditch? 1 *Henry IV*, i, 2.

Another superstition was that hares are sexless, or that they change their sex every year

> Snakes that cast their coats for new,
> Cameleons that alter hue,
> Hares that yearly sexes change
> FLETCHER *Faithful Shepherd*, iii, 1.

And among the Hindus the hare is sacred to the moon because, as they affirm, the outline of a hare is distinctly visible in the full disk.

The Order of the Hare. An order of twelve knights traditionally said to have been created by Edward III in France, on an occasion when he thought that a great shouting raised by the French army heralded the onset of battle, but found afterwards it was on account of a hare running between the two armies.

The quaking hare, in Dryden's *Hind and Panther*, means the Quakers.

> Among the timorous kind, the quaking hare
> Professed neutrality, but would not swear.
> Pt, i, 37, 38.

First catch your hare. *See* CATCH.

Mad as a March hare. Hares are unusually shy and wild in March, which is their rutting season.

Erasmus says "Mad as a marsh hare," and adds, "hares are wilder in marshes from the absence of hedges and cover."

The hare and the tortoise. An allusion to the well-known fable of the race between the hare and the tortoise, won by the latter; and the moral, "Slow and steady wins the race."

To hold with the hare and run with the hounds. To play a double and deceitful game, to be a traitor in the camp To run with the hounds as if intent to catch the hare, all the while being the secret friend of poor Wat. In the American Civil War these double-dealers were called Copperheads (*q.v.*).

To kiss the hare's foot. To be too late for anything, to be a day after the fair. The hare has gone by, and left its footprint for you to salute. A similar phrase is *To kiss the post*

Hare-brained. Mad as a March hare, giddy, foolhardy

> Let's leave this town, for they [the English] are hairbrained slaves,
> And hunger will enforce them to be more eager
> 1 *Henry VI*, i, 2.

Probably from this, in World War II, arose the term **a hare** to denote a baseless idea which, if pursued, would lead to nothing

Harefoot. The surname given to Harold I, youngest son of Canute (1035-40)

Hare-lip. A cleft lip; so called from its resemblance to the upper lip of a hare. It was fabled to be caused at birth by an elf or malicious fairy

> This is the foul fiend Flibbertigibbet He begins at curfew, and walks till the first cock He squints the eye and makes the hare-lip —*King Lear*, iii, 4.

Hare-stone. Another form of *Hoar-stone* (*q v*).

Harem (hâr´ em). The name given by Mohammedans to those apartments (and the occupants) which are appropriated exclusively to the female members of a family The word is Arab *haram*, from *harama*, be prohibited.

Harikiri. *See* HARA-KIRI.

Hark Back, To. To return to the subject. A call to the dogs in fox-hunting, when they have overrun the scent, "Hark [dogs] come back"; so "Hark for'ards!" "Hark away!" etc

Harleian (har lā´ an). Robert Harley, Earl of Oxford (1661-1724) and his son Edward, the second earl (1689-1741) were great collectors of manuscripts, scarce tracts. etc. Their library was purchased by the nation in 1753 and deposited in the British Museum, and the *Harleian MSS.* are amongst its most valuable literary and historical possessions The *Harleian Miscellany* (10 vols, first published 1744-46) contains reprints of nearly 700 tracts, etc, mostly of the 16th and 17th centuries; and since 1870 the Harleian Society has published numerous volumes of Registers, Heralds' Visitations, and Pedigrees

Harlem, New York City, was named after their home town of Haarlem by the early Dutch settlers. It is now the uptown section of New York and is the metropolis of the Negro population of the city.

Harlequin (har´ le kwin). In the British pantomime, a mischievous fellow supposed to be invisible to all eyes but those of his faithful Columbine (*q v*). His office is to dance through the world and frustrate all the knavish tricks of the Clown, who is supposed to be in love with Columbine He wears a tight-fitting spangled or parti-coloured dress and is usually masked. He derives from *Arlecchino*, a stock character of Italian comedy (like Pantaloon and Scaramouch), whose name was in origin probably that of a sprite or hobgoblin One of the demons in Dante is named "Alichino," and another devil of mediæval demonology was "Hennequin."

The old Christmas pantomime or harle-
quinade is essentially a British entertainment,
first introduced by John Weaver (1673-1760),
a dancing-master of Shrewsbury, in 1702.

What Momus was of old to Jove
The same a harlequin is now
The former was buffoon above,
The latter is a Punch below
SWIFT *The Puppet Show*

The prince of Harlequins was John Rich
(1681-1761).

Harlequin. So Charles Quint (1500-58) was
called by François I of France

Harlot. Popular etymology used to trace this
word to Arlotta, mother of William the
Conqueror, but it is O Fr. *herlot* and Ital
arlotto, a base fellow, vagabond, and was
formerly applied to males as well as females.
Hence Chaucer speaks of "a sturdy harlot . . .
that was her hostes man."

He was a gentil harlot, and a kinde,
A bettre felaw shulde man no wher finde
Canterbury Tales, prol 649.
The harlot king is quite beyond mine arm
Winter's Tale, ii, 3.

The earliest sense of the word may have been
"camp-follower," and if so it represents O H
Ger. *hari*, war, and *lotter* (A S *loddere*), a
beggar, wastrel.

Harm. Harm set, harm get. Those who lay
traps for others get caught themselves Haman
was hanged on his own gallows Our Lord says,
"They that take the sword shall perish with
the sword" (*Matt.* xxvi, 52).

Harmattan (har mät' an) A wind which blows
periodically from the interior parts of Africa
towards the Atlantic. It prevails in December,
January, and February, and is generally
accompanied with fog, but is so dry as to
wither vegetation and cause human skin to
peel off.

Harmonia (har mō' ni à) **Harmonia's Necklace.** An unlucky possession, something that
brings evil to all who possess it Harmonia was
the daughter of Mars and Venus On her
marriage with King Cadmus, she received a
necklace which proved fatal to all who possessed it. *Cp.* FATAL GIFTS

On the same occasion Vulcan, to avenge the
infidelity of her mother, made the bride a
present of a robe dyed in all sorts of crimes,
which infused wickedness and impiety into all
her offspring *Cp* NESSUS Both Harmonia and
Cadmus, having suffered many misfortunes,
and seen their children a sorrow to them, were
changed into serpents.

Medea, in a fit of jealousy, sent Creusa a
wedding robe, which burnt her to death

Harmonious Blacksmith, The The name given,
after his death, to a well-known air by Handel
An ingenious story, but a complete and baseless fabrication, ascribed the origin of the
tune to the hammering at his forge of a
blacksmith William Powell (d. 1780), the
ringing of whose hammer set Handel to work
on it. Powell's tomb is still to be seen in the
little churchyard of St. Lawrence at Whitchurch in Edgware.

Harmonists. A sect founded in Wurtemberg by
George and Frederick Rapp about 1780 They
emigrated to the U.S A in 1815 (Indiana, later
Pittsburg, Pa.) They are now extinct and little
is known of their tenets, except that they held
property in common and regarded marriage as
a purely civil contract

Harness. Out of harness Not in practice,
retired A horse out of harness is one not at
work

To die in harness. To continue in one's work
or occupation till death. The allusion is to a
horse working in harness until it falls down
dead, or to soldiers in armour or harness

At least we'll die with harness on our back
Macbeth, v 5.

Harness cask A large cask or tub with a rim
cover, containing a supply of salt meat for
immediate use A nautical term

Harness Prize A prize founded at Cambridge
in memory of William Harness (1790-1869),
editor of a Life of Shakespeare, of the Plays of
Massinger and Ford, etc, for the best essay
connected with Shakespearean literature.
Awarded every third year

Haro (hä' rō). **To cry out haro to anyone** To
denounce his misdeeds, to follow him with hue
and cry "Ha rou" was the ancient Norman
hue and cry, and the exclamation made by
those who wanted assistance, their person or
property being in danger

In the Channel Isles, *Haro !* said to have been
originally *Ha ! ho ! a l'aide, mon prince !* is a
protest still in vogue when one's property is
endangered, and is still a form of legal appeal
It is supposed to have been an appeal to Rollo,
Duke of Normandy

Haroun al Raschid (ha roon' äl räsh' id) Calif
of Bagdad, of the Abbasside line (763-809)
The adventures and stories connected with him
form a large part of the *Arabian Nights Entertainments* (*q.v.*).

Harp. The cognizance of Ireland. According
to tradition, one of the early kings of Ireland
was named David, and this king took the harp
of the Psalmist as his badge But King John, to
distinguish his Irish coins from the English,
had them marked with a triangle, either in
allusion to St Patrick's explanation of the
Trinity, or to signify that he was king of England, Ireland, and France, and the harp may
have originated from this Henry VII was the
first to adopt it as the Irish device, and James I
to place it in the third quarter of the royal
achievement of Great Britain

To harp for ever on the same string. To
reiterate, to return continually to one point
or argument

Still harping on my daughter —*Hamlet*, ii, 1

Harpagon (ar pa gong). A miser, the chief
character in Molière's *L'Avare*, 1668

Harpocrates (har pok' ra tēz) The Greek form
of the Egyptian Heru-P-Khart (Horus the
Child), who is figured as a youth with one
finger pointing to his mouth He was adopted
by them as the god of silence

I assured my mistress she might make herself
perfectly easy on that score for I was the Harpocrates
of trusty valets.—*Gil Blas*, iv, 2.

Harpsichord (harp' si kôrd). The most important of the stringed instruments with key-

boards before the invention of the pianoforte The strings are plucked by quills of leather plectra inserted in "jacks" or uprights, which are caused to pass the strings when the keys are depressed. The harpsichord was universally used in the 16th to 18th centuries. As a distinctive instrument and not merely a crude piano it has been reintroduced for the performance of music originally composed for it.

Harpy. In classical mythology, a winged monster with the head and breasts of a woman, very fierce, starved-looking, and loathsome, living in an atmosphere of filth and stench, and contaminating everything it came near. Homer mentions but *one* harpy, Hesiod gives *two*, and later writers *three*. Their names, Ocypeta *(rapid)*, Celeno *(blackness)*, and Aello *(storm)*, indicate that these monsters were personifications of whirlwinds and storms.

A regular harpy. One who wants to appropriate everything, one who sponges on another without mercy

I will   do you any embassage   rather than hold three words conference with this harpy —*Much Ado*, ii, 1

Harridan (hăr′ i dan). A haggard old beldame. So called from the Fr *haridelle*, a worn-out jade of a horse.

Harrier (hăr′ i ĕr) A dog for hare-hunting, whence the name

Harrington A farthing. So called from John, 1st Lord Harrington (d 1613), to whom James I granted a patent (1613) for making these coins of brass

I will not bate a Harrington of the sum.
BEN JONSON *The Devil is an Ass*, ii, 1.

Harris, Mrs. The fictitious crony of Sarah Gamp *(q.v.)*, to whom the latter referred for the corroboration of all her statements (*Martin Chuzzlewit*)

Harry By the Lord Harry. A mild imprecation, the person referred to being the devil

By the Lord Harry, he says true.
CONGREVE *Old Bachelor*, ii, 1.

Great Harry. *See* GREAT.

Old Harry. A familiar name for the devil; Old Scratch Probably from the personal name (*cp Old Nick*), but perhaps with some allusion to the word *harry*, meaning to plunder, harass, lay waste, from which comes the old *harrow*, as in the title of the 14th-century *estrif*, or miracle-play, *The Harrowing of Hell*

To play Old Harry. To play the devil; to ruin, or seriously damage.

Hart. In Christian art, the emblem of solitude and purity of life. It was the attribute of St Hubert, St Julian, and St Eustace. It was also the type of piety and religious aspiration (*Ps.* xlii, 1). *Cp.* HIND

Hart of grease. A hunter's phrase for a fat venison; a stag full of the pasture, called by Jaques "a fat and greasy citizen" (*As You Like It*, ii, 1)

Hart royal. A male red deer, when the crown of the antler has made its appearance, and the creature has been hunted by a king.

The White Hart, or **Hind**, with a golden

chain, in public-house signs, is the badge of Richard II, which was worn by his adherents. It was adopted from his mother, Joan of Kent, whose cognizance it was.

Harum Scarum (hâr′ üm skâr′ um) Giddy, hare-brained, or a person so constituted. From the old *hare* (*cp* HARRY) to harass, and *scare*, perhaps with the additional allusion to the "madness of a March *hare*."

Who's there? I s'pose young harum-scarum.
Cambridge Facetiæ · Collegian and Porter

Haruspex (pl *haruspices*). Officials among the Etruscans and ancient Romans who interpreted the will of the gods by inspecting the entrails of animals offered in sacrifice (O.Lat *haruga*, a victim, *specio*, I inspect). Cato said, "I wonder how one haruspex can keep from laughing when he sees another "

Harvard University. The senior University in the U S.A , situated at Cambridge, Mass , and founded in 1636 by the general court of the colony in Massachusetts Bay. In 1638 it was named after John Harvard (1607-1638), who had left to it his library and half his estate.

Harvest Moon. The full moon nearest the autumnal equinox, which rises for several days nearly at sunset, and at about the same time

Hash. A mess, a muddle; as, "a pretty hash he made of it."

I'll soon settle his hash for him. I will soon smash him up, ruin his schemes; "cook his goose"; "put my finger in his pie", "make mincemeat of him." Our slang is full of such phrases *See* COOKING

About earls as goes mad in their castles
And females what settles their hash
G R. SIMS, *The Dagonet Ballads.*

Hassan-Ben-Sabah (hăs′ ăn ben sa′ ba) The Old Man of the Mountain, founder of the sect of the Assassins (*q v.*)

Hassock. A footstool, properly one made of coarse grass (A S. *hassuc*), or sedge (Welsh *hesg*)

Hassocks should be gotten in the fens, and laid at the foot of the said bank   where need required.
—DUGDALE *Imbanking*, p 322,

Hat. How Lord Kingsale acquired the right of wearing his hat in the royal presence is this: King John and Philip II of France agreed to settle a dispute respecting the duchy of Normandy by single combat. John de Courcy, conqueror of Ulster and founder of the Kingsale family, was the English champion, and no sooner appeared than the French champion put spurs to his horse and fled. The king asked the earl what reward should be given him, and he replied, "Titles and lands I want not, of these I have enough, but in remembrance of this day I beg the boon, for myself and successors, to remain covered in the presence of your highness and all future sovereigns of the realm " So runs the story.

The privilege was at one time more extensive, Motley informs us that all the Spanish grandees had the privilege of being covered in the presence of the reigning monarch; and to this day, in England, any peer of the realm has the right to sit in a court of justice with his hat on.

In the House of Commons, whilst a division is proceeding a member may speak on a point of order arising out of or during the division, but if he does so he must speak sitting and with his head covered

It was a point of principle with the early Quakers not to remove the hat as a mark of respect but to remain covered, even in the presence of royalty The story goes that on one occasion William Penn came into the room where Charles II was standing and kept his hat on, whereupon Charles removed his own hat "Friend Charles," said Penn, "why dost thou uncover thy head?" "Friend Penn," answered Charles with a smile, "it is the custom here that only one person wears his hat in the king's presence"

A cockle hat. A pilgrim's hat So called from the custom of putting cockle-shells upon their hats, to indicate their intention or performance of a pilgrimage

> How should I your true love know
> From another one?
> By his cockle-hat and staff
> And by his sandal shoon.
> *Old Ballad quoted in Hamlet,* iv, 5

Hat-trick. A cricket phrase for taking three wickets with three successive balls A bowler who did this used to be entitled to a new hat at the expense of his club

Hats and Caps. Two political factions of Sweden in the 18th century, the former favourable to France, and the latter to Russia. Carlyle says the latter were called Caps, meaning night-caps, because they were averse to action and war, but the fact is that the French partisans wore a French *chapeau* as their badge, and the Russian partisans wore a Russian cap.

A white hat A white hat used to be emblematical of radical proclivities, because the Radical reformer, "Orator" Henry Hunt (1773-1835) wore one during the Wellington and Peel administration

Street arabs used to accost a person wearing a white hat with the question, "Who stole the donkey?" and a companion would answer, "Him wi' the white hat on."

Knocked into a cocked hat. *See* COCKED.

Never wear a brown hat in Friesland. When at Rome do as Rome does In Friesland (a province of the Netherlands) the inhabitants used to cover the head first with a knitted cap, a high silk skull-cap, a metal turban, and over all a huge flaunting bonnet A traveller once passed through the province with a common brown wide-awake, and was hustled by the workmen, jeered at by the women, pelted by the boys, and sneered at by the magnates

Pass around the hat. Gather subscriptions into a hat

To eat one's hat. Indicative of strong emphasis "I'd eat my hat first," "I'd be hanged first"

"If I knew as little of life as that, I'd eat my hat and swallow the buckle whole," said the clerical gentleman —DICKENS. *Pickwick Papers,* ch xlii

To hang up one's hat in a house. To make oneself at home, to become one of the family.

You are only fit to wear a steeple-crowned hat. To be burnt as a heretic. The victims of the Inquisition were always decorated with such a headgear

"Where did you get that hat?" a catch-phrase in the early '90s, originating in J. J. Sullivan's comic song, sung in 1888, with the refrain —

> Where did you get that hat?
> Where did you get that tile?
> Isn't it a nobby one
> And just the proper style

Hatches. Put on the hatches. Figuratively, shut the door. (A.S. *hæce,* a gate, *cp haca,* a bar or bolt)

Under hatches Very depressed, down in the world; also, dead and buried The hatches of a ship are the coverings over the hatchways (or openings in the deck of a vessel) to allow of cargo, etc , being easily discharged.

> For though his body's under hatches
> His soul has gone aloft
>   DIBDIN *Tom Bowling.*

These lines were inscribed on Dibdin's tombstone at St Martin-in-the-Fields.

Hatchet. To bury the hatchet *See* BURY.

To throw the hatchet. To exaggerate heavily, tell falsehoods In allusion to an ancient game where hatchets were thrown at a mark, like quoits It means the same as drawing the longbow (*q v.*).

Hatto (hăt'ō) A 10th-century archbishop of Mainz, a noted statesman and councillor of Otho the Great, proverbial for his perfidy, who, according to tradition (preserved in the *Magdeburg Centuries*), was devoured by mice The story says that in 970 there was a great famine in Germany, and Hatto, that there might be better store for the rich, assembled the poor in a barn, and burnt them to death, saying "They are like mice, only good to devour the corn." By and by an army of mice came against the archbishop, who, to escape the plague, removed to a tower on the Rhine; but hither came the mouse-army by hundreds and thousands, and ate him up. The tower is still called Mouse-tower (*q.v.*).

Many similar legends, or versions of the same legend, are told of the mediæval Rhineland

Count Graaf raised a tower in the midst of the Rhine, and if any boat attempted to evade payment of toll, the warders shot the crew with crossbows. One year a famine prevailed, and the count made a corner in wheat and "profiteered" grossly, but an army of rats, pressed by hunger, invaded his tower, and falling on the old baron, worried him to death and then devoured him

Widerolf, bishop of Strasburg (in 997), was devoured by mice because he suppressed the convent of Seltzen, on the Rhine

Bishop Adolf of Cologne was devoured by mice or rats in 1112.

Freiherr von Guttingen collected the poor in a great barn. and burnt them to death, and being invaded by rats and mice, ran to his castle of Guttingen The vermin, however, pursued him and ate him clean to the bones, after which his castle sank to the bottom of the lake, "where it may still be seen."

A similar tale is recorded in the chronicles of William of Mulsburg, Bk. ii; and *cp* PIED PIPER.

Haussmannization. The pulling down of buildings, districts, etc., and the construction on the site of new streets and cities, as Baron Haussmann (1809-91) remodelled Paris. By 1868 he had saddled Paris with a debt of about £35,000,000, and two years later was dismissed from his office of Prefect of the Seine.

Hautville Coit. *See* HACKELL'S COIT.

Havelok the Dane (hăv'lok). A hero of mediæval romance. He was the orphan son of Birkabegn, king of Denmark, was exposed at sea through the treachery of his guardians, and the raft drifted to the coast of Lincolnshire. Here a fisherman named Grim found the young prince, and brought him up as his own son. In due time he became king of Denmark and of part of England, Grim was suitably rewarded, and with the money founded the town of Grimsby (*q v*).

Haver-cakes. Oaten cakes (Scand *hafre*; Ger. *hafer*, oats).

Haversack. Strictly speaking, a bag to carry oats in. *See* HAVER-CAKES. It now means any small canvas bag for rations, etc., slung from the shoulder; a gunner's leather-case for carrying charges.

Havock. An old military command to massacre without quarter. This cry was forbidden in the ninth year of Richard II on pain of death. In a 14th-century tract entitled *The Office of the Constable and Mareschall in the Tyme of Werre* (contained in the Black Book of the Admiralty), one of the chapters is, "The peyne of hym that crieth havock, and of them that followeth him"—*Item si quis inventus fuerit qui clamorem inceperit qui vocatur havok.*

> Cry Havock, and let slip the dogs of war.
> *Julius Cæsar*, iii, 1.

Havre, Le (le avr). A contraction of *Le havre* (the haven, harbour) *de notre Dame de grâce.*

Hawcubites (haw'kū bĭtz). Street bullies in the reign of Queen Anne. It was their delight to molest and ill-treat the old watchmen, women, children, and feeble old men who chanced to be in the streets after sunset. The succession of these London pests after the Restoration was The Muns, the Tityre Tus, the Hectors, the Scourers, the Nickers, then the Hawcubites (1711-14), and then the Mohocks—most dreaded of all.

> From Mohock and from Hawcubite,
>   Good Lord deliver me,
> Who wander through the streets at nighte,
>   Committing cruelty.
> They slash our sons with bloody knives,
>   And on our daughters fall
> And, if they murder not our wives,
>   We have good luck withal.

The name Hawcubite is probably a combination of *Mohawk* and *Jacobite.*

Haw-haw, Lord. The name given (originally by a Fleet St journalist) to William Joyce, who broadcast anti-British propaganda in English from Germany during World War II. He was hanged for treason in 1946.

B D —15

Hawk.

(1) Different parts of a hawk·
Arms The legs from the thigh to the foot.
Beak The upper and crooked part of the bill.
Beams. The long feathers of the wings.
Clap The nether part of the bill.
Feathers summed and unsummed Feathers full *or* not full grown.
Flags The next to the principals.
Glut The slimy substance in the pannel.
Gorge The crow or crop.
Haglurs The spots on the feathers.
Mails The breast feathers.
Nares The two little holes on the top of the beak.
Pannel The pipe next to the fundament.
Pendent feathers Those behind the toes.
Petty singles The toes.
Pounces The claws.
Principal feathers The two longest.
Sails. The wings.
Sear or *sere* The yellow part under the eyes.
Train The tail.

(2) Different sorts of hawk.
Gerfalcon A Gerfalcon (esp the Tercel, or male) is for a king.
Falcon or *Tercel gentle* For a prince.
Falcon of the rock For a duke.
Falcon peregrine For an earl.
Bastard hawk For a baron.
Sacre and a *sacret* For a knight.
Lanare and *Lanret* For a squire.
Merlin For a lady.
Hoby For a young man.
Goshawk For a yeoman.
Tercel For a poor man.
Sparrow-hawk For a priest.
Musket For a holy-water clerk.
Kestrel. For a knave or servant.

Dame Juliana Berners

The "Sore-hawk" is a hawk of the first year so called from the French, *sor* or *saure*, brownish-yellow.

(3) The dress of a hawk.
Bewits The leathers with the hawk-bells, buttoned to the bird's legs.
Creanse. A packthread or thin twine fastened to the leash in disciplining a hawk.
Hood A cover for the head, to keep the hawk in the dark. A *rufter hood* is a wide one, open behind. *To unstrike the hood* is to draw the strings so that the hood may be in readiness to be pulled off.
Jesses The little straps by which the leash is fastened to the legs.
Leash The leather thong for holding the hawk.

(4) Terms used in falconry.
Casting Something given to a hawk to cleanse her gorge.
Cawking Treading.
Cowering When young hawks, in obedience to their elders, quiver and shake their wings.
Crabbing. Fighting with each other when they stand too near.
Hack The place where a hawk's meat is laid.
Imping Repairing a hawk's wing by engrafting a new feather.
Inke or *Ink* The breast and neck of a bird that a hawk preys on.
Intermewing The time of changing the coat.
Lure A figure of a fowl made of leather and feathers.
Make. An old staunch hawk that sets an example to young ones.
Mantling Stretching first one wing and then the other over the legs.
Mew The place where hawks sit when moulting.
Muting The dung of hawks.
Pelf or *pull* What a hawk leaves of her prey.
Pelt The dead body of a fowl killed by a hawk.
Perch The resting-place of a hawk when off the falconer's wrist.
Plumage Small feathers given to a hawk to make her cast.
Quarry The fowl or game that a hawk flies at.
Rangle Gravel given to a hawk to bring down her stomach.

Sharp set Hungry.
Tiring Giving a hawk a leg or wing of a fowl to pull at.
The peregrine when full grown is called a blue-hawk.
The hawk was the symbol of Ra or Horus, the sun-god of the Egyptians
See BIRDS (protected by superstitions)

I know a hawk from a handsaw (*Hamlet*, II, 2). Handsaw is probably a corruption of *hern-shaw* (a heron) I know a hawk from a heron, the bird of prey from the game flown at, I know one thing from another.

Neither hawk nor buzzard. Of doubtful social position—too good for the kitchen, and not good enough for the family, not hawks to be fondled and petted—the "tasselled gentlemen" of the days of falconry—nor yet buzzards—a dull kind of falcon synonymous with dunce or plebeian "Neither flesh, fowl, nor good red herring "

Hawker's News or "Piper's News." News known to all the world. *Un secret de polichinelle.*

Hawk-eye. An inhabitant of the State of Iowa.
It was one of the names of Natty Bumpo in J. Fenimore Cooper's novels. See LEATHER-STOCKING.

Hawse-hole. He has crept through the hawse-hole, or He has come in at the hawse-hole. That is, he entered the service in the lowest grade, he rose from the ranks A naval phrase The hawse-hole of a ship is that through which the cable of the anchor runs

Hawthorn. The symbol of ' Good Hope" in the language of flowers, because it shows that winter is over and spring at hand. The Athenian girls used to crown themselves with hawthorn flowers at weddings, and the marriage-torch was made of hawthorn The Romans considered it a charm against sorcery, and placed leaves of it on the cradles of newborn infants.
The hawthorn was chosen by Henry VII for his device, because the crown of Richard III was discovered in a hawthorn bush at Bosworth.

Hay, Hagh, or Haugh (all pron. hā). An enclosed estate, rich pasture-land, especially a royal park, as Bilhagh (*Billa-haugh*), Beskwood- or Bestwood-hay, Lindeby-hay, Welleyhay or Wel-hay. These were "special reserves" of game for royalty alone

A bottle of hay. See BOTTLE

Between hay and grass. Too late for one and too soon for the other

Neither hay nor grass. That hobbledehoy state when a youth is neither boy nor man

Make hay while the sun shines Strike while the iron is hot, take time by the forelock, one to-day is worth two to-morrows

Hayseed. An American colloquial term for a countryman, a rustic

Haywire. To go haywire is to run riot, to behave in an uncontrolled manner This American phrase probably arises from the difficulty of handling the coils of wire used for binding bundles of hay; if such a coil is unfastened unskilfully it springs out in great loops that quickly become entangled and unmanageable

Hay, Antic. The hay was an old English country dance, somewhat of the nature of a reel, with winding, sinuous movements around other dancers or bushes, etc., when danced in the open
My men like satyrs grazing on the lawn
Shall with their goat feet dance the antic hay.
MARLOWE· *Edward II*, I, 1.

Haysugge. See ISAAC.

Hayward, an official in the old English village whose duty it was to look after the hedges and boundaries and impound any cattle found straying
I haue an horne and be haywarde and liggen oute a nyghtes
And keep my corn in my croft fro pykers and theeves. *Piers Plowman* (C), VI. 16

Hazazel. The scapegoat See AZAZEL

Haze. To bully (first used at sea) "It is very expressive to a sailor, and means to punish by hardwork " R H. DANA *Two Years Before the Mast*, 1840

He Bible, The. See BIBLE, SPECIALLY NAMED

Head. Cattle are counted by the *head*, labourers by *hands*, as "How many hands do you employ?", soldiers by their *arms*, as "So many rifles, bayonets," etc., guests at dinner by the *cover*, as "Covers for ten," etc
Human beings are, in some circumstances, counted as "heads," as, for instance, in contracting for meals the caterer will take the job at so much "a head"—*i e* for each person
Better be the head of an ass than the tail of a horse. Better be foremost amongst commoners than the lowest of the aristocracy; "Better to reign in hell than serve in heav'n" (MILTON· *Paradise Lost*, I, 263)
Get your head shaved. You are a dotard Go and get your head shaved like other lunatics. See BATH
Thou thinkst that monarchs never can act ill,
Get thy head shaved, poor fool, or think so still.
PETER PINDAR *Ode Upon Ode.*

Head and shoulders. A phrase of sundry shades of meaning Thus "head and shoulders taller" means considerably taller; "to turn one out head and shoulders" means to drive one out forcibly and without ceremony

Heads I win, tails you lose. Descriptive of a one-sided arrangement

Heads or tails Guess whether the coin tossed up will come down with head-side uppermost or not. The side not bearing the head has various devices, which are all included in the word tail, meaning opposite to the head The ancient Romans used to play this game, but said, "Heads or ships "

He has quite turned her head. He has so completely enchanted her that she is unable to take a reasonable view of the situation.

He has a head on his shoulders. He is a clever fellow, with brains in his head

He has quite lost his head. He is so excited and confused that he does not know the right thing to do.

I can make neither head nor tail of it. I cannot understand it at all. A gambling phrase

Off one's head. Deranged; delirious, extremely excited.

Over head and ears. *See* EAR.

To come to a head. To ripen, to reach a crisis The allusion is to the ripening, or coming to a head, of a suppurating boil or ulcer.

To eat his head off. To cost more in food than he is worth, to do little or no work. The phrase comes from the stable

To give one his head To allow him complete freedom, let him go just as he pleases. Another "horsey" phrase

To head off. To intercept; get ahead of and force to turn back

To hit the nail on the head. To guess aright; to do the right thing The allusion is obvious. The French say, *Vous avez frappé au but* (You have hit the mark); the Italians have the phrase, *Avete dato in brocca* (You have hit the pitcher), alluding to a game where a pitcher stood in the place of Aunt Sally (*q v*). The Lat *Rem acu tetigisti* (You have touched the thing with a needle), refers to the custom of probing sores

To keep one's head above water. To avoid bankruptcy.

To make head, or headway. To get on, to struggle effectually against something

To take it into one's head. To conceive a notion.

Heady. Wilful; also, affecting the head, as "The wine or beer is heady"

Health. Drinking healths. This custom, of immemorial antiquity, William of Malmesbury says, took its rise from the death of young King Edward the Martyr (979), who was traitorously stabbed in the back while drinking a cup of wine presented to him by his mother Elfrida. According to Rabelais the giant, Gabbara, was "the first inventor of the drinking of healths " He was an ancestor of Gargantua.

It was well known to the ancients. The Greeks handed the cup to the person toasted and said, "This to thee " Our holding out the wineglass is a relic of this Greek custom

The Romans had a curious fashion of drinking the health of a mistress, which was to drink a bumper to each letter of her name Hudibras satirizes this custom, which he calls "spelling names with beer-glasses" (ii, I). In Plautus, we read of a man drinking to his mistress with these words · *Bene vos, bene nos, bene te, bene me, bene nostrum etiam Stephanium* (Here's to you, here's to us all, here's to thee, here's to me, here's to our dear ——). (*Stich* v, 4.) Martial, Ovid, Horace, etc., refer to the same custom.

The Saxons were great health-drinkers, and Geoffrey of Monmouth (Bk. vi, 12) says that Hengist invited King Vortigern to a banquet to see his new levies After the meats were removed, Rowena, the beautiful daughter of Hengist, entered with a golden cup full of wine, and, making obeisance, said, "*Lauerd kining, wacht heil*" (Lord King, your health). The king then drank and replied, *Drinc heil* (Here's to you) *See* WASSAIL

Heap. Struck all of a heap. Struck with astonishment.

Hear, hear! An exclamation used to call attention to the words of a speaker, usually with approbation. Until the late 17th century such approval was shown by a loud humming among the hearers, and "Hear him!" was used to silence interrupters and remind others of the duty of attending to what was being said In the Parliament of 1689 the Whigs greeted every speech by one of their own party with shouts of "Hear, hear him!" to drown any Tory interjections, and from this the phrase grew to its present significance.

Hearse. Originally a framework shaped like an ancient harrow (O Fr *herce*, a harrow), holding candles and placed over a bier or coffin These frames at a later period were covered with a canopy, and lastly were mounted on wheels and became the modern carriage for the dead

Heart. In Christian art the *heart* is an attribute of St Teresa.

The flaming heart is the symbol of charity, and an attribute of St Augustine, denoting the fervency of his devotion The heart of the Saviour is frequently so represented

The Bleeding Heart. *See* BLEEDING

A heart to heart talk A confidential talk in private; generally one in which good advice is offered, or a warning or reprimand given

After my own heart. Just what I like, in accordance with my wish.

Be of good heart. Cheer up.

From the bottom of one's heart. Fervently; with absolute sincerity

His heart is in the right place He is kind and sympathetic in spite, perhaps, of appearances. He is perfectly well disposed

His heart sank into his boots. In Latin, *Cor illi in genua decidit*. In French, *Avoir la peur au ventre* The last two phrases are very expressive: Fear makes the knees shake, and it gives one a stomach ache; but the English phrase suggests that his heart or spirits sank as low as possible short of absolutely deserting him

His heart was in his mouth. That choky feeling in the throat which arises from fear, conscious guilt, shyness, etc

In one's heart of heart. In the farthest, innermost, most secure recesses of one's heart
> Give me that man
> That is not passion's slave, and I will wear him
> In my heart's core, ay, in my heart of heart.
> *Hamlet*, iii, 2

The phrase is often heard as "heart of *hearts*," but this, as will be seen from Shakespeare's very clear reference to the "heart's core," is incorrect. *Cp* also:—
> Even the very middle of my heart
> Is warmed   *Cymbeline*, iii, 6.

Out of heart. Despondent, without sanguine hope

Set your heart at rest. Be quite easy about the matter.

Take heart. Be of good courage. Moral courage at one time was supposed to reside in the heart, physical courage in the stomach, wisdom in the head, affection in the reins or kidneys, melancholy in the bile, spirit in the blood, etc.

To break one's heart. To waste away or die of disappointment. "Broken-hearted," hopelessly distressed. It is not impossible to die "of a broken heart," but it is never caused through grief.

To eat one's heart out. To brood over some trouble to such an extent that one wears oneself out with the worry of it; to suffer from hopeless disappointment in expectations.

To have at heart. To cherish as a great hope or desire, to be earnestly set on.

To learn by heart. *See* LEARN.

To lose one's heart to. To fall in love with somebody.

To take heart of grace. To pluck up courage, not to be disheartened or down-hearted when all seems to be going against one. This expression may be based on the promise, "My grace is sufficient for thee" (2 *Cor* xii, 9), by this grace St. Paul says, "When I am weak then am I strong." Take grace into your heart, rely on God's grace for strength, with grace in your heart your feeble knees will be strengthened.

To set one's heart upon. Earnestly to desire it.

To take to heart. To feel deeply pained at something which has occurred, to appreciate fully the implications of.

To wear one's heart upon one's sleeve. To expose one's secret intentions to general notice, the reference being to the custom of tying your lady's favour to your sleeve, and thus exposing the secret of the heart. Iago says:—

When my outward action doth demonstrate
The native act and figure of my heart
In compliment extern, 'tis not long after
But I will wear my heart upon my sleeve
For daws to peck at: I am not what I am
Othello, i, 6.

With all my heart, or with my whole heart and soul. With all the energy and enthusiasm of which I am capable.

With heart and hand. With enthusiastic energy.

Heartbreaker. A flirt. Also a particular kind of curl. A loose ringlet worn over the shoulders, or a curl over the temples.

Heart of Midlothian. The old jail, the Tolbooth of Edinburgh, taken down in 1817. Sir Walter Scott has a novel so entitled.

Heartsease (harts' ēz). The *viola tricolor*. It has a host of fancy names, as the "Butterfly flower," "Kiss me quick," a "Kiss behind the garden gate," "Love in idleness" (*q v.*), "Pansy," "Three faces under one hood," the "Variegated violet," "Herba Trinitatis," etc.

Hearth Money. *See* CHIMNEY MONEY.

Heat. One course in a race, that part of a race run as "instalment" of the main event. One, two, or more heats make a race. A *dead heat* is a heat in which two or more competitors are tied for the first place.

Feigned Zeal, you saw, set out with speedier pace,
But the last heat Plain Dealing won the race.
DRYDEN *Albion and Albanius, Epilogue*

To turn the heat on. To subject to a severe cross-examination, to grill.

Heath Robinson is a phrase popularly applied to any fantastic but ingenious contraption—usually of bits of string and wood. In a number of amusing drawings in *Punch* and elsewhere W. Heath Robinson (1872-1944) invented the crazy inventors of such needlessly complicated devices to perform simple actions.

Heaven (A S *heofon*). The word properly denotes the abode of the Deity and His angels—"heaven is My throne" (*Is* lxvi, 1, and *Matt* v, 34)—but it is also used in the Bible and elsewhere for the air, the upper heights as "the fowls of heaven," "the dew of heaven," "the clouds of heaven"; "the cities are walled up to heaven" (*Deut.* i, 28), and a tower whose top should "reach unto heaven" (*Gen* xi, 4); the starry firmament, as, "Let there be lights in the firmament of heaven" (*Gen* i, 14).

In the Ptolemaic system (*q v*) the heavens were the successive spheres of space enclosing the central earth at different distances and revolving round it at different speeds. The first seven were those of the so-called Planets, *viz* the Moon, Mercury, Venus, the Sun, Mars, Jupiter, and Saturn; the eighth was the firmament of heaven containing all the fixed stars; the ninth was the crystalline sphere, invented by Hipparchus (2nd cent B C), to account for the precession of the equinoxes. These were known as *The Nine Heavens* (*see* NINE SPHERES). the tenth—added much later—was the primum mobile.

The Seven Heavens (of the Mohammedans)
The first heaven is of pure silver, and here the stars, each with its angel warder, are hung out like lamps on golden chains. It is the abode of Adam and Eve.

The second heaven is of pure gold and is the domain of John the Baptist and Jesus.

The third heaven is of pearl, and is allotted to Joseph. Here Azrael, the angel of death, is stationed, and is for ever writing in a large book or blotting words out. The former are the names of persons born, the latter those of the newly dead.

The fourth heaven is of white gold, and is Enoch's. Here dwells the Angel of Tears, whose height is "500 days' journey," and he sheds ceaseless tears for the sins of man.

The fifth heaven is of silver and is Aaron's. Here dwells the Avenging Angel, who presides over elemental fire.

The sixth heaven is composed of ruby and garnet, and is presided over by Moses. Here dwells the Guardian Angel of heaven and earth, half-snow and half-fire.

The seventh heaven is formed of divine light beyond the power of tongue to describe, and is ruled by Abraham. Each inhabitant is bigger than the whole earth, and has 70,000 heads, each head 70,000 mouths, each mouth 70,000 tongues and each tongue speaks 70,000 languages, all for ever employed in chanting the praises of the Most High.

To be in the seventh heaven. Supremely happy The Cabbalists maintained that there are seven heavens, each rising in happiness above the other, the seventh being the abode of God and the highest class of angels. *See also* PARADISE.

Heaviside Layer The name given to an ionised region of the upper atmosphere having a high degree of electrical conductivity. It is believed to exist about 60 miles above the earth and it reflects radio waves back to the earth, thus enabling reception round the curved surface of the globe. The name is taken from Oliver Heaviside (1850-1925) who suggested its existence in 1901

Heavy. Heavy man In theatrical parlance, an actor who plays foil to the hero, such as the king in *Hamlet*; Iago is another "heavy man's" part as foil to Othello.

Heavy water is the name given to deuterium oxide, a liquid similar to ordinary water but about 10 per cent denser It is largely used in experiments in nuclear physics and its properties and possible uses are still being investigated

Heavies, The. *See* REGIMENTAL NICKNAMES.

Hebe (hē' bi) Goddess of youth, and cup-bearer to the celestial gods She had the power of restoring the aged to youth and beauty (Greek mythology).

> Wreathed smiles
> Such as hang on Hebe's cheek,
> And love to live in dimple sleek.
> MILTON. *L'Allegro.*

Hebron (heb' ron) In Dryden's *Absalom and Achitophel* (*q v.*), in the first part stands for Holland, but in the second part for Scotland.

Hecate (hek' a ti). One of the Titans of Greek mythology, and the only one that retained her power under the rule of Zeus. She was the daughter of Perses and Asteria, and became a deity of the lower world after taking part in the search for Proserpine She taught witch-craft and sorcery, and was a goddess of the dead, and as she combined the attributes of, and became identified with, Selene, Artemis, and Persephone, she was represented as a triple goddess and was sometimes described as having three heads—one of a horse, one of a dog, and one of a lion Her offerings consisted of dogs, honey, and black lambs, which were sacrificed to her at cross-roads. Shakespeare refers to the triple character of this goddess:

> And we fairies that do run
> By the triple Hecate's team
> *Midsummer Night's Dream*, **v**, 2.

Hecatomb (hek' a tom) In Greek antiquities, a sacrifice consisting of a hundred head of oxen (*hekaton*, a hundred); hence, a large number. Keats speaks of "hecatombs of vows," Shelley of "hecatombs of broken hearts," etc.

It is said that Pythagoras, who, we know, would never take life, offered up 100 oxen to the gods when he discovered that the square of the hypotenuse of a right-angled triangle equals the sum of the squares of the other two sides. This is the 47th proposition of Bk. i of "Euclid," called the Dulcarnon (*q.v.*).

Hector (hek' tör) Eldest son of Priam, the noblest and most magnanimous of all the Trojan chieftains in Homer's *Iliad*. After holding out for ten years, he was slain by Achilles, who lashed him to his chariot, and dragged the dead body in triumph thrice round the walls of Troy The *Iliad* concludes with the funeral obsequies of Hector and Patroclus

In modern times his name has somewhat deteriorated, for it is used to-day for a swag-gering bully, and "to hector" means to brow-beat, bully, bluster

The Hector of Germany. Joachim II, Elector of Brandenburg (1514-71)

You wear Hector's cloak. You are paid in your own coin for trying to deceive another When Thomas Percy, Earl of Northumberland, in 1569, was routed, he hid himself in the house of Hector Armstrong, of Harlaw. This villain betrayed him for the reward offered, but never after did anything go well with him till at last he died a beggar on the roadside

Hecuba (hek' û ba) Second wife of Priam, and mother of nineteen children, including Hector. When Troy was taken by the Greeks she fell to the lot of Ulysses She was afterwards metamorphosed into a dog, and threw herself into the sea. Her story has furnished a host of Greek tragedies.

> I have heard my grandsire say full oft,
> Extremity of griefs would make men mad;
> And I have read that Hecuba of Troy
> Ran mad through sorrow
> *Titus Andronicus*, iv, 1.

Hedge. To hedge, in betting, is to protect one-self against loss by cross bets, to prevaricate.

> He [Godolphin] began to think . . that he had betted too deep . . and that it was time to hedge — MACAULAY. *England*, vol iv, ch. xvii

The word is used attributively for persons of low origin, vagabonds who ply their trade in the open, under—or between—the hedges, etc , hence for many low and mean things, as *hedge-priest*, a poor or vagabond parson; *hedge-writer*, a Grub Street author; *hedge-marriage*, a clandestine one, etc ; *hedge-born swain*, a person of mean, or illegitimate, birth (1 *Henry VI*, iv, 1), *hedge-school*, a school kept in the open air, at one time common in Ireland, etc.

To hedge-hop. Airman's term for flying so low as almost to skim the tops of the hedges

Hedonism. The doctrine of Aristippus, that pleasure or happiness is the chief good and chief end of man (Gr *hedone*, pleasure)

Heebie-jeebies (hē' bi jē' biz), an American slang term descriptive of intense nervousness, the jitters.

Heel. In American slang usage a *heel* is a cad, a despicable fellow with no sense of decency or honour

A heeler is the hanger-on of a political boss.

Heeled, in Western U S A. means supplied with all necessities, particularly money and firearms.

Achilles' heel. *See* ACHILLES

Down, or out at heels. In a sad plight, in decayed circumstances, like a beggar whose boots are worn out at the heels.

A good man's fortune may grow out at heels.
King Lear, ii, 2.

To cool or kick one's heels. To be kept waiting a long time, especially after an appointment has been given one.

To lay by the heels. To render powerless. The allusion is to the stocks, in which vagrants and other petty offenders were confined by the ankles.

To lift up the heel against. To spurn, physically or figuratively; to treat with contumely or contempt. to oppose, to become an enemy.

Yea, mine own familiar friend, in whom I trusted, which did eat of my bread, hath lifted his heel against me —*Ps* xli, 9.

To show a clean or fair pair of heels. To abscond, run away and get clear.

To take to one's heels. To run off.

Bumpers all round, and no heel-taps. The bumpers are to be drained to the bottom of the glass.

Heep, Uriah An abject toady and a malignant hypocrite, making great play of being "'umble," but in the end falling a victim to his own malice —DICKENS. *David Copperfield*

Hegemony (he gem' o ni) The hegemony of nations. The leadership (Gr *hegemonia,* from *ago,* to lead)

Hegira (hej' i ra, hē jī' ra) (Arab *hejira,* the departure). The epoch of the flight of Mohammed from Mecca to Medina when he was expelled by the magistrates, July 15th, 622. The Mohammedan calendar starts from this event.

Heimdall (him' dal). One of the gods of Scandinavian mythology, son of the nine virgins, daughters of Ægir, and in many attributes identical with Tiw

Heimskringla (him skring' la) An important collection of sixteen sagas containing an account of the history of Norway—sketched through the medium of biography—and a compendium of ancient Scandinavian mythology and poetry It is probably by Snorri Sturluson (d 1241) *See* EDDA.

Heir-apparent. The actual heir who will succeed if he outlive the present holder of the crown, estate, etc , as distinguished from the **heir-presumptive,** whose succession may be broken by the birth of someone nearer akin to the holder Thus, in the time of Queen Victoria, the Princess Royal was heir-presumptive until the Prince of Wales, afterwards Edward VII, was born and became heir apparent At the death of his predecessor the heir-apparent becomes **heir-at-law.**

Hel. The name in late Scandinavian mythology of the queen of the dead, also of her place of abode, which was the home of the spirits of those who had died in their beds as distinguished from Valhalla, the abode of heroes slain in battle

Heldenbuch (hel' den buk) (Ger , *Book of Heroes*). The name given to the collection of songs, sagas, etc., recounting the traditions and myths of Dietrich of Bern Much of it is ascribed to Wolfram von Eschenbach

Helen. The type of female beauty. She was the daughter of Zeus and Leda, and wife of Menelaos, king of Sparta She eloped with Paris, and thus brought about the siege and destruction of Troy

For which men all the life they here enjoy
Still fight, as for the Helens of their Troy
SIR FULKE GREVILLE, LORD BROOKE *Treatie of Humane Learning*
She moves a goddess and she looks a queen
POPE *Homer's Iliad,* iii

St. Helen's fire. The St Elmo's Fire, or Corpozant (*q v*), occasionally seen on the masts of ships, etc If the flame is single, foul weather is said to be at hand, but if two or more flames appear, the weather will improve *See* CASTOR AND POLLUX.

Helena (hel' en a) The type of a lovely woman, patient and hopeful, strong in feeling, and sustained through trials by her enduring and heroic faith. (*All's Well that Ends Well*)

Helena, St. Mother of Constantine the Great She is represented in royal robes, wearing an imperial crown, because she was empress Sometimes she carries in her hand a model of the Holy Sepulchre, an edifice raised by her in the East, sometimes she bears a large cross, typical of her alleged discovery of Our Lord's Cross (*see Invention of the Cross, under* CROSS), sometimes she also bears the three nails by which the Saviour was affixed to the cross She died about 328, and is commemorated on August 18th.

The island of St Helena (săn' ta iē' nà) in the South Atlantic, discovered by the Portuguese on St. Helena's Day, 1501, was the place of exile of Napoleon from 1815 until his death in 1821.

Helicon (hel' i kon). The home of the Muses, a part of the Parnassus, a mountain range in Greece. It contained the fountains of Aganippe and Hippocrene, connected by "Helicon's harmonious stream " The name is used allusively of poetic inspiration

From Helicon's harmonious springs
A thousand rills their mazy progress take
The laughing flowers, that round them blow
Drink life and fragrance as they flow
GRAY. *The Progress of Poesy*

Helicopter (hel' i kop ter) A flying-machine that can raise itself vertically by means of horizontally revolving propellers. The uses of these aircraft have not yet been fully explored and developed.

Heliopolis (hel i op' ō lis, hē' li op' ō lis), the City of the Sun, a Greek form of (1) Baalbek, in Syria, and (2) of An, in ancient Egypt, noted for its temple of Actis, which may be the Beth Shemesh, or Temple of the Sun, referred to in *Jer* xliii, 13. It is now a pleasant residential suburb of Cairo

Helios (hē' li os) The Greek sun-god, who rode to his palace in Colchis every night in a golden boat furnished with wings He is called Hyperion by Homer, and, in later times, Apollo

Heliotrope (hel' i ō trōp, hē' li ō trōp) Apollo loved Clytie (*q v.*), but forsook her for her sister Leucothoe On discovering this, Clytie pined away; and Apollo changed her at death to a flower, which, always turning towards the sun, is called heliotrope (Gr "turn-to-sun.")

The bloodstone, a greenish quartz with veins and spots of red, used to be called "heliotrope," the story being that if thrown into a bucket of water it turned the rays of the sun to blood-colour This stone also had the power of rendering its bearer invisible.

No hope had they of crevice where to hide,
Or heliotrope to charm them out of view
DANTE: *Inferno*, xxvi

Hell. This word occurs twenty-one times in the Authorized Version of the New Testament In nine instances the Greek word is *Hades*; in eight instances it is *Gehenna*; and in one it is *Tartarus*

According to the Koran, Hell has seven portals leading into seven divisions (*Surah* xv, 44)

True Buddhism admits of no Hell, properly so called (*cp* NIRVANA), but certain of the more superstitious acknowledge as many as 136 places of punishment after death, where the dead are sent according to their degree of demerit.

Classic authors tell us that the Inferno is encompassed by five rivers Acheron, Cocytus, Styx, Phlegethon, and Lethe Acheron, from the Gr *achos-reo*, grief-flowing, Cocytus, from the Gr *kokuo*, to weep, supposed to be a flood of tears, Styx, from the Gr. *stugeo*, to loathe, Phlegethon, from the Gr *phlego*, to burn; and Lethe, from the Gr. *lethe*, oblivion. *See also* INFERNO

Hell and chancery are always open. There's not much to choose between lawyers and the devil An old saying, given in Fuller's *Collection* (1732)

Hell, Hull, and Halifax. *See* HULL.

Hell is paved with good intentions. This occurs as a saying of Dr Johnson (Boswell's *Life*, ann. 1775), but it is a good deal older than his day It is given by George Herbert (*Jacula Prudentum*) (1633) as "Hell is full of good meanings and wishes "

It was hell broken loose. Said of a state of anarchy or disorder

Why, here you have the awfulest of crimes
For nothing! Hell broke loose on a butterfly!
A dragon born of rose-dew and the moon!
BROWNING: *Ring and the Book*, iv, 1601.

The road to hell is easy. *Facilis descensus Averno See* AVERNUS

The Vicar of Hell. *See* VICAR.

To give one hell. To make things very unpleasant for oneself

To Hell or Connaught. This phrase, usually attributed to Cromwell, and common to the whole of Ireland, rose thus: during the Commonwealth all the native Irish were dispossessed of their lands in the other three provinces and ordered to settle in Connaught, under pain of death.

To lead apes in hell. *See* APE.

To ride hell for leather To ride with the utmost speed, "all out "

To work, play, etc, like hell. To do it feverishly, with all the power at one's disposal

Hell broth. A magical mixture prepared for evil purposes (*Macbeth* iv, 1.)

Hell's Corner (World War II) The triangle of Kent about Dover, so called from its being both under fire from German cross-channel guns and the scene of much of the bitterest air fighting during the Battle of Britain, 1940.

Hell Gate. A dangerous passage between Great Barn Island and Long Island The Dutch settlers of New York called it Hoellgat (whirling-gut), corrupted into Hell Gate. Flood Rock, its most dangerous reef, has been blown up.

Hellenes (hel' ēnz) "This word had in Palestine three several meanings. sometimes it designated the pagans, sometimes the Jews, speaking Greek and dwelling among the pagans; and sometimes proselytes of the gate, that is, men of pagan origin converted to Judaism, but not circumcised" (*John* vii, 35, xii, 20, *Acts* xiv. 1, xvii, 4, xviii, 4, xxi, 28) (Renan *Life of Jesus*, xiv)

The Greeks were called *Hellenes*, from Hellen, son of Deucalion and Pyrrha, their legendary ancestor, the name has descended to the modern Greeks, and their ruler is not "King of Greece," but "King of the Hellenes " The ancient Greeks called their country "Hellas", it was the Romans who applied to it the name "Græcia," which, among the inhabitants themselves, referred only to Epirus.

Hellenic. The common dialect of the Greek writers after the age of Alexander. It was based on the Attic

Hellenistic. The dialect of the Greek language used by the Jews It was full of Oriental idioms and metaphors.

Hellenists Those Jews who used the Greek or Hellenic language, also a Greek scholar.

Hellespont (hel' es pont) The "sea of Helle", so called because Helle, the sister of Phryxus, was drowned there She was fleeing with her brother through the air to Colchis on the golden ram to escape from Ino, her mother-in-law, who most cruelly oppressed her, but turning giddy, she fell into the sea It is the ancient name of the Dardanelles and is celebrated in the legend of Hero and Leander (*q v*)

Helmet. The helmets of Saragossa were most in repute in the days of chivalry.

Close helmet. The complete head-piece, having in front two movable parts, which could be lifted up or let down at pleasure

Visor. One of the movable parts; it was to look through

Bever, or **drinking-piece.** One of the movable parts, which was lifted up when the wearer ate or drank It comes from the old Italian verb *bevere* (to drink)

Morion. A low iron cap, worn only by infantry.

Mohammed's helmet. Mohammed wore a double helmet, the exterior one was called *al mawashah* (the wreathed garland).

The helmet of Perseus rendered the wearer invisible This was the "helmet of Hades," which, with the winged sandals and magic wallet, he took from certain nymphs who held them in possession; but after he had slain Medusa he restored them again, and presented the Gorgon's head to Athene (Minerva), who placed it in the middle of her ægis.

The pointed helmet in the bas-reliefs from the earliest palace of Nimroud appears to have been the most ancient   Several were discovered in the ruins They were iron, and the rings which ornamented the lower part .   were inlaid with copper —LAYARD' *Nineveh and its Remains*, vol. ii, Pt ii, ch iv

In heraldry, the helmet, resting on the chief of the shield, and bearing the crest, indicates rank

Gold with six bars, or with the visor raised (in full face), for royalty;

Steel, with gold bars, varying in number (in profile), for a nobleman,

Steel, without bars, and with visor open (in profile), for a knight or baronet,

Steel, with visor closed (in profile), for a squire or gentleman

Helot (hel' ŏt). A slave in ancient Sparta, hence, a slave or serf. The Spartans used to make a helot drunk as an object-lesson to the youths of the evils of intemperance Dr. Johnson said of one of his old acquaintances —

He is a man of good principles, and there would be no danger that a young gentleman should catch his manner, for it is so very bad, that it must be avoided. In that respect he would be like the drunken Helot — Boswell s *Life* ann 1779

Helter-skelter. Higgledy-piggledy, in hurry and confusion A jingling expression, more or less imitating the clatter of swiftly moving feet; post-haste, as Shakespeare uses the expression (*2 Henry IV*, v, 3) —

Sir John I am thy Pistol and thy friend,
And helter-skelter have I rode to thee,
And tidings do I bring

Helve. To throw the helve after the hatchet. To be reckless, to throw away what remains because your losses have been so great. The allusion is to the fable of the wood-cutter who lost the head of his axe in a river and threw the handle in after it.

Helvetia (hel vē' sha) Switzerland. So called from the Helvetii, a powerful Celtic people who dwelt thereabouts

Hemp When hempe is spun England is done Lord Bacon says he heard the prophecy when he was a child, and he interpreted it thus: Hempe is composed of the initial letters of *H*enry, *E*dward, *M*ary, *P*hilip, and *E*lizabeth. At the close of the last reign "England was done," for the sovereign no longer styled himself "King of England," but ' King of Great Britain and Ireland " *See* NOTARIKON.

Hempen caudle, collar, etc. A hangman's rope

Ye shall have a hempen caudle then, and the help of a hatchet.—*2 Henry VI*, iv, 7

Hempen fever. Death on the gallows, the rope being made of hemp

Hempen widow. The widow of a man who has been hanged

Hen. A grey hen. A stone bottle for holding liquor. Large and small pewter pots mixed together are called "hen and chickens "

A dirty leather wallet lay near the sleeper, .   also a grey-hen which had contained some sort of strong liquor —EMMA ROBINSON *Whitefriars*, ch viii

A whistling maid and a crowing hen is fit for neither God nor men. A whistling maid means a witch, who whistles like the Lapland witches to call up the winds; they were supposed to be in league with the devil The crowing of a hen was supposed to forebode a death The usual interpretation is that masculine qualities in women are undesirable

As fussy as a hen with one chick Over-anxious about small matters, over-particular and fussy. A hen with one chick is for ever clucking it, and never leaves it in independence a single moment.

A hen on a hot griddle, a Scottish phrase descriptive of a restless person

Hen and chickens. In Christian art this device is emblematical of God's providence *See Matt* xxiii, 37 *See also* GREY HEN *above.*

Hen-pecked. A man who tamely submits to the lectures and nagging of his wife is said to be "hen-pecked."

Tappit hen. *See* TAPPIT.

Henchman. A faithful follower Originally a squire or attendant, especially one who looked after the horses (A S *hengest*, horse, and *man*)

I do but beg a little changeling boy
To be my henchman.
A Midsummer Night's Dream, ii, 1

Hengist and Horsa The semi-legendary leaders of the Jutes, who landed in England at Ebbsfleet, Kent, in 449 Horsa is said to have been slain at the battle of Aylesford, about 455, and Hengist to have ruled in Kent till his death in 488. Ger *hengst*, a stallion, and Horsa is connected with our word horse The two brothers may have received their names from the devices borne on their arms

Henry Grâce de Dieu *See* GREAT HARRY

Hep, an American slang phrase of uncertain origin meaning "aware of, informed of, wise to "

Hep-cat, one who is fond of and moved by fast and noisy music.

Hephaestos (hē fes' tos) The Greek Vulcan.

Heptameron, The. A collection of Italian and mediæval stories written by—or at any rate ascribed to—Marguerite of Angoulême, Queen of Navarre (1492-1549), and published posthumously in 1558 They were supposed to have been related in seven days, hence the title (Gr. *hepta*, seven, *hemera*, day; *cp* DECAMERON, HEXAMERON)

Heptarchy (Gr , seven governments) The Saxon Heptarchy was the division of England into seven parts, each of which had a separate ruler as Kent, Sussex, Wessex, Essex, East Anglia, Mercia, and Northumbria. It flourished in various periods from the 6th to the 9th centuries under a Bretwalda (*q v*), but seldom consisted of exactly seven members, and the names and divisions were constantly changing

Hera (hē′ rá) The Greek Juno, the wife of Zeus. (The word means "chosen one," *hatreo*)

Heraldry. The herald (O.Fr *heralt*, *heraut*) was an officer whose duty it was to proclaim war or peace, carry challenges to battle, and messages between sovereigns, etc , nowadays war or peace is still proclaimed by the heralds, but their chief duty as court functionaries is to superintend state ceremonies such as coronations, installations, etc , and also to grant arms, trace genealogies, attend to matters of precedence, honours, etc.

Edward III appointed two heraldic kings-at-arms for south and north—Surroy and Norroy—in 1340. The English College of Heralds was incorporated by Richard III in 1483-84. It consists of three kings of arms, and four pursuivants, under the Earl Marshal, which office is hereditary in the line of the Dukes of Norfolk.

The three kings of arms are Garter (blue), Clarenceux, and Norroy (purple)

The six heralds are styled Somerset, Richmond, Lancaster, Windsor, Chester, and York.

The four pursuivants are Rouge Dragon, Blue Mantle, Portcullis, and Rouge Croix

Garter King of Arms is so called from his special duty to attend at the solemnities of election, investiture, and installation of Knights of the Garter; he is Principal King of Arms for all England

Clarenceux King of Arms So called from the Duke of Clarence, brother of Edward IV. His jurisdiction extends over England south of the Trent.

Norroy King of Arms has similar jurisdiction to Clarenceux, only on the north side of the Trent.

The "Bath King of Arms" is not a member of the Heralds' College, and is concerned only with the Order of the Bath

The Scottish and Irish officers of Arms are, unlike those of England, directly under the Government, and are not connected with the Earl Marshal or Garter

In *Scotland* the heraldic college consists of *Lyon King of Arms*, three heralds (*Albany, Ross,* and *Rothesay*), and three pursuivants (*Garrick, March,* and *Unicorn*)

In *Ireland* it consists of *Ulster King of Arms*, two heralds (*Dublin* and *Cork*), and one pursuivant (*Athlone*)

In *Blazonry*, the *coat of arms* represents the knight himself from whom the bearer is descended

The *shield* represents his body, and the *helmet* his head.

The *flourish* is his mantle.

The *motto* is the ground or moral pretension on which he stands

The *supporters* are the pages, designated by the emblems of bears, lions, and so on

There are nine *points* on the *shield* or *escutcheon*, distinguished by the first nine letters of the alphabet—three at top, A, B, C; three down the middle, D, E, F; and three at the bottom, G, H, I The first three are *chiefs*; the middle three are the *collar point, fess point,* and *nombril* or *navel point*; the bottom three are the *base* points

It should be noted that in heraldry the shield

15*

is taken as being held before the wearer, hence the *dexter*, or right side is the left side of the shield as it appears on paper.

The *tinctures* or *colours* used in heraldry are known by distinctive names, also sometimes by equivalents among the planets and precious stones They are.—

Gold or, Sol, topaz.
Silver argent, Luna, pearl.
Red gules, Mars, ruby
Blue. azure, Jupiter, sapphire
Black sable, Saturn, diamond.
Green vert, Venus, emerald
Purple. purpure, Mercury, amethyst

Besides these there are the different furs, as *ermine, vair,* and their arrangements as *erminois, erminites, pean, potent, verry,* etc.

Marshalling is the science of bringing together the arms of several families in one escutcheon

The following are the main terms used in heraldry —

Bend, a diagonal stripe
Bordure, an edge of a different colour round the whole shield.
Chevron, a bent stripe, as worn by non-commissioned officers in the army, but the point upwards
Cinquefoil, a five-petalled formalised flower.
Couchant, lying down
Counter-passant, moving in opposite directions
Couped, cut off straight at the stem or neck.
Coward, coué, with tail hanging between the legs.
Displayed, (of birds) with wings and talons outspread.
Dormant, sleeping
Endorse, a very narrow vertical stripe, *see* Pale.
Erased, with nothing below the stem or neck, which ends roughly as opposed to the sharp edge of *couped*
Fesse, a horizontal stripe across the middle of the shield
File, a horizontal bar from which normally depend one or more smaller bars called *labels*
Gardant, full-faced
Haunant, standing on its tail (of fishes)
Issuant, rising from the top or bottom of an ordinary
Lodged, reposing (of stags, etc.).
Martlet, a swallow, with no feet.
Mullet, a star of a stated number of points.
Naiant, swimming (of fishes).
Nascent, rising out of the middle of an ordinary
Pale, a wide vertical stripe down the centre of the shield.
Pallet, a narrow vertical stripe, *see* Pile
Passant, walking, the face in profile (emblematic of resolution).
Passant gardant, walking, with full face (emblematic of resolution and prudence)
Passant regardant, walking and looking behind
Pile, a narrow triangle
Rampant, rearing, with face in profile (emblematic of magnanimity)
Rampant gardant, erect on the hind legs; full face (emblematic of prudence)

Rampant regardant, erect on the hind legs, side face looking behind (emblematic of circumspection).

Regardant, looking back (emblematic of circumspection).

Salient, springing (emblematic of valour).

Sejant, seated (emblematic of counsel).

Statant, standing still.

Trippant, running (of stags, etc).

Volant, flying

Herb. Herb of grace. Rue is so called probably because (owing to its extreme bitterness) it is the symbol of repentance

> Here did she fall a tear; here in this place,
> I'll set a bank of rue, sour herb of grace;
> Rue, even for ruth, here shortly shall be seen,
> In the remembrance of a weeping queen
> *Richard II*, iii, 4

Jeremy Taylor, quoting from the *Flagellum Dæmonum*, a form of exorcism by Father Jerome Mengus (used in exorcizing Martha Brosser in 1599), says —

> First, they are to try the devil by holy water, incense, sulphur, rue, which from thence, as we suppose, came to be called "herb of grace,"—and especially, St John's wort, which therefore they call "devil's flight," with which if they cannot cast the devil out, yet they may do good to the patient.—*A Dissuasive from Popery, I*, ii, 9 (1664)

Herba Sacra. The "divine weed," vervain, said by the old Romans to cure the bites of all rabid animals, to arrest the progress of venom, to cure the plague, to avert sorcery and witchcraft, to reconcile enemies, etc. So highly esteemed was it that feasts called *Verbenalia* were annually held in its honour Heralds wore a wreath of vervain when they declared war, and the Druids held vervain in similar veneration.

> Lift your boughs of vervain blue,
> Dipt in cold September dew,
> And dash the moisture, chaste and clear,
> O'er the ground, and through the air,
> Now the place is purged and pure
> W MASON *Caractacus* (1759)

Herb Trinity. The popular name for the pansy (*q v*), *Viola tricolor*; also called "Three-faces-under-a-hood"; the markings of the pansy account for both names. *Cp.* HEARTS-EASE

Herculaneum (hẽr kū lā' ni ŭm), one of the ancient towns on the Bay of Naples destroyed in the eruption of A.D 79. But whereas Pompeii was buried in ashes, Herculaneum was overwhelmed with molten lava and its remains have had to be hewn with difficulty from this rock The architectural remains are inferior to those of Pompeii but the works of art are superior.

Hercules (hẽr' kū lēz) A hero of ancient Greek myth, who was possessed of superhuman physical strength and vigour He is represented as brawny, muscular, short-necked, and of huge proportions The Pythian told him if he would serve Eurystheus for twelve years he should become immortal, accordingly he bound himself to the Argive king, who imposed upon him twelve tasks of great difficulty and danger

(1) To slay the Nemean lion
(2) To kill the Lernean hydra.
(3) To catch and retain the Arcadian stag

(4) To destroy the Erymanthian boar.
(5) To cleanse the stables of King Augeas
(6) To destroy the cannibal birds of the Lake Stymphalis
(7) To take captive the Cretan bull.
(8) To catch the horses of the Thracian Diomedes
(9) To get possession of the girdle of Hippolyta, Queen of the Amazons
(10) To take captive the oxen of the monster Geryon
(11) To get possession of the apples of the Hesperides
(12) To bring up from the infernal regions the three headed dog Cerberus.

After death Hercules took his place in the heavens as a constellation, and is still to be seen between Lyra and Corona Borealis.

The Attic Hercules. Theseus, who went about like Hercules, destroying robbers and achieving wondrous exploits

The Farnese Hercules. A celebrated statue, copied by Glykon from an original by Lysippus, and now in the Farnese Palace, Rome It exhibits the hero, exhausted by his toils, leaning upon his club, his left hand rests upon his back, and grasps one of the apples of the Hesperides

Hercules' choice. Immortality the reward of toil in preference to pleasure Xenophon tells us that when Hercules was a youth he was accosted by Virtue and Pleasure, and asked to choose between them Pleasure promised him all carnal delights, but Virtue promised immortality. Hercules gave his hand to the latter, and, after a life of toil, was received amongst the gods

Hercules' horse. Arion, given him by Adrastos It had the power of speech, and its feet on the right side were those of a man.

Hercules' Pillars. *See* PILLARS

Hercules Secundus. Commodus, the Roman Emperor (A D. 180-92), gave himself this title Dissipated and inordinately cruel, he claimed divine honours and caused himself to be worshipped as Hercules It is said that he killed 100 lions in the amphitheatre, and that he slew over a thousand defenceless gladiators.

Herculean knot (hẽr kū lē' ăn). A snaky complication on the rod or caduceus of Mercury, adopted by the Grecian brides as the fastening of their woollen girdles, which only the bridegroom was allowed to untie. As he did so he invoked Juno to render his marriage as fruitful as that of Hercules, whose numerous wives all had families Amongst his wives were the fifty daughters of Thestius, all of whom conceived in one night. *See* KNOT

Herefordshire Kindness. A good turn rendered for a good turn received. Fuller says the people of Herefordshire "drink back to him who drinks to them."

Heretic. From a Greek word meaning "one who chooses," hence *heresy* means simply "a choice." A heretic is one who chooses his own creed instead of adopting one set forth by authority.

The principal heretical sects of the first six centuries were —

FIRST CENTURY The *Simonians* (from Simon Magus), *Cerinthians* (Cerinthus), *Ebionites* (Ebion), and *Nicolaitans* (Nicholas, deacon of Antioch).

SECOND CENTURY: The *Basilidians* (Basilides), *Carpocratians* (Carpocrates), *Valentinians* (Valentinus), *Gnostics* (Knowing Ones), *Nazarenes*, *Millenarians*, *Cainites* (Cain), *Sethians* (Seth), *Quartodecimans* (who kept Easter on the fourteenth day of the first month), *Cerdonians* (Cerdon), *Marcionites* (Marcion), *Montanists* (Montanus), *Alogians* (who denied the "Word"), *Artotyrites* (*q v*), and *Angelics* (who worshipped angels)

Tatianists belong to the 3rd or 4th century The Tatian of the 2nd century was a Platonic philosopher who wrote *Discourses* in good Greek; Tatian the heretic lived in the 3rd or 4th century, and wrote very bad Greek The two men were widely different in every respect, and the authority of the heretic for "four gospels" is of no worth.

THIRD CENTURY: The *Patri-passians*, *Arabaci*, *Aquarians*, *Novatians*, *Origenists* (followers of Origen), *Melchisedechians* (who believed Melchisedec was the Messiah), *Sabellians* (from Sabellius), and *Manicheans* (followers of Mani)

FOURTH CENTURY: The *Arians* (from Arius), *Colluthians* (Colluthus), *Macedonians*, *Agnetæ*, *Apollinarians* (Apollinaris), *Timotheans* (Timothy, the apostle), *Collyridians* (who offered *cakes* to the Virgin Mary), *Seleucians* (Seleucius), *Priscillians* (Priscillian), *Anthropomorphites* (who ascribed to God a human form), *Jovinianists* (Jovinian), *Messalians*, and *Bonosians* (Bonosus).

FIFTH CENTURY: The *Pelagians* (Pelagius), *Nestorians* (Nestorius), *Eutychians* (Eutychus), *Theo-paschites* (who said all the three persons of the Trinity suffered on the cross)

SIXTH CENTURY: The *Predestinarians*, *Incorruptibilists* (who maintained that the body of Christ was incorruptible), the new *Agnoetæ* (who maintained that Christ did not know when the day-of judgment would take place), and the *Monothelites* (who maintained that Christ had but one will)

Heriot (her' i ot) The ancient right of the lord of a manor to the best beast or chattel of a deceased copyhold tenant The word is compounded of the Sax. *here* (army), *geatwe* (equipments), because originally it was military furniture, such as armour, arms, and horses paid to the lord of the fee.

Hermæ *See* HERMES.

Hermaphrodite (her măf' rō dīt). A person or animal with indeterminate sexual organs, or with these organs being of both sexes, a flower containing both the male and female organs of reproduction The word is derived from the fable of Hermaphroditus, son of Hermes and Aphrodite The nymph Salmacis became enamoured of him, and prayed that she might be so closely united that "the twain might become one flesh." Her prayer being heard, the nymph and boy became one body. (Ovid: *Metamorphoses*, IV, 347)

Though hermaphroditism in human beings to the extent of the combination in one person of certain characteristics of the two sexes is not unknown, a *true* hermaphrodite is rare, and the so-called examples are almost invariably merely cases of the malformation of the reproductive organs.

The Jewish Talmud contains several references to hermaphrodites; they are recognized in English law, and an old French law allowed them great latitude. The ancient Athenians commanded that they should be put to death The Hindus and Chinese enact that every hermaphrodite should choose one sex and keep to it. According to fable, all persons who bathed in the fountain Salmãcis, in Caria, became hermaphrodites

Hermes. The Greek Mercury, whose busts, known as *Hermæ*, were affixed to stone pillars and set up as boundary marks at street corners, and so on. The Romans used them also for garden decorations.

Among alchemists Hermes was the usual name for quicksilver or mercury (*q v.*).

See Milton's *Paradise Lost*, III, 603

Hermetic Art or **Philosophy.** The art or science of alchemy; so called from Hermes Trismegistus (the Thrice Greatest Hermes), the name given by the Neo-Platonists to the Egyptian god Thoth, its hypothetical founder.

Hermetic books. Forty-two books fabled to have been written from the dictation of Hermes Trismegistus dealing with the life and thought of ancient Egypt They state that the world was made out of fluid, that the soul is the union of light and life; that nothing is destructible; that the soul transmigrates; and that suffering is the result of motion

Hermetic powder. A sympathetic powder, supposed to possess a healing influence, from a distance, so called by mediæval philosophers out of compliment to Hermes Trismegistus (Sir Kenelm Digby. *Discourse Concerning the Cure of Wounds by the Sympathetic Powder*, 1644)

By his side a pouch he wore
Replete with strange hermetic powder,
That wounds nine miles point-blank would solder.
BUTLER. *Hudibras*, I, 2.

Hermetically sealed. Closed securely, from sealing a vessel *hermetically*, *i.e.* as a chemist, a disciple of Hermes Trismegistus, would, by heating the neck of the vessel till it is soft, and then twisting it till the aperture is closed up.

Hermit. Peter the Hermit (1050-1115). Preacher of the first crusade, which he led as far as Asia Minor.

Hermit's Derby. One of the famous races in the history of the Turf, when Hermit, belonging to Henry Chaplin (1840-1923), later Viscount Chaplin, won the Derby of 1867 against all expectations, and the notorious Marquis of Hastings lost £300,000 in bets

Herne the Hunter. *See* WILD HUNTSMAN.

Hero. No man is a hero to his valet An old saying Plutarch has the idea both in his *De Iside* and *Regum et Imperatorum Apothegmata*

And Montaigne in his *Essays* (Bk III, ch. II) amplifies the idea—

Tel a este miraculeux au monde, auquel sa femme et son valet n'ont rien veu seulement de remarquable, peu d'hommes ont esté admirez par leur domestiques. (Such an one has been, as it were, miraculous in the world in whom his wife and valet have seen nothing even remarkable; few men have been admired by their servants).

Cp the Latin saying frequently quoted by Bacon, *Verior fama e domesticis emanat* (Truer fame comes from one's servants), and *Matt* XIII, 57—

A prophet is not without honour save in . . his own house

Heroic age. That age of a nation which comes between the purely mythical period and the historic This is the age when the sons of the gods were said to take unto themselves the daughters of men, and the offspring partake of the twofold character

Heroic size in sculpture denotes a stature superior to ordinary life, but not colossal

Heroic verse. That verse in which epic poetry is generally written. In Greek and Latin it is hexameter verse, in English it is ten-syllable iambic verse, either in rhymes or not, in Italian it is the *ottava rima*. So called because it is employed to celebrate heroic exploits

Hero and Leander. The old Greek tale is that Hero, a priestess of Venus, fell in love with Leander, who swam across the Hellespont every night to visit her One night he was drowned, and heart-broken Hero drowned herself in the same sea The story is told in one of the poems of Musæus, and in Marlowe and Chapman's *Hero and Leander*

Lord Byron and Lieutenant Ekenhead repeated the experiment of Leander in 1810 and accomplished it in 1 hour 10 minutes The distance, allowing for drifting, would be about four miles. In *Don Juan* Byron says of his hero:—

A better swimmer you could scarce see ever, He could, perhaps, have pass'd the Hellespont, As once (a feat on which ourselves we prided) Leander, Mr Ekenhead, and I did
Canto, II, cv

Herod (her' od). **To out-herod Herod.** To outdo in wickedness, violence, or rant, the worst of tyrants Herod, who destroyed the babes of Bethlehem (*Matt* ii, 16), was made (in the ancient mysteries) a ranting, roaring tyrant, the extravagance of his rant being the measure of his bloody-mindedness *Cp* PILATE

Oh, it offends me to the soul to hear a robustious, periwig-pated fellow tear a passion to tatters, to very rags, to split the ears of the groundlings . . it out-herods Herod —*Hamlet,* III, 2

Herrenvolk (hâr ên fõk), a German word, meaning broadly "master race," used in the Nazi philosophy to describe the superiority of the German peoples

Herring. A shotten herring. One that has shot off or ejected its spawn, and hence is worthless

Go thy ways, old Jack; die when thou wilt If man-hood, good manhood, be not forgot upon the face of the earth, then am I a shotten herring. There live not three good men unhanged in England, and one of them is fat and grows old.—I *Henry IV,* II, 4

Drawing a red herring across the path. Trying to divert attention from the main question by some side issue A red herring (*i e* one dried, smoked, and salted) drawn across a fox's path destroys the scent and sets the dogs at fault.

Neither barrel the better herring. Much of a muchness, not a pin to choose between you, six of one and half a dozen of the other The herrings of both barrels are so much alike that there is no choice whatever

Neither fish, flesh, nor good red herring. Neither one thing nor another

The Battle of the Herrings. A sortie made during the Hundred Years War (February 12th, 1429) by the men of Orléans, during the siege of their city, to intercept a supply of food being brought to the besiegers by the English under Sir John Fastolf The English repulsed the onset, using barrels of herrings, which were among the supplies, as a defence; hence the name

The king of the herrings The *Chimæra,* or sea-ape, a cartilaginous fish which accompanies a shoal of herrings in their migrations.

Herring-bone (in building) Courses of stone laid angularly, thus. ←← ←← Also applied to strutting placed between thin joists to increase their strength.

In needlework an embroidery stitch, or alternatively a kind of cross-stitch used to fasten down heavy material

Herring-pond, The. A name humorously given to various dividing seas, especially to the Atlantic, which separates America from the British Isles The English Channel, the North Sea, and the seas between Australasia and the United Kingdom are also so called.

"I'le send an account of the wonders I meet on the Great Herring Pond "—JOHN DUNTON: *Letters from New England,* 1686

Hershey Bar (hêr' shi) In the U S A. a Hershey Bar is a trade-marked form of sweetmeat, in U.S. army slang the term was applied to the gold narrow bar worn by troops on the left sleeve to indicate that they had done six months' overseas service

Hertha. *See* NERTHUS

Hesperia (hes pêr' i a) (Gr., western) Italy was so called by the Greeks, because it was to them the "Western Land"; and afterwards the Romans, for a similar reason, transferred the name to Spain.

Hesperides (hes per' i dēz). Three sisters who guarded the golden apples which Hera received as a marriage gift They were assisted by the dragon Ladon. Hercules, as the last of his "twelve labours," slew the dragon and carried some of the apples to Eurystheus

Many poets call the place where these golden apples grew the "garden of the Hesperides." Shakespeare (*Love's Labour's Lost,* IV, 3) speaks of "climbing trees in the Hesperides " (*See Comus,* lines 402–6)

Show thee the tree, leafed with refined gold, Whereon the fearful dragon held his seat. That watched the garden called Hesperides.
ROBERT GREENE *Friar Bacon and Friar Bungay* (1589).

Hesperus (hes' per ùs) The evening star, because it sets in the west *See* HESPERIA.

> Ere twice in murk and occidental damp
> Moist Hesperus hath quenched his sleepy lamp.
> *All's Well that Ends Well*, ii, 1.

The Wreck of the Hesperus, a ballad once learned by every child at school, written by H W Longfellow in 1842, and based upon an actual disaster at sea

Hessian. A coarse, strong cloth made from jute or hemp originally made in Hesse in Germany. Hessian boots were first worn by troops in Germany and became fashionable in England in the 19th century.

Hetman. A general or commander-in-chief. (Ger. *hauptmann*, chief man) The chief of the Cossacks of the Don used to be so called. He was elected by the people, and the mode of choice was thus · The voters threw their fur caps at the candidate they voted for, and he who had the largest number of caps at his feet was the successful candidate The last elected Hetman was Count Platoff (1812-14)

Hexameron (hek zăm' er òn) Six days taken as one continuous period, especially the six days of the Creation

Hexameter (hek zăm' e tĕr). The metre in which the Greek and Latin epics were written, and which has been imitated in English in such poems as Longfellow's *Evangeline*, Clough's *Bothie*, Kingsley's *Andromeda* (probably the best), etc.

The line consists, says Professor Saintsbury (*Manual of English Prosody*, iv, 1) —

of six feet, dactyls or spondees at choice for the first four, but normally always a dactyl in the fifth and always a spondee in the sixth—the latter foot being by special licence sometimes allowed in the fifth also (in which case the line is called spondaic), but never a dactyl in the sixth To this metre, and to the attempts to imitate it in English, the term should be strictly confined, and never applied to the Alexandrine or iambic trimeter

Verse consisting of alternate hexameters and pentameters (*q v*) is known as elegiac (*q v*). Coleridge illustrates this in his —

> In the hexameter rises the fountain's silvery column;
> In the pentameter aye falling in melody back

The Authorized Version of the Bible furnishes a number of examples of "accidental" hexameter lines, the following are well known —

> How art thou fallen from Heaven, O Lucifer son of the Morning.
> Why do the heathen rage and the people imagine a vain thing?
> God is gone up with a shout, the Lord with the sound of the trumpet

Hiawatha. The Iroquois name of a hero of miraculous birth who came (under a variety of names) among the North American Indian tribes to bring peace and goodwill to man. In Longfellow's poem (1855) he is an Ojibway, son of Mudjekeewis (the west wind) and Wenonah He represents the progress of civilization among the American Indians. He married Minnehaha "Laughing Water." When the white man landed and taught the Indians the faith of Jesus, Hiawatha exhorted them to receive the words of wisdom, to reverence the missionaries who had come so far to see them

Hibernia (hī bĕr' ni a). The Latin name for Ireland, and hence still used in poetry. It is a variant of the old Celtic *Erin*

Hic Jacet. Tombstones, so called from the first two words of their Latin inscriptions "Here lies   "

> By the cold *Hic Jacet* of the dead.
> TENNYSON *Idylls of the King* (*Vivien*)

Hickathrift, Tom (hik' a thrift). A hero of nursery rhyme, fabled to have been a poor labourer in the time of the Conquest, of such enormous strength that, armed with an axletree and cartwheel only, he killed a giant who dwelt in a marsh at Tilney, Norfolk. He was knighted and made governor of Thanet.

Hickory. Hickory cloth. Cloth dyed with hickory juice

> Fumbling in the breast pocket of his hickery shirt
> *Bret Harte*, 1891

Hickory Mormons. Mormons who are only half-hearted adherents to the religion

Old Hickory. General Andrew Jackson (1767-1845), President of the United States, 1829-37 He was first called "Tough," from his great powers of endurance, then "Tough as hickory," and lastly, "Old Hickory."

Hicksites A sect of Quakers in the U.S.A. who seceded from the main body under the leadership of Elias Hicks in 1827.

Hidalgo (hi dăl' gō) The title in Spain of the lower nobility The word is from Lat *filius de aliquo*, son of someone, or, as we should say, the son of a "somebody " In Portuguese it is *Fidalgo*.

Hide of Land. The term applied in Anglo-Saxon times to a portion of land that was sufficient to support a family; usually from 60 to 100 acres, but no fixed number A hide of good arable land was smaller than a hide of inferior quality

Hieroglyphs (hī er ō glifs) The name applied to the picture characters which the Egyptians used in writing The Egyptians called them, "words of the gods," and coming to us through the Greek, *hiero* means sacred, *glyph*, what is carved For many years these inscribed symbols of beasts and birds, men and women, were undecipherable, but in 1822 a French archæologist, J F. Champollion, pieced together an alphabet from the three-language inscription on the Rosetta Stone (*q.v.*) and from those small beginnings the decipherment of hieroglyphic inscriptions has enabled scholars to elucidate the whole history of Egyptian civilization.

Higgledy-piggledy. In great confusion; at sixes and sevens, perhaps with reference to a higgler or pedlar whose stores are all huddled together. *Higgledy* would then mean after the fashion of a higgler's basket; *piggledy* is a ricochet word suggested by this.

High. High-ball, the American term for a drink of whiskey diluted with water, soda-water or ginger ale and served in a tall glass with ice.

Highbinders. Gangsters in New York City in the first decade of the 19th century

High-brow. A self-consciously cultured person; especially one who, in his own estimation at least, is intellectually superior. The terms *low-brow* and *middle-brow* have developed from this

High Church. *See* CHURCH

High days. Festivals On high days and holidays. Here "high" means grand or great

High falutin. Oratorical bombast, affected pomposity, tall talk The word is perhaps a variant of *high-flown*

High hand. With a high hand. Arrogantly. To carry things with a high hand in French would be. *Faire une chose haut la main*

High Heels and Low Heels. The names of two factions in Swift's tale of Lilliput (*Gulliver's Travels*), satirizing the High and Low Church parties

High Mass. *See* MASS.

High places. In the Authorized Version of the Scriptures this is a literal translation of the Hebrew *bamah*, but actually the word was applied to a tribal or village place of worship because such were usually on hilltops or rises in the ground. Such sites usually had a *stele*, the seat of the local god, and a wooden pole, itself an object of worship and often translated in the Old Testament as a "grove." This worship of a local or tribal Baal was a relic of the ancient Canaanitish religion and was long anterior to the cult of Jahwe It was denounced fiercely by the prophet Hosea as idolatry Hezekiah removed the high places (2 *Kings* xviii, 4), so did Asa (2 *Chron* xiv 3), Jehoshaphat (2 *Chron* xvii, 6), Josiah, and others *Cp* HILLS.

High seas All the sea which is not the property of a particular country The sea up to three miles out from the coast belongs to the country, and is called "territorial waters." High seas, like high-ways, means for public use In both cases the word *high* means "chief," "principal." (Lat. *altum*, "the main sea"; *altus*, "high")

High tea. A meal served about the usual teatime which includes besides tea, fish, cold meats, pastry, etc. It is common in Scotland and the North of England, and generally in agricultural communities.

A well understood "high tea" should have cold roast beef at the top of the table, a cold Yorkshire pie at the bottom, a mighty ham in the middle The side dishes will comprise soused mackerel, pickled salmon (in due season), sausages and potatoes, etc, etc Rivers of tea, coffee and ale, with dry and buttered toast, sally-lunns, scones, muffins and crumpets, jams and marmalade —*Daily Telegraph*, May 9th, 1893

High words. Angry words.

Highgate. A North London suburb, so called from a gate set up there about 400 years ago to receive tolls for the bishop of London, when the old miry road from Gray's Inn Lane to Barnet was turned through the bishop's park The village being perched on a hill explains the first part of the name.

Sworn at Highgate. A custom anciently prevailed at the public-houses in Highgate to administer a ludicrous oath to all travellers who stopped there The party was sworn on a pair of horns fastened to a stick—

(1) Never to kiss the maid when he can kiss the mistress.

(2) Never to eat brown bread when he can get white.

(3) Never to drink small beer when he can get strong—unless he prefers it.

Highlands. That part of Scotland lying north of the line approximately from Dumbarton to Stonehaven. Stirling is known as "the gateway to the Highlands", in the wars between Scotland and England, possession of this strong point carried immense advantage

Highland bail. Fists and cuffs, to escape the constable by knocking him down with the aid of a companion

Highland Mary. The most shadowy of Robert Burns's sweethearts, but the one to whom he addressed some of his finest poetry, including "My Highland Lassie, O," "Highland Mary" ("Ye banks and braes and streams around the castle o' Montgomery"), "Thou Ling'ring Star," and—perhaps—"Will ye go to the Indies, my Mary?"

She is said to have been a daughter of Archibald Campbell, a Clyde sailor, and to have died young about 1784 or 1786

Highness. A title of honour (used with a possessive pronoun) given to royalties and a few others of exalted rank In England the title *Royal Highness* was formerly given to the Sovereign, his consort, his sons and daughters, brothers and sisters, paternal uncles and aunts, grandsons and granddaughters being the children of sons, and great-grandchildren being the children of an eldest son of any Prince of Wales, but by the proclamation of June 17th, 1917 (when the style, the House of Windsor, was adopted), the title *Royal Highness* was confined in future to children of the Sovereign and to grandchildren in the male line.

James I was the first King of England to be styled "Your Royal Highness", Oliver Cromwell and his wife were both called "Your Highness."

Serene Highness was a title of many of the members of the former German Imperial, Royal, and Ducal Houses.

Hijacker (hī' jăk er). In American slang a bandit who preys on such criminals as bootleggers by robbing them of their ill-gotten booty, a parasite on rogues

Hike. To hike is an old English dialect word meaning to walk a long distance; it is now used in the sense of going on a cross-country tramp organized by a club or undertaken by a smaller party of two or three

To **hitch-hike** is to travel from one place to another by getting lifts from cars and lorries

Hilary Term (hil' a ri), in the Law Courts, begins on the day after Plough Monday (*q v.*) and ends the Wednesday before Easter It is so called in honour of St. Hilary, whose day is January 13th

Hildebrand (hil' de brănd). The Nestor of German romance His story is told in the *Hildebrandslied*, an Old High German poem, and he also appears in the *Nibelungenlied*, *Dietrich von Bern*, etc Like Maugis among the heroes of

Charlemagne, he was a magician as well as champion

The name is, however, more commonly associated with the great pope St. Gregory VII (c 1020-85) who was elected to the papal chair in 1073. He curbed the temporal power and reformed the Church from top to bottom, enforced celibacy among the clergy, put down simony, and promoted piety. His uncompromising forcefulness made him many enemies and gained him few friends He was canonized in 1728, his feast day being May 25th

Hildesheim (hil' des him). Legend relates that a monk of Hildesheim, an old city of Hanover, doubting how with God a thousand years could be as one day, listened to the singing of a bird in a wood, as he thought for three minutes, but found the time had been three hundred years. Longfellow introduced this tale in his *Golden Legend*, calling the monk Felix.

Hill. Hill-billy, an American phrase descriptive of a countryman from the hilly or mountainous districts The hill-billy is a distinctive type, whose music and literature are being increasingly studied

Hill folk. So Scott calls the Cameronian Scottish Covenanters, who met clandestinely among the hills Sometimes the Covenanters generally are so called.

A class of beings in Scandinavian tradition between the elves and the human race were known as "hill folk" or "hill people" They were supposed to dwell in caves and small hills, and to be bent on receiving the benefits of man's redemption

Hills. Prayers were offered on the tops of high hills, and temples built on "high places," from the notion that the gods could better hear prayers on such places, as they were nearer heaven It will be remembered that Balak (*Num* xxiii, xxiv) took Balaam to the top of Peor and other high places when Balaam wished to consult God We often read of "idols on every high hill" (*Ezek* vi, 13) *Cp.* HIGH PLACES

Old as the hills. Very old indeed.

Hinc illæ lachrymæ (hingk il ē lăk' ri mē) (Lat , "hence those tears " Terence, *Andria*, I, i, 99) This was the real offence, this was the true secret of the annoyance, the real source of the vexation

Lady Loadstone He keeps off all her suitors, keeps the portion.
Still in his hands, and will not part withal,
On any terms
Palate Hinc illæ lachrymæ
Thence flows the cause of the main grievance
BEN JONSON *Magnetic Lady*, i, 1.

Hind. Emblematic of St. Giles, because "a heaven-directed hind went daily to give him milk in the desert, near the mouth of the Rhone " *Cp* HART

The hind of Sertorius. Sertorius was invited by the Lusitanians to defend them against the Romans. He had a tame white hind, which he taught to follow him, and from which he pretended to receive the instructions of Diana. By this artifice, says Plutarch, he imposed on the superstition of the people.

The milk-white hind, in Dryden's *Hind and the Panther,* means the Roman Catholic Church, milk-white because "infallible " The panther, full of the spots of error, is the Church of England.

Without unspotted, innocent within,
She feared no danger, for she knew no sin
Part i, 3, 4

Hindustan (hin doo stan´) India, properly, the country watered by the river Indus, i e the country known by the ancients as "India " From Pers *hindu,* water, *stan,* district or region The suffix is common in the East, as Afghanistan, Baluchistan, Gulistan (the district of roses), Kafiristan (the country of the unbelievers), etc *See* INDIA

Hindustan Regiment. *See* REGIMENTAL NICKNAMES

Hinny. *See* MULE

Hip. To have one on the hip. To have the mastery over him in a struggle.

"Now, infidel, I have thee on the hip" (*Merchant of Venice*), and again, "I'll have our Michael Cassio on the hip" (*Othello*) The term is derived from a throw in wrestling.

In fine he doth apply one speciall drift,
Which was to get the pagan on the hip,
And having caught him right, he doth him lift
By nimble sleight, and in such wise doth trip,
That down he threw him
SIR J. HARINGTON *Orlando Furioso,* XLVI, cxvii, 4

To smite hip and thigh. To slay with great carnage A Biblical phrase
And he smote them hip and thigh with great slaughter.—*Judges* xv, 8.

Hipped. Melancholy, low-spirited, suffering from a "fit of the blues." The hip was formerly a common expression for morbid depression (now superseded by *the pip*), it is an abbreviation of *hypochondria*

Hip! Hip! Hurrah! The old fanciful explanation of the origin of this cry is that *hip* is a notarikon (q v.), composed of the initials *Hierosolyma est Perdita,* and that when the German knights headed a Jew-hunt in the Middle Ages, they ran shouting "Hip! Hip!" as much as to say "Jerusalem is destroyed "

Hurrah (q v) was derived from Slavonic *hu-raj* (to Paradise), so that *Hip! hip! hurrah!* would mean "Jerusalem is lost to the infidel, and we are on the road to Paradise " These etymons may be taken for what they are worth! The older English form of this cry was Huzza!

Hipper-switches. A dialect name for coarse willow withes A *hipper* is a coarse osier used in basket-making, and an osier field is a *hipper-nolm* A suburb of Halifax, Yorks, is called Hipperholme-with-Brighouse.

Hippo (hip' ō) Bishop of Hippo. A title by which St. Augustine (354-430) is sometimes designated. Hippo was a town in Numidia, N Africa, near the modern Bona It was destroyed by the Vandals in 430

Hippocampus (hip' ō kăm' pus) (Gr *hippos,* horse, *kampos,* sea monster) A seahorse, having the head and forequarters resembling those of a horse, with the tail and hindquarters of a fish or dolphin It was the steed of Neptune (*q v*)

Hippocras (hip' ŏ krăs) A cordial of the late Middle Ages and down to Stuart times made of Lisbon and Canary wines, bruised spices, and sugar, so called from being passed through Hippocrates' sleeve (*q v*)

When these [*i e* other wines] have had their course which nature yeeldeth, sundrie sorts of artificial stuffe as ypocras and wormewood wine, must in like maner succeed in their turnes —*Harrison's Description of England*, II, vi (1577)

Hippocrates (hip ok' rȧ tēz) A Greek physician who lived from *c.* 460-377 B C, and is commonly called the Father of Medicine He was member of the famous family of priest-physicians, the Asclepiadae, and was an acute and indefatigable observer, practising as both physician and surgeon More than seventy of his essays are extant In the Middle Ages he was called "Ypocras" or "Hippocras" Thus

Well knew he the old Esculapius,
And Deiscorides, and eek Rufus,
Old Ypocras, Haly, and Galien
CHAUCER. *Canterbury Tales* (*Prologue*, 431).

Hippocratean School. The "Dogmatic" school of medicine, founded by Hippocrates. *See* EMPIRICS

Hippocrates' sleeve. A woollen bag of a square piece of flannel, having the opposite corners joined, so as to make it triangular Used by chemists for straining syrups, decoctions, etc, and anciently by vintners, whence the name of Hippocras (*q v*)

Hippocratic oath A code of ethics governing the profession and sworn to by physicians upon taking a doctor's degree. The oath relates particularly to the inviolability of secrecy concerning any communication made by a patient in the course of consultation, and enjoins the absolute integrity essential in dealing with problems arising from a patient's confession or revelation

Hippocrene (hip' ŏ krēn) (Gr *hippos*, horse; *krene*, fountain). The fountain of the Muses on Mount Helicon, produced by a stroke of the hoof of Pegasus; hence poetic inspiration.

O for a beaker full of the warm South.
Full of the true, the blushful Hippocrene,
With beaded bubbles winking at the brim
And purple-stained mouth,
That I might drink, and leave the world unseen.
KEATS *Ode to a Nightingale*

Hippodamia. *See* BRISEIS

Hippogriff (hip' ŏ grif) (Gr *hippos*, a horse, *gryphos*, a griffin) The winged horse, whose father was a griffin and mother a filly. A symbol of love (Ariosto: *Orlando Furioso*, iv, 18, 19).

So saying, he caught him up, and without wing
Of hippogrif, bore through the air sublime,
Over the wilderness and o'er the plain
MILTON: *Paradise Regained*, iv, 541-3

Hippolyta (hip ol' i tȧ). Queen of the Amazons, and daughter of Mars Shakespeare has introduced the character in his *A Midsummer Night's Dream*, where he betroths her to Theseus, Duke of Athens. In classic fable it is her sister Antiope who married Theseus, al-

though some writers justify Shakespeare's account Hippolyta was famous for a girdle given her by her father, and it was one of the twelve labours of Hercules to possess himself of this prize

Hippolytus (hip ol' it ŭs) Son of Theseus, King of Athens He was dragged to death by wild horses, and restored to life by Esculapius

Hippomenes (hip om' en ēz). The name given in Boeotian legend to the Greek prince who ran a race with Atalanta (*q v*) for her hand in marriage. He had three golden apples, which he dropped one by one, and which the lady stopped to pick up By this delay she lost the race

Hiram Abif (hī' ram a bif') is a central figure in the legend and ritual of Freemasonry Under the name of Huram he appears in II *Chron.* ii and iii, as the craftsman builder of Solomon's Temple, he must not be confused with Hiram King of Tyre, who supplied much of the material

Hiren. A strumpet She was a character in Greene's lost play (about 1594), *The Turkish Mahomet and Hyren the Fair Greek*, and is frequently referred to by Elizabethan dramatists. *See* 2 *Henry IV*, ii, 4, Dekker's *Satiromastix* IV, iii, Massinger's *Old Law*, IV, i, Chapman's *Eastward Hoe*, II, i, etc The name is a corruption of the Greek "Irene"

Hiroshima (hi rō shē' mȧ), a Japanese army base and a city of 343,000 inhabitants, was the target of the first atomic bomb to be dropped in warfare, August 6th, 1945 The flash of the explosion was seen 170 miles away, and a column of black smoke rose over the city to a height of 40,000 feet The entire business section of Hiroshima disappeared, 60,000 persons were killed, 100,000 injured, and twice that number made homeless

Hispania (his păn' ya) Spain So called from the Phœnician word *Sapan*, or *Span*, the skin of the marten (or perhaps rabbit), which was procured from Spain in great quantities.

Hispaniola (his păn yō' la), the old name for the island of Haiti When Columbus discovered the island on his first voyage, 1492, he named it Española, or Little Spain, which in the maps was Latinized as above It was not until 1844, when the island was divided politically into Haiti and the Dominican Republic, that the old name completely disappeared

History. The Father of History. Herodotus, the Greek historian (5th cent B.C) So called by Cicero.

The Father of Ecclesiastical History. Eusebius of Cæsarea (about 264-340)

Father of French History. André Duchesne (1584-1640).

Father of Historic Painting. Polygnotus of Thaos (fl 463-435. B C)

Happy is the nation that has no history. *See* HAPPY

Histrionic, pertaining to the drama or to theatrical matters, is from the Lat. *histrio*, a stage-player *History* is quite another word, being the Greek *historia*, *histor*, a judge, allied to *histamai*, to know

Hit. A great hit. A piece of good luck From the game *hit and miss*, or the game of backgammon, where "two hits equal a gammon "

Hitting on all six. Doing well, giving a fine performance. The phrase comes from motoring, where an engine which is running well is described as having the pistons in all six cylinders hitting perfectly

To hit it off. To describe a thing tersely and epigrammatically, to make a sketch truthfully and quickly

To hit it off together. To agree together, or suit each other.

To hit the nail on the head *See* HEAD.

To make a hit. To meet with great approval, to succeed unexpectedly in an adventure or speculation

Hitch. Hitch your wagon to a star. Aim high, don't be content with low aspirations The phrase is from Emerson's essay *Civilization*. Young expressed much the same idea in his *Night Thoughts* (VIII) —

Too low they build who build beneath the stars.

There is some hitch. Some impediment. A horse is said to have a hitch in his gait when he is lame

To hitch. To get on smoothly; to fit in consistently, also, to harness as, "You and I hitch on well together", "These two accounts do not hitch in with each other "

To hitch-hike *See* HIKE

Hitlerism, a generic term for the whole doctrine and practice of Fascism, exemplified in the regime of Adolf Hitler (1889-1945)

Hittites built up one of the ancient civilizations of the world. Little is known of their origin, they first appear in eastern Asia Minor where their superior knowledge of implements and weapons of the early copper-age culture enabled them to master all their foes They also bred and harnessed the horse—one of the earliest people to do so The Hittites were well established by the 3rd millennium B.C , they overturned the first dynasty of Babylon in 1925 B C and in one form or another flourished until about 700 B C when Carchemish, their main city fell to the Assyrians.

Hoarstone. A stone marking out the boundary of an estate, properly an old, grey, lichen-covered stone They are also called "Hour-stones" and (in Scotland) "Hare Stanes," and have been erroneously taken for Druidical remains

Hob and nob. *See* HOB-NOB.

Hobbema (hob' e må). Meindert Hobbema (1638-1709) was a Dutch landscape painter

The English Hobbema. John Crome (1768-1821), "Old Crome," of Norwich, whose last words were, "O Hobbema, Hobbema, how I do love thee!"

The Scottish Hobbema. Patrick Nasmyth (born at Edinburgh, 1787, died 1831), the landscape painter, was so called.

Hobbinol (hob' i nol) The shepherd in Spenser's *Shepherd's Calendar* who sings in praise of Eliza, queen of shepherds (Queen Elizabeth). He typifies Spenser's friend and correspondent Gabriel Harvey (c 1545-1630), the poet and writer.

Hobbism. The principles of Thomas Hobbes (1588-1679), author of *Leviathan* (1651) He taught that religion is a mere engine of state, and that man acts wholly on a consideration of self, even his benevolent acts spring from the pleasure he experiences in doing acts of kindness.

Hobbledehoy. A raw, awkward young fellow, neither man nor boy. The word is generally taken as being connected with *hobble*, in reference to an awkward, clumsy gait, but this is hardly borne out by the early forms of the word, which include such spellings as *hobbard de hoy*, *habber de hoy*, *hobet a hoy*, etc The first syllable is probably *hob*, a clown, as seen in *Hobbididance*, *Hobbinol*, etc , and is connected with *Robert* or *Robin*, as in *Robin Goodfellow* There is very little etymological support for the theory that would connect the word with *hobby* hawk

The first seven yeeres bring up as a childe,
The next to learning, for waxing too wide
The next keepe under sir hobbard de hoy,
The next a man, no longer a boy.

TUSSER *Hundred Good Points* (1573)

Hobblers or Hovellers. An old name for long-shoremen—especially on the Kentish coast—who acted as pilots although they were not licensed, and got their living by rendering casual assistance to vessels in distress, plundering wrecks, warning smugglers, etc

The word was also applied to seafaring men whose duties were to reconnoitre, carry intelligence, harass stragglers, act as spies, intercept convoys, pursue fugitives, etc.

Hobblers were another description of cavalry more lightly armed, and taken from the class of men rated at 15 pounds and upwards —LINGARD *History of England*, vol IV, ch II

Hobble Skirts This women's fashion of skirts so tight round the ankles that the wearer was impeded in walking—much as a horse is hobbled—was at its height in 1912 and was gone by 1914

Hobby. A favourite pursuit, a personal pastime that interests or amuses one.

There are two words *hobby*, and they are apt to be confused The earlier, meaning a medium-sized horse, is the M E *hobyn* (cp *Dobbin* as a name for a horse), the later, a small species of falcon, is the O F *hobé* or *hobet*, from Lat *hobetus*, a falcon. It is from the first that our "hobby," a pursuit, comes It is through **hobby-horse**, a light frame of wickerwork, appropriately draped, in which someone performed ridiculous gambols in the old morris dances, and later applied to a child's plaything consisting of a stick across which he straddled, with a horse's head on one end

To ride a hobby-horse was to play an infantile game of which one soon tired, and now implies to dwell to excess on a pet theory, the transition is shown in a sentence in one of Wesley's sermons (No lxxxiii).—

Every one has (to use the cant term of the day) his hobby-horse!

Hobgoblin (hob gob' lin). An impish, ugly, and mischievous sprite particularly Puck or Robin Goodfellow (*q v*) The word is a variant of *Rob-Goblin—i e.* the goblin Robin, just as Hodge is the nickname of Roger

> Those that Hobgoblin call you, and sweet Puck,
> You do their work, and they shall have good luck.
> *A Midsummer Night's Dream*, ii, 1

Hob-nob. A corruption of *hab nab*, meaning "have or not have," hence hit or miss, at random, and, secondarily, give or take, whence also an open defiance

> The citizens in their rage shot habbe or nabbe [hit or miss] at random —HOLINSHED *History of Ireland*

> He writes of the weather hab nab and as the toy takes him, chequers the year with foul and fair.— *Quack Astrologer* (1673)

> He is a devil in private brawls hob nob is his word, give 't or take 't —*Twelfth Night*, iii, 4

> Not of Jack Straw, with his rebellious crew,
> That set king, realm and laws at hab or nab [defiance]　　　SIR J HARINGTON: *Epigram*, iv

To hobnob or hob and nob together To be on intimate terms of good-fellowship, hold close and friendly conversation with, etc ; especially to drink together as cronies—probably with the meaning of "give and take"

> "Have another glass'" "With you Hob and nob," returned the sergeant "The top of mine to the foot of yours—the foot of yours to the top of mine—Ring once, ring twice—the best tune on the Musical Glasses' Your health "—DICKENS *Great Expectations*, ch v

Hobo (hō' bō). Late-19th-century American for a tramp, vagrant

Hobson's Choice. This or none. Thomas Hobson (*c* 1544-1631) was a carrier and innkeeper at Cambridge who erected the handsome conduit there, and settled "seven lays" of pasture ground towards its maintenance "He kept a stable of forty good mounts, always ready and fit for travelling, but when a man came for a horse he was led into the stable, where there was another choice, but he obliged him to take the horse which stood nearest to the stable door, so that every customer was alike well served according to his chance, and every horse ridden with the same justice " (*Spectator*, No 509)

Milton wrote two epitaphs upon this eccentric character

Hob's Pound. Difficulties, great embarrassment To be in Hob's pound is to be in the pound of a *hob* or *hoberd—i e.* a fool or ne er-do-well—paying for one's folly.

Hock. German white wine, so called from Hockheim, on the River Main It used to be called hoccamore

> Restored the fainting high and mighty
> With brandy, wine, and aqua-vitæ,
> And made 'em stoutly overcome
> With Bacrack, Hoccamore, and Mum
> 　　　　　BUTLER *Hudibras*, III, iii, 297

The earlier English name was *Rhenish*

There are several colloquial uses of this word hock. In American slang to hock is to pawn and a **hock-shop** a pawnbroker's

Hock cart. The last cartload of harvest; probably connected with *hockey*

> The harvest swains and wenches bound,
> For joy, to see the hock cart crowned.
> 　　　　　HERRICK *Hesperides*, p 114

Hockey cake. The cake given out to the harvesters when the hock cart (*q v.*) reached home　*Hockey* is the old name in the eastern counties for the harvest-home feast.

Hock-day or **Hock Tuesday.** The second Tuesday after Easter Day, long held as a festival in England, it was the time for paying church dues, and landlords received an annual tribute called Hock-money, for allowing their tenants and serfs to commemorate it. Its origin is unknown; but the old idea that it commemorates the massacre of the Danes in 1002 does not seem to be tenable, as this took place in November.

> Hoke Monday was for the men and Hock Tuesday for the women On both days the men and women alternately, with great merryment, obstructed the public road with ropes, and pulled passengers to them, from whom they exacted money to be laid out in pious uses —BRAND *Antiquities*, vol. i, p 187

Hockey. A game of Indian origin in which each player has a hooked stick with which to strike the ball. Hockey is simply the diminutive of *hook*

Hockley-i'-the-Hole. Public gardens near Clerkenwell Green, famous in Restoration times for bear- and bull-baiting, dog- and cock-fights, etc , and for its butchers. Pope called Colley Cibber—

> This mess, tossed up of Hockley-hole and White's,
> Where dukes and butchers join to wreathe my crown
> At once the bear and fiddle of the town
> 　　　　　*Dunciad*, I, 222

Hocus Pocus (hō' kus pō' kus) The words formerly uttered by conjurers when performing a trick, hence the trick or deception itself, also the juggler himself

The phrase dates from the early 17th century, and is the opening of a ridiculous string of mock Latin used by some well-known performer (*Hocus pocus, toutus talontus, vade celerita jubes*), the first two words of which may have been intended as a parody of *Hoc est corpus*, the words of consecration in the Mass, while the whole was reeled off merely to occupy the attention of the audience

Our word *hoax* is probably a contraction of *hocus pocus*, which also supplies the verb *to hocus*, to cheat, bamboozle, tamper with.

Hodge. A familiar and slightly contemptuous name for a farm labourer or peasant, an abbreviated form of Roger, as Hob is of Robert or Robin.

Hodge-podge. A medley, a mixed dish of "bits and pieces all cooked together " The word is a corruption of *hotch-pot* (*q v*)

Hodmandod. *See* DODMAN.

Hoe-cake (U S.A) Flat cake originally baked on a hoe held over a coal fire.

Hog. Properly a male swine, castrated, and— as it is raised solely for slaughter—killed young. The origin of the word is not certain, but it may originally have referred to age more than to any specific animal Thus, boars of the second year, sheep between the time of their being weaned and shorn, colts, and bullocks a year old, were all called *hogs* or *hoggets*, which name was specially applied to a sheep after its first shearing A boar three years old is a "hog-steer."

In slang use a *hog* is a gluttonous, greedy, or unmannered person, motorists who, caring nothing for the rights or convenience of other travellers, drive in a selfish and reckless manner wanting the whole road to themselves are called *road-hogs*

Hog in armour. A person of awkward manners dressed so fine that he cannot move easily, perhaps a corruption of "*Hodge* in armour" See HODGE

Hog-shearing. Much ado about nothing "It's great cry and little wool, as the Devil said when he sheared his hogs." *See* CRY

To go the whole hog. To do the thing completely and thoroughly, without compromise or reservation; to go the whole way. William Cowper says (*Hypocrisy Detected*, 1779) that the Moslem divines sought to ascertain which part of the hog was forbidden as food by the Prophet Unable to come to a decision, each thought excepted the portion of the meat he most preferred, and as the tastes of the worthy imams differed ·

> The conscience freed from every clog.
> Mohammedans eat up the hog.

A more probable origin of the phrase is that a *hog* was old slang for a shilling—*to go the whole hog* was to spend the whole shilling at one go, to spare nothing

Formerly, any small silver coin, a shilling or sixpence, or (in the U.S.A) a ten-cent piece, was contemptuously styled a *hog*

In U.S A the phrase came into popularity during Andrew Jackson's campaign for the Presidency, in 1828 Hence the expression *whole-hogger*, one who will see the thing through to the bitter end, and "damn the consequences." At the time of Joseph Chamberlain's agitation on behalf of Protection (1903, *et seq*) those who advocated a complete tariff of protective duties regardless of possible reciprocity were called the *whole-hoggers*

As independent as a hog on ice. Supremely confident, cocky, self-assured. A phrase common in the U S.A Its origin is unknown, though it may be Scottish, having some connexion with the hog used in curling The phrase is discussed amusingly and in detail by Charles Earle Funk in his book *A Hog on Ice.*

To drive one's hogs to market. To snore very loudly

To hear as a hog in harvest. In at one ear and out at the other; hear without paying attention Giles Firmin says, "If you call hogs out of the harvest stubble, they will just lift up their heads to listen, and fall to their shack again " (*Real Christian*, 1670)

You have brought your hogs to a fine market. You have made a pretty kettle of fish; said in derision when one's projects turn out ill.

To hog it, in English colloquial usage means to live in a rough, uncouth fashion amid crude surroundings, in American *to hog it* is to act selfishly and greedily, to grasp everything for oneself

Hog and hominy (U.S A) Pork and maize, considered inferior food

Hog-wallows. American prairie which has become a series of mounds and depressions through the alternate action of rain and drought

Hogen Mogen (hō' gen mō' gen) Holland or the Netherlands; so called from *Hooge en Mogende* (high and mighty), the Dutch style of addressing the States-General.

> But I have sent him for a token
> To your low country Hogen-Mogen
> BUTLER *Hudibras* III, i, 1440

Hogmanay (hog ma nā´) The name given in Scotland to the last day of the year, also to an entertainment or present given on that day. It is from the French, and probably represents the O Fr *aiguillanneuf*, which has been (somewhat doubtfully) explained as standing for *au guy l'an neuf*, "(good luck) to the mistletoe of the new year."

It is still the custom in parts of Scotland for persons to go from door to door on New Year's Eve asking in rude rhymes for cakes or money; and in Galloway the chief features are "taking the cream off the water," wonderful luck being attached to a draught thereof, and "the first foot" (*q v*) or giving something to drink to the first person who enters the house

Hogni. *See* HAGEN

Hogshead. A large cask containing approximately 52½ gallons; also, the measure of this, apart from the cask The word dates from the 14th century and is composed of *hog* and *head*, and not of *ox* and *hide*, or of any of the other fancy etymologies that have been proposed. The reason for the name is obscure, but *cp.* the name of a Low German measure for beer, *bullenkop*, bull's head

Hogs-Norton. A village in Oxfordshire, now called Hook Norton I think you were born at Hogs-Norton. A reproof to an ill-mannered person The place has been made famous over the radio by the English comedian Gillie Potter who described in erudite fashion a long series of unlikely events taking place in this village

> I think thou wast born at Hoggs-Norton where piggs play upon the organs —HOWELL. *English Proverbs* (1660)

Hoi Polloi (hoi pol' oi) (Gr , the many). The masses of the people, the majority.

> If by the people you understand the multitude, the *hoi polloi*, 'tis no matter what they think, they are sometimes in the right, sometimes in the wrong, their judgment is a mere lottery —DRYDEN *Essay on Dramatic Poesy* (1668)

At the Universities the poll-men, *i e.* those who take a degree without honours, are colloquially known as the *hoi polloi.*

Hoity-toity. A reduplicated word (like *harum-scarum, mingle-mangle, hugger-mugger,* etc.). probably formed from the obsolete verb *hoit,* to romp about noisily. It is used as an adjective, meaning "stuck up," haughty, or petulant; as a noun, meaning a good romp or frolic, and as an interjection expressing disapproval or contempt of one's airs, assumptions etc.

> "I do not speak on your account, Mrs Honour" [said Mrs Western's maid], "for you are a civilized young woman, and when you have seen a little more of the world, I should not be ashamed to walk with you in St. James Park " "Hoity toity!" cries Honour, "Madam is in her airs, I protest."—FIELDING *Tom Jones.* Bk vii, ch viii

See also the quotation from Selden given under CUSHION DANCE, where *hoyte-cum-toyte* is used of rowdy behaviour

Hokey-pokey (hō' kı pō' kı), the name given to cheap ice-cream as sold in the street The name comes from hocus-pocus (*q.v*) but the connexion is not obvious Also a ludicrous dance popular during the 1940s in English dance-halls

Hokum (hō' kum), an American colloquialism (also deriving from hocus-pocus) for any device employed to create a poignant effect or stimulate easy sentimentality

Holborn. This London name, originally that of the northern portion of the Fleet stream, is not a corruption of Old Bourne, as Stow asserts, but of Holeburne, the *burne* or stream in the *hole* or hollow It is spelt Holeburne in *Domesday Book*, i, 127a, and in documents connected with the nunnery of St Mary, Clerkenwell (during the reign of Richard II).

To ride backwards up Holborn Hill To go to be hanged. The way to Tyburn from Newgate was up Holborn Hill which led steeply from Farringdon Street to what is now Holborn Circus, and criminals used to sit or stand with their backs to the horse when drawn to the place of execution

> I shall live to see you ride up Holborn Hill —CON-GREVE *Love for Love*

The spanning of the valley by Holborn Viaduct (1867-69) did away with the old hill

Hold. Hold hard! Stop; go easy; keep a firm hold, seat, or footing, as there is danger else of being overthrown A caution given when a sudden change of *vis inertiæ* is about to occur.

Hold off! Keep at a distance

Hold the fort! Maintain your position at all costs. Immortalized as a phrase from its use by General Sherman, who signalled it to General Corse from the top of Kenesaw in 1864 during the American Civil War.

To cry hold. To give the order to stop, in the old tournaments, when the umpires wished to stop the contest they cried out "Hold!"

> Lay on Macduff,
> And damn'd be him that first cries, "Hold, enough!"
> *Macbeth*, v, 8.

To hold the candle to one, a candle to the devil *See* CANDLE

To hold forth. To speak in public, to harangue, to declaim. An author holds forth certain opinions or ideas in his book, *i e*. exhibits them or holds them out to view A speaker does the same in an oratorical display.

Hold your horses! Be patient, wait a moment, hold up for a while whatever you are doing

To hold good. To be valid, or applicable. We say "such and such a proverb is very true, but it does not hold good in every case," *i e* it does not always apply.

To hold in. To restrain. The allusion is to horses reined up tightly.

To hold in esteem. To regard with esteem

To hold on one's way. To proceed steadily, to go on without taking notice of interruptions or being delayed.

To hold one guilty To adjudge or regard as guilty.

To hold one in hand or in play To divert one's attention, or to amuse in order to get some advantage.

To hold one's own. To maintain one's own opinion, position, way, etc.

To hold one's tongue. To keep silence In Coverdale's Bible (1535), where the Authorized Version has "But Jesus held his peace" (*Matt.* xxvi, 63) the reading is "Jesus helde his tonge "

To hold out. To endure, persist; not to succumb.

To hold over. To keep back, retain in reserve, defer.

To hold up To stop, as a highwayman does, with the object of robbing In this connexion the order, ' Hold up your hands!" or "Hold 'em up!" means that the victim must hold them above his head to make sure that he is not reaching for a weapon

To hold water. To bear close inspection; to endure a trial; generally used negatively, as "That statement of yours won't hold water," *i e* it will prove false as soon as it is examined. A vessel that will hold water is sound.

Holding the bag. In an awkward predicament, held responsible for faults committed by others.

Holdfast. A means by which something is clamped to another, a support.

Brag is a good dog, but Holdfast is a better. *See* BRAG

Hole. A better 'ole. Any situation that is preferable to that occupied at present The phrase dates from World War I when it originated from a drawing by the humorist Bruce Bairnsfather, depicting "Old Bill" taking cover in a wet and muddy shell-hole and rebutting the complaints of his companion with the remark "If you know a better 'ole, go to it "

Fox-hole. World War II. A phrase of U.S A. origin for a small slit-trench to hold one man.

In a hole. In an awkward predicament; in a difficulty or a position from which it is not easy to extricate oneself

It is a hole and corner business. There's something "fishy" about it—it is underhand, secret for a bad or shady purpose.

To make a hole in anything. To consume a considerable portion of it

To pick holes in. To find fault with; properly, to *cause* some depreciation and then complain of it The older phrase was *to pick a hole in one's coat.*

> And shall such mob as thou, not worth a groat,
> Dare pick a hole in such a great man's coat?
> PETER PINDAR *Epistle to John Nichols*

Holger Danske (hol' ger dān' skē) The national hero of Denmark. *See* OGIER THE DANE.

Holiday. Give the boys a holiday. This custom of marking some specially noteworthy event is of great antiquity, it is said that Anaxagoras, on his death-bed, being asked what honour should be conferred upon him, replied, "Give the boys a holiday"

Holiday speeches. Fine or well-turned speeches or phrases; complimentary speeches. We have also "holiday manners," "holiday clothes," meaning the best we have

With many holiday and lady terms
He questioned me
1 *Henry IV*, i, 3.

Holidays of Obligation, days on which Catholics are bound to hear Mass and rest from servile works They are all Sundays, Christmas Day, the Circumcision (January 1st), the Epiphany (January 6th), Ascension Day (40th day after Easter Sunday), Corpus Christi (Thursday after Trinity Sunday), S S Peter and Paul (June 29th), the Assumption of the B.V M. (August 15th), All Saints (November 1st), the Immaculate Conception (December 8th), St Joseph (March 19th) The last two are not observed in England and Wales; Epiphany, Corpus Christi, St. Peter and Paul, and St. Joseph are not kept in the U S A.

Holland. The country gets its name from the well-wooded (*holt*, wood) land around Dordrecht, to which it was originally applied, the district in South Lincolnshire is called "Holland" from *holl* (*adj.*), lying in a hollow, *i e.* low-lying land

Holland, the cloth, is so called because it was originally manufactured in, and imported from, Holland; its full name was *holland cloth*. **Hollands,** or properly **Hollands gin,** is the Dut. *Hollandsch geneveer.*

Hollow. I beat him hollow. Completely, thoroughly. *Hollow* is, perhaps, here a corruption of *wholly*

Holly. The custom of decking the interiors of churches and houses with holly at Christmastime is of great antiquity, and was probably employed by the early Christians at Rome in imitation of its use by the Romans in the great festival of the Saturnalia, which occurred at the same season of the year

Hollyhock is the A S *holihoc*, the *holy mallow*, *i e.* the marsh-mallow. It is a mistake to derive the second syllable from *oak*.

Holmes. *See* Sherlock Holmes

Holy. Holy Alliance. A league formed by Russia, Austria, and Prussia in 1815 to regulate the affairs of Europe after the fall of Napoleon "by the principles of Christian charity"—meaning that every endeavour would be made to stabilize the existing dynasties and to resist all change It lasted until 1830, and was joined by all the European sovereigns except George III, the Sultan of Turkey and the Pope

Holy Boys, The. The Royal Norfolk Regiment, the 9th Foot The regimental badge is a figure of Britannia, and in the Peninsular War the Spaniards thought this was a representation of the Virgin Mary, hence the nickname. A detachment of the regiment buried Sir John Moore, at Corunna, in 1809, and in full dress all officers still wear a strip of mourning in his memory.

Holy City. That city which the religious consider most especially connected with their faith, thus·

Allahabad is the Holy City of the Moslems of India
Benares of the Hindus
Cuzco of the ancient Incas
Fez of the Western Arabs.
Jerusalem of the Jews and Christians.
Kairwan, near Tunis contains the Okbar Mosque in which is the tomb of the prophet's barber
Mecca and *Medina* as the places of the birth and burial of Mohammed
Moscow and *Kief* of the Russians, the latter being the cradle of Christianity in Russia

Holy Coat. *See* Trèves

Holy Cross (or **Holy Rood**) **Day** September 14th, the day of the Feast of the Exaltation of the Cross, called by the Anglo-Saxons "Roodmass-day," commemorating the return of the true Cross to Jerusalem by the Emperor Heraclius in 627, after retaking it from the Persians who had carried it off thirteen years before.

It was on this day that the Jews in Rome used to be compelled to go to church, and listen to a sermon—a custom done away with about 1840 by Pope Gregory XVI *See* Browning's *Holy Cross Day* (1855)

Holy Family. The infant Saviour and his attendants, as Joseph, Mary, Elizabeth, Anne the mother of Mary, and John the Baptist. All five figures are not always introduced in pictures of the "Holy Family."

Holy Ghost, The. The third Person of the Trinity, the Divine Spirit, represented in art as a dove.

The seven gifts of the Holy Ghost are (1) counsel, (2) the fear of the Lord, (3) fortitude, (4) piety, (5) understanding, (6) wisdom, and (7) knowledge.

The Order of the Holy Ghost A French order of knighthood (*Ordre du Saint-Esprit*), instituted by Henri III in 1578 to replace the Order of St Michael It was limited to 100 knights, and has not been revived since the revolution of 1830

The Procession of the Holy Ghost. *See* Filioque.

Holy Isle. Lindisfarne, in the North Sea, about eight miles from Berwick-upon-Tweed Chosen by St. Aidan in 635 as the head of this diocese, and (685-87) the see of St Cuthbert, it is now in the diocese of Durham. The ruins of the old cathedral are still visible

Ireland was called the Holy Island on account of its numerous saints.

Guernsey was so called in the 10th century in consequence of the great number of monks residing there

Holy Land, The.
(1) Christians call Palestine the Holy Land, because it was the site of Christ's birth, ministry, and death.
(2) Mohammedans call Mecca the Holy Land, because Mohammed was born there
(3) The Chinese Buddhists call India the Holy Land, because it was the native land of Sakya-muni, the Buddha (*q.v*).
(4) The Greeks considered Elis as Holy Land, from the temple of Olympian Zeus and the sacred festival held there every four years

Holy League, The. A combination formed by Pope Julius II in 1511 with Venice, Maximilian of Germany, Ferdinand III of Spain, and various Italian princes, to drive the French out of Italy.

Other leagues have been called by the same name, particularly that formed in the reign of Henri III of France (1576), under the auspices of Henri de Guise, "for the defence of the Holy Catholic Church against the encroachments of the reformers," i.e for annihilating the Huguenots

Holy Maid of Kent, The. Elizabeth Barton (c 1506-34) who incited the Roman Catholics to resist the Reformation, and imagined that she acted under inspiration. Having announced the doom and speedy death of Henry VIII for his marriage with Anne Boleyn, she was hanged at Tyburn in 1534

Holy Office, The. See INQUISITION.

Holy of Holies. The innermost apartment of the Jewish temple, in which the ark of the covenant was kept, and into which only the high priest was allowed to enter, and that but once a year on the Day of Atonement Hence a private apartment, a *sanctum sanctorum* (q v)

Holy Orders. See ORDERS

Holy places. Places in which the chief events of our Saviour's life occurred, such as the sepulchre, Gethsemane, the supper-room, the Church of the Ascension, the tomb of the Virgin and so on

In 1852 a dispute between Greek and Latin religions as to the custody of the holy places at Jerusalem, followed by the diplomatic rivalries of their respective patrons, Russia and France, produced a crisis —MORLEY *Life of Gladstone*, Bk. iv, ch. iii.

Holy Roman Empire, The. The name given to the confederation of Central European States that subsisted, either in fact or in theory, from A D. 800, when Charlemagne was crowned Emperor of the West, until 1806 It was first called "Holy" by Barbarossa, in allusion both to its reputed divine appointment, and to the inter-dependence of Empire and Church, it comprised the German-speaking peoples of Central Europe, and was ruled by an elected Emperor, who claimed to be the representative of the ancient Roman Emperors.

After the defeat of Austerlitz the Habsburg Emperor lost even the semblance of authority over the greater part of the Empire, and the constitution of this ancient estate ceased to exist even in name At Napoleon's bidding Francis II published an Act (1806) declaring himself Emperor of Austria and abdicating from the throne of an outworn and dishonoured fiction—the Holy Roman Empire—which was justly stigmatized by a contemporary as being neither Holy, nor Roman, nor an Empire

Holy Rood Day. See HOLY CROSS DAY

Holy Thursday. An old name in England for Ascension Day (q v), i.e. the Thursday but one before Whitsun By Roman Catholics and others Maundy Thursday (q v.), i e the Thursday before Good Friday, is called "Holy Thursday " See also IN CÆNA DOMINI.

Holy Saturday. See HOLY WEEK.

Holy War. A war in which religious fanaticism plays, or purports to play, a considerable part. The Crusades, the Thirty Years War, the wars against the Albigenses, etc., were so called.

The *Jehad* or Holy War of the Moslems, is a call to the whole Islamic world to take arms against the Unbelievers

John Bunyan's *Holy War*, published in 1682, tells the story of the assault of the armies of Satan against the citadel of Mansoul, despite many excellences it lacks the spontaneity and naïvety of *Pilgrim's Progress*

Holy Water. Water blessed by a priest or bishop for sacramental purposes. Its principal use is at the *Asperges*, or aspersing of the congregation before High Mass, but it is employed in nearly every blessing which the Church gives.

As the devil loves holy water. Not at all.

Holy water sprinkler. A military club of mediæval times, set with spikes So called facetiously because it makes the blood to flow as water sprinkled by an aspergillum

Holy Week. The last week in Lent It begins on Palm Sunday, the fourth day is called "Spy Wednesday" (an allusion to Judas Iscariot's spying on Jesus preparatory to betraying him), the fifth is "Maundy Thursday" (q v); the sixth is "Good Friday", and the last "Holy Saturday" or the "Great Sabbath."

Holy Week has been called *Hebdomada Muta* (Silent Week). *Hebdomada Inofficiosa* (Vacant Week), *Hebdomada Penitentialis*, *Hebdomada Indulgentiæ*, *Hebdomada Luctuosa*, *Hebdomada Nigra*, and *Hebdomada Ultima*

Holy Writ. The Bible

Trifles light as air
Are to the jealous confirmations strong
As proofs of holy writ.   *Othello*, iii, 3.

Homburg. A soft felt hat popularized by Edward VII It was originally made in Homburg in Prussia where the King "took the waters "

Home. At home. At one's own house and prepared to receive visitors An *at home* is a more or less informal reception for which arrangements have been made *To be at home to somebody* is to be ready and willing to receive him, *to be at home with a subject* is to be familiar with it, quite conversant with it

Home, sweet home. This popular English song first appeared in the opera *Clari, the Maid of Milan* (Covent Garden, 1823). The words were by John Howard Payne (an American), and the music by Sir Henry Bishop, who professed to have founded it on a Sicilian air

Not at home A familiar locution for "not prepared to receive visitors"—or the one who is applying for admission, it does not necessarily mean "away from home "

An old story, sometimes attributed to Swift, is that once when Scipio Nasica called on the poet Ennius, the servant said, "Ennius is not at home," but Nasica could see him plainly in the house A few days later Ennius returned the visit, and Nasica called out, "Not at home " Ennius instantly recognized the voice, and remonstrated "You are a nice fellow" (said Nasica), "why, I believed your slave, and you won't believe me "

One's long home. The grave
Man goeth to his long home, and the mourners go
about the streets —*Eccles* xii, 5.

To come home to one. To reach one's heart;
to become thoroughly understood or realized.
I doe now publish my Essayes; which, of all my
other workes, have been most Currant For that, as it
seems they come home, to Mens Businesse, and
Bosomes — BACON· *Epistle Dedicatorie to the
"Essayes"* (1625).

To come home to roost. Usually said of a lie,
fault, hidden sin, etc , which eventually rebounds to the discomfiture of its originator.

To make oneself at home. To dispense with
ceremony in another person's house, to act as
though one were at home

Who goes home? When the House of
Commons breaks up at night the door-keeper
asks this question of the members In bygone
days all members going in the direction of the
Speaker's residence went in a body to see him
safe home The question is still asked, but is
a mere relic of antiquity.

Home Rule, now a mere skeleton in the
British political cupboard, was half a century
ago a problem that called forth the fiercest
passions The Irish movement for constitutional self-government was to the forefront
from 1870 until 1920 The Home Rulers
formed a party in Parliament led by Isaac
Butt (1813-79) and then by C. W Parnell
(1846-91) They were about 80 strong, kept
themselves free from all political alliances or
bonds and pursued a policy of obstruction In
1885 W E Gladstone took up their cause, but
his first Home Rule Bill (1886) was thrown out
by the Commons, his second Bill (1893) was
thrown out by the Lords and it was not until
1914 that a third Home Rule Bill was passed
into law The outbreak of World War I postponed the putting of the Act into operation;
the Easter rising of 1916 and the growth of
Sinn Fein made Home Rule, as such, a thing
of the past, and Eire gained her independence
by a new measure enacted by Parliament in
1920

Homer (hō´ mer). The name given to the entirely unknown poet—or group of poets perhaps
—to whom is assigned the authorship of the
Iliad (q v.) and the *Odyssey* (q.v), the greatest
monuments of ancient or modern epic poetry
Some writers have considered Homer to
have been a mythical figure, but modern
scholarship tends to regard the epics as actually
the work of a blind poet Homer who lived some
time between 1200 and 850 B C.
No doubt was ever entertained by the ancients respecting the personality of Homer Pindar, Aristotle,
Plato, and others, all assumed this fact, nor did they
even doubt that the *Iliad* and *Odyssey* were the work
of one mind —R W BROWNE *Historical Classical
Literature*
Homer's birthplace is unknown. The old
rhyme, founded on an epigram preserved by
Aulus Gellius, says:—
Seven cities warred for Homer being dead,
Who living had no roof to shroud his head.
HEYWOOD· *Hierarchie of the Blessed Angels* (1635).
the "seven cities" being Smyrna, Rhodes,
Colophon, Salamis, Chios, Argos, and Athens
See SCIO's.

Among the many names and epithets that
have been bestowed on him are Melesigenes
the Man of Chios (*see* CHIOS), the Blind
Old Man; and Mæonides (*q v*) He is spoken
of as *Mæonius senex*, and his poems as *Mæoniæ
chartæ* or *Mæonia carmina*
Milton has been called the English Homer,
Ossian the Gaelic Homer, Plato the Homer of
philosophers, Byron called Fielding the prose
Homer of human nature; and Dryden (*Essay
on Dramatic Poesy*) says —
Shakespeare was the Homer, or father of our
dramatic poets, Jonson was the Virgil, the pattern of
elaborate writing, I admire him but I love Shakespeare

The Casket Homer. An edition corrected by
Aristotle, which Alexander the Great always
carried about with him, and laid under his
pillow at night with his sword After the battle
of Arbela, a golden casket richly studded with
gems was found in the tent of Darius, and
Alexander being asked to what purpose it
should be assigned replied, "There is but one
thing in the world worthy of so costly a
depository," saying which he placed therein
his edition of Homer.

Homer a cure for the ague. *See* AGUE

Homer sometimes nods. Even the best of us
is liable to make mistakes The line is from
Horace's *De Arte Poetica* (359):—
Quandoque bonus dormitat Homerus!
Verum operi longo fas est obrepere somnum
(Sometimes good Homer himself even nods; but
in so long a work it is allowable if there should be a
drowsy interval or so)

Homœopathy (hō mi op' à thi) (Gr. *homoios
pathos*, like disease) The plan of curing a
disease by minute doses of a medicine which
would in healthy persons produce the disease.
The theory was first formulated and practised
by Samuel Hahnemann (1755-1843), a German
physician.

Honey. An expression of endearment (with
allusion to sweetness), formerly common, but
now largely confined to the North of England
Him thinketh verraily that he may see
Noe's flood come walwing as the see
To drenchen Alisoun, his hony dere.
CHAUCER *Miller's Tale,* 429

Honeydew. A sweet substance found on the
leaves of lime-trees and some other plants.
Bees and ants are fond of it It is probably the
excretion of the aphis, and gets its popular
name from its great sweetness coupled with its
dew-like appearance
Some framed faire lookes, glancing like evening lights,
Others sweet words, dropping like honny dew
SPENSER· *Faerie Queene,* II, v, 33

Honeymoon. The first month after marriage,
especially that part of it spent away from home.
It appears to have been an ancient custom to
drink a dilution of honey for thirty days after
marriage—*i e* a moon's age, hence the name.
Attila is said to have drunk so liberally of this
potion that he died of suffocation in A D 453

Honeysuckle. *See* MISNOMERS.

Hong Merchants. Those Chinese merchants
who, under licence from the government of
China, held the monopoly of trade with
Europeans until 1842, when the restriction was

abolished by the Treaty of Nanking The Chinese applied the word *hong* to the foreign factories situated at Canton

Honi soit qui mal y pense (on' ē swa kē māl ē pons). The motto of the Most Noble Order of the Garter (*q.v*) The common rendering of the motto as "Evil be to him who evil thinks" has little meaning. A better rendering is, "Shame to him who thinks evil of it."

Honky-tonk (hong' ki tongk), an American slang term for a brothel, a disreputable night-club or low roadhouse.

Honorificabilitudinitatibus (on ôr if i kǎ 'bil i tū' din i tāt' i bus) A made-up word on the Lat *honorificabilitudo*, honourableness, which frequently occurs in Elizabethan plays as an instance of sesquipedalian pomposity.

> Thou art not so long by the head as honorificabili-tudinitatibus —SHAKESPEARE *Love's Labour's Lost*, v, 1

See LONG WORDS.

Honour. In feudal law, a superior seigniory, on which other lordships or manors depended by the performance of customary services At bridge, the *honours* are the five highest trump cards—ace, king, queen, knave, and ten.

An affair of honour. A dispute to be settled by a duel. Duels were generally provoked by offences against the arbitrary rules of etiquette, courtesy, or feeling, called the laws "of honour"; and, as these offences were not recognizable in the law courts, they were settled by private combat.

Crushed by his honours. The allusion is to the legend of the Roman damsel, Tarpeia, who agreed to open the gates of Rome to King Tatius, provided his soldiers should give her the ornaments which they wore on their arms. As they entered they threw their shields on her and crushed her, saying as they did so, "These are the ornaments worn by Sabines on their arms "

Draco, the Athenian legislator, was crushed to death in the theatre of Ægina, by the number of caps and cloaks showered on him by the audience, as a mark of their high apprecia-tion of his merits. A similar story is told of the mad Emperor, Elagabalus (*q.v*), who smothered the leading citizens of Rome with roses

Debts of honour. Debts contracted by betting or gambling, so called because these debts cannot be enforced as such by law

Honours of war. The privilege allowed to an enemy, on capitulation, of being permitted to retain his offensive arms This is the highest honour a victor can pay a vanquished foe Sometimes the troops so treated are allowed to march with all their arms, drums beating, and colours flying

Laws of honour. Certain arbitrary rules which the fashionable world tacitly admits; they wholly regard deportment, and have nothing to do with moral offences Breaches of this code are punished by expulsion or suspension from society, "sending to Coventry" (*q.v.*)

Legion of Honour. *See* LEGION.

Point of honour. An obligation which is binding because its violation would offend some conscientious scruple or notion of self-respect

Word of honour A gage which cannot be violated without placing the breaker of it beyond the pale of respectability and good society

Honourable A title of honour accorded in the United Kingdom to the younger sons of earls and the children of viscounts, of barons and life peers, to maids of honour, the Lord Provost of Glasgow, justices of the High Court except lords justices and justices of appeal. In the House of Commons one member speaks of another as "the honourable member for —" In U S A. *honourable* is a courtesy title applied to persons of distinction in legal or civic life. *See also* RIGHT HONOURABLE.

Honourable Artillery Company, a very ancient regiment in the British Army, having been founded by Henry VIII, in 1537, as the Guild of St George Since 1641 it has occupied its training ground near Bunhill Fields In Tudor and Stuart days the officers for the Trained Bands of London were supplied by the H A C., in whose ranks Milton, Wren, and Samuel Pepys served at one time or another It has the privilege of marching through the City with fixed bayonets

In 1638 Robert Keayne, a member of the London company, founded the Ancient and Honourable Artillery Company of Boston, Mass, the oldest military unit in the U S A.

Hooch, an American slang term for whisky or crude raw spirits, often made surreptitiously or obtained illegally The word comes from the Alaskan Indian *hoochinoo*, a crude distilled liquor

Hood. The hood (or cowl) does not make the monk. It is a man's way of life, not what he professes to be, that really matters; from the Latin *Cucullus non facit monachum*

> *Escalus* Signior Lucio, did not you say you knew that Friar Lodowick to be a dishonest person?
> *Lucio Cucullus non facit monachum* honest in nothing, but in his clothes, and one that hath spoke most villainous speeches of the duke —*Measure for Measure*, v, 1
> They should be good men, their affairs are righteous But all hoods make not monks
> *Henry VIII*, iii 1

The origin of the phrase is probably to be found in these lines from St Anselm's *Carmen de Contemptu Mundi* (11th cent)'—

> Non tonsura facit monachum, non horrida vestis,
> Sed virtus animi, perpetuusque rigori

Hood, Robin. *See* ROBIN HOOD

Hoodlum (American slang) A rough hooligan. The word was originally confined to the particular variety native to San Francisco.

Hoodman Blind. Now called "Blindman's Buff."

> What devil was't
> That thus hath cozened you at hoodman blind?
> *Hamlet*, iii, 4

Hoo-doo, originating from Voodoo (*q v*), this term is applied to any person or object that is supposed to bring bad luck

Hoo-ey, an exclamation of incredulity—nonsense! absurd!

Hook *Above your hook.* Beyond your comprehension, beyond your mark The allusion is perhaps to hat-pegs placed in rows, the higher rows being beyond the reach of small statures

By hook or crook. Either rightfully or wrongfully; somehow, one way or another.
There is more than one attempted explanation of the phrase, it is probable, however, that it derives from an old manorial custom which authorized tenants to take as much firewood from the hedges, etc , as could be cut with a crook or bill-hook, and as much low timber as could be reached down from the boughs by a shepherd's crook.

Dynmure Wood was ever open and common to the . . inhabitants of Bodmin . to bear away upon their backs a burden of lop, crop, hook, crook, and bag wood —*Bodmin Register* (1525).

He is off the hooks. Done for, laid on the shelf, superseded, dead The bent pieces of iron on which the hinges of a gate rest and turn are called *hooks*

Hook, line, and sinker. To swallow a tale, hook, line, and sinker is to be extremely gullible, like the hungry fish that swallows not only the baited hook, but the lead weight and some of the line as well.

A hook-up is a radio term for an arrangement of wiring for extended transmission or reception; it is applied to a network of radio stations connected for the transmission of the same programme

Hook it! Take your hook! Sling your hook! Be off! Be off about your business!

On one's own hook. On one's own responsibility or account An angler's phrase.

With a hook at the end. "My assent is given with a hook at the end" means that it is given with a mental reservation In some parts it is still the custom for a witness when he swears falsely to crook his finger into a sort of hook, and this is supposed sufficient to annul the perjury. It is a crooked oath, an oath "with a hook at the end." *Cp* OVER THE LEFT, *under* LEFT

Hookey Walker. *See* WALKER

Hooky. To play hooky is to play truant, especially from school.

Hooligan. A violent young rough The term originated in the last years of the 19th century from the name of one of this class From it is derived the substantive *hooliganism.*

The original *Hooligans* were a spirited Irish family of that name whose proceedings enlivened the drab monotony of life in Southwark towards the end of the 19th century The word is younger than the Australian *larrikin,* of doubtful origin, but older than Fr *apache.* —ERNEST WEEKLEY· *Romance of Words* (1912)

Hooped Pots. Drinking pots at one time were marked with bands, or hoops, set at equal distances, so that when two or more drank from the same tankard no one should take more than his share. Jack Cade promises his followers that "seven halfpenny loaves shall be sold for a penny; the three-hooped pot

shall have ten hoops, and I will make it felony to drink small beer." (*2 Henry VI*, iv, 2)

I beleeve hoopes in quart pots were invented to that ende, that every man should take his hoope, and no more.—NASH *Pierce Pennilesse* (1592).

Hoosegow (hooz' gou), in American slang, a gaol. The word comes from the Mexican-Spanish *juzgado,* a court of justice

Hoosier (hoo' zhér), an inhabitant of the State of Indiana, the Hoosier State The origin of the name is now unknown, it is doubtless that of some forgotten local magnate or character

Hop. *To hop the twig.* Usually, to die, but sometimes to run away from one's creditors, as a bird eludes a fowler
There are numerous phrases to express the cessation of life, for example, "to kick the bucket", "to lay down one's knife and fork", "to peg out" (from cribbage), "to be snuffed out" (like a candle), "to throw up the sponge"; "to fall asleep", "to enter Charon's boat", "to join the majority"; and "to give up the ghost "

Hop-o'-my-Thumb. A pygmy or midget The name has been given to several dwarfs, as well as being commonly used as a generic term. Tom Thumb in the well-known nursery tale is quite another character He was the son of peasants, knighted by King Arthur, and killed by a spider.

Plaine friend, Hop-o'-my-Thumb, know you who we are?—*Taming of a Shrew* (*Anon* 1594)

Hope. *See* PANDORA'S BOX.
Thomas Campbell (1777-1844) was known as *The Bard of Hope,* on account of his poem, "The Pleasures of Hope" (1799)

Hopkinsians (hop kin' zianz) A sect of Independent Calvinists who followed the teaching of Samuel Hopkins (1721-1803), a minister at Newport, Rhode Island, whose *System of Divinity* was published shortly before his death The particular tenet of the system is that true holiness consists in disinterested benevolence, and that all sin is *selfishness.*

Horace The Roman lyric poet, born 65 B C , died 8 B C.

Horace of England. George, Duke of Buckingham, preposterously declared Cowley to be the Pindar, Horace, and Virgil of England. Ben Jonson was nicknamed Horace by Dekker in the so-called "War of the Theatres "

Horace of France. Jean Macrinus or Salmon (1490-1557), and Pierre Jean de Beranger (1780-1857), also called the French Burns.

Horace of Spain. The brothers Lupercio (1559-1613) and Bartolme Argensola (1562-1631)

Horn. *Astolpho's horn.* Logistilla gave Astolpho at parting a horn that had the virtue of being able to appal and put to flight the boldest knight or most savage beast. (ARIOSTO. *Orlando Furioso,* Bk viii)

Cape Horn. So named by Schouten, a Dutch mariner, who first doubled it (1616). He was a native of Hoorn, in north Holland, and named the cape after his native place.

The Horn gate. *See* DREAMS, GATES OF.

Horn of fidelity. Morgan le Fay sent a horn to King Arthur, which had the following "virtue" —No lady could drink out of it who was not "to her husband true"; all others who attempted to drink were sure to spill what it contained This horn was carried to King Mark, and "his queene with a hundred ladies more" tried the experiment, but only four managed to "drinke cleane" Ariosto's *enchanted cup* possessed a similar spell.

Horn of plenty. Amalthea's horn (*q v*), the cornucopia, an emblem of plenty.

Ceres is drawn with a ram's horn in her left arm filled with fruits and flowers, sometimes they are being poured on the earth, and sometimes they are piled high in the horn as in a basket Diodorus (iii, 68) says the horn is one from the head of the goat by which Jupiter was suckled

King Horn. *See under* KING

Moses' Horns. *See* MOSES

Horn with horn or **horn under horn.** The promiscuous feeding of bulls and cows, or, in fact, all horned beasts that are allowed to run together on the same common.

My horn hath He exalted (1 *Sam.* ii, 10, *Ps.* lxxxix, 24, etc) He has given me the victory, increased my sway. Thus, *Lift not up your horn on high* (*Ps* lxxv, 5) means, do not behave scornfully, maliciously, or arrogantly In these passages "horn" symbolizes power, and its exaltation signifies victory or deliverance. In Daniel's vision (*Dan* vii) the "fourth beast, dreadful and terrible, and strong exceedingly," had ten horns, symbolical of its great might

The horns of a dilemma. *See* DILEMMA.

To come (or **be squeezed**) **out at the little end of the horn.** To come off badly in some affair, get the worst of it; fail conspicuously

To draw in one's horns. To retrench, to curtail one's expenditure; to retract, or mitigate, a pronounced opinion, to restrain pride The allusion is to the snail.

To put to the horn. To denounce as a rebel, or pronounce a person an outlaw, for not answering to a summons In Scotland the messenger-at-arms used to go to the Cross of Edinburgh and give three blasts with a horn before he proclaimed judgment of outlawry

To the horns of the altar. *Usque ad aras amicus* Your friend even to the horns of the altar—*i.e* through thick and thin In swearing, the ancient Romans held the horns of the altar, and one who did so in testimony of friendship could not break his oath without calling on himself the vengeance of the angry gods.
The altar in Solomon's temple had a projection at each of the four corners called "horns"; these were regarded as specially sacred, and probably typified the great might of God (*cp. above*)

To wear the horns. To be a cuckold. This old term is possibly connected with the chase In the rutting season one stag selects several females, who constitute his harem, till another

stag contests the prize with him If beaten he is without associates till he finds a stag feebler than himself, who is made to submit to similar terms As stags are horned, and have their mates taken from them by their fellows, the application is palpable.

Another explanation (*see* N E D) is that it is due
to the practice formerly prevalent of planting or engrafting the spurs of a castrated cock on the root of the excised comb, where they grew and became horns, sometimes of several inches long
In support of this it is noteworthy that *hahnrei*, the German equivalent for *cuckold*, originally signified a capon.

To make horns at To thrust out the fist with the first and fourth fingers extended, the others doubled in This ancient gesture, now more common in Latin countries than in England, was employed as an insult to the person at whom it was directed, as implying that he was a cuckold.
He would have laine withe the Countess of Nottinghame, making horns in derision at her husband the Lord High Admiral —SIR E PEYNTON *The Divine Catastrophe of the . . House of Stuart,* 1652.

To show one's horns To let one's evil intentions appear. The allusion, like that in "to show the cloven hoof," is to the Devil— "Old Hornie."

To take the bull by the horns *See* BULL.

Auld Hornie. The devil, so called in Scotland The allusion is to the horns with which Satan is generally represented
O thou! whatever title suits thee,
Auld Hornie, Satan, Nick, or Clootie
BURNS *Address to the Deil*

Horn-book. A thin board of oak about nine inches long and five or six wide, on which were printed the alphabet, the nine digits, and sometimes the Lord's Prayer, the Creed, and the Angelic Salutation. Horn-books were in use in elementary schools for the poor when books were scarce and expensive, and survived well into the 18th century They had a handle, and were covered in front with a sheet of thin horn; the back was often ornamented with a rude sketch of St George and the Dragon *See* CHRISS-CROSS ROW
Thee will I sing, in comely wainscot bound,
And golden verge inclosing thee around,
The faithful horn before, from age to age
Preserving thy invulnerable page,
Behind, thy patron saint in armour shines,
With sword and lance to guard the sacred lines
TICKELL *The Horn Book.*
Their books of stature small they took in hand
Which with pellucid horn secured are
To save from finger wet the letters fair.
SHENSTONE· *Schoolmistress*

Death and Doctor Hornbook. In this satire by Robert Burns "Doctor Hornbook" stands for John Wilson the apothecary, whom the poet met at the Tarbolton Masonic Lodge

Horner, Little Jack. *See* JACK

Hornpipe. The dance is so called because it used to be danced to the *pib-corn* or *hornpipe*, an instrument consisting of a pipe each end of which was made of horn. In his *Dictionary* Johnson mistakenly said that it was "danced commonly to *a horn*."

Hornswoggle, To U S A slang meaning to cheat Variants are *honeyfackle, honeyfoggle.*

Horoscope The figure or diagram of the twelve houses of heaven, showing the positions of the planets at a given time The horoscope is used by astrologers for calculating nativities and working out the answers to various horary questions *See* HOUSES, ASTROLOGICAL The word (Greek) means the "hour-scrutinized," because it is the disposition of the heavens at the exact hour of birth which is examined.

Hors de combat (ôr de kom' ba) (Fr , out of battle) Incapable of taking any further part in the fight

He (*i e.* Cobbett) levels his antagonists, he lays his friends low, and puts his own party *hors de combat.*— HAZLITT: *Table Talk*

Hors d'œuvre (ôr dĕrvr) (Fr , outside the work) A relish served at the beginning of a dinner as a whet to the appetite, not as an integral part of the meal In French the expression is also used in architecture for an outbuilding or outwork, and as a literary term for a digression or interpolated episode

Horse. A dark horse. A horse whose merits as a racer are not known to the general public, hence, a person who keeps his true capabilities to himself till he can produce them to the best advantage.

A horse of another colour. A different affair altogether.

A nod is as good as a wink to a blind horse. Said of one who is determined not to take a hint, or to see a point; also used with the contrary meaning, viz "I grasp your meaning, though you speak darkly of what you purpose; but mum's the word "

A one-horse show. *See* ONE.

As strong as a horse. Very strong. *Horse* is often used with intensive effect; as, *to work,* or *to eat, like a horse*

A Trojan horse. A deception, a concealed danger *See* WOODEN HORSE OF TROY

Don't look a gift-horse in the mouth. *See* GIFT-HORSE

Flogging the dead horse Trying to revive interest in a subject out of date. Bright said that Earl Russell's Reform Bill (1867) was a "dead horse," and every attempt to create any enthusiasm in its favour was like "flogging the dead horse "

Hold your horses. Don't be in such a hurry, keep your temper

Horse and foot. The cavalry and infantry; hence all one's forces; with all one's might

Cook's son, duke's son, son of a belted earl,
Forty thousand horse and foot going to Table Bay!
RUDYARD KIPLING *The Absent Minded Beggar* (1899)

I will win the horse or lose the saddle. Neck or nothing, double or quits The story is that a man made the bet of a horse that another could not say the Lord's Prayer without a wandering thought The bet was accepted, but before half-way through the person who accepted the bet looked up and said, "By the by, do you mean the saddle also?"

One man may steal a horse, while another may not look over the hedge. Some people are specially privileged, and can take liberties, or commit crimes, etc , with impunity, while others get punished for very trivial offences. An old proverb; given by Heywood (1546)

Riding the wooden horse. Being strapped to a wooden contrivance shaped something like a horse's back and flogged. An old form of military punishment

Straight from the horse's mouth Direct from the highest authority, which can not be questioned The only certain way of discovering the age of a horse is by examining its lower jaw

The grey mare is the better horse. *See* MARE.

They cannot draw (or set) horses together. They cannot agree together.

'Tis a good horse that never stumbles. Everyone makes mistakes sometimes, Homer sometimes nods

To back the wrong horse. To make an error in judgment, and suffer for it. A phrase from the Turf Speaking in the House of Lords (January 19th, 1897), Lord Salisbury said —

I consider that both parties have been mistaken in their policy towards the Turkish Empire, they staked their money on the wrong horse at the time of the Crimean War.

To be on one's high horse, to ride the high horse. To be overbearing and arrogant; to give oneself airs. Formerly people of high rank rode on tall horses or chargers

To ride on the horse with ten toes. To walk, to ride on Shanks's mare (*q.v*).

To set the cart before the horse. *See* CART.

When the horse is stolen, lock the stable door. Said in derision when obvious precautions are taken *after* a loss or disaster The French say, *Après la mort, le medecin*

Working with a dead horse. Doing work which has been already paid for. Such work is a dead horse, because you can get no more out of it.

You can take a horse to the water but you cannot make him drink. There is always *some* point at which it is impossible to get an obstinate man to proceed farther in the desired direction The proverb is an old one, and is found in Heywood (1846).

According to classical mythology, Poseidon (Neptune) created the horse; and, according to Virgil, the first person that drove a four-in-hand was Erichthonius

A horse wins a kingdom. It is said that on the death of Smerdis (522 B.C), the several competitors for the throne of Persia agreed that he should be king whose horse neighed first when they met on the day following The groom of Darius showed his horse a mare on the place appointed, and as soon as it arrived at the spot on the following day the horse began to neigh, and won the crown for its master

Directions for riding and driving.

Up a hill hurry not,
Down a hill flurry not,
On level ground spare him not
On a Milestone near Richmond, Yorks

Flesh-eating horses The horses of Diomed, tyrant of Thrace (not Diomede, son of Tydeus) who fed his horses on the strangers who visited his kingdom Hercules vanquished the tyrant, and gave the carcass to the horses to eat

Like to the Thracian tyrant who, they say,
Unto his horses gave his guests for meat,
Till he himself was made their greedy prey,
And torn in pieces by Alcides great
SPENSER· *Faerie Queene*, V, viii, 31

White horses A poetic phrase for the white-capped breakers as they roll in from the sea

The wild white horses play
Champ and chafe and toss in the spray
M. ARNOLD *The Forsaken Merman*

O'Donohue's white horses Waves which come on a windy day, crested with foam. The hero reappears every seventh year on May-day, and is seen gliding, to sweet but unearthly music, over the lakes of Killarney, on his favourite white horse. He is preceded by groups of fairies, who fling spring flowers in his path

Moore has a poem on the subject in his *Irish Melodies*, it refers to a tradition that a young and beautiful girl became enamoured of O'Donohue, the visionary chieftain, and threw herself into the lake that he might carry her off for his bride

Vale of White Horse *See* WHITE HORSE

The brazen horse. *See* CAMBUSCAN

The fifteen points of a good horse—
A good horse sholde have three propyrtees of a man, three of a woman, three of a foxe, three of a hare, and three of an asse
Of a man Bolde, prowde, and hardye
Of a woman Fayre-breasted, faire of haire, and easy to move.
Of a foxe. A fair taylle, short eers, with a good trotte
Of a hare A grate eye, a dry head, and well ren-nynge
Of an asse A bygge chynn, a flat legge, and a good hoof —*Wynkyn de Worde* (1496)

The Wooden Horse, a nickname for the scaffold, as also

A horse that was foaled of an acorn, as appears in Ray's *Proverbs*, 1678

Famous Horses of Myth and History
In classical mythology the names given by various poets to the horses of Helios, the Sun, are.—

Actæon (effulgence), *Æthon* (fiery red), *Amethea* (no loiterer); *Bronte* (thunder), *Erythreos* (red producer); *Lampos* (shining like a lamp, one of the noontide horses); *Phlegon* (the burning one; noontide), and *Purocis* (fiery hot, also noontide).

Pluto's horses were· *Abaster* (away from the stars), *Abatos* (inaccessible); *Aeton* (swift as an eagle), and *Nonios*, and Aurora's· *Abraxas* (*q.v*), *Eöos* (dawn), and *Phæthon* (the shining one)

Alborak See BORAK, below
Alfana ("mare"). Gradasso's horse, in *Orlando Furioso*

Aquiline ("like an eagle") Raymond's steed, bred on the banks of the Tagus (Tasso. *Jerusalem Delivered*.)

Arion ("martial") Hercules' horse, given to Adrastus. The horse of Neptune, brought out of the earth by striking it with his trident, its right feet were those of a man, it spoke with a human voice, and ran with incredible swiftness

Arundel The horse of Bevis of Hamtown, or Southampton. The word means "swift as a swallow" (Fr *hirondelle*)

Baiardo (the same name as *Bayard* below) Rinaldo's horse, of a bright bay colour, once the property of Amadis of Gaul According to tradition it is still alive, but flees at the approach of man, so that it can never be caught (*Orlando Furioso*)

Balios (Gr "swift") One of the horses given by Neptune to Peleus It afterwards belonged to Achilles Like Xanthos, its sire was the west wind, and its dam Swift-foot the harpy

Barbary See Roan Barbary

Bavieca The Cid's horse He survived his master two years and a half, during which time no one was allowed to mount him, and when he died he was buried before the gate of the monastery at Valencia, and two elms were planted to mark the site

Bayard ("bay coloured"). The horse of the four sons of Aymon, which grew larger or smaller as one or more of the four sons mounted it According to tradition, one of the footprints may still be seen in the forest of Soignes, and another on a rock near Dinant

Black Agnes The palfrey of Mary Queen of Scots, given her by her brother Moray, and named after Agnes of Dunbar

Black Bess The famous mare ridden by the highwayman Dick Turpin, which, tradition says, carried him from London to York

Black Saladin Warwick's famous horse, which was coal-black. Its sire was Malech, and according to tradition, when the race of Malech failed, the race of Warwick would fail also. And it was so.

Borak (Al) The mare which conveyed Mohammed from earth to the seventh heaven It was milk-white, had the wings of an eagle, and a human face, with horse's cheeks Every pace she took was equal to the farthest range of human sight The word is Arabic for "the lightning."

Brigadore or *Brigliadore* ("golden bridle"). Sir Guyon's horse, in Spenser's *Faerie Queene* (V, ii, etc.) It had a distinguishing black spot in its mouth, like a horseshoe.
Orlando's famous charger, second only to Baiardo in swiftness and wonderful power's, had the same name—*Brigliadoro*

Bucephalus ("ox-head"). The celebrated charger of Alexander the Great. Alexander was the only person who could mount him, and he always knelt down to take up his master. He was thirty years old at death, and Alexander built a city for his mausoleum, which he called Bucephala.

Carman. The Chevalier Bayard's horse, given him by the Duke of Lorraine It was a Persian horse from Kerman or Carmen (Laristan)
Celer ("swift"). The horse of the Roman

Emperor Verus It was fed on almonds and raisins, covered with royal purple, and stalled in the imperial palace

Cerus The horse of Adrastus, swifter than the wind (*Pausanias*) The word means "fit."

Copenhagen Wellington's charger at Waterloo It died in 1835 at the age of twenty-seven. *Cp Marengo.*

Cyllaros Named from Cylla in Troas, a celebrated horse of Castor or Pollux.

Dapple Sancho Panza's ass in *Don Quixote.* So called from its colour

Dinos ("the marvel") Diomed's horse

Ethon ("fiery"). One of the horses of Hector.

Fadda. Mohammed's white mule

Ferrant d'Espagne ("the Spanish traveller"). The horse of Oliver, one of Charlemagne's paladins.

Galathe ("cream-coloured"). One of Hector's horses.

Grani ("grey-coloured") Siegfried's horse, of marvellous swiftness

Grizzle Dr Syntax's horse, all skin and bone, in Combe's *Tour of Dr Syntax*, etc (1812)

Hatzum The horse of the archangel Gabriel. (Koran)

Harpagus ("one that carries off rapidly"). One of the horses of Castor and Pollux

Hippocampus One of Neptune's horses It had only two legs, the hinder quarter being that of a dragon or fish.

Hrimfaxi The horse of Night, from whose bit fall the "rime-drops" which every night bedew the earth (Scandinavian mythology.)

Incitatus ("spurred-on"). The horse of the Roman Emperor Caligula, made priest and consul It had an ivory manger, and drank wine out of a golden pail

Kantaka The white horse of Prince Gautama, the Buddha (*q v.*)

Lampon ('the bright one"). One of the horses of Diomed

Lamri King Arthur's mare The word means "the curvetter."

Marengo The white stallion which Napoleon rode at Waterloo It is represented in Vernet's picture of *Napoleon Crossing the Alps. Cp* COPENHAGEN.

Malech See Black Saladin above.

Marocco Banks's performing horse, famous in the late Elizabethan period, and frequently mentioned by the dramatists. Its shoes were of silver, and one of its exploits was to mount the steeple of old St Paul's

The Pale Horse Death *Rev.* vi, 8.

Pegasus ("born near the *pege* or source of the ocean") The winged horse of Apollo and the Muses Perseus rode him when he rescued Andromeda

Phallas ("stallion") The horse of Heraclius

Phrenicos ("intelligent") The horse of Hiero of Syracuse, that won the Olympic prize for single horses in the seventy-third Olympiad.

Podarge ('swift-foot"). One of the horses of Hector.

Roan Barbary. The favourite horse of Richard II.

> When Bolingbroke rode on Roan Barbary
> That horse that thou so often hast bestrid.
> *Richard II,* v, 5.

Rosabelle The favourite palfrey of Mary Queen of Scots.

Rosinante ("formerly a hack") Don Quixote's horse, all skin and bone.

Saladin. See Black Saladin above.

Savoy The favourite black horse of Charles VIII of France, so called from the Duke of Savoy who gave it him It had but one eye, and "was mean in stature "

Shibdiz The Persian Bucephalus, fleeter than the wind It was the charger of Chosroes II of Persia

Sleipnir Odin's grey horse, which had eight legs and could traverse either land or sea. The horse typifies the wind which blows over land and water from eight principal points.

Sorrel The horse of William III, which stumbled by catching his foot in a mole-heap. This accident ultimately caused the king's death. *Sorrel,* like *Savoy,* was blind of one eye, and "mean of stature "

Strymon The horse immolated by Xerxes before he invaded Greece. Named from the river Strymon, in Thrace, from which vicinity it came

Tachebrune The horse of Ogier the Dane.

Trebizond. The grey horse of Guarinos, one of the French knights taken at Roncesvalles

Veghantino ("the little vigilant one") The famous steed of Orlando, called in French romance *Veillantif,* Orlando there appearing as Roland

White Surrey. The favourite horse of Richard III

> Saddle White Surrey for the field to-morrow
> *Richard III,* v, 3

Xanthus ("golden-hued") One of the horses of Achilles, who announced to the hero his approaching death when unjustly chidden by him. Its sire was *Zephyros,* and dam *Podarge.*

USED EMBLEMATICALLY

In Christian art, the horse is held to represent courage and generosity. It is an attribute of St Martin, St. Maurice, St. George, and St. Victor, all of whom are represented on horseback St. Leon is represented on horseback, in pontifical robes, blessing the people

In the catacombs, where the horse is a not uncommon emblem, it probably typifies the transitoriness of life Sometimes a palm-wreath is placed above its head.

The inn-sign of The White Horse in its various forms comes from the heraldic device of the House of Hanover, a white horse courant. During the reigns of the two first Georges a number of country inns and taverns exchanged their Stuart signs of Royal Oak, Rose, etc, to emblems better fitting the new times and dynasty.

Horse-chestnut. In his *Herball* (1597) Gerarde tells us that the tree is so called—

> For that the people of the East countries do with the fruit thereof cure their horses of the cough and such like diseases.

Another explanation is that when a slip is cut off obliquely close to a joint, it presents a miniature of a horse's hock and foot, shoe and nails (*Cp.* HORSE-VETCH) But the use of *horse-* attributively to denote something that is inferior, coarse, or unrefined, is quite common

Horse Latitudes. A region of calms between 30° and 35° North; perhaps so called because sailing-ships carrying horses to America or the West Indies were often obliged to lighten the vessel by casting them overboard when becalmed in these latitudes

Horse-laugh. A coarse, vulgar laugh
He plays rough pranks . . . and has a big horse-laugh in him when there is a fop to be roasted.—
CARLYLE *Frederick the Great,* vol i, Bk iv, ch ii.

Horse-leech. A type of insatiable voracity; founded on the blood-sucking habits of the worm, and the well-known passage in the Bible —
The horseleach hath two daughters, crying Give, give —*Prov* xxx, 15
John Marbeck, the commentator, in 1581, explains the "two daughters"—
that is, two forks in her tongue, which he heere calleth her two daughters, whereby she sucketh the bloud, and is never saciate.

Go and tell that to the horse marines! Said in derision to the teller of some unbelievable yarn or specially "tall" story The point of the jest is that no such force exists, the Royal Marines are confined to artillery and infantry, and naturally do not include cavalry. To belong to the "Horse Marines" means to be an awkward lubberly recruit. Cp MARINE

Horse-milliner. One who makes up and supplies decorations for horses; hence a horse-soldier more fit for the toilet than the battle-field The expression was used by Chatterton in his *Excelent Balade of Charitie* (Rowley Poems), and Scott revived it.

Horse-play Rough play

Horse-power. The standard theoretical unit of rate of work, equal to the raising of 33,000 lb. one foot high in one minute. This was fixed by Watt, who, when experimenting to find some settled way of indicating the power exerted by his steam-engine, found that a strong dray horse working at a gin for eight hours a day averaged 22 000 foot-pounds per minute He increased this by 50 per cent , and this, ever since, has been 1 horse-power.

Horse sense. Practical common sense; the term originated in western U S.A

It is lucky to pick up a horseshoe. This is from the old notion that a horseshoe nailed to the house door was a protection against witches Lord Nelson had one nailed to the mast of the ship *Victory.*
The legend is that the devil one day asked St. Dunstan, who was noted for his skill in shoeing horses, to shoe his "single hoof" Dunstan, knowing who his customer was, tied him tightly to the wall and proceeded with his job, but purposely put the devil to so much pain that he roared for mercy. Dunstan at last consented to release his captive on condition that he would never enter a place where he saw a horseshoe displayed
Straws laid across my path retard,
The horseshoes nailed, each threshold's guard.
GAY *Fable* xxiii, Pt. 1.
In 1251 Walter le Brun, farrier, in the Strand, London, was to have a piece of land in the parish of St Clements, to place there a forge, for which he was to pay the parish six horse-shoes, which rent was paid to the Exchequer every year, and was for some centuries rendered to the Exchequer by the Lord Mayor

and citizens of London, to whom subsequently the piece of ground was granted.

Horse-vetch. The vetch which has pods shaped like a horseshoe, sometimes called the "horseshoe vetch." Cp HORSE CHESTNUT

Horse-wrangler, a Western American term for a breaker-in and herder of horses

Hortus Siccus (hôr' tus sik' us) (Lat , a dry garden) A collection of plants dried and arranged in a book

Horus (hôr' us) One of the major gods of the ancient Egyptians, a blending of Horus the Elder the sun-god (corresponding to the Greek Apollo), and Horus the Child (*see* HARPO-CRATES), the son of Osiris and Isis. He was represented in hieroglyphics by a hawk, which bird was sacred to him, or as a hawk-headed man, and his emblem was the winged sun-disk In many of the myths he is hardly distinguishable from **Ra.**

Hospital (Lat. *hospitale, hospitium,* from *hospes,* a guest), Originally a hospice, or hostel for the reception of pilgrims, the word came to be applied to a charitable institution for the aged and infirm (as in *Greenwich Hospital, Chelsea Hospital*), to similar institutions for the education of the young (as in *Christ's Hospital*), and so, finally, to its present usual sense, a place where the sick and wounded are cared for, and where medical students gain their experience in the treatment of disease, etc The words *hostel* and *hotel* are "doublets" of *hospital* Another common variation is *hospice*

Hospitallers (hos' pit al erz) First applied to those whose duty it was to provide *hospitium* (lodging and entertainment) for pilgrims. The most noted institution of the kind was at Jerusalem, which gave its name to an order called the Knights Hospitallers, or the Knights of St John at Jerusalem, afterwards they were styled the Knights of Rhodes, and then Knights of Malta (*q v*), the island of Rhodes and Malta being conferred on them at different times.
The first crusade . . led to the establishment of the Christian kingdom of Jerusalem, in 1099 The chief strength of the kingdom lay in the two orders of military monks—the Templars and the Hospitallers or Knights of St John —FREEMAN. *General Sketch,* ch xi.
The Grand Priory of the Order of the Hospital of St John of Jerusalem in the British Realm (with headquarters at St John's Gate, Clerkenwell) is not connected with the ancient Order. It received a Royal Charter of Incorporation in 1888, and a supplemental charter (empowering the Grand Prior to establish Priories in any part of the British Dominions) in 1907, and it exists for the purpose of carrying on ambulance and other charitable work
At the beginning of World War II the St John Ambulance Brigade combined with the British Red Cross Society to form a war organization to carry out the work of both bodies in connexion with the war, this did not affect the status or independence of either body in matters unconnected with hostilities, and it ceased with the war

Host. The consecrated bread of the Eucharist is so called in the Latin Church because it is regarded as a real victim consisting of flesh, blood, and spirit, offered up in sacrifice; so called from *hostia*, the Latin word for a lamb when offered up in sacrifice (a larger animal was *victima*) At the Benediction it is exposed for adoration or carried in procession in a transparent vessel called a "monstrance."

The elevation of the Host. The celebrant lifting up the consecrated wafers above his head, that the people may see the paten and adore the Host while his back is turned to the congregation.

Host as an army. a multitude At the breaking up of the Roman Empire the first duty of every subject was to follow his lord into the field, and the proclamation was *bannire in hostem* (to order out against the foe), which soon came to signify "to order out for military service," and *hostem facere* came to mean "to perform military service" *Hostis* (military service) next came to mean the *army* that went against the foe, whence this word *host* Host, one who entertains guests, is from Lat. *hospes*, a guest.

To reckon without your host. To reckon from your own standpoint only; not to take into consideration what the other man may do or think.

> Found in few minutes, to his cost,
> He did but count without his host
> BUTLER *Hudibras*, I, iii, 22

Hostler or **Ostler** (os'lẽr), nowadays the man who looks after the horses of travellers at an inn, was originally the innkeeper, *hosteller*, keeper of an hostelry, himself The so-called derivation of *ostler* from *oat-stealer* is merely a joke

Hot. A phrase used in jazz music to describe a piece played with great spirit; when the players are carried away by the music they "get hot"

Hot air. Empty talk, boasting, threats, etc , bombast Hence, a *hot-air merchant*, one whose "vaporizings" are "full of sound and fury, signifying nothing", a declamatory windbag

Hot and hot. Hot dishes served in succession at a meal

Hot cockles. A Christmas game One blindfolded knelt down, and being struck had to guess who gave the blow

> Thus poets passing time away,
> Like children at hot-cockles play.   (1653.)

Hot cross buns. *See* BUN

Hot-foot. With speed, fast.

Hot-pot. A dish of mutton or beef with sliced potatoes cooked in an oven in a tight-lidded pot. A favourite dish in the North of England.

Hot stuff. Formerly said of a girl or woman who indulged in violent flirtations often carried beyond the limits of good behaviour

I'll make this place too hot to hold him. I'll "show him up," or otherwise make this so unpleasant and disagreeable for him that he will not be able to stand it.

I'll give it him hot and strong. I'll rate him most soundly and severely. *To get it hot*, to get severe punishment.

Like hot cakes. Very rapidly, as in "The goods sold like hot cakes "

Not so hot, a slang phrase meaning not so good, not very satisfactory

To blow hot and cold. *See* BLOW

To get into hot water. To get into difficulties, or in a state of trouble and anxiety.

Hotch-pot. This word is used with the same significance as *hotch-potch* (*q v.*), but it also has a legal use, which descends from Norman times in England, and is, apparently, the earlier. It meant the amalgamating of landed property that had belonged to a person dying intestate for the purpose of dividing the whole between the heirs in equal, or legal, shares

It was also applied to such cases as the following.—

Suppose a father has advanced money to one child, at his death this child receives such sum as, added to the loan, will make his share equal to that of the other members of the family If not content, he must bring into *hotch-pot* the money that was advanced, and the whole is then divided amongst all the children according to the terms of the will

Hotch-potch (Fr. *hochepot; hocher*, to shake together, and *pot*) A hodge-podge (*q v.*); a mixed dish, a confused mixture or jumble; a thick broth containing meat and vegetables.

Hotspur. A fiery person who has no control over his temper Harry Percy (1364–1403), son of the first Earl of Northumberland (*see* 1 *Henry IV*), was so called The 14th Earl of Derby (1799–1869) several times Prime Minister, was sometimes called the "*Hotspur of debate*," though he was more generally known as the "Rupert of debate."

Hound. To hound a person is to persecute him, or rather to set on persons to annoy him, as hounds are let from the slips at a hare or stag

Hour. A bad quarter of an hour. *See* QUART D'HEURE

At the eleventh hour. Just in time not to be too late, only just in time to obtain some benefit The allusion is to the parable of labourers hired for the vineyard (*Matt* xx).

My hour is not yet come. The time for action has not yet arrived, properly, the hour of my death is not yet fully come The allusion is to the belief that the hour of one's death is preordained

> When Jesus knew that his hour was come —
> *John* xiii, 1

In an evil hour. Acting under an unfortunate impulse In astrology we have our lucky and unlucky hours.

In the small hours of the morning. One, two, and three, after midnight.

To keep good hours. To return home early every night; to go to bed betimes Also, to be punctual in attending to one's work

Houri (hoo'ri) One of the black-eyed damsels of the Mohammedan Paradise, possessed of perpetual youth and beauty. whose virginity is renewable at pleasure; hence, in English use, any dark-eyed and attractive beauty.

Every believer will have seventy-two of these *houris* in Paradise, and, according to the Koran, his intercourse with them will be fruitful or otherwise, according to his wish If an offspring is desired, it will grow to full estate in an hour.

House A house of call. Some house, frequently a public-house, that one makes a point of visiting or using regularly, a house where workers in a particular trade meet when out of employment, and where they may be engaged

A house of correction. A jail governed by a keeper Originally it was a place where vagrants were made to work, and offenders were kept in ward for the correction of small offences

House of office, a Stuart term for a privy

House to house. Performed at every house, one after another, as, "a house-to-house canvass"

Like a house afire. Very rapidly. The phrase alludes to the rapidity with which the old wooden houses with their straw-thatched roofs, were burned down once they caught fire

The House. A familiar name for Christ Church, Oxford, the London Stock Exchange, and the deliberative bodies in various forms of government:

House of Lords, the peers of the United Kingdom

House of Commons, the elected representatives of the British people, and those of Canada.

House of Representatives, the lower legislative chamber in U.S.A, Australia, New Zealand.

House of Assembly, South Africa

The House of . . . denotes a royal or noble family with the ancestors and branches, as the *House of Windsor* (the British Royal Family), the *House of Stuart,* the *House of Brunswick,* etc , also a commercial establishment or firm as the *House of Tellson,* the banking firm in Dickens's *Tale of Two Cities,* the *House of Cassell,* the publishers, etc.

The House of God. Not solely a church, or a temple made with hands, but any place sanctified by God's presence Thus, Jacob in the wilderness, where he saw the ladder set up leading from earth to heaven, said, "This is none but the house of God, and this is the gate of heaven" (*Gen* xxviii, 17)

The House that Jack built. There are numerous similar glomerations. For example, the Hebrew parable of *The Two Zuzim.* The summation runs thus —

10 This is Yavah who vanquished
9 Death which killed
8 The butcher which slew
7 The ox which drank
6 The water which quenched
5 The fire which burnt
4 The stick which beat
3 The dog which worried
2 The cat which killed
1 The kid which my father bought for two zuzim.
(A zuzim was about a farthing.)

To bring down the house. *See* BRING

To cry or proclaim from the house-top. To announce something in the most public manner possible. Jewish houses had flat roofs. Here the ancient Jews used to assemble for gossip, here, too, not infrequently, they slept; and here some of their festivals were held. From the housetops the rising of the sun was proclaimed, and public announcements were made.

That which ye have spoken [whispered] in the ear . . . shall be proclaimed upon the housetops —*Luke* xii, 3

To eat one out of house and home. *See* EAT

To keep house. To maintain an establishment "To go into housekeeping" is to start a private establishment

To keep a good house To supply a bountiful table

To keep open house. To give free entertainment to all who choose to come

To throw the house out of the windows. To throw all things into confusion from exuberance of spirit

House-bote. A term in old law denoting the amount of wood that a tenant is allowed to take from the land for repairs to the dwelling and for fuel *Bote* is A.S profit, compensation. *See* BOOT.

House-leek. Grown formerly on house-roofs, from the notion that it warded off lightning, fever, and evil spirits, Charlemagne made an edict that every one of his subjects should have house-leek, or "Jove's beard," as it is also called, on his roof The words are, *Et habet quisque supra domum suum Jovis barbam*

If the herb house-leek or syngreen do grow on the housetop, the same house is never stricken with lightning or thunder —THOMAS HILL: *Natural and Artificiall Conclusions* (16th cent)

Houses, Astrological In judicial astrology the whole heaven is divided into twelve portions by means of great circles crossing the north and south points of the horizon, through which the heavenly bodies pass every twenty-four hours Each of these divisions is called a *house,* and in casting a horoscope (*q v*) the whole is divided into two parts (beginning from the east), six above and six below the horizon. The eastern ones are called the *ascendant,* because they are about to rise, the other six are the *descendant,* because they have already passed the zenith The twelve houses each have their special functions—(1) the house of life; (2) fortune and riches, (3) brethren; (4) parents and relatives, (5) children, (6) health, (7) marriage, (8) death; (9) religion, (10) dignities; (11) friends and benefactors, (12) enemies

Three houses were assigned to each of the four ages of the person whose horoscope was to be cast, and his lot in life was governed by the ascendancy or descendancy of these at the various periods, and by the stars which ruled in the particular "houses"

Household, The. Specifically, the immediate members of the Royal Family but more particularly the retinue of court officials, servants, and attendants attached to the sovereign's and other royal households The principal officials of the sovereign's household are the Lord Chamberlain, Lord Steward, Master of the Horse, Treasurer of the Household, all of whom are personally appointed. The higher members of the Household in Scotland are mostly hereditary

Household gods. The Lares and Penates (*q v*), who presided over the dwellings and domestic concerns of the ancient Romans, hence, in modern use, the valued possessions of home, all those things that go to endear it to one

> Bearing a nation with all its household gods into exile.
> LONGFELLOW *Evangeline*

Household Troops Those troops whose special duty it is to attend the sovereign In time of war they can be used overseas with the King's permission. They consist of the Household Cavalry (1 and 2 Life Guards, *ca* 1650, Royal Horse Guards or Blues, 1661) which in 1939-45 mustered two armoured car Regiments, and the Brigade of Guards (five Regiments of Foot Guards Grenadier, 1660, Coldstream, 1660, Scots 1641, Irish 1902, and Welsh Guards, 1915).

Housel (hou'zel) To give the Sacrament (A S *husel*, connected with Goth *hunsl*, sacrifice) *Cp* UNANELED

> Children were christened, and men houseled and assoyled through all the land, except such as were in the bill of excommunication by name expressed —
> HOLINSHED. *Chronicle*

Houssain (hu sān') Brother of Prince Ahmed in one of the *Arabian Nights* stories He possessed a piece of carpet or tapestry of such wonderful power that he had only to sit upon it, and it would transport him in a moment to any place to which he desired to go

Houyhnhnms (*whinims*, or *whinhims*). A race of horses endowed with reason and all the finer characteristics of man, introduced with caustically satirical effect by Swift in his *Gulliver's Travels* The name was the author's invention, coined in imitation of the "whinny" of a horse

> Nay, would kind Jove my organ so dispose
> To hymn harmonious Houyhnhnms through the nose
> I'd call thee Houhnhnm, that high-sounding name,
> Thy children's noses all should twang the same
> POPE *Mary Gulliver to Capt Lemuel Gulliver, an Epistle*

Howard. The female Howard. Mrs Elizabeth Fry (1780-1845), the Quaker philanthropist and worker in prisons In 1813 she paid her first visit to Newgate Prison, the horror of the conditions prevailing there determined her to devote herself to improving the lot of the prisoners, especially the females In 1817 she formed an association for their improvement, and extended her interests to Continental prisons. She was called The Female Howard in allusion to John Howard (1726-90) who is celebrated for his exertions on behalf of prison reform and for the success which attended his efforts He visited prisons not only in the United Kingdom and Ireland, but all over the Continent, and in 1777 published *The State of Prisons in England and Wales*, etc

> The radiant path that Howard trod to Heaven.
> BLOOMFIELD· *Farmer's Boy, Autumn.*

B D —16

Howdie or **Howdy** The Scottish word for a midwife

> When skirlin weanies see the light,
> Thou maks the gossips clatter bright,
> How fumbling cuffs their dearies slight,
> Wae worth the name!
> Nae howdie gets a social night
> Or plack frae them
> BURNS *Scotch Drink.*

Howleglass An old form of *Owlglass* See EULENSPIEGEL

Hoyle. According to Hoyle According to the best usage, or the highest authority Edmond Hoyle, who wrote in 1742 *A Short Treatise on the Game of Whist*, was for many years quoted as an authority in all disputes over games of whist

Hrimfaxi. See HORSE

Hub The nave of a wheel, a boss; the centre of any form of activity
In the U S A *The Hub* is Boston Mass

> Boston State-house is the hub of the solar system —
> HOLMES *Autocrat of the Breakfast Table* ch vi p 143

Up to the hub. Fully, entirely, as far as possible If a cart sinks in the mud up to the hub, it can sink no lower, if a man is thrust through with a sword up to the hub, the entire sword has passed through him, and if a quoit strikes the hub, it is not possible to do better

Hubba Hubba. An exclamation of enthusiasm of American origin which came into wide prevalence during World War II Like all such expressions its origin is obscure, though it has been ingeniously traced back to an old English expression "Hubba—a cry given to warn fishermen of the approach of pilchards."

Hubert, St. Patron saint of huntsmen (d. 727) He was the son of Bertrand, Duc d'Aquitaine, and cousin of King Pepin Hubert was so fond of the chase that he neglected his religious duties for his favourite amusement, till one day a stag bearing a crucifix menaced him with eternal perdition unless he reformed Upon this he entered the cloister, became in time Bishop of Liege, and the apostle of Ardennes and Brabant Those who were descended of his race were supposed to possess the power of curing the bite of mad dogs
In art he is represented as a bishop with a miniature stag resting on the book in his hand, or as a huntsman kneeling to the miraculous crucifix borne by the stag. His feast day is November 3rd.

Hudibras (hū'di bras) A satirical poem in three parts and nine cantos (published 1663-78) by Samuel Butler, so named from its hero, who is said to be a caricature of Sir Samuel Luke, a patron of Butler The *Grub Street Journal* (1731) maintains it was Colonel Rolle, of Devonshire, with whom the poet lodged for some time, and adds that the name is derived from Hugh de Bras, the patron saint of the county. Hudibras represents the Presbyterian party, and his squire the Independents

> 'Tis sung there is a valiant Mameluke
> In foreign land ycleped——
> BUTLER *Hudibras*, i, 1.

Zachary Grey's notes to *Hudibras* seem to prove conclusively that Sir Samuel Luke is referred to—a not too-honest man of doubtful loyalties

There are two characters of this name in Spenser's *Faerie Queene*: (1) the lover of Elissa (II, ii), typifying rashness, and (2) a legendary king of Britain (II, x, 25)

Hudson, Jeffrey (1619-82). The famous dwarf, at one time page to Queen Henrietta Maria, who caused him to be served up in a pie one day when Charles I was at dinner When he was thirty years old he was 18 in. high, but he later reached 3 ft 6 in or 3 ft 9 in He was a captain of horse in the Civil War, and afterwards was captured by pirates and sold as a slave in Barbary, but managed to escape His portrait by Van Dyck is in the National Portrait Gallery, London.

Hue and Cry. The old legal name for the official outcry made when calling for assistance "with horn and with voice," in the pursuit of a criminal escaping from justice (O Fr *huer*, to shout) Persons failing to respond when the "hue and cry" was raised were liable to penalties, hence, a clamour or outcry, a cry of alarm.

> But now by this, with noyse of late uprore,
> The hue and cry was raysed all about
> SPENSER: *Faerie Queene*, VI, xi, 46.

Hug. To hug the shore. In the case of a ship, to keep as close to the shore as is compatible with the vessel's safety

To hug the wind. To keep a ship close hauled

Hugger-mugger One of a large class of re-duplicated words (i e *namby-pamby, skimble-skamble, flip-flap*, etc) of uncertain origin, but probably an extension of *hug* Clandestinely, secretly, also, in an untidy, disorderly manner

The king in *Hamlet* says of Polonius "We have done but greenly in hugger-mugger to inter him"—i e. to smuggle him into the grave clandestinely and without ceremony

North, in his *Plutarch*, says "Antonius thought that his body should be honourably buried, and not in hugger-mugger" (clandestinely)

Ralpho says·—
> While I, in hugger-mugger hid,
> Have noted all they said and did.
> BUTLER: *Hudibras*, iii, 3.

In modern speech we say—*He lives in a hugger-mugger sort of way; the rooms were all hugger-mugger* (disorderly).

Hugh of Lincoln. It was said that the Jews in 1255 stole a boy of 8 years old named Hugh, whom they tortured for ten days and then crucified or drowned in a well Eighteen of the richest Jews of Lincoln were hanged for taking part in this affair, and more would have been put to death had it not been for the intercession of the Franciscans, the boy was buried in state This is the subject of *The Prioress's Tale* of Chaucer, and it is given in *Alphonsus of Lincoln* (1459), etc In Rymer's *Fœdera* are several documents relating to this event. Cp WILLIAM OF NORWICH

Huguenot (hū' ge not). The French Protestants (Calvinists) of the 16th and 17th centuries The name was first applied to the revolutionaries of Geneva by the adherents of the Duke of Savoy,

about 1560, and is probably an adaptation of the Ger. *eidgenossen*, confederates

Philippe de Mornay (1549-1623), the great supporter of the French Protestants, was nicknamed "the Huguenot Pope "

Huitzilopochtli. *See* MEXITL

Hulda (hūl' da). The old German goddess of marriage and fecundity who sent bridegrooms to maidens and children to the married The name means "the Benignant "

Hulda is making her bed. It snows

Hulking. A great hulking fellow. A great overgrown one A hulk is a large, unwieldy ship, or the body of a superannuated one, that looks very clumsy as it lies ashore Shakespeare says —referring to Falstaff:—
> Harry Monmouth's brawn, the hulk Sir John
> Is prisoner to your son —2 *Henry IV*, i, 1

Hulks, The, or Ship Prisons were old dismasted men-of-war anchored in the Thames and off Portsmouth, used to house prisoners awaiting transportation The principal Hulks, stationed off Woolwich, were the *Warrior*, which accommodated 480 convicts employed in the dockyard, and the *Justitia* with an equal number of men employed in the arsenal An impression of the Hulks is given in the opening chapters of *Great Expectations*

Hull, Hell, and Halifax. An old beggars' and vagabonds' "prayer," quoted by Taylor, the Water Poet (early 17th cent), was
> From Hull, Hell, and Halifax,
> Good Lord, deliver us

"Hell" was probably the least feared as being farthest from them; Hull was to be avoided because it was so well governed that beggars had little chance of getting anything without doing hard labour for it; and Halifax, because anyone caught stealing cloth in that town was beheaded without further ado.

Hullabaloo (hūl a ba loo') Uproar The word is fairly modern (middle of the 17th cent), it is of uncertain origin, but is probably a re-duplicated word formed on *holloa!* or *hullo!* Cp HURLY-BURLY.

Hulled (U.S A). Made a prisoner after capitulating, from the surrender of General Hull at Detroit, August 16th, 1812

Hulsean Lectures (hūl' sē an) Instituted by the Rev John Hulse (1708-90), of Cheshire, in 1777 Some four or six sermons on Christian evidences are preached annually at Great St Mary's, Cambridge, by the Hulsean Lecturer, who, till 1860, was entitled the Christian Advocate. Hulse also bequeathed estates to the University as an endowment for a Hulsean Professor of Divinity, and for certain Hulsean prizes

Hum and Haw, To. To hesitate to give a positive answer, to hesitate in making a speech To introduce *hum* and *haw* between words which ought to follow each other freely

Huma (hū' ma) A fabulous Oriental bird which never alights, but is always on the wing. It is said that every head which it overshadows will wear a crown. The bird suspended over the throne of Tippoo Sahib at Seringapatam represented this poetical fancy

Humanitarians (hū măn ĭ târ' ĭ anz). A name that used to be given to certain Arian heretics who believed that Jesus Christ was only man The disciples of St Simon were so called also, because they maintained the perfectibility of human nature without the aid of grace

Nowadays the term is usually applied to philanthropists whose object is the welfare of humanity at large.

Humanities or Humanity Studies. Grammar, rhetoric and poetry, with Greek and Latin (*literæ humaniores*), in contradistinction to divinity (*literæ divinæ*).

The humanities is used to designate those studies which are considered the most specially adapted for training . . true humanity in every man. —TRENCH *Study of Words*, Lect. III

A degree, L H.D , Litterarum Humaniorum Doctor (Doctor of Humane Letters), is given at some of the American universities

Humanity Martin. Richard Martin (1754-1834) one of the founders of the Royal Society for the Prevention of Cruelty to Animals He secured the passage of several laws making cruelty to certain animals illegal.

Humber. The legendary king of the Huns who are fabled to have invaded Britain about 1000 B C., he was defeated in a great battle by Locrine, and his body was cast into the river Abus, which was forthwith renamed the Humber (*Geoffrey of Monmouth*.)

Their chieftain Humber named was aright
Unto the mighty streame him to betake,
Where he an end of battell and of life did make.
SPENSER. *Faerie Queene*, II, x, 16

Humble. Humble bee. A corruption of the Ger *hummel bee*, the buzzing bee. Sometimes called the Dumble-dor. Also Bumble-bee, from its booming drone.

Humble cow. A cow without horns

To eat humble pie. To come down from a position you have assumed, to be obliged to take "a lower room " Here "humble" is a pun on *umble*, the umbles being the heart, liver, and entrails of the deer, the huntsman's perquisites When the lord and his household dined the venison pasty was served on the dais, but the *umbles* were made into a pie for the huntsman and his fellows, who took the lower seats.

Humbug. A hoax or imposition: also (as verb) to hoax, cajole, impose upon. The word is of unknown origin, but was new in the middle of the 18th century, and the Earl of Orrery, writing in the *Connoisseur* in 1754, called it a—

New-coined expression, which is only to be found in the nonsensical vocabulary and sounds absurd and disagreeable whenever it is pronounced

Humhum. (U S A) A thin cambric material.

Humming Ale. Strong liquor that froths well, and causes a humming in the head of the drinker

Let us fortify our stomachs with a slice or two of hung beef, and a horn or so of humming stingo — PIERCE EGAN· *Tom and Jerry*, ch. VII.

Hummums (hŭm' ŭmz) The hotel of this name in Covent Garden is on the site of an old bathing establishment founded there about 1631, so called from the Pers *humoun* (a sweating or Turkish bath). For many years after the Restoration the Hummums was a fashionable resort In 1708 it was kept by one Small; the rates were 5s for a single person, or 4s each for parties of two or more

"Now," says my friend, "we are so near I'll carry you to see the Hummums . and if you will pay your club towards eight shillings we'll go in and sweat "—NED WARD *The London Spy*

Humour. As good humour, ill or bad humour. etc According to an ancient theory, there are four principal humours in the body phlegm, blood, choler, and black bile. As any one of these predominates it determines the temper of the mind and body, hence the expressions sanguine, choleric, phlegmatic, and melancholic humours. A just balance made a good compound called "good humour", a preponderance of any one of the four made a bad compound called an ill or evil humour. *See* Ben Jonson's *Every Man Out of His Humour* (*Prologue*).

Humpback, The. Geronimo Amelunghi, *Il Gobbo di Pisa*, an Italian burlesque poet of the mid-16th century

Andrea Solario, the Italian painter, *Del Gobbo* (1470-1527).

Humphrey. To dine with Duke Humphrey. To have no dinner to go to Humphrey, Duke of Gloucester, son of Henry IV, the "Good Duke Humphrey" (*see under* GOOD), was renowned for his hospitality. At death it was reported that a monument would be erected to him in St Paul's but his body was interred at St. Albans The tomb of Sir John Beauchamp (d 1358), on the south side of the nave of old St. Paul's, was popularly supposed to be that of the Duke; and when the promenaders left for dinner, the poor stay-behinds who had no dinner to go to, or who feared to leave the precincts of the cathedral because, once outside they could be arrested for debt, used to say to the gay sparks who asked if they were going, that they would "dine with Duke Humphrey" that day

The expression used to be very common, and a similar one was *To sup with Sir Thomas Gresham*, the Exchange built by Sir Thomas being a common lounge

Though little coin thy purseless pocket line,
Yet with great company thou art taken up,
For often with Duke Humphrey thou dost dine,
And often with Sir Thomas Gresham sup
HAYMAN *Quodlibet* (*Epigram on a Loafer*), 1628

Humpty Dumpty. A little deformed dwarf, "humpty" and "dumpty " There used to be a drink of this name, composed of ale boiled with brandy, and it is also applied—in allusion to the old nursery rhyme—to an egg, and to anything that is, or may be, irretrievably shattered

Hunch, a colloquial term—originally American —for a premonition, a shrewd guess

Hundred An English county division dating from pre-Conquest times, and supposed to be so called either because it comprised exactly one hundred hides of land, or one hundred families, grouped together for civil and military purposes, these families being collectively responsible to the authorities in case of crime within the "hundred."

Northumberland, Cumberland, Westmorland, and Durham were divided into "wards" (*q.v*).

Yorkshire, Lincolnshire, and Notts, into "wapentakes" (*q v*) Yorkshire has also three special divisions called "ridings" (*q v*).

Kent was divided into five "lathes" (*q.v*), with subordinate hundreds.

Sussex into six "rapes" (*q v.*), with subordinate hundreds

Great, or long hundreds. Six score, a hundred and twenty

Hero of the hundred fights. Conn, a legendary Irish king, was so called by O'Gnive, the bard of O'Niel: "Conn, of the hundred fights, sleeps in his grass-grown tomb." The epithet has also been applied to Nelson, Wellington, and other famous commanders

Hundreds and thousands. A name given by sweetstuff-sellers to almost any very tiny comfits

It will be all the same a hundred years hence. An exclamation of resignation—it doesn't much matter *what* happens It is an old saying, and occurs in Ray's *Collection*, 1742. A similar one is:—

> A thousand pounds and a bottle of hay
> Is all one thing at Doom's-day —*Ray*

Not a hundred miles off. An indirect way of saying in this very neighbourhood, or very spot The phrase is employed when it would be indiscreet or dangerous to refer more directly to the person or place hinted at.

The Chiltern Hundreds. *See* CHILTERN.

The Hundred Days The days between March 20th, 1815, when Napoleon reached the Tuileries, after his escape from Elba, and June 28th, the date of the second restoration of Louis XVIII. These hundred days were noted for five things:

The additional Act to the constitutions of the empire, April 22,
The Coalition,
The Champ de Mai, June 1;
The battle of Waterloo, June 18,
The second abdication of Napoleon in favour of his son, June 22

Napoleon left Elba February 26th; landed near Cannes March 1st, entered Paris March 20th, and signed his abdication June 22nd

The address of the prefect of Paris to Louis XVIII on his second restoration begins. "A hundred days, sire, have elapsed since the fatal moment when your Majesty was forced to quit your capital in the midst of tears." This is the origin of the phrase.

The Hundred-eyed. Argus, in Greek and Latin fable Juno appointed him guardian of Io (the cow), but Jupiter caused him to be put to death; whereupon Juno transplanted his eyes into the tail of her peacock.

The Hundred-handed. Three of the sons of Uranus, viz Ægæon or Briareus, Kottos, and Gyges or Gyes After the war between Zeus and the Titans, when the latter were overcome and hurled into Tartarus, the Hundred-handed ones were set to keep watch and ward over them.

Sometimes Cerberus (*q v.*) is so called, because from his three necks sprang writhing snakes instead of hair.

The Hundred Years War The long series of wars between France and England, beginning in the reign of Edward III, 1337, and ending in that of Henry VI, 1453.

The first battle was a naval action off Sluys, and the last the fight at Castillon It originated in English claims to the French Crown and resulted in the English being expelled from the whole of France, except Calais

Hungary Water. Made of rosemary flowers and spirit, said to be so called because the receipt was given by a hermit to a Queen of Hungary.

Hungry. Hungry dogs will eat dirty puddings. *See* DOG

There are many common similes expressive of hunger, among which are—hungry as a hawk, a hunter, a church mouse (*cp*. POOR), a dog. James Thomson (*Seasons· Winter*) has "Hungry as the grave," and Oliver Wendell Holmes "Hungry as the chap that said a turkey was too much for one, not enough for two."

The Hungry Forties. A term applied to the period prior to the repeal of the Corn Laws by Sir Robert Peel in 1846, when, owing to the high price of food, distress was very common among the poor.

Hunks. An old hunks. A screw, a hard, selfish, mean fellow The term appears in late Elizabethan times—when it was a name commonly given to performing bears—and probably has its origin in some unknown person of cross (*cp* "Cross as a bear") or miserly character.

Hunky, Hunky dory (hŭng' kı, hŭng' kı dôr' ı), American slang for all's right, satisfactory

Hunt. Like Hunt's dog, he would neither go to church nor stay at home A Shropshire saying. The story is that one Hunt, a labouring man, kept a mastiff, which, on being shut up while his master went to church, howled and barked so as to disturb the whole congregation, whereupon Hunt thought he would take him to church the next Sunday, but the dog positively refused to enter The proverb is applied to a self-willed person, who will neither be led nor driven.

Hunter, Mr. and Mrs. Leo Hunter. Characters in *Pickwick Papers* who hunt up the celebrities, or "lions," to grace their parties and bring them renown and reputation.

The hunter's moon. The month or moon following the "harvest moon" (*q.v*). Hunting does not begin until after harvest.

The mighty hunter. Nimrod is so called (*Gen* x, 9) The meaning seems to be a conqueror Jeremiah says, "I [the Lord] will send for many hunters [warriors], and they shall hunt [chase] them [the Jews] from every mountain . . and out of the holes of the rocks" (xvi, 16).

> Proud Nimrod first the bloody chase began—
> A mighty hunter, and his prey was man
> POPE *Windsor Castle.*

Hunters and Runners of classic renown:—

ACASTUS, who took part in the famous Calydonian hunt (a wild boar).

ACTÆON, the famous huntsman who was transformed by Diana into a stag, because he chanced to see her bathing

ADONIS, beloved by Venus, slain by a wild boar while hunting

ADRASTUS, who was saved at the siege of Thebes by the speed of his horse Arion, given him by Hercules

ATALANTA, who promised to marry the man who could outstrip her in running.

CAMILLA, the swiftest-footed of all the companions of Diana

LADAS, the swiftest-footed of all the runners of Alexander the Great

MELEAGER, who took part in the great Calydonian boar-hunt

ORION, the great and famous hunter, changed into the constellation, so conspicuous in November

PHEIDIPPIDES, who ran 135 miles in two days

He who hunts two hares leaves one and loses the other. No one can do well or properly two things at once, he "falls between two stools " "No man can serve two masters."

Like a man to double business bound,
I stand in pause where I shall first begin
And both neglect —*Hamlet*, III, 3.

Hunting the gouk, snark, etc. See these words

To hunt with the hounds and run with the hare. See HARE.

Huntingdonians Members of "the Countess of Huntingdon's Connexion," a sect of Calvinistic Methodists founded in 1748 by Selina, widow of the ninth Earl of Huntingdon, and George Whitefield, who had become her chaplain. The churches founded by the Countess numbering some 38, are mostly affiliated with the Congregational Union

Hurdy-gurdy A stringed musical instrument, like a rude guitar, the music of which is produced by the friction of a rosined wheel on the strings, which are stopped by means of keys. It had nothing whatever to do with the modern barrel-organ or piano-organ of the streets

Hurlo-Thrumbo. A ridiculous burlesque, which in 1729-30 had an extraordinary run at the Haymarket theatre. So great was its popularity that a club called "The Hurlo-Thrumbo Society" was formed The author was Samuel Johnson (1691-1773), a half-mad dancing master, who put this motto on the title-page when the burlesque was printed —

Ye sons of fire, read my *Hurlo-Thrumbo*,
Turn it betwixt your finger and your thumbo,
And being quite undone, be quite struck dumbo.

Hurly-burly. Uproar, tumult, especially of battle A reduplication of *hurly*. Cp. HULLA-BALOO.

Now day began to break, and the army to fall again into good order, and all the hurly-burly to cease.— *North's Plutarch, Antonius* (1579)

When the hurly-burly's done,
When the battle's lost and won
            The Witches, in *Macbeth*, I, 1

In the *Garden of Eloquence* (1577) the word is given as a specimen of onomatopœia.

Hurra's Nest (U.S A) A mess up, tangle—a phrase of nautical origin.

Hurrah. A later (17th cent) form of the earlier *huzza*, an imitative sound expressing joy, enthusiasm, pleasure at victory, etc The word may be connected with the Low Ger *hurra*, in which case it was probably introduced by soldiers about the time of the Thirty Years War.

The Norman battle-cry was "Ha Rollo!" or "Ha Rou!"

Hurricane (hŭr′ ɪ kan) An 18th-century term for a large private party or rout; so called from its hurry, bustle, and noise. Cp DRUM

There is a squeeze, a fuss, a drum, a rout, and lastly a hurricane, when the whole house is full from top to bottom —*Mrs Barbauld* (1779)

The word is West Indian, and was introduced through Spanish, it means a very violent storm of wind

Hurry An imitative word, probably connected with *hurl* (as in *hurly-burly*), which first appears in Shakespeare —

She spied the hunted boar,
Whose frothy mouth .
A second fear through all her sinews spread,
Which madly hurries her she knows not whither.
            Venus and Adonis, 904.

Don't hurry, Hopkins. A satirical reproof to those who are not prompt in their payments. It is said that one Hopkins, of Kentucky, gave a creditor a promissory note on which was this memorandum, "The said Hopkins is not to be hurried in paying the above "

Husband. The word is Anglo-Saxon, from *hus*, house, and Old Norse *bondi*, a freeholder or yeoman, from *bua*, to dwell, hence the word is literally, a house-owner in his capacity as head of the household, and so came to be applied to a man joined to a woman in marriage, who was, naturally, the head of his household. When Sir John Paston, writing to his mother in 1475, said—

I purpose to leeffe aile heer, and come home to you and be your husbonde and bailyff,

he was proposing to come and manage her household for her. We use the word in the same sense in such phrases as **To husband one's resources.**

Similarly a ship's husband is an official responsible for seeing that all the equipment, etc , necessary for going to sea is placed on board a ship before sailing, that all the regulations relating to the voyage are fulfilled, and that the captain is sufficiently furnished with money, etc , for carrying on business when in foreign or other ports.

Thomas Tusser was in error when he derived the word from "houseband," as in the following distich.—

The name of the husband, what is it to say?
Of wife and of *house*-hold the *band* and the stay.
            Five Hundred Points of Good Husbandry (1557).

Husbandry is merely the occupation of the (original) *husband*, i.e. the management of the household and what pertains thereto, it became restricted later to farm-management, and the *husband* became the *husbandman*.

I commit into your hands
The husbandry and manage of my house
            Merchant of Venice, III, 4.

Hush, Hush-hush, a term that came into use in World War I to describe very secret operations, designs, or inventions.

Hush-money. Money given as a bribe for silence or "hushing" a matter up.

Hushai (hŭsh′ ī). In Dryden's *Absalom and Achitophel* (q.v.) is Laurence Hyde, Earl of Rochester (1641-1711)

Husking, Husking-bee, Husking-frolic. Cornhusking. In N. America in the 18th century this was a gathering for husking Indian corn, which frequently ended in a brawl.

Husky. In American usage this word is applied to a big, burly, strong man As an abbreviation for the word *Eskimo* it is the name used for an Eskimo sledge dog

Hussar (hu zar') An Hungarian word (*huszar*), which is ultimately from the same Greek word that gives us our *corsair* It was applied in the time of Matthias Corvinus (mid-15th cent.), to a body of light horsemen, and was hence adopted in various European armies to denote light cavalry

Hussites (hŭs' ĭtz) Followers of John Huss, the Bohemian reformer, in the 15th century *Cp* BETHLEMENITES

Hussy (hŭz' ı). Nowadays a word of contempt implying an ill-behaved girl, a "jade" or "minx," it is no other than the honourable appellation *housewife* (pron "hussif") Just as *wench* has come down in the world, so has *hussy* been degraded.

Hustings (hŭs' tingz) An Anglo-Saxon word, meaning originally the immediate council of the king, from *hus*, house (*i e.* the royal house), and *thing*, assembly. the *hus-thing* was the assembly of the house as apart from the *thing*, the general assembly of the people London has still its *Court of Hustings*, which is held by the Lord Mayor, Sheriffs, Recorder, and Aldermen to consider gifts offered to the City, this was formerly the supreme court (common pleas, probate, etc) of the City The hustings of elections were, previous to the Ballot Act of 1872, the platforms from which candidates made their election addresses, etc , hence *to be beaten at the hustings* means to lose at an election.
  A realistic impression of the old hustings at a Parliamentary election is given in *Pickwick Papers* (xiii).

Hutin (oo' tan) **Louis le Hutin.** Louis X (1289, 1314-16) was so nicknamed. It means "the quarreller," "the stubborn or headstrong one," and it is uncertain why the name was given to this insignificant king of France

Hutkin. A word in some dialects for a cover for a sore finger, made by cutting off the finger of an old glove, called also, a *hut, hutch*, and *hutchkin*.

Huzza! An exclamation of joy or applause, the forerunner of *Hurrah!* (*q v.*). The word has no etymology, being merely an extension of an involuntary vocable, such as *Chut!* or *Pshaw!*

Hyacinth (hī' a sinth) According to Greek fable, the son of Amyclas, a Spartan king The lad was beloved by Apollo and Zephyr, and as he preferred the sun-god, Zephyr drove Apollo's quoit at his head, and killed him The blood became a flower, and the petals are inscribed with the signature A I, meaning *woe*. (Virgil *Eclogues*, iii, 106)
  The hyacinth bewrays the doleful "A I,"
  And culls the tribute of Apollo's sigh.
  Still on its bloom the mournful flower retains
  The lovely blue that dyed the stripling's veins
                              CAMOENS *Lusiad*, ix

Hyades (hī' a dēz) (Gr. *huein*, to rain). Seven nymphs placed among the stars, in the constellation Taurus, which threaten rain when they rise with the sun The fable is that they wept the death of their brother Hyas so bitterly that Zeus, out of compassion, took them to heaven
  The seaman sees the Hyades
  Gather an army of Cimmerian clouds . .
  All-fearful folds his sails, and sounds the main,
  Lifting his prayers to the heavens for aid
  Against the terror of the winds and waves
                              MARLOWE 1 *Tamburlaine*, III, ii.

Hybla (hib' la) A city and mountain in Sicily, famous for its honey *Cp* HYMETTUS
  For your words, they rob the Hybla bees
  And leave them honeyless
    Ant   Not stingless too
    Bru. O, yes, and soundless too,
  For you have stol'n their buzzing, Antony,
  And very wisely threat before you sting
                              Julius Cæsar, v, 1.

Hydra (hī' dra) A monster of the Lernean marshes, in Argolis. It has nine heads. and it was one of the twelve labours of Hercules to kill it. As soon as he struck off one of its heads. two shot up in its place, hence *hydra-headed* applies to a difficulty which goes on increasing as it is combated

Hyena (hī ē' nå). Held in veneration by the ancient Egyptians. It is fabled that a certain stone, called the "hyæna," is found in the eye of the creature, and Pliny asserts (*Nat. Hist.*, xxxvii, 60) that when placed under the tongue it imparts the gift of prophecy
  The skilful Lapidarists of Germany affirm that this beast hath a stone in his eye (or rather his head) called Hyæna or Hyænius —TOPSELL. *Four-footed Beasts* (1607).

Hygeia (hī jē' å). Goddess of health in Greek mythology, and the daughter of Æsculapius (*q v*) Her symbol was a serpent drinking from a cup in her hand

Hyksos (hik' sos) A line of six or more foreign rulers over Egypt, known as the Shepherd Kings, who reigned for about 250 years between the XIIth and XVIIIth Dynasties, *i e* about 2000 B C. It is uncertain whence they came, who they were, what they did, or whither they went, they left little in the way of records or monuments, and practically all that is known of them is the (historically speaking) very unsatisfactory notice gleaned by Josephus from Manetho
  The exact nationality of the Hyksos is still a matter of dispute All we know for certainty is that they came from Asia, and they brought with them in their train vast numbers of Semites —SAYCE *Races of the Old Testament* (1891)

Hylas (hī' lås). A boy beloved by Hercules, carried off by the nymphs while drawing water from a fountain in Mysia

Hymen (hī' men) Properly, a marriage song of the ancient Greeks, later personified as the god of marriage, represented as a youth carrying a torch and veil—a more mature Eros, or Cupid

Hymettus (hī met' ûs) A mountain in Attica, famous for its honey *Cp.* HYBLA
  There, flowery hill, Hymettus, with the sound
  Of bees' industrious murmur, oft invites
To studious musing.
                              MILTON *Paradise Regained, IV*, 247.

Hymnus Eucharisticus. *See* EUCHARIST.

Hyperbole (hī pĕr′ bō lǐ) The rhetorical figure of speech which consists of exaggeration or extravagance in statement for the purpose of giving effect but not intended to be taken *au pied de la lettre*—*e g*. "the waves were mountains high "

Hyperboles are of two kinds, either such as are employed in description, or such as are suggested by the warmth of passion.—LINDLEY MURRAY· *English Grammar*, I, p 510

Hyperboreans (hī pĕr bôr′ ǐ anz) A happy people of early Greek legend, who were supposed to dwell on the other side of the spot where the North Wind has its birth, and therefore to enjoy perpetual warmth and sunshine They were said to be the oldest of the human race, the most virtuous, and the most happy, to dwell for some thousand years under a cloudless sky, in fields yielding double harvests, and in the enjoyment of perpetual Spring

Later fable held that they had not an atmosphere like our own, but one consisting wholly of feathers Both Herodotus and Pliny mention this fiction, which they say was suggested by the quantity of snow observed to fall in those regions. (*Herodotus*, IV, 31.)

Hyperion (hī pĕr′ ı on) In Greek mythology, one of the Titans, son of Uranus and Ge, and father of Helios, Selene, and Eos (the Sun, Moon, and Dawn) The name is sometimes given by poets to the sun itself, but not by Keats in his wonderful "poetical fragment" of this name (1820)

Hypermnestra (hī pĕrm nes′ trá). Wife of Lynceus and the only one of the fifty daughters of Danaos who did not murder her husband on their bridal night *See* DANAIDES

Hypnotism (hip′ nō ızm). The art of producing trance-sleep, or the state of being hypnotized Dr James Braid of Manchester gave it this name (1843), after first having called it *neurohypnotism*, an inducing to sleep of the nerves (Gr)

The method, discovered by Mr Braid, of producing this state appropriately designated . hypnotism consists in the maintenance of a fixed gaze for several minutes . on a bright object placed somewhat above [the line of sight], at so short a distance [as to produce pain]—CARPENTER. *Principles of Mental Physiology*, II, 1

Hypochondria (hī pō kon′ drı a) (Gr *hypo*, *chrondros*, under the cartilage—*i.e* the spaces on each side of the epigastric region) A morbid depression of spirits for which there is no known or defined cause, so called because it was supposed to be caused by some derangement in these parts, which were held to be the seat of melancholy

Hypocrite (hip′ ō krıt) Prince of hypocrites. Tiberius Cæsar (42 B C , A.D. 14 to 37) was so called because he affected a great regard for decency, but indulged in the most detestable lust and cruelty

Abdallah Ibn Obba and his partisans were called The Hypocrites by Mohammed, because they feigned to be friends, but were in reality foes

Hypocrites' Isle. *See* CHANEPH

Hypodorian Mode. *See* ÆOLIAN.

Hypostatic Union (hī pō stǎt′ ık) The union of the three Persons in the Trinity; also the union of the Divine and Human in Christ The *hypostasis* (Gr *hypo*, under, *stasis*, standing, hence foundation, essence) is the personal existence as distinguished from both *nature* and *substance*.

Hyson (hī′ son). One of the varieties of Chinese green tea; so called from *her-ch'un*, bright spring. *Young hyson*, a still better variety, is *Yu-ch ien*, before the rains, meaning that the leaf is picked before the commencement of the rainy season

Hyssop (his′ op) David says (*Ps* lı, 7). "Purge me with hyssop, and I shall be clean." The reference is to the custom of ceremonially sprinkling the unclean with a bunch of hyssop (marjorum or the thorny caper) dipped in water in which had been mixed the ashes of a red heifer This was done as they left the Court of the Gentiles to enter the Court of the Women (*Numb* xix, 17, 18)

Hysteron Proteron (his′ ter on prō′ ter on), from the Greek meaning "hinder foremost," is a term used in logic and rhetoric to describe a figure of speech in which the word that should come last is placed first, or the second of two consecutive propositions is stated first, *e g* "Let us die, and rush into the midst of the fray."

I

I. The ninth letter of the alphabet, also of the futhorc (*q v.*), representing the Greek *iota* and Semitic *yod*. The written (and printed) *ı* and *j* were for long interchangeable; it was only in the 19th century that in dictionaries, etc , they were treated as separate letters (in Johnson s Dictionary, for instance, *iambic* comes between *iamb* and *jangle*), and hence in many series—such as the signatures of sheets in a book, hallmarks on plate, etc.—either I or J is omitted. *Cp.* U

The dot on the small *ı* is not originally part of the letter, but was introduced about the 11th century as a diacritic in cases where two *ı*'s came together (*e g. filiı*) to distinguish between these and *u*.

To dot the i's and cross the t's To be meticulous, particularly about things of apparently little consequence, to clinch 'an agreement

Iambic (ī ăm′ bik) An *iamb*, or *iambus*, is a metrical foot consisting of a short syllable followed by a long one, as *away*, *deduce*, or an unaccented followed by an accented, as *be gone'* *Iambic* verse is verse based on iambs, as, for instance, the Alexandrine measure, which consists of six iambuses—

I think the thoughts you think, and if I have the knack Of fitting thoughts to words, you peradventure lack, Envy me not the chance, yourselves more fortunate'
BROWNING· *Fifine at the Fair*, lxxvi

Father of Iambic verse, Archilochos of Paros (fl *c* 700 B C)

Ianthe (ĭ ăn′ tnĭ), a Cretan girl who, as told in Ovid's *Metamorphoses*, ix, 5, married Iphis, who had been transformed for the purpose, from a girl into a young man. The Ianthe to whom Lord Byron dedicated his *Childe Harold*, was Lady Charlotte Harley, born 1801, and only eleven years old at the time Shelley gave the name to his infant daughter.

Iapetos (Ĭ ăp′ ĕ tos) Son of Uranus and Ge, father of Atlas, Prometheus, Epimetheus, and Menœtius, and ancestor of the human race, hence called *genus Iapeti*, the progeny of Iapetus.

Iberia (Ĭ bēr′ ı à), Spain; the country of the Iberus, the ancient name of the river Ebro The Iberians were the prehistoric, non-Aryan inhabitants of the peninsula, probably of African origin The Spanish Basques are their nearest modern representatives.

Iberia's Pilot. Christopher Columbus (1446?-1507)

> Launched with Iberia's pilot from the steep,
> To worlds unknown, and isles beyond the deep.
> CAMPBELL: *The Pleasures of Hope*, ii.

Ibid. (ib′ id) A contraction of Lat *ibidem*, in the same place

Ibis (Ī′ bis) A sacred bird of the ancient Egyptians, specially connected with the god Thoth, who in the guise of an Ibis escaped the pursuit of Typhon Its white plumage symbolized the light of the sun, and its black neck the shadow of the moon, its body a heart, and its legs a triangle It was said that it drank only the purest of water, and that the bird was so fond of Egypt that it would pine to death if transported elsewhere The practical reason for the protection of the Ibis—for it was a crime to kill it—was that it devoured crocodiles' eggs, serpents and all sorts of noxious reptiles and insects *Cp* ICHNEUMON

Iblis *See* EBLIS

Ibraham (ib′ rà hìm). The Abraham of the Koran.

Icarius (ı kâr′ ı ũs) In Greek legend an Atherian who was taught the cultivation of the vine by Dionysus (Bacchus) He was slain by some peasants who had become intoxicated with wine he had given them, and who thought they had been poisoned They buried the body under a tree; his daughter Erigone, searching for her father, was directed to the spot by the howling of his dog Mœra, and when she discovered the body she hanged herself for grief. Icarius became the constellation *Boötes*, Erigone the constellation *Virgo*, and Mœra the star *Procyon*, which rises in July, a little before the dog-star.

Icarus (ik′ à rus) Son of Dædalus (*q.v.*) He flew with his father from Crete; but the sun melted the wax with which his wings were fastened on, and he fell into the sea Those waters of the Ægean were thenceforward called the Icarian Sea.

Ice. Ice age. There have been several glacial epochs, but what is commonly known by that name was the earlier part of the existing geological period, the Pleistocene, when a considerable portion of the northern hemis-phere was overwhelmed by ice caps or ice sheets Ice covered large areas of north-western Europe, Canada, and the U S A , and as it melted the included stones were spread out in vast sheets of irregular deposits Man was contemporary with at least the latter periods of the Ice Age, his remains having been found in England and France together with the mammoth and reindeer in beds earlier than the last glacial deposits Science has as yet found no satisfactory explanation of the causes of the Ice Age.

A sword of ice-brook temper. Of the very best quality. The Spaniards used to plunge their swords and other weapons, while hot from the forge, into the brook Salo [Xalon], near Bilbilis, in Celtiberia, to harden them The water of this brook is very cold.

> It is a sword of Spain, the ice-brook temper
> *Othello*, v, 2.

Ice Saints or Frost Saints. Those saints whose days fall in what is called "the black-thorn winter"—that is, the second week in May (between 11 and 14). Some give only three days, but whether 11, 12, 13 or 12, 13, 14 is not agreed. May 11th is the day of St Mamertus, May 12th of St Pancras, May 13th of St. Servatius, and May 14th of St Boniface

The ice-blink. The name given by mariners to a luminous appearance of the sky, caused by the reflection of light from ice If the sky is dark or brown, the navigator may be sure that there is water; if it is white, rosy, or orange-coloured, he may be certain there is ice The former is called a "water sky," the latter an "ice sky"

The Danish name for the great ice-cliffs of Greenland is "The Ice-blink"

To break the ice. To broach a disagreeable subject, to open the way, take the first step, make the plunge

> [We] An' if you break the ice, and do this feat .
> Will not so graceless be, to be ingrate.
> *Taming of the Shrew*, i, 2.

To skate over thin ice. To take unnecessary risks, especially in conversation or argument; to touch on dangerous subjects very lightly.

Iceberg. A mass of ice, broken from a glacier which ends in the sea, and floated about the ocean by the currents The magnitude of some icebergs is considerable One seen off the Cape of Good Hope was two miles in circumference, and a hundred and fifty feet high For every cubic foot above water there must be at least eight cubic feet below, their weight must be enormous, and the danger to shipping—witness the *Titanic* disaster of April, 1912—is very great

Iceland Dogs. Shaggy, white dogs, once great favourites as lap-dogs. Shakespeare mentions them in *Henry V*, where he makes Pistol call Nym in contempt a "prick-eared cur of Iceland."

> Iceland dogges curled and rough all over, wh ch, by reason of the length of their heire make showe neither of face nor of body —FLEMING *Of English Dogges* (1576)

Iceni. *See* WARRIOR QUEEN

Ich Dien (ik dēn) According to a Welsh tradition, Edward I promised to provide Wales with a prince "who could speak no word of English," and when his second son Edward (afterwards Edward II) was born at Carnarvon he presented him to the assembly, saying in Welsh *Eich dyn* (behold the man) The words are actually German, meaning "I serve," and are erroneously said to have been adopted as the Prince of Wales's motto by the Black Prince, together with the three white ostrich plumes, from John, King of Bohemia, who fell at the Battle of Crecy, 1346

Ichabod (ik´ a bod) A son of Phinehas, born just after the death of his father and grandfather (1 *Sam* iv, 21) The name (Heb. I-kabhoth) means "where is the glory ?" It is usually popularly translated by "the glory has departed "

Ichneumon (ik nū´ mon) A weasel-like animal (also called "Pharaoh's rat") found in Egypt and venerated by the ancient Egyptians because, like the ibis (*q.v*), it feeds on serpents, mice, and other vermin, and is especially fond of crocodiles' eggs According to legend, it steals into the mouths of crocodiles when they gape, and eats out their bowels The name is Greek, and means "one who tracks, or traces out "

Ichor (i´ kôr) In classical mythology, the colourless blood of the gods (Gr , juice)

> [St Peter] patter'd with his keys at a great rate,
> And sweated through his apostolic skin.
> Of course his perspiration was but ichor,
> Or some such other spiritual liquor
>   BYRON. *Vision of Judgment*, xxv

Ichthus (ik´ thùs) Greek for "fish," which in primitive times was used as a symbol of Christ because the word is formed of the initial letters *Iesous CH*ristos, *TH*eou *U*ios, *S*oter, Jesus Christ, Son of God, Saviour This notarica is found on many seals, rings, urns, and tombstones belonging to the early times of Christianity, and was supposed to be a "charm" of mystical efficacy.

Icknield Street, or **Way** One of the principal of the old "Roman" roads in Britain It crossed the country from Norfolk to Cornwall, and large parts of it date from pre-Roman times

Its name of the Icknield Way connects this road with the Iceni, whom the Romans found settled in our Norfolk and Suffolk, and points back to days in which this tribe stood supreme in south east Britain —J R GREEN *Making of England*, ch iii.

Icon or **Ikon** (i´ kon), from the Greek *eikon*, an image or likeness, is a representation in the form of painting, low-relief sculpture or mosaic of some sacred personage in the Eastern Church Excepting the face and bands, the whole is often covered with an embossed metal plaque representing the figure and drapery Icons are greatly venerated by the Russian peasantry

Icon Basilike. *See* EIKON BASILIKE

Iconoclasts (Gr , "image breakers") Reformers who rose in the Eastern Church in the 8th century, and were specially opposed to the employment of pictures, statues, emblems, and all visible representations of sacred objects. The crusade against these things began in 726 with the Emperor Leo III (the Isaurian), and

16*

continued for one hundred and twenty years under Constantine Copronymus, Leo the Armenian, Theophilus, and other Byzantine Emperors, who are known as the Iconoclast Emperors

Id, in Freudian psychology is the whole reservoir of impulsive reactions that forms the mind, of which the ego is a superficial layer It is the totality of impulses or instincts comprising the true unconscious mind

Ideal Republics *See* COMMONWEALTHS

Idealism Subjective idealism, taught by Fichte (1762-1814), supposes the object (say a tree) and the image of it on the mind are one. Or rather, that there is no object outside the mental idea

Objective idealism, taught by Schelling (1775-1854), supposes that the tree and the image thereof on the mind are distinct from each other

Absolute idealism, taught by Hegel (1770-1831), supposes there is no such thing as phenomena, that mind, through the senses, creates its own world In fact, that there is no real, but all is ideal

Personal idealism, as expounded by William James (1842-1910), lays special emphasis on the authority of the will and the initiative of the self in experience, as opposed to the tendency of absolute idealism to minimize the working of the individual soul

Idealists. They may be divided into two distinct sections—

(1) Those who follow Plato, who taught that before creation there existed certain types or ideal models, of which *ideas* created objects are the visible images, Malebranche, Kant, Schelling, Hegel, etc , were of this school

(2) Those who maintain that all phenomena are only subjective—that is, mental cognizances only within ourselves, and what we see and what we hear are only brain impressions. Of this school were Berkeley, Hume, Fichte, and many others.

Ides (idz) In the Roman calendar the 15th of March, May, July, and October, and the 13th of all the other months, always eight days after the Nones.

Beware the Ides of March. Said as a warning of impending and certain danger The allusion is the warning received by Julius Cæsar before his assassination.—

Furthermore, there was a certain soothsayer that had given Cæsar warning long time afore, to take heed of the day of the Ides of March (which is the fifteenth of the month), for on that day he should be in great danger That day being come, Cæsar going into the Senate-house and speaking merrily unto the soothsayer, told him, "The Ides of March be come", "So be they," softly answered the soothsayer, "but yet are they not past."—PLUTARCH *Julius Cæsar* (North's *trans*)

See also Julius Cæsar, 1, 2, iii, 1, etc

Idiot. Originally—in Greece—a private person, one not engaged in any public office, hence an uneducated, ignorant person Jeremy Taylor says, "Humility is a duty in great ones, as well as in idiots" (private persons). The Greeks have the expressions, "a priest or an idiot" (layman), "a poet or an idiot" (prose-writer). In 1 *Cor* xiv, 16, where the Authorized Version has "how shall he who occupieth the place of the unlearned say Amen . ?" Wyclif's version reads " . who fillith the place of an idyot, how schal he seie amen . ?"

Idle Bible, The *See* BIBLE, SPECIALLY NAMED

Ido (ē′ dō), an international language invented by Louis Couturat in 1907. It was a modification of Esperanto—indeed, the name is Esperanto for "offspring"—but was said to be simpler and free of many of the defects of that language

Idomeneus (ī dom′ in ūs) King of Crete, an ally of the Greeks at Troy. After the city was burnt he made a vow to sacrifice whatever he first encountered, if the gods granted him a safe return to his kingdom It was his own son that he first met; he offered him up to fulfil his vow, but a plague followed, and the king was banished from Crete as a murderer. (*Iliad*) *Cp* IPHIGENIA

Iduna or **Idun** (ī dū′ nā, ī dūn′) In Scandinavian mythology, daughter of the dwarf Svald, and wife of Bragi She was guardian of the golden apples which the gods tasted as often as they wished to renew their youth.

Ifreet. *See* AFREET.

Ifs and Ans.

If ifs and ans
Were pots and pans
Where would be the tinker?

An old-fashioned jingle to describe wishful thinking The "ans"—often erroneously written "ands"—is merely the old "an" for 'if."

Igerna. *See* IGRAINE

Ignatius, St. (ig nā′ shus) According to tradition, St Ignatius was the little child whom our Saviour set in the midst of His disciples for their example He was a convert of St John the Evangelist, was consecrated Bishop of Antioch by St. Peter, and is said to have been thrown to the beasts in the amphitheatre by Trajan, about 107 He is commemorated on February 1st, and is represented in art accompanied by lions, or chained and exposed to them, in allusion to his martyrdom

Father Ignatius. The Rev. Joseph Leycester Lyne (1837-1908), a deacon of the Church of England, who founded a pseudo-Benedictine monastery at Llanthony, N. Wales He was an eloquent preacher, but his ritualistic practices brought him into conflict with his ecclesiastical superiors He was never ordained priest in the Anglican Church but secured an irregular ordination through a dissident priest of an Oriental rite

The Hon and Rev Geo. Spencer (1799-1864), a clergyman of the Church of England who joined the Roman communion, and became Superior of the English province of the Congregation of Passionists, was also known as "Father Ignatius."

St Ignatius Loyola. *See* LOYOLA.

Ignis Fatuus (ig′ nis făt′ ū ūs) The "Will o' the wisp" or ' Friar's lanthorn" (*q v*), a flame-like phosphorescence flitting over marshy ground (due to the spontaneous combustion of gases

from decaying vegetable matter), and deluding people who attempt to follow it: hence, any delusive aim or object, or some Utopian scheme that is utterly impracticable The name means "a foolish fire", it is also called "Jack o' Lantern," "Spunkie," "Walking Fire," and "Fair Maid of Ireland "

When thou rannest up Gadshill in the night to catch my horse, if I did not think thou hadst been an *ignis fatuus* or a bail of wildfire, there's no purchase in money.—1 *Henry IV*, iii, 3

According to a Russian superstition, these wandering fires are the spirits of still-born children which flit between heaven and the Inferno.

Ignoramus (ig nôr ā′ mus) One who ignores the knowledge of something, one really unacquainted with it It is an ancient law term The grand jury used to write *Ignoramus* on the back of indictments "not found" or not to be sent into court Hence *ignore*

Ignorantines (ig nôr ān′ tīnz). A name given to the Brothers of Charity, or Brethren of Saint Jean-de-Dieu, an order of Augustinian mendicants founded in 1495 in Portugal by John of Monte Major (d 1550) to minister to the sick poor, and introduced into France by Marie de' Medici

It was also given later, to a religious association founded by the Abbé de la Salle in 1724 in France, for educating gratuitously the children of the poor.

Igraine (i grān). Wife of Gorlois (*q v*), Duke of Tintagel, in Cornwall, and mother of King Arthur His father, Uther Pendragon, married Igraine thirteen days after her husband was slain

Iguanodon (i gwān′ ō don), one of the dinosaurs; a land repule from 15 ft. to 25 ft. long with a small head, heavy jaws set with teeth like those of the modern iguana, and flexible lips The creature supported itself on its two hind legs and powerful tail, its front limbs being comparatively small

Ihram (i răm) The ceremonial garb of Mohammedan pilgrims to Mecca, also, the ceremony of assuming it

We prepared to perform the ceremony of *Al-Ihram* (assuming the pilgrim garb) . we donned the attire, which is nothing but two new cotton cloths, each six feet long by three and a half broad, white with narrow red stripes and fringes. One of these sheets, technically armed the *Rida*, is thrown over the back, and, exposing the arm and shoulder, is knotted at the right side in the style of *Wishah* The *Izar* is wrapped round the loins from waist to knee, and, knotted or tucked in at the middle, supports itself—BURTON: *Pilgrimage to Al-Madinah and Mecca*, xxvi.

I.H.S —*i e* the Greek *IHΣ*, meaning *IHΣους* (Jesus), the long e (H) being mistaken for a capital H, and the dash perverted into a cross The letters being thus obtained, St. Bernardine of Siena, in 1347, applied them to *Jesus Hominum Salvator* (Jesus, the Saviour of men), another application being *In hac salus* (safety in this *i e*. the Cross).

Iliad (il′ i ad) (Gr. *Ilias*, gen. *Iliad-os*, the land of Ilium). The tale of the siege of Troy, or Ilium, an epic poem attributed to Homer (*q.v.*), in twenty-four books Menelaus, King of Sparta, received as his guest Paris, a son of Priam,

King of Troy, who ran away with Helen, wife of Menelaus Menelaus induced the Greeks to lay siege to Troy to avenge the perfidy, and the siege lasted ten years The poem begins in the tenth year with a quarrel between Agamemnon, King of Mycenæ and commander-in-chief of the allied Greeks, and Achilles, the hero who had retired from the army in ill temper The Trojans now prevail, and Achilles sends his friend Patroclus to oppose them, but Patroclus is slain Achilles, in a desperate rage, rushes into the battle, and slays Hector, the commander of the Trojan army. The poem ends with the funeral rites of Hector

An Iliad of woes A number of evils falling one after another, there is scarce a calamity in the whole catalogue of human ills that finds not mention in the *Iliad*
Demosthenes used the phrase (*Ilias kakon*), and it was adopted by Cicero (*Ilias malorum*) in his *Ad Atticum*, viii, 11
> It opens another Iliad of woes to Europe
> BURKE. *On a Regicide Peace*, ii.

The Iliad in a nutshell *See* NUTSHELL

The French Iliad. The *Romance of the Rose* (*see* ROSE) has been so called Similarly, the *Nibelungenlied* (*q.v.*) and the *Lusiad* (*q v.*) have been called respectively the *German* and *Portuguese Iliad.*

Ilk (A S *ilca*, the same). Only used—correctly —in the phrase of that ilk, when the surname of the person spoken of is the same as the name of his estate; *Bethune of that ilk* means "Bethune of Bethune." It is a mistake to use the phrase "All that ilk" to signify all of that name or family.

Illegitimates. An old Australian slang phrase applied to early settlers who came to the country voluntarily, and not for "legal" reasons—*i e* as convicts

Illinois. Originally the name of a confederacy of North American Indian tribes who were allied to the French *Illini* means "man," and the French substituted their plural termination *-ois* for the Indian *-uk*.

Illinois nut. The pecan

Ill May-day. *See* EVIL MAY-DAY.

Ill-starred. Unlucky, fated to be unfortunate. Othello says of Desdemona, "O ill-starred wench!" The allusion is to the astrological dogma that the stars influence the fortunes of mankind.

Illuminated Doctor. Raymond Lully (1254-1315), the Spanish scholastic philosopher, also Johann Tauler (1294-1361), the German mystic.

Illuminati. The baptised were at one time so called, because a lighted candle was given them to hold as a symbol that they were illuminated by the Holy Ghost.
The name has been given to, or adopted by, several sects and secret societies professing to have superior enlightenment, especially to a republican society of deists, founded by Adam Weishaupt (1748-1830) at Ingoldstadt in Bavaria in 1776, having for its object the establishment of a religion consistent with "sound reason "

Among others to whom the name has been applied are the Hesychasts; the Alombrados, a Spanish sect founded about 1575 by the Carmelite, Catherine de Jesus, and John of Willelpando, the members of which rejected the sacraments; the French Guerinists, the Rosicrucians (*q v*); and in the U S A. to the Jeffersonians, and (by them) to the Princetonians and opponents of Freemasonry

Illuminator, The. The surname given to St. Gregory of Armenia (257-331), the apostle of Christianity among the Armenians

Illustrious, The.
Albert V, Duke and second Emperor of Austria (1398-1439)
Nicomedes II of Bithynia (d 89 B C).
Ptolemy V, King of Egypt, Epiphanes (210, 205-181 B C)
Jam-shid (Jam the Illustrious), nephew of Tah Omurs, fifth king of the Paisdadian dynasty of Persia (about 840-800 B C)
Kien-long, fourth of the Manchu dynasty of China (1709-99)

Ilokano (ē lō ka' nō), an Indonesian language spoken in Luzon, but the term is also in use since World War II to describe a sort of lingua franca composed of Malay, English, and Spanish, common in the Philippines and adjacent islands of Malaysia.

Image-breakers, The. *See* ICONOCLASTS

Imaum or **Imam** (i' mäm, i mäm') A member of the priestly body of the Mohammedans He recites the prayers and leads the devotions of the congregation The Sultan of Turkey as "head of the Moslems" was an Imaum, and the title is also given to the Sultan of Muscat and to the heads of the four orthodox Moslem sects. The word means *teacher* or *guide. Cp* ULEMA.

Imbrocata (im bro ka' ta) (Ital) An old fencing term for a thrust over the arm.
> If your enemie bee cunning and skilfull, never stand about giving any foine or imbrocata, but this thrust or stoccata alone, neither it also [never attempt] unlesse you be sure to hit him —SAVIOLO *Practise of the Duello* (1595).

Imbroglio (im brō lyō) (Ital) A complicated plot; a misunderstanding of a complicated nature

Immaculate Conception This dogma, that the Virgin Mary was conceived without original sin, was first broached by St Bernard, was stoutly maintained by Duns Scotus and his disciples, but was not declared by the Roman Catholic Church to be an article of faith till 1854 It was proclaimed by Pius IX in the bull *Ineffabilis Deus* in these words.—
> That the most blessed Virgin Mary, in the first moment of her conception, by a special grace and privilege of Almighty God, in virtue of the merits of Christ, was preserved immaculate from all stain of original sin.

The Feast of the Immaculate Conception is celebrated on December 8th, and is a holiday of obligation (*q v.*).

Immolate (im' ō lāt). To sacrifice, literally, "put meal on one" (Lat *immolare*, to sprinkle with meal). The reference is to the ancient Roman custom of sprinkling wine and fragments of the sacred cake (*mola salsa*) on the head of a victim to be offered in sacrifice

Immortal. The Immortal. Yông-Tching (1723-36), third of the Manchu dynasty of China, assumed the title.

The Immortal Tinker. John Bunyan (1628-88), a tinker by trade

The Immortals. The forty members of the French Academy, also the name given to a body of 10,000 foot-soldiers, which constituted the bodyguard of the ancient Persian kings, and to other highly trained troops

In the British Army the 76th Foot were called "The Immortals," because so many were wounded, but not killed, in India (1788-1806) This regiment, with the old 33rd, now forms the two battalions of the West Riding regiment

Imp A graft (A S. *impian*), a shoot; hence offspring, and a child In hawking, "to imp a feather" was to engraft or add a new feather for a broken one The needles employed for the purpose were called "imping needles "

The noun "imp," child, did not formerly connote mischievousness as it now does; Thomas Cromwell, writing to Henry VIII, speaks of "that noble imp your son."

Let us pray for . the king's most excellent majesty and for . his beloved son Edward, our prince, that most angelic imp —*Pathway to prayer*.

Milton calls the serpent "fittest imp of fraud" (*Paradise Lost*, IX, 89).

Lincoln Imp. *See* LINCOLN.

Impanation (im pă nă shon) The Lutheran dogma that the body and soul of Christ are infused into the eucharistic elements after consecration; and that the bread and wine are united with the body and soul of Christ in much the same way as the body and soul of man are united. The word means *putting into the bread*

Imperial. From the Lat *imperialis*, *imperium*, the word really means anything to do with an empire or emperor Following are some of its special and particular applications:—

A standard size of printing paper measuring between 22 × 30 in and 22 × 32 in. Also of writing paper measuring 22 × 30 in.

In Russia there used to be current a gold coin, value 15 roubles, called an "imperial "

A tuft of hair on the chin, all the rest of the beard and all the whiskers being shaved off. So called from the Emperor Napoleon III (1808-73), who set the fashion.

Imperial Conference. The origin of this goes back to Queen Victoria's Jubilee (1887) when the prime ministers of the various dominions were in London and met together to confer. Similar conferences were held in 1897, 1902, 1907, 1911, and since World War I it has met every few years in London or elsewhere.

Imperial Institute. A building erected in S. Kensington to commemorate the jubilee of Queen Victoria (1887) and opened in 1893 The name is also used for the Society which has its headquarters therein, the object of which is to assist in the development of the resources of the British Empire by arranging exhibitions and disseminating information.

The Imperial Service Order was instituted by Edward VII in 1902 for Civil Servants with long and meritorious records

Imperialism, coming from the Latin *imperium* is applied in modern times to the belief in the expansion and development of an empire, more especially the British Empire. It came into use in the latter part of the 19th century, since when the word has gradually come to acquire a somewhat derogatory meaning, suggestive of jingoism

Imposition. A task given in schools, etc , as a punishment The word is taken from the verb *impose*, as the task is imposed In the sense of a *deception* it means to "put a trick on a person," hence, the expression "to put on one," etc

Imposition of hands. The bishop laying his hand on persons confirmed or ordained (*Acts* VI, VIII, XIX) *See* To LAY HANDS ON *under* HAND

Impossibilities (phrases)

> Gathering grapes from thistles
> Fetching water in a sieve
> Washing a blackamoor white
> Catching wind in cabbage nets.
> Flaying eels by the tail
> Making cheese of chalk.
> Squaring the circle.
> Turning base metal into gold
> Making a silk purse of a sow's ear
> (And hundreds more).

Impressionist. An important school in the history of painting As the name implies, it desired to capture the impression of colour of transitory and volatile nature rather than its form. The first phase—the study of light—was headed by Edouard Manet (1832-83), the second, which specialized in "*peinture claire*" —an endeavour to eliminate grey and black from the palette and achieve the effects of light by dabs of pure juxtaposed colour—by Claude Monet (1840-1926).

Imprimatur (im pri mā' tur) An official licence to print a book, especially a licence from the ecclesiastical authorities of the Catholic Church, or—where censorship exists—from the official censor The word is the 3rd sing pres subj of Lat. *imprimere*, "let it be printed "

What advantage is it to be a man, over it is to be a boy at school, if we have only escaped the ferula, to come under the fescue of an Imprimatur? If serious and elaborate writings, as if they were no more than the theme of a grammar-lad under his pedagogue, must not be uttered without the cursory eyes of a temporizing and extemporizing licenser?—MILTON *Areopagitica*.

Impropriation. Profits of ecclesiastical property in the hands of a layman, who is called the *impropriator*. *Appropriation* is the term used when the profits of a benefice are in the hands of a college or spiritual corporation

In Cœna Domini (in chā' na dom' i ni) (Lat., At the Lord's Supper). The papal bull published annually on Maundy Thursday (the Feast of the Lord's Supper) from the 14th century to 1770, fulminating curses and excommunications against all heretics and against all temporal powers and others who wronged the Church by taxing the clergy, levying on ecclesiastical lands, appealing to a general council, etc It was added to and altered from time to time, and its ecclesiastical, as apart from its political, anathemas are included in the *Apostolicæ Sedis*, issued by Pius IX in 1869

In commendam (in kom en' dăm) (Lat , in trust) The holding of church preferment for a time, on the recommendation of the Crown, till a suitable person can be provided Thus a benefice-holder who has become a bishop and is allowed to hold his living for a time is said to hold it *in commendam*

In esse (in es' ĭ) In actual existence (Lat *esse,* to be), as opposed to *in posse,* in potentiality. Thus a living child is "in esse," but before birth is only "in posse "

In extenso (in eks ten' sō) (Lat.) At full length, word for word, without abridgment.

In extremis (in eks trē' mis) (Lat). At the very point of death, *in articulo mortis*

In flagrante delicto (in fla grăn' te de lik' to) Red-handed; in the very fact (Lat , while the offence is flagrant).

In forma pauperis (in fōr' ma paw' per is) (Lat) In the character of a pauper. For many centuries in England persons without money or the means of obtaining it have been allowed to sue in the courts *in forma pauperis,* when the fees are remitted and the suitor is supplied gratis with the necessary legal advice, counsel, etc

In gremio legis (in grē' mi ō lē' jis) (Lat). Under the protection of (literally, at the breast of) the law

In loco parentis (in lō' kō pa ren' tis). (Lat.) In the position of being in a parent's place

In medias res (in mē' di ăs rēz) (Lat.) In the middle of the subject In novels and epic poetry, the author generally begins *in medias re,* and explains the preceding events as the tale unfolds. In history, on the other hand, the author begins *ab ovo (q v)*

In memoriam (in me môr' i ăm) (Lat.). In memory of

In partibus (in par' ti bus) (Lat). A "bishop *in partibus*" was a bishop in any country, Christian or otherwise, whose title was from some old see fallen away from the Catholic faith. The full phrase was *in partibus infidelium,* in the regions of infidels, and the title was generally conferred on a Church dignitary without an actual see. Many of the sees having now again a considerable Christian population, Pope Leo XIII, in 1882, abolished the designation and substituted that of "titular" bishop or see

In petto (in pet' ō) (Ital). Held in reserve, kept back, something done privately, and not announced to the general public. (Lat. *in pectore,* in the breast)

Cardinals in petto. Cardinals chosen by the Pope, but not yet publicly announced Their names are *in pectore* (of the Pope).

In posse. *See* IN ESSE.

In propria persona (in prop' ri a pěr sō' nà) (Lat) Personally, and not by deputy or agents.

In re (in rē) (Lat). In the matter of; on the subject of, as *In re* Jones v Robinson. But **in rem,** against the property or thing referred to.

In situ (in sī' tū) (Lat) In its original place

    I at first mistook it for a rock *in situ,* and took out my compass to observe the direction of its cleavage.—DARWIN *Voyage in the Beagle,* ix

In statu quo (in stăt' ū kwō) or *In statu quo ante* (Lat) In the condition things were before the change took place Thus, two nations arming for war may agree to lay down arms on condition that all things be restored to the same state as they were before they took up arms

In toto (in tō' tō) (Lat.) Entirely, altogether.

In vacuo (in văk' ū ō) (Lat) In a vacuum—*i e.* in a space from which, nominally all, and really almost all, the air has been taken away.

In vino veritas (Lat.). *See* VINO

In-and-In A game for three played with four dice, once extremely common, and frequently alluded to "In" is a throw of doubles, "in-and-in" a throw of double doubles, which sweeps the board

    I have seen . . three persons sit down at twelvepenny In and In, and each draw forty shillings a-piece.—*Nicker Nicked* (1668 *Harl Misc ,* II)

Inaugurate To install into some office with appropriate ceremonies, to open or introduce formally From Lat *inaugurare,* which meant first to take omens from the flight of birds by augury *(q v),* and then to consecrate or install after taking such omens.

Inbread *See* BAKER'S DOZEN.

Inca (ing' ka) A king or royal prince of the ancient Peruvians Of this dynasty Manco Capac was the founder (c A D 1240) and Atahualpa, murdered by the Spaniards in 1533, the last. The Inca Empire covered a wide area extending from Quito southwards into northern Chile, and from the Pacific seaboard to beyond the Andes, a region over 2,000 miles long and 500 miles wide, with its capital at Cuzco. The Incas were skilful agriculturists, and maintained an enlightened social and economic regime that has not been seen in S. America since their time

    The Inca was a war-chief, elected by the Council to carry out its decision —BRINTON *The American Race (South American Tribes),* pt. 1, ch ii, p 211

Inchcape Rock. A rocky reef (also known as the Bell Rock) about 12 miles from Arbroath in the North Sea (Inch or Innis means *island*) It is dangerous for navigators, and therefore the abbot of Arbroath, or "Aberbrothok," fixed a bell on a float, which gave notice to sailors of its whereabouts Southey's ballad tells how Ralph the Rover, a sea pirate, cut the bell from the float, and was wrecked on his return home on the very rock.

    A similar tale is told of St. Gowen's bell, in Pembrokeshire. In the chapel was a silver bell, which was stolen one summer evening by pirates, but no sooner had the boat put to sea than it was wrecked. The silver bell was carried by sea-nymphs to the brink of a well, and whenever the stone of that well is struck the bell is heard to moan.

Incog.—i.e. Incognito (in kog' ni tō) (Ital) Under an assumed name or title When a royal person travels, and does not wish to be treated with royal ceremony, he assumes some inferior title for the nonce, and travels *incog*

Income Tax. From the days of the Revolution of 1688 English statesmen have taken steps in one direction or another to introduce a tax on incomes The first workable tax of this nature was devised by William Pitt, in 1799, to finance the war with France A tax of 10 per cent. was put on all incomes over £200, with a modified charge for those between that sum and £60, beneath which all were exempt. This tax was dropped in 1802 but the next year a new Income Tax was introduced on practically the same system of schedules, etc., as is still in force Though aiming at only 5 per cent of the income, this tax yielded as much as the earlier tax The new tax was dropped in 1815, but it was renewed by Peel in 1842, with an exemption limit of £150 (in 1853 lowered to £100) at a rate varying between 6d and 8d in the £. In 1874-75 this sank so low as 2d. in the £. In the South African war the Income Tax rose to 1s , in World War I to 6s and in World War II to 10s Since World War I a surtax has been charged in addition to the standard rate of Income Tax on incomes over £2,000

In 1944 a system of Pay As You Earn (P.A.Y.E.) was introduced which facilitated the payment and collection of Income Tax by making the employer deduct the tax from the employee's wages

Incorruptible, The. Robespierre *See* SEA-GREEN.

Incubus (ing' kū bus) A nightmare, anything that weighs heavily on the mind In mediæval times it denoted an evil spirit who was supposed to consort with women in their sleep (Lat *incubo*, nightmare, from *incubare*, to lie on)

Merlin was the son of no mortal father, but of an Incubus, one of a class of beings not absolutely wicked, but far from good, who inhabit the regions of the air —BULLFINCH *Age of Chivalry*, pt. 1, ch. iii

Indenture (in den' chur) A written contract, especially one between an apprentice and his master, so called because the identical documents held by each party had their edges indented in such a manner that they would fit precisely into each other.

Independence Day. July 4th, which is kept as a national holiday in the United States of America, because the declaration by the American States, declaring the colonies free and independent and absolved from all allegiance to Great Britain, was signed on that day (1776).

Index. The "Roman Index" includes the *Index Librorum Prohibitorum* and the *Index Expurgatorius*. The former contains a list of such books as are absolutely forbidden to be read by Catholics The latter contains such books as are forbidden till certain parts are omitted or amended Rules for the guidance of the compilers were formulated by the Council of Trent (1563), and the first *Index* was published under Pius IV in 1564 The lists are made out by a board of cardinals (*Congregation of the Index*) Besides the Protestant Bibles, and the works of such schismatics as Arius and Calvin, we find in the lists the following well-known names —

Of English authors: Addison, Bacon, Chaucer, Gibbon, Goldsmith, Hallam, Andrew Lang, Locke, J S Mill, Milton, Robertson, Whately, etc , and even some children's tales

Of French authors Arnauld, Descartes, Dumas, Fenelon, Hugo, Malebranche, Montaigne, Pascal, Renan, Taine, Voltaire, etc Of Italian authors Dante, d'Annunzio, Guicciardini Sismondi

India The independence of India was created by a Bill introduced on July 4th, 1947 and given the Royal Assent on the 19th of the same month On August 15th British India became two dominions—India and Pakistan, the first mainly Hindu and the second almost entirely Moslem Each has its own legislature and Governor General Each independent state was left to decide for itself to which of the two dominions it would belong

India is so named from Indus (the river), in Sanskrit *Sindhu*, in Persic *Hindu* (the water) *Hindustan* is the *stan* or "country" of the river *Hindus*

India paper. A creamy-coloured printing-paper originally made in China and Japan from vegetable fibre, and used for taking off the finest proofs of engraved plates, hence **India proof**, the proof of an engraving on India paper, before lettering

The *India paper* (or *Oxford India paper*) used for printing Bibles and high-class "thin paper" and "pocket" editions, is a very thin, tough, and opaque imitation of this.

Indian. American Indians. When Columbus landed on one of the Bahamas he thought that he had reached India, and in this belief gave the natives the name of Indians Nowadays, in order to avoid ambiguity, the American Indians are known by ethnologists as **Amerinds.**

Indian Congress Party. This was founded in 1885 by A. O Hume, with the object of consolidating union between England and India It split on points of principle in 1907 and in 1920 became a vehicle for the dissemination of Gandhi's views and teachings. In 1927 Congress demanded independence as the goal of India, and to this end it strove until the goal was reached

Indian drug or weed, The. Tobacco Here the reference is, of course, to the *West Indies*.

His breath compounded of strong English beere, And th' Indian drug, would suffer none come neere. TAYLOR, the Water Poet (1630).

Indian file. One after the other, singly The American Indians, when they go on an expedition, march one by one The one behind carefully steps in the footprints of the one before, and the last man of the file is supposed to obliterate the footprints. Thus, neither the track nor the number of invaders can be traced

Indian sugar. West Indian maple sugar

Indian summer. The autumnal summer, occurring as a rule in the early part of October. It is often the finest and mildest part of the whole year, especially in North America

The gilding of the Indian summer mellowed the pastures far and wide The russet woods stood ripe to be stript, but were yet full of leaf The purple of heath-bloom, faded but not withered, tinged the hills. . . Fieldhead gardens bore the seal of gentle decay; . . . its time of flowers and even of fruit was over — C. BRONTË· *Shirley*, ch. xxvii

Indirect Taxation is the levying of a tax on commercial goods, etc , in such a way that the consumer pays both for the article and the tax.

Indo-European, a term invented by Thomas Young the Egyptologist in 1813 and later adopted by scientists to describe the race and language from which the main Indian and European peoples sprang Anthropologists have devoted to the subject much study as yet inconclusive; philologists have classified the Indo-European languages in such broad groups as Greek, Latin; Celtic, Teutonic, Sanskrit and Iranian, Armenian, Slavonic, Albanian.

Indonesia (in dō nē′ zhā), a term that includes the islands of the Malay Archipelago and such islands as Sumatra, Java, Borneo, the Celebes, the Lesser Sunda Islands, the Moluccas, the Philippines

Induction (Lat., the act of leading in). When a clergyman is inducted to a living he is led to the church door, and the ring which forms the handle is placed in his hand The door being opened, he is next led into the church, and the fact is announced to the parish by tolling the bell

Indulgence. In Catholic theology the remission before God of the temporal punishment due for those sins of which the guilt has been forgiven in the sacrament of Penance The competent ecclesiastical authority grants such indulgences out of the Treasury of the Church (*q.v*), they are either plenary or partial, partial remitting a part only of such punishment due for sin at any given moment, the proportion being expressed in terms of time (*e g* thirty days, seven years). The precise meaning of these terms has never been defined, but they date back to the ancient penitential discipline of the Church In the Middle Ages indulgences were of high commercial value, and it was the sale of them that first roused the ire of Luther and prepared the way for the Reformation.

The Declaration of Indulgence. The proclamation of James II in 1687 which annulled religious tests and the penal laws against Roman Catholics and Dissenters The refusal of certain ecclesiastics to read this in their churches led to the Trial of the Seven Bishops

Industrial Revolution is the term applied to the social and economic changes that took place in Britain from the late 18th to the mid-19th century, when the introduction of machinery in manufacture and railways for transport entirely revolutionized the methods of living and the location of industries throughout the country

Ineffable. *See* AFFABLE

Inexpressibles. A euphemism for trousers— also known as *unmentionables*—in use in the 19th century This absurdity is attributed to the satirical poet Peter Pindar, the pen-name of John Wolcot (1738-1819) who used it in a biting lampoon on the dandy Prince Regent (George IV)

Infallibility. The doctrine that the Pope, when speaking *ex cathedra* (*q v*.) on a question of faith or morals, is free from error did not become an accepted dogma of the Church until the Vatican Council of 1870 The promulgation of the dogma, after having been agreed to by the council (many members dissenting or abstaining from voting), was publicly read by Pius IX at St Peter's.

Infallibility does not involve inspiration or universal inerrability, the Pope does not originate new doctrines infallibly, his infallibility preserves him from making errors in defining truths of doctrines or morals

Infant. Literally, one who is unable to speak (Lat *infans*, ultimately from *in*, negative, and *fari*, to speak *Cp.* INFAMOUS *above*) Used as a synonym of "childe," as in *Childe Harold* (*q v*), meaning a knight or youth of gentle birth, the word was once of common occurrence. Thus, as in the following passage, Spenser frequently refers to Prince Arthur in this way —
> The Infant harkened wisely to her tale,
> And wondered much at Cupid's judg'ment wise.
> *Faerie Queene*, VI, viii, 25

Infanta. Any princess of the blood royal, except an heiress of the crown, was so called in Spain and in Portugal

Infante. All the sons of the sovereigns of Spain bore this title, as did those of Portugal, except the crown prince, who was called in Spain the Prince of Asturias

Infantry Foot soldiers This is the same word as *infant* (*q.v*); it is the Italian *infanteria*, a foot soldier, from *infanta*, a youth; hence, one who is too inexperienced to serve in the cavalry

Inferiority Complex. A psycho-analytical term for a complex resulting from a sense of inferiority dating from childhood Over-compensation for that feeling produces, it is suggested, an exaggerated or even abnormal desire for success, power, and accomplishment, and frequently a conceited and pushing attitude

Infernal Column. So the corps of Latour d'Auvergne (1743-1800)—"the First Grenadier of France"—was called, from its terrible charges with the bayonet.

The same name—*Colonnes infernales*—was given, because of their brutality, to the twelve bodies of republican troops which "pacified" La Vendée in 1793, under General Thurreau.

Inferno (in fēr′ nō) We have Dante's notion of the infernal regions in his *Inferno* , Homer's in the *Odyssey*, Bk xi; Virgil's in the *Æneid*, Bk. vi; Spenser's in the *Faerie Queene*, Bk. ii, canto 7; Ariosto's in *Orlando Furioso*, Bk xvii; Tasso's in *Jerusalem Delivered*, Bk iv , Milton's in *Paradise Lost*; Fenelon's in *Télémaque*, Bk xviii, and Beckford's in his romance of *Vathek See* HELL· HADES

Informer. Readers of *Pickwick Papers* and other novels of the period will find references to police informers Before the organization of the police and detective forces a thriving trade used to be driven by a certain class of persons who frequented the streets and public places on the look-out for anyone committing minor illegal acts, which they reported to the authorities for a small fee.

Infra dig. Not befitting one's position and public character Short for Lat *infra dignitatem*, beneath (one's) dignity.

Infralapsarian. The same as a SUBLAPSARIAN (*q v*)

Ingoldsby (ing' gŏldz bi). The pseudonym of the Rev. Richard Harris Barham (1788-1845), as author of the *Ingoldsby Legends*, which appeared in Bentley's *Miscellany* and the *New Monthly Magazine*, and later (1840 and 1847) in book form.

Ingrain Colours. *See* KNAVE IN GRAIN *under* GRAIN

Inhibition, in psychology, is an unconscious force forbidding what would otherwise be an impulse or urge

Injunction. A writ forbidding a person to encroach on another's privileges, as, to sell a book which is only a colourable copy of another author's book, or to infringe a patent, or to perform a play based on a novel without permission of the novelist; or to publish a book the rights of which are reserved. Injunctions are of two sorts—temporary and perpetual The first is limited "till the coming on of the defendant's answer"; the latter is based on the merits of the case, and is of perpetual force.

Ink. From Lat *encaustum* (Gr. *enkaustos*, burnt in), the name given to the purple fluid used by the Roman emperors for writing with.

Inkhorn terms. A common term in Elizabethan times for pedantic expressions which smell of the lamp The inkhorn was the receptacle for ink which pedants and pedagogues wore fastened to the clothing

> I know them that thinke rhetorique to stand wholie upon darke wordes, and hee that can catch an ynke horne terme by the taile, him they coumpt to be a fine Englishman —WILSON *Arte of Rhetorique* (1553).

Shakespeare uses the phrase, an "Inkhorn mate" (1 *Henry VI*, iii, 1)

Ink-slinger (U S A, ink-jerker). A contemptuous name for a writer, especially for a newspaper journalist.

Inn. The word is Anglo-Saxon, and meant originally an ordinary dwelling-house, residence, or lodging. Hence Clifford's Inn, once the mansion of De Clifford, Lincoln's Inn, the abode of the Earls of Lincoln; Gray's Inn, that of the Lords Gray, etc

> Now, whenas Phœbus, with his fiery waine,
> Unto his inne began to draw apace.
> SPENSER *Faerie Queene*, VI, iii, 29.

Inns of Court. The four voluntary societies which have the exclusive right of calling to the English Bar They are all in London, and are the Inner Temple, the Middle Temple, Lincoln's Inn, and Gray's Inn Each is governed by a board of benchers *See* BAR: BENCHER.

Innings. He has had a long, or a good innings. A good long run of luck An innings in cricket is the time that the eleven or an individual is having its turn batting at the wicket

Inniskillings. The 5th and 6th Dragoon Guards. The former was raised by the 12th Earl of Shrewsbury for James II in 1685. The latter was raised by Sir Albert Conyngham for the defence of Enniskillen in the cause of William

III, it was named the 6th Dragoons in 1751. In 1922 the two regiments were amalgamated as the 5th, and granted the title "Royal" in commemoration of George V's silver jubilee

This cavalry regiment must not be confounded with the Inniskillings or Old 27th Foot, now called the "1st battalion of the Royal Inniskilling Fusiliers," which is a foot regiment.

Innocent, An. An idiot or born fool was formerly so called *Cp.* BENET

> Although he be in body deformed, iii minde foolish, an innocent borne, a begger by misfortune, yet doth he deserve a better than thy selfe —LYLY *Euphues* (1579)

The Feast of the Holy Innocents. The 28th December, to commemorate Herod's massacre of the children of Bethlehem under two years old, with the design of cutting off the infant Jesus (*Matt* ii, 16) It used to be the custom on Holy Innocents' Day, or Childermas, to whip the children—and even adults—"that the memory of Herod's murder of the Innocents might stick the closer," and this practice forms the plot of several old tales in the *Decameron* and elsewhere

The massacre of the innocents. The name facetiously given in parliamentary circles (with an allusion to the above) to Bills that are left over at the end of a session for lack of time to deal with them

Innuendo (in ū en' dō). An implied or covert hint of blame, a suggestion that one dare not make openly, so it is made indirectly, as by a nod, originally a law term, meaning the person nodded to or indirectly referred to (Lat, *innuo*, to nod to)

Ino *See* LEUCOTHEA.

Inoculation Originally, the horticultural practice of grafting a *bud* (Lat, *oculus*) into an inferior plant, in order to produce flowers or fruits of better quality, hence, introducing into the body infectious matter which produces a mild form of the disease against which this treatment is counted on to render one immune.

Inquisition. A court instituted to inquire into offences against the Roman Catholic religion, and fully established by Gregory IX in 1229. Torture, as a means of extracting recantations or evidence, was first authorized by Innocent IV in 1252, and those found guilty were handed over to the secular arm to be dealt with according to the secular laws of the land The Inquisition was generally administered by the Dominicans, from which Order came the notorious Torquemada (1420-98), who was Inquisitor-General 1483-94 It was most active in southern Europe, particularly in Spain, where it flourished from 1237 to 1820 It was suppressed in France in 1772. The Inquisition now known as the Holy Office occupies itself with the protection of faith and morals and among other activities examines and, where it considers necessary, prohibits books dangerous to the faithful.

Insane Root, The. A plant which is not positively identified, but which was probably henbane or hemlock, supposed to deprive of his senses anyone who took it Banquo says of the witches.—

> Were such things here as we do speak about?
> Or have we eaten on the insane root
> That takes the reason prisoner?
>
> *Macbeth*, i, 3.

There were many plants to which similar properties were, rightly or wrongly, attributed, such as the mandrake, belladonna (deadly nightshade), poppy, etc ; and *cp* MOLY.

Inscription (*on coins*). *See* LEGEND

Inspired Idiot, The. Oliver Goldsmith (1728-1774) was so called by Horace Walpole.

Institutes. A digest of the elements of a subject, especially of law The most celebrated is the *Institutes of Justinian*, completed in A D 533 at the order of the Emperor It was based on the earlier *Institutes of Gaius*, and was intended as an introduction to the Pandects (*q v.*). Other *Institutes* are those of Florentius, Callistratus, Paulus, Ulpian, and Marcian

Instructions to the Committee. A means empowering a Committee of the House of Commons to do what it would not otherwise be empowered to do

> An "Instruction" must be supplementary and auxiliary to the Bill under consideration.
>
> It must fall within the general scope and framework of the Bill in question
>
> It must not form the substance of a distinct measure.

Insulin (in' su lin), a specific discovered by Sir F G Banting (1891-1941). It is extracted from the pancreatic glands of oxen and its function is to reduce the sugar in the blood, for this reason it is used in the treatment of diabetes

Insult. Literally, to leap on (the prostrate body of a foe), hence, to treat with contumely (Lat *insultare, saltus,* a leap) Terence says, *Insultare fores calcibus* (*Eunuchus*, ii. 2, 54). It will be remembered that the priests of Baal, to show their indignation against their gods, "leaped upon the altar which they had made" (1 *Kings* xviii, 26) *Cp* DESULTORY.

Intaglio (in ta' lyō) (Ital) A design cut into a gem, like a crest or initials in a stamp. The design does not stand out in relief, as in a cameo (*q v.*), but is hollowed in.

Intelligence Quotient, commonly abbreviated to I.Q , is the ratio, expressed as a percentage, of a person's mental age to his actual age, the former being the age for which he scores 100 per cent when tested by the Binet or some similar system. The Binet Tests consist in testing a child's intelligence by asking standard questions adapted to the intelligence of a normal child of that age.

Intelligentsia (in tel i jen' si ä). A Russian term for the educated and cultured classes, which has acquired in English a somewhat derogatory sense

Inter alia (in' ter ä lyä) (Lat). Among other things or matters.

Intercalary (in tĕr kǎl' ä ri) (Lat *inter,* between, *calare,* to proclaim solemnly). An intercalary day is a day thrust in between two others, as February 29th in leap year; so called because, among the Romans, this was a subject for solemn proclamation. *Cp.* CALENDS

Interdict (in' tĕr dikt) In the Roman Catholic Church an Interdict is a sentence of excommunication directed against a place and/or its inhabitants, if the place only is under the interdict the sacraments cannot be administered there, burials with religious ceremonies are prohibited, and all church communion is in abeyance The most remarkable instances are —

586 The Bishop of Bayeux laid an interdict on all the churches of Rouen, in consequence of the murder of the Bishop Prétextat.

1081 Poland was laid under an interdict by Gregory VII, because Bolesfas II had murdered Stanislaus at the altar

1180 Scotland was put under a similar ban by Pope Alexander III

1200 France was interdicted by Innocent III, because Philippe Auguste refused to marry Ingelburge, who had been betrothed to him.

1209 England was under similar sentence for six years (Innocent III), in the reign of King John

Interest (Lat *interesse,* to be a concern to) The *interest* on money is the sum which a borrower agrees to pay a lender for its use. Simple interest is interest on the principal, or money lent, only, compound interest is interest on the principal plus the interest as it accrues

In an interesting condition. Said of a woman who is expecting to become a mother. The phrase came into use in the 18th century.

Interim of Augsburg. *See* AUGSBURG.

Interlard (Fr) Originally to "lard" meat, *i.e.* to put strips of fat between layers of lean meat; hence, metaphorically, to mix irrelevant matter with the solid part of a discourse Thus we say, "To interlard with oaths," to "interlard with compliments," etc.

> They interlard their native drinks with choice
> Of strongest brandy.   PHILIPS *Cider* ii

Interloper. One who "runs" between traders and upsets their business by interfering with their actual or supposed rights. The word came into English through the Dutch trade in the 16th century, and the *lope* is a dialect form of *leap* confused with Dut. *loopen,* to run (as in *elope*)

Interpellation. The equivalent in the French Chamber to "moving the adjournment" in our House of Commons It is an interruption to the order of the day by asking a Minister some question of importance the subject of which would come under his department From Lat *interpellare,* to interrupt by speaking, literally, to drive between.

Interpreter, Mr. The Holy Spirit personified, in Bunyan's *Pilgrim's Progress.*

Interrex (in' tĕr reks) (Lat). A person appointed to hold the office of king during a temporary vacancy.

Intrigue (in trēg') From the Latin *tricae,* trifles, whence the verb *intrico,* to entangle. In its more common use the word means an underhand plot, a piece of crafty manœuvring, or a liaison. Within the 20th century, however, it has come to be used as a transitive verb meaning to rouse the interest of, to awaken curiosity, as one may talk of an intriguing play, or a situation that intrigued one In the 17th and 18th centuries this connotation was not at all rare.

Introvert. The psychological term for an introspective person who instinctively seeks to alter his conception of external realities to make them correspond more closely with his own desires An introvert is interested mainly in his own mental processes and in the way in which he is regarded by others; he is thus retiring in manner and usually shy.

Invalides (an' vä lēd) *Hôtel des Invalides* The great institution founded by Louis XIV at Paris in 1670 for disabled and superannuated soldiers It contains large numbers of military trophies, statues, paintings, etc , and a museum of artillery and mediæval and renaissance armour
The central feature of the church of the Invalides is the tomb of Napoleon, whose body was brought hither from St. Helena in 1840 Close by are the tombs of his son, the Duke of Reichstadt (L'Aiglon) and Marshal Foch (1851-1929) Others buried there are Marshal Turenne (1611-75), General Bertrand (1773-1844), Marshals Duroc (1772-1813) and Grouchy (1766-1847), General Kléber (1753-1800), Joseph Bonaparte, King of Naples and Spain (1768-1844), and Jerome Bonaparte, King of Westphalia (1784-1860).

Inventions. The following are some of the most important inventions in the history of civilized man No date can be given to the most useful invention of all, that of the wheel (involving the use of rollers and pulleys) for in Europe and Asia Minor it dates back to prehistoric times. Yet in America and in early Egypt the pulley was unknown.
Lever and screw Archimedes (c 287-212, B C.)
Printing: from movable type, China, A.D. 1041; in Europe, 1440
Gunpowder (in the Western world) the monk Berthold Schwartz, 1313
Logarithms J. Napier, 1614, J Burgi, 1620
Steam engine. Piston, Newcommen, 1698.
Condenser, Watt, 1769
Locomotive, Trevethick, 1804.
Turbine, Parsons, 1884.
Spinning Jenny Arkwright, 1769
Gas illumination: Murdoch, 1792.
Electricity. Leyden Jar. 1745
Electro-magnetic induction, Faraday, 1831
Steel: Bessemer process, 1856
Anæsthetics: Humphrey Davy, 1799.
Chloroform, Simpson, 1847
Wireless receiving and transmitting apparatus, Marconi, 1895.
Internal combustion engine Gottlieb, 1883.
Aeroplane. Wright Brothers, 1903.
Radiography: Röntgen Rays, 1895
Photography: J. N Niepce, 1817, Daguerre, 1839.
Atomic energy: splitting of the atom by Cockroft and Walton, 1932

Invention of the Cross. *See* CROSS.

Inventors. A curious instance of the *sin* of invention is mentioned in the *Bridge of Allan Reporter*, February, 1803 —
It is told of Mr Ferguson's grandfather, that he invented a pair of fanners for cleaning grain, and for this proof of superior ingenuity he was summoned before the Kirk Session, and reproved for trying to place the handiwork of man above the time-honoured practice of cleaning the grain on windy days, when the current was blowing briskly through the open doors of the barn
It is extraordinary how many inventors have been "hoist with their own petard", the following list—in which some entries will no doubt be found that belong to the realm of fable—is by no means complete.—
Bastille Hugues Aubriot, Provost of Paris, who built the Bastille, was the first person confined therein. The charge against him was heresy.
Brazen Bull. Perillos of Athens made a brazen bull for Phalaris, Tyrant of Agrigentum, intended for the execution of criminals, who were shut up in the bull, fires being lighted below the belly. Phalaris admired the invention, and tested it on Perillos himself, who was the first person baked to death in the horrible monster.
Cannon Thomas Montacute, 4th Earl of Salisbury was the first to use cannon, and was the first Englishman killed by a cannon ball, at Tourelles, 1428
Catherine Wheel. The inventor of St. Catherine's Wheel, a diabolical machine consisting of four wheels turning different ways, and each wheel armed with saws, knives and teeth, was killed by his own machine, for when St Catherine was bound on the wheel, she fell off, and the machine flew to pieces. One of the pieces struck the inventor, and other pieces struck several of the men employed to work it, all of whom were killed (*Metaphrastes*)
Eddystone. Henry Winstanley erected the first Eddystone lighthouse It was a wooden polygon, 100 feet high, on a stone base, but it was washed away by a storm in 1703, and the architect perished in his own edifice
Gallows and *Gibbet* We are told in the book of *Esther* that Haman devised a gallows 50 cubits high on which to hang Mordecai, by way of commencing the extirpation of the Jews; but the favourite of Ahasuerus was himself hanged thereon. We have a repetition of this incident in the case of Enguerrand de Marigni, Minister of Finance to Philippe the Fair, who was hung on the gibbet which he had caused to be erected at Montfaucon for the execution of certain felons, and four of his successors in office underwent the same fate.
Guillotine. J. B V. Guillotin, M D, of Lyons, was guillotined, but it is an error to credit him with the invention of the instrument. The inventor was Dr Joseph Agnace Guillotin.
Iron Cage The Bishop of Verdun, who invented the Iron Cage, too small to allow the person confined in it to stand upright or lie at full length, was the first to be shut up in one; and Cardinal La Balue, who recommended them to Louis XI, was himself confined in one for ten years
Iron Shroud Ludovico Sforza, who invented the Iron Shroud, was the first to suffer death by this horrible torture.

Maiden The Regent Morton of Scotland, who invented the Maiden (*q.v*), was the first to be beheaded thereby.

Ostracism Clisthenes introduced the custom of Ostracism (*q v*), and was the first to be banished thereby.

The *Perriere* was a piece of mediæval artillery for throwing stones of 3,000 lb in weight, and the inventor fell a victim to his own invention by the accidental discharge of a perriere against a wall

Sanctuary. Eutropius induced the Emperor Arcadius to abolish the benefit of sanctuary; but a few days afterwards he committed some offence and fled for safety to the nearest church St. Chrysostom told him he had fallen into his own net, and he was put to death (*Life of St. Chrysostom*)

Turret-ship Cowper Coles, inventor of the Turret-ship, perished in the *Captain* off Finisterre September 7th, 1870.

Witch-finding Matthew Hopkins, the witch-finder, was himself tried by his own tests, and put to death as a wizard in 1647.

Investiture. The ceremonial clothing (Lat. *vestire*, to clothe) or investing of an official, dignitary, sovereign, etc , with the special robes or insignia of his office Thus, a pair of gloves is given to a Freemason in France, a cap is given to a graduate, a crown, etc , to a sovereign, etc , and a crosier and ring are placed in the hands of a church dignitary on his induction into tne office of bishop

In the 11th and 12th centuries the kings of Europe and the popes were perpetually at variance about the right of investiture; the question was, did the right of appointing to vacant bishoprics and other ecclesiastical dignities belong to the spiritual or to the temporal power, the pope or the king? The Emperor Henry V relinquished his claim in 1111, but his action was not followed by the other European sovereigns

Invincible Doctor. William of Occam (d. 1347), or Ockham (a village in Surrey), Franciscan friar and scholastic philosopher. He was also called *Doctor Singularis*, and *Princeps Nominalium*, for he was the reviver of nominalism

Invincibles, The Irish A Fenian secret society founded in Dublin in 1881 with the object of doing away with the English "tyranny" and killing the "tyrants " Members of this society were responsible for the Phœnix Park murders in 1882

Invisible Empire. *See* KU KLUX KLAN

Invisibility, according to fable, might be obtained in a multitude of ways. For example —

Alberich's cloak, "Tarnkappe," which Siegfried got possession of, rendered him invisible (*Nibelungenlied*)

A *dead hand* It was believed that a candle placed in a dead man's hand gives no light to any but those who use it. *See* HAND.

The *helmet* of Perseus and the helmet that Pluto gave to the Cyclops (*Orci Galea*) both rendered the wearers invisible

Jack the Giant-killer had a cloak of invisibility as well as a cap of knowledge

Otnit's ring The ring of Otnit, King of Lombardy, according to the *Heldenbuch*, possessed a similar charm.

Reynard's wonderful ring had three colours, one of which (green) caused the wearer to become invisible (*Reynard the Fox, q v.*)

See also FERN SEED; GYGES' RING; HELIOTROPE

The Druids were supposed to possess the power of making themselves invisible by producing a magic mist, and this spell, the *faeth fiadha*, appears in the stories of St Patrick and other early British saints.

Invulnerability. There are many fabulous instances of this having been acquired According to ancient Greek legend, a dip in the river Styx rendered Achilles invulnerable, and Medea rendered Jason, with whom she had fallen in love, proof against wounds and fire by anointing him with the Promethean unguent

Siegfried was rendered invulnerable by anointing his body with dragon's blood. (*Nibelungenlied.*)

Ionian Mode (I ō' ni ăn) A species of mediæval church music in the key of C major, in imitation of the ancient Greek mode so called It was the last of the "authentic" church modes, and corresponded to the modern major diatonic scale *Cp* GREGORIAN

Ionic (I on' ik) **Ionic Architecture.** So called from Ionia, where it took its rise The capitals are decorated with volutes, and the cornice with dentils. The shaft is fluted, the entablature either plain or embellished.

The people of Ionia formed their order of architecture on the model of a young woman dressed in her hair, and of an easy, elegant shape, whereas the Doric had been formed on the model of a robust, strong man.—*Vitruvius.*

Ionic School. The school of philosophy that arose in Ionia in the 6th century B C , and which formed the starting-point of the whole of Greek philosophy It included Thales, Anaximander, Anaximenes, Heraclitus, and Anaxagoras, and the great advance they made was the recognition that matter, motion, and physical causation were themselves manifestations of the Absolute Reality. They also tried to show that all created things spring from one universal physical cause, Thales said it was water, Anaximenes thought it was air, Anaxagoras that it was atoms, Heraclitus maintained that it was fire or caloric while Anaximander insisted that the elements of all things are eternal, for *ex nihilo nihil fit*

Iota. *See* I; JOT.

IOU, *i e.* "I owe you " The memorandum of a debt given by the borrower to the lender It requires no stamp unless it specifies a day of payment, when it becomes a *bill*, and must be stamped.

Iphigenia (if i jen ē' a, if i je nī' a). In classical legend, the daughter of Agamemnon and Clytemnestra. One account says that her father, having offended Artemis by killing her favourite stag, vowed to sacrifice to the angry goddess the most beautiful thing that came into his possession in the next twelve months, this was an infant daughter. The father deferred the sacrifice till the fleet of the combined Greeks that was proceeding to Troy reached Aulis and Iphigenia had grown to womanhood The Calchas told him that the fleet would be wind-bound till he had fulfilled his vow; accordingly the king prepared to sacrifice his daughter, but Artemis at the last moment snatched her from the altar and carried her to heaven, substituting a hind in her place Euripides, Æschylus, and Sophocles all wrote tragedies on Iphigenia. *Cp* IDOMENEUS.

Ipse dixit (ip′ se diks′ it) (Lat , he himself said so) A mere assertion, wholly unsupported "It is his *ipse dixit*," implies that there is no guarantee that what he says is so.

Ipso facto (Lat., by the very fact). Irrespective of all external considerations of right or wrong; absolutely It sometimes means the act itself carries the consequences (as excommunication without the actual sentence being pronounced)

By burning the Pope's bull, Luther *ipso facto* [by the very deed itself] denied the Pope's supremacy Heresy carries excommunication *ipso facto*

I.R.A. The Irish Republican Army, which opposed the Crown forces, the Royal Irish Constabulary, the "Black and Tans," etc , in the rebellion that preceded the grant of dominion status in 1921.

Irak (ē răk′) The name given at different times to varying portions of Mesopotamia (*q v*), Babylonia, and the surrounding country It is now the official name of that portion of the country ruled by the king of Irak with his capital at Bagdad.

Iram (ē răm′). An enchanted garden of old Persian legend, planted by the mythological king Shaddad, and for centuries sunk deep in the sands of Arabia. *See* JAMSHID.

Iran (ē ran′), since March, 1935, the official Persian name of modern Persia, though in 1949 it was announced that foreigners might use the name of Persia. The Iranian languages, including Zend and Old Persian, form a branch of the great Indo-European family.

I.R.B. Irish Republican Brotherhood, the Fenians of the 1860s, etc

Ireland. Called by the natives Erin, *i e Erinius*, or *Iar-innis* (west island)
By the Welsh, **Yver-den** (west valley)
By Apuleius, Hibernia, which is *Ierna*, a corruption of *Iar-inni-a*.
By Juvenal (ii, 260), Juverna or Juberna, the same as *Ierna* or *Iernia*.
By Claudian, Ouernia, the same.
By moderns, Ireland, which is *Iar-en-land* (land of the west)

After many struggles throughout the 19th century Ireland was given Home Rule (*q v.*) in 1914, though the Act was not put into operation until 1920 After much unrest the country was divided into Eire and Northern Ireland in 1921, the former being a sovereign democratic State with a constitution (remodelled in 1937), while Northern Ireland consisting of the counties of Antrim, Armagh, Down, Fermanagh, Londonderry and Tyrone, and the boroughs of Belfast and Londonderry remains

an integral part of the British Empire, with a parliament of its own, returning 12 members to the House of Commons in Westminster

The fair maid of Ireland Ignis fatuus (*q v.*)
He had read in former times of a Going Fire, called "Ignis Fatuus," the fire of destiny, by some, "Will with the Wisp," or "Jack with the Lantern", and likewise, by some simple country people, "The Fair Maid of Ireland" which used to lead wandering travellers out of their way —*The Seven Champions of Christendom*, i, 7

The three great saints of Ireland. St. Patrick, St. Columba, and St Bridget

Ireland Scholarships. Four scholarships of £30 a year in the University of Oxford, founded by Dr. John Ireland (1761-1842), Dean of Westminster, in 1825, for Latin and Greek They are tenable for four years He also founded an "Exegetical Professorship" of £800 a year.

Iris (ī′ ris) Goddess of the rainbow, or the rainbow itself. In classical mythology she is called the messenger of the gods when they intended *discord*, and the rainbow is the bridge or road let down from heaven for her accommodation. When the gods meant *peace* they sent Mercury.
I'll have an Iris that shall find thee out
2 *Henry VI*, iii, 2.

Besides being poetically applied to the rainbow the name, in English, is given to the coloured membrane surrounding the pupil of the eye, and to a family of plants (Iridaceæ) having large, bright-coloured flowers and tuberous roots

Iron. The Iron Age. An archæological term denoting the cultural phase conditioned by the discovery of the use of iron for edged tools, weapons, etc Iron was known as a curiosity by the builders of the pyramids, but it was not until 1000 B C that iron-working became general in the Mediterranean basin. Its gradual development from the bronze age precursors is traceable at Hallstatt, and its fuller development at La Tène, these places give their names to the first and second periods of the early Iron Age.

The era between the death of Charlemagne and the close of the Carlovingian dynasty (728-987) is sometimes so called from its almost ceaseless wars It is sometimes called the *leaden* age for its worthlessness, and the *dark* age for its barrenness of learned men *See* also AGE.

Iron-arm. François de la Noue (1531-91), the Huguenot soldier, *Bras de Fer*, was so called **Fierabras** (*q v.*). is another form of the same

Iron Chancellor, the name given to Prince Bismarck (1815-98), the great statesman who created the German Empire.

The Iron Cross. A Prussian military decoration (an iron Maltese cross, edged with silver). It was instituted by Frederick William III in 1813 during the struggle against Napoleon, and was remodelled by William I in 1870, with three grades, in civil and military divisions. In World War I some 3,000,000 Iron Crosses were awarded; there are no figures for World War II

The Iron Crown of Lombardy. *See* CROWN.

Iron Curtain. A phrase used to describe the almost impenetrable secrecy with which all happenings in the U.S.S.R. or countries dominated by Russia are concealed from the rest of the world. The phrase was first used by Count Schwerin von Krosigk, the German statesman, in 1945.

The Iron Duke. The Duke of Wellington (1769-1852) was so called from his iron will.

The iron entered into his soul. When anguish or annoyance is felt most keenly. The phrase arose in a mistranslation from the Hebrew of Psalm cv, 18, which appeared in the Vulgate and was copied in some of the earlier English translations, and is perpetuated in the Prayer Book version, though it was corrected in the Authorized Version. The Hebrew says "his person entered into the iron" (*i.e.* he was laid in irons), but Coverdale and some others—following the Vulgate—have "They hurte his fete in the stockes, the yron pearsed his herte."

Iron-hand or the Iron-handed. Goetz von Berlichingen (about 1480-1562), a German baron, who lost his right hand and had one made of iron to supply its place. Some accounts say that it was lost at the siege of Landshut, others that it was struck off in consequence of his having disregarded a law prohibiting duels.

Iron Gates. The narrowing of the Danube between Orsova and Turnu Severin in S.W. Rumania. It is about 2 miles long, with great rapids and an island in mid-stream. Between 1890 and 1900 a navigable way was made.

Iron Guard. The title adopted by the Fascist party in Rumania.

The iron horse. The railway locomotive.

The Iron Maiden of Nuremberg. A mediæval instrument of torture used in Germany for "heretics," traitors, parricides, etc. It was a box big enough to admit a man, with folding-doors, the whole studded with sharp iron spikes. When the doors were closed on him these spikes were forced into the body of the victim, who was left there to die in horrible torture.

Iron-man. An American colloquialism for a dollar.

Man in the iron mask. *See* MASK.

Iron rations. Bully beef; tinned meat. Also emergency rations (*q.v.*).

Shooting-iron. Slang for a small firearm, especially a pistol or revolver.

To rule with a rod of iron. To rule tyrannically.

Ironside. Edmund II (about 989-1016), King of the West Saxons from April to November, 1016, was so called, from his iron armour.

Nestor Ironside. Sir Richard Steele assumed the name in *The Guardian*.

Ironsides. The soldiers that served under Cromwell were so called, especially after the battle of Marston Moor (1644), where they displayed an iron resolution. The name had first been applied only to a special regiment of stalwarts.

Iron-tooth. Frederick II, Elector of Brandenburg (1440-1470).

Too many irons in the fire. More affairs in hand than you can properly attend to. The allusion is to a smithy where the smith has a number of irons heating to red heat.

In irons. In fetters. A square-rigged sailing vessel is said to be in irons when the yards are so braced that some sails being full of wind and others aback, the vessel is temporarily unmanageable.

Strike while the iron is hot. Don't miss a good opportunity; seize time by the forelock; make hay while the sun shines.

Irony (I'ron i). A dissembling (Gr. *eiron*, a dissembler, *eironeia*), hence, subtle sarcasm, language having a meaning different from the ostensible one but understood correctly by the initiated. Socratic irony is an assumption of ignorance, as a means of leading on and eventually confuting an opponent.

The irony of fate. A strange fatality which has brought about something quite the reverse of what might have been expected.

By the irony of fate the Ten Hours Bill was carried in the very session when Lord Ashley, having changed his views on the Corn Laws, felt it his duty to resign his seat in Parliament.—*The Leisure Hour*, 1887.

Iroquois (ir'ō kwa). The name given by the French to the five (later six) confederate tribes of North American Indians, viz. the Mohawks, Oneidas, Onondagas, Cayugas, Senecas, and sixth the Tuscaroras, added in 1712, forming "The Six Nations of the Iroquois Confederacy."

Irredentism (ir rē dent' izm). The name of a movement in Italy which aimed at delivering all Italian-speaking peoples from foreign rule. The party cry was "Italia Irredenta" (unredeemed Italy), and the party came into existence soon after the formation of the kingdom of Italy in 1860, when Venetia, Rome, and certain other territories were still under foreign rule. By 1920 most of the Irredentist demands had been met.

Irrefragable Doctor. Alexander of Hales (d. 1245), an English Franciscan, author of *Summa Theologiæ*.

Irresistible. Alexander the Great went to consult the Delphic oracle before he started on his expedition against Persia. He chanced, however, to arrive on a day when no responses were made. Nothing daunted, he went in search of the Pythia, and when she refused to attend, took her to the temple by force. ' Son," said the priestess, "thou art irresistible." "Enough," cried Alexander; "I accept your words as an answer."

Irus (I'rus). The beggar of gigantic stature, who waited on the suitors of Penelope. Ulysses, on his return, felled him to the ground with a single blow, and flung his corpse out of doors.

Poorer than Irus. A Greek proverb, adopted by the Romans and the French, alluding to the beggar referred to above.

Irvingites. Members of the Catholic Apostolic Church founded about 1829 by Edward Irving, a Presbyterian minister and a friend of the Carlyles Irving claimed to revive the college of the Apostles and established a complex hierarchy with such symbolical titles as "Angel," "Prophet," etc In their early days they claimed to have manifested the gift of tongues.

Isaac. A hedge-sparrow; a dialect form of *haysugge*, or *haysuck*, an obsolete name for the bird (used by Chaucer). The name meant a *sucker* (small thing) that lived in a *hay* or hedge, a corruption of Chaucer's word, *heisuagge*

Isabelle. The *colour* so called is the yellow of soiled calico. A yellow-dun horse is, in France, *un cheval isabelle* According to Isaac D'Israeli (*Curiosities of Literature*) Isabel of Austria, daughter of Philip II, at the siege of Ostend vowed not to change her linen till the place was taken As the siege lasted three years, we may suppose that it was somewhat soiled by three years' wear.

Another story, equally unwarranted, attaches it to Isabella of Castile, who, we are told, made a vow to the Virgin not to change her linen till Granada fell into her hands

There is, however, no reason for accepting these very fanciful derivations The word appears in an extant list of Queen Elizabeth's clothes of July, 1600 ("one rounde gowne of Isabella-colour satten")

Isaiah (I zī' a) Great controversy has raged round the ascribed author of this book It seems certain that he was a man of rank and influence, between 735 B C and the invasion of Sennacherib in 701 His great task was to warn the Hebrews of the impending Assyrian invasion and recall them to the true worship of Jahveh In its English version the book of Isaiah contains some of the finest writing in the language

Isenbras or **Isumbras**, Sir (I' zen brǎs). A hero of mediæval romance (including, as usual, visits to the Holy Land and the slaughter of thousands of "Saracens"), first proud and presumptuous, when he was visited by all sorts of punishments, afterwards, penitent and humble, his afflictions were turned into blessings It was in this latter stage that he one day carried on his horse two children of a poor woodman across a ford

Iseult. *See* YSOLDE.

Ishbosheth (ish bō' sheth), in Dryden's *Absalom and Achitophel*, is meant for Richard Cromwell His father, Oliver, is Saul

The actual Ishbosheth (man of shame) was the son of Saul, who was proclaimed King of Israel at his father's death (*see* 2 *Sam* iv) and was almost immediately superseded by David

Ishtar (ish' tar) The Babylonian goddess of love and war (Gr *Astarte*), corresponding to the Phœnician Ashtoreth (*q v.*), except that while the latter was identified with the moon Ishtar was more frequently identified with the planet Venus She was the wife of Bel

Isiac Tablet (ı e tablet of Isis) A spurious Egyptian monument sold by a soldier to Cardinal Bembo in 1527, and preserved at Turin It is of copper, and on it are represented most of the Egyptian deities in the mysteries of Isis It was said to have been found at the siege of Rome in 1525.

Isidorian Decretals. *See* DECRETALS

Isinglass (I' zing glas) A corruption of the Dutch *huyzenblas*, a sturgeon's bladder (Ger. *hausen*, sturgeon): it is prepared from the bladders and sounds of sturgeon, and was introduced from Holland in the 16th century.

Isis (I' sis) The principal goddess of ancient Egypt, sister and wife of Osiris, and mother of Horus She was identified with the moon (Osiris being a sun-god), and the cow was sacred to her, its horns representing the crescent moon

Her chief temples were at Abydos, Busiris, and Philæ, she is represented as a queen, her head being surmounted by horns and the solar disk or by the double crown Proclus mentions a statue of her which bore the inscription—

I am that which is, has been, and shall be. My veil no one has lifted. The fruit I bore was the Sun—

hence to lift the veil of Isis is to pierce to the heart of a great mystery

She was identified with Io, Aphrodite, and others by the Greeks; with Selene, Ceres, Venus, Juno, etc, by the Romans, and the Phœnicians confused her with Ashtoreth Her worship as a nature goddess was very popular among the later Greeks and with the Romans of republican times Milton, in *Paradise Lost* (I, 478), places her among the fallen angels

Isis, River. *See* THAMES

Islam (iz lam') The Mohammedan religion, the whole body of Mohammedans, the true Mohammedan faith The Moslems say every child is born in Islam, and would continue in the true faith if not led astray The word means *resignation* or *submission to the will of God* Islam consists of five duties'—

(1) Bearing witness that there is but one God.
(2) Reciting daily prayers
(3) Giving the appointed and legal alms
(4) Observing the Ramazan (a month's fast).
(5) Making a pilgrimage to Mecca at least once in a lifetime

Islands of the Blest. *See* FORTUNATE ISLANDS

Isle of Dogs A peninsula on the left bank of the Thames between the Limehouse and Blackwall reaches, opposite Greenwich It is said to be so called because it was here that Edward III kept his greyhounds; but another explanation is that it is a corruption of *Isle of Ducks*, from the number of wild fowl anciently inhabiting the marshes

Ismene. In Greek legend, daughter of Œdipus and Jocasta Antigone was buried alive by the order of King Creon, for burying her brother Polynices, slain in combat by his brother Eteocles. Ismene declared that she had aided her sister, and requested to be allowed to share the same punishment

Isocrates (I sok' rǎ tēz), was one of the great orators of Athens and was distinguished as a teacher of eloquence He died 338 B.C.

The French Isocrates. Esprit Fléchier (1632-1710), Bishop of Nismes, specially famous for his funeral orations

Isolationism. A nationalistic philosophy opposed to political co-operation with any other nation or group of nations, the term is especially applied to a school of thought in U.S.A which repudiates any foreign alliances, friendships, connexions or commitments

Israel (iz räl), in Dryden's *Absalom and Achitophel* (q v), stands for England

Israfel (is' râ fel) The angel of music of the Mohammedans He possesses the most melodious voice of all God's creatures, and is to sound the Resurrection Trump which will ravish the ears of the saints in paradise. Israfel, Gabriel, and Michael were the three angels that, according to the Koran, warned Abraham of Sodom's destruction

> In Heaven a spirit doth dwell
>   Whose heart-strings are a lute;
> None sing so wildly well
> As the angel Israfel,
> And the giddy Stars (so legends tell),
> Ceasing their hymns, attend the spell
>   Of his voice, all mute   E A POE: *Israfel*

Issachar (is' a kar), in Dryden's satire of *Absalom and Achitophel* (q.v), means Thomas Thynne (1648-82), of Longleat, known as "Tom of Ten Thousand."

Issachar's ears. Ass's ears The allusion is to *Gen.* xlix, 14: 'Issachar is a strong ass couching down between two burdens."

> Is't possible that you, whose ears
> Are of the tribe of Issachar's   ..
> Should yet be deaf against a noise
> So roaring as the public voice?
>   SAMUEL BUTLER. *Hudibras to Sidrophel.*

Issei (ĕ' sā) A Japanese word meaning "first born" or "first generation," applied to a person of Japanese ancestry, born in Japan, but taking up residence in U S A, though retaining allegiance to Japan A Japanese born in U S.A. and loyal to that country is called a Nisei

Issue. The point of law in debate or in question "At issue," under dispute

To join issue. To take opposite views of a question, or opposite sides in a suit.

To join issues. To leave a suit to the decision of the court because the parties interested cannot agree.

Istar. *See* ISHTAR.

Isthmian Games (is' mi ån) Games consisting of chariot races, running, wrestling, boxing, etc., held by the ancient Greeks in the Isthmus of Corinth every alternate spring, the first and third of each Olympiad. Epsom races, and other big sporting events, have been called our "Isthmian games" in allusion to these

Istanbul (is tän bul') the name by which old Constantinople, until 1923 the capital of the Turkish Empire, is now known.

Isumbras. *See* ISENBRAS.

It. I'm it! I'm a person of some importance.

In for it. About "to catch it", on the point of being in trouble
In such phrases as this, and as to come it strong, to rough it, etc, it is the definite object of the transitive or intransitive verb

It, is used in U S A. as "He" is in England to denote the child who must catch the others at tag, or find them at hide-and-seek The word was also used at one time as a humorous euphemism for sex appeal.

Its. One of the words by the use of which Chatterton betrayed his forgeries. He wrote in a poem purporting to be the work of a 15th-century priest, "Life and its goods I scorn," but the word was not in use till more than two centuries later than his supposed time, it (*hit*) and *his* being the possessive case

For love and devocioun towards god also hath *it* infancie and it hath *it* comyng forewarde in groweth of age —*Udal's Erasmus Luke*, vii (1548).

Learning hath *his* infancy, when it is but beginning and almost childish, then *his* youth .   then *his* strength of yeares . . and lastly, *his* old age —BACON. *Essays of Vicissitude of Things* (1625)

Its does not occur in any play of Shakespeare published in his lifetime, but there is one instance in the First Folio of 1623 (*Measure for Measure* i, 2), as well as nine instances of *it's*. Nor does *its* occur in the Authorized Version of the Bible (1611), the one instance of it in modern editions (*Lev.* xxv, 5) having been substituted for *it* in the Bible printed for Hills and Field in 1660

Italian hand. I see his fine Italian hand in this may be said of a picture in which the beholder can discern the work of a particular artist through certain characteristics of his which appear Or it may be remarked of an intrigue, in which the characteristics of a particular plotter are apparent The Italian hand was originally the *cancelleresca* type of handwriting, used by the Apostolic Secretaries, and distinguishable by its grace and fineness from the Gothic styles of Northern Europe.

Italic. Pertaining to Italy, especially ancient Italy and the parts other than Rome

Italic type or **italics** (the type in which the letters, instead of being erect—as in roman—slope from left to right, *thus*) was first used by Aldo Manuzio in 1501 in an edition of Virgil, and was dedicated by him to Italy—hence its name It has been said that italic type was based on the beautiful handwriting of the poet Petrarch. Francesco of Bologna cast it

The words italicized in the Bible have no corresponding words in the original The translators supplied these words to render the sense of the passage more full and clear.

Italic School of Philosophy. The Pythagorean (6th cent. B.C.), so called because Pythagoras taught in Italy.

Italic version. An early Latin version of the Bible, prepared from the Septuagint. It preceded the Vulgate, or the version by St Jerome.

Itch, To. Properly, to have an irritation of the skin which gives one a desire to scratch the part affected, hence, figuratively, to feel a constant teasing desire for something The figure of speech enters into many phrases, as, *to itch* or *to have an itch for gold*, to have a longing desire for wealth; *an itching palm* means the same —

> Let me tell you, Cassius, you yourself
> Are much condemned to have an itching palm.
>   *Julius Cæsar*, iv, 3

Similarly, **to have itching ears,** is to be very desirous for news or novelty:—

The time will come when they will not endure the sound doctrine; but, having itching ears, will heap to themselves teachers after their own lusts.—*2 Tim* iv, 3 (R V)

To have an itching foot is to have a craving for travel

And **My fingers itch to be at him** means, "I am longing to give him a sound thrashing"

It was formerly a popular idea that the itching of various parts foretold various occurrences; for instance, if your right palm itched you were going to receive money, the itching of the left eye betokened grief, and of the right pleasure —

My right eye itches now, so I shall see
My love.   *Theocritus*, i, 37.

Itching of the lips of course foretold that they were shortly to kiss or be kissed; of the nose, that strangers were at hand —

We shall ha' guests to-day
. . My nose itcheth so,
         DEKKER *Honest Whore.*

And the thumb, that evil approaches

By the pricking of my thumbs,
Something evil this way comes
         SHAKESPEARE: *Macbeth*, iv, 1.

Ithuriel (ith û' ri el). The angel who, with Zephon (*q v*), was, in Milton's *Paradise Lost*, commissioned by Gabriel to search for Satan, after he had effected his entrance into Paradise The name is Rabbinical, and means "the discovery of God"

Ithuriel and Zephon, with winged speed
Search through this garden, leave unsearched no nook.
         Paradise Lost, Bk iv, 788

He was armed with a spear, the slightest touch of which exposed deceit

Him [i e Satan], thus intent Ithuriel with his spear
Touched lightly, for no falsehood can endure
Touch of celestial temper, but returns
Of force to its own likeness   *Paradise Lost*, iv, 810.

Itinerary. The account of a route followed by a traveller. The Itinerary of Antoninus marks out all the main roads of the Roman Empire, and the stations of the Roman army. The Itinerary of Peutinger (*Tabula Peutingeriana*) is also an invaluable document of ancient geography, executed A D 383, in the reign of Theodosius the Great, and hence called sometimes the *Theodosian Table.*

Ivan (I' van). The Russian form of John, called *Juan* in Spain, *Giovanni* in Italian.

Ivan the Terrible. Ivan IV of Russia (1530, 1533-84), infamous for his cruelties, but a man of great energy He first adopted the title of Tsar.

Ivanhoe (I' van hō) Sir Walter Scott took the name of his hero from the village of Ivanhoe, or Ivinghoe, in Bucks, a line in an old rhymed proverb—"Tring, Wing, and Ivanhoe"—attracted his attention

Ivanovitch (ē văn' ō vich) The national impersonation of the Russians as a people, as *John Bull* is of the English,

Ivory. Ivory Gate. *See* DREAMS, GATES or.

Ivory shoulder. *See* PELOPS.

Ivory tower. A place of refuge from the world and its strivings and posturings The

phrase is a symbol first used by Sainte-Beuve as *un tour d'ivoire*

Ivories Teeth, also dice, keys of the piano, billiard balls, dominoes, etc

Ivy (A S , *ifig*) Dedicated to Bacchus from the notion that it is a preventive of drunkenness But whether the Dionysian ivy is the same plant as that which we call *ivy* is doubtful, as it was famous for its golden berries, and was termed *chryso-carpos* An ivy wreath was the prize of the Isthmian games, until it was superseded by a pine garland.

In Christian symbolism ivy typifies the everlasting life, from its remaining continually green

Like an owl in an ivy-bush. *See* OWL

I.W.W., initials of Industrial Workers of the World, an international industrial union founded in Chicago in 1905. After World War I it fell to pieces.

Ixion. In Greek legend, a king of the Lapithæ who was bound to a revolving wheel of fire in the Infernal regions, either for his impious presumption in trying to imitate the thunder of heaven, or for boasting of the favours of Hera, Zeus having sent a cloud to him in the form of Hera, and the cloud having become by him the mother of the Centaurs (*q v*).

J

J. The tenth letter of the alphabet, a modern letter, only differentiated from *I* (*q v*.), the consonantal functions of which it took, in the 17th century, and not completely separated till the 19th. There is no roman J or j in the 1611 Authorized Version of the Bible In the Roman system of numeration it was (and in medical prescriptions still is) used in place of i as the final figure in a series—iij, vij, etc , for iii, vii

Jabberwocky (jăb' er wok' i), the eponymous central figure of a strange, almost gibberish poem in Lewis Carroll's *Through the Looking-glass*. It contains many significant "portmanteau words," as subsequently explained to Alice by Humpty Dumpty.

Jachin and Boaz (jā' kin, bō' ăz) The two great bronze pillars set up by Solomon at the entrance of his Temple—*Jachin* being the right-handed (southern) pillar, and the name probably expressing permanence, immovability, and *Boaz* being the left-hand (northern) pillar typifying the Lord of all strength. *See* 1 *Kings* vii, 21, *Ezek.* xl, 49

Jack. A personal name, probably a diminutive of *John*, but confused with the French *Jacques* (*q v.*)

A **good Jack makes a good Jill.** A good husband makes a good wife, a good master makes a good servant Jack, a generic name for man, husband, or master; and Jill for a woman. *See* JACKEROO.

Before you can say Jack Robinson. Immediately Grose says that the saying had its birth from a very volatile gentleman of that name, who used to pay flying visits to his neighbours, and was no sooner announced than he was off again; Halliwell says (*Archaic Dictionary*, 1846):—

> The following lines from "an old play" are elsewhere given as the original phrase—
> A warke it ys as easie to be done
> As tys to saye *Jacke' robys on*

But the "old play" has never been identified, and both these accounts are palpably *ben trovato*. The phrase was in use in the 18th century, and is to be found in Fanny Burney's *Evelina* (1778), II, xxxvii.

"Before you could say Jack Robinson" was the refrain of an immensely popular song sung by Thomas Hudson at the Cyder Cellars in the early 19th century

Every Jack shall have his Jill. Every man shall have a wife of his own

> Jack shall have his Jill,
> Nought shall go ill:
> The man shall have his mare again, and all shall be
> well.   *Midsummer Night's Dream*, iii, 2.

Every man Jack of them. All without exception, even the most insignificant Shakespeare uses the word in the same sense in *Cymbeline*, ii, 1—"Every Jack-slave hath his bellyful of fighting."

Jack Drum's Entertainment. *See* DRUM.

Jack of all trades and master of none. One who can turn his hand to anything is not usually an expert in any one branch *Jack of all trades* is a contemptuous expression—more grandiloquently he is a sciolist.

Jack's as good as his master. An old proverb (like "When Adam delve'd and Eve span"; *see* ADAM) indicating the equality of man It was the wise Agur (*see Proverbs*, xxx, 22) who placed "a servant when he reigneth" as the first of the four things that the earth cannot bear.

To be upon their jacks. To have the advantage over one The reference is to the jack, or jerkin, a coat of mail quilted with stout leather.

To make one's jack. To be successful The allusion is to the jack in games, such as bowls.

To play the Jack. To play the rogue, the knave. To deceive or lead astray like Jack-o'-lantern, or *ignis fatuus*

> —your fairy, which you say, is a harmless fairy, has done little better than played the Jack with us — *Tempest*, iv, 1

Cheap jack *See* CHEAP.

Cousin Jack. *See* COUSIN.

Jack Adams. A fool.

Jack-a-dandy. A term of endearment for a smart, bright little fellow,

> Smart she is, and handy, O!
> Sweet as sugar-candy, O! .
> And I'm her Jack-a-dandy, O!

Jack-a-dandy is also rhyming-slang for brandy

Jack-a-dreams. *See* JOHN-A-DREAMS.

Jack-a-Lent. A kind of Aunt Sally which was thrown at in Lent, hence, a puppet, a sheepish booby Shakespeare says: "You little

Jack-a-Lent, have you been true to us?" (*Merry Wives*, ii, 3).

> Thou, that when last thou wert put out of service,
> Travell'dst to Hampstead Heath on an Ass Wednesday
> Where thou didst stand six weeks the Jack of Lent,
> For boys to hurl, three throws a penny, at thee,
> To make thee a purse
>   BEN JONSON *Tale of a Tub*, IV, iii

Jack among the maids A favourite with the ladies, a ladies' man.

Jackanapes. A pert, vulgar, apish little fellow, a prig. Jackanapes must, however, have been in use before it became a nickname, and it is uncertain whether the *-napes* is connected originally with *ape* or with *Naples*, *Jackanapes* being a *Jack* (monkey) of (imported from) *Naples*, just as *fustian-a-napes* was fustian from Naples. There is an early 15th-century record of monkeys being sent to England from Italy, and by the 16th century, at all events, *Jackanapes* was in use as a proper name for a tame ape

> I will teach a scurvy jackanape priest to meddle or make —*Merry Wives of Windsor*, i, 4.

Jack-a-Napes. The nickname of William de la Pole, Duke of Suffolk, who was beheaded at sea (off Dover), possibly at the instigation of the Duke of York (1450) The name was given to him on account of his device, the clog and chain of an ape, which was also the cause of another of his names—"Ape-clogge."

Jackass. An unmitigated fool

Jack-at-a-pinch. One who lends a hand in an emergency; a clergyman, for instance, who has no cure, but officiates for a fee in any church where his assistance is required

Jack Brag. *See* BRAG.

Jackdaw. A prating nuisance

Jack-knife. Phrases from the similitude of a jack-knife in which the big blade doubles up into the handle

(i) In logging, where two logs jam end to end and hold up the rest,

(ii) In swimming a form of fancy dive.

Jack-pot. In poker, a pot which cannot be opened until a player has a pair of jacks, or better.

Jack Pudding. A buffoon, a mountebank; perhaps originally one who performed tricks, such as swallowing a certain number of yards of black pudding.

Jack Rice. An Australian race-horse once noted for his performance over the hurdles, hence **to have a roll Jack Rice couldn't jump over** is to have a lot of money

Jack-sauce. An insolent sauce-box, "the worst Jack of the pack."

Jackstones. A game played with six small stones or specially shaped pieces of metal, and a rubber ball.

Jackstraws. The American name for the game of spillikins

Jack-in-office. A conceited official or upstart, who presumes on his appointment to give himself airs.

Jack-in-the-green. A youth or boy who moves about concealed by a wicker framework covered with leaves and boughs as part of the chimney-sweeps' revels on May Day An old English custom now dead.

Jack of both sides One who tries to favour two antagonistic parties, either from fear or for profit.

Jack out of office One no longer in office, one dismissed from his employment

I am left out, for me nothing remains,
But long I will not be Jack-out-of-office.
1 *Henry VI*, i, 1

Jack is applied to animals and plants usually with reference to the male sex, smallness, or inferiority

Jackass, Jack-baker (a kind of owl), **Jack or dog fox, Jack hare, Jack rat, Jack shark, Jack snipe,** a young pike is called a *Jack,* so also were the male birds used in falconry.

Jack-in-the hedge, Jack-go-to-bed-at-noon, Jack-jump-about, and **Jack-in-the-bush,** are names of various common wild flowers **Jack-in-the-pulpit,** a North American woodland plant, *Arisaema triphyllum,* with an upright club-shaped spike, or spadix within an over-arching green or purple sheath

Jack-curlew. The whimbrel, a small species of curlew

Jack-in-a-bottle. The long-tailed tit-mouse, or bottle-tit, so called from the shape of its nest

Jack-rabbit. A large prairie-hare of North America, shortened from Jackass-rabbit, a name given to it on account of its very long ears and legs.

Jack Amend-All. One of the nicknames given to Jack Cade (killed 1450), the leader of "Cade's Rebellion." He promised to remedy all abuses.

Jack and the Beanstalk. A nursery tale found among all sorts of races from Icelanders to Zulus.

Jack and Jill. It has been suggested that the well-known nursery rhyme is a relic of a Norse myth, the two children are said to have been kidnapped by the moon while drawing water, and they are still to be seen with the bucket hanging from a pole resting on their shoulders.
An otherwise unknown comedy *Jack and Jill* is mentioned in the Revels Accounts as having been played at court in 1567-8 *Jill* or *Gill,* is an abbreviation of *Gillian,* for *Juliana.*

Jack the Giant-killer. The hero of this old nursery tale owed much of his success to his four marvellous possessions—an invisible coat, a cap of wisdom, shoes of swiftness, and a resistless sword When he put on his coat no eye could see him; when he had his shoes on no one could overtake him, his sword would cut through everything, and when his cap was on he knew everything he required to know. The story is given by Walter Map (and later by Geoffrey of Monmouth), who obtained it in the early 13th century from a French chronicle

Jack Horner. A very fanciful explanation of the old nursery rhyme "Little Jack Horner" is that Jack was steward to the Abbot of Glastonbury at the time of the Dissolution of the Monasteries, and that he, by a subterfuge, became possessed of the deeds of the Manor of Mells, which is in the neighbourhood and which is still owned by his descendants of the same name Some say that these deeds with others were sent to Henry VIII concealed, for safety, in a pasty, that "Jack Horner" was the bearer, and that on the way, he lifted the crust and extracted this "plum"

Jack Ketch. A hangman and executioner, notorious for his barbarity, who was appointed about 1663 and died in 1686. He was the executioner of William, Lord Russell, for his share in the Rye House Plot (1683) and of Monmouth (1685) In 1686 he was turned out of office for insulting one of the sheriffs, and was succeeded by a butcher named Rose Rose, however, was himself hanged within four months, whereupon Ketch was reinstated. As early as 1678 his name had appeared in a ballad, and by 1702 it was associated with the Punch and Judy puppet-play, which had recently been introduced from Italy

Ketch the executioner, a wretch who had butchered many brave and noble victims, and whose name has, during a century and a half, been vulgarly given to all who have succeeded him in his odious office — MACAULAY *History of England,* vol i, ch. V.

Jack of Newbury. John Winchcombe alias Smallwood (d 1520), a wealthy clothier in the reign of Henry VIII He was the hero of many chap-books, and is said to have kept 100 looms in his own house at Newbury, while legend relates that he equipped at his own expense 100 to 200 of his men to aid the king against the Scots in Flodden Field

Jack the Ripper. An unknown person who committed a series of murders on prostitutes in the East End of London in 1888-89 He gave himself the name, and the mystery surrounding his crimes made it very widely known

The first murder was April 2nd, 1888, the next was August 7th; the third was August 31st, the fourth was September 8th, the fifth was September 30th, when two women were murdered, the sixth was November 9th, the seventh was December 20th, in a builder's yard, the eighth was July 17th, 1889, at Whitechapel, the ninth was September 17th

Jack Straw The name (or nickname) of one of the leaders in the Peasants' Revolt of 1381 There is an allusion to him in Chaucer's *Nun's Prologue* (1386), and the name soon came to signify a man of straw, a worthless sort of person

It shall be but the weight of a strawe, or the weight of Jack Strawe more —THOS NASH *Nashe's Lenten Stuffe* (1598)

Jacky Howe (Austr.) A short-sleeved shirt worn by shearers, called after Jack Howe, whose 320 sheep sheared in eight hours—a feat performed in Queensland about 1900—still holds the world's record.

Jack-snip. A botching tailor.

Jack Sprat. A dwarf, as if sprats were dwarf mackerels Children, by a similar metaphor, are called small fry

Jack Tar. A common sailor, whose hands and clothes are tarred by the ship's tackling

Jack-o'-lantern. A will-o'-the-wisp. *See* IGNIS FATUUS

Jack Drum. *See* DRUM

Jack Frost. The personification of frost or frosty weather.

Jack-in-the-box. A toy consisting of a box out of which, when the lid is raised, a figure springs

Jack in the cellar. Old slang for an unborn child: a translation of the Dutch expression for the same *Hans in kelder*

Jack of cards. The knave or servant of the king and queen of the same suit.

Jack o' the bowl The brownie or house spirit of Switzerland: so called from the custom of placing for him every night on the roof of the cowhouse a bowl of fresh sweet cream. The contents are sure to disappear before morning.

Jackey. A monkey. *Cp.* JACKANAPES *above.*

Yellow jack. The yellow fever.

A very large number of appliances and parts of appliances are called by this name, such as the jack, bottle-jack, or roasting-jack, used for turning the meat when roasting before an open fire, the jack used for lifting heavy weights, the rough stool or wooden horse used for sawing timber on, etc Other instances of this use are ⸱

Boot-jack. An instrument for drawing off boots

Jack-block. A block attached to the top-gallant-tie of a ship.

Jack-in-the-basket. The cap or basket on the top of a pole to indicate the place of a sand-bank at sea, etc

Jack-o'-the clock or clock-house. The figure which, in some old public clocks, comes out to strike the hours on the bell

Strike like Jack o' the clock-house, never but in season —WM STRODE *Floating Island* (1655).
King Richard   Well, but what's o'clock?
Buckingham Upon the stroke of ten.
K R   Well, let it strike
B ⸱ Why let it strike?
K R Because that, like a jack, thou keep'st the stroke
Betwixt thy begging and my meditation.
Richard III, IV, 2.

Jack-roll. The cylinder round which the rope of a well coils

Jack-screw. A large screw rotating in a threaded socket, used for lifting heavy weights

Lifting-jack. A machine for lifting the axle-tree of a vehicle when the wheels are cleaned or the tires require attention

Smoke-jack. An apparatus in a chimney-flue for turning a spit It is made to revolve by the upward current of smoke and air.
The JACK is also applied to the small flag flown at the bow in ships (*cp* UNION JACK); a small drinking vessel made of waxed leather, the large one being called a *black jack* (*q v.*), and to an inferior kind of armour consisting of a leather surcoat worn over the hauberk, from the 14th to the 17th century It was formed by overlapping pieces of steel fastened by one edge upon canvas, coated over with cloth or velvet, and was worn by the peasantry of the English borders in their skirmishes with moss-troopers, etc North, in his translation of *Plutarch* (1579, *Life of Crassus*), applies the word to the armour of the Parthians:—

For himself [*i e* Crassus] and his men with weak and light staves, brake upon them that were armed with curaces of steel, or stiff leather jacks.

And the "jack" at bowls is so called because it is very small in comparison with the bowls themselves.

A Jack and a half-jack. Counters resembling a sovereign and a half-sovereign, used at gaming-tables.

Jack boots. Cumbrous boots of thick leather worn by fishermen, cavalrymen, etc

Jack of Dover. Some unidentified eatable mentioned by Chaucer in the *Cook's Prologue.* "Our host," addressing the cook, says.—

Now telle on, Roger, loke that it be good;
For many a pastee hastow laten blood,
And many a Jakke of Dover hastow sold
That hath been twyes hoot and twyes cold

Professor Skeat says that this is ' probably a pie that had been cooked more than once", another suggestion is that it means some sea-fish (*cp.* JOHN DORY), while another is that it is the heel-taps of bottles of wine collected into a *jack*, and, by being served to customers made to "do over" (*Dover*) again!

Jack plane, Jack saw. A plane or saw to do rough work before the finer instruments are used

Jack rafter. A rafter in a hipped roof, shorter than a full-sized one.

Jack rib. An inferior rib in an arch, being shorter than the rest.

Jack timbers. Timbers in a building shorter than the rest

Jack towel. A long towel hung on a roller

Jackal. A toady. One who does the dirty work of another. It was once thought that the jackals hunted in troops to provide the lion with prey, hence they were called the "lion's providers" No doubt the lion will at times avail himself of the jackal's assistance by appropriating prey started by these "hunters," but it would be folly to suppose that the jackal acted on the principle of *vos non vobis.* *See* LION'S PROVIDER

Jackeroo, a name used in Australia in the first half of the 19th century to describe a young Englishman newly arrived to learn farming It was said by some to be derived from the Queensland *tchaceroo*, the shrike, noted for its garrulity Later the name was applied simply to a station hand. Jilleroo, a feminine adaptation of Jackeroo, used for land girls in Australia during World War II

Jacket. Diminutive of *jack*, a surcoat (whence the armour
The skin of a potato is called its "jacket" Potatoes brought to table unpeeled are said to be "with their jackets on"

To dust one's jacket, or to give one a good jacketing. *See* DUST.

Jacksonian Professor. The professor of natural and experimental philosophy at Cambridge The professorship was founded in 1782 by the Rev. Richard Jackson (1700-82), a fellow of Trinity

Jacob. Jacob's ladder The ladder seen by the patriarch Jacob in a vision (*Gen* xxviii, 12) *Jacob* is, on this account, a cant name for a ladder, and steep and high flights of steps going up cliffs, etc , are often called *Jacob's ladders*, as is a flaw in a stocking where only the weft threads are left, giving a ladder-like appearance There is a garden flower also so called

Jacob's staff. A pilgrim's staff; from the Apostle James (Lat *Jacobus*), who is usually represented with a staff and scallop shell

As he had travelled many a summer's day
Through boiling sands of Arabie and Ynd,
And in his hand a Jacob's staff to stay
His weary limbs upon.
SPENSER· *Faerie Queene*, Bk. i, canto vi, 32-35

Also the name of an obsolete instrument for taking heights and distances

Reach then a soaring quill, that I may write
As with a Jacob's staff to take her height
CLEVELAND· *The Hecatomb to his Mistress*

Jacob's stone. The Coronation Stone (*see* SCONE) is sometimes so called, because of the legend that it was on this stone that Jacob's head rested when he had the vision of the angels ascending and descending the ladder (*Gen.* xxviii, 11)

Jacobins The Dominicans were so called in France from the "Rue St. Jacques," Paris, where they first established themselves in 1219; and the French Revolutionary club (known as the "Society of Friends of the Constitution" when founded at Versailles in 1789) took the name because, on their removal to Paris, they met in the hall of an ex-convent of Jacobins, in the Rue St Honoré The Jacobins were at first constitutional monarchists, with Mirabeau as one of their leading members After the king's flight to Varennes in 1791 there was a schism in the party and the main body became extreme republicans, swayed by Robespierre, St Just, Marat, and Couthon During the Terror they had unrivalled power, but the fall of Robespierre in 1794 brought their reign to an end and in November of that year the club was suppressed. Their badge was the Phrygian Cap of Liberty

Jacobites (jăk' ō bīts) The supporters of the right of James II and his descendants to the throne of Great Britain and Ireland. They came into existence after the flight of James II in 1688, and were strong in Scotland and the North of England They were responsible for two risings, in 1715 and 1745, the latter marking the virtual end of Jacobitism as a political force The last male descendant of James II, Henry Cardinal of York, died in 1807; a certain number of sentimental adherents to the lost cause are still to be found here and there

Jacobites. An Oriental sect of Monophysites, so called from Jacobus Baradæus, Bishop of Edessa, in Syria, in the 6th century. The Jacobite Church comprises three Patriarchates, viz , those of Alexandria, Antioch, and Armenia.

Jacobus (ja kō' bus) The unofficial name of a gold coin of the value of from 20s to 24s , struck in the reign of James I

Jacquard Loom (jăk' ard) So called from Jos Marie Jacquard (1752-1834), of Lyons, its inventor It is a machine for weaving figures upon silks and muslins

Jacques (zhak) (Fr) A generic name for the poor artisan class in France (*see* JACQUERIE, LA, *below*), so called from the *jaque*, a rough kind of waistcoat, sleeved, and coming almost to the knees, that they used to wear.

Jaques, il me faut troubler ton somme,
Dans le village, un gros huissier
Rude et court, suivi du messier.
C'est pour l'impôt, las! mon pauvre homme,
Lève-toi, Jacques, leve-toi,
Voici venir l'huissier du roi
Béranger (1831)

Jacquerie, La (zhăk' e rē). An insurrection of the peasantry of France in 1358, excited by the oppressions of the privileged classes and Charles the Bad of Navarre, while King John II was a prisoner in England, so called from *Jacques*, or **Jacques Bonhomme**, the generic name given to the French peasantry They banded together, fortified themselves and declared war to the death against every gentleman in France, but in six weeks some 12,000 of the insurgents were cut down, and the rebellion suppressed with the greatest determination

Jactitation of Marriage. A false assertion by a person of being married to another This is actionable. *Jactitation* means literally "a throwing out," and here means "to utter," i.e "to throw out publicly " The term comes from the old Canon Law

Jade. The fact that in mediæval times this ornamental stone was supposed, if applied to the side, to act as a preservative against colic is enshrined in its name, for *jade* is from the Spanish *piedra de ijada*, stone of the side, and its other name, *nephrite*, is from Gr. *nephros*, kidney Among the North American Indians it is still worn as an amulet against the bite of venomous snakes, and to cure the gravel, epilepsy, etc

Jade A worthless horse. An old woman (used in contempt) A young woman (not necessarily contemptuous)

Jagannath. *See* JUGGERNAUT

Jahveh. *See* JEHOVAH

Jains. A sect of dissenters from Hinduism of great antiquity, its known history going back beyond 477 B C. Its differences from Hinduism are theological and too abstruse for expression in brief. Jains being largely traders the sect is wealthy though comparatively small in size and influence

Jalopy (jăl ō' pi or jă lop' i), an American colloquial term for an old, decrepit automobile

Jam. Used in a slang way for something really nice, especially if unexpected, something delightful, tip-top

There must have been a charming climate in Paradise and [the] connubial bliss [there] . . was real jam.—SAM SLICK. *Human Nature.*

Money for jam. Money (or money's worth) for nothing; an unexpected bit of luck.

Jam session. A meeting of jazz musicians improvising spontaneously, without rehearsal.

Jamboree (jăm bŏ rē'), originally meaning a noisy merry-making, this word is now more usually applied to a large rally of Boy Scouts, usually of an international scope

Jambres. See JANNES

James. A sovereign, a jacobus (*q v*), also called a "jimmy." *Half a jimmy* is half a sovereign.

James, St. The Apostle St. James the Great is the patron saint of Spain Legend states that after his death in Palestine his body was placed in a boat with sails set, and that next day it reached the Spanish coast; at Padron, near Compostella, they used to show a huge stone as the veritable boat According to another legend, it was the *relics* of St James that were miraculously conveyed to Spain in a ship of marble from Jerusalem, where he was bishop A knight saw the ship sailing into port, his horse took fright, and plunged with its rider into the sea. The knight saved himself by "boarding the marble vessel," but his clothes were found to be entirely covered with scallop shells.

The saint's body was discovered in 840 by divine revelation to Bishop Theodomirus, and a church was built at Compostella for its shrine.

St James is commemorated on July 25th, and is represented in art sometimes with the sword by which he was beheaded, and sometimes attired as a pilgrim, with his cloak covered with shells.

St. James the Less. His attribute is a fuller's club, in allusion to the instrument by which he was put to death after having been precipitated from the summit of the temple at Jerusalem in A.D. 62. He is commemorated on May 1st. *Less* means the shorter of stature.

The Court of St. James's. The British court, to which foreign ambassadors are officially accredited. St James's Palace, Pall Mall, stands on the site of a 12th-century leper hospital dedicated to St James the Less. The Palace was a royal residence from 1698 until 1837, and since then has been used for levees and drawing-rooms

Jameson Raid, a coup d'etat attempted in S. Africa by Dr. L. S. Jameson in 1895 With the connivance of Cecil Rhodes he organized a force of some 500 men to invade the Transvaal simultaneously with a rising of Uitlanders in Johannesburg. Jameson crossed the Bechuanaland border but was met by a Boer force at Doornkop and compelled to surrender The Boers handed the invaders over to the British authorities and Jameson and others were tried for treason and sentenced to various terms of imprisonment.

Jamshid (jăm shid') In Persian legend, the fourth king of the Pishdadian Dynasty, *i e* the earliest, who is fabled to have reigned for 700 years and to have had the Deevs, or Genii, as his slaves. He possessed a sevenringed golden cup, typical of the seven heavens, the seven planets, the seven seas, etc., which was full of the elixir of life, it was hidden by

the genii and was said to have been discovered while digging the foundations of Persepolis.
Iram indeed is gone with all his rose,
And Jamshyd's Sev'n-ring'd Cup where no one knows.
FitzGerald *Rubaiyat of Omar Khayyam.*

Jane. A small Genoese silver coin, so called from Fr. *Genes,* Genoa.
Because I could not give her many a jane
SPENSER *Faerie Queene,* III, vii, 58

In American slang a *jane* is a derogatory term for a woman. She is also the heroine of a strip cartoon by Petty, that began in the London *Daily Mirror* during the 1930s—a great favourite with the British armed forces in World War II

Janissaries or **Janizaries** (jăn' i săr iz) (Turk. *yeni-tscheri,* new corps) A celebrated militia of the Ottoman Empire, raised by Orchan in 1326, originally, and for some centuries, compulsorily recruited from the Christian subjects of the Sultan It was blessed by Hadji Becktash, a saint, who cut off a sleeve of his fur mantle and gave it to the captain. The captain put the sleeve on his head, and from this circumstance arose the fur cap worn by these foot-guards In 1826, having become too formidable to the state, they were abolished after a massacre in which many thousands of the Janissaries perished.

Jannes and Jambres (jăn' ēz, jăm' brēz) The names under which St. Paul (2 *Tim.* iii, 8) referred to the two magicians of Pharaoh who imitated some of the miracles of Moses (*Exod.* vii) The names are not mentioned in the Old Testament, but they appear in the Targums and other rabbinical writings, where tradition has it that they were sons of Balaam, and that they perished either in the crossing of the Red Sea, or in the tumult after the worship of the golden calf

Jansenists (jăn' sen ists). A sect of Christians, who held the doctrines of Cornelius Jansen, (1585-1638), Bishop of Ypres Jansen professed to have formulated the teaching of Augustine, which resembled Calvinism in many respects. He taught the doctrines of ' irresistible grace,'' "original sin," and the "utter helplessness of the natural man to turn to God " Louis XIV took part against them, and they were put down by Pope Clement XI, in 1705, in the famous bull Unigenitus (*q v.*).

Januarius, St. (jăn ū âr' i us) The patron saint of Naples, a bishop of Benevento who was martyred during the Diocletian persecution, 304 He is commemorated on September 19th, and his head and two vials of his blood are preserved in the cathedral at Naples. This congealed blood is said to liquefy several times a year.

January. The month dedicated by the Romans to Janus (*q.v.*), who presided over the entrance to the year and, having two faces, could look back to the year past and forward on the current year.
The Dutch used to call this month *Louw-maand* (frosty-month), the Saxons, *Wulf-monath,* because wolves were very troublesome then from the great scarcity of food After the introduction of Christianity, the name was changed to *Se æftera geola* (the afteryule), it was also called *Forma monath* (first month) In the French Republican calendar it was called *Nivose* (snow-month, December 20th to January 20th).

It's a case of January and May. Said when an old man marries a young girl The allusion is to the Merchant's Tale in Chaucer's *Canterbury Tales,* in which May, a lovely girl, married January, a Lombard baron sixty years of age

Janus (jā' nus) The ancient Roman deity who kept the gate of heaven, hence the guardian of gates and doors He was represented with two faces, one in front and one behind, and the doors of his temple in Rome were thrown open in times of war and closed in times of peace The name is used allusively both with reference to the double-facedness and to war Thus Milton says of the Cherubim:—

Four faces each
Had, like a double Janus
Paradise Lost, xi, 129

And Tennyson—

State-policy and church-policy are conjoint,
But Janus-faces looking diverse ways
Queen Mary, III, ii.

While Dante says of the Roman eagle that it—

composed the world to such a peace,
That of his temple Janus barr'd the door.
Paradiso, vi, 83 (*Cary's tr.*).

Japanese Vellum. An extremely costly hand-beaten Japanese paper manufactured from the inner bark of the mulberry tree.

Japhetic. An adjective sometimes applied to the Aryan family

The Indo-European family of languages as known by various designations Some style it *Japhetic,* as if it appertained to the descendants of the patriarch Japheth [son of Noah] as the *Semitic* tongues [appertain] to the descendants of Shem —WHITNEY *Languages, etc ,* lect v

Jarkman. Sixteenth-century slang for an Abram-man (*q.v.*), especially one who was able to forge passes, licences, etc. *Jark* was rogues' cant for a seal, whence also a licence of the Bethlehem Hospital to beg.

Jarnac. Coup de Jarnac. A treacherous and unexpected attack, so called from Guy Chabot, Sieur de Jarnac, who, in a duel with La Châteignerate, on July 10th, 1547, in the presence of Henri II, first "hamstrung" his opponent and then, when he was helpless, slew him.

Jarndyce v. Jarndyce (jarn dīs'). An interminable Chancery suit, in *Bleak House.* Dickens probably founded his story on the long drawn-out Chancery suit of Jennens v. Jennens, which related to property in Nacton, Suffolk, belonging to an intestate miser who died in 1798 The case was only finally concluded more than eighty years after its start

Jarvey. Old slang for a hackney-coach driver; from the personal name *Jarvis,* with a possible allusion to St. Gervaise, whose symbol in art is a whip

I pity them ere Jarvies a sitting on their boxes all night and waiting for the nobs what is dancing — DISRAELI *Sybil,* V, vii (1845)

Jason (jā' sòn) The hero of Greek legend who led the Argonauts (*q v*) In the quest for the Golden Fleece. He was the son of Æson, king of Ioclus, was brought up by the centaur, Chiron, and when he demanded his kingdom from his half-brother, Pelias, who had deprived him of it, was told he could have it in return for the Golden Fleece Jason thereupon

gathered together the chief heroes of Greece and set sail in the *Argo* After many tests and trials he, through the help of Medea (*q v*), was successful He married Medea, but later deserted her, and, according to one account, he killed himself with grief, according to another was crushed to death by the keel of his old ship, *Argo,* while resting beneath it.

Jaundice (Fr *jaune,* yellow). *A jaundiced eye.* A prejudiced eye which sees only faults It was a popular belief that to the eye of a person who had the jaundice everything looked of a yellow tinge.

All seems infected that th' infected spy,
As all seems yellow to the jaundiced eye
POPE *Essay on Criticism,* ii, 359

Javan (jā' van). In the Bible the collective name of the Greeks (*Is* lxvi, 19, and *Ezek* xxvii, 13 and elsewhere), who were supposed to be descended from Javan, the son of Japheth (*Gen* x, 2).

Jaw To jaw, to annoy with words, to jabber, wrangle, or abuse

A break-jaw word; a jaw-breaker. A very long word, or one hard to pronounce

Pi jaw. A contemptuous term for *pious* talk, or for an ostentatiously pious or goody-goody person

Jay Old slang for a frivolous person, a wanton

This jay of Italy . . . hath betrayed him —*Cymbeline,* iii, 4

Jay hawker. In older American slang, a bandit

Jaywalker. One who crosses a street regardless of traffic regulations

Jazey. A wig, a corruption of Jersey, and so called because they used to be made of Jersey flax and fine wool

Jazz (jăz) The folk-music of the American Negro Originating in the cotton-fields, it was developed in New Orleans and thence spread up the Mississippi in the river boats to Chicago. Now world-wide, this type of music, originally and sometimes still the expression of a naturally musical people is too often confused with insipid dance tunes. One of its earliest exponents was "Jelly Roll" Morton who introduced the Blues Buddy Bolden, the great trumpet-player, was playing in New Orleans in the 1880s The music started up the river in 1915, and in March, 1916, Bert Kelly's "Jazz Band" (the first to be so called) was engaged by the Boosters' Club, of Chicago, scored an immediate success, and started jazz on its conquering career

The origin of the name is uncertain. One account is that it is an adaptation of the name of one *Razz,* who was a band conductor in New Orleans about 1904, another that it has long been a common word to the Negro and on the Barbary coast, and means simply "to mess 'em up and slap it on thick," and another that it was the spontaneous production of a brain-wave on the part of Bert Kelly.

Je ne sais quoi (zhe ne sä kwa) (Fr , I know not what). An indescribable something, as "There was a *je ne sais quoi* about him which made us dislike him at first sight"

Jeames (jēmz). A flunkey The *Morning Post* used sometimes to be so called, because of its never failing solicitude for the flunkey-employing classes and its flunkey-like attitude towards them

Thackeray wrote *Jeames's Diary* (published in *Punch*), of which Jeames de la Pluche—a "super" flunkey—was the hero.

Jean Crapaud. A Frenchman *See* CRAPAUD.

Jedwood Justice Putting an obnoxious person to death first, and trying him afterwards This sort of justice was dealt to moss-troopers. Same as *Jedburgh justice*, *Jeddart justice*. We have also "Cupar justice" and "Abingdon law"

Jedwood justice—hang in haste and try at leisure — SCOTT. *Fair Maid of Perth*, ch xxxii

Jeep (jēp) A small all-purpose car developed by the U S A. during World War II. Its 4-wheel drive and high and low gear-boxes gave it astonishing cross-country performances Its value to the Allied armed forces was inestimable The experimental models were called Beeps, Peeps and Blitz Buggies, but the name Jeep had been coined and had stuck by early 1941.

Jehennam *See* JAHANNAM.

Jehovah (je hō' vȧ) The name JEHOVAH itself is an instance of the extreme sanctity with which the name of God was invested, for this is a disguised form of the name. This word JHVH, the sacred tetragrammaton (*q v*), was too sacred to use, so the scribes added the vowels of *Adonai*, thereby indicating that the reader was to say *Adonai* instead of JHVH. At the time of the Renaissance these vowels and consonants were taken for the sacred name itself and hence *Jehovah* or *Yahwe*.

Jehovistic *See* ELOHISTIC

Jehovah's Witnesses, a sect of religious pacifists who refuse to acknowledge the authority of the State when it crosses their religious views or doctrines.

Jehu (jē' hū) A coachman, especially one who drives at a rattling pace

The watchman told, saying, . . The driving is like the driving of Jehu the son of Nimshi, for he driveth furiously —2 *Kings* ix, 20

Jekyll (jek' il). **Dr Jekyll and Mr. Hyde.** Two phases of one man. Jekyll is the "would do good," Hyde is "the evil that is present " The phrase comes from R L Stevenson's *The Strange Case of Dr Jekyll and Mr. Hyde*, first published in 1886

Jellyby, Mrs. (jel' i bi) The type of the enthusiastic, unthinking philanthropist who forgets that charity should begin at home Dickens, *Bleak House*

Jemmy (the diminutive or pet form of *James*). Slang for a number of different things, as a burglar's crowbar; a sheep's head, boiled or baked, said to be so called from the tradition that James IV of Scotland breakfasted on a sheep's head just before the battle of Flodden Field (September 9th, 1513), also, a greatcoat,

and—as an adjective—spruce, dandified *See* JEMMY JESSAMY

She presently returned with a pot of porter and a dish of sheep's heads, which gave occasion to several pleasant witticisms on the part of Mr Sikes, founded upon the singular coincidence of jemmies, being a cant name, common to them, and also to an ingenious instrument much used in his profession —DICKENS *Oliver Twist*, ch xx.

Jemmy Dawson. *See* DAWSON

Jemmy Jessamy. A Jack-a-dandy, a lady's fondling, "sweet as sugar-candy "

This was very different language to that she had been in the habit of hearing from her Jemmy Jessamy adorers —THACKERAY. *Barry Lyndon*, ch xiii

Jemmy O'Goblin. Slang for a sovereign *Cp* JAMES.

Jenkins's Ear The name given to an incident that helped largely to bring about the war between England and Spain in 1739 that eventually developed into the War of the Spanish Succession. Captain Robert Jenkins, skipper of the brig *Rebecca* was homeward bound from the West Indies when he was attacked by a Spanish *guarda costa* off Havana on 9th April, 1731 The Spaniards plundered his ship and ended by cutting off one of Jenkins's ears. On reaching London Jenkins carried his complaint (and his severed ear in a leather case) to the king and demanded reparation. At the time little notice was taken of the incident, but some years later, in 1738, the matter was brought up again, Jenkins and his ear were examined by a committee of the House of Commons and his case became an added grievance to the many others that culminated in war.

Jenny Wren. The sweetheart of Robin Redbreast in the old nursery rhyme

Robin promised Jenny, if she would be his wife. she should "feed on cherry-pie and drink currant-wine"; and he says —

"I'll dress you like a goldfinch,
Or any peacock gay,
So, dearest Jen, if you'll be mine,
Let us appoint the day."

Jenny replies —

"Cherry-pie is very nice,
And so is currant wine;
But I must wear my plain brown gown
And never go too fine "

Jeofail (jō' fāl) The old legal term for an error, omission, or oversight in proceedings at law The word is the Anglo-Fr *jeo fail*, O.Fr *je faille*, I am at fault. There were several statutes of Jeofail for the remedy of slips or mistakes

Jeopardy (jep' ar di). Hazard, danger It originally signified an even chance, hence an uncertain chance, something hazardous It has since been extended to mean exposure to the risk of death, loss, or injury The word is French in derivation—*jeu*, game, *parti*, divided.

Jeremiah (jer e mī' ȧ). **The British Jeremiah.** Gibbon so calls Gildas (fl 6th cent), author of *Lamentations over the Destruction of Britain*

Jeremiad (jer e mī' ad) A pitiful tale, a tale of woe to produce compassion, so called from the "Lamentations" of the prophet Jeremiah.

Jericho (jer'ı kō) Used in a number of phrases for the sake of giving verbal definition to some altogether indefinite place The reason for fixing on this particular town is possibly to be found in *2 Sam* x, 5, and *1 Chron.* xix, 5

Go to Jericho. A euphemistic turn of phrase for "Go and hang yourself," or something more offensive still

Gone to Jericho. No one knows where.

I wish you were at Jericho Anywhere out of my way

Jerked Beef. "Jerked" is here a corruption of Peruvian *charqui*, meat cut into strips and dried in the sun

Jerkin. A short coat or jacket, formerly made of leather, a close waistcoat
A plague of opinion, one may wear it on both sides, like a leather jerkin —*Troilus and Cressida*, iii, 3

Jerkwater. An early American term for a small train on a branch railway line.

Jeroboam (jer ō bō' am) A very large wine bottle or flagon, so called in allusion to the "mighty man of valour" who "made Israel to sin" (*1 Kings* xi, 28, xiv, 16) Its capacity is not very definite; some say it is from ten to twelve quarts, but the more usual allowance is eight. A *magnum* = 2 quart bottles; a *tappit hen* = 2 magnums, a *jeroboam* = 2 tappit hens, and a *rehoboam* = 2 jeroboams or 16 quart bottles. *See these names*, and *cp* JORUM.

Jerome, St (jer' ōm) A father of the Western Church, and translator of the Vulgate (*q v.*) He was born about 340, and died at Bethlehem in 420 He is generally represented as an aged man in a cardinal's dress, writing or studying, with a lion seated beside him. His feast is kept on September 30th

Jeronimo (je ron' imō). The chief character in the *Spanish Tragedy* by Thomas Kyd (acted about 1590) On finding his application to the king ill-timed, he says to himself, "Go by, Jeronimo," which tickled the fancy of the audience so that it became for a time a street jest, and was introduced into many contemporary plays, as in Shakespeare's *Taming of the Shrew* (*Induction*), Jonson's *Every Man in his Humour* (I, v), Dekker's *Shoemaker's Holiday* (II, i), etc *See also* GERONIMO.

Jerrican (World War II) A 4½-gallon petrol or water container which would stand rough handling and stack easily, developed by the Germans for the Afrika Korps. Borrowed by the British in Libya (hence its name), it became the standard unit of fuel replenishment throughout the Allied armies

Jerry. In World War I this was an army nickname for a German, or Germans collectively.

Jerry-built. Unsubstantial. A "jerry-builder" is a speculative builder who runs up cheap, unsubstantial houses, using materials of the commonest kind. The name is probably in some way connected with *Jeremiah*

Jerry Diddler. *See* DIDDLE

Jerry-shop, or Tom and Jerry shop. A low-class beerhouse. Probably the *Tom and Jerry* was a public-house sign when Pierce Egan's

Life in London (1821), in which these are leading characters, was popular

Jerrymander. *See* GERRYMANDER

Jerry Twitcher. *See* TWITCHER.

Jersey is Cæsar's-ey—i e Cæsar's island, so called in honour of Julius Cæsar In U S.A Jersey is often used to indicate the State of New Jersey.

Jerusalem. Julian the Apostate, the Roman Emperor (d 363), with the intention of pleasing the Jews and humbling the Christians, said that he would rebuild the temple and city, but was mortally wounded before the foundation was laid, and his work set at naught by "an earthquake, a whirlwind, or a fiery eruption" (*see* Gibbon's *Decline and Fall*, ch xxiii).
Much has been made of this by early Christian writers, who dwell on the prohibition and curse pronounced against those who should attempt to rebuild the city, and the fate of Julian is pointed out as an example of Divine wrath

Jerusalem, in Dryden's *Absalom and Achitophel* (*q v.*), means London (Pt 1, v. 86, etc.)

The New Jerusalem. The paradise of Christians, in allusion to *Rev* xxi.

Jerusalem artichoke. Jerusalem is here a corruption of Ital. *Girasole* Girasole is the sunflower, which this vegetable resembles both in leaf and stem

Jerusalem Chamber. The Chapter-house of Westminster Abbey Henry IV died there, March 20th, 1413
It hath been prophesied to me many years,
I should not die but in Jerusalem.
2 Henry IV, iv, 5
Pope Silvester II was told the same thing, and he died as he was saying Mass in a church so called (Bacon, *Tusculum*)
The Lower House of Convocation usually meets in the Jerusalem Chamber.

Jerusalem Cross A cross potent *See* POTENT

Jerusalem Delivered. An Italian epic poem in twenty books, by Torquato Tasso (1544-95) It was published in 1581, and was translated into English by Edward Fairfax in 1600 It tells the story of the First Crusade and the capture of Jerusalem by Godfrey of Bouillon, 1099.

Jess (through Fr from Lat *jactus*, a cast, throw). A short strap of leather tied about the legs of a hawk to hold it on the fist. Hence, metaphorically. a bond of affection, etc
If I prove her haggard,
Though that her jesses were my dear heart-strings
I'd whistle her off. *Othello*, iii, 3

Jessamy Bride The fancy name given by Goldsmith to Mary Horneck when he fell in love with her in 1769 *Cp* JEMMY JESSAMY

Jesse, or Jesse Tree (jes' i) A genealogical tree, usually represented as a vine or as a large brass candlestick with many branches, tracing the ancestry of Christ, called a "rod out of the stem of Jesse" (*Is* xi 1) Jesse is himself sometimes represented in a recumbent position with the vine rising out of his loins, hence a stained-glass window representing him thus with a tree shooting from him containing the pedigree of Jesus is called a *Jesse window*

Jesters. *See* COURT FOOLS, *under* FOOLS

Jesuit (jez' ū it) The popular name of members of the Society of Jesus, founded by St Ignatius Loyola in 1533, who, when asked what name he would give his order, replied, "We are a little battalion of Jesus." The order was founded to combat the Reformation and to propagate the faith among the heathen, but through its discipline, organization, and methods of secrecy, it acquired such political power that it came into conflict with both the civil and religious authorities; it was driven from France in 1594, from England in 1579, from Venice in 1607 from Spain in 1767, from Naples in 1768, in 1773 it was altogether suppressed by Pope Clement XIV, but was revived in 1814

Owing to the casuistical principles maintained by many of its leaders and attributed to the order as a whole the name *Jesuit* has acquired a very opprobrious signification in both Protestant and Roman Catholic countries, and a *Jesuit*, or *Jesuitical person* means (secondarily) a deceiver, prevaricator, one who "lies like truth," or palters in a double sense, that "keeps the word of promise to our ear, and breaks it to our hope"

Jesuit's bark. *See* PERUVIAN

Jesus Paper Paper of large size (about 28¼ in by 21½) chiefly used for engravings Originally it was stamped with the initials I H S

Jetsam or **Jetson** (jet' sam) Goods cast into the sea to lighten a ship (Fr *jeter*, to cast out). *See* FLOTSAM. LIGAN

Jettatura (yet à too' ra) The Italian phrase for the evil eye, a superstition that certain persons have the power, by looking at one, to cast a malevolent spell This can be countered only by various gestures, chief among which is the extending of the clenched fist with the index and little fingers stuck out like horns The superstition and all connected with it is of extreme antiquity.

Jeu d'esprit (je des prē) (Fr) A witticism

Jeu de mot (je de mō) (Fr) A pun; a play on some word or phrase

Jeunesse Dorée (je nes' dôr ā) (Fr) The "gilded youth" of a nation, that is, the rich and fashionable young unmarried men.

There were three of the *jeunesse dorée*, and, as such, were pretty well known to the ladies who promenade the grand circle.—T. TERREL. *Lady Delmar*, ix.

Jew. In Dryden's *Absalom and Achitophel* (*q v.*) the *Jews* stand for those English who were loyal to Charles II, called David.

Jews born with tails. *See* RABBIN.

Rich as a Jew. This expression arose in the Middle Ages, when Jews were almost the only money-lenders, and were certainly the most wealthy of the people

Jew's-harp. It is not known how or why this very simple musical instrument got its name (known from the 16th cent); it has no special connexion with the Jews, and is not like a harp

B.D.—17

It was called by Bacon *jeutrompe*, by Beaumont and Fletcher, *jew-trump*, and in Hakluyt's *Voyages* (1595), *jew's-harp*

Jew's ear. A fungus that grows on the Judas-tree (*q v*), its name is due to a mistranslation of its Latin name, *Auricula Judæ*, i.e. Judas's ear

Jew's myrtle Butcher's broom is so called, from the popular notion that it formed the crown of thorns placed by the Jews on the Saviour's head.

Worth a Jew's-eye. According to fable, this expression arose from the custom of torturing Jews to extort money from them. The expedient of King John is well known, he demanded 10,000 marks of a rich Jew of Bristol, the Hebrew resisted, but the tyrant ordered that one of his teeth should be tugged out every day till the money was forthcoming In seven days the sufferer gave in, and John jestingly observed, "A Jew's eye may be a quick ransom, but Jew's teeth give the richer harvest."

Launcelot, in the *Merchant of Venice*, ii, 5, puns upon this phrase when he says to Jessica —

There will come a Christian by
Will be worth a Jew.ess' eye.

Jewels have (or had) in the popular belief special significations in various ways. For instance, each month was supposed to be under the influence of some precious stone—

January	. Garnet	Constancy.
February	.. Amethyst	Sincerity.
March	. Bloodstone	Courage.
April	.. . Diamond	Innocence.
May	.. Emerald	Success in love.
June	.. Agate ..	Health and long life
July	Cornelian	.. Content
August	. Sardonyx	Conjugal fidelity.
September	.. Sapphire	.. Antidote to madness
October	Opal	. Hope
November	. Topaz ..	Fidelity
December	Turquoise	. Prosperity.

The signs of the zodiac were represented by—

Aries	. Ruby.	*Libra* .. . Jacinth.
Taurus	Topaz	*Scorpio* . Agate
Gemini	Carbuncle	*Sagittarius* Amethyst
Cancer	Emerald	*Capricornus* Beryl
Leo.	. Sapphire	*Aquarius* . Onyx
Virgo	Diamond.	*Pisces* Jasper.

And among heralds and astrologists jewels represented special tinctures or planets, as the topaz "or" (*gold*), and *Sol*, the sun, the pearl or crystal, "argent" (*silver*), and the moon, the ruby, "gules" (*red*), and the planet Mars, the sapphire, "azure" (*blue*), and Jupiter, the diamond, "sable" (*black*), and Saturn, the emerald, "vert" (*green*), and Venus, the amethyst "purpure" (*purple*), and Mercury.

These are my jewels! *See* TREASURES

Jezebel (jez' ē bel). **A painted Jezebel.** A flaunting woman of bold spirit but loose morals, so called from Jezebel, wife of Ahab, King of Israel (*see* 2 *Kings*, ix, 31).

Jezreelites (jez' rē litz) A small sect, with headquarters at Gillingham, Kent, believing that Christ redeemed only *souls*, and that the *body* is saved by belief in the Law It was founded in 1876 by James White (1840-85), who had been a private in the Army, and took the name James Jershom Jezreel. They are also called the "New and Later House of Israel" their object is to be numbered among the 144,000 (*see Rev* vii, 4) who at the Last Judgment will be endowed with immortal bodies.

Jib. A triangular sail borne in front of the foremast. It has the bowsprit for a base in small vessels, and the jib-boom in larger ones, and exerts an important effect, when the wind is abeam, in throwing the ship's head to leeward The **jib-boom** is an extension of the bowsprit by the addition of a spar projecting beyond it Sometimes the boom is further extended by another spar called the *flying jib-boom* The *jib-topsail* is a light sail flying from the extreme forward end of the flying jib-boom, and set about half-way between the mast and the boom.

The cut of his jib. A sailor's phrase, meaning the expression of a person's face Sailors recognize vessels at sea by the cut of the jibs, and in certain dialects the *jib* means the lower lip. Thus, *to hang the jib* is to look ill-tempered, or annoyed

To jib To start aside, to back out, a "jibbing horse" is one that is easily startled. It is probably from the sea-term, to *gybe*, *i e* to change tacks by bearing away before the wind.

Jiffy. In a jiffy. In a minute; in a brace of shakes; before you can say "Jack Robinson" The origin of the word is unknown, but it is met with as early as the late 18th century

Jig, from *gigue.* A short piece of music much in vogue in olden times, of a very lively character, either six-eight or twelve-eight time, and used for dance-tunes It consists of two parts, each of eight bars Also the dance itself
You jig, you amble, and you lisp —*Hamlet,* iii, 1.

The jig is up. Your trickery is discovered "Jig" was old slang for a joke or trick.

Jiggery. An American slang term for a dance-hall.

Jiggery-pokery Fraud, "wangling" of accounts, etc.

Jigot (jig' ot) A Scots term for a leg of mutton or lamb. It is the French *gigot*, and is one of the Scots words arising from the close connexion between the two countries in the 16th and 17th centuries.

Jill. A generic name for a lass, a sweetheart *See* JACK AND JILL *under* JACK

Jilleroo *See* JACKAROO

Jim Crow. A popular Negro song and dance of last century, introduced by T D. Rice, the original "nigger minstrel," at Washington in 1835, and brought to the Adelphi, London, in the following year A renegade or turncoat was called a "Jim Crow," from the burden of the song.—

Wheel about and turn about
And do jis so,
Ebry time I wheel about
I jump Jim Crow.

Jim Crow cars. Railway coaches set apart for the sole use of Negroes

Jim Crow regulations. Any rules which prohibit Negroes from associating with or enjoying the same privileges as white people

Jimmie's or the St James's (later the Piccadilly Hotel) was a famous, rowdy, fast-going restaurant in the last half of the 19th century, it figures in many society and London novels and memoirs In it was to be found any night of the week everything that was blasé, belladonna'ed and often beautiful in the lower strata of female Bohemianism Its proximity to Vine Street police station was not infrequently a matter of congratulation to the authorities.

Jimmy Woodser (Austr). A solitary drinker In Victoria a solitary drinker *goes Ballarat* Jimmy Warder is an habitual drunk who goes about cadging drinks where he can.

Jingo (jing' gō) A word from the unmeaning jargon of the 17th-century conjurers (*cp* HOCUS-POCUS), probably substituted for *God,* in the same way as *Gosh, Golly* etc , are In Motteux's translation of Rabelais (1694), where the original reads *par Dieu* (Bk iv, lvi), the English rendering is "By jingo", but there is a possibility that the word is Basque *Jinko* or *Jainko,* God, and was introduced by sailors.
Hey, Jingo! What the de'il's the matter?
Do mermaids swim in Dartford water?
SWIFT *Actæon or The Original Horn Fair.*
The modern meaning of the word, a blustering so-called "patriot" who is itching to go to war on the slightest provocation—a *Chauvinist* in France—is from a music-hall song by G W Hunt, which was popular in 1878 when the country was supposed to be on the verge of intervening in the Russo-Turkish War on behalf of the Turks —
We don't want to fight, but, by Jingo, if we do,
We've got the ships, we've got the men, and got the money too
The Russophobes became known as the *Jingoes,* and a noisy, war-mongering policy has been labelled *Jingoism* ever since

Jinks (jingks) **High jinks.** The present use of the phrase expresses the idea of pranks, fun, and jollity
The frolicsome company had begun to practise the ancient and now forgotten pastime of *High Jinks* The game was played in several different ways Most frequently the dice were thrown by the company, and those upon whom the lot fell were obliged to assume and maintain for a time a certain fictitious character, or to repeat a certain number of fescennine verses in a particular order If they departed from the character assigned . . . they incurred forfeits, which were compounded for by swallowing an additional bumper.—SCOTT *Guy Mannering,* xxxvi.

Jinn (jin) Demons of Arabian mythology, according to fable created from fire two thousand years before Adam was made of earth, and said to be governed by a race of kings named Suleyman, one of whom "built the pyramids" Their chief abode is the mountain Kâf, and they assume the forms of serpents, dogs, cats, monsters, or even human beings, and become invisible at pleasure The evil jin are hideously ugly, but the good are exquisitely beautiful The word is plural, its singular is *jinnee*

Jinx (jingks) A colloquial term in U.S A. for a person or thing supposed to bring ill luck

Jitney (jit' ni). An American term for an automobile plying for hire or hired to carry passengers The name comes from the slang word for a five-cent piece—a jitney—as this was the fare originally charged for each passenger

Jitters. An American phrase for nervousness, apprehensiveness, hence *jittery* is nervous, jumpy.

Jitterbug is one whose responses to the rhythm of swing music take the form of violent and unexpected dance movements, making him (or her) dance in an unpredictable, often acrobatic fashion

Jiujitsu, Jujitsu (joo jit′ soo) The Japanese art of self-defence It is based on leverage applied to the assailant's limbs which are forced into unnatural positions, called locks, to which there is no key, the victim must either give in or have the limb broken The neck, body and hip joints are all susceptible to such attack, the spine can be injured and the hips dislocated

Jive A canting name for the livelier and debased forms of jazz music, largely accomplished by uninspired improvisations of short phrases The adepts have developed a vocabulary of their own, known as *jive-talk*.

Joachim, St (jo′ á kim). The father of the Virgin Mary Generally represented as an old man carrying in a basket two turtledoves, in allusion to the offering made for the purification of his daughter His wife was St. Anne

Joan, Pope A supposed female "pope" between Leo IV and Benedict III in the 9th century She is said to have been born in England and educated at Cologne, passing under the name of Joannes Anglicus. Blondel, a Calvinist, wrote a book in 1640 to prove that no such person ever occupied the papal chair, but at least a hundred and fifty authors between the 13th and 17th centuries repeat the tale as an historic fact Dollinger critically examined the question in 1868, but the entire mythicality of the legend has long been recognized.

Job (jōb). The personification of poverty and patience, in allusion to the patriarch whose history is given in the Bible.

I am as poor as Job, my lord, but not so patient.—
2 *Henry IV*, i, 2.

In the Koran Job's wife is said to have been either Rahmeh, daughter of Ephraim, son of Joseph, or Makhir, daughter of Manasses, and the tradition is recorded that Job, at the command of God, struck the earth with his foot from the dunghill where he lay, and instantly there welled up a spring of water with which his wife washed his sores, and they were miraculously healed.

Job's comforter. One who means to sympathize with you in your grief, but says that you brought it on yourself; thus in reality adding weight to your sorrow.

Job's post. A bringer of bad news.

Job's pound. Bridewell; prison.

As poor as Job's turkey. An expression invented by "Sam Slick" (Thomas Chandler Haliburton) an early 19th-century American humorous writer, to denote someone even poorer than Job.

Jobation. A scolding, so called from the patriarch Job

Jobation . means a long, dreary homily, and has reference to the tedious rebukes inflicted on the patriarch Job by his too obliging friends —G. A SALA. (*Echoes*), Sept 6th, 1884.

Job (job) A piece of chance work, a public work or office not for the public benefit, but for the profit of the person employed; a misfortune, an untoward event, a "jab"; also, among printers, all kinds of work not included in the term "book-work" or newspapers.

A bad job. An unfortunate happening; a bad speculation.

A job lot. A lot of miscellaneous goods.

A ministerial job Sheridan says·—"Whenever any emolument, profit, salary, or honour is conferred on any person not deserving it—that is a job, if from private friendship, personal attachment, or any view except the interest of the public, anyone is appointed to any public office . that is a job."

No cheek is known to blush, or heart to throb,
Save when they lose a question or a job
         POPE *Essay on Criticism*, i, 104.

Jobber One who does small jobs; one who buys from merchants to sell to retailers, a middle-man. A "stock-jobber" is a member of the Stock Exchange who acts as an intermediary between buying and selling stockbrokers, only a jobber can actually buy and sell shares in the Stock Exchange itself The relationship between the *jobber* and the *broker* is much the same as that between the wholesaler and the retailer in trade

Jock. Popular nickname for a Scotsman.

Jockey. Properly, "a little Jack" (*q.v*). So in Scotch, "Ilka Jeanie has her Jockie"

All fellows, Jockey and the laird (man and master). (*Scots proverb*)

To jockey. To deceive in trade; to cheat, to indulge in sharp practice.

Jockey of Norfolk. Sir John Howard (*c.* 1430–85), the first Howard to be Duke of Norfolk, and a firm adherent of Richard III. On the night before the battle of Bosworth, where he was slain, he found in his tent the warning couplet

Jockey of Norfolk, be not too bold,
For Dickon thy master, is bought and sold.

Joe. The American equivalent of the British "Tommy," an enlisted soldier. The full phrase is G I Joe, the initials standing for "Government Issue," as stamped on all U S.A. military equipment.

Joe in Australian usage was formerly a term of the greatest insult. Charles Joseph Latrobe was governor of Victoria in 1851 and set the police to checking up every gold-miner to see that he had a licence Hence "Joe!" was a warning cry at the approach of the Law

Joe Miller. *See* MILLER

Joey. A groat; so called from Joseph Hume (1777–1855), M P for Kilkenny at the time, who, about 1835, strongly recommended the coinage of groats for the sake of paying short cab-fares, etc.

In Australia a young kangaroo is called a *joey*.

Jog. Jog away; jog off; jog on. Get away; be off, keep moving. Shakespeare uses the word *shog* in the same sense—as, "Will you shog off?" (*Henry V*, ii, 1); and again in the same play, "Shall we shog?" (ii, 3). Beaumont and Fletcher use the same expression in *The Coxcomb*—"Come, prithee, let us shog off." In the *Morte d'Arthur* we have another variety— "He shokkes in sharpely" (rushes in). The words are connected with *shock*, and *shake*

> Jog on a little faster, pri'thee,
> I'll take a nap and then be wi' thee
>   R LLOYD. *The Hare and the Tortoise.*

Give his memory a jog. Remind him of something.

Jog-trot. A slow but regular pace.

Joggis or **Jogges.** *See* JOUGS.

John. The English form of Lat. and Gr *Johannes*, from Heb. *Jochanan*, meaning "God is gracious." The feminine form, *Johanna*, or *Joanna*, is nearer the original. The French equivalent of "John" is *Jean* (formerly *Jehan*), the Italian *Giovanni*, Russian *Ivan*, Gaelic *Ian*, Irish, *Sean* or *Shaun*, German *Johann* or *Johannes*, which is contracted to *Jan, Jahn*, and *Hans*.

For many centuries John has been one of the most popular of masculine names in England —probably because it is that of St. John the Evangelist, St. John the Baptist and many other saints.

There have been twenty-three Popes of this name, nearly all of whom were bad, unfortunate, or mere nonentities, England has had one King John (also unfortunate) The most famous "Johns" of history are probably *John of Gaunt* (1340-99), the fourth son of Edward III, and *Don John of Austria* (1547-78), illegitimate son of the Emperor Charles V, celebrated as a military leader, for his naval victory over the Turks at Lepanto (1571), and as Governor of the Netherlands.

The principal SAINTS of the name are:—

St. John the Evangelist or the Divine. His day is December 27th, and he is usually represented bearing a chalice from which a serpent issues, in allusion to his driving the poison from a cup presented to him to drink Tradition says that he took the Virgin Mary to Ephesus after the Crucifixion, that in the persecution of Domitian (96) he was plunged into a cauldron of boiling oil, but was delivered unharmed, and was afterwards banished to the isle of Patmos (where he is said to have written the Book of Revelation), but shortly returned to Ephesus, where he died

St. John the Baptist. Patron saint of missionaries, because he was sent "to prepare the way of the Lord." His day is June 24th, and he is represented in a coat of sheepskin (in allusion to his life in the desert), either holding a rude wooden cross, with a pennon bearing the words, *Ecce Agnus Dei*, or with a book on which a lamb is seated; or holding in his right hand a lamb surrounded by a halo, and bearing a cross on the right foot.

St. John of Beverley. Bishop of Hexham, and later of York (d. 721), his name formed the war-cry of the English in the border warfare of the Middle Ages It was he who ordained the Venerable Bede. He was canonized in 1037. He is commemorated on May 7th

St. John Chrysostom, who was bishop of Constantinople from 398 till he was deposed by the Arians in 403. Four years later he was slain by his enemies in Pontus His day is January 27th

St. John of the Cross Founder of the Discalced Carmelites (1568) A friend and co-worker with St. Teresa in the reform of the Carmelites, he is now better known for his mystical writings *The Dark Night of the Soul, Spiritual Canticles*, etc. St. John of the Cross was one of the greatest mystics the Christian Church has known. He died in 1591 and was canonized in 1726, his feast day being November 24th

St. John Damascene. One of the Fathers of the Church He was born at Damascus, opposed the Iconoclasts (*q v*), and died about 770. He is commemorated on March 27th

St. John of Nepomuk. Patron Saint of Bohemia, a priest who was drowned in 1393 by order of the brutal Wenceslaus IV, partly because he tried to restrain the licentiousness of the king, partly because he refused to reveal to him the confessions of the queen *Nepomuk*, or *Nepomuk* is the French *ne*, born, and Pomuk, the village of his birth His day is May 16th.

John-a-Dreams. A stupid, dreamy fellow, always in a brown study and half asleep

> Yet I,
> A dull and muddy-mettled rascal, peak,
> Like John-a-dreams, unpregnant of my cause,
> And can say nothing.   *Hamlet*, ii, 2.

John-a-Droynes. An Elizabethan term for a country bumpkin There is a foolish character in Whetstone's *Promos and Cassandra* (1578), who, being seized by informers, stands dazed, and suffers himself to be quietly cheated out of his money. In *Superbiæ Flagellum*, by John Taylor, the Water Poet (1621), we read of "Jack and Jill, and John a Drones his issue," the meaning evidently being "the rag, tag, and bobtail."

John Anderson, my Jo. Burns's well-known poem is founded on an 18th-century song which, in its turn, was a parody of a mid-16th century anti-Roman Catholic song in ridicule of the Sacraments of the Church The whole is given in the *Percy Folio MS* The first verse is:—

> John Anderson, my Jo, cum in as ye gae by,
> And ye sall get a sheip's heid weel baken in a pye,
> Weel baken in a pye, and the haggis in a pat.
> John Anderson, my Jo, cum in, and ye's get that.

Jo is an old Scottish word for a sweetheart.

John-a-Nokes and **John-a-Stiles.** Names formerly given, instead of the very impersonal "A and B," to fictitious persons in an imaginary action at law: hence either name may stand for "just anybody." *Cp* DOE.

> Poets gyve names to men they write of, which argueth a conceite of an actuall truth, and so, not being true, prooves a falshood. And doth the Lawyer lye then, when under the names of *John a stile* and *John a noakes*, hee puts his case?—SIR PHILIP SIDNEY: *An Apologie for Poetrie* (1595)

John Audley. *See* AUDLEY

John Brown (1800-59). An American abolitionist who led a body of men to free Negro slaves at Harper's Ferry, Virginia, October 16th, 1859 The famous Union song of the Civil War, "John Brown's Body," made him a legend

John Bull. The national nickname for an Englishman, represented as a bluff, kind-hearted, bull-headed farmer The character is from Dr. John Arbuthnot's satire *The History of John Bull*, which was originally published in 1712 as *Law in a Bottomless Pit* "John Bull" is the Englishman, the Frenchman is termed *Lewis Baboon*, the Dutchman *Nicholas Frog*, etc

John Chinaman. A Chinaman or the Chinese as a people

John Company. The old Honourable East India Company It is said that "John" is a perversion of "Hon", no doubt *Hon*, like *Hans*, may be equal to *John*, but probably "John Company" is allied to the familiar "John Bull"
By 1765 the Company had become the official administrators of Bengal Pitt's India Act of 1784 instituted a dual control between the Company and Parliament, but after the Indian Mutiny of 1857 the government of India was transferred to the Crown, and the East India Company was abolished in 1858.

John Doe. *See* DOE

John dory (dōr′i) A golden yellow fish, the *Zeus faber*, common in the Mediterranean and round the south-western coasts of England. Its name was *dory* (Fr. *dorée*, golden) long before the *John* was added, this was probably a humorous amplification—from the name of some real or imaginary person—with, perhaps, a side allusion to Fr, *jaune*, yellow.
There is a tradition that it was from this fish (*but see* HADDOCK) that St Peter took the stater or shekel Hence it is called in French *le poisson de St Pierre*, and in Gascon, the *golden* or *sacred cock*, meaning St Peter's cock. Like the haddock, it has an oval black spot on each side, said to be the finger-marks of St. Peter, when he held the fish to extract the coin.

John Drum's Entertainment. *See* DRUM

John in the Wad. Another name for the will-o'-the-wisp *See* IGNIS FATUUS.

To wait for John Long, the carrier. To wait a long time, to wait for John, who keeps us a long time.

John o' Groat's The story is that John o' Groat (or Jan Groot) came with his two brothers from Holland in the reign of James IV of Scotland, and purchased lands on the extreme north-eastern coast of Scotland In time the o' Groats increased, and there came to be eight families of the name They met regularly once a year in the house built by the founder, but on one occasion a question of precedency arose, and John o' Groat promised them the next time they came he would contrive to satisfy them all Accordingly he built an eight-sided room, with a door to each side, and placed an octagonal table therein. This building went ever after with the name of

John o' Groat's House, its site is the Berubium of Ptolemy, in the vicinity of Duncansby Head.

From John o' Groat's to the Land's End. From Dan to Beersheba, from one end of Great Britain to the other

John Roberts. Obsolete slang for a very large tankard, supposed to hold enough drink for any ordinary drinker to last through Saturday and Sunday This measure was introduced into Wales in 1886 to compensate topers for the Sunday closing, and derived its name from John Roberts, M P., author of the Sunday Closing Act

John Tamson's man. A henpecked husband; one ordered here, there, and everywhere Tamson—*i.e.* spiritless, a *Tame-son*

John with the Leaden Sword. John of Lancaster, Duke of Bedford (1389-1435), third son of Henry IV, who acted as regent in France from 1422 to 1429, was so called by Earl Douglas.

Johnny. A superfine, dandified youth, was known as a *Johnny* in the latter part of last century, but from earlier times it has been applied indiscriminately to the British bourgeois Byron, February 23rd, 1824, writes to Murray his publisher respecting an earthquake —
> If you had but seen the *English Johnnies*, who had never been out of a cockney workshop before . . . [running away . . .].

Johnny-cake. An American name for a cake made of maize-meal, formerly much esteemed as a delicacy. It is said to be a corruption of *journey*-cake

Johnny Raw. A nervous novice, a newly enlisted soldier; an adult apprentice in the ship trade

Johnny Reb. In the American Civil War a Federal name for a Confederate soldier—from the Northern point of view, a rebel.

Joint, in U S A slang originally meant a sordid place where illicit spirits could be bought and drunk, opium smoked, etc. From that it has come to be applied, disparagingly, to any place of common resort, restaurant, etc.

To case a joint. To inspect a place with a view to committing robbery there.

Jolly. A sailor's nickname for a marine, a militiaman being a *tame jolly*
> To stand and be still to the Birken'ead drill is a damn
>   tough bullet to chew,
> An' they done it, the Jollies,—'Er Majesty's Jollies—
>   soldier an' sailor too!
>   KIPLING: *Soldier an' Sailor Too*.

The noun is also slang for a man who bids at auction with no intention of buying, but merely to force up the price
As an adjective and adverb, *jolly* frequently has an intensive, approving, or ironical effect:—
> All was jolly quiet at Ephesus before St Paul came thither—JOHN TRAPP *Commentary* (1656).
> 'Tis likely you'll prove a jolly surly groom.
>   *Taming of the Shrew*, iii, 2.

Jolly-boat. A small boat usually hoisted at the stern of a ship. *Jolly* here is probably connected with the Danish *jolle*, Dut. *jol*, and our *yawl*.

A jolly dog. A *bon vivant*, a jovial fellow

The jolly god Bacchus The Bible speaks of wine which "maketh glad the heart of man."

A jolly good fellow. A very social and popular person When toasts are drunk "with musical honours" the chorus usually is—

> For he's a jolly good fellow [three times]
> And so say all of us,
> With a hip, hip, hip, hooray!

The Jolly Roger. *See* ROGER

Jonathan. Collective term for the people of the U S A, equivalent to the British John Bull.

Brother Jonathan. *See* BROTHER.

Jonathan's. A noted coffee-house in Change Alley, described in the *Tatler* as the general mart of stock-jobbers.

> Yesterday the brokers and others   came to a resolution that [the new building] instead of being called "New Jonathan's," should be called "The Stock Exchange." . . . The brokers then collected sixpence each, and christened the house with punch — Newspaper par (July 15, 1773)

Jonathan's arrows. They were shot to give warning, and not to hurt (1 *Sam* xx, 36.)

Jones, Davy, *See* DAVY

Jongleur (zhong′ gler) A mediæval minstrel who recited verses, while accompanying himself on a musical instrument. Jongleurs formed a branch of the Troubadours—a force which permeated culture throughout Europe Petrarch compared the function of the Jongleur in the spread of literature and education to that of the book-publisher.

Jordan (jôr′ dan) A name anciently given to a pot used by alchemists and doctors, then transferred to a chamber-pot The word is thought to have been originally *Jordan-bottle*, *i e.* a bottle in which pilgrims and crusaders brought back water from the River Jordan.

> Why, they will allow us ne'er a jordan, and then we leak in the chimney, and your chamber-lie breeds fleas like a loach —1 *Henry IV*, ii, 1.

Jordan almond. Here *Jordan* has nothing to do with the river (*cp.* JERUSALEM ARTICHOKE), but is a corruption of Fr *jardin*, garden. The Jordan almond is a fine variety which comes chiefly from Malaga.

Jordan passed. Death over. The Jordan separated the wilderness [of the world] from the Promised Land, and thus came to be regarded almost as the Christian "Styx" (*q.v*)

Jorum. A large drinking-bowl, intended specially for punch The name is thought to be connected with King *Joram* (*cp.* JEROBOAM), who " brought with him vessels of silver, and vessels of gold, and vessels of brass" (2 *Sam* viii, 10).

Josaphat. An Indian prince converted by the hermit Barlaam. *See* BARLAAM AND JOSAPHAT.

Joseph. One not to be seduced from his continency by the severest temptation is sometimes so called. The reference is to Joseph in Potiphar's house (*Gen* xxxix) *Cp* BELLEROPHON.

A great-coat used to be known by the same name, in allusion to Joseph, who left his garment, or upper coat, behind him.

Joseph, St. Husband of the Virgin Mary, and the reputed father of Jesus He is patron saint of carpenters, because he was of that craft.

In art Joseph is represented as an aged man with a budding staff in his hand His day is March 19th.

Joseph of Arimathea. The rich Jew, probably a member of the Sanhedrin, who believed in Christ but feared to confess it, and, after the Crucifixion, begged the body of the Saviour and deposited it in his own tomb (*see Matt* xxvii, 57-60, *Mark* xv, 42). Legend relates that he was imprisoned for 42 years, during which time he was kept alive miraculously by the Holy Grail (*see* GRAIL), and that on his release by Vespasian, about 63 A D , he brought the Grail and the spear with which Longinus wounded the crucified Saviour, to Britain, and there founded the abbey of Glastonbury (*q v*), whence he commenced the conversion of Britain

The origin of these legends is to be found in a group of apocryphal writings of which the *Evangelium Nicodemi* is the chief, these were worked upon at Glastonbury between the 8th and 11th centuries, were further embellished by Robert de Borron in the 13th, the latter version (by way of Walter Map) being woven by Malory into his *Morte d'Arthur*

Josh. An American slang term meaning to chaff, to banter or tease

Joshua tree. The *Yucca brevifolia*, a spiky-leaved tree growing in the desert areas of the south-western regions of the U S A. and in Mexico

Joss. An idol or house-god of the Chinese; every family has its joss A temple is called a *joss-house*, and a *joss-stick* is a stick of scented wood which is burnt as incense in a joss-house

Jot. A very little, the least quantity possible The iota [ι] (see I) is the smallest letter of the Greek alphabet, called the Lacedemonian letter.

> Heven and erthe shal soner passe away then one iote of goddis worde shal passe unfulfilled —GEO. JOY *An Apology to W. Tindale* (1535)
> This bond doth give thee here no jot of blood *Merchant of Venice*, iv, 1.

Jot or tittle. A tiny amount. The jot is i or iota, and the tittle, from Lat *titulus*, is the mark, or dot over the i.

Jotunheim (jö′ tùn hîm) Giant land. The home or region of the Scandinavian giants or *Jotunn*

Jougs (joogz). The Scottish pillory, or, more properly, an iron ring or collar fastened by a short chain to a wall, and used as a pillory. Jamieson says, "They punish delinquents, making them stand in 'jogges,' as they call their pillories "

Jourdain, Monsieur. The type of the bourgeois placed by wealth in the ranks of gentlemen, who makes himself ridiculous by his endeavours to acquire their accomplishments He is chiefly remembered from the delight he felt when he discovered that whereas some men wrote poetry, he had been speaking prose all his life without knowing it The character is from Molière's comedy *Le Bourgeois Gentilhomme* (1670).

Journal (O Fr , from Lat *diurnalis*, diurnal, *dies*, a day)
Applied to newspapers, the word strictly means a daily paper; but the extension of the term to weekly and other periodicals is sanctioned by custom

Journey-weight. The weight of certain parcels of gold and silver in the mint A *journey of gold* is fifteen pounds troy, which was coined into 701 sovereigns, or double that number of half-sovereigns, A *journey of silver* is sixty pounds troy, which, before the alteration in the silver coinage (1920), was coined into 3,960 shillings. So called because this weight of coin was at one time esteemed a day's mintage (Fr *journée*

Jove (jōv) Another name of Jupiter (*q v*), the later being *Jovis pater*, father Jove The Titans made war against Jove, and tried to dethrone him
Milton, in *Paradise Lost*, makes Jove one of the fallen angels (i, 512)

Jovial (jō' vi al) Merry and sociable, like those born under the planet Jupiter, which astrologers considered the happiest of the natal stars
Our jovial star reigned at his birth
        Cymbeline, v, 4.

Joy. The seven joys of the Virgin. *See* MARY.

Joy-ride. A ride in a motor-car, especially when it is driven fast and somewhat recklessly and more particularly still when it is done without the owner's knowledge or permission

Joy stick The control column of an aeroplane or glider, which is linked to the elevators and ailerons to control them.

Joyeuse (zhwa' yerz). A name given to more than one sword famous in romance, but especially to Charlemagne's, which bore the inscription *Decem præceptorum custos Carolus*, and was buried with him

Joyeuse Garde or **Garde-Joyeuse.** The estate given by King Arthur to Sir Launcelot of the Lake for defending the Queen's honour against Sir Mador It is supposed to have been at Berwick-on-Tweed, but the Arthurian topography is all very indefinite

Juan Fernandez. *See* ROBINSON CRUSOE

Jubilate (joo bi la' ti). Latin for "Cry aloud," is the name given to two Psalms which begin with this word in the Vulgate version In the English psalter they are Psalms lxvi and c; in the Vulgate lxv and xcix respectively

Jubilate Sunday is the third Sunday after Easter, when the introit begins with two verses of the former of the above psalms

Jubilee. In Jewish history the year of *jubilee* was every fiftieth year, which was held sacred in commemoration of the deliverance from Egypt In this year the fields were allowed to lie fallow, land that had passed out of the possession of those to whom it originally belonged was restored to them, and all who had been obliged to let themselves out for hire were released from bondage. The year of jubilee was proclaimed with trumpets of ram's horn, and takes its name from *jobil*, a ram's

horn (*See Lev* xxv, 11-34, 39-54; and xxvii, 16-24)
Hence any fiftieth anniversary, especially one kept with great rejoicings, is called a *Jubilee*, and the name has been applied to other outbursts of joy or seasons of festivity, such as the *Shakespeare Jubilee*, which was held at Stratford-on-Avon in September, 1769, and the *Protestant Jubilee*, celebrated in Germany in 1617 at the centenary of the Reformation
King George III held a *Jubilee* on October 25th, 1809, that being the day before he *commenced* the fiftieth year of his reign, and Queen Victoria celebrated hers on June 21st, 1887, two days after she had *completed* her fiftieth year on the throne Ten years later Queen Victoria kept her *Diamond Jubilee* as a thanksgiving for sixty years of queenhood, and a reign the length of which exceeded that of any of her predecessors The only other English monarchs to have *Jubilees* were Henry III (who reigned for 56 years and 6 weeks), and Edward III (51 years and nearly 5 months). On May 6th, 1935, George V celebrated the *Silver Jubilee* (twenty-five years) of his accession to the throne
In the Catholic Church Pope Boniface VIII instituted a *Jubilee* or Holy Year in 1300 for the purpose of granting indulgences, and ordered it to be observed every hundred years. Clement VI reduced the interval to fifty years. Urban IV to thirty, Sixtus IV to the present interval of twenty-five There was a Jubilee in 1950 It is only on the occasion of a Jubilee that the Porta Santa (Holy Door) in St. Peter's, Rome, is opened

Jubilee Juggins. A nickname given to Ernest Benzon, a foolish and wealthy young man about Town who squandered a fortune on horse-racing about the time of Queen Victoria's Jubilee (1887).

Judas. Judas Iscariot, who betrayed his Master.

Judas kiss. A deceitful act of courtesy or simulated affection. Judas betrayed his Master with a kiss (*Matt* xxvi, 49)
 So Judas kissed his Master,
And cried, "All hail!" whenas he meant *all harm*
        3 Henry VI, v, 7

Judas slits or **holes.** The peep-holes in a prison door, through which the guard looks into the cell to see if all is right; when not in use, the holes are covered up.

Judas tree. A leguminous tree of southern Europe (*Cercis siliquastrum*) which flowers before the leaves appear, so called because of a Greek tradition that it was upon one of these trees that Judas Iscariot hanged himself But *see* ELDER-TREE, which is also sometimes called by the same name. *See also* MARSIGLIO

Judas-coloured hair. Fiery red. In the Middle Ages Judas Iscariot was represented with red hair and beard, as also was Cain.
 His very hair is of the dissembling colour, something browner than Judas's —*As You Like It*, iii, 4.

Jude, St. Represented in art with a club or staff, and a carpenter's square, in allusion to his trade. His day is celebrated with that of St. Simon on October 28th

Judge. Judge's black cap *See* BLACK CAP

Judges' robes. In the criminal courts, where the judges represent the sovereign, they appear in full court dress, and wear a scarlet robe, but in nisi prius courts the judge sits merely to balance the law between civilians, and therefore appears in his judicial undress, or violet gown.

Judge Lynch. In the U S A , a lynching, or the personification of lynch law

Judica Sunday (joo' di ka) The fifth Sunday after Lent (also known as Passion Sunday) is so called from the first word of the Introit, *Judica me, Deus*, Judge me, O Lord. (*Ps.* xliii).

Judicial Committee. A committee of the Privy Council and the final court of appeal in the British Empire, except in Great Britain itself. Constituted by an Act of 1833, it hears appeals from the courts of law throughout the Empire, the members being the Lord Chancellor and persons who hold or have held high judicial office in Great Britain or the Overseas Dominions. They do not deliver a judgment but state that they will advise His Majesty to allow or disallow an appeal.

Judicium Crucis (jū dis' i um kroo' sis). A form of ordeal which consisted in stretching out the arms before a cross, till one party could hold out no longer, and lost his cause It is said that a bishop of Paris and abbot of St. Denis appealed to this judgment in a dispute they had about the patronage of a monastery, each of the disputants selected a man to represent him, and the man selected by the bishop gave in, so that the award was given in favour of the abbot.

Jug or Stone Jug A prison It is curious that Gr. *keramos*, potter's earth and anything made with it, as a jug, also meant a prison or dungeon. *See* JOUGS

Jug-band A jazz band in the Deep South, in which one of the players blew a trombone or cornet into a large whiskey jug, so producing a deep resonant beat.

Jugged hare. Hare stewed in a jug or jar

To be jugged. To be put in prison.

Juggernaut or Jagganath. A Hindu god, "Lord of the World," having his temple at Puri, in Orissa. The legend, as told in the *Ayeen-Akbery*, is that a learned Brahman was sent to look out a site for a temple The Brahman wandered about for many days, and then saw a crow dive into the water; he then washed and made obeisance to the element This was selected as the site of the temple While the temple was a-building the king, Indica Dhumna, had a prophetic dream, telling him that the true form of Vishnu should be revealed to him in the morning. When the king went to see the temple he beheld a log of wood in the water, and this log he accepted as the realization of his dream, enshrining it in the temple

Jagganath is regarded as the remover of sin. His image is on view three days in the year: the first day is the Bathing Festival, when the god is washed, he is then supposed to have a cold for ten days, at the end of which he is again brought out and taken in his car to the nearest temple, a week later the car is pulled back amid the rejoicings of the multitude at his recovery. It was on the final day that fanatical devotees used to throw themselves to be crushed beneath the wheels of the enormous, decorated machine, in the idea that they would thus obtain immediate admission to Paradise Hence the phrase *the car of Juggernaut* is used of customs, institutions, etc , beneath which people are ruthlessly and unnecessarily crushed

Juggins. *See* JUBILEE JUGGINS

Juggler (Lat *joculator*, a player) In the Middle Ages, jugglers accompanied the minstrels and troubadours, and added to their musical talents sleight of hand, antics, and feats of prowess to amuse the company assembled In time the music was dropped, and tricks became the staple of wandering performers.

Juke Box. An American term for a gramophone or automatic musical box that plays a selection of pieces when a coin is inserted.

Julep. A long drink flavoured with mint, a great favourite in the Southern States of the U.S.A.

Julian. Pertaining to Julius Cæsar (100–44 B C), particularly with reference to the Calendar (*i e.* the "Old Style") instituted by him in 46 B C. (the *Julian Year* consisting of 365¼ days), which was in general use in Western Europe until it was corrected by Gregory XIII in 1582, in England until 1752, and until 1918 in use in Russia. To allow for the odd quarter day Cæsar ordained that every fourth year should contain 366 days, the additional day being introduced after the 6th of the calends of March, *i e* February 24th Cæsar also divided the months into the number of days they at present contain, and July (*q v.*) is named in his honour

Julian, St. Patron saint of travellers and of hospitality, looked upon in the Middle Ages as the epicure of saints Thus, after telling us that the Frankleyn was "Epicurus owne sone," Chaucer says :—

> An householdere, and that a greet was he,
> Seint Julian he was in his contree
> *Canterbury Tales Prologue*, 339

In art he is represented as accompanied by a stag in allusion to his early career as a hunter, and either receiving the poor and afflicted, or ferrying travellers across a river.

Julium Sidus (joo' li um si' dus) The comet which appeared at the death of Julius Cæsar, and which in court flattery was called the apotheosis of the murdered man.

Jullien's Concerts were features of the London season from 1840 until the middle 50s. Louis Antoine Jullien (1812-60) came to London from Paris in 1840 and began a series of summer concerts at Drury Lane, and two years later winter concerts at which the best artists were engaged to perform and sing classical music. He invented the promenade concert, and though much derided for his eccentric methods of conducting and his often garish ways of advertising, he undoubtedly raised the level of musical appreciation in London.

July. The seventh month, named by Mark Antony, in honour of Julius Cæsar, who was born in it. It was previously called *Quintilis*, as it was the fifth month of the Roman year, its Anglo-Saxon name was *litha se æfterra* (lithe, mild)

The old Dutch name for it was *Hooy-maand* (hay-month), the old Saxon, *Mædd-monath* (because the cattle were turned into the meadows to feed), and *Lida æftevr* (the second mild or genial month) In the French Republican calendar it was called *Messidor* (harvest-month, June 19th to July 18th)

Until the late 18th century, *July* was accented on the first syllable; why the change took place no one seems to know.

> Her lips were red, and one was thin,
> Compar'd to that was next her chin
> (Some bee had stung it newly)
> But, Dick, her eyes so guard her face,
> I durst no more upon them gaze
> Than on the sun in July
>   SUCKLING *Ballad Upon a Wedding* (1646)

And even as late as 1798 Wordsworth wrote.—

> In March, December, and in July,
> 'Tis all the same with Harry Gill,
> The neighbours tell, and tell you truly,
> His teeth they chatter, chatter still.
>   *Goody Blake and Harry Gill.*

Jumbo. The name of an exceptionally large African elephant which, after giving rides to many thousands of children in the London Zoo, was sold, in 1882, to Barnum's Greatest Show on Earth He weighed 6½ tons He was accidentally killed by a railway engine in 1885, but his name is still synonymous with the idea of an elephant in children's minds

Jump To fit or unite with like a graft; as, *our inventions meet and jump in one.* Hence exactly, precisely

> Good advice is easily followed when it jumps with our own . . inclinations —LOCKHART. *Sir Walter Scott*, ch x

In jazz when the music is of an exciting and lively tempo it is said *to jump*

To jump a claim. An expression from the miners' camps, meaning to seize somebody else's "claim," *i e* his diggings, in his absence and work it oneself; or, to take his mine by force, hence, to annex property by stealing a march on the owner.

To jump at an offer To accept eagerly.

To jump over the broomstick. To marry in an informal way A "brom" is the bit of a bridle; to "jump the brom" is to skip over the marriage restraint, and "broomstick" is a mere corruption

To jump the gun. To start ahead of time, as a nervous competitor in a race, who starts before the gun is fired

Jumping-off place. The edge of the earth, from which one leaped into nothingness. Applied by American pioneers to any remote, desolate spot.

Counter-jumper. *See* COUNTER.

Jumper. Originally a coarse canvas or hard-material sort of shirt reaching to the hips, and worn by sailors and other heavy labourers. The use of the word for the woollen garment worn by women is of fairly recent growth. It is from the obsolete *jump*, a short coat worn by men two hundred years ago, connected with Fr *jupe*, and *jupon*, a petticoat.

17*

June. The sixth month, named from the Roman *Junius* gens Ovid says, *Junius a juvenum nomine dictus* (*Fasti*, v, 78.)

The old Dutch name was *Zomer-maand* (summer-month), the old Saxon, *Sere-monath* (dry-month), and *Lida-ærra* (joy time) In the French Republican calendar the month was called *Prairial* (meadow-month, May 20th to June 18th).

June marriages lucky. "Good to the man and happy to the maid " This is an old Roman superstition. The festival of Juno moneta was held on the calends of June, and Juno was the great guardian of women from birth to death

Junius (jōō′ ni ŭs). *The Letters of Junius* are a series of anonymous letters, the authorship of which has never been finally settled, which appeared in the London *Public Advertiser* from November 21st, 1768, to January 21st, 1772, and were directed against Sir William Draper, the Duke of Grafton, and the Ministers generally The author himself said, "I am the sole depositary of my secret, and it shall die with me", they were probably by Sir Philip Francis (1740-1818). Mr. Pitt told Lord Aberdeen that he knew who wrote them, and that it was not Francis, and Edmund Burke, his brother William, Earl Temple, Charles Lloyd, and John Roberts (clerks at the Treasury), John Wilkes, Dr Butler, Bishop of Hereford, Lord George Sackville, and even Gibbon are among those to whom they have been credited The following extract from Letter LXVII, addressed to the Duke of Grafton, may be taken as a specimen of the literary and vitriolic excellence of the *Letters of Junius*:

> The unhappy baronet [Sir Jas. Lowther] has no friends even among those who resemble him You, my Lord, are not yet reduced to so deplorable a state of dereliction. Every villain in the kingdom is your friend and, in compliment to such amity, I think you should suffer your dismal countenance to clear up Besides, my Lord, I am a little anxious for the consistency of your character, You violate your own rules of decorum, when you do not insult the man whom you have betrayed

Junk. Salt meat supplied to vessels for long voyages (*cp* HARNESS CASK), so called because it is hard and tough as old rope-ends, which may have got the name *junk* from the rush-like shore plant, *Juncus maritimus.* Junk is often called "salt horse " The word is more usually applied to cast-off broken things, valueless odds and ends of lumber

Junk shop. A shop where such stuff is sold

Junker (yŭng′ ker) A landowner of East Prussia The junker families provided the greatest proportion of regular army officers, and hence the name has become identified with the worst elements of German militarism

> He gives himself the airs of a demi-god walking the pavement—civilians and their wives swept into the gutter; they have no right to stand in the way of the great Prussian Junker . The Prussian Junker is the road hog of Europe Small nationalities in his way hurled to the roadside, bleeding and broken; women and children crushed under the wheels of his cruel car, Britain ordered out of his road —D LLOYD GEORGE

Junket (jŭng′ ket). Curdled cream with spice, etc ; any dainty. So called because it was originally made in a rush basket (Ital. *giuncata*, from Lat. *juncus*, a rush)

> You know there wants no junkets at the feast
> *Taming of the Shrew*, ii, 2.

Junketing. Feasting, merrymaking

> But great is song
> Used to great ends .   for song
> Is duer unto freedom, force and growth
> Of spirit than to junketing and love
> TENNYSON *Princess*, Pt. iv

Juno (joo′ nō) In Roman mythology the "venerable ox-eyed" wife of Jupiter, and queen of heaven She is identified with the Greek Hera, was the special protectress of marriage and of woman, and was represented as a war goddess

Junonian Bird. The peacock, dedicated to the goddess-queen

Junta (jŭn′ tà). In Spain a council or legislative assembly other than the Cortes (*q v*), which may be summoned either for the whole country, for one of its separate parts, or for some special object only. The most famous was that called together by Napoleon in 1808

> I had also audience of the King, to whom I deliver'd two Memorials since, in His Majesty's name of *Great Britain*, that a particular Junta of some of the Council of State and War might be appointed to determine the business—*Howell's Letters*, Bk. i, sect. iii, 10 (*Madrid*, Jan 5th, 1622).

Junto. In English history, the name given to a faction that included Wharton, Russell, Lord-Keeper Somers, Charles Montague, and several other men of mark, who ruled the Whigs in the reign of William III and exercised a very great influence over the nation The word is a corruption of *junta* (*q v*)

Jupiter (joo′ pi ter). The supreme deity of Roman mythology, corresponding to the Greek Zeus (*see* JOVE), son of Cronos, or Saturn (whom he dethroned) and Rhea He was the special protector of Rome, and as Jupiter Capitolinus—his temple being on the Capitoline Hill—presided over the Roman games He determined the course of all human affairs and made known the future to man through signs in the heavens, the flight of birds (*see* AUGURY), etc

As Jupiter was lord of heaven and prince of light, *white* was the colour sacred to him; hence among the mediæval alchemists *Jupiter* designated tin In heraldry Jupiter stands for *azure*, the blue of the heavens.

His statue by Phidias (taken to Constantinople by Theodosius I and there destroyed by fire in A D. 475) was one of the Seven Wonders of the World.

Jupiter Scapin. A nickname of Napoleon Bonaparte, given him by the Abbe de Pradt Scapin is a valet famous for his knavish tricks, in Molière's comedy of *Les Fourberies de Scapin*

Jupiter tonans (the thundering Jupiter) A complimentary nickname given to the London *Times* about the middle of the 19th century

Jupiter's beard. House leek Supposed to be a charm against evil spirits and lightning Hence grown at one time very generally on the thatch of houses.

Jurassic Rocks (joo răs′ ik) The group of limestone rocks embracing the strata between the top of the Rhætic Beds and the base of the Purbeckian Rocks, thus including the Lias and Oolites So named from the Swiss *Jura*, where they are typically developed

Jury mast. A temporary mast, a spar used for the nonce when the mast has been carried away The origin of the term is unknown, it has been in use for certainly over three hundred years

"Jury" has been humorously tacked on to other nouns, giving to the word a makeshift or temporary significance. *e g Jury-leg*, a wooden leg

Jus Latin for law

  Jus civile (Lat) Civil law

  Jus divinum (Lat) Divine law

  Jus gentium (Lat) International law

  Jus mariti (Lat) The right of the husband to the wife's property

Just, The. Among rulers and others who have been given this surname are —

Aristides, the Athenian (d 468 B C.).

Baharam, styled *Shah Endeb*, fifth of the Sassanidæ (276-96).

Casimir II, King of Poland (1117, 1177-94).

Ferdinand I, King of Aragon (1373, 1412-16).

Haroun al-Raschid The most renowned of the Abbasside califs, and the hero of several of the *Arabian Nights* stories (765, 786-808).

James II, King of Aragon (1261-1327)

Khosru or Chosroes I of Persia (531-79), called by the Arabs *Malk al Adel* (the Just King)

Pedro I of Portugal (1320, 1357-67).

Juste milieu (zhust mē lye) (Fr). The golden mean

> The Church of England is the *juste milieu*.
> LADY BLOOMFIELD *Reminiscences*, II, p. 18 (1883)

Justice *See* JEDWOOD JUSTICE

  Justices in Eyre *See* EYRE

Poetic justice. That ideal justice which poets exercise in making the good happy, and the bad unsuccessful in their evil schemes

Juvenal (joo′ ve năl) (Lat , from *juvenis*). A youth; common in Shakespeare, thus —

> The juvenal, the prince your master, whose chin is not yet fledged —*2 Henry IV*, i, 2

Juveniles. In theatrical parlance, those actors who play young men's parts; in the journalistic and book-trade, periodicals or books intended for the young.

K

K. The eleventh letter of the alphabet, representing the Greek *kappa*, and Hebrew *kaph*. The Egyptian hieroglyphic for *k* was a bowl. The Romans, after the C was given the K sound, gave up the use of the letter, except in abbreviated forms of a few words from Greek, thus, false accusers were branded on the forehead with a K (*kalumnia*), and the Carians,

Cretans, and Cilicians were known as *the three bad K's*

K is the recognized abbreviation of *Knight* in a large number of British Orders (but the abbreviation of "Knight" *per se* is *Kt.*).

In order of precedence these are:

K G	Knight of the Garter.		
K T., *K P.*	Knight of the Thistle, Knight of St Patrick.		
K C B	Knight Commander of the Bath		
K C S I	„	„	„ Star of India
K C M G	„	„	„ St. Michael & St. George
K C.I E	„	,	„ Indian Empire
K C V O	„	„	„ Victorian Order
K B E.	„	„	„ British Empire
Kt	Knight Bachelor		

K. K. K. The initials branded by the Ku Klux Klan (*q.v*) on their victims

K. of K. A familiar way of referring to Earl Kitchener of Khartoum (1850-1916).

Ka me, ka thee. You scratch my back and I'll scratch yours, one good turn deserves another; do me a service, and I will give you a helping hand when you require one It is an old proverb, and appears in Heywood's collection (1546)

Kaaba (ka' ba) (Arabic, *kabah*, a square house) A shrine of Mecca, said to have been built by Ishmael and Abraham on the spot where Adam first worshipped after his expulsion from Paradise. The building which stands in the centre of the court is about 50 ft. high, its peculiar sanctity is due to the Black Stone, which is built into the N E. corner This stone, about 6 in. in diameter is kissed by every pilgrim The present Kaaba was built in 1626; it is covered with a cloth of black brocade that is replaced with considerable ceremony every year

Kaf, Mount. The huge mountain in the middle of which, according to Mohammedan myth, the earth is sunk, as a night light is placed in a cup. Its foundation is the emerald *Sakhrat*, the reflection of which gives the azure hue to the sky.

Kaffir (kăf' ir) (Arabic, *Kafir*, an infidel). A name formerly given to Hottentots who rejected the Moslem faith, also to the natives of *Kafiristan* ("the country of the infidels"), in northern Afghanistan; but now restricted to the Bantu races of South Africa, especially the Xosa tribe.

Kaffirs, Kaffir market. The Stock Exchange names for shares in South African mines, and for the market in which they are dealt

Kailyard School. A school of writers, who took their subjects from Scottish humble life; it flourished in the 'nineties of last century, and included such writers as Ian Maclaren, J. J. Bell, S. R Crockett, and J. M. Barrie The name is due to the motto—"There grows a bonnie brier bush in our kailyard"— used by Ian Maclaren for his *Beside the Bonnie Brier Bush* (1894)

Kaiser (kī' zer) The German form of *Cæsar*; the title formerly used by the head of the Holy Roman Empire, and by the Emperors of Germany and Austria It was Diocletian who (about 284) ordained that *Cæsar* should be the title of the Emperor of the West, and it is thence that the modern *Kaiser* takes its rise.

Kalevala (ka le va' là) The national epic of the Finns, compiled from popular songs and oral tradition by the Swedish philologist, Elias Lonnrott (1802-1884), who published his first edition of 12,000 verses in 1835, and a second, containing some 22,900 verses, in 1849

The hero is a great magician, Wainamoinen, and a large part of the action turns on Sampo, an object that gives one all his wishes

The epic is influenced by, but by no means dependent upon, Teutonic and Scandinavian mythology, and, to a less extent, by Christianity. It is written in unrhymed alliterative trochaic verse, and is the prototype, both in form and content, of Longfellow's *Hiawatha*

Kali (ka' lē) The Hindu goddess after whom Calcutta receives its name, Kali-ghat, the steps of Kali, *i.e* those by which her worshippers descended from the bank to the waters of the Ganges She was the wife of Siva (*q.v.*), was the acme of bloodthirstiness, many human sacrifices being made to her, and it was to her that the Thugs sacrificed their victims Her idol is black, besmeared with blood, she has red eyes, four arms with blood-stained hands, matted hair, huge fang-like teeth, and a protruding tongue that drips with blood. She wears a necklace of skulls, ear-rings of corpses, and is girdled with serpents

Kaliyuga (kăl yū ga) The last of the four Hindu periods contained in the great Yuga (*q.v.*).

Kalki. *See* Avatar.

Kalmar. The Union of Kalmar. A treaty made on July 12th, 1397, uniting the kingdoms of Norway, Sweden and Denmark This union lasted till it was dissolved by Gustavus Vasa in 1523

Kalmucks—*i e. Khalmuku* (apostates) from Buddhism A race of nomadic Mongols, extending from western China to the valley of the Volga, and adhering to a debased form of Buddhism

Kalyb (kă' lib) The "Lady of the Woods," who stole St. George from his nurse, brought him up as her own child, and endowed him with gifts St. George enclosed her in a rock, where she was torn to pieces by spirits. (*Seven Champions of Christendom*, Pt. i.)

Kam. Crooked; a Celtic word. *Clean kam*, perverted into *kim kam*, means wholly awry, clean from the purpose.

This is clean kam—merely awry.
Coriolanus, iii, 1

Kama (ka' ma) The Hindu god of love. *See* Cama

Kamerad (ka' mě rad). (Ger., comrade, mate.) A word used by the Germans in World War I as an appeal for quarter It is now used in English with the meaning "I surrender."

Kami (ka' mē). A god or divinity in *Shinto*, the native religion of Japan; also the title given to daimios and governors, about equal to our "lord."

Kamikaze (ka mi ka zi) (World War II) Japanese word meaning "divine wind" and applied to suicide squadrons and suicide resistance.

Kamsin (kăm' sin) A simoom or hot, dry, southerly wind, which prevails in Egypt and the deserts of Africa from about the middle of March to the first week in May.

Kansa. See KRISHNA.

Karma (kar' mà) (Sans , action, fate) In Buddhist philosophy, the name given to the results of action, especially the cumulative results of a person's deeds in one stage of his existence as controlling his destiny in the next.

Among Theosophists the word has a rather wider meaning, viz the unbroken sequence of cause and effect; each effect being, in its turn, the cause of a subsequent effect. It is a Sanskrit word, meaning "action" or "sequence."

Karmathians (kar mā 'thi ánz) A Mohammedan sect which rose in Irak in the 9th century Its founder was Karmat, a labourer who professed to be a prophet; they were communistic pantheists and rejected the forms and ceremonies of the Koran, which they regarded as a purely allegorical work

Karttikeya (kar ti kĕ' yá) The Hindu Mars, and god of war He is shown riding on a peacock, with a bow in one hand and an arrow in the other, and is known also as *Skanda* and *Kumara*.

Kaswa, Al. (kăs' wà) Mohammed's favourite camel, which fell on its knees in adoration when the prophet delivered the last clause of the Koran to the assembled multitude at Mecca

Katerfelto (kăt er fel' tō). A generic name for a quack or charlatan, Gustavus Katerfelto was a celebrated quack who became famous during the influenza epidemic of 1782, when he exhibited in London his solar microscope and created immense excitement by showing the infusoria of muddy water. The doctor used to aver that he was the greatest philosopher since the time of Sir Isaac Newton. He was a tall man, dressed in a long, black gown and square cap, and died in 1799.

> Katerfelto with his hair on end,
> At his own wonders wondering for his bread.
> COWPER *Task, The Winter Evening* (1782).

Kathay. China. See CATHAY.

Katmir. See KETMIR.

Kay, Sir. In Arthurian romance, son of Sir Ector and foster-brother of King Arthur, who made him his seneschal.

Keblah (keb' la) The point towards which Mohammedans turn when they worship, *i e.* the Kaaba (*q.v*) at Mecca; also the niche or slab (called the *mihrab*) on the interior wall of a mosque indicating this direction.

Kedar's Tents (kĕ' dá). This world. Kedar was a son of Ishmael (*Gen.* xxv, 15), and was the ancestor of an important tribe of nomadic Arabs. The phrase means houses in the wilderness of this world, and comes from *Ps.* cxx, 5. "Woe is me, that I sojourn in Mesech, that I dwell in the tents of Kedar."

Kedgeree (kej' er ĕ) (Hindi, *khichri*) In India a stew of rice, vegetables, eggs, butter, etc , but in England a dish of re-cooked fish with boiled rice, eggs, sauce, etc , is so called.

Keel. Keel-hauling or -haling Metaphorically, a long, troublesome, and vexatious examination or repetition of annoyances from one in authority The term comes from a practice that was formerly common in the Dutch and many other navies of tying delinquents to a yardarm with weights on their feet, and dragging them by a rope under the keel of a ship, in at one side and out at the other. The result was often fatal

Keelson or **Kelson.** A beam running lengthwise above the keel of a ship, and bolted to the middle of the floor-frames, in order to stiffen the vessel.

Keening A weird lamentation for the dead, common in Galway The coffin is carried to the burying place, and while it is carried three times round, the mourners go to the graves of their nearest kinsfolk and "keen " The word is Ir. *cacoine*, from *caoinim*, to weep.

Keep. One's *keep* is the amount that it takes to maintain one; heard in such phrases as You're not worth your keep. The *keep* of a mediæval castle was the main tower or stronghold, the donjon.

Keep your breath to cool your porridge. Look after your own affairs, and do not put your spoke in another person's wheel

Keep your hair on! See HAIR.

Keep your powder dry Keep yourself prepared for action, keep your courage up The phrase comes from a story told of Oliver Cromwell During his campaign in Ireland he concluded an address to his troops, who were about to cross a river before attacking, with the words— "Put your trust in God, but be sure to keep your powder dry "

To keep a stiff upper lip. To preserve a resolute appearance, not to give way to grief.

To keep at arm's length. To prevent another from being too familiar.

To keep body and soul together See BODY.

To keep company with. A phrase formerly commonly used to describe a friendship preliminary to courtship.

To keep down. To prevent another from rising to an independent position, to keep in subjection; also to keep expenses low.

To keep good hours. See HOUR

To keep house, open house, etc See HOUSE.

To keep in. To repress, to restrain; also, to confine boys in the classroom after school hours as a punishment.

To keep in with. To continue to maintain friendly relations with

To keep it dark. See DARK.

To keep one's countenance. See COUNTENANCE.

To keep one's terms. To reside in college, attend the Inns of Court, etc., during the recognized term times.

To keep the pot a-boiling. *See* POT

To keep tab. To keep a record or note.

To keep touch. *See* TOUCH.

To keep up. To continue, as, "to keep up a discussion", to maintain, as, "to keep up one's courage," "to keep up appearances"; to continue *pari passu,* as "Keep up with the rest."

Keeping-room. In 18th-century American parlance, the second-best room in the house

Kehama (ke ha′ ma) The Hindu rajah in Southey's epic, *The Curse of Kehama* (1810), who obtains and sports with supernatural powers.

Kells, The Book of. Kells is an ancient Irish town in county Meath, once the residence of the kings of Ireland and the see of a bishop until 1300 Among its antiquities, but now preserved in Trinity College, Dublin, is the finest extant early Irish illuminated MS of the Gospels, dating from the 8th century.

Kelly. As game as Ned Kelly. An Australian phrase referring to a noted desperado, who became something of a folk-hero Ned Kelly (1854-80), after enormous depredations, was captured in a suit of armour made by himself, and hanged at Melbourne.

Kelmscott Press, was a private printing press founded in 1890 by William Morris in a cottage adjoining his residence, Kelmscott House, Hammersmith, with the assistance of Emery Walker and Sidney Cockerell. The object was to return to the finest principles of printing in the 15th century.

Kelpie or **Kelpy.** A spirit of the waters in the form of a horse, in Scottish fairy-lore It was supposed to take a delight in the drowning of travellers, but also occasionally helped millers by keeping the mill-wheel going at night.

Every lake has its Kelpie or Water-horse, often seen by the shepherd sitting upon the brow of a rock, dashing along the surface of the deep, or browsing upon the pasture on its verge.—GRAHAM *Sketches of Perthshire*

Kendal Green. Green cloth for foresters; so called from Kendal, Westmorland, famous at one time for this manufacture. Kendal green was the livery of Robin Hood and his followers. In Rymer's *Fœdera* (ii, 83) is a letter of protection, dated 1331, and granted by Edward III to John Kempe of Flanders, who established cloth-weaving in the borough Lincoln was also famous at one time for dyeing green

How couldst thou know these men in Kendal green when it was so dark thou couldst not see thy hand? —1 *Henry IV,* ii, 4.

Kenelm, St. An English saint, son of Kenwulf, King of Wessex in the early 9th century. He was only seven years old when, by his sister's order, he was murdered at Clente-in-Cowbage, Gloucestershire. The murder, says Roger of Wendover, was miraculously notified at Rome by a white dove, which alighted on the altar of St Peter's, bearing in its beak a scroll with these words:—

In Clent cow pasture, under a thorn,
Of head bereft, lies Kenelm king-born.

St. Kenelm's feast day is July 17th

Kenna. *See* KENSINGTON GARDEN.

Kenne. A stone that by mediæval naturalists was fabled to be formed in the eye of the stag. It was used as an antidote to poison. *Cp* HYENA.

Kennel. A dog's shelter; from Lat. *canis* (a dog), Ital *canile,* but *kennel,* a gutter, is, like *channe* and *canal,* from Lat. *canalis,* a pipe (our *cane*) through which water was conveyed.

Kenno (ken′ ō). The dialect name of a large rich cheese, made by the women of the family, with a great affectation of secrecy, for the refreshment of the gossips who were in the house at the birth of a child After all had eaten their fill what was left was divided among the gossips and taken home The Kenno is supposed to be a relic of the secret rites of the *Bona Dea.*

Kensington Garden. A mock-heroic poem by Thomas Tickell (pub 1722) peopling Kensington Gardens, which a few years before had been laid out, with fairies The gardens were the royal domain of Oberon, and the hero is Albion, son of "Albion's royal blood," who was stolen thence by a fairy named Milkah He later fell in love with Kenna, daughter of Oberon, and after many adventures and a war caused by Oberon's opposition they were married and "lived happy ever after "

Kent (Lat. *Cantium*), the territory of the Kantii or Cantii; Old British, *Kant,* a corner or headland. In the reign of Queen Elizabeth Kent was so notorious for highway robbery that the word signified a "nest of thieves."

Some bookes are arrogant and impudent,
So are most thieves in Christendome and Kent.
            TAYLOR, *the Water Poet* (1630).

"Kent" and "Christendom" have been verbally associated from very early times, partly, no doubt, because of the alliteration, partly, perhaps, because it was to Kent that St Augustine first brought Christianity

A man of Kent. One born east of the Medway. These men went out with green boughs to meet the Conqueror, and obtained in consequence a confirmation of their ancient privileges from the new king They call themselves the *invicti*

A Kentish man. A resident of West Kent.

The Fair Maid of Kent. *See* FAIR.

The Holy Maid of Kent *See* HOLY.

Kent cap. A standard size of brown paper measuring 22 by 18 in.

Kentish Fire. Rapturous applause, or three times three and one more. The expression originated with the protracted cheers given in Kent to the No-Popery orators in 1828-29 Lord Winchilsea, who proposed the health of the Earl of Roden on August 15th, 1834, said: "Let it be given with the 'Kentish Fire.' "

Kentishmen's Tails. *See* TAILS

Kent's Cavern, a mile or so out of Torquay, is a limestone cave in which a great number of bones and flint implements have been discovered. There appear to have been two different periods of occupation in prehistoric times, and the objects found in the cave throw important light on the civilization of those ages

Kentigern, St. (kent' i jĕrn) The patron saint of Glasgow, born of royal parents about 510 He is said to have founded the cathedral at Glasgow, where he died in 601 He is represented with his episcopal cross in one hand, and in the other a salmon and a ring, in allusion to the well-known legend —

Queen Langoureth had been false to her husband, King Roderich, and had given her lover a ring The king, aware of the fact, stole upon the knight in sleep, abstracted the ring, threw it into the Clyde, and then asked the queen for it The queen, in alarm, applied to St. Kentigern, who after praying, went to the Clyde, caught a salmon with the ring in its mouth, handed it to the queen and was thus the means of restoring peace to the royal couple, and of reforming the repentant queen.

The Glasgow arms include the salmon with the ring in its mouth, and also an oak tree, a bell hanging on one of the branches, a bird at the top of the tree —

> The tree that never grew,
> The bird that never flew,
> The fish that never swam,
> The bell that never rang

The oak and bell are in allusion to the story that St. Kentigern hung a bell upon an oak to summon the wild natives to worship

St Kentigern is also known as "St Mungo," for *Mungho* (i e dearest) was the name by which St. Servan, his first preceptor, called him His day is January 13th

Kentucky Pill. A bullet.

Kepler's Laws. Astronomical laws first enunciated by Johann Kepler (1571-1630) They formed the basis of Newton's work, and are the starting-point of modern astronomy. They are:—

(1) That the orbit of a planet is an ellipse, the sun being in one of the foci

(2) That every planet so moves that the line drawn from it to the sun describes equal areas in equal times.

(3) That the squares of the times of the planetary revolutions are as the cubes of their mean distances from the sun

Kermess (ker mes') Several of the Dutch and Flemish painters depicted scenes of a kermess This was an annual fair or festival popular in most towns of the Low Countries and the occasion for open-air sports and games often of a somewhat riotous nature. The kermess (kirk mass, church mass) was usually held on the anniversary of the dedication of the parish church.

Kernel. The kernel of the matter; its gist, true import, the core or central part of it. The word is the A S *cyrnel*, diminutive of *corn*.

Kersey. A coarse cloth, usually ribbed, and woven from long wool, said to be so named from Kersey, in Suffolk, where it was originally made. Shakespeare uses the word figuratively ("russet yeas and honest kersey noes," *Love's Labour's Lost*, v, 2), with the meaning plain or homely.

Kerseymere. A twilled fine woollen cloth of a particular make, formerly called *cassimere*, a variation of *cashmere*, its present name being due to confusion with *kersey* (*see above*). *Cashmere*, a fine woollen material, is so called because it is made from hair of the goats of *Kashmir*

Kerton. *See* EXETER.

Kestrel. A hawk of a base breed, hence a worthless fellow.

> No thought of honour ever did assay
> His baser brest; but in his kestrell kynd
> A pleasant veine of glory he did find   .
> SPENSER *Faerie Queene*, II, iii, 4

Ketch. *See* JACK KETCH, under JACK.

Ketchup. A sauce made from mushrooms, tomatoes, etc , which originally, with its name, came from the Far East

Soy comes in Tubbs from Jappan, and the best ketchup from Tonquin, yet good of both sorts are made and sold very cheap in China —LOCKYER *Trade with India* (1711).

The word is from Chinese, through Malay, *kechap*

Ketmir or **Katmir.** The dog of the Seven Sleepers (*q v*), called in the Mohammedan version "Al Rakhim "

Kettle. Old thieves' slang for a watch; a **tin kettle** is a silver watch and a **red kettle** a gold one

A kettle of fish. An old Border name for a kind of *fête champêtre*, or picnic by the riverside in which newly caught salmon is the chief dish Having thickened some water with salt to the consistency of brine, the salmon is put therein and boiled, and when fit for eating, the company partake in gipsy fashion. The discomfort of this sort of picnic probably gave rise to the phrase "A pretty kettle of fish," meaning an awkward state of affairs, a mess, a muddle

The surgeon . . . was now come to acquaint Mr. Tow-wouse that his guest was in such extreme danger of his life, that he scarce saw any hopes of his recovery. "Here's a pretty kettle of fish," cried Mrs Towwouse, "you have brought upon us' We are like to have a funeral at our own expense "—FIELDING. *Joseph Andrews*, I, xii

Kettledrum. A drum made of a thin hemispherical shell of brass or copper with a parchment top

Also, an obsolete name for an afternoon tea-party, so called because it was on a somewhat smaller scale than the regular "drum" (*q v.*), and also in playful allusion to the presence of the tea *kettle*.

Kevin, St. (kev' in). An Irish saint of the 6th century, of whom legend relates that, like St. Senanus, he retired to an island where he vowed no woman should ever land A girl named Kathleen followed him, but the saint hurled her from a rock, and her ghost never left the place while he lived A rock at Glendalough (Wicklow) is shown as the bed of St. Kevin. Moore has a poem on this tradition (*Irish Melodies*, iv)

Kex. The dry, hollow stem of umbelliferous plants, like the hemlock Tennyson says in *The Princess*, "Though the rough kex break the starred mosaic " Nothing breaks a pavement like the growth of grass or lichen through it

Key. Metaphorically, that which explains or solves some difficulty, problem, etc , as *the key to a cipher*, the means of interpreting it, *the key to a "roman à clef*," the list showing whom the fictional characters represent in actual life. Also, a place which commands a large area of land or sea, as Gibraltar is the key to the Mediterranean, and, in the Peninsular War, Ciudad Rodrigo (taken by Wellington, 1812) was known as the **key to Spain**.

In music the lowest note of a scale is the **keynote**, and gives its name to the scale, or key, itself: hence the figurative phrases *in key, out of key*, in or out of harmony with.

St. Peter's keys. The cross-keys on the papal arms symbolizing.

The power of the keys. The supreme ecclesiastical authority claimed by the pope as successor of St. Peter. The phrase is derived from *St Matt* xvi, 19:—

And I will give unto thee the keys of the kingdom of heaven and whatsoever thou shalt bind on earth shall be bound in heaven· and whatsoever thou shalt loose on earth shall be loosed in heaven

The Gold Key. The office of Groom of the Stole (*see* STOLE), the holder of which had a golden key as his emblem

The key shall be upon his shoulder. He shall have the dominion, shall be in authority, have the keeping of something. It is said of Eliakim that God would lay upon his shoulder the key of the house of David (*Is* xxii, 22) The chamberlain of the court used to bear a key as his insignia, and on public occasions the steward slung his key over his shoulder, as our mace-bearers carry their mace

The queen's keys. An old legal phrase for the crowbars, hammers, etc, used to force an entrance so that a warrant could be executed

At the ceremony of locking up the Tower of London at night, the keys are brought to the main guard house, where the sentry demands, "Who goes there?" "Keys," is the answer. "Whose keys?" "Queen Elizabeth's keys" "Advance Queen Elizabeth's keys, and all's well "

To have the key of the street. To be locked out of doors, to be turned out of one's home

Keys of stables and cowhouses are not infrequently, even at the present day, attached to a stone with a hole through it with a piece of horn attached to the handle This is a relic of an ancient superstition The *halig*, or holy stone, was looked upon as a talisman which kept off the fiendish Mara (nightmare); and the horn was supposed to ensure the protection of the god Pan

Key and Bible. Formerly employed as a method of divination. The Bible is opened either at *Ruth*, ch i, or at *Psalm* li, and a door-key is placed inside the Bible, so that the handle projects beyond the book. The Bible is then tied with a piece of string and held by the fourth fingers of the accuser and defendant, who must repeat the words touched by the wards of the key The key was then supposed to turn towards the guilty person, and the Bible fall to the ground

The Cross Keys as a public-house sign has an ecclesiastical origin (*see St. Peter's keys, above*). St Peter is always represented in art with two keys in his hand, they are consequently the insignia of the papacy, and are borne saltire-wise, one of gold and the other of silver. They also form the arms of the Archbishop of York;

the Bishop of Winchester bears two keys and sword in saltire, and the bishops of St Asaph, Gloucester, Exeter, and Peterborough bear two keys in saltire The *cross-keys* are also the emblem of St Servatius, St Hippolytus, St. Geneviève, St Petronilla, St Osyth, St. Martha, and St. Germanus of Paris

Key-cold. Deadly cold, lifeless A key, on account of its coldness, is still sometimes employed to stop bleeding at the nose

Poor key-cold figure of a holy king!
Pale ashes of the house of Lancaster!
Thou bloodless remnant of that royal blood
Richard III, i, 2.

Keys, The House of. The representative branch of the Legislature, or Tynwald, in the Isle of Man, which consists of two branches, viz. the Governor and Council, and this House Since 1866 the twenty-four members of the House of Keys have been popularly elected every seven years, previous to that date the House was self-elected, vacancies being filled by the House presenting to the governor "two of the eldest and worthiest men of the isle," one of which the governor nominated

The governor and his council consists of the governor, the bishop, the attorney-general, two deemsters (or judges), members appointed by the governor and four members appointed by the House of Keys

The Keystone State. Pennsylvania, so called from its position and importance

Keystone Comedies. Early film comedies at Hollywood made between 1916 and about 1926 by the Keystone Company, featuring Mack Sennett.

Keyne, St. (kān) A Celtic saint, daughter of Brychan, King of Brecknock in the 5th century. Concerning her well, near Liskeard, Cornwall, it is said that if a bridegroom drinks therefrom before his bride, he will be master of his house; but if the bride gets the first draught, the grey mare will be the better horse.

Khaki (ka' ki) A Hindu word, meaning *dusty*, or *dust-coloured*, from *khak*, dust. Khaki was first used by British troops at the time of the Indian Mutiny, when it was adopted as the uniform for an irregular corps of Guides, raised at Meerut, hence called the *Khaki Risala* (*Risala* = squadron). In 1882 the War Office discussed the question of adopting it as the general active service uniform, but, though certain regiments wore it then, and in the Omdurman campaign in Egypt sixteen years later, on the North-West Frontier, etc., it was not generally introduced until the Boer War of 1899-1902

Khalifa (ka lē' fa) An Arabic word meaning "successor" and the title adopted by Abdullah el Tashi, the successor in 1885 of the Mahdi (*q.v.*). Much was heard of the Khalifa in late Victorian days, for it was against him that the British expedition went under Lord Kitchener in 1898, when his power was broken at the battle of Omdurman.

Khamsin. *See* KAMSIN.

Khedive (ke dēv'). The title by which, from 1867 to 1914, the ruler of Egypt, as viceroy of the Sultan of Turkey, was known, The word is Turkish (from Persian) and means a prince, or viceroy.

In 1914 Egypt was a semi-independent tributary state of Turkey, occupied by British troops. The then Khedive, Abbas II, joined the Central Powers, and was deposed, a British Protectorate being declared. The title then disappeared, and the new ruler, Hussein Kamil, became King of Egypt

Kibitzer (kĭb′ ĭt zĕr) An American colloquial term to describe, originally, a spectator at a card game who looks over the players' shoulders and as often as not gives unwanted advice. The word is of Yiddish-German derivation

Kibosh (kī′ bosh) To put the kibosh on To put an end to, dispose of Mr Charles Funk received the following explanation of its origin from Mr Padraic Colum " 'Kibosh,' I believe, means 'the cap of death' and it is always used in that sense—'He put the kibosh on it ' In Irish it could be written 'cie bais'—the last word pronounced 'bosh,' the genitive of 'bas,' death."

Kiblah. *See* KEBLAH.

Kick. Slang for a sixpence, but only in compounds. "Two-and-a-kick" is two shillings and sixpence

He's not got a kick left in him. He's done for, "down and out " The phrase is from pugilism

More kicks than ha'pence. More abuse than profit Called "monkey's allowance" in allusion to monkeys led about to collect ha'pence by exhibiting "their parts " The poor brutes get the kicks if they do their parts in an unsatisfactory manner, but the master gets the ha'pence collected

Quite the kick. Quite a dandy The Italians call a dandy a *chic*. The French *chic* means knack, as *avoir le chic*, to have the knack of doing a thing smartly
> I cocked my hat and twirled my stick,
> And the girls they called me quite the kick.
> *George Colman the Younger*

To get the kick out. To be summarily dismissed; given the sack or "the Order of the Boot "

To kick one's heels. *See* HEEL.

To kick against the pricks. To protest when all the odds are against one, to struggle against overwhelming opposition *See Acts* ix, 5, and xxvi, 14, where the reference is to an ox kicking when goaded, or a horse when pricked with the rowels of a spur. *Cp.* also 1 *Sam* ii, 29—"Wherefore kick ye at my sacrifice and at mine offering," why do you protest against them?

Kick-off, in football, the start or resumption of a game by kicking the ball from the centre of the field.

To kick over the traces. Not to follow the leader, but to act independently, as a horse refusing to run in harness kicks over the traces

To kick the beam. To be of light weight; to be of inferior consequence. When one pan of a pair of scales is lighter than the other, it flies upwards and "kicks the beam" of the scales.

To kick the bucket. *See* BUCKET.

To kick up a dust, a row, etc To create a disturbance The phrase "to kick up the dust" explains the other phrases.

Kickshaws. Made dishes, odds and ends, and dainty trifles of small value Formerly written "kickshose." (Fr. *quelque chose*)
> Some pigeons, Davy, a couple of short-legged hens, joint of mutton, and any pretty little tiny kickshaws
> —2 *Henry IV*, v, 1.

Kicksy-wicksy. Full of whims and fancies, uncertain, hence, figuratively, a wife. Taylor, the water poet, calls it *kicksie-winsie*, but Shakespeare spells it *kicky-wicky*
> He wears his honour in a box unseen
> That hugs his kicky-wicky here at home,
> Spending his manly marrow in her arms,
> Which should sustain the bound and high curvet
> Of Mars's fiery steed
> *All's Well that Ends Well*, ii, 3.

Kid. A faggot or bundle of firewood. To kid is to bind up faggots. In the parish register of Kneesal church there is the following item "Leading kids to church, 2s. 6d.," that is, carting faggots to church.

Kid. A young child, in allusion to kid, the young of the goat, a very playful and frisky little animal
The verb to kid, means to make a fool of

Kiddies, The. The Scots Guards, raised in the reign of Charles I. When James II attempted to overawe the City of London by forming a large camp on Hounslow Heath, the three regiments of Guards then in existence were present, and the Scots Guards, being the junior, gained this disrespectful nickname

Kidnapping is a slang word imported into the language in the 17th century. "Nabbing" a "kid,' or a child was the popular term for the abominable offence of stealing young children and selling them to sea captains and others who bore them off to work on the plantations in America The most notorious instance of kidnapping in modern times was the stealing and murder of Colonel Lindbergh's infant son in 1932.

Kidney. Temperament, disposition; stamp.

Men of another kidney or of the same kidney. The *reins* or *kidneys* were even by the Jews supposed to be the seat of the affections

Kildare's Holy Fane. Famous for the "Fire of St. Bridget," which was inextinguishable, because the nuns never allowed it to go out Every twentieth night St. Bridget was fabled to return to tend the fire Part of the chapel still remains, and is called "The Firehouse."

Kill. To kill two birds with one stone *See* BIRD

Killed by Kindness. It is said that Draco, the Athenian legislator, met with his death from his popularity, being smothered in the theatre of Ægina by the number of caps and cloaks showered on him by the spectators (590 B C). Thomas Heywood wrote a play called *A Woman Killed with Kindness* (1603).

Killing. Irresistible, overpowering, fascinating, or bewitching; so as to compel admiration and notice.
> Those eyes were made so killing.
> POPE· *Rape of the Lock*, v, 64.

A killing pace. Too hot or strong to last, exceptionally great, exhausting.

Killing no murder. A pamphlet published in
Holland and sent over to England in 1657
advising the assassination of Oliver Cromwell
It purported to be by one William Allen, a
Jesuit, and has frequently been attributed to
Silas Titus (later made a colonel and Groom of
the Bedchamber by Charles II), but it was
actually by Col Edward Sexby, a Leveller,
who had gone over to the Royalists, and who,
in 1657, narrowly failed in an attempt to
murder Cromwell

The texts on the title-page are —

And all the People of the Land rejoiced and the
City was quiet, after that they had slain Athaliah with
the Sword.—*2 Chron* xxiii, 21

Now after the time that Amaziah did turn away
from following the Lord, they made a conspiracy
against him in Jerusalem, and he fled to Lachish;
but they sent to Lachish after him, and slew him there.
—*2 Chron.* xxv, 27

Kilroy. (World War II) The phrase "Kilroy
was here" was found written up wherever the
Americans (particularly Air Transport Command) had been, somewhat like "Chad" (*q v*)
in Britain. Various theories have been put forward as to its origin—one being that a certain
Kilroy was inspector in a shipyard at Quincy,
Mass , and wrote the words in chalk on equipment to indicate that he had inspected it—but
it seems more likely that the phrase grew by
accident. Imitations such as "Clem" did not
become so fashionable.

Kilter. Out of kilter. Out of order.

Kin, Kind.

King But now, my cousin Hamlet, and my son—
Ham · A little more than kin, and less than kind.
Hamlet, i, 2.

Kin or **kinsman** is a relative by marriage or
blood more distant than father and son.
Kind means of the same sort or genus, as
man-kind or man-genus
Hamlet says he is more than *kin* to Claudius
(as he was stepson), but still he is not of the
same *kind*, the same class, He is not a bird of
the same feather as the king.

Kindhart. A jocular name for a tooth-
drawer in the time of Queen Elizabeth.
Kindhart, the dentist, is mentioned by Row-
land in his *Letting of Humours-Blood in the
Bead-vaine* (1600); and in Rowley's *New
Wonder.*

Mistake me not, Kindhart . .
He calls you tooth-drawer   Act i, 1

The dedication in Chettle's *Kind-heartes
Dreame* (which contains a reference to Shakespeare and was published in 1592) begins.—

Gentlemen and good-fellowes, (whose kindnes
having christened mee with the name of kind-heart,
bindes me in all kind course I can to deserve the continuance of your love) let it not seeme strange (I
beseech ye) that he that all dayes of his life hath beene
famous for drawing teeth, should now in drooping
age hazard contemptible mfamie by drawing himselfe
into print.

Kindergarten (kin′ dĕr gar′ tĕn) meaning in
German a children's garden, is the term
applied to schools in which very young
children are taught by the use of objects,
games and songs. The system was initiated in
Germany by Friederich Froebel (1782-1852)
in 1840.

King. The A S *cyning*, from *cyn*, a nation or
people, and the suffix *-ing*, meaning "of," as
"son of," "chief of," etc In Anglo-Saxon
times the king was elected by the Witenagemot, and was therefore the *choice of the
nation*

King Franconi. Joachim Murat (1767-1815)
was so called because of his resemblance to
the mountebank Franconi.

King of Kings. In the Prayer Book the term,
of course, refers to the Deity, but it has been
assumed by many Eastern rulers, especially by
the sovereigns of Abyssinia

King of the King. Cardinal Richelieu (1585-
1642) was so called, because of his influence
over Louis XIII of France.

The Factory King. Richard Oastler, of
Bradford (1789-1861), the successful advocate
of the Ten Hours Bill.

The King of Bath. *See* BATH

The King of the Beggars. *See* BEGGARS

The King of the Border. A nickname of
Adam Scott of Tushielaw (executed 1529), a
famous border outlaw and chief.

The King of Dunces. In his first version of
the *Dunciad* (1712), Pope gave this place of
honour to Lewis Theobald (1688-1744): but
in the edition of 1742 Colley Cibber (1671-
1757) was put to reign in his stead.

The King of Men. A title given both to Zeus
and Agamemnon.

The King of Painters. A title assumed by
Parrhasius, the painter, a contemporary of
Zeuxis (400 B.C.). Plutarch says he wore a
purple robe and a golden crown.

The King of Preachers. Louis Bourdaloue
(1632-1704), the eloquent French Jesuit.

The King of Rome. A title conferred by
Napoleon I on his son François Charles Joseph
Napoleon, Duke of Reichstadt (1811-32), on
the day of his birth. He was called *L'Aiglon*
(the young eagle) by Edmond Rostand in his
play.

The King of Waters. The river Amazon, in
South America.

The King of the World. The title (in Hindi
Shah Jehan) assumed by Khorrum Shah, third
son of Selim Jehan Ghir, and fifth of the Mogul
emperors of Delhi (reigned 1628-58).

The King over the water. The name given by
Jacobites to James II after his flight to France:
to his son the Old Pretender (James III), and
to his grandsons Charles Edward the Young
Pretender (Charles III), and Henry, Cardinal
of York (Henry IX).

My father so far compromised his loyalty as to
announce merely "The king," as his first toast after
dinner, instead of the emphatic "King George " . . .
Our guest made a motion with his glass, so as to pass
it over the water-decanter which stood beside him,
and added, "Over the water."—SCOTT *Redgauntlet*,
letter v.

King's Cave. Opposite to Campbelton; so
called because it was here that King Robert
Bruce and his retinue lodged when they landed
on the mainland from the Isle of Arran.

King's Crag. Fife, in Scotland. So called because Alexander III of Scotland was killed there (1286)

As he was riding in the dusk of the evening along the sea-coast of Fife, betwixt Burnt-island and King-horn, he approached too near the brink of the precipice, and his horse, starting or stumbling, he was thrown over the rock and killed on the spot   . The people of the country still point out the very spot where it happened, and which is called "The King's Crag"—
SCOTT: *Tales of a Grandfather,* vi

King's Cross Up to the accession of George IV this London locality was called "Battle Bridge" and had an infamous notoriety. The name was changed in 1821, when the neighbourhood was being developed by speculating builders. A battle is said to have been fought on this site between King Alfred and the Danes, but it is mostly a matter of legend, no facts having yet been discovered to substantiate the story. There was never any cross here, only a singularly bad statue of George IV which was taken down in 1842.

King's Lynn (*Lynn Regis*) The town in Norfolk has been so called since the time of the dissolution of the monasteries, when certain Church property fell into the hands of King Henry VIII. Previously its name was *Lynn Episcopi* (Bishop's Lynn) *Lynn* is Celtic for a deep pool.

A cat may look at a king. *See* CAT.

King of Arms. The official title of the chief heralds In England there are three kings of arms, Garter, Clarenceux, and Norroy and Ulster; in Scotland there is the Lord Lyon King of Arms. The Order of the Bath has its own Bath King of Arms, instituted in 1725. In Ireland the office of Ulster King of Arms is now associated with the Norroy King of Arms in England.

A king's bad bargain. Said of a soldier (or sailor) who turns out a malingerer or to be of no use, in allusion to the shilling formerly given by the recruiting sergeant to a soldier on enlistment.

A king of shreds and patches. In the old mysteries Vice used to be dressed as a mimic king in a parti-coloured suit (*Hamlet*, iii, 4) The phrase has been applied to hacks who compile books for publishers but supply no originality of thought or matter.

A king should die standing. The reputed dying saying of Louis XVIII

King Charles's head A phrase applied to an obsession, a fixed fancy It comes from Mr Dick, the harmless half-wit in *David Copperfield*, who, whatever he wrote or said always got round to the subject of King Charles's head, about which he was composing a memorial—he could not keep it out of his thoughts

King Charles's Spaniel. A small black-and-tan spaniel with a rounded head, short muzzle, full, rather protruding eyes. This variety came into favour at the Restoration, but the colour of the dogs at that time was liver and white

King Cotton. Cotton, the staple of the Southern States of America, and one of the chief articles of manufacture in England. The

expression was first used by James H. Hammond in the United States Senate in 1858.

King's County in the province of Leinster in Eire is now called Offaly, and Queen's County is now Leix

King's Cup Air Race was instituted in 1922 for a cup presented by George V. It is a handicap air race open only to British and Empire pilots flying British or Dominion aeroplanes The winner in 1950 was E Day, at a speed of 138 m.p.h

King James's Bible. *See* BIBLE, THE ENGLISH

King Log and King Stork *See* LOG

King's (or Queen's) Messenger is an official of the British Foreign Office whose duty it is to carry personally confidential messages from London to any embassy or legation abroad He carries as his badge of office a silver greyhound, and though he naturally receives courtesies and help in the countries across which he travels, he enjoys no diplomatic immunities or privileges save that of passing through the customs the "diplomatic bag" he is carrying.

King of Misrule. In mediæval and Tudor times, the director of the Christmas-time horseplay and festivities, called also the *Abbot,* or *Lord, of Misrule,* and in Scotland the *Master of Unreason* At Oxford and Cambridge one of the Masters of Arts superintended both the Christmas and Candlemas sports, for which he was allowed a fee of 40s. A similar "lord" was appointed by the lord mayor of London, the sheriffs, and the chief nobility Stubbs tells us that these mock dignitaries had from twenty to sixty officers under them, and were furnished with hobbyhorses, dragons, and musicians They first went to church with such a confused noise that no one could hear his own voice. Polydore Vergil says of the Feast of Misrule that it was "derived from the Roman Saturnalia," held in December for five days (17th to 22nd) The Feast of Misrule lasted twelve days.

If we compare our Bacchanalian Christmases and New Year-tides with these Saturnalia and Feasts of Janus, we shall finde such near affinitye between them ... that wee must needs conclude the one to be the very ape or issue of the other —PRYNNE *Histrio-Mastix* (1632)

King-maker, The. Richard Neville, Earl of Warwick (1420-71), so called because, when he sided with Henry VI, Henry was king, but when he sided with Edward IV, Henry was deposed and Edward crowned. He was killed at the battle of Barnet He was first called "the king-maker" by John Major in his *History of Greater Britain, England and Scotland,* 1521.

King's (or Queen's) Bench. The Supreme Court of Common Law, so called because at one time the sovereign presided in this court, and the court followed the sovereign when he moved from one place to another. Originally called the *Aula Regia,* it is now a division of the High Court of Judicature

King-pin, in skittles, etc, the pin in the centre when all the pins are in place, or the pin at the front apex. Figuratively the word is used to describe the principal person in a company, cast, etc

King's (or Queen's) Remembrancer. An officer of the High Court who represents the Exchequer with the duty of collecting debts and dues on behalf of the Crown

The King's (or Queen's) Speech with which each session of the British Parliament is opened is prepared by the cabinet and outlines their programme It is always addressed to both Houses but the special clause relating to finance is addressed to the Commons alone.

King of the Bean. See BEAN-KING

King of Yvetot. See YVETOT

King Pétaud. See PÉTAUD

Kings are above grammar. See GRAMMAR

Kings have long hands Do not quarrel with a king, as his power and authority reach to the end of his dominions The Latin proverb is, *An nescis longas regibus esse manus* (Ovid), *Heroides,* 17, 166).

> There's such divinity doth hedge a king,
> That treason can but peep to what it would.
> *Hamlet,* iv, 5

King's (or Queen's) evidence. See EVIDENCE.

King Horn. The hero of a French metrical romance of the 13th century, and the original of our *Horne Childe,* generally called *The Geste of Kyng Horn* The nominal author is a certain *Mestre Thomas.*

Like a king. When Porus, the Indian prince, was taken prisoner, Alexander asked him how he expected to be treated "Like a king," he replied, and Alexander made him his friend.

Pray aid of the king (or queen). When someone, under the belief that he has a right to the land, claims rent of the king's tenants, they appeal to the sovereign, or "pray aid of the king "

The books of the four kings. A pack of cards. After supper some were brought in the books of the four kings.—RABELAIS *Gargantua and Pantagruel,* i, 22

The king of beasts. The lion.

The King of Spain's trumpeter. A donkey. A pun on the word *don,* a Spanish magnate.

The King of Terrors. Death.

The king of the forest. The oak, which not only braves the storm, but fosters the growth of tender parasites under its arms.

The king's cheese goes half in paring. A king's income is half consumed by the numerous calls on his purse

The King's English. See ENGLISH

The King's Oak. The oak under which Henry VIII sat, in Epping Forest, while Anne (Boleyn) was being executed

The King's (or Queen's) picture. Money; so called because coin is stamped with "the image" of the reigning sovereign

The Three Kings of Cologne. The Magi (*q v*).

King's (or Queen's) Counsel. In England a member of the Bar appointed by the Crown on the nomination of the Lord Chancellor, in Scotland on the recommendation of the Lord Justice-General. A K.C wears a silk gown and

is thus often called a silk He takes precedence over the junior Bar, and in a case must have a junior barrister with him

King's Evil Scrofula; so called from a notion which prevailed from the reign of Edward the Confessor to that of Queen Anne that it could be cured by the royal touch The Jacobites considered that the power did not descend to William III and Anne because the "divine" hereditary right was not fully possessed by them, but the office remained in our Prayer-Book till 1719 Prince Charles Edward, when he claimed to be Prince of Wales, touched a female child for the disease in 1745. One of the last persons touched in England was Dr Johnson, in 1712, when less than three years old, by Queen Anne The practice was introduced by Henry VII of presenting the person "touched" with a small gold or silver coin, called a touchpiece The one presented to Dr Johnson has St George and the Dragon on one side and a ship on the other; the legend of the former is *Soli deo gloria,* and of the latter *Anna D · G M.B R F: ET H REG* (Anne, by the Grace of God, of Great Britain, France, and Ireland Queen)

We are told that Charles II touched 92,107 persons. The smallest number in one year was 2,983, in 1669; and the largest number was in 1684, when many were trampled to death *(See* Macaulay's *History of England,* ch. xiv) John Brown, a royal surgeon, had to superintend the ceremony.

Cp. Macbeth, iv, 3:—

> *Malcolm* Comes the king forth, I pray you?
> *Doctor:* Ay, sir; there are a crew of wretched souls
> That stay his cure, their malady convinces
> The great assay of art, but, at his touch
> Such sanctity hath heaven given his hand,
> They presently amend.

The French kings laid claim to the same divine power from the time of Clovis, A D 481, and on Easter Sunday, 1686, Louis XIV touched 1,600 persons, using these words *Le roy te touche, Dieu te guerisse.*

Days fatal to Kings. Much foolish superstition has been circulated respecting certain days supposed to be "fatal" to the crowned heads of Great Britain The following notes will help the reader to discriminate truth from fiction —

Of the sovereigns who have died since 1066 *Sunday* has been the last day of the reign of seven, *Monday, Tuesday* and *Thursday* that of six each, *Friday* and *Wednesday* of five, and *Saturday* of four.

Sunday. Henry I, Edward III, Henry VI, James I, William III, Anne, George I.

Monday: Stephen, Richard II, Henry IV, Henry V, Richard III, George V.

Tuesday: Richard I, Edward II, Charles I, James II, William IV, Victoria.

Wednesday: John, Henry III, Edward IV, Edward V, George VI.

Thursday. William I, William II, Henry II, Edward VI, Mary I, Elizabeth.

Friday: Edward I, Henry VIII, Charles II, Mary II, Edward VII.

Saturday: Henry VII, George II, George III, George IV.

Kingdom Come. Death, the grave, execution, the next world.

> And forty pounds be theirs, a pretty sum,
> For sending such a rogue to kingdom come
> PETER PINDAR *Subjects for Painters.*

Kingsale. The premier baron of Ireland, Lord Kingsale, is one of the two British subjects who claim the right of wearing a hat in the presence of royalty. *See* HAT

Kingston Bridge. A card bent so that when the pack is cut it is cut at this card

Kingston-on-Thames. Named *King's stone* from a large square block of stone near the town hall, on which the early Anglo-Saxon monarchs knelt when they were appointed to the kingly office. Edward the Elder, Athelstan, Edmund, Ethelred, Edred, Edwy, and Edward the Martyr received on this stone the royal unction. The stone is now enclosed

Kingstown (Eire), by the Irish called Dunleary. The name was changed in 1821 out of compliment to George IV, who visited Ireland that year, and left Dunleary harbour for his return home on September 5th

Kinless Loons. The judges whom Cromwell sent into Scotland were so termed, because they had no relations in the country and so were free from temptation to nepotism. They tried the accused on the merits of the case.

Kiosk (kē' osk) A Turkish summer-house or pavilion supported by pillars which were usually covered with vines or flowering creepers and often enclosed a fountain In England and western Europe the name is given to bandstands, pavilions for the sale of refreshments, etc , and to small enclosed stalls for the sale of newspapers in the street; booths for public telephones, etc

Kirk of Skulls. Gamrie Church, in Banffshire; so called because the skulls and other bones of the Norsemen who fell in the neighbouring field, the *Bloody Pots*, were built into its walls.

Kirke's Lambs. *See* REGIMENTAL NICKNAMES.

Kismet (kis' met). Fate, destiny; or the fulfilment of destiny, from Turk *quismat*, portion, lot (*qasama*, to divide).

Kiss. A very ancient and widely spread mode of salutation, frequently mentioned in the Bible, both as an expression of reverence and adoration and as a greeting or farewell between friends Esau embraced Jacob, "fell on his neck and kissed him" (*Gen* xxxiii, 4), the repentant woman kissed the feet of Christ (*Luke* vii, 45), and the disciples from Ephesus "fell on Paul's neck and kissed him" (*Acts* xx, 37). But kissing between the sexes was unknown among the ancient Hebrews, and while the cheeks, forehead, beard, hands, and feet might be kissed the lips might not, the passage in the Bible (*Prov* xxiv, 26, *see* marginal note in Revised Version) that seems to contradict this being a mistranslation. "Kiss the Son, lest He be angry" (*Ps.* ii, 12), means worship the Son of God This is the only reference in the Bible to the Kiss of Homage.

The old custom of ' kissing the bride" comes from the Salisbury rubric concerning the Pax (*q v*).

In billiards (and also bowls) a *kiss* is a very slight touch of one moving ball on another, especially a second touch, accidental or designed, and the name also used to be given to a little drop of sealing-wax accidentally let fall beside the seal

Kiss-behind-the-garden-gate. A country name for a pansy.

Kiss the place to make it well. Said to be a relic of the custom of sucking poison from wounds. St Martin of Tours, when he was at Paris, observed at the city gates a leper full of sores, and, going up to him, he kissed the sores, whereupon the leper was instantly made whole (Sulpicius Severus . *Dialogues*). Similar stories are told of St. Mayeul, and quite a number of saints

> Who ran to help me, when I fell,
> And would some pretty story tell,
> Or kiss the place to make it well?
> 　　　　　　ANN TAYLOR: *My Mother*

Kissing the Pope's toe. Matthew of Westminster says it was customary formerly to kiss the hand of his Holiness, but that a certain woman, in the 8th century, not only kissed the Pope's hand, but "squeezed it " The Church magnate, seeing the danger to which he was exposed, cut off his hand, and was compelled in future to offer his foot In reality, the Pope's foot (*i e.* the cross embroidered on his right shoe) may be kissed by the visitor, bishops kiss his knee as well This sign of respect was formerly given to other patriarchs and even to temporal sovereigns and, needless to say, implies no servility It is customary to bend the knee and kiss the ring of a cardinal, bishop, or abbot.

To kiss the book. To kiss the Bible, or the New Testament, after taking an oath, the kiss of confirmation or promise to act in accordance with the words of the oath and a public acknowledgment that you adore and fear to offend, by breaking your oath, the God whose book you reverence.

In the English Courts, the Houses of Parliament, etc., non-Christians and others who have scruples are now permitted to affirm without going through this ceremony

To kiss or lick the dust. To be completely overwhelmed or humiliated, to be slain. In *Ps* lxxii, 9, it is said, "his enemies shall lick the dust."

To kiss hands. To kiss the hand of the sovereign either on accepting or retiring from office.

Kissing the hand of, or one's own hand to, an idol was a usual form of adoration, if the statue was low enough the devotee kissed its hand, if not, kissed his own hand and waved it to the image God said he had in Israel seven thousand persons who had not bowed unto Baal, "every mouth which hath not kissed him" (1 *Kings* xix, 18).

To kiss the gunner's daughter. *See* GUNNER.

To kiss the hare's foot. *See* HARE.

To kiss the rod. *See* ROD

Kissing-comfit. The candied root of the Sea Holly (*eryngium maritimum*) prepared as a lozenge, to perfume the breath.

Kissing-crust. The crust where the lower lump of a cottage loaf kisses the upper. In French, *baisure de pain*

Kist of Whistles. A church-organ (Scotch). *Kist* is the same word as *cist* (*q.v.*), a chest

Kit. From Dut. *kitte*, a wooden receptacle made of hooped staves; hence that which contains the necessaries, tools, etc, of a workman, and hence the articles themselves collectively

A **soldier's kit.** His outfit.

A small three-stringed fiddle, formerly used by dancing masters, was called a *kit.* The word is from the obsolete *gitterne* (Fr. *quitterne*), a sort of guitar.

Kit-cat Club. A club formed about the beginning of the 18th century by the leading Whigs of the day, and held in the house of Christopher Catt, a pastrycook of Shire Lane, which used to run north from Temple Bar to Carey Street (its site is now covered by the Law Courts). Christopher Catt's mutton pies, which were eaten at the club, were also called *kit-cats*, and in the *Spectator* (No IX) we are told that it was from these the club got its name.

Steele, Addison, Congreve, Garth, Vanbrugh, Manwaring, Stepney, Walpole, and Pulteney were of it; so was Lord Dorset and the present Duke Manwaring . . was the ruling man in all conversation . . Lord Stanhope and the Earl of Essex were also members. . . Each member gave his [picture] —
Pope to Spence

Sir Godfrey Kneller painted forty-two portraits of the club members for Jacob Tonson, the secretary, whose villa was at Barn Elms, where latterly the club was held In order to accommodate the paintings to the height of the club-room, he was obliged to make them three-quarter lengths (28 in by 36 in), hence a three-quarter portrait is still called a *kit-cat* The set of portraits is now in the National Portrait Gallery, London.

Kit's Coty House. A great cromlech, 3½ m. N.W of Maidstone on the Rochester road. consisting of a vast block of sandstone resting on three other blocks It is near the ancient battlefield of Aylesford, where the Saxons under Hengist and Horsa fought the Britons, whose chieftain was, according to the Chronicles, named Catigern, and some authorities derive the name from him The dolmen is undoubtedly much older than his day, and the name may be British for "the tomb in the woods" (Wel. *coed*, a wood)

Kitchen. An old term, still used in some parts of rural Scotland, for a cooked relish as toasted cheese, eggs, sausages, bacon, etc

Kitchen-middens. Prehistoric mounds (referred to the Neolithic Age) composed of seashells, bones, kitchen refuse, rude stone implements, and other relics of early man. They were first noticed on the coast of Denmark, but have since been found in the British Isles, North America, etc.

Kite. In lawyer's slang, a junior counsel who is allotted at an assize court to advocate the cause of a prisoner who is without other defence

In R A.F. slang, any aircraft.

In Stock Exchange slang, a worthless bill.

To fly the kite. To "raise the wind" by questionable methods, such as by sending begging letters to persons of charitable reputation or by means of worthless bills.

Kiwanis (kı wa′ nıs). An organization founded in U S.A. in 1915 aiming to improve business ethics and provide leadership for raising the level of business and professional ideals There are many Kiwanis clubs in U.S.A and Canada.

Kiwi (kē′ wē) A New Zealand bird incapable of flight. In flying circles the word is applied to a man of the ground staff at an aerodrome In Australia it is often used to denote a New Zealander

Klepts (Gr, robbers) The name given to those Greeks who, after the conquest of their country by the Turks in the 15th century, refused to submit and maintained their independence in the mountains. They degenerated—especially after the War of Independence (1821-28)—into brigands, hence the word is often used for a lawless bandit or brigand.

Klondike (klon′ dık). A river and district of Yukon Territory in Canada In 1896 placer gold was discovered in the creeks that flow into the river and for some years much gold was produced. The famous Gold Rush took place 1897-98.

Knave (A S. *cnafa*, Ger. *knabe*) Originally merely a boy or male-child, then a male servant or one in low condition and finally—its present sense—an unprincipled and dishonourable rascal

The tyme is come, a knave-child she ber;
Mauricius at the font-stoon they him calle
CHAUCER *Man of Lawe's Tale*, 722.

And sche bare a knave child that was to reulynge alle folkis in an yrun gherde (*Auth Ver* —And she brought forth a man child, who was to rule all nations with a rod of iron) —*Wyclif's Bible. Rev.* xii, 5.

In cards the *knave* (or *jack*), the lowest court card of each suit, is the common soldier or servant of the royalties.

He lived like a knave, **and died like a fool.** Said by Warburton of Henry Rich, first Earl of Holland (1590-1649), the turncoat. He went to the scaffold dressed in white satin, trimmed with silver.

Knave of hearts. A flirt.

Knee. Knee tribute. Adoration or reverence, by prostration or bending the knee *Cp* LIP-SERVICE.

Coming to receive from us
Knee-tribute yet unpaid, prostration vile.
MILTON: *Paradise Lost*, v, 782

Weak-kneed. Irresolute, not thorough; as, *a weak-kneed Christian*, a Laodicean, neither hot nor cold

Kneph. Another name of the Egyptian god Amen-Ra (*q v*).

Knickerbockers, or **Knickers.** Loose-fitting breeches, gathered in below the knee, and worn by boys, cyclists, sportsmen, tourists, etc, and by women as an undergarment So named from George Cruikshank's illustrations of *Knickerbocker's History of New York*, a burlesque published in 1809 by Washington Irving, where the Dutch worthies are drawn with very loose knee-breeches. The name *Knickerbacker* is found among the old Dutch inhabitants of

New York a century and more earlier, it probably signified a *baker* of *knickers, i e.* clay marbles.

Knife. The emblem of St Agatha, St. Albert, and St. Christina

The **flaying knife** is the emblem of St. Bartholomew, because he was flayed.

He is a capital knife-and-fork, he has a good appetite

War to the knife. Deadly strife.

Knifeboard. The long, back-to-back benches that used to run longitudinally down the middle of the roof of the old horse omnibuses In the 'nineties of last century transverse "garden seats" gradually took their place The allusion is to the board covered with knife-powder on which steel table knives were made bright

Knight (A S *cniht*). Originally meaning merely a boy or servant, the word came to denote a man of gentle birth who, after serving at court or in the retinue of some lord as a page and esquire, was admitted with appropriate ceremonies to an honourable degree of military rank and given the right to bear arms.

The **Knight, or Knight Bachelor,** of to-day is a commoner who is the possessor of a personal and non-hereditary dignity conferred by the sovereign, carrying with it the prefix "Sir" and a place in the Table of Precedence next above County Court Judges and next below Knight Commanders of the Order of the British Empire The wife of a Knight is usually entitled "Lady" or "Dame," but this, as in the case of Baronets, is a matter of courtesy only, not of right

There are nine *Orders of Knighthood* in the British Empire, viz (in the following order of precedence) the Garter, the Thistle, St. Patrick, the Bath, the Star of India, St Michael and St George, the Indian Empire, the Royal Victorian Order, and the British Empire After these come the Knights Bachelor, who are members of no Order and who do not constitute an order *Bachelor* here is Fr *bas chevalier,* signifying "lower than the Knight of an order."

The word *knight* is used in various slang or jocular phrases denoting a member of some trade or profession, follower of some calling or occupation, etc Thus we have *Knight of the blade,* a roystering bully, *Knight of the cleaver,* a butcher, *Knight of the cue,* a billiard player, *Knight of the needle,* a tailor, *Knight of the pestle,* a druggist, *Knight of the road,* a footpad, *Knight of the spigot,* a tapster, *Knight of the wheel,* a cyclist, etc , etc.

Cross-legged Knights. *See* CROSS-LEGGED.

Knight Bachelor. *See* KNIGHT, *above*

Knight Banneret. *See* BANNERET

Knight Baronet. The title originally given to Baronets (*q.v.*) when the degree was instituted by James I in 1611.

Knights of Columbus A Roman Catholic fraternal and philanthropic society in U S A , founded in 1882 with the aim of uniting lay-men of the Church in corporate religious and civic unity and usefulness.

Knight errant. A mediæval knight, especially a hero of those long romances satirized by Cervantes in *Don Quixote,* who wandered about the world in quest of adventure and in search of opportunities of rescuing damsels in distress and performing other chivalrous deeds.

It seemed unto him [Don Quixote] very requisite and behooveful that he himself should become a knight-errant, and go throughout the world, with his horse and armour, to seek adventures, and practise in person all that he had read was used by knights of yore, revenging all kinds of injuries, and offering himself to occasions and dangers, which, being once happily achieved, might gain him eternal renown — CERVANTES *Don Quixote (Shelton's tr* 1612)

Knight Marshal. *See* MARSHALSEA.

Knight of Grace. A member of the lower order of the Knights of Malta *See* MALTA

Knight of industry. Slang for a sharper, one who lives on his wits.

Knight of the post. A man who had stood in the pillory or had been flogged at the whipping-post was so called, hence, one who haunted the purlieus of the courts, ready to be hired for a bribe to give false witness, go bail for a debtor for pay, etc.

"A knight of the post," quoth he, "for so I am termed, a fellow that will sweare you anything for twelve pence "—NASH *Pierce Penilesse* (1592)

These perjured knaves be commonly old knightes of the post, that are foisted off from being taken for bale at the king's bench, or other places, and seeing for open perjuries they are refused there, they take that course of life —GREENE· *Second Part of Cony-catching* (1591).

The Knight of the Rueful Countenance. *Don Quixote* (*q v*).

Knight of the Shire. The old name for one of the two gentlemen of the rank of knight who represented a county or shire in the English Parliament, a member elected by a county, in contradistinction to a borough member.

Knight of the square flag A knight banneret, in allusion to cutting off the points of his pennon when he was raised to this rank on the battlefield

The Knight of the Swan. Lohengrin (*q.v.*).

Knight service. The tenure of land, under the feudal system, on the condition of rendering military service to the Crown.

Knight's fee. The amount of land for which, under the feudal system, the services of a knight were due to the Crown. There was no fixed unit, some were larger than others; William the Conqueror created 60,000 such fees when he came to England, and in his time all who had £20 a year in lands or income were compelled to be knights

Knights of Labour. An organization of working men, founded at Philadelphia in 1869. At first secret, it later emerged to play an important part in the American Trade Union movement Its objects were to regulate wages, hours of work, etc , and to control strikes. It secured the establishment of Labour Day (*q.v.*) as a national holiday In the early 20th century it ceased to exist, being unable to compete with the more powerful American Federation of Labour (founded 1886).

Knights of the Round Table. *See* ROUND TABLE

Knights of Windsor. A small order of knights, originally founded by Edward III in 1349 as the "Poor Knights of the Order of the Garter." It was at first formed of 26 veterans, but since the time of Charles I the numbers have been fixed at 13 for the Royal Foundation and 5 for the Lower (since abolished) with a Governor. The members are retired meritorious military officers. They are granted apartments in Windsor Castle and pensions ranging from £50 to £130 a year They must be in residence for at least nine months in the year, must attend St. George's Chapel on saints' days, and occasionally act as guards of honour. Their present uniform was assigned by William IV, who made their title the "Military Knights of Windsor", and their early connexion with the Order of the Garter is still retained in many ways, as, for instance, every K G on appointment has to give a sum of money for distribution among them, and the Sovereign appoints members in his capacity as head of the Order of the Garter.

Knights Templar. *See* TEMPLAR.

Knightenguild. The Guild of thirteen "cnihts" (probably youthful scions of noble houses attached to the court) to which King Edgar, or, according to other accounts, Canute, gave that easternmost portion of the City of London now called *Portsoken Ward*, on the following conditions. (1) Each knight was to be victorious in three combats—one on the earth, and one under, and one in the water; and (2) each was, on a given day, to run with spears against all comers in East Smithfield. William the Conqueror confirmed the same unto the heirs of these knights, whose descendants, in 1125, gave all the property and their rights to the newly founded Priory of Holy Trinity

Knipperdollings (nip er dol' ingz) A sect of 16th-century German Anabaptists, so called from their leader, Bernard Knipperdolling, who was active about 1530-35, and was one of the leaders of the insurrection of Münster

Knock, To. Slang for to create a great impression, to be irresistible; as in Albert Chevalier's song, "Knocked 'em in the Old Kent Road" (1892), i e astonished the inhabitants, filled them with admiration

To knock about or **around.** To wander about town "seeing life" and enjoying oneself

A knock-about turn. A music-hall term for a noisy, boisterous act in which (usually) a couple of red-nosed comedians indulge in violent horseplay

Knock-kneed. With the knees turned inwards so that they knock together in walking

To be knocked into a cocked hat, or into the middle of next week. To be thoroughly beaten. *See* COCKED.

To get the knock (or **the nasty knock**). To have a blow (actual or figurative) that finishes one off.

To knock out of time. To settle one's hash for him, double him up The phrase is from pugilism, and refers to disabling an opponent so that he is unable to respond when the referee calls "Time "

To knock spots off someone or **something** To beat him soundly, get the better of it, do the job thoroughly The allusion is probably to pistol-shooting at a playing-card, when a good shot will knock out the pips or spots.

To knock the bottom or **the stuffing out of anything.** To confound, bring to naught, especially to show that some argument or theory is invalid and "won't hold water."

To knock under. To acknowledge oneself defeated, in argument or otherwise, to knuckle under. Perhaps from the old custom of a disputant who gets the worst of it tapping the under side of the table or from the habit, in hard-drinking days, of subsiding under the table

> He that flinches his Glass, and to Drink is not able,
> Let him quarrel no more, but knock under the table.
> *Gentleman's Journal. March,* 1691-2.

Knock-out. Primarily, a disabling blow, especially (in pugilism) one out of guard on the point of the chin, which puts the receiver to sleep and so finishes the fight Hence, a complete surprise is "a fair knock-out."

In the auction room a *knock-out* is a sale at which a ring of dealers combine to keep prices artificially low, so that they obtain the goods and afterwards sell them among themselves, dividing the profits.

Knockers. Goblins, or kobolds (*q* v.), who dwell in mines, and indicate rich veins of ore by their presence In Cardiganshire and elsewhere miners attribute the strange noises so frequently heard in mines to these spirits.

Knot. (Lat. *nodus*, Fr *næud*, Dan *knude*, Dut *knot*, A S *cnotta*, allied to *knit*)

He has tied a knot with his tongue he cannot untie with his teeth. He has got married He has tied the marriage-knot (*q* v) by saying, "I take thee for my wedded wife," etc , but it is not to be untied so easily

Gordian knot. *See* GORDIAN.

Knots of May. *See* NUT

She was making 15 knots. The measurement of speed for ocean-going vessels is the knot, i.e. the speed of one mile in one hour; 15 knots is therefore the rate of 15 nautical miles an hour The log-line is divided into lengths by knots, and is run out while a sand-glass runs for either 28 or 30 seconds.

True lovers' knot. Sir Thomas Browne thinks the knot owes its origin to the *nodus Herculanus*, a snaky complication in the caduceus or rod of Mercury, in which form the woollen girdle of the Greek brides was fastened (*Pseudodoxia Epidemica,* V, XXII)

To seek for a knot in a rush Seeking for something that does not exist Not a very wise phrase, seeing there are jointed rushes, probably not known when the proverb was first current

Knotgrass. This grass, *Polygonum aviculare*, was formerly supposed, if taken in an infusion, to stop growth

> Get you gone, you dwarf;
> You minimus, of hindering knotgrass made
> *Midsummer Night's Dream*, iii, 2

The child's a fatherless child, and say they should put him into a straight pair of gaskins (breeches], 'twere worse than knot-grass; he would never grow after it —BEAUMONT AND FLETCHER *Knight of the Burning Pestle*, ii, 2

Knout (Russ., *knut*, probably connected with *knot*). A long, hard leather thong or a knotted bunch of thongs formerly used in Russia for corporal punishment on prisoners, hence, a symbol of supremely autocratic rule

Know Thyself. The admonition of the oracle of Apollo at Delphi, also attributed (by Diogeneus Laertius, i, 40) to Thales, also to Solon the Athenian lawgiver, Socrates, Pythagoras, and others

Know-Nothings. A secret political society in the U S.A , also called the "American party." It arose in 1853, and its members replied to every question about their society, "I know nothing about it " Their object was to accomplish the repeal of the naturalization laws, and of the law which excluded all but natives from holding office It split on the slavery question and died out in 1859

Knuckle. To knuckle under. To acknowledge oneself beaten, to sue for pardon; in allusion to the old custom of striking the under side of a table with the knuckles when defeated in an argument. *Cp* To KNOCK UNDER

To knuckle down to. To submit to

To knuckle down to it. To work away at it, heart and soul, to do one's best.

Knuckle-duster. A brass sheath fitting over the knuckles Its origin goes back to the times of Roman pugilism, but to-day its use is confined to thugs the world over.

Knurr and Spell (nêr, spel) A game resembling trapball, and played with a wooden ball (the *knurr*) which is released by means of a spring from a little brass cup at the end of a tongue of steel called a *spell* or *spill* After the player has touched the spring, the ball flies into the air, and is struck with a bat.

Knut. *See* NUT.

Kobold (kob' ōld). A house-spirit in German superstition, similar to our Robin Goodfellow, and the Scots brownie. Also a gnome who works in the mines and forests.

Kochlani (kok la' ni). Arabian horses of royal stock, of which genealogies have been preserved for more than 2,000 years. It is said that they are the offspring of Solomon's stud. (*Niebuhr*)

Koheleth. *See* ECCLESIASTES.

Koh-i-Nur (kō i nôr) (Pers , mountain of light) A large diamond which, since 1849, has been among the British Crown Jewels It is said to have been known 2,000 years ago, but its authentic history starts in 1304, when it was wrested by the Sultan, Al-eddin, from the Rajah of Malwa. From his line it passed in 1526 to Humaiun, the son of Sultan Baber,

and thence to Aurungzebe (d. 1707), the Mogul Emperor, who used it for the eye of a peacock in his famous peacock throne at Delhi In 1739 it passed into the hands of Nadir Shah, who called it the Koh-i-nur It next went to the monarchs of Afghanistan, and when Shah Sujah was deposed he gave it to Runjit Singh, of the Punjab, as the price of his assistance towards the recovery of the throne of Cabul After Runjit's death (1839) it was kept in the treasury at Lahore, and when the Punjab was annexed to the British Crown, in 1849, it was, by stipulation, presented to Queen Victoria. At this time it weighed 186$\frac{1}{16}$ carats, but after its acquisition it was cut down to 106$\frac{1}{16}$ carats There is a tradition that it always brings ill luck to its possessor.

Kohl or **Kohol** (kōl) Finely powdered antimony, used by women in Persia and the East to blacken the inside of their eyelids.

> And others mix the Kohol's jetty dye
> To give that long, dark languish to the eye
> THOMAS MOORE *Lalla Rookh*, Pt i.

Konx Ompax (kongks om' paks). The words of dismissal in the Eleusinian Mysteries. *Konx* is the sound made by a pebble as it falls into the voting urn, *ompax* is a compound of two words meaning *like* or *resembling*, and the Latin *pax* (Ital *basta*) an exclamation of dismissal, signifying that the proceedings have come to an end

Köpenick is a suburb of Berlin and the scene of a famous imposture On October 16th, 1906, a cobbler named Wilhelm Voigt donned the uniform of a captain of a Guards regiment and accompanied by two privates entered the burgomaster's office at Kopenick, appropriated all the cash that happened to be there, and sent the burgomaster, terrified at having committed some unspecified crime, to the guard-house at Berlin in charge of the grenadier guardsman The discovery of the hoax caused a great sensation, chiefly because of the effrontery of anyone daring to make fun of the all-powerful Army.

Koppa. An ancient Greek letter, disused as a letter in classical Greek, but retained as the sign for the numeral 90

Korah. *See* ASAPH.

Koran (ko rän'), or, with the article, *Al Koran*. The bible or sacred book of the Mohammedans, containing the religious, social, civil, commercial, military, and legal code of Islam The Koran, which contains 114 chapters, or *Surahs*, is said to have been communicated to the prophet at Mecca and Medina by the angel Gabriel, with the sound of bells. It is written in Arabic and was compiled from Mohammed's own lips.

Korrigans (kor' i gänz) Nine fays of Breton folklore, who can predict future events, assume any shape they like, move quick as thought from place to place, and cure diseases or wounds

Kosher (kō' sher) A Hebrew word denoting that which is permitted by, or fulfils the requirements of, the law; applied usually to food—especially to meat which has been slaughtered and prepared in the prescribed manner

Kraken (kra´ ken) A sea-monster of vast size, supposed to have been seen off the coast of Norway and on the North American coasts, and probably founded on a hurried observation of one of the gigantic squids or cuttlefish It was first described (1752) by Pontoppidan in his *History of Norway* Pliny speaks of a sea-monster in the Straits of Gibraltar, which blocked the entrance of ships

The shoal called the Shambles at the entrance of Portland Roads was very dangerous before the breakwater was constructed. According to local legend, at the bottom of the gigantic shaft are the wrecks of ships seized and sunk by the huge spider *Kraken*, called also the *fish-mountain*

Kralitz Bible, The. *See* BIBLE, SPECIALLY NAMED

Kratim The dog of the Seven Sleepers. More correctly called Katmir or Ketmir (*q.v.*).

Kremlin, The. A gigantic pile of buildings in Moscow of every style of architecture: Arabesque, Gothic, Greek, Italian, Chinese, etc , enclosed by battlemented and many-towered walls 1½ miles in circuit It contains palaces and cathedrals churches, convents, museums and barracks, arcades and shops, the great bell, and, before the Revolution, the Russian treasury, government offices, the ancient palace of the patriarch, a throne-room, etc. It was built by two Italians, Marco and Pietro Antonio, for Ivan III in 1485 to 1495, but the Great Palace, as well as many other buildings, dates only from the middle of the 19th century, previous palaces, etc , having been destroyed at various times. There had been previously a wooden fortress on the spot As the seat of government of the U S S R. the word "Kremlin" is often used symbolically of that government, just as the Vatican is for the Papacy, or Quai D'Orsay for the French government.

The name is from Russ *kreml*, a citadel, and other towns beside Moscow possess kremlins, but none on this scale.

Kreuzer (kroit´ zer) A small copper coin in Southern Germany and Austria, formerly of silver and marked with a cross (Ger. *kreuz*, Lat. *crux*) It is worth (nominally) one-third of a penny.

Kreig-spiel. *See* WAR GAME

Kriemhild (krēm´ hild) The legendary heroine of the Nibelungenlied (*q v.*), a woman of unrivalled beauty, daughter of the Burgundian, King Gibich, and sister of Gunther, Gernot, and Giselher She first married Siegfried (*q.v.*), and next Etzel (Attila), king of the Huns.

Krishna (krish´ nà) (*the black one*). One of the greatest of the Hindu deities, the god of fire, lightning, storms, the heavens, and the sun, usually regarded as the eighth avatar (*q v*) of Vishnu One story relates that Kansa, demon-king of Mathura, having committed great ravages, Brahma prayed to Vishnu to relieve the world of its distress, whereupon Vishnu plucked off two hairs, one white and the other black, and promised they should revenge the wrongs of the demon-king. The black hair became Krishna.

Another myth says that Krishna was the son of Vasudeva and Devaki, and when he was born among the Yadavas at Mathura, between Delhi and Agra, his uncle, King Kansa, who had been warned by heaven that this nephew was to slay him, sought to kill Krishna, who was, however, smuggled away He was brought up by shepherds, and later killed his uncle and became King of the Yadavas in his stead. He was the Apollo of India and the idol of women. His story is told in the Bhagavadghita and Bhagavatapurana

Kronos or **Cronus** (krō´ nos) One of the Titans of Greek mythology, son of Uranus and Ge, father (by Rhea) of Hestia, Demeter, Hera, Hades, Poseidon, and Zeus He dethroned his father as ruler of the world, and was in turn dethroned by his son, Zeus By the Romans he was identified with Saturn (*q v.*)

Ku Klux Klan (kū klüks klăn) A secret society in the southern U S A. that was founded in Pulaski, Tenn , in 1865, at the close of the Civil War It was originally a social club with a fanciful ritual and uniform that easily terrified the Negroes The organization rapidly increased in numbers and, together with a similar society known as the White Camelias (1867) it overawed the whole black population of the South until 1870 Its policy for securing white supremacy was carried to the most extreme lengths and its murders and terrorism grew so numerous and formidable that in 1871 an Act of Congress was passed suppressing it.

The Ku Klux Klan was fully organized, the whole of the South forming its Invisible Empire under a Grand Wizard Each State was a Realm under a Grand Dragon , a number of counties made a Dominion ruled by a Grand Titan; each county was a Province under a Grand Giant, the Provinces themselves being divided into Dens, each under a Grand Cyclops Private members were called Ghouls and the minor officials had fantastic titles such as Furies, Goblins, Night Hawks, etc.

In 1915 the Knights of the Ku Klux Klan came into existence at Atlanta, Georgia, and in the hysteria following World War I the movement swept the South It admitted to membership only native-born, white, Gentile, Protestant Americans and from 1922 until 1925 it controlled elections and politics in several of the Southern States. But its violent views defeated its own ends and by 1927 the society was moribund.

Kudos (kū´ dos) (Gr., renown) A slang or colloquial phrase for credit, fame, glory.

Kufic (kū´ fik) Ancient Arabic letters , so called from Kufa, a town in the pashalic of Bagdad, noted for expert copyists of the ancient Arabic MSS.

Kufic coins. Mohammedan coins with Kufic or ancient Arabic characters. The first were struck in the eighteenth year of the Hegira (A D. 638)

Kultur (kul tur´). The German system of intellectual, moral, æsthetic, economic, and political progress, which is characterized by the subordination of the individual to the State, and through the power of which it was hoped that "kultur" would be imposed on the rest of the world

It does not mean the same as English *culture*, which is translated by *bildung*

Kulturkampf In German history, the long and bitter struggle (G● *kampf*) which took place in the 'seventies of last century between Bismarck and the Vatican, with the idea of ensuring the unity of the new Empire and protecting the authority of its government against outside interference Many laws were passed against the Catholic hierarchy, but political complications very soon brought about the repeal of the more oppressive, and the Catholics were left practically in their old position.

Kuomintang (kwō' min' tăng'). A Chinese political party formed by Sun Yat-sen in 1912 on the foundation of the Chinese Republic. A combination of several political groups, it came into power in 1927 under the leadership of General Chiang Kai-shek The three Chinese words mean "nation," "people," "party" and may be translated as "National Party"

Kurma. *See* AVATAR.

Kursaal (kur' sal) (Ger *kur*, cure, *saal*, room). A public room or building for the use of visitors, especially at German watering places and health resorts

Kuru (koo' roo). A noted legendary hero of India, the contests of whose descendants form the subject of two Indian epics He was a prince of the lunar race, reigning over the country round Delhi.

Kyle (kil). The central district of Ayrshire

Kyle for a man, Carrick for a coo [cow],
Cunningham for butter, Galloway for woo' [wool].

Kyle, a strong corn-growing soil; Carrick, a wild hilly portion, only fit for feeding cattle, and Cunningham, a rich dairy land

Kyrie Eleison (ki ri e e li' son) (Gr , "Lord have mercy"). The short petition used in the liturgies of the Eastern and Western Churches, as a response at the beginning of the Mass and in the Anglican Communion Service Also, the musical setting for this.

Kyrle Society, The (kĕrl). Founded 1877 for decorating the walls of hospitals, schoolrooms, mission-rooms, cottages, etc., for the cultivation of small open spaces, window gardening, the love of flowers, etc , and improving the artistic taste of the poorer classes. It was named in memory of John Kyrle (1637-1724), Pope's "Man of Ross." *See* Ross.

L

L. This letter, the twelfth of the alphabet, in Phœnician and Hebrew represents an ox-goad, *lamed*, and in the Egyptian hieroglyphic a lioness.

L, for a pound sterling, is the Lat. *libra*, a pound. In the Roman notation it stands for 50, and with a line drawn above the letter, for 50,000.

LL D. Doctor of Laws—*i e* both civil and canon. The double L is the plural, as in MSS , the plural of MS (manuscript), pp , pages, etc.

L.S. Lat. *locus sigilli*, that is, the place for the seal

L S D. Lat *libra* (a pound); *solidus* (a shilling); and *denarius* (a penny), introduced by the Lombard merchants, from whom also we have *Cr.* (creditor), *Dr.* (debtor), *bankrupt*, *do* or *ditto*, etc.

L.S.T. Landing Ship Tank. A form of vessel developed in World War II which was of sufficiently shallow draught to carry its cargo of tanks near enough inshore for them to drive out of the bows, which opened, and get ashore under their own power.

La Belle Sauvage (la bel sō vazh'). The site on the north side of Ludgate Hill occupied by the House of Cassell from 1852 until May 11th, 1941, when the whole area was demolished in an air raid It took its name from the inn that stood there, noted for the dramatic performances that took place in its courtyard in the 16th and early 17th centuries, and as the starting-place for coaches to the eastern counties in the 18th century, and until the advent of railways. As early as 1530 it appears as "The Belle Savage," and in 1555 as " 'la Bell Savage' otherwise 'le Bell Savoy.' " The inn would seem to have been originally called "The Bell," or "The Bell on the Hoop" (the latter was common as part of inn names) and, at some early date, to have been owned by one "Savage", for, in a deed enrolled in the Close Rolls of 1453 John Frensh confirms to his mother Joan Frensh

all that tenement or inn with its appurtenance called Savages ynn, alias vocat "le Belle on the Hope," in the parish of St Bridget in Fleet Street.

(Fleet Street at that time extended up Ludgate Hill as far as the Old Bailey)

La Mancha, the Knight of (la man' cha) Don Quixote de la Mancha, the hero of Cervantes' romance *Don Quixote*. La Mancha, an old province of Spain, is now a part of Ciudad Real

La-di-da (la' dĕ da'). A yea-nay sort of fellow, with no backbone; an affected fop with a drawl in his voice Also used adjectivally, as "in a la-di-da" sort of way.

The phrase was popularized by a song sung by the once-famous Arthur Lloyd, the refrain of which was —

La-di-da, la-di-do, I'm the pet of all the ladies,
The darlings like to flirt with Captain La-di-da-di-do.

Labarum (lăb' á rum). The standard borne before the Roman emperors. It consisted of a gilded spear, with an eagle on the top, while from a cross-staff hung a splendid purple streamer, with a gold fringe, adorned with precious stones. Constantine substituted a crown for the eagle, and inscribed in the midst the mysterious monogram. *See* CROSS.

Labour Party. One of the great political parties of Great Britain It was founded in 1900 for the express purpose of securing the representation of the working classes in Parliament. At the General Election of 1906 29 out of 50 candidates were successful; in 1924 the first Labour government was formed under Ramsay MacDonald, though it lasted only 9 months.

In 1929 Labour came once again into power; forming a coalition with the Tories in 1931 and itself giving way to a Tory government in 1935. After World War II Labour swept the country in the General Election of 1945, was returned again in 1950 with a majority over all the other parties, and gave way to a Tory government in October 1951.

Labour Day is a legal holiday in the U.S.A. and some provinces of Canada It is held on the first Monday in September "in honour of the labouring class."

The labourer is worthy of his hire (*Luke* x 7). In Latin. *Digna canis pabulo* "The dog must be bad indeed that is not worth a bone." Hence the Mosaic law, "Thou shalt not muzzle the ox that treadeth out the corn"

The Statute of Labourers. An attempt made in 1349 to fix the rate of wages at which labourers should be compelled to work. It followed the "Black Death," and decreed that the men must work for their former employers, and at the old wages

Labyrinth (lăb' ı rinth) A Greek word of unknown (but probably Egyptian) origin, denoting a mass of buildings or garden walks, so complicated as to puzzle strangers to extricate themselves, a maze The maze at Hampton Court, formed of high hedges, is a labyrinth on a small scale. The chief labyrinths of antiquity are:—

(1) The Egyptian, by Petesuchis or Tithoes, near the Lake Mœris It had 3,000 apartments, half of which were underground (1800 B C.).—*Pliny*, xxxvi, 13, and *Pomponius Mela*, 1, 9

(2) The Cretan, by Dædalus, for imprisoning the Minotaur The only means of finding a way out of it was by help of a skein of thread (*See Virgil Æneid*, v)

(3) The Cretan conduit, which had 1,000 branches or turnings.

(4) The Lemnian, by the architects Smilis, Rholus, and Theodorus. It had 150 columns, so nicely adjusted that a child could turn them Vestiges of this labyrinth were still in existence in the time of Pliny

(5) The labyrinth of Clusium, made by Lars Porsena, King of Etruria, for his tomb

(6) The Samian, by Theodorus (540 B C) Referred to by Pliny; by Herodotus, ii, 145, by Strabo, x; and by Diodorus Siculus, i

(7) The labyrinth at Woodstock, built by Henry II to protect Fair Rosamund

Lac of Rupees. One hundred thousand rupees. The nominal value of the Indian rupee is 2s, and at this rate of exchange a lac of rupees is equivalent to £10,000. Its value varies, however, according to the market value of silver.

Lace. I'll lace your jacket for you, beat you, flog you severely. Perhaps a play on the word *lash*.

Laced Mutton. *See* MUTTON.

Tea or coffee laced with spirits, a cup of tea or coffee qualified with brandy or whisky.

Deacon Bearcliff . had his pipe and his teacup the latter being laced with a little spirits.—SCOTT *Guy Mannering*, ch xi.

Lacedæmonians, The. *See* REGIMENTAL NICKNAMES.

Lacedæmonian Letter. The Greek ι (*iota*), the smallest of the letters *See* JOT.

Laches (lăsh' ız) A legal term, from the Old French *laschesse*, meaning negligence, especially any inexcusable delay in making a claim.

Lachesis (lăk' e sis). The Fate who spins life's thread, working into the woof the events destined to occur *See* FATE

Lackadaisical. Affectedly languid, pensive, sentimental The word is an extension of the old *lackadaisy*, which, in its turn, is an extended form of *lackaday!* or *alackaday!* an exclamation of regret, sorrow, or grief

Lack-learning or **Unlearned Parliament** was the name given to the Parliament which met at Coventry in 1404 It was so called because Edward III, in 1372, had directed that no lawyers should be returned to Parliament as members

Laconic (la con' ık). Pertaining to Laconia or Sparta, hence very concise and pithy, for the Spartans were noted for their brusque and sententious speech When Philip of Macedon wrote to the Spartan magistrates, "If I enter Laconia, I will level Lacedæmon to the ground," the ephors sent back the single word, "If." Cæsar's dispatch *Veni, vidi, vici* (*q v*) and Sir Charles Napier's apocryphal "Peccavi" (*q.v*) are well-known examples of laconicisms.

Lacrosse (la kros) A ball game originally played by N. American Indians and now the national game of Canada. The ball is of rubber; it is caught in a net-like racket and thrown through a goal The playing space between the goals varies from 100 to 150 yards; the goal posts at either end are 6 ft. apart and 6 ft high There are twelve players on a side, and the object of the game is to score goals by kicking, striking or carrying the ball on the crosse, in which lies the great art of the game.

Ladas (lă' dăs) Alexander's messenger, noted for his swiftness of foot, mentioned by Catullus, Martial, and others.

Ladon (lă' don) The name of the dragon which guarded the apples of the Hesperides (*q.v*), also of one of the dogs of Actæon

Ladrones (la' drōnz) The island of thieves; so called, in 1519, by Magellan, on account of the thievish habits of the aborigines.

Lady. Literally "the bread-maker," as *lord* (*q v*) is "the bread-guarder" A S *hlæfdige*, from *hlaf*, loaf, and a supposed noun *dige*, a kneader, connected with Gothic *deigan*, to knead The original meaning was simply the female head of the family, the "house-wife."

Ladybird, Ladyfly, or **Ladycow.** The small red coleopterous insect of the genus *Coccinella* with black spots, called also Bishop Barnaby (*q.v*), and, in Yorkshire, the Cushcow Lady.

Lady Bountiful. The benevolent lady of a village The character is from Farquhar's *Beaux Stratagem* (1707).

Lady Chapel The small chapel east of the altar, or behind the screen of the high altar; dedicated to the Virgin Mary.

Lady Day. March 25th, to commemorate the Annunciation of Our Lady, the Virgin Mary It used to be called "St Mary's Day in Lent" to distinguish it from other festivals in honour of the Virgin, which were also, properly speaking, "Lady Days" Until 1752 Lady Day was the legal beginning of the year, and dates between January 1st and that day were shown with the two years, *e g.* January 29th, 1648/9, *i e.* January 29th, 1649.

Lady-killer. A male flirt; a great favourite with the ladies or one who devotes himself to their conquest

Lady Margaret Professor. The holder of the Chair of Divinity, founded in 1502, at Cambridge by Lady Margaret Beaufort (1443-1509), the mother of Henry VII, who also founded Christ's (1505) and St. John's Colleges (1508).

The Lady of England and Normandy. The Empress Maud, or Matilda (1102-67), daughter of Henry I of England, and wife of the Emperor Henry V of Germany The title of *Domina Anglorum* was conferred upon her by the Council of Winchester, April 7th, 1141. (Rymer: *Fœdera,* i.)

Charlotte M. Tucker (1823-93), a writer for children, used the signature "A.L O.E.," meaning "A Lady of England "

The Lady of the Lake. In the Arthurian legends, Vivien, the mistress of Merlin. She lived in the midst of an imaginary lake surrounded by knights and damsels *See* LANCELOT.

In Scott's poem of this name (1810) the lady is Ellen Douglas, who lived with her father near Loch Katrine

The Lady of the Lamp. A name given to Florence Nightingale (1820-1910) because she went the rounds of the hospital wards in the Crimea carrying a lighted lamp.

Our Lady of Mercy. A Spanish order of knighthood, instituted in 1218 by James I of Aragon, for the deliverance of Christian captives amongst the Moors. Within the first six years, as many as 400 captives were rescued by these knights.

Our Lady of the Rock. A miraculous image of the Virgin found by the wayside between Salamanca and Ciudad Rodrigo in 1409.

The Lady of Shallott. *See* SHALLOTT.

Our Lady of the Snows. A fanciful name, given by Kipling in *The Five Nations* (1903) to Canada

Lady's Mantle. *See* ALCHEMILLA.

Lady's Smock. A common name for the Cuckoo-flower or garden cress (*Cardamine pratensis*), also sometimes applied to the convolvulus, Canterbury bells, and other flowers.

> When daisies pied and violets blue
> And lady-smocks all silver-white
> And cuckoo-buds of yellow hue
> Do paint the meadows with delight,
> The cuckoo then, on every tree,
> Mocks married men for thus sings he,
> Cuckoo,
> Cuckoo, cuckoo O, word of fear,
> Unpleasing to a married ear!
> *Love's Labour's Lost*, v, 2

So-called because the flowers are supposed to resemble linen exposed to bleach on the grass

The Ladies' Mile. A stretch of the road on the north side of the Serpentine, Hyde Park, much favoured in Victorian days by "equestriennes." The Coaching and Four-in-Hand Clubs held their meets there in spring.

Ladies' Plate. Formerly, a horse-race in which the riders were women.

Naked Lady. *See* NAKED.

Læstrygones. *See* LESTRIGONS

Lætare Sunday (lē ta' ri) (*i e* Rejoice Sunday, Lat.). The fourth Sunday in Lent, so called from the first word of the Introit, which is from *Is.* lxvi, 10 "*Rejoice* ye with Jerusalem, and be glad with her all ye that love her." It is on this day that the Pope blesses the Golden Rose

It is also known as Mothering Sunday, from the indulgence granted by Mother Church at mid-Lent, or to the old custom of visiting the cathedral or mother church on that day.

Lag. An old English slang term for a convict, especially one under sentence of transportation An *old lag* was a phrase used in Australia to describe a convict who had served his sentence, or a ticket-of-leave man.

Lagado (lá ga' dō) In Swift's *Gulliver's Travels*, the capital of Balnibarbi, celebrated for its grand academy of projectors, where the scholars spend their time in such projects as making pincushions from softened rocks, extracting sunbeams from cucumbers, and converting ice into gunpowder.

Lagan, or **Ligan** (lăg' àn, lig' an). Goods thrown overboard, but marked by a buoy in order to be found again. An Anglo-Fr word, probably connected with Icel. *lagnir*, a sea-net

Lagniappe (lăn yăp') A phrase from the Southern States of U S A meaning a sort of token gift given to a customer with his purchase, by way of compliment or as good measure. The word comes from the Am - Spanish *la ñapa*, the gift.

Laid. The term used in the paper trade for the ribbed appearance in papers, due to manufacture on a mould or by a dandy on which the wires are *laid* side by side instead of being *woven* transversely.

Lais (lā' is). The name of two celebrated Greek courtezans; the earlier was the most beautiful woman of Corinth, and lived at the time of the Peloponnesan War. The beauty of Lais the Second so excited the jealousy of the Thessalonian women that they pricked her to death with their bodkins. She was the contemporary and rival of Phryne and sat to Apelles as a model. Demosthenes tells us that Lais sold her favours for 10,000 (Attic) drachmæ (about £300)

Laissez faire (lā zā făr) (Fr., let alone). The principle of allowing things to look after themselves, especially the policy of non-interference by Government in commercial affairs. The phrase comes from the motto of the mid-18th century "Physiocratic" school of French economists, *Laissez faire, laissez passer* (let us alone, let us have free circulation for our goods), who wished to have all customs duties abolished and thus anticipated the later Free-traders.

Lake Dwellings. Prehistoric human dwellings on certain lakes in Switzerland, Ireland, etc , built on piles at their shallow edges. The remains found in various examples show that they date from the Neolithic and early metallic periods.

Lake School, The. The name applied in derision by the *Edinburgh Review* to Wordsworth, Coleridge, and Southey, who resided in the Lake District of Cumberland and Westmorland, and sought inspiration in the simplicity of nature, it was also applied to the poets who followed them Charles Lamb, Charles Lloyd, and "Christopher North" (John Wilson) are sometimes placed among the "Lake Poets" or "Lakers."

Lakin. By'r lakin. An oath, meaning "By our Ladykin," or Little Lady, where little does not refer to size, but is equivalent to *dear*

By'r lakin, a parlous [perilous] fear.—*A Midsummer Night's Dream*, iii, 1

Laksmi or **Lakshmi.** One of the consorts of the Hindu god Vishnu, and mother of Kama (*q v*). She is goddess of beauty, wealth, and pleasure, and the Ramayana describes her as springing, like Venus, from the foam of the sea

Lalla Rookh (*tulip cheek*) In Thomas Moore's poem of that name (1817), the supposed daughter of Aurungzebe, Emperor of Delhi, betrothed to Aliris, Sultan of Lesser Bucharia.

Lama. The Tibetan word *blama* (*b* silent) for a Buddhist priest or monk The Grand Lama or Dalai Lama (the Sacred Lama) was the ruler of Tibet, under the more or less nominal suzerainty of China. In 1910 he fled to India before an invading Chinese army, was deposed, and Tibet has since been in an unsettled state. The Teshu, or Tashi, Lama is the chief lama of Mongolia. The religion of both Mongolia and Tibet is called Lamaism and is a corrupt form of Buddhism The priests are housed in great monasteries known as lamaseries.

Lamb. In Christian art, an emblem of the Redeemer, in allusion to *John* i, 29, "Behold the Lamb of God, which taketh away the sin of the world."

It is also the attribute of St. Agnes, St. Geneviève, St. Catherine, and St Regina. John the Baptist either carries a lamb or is accompanied by one. It is also introduced symbolically to represent any of the "types" of Christ; as Abraham, Moses, and so on.

Lamb-ale. The "ale," or merry-making formerly given by the farmer when his lambing was over. *Cp.* CHURCH-ALE

Lamb's wool. A beverage consisting of the juice of apples roasted with spiced ale.

The pulpe of the roasted apples, in number foure or five . . . mixed in a wine quart of faire water, laboured together untill it come to be as apples, and ale, which we call lambes wool.—*Johnson's Gerard*, p. 1460

The Vegetable, Tartarian, or Scythian Lamb. The woolly rootstalk of a polypodiaceous fern (*Dicksonia barometz*), found in the Far East, and supposed in mediæval times to be a kind of hybrid animal and vegetable The down is used in India for stanching wounds

And there groweth a maner of Fruyt, as thoughe it weren Gowrdes, and whan thei ben rype, men kutten hem a to, and men fynden with inne a lytylle Best, in Flessche, in Bon and Blode, as though it were a lytylle Lomb, withouten Wolle. And men eten bothe the Frut and the Best, and that is a gret Marveylle.—*Travels of Sir John Mandeville, Kt.* (Mid-14th cent.).

Lambeth. A London district on the South side of the River.

Lambeth Palace. The official residence of the archbishops of Canterbury since 1197. The palace was built by Hubert Walter, Archbishop of Canterbury, 1193-1205. The followers of Wat Tyler raided the palace on June 14th, 1381, destroyed many valuable books and papers and ended by beheading the archbishop, John of Sudbury. The library and chapel were damaged in an air-raid in 1941.

Lambeth Conferences of Church of England bishops from all over the world have been held at intervals since 1867.

Lambeth Walk is a thoroughfare in Lambeth leading from Broad Street to the Lambeth Road. It gave its name to a Cockney dance that became immensely popular in the early 1940s, introduced by Lupino Lane in a show entitled "Me and my Gal."

Lambert's Day, St. September 17th. St. Lambert, a native of Maestricht, lived in the 7th century.

Be ready, as your lives shall answer it,
At Coventry, upon St. Lambert's day.
Richard II, i, 1.

Lamia (lā´ mi a). A female phantom, whose name was used by the Greeks and Romans as a bugbear to children She was a Libyan queen beloved by Jupiter, but robbed of her offspring by the jealous Juno; and in consequence she vowed vengeance against all children, whom she delighted to entice and devour.

. . a troop of nice wantons, fair women, that like to Lamiæ had faces like angels, eies like stars, brestes like the golden front in the Hesperides, but from the middle downwards their shapes like serpents.—GREENE. *A Quip for an Upstart Courtier* (1592)

Witches in the Middle Ages were called *Lamiæ*, and Keats's poem *Lamia* (1820), which relates how a bride when recognized returned to her original serpent form, represents one of the many superstitions connected with the race Keats's story came (through Burton) from Philostratus' *De Vita Apollonii*, Bk. iv In Burton's rendering, the sage Apollonius, on the wedding night—

found her out to be a serpent, a lamia . . . When she saw herself descried, she wept, and desired Apollonius to be silent, but he would not be moved, and thereupon she, plate, house, and all that was in it, vanished in an instant; many thousands took notice of this fact, for it was done in the midst of Greece.—*Anatomy of Melancholy*, Pt. iii, sect. ii, memb i, subsect. i.

Lammas Day (lăm´ as). August 1st; one of the regular quarter days in Scotland, and in England the day on, which, in Anglo-Saxon times, the first-fruits were offered. So called from A S *hlafmæsse*, the loaf-mass. *See also* LLEW LLAW GYFFES.

At latter Lammas. A humorous way of saying "Never."

Lamourette's Kiss (la moo ret´). A term used in France (*baiser Lamourette*) to denote an insincere or ephemeral reconciliation On July 7th, 1792, the Abbé Lamourette induced the different factions of the Legislative Assembly to lay aside their differences and give the kiss of peace, but the reconciliation was unsound and very short-lived.

Lamp   The Lamp of Heaven. The moon. Milton calls the stars "lamps."

> Why shouldst thou . . .
> In thy dark lantern thus close up the stars,
> That Nature hung in heaven, and filled their lamps
> With everlasting oil, to give due light
> To the misled and lonely traveller?
> *Comus*, 200-204.

The Lamp of Phœbus The sun. Phœbus is the mythological personification of the sun.

The Lamp of the Law. Irnerius the Italian jurist was so called. He was the first to lecture on the Pandects of Justinian after their discovery at Amalfi in 1137.

Sepulchral lamps. The Romans are said to have preserved lamps in some of their sepulchres for centuries, and many legends are told of their never dying. In the papacy of Paul III (1534-40) one was found in the tomb of Tullia (Cicero's daughter), which had been shut up for 1,550 years, and at the dissolution of the monasteries a lamp was found which is said to have been burning 1,200 years. Two are preserved in Leyden museum.

> Nor can thy flame immortal burn
> Like monumental fires within an urn
>   T. STANLEY (1625-78).

It smells of the lamp. Said of a literary composition that bears manifest signs of midnight study, one that is over-laboured. In Lat. *olet lucernam.*

Lampadion (lăm pä' di on) The received name of a lively, petulant courtesan, in the later Greek comedy.

Lampoon. A sarcastic or scurrilous personal satire, so called from Fr. *lampons*, let us drink, which formed part of the refrain of a 17th-century French drinking song.

These personal and scandalous libels, carried to excess in the reign of Charles II, acquired the name of lampoons from the burden sung to them "Lampone, lampone, camerada lampone"—Guzzler, guzzler, my fellow guzzler

Lampos and Phæton (lăm' pos, fā' ton) The two steeds of Aurora. One of Actæon's dogs was also called Lampos

Lancasterian (lăn kăs tēr' i ån) Of or pertaining to Joseph Lancaster (1778-1838), an educational reformer who introduced the monitorial system into schools.

Lancastrian (lăn kăs' tri ån) An adherent of the Lancastrian line of kings, or one of these kings (Henry IV, V, VI), who were descended from John of Gaunt, Duke of Lancaster third son of Edward III, as opposed to the *Yorkists*, who sprang from Edmund, Duke of York, Edward III's fourth son. The Lancastrian badge was the red rose and the Yorkist the white.

Lance. An attribute in Christian art of St. Matthew and St. Thomas, the apostles; also of St. Longinus, St. George, St. Adalbert, St Barbara, St. Michael, and several others.

A free lance. One who acts on his own judgment, and not from party motives, a journalist who is not definitely attached to, or on the salaried staff of, any one paper.

The reference is to the Free Companies of the Middle Ages, called in Italy *condottieri,* and in France *compagnies grandes,* which were

free and willing to sell themselves to any master and any cause, good or bad.

Lance-corporal. A private soldier acting as a corporal, usually as a first step to being promoted to that rank. Similarly, a lance-sergeant is a corporal who performs the duties of a sergeant on probation.

Lance-knight. An old term for a foot-soldier, a corruption of *lansquenet* or *lance-quenet,* a German foot-soldier.

Lancers. The dance so called, an amplified kind of quadrille, was introduced by Laborde from Paris in 1836. It is in imitation of military evolutions in which men used lances.

Lancelot du Lac. One of the earliest romances of the Round Table (1494)

Sir Lancelot was the son of King Ban of Brittany, but was stolen in infancy by Vivienne, the Lady of the Lake (*q.v*), she plunged with the babe into the lake (whence the cognomen of *du Lac*), and when her *protége* was grown into man's estate, presented him to King Arthur. Sir Lancelot went in search of the Grail (*q v.*), and twice caught sight of it. Though always represented in the Arthurian romances as the model of chivalry, bravery, and fidelity, Sir Lancelot was the adulterous lover of Guinevere, wife of King Arthur, his friend, and it was through this love that the war, which resulted in the disruption of the Round Table and the death of Arthur, took place.

Land. The Land of Beulah (*Is.* lxii, 4). In *Pilgrim's Progress* it is that land of heavenly joy where the pilgrims tarry till they are summoned to enter the Celestial City

The Land of Cakes. *See* CAKE.

The Land of Nod. To go to the land of Nod is to go to bed. There are many similar puns, and more in French than in English.

The Land o' the Leal. The land of the faithful or blessed, a Scotticism for a hypothetical land of happiness, loyalty, and virtue, hence heaven, as in Lady Nairn's song—

> I'm wearin' awa'
>   To the land o' the leal.

The Land of Promise, or the Promised Land. Canaan, which God promised to give to Abraham for his obedience *See Ex.* xii, 25, *Deut.* ix, 28, etc.

The Land of Steady Habits. A name given to the State of Connecticut, which was the original stronghold of Presbyterianism in America and the home of the notorious Blue Laws (*q v.*)

See how the land lies. See whether things are propitious or otherwise, see in what state the land is that we have to travel over.

Land-damn. A term of uncertain meaning and origin used (possibly inadvertently) by Shakespeare and, apparently, by no one else.

> You are abus'd, and by some putter-on
> That will be damn'd for't, would I knew the villain,
> I would land-damn him.   *Winter's Tale*, ii, 1

Land-hunger. A craving for the ownership of land; also the state in which the progress of a community is retarded because it has not sufficient land with which to support itself

Land League. An association of Irish extremists formed in Ireland in 1879 to agitate for the reduction, or abolition, of rent, introduction of peasant proprietorship, and the settlement of the land question generally.

Land-loupers, vagrants *Louper* is from the Dutch *looper,* to run Persons who fly the country for crime or debt. Louper, loper, loafer, and luffer are varieties of the German *laufer,* a vagrant, a runner

Land-lubber. An awkward or inexpert sailor on board ship

Land Office Business. The U S government in the last century set up offices for the allotment of Government land The rush of citizens to claim land at these offices led to the use of the above phrase, meaning a tremendous amount of business, or a rush of business.

Land-slide. Used metaphorically of a crushing defeat at the polls, or of a complete reversal of the votes.

Landau (lăn dō). A four-wheeled carriage, the top of which may be thrown back, first made at Landau, in Bavaria, in the 18th century.

Landscape. A country scene, or a picture representing this The word comes from Dutch *scape* being connected with our *shape,* and the A S. *scap-an,* to shape, to give a form to The old word in English was *Landskip.*

Father of landscape gardening André Lenôtre (1613-1700)

Landwehr (lănd' văr), in Germany and Switzerland, troops composed of men in civil life who have had an army training and are liable to be called to the colours in times of national emergency

Lane. 'Tis a long lane that has no turning. Every calamity has an ending

> Hope peeps from a cloud on our squad,
> Whose beams have been long in deep mourning;
> 'Tis a lane, let me tell you, my lad,
> Very long that has never a turning.
> PETER PINDAR　*Great Cry and Little Wool,* epist 1.

Lang Syne (*Scots,* long since). In the olden time, in days gone by.

Auld Lang Syne, usually attributed to Robert Burns, is really a new version by him of a very much older song in Watson's Collection (1711) it is attributed to Francis Sempill (d 1682), but it is probably even older Burns says in a letter to Thomson, "It is the old song of the olden times, which has never been in print. . . . I took it down from an old man's singing," and in another letter, "Light be the turf on the heaven-inspired poet who composed this glorious fragment "

Language. Language was given to men to conceal their thoughts　*See* SPEECH

The three primitive languages. The Persians say that Arabic, Persian, and Turkish are three primitive languages. Legend has it that the serpent that seduced Eve spoke Arabic, the most suasive language in the world, that Adam and Eve spoke Persian, the most poetic of all languages, and that the angel Gabriel spoke Turkish, the most menacing

Langue d'oc ; langue d'oïl (lang dok , lang do il). The former is the old Provençal language, spoken on the south of the River Loire, the latter Northern French, spoken in the Middle Ages on the north of that river, the original of modern French So called because our "yes" was in Provençal *oc* (from Latin *hoc illud*) and in the northern speech *oïl* (*oui*).

Lansquenet. *See* LANCE-KNIGHT.

Lantedo *See* ADELANTADO.

Lantern In Christian art, the attribute of St Gudule and St Hugh

A la lanterne! Hang him from the lamp-post! A cry and custom introduced into Paris during the French revolution Many of the street lamps in old Paris were hung from iron brackets very suitable for the purpose.

Lantern jaws. Cheeks so thin and hollow that one may almost see daylight through them, as light shows through the horn of a lantern.

The feast of lanterns. A popular Chinese festival, celebrated at the first full moon of each year Tradition says that the daughter of a famous mandarin one evening fell into a lake. The father and his neighbours went with lanterns to look for her, and happily she was rescued In commemoration thereof a festival was ordained, and it grew in time to be the celebrated "feast of lanterns."

Lantern Land. The land of literary charlatans, pedantic graduates in arts, doctors, professors, prelates, and so on ridiculed as "Lanterns" by Rabelais (with a side allusion to the divines assembled in conference at the Council of Trent) in his *Pantagruel,* v, 33, *Cp.* CITY OF LANTERNS

Laocoon (lā ok' ō on) A son of Priam and priest of Apollo of Troy, famous for the tragic fate of himself and his two sons, who were crushed to death by serpents while he was sacrificing to Poseidon, in consequence of his having offended Apollo The group representing these three in their death agony, now in the Vatican, was discovered in 1506, on the Esquiline Hill (Rome) It is a single block of marble, and is attributed to Agesandrus, Athenodorus, and Polydorus of the School of Rhodes in the 2nd century B.C. It has been restored

Lessing called his treatise on the limits of poetry and the plastic arts (1766) *Laocoon* because he uses the famous group as the peg on which to hang his dissertation

> Since I have, as it were, set out from the Laocoon, and several times return to it, I have wished to give it a share also in the title —*Preface*

Laodamia (lā ō dăm I' ā) The wife of Protesilaus, who was slain before Troy She begged to be allowed to converse with her dead husband for only three hours, and her request was granted; when the respite was over, she voluntarily accompanied the dead hero to the shades. Wordsworth has a poem on the subject (1815)

Laodicean (lā ō di sē' an) One indifferent to religion, caring little or nothing about the matter, like the Christians of that church, mentioned in the book of *Revelation* (iii, 14-18).

Lapithæ (lăp´ĭ thē). A people of Thessaly, noted in Greek legend for their defeat of the Centaurs at the marriage-feast of Hippodamia, when the latter were driven out of Pelion The contest was represented on the Parthenon, the Theseum at Athens, the Temple of Apollo at Basso, and on numberless vases.

Lapsus Linguæ (lăp´sus ling´gwē) (Lat) A slip of the tongue, a mistake in uttering a word, an imprudent word inadvertently spoken

We have also adopted the Latin phrases *lapsus calami* (a slip of the pen), and *lapsus memoriæ* (a slip of the memory).

Laputa (la pū´ta) The flying island inhabited by scientific quacks, and visited by Gulliver in his "travels" These dreamy philosophers were so absorbed in their speculations that they employed attendants called "flappers," to flap them on the mouth and ears with a blown bladder when their attention was to be called off from "high things" to vulgar mundane matters.

Lapwing. Shakespeare refers to two peculiarities of this bird · (1) to allure persons from its nest, it flies away and cries loudest when farthest from its nest, and (2) the young birds run from their shells with part thereof still sticking to their heads.

> Far from her nest the lapwing cries away
> *Comedy of Errors*, iv, 2.
> This lapwing runs away with the shell on his head.
> —*Hamlet*, v, 2

The first peculiarity, referred to in Ray's *Proverbs*, as well as by other dramatists and also by Shakespeare himself in other passages, made the lapwing a symbol of insincerity, and the second that of a forward person, one who is scarcely hatched.

> *Giov*   If I live,
> I'll charge the French foe in the very front
> Of all my troops, the foremost man.
> *Fran. de Med*   What! What!
> *Giov* . And will not bid my soldiers up, and follow,
> But bid them follow me
> *Brach.* Forward lapwing!
> He flies with the shell on's head.
> WEBSTER. *The White Devil*, ii, 1.

Lar. *See* LARES.

Larboard. *See* STARBOARD.

Larder. A place for keeping bacon (Lat. *laridum*), from O Fr. *lardier* or *lardoir*, a storeroom for bacon This shows that swine were the chief animals salted and preserved in olden times.

The Douglas Larder. The English garrison and all its provisions in Douglas Castle, Lanark, seized by "the Good" Lord James Douglas, in 1307.

> He caused all the barrels containing flour, meat, wheat, and malt to be knocked in pieces, and their contents mixed on the floor, then he staved the great hogsheads of wine and ale, and mixed the liquor with the stores, and last of all, he killed the prisoners, and flung the dead bodies among this disgusting heap, which his men called, in derision of the English, "The Douglas Larder"—SCOTT. *Tales of a Grandfather*, ix

Robin Hood's Larder. *See* OAKS.

Wallace's Larder is very similar to Douglas's. It consisted of the dead bodies of the garrison of Ardrossan, in Ayrshire, cast into the dungeon keep. The castle was surprised by Wallace in the reign of Edward I

Lares and Penates. Used as a collective expression for home, and for those personal belongings that make home homely and individual In ancient Rome the *lares* (sing *lar*) were the household gods, usually deified ancestors or heroes, the *penates* were also guardian deities of the household (and the State), but were more in the nature of personifications of the natural powers, their duty being to bring wealth and plenty rather than to protect and ward off danger The *Lar familiaris* was the spirit of the founder of the house, which never left it, but accompanied his descendants in all their changes

Large. A vulgarism for excess, as That's all very fine and large, that's a trifle steep, "coming it a bit thick," etc , *To talk large*, to brag, "swank" in conversation, talk big, *a large order*, an exaggerated claim or statement, a difficult undertaking

To sail large. A nautical phrase for to sail with the wind not straight astern, but "abaft the beam."

Set at large. At liberty It is a French phrase, *prendre la large* is to stand out to sea, or occupy the main ocean, so as to be free to move Similarly, to be set at large is to be placed free in the wide world.

Lark A spree or frolic The word is a modern adaptation (about 1800) of the dialectal *lake*, sport, from M E *laik*, play, and A S *lac*, contest. *Skylark*, as in *skylarking* about, etc , is a still more modern extension Hood plays on the two words—for the name of the bird, the old *laverock*, A S. *laferce*, is in no way connected with this—in his well-known lines:

> So, Pallas, take thine owl away
> And let us have a lark instead'

When the sky falls we shall catch larks. *See* SKY.

Larrikin (lă´ri kin). An Australian term dating from the early 19th century used to describe a young ruffian given to brutal lawlessness. These lads formed a recognized stratum of society in the country They flourished particularly in the 1880s, had their own language and their own style of dress which, oddly enough, was recognizable by its excessive neatness and severe colours. Larrikins still exist, they are obviously distant relatives of the Glasgow corner-boy who spends all his money on dress and carries a razor in his pocket. They are also known as *pushers*, and *currency lads*

Larvæ. A name among the ancient Romans for malignant spirits and ghosts. The *larva* or ghost of Caligula was often seen (according to Suetonius) in his palace

> [Fear] sometimes representeth strange apparitions, as their fathers and grandfathers ghosts, risen out of their graves, and in their winding-sheets . and to others it sometimes sheweth Larves, Hobgoblins, Robbingood-fellowes, and such other Bug-beares and Chimeraes —*Florio's Montaigne*, I, xvii

Lascar. An East Indian sailor employed on European vessels The natives of the East Indies call camp-followers *lascars* (Hindu *lashkar*, a soldier)

Last. Last Light. *See* FIRST LIGHT

Last Man, The. Charles I was so called by the Parliamentarians, meaning that he would be the last king of Great Britain His son, Charles II, was called *The Son of the Last Man.*

Last of the Barons, The Another name given to Warwick, the King-maker (*q v*)

Last of the Fathers, The. St. Bernard (1091-1153), Abbot of Clairvaux

Last of the Goths, The Roderick, who was the last of the kings of the Visigoths in Spain, and died in 711 Southey has a tale in blank verse on him.

Last of the Greeks, The. The general, Philopœmen of Arcadia (253-183 B C)

Last of the Knights, The. The Emperor Maximilian I (1459-1519)

Last of the Romans. A title, or sobriquet, given to a number of historical characters, among whom are—
Marcus Junius Brutus (85-42 B C), one of the murderers of Cæsar.
Caius Cassius Longinus (d 42 B C), so called by Brutus
Stilicho, the Roman general under Theodosius
Aetius, the general who defended the Gauls against the Franks and other barbarians, and defeated Attila near Châlons in 451. So called by Procopius
François Joseph Terasse Desbillons (1711-89), a French Jesuit, so called from the elegance and purity of his Latin.
Pope called Congreve *Ultimus Romanorum,* and the same title was conferred on Dr. Johnson, Horace Walpole, and C J Fox.

Last of the Saxons, The King Harold (1022-66), who was defeated and slain at the Battle of Hastings

Last Supper. Leonardo da Vinci's famous picture of this was painted on a wall of the refectory of the convent of Santa Maria delle Grazie, Milan, in 1494-97. The artist varied the normal tempera with a formula of his own which was not a success, hence the painting wore badly with time Although the refectory was reduced to ruins by Allied bombs in August, 1943, the wall on which the Last Supper is painted remained practically unharmed—the picture itself quite undamaged It is now hermetically sealed behind glass and thermostatically controlled to prevent further deterioration.

Last of the Tribunes, The. Cola di Rienzi (1314-54), who led the Roman people against the barons

Last of the Troubadours, The. Jacques Jasmin, of Gascony (1798-1864)

Last Words. *See* DYING SAYINGS.

La Tene (la tän), or The Shallows is a site at the eastern end of the Lake of Neuchatel, Switzerland, where extensive remains of the Second Iron Age have been found. It was discovered when the level of the lake was lowered, and a number of weapons, ornaments,

B.D.—18

pieces of jewellery, etc , from about 550 B C until the Christian era were brought to light.

Lateran (lăt′ e răn) The ancient palace of the Laterani, which was appropriated by Nero and later given by the Emperor Constantine to the popes Fable derives the name from *lateo*, to hide, and *rana*, a frog, and accounts for it by saying that Nero once vomited a frog covered with blood, which he believed to be his own progeny, and had it hidden in a vault. The palace built on its site was called the "Lateran," or the palace of the *hidden frog.*

Lateran Council Name given to each of the five œcumenical councils held in the Lateran Church at Rome They are (1) 1123, held under Calixtus II, it confirmed the Concordat of Worms, (2) 1139, when Innocent II condemned Anacletus II and Arnold of Brescia, (3) 1179, under Alexander III; it was concerned with the election of popes, (4) 1215, when Innocent III condemned the Albigenses, and (5) 1512-17, under Julius II and Leo X, when the Canons of the Council of Pisa were abrogated
The locality in Rome so called contains the Lateran palace, the Piazza, and the Basilica of St John Lateran The Basilica is the Pope's cathedral church. The palace (once a residence of the popes) is now a museum

Lateran Treaty, a treaty concluded between the Holy See and the Kingdom of Italy in 1929, granting the Pope jurisdiction over territory on the right bank of the Tiber, to be known as Vatican City Thus ended the sixty-years' quarrels between the Papacy and the State, and the "Roman Question" was finally answered

St. John Lateran is called the *Mother and Head of all Churches* It occupies part of the site of the palace, which was escheated to the Crown through treason, and given to the Church by the Emperor Constantine.

Lathe. An old division of a county, containing a number of hundreds The term is now confined to Kent, which is divided into five *lathes.* In Sussex similar county divisions are called *rapes*
Spenser, in his *Description of Ireland* (1596), uses *lathe* or *lath* for the division of a hundred.—
If all that tything failed, then all that lath was charged for that tything, and if the lath failed, then all that hundred was demanded for them [i e turbulent fellows], and if the hundred, then the shire.

Latin. The language spoken by the ancient inhabitants of Latium, in Italy, and by the ancient Romans Alba Longa was head of the Latin League, and, as Rome was a colony of Alba Longa, it is plain to see how the Roman tongue was Latin
The tale is that the name *Latium* is from *lateo*, to lie hid, and was so called because Saturn lay hid there, when he was driven out of heaven by the gods
According to Roman tradition the Latini were the aborigines, and Romulus and Remus were descended from Lavinia, daughter of their king, Latinus (*q v*).

The earliest known specimen of the Latin language is an inscription of the 5th century B C , or even earlier, found in the Forum in 1899 on a pyramidal stone. This, unfortunately, was broken and the upper half missing; as the lines were written alternately from the bottom upwards and the top downwards, the meaning of the inscription cannot be ascertained

The fragment of a hymn of the Arval Brethren, formerly thought to be very ancient, dates only from the early part of the 3rd cent A D The *hymn* itself, of which this is a corrupt form, is of very great antiquity, but the tablet is comparatively modern. It was discovered in 1778 in the grove of the *Dea Dia*, five miles from Rome on the Via Campana

Classical Latin. The Latin of the best authors of the Golden or Augustan Age (about 75 B C to A D 145), as Livy, Tacitus, and Cicero (prose), Horace, Virgil, and Ovid (poets)

Dog Latin *See* DOG-LATIN

Late Latin. The period which followed the Augustan Age, to about A D 600, it includes the Church Fathers.

Low Latin. Mediæval Latin, mainly early French, Italian, Spanish, and so on

Middle, or Mediæval, Latin Latin from the 6th to the 16th century, both inclusive. In this Latin, prepositions frequently supply the cases of nouns

Thieves' Latin Cant or jargon employed as a secret language by rogues and vagabonds.

The Latin Church. The Western Church, in contradistinction to the Greek or Eastern Church.

The Latin cross. Formed thus · † The Greek cross has four equal arms, thus +.

The Latin races The peoples the basis of whose language is Latin; *i e* the Italians, Spanish, Portuguese, French, Rumanians, etc

Latinus (la tī′ nus). Legendary king of the Latini, the ancient inhabitants of Latium *See* LATIN. According to Virgil, he opposed Æneas on his first landing, but subsequently formed an alliance with him, and gave him his daughter, Lavinia, in marriage Turnus, King of the Rutuli, declared that Lavinia had been betrothed to him; the issue was decided by single combat, and Æneas being victor, obtained Lavinia for his wife and became by her the ancestor of Romulus, the mythical founder of Rome.

Latitudinarians (lăt ɪ tū dɪ nâr′ ɪ anz). A Church of England party in the time of Charles II, opposed both to the High Church party and to the Puritans The term is now applied to those persons who attach little importance to dogma and what are called orthodox doctrines

Latium. *See* LATIN

Latona (la tō′ na). The Roman name of the Greek Leto, mother by Jupiter of Apollo and Diana. Milton, in one of his sonnets, refers to the legend that when she knelt with her infants in arms by a fountain in Delos to quench her thirst, some Lycian clowns insulted her and were turned into frogs

As when those hinds that were transformed to frogs
Railed at Latona's twin-born progeny,
Which after held the sun and moon in fee

Latria and Dulia (lăt′ rɪ a, dū′ lɪ a) Greek words adopted by the Roman Catholics, the former to express that supreme reverence and

adoration which is offered to God alone, and the latter, that secondary reverence and adoration which is offered to saints *Latria* is from the Greek suffix -*latreia*, worship, as in our i*dolatry*, *dulia* is the reverence of a *doulos* or slave Hyperdulia is the special reverence paid to the Virgin Mary

Latter-day Saints. *See* MORMONISM

Lattice. *See* RED LATTICE

Laugh. He laughs best that laughs last. A game's not finished till it's won In Ray's *Collection* (1742) is "Better the last smile than the first laughter," and the French have the proverb *Il rit bien qui rit le dernier*

It's no laughing matter It's really serious, it's no subject for merriment

Laugh and grow fat. An old saw, expressive of the wisdom of keeping a cheerful mind One of the works of Taylor, the Water Poet, has the title *Laugh and be Fat* (about 1625), and in Trapp's *Commentaries* (1647), on 2 *Thess* iii, 11, he says, "Whose whole life is to eat and drink　　and laugh themselves fat "

To have the laugh of one. To be able to make merry at another's expense, generally to that other's surprise and confusion.

To laugh in one's sleeve *See* SLEEVE

To laugh on the wrong, or the other side of one's mouth. To be made to feel vexation and annoyance after mirth or satisfaction, to be bitterly disappointed, to cry

To laugh out of court. To cover with ridicule and so treat as not worth considering

To laugh to scorn. To treat with the utmost contempt

All they that see me laugh me to scorn, they shoot out the lip, they shake the head —*Ps* xxii, 7

Laughing Philosopher. Democritus of Abdera (5th cent. B C), who viewed with supreme contempt the feeble powers of man. *Cp.* WEEPING PHILOSOPHER.

Laughing-stock. A butt for jokes

Launcelot. *See* LANCELOT.

Launfal, Sir (lawn′ fal) One of the Knights of the Round Table His story is told in a metrical romance written by Thomas Chestre in the reign of Henry VI

Laura. The girl of this name immortalized by Petrarch is generally held to have been Laure de Noves, who was born at Avignon in 1308, was married in 1325 to Hugues de Sede, and died of the plague in 1348, the mother of eleven children It was Petrarch's first sight of her, in the church of St Clara, Avignon, on April 6th, 1327 (exactly 21 years before her death) that, he says, made him a poet

Laura (Gr *laura*), an alley An aggregation of separate cells under the control of a superior In monasteries the monks live under one roof, in lauras they live each in his own cell apart, but on certain occasions they assemble and meet together, sometimes for a meal, and sometimes for a religious service

Laureate, Poet *See* POET LAUREATE.

Laurel. The Greeks gave a wreath of laurels to the victor in the Pythian games, but the victor in the Olympic games had a wreath of wild olives, in the Nemean games a wreath of green parsley, and in the Isthmian games a wreath of dry parsley or green pine-leaves

The ancients believed that laurel communicated the spirit of prophecy and poetry. Hence the custom of crowning the pythoness and poets, and of putting laurel leaves under one's pillow to acquire inspiration Another superstition was that the bay laurel was antagonistic to the stroke of lightning, but Sir Thomas Browne, in his *Vulgar Errors*, tells us that Vicomereatus proves from personal knowledge that this is by no means true

Laurel, in modern times, is a symbol of victory and peace, and of excellence in literature and the arts. St Gudule, in Christian art, carries a laurel crown.

Laurin (law' rin) The dwarf-king in the German folk-legend *Laurin*, or *Der Kleine Rosengarten* He possesses a magic ring, girdle, and cap, and is attacked in his rose-garden, which no one may enter on pain of death, by Dietrich of Bern. The poem belongs to the late 13th century, and is attributed to Heinrich von Offerdingen.

Lavender. The earliest form of the word is Med Lat *lιvendula*, and it is probably, like our *lιvid*, from *lιvere*, to make bluish, as, however, the plant has for centuries been used by laundresses for scenting linen, and in connexion with the bath, later forms of the word are associated with *lavare*, to wash. The modern botanical name is *Lavandula* It is a token of affection

> He from his lass him lavender hath sent,
> Showing his love and doth requital crave
>   DRAYTON *Eclogue.*

Laid up in lavender. Taken great care of, laid away, as things are put in lavender to keep off moths.

> The poore gentleman paies so deere for the lavender it is laid up in, that if it lies long at the broker's house he seems to buy his apparel twice.—GREENE *A Quip for an Upstart Courtier* (1592)

Lavinia (läv in' i a) Daughter of Latinus (*q v*). betrothed to Turnus, King of the Rutuli. When Æneas landed in Italy, Latinus made an alliance with the Trojan hero, and promised to give him Lavinia to wife This brought on a war between Turnus and Æneas, which was decided by single combat, in which Æneas was victor (Virgil. *Æneid*, vi)

Shakespeare gives the name to the daughter of Titus Andronicus in the play of that name

Lavolta (la vol' tä) (Ital , the turn) A lively dance, in which was a good deal of jumping or capering, whence its name Troilus says, "I cannot sing, nor heel the high lavolt" (*Troilus and Cressida*, iv, 4). It originated in the 16th century in Provence or Italy, and is thus described —

> A lofty jumping or a leaping round,
> Where arm in arm two dancers are entwined,
> And whirl themselves with strict embracements bound,
> And still their feet an anapest do sound
>   SIR JOHN DAVIES *The Orchestra* (1594)

Law In-laws. A way of referring to one's relations by marriage—mother-in-law, sisters-in-law, etc *In-law* is short for *in Canon law*, the reference being to the degrees of affinity within which marriage is allowed or prohibited

Law-calf A bookseller's term for a special kind of binding in plain sheep or calf used largely for law-books

> Gentlemen who had no briefs to show carried under their arms goodly octavos, with a red label behind, and that underdone-pie-crust-coloured cover, which is technically known as "law calf."—DICKENS *Pickwick Papers*, ch. xxxiv

Law Latin. The debased Latin used in legal documents *Cp* DOG LATIN

Law Lords. Members of the House of Lords who are qualified to deal with the judicial business of the House, i e the Lord High Chancellor, the Lord Chief Justice, the Master of the Rolls, the Lords of Appeal in Ordinary, and such peers as are holding or have held high judicial office

Possession is nine points of the law. See NINE.

Quips of the law *See* CEPOLA

The laws of the Medes and Persians. Unalterable laws.

> Now, O king . sign the writing, that it be not changed, according to the law of the Medes and Persians which altereth not —*Dan* vi, 8

To give one law. A sporting term "law," meaning the chance of saving oneself Thus a hare or a stag is allowed "law"—i e a certain start before any hound is permitted to attack it, and a tradesman allowed "law" is one to whom time is given to "find his legs."

To have the law of one. To take legal proceedings against him.

To lay down the law. To speak in a dictatorial manner, to give directions or order in an offensive and high-handed way.

To take the law into one's own hands. To try to secure satisfaction by force, to punish, reward, etc , entirely on one's own responsibility without obtaining the necessary authority

Law's Bubble. *See* MISSISSIPPI BUBBLE.

Lawless Parliament, The. Another name for the Unlearned Parliament (*q v*).

Lawn. Fine, thin cambric, used for the rochets of Anglican bishops, ladies' handkerchiefs, etc. So called from *Laon* (O.Fr. *Lan*), a town in the Aisne department of France, which used to be famous for its linen factories.

Man of lawn. A bishop.

Lawn-market. The higher end of the High Street, Edinburgh, and the old place for executions, hence, to go **up the Lawn-market,** in Scots parlance, means to go to be hanged.

> Up the Lawn-market, down the West Bow,
> Up the lang ladder, down the short low
>   *Schoolboy Rhyme (Scotland)*

Lawn-tennis. The game of tennis greatly simplified and played on an open lawn It was introduced in England in 1877 and has acquired universal popularity. *See* TENNIS

Lawrence, St. The patron saint of curriers, who was broiled to death on a gridiron. He was deacon to Sixtus I and was charged with the care of the poor, the orphans, and the widows In the persecution of Valerian (258), being summoned to deliver up the treasures of the church, he produced the poor, etc , under his charge, and said to the prætor, "These are the church's treasures." He is generally represented as holding a gridiron, and is commemorated on August 10th

The phrase **Lazy as Lawrence** is said to take its origin from the story that when being roasted over a slow fire he asked to be turned, "for," said he, "that side is quite done " This expression of Christian fortitude was interpreted by his torturers as evidence of the height of laziness, the martyr being too indolent even to wriggle

St. Lawrence's tears or **The fiery tears of St. Lawrence** *See* SHOOTING STARS

Lawyers' Bags. Some red, some blue. In the Common Law, *red* bags are reserved for Q C s, but a stuffgownsman may carry one "if presented with it by a silk " Only *red* bags may be taken into Common Law Courts, *blue* must be carried no farther than the robing-room In Chancery Courts the etiquette is not so strict.

Lay. Pertaining to the people, or laity (Lat. *laicus*) as distinguished from the clergy Thus, a *lay brother* is one who, though not in holy orders, is received into a monastery and is bound by its vows.

A **layman** is, properly speaking, anyone not in holy orders, but the term is also used by professional men—especially doctors and lawyers—to denote one not of their particular profession

Lay figures. Wooden figures with free joints, used by artists chiefly for the study of how drapery falls. The word was earlier *layman*, from Dut *leeman*, a contraction of *ledenman*, i e. led (now lid), a joint, and *man*, man. Horace Walpole uses *layman* (1762), but *lay figure* had taken its place by the end of the 18th century

Lay (the verb). **To lay about one.** To strike out lustily on all sides.

He'll lay about him to-day.—*Troilus and Cressida,* i, 2

To lay it on thick. To flatter or over-praise.

To lay out. (*a*) To disburse.
(*b*) To display goods; place in convenient order what is required for wear.
(*c*) To prepare a corpse for the coffin, by placing the limbs in order, and dressing the body in its grave-clothes

To lay to one's charge. To attribute an offence to a person

And he [Stephen] kneeled down, and cried with a loud voice, Lord lay not this sin to their charge.—*Acts,* vii, 60 The phrase occurs again in the Bible, e g *Deut* xxi, 8, *Rom.* viii, 33, etc.

Laylock. Ancient rustic name for lilac

Lazar House or **Lazaretto.** A house for lazars, or poor persons affected with contagious diseases. So called from the beggar Lazarus (*q v.*)

Lazarillo de Tormes (lăz a ril' yo de tôrm' ez). A romance, something in the *Gil Blas* style, satirizing all classes of society. Lazarillo, a

light, jovial, audacious manservant, sees his masters in their undress, and exposes their foibles It was by Diego Hurtado de Mendoza, general and statesman of Spain, and was published in 1553

Lazarone (lăts ă rō ni) (Ital) Originally applied to Neapolitan vagrants who lived in the streets and idled about, begging, now and then doing odd jobs So called from the hospital of St Lazarus, which served as a refuge for the destitute of Naples Every year they elected a chief, called the *Capo Lazzaro* Masaniello, in 1647, with these vagabonds accomplished a revolution, and in 1798 Michele Sforza, at the head of the Lazzaroni, successfully resisted the French general Championnet

Lazarus (lăz' ă rus) Any poor beggar, so called from the Lazarus of the parable, who was laid daily at the rich man's gate (*Luke* xvi)

Lazy. Lazy as Ludlam's dog, which leaned his head against the wall to bark. Fable has it that Ludlam was a sorceress who lived in a cave near Farnham, Surrey Her dog was so lazy that when the rustics came to consult her it would hardly condescend to give notice of their approach, even with the ghost of a bark. (Ray. *Proverbs*)

Lazy as Lawrence's dog is a similar old saying *See* LAWRENCE.

Lazy-bones. A lazy fellow, a regular idler The expression is some hundreds of years old.

Go tell the Labourers, that the lazie bones
That will not worke, must seeke the beggars gaines.
NICHOLAS BRETON *Pasquil's Madcap* (1600)

Lazy man's load. One too heavy to be carried, so called because lazy people, to save themselves the trouble of coming a second time, are apt to overload themselves

Lazzaroni. *See* LAZARONE.

L'état c'est moi (lā ta sā mwa) (Fr , I am the State) The reply traditionally ascribed to Louis XIV when the President of the Parlement of Paris offered objections "in the interests of the State" to the king's fiscal demands This was in 1655, when Louis was only 17 years of age, on this principle he acted with tolerable consistency throughout his long reign

Le roi (La reine) le veut (Fr , The king (queen) wills it). The form of royal assent to Bills submitted to the Crown. The dissent is expressed by *Le roi (La reine) s'avisera* (the king (queen) will give it his consideration).

Leach. *See* LEECH.

Lead (led) was, by the ancient alchemists, called Saturn.

The *lead*, or *blacklead*, of a *lead* pencil contains no lead at all, but is composed of plumbago or graphite, an almost pure carbon with a touch of iron It was so named in the 16th century, when it was thought to be or to contain the metal

Swinging the lead. Navy slang for concocting a plausible yarn to enable one to malinger.

To strike lead. To make a good hit
That, after the failure of the king, he should "strike lead" in his own house seemed . . an inevitable law.
—BRET HARTE *Fool of Five Forks.*

Leads, The. Famous prison in Venice, in which Casanova was incarcerated and from which he escaped

Lead (lĕd) (the verb.) (A S. *lædan*).

To lead apes in hell. *See* APE.

To lead by the nose. *See* NOSE

To lead one a pretty dance. *See* DANCE

Leader. The first violin of an orchestra, the first cornet of a military band, etc , is called the leader.

Leading article, or **Leader.** A newspaper article by the editor or a special writer. So called because it takes the lead or chief place in the summary of current topics, and expresses the policy of the paper

Leading case. A lawsuit that forms a precedent in deciding others of a similar kind

Leading counsel in a case, the senior counsel on a circuit.

Leading lady or **man** The actress or actor who takes the chief rôle in a play.

Leading note (*music*) The seventh of the diatonic scale, which *leads* to the octave, only half a tone higher

Leading question A question so worded as to suggest an answer "Was he not dressed in a black coat?" leads to the answer "Yes " In cross-examining a witness, leading questions are permitted, because the chief object of a cross-examination is to obtain contradictions

Men of light and **leading.** Men capable of illuminating the way and guiding the steps of others The phrase is Burke's.—

The men of England, the men, I mean, of light and leading in England, . . . would be ashamed   to profess any religion in name, which, by their proceedings, they appear to contemn —*Reflections on the Revolution in France*

But he seems to have derived it from Milton, who, in his *Address to the Parliament*, prefixed to his notes on the *Judgment of Martin Bucer Concerning Divorce*, says :—

I owe no light, or leading received from any man in the discovery of this truth, what time I first undertook it in "the Doctrine and Discipline of Divorce "

Disraeli was rather fond of the phrase. he used it in *Sybil*—"A public man of light and leading" (Bk. v , ch 1)—as well as in speeches.

To be in leading-strings is to be under the control of another Leading-strings are those strings used for holding up infants just learning to walk.

Leaf. Before the invention of paper one of the substances employed for writing upon was the leaves of certain plants The reverse and obverse pages of a book are still called leaves; and the double page of a ledger is termed a "folio," from *folium*, a leaf Cp the derivation of *paper* itself, from *papyrus*, and *book*, from *boc*, a beech-tree There are still extant many ancient MSS. written on palm or other leaves.

To take a leaf out of my book. To imitate me, to do as I do The allusion is to literary plagiarisms

To turn over a new leaf. To amend one's ways, to start afresh.

League The Holy League. Several leagues are so denominated The three following are the most important 1511, by Pope Julius II, Ferdinand the Catholic, Henry VIII, the Venetians, and the Swiss against Louis XII; and that of 1576, founded at Péronne for the maintenance of the Catholic Faith and the exclusion of Protestant princes from the throne of France This league was organized by the Guises to keep Henri IV from the throne. The struggle that ensued formed the subject of Voltaire's epic known first as *La Ligue* and subsequently as *La Henriade*, 1724.

The League of Nations. A league, having headquarters at Geneva, formed after the close of World War I, largely through the exertions of Woodrow Wilson, President of the United States 1913-21, whose action was, however, repudiated by the United States At one time or another some 44 nations were members of the League The League was founded on a Covenant and a Charter of XXVI Articles, the High Contracting Parties agreeing to the Covenant in order to promote International Co-operation and to achieve International Peace and Security, by the acceptance of obligations not to resort to War The final session of the League was on April 18th, 1946, the United Nations having come into existence on the 24th October, 1945.

Leak. To leak out. To come clandestinely to public knowledge As a liquid leaks out of an unsound vessel, so the secret oozes out unawares

To spring a leak. Said of ships, etc., that open or crack so as to admit the water.

Leal Anglo-Fr and O.Fr *leel*, our loyal, trusty, law-abiding; now practically confined to Scotland.

Land of the leal. *See* LAND.

Leander. *See* HERO AND LEANDER.

Leaning Tower. The campanile or bell-tower of the cathedral of Pisa stands apart from the cathedral itself It is 181 ft high, 57½ ft. in diameter at the base, and leans about 14 ft. from the perpendicular. It was begun in 1174 and the sinking commenced during construction Galileo availed himself of the overhanging tower to make his experiments in gravitation At Caerphilly, Glamorganshire, there is a tower which leans 11ft in 80. This was caused by an attempt to blow it up with gunpowder during the Civil Wars.

The Leaning Tower of Pisa continues to stand because the vertical line drawn through its centre of gravity passes within its base —GANOT: *Physics.*

Leap Year A year of 366 days, a *bissextile* year (*q.v*), i e. in the Julian and Gregorian calendars any year whose date is exactly divisible by four except those which are divisible by 100 but not by 400. Thus 1900 (though exactly divisible by 4) was not a leap year, but 2000 will be

In ordinary years the day of the month which falls on Monday this year will fall on Tuesday next year, and Wednesday the year after; but the fourth year will leap over Thursday to Friday This is because a day is added to February, the reason being that the astronomical year (*i e.* the time that it takes the earth to go round the sun) is approximately 365¼ days (365-2422), the difference between ·25 and 2422 being righted by the loss of the three days in 400 years

It is an old saying that during leap year the ladies may propose, and, if not accepted, claim a silk gown. The origin of this cannot now be traced. there is, however, an Act of the Scottish parliament, passed in 1288, which says "it is statut and ordaint that during the rein of hir maist blissit Megeste, for ilke year known as lepe yeare, olk mayden ladye of bothe highe and lowe estait shall hae liberte to bespeke ye man she like, albeit he refuses to taik hir to be his lawful wyfe, he shall be mulcted in ye sum of ane pundis or less, as his estait may be, except and awis gif he can make it appeare that he is betrothit ane ither woman he then shall be free " A few years later than this a somewhat similar law was passed in France In the 15th century the custom was legalized in both Genoa and Florence.

Lear, King. A legendary king of Britain whose story is told by Shakespeare In his old age he divided his kingdom between Goneril and Regan, two of his daughters, who professed great love for him. These two daughters drove the old man mad by their unnatural conduct, while the third, Cordelia (*q v.*), who had been left portionless, succoured him and came with an army to dethrone her two sisters, but was captured and slain in prison. King Lear died over her body.

Camden tells a similar story of Ina, King of the West Saxons The story of King Lear is given in the *Gesta Romanorum* (of a Roman emperor), in the old romance of *Perceforest*, and by Geoffrey of Monmouth in his *Chronicles*, whence Holinshed, Shakespeare's immediate source, transcribed it. Spenser introduced the same story into his *Faerie Queene* (II, x). *See* LIR.

Learn. To learn a person a thing, or to do something is now a provincialism, but was formerly quite good English. Thus, in the Prayer Book version of the *Psalms* we have "Lead me forth in thy truth and learn me," and ' such as are gentle them shall he learn his way" (xxv, 4, 8), and other examples of this use of *learn* as an active verb will be found at *Ps.* cxix, 66 and cxxxii, 13.

> The red plague rid you
> For learning me your language
>   *Tempest*, i, 2

To learn by heart. The heart is the seat of understanding; thus the Scripture speaks of men "wise in heart"; and "slow of heart" means dull of understanding To learn by *heart* is to learn and understand, but we commonly employ the phrase as a synonym for committing to memory, to learn by *rote* is to learn so as to be able to repeat

Learned (lērn' ed) Colman, king of Hungary (1095-1114), was called *The Learned. Cp.* BEAUCLERC.

The learned Blacksmith. Elihu Burritt (1811-79), the American linguist, who was at one time a blacksmith

The learned Painter. Charles Lebrun (1619-90), so called from the great accuracy of his costumes

The learned Tailor. Henry Wild, of Norwich (1684-1734), who mastered, while he worked at his trade, the Greek, Latin, Hebrew, Chaldaic, Syriac, Persian, and Arabic languages.

Leather Nothing like leather. The story is that a town in danger of a siege called together a council of the chief inhabitants to know what defence they recommended. A mason suggested a strong wall, a shipbuilder advised "wooden walls," and when others had spoken, a currier arose and said, "There's nothing like leather "

Another version is, "Nothing like leather to administer a thrashing "

It is all leather or prunella. Nothing of any moment, all rubbish, through a misunderstanding of the lines by Pope, who was drawing a distinction between the work of a cobbler and that of a parson

> Worth makes the man, and want of it the fellow,
> The rest is all but leather or prunella
>   POPE *Essay on Man*

Prunella is a worsted stuff, formerly used for clergymen's gowns, etc , and for the uppers of ladies' boots, and is probably so called because it was the colour of a *prune*.

Leather medal. A U S A colloquial term for a booby prize.

To give one a leathering. To beat him with a leather belt, hence, to give him a drubbing.

Leatherneck. A nickname in the U.S.A. forces for a Marine

Leatherstocking Novels. The novels by Fenimore Cooper in which Natty Bumpo. nicknamed *Leatherstocking* and *Hawkeye*, is a leading character. They are *The Pioneers* (1823), *The Last of the Mohicans* (1826), *The Prairie* (1826), *The Pathfinder* (1840), and *The Deerslayer* (1841) "Leatherstocking" was a hardy backwoodsman, a type of North American pioneer

Leave in the lurch. *See* LURCH.

Lebensraum (lā bĕnz roum') A German phrase (room for living) somewhat akin to Land Hunger (*q.v*). It is applied especially to the additional territory required by a nation for the expansion of its trade and the settlement of a population growing too numerous to be sustained in the mother country ,

Leda. In Greek mythology, the mother by Zeus (who is fabled to have come to her in the shape of a swan) of two eggs, from one of which came Castor and Clytemnestra, and from the other Pollux and Helen

Leda Bible, The. *See* BIBLE, SPECIALLY NAMED

Lee. In nautical language, the side or quarter opposite to that against which the wind blows, the sheltered side, the side away from the windward or weather side. From A S *hleo*, *hleow*, a covering or shelter

Lee shore. The shore under the lee of a ship, or that towards which the wind blows

Lee side. *See* LEEWARD.

Lee tide. A tide running in the same direction as the wind blows, if in the opposite direction it is called *a tide under the lee*

Leeward (loo' ard) Toward the lee (*q v*), or that part towards which the wind blows; *windward* is in the opposite direction, viz, in the teeth of the wind *See* A-WEATHER, LEE

Take care of the lee hatch. A warning to the helmsman to beware lest the ship goes to the leeward of her course—*i e*. the part towards which the wind blows

To lay a ship by the lee. An obsolete phrase for to heave to, *i e* to arrange the sails of a ship flat against the masts and shrouds so that the wind strikes the vessel broadside and thus causes her to make little or no headway.

Under the lee of the land. Under the shelter of the cliffs which break the force of the winds.

Under the lee of a ship. On the side opposite to the wind, so that the ship shelters or wards it off

Leech. One skilled in medicine or "leech-craft", the word, which is now obsolete, is the A S *læce*, one who relieves pain, from *lacnian*, to heal. The blood-sucking worm, the *leech*, gets its name probably from the same word, *the healer*

> And straightway sent, with carefull diligence,
> To fetch a leach the which had great insight
> In that disease.
>
> SPENSER *Faerie Queene*, I, x, 23.

Leech-finger. *See* MEDICINAL FINGER.

Leek. The national emblem of Wales The story is that St David, patron saint of the Welsh, on one occasion caused his countrymen under King Cadwallader to distinguish themselves from their Saxon foes by wearing a leek in their caps

Shakespeare makes out that the Welsh wore leeks at the battle of Poitiers, for Fluellen says —

> If your majesty is remembered of it, the Welshmen did goot service in a garden where leeks grow, wearing leeks in their Monmouth caps, which, your majesty know, to this hour is an honourable padge of the service, and I do believe your majesty takes no scorn to wear the leek upon St Tavy's Day —*Henry V*, iv, 7

To eat the leek To be compelled to eat your own words, or retract what you have said Fluellen (in *Henry V*) is taunted by Pistol for wearing a leek in his hat "Hence," says Pistol, "I am qualmish at the smell of leek " Fluellen replies, "I beseech you . at my desire . . . to eat this leek " The ancient answers, "Not for Cadwallader and all his goats " Then the peppery Welshman beats him, nor desists till Pistol has swallowed the entire abhorrence

Lees. There are lees to every wine. The best things have some defect A French proverb.

> Doubt is the lees of thought.
>
> BOKER *Doubt*, etc , i, 11.

Settling on the lees. Making the best of a bad job, settling down on what is left, after having squandered the main part of one's fortune.

Leet or **Court-leet.** A manor court for petty offences, held once a year; the day on which it was held The word is probably connected with A S *lathe* (*q v*), a division of a county.

> Who has a breast so pure,
> But some uncleanly apprehensions
> Keep leets and law-days and in session sit
> With meditations lawful?
>
> *Othello*, iii, 3

Left. The *left* side of anything is frequently considered to be unlucky, of bad omen (*cp* AUGURY, SINISTER), the *right* the reverse

In politics the *left* is the opposition, the party which, in a legislative assembly, sits on the left of the Speaker or President The *left wing* of a party is composed of its extremists, the "irreconcilables The term *leftist* has been used since *c* 1930 to denote a person of Socialist or Communist tendencies

A left-handed compliment. A compliment which insinuates a reproach.

A left-handed marriage. A morganatic marriage (*q v*), in which the husband gave his *left* hand to the bride instead of the right, when saying, "I take thee for my wedded wife "

A left-handed oath. An oath not intended to be binding

Over the left. In early Victorian time a way of expressing disbelief, incredulity, or a negative.

> Each gentleman pointed with his right thumb over his left shoulder. This action, imperfectly described in words by the very feeble term of "over the left", when performed by any number of ladies or gentlemen who are accustomed to act in unison, has a very graceful and airy effect; its expression is one of light and playful sarcasm.—DICKENS *Pickwick Papers*.

Leg. In many phrases, *e g*. "to find one's legs," "to put one's best leg foremost," *leg* is interchangeable with *foot* (*q.v*)

Leg and leg. Equal, or nearly so, in a race, game, etc *Cp* NECK AND NECK

On its last legs. Moribund, obsolete; ready to fall out of cognisance.

Show a leg, there! Jump out of bed and be sharp about it! A phrase from the Navy.

To give a leg up. To render timely assistance, "to help a lame dog over a stile," Originally from horsemanship—to help one into the saddle

To have good sea legs. To be a good sailor; to be able to stand the motion of the ship without getting sea sick.

To make a leg. To make a bow, especially an old-fashioned obeisance, drawing one's leg backward.

> The pursuivant smiled at their simplicitye,
> And making many leggs, tooke their reward
> *The King and Miller of Mansfield*.

Leg-pulling, in England, means teasing or chaffing (*see* PULL), in USA it means toadying, intriguing, or blackmailing

To set on his legs So to provide for a man that he is able to earn his living without further help.

To stand on one's own legs. To be independent, to be earning one's own living Of course, the allusion is to being nursed and standing "alone "

Without a leg to stand on. Having no excuse, divested of all support, with no chance of success

Leg-bail. A runaway To give leg-bail, to abscond, make a "get-away."

Leg bye. In cricket a run scored from a ball which has glanced off any part of a batsman's person except his hand

Legal tender Money which, by the law of the particular country, a creditor is bound to accept in discharge of a debt. In England the tender of gold, Treasury notes, and Bank of England notes (except for £10 and upwards) is legal up to any amount, with the one exception that a creditor of the Bank of England cannot be compelled to receive his money in Bank of England notes. Silver is not legal tender for sums over forty shillings, nor bronze for sums over one shilling

Legem Pone (lē' jem pō ne) Old slang for money paid down on the nail, ready money; from the opening words of the first of the psalms appointed to be read on the twenty-fifth morning of the month—*Legem pone mihi, Domine, viam justificationum tuarum* (Teach me, O Lord, the way of thy statutes, *Ps* cxix, 33) March 25th is the first pay-day of the year, and thus the phrase became associated with cash down

> Use *legem pone* to pay at thy day,
> But use not *oremus* for often delay
> TUSSER *Good Husbandry* (1557)

Oremus (let us pray) occurs frequently in the Roman Catholic liturgy Its application to a debtor who is suing for further time is obvious.

Legend Literally and originally, "something to be read" (Lat *legenda*, from *legere*, to read); hence the narratives of the lives of saints and martyrs were so termed from their being read, especially at matins, and after dinner in the refectories. Exaggeration and a love for the wonderful so predominated in these readings, that the word came to signify a traditional story, especially one popularly regarded as true, a fable, a myth.

In Numismatics the legend is the inscription impressed in letters on a coin or medal Formerly the words on the obverse only (*i e.* round the head of the sovereign) were called the legend, the words on the reverse being the inscription, but this distinction is no longer recognized by numismatists It is also properly applied to the title on a map or under a picture

Legenda Aurea. *See* GOLDEN LEGEND

Leger. *See* ST LEGER.

Legion. My name is Legion: for we are many (*Mark* v, 9) A proverbial expression somewhat similar to hydra-headed. Thus, we say of a plague of rats, "Their name is Legion"

Foreign Legion. A body of highly-trained mercenaries of any nationality, the French and Spanish armies include such bodies.

The Thundering Legion. *See* THUNDERING.

Legion of Honour. An order of distinction and reward instituted by Napoleon in 1802, for either military or civil merit.

It was, at the outset, limited to 15 *cohortes*, each composed of 7 *grands officiers*, 20 *commandants*, 30 *officiers*, and 350 *legionnaires*, making in all 6,105 members, it was reorganized by Louis XVIII in 1814, and again by Napoleon III in 1852, and now comprises 80 *grands croix*, 200 *grands officiers*, 1,000 *commandeurs*, 4,000 *officiers*, with *chevaliers* to whose creation there is no fixed limit

The badge is a five-branched cross with a medallion bearing a symbolical figure of the republic and round it the legend, 'République Française, 1870 " This is crowned by a laurel wreath and the ribbon is of red watered silk

The order holds considerable property, out of which it distributes pensions to members and maintains schools for their daughters

Leglen-girth. To cast a leglen-girth. To have made a *faux pas*, particularly by having an illegitimate child; to have one's reputation blown upon *Leglen* is Scottish for a milk-pail, and a *leglen-girth* is its lowest hoop

Leicester. The town gets its name from Lat. *Legionis castra*, the camp of the legion, it having been the headquarters of a legion during the Roman occupation of Britain *Caerleon*, in Wales, *Leon*, Spain, and *Ledjun*, in Palestine, owe their names to the same cause.

Leicester Square (London) So called from the family mansion of the Sydneys, Earls of Leicester, which stood on the north-east side in the 17th century

Leipzig Fairs. These were sample fairs to which commercial agents used to flock from all parts of the world The Spring Fair opened the first week in March, the Autumn Fair the last week in August, and each lasted three weeks All sorts of wares including pottery, textiles, glass, machinery, books, etc , were on sale

Leitmotiv (līt' mō tēf') This is a German word meaning the leading motive, and is applied in music to a theme associated with a personage, etc , in an opera or similar work which is quoted at appropriate times and worked up symphonically The term has got into general usage to describe any phrase or turn of thought or speech that continually recurs with a certain association

Lely (Sir Peter) (lē' li), the painter, was the son of Vander Vaas or Faes, of Westphalia, whose house had a lily for its sign Both father and son went by the nickname of Le-lys (the Lily), a sobriquet which Peter afterwards adopted as his cognomen

Lemmings are one of the curiosities of nature, and their blind instinct is the origin of several fables The lemming is a mouse-like rodent, some five inches long, that lives in the grass and bushes in the higher lands of the great mountain ranges of Scandinavia Lemmings multiply at such a rate that every three or four years they make a vast migration, coming down the mountain slopes, swimming rivers and lakes, but always descending As they pass on their way, devastating the countryside, they are harassed by man, birds of prey and beasts, but undeterred they push in their millions ever onwards and downwards until they reach the sea, into which they plunge and are drowned

Various theories have been advanced to account for their behaviour It would seem that lemmings are obeying a blind instinct, inherited maybe from Miocene days when the Baltic and North Sea were dry land which could offer a refuge for their overcrowded, teeming hosts

Lemnos The island where Vulcan fell when Jupiter flung him out of heaven One myth connected with Lemnos tells how the women of the island, in revenge for their ill-treatment, murdered all the men The Argonauts (*q v.*) were received with great favour by the women, and as a result of their few months' stay the island was repopulated the queen, Hypsipyle, became the mother of twins by Jason.

Lemnian earth. A kind of bole, or clayey earth, of a reddish or yellowish grey colour, found in the island of Lemnos, said to cure the bites of serpents and other wounds It was made into cakes, and was called *terra sigillata*, because these were sealed by a priest before being vended

Lemon. Lemon, Salts of. *See* MISNOMERS.

Lemon sole. The name of the flat-fish has nothing to do with the fruit but is from *limande*, a dab or flat-fish This may be connected with O Fr *limande*, a flat board, but may also be from Lat *limus*, mud, the fish being essentially a bottom fish

The answer's a lemon. A senseless and ridiculous repartee, used as a form of reply to some particularly silly or unanswerable conundrum.

Lemures (lem' ū rēz) The name given by the Romans to the spirits of the dead, especially spectres which wandered about at night-time to terrify the living *Cp.* LARVÆ. (Ovid. *Fasti* v.)

> The lars and lemures moan with midnight plaint
> MILTON *Ode on the Nativity*.

Lemuria (le mū' rı à). The name given to a lost land that is supposed to have connected Madagascar with India and Sumatra in prehistoric times *See* W Scott Elliott's *The Lost Lemuria* (1904) *Cp.* ATLANTIS.

Lend Lease. On March 11th, 1942, President Roosevelt signed the Lend-Lease Act whereby U.S A was committed to lend or lease military equipment, stores, food, etc., to the governments of the powers fighting Fascism in the name of democracy Fifteen powers in addition to the twenty Latin-American Republics benefited by Lend-Lease, and over £1,000,000,000 was expended by U.S.A. It was ended by President Truman on the conclusion of hostilities in 1945.

Leningrad (len' ın grăd). The present name of what was once known as St Petersburg, the capital city of Tsarist Russia. It was founded by Peter the Great in 1703; the name was changed to Petrograd in 1914, and to Leningrad in 1924

Lens (Lat , a lentil or bean). Glasses used in optical instruments are so called because the

double convex one, which may be termed the perfect lens, is of a bean shape.

Lent (A S *lencten*) *Lenctentid* (spring tide) was the Saxon name for March, because in this month there is a manifest lengthening of the days As the chief part of the great fast, from Ash Wednesday to Easter, falls in March, this period received the name of the *Lenctenfæsten*, or Lent

The fast of thirty-six days was introduced in the 4th century Felix III (483-492) added four days in 487 to make it correspond with Our Lord's fast in the wilderness.

Galeazzo's Lent. A form of torture devised by Galeazzo Visconti, Duke of Milan, 1395-1402, calculated to prolong the unfortunate victim's life for forty days.

Lent lily. The daffodil, which blooms in Lent.

Lenten. Frugal, stinted, as food in Lent. Shakespeare has "lenten entertainment" (*Hamlet*, ıı, 2), "a lenten answer" (*Twelfth Night*, ı, 5), "a lenten pye" (*Romeo and Juliet*, ıı, 4)

> And with a lenten salad cooled her blood
> DRYDEN· *Hind and Panther*, ııı, 27

Leonard, St A Frank at the court of Clovis in the 6th century He founded the monastery of Noblac, and is the patron saint of prisoners, Clovis having given him permission to release all whom he visited. He is usually represented as a deacon, and holding chains or broken fetters in his hand His feast day is November 6th

Leonidas of Modern Greece (lē on' ı dăs) Marco Bozzaris, who with 1,200 men put to rout 4,000 Turco-Albanians, at Kerpenisi, but was killed in the attack (1823) He was buried at Missolonghi.

Leonine (lē' ō nīn) Lion-like, also, relating to one of the popes named *Leo*, as the **Leonine City**, the part of Rome surrounding the Vatican, which was fortified by Leo IV in the 9th century

Leonine contract. A one-sided agreement; so called in allusion to the fable of *The Lion and his Fellow-Hunters Cp* GLAUCUS SWOP, *under* GLAUCUS.

Leonine verses Latin hexameters, or alternate hexameters and pentameters, rhyming at the middle and end of each respective line. These fancies were common in the 12th century, and are said to have been popularized by and so called from Leoninus, a canon of the church of St Victor, in Paris; but there are many such lines in the classic poets, particularly Ovid In English verse, any metre which rhymes middle and end may be called Leonine verse.

Leopard. So called because it was thought in mediæval times to be a cross between the lion (*leo*), or lioness, and the *pard*, which was the name given to a panther that had no white specks on it.

References to the impossibility of a leopard changing its spots are frequent; the allusion is to *Jeremiah*, xiii, 23

> Lions make leopards tame.
> Yea, but not change his spots.
> *Richard II*, i, 1

In Christian art the leopard represents that beast spoken of in *Revelation* xiii, 1-8, with seven heads and ten horns, six of the heads bear a nimbus, but the seventh, being "wounded to death," lost its power, and consequently is bare

> And the beast which I saw was like unto a leopard, and his feet were as the feet of a bear, and his mouth as the mouth of a lion —*Rev* xiii, 2

The lions in the coat of arms of England. *See* LION

The leopard's head, or King's Mark, on silver is really a lion's head It is called a leopard, because the O Fr. heraldic term *Leopart* means a lion passant guardant

Leopolita Bible. *See* BIBLE, SPECIALLY NAMED

Leprachaun (lep'ra kawn) The fairy shoemaker of Ireland, so called because he is always seen working at a single shoe (*leith*, half, *brog*, a shoe or brogue) Another of his peculiarities is that he has a purse that never contains more than a single shilling

> Do you not catch the tiny clamour,
> Busy click of an elfin hammer,
> Voice of the Leprachaun singing shrill,
> As he merrily plies his trade?
> W B YEATS *Fairy and Folk Tales.*

He is also called lubrican, cluricaune (*q v.*), etc In Dekker and Middleton's *Honest Whore* (Pt II, III, i) Hippolito speaks of Bryan, the Irish footman, as "your Irish lubrican "

Lesbian (lez' by an) Pertaining to Lesbos, one of the islands of the Greek Archipelago, or to Sappho, the famous poetess of Lesbos, and to the homosexual practices attributed to her.

The Lesbian Poets. Terpander, Alcæus, Arion, and Sappho, all of Lesbos

The Lesbian rule. A flexible rule used by ancient Greek masons for measuring curved mouldings, etc , hence, figuratively, a pliant and accommodating principle or rule of conduct.

Lèse-majesté (lēz mǎj' es ti) High treason, a crime against the sovereign (Lat. *læsa majestas*, hurt or violated majesty).

Lestrigons (les' tri gonz). A fabulous race of cannibal giants who lived in Sicily Ulysses (*Odyss* x) sent two of his men to request that he might land, but the king of the place ate one for dinner and the other fled The Lestrigons assembled on the coast and threw stones against Ulysses and his crew, they fled with all speed, but many men were lost. *Cp.* POLYPHEMUS

Let, to permit, is the A S *læt-an*, to suffer or permit; but *let*, to hinder, now obsolete or archaic, is the verb *lett-an* From this comes a *let* in ball games such as lawn-tennis, where a point is played again because there has been a hindrance

> Oftentimes I purposed to come unto you, but was let hitherto.—*Rom.* i, 13

> Yf any man had rathere bestowe thys tyme upon hys owne occupatyon   he is not letted nor prohibited —MORE *Utopia*, II, iv

Lethe (lē' thī) In Greek mythology, one of the rivers of Hades, which the souls of all the dead are obliged to taste, that they may forget everything said and done when alive (Gr.

letho, latheo, lanthano, to cause persons not to know)

> Here, in a dusky vale where Lethe rolls
> Old Bavius sits, to dip poetic souls,
> And blunt the sense
> POPE *Dunciad*, iii, 23

Letter. The name of a character used to represent a sound, and of a missive or written message Through O Fr *lettre*, from Lat *littera*, a letter of the alphabet, the plural of which (*litteræ*) denoted an epistle The plural, with the meaning literature, learning, erudition (as in *man of letters*, *republic of letters*, etc), dates in English from at least the time of King Alfred, and is seen in Cicero's *otium literatum*, lettered ease

The number of letters in the English alphabet is 26, but in a fount of type 206 characters are required, these are made up of Roman lower case (*i e* small letters), capitals, and small capitals; included are the diphthongs (Æ, æ, etc.) and ligatures (ff, fi, fl, ffi, ffl), the remaining characters being the accented letters, *i e* those with the grave ('), acute ('), circumflex ( ), diæresis ( ), or tilde (~), and the "cedilla *c*" (ç) To these characters must be added the figures, fractions, points (, !, etc), brackets, reference marks (*, §, etc), and commercial and mathematical signs (£, %, +, etc) in common use *Cp* TYPOGRAPHICAL SIGNS, FONT.

The proportionate use of the letters of the alphabet is given as follows —

E	1,000	H	540	F	236	K		88
T	770	R	528	W	190	J	.	55
A	728	D	. 392	Y	184	Q		50
I	704	L	360	P	168	X		46
S	680	U	. 296	G	. 168	Z		22
O	. 672	C	. 280	B	. 158			
N	670	M	272	V	120			

Consonants, 5,977   Vowels, 3,400.

Another "fount-scheme" gives a rather different order, viz e, t, a, o, i, n, s, r, h, d, l, u, c, m, f, w, y, p, g, b, v, k, j, q, x, fi, ff, fl, z, ffi, ffl. "e" accounts for 7 83 per cent. of the fount, "z" for 0 17, and the first twelve characters here given for 50 per cent of the whole The least wanted character is the italic capital Ç, of which it has been calculated that only five are necessary for a million type

As initials the order of frequency is very different, the proportion being —

S	.	1,194	M	439	W	. 272	Q	. 58
C	.	937	F	.. 388	G	. 266	K	47
P	..	804	I	377	U	. 228	Y	23
A	..	574	E	.. 340	O	206	Z	18
T	..	571	H	308	V	172	X	.. 4
D	..	505	L	.. 298	N	. 153		
B	..	463	R	291	J	69		

See also TYPE; FONT

Letter-Gae. A jocular Scottish name (after Allan Ramsay, 1686-1758) for the precentor of a kirk, he who leads off the singing, and *lets go*

> There were no sae mony hairs on the warlock's face as there's on Letter-gae's ain at this moment.—SCOTT. *Guy Mannering*, ch xi.

Letter-lock. A lock that cannot be opened unless letters on exterior movable rings are arranged in a certain order

> A strange lock that opens with A M E N
> BEAUMONT AND FLETCHER *Noble Gentleman*

Letter of Bellerophon. *See* BELLEROPHON

Letter of credence, or **letters credential,** formal documents with which a diplomatic agent is furnished accrediting him on his appointment to a post at the seat of a foreign government.

Letter of Credit. A letter written by a merchant or banker to another, requesting him to credit the bearer with certain sums of money *Circular Notes* are letters of credit carried by travellers

Letter of Licence. An instrument in writing made by a creditor, allowing a debtor longer time for the payment of his debt.

Letter of Marque A commission authorizing a privateer to make reprisals on a hostile nation till satisfaction for injury has been duly made. *Marque* is from Provençal *marcar*, Med. Lat *marcare*, to seize as a pledge

Letter of Safe Conduct. A writ under the Great Seal, guaranteeing safety to and fro to the person named in the passport.

Letter of Slains In old Scottish law a petition to the Crown from the relatives of a murdered person, declaring that they have received satisfaction (*assythment*), and asking pardon for the murderer.

Letter of Uriah. *See* URIAH

Letters Missive. An order from the Lord Chancellor to a peer to put in an appearance to a bill filed in chancery.

Letters of Administration. The legal instrument granted by the Probate Court to a person appointed administrator to one who has died intestate

Letters of Horning. In Scottish history, signed orders putting rebels to the horn. *See* HORN

Letters of Junius. *See* JUNIUS.

Letters Patent, or **Overt.** *See* PATENT.

Lettres de Cachet. *See* CACHET.

Leucadia or **Leucas** (lū kā´ di a) One of the Ionian Islands, now known as Santa Maura. Here is the promontory from which Sappho threw herself into the sea when she found her love for Phaon was in vain

> Haste, Sappho, haste, from high Leucadia throw
> Thy wretched weight, nor dread the deeps below!
> There injured lovers, leaping from above,
> Their flames extinguish, and forget to love
> POPE *Sappho to Phaon.*

Leucothea (lū kōth´ ē a) (*The White Goddess*). So Ino, the mortal daughter of Cadmus and wife of Athamas, was called after she became a sea goddess Athamas in a fit of madness slew one of her sons, she threw herself into the sea with the other, imploring assistance of the gods, who deified both of them. Her son, Melicertes, then renamed Palæmon, was called by the Romans Portunus, or Portumnus, and became the protecting genius of harbours.

Levant (le vănt´) He has **levanted**—i e made off, decamped A *levanter* is an absconder, especially one who makes a bet, and runs away without paying his bet if he loses. From Span *levantar el campo*, or *la casa*, to break up the camp or house

Levant and Ponent Winds The east wind is the Levant, and the west wind the Ponent. The former is from Lat. *levare*, to raise (sunrise), and the latter from *ponere*, to set (sunset)

> Forth rush the Levant and the Ponent winds
> MILTON *Paradise Lost*, x, 704

Levant, the region, strictly speaking, means the eastern shore of the Mediterranean, but is often applied to the whole East

Levant and Couchant (lev´ ânt, kou´ chant) Applied in legal phraseology to cattle which have strayed into another's field, and have been there long enough to lie down and sleep The owner of the field can demand compensation for such intrusion. (Lat *levantes et cubantes,* rising up and going to bed.)

Levee (le´ vi) (Fr , *lit* , a rising, i e from bed) An official reception of men only by the sovereign or his representative, held usually in the afternoon

It was customary for the queens of France to receive at the hour of their *levée*—i e while making their toilet—the visits of certain noblemen The court physicians, messengers from the king, the queen's secretary, and some few others demanded admission as a right, so ten or more persons were often in the dressing-room while the queen was making her toilet and sipping her coffee.

In the Southern U S A. the word *levee* is used for an earth or masonry embankment for preventing the overflowing of a river

Levée en masse (Fr) A patriotic rising of a whole nation to defend their country

Level. Level-headed. Shrewd, business-like, characterized by common sense, said of one who "has his head screwed on the right way."

To do one's level best. To exert oneself to the utmost. This term, and that above, were originally American slang, and came from the gold-diggings of California

To find one's own level. Said of a person who, after making an unsuccessful start, arrives at the position in society, business, etc , for which his gifts or attainments qualify him.

To level up, or **down.** To bring whatever is being spoken of—as the state of some class of society, the standard of wages, and so on—up or down to the level of some similar thing.

> Your levellers wish to level *down* as far as themselves, but they cannot bear levelling *up* to themselves.
> —DR. JOHNSON. *Remark to Boswell,* 1763

On the level. Honest and sincere in whatever one is doing or saying. A term from Freemasonry.

Levellers. In English history, a body of ultra-Republicans in the time of Charles I and the Commonwealth, who wanted all men to be placed on a level, particularly with respect to their eligibility to office John Lilburne was one of the leaders of the sect, which was active from 1647 to 1649, when it was suppressed.

In Irish history the name was given to the 18th century agrarian agitators, afterwards called Whiteboys (*q v*) Their first offences were levelling the hedges of enclosed commons, but their programme developed into a demand for the general redress of all agrarian grievances.

Lever de Rideau (lev' ā de rē' dō) (Fr , curtain-raiser). A short sketch performed on the stage before drawing up the curtain on the real play of the evening

Leviathan (le vī' a than). The name (Hebrew for "that which gathers itself together in folds," *Cp Is* xxvii, 1) given in the Bible to a sea-serpent, though in *Job* xli, 1, it is possible that the reference is to the crocodile *Cp.* BEHEMOTH

The name is applied to a ship of great size from the reference in *Ps* civ, 25, 26—

This great and wide sea, wherein are things creeping innumerable both small and great beasts There go the ships, there is that leviathan, whom thou hast made to play therein.

But this is a mistranslation of the Hebrew, the correct rendering being—according to Dr. Cheyne—

. . . There dragons move along, (yea), Leviathan whom thou didst appoint ruler therein.

Hobbes took the name as the title for his treatise on "the Matter, Forme, and Power of a Commonwealth Ecclesiasticall and Civil" (1651), and applied it to the Commonwealth as a political organism. He says:—

I have set forth the nature of man, (whose Pride and other Passions have compelled him to submit himselfe to Government,) together with the great power of his Governour, whom I compared to *Leviathan*, taking that comparison out of the two last verses of the one and fortieth of *Job*; where God having set forth the great power of *Leviathan*, calleth him King of the Proud.—*Leviathan*, Pt ii, ch xxviii

The **Leviathan of Literature** Dr. Johnson (1709-84).

Levitation is a term applied to the phenomenon of heavy bodies rising and floating in the air It is frequently mentioned in the Hindu scriptures and other writings, and it is a not-uncommon attribute of Catholic saints. Joseph of Cupertino (1603-66) was the subject of such frequent levitation that he was forbidden by his superiors to attend choir and performed his devotions in a special chapel where his levitation would cause no distraction to other worshippers. D. D. Home was alleged by Sir W Crookes to have had this power or gift Scientific research has not yet found an explanation

Levites (lē' vīts) In Dryden's *Absalom and Achitophel* (*q v*), the Dissenting clergy who were expelled by the Act of Conformity.

Lewis Machine-gun. Named after an American Army officer and inventor, Isaac Newton Lewis (1858-1931), whose organizational system still dominates the artillery corps.

Lex. (Lat., law).

Lex non scripta (leks non skrip' ta) (Lat., unwritten law) The common law, as distinguished from the statute or written law. Common law does not derive its force from being recorded, and though its several provisions have been compiled and printed, the compilations are not statutes, but simply remembrancers.

Lex talionis (Lat) The law of retaliation, tit for tat

Leyden Jar A glass vessel partly coated, inside and out, with lead foil, and used to accumulate electricity, invented by Vanleigh, of Leyden, Holland, in 1745

Lia-fail. The Irish name of the Coronation Stone, or Stone of Destiny, of the ancient Irish kings. *See* SCONE; TANIST STONE.

Liar. Liars should have good memories. This old proverb, which is found in many languages and was quoted by St. Jerome in the 4th century, has been traced to Quintillian's *Mendacem memorem esse oportet* "It is fitting that a liar should be a man of good memory" (*Institutes*, IV, ii, 91) It occurs in Taverner's translation of Erasmus's *Proverbs* (1539)—

A lyer ought not to be forgetfull.

And Montaigne says (*Essayes*, I, ix):—

It is not without reason, men say, that *he who hath not a good and readie memorie, should never meddle with telling of lies, and feare to become a lar*

Libel (Lat. *libellus*, a little book). A writing of a defamatory nature, one which contains malicious statements ridiculing someone or calculated to bring him into disrepute, etc ; a lampoon, a satire Originally a plaintiff's statement of his case, which usually "defames" the defendant, was called a "libel," for it made a "little book "

. Malicious intention is not necessary to make a written or printed statement libellous if it reflects on the character of another and is published without lawful justification or excuse, and the use of the name of a real person in a work of fiction has been held to constitute a libel

In legal phraseology a libel is the written statement commencing a suit, containing the plaintiff's allegations

The greater the truth, the greater the libel, a dictum of Lord Ellenborough (1750-1818), who amplified it by the explanation—"if the language used were true, the person would suffer more than if it were false"

Burns, in some lines written at Stirling, attributes the saying to the Earl of Mansfield—

Dost not know that old Mansfield, who writes like the Bible,
Says. "The more 'tis a truth, sir, the more 'tis a libel"?

Liber (Lat , a book)

Liber Albus (Lat , the white book). A compilation of the laws and customs of the City of London, made in 1419, by John Carpenter, town clerk.

Liber Niger. *The Black Book of the Exchequer*, compiled by Gervase of Tilbury, in the reign of Henry II. It is a roll of the military tenants

Liberal. A political term introduced in the early 19th century from Spain and France (where it denoted "advanced" or revolutionary politicians), and employed in 1815 by Byron, Leigh Hunt, and others as the title of a periodical representing their views in politics, religion, and literature It was originally bestowed upon the advanced Whigs as a term of reproach but when the moderate Whigs formed a coalition with the Tories and the advanced Whigs with the Radicals, it was adopted by the latter party; it came into general use about 1831, when the Reform Bill, in Lord Grey's Ministry, gave it prominence

Influenced in a great degree by the philosophy and the politics of the Continent, they [the Whigs] endeavoured to substitute cosmopolitan for national principles, and they baptized the new scheme of politics with the plausible name of "Liberalism."— DISRAELI, June 24, 1872

Liberal Unionists. Those Liberals who united, in 1886, with Lord Salisbury and the Conservative party to oppose Home Rule for Ireland Lord Hartington, afterwards Duke of Devonshire, and Joseph Chamberlain were the chiefs of the party.

Liberate. At a press conference in May, 1944, President Roosevelt said that the Allied campaigns in Europe were a liberation, not an invasion This gave rise to a sarcastic use of the verb "to liberate" as a synonym for "to loot"

Liberator, The. The Peruvians so call Simon Bolivar (1783-1830), who established the independence of Peru Daniel O'Connell (1775-1847) was also so called, because he led the agitation which resulted in the repeal of the Penal Laws and the Emancipation of the Irish Roman Catholics

Liberator was the name associated with a famous financial crash at the close of last century. In 1868 Jabez Balfour promoted the Liberator Building Society in which a great number of small investors embarked their entire capital. The crash came in 1892, owing to the systematic fraud whereby Balfour had applied the funds to all manner of wild speculation Balfour, at the time M.P. for Burnley, was sentenced to 14 years penal servitude.

Liberator of the World. So Benjamin Franklin (1706-90) has been called

Libertarians. *See* AGENT.

Libertine. A debauchee, a dissolute person, one who puts no restraint on his personal indulgence

A libertine, in earlier use, was a speculative freethinker in matters of religion and in the theory of morals but [it has come] to signify a profligate — TRENCH *On the Study of Words*, lecture iii

In the New Testament the word is used to mean a freedman (Lat *Libertinus*).

Then there arose certain of the synagogue, which is called the synagogue of the Libertines, disputing with Stephen —*Acts* vi, 9

There was a sect of heretics in Holland, about 1525, who maintained that nothing is sinful but to those who think it sinful, and that perfect innocence is to live without doubt

Liberty means "to do what one likes" (Lat. *liber*, free.)

Civil liberty. The liberty of a subject to conduct his own affairs as he thinks proper, provided he neither infringes on the equal liberty of others, nor offends against the good morals or laws under which he is living

Moral liberty. Such freedom as is essential to render a person responsible for what he does, or what he omits to do.

Natural liberty. Unrestricted freedom to exercise all natural functions in their proper places; the state of being subject only to the laws of nature

Political liberty. The freedom of a nation from any unjust abridgment of its rights and independence; the right to participate in political elections and civil offices, and to have a voice in the administration of the laws under which one lives.

Religious liberty. Freedom in religious opinions, and in both private and public worship, provided such freedom in no wise interferes with the equal liberty of others.

The liberty of the press. The right to publish what one pleases, subject only to penalty if the publication is mischievous, hurtful, or libellous to the state or individuals

Cap of Liberty. *See* CAP

Liberty Enlightening the World. The colossal statue standing on Bedloe's (or Liberty) Island, at the entrance of New York Harbour, presented to the American people by France in commemoration of the centenary of the American Declaration of Independence, and inaugurated in 1886 It is of bronze, 155 ft in height (standing on a pedestal 135 ft high), and represents a woman, draped, and holding a lighted torch in her upraised hand. It is the work of the Alsatian sculptor, Auguste Bartholdi (1834-1904).

The statue of Liberty, placed over the entrance of the Palais Royal, Paris, was modelled from Mme Tallien.

The liberties of the Fleet. The district immediately surrounding the Fleet, the old debtors' prison in the City of London, in which prisoners were sometimes allowed to reside, and beyond which they were not allowed to go They included the north side of Ludgate Hill and the Old Bailey to Fleet Lane, down the lane to the market, and on the east side along by the prison wall to the foot of Ludgate Hill

The word **liberty** was also used to denote the areas belonging to the City of London, but lying immediately without the City walls which, in course of time, were attached to the nearest ward within the walls, and to the surroundings of the Tower of London. *See* TOWER LIBERTY

Liberty Ship. A name given to a type of merchant vessel of some 10,000 tons built in numbers by U S A during World War II.

In the Royal Navy it is the name given to the boat taking men off a warship for shore leave

Liberty Tree, or Pole (U S A) The first so called was an elm on Boston Common. A pole inscribed "To his Gracious Majesty George III, Mr. Pitt, and Liberty" was set up in New York in 1766. It was cut down by the British four times, but the fifth remained for ten years

Libido (li bē' dō) A term used by Freud to designate "the energy of those instincts which have to do with all that may be comprised under the word 'Love'" More simply, it is applied to the innate impelling force of sex urge.

Libitina (lĭb ĭ tĭ′ na). The goddess who, in ancient Italy, presided over funerals She was identified by the Romans with Proserpina, and her name was frequently used as a synonym for death itself.

Libra (Lat , the balance) The seventh sign of the Zodiac (and the name of one of the ancient constellations), which the sun enters about September 22nd and leaves about October 22nd At this time the day and night being weighed would be found equal.

Library. Before the invention of paper the thin rind between the solid wood and the outside bark of certain trees was used for writing on, this was in Lat called *liber*, which came in time to signify also a "book " Hence our *library*, the place for books, *librarian*, the keeper of books, and the French *livre*, a book

Famous libraries —

Athens public library, founded 540 B C.
The first private library was that of Aristotle, 334 B.C.
Alexandrian Library, burned A D 640
St. Mark's, Venice, founded with gifts from Petrarch, 1468
Vatican Library, 1450.
Matthias Corvinus's Library (500,000 vols)
He was King of Hungary, died 1490
Bibliothèque Nationale, Paris, founded 1350
University Library, St. Andrews, founded 1411.
Cambridge University Library, founded 1475
Bodleian Library, Oxford, founded 1598.
British Museum Library, became important with the gift of George III's books, 1823
New York Public Library
Morgan Library
Henry E Huntington Library.
John Rylands Library, Manchester

A circulating library. A library from which the books may be borrowed and taken by readers to their homes.

Libya The north of Africa between Egypt and the Atlantic Ocean. It was the Greek name for Africa in general. The Romans used the word sometimes as synonymous with Africa, and sometimes for the fringe containing Carthage.

Libya was occupied by the Italians in 1911-12, and by the Treaty of Ouchy (1912) the sovereignty of the province was transferred from Turkey to Italy. The Italians began its colonization, and so late as 1938 some 16,000 emigrants left Genoa for the province In 1942-43 the Germans and Italians were driven from Libya in the British advance from El Alamein In 1949 the General Assembly of the United Nations decreed that Libya should become an independent state by January 1st, 1952. On this date Libya became a kingdom under Sayed Mohammed Idris.

Lich. A dead body (A S *lie*, Ger. *leiche*)

Lich-fowls. Birds that feed on carrion, as night-ravens, etc.

Lich-gate The shed or covered place at the entrance of churchyards, intended to afford shelter to the coffin and mourners, while they wait for the clergyman to conduct the cortege into the church.

Lich-owl. The screech-owl, superstitiously supposed to foretell death

Lich-wake or **Lyke-wake.** The funeral feast or the waking of a corpse, *i.e.* watching it all night

In a pastoral written by Ælfric in 998 for Wilfsige, Bishop of Sherborne, the attendance of the clergy at lyke-wakes is forbidden.

Lich-way. The path by which a funeral is conveyed to church, which not infrequently deviates from the ordinary road It was long supposed that wherever a dead body passed became a public thoroughfare

Lick. I licked him. I flogged or beat him A licking is a thrashing, or—in games—a defeat, as *I gave him a good licking at billiards.*

A lick and a promise. To give a lick and a promise to a piece of work is to do it in a hasty and superficial way—as a cat might give its dirty face one quick lick of its tongue with a promise of more cleaning later

To go at a great lick. To run, ride, etc , at great speed, to put on a spurt

To lick into shape. To make presentable, to give a good appearance, decent manners, etc , to In allusion to the tradition that the cubs of bears are cast shapeless, and remain so till the dam has licked them into proper form *See* BEAR

So watchful Bruin forms, with plastic care,
Each growing lump, and brings it to a bear
POPE *Dunciad*, i, 101

To lick one's lips To give evident signs of the enjoyment of anticipation

To lick a man's shoes To be humble or abjectly servile towards him *Cp* LICKSPITTLE.

To lick the dust or the ground *See* TO KISS THE DUST *under* KISS

Lickpenny. Something or someone that makes the money go—that "licks up" the pennies Lydgate (about 1425) wrote a humorous poem called *London Lyckpenny* in which he shows that life in London makes the money fly

Lickspittle A toady, the meanest of sycophants.

Lictors. Binders (Lat *ligo*, to bind or tie). These Roman officers were so called because they bound the hands and feet of criminals before they executed the sentence of the law.

Lidice (lĭd′ ĭ si). Once a mining village in Czechoslovakia. In 1942 the German authorities asserted that the inhabitants had helped the patriots who had assassinated the atrocious Reinhard Heydrich, Nazi governor of Bohemia All the adult inhabitants of Lidice were shot and the children taken away none have ever known where; the village was then utterly rased to the ground This example of German ferocity aroused such indignation throughout the civilized world that in U S A , Mexico, and elsewhere a number of towns and villages were renamed Lidice in its memory.

Lido (lē′ dō) An outdoor bathing-pool, usually with a place for sunbathing and often with accommodation for concerts or other amusements The name is taken from the sandy island called the Lido, facing the Adriatic outside Venice, and a fashionable bathing resort

Lie. A falsehood (A S *lyge*, from *leogan*, to lie)

A lie hath no feet. Because it cannot stand alone. In fact, a lie wants twenty others to support it, and even then is in constant danger of tripping. *Cp* LIAR (*Liars should have good memories*)

A white lie. A conventional lie, such as telling a caller that Mrs A or Mrs B is not at home, meaning not "at home" to that particular caller.

It is said that Dean Swift called on a friend, and was told "master is not at home." The friend called on the dean, and Swift, opening the window, shouted, "Not at home." When the friend expostulated, Swift said, "I believed your footman when he said his master was not at home, surely you can believe the master himself when he tells you he is not at home"

Lie detector An American invention which records the heart-beats of a man under questioning It has been found that a human being cannot tell a lie without the pulse of his heart increasing, and this increase of pulsation is recorded. In some States of the Union the findings of this machine are accepted as legal evidence

The Father of lies. Satan (*John* viii, 44).

The greatest lie. In Heywood's *Four P's*, an interlude of about 1543, a Palmer, a Pardoner, a Poticary, and a Pedlar disputed as to which could tell the greatest lie. The Palmer said he had never seen a woman out of patience, whereupon the other three P's threw up the sponge, saying such a falsehood could not possibly be outdone.

The lie circumstantial, direct, etc. *See* COUNTERCHECK.

To give one the lie. To accuse him to his face of telling a falsehood

To give the lie to. To show that such and such a statement is false, to belie

Lie (A.S *licgan*, to 'bide or rest).
Lie heavy on him, earth, for he
Laid many a heavy load on thee.

This is part of Dr. Evan's epitaph on Sir John Vanbrugh (1664-1726), the dramatist, herald, and architect The "heavy loads" referred to were Blenheim, Greenwich Hospital (which he finished), Castle Howard in Yorkshire, and other massive buildings

To lie at the catch. In Bunyan's *Pilgrim's Progress* Talkative says to Faithful, "You lie at the catch, I perceive" To which Faithful replies, "No, not I, I am only for setting things right" *To lie at* or *on the catch* is to lie in wait or to lay a trap to catch one

To lie in. To be confined in childbirth

To lie in state. Said of a corpse of a royal or distinguished person that is displayed to the general public

To lie low. To conceal oneself or one's intentions
All this while Brer Rabbit lay low.—JOEL CHANDLER HARRIS *Uncle Remus*

To lie over. To be deferred, as, this question must lie over till next sessions

To lie to. To stop the progress of a vessel at sea by reducing the sails and counterbracing the yards; hence, to cease from doing something
We now ran plump into a fog, and were obliged to lie to —LORD DUFFERIN *Letters from High Latitudes*

To lie to one's work. To work energetically.

To lie with one's fathers. To be buried in one's native place
I will lie with my fathers, and thou shalt carry me out of Egypt —*Gen* xlvii, 30.

To lie up. To refrain from work, especially on account of ill health, to rest

Liege (lēj). The word means one bound, a bondsman (O.Fr *lige*, connected with O H - Ger *ledig*, free), hence, vassals were called *liege-men*—i e. men bound to serve their lord, or *liege lord*
Unarmed and bareheaded, on his knees, and with his hands placed between those of his lord, he [the military tenant] repeated these words "Hear, my lord, I have become your liegeman of life and limb, and earthly worship, and faith and truth I will bear to you to live and die —LINGARD *History of England*, vol ii, ch 1

Lieutenant (in the British Navy and Army, lef ten' ant, American usage, loo ten' ánt), is the Latin *locum-tenens*, through the French A *Lieutenant-Colonel* is the colonel's deputy The *Lord-Lieutenant* of Ireland was the representative of the Crown in that country.

Life (A S. *lif*) Drawn from life. Drawn or described from some existing person or object.

For life. As long as life continues.

For the life of me. True as I am alive Even if my life depended on it. A strong asseveration, originally "under pain of losing my life"
Nor could I, for the life of me, see how the creation of the world had anything to do with what I was talking about —GOLDSMITH· *Vicar of Wakefield*

Large as life Of the same size as the object represented

On my life. I will answer for it by my life

People of high life. The upper ten, the *haut monde*.

To bear a charmed life To escape accidents in a marvellous manner.

To know life To be well versed in the niceties of social intercourse, good breeding, manners, etc., to be up to all the dodges by which one may be imposed upon

To see life. To "knock about" town, where life may be seen at its fullest, to move in smart or fast society

To the life. In exact imitation "Done to the life"

Life Guards. The two senior cavalry regiments of the Household Troops (*q v*), the members of which are not less than six feet high; hence, a fine, tall, manly fellow is called "a regular Life Guardsman"

Life preserver. A buoyant jacket, belt, or other appliance, to support the human body in water, also a loaded staff or knuckle-duster for self-defence.

Lift To have one at a lift is to have one in your power When a wrestler has his antagonist in his hands and lifts him from the ground, he has him "at a lift," or in his power

"Sirra," says he, "I have you at a lift
Now you are come unto vour latest shift "
PERCY. *Reliques Guy and Amarant.*

Air-lift. Organized manœuvre to transport a quantity of troops or stores to a destination by air The *Berlin air-lift*, to victual the British and American zones of the city after the Russian embargo on all land transport, began June 28th, 1948 and ended May 12th, 1949, having made in all 195,530 flights and carried 1,414,000 tons of food, coal and other stores

Lifter. A thief. We still call one who plunders shops a "shop-lifter."

Is he so young a man, and so old a lifter?
Troilus and Cressida, 1, 2

Lifting. In Scotland, the raising of the coffin on to the shoulders of the bearers Certain ceremonies preceded the funeral

At the first service were offered meat and ale, at the second, shortbread and whisky, at the third, seed-cake and wine, at the fourth, currant-bun and rum, at the last, sugar-biscuits and brandy.

Lifting the little finger. *See* FINGER

Ligan. *See* LAGAN.

Light. The A S of this word in both senses, *i e* illumination and smallness of weight, is *leoht,* but in the former sense it is connected with Ger *licht,* Lat *lux,* and Gr *leukos* (white), and in the latter with Ger *leicht,* Gr *elachus* (not heavy), and Sansk *laghu* The verb *to light,* to dismount, to settle after flight, is A S *lihtan,* from the last mentioned *leont,* originally meaning to lighten, or relieve of a burden

According to his lights. According to his information or knowledge of the matter, or, according to the capacity he has for forming opinions on it.

Ancient lights. A sign put up on a building to show the owner thereof has a right to the light coming from adjacent property, and consequently, no building may be erected there without his consent, if it would interfere with his light By the Prescription Act of 1832 a light is ancient if it has been uninterrupted for a period of twenty years.

Before the lights In theatrical parlance, on the stage, *i e* before the foot-lights

Light comedian. One who takes humorous, but not *low,* parts Orlando, in *As You Like It,* might be taken for a "light comedian", Tony Lumpkin (*She Stoops to Conquer*), and Paul Pry (in Poole's comedy of that name, 1825) are parts for a "low comedian "

Light and leading. *See* LEADING

Light-fingered. *See* FINGER.

Light gains make a heavy purse. Small profits and a quick return, is the best way of gaining wealth

Light Infantry. In the British Army, infantry carrying less equipment than normal and trained to move at high speed in manœuvring round the flanks of an enemy They were introduced into the British Army by Sir John Moore (1761-1809) The regiments so designated still march at a high speed, with short paces and with arms trailed instead of carried at the slope

Light o' love. An inconstant or loose-principled woman, a harlot

Light troops. A term formerly applied to light cavalry, *i e.* lancers and hussars, who are neither such large men as the "Heavies," nor yet so heavily equipped

The light of Thy countenance. God's smile of approbation and love.
Lift up the light of Thy countenance on us —*Ps* iv, 6.

The light of the age. Maimonides or Rabbi Moses ben Maimon, of Cordova (1135-1204).

To bring to light. To discover and expose.
The duke yet would have dark deeds darkly answered, he would never bring them to light, would he were returned[1]—*Measure for Measure,* iii, 2

To light upon. To discover by accident, to come across by a lucky chance Thus, Dr Johnson wrote to Mrs. Thrale "How did you light on your specifick for the tooth-ach?"

To make light of To treat as of no importance, to take little notice of
Behold, I have prepared my dinner my oxen and my fatlings are killed, and all things are ready; come unto the marriage
But they made light of it, and went their ways, one to his farm, another to his merchandise —*Matt* xxii, 4, 5.

To put out one's light. To kill him, "send him into the outer darkness " Othello says, "Put out the light and then put out the light."

To stand in one's own light To act in such a way as to hinder advancement

To throw or shed light upon. To elucidate, to explain.

Lighthouse *See* PHAROS

Light year. This is a term used by scientists as a unit in measuring stellar distances. Light travels at the rate of 186,000 miles a second, a light year, or the distance travelled by light in a year, is, therefore, 5,876,068,880,000 miles.

Lightning. Hamilcar (d. 228 B.C), the Carthaginian general, was called "Barca," the Phœnician for "lightning" (Heb *Barak*), both on account of the rapidity of his march and for the severity of his attacks.

Chain lightning. Two or more flashes of lightning repeated without intermission.

Forked lightning. Zig-zag lightning

Globular lightning. A meteoric ball (of fire), which sometimes falls on the earth and flies off with an explosion.

Lightning conductor. A metal rod raised above a building with one end in the earth, to carry off the lightning and prevent its injuring the building.

Lightning preservers. The most approved classical preservatives against lightning were the eagle, the sea-calf, and the laurel Jupiter chose the first, Augustus Cæsar the second, and Tiberius the third (*Columella*, x; *Sueton* in *Vit Aug*, xc., ditto in *Vit Tib*, lxix) *Cp.* HOUSE-LEEK.

Bodies scathed and persons struck dead by lightning were said to be incorruptible, and anyone so distinguished was held by the ancients in great honour. (J C. Bullenger: *De Terrae Motu*, etc, v, 11.)

Liguria (li gū' ri a) The ancient name of a part of Cisalpine Gaul, including the modern Genoa, Piedmont, some of Savoy, etc In 1797 Napoleon founded a "Ligurian Republic," with Genoa as its capital, and embracing also Venetia and a part of Sardinia. It was annexed to France in 1805.

The **Ligurian Sage** Aulus Persius Flaccus (A D 34-62), born at Volaterræ, in Etruria, famous for his *Satires*

Lilburne. If no one else were alive, John would quarrel with Lilburne John Lilburne (1614-57) was a contentious Leveller (*q.v*) in the Commonwealth, so rancorous against rank that he could never satisfy himself that any two persons were exactly on the same level

Is John departed? and is Lilburne gone?
Farewell to both—to Lilburne and to John.
Yet, being gone, take this advice from me
Let them not both in one grave buried be.
Here lay ye John, lay Lilburne thereabout.
For if they both should meet, they would fall out.
Epigrammatic Epitaph.

Lilith (lil' ith) A Semitic (in origin probably Babylonian) demon supposed to haunt wildernesses in stormy weather, and to be specially dangerous to children and pregnant women. She is referred to in *Is* xxxiv, 14, as the "screech-owl" (Revised Version, "night monster," and in margin "Lilith"), and the Talmudists give the name to a wife that Adam is fabled to have had before Eve, who, refusing to submit to him, left Paradise for a region of the air, and still haunts the night Superstitious Jews put in the chamber occupied by their wife four coins inscribed with the names of Adam and Eve and the words "Avaunt thee, Lilith!" Goethe introduced her in his *Faust*, and Rossetti in his *Eden Bower* adapted the Adamitic story, making the Serpent the instrument of Lilith's vengeance *See* THE DEVIL AND HIS DAM *under* DEVIL, and *Cp* LAMIA

Lilli-Burlero (lil' i bêr lēr' ō) Said to have been the watchword of the Irish Roman Catholics in their massacres of the Protestants in 1641, the words were adopted as the refrain of a piece of political doggerel (written by Lord Wharton) satirizing James II, which contributed not a little to the success of the great revolution of 1688. Burnet says, "It made an impression on the (king's) army that cannot be imagined . The whole army, and at last the people, both in city and country, were singing it perpetually . never had so slight a thing so great an effect "

The song is referred to in *Tristram Shandy*, and is given in Percy's *Reliques* (series ii, Bk 3). Chappell attributes the air to Henry Purcell.

Wharton afterwards boasted that he had sung a king out of three kingdoms But in truth, the success of Lilliburlero was the effect, not the cause, of that excited state of public feeling which produced the Revolution —MACAULAY *History.*

In World War II the tune of *Lilliburlero* was revived in certain official broadcasts on military matters.

Lilli Marlene. A song composed by Norbert Schultze, in 1938, and sung by the Swedish singer Lala Anderson. It was broadcast by the German radio on the capture of Belgrade, 1941, and became a favourite song of the Afrika Korps From them it was caught up by the British 8th Army In 1944 a documentary film, *The True Story of Lilli Marlene* appeared, featuring Lala Anderson herself.

Lilliput. The country of pigmies ("Lilliputians") to whom Captain Lemuel Gulliver was a giant. (Swift: *Gulliver's Travels*)

Lily, The. There is a tradition that the lily sprang from the repentant tears of Eve as she went forth from Paradise

In Christian art, the lily is an emblem of chastity, innocence, and purity. In pictures of the Annunciation, Gabriel is sometimes represented as carrying a lily-branch, while a vase containing a lily stands before the Virgin, who is kneeling in prayer St Joseph holds a lily-branch in his hand, indicating that his wife Mary was a virgin.

Lily of France. The device of Clovis was three black toads (*see* CRAPAUD), but the story goes that an aged hermit of Joye-en-valle saw a miraculous light stream one night into his cell, and an angel appeared to him holding an azure shield of wonderful beauty, emblazoned with three gold lilies that shone like stars, which the hermit was commanded to give to Queen Clotilde, she gave it to her royal husband, whose arms were everywhere victorious, and the device was thereupon adopted as the emblem of France (*See Les Petits Bollandistes*, vol vi, p 426) It is said the people were commonly called *Liliarts*, and the kingdom *Lilium* in the time of Philippe le Bel, Charles VIII, and Louis XII *See* FLEUR-DE-LYS

Florence is "The City of Lilies "

By "the lily in the field" in *Matt.* vi, 28, which is said to surpass Solomon in all his glory, is meant simply the wild lily, probably a species of iris Our "lily of the valley"—with which this is sometimes confused—is one of the genus *Convallaria*, a very different plant

To paint the lily. *See* PAINT.

Limb. Slang for a mischievous rascal, a young imp, it is short for the older *Limb of the devil*, where the word implies "agent" or "scion " Dryden called Fletcher "a limb of Shakespeare."

Limb of the law. A clerk articled to a lawyer, a sheriff's officer, a policeman, or other legal assistant Just as the *limbs* of the body do what the *head* directs, so these obey the commands of the *head* of the office

Limbo (Lat., border, fringe, edge). The borders of hell; the portion assigned by the Schoolmen to those departed spirits to whom the benefits of redemption did not apply through no fault of their own

The **Paradise of Fools.** As fools or idiots are not responsible for their works, the old Schoolmen held that they are not punished in purgatory and cannot be received into heaven, so they go to a special "Paradise of Fools "

> Then might you see
> Cowls, hoods, and habits, with their wearers tossed
> And fluttered into rags, then relics, beads,
> Indulgences, dispenses, pardons, bulls,
> The sport of winds All these, upwhirled aloft,
> Into a Limbo large and broad, since called
> The Paradise of Fools
> MILTON *Paradise Lost*, iii, 489.

Cp FOOL'S PARADISE *under* FOOL

Limbo of the Fathers. The half-way house between earth and heaven, where the patriarchs and prophets who died before the death of the Redeemer await the Last Day, when they will be received into heaven. Some hold that this is the "hell" into which Christ descended after He gave up the ghost on the cross.

Shakespeare uses *limbo patrum* for "quod," jail, confinement

> I have some of them in limbo patrum, and there they are like to dance these three days —*Henry VIII*, v, 4

The **Limbo** of **Children**, for children who die before they are baptized or are responsible for their actions

Limbus of the Moon. *See* MOON.

Limehouse. At one time descriptive of violent abuse of one's political opponents so called out of compliment to a speech by Lloyd George at Limehouse, London, on July 30th, 1909, when he poured forth scorn and abuse on dukes, landlords, financial magnates, etc.

Lime-light. A vivid light, giving off little heat, produced by the combustion of oxygen and hydrogen on a surface of lime It is also called Drummond Light, after Thomas Drummond (1797-1840), who invented it in 1826 It was tried at the South Foreland lighthouse in 1861. But its main use developed in the theatre, where it could be used to throw a powerful beam upon one player to the exclusion of others on the stage Hence the phrase to be **in the lime-light**, to be in the full glare of public attention.

Limerick. A nonsense verse in the metre, popularized by Edward Lear in his *Book of Nonsense* (1846), of which the following is an example :—

> There was a young lady of Wilts,
> Who walked up to Scotland on stilts,
> When they said it was shocking
> To show so much stocking
> She answered, "Then what about kilts?""

The name was not given till much later, and comes from the chorus, "We'll all come up, come up to Limerick," which was interposed after each verse as it was improvised and sung by a convivial party

Limey (li'mi) In American and Australian slang this means a British sailor or ship, or just a Briton It comes from the old system of taking steps to prevent scurvy by making the crew take lime water

Limp A word formed of the initials of Louis (XIV), James (II), his wife Mary of Modena, and the Prince (of Wales), and used as a Jacobite toast in the time of William III *Cp* NOTARIKON.

Lincoln. A hybrid Celtic and Latin name, *Lindumcolonia*, *Lindum*, the name of the old British town, meaning "the hill fort on the pool "

Lincoln green. Lincoln, at one time, was noted for its light green, as was Coventry for its blue, and Yorkshire for its grey cloth *Cp.* KENDAL GREEN

> Swains in shepherds' gray, and girls in Lincoln green
> DRAYTON *Polyolbion*, xxv 262

Lincoln College (Oxford) Founded by Richard Fleming, Bishop of Lincoln, in 1427, and completed by Thomas Rotherham, Bishop of Lincoln (afterwards Archbishop of York and Lord Chancellor), in 1479.

Lincoln Imp. A grotesque carving, having long ears and only one leg, in the Angel Choir of Lincoln Cathedral.

The devil looking over Lincoln. *See* DEVIL.

Lincoln's Inn. One of the four Inns of Court (*q v.*), in London Henry Lacy, Earl of Lincoln, built a mansion here in the 14th century on ground which had belonged to the Black Friars, but was granted to him by Edward I. A Bishop of Chichester, in the reign of Henry VII, granted leases here to certain students of law

Lindabrides (lin da bri' děz) A heroine in *The Mirror of Knighthood*, whose name at one time was a synonym for a kept mistress

Linden. The German name (largely used in England) for lime trees *Unter den Linden* ("under the limes") is the name of the principal street in Berlin. It is about 1,100 yd in length

Baucis (*see* PHILEMON) was converted into a linden tree.

Lindor. One of the conventional names given by the classical poets to a rustic swain, a lover *en bergere*

Line All along the line. In every particular, as in such phrases as—

> The accuracy of the statement is contested all along the line by persons on the spot

Crossing the line. Sailing across the Equator. Advantage is usually taken of this for all sorts of sports aboard ship, playing great practical jokes on those who have never crossed the Line before The custom was at its prime in the old sailing-ship days A sailor crudely dressed as Father Neptune, accompanied by a yet cruder Amphitrite appeared over the ship's side, followed by yet others, naked to the waist and painted with red ochre or the like The neophytes were then seized, lathered with some horrible compound and while still struggling were forcibly shaved with a piece of rusty hoop iron This was the usual procedure, accompanied by much horseplay and licence

The line. In the British Army all regular infantry regiments except the Foot Guards, the Rifle Brigade, and the Marines are line regiments

Line of battle. The order of troops in the old set-piece battle, drawn up so as to present a battle-front There were three lines—the van, the main body, and the rear A fleet drawn up in *line of battle* is so arranged that the ships are ahead and astern of each other at stated distances

To break the enemy's line is to derange his order of battle, and so put him to confusion

Line of beauty. According to Hogarth, a curve thus ∼

Line of direction. The line in which a body moves, a force acts, or motion is communicated In order that a body may stand without falling, a line let down from the centre of gravity must fall within the base on which the object stands Thus the leaning tower of Pisa does not fall, because this rule is preserved

Line of life. In palmistry, the crease in the left hand beginning above the web of the thumb, and running towards or up to the wrist.

The nearer it approaches the wrist the longer will be the life, according to palmists If long and deeply marked, it indicates long life with very little trouble; if crossed or cut with other marks, it indicates sickness.

Line upon line. Admonition or instruction repeated little by little (a line at a time).

Line upon line, line upon line, here a little and there a little —*Is* xxviii, 10

Hard lines. Hard luck, a hard lot Here *lines* means an allotment measured out

No day without its line. A saying attributed by Pliny to the Greek artist Apelles (*nulla dies sine linea*), who said he never passed a day without doing at least one line, and to this steady industry owed his great success The words were adopted as his motto by Anthony Trollope

On the line. Said of a picture that at the Royal Academy is hung in a position that places its centre about the level of the spectator's eye

The lines have fallen to me in pleasant places (*Ps* xvi, 6) The part allotted to me and measured off by a measuring line The allusion is to drawing a line to mark out the lot of each tribe, hence line became the synonym of lot, and lot means position or destiny

The thin red line. British infantrymen in action The old 93rd Highlanders were so described at the battle of Balaclava by W. H Russell, because they did not take the trouble to form into square, their regimental magazine is named *The Thin Red Line*

˙ To read between the lines. To discern the secret meaning One method of cryptography is to write so that the hidden message is revealed only when alternate lines are read

What line are you in? What trade or profession are you of? Commercial travellers use the word frequently to signify the sort of goods which they have to dispose of, as, one travels

"in the hardware line," another "in the drapery line," or "grocery line," etc.

Line-up. A phrase with a variety of meanings, a parade of persons, especially criminals, for inspection or recognition, an arrangement of players at the start of a game, the deploying of opposing forces before a battle.

To shoot a line. An R A F phrase meaning to exaggerate, to tell a tall story.

Lingo. Talk, language, especially some peculiar or technical phraseology, from *lingua*, tongue

Lingua Franca (ling' gwa fräng' ka) A species of Italian mixed with French, Greek, Arabic, etc , spoken on the coasts of the Mediterranean Also, any jumble of different languages

Lining of the Pocket. Money.

My money is spent Can I be content
With pockets deprived of their lining?
The Lady's Decoy, or Man Midw.fe's Defence, 1738,
p. 4.

When the great court tailor wished to obtain the patronage of Beau Brummel, he made him a present of a dress-coat lined with bank-notes Brummel wrote a letter of thanks, stating that he quite approved of the coat, and he especially admired the lining

Linnæan System (lin ē' an) The artificial classification adopted by the great Swedish naturalist Linnæus (1707-78), who arranged his three kingdoms of animals, vegetables, and minerals into classes, orders, genera, species, and varieties, according to certain characteristics.

Linne, The Heir of (lin) The hero of an old ballad, given in Percy's *Reliques*, which tells how he wasted his substance in riotous living, and, having spent all, sold his estates to his steward, reserving only a poor lodge in a lonely glen When no one would lend him money, he retired to the lodge, where was dangling a rope with a running noose He put it round his neck and sprang aloft, but he fell to the ground, and when he came to espied two chests of beaten gold, and a third full of white money, over which was written—

Once more, my sonne, I sette thee clere,
Amend thy life and follies past,
For but thou amend thee of thy life,
That rope must be thy end at last.

The heir of Linne now returned to his old hall, where he was refused the loan of forty pence by his quondam steward, one of the guests remarked that he ought to have lent it, as he had bought the estate cheap enough. "Cheap call you it?" said the steward; "why, he shall have it back for 100 marks less " "Done," said the heir of Linne, and recovered his estates.

Lion As an agnomen

Alp Arslan, son of Togrul Beg, the Perso-Turkish monarch (reigned 1063-72) was surnamed *The Valiant Lion*

Ali Pasha, called *The Lion of Janina*, overthrown in 1822 by Ibrahim Pasha. (1741, 1788-1822)

Arioch (fifth of the dynasty of Ninu, the Assyrian), called Arioch Ellasar—*i e* Arioch Melech al Asser, *the Lion King of Assyria* (1927-1897 B C)

Damelowicz, Prince of Halicz, who founded Lemberg (*Lion City*) in 1259

Gustavus Adolphus, called *The Lion of the North.* (1594, 1611-32)

Hamza, called *The Lion of God and His Prophet.* So Gabriel told Mohammed that his uncle was enregistered in heaven

Henry, Duke of Bavaria and Saxony, was called *The Lion* for his daring courage (1129-95)

Louis VIII of France was called *The Lion* because he was born under the sign Leo (1187, 1223-26)

Richard I Cœur de Lion (*Lion's heart*), so called for his bravery (1157, 1189-99)

William of Scotland, so called because he chose a red lion *rampant* for his cognizance (Reigned 1165-1214)

See LION OF GOD *below*

A lion is emblem of the tribe of Judah. Christ is called "the lion of the tribe of Judah"

Judah is a lion's whelp: . . he couched as a lion, and as an old lion, who shall rouse him up?—*Gen xlix, 9*

Among the titles of the Emperor of Abyssinia are Conquering Lion of the Tribe of Judah, Elect of God, King of the Kings of Ethiopia

The Lion in Story and Legend

Cybele is represented as riding in a chariot drawn by two tame lions

Pracriti, the goddess of nature among the Hindus, is represented in a similar manner

Hippomenes and *Atalanta* (fond lovers) were metamorphosed into lions by Cybele

Hercules is said to have worn over his shoulders the hide of the Nemean lion (*see* NEMEAN), and the personification of Terror is also arrayed in a lion's hide

The story of Androcles and the lion (*see* ANDROCLES) has many parallels, the most famous of which are those related of St. Jerome and St. Gerasimus —

While St. Jerome was lecturing one day, a lion entered the schoolroom, and lifted up one of its paws All the disciples fled; but Jerome, seeing that the paw was wounded, drew out of it a thorn and dressed the wound The lion, out of gratitude, showed a wish to stay with its benefactor. Hence the saint is represented as accompanied by a lion

St. Gerasimus, says the story, saw, on the banks of the Jordan, a lion coming to him, limping on three feet When it reached the saint it held up to him the right paw, from which Gerasimus extracted a large thorn The grateful beast attached itself to the saint, and followed him about as a dog

Half a score of such tales are told by the Bollandists in the *Acta Sanctorum,* and in more recent times a similar one was told of Sir George Davis, an English consul at Florence at the beginning of the 19th century One day he went to see the lions of the great Duke of Tuscany. There was one which the keepers could not tame, but no sooner did Sir George appear than it manifested every symptom of joy. Sir George entered its cage, when the lion leaped on his shoulder, licked his face, wagged its tail, and fawned on him like a dog Sir George told the great duke that

he had brought up the creature, but as it grew older it became dangerous, and he sold it to a Barbary captain. The duke said that he had bought it of the very same man, and the mystery was solved.

Sir Iwain de Galles, a hero of romance, was attended by a lion, which, in gratitude to the knight who had delivered it from a serpent with which it had been engaged in deadly combat, ever after became his faithful servant, approaching the knight with tears, and rising on its hind-feet like a dog

Sir Geoffrey de Latour was aided by a lion against the Saracens, but the faithful brute was drowned in attempting to follow the vessel in which the knight had embarked on his departure from the Holy Land.

The lion will not touch the true prince (1 *Henry IV,* ii, 4) This is an old superstition, and has been given a Christian significance, the "true prince" being the Messiah, It is applied to any prince of blood royal, supposed at one time to be hedged around with a sort of divinity

Fetch the Numidian lion I brought over,
If she be sprung from royal blood, the lion
He'll do her reverence, else . . .
He'll tear her all to pieces
FLETCHER· *The Mad Lover,* iv, 5.

The lion in Heraldry

Ever since 1164, when it was adopted as a device by Philip I, Duke of Flanders, the lion has figured largely and in an amazing variety of positions as an heraldic emblem, and, as a consequence, in public-house signs The earliest and most important attitude of the heraldic lion is *rampant* (the device of Scotland), but it is also shown as *passant, passant gardant* (as in the shield of England), *salient, sejant,* etc , and even *dormant* For these terms *see* HERALDRY

The lions in the arms of England They are three lions passant gardant, i e walking and showing the full face The first was that of Rollo, Duke of Normandy, and the second represented the country of Maine, which was added to Normandy These were the two lions borne by William the Conqueror and his descendants. Henry II added a third lion to represent the Duchy of Aquitaine, which came to him through his wife Eleanor Any lion not rampant is called a *lion leoparde,* and the French heralds call the lion passant a *leopard;* accordingly Napoleon said to his soldiers, "Let us drive these leopards (the English) into the sea "

Since 1603 the royal arms have been supported as now by (dexter) the English lion and (sinister) the Scottish unicorn (*see* UNICORN), but prior to the accession of James I the sinister supporter was a family badge. Edward III, with whom supporters began, had a lion and eagle, Henry IV, an antelope and swan; Henry V, a lion and antelope, Edward IV, a lion and bull; Richard III, a lion and boar; Henry VII, a lion and dragon, Elizabeth, Mary, and Henry VIII, a lion and greyhound.

The lion in the arms of Scotland is derived from the arms of the ancient Earls of Northumberland and Huntingdon, from whom some of the Scottish monarchs were descended The *tressure* is referred to the reign of Achaius (d.

about 819), who made a league with Charlemagne, "who did augment his arms with a double trace formed with Floure-de-lyces, signifying thereby that the lion henceforth should be defended by the ayde of Frenchemen." (Holinshed *Chronicles*)

Sir Walter Scott says —

William, King of Scotland, having chosen for his armorial bearing a Red Lion *rampant*, acquired the name of William the Lion, and this rampant lion still constitutes the arms of Scotland, and the president of the heraldic court . . is called Lord Lion King-at-Arms.—*Tales of a Grandfather*, iv.

The lion an emblem of the resurrection. According to tradition, the lion's whelp is born dead, and remains so for three days, when the father breathes on it and it receives life. Another tradition is that the lion is the only animal of the cat tribe born with its eyes open, and it is said that it sleeps with its eyes open This is not a fact.

St Mark the Evangelist is symbolized by a *lion* because he begins his gospel with the scenes of St. John the Baptist and Christ in the wilderness *See* EVANGELISTS.

A lion at the feet of crusaders or martyrs, in effigy, signifies that they died for their cause

The Lion of St Mark, or *of Venice* A winged lion *sejant*, holding an open book with the inscription *Pax tibi, Marce, Evangelista Meus* A sword-point rises above the book on the dexter side, and the whole is encircled by an aureola

Among other distinctive lions that appear in blazonry and on the signs of inns, etc , may be mentioned —

Blue, the badge of the Earl of Mortimer, also of Denmark

Crowned, the badge of Henry VIII.

Golden, the badge of Henry I, and also of Percy, Duke of Northumberland.

Rampant, with the tail between its legs and turned over its back, the badge of Edward IV as Earl of March

Red, of Scotland, also the badge of John of Gaunt, Duke of Lancaster, who assumed this badge as a token of his claim to the throne of Castile

Sleeping, the device of Richard I.

Statant gardant (i e standing and showing a full face), the device of the Duke of Norfolk.

White, the device of the Duke of Norfolk; also of the Earl of Surrey, Earl of Mortimer, and the Fitz-Hammonds

Lion of God. Ali-Ben-Abou-Thaleb (602-61), the son-in-law of Mohammed, was so called because of his zeal and his great courage His mother called him at birth *Al Haidara*, "the Rugged Lion"

Lion-hunter. One who hunts up a celebrity to adorn or give prestige to a party. Mrs Leo Hunter, in *Pickwick*, is a good satire on the name and character of a lion-hunter.

Lion of St. Mark. *See* above.

Lion Sermon, The. Preached annually in St. Katharine Cree Church, Leadenhall Street, London, in October, to commemorate ' the wonderful escape" of Sir John Gayre, about 300 years ago, from a lion which he met with

on being shipwrecked on the coast of Africa. Sir John was Lord Mayor in 1647.

Sir John Gayre bequeathed £200 for the relief of the poor on condition that a commemorative sermon was preached annually at St Katharine Cree It is said that Sir John was on his knees in prayer when the lion came up, smelt about him, prowled round and round him, and then stalked off.

Lions. The lions of a place are sights worth seeing, or the celebrities, so called from the ancient custom of showing strangers, as chief of London sights, the lions at the Tower. The Tower menagerie was abolished in 1834.

Lion's Head. In fountains the water is often made to issue from the mouth of a lion. This is a very ancient custom. The Egyptians thus symbolized the inundation of the Nile, which happens when the sun is in Leo (July 28th to August 23rd), and the Greeks and Romans adopted the device for their fountains.

To place one's head in the lion's mouth. To expose oneself needlessly and foolhardily to danger.

Lion's Provider. A jackal; a foil to another man's wit, a humble friend who plays into your hand to show you to best advantage. The jackal (*q v*) feeds on the lion's leavings, and is said to yell to advise the lion that it has roused up his prey, serving the lion in much the same way as a dog serves a sportsman.

. the poor jackals are less foul,
As being the brave lion's keen providers,
Than human insects catering for spiders.
BYRON, *Don Juan*, ix, 27

Lion's share. The larger part all or nearly all. In *Æsop's Fables*, several beasts joined the lion in a hunt, but, when the spoil was divided, the lion claimed one quarter in right of his prerogative, one for his superior courage, one for his dam and cubs, "and as for the fourth, let who will dispute it with me " Awed by his frown, the other beasts yielded and silently withdrew. *Cp* MONTGOMERY.

Lionize a person, To, is either to show him the *lions,* or chief objects of attraction, or to make a lion of him by fêting him and making a fuss about him

Lip. Lip homage or **service** Verbal devotion. Honouring with the lips while the heart takes no part nor lot in the matter. *See Matt* xv, 8; *Is* xxix, 13

To bite one's lip. To express vexation and annoyance, or to suppress some unwanted emotion as laughter or anger.

To carry a stiff upper lip. To be self-reliant; to bear oneself courageously in face of difficulties or danger

To curl the lip. To express contempt or disgust with the mouth.

To hang the lip. To drop the under lip in sullenness or contempt Thus in *Troilus and Cressida* (iii, 1) Helen explains why her brother Troilus is not abroad by saying, "He hangs the lip at something "

A foolish hanging of thy nether lip.—1 *Henry IV,* i, 4

To shoot out the lip. To show scorn

All they that see me laugh me to scorn They shoot out the lip, they shake the head . . .—*Ps* xxii, 7

Liqueur (lı kū′ er) An aromatic and usually sweetened drink combined with various flavourings to give a distinctive character. Liqueurs generally consist of equal portions of alcohol and syrup made from cane sugar mixed with essences and herbs. Some of the most renowned liqueurs originated in monasteries, and the secret of their recipe has been and still is jealously guarded. Among the chief of these are the green and yellow Chartreuse, now made at Tarragona by paid servants and lay brothers. The great profits help to keep up the monasteries and maintain considerable charities. Benedictine, although made on the site of the great monastery of Fecamp, has nothing whatever to do with the monastic order—it is an ordinary commercial product.

Liquidate. In the sinister slang introduced by Fascism, this means to kill, to get out of the way by murder.

Lir, King. The earliest known original of the King in *King Lear*, an ocean god of early Irish and British legend. He figures in the romance *The Fate of the Children of Lir* as the father of Fionnuala (*q v*). On the death of Fingula, the mother of his daughter, he married the wicked Aoife, who, through spite, transformed the children of Lir into swans, doomed to float on the water till they heard the first mass-bell ring.
Lir was fabled to be a descendant of Brutus, and appears in early Welsh chronicles as *Lear*, or *Leyr* (the founder of Leicester), whence—through Geoffrey of Monmouth, by whose time other legends had crystallized round him—Shakespeare obtained the framework of his plot.

Lisbon. Camoëns, in the *Lusiad*, derives the name from '*Ulyssippo* (Ulysses' polis or city), and says that it was founded by Ulysses, but it is in fact the old Phœnician *Olisippo*, the walled town. The root *Hippo* appears as the name of more than one ancient African city, also in Orippo, Lacippo, and other Spanish towns.

Lismahago (lıs má hã′ gō). A proud but poor, and very conceited, Scots captain, in Smollett's *Humphrey Clinker*. Fond of disputation, jealous of honour, and brimful of national pride, he marries Miss Tabitha Bramble.

Lit de Justice (lē de zhus tēs) Properly the seat occupied by the French king when he attended the deliberations of his *parlement*, hence, the session itself, any arbitrary edict. As the members derived their power from the king, when the king was present their power returned to the fountain-head, and the king was arbitrary. What he then proposed could not be controverted, and had the force of law. The last *lit de justice* was held by Louis XVI in 1787.

Little. Little by little Gradually; a little at a time.

Many a little makes a mickle. The real Scottish proverb is: "A wheen o 'mickles mak's **a** muckle," where *mickle* means *little*, and *muckle much*, but the Anglo-Saxon *micel* or *mycel* means "much," so that, if the Scots proverb is accepted, we must give a forced meaning to the word "mickle."

Little Britain. The name given in the old romances to Armorica, now Brittany, also called Benwic.
The street in the City of London of this name was first so called in the time of Queen Elizabeth, previously it was known as *Britten* or *Brettone Street*, and is said to have been so called because the Dukes of Brittany had had a mansion on this site. The old name of the northern part of Little Britain was *Duke Street*.

Little Corporal, The. Napoleon Bonaparte. So called after the battle of Lodi, in 1796, from his low stature, youthful age, and amazing courage. He was barely 5 ft. 2 in in height.

Little-endians. In Swift's *Gulliver's Travels* (*Voyage to Lilliput*) the faction which insisted on interpreting the vital direction contained in the 54th chapter of the Blundecral: "All true believers break their eggs at the convenient end," as meaning the *little end*, and waged a destructive war against those who adopted the alternative (*cp.* BIG-ENDIANS).
The terms are still used in connexion with hostilities or arguments arising out of trifling differences of opinion, etc, especially in matters of doctrine. In Swift's satire the Big-endians typify the Catholics, and the Little-endians the Protestants.

Little Englanders An opprobrious name which became popular about the time of the last Boer War for those who upheld the doctrine that the English should concern themselves with England only, and were opposed to any extension of the Empire.

Little Entente was the name given to some of the Near Eastern countries before World War II. Czechoslovakia, Yugoslavia, and Rumania signed formal treaties of alliance in 1920 and again in 1929, one of the chief objects being to prevent the restoration of the Hapsburgs to the throne of Hungary.

Little Gentleman in Velvet. "The little gentleman in velvet," *i.e* the mole, was a favourite Jacobite toast in the reign of Queen Anne. The reference was to the mole that raised the molehill against which the horse of William III stumbled at Hampton Court. By this accident the king broke his collar-bone, and after a severe illness died early in 1702.

Little-go A preliminary examination at Cambridge which all undergraduates must pass (unless excused on account of having passed certain other exams.) before proceeding to take any examination for a degree. The *Little-go* is almost invariably taken in or before the first term. The examination at Oxford corresponding with this is Responsions.

Little Jack Horner. *See* JACK.

Little John. A semi-legendary character in the Robin Hood cycle, a big stalwart fellow, first named John Little (or John Nailor), who encountered Robin Hood, and gave him a sound thrashing, after which he was re-christened, and Robin stood godfather

"This infant was called John Little," quoth he,
"Which name shall be changed anon
The words we'll transpose, so wherever he goes,
His name shall be called Little John"
RITSON · *Robin Hood*, xxi.

Little Mary. *See* MARY.

Little Masters. A name applied to certain designers who worked for engravers, etc , in the 16th and 17th centuries, because their designs were on a small scale, fit for copper or wood The most famous are Jost Amman, Hans Burgmair (who made drawings in wood illustrative of the triumph of the Emperor Maximilian), Albert Altdorfer, and Heinrich Aldegraver Albert Durer and Lucas van Leyden made the art renowned and popular

Little Parliament, The Another name for the Barebones Parliament (*q v*)

Little Red Ridinghood. This nursery tale is, with slight alterations, common to Sweden, Germany, and France. It comes to us from the French *Le Petit Chaperon Rouge*, in Charles Perrault's *Contes des Temps*, and was probably derived from Italy The *finale*, which tells of the arrival of a huntsman who slits open the wolf and restores little Red Ridinghood and her grandmother to life, is a German addition.

Little Rhody The State of Rhode Island, U S A.

Liturgy. The Greek word from which this comes means *public service*, or *worship of the gods*, and the arranging of the dancing and singing on public festivals, the equipping and manning of ships, etc In the Church of England it means the religious forms prescribed in the Book of Common Prayer.

Liver. The liver was anciently supposed to be the seat of love, hence, when Longaville reads the verses, Biron says, in an aside, "This is the liver-vein, which makes flesh a deity" (*Love's Labour's Lost*, iv, 3), and in *The Merry Wives of Windsor* (ii, 1) Pistol speaks of Falstaff as loving Ford's wife "with liver burning hot "

Another superstition concerning this organ was that the liver of a coward contained no blood, hence such expressions as white-livered, lily-livered, and Sir Toby's remark in *Twelfth Night* (ii, 2) —

For Andrew, if he were opened, and you find so much blood in his liver as will clog the foot of a flea, I'll eat the rest of the anatomy

In the auspices taken by the Greeks and Romans before battle, if the liver of the animals sacrificed was healthy and blood-red, the omen was favourable, but if pale, it augured defeat.

Liverpool. There have been many guesses at the origin of this place-name (which was first recorded about 1190, as *Leverpol*), the most probable deriving it from Welsh *Llyr-pwl*, the sea-pool, though both the Norse *hlithar polir*, the pool of the slape, and Eng *lither* (stagnant) *pool* have something to recommend them.

It was in the 17th century that antiquarians invented the *liver*, a mythical bird, to account for the name They evolved it from the bird in the arms of the city, which was intended for an heraldic representation of the eagle of St John the Evangelist

A native of Liverpool is called a **Liverpudlian** or a **Dicky Sam**

Livery. What is delivered The clothes of a manservant delivered to him by his master The stables to which your horse is delivered for keep. Splendid dresses were formerly given to all the members of royal households, barons and knights gave uniforms to their retainers, and even a duke's son, serving as a page, was clothed in the *livery* of the prince he served.

What livery is we know well enough, it is the allowance of horse-meate to keepe horses at livery, the which word, I guess, is derived of delivering forth their nightly food —*Spenser on Ireland*

The colours of the livery of menservants should be those of the field and principal charge of the armorial shield, hence the royal livery is scarlet trimmed with gold

Livery Companies. The modern representatives in the City of London of the old City Guilds (*see* GUILDHALL), so called because they formerly wore distinctive costumes, or *liveries* (*see above*) for special occasions The names of the companies are not, to-day, any guide to the profession or occupation of the "liverymen" (except, perhaps, in a few cases, such as the Stationers'), but they show the origin of the company, and many of the present members are descendants of prominent men in the particular business

The twelve "great" companies, in order of civic precedence, with the date of their formation or incorporation, are.—

Mercers (1393).	Merchant Taylors (1326).
Grocers (1345).	Haberdashers (1448)
Drapers (1364)	Salters (1394).
Fishmongers (1384)	Ironmongers (1463)
Goldsmiths (1327).	Vintners (1437)
Skinners (1319)	Clothworkers (1527)

The Grocers' were originally known as the *Pepperers*, and the Haberdashers' the *Hurrers* Samuel Pepys was Master (1677) of the Clothworkers, which was a 16th-century incorporation of the Shearmen and Fullers' Guild

The first twelve of the lesser livery companies, in order of civic precedence, are —

Dyers	Barbers.	Tallowchandlers.
Brewers	Cutlers	Armourers & Braziers.
Leathersellers	Bakers	Girdlers
Pewterers.	Waxchandlers.	Butchers.

There are about 90 City companies of old standing, nearly all of which contribute largely from their funds to charities (especially in the matter of education), and about 40 of which have their own "Halls" in the City

Liverymen. The freemen of the London livery companies are so called because they were entitled to wear the livery of their respective companies.

Livy. Livy of France, The. Juan de Mariana (1537-1624)

Livy of Portugal, The. João de Barros, the chief of the Portuguese historians (1496-1570).

Lizard. Supposed, at one time, to be venomous, and hence a "lizard's leg" was an ingredient of the witches' cauldron in *Macbeth*

Poison be their drink!
Their chiefest prospect murdering basilisks!
Their softest touch as smart as lizard's stings!
2 *Henry VI*, iii, 2.

Lizard Point (Cornwall) Gaelic, "the point of the high (*ard*) fort (*lis*) " *Ard* appears in a large number of place names—*Ardrossan* (the little high point), *Ardwick* (the high town), the *Ardennes* (high valleys), etc , and *Lis* in *Lismore*, *Liskeard*, *Ballylesson* (the town of the little fort), etc

Lounge lizard. A phrase current in the 1920s to describe a young man who spent his time, or, often made his living, by dancing and waiting upon elderly women

Llew Llaw Gyffes, or the Lion with the Steady Hand, a hero of the type of Hercules, was worshipped in ancient Britain and until the 19th century in some parts of Wales His death on the first Sunday in August, was celebrated by a feast called Lugh-mass, sometimes confounded with Lammas

Lloyd's. An association of underwriters, merchants, shipowners, brokers, etc , principally dealing with ocean-borne commerce, marine insurance, and the publication of shipping intelligence. So called because the society was founded (1689) in Tower Street, and moved (1691) to a coffee-house kept in Lombard Street by one Edward Lloyd In 1774 the offices, or *Lloyd's Rooms*, were removed to the Royal Exchange, in 1928 to Leadenhall Street

Lloyd's books. Two enormous ledger-like volumes, placed on desks at the entrance (right and left) of Lloyd's Rooms They give the principal arrivals, and all losses by wrecks, fire, or other accidents at sea The entries are written in a fine, bold Roman hand, legible to all.

Lloyd's List A periodical, in which the shipping news received at Lloyd's Rooms is published It has been issued regularly from 1726, since 1800 as a daily

Lloyd's Register. A register of ships, British and foreign, published yearly

Load Line is another name for the Plimsoll Mark (*q v*) that is carried amidships by every vessel of the Merchant Navy. It shows the maximum depth to which she may be loaded in salt water, in fresh water, at different times of the year, in different oceans, etc

Loaf. In sacred art a loaf held in the hand is an attribute of St. Philip the Apostle, St. Osyth, St Joanna, St Nicholas, St. Godfrey, and of many other saints noted for their charity to the poor.

Half a loaf is better than no bread. An old saying, if you can't get all you want, try to be content with what you do get. Heywood (1546) says —

> Throw no gift at the giver's head;
> Better is half a loaf than no bread.

Never turn a loaf in the presence of a Menteith. An old Scottish saying It was Sir John Stewart de Menteith who betrayed Wallace to the English When he turned a loaf set on the table, his guests were to rush upon the patriot and secure him. (Scott. *Tales of a Grandfather*, vii.)

With an eye to the loaves and fishes. With a view to the material benefits to be derived. The allusion is to the Gospel story of the crowd following Christ, not for the spiritual doctrines

He taught, but for the loaves and fishes distributed by Him amongst them

> Jesus answered them and said, Verily, verily, I say unto you, Ye seek Me, not because ye saw the miracles, but because ye did eat of the loaves, and were filled — *John* vi, 26.

Loafer One who idles away his time, or saunters about as though he had all his life to do it in, a lazy "do-nothing." The word was originally American slang (about 1830), and was probably German—either a mispronunciation of *lover*, or from *laufen*, to run, go, move

Loathly Lady. A stock character of the old romances who is so hideous that everyone is deterred from marrying her When, however, she at last finds a husband her ugliness—the effect of enchantment—disappears, and she becomes a model of beauty Her story—a very common one, in which sometimes the enchanted beauty has to assume the shape of a serpent or some hideous monster—is the feminine counterpart of that of "Beauty and the Beast" (*q v.*).

Lob. Old thieves' slang for a till Hence *lobsneak*, one who robs the till, *lob-crawling*, on the prowl to rob tills

Lob's Pound Old slang for prison, the stocks, or any other place of confinement

Lobby A vestibule or corridor, usually giving access to several apartments, from Med. Lat. *lobia*, a word used in the monasteries for the passages (connected with *lodge*) In the Houses of Parliament the name is given to the corridors ("Division Lobbies") to which members of the Commons go to vote, and also to the large anteroom to which the public are admitted The latter gives us the verb **to lobby**, to solicit the vote of a member or to seek to influence members, and the noun **lobbyist**, one who does this

> The Bill will cross the lobbies. Be sent from the House of Commons to the House of Lords

Loblolly. A sailors' term for spoon-victuals, pap, water-gruel, and so on

Loblolly boy A surgeon's mate in the Navy, a lad not yet out of his spoon-meat.

> Loblolly-boy is a person on board a man-of-war who attends the surgeon and his mates, but knows as much about the business of a seaman as the author of this poem.—*The Patent* (1776)

Lobsters. Soldiers used to be popularly called lobsters, because they were "turned red" when enlisted into the service But the term was originally applied to a troop of horse soldiers in the Great Rebellion, clad in armour which covered them as a shell.

> Sir William Waller received from London (in 1643) a fresh regiment of 500 horse, under the command of Sir Arthur Haslerig, which were so prodigiously armed that they were called by the king's party "the regiment of lobsters," because of their bright iron shells with which they were covered, being perfect cuirassiers, and were the first seen so armed on either side —CLARENDON· *History of the Rebellion*, iii, 91.

Died for want of lobster sauce. Sometimes said of one who dies or suffers severely because of some trifling disappointment, pique, or wounded vanity At the grand feast given by the great Condé to Louis XIV, at Chantilly, Vatel, the *chef*, was told that the lobsters intended for sauce had not arrived, whereupon he retired to his private room, and, leaning on his sword, ran it through his body, unable to survive the disgrace thus brought upon him

Local, in colloquial parlance, means the nearest or the most frequented public house

Local option is the choice allowed to a town, county, or other locality to decide what course it shall take on a given question, specifically the sale of liquor. In 1913 Carlisle was given local option in this sense, in each area the electors having the decision as to whether or not intoxicating liquor should be sold

Lochiel (loch ēl') The title of the head of the clan Cameron

The hero of Campbell's poem, *Lochiel's Warning* (1802), is Donald Cameron, known as *The Gentle Lochiel* He was one of the Young Pretender's staunchest adherents, and escaped to France with him after Culloden (1746) He took service in the French army, but died two years later.

Lochinvar (lok in var'), being in love with a lady at Netherby Hall, persuaded her to dance one last dance She was condemned to marry a "laggard in love and a dastard in war," but her young chevalier swung her into his saddle and made off with her, before the "bridegroom" and his servants could recover from their astonishment (Scott. *Marmion.*)

Loch Ness Monster. In April, 1933, a motorist driving along the shore of Loch Ness, Scotland, saw at some distance from the land what seemed a strange object, subsequently described as being 30 ft long, with two humps, a snake-like head at the end of a long neck, and two flippers about the middle of the body It was "seen" by others, and a brisk tourist trade began to centre around its movements Public interest and excitement were worked up by newspaper reports, and the question of an official investigation was raised in Parliament, but negatived A well-known circus proprietor offered £20,000 for the monster, but it resisted all baits and allurements. From time to time fresh evidences of its presence have been reported, but scientists have found few details to arouse their interest The popular theory is that the creature is a diplodoccus or some prehistoric survival, but scientists preserve an open mind on the existence or nature of the Loch Ness Monster.

Lockhart Legend has it that when the good Lord James, on his way to the Holy Land with the heart of King Robert Bruce, was slain in Spain fighting against the Moors, Sir Simon Locard, of Lee, was commissioned to carry back to Scotland the heart, which was interred in Melrose Abbey. In consequence thereof he changed his name to Lock-heart, and adopted the device of *a heart within a fetterlock*, with this motto: "*Corda serrata pando*" (Locked hearts I open.)

Locksley Hall. Tennyson's poem of this name (1842) deals with an imaginary place and an imaginary hero The Lord of Locksley Hall

fell in love with his cousin Amy, she married a rich clown, and he, indignant at this, declared he would wed a savage, he changed his mind, however, and decided, "Better fifty years of Europe than a cycle of Cathay"

In 1886 Tennyson published *Locksley Hall Sixty Years After*, another dramatic poem.

Locksmith's Daughter. A key

Lock, Stock, and Barrel The whole of anything The lock, stock, and barrel of a gun is the complete firearm

Locofoco (lō' kō fō' kō) A trade-name coined in America as that of a self-igniting cigar (patented in New York, 1834), but quickly transferred to lucifer matches, and then to the Democratic Party in America, because, at a meeting in Tammany Hall (1835), when the chairman left his seat, and the lights were suddenly extinguished with the hope of breaking up the turbulent assembly, those of the opposition faction drew from their pockets their *locofocos*, re-lighted the gas, and got their way

Here's full particulars of the patriotic loco-foco movement yesterday, in which the whigs was so chawed up —DICKENS *Martin Chuzzlewit* (1843).

Locrine (lok rīn'). Father of Sabrina, and eldest son of the mythical Brutus, King of ancient Britain On the death of his father he became king of Loegria (Geoffrey: *Brit. Hist*, ii, 5)

> Virgin daughter of Locrine,
> Sprung from old Anchises' line
> MILTON · *Comus*, 942-3.

An anonymous tragedy, based on Holinshed and Geoffrey of Monmouth, was published under this name in 1595 As the words "Newly set foorth, overseene and corrected, By *W. S*" appear on the title-page, it was at one time ascribed to Shakespeare It has also been ascribed to Marlowe, Greene, and Peele—the weight of evidence being rather in favour of the last named

Locum tenens (lō' kum tē' nens) (Lat) One (especially a doctor) acting temporarily for another.

Locus Latin for a place.

Locus delicti. The place where a crime was committed

Locus in quo (Lat.). The place in question, the spot mentioned.

Locus pœnitentiæ (Lat) Place for repentance —that is, the licence of drawing back from a bargain, which can be done before any act has been committed to confirm it In the interview between Esau and his father Isaac, St Paul says that the former "found no place for repentance, though he sought it carefully with tears" (*Heb.* xii, 17)—i e no means whereby Isaac could break his bargain with Jacob.

Locus sigilli (Lat). The place where the seal is to be set, usually abbreviated in documents to "L.S."

Locus standi (Lat) Recognized position, acknowledged right or claim, especially in courts of law We say such-and-such a one has no *locus standi* in society

Locusta (lŏ kŭs' tå). A woman who murders those she professes to nurse, or those whom it is her duty to take care of. Locusta lived in the early days of the Roman Empire, poisoned Claudius and Britannicus, and attempted to destroy Nero, but, being found out, she was put to death.

Lode. Originally a ditch that guides or leads water into a river or sewer, from A S *lad*, way, course (connected with *to lead*), hence, in mines, the vein that leads or guides to ore

Lodestar. The North Star or Pole Star, the *leading-star* by which mariners are guided (*see* LODE)
Your eyes are lodestars.—*Midsummer Night's Dream*, i, 1

Lodestone, Loadstone. The magnet or stone that guides

Lodona (lo dō' na) The Lodden, an affluent of the Thames in Windsor Forest. Pope, in *Windsor Forest*, says it was a nymph, fond of the chase, like Diana It chanced one day that Pan saw her, and tried to catch her, but Lodona fled from him, imploring Cynthia to save her from her persecutor. No sooner had she spoken than she became "a silver stream which ever keeps its virgin coolness."

Loegria or **Logres** (lŏ eg' ri å, lō' gres) England is so called by Geoffrey of Monmouth, from Locrine (*q v*)
His [Brute's] three sons divide the land by consent, Locrine had the middle part, Loegra —MILTON *History of England*, Bk i
Thus Cambria to her right, what would herself restore,
And rather than to lose Loegria, looks for more
DRAYTON. *Polyolbion*, iv

Log. Instrument for measuring the velocity of a ship in motion. In its simplest form it is a flat piece of wood, some six inches in radius, in the shape of a quadrant, and made so that it will float perpendicularly. To this is fastened the log-line, knotted at intervals *See* KNOT

A King Log. A king who rules in peace and quietness, but never makes his power felt. In allusion to the fable of the frogs asking for a king. Jupiter first threw them down a log of wood, but they grumbled at so spiritless a king. He then sent them a stork, which devoured them eagerly

Log-book. On board ship, the journal in which the "logs" are entered. It contains also all general transactions pertaining to the ship and its crew, such as the strength and course of the winds, everything worthy of note

Log-cabin Campaign (U S A). Political campaign in 1840, in which Gen. W H Harrison is said to have lived in a log-cabin and subsisted mainly on hard cider

Log-rolling. Applied in politics to the ' give and take" principle, by which one party will further certain interests of another in return for assistance given in passing their own measures, in literary circles it means mutual admiration. The mutual admirers are called "log-rollers," and the allusion (originally American) is to neighbours who assist a new settler to roll away the logs of his "clearing."

Logs. An early Australian name for prison, changed with time and circumstances to *The Bricks*.

Loganberry. A cross between the raspberry and blackberry, so called from Judge Logan, of California, who was the first to cultivate it

Logan Stones. Rocking stones, large masses of stone so delicately poised by nature that they will rock to and fro at a touch There are many logan stones in Cornwall, Derbyshire, Yorkshire, and Wales, and some well-known specimens in Scotland and Ireland, they were formerly used in connexion with Druidical rites. When the Logan Rock (about 70 tons) at Land's End was displaced by a naval lieutenant (1824), he was ordered to replace it, which he did at a cost of some £2,000.
Pliny tells of a rock near Harpasa which might be moved with a finger
Ptolemy says the Gygonian rock might be stirred with a stalk of asphodel
Half a mile from St. David's is a Logan stone, mounted on divers other stones, which may be shaken with one finger
In Pembrokeshire is a rocking stone, rendered immovable by the soldiers of Cromwell, who held it to be an encouragement to superstition.
The stone called Menamber in Sithney (Cornwall) was also rendered immovable by the soldiers, under the same notion

Loggerheads. Fall to loggerheads: to squabbling and fisticuffs The word is used by Shakespeare *Logger* was the name given to the heavy wooden clog fastened to the legs of grazing horses to prevent their straying.

Logres, Logria *See* LOEGRIA.

Logris. Same as Locrine (*q v*).

Lohengrin (lō' en grin) A son of Percival, in German legend, attached to the Grail Cycle, and Knight of the Swan He appears at the close of Wolfram von Eschenbach's *Parzival* (about 1210), and in other German romances, where he is the deliverer of Elsa, Princess of Brabant, who has been dispossessed by Tetramund and Ortrud. He arrives at Antwerp in a skiff drawn by a swan, champions Elsa, and becomes her husband on the sole condition that she shall not ask his name or lineage. She is prevailed upon to do so on the marriage-night, and he, by his vows to the Grail, is obliged to disclose his identity, but at the same time disappears. The swan returns for him, and he goes; but not before retransforming the swan into Elsa's brother Gottfried, who, by the wiles of the sorceress Ortrud, had been obliged to assume that form Wagner's opera of this name was composed in 1847.

Loins. Gird up your loins. Brace yourself for vigorous action, or energetic endurance. The Jews wore loose garments, which they girded about their loins when they travelled or worked
Gird up the loins of your mind —1 *Pet* i, 13.

My little finger shall be thicker than my father's loins (1 *Kings* xii, 10). My lightest tax shall be heavier than the most oppressive tax of my predecessor. The arrogant answer of Rehoboam to the deputation which waited on him to entreat an alleviation of "the yoke" laid on them by Solomon. The reply caused the revolt of all the tribes, except those of Judah and Benjamin

Loki (lō´kĭ) The god of strife and spirit of evil in Norse mythology, son of the giant Firbauti and Laufey, or Nal, the friend of the enemy of the gods, and father of the Midgard Serpent, Fenrir, and Hel It was he who artfully contrived the death of Balder (*q.v*) He was finally chained to a rock with ten chains, and—according to one legend—will so continue till the Twilight of the Gods, when he will break his bonds, the heavens will disappear, the earth be swallowed up by the sea, fire shall consume the elements, and even Odin, with all his kindred deities, shall perish Another story has it that he was freed at Ragnarok, and that he and Heimdall fought till both were slain

Lollards. The early German reformers and the followers of Wyclif were so called An ingenious derivation is given by Bailey, who suggests the Latin word *lolium* (darnel), because these reformers were deemed ' tares in God's wheat-field," but the name is from Mid. Dut *lollaerd*, a mutterer, one who mumbles over prayers and hymns

Gregory XI, in one of his bulls against Wyclif, urged the clergy to extirpate this *lolium*

Lombard. A banker or moneylender, so called because the first bankers were from Lombardy, and set up in Lombard Street (London), in the Middle Ages

I am an honester man than Will Coppersmith, for all his great credit among the Lombards —STEELE *The Tatler* No lvii.

The business of lending money on pawn was carried on in England by Italian merchants or bankers as early as the reign of Richard I By the 12 Edward I, a messuage was confirmed to these traders where Lombard Street now stands; they exercised a monopoly in pawnbroking till the reign of Queen Elizabeth, but the trade was first recognized in law by James I Among the richest of the Lombard merchant princes was the celebrated Medici family, from whose armorial bearings the insignia of three golden balls has been derived

All Lombard Street to a China orange An old saying, implying very long odds Lombard Street, London, is the centre of great banking and mercantile transactions To stake the wealth of London against a common orange is to stake what is of untold value against a mere trifle.

"It is Lombard Street to a China orange," quoth Uncle Jack —BULWER LYTTON *The Caxtons*

London. The origin of the name is uncertain, but it first appears in *Tacitus* (Lib. XIV, ch xxxiii, 61 A.D).

At Suetonius mira constantia medios inter hostes Londinium perrexit, cognomento quidem coloniæ non insigne, sed copia negotiatorum et commeatum maxime celebre

Stow, following Geoffrey of Monmouth, says that it was originally called Troynovant (*q.v*), and that Cæsar's "cittie of the Trinobantes" meant London By later Latin writers it was frequently called "Londinium Augusta."

The first syllable may represent Welsh *llŷ*, water, and the second be the Celtic *dun*, a hillfort—the fort on the water; *lon*- may equally

well be Celtic *lon*, a marsh, or *llwyn*, a grove, while another authority says that it is Welsh *llong*, a ship—the City of Ships.

Francis Crossley derives the name from *Luan-dun* (Celtic), City of the Moon, and tradition says there was once a temple to Diana (the Moon) where St Paul's now stands; but he says that Greenwich (*q v*) is *Grianwich* (City of the Sun), also Celtic It would fill a page to give a list of guesses made at the derivation of the word London.

London Bridge. There was a bridge over the Thames in the 10th century There was a new one of wood in 1014 The stone bridge (1176-1209) was by Peter of Colechurch The present London Bridge, constructed of granite, was begun in 1824. and finished in seven years It was built some 50 yards west of the old bridge, which started from Fish Street Hill It was designed by Sir John Rennie, and cost £1,458,000. Till 1750 London Bridge was the only bridge crossing the Thames in London

London Bridge was built upon woolpacks. An old saying commemorating the fact that in the reign of Henry II the new stone bridge over the Thames was paid for by a tax on wool.

London Gazette is the official organ of the British Government and the appointed medium for all official announcements It dates from 1665 when Henry Muddiman started it as a daily newsletter or newspaper. It is now published on Tuesdays and Fridays The *Irish Free State Gazette* (Dublin), the *Belfast Gazette* are similar official organs.

London Pride is the little red-and-white *Saxifraga umbrosa* also called None-so-pretty and St. Patrick's Cabbage.

London Regiment consists of two regular battalions of the City of London Regiment (Royal Fusiliers) and a number of territorial battalions including the London Rifle Brigade, Kensingtons, Artists Rifles, London Scottish, etc

London Stone The ancient Roman stone now fixed for security in the wall of St. Swithin's church, facing Cannon Street station, and guarded by an iron grille It has two inscriptions, one in Latin and one in English. The latter runs thus —

London stone Commonly believed to be a Roman work, long placed about xxxv feet hence towards the south-west, and afterwards built into the wall of this church, more for carefvl protection and transmission to future ages, better secured by the churchwardens in the year of OVR LORD MDCCCLXIX.

It is supposed to have been the central milliarium (*milestone*) of Roman London, similar to that in the Forum of Rome, from which the high roads radiated and were measured.

Londonderry. This Northern Ireland county took its prefix of "London" when, in 1609, much of the land was made over to the corporation of London. The capital city, long known as Derry, was besieged for 15 weeks by James II in 1689 and its citizens were reduced to great distress before the relieving fleet broke the boom across the harbour, June 30th, 1689

Lone Star State. The state of Texas, U.S A.

Long. For **Long** chalks, dozen, odds, etc , *see* these words

So long. Good-bye, till we meet again

Longboat. Formerly the largest boat carried by a sailing ship, built so as to take a great weight A longboat is often from 30 to 40 feet long, having a beam from 29 to 25 of its length. It has a heavy flat floor, and is carvel-built

To draw the longbow. *See* Bow.

Long-headed. Clever, sharp-witted. Those who believe in the shape and bumps of the head think that a long head indicates shrewdness

Long Meg of Westminster. A noted virago in the reign of Henry VIII, around whose exploits a comedy (since lost) was performed in London in 1594

> *Lord Proudly.* What d'ye this afternoon?
> *Lord Feesimple* Faith, I have a great mind to see *Long Meg* and *The Ship* at the Fortune.
> FIELD. *Amends for Ladies*, II, 1 (1618)

Her name has been given to several articles of unusual size Thus, the large blue-black marble in the south cloister of Westminster Abbey, over the grave of Gervasius de Blois, is called "Long Meg of Westminster." Fuller says the term is applied to things "of hop-pole height, wanting breadth proportionable thereunto," and refers to a great gun in the Tower so called, taken to Westminster in troublesome times, and in the *Edinburgh Antiquarian Magazine* (September, 1769) we read of Peter Branan, aged 104, who was 6 ft. 6 in high, and was commonly called *Long Meg of Westminster.* Cɒ MEG

Long Meg and her daughters. In the neighbourhood of Penrith, Cumberland, is a circle of 67 (Camden says 77) stones, some of them 10 ft high, ranged in a circle Some seventeen paces off, on the south side, is a single stone, 15 ft high, called *Long Meg*, the shorter ones being called *her daughters.*

> This, and the Robrick stones in Oxfordshire, are supposed to have been erected at the investiture of some Danish kings, like the Kingstoler in Denmark and the Moresteen in Sweden —CAMDEN. *Britannia.*

Long Melford. A long, stocking purse, such as was formerly carried by country folk. In boxing, according to Isopel Berners, a Long Melford was a straight blow with the right hand (*Lavengro*, lxxxv.)

Long Parliament. The parliament that sat 12 years and 5 months, from November 2nd, 1640, to April 20th, 1653, when it was dissolved by Cromwell A fragment of it called "The Rump" (*q v*), continued till the Restoration, in 1660.

Long Range Desert Patrol. A British military organization of volunteers in World War II who, in N. Africa, penetrated behind the enemy's lines to do as much damage as possible Their most celebrated exploit was the raid on Field Marshal Rommel's headquarters, carried out by a small group under Lieut-Col Keyes, who was posthumously awarded the V C.

Long-Sword (*Longue epee*) The surname of William, the first Duke of Normandy (d 943). He was the great-great-grandfather of William the Conqueror, and so a direct ancestor of our reigning House The name was also given to William, third Earl of Salisbury (d 1226), a natural son of Henry II and (probably) the Fair Rosamund

Cut and long tail. One and another, all of every description The phrase had its origin in the practice of cutting the tails of certain dogs and horses, and leaving others in their natural state, so that cut and long tail horses or dogs included all the species, Master Slender says he will maintain Anne Page like a gentlewoman "Ah!" says he—

> That I will, come cut and long tail under the degree of a squire [*i e* as well as any man can who is not a squire]—SHAKESPEARE *Merry Wives of Windsor*, iii, 4.

How about the **long-tailed beggar?** A reproof given to one who is drawing the longbow too freely The tale is that a boy who had been a short voyage pretended on his return to have forgotten everything belonging to his home, and asked his mother what she called that "long-tailed beggar," meaning the cat

Long words. "Honorificabilitudinitatibus," (*q v*) has often been called the longest word in the English language; "quadradimensionality" is almost as long, and "antidisestablishmentarianism" beats it by one letter

While there is some limit to the coining of polysyllabic words by the conglomeration of prefixes, combining forms, and suffixes (*e g* "deanthropomorphization," "inanthropomorphizability"), there is little to the length to which chemists will go in the nomenclature of compounds, and none at all to that indulged in by facetious romancers like Rabelais, the author of *Croquemitaine* The chemists furnish us with such concatenations (for they are scarcely *words*) as " nitrophenylenediamine," and "tetramethyldiamidobenzhydrols", but the worst in this sort are far surpassed by the nonsense words found in Urquhart and Motteux's translation of Rabelais The following come from a single chapter (Bk. IV, ch xv) —

> He was grown quite esperruquanchurelubelouzerirelieced down to his very heel .

Long place-names in Britain include Drimtaidhvrickhillichattan, in the Isle of Mull, Argyllshire, and the famous village in Anglesea, Llanfairpwllgwyngyllgogerychwyrndrobwllllandysiliogogogoch (usually called Llanfairpwll) In the postal directory the first twenty letters only are given as a sufficient address for practical purposes, but the full name contains 59 letters The meaning is, "The church of St. Mary in a hollow of white hazel, near to the rapid whirlpool, and to St Tisilio church, near to a red cave "

The longest English surname is said to be Featherstonehaugh, often pronounced făn'-shaw

The longest English monosyllables are probably "stretched" and "screeched"

The German language lends itself to very extensive agglomerations of syllables, but the following official title of a North Bohemian official— "Lebensmittelzuschusseinstellungs-kommissionsvorsitzenderstellvertreter," *i e.* Deputy-President of the Food-Rationing-Winding-up-Commission—would be hard to beat

Longchamps (long shong) The racecourse at the end of the Bois de Boulogne, Paris. An abbey formerly stood there, and it was long celebrated for the promenade of smartly dressed Parisians which took place on the Wednesday, Thursday, and Friday of Holy Week

The custom dates from the time when all who could do so went to the abbey to hear the Ténèbres sung in Holy Week, and it survives as an excellent opportunity to display the latest spring fashions.

Longevity (lon jev' i ti) The oldest man of modern times was Thomas Carn, if we may rely on the parish register of St Leonard's, Shoreditch, where it is recorded that he died in the reign of Queen Elizabeth, aged 207 He was born in 1381, in the reign of Richard II, lived in the reigns of ten sovereigns, and died in 1588. Henry Jenkins was only 160 when he died in 1670 and remembered going (when he was a boy of twelve) with a load of arrows, to be used in the battle of Flodden Field. Thomas Parr died in 1635 at the age of 152 William Wakley (according to the register of St Andrew's Church, Shifnal, Salop) was at least 124 when he died He was baptized at Idsal 1590, and buried at Adbaston, November 28th, 1714, and he lived in the reigns of eight sovereigns. Mary Yates, of Lizard Common, Shifnal, married her third husband at the age of 92, and died in 1776, at the age of 127.

Longinus, or **Longius** (lon ji' nus) The traditional name of the Roman soldier who smote Our Lord with his spear at the Crucifixion. The only authority for this is the apocryphal Gospel of Nicodemus, dating from the 5th century In the romance of King Arthur, this spear was brought by Joseph of Arimathea to Listenise, when he visited King Pellam, "who was nigh of Joseph's kin " Sir Balin the Savage, being in want of a weapon, seized this spear, with which he wounded King Pellam "Three whole countries were destroyed" by that one stroke, and Sir Balin saw "the people thereof lying dead on all sides "

Longwood. The residence on the island of St. Helena where the Emperor Napoleon passed the last years of his life in exile, dying there May 5th, 1821.

Look. To look black, blue, daggers, a gift-horse, etc , *see* these words.

Look before you leap. Consider well before you act.

And look before you ere you leap,
For, as you sow, you're like to reap
BUTLER *Hudibras,* canto ii, Pt ii, 502.

To look one way and row another. To aim apparently at one thing, but really to be seeking something quite different In *Pilgrim's Progress* Mr By-ends told Christian and Hopeful, "my great-grandfather was but a waterman, looking one way and rowing another, and I got most of my estate by the same occupation."

To look through blue glasses or coloured spectacles. To regard actions in a wrong light; to view things distorted by prejudice.

It is unlucky to break a looking-glass. The nature of the ill-luck varies, thus, if a maiden, she will never marry; if a married woman, it betokens a death, etc. This superstition arose from the use made of mirrors in former times by magicians If in their operations the mirror used was broken, the magician was obliged to give over his operation, and the unlucky inquirer could receive no answer

Looping the Loop. The airman's term for the evolution which consists of describing a perpendicular circle in the air; at the top of the circle, or "loop," the airman and the aeroplane are, of course, upside down. The term comes from a kind of switchback that used to be popular at fairs, etc , in which a rapidly moving car or bicycle performed a similar evolution on a perpendicular circular track

Loose. Figuratively—of lax morals, dissolute, dissipated.

Drummond was a loose and profane man but a sense of honour which his two kinsmen wanted restrained him from a public apostasy.—MACAULAY: *Hist of Eng , ch. iI.*

A loose fish. *See* FISH.

At a loose end. Without employment, or uncertain what to do next

Having a tile loose. *See* TILE.

On the loose. Dissolute (which is *dis-solutus*). *Living on the loose* is leading a dissolute life.

To play fast and loose. *See* FAST.

Loose-strife. The name of this plant is an instance of erroneous translation The Greeks called it *lusimachion,* from the personal name *Lusimachos,* and this was treated as though it were *lusi-,* from *luein,* to loose, and *mache,* strife. Pliny refers the name to one of Alexander's generals, said to have discovered its virtues, but the mistake obtained such currency that the author of *Flora Domestica* tells us that the Romans put these flowers under the yokes of oxen to keep them from quarrelling with each other; for (says he) the plant keeps off flies and gnats and thus relieves horses and oxen from a great source of irritation Similarly in Fletcher's *Faithful Shepherdess* (II, ii), we read—

Yellow Lysimachus, to give sweet rest,
To the faint shepherd, killing, where it comes,
All busy gnats, and every fly that hums.

Lope. *See* SLOPE.

Lord. A nobleman, a peer of the realm; formerly (and in some connexions still), a ruler, a master, the holder of a manor

The word is a contraction of A S. *hlaford, hlaf,* loaf, and modern *ward, i e.* the bread-guardian, or *-keeper,* the head of the household (cp. LADY); all members of the House of Lords are Lords (the Archbishops and Bishops being Lords Spiritual, and the lay peers Lords Temporal), and the word is given as a courtesy title as a prefix to the Christian and surname of the younger sons of dukes and marquises, and to the eldest sons of viscounts and earls when the fathers hold subordinate titles as barons, and as a title of honour to certain official personages, as the Lord Chief Justice and other Judges, the Lord Mayor, Lord Advocate, Lord Rector, etc. A baron is called by his title of peerage (either a surname or territorial designation), prefixed by the title "Lord," as "Lord Dawson," "Lord Islington," and it may also be substituted in other than strictly ceremonial use for "Marquis," "Earl," or "Viscount," the *of* being dropped, as "Lord Salisbury" (for "the Marquis of Salisbury"), "Lord Derby" ("The Earl of Derby"), etc ; this cannot be done in the case of dukes

Drunk as a lord *See* DRUNK.

In the Year of our Lord. *See* ANNO DOMINI.

Lord Harry. *See* HARRY

Lord Major. *See* ALDERMAN.

Lord Mayor's Day. November 9th. So called because the Lord Mayor of London enters office on that day, and inaugurates his official dignity with a procession through the City to the Royal Courts of Justice, followed by a banquet at the Guildhall at which it is the custom for the Prime Minister to make a political speech.

Lord of the Ascendant. *See* ASCENDANT.

Lord of Creation. Man
Replenish the earth, and subdue it· and have dominion over the fish of the sea, and over the fowl of the air, and over every living thing that moveth upon the earth . Behold, I have given you every herb bearing seed .. and every tree . *—Gen* i, 28, 29

Lord of the Isles. Donald of Islay, who in 1346 reduced the Hebrides under his sway The title had been borne by others for centuries before, and is now borne by the Prince of Wales One of Scott's metrical romances is so called.

Lord of Misrule. *See* KING OF MISRULE.

Lords and ladies The popular name of the wild arum, *Arum maculatum*

My Lord. The correct form to use in addressing Judges of the Supreme Court (usually slurred to "M'Lud"), also the respectful form of address to bishops, noblemen under the rank of a Duke, Lord Mayors, Lord Provosts, and the Lord Advocate

The Lord knows who, what, where, etc Flippant expressions used to denote one's own entire ignorance of the matter.
Great families of yesterday we show,
And lords, whose parents were the Lord knows who
    DEFOE *The True-Born Englishman,* 374.
Ask where's the north? At York, 'tis on the Tweed;
In Scotland, at the Orcades, and there,
At Greenland, Zembla, or the Lord knows where
    POPE *Essay on Man,* ii, 217.

The Lord's Day. Sunday

To live like a lord. To fare luxuriously, live like a fighting-cock (*q v*).

To lord it, or lord it over. To play the lord, to rule tyrannically, to domineer.
Yon grey towers that still
Rise up as if to lord it over air
WORDSWORTH *The Punishment of Death,* Sonn i

When our Lord falls in our Lady's lap When Easter Sunday falls on the same date as Lady Day (March 25th) This is said to bode ill for England In the 19th century the combination occurred only twice (1883 and 1894), in the 20th its sole occurrence was in 1951.

Lord's Cricket Ground The headquarters of the Marylebone Cricket Club (M C C) and of cricket generally, is at St John's Wood, London Its founder, Thomas Lord (1757-1832), was groundsman at the White Conduit Club, London, in 1780. In 1797 he started a cricket ground of his own on the site of what is now Dorset Square, moving the turf in 1811 to a new site near Regent's Canal whence, in 1814, he transferred it to the present position.

Lorel. A worthless person, a rogue or blackguard The word is from *loren,* the past part of the old verb *leese,* to lose, and is chiefly remembered through "Cock Lorell". *See* COCK LORELL'S BOTE
Here I set before the good Reader the lewd, lousey language of these lewtering Luskes and lasy Lorrels, wherewith they bye and sell the common people as they pas through the countrey Whych language they terme Peddelar's Frenche *—Harman's Caveat* (1567)

Lorelei (lō´ rē lī) The name of a steep rock on the right bank of the Rhine, near St Goar, some 430 ft high. It is noted for its remarkable echo and is the traditional haunt of a siren who lures boatmen to their death Heine and others have written poems on it, and Max Bruch made it the subject of an opera (*Die Lorelei*) produced in 1864 Mendelssohn began an uncompleted opera with the same title in 1847.

Loreto (lo re´ tō) The house of Loreto. The Santa Casa, the reputed house of the Virgin Mary at Nazareth It was said to have been translated to Fiume in Dalmatia in 1291, thence to Recanati in 1294, and finally to a plot of land belonging to a certain Lady Lauretta, situated in Italy, 3 m from the Adriatic, and about 14 SSE from Ancona, round which the town of Loretto sprang up The chapel contains bas-reliefs showing incidents in the life of the Virgin, and a rough image which is traditionally held to have been carved by St. Luke The tradition has been approved by many popes and theologians and numerous miracles are recorded of the place, but the most recent research tends to show that the tradition rests on some unexplained misunderstanding
There is a Loretto in Styria — Mariazel (*Mary in the Cell*), so called from the miracleworking image of the Virgin, made of ebony, and very ugly, another in Bavaria (*Altötting*), near the river Inn, where there is a shrine of the Black Virgin; and one in Switzerland, at Einsiedeln, a village containing the shrine of the "Black Lady of Switzerland," a church of black marble with an image of ebony.

Loss To be at a loss To be unable to decide To be puzzled or embarrassed As: "I am at a loss for the proper word "

Lost Tribes The term used for that portion of the Hebrew race that disappeared from North Palestine about 140 years before the dispersion of the Jews This disappearance has caused much speculation, especially among those who look forward to a restoration of the Hebrews as foretold in the O T In 1649 John

Sadler suggested tnat the English were of Israelitish origin This suggestion was developed by Richard Brothers, the half-crazy enthusiast who declared himself Prince of the Hebrews and Ruler of the World (1792). The theory has since been developed by other writers

Lothair (lō thâr) A novel by Benjamin Disraeli (Lord Beaconsfield), pubd 1870 The characters are supposed to represent the following persons —

    The Oxford Professor, Goldwin Smith.
    Grandison, Cardinals Manning and Wiseman
    Lothair, Marquis of Bute
    Catesby, Monsignor Capel
    The Duke and Duchess, the Duke and Duchess of Abercorn.
    The Bishop, Bishop Wilberforce.
    Corisande, one of the Ladies Hamilton.

Lothario (lo thâr' ɪ ō) **A gay Lothario. A gay** libertine, a seducer of women, a debauchee The character is from Rowe's tragedy *The Fair Penitent* (1703), which is founded on Massinger's *Fatal Dowry*, though Rowe probably got the name from Davenant's *Cruel Brother* (1630), where is a similar character with the same name
   " Is this that haughty, gallant, gay Lothario?
                           Fair Penitent, v, 1.

Lothian (lōth' ɪ an) (Scotland). So named, according to tradition, from King Lot, or Lothus, Llew, the second son of Arthur, also called Lothus He was the father of Modred, leader of the rebellious army that fought at Camlan, 537 A D.

Lotus (lō' tus) A name given to many plants, *e g* by the Egyptians to various species of water-lily, by the Hindus and Chinese to the Nelumbo (a water-bean, *Nymphæaceæ speciosum*), their "sacred lotus," and by the Greeks to *Zizyphus Lotus,* a north African shrub of the natural order Rhamneæ, the fruit of which was used for food

According to Mohammed a lotus-tree stands in the seventh heaven, on the right hand of the throne of God, and the Egyptians pictured God sitting on a lotus above the watery mud. Jamblichus says the leaves and fruit of the lotus-tree being *round* represent "the motion of intellect", its towering up through mud symbolizes the eminency of divine intellect over matter; and the Deity sitting on it implies His intellectual sovereignty. (*Myster Egypt*, sec 7, cap ɪɪ, p 151.)

The classic myth is that *Lotis,* a daughter of Neptune, fleeing from Priapus was changed into a tree, which was called *Lotus* after her, while another story goes that *Dryope* of Œchalia was one day carrying her infant son, when she plucked a lotus flower for his amusement, and was instantaneously transformed into a lotus.

Lotus-eaters or **Lotophagi,** in Homeric legend, are a people who ate of the lotus-tree (thought to be intended for *Zizyphus Lotus, see above*), the effect of which was to make them forget their friends and homes, and to lose all desire of returning to their native country, their only wish being to live in idleness in

Lotus-land (*Odyssey*, xɪ) ɪɪɪɪɪɪɪɪ, a *lotus-eater* is one living in ease and luxury

Louis, St. (Louis IX of France, 1215, 1226-70), is usually represented as holding the Saviour's crown of thorns and the cross, sometimes, however, he is pictured with a pilgrim's staff, and sometimes with the standard of the cross, the allusion in all cases being to his crusades He was canonized in 1297, his feast day being August 25th

Louisette. *See* GUILLOTINE

Louisiana (loo ēz 'ɪ ăn á) U S A So named in compliment to Louis XIV of France. The name originally applied to the French possessions in the Mississippi Valley

The **Louisiana Purchase** was the acquisition by the U S. Government in 1803 of New Orleans and a vast tract of territory extending westward from the Mississippi to the Rockies, and northward from the Gulf of Mexico to the Canadian border, from the French under Napoleon (then First Consul) for the sum of $15,000,000

Lounge Lizard. *See* LIZARD

Lourdes (loord) A famous scene of pilgrimage, situated in the south-west of France In 1858 Bernadette Soubirous, a simple peasant girl, claimed that the Virgin Mary had appeared to her on eighteen occasions. Investigation failed to shake her narrative, and a spring with miraculous healing properties that appeared at the same time began to draw invalids from all parts of the world. Lourdes became the greatest sanctuary in Christendom and is resorted to by thousands, sick and well, every year.

Louver or **Louvre.** The tower or turret of mediæval buildings, originally designed for a sort of chimney to let out the smoke by means of *louvre boards, ɪ e* narrow sloping and overlapping boards which, while allowing smoke to emerge, prevented the entrance of rain *Louvre* is the old Fr *lover* or *lovier,* probably from Old High Ger *lauba,* whence our *lodge.*

Louvre (loo' vre) The former royal palace of the French kings in Paris.

Dagobert is said to have built here a hunting-seat, but the present buildings were begun by Francis I in 1541. Since the French Revolution the greater part of the Louvre has been used for the national museum and art gallery.
    He'll make your Paris Louvre shake for it
                       Henry V, ɪɪ, 4.

Love. The word is connected with Sanskrit *lubh,* to desire (Lat *lubet,* it pleases), and was *lufu* in A S.

A labour of love. Work undertaken for the love of the thing, without regard to pay

Love and lordship never like fellowship. Neither lovers nor princes can brook a rival.

Love in a cottage. A marriage for love without sufficient means to maintain one's social status "When poverty comes in at the door, love flies out of the window "
    Love in a hut, with water and a crust,
    Is—Love, forgive us!—cinders, ashes, dust;
    Love in a palace is, perhaps, at last
    More grievous torment than a hermit's fast.
                KEATS *Lamia,* Pt. ɪɪ.

Love me, love my dog If you love anyone you will like all that belongs to him St Bernard quotes this proverb in Latin, *Qui me amat, amat et canem meam*

Love's Girdle. *See* CESTUS

Not for love or money. Unobtainable, either for payment or for entreaties

The abode of Love. *See* AGAPEMONE.

The family of love. Certain fanatics in the 16th century, holding tenets not unlike those of the Anabaptists They were founded by David Joris (or George), a Dutchman (1501-65), and in England formed a sect of the Puritans in the reign of Queen Elizabeth They are also known as the "Familists"

The god of love. Generally meaning either Eros (Gr) or Cupid (Roman mythology) Among the Scandinavians Freyja was the goddess of sexual love, and among the Hindus Kama more or less takes the place of Eros.

There is no love lost between so and so. The persons referred to have no love for each other. Formerly the phrase was used in exactly the opposite sense—it was *all* love between them, and none of it went a-missing In the old ballad *The Babes in the Wood* we have—

No love between these two was lost
Each was to other kind.

To play for love. To play without stakes, for nothing.

Love-lock. A small curl worn by women, plastered to the temples, sometimes called a *beau* or *bow* catcher A man's "love-lock" is called a *bell-rope* At the latter end of the 16th century the love-lock was a long lock of hair hanging in front of the shoulders, curled and decorated with bows and ribbons

Love-powders or **Potions** were drugs to excite lust. Once these love-charms were generally believed in, thus, Brabantio accuses Othello of having bewitched Desdemona with "drugs to waken motion"; and Lady Grey was accused of having bewitched Edward IV "by strange potions and amorous charms" (*Fabian*, p. 495).

Love-in-Idleness. One of the numerous names of the pansy or heartsease (*q.v*). Fable has it that it was originally white, but was changed to purple by Cupid

Yet marked I where the bolt of Cupid fell,
It fell upon a little Western flower.
Before, milk-white, now purple with love's wound,
The maidens call it Love-in-idleness
Midsummer Night's Dream, ii, 1

Love's Labour's Lost. The exact form of the title of this, probably the first of Shakespeare's plays (1588), cannot be ascertained, but the above is the generally accepted form, the first "'s" denoting the possessive, and the second the contraction of "is" On the title-page of the first quarto it is given as "A Pleasant Conceited Comedie called, Loves labors lost," with no apostrophes; the running head-line of this edition, however, is "Love's Labour's Lost," while the title given to the play in the first folio (1623) is "Loves Labour's Lost."

Other variants are Mere's "Love labors lost" and Robert Tofte's "Loves Labour Lost" (both 1598), Sir Walter Cope's "Loves Labore lost" (1604), Drummond of Hawthornden's "Loves Labors Lost" (1606), and Dryden's 'Love's labour lost" (1672)

Loving or **Grace Cup.** A large cup passed round from guest to guest at formal banquets, especially at College, Court, and in the City of London Miss Strickland says that Margaret Atheling, wife of Malcolm Canmore, in order to induce the Scots to remain for grace, devised the grace cup, which was filled with the choicest wine, and of which each guest was allowed to drink *ad libitum* after grace had been said (*Historic Sketches*)

On the introduction of Christianity, the custom of wassailing was not abolished, but it assumed a religious aspect The monks called the wassail bowl the *poculum caritatis* (loving cup), a term still retained in the London companies, but in the universities the term *Grace Cup* is more general

At the Lord Mayor's or City companies' banquets the loving-cup is a silver bowl with two handles, a napkin being tied to one of them Two persons stand up, one to drink and the other to defend the drinker Having taken his draught, the first wipes the cup with the napkin, and passes it to his "defender," when the next person rises to defend the new drinker, and so on to the end.

Lovel, the Dog. *See* RAT, CAT, etc.

Lovelace. The principal male character of Richardson's novel *Clarissa Harlowe* (1748) He is a selfish voluptuary, a man of fashion, whose sole ambition is to seduce young women, and he is—like Lothario (*q v*)—often taken as the type of a libertine Crabbe calls him "rich, proud, and crafty, handsome, brave, and gay."

Low. To lay low is transitive, and means to overthrow or to kill, to lie low is intransitive, and means to be abased, or dead, and (in slang use) to bide one's time, to do nothing at the moment

In low water. Financially embarrassed; or, in a bad state of health The phrase comes from seafaring men, *cp.* "stranded," "left high and dry."

Low-bell. A bell formerly used in night-fowling. The birds were first roused from their slumber by its tinkling, and then dazzled by a *low* (Sc for "a blaze" or "flame") so as to be easily caught The word *low-bell* was, however, in earlier use for any small bell, such as a sheep-bell, without any connexion with lights or fowling.

The sound of the low-bell makes the birds lie close, so that they dare not stir whilst you are pitching the net for the sound thereof is dreadful to them; but the sight of the fire, much more terrible, makes them fly up, so that they become instantly entangled in the net —*British Sportsman* (1792)

Low Church. The popular name given to the evangelical party in the Church of England which maintains the essential Protestantism of that institution, adheres to the doctrinal and devotional formulas of the Book of Common Prayer, and regards the Bible as the ultimate rule of faith

Low Sunday The Sunday next after Easter The popular English name of Low Sunday has probably arisen from the contrast between the joys of Easter and the first return to ordinary Sunday services On this Sunday, or sometimes on the fourth Sunday after Easter, it was the custom, in primitive days, for those who had been baptized the year before to keep an anniversary of their baptism, which was called the *Annotine Easter*, although the actual anniversary of the previous Easter might fall on another day.— *Blunt's Annotated Book of Common Prayer.*

Lower case. The printer's name for the small letters (minuscules) of a fount of type, as opposed to the capitals; these are, in a type-setter's "case," on a *lower* level than the others.

Lower Empire. The later Roman, especially the Western Empire, from about the foundation of the Eastern Empire in 364 to the fall of Constantinople in 1453

Lower House, The. The second of any two legislative chambers; in England, the House of Commons.

Lower your sail, To. To salute; to confess yourself submissive or conquered; to humble oneself A nautical phrase.

Lowndean Professor. The professor of astronomy and geometry at Cambridge, so called from Thomas Lowndes (1692-1748) who bequeathed all his property for the founding of the chair.

Loyal. Only one regiment of all the British army is so called, and that is the Loyal North Lancashire It was so called in 1793, and probably had some allusion to the French revolutionists

Loyola, St. Ignatius (ig nā′ shŭs loi ō′ la) (1491-1556) Founder of the Society of Jesus (the order of Jesuits), is depicted in art with the sacred monogram I H S. on his breast, or as contemplating it, surrounded by glory in the skies, in allusion to his claim that he had a miraculous knowledge of the mystery of the Trinity vouchsafed to him He was a son of the Spanish ducal house of Loyola, and after being severely wounded at the siege of Pampeluna (1521) left the army and dedicated himself to the service of the Virgin The society of Jesus (*see* JESUITS), which he projected in 1534, was confirmed by Paul III in 1540

Luath (loo′ ath) The name of Burns's favourite dog, and that which he gave to the poor man's dog representing the peasantry in his poem *The Twa Dogs* Burns got the name from Macpherson's *Ossian*, where it is borne by Cuchullin's dog

A ploughman's collie,
A rhyming, ranting, raving billie,
Wha for his friend and comrade had him,
And in his freaks had Luath ca'd him
After some dog in Highland sang
Was made lang syne—Lord knows how lang
BURNS. *The Twa Dogs.*

Lubber's Hole. In sailing ships a seaman's name for the vacant space between the head of a lower mast and the edge of the top, because timid boys, or "lubbers," got through it to the top, to avoid the danger and difficulties of the "futtock shrouds." Hence, some means for, or method of, wriggling through one's difficulties

B D.—19

Lubberkin or **Lubrican**. *See* LEPRACHAUN.

Lucasian Professor. A professor of mathematics at Cambridge The professorship was endowed by a bequest from Henry Lucas (d 1663), M P for the University.

Lucasta (lū kās′ tá), to whom Richard Lovelace sang (1649), was Lucy Sacheverell, called by him *lux casta, i e* Chaste Lucy.

Luce. The full-grown pike (*Esox lucius*), from Gr *lukos*, a wolf, meaning the wolf of fishes.

Shakespeare plays upon the words *luce* and *louse* (*Merry Wives*, I, 1) at the expense of Justice Shallow, who stands for his old enemy, Sir Thomas Lucy According to Ferne's *Blazon of Gentry* (1586) the arms of the Lucy family were "Gules, three lucies hariant, argent " but Dugdale (*Warwickshire*, 1656) gives a representation of a quartering of the Lucy arms where the "dozen white luces" are shown.

They may give the dozen white luces in their coat.—
Merry Wives, 1, 1

Luce was also formerly used as a contraction of *fleur-de-lys* (*q v*) The French messenger says to the Regent Bedford—

Cropped are the flower de luces in your arms,
Of England's coat one-half is cut away
1 *Henry VI,* i, 1.

Referring of course to the loss of France

Lucian (loo′ si an). The chief character in the *Golden Ass* of Apuleius (2nd cent A.D.), a work which is in part an imitation of the *Metamorphoses* by Lucian, the Greek satirist who lived about 120 to 200 In the *Golden Ass* Lucian, changed into an ass, is the personification of the follies and vices of the age.

Lucifer (loo′ si fēr) Venus, as the morning star. When she *follows* the sun and is an evening star, she is called *Hesperus*

Isaiah applied the epithet "Day-star" to the king of Babylon who proudly boasted he would ascend to the heavens and make himself equal to God, but who was fated to be cast down to the uttermost recesses of the pit This epithet was translated into "Lucifer"—

Take up this proverb against the king of Babylon, and say, . . How art thou fallen, from heaven, O Lucifer, son of the morning!—*Is.* xiv, 4, 12

By St Jerome and other Fathers the name was applied to Satan Hence poets feign that Satan, before he was driven out of heaven for his pride, was called Lucifer, and Milton, in *Paradise Lost*, gives this name to the demon of "Sinful Pride," and hence, too, the phrase *Proud as Lucifer*

Lucifer-match, or Lucifer. The name given by the inventor to one of the earliest forms (about 1832) of matches tipped with a combustible substance and ignited by friction, an improvement on the Congreves and Prometheans (*qq v.*), hence, any match igniting by friction.

Luciferians. A sect of the 4th century, who refused to hold any communion with the Arians, who had renounced their "errors" and been readmitted into the Church. So called from Lucifer, Bishop of Cagliari, in Sardinia, their leader.

Lucius. One of the mythical kings of Britain, placed as the great-great-grandson of Cymbeline (*q.v.*), and fabled as the first Christian king. He is supposed to have died about 192 *See* PUDENS.

Luck. Accidental good fortune. (Dut., *luk*, Ger *glück* verb *glucken*, to succeed, to prosper)

Down on one's luck. Short of cash and credit

He has the luck of the devil, or the devil's own luck. He is extraordinarily lucky, everything he attempts is successful

Give a man luck and throw him into the sea. Meaning that his luck will save him even in the greatest extremity Jonah and Arion were cast into the sea, but were carried safely to land, the one by a whale and the other by a dolphin.

Luck or lucky penny. A trifle returned to a purchaser for good luck; also a penny with a hole in it, supposed to ensure good luck

Not in luck's way. Not unexpectedly promoted, enriched, or otherwise benefited

The Luck of Eden Hall. *See* EDEN HALL.

There's luck in odd numbers. *See* ODD.

Lucky. In Scotland a term of familiar but respectful endearment for any elderly woman; often used of the landlady of an ale-house.

A lucky dip, or bag. A tub or other receptacle in which are placed a number of articles covered with bran or the like Much in request at bazaars and so on, where the visitors pay so much for a "dip" and take what they get

A lucky stone. A stone with a natural hole through it. *Cp.* LUCK PENNY.

The lucky bone. The small bone of a sheep's head; prized by beggars and tramps, as it is supposed to bring luck for the whole day on which it is received

To cut one's lucky (old slang) To decamp or make off quickly. to "cut one's stick" (*q v*) As *luck* means chance, the phrase may signify, "I must give up my chance and be off."

To strike lucky. *See* STRIKE.

Lucullus sups with Lucullus (lūk ŭl' ŭs) Said of a glutton who gormandizes alone. Lucullus was a rich Roman, noted for his magnificence and self-indulgence Sometimes above £1,700 was expended on a single meal, and Horace tells us he had 5,000 rich purple robes in his house On one occasion a very superb supper was prepared, and when asked who were to be his guests the "rich fool" replied, "Lucullus will sup to-night with Lucullus" (110-57 B C).

Lucus a non lucendo (lū' kŭs ā non loo sen' dŏ). An etymological contradiction, a phrase used of etymologists who accounted for words by deriving them from their opposites It means literally "a grove (called *lucus*) from not being lucent" (*lux*, light, *luceo*, to shine). It was the Roman grammarian Honoratus Maurus Servius (fl. end of 4th cent. A D) who provided this famous etymology In the same way *ludus*, a school, may be said to come from

ludere, to play, and our word *linen*, from *lining*, because it is used for linings

One *Triphiodorus* . composed an Epick Poem of four and twenty books, having entirely banished the letter *A* from his first Book, which was called *Alpha* (as *Lucus a non Lucendo*) because there was not an *Alpha* in it —ADDISON *Spectator*, No 59

Lucy, St. Patron saint for those afflicted in the eyes. She is supposed to have lived in Syracuse and to have suffered martyrdom there about 303 One legend relates that a nobleman wanted to marry her for the beauty of her eyes, so she tore them out and gave them to him, saying, "Now let me live to God " Hence she is represented in art carrying a palm branch and a platter with two eyes on it Her day is December 13th

Lud (lŭd). A mythical king of Britain, stated by the old chronicles to have been the eighth in succession from Brute and to have died in 862 B.C. He was the father of Bladud, founder of Bath. This King Lud must either have started as a deity or have been early euhemerized, for temples to him existed both on the Severn and the Thames (LUDGATE): but the King Lud whom Geoffrey of Monmouth supposes to have founded London was a king of the Trinobantes, a brother of Cassivelaunus, and is dated about 66 B C

General Lud. *See* LUDDITES

Lud's Town. London, so called from King Lud

And on the gates of Lud's town set your heads.
SHAKESPEARE *Cymbeline*, IV, 2

Luddites. Discontented workmen who, from 1811 to 1816, went about the manufacturing districts (especially Nottingham) breaking machines, under the impression that machinery threw men out of work. So called from Ned Lud, of Leicestershire, who forced his way into a house, and broke two stocking-frames, whence the leader of these rioters was called *General Lud.*

In the winter of 1811 the terrible pressure of this transition from handicraft to machinery was seen in the Luddite, or machine-breaking, riots which broke out over the northern and midland counties, and which were only suppressed by military force —J R GREEN. *Short History*, x, § IV.

Ludgate. One of the gates in the old City walls of London standing (till 1760) on Ludgate Hill, a few yards above the Old Bailey It was probably on the site of a gate in the later Roman wall, but its first mention (as *Ludgata*) occurs in the early 12th century. Suggestions have been made that the true origin of the name is to be found in *Floodgate* (or *Fleetgate*, *cp. Fleet Street*, which at one time extended to Ludgate), or in A S *leode*, people, nation (*cp.* the *Porto del populi* of Rome)

Ludgate was used as a free prison in 1373, but soon lost that privilege A romantic story is told of Sir Stephen Forster, who was Lord Mayor in 1454 He had been a prisoner at Ludgate, and begged at the gate, where he was seen by a rich widow, who bought his liberty, took him into her service, and afterwards married him To commemorate this, Sir Stephen enlarged the prison accommodation, and added a chapel. The old gate was taken down and rebuilt in 1586 The new-built gate was destroyed in the Great Fire of London, and the next gate (used also as a prison for debtors) was pulled down in 1760

Stow says·

King Lud, repairing the city, called it after his name *Lud's town* the strong gate which he built in the west part he likewise named Lud-gate In the year 1260 the gate was beautiful with images of Lud and other kings. Those images, in the reign of Edward VI, had their heads smitten off   Queen Mary did set new heads on their old bodies again

Survey of London

[Lud] Built that gate of which his name is hight, By which he lies entombed solemnly.

Spencer: *Faerie Queene*, ii, x, 46

The statue of Queen Elizabeth I formerly on old Lud Gate is now built into the façade of St Dunstan's Church, Fleet Street

Ludlum. See LAZY.

Luez. *See* LUZ

Luff. The weather-gauge; the part of a vessel towards the wind (Dut *loef*, a weather-gauge)

Luff! Put the tiller on the lee-side. This is done to make the ship sail nearer the wind

A ship is said to **spring her luff** when she yields to the helm by sailing nearer the wind

Luggnagg. In *Gulliver's Travels*, an island where people live for ever Swift shows the evil of such a destiny, unless accompanied with eternal youth *See* STRULDBRUGS.

Lugs. To put on the lugs. 19th-century American slang for conceit, swank

Luke, St. Patron saint of painters and physicians Tradition says he painted a portrait of the Virgin Mary. *Col.* iv, 14, states that he was a physician, but the word may have been used in a metaphorical sense His day is October 18th

In art St Luke is usually represented with an ox lying near him, and often with painting materials Sometimes he is pictured as painting the Virgin and infant Saviour. Metaphrastus mentions his skill in painting, and John of Damascus speaks of his portrait of the Virgin (*cp* LORETO). Many pictures still extant are attributed to St Luke; but the artist was probably St. Luke, the Greek hermit, for certainly these meagre Byzantine productions were not the work of the evangelist

St. Luke's Club or **The Virtuosi.** An artists' club, established in England by Vandyck about 1638, and held at the Rose Tavern, Fleet Street. There was an academy of St Luke founded by the Paris artists in 1391, one at Rome, founded in 1593, but based on the "Compagnia di San Luca" of Florence, founded in 1345; a similar one was established at Siena in 1355.

St. Luke's Summer. The latter end of autumn, called by the French *l'été de S Martin.*

As light as St. Luke's bird. Not light at all, but quite the contrary.

Luke's Iron Crown. A symbol of political tyranny

The lifted axe, the agonising wheel,
Luke's iron crown, and Damien's bed of steel,
To men remote from power but rarely known,
Leave reason, faith, and conscience all our own.
GOLDSMITH *The Traveller*, 435

George and Luke Dosa headed an unsuccessful revolt in Hungary in the early part of the 16th century. *George* underwent the torture of the red-hot iron crown, as a punishment for allowing himself to be proclaimed king, Goldsmith slips in attributing the incident to *Luke*

Lumber. Formerly a pawnbroker's shop (from *Lombard, q.v*) Thus Lady Murray (*Lives of the Baillies*, 1749) writes· "They put all the little plate they had in the lumber, which is pawning it, till the ships came home "

From its use as applied to old broken boards and bits of wood the word was extended to mean timber sawn and split, especially when the trees have been felled and sawn *in situ.*

Lump. If you don't like it, you may lump it Whether you like to do it or not, no matter, you must take it without choice, it must be done

Lumpkin, Tony (Goldsmith's *She Stoops to Conquer*) A sheepish, mischievous, idle, cunning lout, "with the vices of a man and the follies of a boy "

Lunar Month. From new moon to new moon, i e. the time taken by the moon to revolve round the earth, about 29½ days Popularly, the lunar month is 28 days In the Jewish and Mohammedan calendars, the lunar month commences at sunset of the day when the new moon is first seen after sunset, and varies in length, being sometimes 29 and sometimes 30 days. **Lunar Year.** Twelve lunar months, i e. about 354½ days

Lunatics. Literally, moon-struck persons. The Romans believed that the mind was affected by the moon, and that ' lunatics" grew more and more frenzied as the moon increased to its full.

The various mental derangements .   which have been attributed to the influence of the moon, have given to this day the name *lunatics* to persons suffering from serious mental disorders.—CROZIER *Popular Errors*, ch iv.

Lunch, Luncheon. *Lunch* was originally a variant of *lump*, meaning a piece or slice of bread, etc The *-eon* is a later extension, perhaps representing *-ing* ("Noonings and intermealiary Lunchings," Brome's *Mad Couple*, about 1650), but affected by the suffix of *nuncheon* This *-eon* has now been dropped except as an affectation of gentility

Luni (loo' nē) The ancient Etruscan town of Luna some 70 miles from Genoa The quarries nearby furnish a beautiful white marble which takes its name from the place "marmo lunese" and the whole district is called La Lunigiana

Lupercal, The (lū' pĕr kāl) In ancient Rome, an annual festival held on the spot where Romulus and Remus were suckled by the wolf (*lupus*), on February 15th, in honour of Lupercus, the Lycæan Pan (so called because he protected the flocks from wolves) It was on one of these occasions that Antony thrice offered Julius Cæsar the crown, and Cæsar refused, saying, "Jupiter alone is king of Rome "

You all did see that on the Lupercal,
I thrice presented him a kingly crown,
Which he did thrice refuse

Julius Cæsar, iii, 2

Lurch. To leave in the lurch. To leave a person in a difficulty. In cribbage one is *left in the lurch*

when his adversary has run out his score of sixty-one holes before he himself has turned the corner (or pegged his thirty-first) hole In some card-games it is a *slam*, that is, when one side wins the entire game before the other has scored a point.

Lush. Beer and other intoxicating drinks The word is well over a century old, and is of uncertain origin Up to about 1895 there was a convivial society of actors called "The City of Lushington," which met in the Harp Tavern, Russell Street, and claimed to have been in existence for 150 years. *Lush* may have come from the name of this club, though it is just as likely that the club took its name from the *lush*—for which it was famous

Lusiad, The (loo' si ăd) The Portuguese national epic, written by Camoens, and published in 1572 It relates the stories of illustrious actions of the *Lusians*, or Portuguese, of all ages, but deals principally with the exploits of Vasco da Gama and his comrades in their "discovery of India " Gama sailed three times to India:—(1) with four vessels, in 1497, returning to Lisbon in two years and two months; (2) in 1502, with twenty ships, when he was attacked by the Zamorin or king of Calicut, whom he defeated, and returned to Lisbon the year following; and (3) when John III appointed him viceroy of India He established his government at Cochin, where he died in 1525 It is the first of these voyages which is the groundwork of the epic, but its wealth of episode, the constant introduction of mythological "machinery," and the intervention of Bacchus, Venus, and other deities, make it far more than a mere chronicle of a voyage.

Lusitania (loo si tăn' yà) The Cunard liner that was torpedoed and sunk by a German submarine off the Old Head of Kinsale on May 7th, 1915, with the loss of 1198 lives. The sinking of the *Lusitania* was notorious as the first of many subsequent examples of German atrocities. The Germans struck a medal to celebrate this feat

Lustrum (lŭs' trŭm) In ancient Rome the purificatory sacrifice made by the censors for the people once in five years, after the census had been taken (from *luere*, to wash, to purify); hence, a period of five years

Lustral (lŭs' tral) Properly, pertaining to the *Lustrum* (q v), hence, purificatory, as *lustral water*, the water used in Christian as well as many pagan rites for aspersing worshippers. In Rome the priest used a small olive or laurel branch for sprinkling infants and the people.

Lusus. Pliny (iii, 1) tells us that Lusus was the companion of Bacchus in his travels, and settled a colony in Portugal; whence the country was termed *Lusitania*, and the inhabitants *Lusians*, or *the sons of Lusus*

Lutestring. A glossy silk fabric; the French *lustrine* (from *lustre*)

Speaking in lutestring. Flash, highly polished oratory The expression was used more than once by Junius Shakespeare has "taffeta phrases and silken terms precise " We call

inflated speech ' fustian'' (*q v*) or "bombast" (*q v*), say a man talks *stuff*, term a book or speech made up of other men's brains, *shoddy* (*q v*), sailors call telling a story "spinning a yarn," etc , etc

Lutetia (Lat *lutum*, mud) The ancient name of Paris, which, in Roman times, was merely a collection of mud hovels. Cæsar called it *Lutetia Parisiorum* (the mud-town of the Parisii), which gives the present name *Paris*.

Lutin A goblin in the folklore of Normandy; similar to the house-spirits of Germany The name was formerly *netun*, and is said to come from the Roman sea-god *Neptune* When the *lutin* assumes the form of a horse ready equipped it is called *Le Cheval Bayard*

To lutin. To twist hair into elf-locks These mischievous urchins are said to tangle the mane of a horse or head of a child so that the hair must be cut off

Lutine Bell (loo' tēn) H.M S. *Lutine*, a French warship that had been captured and put into service by the British, sailed from Yarmouth for Holland on October 9th, 1799, with bullion and specie to the value of some £500,000. That same night she was wrecked on a sandbank off the Zuyder Zee, with the loss of every soul on board save one, who died as soon as rescued It was a black day for Lloyd's underwriters In 1858 some £50,000 was salvaged, and among other things the *Lutine*'s bell and rudder were brought back to England The latter was made into the official chair for Lloyd's chairman and a secretary's desk, the bell was hung up at Lloyd's and is rung once whenever a total wreck is reported, and twice when an overdue ship is reported

Luz or **Luez** (lŭz) The indestructible bone the nucleus of the resurrection body of Rabbinical legend

> The learned rabbins of the Jews
> Write there's a bone which they call luez .
>   BUTLER *Hudibras*, iii, 2

"How doth a man revive again in the world to come?" asked Hadrian, and Joshua Ben Hananiah made answer "From luz in the backbone " He then went on to demonstrate this to him, He took the bone luz, and put it into water, but the water had no action on it, he put it in the fire, but the fire consumed it not, he placed it in a mill, but could not grind it, and laid it on an anvil, but the hammer crushed it not.— *Lightfoot.*

LXX. *See* SEPTUAGINT

Lycanthropy (li kăn' thrŏ pi) The insanity afflicting a person who imagines himself to be some kind of animal and exhibits the tastes, voice, etc , of that animal; formerly the name given by the ancients to those who imagined themselves to be wolves (Gr. *lukos*, wolf, *anthropos*, man) The *werewolf* (*q v*) has sometimes been called a *lycanthrope*, and *lycanthropy* was sometimes applied to the form of witchcraft by which witches transformed themselves into wolves

Lycaon (li kā' on). In classical mythology, a king of Arcadia, who, desirous of testing the divine knowledge of Jove, served up human flesh on his table, for which the god changed him into a wolf. His daughter, Callisto, was changed into the constellation the Bear, which is sometimes called *Lycaonis Arctos*.

Lycidas (lĭs' ĭ dăs) The name under which Milton celebrated the untimely death of Edward King, Fellow ôf Christ's College, Cambridge, who was drowned in his passage from Chester to Ireland, August 10th, 1637. He was the son of Sir John King, Secretary for Ireland

Lycopodium (lĭ kō pō' dĭ um) A genus of perennial plants comprising the club-mosses, so called from their fanciful resemblance to a wolf's foot (Gr *lukos*, wolf, *pous, podos*, foot), the powder from the spore-cases of some of these is used in surgery as an absorbent and also—as it is highly inflammable—for stage-lightning

Lyddite (lĭd' ĭt) A high-explosive composed mainly of picric acid, so called from Lydd, in Kent, where are situated the artillery ranges on which it was first tested in 1888.

Lydford Law. Punish first and try afterwards Lydford, in the county of Devon, was a fortified town, where were held the courts of the Duchy of Cornwall. Offenders against the stannary laws were confined before trial in a dungeon so loathsome and dreary that they frequently died before they could be brought to trial. *Cp.* CUPAR JUSTICE

Lydia (lĭd' ĭ à). The ancient name of a district in the middle of Asia Minor which was an important centre of early civilization and exerted much influence on Greece Gyges (716 B C) was one of its most famous rulers, and the Empire flourished until its overthrow by the Persians under Cyrus (546 B C.).

Lydian Poet, The. Alcman of Lydia (fl 670 B C)

Lying for the Whetstone. *See* WHETSTONE.

Lyke-wake. *See* LICH-WAKE (LICH)

Lyme-, or **Lyam-hound** (līm) The bloodhound, so called from *lyme*, or *lyam*, the leash (Lat *ligare*, to tie) By mediæval huntsmen the lyme-hound was used for tracking down the wounded buck, and the *gaze-hound* for killing it

> Thou art the lyme-hound, I am the gaze-hound
> . . Thou hast deep sagacity and unrelenting purpose,
> a steady, long-breathed malignity of nature, that sur-
> passes mine But then, I am the bolder, the more ready,
> both at action and expedient I say . . shall we
> hunt in couples?—SCOTT *Kenilworth*, ch iv.

Lynceus (lĭn' sūs) One of the Argonauts (*q.v*). He was so sharp-sighted that he could see through the earth, and distinguish objects nine miles off

> Non possis oculo quantum contendere Lynceus.
> HORACE· 1 *Epistle*, i, 28.

Lynch Law (linch). Mob-law, law adminis-tered by private persons. The origin of the term is unknown; none of the suggested derivations from James Lynch or Justice Lynch having any foundation in fact

The term is first recorded in 1817, and is certainly American in origin, though there is an old northern English dialect word *linch*, meaning to beat or maltreat.

In the U S A. the drastic justice of Lynch Law—usually true justice, it must be observed—was effective where the civil law failed in clearing the West of outlaws, cattle-thieves, and rogues in general

Lynx (lĭngks). The animal proverbial for its piercing eyesight is a fabulous beast, half dog and half panther, but not like either in character The cat-like animal now called a lynx is not remarkable for keen-sightedness The word is probably related to Gr *lussein*, to see. *Cp* LYNCEUS

> Oh, I must needs o' the sudden prove a lynx
> And look the heart, that stone-wall, through and
> through
> Such an eye, God's may be,—not yours nor mine.
> BROWNING *The Ring and the Book*, xi, 917

Lyon King-of-Arms. The chief heraldic officer for Scotland, so called from the lion rampant in the Scottish regal escutcheon *See* HERALDRY, *also* LION

Lyonesse (lī on es') "That sweet land of Lyonesse"—a tract of land fabled to stretch between the Land's End and the Scilly Isles now submerged full "forty fathoms under water" Arthur came from this mythical country

> Faery damsels met in forest wide
> By knights of Logres, or of Lyones,
> Lancelot, or Pelleas, or Pellenore.
> MILTON *Paradise Regained*, ii, 359

Lyre (līr). That of Terpander and Olympus had only three strings, the Scythian lyre had five; that of Simonides had eight, and that of Timotheus had twelve It was played either with the fingers or with a plectrum. The lyre is called by poets a "shell," because the cords of the lyre used by Orpheus, Amphion, and Apollo were stretched on the shell of a tortoise Hercules used boxwood.

Amphion built Thebes with the music of his lyre, for the very stones moved of their own accord into walls and houses.

Arion charmed the dolphins by the music of his lyre, and when the bard was thrown over-board one of them carried him safely to Tænarus

Hercules was taught music by Linus One day, being reproved, the strong man broke the head of his master with his own lyre.

Orpheus charmed savage beasts, and even the infernal gods, with the music of his lyre, or —as some have it, lute.

M

M. The thirteenth letter of the English alphabet (the twelfth of the ancient Roman, and twentieth of the *futhorc*), M in the Phœnician character represented the wavy appearance of water, and is called in Hebrew *mem* (water) The Egyptian hieroglyphic represented the owl. In English M is always sounded, except in words from Greek in which it is followed by *n*, as *mnemonics*, *Mnason* (Acts xxi, 16)

In Roman numerals M stands for 1,000 (Lat. *mille*): MCMLII = one thousand, nine hundred and fifty-two.

Persons convicted of manslaughter, and admitted to the benefit of clergy, used to be branded with an M It was burnt on the brawn of the left thumb

What is your name? N or M. (Church Catechism) *See* N.

M, to represent the human face Add two dots for the eyes, thus, .M These dots being equal to O's, we get OMO (*homo*) Latin for man

> Who reads the name,
> For *man* upon his forehead, there the M
> Had traced most plainly
>   DANTE· *Purgatory*, XXIII

M'. The first letter of certain Celtic surnames (*M'Cabe, M'Ian, M'Mahon*, etc) represents *Mac*, and should be so pronounced

M B. Waistcoat. A clerical cassock waistcoat was so called (about 1830) when first introduced by the High Church party M B means "mark of the beast "

> He smiled at the folly which stigmatised an M B waistcoat."—MRS OLIPHANT *Phœbe Juno*, ii, 3

M P. Member of Parliament

MS (pl MSS) Manuscript; applied to literary works either in handwriting or typescript (Lat. *manuscriptum*, that which is written by the hand.)

Mab (perhaps the Welsh *mab*, a baby). The "fairies' midwife"—*i e.* employed by the fairies as midwife to deliver man's brain of dreams Thus when Romeo says, "I dreamed a dream to-night," Mercutio replies, "Oh, then, I see Queen Mab hath been with you " When Mab is called "queen," it does not mean sovereign, for Titania as wife of King Oberon was Queen of Faery, but simply female. A S. *quen* or *cwén* (modern *quean*) meant neither more nor less than *woman*, so "elf-queen," and the Danish *ellequinde*, mean *female elf*; and not "queen of the elves "

Excellent descriptions of Mab are given by Shakespeare (*Romeo and Juliet*, i, 4), by Ben Jonson, by Herrick, and by Drayton in *Nymphidea*

Macaber (or **Macabre**), **the Dance.** *See* DANCE OF DEATH

Macadamize (ma kăd' à mīz). A method of road-making introduced about 1820 by John L. Macadam (1756-1836), consisting of layers of broken stones of nearly uniform size, each layer being separately crushed into position by traffic, or (later) by a heavy roller.

Macaire, Robert (ma kâr') The typical villain of French comedy, from the play of this name (a sequel to *L'Auberge des Adrets*) by Frédéric Lemaître and Benjamin Antier (1834) Macaire is—

> le type de la perversité, de l'impudence, de la friponnerie audacieuse, le héros fanfaron du vol et de l'assassinat

"Macaire" was the name of the murderer of Aubrey de Montdidier in the old French legend, he was brought to justice by the sagacity of Aubrey's dog, the Dog of Montargis. *See* DOG.

Macaroni (măk' à rō ni). A coxcomb (Ital *un maccherone*, see next entry). The word is derived from the Macaroni Club, instituted in London about 1760 by a set of flashy men who had travelled in Italy, and introduced at Almack's subscription table the new-fangled Italian food, *macaroni*. The Macaronies were

the most exquisite fops, vicious, insolent, fond of gambling, drinking, and duelling, they were (about 1773) the curse of Vauxhall Gardens.

An American regiment raised in Maryland during the War of Independence was called The Macaronies from its showy uniform

Macaronic Latin. Dog Latin (*q v*), modern words with Latin endings, or a mixture of Latin and some modern language From the Italian *macheroni* (macaroni), a mixture of coarse meal, eggs, and cheese The law pleadings of G Steevens, as *Daniel* v *Dishclout* and *Bullum* v. *Boatum*, are excellent examples

Macaronic verse. Verses in which foreign words are ludicrously distorted and jumbled together, as in Porson's lines on the threatened invasion of England by Napoleon or J A Morgan's "translation" of Canning's *The Elderly Gentleman*, the first two verses of which are—

> Prope ripam fluvi solus
>   A senex silently sat
> Super capitum ecce his wig
>   Et wig super, ecce his hat
> Blew Zephyrus alte, acerbus,
>   Dum elderly gentleman sat,
> Et a capite took up quite torve
>   Et in rivum projecit his hat

It seems to have been originated by Odaxius of Padua (born *c* 1450), but was popularized by his pupil, Teofilo Folengo (Merlinus Coccaius), a Mantuan monk of noble family, who published a book entitled *Liber Macaronicorum*, a poetical rhapsody made up of words of different languages, and treating of ' pleasant matters'' in a comical style (1520).

In England a somewhat similar kind of verse was practised rather earlier Skelton's *Phyllyp Sparowe* (1512), which contains a good deal of it, begins—

> Pla ce bo,
> Who is there, who?
> Di le xi,
> Dama Margery

and Dunbar's *Testament of Andrew Kennedy* (1508)—

> I will na priestis for me sing,
>   Dies illa, Dies iræ,
> Na yet na bellis for me ring,
>   Sicut semper solet fieri—

though not true macaronic, is a near approach

A Cunningham in 1801 published *Delectus Macaronicorum Carminum*, a history of macaronic poetry

Macbeth (mac beth') The story of Shakespeare's tragedy (written 1605-6, acted certainly in 1610 and probably four years earlier, and first printed in the First Folio, 1623) is taken from Holinshed, who copied it from the *History of Scotland*, by Hector Boece (1527).

History states that Macbeth slew Duncan at Bothgown, near Elgin, in 1039, and not, as Shakespeare says, at his castle of Inverness, the attack was made because Duncan had usurped the throne, to which Macbeth had the better claim As a king Macbeth proved a very just and equitable prince, but the partisans of Malcolm got head, and succeeded in deposing Macbeth, who was slain in 1056, at Lumphanan He was thane of Cromarty [Glamis] and afterwards of Moray [Cawdor]—LARDNER. *Cabinet Cyclopædia.*

Ambition is the dominant trait in the character of Lady Macbeth, and to gain her ends she hesitates at nothing Her masterful mind sways the weaker Macbeth to "the mood of what she liked or loathed " She is a Medea. or Catherine de' Medici, or Cæsar Borgia in female form.

The real name of Lady Macbeth was Graoch, and instead of being urged to the murder of Duncan through ambition, she was goaded by deadly injuries She was, in fact, the granddaughter of Kenneth IV, killed in 1003, fighting against Malcolm II —LARD-NER. *Cabinet Cyclopædia*, vol i, p 17.

Maccabæus (măk a bē' us). The surname given to Judas (the central figure in the struggle for Jewish independence, about 170-160 B C), third son of Mattathias, the Hasmonæan, and hence to his family or clan It has generally been supposed that the name is connected with Heb *Makkébeth*, hammer (Judas being the *Hammerer* of the Syrians just as Charles *Martel* was of the Saracens), but this view is open to many weighty objections, and the origin of the name is wholly obscure

Maccabees, The The family of Jewish heroes, descended from Mattathias the Hasmonæan (*see above*) and his five sons, John, Simon, Judas, Eleazar, and Jonathan, which delivered its race from the persecutions of the Syrian king Antiochus Epiphanes (175-164 B C), and established a line of priest-kings which lasted till supplanted by Herod in 40 B C Their exploits are told in the two *Books of the Maccabees*, the last books in the Apocrypha

Macdonald. Lord Macdonald's breed. Parasites. It is said that a Lord Macdonald (son of the Lord of the Isles) once made a raid on the mainland He and his followers, with other plunder, fell on the clothes of the enemy, and stripping off their own rags, donned the smartest and best they could lay hands on, with the result of being overrun with parasites

Macduff (mac dŭf'). The thane of Fife in *Macbeth* (*q.v*) His castle of Kennoway was surprised by Macbeth, and his wife and babes "savagely slaughtered " Macduff vowed vengeance and joined the main army of Siward, to dethrone the tyrant. On reaching the royal castle of Dunsinane they fought, and Macbeth was slain.

History states that Macbeth was defeated at Dunsinane, but escaped from the battle and was slain at Lumphanan in 1056 —LARDNER. *Cabinet Cyclopædia*, vol i, p 17

Mace. Originally a club armed with iron, and used in war; now a staff of office pertaining to certain dignitaries, as the Speaker of the House of Commons, Lord Mayors and Mayors, etc Both sword and mace are symbols of dignity, suited to the times when men went about in armour, and sovereigns needed champions to vindicate their rights.

Macedon (măs' e dŏn). Macedon is not worthy of thee, is what Philip said to his son Alexander, after his achievement with the horse Bucephalus, which he subdued to his will, though only eighteen years of age

Macedonian Madman, The. *See* MADMAN.

Macedonians. A religious sect, so named from Macedonius, an Arian patriarch of Constantinople, in the 4th century. They

denied the divinity of the Holy Ghost, and that the essence of the Son is the same in kind with that of the Father

MacFarlane's Geese. The proverb is that "MacFarlane's geese like their play better than their meat " The wild geese of Inch-Tavoe (Loch Lomond) used to be called *MacFarlane's Geese* because the MacFarlanes had a house on the island, and it is said that the geese never returned after the destruction of that house One day James VI visited the chieftain, and was highly amused by the gambols of the geese, but the one served at table was so tough that the king exclaimed, "Mac-Farlane's geese like their play better than their meat."

MacFlecknoe (măc fiek' nō), in Dryden's famous satire (1682), is Thomas Shadwell (1640-92), poet laureate in succession to his attacker (1688) when Dryden, having become a Catholic, refused to take the oath

The original Flecknoe (Richard, d about 1678) was an Irish Roman Catholic priest, doggerel sonneteer, and playwright Shadwell, according to Dryden, was his double.

The rest to some slight meaning make pretence,
But Shadwell never deviates into sense
MacFlecknoe, 19.

MacGirdie's Mare, used by degrees to eat less and less, but just as he had reduced her to a straw a day the poor beast died This is an old Greek joke, which is well known to schoolboys who have been taught the *Analecta Minora*

MacGregor (mà greg' or) The motto of the MacGregors is, "E'en do and spair nocht," said to have been given them in the 12th century by a king of Scotland While the king was hunting he was attacked by a wild boar, when Sir Malcolm requested permission to encounter the creature, "E'en do," said the king, "and spair nocht " Whereupon the strong baronet tore up an oak sapling and dispatched the enraged animal For this defence the king gave Sir Malcolm permission to use the said motto, and, in place of a Scotch fir, to adopt for crest *an oak-tree eradicate, proper.*

Another motto of the MacGregors is *Sriogal mo dhream, i e* "Royal is my tribe "

The MacGregors furnish the only instance of a race being forbidden to bear its family name It was proscribed by James VI owing to the treachery of the family, who then took the name of Murray Charles II restored them to their estates and name in 1661, but under William and Mary the law of proscription again came into force, and it was not till 1822 that Sir John Murray, as he then was, obtained by royal licence the right to resume the ancient name of his family, MacGregor

Rob Roy MacGregor. *See* ROB ROY

Macheath, Captain (măk hēth'). A highwayman, hero of *The Beggar's Opera* by John Gay (1685-1732), which was produced as a satire on and protest against the fashionable Italian opera, based on classical subjects It took London by storm when produced in 1727

Machiavelli, Niccolo (nik ō lō' ma kyà vel' i) (1469-1527) The celebrated Florentine statesman, and author of *Il Principe*, an exposition of unscrupulous statecraft, whose name has long been used as an epithet or synonym for an intriguer or for an unscrupulous politician, while political cunning and overreaching by diplomacy and intrigue are known as *Machiavellianism* or *Machiavellism*. The general trend of *Il Principe* is to show that rulers may resort to any treachery and artifice to uphold their arbitrary power, and whatever dishonourable acts princes may indulge in are fully set off by the insubordination of their subjects.

The Imperial Machiavelli. Tiberius, the Roman emperor (42 B.C to A D. 37). His political axiom was "He who knows not how to dissemble knows not how to reign." It was also the axiom of Louis XI of France

Macintosh. Cloth waterproofed with rubber by a process patented in 1823 by Charles Macintosh (1766-1843), also a coat made of this

Mackerel Sky. A sky dappled with detached rounded masses of white cloud, something like the markings of a mackerel

To throw a sprat to catch a mackerel. *See* SPRAT

Mackworth's Inn. *See* BARNARD'S INN

Macmillanites. A religious sect of Scotland, who in 1743 seceded from the Cameronians because they wished to adhere more strictly to the principles of the Reformation in Scotland, so named from John Macmillan (1670-1753), their leader They called themselves the ' Reformed Presbytery "

MacPherson (mac fer´ son) Fable has it that during the reign of David I of Scotland, a younger brother of the chief of the powerful clan Chattan became abbot of Kingussie His elder brother died childless, and the chieftainship devolved on the abbot He procured the needful dispensation from the Pope (a dispensation, by the way, that no pope would ever give), married the daughter of the thane of Calder, and a swarm of little "Kingussies" was the result The people of Inverness-shire called them the *Mac-phersons*, *i e.* the sons of the parson.

Macrocosm (Gr , the *great world*), in opposition to the microcosm, the *little world*. The ancients looked upon the universe as a living creature, and the followers of Paracelsus considered man a miniature representation of the universe. The one was termed the Macrocosm, the other the Microcosm (*q v.*)

Mad. Mad as a hatter. The probable origin of this phrase is "Mad as an *adder*" (A S *nœddre*, A S *atter* being "poison"), but evidence is wanting It was popularized by Lewis Carroll (*Alice in Wonderland*, 1865), but was well known earlier, and was used by Thackeray (*Pendennis*, ch x) in 1849

Mad as a March hare. *See* HARE.

The Mad Cavalier. Prince Rupert (1619-82), noted for his rash courage and impatience of control He was a grandson of James I, through his mother, Elizabeth, and was famous as a cavalry leader on the Royalist side during the English Civil War

The Mad Parliament. The Parliament which assembled at Oxford in 1258, and broke out into open rebellion against Henry III It confirmed the Magna Charta, the king was declared deposed, and the government was vested in the hands of twenty-four councillors, with Simon de Montfort at their head

The Mad Poet Nathaniel Lee (about 1653-92), who towards the end of his life lost his reason through intemperance and was confined for four years in Bedlam

Macedonia's Madman. Alexander the Great (356, 336-323 B C)

The Brilliant Madman or **Madman of the North.** Charles XII of Sweden (1682, 1697-1718)

> Heroes are much the same, the point's agreed
> From Macedonia's madman to the Swede
>   POPE *Essay on Man*, IV

Madame. The wife of Philippe Duc d'Orleans, brother of Louis XIV, was so styled, other ladies were only Madame This or That.

Madame la Duchesse. Wife of Henri Jules de Bourbon (1627-93), eldest son of the Prince de Condé

Mademoiselle. The daughter of Philippe, Duc de Chartres, grandson of Philippe, Duc d'Orléans, brother of Louis XIV

La Grande Mademoiselle The Duchesse de Montpensier, cousin to Louis XIV, and daughter of Gaston, Duc d'Orléans

Madge A popular name for the barn owl

> 'Sdeins, an I swallow this, I'll ne'er draw my sword
> in the sight of Fleet-street again while I live, I'll sit in
> a barn with madge-howlet, and catch mice first —BEN
> JONSON *Every Man in his Humour*, II, 1

Madoc (mad´ ok) A legendary Welsh prince, youngest son of Owain Gwyneth, king of North Wales, who died in 1169 According to tradition he sailed to America, and established a colony on the southern branches of the Missouri About the same time the Aztecs forsook Aztlan, under the guidance of Yuhidthiton, and founded the empire called Mexico, in honour of Mexitli, their tutelary god. Southey's poem, *Madoc* (1805), harmonizes these two events.

Madonna (Ital , my lady) A title specially applied to the Virgin Mary

Mæander. *See* MEANDER.

Mæcenas (mē sē´ nas) A patron of letters, so called from C. Cilnius Mæcenas (d. 8 B.C), a Roman statesman in the reign of Augustus. who kept open house for all men of letters. and was the special friend and patron of Horace and Virgil Nicholas Rowe so called the Earl of Halifax on his installation to the Order of the Garter (1714).

The last English Mæcenas. Samuel Rogers (1763-1855), poet and banker

Maelstrom (mäl´ strom) (Norw , whirling stream) A dangerous whirlpool off the coast of Norway, between the islands of Moskenaso and Varo (in the Lofoten Islands), where the water is pushed and jostled a good deal, and where, when the wind and tide are contrary, it is not safe for small boats to venture.

It was anciently thought that it was a subterranean abyss, penetrating the globe, and communicating with the Gulf of Bothnia.

The name is given to other whirlpools, and also, figuratively, to any turbulent or overwhelming situation.

Mæonides (mē on' ĭ dēz), or **The Mæonian Poet.** Homer (q v), either because he was the son of Mæon or because he was born in Mæonia (Asia Minor).

Mæra. The dog of Icarius (q v).

Mæviad. See BAVIAD

Mae West (mā west) The name given by flying men in World War II to the inflatable life-preserver vest or jacket worn when there was a possibility of their being forced into the sea The name was given in compliment to the figure and charms of the famous film star

Mafflick. To celebrate an event, especially an occasion of national rejoicing, with wild and extravagant exuberance From the uproarious scenes and unrestrained exultation that took place in London on the night of May 18th, 1900, when the news of the relief of Mafeking (besieged by the Boers since the previous November) became known.

Mafia (mä fē' a) In Sicily, those who take part in active hostility to the law, viz the greater part of the population *Mafia* is often erroneously stated to denote an organized secret society.

Mag A contraction of magpie **What a mag you are!** You chatter like a magpie A prating person is called "a mag."

Not a mag to bless myself with. Not a halfpenny

Maga (mä' ga). A familiar name for *Blackwood's Magazine*

Magazine. A place for stores (Arab *makhzan*, a storehouse) This meaning is still retained for military and some other purposes, but the word now commonly denotes a periodical publication containing contributions by various authors. How this came about is seen from the *Introduction* to the *Gentleman's Magazine* (1731)—the first to use the word in this way —
This Consideration has induced several Gentlemen to promote a Monthly Collection to treasure up, as in a Magazine, the most remarkable Pieces on the Subjects above mention'd

Magdalene (măg' da lēn). An asylum for the reclaiming of prostitutes, so called from Mary Magdalene or Mary of Magdala, "out of whom He had cast seven devils" (*Mark* xvi, 9)

Magdalen College, Oxford (1458) and

Magdalene College, Cambridge (1542), are pronounced mawd' lin

Magdalenian (măg dē lē' nyan) The name given to a late period of the Stone Age, during which the climate was cold and reindeer, bison, and wild horses roamed over all Europe. It was at this time that the mammoth became extinct Stone Age man attained his highest degree of civilization in the Magdalenian period, the finest examples of which are found in the district of La Madeleine, Dordogne, France

19 *

Magdeburg Centuries. The first great work of Protestant divines on the history of the Christian Church It was begun at Magdeburg by Matthias Flacius, in 1552, and published at Basle (13 volumes), 1560-74. As each century occupies a volume, the thirteen volumes complete the history to 1300

Magellan, Straits of (ma jel' an). So called after Fernão de Magelhaes (c. 1480-1521), the Portuguese navigator, and first circumnavigator of the globe, who discovered them in 1520.

Magenta (ma jen' ta) A brilliant red aniline dye derived from coal-tar, named in commemoration of the bloody battle of Magenta, when the Austrians were defeated by the French and Sardinians This was just before the dye was discovered, in 1859

Maggot. There was an old idea that whimsical or crotchety persons had maggots in their brains—

Are you not mad, my friend? What time o' th' moon is't?

Have not you maggots in your brains?
　　　FLETCHER *Women Pleased*, iii, 4 (1620)

Hence we have the adjective *maggoty*, whimsical, full of fancies Fanciful dance tunes used to be called *maggots*, as in *The Dancing Master* (1716) there are many such titles as "Barker's maggots," "Cary's maggots," "Draper's maggots," etc , and in 1685 Samuel Wesley father of John and Charles Wesley, published a volume with the title *Maggots, or Poems on Several Subjects*

When the maggot bites. When the fancy takes us Swift, making fun of the notion, says that if the bite is hexagonal it produces poetry, if circular, eloquence; if conical, politics

Instead of maggots the Scots say, "His head is full of bees", the French, *Il a des rats dans la tête* (cp. our slang "Rats in the garret"); and in Holland, "He has a mouse's nest in his head."

Magi (mā' jī) (Lat ; pl of *magus*) Literally "wise men", specifically, the Three Wise Men of the East who brought gifts to the infant Saviour Tradition calls them Melchior, Gaspar, and Balthazar three kings of the East The first offered gold, the emblem of royalty, the second, frankincense, in token of divinity; and the third, myrrh, in prophetic allusion to the persecution unto death which awaited the "Man of Sorrows."

　　MELCHIOR means "king of light "
　　GASPAR, or CASPAR, means "the white one "
　　BALTHAZAR means "the lord of treasures."

Mediæval legend calls them the Three Kings of Cologne, and the Cathedral there claims their relics They are commemorated on January 2nd, 3rd, and 4th, and particularly at the Feast of the Epiphany.

Among the ancient Medes and Persians the Magi were members of a priestly caste credited with great occult powers. and in Camoens' *Lusiad* the term denotes the Indian Brahmins. Ammianus Marcellinus says that the Persian *magi* derived their knowledge from the Brahmins of India (i, 23) and Arianus expressly calls the Brahmins "magi" (i, 7)

Magic Rings, Wands, etc. *See these words*

The Great Magician or Wizard of the North. Professor Wilson ("Christopher North ') gave Sir Walter Scott the name, because of the wonderful fascination of his writings.

Magician of the North. The title assumed by Johann Georg Hamann (1730-88), a German philosopher and theologian.

Maginot Line (ma′ zhi no). A zone of fortifications, mostly of concrete, with impregnable gun-positions, shelters, etc , built along the eastern frontier of France between 1929 and 1934, and named after André Maginot (1877-1932), Minister of War, who was responsible for their construction The line extended from the Swiss border to that of Belgium, and for long it deluded the French into the belief that it would make a German invasion impossible This might have been true, had the Germans not entered France through Belgium in 1940, turning the Maginot Line, which thus served no purpose whatever.

Magna Charta. The *Great Charter* of English liberty extorted from King John, 1215.

It contained (in its final form) 37 clauses and is directed principally against abuses of the power of the Crown and to guaranteeing that no subject should be kept in prison without trial and judgment by his peers

Magnanimous, The. Alfonso V of Aragon (1385, 1416-58).

Chosroes or Khosru, King of Persia, twenty-first of the Sassanides, surnamed *Noushirwan* (the Magnanimous) (531-579)

Magnet. The loadstone; so called from Magnesia, in Lydia, where the ore was said to abound Milton uses the adjective for the substantive in the line "As the magnetic hardest iron draws" (*Paradise Regained*, ii, 168).

Magnetic Mountain. A mountain of mediæval legend which drew out all the nails of any ship that approached within its influence It is referred to in Mandeville's Travels and in many stories, such as the tale of the Third Calender and one of the voyages of Sinbad the Sailor in the *Arabian Nights*

Magnificat. The hymn of the Virgin (*Luke* i 46-55) beginning "My soul doth magnify the Lord" (*Magnificat anima mea Dominum*), used as part of the daily service of the Church since the beginning of the sixth century, and at Evening Prayer in England for over 800 years

To correct Magnificat before one has learnt Te Deum. To try to do that for which one has no qualifications; to criticize presumptuously

To sing the Magnificat at matins. To do things at the wrong time, or out of place The Magnificat belongs to vespers, not to matins

Magnificent, The. Chosroes of Persia. *See* MAGNANIMOUS.

Lorenzo de Medici (1448-92), *Il Magnifico*, Duke of Florence

Robert, Duke of Normandy, also called *Le Diable* (1028-35).

Soliman I, greatest of the Turkish sultans (1490, 1520-66)

C'est magnifique, mais ce n'est pas la guerre. A magnificent gesture, but not real warfare Admirable, but not according to rule The comment on the field made by the French General Bosquet to A H Layard on the charge of the Light Brigade at Balaclava It has frequently been attributed to Marshal Canrobert

Magnolia (măg nō′ li a) A genus of North American flowering trees so called from Pierre Magnol (1638-1715), professor of botany at Montpellier

Magnum (măg′ num) A wine bottle, double the size of the ordinary bottle—holding two quarts or thereabouts. *Cp* JEROBOAM

Magnum bonum (Lat , "great and good') A name given to certain choice potatoes, and also plums Burns, in the following extract, evidently meant by it a magnum (*see above*) —

> And Welsh, who ne'er yet flinch'd his ground,
> High-way'd his magnum-bonum round
> > With Cyclopean fury
> > > *An Election Ballad Dumfries Burghs*

Magnum opus. The chief or most important of one's literary works

> My magnum opus, the "Life of Dr Johnson" is to be published on Monday, 16th May —BOSWELL *Letter to Rev. W. Temple*, 1791

Magpie. Formerly "maggot-pie," *maggot* representing *Margaret* (*cp. Robin* redbreast, *Tom*-tit, and the old *Phyllyp*-sparrow), and *pie* being *pied*, in allusion to its white and black plumage

> Augurs and understood relations have
> (By magotpies, and choughs, and rooks) brought forth
> The secret'st man of blood
> > *Macbeth*, iii, 4.

The magpie has generally been regarded as an uncanny bird· in Sweden it is connected with witchcraft, in Devonshire if a peasant sees one he spits over his shoulder three times to avert ill luck, and in Scotland magpies flying near the windows of a house foretell the early death of one of its inmates

The following rhyme about the number of magpies seen in the course of a walk is old and well known.—

> One's sorrow, two's mirth,
> Three's a wedding, four's a birth,
> Five's a christening, six a dearth,
> Seven's heaven, eight is hell,
> And nine's the devil his ane sel '

In target-shooting the score made by a shot striking the outermost division but one is called a *magpie* because it was customarily signalled by a black and white flag, and formerly bishops were humorously or derisively called magpies because of their black and white vestments

> Lawyers, as Vultures, had soared up and down,
> Prelates, like Magpies, in the Air had flown.
> > *Howell's Letters Lines to the Knowing Reader* (1645)

Magus. *See* SIMON MAGUS

Magyar (mâ jar′). The dominant race in Hungary Magyars are not of Aryan stock but of the Finno-Ugrian peoples, who invaded Hungary about the end of the 9th century and settled there. The Hungarian language is one of the most difficult to master in Europe.

Mahabharata (ma ha ba ra′ ta). One of the two great epic poems of ancient India (*cp.*

RAMAYANA), about eight times as long as the *Iliad* and *Odyssey* together. Its main story is the war between descendants of Kuru and Pandu, but there are an immense number of episodes

Maha-pudma. *See* TORTOISE.

Maharajah (ma ha ra' ja) (Sansk , "great king") The title of certain native rulers of India whose territories are very extensive The wife of a Maharajah is a *Maharanee.*

Mahâtma (ma hät' ma) (Sansk , "great soul") Max Muller tells us that.—

Mahâtma is a well-known Sanskrit word applied to men who have retired from the world, who, by means of a long ascetic discipline, have subdued the passions of the flesh, and gained a reputation for sanctity and knowledge That these men are able to perform most startling feats, and to suffer the most terrible tortures, is perfectly true —*Nineteenth Century*, May, 1893

By the Esoteric Buddhists the name is given to adepts of the highest order, a community of whom is supposed to exist in Tibet, and by Theosophists to one who has reached perfection spiritually, intellectually, and physically As his knowledge is perfect he can produce effects which, to the ordinary man, appear miraculous

The title was later associated with Mohandas Gandhi, the Hindu leader of revolt against British rule in India. A preacher and unceasing practiser of the doctrine of non-violence, by his life of pure simplicity and his intercessory fasts—often carried to the verge of death—he acquired an immense influence over Indians of all creeds and races Gandhi was assassinated by a fanatical Hindu at the age of 78, on January 30th, 1948.

Mahdi (ma' di) (Arab , "the divinely directed one"). The expected Messiah of the Mohammedans, a title often assumed by leaders of insurrection in the Sudan, especially Mohammed Ahmed (1843-85) who led the rising of 1883, and who, say some, is not really dead, but sleeps in a cavern near Bagdad, and will return to life in the fullness of time to overthrow Dejal (anti-Christ) The Shiahs believe that the Mahdi has lived (some sects maintaining that he is in hiding), but the Sunnis hold that he is still to appear.

Mah-jongg (ma jong'). A Chinese game played with dominoes made of ivory and bamboo. There are usually four players at a table, each acting for himself The dominoes, which number 136, are arranged in three suits, and there are four sets of each One consists of three honours—red, white, and green, another represents the four winds, north, south, east, and west, the third consists of three sets of nine dominoes named characters, circles, and bamboos The object of each player is to obtain the highest scoring hand, known as Mah-jongg

Mahomet. *See* MOHAMMED.

Mahoun, Mahound. Names of contempt for Mohammed, a Moslem, a Moor, particularly in romances of the Crusades The name is sometimes used as a synonym for "the Devil "

Oft-times by Termagant and Mahound swore
SPENSER *Faerie Queene*, VI, vii, 47.

Maid. Maid Marian A female character in the old May games and morris dances, in the former usually being Queen of the May. In the later Robin Hood ballads she became attached to the cycle as the outlaw's sweetheart, probably through the performance of Robin Hood plays at May-day festivities The part of Maid Marian both in the games and the dance was frequently taken by a man dressed as a woman

[The Courtier] must, if the least spot of morphew come on his face, have his oyle of tartar, his *lac virginis*, his camphir dissolved in verjuice, to make the foole as faire, for sooth, as if he were to playe Maid Marian in a May-game or moris-dance — GREENE *Quip for an Upstart Courtier* (1592)

Maid of Athens. The girl immortalized by Byron, was Theresa Macri.

Maid of Norway. Margaret (1283-90), daughter of Eric II and Margaret of Norway. On the death of Alexander III of Scotland (1285), her maternal grandfather, she was acknowledged Queen of Scotland, and was betrothed to Edward, son of Edward I of England, but she died on her passage to Scotland

Maid of Orleans. Joan of Arc (1412-31), who raised the siege of Orleans in 1429 She was canonized in 1920, her feast day being May 8th

Maid of Saragossa Augustina Zaragoza, distinguished for her heroism when Saragossa was besieged in 1808 and 1809, and celebrated by Byron in his *Childe Harold* (I, liv-lvi)

Maiden. A machine resembling the guillotine, used in Scotland in the 16th and 17th centuries for beheading criminals, and introduced there by the Regent Morton for the purpose of beheading the laird of Pennycuik It was also called "the widow "

He who invented the maiden first hanselled it Morton is erroneously said to have been the first to suffer by it. Thomas Scott, one of the murderers of Rizzio, was beheaded by it in 1566, fifteen years before the Regent's execution.

Maiden Assize One in which there is no person to be brought to trial. We have also the expressions maiden tree, one never lopped, maiden fortress one never taken, maiden speech, the first delivered, etc In a maiden assize, the sheriff of the county presents the judge with a pair of white gloves. *Maiden* conveys the sense of unspotted, unpolluted, innocent; thus Hubert says to the king—

This hand of mine
Is yet a maiden and an innocent hand,
Not painted with the crimson spots of blood
King John, iv, 2

Maiden King, The. Malcolm IV of Scotland (1141, 1153-65)

Malcolm . . . son of the brave and generous Prince Henry . was so kind and gentle in his disposition, that he was usually called Malcolm the Maiden — SCOTT *Tales of a Grandfather*, iv

Maiden over. A cricket term for an over in which no runs are made.

Maiden or Virgin Queen Elizabeth I, Queen of England, who never married. (1533, 1558-1603.)

Maiden Town. A town never taken by the enemy (cp MAIDEN ASSIZE above). Also, specifically, Edinburgh, from tradition that the maiden daughters of a Pictish king were sent there for protection during an intestine war.

Mail Order. The carrying on of business by post, that is of receiving orders and cash by post and sending on the goods purchased by the customer also by post, grew to enormous dimensions in U S A where, in great agricultural areas, it was the only method whereby people could obtain other than the mere necessaries of life.

Mailed Fist, The. Aggressive military might, from a phrase (*gepanzerte Faust*) made use of by William II of Germany when bidding adieu to Prince Henry of Prussia as he was starting on his tour to the Far East (December 16th, 1897):—

Should anyone essay to detract from our just rights or to injure us, then up and at him with your mailed fist

Maillotins (mī yŏ tan) Insurgents in Paris who, in 1382, rose against the taxes imposed by the Regent, the Duc d'Anjou. They seized iron mallets (maillotins) from the Arsenal and killed the tax collectors.

Main. To splice the mainbrace. A nautical phrase meaning to serve out grog, hence to indulge freely in strong drink Literally, the *mainbrace* is the rope by which the mainyard of a ship is set in position, and to *splice* it would be to join the two ends together again when broken

Main, chance, The. Profit or money, probably from the game called hazard, in which the first throw of the dice is called the *main*, which must be between four and nine, the player then throwing his *chance*, which determines the main

To have an eye to the main chance. To keep in view the money or advantage to be made out of an enterprise.

Main Street. The principal thoroughfare in many of the smaller towns and cities of U S A The novel of this name, by Sinclair Lewis (1920) epitomized the social and cultural life of these towns, and gave the phrase a significance of its own.

Maintenance (Fr. *main, tenir,* to hold in the hand, maintain) Means of support or sustenance in *legal* phraseology, officious intermeddling in litigation with which one has rightfully nothing whatever to do Cp CHAMPERTY Actions for maintenance are rare, but damages can be recovered for this abuse of legal process.

Cap of Maintenance. See CAP

Maitland Club. A club of literary antiquaries, instituted at Glasgow in 1828 It published or reprinted a number of works of Scottish historical and literary interest

Maize. American superstition had it that if a damsel found a blood-red ear of maize, she would have a suitor before the year was over.

Even the blood-red ear to Evangeline brought not her lover   LONGFELLOW· *Evangeline*

Majesty. Henry VIII was the first English sovereign who was styled "His Majesty," though it was not till the time of the Stuarts that this form of address had become stereotyped, and in the Dedication to James I prefixed to the Authorized Version of the Bible (1611) the King is addressed both in this way and as "Your Highness "

The Lord of Heaven and earth blesse your Majestie with many and happy dayes, that as his Heavenly hand hath enriched your Highnesse with many singular and extraordinary Graces, etc

Henry IV was "His Grace"; Henry VI, "His Excellent Grace", Edward IV, "High and Mighty Prince", Henry VII, "His Grace" and "His Highness", Henry VIII, in the earlier part of his reign, was styled "His Highness " "His Sacred Majesty" was a title assumed by subsequent sovereigns, but was afterwards changed to "Most Excellent Majesty " "His Catholic Majesty" was the king of Spain, and "His Most Christian Majesty" the king of France

In heraldry, an eagle crowned and holding a sceptre is said to be "an eagle in his majesty "

Majolica Ware. A pottery originally made in the island of Majorca or Majolica See FAIENCE

Major-General. A rank in the British Army above that of Brigadier and below that of Lieutenant-General The distinguishing badge is a crossed sword and baton with one star The rank was first instituted by Cromwell in 1655, after his quarrel with the Parliament; each major-general was to govern a military district with civil and military powers As such the scheme was in force until 1657, when the civil side was dropped and the rank became purely military.

Majority He has joined the majority. He is dead Blair says, in his *Grave*, "'Tis long since Death had the majority "

Make. In America this word is much more frequently used with the meaning put ready for use than it is with us; we have the phrase *to make the bed*, and Shakespeare has *make the door* (see DOOR), but in the States such phrases as *Have you made my room?* (i.e put it tidy), are common. *To make good, to make one's pile, to make a place* (i e to arrive there), are among the many Americanisms in which this word is used *To make a die of it*, to die, is another

Why, Tom, you don't mean to make a die of it?—R. M BIRD *Nick of the Woods* (1837)

On the make. Looking after one's own personal advantage, intent on the "main chance."

Make and mend. A term used in the Royal Navy for a period of time devoted to sewing and general repairs on board ship

To make it. To succeed in catching a train, keeping an appointment, etc

To make away with. To put or take out of the way, run off with, to squander, also to murder, *to make away with oneself* is to commit suicide

To make believe. To pretend, to play a game at.

We will make believe that there are fairies in the world   KINGSLEY *Water Babies,* ch. ii

Make-believe is also used as a noun

To make bold. *See* BOLD

To make for To conduce, as, "His actions make for peace", also to move towards, hence, in slang use, to attack

To make free with. To take liberties with, use as one's own

To make good. To fulfil one's promises or to come up to expectations, to succeed
     Whether or not the new woman Mayor would "make good" was of real interest to the country at large —*Evening Post (New York)*, Sept 14th, 1911

Also to replace, repair, or compensate for, as, "My car was damaged through your carelessness, so now you'll have to make it good"

To make it up To become reconciled

To make off. To run away, to abscond.

To make out. To manage, to contrive, to assert

To make tracks. To hurry away.

What make you here? What do you want? What are you come here for?
     Now, sir, what make you here?—*As You Like It*, I 1
     'Twas in Margate last July, I walk'd upon the pier, I saw a little vulgar boy—I said, "What make you here?"
     INGOLDSBY LEGENDS *Misadventures at Margate*

Makeshift. A temporary arrangement during an emergency.

Make-up The general use of this term as noun and verb to describe face cosmetics and their application is of theatrical origin, being employed to describe the materials used by an actor for painting his face and otherwise transforming his appearance to suit a character on the stage, the manner in which he is *made up*; hence, in colloquial use, the sum of one's characteristics, idiosyncrasies, etc In *printing* the *make-up* is the arrangement of the printed matter in columns, pages, etc.

Make-weight A small addition as compensation or an "extra," as a piece of meat, cheese, bread, etc , thrown into the scale to make the weight correct.

Malagrowther, Malachi. The signature of Sir Walter Scott to a series of letters contributed in 1826 to the *Edinburgh Weekly Journal* upon the lowest limitation of paper money to £5. They caused an immense sensation, similar to that produced by *Drapier's Letters* (*q v*), or Burke's *Reflections on the French Revolution*.

Malakoff (măl' á kof) This fortification, which was carried by storm by the French, September 8th, 1855 was named from a drunken Russian sailor who lived at Sebastopol, and, being dismissed the dockyards in which he had been employed, opened a liquor-shop on the hill outside the town. His old friends gathered round, other houses sprang up, and "Malakoff," as it came to be called, was ultimately fortified.

Malaprop, Mrs. (măl' á prop). The famous character in Sheridan's *The Rivals*. Noted for her blunders in the use of words (Fr *mal à*

propos) "As headstrong as an *allegory* on the banks of the Nile" is one of her grotesque misapplications, and she has given us the word *malapropism* to denote such mistakes.

Malaysia (ma lā' zya). The collective name given to the whole Malay Archipelago, as opposed to Malaya, which is applied to the southern and greater portion of the Malay Peninsula Amongst other islands Malaysia includes the Sunda Islands, the Moluccas, Borneo, and the Philippines

Malbecco (măl bek' ō) A "cankered, crabbed carle" in Spenser's *Faerie Queene* (III, x) wealthy, very miserly, and the personification of self-inflicted torments. His young wife, Helenore, set fire to his house, and eloped with Sir Paridel, whereupon Malbecco cast himself from a rock, and his ghost was metamorphosed into Jealousy.

Malbrouk or Marlbrough. The old French song, "*Malbrouk s'en va-t-en guerre*" (Marlborough is off to the wars), is said to date from 1709, when the Duke of Marlborough was winning his battles in Flanders, but it did not become popular till it was applied to Charles Churchill, 3rd Duke of Marlborough, at the time of his failure against Cherbourg (1758), and was further popularized by its becoming a favourite of Marie Antoinette about 1780, and by its being introduced by Beaumarchais into *Le Mariage de Figaro* (1784). The air, however (the same as our "We won't go home till morning"), is of far older date, was well known in Egypt and the East, and is said to have been sung by the Crusaders According to a tradition recorded by Châteaubriand, the air came from the Arabs, and the tale is a legend of Mambron, a crusader.

     Malbrouk s'en va-t-en guerre,
     Mironton, mironton, mirontaine,
     Malbrouk s'en va-t-en guerre,
     Nul sait quand reviendra.
     Il reviendra z'à pâques—
     Mironton, mironton, mirontaine . . .
     Ou à la Trinite.

Male. Applied in the vegetable kingdom to certain plants which were supposed to have some masculine property or appearance, as the *male fern* (*Nephrodium filix-mas*), the fronds of which cluster in a kind of crown; and to precious stones—particularly sapphires—that are remarkable for their depth or brilliance of colour.

Malebolge (măl ē bolj'). The eighth circle of Dante's *Inferno* (Canto xviii), containing ten *bolgi* or pits The name is used figuratively of any cesspool of filth or iniquity

Malice. In addition to its common meaning malice is a term in English law to designate either actual ill-will formed against another in the mind of the person charged with malice or the doing of some deliberate act so injurious to another that the law will imply evil intent—this is commonly known as malice prepense, or malice aforethought Malicious damage is a legal term meaning damage done to property wilfully and purposely, malicious prosecution means the preferring a criminal prosecution or the presentation of a bankruptcy petition maliciously and without reasonable cause

Malkin (mol' kin). An old diminutive of Matilda; formerly used as a generic term for a kitchen-wench or untidy slut; also for a cat (*see* GRIMALKIN), and for a scarecrow or grotesque puppet

> All tongues speak of him . .
> The kitchen malkin pins
> Her richest lochram 'bout her reechy neck,
> Clambering the walls to eye him
> *Coriolanus*, ii, 1.

The name was also sometimes given to the Queen of the May (*see* MAID MARIAN) —

> Put on the shape of order and humanity,
> Or you must marry Malkin, the May lady.
> BEAUMONT AND FLETCHER *Monsieur Thomas*, ii, 2.

Mall, The (mǎl) A broad promenade in St James's Park, London, so called because the game of *Pall-mall* (*q* v.) used to be played there. The *mall* was the mallet with which the ball was struck

> Noe persons shall after play carry their malls out of St James's Parke without leave of the said keeper.— *Order Book of General Monk* (1662)

Malmesbury, The Philosopher of (mamz' be ri) Thomas Hobbes (1588-1679), author of *Leviathan* (*q.v*), from his birthplace

Malmsey Wine (mam' zi) is the wine of Malvasia, in the Morea, and is the same name as *Malvoisie*

George, Duke of Clarence, son of Richard, Duke of York, was, according to tradition, drowned in a butt of malmsey in 1477-8, by order of his brother, Richard III. Holinshed says, "finallie the duke was cast into the Tower, and therewith adjudged for a traitor, and privily drowned in a butt of malmesie, the eleventh of March, in the beginning of the seventeenth yeare of the kinge's reigne "

See Shakespeare's *Richard III*, i, 4

Malt. A malt worm. A toper, especially a well-soaked beer-drinker.

> I am joined with no foot-landrakers, no long-staff sixpenny strikers, none of these mad mustachio-purple-hued malt worms; but with nobility and tranquillity —1 *Henry IV*, ii, 1.

In meal or malt. *See* MEAL.

When the malt gets aboon the meal. When persons, after dinner, get more or less fuddled

The famous **Sermon on Malt** is generally credited to the Puritan divine John Dod (about 1549-1645), rector of Fawsley, Northants, called *the Decalogist*, from his exposition of the Ten Commandments (1604)

Malta After a varied and eventful history this island became a British possession in 1814 since when it has been almost impregnably fortified as a naval base, commanding the Mediterranean and the approaches to the Suez Canal For its resistance and suffering under aerial bombardment the island was awarded the George Cross in 1942.

Malta, Knights of, or *Hospitallers of St John of Jerusalem* Some time after the first crusade (1042), some Neapolitan merchants built at Jerusalem a hospital for sick pilgrims and a church which they dedicated to St John; these they committed to the charge of certain knights, called *Hospitallers of St John* In 1310 these Hospitallers, having developed into a military Order, took the island of Rhodes,

and changed their title into *Knights of Rhodes* In 1522 they were expelled by the Turks, and took up their residence in Malta, which was ruled by the Grand Master until the island was taken by the French in 1798 The Order is now extinct as a sovereign body, but maintains a lingering existence in Italy, Germany, France, etc , and in Malta, where it still confers titles of "Marquis" and "Count " *See* HOSPITALLERS

Maltese Cross. Made thus ✠ Originally the badge of the Knights of Malta, formed of four barbed arrow-heads with their points meeting in the centre In modified and elaborated forms it is the badge of many well-known Orders, etc., as the British Victoria Cross and Order of Merit, and the German Iron Cross.

Maltese terrier. An ancient breed of lap-dog, somewhat resembling a Skye terrier though not really a terrier at all In colour it is pure white, though occasionally marked with fawn; the face and sides are clothed with long, silky hair and the highly-plumed tail usually curves over the back.

Malthusian Doctrine was that population increases more than the means of subsistence does, so that in time, if no check is put upon the increase of population, many must starve or all be ill fed It was promulgated by T R. Malthus (1766-1835), especially in his *Essay on Population* (1798). Applied to individual nations, such as Britain, it intimated that something must be done to check the increase of population, as all the land would not suffice to feed its inhabitants.

Malum (mã' lum), in Latin, means *an apple*, and *malus, mala, malum* means *evil* Southey, in his *Commonplace Book*, quotes as its etymon given by Nicolson and Burn, making the noun derived from the adjective, in allusion, possibly, to the apple eaten by Eve; and there is the schoolboy joke showing how *malo* repeated four times can be translated into a tolerable and fairly lengthy quatrain:—

> *Malo*, I would rather be
> *Malo*, Up an apple tree
> *Malo*, Than a bad man
> *Malo*, In adversity.

Malum in se (Lat) What is of itself wrong, and would be so even if no law existed against its commission, as lying, murder, theft

Malum prohibitum (Lat) What is wrong merely because it is forbidden, as eating a particular fruit was wrong in Adam and Eve, because they were commanded not to do so.

Malvern Hills (mawl' věrn) A range of hills or downs extending for some nine miles between Worcestershire and Herefordshire Worcester Beacon and Hereford Beacon are both nearly 1,400 ft high, from the former can be seen fifteen counties, the cathedrals of Hereford, Worcester, and Gloucester and five abbeys

> On a May morwenynge on Malverne hilles
> Me befel a ferly, of fairye me thogte.
> I was wery for-wandred, and wente me to reste
> Under a brood bank by a bournes syde,
> And as I lay and lenede, and loked on the watres
> I slombred into a slepyng, it sweyed so murye
> LANGLAND · *Piers Plowman*

Mambrino (măm brē nō) A pagan king of old romance, introduced by Ariosto into *Orlando*

Furioso He had a helmet of pure gold which rendered the wearer invulnerable, and was taken possession of by Rinaldo. This is frequently referred to in *Don Quixote*, and we read that when the barber was caught in a shower and clapped his brazen basin on his head, Don Quixote insisted that this was the enchanted helmet of the Moorish king.

Mamelukes (măm′ e lookz) (Arab. *mamluc*, a slave) The slaves brought from the Caucasus to Egypt, and formed into a standing army, who, in 1254, raised one of their body to the supreme power They reigned over Egypt till 1517, when they were overthrown by the Turkish Sultan, Selim I. The country, though nominally under a Turkish viceroy, was subsequently governed by twenty-four Mameluke beys In 1811 the Pasha of Egypt, Mohammed Ali, by a wholesale massacre annihilated the Mamelukes.

Mammet, or Maumet. An idol; hence a puppet or doll (as in *Romeo and Juliet*, iii, 5, and 1 *Henry IV*, ii, 3) The word is a corruption of *Mahomet*. Mohammedanism being the most prominent non-Christian religion with which Christendom was acquainted before the Reformation, it became a generic word to designate any false faith; even idolatry is called *mammetry*; and in a 14th-century MS. Bible (first edited by A C. Paues, 1904) 1 *John* v, 21, reads—

My smale children, kepe ye you from mawmetes and symulacris

Mammon (măm′ on) The god of this world. The word in Syriac means riches, and it occurs in the Bible (*Matt.* vi, 24, *Luke* xvi, 13) "Ye cannot serve God and mammon." Spenser (*Faerie Queene*, II, vii) and Milton (who identifies him with Vulcan or Mulciber, *Paradise Lost*, i, 738-51) both make Mammon the personification of the evils of wealth and miserliness

> Mammon led them on—
> Mammon, the least erected Spirit that fell
> From Heaven; for even in Heaven his looks and thoughts
> Were always downward bent, admiring more
> The riches of Heaven's pavement, trodden gold,
> Than aught divine or holy
> MILTON *Paradise Lost*, i, 678

The Mammon of Unrighteousness. Money, see *Luke* xvi, 9.

Sir Epicure Mammon. A worldly sensualist in Ben Jonson's *Alchemist*.

Mammoth Cave. In Edmonson county, Kentucky; the largest known in the world, discovered in 1809 It comprises a large number of chambers, with connecting passages said to total 150 miles, and covers an area of nearly 10 miles in diameter.

Man. Man in the Moon, Man of Blood, Brass, December, Sin, Straw, War, etc *See these words.*

Man about town. A fashionable idler

Man Friday. *See* FRIDAY.

Man-Mountain. *See* QUINBUS FLESTRIN.

Man of letters. An author, a literary scholar.

Man of the world. One "knowing" in world-craft, no greenhorn. Charles Macklin brought out a comedy (1704), and Henry Mackenzie a novel (1773) with the title

Man of war. A warship in the navy of a government; though the name is masculine, always spoken of as "she " Formerly the term was used to denote a fighting man ("the Lord is a man of war," *Ex.* xv, 3).

The name of the "Man of War Rock," in the Scilly Islands, is a corruption of Cornish *men* (or *maen*) *an vawr*, meaning "big rock "

The popular name of the marine hydrozoan, *Physalia pelagica*, is the *Portuguese man of war*, or, simply, *man of war*

Man-of-war bird. The frigate-bird.

Man proposes, but God disposes So we read in the *Imitatio Christi* (*Homo proponit, sed Deus disponit*, I, xix, 2) Herbert (*Jacula Prudentum*) has nearly the same words; as also has Montluc: *L'homme propose et Dieu dispose* (*Comedie de Proverbes*, iii, 7)

The Man in Black. A well-known character in Goldsmith's *Citizen of the World*; supposed to have been drawn from the author's father

The Man in the Iron Mask. *See* MASK.

Man in the street. The ordinary citizen, the man or woman who, in the aggregate, makes public opinion According to Charles Greville (1794-1865) this was originally a racing term— " 'the man in the street,' as we call him at Newmarket." *Diary, s.d.* March 22nd, 1831.

The Man of Destiny. Napoleon I (1761-1821). He looked on himself as an instrument in the hands of destiny.

G. B. Shaw used the epithet as the title of a play about Napoleon.

The Man of Ross. *See* ROSS

The New Man The regenerated man In Scripture phrase the unregenerate state is called *the old man.*

The Threefold Man. According to Diogenes Laertius, the body was composed of (1) a mortal part; (2) a divine and ethereal part, called the *phren*, and (3) an aerial and vaporous part, called the *thumos*

According to the Romans, man has a threefold soul, which at the dissolution of the body resolves itself into (1) the *Manes*; (2) the *Anima* or Spirit, (3) the *Umbra* The Manes went either to Elysium or Tartarus; the Anima returned to the gods; but the Umbra hovered about the body as unwilling to quit it.

According to the Jews, man consists of body, soul, and spirit.

Man, Isle of. The origin of the name is doubtful, but it may be O Celt. *man*, a place The *Old English Chronicle* calls it *Mon ege* (Mona's Isle), Orderic (about 1100) *Insula Man*, while Cæsar called it *Mona*, Pliny *Monapia*, and Ptolemy *Monarina*. To Bede the island was *Mevaniæ Insulæ*, and Nennius gives it its current Latin name as well as its native name—*Eubonia, id est Manau* The Manx form is *Eilan Mhannin*.

Mancha, La (la man′ cha) was a province of Spain almost identical with the modern province of Ciudad Real It is celebrated as the country of Don Quixote. It is a land of arid steppes and wide expanses of heath and waste, and is the least populated area of Spain.

Manchester. The name—which is given in Domesday Book as *Mamecestre*, and in the *Old English Chronicle* as *Mameceaster*—is of doubtful origin, but the *mam-* is probably Celtic *mam*, rounded, breast-like, in which case the word would be a Latin and Celtic hybrid denoting "the camp by the round hill" A native of Manchester is a Mancunian, from *Mancunium*, the mediæval Latin name of the city.

The Manchester Massacre. See PETERLOO.

The Manchester Poet. Charles Swain (1803-74)

The Manchester School. The name given in derision by Disraeli to the Cobden-Bright group of Free Trade economists in 1848 Hence, Free Traders, and Free Trade principles generally.

Manchukuo (măn choo kwŏ'). This was the name given to a country formed of Manchuria and parts of Inner Mongolia, under the control of Japan, incorporated in 1932. In 1945 it was restored to China under the old name of Manchuria.

Manciple A purveyor of food, a steward, or clerk of the kitchen Chaucer has a "manciple" in his *Canterbury Tales* (Lat *manceps, mancipis,* a buyer, manager)

Mancus. An Anglo-Saxon coin worth thirty pence In the reign of Ethelbert, King of Kent, money accounts were kept in *pounds, mancuses, shillings,* and *pence* Five pence = one shilling, 30 pence = one mancus Mancuses were in gold and silver also

Mandamus (Lat , we command) A writ of Queen's Bench, commanding the person or corporation, etc , named to do what the writ directs. So called from the opening word.

Mandarin is not a Chinese word, but one given by the Portuguese colonists at Macao to the officials called by the natives *Kwan* It is from Malay and Hindi *mantri,* counsellor, from Sansk *mantra,* counsel (*man,* to think).

The word is sometimes used derisively for over-pompous officials, as, "The mandarins of our Foreign Office."

The mandarin orange is probably so called from the resemblance of its colour to that of a mandarin's robe.

The nine ranks of mandarins were distinguished by the button in their cap'—1, ruby, 2, coral; 3, sapphire, 4, an opaque blue stone, 5, crystal, 6, an opaque white shell; 7, wrought gold, 8, plain gold; and 9, silver.

The whole body of Chinese mandarins consists of twenty-seven members. They are appointed for (1) imperial birth, (2) long service; (3) illustrious deeds, (4) knowledge, (5) ability; (6) zeal, (7) nobility, and (8) aristocratic birth —GUTZLAY

Mandate (Lat *mandatum, mandare,* to command). An authoritative charge or command, in law, a contract of bailment by which the mandatory undertakes to perform gratuitously a duty regarding property committed to him

After World War I it was decided by the victorious Powers that the former extra-European colonies and possessions of Germany and Turkey should be governed under *mandate* by one or other of the Powers Thus, the German colonies in West Africa and parts of the Turkish possessions in Palestine and Mesopotamia became *mandatory spheres* under Great Britain

Mandeville, Sir John. *See* MAUNDREL

Mandrake. The root of the mandrake, or mandragora, often divides in two, and presents a rude appearance of a man In ancient times human figures were cut out o the root, and wonderful virtues ascribed to them, such as the production of fecundity in women (*Gen* xxx, 14-16) It was also thought that mandrakes could not be uprooted without producing fatal effects, so a cord used to be fixed to the root, and round a dog's neck, and the dog being chased drew out the mandrake and died Another fallacy was that a small dose made a person vain of his beauty, and a large one made him an idiot, and yet another that when the mandrake is uprooted it utters a scream, in explanation of which Thomas Newton, in his *Herball to the Bible,* says, "It is supposed to be a creature having life, engendered under the earth of the seed of some dead person put to death for murder "

Shrieks like mandrakes, torn out of the earth.
Romeo and Juliet, iv, 3

Mandrakes called love-apples. From the old notion that they were aphrodisiacs Hence Venus is called *Mandragoritis,* and the Emperor Julian, in his epistles, tells Calixenes that he drank its juice nightly as a love-potion.

He has eaten mandrake. Said of a very indolent and sleepy man, from the narcotic and stupefying properties of the plant, well known to the ancients

Give me to drink mandragora
That I might sleep out this great gap of time
My Antony is away
Antony and Cleopatra, i, 5

Not poppy, nor mandragora
Nor all the drowsy syrops of the world,
Shall ever medicine thee to that sweet sleep
Which thou owedst yesterday
Othello, iii, 3

Manes (mā' nēz) To appease his Manes. To do when a person is dead what would have pleased him or was due to him when alive The spirit or ghost of the dead was by the Romans called his *Manes,* which never slept quietly in the grave so long as survivors left its wishes unfulfilled February 19th was the day when all the living sacrificed to the shades of dead relations and friends—a kind of pagan All Souls' Day

Manes is probably from the old word *manis, i e* "bonus," "quod eos venerantes manes vocarent, ut Græci *chrestous.*" (*See Lucretius,* iii, 52.)

Manfred. Count Manfred, the hero of Byron's dramatic poem of this name (1817), sold himself to the Prince of Darkness, was wholly without human sympathies, and lived in splendid solitude among the Alps. He loved the Lady Astarte (*q v*), who died, but Manfred went to the hall of Arimanes to see her, and was told that he would die the following day The next day the Spirit of his Destiny came to summon him, the proud count scornfully dismissed it, and died.

Mani (ma′ nē). The moon, in Scandinavian mythology, the son of Mundilfœri (*q v*), taken to heaven by the gods to drive the moon-car He is followed by a wolf, which, when time shall be no more, will devour both Mani and his sister Sol.

Mani, Manes, or **Manichæus.** The founder of Manichæanism (*see below*), born in Persia probably about 216, prominent at the court of Sapor I (240-72), but crucified by the Magians in 277

Manichæans or **Manichees** The followers of Mani who taught that the universe is controlled by two antagonistic powers, viz light or goodness (identified with God), and darkness, chaos, or evil The system was the old Babylonian nature-worship modified by Christian and Persian influences, and its own influence on the Christian religion was, even so late as the 13th century, deep and widespread St Augustine was a member of the body for some nine years One of Mani's claims was that though Christ had been sent into the world to restore it to light and banish the darkness His apostles had perverted his doctrine and he, Mani, was sent as the Paraclete to restore it The headquarters of Manichæanism were for many centuries at Babylon, and later at Samarkand

Manitou (măn′ i too) The Great Spirit of the American Indians The word is Algonkin, and means either the Great Good Spirit or the Great Evil Spirit.

Manna (*Ex.* xvi, 15), popularly said to be a corrupt form of *man-hu* (What is this?) The marginal reading gives—"When the children of Israel saw it [the small round thing like hoar-frost on the ground], they said to one another, What is this? for they wist not what it was "

And the house of Israel called the name thereof manna, and it was like coriander seed, white, and the taste of it was like wafers made with honey

The word is more probably the Egyptian *mennu,* a waxy exudation of the tamarisk (*Tamarix gallica*).

Manna of St Nicholas of Bari. The name given to a colourless and tasteless poison, sold by a notorious female poisoner of 16th-century Italy named Tofana, who confessed to having poisoned six hundred persons by its means Also called Aqua Tofana.

Manningtree (Essex). Noted for its Whitsun fair, where an ox was roasted whole Shakespeare makes Prince Henry call Falstaff "a roasted Manningtree ox, with the pudding in his belly" (1 *Henry IV*, ii, 4).

Manoa (mä nō′ ä). The fabulous capital of El Dorado (*q v.*), the houses of which city were said to be roofed with gold.

Manon Lescaut (mä nong les kō) A novel by the Abbé Prevost (1733) It is the history of a young man, the Chevalier des Grieux, possessed of many brilliant and some estimable qualities, who being intoxicated by a fatal

attachment to Manon, a girl who prefers luxury to faithful love, sets his love against the claims of society

Manor. *Demesne* (*i e.* "domain") land is that near the demesne or dwelling (*domus*) of the lord, and which he kept for his own use *Manor* land was all that remained (*maneo*), and was let to tenants for money or service, originally, a barony held by a lord and subject to the jurisdiction of his court-baron

In some manors there was *common land* also, *i e* land belonging in common to two or more persons, to the whole village, or to certain natives of the village.

Lord of the manor. The person of corporation in whom the rights of a manor are vested

Mansard Roof, also called the *curb roof.* A roof in which the rafters, instead of forming a ∧, are broken on each side into an elbow, the lower rafters being nearly vertical and the upper much inclined It was devised by François Mansard (1598-1666), the French architect, to give height to attics Mansard's nephew, Jules Hardouin Mansard (1645-1708) was the architect of the palace of Versailles, and the magnificent dome of the Invalides, among many great works of French architecture

Mansfield. The Miller of Mansfield. The old ballad (given in Percy's *Reliques*) tells how Henry II, having lost his way, met a miller, who took him home to his cottage Next morning the courtiers tracked the king, and the miller discovered the rank of his guest, who, in merry mood, knighted his host as "Sir John Cockle " On St. George's Day, Henry II invited the miller, his wife and son, to a royal banquet, and after being amused with their rustic ways, made Sir John "overseer of Sherwood Forest, with a salary of £300 a year "

Mansion. The Latin *mansio* (from *manere*, to remain, dwell) was simply a tent pitched on the march, hence sometimes a "day's journey" (*Pliny*, xii, 14) Subsequently the word was applied to a roadside house for the accommodation of strangers (Suetonius *Tit.* 10).

Mansion House, now the name of the official residence of a Lord Mayor. It was formerly used of any important dwelling, especially the houses of lords of the manor and of high ecclesiatics

Mantalini, Madame (măn ta lin′ i). A fashionable milliner in Dickens's *Nicholas Nickleby*, near Cavendish Square. Her husband, whose original name was "Muntle," noted for his white teeth, minced oaths, and gorgeous morning gown, lives on his wife's earnings, and ultimately goes to "the demnition bow-wows."

Mantle of Fidelity The old ballad "The Boy and the Mantle," in Percy's *Reliques*, tells how a little boy showed King Arthur a curious mantle, "which would become no wife that was not leal " Queen Guinever tried it, but it changed from green to red, and red to black, and seemed rent into shreds Sir Kay's lady tried it, but fared no better, others followed, but only Sir Cradock's wife could wear it. The theme is a very common one in old story, and was used by Spenser in the incident of Florimel's girdle.

Mantuan Swan, Bard, (măn' tū ăn) etc. Virgil, a native of Mantua, in Italy Besides his great Latin epic, he wrote pastorals and Georgics

Ages elapsed ere Homer's lamp appeared,
And ages ere the Mantuan Swan was heard
COWPER. *Table-Talk*, 557.

Manu. *See* MENU

Manufacturer. *See* SURGEON.

Manumit (măn' ū mit) To set free; properly "to send from one's hand" (*e manu mittere*) One of the Roman ways of freeing a slave was to take him before the chief magistrate and say, "I wish this man to be free." The lictor or master then turned the slave round in a circle, struck him with a rod across the cheek, and let him go. The ancient ceremony subsists to this day in the R C rite of Confirmation when the bishop strikes the confirmand lightly on the cheek with the words, "Peace be with thee"

Manure (Fr. *main-œuvre*) Literally "handwork," hence tillage by manual labour, hence the dressing applied to lands Milton uses the word in its original sense in *Paradise Lost*, IV, 628·—

You flowery arbours . with branches overgrown
That mock our scant manuring

And in XI, 28, says that the repentant tears of Adam brought forth better fruits than all the trees of Paradise that his hands "manured" in the days of innocence.

Manx cat. A tailless species of cat found in the Isle of Man

Many a little makes a mickle. Little and often fills the purse *See* LITTLE

Many men, many minds, *i e.* as many opinions as there are persons to give them, an adaptation of Terence's *Quot homines tot sententiæ* (*Phormio*, II, IV, 14)

Too many for me or One too many for me. More than a match *Il est trop fort pour moi*.
The Irishman is cunning enough, but we shall be too many for him.—MRS EDGEWORTH.

Maori (mou' ri). The aboriginal Polynesian inhabitants of New Zealand, a native word meaning *indigenous*.

Maple Leaf. The emblem of Canada.

Maquis (ma' kë) The thick scrub in Corsica to which bandits retire and resist by arms any attempt to apprehend them. A bandit so on the run is called a *maquisard See also* F.F.I.

Marabou. A large stork or heron of western Africa, so called from Arab *murabit*, a hermit, because among the Arabs these birds were held to be sacred Its feathers are used by ladies for headgear, neck-wraps, etc

Marabouts. A priestly order of Morocco (Arab. *murabit*, a hermit) which, in 1075, founded a dynasty and ruled over Morocco and part of Spain till it was put an end to by the Almohads in the 12th century

Marais, Le. *See* PLAIN

Maranatha (Syriac, *the Lord will come—i e* to execute judgment). A word which, with

Anathema (*q v*), occurs in 1 *Cor* XVI, 22, has been erroneously taken as a form of anathematizing among the Jews, hence, used for a terrible curse

Marathon Race (măr' a thon) A long-distance running race, named after the Battle of Marathon (490 B C) the result of which was announced at Athens by a courier, sometimes called Pheidippides, who fell dead on his arrival. The race, properly of 26 miles, 385 yards, is one of the events at the modern Olympic games The record (1948) was held by K Son, of Japan, who in 1936 ran the course in 2 hours, 29 mins, 19 2 secs.

Maravedi or **Marvedie** (mar a ve' di). A very small Spanish copper coin, worth less than a farthing and long obsolete There are frequent references to it in Elizabethan and 17th-century literature In the 11th and 12th centuries there was a Portuguese gold coin of the same name, equivalent to about 14s

Marbles. *See* ARUNDELIAN, ELGIN.

March. The month is so called from "Mars," the Roman war-god and patron deity

The old Dutch name for it was *Lent-maand* (lengthening-month), because the days sensibly lengthen, the old Saxon name was *Hreth-monath* (rough month, from its boisterous winds), the name was subsequently changed to *Length-monath* (lengthening month); it was also called *Hlyd-monar't* (boisterous month); In the French Republican calendar it was called *Ventose* (windy month, February 20th to March 20th)

A bushel of March dust is worth a king's ransom. Because we want plenty of dry, windy weather in March to ensure good crops The fine for murder used to be proportioned to the rank of the person killed The lowest was £10, and the highest £60; the former was the ransom of a churl, and the latter of a king

He may be a rogue, but he's no fool on the march Though his honesty may be in question he is a useful sort of person to have about

March borrows three days from April. *See* BORROWED DAYS

Mad as a March hare. *See* HARE.

To steal a march on. *See* STEAL.

March table. British military term denoting a direction setting out the order in which the elements of a convoy should proceed, the exact minute at which each should pass a given starting point, and the average speed at which each should proceed.

Marching Watch The guard of civilians enrolled in London during the Middle Ages to keep order in the streets on the Vigils of St Peter and St John the Baptist during the festivities then held, used also of the festivities themselves Henry VIII approved of the pageants, etc, and on one occasion, to encourage them, took his queen, Katharine of Aragon, to witness the proceedings at "the King's Heade in Cheape." The custom fell into abeyance in 1527 on account of the sweating sickness, but was revived a few years later.

Marches. The A S *mearc*, a mark, by way of Fr. *marche*, a frontier. The boundaries between England and Wales, and between England and

Scotland, were called "marches," and the word is the origin of our *marquis*, the lord of the march.

The word is still applied in the sense that a boundary is shared, *e g* Kent marches with Sussex, that is, the two counties are contiguous.

Riding the marches—*i e* beating the bounds of the parish (Scots) *See* BOUNDS, BEATING THE

Marchington (Staffordshire) Famous for a crumbling short cake Hence the saying that one of crusty temper is "as short as Marchington wake-cake "

Marchioness, The. The half-starved girl-of-all-work in Dickens's *Old Curiosity Shop* As she has no name of her own Dick Swiveller gives her that of "Sophronia Sphynx," and eventually marries her

Marchpane (march' pān) The old name for the confection of almonds, sugar, etc , that we call *marzipan*, this being the German form of the original Ital *marzapane*, and adopted by us in the 19th century in preference to our own well-established word, because we imported the stuff largely from Germany.

First Serv · Away with the joint-stools, remove the court-cupboard, look to the plate Good thou, save me a piece of marchpane —*Romeo and Juliet*, i, 5

Marcionites (mar' si on itz). An ascetic Gnostic sect, founded by Marcion of Sinope in the 2nd century, and surviving till the 7th or even later They believed in a good God, first revealed by Christ (whose incarnation and resurrection they rejected), in an evil God, *i.e* the Devil, and in "Demiurge," the name they gave to the imperfect God of the Jews

Marcley Hill. Legend states that this hill in Herefordshire, on February 7th, 1571, at six o'clock in the evening, "roused itself with a roar, and by seven next morning had moved 40 paces " It kept on the move for three days, carrying all with it, it overthrew Kinnaston chapel, and diverted two high roads at least 200 yards from their former route. Twenty-six acres of land are said to have been moved 400 yards. (Speed *Herefordshire*)

Marconigram. A radiogram named after Marconi (1874-1937) who invented wireless telegraphy.

Mardi Gras (mar dē gra') (Fr , "fat Tuesday") The last day of the Lent carnival in France, Shrove Tuesday, which is celebrated with all sorts of festivities In Paris a fat ox used to be paraded through the principal streets, crowned with a fillet, and accompanied by mock priests and a band of tin instruments· in imitation of a Roman sacrificial procession.

Mare. The Cromlech at Gorwell, Dorsetshire, is called the White Mare; the barrows near Hambleton, the Grey Mare.

Away the mare. Off with the blue devils, good-bye to care This mare is the incubus called the nightmare

To cry the mare (Herefordshire and Shropshire) In harvesting, when the ingathering is complete, a few blades of corn left for the purpose have their tops tied together. The reapers then place themselves at a certain distance, and fling their sickles at the "mare " He who succeeds in cutting the knot cries out "I have her!" "What have you?" "A mare " "Whose is she?" The name of some farmer whose field has been reaped is here mentioned "Where will you send her?" The name of some farmer whose corn is not yet harvested is here given, and then all the reapers give a final shout

To win the mare or lose the halter. To play double or quits, all or nothing.

The grey mare is the better horse. The woman is paramount, said of a wife who "bosses" her husband Macaulay says (*Hist Eng.* I, iii).— "I suspect (the proverb) originated in the preference generally given to the grey mares of Flanders over the finest coach-horses of England", but as the saying is recorded in England from earlier than the date of importation of Flemish horses this explanation is probably incorrect

> As long as we have eyes, or hands, or breath,
> We'll look, or write, or talk you all to death,
> Yield, or she-Pegasus will gain her course
> And the grey mare will prove the better horse
> PRIOR: *Epilogue to Mrs Manley's "Lucius "*

The grey mare's tail. A cataract that is made by the stream which issues from Lochskene, in Scotland, so called from its appearance.

The two-legged mare. The gallows

Shanks's mare. One's legs or shanks.

Money will make the mare to go. You can do anything if only you have the money.

> "Will you lend me your mare to go a mile?"
> "No, she is lame leaping over a stile "
> "But if you will her to me spare,
> You shall have money for your mare."
> "Oh, ho! say you so?
> Money will make the mare to go "
> *Old Glees and Catches.*

Whose mare's dead? What's the matter? Thus, in 2 *Henry IV*, when Sir John Falstaff sees Mistress Quickly with the sheriff's officers, evidently in a state of great discomposure, he cries,

> How now? Whose mare's dead? What's the matter?
> —*Act* ii, 1

To find a mare's nest is to make what you suppose to be a great discovery, but which turns out to be either no discovery at all or else all moonshine.

> Why dost thou laugh?
> What mare's nest hast thou found?
> BEAUMONT AND FLETCHER *Bonduca*, v, 2

In some parts of Scotland the expression is *a skate's nest*, and in Cornwall they say, *You have found a wee's nest, and are laughing over the eggs* In Devon, nonsense is called a *blind mare's nest*

Mare (mār' i) The Latin word for *sea Mare clausum* is a sea that is closed by a certain Power or Powers to the unrestricted trade of other nations *Mare liberum* is a free and open sea In 1635 John Selden (1584-1654) published a treatise entitled *Mare Clausum Mare nostrum*, "our sea" was a term applied by Italian Fascists to the Mediterranean at the height of their imperial ambitions.

Marforio. *See* PASQUINADE

Margaret. A country name for the magpie (*q.v*), also for the daisy, or marguerite, so called from its pearly whiteness, *marguerite* being Old French for a pearl.

> The daise, a flour white and redde,
> In French called "la belle Marguerite"

Lady Margaret Professor. A professor of divinity both at Oxford and Cambridge, the professorship being founded in 1502 by Lady Margaret Beaufort (1443-1509), mother of Henry VII, who also endowed Christ's and St John's College at Cambridge These lectures are given for the "voluntary theological examination," and treat upon the *Fathers*, the *Liturgy*, and the *priestly duties*, *Cp* NORRISIAN

Lady Margaret Hall, a college for women at Oxford, was founded in her memory in 1878

Margaret, St. The chosen type of female innocence and meekness, represented as a young woman of great beauty, bearing the martyr's palm and crown, or with the dragon as an attribute Sometimes she is delineated as coming from the dragon's mouth, for legend says that the monster swallowed her, but on her making the sign of the cross he suffered her to quit his maw

Another legend has it that Olybrius, governor of Antioch, captivated by her beauty, wanted to marry her, and, as she rejected him with scorn, threw her into a dungeon, where the devil came to her in the form of a dragon Margaret held up the cross, and the dragon fled

St Margaret, whose feast is held on July 20th, is the patron saint of the ancient borough of Lynn Regis, and on the corporation seal she is represented as standing on a dragon and wounding it with the cross The inscription is "SVB MARGARETA TERITUR . DRACO . STAT CRUCE . LÆTA."

St. Margaret of Scotland, whose feast is kept on June 10th in the Western Church except in Scotland where it is observed on November 16th, was the daughter of Edmund Ironside, King of England, and the wife of Malcolm III of Scotland She died in 1093 and was canonized in 1250.

Margarine (there are two pronunciations of this mar′ ja rēn, mar′ gā rēn) It is a well-known butter substitute made of a great variety of vegetable and animal fats and oils It takes its names from the Greek *margaron*, a pearl.

Margin. In many old books a commentary was printed in the margin (as in our Bible of the present day), hence the word was often used for a commentary itself, as in Shakespeare's—

> His face's own margent did quote such amazes
> *Love's Labour's Lost*, ii, 1
> I knew you must be edified by the margent
> *Hamlet*, v, 2

And Lyly's—

> Beware my Comment, tis odds the margent shall bee as full as the text.—*Pappe with a Hatchet* (1589)

Marguerite des Marguerites (*the pearl of pearls*) So Francis called his sister, Mar-

guerite de Valois (1492-1549), authoress of the *Heptameron* She married twice, first, the Duc d'Alençon, and then Henri d'Albret, king of Navarre, and was the mother of Henry IV of France

Sylvius de la Haye published (1547) a collection of her poems with the title *Marguerites de la marguerite des princesses*, etc.

Marigold. The plant *Calendula officinalis* and its bright yellow flower are so called in honour of the Virgin Mary

> This riddle, Cuddy, if thou canst, explain .
> What flower is that which bears the Virgin's name,
> The richest metal added to the same?
> GAY *Pastoral*

In 17th-century slang a marigold (or "marygold") meant a sovereign

Marimba (ma rim′ bà) A musical instrument formed of strips of wood struck by hammers or sticks It is of African origin but it has been improved upon and popularized in Central America, where it got its present name

Marine. The female Marine. Hannah Snell, of Worcester (1723-92), who (according to tradition), passing herself off as a Marine, took part in the attack on Pondicherry It is said that she ultimately opened a public-house in Wapping, but retained her male attire.

Tell that to the Marines. *See* HORSE MARINES. In nautical parlance a greenhorn or a land-lubber afloat is often called "a marine" in contempt *See* JOLLY.

Empty bottles were at one time called "marines," because the Royal Marines were looked down upon by the regular seamen, who considered them useless A marine officer was once dining at a mess-table, when the Duke of York said to the man in waiting, "Here, take away these marines." The officer demanded an explanation, when the duke replied, "They have done their duty, and are prepared to do it again."

Mariner's compass. Traditionally claimed by the Chinese to have been in use as early as 2364 B.C , but first recorded as being used for sea travel by a Chinese writer of about A.D 800 It was introduced to Europe by Marco Polo, but it is probable that it was known—as the result of independent discovery —in the 12th century *See* FLEUR-DE-LIS

Marinism. Excessive literary ornateness and affectation So named from Giambattista Marini (1569-1625), the Neapolitan poet, famous for his whimsical comparisons, pompous and overwrought descriptions, and "conceits."

Marino Faliero (ma rē′ nō fäl yer′ ō) The forty-ninth doge of Venice, elected 1354 He joined a conspiracy to overthrow the republic, under the hope and promise of being made a king, but was betrayed by Bertram, one of the conspirators, and was beheaded on the "Giant's Staircase," the place where the doges were wont to take the oath of fidelity. A different story is told in Byron's tragedy of this name (1820)

Marivaudage (ma rē vō daj). An imitation of the style of Marivaux (1688-1763), author of several comedies and novels *Il tombe souvent dans une métaphysique alambiquee* (far-fetched, over-strained) *pour laquelle on a cree le nom de marivaudage*

Ce qui constitue le marivaudage, c'est une recherche affectée dans le style, une grande subtilite dans les sentiments, et une grande complication d'intrigues.— BOUILLET. *Dict Universel*, etc.

Marjoram (mar' jŏr ảm) **As a pig loves marjoram.** Not at all "How did you like so-and-so?" 'Well, as a pig loves marjoram" Lucretius tells us (vi, 974), *Amaricinum fugitat sus*, swine shun marjoram, but it is not at all certain that the Latin *amaricus* is identical with our *marjoram*.

Mark. A man of mark. A notable or famous man, one who has "made his mark" in some walk of life

Beside the mark. Not to the point, a phrase from archery, in which the *mark* was the target

God bless or **save the mark!** An ejaculation of contempt or scorn Hotspur, apologizing to the king for not sending the prisoners according to command (Shakespeare, 1 *Henry IV*, 1, 3), says the messenger was a "popinjay," who made him mad with his unmanly ways, and who talked "like a waiting gentlewoman of guns, drums, and wounds (God save the mark!)", and in *Othello* (I, 1) Iago says he was "his Moorship's ancient, God bless the mark!" expressive of derision and contempt

Sometimes the phrase is used to avert ill fortune or an evil omen, as in—

To be ruled by my conscience, I should stay with the Jew my master, who, God bless the mark! is a kind of devil —*Merchant of Venice*, ii, 2

I saw the wound, I saw it with mine eyes (God save the mark!) upon his manly breast —*Romeo and Juliet*, iii, 2

And sometimes it refers simply to the perverted natural order of things, as "travelling by *night* and resting (save the mark!) by day"

Its origin is unknown, and there is no evidence in favour of the widely quoted assumption that it arose from archery. It seems to have been originally a formula used for averting evil omens, and was in early use by midwives at the delivery of a child with a "birth-mark"

Mark time! Move the feet alternately as in marching, but without advancing or retreating from the spot

The mark of the beast. To set the "mark of the beast" on an object or pursuit (such, for instance, as dancing, theatres, gambling, etc) is to denounce it, to run it down as unorthodox. The allusion is to *Rev.* xvi, 2, xix, 20.

A certain kind of clerical waistcoat that used to be considered "Popish" in the 60s and 70s of last century was known as the "Mark of the Beast," or "M B." waistcoat

Mark is also a British military term denoting a version or issue of a piece of equipment The first issue of a new weapon, for example, is Mark I, which continues until any alteration or improvement, however small, is made in the design Subsequent issues are known as Mark II until any further alteration is made, and so on

To make one's mark To distinguish oneself. To write one's name (or make one's mark) on the page of history

In olden times persons who could not write "made their mark" as they do now, but we find in ancient documents words such as these "This (grant) is signed with the sign of the cross for its greater assurance (or) greater inviolability," and after the sign follows the name of the donor.

To toe the mark. To line up abreast of the others, so, to 'fall in" and do one's duty

Up to the mark. Generally used in the negative, as, "Not quite up to the mark," not good enough, not up to the standard fixed by the assay office for gold and silver articles, not quite well

Marks of gold and silver. *See* HALL MARK.

Marks in printing *See* TYPOGRAPHICAL SIGNS

Mark, as a name

Mark Banco. *See* BANCO

Mark, King. A king of Cornwall in the Arthurian romances, Sir Tristram's uncle He lived at Tintagel, and is principally remembered for his treachery and cowardice, and as the husband of Isolde the Fair, who was passionately enamoured of his nephew, Tristram (*q v*)

Mark Twain. The pseudonym of the American novelist and humorist, Samuel L. Clemens (1835-1910) who adopted it from the Mississippi river pilots' cry, "Mark twain!" when taking soundings.

Mark, St., in art, is represented as being in the prime of life, sometimes habited as a bishop, and, as the historian of the resurrection, accompanied by a winged lion He holds in his right hand a pen, and in his left the Gospel. His day is April 25th.

St. Mark's Eve. An old custom in North-country villages is for people to sit in the church porch on this day (April 24th) from 11 at night to 1 in the morning for three years running, and the third time they will see the ghosts of those who are to die that year pass into the church.

Poor Robin's Almanack for 1770 refers to another superstition —

On St Mark's Eve, at twelve o'clock,
The fair maid will watch her smock,
To find her husband in the dark,
By praying unto good St Mark

Keats has an unfinished poem on the subject, and he also refers to it in *Cap and Bells* (lvi) —

Look in the Almanack—Moore never lies—
April the twenty-fourth,—this coming day
Now breathing its new bloom upon the skies,
Will end in St Mark's Eve, you must away,
For on that eve alone can you the maid convey

Market-penny. A toll surreptitiously exacted by servants sent out to buy goods for their master, secret commission on goods obtained for an employer.

Marlborough (mawl' brŏ). **Statutes of Marlborough.** Laws passed in 1267 by a parliament held in Marlborough Castle They reaffirmed in more formal fashion the Provisions of Westminster of a few years earlier

Marmion (mär' mı on) A romantic poem by Scott (pubd 1808), telling the story of Lord Marmion, an entirely fictional character, who lived in the Border Country in the time of Henry VIII and James IV of Scotland He was slain at the battle of Flodden

Maro (mâr' ō) Virgil (70-19 B C), whose full name was Publius Virgilius Maro, born on the banks of the river Mincio, at the village of Andes, near Mantua.

Marocco or **Morocco**. The name of Banks's horse (*q v*)

Maronites (mär' ō nītz) A nation and Church of Arabic-speaking Syrian Christians, united to the Roman Catholic Church but still retaining the Syrian liturgy and many of their peculiarities They descend from a sect of Monothelites of the 8th century, and are so called from their chief seat, the monastery of Maron, on the slopes of Lebanon, which was named from Maron (Syriac, "my lord," or "master"), Patriarch of Antioch in the 6th century

Maroon (må roon'). To set a person on an in-hospitable shore and leave him there (a practice common with pirates and buccaneers); a corruption of *Cimarron*, a word applied by Spaniards to anything unruly, whether man or beast. As a noun the word denotes runaway slaves or their descendants who live in the wilds of Dutch Guiana, Brazil, etc Those of Jamaica are the offspring of runaways from the old plantations or from Cuba, to whom, in 1738, the British Government granted a tract of land, on which they built two towns.

Maroon, the firework that explodes like a cannon going off, is so called from Fr *marron*, a chestnut, probably with reference to the popping of chestnuts when being roasted

In World War I air-raid warnings and all-clear signals were made by means of maroons.

In the U S A the term was also applied to a hunting or fishing expedition in the form of a prolonged picnic lasting several days.

Marplot. An officious person who defeats some design by gratuitous meddling The name is given to a silly, cowardly, inquisitive Paul Pry, in *The Busybody* (1710), by Mrs. Centlivre Similarly we have Shakespeare's "Sir Oliver *Mar-text*," the clergyman in *As You Like It*, and "Sir Martin *Mar-All*, the hero of the Duke of Newcastle's comedy of that name, which was founded on Molière's *L'Etourdi*

Marprelate Controversy. The name given to the vituperative paper war of about 1589, in which the Puritan pamphleteers attacked the Church of England under the pseudonym "Martin Marprelate " Thomas Cooper, Bishop of Winchester, defended the Church, and the chief of the "Martinists" were probably Udall, Throckmorton, Penry, and Barrow Udall died in prison (1592), Penry and Barrow were executed in 1593 Some thirty pamphlets are known to have been published in this controversy

Marque. *See* LETTER OF.

Marquess or **Marquis** (O Fr *marchis*, warden of the marches) A title of nobility, in England ranking next below that of Duke (*q.v*) It

was first conferred on Richard II's favourite, Robert de Vere, Earl of Oxford, who was created Marquess of Dublin in 1385 A marquess is addressed as "The Most Honourable the Marquess of —", his younger sons and daughters bear the honorary titles of Lord and Lady

Marriage. Marriage knot, The. The bond of marriage effected by the legal marriage service. The Latin phrase is *nodus Herculeus*, and part of the marriage service was for the bridegroom to loosen (*solvere*) the bride's girdle, not to *tie* it In the Hindu marriage ceremony the bridegroom hangs a ribbon on the bride's neck and ties it in a knot Before the knot is tied the bride's father may refuse consent unless better terms are offered, but immediately the knot is tied the marriage is indissoluble The Parsees bind the hands of the bridegroom with a sevenfold cord, seven being a sacred number. The ancient Carthaginians tied the thumbs of the betrothed with a leather lace.

The practice of throwing rice (*see* RICE) is also Indian.

Marriages are made in heaven This does not mean that persons in heaven "marry and are given in marriage," but that the partners joined in marriage on earth were foreordained to be so united E Hall (1499-1547) says, "Consider the old proverbe to be true that saieth Marriage is destinie." *Cp.* "Hanging and wiving, etc " *under* HANG.

Married women take their husband's surname This was a Roman custom. Thus Julia, Octavia, etc , married to Pompey, Cicero, etc., would be called Julia of Pompey, Octavia of Cicero. Our married women are named in the same way, omitting "of "

Marrow. A Scots and North-country word (obsolete except in dialect) for a mate or companion, hence a husband or wife, and (of things) an article that makes a pair with another The origin of the word is unknown.

> Busk ye busk ye, my bonnie bonnie bride,
> Busk ye, busk ye, my winsome marrow
> W. HAMILTON *The Braes of Yarrow* (1774)

Down on your marrow-bones! Down on your knees! A humorous way of telling a person he had better beg pardon.

The marrow-bone stage. Walking The leg-bone is the marrow-bone of beef and mutton, and the play is on Marylebone (London), formerly pronounced "Marrybun."

Marrow Controversy. A memorable struggle in Scotland about 1719 to 1722, between Puritanism and Presbyterianism; so called from Edward Fisher's *Marrow of Modern Divinity*, a book of ultra-evangelical tendency (pubd 1644), which was condemned by the General Assembly in 1720.

Abelli, Bishop of Rhodes (d. 1691), wrote the *Medulla Theologica*

Marrow-men. The twelve ministers who signed the remonstrance to the General Assembly for condemning the evangelical doctrines of the "Marrow" (*see above*); the chief were Thomas Boston and Ralph and Ebenezer Erskine

Marry! An oath, meaning by Mary, the Virgin

Marry come up! An exclamation of disapproval or incredulity May Mary come up to my assistance, or to your discomfort!

> Marry come up, you saucy jade!

Mar's Year. The year 1715, noted for the Jacobite rebellion of the Earl of Mar on behalf of the Old Pretender

> Auld uncle John wha wedlock's joys
> Sin Mar's year did desire
> BURNS *Hallowe'en*, 27.

Mars. The Roman god of war, identified in certain aspects with the Greek Ares He was also the patron of husbandmen.

The planet of this name was so called from early times because of its reddish tinge, and under it, says the *Compost of Ptholomeus*, "is borne theves and robbers . nyght walkers and quarell pykers, bosters, mockers, and skoffers; and these men of Mars causeth warre, and murther, and batayle They wyll be gladly smythes or workers of yron . lyers, gret swerers. . He is red and angry . a great walker, and a maker of swordes and knyves, and a sheder of mannes blode . . . and good to be a barboure and a blode letter, and to drawe tethe "

Among the alchemists Mars designated iron, and in Camoen's *Lusiad* typified divine fortitude As Bacchus, the evil demon, is the guardian power of Mohammedanism, so Mars is the guardian of Christianity.

The Mars of Portugal. Alfonso de Albuquerque, Viceroy of India (1452-1515).

See also MARTIANS

Marseillaise (*Eng* mar se läz', *Fr.* mar sã yãz') The hymn of the French revolution. Claude Joseph Rouget de Lisle (1760-1835), an artillery officer in garrison at Strasbourg, composed both the words and the music (April 24th, 1792). On July 30th, 1792, the Marseilles volunteers entered Paris singing the song; and the Parisians, enchanted with it, called it the *Hymne des Marseillais*

Marshal (A S *mere*, mare, *scealc*, servant; O Fr *mareschal*) Originally one who tended horses, either as a groom or farrier, now the title of high officials about the Court, in the armed forces, etc In the Army Field-Marshal (*q v.*) is the highest rank; in the Royal Air Force Marshal of the R A F, Air Chief Marshal, Air Marshal, and Air Vice-Marshal, correspond to Field-Marshal, General, Lieutenant-General, and Major-General respectively. The military rank of Marshal of France was revived by Napoleon I, who gave the baton to a number of his most able generals No Marshals were created after 1870 until 1916 when the title was given to General Joffre (1852-1931) Generals Foch (1851-1929), Lyautey (1854-1934), and Pétain (1856-1951) were also Marshals of France

Marshal Vorwärts (Ger, forward) Blucher; so called for his persistence in attacking and pursuing the French during the campaign of 1813

Marshal of the Army of God, and of Holy Church. The Baron Robert Fitzwalter, appointed by his brother barons to lead their forces in 1215 to obtain from King John redress of grievances Magna Charta was the result

Marshall Plan. This was a plan for aiding the stricken European states after World War II On June 5th, 1947, G C. Marshall, Secretary of State for the U S A, called upon the countries of Europe to work out a programme of reconstruction for which he promised American assistance "so far as it may be practicable " After consultation together most of the powers concerned, with the exception of Russia and the eastern European states under her tutelage, agreed to participate and on April 3rd, 1948 the scheme came into force by Congress passing a Foreign Aid Bill of $3,800,000,000 Britain ceased to receive Marshall Aid in 1950

Marshalsea Prison. An old prison in Southwark, London (demolished in 1849), so called because it was formerly governed by a *Knight Marshal*, i e an official of the Royal Household who took cognizance of offences committed within the royal verge and who presided over the *Marshalsea Court* (amalgamated with the Queen's Bench in 1842). It was the Marshal of this prison who was beheaded by the rebels under Wat Tyler in 1381.

Marsyas (mar' si ås). The Phrygian fluteplayer who challenged Apollo to a contest of skill, and, being beaten by the god, was flayed alive for his presumption. From his blood arose the river so called The flute on which Marsyas played was one Athene had thrown away, and, being filled with the breath of the goddess, discoursed most excellent music The interpretation of this fable is as follows: A contest long existed between the lutists and the flautists as to the superiority of their respective instruments The Dorian mode, employed in the worship of Apollo, was performed on lutes, and the Phrygian mode, employed in the rites of Cybele, was executed by flutes, the reeds of which grew on the banks of the river Marsyas As the Dorian mode was preferred by the Greeks, they said that Apollo beat the flute-player.

Martel (mar' tel) The surname given to Charles, son of Pépin d'Heristal (about 690-791), probably because of his victory over the Saracens, who had invaded France under Abd-el-Rahman in 732 It is said that Charles "knocked down the foe, and crushed them beneath his axe, as a *martel* or hammer crushes what it strikes " Another suggestion is that he was so called because his patron saint (and the patron saint of Tours, near which he gained his great victory) was *St Martellus* (or *Martin*).

Martello Towers. Round towers about forty feet in height, of great strength, and situated on a coast or river-bank. Many of them were built on the south-eastern coasts of England about 1804, to repel the threatened Napoleonic invasion, and they took their name from *Mortella* (Corsica), where a tower from which these were designed had proved, in 1794, extremely difficult to capture

Mar-text. *See* MARPLOT.

Martha, St., patron saint of good housewives, is represented in art in homely costume bearing at her girdle a bunch of keys, and holding a ladle or pot of water in her hand Like St Margaret, she is accompanied by a dragon bound, for she is said to have destroyed one that ravaged the neighbourhood of Marseilles, but she has not the palm and crown of martyrdom. She is commemorated on July 29th, and is patron of Tarascon

Martha's Vineyard. An island, some 100 sq miles in area, off the S E. coast of Massachusetts It was discovered in 1602 by Bartholomew Gosnold, the discoverer of Cape Cod and the adjacent coasts, and so named by him Martha's Vineyard is now a popular summer resort with a population, in 1940, of over 5,000.

Martian Laws. Laws traditionally said to have been compiled by Martia, wife of Guithelin, great-grandson of Mulmutius, who established in England the Mulmutine Laws (*q v*). Alfred translated both these codes into Saxon-English

Guyntelme   whose queen, .   to show her up-
right mind,
To wise Malmutius' laws her Martian first did frame
DRAYTON *Polyolbion,* viii

Martians (mar'shanz) The hypothetical inhabitants of the planet Mars This planet has an atmosphere of much less density than that of the earth, but it has clouds and seasonal changes which have led some observers to presume that there is vegetation of a sort. From this it was an easy step to imagine life on its surface and in 1898 H. G Wells wrote *The War of the Worlds* in which he recounted the adventures and horrors of a war between the fabulous men of Mars and the dwellers on Earth.

Martin. One of the swallow tribe, probably so called from the Christian name *Martin* (St Martin's bird is the *goose*), but possibly because it appears in England about March (the *Martian* month) and disappears about Martinmas.

In *Reynard the Fox* (*q v*) Martin is the Ape, Rukenaw was his wife, Fubrumpe his son, and Byteluys and Hattenette his two daughters; and in Dryden's *Hind and the Panther,* an allegory, *Martin* means the Lutheran party, so called by a pun on the name of Martin Luther.

Martin, St. The patron saint of innkeepers and drunkards, usually shown in art as a young mounted soldier dividing his cloak with a beggar He was born of heathen parents but was converted in Rome, and became Bishop of Tours in 371, dying at Caudes forty years later His day is November 11th, the day of the Roman *Vinalia,* or Feast of Bacchus, hence his purely accidental patronage (as above), and hence also the phrase *Martin drunk.*

The usual illustration of St Martin is in allusion to the legend that when he was a military tribune stationed at Amiens he once, in midwinter, divided his cloak with a naked beggar, who craved alms of him before the city gates At night, the story says, Christ Himself appeared to the soldier, arrayed in this very garment.

Martin drunk. Very intoxicated indeed, a drunken man "sobered" by drinking more. Baxter uses the name as a synonym of a drunkard —
The language of Martin is there [in heaven] a stranger—*Saint's Rest*

St. Martin's bird. The goose, whose blood was shed "sacrificially" on November 11th, in honour of that saint *See below*

St. Martin's heads, jewellery, lace, rings, etc Cheap, counterfeit articles When the old collegiate church of St Martin's le Grand was demolished at the Dissolution of the Monasteries, hucksters established themselves on the site and carried on a considerable trade in artificial jewels, Brummagem ornaments, and cheap ware generally Hence the use of the saint's name in this connexion in Elizabethan and 17th-century writings

Certayne lyght braynes .   . wyll rather weare a Marten chayne, the pryce of vind, then they woulde be unchayned   BECON *Jewel of Joy* (*about* 1558)
This kindnesse is but like Alchimy or Saint Martin's rings, that are faire to the eye, and have a rich outside, but if a man breake them asunder and looke into them (etc)—FENNER *Compter's Commonwealth* (1618)

St. Martin's goose. November 11th, St Martin's Day, was at one time the great goose feast of France The legend is that St. Martin was annoyed by a goose, which he ordered to be killed and served up for dinner. He died from the repast, and the goose was "sacrificed" to him on each anniversary

St. Martin of Bullions The St Swithin of Scotland His day is July 4th, and the saying is that if it rains then, rain may be expected for forty days

St. Martin's running footman. The devil, traditionally assigned to St Martin for such duties on a certain occasion
Who can tell but St Martin's running footman may still be hatching us some further mischief —RABELAIS' *Pantagruel,* iv, 23.

St. Martin's summer. *See* SUMMER

Martinmas. The feast of St. Martin, November 11th. *His Martinmas will come, as it does to every hog*—i e. all must die. November was the great slaughtering time of the Anglo-Saxons, when oxen, sheep, and hogs, whose food was exhausted, were killed and salted Thus the proverb intimates that our day of death will come as surely as that of a hog at St Martin's-tide

Martinet. A strict disciplinarian, so called from the Marquis de Martinet, colonel commanding Louis XIV's own regiment of infantry All young noblemen were obliged, by direction of the king, to command a platoon in this unit before purchasing command of an infantry regiment, and Martinet's own system for inculcating in these wild young men the principles of military discipline earned him immortal fame He was slain at the siege of Doesbourg, in 1672 (Voltaire, *Louis XIV,* c 10)

Martyr (Gr), simply means a witness, but is applied to one who witnesses a good confession with his blood

The Martyr King. Charles I of England, beheaded January 30th, 1649

Martyr to science. A title conferred on anyone who loses his health or life through his devotion to science, especially Claude Louis, Count Berthollet (1748-1822), who tested in his own person the effects of carbolic acid on the human frame, and died under the experiment

Marvedie. *See* MARAVEDI.

Mary. As *the Virgin*, she is represented in art with flowing hair, emblematical of her virginity.

As *Mater Dolorosa*, she is represented as somewhat elderly, clad in mourning, head draped, and weeping over the dead body of Christ.

As *Our Lady of Dolours*, she is represented as seated, her breast being pierced with seven swords, emblematic of her seven sorrows

As *Our Lady of Mercy*, she is represented with arms extended, spreading out her mantle, and gathering sinners beneath it

As *The glorified Madonna*, she is represented as bearing a crown and sceptre, or a ball and cross, in rich robes and surrounded by angels.

Her seven joys The Annunciation, Visitation, Nativity, Epiphany, Finding in the Temple, Resurrection, Ascension

Her seven sorrows Simeon's Prophecy, the Flight into Egypt, Christ Missed, the Betrayal, the Crucifixion, the Taking Down from the Cross, and the Entombment

Little Mary. A euphemism for the stomach; from the play of that name by J. M. Barrie (1903).

The four Marys. Mary Beaton (or *Bethune*), Mary Livingston (or *Leuson*), Mary Fleming (or *Flemyng*), and Mary Seaton (or *Seyton*), called the "Queen's Marys," that is, the ladies of the same age as Mary, afterwards Queen of Scots, and her companions Mary Carmichael was not one of the four, although introduced in the well-known ballad.

> Yestre'en the queen had four Marys,
> This night she'll hae but three
> There was Mary Beaton, and Mary Seaton,
> Mary Carmichael, and me

Mary Ann or **Marianne.** A slang name for the guillotine *See below*.

Mary Anne Associations. Secret republican societies in France The name was adopted by the Republican party because Ravaillac was instigated to assassinate Henri IV (1610) by reading the treatise *De Rege et Regio Institutione*, by *Mariana*

The Mary Annes, which are essentially republicans, are scattered about all the French provinces — DISRAELI *Lothair*

Mary of Arnhem. Name used by Helen Sensburg in Nazi propaganda broadcasts to British troops in North-west Europe, 1944-45 Her melting voice made her programmes very popular with the British, but without the results for which she hoped

Mary, Highland. *See* HIGHLAND MARY

Mary Magdalene, St. Patron saint of penitents, being herself the model penitent of Gospel history. Her feast is July 22nd.

In art she is represented either as young and beautiful, with a profusion of hair, and holding a box of ointment, or as a penitent, in a sequestered place, reading before a cross or skull

Mary Queen of Scots. Shakespeare being under the patronage of Queen Elizabeth, and knowing her jealousy, would not, of course, praise openly her rival queen, but in the *Midsummer Night's Dream* (ii, 1) composed in 1592, five years after the execution of Mary, he wrote these exquisite lines —

> Thou rememberest
> Since once I sat upon a promontory,
> And heard a *mermaid* on a *dolphin's* back
> Uttering such dulcet and harmonious breath
> That the *rude sea* grew civil at her song,
> And *certain stars* shot *madly from their spheres,*
> To hear the sea-maid's music   *Act* ii, 1.

These have been conjectured to refer to the ill-fated queen on the following grounds —

Mermaid and *sea-maid*, Mary, on the *dolphin's* back, she married the *Dolphin* or *Dauphin* of France, *the rude sea grew civil*, the Scottish rebels, *certain stars*, the Earl of Northumberland, the Earl of Westmoreland, and the Duke of Norfolk; *shot madly from their spheres*, that is, revolted from Queen Elizabeth, bewitched by the *sea-maid's* sweetness.

The Queen of Scot's pillar is a column in the Peak Cavern, Derbyshire, as clear as alabaster, and so called because on one occasion, when going to throw herself on the mercy of Elizabeth, the Queen of Scots proceeded thus far, and then returned.

Marybuds. The flower of the marigold (*q v*) Like many other flowers, they open at daybreak and close at sunset

> And winking marybuds begin
> To ope their golden eyes
> *Cymbeline*, ii, 3.

Marygold. *See* MARIGOLD

Maryland (U S A) was so named in compliment to Henrietta Maria, Queen of Charles I In the Latin charter it is called *Terra Mariæ*

Marylebone (London) is not a corruption of *Marie la bonne*, but "Mary on the bourne," i e the Tyburn (*q v*), as Holborn is "Old Bourne"

Masaniello (măs án yel' ō). A corruption of TOMMASO ANIELLO, a Neapolitan fisherman, who led the revolt of July, 1647. The great grievance was heavy taxation, and the immediate cause of Masaniello's interference was the seizure of his property because his wife had smuggled flour He obtained a large following, was elected chief of Naples, and for nine days ruled with absolute control; but he was betrayed by his own people, shot, and his body flung into a ditch. It was reclaimed and interred with a pomp and ceremony never equalled in Naples

Auber's opera *La Muette de Portici* (1828) takes the story for its groundwork

Mascot. A person or thing that is supposed to bring good luck (*cp* JETTATURA) The word is French slang (perhaps connected with

Provençal *masco*, a sorcerer), and was popularized in England by Audran's opera, *La Mascotte*, 1880

    Ces envoyes du paradis,
    Sont des Mascottes, mes amis,
    Heureux celui que le ciel dote d'une Mascotte
                      La Mascotte.

Masher. An old-fashioned term for a "nut" or dude (*q v*), an exquisite; a lardy-dardy swell This sort of thing used to be called "crushing" or killing, and, as mashing is crushing, the synonym was substituted about 1880 A ladykiller, a crusher, a masher, all mean the same thing

Mask, The Man in the Iron. A mysterious individual held for over forty years as a State prisoner by Louis XIV at Pignerol and other prisons, ultimately dying in the Bastille, Nov 19th, 1703, with his identity still undisclosed His name was given as "Marchiali" when he was buried, but despite the numerous conjectures and wide research that have been made, no one to this day knows for certain who he was. One name put forward is that of General du Bulonde, who, in 1691, raised the siege of Cuneo against the orders of Catinat. In 1891 Capt Bazeriès published in *Le Temps* translations of some cipher dispatches, apparently showing that this is the solution.

Other persons who have been suggested are.—

A twin brother of Louis XIV, or, perhaps, an elder brother, whose father is given as Cardinal Mazarin or the Duke of Buckingham.

Louis Duc de Vermandois, natural son of Louis XIV by De la Vallière, who was imprisoned for life because he gave the Dauphin a box on the ears

It is now considered probable that he was Count Girolamo Mattioli, Minister to the Duke of Mantua, who had acted treacherously towards Louis in refusing to give up the fortress of Casale—the key of Italy—after signing a treaty promising to do so, and in consequence was lured on to French soil, captured, and imprisoned at Pignerol.

Among the less likely names that have been put forward are the Duke of Monmouth, Avedick (an Armenian patriarch), Fouquet (the disgraced Minister of Finance), the Duc de Beaufort (who disappeared at the siege of Candia in 1669), and Mattioli's secretary, Jean de Gonzague.

Masochism (mãs′ ō kizm). A psychological term for the condition in which sexual gratification depends on the subject's self-humiliation and self-inflicted physical pain It takes its name from Leopold von Sacher-Masoch (1836-95) the Austrian novelist who first described this aberration

Mason and Dixon's Line. The southern boundary line which separated the free state of Pennsylvania from what were at one time the slave states of Maryland and Virginia It lies in 39° 43′ 26″ north latitude, and was fixed by Charles Mason and Jeremiah Dixon, English astronomers and surveyors (1763-67)

Mass (mãs, mas) The R C name for the Eucharist There are several kinds of Mass, the principal being High Mass, or *Missa solemnis* in which the celebrant is assisted by a deacon and subdeacon—it requires the presence of a choir, a number of acolytes or servers, and the use of incense, Sung Mass, said and sung by the celebrant alone, Low Mass, which is said by the celebrant alone in four tones of voice; clear, medium, low, and inaudible (secret). There is also Pontifical Mass, sung by a cardinal, bishop in his own diocese, or abbot in his own abbey, with a very full ritual, three assistants and at least nine acolytes

There are also a number of special masses, as the *mass of the Beatæ, mass of the Holy Ghost, mass of the dead, of a saint, of security, dry mass, votive mass, holiday mass, Ambrosian mass, Gallic mass, mass of the presanctified* (for Good Friday), etc.

  Pope Celestinus ordained the *introit* and the *gloria in excelsis*
  Pope Gregory the Great ordered the *kyrie eleison* to be repeated nine times, and introduced the prayer
  Pope Gelasius ordained the Epistle and Gospel
  Pope Damasus introduced the *Credo.*
  Pope Alexander put into the canon the following clause *"Qui pridie quam pateretur."*
  Pope Sextus introduced the *Sanctus*
  Pope Innocent the *pax*
  Pope Leo the *Orate Fratres*, and the words in the canon; *"Hostiam sanctam, hostiam immaculatum "*
     E. KINESMAN. *Lives of the Saints*, p 187 (1623)

Mass observation is a British trade-mark name for a system of obtaining information as to popular sentiment and opinion similar to the Gallup Poll (*q.v*).

Massachusetts (mãs à choo′ sets) (U S A) So called from the tribe of Indians of that name Its origin is not clear, one suggestion is that it means "the Blue Mountains," and another that it is *massa*, great, *wadehuash*, mountains, *et*, near, *i e*. near-the-great-mountain.

Massacre of the Innocents. The slaughter of the male children of Bethlehem "from two years old and under," when Jesus was born (*Matt* ii, 16) This was done at the command of Herod the Great in order to cut off "the babe" who was destined to become "King of the Jews."

In parliamentary phraseology, the phrase denotes the withdrawal at the close of a session of the bills which there has been no time to consider and pass

Mast. To serve before the mast. To be one of the common sailors, whose quarters are in the forward part of the ship In an old sailing-ship the half-deck was the sanctum of the second mate, and, in Greenland fishers, of the spikeoneer, harpooners, carpenters, coopers, boatswains, and all secondary officers.

Master (through O Fr *maistre*, or A S *mægester*, from Lat *magister*)

Little Masters. See LITTLE.

Master-at-arms The first-class petty officer in the Navy who acts as head of the ship's police

Master Mason. A Freemason who has been raised to the third degree

Master of sentences. See SENTENCES

Master of the Rolls *See* ROLLS

Old Masters The great painters (especially of Italy and the Low Countries) who worked from the 13th century to about the end of the 16th, or a little later. Also their paintings

Mastic. A kind of chewing-gum made of the resin of *Pistachia Lentiscus*, a tree of the Levant and other Eastern parts, formerly much used in medicine It was said to promote appetite, and therefore only increased the misery of a hungry man.

> Like the starved wretch that hungry mastic chews,
> But cheats himself and fosters his disease
> WEST *Triumphs of the Gout (Lucian).*

Matador (măt′ a dôr). In Spanish bull-fights the star or leader of each team, who has to play the bull alone and finally kill it

In the game of ombre, *Spadille* (the ace of spades), *Manille* (the seven of trumps), and *Basto* (the ace of clubs) are called "Matadors."

> Now move to war her sable Matadores . .
> Spadillo first, unconquerable lord,
> Led off two captive trumps, and swept the board,
> As many more Manillo forced to yield,
> And marched a victor from the verdant field
> Him Basto followed   "
> POPE. *Rape of the Lock*, canto iii.

In the game of dominoes of this name the double-blank and all the "stones" that of themselves make seven (6-1, 5-2, and 4-3) are "matadors," and can be played at any time.

Matamore (măt à môr) A poltroon, a swaggerer, a Bobadil (*q v*) It is composed of two Spanish words, *matar-Moros* (a slayer of Moors). *See* MOOR-SLAYER.

Matapan Stew (Austr) A meal concocted of left-overs, and so called from the fact that the cooks of H M A.S *Perth* served a scratch hot meal during the Battle of Matapan, March 28th, 1941.

Mate. A man does not get his hands out of the tar by becoming second mate. In long-past days of sailing-ships the second mate was expected to put his hands into the tar bucket for tarring the rigging, like the men below him. The first mate was exempt from this dirty work

Maté (măt′ ä) Paraguay tea, made from the leaves of the Brazilian holly (*Ilex Paraguayensis*), is so called from the vessel in which it is infused. The vessels are generally hollow gourds

Materialism. The doctrines of a *Materialist*, who maintains that there is nothing in the universe but matter, that mind is a phenomenon of matter, and that there is no ground for assuming a spiritual First Cause, as against the orthodox doctrine that the soul is distinct from the body, and is a portion of the Divine essence breathed into the body Materialism is opposed to Idealism, in the ancient world its chief exponents were Epicurus and Lucretius, in modern times the 18th-century French philosophers, Helvetius, d'Holbach, and Lamettrie

Materialize. A word used in psychical research to describe the assumption of bodily form of psychical phenomena The principles governing materialization are as yet unknown, and little progress has been made in discovering them

Matriculate means to enrol oneself in a society (Lat *matricula*, a roll or register) The University is called our *alma mater* (propitious mother) The students are her *alumni* (foster-children), and become so by being enrolled in a register after certain forms and examinations

In common parlance it used to mean to pass the entrance examination that permits one to be entered as a student at a university Many, however, sat for the matriculation examinations who had no intention of proceeding to a university. It has now been abolished.

Matsya. *See* AVATAR.

Matter-of-fact. Unvarnished truth; prosaic, unimaginative, as a "matter-of-fact swain "

Matterhorn. The German name of the mountain in the Pennine Alps known to the French as *Mont Cervin* and to the Italians as *Monte Silvio*, so called from its peak (*horn*) and the scanty patches of green meadow (*matter*) which hang around its base Above a glacier-line 11,000 feet high, it rises in an almost inaccessible obelisk of rock to a total elevation of 14,703 feet It was first scaled in 1865 by Edward Whymper (1840-1911), when four of his party lost their lives.

Figuratively any danger, desperate situation threatening destruction, or leap in the dark, as *the matrimonial Matterhorn*

Mathew, Father. Theobald Mathew (1790-1856), called *The Apostle of Temperance*. He was an Irish priest, and in his native country the success of his work on behalf of total abstinence was almost miraculous

> O Father Matthew!
> Whatever path you
> In life pursue
> God grant your Reverence
> May brush off never hence
> Our mountain dew!
> *An Irishman to Father Mathew* WALTER SAVAGE LANDOR

Matthew, St. Represented in art (1) as an evangelist—an old man with long beard—an angel generally standing near him dictating his Gospel, (2) As an apostle, in which capacity he bears a purse, in reference to his calling as a publican; sometimes he carries a spear, sometimes a carpenter's rule or square. His symbol is an angel, or a man's face (*see* EVANGELISTS), and he is commemorated on September 21st

Legend has it that St Matthew preached for 15 years in Judæa after the Ascension, and then carried the Gospel to Ethiopia, where he was martyred

In the last of Matthew. At the last gasp, on one's last legs. This is a German expression, and arose thus· a Catholic priest said in his sermon that Protestantism was in the last of Matthew, and, being asked what he meant, replied, "The last five words of the Gospel of St Matthew are these. 'The end of this dispensation ' " He quoted the Latin version; ours is less correctly translated "the end of the *world*."

Matthew Parker's Bible: Matthew's Bible. *See* BIBLE, THE ENGLISH

Maudlin Stupidly sentimental *Maudlin drunk* is the drunkenness which is sentimental and inclined to tears *Maudlin slip-slop* is sentimental chit-chat. The word is derived from Mary Magdalen, who is drawn by ancient painters with a lackadaisical face, and eyes swollen with weeping.

Maul of Monks, The. Thomas Cromwell (1485-1540), visitor-general of English monasteries, many of which he summarily suppressed

Maumet, Maumetry. See MAMMET.

Maundrel. A foolish, vapouring gossip The Scots say, "Haud your tongue, maundrel" As a verb it means to babble, to prate, as in delirium, in sleep, or intoxication. The term is said to be from Sir John *Mandeville*, well-known 14th-century traveller in the Far East, the account of whose adventures (earliest MS., 1371) is full of strange stories and unverified events

Maundy Thursday. The day before Good Friday is so called from the first words of the antiphon for that day being *Mandatum novum do vobis*, a new commandment I give unto you (*St. John* xiii, 34), with which the ceremony of the washing of the feet begins. This is still carried out in R C. cathedral churches and monasteries. In the monasteries it was the custom to wash the feet of as many poor people as there were monks, and for centuries in England the sovereign, as a token of humility, did the same Mention is made in the Wardrobe Book of Edward I of money being given on Easter Eve to thirteen poor people whose feet the Queen had washed, the custom is said to have been kept up even as late as the time of James II, but for long now the distribution of money (*see* MAUNDS) is all that is left of it

The word has been incorrectly derived from *maund* (a basket), because on the day before the great fast Catholics brought out their broken food in *maunds* to distribute to the poor. This custom in many places gave birth to a fair, as the Tombland Fair of Norwich, held on the plain before the Cathedral Close

Maunds, the Royal, or **Maundy Money.** Gifts in money given by the sovereign on Maundy Thursday to the number of aged poor persons that corresponds with his age It used to be distributed by the Lord High Almoner, but since 1883 the Clerk of the Almonry Office has been responsible for the distribution which takes place in Westminster Abbey, and for which special money (silver pennies, fourpenny pieces, etc) is usually coined. These amount in value to £50 or £60 The custom began in 1368, in the reign of Edward III, and is a relic of the "washing of the feet" (*see* MAUNDY THURSDAY) James II was the last sovereign to distribute the doles personally, until George V did so in 1932 Edward VIII distributed the purses also, in 1936 Since then the sovereign has been present on most occasions at the distribution

Entries of "al maner of things yerly yevin by my lorde of his Maundy, and my laidis, and his lordshippis children"—*Household Book of the Earl o Northumberland,* 1512.

Mauritania (maw ri tā´ nya). Morocco and Algiers, the land of the ancient Mauri or Moors. The kingdom of Mauritania was annexed to the Roman Empire in A.D. 42, and was finally disintegrated when overrun by the Vandals in 429

Mausoleum. Originally the name of the tomb of Mausolus, King of Caria, to whom Artemisia (his wife) erected at Halicarnassus a splendid sepulchral monument (353 B C) Parts of this sepulchre, which was one of the Seven Wonders of the World, are now in the British Museum The name is now applied to any sepulchral monument of great size or architectural quality.

The chief mausoleums are that of Augustus; of Hadrian, *i e* the castle of St. Angelo, at Rome, that erected in France to Henry II by Catherine de' Medicis, that of St. Peter the Martyr in the church of St Eustatius, by G Balduccio in the 14th century

Mauthe Dog. A ghostly black spaniel that for many years haunted Peel Castle, in the Isle of Man. It used to enter the guardroom as soon as candles were lighted, and leave it at daybreak While this spectre dog was present the soldiers forbore all oaths and profane talk. One day a drunken trooper entered the guardhouse alone out of bravado, but lost his speech and died in three days Scott refers to it in his *Lay of the Last Minstrel,* vi stanza, 26, and again in a long note to ch. xv of *Peveril of the Peak.*

Mauther, mawther (maw´ ther) An old dialect word in East Anglia for a young girl, frequently altered to *Modder, Morther, Mor,* etc Its etymology is obscure, but the word does not seem to be connected with *mother.*

Kastril (to his sister) Away' you talk like a foolish mauther —BEN JONSON. *Alchemist,* iv, 4
> When once a giggling morther you,
> And I a red-faced chubby boy,
> Sly tricks you played me not a few,
> For mischief was your greatest joy
> BLOOMFIELD. *Richard and Kate*

Well, Mor, where have you been this long while? and I s'y, Mor, come hither! are, in Norfolk, still common modes of addressing a young girl

Mauvais, mauvaise (mō vä, mo väz). French, bad

Mauvais ton. Bad manners. Ill-breeding, vulgar ways.

Mauvaise honte. Bad or silly shame. Bashfulness, sheepishness

Mauvaise plaisanterie. A rude or ill-mannered jest, a jest in bad taste

Maverick. *See* BRAND.

Mavournin (ma voor´ nin) Irish (*mo mhurnin*) for "My darling " Erin mavournin = Ireland, my darling, Erin go bragh = Ireland for ever!
> Land of my forefathers, Erin go bragh! . .
> Erin mavournin, Erin go bragh!
> CAMPBELL *Exile of Erin*

Mawworm (maw´ wērm) A hypocritical pretender to sanctity, a pious humbug. From the character of this name in Isaac Bickerstaffe's *The Hypocrite* (1769)

Maximum and Minimum (Lat.) The *greatest* and the *least* amount; as, the maximum profits or exports and the minimum profits or exports, the maximum and minimum price of corn during the year The terms are also employed in mathematics, etc , a *maximum and minimum*

thermometer is one that indicates the highest and lowest temperatures during a specified period

May. The Anglo-Saxons called this month *thrimilce*, because then cows can be milked three times a day, the present name is the Latin *Maius* from *Maia*, the goddess of growth and increase, connected with *major*

The old Dutch name was *Blou maand* (blossoming month) In the French Republican calendar the month was called *Floreal* (the time of flowers, April 20th to May 20th)

Here we go gathering nuts in May. *See* NUTS

It's a case of January and May *See* JANUARY

May unlucky for weddings. This is a Roman superstition, and is referred to by Ovid In this month were held the festivals of *Bona Dea* (the goddess of chastity), and the feasts of the dead called *Lemuralia*

Nec viduæ tædis eadem, nec virginis apta
Tempora, quæ nupsit, non diuturna fuit,
Hæc quoque de causa, si te proverbia tangunt,
Mente malum Maio nubere vulgus ait
            OVID *Fasti*, v, 496, etc

May meetings. The annual gatherings, usually held in London in May and June, of religious and charitable societies, to hear the annual reports and appeals for continued or increased support, etc

May-day. Polydore Virgil says that the Roman youths used to go into the fields and spend the calends of May in dancing and singing in honour of Flora, goddess of fruits and flowers The English consecrated May-day to Robin Hood and Maid Marian, because the favourite outlaw died on that day, and villagers used to set up Maypoles (*q.v*), and spend the day in archery, morris dancing, and other amusements.

The old custom of singing the *Hymnus Eucharisticus* on the top of Wolsey's Tower, Oxford, as the clock strikes five on May Morning is still kept up by the choristers of Magdalen This is a relic of the requiem mass that, before the Reformation, was sung at this spot and time for the repose of the soul of Henry VII The opening lines of the hymn are —

Te Deum Patrem colimus,
Te laudibus prosequimur,
Qui corpus cibo reficis,
Cœlesti mentem gratia

Evil May Day. *See* EVIL

Maypole, Queen, etc. Dancing round the Maypole on May Day, "going a-Maying," electing a May Queen, and lighting bonfires, are all remnants of nature-worship, and may be traced to the most ancient times The chimney-sweeps used to lead about a Jack-i'-the-green, and the custom is not yet quite extinct, especially in country towns

Any very tall, ungainly woman is sometimes called a "Maypole," a term which was bestowed as a nickname on the Duchess of Kendal, one of George I's mistresses.

The Maypole in the Strand. This ancient London landmark, referred to more than once by 18th-century writers, stood on a spot now occupied by St Mary-le-Strand, where formerly stood a cross In place of this a May-pole was set up by John Clarges, the blacksmith, whose daughter Ann became the wife of Monk, Duke of Albemarle It was taken down in 1713, and replaced by a new one erected opposite Somerset House This had two gilt balls and a vane on its summit, and on holidays was decorated with flags and garlands It was removed in 1718, and sent by Sir Isaac Newton to Wanstead Park to support the largest telescope in Europe

Captain Baily   employed four hackney coaches, with drivers in liveries, to ply at the Maypole in the Strand, fixing his own rates, about the year 1634 — Note 1, *The Tatler*, iv, p 415

Amid that area wide they took their stand,
Where the tall maypole once o'erlooked the Strand,
But now (so Anne and piety ordain)
A church collects the saints of Drury Lane.
          POPE *Dunciad* II, 217 (1728)

What's not destroyed by Time's devouring hand?
Where's Troy, and where's the Maypole in the Strand?
      J BRAMSTON (*d* 1744): *The Art of Politics*

Maya Civilization. The Mayas were an American Indian race who possessed an advanced civilization at the time of the Spanish conquest of Central America. The oldest dated monument approximates to A D 50, when the race centre was in the neighbourhood of Yucatan A general decay in art and the building of the great pyramidal temples set in in the 15th century and the Maya civilization was gradually absorbed into the Aztec of S Mexico Little progress has been made in the decipherment of the Maya inscriptions and the history and mode of life of this ancient people is still largely conjectural.

Mayduke Cherries. So called from Médoc, a district of France, whence the cherries first came to us.

Mayflower The name of the ship that took the Pilgrim Fathers (*q v*) from Southampton to Massachusetts in 1620. It was about 180 tons. Some of the timbers of the old *Mayflower* are said to have been discovered as forming part of a barn at Jordans, Bucks

Mayonnaise. A sauce made with pepper, salt, oil, vinegar, and the yolk of an egg beaten up together The word is French, its origin is unknown, but it has been conjectured that it was originally called *mahonnaise* in honour of the capture of Mahon, Minorca, by the Duc de Richelieu in 1756

Mayor. The chief magistrate of a city, elected by the citizens, and holding office for twelve months

The chief magistrate of London is The Right Hon the Lord Mayor, one of the Privy Council Since 1389 the magistracy of York has been headed by a Lord Mayor, and the other English towns in which the chief magistrate is Lord Mayor are Birmingham, Liverpool, Manchester, Leeds, Sheffield, Bristol, Hull, Bradford and Newcastle-on-Tyne

At the Conquest the sovereign appointed the chief magistrates of cities That of London was called the Port-Reeve, but Henry II changed the word to the Norman *maire* (our mayor). John made the office annual, and Edward III (in 1354) conferred the title of "The Right Hon. the Lord Mayor of London " The first Lord Mayor's Show was in 1458, when Sir John Norman went by water in state, to be sworn in at Westminster; and the cap and sword were given by Richard II to Sir William Walworth, for killing Wat Tyler

Mayor of Garratt. *See* GARRATT.

Mayor of the Bull-ring (Old Dublin) This official and his sheriffs were elected on May Day and St Peter's Eve "to be captaine and gardian of the batchelers and the unwedded youth of the civitie " For the year the "Mayor" had authority to punish those who frequented houses of ill-fame He was termed "Mayor of the Bull-ring" because he conducted any bachelor who married during his term of office to an iron ring that used to hang in the market place and to which bulls were tied for baiting, and make him kiss it

Mayor of the Palace (*Maire du Palais*). The superintendent of the king's household, and steward of the royal *leudes* (companies) of France, before the accession of the Caroving-ian dynasty

Mazarin, Cardinal Jules (1602-61), was an Italian-born French stateman, trained by and successor to Cardinal Richelieu, and minister to the Queen-Regent during the minority of Louis XIV

Mazarine Bible, The. *See* BIBLE, SPECIALLY NAMED.

Mazarin Library. The first public Library in Paris The great Cardinal Mazarin left his collection of 40 000 books to the city on his death in 1661, and himself composed the rules for its conduct

Mazarinades. Pamphlets in prose or verse published against Cardinal Mazarin by supporters of the Fronde (the armed opposition to Louis XIV during his minority, 1648-53).

Mazeppa, Ivan (mǎ zep' a) (1644-1709) The hero of Byron's poem was born of a noble Polish family in Podolia, became a page in the court of John Casimir, King of Poland, but intrigued with Theresia, the young wife of a Podolian count, who had the young page lashed naked to a wild horse, and turned adrift. The horse dropped dead in the Ukraine, where Mazeppa was released and cared for by Cossacks He became secretary to the hetman, and at his death was appointed his successor Peter I created him Prince of the Ukraine, but in the wars with Sweden Mazeppa deserted to Charles XII and fought against Russia at Pultowa After the loss of this battle, Mazeppa fled to Valentia, and then to Bender, where he committed suicide. Byron makes Mazeppa tell his tale to Charles after the battle of Pultowa

Adah Isaacs Menken (1835-68) was famous for her equestrian performance in the stage version of *Mazeppa* at Astley's, in 1844

Mazer (mǎ' zer) A large drinking vessel originally made of maple-wood, and so called from O Fr *masere*, O H Ger *masar*, a knot in wood, maple wood.

A mazer wrought of the maple ware
SPENSER *Shepheard's Calendar* (August).

Mazikeen or **Shedeem** (mǎz' i kēn) A species of beings in Jewish mythology resembling the Arabian Jinn (*q v.*), and said to be the agents of magic and enchantment. When Adam fell, says the Talmud, he was excommunicated for 130 years, during which time he begat demons

and spectres, for, it is written "Adam lived 130 years and (i e before he) begat children in his own image" (*Gen* v, 3) (*Rabbi Jeremiah ben Eliezar*.)

And the Mazikeen shall not come nigh thy tents.— *Ps* xci, 5 (Chaldee version)

Swells out like the Mazikeen ass. The allusion is to a Jewish tradition that a servant, whose duty it was to rouse the neighbourhood to midnight prayer, one night mounted a stray ass and neglected his duty As he rode along the ass grew bigger and bigger, till at last it towered as high as the tallest edifice where it left the man, and there next morning he was found

McCoy. The real McCoy. Something excellent, something genuine From an early 20th-century American prize-fighter known as "Kid Mc-Coy," whose fame was so great that other less able fighters adopted his name to gain some of his glory There were many McCoys but only one "real" one

Meal. In meal or in malt. Directly or indirectly, in one way or another If much money passes through the hand, some profit will be sure to accrue either "in meal or in malt," and a certain percentage of one or the other is the miller's perquisite.

Meal-tub Plot. A pretended conspiracy against Protestants, fabricated by Thomas Dangerfield (*c.* 1650-85) in 1679, so called because he said that the papers relating to it were concealed in a meal-tub in the house of Mrs Elizabeth Cellier, a Roman Catholic She was tried for high treason and acquitted, while Dangerfield was convicted of libel, whipped, and pilloried

Mealy-mouthed is the Greek *meli-muthos* (honey-speech), and means velvet-tongued, afraid of giving offence, hypocritical, "smarmy"

Meander (mē ǎn' der) To wind, to saunter about at random, so called from the Mæander, a winding river of Phrygia The term is also applied to an ornamental pattern of winding lines, used as a border on pottery, wall decorations, etc

Means Test. By the 1934 revision of the Unemployment Act, the claimant for insurance benefit was called upon to undergo an inquisition, known as the Means Test, and furnish information as to the total amount of money coming into the household from any source whatsoever, thus laying before the officials the private affairs of every member of his family The purpose of this was, of course, to safeguard public funds and ensure that the minimum relief should be furnished, but its application was felt by the unemployed to attach an odious stigma to an already unfortunate situation. The Means Test was abolished by the Labour Government in the National Insurance Act that came into force in 1948

Measure (O Fr *mesure*, Lat *mensura*, *metiri*, to measure) **Beyond measure**, or **out of all measure.** Beyond all reasonable degree, exceedingly, excessively.

Thus out of measure sad.—*Much Ado About Nothing*, i, 3

To measure one's length on the ground To fall flat on the ground, to be knocked down
If you will measure your lubber's length, tarry.—
King Lear, i, 4

To measure other people's corn by one's own bushel. *See* BUSHEL.

To measure strength. To wrestle together, to fight, to contest

To measure swords. To try whether or not one is strong enough or sufficiently equally matched to contend against another The phrase is from duelling, in which the seconds measure the swords to see that both are of one length
So we measured swords and parted —*As You Like It*, v, 4

To take the measure of one's foot To ascertain how far a person will venture, to make a shrewd guess of another's character. The allusion is to "*Ex pede Herculem*"

Measure for Measure The plot of Shakespeare's play (acted 1604, first printed 1623) is founded on Whetstone's *Promos and Cassandra* (1582), which was taken from the 85th tale in Cinthio's *Hecatommithi* (1565) Promos is called by Shakespeare, "Lord Angelo"; and Cassandra is ' Isabella " Her brother, called by Shakespeare "Claudio," is named Andrugio in the story.

Meat, Bread. These words tell a tale, for both can connote food in general. The Italians and Asiatics eat little animal food, and with them the word *bread* stands for food, so also with the poor, whose chief diet it is, but the English once consumed meat very plentifully, and this word, which simply means food, almost exclusively implies animal food. In the banquet given to Joseph's brethren, the viceroy commanded the servants "to set on *bread*" (*Gen* xliii, 31) In *Ps* civ, 27, it is said of fishes, creeping things, and crocodiles, that God giveth them their *meat* in due season.

To carry off meat from the graves. To be as poor as a church mouse; to be so poor as to descend to robbing the tombs of offerings. The Greeks and Romans used to make feasts at certain seasons, when spirits were supposed to return to their graves, and the fragments were left on the tombs for the use of the ghosts Hence the Latin proverb *Eleemosynam sepulcri patris tui* (Alms on your father's grave).

Mecca. The birthplace of Mohammed in Arabia. It is one of the two holy cities, the other being Medina. Derivatively it means "a place one longs to visit."

Mecklenburg Declaration. The first declaration of independence in the U S A, made at Mecklenberg, N Carolina, on May 20th, 1775

Medal of Honor. A U S A medal awarded by Congress to soldiers, sailors, and marines who have shown conspicuous gallantry in the face of the enemy and have risked their lives beyond any call that duty may have made upon their services.

Médard, St (mā´ dar). The French "St. Swithin"; his day is June 8th.
Quand il pleut à la Saint-Médard
Il pleut quarante jours plus tard.

He was Bishop of Noyon and Tournai in the 6th century, and founded the Festival of the Rose at Salency, which is kept up to this day, the most virtuous girl in the parish receiving a crown of roses and a purse of money
Legend says that a sudden shower once fell which wetted everyone to the skin except St. Médard, he remained dry as toast, for an eagle had spread its wings over him, and ever after he was termed *maître de la pluie*.

Medea (me dē´ a) In Greek legend, a sorceress, daughter of Ætes, King of Colchis She married Jason, the leader of the Argonauts, whom she aided to obtain the golden fleece, and was the mother of Medus, whom the Greeks regarded as the ancestor of the Medes. *See* HARMONIA.

Medea's kettle or **cauldron.** A means of restoring lost youth. Medea cut an old ram to pieces, threw the pieces into her cauldron, and a young lamb came forth. The daughters of Pelias thought to restore their father to youth in the same way, but Medea refused to utter the magic words, and the old man ceased to live
Get thee Medea's kettle and be boiled anew —
CONGREVE *Love for Love*, iv

Medes and Persians. *See* LAW

Mediæval Ages. *See* MIDDLE AGES.

Medici (med´ i chi) A great and powerful family that ruled in Florence in the 15th and 16th centuries. It was founded by Giovanni Medici, a banker, whose son, Cosimo (1389-1464) was famous as a patron of art and learning His grandson, Lorenzo the Magnificent (1448-92) was one of the outstanding figures of the Renaissance His illegitimate son Alessandro (1492-1519) was made Duke of Florence in 1530, and in 1569 his son Cosimo became Grand Duke of Tuscany
His granddaughter, Marie de Medici (1573-1642) was Queen Consort of Henry IV of France and one of the great and sinister figures of French history. The Medici family gave three Popes to the Church, Leo X (1475-1521, pope 1513-21) in whose reign the Reformation began under Martin Luther; Leo XI who reigned as Pope only a few months in 1605; and Clement VII (1478-1534, pope 1523-34) who refused to grant Henry VIII a divorce from Catherine of Aragon.

Medicine. From the Lat *medicina*, which meant both the physician's art and his laboratory, and also a medicament The alchemists applied the word to the philosopher's stone, and the elixir of life; hence Shakespeare's
How much unlike art thou, Mark Antony!
Yet, coming from him, that great medicine hath
With his tinct gilded thee.
Antony and Cleopatra, i, 5
And the word was—and is—frequently used in a figurative sense, as—
The miserable have no other medicine
But only hope   *Measure for Measure*, iii, 1
Among the North American Indians *medicine* is a spell, charm, or fetish, and sometimes even Manitou (*q.v*) hence *Medicine-man*, a witch-doctor or magician.

The Father of Medicine. Aretæus of Cappadocia, who lived at the close of the first and beginning of the second centuries, and Hippocrates of Cos (460-377 B C) are both so called

Medicine ball. A large, leather-covered ball —usually of some weight—tossed from one person to another as a form of exercise.

Medicine lodge. A tent or other form of structure used by North American Indians for ceremonial purposes

Medicinal days In ancient practice the sixth, eighth, tenth, twelfth, sixteenth, eighteenth, etc., of a disease, so called because, according to Hippocrates, no "crisis" (*q v*) occurs on these days, and medicine may be safely administered

Medicinal-finger. Also the *leech-finger* or *leechman* The finger next to the little finger, the ring finger, so called in mediæval times because of the notion that it contained a vein that led direct to the heart

Medina (me dī′ nä) In Spenser's *Faerie Queene* (II, ii) the typification of "the golden mean" (Lat. *medium*) She was step-sister of Perissa (*excess*) and Elissa (*deficiency*), who could never agree upon any subject.

The Arabian city of *Medina* (mē dē′ na) is the second holy city of the Mohammedans, called "Yathrib" before Mohammed fled thither from Mecca, but afterwards Medina-al-Nabi (the city of the prophet), whence its present name In Spain there are four or five Medinas, *Medina-Sidonia* was so called by the Moors because it was believed to be on the site of the city Asidur, which was founded by Phœnicians from Sidon.

Mediterranean. The midland sea, the sea in the middle of the (Roman) earth (Lat *medius*, middle, *terra*, land).

The Key of the Mediterranean The Rock of Gibraltar, which commands the entrance between Europe and Africa It was taken from the Spaniards by a combined British and Dutch force under Sir George Rooke, July 24th, 1704 Spain attempted to retake the Rock in 1705, 1736, and 1779-83 when it was held throughout the lengthy siege by Lord Heathfield (1717-90). *See also* MARE NOSTRUM.

Medusa (me dū′ zá). The chief of the Gorgons, (*q v*) of Greek mythology Legend says that she was a beautiful maiden, specially famous for her hair but that she violated the temple of Athene, who thereupon transformed her hair into serpents and made her face so terrible that all who looked on it were turned to stone Perseus, assisted by Athene (who lent him her shield wherein he looked only on the *reflection* of Medusa during his attack), struck off her head, and by its means rescued Andromeda (*q v*) from the monster Medusa was the mother by Poseidon of Chrysaor and Pegasus. The story of Perseus is well told in Charles Kingsley's *Heroes*

Meerschaum (mēr′ shawm) (Ger., sea-froth) This mineral (used for making tobacco-pipes), from having been found on the seashore in rounded white lumps, was ignorantly supposed to be sea-froth petrified, but it is a compound of silica, magnesia, lime, water, and carbonic acid When first dug it lathers like soap, and is used as a soap by the Tartars.

Meg. Formerly slang for a guinea, but now signifying a halfpenny. *Cp* MAG.

No, no, Meggs are Guineas Smelts are half-guineas —SHADWELL *Squire of Alsatia*, I, i (1688)

Mons Meg. A great 15th-century piece of artillery in Edinburgh Castle, made at Mons, in Flanders. It was considered a palladium by the Scotch *Cp.* LONG MEG

Roaring Meg. Formerly any large gun that made a great noise when let off was so called, as Mons Meg herself and a cannon given by the Fishmongers of London, and used in 1689 Burton says: "Music is a roaring Meg against melancholy"

Drowning the noise of their consciences by ringing their greatest Bells, discharging their roaring-megs —TRAPP *Comment on Job* (1656)

Megarians. The inhabitants of Megara and its territory, Megaris, Greece, proverbial for their stupidity, hence the proverb, "Wise as a Megarian"—*i e.* not wise at all, yet *see below*

Megarian School (me gâr′ i an) A philosophical school, founded by Euclid, a native of Megara, and disciple of Socrates It combined the ethical doctrines of Socrates with the metaphysic of the Eleatics (*q v*)

Megrims (mē′ grimz) A corruption of the Greek *hemi-crania* (half the skull), through the French *migraine*. A neuralgic affection generally confined to one brow, or to one side of the forehead, whims, fancies

Meinie, or **Meiny** (mī′ ni) A company of attendants, a household, from O Fr *meyne*, *mesnie*, from Lat *mansionem*, *mansio*, a house. Our word *menial* has much the same derivation and significance

With that the smiling Kriemhild forth stepped a little space
And Brunhild and her meiny greeted with gentle grace
Lettsom's Nibelungenlied, stanza 604

Mein Kampf (mīn kämf) The political and half mystical thesis in which Adolf Hitler embodied his social and racial theories, his doctrine of anti-Semitism; and his call for revenge for the disasters of 1918 and the revision of the Versailles treaty. He wrote *My Fight*—as the title may be translated—while undergoing a sentence of imprisonment at Landeck-am-Lech for his part in the abortive "Beer Hall Putsch" of 1923, it was published in 1925 and as he increased in power so did *Mein Kamp* become increasingly the Nazi bible.

Meiosis (mī ō′ sis). This word, coming from the Greek and meaning "lessening" is applied to the ironical form of speech in which a negative is used for the affirmation of its contrary, as "no small quantity" meaning "a considerable quantity," or "not so bad," meaning "quite good." It is also known as litotes

Meistersingers (mī′ ster sing′ erz) Burgher poets of Germany, who attempted, in the 14th to 16th centuries, to revive the national minstrelsy of the *Minnesingers* (*q v*), which had fallen into decay Hans Sachs, the cobbler (1494-1576), was the most celebrated.

Die Meistersinger von Nurnberg. An opera by Wagner (1868) in which he satirized his critics

Melampod (mel' am pod) Black hellebore, so called from Melampus, a famous soothsayer and physician of Greek legend, who with it cured the daughters of Prætus of their melancholy (Virgil *Georgics*, iii, 550).

> My seely sheep, like well below,
> They need not melampode,
> For they been hale enough I trow,
> And liken their abode
> SPENSER *Eclogue*, vii

Melancholy. Lowness of spirits, supposed at one time to arise from a redundance of black bile (Gr *melas chole*)

Melancholy Jacques. So Jean Jacques Rousseau (1712-78) was called for his morbid sensibilities and unhappy spirit The expression is from *As You Like It*, ii, 1.

Melanchthon (me lăngk' thon) is the Greek for *Schwarzerde* (black earth), the real name of this reformer (1497-1560) Similarly, *Œcolampadius* is the Greek version of the German name *Hauschein*, and *Desiderius Erasmus* is one Latin and one Greek rendering of the name *Gheraerd Gheraerd*

Melba. Pêche Melba, a confection of fruit (usually peach), cream and icecream **Melba toast,** narrow slices of thin toast. These take their name from Dame Nellie Melba (1861-1931) the great Australian operatic soprano.

Meleager (mel ĕ ā' ger). A hero of Greek legend, son of Œneus of Calydon and Althæa, distinguished for throwing the javelin, for slaying the Calydonian boar, and as one of the Argonauts It was declared by the Fates that he would die as soon as a piece of wood then on the fire was burnt up; whereupon his mother snatched the log from the fire and extinguished it; but after Meleager had slain his maternal uncles, his mother threw the brand on the fire again, and Meleager died.

The death of Meleager was a favourite subject in ancient reliefs The famous picture of Charles le Brun is in the Musee Imperiale of Paris

Melibœus or **Melibe** (mel i bē' us, mel' i bi) The central figure in Chaucer's prose *Tale of Melibæus* (*Canterbury Tales*), which is a translation of a French rendering of Albertano da Brescia's Latin *Liber Consolationis et Concilii.* Melibœus is a wealthy young man, married to Prudens One day, when gone "into the fields to play," enemies beat his wife and left his daughter for dead. Melibœus resolved upon vengeance, but his wife persuaded him to call together his enemies, and he told them he forgave them "to this effect and to this ende, that God of His endeles mercy wole at the tyme of oure deyinge forgive us oure giltes that we have trespassed to Him in this wreeched world"

Melibœan Dye. A rich purple Melibœa, in Thessaly, was famous for the *ostrum*, a fish used in dyeing purple

> A military vest of purple flowed,
> Lovelier than Melibœan.
> MILTON *Paradise Lost*, xi, 242.

Melicertes (mel i sĕr' tēz) Son of Ino, a sea deity of Greek legend (*see* LEUCOTHEA) Athamas imagined his wife to be a lioness, and her two sons to be lion's cubs In his frenzy

B D —20

he slew one of the boys, and drove the other (named Melicertes) with his mother into the sea The mother became a sea goddess, and the boy the god of harbours.

Melisande (mel' i sănd) The same as Melusina (*q v*)

Mell Supper. Harvest supper, in Scotland and the northern counties the last sheaf of corn cut is called the *mell*, and when the harvest is borne a woman carries a *mell-doll*, i e a straw image dressed up like a young girl, on top of a pole among the reapers

Mellifluous Doctor, The. St Bernard (1091-1153), whose writings were called a "river of Paradise"

Melodrama. Properly (and in the early 19th cent) a drama in which song and music were introduced (Gr *melos*, song), an opera. These pieces were usually of a sensational character, and now—the musical portions having been gradually dropped—the word denotes a lurid, sensational play, highly emotional, and with a happy ending in which the villain gets all he so richly deserves

Melon. The Mohammedans say that the eating of a melon produces a thousand good works. There are certain stones on Mount Carmel called *Stone Melons*. The tradition is that Elijah saw a peasant carrying melons, and asked him for one. The man said they were not melons but stones, and Elijah instantly converted them into stones.

A like story is told of St. Elizabeth of Hungary She gave so bountifully to the poor as to cripple her own household. One day her husband met her with her lap full of something, and demanded of her what she was carrying. "Only flowers, my lord," said Elizabeth, and to save the lie God converted the loaves into flowers

Melpomene (mel pom' e ni). The muse of tragedy

> Up then Melpomene, thou mournfullest Muse of mine
> Such cause of mourning never hadst afore
> SPENSER *Shepherd's Calendar, November*.

Melusina, or **Melisande** (mel ūs' i na, mel' i sănd) The most famous of the *fees* of French romance, looked upon by the houses of Lusignan, Rohan, Luxembourg, and Sassenaye as their ancestor and founder Having enclosed her father in a high mountain for offending her mother, she was condemned to become every Saturday a serpent from her waist downward She married Raymond, Count of Lusignan, and made her husband vow never to visit her on a Saturday; but the count hid himself on one of the forbidden days, and saw his wife's transformation. Melusina was now obliged to quit her husband, and was destined to wander about as a spectre till the day of doom, though some say that the count immured her in the dungeon of his castle. Cp UNDINE

A sudden scream is called *un cri de Melusine*, in allusion to the scream of despair uttered by Melusina when she was discovered by her husband, and in Poitou certain gingerbread cakes bearing the impress of a beautiful woman "*bien coiffee*," with a serpent's tail, made by confectioners for the May fair in the neighbourhood of Lusignan, are still called Melusines

Memento mori (me men' tŏ môr' ĭ) (Lat, remember you must die) An emblem of mortality, such as a skull, something to put us in mind of the shortness and uncertainty of life

I make as good use of it [Bardolph's face] as many a man doth of a death's head or a memento mori — *Henry IV*, iii, 3

Memnon. The Oriental or Ethiopian prince who, in the Trojan War, went to the assistance of his uncle Priam and was slain by Achilles His mother Eos (the Dawn) was inconsolable for his death, and wept for him every morning

The Greeks called the statue of Amenophis III, in Thebes, that of Memnon. When first struck by the rays of the rising sun it is said to have produced a sound like the snapping asunder of a cord Poetically, when Eos kissed her son at daybreak, the hero acknowledged the salutation with a musical murmur

Memnon's sister, in *Il Penseroso*, is perhaps the Himera, mentioned by Dictys Cretensis, but Milton is supposed to have invented her, because it might be presumed that any sister of the black but comely Memnon would be likewise

Black, but such as in esteem
Prince Memnon's sister might beseem
Il Penseroso, 18.

Probably all that is meant is this Black so delicate and beautiful that it might beseem a sister of Memnon the son of Aurora or the early day-dawn

The legend given by Dictys Cretensis (Bk vi) is that Himera, on hearing of her brother's death, set out to secure his remains, and encountered at Paphos a troop laden with booty, and carrying Memnon's ashes in an urn. Pallas, the leader of the troop, offered to give her either the urn or the booty, and she chose the urn.

Memory. The Bard of Memory. Samuel Rogers (1763-1855), the banker-poet, author of *The Pleasures of Memory* (1792).

Memory Woodfall, Wilham Woodfall (1746-1803), brother of the Woodfall of *Junius*, and editor of the *Morning Chronicle*, would attend a debate, and, without notes, report it accurately next morning

The ever memorable. John Hales, of Eton (1584-1656), scholar and Arminian divine

Memorial Day, also known as Decoration Day, May 30th, observed in U S A since the Civil War to commemorate the soldiers and sailors who fell in action In some of the Southern States April 26th, May 10th or June 3rd are kept as Memorial Day

Menah (mē' nä) A large stone worshipped by certain tribes of Arabia between Mecca and Medina. Like most other Arabian idols it was demolished in the eighth year of "the flight." It is, in fact, a rude stone brought from Mecca, the sacred city, by pilgrims who wished to

carry away with them some memento of their Holy Land

Menalcas (me näl' käs) Any shepherd or rustic The name figures in the *Eclogues* of Virgil and the *Idyls* of Theocritus

Menamber (me näm' ber). A rocking-stone in the parish of Sithney (Cornwall) which at one time a little child could move Cromwell's soldiers thought it fostered superstition, and rendered it immovable

Mendelism. The theory of heredity promulgated by Gregor Johann Mendel (1822-84), the Austrian scientist and Abbot of Brunn, showing that the characters of the parents of cross-bred offspring reappear in certain proportions in successive generations according to definite laws Mendel's Law was discovered by him in 1865 through experiments with peas.

Mendicant Orders, or **Begging Friars.** The orders of the Franciscans (*Grey Friars*), Augustines (*Austin Friars*), Carmelites (*White Friars*), and Dominicans (*Black Friars*)

Menechmians (me nek' mi anz) Persons exactly like each other, so called from the *Menæchmi* of Plautus, the basis of Shakespeare's *Comedy of Errors*, in which not only the two Dromios are exactly like each other, but Antipholus of Ephesus is the facsimile of his brother, Antipholus of Syracuse

Menelaus (men e lā' ŭs) Son of Atreus, brother of Agamemnon, and husband of Helen, through whose desertion of him was brought about the Trojan War He was the King of Sparta or of Lacedæmon.

Menevia (me nē' vi a) A form of the old name, *Mynyw*, of St David's (Wales) Its present name is from Dewi or David, the founder of the episcopal see in the 6th century.

Meng-tse. The fourth of the sacred books of China, so called from the name of its author (d. about 290 B C), Latinized into Mencius. It was written in the 4th century B C Confucius or Kung-fu-tse wrote the other three, viz. Ta-heo (*School of Adults*), Chong-yong (*The Golden Mean*), and Lun-yu (or *Book of Maxims*)

Mother of Meng A Chinese expression, meaning "an admirable teacher" Meng's father died soon after the birth of the sage, and he was brought up by his mother

Menippus (men ip' ŭs), the cynic, was born at Gadara, Syria, in the 3rd century B C He was called by Lucian "the greatest snarler and snapper of all the old dogs" (*cynics*)

Varro wrote the *Satyræ Menippeæ*, and in imitation of it a political pamphlet, in verse and prose, designed to expose the perfidious intentions of Spain in regard to France, and the criminal ambition of the Guise family, was published in 1593 as *The Menippean Satire* The authors were Pierre Leroy (d 1593), Pithou (1539-96), Passerat (1534-1602), and Rapin, the poet (1540-1608)

Mennonites. Followers of Simon Menno (1492-1559), a native of Friesland, who modified the fanatical views of the Anabaptists. The sect still survives, in the United States as well as in Holland and Germany

Mensheviks (men' she viks) A Russian word for a minority party After the Russian Revolution of November, 1917, the less radical socialists who were in opposition to the more violent Bolshevik government, took this name

Menthu. *See* BAKHA

Mention in Dispatches British term given to a reference by name in official dispatches to an officer who has done well in battle An officer so mentioned is entitled to wear a small bronze oak leaf on the left breast or upon the medal ribbon for that particular campaign.

Mentor. A guide, a wise and faithful counsellor, so called from Mentor, a friend of Ulysses, whose form Minerva assumed when she accompanied Telemachos in his search for his father

Menu or Manu (mĕ' nū) In Hindu philosophy, one of a class of Demiurges of whom the first is identified with Brahma Brahma divided himself into male and female, these produced *Viraj*, from whom sprang the first *Menu*, a kind of secondary creator He gave rise to ten *Prajapatis* ("lords of all living"); from these came seven *Menus*, each presiding over a certain period, the seventh of these being *Menu Vaivasvata* ("the sun-born") who is now reigning and who is looked upon as the creator of the living races of beings To him are ascribed the *Laws of Menu*, now called the *Manavadharmashastra*, a section of the Vedas containing a code of civil and religious law compiled by the Manavans

Meo periculo (mē ŏ per ik' ū lō) (Lat at my own risk) On my responsibility; I being bond.

Mephibosheth (me fib' ŏ sheth), in Dryden's *Absalom and Achitophel*, Pt ii, (*q.v*) is meant for Samuel Pordage (d 1691), a poetaster

Mephistopheles (mef is tof' e lēz) A manufactured name (possibly from three Greek words meaning "not loving the light") of a devil or familiar spirit which first appears in the late mediæval Faust legend, he is well known as the sneering, jeering, leering tempter in Goethe's *Faust* He is mentioned by Shakespeare (*Merry Wives*, i, 1) and Fletcher as *Mephostophilus*, and in Marlowe's *Faustus* as *Mephostopilis*

Mercator's Projection is Mercator's chart or map for nautical purposes The meridian lines are at right angles to the parallels of latitude. It is so called because it was devised by Gerhard Kremer (= merchant, pedlar) (1512-94), whose surname Latinized is *Mercator*.

Merchant Adventurers were a guild of traders originally established in Brabant in 1296 Henry VII granted a patent for the Adventurers in England in 1505 and they were incorporated in 1564

Merchant of Venice. The interwoven stories of Shakespeare's comedy (written 1598, published 1600) are drawn from mediæval

legends the germs of which are found in the *Gesta Romanorum*. The tale of the bond is ch xlviii, and that of the caskets is ch. xcix Much of the plot is also given in the 14th century *Il Pecorone* of Ser Giovanni, but Shakespeare could not read Italian, there was no translation in his day, and it is more than doubtful whether he ever saw or was aware of it.

Mercia (mĕr' si a) One of the ancient Anglian kingdoms of the Heptarchy, founded soon after the middle of the 6th century. It flourished under Penda in the 7th century; in the 8th, under Ethelbald and Offa, it became overlord, but in 827 was incorporated with Wessex, to be revived again as an earldom until the Norman Conquest It embraced a large part of the Midlands, stretching from the Humber to the Thames, and westward to the Welsh Marches

Mercilla *See* SOLDAN.

Mercury (mĕr' kū ri) The Roman equivalent of the Greek Hermes (*q v*), son of Maia and Jupiter, to whom he acted as messenger He was the god of science and commerce, the patron of travellers and also of rogues, vagabonds, and thieves Hence, the name of the god is used to denote both a messenger and a thief—

> Delay leads impotent and snail-pac'd beggary
> Then fiery expedition be my wing,
> Jove's Mercury, and herald for a king
> *Richard III*, iv, 3

> My father named me Autolycus; who being, as I am, littered under Mercury, was likewise a snapper-up of unconsidered trifles.—*Winter's Tale*, iv, 2.

Mercury is represented as a young man with winged hat and winged sandals (*talaria*), bearing the *caduceus* (*q.v.*), and sometimes a purse

Posts with a marble head of Mercury on them used to be erected where two or more roads met, to point out the way. (*Juvenal*, viii, 53)

In astrology, Mercury ' signifieth subtill men, ingenious, inconstant rymers, poets, advocates, orators, phylosophers, arithmeticians, and busie fellowes," and the alchemists cred.ted it with great powers and used it for a large number of purposes *See* Ben Jonson's masque, *Mercury Vindicated.*

Mercury fig (Lat *Ficus ad Mercurium*). The first fig gathered off a fig-tree was by the Romans devoted to Mercury. The proverbial saying was applied generally to all first fruits or first works.

You cannot make a Mercury of every log Pythagoras said *Non ex quovis ligno Mercurius fit* That is, "Not every mind will answer equally well to be trained into a scholar." The proper wood for a statue of Mercury was box—*vel quod hominis pultorem præ se ferat, vel quod materies sit omnium maxime æterna* (*Erasmus*)

Mercurial (mer kū' ri ál) Light-hearted, gay, volatile; because such were supposed by the astrologers to be born under the planet Mercury

Mercurial finger The little finger, which, if pointed denotes eloquence, if square sound judgment
> The thumb, in chiromancy, we give to Venus,
> The forefinger to Jove, the midst to Saturn,
> The ring to Sol, the least to Mercury
> BEN JONSON *Alchemist*, i, 1

Mercy. The seven corporal works of mercy are —
(1) To tend the sick
(2) To feed the hungry
(3) To give drink to the thirsty
(4) To clothe the naked
(5) To house the homeless.
(6) To visit the fatherless and the afflicted
(7) To bury the dead *Matt* xxv, 35-40

Merciless (or Unmerciful) Parliament, The (from February 3rd to June 3rd, 1388) A junto of fourteen tools of Thomas, Duke of Gloucester, which assumed royal prerogatives, and attempted to depose Richard II.

Meridian. Sometimes applied, especially in Scotland, to a noonday dram of spirits.
> He received from the hand of the waiter the meridian, which was placed ready at the bar —SCOTT *Redgauntlet*, ch i.

Merino Sheep (me rē' nō) A Spanish breed of sheep, very valuable for their wool The word is the Latin *majorinus*, and may originally have indicated a specially large breed of sheep, or have been the official designation of the overseer of the pastures

Merit, Order of. This is a British order for distinguished service in all callings It was founded by Edward VII in 1902, with two classes civil and military The Order is limited to 24 members—men and women—and confers no precedence; it is designated by the letters O M , following the first class of the Order of the Bath and precedes all letters designating membership of other Orders The badge is a red and blue cross pattee, with a blue medallion in the centre surrounded by a laurel wreath, and bears the words "For Merit"; the ribbon is blue and crimson Crossed swords are added to the badge for military members

Merlin The historical Merlin was a Welsh or British bard, born towards the close of the 5th century, to whom a number of poems have been very doubtfully attributed He is said to have become bard to King Arthur, and to have lost his reason and perished on the banks of the river after a terrible battle between the Britons and their Romanized compatriots about 570

His story has been mingled with that of the enchanter Merlin of the Arthurian romances, which, however, proceeds on different lines This Prince of Enchanters was the son of a damsel seduced by a fiend, but was baptized by Blaise, and so rescued from the power of Satan He became an adept in necromancy, but was beguiled by the enchantress Nimue, who shut him up in a rock, and later Vivien, the Lady of the Lake, entangled him in a thornbush by means of spells, and there he still sleeps, though his voice may sometimes be heard

He first appears in Nennius (as Ambrosius), Geoffrey of Monmouth wrote the *Vita Merlini* (about 1145), this was worked upon by Wace and Robert de Borron, and formed the basis of the English prose romance *Merlin*, and of most of the Merlin episodes in the Arthurian cycle. *See also* Spenser's *Faerie Queene* (III, iii), and Tennyson's *Idylls*
> Now, though a Mechanist, whose skill
> Shames the degenerate grasp of modern science,
> Grave Merlin (and behke the more
> For practising occult and perilous lore)
> Was subject to a freakish will
> That sapped good thoughts, or scared them with
> defiance WORDSWORTH *The Egyptian Maid*

The English Merlin. William Lilly (1602-81), the astrologer, who published two tracts under the name of "Merlinus Anglicus" and was the most famous charlatan of his day

Merlin chair An invalid's chair, which can be propelled by the hands of the occupant. So called from the inventor, J J Merlin (d 1803).

Mermaid. The popular stories of the mermaid, a fabulous marine creature half woman and half fish—allied to the Siren (*q v*) of classical mythology—probably arose from sailors' accounts of the dugong, a cetacean whose head has a rude approach to the human outline The mother while suckling her young holds it to her breast with one flipper, as a woman holds her infant in her arm If disturbed she suddenly dives under water, and tosses up her fish-like tail

In Elizabethan plays the term is often used for a courtesan *See* Massinger's *Old Law*, iv, 1, Shakespeare's *Comedy of Errors*, iii, 2, etc

The Mermaid Tavern. The famous meeting-place (in Bread Street, Cheapside) of the wits, literary men, and men about town in the early 17th century Among those who met there at a sort of early club were Ben Jonson, Sir Walter Raleigh, Beaumont, Fletcher, John Selden, and in all probability Shakespeare
> What things have we seen
> Done at the Mermaid! Heard words that have been
> So nimble, and so full of subtile flame,
> As if that everyone from whence they came
> Had meant to put his whole wit in a jest
> BEAUMONT *Lines to Ben Jonson.*

Mermaid's glove The largest of the British sponges (*Halichondria palmata*), so called because its branches resemble fingers.

Mermaid's purses. The horny cases of the eggs of the ray, skate, or shark, frequently cast up by the waves on the sea-beach

Merope (mer' ō pe). One of the Pleiades, dimmer than the rest, because, according to Greek legend, she married a mortal She was the mother of Glaucus

Merops' Son. One who thinks he can set the world to rights, but can't Agitators demo-gogues, and Bolsheviks, are sons of Merops The allusion is to Phæton, son of Merops, who thought himself able to drive the car of Phœbus, but, in the attempt, nearly set the world on fire

Merovingian Dynasty (mer ō ving' gi an) The dynasty of Merovius, a Latin form of *Merwig* (great warrior), who is said to have ruled over the Franks in the 5th century The dynasty rose to power under Clovis (d 511), and gradually gave way before the Mayors of the

Palace (*q v*), until in 751 the Merovingians were deposed by Pepin the Short, grandson of Pepin of Heristal

Merrie England. *See* MERRY.

Merrow (Irish, *muirruhgach*) A mermaid, believed by Irish fishermen to forebode a coming storm

It was rather annoying to Jack that, though living in a place where the merrows were as plenty as lobsters, he never could get a right view of one — W B YEATS *Fairy and Folk Tales*, p 63

Merrows are of human shape above but from the waist like a fish The females are attractive, but the males have green teeth, green hair, pig's eyes, and red noses Fishermen dread to meet them

Merry The original meaning is *pleasing*, *delightful*, hence *giving pleasure*, hence *mirthful, joyous*

The old phrase *Merrie England* (*Merry London*, etc.) merely signified that these places were pleasant and delightful, not necessarily bubbling over with merriment, and so with *the merry month of May*

Thou Saint George shalt called bee,
Saint George of mery England, the signe of victoree.
SPENSER *Faerie Queene*, I, x, 61.
Thus all through merry Islington
These gambols did he play
COWPER *John Gilpin*

The phrase *merry men*, meaning the companions at arms of a knight or outlaw (especially Robin Hood), is really for *merry meinie See* MEINIE

Merry Andrew. A buffoon, jester, or attendant on a quack doctor at fairs Said by Thomas Hearne (1678-1735)—with no evidence —to derive from Andrew Boorde (*c* 1490-1549), physician to Henry VIII, who to his vast learning added great eccentricity Prior has a poem on "Merry Andrew." Andrew is a common name in old plays for a manservant, as Abigail is for a waiting-woman

Merry as a cricket, grig. *See* GRIG.

Merry Dancers. The northern lights, so called from their undulatory motion. The French also call them *chevres dansantes* (dancing goats)

Merry Dun of Dover. In Scandinavian folktale, an enormous ship which knocked down Calais steeple in passing through the Straits of Dover, while the pennant swept a flock of sheep off Dover cliffs into the sea The masts were so lofty that a boy who ascended them would grow grey before he could reach deck again.

Merry Greek. *See* GRIG.

Merry Maidens. The ancient stone circle (of 19 stones) in St Buryan parish, 5 miles from Penzance, Cornwall It is 76 ft. in diameter Also called *Rosemodris Circle*.

Merry men. *See* MERRY, *above*.

Merry Men of Mey. An expanse of broken water which boils like a cauldron in the southern side of the Stroma channel, in the Pentland Firth.

Merry Monarch Charles II

Merry Monday. An old name for the day before Shrove Tuesday

Merrythought. The furcula or wishing-bone in the breast of a fowl, sometimes broken by two persons, when the one who holds the larger portion has his wish, as it is said

'Tis merry in hall, when beards wag all (2 *Henry IV*, v, 3) It is a sure sign of mirth when the beards of the guests shake with laughter

To make merry. To be jovial, festive; **to make merry over,** to treat with amusement or ridicule, to make fun of.

Merse. The south-easterly part of Berwickshire was so called because it was the *mere, march,* or frontier of England and Scotland It gives the second half of the title, to the Earl of Wemyss and March.

Merton College. Founded by Walter de Merton (d 1277), Bishop of Rochester, and Lord High Chancellor in 1264 He was, through this foundation, the originator of the collegiate system still maintained in the older English Universities

Meru (me' roo). The "Olympus" of the Hindus, a fabulous mountain in the centre of the world, 80,000 leagues high, the abode of Vishnu, and a perfect paradise

Merveilleuse (mâr vi yers) (Fr, marvellous) The sword of Doolin of Mayence (*q.v*) It was so sharp that when placed edge downwards it would cut through a slab of wood without the use of force.

The term is also applied to the dress worn by the fops and ladies of the Directory period in France, who were noted for their extravagance and aping of classical Greek modes

Mesa Spanish and Mexican term for grassy table-land.

Meschino. *See* GUERINO MESCHINO

Mesmerism (mez' mēr izm). So called from Friedrich Anton Mesmer (1733-1815), of Meersburg, Baden, who introduced his theory of "animal magnetism" into Paris, in 1778 It is the basis or forerunner of hypnotism, the therapeutic employment of which is being increasingly studied by the medical and psychiatric professions

Mesopotamia (mes ŏ pot ām' i à) (Gr, the land between the rivers, *i e.* the Euphrates and Tigris) The territory bounded by Kurdistan on the N. and NE, the Persian Gulf on the S and SE, Persia on the E, and Syria and the Arabian Desert on the W. Since World War I —as a consequence of which it was freed from Turkish rule and constituted a separate kingdom—its name has been changed to *Irak* (*q.v.*), or *Iraq*

The true "Mesopotamia" ring. Something high-sounding and pleasing, but wholly past comprehension. The allusion is to the story of an old woman who told her pastor that she "found great support in that blessed word *Mesopotamia*"

Mess. The usual meaning to-day is a dirty, untidy state of things, a muddle, a difficulty (*to get into a mess*), but the word originally signified a portion of food (Lat *missum,* *mittere*, to send, *cp*. Fr *mets*, viands, Ital *messo*, a course of a meal), thence it came to mean mixed food—especially for an animal—and so a confusion, medley, jumble.

Another meaning was a small group of persons (usually four) who at banquets sat together and were served from the same dishes This use gave rise not only to the army and navy *mess* (used also at the Inns of Court), but to the Elizabethans using it in place of "four" or "a group of four " Thus, Lyly says, "Foure makes a messe, and we have a messe of masters " (*Mother Bombie* ii, 1), and Shakespeare calls the four sons of Henry his "mess of sons" (2 *Henry VI*, i, 4); and says (*Love's Labour's Lost*, iv, 3), "You three fools lacked me .. to make up the mess "

Messalina (mes a lē′ na). Wife of the Emperor Claudius of Rome; she was executed by order of her husband in A D 48. Her name has become a byword for lasciviousness and incontinency. Catherine II of Russia (1729-96) has sometimes been called *The Modern Messalina*.

Messiah (me sī′ á), from the Hebrew *mashiach*, one anointed It is the title of an expected leader of the Jews who shall deliver the nation from its enemies and reign in permanent triumph and peace. Equivalent to the Greek word Christ, it is applied by Christians to Jesus *Messiah* (incorrectly *The Messiah*) is the title of an oratorio by Handel, first produced in Dublin in 1742.

Mestizo Spanish-Mexican phrase for a half-breed

Metals. Metals used to be divided into two classes—*Noble*, and *Base*. The *Noble*, or *Perfect*, *Metals* were gold and silver, because they were the only two known that could be not changed or "destroyed" by fire, the remainder were *Base*, or *Imperfect*.

The seven metals in alchemy.
Gold, Apollo or the sun.
Silver, Diana or the moon.
Quicksilver, Mercury.
Copper, Venus.
Iron, Mars
Tin, Jupiter.
Lead, Saturn

The only metals used in heraldry are *or* (gold) and *argent* (silver)

Metamorphic Rocks (met á môr ′fik) Sedimentary or eruptive rocks whose original character has been more or less altered by changes beneath the surface of the earth. These include gneiss, mica-schist, clay-slate, marble, and the like, which have become more or less crystalline.

Metaphysics (met á fiz′ iks) (Gr., after-physics, so called because the disciples of Aristotle held that matter or nature should be studied before mind) The science of metaphysics is the consideration of things in the abstract—that is, divested of their accidents, relations, and matter; the philosophy of being and knowing, the theoretical principles forming the basis of any particular science, the philosophy of mind

Metathesis (met a thē′ sis) A figure of speech in which letters or syllables are transposed, as "You occupew my pie [py]," instead of "You *occupy my pew*", *daggle-trail* for "draggle-tail," etc , the same as a Spoonerism (*q v*).

Methodists. A name given (1729) by a student of Christ Church to the brothers Wesley and their friends, who used to assemble on given evenings for religious conversation, because of the methodical way in which they observed their principles The word was in use many centuries earlier for those (especially physicians) who attached great importance to method, and the name was at one time applied to the Jesuits, because they were the first to give systematic representations of the method of polemics Theophilus Gale (1628-78) speaks of a religious sect called "the New Methodists" (*Court of the Gentiles*).

Primitive Methodists. A secession from the Methodists, led by Hugh Bourne in 1810 They adopted this name because they reverted to the original methods of preaching of the Wesleys

Methuselah (me′ thū zē lá). **Old as Methuselah.** Very old indeed, almost incredibly old He is the oldest man mentioned in the Bible, where we are told (*Gen* v, 27) that he died at the age of 969.

Metonic Cycle, The (me ton′ ik) A cycle of nineteen years, at the end of which period the new moons fall on the same days of the year, so-called because discovered by the Greek astronomer, Meton, 432 B C. In 330 a slight error in it was put right by Calippus, who, to allow for odd hours, laid down that at the end of four cycles (76 years) one day was to be omitted

Metonymy (me ton′ i mi) The use of the name of one thing for another, as "the Bench" for the magistrates or judges sitting in court, "a silk" for a King's Counsel, "the bottle" for alcoholic liquor The word is Greek, meaning a change of name

Metropolitan. A prelate who has suffragan bishops subject to him. The two metropolitans of England are the archbishops of Canterbury and York, and the two of Ireland the archbishops of Armagh and Dublin The word does not mean the prelate of the metropolis (Gr *meter*, mother, *polis*, city) in a secular sense, but the prelate of a "mother city" in an ecclesiastical sense—*i e* a city which is the mother or ruler of other cities Thus, the Bishop of London is not a metropolitan, but the Archbishop of Canterbury is *metropolitanus et primus totius Angliæ*, and the Archbishop of York *primus et metropolitanus Angliæ*.

In the Greek Church a metropolitan ranks next below a patriarch and next above an archbishop

Meum and tuum (mē′ um, tū′ um). That which belongs to me and that which is another's *Meum* is Latin for "what is mine," and *tuum* is Latin for "what is thine." If a man is said not to know the difference between *meum* and *tuum*, it is a another way of saying he is a thief.

"Meum est propositum in taberna mori" A famous drinking song usually credited to Walter Map, who died in 1210

Meum est propositum in taberna mori;
Vinum sit oppositum morientis ori
Ut dicant cum venerint angelorum chori
Deus sit propitius huic potatori (etc.)

It is my intention to die in a tavern May wine be placed to my dying lips, that when the choirs of angels shall come they may say, God be merciful to this drinker "

Mews. Stables, but properly a cage for hawks when moulting (O F *mue*, Lat. *mūtāre*, to change) The word has acquired its present meaning because (in the 17th cent.) the royal stables were built upon the site (now occupied by the National Gallery) where formerly the king's hawks were kept, and the name was transferred from the establishment for hawks to that of horses

Mexitl, or **Mextli** (meks' itl) The principal god of the ancient Mexicans (whence the name of their country), to whom enormous sacrifices, running into many thousands of human beings, were offered at a time. Also called *Huitzilopochtli*.

Mezzotint, or **Mezzo tinto** (Ital., medium tint). A process of engraving in which a copper plate is uniformly roughened so as to print a deep black, lights and half-lights being then produced by scraping away the burr; also a print from this, which is usually a good imitation of an Indian-ink drawing

Micah Rood's Apples. Apples with a spot of red in the heart. The story is that Micah Rood was a prosperous farmer at Franklin, Pa In 1693 a pedlar with jewellery called at his house, and next day was found murdered under an apple-tree in Rood's orchard The crime was never brought home to the farmer, but next autumn all the apples of the fatal tree bore inside a red blood-spot, called "Micah Rood's Curse," and the farmer died soon afterwards

Micawber (mi caw' ba). An incurable optimist, from Dickens's Mr. Wilkins Micawber (*David Copperfield*), a great speechifier and letter-writer and projector of bubble schemes sure to lead to fortune, but always ending in grief Notwithstanding his ill success, he never despaired, but felt certain that something would ' turn up" to make his fortune Having failed in every adventure in the old country, he emigrated to Australia, where he became a magistrate

Michael, St. The great prince of all the angels and leader of the celestial armies

And there was war in heaven: Michael and his angels fought against the dragon, and the dragon fought and his angels, and prevailed not.—*Rev.* xii, 7, 8

Go, Michael, of celestial armies prince,
And thou, in military prowess next,
Gabriel, lead forth to battle these my sons
Invincible, lead forth my armed Saints
By thousands and by millions ranged for fight.
MILTON: *Paradise Lost,* vi, 44.

His day ("St Michael and All Angels") is Sept 29th (*see* MICHAELMAS), and in the Roman Catholic Church he is also commemorated on May 8th, in honour of his apparition in 492 to a herdsman of Monte Gargano. In the Middle Ages he was looked on as the presiding spirit of the planet Mercury, and bringer to man of the gift of prudence

The planet Mercury, whose place '
Is nearest to the sun in space,
Is my allotted sphere,
And with celestial ardour swift
I bear upon my hands the gift
Of heavenly *prudence* here.
LONGFELLOW *Golden Legend, The Miracle Play,* iii.

In art St Michael is depicted as a beautiful young man with severe countenance, winged, and clad in either white or armour, bearing a lance and shield, with which he combats a dragon In the final judgment he is represented with scales, in which he weighs the souls of the risen dead

St. Michael's chair It is said that any woman who sits on St Michael's Chair, Cornwall, will rule the roost as long as she lives.

The Order of St. Michael and St. George A British order of knighthood, instituted in 1818 (enlarged and extended on four occasions since), and conferred on natural-born British subjects who hold, or have held, high official rank in the Colonies, or as a reward for services in relation to the foreign affairs of the Empire It is limited to one hundred Knights Grand Cross, three hundred Knights Commanders, and six hundred Companions; and its chapel is in St. Paul's Cathedral

Michael Angelo The celebrated painter, born 1474, died 1564, his full name was Michelangelo Buonarroti.

The Michael-Angelo of battle-scenes Michael-Angelo Cerquozzi (1600-60), a native of Rome, famous for his battle scenes and shipwrecks.

Michel-Ange des Bamboches Peter van Laar (1613-73), the Dutch painter

Michael-Angelo of Music. Christoph Willibald von Gluck (1714-87), the German musical composer

Michael-Angelo of Sculptors. Pierre Puget (1622-94), the French sculptor Also René Michael Slodtz (1705-64)

Michaelmas Day. September 29th, the Festival of St Michael and All Angels (*see* MICHAEL, *above*), one of the quarter-days when rents are due, and the day when magistrates are elected.

The custom of eating goose at Michaelmas (*see also* ST. MARTIN'S GOOSE) is many centuries old, and probably arose solely because geese were plentiful and in good condition at this season, and we are told that tenants formerly presented their landlords with one to keep in their good graces The popular story, however, is that Queen Elizabeth, on her way to Tilbury Fort on September 29th, 1588. dined at the seat of Sir Neville Umfreyville, and partook of geese, afterwards calling for a bumper of Burgundy, and giving as a toast, "Death to the Spanish Armada!" Scarcely had she spoken when a messenger announced the destruction of the fleet by a storm The queen demanded a second bumper, and said, "Henceforth shall a goose commemorate this great victory " This tale is marred by the awkward circumstances that the fleet was dispersed by the winds in July, and the thanksgiving sermon for the victory was preached at St Paul's on August 20th Gascoigne, who died 1577, refers to the custom of goose-eating at Michaelmas as common.—

At Christmas a capon, at Michaelmas a goose,
And somewhat else at New Yere's tide, for feare the lease flies loose

Miching Malicho (mich' ing măl' i kō)

Oph What means this, my lord?
Ham · Marry, this is Miching Malicho, it means mischief
Oph : Belike this show imports the argument of the play. *Hamlet*, iii, 2.

The meaning of this phrase is not at all certain, but it is usually taken that *miching* is "skulking" (*miche*, from O Fr. *muchier*, *mucier*, to hide), and *malicho* is a form of Span. *malhecco*, a misdeed, mischief, hence skulking or sneaking mischief The form we give is that of the First Folio, in the First Quarto the words appear as *myching Mallico*, and in the Second Quarto *munching Mallico*

Michon (mi' shon), according to Cotgrave, is a "block, dunce, dolt, jobbernol, dullard, loggerhead" *Michon, mikel,* and *Cousin Michel,* are the Italian *muccio*, an ass.

Mickey Mouse, one of the most famous and popular characters of Walt Disney's animated cartoons. *Steamboat Willie* (1928) starring Mickey Mouse was the first animated cartoon in colours

Mickleton Jury. A corruption of mickle-tourn (*magnus turnus*), i e the jury of court leets, which were visited at Easter and Michaelmas by the county sheriffs in their *tourns* In Anglo-Saxon times the great council of the kings was known as the *Micklemoot* (great assembly)

Microcosm (mī krō kozm) (Gr, little world) So man is called by Paracelsus The ancients considered the world (*see* MACROCOSM) as a living being; the sun and moon being its *two eyes,* the earth its *body,* the ether its *intellect,* and the sky its *wings.* When man was looked on as the world in miniature, it was thought that the movements of the world and of man corresponded, and if one could be ascertained, the other could be easily inferred, hence arose the system of astrology, which professed to interpret the events of a man's life by the corresponding movements, etc, of the stars. *Cp.* DIAPASON.

Micronesia (mī krō nē' zhȧ) The name given to the groups of small Pacific islands north of the Equator and east of the Philippines, including the Marianas, the Caroline and the Marshall Islands.

Midas (mī' dăs). A legendary king of Phrygia who requested of the gods that everything he touched might be turned to gold His request was granted, but as his food became gold the moment he touched it, he prayed the gods to take their favour back He was then ordered to bathe in the Pactolus, and the river ever after rolled over golden sands

Another story told of him is, that when appointed to judge a musical contest between Apollo and Pan, he gave judgment in favour of the satyr, whereupon Apollo in contempt gave the king a pair of ass's ears Midas hid them under his Phrygian cap, but his barber discovered them, and, not daring to mention the matter, dug a hole and relieved his mind by whispering in it "Midas has ass's ears," then covering it up again Budæus gives a different version He says that Midas kept spies to tell him everything that transpired throughout his kingdom, and the proverb "kings have long arms" was changed to "Midas has long ears"

A parallel of this tale is told of Portzmach, king of a part of Brittany He had all the barbers of his kingdom put to death, lest they should announce to the public that he had the ears of a horse An intimate friend was found willing to shave him, after swearing profound secrecy, but not able to contain himself, he confided his secret to the sands of a river bank The reeds of this river were used for pan-pipes and hautbois, which repeated the words "Portzmach—King Portzmach has horse's ears"

Midden. The midden or refuse heaps of prehistoric and other ancient encampments have yielded a great amount of archæological information as to the habits and state of civilization of the people who made them

Better marry over the midden than over the moor. Better seek a wife among your neighbours whom you know than among strangers of whom you know nothing.

Ilka cock craws loodest on its ain midden. In English, "Every cock crows loudest on his own dunghill"

Kitchen midden. *See* KITCHEN.

Middle. Middle Ages. The period from about 476 (the fall of the Roman Empire) to 1453 (the capture of Constantinople by the Turks). It varies a little with almost every nation, in France it is usually dated from Clovis to Louis XI (481 to 1461); in England, from the Heptarchy to the accession of Henry VII (409 to 1485). The earlier part of this time (to about 1200) is usually referred to as the Dark Ages (*q v*)

Middle Kingdom is the Chinese term for China proper, the eighteen inner provinces, anciently for the Chinese Empire as being situated in the centre of the world The Middle Empire in Egyptian history is the great period from 2200 to 1690 B C comprising the XI to the XIV Dynasties

Middlesex. The territory of the Middle Saxons—that is, between Essex, Sussex, and Wessex

Midgard. In Scandinavian mythology, the abode of the first pair, from whom sprang the human race. It was made of the eyebrows of Ymer, and was joined to Asgard by the rainbow bridge called Bifrost

Asgard is the abode of the celestials
Utgard is the abode of the giants
Midgard is between the two—better than Utgard, but inferior to Asgard.

Mid-Lent Sunday The fourth Sunday in Lent. It is called *dominica refectionis* (Refection Sunday), because the first lesson is the banquet given by Joseph to his brethren, and the gospel of the day is the miraculous feeding of the five thousand It is the day on which simnel cakes (*q v.*) are eaten, and it is also called Mothering Sunday (*q v*)

Midnight Oil. Late hours

Burning the midnight oil. Sitting up late, especially when engaged on literary work.

Smells of the midnight oil *See* IT SMELLS OF THE LAMP *under* LAMP

Midrash (mid' rasn) The rabbinical investigation into and interpretation of the Old Testament writings, which began when the Temple at Jerusalem was destroyed and was committed to writing in a large number of commentaries between the 2nd and 11th centuries A D The three ancient *Midrashim* (*Mechiltha, Sifre*, and *Sifra*—first half of the 2nd century) contain both the Halachah and the Haggadah (*q v*)

Midsummer. The week or so round about the summer solstice (June 21st) **Midsummer Day** is June 24th, St John the Baptist's Day, and one of the quarter days

Midsummer ale. Festivities which used to take place in rural districts at this season Here *Ale* has the same extended meaning as in "Church-ale" (*q v.*)

Midsummer madness Olivia says to Malvolio, "Why, this is very midsummer madness" (*Twelfth Night*, III, 4) The reference is to the rabies of dogs, which was supposed to be brought on by midsummer heat People who were a bit inclined to be mad used to be said *to have but a mile to midsummer.*

Midsummer men. Orpine or Live-long, a plant of the Sedum tribe; so called because it used to be set in pots or shells on midsummer eve, and hung up in the house to tell damsels whether their sweethearts were true or not. If the leaves bent to the right, it was a sign of fidelity; if to the left, the "true-love's heart was cold and faithless."

Midsummer moon " 'Tis *midsummer moon with you*", you are stark mad. Madness was supposed to be affected by the moon, and to be aggravated by summer heat, so it naturally follows that the full moon at midsummer is the time when madness would be most outrageous

What's this midsummer moon?
Is all the world gone a-madding?
DRYDEN *Amphitryon*, IV, 1.

Midsummer Night's Dream, A. Shakespeare's comedy (acted 1595, first printed 1600) is indebted to Chaucer's *Knight's Tale* for the Athenian setting, and to Ovid's *Metamorphoses* for the Pyramus and Thisbe interlude, but its airy grace and the ingenious inter-weaving of the four separate threads are all Shakespeare's own

Midway Islands are a cluster of islands in the North Pacific, about 1200 miles NW. of Hawaii and forming part of that Territory The Japanese suffered a heavy naval defeat near the islands in June, 1942.

Midwife (A S , *mid*, with; *wif*, woman). The nurse who is *with* the mother in her labour

Midwife of men's thoughts. So Socrates termed himself, and, as Mr. Grote observes, "No other man ever struck out of others so many sparks to set light to original thought." Out of his intellectual school sprang Plato and
20*

the Dialectic system, Euclid and the Megaric; Aristippus and the Cyrenaic; Antisthenes and the Cynic.

Mihrab. *See* KEBLAH

Mikado (mik a 'dō) (Jap. *mi*, exalted; *kado*, gate or door). The title of the Emperor of Japan (*cp* SHOGUN)

Mike. To mike, or to do a mike To idle away one's time, pretending to be waiting for a job, or just hanging about and avoiding one The word may be from *miche*, to skulk (*see* MICHING MALICHO). More recently *mike* has been a short name for the microphone.
Shall the blessed sun of heaven prove a mucher [truant loiterer]?—1 *Henry IV*, II, 4.

Milan (mi làn') The English form of Milano, the capital city of Lombardy, in Latin *Mediolanum*, in the middle of the plain, *i e* the Plain of Lombardy In the Middle Ages Milan was famous for its steel, used for making swords, chain armour, etc

The edict of Milan. Proclaimed by Constantine, after the conquest of Italy (313), to secure to Christians the restitution of their civil and religious rights.

The Milan Decree A decree made by Napoleon, dated "Milan, Dec. 27th, 1807," declaring "the whole British Empire to be in a state of blockade, and forbidding all countries either from trading with Great Britain or from even using an article of British manufacture."
This decree was killing the goose which laid the golden eggs, for England was the best customer of the very countries thus restricted from dealing with her

Milanion. *See* ATALANTA'S RACE.

Mile. A measure of length; in the British Empire and the United States, 1,760 yd , so called from Lat. *mille*, a thousand, the Roman lineal measure being 1,000 paces, or about 1,680 yds The old Irish and Scottish miles were a good deal longer than the standard English, that in Ireland (still in use in country parts) being 2,240 yd

The *Nautical* or *Geographical Mile*, is supposed to be one minute of a great circle of the earth, but as the earth is not a true sphere the length of a minute is variable, so a mean length—6,080 ft. (2,026 yd. 2 ft)—has been fixed by the British Admiralty. The Geographical Mile varies slightly with different nations, so there is a further *International Geographical Mile*, which is invariable at one-fifteenth of a degree of the earth's equator, equal to about 4 61 statute miles of 5,280 ft.

Milesian Fables (mi lē' zi àn) A Greek collection of witty but obscene short stories by Antonius Diogenes, and compiled by Aristides, of *Miletus* (2nd cent B C), whence the name. They were translated into Latin by Sidenna about the time of the civil wars of Marius and Sylla, and were greedily read by the luxurious Sybarites, but are no longer extant Similar stories however, are still sometimes called *Milesian Tales*

Milesians. Properly, the inhabitants of Miletus, but the name has been given to the ancient Irish because of the legend that two sons of Milesius, a fabulous king of Spain, conquered the country and repeopled it after exterminating the Firbolgs—the aborigines

My family, by my father's side, are all the true ould Milesians, and related to the O'Flahertys, and O'Shaughnesses, and the M'Lauchlins, the O'Donnaghans, O'Callaghans, O'Geogaghans, and all the thick blood of the nation, and I myself am an O'Brallaghan, which is the ouldest of them all—
MACKLIN: *Love a la Mode.*

Milk, To. Slang for to get money out of somebody in an underhand way, also, to plunder one's creditors, and (in mining) to exhaust the veins of ore after selling the mine.

A land of milk and honey. One abounding in all good things, or of extraordinary fertility *Joel* iii, 18, speaks of "the mountains flowing with milk and honey." Figuratively used to denote the blessings of heaven

> Jerusalem the golden,
> With milk and honey blest.

Milk and water. Insipid, without energy or character, baby-pap (of literature, etc.),

Milk teeth. The first, temporary, teeth of a child

The milk of human kindness. Sympathy, compassion. The phrase is from *Macbeth*, i, 5

> . . . . yet I do fear thy nature
> It is too full o' th' milk of human kindness.

So that accounts for the milk in the coconut! Said when a sudden discovery of the reason for some action or state of things is made

To cry over spilt milk. *See* CRY

Milk-run. R A F and A.A.F. expression during World War II for any sortie flown regularly day after day, or a sortie against an easy target on which inexperienced pilots could be used with impunity

Milksop. An effeminate person; one without energy, one under petticoat government. The allusion is to young, helpless children, who are fed on pap.

Milky Way A great circle of stars entirely surrounding the heavens, apparently so crowded together that they look to the naked eye like a "way" or stream of faint "milky" light. *See* GALAXY.

> A broad and ample road, whose dust is gold
> And pavement stars, as stars to thee appear,
> Seen in the galaxy—that Milky Way,
> Thick, nightly, as a circling zone, thou seest
> Powdered with stars.
> MILTON: *Paradise Lost*, vii, 577, etc.

Mill. To fight, or a fight. It is the same word as the mill that grinds flour (from Lat. *molere*, to grind). Grinding was anciently performed by pulverizing with a stone or pounding with the hand *To mill* is to beat with the fist, as persons used to beat corn with a stone

To mill about is to move aimlessly in a circle, like a herd of cattle

The mill cannot grind with water that is past. An old proverb, given in Herbert's *Collection* (1639) It implies both that one must not miss one's opportunities and that it is no good crying over spilt milk

> And a proverb haunts my mind,
> As a spell is cast;
> "The mill cannot grind
> With the water that is past."
> SARAH DOUDNEY *Lesson of the Watermill.*

The mills of God grind slowly. Retribution may be delayed, but it is sure to overtake the wicked The *Adagia* of Erasmus puts it, *Sero molunt deorum molæ*, and the sentiment is to be found in many authors, ancient and modern. The mills of God grind slowly, yet they grind exceeding small,

> Though with patience He stands waiting, with exactness He grinds all.   LONGFELLOW *Retribution*

Millennium (mi len´ i um) A thousand years (Lat., *mille annus*) In *Rev*, xx, 2, it is said that an angel bound Satan a thousand years, and in verse 4 we are told of certain martyrs who will come to life again, and "reign with Christ a thousand years " "This," says St. John, "is the first resurrection", and this is what is meant by the millennium.

Millenarians, or Chiliasts, is the name applied to an early Christian sect who held this opinion strongly In the 19th century belief in this doctrine was revived by various sects such as the Plymouth Brethren

Millennial Church. *See* SHAKERS.

Miller. A Joe Miller. A stale jest. A certain John Mottley compiled a book of facetiæ in 1739, which he, without permission, entitled *Joe Miller's Jests*, from Joseph Miller (1684-1738), a popular comedian of the day who could neither read nor write. A stale jest is called a "Joe Miller," implying that it is stolen from Mottley's compilation

> A man must serve his time to every trade
> Save censure—critics all are ready made,
> Take hackney'd jokes from Miller, got by rote,
> With just enough of learning to misquote . . .
> Care not for feeling—pass your proper jest,
> And stand a critic, hated yet caress'd.
> BYRON: *English Bards and Scotch Reviewers.*

More water glideth by the mill than wots the miller of (*Titus Andronicus*, ii, 1) Many things are done in a house which the master and mistress never dream of

To drown the miller. To put too much water into spirits, or tea The idea is that the supply of water is so great that even the miller, who uses a water wheel, is drowned with it.

To give someone to the miller. To engage him in conversation till enough people have gathered round to set upon the victim with stones, dirt, garbage, and all the arms which haste supplied a mob with (*see* MILL).

Miller's thumb. A small freshwater fish four or five inches long *Cottus gobio*, also called the *Bullhead*, from its large head

To put the miller's eye out. To make broth or pudding so thin that even a miller's eye would be puzzled to find the flour.

Lumps of unleavened flour in bread are sometimes called *miller's eyes*.

Millerites. Followers of William Miller of Massachusetts (1782-1849) who in 1831 preached that the end of the world would come in 1843—now called Adventists

Milliner. A corruption of *Milaner*, so called from Milan, in Italy, which at one time gave the law to Europe in all matters of taste, dress, and elegance.

Nowadays one nearly always means a woman when one speaks of a milliner, but it was not always so, Ben Jonson, in *Every Man in his Humour*, i, 3, speaks of a "milliner's wife," and the French have still *une modiste* and *un modiste*.

Man-Milliner An effeminate fellow, or one who busies himself over trifles

The Morning Herald sheds tears of joy over the fashionable virtues of the rising generation, and finds that we shall make better man-milliners, better lacqueys, and better courtiers than ever —HAZLITT: *Political Essays* (1814)

Millstone. Hard as the nether millstone. Unfeeling, obdurate The lower or "nether" of the two millstones is firmly fixed and very hard, the upper stone revolves round it on a shaft, and the corn, running down a tube inserted in the upper stone, is ground by the motion of the upper stone upon the lower one.

The millstones of Montisci. They produce flour of themselves, whence the proverb, "Grace comes from God, but millstones from Montisci." (Boccaccio *Decameron*, day viii, novel 3)

To look (or see) through a millstone. To be wonderfully sharpsighted

Then . since your eies are so sharp that you can not only looke through a milstone, but cleane through the minde . . .—LYLY *Euphues*

To see through a millstone as well as most means that in a complicated problem one can see as reasonable a solution as the most clear-sighted person, though that may not be far.

To weep millstones. Not weep at all
Bid Glos'ter think on this, and he will weep—
Aye, millstones, as he lessoned us to weep.
SHAKESPEARE *Richard III*, i, 6

Millwood, Sarah. *See* BARNWELL.

Milo (mi' lō) A celebrated Greek athlete of Crotona (*q v*) in the late 6th cent B C It is said that he carried through the stadium at Olympia a heifer four years old, and ate the whole of it afterwards When old he attempted to tear in two an oak-tree, but the parts closed upon his hands, and while held fast he was devoured by wolves *See* POLYDAMUS.

Milton. "Milton," says Dryden, in the preface to his *Fables*, "was the poetical son of Spenser Milton has acknowledged to me that Spenser was his original."

Milton of Germany. Friedrich G. Klopstock (1724-1803), author of *The Messiah* (1773). Coleridge says he is "a very German Milton indeed "

Mimosa (mi mō' za) Niebuhr says the Mimosa "droops its branches whenever anyone approaches it, seeming to salute those who retire under its shade " The name reflects this notion, as the plant was thought to *mimic* the motions of animals, as does the Sensitive Plant.

Mince Pies at Christmas time are said to have been emblematical of the manger in which our Saviour was laid. The paste over the "offering" was made in form of a *cratch* or *hay-rack* Southey speaks of—

Old bridges dangerously narrow, and angles in them like the corners of an English mince-pie, for the foot-passengers to take shelter in.—*Esprinella's Letters*, III 384 (1807)

Mince pies. Rhyming slang for "the eyes."

To make mincemeat of. Utterly to demolish; to shatter to pieces Mincemeat is meat minced, *i e* cut up very fine.

Mincing Lane (London) Called in the 13th century *Menechinelane, Monechenlane*, etc., and in the time of Henry VIII *Mynchyn Lane* The name is from A S *mynechenn*, a nun (fem. of *munuc*, monk), and the street is probably so called from the tenements held there by the nuns of St Helen's, in Bishopsgate Street. Mincing Lane is the centre of the tea trade, for which it is often used as a generic term.

Mind. Mind your own business; mind your eye, etc *See these words*

To have a mind for it. To desire to possess it, to wish for it Mind meaning desire, intention, is by no means uncommon· "I mind to tell him plainly what I think " (2 *Henry VI*, iv, 1) "I shortly mind to leave you " (2 *Henry VI*, iv, 1)

Minden Boys. The 20th Foot, now the Lancashire Fusiliers, so called from their noted bravery at Minden, Prussia, Aug. 1st, 1759, when the British and Hanoverian army under Prince Ferdinand of Brunswick defeated the French

Minerva (mi nēr' va) The Roman goddess of wisdom and patroness of the arts and trades, fabled to have sprung, with a tremendous battle-cry, fully armed from the head of Jupiter. She is identified with the Greek Athene, and was one of the three chief deities, the others being Jupiter and Juno She is represented as grave and majestic, clad in a helmet and with drapery over a coat of mail, and bearing the ægis on her breast. The most famous statue of this goddess was by Phidias, and was anciently one of the Seven Wonders of the World

Invita Minerva Against the grain Thus, Charles Kean acted comedy *invita Minerva*, his *forte* lying another way Sir Philip Sidney attempted the Horatian metres in English verse *invita Minerva* The phrase is from Horace's *Ars Poetica*, 1, 385—*Tu nihil invita dices faciesve Minerva* (Beware of attempting anything for which nature has not fitted you)

The Minerva Press A printing establishment in Leadenhall Street, London, famous in the late 18th century for its trashy, ultra-sentimental novels, which were characterized by complicated plots, and the labyrinths of difficulties into which the hero and heroine got involved before they could be married.

Miniature. Originally, a rubrication or a small painting in an illuminated MS , which was done with *minium* or red lead. Hence, the word came to express any small portrait or picture on vellum or ivory; but it is in no way connected with the Latin *minor* or *minimus*

Minimalist is a term applied in Russian politics to a less radical member of the Social Revolutionary party

Minims (Lat *Fratres Minimi*, least of the brethren) A term of self-abasement assumed by a mendicant order founded by St Francis of Paula, in 1453, they went bare-footed, and wore a coarse, black woollen stuff, fastened with a woollen girdle, which they never put off, day or night. The order of St. Francis of Assisi had already engrossed the "humble" title of *Fratres Minores* (inferior brothers). The superior of the minims is called *corrector*.

Minister. Literally, an inferior person, in opposition to *magister*, a superior. One is connected with the Latin *minus*, and the other with *magis*. Our Lord says, "Whosoever will be great among you, let him be your minister," where the antithesis is well preserved, and Gibbon mentions—
a multitude of cooks, and inferior ministers, employed in the service of the kitchens —*Decline and Fall*, ch. xxxi

The minister of a church is a man who *serves* the parish or congregation, and the minister of the Crown is the sovereign's or state's servant.

Florimond de Remond, speaking of Albert Babinot, one of the disciples of Calvin, says, "He was a student of the Institutes, read at the hall of the Equity school in Poitiers, and was called *la Ministerie*." Calvin, in allusion thereto, used to call him "Mr. Minister," whence not only Babinot but all the other clergy of the Calvinistic Church were called *ministers*

Minnehaha (min e ha' ha) (*Laughing-water*). The lovely daughter of the old arrow-maker of the Dacotahs, and wife of Hiawatha in Longfellow's poem. She died of famine

Minnesingers (min' e sing erz) Minstrels. The lyric poets of 12th- to 14th-century Germany were so called, because the subject of their lyrics was *minne-sang* (love-ditty). The chief *minnesingers* were Heinrich von Ofterdingen, Wolfram von Eschenbach, Walther von der Vogelweide, and (the earliest) Heinrich von Veldeke All of them were men of noble birth, and they were succeeded by the Meistersingers (*q v*)

Minoan. *See* MINOS

Minories (min' ôr iz) (London). So called from the Abbey of the *Minoresses* of St Mary of the Order of St Clare which, till the Dissolution of the Monasteries, stood on the site

Minorites, or **Minors**. *See* FRANCISCANS.

Minos (mī' nos). A legendary king and lawgiver of Crete, made at death supreme judge of the lower world, before whom all the dead appeared to give an account of their stewardship, and to receive the reward of their deeds. He was the husband of Pasiphæ and the owner of the labyrinth constructed by Dædalus. From his name we have the adjective *Minoan*, pertaining to Crete the *Minoan period* is the Cretan bronze age, roughly about 2500-1200 B C

Minotaur (min' ô tôr) A mythical monster with the head of a bull and the body of a man, fabled to have been the offspring of Pasiphæ and a bull that was sent to her by Poseidon Minos kept it in his labyrinth and fed it on human flesh, 7 youths and 7 maidens being sent as tribute from Athens every year for the purpose Theseus slew this monster

Minstrel. Originally, one who had some official duty to perform (Lat. *ministerialis*), but quite early in the Middle Ages restricted to one whose duty it was to entertain his employer with music, story-telling, juggling, etc., hence a travelling gleeman and entertainer

Mint. The name of the herb is from Lat *menth* (Gr *mintha*), so called from Minthe, daughter of Cocytus, and a favourite of Pluto This nymph was metamorphosed by Pluto's wife (Proserpine) out of jealousy, into the herb called after her name The fable means that mint is a capital medicine. Minthe was a favourite of Pluto, or death, that is, was sick and on the point of death; but was changed into the herb mint, that is, was cured thereby.
Could Pluto's queen, with jealous fury storm
And Minthe to a fragrant herb transform? OVID

Mint sling. A mixed drink found in the U S A as early as 1804

The **Mint**, a place where money is coined, gets its name from A S *mynet*, representing Lat. *moneta*, money

Minute. A minute of time (one-sixtieth part of an hour) is so called from the mediæval Latin *pars munuta prima*, which, in the old system of sexagesimal fractions, denoted *one-sixtieth* part of the unit In the same way, in Geometry, etc , a minute is *one-sixtieth* part of a degree

A **minute** of a speech, meeting, etc , is a rough draft taken down in *minute* or small writing, to be afterwards *engrossed*, or written larger It is from the Fr. *minute*.

Minute gun. A signal of distress at sea, or a gun fired at the death of a distinguished individual; so called because a minute elapses between the discharges

Minute-men. Men who are ready to turn out and fight at a minute's notice The expression was first generally used in connexion with the Connecticut farmers who fought against the British in 1775.

Minute (mī nūt'), from the same Latin word, describes something very small

Miocene (mī' ô sēn). The geological period immediately preceding the Pliocene, when the mastodon, dinotherium, protohippus and other creatures flourished.

Miramolin. The title in the Middle Ages of the Emperor of Morocco.

Mirror Alasnam's mirror. The "touchstone of virtue," showed if the lady beloved was chaste as well as beautiful. (*Arabian Nights, Prince Zeyn Alasnam*)

Cambuscan's mirror. Sent to Cambuscan by the King of Araby and Ind, it warned of the approach of ill fortune, and told if love was returned (Chaucer *Canterbury Tales; The Squire's Tale*)

Lao's mirror reflected the mind and its thoughts, as an ordinary mirror reflects the outward seeming (Goldsmith *Citizen of the World*, xlv)

Merlin's magic mirror, given by Merlin to King Ryence It informed the king of treason, secret plots, and projected invasions. (Spenser *Faerie Queene*, iii, 2)

Reynard's wonderful mirror. This mirror existed only in the brain of Master Fox; he told the queen lion that whoever looked in it could see what was done a mile off The wood of the frame was not subject to decay, being made of the same block as King Crampart's magic horse (*Reynard the Fox*, ch xii)

Vulcan's mirror showed the past, the present, and the future Sir John Davies tells us that Cupid gave it to Antinous, and Antinous gave it to Penelope, who saw therein "the court of Queen Elizabeth."

The Mirror for Magistrates. A large collection of poems, published 1555-59, by William Baldwin, George Ferrers, and many others, with an "Induction" (1563) by Thomas Sackville. It contained in metrical form biographical accounts of the Falls of Princes. It was much extended in four later editions up to 1587

The Mirror of Human Salvation. *See* SPECULUM, etc

The Mirror of Knighthood. One of the books in Don Quixote's library, a Spanish romance (*Cavallero del Febo*, "The Knight of the Sun"), one of the Amadis group It was at one time very popular

The barber, taking another book, said, "This is the *Mirror of Knighthood*"—Pt. 1, bk i, 6.

Butler calls *Hudibras* "the Mirror of Knighthood" (bk 1, 15).

Mirza (mër′ zà) (Pers , royal prince). The term is used in two ways by the Persians; when *prefixed* to a surname it is simply a title of honour. but when *annexed* to the surname, it means a prince of the blood royal.

Miscreant means a false believer. (Fr , *mis-créance*) A term first applied to the Mohammedans, who, in return, call Christians *infidels*, and associate with the word all that we mean by "miscreants "

Mise (mēz) (O Fr., expenses), means an honorarium, especially that given by the people of Wales to a new Prince of Wales on his entrance upon his principality, or by the people of the county palatine of Chester on change of an Earl (the Prince of Wales is Earl of Chester) At Chester a misc-book is kept, in which every town and village is rated to this honorarium

Littleton (*Dict*) says the usual sum is £500.

Mise en scène (Fr., setting on stage). The stage setting of a play, including the scenery, properties, etc , and the general arrangement of the piece Also used metaphorically

Misère (mi zâr′) (Fr , misery, poverty) In solo whist and some other card games the declaration made when the caller undertakes to lose every trick.

Miserere (miz e rē′ re). The fifty-first psalm is so called because its opening words are *Miserere mei Deus* (Have mercy upon me, O God *See* NECK-VERSE). One of the evening services of Lent is called *miserere*, because this penitential psalm is sung, after which a sermon is delivered The under side of a folding seat in choir-stalls is called a *miserere*, or, more properly, a *misericord*, when turned up it forms a ledge-seat sufficient to rest the aged in a kneeling position.

Misers. The most renowned are·—

Baron Aguilar or Ephraim Lopes Pereira d'Aguilar (1740-1802), born at Vienna and died at Islington, worth £200,000.

Daniel Dancer (1716-94) His sister lived with him, and was a similar character, but died before him, and he left his wealth to the widow of Sir Henry Tempest, who nursed him in his last illness.

Sir Harvey Elwes, who died worth £250,000, but never spent more than £110 a year. His sister-in-law inherited £100,000, but actually starved herself to death, and her son *John* (1714-89), M P., an eminent brewer in Southwark, never bought any clothes, never suffered his shoes to be cleaned, and grudged every penny spent in food

Thomas Guy, founder of Guy's Hospital (*q v*).

William Jennings (1701-97), a neighbour and friend of Elwes, died worth £200,000 *See* HARPAGON.

Mishna (mish′ nà) (Heb , repetition or instruction). The collection of moral precepts, traditions, etc , forming the basis of the Talmud, the second or oral law (*see* GEMARA) It is divided into six parts (1) agriculture, (2) Sabbaths, fasts, and festivals, (3) marriage and divorce; (4) civil and penal laws, (5) sacrifices, (6) holy persons and things

Misnomers In English nomenclature we have many words and short phrases that can be called "misnomers", some of these have arisen through pure ignorance (and when once a useful word has been adopted and taken to our bosoms nothing—not even conviction of etymological errors—will eradicate it), some through confusion of ideas or the taking of one thing for another, and some through the changes that time brings about. *Catgut*, for instance, was in all probability, at one time made from the intestines of a *cat*, and now that sheep, horses, asses, etc., but never *cats*, are used for the purpose the name still remains

A large number of these "misnomers" will be found scattered throughout this book (*see especially* CLEOPATRA'S NEEDLE, GERMAN SILVER, HONEYDEW, HUMBLE PIE, INDIANS (AMERICAN), JERUSALEM ARTICHOKE, MEERSCHAUM, MOTHER OF PEARL, POMPEY'S PILLAR, SAND-BLIND, SLUG-HORN, VENTRILOQUISM, WOLF'S-BANE, and WORMWOOD); and we give a few more below.—

Black beetles are neither black nor beetles; their alternative name, *cockroach*, is from the Span *cucaracha*

Blacklead is plumbago or graphite, a form of carbon, and has no lead in its composition. *See under* LEAD.

Blind worms are no more blind than *moles* are, they have very quick and brilliant eyes, though somewhat small

Brazilian grass does not come from Brazil or even grow in Brazil, nor is it a grass. It consists of strips of a palm-leaf (*Chamærops argentea*), and is chiefly imported from Cuba.

Burgundy pitch is not pitch, nor is it manufactured or exported from Burgundy. The best is a resinous substance prepared from common frankincense, and brought from Hamburg but by far the larger quantity is a mixture of resin and palm oil

China, as a name for porcelain, gives rise to the contradictory expressions British china, Sèvres china, Dresden china, Dutch china, Chelsea china, etc ; like wooden or iron mile-stones, brass shoe-horns, coppers for our bronze coinage, etc.

Dutch clocks are not of Dutch but German (*Deutsch*) manufacture

Elements. Fire, air, earth, and water, still often called "the four elements," are not elements at all.

Forlorn hope (*q.v.*) is not etymologically connected with *hope*, though the term is usually employed in connexion with almost hopeless enterprises. The actual derivation is the Dutch *verloren houp*, a lost troop.

Galvanized iron is not galvanized It is simply iron coated with zinc, and this is done by dipping the iron into molten zinc.

Guernsey lily (*Nerine* or *Imbrofia sarniensis*) is not a native of Guernsey but of Japan and South Africa. It was discovered by Kæmpfer in Japan, and the ship which was bringing specimens of the new plant to Europe was wrecked on the coast of Guernsey: some of the bulbs that were washed ashore took root and germinated, hence the misnomer

Guinea-pigs (*q v*) have no connexion with the pig family, nor do they come from Guinea.

Honeysuckle So named because of the old but entirely erroneous idea that bees extracted honey therefrom The honeysuckle is useless to the bee.

Indian ink comes from China, not from India.

Rice paper is not made from rice, but from the pith of the Formosan plant, *Aralia papyrifera*, or hollow plant, so called because it is hollow when the pith has been pushed out

Running the gauntlet (see GAUNTLET) has nothing to do with gauntlets (gloves), though these may be used in the process.

Salt of lemon is in reality potassium acid oxalate, or potassium quadroxalate

Silver paper, in which chocolates, etc., are sometimes wrapped, is not, of course, made from silver. It is usually composed of tin-foil

Slow-worm Not so called because it is *slow*; the first syllable is corrupted from *slay* and it was called the *slay-worm* (= serpent) from the idea that this perfectly harmless creature was venomous

Titmouse. Nothing to do with *mouse*, though the erroneous plural *titmice*—has now probably come to stay The second syllable represents A.S. *mase*, used of several small birds. *Tit* is Scandinavian, and also implies "small," as in *titbit*

Tonquin beans. A geographical blunder, for they are the seeds, the *Dipteryx odorata*, from Tonka, in Guiana, not Tonquin, in Asia

Turkeys do not come from Turkey, but North America, through Spain, or India. The French call them "dindon," i e. *d'Inde* or *coq d'Inde*, a term equally incorrect

Turkey rhubarb neither grows in Turkey, nor is it imported from Turkey. It grows in the great mountain chain between Tartary and Siberia, and is a Russian monopoly

Turkish baths are not of Turkish origin though they were introduced from the Near East, popularly associated with Turkish rule and customs. The correct name of Hammam was commonly used in England in the 17th century, and for many years there was a Hummum's Hotel in Covent Garden on the site of a 17th-century Turkish Bath

Whalebone is no bone at all, nor does it possess any properties of bone It is a substance attached to the upper jaw of the whale, and serves to strain the algæ and small life from the water which the creature takes up in large mouthfuls.

Misprision. (Fr *mépris*) Concealment, neglect of; in law, an offence bordering on a capital offence

Misprision of felony. Neglecting to reveal a felony when known.

Misprision of treason Neglecting to' disclose or purposely concealing a treasonable design

Misrule, Feast of. *See* KING OF MISRULE

Miss, Mistress, Mrs (masteress, lady-master) Miss used to be written Mis, and is the first syllable of Mistress, Mrs is the contraction of *mistress*, called Mis'ess. So late as the reign of George II unmarried women used to be styled Mrs., as, Mrs Lepel, Mrs Bellenden, Mrs. Blount, all unmarried women. (*See* Pope's *Letters*)

Mistress was originally an honourable term for a sweetheart or lover—"Mistress mine, where are you roaming" It has since come to mean a woman who lives with a man as his wife but without being so

Mistress Roper. The Marines, or any one of them; so called by the regular sailors, because they handle the ropes as unhandily as girls.

The mistress of the night. The tuberose is so called because it emits its strongest fragrance after sunset

In the language of flowers, the tuberose signifies "the pleasures of love "

The mistress of the world. Ancient Rome was so called, because all the known world gave her allegiance.

To kiss the mistress. To make a good hit, to shoot right into the eye of the target; in bowls to graze another bowl with your own; the *Jack* used to be called the "mistress," and when one ball just touches another it is said "to kiss it "

Rub on, and kiss the mistress.—*Troilus and Cres-sida*, iii, 2.

Miss To fail to hit, or—in such phrases as I miss you now you are gone—to lack, to feel the want of

A miss is as good as a mile. A failure is a failure be it ever so little, and is no more be it ever so great, a narrow escape is an escape. An old form of the phrase was *An inch in a miss is as good as an ell.*

The missing link. A popular term for the hypothetical being that is supposed, according to the theory of evolution, to bridge the gap between man and the anthropoid apes Haeckel held it to be *Pithecanthropus erectus*; but scientists are not agreed, either on this or on the number of "missing links" there may be Professor Woodward, in a lecture on the Rhodesian skull discovered at Broken Hill in 1921, said—

The Rhodesian man was one of the links in the chain of which many species would be found It would be a long time before a connecting series of missing links would be discovered which would be convincing

Mississippi Bubble. The French "South Sea Scheme," and equally disastrous It was projected by the Scots financier, John Law (1671-1729), and had for its object the payment of the National Debt of France, which amounted to 208 millions sterling, on being granted the exclusive trade of Louisiana, on the banks of the Mississippi Inaugurated in 1717, it was taken up by the French Government, and in 1719 the shares were selling at forty times their original value But in 1720 the "bubble" burst, France was almost ruined, Law fled to Russia, and his estates were confiscated.

Missouri (mis oo′ ri, ra miz oo′). **I'm from Missouri** is equivalent to "I'm hard-headed and you have to show me" or "I won't believe anything without proof." First used in a speech in 1899 by Willard D. Vandiver, Congressman from Missouri

Missouri Compromise. An arrangement whereby Missouri was in 1820 admitted to the Union as a Slave State, but that at the same time there should be no slavery in the state north of 36° 30′.

Mistletoe (mis′ él tō) (A S *mistiltan*; *mist*, being both basil and mistletoe, and *tan*, a twig) The plant grows as a parasite on various trees, especially the apple tree, and was held in great veneration by the Druids when found on the oak Shakespeare calls it "the *baleful* mistletoe" (*Titus Andronicus*, ii, 3), perhaps in allusion to the Scandinavian legend that it was with an arrow made of mistletoe that Balder (*q v.*) was slain, but probably with reference either to the popular but erroneous notion that mistletoe berries are poisonous, or to the connexion of the plant with the human sacrifices of the Druids It is in all probability for this latter reason that mistletoe is rigorously excluded from church decorations

Kissing under the mistletoe. An English Christmas-time custom, dating back at least to the early 17th century The correct procedure, now rarely observed, is that as the young man kisses a girl under the mistletoe he should pluck a berry, and that when the last berry is gone there should be no more kissing

The Mistletoe Bough. This old song is about the daughter of a Lord Lovel who, on her wedding-day, was playing at hide and seek, and selected an old oak chest for her hiding-place The chest closed with a spring lock, and many years later her skeleton was discovered

Marwell Old Hall, once the residence of the Seymours and afterwards of the Dacre family, has a similar tradition attached to it.

Mistpoeffers. *See* BARISAL GUNS.

Mistral, The. A violent north-west wind blowing down the Gulf of Lyons; felt particularly at Marseilles and the south-east of France.

Mistress. *See* MISS.

Mithra or **Mithras** (mith′ ra). The god of light of the ancient Persians, one of their chief deities, and the ruler of the universe Sometimes used as a synonym for the sun. The word means *friend*, and this deity is so called because he befriends man in this life, and protects him against evil spirits after death. He is represented as a young man with a Phrygian cap, a tunic, a mantle on his left shoulder, and plunging a sword into the neck of a bull (*see Thebais*, i). The Mithraic rites—

have been maintained by a constant tradition, with their penances and tests of the courage of the candidate for admission, through the Secret Societies of the Middle Ages and the Rosicrucians, down to the modern faint reflex of the latter, the Freemasons — KNIGHT: *Symbolical Language*

Sir Thomas More called the Supreme Being of his *Utopia* "Mithra."

Mithridate (mith′ ri dāt). A confection named from Mithridates IV, King of Pontus and Bithynia (d about 63 B C), who is said to have made himself immune from poisons by the constant use of antidotes It was supposed to be an antidote to poison, and contained seventy-two ingredients.

What brave spirit could be content to sit in his shop selling Mithridatum and dragon's water to infected houses?—BEAUMONT AND FLETCHER: *Knight of the Burning Pestle* (1608).

Mitre (mi′ ter) (Gr. and Lat *mitra*, a head-band, turban) The episcopal mitre symbolizes the cloven tongues of fire which descended on the apostles on the day of Pentecost (*Acts* ii, 1-12) Dean Stanley tells us that the cleft represents the crease made when the mitre is folded and carried under the arm, like an opera hat.

The Mitre Tavern. A place of resort in the time of Shakespeare, it was in Mitre Court, leading south of Cheapside, and was in existence from before 1475 till the Great Fire (1666), when it was destroyed and not rebuilt There are several other taverns of the same name in London (*see* Barrey's *Ram Alley*, v 1611)

Mitten. To give one the mitten. To reject a sweetheart; to jilt Possibly with punning allusion to Lat *mitto*, to send (about your business), whence dismissal, to get your dismissal.

There is a young lady I have set my heart on, though whether she is going to give me hern, or give me the mitten I ain't quite satisfied —SAM SLICK *Human Nature*, p 90

Mittimus (mit′ i mus) (Lat., we send) A command in writing to a jailer, to keep the person named in safe custody. Also a writ for removing a record from one court to another. So called from the first word of the writ

Mitton. The Chapter of Mitton. So the battle of Mitton was called, because so many priests took part therein It was fought in 1319, and the Scots defeated the forces of the Archbishop of York

Mizentop, maintop, foretop. A "top" is a platform fixed over the head of a lower mast, resting on the trestle-trees, to spread the rigging of the topmast The mizenmast is the aftermost mast of a ship; the foremast is in the forward part of a ship, the mainmast is between these two

He was put into the mizentop, and served three years in the West Indies, then he was transferred to the maintop, and served five years in the Mediterranean, and then he was made captain of the foretop, and served six years in the East Indies, and at last he was rated captain's coxswain in the *Druid* frigate — CAPT MARRYAT *Poor Jack*, ch 1

Mnemonics (ne mon' iks) The art of improving the memory by artificial aids and methods Such methods usually depend on the association of ideas and are chiefly based on the principles of localization and analogy. The word comes from the Greek *mnemonikos*, of memory

Mnemosyne (ne mos' i ni). Goddess of memory and mother by Zeus of the nine Muses of Greek mythology. She was the daughter of Heaven and Earth (Uranus and Ge).

To the Immortals every one
A portion was assigned of all that is;
But chief Mnemosyne did Maia's son
Clothe in the light of his loud melodies
SHELLEY *Homer's Hymn to Mercury*, lxxiu

Moabite Stone, The. An ancient *stele*, bearing the oldest extant Semitic inscription, now in the Louvre, Paris The inscription, consisting of thirty-four lines in Hebrew-Phœnician characters, gives an account of the war of Mesha, King of Moab, who reigned about 850 B C, against Omri, Ahab, and other kings of Israel (*see* 2 *Kings*, iii) Mesha sacrificed his eldest son on the city wall in view of the invading Israelites The stone was discovered by F. Klein at Dibhan in 1868, and is 3 ft. 10 in. high, 2 ft broad and 14½ in thick. The Arabs resented its removal, and splintered it into fragments, but it has been restored.

Moaning Minnie. World War II term for a six-barrelled German mortar, so named from the rising shriek it gave when the six projectiles were simultaneously released The name was also given popularly to the air-raid warning siren.

Mob. A contraction of the Latin *mobile vulgus* (the fickle crowd) The term was first applied to the people by the members of the Green-ribbon Club, in the reign of Charles II (*Northern Examiner*, p 574)
In subsequent years the word was applied to an organized criminal gang.

Mob-cap. A cap worn indoors by women and useful for concealing hair that is not yet "done." It was formerly called *mab-cap*, from the old verb *mab*, to dress untidily

Mock. Mock-beggar Hall or **Manor.** A grand, ostentatious house, where no hospitality is afforded. neither is any charity given

No times observed, nor charitable lawes,
The poor receive their answer from the dawes
Who, in their cawing language, call it plaine
Mock-beggar Manour, for they come in vaine
TAYLOR *The Water Cormorant* (1622)

Mockery. "It will be a delusion, a mockery, and a snare." Thomas, Lord Denman, observed this in his judgment on the case of The Queen *v* O'Connell (1844)

Mock-up. Phrase originating in World War II for a model or any full-size working model. (2) American phrase for panels mounted with models of aircraft parts used by the A A F. for instructional purposes

Modality, in scholastic philosophy, means the *mode* in which anything exists Kant divides our judgment into three modalities: (1) *Problematic*, touching possible events, (2) *Assertoric*, touching real events, (3) *Apodictic*, touching necessary events

Modernism. A movement in the Catholic Church which sought to interpret the ancient teachings of the Church in the light of the scientific knowledge of modern times It was condemned by Pope Pius X in 1907 in the encyclical *Pascendi*, which stigmatized it as the "synthesis of all heresies."

Modred. One of the Knights of the Round Table in Arthurian romance, nephew and betrayer of King Arthur. He is represented as the treacherous knight He revolted from the king, whose wife he seduced, was mortally wounded in the battle of Camlan, in Cornwall, and was buried in the island of Avalon. The story is told, with a variation, in Tennyson's *Guinevere* (*Idylls of the King*).

Mods. In Oxford a contracted form of moderations The three necessary examinations in Oxford are the Smalls, the Mods, and the Greats. No one can take a class till he has passed the Mods.

Modus operandi (Lat) The mode of operation; the way in which a thing is done or should be done **Modus vivendi** (Lat, way of living). A mutual arrangement whereby persons not at the time being on friendly terms can be induced to live together in harmony The term may be applied to individuals, to societies, or to peoples

Mofussil (East Indies) The subordinate divisions of a district; the rural divisions of a district, the rural districts as apart from the chief city or seat of government, which is called the *sudder*, provincial

To tell a man that fatal charges have been laid against him, and refuse him an opportunity for explanation, this is not even Mofussil justice —*The Times*

Mogul (mō' gŭl) **The Mogul Empire.** The Mohammedan-Tartar Empire in India which began in 1526 with Baber, great-grandson of Timur, or Tamerlane, and split up after the death of Aurungzebe in 1707, the power passing to the British and the Mahrattas The Emperor was known as the *Great* or *Grand Mogul*, besides those mentioned, Akbar, Jahangir, and Shah Jehan are the most noteworthy.

Mogul cards. The best-quality playing-cards were so called because the wrapper, or the "duty-card" (cards are subject to excise duty) was decorated with a representation of the

Great Mogul Inferior cards were called "Harrys," "Highlanders," and "Merry Andrews" for a similar reason.

Mohair (mō'hâr) (Probably the Arabic *mukhayyar*, goat's-hair cloth) It is the hair of the Angora goat, introduced into Spain by the Moors, and thence brought into Germany.

Mohammed, Mahomet (Arab , "the praised one"). The titular name of the founder of Islam (*q v*), or Mohammedanism (born at Mecca about 570, died at Medina, 632), which was adopted by him about the time of the Hegira to apply to himself the Messianic prophecies in the Old Testament (*Haggai* ii, 7, and elsewhere) His original name is given both as Kotham and Halabi

Angel of When Mohammed was transported to heaven, he says "I saw there an angel, the most gigantic of all created beings It had 70,000 heads, each had 70,000 faces, each face had 70,000 mouths, each mouth had 70,000 tongues, and each tongue spoke 70,000 languages, all were employed in singing God's praises " This must not, of course, be taken as a definition of belief, but as a mode of Oriental emphasis

Banner of Sanjaksherif, kept in the Eyab mosque, at Constantinople

Bible of The Koran.

Camel (swiftest) Adha

Cave The cave in which Gabriel appeared to Mohammed (610) was in the mountain of Hirâ, near Mecca

Coffin Legend used to have it that Mohammed's coffin is suspended in mid-air at Medina without any support

> Sp'ritual men are too transcendent . . .
> To hang, like Mahomet, in the air,
> Or St. Ignatius at his prayer,
> By pure geometry
> BUTLER. *Hudibras*, III, ii, 602.

Daughter (favourite) Fatima

Dove Mohammed had a dove which he fed with wheat out of his ear When it was hungry it used to light on the prophet's shoulder, and thrust its bill into his ear to find its meal. Mohammed thus induced the Arabs to believe that he was divinely inspired.

> Was Mahomet inspired with a dove?
> 1 *Henry VI*, i, 2

Father Abdallah, of the tribe of Koreish He died a little before or a little after the birth of Mohammed

Father-in-law (father of Ayesha), Abu-Bekr He succeeded Mohammed and was the first calif

Flight from Mecca (called the Hegira), A D 622 He retired to Medina

Hegira See above, Flight.

Horse Al Borak (*The Lightning*). It conveyed the prophet to the seventh heaven.

Miracles Several are traditionally mentioned, but many of the True Believers hold that he performed no miracle That of the moon is best known

Habib the Wise asked Mohammed to prove his mission by cleaving the moon in two Mohammed raised his hands towards heaven, and in a loud voice summoned the moon to do Habib's bidding Accordingly, it descended to the top of the Kaaba (*q v*), made seven circuits, and, coming to the prophet, entered

his right sleeve and came out of the left. It then entered the collar of his robe, and descended to the skirt, clove itself into two parts, one of which appeared in the east of the skies and the other in the west, and the two parts ultimately reunited and resumed their usual form

Mother of Amina, of the tribe of Koreish. She died when Mohammed was six years old.

Paradise of The ten animals admitted to the Moslem's paradise are —

(1) The dog Kratim, which accompanied the Seven Sleepers

(2) Balaam's ass, which spoke with the voice of a man to reprove the disobedient prophet

(3) Solomon's ant, of which he said, "Go to the ant, thou sluggard   "

(4) Jonah's whale

(5) The ram caught in the thicket, and offered in sacrifice in lieu of Isaac.

(6) The calf of Abraham.

(7) The camel of Saleh.

(8) The cuckoo of Bilkis

(9) The ox of Moses

(10) Mohammed's horse, Al Borak.

Stepping-stone The stone upon which the prophet placed his foot when he mounted Al Borak on his ascent to heaven. It rose as the beast rose, but Mohammed, putting his hand upon it, forbade it to follow him, whereupon it remained suspended in mid-air, where the True Believer, if he has faith enough, may still behold it

Tribe. On both sides, the Koreish.

Uncle, who took charge of Mohammed at the death of his grandfather, Abu Tâlib.

Wives. Ten in number, viz (1) Kadija, a rich widow of the tribe of Koreish, who had been twice married already, and was forty years of age For twenty-five years she was his only wife, but at her death he married nine others, all of whom survived him

The nine wives. (1) Ayesha, daughter of Abu Bekr, only nine years old on her wedding-day. This was his youngest and favourite wife

(2) Sauda, widow of Sokram, and nurse to his daughter Fatima

(3) Hafsa, a widow twenty-eight years old, who also had a son She was daughter of Omeya.

(4) Zeinab, wife of Zaid, but divorced in order that the prophet might take her to wife.

(5) Barra, wife of a young Arab and daughter of Al Hareth, chief of an Arab tribe. She was a captive

(6) Rehana, daughter of Simeon, and a Jewish captive

(7) Safiya, the espoused wife of Kenana Kenana was put to death. Safiya outlived the prophet forty years

(8) Omm Habiba—*i e.* mother of Habiba; the widow of Abu Sofian

(9) Maimuna, fifty-one years old, and a widow, who survived all his other wives

Also ten or fifteen concubines, chief of whom was Mariyeh, mother of Ibrahim, the prophet's only son, who died when fifteen months old.

Year of Deputations A D 630, the 8th of the Hegira.

If the mountain will not come to Mohammed, Mohammed must go to the mountain. When

Mohammed introduced his system to the Arabs, they asked for miraculous proofs. He then ordered Mount Safa to come to him, and as it did not move, he said, "God is merciful. Had it obeyed my words, it would have fallen on us to our destruction I will therefore go to the mountain, and thank God that He has had mercy on a stiffnecked generation." The phrase is often used of one who, not being able to get his own way, bows before the inevitable.

Mohocks (mō' hocks) A class of ruffians who in the 18th century, infested the streets of London. So called from the Indian Mohawks One of their "new inventions" was to roll persons down Snow Hill in a tub, another was to overturn coaches on rubbish-heaps (*See* Gay: *Trivia*, iii)
A vivid picture of the misdoings in the streets of London by these and other brawlers is given in *The Spectator*, No 324
> You sent your Mohocks next abroad,
> With razors armed, and knives;
> Who on night-walkers made inroad,
> And scared our maids and wives;
> They scared the watch, and windows broke . .
> *Plot upon Plot* (about 1713)

Moira. Fate, or Necessity, supreme even over the gods of Olympus.

Molinism (mol' i nizm) The system of grace and election taught by Louis Molina, the Spanish Jesuit (1535-1600)
> The Pope's great self—Innocent by name .
> 'Twas he who first bade leave those souls in peace
> Those Jansenists, renicknamed Molinists
> "Leave them alone," bade he, "those Molinists!
> Who may have other light than we perceive,
> Or why is it the whole world hates them thus?'"
> BROWNING *The Ring and the Book*, I, 300-17

His doctrine was that grace is a free gift to all, but that the consent of the will must be present before that grace can be effective

Moll, Molly. Moll Cutpurse. *See* CUTPURSE.

Take away this bottle, it has Moll Thomson's mark on it. Moll Thomson is M.T. (*empty*).

Molly coddle. A pampered creature, afraid that the winds of heaven should visit him too roughly.

Molly Maguires. An Irish secret society organized in 1843. Stout, active young Irishmen dressed up in women's clothes and otherwise disguised themselves to surprise those employed to enforce the payment of rents. Their victims were ducked in bog-holes, and many were beaten most unmercifully
A similar secret society in the mining districts of Pennsylvania was (about 1877) known by the same name.
> The judge who tried the murderer was elected by the Molly Maguires, the jurors who assisted him were themselves Molly Maguires A score of Molly Maguires came forward to swear that the assassin was sixty miles from the spot on which he had been seen to fire at William Dunn . . and the jurors returned a verdict of Not Guilty —W HEPWORTH DIXON *New America*, ii, 28

Molly Mog. This celebrated beauty was an innkeeper's daughter, at Oakingham, Berks She was the toast of the gay sparks of the first half of the 18th century, and died unmarried in 1766, at the age of sixty-seven Gay has a ballad on this *Fair Maid of the Inn*, in which

the "swain" alluded to is Mr Standen, of Arborfield, who died in 1730 It is said that Molly's sister Sally was the greater beauty A portrait of Gay still hangs in the inn

Molmutius or **Mulmutius.** *See* MULMUTINE LAWS

Moloch (mō' lok) Any influence which demands from us the sacrifice of what we hold most dear Thus, *war* is a Moloch, *king mob* is a Moloch, the *guillotine* was the Moloch of the French Revolution, etc The allusion is to the god of the Ammonites, to whom children were "made to pass through the fire" in sacrifice (*see* 2 *Kings*, xxiii, 10) Milton says he was worshipped in Rabba, in Argob, and Basan, to the stream of utmost Arnon (*Paradise Lost*, i, 392-398)

Molloch, May, or **The Maid of the Hairy Arms** An elf of folklore who mingles in ordinary sports, and will even direct the master of the house how to play dominoes or draughts Like the White Lady of Avenel, May Molloch is a sort of banshee

Molotov. The name of Vyacheslav Mikhailovich Molotov, the Russian diplomat, was adopted in World War II in several ways —

Molotov breadbasket. A canister of incendiary bombs which, on being launched from a plane, opened and showered the bombs over a wide area.

Molotov cocktail. A home-made anti-tank bomb, invented and first used by the Finns against the Russians (1940) and developed in England as one of the weapons of the Home Guard. It consisted of a bottle filled with inflammable and glutinous liquid, with a slow match protruding from the top. When thrown at a tank the bottle burst, the liquid ignited and spread over the plating of the tank

Moly (mō' li). The mythical herb given, according to Homer, by Hermes to Ulysses as an antidote against the sorceries of Circe.
> Black was the root, but milky white the flower,
> Moly the name, to mortals hard to find
> *Pope's Odyssey*, x, 365.
> That moly
> That Hermes once to wise Ulysses gave
> MILTON *Comus*, 655

The name is given to a number of plants, especially of the *Allium* (garlic) family, as the wild garlic, the Indian moly, the moly of Hungary, serpents moly, the yellow moly, Spanish purple moly, Spanish silver-capped moly, and Dioscorides' moly
They all flower in May, except "the sweet moly of Montpelier," which blossoms in September.

Momus (mō' mus) One who carps at everything. Momus, the sleepy god of the Greeks, son of Nox (Night), was always railing and carping.
> Momus, being asked to pass judgment on the relative merits of Neptune, Vulcan, and Minerva, railed at them all He said the horns of a bull ought to have been placed in the shoulders, where they would have been of much greater force, as for man, he said Jupiter ought to have made him with a window in his breast, whereby his real thoughts might be revealed.
Hence Byron's—
> Were Momus' lattice in our breasts .
> *Werner*, iii, 1.

Monday. The second day of the week; called by the Anglo-Saxons Monandæg, i e. the day of the Moon

That Monday feeling. Disinclination to return to work after the week-end break.

Money. Shortly after the Gallic invasion of Rome, in 344 B C , Lucius Furius (or according to other accounts, Camillus), built a temple to Juno Moneta (the *Monitress*) on the spot where the house of Manlius Capitolinus stood, and to this temple was attached the first Roman mint, as to the temple of Saturn was attached the *aerarium* (public treasury) Hence the "ases" there coined were called *moneta*, and hence our word *money*

Juno is represented on medals with instruments of coinage, as the hammer, anvil, pincers, and die *See Livy*, vii, 28, and Cicero, *De Divinitate*, i, 15

The oldest coin of Greece bore the impress of an ox Hence a bribe for silence was said to be an "ox on the tongue" Subsequently each province had its own impress —

Athens, an owl (the bird of wisdom)
Bœotia, Bacchus (the vineyard of Greece).
Delphos, a dolphin.
Macedonia, a buckler (from its love of war).
Rhodes, the disc of the sun (the Colossus was an image to the sun)

Rome had a different impress for each coin —

For the *As*, the head of Janus on one side, and the prow of a ship on the reverse
The *Semi-as*, the head of Jupiter and the letter S
The *Sextans*, the head of Mercury, and two points to denote two ounces.
The *Triens*, the head of a woman (? Rome or Minerva) and three points to denote three ounces.
The *Quadrans*, the head of Hercules, and four points to denote four ounces.

In every country there are familiar phrases and words for the more commonly used coins and sums of money. The most usual are.—

A bawbee in Scotland means a halfpenny and is applied to money generally In England·

1d A copper
4d When there was a coin for this sum it was often called a joey
6d A tanner, a tizzy.
1s A bob.
2s. A florin
2s. 6d. Half a crown, half a dollar, two and a kick.
5s A crown, a cartwheel
20s A quid, a sovereign (esp the gold coin), a jimmy o'goblin, thick 'un.
21s A guinea
£5. A fiver
£10 A tenner.
£25. A pony.
£500 A monkey

In North America —

1c. A penny, a Red Indian
5c A nickel.
10c A dime
25c A quarter, two bits
50c Four bits
$1 00 A buck (In silver, a cartwheel, or a smacker.)
$10 00 A sawbuck.
$100 00 A century
$1000,00 A grand, a G.

Money makes the mare to go. *See* MARE

Money of account is a monetary denomination used in reckoning and often not employed as actual coin For example, a guinea is in Britain money of account, though no coin of this value is in circulation. The U S A mill, being one-thousandth of a dollar or one-tenth of a cent is money of account

Money for old rope, or money for jam An easy job, yielding extravagant reward for very little expenditure of effort.

Mongrel Parliament. The Parliament that met at Oxford in 1681 and passed the Exclusion Bill

Monism (mō′ nizm). The doctrine of the oneness of mind and matter, God and the universe. It ignores all that is supernatural, any dualism of mind and matter, God and creation: and there can be no opposition between God and the world, as unity cannot be in opposition to itself Monism teaches that "all are but parts of one stupendous whole, whose body nature is, and God the soul", hence, whatever is, only conforms to the cosmical laws of the universal ALL.

Haeckel explained it thus in 1866 "Monism (the correlative of Dualism) denotes a unitary conception, in opposition to a supernatural one Mind can never exist without matter, nor matter without mind" As God is the same "yesterday, to-day, and for ever," creation must be the same, or God would not be unchangeable

Monitor. So the Romans called the nursery teacher. The *Military Monitor* was an officer to tell young soldiers of the faults committed against the service The *House Monitor* was a slave to call the family of a morning, etc

A shallow-draught ironclad with a flat deck, sharp stern, and one or more movable turrets, was so called They were first used in the American War of Secession, and were so named by the inventor, Captain Ericsson, because they were to be "severe monitors" to the leaders of the Southern rebellion.

The word is also used to designate a broadcasting official employed to listen in to foreign (esp enemy) radio transmissions in order to analyse the news announced and to study propaganda In normal circumstances the duties of a monitor include checking the quality of transmissions.

Monk. The word *monk* is often employed loosely and incorrectly for any religious living in community or belonging to an order In the Western Church only members of the following orders are monks: Benedictines, Cistercians, Carthusians, and four smaller orders Members of the great orders of Dominicans. Franciscans, Carmelites, and Augustinians are friars.

In printing, a black smear or blotch made by leaving too much ink on the part. Caxton set up his printing-press in the *scriptorium* of Westminster Abbey (*see* CHAPEL), and the association gave rise to the slang expressions *monk* and *friar* (q v.) for black and white defects.

Monk Lewis. Matthew Gregory Lewis (1775-1818) is so called from his highly coloured "Gothic" novel *Ambrosio, or the Monk* (1795)

Monkey. Slang for £500 or (in America) $500, also for a mortgage (sometimes extended to *a monkey with a long tail*), and among sailors the vessel which contains the full allowance of grog for one mess A child, especially an active, meddlesome one, is often called "a little monkey"—for obvious reasons.

Monkey's allowance. More kicks than halfpence The allusion is to the monkeys formerly carried about for show, they picked up the halfpence, but carried them to the master, who kept kicking or ill-treating the poor creatures to urge them to incessant tricks

Monkey board In the old-fashioned horsed knifeboard omnibuses, the step on which the conductor stood, and on which he often skipped about like a monkey.

Monkey jacket. A short coat worn by seamen, so called because it has "no more tail than a monkey," or, more strictly speaking, an ape

Monkey puzzle. The Chilean pine, *Araucaria imbricata*, whose twisted and prickly branches puzzle even a monkey to climb.

Monkey spoons. Spoons having on the handle a heart surmounted by a monkey, at one time given in Holland at marriages, christenings, and funerals At weddings they were given to some immediate relative of the bride; at christenings and funerals to the officiating clergyman Among the Dutch, drinking is called "sucking the monkey," because the early morning appetizer of rum and salt was taken in a monkey spoon

Monkey tricks Mischievous, illnatured, or deceitful actions

To get one's monkey up. To be riled or enraged, monkeys are extremely irritable and easily provoked.

To monkey with or about. To tamper with or play mischievous tricks *To monkey with the cords* is to try to arrange them so that the deal will not be fair; *to monkey with the milk* is to add water to it and then sell it as pure and unadulterated

To pay in monkey's money (*en monnaie de singe*)—in goods, in personal work, in mumbling and grimace In Paris when a monkey passed the Petit Pont, if it was for sale four deniers' toll had to be paid; but if it belonged to a showman and was not for sale, it sufficed if the monkey went through his tricks

It was an original by Master Charles Charmois, principal painter to King Megistus, paid for in court fashion with monkey's money —RABELAIS *Gargantua and Pantagruel*, IV, 3

To suck the monkey. Sailor's slang for surreptitiously sucking liquor from a cask through a straw (*see* MONKEY, *above*); and when milk has been taken from a coconut, and rum has been substituted, "sucking the monkey" is drinking this rum.

What the vulgar call "sucking the monkey"
Has much less effect on a man when he's funky
    Ingoldsby Legends The Black Mousquetaire

Monkey suit, in the U S A services, is the term applied to full dress uniform, also to an aviator's overalls The phrase is often used for men's formal dress on important occasions

Monmouth. The town at the mouth of the Monnow, surname of Henry V of England, who was born there

Monmouth cap A soldier s cap
    The soldiers that the Monmouth wear,
    On castles' tops their ensigns rear
The best caps were formerly made at Monmouth, where the cappers' chapel doth still remain —FULLER *Worthies of Wales*, p 50

Monmouth Street (London) takes its name from the unfortunate son of Charles II, executed for rebellion in 1685 Later Dudley Street, St Giles, and now forming part of Shaftesbury Avenue close to Soho Square, where the Duke of Monmouth had his town house, it was formerly noted for its secondhand clothes shops, hence the expression *Monmouth Street finery* for tawdry, pretentious clothes.

[At the Venetian carnival] you may put on whate'er
    You like by way of doublet, cape, or cloak,
Such as in Monmouth-street, or in Rag Fair
Would rig you out in seriousness or joke
                        BYRON *Beppo*, V

Monongahela (mo nong' ga hē' la)   A river flowing into the Ohio at Pittsburgh, Pa , near which whisky is distilled. The term is sometimes applied to American whisky generally.

Monophysites (mo nof' i sitz) (Gr *monos phusis*, one nature) A religious sect in the Levant who maintained that Jesus Christ had only one nature, and that divine and human were combined in much the same way as the body and soul in man They arose upon the condemnation of the Eutychian heresy at the Council of Chalcedon, 451, and are still represented by the Coptic, Armenian, Abyssinian, and Jacobite Churches

Monotheism (mon' ō thē izm) (Gr. *monos theos*, one God) The doctrine that there is but one God

The only large monotheism known to historic times is that of Mahomet —GLADSTONE, in *Contemporary Review*, June, 1876

Monroe Doctrine (mùn rō'). The doctrine first promulgated in 1823 by James Monroe (President of the U S A , 1817-25), to the effect that the American States are never to entangle themselves in the broils of the Old World, nor to suffer it to interfere in the affairs of the New, and they are to account any attempt on the part of the Old World to plant their systems of government in any part of North America not at the time in European occupation dangerous to American peace and safety. The capture of Manila and the cession of the Philippine Islands to the United States in 1898, and still more the part the States took in the two World Wars has abrogated a large part of this famous Doctrine

Mons Meg. *See* MEG

Monsieur. The eldest brother of the king of France was formerly so called, especially Philippe, Duc d'Orléans, brother to Louis XIV (1640-1701)

Monsieur de Paris The public executioner or Jack Ketch of France

Riccardo de Albertes was a personal friend of all the "Messieurs de Paris," who served the Republic. He attended all capital executions —*Newspaper Paragraph*, January 25th, 1893

Monsieur le Grand. The Great Equerry of France

The Peace of Monsieur. The peace that the Huguenots, the Politiques, and the Duke d'Alençon ("Monsieur") obliged Henri III of France to sign in 1576 By it the Huguenots and the Duke gained great concessions.

Monsignor (mon sē' nyôr) (pl *monsignori*) A title pertaining to all prelates in the R.C Church, which includes all prelates of the Roman court, active or honorary Used with the surname, as Monsignor So-and-so it does away with the barbarism of speaking of Bishop So-and-so, which is as incorrect as calling the Duke of Marlborough 'Duke Churchill.'

Monsoon (Arab *mausim*, time, season) A periodical wind; especially that which blows off S W Asia and the Indian Ocean from the south-west from April to October, and from the north-east during the rest of the year

Mont (Fr , hill) The technical term in palmistry for the eminences at the roots of the fingers.

That at the root of the
  thumb is the Mont de Mars
  index finger is the Mont de Jupiter
  long finger is the Mont de Saturne.
  ring finger is the Mont de Soleil
  little finger is the Mont de Venus.
The one between the thumb and index finger is called the Mont de Mercure and the one opposite the Mont de Lune.

Mont de Piété. A pawnshop in France; first instituted as *monti di pieta* (charity loans) under Leo X (reigned 1513-21), at Rome, by charitable persons who wished to rescue the poor from usurious moneylenders. They advanced small sums of money on the security of pledges, at a rate of interest barely sufficient to cover the working expenses of the institution. Both the name and system were introduced into France and Spain Public granaries for the sale of corn are called in Italian *Monti frumentari* "Monte" means a public or state loan; hence also a "bank."

Montage (mon' tazh) In cinematography the final arrangement and assembling of photos to make a continuous film; also the art of film-cutting

Montagnards. See MOUNTAIN, THE

Montanists (mon ta' nists). Heretics of the 2nd century, so called from Montanus, a Phrygian, who asserted that he had received from the Holy Ghost special knowledge that had not been vouchsafed to the apostles They were extremely ascetic, believed in the speedy coming of the Second Advent, and quickly died out

Monteer Cap. See MONTERO

Monteith (mon tēth) A scalloped basin to cool and wash glasses in, a sort of punch-bowl made of silver or pewter, with a movable rim scalloped at the top, so called, according to Anthony Wood, in 1683 from "a fantastical Scot called 'Monsieur Monteigh' who at that time or a little before wore the bottome of his coate so notched ⌣ ⌣ ⌣ ⌣ ⌣."
New things produce new names, and thus Monteith
Has by one vessel saved his name from death —KING

Montem (mon' tem) A custom observed every three years till 1847 by the boys of Eton College, who proceeded on Whit Tuesday *ad montem* (to a mound called Salt Hill), near Slough, and exacted a gratuity called *salt money* from all who passed by Sometimes as much as £1,000 was thus collected, and it was used to defray expenses of the senior scholar at King's College, Cambridge

Montero or **Monteer Cap** (mon tē' rō). So called from the headgear worn by the *monteros d'Espinoza* (mountaineers), who once formed the interior guard of the palace of the Spanish king It had a spherical crown, and flaps that could be drawn over the ears, not unlike a Victorian shooting-cap.

Montgomery (mŭn gŭm' er i). A Norman name, not Welsh The town was founded by a Norman named Baldwin, and was in Welsh called *Trefaldwyn*, "house of Baldwin": in 1086 it was taken by Roger Montgomery, Earl of Shrewsbury, Count of the Marches to William the Conqueror, and it was given his name—which is a French place-name, the *Hill of Gomerie.*

Montgomery's division, all on one side. This is a French proverb, and refers to the Free Companies of the 16th century, of which a Montgomery was a noted chief The booty he took he kept himself.

Month. One of the twelve portions into which the year is divided Anciently a new month started on the day of the new moon, or the day after, hence the name (A.S *monath*), which is connected with *moon.* See LUNAR MONTH; and, for the months themselves *see* their names throughout this DICTIONARY.

The old mnemonic for remembering the number of days in each month runs—

  Thirty days hath September,
  April, June, and November,
  February eight-and-twenty all alone
  And all the rest have thirty-one,
  Unless that Leap Year doth combine
  And give to February twenty-nine.

This, with slight variations, is to be found in Grafton's *Chronicles* (1590), the play *The Return from Parnassus* (1606), etc. In Harrison's *Description of England* (prefixed to Holinshed's *Chronicle*, 1577) is the Latin version —

  Junius, Aprilis, Septemq; Novemq; tricenos,
  Unum plus reliqui, Februs tenet octo vicenos,
  At si bissextus fuerit superadditur unus

A month of Sundays. An indefinite long time, never. See NEVER

A month's mind. Properly the Mass, or lesser funeral solemnities, that in pre-Reformation days was said for a deceased person on the day one month from his death The term often occurs in old wills in connexion with charities to be disbursed on that day.

Shakespeare uses the term figuratively for an irresistible longing (for something); a great desire —

I see you have a month's mind for them.—*Two Gentlemen of Verona,* i, 2

As also does Samuel Butler —

For if a trumpet sound or drum beat,
Who hath not a month's mind to combat?
  Hudibras, I, ii, 111

And others; and it has been conjectured that here the allusions are to the *longings* of a pregnant woman, which start in the first month of pregnancy.

Montjoie St. Denis. The war-cry of the French. *Montjoie* is a corruption of *Mons Jovis*, as the little mounds were called which served as direction-posts in ancient times, hence it was applied to whatever showed or indicated the way, as the banner of St Denis called the Oriflamme. The Burgundians had for their war-cry. 'Montjoie St André', the dukes of Bourbon, "Montjoie Notre Dame", and the kings of England used to have "Montjoie St. George."

Montjoie was also the cry of the French heralds in the tournaments, and the title of the French king of arms

> Where is Mountjoy the herald? speed him hence
> Let him greet England with our sharp defiance
>   SHAKESPEARE *Henry V*, III, 5

Montserrat (mont ser ät'). The Catalonians aver that this mountain was riven and shattered at the Crucifixion. Every rift is filled with evergreens (Lat, *mons serratus*, the mountain jagged like a saw) The monastery of Montserrat is famous for its printing-press and for its Black Virgin.

Monument. The fluted Roman-Doric column of Portland stone (202 ft. high) built by Sir Christopher Wren to commemorate the Great Fire of London in 1666 is known as The Monument It stands near the north end of London Bridge, about the spot where the fire started

The old inscription (effaced in 1831) maintained that the fire had been caused—
by ye treachery and malice of ye popish faction, in order to ye carrying on their horrid plott for extirpating the Protestant religion and old English liberty, and the introducing popery and slavery

and it was this that made Pope refer to it as—
> London's column, pointing at the skies
> Like a tall bully, lifts the head, and lies
>   *Moral Essays*, III, 339

When looking at monuments and effigies, etc, in our churches it may be useful to remember the following points which must not, however, be taken as invariable rules —

Founders of chapels, etc, lie with their monument built into the wall.

Figures with their hands on their breasts, and chalices, represent *priests*.

Figures with crozier, mitre, and pontificals, represent *prelates*

Figures with armour represent *knights*.

Figures with legs crossed represent either *crusaders* or *married men*, but those with a scallop shell are certainly *crusaders*

Female figures with a mantle and large ring represent *nuns*

In the age of chivalry the woman was placed on the man's right hand, but when chivalry declined she was placed on his left hand

It may usually be taken that inscriptions in Latin, cut in capitals, are of the first twelve centuries, those in Lombardic capitals and French, of the 13th, those in Old English text, of the 14th, while those in the English language and Roman characters are subsequent to the 14th century

Tablets against the wall came in with the Reformation, and brasses are for the most part subsequent to the 13th century.

Monumental City. Baltimore, Maryland, is so called because it abounds in monuments, witness the obelisk, the 104 churches, etc.

Moon. The word is probably connected with the Sanskrit root *me-*, to measure (because time was measured by it) It is common to all Teutonic languages (Goth *mena*, O Frisian *mona*, O.Norm *mane*, A S *mona*, etc), and is almost invariably masculine In the Edda the *son* of Mundilfœri is Mani (moon), and *daughter* Sôl (*sun*), so it is still with the Lithuanians and Arabians, and so was it with the ancient Slavs, Mexicans, Hindus, etc, and the Germans to this day have *Frau Sonne* (Mrs Sun) and *Herr Mond* (Mr Moon)

The Moon is represented in five different phases: (1) new, (2) full; (3) crescent or descrescent; (4) half, and (5) gibbous, or more than half In pictures of the Assumption it is shown as a crescent under Our Lady's feet, in the Crucifixion it is eclipsed, and placed on one side of the cross, the sun being on the other, in the Creation and Last Judgment it is also introduced by artists.

In classical mythology the moon was known as *Hecate* before she had risen and after she had set, as *Astarte* when crescent, as *Diana* or *Cynthia* (she who "hunts the clouds") when in the open vault of heaven; as *Phœbe* when looked upon as the sister of the sun (i e. *Phœbus*) and was personified as *Selene* or *Luna*, the lover of the sleeping *Endymion*, i e moonlight on the fields (*see these names*).

The moon is called *triform*, because it presents itself to us either *round*, or *waxing* with horns towards the east, or *waning* with horns towards the west

One legend connected with the moon was that there was treasured everything wasted on earth, such as misspent time and wealth, broken vows, unanswered prayers fruitless tears, abortive attempts unfulfilled desires and intentions, etc. In Ariosto's *Orlando Furioso* Astolpho found on his visit to the Moon (Bk. XVIII and XXXIV, 70) that bribes were hung on gold and silver hooks; princes' favours were kept in bellows; wasted talent was kept in vases, each marked with the proper name, etc.; and in *The Rape of the Lock* (canto v) Pope tells us that when the Lock disappeared—

> Some thought it mounted to the lunar sphere,
> Since all things lost on earth are treasured there,
> There heroes' wits are kept in pond'rous vases,
> And beaux' in snuff-boxes and tweezer-cases
> There broken vows and death-bed alms are found
> And lovers' hearts with ends of ribbon bound,
> The courtier's promises, and sick man's prayers,
> The smiles of harlots, and the tears of heirs
> Cages for gnats, and chains to yoke a flea,
> Dried butterflies, and tomes of casuistry

Hence the phrase, *the limbus of the moon.*

I know no more about it than the man in the moon. I know nothing at all about the matter

It's all moonshine Bunkum, nonsense. The light of the moon was formerly held to have very deleterious effects on mental stability *See* LUNATIC

Mahomet and the Moon. *See* MOHAMMED.

Minions of the moon. Thieves who rob by night (*see* 1 *Henry IV*, i, 2).

Moon-calf An inanimate, shapeless abortion formerly supposed to be produced prematurely by the cow owing to the malign influence of the moon

A false conception, called *mola*, *i e* moon-calf . a lump of flesh without shape or life —HOLLAND *Pliny*, vii, 15

Moon-drop. In Latin, *virus lunare*, a vaporous foam supposed in ancient times to be shed by the moon on certain herbs and other objects, when influenced by incantations.

Upon the corner of the moon,
There hangs a vaporous drop profound;
I'll catch it ere it come to ground
Macbeth, iii, 5

Cp. Lucan's *Pharsalia*, vi, 669, where Erichtho is introduced using it —

Et virus large lunare ministrat.

Moonlight flit. A clandestine removal of one's furniture during the night, to avoid paying one's rent or having the furniture seized in payment thereof

Moon-rakers. A nickname of people of Wiltshire The absurd story offered to account for the name is that in the "good old times" they were noted smugglers, and one night, seeing the coastguard on the watch, they sank some smuggled whisky in the sea. When the coast was clear they employed rakes to recover their goods, when the coastguard reappeared and asked what they were doing Pointing to the reflection of the moon in the water, they replied, "We are trying to rake out that cream cheese yonder "

Moon's men. Thieves and highwaymen who ply their trade by night

The fortune of us that are but Moon's-men doth ebb and flow like the sea —1 *Henry IV*, i, 2

Moonstone. A variety of feldspar, so called on account of the play of light which it exhibits It contains bluish white spots, which, when held to the light, present a silvery play of colour not unlike that of the moon

Once in a blue moon. *See* BLUE MOON

The cycle of the moon. *See* CYCLE

The Island of the Moon. Madagascar is so named by the natives

The limbus of the moon. *See above*

The man in the moon. Some say it is a man leaning on a fork, on which he is carrying a bundle of sticks picked up on a Sunday The origin of this fable is from *Numb.* xv, 32-36 Some add a dog also, thus the prologue in *Midsummer Night's Dream* says, "This man with lantern, dog, and bush of thorns, presenteth moonshine"; Chaucer says "he stole the bush" (*Test. of Cresseide*) Another tradition says that the man is Cain, with his dog and thorn bush; the thorn bush being emblematical of the thorns and briars of the fall, and the dog being the "foul fiend " Some poets make out the "man" to be Endymion, taken to the moon by Diana

The Mountains of the Moon means simply White Mountains The Arabs call a white horse "moon-coloured."

To aim or level at the moon. To be very ambitious, to aim in shooting at the moon.

To cast beyond the moon. *See* CAST.

To cry for the moon. To crave for what is wholly beyond one's reach The allusion is to foolish children who want the moon for a plaything The French say, "He wants to take the moon between his teeth" (*Il veut prendre la lune avec les dents*), alluding to the old proverb about "the moon," and a "green cheese."

You have found an elephant in the moon—found a mare's nest Sir Paul Neal, a conceited virtuoso of the 17th century, gave out that he had discovered "an elephant in the moon." It turned out that a mouse had crept into his telescope, and had been mistaken for an elephant in the moon Samuel Butler has a satirical poem on the subject called *The Elephant in the Moon*

You would have me believe that the moon is made of green cheese—*i e* the most absurd thing imaginable

You may as soon persuade some Country Peasants, that the Moon is made of Green-Cheese (as we say) as that 'tis bigger than his Cart-wheel —WILKINS: *New World*, i (1638)

Moonlighting. Riding after cattle by night in Australia

Moonshine. A U.S.A colloquial term for illicitly distilled liquor.

Moor. The word comes from Gr. and Lat. *Mauros*, an inhabitant of Mauretania (*q.v.*). In the Middle Ages, the Europeans called all Mohammedans *Moors*, in the same manner as the Eastern nations called all inhabitants of Europe *Franks* Camoens, in the *Lusiad* (Bk. viii), gives the name to the Indians.

Moor-slayer or Mata-moros. A name given to St James, the patron saint of Spain, because, as the legends say, in encounters with the Moors he came on his white horse to the aid of the Christians.

Moot. In Anglo-Saxon times, the assembly of freemen in a township, tithing, etc. *Cp.* WITENAGEMOT In legal circles the name is given to the students' debates on supposed cases which formerly took place on the halls of Inns of Court. The benchers and the barristers, as well as the students, took an active part In a few towns, *e g.* Aldeburgh, Suffolk, the town hall is still called the Moot Hall

Hence, **moot case** or **moot point**, a doubtful or unsettled question, a case that is open to debate.

Mop. A statute fair at which servants seek to be hired Carters fasten to their hats a piece of whipcord, shepherds, a tuft of wool, grooms, a piece of sponge, and others a broom, pail, or *mop*, etc When hired a cockade with streamers is mounted. The origin of the name—which was in use in the 17th century—is not certain, but is probably an allusion to the mops carried by domestics

Mop. One of Queen Mab's attendants.

All mops and brooms. Intoxicated

Mops and mows. Grimaces; here *mop* is connected with the Dutch *mopken*, to pout.

Moral. The moral Gower. John Gower (*c* 1325-1408), the poet, is so called by Chaucer (*Troilus and Criseyde*, v, 1, 1856)

Father of moral philosophy. St. Thomas Aquinas (1227-74)

Morality Play. An allegorical dramatic form in vogue from the 14th to the 16th centuries in which the vices and virtues were personified and the victory of the last clearly established One of the best known morality plays was *Everyman*, a 15th-century English play translated from the Dutch *Elkerlyk*.

Moran's Collar. In Irish folk-tale, the collar of Moran, the wise councillor of Feredach the Just, an early king of Ireland, before the Christian era, which strangled the wearer if he deviated from the strict rules of equity.

Moratorium (mor à tôr' i um) (Lat *morari*, to delay) A legal permission to defer for a stated time the payment of a bond, debt, or other obligation. This is done to enable the debtor to pull himself round by borrowing money, selling effects, or otherwise raising funds to satisfy obligations. The device was adopted in 1891 in South America during the panic caused by the Baring Brothers' default of some twenty millions sterling, and the word came into popular use during World War I, and afterwards in connexion with the inability of Germany to pay to date the stated amount due as reparations under the Treaty of Versailles.

In Great Britain, on Aug 6th, 1914, a moratorium was proclaimed giving the banks power to retain certain sums credited to them and putting off the payment of Bills of Exchange and other debts for a month, this was later extended to Oct 4th, and a partial renewal to assist certain interests was allowed to Nov 4th

Moravians (mo rā' vi anz) A religious community tracing its origin to John Huss (*see* BOHEMIAN BRETHREN), expelled by persecution from Bohemia and Moravia in the 17th century. They are often called *The Bohemian Brethren*

More. More or less. Approximately; in round numbers; as "It is ten miles, more or less, from here to there," *i e* it's about ten miles

The more one has, the more he desires In French, *Plus il en a, plus il en veut* In Latin, *Quo plus habent, eo plus cupiunt.*

My more having would be a source
To make me hunger more
                                Macbeth, iv, 3

The more the merrier, the fewer the better cheer, or fare. The proverb is found in Ray's *Collection* (1742), and in Heywood's (1548)

To be no more. To exist no longer, to be dead

Cassius is no more
                                Julius Cæsar

More of More Hall. *See* WANTLEY, DRAGON OF

Morgan le Fay (môr' gàn le fā) The fairy sister of King Arthur, one of the principal characters in Arthurian romance and in Celtic legend generally; also known as *Morgaine* and (especially in *Orlando Furioso*) as *Morgana* (*see* FATA MORGANA)

In the Arthurian legends it was Morgan le Fay who revealed to the King the intrigues of Lancelot and Guinevere She gave him a cup containing a magic draught, and Arthur had no sooner drunk it than his eyes were opened to the perfidy of his wife and friend

In *Orlando Furioso* she is represented as living at the bottom of a lake, and dispensing her treasures to whom she liked, and in *Orlando Innamorato*, she first appears as "Lady Fortune," but subsequently assumes her witch-like attributes In Tasso her three daughters, Morganetta, Nivetta, and Carvilia, are introduced

In the romance of *Ogier the Dane* Morgan le Fay receives Ogier in the Isle of Avalon when he is over one hundred years old, restores him to youth, and becomes his bride

Morganatic Marriage (môr gan ăt' ik) A marriage between a man of high (usually royal) rank and a woman of inferior station, by virtue of which she does not acquire the husband's rank and neither she nor the children of the marriage are entitled to inherit his title or possessions, often called a "left-handed marriage" (*q v.*) because the custom is for the man to pledge his troth with his left hand instead of the right George Wilham, Duke of Zell, married Eleanora d'Esmiers in this way, and she took the name and title of Lady of Harburg, her daughter was Sophia Dorothea, the wife of George I. An instance of a morganatic marriage in the British Royal Family is that of George, Duke of Cambridge (1819-1904), cousin of Queen Victoria, who married morganatically in 1840 His children took the surname Fitz-George

The word comes from the mediæval Latin phrase *matrimonium ad morganaticam*, the last word representing the O H.Ger *morgan geba*, morning-gift, from husband to wife on the morning after the consummation of the marriage, hence the wife's only claim to her husband's possessions

Morgane: Morganetta. *See* MORGAN LE FAY.

Morgante Maggiore (môr gan' te mà jōr' ĕ) A serio-comic romance in verse, by Pulci of Florence (1485) The characters had appeared previously in many of the old romances, Morgante is a ferocious giant, converted by Orlando (the real hero) to Christianity After performing the most wonderful feats, he dies at last from the bite of a crab.

Pulci was practically the inventor of this species of poetry, called by the French *bernesque*, from Berni, who greatly excelled in it

Morgiana (môr ji än' à) The clever, faithful, female slave of Ali Baba, who pries into the forty jars, and discovers that every jar, but one contains a man She takes oil from the only one containing it, and, having made it boiling hot, pours enough into each jar to kill the thief concealed there At last she kills the captain of the gang, and marries her master's son (*Arabian Nights, Ali Baba and the Forty Thieves*)

Morgue (môrg) A mortuary, a building, especially that in Paris, where the bodies of persons found dead are exposed to view so that people may come and identify them. The origin of the name is unknown, it does not seem to be connected in any way with *mors*, death, and is probably the same word as *morgue*, meaning of stately or haughty mien. It was formerly applied to prison vestibules, where new criminals were placed to be scrutinized, that the prison officials might become familiar with their faces and general appearance

On me conduit donc au petit chastelet, ou du guichet estant passé dans la morgue, un homme gros, court, et carre, vint à moy.—ASSOUCY: *La Prison de M Dassouch* (1674), p 35

Morgue Endroit ou l'on tient quelque temps ceux que l'on ecroue, afin que les guichetiers puissent les reconnaitre ensuite —*Fleming and Tibbins*, vol ii, p 688

Morgue la Faye. The form taken by the name Morgan le Fay (*q v.*) in *Ogier the Dane*

Morley, Mrs The name under which Queen Anne corresponded with "Mrs. Freeman" (Sarah Churchill, Duchess of Marlborough)

Mormonism. The religious and social system of the Mormons, or Latter-day Saints, largely connected in the minds of most people with the practice of polygamy, which became part of the Mormon code in 1852, but is now a diminishing—if not vanished—quantity Hence the phrase *a regular Mormon*, for a flighty person who cannot keep to one wife or sweetheart.

The fraternity takes its name from *The Book of Mormon*, or *Golden Bible*, which is alleged to have been written on golden plates by the angel Mormon, but was possibly abstracted from a romance (1811) by the Rev Solomon Spaulding (1761-1816) Joseph Smith (1805-44), adapted this and claimed it as a direct revelation. Smith was born in Sharon, Windsor county, Vermont, and founded the denomination in 1830 He was cited thirty-nine times into courts of law, and was at last assassinated by a gang of ruffians while in prison at Carthage, Ill. His successor was Brigham Young (1801-77), a carpenter, who led the "Saints," driven from home by force, to the valley of the Salt Lake, 1,500 miles distant, generally called Utah, but by the Mormons themselves *Deseret* (Bee-country), the New Jerusalem, where they have been settled, despite many disputes with the United States Government, since 1848.

The Mormons accept the Bible as well as the *Book of Mormon* as authoritative, they hold the doctrines of repentance and faith (putting a curious construction on the latter); and they believe in baptism, the Eucharist, the physical resurrection of the dead, and in the Second Coming, when Christ will have the seat of His power in Utah Marriage may be either for time or for eternity; in the latter case consummation is unnecessary, for the man and the wife or wives he has taken in this way will spend the whole of the afterlife together, in the former case the rite is gone through solely that the community may be increased and multiplied

Morning The first glass of whisky drunk by Scottish fishermen in salutation to the dawn. One fisherman will say to another, "Hae ye had your morning, Tam?"

Morning Star, The. Byron's name for Mary Chaworth, his charming neighbour at Newstead, with whom he was in love early in his life

Morning Star of the Reformation. John Wyclif (1324-84).

Morocco (mo rŏk' ō). Strong ale made from burnt malt, used in the annual feast at Levens Hall, Westmorland (the seat of Sir Alan Desmond Bagot), on the opening of Milnthorpe Fair. It is put into a large glass of unique form, and the person whose turn it is to drink is called the "colt" He has to "drink the constable," *i e.* stand on one leg and say "Luck to Levens as long as Kent flows," then drain the glass or forfeit one shilling *See also* MAROCCO

Morocco men. Men who, about the end of the 18th century, used to visit public-houses touting for illegal lottery insurances Their rendezvous was a tavern in Oxford Market, at the Oxford St end of Great Portland Street

Morpheus (môr' fūs) Ovid's name for the son of Sleep, and god of dreams, so called from Gr *morphe*, form, because he gives these airy nothings their form and fashion Hence the name of the narcotic, *morphine*, or *morphia*

Morrice, Gil (or **Childe**). The hero of an old Scottish ballad, a natural son of an earl and the wife of Lord Barnard, and brought up "in the gude grene wode." Lord Barnard, thinking the Childe to be his wife's lover, slew him with a broad-sword, and setting his head on a spear gave it to "the meanest man in a' his train" to carry to the lady. When she saw it she said to the baron, "Wi' that same spear, O pierce my heart, and put me out o' pain"; but the baron replied, "Enouch of blood by me's bin spilt, sair, sair I rew the deid," adding—

> I'll ay lament for Gil Morice,
> As gin he were mine ain,
> I'll neir forget the dreiry day
> On which the youth was slain.
> *Percy's Reliques*, ser. iii, 1.

Percy says this pathetic tale suggested to Home the plot of his tragedy, *Douglas*.

Morris Dance. A dance, popular in England in the 15th century and later. in which the dancers usually represented characters from the Robin Hood stories (*see* MAID MARIAN). Other stock characters were Friar Tuck, Bavian the fool, hobby horse and foreigners, probably Moors or Moriscos It was brought from Spain in the reign of Edward III, and was originally a military dance of the Moors, or Moriscos—hence its name

Morse Code. A system of sending messages by telegraph, heliograph, flags, etc., invented in 1835 by the American S. F. B. Morse (1791-1872). Each letter, figure, and punctuation mark is represented by dots, dashes, or a combination of them, thus dot, dash (· —) stands for *a*, dash, dot, dot, dot (— · · ·) for *b*, a single dot for *e*, four dots and a dash (· · —) for 4, etc The first message in Morse code was sent May 24th, 1844, from Washington to New York, reading, "What hath God wrought?" In visual signalling a short flash or a rapid dip of the flag corresponds with the dot, and a long or slow with the dash.

Mortal A **mortal sin.** A "deadly" sin, one which deserves everlasting punishment, opposed to *venial*

> Earth trembled from her entrails,   some sad drops
> Wept at completing of the mortal Sin
> Original, while Adam took no thought
> MILTON *Paradise Lost*, ix, 1003

In slang and colloquial speech the word is used to express something very great—as "He's in a mortal funk," "There was a mortal lot of people there," or as an emphatic expletive—"You can do any mortal thing you like "

Mortar. Originally a short gun with a large bore for throwing bombs Said to have been used at Naples in 1435; first made in England in 1543 To-day mortars take the form of a long smooth-bored pipe which throws a bomb with a high trajectory with extreme accuracy

Mortar-board A college cap surmounted by a square "board" covered with black cloth The word is possibly connected with Fr. *mortier*, the cap worn by the ancient kings of France, and still used officially by the chief justice or president of the court of justice, but is more likely an allusion to the small square board on which a bricklayer carries his mortar—frequently balanced on his head.

Morte d'Arthur, Le (môrt dar' ther) (*see* Arthurian romances), was compiled by Sir Thomas Malory from French originals, and printed by Caxton in 1485 It contains—

> *The Prophecies of Merlin*
> *The Quest of the St Graal*
> *The Romance of Sir Lancelot of the Lake*
> *The History of Sir Tristram*, etc , etc.

Tennyson's *Morte d'Arthur* gives a poetic version of some of these poems, not always following the originals and rarely preserving their mediæval atmosphere.

Morther. *See* MAUTHER.

Mortimer. Fable has it that this family name derives from an ancestor in crusading times, noted for his exploits on the shores of the Dead Sea (*De Mortuo Mari*). Fact, however, is not so romantic *De Mortemer* was one of William the Conqueror's knights and is mentioned in the Roll of Battle Abbey, he was tenant in chief of *Mortemer*, a township in Normandy.

Mortmain (môrt' mān) (O Fr , Lat. *mortua manus*, dead hand). A term applied to land that was held inalienably by ecclesiastical or other corporations, In the 13th century it was common for persons to make over their land to the Church and then to receive it back as tenants, thus escaping their feudal obligations to the king In 1279 the *Statute of Mortmain* prohibiting grants of land to the "dead hand" of the Church was passed

Morton's Fork. John Morton (*c* 1420-1500), Cardinal Archbishop of Canterbury, introduced a plan for increasing the royal revenues, in the time of Henry VII, so arranged that nobody should escape. Those who were rich were forced to contribute on the ground that they could well afford it, those who lived

without display on the ground that their economies must mean that they were saving money

Mortstone. A rock of Morte Point, Devon.

He may remove Mortstone A Devonshire proverb, said incredulously of husbands who pretend to be masters of their wives It also means, "If you have done what you say, you can accomplish anything "

Morven (môr' ven). The Scottish mainland over the sound from Mull Much mentioned in the Ossian legends

Moses. The horns of Moses' face Moses is conventionally represented with horns, owing to a blunder in translation In *Ex* xxxiv, 29, 30, where we are told that when Moses came down from Mount Sinai ' the skin of his face shone," the Hebrew for this *shining* may be translated either as "sent forth *beams*" or "sent forth *horns*"; and the Vulgate took the latter as correct, rendering the passage— *quod cornuta esset facies sua. Cp Hab.* iii, 4, "His brightness was as the light, He had horns [*rays of light*] coming out of His hand "

Michael Angelo followed the earlier painters in depicting Moses with horns.

Moses boat. U S A. A type of boat made at Salisbury, Mass , by a famous boat-builder, Moses Lowell, in the 18th century Farther south (in the West Indies), it is said to have been a boat of sufficient capacity to take a hogshead of sugar from shore to ship in one trip

Moses' rod The divining-rod (*q v*) is sometimes so called, after the rod with which Moses worked wonders before Pharaoh (*Ex* vii, 9), or the rod with which he smote the rock to bring forth water (*Ex*. xvii, 6)

Moslem or **Muslim** (moz' lem, mŭz' lim) A Mohammedan, the pres part. of Arab *aslama*, to be safe or at rest, whence Islam (*q v*) The Arabic plural *Moslemin* is sometimes used, but *Moslems* is more common, and in English more correct.

Mosstrooper. A robber, a bandit; applied especially to the marauders who infested the borders of England and Scotland, who encamped on the *mosses* (A S *mos*, a bog.)

Mother. Properly a female parent (Sansk *mātr*, Gr. *mèter*, Lat *mater*, A S *mōdor*, Ger *mutter*, Fr *mère*, etc.), hence, figuratively, the source or origin of anything, the head or headquarters of a religious or other community, etc.

Mother Ann, Bunch, Goose, Shipton, etc *See* these names.

Mother Carey's chickens. Stormy petrels Mother Carey is *mata cara*, dear mother The French call these birds *oiseaux de Notre Dame* or *aves Sanctæ Mariæ See* Captain Marryat's *Poor Jack,* where the superstition is fully related

Mother Carey's Goose. The great black petrel or fulmar of the Pacific

Mother Carey is plucking her goose. It is snowing. *Cp* HULDA. Sailors call falling snow *Mother Carey's chickens*

Mother Church. The Church considered as the central fact, the head, the last court of appeal in all matters pertaining to conscience or religion St. John Lateran, at Rome (*see* LATERAN), is known as the Mother and Head of all Churches Also, the principal or oldest church in a country or district, the cathedral of a diocese.

Mother country. One's native country; or the country whence one's ancestors have come to settle England is the *Mother country* of Australia, New Zealand, Canada, etc The German term is *Fatherland*.

Mother's Day In U S A the second Sunday in May is observed as an occasion for each person to remember his mother by some act of grateful affection In schools Mother's Day is observed on the Friday preceding the above date

Mothering Sunday Mid-Lent Sunday, a great holiday, when the Pope blesses the golden rose, children go home to their mothers to feast on "mothering cakes," and "simnel cakes" (*q v.*) are eaten It is said that the day received its appellation from the ancient custom of visiting the "mother church" on that day, but to school-children it always meant a holiday, when they went home to spend the day with their mother or parents.

Mother Earth. When Junius Brutus (after the death of Lucretia) formed one of the deputation to Delphi to ask the Oracle which of the three would succeed Tarquin, the response was, "He who should first kiss his mother" Junius instantly threw himself on the ground, exclaiming, "Thus, then, I kiss thee, Mother Earth," and he was elected consul

Mother-of-pearl. The inner iridescent layers of the shells of many bivalve molluscs, especially that of the pearl oyster

Mother-sick. Hysterical Hysteria in women used to be known as "the mother."

She [Lady Bountiful] cures rheumatisms, ruptures and broken shins in men; green-sickness, obstructions, and fits of the mother in women, the king's evil, ... etc —FARQUHAR *The Beaux Stratagem*, I, 1

Mother-wit. Native wit, a ready reply; the wit which "our mother gave us"

Mother's meeting. A meeting of mothers held periodically in connexion with some church or denomination, at which the women can get advice or religious instruction, drink tea, gossip, and sometimes do a little needlework. Hence, applied facetiously to any gossiping group of people—men, as well as women.

The Mother of Believers. Among Mohammedans, Ayeshah, the second and favourite wife of Mohammed, who was called the "Father of Believers"

The Mother of Cities (*Amu-al-Bulud*). Balkh is so called.

Mother of Presidents. The State of Virginia

Does your mother know you're out? A jeering remark addressed to a presumptuous youth or to a simpleton The phrase is the title of a comic poem published in the *Mirror*,

April 28th, 1838. It became a catch phrase both in England and in America, and occurs in the *Ingoldsby Legends*, "Misadventures at Margate"

Oh, mother, look at Dick! Said in derision when someone is showing off, or doing something easy with the idea of being applauded for his skill

Tied to one's mother's apron-strings. *See* APRON.

Mother, a stringy, gummy substance, sometimes called mother of vinegar which forms on the surface of a liquor undergoing acetous fermentation, consisting of the bacteria which are causing that fermentation

Motion. The laws of motion, according to Galileo and Newton

(1) If no force acts on a body in motion, it will continue to move uniformly in a straight line.

(2) If force acts on a body, it will produce a change of motion proportionate to the force, and in the same direction (as that in which the force acts)

(3) When one body exerts force on another, that *other* body reacts on it with equal force.

Motley. Men of motley Licensed fools; so called because of their dress

Motley is the only wear
As You Like It, ii, 7.

Motu proprio (mō′ tū prop′ ri ō) (Lat) Of one's own motion; of one's own accord Always applied to a rescript drawn up and issued by the pope on his own initiative without the advice of others, and signed by him

Mountain Mountain ash. *See* ROWAN-TREE.

Mountain dew. Scotch whisky, formerly that from illicit stills hidden away in the mountains.

If the mountain will not come to Mohammed, etc. *See* MOHAMMED.

The mountain (*La Montagne*) The extreme democratic party in the French Revolution, the members of which were known as *Les Montagnards* because they seated themselves on the highest benches of the hall in which the National Convention met. Their leaders were Danton and Robespierre, Marat, St. Andre, Legendre, Camille Desmoulins, Carnot, St. Just, and Collot d'Herbois, the men who introduced the "Reign of Terror." Extreme Radicals in France are still called *Montagnards*

The mountain in labour. A mighty effort made for a small effect The allusion is to the celebrated line "*Parturiunt montes, nascetur ridiculus mus* (*Ars Poetica*, 139), which Horace took from a Greek proverb preserved by Athenæus.

The story is that the Egyptian King Tachos sustained a long war against Artaxerxes Ochus, and sent to the Lacedemonians for aid. King Agesilaus went with a contingent, but when the Egyptians saw a little, illdressed lame man, they said "*Parturiebat mons, formidavat Jupiter, ille vero murem peperit.*" ("The mountain laboured, Jupiter stood aghast, and a mouse ran out.") Agesilaus replied, "You call me a mouse, but I will soon show you I am a lion "

Creech translates Horace, "The travailing

mountain yields a silly mouse"; and Boileau, "*La montagne en travail enfante une souris*"

The Old Man of the Mountains (*Sheikh-al-Jebal*). Hassan ben Sabbah, the founder of the Assassins (*q v*), who made his stronghold in the mountain fastnesses of Lebanon He died in 1124, and in 1256 his dynasty, and nearly all the Assassins, were exterminated by the Tartar prince, Hulaku

To make mountains of molehills To make a difficulty of trifles. *Arcem ex cloaca facere.* The corresponding French proverb is, *Faire d'un mouche un eléphant.*

Mountebank (mount′ e băngk). A vendor of quack medicines at fairs, etc, who attracts the crowd by doing juggling feats or other antics from the tail of a cart or other raised platform, hence, any charlatan or self-advertising pretender The *bank* or bench was the counter on which shopkeepers displayed their goods, and street-vendors used to *mount* on their *bank* to patter to the public The Italian word, from which ours comes, is *montambanco*, and the French *saltimbanque.*

Mourning (môrn′ ing). *Black* To express the privation of light and joy, the midnight gloom of sorrow for the loss sustained. The colour of mourning in Europe; also in ancient Greece and the Roman Empire

Black and white striped. To express sorrow and hope. The mourning of the South Sea Islanders

Greyish brown. The colour of the earth, to which the dead return; used for mourning in Ethiopia

Pale brown The colour of withered leaves The mourning of Persia.

Sky blue To express the assured hope that the deceased has gone to heaven, used in Syria, Armenia, etc.

Deep blue The colour of mourning in Bokhara, also that of the Romans of the Republic

Purple and violet. To express royalty, "kings and priests to God." The colour of mourning for cardinals and the kings of France; in Turkey the colour is violet

White Emblem of "white-handed hope" Used by the ladies of ancient Rome and Sparta, also in Spain till the end of the 15th century Henry VIII wore white for Anne Boleyn.

Yellow The sear and yellow leaf. The colour of mourning in Egypt and in Burma, where also it is the colour of the monastic order In Brittany, widows' caps among the *paysannes* are yellow Anne Boleyn wore yellow mourning for Catherine of Aragon Some say yellow is in token of exaltation. *See also* BLACK CAP.

Mournival *See* GLEEK.

Mouse. The soul was often supposed in olden times to make its way at death through the mouth of man in the form of some animal, sometimes a pigeon, sometimes a mouse or rat A red mouse indicated a pure soul, a black mouse, a soul blackened by pollution; a pigeon or dove, a saintly soul

Exorcists used to drive out evil spirits from the human body, and Harsnet gives several instances of such expulsions in his *Popular Impositions* (1604)

Mouse is slang for a black eye, and was formerly in common use as a term of endearment Similar terms from animals are, *bird* or *birdie*, *duckie*, and *lamb* "You little monkey" is an endearing reproof to a child Dog and pig are used in a bad sense, as "You dirty dog", "You filthy pig" Brave as a lion, surly as a bear, crafty as a fox, proud as a peacock, fleet as a hare, and several phrases of a like character are in common use

"God bless you, mouse," the bridegroom said,
And smakt her on the lips
WARNER *Albion's Eng* , p 17

It's a bold mouse that nestles in the cat's ear. Said of one who is taking an unnecessary risk An old proverb, given by Herbert (1639)

Poor as a church mouse *See* POOR

The mouse that hath but one hole is quickly taken. Have two strings to your bow The proverb appears in Herbert's *Collection* (1639), and is found in many European languages. In Latin it was *Mus non uni fidit antro*, the mouse does not trust to one hole.

When the cat's away the mice will play. *See* CAT.

Mouse Tower, The. A mediæval watch-tower on the Rhine, near Bingen, so called because of the tradition that Archbishop Hatto (*q v*) was there devoured by mice The tower, however, was built by Bishop Siegfried, two hundred years after the death of Hatto, as a toll-house for collecting the duties upon all goods which passed by. The German *maut* means "toll," (mouse is *maus*), and the similarity of the words together with the great unpopularity of the toll on corn gave rise to the tradition

Mouth. Down in the mouth. *See* DOWN

His mouth was made He was trained or reduced to obedience, like a horse trained to the bit

At first, of course, the fireworker showed fight but in the end "his mouth was made," his paces formed, and he became a very serviceable and willing animal —LE FANU *House in the Churchyard*, ch xcix

That makes my mouth water. The fragrance of appetizing food excites the salivary glands The phrase means—that makes me long for or desire it.

Hold your mouth! A rougher equivalent of "hold your tongue!", keep silent

To laugh on the wrong side of one's mouth. *See* LAUGH

To mouth one's words To talk affectedly or pompously, to declaim
He mouths a sentence as curs mouth a bone
CHURCHILL. *The Rosciad*, 322.

To open one's mouth wide. To name too high a price, to strain after too big a prize

Moutons (moo′ tong). **Revenons à nos moutons** (Fr.). Literally "Let us come back to our sheep," but used to express "let us return to the subject" The phrase is taken from the 14th-century French comedy *La Farce de Maître Pathelin*, or *l'Avocat Pathelin* (line 1282), in which a woollen-draper charges a shepherd with ill-treating his sheep In telling his story he kept for ever running away from his subject, and to throw discredit on the defendant's attorney (Pathelin), accused him of stealing a piece of cloth The judge had to pull him up every moment, with *"Mais, mon ami, revenons a nos moutons."* The phrase is frequently quoted by Rabelais. *See* PATELIN SANS SOUCI.

Move **Give me where to stand, and I will move the world.** So said Archimedes of Syracuse, and the instrument he would have used is the lever

The first movable. *See* PRIMUM MOBILE.

To move the adjournment of the House (i e the House of Commons) To bring forward a motion of adjournment, which can only be done in certain special circumstances This is the only method by which the rules of the House allow a member to bring up, without notice, business which is not on the order paper.

To move the previous question *See* QUESTION.

Mow (mō) The three *mows* in English are altogether different words, though spelt alike *Mow*, a heap of hay, etc ("the barley-mow") is A.S *mūga*, connected with Icel *muge*, a swath *Mow* to cut down grass, corn, and so on, is A S *māwan*, connected with Ger. *mahen*, Gr. *amān*, and Lat *mēlere*, to reap, and *Mow* a grimace (in "mops and mows," *q.v*) is Fr *moue*, a pout or grimace.

Much The miller's son in the Robin Hood stories In the morris-dances he played the part of the Fool, and his great feat was to bang the head of the gaping spectators with a bladder of peas.

Much Ado about Nothing. Shakespeare's comedy, named from a proverbial saying of the time, and with only the slightest relevance to the plot, was probably written in 1599, and was published in 1600

The story first appears (about 1550) in Bandello's *Novelle* (No. xxii), where the slandered heroine is Fenicia, and a French translation of this was given in Belleforest's *Les Histoires Tragiques* (1559), with which Shakespeare was well acquainted Ariosto also, calling the injured bride Ginevra and her lover Ariodante, used the story in his *Orlando Furioso* (canto v), and it appears again in Spenser's *Faerie Queene* (II, iv), where Claribell is the name of the heroine A lost play called *A Historie of Ariodante and Ginevra* was given at Court by the boys of Merchant Taylors' School in 1583, this may have formed the groundwork of Shakespeare's comedy, but many of the episodes—especially those in which Dogberry and the rustic watchmen are concerned—bear all the marks of originality

Muckle. Many a mickle makes a muckle. *See under* LITTLE.

Muff. A person who is awkward at outdoor sports, or who is effeminate, dull, or stupid, probably so called as a sneering allusion to the use of muffs to keep one's hands warm The term does not seem to be older than the early part of last century but there is a Sir Henry Muff in Dudley's interlude, *The Rival Candidates* (1774), a stupid, blundering dolt,

who is not only unsuccessful at the election but finds that his daughter has engaged herself during his absence

Muffins and Crumpets. Muffins is probably *pain-moufflet*, soft bread. Du Cange describes the *panis mofletus* as bread of a more delicate nature than ordinary, for the use of prebends, etc , and says it was made fresh every day Crumpets is a word of ancient but unknown origin *Crumpet* is also slang for the head— *I caught him one on the crumpet*—I gave him a blow on the head.

Mufti (mŭf′ ti). An Arabic word meaning an official expounder of the Koran and Mohammedan law, but used in English to denote *civil*, as distinguished from *military* or official costume Our meaning dates from the early 19th century, and probably arose from the resemblance that the flowered dressing-gown and tasselled smoking-cap worn by officers at that time when in their quarters off duty bore to the stage get-up of an Eastern muftı.

Mug. This word, used as slang for a face, is of obscure origin, possibly coming from the gypsy meaning a simpleton or muff **To mug up**, meaning to study hard for a specific purpose, e g to pass an examination, is an old university phrase; it has been suggested that it comes from the theatre where an actor, while making up his face or "mug," would hurriedly con over his words.

Mug-house. An ale-house was so called in the 18th century where some hundred persons assembled in a large tap-room to drink, sing, and spout. One of the number was made chairman Ale was served to the guests in their own mugs, and the place where the mug was to stand was chalked on the table.

Muggins. Slang for a fool or simpleton—a *Jiggins* is the same thing; also for a pettifogging magnate, a village leader Muggins is a surname, and those bearing it sometimes like to hear it pronounced mū′ ginz.

Muggletonian (mŭg el tō′ ni an) A follower of Lodovic Muggleton (1609-98), a journeyman tailor, who, about 1651, set up for a prophet He was sentenced for blasphemous writings to stand in the pillory, and was fined £500 The members of the sect—which maintained a sort of existence till about 1865—believed that their two founders, Muggleton and John Reeve, were the "two witnesses" spoken of in *Rev*. xi, 3.

Mugwump (mŭg′ wŭmp) An Algonquin word meaning a chief, in Eliot's Indian Bible the word "centurion" in the *Acts* is rendered *mugwump*. It is now applied in the United States to independent members of the Republican party, those who refuse to follow the dictum of a caucus, and all political Pharisees whose party vote cannot be relied on.

"I suppose I am a political mugwump," said the Englishman "Not yet," replied Mr Reed. "You will be when you have returned to your allegiance "— *The Liverpool Echo*, July 19th, 1886.

Mulatto (mū lăt′ ō) (Span , from *mulo*, a mule). The offspring of a negress by a white man; loosely applied to any halfbreed. *Cp.* CREOLE.

Mulberry. Fable has it that the fruit was originally white, and became blood-red from the blood of Pyramus and Thisbe (*se* Py-RAMUS) The botanical name is Morus, from the Greek *moros* (a fool), so called, we are told in the *Hortus Anglicus*, because "it is reputed the wisest of all flowers, as it never buds till the cold weather is past and gone" Ludovic Sforza, who prided himself on his prudence, chose a mulberry-tree for his device, and was called "*Il Moro* "

In the *Seven Champions* (Pt i, ch iv) Eglantine. daughter of the King of Thessaly, was transformed into a mulberry-tree.

Here we go round the mulberry bush. An old game in which children take hands and dance round in a ring, singing a song of which this is the refrain.

In World War II *Mulberry* was the code name given to the engineering feat of making a pre-fabricated port and towing it across to the Normandy coast to make possible the supply of the Allied armies in France in 1944. Submersible sections of concrete formed a breakwater and quay alongside which the transports were tied up for the stores to be unloaded. The name was chosen because at the time it was the next in rotation on the British Admiralty's list of names available for war ships

Mulciber (mŭl' si ber)　A name of Vulcan (q 1) among the Romans, it means *the softener*, because he softened metals

Round about him [Mammon] lay on every side
Great heaps of gold that never could be spent
Of which some were rude ore, not purified
Of Mulciber's devouring element
　　　　　　　SPENSER. *Faerie Queene*, II, vii, 5

Mule. The offspring of a male ass and a mare, hence, a hybrid between other animals (or plants), as a *mule canary*, a cross between a canary and a goldfinch The offspring of a stallion and a she-ass is not, properly speaking, a mule, but a *hinny*.

Very stubborn or obstinate people are sometimes called *mules*, in allusion to the well-known characteristic of the beast; and the *spinning-mule* was so called because it was—a kind of mixture of machinery between the warp-machine of Mr Arkwright and the woof-machine or hand-jenny of Mr Hargrave —*Encyc Britannica*, 1797

To shoe one's mule. To appropriate moneys committed to one's trust

He had the keeping and disposal of the moneys, and yet shod not his own mule.—*History of Francion* (1655)

Mull. *To make a mull of a job* is to fail to do it properly It is either a contraction of *muddle*, or from the old verb *to mull*, to reduce to powder

Among Anglo-Indians members of the service in the Madras Presidency were known as *Mulls* Here the word stands for *mulligatawny*.

Mulla. The Bard of Mulla's silver stream. So Spenser was called by Shenstone, because at one time his home in Ireland was on the banks of the Mulla, or Awbeg, a tributary of the Blackwater

Mulmutine Laws (mŭl' mū tin)　The code of Dunvallo Mulmutius, the sixteenth legendary King of the Britons (about 400 B C.), son of Cloten, King of Cornwall It is said to have been translated by Gildas from British into Latin, and to have formed the basis of King Alfred's code, which obtained in England till the Conquest (Holinshed *History of England*, III, 1.)

Mulmutius made out laws,
Who was the first of Britain which did put
His brows within a golden crown, and called
Himself a king.　　　　*Cymbeline*, III, 1

Mulready Envelope (mŭl red' i)　An envelope resembling a half-sheet of letter-paper, when folded, having on the front an ornamental design by William Mulready (1786-1863), the artist When the penny postage envelopes were first introduced (1840), these were the stamped envelopes of the day, they remained in circulation for one year only. They are prized by stamp-collectors

A set of those odd-looking envelope-things,
Where Britannia (who seems to be crucified) flings
To her right and her left, funny people with wings
Amongst elephants, Quakers, and Catabaw kings,—
And a taper and wax, and small Queen's-heads in packs,
Which, when notes are too big you must stick on their
　　　backs　　　　　*Ingoldsby Legends.*

Multipliers. So alchemists, who pretended to multiply gold and silver, were called An Act was passed (2 Henry IV, c iv) making the "art of multiplication" felony In the *Canterbury Tales*, the Canon's Yeoman (*see Prologue* to his *Tale*) says he was reduced to poverty by alchemy, adding. "Lo, such advantage is't to multiply "

Multitude, Nouns of. Dame Juliana Berners, in her *Booke of St. Albans* (1486), says, in designating companies we must not use the names of multitudes promiscuously, and examples her remark thus —

"We say a *congregacyon* of people, a *hoost* of men, a *felyshyppynge* of yeomen, and a *bevy* of ladyes; we must speak of a *harde* of dere, swannys, cranys, or wrenys, a *sege* of herons or bytourys, a *muster* of pecockes, a *watche* of nyghtyngales, a *flyghte* of doves, a *claterynge* of choughes, a *pryde* of lyons, a *slewthe* of beeres, a *gagle* of geys, a *skulke* of foxes, a *sculle* of frerys, a *pontificalitye* of prestys, and a *superfluyte* of nonnes —*Booke of St. Albans* (1486).

She adds, that a strict regard to these niceties better distinguishes "gentylmen from ungentylmen," than regard to the rules of grammar, or even to the moral law (*See* ASSEMBLAGE, NOUNS OF

Multum in parvo (mŭl 'tum in par' vō) (Lat)　Much "information" condensed into few words or into a small compass.

Mum. A strong beer made in Brunswick; said to be so called from Christian Mumme, by whom it was first brewed in the late 15th century

Mum's the word. Keep what is told you a profound secret *See* MUMCHANCE

Seal up your lips, and give no words but—mum
　　　　　　　　　　　　　2 Henry VI, i, 2

Mumbudget An old exclamation meaning "Silence, please"; perhaps from a children's game in which silence was occasionally necessary *Cp* BUDGET, CRY, *and* MUMCHANCE, *below*

> Have these bones rattled, and this head
> So often in thy quarrel bled?
> Nor did I ever winch or grudge it,
> For thy dear sake Quoth she, Mumbudget
> > BUTLER' *Hudibras*, I, iii, 208.

Mumchance. Silence Mumchance was a game of chance with dice, in which silence was indispensable *Mum* is connected with *mumble* (Ger *mummeln*; Dan. *mumle*, to mumble) *Cp* MUMBUDGET

> And fro "mumchance," howe'er the *chance* may fall
> You must be *mum* for fear of spoiling all
> > *Machiavell's Dogg*

Mumbo Jumbo (mŭm' bō jŭm' bō) The name given by Europeans (possibly from some lost native word) to a bogy or grotesque idol venerated by certain African tribes; hence, any object of blind and unreasoning worship

Mungo Park in his *Travels in Africa* says that Mumbo Jumbo is not an idol, any more than the American *Lynch*, but merely one disguised to punish unruly wives It not infrequently happens that a house which contains many wives becomes unbearable. In such a case, either the husband or an agent disguises himself as "Mumbo Jumbo" and comes at dusk with a following, making the most hideous noises possible When the women have been sufficiently scared, "Mumbo" seizes the chief offender, ties her to a tree, and scourges her, amidst the derision of all present

Mummer. A contemptuous name for an actor, from the parties that formerly went from house to house at Christmas-time *mumming*, *i e* giving a performance of St George and the Dragon and the like, in dumb-show

> Peel'd, patch'd, and piebald, linsey-woolsey brothers
> Grave mummers! sleeveless some, and shirtless others
> > POPE. *Dunciad*, III, 115

Mummy is the Arabic *mum*, wax used for embalming, from the custom of anointing the body with wax and wrapping it in cerecloth

Mummy wheat. Wheat said to have been taken from ancient Egyptian tombs, which, when sown, fructifies No seed, however, will preserve its vitality for centuries, and what is called *mummy wheat* is a species of corn commonly grown on the southern shores of the Mediterranean

Mumpers. Beggars; from the old slang to *mump*, to cheat or to sponge on others, probably from Dutch *mompen* to cheat In Norwich, Christmas waits used to be called "Mumpers."

A parcel of wretches hopping about by the assistance of their crutches, like so many Lincoln's Inn Fields mumpers, drawing into a body to attack the coach of some charitable lord —NED WARD *The London Spy*, Pt v

Mumping day. St Thomas's Day, December 21st, is so called in some parts of the country, because on this day the poor used to go about begging, or, as it was called, "a-gooding," that is, getting gifts to procure *good things* for Christmas

In Lincolnshire the name used to be applied to Boxing Day (*q v*), in Warwickshire the term used was "going a-corning," *i e* getting gifts of corn

Mumpsimus. Robert Graves, in *Impenetrability*, gives this word as an example of the practice of making new words by declaration. With the meaning, "an erroneous doctrinal view obstinately adhered to," mumpsimus was put into currency by Henry VIII in a speech from the throne in 1545 He remarked, "Some be too stiff in their old mumpsimus, others be too busy and curious in their sumpsimus " He referred to a familiar story in the jest-books of a priest who always read in the Mass "quod in ore mumpsimus" instead of "sumpsimus," as his Missal was incorrectly copied When his mistake was pointed out he said that he had read it with an *m* for forty years, "and I will not change my old mumpsimus for your new sumpsimus " The word no longer has its doctrinal meaning, and is now used to mean "an established manuscript-reading that, though obviously incorrect, is retained blindly by old-fashioned scholars "

Munchausen, Baron (mŭn' chou zen) A traveller who meets with the most marvellous adventures, the hero of a collection of stories by Rudolph Erich Raspe, published in English in 1785 The incidents were compiled from various sources, including the adventures of an actual Hieronymus Karl Friedrich von Munchhausen (1720-97), a German officer in the Russian army, noted for his marvellous stories, Bebel's *Facetiæ*, Castiglione's *Cortegiano*, Bildermann s *Utopia*, etc. The book is a satire either on Baron de Tott, or on Bruce, whose *Travels in Abyssinia* were looked upon as mythical when they first appeared.

Mundane Egg. *See* EGG.

Mundungus (mŭn dŭng' gus) Bad tobacco, originally offal, or refuse, from Span. *mondongo*, black pudding

In Sterne's *Sentimental Journey* (1768) the word is used as a name for Samuel Sharp, a surgeon, who published *Letters from Italy*; and Smollett, who published *Travels through France and Italy* (1766), "one continual snarl," was called "Smelfungus "

Mungo, St (mŭng' gō). An alternative name for St Kentigern (*q v*)

A superior kind of shoddy, made from second-hand woollens, is known as *mungo*

Munich Pact or Agreement. The pact signed by Germany, France, Great Britain, and Italy on September 29th, 1938, whereby the Sudetenland of Czechoslovakia was ceded to Germany From this unfortunate act of appeasement the phrase has come to mean any dishonourable appeasement.

Murderer's Bible, The. *See* BIBLE, SPECIALLY NAMED.

Murrumbidgee Whaler (mǔ rǔm' bi jē) The Australian term for a tramp, the origin of which is obscure Many derive the term from the fact that tramps camped for long periods by rivers such as the Murrumbidgee and then told lies about the fish or "whales" they had caught It may be connected more specifically with New South Wales where horses exported to the Indian Army were called "walers."

Muscadins (mŭs' kà dinz) Parisian exquisites who aped those of London about the time of the French Revolution They wore top-boots with thick soles, knee-breeches, a dress-coat with long tails, and a high stiff collar, and carried a thick cudgel called a *constitution* It was thought "John Bullish" to assume a huskiness of voice, a discourtesy of manners, and a swaggering vulgarity of speech and behaviour

> Cockneys of London, Muscadins of Paris
> BYRON *Don Juan*, viii, 124

Muscular Christianity. Hearty or strong-minded Christianity, which braces a man to fight the battle of life bravely and manfully The term was applied to the teachings of Charles Kingsley—somewhat to his annoyance

> It is a school of which Mr Kingsley is the ablest doctor, and its doctrine has been described fairly and cleverly as "muscular Christianity."—*Edinburgh Review*, Jan., 1858

Muses. In Greek mythology the nine daughters of Zeus and Mnemosyne, originally goddesses of memory only, but later identified with individual arts and sciences The paintings of Herculaneum show all nine in their respective attributes They are —

> *Calliope* the chief of the Muses
> *Clio* heroic exploits and history
> *Euterpe* Dionysiac music and the double flute
> *Thalia·* gaiety, pastoral life, and comedy
> *Melpomene.* song, harmony, and tragedy
> *Terpsichore·* choral dance and song
> *Erato* the lyre and erotic poetry
> *Polyhymnia* the inspired and stately hymn
> *Urania* celestial phenomena and astronomy

See these names

Museum. Literally, a home or seat of the Muses The first building to have this name was the university erected at Alexandria by Ptolemy Soter about 300 B C.

Mushroom Slang for an umbrella, on account of the similarity in shape; and as mushrooms are of a very rapid growth, applied figuratively to almost anything that "springs up in the night," as a new, quickly built suburb, an upstart family, and so on In 1787 Bentham said—somewhat unjustly—"Sheffield is an oak, Birmingham is a mushroom "

To mushroom. To expand into a mushroom shape; said especially of certain soft-nosed rifle-bullets used in big-game shooting, or of a dense cloud of smoke that spreads out high in the sky

Music Father of modern music Mozart (1756-91) has been so called

> Father of Greek music Terpander (fl 676 B C)

The prince of music. Giovanni Pierluigi da Palestrina (1524-94)

Music hath charms, etc. The opening line of Congreve's *Mourning Bride*

> Music hath charms to soothe a savage breast,
> To soften rocks, or bend a knotted oak.

The allusion is to Orpheus (*q v*), who—

> With his lute made trees,
> And the mountain tops that freeze,
> Bow themselves when he did sing
> *Henry VIII*, iii, 1

And the lines are among those most frequently misquoted in the whole of English poetry, the words "a savage breast" being turned into "the savage beast " James Bramston, in his *Man of Taste* (1733), wittily substituted for the second line "And therefore proper at a sheriff's feast "

The music of the spheres *See* SPHERES

To face the music *See* FACE.

Musical Notation. *See* DOH

Musical Small-coal Man. Thomas Britton (1654-1714), a coal-dealer of Clerkenwell, who established a musical club in a loft over his shop in which all the musical celebrities of the day took part. The club met every Thursday night and was frequented by professional musicians such as Handel, talented amateurs such as Roger L'Estrange, and lovers of music generally

Father of musicians. Jubal, "the father of all such as handle the harp and organ" (*Gen* iv, 21)

Musits or Musets. Gaps in a hedge, places through which a hare makes his way to escape the hounds.

> The many musits through the which he goes
> Are like a labyrinth to amaze his foes.
> SHAKESPEARE *Venus and Adonis*.

The passing of the hare through these gaps is termed *musing*. The word is from O.Fr *muce*, a hiding-place

Muslim. *See* MOSLEM

Muslin. So called from Mosul, in Asia, where it was first manufactured (Fi *mousseline*, Ital *mussolino*)

Mustang (U.S A.). A wild horse

Mustard. So called because originally *must*, new wine (Lat. *mustus*, fresh, new) was used in mixing the paste Fable, however, alleges that the name arose because in 1382 Philip the Bold, Duke of Burgundy, granted to the town of Dijon, noted for its mustard, armorial bearings with the motto MOULT ME TARDE '*Multum ardeo*, I ardently desire' The arms and motto, engraved on the principal gate, were adopted as a trade-mark by the mustard merchants, and got shortened into Moulttarde (to burn much)

Mustard, ground and sifted to a flour, is said to have been the invention of an old Durham woman named Clements, who came to London in 1720 with her concoction, which pleased the palate of George I and hence became popular

After meat, mustard. Expressive of the sentiment that something that would have been welcome a little earlier has arrived too late, I have now no longer need of it *C'est de la moutarde apres diner.*

Mussulman. A Mohammedan, a Moslem (*q v*) The plural is Mussulmans

Mutantur. *See* TEMPORA MUTANTUR

Mute, To stand. An old legal term for a prisoner who, when arraigned for treason or felony, refused to plead or gave irrelevant answers

Mutton (Fr *mouton*, a sheep) In old slang, a prostitute, frequently extended to *laced mutton*

> *Speed* Ay, sir I, a lost mutton, gave your letter to her, a laced mutton, and she, a laced mutton, gave me, a lost mutton, nothing for my labour —SHAKE-SPEARE *Two Gentlemen of Verona*, i, 1.

> The old lecher hath gotten holy mutton to him, a Nunne, my lord —GREENE *Friar Bacon*

It was with this suggestion that Rochester wrote his mock epitaph on Charles II —

> Here lies our mutton-eating king,
> Whose word no man relies on,
> He never *said* a foolish thing,
> And never *did* a wise one

Come and eat your mutton with me Come and dine with me

Dead as mutton. Absolutely dead

Mutton fist. A large, coarse, red fist

To return to our muttons. To come back to the subject *See* MOUTONS

Mutton Lancers The Queen's Royal Regiment (West Surrey), the 2nd Foot, raised in 1661 The nickname comes from the regimental badge—the Pascal Lamb bearing a lance

Mutual Friends. Can people have mutual friends? Strictly speaking *not*, but since Dickens adopted the solecism in the title of his novel, *Our Mutual Friend* (1864), many people have objected to the correct term, *common friends Mutual* implies reciprocity from one to the other (Lat. *mutare*, to change), the friendship between two friends should be mutual, but this mutuality cannot be extended to a third party

> A mutual flame was quickly caught,
> Was quickly, too, revealed,
> For neither bosom lodged a thought
> Which virtue keeps concealed
> *Edwin and Emma.*

Mynheer (min hēr') The Dutch equivalent for "Mr", hence, sometimes used for a Dutchman

> 'Tis thus I spend my moments here,
> And wish myself a Dutch mynheer.
> COWPER *To Lady Austin*

Myrmidons of the Law. Bailiffs, sheriffs' officers, and other law servants Any rough fellow employed to annoy another is the employer's myrmidon

The Myrmidons were a people of Thessaly who followed Achilles to the siege of Troy, and were distinguished for their savage brutality, rude behaviour, and thirst for rapine

Myrrha. The mother of Adonis, in Greek legend She is fabled to have had an unnatural love for her own father, and to have been changed into a myrtle tree

Myrrophores (Gr, myrrh bearers) The three Marys who went to see the sepulchre, bearing myrrh and spices (*see Mark* xvi, 1) In Christian art they are represented as carrying vases of myrrh in their hands.

Myrtle. If you look at a leaf of myrtle in a strong light, you will see that it is pierced with innumerable little punctures According to fable, Phædra, wife of Theseus, fell in love with Hippolytus, her stepson, and when Hippolytus went to the arena to exercise his horses, Phædra repaired to a myrtle-tree in Trœzen to await his return, and beguiled the time by

piercing the leaves with a hairpin The punctures referred to are an abiding memento of this legend

In *Orlando Furioso* Astolpho is changed into a myrtle-tree by Acrisia. *See also* MYRRHA *above*

The ancient Jews believed that the eating of myrtle leaves conferred the power of detecting witches, and it was a superstition that if the leaves crackled in the hands the person beloved would prove faithful

The myrtle which dropped blood. Æneas (*Æneid*, Bk iii) is represented as tearing up the myrtle which dropped blood. Polydorus tells us that the barbarous inhabitants of the country pierced the myrtle (then a living being) with spears and arrows The body of the myrtle took root and grew into the bleeding tree

Mysterium The letters of this word which, until the time of the Reformation, was engraved on the Pope's tiara, are said to make up the number 666 (*see* NUMBER OF THE BEAST) *See also* Rev xvii, 5

Mystery. In English two totally distinct words have been confused here *mystery*, the archaic term for a handicraft, as in *the art and mystery of printing*, is the same as the French *métier* (trade, craft, profession), and is the M E *mistere*, from mediæval Lat *misterium*, *ministerium*, ministry

Mystery, meaning something beyond human comprehension, is (through French) from the Lat *mysterium* and Gr. *mustes*, from *muen*, to close the eyes or lips It is from this sense that the old miracle-plays, mediæval dramas in which the characters and story were drawn from sacred history, were called *Mysteries*, though, as they were frequently presented by members of some single guild, or *mystery* in the handicraft sense, even here the words were confused and opening made for many puns

The three greater mysteries. In ecclesiastical language, the Trinity, Original Sin, and the Incarnation.

N

N. The fourteenth letter of our alphabet; represented in Egyptian hieroglyph by a water-line (〰). It was called *nun* (a fish) in Phœnician, whence the Greek *nu.*

N, a numeral Gr. $\nu = 50$, but $\nu = 50,000$ N (Lat) = 90, or 900, but $\bar{N} = 90,000$, or 900,000

n. The sign ~ (*tilde*) over an "n" indicates that the letter is to be pronounced as though followed by a "y," as *cañon* = *canyon* It is used thus almost solely in words from Spanish. In Portuguese the accent (called *til*) is placed over vowels to indicate that they have a nasal value

nth, or **nth plus one.** The expression is taken from the index of a mathematical formula, where *n* stands for any number, and $n+1$, one more than any number Hence, *n-dimensional*, having an indefinite number of dimensions.

n-tuple (on the analogy of *quadruple, quintuple*, etc), having an indefinite number of duplications

n ephelkustic. The Greek nu (*v*) added for euphony to the end of a word that terminates with a vowel when the next word in the sentence begins with a vowel.

N or M. The answer given to the first question in the Church of England Catechism, and it means that here the person being catechized gives his or her *name* or *names* Lat *nomen vel nomina* The abbreviation for the plural *nomina* was—as usual—the doubled initial (*cp* "LL D " for Doctor of Laws); and this, when printed (as it was in old Prayer Books) in black-letter and close together, 𝔫.𝔫. came to be taken for 𝔪.

In the same way the *N* in the marriage-service ("I *M.* take thee *N* to my wedded wife ') merely indicates that the *name* is to be spoken in each case, but the *M* and *N* in the publication of banns ("I publish the Banns of Marriage between *M* of —— and N of ——") stand for *maritus*, bridegroom, and *nupta*, bride

Nab. Colloquial for to seize suddenly, without warning (*Cp* Norw. and Swed *nappa*, Dan , *nappe*). Hence *nabman*, a sheriff's officer or police-constable.

> Ay, but so be if a man's nabbed, you know
> GOLDSMITH *The Good-natured Man*

Nabob (nā' bob). Corruption of the Hindu *nawab*, plural of *naib*, a deputy-governor under the Mogul Empire These men acquired great wealth and lived in splendour; hence, *Rich as a nabob* came to be applied to a merchant who had attained great wealth in the Indies, and returned to live in his native country

Nabonassar, Era of (năb on ăs' ăr). An era that was in use for centuries by the Chaldean astronomers, and was generally followed by Hipparchus and Ptolemy It commenced at midday, Wed , Feb 26th, 747 B C , the date of the accession of Nabonassar (d. 733 B C), as King of Babylonia. The year consisted of 12 months of 30 days each, with 5 complementary days added at the end As no intercalary day was allowed for, the first day of the year fell one day earlier every four years than the Julian year, consequently, to transpose a date from one era to another it is necessary to know the exact day and month of the Nabonassarian date, and to remember that 1460 Julian years are equal to 1461 Babylonian

Naboth's Vineyard (nā' both) The possession of another coveted by one able to possess himself of it. (1 *Kings* xxi)

Nabu. See NEBO.

Nacelle (nā sel'). This French word meaning a skiff or wherry is applied to the body of an aircraft—aeroplane, glider, or airship—which holds the crew, load, or motors.

Nadir (năd' ir). An Arabic word, signifying that point in the heavens which is directly opposite to the zenith, i e. directly under our feet; hence, figuratively, the lowest depths of degradation. *See also* ZENITH

Nævius. *See* ACCIUS NÆVIUS

Nag, Nagging. Constant fault-finding (A S. *gnag-an*, to gnaw, bite) We call a slight but constant pain, like a toothache, a *nagging pain*

Nag's Head Consecration. On the passing of the second Act of Uniformity in Queen Elizabeth's reign (1559), fourteen bishops vacated their sees, and all the other sees, except Llandaff, were at the time vacant The question was how to obtain consecration so as to preserve the apostolic succession unbroken, as Llandaff refused to officiate at Matthew Parker's consecration as Archbishop of Canterbury In this dilemma (the story runs) John Scory, the deposed Bishop of London, was sent for, and officiated at the Nag's Head tavern, in Cheapside, thus transmitting the succession. This is the story that was circulated some forty years later by certain Roman Catholics.

Strype refutes it, and so does Dr Hook We are told that it was not the *consecration* which took place at the Nag's Head, but only that those who took part in it dined there subsequently Bishops Barlow, Scory, Coverdale, and Hodgkins, all officiated at the consecration which was properly performed at Lambeth Palace on December 17th, 1559

Naiad (nī' ăd) Nymph of lake, fountain, river, or stream in classical mythology.
> You nymphs, call'd Naiads, of the wand'ring brooks,
> With your sedg'd crowns, and ever-harmless looks,
> Leave your crisp channels, and on this green land
> Answer your summons· Juno does command
> *Tempest*, iv, 1

Nail. The nails with which Our Lord was fastened to the cross were, in the Middle Ages, objects of great reverence Sir John Mandeville says, "He had two in his hondes, and two in his feet, and of on of theise the emperour of Constantynoble made a brydille to his hors, to bere him in bataylle; and throghe vertue thereof he overcam his enemyes" (c. vii). Fifteen are shown as relics. *See* IRON CROWN

In ancient Rome a nail was driven into the wall of the temple of Jupiter every 13th September This was originally done to tally the year, but subsequently it became a religious ceremony for warding off calamities and plagues from the city. Originally the nail was driven by the *prætor maximus*, subsequently by one of the consuls, and lastly by the dictator (*see Livy*, vii, 3).

A somewhat similar ceremony took place in Germany in World War I when patriotic Germans drove nails into a large wooden statue of Field-Marshal Hindenburg, buying each nail in support of a national fund

A nail was formerly a measure of weight of 8 lb It was used for wool, hemp, beef, cheese, etc. It was also a measure of length, = 2¼ in

> *Motto·* You shall have . a dozen beards, to stuffe two dozen cushions.
> *Lucio* Then they be big ones
> *Dello* They be halfe a yard broad, and a nayle, three quarters long, and a foote thick
> LYLY *Midas*, V, ii (1589).

For want of a nail. "For want of a nail, the shoe is lost, for want of a shoe, the horse is lost, and for want of a horse, the rider is lost " (Herbert *Jacula Prudentum.*)

Hard as nails. Stern, hard-hearted, unsympathetic, able to stand hard blows like nails The phrase is used with both a physical and a figurative sense, a man in perfect training is "as hard as nails," and bigotry, straitlacedness, rigid puritanical pharisaism, make people "hard as nails "

I know I'm as hard as nails already; I don't want to get more so —EDNA LYALL *Donovan*, ch. xxiii

Hung on the nail. Put in pawn The custom referred to is the old one of hanging each pawn on a nail, with a number attached, and giving the customer a duplicate thereof.

I nailed him (or it) I pinned him, meaning I secured him *Is* (xxii, 23) says, "I will fasten him as a nail in a sure place "

On the nail. At once, without hesitation, as, "to pay down on the nail "

In O'Keefe's *Recollections* we are told that in the centre of Limerick Exchange is a pillar with a circular plate of copper about 3 ft in diameter, called *The Nail*, on which the earnest of all Stock Exchange bargains has to be paid, there were four pillars called *Nails* and used for a similar purpose at Bristol, and at the Liverpool Exchange there was a plate of copper called *The Nail* on which bargains were settled But the phrase cannot come from any such source, as it was common in England by the 16th century, long before Exchanges were in existence *Cp* SUPERNACULUM

To drive a nail into one's coffin. *See* COFFIN

To hit the nail on the head. To come to a right conclusion In Latin, *Rem tenes.*

To nail to the counter. To convict and expose as false or spurious, as, "I nailed that lie to the counter at once " From the custom of shopkeepers nailing to the counter false money that is passed to them as a warning to others

Tooth and nail. *See* TOOTH

With colours nailed to the mast. *See* COLOURS

Nail-paring. Superstitious people are very particular as to the day on which they cut their nails. The old rhyme is

Cut them on Monday, you cut them for health,
Cut them on Tuesday, you cut them for wealth,
Cut them on Wednesday, you cut them for news;
Cut them on Thursday, a new pair of shoes,
Cut them on Friday, you cut them for sorrow,
Cut them on Saturday, you see your true love to-morrow;
Cut them on Sunday, your safety seek
The devil will have you the rest of the week.

Another rhyme conveys an even stronger warning on the danger of nail-cutting on a Sunday —

A man had better ne'er be born
As have his nails on a Sunday shorn

Nain Rouge (nān roozh) (Fr, red dwarf) A lutin or house spirit of Normandy, kind to fishermen. There is another called *Le petit homme rouge* (the little red man)

Naked. A.S *nacod*, a common Teutonic word, connected with Lat *nudus*, nude Destitute of covering, hence, figuratively, defenceless, exposed; without extraneous assistance, as *with the naked eye,* i e. without a telescope or other optical aid.

Naked boy, or lady. The meadow saffron (*Colchicum autumnale*), so called because, like the almond, peach, etc , the flowers come out before the leaves It is poetically called ' the leafless orphan of the year," the flowers being orphaned or destitute of foliage

The Naked Boy Courts and Alleys, of which there are more than one in the City of London, are named from the public-house sign of Cupid

The naked truth. The plain, unvarnished truth, truth without trimmings The fable says that Truth and Falsehood went bathing, Falsehood came first out of the water, and dressed herself in Truth's garments Truth, unwilling to take those of Falsehood, went naked.

Namby-pamby. Wishy-washy, insipid, weakly sentimental, said especially of authors It was the nickname of Ambrose Philips (1671-1749), bestowed upon him by Harry Carey, the dramatist, for his verses addressed to Lord Carteret's children, and was adopted by Pope.

Name.
What's in a name? That which we call a rose,
By any other name would smell as sweet
     Romeo and Juliet, ii, 2

Give a dog a bad name *See* DOG

Give it a name Tell me what it is you would like, said when offering a reward, a drink, etc

In the name of In reliance upon, or by the authority of

Their name liveth for evermore. These consolatory words, so often seen on war memorials are from the Apocrypha —

Their bodies are buried in peace, but their name liveth for evermore —*Ecclus* xliv, 14.

To call a person names. To blackguard him by calling him nicknames, or hurling opprobrious epithets at him.

Sticks and stones
May break my bones,
But names can never hurt me
     Old Rhyme.

To name the day To fix the day of the wedding—which is a privilege belonging to the bride to be

To take God's name in vain. To use it profanely, thoughtlessly, or irreverently

Thou shalt not take the name of the Lord thy God in vain —*Exod* xx, 7

Among all primitive peoples, and the ancient Hebrews were no exception, the *name* of a deity is regarded as his manifestation, and is treated with the greatest respect and veneration, and among savage tribes there is a widespread feeling of the danger of disclosing one's name, because this would enable an enemy by magic means to work one some deadly injury; the Greeks were particularly careful to disguise or reverse uncomplimentary names (*see* ERINYES, EUMENIDES, EUXINE).

Nancy, Miss. An effeminate, foppish youth The celebrated actress, "Mrs " Anne Oldfield (*see* NARCISSA) was nicknamed "Miss Nancy."

Nancy Boy is applied to a homosexual

Nankeen. So called from Nankin, in China It is the natural yellow colour of Nankin cotton

Nansen (nän' sen) Fridtjof Nansen (1861-1930) was a prominent figure at the close of the 19th and beginning of the present centuries In 1888-89 he was the first to cross the continent of Greenland, and four years later made an attempt to reach the North Pole in the *Fram*, reaching the farthest north recorded at that time, 86° 14' He is now chiefly remembered for the work he did in repatriating prisoners and displaced persons in 1919-20. Under the League of Nations he devised a comprehensive scheme, called the Nansen Scheme, for this purpose which gained international support and did great ameliorative work. For this he received the Nobel Prize in 1922

Nantes (näntz) **Edict of Nantes.** The decree of Henri IV of France, published from Nantes in 1598, securing freedom of religion to all Protestants. Louis XIV revoked it in 1685

Nap. The doze or short sleep gets its name from A S *hnæppian*, to sleep lightly the surface of cloth is probably so called from Mid. Dutch *noppe*; and *Nap*, the card game, is so called in honour of Napoleon III

To catch one napping. *See* CATCH.

To go nap. To set oneself to make five tricks (all one can) in the game of Nap; hence, to risk all you have on some venture, to back it through thick and thin

Naphtha (näf' tha). The Greek name for an inflammable, bituminous substance coming from the ground in certain districts, in the Medea legend it is the name of the drug used by the witch for anointing the wedding robe of Glauce, daughter of King Creon, whereby she was burnt to death on the morning of her marriage with Jason

Napier's Bones (nä' pēr) The little slips of bone or ivory invented in 1615 by John Napier of Merchiston (1550-1617) He had, the previous year, invented logarithms, and by the use of these on his strips of ivory, he shortened the labour of trigonometrical calculations By shifting these rods the result required is obtained

Napoleon Bonaparte. For all his many glaring faults and ambitions, Napoleon was one of the greatest men modern civilization has produced Within the short space of 15 years his campaigns and victories changed the aspect of Europe and made him the master of kings and peoples from Spain to the borders of Russia His influence is felt to this day in the Code Napoleon, the code of laws prepared under his direction, which forms the substance of the laws of France and Belgium and in importance is only second to the code of Justinian Equality in the eyes of the Law, justice, and common sense may be called its keynotes.

Napoleon III Few men have had so many nicknames

MAN OF DECEMBER, so called because his *coup d'etat* was December 2nd, 1851, and he was made emperor December 2nd, 1852.

MAN OF SEDAN, and, by a pun, *M Sedantaire*. It was at Sedan he surrendered his sword to William I King of Prussia (1870)

MAN OF SILENCE, from his great taciturnity

COMTE D'ARENENBERG, the name and title he assumed when he escaped from the fortress of Ham

BADINGUET, the name of the mason who changed clothes with him when he escaped from Ham The emperor's partisans were called *Badingueux*, those of the empress were *Montijoyeaux*

BOUSTRAPA is a compound of Bou[logne], Stra-[sbourg], and Pa[ris] the places of his noted escapades

RANTIPOLE, harum-scarum, half-fool and half-madman

There are some curious numerical coincidences connected with Napoleon III and Eugenie The last complete year of their reign was 1869 (In 1870 Napoleon was dethroned and exiled)

Now, if to the year of coronation (1852), you add either the birth of Napoleon, or the birth of Eugénie, or the capitulation of Paris, or the date of marriage, the sum will always be 1869 For example —

1852 {Coronation.}	1852	1852	1852
1 Birth 8 of 0 Napo- 8 leon.	1 Birth 8 of 2 Eugé- 6 nie	1 Date 8 of 5 mar- 3 riage	1 Capit- 8 ulat'n 7 of 1 Paris
1869	1869	1869	1869

And if to the year of *marriage* (1853) these dates are added, they will give 1870, the fatal year.

Napoleon of the Ring. James Belcher, the pugilist (1781-1811), who was remarkably like Napoleon in looks.

Napoo (na poo') Soldier slang introduced during World War I for something that is of no use or does not exist It represents the French phrase *il n'y en a plus*, there is no more of it

Nappy Ale. Strong ale has been so called for many centuries, probably because it contains a *nap* or frothy head

Naraka (nar' a kä) The hell of Hindu mythology It has twenty-eight divisions, in some of which the victims are mangled by ravens and owls, in others they are doomed to swallow cakes boiling hot, or walk over burning sands

Narcissa (nar sis' ä), in the *Night Thoughts*, was Elizabeth Lee, Dr Young's stepdaughter

In Pope's *Moral Essays* "Narcissa" stands for the actress, Anne Oldfield (1683-1730) When she died her remains lay in state attended by two noblemen She was buried in Westminster Abbey in a very fine Brussels lace head-dress, a holland shift, with a tucker and double-ruffles of the same lace, new kid gloves, etc

"Odious! In woollen? 'Twould a saint provoke!"
Were the last words that poor Narcissa spoke

POPE *Moral Essays*, i, 246

"In woollen" is an allusion to a law enacted for the benefit of the wool trade, that all shrouds were to be made of wool

Narcissus (nar sis' us) The son of Cephisus in Greek mythology, a beautiful youth who saw his reflection in a fountain, and thought it the presiding nymph of the place. He tried to reach it, and jumped into the fountain, where he died The nymphs came to take up the body that they might pay it funeral honours, but found only a flower, which they called by his name (Ovid's *Metamorphoses*, iii, 3⁴6, etc)

Plutarch says the plant is called Narcissus from the Greek *narke* (numbness), and that it is properly *narcosis*, meaning the plant which produces numbness or palsy

Echo fell in love with Narcissus.

Sweet Echo, sweetest nymph that liv'st unseen . -
Canst thou not tell me of a gentle pair,
That likest thy Narcissus are'
　　　　　　　MILTON *Comus*, 235.

Narcissism is the psychoanalytical term for sexual excitement through admiration of one's own body

Nark A police spy or informer, from a Romany word *nak*, a nose, on the analogy of Nosey Parker

Narrowdale Noon. To defer a matter *till Narrowdale noon* is to defer it indefinitely Narrowdale is the local name for the narrowest part of Dovedale, Derbyshire, in which dwell a few cotters, who never see the sun all the winter, and when its beams first pierce the dale in the spring it is only for a few minutes in the afternoon

Nary U S A colloquial expression for "never" or "never a", as in "They take everything, and nary dollar do you get " *Nary a red* is "never a red cent "

Naseby (nāz' bi) Fable has it that this town in Northamptonshire is so called because it was considered the *navel* (A S *nafela*) or centre of England, just as Delphi (*q v*) was considered "the navel of the earth " Fact, however, must destroy the illusion the town's name in Domesday Book is *Navesberi*, showing that it was the *burgh* or dwelling of Hnæf, a Dane

Naso (nā' zō) Ovid (Publius Ovidius Naso, 43 B C -A D 18), the Roman poet, author of *Metamorphoses* Naso means "nose," hence Holofernes' pun, "And why Naso, but for smelling out the odoriferous flowers of fancy " (Shakespeare *Love's Labour's Lost*, iv, 2)

Natheless (nāth' les) An archaic form of nevertheless

Smote on him sore besides, vaulted with fire
Natheless he so endured
　　　　　　　MILTON *Paradise Lost*, i.

National Anthem It is said by some that both the words and music of "God save the Queen," the British national anthem, were composed by Dr. John Bull (d 1628), organist at Antwerp cathedral 1617-28, where the original MS is still preserved Others attribute them to Henry Carey, author of *Sally in our Alley* The words, "Send her victorious," etc , look like a Jacobite song, and Sir John Sinclair tells us he saw that verse cut in an old glass tankard, the property of P Murray Threipland, of Fingask Castle, whose predecessors were staunch Jacobites.

No doubt the words have often been altered. The air and opening words were probably suggested by the *Domine Salvum* of the Catholic Church In 1605 the lines, "Frustrate their knavish tricks," etc , were perhaps added in reference to Gunpowder Plot, and in 1740

Henry Carey reset both words and music for the Mercers' Company on the birthday of George II.

The National Anthems or principal patriotic songs of the leading nations follow —

Argentine *Oid mortales, el grito sagrado Libertad*

Australia. *Advance Australia.*

Austria (Republic) *Osterreichische Bundeshymne* (Nazi) *Lied der Jugend*

Belgium The *Brabançonne* (q v.)

Brazil: *Ouviram do Yspiranga as margens placidas.*

Canada *The Maple Leaf Forever*. (French) *O Canada terre de nos aieux.*

Chile *Dulce patria*

Denmark *The Song of the Danebrog* (see DANEBROG), *Kong Christian stod ved hoien Mast, Rog og Damp* (King Christian stood beside the lofty mast, In mist and smoke)

Eire *Let Erin remember the days of old.*

France The *Marseillaise* (q v)

Germany *Deutschland über alles* (Germany over all), and *Die Wacht am Rhein* (The watch —or guard—on the Rhine) (Nazi) *Horst Wessel Lied*

Greece *Se gnorizo apo ten kopsi tu spati'iu ten tromere.*

Holland. *Wien Neerlandsch bloed in de aders vloeit, Van vreemde smetten vrij* (Let him in whose veins flows the blood of the Netherlands, free from an alien strain . .)

Italy (Kingdom) *Marcia Reale*, (Fascist) *Giovinezza*, (Republic) Garibaldi's Hymn.

Mexico *Mexicanos al grito guerra.*

New Zealand: *God defend New Zealand*

Norway *Ja, vi elsker det te Landet som det stiger frem* (Yes, we love our country, just as it is)

Peru *Somos libros, seamos lo siempre*

Portugal *Heiros do mar*

Russia· (1917-44) The Internationale, (since 1944) *Gymn Sovietskogo Soiusa*

Scotland *Scots wha hae wi' Wallace bled*

South Africa *Die Stem van Suid-Afrika*

Spain *Marcha grandera.*

Sweden *Du gamla du friska, du fjellhog Nord, Du tysta, du gladjerika skòna'* (Thou ancient, free, and mountainous North' Thou silent, joyous, and beautiful North')

Switzerland *Rufst du, mein Vaterland Sieh uns mit Herz und Hand, All dir geweiht'* (Thou call'st, my Fatherland! Behold us, heart and hand, all devoted to thee!)

The United States *The Star-spangled Banner.* See STARS AND STRIPES.

Wales *Mae hen wlad fy nhadau* (Land of my fathers), also *Men of Harlech.*

National Colours (*See* COLOURS.)

National Convention. The assembly of deputies which assumed the government of France on the overthrow of the throne in 1792 It succeeded the National Assembly (*cp* CONSTITUENT ASSEMBLY)

National Debt. Money borrowed by a Government, on the security of the taxes, which are pledged to the lenders for the payment of interest The portion of our National Debt which is converted into bonds or annuities is known as the *Funded Debt*, and the portion that is repayable at a stated time or on demand as the *Floating Debt*

The National Debt in William III's reign was £15,730,439

At the commencement of the American war, £128,583,635.

At the close thereof, £249,851,628

At the close of the French war. £840,850,491

The existence of National Debts is almost entirely due to wars, as the following figures will show in the case of the British Debt.

Just before the Revolution of 1688 it stood at £664,263, the Revolution added nearly £16,000,000, the Marlborough campaigns in Queen Anne's reign added nearly £38,000,000, the American War, in George III's, £121,000,-000, and the Napoleonic Wars (1793-1816) over £600,000,000, bringing the total debt in 1816 to £900,436,000 At Queen Victoria's accession (1837) this had been reduced to £788,000,000, the Crimean War added £33,000,000 and thereafter reductions were made annually (with only five exceptions) till 1899, the year of the outbreak of the Boer War, when the Debt stood at £628,021,572 This war added over £160,000,000, but from 1904 to the outbreak of World War I reductions were made annually (with one exception), so that in 1914 the Debt was £651,270,091 On March 31st, 1951, the British National Debt stood at £26,000,000,000

National Guard Military forces raised in each State but partly trained, equipped and quartered by the U S A Federal government When called up by the President these forces become an integral part of the armed forces.

Nations, Battle of the. A name given to the great battle of Leipzig in the Napoleonic wars (Oct 16th-19th, 1813), when the French under Napoleon were defeated by the coalition armies, consisting of the Prussians, Russians, Austrians, and Swedes

Native (Lat, *nativus*, produced by birth, natural) In feudal times, one born a serf After the Conquest, the natives were the serfs of the Normans Wat Tyler said to Richard II

The first peticion was that he scholde make alle men fre thro Ynglonde and quiete, so that there scholde not be eny native man after that time —HIGDEN *Polychronicon*, VIII, 457.

Legally, a person is a native of the place of his parents' domicile, wherever he himself may have happened to be born

Oysters raised in artificial beds are called *natives*, though they may be, and frequently are, imported This is because artificially reared oysters are the best, and for centuries the best oysters were those actually taken from British waters. It is a case of the transference of a convenient name

Nativity, The Christmas Day, the day set apart in honour of the Nativity or Birth of Christ.

The Cave of the Nativity. The tradition that the rock cave near Constantine's basilica, S Maria a Præsepio, is the birthplace of the Saviour dates from the time of St Jerome (d 420), when Bethlehem had been a wood-covered wilderness since it was devastated by Hadrian three hundred years earlier The

chancel of the basilica was subsequently built over it. In the recess, a few feet above the ground is a stone slab with a star cut in it, to mark the supposed spot where Christ was born. and near it is a hollow scraped out of the rock, said to be the place where the Infant was laid

To cast a man's nativity. The astrologers' term for constructing a plan or map of the position, etc, of the twelve "houses" which belong to him, and explaining the significance.

Natter, To To talk aimlessly, foolishly or without sense It is a Scots word of long standing, probably deriving from the Icelandic *knetta*, to grumble

Nature In a state of nature. Nude or naked.

Natural. A born idiot, one on whom education can make no impression As nature made him, so he remains

A natural child. One not born in lawful wedlock The Romans called the children of concubines *naturales*, children according to nature, and not according to law

Cui pater est populus, pater est sibi nullus omnes,
Cui pater est populus non habet ille patrem —OVID.

In Music a **natural** is a white key on the pianoforte, etc, as distinguished from a black key. In musical notation the sign ♮ is employed to counteract the following note from a sharp or flat in the signature.

Natural Philosophy. *See* EXPERIMENTAL.

Naught, Nought. These are merely variants of the same word, *naught* representing A S *na whil* and *nought*, *no whit* In most senses they are interchangeable, but nowadays *naught* is the more common form, except for the name of the cipher, which is usually *nought*

Naught was formerly applied to things that were bad or worthless, as in 2 *Kings* II, 19, "The water is naught and the ground barren," and it is with this sense that Jeremiah (XXIV, 2) speaks of "naughty figs" —

One basket had very good figs, even like the figs that are first ripe .. The other basket had very naughty figs which could not be eaten.

The Revised Version did away with the old "naughty" and substituted "bad", and in the next verse, where the Authorized calls the figs "evil," the Douai Version has —

The good figges, exceeding good, and the naughtie figges, exceeding naught which can not be eaten because they are naught

Nausicaa (naw sik ā′ a). The Greek heroine whose story is told in the Odyssey She was the daughter of Alcinous, king of the Phæacians, and the shipwrecked Odysseus found her playing at ball with her maidens on the shore Pitying his plight she conducted him to her father, by whom he was entertained.

Nautical Mile. *See* MILE

Navaho (năv′ á hō) The largest tribal group of N American Indians in the U S A Their reservations are in New Mexico and Arizona, where they retain much of their traditional way of life and eschew contact with the white men. The Navahos belong to the southern division of the Athapascan stock, to which belong the Apache tribes.

Navicert. Contraction of Navigation Certificate, issued by the British authorities to merchant ships carrying non-contraband cargo to facilitate their passage through the blockade First used (at any rate in modern times) during the Spanish Civil War, and continued during World War II.

Navvy. A contraction of navigator One employed to make railways.

Canals were thought of as lines of inland navigation, and a tavern built by the side of a canal was called a "Navigation Inn" Hence it happened that the men employed in excavating canals were called "navigators," shortened into navvies —SPENSER *Principles of Sociology*, vol i, appendix C, p. 834

Nay-word. Password Slender, in *The Merry Wives of Windsor*, says —

We have a nay-word how to know each other. I come to her in white and cry *Mum*, she cries *Budget*, and by that we know one another

Nazaraeans or **Nazarenes** (năz' à rēnz) A sect of Jewish Christians, who believed Christ to be the Messiah, that He was born of the Holy Ghost, and that He possessed a Divine nature, but who, nevertheless, conformed to the Mosaic rites and ceremonies

Nazarene. A native of Nazareth, Our Lord is so called (*John* xviii, 5, 7, *Acts* xxiv, 5), though He was born in Bethlehem

Can any good thing come out of Nazareth? (*John* i, 46) A general insinuation against any family or place of ill repute Can any great man come from such an insignificant village as Nazareth?

Nazarite (năz' a rīt) One separated or set apart to the Lord by a vow They refrained from strong drink, and allowed their hair to grow. (Heb *nazar*, to separate *Numb* vi, 1-21)

Nazi (nat' zi, naz' i). The shortened form of *Nazional-Sozialist*, the name given to the party of Adolf Hitler and its members

Ne plus ultra (nē plŭs ŭl' trà) (Lat., nothing further, i e. perfection) The most perfect state to which a thing can be brought. *See* PLUS ULTRA

Neaera (ne ē' ra) Any sweetheart or ladylove She is mentioned by Horace, Virgil, and Tibullus

To sport with Amaryllis in the shade,
Or with the tangles of Neaera's hair.
MILTON. *Lycidas*

Neanderthal Man (ni ăn' dèr tal) A palaeolithic race inhabiting Europe during the Mousterian period It was first revealed by the discovery of a human burial in a grotto of the Neanderthal ravine near Düsseldorf, in 1856. Its fossil remains have since been found in widely scattered caves

Neap Tide. The tide between spring tides which attains the least height at or near the first and last quarters of the moon The high water rises little more than half as high above the mean level as it does at spring tide, and the low water sinks about half as little below it.

Near, meaning *mean,* is rather a curious play on the word *close* (close-fisted). What is "close by" is near

Near Side and Off Side. Left side and right side. "Near wheel" means that to the driver's left hand, and "near horse" (in a pair) means that to the left hand of the driver In a four-in-hand the two horses on the left side of the coachman are the near wheeler and the near leader Those on the right-hand side are "off" horses. This, which seems an anomaly, arose when the driver *walked* beside his team The teamster always walks with his right arm nearest the horse, and therefore, in a pair of horses, the horse on the left side is nearer than the one on his right *See also* OFF-SIDE

Nebo (nē' bō) A god of the Babylonians (properly, *Nabu*) mentioned in *Is* xlvi, 1, and corresponding more or less with the classical Hermes He was the patron of Borsippa, near Babylon, and was regarded as the inventor of the art of writing, as well as the god of wisdom and the herald of the gods The name occurs in many Babylonian royal names (Nebuchadrezzar, Nebushasban [*Jer* xxxix, 13], Nebuzaradan [2 *Kings,* xxv, 8], etc), but it is very doubtful whether it is present, as has been stated, in the place-name *Nebo*, or the personal name *Barnabas.*

Nebuchadnezzar (neb û kăd nez' år) This name which is now firmly fixed in English, is a mistake, for it is a misrendering in the Hebrew of Daniel (and consequently in English and other translations) of the Babylonian *Nabu-kudur-usur,* and should be *Nebuchadrezzar,* as indeed it is given in *Jer* xxi, 2, etc The French call him *Nabuchodonosor,* or *Nabuchodoroser,* which are nearer the Greek transliteration The name means *Nebo protects the crown See* NEBO

Nebuchadnezzar was the greatest king of Assyria, and reigned for forty-three years (604-561 B C) He restored his country to its former prosperity and importance, practically rebuilt Babylon, restored the temple of Bel, erected a new palace, embanked the Euphrates, and probably built the celebrated Hanging Gardens His name became the centre of many legends, and of the story related by Daniel (iv, 29-33) that he was one day walking—

in the palace of the kingdom of Babylon and said, "Is not this great Babylon that I have built by the might of my power, and for the honour of my majesty?" And "the same hour he was driven from men, and did eat grass as oxen, and his body was wet with the dew of heaven, till his hairs were grown like eagles' feathers, and his nails like birds' claws"

This is an allusion to the suspension of his interest in public affairs, which lasted, as his inscription records, for four years

Necessary. The 17th- and 18th-century term for a privy In large houses the emptying and cleaning of this was carried out by a servant known as the *Necessary Woman*

Necessitarians. *See* AGENT.

Necessity. Necessity knows no law. These were the words used by Dr von Bethmann-Hollweg, the German Imperial Chancellor, in the Reichstag on August 4th, 1914, as a justification for the German infringement of Belgian neutrality —

Gentlemen, we are now in a state of necessity (*Notwehr*), and necessity (*Not*) knows no law Our troops have occupied Luxemburg and perhaps have already entered Belgian territory

To quote Milton—

So spake the Fiend, and with necessity,
The tyrant s plea excused his devilish deeds
Paradise Lost, iv, 393

The phrase is, of course, not original Cromwell used it in a speech to Parliament on September 12th, 1654, but to very different purpose —

Necessity hath no law Feigned necessities, imaginary necessities, are the greatest cozenage men can put upon the Providence of God, and make pretences to break known rules by.

It is common to most languages. Publius Syrus has *Necessitas dat legem, non ipsa accipit* (Necessity gives the law, but does not herself accept it), and the Latin proverb *Necessitas non habet legem* appears in *Piers Plowman* (14th century) as "Neede hath no lawe."

To make a virtue of necessity. To "grin and bear it", what can't be cured must be endured"

Thanne is it wisdom, as it thinketh me
To maken vertu of necessitee
CHAUCER· *Knightes Tale*, 3041

Are you content to be our general?
To make a virtue of necessity
And live, as we do, in this wilderness?
Two Gentlemen of Verona, iv, 1

Quintilian has *laudem virtutis necessitati damus*, St Jerome (epistle 54, section 6), *Fac de necessitate virtutem*. In the *Roman de la Rose*, line 14058, we find *S'il ne fait de necessite virtu*, and Boccaccio has *Si come savia fatta della necessita*.

Neck. Slang for brazen impudence, colossal cheek

Neck and crop. Entirely The crop is the gorge of a bird; a variant of the phrase, is, *neck and heels*, as I bundled him out neck and heels. There was a punishment formerly in vogue which consisted in bringing the chin and knees of the culprit forcibly together, and then thrusting him into a cage.

Neck and neck. Very near in merit, very close competitors A phrase used in horse races, when two or more horses run each other very closely.

Neck of woods. (U.S A) A settlement in the forest.

Neck or nothing. Desperate A racing phrase, to win by a neck or to be nowhere—*i.e.* not counted at all because unworthy of notice

Oh that the Roman people had but one neck! The words of Caligula, the Roman emperor He wished that he could slay them all with one stroke.

Stiff-necked. Obstinate and self-willed In the *Psalms* we read· "Speak not with a stiff neck" (lxxv, 5); and *Jer* xvii, 23, "They obeyed not, but made their necks stiff", and Isaiah (xlviii, 4) says "Thy neck is an iron sinew." The allusion is to a wilful horse, ox, or ass, which will not answer to the reins.

To break the neck of an enterprise. To begin it successfully, and overcome the first difficulties Well begun is half done.

To get it in the neck. To be completely defeated, thoroughly castigated, soundly rated, etc The phrase is an Americanism, from the picturesque expression of one who has just been "through it"— *I got it where the chicken got the axe*—which, of course, is "in the neck."

To stick one's neck out. To expose oneself to being hurt, as a chicken might stick out its neck for the axe

Neck-tie party (U S A.) A hanging, particularly by lynch law (*q.v*)

Neck-verse. The first verse of *Ps* li. *See* MISERERE "Have mercy upon me, O God, according to Thy loving-kindness according unto the multitude of Thy tender mercies blot out my transgressions"

He [a treacherous Italian interpreter] by a fine cunny-catching corrupt translation, made us plainly to confesse, and cry *Miserere*, ere we had need of our necke-verse.—NASH. *The Unfortunate Traveller* (1594).

This verse was so called because it was the trial-verse of those who claimed Benefit of Clergy (*q v*), and if they could read it, the ordinary of Newgate said, *"Legit ut clericus,"* and the prisoner *saved his neck*, being only burnt in the hand and set at liberty.

If a clerk had been taken
For stealing of bacon,
For burglary, murder, or rape
If he could but rehearse
(Well prompt) his neck-verse,
He never could fail to escape
British Apollo (1710)

Necklace. A necklace of coral or white bryony beads used to be worn by children to aid their teething Necklaces of hyoscyamus or henbane-root have been recommended for the same purpose

Diamond necklace. *See* DIAMOND

The fatal necklace. Cadmus received on his wedding-day the present of a necklace, which proved fatal to everyone who possessed it. Some say that Vulcan, and others that Europa, gave it to him Harmonia's necklace (*q.v*) was a similar fatal gift.

Necromancy (nek' rō mǎn' si) Prophesying by calling up the dead, as the witch of Endor called up Samuel (1 *Sam* xxviii, 7 ff) (Gr. *nekros*, the dead, *manteia*, prophecy)

Nectar (Gr) The drink of the gods of classical mythology Like their food, *Ambrosia*, it conferred immortality Hence the name of the *nectarine*, so called because it is "as sweet as nectar"

The Koran tells us "the righteous shall be given to drink pure wine sealed with musk."

Neddy. An old familiar name for a donkey

Needfire. Fire obtained by friction; formerly supposed to defeat sorcery, and cure diseases ascribed to witchcraft, especially cattle diseases In Henderson's *Agricultural Survey of Caithness* (1812) we are told that as late as 1785—

when the stock of any considerable farmer was seized with the murrain, he would send for one of the charm doctors to superintend the raising of a need-fire.

Needful, The. Ready money, cash

Needham. You are on the high-road to Needham—to ruin or poverty The pun is on the *need*, and there is no reference to Needham in Suffolk Cp. LAND OF NOD.

Needle. Looking for a needle, etc. *See* BOTTLE

The eye of a needle. *See* EYE

To get the needle To become thoroughly vexed, or even enraged, and to show it A variant of the phrase is *to get the spike*

To hit the needle. Hit the right nail on the head, to make a perfect hit A term in archery, equal to hitting the bull's-eye

Negative. The answer is in the negative The circumlocutory Parliamentary way of enouncing the monosyllable *No*

Negro. Negro offspring. White father and negro mother mulatto

White father and mulatto mother· quadroon White father and quadroon mother quintero

White father and quintero mother, white

Negro drunk (U.S A) Very drunk indeed

Negus (nē′ gus). The drink—port or sherry, with hot water, sugar, and spices—is so called from a Colonel Francis Negus (d 1732), who first concocted it

The supreme ruler of Abyssinia is entitled *the Negus*, from the native *n′gus*, meaning crowned

Neiges d'Antan, Les (nāzh don tan) (Fr). A thing of the past Literally, "last year's snows," from the refrain of Villon's well-known *Ballade des Dames du Temps Jadis*—

Prince, n'enquerez de semaine
Ou elles sont, ni de cet an,
Que ce refrain ne vous remaine,
Mais où sont les neiges d'antan]
(Where are the snows of yester-year?)

Nemean (nem′ ē ἀn). Pertaining to Nemea, the ancient name of a valley in Argolis, Greece, about 10 m SW of Corinth

The Nemean Games One of the four great national festivals of Greece, celebrated at Nemea every alternate year, the second and fourth of each Olympiad Legend states that they were instituted in memory of Arche-morus, who died from the bite of a serpent as the expedition of the Seven against Thebes was passing through the valley

The victor's reward was at first a crown of olive leaves, but subsequently a garland of ivy. Pindar has eleven odes in honour of victors

The Nemean Lion. A terrible lion which kept the people of the valley in constant alarm. The first of the twelve Labours of Hercules was to slay it, he could make no impression on the beast with his club, so he caught it in his arms and squeezed it to death Hercules ever after wore the skin as a mantle

My fate cries out,
And makes each petty artery in this body
As hardy as the Nemean lion's nerve
Hamlet, i, 4

Nemesis (nem′ ė sis). The Greek goddess who allotted to men their exact share of good, or bad fortune, and was responsible for seeing that everyone got his due and deserts, the personification of divine retribution Hence, retributive justice generally, as **the Nemesis** of **nations**, the fate which, sooner or later, has overtaken every great nation of the ancient and modern world.

And though circuitous and obscure
The feet of Nemesis how sure!
SIR WILLIAM WATSON *Europe at the Play*

21*

Nemine contradicente (usually contracted to **nem. con.**) No one opposing

Nemine dissentiente (nem. diss.). Without a dissentient voice

Nemo me impune lacessit (nē′ mō mē im pū ni la ses′ it) (Lat) No one injures me with impunity The motto of the Order of the Thistle (*q v*)

Neolithic Age, The (nē ō lith′ ik) (Gr *neos*, new, *lithos*, a stone) The later Stone Age of Europe, the earlier being called the Palæolithic (Gr *palaios*, ancient) Stone implements of the Neolithic age are polished, more highly finished, and more various than those of the Palæolithic, and are found in kitchen-middens and tombs, with the remains of recent and extinct animals, and sometimes with bronze implements Neolithic man knew something of agriculture, kept domestic animals, used boats, and caught fish.

Nepenthe or **Nepenthes** (ne pen′ thē) (Gr *ne*, not, *penthos*, grief) An Egyptian drug mentioned in the *Odyssey* (iv, 228) that was fabled to drive away care and make persons forget their woes Polydamna, wife of Thonis, king of Egypt, gave it to Helen, daughters of Jove and Leda

That nepenthes which the wife of Thone
In Egypt gave the Jove-born Helena
MILTON *Comus*, 695-6

Nephew (Fr *neveu*, Lat. *nepos*) Both in Latin and in archaic English the word means a grandchild, or descendant Hence, in the Authorized Version of I *Tim*. v, 4, we read— "If a widow have children or nephews," but in the Revised "grandchildren " Propertius has it, *Me inter seros laudabit Roma nepotes* (posterity)

Niece (Lat *neptis*) also means a grand-daughter or female descendant *See* NEPOTISM.

Nepman. This is the term applied in the U.S.S R to a man who engaged in private business under the New Economic Policy (N E P.) This was a programme begun in 1921 to revive the wage system and private owner-ship of certain factories and businesses, at the same time relinquishing the requisitions of grain

Nepomuk. *See* ST JOHN OF NEPUMUK, *under* JOHN

Nepotism (Lat *nepos*, a nephew or kinsman). An unjustifiable elevation of one's own relations to places of wealth and trust at one's disposal

Neptune (nep′ tūn) The Roman god of the sea, corresponding with the Greek Poseidon (*q v*), hence used allusively for the sea itself Neptune is represented as an elderly man of stately mien, bearded, carrying a trident, and sometimes astride a dolphin or a horse *See* HIPPOCAMPUS.

great Neptune with this threeforkt mace,
That rules the Seas, and makes them rise or fall;
His dewy lockes did drop with brine apace,
Under his Diademe imperiall
SPENSER· *Faerie Queene*, IV, xi, 11

Neptunian or **Neptunist.** The name given to certain 18th-century geologists, who held the opinion of Werner (1750-1817), that all the great rocks of the earth were once held in solution in water, and were deposited as sediment. The *Vulcanists* or *Plutonians* ascribed them to the agency of fire

Nereus (nē′ rūs). A sea-god of Greek mythology, represented as a very old man. He was the father of the fifty Nereids (*q v.*), and his special dominion was the Ægean Sea

Nereids were the sea-nymphs of Greek mythology, the fifty daughters of Nereus and "grey-eyed" Doris The best known are Amphitrite, Thetis, and Galatea, Milton refers to another, Panope—in *Lycidas* (line 99)—

> The air was calm, and on the level brine
> Sleek Panope with all her sisters played

And the names of all will be found in Spenser's *Faerie Queene*, Bk iv, c. xi, verses 48-57.

Neri. *See* BIANCHI

Nero, A. Any bloody-minded man, relentless tyrant, or evil-doer of extraordinary savagery, from the depraved and infamous Roman Emperor, C Claudius Nero (A D 54-68), who set fire to Rome to see, it is said, "what Troy would have looked like when it was in flames," and is reported to have fiddled as he watched the conflagration

Nero of the North. Christian II of Denmark (1481-1559), also called "The Cruel" He massacred the Swedish nobility at Stockholm in 1520, and thus prepared the way for Gustavus Vasa and Swedish freedom

Nerthus or **Hertha.** The name given by Tacitus to a German or Scandinavian goddess of fertility, or "Mother Earth," who was worshipped on the island of Rugen She roughly corresponds with the classical Cybele, and is probably confused with the Scandinavian god *Njorthr* or *Niordhr*, the protector of sailors and fishermen *Nerthus* and *Njorthr* alike mean "benefactor"

Nessus. Shirt of Nessus. A source of misfortune from which there is no escape, a fatal present. The legend is that Hercules ordered Nessus (the centaur) to carry his wife Dejanira across a river. The centaur attempted to carry her off, and Hercules shot him with a poisoned arrow. Nessus, in revenge, gave Dejanira his tunic, deceitfully telling her that it would preserve her husband's love, and she gave it to her husband, who was devoured by the poison still remaining in it from his own arrow as soon as he put it on He was at once taken with mortal pains; Dejanira hanged herself from remorse, and the hero threw himself on a funeral pile, and was borne away to Olympus by the gods *Cp.* HARMONIA'S ROBE.

> While to my limbs th' envenomed mantle clings,
> Drenched in the centaur's black, malignant gore
> WEST *Triumphs of the Gout (Lucian)*

Nest-egg. Money laid by. The allusion is to the custom of placing an egg in a hen's nest to induce her to lay her eggs there. If a person has saved a little money, it serves as an inducement to him to increase his store

Nestor. King of Pylos, in Greece, the oldest and most experienced of the chieftains who went to the siege of Troy. Hence the name is frequently applied as an epithet to the oldest

and wisest man of a class or company Samuel Rogers, for instance, who lived to be 92, was called "the Nestor of English poets"

Nestorians. Followers of Nestorius, Patriarch of Constantinople, 428-431 He maintained that Christ had two distinct natures, and that Mary was the mother of His human nature, which was the mere shell or husk of the divine. They spread in India and the Far East, and remains of the Nestorian Christians, their inscriptions, etc , are still found in China, but the greater part of their churches were destroyed by Timur (Tamerlane) about 1400

Net. On the Old Boy net. To arrange something through a friend (originally, someone known at school) instead of through the usual channels—a British military expression in World War II

Neustria (nū′ stria) The western portion of the ancient Frankish kingdom, corresponding roughly to the northern and north-western provinces of France

Never. There are numerous locutions to express this idea; as—

> At the coming of the Coquecigrues (RABELAIS' *Pantagruel*)
> At the Latter Lammas.
> On the Greek Calends
> In the reign of Queen Dick
> On St Tib's Eve
> In a month of five Sundays
> When two Friday s or three Sundays come together
> When Dover and Calais meet
> When Dudman and Ramehead meet
> When the world grows honest
> When the Yellow River runs clear

Never Never Land. An Australian term for North Queensland.

New. New Deal. The name given to President Roosevelt's policy, announced in his first presidential campaign (1932) when he said "we are going to think less about the producer and more about the consumer . and bring about a more equitable distribution of the national income" The New Deal took shape in the National Industrial Recovery Act which empowered the President to lay down codes regulating industry, child labour, minimum wages and maximum hours In 1935 these codes were judged unconstitutional by the U.S Supreme Court

Newfangled. Applied to anything of a quite new or different fashion; a novelty The older word was *newfangle*—

> Men loven of propre kinde newfangelnesse
> As briddes doon that men in cages fede .
> So newfangel ben they of hir mete,
> And loven novelryes of propre kinde
> CHAUCER *Squire's Tale*, 602, 610

M E *fangel*, from A S *fang*, past part of *fōn*, to take, meaning "always ready to take, or grasp at, some new thing"

New Learning. The name sometimes given to the revival of Greek and Latin classical learning during the 15th and 16th centuries. It was the chief motive of the Renaissance and was at its zenith from the fall of Constantinople in 1453 to the sack of Rome in 1527.

New Lights. *See* CAMPBELLITES.

New Style. The reformed or Gregorian Calendar, adopted in England in 1752 *See* GREGORIAN YEAR

New Theology. An interpretation of Christian teaching based on broader views than that of the older fundamental reading of the Bible It was first expounded in 1907 by R J Campbell, at the time Congregational minister at the City Temple He later entered the Church of England

New Thought A general term for a system of therapeutics based on the theory that the mental and physical problems of life should be met, regulated and controlled by the suggestion of right thoughts This system has nothing in common with Christian Science, auto-suggestion or psycho-therapy

New World America the Eastern Hemisphere is called the Old World

New Year's Day. January 1st The Romans began their year in March, hence *September*, *October*, *November*, *December* for the 7th, 8th, 9th, and 10th months Since the introduction of the Christian era, Christmas Day, Lady Day, Easter Day, March 1st and March 25th have in turns been considered as New Year's Day; but at the reform of the calendar in the 16th century (*see* CALENDAR), January 1st was accepted by practically all Christian peoples
In England the civil and legal year began on March 25th till after the alteration of the style, in 1752, when it was fixed, like the historic year, to January 1st In Scotland the legal year was changed to January 1st as far back as 1600.

New Year's gifts The giving of presents at this time was a custom among both the Greeks and the Romans, the latter calling them *strenæ*, whence the French term *étrenne* (a New Year's gift) Nonius Marcellus says that Tatius, King of the Sabines, was presented with some branches of trees cut from the forest sacred to the goddess Strenia (*strength*), on New Year's Day, and from this incident the custom arose
Our forefathers used to bribe the magistrates with gifts on New Year's Day—a custom abolished by law in 1290, but even down to the reign of James II the monarchs received their tokens

Newcastle upon Tyne was so called (*Noef-Chastel-sur-Tine*, or *Novum Castellum*) from the castle built there by Robert, son of the Conqueror, in 1080, to defend the neighbourhood from the Scots Previous names were, in Roman times, *Pons Ælii*, and, by the Anglo-Saxons, *Munechecaster* (Monks' castle)
Newcastle was the first coal port in the world and the first charter granted to the town for the digging of coal was given by Henry III in 1239

To carry coals to Newcastle. *See* COAL

Newcastle under Lyme was known as *Novum Oppidum* (Lat., New Town) till about 1200, when the new castle was built to supply the place of an older one which stood at Chesterton-under-Lime, about two miles distant

New England The name given collectively to the north-eastern States of the USA— Connecticut, Massachusetts, Rhode Island, Vermont, New Hampshire and Maine The name was given by Captain John Smith to what was then part of "North Virginia," granted to the Plymouth Company by James I, in 1606 Between 1643 and 1684 the New England Confederation of the colonies of Massachussetts Bay, Plymouth, Connecticut, and New Haven was in force to secure a united defence against the Dutch and the Indians

Newgate. According to Stow this was first built in the city wall of London in the time of Henry I, but excavations have shown that there was a Roman gate here, about 31 ft in width It may have fallen into disuse, and have been repaired by Henry I, the present name being given at the time

Newgate Gaol was originally merely a few cells over the gate; the first great prison here was built in 1422, and the last in 1770-83 For centuries it was the gaol for the City and for the County of Middlesex, it was demolished in 1902, and the Central Criminal Court (opened 1905) erected on its site
From its prominence, Newgate came to be applied as a general name for gaols, and Nash, in his *Pierce Penilesse* (1592) says it is "a common name for all prisons, as *homo* is a common name for a man or woman "

Newgate Calendar, The. A biographical record of the more notorious criminals confined at Newgate, begun in 1773 and continued at intervals for many years In 1824-28 A Knapp and Wm Baldwin published, in 4 vols , *The Newgate Calendar, comprising Memoirs of Notorious Characters*, partly compiled by George Borrow; and in 1886 C. Pelham published his *Chronicles of Crime, or the New Newgate Calendar* (2 vols) The term is often used as a comprehensive expression embracing crime of every sort
I also felt that I had committed every crime in the Newgate Calendar —DICKENS *Our Mutual Friend*, ch xiv

Newgate fashion. Two by two Prisoners used to be conveyed to Newgate coupled together in twos.
Must we all march?
Yes, two and two, Newgate fashion
SHAKESPEARE 1 *Henry IV*, iii, 3.

Newgate fringe. The hair worn under the chin, or between the chin and the neck So called because it occupies the position of the rope when men are about to be hanged

Newgate knocker. A lock of hair twisted into a curl, worn by costermongers and persons of similar status So called because it resembles a knocker, and the wearers were too often inmates of Newgate

New Jerusalem. The city of heaven foretold in *Rev* xxi, "coming down from God out of heaven, prepared as a bride adorned for her husband."

The New Jerusalem Church was the name chosen by Richard Hindmarsh in 1787 for the sect founded by him on the doctrines of Emanuel Swedenborg

New South Wales is the oldest state in the Commonwealth of Australia It was so named in 1770 by Captain Cook from its fancied resemblance from the sea to the northern shores of the Bristol Channel. The famous penal settlement of Botany Bay was founded there in 1787, five miles south of the present city of Sydney, itself named after Thomas Townshend, 1st Viscount Sydney, at that time secretary of state in charge of colonial affairs

New York The first settlements here were made on Manhattan Island by the Dutch in 1614 Manhattan Island was bought from the Indians for cloth and trinkets to the total value of about £5 Under the name of New Amsterdam it was held by the Dutch until 1644. In that year the whole of the Atlantic seaboard was granted by Charles II to his brother James, Duke of York. Col Richard Nicolls sailed there at once with four ships and 30 soldiers, and overcoming the gallant resistance of the Dutch governor, Peter Stuyvesant, captured the place and renamed it after his patron, New York It has thus no connection with the English city of York.

News. The letters E W used to be prefixed to
S
newspapers to show that they obtained information from the four quarters of the world, and the supposition that our word *news* is thence derived is at least ingenious, the old-fashioned way of spelling the word, *newes*, is alone fatal to the conceit. Fr *nouvelles* is the real source

> News is conveyed by letter, word or mouth
> And comes to us from North, East, West and South
> *Wit's Recreations*

The word is now nearly always construed as singular ("the news *is* very good this morning"), but it was formerly treated as a plural, and in the *Letters of Queen Victoria* the Queen, and most of her correspondents, followed that rule —

> The news from Austria are very sad, and make one very anxious —*To the King of the Belgians*, 20 Aug., 1861

Newscast. The American term for the radio broadcast of news.

Newt. *See* NICKNAMES

Newtonian Philosophy. The astronomical system that in the late 17th century displaced the Copernican (*see* COPERNICANISM), together with the theory of universal gravitation. So called after Sir Isaac Newton (1642-1727), who established the former and discovered the latter.

> Nature and Nature's laws lay hid in night
> God said "Let Newton be," and all was light
> POPE.

Next of Kin. The legal term for a person's nearest relative, more especially where estate is left by an intestate. In English law the next of kin in priority is —

> Husband or wife; children, father or mother (equally if both alive), brothers and sisters, half brothers and sisters, grandparents; uncles and aunts, half uncles and aunts, the Crown.

Next Friend, in law, is an adult who brings an action in a court of law on behalf of a minor

Nibelungenlied, The (nē be lung' en lēd) A Middle High German poem, the greatest monument of early German literature, founded on old Scandinavian legends contained in the *Volsunga Saga* and the *Edda*, and written in its present form by an anonymous South German of the early part of the 13th century

Nibelung was a mythical king of a race of Scandinavian dwarfs dwelling in *Nibelheim* (*i.e.* 'the home of darkness, or mist"). These *Nibelungs*, or *Nibelungers*, were the possessors of the wonderful "Hoard" of gold and precious stones guarded by the dwarf Alberich, and their name passed to later holders of the Hoard, Siegfried's following and the Burgundians being in turn called "the Nibelungs."

Siegfried, the hero of the first part of the poem, became possessed of the Hoard and gave it to Kriemhild as her marriage portion After his murder Kriemhild carried it to Worms, where it was seized by Hagen and Gunther They buried it in the Rhine, intending later to enjoy it; but they were both slain for refusing to reveal its whereabouts, and the Hoard remains for ever in the keeping of the Rhine Maidens. The second part of the Nibelungenlied tells of the marriage of the widow Kriemhild with King Etzel (Attila), the visit of the Burgundians to the court of the Hunnish king, and the death of all the principal characters, including Gunther, Hagen, and Kriemhild.

Nic Frog. *See* FROG

Nice, Nicæa, Nicene (nī' si, ni sē' à, nī sēn) An ancient city of Asia Minor, now known as Isnik.

This ancient city should be distinguished from *Nice* (nēs) on the French Riviera, an old port and modern holiday resort that until 1860 formed part of the kingdom of Sardinia

The Council of Nice. The first œcumenical council of the Christian Church, held under Constantine the Great in 325 at Nice, or Nicæa, in Bithynia, Asia Minor, to condemn the Arian heresy, to affirm the consubstantiality of the Son of God, and to deal with points of discipline. The seventh œcumenical council was also held at Nice (787).

Nicene Creed. The Creed formulated at the great Council of Nice (325) It is used in the Holy Communion Service of the Church of England, and was first adopted in the Roman Church in 1014 In the Eastern Church it was first introduced in 471, and still forms part of the Baptism Service as well as of the Eucharist

> The Nicene, or more correctly, the Niceno-Constantinopolitan Creed, from the solemn sanction thus given to it by the great Œcumenical Councils, stands in a position of greater authority than any other, and amid their long-standing divisions is a blessed bond of union between the three great branches of the one Catholic Church—the Eastern, the Roman, and the Anglican, of all whose Communion Offices it forms a part —J H BLUNT *Annotated Book of Common Prayer.*

Nicholas, St. One of the most popular saints in Christendom, especially in the East He is the patron saint of Russia, of Aberdeen, of parish clerks, of scholars (who used to be called *clerks*), of pawnbrokers (because of the three bags of gold—transformed to the three gold balls—that he gave to the daughters of a poor man to save them from earning their dowers in a disreputable way), of little boys (because he once restored to life three little boys who had been cut up and pickled in a salting-tub to serve for bacon), and is invoked by sailors (because he allayed a storm during a voyage to the Holy Land) and against fire Finally, he is the original of Santa Claus (*q v*)

Little is known of his life, but he is said to have been Bishop of Myra (Lycia) in the early 4th century, and one story relates that he was present at the Council of Nice (325) and there buffeted Arius on the jaw His day is December 6th, and he is represented in episcopal robes with either three purses of gold, three gold balls, or three small boys, in allusion to one or other of the above legends

St Nicholas's Clerks Old slang for thieves, highwaymen St. Nicholas was the patron saint of scholars

Gadshill Sirrah, if they meet not with Saint Nicholas' clerks, I'll give thee this neck

Chamberlain No I'll none of it, I prithee, keep that for the hangman, for I know thou worship'st Saint Nicholas as truly as a man of falsehood may
   SHAKESPEARE 1 *Henry IV*, ii, 1

I think there came prancing down the hill a couple of St Nicholas's clerks —ROWLEY *Match at Midnight*, 1633

St. Nicholas's Bishop *See* BOY BISHOP.

Nick. Slang for to pilfer, and, in the 18th century, for to break windows by throwing coppers at them —

His scattered pence the flying Nicker flings,
And with the copper shower the casement rings
   GAY *Trivia*, iii

He nicked it. Won, hit, accomplished it A nick is a winning throw of dice in the old game of "hazard."

In the nick of time. Just at the right moment The allusion is to tallies marked with nicks or notches *Cp* PRICK OF NOON

To nick the nick. To hit the exact moment Tallies used to be called "nicksticks " Hence, to make a record of anything is "to nick it down," as publicans nick a score on a tally

Old Nick The Devil The term was in use in the 17th century, and is perhaps connected with the German *Nickel*, a goblin (*see* NICKEL), or in some forgotten way with St Nicholas Butler's derivation from Nicholas Machiavelli is, of course, poetical licence —

Nick Machiavel had ne'er a trick
(Though he gives name to our old Nick)
But was below the least of these
   Hudibras, iii, 1.

Nicka-Nan Night. The night preceding Shrove Tuesday is so called in Cornwall, because boys play tricks and practical jokes on that night On the following night they go round again from house to house singing—

Nicka, nicka nan,
Give me some pancake and then I'll be gone;
But if you give me none
I'll throw a great stone
And down your doors shall come.

Nickel. The metal is so called from the German *kupfernickel*, the name given to the ore from which it was first obtained (1754) by

Axel F von Cronstedt *Kupfer* means copper, and *Nickel* is the name of a mischievous goblin fabled to inhabit mines in Germany, the name was given to it because, although it was copper-coloured, no copper could be got from it, and so the *Nickel* was blamed.

In U S A a *nickel* is a coin of 5 cents, and is so termed from being composed of an alloy of nickel and copper

Nicker, or **Nix.** In Scandinavian folklore, a water-wraith, or kelpie, inhabiting sea, lake, river, and waterfall They are sometimes represented as half-child, half-horse, the hoofs being reversed, and sometimes as old men sitting on rocks wringing the water from their hair The female nicker is a *nixy*

Another tribe of water-fairies are the Nixes, who frequently assume the appearance of beautiful maidens —DYER: *Folk-lore of Plants*, ch vii.

Nickname. Originally *an eke-name*, *eke* being an adverb meaning "also," A S *eac*, connected with *iecan*, to supply deficiencies in or to make up for. *A newt* in the same way was originally "an eft" or "an evt", "v" and "u" being formerly interchangeable gave us "neut," or "newt "

The "eke" of a beehive is the piece added to the bottom to enlarge the hive.

National Nicknames.

For an American of the United States, "Brother Jonathan " For America as a national entity, "Uncle Sam "

For a Dutchman, "Nic Frog" and "Mynheer Closh."

For an Englishman, "John Bull."

For a Frenchman, "Crapaud," "Johnny" or "Jean," "Robert Macaire."

For French Canadians, "Jean Baptiste "

For French reformers, "Brissotins "

For French peasantry, "Jacques Bonhomme."

For a German, "Cousin Michael" or "Michel"; "Hun", "Jerry"; "Fritz."

For an Irishman, "Paddy."

For an Italian, "Antonio," or "Tony "

For a Scot, "Sandy" or "Mac."

For a Spaniard or Portuguese, "Dago" (Diego)

For a Welshman, "Taffy "

Nickneven (nik' nev en). A gigantic malignant hag of Scotch superstition Dunbar has well described this spirit in his *Flyting of Dunbar and Kennedy*

Nicodemus, Gospel of (nik ō dē' mus) *See* GOSPEL

Nicodemused into nothing. To have one's prospects in life ruined by a silly name; according to the proverb, "Give a dog a bad name and hang him " It is from Sterne's *Tristram Shandy* (vol i, 19):—

How many Cæsars and Pompeys .. by mere inspiration of the names have been rendered worthy of them, and how many . might have done . . well in the world ... had they not been Nicodemused into nothing

Nicotine (nik' ō tēn). So named from *Nicotiana*, the Latin name of the tobacco-plant, given to it in honour of Jean Nicot (*c* 1530-1600), Lord of Villemain, who was French ambassador in Madrid and introduced tobacco into France in 1560

Niflheim (nif' el him) (i e mist-home) The region of endless cold and everlasting night of Scandinavian mythology, ruled over by Hela. It consisted of nine worlds, to which were consigned those who die of disease or old age, it existed "from the beginning" in the North, and in its middle was the well Hvergelmir, from which flowed the twelve rivers

Nigger. An offensive—and obsolescent—term for a Negro or any member of a dark-skinned race.

A nigger in the woodpile. Originally a way of accounting for the disappearance of fuel, this phrase now denotes something underhanded or wrong, or a concealed motive

Nightcap. A drink before going to bed.

Nightingale. The Greek legend is that Tereus, King of Thrace, fetched Philomela to visit his wife, Procne, who was her sister, but when he reached the "solitudes of Heleas" he dishonoured her, and cut out her tongue that she might not reveal his conduct. Tereus told his wife that Philomela was dead, but Philomela made her story known by weaving it into a peplus, which she sent to Procne. Procne, in revenge, cut up her own son and served it to Tereus, and as soon as the king discovered it he pursued his wife, who fled to Philomela, whereupon the gods changed all three into birds, Tereus became the *hawk*, his wife, the *swallow*, and Philomela the *nightingale*, which is still called Philomel (*lit* lover of song) by the poets

> Youths and maidens most poetical
> Full of meek sympathy must heave their sighs
> O'er Philomela's pity-pleading strains
>   COLERIDGE *The Nightingale.*

The Swedish Nightingale. The operatic singer, Jenny Lind (1820-87), afterwards Mme Goldschmidt She was a native of Stockholm.

Nightmare. A sensation in sleep as if something heavy were sitting on one's breast, formerly supposed to be caused by a monster (*see* INCUBUS) who actually did this; it was not unfrequently called the *night-hag*, or the *riding of the witch* The second syllable is the A S *mare* (old Norse *mara*), an incubus, and appears again in the French equivalent *cauchemar*, "the fiend that tramples" The word is now more often employed to describe a frightening dream, a night terror

Nightmare of Europe, The. Napoleon Bonaparte was so called

Nihilism (ni' hil izm) (Lat *nihil*, nothing) An extreme form of Socialism, the prelude to Bolshevism (*see* BOLSHEVIST), which took form in Russia in the 50s of last century, and was specially active in the 70s, and later, under Bakounin It aimed at the complete overthrow of law, order, and all existing institutions, with the idea of re-forming the world *de novo*
The name was given by the novelist, Ivan Turgenieff (1818-83)

Nil admirari (Lat) To be stolidly indifferent Neither to wonder at anything nor yet to admire anything The tag is from Horace (*Ep* I, vi, 1) —

> Nil admirari prope res est una, Numici,
> Solaque, quæ possit facere et servare beatum.
> (Not to admire, Numicius, is the best—
> The only way to make and keep men blest)
>   *Connington*

Nil desperandum Never say die, never give up in despair, another tag from Horace (*Carmen*, I, vii, 27) —
Nil desperandum Teucro duce et auspice Teucro (There is naught to be despaired of when we are under Teucer's leadership and auspices).

Nile The Egyptians used to say that the rising of the Nile was caused by the tears of Isis The feast of Isis was celebrated at the anniversary of the death of Osiris, when Isis was supposed to mourn for her husband

The hero of the Nile. Horatio, Lord Nelson (1758-1805)

Nimbus (nim' bus) (Lat., a cloud) In Christian art a halo of light placed round the head of an eminent personage There are three forms: (1) *Vesica piscis*, or fish form (*cp* ICHTHUS), used in representations of Christ and occasionally of the Virgin Mary, extending round the whole figure, (2) a circular halo, (3) radiated like a star or sun The enrichments are: (1) for Our Lord, a cross, (2) for the Virgin, a circlet of stars, (3) for angels, a circlet of small rays, and an outer circle of quatrefoils, (4) the same for saints and martyrs, but with the name often inscribed round the circumference, (5) for the Deity the rays diverge in a triangular direction Nimbi of a square form signify that the persons so represented were living when they were painted
The nimbus was used by heathen nations long before painters introduced it into sacred pictures of saints, the Trinity, and the Virgin Mary. Proserpine was represented with a nimbus, the Roman emperors were also decorated in the same manner, because they were *divi*

Nimini-pimini (nim' i ni pim' i ni) Affected simplicity Lady Emily, in General Burgoyne's *The Heiress*, III, ii (1786), tells Miss Alscrip to stand before a glass and keep pronouncing *nimini-pimini*—"The lips cannot fail to take the right plie "
The conceit was borrowed by Dickens in *Little Dorrit*, where Mrs General tells Amy Dorrit—
Papa gives a pretty form to the lips *Papa, potatoes, poultry, prunes*, and *prism* are all very good words for the lips, especially *prunes* and *prism*

The form mimini-pimini is also in use —
A mimini-pimini, *Je-ne-sais-quoi* young man —
W S GILBERT *Patience*, II

Nimrod (nim' rod) Any daring or outstanding hunter, from the 'mighty hunter before the Lord" (*Gen* x, 9), which the Targum says means a "sinful hunting of the sons of men " Pope says of him, he was "a mighty hunter, and his prey was man" (*Windsor Forest*, 62), so also Milton interprets the phrase (*Paradise Lost*, xii, 24, etc.)
The legend is that the tomb of Nimrod still exists in Damascus, and that no dew ever falls upon it, even though all its surroundings are saturated.

C. J. Apperley (1779-1843), a well-known sporting writer, used **Nimrod** as his pseudonym in widely-read books and essays on racing

Nincompoop (nĭn′ kŏm poop) A poor thing of a man Said to be a corruption of the Latin *non compos* (*mentis*), but of this there is no evidence The last syllable is probably connected with Dut *poep*, a fool

Nine. Nine, five, and three are mystical numbers—the *diapason* (*q v.*), *diapente*, and *diatrion* of the Greeks Nine consists of a trinity of trinities According to the Pythagoreans man is a full chord, or eight notes, and Deity comes next Three, being the trinity, represents a perfect *unity*, twice three is the perfect *dual*, and thrice three is the perfect *plural*. This explains why nine is a mystical number.

From the earliest times the number nine has been regarded as of peculiar significance Deucalion's ark, made by the advice of Prometheus, was tossed about for *nine* days, when it stranded on the top of Mount Parnassus There were the *nine* Muses (*q.v*), frequently referred to as merely "the Nine"—

> Descend, ye Nine! Descend and sing
> The breathing instruments inspire
> POPE *Ode on St Cecilia's Day*

There were **nine Gallicenæ** or virgin priestesses of the ancient Gallic oracle, and Lars Porsena swore by the *nine* gods—

> Lars Porsena of Clusium
> By the nine gods he swore
> That the great house of Tarquin
> Should suffer wrong no more.
> MACAULAY *Lays of Ancient Rome* (*Horatius*, 1).

who were Juno, Minerva, and Tinia (*the three chief*), Vulcan, Mars, Saturn, Hercules, Summanus, and Vedius, while the *nine* of the Sabines were Hercules, Romulus, Esculapius, Bacchus, Æneas, Vesta, Santa, Fortuna, and Fides

Niobe's children lay *nine* days in their blood before they were buried, the Hydra had *nine* heads; at the *Lemuria*, held by the Romans on May 9th, 11th, and 13th, persons haunted threw black beans over their heads, pronouncing nine times the words "Avaunt, ye spectres, from this house!" and the exorcism was complete (*see* Ovid's *Fasti*).

There were *nine* rivers of hell, or, according to some accounts the Styx encompassed the infernal regions in *nine* circles, and Milton makes the gates of hell "thrice three-fold, three folds are brass, three iron, three of adamantine rock" They had nine folds, nine plates, and nine linings (*Paradise Lost*, ii, 645).

Vulcan, when kicked from Olympus, was *nine* days falling to the island of Lemnos, and when the fallen angels were cast out of heaven, Milton says "*Nine* days they fell" (*Paradise Lost*, vi 871)

In the early Ptolemaic system of astronomy, before the Primum Mobile (*q v*) was added, there were *nine* spheres, hence Milton, in his *Arcades*, speaks of the "celestial syrens' harmony that sit upon the *nine* enfolded spheres ' They were those of the Moon, Mercury, Venus, the Sun, Mars, Jupiter, Saturn, and the Firmament or that of the fixed stars, and the Crystalline Sphere In Scandinavian mythology there were *nine* earths, Hel (*q v*) being the goddess of the ninth, there were *nine* worlds in Nilheim, and Odin's ring dropped eight other rings (*nine* rings of mystical import) every *ninth* night.

In folk-lore *nine* appears many times. The Abracadabra was worn *nine* days, and then flung into a river, in order to see the fairies one is directed to put "*nine* grains of wheat on a four-leaved clover", *nine* knots are made on black wool as a charm for a sprained ankle, if a servant finds *nine* green peas in a peascod, she lays it on the lintel of the kitchen door, and the first man that enters in is to be her cavalier, to see *nine* magpies is most unlucky, a cat has *nine* lives (*see also* CAT O' NINE TAILS); and the *nine* of Diamonds is known as the Curse of Scotland (*q.v*).

The weird sisters in *Macbeth* sang, as they danced round the cauldron, "Thrice to thine, and thrice to mine, and thrice again to make up *nine*", and then declared "the charm wound up"; and we drink a *Three-times-three* to those most highly honoured.

Leases are sometimes granted for 999 years, that is *three* times *three-three-three* Even now they run for ninety-nine years, the dual of a trinity of trinities

See also the *Nine Points of the Law*, in PHRASES, *below*, and the *Nine Worthies*, under WORTHIES.

There are *nine* orders of angels (*see* ANGELS); in Heraldry there are *nine* marks of cadency and *nine* different crowns recognized, and among ecclesiastical architects there are *nine* crosses, viz, altar, processional, roods on lofts, reliquary crosses, consecration, marking, pectoral, spire crosses, and crosses pendent over altars.

A nine days' wonder. Something that causes a great sensation for a few days, and then passes into the limbo of things forgotten An old proverb is "A wonder lasts nine days, and then the puppy's eyes are open," alluding to dogs which, like cats, are born blind As much as to say, the eyes of the public are blind in astonishment for nine days, but then their eyes are open, and they see too much to wonder any longer

> *King* You'd think it strange if I should marry her
> *Gloster* That would be ten days' wonder, at the least
> *King* That's a day longer than a wonder lasts.
> 3 *Henry VI*, iii, 2

Dressed up to the nines To perfection from head to foot.

Nine-tail bruiser. Prison slang for the cat-o'-nine-tails (*q.v*).

Nine tailors make a man *See* TAILORS

Nine times out of ten Far more often than not, in a great preponderance

Possession is nine points of the law. It is every advantage a person can have short of actual right. The "nine points of the law" have been given as—

(1) A good deal of money, (2) a good deal of patience, (3) a good cause, (4) a good lawyer, (5) a good counsel; (6) good witnesses, (7) a good jury; (8) a good judge, and (9) good luck.

To look nine ways. To squint

Nice as ninepence. A corruption of "Nice as nine-pins" In the game of nine-pins, the "men" are set in three rows with the utmost exactitude or nicety

Nimble as ninepence. Silver ninepences were common till the year 1696, when all unmilled coin was called in. These ninepences were very *pliable* or "nimble," and, being bent, were given as love tokens, the usual formula of presentation being *To my love, from my love* There is an old proverb, *A nimble ninepence is better than a slow shilling*

Right as ninepence. Perfectly well, in perfect condition

Ninus Son of Belus, husband of Semiramis, and the reputed builder of Nineveh It is at his tomb that the lovers meet in the Pyramus and Thisbe travesty —

Pyr Wilt thou at Ninny's tomb meet me straight way?
This.. 'Tide life, 'tide death, I come without delay.
Midsummer Night's Dream, v, 1.

Niobe. The personification of maternal sorrow According to Grecian fable Niobe, the daughter of Tantalus and wife of Amphion, King of Thebes, was the mother of twelve children, and taunted Latona because she had only two— Apollo and Diana Latona commanded her children to avenge the insult, and they caused all the sons and daughters of Niobe to die. Niobe was inconsolable, wept herself to death, and was changed into a stone, from which ran water, "Like Niobe, all 'ears" (*Hamlet*, i, 2).

The Niobe of nations. So Byron styles Rome, the "lone mother of dead empires," with "broken thrones and temples", a "chaos of ruins", a "desert where we steer stumbling o'er recollections." (*Childe Harold*, iv, 79)

Nip. Nip of whisky, etc. Short for **Nipperkin** A small wine and beer measure containing about half a pint, or a little under, now frequently called "a nip "
His hawk-economy won't thank him for't
Which stops his petty nipperkin of port
PETER PINDAR *Hair Powder*

The traditional Devon and Cornish song *The Barley Mow* starts with drinking the health out of the "jolly brown bowl," and at each chorus increases the size of the receptacle until in the sixteenth and last we have—
We'll drink it out of the ocean, my boys,
Here's a health to the barley-mow!
The ocean, the river, the well, the pipe, the hogshead, the half-hogshead, the anker, the half-anker, the gallon, the half-gallon, the pottle, the quart, the pint, the half a pint, the quarter-pint, the nipperkin, *and* the jolly brown bowl!

Nip and tuck. A neck-and-neck race; a close fight

Number Nip Another name for Rübezahl (*q v*)

To nip in the bud To destroy before it has had time to develop; usually said of bad habits, tendency to sin, etc. Shakespeare has—
The third day comes a frost, a killing frost;
And, when he thinks, good easy man, full surely
His greatness is a-ripening, nips his root,
And then he falls as I do *Henry VIII*, iii, 2

Nip-cheese or **Nip-farthing.** A miser, who nips or pinches closely his cheese and farthings

Among sailors the purser is nicknamed "Nipcheese " (Dutch, *nypen*)

Nipper. Slang for a small boy

Nippon (ni pon'). The Japanese name of Japan

Nirvana (ner van' à) (Sansk , a blowing out, or extinction) Annihilation, or rather the final deliverance of the soul from transmigration (*see* BUDDHISM).

Nisei (nē' sā) A person born in the U.S A of Japanese descent but a loyal American

Nisi (ni' si) (Lat , unless) In Law a "rule *nisi*" is a rule *unless* cause be shown to the contrary

Decree nisi. A decree of divorce granted on. the condition that it does not take effect until made *absolute*, which is done in due course *unless* reasons why it should not have meantime come to light. Every decree of divorce is, in the first instance, a *decree nisi.*

Nisi prius (unless previously) Originally a writ commanding a sheriff to empanel a jury which should be at the Court of Westminster on a certain day *unless* the judge of assize *previously* come to his county, as—
"We command you to come before our justices at Westminster on the morrow of All Souls', NISI PRIUS justiciarii domini regis ad assisas capiendas venerint—*i e* unless previously the justices of our lord the king come to hold their assizes at (the court of your own assize town)

The second Statute of Westminster (1285) instituted Judges of *nisi prius*, who were appointed to travel through the shires three times a year to hear civil causes, and such causes tried before Judges of Assize are still known as "Causes of nisi prius "

Nisroch (nis' rok) The Assyrian god in whose temple Sennacherib was worshipping when he was slain (2 *Kings* xix, 37) Nothing is known of the god, and the name is probably a corruption either of Asur or of Nusku, a god connected with Nebo (*q v*).

Nissen hut A long, iron-roofed hut, semicircular in section, easily portable and largely used by armies, etc The name comes from the original designers and makers

Nitouche (ni toosh') *Faire la Sainte Nitouche,* to pretend to great sanctity, to look as though butter would not melt in one's mouth. Sainte Nitouche is the name given in France to a hypocrite, it is a contraction of *n'y touche.*

Nitwit. A slow-witted person, one who is irresponsible and is liable to say or do foolish and irrelevant things

Nivetta. *See* MORGAN LE FAY

Nix. *See* NICKER The word is also slang for "nothing." "You can't get him to work for nix," *i e* without paying him In this sense it is from Ger *nichts*, nothing.

Nizam (ni zăm') A title of sovereignty in Hyderabad (India), contracted from *Nizam-ul-mulk* (regulator of the state), the style adopted by Asaf Jah, who obtained possession of the Deccan in 1713

Njorthr. *See* NERTHUS.

No. No dice (U S.A). Nothing doing.

No Man's Land. The name applied to the area between hostile entrenched lines or to any space contested by both sides and belonging to neither

No-popery Riots. Those of Edinburgh and Glasgow, February 5th, 1779, and those of London instigated by Lord George Gordon, of 1780 A stirring account of these is given in Dickens's *Barnaby Rudge.*

Noachian (nō ā' ki an). The adjective formed from the name of the patriarch Noah, hence the Noachian deluge, *i e.* The Flood

Noah's Ark. A name given by sailors to a white band of cloud spanning the sky like a rainbow and in shape something like the hull of a ship If east and west expect dry weather, if north and south expect wet

Noah's Wife. According to legend she was unwilling to go into the ark, and the quarrel between the patriarch and his wife forms a prominent feature of *Noah's Flood,* in the Chester and Townley Mysteries

Hastow nought herd, quod Nicholas, also
The sorwe of Noe with his felawshipe
Er that he mighte gete his wyf to shipe?
                            CHAUCER *Miller's Tale,* 352

Nob. Slang for the head (probably from *knob*); also for a person of rank and position (contraction of *noble* or *nobility*) *Cp* SNOB

Nobbler. Australian colloquial term for a short drink, one-fifth of a gill or a fluid ounce

Nobel Prizes Prizes established by the will of Alfred Bernard Nobel (1833-96), the Swedish chemist and inventor of dynamite, etc , to encourage work in the cause of humanity There are five prizes given annually, each of about £7,000, as follows· (1) for the most noteworthy work in *physics,* (2) in *chemistry,* (3) in *medicine* or *physiology,* (4) in *idealistic literature,* and (5) in the furtherance of universal peace W C Rontgen, Mme. Curie, A Carrel, Rudyard Kipling, Maeterlinck, Hauptmann, Rabindranath Tagore, Romain Rolland, Elihu Root, Woodrow Wilson, F G. Banting, W B Yeats, Albert Einstein, Sir A. Fleming, Luigi Pirandello, Sinclair Lewis, G B. Shaw, Pearl Buck, Sir Norman Angell, The Society of Friends (Quakers), T. S Eliot, Earl Russell, Mr Ralph Bunche, are among those to whom the prizes have been awarded

Noble. A former English gold coin, so called on account of the superior excellency of its gold. Nobles were originally disposed of as a reward for good news, or important service done, first minted by Edward III, they remained in use till the time of Henry VIII; their nominal value was 6s 8d to 10s.

Noble. The Lion, the King of all the Beasts, in Caxton's edition of *Reynard the Fox* (*q v.*)

The Noble. Charles III of Navarre (1361-1425). Soliman *Tchelibi,* Turkish prince at Adrianople (d 1410)

The Noble Science The old epithet for

fencing or boxing, now usually called "The Noble Art of Self-Defence."
    . a bold defiance
    Shall meet him, were he of the noble science.
BEAUMONT AND FLETCHER *Knight of the Burning Pestle,* ii, 1.

Noblesse oblige (nō bles' ō blēzh) (Fr) Noble birth imposes the obligation of high-minded principles and noble actions.

Noctes Ambrosianæ (nok' tēz am bro zi ā' nē) A series of papers on literary and topical subjects, in the form of dialogues, contributed to *Blackwood's Magazine,* 1822-35 They were written principally by Professor Wilson, "Christopher North " *See* AMBROSIAN NIGHTS

Nod A nod is as good as a wink to a blind horse However obvious a hint or suggestion may be it is useless if the other person is unable to see it

On the nod. On credit. To get a thing on the nod is to get it without paying for it at the time—and often without any definite intention of paying for it at all. The phrase is from the auction-room, one buys articles by a mere nod of the head to the clerk, and the formalities are attended to later

The Land of Nod. *See* LAND

Noddy. A Tom Noddy is a very foolish or half-witted person, "a noodle " The marine birds called noddies are so silly that anyone can go up to them and knock them down with a stick It seems more than likely that the word is connected with *to nod,* but it has been suggested that it was originally a pet form of *Nicodemus.*

Noel (nō' el) In English (also written *Nowell*), a Christmas carol, or the shout of joy in a carol, in French, Christmas Day. The word is Provençal *nadal,* from Lat *natalem,* natal
    Nowells, nowells, nowells'
      Sing all we may,
    Because that Christ, the King,
      Was born this blessed day —*Old Carol.*

Nokes *See* JOHN-A-NOKES

Nolens volens (nō' lenz vō' lenz) Whether willing or not. Two Latin participles meaning "being unwilling (or) willing " *Cp* WILLY-NILLY

Noli me tangere (nol' i me tǎn' jer i) (Lat , touch me not). The words Christ used to Mary Magdalene after His resurrection (*John* xx, 17), and given as a name to a plant of the genus *Impatiens* The seed-vessels consist of one cell in five divisions, and when the seed is ripe each of these, on being touched, suddenly folds itself into a spiral form and leaps from the stalk *See* Darwin's *Loves of the Plants,* ii, 3

Noll. Old Noll. Oliver Cromwell was so called by the Royalists. Noll is a familiar form of *Oliver.*

Nolle prosequi (nol' i prō sek' wi) (Lat , to be unwilling to prosecute) A petition from a plaintiff to stay a suit. *Cp.* NON PROS

Nolo episcopari (nō' lō ep isk ō pā' ri) (Lat , I am unwilling to be made a bishop) The formal reply supposed to be returned to the royal offer of a bishopric. Chamberlayne says (*Present*

State of England, 1669) that in former times the person about to be elected modestly refused the office twice, and if he did so a third time his refusal was accepted.

Nom. Nom de guerre is French for a "war name," but really means an assumed name It was customary at one time for everyone who entered the French army to assume a name; this was especially the case in the times of chivalry, when knights were known by the device on their shields

Nom de plume. English-French for "pen name," or pseudonym, the name assumed by a writer, cartoonist, etc , who does not choose to give his own to the public, as *Currer Bell* (Charlotte Bronte), *Fiona McLeod* (William Sharp), *Henry Seton Merriman* (Hugh Stowell Scott), etc. Occasionally, as in the case of *Voltaire* (François Marie Arouet) and *De Stendhal* (Marie Henri Beyle), the assumed name quite replaces the true name

Nominalist (nom' i nal ist) The schoolmen's name for one who—following William of Occam—denied the objective existence of abstract ideas, also, the name of a sect founded by Roscelin, Canon of Compiegne (1040-1120), who maintained that if the Father, Son, and Holy Ghost are *one God*, they cannot be three distinct *persons*, but must be simply three *names* of the same being, just as father, son, and husband are three distinct names of one and the same man under different conditions. Abélard, Hobbes, Locke, Bishop Berkeley, Condillac, and Dugald Stewart are noted Nominalists *Cp.* REALISTS

Non. The Latin negative, *not*; adopted in English, and very widely employed, as a prefix of negation, *e g.* in *non-abstainer*, *non-conformist*, *non-existent*, *non-resident*, *non-sense*, *nonsuit*, etc.

Non amo te, Sabidi. *See* I DO NOT LIKE THEE, DR FELL, *under* DOCTOR.

Non Angli sed angeli (Lat , Not Angles, but angels) *See* ANGELS

Non assumpsit (Lat , he has not undertaken) The legal term for a plea denying promise or undertaking by the defendant

Non compos mentis (Lat , not of sound mind) Said of a lunatic, idiot, drunkard, or one who has lost memory and understanding by accident or disease
The prisoner not denying the fact, and persisting before the court that he looked upon it as a compliment, the jury brought him in *non compos menns.*— ADDISON *Tatler*, 5 Dec , 1710.

Non dolet. *See* ARRIA.

Non-ego. *See* EGO

Non est. A contraction of Lat *non est inventus* (not to be found). They are the words which the sheriff writes on a writ when the defendant is not to be found in his bailiwick

Non mi ricordo (Ital , I do not remember) A shuffling way of saying "I don't choose to answer that question " It was the usual answer of the Italian witnesses when under examination at the trial of Queen Caroline, wife of George IV, in 1820

Non placet (Lat , it is unpleasing). The formula used, especially by the governing body of a University, for expressing a negative vote.

Non pros. for Lat *non prosequi* (not to prosecute) The judgment of *non pros* is one for costs, when the plaintiff stays a suit.

Non sequitur (Lat., it does not follow). A conclusion which does not follow from the premises stated, an inconsequent statement, such as Artemus Ward's—
I met a man in Oregon who hadn't any teeth—not a tooth in his head,—yet that man could play on the bass drum better than any man I ever met

Non-com. A non-commissioned officer in the army

Nonconformists. In England, members of Protestant bodies who do *not conform* to the doctrines of the Church of England (also called *Dissenters*); especially the 2,000 clergy who, in 1662, left the Church rather than submit to the conditions of the Act of Uniformity—*i e* "unfeigned assent to all and everything contained in the Book of Common Prayer."

Nonjurors. Those clergymen who refused to take the oath of allegiance to the new government after the Revolution (1690) They were Archbishop Sancroft with eight bishops, and four hundred clergymen, all of whom were ejected from their livings The non-juring bishops ordained clergy and kept up the "succession" until the death of the last "bishop" in 1805. *Cp* SEVEN BISHOPS, THE.

Nonplus (Lat , no more) A quandary a state of perplexity when "no more" can be said on the subject When a man is *nonplussed* or has *come to a nonplus* in an argument, it means that he is unable to deny or controvert what is advanced against him *To nonplus* a person is to put him into such a fix.

Nonce-word A temporary word that is coined for the occasion *Burrelism*, *couponeer*, *Limehouse*, *Puseyite*, and many others to be found throughout this DICTIONARY, are examples

Nones (nōnz) In the ancient Roman calendar, the *ninth* (Lat *nonus*) day before Ides; in the Roman Catholic Church, the office for the *ninth* hour after sunrise, i e. between noon and 3 p m.

Norfolk Island. A South Pacific island belonging to Australia It was discovered by Captain Cook in 1774 and was for many years a penal settlement for the most desperate convicts who had to be segregated from the other penal transportees in Australia. In 1856 Norfolk Island was colonized by the people from Pitcairn Island who were descended from the mutineers of the *Bounty* (*q.v.*)

Norman French. The Old French dialect spoken in Normandy at the time of the conquest of England and spoken by the dominant class in the latter country for some two centuries after the conquest Vestiges of it remain in the formal words of the royal assent given to Bills that have passed through Parliament—"La

Reine le veult"— and in the "Fitz" (*fils*, son) that precedes certain family surnames

Norns, The The three giant goddesses who, in Scandinavian mythology, presided over the fates of both men and gods.

Norrisian Professor (nor is' i an) A Professor of Divinity in Cambridge University This professorship was founded in 1760 by John Norris (1734-77), of Whitton, Norfolk The four divinity professors are Lady Margaret's, the Regius, the Norrisian, and the Hulsean

Norroy (*i e* north roy, or king) The third king of arms is so called, because his office is on the north side of the river Trent, that of the south side is called Clarenceux (*q v.*)

North It is said that villagers have a great objection to being buried on the north side of a churchyard They seem to think only evildoers should be there interred Probably the chief reason is the want of sun, but the old idea is that the east is *God's* side, where His throne is set, the west, *man's* side, the Galilee of the Gentiles, the south, the side of the "*spirits made just*" *and angels*, where the sun shines in his strength, and the north, the *devil's* side Cp THE DEVIL'S DOOR, *under* DEVIL

As men die, so shall they arise; if in faith, in the Lord, towards the south . and shall arise in glory; if in unbelief . towards the north, then are they past all hope.—COVERDALE *Praying for the Dead*

He's too far north for me. Too canny, too cunning to be taken in, very hard in making a bargain The inhabitants of Yorkshire are supposed to be very canny, especially in driving a bargain; and when you get to Aberdeen——'

North Briton A periodical founded in 1762 by John Wilkes (1727-97) to air his animosity against Lord Bute and the Scottish nation On April 23rd, 1763 appeared No 45 which attacked the royal speech at the close of the late session of Parliament Wilkes was arrested and sent to the Tower, but claiming his prerogative as a member of Parliament he obtained his release and went to Paris The House passed a resolution that No 45 was a "false, scandalous and malicious libel," and in his absence Wilkes was expelled the House

North-east Passage, The. A way to India from Europe round the north extremity of Asia It had been often attempted even in the 16th century Hence Beaumont and Fletcher

That everlasting cassock, that has worn
As many servants out as the North-east Passage
Has consumed sailors *The Woman's Prize*, ii, 2

North Pole. For two or three centuries men tried to reach the North Pole, and many were the speculations as to what would be found when they got there It was not until April 6th, 1909, that the American sailor and explorer Robert Edwin Peary (1856-1920) reached the Pole, by that time known to be the central point of the shallow Arctic basin wherein lies the Arctic Ocean, of which the surface near the Pole is floating and moving ice In May, 1933, the North Pole was claimed by the Russians as a Soviet possession and four years later they established a Polar station there, under Prof Otto Schmidt

North-west Passage The name given to an assumed passage to China and the Orient round the north of the American continent. Attempts to find it were made in the 16th and 17th century by such sailors as the Cabots, Frobisher, Gilbert, Davis, Hudson and Baffin In the 19th century the quest was followed by Ross, Parry, and Sir John Franklin who lost his life and the lives of his crew in the attempt It was not until 1903-05 that Roald Amundsen made the complete voyage

The Northern Bear. Tsarist Russia was so called

The Northern Gate of the Sun. The sign of Cancer, or summer solstice; so called because it marks the northern tropic.

The Northern Lights The Aurora Borealis (*q v*)

℣ **The Northern Wagoner** The genius presiding over the Great Bear, or Charles's Wain (*q v.*), which contains seven large stars

By this the northern wagoner has set
His sevenfold team behind the stedfast star [*the pole-
star*] SPENSER *Faerie Queene*, I, ii, 1

Dryden calls the Great Bear *the Northern Car*, and similarly the crown in Ariadne has been called *the Northern Crown*

Northamptonshire Poet. John Clare (1793-1864), son of a farmer at Helpstone

Norway, Maid of. *See* MAID

Nose. A nose of wax. *See* WAX

As plain as the nose on your face. Extremely obvious, patent to all

Bleeding of the nose. According to some, a sign that one is in love Grose says if it bleeds one drop only it forebodes sickness, if three drops the omen is still worse, but Melton, in his *Astrologaster*, says, "If a man's nose bleeds one drop at the *left* nostril it is a sign of good luck, and *vice versa*"

Cleopatra's nose. *See* CLEOPATRA.

Golden nose Tycho Brahe (d. 1601), the Danish astronomer He lost his nose in a duel, so adopted a golden one, which he attached to his face by a cement which he carried about with him

The bloodthirsty emperor Justinian II, nicknamed Rhinotmetus, had a golden nose in place of the nose that had been cut off by his general Leontius before he ascended the imperial throne It used to be said that when Justinian cleansed this golden nose, those who were present knew that the death of someone had been decided upon

Led by the nose. Said of a person who has no volition of his own but follows with docility the guidance of a stronger character In another sense it appears in *Isaiah* xxxvii, 29 —— "Because thy rage against me . is come up into mine ears, therefore will I put my hook in thy nose and will turn thee back . " Horses, asses, etc , led by bit and bridle, are led by the nose Hence Iago says of Othello, he was "led by the nose as asses are" (i, 3) But buffaloes, camels, and bears are actually led by a ring inserted in their nostrils.

Though authority be a stubborn bear, yet he is often led by the nose with gold.—*Winter's Tale*, iv, 4.

Nose tax. It is said that in the 9th century the Danes imposed a poll tax in Ireland, and that this was called the "Nose Tax," because those who neglected to pay were punished by having their noses slit

On the nose. An American expression meaning exactly on time It originated in the broadcasting studio, where the producer, when signalling to the performers, puts his finger on his nose when the programme is running to schedule time

The Pope's nose. The rump of a fowl, which is also called the parson's nose The phrase is said to have originated during the years following James II's reign, when anti-Catholic feeling was high.

To count noses. A horse-dealer counts horses by the *nose*, as cattle are counted by the *head*, hence, the expression is sometimes ironically used of numbering votes, as in the Division lobbies

To cut off your nose to spite your face, or **to be revenged on your face.** To act out of pique in such a way as to injure yourself.

To follow one's nose. To go straight ahead, to proceed without deviating from the path

> Juan, following honour and his nose,
> Rush'd where the thickest fire announced most foes
> > BYRON *Don Juan,* VIII, xxxii

To keep one's nose to the grindstone. To keep hard at work. Tools, such as scythes, chisels, etc , are constantly sharpened on a stone or with a grindstone.

> Be to the poor like one whunstane,
> And haud their noses to the grunstane
> > BURNS' *Dedication to Gavin Hamilton*

To pay through the nose. To pay an excessive price, or at an exorbitant rate There may be some connexion between this old phrase, 'rhino" (*q v*), slang for money, and Gr *rhinos,* the nose, or there may be an allusion to nosebleeding and being *bled* for money.

To poke or **thrust one's nose in.** Officiously to intermeddle with other people's affairs, to intrude where one is not wanted

To put one's nose out of joint. To supplant a person in another's good graces, to upset one's plans; to humiliate a conceited person

To snap one's nose off. To speak snappishly. To *pull* (or *wring*) *the nose* is to affront by an act of indignity; to *snap one's nose* is to affront by speech Snarling dogs snap at each other's noses

To take pepper in the nose. *See* PEPPER.

To turn up one's nose. To express contempt When a person sneers he turns up the nose by curling the upper lip

To wipe one's nose. *See* WIPE.

Under one's very nose. Right before one; in full view

Nosey. Very inquisitive, given to overmuch poking of the nose into other people's business One who does this is often called a Nosey Parker, an epithet of unknown origin.
The Duke of Wellington was familiarly called "Nosey" by the soldiery His "commander's face" with its strongly accentuated aquiline nose, was a very distinguishing feature of the Iron Duke The nickname was also given to Oliver Cromwell *See* COPPER-NOSE.

Nostradamus, Michel (nos´ trä dä´ mus) A French astrologer (1503-66) who published an annual "Almanack" as well as the famous *Centuries* (1555) containing prophecies which, though the book suffered papal condemnation in 1781, still occasion controversy from time to time His prophecies are couched in most ambiguous language, hence the saying *as good a prophet as Nostradamus—i e* so obscure that none can make out your meaning

Nostrum (nos´ trum) (Lat , our own) A term applied to a quack medicine, the ingredients of which are supposed to be a secret of the compounders, also, figuratively, to any political or other scheme that savours of the charlatan.

Notables An assembly of nobles or notable men, in French history, selected by the king to form a parliament. They were convened in 1626 by Richelieu, and not again till 1787 when Louis XVI called them together with the view of relieving the nation of some of its pecuniary embarrassments The last time they ever assembled was November 6th, 1788.

Notarikon (nō tär´ i kon) A cabalistic word (Gr *notarikon,* Lat. *notarius,* a shorthand-writer) denoting the old Jewish art of using each letter in a word to form another word, or using the initials of the words in a sentence to form another word, etc , as *Cabal* itself (*q.v*) was fabled to have been formed from Clifford, Ashley, Buckingham, Arlington, and Lauderdale, and as the term *Ichthus* (*q v*) was applied to the Saviour Other instances will be found under A E I O U., CLIO; HEMPE, LIMP; and SMECTYMNUUS, *cp. also* HIP

Notch Out of all notch. *See* SCOTCH

Note-sharer (U S A). A bill discounter, usurer

Nothing. Mere nothings. Trifles, unimportant things or events.

> You shapeless nothing in a dish,
> You that are but almost a fish—
> > COWPER *The Poet, the Oyster,* etc

Next to nothing. A very little As "It will cost next to nothing," "He eats next to nothing "

Nothing doing! A slang expression, generally implying that you are disappointed in your expectations, or refuse some request

Nothing venture, nothing have. If you daren't throw a sprat you mustn't expect to catch a mackerel, don't be afraid of taking a risk now and then A very old proverb

Out of nothing one can get nothing; the Latin *Ex nihilo nihil fit—i e* every effect must have a cause. It was the dictum by which Xenophanes, founder of the Eleatic School (*q v*), postulated his theory of the eternity of matter. Persius (*Satires,* iii, 84) has *De nihilo nihilum, in nihilum nil posse reverti,* From nothing nothing, and into nothing can nothing return
We now use the phrase as equivalent to "You cannot get blood from a stone," or expect good work from one who has no brains.

That's nothing to you, or to do with you. It's none of your business.

There's nothing for it but . There's no alternative, take it or leave it

To come to nothing. To turn out a failure, to result in naught.

To make nothing of. To fail to understand; not to succeed in some operation.

Nourmahal (noor ma hal') (Arab , The Light of the Harem) One of the women in the harem of the Caliph Haroun-al-Raschid, afterwards called Nourjehan (Light of the World) The story of her love for Selim and how she regained his lost affections by means of a love-spell is told in Moore's *Lalla Rookh*

Nous (nous) (Gr , mind, intellect) Adopted in English and used more or less loosely for intelligence, "horse-sense "

> This is the genuine head of many a house,
> And much divinity without a NOUS
> POPE *Dunciad*, IV, 244

Nous was the Platonic term for mind, or the first cause, and the system of divinity here referred to is that which springs from blind nature.

Nous avons changé tout cela (noo zăv ong shon' jă too sla) (Fr , we have changed all that) A facetious reproof to one who lays down the law upon everything, and talks contemptuously of old customs, old authors, old artists, and old everything The phrase is taken from Molière's *Médecin Malgré Lui*, ii, 6 (1666)

Nova Scotia. *See* ACADIA

Novatians (nō vā' shanz) Followers of Novatianus, a presbyter of Rome in the 3rd century They differed little from the orthodox Catholics, but maintained that the Church had no power to allow one who had lapsed to be readmitted

Novella (nō vel' la) A short story of the kind contained in Boccaccio's *Decameron* These *novelle* were immensely popular in the 16th and 17th centuries and were the forerunners of the long novel that later developed from them, as also of the short story of more recent times

November (Lat *novem*, nine) The ninth month in the ancient Roman calendar, when the year began in March, now the eleventh The old Dutch name was *Slaght-maand* (slaughter-month, the time when the beasts were slain and salted down for winter use); the old Saxon, *Wind-monath* (wind-month, when the fishermen drew their boats ashore, and gave over fishing till the next spring); it was also called *Blot-monath*—the same as *Slaght-maand* In the French Republican calendar it was called *Brumaire* (fog-month, October 22nd to November 21st).

Novena (nō vē' ná) In R C devotions a prayer for some special object or occasion extended over a period of nine days Various reasons have been adduced for the choice of nine days, but at root the custom seems to have been taken over from Roman paganism.

Nowell. *See* NOEL

Noyades (nwa' yad) (Fr., drownings) A means of execution adopted by Carrier at Nantes, in the French Revolution (1793-4). Prisoners to be "removed" were first bound and then stowed in the hold of a vessel which had a movable bottom This was sent to the middle of the Loire, the vessel was scuttled, and the victims drowned Nero, at the suggestion of Anicetus, attempted to drown his mother in the same manner

Nubbin (U S A) A spoiled ear of corn.

Nude Naked. Rabelais (IV, XXIX) says that a person without clothing is dressed in "grey and cold" of a comical cut, being "nothing before, nothing behind, and sleeves of the same " King Shrovetide, monarch of Sneak Island, was so arrayed

Nulla linea. *See* NO DAY WITHOUT ITS LINE *under* LINE

Nulli secundus (nŭl' I se kŭn' dus) (Lat , second to none) The motto of the Coldstream Guards. which regiment is hence sometimes spoken of as the *Nulli Secundus Club.*

Nullification (U S A.) In a political sense this term is said to have first been used by Thomas Jefferson in 1798 In 1832 South Carolina said they would *nullify* tariffs by not allowing duty to be collected at Charleston, hence those who set State rights above Federal Law are called *nullifiers*

Numbers, Numerals. Pythagoras looked on numbers as influential principles; in his system—

1 was Unity, and represented Deity, which has no parts

2 was Diversity, and therefore disorder; the principle of strife and all evil.

3 was Perfect Harmony, or the union of unity and diversity

4 was Perfection, it is the first square (2 < 2 = 4)

5 was the prevailing number in Nature and Art

6 was Justice

7 was the climacteric number in all diseases, called the *Medical Number* See CLIMACTERIC.

With the ancient Romans 2 was the most fatal of all the numbers, they dedicated the second month to Pluto, and the second day of the month to the Manes

In old ecclesiastical symbolism the numbers from 1 to 13 were held to denote the following —

1 The Unity of God

2 The hypostatic union of Christ, both God and man

3 The Trinity

4 The number of the Evangelists

5 The wounds of the Redeemer two in the hands, two in the feet, one in the side

6 The creative week

7 The gifts of the Holy Ghost (*Rev* i, 12), and the seven times Christ spoke on the cross

8 The number of beatitudes (*Matt* v, 3-11)

9 The nine orders of angels

10 The number of the Commandments

11 The number of the Apostles who remained faithful

12 The original college

13 The final number after the conversion of Paul

Apocalyptic number, 666 *See* NUMBER OF THE BEAST *below*

Back number A number of a paper or periodical issued previously to the current one; hence an out-of-date or old-fashioned person or thing

Cyclic number. A number the final digit of whose square is the same, 5 (25) and 6 (36) are examples

Golden number. *See* GOLDEN.

His days are numbered. They are drawing to a close; he is near death

God hath numbered thy kingdom, and finished it — *Dan* v, 26.

Irrational number. A definite number not expressible in a definite number of digits, as the root of a number that cannot be exactly extracted.

Medical number. In the Pythagorean system (*see above*), 7.

Number of the Beast, The. 666, a mystical number of unknown meaning but referring to some man mentioned by St John

Let him that hath understanding count the number of the beast; for it is the number of a man, and his number is Six hundred threescore and six —*Rev* xiii, 18.

One of the most plausible suggestions is that it refers to Neron Cæsar, which in Hebrew characters with numerical value gives 666, whereas Nero, without the final "n," as in Latin, gives 616 (n = 50), the number given in many early MSS, according to Irenaeus

Among the Cabalists every letter represented a number, and one's number was the sum of these equivalents to the letters in one's name If, as is probable, the *Revelation* was written in Hebrew, the number would suit either Nero, Hadrian, or Trajan—all persecutors, if in Greek, it would fit Caligula or *Lateinos*, i e the Roman Empire, but almost any name in any language can be twisted into this number, and it has been applied to many persons assumed to have been Antichrist, or Apostates, Diocletian, Evanthas, Julian the Apostate, Luther, Mohammed, Paul V, Silvester II, Napoleon Bonaparte, Charles Bradlaugh, Wilham II of Germany, and several others, as well as to certain phrases supposed to be descriptive of "the Man of Sin," as Vicar-General of God, Kakos Odegos (bad guide), Abinu Kadescha Papa (our holy father the pope), e g —

M	a	o	m	e	t	i	s
40,	1,	70,	40,	5,	300,	10,	200	= 666
L	a	t	e	i	n	o	s
30,	1,	300,	5,	10,	50,	70,	200	= 666

One suggestion is that St John chose the number 666 because it just fell short of the holy number 7 in every particular, was straining at every point to get there, but never could, *See also* MYSTERIUM

Odd numbers. *See* ODD

To consult the Book of Numbers A facetious way of saying, "to put it to the vote," "to call for a division"

Your number's up. You are in a very serious position or, sometimes, about to die A soldier's phrase; in the American army a soldier who has just been killed or has died is said to have "lost his mess number" An older phrase used in the British Navy was "to lose the number of his mess."

Numerals. All our numerals and ordinals up to a million (with one exception) are Anglo-Saxon. The one exception is *Second*, which is French The Anglo-Saxon word was *other*, as First, Other, Third, etc, but as this was ambiguous the Fr *seconde* was early adopted. Million is from Lat *mille*, a thousand

The primitive method of counting was by the fingers (*cp* DIGIT), thus in the Roman system of numeration the first four were simply I, II, III, IIII, five was the outline of the hand simplified into a v, the next four figures were the two combined, thus, vi, vii, viii, viiii, and ten was a double v, thus, x. At a later period iiii and viiii were expressed by one less than five (i-v) and one less than ten (i-x); nineteen was· ten-plus-nine (x + ix), etc. *See also* ARABIC FIGURES

Nunawadding Messiah. This was Andrew Fisher, of Nunawadding, Victoria, Australia, who declared himself to be the Messiah, in 1871 His hundred followers were polygamous, he himself having three wives

Nunc dimittis (nŭngk di mit' is) The Song of Simeon (*Luke* ii, 29), "Lord, now lettest thou thy servant depart in peace," so called from the opening words of the Latin version, *Nunc dimittis servum tuum, Domine*

Hence, *to receive one's Nunc dimittis*, to be given permission to go, *to sing one's Nunc dimittis*, to show satisfaction at departing.

The Canticle is sung in the Evening Service of the Church of England, and has been used at Compline or Vespers throughout the Church from the earliest times

Nuncheon (nŭn' chun) Properly, "the noon-tide draught", M E *noneschenh* (*none*, noon, and *schench*, a cup or draught), hence, light refreshments between meals, lunch The word *luncheon* has been affected by the older *nuncheon Cp* BEVER

Laying by their swords and truncheons,
They took their breakfasts, or their nuncheons
                              BUTLER *Hudibras*, I, i, 345

Nunky. Slang for "Uncle" (*q v*), especially as meaning a pawnbroker, or for "Uncle Sam" (*see* SAM)

Nunky pays for all The American Government (*see* SAM) has to "stand the racket"

Nuremberg (nū' rem bĕrg) One of the principal cities of Bavaria (in German Nuernberg), with a long and honorable history, among other things famous as the home of Albrecht Durer. After 1933 the Nazi party held its annual September conventions there, and in 1935 the infamous *Nuremberg Laws* were promulgated, dividing the people of Germany into three classes Aryans (with full civic rights), Jews (with no rights), and mixed Aryans and Jews (who might acquire Aryan rights by marrying Germans) As the centre of Nazi Germany Nuremberg was chosen as the venue for the trial of the 23 chief Nazi leaders which opened November 21st, 1945 and concluded October 1st, 1946, when 3 were acquitted, 11 were condemned to death and the remainder sentenced to various terms of imprisonment.

Nuremberg Eggs. Watches, which were invented at Nuremberg about 1500, and were egg-shaped

Nurr and Spell. *See* KNURR

Nursery. A room set apart for the use of young children (Lat *nutrire*, to nourish), hence, a garden for rearing plants (tended by a *nursery-man*).

In horse-racing, *Nurseries* are races for two-year-olds; and figuratively the word is used of any place or school of training for the professions, etc

Under William Rufus the Chancery became a nursery of clever and unscrupulous churchmen — FREEMAN *The Norman Conquest*, V, 135

Nursery cannons. In billiards, a series of cannons played so that the balls move as little as possible

Nursery slopes. Easy hillsides on which beginners learn to ski.

Nut. Slang for the head, perhaps so called from its resemblance to a nut

Also slang for a swell young man about town, a dude (in this sense frequently written—and pronounced—with an initial *k*, *knut*); from a music-hall song of the early 20th century, sung by Basil Hallam, "I'm Gilbert the Filbert, the colonel of the K-nuts"

A hard nut to crack. A difficult question to answer, a hard problem to solve

He who would eat the nut must first crack the shell. The gods give nothing to man without great labour.

To lie in a nutshell. To be explained in a few words; to be capable of easy solution

Here we go gathering nuts in May. This burden of the old children's game is a perversion of "Here we go gathering *knots* of may," referring to the old custom of gathering knots of flowers on May-day, or, to use the ordinary phrase, "to go a-maying" There are no nuts to be gathered in May

It is time to lay our nuts aside (Lat *relinquere nuces*). To leave off our follies, to relinquish boyish pursuits The allusion is to an old Roman marriage ceremony, in which the bridegroom, as he led his bride home, scattered nuts to the crowd, as if to symbolize to them that he gave up his boyish sports

Off one's nut. Crazy, daft

That's nuts to him. A great pleasure, a fine treat.

To edge his way along the crowded paths of life, warning all human sympathy to keep its distance, was what the knowing ones call nuts to Scrooge — DICKENS· *A Christmas Carol*, 1

To be dead nuts on To be very much pleased with, highly gratified with

My aunt is awful nuts on Marcus Aurelius, I beg your pardon, you don't know the phrase, my aunt makes Marcus Aurelius her Bible —WM BLACK *Princess of Thule*, xl

To be off one's nut, to be nuts. Crazy, demented Hence, Nut house. A lunatic asylum

Nut-brown Maid, The. An English ballad, dating (probably) from the late 15th century, first printed in *Arnolde's Chronicle* (Antwerp, 1502) It tells how the "Not-browne Mayd" was wooed and won by a knight who gave out that he was a banished man. After describing the hardships she would have to undergo if she married him, and finding her love true to the test, he revealed himself to be an earl's son, with large hereditary estates in Westmorland.

The ballad is given in Percy's *Reliques*, and forms the basis of Prior's *Henry and Emma*.

Nutcrack Night. All Hallows' Eve, when it is customary in some places to crack nuts in large quantities

Nutcrackers. The East Kent Regiment, the old 3rd Foot, so called because at Albuera (1811) they opened and retreated, but in a few minutes came again into the field, cracked the heads of the Polish Lancers, and did most excellent service

The "Iliad" in a nutshell. Pliny (vii, 21) tells us that the *Iliad* was copied in so small a hand that the whole work could lie in a walnut shell, his authority is Cicero (*Apud Gellium*, ix, 421)

Whilst they (as Homer's *Iliad* in a nut)
A world of wonders in one closet shut
On the Tradescants' Monument, Lambeth Churchyard.

Huet, Bishop of Avranches (d. 1721), proved by experiment that a parchment 27 by 21 centimetres would contain the entire *Iliad*, and that such a parchment would go into a common-sized nut; he wrote eighty verses of the *Iliad* (which contains in all 501,930 letters) on a single line of a page similar to this DICTIONARY This would be 19,000 verses to the page, or 2,000 more than the *Iliad* contains

In the Harleian MSS (530) is an account of Peter Bales, a clerk of the Court of Chancery about 1590, who wrote out the whole Bible so small that he inclosed it in a walnut shell of English growth Lalanne describes, in his *Curiosités Bibliographiques*, an edition of Rochefoucault's *Maximes*, published by Didot in 1829, on pages one inch square, each page containing 26 lines, and each line 44 letters Charles Toppan, of New York, engraved on a plate one-eighth of an inch square 12,000 letters, the *Iliad* would occupy 42 such plates engraved on both sides. George P. Marsh says, in his *Lectures*, he has seen the entire Koran in a parchment roll four inches wide and half an inch in diameter

Nutmeg State The nickname of Connecticut The story is that the inhabitants at one time manufactured wooden nutmegs for export

O

O The fifteenth letter of our alphabet, the fourteenth of the ancient Roman, and the sixteenth of the Phœnician and Semitic—in which it was called "the eye." Its name in Anglo-Saxon was *oedel*, home

A headless man had a letter [o] to write,
He who read it [naught] had lost his sight
The dumb repeated it [naught] word for word,
And deaf was the man who listened and heard [naught]

Dr. Whewell

Round as Giotto's O. Said of work that is perfect and complete, but done with little labour. *See* GIOTTO

The Fifteen O's, or the O's of St. Bridget. Fifteen meditations on the Passion, composed by St Bridget. Each begins with *O Jesu*, or a similar invocation.

The Seven O's, or the **Great O's** of Advent. The seven antiphons to the Magnificat sung during the week preceding Christmas They commence respectively with *O Sapientia, O Adonai, O Radix Jesse, O Clavis David, O Oriens Splendor, O Rex gentium,* and *O Emmanuel* They are sometimes called *The Christmas O's*

O'. An Irish patronymic. (Gael *ogha,* Ir. *oa,* a descendant)

O' in *tam-o'-shanter, what's o'clock? cat-o'-nine-tails,* etc. stands for *of;* but in such phrases as *He comes home late o' night, I go to church o' Sundays,* it represents M.E. *on*

O.K. All correct, all right, a reassuring affirmative that, coming from the U S A to England has spread colloquially throughout several European languages. It derives probably from the Choctaw *oke,* meaning, "It is so " Andrew Jackson (1767-1845), who was notoriously illiterate, used the phrase In the presidential campaign of 1828 Jackson's opponents asserted that he derived the abbreviation from his own spelling "orl korrect "

O P. Riots. When Covent Garden Theatre was reopened in 1809 after the disastrous fire of the preceding year, the charges of admission were increased, but night after night for three months a throng crowded the pit, shouting "O P." (*old prices*), much damage was done, and the manager was obliged at last to give way.

O tempora! O mores! (ō tem' pôr a ō môr'ēz) (Lat from Cicero's *In Catilinam* 1, 2) Alas! how the times have changed for the worse! Alas! how the morals of the people are degenerated!

O Yes! O Yes! O Yes! *See* OYEZ

Oaf. A corruption of *ouph* (elf) A foolish lout or dolt is so called from the notion that idiots are changelings, left by the fairies in place of the stolen ones

> This guiltless oaf his vacancy of sense
> Supplied, and amply too, by innocence
> BYRON. *Verses found in a Summer-house*

> Then ye returned to your trinkets, then ye contented
>   your souls
> With the flannelled fools at the wicket, or the muddied
>   oafs at the goals
>   RUDYARD KIPLING *The Islanders*

Oak The oak was in ancient times sacred to the god of thunder because these trees are said to be more likely to be struck by lightning than any other Among the Druids the oak was held in the greatest veneration

Royal Oak Day. *See* OAK-APPLE DAY.

To sport one's oak. To be "not at home " At the Universities, chambers have two doors, the usual room-door and another, made of oak, outside it; when the "oak" is shut or "sported" it indicates either that the occupant of the room is out, or that he does not wish to be disturbed by visitors

Oak before ash, in for a splash; Ash before oak, in for a soak. The intuition is, if the oak gets into leaf before the ash we may expect a fine and productive year, if the ash precedes the oak in foliage, we may anticipate a wet summer and unproductive autumn

Some Famous Oaks:

The *Abbot's Oak,* near Woburn Abbey, is so called because the Woburn abbot was hanged on one of its branches, in 1537, by order of Henry VIII.

The *Bull Oak,* Wedgenock Park, was growing at the time of the Conquest

Cowthorpe Oak, near Wetherby, in Yorkshire, will hold seventy persons in its hollow It is said to be over 1,600 years old

The *Ellerslie Oak,* near Paisley, is reported to have sheltered Sir William Wallace and 300 of his men

Fairlop Oak, in Hainault Forest, was 36 ft in circumference a yard from the ground It was blown down in 1820

Owen Glendower's Oak, at Shelton, near Shrewsbury, was in full growth in 1403, for in this tree Owen Glendower witnessed the great battle between Henry IV and Henry Percy Six or eight persons can stand in the hollow of its trunk Its girth is 40$\frac{1}{2}$ ft.

The *Major Oak,* Sherwood Forest, Edwinstowe, according to tradition, was a full-grown tree in the reign of King John. The hollow of the trunk will hold fifteen persons, but a new bark has considerably diminished the opening Its girth is 37 or 38 ft , and the head covers a circumference of 240 ft

The *Parliament Oak,* Clipston, in Sherwood Forest, was the tree under which Edward I, in 1282, held his parliament He was hunting when a messenger came to tell him of the revolt of the Welsh He hastily convened his nobles under the oak, and it was resolved to march at once against Llewelyn, who was slain It was standing until early in this century

The *Oak of the Partisans,* in Parcy Forest, St Ouen, in the department of the Vosges, is 107 ft in height At the beginning of this century it was 706 years old

Queen's Oak, Huntingfield, Suffolk, is so named because near this tree Queen Elizabeth I shot a buck.

The *Reformation Oak,* on Mousehold Heath, near Norwich, is where the rebel Ket held his court in 1549, and when the rebellion was stamped out nine of the ringleaders were hanged on this tree

Robin Hood's Larder is an oak in Sherwood Forest The tradition is that Robin Hood used its hollow trunk as a hiding-place for the deer he had slain Late in the last century some schoolgirls boiled their kettle in it, and burnt down a large part of the tree, but every effort was made to preserve what remained

The Royal Oak. See OAK-APPLE DAY

Sir Philip Sydney's Oak, near Penshurst, was planted at his birth in 1554, and was commemorated by Ben Jonson and Waller

The *Swilcar Oak,* in Needwood Forest, Staffordshire, is between 600 and 700 years old

William the Conqueror's Oak, in Windsor Great Park, is 38 feet in girth

The *Winfarthing Oak* is said to have been 700 years old at the time of the Conquest

Oak-apple Day (also called *Royal Oak Day*). May 29th, the birthday of Charles II, commanded by Act of Parliament in 1664 to be observed as a day of thanksgiving. A special service—expunged only in 1859—was inserted in the Book of Common Prayer

It was in the month of September that Charles concealed himself in an oak (the "Royal Oak") at Boscobel The battle of Worcester was fought on Wednesday, September 3rd, 1651, and Charles arrived at Whiteladies, about three-quarters of a mile from Boscobel House, early the next morning He returned to England on his birthday, when the Royalists displayed a branch of oak in allusion to his hiding in this tree

Oakes's Oath (Austr) Unreliable testimony delivered on oath The phrase is said to derive from one Oakes who was asked in a Court of Law if he could identify a pair of horns as belonging to one of his own cattle After hesitating a moment he is reported to have said, 'I'll chance it, Yes!'

Oakley, Annie. An expert American markswoman (1860-1926), who in Buffalo Bill's Wild West Show, using a playing card as a target, centred a shot in each of the pips From this performance of hers, and the resemblance of the card to a punched ticket, springs the American use of the name "Annie Oakley" to mean a complimentary ticket to a show, a meal ticket, or a pass on a railway

Oaks, The. One of the "classic" horse-races, it is for three-year-old fillies, and is run at Epsom shortly before or after the Derby (q v) So called by the twelfth Earl of Derby, who established the race in 1779, from an estate of his near Epsom named "The Oaks "

Oakum is the fibre obtained by unravelling and unpicking old rope It was formerly used for caulking the seams in the timbers of wooden ships The picking of oakum was once a form of employment forced upon prisoners, the plucking of old, tarred rope with the bare fingernails was little short of a form of torture, and a more sensible attitude towards imprisonment and punishment has made it obsolete.

Oannes (ō ăn' ēz) A Babylonian god having a fish's body and a human head and feet In the daytime he lived with men to instruct them in the arts and sciences, but at night retired to the depths of the Persian Gulf He has been identified with Ea of the cuneiform inscriptions.

Oar. To put your oar into my boat To interfere with my affairs "Paddle your own canoe, and don't put your oar into my boat "

To rest on one's oars. To take an interval of rest after hard work A boating phrase

To toss the oars. To raise them vertically, resting on the handles It is a form of salute

Oasis (ō ā' sis) (Coptic, *ouahe*, from *ouh*, to dwell) A fertile spot in the midst of a desert country, especially in the deserts of Africa where wells of water or small lakes are to be found, and vegetation is pretty abundant Hence a sudden cessation of pain, or a sudden pleasure in the midst of monotonous existence, is sometimes called "a perfect oasis "

Oaten pipe. A rustic musical pipe made of an oat straw so cut as to be stopped at one end with a knot, the other end being left open A

slit made in the straw near the knot was so cut as to form a reed

> Meanwhile the rural ditties were not mute,
> Temper'd to th' oaten flute
> MILTON: <i>Lycidas.</i>

Oath *See* SWEAR

Oats He has sown his wild oats. He has left off his gay habits and is become steady The reference is to the folly of sowing wild, *i e.* bad, grain instead of good; but it is worth noting that in Denmark the thick vapours which rise just before the land bursts into vegetation are called *Lokkens havre* (Loki's wild oats), and when the fine weather succeeds, the Danes say, "*Loki has sown his wild oats.*"

Obadiah (ō be di' ȧ). A slang name for a Quaker

Obeah, Obi (ō 'be a) The belief in and practice of obeah, *i e* , a kind of sorcery or witchcraft prevalent in West Africa and formerly in the West Indies *Obeah* is a native word, and signifies something put into the ground, to bring about sickness, death. or other disaster

Obelisk. A tapering pillar stone, originally erected by the Egyptians, who placed them in pairs before temple portals They were usually monoliths of pink syenite, with a base width one-tenth of the height and a copper-sheathed, pyramidal apex Each of the obelisk's four faces bore incised hieroglyphs The best known in England is Cleopatra's Needle, placed on the Victoria Embankment, London, in 1878, its partner being set up in Central Park, New York These granite obelisks were erected in Heliopolis by Thothmes III, about 1475 B C , and removed to Alexandria by Augustus Cæsar in 12 B C.

The tallest of all obelisks is at Rome, taken there from Heliopolis by the Emperor Caligula and erected in the circus that is now the Piazza of St Peter's Although weighing some 320 tons, it was moved bodily on rollers by Pope Sixtus V, in 1586—an astonishing engineering feat, considering the appliances then available The task was so tricky that spectators were forbidden to utter a sound on pain of death But at a critical moment, when the immense weight of stone appeared to be straining the ropes to breaking point, one of the workmen, a sailor from San Remo, called "Acqua alle fune"—Water on the ropes—and saved the situation at the risk of his life

The Obelisk of Luxor, in the Place de la Concorde, Paris, came from Thebes and was presented to Louis Philippe, in 1831, by the then Khedive of Egypt Its hieroglyphs record the deeds of Rameses II (13th century, B C)

Oberammergau. *See* PASSION PLAY.

Obermann (ō' bĕr măn) The impersonation of high moral worth without talent, and the tortures endured by the consciousness of this defect From Senancour's psychological romance of this name (1804), in which Obermann, the hero, is a dreamer perpetually trying to escape from the actual.

Oberon (ō' bĕr on) King of the Fairies, husband of Titania Shakespeare introduces them in his *Midsummer Night's Dream* The name is probably connected with Alberich (*q v.*), the king of the elves.

He first appears in the mediæval French romance, *Huon de Bordeaux*, where he is a son of Julius Cæsar and Morgan le Fay He was only three feet high, but of angelic face, and was lord and king of Mommur. At his birth the fairies bestowed their gifts—one was insight into men's thoughts, and another was the power of transporting himself to any place instantaneously, and in the fullness of time legions of angels conveyed his soul to Paradise

Obi. *See* OBEAH.

Obiter dictum (ob' i tér dik' tum) (Lat) An incidental remark, an opinion expressed by a judge, but not judicially. An *obiter dictum* has no authority beyond that of deference to the wisdom, experience, and honesty of the person who utters it, but a judicial sentence is the verdict of a judge bound under oath to pronounce judgment only according to law and evidence.

Object; Objective. *See* SUBJECT

Oblong (U S A). A late 19th-century slang term for a bank note

Obolus (ob' ō lus) An ancient Greek copper coin worth five lepta, or about a halfpenny Also a silver coin of the Byzantine Empire, worth about three times as much It is to this latter that the phrase "Give an obolus to poor old Belisarius" (*see* BELISARIUS) refers

Observantins. *See* FRANCISCANS

Obverse. That side of a coin or medal which contains the principal device Thus, the obverse of our coins is the side which contains the sovereign's head, the other side is the "reverse"

Occam's Razor. *Entia non sunt multiplicanda* (entities are not to be multiplied). With this axiom, which means that all unnecessary facts or constituents in the subject being analysed are to be eliminated, Occam dissected every question as with a razor.

William of Occam, the *Doctor Singularis et Invincibilis* (d. 1347), was a scholastic philosopher, famous as the great advocate and reviver of nominalism (*q v*)

Occasion. A lame old hag in Spenser's *Faerie Queene* (II, iv), mother of Furor, and symbolical of the cause of anger.

To improve the occasion. To draw a moral lesson from some event which has occurred

Occult Sciences (Lat *occultus*, related to *celāre*, to hide). Magic, alchemy, and astrology, so called because they were hidden mysteries

Oceana (ō sē' a na) A philosophical treatise on the principles of government by James Harrington (1656). *See* COMMONWEALTHS, IDEAL

Octavo (ok tā' vō) A book in which each sheet of paper is folded into eight leaves (16 pages), contracted thus—8vo (Ital *un' ottavo*, Fr. *in octavo*, Lat *octo*, eight) An octavo can be of almost any size, dependent entirely on the size of the sheets before folding.

October. The eighth month of the ancient Roman calendar (Lat. *octo*, eight) when the year began in March, the tenth of ours. The old Dutch name was *Wyn-maand*, the Anglo-Saxon, *Winmonath* (wine-month, or the time of vintage), also *Teo-monath* (tenth-month) and *Winter-fylleth* (winter full-moon). In the French Republican calendar it was *Vendemiaire* (time of vintage, September 22nd to October 21st)

A tankard of October A tankard of the best and strongest ale, brewed in October.

October Club A club of extreme Tories founded in 1710, with the password "October" —easily remembered "by a country gentleman who loved his ale " In the last years of Queen Anne's reign the October Club was a staunch supporter of the Jacobites.

Od *See* ODYLE.

Odal *See* UDAL

Odd. There's luck in odd numbers This is a very ancient fancy According to the Pythagorean system, "all nature is a harmony," man is a full chord, and all beyond is Deity, so that *nine* represents Deity. A major chord consists of a fundamental or tonic, its major third, and its just fifth. As the odd numbers are the fundamental notes of nature, the last being Deity, it will be easy to see how they came to be considered the great or lucky numbers. *Cp.* DIAPASON, NUMBER

Good luck lies in odd numbers   They say, there is divinity in odd numbers, either in nativity, chance, or death—*Merry Wives of Windsor*, v, 1

The odd numbers 1, 3, 5, 7, 9 (*which see*) seem to play a far more important part than the even numbers. *One* is Deity, *three* the Trinity, *five* the chief division, *seven* is the sacred number, and *nine* is three times three, the great climacteric

Numero Deus impare gaudet (the god delights in odd numbers—Virgil, *Eclogues*, VIII, 75) Three indicates the "beginning, middle, and end " The Godhead has three persons, so in classic mythology Hecate had threefold power, Jove's symbol was a triple thunderbolt, Neptune's a sea-trident, Pluto's a three-headed dog, the Fates were three, the Furies three, the Graces three, the Horæ three, the Muses three-times-three There are seven notes, nine planets, nine orders of angels, seven days a week, thirteen lunar months, or 365 days a year, etc , five senses, five fingers on the hand and toes on the foot, five continents, etc.

Odd Volumes, Sette of A literary dining Society in London, founded in 1884

At odds At variance

By long odds. By a great difference, as, "He is the best man by long odds " In horse-racing, *odds* are the ratio by which the amount staked by one party to a bet exceeds that of the other, hence long odds indicates a big variance in this ratio

Odds and Ends. *See* END

That makes no odds. No difference; never mind, that is no excuse An application of the betting phrase

Odd Fellows A secret society with benevolent aims and of uncertain antiquity. Records go back to 1745, and in the following years it flourished despite considerable persecution on account of its alleged "seditiousness." In 1813 it awakened to new vigour as the Independent Order of Odd Fellows, in Manchester it has since then become the greatest of such benevolent orders, spreading into most of the countries of North Europe and into North America In 1950 it numbered some 685,000 members in Great Britain alone

Odin (ō' din) The Scandinavian name of the god called by the Anglo-Saxons Woden (*q v*). Odin was god of wisdom, poetry, war, and agriculture He was god of the dead, also, and presided over banquets of those slain in battle *See* VALHALLA He became the *All-wise* by drinking of Mimir's fountain, but purchased the distinction at the cost of one eye, and is often represented as a one-eyed man wearing a hat and carrying a staff His remaining eye is the Sun

The promise of Odin The most binding of all oaths to a Norseman In making it the hand was passed through a massive silver ring kept for the purpose, or through a sacrificial stone, like that called the ' Circle of Stennis "

The vow of Odin. A matrimonial or other vow made before the 'Stone of Odin," in the Orkneys. This was an oval stone, with a hole in it large enough to admit a man's hand Anyone who violated a vow made before this stone was held infamous.

Odium theologicum (ō' di um thē ō loj' i kum) (Lat) The bitter hatred of rival theologians No wars so sanguinary as holy wars, no persecutions so relentless as religious persecutions, no hatred so bitter as theological hatred

Odor lucri (ō' dôr lū' krī) (Lat.) The sweets of gain, the delights of money-making

Odour. In good odour, in bad odour In favour, out of favour, in good repute, in bad repute

The odour of sanctity In the Middle Ages it was held that a sweet and delightful odour was given off by the bodies of saintly persons at their death, and also when their bodies, if "translated," were disinterred Hence the phrase, *he died in the odour of sanctity, i e* he died a saint. The Swedenborgians say that when the celestial angels are present at a deathbed, what is then cadaverous excites a sensation of what is aromatic

There is an "odour of iniquity" as well as an "odour of sanctity," and Shakespeare has a strong passage on the odour of impiety Antiochus and his wicked daughter were killed by lightning, and the poet says —

A fire from heaven came and shrivelled up
Their bodies, e'en to loathing, for they so stunk
That all those eyes adored them ere their fall
Scorned now their hand should give them burial
Pericles, ii, 4

Od's, used in oaths, as '—
Od's bodikins! or *Odsbody'* means "God's body "
Od's pittikins! God's pity.
Od's plessed will! (*Merry Wives of Windsor*, i, 1.)
Od rot 'em! See DRAT
Od-zounds! God's wounds

Odyle (od' il) The name formerly given to the hypothetical force which emanates from a medium to produce the phenomena connected with mesmerism, spirit-rapping, table-turning, and so on Baron von Reichenbach (1788-1869) called it *Od force*, and taught that it pervaded all nature especially heat, light, crystals, magnets, etc., and was developed in chemical action, and also that it streamed from the fingers of specially sensitive persons.

That od-force of German Riechenbach
Which still from female finger-tips burns blue
MRS. BROWNING *Aurora Leigh*, vii, 295

Odyssey (od' i si) The epic poem of Homer which records the adventures of *Odysseus* (Ulysses) on his home-voyage from Troy. The word is an adjective formed out of the hero's name, and means the *things* or *adventures* of Ulysses

Œcumenical Councils (ē kū men' ik al) Ecclesiastical councils whose findings are—or were —recognized as applying to the whole of the Christian world (Gr *oikoumenikos*, the inhabited—*ge*, earth being understood), and the members of which were drawn from the whole Church They are —

Nicæa, 325, 787; Constantinople, 381, 553, 680-1, 869, Ephesus, 431, Chalcedon, 451, Lateran, 1123, 1139, 1179, 1215, 1512-17, Lyons, 1245, 1274, Vienne, 1311-13, Constance, 1414-18, Basle-Ferrara-Florence, 1431-43, Trent, 1545-1563, Vatican, 1869 (adjourned 1870 and still unfinished)

Of these the Church of England recognizes only six —

Nicæa, 325, against the Arians
Constantinople, 381, against "heretics "
Ephesus, 431, against the Nestorians and Pelagians
Chalcedon, 451, when Athanasius was restored.
Constantinople, 553, against Origen.
Constantinople, 680, against the Monothelites

Œdipus (ē' di pūs) was the son of Laius, King of Corinth, and of Jocasta his wife. To avert the fulfilment of a prophecy Œdipus was exposed on the mountains as an infant and taken in and reared by the shepherds When grown to manhood he unwittingly slew his father, then, having solved the riddle of the Sphinx, he became King of Thebes, thereby gaining the hand in marriage of Jocasta, his mother, of whose relationship to himself they were both ignorant When the facts came to light Jocasta hanged herself and Œdipus tore out his own eyes

An **Œdipus complex** is the psychoanalytical term for the sexual desire (usually unrecognized by himself) of a son for his mother and conversely an equally unrecognized jealous hatred of his father

Œil de Bœuf (ō ē de bêrf) (Fr , "bull's-eye"). A large reception room (*salle*) in the palace of Versailles, lighted by a round, "bull's-eye" window. The ceiling, decorated by Van der Mulen, contains likenesses of the children of Louis XIV It was the ante-room where courtiers waited and gossiped, and hence the name became associated with backstairs intrigue

Les Fastes de l'Œil de Bœuf. The annals of the courtiers of the Grand Monarque, hence, anecdotes of courtiers generally

Off (Lat *ab*, from, away). The house is a *mile* off—*i e* is "away" or "from" us a mile The word preceding off defines its scope To be '*well* off" is to be away or on the way towards well-being, to be *badly* off is to be away or on the way to the bad

The **off-side** of horses when in pairs is that to the *right* hand of the coachman (*cp* NFAR), and a "Soccer" football referee signals *Off-side* and awards a free kick when a player has kicked the ball—there being none of his opponents except the goal-keeper between himself and his opponents' goal—unless he himself has taken the ball there The off-side rules vary with the different varieties of football.

An act of behaviour, a thing, a person, etc , is said to be *a bit off* when it is not quite up to the mark—it is a bit "off colour" (*see* COLOUR), and a girl is said "to get off with a man" when she sets out to attract him and succeeds

Offa's Dyke. An entrenchment which runs from Beachley, near the mouth of the Wye, to Flintshire If not actually the work of Offa, King of Mercia (about 757-96) it was repaired by him, and he availed himself of it as a line of demarcation between him and the Welsh, though it by no means tallied with his territory either in extent or position

Office, The Divine *See* BREVIARY

Office, The Holy. The Inquisition (*q v*)

Og, King of Bashan, according to Rabbinical mythology was an antediluvian giant, saved from the flood by climbing on the roof of the ark. After the passage of the Red Sea, Moses first conquered Sihon, and then advanced against the giant Og (whose bedstead, made of iron, was above 15 ft long and nearly 7 ft broad (*Deut* iii, 11) The legend says that Og plucked up a mountain to hurl at the Israelites, but he got so entangled with his burden that Moses was able to kill him without much difficulty

In Dryden's *Absalom and Achitophel* (*q.v*), Og stands for Thomas Shadwell (*see* MAC-FLECKNOE) He was very large and fat.

Ogham (og' am). The alphabet in use among the ancient Irish and British nations There were twenty characters, each of which was composed of any number of thin strokes from one to five, which were arranged and grouped above, below, or across a horizontal line

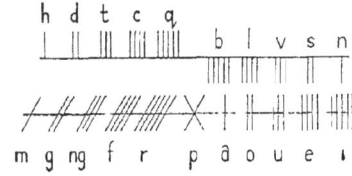

The word is connected with *Ogmius*, the name, according to Lucian, of a Gaulish god who presided over speech

Ogier the Dane (ō' ji ēr) One of the great heroes of mediæval romance, a paladin of Charlemagne, and son of Geoffrey, King of

Denmark, of which country (as Holger Danske) he is still the national hero. Fairies attended at his birth, and bestowed upon him divers gifts Among these fairies was Morgan le Fay (*q v.*), who when the knight was a hundred years old embarked him for Avalon, "hard by the terrestrial paradise " On reaching the island he entered the castle, where he found a horse sitting at a banquet-table The horse, who had once been a mighty prince, conducted him to Morgan le Fay, who gave him a ring which removed all infirmities and restored him to ripe manhood, and a crown which made him forget his country and past life, and introduced him to King Arthur Two hundred years rolled on, and France was invaded by the Paynims Morgan le Fay now sent Ogier to defend "*le bon pays de France*", and when he had routed the invaders she took him back to Avalon, where he remains until the time for him to reappear on this earth of ours has arrived William Morris gives a rendering of the romance in his *Earthly Paradise (August)*

Ogpu (og'poo) or G P U (gā pā oo), the secret political police of the U S S R , employed to suppress political crime and root out disaffection among the proletariat It succeeded the dreaded Cheka in 1922, but proved itself no less tyrannical and feared. The initials stand for Russian Obedinennoe Gosudarstvennoe Politicheskoe Upravlenie, State Political Control.

Ogres of nursery story are giants of very malignant disposition, who live on human flesh The word was first used (and probably invented) by Perrault in his *Contes* (1697), and is thought to be made up from *Orcus*, a name of Pluto, the god of Hades

Ogygia (ō jij' i a) *See* CALYPSO

Ogygian Deluge. In Greek legend a flood supposed to have taken place two hundred years before Deucalion's flood, when Ogyges was King of Bœotia

Varro tells us that the planet Venus underwent a great change in the reign of Ogyges It changed its diameter, its colour, its figure, and its course

Oi Polloi, properly *Hoi Polloi* (*q v*) The commonalty, the many. In University slang the "poll men," or those who take degrees without "honours "

Oil. Oil of palms *See* PALM-OIL

To oil the knocker. To fee the porter The expression is from Racine's *Les Plaideurs* "*On n'entre point chez lui sans graisser le marteau*" ("No one enters *his* house without oiling the knocker")

To pour oil on troubled waters. To soothe by gentle words; to bring about a state of calm after great anger or excitement, etc , by tact and diplomacy

The allusion is to the well-known fact that during a storm at sea the force of the waves striking against a ship is very much lessened by pouring out oil In Bede's *Ecclesiastical History* (735) it is said that St Aidan gave a young priest who was to convoy a maiden destined for the bride of King Oswin a cruse of oil to pour on the sea if the waves became stormy A storm did arise, and the priest, pouring the oil on the waves, actually reduced them to a calm.

To strike oil. To make a happy hit or valuable discovery The phrase refers to hitting upon or discovering a bed of petroleum or mineral oil.

Old. Used in slang and colloquial talk as a term of endearment or friendship, as in *My dear old chap, my old man (i.e* my husband), as a general disparagement, as in *Old cat, old fogy, old geezer, old stick-in-the-mud,* and as a common intensive, as in Shakespeare's "Here will be an old abusing of God's patience and the king's English," and in the modern *Any old thing will do*

For names such as Old Grog, Harry, Noll, Rowley, Scratch, Tom, etc , *see these words*

Old and Bold. *See* REGIMENTAL NICKNAMES

Old Bags. John Scott, Lord Chancellor Eldon (1751-1838), so called from his carrying home with him in different bags the cases still pending his judgment.

Old Blood-and-Guts Nickname of American General George S. Patton (World War II)

Old Bold. *See* REGIMENTAL NICKNAMES

Old Bold Fifth. *See* REGIMENTAL NICKNAMES

Old Bona Fide. Louis XIV (1638, 1643-1715)

Old boots. *See* BOOTS

Old Boy Net. *See* NET

Old Braggs. The Gloucestershire Regiment, the 28th Foot, raised in 1694 The name is derived from General Philip Bragg, who was colonel of the regiment from 1734 to 1759

Old Contemptibles The British Expeditionary Force that crossed to France in 1914 and fought in the battle and retreat from Mons The phrase originated in the alleged comment of the Kaiser about "the contemptible British army "

Old Cracow Bible. *See* BIBLE, SPECIALLY NAMED

Old Dominion Virginia Every Act of Parliament up to the Declaration of Independence designated Virginia "the Colony and Dominion of Virginia " Captain John Smith, in his *History of Virginia* (1629), calls this "colony and dominion" *Ould Virginia,* in contradistinction to *New England,* and other British settlements

Old Dozen. *See* REGIMENTAL NICKNAMES

Old Fogs. *See* REGIMENTAL NICKNAMES

Old Glory The United States Flag *See* STARS AND STRIPES

Old Guard The Imperial Guard created by Napoleon in 1804 and composed of picked men, the flower of the French army Devoted to the Emperor, with a magnificent uniform including a huge bearskin hat, with better pay and rationing than the rest of the army, the Old Guard were to be relied upon in any desperate strait of battle, and it was they who made the last charge of the French at Waterloo Figuratively the phrase Old Guard is used for the stalwarts of any party or movement

Old Hickory. The nickname of General Andrew Jackson (1767-1845), 7th President of

the U S A , it arose from the staunchness and strength of his character.

Old King Cole. *See* COLE.

Old Lady of Threadneedle Street. *See* THREADNEEDLE

Old Man Eloquent. Isocrates; so called by Milton When he heard of the result of the battle of Chæronea, which was fatal to Grecian liberty, he died of grief.

> That dishonest victory
> At Chæronea, fatal to liberty,
> Killed with report that Old Man Eloquent.
> MILTON: *Sonnets*

This name was also applied to John Quincy Adams (1767-1848), 6th President of the U S A , 1825-29

Old Man of the Mountain. Hassan-ben-Sabah, the sheikh Al Jebal, and founder of the sect called Assassins (*q v*).

Old Man of the Sea. In the *Arabian Nights* story of *Sinbad the Sailor,* the Old Man of the Sea hoisted himself on the shoulders of Sinbad and clung there for many days and nights, much to the discomfort of Sinbad, who finally released himself by making the Old Man drunk Hence, any burden, figurative or actual, of which it is impossible to free oneself without the greatest exertions is spoken of as an Old Man of the Sea

Old Pretender. James Stuart (1688-1760), son of James II the last Stuart king of Great Britain and Ireland He was also called the Old Chevalier, and on the death of his father was proclaimed king by his adherents, under the title of James III The word "Pretender" in this context has its old connotation of one who makes a baseless claim to a title, etc There was a popular Jacobite toast

> God bless the king, I mean the Faith's Defender;
> God bless (no harm in blessing) the Pretender
> But who that Pretender is, and who that king,
> God bless us all' is quite another thing

Old Reekie. *See* AULD REEKIE

Old Rough and Ready. General Zachary Taylor (1784-1850), 12th President of the U S A , 1849-50

Old School Tie. Literally a necktie of the colours of the wearer's public school, but more often used figuratively in a pejorative sense as a symbol of the class distinction allegedly assumed by those who went to a public school

Old Style—New Style. Terms used in chronology, the *Old Style* being the Julian Calendar (*q v.*), and the *New Style* the Gregorian (*q v*) *See also* CALENDAR.

Old World So Europe, Asia, and Africa are called when compared with North and South America (the New World).

Oldenburg Horn A horn long in the possession of the reigning princes of the House of Oldenburg, but now in the collection of the King of Denmark According to tradition, Count Otto of Oldenburg, in 967, was offered drink in this silver-gilt horn by a "wild woman," at the Osenborg As he did not like the look of the liquor, he threw it away, and rode off with the horn

'Ole, A Better. Old Bill, a walrus-moustached, disillusioned old soldier in the days of trench warfare was the creation of Capt Bruce Bairnsfather, who was doing drawings for London illustrated papers in 1914-18 Cowering in a muddy shell-hole in the midst of a withering bombardment, he says to his grousing pal Bert, "If you know of a better 'ole, go to it" The joke and Old Bill struck the public fancy Old Bill became a national figure—the embodiment of a familiar type of simple, cynical, long-suffering, honest old grumbler

Olet lucernam (ō 'let loo sĕi' năm) (Latin proverb). It smells of the lamp See LAMP

Oligarchy (ol' i gar ki) (Gr *oligos*, the few, *archē*, rule). A government in which the supreme power is vested in a small number of families or a few members of a class

Olio (ō' li ō) (Span *olla*, a stew, or the pot in which it is cooked, from Lat *olla*, a pot) In Spain a mixture of meat, vegetables, spices, etc, boiled together and highly seasoned, hence, any hotchpotch of various ingredients, as a miscellaneous collection of verses, drawings, pieces of music, etc

Olive. In ancient Greece the olive was sacred to Pallas Athene, in allusion to the story (*see* ATHENS) that at the naming of Athens she presented it with an olive tree. It was the symbol of peace, and also an emblem of fecundity, brides wearing or carrying an olive garland as ours do a wreath of orange blossom A crown of olive was the highest distinction of a citizen who had deserved well of his country, and was the highest prize in the Olympic Games.
In the O T the subsiding of the Flood was demonstrated to Noah by the return of a dove bearing an olive leaf in her beak (*Gen.* viii, 11)

To hold out the olive branch To make overtures for peace, in allusion to the olive being an ancient symbol of peace In some of Numa's medals the king is represented holding an olive twig, indicative of a peaceful reign

Olive branches. A facetious term for children in relation to their parents, the allusion is to "Thy wife shall be as a fruitful vine . . thy children like olive plants round about thy table" (*Ps* cxxviii, 3)
The wife and olive branches of one Mr Kenwigs — DICKENS. *Nicholas Nickleby*, xiv.

Oliver. Charlemagne's favourite paladin, who, with Roland, rode by his side. He was the son of Regnier, Duke of Genoa (another of the paladins), and brother of the beautiful Aude His sword was called *Hauteclaire*, and his horse *Ferrant d'Espagne*

A Roland for an Oliver See ROLAND

Olivetans (ol i vet' anz) Brethren of "Our Lady of Mount Olivet," and offshoot of the Benedictines. The order was founded in 1313 by Bernard Tolomei, of Siena.

Olla Podrida (ol 'yà pod rē' dà) (Span., putrid pot) Odds and ends, a mixture of scraps or *pot au feu*, into which every sort of eatable is thrown and stewed. *Cp* OLIO. Figuratively, the term means an incongruous mixture, a miscellaneous collection of any kind, a medley

Olympia. The ancient name of a valley in Elis, Peloponnesus, so called because here were held the famous games in honour of the Olympian Zeus (*see below*) In the valley was built the Altis, an enclosure of about 500 ft by 600 ft, which contained, besides the temple of Zeus, the Herœum, the Metroum, etc, the Stadium, with gymnasia, baths, etc. Hence, the name has been given to large buildings (more particularly the great halls and amphitheatre near Hammersmith, London) in which sporting events, spectacles, exhibitions, and so on can be presented under cover

Olympiad. Among the ancient Greeks, a period of four years, being the interval between the celebrations of the Olympic Games (*q.v*). The first Olympiad began in 776 B C, and the last (the 23rd) in A D 393

Olympian Zeus or Jove. A statue by Phidias, one of the "Seven Wonders of the World" Pausanias (vii, 2) says when the sculptor placed it in the temple at Olympia (433 B C), he prayed the god to indicate whether he was satisfied with it, and immediately a thunderbolt fell on the floor of the temple without doing the slightest harm.
It was a chryselephantine statue, i e. made of ivory and gold, and though seated on a throne, was 60 ft in height The left hand rested on a sceptre, and the right palm held a statue of Victory in solid gold The robes were of gold, and so were the four lions which supported the footstool. The throne was of cedar, embellished with ebony, ivory, gold, and precious stones
It was removed to Constantinople in the 5th century A D, and perished in the great fire of 475.

Olympic Games. The greatest of the four sacred festivals of the ancient Greeks, held at Olympia (*q v*) every fourth year, in the month of July The festival began with sacrifices and included racing, wrestling, and all kinds of contests, ending on the fifth day with processions, sacrifices, and banquets to the victors —who were garlanded with olive leaves
The Olympic Games were revived in 1896, the first meeting being held at Athens in that year. These were followed at four-yearly intervals. 1900 (Paris), 1904 (St Louis). 1908 (London), 1912 (Stockholm), 1920 (Antwerp), 1924 (Paris), 1928 (Amsterdam), 1932 (Los Angeles), 1936 (Berlin), 1948 (London), 1952 (Helsinki) The games in 1916, 1940, and 1944 were not held on account of World Wars I and II

Olympus. The home of the gods of ancient Greece, where Zeus held his court, a mountain about 9,800 ft. high on the confines of Macedonia and Thessaly The name is used for any pantheon, as "Odin, Thor, Balder, and the rest of the Northern Olympus"

Om. Among the Brahmans, the mystic equivalent for the name of the Deity, it has been adopted by modern occultists to denote absolute goodness and truth or the spiritual essence

Om mani padme hum ("Om, the jewel, is in the lotus: amen"). The mystic formula of the Tibetans and northern Buddhists used as a charm and for many religious purposes They are the first words taught to a child and the last uttered on the death-bed of the pious The lotus symbolizes universal being, and the jewel the individuality of the utterer

Omar Khayyam (ō' mar kī yăm'), Persian poet, astronomer, and mathematician, lived at Nishapur, where he died about the age of 50 in A D 1123. He was known chiefly for his work on algebra until Edward Fitzgerald published a poetical translation of his poems in 1859 Little notice of this was taken, however, until the early '90s when the Rubaiyat took Britain and America by storm It is frankly hedonistic in tone, but touched with a melancholy that attunes with eastern and western pessimism alike Fitzgerald never pretended that his work was other than a free version of the original; he made several revisions, but did not improve on his first text.

Ombre (om' ber). A card-game, introduced into England from Spain in the 17th century, and very popular till it was supplanted by quadrille, about 1730 It was usually played by three persons, and the eights, nines, and tens of each suit were left out Prior has an epigram on the game; he was playing with two ladies, and Fortune gave him "success in every suit but hearts " Pope immortalized the game in his *Rape of the Lock*.

Omega (ō 'meg ȧ) The last letter of the Greek alphabet *See* ALPHA

Omelet (om' lĕt) **You can't make omelets without breaking eggs**. Said by way of warning to one who is trying to "get something for nothing"—to accomplish some desired object without being willing to take the necessary trouble or make the necessary sacrifice The phrase is a translation of the French *On ne saurait faire une omelette sans casser des œufs*.

Omen (ō' men) Some phenomenon or un-usual event taken as a prognostication either of good or evil, a prophetic sign or augury The Latin word was adopted in the 16th century, its origin is unknown, but it is thought to be connected with *audire*, to hear Some well-known examples of accepting omens, ap-parently evil, as of good augury, are —

Leotychides II, of Sparta, was told by his augurs that his projected expedition would fail, because a viper had got entangled in the handle of the city key. 'Not so," he replied "The key caught the viper "

When Julius Cæsar landed at Adrumetum he hap-pened to trip and fall on his face. This would have been considered a fatal omen by his army; but, with admirable presence of mind, he exclaimed, "Thus I take possession of thee, O Africa!" Told of Scipio also

When William the Conqueror leaped upon the English shore he fell on his face and a great cry went forth that it was an ill-omen; but the duke exclaimed "I have taken seisin of this land with both my hands."

Omnibus (om' ni bus) (dative pl. of Lat *omnis*, all, for all) The name was first applied to the public vehicle in France in 1828 In the following year it was adopted by Shillibeer for the vehicles which he started on the Padding-ton (now Marylebone) Road, London The plural is *omnibuses*, and the word is generally abbreviated to *bus*, without any initial apos-trophe—just as *cabriolet* became *cab*, not *cab'*

Omnibus Bill. The Parliamentary term for a Bill embracing clauses that deal with a number of different subjects, as a Revenue Bill dealing with Customs, Taxes, Stamps, Excise, etc.

Omnibus box A box at a theatre for which the subscription is paid by several different parties, each of which has the right of using it.

Omnibus train. An old name for a train that stops at all stations—a train *for all*, as apart from the specials and the expresses that ran between only a few stations

Omnibus volume. A collection in one volume of an author's works, of short stories, essays, etc.

Omnium (om' ni um) (Lat , of all) The par-ticulars *of all* the items, or the assignment *of all* the securities, of a government loan.

Omnium gatherum. Dog Latin for a *gathering* or collection *of all* sorts of persons and things; a miscellaneous gathering together without regard to suitability or order

Omphale (om' fa lē) In Greek legend, the masculine but attractive Queen of Lydia, to whom Hercules was bound a slave for three years He fell in love with her, and led an effe-minate life spinning wool, while Omphale wore the lion's skin and was lady paramount

On A little bit on Slightly drunk.

It's not on to-day. It's not on the menu, it's not available.

It's not on Impossible A phrase from snooker, used when the object ball is obscured.

On dit (ong dē) (Fr., they say) A rumour, a report, a bit of gossip "There is an *on dit* that the prince is to marry soon "

One The word has a good many indefinite applications, as a person or thing of the kind implied or already mentioned (*I like those hats, I must buy one*), an unspecified person (*One doesn't do that sort of thing*), someone or some-thing, anyone or anything.

There is One above is a reference to the Deity, *the Evil One* is the Devil.

By one and one Singly, one at a time; en-tirely by oneself

He was one too many for me. He was a little bit too clever, he outwitted me

Number one. Oneself; hence, to take care of number one, to look after oneself, to seek one's own interest, to be selfish

One and all. Everybody individually and jointly The phrase is the motto of Cornishmen

One-horse. Third-rate, petty, insignificant; as, *a one-horse show*, *a one-horse town*, etc The phrase is of American origin, and the allusion was to a town so poor and idle that one horse was enough for all its transportation.

One in the eye, on the nose, in the bread-basket, etc. A blow on the spot indicated—the last being slang for the stomach.

One of these days. At some unspecified time in the future, generally the rather remote and uncertain future

To go one better than he did. To do a little more, etc., than he did. The phrase is from card-playing, at poker if one wishes to continue betting one has to "go" at least "one better," i.e. raise the stake.

Oneida Community, The See PERFECTIONISTS.

Onomatopeia (on ŏ măt ŏ pē' ä) The grammatical term for forming a word by imitating the sound associated with the object designated, or for a word that appears to suggest its nature or qualities "Cuckoo" and "tingle" are examples of onomatopeia The word itself comes from the Greek for "making of words."

Onus (ō' nus) (Lat) The burden, the responsibility, as, "The whole onus must rest on your own shoulders."

Onus probandi (Lat , the burden of proving) The obligation of proving some proposition, accusation, etc , as, "The onus probandi rests with the accuser."

Onyx (on 'iks) is Greek for a finger-nail, so called because the colour of an onyx resembles that of the finger-nail

Oom Paul "Uncle" Paul, the name familiarly applied to Paul Kruger (1825-1902), President of the Transvaal Republic and inspirer of the Dutch resistance to the British rule in South Africa.

Opal (Gr opallios, probably from Sansk upala, a gem) This semi-precious stone—a vitreous form of hydrous silica—is well known for its play of iridescent colours, and has long been considered to bring ill luck Alphonso XII of Spain (1874-85) is said to have had one that seemed to be fatal. On his wedding-day he presented it in a ring to his wife, and her death occurred soon afterwards Before the funeral he gave the ring to his sister, who died a few days later The king then presented it to his sister-in-law, and she died within three months. Alphonso, astounded at these fatalities, resolved to wear the ring himself, and within a very short time he too was dead The Queen Regent then suspended it from the neck of the Virgin of Almudena of Madrid

> Not an opal
> Wrapped in a bay-leaf in my left fist,
> To charm their eyes with
>   BEN JONSON New Inn, 1, 6

Open. Open city. A military term for a city which the occupying army declares it will not defend, and from which it guarantees it has withdrawn its armed forces—either because of the place's great historical importance (e g Rome), or because it is full of hospitals and wounded

Open door. In political parlance the principle of admitting all nations to a share in a country's trade, etc. The phrase is also applied to any loophole being left for the possibility of negotiation between contending parties, nations, etc

Open question. See QUESTION.

Open secret See SECRET DE POLICHINELLE.

Open, Sesame. See SESAME

Opera. A production for the stage composed of music and drama. The dialogue is mostly in verse and is sung to orchestral accompaniment, lyrics are an important element and in older operas a ballet was often included The rise of opera began about 1582, but it was not until the first opera house was opened in Venice, in 1637, that it became popular as a form of entertainment Alessandro Scarlatti (1659-1725) established the aria as a legitimate form of expressing soliloquy, and introduced the recitativo In England Henry Purcell (c. 1658-95) was the father of opera, writing some 42 musical works for the stage, some of them, such as Dido and Æneas (1689) being full operas In 1930 the British Government allocated a yearly sum of £17,000 for subsidizing opera in London and the provinces.

Opera bouffe is a form of French comic opera or operetta light in construction and of slight musical value It should be distinguished from —

Opera buffa, a form of light Italian comedy with musical numbers and dialogue in recitative.

Opera comique is a French type of opera, not necessarily comic, with spoken dialogue and musical numbers The dialogue is sometimes recitative, as in Bizet's Carmen.

Operetta is a very light opera with spoken dialogue, such as the Gilbert and Sullivan works

Operations. In World War II operations were given code-names by which they could be known, for reasons of convenience and security These should be differentiated from names, such as FIDO and PLUTO, which were made up of initials and had a special meaning, these will be found under their separate headings Among the most important Allied operations were.—

Anvil American and French landing in Southern France

Capital The investing of North and Central Burma by Admiral Lord Mountbatten and General Stilwell

Crossroads. First atom bomb test at Bikini, May 1946

Dynamo. British evacuation from Dunkirk

Eclipse First plan for Allied occupation of Germany.

Epsom. Major British operation south of Caen to break out of the beachhead, June 1944

Goldflake Large-scale switch of British and Canadian troops from the Italian front to that in North-west Europe, February 1945

Neptune Naval name for the operations against North-west France, 1944

Overlord Allied invasion of North-west Europe, 1944 First known as Roundup

Torch Allied invasion of North-west Africa, 1942

Operations, Base of, Line of See BASE

Opinicus (op in' i kus) A fabulous monster, composed of dragon, camel, and lion, used in heraldry It forms the crest of the Barber Surgeons of London. The name seems to be a corruption of Ophincus, the classical name of the constellation, the serpent (Gr ophis)

Opium-eater. Thomas De Quincey (1785-1859), author of The Confessions of an English Opium-Eater (1821).

Oppidan (op' i dan) At Eton College, a student not on the foundation, but who boards in the town (Lat oppidum, town).

Opponency. See ACT AND OPPONENCY

Opposition. The constitutional term for whichever of the great political parties is not in power In the House of Commons the Opposition sits on the benches on the Speaker's left, on the front bench being the leaders who are, generally, ministers-elect waiting for a change of Government The Leader of the Opposition, elected by his Party, receives an official salary from the State of £2,000 a year.

Optime (op' tǐ mē) In Cambridge phraseology a graduate in the second or third division of the Mathematical Tripos, the former being *Senior Optimes* and the latter *Junior Optimes* The term comes from the Latin phrase formerly used—*Optime disputasti* (You have disputed very well) The class above the Optimes is composed of Wranglers (*q v*)

Optimism The doctrine that "whatever is, is right," that everything which happens is for the best. It was originally set forth by Leibnitz (1646-1716) from the postulate of the omnipotence of God, and is cleverly travestied by Voltaire in his *Candide, ou l Optimisme* (1759), where Dr. Pangloss continually harps on the maxim that "all is for the best in this best of all possible worlds "

Opus (ō' pus) (Lat., a work) *See* MAGNUM OPUS

Opus operantis. Ex opere operato is a phrase used by theologians to express the efficiency of acts irrespective of the intention of the agent or patient *Ex opere operantis* implies the concurrence of intention on the part of the agent; it is the personal piety of the person who does the act, and not the act itself, that causes it to be an instrument of grace Thus in the Eucharist, it is the faith of the recipient which makes it efficient for grace

Opus operatum. The thing done, the theologian's term for expressing the effect of sacraments irrespective of the disposition of the receivers of them Thus, baptism is said by many to convey regeneration to an infant in arms.

Or. The heraldic term for the metal gold *See* HERALDRY

Oracle (Lat *oraculum*, from *orāre*, to speak, to pray) The answer of a god or inspired priest to an inquiry respecting the future, the deity giving responses, the place where the deity could be consulted, etc , hence, a person whose utterances are regarded as profoundly wise, an infallible, dogmatical person—

I am Sir Oracle,
And when I ope my lips let no dog bark.
Merchant of Venice, i, 1

In ancient Greece oracles were extremely numerous, and very expensive to those who consulted them The most famous were the—

Oracle of APOLLO, at Delphi, the priestess of which was called the Pythoness, at Delos, and at Claros.

Oracle of DIANA, at Colchis, of ESCULAPIUS, at Epidaurus, and another in Rome

Oracle of HERCULES, at Athens, and another at Gades

Oracle of JUPITER, at Dodona (the most noted), another at Ammon, in Libya, another in Crete

Oracle of MARS, in Thrace, MINERVA, in Mycenæ, PAN, in Arcadia

Oracle of TRIPHONIUS, in Bœotia, where only men made the responses

Oracle of VENUS, at Paphos, another at Aphaca, and many others

B D.—22

In most of the temples women, sitting on a tripod, made the responses, many of which were either ambiguous or so obscure as to be misleading to this day, our word *oracular* is still used of obscure as well as of authoritative pronouncements

The difficulty of making head or tail of oracles is well illustrated by the following classic examples —

When Crœsus consulted the Delphic oracle respecting a projected war, he received for answer, "*Crœsus Halyn peretrans magnum, pervertet opum vim*" (When Crœsus passes over the river Halys, he will overthrow the strength of an empire) Crœsus supposed the oracle meant he would overthrow the enemy's empire, but it was his own that he destroyed

Pyrrhus, being about to make war against Rome, was told by the oracle "*Aio te, Æacide, Romanos vincere posse*" (I say, Pyrrhus, that you the Romans can conquer), which may mean either *You, Pyrrhus, can overthrow the Romans*, or *Pyrrhus, the Romans can overthrow you*

Another prince, consulting the oracle on a similar occasion, received for answer, "*Ibis redibis nunquam per bella peribis*" (You shall go you shall return never you shall perish by the war), the interpretation of which depends on the position of the comma, it may be *You shall return, you shall never perish in the war*, or *You shall return never, you shall perish in the war*, which latter was the fact

Philip of Macedon sent to ask the oracle of Delphi if his Persian expedition would prove successful, and received for answer—

The ready victim crowned for death
Before the altar stands

Philip took it for granted that the "ready victim" was the King of Persia, but it was Philip himself

When the Greeks sent to Delphi to know if they would succeed against the Persians, they were told—

Seed-time and harvest, weeping sires shall tell
How thousands fought at Salamis and fell

But whether the Greeks or the Persians were to be "the weeping sires," no indication was given, nor whether the thousands "about to fall" were to be Greeks or Persians

When Maxentius was about to encounter Constantine, he consulted the guardians of the Sibylline Books as to the fate of the battle, and the prophetess told him, "*Illo die hostem Romanorum esse periturum*," but whether Maxentius or Constantine was "the enemy of the Roman people" the oracle left undecided

In the Bible we have a similar equivoque When Ahab, King of Israel, was about to wage war on the king of Syria, and asked Micaiah if Ramoth-Gilead would fall into his hands, the prophet replied, "Go, for the Lord will deliver the city into the hands of the king" (1 *Kings* xxii, 15, 35)

The Oracle of the Church. St Bernard of Clairvaux (1091-1153).

The Oracle of the Holy Bottle The oracle to which Rabelais (Bks iv and v) sent Panurge and a large party to obtain an answer to a question which had been put to sibyl and poet, monk and fool, philosopher and witch, judge and fortune-teller. "whether Panurge should marry or not?" The oracle was situated at Bacbuc (*q v*), "near Cathay in Upper Egypt," and the story has been interpreted as a satire on the Church The celibacy of the clergy was for long a moot point, and the "Holy Bottle" or cup to the laity was one of the moving causes of the schisms from the Church The crew setting sail for the Bottle refers to Anthony, Duke of Vendôme, afterwards king of Navarre, setting out in search of religious truth.

The oracle of the sieve and shears. *See* SIEVE.

To work the oracle. To induce another to favour some plan or to join in some project, generally by manœuvring behind the scenes. Also—in slang—to raise money

They fetched a rattling price through Starlight's working the oracle with those swells —BOLDREWOOD: *Robbery Under Arms*, ch xii

Orange William III's territorial name came from Orange (anciently Arausio), a town on the Rhone 13 miles north of Avignon, and capital of the former principality of the same name, which dated from the 11th century. From 1373 to 1530 it belonged to the House of Châlons; through failure of male heirs it then fell through a sister of Philibert, the last prince of that House, to William the Silent, Prince of Nassau, who thereupon became Prince of Orange-Nassau, or simply "of Orange " His grandson, William II, married Mary, daughter of our Charles I, and they were the parents of William of Orange, our William III, husband of Mary, daughter of his uncle and enemy, James II

The principality remained in the hands of the House of Orange-Nassau till 1702, and was finally annexed to France by the Treaty of Utrecht, 1713 The title "Prince of Orange" is still borne by the heir-presumptive to the throne of Holland, which is occupied by the House of Nassau.

Orange. This distinctive epithet of the ultra-Protestants of Northern Ireland and of Ulstermen generally, it is said, became attached to them because in 1795 two members of the famous "Orange Lodge" of Freemasons (which had been revived in Belfast about 1780) were active in raising the Orange Lodges (*see below*), an armed force of Protestant volunteers —hence called ' Orange boys"—in defence of civil and religious liberty.

The Orange Lodge was named in honour of William of Orange (William III), the Protestant opposer of James II in the "Glorious Revolution" of 1689, and the victor at the Battle of the Boyne (1690).

Orange Lodges or Clubs are referred to in print as early as 1769 Thirty years later the Orangemen were a very powerful society, having a "grand lodge" extending over the entire province of Ulster and through all the centres of Protestantism in Ireland.

Orangemen. A name given to the members of an Orange Lodge, originating in their respect for the memory of William III of the House of Orange

Orange blossom. The conventional decoration for the bride at a wedding, introduced as a custom into England from France about 1820 The *orange* is said to indicate the hope of fruitfulness, as few trees are more prolific, while the *white blossoms* are symbolical of innocence.

Hence the phrase, **to go gathering orange blossoms,** to look for a wife.

Orange Free State. This province of the Union of South Africa originated in 1824 when some Dutch farmers from Cape Colony settled across the Orange River. They had trouble with the Basutos, but they held on and in

1854 formed a republic with this name In 1899 the Orange Free State joined the Transvaal in making war on Great Britain and it was consequently annexed in 1900. In 1907 it was given responsible government and three years later it joined the Union

Orange Lilies. *See* REGIMENTAL NICKNAMES

Orange Peel. A nickname given to Sir Robert Peel when Chief Secretary for Ireland (1812-18), on account of his strong anti-Catholic proclivities

Orange-tawny. The ancient colour appropriated to clerks and persons of inferior condition. It was also the colour worn by the Jews Hence Bacon says, "Usurers should have orange-tawny bonnets, because they do Judaise" (*Essay* xli) Bottom the weaver asked Quince what colour beard he was to wear for the character of Pyramus —

I will discharge it in either your straw-colour beard, your orange-tawny beard, your purple-in-grain beard, or your French-crown-colour beard, your perfect yellow "—*Midsummer Night's Dream*, i, 2

Orator. Orator Henley. John Henley (1692-1756), who for about thirty years delivered lectures on theological, political, and literary subjects

Orator Hunt. Henry Hunt (1773-1835), a politician and radical reformer was so named He presided at the famous "Peterloo" meeting (*q v*) and as M P for Preston (1830-33) presented the first petition to Parliament in favour of woman's rights

Orator of the Human Race, The. *See* ANACHARSIS

Oratorio is sacred story or drama set to music, in which solo voices, chorus, and instrumental music are employed In 1574 St. Philip Neri introduced the acting and singing of sacred dramas in his Oratory at Rome, and it is from this that the term comes Oratorio has appealed to many of the greatest composers of the past, outstanding among them being Handel

Orc. A sea-monster fabled by Ariosto, Drayton, Sylvester, etc , to devour men and women The name was sometimes used for the whale Milton speaks of the Mount of Paradise being "pushed by the horned flood":—

Down the great river to the opening Gulf,
And there take root, an island salt and bare,
The haunt of seals, and orcs, and sea-mews' clang
Paradise Lost, xi, 833

Orchard properly means a garden-yard. *Hort-yard* was one of the old spellings, and in this form its connexion with Lat *hortus*, a garden, is clear.

The hortyard entering [he] admires the fair
And pleasant fruits   GEORGE SANDYS

Orcus (ôr' kŭs). A Latin name for Hades, the abode of the dead Spenser speaks of a dragon whose mouth was—

All set with iron teeth in ranges twain,
That terrified his foes, and armed him,
Appearing like the mouth of *Orcus* grisely grim
Faerie Queene, VI, xii, 26

Ordeal (A S *ordel*, related to *adælan*, to deal, allot, judge) The ancient Anglo-Saxon and Teutonic practice of referring disputed questions of criminality to supernatural decision, by subjecting the suspected person to physical tests by fire, boiling water, battle, etc , hence, figuratively, an experience testing endurance, patience, courage, etc

This method of ' trial" was based on the belief that God would defend the right, even by miracle if needful All ordeals, except the ordeal of battle, were abolished in England by law in the early 13th century

In **Ordeal of battle** the accused person was obliged to fight anyone who charged him with guilt This ordeal was allowed only to persons of rank

Ordeal of fire was also for persons of rank only The accused had to hold in his hand a piece of red-hot iron, or to walk blindfold and barefoot among nine red-hot plough-shares laid at unequal distances If he escaped uninjured he was accounted innocent, otherwise not. This might be performed by deputy.

Ordeal of hot water was for the common people The accused was required to plunge his arm up to the elbow in boiling water, and was pronounced guilty if the skin was injured in the experiment

Ordeal of cold water was also for the common people The accused, being bound, was tossed into a river; if he *sank* he was acquitted, but if he *floated* he was accounted guilty. This ordeal remained in use for the trial of witches to comparatively recent times.

In the **Ordeal of the bier** a person suspected of murder was required to touch the corpse; if guilty the "blood of the dead body would start forth afresh."

In that of the **cross** plaintiff and defendant had to stand with their arms crossed over their breasts, and he who could endure the longest won the suit *See also* JUDICIUM CRUCIS

The **Ordeal of the Eucharist** was for priests. It was supposed that the elements would choke him if taken by a guilty man

In the **Ordeal of the Corsned** (*q v*) consecrated bread and cheese was similarly given Godwin, Earl of Kent, is said to have been choked when, being accused of the murder of the king's brother, he submitted to this ordeal,

In Ceylon, a man suspected of theft is required to bring what he holds dearest before a judge, and placing a heavy stone on the head of his substitute, says, "May this stone crush thee to death if I am guilty of this offence "

In Tartary, an ostiack sets a wild bear and a hatchet before the tribunal, saying, as he swallows a piece of bread, "May the bear devour me, and the hatchet chop off my head, if I am guilty of the crime laid to my charge."

Order! When members of the House of Commons and other debaters call out *Order!* they mean that the person speaking is in some way breaking the rule or *order* of the assembly, and has to be *called to order*

Architectural orders. *See* ARCHITECTURE

Holy orders. A clergyman is said to be *in holy orders* because he belongs to one of the *orders* or ranks of the Church In the Church of England these are three, viz , Deacon, Priest, and Bishop; in the Roman Catholic Church there is a fourth, that of Sub-deacon

In ecclesiastical use the term also denotes a fraternity of monks or friars (as the *Franciscan Order*), and also the Rule by which the fraternity is governed

The order of the day. In the House of Commons the ordinary public business of each day is classified as consisting of notices of motions and orders of the day A motion becomes an order of the day as soon as the debate on it has been adjourned by order of the House to a particular day *See* QUESTION.

To move for the Order of the Day is a proposal to set aside a government measure on a private members' day (Friday), and proceed to the agenda prearranged This is done by the member concerned raising his hat without rising to address the chair If the motion is carried, the agenda must be proceeded with, unless a motion "to adjourn" is carried.

Ordinary In Law an ordinary is one who has an "ordinary or regular jurisdiction" in his own right, and not by depute Thus a judge who has authority to take cognizance of causes in his own right is an ordinary A bishop is an ordinary in his own diocese, because he has authority to take cognizance of ecclesiastical matters therein, an archbishop is the ordinary of his province, having authority in his own right to receive appeals therein from inferior jurisdictions The chaplain of Newgate was also called the ordinary thereof

A meal prepared at an inn at a fixed rate for all comers is called an "ordinary"; hence, also, the inn itself —

'Tis almost dinner, I know they stay for you at the ordinary —BEAUMONT AND FLETCHER *Scornful Lady,* IV, I

And in Heraldry the "ordinary" is a simple charge, such as the chief, pale, fesse, bend, bar, chevron, cross, or saltire.

Oread (ôr' ē ad) (pl *Oreads* or *Oreades*). Nymphs of the mountains (Gr. *oros*, a mountain)

The Ocean-nymphs and Hamadryades,
Oreads and Naiads, with long weedy locks,
Offered to do her bidding through the seas,
Under the earth, and in the hollow rocks
SHELLEY *Witch of Atlas,* xxii.

Oregon Trail. This was the old American transcontinental route from Independence, Missouri, to The Dalles, on Columbia River, Oregon, a distance of some 2,000 miles. The route was principally used by immigrants to the North-west from the Southern states It was originally blazed by trappers and the Lewis and Clarke Expedition, and crossed the Rockies at South Pass

Orellana (or el ā' nä) The name formerly used for the river Amazon, so called from Francisco de Orellana, lieutenant of Pizarro, who was the first to explore it (about 1537–41)

Oremus. *See* LEGEM PONE

Orestes. *See* PYLADES

Orgies (ôr' jez) Drunken revels, riotous feasts, hence, figuratively, wild or licentious extravagance So called from the Gr *orgia,* the secret, nocturnal festivals in honour of Bacchus (*q v*).

Orgoglio (ôr gō' lyō) (Ital., Arrogant Pride, or Man of Sin) In Spenser's *Faerie Queene* (I, vii, and viii), a hideous giant as tall as three men, son of Earth and Wind

He typifies the tyrannical power of the Church of Rome, in slaying him Arthur first cut off his *left arm—i e* Bohemia was first cut off from the Church of Rome, then the giant s *right leg—l e* England, when Orgoglio fell to earth, and was easily dispatched.

Oriana (ôr i än' a) The beloved of Amadis of Gaul, who called himself Beltenebros when he retired to the Poor Rock (*Amadis de Gaul*, ii, 6)

Queen Elizabeth I is sometimes called the "peerless Oriana," especially in the madrigals entitled the *Triumphs of Oriana* (1601)

Oriel College, Oxford (ôr' i el) The fifth in age of the Oxford Colleges, founded in 1326 by Edward II and his almoner, Adam de Brome, who was its first Provost The name comes from a messuage in Oxford called *La Oriole*, which was granted to the College at its foundation, but the origin of this name is unknown

Oriel window is also obscure The name originally denoted a gallery or balcony, then a gallery in a private chapel, then a small private apartment which had a window looking into the chapel It may be connected with Late Lat *aulæum*, a curtain (*aula*, hall), but this is by no means certain

Orientation. The placing of the east window of a church due east (Lat *oriens*), that is, so that the rising sun may shine on the altar Anciently, churches were built with their axes pointing to the rising sun on the saint's day, so that a church dedicated to St John was not parallel to one dedicated to St Peter, but in the building of modern churches the saint's day is not, as a rule, regarded

Figuratively, orientation is the correct placing of one's ideas, mental processes, etc , in relation with themselves and with current thought—the ascertainment of one's "bearings."

Oriflamme (ôr' i flåm) (Fr , "flame of gold"). The ancient banner of the kings of France, first used as a national banner in 1119. It was a crimson flag cut into three "vandykes" to represent "tongues of fire," with a silken tassel between each, and was carried on a gilt staff (*un glaive tout doré où est attaché une bannière vermeille*) This celebrated standard was the banner of St. Denis, but when the Counts of Vexin became possessed of the abbey it passed into their hands In 1082 Philippe I united Vexin to the crown, and the sacred Oriflamme fell to the king. It was carried to the field after the battle of Agincourt, in 1415. The romance writers say that 'mescreans" (infidels) were blinded by merely looking on it In the *Roman de Garin* the Saracens cry, "If we only set eyes on it we are all dead men", and Froissart records that it was no sooner unfurled at Rosbecq than the fog cleared away from the French, leaving their enemies in misty darkness.

In the 15th century the Oriflamme was succeeded by the blue standard powdered with fleurs-de-lis, and the last heard of the original Oriflamme is a mention in the inventory of the Abbey of St Denis dated 1534

Original Sin. *See* SIN.

Orinda the Matchless (o rin' da) Katherine Philips (1631-64), the poetess and letter-writer She first adopted the signature "Orinda" in her correspondence with Sir Charles Cotterell, and afterwards used it for general purposes. Her praises were sung by Cowley, Dryden, and others

Dryden's lines—
O double sacrilege on things divine,
To rob the relic and deface the shrine!
But thus Orinda died
Eleg.) on Mrs. Anne Killigrew.

refer to the fact that both women died of small-pox

Orion (o rī' on) A giant hunter of Greek mythology, noted for his beauty He was blinded by Œnopion, but Vulcan sent Cedalion to be his guide, and his sight was restored by exposing his eyeballs to the sun Being slain by Diana, he was made one of the constellations, and is supposed to be attended with stormy weather His wife was named Sidē, and his dogs Arctophonus and Ptoophagus
With fierce winds Orion armed
Hath vexed the Red-Sea coast
MILTON *Paradise Lost*, I, 305.

The constellation Orion is the clearest defined in the northern winter sky Below the "shoulder" stars, Betelgeuse and Bellatrix, are the three stars forming the "sword," close to which is the nebula The "feet," Rugel and Salph, point to Sirius, the brightest star in the heavens

Orkneys. The name is probably connected with the old *orc* (*q v*), a whale, and either Gaelic *innis* or Norse *ey*, an island—"the isles of whales " For centuries the Orkneys were a jarldom of Norway or Denmark, and it was not till 1590 that the latter renounced its claim to sovereignty They had passed to the Scottish crown in 1468 after having been in the possession of the Earls of Angus for nearly 250 years.

Orlando. The Italian form of "Roland" (*q v*), one of the great heroes of mediæval romance, and the most celebrated of Charlemagne's paladins He appears under this name in the romances mentioned below, and in other works

Orlando Furioso (Orlando mad) An epic poem in 45 cantos, by Ariosto (published 1515-33) Orlando's madness is caused by the faithlessness of Angelica, but the main subject of the work is the siege of Paris by Agramant the Moor, when the Saracens were overthrown.

The epic is full of anachronisms We have Charlemagne and his paladins joined by King Edward of England, Richard Earl of Warwick, Henry Duke of Clarence, and the Dukes of York and Gloucester (Bk vi) Cannon are employed by Cymosco, King of Friza (Bk iv), and also in the siege of Paris (Bk vi) We have the Moors established in Spain, whereas they were not invited over by the Saracens for nearly 300 years after Charlemagne's death In Bk. xvii the late mediæval Prester John (*q v*) appears, and in the last three books Constantine the Great, who died 337.

There are English translations by Sir John Harrington (1591), John Hoole (1783), and W. S. Rose (1823-31)

About 1589 a play (printed 1594) by Robert Greene entitled *The History of Orlando Furioso* was produced In this version Orlando marries Angelica

Orlando Innamorato (Orlando in love) A romance in verse by Boiardo telling the love of Roland (*q v*) and Angelica Boiardo died in 1494, not having finished the work, and Ariosto wrote his *Orlando Furioso (see above)* as a sequel to it In 1541 Berni turned it into burlesque

Orleans, The House of There are several younger sons of the great French family of Bourbon who bore this title, but the main branch stems from Philip, son of Louis XIII, who married Henrietta, the daughter of the English King Charles I By his second wife Philip had a son Philip (1674-1723) known as the Regent Orleans as he acted in that capacity to Louis XV in his minority His great-grandson became notorious for his career in the French Revolution when he assumed the name of Philippe Egalité and voted for the death of his kinsman Louis XVI He was guillotined in 1793, at the age of 46 His son, after many vicissitudes, became King of the French in 1830, but was deposed and sought refuge in England in 1848 In 1883 the older branch of the Bourbon family became extinct and since that date the Orleans family are the "legitimate" claimants to the throne of France

Orlop Deck. The lowest deck in an old sailing ship, and so called from the Dutch *overloopen*, or spread over, because it covered the ship's hold

Ormandine (ôr' mân dîn) The necromancer who by his magic arts threw St David for seven years into an enchanted sleep, from which he was redeemed by St George (*The Seven Champions of Christendom*, i, 9)

Ormulum (ôrm' û lum) A long poem in Transition, or Early Middle, English, of which only a "fragment" of some 10,000 lines is extant It is so called from the author, Orm, or Ormin, an Augustinian canon—

> This boc iss nemmed Ormulum
> Forrthi that Orm itt wrohhte—

and in it the Gospel for each day is versified and elaborated with expositions out of Aelfric, Bede, and Augustine It was written in the early 13th century

Ormuzd or **Ahura Mazda** (ôr 'mûzd, a hûr a mäz' dá) The principle or angel of light and good, and creator of all things, according to the Magian system He is in perpetual conflict with Ahriman (*q v*), but in the end will triumph The Latin form of the name is *Oromasdes.*

> And Oromaze, Joshua, and Mahomet,
> Moses and Buddh, Zerdusht, and Brahm, and Foh,
> A tumult of strange names, which never met
> Before, as watchwords of a single woe
> Arose   SHELLEY *Revolt of Islam*, X, xxxi

Ornery (U S A) Mean, purposely difficult

Orosius (o rō' si us) A Latin writer of the early 5th century A.D , whose *General History*,

from the Creation to A D 417, is frequently referred to by historians and was translated into Anglo-Saxon by Alfred the Great. Orosius was a native of Tarragona, in Spain, and a friend of St Augustine's

Orpheus (ôr' fûs) A Thracian poet of Greek legend (son of Apollo and Calliope), who could move even inanimate things by his music—a power that was also claimed for the Scandinavian Odin When his wife Eurydice (*q v*) died he went into the infernal regions, and so charmed Pluto that she was released on the condition that Orpheus would not look back till they reached the earth He was just about to place his foot on the earth when he turned round, and Eurydice vanished from him in an instant

> Orpheus' self may   hear
> Such strains as would have won the ear
> Of Pluto to have quite set free
> His half-regained Eurydice
>   MILTON *L'Allegro*, 145-50

The prolonged grief of Orpheus at his second loss so enraged the Thracian women that in one of their Bacchanalian orgies they tore him to pieces The fragments of his body were collected by the Muses and buried at the foot of Mount Olympus, but his head had been thrown into the river Hebrus, whither it was carried into the sea, and so to Lesbos, where it was separately interred.

> What could the Muse herself that Orpheus bore,
> The Muse herself, for her enchanting son,
> Whom universal nature did lament,
> When, by the rout that made the hideous roar
> His gory visage down the stream was sent,
> Down the swift Hebrus to the Lesbian shore?
>   MILTON *Lycidas*, 58

Orpheus of Highwaymen. So John Gay (1685-1732) has been called on account of his *Beggar's Opera* (1728)

Orphic. Connected with Orpheus, the mysteries associated with his name, or the doctrines ascribed to him, similar to his music in magic power Thus, Shelley says—

> Language is a perpetual Orphic song,
> Which rules with Dædal harmony a throng
> Of thoughts and forms, which else senseless and shapeless were   *Prometheus Unbound*, IV, i, 415

The **Orphic egg** *See* EGG, THE MUNDANE.

Orrery (or' ër i) A complicated piece of mechanism showing by means of clockwork the movements of the planets, etc , round the sun. It was invented about 1700 by George Graham, who sent his model to Rowley, an instrument maker, to make one for Prince Eugene Rowley made a copy of it for Charles Boyle (1636-1731), third Earl of Orrery, in whose honour it was named One of the best is Fulton's, in Kelvin Grove Museum, Glasgow

Orson. Twin brother of Valentine in the old romance *Valentine and Orson* (*q v*) The twins were born in a wood near Orleans, and Orson (Fr *ourson*, a little bear) was carried off by a bear, which suckled him with her cubs. When he grew up he was the terror of France, and was called the *Wild Man of the Forest* He was reclaimed by Valentine, overthrew the Green Knight, and married Fezon, the daughter of Duke Savary of Aquitaine.

Orthodox. The Orthodox Church. *See* GREEK CHURCH.

Orthodox Sunday, in the Eastern Church, is the First Sunday in Lent, to commemorate the restoration of images in 843

Orts Crumbs, refuse (Low Ger *ort—i e* what is left after eating)

> I shall not eat your orts—*i e* your leavings.
> Let him have time a beggar's orts to crave
> *Rape of Lucrece,* 985

Ortus (ôr' tu) *Ortus a quercu, non a salice* Latin for "sprung from an oak, and not from a willow"—*i.e* stubborn stuff; one that cannot bend to circumstances

Orvietan or **Venice Treacle** (ôr vi et' an), once believed to be a sovereign remedy against poison, hence sometimes used of an antidote It is not now known of what this electuary was concocted, it took its name from a charlatan of Orvieto, Italy, who used to pretend to take poison and cure himself by means of his potion

Os Sacrum. *See* LUZ. A triangular bone situate at the lower part of the vertebral column, of which it is a continuation Some say that this bone was so called because it was in the part used in sacrifice, or the sacred part; Dr Nash says it is so called "because it is much bigger than any of the vertebræ", but the Jewish rabbins say the bone is called sacred because it resists decay, and will be the germ of the "new body" at the resurrection (*Hudibras,* pt iii, canto 2.)

Osiris (ô si' ris) One of the chief gods of Egyptian mythology judge of the dead, ruler of the kingdom of ghosts, the Creator, the god of the Nile, and the constant foe of his brother (or son), Set, the principle of evil He was the husband of Isis (*q.v*), and represents the setting sun (*cp* RA) He was slain, but came to life again and was revenged by Horus and Thoth

The name means *Many-eyed* Osiris was usually depicted as a mummy wearing the crown of Upper Egypt, but sometimes as an ox

> Nor is Osiris seen
> In Memphian grove or green,
> Trampling the unshowered grass with lowings loud
> MILTON *Christ's Nativity,* 213

Osmand A necromancer in *The Seven Champions of Christendom,* i, 19, who by enchantment raised an army to resist the Christians Six of the Champions fell, whereupon St George restored them, Osmand tore out his own hair, in which lay his magic power, bit his tongue in two, disembowelled himself, cut off his arms, and then died.

OSS. The U S. Office of Strategic Services in World War II. It covered and directed all espionage and co-operation with resistance movements in enemy-occupied countries

Ossa. *See* PELION.

Ossian (Oisin) (os' i an) The legendary Gaelic bard and warrior of about the end of the 3rd century, son of Finn (Fingal), and reputed author of *Ossian's Poems,* published 1760-63, by James Macpherson, who professed that he had translated them from MSS collected in the Highlands A great controversy as to the authenticity of the supposed originals was

aroused, the question has not yet been finally settled, but it is generally agreed that Macpherson, while compiling from ancient sources, was the principal author of the poems as published The poems are full of Celtic glamour and charm, but are marred by rant and bombast

Ostend Manifesto. A declaration made in 1857 by the Ministers of the United States in England, France, and Spain, "that Cuba must belong to the United States " Notwithstanding this, until 1898 the island belonged to Spain, when, as one of the results of the Spanish American War, it was freed and was for four years under the military rule of the United States In 1902 Cuba was formed into an autonomous republic

Ostler. *See* HOSTLER.

Ostracism (os' trà sizm) (Gr *ostrakon,* an earthen vessel) Black-balling, boycotting, expelling, exclusion from society or common privileges, etc The word arose from the ancient Greek custom of banishing one whose power was a danger to the state, the voting for which was done by the people recording their votes on tiles or potsherds. The custom of ostracizing is widespread St Paul exhorts Christians to "come out from" idolaters (2 *Cor* vi, 17); and the Jews ostracized the Samaritans The Catholic Church anathematizes and interdicts

Ostrich. At one time the ostrich was fabled, when hunted, to run a certain distance and then thrust its head into the sand, thinking, because it cannot see, that it cannot be seen (*cp* CROCODILES), this supposed habit is the source of many allusions, *e g* —

> Whole nations, fooled by falsehood, fear, or pride,
> Their ostrich-heads in self-illusion hide,
> MOORE *Sceptic*

Another source of literary allusion to the bird is its habit of eating indigestible things such as stones and metals to assist the functions of the gizzard—

> Ah, villain ! thou wilt betray me, and get a thousand crowns of the king by carrying my head to him but I'll make thee eat iron like an ostrich, and swallow my sword like a great pin, ere thou and I part.—2 *Henry VI,* iv 10

Hence, **ostrich-stomachs,** stomachs that will digest anything.

Ostrich eggs are often suspended in Eastern churches as symbols of God's watchful care It used to be thought that the ostrich hatches her eggs by gazing on them, and if she suspends her gaze even for a minute or so, the eggs are addled Furthermore, we are told that if an egg is bad the ostrich will break it, so will God deal with evil men

> Oh ! even with such a look as fables say
> The mother ostrich fixes on her eggs,
> Till that intense affection
> Kindle its light of life.
> SOUTHEY *Thalaba.*

Ostrog Bible, The. *See* BIBLE, SPECIALLY NAMED

Othello (o thel' ō) Shakespeare's tragedy (written and performed in 1604, first printed 1622) is founded on a tale in Cithio's *Hecatommithi* (1565)—*Un Capitano Moro* (decad. iii, Nov vii)

Othello's occupation's gone (iii, 3) A phrase sometimes used when one is "laid on the shelf," no longer "the observed of all observers "

Other Day, The. Originally this meant "the second day," either forward or backward, *other* being the Anglo-Saxon equivalent for *second*, as in Latin *unus, alter, tertius*, or *proximus, alter, tertius* Starting from to-day, and going backwards, yesterday was the *proximus ab illo*, the day before yesterday was the *altera ab illo*, or the other day, and the day preceding that was *tertius ab illo*, or three days ago Now the phrase is used to express "a few days ago," "not so long since "

Otium cum dignitate (ō' ti um kŭm dig ni tā' ti) (Lat , leisure with dignity) Retirement after a person has given up business and has saved enough to live upon in comfort The words were taken as a motto by Cicero
Otium cum dignitate is to be had with £500 a year as well as with 5,000 —POPE· *Letters* (Wks vol x, p 110)

Ottava Rima (o ta' vä rē' ma) A stanza of eight ten-syllabled lines, rhyming *a b a b a b c c*, used by Keats in . is *Isabella*, Byron in *Don Juan*, etc It was originally Italian and was employed by Tasso (the lines were elevensyllabled), Ariosto, and many others

Ottoman Empire The Turkish Empire, so called from Othman, or Osman, I, the founder, about 1300, of the dynasty. Our *ottoman*, a kind of sofa having some resemblance to an oriental couch, is, of course, the same word

Oubliette (oo bli et'). Traditionally a secret dungeon in a mediæval castle or monastery, only accessible from a hole in the roof It used to be supposed that certain prisoners or refractory monks or nuns were incarcerated in these oubliettes and on occasions sealed up in them The real use of these cells is a debated point with archæologists.

Ouija (wē' ja) A device employed by spiritualists for receiving spirit messages It consists of a small piece of wood on wheels, placed on a board marked with the letters of the alphabet and certain commonly-used words. When the fingers of the communicators are placed on the ouija board it moves from letter to letter and thus spells out sentences The word is a combination of Fr *oui* and German *ja*, both meaning "yes "

Out. Murder will out. The secret is bound to be revealed, "be sure your sin will find you out "
> O blisful god, that art so just and trewe!
> Lo, how that thou biwreyest mordre alway,
> Mordre wol out, that see we day by day
> CHAUCER *Nun's Priest's Tale*, 232

Out and out. Incomparably, by far, or beyond measure, as, "He was out and out the best man "

Out of it. Left on one side, not included

Outed. Expelled, ejected

To go all out. In sport, racing, etc , to do one's very best—to put out every effort to win

To have it out. To contest either physically or verbally with another to the utmost of one's ability; as, "I mean to have it out with him one of these days", "I had it out with him"—*i e* "I spoke my mind freely and without reserve." The idea is that of letting loose pent-up disapprobation

To out-Herod Herod. *See* HEROD

To outrun the constable *See* CONSTABLE

Ovation. An enthusiastic display of popular favour, so called from the ancient Roman *ovatio* or minor triumph, in which the general after a bloodless victory or one over slaves entered the city on horseback or on foot, instead of in a chariot as in the greater triumph, and was crowned with myrtle instead of with gold.

Oven wood. Small firewood Of English origin, the phrase is there long obsolete, but it survived in the U S A. into the 19th century.

Over. Half seas over. *See* HALF

It's all over with him. He's finished, he can't go any farther, he's "shot his bolt " Said also of one who has been given up by the doctors

Over and over again. Very frequently (In Lat , *Iterum iterumque*)

Over the left. *See* LEFT.

Overlanders. An Australian term for those who drove cattle across country to their destination, as opposed to transporting them by sea The word is applied particularly to the heroic drive of large herds across the desert into safety during World War II, when a Japanese invasion of N Australia was expected

Overture (Fr. *ouvert*, O F. *overt*, past part. of *ouvrir*, to open). An opening, a preliminary proposal, a piece of music for the opening of an opera. To make *overtures* is to be the first to make an advance, as with a view to acquaintanceship, some business deal, or a reconciliation

Overy. The church of St Mary Overy, Southwark, was, according to Stow, founded by a ferry-woman named Mary Overy, who, long before the age of bridges, devoted her savings to this purpose This is fable, the name is a contraction of *St Mary's over the river.*

Owain (o wǎn') The hero of a 12th-century legend *The Descent of Owain*, written by Henry of Saltrey, an English Benedictine monk Owain (the name is a form of Welsh *Owen*) was an Irish knight of Stephen's court who, by way of penance for a wicked life, entered and passed through St Patrick's Purgatory (*q.v*)

Owl, the emblem of Athens, where owls abounded As Athene (Minerva) and Athenæ (Athens) are the same word, the owl was given to Minerva for her symbol also
The Greeks had a proverb, **To send owls to Athens**, which meant the same as our *To carry coals to Newcastle* (*q v*) *See also* MADGE

I live too near a wood to be scared by an owl. I am too old to be frightened by a bogy.

Like an owl in an ivy-bush. Having a sapient, vacant look, as some persons have when in their cups; having a stupid vacant stare Owls are proverbial for their judge-like solemnity, ıvy ıs the favourite plant of Bacchus, and was supposed to be the favourite haunt of owls

> Good ıvy, say to us what bırds hast thou?
> None but the owlet that cries "How how!"
> *Carol* (tıme Henry VI).

Gray, ın hıs *Elegy*, and numerous other poets bracket the two:—

> From yonder ıvy-mantled tower
> The mopıng owl doth to the moon complaın.

Owl light. Dusk, the gloamıng, "blınd man's holıday." Fr *Entre chıen et loup*

The owl was a baker's daughter. Accordıng to a Gloucestershire legend, our Savıour went ınto a baker's shop for somethıng to eat The mıstress put a cake ınto the oven for Hım, but her daughter saıd ıt was too large, and reduced ıt by half The dough, however, swelled to an enormous sıze, and the daughter crıed out, "Heugh! heugh! heugh!" and was transformed ınto an owl Ophelıa alludes to the tradıtion—

> Well, God 'ıeld you! They say the owl was a baker's daughter —SHAKESPEARE *Hamlet*, ıv, 5

Owlglass. *See* EULENSPIEGEL

Ox. One of the four fıgures whıch made up Ezekıel's cherub (ı, 10) It ıs the emblem of the prıesthood, and was assıgned to St Luke (*q v*) as hıs symbol because he begıns hıs gospel wıth the Jewısh prıest sacrıficıng ın the Temple

In early art the ox ıs usually gıven as the emblem of St Frıdeswıde, St Leonard, St Sylvester, St Medard, St Julıetta, and St Blandına

He has an ox on hıs tongue. *See under* MONEY.

Off-ox. A stupıd or clumsy person In an ox-team the off-ox ıs the one faıthest away from the drıver

Ox-bow (U.S.A.). A horseshoe bend ın a rıver.

Ox-eye. A saılor's name for a cloudy speck whıch ındıcates the approach of a storm When Elıjah heard that a speck no bıgger than a "man's hand" mıght be seen ın the sky, he told Ahab that a torrent of raın would over-take hım before he could reach home (1 *Kıngs* xvıı, 44, 45) Thomson alludes to thıs storm sıgnal ın hıs *Summer*

The black ox hath trod on your foot, or hath tampled on you. Mısfortune has come to you or your house, sometımes, you are henpecked A black ox was sacrıficed to Pluto, the ınfernal god, as a whıte one was to Jupıter

> Venus waxeth old, and then she was a pretıe wench, when Juno was a young wıfe, now crowes foote ıs on her eye, and the blacke ox hath trod on her foot —LYLY *Sapho and Phao*, IV, ıı

The dumb ox. St Thomas Aquınas (1227-74), so named by hıs fellow students at Cologne, on account of hıs dullness and tacıturnıty Alber-tus saıd "We call hım the dumb ox, but he wıll gıve one day such a bellow as shall be heard from one end of the world to the other."

Thou shalt not muzzle the ox when he treadeth out the corn (*Deut.* xxv, 4) In other words, do not grudge hım the mouthful he may snatch when workıng for you, do not deprıve a man of hıs lıttle perquısıtes.

To play the gıddy ox. To act the fool gene-rally; to behave ın an ırresponsıble or over-hılarıous manner There was an old phrase, *to make an ox of one*, meanıng the same as the modern *to make a fool of one*; and ın the *Merry Wıves of Wındsor* (v, 5) we have—

> Fal I do not begın to perceıve that I am made an ass
> Ford Ay, and an ox too, both the proofs are extant

Oxgang. An Anglo-Saxon land measure of no very defınıte quantıty, but as much as an ox could *gang* over or cultıvate Also called a *bovate* The Latın *jugum* was a sımılar term, whıch Varro defınes "*Quod juncti boves uno die exarăre possunt.*"

Eıght oxgangs made a carucate. If an oxgang were as much as one ox could cultıvate, ıts average would be about fıfteen acres.

Oxford Oxford bags Wıde-bottomed flannel trousers fashıonable ın Oxford ın the 1920s

Oxford Blues The Royal Horse Guards were so called ın 1690 because of theır blue facıngs

Oxford frame. A pıcture frame made so that the wooden sıdes cross each other at the corners and project an ınch or two, much used for photographs of college groups and so on

Oxford Group or Buchmanıtes A relıgıous group named after ıts founder, Frank Buch-man, and ın no way connected wıth Oxford In maın ıts prıncıples are Chrıstıan fellowshıp, publıc confessıon of sıns, group "sharıngs" of spırıtual experıences, and dependence on dıvıne guıdance ın the everyday affaırs of lıfe.

Oxford Movement A successful effort to arouse the Church of England from a perıod of ınertıa and ındıfference that had lasted through much of the 18th century It was begun ın 1833 at Oxford by Dr. Keble and carrıed on there by Hurrell Froude, Dr. Pusey, Isaac Wıllıams, Charles Marrıott, J. H Newman, F W Faber, J D Dalgaırns, and W. G Ward (the last four afterwards went over to the Church of Rome). The Movement ınsısted on the Catholıc charac-ter of the Church of England and the resultıng necessıty for a reformatıon ın ıts faıth and worshıp The Movement was condemned by the Church authorıtıes and after the secessıon of some of ıts leaders ıt may be saıd to have ended, but the results were very great, the Church was transformed and ıts lıfe renewed, a large and powerful Anglo-Catholıc party beıng formed *See* TRACTS FOR THE TIMES.

Oxymoron (oks ı môr' on) A rhetorıcal fıgure ın whıch effect ıs produced by apparent self-contradıctions, such as "More haste less speed," "Cruel to be kınd " The word ıs the Gr. for poıntedly foolısh

Oyer and termıner (oı' ĕr, tĕr' mın ĕr). An Anglo-French legal phrase meanıng "to hear and determıne " *Commıssıons* or *Wrıts of oyer and termıner* as ıssued to judges on cırcuıt twıce a year ın every county dırectıng them to hold courts for the trıal of offences.

Oyez! Oyez! Oyez! (ō yes') (O.Fr , *hear ye!*), The call made by a publıc crıer, court offıcer. etc , to attract attentıon when a proclamatıon is about to be read out. Sometimes written *O yes!*

> Fame with her loud'st O yes'
> Cries, "This is he "
> SHAKESPEARE *Troilus and Cressida*, IV, 5
> But when the Crier cried "O Yes'" the people cried
> "O No'"—BARHAM *Misadventures at Margate*

Oyster And did you ever see an oyster walk upstairs? A satirical query sometimes addressed to one who has been telling unbelievable yarns about his own experiences

Close as a Kentish oyster Absolutely secret; hermetically sealed Kentish oysters are proverbially good, and all good oysters are fast closed

Never eat an oyster unless there's an R in the month. Good advice, which limits the eating of oysters to the months from September to April inclusive The legal close-time for oysters in England and Scotland, however, extends only from June 15th to Aug 4th, thus freeing all May and parts of June and August

Who eats oysters on St. James's Day will never want. St James's Day is the first day of the oyster season (August 5th), when oysters are an expensive luxury eaten only by the rich.

Oz. The abbreviation for an ounce is the 15th-century contraction of Ital *onza* The "z" here does not play the same part as that in "viz " (*q v*). *See also* WIZARD OF OZ.

P

P. The sixteenth letter in the English alphabet; called *pe*, "mouth," by the Phœnicians and ancient Hebrews, and represented in Egyptian hieroglyph by a shutter

In the 16th century Placentius, a Dominican monk, wrote a poem of 253 hexameter verses called *Pugna Porcorum*, every word of which begins with the letter *p* It opens thus —

> Plaudite, Porcelli, porcorum pigra propago—

which may be translated—

> Praise Paul's prize pig's prolific progeny

The Four P's. A "merry interlude" by John Heywood, written about 1540 The four principal characters are "a Palmer, a Pardoner, and a Poticary (apothecary), and a Pedlar "

The five P's William Oxberry (1784-1824) was so called, because he was Printer, Poet, Publisher, Publican, and Player

P C. The Roman *patres conscripti See* CONSCRIPT FATHERS

P , PP , P.P.P. (in music) P=piano, pp= pianissimo, and ppp=pianississimo Sometimes pp means *piu piano* (more softly)

So f=forte, ff=fortissimo, and fff=fortississimo

P.P C. *See* CONGÉ

P S. (Lat , *post-scriptum*) Written afterwards —*i e* after the letter or book was finished

P's and Q's Mind your P's and Q's Be very circumspect in your behaviour

Several explanations have been suggested, but none seems to be wholly satisfactory. One

22*

is that it was an admonition to children learning the alphabet—and still more so to printers' apprentices sorting type—because of the similar appearance of these tailed letters, another that in old-time bar-parlours in the accounts that were scored up for beer "P" stood for ' pints" and "Q" for "quarts," and of course the customer when settling up would find it necessary "to mind his P's and Q's," or he would pay too much; and yet another—from France—is that in the reign of Louis XIV, when huge wigs were worn, and bows were made with great formality, two things were specially required a "step" with the feet, and a low bend of the body In the latter the wig would be very apt to get deranged, and even to fall off The caution, therefore, of the French dancing-master to his pupils was, "Mind your P's (*i e pieds*, feet) and Q's (*i e. queues*, wigs) "

Pace (pā' si) From the Latin *pax*, meaning peace or pardon, this word is used in the sense of 'with the permission of" when preceding the mention of some person who disagrees with what is being said or done

Pacific Ocean So named by Magellan in 1520, because there he enjoyed calm weather and a placid sea after the stormy and tempestuous passage of the adjoining straits

The Pacific
Amadeus VIII, Duke of Savoy (1383, 1391-1439, d 1451) He was an anti-pope, as Felix V, from 1440 to 1449
Frederick III, Emperor of Germany (1415, 1440-93)
Olaf III of Norway (1030-93).

Pacifico, Don. In 1850 the name of Don Pacifico was on everyone's lips David Pacifico was a Portuguese Jew born at Gibraltar but in trade at Athens In the course of some religious commotions his house was burned down by the mob Don Pacifico thereupon claimed from the Greek government the exorbitant sum of £26,618 as damages. On their refusal to pay this Pacifico fell back on his British citizenship and in January, 1850, Palmerston sent the Mediterranean fleet to the Piræus The French government then instructed their ambassador in Athens to patch matters up, with the result that Britain and France fell out and the French ambassador to Queen Victoria was recalled to Paris The House of Lords passed a vote of censure on Palmerston, but in the Commons he replied in his most famous speech claiming that British citizenship was a protection throughout the world (*See* CIVIS ROMANUS) In the end Pacifico received some £5,000 for his lost house and injured feelings

Pack (U.S A) To carry, as *to pack a gun* "We packed the hams and shoulders to camp" (1857).

Packing a jury Selecting on a jury persons whose verdict may be relied on from proclivity, far more than from evidence.

To pack up Slang for to take one's departure, to have no more to do with the matter, also to die

To send one packing To dismiss him summarily and without ceremony.

Packstaff. *See* PIKESTAFF.

Pactolus (păk tō′ lŭs) The golden sands of the Pactolus. The Pactolus is a small river in Lydia, Asia Minor, long famous for its gold which, according to legend, was due to Midas (*q.v*) having bathed there. Its gold was exhausted by the time of Augustus

Paddington Fair. A public execution. Tyburn, where executions formerly took place, is in the parish of Paddington Public executions were abolished in England in 1868

Paddock. Cold as a paddock. A paddock is a toad or frog; and we have the corresponding phrases "cold as a toad," and "cold as a frog "

> Here a little child I stand,
> Heaving up my either hand,
> Cold as Paddocks though they be,
> Here I lift them up to Thee,
> For a Benizon to fall
> On our meat and on us all.
> HERRICK *Grace for a Child*

Paddy, Paddywhack. An Irishman, from Patrick (Ir *Padraig*) In slang both terms are used for a loss of temper, a rage on a small scale, and the latter also denotes the gristle in roast meat.

Padishah (păd′ i sha) is the Turkish form of the Persian Padshah, a king or reigning sovereign It was formerly applied exclusively to the Sultan of Turkey.

Padre (pa′ drä). The name given by soldiers and sailors to a chaplain. It is Spanish and Portuguese for "father," and was adopted in the British Army in India from the natives, who had learned the term from the Portuguese

Padua (păd′ ū a) was long supposed by the Scottish to be the chief school of necromancy, hence Scott says of the Earl of Gowrie—

> He learned the art that none may name
> In Padua, far beyond the sea
> *Lay of the Last Minstrel*

Paduasoy (păd′ ū a soi) A silk stuff, the French *pou-* or *pout-de-soie*, introduced into England in the 17th century and for 150 years or so called *poudesoy* or *poodesoy* The material had no connexion with Padua, but there was a "say" or serge manufactured there which was known as *Padua say*, and the name *Paduasoy* is due to confusion with this

Pæan (pē′ ăn) The name, according to Homer, of the physician to the gods. It was used in the phrase *Io Pæan* as the invocation in the hymn to Apollo, and later in hymns of thanksgiving to other deities, hence *pæan* has come to mean any song of praise or thanksgiving, any shout of triumph or exultation.

> Io pæans let us sing,
> To physicke's and to poesie's king
> LYLY. *Midas*, v, 3.

Pagan (pā′ gan) The long held idea that this word—which etymologically means a villager, a rustic (Lat *paganus*)—acquired its present meaning because the Christian Church first established itself in the cities, the village dwellers continuing to be heathen, has been shown by recent research to be incorrect The name arose from a Roman military colloquialism. *Paganus* (rustic) was the soldier's contemptuous name for a civilian or for an incompetent soldier, and when the early Christians called themselves *miles Christi* (soldiers of Christ) they adopted the soldier-slang, *paganus*, for those who were not "soldiers of Christ " *See* the last note but one to ch. xxi of Gibbon's *Decline and Fall.*

Pageant. A performance, usually in the open air, of a series of dramatic scenes representing outstanding events in the history of a town or building The fashion for pageants was inaugurated in England by the Sherborne Pageant of 1905 Outstanding pageants were those of Bury St Edmunds (1907), Oxford (1907), Winchester (1908), Chelsea (1908), Dover (1908) One of the principal producers of pageants was Louis N Parker (1852-1944)

Pagoda (pá gō′ da) A Buddhist temple or sacred tower in India, China, etc , especially a slender, storied tower built over the relics of a saint The word is Portuguese, and was formed by them in the 16th century on some now unknown native word which may have been the Persian *but-kadah*, idol-house, or some form of *bhagavat*, holy.

Pagoda was also the name of a gold coin, value about 7s , formerly current in Southern India. Hence the phrase—

To shake the pagoda-tree To make money readily in the Far East.

> I have granted a pension of 400 pagodas *per annum* to the family of the late Reza Saheb —*Wellington's Dispatches*, I, p 31 (1799)
> The amusing pursuit of "shaking the pagoda-tree" once so popular in our Oriental possessions — THEODORE HOOK *Gilbert Gurney*, I, p 45

Paid *See* PAY.

Paiforce. The short name for the Persia and Iraq Command (P A I. Force) Constituted in Sept. 1942, with headquarters at Baghdad, its functions were (*a*) to stand as a bulwark against a possible German drive through the Caucasus, and (*b*) to protect and operate the routes by which supplies were sent to Russia The Command was wound up in 1946

Paint. To paint the lily. To indulge in hyperbolical praise, to exaggerate the beauties, good points, etc., of the subject to a very considerable extent

> To gild refined gold, to paint the lily,
> To throw a perfume on the violet, .
> Is wasteful and ridiculous excess
> *King John*, IV, 2.

To paint the lion. A sailor's term, meaning to strip a person naked and then smear the body all over with tar.

To paint the town red To have a gay, noisy time; to cause some disturbance in town by having a noisy spree. Possibly from the frequent firing of towns by Indians on the warpath.

Painting. It is said that Apelles, being at a loss to delineate the foam of Alexander's horse, dashed his brush at the picture in despair, and did by accident what he could not accomplish by art.

This story is related of many other artists, and the incident is said actually to have occurred to Michael Angelo when painting the interior of the dome of St. Peter's at Rome

Many legends are told of pictures so painted that the objects depicted have been taken for the things themselves It is said, for instance, that Apelles painted Alexander's horse so realistically that a living horse mistook it and began to neigh Velasquez painted a Spanish admiral so true to life that Philip IV mistook the painting for the man and reproved it severely for not being with the fleet Zeuxis painted some grapes so well that birds flew at them to peck them Quentin Matsys painted a fly on a man's leg so inimitably that Mandyn, the artist, tried to brush it off with his hand-kerchief Parrhasios, of Ephesus, painted a curtain so well that Zeuxis was deceived by it, and told him to draw it aside that he might see the picture behind it, and Myron, the Greek sculptor, is said to have fashioned a cow so true to nature that a bull mistook it for a living animal

Painter. The rope by which a ship's boat can be tied to the ship, a buoy, mooring-post, etc. The word is probably an extended sense of the 14th-century *peyntour*, the rope which held the anchor to the ship's side (now called the *shank-painter*), which was from Fr *pendre*, Lat *pendere*, to hang.

To cut the painter. To sever connexion, to send one to the right about in double quick time In the late 19th century the phrase was much used in reference to a possible severance between her Colonial Empire and Great Britain

On the contrary, the idea of "cutting the painter" is not popular —E KINGLAKE *The Australian at Home* (1891)

Pair Off. When two members of Parliament of opposite parties agree to absent themselves, so that when a vote is taken the absence of one neutralizes the missing vote of the other, they are said to *pair off*. In the House of Commons this is usually arranged by the Whips

Paix (pā). **La Paix des Dames** The treaty concluded at Cambray, in 1529, between Francis I and Charles V of Germany, so called because it was brought about by Louise of Savoy (mother of the French king) and Margaret, the emperor's aunt

Pakistan The name of the present Dominion was coined by Chaudhrie Rahmat Ali in 1933 to represent the units which should be included when the time came P-Punjab, A-Afghan border states, K-Kashmir; S-Sind, TAN for Baluchistan

Pal. A good friend, a mate, boon companion It is a gipsy word meaning a brother or mate

Palace originally meant a dwelling on the Palatine Hill (*See* PALATINATE) of Rome, where Augustus and, later, Tiberius and Nero built their mansions. The word was hence transferred to other royal and imperial residences; then to similar buildings, such as *Blenheim Palace, Dalkeith Palace,* and to the official residence of a bishop, and finally to a place of amusement as the *Crystal Palace,* the *People's Palace,* and—in irony—to a *gin palace.*

In parts of Devonshire cellars for fish, store-houses cut in the rock, etc , are called *palaces*

or *pallaces,* but this may be from the old word *palis* a space enclosed by a palisade

All that cellar and the chambers over the same, and the little pallace and landing-place adjoining the River Dart —*Lease granted by the Corporation of Totnes in* 1703

Paladin (păl' a din) Properly, an officer of, or one connected with, the palace (*q v*), palatine (*q v*), usually confined in romance to the Twelve Peers of Charlemagne's court, and hence applied to any renowned hero or knight-errant.

The most noted of Charlemagne's paladins were Allory de l'Estoc, Astolfo; Basin de Genevois, Fierambras or Ferumbras, Floris-mart, Ganelon, the traitor, Geoffroy, Seigneur de Bordelois, and Geoffroy de Frises, Guerin, Duc de Lorraine, Guillaume de l'Estoc, brother of Allory, Guy de Bourgogne; Hoel, Comte de Nantes, Lambert, Prince de Bruxelles, Malagigi, Nami or Nayme de Bavière, Ogier the Dane, Oliver (*q v*), Otuel, Richard, Duc de Normandie, Rinaldo, Riol du Mans, Roland (*q v*), otherwise Orlando, Samson, Duc de Bourgogne, and Thiry or Theiry d'Ardaine Of these, twelve at a time seemed to have formed a special bodyguard to the king.

Who bear the bows were knights in Arthur's reign,
Twelve they, and twelve the peers of Charlemain
DRYDEN *The Flower and the Leaf*

Palæmon (păl ē' mon) In Roman legend, a son of Ino (see LEUCOTHEA), and originally called Melicertes Palæmon is the name given to him after he was made a sea-god, and as Por-tumnus he was the protecting god of harbours. The story is given in Spenser's *Faery Queene* (IV, xi), in the same poet's *Colin Clout* his name is used for Thomas Churchyard (*c* 1520-1604) the poet

Palæography. *See* DIPLOMATICS

Palæolithic Age, The (pā li ō lith' ik) (Gr. *palaios,* old, *lithos,* a stone) The earlier of the two periods into which the Stone Age of Europe is divided (*cp* NEOLITHIC)

Palamedes (păl a mē' dēz) In Greek legend, one of the heroes who fought against Troy. He was the son of Nauplios and Clymene, and was the reputed inventor of lighthouses, scales and measures, the discus, dice, etc , and was said to have added four letters to the original alphabet of Cadmus It was he who detected the as-sumed madness of Ulysses, in revenge for which the latter encompassed his death The phrase, *he is quite a Palamedes,* meaning "an ingenious person," is an allusion to this hero

In Arthurian romance, *Sir Palamedes* is a Saracen knight who was overcome in single combat by Tristram Both loved Isolde, the wife of King Mark, and after the lady was given up by the Saracen, Tristram converted him to the Christian faith, and stood his god-father at the font.

Palamon and Arcite (păl' à mon, ar si' tē) Two young Theban knights of romance whose story (borrowed from Boccaccio's *Le Teseide*) is told by Chaucer in his *Knight's Tale,* by Fletcher and (probably) Shakespeare in *The Two Noble Kinsmen* (1634) and elsewhere Both were in love with Emilia, sister-in-law to the

Duke of Athens, in whose hands they were prisoners In time they obtained their liberty, and the Duke appointed a tournament, promising Emilia to the victor Arcite prayed to Mars to grant him victory, Palamon prayed to Venus to grant him Emilia Arcite won the victory, but, being thrown from his horse, died, and Palamon, though not the winner, won the prize

Palatinate (pă lăt' in ăt) The province of a *palatine* who originally was an officer of the imperial palace at Rome (*cp* PALACE) This was on the *Palatine Hill*, which was so called from Pales, a pastoral deity, whose festival was celebrated on April 21st, the "birthday of Rome" to commemorate the day when Romulus, the wolf-child, drew the first furrow at the foot of the hill, and thus laid the foundation of the "Roma Quadrata," the most ancient part of the city.

In Germany *The Palatinate* was the name of a former very powerful and extensive state on the Rhine, and it is still that of the detached portion of Bavaria to the west of the Rhine bounded by Baden, Alsace, Rhenish Prussia, and Hesse.

In England Cheshire and Lancashire are *palatine* counties. *See* COUNTY PALATINE

Pale, The English. The name given in the 15th century to that part of Ireland which had been colonized in the 12th century by Henry II, viz, the districts of Cork, Dublin, Drogheda, Waterford, and Wexford It was only in these districts that the English law prevailed, hence the phrases, **Within the pale, and Outside the pale** By the 16th century the English Pale had so much contracted that it embraced only the district about 20 miles round Dublin

Paleface. A name for a white man attributed to the North American Indians as if translated from a term in their languages Its popularity is largely due to the novels of Fenimore Cooper, but the term became notorious through an earlier connexion with an incident that occurred in 1799. A junior officer named Sterrett, serving on the *Constellation* frigate, wrote home "we would put a man to death for even looking pale on this ship " This letter was published in a Philadelphia paper on March 13th, by early April the affair had become magnified to the point where it was said that Sterrett himself had killed a man for looking pale

Pales (pā' lēz). The Roman god of shepherds and their flocks. *See* PALATINATE *above*

Palimpsest (păl' imp sest) (Gr *palin*, again, *psestos*, scraped) A parchment on which the original writing has been effaced and something else has been written When parchment was scarce the scribes used to erase what was written on it and use it again As sometimes they did not rub it out entirely, many works that would otherwise have been lost have been recovered Thus Cicero's *De Republica*, which was partially erased to make room for a commentary of St Augustine on the Psalms, has been restored

Palindrome (păl' in drōm) (Gr *palin dromo*, to run back again) A word or line which reads

backwards and forwards alike, as *Madam*, also *Roma tibi subito motibus ibit amor* They had also been called *Sotadics*, from their reputed inventor, Sotades, a scurrilous Greek poet of the 3rd century B C

Probably the longest palindrome in English is—

Dog as a devil deified
Deified lived as a god—

and another well known is Napoleon's reputed saying—

Able was I ere I saw Elba

A good palindrome is attributed to Adam who thus introduced himself to Eve

Madam, I'm Adam.

The following Greek palindrome is very celebrated —

ΝΙΨΟΝΑΝΟΜΗΜΑΤΑΜΗΜΟΝΑΝΟΨΙΝ

i e wash my transgressions, not only my face It appears as the legend round many fonts, notably that in the basilica of St Sophia, Constantinople, those at St Stephen d'Egres, Paris, and St Menin's Abbey, Orleans, and, in England, round the fonts of St Martin's, Ludgate Hill, St Mary's, Nottingham, at Dulwich College, and in churches at Worlingworth (Suffolk), Harlow (Essex), Knapton (Norfolk), and Hadleigh (Suffolk)

Palinode (păl' i nōd) (Gr , a singing again) A song or discourse recanting a previous one, such as that of Stesichorus to Helen after he had been struck blind for singing evil of her, or Horace's *Ode* (Bk I, xvi), which ends—

nunc ego mitibus
Mutare quero tristia, dum mihi
fias recentatis amica
obprobriis animumque reddas

It was a favourite form of versification among Jacobean poets, and the best known is that of Francis Quarles (1592-1644) in which man's life is likened to all the delights of nature, all of which fade, and man too dies

Isaac Watts (1674-1748) has a palinode in which he retracts the praise bestowed upon Queen Anne. In the first part of her reign he wrote a laudatory poem to the queen, but he says that the latter part deluded his hopes and proved him a false prophet

Palinurus (păl i nū' rus) (in English *Palinure*) Any pilot, especially a careless one, from the steersman in Virgil's *Æneid*, who went to sleep at the helm and fell overboard and was drowned

Lost was the nation's sense, nor could be found,
While the long solemn unison went round
Wide and more wide, it spread o'er all the realm,
Even Palinurus nodded at the helm
POPE: *Dunciad*, iv, 611

Palissy Ware (păl' i si) Dishes and similar articles of pottery covered with models of fish, reptiles, shells, flowers leaves, etc , carefully coloured and enamelled in high relief, so called after Bernard Palissy (1510-89), the French potter and enameller

Pall (pawl). The covering thrown over a coffin is the Latin *pallium*, a square piece of cloth used by the Romans to throw over their shoulders, or to cover them in bed, hence a coverlet

Pall, the long sweeping robe worn by sovereigns at their coronation, by the Pope, archbishops, etc , is the Roman *palla*, which was only worn by princes and women of honest fame This differed greatly from the *pallium* (*q v*), which was worn by freemen and slaves, soldiers, and philosophers

> Sometimes let gorgeous Tragedy
> In sceptred pall come sweeping by
> MILTON *Il Penseroso.*

Pall-bearers. The custom of appointing men of mark for pall-bearers came to us from the Romans Julius Cæsar had magistrates for his pall-bearers, Augustus Cæsar had senators, Germanicus had tribunes and centurions, Æmilis L Paulus had the chief men of Macedonia who happened to be at Rome at that time, but the poor were carried on a plain bier on men's shoulders.

Pall Mall (păl măl) This fine thoroughfare in the West End of London has been so called since the early 18th century because it is the place where formerly the game of Palle malle (Ital. *palla*, ball, *maglia*, mallet) was played When first built, about 1690, it was named Catherine Street, in honour of Catherine of Braganza "Pale malle," says Cotgrave—

> is a game wherein a round boxball is struck with a mallet through a high arch of iron He that can do this most frequently wins

The game was fashionable in the reign of Charles II, and the walk called the Mall in St James's Park was appropriated to it for the king and his court

> In town let me live then, in town let me die,
> For in truth I can't relish the country, not I.
> If one must have a villa in summer to dwell,
> O, give me the sweet shady side of Pall Mall!
> CHAS MORRIS (d 1832) *The Contrast*

Palladian. An architectural term for a heavy, classic style based on the work of the Italian architect Andrea Palladio (1518-80) It was introduced into England by Inigo Jones, and the Banqueting Hall, Whitehall, is an example of his Palladian work

Palladium (pa lã′ di um) In classical story, the colossal wooden statue of Pallas in the citadel of Troy, which was said to have fallen from heaven, and on the preservation of which it was believed that the safety of the city depended It was carried away by the Greeks, and the city burnt to the ground, and later it was said to have been taken to Rome

Hence, the word is now figuratively applied to anything on which the safety of a people, etc , is supposed to depend

> The liberty of the press is the palladium of all the civil, political, and religious rights of an English man.
> —*Letters of Junius Dedication*

See also ABATON, ANCILE, EDEN HALL

The rare metallic element found associated with platinum and gold was named *palladium* by its discoverer. Wollaston (1803) from the newly discovered asteroid, *Pallas*, and the same name has been given to a place of amusement in London, apparently through the mistaken idea that the ancient Palladium, like the Colosseum (*q v*), was something akin to a circus

Pallas. A name of Minerva (*q v*), sometimes called *Pallas Minerva* According to fable, Pallas was one of the Titans, and was killed by Minerva, who flayed him, and used his skin for armour More likely the word is either from *pallo*, to brandish, the compound implying "Minerva who brandishes the spear," or simply *pallax*, virgin

Pallium (păl′ i um) The square woollen cloak worn by men in ancient Greece, corresponding to the Roman *toga* Hence the Romans called themselves *gens togata*, and the Greeks *gens palliata*

At the present time the scarf-like vestment of white wool with red crosses, worn by the Pope and archbishops, is called the *pallium* It is made from the wool of lambs blessed in the church of St Agnese, Rome, and until he has received his pallium no archbishop can exercise his functions It is still displayed heraldically in the arms of the Archbishop of Canterbury

Palm The well-known tropical and subtropical tree gets its name from the Latin *palma*, which was a transferred use of *palma*, the palm of the hand, applied to the tree because of the spread-hand or open fan-like appearance of the fronds The English *palm* (of the hand) represents M E (and Fr) *paume*

The palm tree is said to grow faster for being weighed down Hence it is the symbol of resolution overcoming calamity It is believed by Orientals to have sprung from the residue of the clay of which Adam was formed

An itching palm. A hand ready to receive bribes The old superstition is that if your palm itches you are going to receive money.

> Let me tell you, Cassius, you yourself
> Are much condemned to have an itching palm
> *Julius Cæsar*, iv. 3

Palm oil. Bribes, or rather money for bribes, fees, etc

> In Ireland the machinery of a political movement will not work unless there is plenty of palm-oil to prevent friction —*Irish Seditions from 1792 to 1880,* p 39

> The rich may escape with whole skins, but those without "palm-oil" have scant mercy —*Nineteenth Century*, Aug , 1892, p 312

Palm Sunday. The Sunday next before Easter So called in memory of Christ's triumphant entry into Jerusalem, when the multitude strewed the way with palm branches and leaves (*John* xii, 12–19).

Sad Palm Sunday. March 29th, 1463, the day of the battle of Towton, the most fatal of all the battles in the War of the Roses It is said that over 30,000 Englishmen were slain

> Whose banks received the blood of many thousand men,
> On "Sad Palm Sunday" slain, that Towton field we call
> The bloodiest field betwixt the White Rose and the Red
> DRAYTON *Polyolbion*, xxviii

Palmy days Prosperous or happy days, as those were to a victorious gladiator when he went to receive the palm branch as the reward of his prowess

To bear the palm. To be the best The allusion is to the Roman custom of giving the victorious gladiator a branch of the palm tree

To palm off To pass off fraudulently. The allusion is to jugglers, who conceal in the palm of their hand what they pretend to dispose of in some other way

> You may palm upon us new for old —DRYDEN.

Palmam qui meruit ferat (Let him bear the palm who has deserved it) was Nelson's motto, and is that of the Royal Naval College The line comes from Jortin's *Lusus Poetici* (1748), *Ad ventos,* stanza iv —

> Et nobis faciles parcite et hostibus,
> Concurrant pariter cum ratibus rates
>   Spectent numina ponti, et
>   Palmam qui meruit, ferat

Palmer A pilgrim to the Holy Land who was privileged to carry a palm staff, and who spent all his days in visiting holy shrines, living on charity

> His sandals were with travel tore,
> Staff, budget, bottle, scrip he wore;
> The faded palm-branch in his hand
> Showed pilgrim from the Holy Land
>   SCOTT *Marmion*, i, 27

At the dedication of palmers prayers and psalms were said over them as they lay prostrate before the altar, they were sprinkled with holy water, and received a consecrated palm branch

Palmerin (păl´mer in) The hero of a number of 16th-century Spanish romances of chivalry, on the lines of *Amadis of Gaul* The most famous are *Palmerin de Oliva,* and *Palmerin of England* Southey published an abridged translation of the latter.

Palmetto State. The State of South Carolina The palmetto is a fan-leafed palm.

Palmy. *See* PALM.

Paludament (pa lū´ da ment) A distinctive mantle worn by a Roman general in the time of war This was the "scarlet robe" in which Christ was invested (*Matt.* xxvii, 28)

> They flung on him an old scarlet paludamentum—some cast-off war-cloak with its purple laticlave from the Prætorian wardrobe —FARRAR *Life of Christ,* ch lx

Pam (păm). The knave of clubs in certain card-games, also the name of a card-game, short for *Pamphile,* French for the knave of clubs

This word is sometimes given as an instance of Johnson's weakness in etymology He says it is "probably from *palm,* victory, as *trump* from *triumph.*"

Pam was the usual nickname of the great Victorian statesman Viscount Palmerston (1784-1865)

Pampas (păm´pås) Treeless plains, some 2,000 miles long and from 300 to 500 broad, in South America They cover an area of 750,000 sq miles. It is the Spanish form of Peruvian *bamba,* meaning *flats* or *plains*

Pampero, The (păm pĕ´ro) A dry, north-west wind that blows in the summer season from the Andes across the pampas to the sea-coast

Pamphlet. A small unbound book of a few sheets stitched together, usually on some subject of merely temporary interest, so called from O Fr *Pamphilet,* the name of a 12th-century erotic Latin poem which was very popular in the Middle Ages

This word has been the subject of much etymological guesswork One "authority" derived it from a supposed Pamphila, a Greek lady, whose chief work was said to be a commonplace book of anecdotes, epitomes, notes, etc ; Johnson suggested *par-un-filet* (he'd "by a thread")—*i e* stitched, but not bound, while another "derivation is *paginæ filatæ* (pages tacked together).

Pan (Gr , all, everything) The god of pastures, forests, flocks, and herds of Greek mythology; also the personification of deity displayed in creation and pervading all things He is represented with lower part of a goat and the upper part of a man, his lustful nature symbolized the spermatic principle of the world, the leopard's skin that he wore indicated the immense variety of created things, and his character of "blameless" symbolized that wisdom which governs the world

>   Universal Pan,
> Knit with the Graces and the Hours in dance,
> Led on the eternal spring
>   MILTON *Paradise Lost,* iv, 266

Legend has it that at the time of the Crucifixion, just when the veil of the Temple was rent in twain, a cry swept across the ocean in the hearing of many, ' Great Pan is Dead," and that at the same time the responses of the oracles ceased for ever *See* E B Browning's poem of this name

Pan-pipes. A wind instrument of great antiquity, consisting of a series of pipes of graduated length, across the upper ends of which the player blows, obtaining a scale of thin, reedy notes Pan-pipes are associated by name and picture with the rural god Pan who, according to Greek legend, invented them and played them to the nymphs and dryads of the mountainside

Panacea (păn a sē´ a) (Gr , all-healing). A universal cure Panacea was the daughter of Æsculapius (god of medicine), and the medicine that cures is the daughter or child of the healing art

In the Middle Ages the search for the panacea was one of the alchemists' self-imposed tasks, and fable tells of many panaceas, such as the Promethean unguent which rendered the body invulnerable, Aladdin's ring, the balsam of Fierabras (*q v*), and Prince Ahmed's apple (*see* APPLE) *Cp also* ACHILLES' SPEAR, MEDEA'S KETTLE, etc

Panache (pan ash´) The literal meaning of this French word is a plume of feathers flying in the wind as from the crest of a helmet. Figuratively, however, "panache" is applied to one's courage or spirit, to keeping one's end up It is in this sense familiar to those who have read or seen *Cyrano de Bergerac*

Panama Hat A light, broad-brimmed hat made of the young leaves of *Carludovica palmata,* a palm-like tree indigenous to Central America

Pancake A thin, flat ' cake" made in a frying-pan These pancakes were made from the necessity in the past, when conditions of fasting were more strict, of using up eggs and fat before the beginning of Lent Shrove Tuesday (*q v*), a special day for these, came to be called **Pancake Day,** and the Shrove-bell the **Pancake Bell.**

Panchæa (păn kē´ å). A fabulous land, possibly belonging to Arabia Felix, renowned among the ancients for the quality and quantity of its perfumes, such as myrrh and incense

Pancras, St. One of the patron saints of children (*cp* NICHOLAS), martyred in the Diocletian persecution (304) at Rome at the age of

13 His day is May 12th, and he is usually represented as a boy, with a sword in one hand and a palm-branch in the other.

The first church to be consecrated in England (by St Augustine, at Canterbury) was dedicated to St Pancras

Pandarus (păn' da rus). A Lycian leader and ally of the Trojans in Greek legend Owing to his later connexion with the story of Troilus and Cressida, he was taken over by the romance writers of the Middle Ages as a procurer. *See* PANDER.

Pandects of Justinian (Gr *pandektes*, all receiver or encloser) A compendium of Roman civil law made in the 6th century by order of the Emperor Justinian. It comprises 50 books, and contains the decisions to which Justinian gave the force of law The story that the copy now in the Laurentian Library at Florence was found at Amalfi (1137), and gave a spur to the study of civil law which changed the whole literary and legal aspect of Europe, is not now credited

Pandemonium (păn de mō' ni um) (Gr , all the demons) A wild, unrestrained uproar, a tumultuous assembly The word was first used by Milton as the name of the principal city in Hell It was formed on the analogy of *Pantheon* (*q v*)

> The rest were all
> Far to the inland retired, about the walls
> Of Pandemonium city and proud seat
> Of Lucifer
> *Paradise Lost*, x, 424 (*see also* i, 756)

Pander. To pander to one's vices is to act as an agent to them, and such an agent is termed a pander from *Pandarus*, who procures for Troilus (*q v*) the love of Cressida In *Much Ado About Nothing* it is said that Troilus was "the first employer of pandars" (v, 2)

> Let all pitiful goers-between be called to the world's end after my name, call them all "Pandars" Let all constant men be "Troiluses," all false women be "Cressids," and all brokers-between, "Pandars"
> Say, Amen —SHAKESPEARE. *Troilus and Cressida*, iii, 2

Pandora's Box (păn dôr' a) A present which seems valuable, but which is in reality a curse; like that of Midas (*q v*), who found his very food became gold, and so uneatable

Prometheus made an image and stole fire from heaven to endow it with life In revenge, Jupiter told Vulcan to make the first woman, who was named Pandora (i e the All-gifted), because each of the gods gave her some power which was to bring about the ruin of man Jupiter gave her a box which she was to present to him who married her Prometheus distrusted Jove and his gifts, but Epimetheus, his brother, married the beautiful Pandora, and—against advice—accepted the gift of the god. Immediately he opened the box all the evils flew forth and have ever since continued to afflict the world According to some accounts the last thing that flew out was Hope, but others say that Hope alone remained

Pangloss, Dr. (păn' gloss) (Gr , all tongues) The pedantic old tutor to the hero in Voltaire's *Candide, ou l'Optimisme* (1759) His great point was his incurable and misleading optimism; it did him no good and brought him

all sorts of misfortune, but to the end he reiterated "all is for the best in this best of all possible worlds " This was an attack upon the current theories of J J Rousseau

Panhandle. In the United States a narrow strip of territory belonging to one State which runs between two others, such as the Texas Panhandle, the Panhandle of Idaho, etc West Virginia is known as **the Panhandle State**

Panic The word comes from the god Pan (*q v*), because sounds heard by night in the mountains and valleys, which gave rise to sudden and groundless fear, were attributed to him There are various legends accounting for the name, one is that Bacchus, in his eastern expeditions, was opposed by an army far superior to his own, and Pan advised him to command all his men at dead of night to raise a simultaneous shout This was rolled from mountain to mountain by innumerable echoes, and the enemy, thinking they were surrounded on all sides, took to sudden flight. *Cp Judges* vii, 18-21.

Panjandrum (păn jăn' drŭm). A village boss, who imagines himself the "Magnus Apollo" of his neighbours The word occurs in Foote's farrago of nonsense which he composed to test old Macklin, who said he had brought his memory to such perfection that he could remember anything by reading it over once. There is more than one version of the test passage; the following is as well authenticated as any —

> So she went into the garden to cut a cabbage-leaf to make an apple-pie, and at the same time a great she-bear came running up the street and popped its head into the shop "What! no soap?" So he died, and she —very imprudently—married the barber And there were present the Picninnies, the Joblillies, the Garyulies, and the Grand Panjandrum, himself with the little red button a-top, and they all fell to playing the game of catch-as-catch-can till the gunpowder ran out at the heels of their boots.

It is said that Macklin was so indignant at this nonsense that he refused to repeat a word of it

Panope *See* NEREIDS.

Panopticon (păn op' ti kon). The Royal Panopticon of Science and Art, in Leicester Square, was opened in 1852-53 as a place of popular instruction and a home for the sciences and music. It was built in the Moorish style and awakened great admiration. It failed in its original intention, however, and after being closed some years was reopened in 1858 as a place of entertainment, under the name of The Alhambra For many years this was one of the landmarks of London

Pan-piper. *See* PAN

Pantables. *See* PANTOFLES

Pantagruel (păn ta groo' el) The principal character in Rabelais' great satire *The History of Gargantua and Pantagruel* (the first part published in 1532, the last posthumously in 1565), King of the Dipsodes, son of Gargantua (*q v*), and by some identified with Henri II of France. He was the last of the giants, and Rabelais says he got his name from the Greek *panta*, all, and Arab *gruel*, thirsty, because he was born during the drought which lasted thirty and six months, three weeks, four days, thirteen hours, and a little more, in that year of grace noted for having "three Thursdays in one week " He was covered with hair at birth, "like a young bear," and was so strong that though he was chained in his cradle with four great iron chains, like those used in ships of the largest size, he stamped out the bottom, which was made of weavers' beams, and, when loosed by the servants, broke his bonds into five hundred thousand pieces with one blow of his infant fist When he grew to manhood he knew all languages, all sciences, and all knowledge of every sort, out-Solomoning Solomon in wisdom His immortal achievement was his voyage from Utopia in quest of the "oracle of the Holy Bottle" (*q v*)

Wouldst thou not issue forth
To see the third part in this earthy cell
Of the brave acts of good Pantagruel
RABELAIS *To the Spirit of the Queen of Navarre.*

Pantagruelism. Coarse and boisterous buffoonery and humour, especially with a serious purpose—like that for which Pantagruel was famous

Pantaloon The breeches, trousers, or underdrawers of various kinds (now often called *pants*) get their name from Pantaloon, a Venetian character in 16th-century Italian comedy, a lean and foolish old man dressed in loose trousers and slippers His name is said to have come from San Pantaleone (a patron saint of physicians and very popular in Venice), and he was adopted by the later harlequinades and pantomimes as the butt of the clown's jokes.

The sixth age shifts
Into the lean and slipper'd pantaloon,
With spectacles on nose and pouch on side,
His youthful hose well sav'd, a world too wide
For his shrunk shank, and his big manly voice,
Turning again toward childish treble, pipes
And whistles in his sound
As You Like It, ii 7

Playing Pantaloon. Playing second fiddle, being the cat's-paw of another, servilely imitating

Pantechnicon (păn tek′ ni kon) (Gr , belonging to all the arts) The name was originally coined for a bazaar for the sale of artistic work built about 1830 in Motcomb Street, Belgrave Square, as this was unsuccessful the building was converted into a warehouse for storing furniture, and the name retained. It is now often used in place of *pantechnicon van*, a furniture-removing van

Pantheism (păn′ thē izm) The doctrine that God is everything and everything is God, a monistic theory elaborated by Spinoza, who, by his doctrine of the Infinite Substance, sought to overcome the opposition between mind and matter, body and soul

Pantheon (păn′ thē on) A temple dedicated to all the gods (Gr *pan,* all, *theos,* god), specifically, that erected at Rome by Agrippa, son-in-law to Augustus It is circular, nearly 150 ft in diameter, and of the same total height, in the centre of the dome roof is a space open to the sky. Since the early 7th century, as Santa Maria Rotunda, it has been used as a Christian church. Among the national heroes buried there are Raffaele, Victor Emmanuel II, and Humbert I

The Pantheon at Paris was originally the church of St Geneviève, started by Louis XV and completed in 1790 In 1791 the Convention changed its name to the Pantheon and decreed that men who had deserved well of their country should be buried there. Among them are Rousseau, Voltaire, and Victor Hugo

Panther (earlier **Panthera**) In mediæval times this animal was supposed to be friendly to all beasts except the dragon, and to attract them by a peculiarly sweet odour it exhaled Swinburne, in *Laus Veneris,* makes use of this tradition, but gives it a rather different significance —

As one who hidden in deep sedge and reeds
Smells the rare scent made where a panther feeds,
And tracking ever slotwise the warm smell
Is snapped upon by the warm mouth and bleeds,
His head far down the hot sweet mouth of her—
So one tracks love, whose breath is deadlier

In the old *Physiologus* the panther was the type of Christ, but later, when the savage nature of the beast was more widely known, it became symbolical of evil and hypocritical flattery; hence Lyly's comparison (in *Euphues, the Anatomy of Wit*) of the beauty of women to a delicate bait with a deadly hook, a sweet panther with a devouring paunch, a sour poison in a silver pot

The mediæval idea is reflected in (or perhaps arose from) the name, which is probably of Oriental origin but was taken from Gr *panther,* all beasts

In *Reynard the Fox (q v)* Reynard affirms that he sent the queen a comb made of panther's bone, "more lustrous than the rainbow, more odoriferous than any perfume, a charm against every ill, and a universal panacea "

The **Spotted Panther** in Dryden's *Hind and Panther* (1687) typifies the Church of England as being full of the spots of error, whereas the Church of Rome is faultless as the milk-white hind.

The panther, sure the noblest next the hind,
And fairest creature of the spotted kind,
Oh, could her inborn stains be washed away
She were too good to be a beast of prey   Pt i

Pantile A roofing-tile curved transversely to an ogee shape In the 18th century as Dissenters' chapels were—like cottages—frequently roofed with these, such meeting-houses were sometimes called *pantile-shops,* and the word was used in the sense of dissenting Mrs Centlivre, in *A Gotham Election* (1715), contrasts the *pantile crew* with a good churchman

The Parade at Tunbridge Wells, known as the *Pantiles,* was so called because the name was erroneously applied in the 18th century to such flat Dutch tiles as those with which it is paved

Pantisocracy (păn ti sok′ ra si) (Gr , all of equal power) The name given by Coleridge to the communistic, Utopian society that he, with Southey, George Burnett, and others intended (about 1794) to form on the banks of the Susquehannah River. The scheme came to nothing owing chiefly to the absence of funds

All are not moralists, like Southey, when
He prated to the world of "Pantisocrasy "
BYRON *Don Juan,* iii, 93

Pantofles, or **Pantubles** (păn' toflz, păn' tab lz) Slippers, especially loose ones worn by Orientals.

To stand upon one's pantofles To stand on one's dignity, get on the high horse. It was a common proverbial phrase from the 16th to the 18th century

I note that for the most part they stand so on their pantofles that they be secure of perils, obstinate in their own opinions . ready to shake off their old acquaintance without cause, and to condemn them without colour.—LYLY· *Euphues, The Anatomy of Wit* (1578).

Richard Puttenham (*c* 1520-1601), in his *Arte of English Poesie* (1589), shows how the phrase probably arose "The actor," he says, "did walk upon those high-corked shoes or pantofles, which now they call in Spain and Italy *Shoppini* "

Pantomime (păn' tŏ mīm) According to etymology this should be all dumb show, but the word was commonly applied to an adaptation of the old Commedia dell'arte that lasted down to the 19th century The principal characters are Harlequin (*q v*) and Columbine, who never speak, and Clown and Pantaloon, who keep a constant fire of joke and repartee. This once popular pantomime has since devolved into a Christmas theatrical entertainment, usually based on a nursery tale, *e g Cinderella, Mother Goose,* or even *Robinson Crusoe,* enlivened by catchy songs, pretty girls, and considerable buffooning

Panurge (Gr *pan,* all, *ergos,* worker, the "all-doer," *i e* the rogue, he who will "do anything or anyone") The roguish companion of Pantagruel, and one of the principal characters in Rabelais' satire, He was a desperate rake, was always in debt, had a dodge for every scheme, knew everything and something more, was a boon companion of the mirthfullest temper and most licentious bias, but was timid of danger, and a desperate coward. Panurge consulted lots, dreams, a sibyl, etc , and, lastly, the Oracle of the Holy Bottle, and to every one of the obscure answers Panurge received, whether it seemed to point to "Yes" or to "No," he invariably found insuperable objections

Some "commentators" on Rabelais have identified Panurge with Calvin, others with Cardinal Lorraine, and this part of the satire seems to be an echo of the great Reformation controversy on the celibacy of the clergy

Panzer (păn' tzer) German term used in World War II meaning "armoured", Panzer division, as a term, applied to all the troops in or attached to that armoured division, whether actually riding in tanks or not

Pap. He gives pap with a hatchet He does or says a kind thing in a very brusque and ungracious manner One of the scurrilous tracts against Martin Marprelate (*see* MARPRELATE), published in 1589, was entitled *Pap with a Hatchet.*

Papal States or **States of the Church,** were the Italian territories under the temporal sovereignty of the Popes until 1860 when, with the exception of the city of Rome and a few outlying possessions, the States were incorporated in the Kingdom of Italy In 1870, with the withdrawal of the French garrison that had alone enabled the enfeebled Papal government to exist, the Italians entered Rome and the Pope made himself a voluntary "prisoner" in the Vatican. In 1929 the Lateran Treaty was signed between the Holy See and Mussolini's Italian government whereby *de jure* and *de facto* sovereignty was accorded to the Papal authorities in the Vatican City, which includes the Palace, the church and piazza of St. Peter's, and contiguous buildings to the extent of a little under a square mile, with a population of some 600 souls. The Pope's country seat at Castel Gandolfo is also included in the Vatican City

Paper. So called from the *papyrus,* the giant water reed from which the Egyptians manufactured a material for writing on

Not worth the paper it's written on Said of an utterly worthless statement, promise, etc

Paper blockade A blockade proclaimed but not put into force

Paper credit. Credit allowed on the score of bills, promissory notes etc , that show that money is due to the borrower.

Paper money or **currency** Bank notes as opposed to coin, or bills used as currency.

Paper profits Hypothetical profits shown on a company's prospectus, etc

The Paper King John Law, the projector of the Mississippi Scheme (*q v*).

To paper a house. In theatrical phraseology, to fill the theatre with "deadheads," or non-paying spectators, admitted by paper orders

To send in (or **to receive**) **one's papers.** To resign one's appointment, commission, etc , *or* to receive one's dismissal.

Paphian (pā' fi án). Relating to Venus, or rather to Paphos, a city of Cyprus, where Venus was worshipped, a Cyprian, a prostitute

Papier mâche (păp' yer mäsh' ă). Pulped paper mixed with glue, or layers of paper glued together and while pliable moulded to form various articles and ornaments When dry the material becomes hard and strong. Lacquered, and often inlaid with mother o' pearl, papier maché articles were greatly in vogue in early and mid-Victorian times. In 1772 Henry Clay, of Birmingham, used it in coach-building, in 1845 it was first employed for architectural mouldings, etc

Papyrus. *See* PAPER The written scrolls of the ancient Egyptians are called *papyri,* because they were written on this.

Par (Lat., equal) Stock *at par* means that it is to be bought at the price it represents Thus, £100 stock if quoted at £105 would be £5 *above par,* if at £95, it would be £5 *below par* A person in low spirits or ill health is said to be "below par "

In journalism *a par* is a paragraph, a note of a few lines on a subject of topical interest

Paraclete (păr' a klēt) The advocate; one *called to* aid or support another, from the Gr *para-kaleō*, to call to The word is used as a title of the Holy Ghost, the Comforter.

> O source of uncreated Light,
> The Father's promised Paraclete!
> DRYDEN *Veni, Creator Spiritus*

Paradise. The Greeks borrowed this word from the Persians, among whom it denoted the enclosed and extensive parks and pleasure grounds of the Persian kings The Septuagint translators adopted it for the garden of Eden, and in the New Testament and by early Christian writers it was applied to Heaven, the abode of the blessed dead.

A fool's paradise. *See* FOOL

Paradise and the Peri. *See* PERI.

Paradise Lost. Milton's epic poem was published in 12 books in 1667. It tells the story—

> Of Man's first disobedience and the fruit
> Of that forbidden tree whose mortal taste
> Brought death into the World, and all our woe
> With loss of Eden

Satan rouses the panic-stricken host of fallen angels with tidings of a rumour current in Heaven of a new world about to be created. He calls a council to deliberate what should be done, and they agree to send him to search for this new world. Seating himself on the Tree of Life, **Satan** overhears Adam and Eve talking about the prohibition made by God, and at once resolves upon the nature of his attack. He takes the form of a mist, and, entering the serpent, induces Eve to eat of the forbidden fruit Adam eats "that he may perish with the woman whom he loved " Satan returns to Hell to tell his triumph, and Michael is sent to lead the guilty pair out of the Garden.

Milton borrowed largely from the epic of Du Bartas (1544-90), entitled *The Week of Creation* which was translated into almost every European language; and he was indebted to St Avitus (d 523), who wrote in Latin hexameters *The Creation, The Fall,* and *The Expulsion from Paradise,* for his description of Paradise (Bk I), of Satan (Bk. II), and other parts.

In 1671 *Paradise Regained* (in four books) was published. The subject is the Temptation Eve, being tempted, fell, and lost Paradise, Jesus, being tempted, resisted, and regained Paradise

Paradise shoots. The lign aloe, said to be the only plant descended to us from the Garden of Eden. When Adam left Paradise he took a shoot of this tree, and from it the lign aloes have been propagated.

The Earthly Paradise. In mediæval times it was a popular belief that paradise, a land—or island—where everything was beautiful and restful, and where death and decay were unknown, still existed somewhere on earth and was to be found for the searching. It was usually located far away to the east; Cosmas (7th century) placed it beyond the ocean east of China, in 9th-century maps it is shown in China itself, and the fictitious letter of Prester John to the Emperor Emmanuel Comnenus states that it was within three days' journey of his own territory—a "fact" that is corroborated by Mandeville The Hereford map (13th century) shows it as a circular island near India, from which it is separated not only by the sea, but also by a battlemented wall *Cp* BRANDAN, ST.

Paraguay, The Reductions of, were a Jesuit mission in Paraguay established in 1607. Basing their rule on the principle that they were the guardians and trustees of the Indians, the Jesuit fathers established a colony of a model nature When the cupidity of the Spanish government closed the Reductions and expelled the Jesuits, Voltaire, a by-no-means uncritical observer, wrote "When the Paraguay mission left the hands of the Jesuits in 1768 they had arrived at what is perhaps the highest degree of civilization to which it is possible to lead a young people . . Laws were there respected, morals were pure, a happy brotherhood bound men together, the useful arts flourished, and there was abundance everywhere."

Parallel. None but himself can be his parallel. Wholly without a peer The line occurs in Lewis Theobald's *The Double Falsehood* (1727), III, I, a play which Theobald tried to palm off on the literary world as by Shakespeare. There are many similar sentences, for example —

> And but herself admits no parallel
> MASSINGER *Duke of Millaine,* III, 4 (1662)
> None but himself can parallel
> *Anagram on John Lilburn* (1658).

Paraphernalia (păr a fēr nā' lya) Literally, all that a woman can claim at the death of her husband beyond her jointure (Gr *para,* beside, *pherne,* dowry) In the Roman law her paraphernalia included the furniture of her chamber, her wearing apparel, her jewels, etc. Hence personal attire, fittings generally, anything for show or decoration

Parasite (păr' a sīt) (Gr *para sitos,* eating at another's cost). A plant or animal that lives on another; hence a hanger-on. one who fawns and flatters for the sake of what he can get out of it—a "sponger "

Parcheesi (par chē' zi) A game resembling backgammon, played mostly in U S A

Parchment So called from Pergamum, in Mysia, Asia Minor, where it was used for the purpose of writing when Ptolemy prohibited the exportation of papyrus from Egypt.

Pardon Bell. The Angelus bell So called because of the indulgence once given for reciting certain prayers forming the Angelus (*q.v*)

Pardoner's Tale, in Chaucer's *Canterbury Tales,* is that of *Death and the Rioters,* which comes from an Oriental source through the Italian *Cento Novelle Antiche.*

A pardoner was a cleric licensed to preach and collect money for a definite object such as a crusade or the building of a church, for contributing to which an indulgence was attached The pardoner's mitten Whoever put this mitten on would be sure to thrive in all things.

> He that his honde put in this metayn,
> He shal have multiplying of his grayn,
> Whan he hath sowen, be it whete or otes,
> So that ye offre pans [pence] or elles grootes.
> CHAUCER *Prologue to the Pardoner's Tale.*

Pargetting (par' jit ing) The ornamental plaster facing of exterior walls, usually in a simple pricked or traced design, and commonly found in Essex. Parget is a plaster made of lime, hair, and cow dung.

Pari mutuel (pa' rı mü tü el') was the name first given to the totalizator. which ensures that the winners of a race share the money staked on the horses, etc , after the cost of management, taxes, etc , have been deducted

Pari passu. At the same time, in equal degrees, two or more schemes carried on at once and driven forward with equal energy, are said to be carried on *pari passu*, which is Latin for *equal strides* or the equally measured pace of persons marching together

The cooling effects of surrounding matter go on nearly *pari passu* with the heating —GROVE *Correlation of Physical Forces*, p 64

Pariah. A member of the lowest caste of Hindu in Southern India, from a native word meaning "a drummer," because it was those who beat the drums at certain festivals

Europeans often extend the term to those of no caste at all, hence it is applied to outcasts generally, the lowest of the low.

There was no worst
Of degradation spared Fifine, ordained from first
To last, in body and soul, for one life-long debauch,
The Pariah of the North, the European Nautch !
BROWNING *Fifine at the Fair*, xxxi.

Parian. A name given to a fine statuary porcelain manufactured in the mid-19th century, and used for small figures, vases, chessmen, jewellery, etc

Parian Chronicle. One of the Arundelian Marbles (*q v*), found in the island of Paros, and bearing an inscription which contains a chronological register of the chief events in the mythology and history of ancient Greece during a series of 1,318 years, beginning with the reign of Cecrops (about 1580 B C), and ending with the archonship of Diognetus (264 B C), of which nearly the last hundred years is now lost

Paris (păr' is) In Greek legend, the son of Priam, King of Troy and Hecuba, and through his abduction of Helen (*q.v*) the cause of the siege of Troy Before his birth Hecuba dreamed that she was to bring forth a firebrand, and, as this was interpreted to mean that the unborn child would bring destruction to his house, the infant Paris was exposed on Mount Ida He was, however, brought up by a shepherd, and grew to perfection of beautiful manhood When the golden Apple of Discord (*see under* APPLE) was thrown on the table of the gods it was Paris who had to judge between the rival claims of Hera (Juno), Aphrodite (Venus), and Athene (Minerva), each goddess offered him bribes—the first power, the second the most beautiful of women, and the third martial glory He awarded the Apple and the title of "Fairest" to Aphrodite, who in return assisted him to carry off Helen, for whom he deserted his wife, Œnone, daughter of the river-god, Cebren At Troy Paris earned the contempt of all by his cowardice, and he was fatally wounded with a poisoned arrow by Philoctetes at the taking of the city.

Paris (păr' is), the capital of France. So called from the ancient Celtic tribe, the *Parisii*, whose capital—the modern *Paris*—was known to the Romans as *Lutetia Parisiorum*, the mud-town of the Parisii See LUTETIA Rabelais

gives a whimsical derivation of the name He tells (I, xvii) how Gargantua played a disgusting practical joke on the Parisians who came to stare at him, and the men said it was a sport "par ris" (to be laughed at); wherefore the city was called Par-'is.

The heraldic device of the city of Paris is a ship As Sauval says, *"L'ile de la cité est faite comme un grand navire enfoncé dans la vase, et échoue au fil de l'eau vers le milieu de la Seine "* This form of a ship struck the heraldic authorities, who, in the latter half of the Middle Ages, emblazoned it in the shield of the city

Monsieur de Paris. The public executioner of Paris.

Plaster of Paris. Gypsum, especially calcined gypsum used for making statuary casts, keeping broken limbs rigid for setting, etc. It is found in large quantities in the quarries of Montmartre, near Paris

Paris-Garden. A bear-garden; a noisy, disorderly place. In allusion to the famous bull-and bear-baiting gardens of that name at Bankside, Southwark, on the site of a house owned by Robert de Paris in the reign of Richard II In 1504 the Swan Theatre was erected here, and in 1613 this gave way to The Hope.

Do you take the court for a Paris-garden?—*Henry VIII*, v, 3

Parisian Wedding, The. The massacre of St. Bartholomew, which took place (Aug. 24th, 1572) during the festivities at the marriage of Henri of Navarre and Margaret of France

Charles IX, although it was not possible for him to recall to life the countless victims of the Parisian Wedding, was ready to explain those murders — MOTLEY *Dutch Republic*, iii, 9.

Parlement. Under the old *régime* in France, the sovereign court of justice where councillors were allowed to plead, and where justice was administered in the king's name The Paris Parlement received appeals from all inferior tribunals, but its own judgments were final It took cognizance of all offences against the crown, the peers, the bishops, the corporations, and all high officers of state, and, though it had no legislative power, had to *register* the royal edicts before they could become law. The Parlements were abolished by the Constituent Assembly in 1790

Parliament From the French *Parlement* (*see above*), from *parler*, to speak, with the suffix *-ment*, denoting action, etc.

My Lord Coke tells us *Parliament* is derived from "parler le ment" (to speak one's mind) He might as honestly have taught us that *firmament* is "firma mentis" (a farm for the mind), or "fundament" the bottom of the mind.—RYMER *On Parliaments*

A number of English Parliaments have received special characteristic names, and the more important of these will be found in their alphabetical places See, for instance, *under* ADDLED; BAREBONES, CONVENTION, DEVIL'S, DRUNKEN, DUNCES, GOOD, GRATTAN'S, LONG, MAD, MONGREL, PENSIONER, RUMP, USELESS, WONDERMAKING

Parliamentary language, i e restrained and seemly language such as is required of any member speaking in Parliament, is now applied to a civil and courteous mode of addressing an opponent in an argument

Parliamentary Train. By the Regulation of Railways Act of 1844 every railway in Great Britain was obliged to run at least one train a day over its system, at a minimum speed of 12 m p h , calling at every station, at a fare not greater than 1d. a mile This was repealed in 1915

Parlour. Originally the reception room in a monastery, etc , where the inmates could see and speak to (Fr *parler*) their friends

Parlour boarder. A pupil at a boarding-school who lives with the principal and receives extra care and attention Hence, used of one in a privileged position

Parlour tricks. Accomplishments that are useful in company, at At Homes, etc , such as singing, witty conversation, and so on

Parlous. A corrupt form of *perilous*
> Oh! 'tis a parlous lad
> *As You Like It*, iii, 2.

Parmesan (par' me zăn') A dry, hard cheese, originally made in Parma, Italy, from skim milk and especially suitable for grating

Parnassus. A mountain near Delphi, Greece, with two summits, one of which was consecrated to Apollo and the Muses, the other to Bacchus. It is said to have been anciently called *Larnassus*, because Deucalion's ark, *larnax*, stranded there after the flood After the oracle of Delphi was built at its foot it received the name of Parnassus, which Peucerus says is a corruption of *Har Nahas* (hill of divination).

Owing to its connexion with the Muses, Parnassus came to be regarded as the seat of poetry and music, and we still use such phrases as *To climb Parnassus*, meaning "to write poetry "
> O, were I on Parnassus hill,
> Or had o' Helicon my fill,
> That I might catch poetic skill,
> To sing how dear I love thee!
> BURNS *Song*

The Legislator or **Solon of Parnassus** Boileau (1636-1711) was so called by Voltaire, because of his *Art of Poetry*, a production unequalled in the whole range of didactic poetry

Gradus ad Parnassum (Lat , steps to Parnassus) The title applied to a dictionary of Latin prosody formerly used in schools for teaching the writing of Latin verse.

Parnassian School The name given to a group of French poets flourishing from about 1850 to 1890, from a collection of their poems entitled *Parnasse contemporain* (1866). They were followers of De Musset, and include Leconte de Lisle, Baudelaire, François Coppée, and Sully-Prudhomme

In England the group of poets following Rossetti and William Morris have sometimes been referred to as "the Parnassians "

Parody. Father of Parody Hipponax of Ephesus (6th century B C) *Parody* means an ode which perverts the meaning of another ode (Gr *para ode*)

Parole (pa rōl') (Fr) A verbal promise given by a soldier that he will not abuse his leave of absence or by a prisoner of war that he will not attempt to escape

Parolles (pa rōl' ĕz) He was a mere Parolles. A pretender, a man of words, and a pedant The allusion is to the faithless, bragging, slandering villain who dubs himself "captain," pretends to knowledge which he has not, and to sentiments he never feels, in Shakespeare's *All's Well that Ends Well*
> I know him a notorious liar,
> Think him a great way fool, solely a coward,
> Yet these fixed evils sit so fit on him
> That they take place Act i, 1

Parr. Thomas Parr, the "old, old, very old man," was said to have lived in the reigns of ten sovereigns, to have married a second wife when he was 120 years old, and to have had a child by her He was a husbandman, born—by repute—at Alberbury, near Shrewbury, in 1483, and died 1635, aged 152 years William Thoms, founder of *Notes and Queries*, examined the evidence in his *Records of Longevity*, and, though Parr certainly lived to a great age, found no confirmation for the generally accepted dates

Parsees (par sēz) Guebres or fire-worshippers (*q.y*), descendants of Persians who fled to India during the Mohammedan persecutions of the 7th and 8th centuries, and still adhere to their Zoroastrian religion See also SILENCE (*Towers of Silence*) The word means *People of Pars—i e* Persia

Parsifal. *See* PERCIVAL

Parsley. He has need now of nothing but a little parsley—*i e* he is dead A Greek saying, the Greeks decked tombs with parsley, because it keeps green a long time

Parson. *See* CLERICAL TITLES

Parson Adams A leading character in Fielding's *Joseph Andrews* (1742), often taken as the type of the simple-minded, hard-working, and learned country curate who is totally ignorant of "the ways of the world "
> As he never had any intention to deceive, so he never suspected such a design in others He was generous, friendly, and brave to an excess, but simplicity was his characteristic, he did, no more than Mr Colley Cibber, apprehend any such passions as malice and envy to exist in mankind—*Joseph Andrews*, ch i.

He was drawn from Fielding's friend, the Rev William Young, who edited Ainsworth's *Latin Dictionary* (1752)

Part. A portion, piece, or fragment.

For my part. As far as concerns me

For the most part. Generally, as a rule.

In good part. Favourably

Part and parcel. An essential part, portion, or element
> "Well, Mr Squeers," he said, welcoming that worthy with his accustomed smile, of which a sharp look and a thoughtful frown were part and parcel, "how do you do?"—DICKENS *Nicholas Nickleby*

Part of speech A grammatical class of words of a particular character The old rhyme by which children used to be taught the parts of speech is —

Three little words you often see
Are ARTICLES, *a*, *an*, and *the*
A NOUN's the name of anything,
As *school* or *garden*, *hoop* or *swing*.
ADJECTIVES tell the kind of noun,
As *great*, *small*, *pretty*, *white*, or *brown*
Instead of nouns the PRONOUNS stand,
Her head, *his* face, *our* arms, *your* hand
VERBS tell of something being done,
To *read*, *count*, *sing*, *laugh*, *jump*, or *run*.
How things are done the ADVERBS tell,
As *slowly*, *quickly*, *ill*, or *well*
CONJUNCTIONS join the words together,
As, men *and* women, wind *or* weather
The PREPOSITION stands before
A noun, as *in* or *through* a door.
The INTERJECTION shows surprise,
As, *oh !* how pretty! *ah !* how wise!
The whole are called nine parts of speech,
Which reading, writing, speaking teach

Part up! Slang for "hand over," as in "If you don't soon part up with the money you owe me there'll be trouble." An extension of the use is the old saying (Tusser, 1573), *A fool and his money are soon parted*

Till death us do part. *See* DEPART.

To play a part. To perform some duty or pursue some course of action; also, to act deceitfully The phrase is from the stage, where an actor's *part* is the words or the character assigned to him

All the world's a stage,
And all the men and women merely players
They have their exits and their entrances;
And one man in his time plays many parts
As You Like It, ii, 7
Why is the Past belied with wicked art,
The Future made to play so false a part?
WORDSWORTH *The Warning*, 140.

To take part. To assist, to participate
But Lilia pleased me, for she took no part
In our dispute
TENNYSON *The Princess, Conclusion*, 29

To take the part of To side with, to support the cause of

A man of parts An accomplished man, one who is clever, talented, or of high intellectual ability

Low in the world, because he scorns its arts.
A man of letters, manners, morals, parts,
Unpatronised, and therefore little known
COWPER *Tirocinium*, 672

Parting cup. *See* STIRRUP CUP

The parting of the ways. Said of a critical moment when one has to choose between two different courses of action. The allusion of course, is to a place at which a road branches off in different directions.

For the difficulties in which we find ourselves now, the parting of the ways was in 1853, when the Emperor Nicholas's proposals were rejected —LORD SALISBURY *Speech* (Jan 19th, 1897).

Partant pour la Syrie (par' tong poor la sir' ē) The favourite march of the French troops in the Second Empire The words were by Count Alexander de Laborde (1810), and the music—attributed to Queen Hortense, mother of Napoleon III—was probably by the flautist Philippe Drouet The ballad tells how young Dunois followed his lord to Syria, and prayed the Virgin "that he might prove the bravest warrior, and love the fairest maiden " Afterwards the count said to Dunois, "To thee we owe the victory, and my daughter I give to thee " The refrain was *Amour a la plus belle, honneur au plus vaillant*

Parthenon (par' thé non). The great temple at Athens to Athene *Parthenos* (*i.e.* the Virgin), many of the sculptured friezes and fragments of pediments of which are now in the British Museum among the Elgin Marbles (*q v*) The Temple was begun by the architect Ictinus about 450 B C , and the embellishment of it was mainly the work of Phidias, whose colossal chryselephantine statue of Athene was its chief treasure.

Parthenope (par then' ō pǐ). Naples, so called from Parthenope, the siren, who threw herself into the sea out of love for Ulysses, and was cast up in the bay of Naples.

Parthenopean Republic The transitory Republic of Naples, established with the aid of the French in Jan. 1799, and overthrown by the Allies in the following June, when the Bourbons were restored.

Particularists. Those who hold the doctrine of *particular* election and redemption, *i e.* the election and redemption of some, not all, of the human race

Partington. Dame Partington and her mop. A taunt against those who try to withstand progress Sydney Smith, speaking on the Lords' rejection of the Reform Bill, October, 1831, compares them to Dame Partington with her mop, trying to push back the Atlantic. "She was excellent," he says, 'at a slop or puddle, but should never have meddled with a tempest "

The story is that a Mrs Partington had a cottage on the shore at Sidmouth, Devon In November, 1824, a heavy gale drove the waves into her house, and the old lady laboured with a mop to sop the water up

B. P. Shillaber, the American humorist, published the *Life and Sayings of Mrs Partington* (1854), the old lady—like Mrs Malaprop—constantly misusing words

Partition of Poland. *See* POLAND.

Partlet. The hen in Chaucer's *Nun's Priest's Tale*, and in *Reynard the Fox* (*q v*) A partlet was a ruff worn in the 16th century by women, and the reference is to the frill-like feathers round the neck of certain hens

In the barn the tenant cock
Close to partlet perched on high.
CUNNINGHAM.

Sister Partlet with her hooded head, allegorizes the cloistered community of nuns in Dryden's *Hind and Panther*, where the Roman Catholic clergy are likened to barnyard fowls

Partridge. Always partridge! *See* PERDRIX

St. Partridges' Day September 1st, the first day of partridge shooting

Parturiunt montes (par tū' ri ent mon' tēz). *Parturiunt montes, nascetur ridiculus mus.* The mountain was in labour, etc. *See under* MOUNTAIN

Party. Person or persons under consideration ' This is the next party, your worship"—*i.e* the next case to be examined "This is the party that stole the things"—the person or persons accused.

If an evil spirit trouble any, one must make a smoke . and the party shall be no more vexed.—*Tobit* vi, 7,

As a Victorian colloquialism party was synonymous with *person*, as—' That dull old party in the corner "

Parvenu (par' ve nū) (Fr , arrived) An upstart, one who has risen from the ranks. The word was made popular in France by Marivaux' *Paysan Parvenu* (1735)

The insolence of the successful *parvenu* is only the necessary continuance of the career of the needy struggler.—THACKERAY: *Pendennis*, II, xxi.

Parvis (par' vis) (*Paravisus*, a Low Latin corruption of *paradisus*, a church close, especially the court in front of St Peter's at Rome in the Middle Ages) The "place" or court before the main entrance of a cathedral In the parvis of St. Paul's lawyers used to meet for consultation, as brokers do in exchange The word is now applied to the room above the church porch.

> A sergeant of lawe, war and wys,
> That often hadde ben atte parvys.
> CHAUCER. *Canterbury Tales.*

Parsival. *See* PERCIVAL.

Pasch. Easter, from the Greek form of the Hebrew *Pesatch*, passover

Pasch eggs. Easter eggs, given as an emblem of the Resurrection

Pasha (päsh' a) A Turkish title borne by governors of provinces and certain military and civil officers of high rank There were three grades of pashas, which were distinguished by the number of horse-tails carried before them and planted in front of their tents The highest rank were those of *three tails*, the grand vizier was always such a pasha, as also were commanding generals and admirals, generals of division, etc , were pashas of *two tails*, and generals of brigades, rear admirals, and petty provincial governors were pashas of *one tail*

Pasht. *See* BUBASTIS

Pasiphæ (päs' i fē). In Greek legend, a daughter of the Sun and wife of Minos, King of Crete She was the mother of Ariadne, and also through intercourse with a white bull (given by Poseidon to Minos) of the Minotaur (*q v.*).

Pasque Eggs *See* PASCH EGGS.

Pasquinade (pas kwin ād') A lampoon or political squib, having ridicule for its object, so called from Pasquino, an Italian tailor of the 15th century, noted for his caustic wit Some time after his death, a mutilated statue was dug up, representing Ajax supporting Menelaus, or Menelaus carrying the body of Patroclus, or else a gladiator, and was placed at the end of the Braschi Palace near the Piazza Navona As it was not clear what the statue represented, and as it stood opposite Pasquin's house, it came to be called "Pasquin." The Romans affixed their political, religious, and personal satires to it, hence the name. At the other end of Rome was an ancient statue of

Mars, called *Marforio*, to which were affixed replies to the Pasquinades

> Then the procession started, took the way
> From the New Prisons by the Pilgrim's Street
> The street of the Governo, Pasquin's Street
> (Where was stuck up, 'mid other epigrams,
> A quatrain   but of all that, presently!)
> BROWNING   *The Ring and the Book*, xii, 137.

Pass A pass or A common pass. At the Universities, an ordinary degree, without honours A candidate getting this is called a *passman*.

To pass the buck. To evade responsibility An American phrase, coming from the game of poker The "buck," perhaps a piece of buckshot or a bucktail, was passed from one player to another as a reminder that the recipient was to be the next dealer The earliest recorded use of the phrase is by Mark Twain in 1872

Passing Bell. *See* BELL

Passepartout (pas' par too) (Fr , pass everywhere) A master-key, also a simple kind of picture-frame in which the picture is placed between a sheet of cardboard and a piece of glass, the whole being held together by strips of paper pasted over the edges

Passim (päs' im) (Lat , here and there, in many places) A direction often found in annotated books which tells the reader that reference to the matter in hand will be found in many passages in the book mentioned

Passion, The. The sufferings of Jesus Christ which had their culmination in His death on the cross

Passion Flower. A plant of the genus *Passiflora*, whose flowers bear a fancied resemblance to the instruments of the Passion *Cp* PIKE'S HEAD It seems to have first got its name in mediæval Spain

> The *leaf* symbolizes the spear
> The *five anthers*, the five wounds
> The *tendrils*, the cords or whips.
> The column of the *ovary*, the pillar of the cross
> The *stamens*, the hammers
> The three *styles*, the three nails
> The *fleshy threads* within the flowers, the crown of thorns
> The *calyx*, the glory or nimbus
> The *white* tint, purity
> The *blue* tint, heaven.

It keeps open three days, symbolizing the three years' ministry.

Passion Play A development of the mediæval mystery play with especial reference to the story of Our Lord's passion and death The best known survival of such plays, which were common in France in the 14th century, is the Oberammergau Passion Play which takes place every ten years In 1633 the Black Death swept over the village of Oberammergau; when it abated the inhabitants vowed to enact the scenes of the Passion every ten years. This has been done at the end of every decade with only one or two failures. Though the cast is still chosen exclusively from inhabitants of the village, the play is no longer the simple expression of piety but has become a highly commercial undertaking, in a special theatre with all the embellishments of costume and properties and an audience drawn thither from all parts of the world.

Passion Sunday. *See* JUDICA.

Passionists. Members of the Congregation of Discalced Clerks of the Passion of Our Lord, founded by St Paul of the Cross in 1728 at Monte Argentoro, an island off the coast of Tuscany, for the purpose of giving retreats and holding missions. The monks wear on the breast of their black cassocks a heart surmounted by a cross and the inscription *Jesu Xpi Passio*, worked in white

Passover (pas' ō ver). A Jewish festival to commemorate the deliverance of the Israelites, when the angel of death (that slew the firstborn of the Egyptians) *passed over* their houses, and spared all who did as Moses commanded them It is held from the 15th to the 22nd of the first month, Nisan, i e about April 13th to 20th

Passport. A safe conduct issued by the authorities of a nation to its citizens, and required to be produced when crossing national frontiers Passports were in wide use by the 18th century, but by the mid-19th century were almost obsolete They were re-introduced with the outbreak of World War I in 1914

Passy-measure Pavin. *See* PAVAN.

Paston Letters. A series of letters (with wills, leases, and other documents) written by or to members of the Paston family in Norfolk between the years 1440 and 1486 They passed from the Earl of Yarmouth to Peter le Neve, antiquary, then to Thomas Martin (1697-1771), known as Honest Tom Martin, of Palgrave, Suffolk, and eventually passed to Sir John Fenn, who, in 1787, edited two volumes of them as *Original Letters written during the Reigns of Henry VI, Edward IV, and Richard III by various Persons of Rank* In 1872-5 James Gairdner re-edited them in three volumes, and included some 500 additional letters besides a voluminous introduction and notes The *Letters* are an invaluable source of information concerning the customs and business methods of the upper middle classes of 15th-century England

Patch. A fool, so called originally from the nickname of Cardinal Wolsey's jester, Sexton, who got this nickname either from Ital *pazzo*, a fool, or from the motley or patched dress worn by licensed fools

> What a pied ninny's this' thou scurvy patch'
> *The Tempest*, iii, 2.

Cross-patch. An ill-tempered person.

Not a patch upon. Not to be compared with, as, "His horse is not a patch upon mine."

To patch up a quarrel To arrange the matter in a not very satisfactory way, a coat that has been torn and then "patched up" is pretty sure to break out again, so is a quarrel.

Patent (through Fr from Lat. *patentem*, lying open) Open to the perusal of anybody. A thing that is *patented* is protected by letters patent

Letters patent. Documents from the sovereign or a crown office conferring a title, right, privilege, etc , such as a title of nobility, or the exclusive right to make or sell for a given number of years some new invention. So called because they are written upon open sheets of parchment, with the seal of the sovereign or party by whom they were issued pendent at the bottom

Patent Rolls Letters patent collected together on parchment rolls They extend from 1210, and each roll contains a year, though in some cases the roll is subdivided into two or more parts Each sheet of parchment is numbered, and called a *membrane*; for example, the 8th sheet, say, of the 10th year of Henry III is cited thus. "Pat 10 Hen. III, m. 8 " If the document is on the back of the roll it is called dorso, and "d" is added to the citation. *Cp.* CLOSE ROLLS

Paternoster (păt' ĕr nos' tĕr) ‾ (Lat , Our Father) The Lord's Prayer, from the first two words in the Latin version Every tenth bead of a rosary is so called, because at that bead the Lord's Prayer is repeated; and the name is also given to a certain kind of fishing tackle, in which hooks and weights to sink them are fixed alternately on the line, somewhat in rosary fashion

A paternoster-while. Quite a short time; the times it takes one to say a paternoster.

To say the devil's paternoster. *See* DEVIL

Paternoster Row (London) was probably so named from the rosary or paternoster makers There is mention as early as 1374 of a Richard Russell, a "paternosterer," who dwelt there, and we read of "one Robert Nikke, a paternoster maker and citizen," in the reign of Henry IV. Another suggestion is that it was so called because funeral processions on their way to St. Paul's began their *pater noster* at the beginning of the Row For over three centuries Paternoster Row was the home of publishers and booksellers It was totally destroyed in an air raid at the end of December, 1940.

Pathfinder. One of the names of Natty Bumpo (q v) in Fenimore Cooper's Leatherstocking Novels (*q.v.*). It was given to the American Major-General John Charles Fremont (1813-90), who conducted four expeditions across the Rocky Mountains.

Pathfinders. In World War II a R.A.F. term for specially skilled pilots and navigators who flew in first and dropped flares to identify the target for the benefit of the attacking force which followed them

Patient Grisel. *See* GRISELDA.

Patmos (păt' mos) The island of the Sporades in the Ægean Sea (now called *Patmo* or *Patino*) to which St. John retired—or was exiled (*Rev.* i, 9) Hence the name is used allusively for a place of banishment or solitude

Patois (păt' wa) Dialect peculiarity, provincialism in speech It is a 13th-century French word of unknown origin

Patres Conscripti. *See* CONSCRIPT FATHERS.

Patriarch (Gr. *patria*, family, *archean*, to rule) The head of a tribe or family who rules by paternal right, applied specially (after *Acts* vii, 8) to the twelve sons of Jacob, and to Abraham,

Isaac, and Jacob and their forefathers In one passage (*Acts* 11, 29) David also is spoken of as a patriarch

In the early Church "Patriarch," first mentioned in the council of Chalcedon, but virtually existing from about the time of the council of Nice, was the title of the highest of Church officers. He ordained metropolitans, convened councils, received appeals, and was the chief bishop over several countries or provinces, as an archbishop is over several dioceses It was also the title given by the popes to the archbishops of Lisbon and Venice, in order to make the patriarchal dignity appear distinct from and lower than the papal, and is that of the chief bishop of various Eastern rites, as the Jacobites, Armenians, and Maronites

In the Orthodox Eastern Church the bishops of Constantinople, Alexandria, Antioch, and Jerusalem are patriarchs Within a religious order the title is given to the founder, as St Benedict, St Francis, and St Dominic

Patrician. Properly speaking, one of the *patres* (fathers) or senators of Rome (*see* PATRES CONSCRIPTI), and their descendants As they held for many years all the honours of the state, the word came to signify the magnates or nobility of a nation, the aristocrats.

Patrick, St. The apostle and patron saint of Ireland (commemorated on March 17th) was not an Irishman, but was born at what is now Dumbarton (about 373), his father, Calpurnius, a deacon and Roman official, having come from "Bannavem Taberniæ," which was probably near the mouth of the Severn. As a boy he was captured in a Pictish raid and sold as a slave in Ireland. He escaped to Gaul about 395, where he studied under St Martin at Tours before returning to Britain There he had a supernatural call to preach to the heathen of Ireland, so he was consecrated and in 432 landed at Wicklow He at first met with strong opposition, but, going north, he converted first the chiefs and people of Ulster, and later those of the rest of Ireland He founded many churches, including the cathedral and monastery of Armagh, where he held two synods He is said to have died at Armagh (about 464) and to have been buried either at Down or Saul—though one tradition gives Glastonbury as the place of his death and burial Downpatrick cathedral claims his supposed grave which is covered with a massive slab of granite, for which Irishmen of every creed subscribed.

St Patrick left his name to countless places in Great Britain and Ireland, and many legends are told of his miraculous powers—healing the blind, raising the dead, etc Perhaps the best known tradition is that he cleared Ireland of its vermin.

The story goes that one old serpent resisted him, but he overcame it by cunning He made a box, and invited the serpent to enter it The serpent objected, saying it was too small, but St Patrick insisted it was quite large enough to be comfortable After a long contention, the serpent got in to prove it was too small, when St Patrick slammed down the lid, and threw the box into the sea

In commemoration of this St Patrick is usually represented banishing the serpents, and with a shamrock leaf, in allusion to the tradition that when explaining the Trinity to the heathen priests on the hill of Tara he used this as a symbol

St Patrick's Cross. The same shape as St Andrew's Cross (X), only different in colour, viz red on a white field.

St. Patrick's Purgatory. A cave in a small island in Lough Derg (between Galway, Clare, and Tipperary) In the Middle Ages it was a favourite resort of pilgrims who believed that it was the entrance to an earthly purgatory. The legend is that Christ Himself revealed it to St Patrick and told him that whoever would spend a day and a night therein would witness the torments of hell and the joys of heaven Henry of Saltrey tells how Sir Owain (*q v*) visited it, and Fortunatus, of the old legend, was also one of the adventurers. It was blocked up by order of the Pope on St Patrick's Day, 1497, but the interest in it long remained, and the Spanish dramatist Calderon (d 1681) has a play on the subject—*El Purgatorio de San Patricia*

Why should all your chimney-sweepers be Irishmen?

Faith, that's soon answered, for St Patrick, you know, keeps purgatory, he makes the fire, and his countrymen could do nothing if they cannot sweep the chimneys —DEKKER: *Honest Whore*, Pt II, I, 1

The Order of St Patrick. A British order of knighthood, instituted by George III in 1783 and revised in 1905, consisting of the Sovereign, the Lord Lieutenant (as Grand Master), and twenty-two knights Its motto is *Quis Separabit?* In 1952 the Order consisted of the Sovereign and five knights

Patriots' Day, in U S A the anniversary of the battle of Lexington, April 19th, 1775, the first battle in the War of Independence It is a public holiday in Massachusetts and Maine.

Patroclus (pá trok' lůs) The gentle and amiable friend of Achilles, in Homer's *Iliad* When Achilles refused to fight in order to annoy Agamemnon, Patroclus appeared in Achilles's armour at the head of the Myrmidons, and was slain by Hector.

Patroon (pa troon') An old term for a landowner in New Jersey and New York when they belonged to the Dutch The patroon had certain manorial rights and privileges under a government grant

Patter. To chatter, to clack, also the running talk of cheap Jacks, conjurers, etc , is from *Paternoster* (*q v.*) When saying Mass the priest recites it in a low, rapid, mechanical way till he comes to the words, "and lead us not into temptation," which he speaks aloud, and the choir responds, "but deliver us from evil " In the Anglican Prayer Book, the priest is directed to say the whole prayer "with a *loud* voice."

Patter, the patter of feet, of rain, etc , is not connected with the above It is a frequentative of *pat*, to strike gently

Pattern. From the same root as *patron* (Lat. *pater*, father) As a *patron* ought to be an example, so pattern has come to signify a model

Paul. St Paul. Patron saint of preachers and tentmakers (*see Acts* xviii, 3). Originally called

Saul, his name, according to tradition, was changed in honour of Sergius Paulus, whom he converted (*Acts* xiii, 6-12).

His symbols are a sword and open book, the former the instrument of his martyrdom, and the latter indicative of the new law propagated by him as the apostle of the Gentiles He is represented of short stature, with bald head and grey, bushy beard, and legend relates that when he was beheaded at Rome (A D 66), after having converted one of Nero's favourite concubines, milk instead of blood flowed from his veins. He is commemorated on June 29th

A Paul's man. A braggart; a captain out of service, with a long rapier, so called because the Walk down the centre of old St Paul's, London, was at one time the haunt of stale knights These loungers were also known as *Paul's Walkers* Jonson called Bobadil (*q v*) a Paul's man, and in his *Every Man out of his Humour* (1599) is a variety of scenes in the interior of St Paul's

Paul's Cross A pulpit in the open air situated on the north side of old St Paul's Cathedral, in which, from 1259-1643, eminent divines preached in the presence of the Lord Mayor and Aldermen every Sunday Upon its site a new pulpit and cross were erected in 1910

St Paul the Hermit. The first of the Egyptian hermits When 113 years old he was visited by St Antony, himself over 90, and when he died in 341 St Antony wrapped his body in the cloak given to him by St. Athanasius, and his grave was dug by two lions His day is Jan. 15th, and he is represented as an old man, clothed with palm-leaves, and seated under a palm-tree, near which are a river and loaf of bread

Paul Pry. *See* PRY.

Pavan or **Pavin** (pa'van) A stately Spanish dance of the 16th and 17th centuries, said to be so called because in it the dancers stalked like peacocks (Lat *pavones*), the gentlemen with their long robes of office, and the ladies with trains like peacocks' tails. The pavan, like the minuet, ended with a quick movement called the *galliard*, a sort of gavotte

Every pavan has its galliard. Every sage has his moments of folly. Every white must have its black, and every sweet its sour

Passy-measures pavin. A reeling dance or motion, like that of a drunken man, from side to side The tipsy Sir Toby Belcher says of "Dick surgeon"—

He's a rogue and a passy-measures pavin I hate a drunken rogue —*Twelfth Night*, v, 1

The **passy-measure** was a slow dance, the Italian *passamezzo* (a middle pace or step) Also called a *cinque measure*, because it consisted of five measures—"two singles and a double forward, with two singles side "

Pawnbroker's Sign, The *See* BALLS, THE THREE GOLDEN

Pawnee (paw' nee) Anglo-Indian for water (Hind *pani*, water)

Brandy pawnee. Brandy and water

Pax (päks) (Lat , peace). The "kiss of peace," which is given at High Mass It is omitted on Maundy Thursday

Also a sacred utensil used when mass is celebrated by a high dignitary. It is sometimes a crucifix, sometimes a tablet, and sometimes a reliquary, and is handed round to be kissed as a symbolic substitute for the "kiss of peace "

The old custom of "kissing the bride," which took place immediately before the Communion of the newly married couple and still obtains in some churches, is derived from the Salisbury rubric concerning the Pax in the Missa Sponsalium —

Tunc amoto pallio, surgant ambo sponsus et sponsa, et accipiat sponsus pacem a sacerdote, et ferat sponsæ osculans eam et neminem alium, nec ipse, nec ipsa, sed statim diaconus vel clericus a presbytero pacem accipiens, ferat aliis sicut solitum est.

Pax! The schoolboy's cry of truce

Pax Britannica. The peace imposed by British rule The phrase is modelled on the Latin *Pax Romana*, the peace existing between the different members of the Roman empire

Pax vobis (cum) (Peace be unto you) The formula used by a bishop instead of "The Lord be with you," wherever this versicle occurs in Divine service They are the words used by Christ to His Apostles on the first Easter morning.

Pay, to discharge a debt, is through O Fr. *paier*, from the Latin *pax*, peace, by way of *pacare*, to appease The nautical *pay*, to cover with hot tar for waterproofing, represents Lat. *picare*, from *pix*, pitch

Here's the devil to pay, and no pitch hot. *See* DEVIL

I'll pay him out. I'll be a match for him, I'll punish him

They with a foxe-tale him soundly did paye
The King and Northern Man (1640).

To pay out a rope is to let it out gradually by slackening it

To pay off old scores *See* SCORE

To pay with the roll of the drum. Not to pay at all No soldier can be arrested for debt when on the march

How happy the soldier who lives on his pay,
And spends half-a-crown out of sixpence a day,
He cares not for justices, beadles, or bum,
But pays all his debts with the roll of the drum
O'KEEFE

Who's to pay the piper? Who is to pay the score ? The phrase may come from the story of the Pied Piper (*q v*), who agreed to rid Hamelin city of rats and mice, and when he had done so was refused his pay An older and more probable derivation goes back to the piper who used to amuse guests at inns or on the green, and expected his payment for the entertainment

You can put paid to that. You can treat it as finished, it's all over, done with. A phrase from the counting-house; when "Paid" is put to an account it is finished with

Pay dirt. A mining term for ground which pays for working

P.A.Y.E. The initials of Pay As You Earn, a system of collecting Income Tax from weekly earnings, introduced in Britain in 1944. The employer is furnished with a guiding table in accordance with which the proper tax is deducted before wages or salary are paid, and he is responsible to the Income Tax authorities for the sum thus collected

Paynim (pā' nim), from the O Fr *paienime*, Lat *paganismus*, a heathen, was the recognized chivalric term for a Moslem

Peabody Buildings or Dwellings. In 1843 George Peabody (1795-1869), a successful American dealer in dry goods, set up in London as a banker and merchant He amassed a fortune and founded in London the Peabody Dwellings for workmen and their families These were a great boon to the overcrowded slum-dwellers who in the accommodation thus offered them found an opportunity of retaining their self-respect and bringing up a family in comparative comfort and decent surroundings

Peace. A Bill of Peace. A Bill intended to secure relief from perpetual litigation It is brought by one who wishes to establish and perpetuate a right which he claims, but which, from its nature, is controversial

Peace Ballot. On June 27th, 1935, the League of Nations Union took a national ballot in Britain on certain questions regarding peace and disarmament 11,640,066 votes were recorded in favour of adherence to the League of Nations, and over ten million voted for a reduction of armaments The ballot was interpreted by the Axis powers as a sign of weakness indicating the unwillingness of the British people to go to war in any circumstances and this strengthened the determination of Hitler to stand out for his territorial and other demands

If you want peace, prepare for war A translation of the Latin proverb, *Si vis pacem, para bellum* It goes a step farther than the advice given by Polonius to his son (*Hamlet*, I, iii), for you are told, whether you are "in a quarrel" or not, always to bear yourself so that all possible opposers "may beware of thee."

Peace at any price. Lord Palmerston sneered at the Quaker statesman, John Bright, as a "peace-at-any-price man " *Cp* CONCHY
> Though not a "peace-at-any-price" man, I am not ashamed to say I am a peace-at-almost-any-price man
> —LORD AVEBURY *The Use of Life*, xi (1849)

Peace with honour. A phrase popularized by Lord Beaconsfield on his return from the Congress of Berlin (1878), when he said —
> Lord Salisbury and myself have brought you back peace—but a peace I hope with honour, which may satisfy our Sovereign and tend to the welfare of the country.

It is, of course, much older than this Shakespeare uses it more than once, *e g* .—
> We have made peace
> With no less honour to the Antiates
> Than shame to the Romans
> *Coriolanus*, v, 5.

And Pepys writes in his *Diary* on May 25th, 1663 —
> With peace and honour I am willing to spare anything so as to keep all ends together

Peace in our time. Phrase used by Neville Chamberlain, Prime Minister, on his return from Munich on September 30th, 1938, when he imagined that by giving way to Hitler he had averted war

The King's peace. The general peace of law-abiding subjects, originally the protection secured by the king to those employed on his business.
> To kill an alien, a Jew, or an outlaw, who are all under the king's peace or protection, is as much murder as to kill the most regular born Englishmen —
> *Blackstone's Commentaries*, IV, xiv

The kiss of peace. *See* PAX

The Perpetual Peace. The peace concluded June 24th, 1502, between England and Scotland, whereby Margaret, daughter of Henry VII, was betrothed to James IV, a few years afterwards the battle of Flodden Field was fought The name has also been given to other treaties, as that between Austria and Switzerland in 1474, and between France and Switzerland in 1516

To keep the peace. To refrain from disturbing the public peace or doing anything that might result in strife or commotion Wrong-doers are sometimes bound over to keep the peace for a certain time by a magistrate; a specified sum of money is deposited, and if the man commits a breach of the peace during that time he is not only arrested but his deposit is forfeit.

Peach. To inform, to "split", a contraction of *impeach*. The word is one of those that has degenerated into slang after being in perfectly good use

Peacock. By the peacock! An obsolete oath which at one time was thought blasphemous. The fabled incorruptibility of the peacock's flesh caused the bird to be adopted as a type of the resurrection
There is a story that when George III had partly recovered from one of his attacks of insanity his Ministers got him to read the King's Speech, and he ended every sentence with the word *peacock*. The Minister who drilled him said that *peacock* was an excellent word for ending a sentence, only kings should not let subjects hear it, but should whisper it softly The result was a perfect success, and the pause at the close of each sentence had an excellent effect

The peacock's feather. An emblem of vain-glory, and in some Eastern countries a mark of rank.
As a literary term the expression is used of a borrowed ornament of style spatchcocked into the composition, the allusion being to the fable of the jay who decked herself out in peacock's feathers, making herself an object of ridicule
The peacock's tail is an emblem of an Evil Eye, or an ever-vigilant traitor hence the feathers are considered unlucky, and the superstitious will not have them in the house The classical legend is that Argus (*see* ARGUS-EYED), who had 100 eyes, was changed into a peacock by Juno, the eyes forming the beautifully coloured disks in the tail.

Pea-jacket. A rough overcoat worn by seamen, etc ; probably from the Dutch *pig* or *pije*, a coarse thick cloth or felt The "courtepy," the short (Fr *court*) jacket worn by Chaucer's "Clerk of Oxenford," is from the same word —

> Ful thredbare was his overest courtepy,
> For he had getten him yet no benefyce
> *Canterbury Tales Prologue*, 290

Peal To ring a peal is to ring 5,040 changes on a set of 8 bells , any number of changes less than that is technically called a *touch* or *flourish* Bells are first *raised*, and then *pealed*.

> This society rung . a true and complete peal of 5,040 grandsire triples in three hours and fourteen minutes —*Inscription in Windsor Curfew Tower*

Pearls. Dioscorides and Pliny mention the belief that pearls are formed by drops of rain falling into the oyster-shells while open, the raindrops thus received being hardened into pearls by some secretions of the animal

Cardan says (*De Rerum Varietate*, vii, 34) that pearls are polished by being pecked and played with by doves

> The liquid drops of tears that you have shed
> Shall come again, transform'd to orient pearl
> *Richard III*, iv, 4

Pearls are believed to be the result of an abnormal secretory process caused by an irritation of the mollusk consequent on the intrusion into the shell of some foreign body, as a grain of sand, an egg of the mollusk itself, or perhaps some cercarian parasite — G F KING *Gems, etc* , ch xii.

Cleopatra (*q.v*) and Sir Thomas Gresham are said to have dissolved pearls in wine by way of making an ostentatious display of wealth, and a similar act of vanity and folly is told by Horace (2 *Satire*, iii, 239). Clodius, son of Æsop the tragedian, drew a pearl of great value from his ear, melted it in vinegar, and drank to the health of Cecilia Metella This story is referred to by Valerius Maximus, Macrobius, and Pliny. Horace says,

> Qui sanior, ac si
> Illud idem in rapidum flumen jaceretve cloacam?

> How say you? had the act been more insane
> To fling it in a river or a drain?
> CONINGTON's *tr*

The Pearl Coast So the early Spanish explorers named the Venezuelan coast from Cumana to Trinidad, the islands off this coast were called the *Pearl Islands* This district was the site of large pearl-fisheries

Peasants' War, The. The name given to the insurrections of the peasantry of southern Germany in the early 16th century, especially to that of 1524 in Swabia, Franconia, Saxony, and other German states, in consequence of the tyranny and oppression of the nobles, which was ended by the battle of Frankenhausen (1525), when many thousands of the peasants were slain In 1502 was the rebellion called the *Laced Shoe*, from its cognizance, in 1514, the *League of Poor Conrad*, in 1523, the *Latin War*

Peascod. Winter for shoeing, peascod for wooing. The allusion in the latter clause is to the custom of placing a peascod with nine peas in it on the door-lintel, under the notion that the first man who entered through the door would be the husband of the person

who did so Another custom is alluded to by Browne—

> The peascod greene oft with no little toyle
> Hee'd seeke for in the fattest, fertil'st soile,
> And rend it from the stalke to bring it to her
> And in her bosome for acceptance woo her
> *Britannia's Pastoral*

Pec. Old Eton slang for money. A contraction of the Latin *pecunia*.

Peccavi (pe kā´ vī) **To cry peccavi.** To acknowledge oneself in the wrong It is said that Sir Charles Napier, after the battle of Hyderabad, in 1843, sent a preliminary despatch with the single word "Peccavi" (I have sinned, *i.e* Sinde)

Peckish Hungry, or desirous of something to eat Of course "peck" refers to fowls, etc., which peck their food

> When shall I feel peckish again —DISRAELI *Sybil*, Bk vi, ch iii

Pecker. Keep your pecker up. As the mouth is in the head, *pecker* (the mouth) means the head; and to "keep your pecker up," means to keep your head up, or, more familiarly, "keep your chin up", "never say die."

Peckham. All holiday at Peckham—*i e* no appetite, not peckish, a pun on the word peck, as going to Bedfordshire is a pun on the word bed.

Going to Peckham. Going to dinner

Pecksniff. A canting hypocrite, who speaks homilies of morality, does the most heartless things "as a duty to society," and forgives wrongdoing in nobody but himself. (Dickens *Martin Chuzzlewit*)

Pecos Bill (pe´ kos) A cowboy of American legend who performed superhuman prodigies on the frontier in early days One of his feats was to dig the Rio Grande river.

Pectoral Cross. *See* CRUX PECTORALIS

Peculiar. A parish or church which was exempt from episcopal jurisdiction, as a royal chapel, etc Peculiars were abolished in 1849

The Court of Peculiars A branch of the Court of Arches which had jurisdiction over the "peculiars" of the archbishop of Canterbury *See above*

The Peculiar People Properly, the Jews— the ' Chosen people", but taken as a title by a sect founded in 1838, the chief characteristic of which is that its members refuse all medical aid and, as a consequence, are frequently in conflict with the authorities They have a strong belief in the efficacy of prayer, subscribe to no creed and have no recognized preachers or clergy The name is based on *Titus* ii, 14—"to purify unto himself a peculiar people "

Pecuniary. From *pecus*, cattle, especially sheep. Varo says that sheep were the ancient medium of barter and standard of value Ancient coin was marked with the image of an ox or sheep

Pedagogue (Gr. *pais*, boy, *agein*, to lead) A "boy-leader," hence, a schoolmaster—now usually one who is pompous and pedantic In ancient Greece the *pedagogos* was a slave whose duty it was to attend his master's son whenever he left home

Pedlar is not a tramp who goes on his feet, as if from the Lat *pedes*, feet The name is probably from the *ped*, a hamper without a lid in which are stored fish or other articles to hawk about the streets In Norwich there is a place called the Ped-market, where women used to expose eggs, butter, cheese, etc, in open hampers

Pedlar's Acre. According to tradition, a pedlar of Lambeth parish left a sum of money, on condition that his picture, with a dog, should be preserved for ever in glass in one of the church windows In the south window of the middle aisle, sure enough, such a picture exists, but probably it is a rebus on *Chapman*, the name of some benefactor In Swaffham church there is a portrait of one John Chapman, a great benefactor, who is represented as a pedlar with his pack, and in that town a similar tradition exists.

Pedlars' French The jargon or cant of thieves, rogues, and vagabonds "French" was formerly widely used to denote anything or anyone that was foreign, and even Bracton uses the word "Frenchman" as a synonym of foreigner

Instead of Pedlars' French, gives him plain language —BEAUMONT AND FLETCHER *Faithful Friends*, i, 2

Peeler Slang for a policeman; first applied to the Irish Constabulary founded when Sir Robert Peel was Chief Secretary (1812-18), and afterwards, when Peel as Home Secretary introduced the Metropolitan Police Act (1829), to the English policeman. *Cp* BOBBY In the 16th century the word was applied to robbers, from *peel* (later *pill*), to plunder, strip of possessions, rob Holinshed, in his *Scottish Chronicle* (1570), refers to Patrick Dunbar, who "delivered the countrie of these peelers" *Cp* also Milton s *Paradise Regained*, iv 136 —

That people   . who, once just,
Frugal, and mild, and temperate, conquered well
But govern ill the nations under yoke,
Peeling their provinces, exhausted all
By lust and rapine

Peelites was the name given to the Conservative adherents of Sir Robert Peel when he introduced a Bill for the repeal of the Corn Laws in 1846.

Peep-o'-Day Boys. The Irish Protestant faction in Ulster of about 1786; they were precursors of the Orangemen (*q v*), and were active from the period mentioned, so called because they used to visit the houses of their Roman Catholic opponents (called *Defenders*) at "peep of day" searching for arms or plunder

Peeping Tom of Coventry. *See* GODIVA, LADY

Peers of the Realm. The five orders of Duke, Marquess, Earl, Viscount, and Baron (*see these names*) The word peer is from the Latin *pares* (equals), and in feudal times all great vassals were held equal in rank

The Twelve Peers of Charlemagne. *See* PALADINS

Peg. A square peg in a round hole One who is doing (or trying to do) a job for which he is not suited, *e g* a bishop refereeing a prize-fight.

I am a peg too low. I am low-spirited, moody, I want another draught to cheer me up Our Saxon ancestors used tankards with pegs inserted at equal intervals, so that when two or more drank from the same bowl no one might exceed his fair proportion (*cp* PIN—*In merry pin*) We are told that St. Dunstan introduced the fashion to prevent brawling

Come, old fellow, drink down to your peg'
But do not drink any farther, I beg
LONGFELLOW *Golden Legend*, iv.

To peg away at it. To stick at it persistently, in spite of difficulties and discouragement

To take one down a peg. To take the conceit out of a braggart or pretentious person The allusion here is not to peg-tankards, but to a ship s colours, which used to be raised and lowered by pegs; the higher the colours are raised the greater the honour, and to take them down a peg would be to award less honour

Trepanned your party with intrigue,
And took your grandees down a peg
BUTLER *Hudibras*, ii, 2

Well, he has come down a peg or two, and he don't like it —HAGGARD

Pegasus (peg' a sus) The winged horse on which Bellerophon (*q v*) rode against the Chimæra When the Muses contended with the daughters of Pieros, Helicon rose heavenward with delight, but Pegasus gave it a kick, stopped its ascent, and brought out of the mountain the soul-inspiring waters of Hippocrene, hence, the name is used for the inspiration of poetry

Then who so will with vertuous deeds assay
To mount to heaven, on Pegasus must ride,
And with sweete Poets verse be glorified
SPENSER *Rumes of Time*, 425

Now, if my Pegasus should not be shod ill,
This poem will become a moral model
BYRON *Don Juan*, V, ii

In World War II the horse, with Bellerophon on his back, in pale blue on a maroon ground, was adopted as the insignia of all British Airborne troops

Peine forte et dure (pān fort ā dūr) A species of torture applied to contumacious felons who refused to plead, it usually took the form of pressing the accused to death by weights The following persons were executed in this way — Juliana Quick, in 1442, Anthony Arrowsmith, in 1598, Walter Calverly, 1605, Major Strangways, in 1657, and even in 1741 a person was condemned to this death at the Cambridge assizes. Abolished 1772

Peking Man, The (*Sinanthropos pekinensis*), is the name given to a suppositional primitive man, based on remains found in caves near Pekin in 1927 Bones of some forty individuals were found, showing considerable resemblance to the Pithecanthropos or ape man supposed to have been in some way connected with primitive man, *Homo sapiens* The date of Pekin man is about 1,000,000 years ago, but whether he was an ancestor of the human race is still a matter of conjecture and dispute among anthropologists

Pelagians (pe lā janz) Heretical followers of the British monk Pelagius (a Latinized form of his native Welsh name, *Morgan*, the sea), who in the 4th and early 5th centuries was fiercely opposed by St Augustine, and was condemned by Pope Zosimus in 418 They denied the doctrine of original sin or the taint of Adam, and maintained that we have power of ourselves to receive or reject the Gospel

Pelf. Filthy pelf. Money, usually with a contemptuous implication—as we speak of "filthy lucre," or "Who steals my purse steals *trash* "

> How blest the maid
> Who knows not pomp, who heeds not pelf,
> Whose heaviest sin it is to look
> Askance upon her pretty Self
> Reflected in some crystal brook
>   WORDSWORTH *The Three Cottage Girls.*

The word is from O Fr *pelfre*, connected with our *pilfer*, and was originally used of stolen or pilfered goods, ill-gotten gains

Pelican (pel' ı kan). In Christian art, a symbol of charity, also an emblem of Jesus Christ, by "whose blood we are healed." St. Jerome gives the story of the pelican restoring its young ones destroyed by serpents, and his own salvation by the blood of Christ, and the popular fallacy that pelicans fed their young with their blood arose from the fact that when the parent bird is about to feed its brood, it macerates small fish in the large bag attached to its under bill, then pressing the bag against its breast, transfers the macerated food to the mouths of the young The correct term for the heraldic representation of the bird in this act is a **pelican in her piety**, *piety* having the classical meaning of filial devotion

The mediæval *Bestiary* tells us that the pelican is very fond of its brood, but when the young ones begin to grow they rebel against the male bird and provoke his anger, so that he kills them, the mother returns to the nest in three days, sits on the dead birds, pours her blood over them, revives them, and they feed on the blood

> Than sayd the Pellycane,
> When my byrdis be slayne
> With my bloude I them reuyue [revive]
> Scrypture doth record,
> The same dyd our Lord,
> And rose from deth to lyue
>   SKELTON *Armoury of Birdis*

The **Pelican State** Louisiana, U S A , which has a pelican in its device

Pelion (pē' lı on) **Heaping Pelion upon Ossa.** Adding difficulty to difficulty, embarrassment to embarrassment, etc When the giants tried to scale heaven, they placed Mount Pelion upon Mount Ossa, two peaks in Thessaly, for a scaling ladder (*Odyssey*, xı, 315).

I would have you call to mind the strength of the ancient giants, that undertook to lay the high mountain Pelion on the top of Ossa, and set among those the shady Olympus.—*Rabelais* IV, xxxvııı

Pell-mell Headlong, in reckless confusion From the players of pall-mall (*q v*), who rushed heedlessly to strike the ball

Pelleas, Sir (pel' ē äs) One of the Knights of the Round Table, famed for his great strength. He is introduced into the *Faerie Queene* (VI, xıı) as going after the "blatant beast" when it breaks the chain with which it had been bound by Sir Calidore See also Tennyson's *Pelleas and Ettare.*

Pells. Clerk of the Pells. An officer of the Exchequer, whose duty it was to make entries on the *pells* or parchment rolls. Abolished in 1834

Pelmanism A system of mind and memory training originated by W J. Ennever in the closing years of last century, and so called because it was an easy name to remember Owing to its very extensive advertising, the verb *to pelmanize*, meaning to obtain good results by training the memory, was coined

Pelops (pel' ops) Son of Tantalus, and father of Atreus and Thyestes He was king of Pisa in Elis, and was cut to pieces and served as food to the gods The Morea was called Peloponnesus, the "island of Pelops," from this mythical king.

The ivory shoulder of Pelops The distinguishing or distinctive mark of anyone The tale is that Demeter ate the shoulder of Pelops when it was served up by Tantalus , when the gods put the body back into the cauldron to restore it to life, this portion was lacking, whereupon Demeter supplied one of ivory

> Not Pelops' shoulder whiter than her hands
>   W BROWNE. *Britannia's Pastorals*, ıı, 3.

P E.N. The initials of an international association of poets, playwrights, editors, essayists, and novelists Its principal activity is the organization of annual reunions of literary and artistic men and women in one or other of the European countries.

Pen An interesting word etymologically, for it is the Latin *penna*, a feather, both of which words are derived from the Sanskrit root *pet-*, to fly *Pet-* gave Sansk. *patra* (feather), this became in Lat *penna* (Eng *pen*), and in O Teut *fethro* (Ger. *feder*, Dut *veder*, Eng *feather*) Also, in O Fr *penne* meant both *feather* and *pen*, but in Mod Fr it is restricted to the long wing- and tail-feathers and to heraldic plumes on crests, while *pen* is *plume* Thus, the French and English usage has been vice versa, English using *plume* in heraldry, French using *penne*, the English writing implement being named *pen*, and the French *plume*

Pen-name. A pseudonym *See* NOM DE GUERRE

Penates. *See* DıI PENATES

Pencil. Originally, a painter's brush, and still used of very fine paint-brushes, from Lat. *penicillum*, a paint-brush, diminutive of *peniculus*, a brush, which itself is a diminutive of *penis*, a tail When the modern pencil came into use in the early 17th century it was known as a *dry pencil* or a *pencil with black lead* ¶

Knight of the pencil. A bookmaker, a reporter, also anyone who makes his living by scribbling

Pencil of rays. All the rays that issue from one point or can be formed at one point, so called because a representation of them has the appearance of a pointed pencil

Pendente lite (penden' tı lı' te) (Lat). Pending the trial, while the suit is going on

Pendragon (pen drăg' ŏn) A title conferred on several British chiefs in times of great danger, when they were invested with supreme power, especially (in the Arthurian legends) to Uther

Pendragon, father of King Arthur The word is Welsh *pen*, head. and *dragon* (the reference being to the war-chief's dragon standard), and it corresponded to the Roman *dux bellorum*

A legend recorded by Geoffrey of Monmouth relates that when Aurelius, the British king, was poisoned by Ambron, during the invasion of Pascentius, son of Vortigern, there "appeared a star at Winchester of wonderful magnitude and brightness, darting forth a ray, at the end of which was a globe of fire in form of a dragon, out of whose mouth issued forth two rays, one of which extended to Gaul and the other to Ireland " Uther ordered two golden dragons to be made, one of which he presented to Winchester, and the other he carried with him as his royal standard, whence he received the title "Pendragon."

Penelope (pe nel' ŏ pi) The wife of Ulysses and mother of Telemachus in Homeric legend She was a model of all the domestic virtues.

The Web of Penelope. A work "never ending, still beginning", never done, but ever in hand Penelope, according to Homer, was pestered by suitors at Ithaca while Ulysses was absent at the siege of Troy To relieve herself of their importunities, she promised to make a choice of one as soon as she had finished weaving a shroud for her father-in-law Every night she unravelled what she had done in the day, and so deferred making any choice until Ulysses returned and slew the suitors

Penetralia (pen e trā' li a) (Lat , the innermost parts) The private rooms of a house, the secrets of a family. Properly, the part of a Roman temple to which the priest alone had access, where the sacred images were housed, the responses of the oracles made, and the sacred mysteries performed The Holy of Holies was the *penetralia* of the Jewish Temple

Peninsular War. The war carried on, under the Duke of Wellington, against the French in Portugal and Spain, between 1808 and 1814 It was brought about through the French attack on Spain and Portugal, and, so far as Britain was concerned, was the most important of the Napoleonic Wars. It resulted in the French being driven from the Peninsula

Penitential Psalms The seven psalms expressive of contrition—viz the vi, xxxii, xxxviii, li, cii, cxxx, cxliii From time immemorial they have all been used at the Ash Wednesday services, the first three at Matins, the 51st at the Commination, and the last three at Evensong.

Pennant, Pennon. The former—the long narrow streamer borne at the masthead of warships—is the nautical form of the latter, which was the name of the small pointed or swallow-tailed flag formerly borne on knights' spears, and still carried by lancer regiments on their lances and as their ensign. *Pennon* is from Lat *penna*, a feather (*see* PEN), and *pennant* was formed on it through a confusion with *pendant* (Lat *pendere*, to hang), because it *hangs* from the masthead It is sometimes, but erroneously, taken as representing the "whip" with which, according to the popular story, the English admiral was to defeat Van Tromp when he hoisted a broom to signify his intention of sweeping the ships of England off the seas.

Pennsylvania Dutch is the name given to the descendants of the settlers from South-west Germany who took up their abode in Pennsylvania in the mid-18th century A German dialect is still spoken by them in East Pennsylvania.

Penny (A.S *pening*) The English bronze coin worth one-twelfth of a shilling—often called a *copper*, because from 1797 to 1860 pennies were made of copper From Anglo-Saxon times till the reign of Charles II pennies were of silver, and between that time and 1797 none were coined, though copper halfpence and farthings were Silver pennies are still coined, but only in very small quantities and solely for use as Maundy Money (*q v*) The weight of a new penny is one-third of an ounce avoirdupois, and it is legal tender up to twelve pence

The plural *pennies* is used of the number of coins, and *pence* of value, and the word is sometimes used to denote coins of low value of other nations, such as in *Luke* xx, 24, where it stands for the Roman denarius

A pretty penny. A considerable sum of money, an unpleasantly large sum

A penny for your thoughts! Tell me what you are thinking about Addressed humorously to one in a "brown study " The phrase occurs in Heywood's *Proverbs* (1546)

A penny saved is a penny earned (or **gained**, etc) An old adage intended to encourage thrift in the young

He has got his pennyworth. He has got good value for his money, sometimes said of one who has received a good drubbing

In for a penny, in for a pound. Another way of saying "having put your hand to the plough " Once a thing has been started it must be carried through, no matter what difficulties arise or what obstacles have to be overcome—one is in it and there can be no drawing back.

My penny of observation (*Love's Labour's Lost*, iii, 1) My pennyworth of wit, my natural observation or mother-wit Perhaps there is some pun on *penny* and *penetration*.

No penny, no paternoster. No pay, no work, you'll get nothing for nothing The allusion is to pre-Reformation days, when priests would not perform services without payment

Penny a liner. The old name for a contributor to the newspapers who was not on the staff and used to be paid a penny a line As it was to his interest to "pad" as much as possible the word is still used in a contemptuous way for a second-rate writer or newspaper hack

Penny-dreadful, or **-horrible.** A cheap boys' paper, full of crude situations and highly coloured excitement "Shilling shocker" is a name for a similar article of higher price, but no higher literary value

A penny-father. A miser, a penurious person, who "husbands" his pence

To nothing fitter can I thee compare
   Than to the son of some rich penny-father,
   Who having now brought on his end with care,
   Leaves to his son all he had heap'd together.
                                     'DRAYTON *Idea*, X, 2.

Penny farthing. The nickname of what was also called the "ordinary" bicycle that came into vogue in 1872 The front wheel was much larger than the back wheel, sometimes being as much as 5 ft in diameter while the rear was only 12 in The drive was directly on the front wheel, the seat being above it and set only slightly back from the perpendicular of its axle The penny farthing lasted until the late 80s, but the Safety, which was introduced in 1885 and was much on the lines of the bicycle now built, ousted it from ordinary use

Penny fish. A name given to the John Dory (*q.v.*) because of the round spots on each side left by St Peter's fingers

Penny gaff. A concert or crude music-hall entertainment for which the entrance charge is one penny *See* GAFF

Penny-leaf. A country name for the navelwort or wall pennywort (*Cotyledon umbilicus*), from its round leaves

Penny-pies. A name given to the above and also to the moneywort (*Sibthorpia europæa*).

Penny Plain, Twopence Coloured. A phrase originating in the shop of a maker of toy theatres in East London The scenery and characters for the plays to be acted on these theatres were printed on sheets of thick paper ready to be cut out, the sheets being sold at 1d if plain but 2d each if coloured

Penny readings. Parochial entertainments, consisting of readings, music, etc , for which one penny admission is charged.

Penny weddings. Weddings formerly in vogue among the poor in Scotland and Wales at which each of the guests paid a small sum of money not exceeding a shilling After defraying the expenses of the feast, the residue went to the newly married pair, to aid in furnishing their house

Vera true, vera true We'll have a' to pay . a sort of penny-wedding it will prove, where all men contribute to the young folk's maintenance —SCOTT *Fortunes of Nigel,* ch xxvii

Penny wise and pound foolish Said of one who is in danger of "spoiling the ship for a ha'porth of tar," like the man who lost his horse from his penny wisdom in saving the expense of shoeing it afresh when one of its shoes was loose, hence, one who is thrifty in small matters and careless over large ones is said to be *penny wise*

Take care of the pence and the pounds will take care of themselves An excellent piece of advice, which Chesterfield records in his *Letters to his son* (Feb 5th, 1750) as having been given by "old Mr Lowndes, the famous Secretary of the Treasury, in the reigns of King William, Queen Anne, and George I " Chesterfield adds—

To this maxim, which he not only preached, but practised, his two grandsons, at this time, owe the very considerable fortunes that he left them

The saying was parodied in the *Advice to a Poet,* which goes "Take care of the *sense* and the *sounds* will take care of themselves."

To turn an honest penny. To earn a little money by working for it.

Pennyroyal. The name of this herb (*Mentha pulegium*), a species of mint, is not connected with the coin, but is a corruption of *pulyole ryale,* from the Latin *pulegium,* thyme (so called from *pulex,* a flea, because it was supposed to be harmful to fleas), and Anglo-French *réal,* royal The French call the herb *pouliot,* from *pou,* a louse

Pennyweight. 24 grains, *i e.* one-two-hundred-and-fortieth of a pound troy, so called because it was formerly the same proportion of the old "Tower pound" (*i e* 22½ grains), which was the exact weight of a new silver penny.

Pension. Etymologically, that which is *weighed out* (Lat. *pensionem,* payment, from *pendĕre,* to weigh, also to pay, because payment was originally weighed out *Cp* our *pound,* both a weight and a piece of money).

Pension, a boarding-house (to live *en pension, i e* as a boarder), though now pronounced and treated as though French, was, in the 17th century, ordinary English; this use arose because *pension* was the term for any regular payment made for services rendered, such as payment for board and lodging

Pensioner. The counterpart at Cambridge of the Oxford commoner, *i e* an undergraduate who pays for his own commons, etc., and is neither a sizar nor on the foundation of a college

At the Inns of Court the *pensioner* is the officer who collects the periodical payments made by the members for the upkeep of the Inn

Gentlemen Pensioners. The old name for the members of the Honourable Corps of Gentlemen-at-arms (*q.v.*).

The Pensioner (or Pensionary) Parliament. That from May 8th, 1661, to Jan 24th, 1679; convened by Charles II, and so called because of the many pensions it granted to adherents of the king

Pentacle (pen' takl) A five-pointed star, or five-sided figure, used in sorcery as a talisman against witches, etc , and sometimes worn as a folded headdress of fine linen, as a defence against demons in the act of conjuration It is also called the Wizard's Foot, and Solomon's Seal (*signum Salamonis*), and is supposed to typify the five senses, though, as it resolves itself into three triangles, its efficacy may spring from its being a triple symbol of the Trinity

And on her head, lest spirits should invade,
A pentacle, for more assurance, laid.
ROSE *Orlando Furioso,* iii, 21.
The Holy Pentacles numbered forty-four, of which seven were consecrated to each of the planets Saturn Jupiter, Mars, and the Sun, five to both Venus and Mercury, and six to the Moon The divers figures were enclosed in a double circle, containing the name of God in Hebrew, and other mystical words

Pentagon (pen' ta gon) A vast five-sided building erected in Washington, D.C , to house government officials It is said to be so great that newcomers who leave their offices never find them again

Pentameron (pen tăm' er on). A collection of stories written in the Neapolitan dialect in 1672 by Giovanni Battista Basile. It is modelled on the Decameron but consists of five days of ten stories each and was based on—in some instances was the foundation of—French fairy tales

The Pentameron (1837) of Walter Savage Landor (1775-1864) was a collection of five long imaginary conversations

Pentameter (pen tăm' e tĕr). In prosody, a line of five feet, dactyls or spondees divided by a cæsura into two parts of two and a half feet each—the line used in alternation with the hexameter (*q v*) in Latin elegiac verse The name is sometimes wrongly applied to the English five-foot iambic line

> In the hexameter rises the fountain's silvery column,
> In the pentameter aye falling in melody back
> COLERIDGE *Example of Elegiac metre.*

Pentateuch (pen' ta tūk) The first five books of the Old Testament, anciently attributed to Moses. (Gr *penta*, five, *teuchos*, a tool, book)

The Samaritan Pentateuch. The Hebrew text as preserved by the Samaritans, it is said to date from 400 B C

Pentathlon (pen tăth' lon) An athletic contest of five events, usually the running broad jump, javelin throw, 200-metre race, discus throw, and 1,500-metre flat race

Pentecost (pen' te kost) (Gr *pentecoste*, fiftieth) The festival held by the Jews on the fiftieth day after the second day of the Passover; our Whit Sunday, which commemorates the descent of the Holy Spirit on the Apostles on the Day of Pentecost (*Acts* ii)

Penthesilea (pen the sil ē' a) Queen of the Amazons who, in the post-Homeric legends, fought for Troy; she was slain by Achilles Hence, any strong, commanding woman, Sir Toby Belch, in *Twelfth Night* (ii, 3), calls Maria by this name

Pent-house. Originally any smaller building with a sloping roof erected against the wall of a house, the word has now become associated chiefly with the dwelling houses built on the roofs of skyscrapers, etc , above the main roof line, but recessed behind the main wall line

Peony (pē' ō ni) So called, according to fable, from Pæon, the physician who cured the wounds received by the gods in the Trojan war. The seeds were, at one time, worn round the neck as a charm against the powers of darkness

> About an Infant's neck hang Peonie,
> It cures Alcydes cruell Maladie
> *Sylvester's Du Bartas*, I, iii 712

People. People of God. *See* SHAKERS.

Peoples' Charter. *See* CHARTISM.

Pepper. To pepper one well. To give one a good basting or thrashing

To take pepper i' the nose. To take offence The French have a similar locution, *La moutarde lui monte au nez*

> Take you pepper in the nose, you mar our sport —
> MIDDLETON *The Spanish Gipsy*, IV, iii.

When your daughter is stolen close Pepper Gate. Pepper Gate used to be on the east side of the city of Chester. It is said that the daughter of the mayor eloped, and the mayor ordered the gate to be closed up "Lock the stable-door when the steed is stolen."

Pepper-and-salt. A light grey colour, especially applied to cloth for dresses

Peppercorn Rent. A nominal rent A pepperberry is of no appreciable value, and given as rent is a simple acknowledgment that the tenement virtually belongs to the person by whom the peppercorn is given, though the freehold belongs to him who receives it

Cowper makes a figurative use of the custom—

> True While they live, the courtly laureate pays
> His quit-rent ode, his pepper-corn of praise
> *Table-talk*, 110

Pepperpot. A stew of tripe, dumplings, and vegetables, originating in Philadelphia.

Per contra (pĕr kon' tra) (Lat) A commercial term for on the opposite side of the account Used also of arguments, etc **Per saltum** (Lat , by a leap) A promotion or degree given without going over the ground usually prescribed Thus, a clergyman on being made a bishop may have the degree of D D given him *per saltum* —*i e*. without taking the B D degree, and waiting the usual period

Perceforest (pĕrs' for est) An early 14th-century French prose romance (said to be the longest in existence), belonging to the Arthurian cycle, but mingling with it the Alexander romance After Alexander's war in India he comes to England, of which he makes Perceforest, one of his knights, king The romance tells how Perceforest establishes the Knights of the Franc Palais, how his grandson brings the Grail to England, and includes many popular tales, such as that of the Sleeping Beauty

Percival, Sir (pĕr' si vàl). The Knight of the Round Table who, according to Malory's *Morte d'Arthur* (and Tennyson's *Idylls of the King*), finally won a sight of the Holy Grail (*q v*) He was the son of Sir Pellinore and brother of Sir Lamerocke, but in the earlier French romances based probably on the Welsh *Mabinogion* and other Celtic originals— he has no connexion with the Grail, but here (as in the English also) he sees the lance dripping blood, and the severed head surrounded by blood in a dish The French version of the romance is by Chrétien de Troies (12th century), which formed the basis of Sebastian Evans's *The High History of the Holy Graal* (1893) The German version, *Parsifal* or *Parzival*, was written some 50 years later by Wolfram von Eschenbach, and it is principally on this version that Wagner drew for his opera, *Parsifal* (1882)

Percy When Malcolm III of Scotland invaded England, and reduced the castle of Alnwick, Robert de Mowbray brought to him the keys of the castle suspended on his lance, and, handing them from the wall, thrust his lance into the king's eye, from which circumstance, the tradition says, he received the name of "Pierce-eye," which has ever since been borne by the Dukes of Northumberland.

> This is all a fable The Percies are descended from a great Norman baron, who came over with William, and who took his name from his castle and estate in Normandy.—SCOTT *Tales of a Grandfather*, IV.

Perdita (pĕr' dı tả) In *A Winter's Tale*, the daughter of Leontes and Hermione of Sicily She was abandoned by order of her father, and put in a vessel which drifted to "the sea-coast of Bohemia," where the infant was discovered by a shepherd, who brought her up as his own daughter In time Florizel, the son and heir of the Bohemian king Polixenes, fell in love with the supposed shepherdess The match was forbidden by Polixenes, and the young lovers fled to Sicily Here the story is cleared up, and all ends happily in the restoration of the lost (Fr *perdu*) Perdita to her parents, and her marriage with Florizel

Mrs Robinson, the actress and mistress of George IV when Prince of Wales, was specially successful in the part of Perdita, and she assumed this name, the Prince being known as Florizel

Perdrix, toujours perdrix (pâr' drē too zhoor pâr' drē). Too much of the same thing Walpole tells us that the confessor of one of the French kings reproved him for conjugal infidelity, and was asked by the king what he liked best "Partridge," replied the priest, and the king ordered him to be served with partridge every day, till he quite loathed the sight of his favourite dish After a time, the king visited him, and hoped he had been well served, when the confessor replied, *Mais oui, perdrix, toujours perdrix* "Ah! ah!" replied the amorous monarch, "and one mistress is all very well, but not *'perdrix, toujours perdrix'* "

Soup for dinner, soup for supper, and soup for breakfast again —FARQUHAR *The Inconstant,* iv, 2

Père la Chaise (pâr la shâz) This great Parisian cemetery is on the site of a religious settlement founded by the Jesuits in 1626, and later enlarged by Louis XIV's confessor, Père la Chaise After the Revolution, the grounds were laid out for their present purpose, and were first used in May, 1804.

Peregrine Falcon A falcon of wide distribution, formerly held in great esteem for hawking, and so called (13th century) because taken when on their passage or *peregrination*, from the breeding place, instead of straight off the nest, as was the case with most other hawks (Lat. *peregrinus*, a foreigner, one coming from foreign parts)

Dame Juliana Berners in the *Book of St Albans* (see HAWK) tells us that the peregrine was for an earl The hen is the *falcon* of falconers, the cock the tercel

The word was formerly used as synonymous with *pilgrim*, and (adjectivally) for one travelling abroad.

Perfect Perfect number. One of which the sum of all its divisors exactly measures itself, as 6, the divisors of which are 1, 2, 3=6 These are very scarce, indeed, from 1 to forty million there are only seven, viz 6, 28, 496, 8,128, 130,816, 2,096,128, and 33,550,336

Perfect rhyme is a rhyme of two words pronounced and often spelled alike but with different meanings, as "rain" and "reign," "thyme" and "time."

Perfectionists Members of a communistic sect founded by J H Noyes (1811-86) in Vermont about 1834, and removed by him and

R D —23

settled at Oneida, New York, 1847-8 Its chief features were that the community was held to be one family, mutual criticism and public opinion took the place of government, and wives were—theoretically, at least—held in common, till 1879, when, owing to opposition, this was abandoned In 1881 the sect, which had prospered exceedingly through its thrift and industry, voluntarily dissolved and was reorganized as a joint-stock company

Perfume means simply "from smoke" (Lat *per fumum*), the first perfumes having been obtained by the combustion of aromatic woods and gums Their original use was in sacrifices, to counteract the offensive odours of the burning flesh

Peri (pē' rı). Originally, a beautiful but malevolent sprite of Persian myth, one of a class which was responsible for comets, eclipses, failure of crops, etc ; in later times applied to delicate, gentle, fairy-like beings, begotten by fallen spirits who direct with a wand the pure in mind the way to heaven These lovely creatures, according to the Koran, are under the sovereignty of Eblis, and Mohammed was sent for their conversion, as well as for that of man

> Like peris' wands, when pointing out the road
> For some pure spirit to the blest abode
> THOMAS MOORE *Lalla Rookh,* Pt ı.

The name used sometimes to be applied to any beautiful, fascinating girl

Paradise and the Peri. The second tale in Moore's *Lalla Rookh* The Peri laments her expulsion from heaven, and is told she will be readmitted if she will bring to the gate of heaven the "gift most dear to the Almighty." After a number of unavailing offerings she brought a guilty old man, who wept with repentance, and knelt to pray The Peri offered the *Repentant Tear*, and the gates flew open.

Pericles, Prince of Tyre (per' ı klēz) According to Sir Sidney Lee, the greater portion of this play, which was ascribed to Shakespeare in all the Quartos (1st, 1608), but was not admitted to the collected works before the Third Folio (1664), was by George Wilkins, author of *The Miseries of Inforst Marriage* (1607), etc The original story was the work of a late Greek romance writer and was extremely popular in mediæval times The hero was *Apollonius* of Tyre, and under this name the story occurs in the *Gesta Romanorum*, Gower's *Confessio Amantis* (Bk vııı), and elsewhere

Perillos and the Brazen Bull. See *under* INVENTORS.

Perilous Castle. The castle of "the good" Lord Douglas was so called in the reign of Edward I, because Douglas destroyed several English garrisons stationed there, and vowed to be revenged on anyone who should dare to take possession of it. Scott calls it "Castle Dangerous" (*see* Introduction of *Castle Dangerous*)

Peripatetic School (per ı pa tet' ık) The school or system of philosophy founded by Aristotle, who used to walk about (Gr *peri*, about, *patein*, to walk) as he taught his disciples in the covered walk of the Lyceum This colonnade was called the *peripatos*

Periphrasis (pe rif' rà sis). The rhetorical term for using more words than are necessary in an explanation or description. A fair example is "Persons prejudicial to the public peace may be assigned by administrative process to definite places of residence," i.e breakers of the law may be sent to gaol.

Perissa (per is' à). The typification of excessive exuberance of spirits in Spenser's *Faerie Queene* (II, ii). She was the mistress of Sansloy and a step-sister of Elissa (*q v.*)

In wine and meats she flowed above the bank,
And in excess exceeded her own might,
In sumptuous tire she joyed herself to prank,
But of her love too lavish
Faerie Queene, II, ii, 26

Periwig. *See* PERUKE

Periwinkle. The plant gets its name from Lat *Pervinca*, which may mean either to conquer completely or to bind around, but *why* it should have received this name is unknown, though it may earlier have been applied to some climbing plant In Italy it used to be wreathed round dead infants, and hence its Italian name, *fiore di morto*

The sea-snail of this name was called in A.S *pinewinkle*, the first syllable probably being cognate with Lat *pina*, a mussel, and *winkle* from A S. *wincel*, a corner, with reference to its much convoluted shell

Perk. The derivation of the word is unknown, but as it is first met with (14th century) in connexion with the popinjay (parrot) it may have something to do with *perch*, the parrot bearing itself on its perch in a *perky* or jaunty way, and in some instances (e g "The eagle and the dove pearke not on one branch," Greene's *Perimedes*, and "Cæsar's crowe durst never cry *Ave* but when she was pearked on the Capitoli," Greene's *Pandosto*) it is not always easy to differentiate the two meanings

To perk up To get more lively, to feel better

Permian Strata (pĕr' mi an) The uppermost strata of the Palæozoic series, consisting chiefly of red sandstone and magnesian limestone, which rest on the carboniferous strata, so called by Sir Roderick Murchison (1841) from Perm, in Russia, where they are most distinctly developed.

Perpetual Motion. The term applied to some theoretical force that will move a machine forever of itself—a mirage which holds attractions for some minds much as did the search for the philosophers' stone, the elixir of life, and the fountain of perpetual youth in less enlightened times

It is quite possible, theoretically, at least, to eliminate all friction, air resistance, and wear and tear, and if this were done a body to which motion had been given would, unless interfered with, retain it for ever, but *only on the condition that it were given no work to do*, once connect the ideal spinning top with a wheel or crank and the spin would inevitably come to an end

Persecutions, The Ten Great. (1) Under Nero, A D 64, (2) Domitian, 95, (3) Trajan, 98, (4) Hadrian, 118, (5) Pertinax, 202, chiefly in Egypt, (6) Maximin, 236, (7) Decius, 249, (8)

Valerian, 257, (9) Aurelian, 272, (10) Diocletian, 302

It would be well if these were the only religious persecutions, but, alas' those on the other side prove the truth of the Founder "I came not to send peace, but a sword" (*Matt* x, 34) Witness the long persecutions of the Wilderness and Albigenses, the thirty years' war of Germany, the persecution of the Guises, the Bartholomew slaughter, the wars of Louis XIV on the revocation of the Edict of Nantes, the Dragonnades, and the wars against Holland Witness the bitter persecutions stirred up by Luther, which spread to England and Scotland, the ferocious persecution of the Jews by Germans

Persepolis (pĕr sep' ō lis) The capital of the ancient Persian empire It was situated some 35 miles NE of Shiraz The palaces and other public buildings were some miles from the city, and were approached by magnificent flights of steps

Perseus (pĕr' sūs) In Greek legend, the hero son of Zeus and Danae. (*q v*) He and his mother were set adrift in a chest, but were rescued through the intervention of Zeus, and he was brought up by King Polydectes, who, wishing to marry his mother, got rid of him by giving him the almost hopeless task of obtaining the head of Medusa (*q.v.*). He, with the help of the gods, was successful, and with the head (which turned all that looked on it to stone) he rescued Andromeda (*q v*), and later metamorphosed Polydectes and his guests to stone

Before his birth an oracle had foretold that Acrisius, Danae's father, would be slain by Danae's son, and this came to pass, for, while taking part in the games at Larissa, Perseus accidentally slew his grandfather with a discus

Person From Lat *persona*, which meant originally a mask worn by actors (perhaps from *per sonare*, to sound through), and later was transferred to the character or personage represented by the actor (cp our *dramatis personæ*), and so to any human being in his definite character, at which stage the word was adopted in English through the O Fr *persone*

Confounding the Persons. The heresy of Sabellius (*see* SABELLIANISM), who declared that Father, Son, and Holy Ghost were but three names, aspects, or manifestations of one God, the orthodox doctrine being that of the Athanasian Creed—

We worship one God in Trinity, and Trinity in Unity, Neither confounding the Persons, nor dividing the Substance (Neque confundentes personas, neque substantiam separantes).

Persona grata (Lat.) An acceptable person, one liked

The Count [Munster] is not a *persona grata* at court, as the royal family did not relish the course he took in Hanoverian affairs in 1866 —*Truth*, Oct 22, 1885

Perth is Celtic for a bush The county of Perth is the county of bushes

The Five Articles of Perth Those passed in 1618 by order of James VI, enjoining the attitude of kneeling to receive the elements, the observance of Christmas, Good Friday, Easter, and Pentecost, the rite of confirmation, etc They were ratified August 4th, 1621, called *Black Saturday*, and condemned in the General Assembly of Glasgow in 1638

Peru (per oo') **From China to Peru.** From one end of the world to the other, world-wide Equivalent to the biblical "from Dan to Beersheba" The phrase comes from the opening of Johnson's *Vanity of Human Wishes*—

Let observation with extensive view
Survey mankind from China to Peru.

Boileau (*Sat* viii, 3) had previously written '—

De Paris au Pérou, du Japon jusqu'à Rome

Peruvian Bark, called also **Jesuit's Bark,** because it was introduced into Spain by the Jesuits. "Quinine," from the same tree, is called by the Indians *quinquina*. *See* CINCHONA.

Peruke (per ûk') (Fr *perruke*, the origin of which is unknown though the word has been conjecturally derived from Lat *pilus*, hair). The wigs are first mentioned in the 16th century, in the next century they became very large, and the fashion began to wane in the reign of George III *Periwig*, which has been further corrupted into *wig*, is a corrupt form of *peruke*

Petard (pe tard') **Hoist with his own petard.** Beaten with his own weapons, caught in his own trap; involved in the danger intended for others, as were many designers of instruments of torture *See list under* INVENTORS The petard was a thick iron engine of war, filled with gunpowder, and fastened to gates, barricades, and so on, to blow them up The danger was lest the engineer who fired the petard should be blown up in the explosion

Let it work,
For 'tis the sport, to have the engineer
Hoist with his own petard, and it shall go hard
But I will delve one yard below their mines,
And blow them at the moon

Hamlet, iii, 4.

Pétaud (pā' tō) **'Tis the court of King Pétaud,** where everyone is master There is no order or discipline at all This is a French proverb *Le roi Petaud* (Lat. *peto*, I beg) was the title of the chief who was elected by the fraternity of beggars in mediæval France, in whose court all were equal

Peter St. Peter. The patron saint of fishermen, being himself a fisherman, the "Prince of the Apostles" His feast is kept universally with that of St. Paul on June 29th, and he is usually represented as an old man, bald, but with a flowing beard, dressed in a white mantle and blue tunic, and holding in his hand a book or scroll His peculiar symbols are the keys, and a sword (*Matt* xvi, 19 and *John* xviii, 10)

Tradition tells that he confuted Simon Magus, who was at Nero's court as a magician, and that in A D 66 he was crucified with his head downwards at his own request, as he said he was not worthy to suffer the same death as Our Lord The location of his tomb under the high altar of St Peter's, Rome, was verified in 1950

St. Peter's fingers. The fingers of a thief The allusion is to the fish caught by St Peter with a piece of money in its mouth They say that a thief has a fish-hook on every finger.

St Peter's fish The John Dory (*q v*), also, the haddock

Great Peter. A bell in York Minster, weighing 10¾ tons, and hung in 1845

Lord Peter The Pope in Swift's *Tale of a Tub*

To peter out. To come gradually to an end, to give out The phrase came from the American mining camps of about '49, but its origin is not known

To rob Peter to pay Paul. *See* ROB

Peter-boat: Peterman. A fishing-boat made to go either way, the stem and stern being alike They are still in common use round the mouth of the Thames, and were so called from *Peterman*, a term up to the 17th century for a fisherman

I hope to live to see dog's meat made of the old usurer's flesh, his skin is too thick to make parchment, 'twould make good boots for a peterman to catch salmon in —CHAPMAN *Eastward Ho,* II, ii

Peter Funk. (U S A) A swindle. A *Peter Funk Auction* is one that has been rigged

Peterhouse, or St Peter's College The oldest of the Cambridge Colleges, having been founded in 1257 by Hugo de Balsham, Bishop of Ely

Peter the Hermit. *See* HERMIT.

Peter's Pence. An annual tribute of one penny, paid at the feast of St. Peter to the see of Rome, collected at first from every family, but afterwards restricted to those "who had the value of thirty pence in quick or live stock" This tax was collected in England from about the middle of the 8th century till it was abolished by Henry VIII in 1534. Peter's Pence now consists of voluntary contributions of any amount made by Catholics in all parts of the world, and it is a considerable source of income to the Holy See

Peter-see-me. A favourite Spanish wine was so called in the 17th century The name is a corruption of *Pedro Ximenes*, the name of a grower who introduced a special grape

Peter-see-me shall wash thy noul
And malaga glasses fox thee,
If, poet, thou toss not bowl for bowl
Thou shalt not kiss a doxy.
MIDDLETON *Spanish Gipsy,* III, i.

Peterloo or the **Manchester Massacre.** The dispersal by the military on August 16th, 1819, of a large crowd of operatives who had assembled at St Peter's Field, Manchester, to hear "Orator" Hunt speak in favour of Parliamentary Reform The arrest of Hunt was ordered, but as this was impossible and riot was feared, the magistrates gave the hussars orders to charge Some six persons were killed in the charge, many were injured, and the arrest of Hunt (who was given two years' imprisonment) was effected

The name was founded on *Waterloo*, then fresh in the popular mind

Petit Sergeanty *See* SERGEANTY

Petitio principii (pe tish' yo prin sip' i I) A begging of the question, or assuming in the premises the question you undertake to prove In mediæval logic a *principium* was an essential, self-evident principle from which particular truths were deducible, the assumption of this principle was the *petitio, i e* begging, of it It is the same as "arguing in a circle "

Petitio Principii, as defined by Archbishop Whately, is the fallacy in which the premise either appears manifestly to be the same as the conclusion, or is actually proved from the conclusion, or is such as would naturally and properly so be proved —J S MILL *System of Logic,* II, p 389

Petitioners and Abhorrers Two political parties in the reign of Charles II The former were those members of the Opposition or 'Country" party who, in 1679, presented petitions to the King asking him to summon a Parliament in 1680 Their opponents presented counter-petitions expressing their abhorrence of the attempt to encroach on the royal prerogative, and were thus called Abhorrers

Petrel The stormy petrel. A small sea-bird (*Procellaria pelagica*), so named, according to tradition, from the Ital *Petrello*, little Peter, because during storms these birds seem to fly patting the water with each foot alternately as though walking on it, reminiscently of St Peter, who walked on the Lake of Gennesareth Sailors call them "Mother Carey's chickens." The term is used figuratively of one whose coming always portends trouble

Petticoat Government is management by women, in another phrase, wearing the breeches

Petto. In petto. In secrecy, in reserve (Ital, in the breast) The pope creates cardinals *in petto*—i e in his own mind—and keeps the appointment to himself till he thinks proper to announce it. On the declaration of their names their seniority in the college of cardinals dates from their appointment *in petto* It is claimed that the English historian Lingard was made cardinal *in petto* by Leo XII who died before announcing the fact.

Petty Cury (Cambridge) means "The Street of Cooks," from Lat. *curare*, to cure or dress food It is called *Parva Cokeria* in a deed dated 13 Edward III. Probably at one time it was part of the Market Hall

Peutingerian Map A map of the roads of the ancient Roman world, constructed in the time of Alexander Severus (A.D 226), discovered in the early 16th century by Conrad Peutinger, of Augsburg.

Pewter. To scour the pewter. To do one's work

> But if she neatly scour her pewter,
> Give her the money that is due t' her
> KING *Orpheus and Eurydice.*

Pfister's Bible. *See* BIBLE, SPECIALLY NAMED

Phædria (fē' dri a). The typification in Spenser's *Faerie Queene* (II, vi) of wantonness, she was handmaid to Acrasia the enchantress, and sailed about Idle Lake in a gondola

Phaeton (fā' ton) In classical myth, the son of Phœbus (the Sun), he undertook to drive his father's chariot, and was upset and thereby caused Libya to be parched into barren sands, and all Africa to be more or less injured, the inhabitants blackened, and vegetation nearly destroyed, and would have set the world on fire had not Zeus transfixed him with a thunderbolt

> Gallop apace, you fiery-footed steeds,
> Towards Phœbus' mansion, such a waggoner
> As Phæton would whip you to the west,
> And bring in cloudy night immediately.
> *Romeo and Juliet,* iii, 2

The name is given to a light, four-wheeled open carriage usually drawn by two horses

Phaeton's bird. The swan Cygnus, son of Apollo, was the friend of Phaeton and lamented his fate so grievously that Apollo changed him into a swan, and placed him among the constellations

Phalanx (făl' ăngks) The close order of battle in which the heavy-armed troops of a Grecian army were usually drawn up Hence, any number of people distinguished for firmness and solidity of union

Phalaris (făl' a ris) The brazen bull of Phalaris *See under* INVENTORS

The epistles of Phalaris. A series of 148 letters said to have been written by Phalaris, Tyrant of Agrigentum, Sicily, in the 6th century B C, and edited by Charles Boyle in 1695 Boyle maintained them to be genuine, but Richard Bentley, applying methods of historical criticism, proved that they were forgeries of about the 7th or 8th centuries, A D *See* BOYLE CONTROVERSY

Phallicism or Phallic Worship is the term applied to the primitive worship of fertility as symbolized in the phallus, or male generative organ Phallic emblems are found in most parts of the world, but there is no reason to suppose that obelisks, church spires, and other suggestive objects are the vestiges of phallic worship

Phantom. A spirit or apparition, an illusory appearance, from M E and O Fr *fantosme,* Gr *phantasma* (*phanein,* to show)

Phantom corn. The mere ghost of corn, corn that has as little body as a spectre.

Phantom fellow. One who is under the ban of some hobgoblin, a half-witted person

Phantom flesh. Flesh that hangs loose and flabby, formerly supposed to be bewitched

The Phantom Ship The "Flying Dutchman" (*q v*)

Phaon (fā' on) In Spenser s *Faerie Queene* (II, iv), a young man ill-treated by Furor, and rescued by Sir Guyon The tale is designed to show the evil of intemperate revenge In some editions of the poem *Phedon* is the name, not *Phaon*

Pharamond (făr' a mond) In the Arthurian romances, a Knight of the Round Table, who is said to have been the first king of France, and to have reigned in the early 5th century He was the son of Marcomir and father of Clodion

La Calprenede's novel *Pharamond, ou l'Histoire de France,* was published in 1661.

Pharaoh (făr' ō) The title or generic appellation of the kings in ancient Egypt The word originally meant "the great house," and its later use arose much in the same way as, in modern times, "the Holy See" for the Pope, or "the Sublime Porte" for the Sultan of Turkey

None of the Pharaohs mentioned in the Old Testament has been certainly identified, owing to the great obscurity of the references and the almost entire absence of reliable chronological data

According to the Talmud, the name of Pharaoh's daughter who brought up Moses was *Bathia*

In Dryden's satire *Absalom and Achitophel* (*q v.*) "Pharaoh" stands for Louis XIV of France.

Pharaoh's chicken, or hen. The Egyptian vulture, so called from its frequent representation in Egyptian hieroglyphics

Pharaoh's corn. The grains of wheat sometimes found in mummy cases *See* MUMMY-WHEAT

Pharaoh's rat *See* ICHNEUMON

Pharaoh's serpent. A chemical toy consisting of sulpho-cyanide of mercury, which fuses into a serpentine shape when lighted; so called in allusion to the magic serpents of *Exod.* vii, 9-12.

Pharisees (făr' ĭ sēs) (Heb *perusim*, from *perash*, to separate) means "those who have been set apart," not as a sect but as a school of ascetics who attempted to regulate their lives by the letter of the Law The opprobrious sense of the word was given it by their enemies, because the Pharisees came to look upon themselves as holier than other men, and refused to hold social intercourse with them The Talmud mentions the following classes —

(1) The "Dashers," or "Bandy-legged" (*Nikfi*), who scarcely lifted their feet from the ground in walking, but "dashed them against the stones," that people might think them absorbed in holy thought (*Matt* xxi, 44)

(2) The "Mortars," who wore a "mortier," or cap, which would not allow them to see the passers-by, that their meditations might not be disturbed Having eyes, they saw not (*Matt* viii, 18)

(3) The "Bleeders," who inserted thorns in the borders of their gaberdines to prick their legs in walking

(4) The "Cryers," or "Inquirers," who went about crying out, "Let me know my duty; and I will do it" (*Matt* xix, 16-22)

(5) The ' Almsgivers," who had a trumpet sounded before them to summon the poor together (*Matt* vi, 2)

(6) The "Stumblers," or "Bloody-browed" (*Kizai*), who shut their eyes when they went abroad that they might see no women, being "blind leaders of the blind" (*Matt* xv, 14) Our Lord calls them "blind Pharisees," "fools and blind "

(7) The "Immovables," who stood like statues for hours together, "praying in the market places" (*Matt* vi, 5),

(8) The "Pestle Pharisees" (*Medinkia*), who kept themselves bent double like the handle of a pestle

(9) The "Strong-shouldered" (*Shikmi*), who walked with their back bent as if carrying on their shoulders the whole burden of the law

(10) The "Dyed Pharisees," called by Our Lord "Whited Sepulchres," whose externals of devotion cloaked hypocrisy and moral uncleanliness (*Talmud of Jerusalem, Berakoth,* ix, *Sota,* v, 7, *Talmud o Babylon, Sota,* 22 b)

Pharos (făr' os) A lighthouse, so called from the lighthouse—one of the Seven Wonders of the World—built by Ptolemy Philadelphus in

the island of Pharos, off Alexandria, Egypt It was 450 feet high, and according to Josephus, could be seen at the distance of 42 miles Part was blown down in 793

Pharsalia (far sā' lia) An epic in Latin hexameters by Lucan It tells of the civil war between Pompey and Cæsar, and of the battle of Pharsalus (48 b c) in which Pompey, with 45,000 legionaries, 7,000 cavalry, and a large number of auxiliaries, was decisively defeated by Cæsar, who had only 22,000 legionaries and 1,000 cavalry Pompey s battle-cry was *Hercules invictus*, that of Cæsar, *Venus victrix*.

Pheasant. The "Phasian bird", so called from Phasis, a river of Colchis, whence the bird is said to have spread westward

Phedon (fē' don) An alternative name of Phaon (*q v*)

Phenomenon (fe nom' e non) (pl phenomena) means simply what has appeared (Gr *phainomai*, to appear) It is used in science to express the visible result of an experiment. In popular language it means a prodigy, and *phenomenal* (as "a phenomenal success") is colloquial for prodigious

Phenomenal, soon, we hope, to perish, unregretted, is (at least indirectly, through the abuse of *phenomenon*) from Metaphysics, [such words are] at present, enjoying some vogue as slang, and come from regions that to most of us are overhead —H. W AND F. G FOWLER *The King's English*, ch 1 (1906)

Phigalian Marbles (fi gā' li an) A series of twenty-three sculptures in alto-relievo, discovered in 1812 at Phigalia, in Arcadia, forming part of the Elgin Marbles (*q v*), now in the British Museum They represent the combat of the Centaurs and Lapithæ, and that of the Greeks and Amazons

Philadelphia (fil a del' fi ȧ) The first city of the State of Pennsylvania, was founded in 1582 by William Penn (1644-1718) and others of the Society of Friends, and so named from the Greek *Philadelpheia*, brotherly love It was also the name of an ancient city in Asia Minor, the seat of one of the Seven Churches (*Rev* iii, 7)

Philadelphia lawyer. A lawyer of outstanding ability, with a keen scent for the weaknesses in an adversary's case and a thorough knowledge of the intricacies of the law. "You will have to get a Philadelphia lawyer to solve that" is a familiar American phrase It is said that in 1735, in a case of criminal libel, the only counsel who would undertake the defence was Andrew Hamilton, the famous Philadelphia barrister, who obtained his client's acquittal in face of apparently irrefutable evidence, and charged no fee In New England there was a saying that three Philadelphia lawyers were a match for the Devil

Philadelphists *See* BEHMENISTS.

Philandering (fi lan' der ing). Coquetting with a woman, paying court, and leading her to think you love her, but never declaring your preference *Philander* literally means "a lover of men" (Gr *philos,* loving, *andros,* man), but as the word was made into a proper noun and used for a lover by Ariosto in *Orlando Furioso* (followed by Beaumont and Fletcher in *The*

Laws of Candy), it obtained its present signification In Norton and Sackville's *Gorboduc* (1561) Philander is the name of a staid old counsellor.

Philemon and Baucis (fĭ lē′ mon, baw′ sĭs) Poor cottagers of Phrygia (husband and wife), who, in Ovid's story (*Metamorphoses*, iii, 631), entertained Jupiter so hospitably that he promised to grant them whatever request they made They asked that both might die together, and it was so. Philemon became an oak, Baucis a linden tree, and their branches intertwined at the top

Philip. Philip, remember thou art mortal. A sentence repeated to the Macedonian king every time he gave an audience.

Philip sober. When a woman who asked Philip of Macedon to do her justice was snubbed by the petulant monarch, she exclaimed, "Philip, I shall appeal against this judgment" "Appeal!" thundered the enraged king, "and to whom will you appeal?" "To Philip sober," was her reply.

St. Philip is usually represented bearing a large cross, or a basket containing loaves, in allusion to *John* vi, 5-7 He is commemorated with St. James on May 1st

Philippic (fĭ lĭp′ ĭk). A severe scolding, a speech full of acrimonious invective So called from the orations of Demosthenes against Philip of Macedon, to rouse the Athenians to resist his encroachments The orations of Cicero against Antony are called "Philippics "

Philistines (fĭl′ ĭs tīnz) The ill-behaved and ignorant; persons lacking in liberal culture or of low and materialistic ideas This meaning of the word is due to Matthew Arnold, who adapted it from *Philister*, the term applied by students at the German universities to the townspeople, the "outsiders " This is said to have arisen at Jena, because, after a-"town and gown" row in 1689, which resulted in a number of deaths, the university preacher took for his text "The Philistines be upon thee" (*Judges* xvi)

The people who believe most that our greatness and welfare are proved by our being very rich, and who most give their lives and thoughts to becoming rich, are just the very people whom we call the Philistines.
—M Arnold *Culture and Anarchy* (1869).

Philoctetes (fĭl ok tē′ tēz) The most famous archer in the Trojan war, to whom Hercules, at death, gave his arrows In the tenth year of the siege Ulysses commanded that he should be sent for, as an oracle had declared that Troy could not be taken without the arrows of Hercules Philoctetes accordingly went to Troy, slew Paris, and Troy fell

The *Philoctetes* of Sophocles is one of the most famous Greek tragedies.

Philomel *See* Nightingale

Philopena (fĭl ŏ pē′ na) From the German *vielliebchen*, darling, sweetheart A philopena is a double almond

One evening we invited him to dine at our table, and we ate a philopena together —Mrs Mackin *Two Continents* (1898).

The word is also applied to a game in which each of two persons tries to inveigle the other into paying a forfeit.

Philosopher. The sages of Greece used to be called *sophoi* (wise men), but Pythagoras thought the word too arrogant and adopted the compound *Philosophie* (lover of wisdom), whence "philosopher," one who courts or loves wisdom

Marcus Aurelius (121-80) was surnamed *The Philosopher* by Justin Martyr, and the name was also conferred on Leo VI, Emperor of the East (d. 911), and Porphyry, the Neoplatonic opponent of Christianity (d. 305).

The leading philosophers and Schools of Philosophy in Ancient Greece were—

Philosophers of the Academic sect Plato, Speusippos, Xenocrates, Polemo, Crates, Crantor, Arcesilaos, Carneades, Clitomachos, Philo, and Antiochos.

Philosophers of the Cynic sect. Antisthenes, Diogenes of Sinope, Monimos, Onesicritos, Crates, Metrocles, Hipparchia, Menippos, and Menedemos of Lampsacos

Philosophers of the Cyrenaic sect. Aristippos, Hegesias, Anniceris, Theodoros, and Bion

Philosophers of the Eleac and Eretriac sects Phædo, Plisthenes, and Menedemos of Eretria

Philosophers of the Eleatic sect Xenophanes, Parmenides, Melissos, Zeno of Tarsos, Leucippos, Democritos, Protagoras, and Anaxarchos

Philosophers of the Epicurean sect Epicuros, and a host of disciples

Philosophers of the Heraclitan sect. Heraclitos; the names of his disciples are unknown.

Philosophers of the Ionic sect Anaximander, Anaximenes, Anaxagoras, and Archelaos.

Philosophers of the Italic sect Pythagoras, Empedocles, Epicharmos, Archytas, Alcmæon, Hippasos, Philolaos, and Eudoxos.

Philosophers of the Megaric sect Euclid, Eubulides, Alexinos, Euphantos. Apollonius Chronosis, Diodoros, Ichthyas, Clinomachos, and Stilpo

Philosophers of the Peripatetic sect Aristotle, Theophrastos, Strato, Lyco, Aristo, Critolaos, and Diodoros.

Philosophers of the Sceptic sect Pyrrho and Timon

Philosophers of the Socratic sect Socrates, Xenophon, Æschines, Crito, Simon, Glauco, Simmias, and Cebes

Philosophers of the Stoic sect Zeno, Cleanthes, Chrysippos, Zeno the Less, Diogenes of Babylon, Antipater, Panætios, Epictetus, Marcus Aurelius, and Posidonios.

Philosopher's Egg. A mediæval preservative against poison and a cure for the plague The shell of a new egg was pricked, the white blown out, and the place filled with saffron or a yolk of an egg mixed with saffron

Philosophers' Stone. The hypothetical substance which, according to the mediæval alchemists, would convert all baser metals into gold Its discovery was the prime object of all the alchemists; and to the wide and unremitting search that went on for it we are indebted for the birth of the science of Chemistry, as well as for many inventions It was in searching for this treasure that Botticher stumbled on the manufacture of Dresden porcelain; Roger Bacon on the composition of gunpowder, Geber on the properties of acids, Van Helmont on the nature of gas, and Dr Glauber on the "salts" which bear his name.

In Ripley's treatise, *The Compound of Alchymy* (*temp* Edward IV), we are told the twelve stages, or "gates," in the transmutation of metals These are —(1) Calcination, (2) Dissolution, (3) Separation; (4) Conjunction; (5) Putrefaction, (6) Congelation, (7) Cibation, (8) Sublimation, (9) Fermentation, (10) Exaltation, (11) Multiplication, and (12) Projection Of these the last two were of much the greatest importance, the former consisted in the "augmentation" of the elixir, the latter in the penetration and transfiguration of metals in fusion by casting the powder of the philosophers' stone upon them, which is then called the "powder of projection " According to one legend, Noah was commanded to hang up the true and genuine philosophers' stone in the ark, to give light to every living creature therein, while another related that Deucalion (*q v*) had it in a bag over his shoulder, but threw it away and lost it

Philosophers' Tree or Diana's Tree. An amalgam of crystallized silver, obtained from mercury in a solution of silver, so called by the alchemists, with whom Diana stood for silver

Philter (Gr *philtron*, from *philein*, to love). A draught or charm to incite in another the passion of love The Thessalian philters were the most renowned, but both the Greeks and Romans used these dangerous potions, which sometimes produced insanity Lucretius is said to have been driven mad by a love-potion, and Caligula's death is attributed to some philters administered to him by his wife, Cæsonia Brabantio says to Othello —

> Thou hast practised on her [Desdemona] with foul charms,
> Abused her delicate youth with drugs or minerals
> That weaken motion
>
> SHAKESPEARE *Othello*, 1, 1

Phiz, the face, is a contraction of physiognomy.

> Th' emphatic speaker dearly loves t' oppose,
> In contact inconvenient, nose to nose,
> As if the gnomon on his neighbour's phiz,
> Touch'd with a magnet, had attracted his.
>
> COWPER *Conversation*, 269.

Phlegethon (fleg' e thon) (Gr *phlego*, to burn). A river of liquid fire in Hades It flowed into the river Acheron

> Fierce Phlegethon,
> Whose waves of torrent fire inflame with rage
> MILTON *Paradise Lost*, 11

Phlogiston (flō jis' ton) (Gr., burnt up) The name used by early chemists to denote the principle of inflammability that was supposed to be a necessary constituent of combustible material It was introduced by the German chemist Georg Ernst Stahl, in 1702, and belief in the theory lasted for nearly a century.

Phœbe (fē' bi) A female Titan of classical myth, daughter of Uranus and Ge, also a name of Diana as goddess of the moon

Phœbus (Gr , the Shining One) An epithet of Apollo, god of the sun. In poetry the name is sometimes used of the sun itself, sometimes of Apollo as the leader of the Muses.

> The rays divine of vernal Phœbus shine
> THOMSON *Spring*
> Blind Melesigenes, thence Homer called,
> Whose poem Phœbus challenged for his own
> MILTON *Paradise Regained*, IV, 260

Phœnix (fē' niks) A fabulous Arabian bird, the only one of its kind, that is said to live a certain number of years, at the close of which it makes in Arabia a nest of spices, sings a melodious dirge, flaps its wings to set fire to the pile, burns itself to ashes, and comes forth with new life

It is to this bird that Shakespeare refers in *Cymbeline* (1, 7) —

> If she be furnished with a mind so rare,
> She is alone the Arabian bird

He also wrote the beautiful *Phœnix and Turtle*, based on the legendary love and death of this bird and the turtle-dove

The phœnix was adopted as a sign over chemists' shops through the association of this fabulous bird with alchemy Paracelsus wrote about it, and several of the alchemists employed it to symbolize their vocation

Phœnix dactylifera. The date-palm; so called because of the ancient idea that this tree, if burnt down or if it falls through old age, will rejuvenate itself and spring up fairer than ever Shakespeare may be referring to it in *The Tempest* (III, 3) —

> Now I will believe
> That there are unicorns, that in Arabia
> There is one tree, the phœnix' throne; one phœnix
> At this hour reigning there

Phœnix period or cycle, generally supposed to be 500 years, Tacitus tells us it was 500 years, R Stuart Poole that it was 1,460 Julian years, like the Sothic Cycle, and Lipsius that it was 1,500 years Now, the phœnix is said to have appeared in Egypt five times (1) in the reign of Sesostris, (2) in the reign of Amasis; (3) in the reign of Ptolemy Philadelphus, (4) a year or two prior to the death of Tiberius; and (5) in A.D. 334, during the reign of Constantine The Phœnix Cycle is therefore irregular, the reign or existence of Sesostris being doubtful, Amasis, 566 B C Ptolemy, 266 B C , Tiberius, A D 34; Constantine, A.D 334 In corroboration of this suggestion it must be borne in mind that Jesus Christ, who died A D 34, is termed *the Phœnix* by monastic writers Tacitus (*Annales*, VI, 28) mentions the first four of these appearances

Phœnix Park (Dublin) A corruption of the Gaelic *Fionn-uisge*, the clear water, so called from a spring at one time resorted to as a chalybeate spa

The Phœnix Park Murders, which created an enormous sensation at the time, were the assassination by Fenians (May 6th, 1882) of Lord Frederick Cavendish and Thomas Henry Burke, Chief and Under Secretaries of Ireland The following year one Thomas Carey turned informer and on his largely unsupported evidence five men were hanged for the crime Carey was shipped for safety to South Africa but was murdered on the voyage out

Phonograph. In Britain this word is applied to the old-fashioned sound-reproducing machine with cylindrical records that has now given place to the gramophone In American the flat-disk gramophone is called a phonograph

Phony. An American slang term originating about 1930 for something not genuine, bogus The word probably comes from the "fawney" ring of imitation gold used by confidence-trick men The period of more or less inactivity that elapsed between the declaration of war in 1939 and the invasion of Norway, Denmark, Belgium, Holland, and France in 1940 was called the "Phony War" by American journalists disappointed of sensational events.

Phrygians (frij' yanz) An early Christian sect, so called from Phrygia, where they abounded They regarded Montanus as their prophet, and laid claim to the spirit of prophecy

Phrygian cap The cap of liberty (*q v*)

Phrygian mode In music, the second of the 'authentic'' ecclesiastical modes It had its "final" on E and its "dominant" on C, and was derived from the ancient Greek mode of this name, which was warlike. It was used for hymns and anthems.

Phryne (fri' nē) A famous Athenian courtesan of the 4th century B C , who acquired so much wealth by her beauty that she offered to rebuild the walls of Thebes if she might put on them this inscription. "Alexander destroyed them, but Phryne the hetæra rebuilt them " It is recorded of her that when she was being tried on a capital charge her defender who had failed to move the judges by his eloquence, asked her to uncover her bosom She did so, and the judges, struck by such astounding beauty, acquitted her on the spot

She is said to have been the model for Praxiteles' Cnidian Venus, and also for Apelles' picture of Venus Rising from the Sea

Phylactery (fi läk' ter i) (Gr *phylacterion*, from *phylasso*, to watch). A charm or amulet worn by the ancient Jews on the wrist or forehead It consisted of four slips of parchment, each bearing a text of Scripture, enclosed in two black leather cases One case contained *Exod* xiii, 1-10, 11-16; and the other case *Deut* vi, 4-9, xi, 13-21 The idea arose from the command of Moses, "Therefore shall ye lay up these my words in your heart and bind them for a sign upon your hand as frontlets between your eyes" (*Deut.* xi, 18)

Physician (Gr. *phusis*, nature)

Every man a fool or a physician *See* FOOL

The Physician finger. The third, *See* MEDICINAL FINGER.

The Beloved Physician St Luke (*q v*), so called by St. Paul in *Col* iv, 14

The Prince of Physicians. Avicenna, the Arabian (980-1037)

Piazza (pi ăt' zä) An Italian word meaning an open place or square in a town In America the word has come to mean the verandah of a dwelling-house

Picador (pik' ä dôr) (Span) An agile horseman, who, in bull fights, is armed with a gilt spear (*pica dorada*), with which he pricks the bull to madden him for the combat. Hence, a skilful debater or one who excels at rapid repartee is sometimes called a picador

Picards. A sect of fanatics prevalent in Bohemia and the Vaudois in the early 15th century, said to be so called from Picard of Flanders, their founder, who called himself the New Adam, and tried to introduce the custom of living nude, like Adam in Paradise They were suppressed by Ziska in 1421

Picaresque (pik ā resk') The term applied to the class of literature that deals sympathetically with the adventures of clever and amusing rogues (Span. *picaresco*, roguish, knavish) The earliest example of the picaresque novel is Mendoza's *Lazarillo de Tormes* (1554). Le Sage's *Gil Blas* (1715) is perhaps the best known Nash's *Jack Wilton* (1594) is the earliest English example, and others are Defoe's *Moll Flanders* and *Colonel Jack*

Picayune. In the days of the French occupation of Florida and Louisiana the Spanish half-real (2½d) was known as a picayune, from Fr *picaillon*, an old Piedmontese coin The word is now used in America for anything of trifling value or of a contemptible character

Piccadilly. This well-known London thoroughfare is named from a house that stood near the corner of Sackville Street and, in the early 17th century, was nicknamed *Pickadilly Hall* One early account (1656) says the house was so called because it was the "outmost or skirt house of the Suburbs that way", another—of the same date—because it was built by one Higgins, a tailor, who made his fortune by selling "piccadilles."

The "piccadille" was originally "the round hem or the several divisions set together about the skirt of a Garment," and was so called because it was pierced (Sp *picado*) or slashed, thence it came to be applied to the stiff collar that supported the ruff of 17th-century gallants

Piccadilly Weepers. *See* WEEPERS

Piccaninny, or **Piccanin** (West Indian Negro, from Sp *pequeño*, small). A little Negro child of the West Indies and southern U S A , also, in South Africa, applied to small Kafir children, and sometimes to native children in Australia

Pick-a-back. On the back or shoulders, as a pack is carried The term dates at least from the early 16th century, but its precise origin, and the force of the *pick*-, are unknown. Other forms of it are *a-pigga-back, piggy-back, pickback,* etc

Pickle. A rod in pickle One ready to chastise with at any moment, one "preserved ' for use

I'm in a pretty pickle. In a sorry plight, or state of disorder
How cam'st thou in this pickle ?
Tempest v, 1

Pickle-herring. The German term for a clown or buffoon, from a humorous character of that name in an early 17th-century play It was adopted in England through Addison's mention in the *Spectator* (No. 47, 1711), where he wrongly attributes it to the Dutch

Pickwickian. In a Pickwickian sense. Said of words or epithets, usually of a derogatory or insulting kind, that, in the circumstances in which they are employed, are not to be taken as having quite the same force or implication as they naturally would have The allusion is to the scene in ch 1 of *Pickwick Papers* when Mr Pickwick accused Mr Blotton of acting in "a vile and calumnious manner," whereupon Mr Blotton retorted by calling Mr Pickwick "a humbug " It finally was made to appear that both had used the offensive words only in a Pickwickian sense, and that each had, in fact, the highest regard and esteem for the other

Picnic. The word came into use in England about 1800 to denote a fashionable party, often but not always in the open air, at which each guest contributed towards the provisions It is a translation of Fr *pique-nique* (which had much the same meaning), the origin of which is uncertain

Picts The ancient inhabitants of Scotland, of unknown race They were gradually dispossessed after the coming of the Scots (Goidels) from northern Ireland, about A D 500, and after the union of the Pictish kingdom with that of the Scots under Kenneth Mac-Alpin (844) the remnant was driven to the far north-east The name is probably not native, but was given them by the Romans because they tattooed their bodies (Lat *picti*, painted).

Picts' houses. Underground prehistoric dwellings found in the Orkneys and on the east coast of Scotland, and attributed to the Picts.

Picture (Lat *pictura*, from *pictus*, past part of *pingere*, to paint) A model, or beau-ideal, as, *He is the picture of health*, *A perfect picture of a house*

Picture Bible. A name given to the *Biblia pauperum* (*q v*)

The pictures. A colloquial and convenient way of referring to a cinematograph entertainment

Picture hat. A woman's hat, with wide drooping brim, such as was worn by many of the sitters to Reynolds and Gainsborough

Pidgin-English. The semi-English lingua franca used in China and the Far East, consisting principally of mispronounced English words with certain native grammatical constructions For instance, the Chinese cannot pronounce *r*, so replace it with *l—te-le* for "three," *solly* for "sorry," etc —and, in Chinese, between a numeral and its noun there is always inserted a word (called the "classifier") and this, in Pidgin-English, is replaced by piece—*e g one piece knifee*, *two piece hingkichi* (handkerchiefs) *Pidgin* is a corruption of *business*.

Hence, this is not my pidgin, this is not my business, it is not strictly my affair.

Pie or **Pi** (pī) A printing term used to describe the mix-up of types (for instance, when dropped) or a jumble of letters when a word or sentence is badly printed The origin of the word is obscure, possibly it comes from the analogy of the mixed ingredients in a pie, or it may come from the assortment of types used in the old *pie* or pre-Reformation books of rules for finding the prayers, etc , proper for the day

Piebald. Parti-coloured (especially black and white like a magpie), usually of horses The word is from *pie*, the magpie (*q v*), and *bald*, of which one of the meanings was "streaked with white," as in the "bald-faced stag "

Piece goods are fabrics woven in the proper lengths for certain purposes rather than lengths cut off from a long bolt

23*

Pieces of Eight. The old Spanish silver *peso* (piastre) or dollar of 8 reals, equivalent to about 1s 8d It was marked with an 8, and was in use in the 17th and 18th centuries

Pied (pē' ā) Fr , foot **Pied-a-terre** (pē ā da târ') (Fr , foot on the ground) A temporary lodging, or a country residence, a footing

Mr Harding, however, did not allow himself to be talked over into giving up his own and only *pied-à-terre* in the High Street —ANTHONY TROLLOPE *Barchester Towers*.

Pied de la lettre, Au (Fr , to the foot of the letter) Quite literally—close to the letter

A wild enthusiastic young fellow, whose opinions one must not take *au pied de la lettre*.—THACKERAY. *Pendennis*, I, xi.

Pied Piper of Hamelin The legend is that the town of Hamelin (Westphalia) was infested with rats in 1284, that a mysterious Piper, clad in a parti-coloured suit, appeared in the town and offered to rid it of the vermin for a certain sum, that the townspeople accepted the offer, the Pied Piper fulfilled his contract, and that then the payment was withheld On the following St John's Day he reappeared, and again played his pipe. This time all the children of the town, in place of the rats, followed him, he led them to a mountain cave where all disappeared save two—one blind, the other dumb, or lame; and one legend adds that the children did not perish in the mountain, but were led over it to Transylvania, where they formed a German colony The story is familiar from Robert Browning's poem

> To blow the pipe his lips he wrinkled,
> And green and blue his sharp eyes twinkled . . .
> And ere three notes his pipe had uttered   .
> Out of the houses rats came tumbling—
> Great rats, small rats, lean rats, brawny rats,
> Brown rats, black rats, grey rats, tawny rats . . .
> And step by step they followed him dancing,
> Till they came to the river Weser

Piepowder Court. A court of justice formerly held at fairs, which had summary powers in cases of dispute between those buyers and sellers who were there temporarily Literally, a "wayfarer's court," *piepowder* being from Fr. *pied-poudreux*, dusty-footed (also, a vagabond). The duties of these old Courts of Piepowder are now performed at the Petty Sessions

Is this well, goody Joan, to interrupt my market in the midst, and call away my customers? Can you answer this at the pie-poudres?—BEN JONSON *Bartholomew Fair*, iii, 1

Pierrot (pēr' ō) (*i e* "Little Peter") A character originally in French mime, representing a man in growth and a child in mind and manners He is generally the tallest and thinnest man that can be got, has his face and hair covered with white powder or flour, and wears a long gown with very long sleeves and a row of big buttons down the front

Piers Plowman. *See* VISION OF PIERS PLOWMAN

Pietá (pē ā ta') A representation of the Virgin embracing the dead body of her Son Filial or parental love was called *pietas* by the Romans

Pietists (pī' e tists) A 17th-century sect of Lutherans who sought to introduce a more moral life and a more "evangelical" spirit of doctrine into the reformed church In Germany the word is about equal to our common use of Methodist

Pig (*see also* Hog) The pig was held sacred by the ancient Cretans because Jupiter was suckled by a sow, it was immolated in the mysteries of Eleusis, was sacrificed to Hercules, to Venus, and to the Lares by all those who sought relief from bodily ailments. The sow was sacrificed to Ceres 'because it taught men to turn up the earth", and in Egypt it was slain at grand weddings on account of its fecundity.

In the forefeet of pigs are very small holes which may be seen when the hair has been carefully removed. The tradition is that the legion of devils entered by these apertures There are also round it some six rings, the whole together not larger than a small spangle, they look as if burnt or branded into the skin, and the tradition is that they are the marks of the devil's claws when he entered the swine (*Mark* v, 11-15).

A pig in a poke. A blind bargain The reference is to a common trick in days gone by of trying to palm off on a greenhorn a cat for a sucking-pig. If he opened the poke or sack he "let the cat out of the bag," and the trick was disclosed. The French *chat en poche* (from which the saying may have come) refers to the fact, while our proverb regards the trick *Pocket* is diminutive of *poke.*

A pig's whisper. A very short space of time, properly a grunt—which doesn't take long

You'll find yourself in bed in something less than a pig's whisper.—Dickens *Pickwick*, ch xxxii

Bartholomew pigs. *See* Bartholomew

He has brought his pigs to a pretty market. He has made a very bad bargain, he has managed his business in a very bad way Pigs were for long a principal article of sale with rustics, and till recently the cottager looked to pay his rent by the sale of his pigs.

Pig-a-back. *See* Pick-a-back

Pig-headed. Obstinate, contrary.

Pig iron. Iron cast in oblong ingots now called *pigs* but formerly *sows. Sow* is now applied to the main channel in which the molten liquid runs, the smaller branches which diverge from it being called pigs, and it is the iron from these which is called *pig iron.*

Pigs and whistles Trifles *To go to pigs and whistles* is to be ruined, to go to the deuce

I would be nane surprised to hear the morn that the Nebuchadnezzar was a' gane to pigs and whistles, and driven out with the divors bill to the barren pastures of bankruptcy —Galt. *The Entail*, I, ix

Pigs in clover. People who have money but don't know how to behave themselves decently Also, a game consisting of a box divided into recesses into which one has to roll marbles by tilting the box.

Please the pigs "I'll come on Tuesday—please the pigs", i e if circumstances permit *Deo volente* The suggestions that this phrase was originally "please the pyx" or "please the pixies," are ingenious, but there is no evidence to back them.

St. Anthony's pig. *See* Anthony

The Pig and Tinderbox. An old colloquial name for the Elephant and Castle public-house, in allusion to its sign of a pig-like elephant surmounted by an erection intended to represent a castle but which might pass as a tinderbox.

To drive one's pigs to market. *See* Hog.

To drive pigs. To snore

To pig together To huddle together like pigs in a sty To share and share alike, especially in lodgings in a small way, formerly it meant to sleep two (or more) in the same bed

To stare like a stuck pig. With open mouth and staring eyes, as a pig that is being killed, in the utmost astonishment, mingled sometimes with fear

When pigs fly: Never *See also* Sow.

Pigskin A saddle, the best being made of pigskin. "To throw a leg across a pigskin" is to mount a horse.

Pigtail. In England the word first appeared (17th century) as the name of a tobacco that was twisted into a thin rope, and it was used of the plait of twisted hair worn by sailors till the early 19th century, as it still is used of that worn by schoolgirls

When the Mongols invaded and conquered China (c 1660) they imposed on the Chinese as a sign of servitude the obligation of wearing their hair in a pigtail. This custom was observed by Chinese of whatever grade or class until the fall of the Empire in 1912, when their freedom from this vassalage was symbolized by the abolition of the pigtail.

Pig-wife. A woman who sells crockery. A *piggin* was a small pail, especially a milk-pail; and a *pig* a small bowl, cup, or mug

Pigeon. Slang for a dupe, an easily gullible person, a gull (*q.v*). To pigeon is to cheat or gull one out of his money by almost self-evident hoaxes. Pigeons are very easily caught by snares, and in the sporting world rogues and their dupes are called "rooks and pigeons." Thackeray has a story entitled "Captain Rook and Mr. Pigeon."

To pluck a pigeon. To cheat a gullible person of his money, to fleece a greenhorn

Flying the pigeons. Stealing coals from a cart or sack between the coal-dealer's yard and the house of the customer.

Pigeon English. An incorrect form of "Pidgin-English" (*q v*).

Pigeon-hole. A small compartment for filing papers, hence, a matter that has been put on one side and forgotten is often said to have been *pigeonholed* In pigeon-lockers a small hole is left for the pigeons to walk in and out

Pigeon-livered. Timid, easily frightened, like a pigeon

> It cannot be
> But I am pigeon-liver'd, and lack gall
> To make oppression bitter, or ere this
> I should have fatted all the region kites
> With this slave's offal.   *Hamlet*, ii, 2.

Pigeon pair Boy and girl twins It was once supposed that pigeons always sit on two eggs which produce a male and a female, and these twin birds live together in love the rest of their lives.

The black pigeons of Dodona Two black pigeons, we are told, took their flight from Thebes, in Egypt, one flew, to Libya, and the other to Dodona (*q v*) On the spot where the former alighted, the temple of Jupiter Ammon was erected, in the place where the other settled, the oracle of Jupiter was established, and there the responses were made by the black pigeons that inhabited the surrounding groves This fable is probably based on a pun upon the word *peleiai*, which usually meant "old women," but in the dialect of the Epirots signified pigeons or doves

Piggin. *See* PIG-WIFE *above.*

Pigmies. *See* PYGMIES

Pigwiggen. An elf in Drayton's *Nymphidia* (1627), in love with Queen Mab He combats the jealous Oberon with great fury

> Pigwiggen was this Fairy Knight,
> One wond'rous gracious in the sight
> Of fair Queen Mab, which day and night
> He amorously observed

Pike. The Germans have a tradition that when Christ was crucified all fishes dived under the waters in terror, except the pike, which, out of curiosity, lifted up its head and beheld the whole scene, hence the fancy that in a pike's head all the parts of the Crucifixion are represented, the cross, three nails, and a sword being distinctly recognizable *Cp* PASSION-FLOWER

Pikestaff. Plain as a pikestaff. Quite obvious and unmistakable The earlier form of the phrase (mid-16th century) was *plain as a packstaff*, *i e* the staff on which a pedlar carried his pack, which was worn plain and smooth

> O Lord' what absurdities! as plain as any packstaff
> —DRYDEN *Amphitryon*, III, 1

Pilate. Tradition has it that Pontius Pilate's later life was so full of misfortune that, in Caligula's time, he committed suicide in Rome His body was cast into the Tiber, but evil spirits disturbed the water so much that it was retrieved and taken to Vienne, where it was thrown into the Rhone, eventually coming to rest in the recesses of a lake on Mount Pilatus (*q v*) opposite Lucerne Another legend states that the suicide occurred so that he might escape the sentence of death passed on him by Tiberius because of his having ordered the crucifixion of Christ, and yet another that both he and his wife became penitent, embraced Christianity, and died peaceably in the faith

Tradition gives the name Claudia Procula, or Procla, to Pilate's wife, and by some she has been identified with the Claudia of 2 *Tim* iv, 21

Pilate voice. A loud, ranting voice In the old mysteries all tyrants were made to speak in a rough, ranting manner. Thus Bottom the Weaver (*q.v.*), after a rant "to show his quality," exclaims, "That's 'Ercles' vein, a tyrant's vein", and Hamlet describes a ranting actor as "out-heroding Herod"

> The Miller, that for-drunken was al pale . .
> in Pilates vois he gan to crye,
> And swoor by armes and by blood and bones,
> "I can a noble tale for the nones
> With which I wol now quyte the Knightes tale"
> CHAUCER. *Miller's Prologue*, 12-19

Pilatus, Mount. In Switzerland, between the canton of Lucerne and Unterwalden So called because during westerly winds it is covered with a white "cap" of cloud (Lat *pileatus*, covered with the *pileus*, or felt cap) The similarity of the name with that of Pilate (*q v.*) gave rise to one of the legends mentioned above, another tradition has it that Pilate was banished to Gaul by Tiberius, wandered to this mount and threw himself into a black lake on its summit, and it is further stated that once a year Pilate appears on the mountain and that whoever sees the ghost will die before the year is out In the 16th century a law was passed forbidding anyone to throw stones into the lake, for fear of bringing a tempest on the country

Pilgarlic or **Pill'd Garlic** (pil' gar lik). A 16th-century term for a bald-headed man, especially one whose hair had fallen off through disease, and had left a head that was suggestive of a bit of peeled garlic Stow says of one getting bald "He will soon be a peeled garlic like myself", and the term was later used of any poor wretch avoided and forsaken by his fellows, and, in a humorous or self-pitying way, of oneself

> After this [feast] we jogged off to bed for the night, but never a bit could poor pilgarlic sleep one wink, for the everlasting jingle of bells —RABELAIS *Pantagruel*, v, 7

Pilgrim Fathers. The term applied to the English founders of Plymouth Colony, Massachusetts, in 1620 They belonged to the church founded at Leyden by John Robinson Having obtained a grant of land in New Jersey they came over from Holland and sailed from Plymouth in the *Mayflower* on September 6th, 1620. The party consisted of 78 men and 24 women By stress of weather they were compelled to land on the coast of Massachusetts on December 21st, far north of the territory granted to them, and here they founded Plymouth Colony

The Pilgrims is a club founded in their honour in 1902, with two branches, one in London and the other in New York.

Pilgrimage A journey to a sacred place undertaken as an act of religious devotion, either simply to venerate it or to ask for the fulfilment of some prayer, or as an act of penance. It is not penitential necessarily, nor need it be performed under conditions of physical discomfort or with great solemnity, hence it can be performed by train or motor with as great reverence as if done barefoot The chief places in the West were Walsingham and Canterbury (England), Fourvière, Puy, and St Denis (France); Rome, Loretto, and Assisi (Italy), Compostella, Guadalupe, and Montserrat (Spain), Oetting, Zell, Cologne, Trier, and Einsiedeln (Germany)

The Pilgrimage of Grace The rising on behalf of the Catholics that broke out in Lincolnshire in the autumn of 1536 It quickly assumed large proportions, but was finally extinguished in March, 1537, by the Council of the North, over 70 of the rebels being executed Robert Aske, the Archbishop of York, Lord Darcy, and the Percys were the principal leaders.

Pill To gild the pill. To soften the blow; to make a disagreeable task less offensive, as pills used to be gilded (and as now sugar-coated) to make them more pleasant to the taste and sight

Pillar. From pillar to post Hither and thither, from one thing to another without any definite purpose; harassed and worried. The phrase was originally *from post to pillar*, and comes from the old tennis-courts in allusion to the banging about of the balls

Pillar Saints. *See* STYLITES.

The Pillars of Hercules The opposite rocks at the entrance of the Mediterranean, one in Spain and the other in Africa The tale is that they were bound together till Hercules tore them asunder in order to get to Gades (Cadiz) The ancients called them Calpe and Abyla, we call them Gibraltar and Mount Hacho, on which stands the fortress of Ceuta. Macrobius ascribes the feat of making the division to Sesostris (the Egyptian Hercules), Lucan follows the same tradition, and the Phœnicians are said to have set on the opposing rocks two large pyramidal columns to serve as seamarks, one dedicated to Hercules and the other to Astarte

I will follow you even to the pillars of Hercules To the end of the world. The ancients supposed that these rocks marked the utmost limits of the habitable globe.

Pillory (pil' ŏr ı) Punishment by the pillory was not finally abolished in England till 1837, but since 1815 it had been in force only for perjury In Delaware, U.S A , it was a legal punishment down to 1905 In France it was abolished in 1848

The following eminent men have been put in the pillory for literary offences —Leighton, for tracts against Charles I, Lilburn, for circulating the tracts of Dr. Bastwick, Bastwick, for attacking the Church of England; Wharton the publisher, Prynne, for a satire on the wife of Charles I, Daniel Defoe, for a pamphlet entitled *The Shortest Way with Dissenters*, etc.

Pilot. Through Fr from Ital *pilota*, formerly *pedota*, which is probably connected with Gr. *pēdon*, a rudder.

Pilot balloon. A small balloon sent up to try the wind, hence, figuratively, a feeler, a hint thrown out to ascertain public opinion on some point

Pilot engine The leading engine when two are needed to draw a railway train, also an engine sent ahead of a train carrying important personages, etc , to ensure that the line is clear

Pilot fish. The small sea-fish, *Naucrates ductor*, so called because it is supposed to pilot the shark to its prey

The pilot that weathered the storm. William Pitt, son of the first Earl of Chatham George Canning, in 1802, wrote a song so called in compliment to him, for his having steered his country safely through the European storm stirred up by Napoleon

Pilpay or **Bidpay** (pil pā'). The name given as that of the author of *Kalilah and Dimnah* (otherwise known as *The Fables of Pilpay*), which is the 8th-century Arabic version of the

Sanskrit *Panchatantra* The word is not a true name, but means 'wise man'' (Arab *bidbah*), and was applied to the chief scholar at the court of an Indian prince.

Pimlico (pim' lı kō) (London) At one time a district of public gardens much frequented on holidays It received its name from Ben Pimlico, famous in the late 16th and early 17th centuries for his nut-brown ale, who had a tavern at Hoxton and, later, one in the neighbourhood of Chelsea

Have at thee, then, my merrie boyes, and beg for old Ben Pimlico's nut-brown ale —*Newes from Hogsdon* (1598)

Pin. The original *pin* (A S *pinn*, connected with *punnacle*) was a small tapered peg of wood, horn, metal, etc In various forms pins were used by all peoples of antiquity, and it is a mistake to suppose that pins were invented in the reign of François I, and introduced into England by Catherine Howard, fifth wife of Henry VIII In 1347, 200 years before the death of François, 12,000 pins were delivered from the royal wardrobe for the use of the Princess Joan

At a pin's fee. At an extremely low estimate, valueless

I do not set my life at a pin's fee
Hamlet, ı, 4

I don't care a pin, or a pin's point In the least.

[the Red-cross Knight] not a pin
Does care for look of living creature's eye
SPENSER *Faerie Queene*, I, v, 4

I do not pin my faith upon your sleeve. I am not going to take your *ipse dixit* for gospel. In feudal times badges were worn, and the partisans of a leader used to wear his badge, which was pinned on the sleeve Sometimes these badges were changed for some reason, hence, people learned to be chary of judging by appearances, and would say—''You wear the badge, but I do not intend to pin my faith on your sleeve.''

In merry pin In merry mood, in good spirits

The Callender, right glad to find
His friend in merry pin.
Return'd him not a single word,
But to the house went in.
COWPER *John Gilpin*, st 45

The origin of the term is not certain, it may be in reference to the *pin* or key of a stringed instrument by which it is kept to the right pitch, or it may be an allusion to the *pins* or pegs of peg-tankards (*see* PEG—*I am a peg too low*). By the rules of ''good fellowship'' a drinker was supposed to stop drinking *only at a pin*, and if he went beyond it, was to drink to the next one As it was hard to stop exactly at the pin, the effort gave rise to much mirth, and the drinker had generally to drain the tankard

No song, no laugh, no jovial din
Of drinking wassail to the pin.
LONGFELLOW *Golden Legend*

Not worth a pin. Wholly worthless

Pin money A woman's allowance of money for her own personal expenditure At one time pins were a great expense, and in 14th- and 15th-century wills there are often special bequests for the express purpose of buying pins, when they became cheap and common the women spent their allowance on other fancies, but the term *pin money* remained in vogue

Miss Hoyden Now, nurse, if he gives me two hundred a year to buy pins, what do you think he'll give me to buy fine petticoats?

Nurse Ah, my dearest, he deceives thee foully, and he's no better than a rogue for his pains! These Londoners have got a gibberage with 'em would confound a gipsy That which they call pin-money is to buy their wives everything in the varsal world, down to their very shoe-ties.—VANBRUGH *The Relapse*, v, 5 (1697)

Pins and needles The tingling sensation that comes over a limb when it has been numbed, or "asleep"

On pins and needles "On thorns," "on edge", in a state of fearful expectation or great uneasiness.

Policy of pin pricks. A policy of petty annoyances The term came into prominence during the strained relations between England and France in 1898, and is an Anglicization of the very much older French phrase, *un coup d'epingle*

There's not a pin to choose between them. They're as like as two peas, practically no difference

To tirl at the pin. *See* TIRL.

Weak on his pins. Weak in his legs, the legs being a man's "pegs" or supporters.

You could have heard a pin drop. Said of a state—especially a sudden state in the midst of din—of complete silence Leigh Hunt speaks of "a pin-drop silence" (*Rimini*, I, 144)

Pin-table A popular game depending partly on skill but mostly on chance in which balls are shot up an inclined table and touch various pins when rolling back, scoring points according to the pins they strike It is usually combined with a penny-in-the-slot machine which deals the players an allotted number of balls

Pin-up Girl In World War II the forces used to pin up in their billets, etc , pictures of film stars, actresses, or their own particular girls The phrase seems to have come into use in the U S.A in 1941

Pinch. A pinch for stale news. A punishment for telling news what is well known.

At a pinch. In an urgent case, if hard pressed. There are things that one cannot do in the ordinary way, but that one may manage "at a pinch "

To be pinched for money. To be in financial straits, hard up Hence to *pinch and scrape*, or *to pinch it*, to economize

To pinch. Slang for to steal

Where the shoe pinches. *See* SHOE.

Pinch-hitter. A person who substitutes for another in a crisis The term is from the game of Baseball where the pinch-hitter—a man who always hits the ball hard—is put in to bat when his team is in desperate straits

Pinchbeck. An alloy of copper (5 parts) and zinc (1 part), closely resembling gold So called from Christopher Pinchbeck (1670-1732), a

manufacturer of trinkets, watches and jewellery in Fleet Street, London. The term is used figuratively of anything spurious, of deceptive appearance, or low quality

Pindar (Pinder or **Pinner) of Wakefield.** *See* GEORGE-A-GREEN A *pinder* was one who impounded straying cattle and looked after the pound.

Pindaric Verse (pin dar' ik). Irregular verse; a poem of various metres, and of lofty style, in imitation of the odes of Pindar *Alexander's Feast*, by Dryden, and *The Bard*, by Gray, are examples

Pine-tree State. Maine, which has forests of these trees, and bears a pine-tree on its coat of arms

Pink. The flower is so called because the edges of the petals are *pinked* or notched The verb *to pink* means to pierce or perforate, also to ornament dress material by punching holes in it so that the lining can be seen, scalloping the edges, etc In the 17th century it was commonly used of stabbing an adversary, especially in a duel

In pink. In the scarlet coat of a fox-hunter The colour is not pink, but no hunting man would call it anything else *Cp* REDCOATS.

In the pink. In a first-rate state of health, flourishing (*cp. next*)

The pink of perfection. The flower or very acme of perfection In the same way Shakespeare (*Romeo and Juliet*, ii, 4) has "the pink of courtesy "

Pinkerton. Pinkerton's National Detective Agency was founded in Chicago, in 1852, by Allan Pinkerton, a deputy sheriff of Kane County, Ill , who had proved himself a detective of some resource The Agency became well known through investigating industrial disputes, but it was in the Civil War that it came to the forefront of such activities In 1861 a plot to assassinate President-Elect Lincoln at Baltimore was laid bare by Pinkerton's men During this war Pinkerton devised a method of obtaining military and political information from the Southern States, and eventually organized the Federal Secret Service Pinkerton's most sensational coups were the discovery of the thieves of $700,000 stolen from the Adams Express in 1866, and the breaking-up of the Molly Maguires (1877), an Irish-American secret society with many subversive and lawless deeds to their discredit.

Pious. The Romans called a man who revered his father *pius*, hence Antoninus was called *Pius*, because he requested that his adoptive father (Hadrian) might be ranked among the gods Æneas was called *Pius* because he rescued his father from the burning city of Troy. The Italian word *pieta* (*q v*) has a similar meaning.

The Pious. Ernest I, founder of the House of Gotha (1601-74)

Robert, son of Hugues Capet (971, 996-1031)

Louis I of France *See* DEBONAIR

Eric IX of Sweden (d 1161)

Frederick III, Elector Palatine (1575-76)

Pip. The pips on cards and dice were named from the seeds of fruit (earlier *peep*, origin obscure). This is merely an abbreviated form of *pippin*, which denoted the seed long before it denoted apples raised from seed *To be pipped* is to be blackballed or defeated, the black ball being the "pip"

Pip emma. Soldier slang in World War I for P.M Originally telephonese, as on the phone "twelve pip emma" cannot be misunderstood, whereas "twelve p.m." might be In the same way *ack emma* stands for A.M

To have or get the pip. To be thoroughly "fed up," downhearted, and miserable Probably connected with the poultry disease which causes fowls to pine away

To get one's second pip. To be promoted from second to first lieutenant These army ranks are marked by "pips" on the shoulder-straps

Pipe. As you pipe, I must dance. I must accommodate myself to your wishes. "He who pays the piper calls the tune."

Piping hot. Hot as water which pipes or sings, hence, new, only just out

Piping times of peace (Shakespeare, *Richard III*, i, 1). Times when there was no thought of war, and the pastoral pipe instead of the martial trumpet was heard on the village greens

Put that in your pipe and smoke it. Digest that, if you can An expression used by one who has given an adversary a severe rebuke

The pipe of peace *See* CALUMET

To pipe one's eye. To snivel, weep

To put one's pipe out. To spoil his piping, to make him change his key or sing a different tune; to "take his shine out."

Pipeclay. Routine, fossilized military dogmas of no real worth, such as excessive attention to correctness in dress, drill, etc (*Cp* RED TAPE.) Pipeclay was at one time largely used by soldiers for whitening their gloves, belts and other accoutrements

Pipe-laying (U S A) Swaying the issue in an election by slipping in voters who are not on the electoral roll

Pipe Rolls or Great Rolls of the Pipe. The series of Great Rolls of the Exchequer, beginning 2 Henry II, and continued to 1834, and probably so called either because of the cylindrical shape of the Rolls, or because they were kept in pipe-like cases The Pipe Rolls form a magnificent series of documents, and contain complete accounts of the Crown revenues as rendered by the Sheriffs of the different counties. They are now in the Public Record Office, Chancery Lane

Office of the Clerk of the Pipe. A very ancient office in the Court of Exchequer, where leases of Crown lands, sheriffs' accounts, etc , were made out It existed in the reign of Henry II, and was abolished in the reign of William IV

Piper. Piper's news. Stale news; "fiddler's news" (*q v*).

The Pied Piper. *See* PIED.

Tom Piper. So the piper is called in the morris dance
The Piper referred to by Drayton seems to have been a sort of jongleur or *raconteur* of short tales

Tom Piper is gone out, and mirth bewailes,
He never will come in to tell us tales.

Who's to pay the piper? *See* PAY.

Pippin *See* PIP

Piqué (pē' kā) The art of inlaying gold or silver in another material, such as tortoiseshell or ivory

Pirie's Chair. "The lowest seat o' hell."

In Pirie's chair you'll sit, I say,
The lowest seat o' hell,
If ye do not amend your ways,
It's there that ye must dwell.
Child's English and Scottish Ballads:
The Courteous Knight

Pis-aller (pēs äl' ā) (Fr , worst course). A makeshift, something for want of a better, a *dernier ressort*.

Piso's Justice (pī' zō). Verbally right, but morally wrong. Seneca tells us that Piso condemned a man on circumstantial evidence for murder, but when the suspect was at the place of execution, the man supposed to have been murdered appeared The centurion sent the prisoner to Piso, and explained the case to him, whereupon Piso condemned all three to death saying, *Fiat justitia* (Lat , let justice be done). The condemned man was executed because sentence of death had been passed upon him, the centurion because he had disobeyed orders, and the man supposed to have been murdered because he had been the cause of death to two innocent men, and *fiat justitia ruat cælum* (let justice be done though the heavens should fall)

Pistol. Formerly *pistolet*, so called from the old *pistolese*, a dagger or hanger for the manufacture of which Pistoia, in Tuscany, was famous

Pocket pistol *See* POCKET

To fire one's pistol in the air. Purposely to refrain from injuring an adversary The phrase is often used of argument, and refers to the old practice of duellers doing this when they wished to discharge a "debt of honour" without incurring risks

Pit-a-pat. My heart goes pit-a-pat. Throbs, palpitates An echoic or a mere ricochet word, of which there are a great many in English—as "fiddle-faddle," "harum-scarum," "ding-dong," etc.

Anything like the sound of a rat
Makes my heart go pit-a-pat.
BROWNING *Pied Piper of Hamelin*

Pitcairn Island, in the South Pacific, was the first home of the mutineers of the *Bounty* (*q.v*).

Pitch. The black resinous substance gets its name from Lat *pix*, the verb (to fling, settle, etc) is the M.E *pichen, pykken*

A pitched battle. One for which both sides have made deliberate preparations

Pitch and pay. Pay up at once There is a suppressed pun in the phrase "to pay a ship" is to pitch it

The word is pitch and pay—trust none
Henry V, ii, 3.

Pitch and toss. A game in which coins are pitched at a mark, the player getting nearest having the right to toss all the others' coins into the air and take those that come down with heads up Hence, *to play pitch and toss* with one's money, prospects, etc , is to gamble recklessly, to play ducks and drakes

> The bounding pinnace played a game
> Of dreary pitch and toss,
> A game that, on the good dry land,
> Is apt to bring a loss
> THOS. HOOD *The Sea Spell*

To pitch into one To assail him vigorously, to give it him hot

Touch pitch, and you will be defiled. "The finger that touches rouge will be red " "Evil communications corrupt good manners " "A rotten apple injures its companions " Shakespeare introduces the proverb in *Much Ado* (iii, 3).

Pitcher. From Lat *picarium* or *bicarium*, the word is a doublet of BEAKER (*q v*).

Little pitchers have long ears. Little folk or children hear what is said when you little think it The ear of a pitcher is the handle, made somewhat in the shape of a man's ear

The pitcher went once too often to the well. The dodge was tried once too often, and utterly failed. The sentiment is proverbial in most European languages

Pithecanthrope (pith e kǎn' thrōp) The name given by Haeckel in 1868 to the hypothetical "missing link" (*q v*), from Gr *pithekos*, ape, and *anthropos*, man. Later, *Pithecanthropus* was the generic name given to the remains of the extinct man-like ape discovered in the Pliocene of Java in 1891

Pitt Diamond A diamond of just under 137 carats found at the Parteal mines, India, and bought by Thomas Pitt (*see* DIAMOND PITT) in 1702 from a thief for a sum (said to have been £20,400) far below its real value Hence Pope's reference—

> Asleep and naked as an Indian lay,
> An honest factor stole a gem away
> *Moral Essays*, Ep iii, 361

Pitt sold the diamond in 1717 to the Regent Orleans (hence it is also called the "Regent Diamond") for £135,000, it later adorned the sword-hilt of Napoleon, and is still in the possession of France Its original weight before cutting was 410 carats.

Pitt's Pictures. "Blind" windows used to be so called, because many windows were blocked up when William Pitt augmented the window tax in 1784, and again in 1797.

Pixie or **Pixy** (pik' si) A sprite or fairy of folklore, especially in Cornwall and Devon, where some hold pixies to be the spirits of infants who have died before baptism The Pixy monarch has his court like Oberon, and sends his subjects on their several tasks The word is probably Celtic, but its history is unknown

Place. Place-maker's Bible. *See* BIBLE.

Placer. An area where surface mining (for gold or silver) is carried out The word is of Spanish origin, the plural being *placeres*.

Place aux dames (Fr) Make way for the ladies; ladies first

Placebo (plǎs ē' bō) (Lat., I shall please, *or* be acceptable) Vespers for the dead, because the first antiphon at Vespers of the Office of the Dead began with the words *Placebo Domino in regione vivorum*, I will walk before the Lord in the land of the living (*Ps* cxvi, 9).

As sycophants and those who wanted to get something out of the relatives of the departed used to make a point of attending this service and singing the *Placebo* the phrase *to sing Placebo* came to mean "to play the flatterer or sycophant", and Chaucer (who in the *Merchant's Tale* gives this as a name to a parasite) has—

> Flatereres been the develes chapelleyns that singen
> evere *Placebo* —*Parson's Tale*, § 40

Plagiarist (plā' ja rist), one who appropriates another's ideas, etc , in literature, music, and so on, means strictly one who kidnaps a slave (Lat *plagiarius*) Martial applies the word to the kidnappers of other men's brains.

Plain, The The Girondists were so called in the French Revolutionary National Convention, because they sat on the level floor or plain of the hall After their overthrow this part of the House was called the *marais* or swamp, and included such members as were under the control of the Mountain (*q v*)

It's all plain sailing. It's perfectly straightforward, there need be no hesitation about the course of action A nautical phrase which should be written *plane*, not *plain* Plane sailing is the art of determining a ship's position on the assumption that the earth is flat and she is sailing, therefore, on a plane, instead of a spherical surface, which is a simple and easy method of computing distances

Plains Indians is the name given by ethnographers to the Indian tribes of the central prairie areas of North America from Alberta to Texas—the land, indeed, once ranged over by the American bison or buffalo on which the Plains Indians largely subsisted The Plains Indians are the Redskins of romance, with their feather bonnets, tepees, and pipes of peace—the Dakotas, Blackfeet, Cheyennes, Comanches, Pawnees, Apaches, and many others.

Planets. The heavenly bodies that revolve round the sun in approximately circular orbits; so called from Gr (through Lat. and O Fr) *planasthai*, to wander, because, to the ancients, they appeared to wander about among the stars instead of having fixed places

The *primary planets* are Mercury, Venus, the Earth, Mars, Jupiter, Saturn, Neptune, Uranus, and Pluto (disc in 1930), these are known as the *major planets*, the asteroids between the orbits of Mars and Jupiter being the *minor planets*.

The *secondary planets* are the satellites, or moons, revolving round a primary.

Mercury and Venus are called *Inferior Planets* because their orbits are nearer to the sun than the Earth's, the remaining planets are *Superior Planets*

Only five of the planets were known to the ancients (the Earth, of course, not being reckoned), viz Mercury, Venus, Mars, Jupiter, and Saturn, but to these were added the Sun and the Moon, making seven in all Among the astrologers and alchemists

THE SUN (APOLLO) represented		Gold
THE MOON (DIANA)	,,	Silver
MERCURY	,,	Quicksilver.
VENUS	,,	Copper
MARS	,,	Iron
JUPITER	,,	Tin
SATURN	,,	Lead

In heraldry the arms of royal personages used to be blazoned by the names of planets (see HERALDRY)

Planet-struck. A blighted tree is said to be planet-struck Epilepsy, paralysis, lunacy, etc , are attributed to the malignant aspects of the planets Horses are said to be planet-struck when they seem stupefied, whether from want of food, colic, or stoppage

> They with speed
> Their course through thickest constellations held,
> Spreading their bane, the blasted stars looked wan,
> And planets, planet-strook, real eclipse
> Then suffered   MILTON *Paradise Lost*, x, 410

To be born under a lucky (or unlucky) planet. According to astrology, some planet, at the birth of every individual, presides over his destiny. Some of the planets, like Jupiter, are lucky, and others, like Saturn, are unlucky *See* HOUSES, ASTROLOGICAL.

Plank, A Any one portion or principle of a political *platform* (*q v*)

To walk the plank. To be put to the supreme test, also, to be about to die Walking the plank was a mode of disposing of prisoners at sea, much in vogue among pirates in the 17th century

Plantagenet (plăn tăj' e net), from *planta genista* (broom-plant), the family cognizance first assumed by Geoffrey, Count of Anjou (d 1151), during a pilgrimage to the Holy Land, as a symbol of humility By his wife Matilda, daughter of Henry I of England, he was father of Henry II, the founder of the House of Plantagenet

The House of Plantagenet Henry II and the English kings descended in the direct male line from him, viz —

Henry II	Edward I
Richard I	Edward II
John	Edward III
Henry III	Richard II

They reigned from 1154 to 1399 *Cp* ANGEVIN

Plate. In horse-racing, the gold or silver cup forming the prize, hence the race for such a prize.

Selling plate. A race in which owners of starters have to agree beforehand that the winner shall be sold at a previously fixed price.

Plates of meat. Rhyming slang for "feet", often abbreviated to *plates*

Platform. The policy or declaration of the policy of a political party, that on which the party stands, each separate principle being called a *plank* of the platform

In this sense the word is an Americanism dating from rather before the middle of last century, but in earlier Elizabethan times and later it was used of a plan or scheme of Church government and of political action

Queen Elizabeth, in answer to the *Supplication* of the Puritans (offered to the Parliament in 1586), said she "had examined the platform and accounted it most prejudicial to the religion established, to her crown, her government, and her subjects "

Platonic (pla ton' ik) Pertaining to or ascribed to Plato, the great Greek philosopher (d about 347 B C) who taught a form of Idealism that attributed real Being to general concepts or Ideas and denied the existence of individual things, the world of *sense* being an illusion, the world of *thought* all

Platonic bodies. An old name for the five regular geometric solids described by Plato— viz the tetrahedron hexahedron, octahedron, dodecahedron, and icosahedron, all of which are bounded by like, equal, and regular planes

Platonic love Spiritual love between persons of opposite sexes, the friendship of man and woman, without anything sexual about it The phrase is founded on a passage towards the end of the *Symposium* in which Plato was extolling not the non-sexual love of a man for a woman but the loving interest that Socrates took in young men—which was pure, and therefore noteworthy in the Greece of the period

> I am convinced, and always was, that Platonic Love is Platonic nonsense —RICHARDSON. *Pamela*, I, lxxviii

The Platonic Year The same as the Platonic Cycle *See under* CYCLE.

Platonism is characterized by the doctrine of pre-existing eternal ideas, and teaches the immortality and pre-existence of the soul, the dependence of virtue upon discipline, and the trustworthiness of cognition

Platt Deutsch (plăt doich) The colloquial German common to most points of Northwest Germany, bearing some relationship to Dutch

Plaudite (plaw' dit i) (Lat , "applaud, ye!"')— hence our word *plaudit*) The appeal for applause at the conclusion of Roman plays, especially the comedies of Terence; hence the end of a play

> Here we may strike the *Plaudite* to our play; my lord Fool's gone, all our audience will forsake us — CHAPMAN *Monsieur D'Olive*, IV, ii.

Play "This may be play to you, 'tis death to us " The allusion is to Æsop's fable of the boys throwing stones at some frogs

As good as a play. Intensely amusing It is said to have been the remark of Charles I when he attended the debate on Lord Ross's "Divorce Bill "

Played out Exhausted; out of date, no longer in vogue

Playing to the gallery, or to the gods. Appealing to the less cultured taste attributed to the common people, appealing to sensational rather than artistic taste

The "gods" in theatrical phrase are the spectators in the uppermost gallery The ceiling of Drury Lane Theatre—only just above the gallery—was at one time painted in imitation of the sky, with cupids and deities In French this gallery is nicknamed *paradis*

Playing possum. *See* POSSUM

Pleader, Pleading *See* SPECIAL PLEADING

Plebeian (ple bē′ an) One of, or appertaining to, the common people, properly a free citizen of Rome, neither patrician nor client Plebeians were, however, free landowners, and had their own "gentes."

Plebiscite (pleb′ i sit) In Roman history, a law enacted by the "comitia" or assembly of tribes, nowadays it means the direct vote of the whole body of citizens of a State on some definite question
In France, the resolutions adopted in the Revolution by the voice of the people, and the general votes given during the Second Empire—such as the general vote to elect Napoleon III emperor of the French were by plebiscite

Pledge To guarantee, to assign as security, hence, in drinking a toast, to give assurance of friendship by the act of drinking
Drink to me only with thine eyes,
And I will pledge with mine
BEN JONSON.

To take the pledge. To bind oneself by a solemn undertaking to abstain from intoxicating liquors, the *pledge* being the guarantee or security—one's pledged word

Pleiades (plī′ a dēz) The cluster of stars in the constellation Taurus, especially the seven larger ones out of the great number that compose the cluster, so called by the Greeks, possibly from *plein*, to sail, because they considered navigation safe at the return of the Pleiades, and never attempted it after those stars disappeared

The Pleiades were the seven daughters of Atlas and Pleione They were transformed into stars, one of which, Electra (*q v*), is invisible, some said out of shame, because she alone married a human being, while others held that she hides herself from grief for the destruction of the city and royal race of Troy. She is known as "the lost Pleiad" —
One of those forms which flit by us, when we
Are young, and fix our eyes on every face;
Whose course and home we know not, nor shall know
Like the lost Pleiad seen no more below
BYRON *Beppo*, xiv.

The name The Pleiad has frequently been given to groups of seven specially illustrious persons, *e g* —
The Seven Wise Men of Greece (*q v*), sometimes called the *Philosophical Pleiad*

The Pleiad of Alexandria. A group of seven contemporary poets in the 3rd century B.C , viz. Callimachus, Apollonius of Rhodes, Aratus, Philiscus (called *Homer the Younger*), Lycophron, Nicander, and Theocritus

Charlemagne's Pleiad, the group of scholars with which the Emperor surrounded himself, viz Charlemagne (who, in this circle, was known as "David"), Alcuin ("Albinus"), Adelard ("Augustine"), Angilbert ("Homer"), Riculfe ("Damætas"), Varnefrid, and Eginhard

The French Pleiad of the 16th century, who wrote poetry in the metres, style, etc., of the ancient Greeks and Romans Of these, Ronsard was the leader, the others being Dorat, Du Bellay, Remi Belleau, Jodelle, Baif, and Ponthus de Thyard.

The second French Pleiad Seven contemporary poets in the reign of Louis XIII, very inferior to the "first Pleiad " They are Rapin, Commire, Larue, Santeuil, Menage, Duperier, and Petit.

Plimsoll Line or **Mark.** A circle with a horizontal line drawn through it, carried on both sides of all British merchant vessels It indicates the maximum depth to which a vessel may be loaded and is named after Samuel Plimsoll (1824-98), M P for Derby, who brought about its compulsory adoption in view of the great loss of life at sea owing to overloaded vessels

Plon-plon The sobriquet of Prince Napoleon Joseph Charles Bonaparte (1822-91), son of Jerome Bonaparte, an adaptation of *Craint-plon* (Fear-bullet), the nickname he earned in the Crimean War

Plough Another name for the "Great Bear" (*q v*)

Fond, Fool, or **White Plough** The plough dragged about a village on Plough Monday Called *white*, because the mummers who drag it about are dressed in white, gaudily trimmed with flowers and ribbons Called *fond* or *fool*, because the procession is fond or foolish—not serious, or of a business character.

Plough Monday. The first Monday after Twelfth Day is so called because it is the end of the Christmas holidays, and the day when men return to their plough or daily work. It was customary on this day for farm labourers to draw a plough from door to door of the parish, and solicit "plough-money" to spend in a frolic The queen of the banquet was called Bessy Cp. DISTAFF

Speed the plough, or **God speed the plough** A wish for success and prosperity in some undertaking It is a very old phrase, and occurs as early as the 15th century in the song sung by the ploughmen on Plough Monday

To be ploughed. To be ′plucked" at an examination, to fail to pass

To plough the sands. To engage in some altogether fruitless labour.

To plough with another's heifer. To use information obtained by unfair means, *e g* through a treacherous friend A biblical phrase When the men of Timnath gave Samson the answer to his riddle, he replied —
If ye had not plowed with my heifer, ye had not found out my riddle—*Judges* xiv, 18

To put one's hand to the plough. To undertake a task, to commence operations in earnest. The man who starts ploughing and looks back is unable to plough a straight furrow; only by keeping one's eyes on an object ahead is it possible to plough straight
And Jesus said unto him, No man, having put his hand to the plough, and looking back, is fit for the kingdom of God —*Luke* ix, 62

Plover Another old synonym for a dupe or "gull" (*q v.*), also for a courtesan

To live like a plover. To live on nothing, to live on air Plovers, however, live on small insects and worms, which they hunt for in newly ploughed fields

Plowden. "The case is altered," quoth Plowden. There is more than one story given by way of accounting for the origin of this old phrase—used by Jonson as the title of one of his comedies (1598) One of them says that Plowden was an unpopular priest, and, to get him into trouble, he was inveigled into attending mass performed by a layman. When impeached for so doing, the cunning priest asked the layman if it was he who officiated "Yes," said the man "And are you a priest?" said Plowden "No," said the man "Then," said Plowden, turning to the tribunal, "*the case is altered,* for it is an axiom with the Church, 'No priest, no mass.'"

Another story fathers the phrase on Edmund Plowden (1518-85), the great lawyer He was asked what legal remedy there was against some hogs that had trespassed on complainant's ground. "There is very good remedy," began Plowden, but when told that they were his own hogs, said, "*Nay, then, the case is altered.*"

Pluck, meaning courage, determination, was originally pugilistic slang of the late 18th century, and meant much the same as *heart* A "pug" who was lacking in pluck was a coward, he hadn't the heart for his job; the *pluck* of an animal is the heart, liver, and lungs, that can be removed by one pull or *pluck* Cp the expressions bold *heart,* lily-*livered,* a man of another *kidney, bowels* of mercy, a *vein* of fun, it raised his *bile,* etc

A rejected candidate at an examination is said to be *plucked,* because formerly at the Universities, when degrees were conferred and the names were read out before presentation to the Vice-Chancellor, the proctor walked once up and down the room, and anyone who objected might signify his dissent by *plucking* the proctor's gown This was occasionally done by tradesmen to whom the candidate was in debt

A plucked pigeon. One fleeced out of his money, one plucked by a rook or sharper

There were no smart fellows whom fortune had troubled no plucked pigeons or winged rooks, no disappointed speculators, no ruined miners —SCOTT *Peveril of the Peak,* ch xi

He's a plucked 'un. He's a plucky chap, there's no frightening *him*

I'll pluck his goose for him. I'll cut his crest, lower his pride, make him eat humble pie Comparing the person to a goose, the threat is to pluck off his feathers in which he prides himself

Plug. Plug song. A song given publicity, *e g.* on the wireless *To plug,* in this connexion, is to publicize—sometimes to an extreme degree

Plug ugly. A rowdy, unpleasant character, a term said to have originated in Baltimore

Plum. Old slang for a very large sum of money (properly £100,000), or for its possession Nowadays the figurative use of the word means the very best part of anything, the "pick of the basket," a windfall, or one of the prizes of life, as "The plums (*i e.* the chief and highly paid positions) of the Civil Service should go by merit, not influence"

Plumes. In borrowed plumes. Assumed merit; airs and graces not merited The allusion is to the fable of the jackdaw who dressed up in peacock's feathers

To plume oneself on something. To be proud of it, conceited about it, to boast of it A plume is a feather, and to plume oneself is to feather one's own conceit

Mrs Bute Crawley plumed herself upon her resolute manner of performing [what she thought right] —THACKERAY *Vanity Fair*

Plump. To give all one's votes to a single candidate, or to vote for only one when one has the right to vote for more The earlier phrase was to give a plumper, or to vote plump

Plunger. One who *plunges, i e.* gambles recklessly, and goes on when he can't afford it in the hope that his luck will turn. The 4th and last Marquis of Hastings was the first person so called by the turf He was the original of Champagne Charlie and the most notorious spendthrift and wastrel of the mid-19th century, whose folly of squandering has become almost legendary One night he played three games of draughts for £1,000 a game, and lost all three He then cut a pack of cards for £500 a cut, and lost £5,000 in an hour and a half He paid both debts before he left the room

Plus ultra (plŭs ûl' trä). The motto in the royal arms of Spain It was once *Ne plus ultra* ("thus far and no farther"), in allusion to the pillars of Hercules, the *ne plus ultra* of the world, but after the discovery of America, and when Charles V inherited the crown of Aragon and Castile, with all the vast American possessions, he struck out *ne,* and assumed the words *plus ultra* for the national motto, the suggestion being that Spain *can* go farther

Pluto (ploo' tō) The ruler of the infernal regions in Roman mythology, son of Saturn, brother of Jupiter and Neptune, and husband of Proserpine (*q v*), hence, the grave, the place where the dead go to before they are admitted into Elysium or sent to Tartarus.

Brothers, be of good cheer, this night we shall sup with Pluto —*Leonidas to the three hundred Spartans before the battle of Thermopylæ*

Th' infernal powers
Covering your foe with cloud of deadly night,
Have borne him hence to Pluto's baleful bowers
SPENSER· *Faerie Queene,* I, v, 14

A *Pluto* of the 20th century is the large, amiable, and stupid dog who is the companion of Mickey Mouse in Walt Disney's animated cartoons

In World War II *Pluto* was the code name (from the initials of Pipe Line Under The Ocean) given to the pipelines to carry petrol which were laid across the bed of the English Channel from England to France—from Sandown to Cherbourg and from Dungeness to Boulogne In all, these Pluto lines covered a distance of 770 miles, and consisted of 23,000 tons of lead piping and 5,500 tons of steel piping Much of this was recovered in 1949.

Plutonian or **Plutonist.** *See* VULCANIST.

Plutonic Rocks. Granites, certain porphyries and other igneous unstratified crystalline rocks, supposed to have been formed at a great depth and pressure, as distinguished from the volcanic rocks, which were formed near the surface So called by Lyell from *Pluto*, as the lord of elemental fire.

Plutus (ploo´tus) In Greek mythology, the god of riches Hence, **Rich as Plutus**, and *plutocrat*, one who exercises influence or possesses power through his wealth The legend is that he was blinded by Zeus so that his gifts should be equally distributed and not go only to those who merited them

Plymouth Brethren. A sect of Evangelical Christians that arose at Plymouth about 1830. They have no regular ministry, holding that national churches are too lax and dissenters too sectarian Sometimes called "Darbyites" (*q v.*) from John Nelson Darby (1800-82), their founder.

Pocahontas (pok a hon´ tăs) Daughter of Powhatan, an Indian chief of Virginia, born about 1595 She is said to have rescued Captain John Smith when her father was on the point of killing him She subsequently married John Rolfe, one of the settlers at Jamestown, was baptized under the name of Rebecca, and in 1616 was brought to England, where she became an object of curiosity and frequent allusion in contemporary literature She died at Gravesend in 1617.

> The blessed
> Pocahontas, as the historian calls her,
> And great king's daughter of Virginia .
> BEN JONSON *Staple of News*, II, 1 (1625)

Pocket. The word is used by airmen to denote a place where a sudden drop or acceleration is experienced, owing to a local variation in air-pressure

Pocket battleship. A small, heavily armoured warship built in accordance with the limiting terms of a treaty By the Treaty of Versailles Germany was forbidden to build battleships of over 10,000 tons In consequence she constructed several formidable battleships which purported to be within this limit, though it was discovered later that they were not

Pocket borough. A parliamentary borough where the influence of the magnate was so powerful as to be able to control the election of any candidate

Pocket judgment. A bond under the hand of a debtor, countersigned by the sovereign. It could be enforced without legal process, but for long has fallen into disuse

Pocket pistol. Colloquial for a flask carried in "self-defence," because we may be unable to get a dram on the road

Pocket veto. When the President of the U S A refuses to ratify a Bill which has passed both Houses, he is said to *pocket* it

Queen Elizabeth's pocket pistol. A formidable piece of ordnance given to Queen Elizabeth I by the Low Countries in recognition of her efforts to protect them in their reformed religion It used to overlook the Channel from Dover cliffs, but in 1834 was removed to make room for a modern battery It bore the following inscription (in Flemish) —

> Load me well and keep me clean,
> And I'll carry a ball to Calais Green

Put your pride in your pocket. Lay it aside for the nonce.

To be in, or **out of pocket.** To be a gainer or a loser by some transaction.

To pocket an insult. To submit to an insult without showing annoyance

To put one's hand in one's pocket To give money (generally to some charity).

Pococurante (pŏ kŏ kū răn´ tı) (Ital , *poco curante*, caring little). Insouciant, devil-may-care, easy-go-lucky Hence, *pococurantism*, indifference to matters of importance but concern about trifles Also used for one who in argument leaves the main gist and rides off on some minor and indifferent point

Podsnap. A pompous, self-satisfied man in Dickens's *Our Mutual Friend*, the type of one who is overburdened with stiff-starched etiquette and self-importance Hence, *Podsnappery*

> He always knew exactly what Providence meant Inferior and less respectable men might fall short of that mark, but Mr Podsnap was always up to it. And it was very remarkable (and must have been very comfortable) that what Providence meant was invariably what Mr. Podsnap meant —*Our Mutual Friend*, Bk I, ch ii

Poet. Poet Laureate. A court official, appointed by the Prime Minister, whose duty it is (or was) to compose odes in honour of the sovereign's birthday and in celebration of State occasions of importance

The first Poet Laureate officially recognized as such was Ben Jonson, but in earlier times there had been an occasional *Versificator Regis*, and Chaucer, Skelton, Spenser, and Daniel were called "Laureates" though not appointed to that office The following is the complete list of Poets Laureate —

> Ben Jonson, 1619-1637
> Sir William Davenant, 1660-1668.
> John Dryden, 1670-1688
> Thomas Shadwell, 1688-1692.
> Nahum Tate, 1692-1715
> Nicholas Rowe, 1715-1718
> Laurence Eusden, 1718-1730
> Colley Cibber, 1730-1757
> William Whitehead, 1757-1785.
> Thomas Warton, 1785-1790
> Henry James Pye, 1790-1813
> Robert Southey, 1813-1843
> William Wordsworth, 1843-1850
> Alfred Tennyson, 1850-1892.
> Alfred Austin, 1896-1913.
> Robert Bridges, 1913-1930
> John Masefield, 1930-

The term arose from the ancient custom in the universities of presenting a laurel wreath to graduates in rhetoric and poetry There were at one time "doctors laureate," "bachelors laureate," etc , and in France authors of distinction are still at times "crowned" by the Academy.

Poeta nascitur non fit. Poets are born, not made. *See* BORN

Poets' Corner, The. The southern end of the south transept of Westminster Abbey, first so called by Oliver Goldsmith because it contained the tomb of Chaucer Addison had previously (*Spectator*, No 26, 1711) alluded to it as the "poetical Quarter," in which, he says—

I found there were Poets who had no Monuments, and Monuments which had no Poets

Besides Chaucer's tomb it contains that of Spenser, and either the tombs of or monuments to Drayton, Ben Jonson, Shakespeare (a statue), Milton (bust), Samuel Butler, Davenant, Cowley, Prior, Gay, Addison, Thomson, Goldsmith, Dryden, Dr Johnson, Sheridan, Burns, Southey, Coleridge, Campbell, Macaulay, Longfellow, Dickens, Thackeray, Tennyson, Browning, and Hardy

The term *Poet's Corner* is also facetiously applied to the part of a newspaper in which poetical contributions are printed

Pogrom. an organized massacre, espec ally one of those directed against the Jews in Russia in 1905 and later. The word is Russian, and means devastation (*gromit*, to thunder, to destroy unmercifully)

Poilu (pwa' lū). The popular name for the French private soldier, equivalent to our "Tommy Atkins." It means literally "hairy," but it had been used by Balzac as meaning "brave."

Point. Defined by Euclid as "that which hath no parts " Playfair defines it as "that which has position but not magnitude," and Legendre says it "is a limit terminating a line," which suggests that a point could not exist, even in imagination, without a line, and presupposes that we know what a *line* is

A point of honour. *See* HONOUR

A point-to-point race. A race, especially a steeplechase, direct from one point to another, a cross-country race

Armed at all points. Armed to the teeth, having no parts undefended

A figure like your Father,
Arm'd at all points exactly, *Cap a Pe,*
Appears before them

                     Hamlet, i, 2

Come to the point! Speak out plainly what you want, don't beat about the bush, but avoid circumlocution and get to the gist of the matter

In point of fact. A stronger way of saying "As a fact," or "As a matter of fact "

Not to put too fine a point upon it. Not to be over delicate in stating it, the prelude to a blunt though truthful remark.

To carry one's point. To attain the desired end, to get one's way

To dine on potatoes and point. To have potatoes without any relish or extras, a very meagre dinner indeed When salt was dear and the cellar was empty parents used to tell their children to *point* their potato to the salt cellar, and eat it This was potato and point, and the "joke" lies in the allusion to a *point-steak*, which is the best portion

To give one points To be able to accord him an advantage and yet beat him, to be considerably better than he

To make a point of doing something. To treat it as a matter of duty, or to make it a special object The phrase is a translation of the older French *faire un point de*

To stand on points. On punctilios; delicacy of behaviour In the following quotation Theseus puns on the phrase, the side allusion being that Quince in the delivery of his Prologue had taken no notice of the stops, or *points* —

This fellow doth not stand upon points *—Midsummer Night's Dream, v, 1*

To stretch a point. To exceed what is strictly right There may be an allusion here to the tagged laces called *points*, formerly used in costume, to "truss a point" was to tie the laces which held the breeches, to "stretch a point" to stretch these laces, so as to adjust the dress to extra growth, or the temporary fullness of good feeding

To truss his points. To tie the points of hose The points were the cords pointed with metal, like shoe-laces, attached to doublets and hose; being very numerous, some second person was required to "truss" them or fasten them properly

Point-blank. Direct A term in gunnery, when a cannon is so placed that the line of sight is parallel to the axis and horizontal the discharge is point-blank, and was supposed to go direct, without curve, to an object within a certain distance In French *point blanc* is the white mark or bull's-eye of a target, to hit which the ball or arrow must not deviate in the least from the exact path

Now art thou within point-blank of our jurisdiction regal —2 *Henry VI*, iv, 7

Point d'appui (Fr). A standpoint, a fulcrum, a position from which you can operate, a pretext to conceal the real intention Literally the point of support.

The material which gives name to the dish is but the *point d'appui* for the literary cayenne and curry-powder, by which it is recommended to the palate of the reader *—The Athenæum*

Point-devise (Fr , the point devised, the desired object) Punctilious, minutely exact. Holofernes says, "I abhor such insociable and *point de vise* companions, such rackers of orthography "

You are rather *point de vise* in your accoutrements. —*As You Like It,* iii, 2

Point of No Return. In an aeroplane flight, that point at which it is just as safe, or close, to go forward as to turn back

Poison It is said that poisons had no effect on Mithridates, King of Pontus This was Mithridates VI (d 63 B C), called the Great, who succeeded his father at the age of eleven, and fortified his constitution by drinking antidotes to poisons which might at any moment be administered to him by persons about the court *See* MITHRIDATE

Poisson d'Avril (pwa' son da vrīl) (Fr., April fish) The French equivalent for our "April fool" (*q v.*)

Poke. A bag, pouch, or sack—from which comes our *pocket*, a little poke The word is rarely used nowadays, except in the phrase **To buy a pig in a poke** (*see* PIG). The word is not connected with the verb *to poke*

Poke bonnet. A long, straight, projecting bonnet, commonly worn by women in the early 19th century, and still worn by Salvation Army lasses and old-fashioned Quaker women Why it was so called is not clear—probably because it projects or *pokes* out

To poke fun at one. To make one a laughing-stock

Poker Face. An expressionless face characteristic of the good poker-player who assumes it to conceal from his adversaries any idea of what cards he may be holding

Poky. Cramped, narrow confined, as, a poky corner. Also poor and shabby.
  The ladies were in their pokiest old headgear,—
  THACKERAY. *The Newcomes*, ch lvii

Polack (pō'lăk) An inhabitant of Poland. The term is not used now, except jokingly in U.S.A. *Pole* having for long taken its place
  So frowned he once, when, in an angry parle,
  He smote the sledded Polacks on the ice
      Hamlet, i, 1

Poland. The Partition of Poland This country, situated between the leading military powers of Eastern Europe—Russia, Austria, and Prussia —has for the last two centuries been subject to invasion by, and division between, those countries The first partition between the three was in 1772, the second in 1793, the final partition in 1796 The kingdom was reconstituted under Napoleon's authority, but was annexed to the Russian crown in 1832 It was again set up, as a republic, in 1919, but partitioned between Germany and Russia in 1939 In 1945 it was again reconstituted as a separate state under Russian dominance

Polish Corridor. The territory given to Poland by the Treaty of Versailles to enable her to have access to the Baltic Sea It followed roughly the line of the Vistula and reached the sea to the west of Danzig (declared a free city) and the port of Gdynia was built by Poland for her commerce. The Corridor cut off East Prussia from the rest of Germany and was one of the causes of irritation which eventually led to World War II.

Pole. The stake, mast, measure (16½ ft), etc , gets its name from Lat *palus*, a pale or stake, *pole*—the *North Pole, magnetic pole*, etc —is from Gr *polos*, an axis, pivot

Barber's pole. *See* BARBER

The Poles are the vintagers in Normandy. The Norman vintage consists of apples beaten down by poles The French say, *En Normandie l'on vendage avec la gaule*, where *gaule* is a play on the word gaul, but really means a pole In this connexion it is interesting to record that during the German occupation of Paris in 1941-43 the students once marched through the streets as a demonstration carrying two posts (*deux gaules*) and it took the German authorities some time to grasp that this was a play on the name De Gaulle—then the symbol of French nationality and liberty.

Under bare poles. *See* BARE

Polichinelle *See* SECRET

Polish Off. To finish out of hand In allusion to articles polished

I'll polish him **off** in no time. I'll set him down, give him a drubbing

To polish off a meal To eat it quickly, and not keep anyone waiting

Polixenes (pol ix' e nēz) Father of Florizel and King of Bohemia in Shakespeare's *Winter's Tale* (q v)

Polka. (q v). A round dance said to have been invented about 1830 by a Bohemian servant girl In a few years it took Europe by storm The polka is danced in couples in 2-4 time, the characteristic feature being the rest on the second beat

Poll (pōl) (of Teutonic origin), means the head; hence, the number of persons in a crowd ascertained by counting heads, hence the counting of voters at an election, and such phrases as to go to the **polls**, to stand for election, and **poll** tax, a tax levied on everybody
  The Cambridge term, **the Poll**, meaning students who obtain only a pass degree, *i e.* a degree without honours, is probably from Gr *hoi polloi*, the common herd These students— *poll men*, are said to *go out in the poll*, and to take a *poll degree*

Pollux (pol' ŭks) In classical mythology the twin brother of Castor (q v)

Polly Mary The change of M for P in pet names is by no means rare, *e g* —
  Margaret Maggie or Meggy, becomes Peggie, and Pegg or Peg
  Martha Matty becomes Patty
  In the case of *Mary*—*Polly* we see another change by no means unusual—that of *r* into *l* or *ll* Similarly, *Sarah* becomes **Sally**, *Dorothea*, *Dora*, becomes Dolly, *Harry*, Hal

Polonius (pol ō' ni ŭs) A garrulous old courtier, in *Hamlet*, typical of the pompous, sententious old man He was father of Ophelia, and lord chamberlain to the king of Denmark

Polony (po lō' ni) A corruption of *Bologna* (*sausage*)

Poltergeist (pol tĕr gīst) A household spirit, well known to spiritualists, remarkable for throwing things about, plucking the bedclothes, making noises, etc. It is a German term—*polter*, noise, *geist*, spirit

Polt-foot. A club-foot Ben Jonson calls Vulcan, who was lame, the "polt-footed philosopher"
  Venus was content to take the blake Smith (*i e.*, blacksmith Vulcan) with his powlt foote—LYLY *Euphues*

Poltroon. A coward; from Ital *poltro*, a bed, because cowards are sluggards and feign themselves sick a-bed in times of war
  In falconry the name was given to a bird of prey, with the talons of the hind toes cut off to prevent its flying at game, probably owing to the old idea that the word was derived from Lat *pollice truncus*, maimed in the thumb, because conscripts who had no stomach for the field used to disqualify themselves by cutting off their right thumb

Polycrates (pol i krā' tēz), Tyrant of Samos, was so fortunate in all things that Amasis, King of Egypt, advised him to chequer his pleasures by relinquishing something he greatly prized. Whereupon Polycrates threw into the sea a beautiful seal, the most valuable of his jewels A few days afterwards a fine fish was sent him as a present, and in its belly was found the jewel. Amasis, alarmed at this good fortune, broke off his alliance, declaring that sooner or later this good fortune would fail, and not long afterwards Polycrates was shamefully put to death by Orœtes, who had invited him to his court.

Polydore (pol' ı dôr) The name assumed by Guiderius in Shakespeare's *Cymbeline.*

Polyhymnia (pol ı hım' nı a) The Muse of lyric poetry, and inventor of the lyre *See* MUSES

Polyphemus (pol i fē' mùs). One of the Cyclops, an enormous giant, with only one eye, and that in the middle of his forehead, who lived in Sicily. When Ulysses landed on the island, this monster made him and twelve of his crew captives; six of them he ate, and then Ulysses contrived to blind him, and escape with the rest cf the crew (*cp.* LESTRIGONS) Polyphemus was in love with Galatea, a sea-nymph who had set her heart on the shepherd Acis, Polyphemus, in a fit of jealousy, crushed him beneath a rock.

Poma Alcinoo dare. *See* ALCINOO.

Pomander (pom än' dër). From the French *pomme d'ambre,* apple of amber, or ambergris A ball made of perfume, such as ambergris or musk, which was worn or carried in a perforated case in order to ward off infection or counteract bad smells The cases, usually of gold or silver, were also called "pomanders "

Pomatum (po mä' tum) Another name for *pomade,* which was so called because it was originally made by macerating over-ripe apples (Fr. *pommes*) in grease.
> There is likewise made an ointment with the pulpe of Apples and Swines grease and Rose water, which is used to beautifie the face   called in shops *pomatum,* of the Apples whereof it is made —GERARDE *Herbal,* III, xcv (1597)

Pomfret Cakes. *See* PONTEFRACT.

Pommard A red Burgundy wine, so called from a village of that name in the Côte d'Or, France In France the word is sometimes colloquially used for cider (or beer), the pun being on *pomme,* apple

Pommel. The pommel of a sword is the rounded knob terminating the hilt, so called on account of its apple-like shape (Fr. *pomme,* apple), and *to pommel one,* now to pound him with your fists, was originally to beat him with the pommel of your sword.

Pomona (po mō' na) The Roman goddess of fruits and fruit-trees (Lat *pomum*), hence fruit generally
> Bade the wide fabric unimpaired sustain
> Pomona's store, and cheese, and golden grain
>   BLOOMFIELD *Farmer's Boy.*

Pompadour (pom' pa dôr), as a colour, is claret purple, so called from Louis XV's mistress, the Marquise de Pompadour (1721-64) The 56th Foot is called the Pompadours, from the claret facings of their regimental uniforms

The Essex Regiment, the 44th Foot. So named from the 2nd Battalion (raised in 1755)

which wore facings of purple, the favourite colour of Mme de Pompadour

There is an old song supposed to be an elegy on John Broadwood, a Quaker, which introduces the word —
> Sometimes he wore an old brown coat,
>   Sometimes a pompadore,
> Sometimes 'twas buttoned up behind,
>   And sometimes down before

The word is also applied to a fashion of hair-dressing in which the hair is raised (often on a pad) in a wave above the forehead.

Pompey (pom' pı) The familiar name in the British Navy for Portsmouth is Pompey It is also a generic name formerly used of a black footman, as *Abigail* used to be of a lady's maid. One of Hood's jocular book-titles was *Pompeii, or, Memoirs of a Black Footman,* by Sir W. Gill (Sir W Gell wrote a book on Pompeii)

Pompey's Pillar. A Corinthian column of red granite, nearly 100 ft high, erected at Alexandria by Publius, Prefect of Egypt, in honour of Diocletian and to record the conquest of Alexandria in 296 It has about as much right to be called *Pompey's* pillar as the obelisk of Heliopolis, re-erected by Rameses II at Alexandria, has to be called *Cleopatra's Needle*

Pone, from an Indian word meaning something baked, in the Southern U S A it is used for maize bread

Pons Asinorum (ponz äs ı nôr' um) (Lat , the asses' bridge) The fifth proposition, Bk 1, of Euclid—the first difficult theorem, which dunces rarely get over for the first time without stumbling It is anything but a "bridge", it is really *pedica asinorum,* the "dolt's stumbling-block "

Pontefract or **Pomfret Cakes** Liquorice lozenges impressed with a castle, so called from being made at Pontefract The name of the town is still frequently pronounced *pum-fret,* representing the Anglo-Norman and Middle English spelling *Pontfret* The place was called *Fractus Pons* by Orderic (1097) and *Pontefractus* by John of Hexham (about 1165), in allusion to the old Roman bridge over the Aire, broken down by William I in 1069, remains of which were still visible in the 16th century

Pontiff. The term was formerly applied to any bishop, but now only to the Bishop of Rome—the Pope—*i e* the Sovereign Pontiff. It means literally one who has charge of the bridges, as these were in the particular care of the principal college of priests in ancient Rome, the head of which was the Pontifex Maximus (Lat. *pons, pontis,* a bridge)

Pontius Pilate's Body-guard. The 1st Foot Regiment, now called the Royal Scots, the oldest regiment in the British Army The fable is that when in the French service as *Le Régiment de Douglas* they had a dispute with the Picardy regiment about the antiquity of their respective corps. The Picardy officers declared they were on duty on the night of the Crucifixion, when the colonel of the 1st Foot replied, "If we had been on guard, we should not have slept at our posts "

Pony, Slang for £25, also (especially in the U S A) for a translation crib, also for a small beer-glass holding a little under a gill

In card games the person on the right hand of the dealer, whose duty it is to collect the cards for the dealer, is called the *pony*, from Lat *pone*, "behind," being behind the dealer.

Pony Express This was the U.S government mail system across the continent just before the days of railways and telegraphs It ran from St Joseph, Missouri, to the Pacific Coast and was inaugurated in 1860, less than two years later it was superseded by the electric telegraph Pony Express is a misnomer, as fleet horses were used, ridden for stages of 10 to 15 miles by men who did three stages, or over 30 miles, before passing on the wallet to the next rider The schedule time for the whole distance was ten days, but Lincoln's inaugural address was taken across the continent in 7 days 17 hours. The fame of the Pony Express rests largely on the hardihood and courage of the riders, who braved storms, landslides, and Indian ambushes to get their mail through on time

Poor. Poor as a church mouse. In a church there is no cupboard or pantry where even so little a creature as a mouse could find a crumb

Poor as Job. The allusion is to Job being deprived by Satan of everything he possessed

Poor as Lazarus. This is the beggar Lazarus, full of sores, who was laid at the rich man's gate, and desired to be fed from the crumbs that fell from Dives' table (*Luke* xvi, 19-31)

Poor Clares. *See* FRANCISCANS

Poor Jack or **John** Dried hake We have "john dory," a "jack" (pike), a "jack shark," etc , and *Jack* may here be a play on the word "Hake," and John a substitute for Jack

Tis well thou art not fish, if thou hadst, thou hadst been poor-john —*Romeo and Juliet*, i, 1

Cp the jocular proof that an eel pie is a pigeon pie An eel pie is a fish pie, a fish pie may be jack pie, a jack pie is a john pie, and a john pie is a pie john (pigeon)

Poor man The blade-bone of a shoulder of mutton is so called in Scotland In some parts of England it is termed a "poor knight of Windsor," because it holds the same relation to "Sir Loin" as a Windsor knight does to a baronet Scott (*Bride of Lammermoor*, ch. xix) tells of a laird who, being asked by an English landlord what he would have for dinner, produced the utmost consternation by saying, "I think I could relish a morsel of a poor man"

Poor Richard. The assumed name of Benjamin Franklin in a series of almanacks from 1732 to 1757 They contained maxims and precepts on temperance, economy, cleanliness, chastity, and other virtues, and several ended with the words, "as poor Richard says"

Poor Robin's Almanack. A farcical almanack, parodying those who seriously indulged in prophecy, published at intervals from 1664 to as late as 1828 The early issues have often been attributed to Herrick, but they were the work of one (or both) of the brothers Robert ("Robin") and William Winstanley The original title was —

POOR ROBIN AN ALMANACK After a New Fashion Wherein the Reader may see (if he be not blinde) many remarkable things worthy of Observation Containing a two-fold Kalendar, viz , the Julian or English, and the Roundheads or Fanaticks, several Saints' days, and Observations upon every Month Written by POOR ROBIN, Knight of the Burnt-Island, a well-wisher to the Mathematicks Calculated for the Meridian of Limehouse, over against Cuckolds-haven, the Longitude and Latitude whereof is set down in the Foreheads of all jealous-pated Husbands

As a specimen of the "predictions," the following, for January, 1664, may be taken as an example —

Strong Beer and good Fires are as fit for this Season as a Halter for a Thiefe, and, when every Man is pleas'd, then 'twill be a Merry World indeed This Month we may expect to hear of the Death of some Man, Woman, or Child, either in Kent or Christendom

There are none poor but those whom God hates. This does not mean that poverty is a punishment, but that those whom God loves are rich in His love. In this sense Dives may be the poor man, and Lazarus abounding in that "blessing of the Lord which maketh rich"

Pope. The word represents the A S *papa*, from ecclesiastical Latin, and Gr. *pappas*, the infantile word for *father* (*cp* modern "papa"), it is not connected with Lat *popa*, which denoted an inferior Roman (pagan) priest who brought the victim to the altar and felled it with an axe In the early Church the title was given to many bishops, Leo the Great (440-61) was the first to use it officially, and in the time of Gregory VII (1073-85) it was, by decree, specially reserved to the Bishop of Rome. *Cp* PONTIFF.

According to Platina, Sergius II (844-6) was the first pope who changed his name on ascending the papal chair Some accounts have it that his name was Hogsmouth, others that it was "Peter di Porca," and he changed it out of deference to St Peter, thinking it arrogant to style himself Peter II.

Gregory the Great (591) was the first pope to adopt the title *Servus Servorum Dei* (the Servant of the Servants of God) It is founded on *Mark* x, 44

Fye upon all his jurisdictions
And upon those whiche to hym are detters;
Fye upon his bulles breves and letters
Wherein he is named *Servus Servorum*
Rede Me and be nott Wrothe, v, 13 (1528).

The title *Vicar of Christ*, or *Vicar of God*, was adopted by Innocent III, 1198. *See also* TIARA

The number of popes is not certain, there are, however, with the election of Pius XII (1939) 262 commonly enumerated Of these 204 were Italians, 15 Frenchmen, 15 Greeks, 7 Syrians, 6 Germans, 3 Spaniards, 2 Dalmatians, 2 Africans, and 1 each English, Portuguese, Cretan, Thracian, Sardinian, Jew (St Peter)

The Black Pope The General of the Jesuits

The Pope of Geneva. A name given to Calvin (1509-64)

The Pope's eye. The tender piece of meat (the lymphatic gland) surrounded by fat in the middle of a leg of mutton The French call it *Judas's eye*, and the Germans *the priest's tit-bit*

The Pope's slave. So Cardinal Cajetan (d 1534) called the Church.

The Red Pope. The Prefect of the Propaganda (*q v*).

Pope Joan. A mythical female pope, fabled in the Middle Ages to have succeeded Leo IV (855) The vulgar tale is that Joan conceived a violent passion for the monk Folda and in order to get admission to him assumed the monastic habit Being clever and popular, she was elected pope, but was discovered through giving birth to a child during her enthronization The whole story has long since been exploded

The name was given to a once popular card-game played with an ordinary pack *minus* the eight of diamonds (called the "Pope Joan"), also to a circular revolving tray divided into eight compartments.

Popish Plot. A fictitious plot implicating the Duke of York and others in high place, invented in 1678 by Titus Oates (1649-1705) who alleged that the Catholics were about to massacre the Protestants, burn London, and assassinate the king Some thirty innocent persons were executed, and Oates obtained great wealth by revealing the supposed plot, but ultimately he was pilloried, whipped, and imprisoned

Popinjay (pop' in jay) An old name for a parrot (ultimately of Arabic origin, Gr *papagos*), hence a conceited or empty-headed fop.

> I then, all smarting with my wounds being cold,
> To be so pestered with a popinjay,
> Answered neglectingly I know not what,
> He should or he should not.
>
> 1 *Henry IV*, i, 3

The Festival of the Popinjay. The first Sunday in May, when a figure of a popinjay, decked with parti-coloured feathers and suspended from a pole, served as a target for shooting practice He whose ball or arrow brought down the bird by cutting the string by which it was hung, received the proud title of "Captain Popinjay," or "Captain of the Popinjay," for the rest of the day, and was escorted home in triumph

Poplar. The poplar was consecrated to Hercules, because he destroyed Kakos in a cavern of Mount Aventine, which was covered with poplars In the moment of triumph the hero plucked a branch from one of the trees and bound it round his head When he descended to the infernal regions, the heat caused a profuse perspiration which blanched the under surface of the leaves, while the smoke of the eternal flames blackened the upper surface Hence the leaves of the poplar are dark on one side and white on the other

The white poplar is fabled to have originally been the nymph Leuce, beloved by Pluto He changed her into this at death

Poplin. This silk and worsted material, now made chiefly in Ireland, gets its name from the old *papil* (Ital *papalino*) city of Avignon, because up to the 17th century that was the chief seat of its manufacture

Popski's Private Army A British volunteer force in World War II operating under the orders of Lieut -Col Peniakoff in a series of daring and highly successful raids in North Africa and Southern Europe The Colonel was familiarly known as "Popski" and his irregular forces wore the initials *P P A* on their shoulders much to the chagrin of conservative military circles.

Popular Front A political alliance by all Left Wing parties (Labour, Liberal, Socialist, but not necessarily Communist) against reactionary government and especially dictatorship

Populist A term applied in U S A. to a member of the People's Party, a political party formed in 1891 and committed to the expansion of the currency, the restriction of land ownership, the state control of transport, etc

Porcelain, from Ital *porcellana*, "a little pig," the name given by the early Portuguese traders, to cowrie-shells, the shape of which is not unlike a pig's back, and later to Chinese earthenware, which is white and glossy, like the inside of these shells

Porch, The A philosophic sect, generally called Stoics (Gr *stoa*, a porch), because Zeno, the founder, gave his lectures in the public ambulatory, *Stoa pœcile*, in the agora of Athens.

> The successors of Socrates formed societies which lasted several centuries, the Academy, the Porch, the Garden —SEELEY *Ecce Homo*

Pork, pig. The former is Norman, the latter Saxon As in the case of most edible domestic animals the Norman word is used for the meat and the Saxon for the live animal

Porphyrogenitus (pôr fi rō jen' i tus) A surname of the Byzantine Emperor, Constantine VII (911-59) It signifies "born in the purple" (Gr. *porphuros*, purple, *genetos*, born), and a son born to a sovereign after his accession is called a *porphyrogenito. Cp* PURPLE

Porridge. Everything tastes of porridge However we may deceive ourselves, whatever castles in the air we may construct, the fact of home life will always intrude

He has supped all his porridge. Eaten his last meal, he is dead

Keep your breath to cool your porridge. A rude remark made to one who is giving unwanted or unsought advice

> Well, Friar, spare your breath to cool your porridge, come, let us now talk with deliberation, fairly and softly —RABELAIS *Pantagruel*, etc , V, xxviii

Not to earn salt to one's porridge. To earn practically nothing, to be a "waster "

Port. The origin of the nautical term, meaning the left-hand side of a ship when looking forward, is not certain, but it is probably from *port*, a harbour The word has been in use for over three centuries, and in course of time took the place of the earlier *larboard* which was so easily confused with *starboard* When the steering-gear was on the starboard (i e *steer-board*) side it was almost a necessity to enter port and tie up at the harbour with the larboard side towards the *port*, and this probably accounts for the name

In the days when a ship was steered by a tiller it was necessary to put the tiller to port in order to make the rudder—and thus the vessel —go to starboard Thus it came that "port the helm" meant really "steer the ship to starboard " To do away with this anomaly, after World War I the rule was introduced universally that "Port the helm" should mean "Turn to port," and "Starboard the helm," to starboard.

A vessel's **port-holes** are so called from Lat *porta*, a door, the harbour is called a *port* from Lat *portus*, a haven, the dark red wine gets its name *port* from *Oporto*, Portugal, whence it is exported, and *port*, the way of bearing oneself, etc (Queen Elizabeth I. says Speed, daunted the Ambassador of Poland "with her stately port and majestical deporture") from Lat *portare*, to carry

Any port in a storm. Said when one is in a difficulty and some not particularly good way out offers itself, a last resource.

Port Royal A convent about 8 miles SW of Versailles which in the 17th century became the headquarters of the Jansenists (*q v*) The community was suppressed by Louis XIV in 1660 but later again sprang into prominence and was condemned by a bull of Clement XI in 1713 Two years later the convent, which had been removed to Paris about 1637, was razed to the ground.

Portage. A place where canoes or boats must be carried overland from one stretch of navigable water to another.

Porte, The Sublime The central office of the Ottoman Government of the Sultans in Constantinople, hence, the Government or the Empire itself The term is French in origin, *sublime* signifying "lofty" or "high and mighty"

Porteous Riot. At Edinburgh in September, 1736 John Porteous was captain of the city guard, and, at the execution of a smuggler named Andrew Wilson, ordered the guards to fire on the mob, which had become tumultuous, six persons were killed, and eleven wounded Porteous was condemned to death, but reprieved, whereupon the mob burst into the jail where he was confined, and, dragging him to the Grassmarket (the usual place of execution), hanged him by torchlight on a barber's pole

Portia (pôr′shà) A rich heiress and "lady barrister" in Shakespeare's *Merchant of Venice* (*q v*), in love with Bassanio Her name is often used allusively for a female advocate.

Portland Vase. A cinerary urn of transparent dark blue glass, coated with opaque white glass cut in cameo fashion, found in a tomb (supposed to be that of Alexander Severus) near Rome in the 17th century In 1770 it was purchased from the Barberini Palace by Sir William Hamilton for 1,000 guineas, and came afterwards into the possession of the Duke of Portland, one of the trustees of the British Museum, who placed it in that institution for exhibition In 1845 a lunatic named Lloyd dashed it to pieces, but it was so skilfully re-paired that the damage is barely visible. It is ten inches high, and six in diameter at the broadest part

Portmanteau Word. An artificial word made up of parts of others, and expressive of a combination denoted by those parts—such as *squarson*, a cross between a *squire* and a *parson* Lewis Carroll invented the term in *Through the Looking-Glass*, ch. vi, *slithy*, he says. means *lithe* and *slimy*, *mimsy* is *flimsy* and *miserable*, etc So called because there are two meanings "packed up" in the one word.

Portsoken Ward (pôrt sō′ ken) The most easterly of the City of London wards—the old *Knighten Guild* (*q v*)—lying outside the wall in the parish of St Botolph, Aldgate. Its name indicates the *soke* or franchise of the city (*not* of the gate) *Port* is an old name for any city, and occurs in *Portreeve*, the chief city officer

Poseidon (po sī′ don) The god of the sea in Greek mythology the counterpart of the Roman Neptune (*q v*) He was the son of Cronos and Rhea, brother of Zeus and Pluto, and husband of Amphitrite It was he who, with Apollo, built the walls of Troy, and as the Trojans refused to give him his reward he hated them and took part against them in the Trojan War Earthquakes were attributed to him, and he was said to have created the first horse

Poser. Formerly used of an examiner, one who *poses* (i e "opposes") questions, especially a bishop's examining chaplain and the examiner at Eton for the King's College fellowship Nowadays the word usually denotes a puzzling question or proposition

Posh Onomatopœic slang for smart, swagger well-turned-out; as, "You're looking very posh to-day," spruce and well groomed

Posse (pos′ i) (Lat , to be able) A body of men —especially constables—who are armed with legal authority

Posse Comitatus. The whole force of the county—that is, all the male members of a county over fifteen, who may be summoned by a sheriff to assist in preventing a riot, the rescue of prisoners, or other unlawful disorders Clergymen, peers, and the infirm are exempt

Possum To play possum is to lie low, to feign quiescence, to dissemble The phrase comes from the opossum's habitual attempt to avoid capture by pretending to be dead.

Post. Beaten on the post. Only just beaten, a racing term, the "post" being the winning-post

By return of post. By the next mail in the opposite direction; originally the phrase referred to the messenger, or "post" who brought the dispatch and would return with the answer

From pillar to post. *See* Pillar.

Knight of the post. *See* Knight

Post-and-rail. Wooden fencing made of posts and rails In Australia roughly made tea in which the stalks are floating is called *post-and-rail tea*

Post captain. A term used in the Navy from about 1730 to 1830 to distinguish an officer who held a captain's commission from one of inferior rank who was given the title by courtesy because he was in command of a small ship or was acting as captain, etc. A ship of under 20 guns was not entitled to a full—or post—captain.

Post haste. With great speed or expedition. The allusion is to the old coaching days, when travelling by relays of horses, or with horses placed on the road to expedite the journey, was the rule in cases of urgency

Post-Impressionism. Name applied to the group of French painters, headed by Cézanne, Gauguin, and Van Gogh, stemming from *Impressionism* (*q v*)

Post paper A standard size of paper measuring 15 × 19¼ in in writing papers, and 15½ × 19¼ in. in printings, so called from an ancient watermark which has been supposed to represent a post-horn This horn or bugle mark was, however, in use as early as 1314 long before anything in the nature of a postman or his horn existed It is probably the famous horn of Roland (*q v.*)

Post term (Lat *post terminum*, after the term) The legal expression for the return of a writ after the term, and for the fee that then is payable for its being filed.

To be posted in a club is to have one's name put upon the notice board as no longer a member, for non-payment of dues, or other irregularity In the British armed forces it means to be assigned to a specific rank, position, or post.

To be well posted in a subject. To be thoroughly acquainted with it, well informed Originally an American colloquialism, probably from the counting-house, where ledgers are *posted.*

To run your head against a post. To go ahead heedlessly and stupidly, or as if you had no eyes

Poste restante (Fr., remaining post) A department at a post office to which letters may be addressed for callers, and where they will remain (with certain limits) until called for.

Post (Lat ; in compounds). *Post factum* (Lat). After the act has been committed.

Post hoc, ergo propter hoc (Lat) *After this,* therefore *because of* this; expressive of the fallacy that a sequence of events is always the result of cause and effect The swallows come to England in the spring, but do not bring the spring

Post meridian (Lat) After noon; usually contracted to "P M "

> 'Twas post meridian half-past four,
> By signal I from Nancy parted
> > DIBDIN *Sea Songs*

Post mortem (Lat) After death, as a post-mortem examination for the purpose of ascertaining the cause of death

A post-mortem degree. In old University slang, a degree given to a candidate after having failed at the poll

Post obit (Lat *post obitum*, after the death, *i e* of the person named in the bond) An agreement to pay for a loan a larger sum of money, together with interest at death

Posteriori. *See* A POSTERIORI

Posy properly means a copy of verses presented with a bouquet It now means the verses without the flowers, as the "posy of a ring," or the flowers without the verses, as a "pretty posy "

> He could make anything in poetry, from the posy of a ring to the chronicle of its most heroic wearer —
> STEDMAN *Victorian Poets* (Landor), p 47

Pot. A big pot An important person, a personage, a leader of his class or group

A pot of money. A large amount of money; especially a large stake on a horse

A little pot is soon hot A small person is quickly "riled " Grumio makes humorous use of the phrase in *The Taming of the Shrew* (iv, 1)

A watched pot never boils. Said as a mild reproof to one who is showing impatience, watching and anxiety won't hasten matters.

Gone to pot Ruined, gone to the bad The allusion is to the pot into which bits of already cooked meat are cast prior to their making their last appearance as hash.

The pot calls the kettle black. Said of a person who accuses another of faults similar to those committed by himself.

The pot of hospitality. The pot or cauldron always hanging over the open fire which in Ireland used to be dipped into by anyone who dropped in at meal-times, or required refreshment

> And the "pot of hospitality" was set to boil upon the fire, and there was much mirth and heartiness and entertainment —*Nineteenth Century*, Oct., 1891, p 643.

To keep the pot a-boiling. To go on paying one's way and making enough to live on, also, to keep things going briskly, to see that the interest does not flag

Pot-boiler. Anything done merely for the sake of the money it will bring in—because it will "keep the pot a-boiling," *i.e* help to provide the means of livelihood, applied specially to work of small merit by artists or literary men.

Pot-hook. The hook over an open fire on which hung the pot The term was applied to the shaky curves and loops made by the beginner in handwriting

Pot-hunter. One who in athletic contests, etc , is keener on winning prizes (often silver cups, or *pots*) than on the sport, it is, of course, a term of reproach among sportsmen

Come and take pot-luck with me Come and take a family dinner at my house; we'll all ' dip into the pot" and share anything that's going

Pot valiant. Made courageous by liquor.

Pot-wallopers, before the passing of the Reform Bill (1832), were those who claimed a vote as householders, because they had boiled their own pot at their own fireplace in the parish for six months. The earlier form was *pot-waller*, from A S *weallan*, to boil.

Potato. This very common vegetable (*Solanum tuberosum*) was introduced into Ireland (and thence into England) from America by Sir Walter Raleigh about 1584, but the name (from Haitian *batata*) properly belonged to another tuberous plant (*Batata edulis*, of the natural order *Convolvulaceæ*), now known as the *sweet potato*, which was supposed to have aphrodisiac qualities It is to this latter that Falstaff refers when he says "Let the sky rain potatoes" (*Merry Wives*, v, 5), and there are many allusions to it in contemporary literature

Potato-bogle. So the Scots call a scarecrow, the head of these bird-bogies being a big potato or turnip

To think small potatoes of it To think very little of it, to account it of very slight worth, or importance.

Poteen (po tēn') (Irish *poitin*, little pot) Whisky that is produced privately in an illicit still, and so escapes duty

Potent. Cross potent. An heraldic cross, each limb of which has an additional cross-piece like the head of an old-fashioned crutch, so called from Fr *potence*, a crutch. It is also known as a *Jerusalem cross*

Potiphar's Wife (pot' i far) is unnamed both in the Bible and the Koran Some Arabian commentators have called her Rahil, others Zuleika, and it is this latter name that the 15th-century Persian poet gives her in his *Yusuf and Zulaikha*

In C J Wells's poetic drama *Joseph and His Brethren* (1824), of which she is the heroine, she is named Phraxanor

Potlatch A North American Indian feast at which gifts are distributed lavishly to the guests, while the hosts destroy much of their own property in a magnificent ostentation of wealth and possessions It is a social barbarity to refuse an invitation to a potlatch, or, having been to one, to neglect to give a potlatch in return, rivalry in this insensate feast-giving often reduced the givers to ruin

Potpourri (pō poo' rē) (Fr) A mixture of dried sweet-smelling flower-petals and herbs preserved in a vase Also a hotch-potch or olla podrida In music, a medley of favourite tunes strung together

Pourri means rotting [flowers], and potpourri, strictly speaking, is the vase containing the sweet mixture

Pott. A size of printing and writing paper (15½ × 12¼ in), so called from its original watermark, a pot, which really represented the Holy Grail

Poulaines (poo' lānz) The long pointed toes of the 14th century They were put on the feet of suits of armour for purposes of defence They appeared also on the fashionable *souliers à la poulaine* The fashion is thought to have come from Poland—whence the name

Poult (pōlt) A chicken, or the young of the turkey, guinea-fowl, etc The word is a contraction of *pullet*, from late Lat *pulla*, a hen, whence *poultry, poulterer*, etc

Poulter's Measure In prosody, a metre consisting of alternate Alexandrines and fourteeners, i e twelve-syllable and fourteen-syllable lines. The name was given to it by

Gascoigne (1576) because, it is said, poulterers —then called *poulters*—used sometimes to give twelve to the dozen and sometimes fourteen It was a common measure in early Elizabethan times, the following specimen is from a poem by Surrey —

Good ladies, ye that have your pleasures in exile,
Step in your foot, come take a place, and mourn with
me a while,
And such as by their lords do set but little price
Let them sit still, it skills them not what chance come
on the dice

Pound. The unit of weight (Lat *pondus*, weight), also cash to the value of twenty shillings sterling, because in the Carlovingian period the Roman pound (twelve ounces) of pure silver was coined into 240 silver pennies The symbols £ and *lb* are for *libra*, the Latin for a pound

In for a penny, in for a pound. *See* PENNY.

Pound of flesh. The whole bargain, the exact terms of the agreement, the bond *literatim et verbatim* The allusion is to Shylock, in *The Merchant of Venice*, who bargained with Antonio for a "pound of flesh," but was foiled in his suit by Portia, who said the bond was expressly a pound of flesh, and therefore (1) the Jew must cut the exact quantity, neither more nor less than a just pound, and (2) in so doing he must not shed a drop of blood

Poverty. When poverty comes in at the door, love flies out at the window An old proverb, given in Ray's *Collection* (1742), and appearing in many languages Keats says much the same in *Lamia* (Pt ii).—

Love in a hut, with water and a crust,
Is—Love forgive us—cinders, ashes, dust

Powder. I'll powder your jacket for you. A corruption of Fr *poudrer*, to dust

Not worth powder and shot. Not worth the trouble, the thing shot won't pay the cost of the ammunition.

Pow-wow. A consultation. Derived from the North American Indians

Poynings' Law or Statute of Drogheda. An Act of Parliament passed in Ireland in 1495 (10 *Henry VII*, ch 22) at the summons of Sir Edward Poynings (d 1521), then Lord Deputy, providing that no Parliament could be called together in Ireland except under the Great Seal of England, that its Acts must be submitted to the English Privy Council before becoming law, and declaring all general statutes hitherto made in England to be in force in Ireland also It was repealed in 1782

Practical and Practicable. These two words are often confused in common usage Practical means adapted to actual conditions, pertaining to action not theory or speculation A practical man is one better adapted to doing manual jobs than to speculating about them A practical joke (rarely a joke to its victim, be' it observed) is a piece of humour that depends on some action on the part of the perpetrator, usually to the discomfiture of the subject.

Practicable is applied to something capable of being done, feasible In theatrical usage a practicable door or window in a piece of stage scenery is one that can be actually opened and shut.

Præmonstratensian. *See* PREMONSTRATENSIAN.

Præmunire (prē mū nī´ re) A writ charging a sheriff to summon one accused of an indictable offence committed overseas, authorized by the *Statute of Præmunire* (1392), so called from the words *præmunire facias*, cause thou to warn (so and so) that appear in the opening sentence The Statute was soon used specially to prevent the purchase in Rome of excommunications, etc , and to stop the assertion or maintenance of papal jurisdiction in England and the denial of the ecclesiastical supremacy of the Crown Offenders could be punished by outlawry, forfeiture of goods, and attachment.

Praetorian Guard (pre tôr´ i ân) The household troops of the Roman Empire *Praetor* was the title given to the consul who had supreme command of the army, his bodyguard was the Praetorian Guard

Pragmatic Sanction. *Sanctio* in Latin means a "decree or ordinance with a penalty attached," or, in other words, a "penal statute." *Pragmaticus* means "relating to state affairs," so that Pragmatic Sanction is a penal statute bearing on some important question of state The term was first applied by the Romans to those statutes which related to their provinces The French applied the phrase to certain statutes which limited the jurisdiction of the Pope, but generally it is applied to an ordinance fixing the succession in a certain line

Pragmatic Sanction of St. Louis, 1268, forbade the court of Rome to levy taxes or collect subscriptions in France without the express sanction of the king It also gave plaintiffs in the ecclesiastical courts the right to appeal to the civil courts The "Constitutions of Clarendon" were to England what the "Pragmatic Sanction" was to France

Pragmatic Sanction of Charles VII (of France), 1438, defining and limiting the power of the Pope in France. By this ordinance the authority of a general council was declared superior to the dictum of the Pope; the clergy were forbidden to appeal to Rome on any point affecting the secular condition of the nation, and the Roman pontiff was forbidden to appropriate a vacant benefice, or to appoint either bishop or parish priest

Pragmatic Sanction of 1713. Whereby the succession of the Austrian Empire was made hereditary in the female line, in order to transmit the crown to Maria Theresa, the daughter of Charles VI This is emphatically *the* Pragmatic Sanction, unless some qualification is added restricting the term to some other instrument

Pragmatic Sanction of Naples, 1759, whereby Carlos II of Spain ceded the succession to his third son and his heirs forever

Pragmatism (Gr *pragma*, deed) The philosophical doctrine that the only test of the truth of human cognitions or philosophical principles is their practical results, i e their workableness It does not admit "absolute" truth, as all truths change their trueness as their practical utility increases or decreases The word was introduced in this connexion about

1875 by the American logician C. S Peirce (1839-1914) and was popularized by William James, whose *Pragmatism* was published in 1907

Prairie Schooner. A large covered wagon, drawn by oxen or mules, used to transport settlers across the North American continent

Praise the Lord and Pass the Ammunition (World War II) Phrase used by an American Naval chaplain during the Japanese attack on Pearl Harbour, though the actual identity of the chaplain has since been in dispute Made the subject of a popular song in 1942.

Prajapatis. *See* MENU.

Prang R.A F slang in World War II, meaning to bomb a target with evident success, or to crash one's aircraft

Pratique (prät ēk´) The licence given to an incoming vessel when she can show a clean bill of health or has fulfilled the necessary quarantine regulations

Prayer-wheel. A device used by the Tibetan Buddhists as an aid or substitute for prayer, the use of which is said to be founded on a misinterpretation of the Buddha's instructions to his followers, that they should "turn the wheel of the law"—i e. preach Buddhism incessantly —we should say as a horse in a mill It consists of a pasteboard cylinder inscribed with—or containing—the mystic formula *Om mani padme hum* (*q v*) and other prayers, and each revolution represents one repetition of the prayers

Pre-Adamites. The name given by Isaac de la Peyrere (1655) to a race of men whom he supposed to have existed before the days of Adam. He held that only the Jews are descended from Adam, and that the Gentiles derive from these "Pre-Adamites"

Prebend (preb´ end) (O Fr from late Lat. *præbenda*, a grant, pension) The stipend given out of the revenues of the college or cathedral to a canon, he who enjoys the prebend is the *prebendary*, though he is sometimes wrongly called the *prebend*

Precarious (Lat. *precarius*, obtained by prayer) is applied to what depends on our prayers or requests. A *precarious tenure* is one that depends solely on the will of the owner to concede to our prayer, hence uncertain, not to be depended on

Preceptor Among the Knights Templar a *preceptory* was a subordinate house or community (the larger being *commanderies*), and the *Preceptor* or *Knight Preceptor* was the superior of a preceptory, the *Grand Preceptor* being the head of all the preceptories in a province The three of highest rank were the Grand Preceptors of Jerusalem, Tripolis, and Antioch.

Précieuses, Les (prā sē ērz). The intellectual circle that centred about the Hotel de Rambouillet in 17th-century Paris It may be interpreted as "persons of distinguished merit " Their affected airs were the subject of Molière's comedy *Les Précieuses Ridicules*, 1659

Precious Stones. The ancients divided precious stones into male and female The darker stones were called the males, and the light ones were called the females Male sapphires approach indigo in colour, but the female ones are sky-blue. Theophartus mentions the distinction

The tent shook, for mighty Saul shuddered, and sparkles 'gan dart
From the jewels that woke in his turban, at once with a start,
All its lordly male-sapphires, and rubies courageous at heart
      BROWNING *Saul,* viii

Each month, according to the Poles, is under the influence of a precious stone —

January	Garnet	*Constancy*
February . .	Amethyst	*Sincerity*
March	Bloodstone	*Courage*
April	Diamond	*Innocence*
May .	Emerald	*Success in love*
June . .	Agate	*Health and long life*
July . .	Cornelian	*Content*
August	Sardonyx	*Conjugal felicity*
September	Chrysolite	*Antidote to madness*
October	Opal .	*Hope*
November	Topaz	*Fidelity*
December	Turquoise	*Prosperity*

In relation to the signs of the Zodiac—

Aries	. Ruby		Libra .	. Jacinth
Taurus	. Topaz.		Scorpio .	Agate
Gemini	. Carbuncle		Sagittarius	Amethyst
Cancer	. Emerald		Capricornus	Beryl
Leo .	. Sapphire		Aquarius .	Onyx
Virgo .	Diamond		Pisces .	Jasper

In relation to the planets—

Saturn .	Turquoise .	. *Lead*
Jupiter	Cornelian	*Tin*
Mars . . .	Emerald	*Iron*
Sun .	Diamond	*Gold*
Venus . .	Amethyst	*Copper*
Moon .	Crystal	*Silver*
Mercury	Loadstone .	. *Quicksilver.*

It was an idea of the ancients that precious stones were dewdrops condensed and hardened by the sun.

Precocious means ripened by the sun before it has attained its full growth (Lat *præ,* before, *coquere,* to cook); hence, premature, development of mind or body beyond one's age

Many precocious trees, and such as have their spring in winter, may be found —BROWN

Prelate (prel' at) (Lat. *prælatus,* carried before) means simply a man preferred, a man promoted to an ecclesiastical office which gives him jurisdiction over other clergymen In the Catholic Church cardinals, bishops, and many other ecclesiastical dignitaries enjoy that title and rank, with the style of *Monsignore,* in the Church of England the term is restricted to bishops

Premier The *Prime Minister,* or *first* minister of the Crown, formerly (17th century) called the *Premier Minister,* from Fr *Ministre premier,* first minister The first British prime minister was Sir Robert Walpole (1676-1745), chief political adviser to George I and II

Première, the feminine of Fr. *premier,* is used in English for that first performance of a play or showing of a cinematograph film

Ce n'est que le premier pas qui coûte It is only the first step that costs anything Pythagoras used to say, "The beginning is half the whole "

Incipe dimidium facti est cœpisse —*Ausonius*
Dimidium facti, qui cœpit, habet —*Horace,* Ep , I, ii, 41
Well begun is half done.

Premillenarians. *See* SECOND (*Second Adventists*).

Premonstratensian (prē mon strā ten' sian) or *Norbertine Order* An order of Augustinians founded by St Norbert in 1120 in the diocese of Laon, France A spot was pointed out to him in a vision, and he termed the spot *Pré Montré* or *Pratum Monstratum* (the meadow pointed out) The order possessed thirty-five monasteries in England—where they were known as the White Canons of the rule of St. Augustine—at the time of the Dissolution

Prepense (prē pens') **Malice prepense.** Malice designed or deliberate, "malice aforethought" (Lat *præ,* before, Fr *penser,* to think)

Preposterous (Lat *præ,* before, *posterus,* coming after) Literally, "putting the cart before the horse", hence, contrary to reason or common sense

Your misplacing and preposterous placing is not all one in behaviour of language, for the misplacing is alwaies intollerable, but the preposterous is a pardonable fault, and many times gives a pretie grace unto the speech We call it by a common saying to *set the carte before the horse* —PUTTENHAM *Arte of English Poesie,* Bk iii, ch xxii (1589).

Pre-Raphaelite Brotherhood, The A group of artists formed in London in 1848, consisting originally of Holman Hunt, Millais, and Rossetti, having for its objects a closer study of nature than was practised by those bound by the academical dogmas, and the cultivation of the methods and spirit of the early Italian (the "pre-Raphael") painters. The group was championed by Ruskin, but was attacked by many artists and critics, and after its second exhibition (1850) Rossetti gave up exhibiting. Millais resigned, and Holman Hunt's methods underwent a change The term *Pre-Raphaelite* was later applied to work characterized by exaggerated attention to detail, and high finish or "finnickiness "

. a society which unfortunately, or rather unwisely, has given itself the name of "Pre-Raphaelite", unfortunately, because the principles on which its members are working are neither pre- nor post-Raphaelite, but everlasting They are endeavouring to paint with the highest possible degree of completion, what they see in nature, without reference to conventional or established rules, but by no means to imitate the style of any past epoch —RUSKIN *Modern Painters,* pt ii, sect vi, ch iii, § 16, *n*

Presbyterian Church A Church governed by elders or presbyters (Gr. *presbuteros,* elder), and ministers, all of equal ecclesiastical rank , especially the United Presbyterian Church of Scotland, which was formed in 1847 by the union of the United Secession and Relief Churches, and which in 1900 united with the Free Church of Scotland.

Presence. *See* REAL PRESENCE

Presents (prez' ents) **Know all men by these presents**—*i e* by the writings or documents now present (Lat *per presentes,* by the [writings] present)

Press-gang. The name given to the bodies of men who formerly carried out the impressment of those liable to forced service in the Army or Navy It was almost entirely used to get men for the Navy Edward III set up a Commission of Empressment, 1355 In 1641 Parliament declared the system illegal, but it was later used by Cromwell to obtain men for his land forces and in the latter half of the 18th century it was used with much harshness and scandal to recruit men for the Navy

Prester John (*i e.* John the Presbyter) A fabulous Christian king and priest supposed in mediæval times to have reigned somewhere in the heart of Asia in the 12th century He figures in Ariosto (*Orlando Furioso*, Bks xvii-xix), and has furnished materials for a host of mediæval legends.

> I will fetch you a toothpicker now from the farthest inch of Asia, bring you the length of Prester John's foot, fetch you a hair off the great Cham s beard .
> —*Much Ado About Nothing*, ii, 1

According to "Sir John Mandeville" he was a lineal descendant of Ogier the Dane (*q v.*), who penetrated into the north of India with fifteen of his barons, among whom he divided the land John was made sovereign of Teneduc, and was called *Prester* because he converted the natives Another tradition says he had seventy kings for his vassals, and was seen by his subjects only three times in a year So firm was the belief in his existence that Pope Alexander III (d 1181) sent him letters by a special messenger. The messenger never returned.

Prestige (pres tēzh). This word has a strangely metamorphosed meaning The Lat *præstigiæ* means juggling tricks, hence *prestidigitateur* (Fr), one who juggles with his fingers We use the word for that favourable impression which results from good antecedents The history of the change is this Juggling tricks were once considered a sort of enchantment, to enchant is to charm, and to charm is to win the heart

Presto. The name frequently applied to himself by Swift in his *Journal to Stella* According to his own account (*Journal*, August 1st, 1711) it was given him by the notorious Duchess of Shrewsbury, an Italian —

> The Duchess of Shrewsbury asked him, was not that Dr ——, Dr ——, and she could not say my name in English, but said Dr Presto, which is Italian for Swift

Preston and his Mastiffs. To oppose Preston and his mastiffs is to be foolhardy, to resist what is irresistible Christopher Preston established the Bear Garden at Hockley-in-the-Hole in the time of Charles II, and was killed in 1700 by one of his own bears

> I'd as good oppose
> Myself to Preston and his mastiffs loose
> OLDHAM. *III Satire of Juvenal*

Pretender. The Old Pretender James Francis Edward Stuart (1688-1766), son of James II

The Young Pretender. Charles Edward Stuart (1720-88), son of the "Old Pretender." *See* JACOBITES

Pretext (prē' tekst) A pretence or excuse From the Latin *prætexta*, a dress embroidered in the front worn by Roman magistrates, priests, and children of the aristocracy between the age of thirteen and seventeen. The *prætextatæ* were dramas in which actors personated those who wore the pretexta, hence persons who pretend to be what they are not.

Prevarication The Latin word *varico* is to straddle, and *prævaricoi*, to go zigzag or crooked The verb, says Pliny, was first applied

to men who ploughed crooked ridges, and afterwards to men who gave crooked answers in the law courts, or deviated from the straight line of truth Cp. DELIRIUM

Prevent. Precede, anticipate (Lat *præ-venio*, to go before) And as what goes before us may hinder us, so prevent means to hinder or keep back

> My eyes prevent the night watches —*Ps* cxix, 148
> Prevent us, O Lord, in all our doings —*Book of Common Prayer*

Previous Question. *See* QUESTION

Priam (prī' am) King of Troy when that city was sacked by the Greeks, husband of Hecuba, and father of fifty children, the eldest of whom was Hector When the gates of Troy were thrown open by the Greeks concealed in the wooden horse, Pyrrhus, the son of Achilles, slew the aged Priam

Priapus (prī ā' pus) In Greek mythology, the god of reproductive power and fertility (hence of gardens), and protector of shepherds, fishermen, and farmers He was the son of Dionysus and Aphrodite, and in later times was regarded as the chief deity of lasciviousness and obscenity *See* PHALLICISM

Prick. Shakespeare has, "'Tis now the prick of noon" (*Romeo and Juliet*, ii, 4), in allusion to the mark on the dial—made by pricking or indenting with a sharp instrument—that indicated 12 o'clock

The annual choosing of sheriffs used to be done by the king, who pricked the names on a list at haphazard Sheriffs are still "pricked" by the sovereign, but the names are chosen beforehand.

Prick-eared. Said of a dog with up-standing ears The Puritans and Roundheads were so called, because they had their hair cut short and covered their heads with a black skull-cap drawn down tight, leaving the ears exposed

Pricklouse. An old contemptuous name for a tailor.

Prick-song. Written music for singing, as distinguished from music learnt by ear So called because the notes were originally pricked in on the parchment. The term has long been obsolete

Prick the garter. *See* GARTER.

The prick of conscience. Remorse, tormenting reflection on one's misdeeds In the 14th century Richard of Hampole wrote a devotional treatise with this title

To kick against the pricks To strive against odds, especially against authority *Prick*, here, is an ox-goad, and the allusion is to *Acts* ix, 5— "It is hard for thee to kick against the pricks "

To prick up one's ears To pay particular attention; to do one's best to follow what is going on In allusion to the twitching of a horse's ears when its attention is suddenly attracted

Pride, meaning ostentation, finery, or that which persons are proud of Spenser talks of "lofty trees yclad in summer's pride" (verdure). Pope, of a "sword whose ivory sheath (was)

inwrought with envious pride" (ornamentation), and in this sense the word is used by Jacques in that celebrated passage—

> Why, who cries out on pride [dress]
> That can therein tax any private party?
> What woman in the city do I name
> When that I say "the city woman bears
> The cost of princes on unworthy shoulders"?
>   What is he of baser function
> That says his bravery [finery] is not of my cost?"
>   *As You Like It*, ii, 7

Fly pride, says the peacock, a bird proverbial for pride (*Comedy of Errors*, iv, 3). The pot calling the kettle black

The heraldic peacock is said to be in *his pride* when depicted with the tail displayed and the wings drooping

The pride of the morning That early mist or shower which promises a fine day The morning is too proud to come out in her glory all at once—or the proud beauty being thwarted weeps and pouts awhile Keble uses the phrase in a different sense when he says —

> Pride of the dewy Morning,
> The swain's experienced eye
> From thee takes timely warning,
> Nor trusts the gorgeous sky
>   KEBLE 25*th Sunday after Trinity*

Pride's Purge. The Long Parliament, not proving itself willing to condemn Charles I, was *purged* of its unruly members by Colonel Thomas Pride (d 1658), who entered the House with a body of soldiers (December 6th, 1648), arrested 47 members, excluded 96 more, and left the House consisting of less than 80 members—the "Rump" (*q v*)

Prig. An old cant word (probably a variant of PRICK) for to filch or steal, also for a thief In the *Winter's Tale* the clown calls Autolycus a "prig that haunts wakes, fairs, and bearbaitings "

Shadwell uses the term for a pert coxcomb, and nowadays it denotes a conceited, formal, or didactic person—one who tries to teach others how to comport themselves, etc , without having any right to do so

> *Shamwell* Cheatly will help you to the ready; and thou shalt shine, and be as gay as any spruce prig that ever walked the street.
> *Belford Senior* Well, adad, you are pleasant men, and have the neatest sayings with you, "ready," and "spruce prig," and abundance of the prettiest witty words —SHADWELL *The Squire of Alsatia*, I, i (1688)

Prima Donna (prī' má don' a) (Ital , first lady). The principal female singer in an opera

Prima facie (Lat) At first sight A *prima facie* case is a case or statement which, without minute examination into its merits, seems plausible and correct

> It would be easy to make out a strong *prima facie* case, but I should advise the more cautious policy of *audi alteram partem*

Primary Colours. *See* COLOURS.

Prime (Lat *primus*, first) In the Catholic Church the first canonical hour of the day, beginning at 6 a m Milton terms sunrise "that sweet hour of prime" (*Paradise Lost*, v, 170), and the word is used in a general way of the first beginnings of anything, especially of the world itself *Cp* Tennyson's "dragons of the prime" (*In Memoriam*, lvi).

Prime Minister. The first minister of the Crown, the Premier (*q v*).

Prime Number. The Golden Number; also called simply "the Prime."

Primed. Full and ready to deliver a speech We say of a man whose head is full of his subject, "He is primed to the muzzle " Also a euphemism for "drunk " The allusion is to firearms.

Primer (prī' mer) Originally the name of the Prayer-book used by laymen in pre-Reformation England, as this was used as a child's first reading-book—generally with the addition of the ABC, etc—the name was transferred to such books, and so to elementary books on any subject.

Great primer (pron prim' er) A large-sized type, rather smaller than eighteen-point, 4¼ lines to the inch.

As This,

Long primer. A smaller-sized type, 9½-point, 7¼ lines to the inch.

As this,

Primero (prim ēr ō) A very popular card-game for about a hundred years after 1530, in which the cards had three times their usual value, four were dealt to each player, the principal groups being flush, prime, and point. *Flush* was the same as in poker, *prime* was one card of each suit, and *point* was reckoned as in piquet

> I left him at primero with the Duke of Suffolk —
> *Henry VIII*, i, 2

Primrose. A curious corruption of the French *primerole*, which is the name of the flower in M E This is from the late Lat *primula*, and the *rose* (as though from *prima rosa*, the first, or earliest, rose) is due to a popular blunder.

Primum mobile (prī' mum mō' bile) (Lat., the first moving thing), in the Ptolemaic system of astronomy, was the ninth (later the tenth) sphere, supposed to revolve round the earth from east to west in twenty-four hours, carrying with it all the other spheres (*q v*) Milton refers to it as "that first mov'd" (*Paradise Lost*, iii, 483), and Sir Thomas Browne (*Religio Medici*) uses the phrase, "Beyond the first movable," meaning outside the material creation According to Ptolemy the *primum mobile* was the boundary of creation, above which came the empyrean (*q.v.*), or seat of God

The term is figuratively applied to any machine which communicates motion to others, and also to persons and ideas suggestive of complicated systems Thus, Socrates may be called the *primum mobile* of the Dialectic, Megaric, Cyrenaic, and Cynic systems of philosophy.

Primus (prī' mus) (Lat , first) The archbishop, or rather "presiding bishop," of the Episcopal Church of Scotland He is elected by the other six bishops, and presides in Convocation, or meetings relative to Church matters

Primus inter pares The first among equals.

Prince (Lat *princeps*, chief, leader) A royal title which, in England, is now limited to the sons of the sovereign and their sons *Princess* is similarly limited to the sovereign's daughters and his sons' (but not daughters') daughters

Crown Prince. The title of the heir-apparent to the throne in some countries, as Sweden, Denmark, and Japan (formerly also in Germany)

Prince Consort. A prince who is the husband of a reigning queen

Prince Imperial The title of the heir-apparent in the French Empire of 1852-70

Prince of Asturias. The title of the heir-apparent to the former Spanish throne

Prince of Piedmont. The heir-apparent to the House of Savoy, former kings of Italy.

Prince of the Church. A cardinal

Prince of the Peace. The Spanish statesman Manuel de Godoy (1767-1851) was granted this title for having negotiated peace with France in the Treaty of Basel, 1795

Prince of Wales. See WALES

Prince Rupert's drops. See RUPERT

Princess Royal, the title of an eldest daughter of a British sovereign On the death of a Princess Royal the eldest daughter of the then reigning monarch automatically receives the title and retains it for life, no matter how many sovereigns with daughters may occupy the throne during her lifetime George III's daughter Charlotte, Queen of Wurtemberg, was Princess Royal until her death in 1828, neither George IV nor William IV having daughters the title was in abeyance until 1840 when Queen Victoria's daughter, Princess Victoria (later the Empress Frederick of Germany) succeeded to it She remained Princess Royal until her death in 1901, when King Edward's daughter, Princess Louise, Duchess of Fife, succeeded On her death in 1931 the title passed to Princess Mary, Countess of Harewood, daughter of George V.

Principalities. Members of one of the nine orders of angels in mediæval angelology *See* ANGEL.

> In the assembly next upstood
> Nisroch, of Principalities the prime
> MILTON *Paradise Lost,* vi, 447

Printing. Wood blocks for printing were first used by the Chinese *c.* A D 600, and movable type was employed *c.* 1000 In the Western World there is no evidence successfully to refute the claim of Johann Gutenberg (*c* 1400-68) who set up a press at Mainz *c* 1450.

Printers' Bible, The. See BIBLE, SPECIALLY NAMED

Printers' marks

? is $\frac{q}{o}$—that is, the first and last letters of *quæstio* (question).

! is $\frac{I}{o}$ *Io* in Latin is the interjection of joy.

¶ is the initial letter of *paragraph* (reversed)

§ the S-mark or section mark

* is used by the Greek grammarians to arrest attention to something striking (*asterisk* or star)

† is used by the Greek grammarians to indicate something objectionable (*obelisk* or dagger). Both marks are now used to indicate footnotes

Priori. See A PRIORI.

Priscian's Head (prish'an) **To break Priscian's head** (in Latin, *Diminuere Prisciani caput*) To violate the rules of grammar Priscian was a great grammarian of the early 6th century, whose name is almost synonymous with grammar

> And held no sin so deeply red
> As tha: of breaking Priscian's head
> BUTLER *Hudibras,* pt ii, 2

Sir Nathaniel Laus Deo, bone intelligo
Holofernes Bone!—*bone* for *bene* Priscian a little scratch'd, 'twill serve
> *Love's Labour's Lost,* v, 1

Prisoner of Chillon, The. See CHILLON.

Privateer. A privately owned vessel commissioned by a belligerent state to wage war on the enemy's commerce The commission, known as letters of marque, was formerly given to a ship-owner who could arm and send out ships to harass the enemy, and important prizes were often captured by privateers The practice of issuing letters of marque ceased as a result of the Declaration of Paris, 1856 At times it required some ingenuity to discriminate between privateering and piracy

Privilege In a Parliamentary sense this applies to the rights enjoyed by Members as such Both Houses have the right of committing to prison an offender against their privilege, nor, unless the commitment be for some other offence than contempt, can the civil courts inquire into the matter Contempts include disobedience to orders of the House, indignities offered to it, assaults, insults or libels on Members, interference with officers of the House or tampering with witnesses Freedom of speech is a dearly bought and much cherished privilege, as also is freedom from arrest

Privy Council. The council chosen by the sovereign originally to administer public affairs, but now never summoned to assemble as a whole except to proclaim the successor to the Crown on the death of the Sovereign It usually includes Princes of the Blood, the two Primates, the Bishop of London, the great officers of State and of the Royal Household, the Lord Chancellor and Judges of the Courts of Equity, the Chief Justices of the Courts of Common Law, the Judge Advocate, some of the Puisne Judges, the Speaker of the House of Commons, the Lord Mayor of London, Ambassadors, Governors of Colonies, the Commander-in-Chief, and many politicians The business of the Privy Council is now performed by Committees (of which the Cabinet is technically one), such as the Judicial Committee of the Privy Council, and the great departments of State—the Board of Trade, Local Government, etc , are, in theory, merely committees of the Privy Council Privy Councillors are entitled to the prefix "the Right Honourable," and rank next after Knights of the Garter who may be commoners

Privy Seal. The seal which the sovereign uses in proof of assent to a document, kept in the charge of a high officer of State known as the Lord Privy Seal, In matters of minor importance it is sufficient to pass the Privy Seal, but instruments of greater moment must have the Great Seal also

Prize Court. A court of law set up in time of war to examine the validity of capture of ships and goods made at sea by the navy

Prize money is the name given to the net proceeds of the sale of enemy property, etc , thus captured at sea Prior to 1914 the distribution of prize money was confined to those ships actually making the capture; since that date the whole prize money is paid into a common fund

The **prize ring** is the boxing ring in which a prize fight takes place, a prize fight being a boxing match for a money prize or trophy

Pro Latin for, on behalf of

Pro and con (Lat) For and against "Con" is a contraction of *contra The pros and cons* of a matter is all that can be said for or against it

Pro tanto (Lat) As an instalment, good enough as far as it goes, but not final, for what it is worth

I heard Mr Parnell accept the Bill of 1886 as a measure that would close the differences between the two countries, but since then he stated that he had accepted it as a *pro tanto* measure . It was a parliamentary bet, and he hoped to make future amendments on it.—*Joseph Chamberlain*, April 10th, 1893

Pro tempore (Lat). Temporarily, for the time being, till something is permanently settled Contracted into *pro tem*

Probate (prō′ bāt) (Lat , proved) The probate of a will is the official proving of it, and a copy certified by an officer whose duty it is to attest it The original is retained in the court registry, and executors cannot act until probate has been obtained

Proces-verbal (prō sā vâr′ bal) (Fr). A detailed and official statement of some fact, especially a written and authenticated statement of facts in support of a criminal charge.

Procne. *See* NIGHTINGALE

Proconsul. A magistrate of Ancient Rome who was invested with the power of a consul and charged with the command of an army or the administration of a province The name is now often applied to a colonial governor or administrator

Procris (prok′ ris) Unerring as the dart of Procris. When Procris fled from Cephalus out of shame, Diana gave her a dog (Lælaps) that never failed to secure its prey, and a dart which not only never missed aim, but which always returned of its own accord to the shooter. *See* CEPHALUS

Procrustes' Bed (prō krus′ tēz) Procrustes, in Greek legend, was a robber of Atica, who placed all who fell into his hands upon an iron bed If they were longer than the bed he cut off the redundant part, if shorter he stretched them till they fitted it, he was slain by Theseus. Hence, any attempt to reduce men to one standard, one way of thinking, or one way of acting, is called placing them on Procrustes' bed

Tyrant more cruel than Procrustes old,
Who to his iron-bed by torture fits
Their nobler parts, the souls of suffering wits
        MALLET. *Verbal Criticism.*

B D —24

Proctor. Literally this is one who manages the affairs of another, the word being a contraction of "procurator " At the universities of Oxford and Cambridge the proctors are two officials whose duties include the maintaining of discipline. Representatives of ecclesiastical bodies in Convocation are called Proctors The **Queen's Proctor** is a law official entitled to intervene in a divorce or nullity suit where collusion or fraud is suspected

Procyon (prō′ si on) The Lesser Dog-star, *alpha in Canis Minoris* It is the eighth brightest star in the heavens. *See* ICARIUS.

Prodigal. Festus says the Romans called victims wholly consumed by fire *prodigæ hostiæ* (victims prodigalized), and adds that those who waste their substance are therefore called prodigals. This derivation is incorrect Prodigal is Lat *pro-ago* or *prod-igo*, to drive forth, and persons who had spent all their patrimony were "driven forth" to be sold as slaves to their creditors

The **Prodigal.** Albert VI, Duke of Austria (1418-63)

Prodigious! *See* DOMINIE SAMPSON

Prodigy (Lat *prodigium*, a portent, prophetic sign) *The prodigy of France* Guillaume Bude (1467-1540), so called by Erasmus.

The **Prodigy of Learning.** Samuel Hahnemann (1755-1843), the German, was so called by J Paul Richter.

Producer's Goods. An economic term for goods, such as tools and raw material, which satisfy needs only indirectly, through making other goods.

Profane means literally before or outside the temple (Lat. *pro fanum*), hence *profanus* was applied to those persons who came to the temple and remaining outside and unattached, were not initiated

Profile (prō′ fil) means shown by a thread (Ital. *profilo*, Lat *filum*, a thread) A profile is an outline, but especially a view, or drawing or some other representation, of the human face outlined by the median line The term "profile," for an essay setting forth the outstanding characteristics of an individual—a verbal outline, so to speak—came into use in the 1940s

Profound. The **Profound Doctor.** Thomas Bradwardine, Richard Middleton, and other 14th-century scholastic philosophers were given this title

Most Profound Doctor. Ægidius de Columna (d 1316), a Sicilian schoolman

Prog. The verb was used in the 16th century for to poke about for anything, especially to forage for food, hence the noun is slang for food, but its origin is unknown Burke says, "You are the lion, and I have been endeavouring to prog for you "

So saying, with a smile she left the rogue
To weave more lines of death, and plan for prog
        DR WOLCOT *Spider and Fly*

Prog is also university slang for proctor (*q v*).

Programme Music is instrumental music based on a literary, historical, or pictorial subject and intended to describe or illustrate this theme musically

Progress. To report progress, in parliamentary language, is to conclude for the night the business of a bill, and defer the consideration of all subsequent items thereof till the day nominated by the Prime Minister, hence, to put off anything till a more convenient time.

Projection. Powder of projection. A form of the "Philosopher's Stone" (q v), which was supposed to have the virtue of changing baser metals into gold. A little of this powder, being cast into the molten metal, was to *project* from it pure gold.

Proletariat (prō le târ' ı ăt). The class of the community, labourers and wage-earners, who are destitute of property. In ancient Rome the *proletarii* contributed nothing to the state but their *proles*, i.e. offspring, they could hold no office, were ineligible for the army, and were useful only as breeders of the race.

Promenade Concert. A type of concert in which a considerable portion of the audience stand in an open area in the concert-room floor. Promenade Concerts (Proms, as they are familiarly called) were started at Drury Lane and Covent Garden in 1840, but it was not until 1895 that they became a feature of London musical life under the conductorship of Sir Henry Wood (1869-1944) at the Queen's Hall. The destruction of the Hall in 1941 caused a break in the concerts but they were renewed at the Albert Hall under the management of the B B C.

Prometheus (prō mē' thūs) (Gr , Forethought). One of the Titans of Greek myth, son of Iapetus and the ocean-nymph Clymene, and famous as a benefactor to man. It is said that Zeus employed him to make men out of mud and water, and that then, in pity for their state, he stole fire from heaven and gave it to them. For this he was chained by Zeus to Mount Caucasus, where an eagle preyed on his liver all day, the liver being renewed at night. He was eventually released by Hercules, who slew the eagle. It was to counterbalance the gift of fire to mankind that Zeus sent Pandora (q v) to earth with her box of evils.

Promethean. Capable of producing fire, pertaining to Prometheus (q v). The earliest "safety" matches, made in 1805 by Chancel, a French chemist, who tipped cedar splints with paste of chlorate of potash and sugar, were known as "Prometheans." They were dipped into a little bottle containing asbestos wetted with sulphuric acid. and burst into flame on being withdrawn.

Promethean fire. The vital principle, the fire with which Prometheus quickened into life his clay images.

> I know not where is that Promethean heat
> That can thy light relume.
> *Othello*, v, 2

The Promethean unguent. Made from a herb on which some of the blood of Prometheus had fallen. Medea gave Jason some of it, and thus rendered his body proof against fire and warlike instruments.

Promised Land or **Land of Promise.** Canaan, so called because God promised Abraham,

Isaac, and Jacob that their offspring should possess it.

Proof. A printed sheet to be examined and approved before it is finally printed. The first, or *foul*, proof is that which contains all the compositor's errors, when these are corrected the impression next taken is called a *clean* proof and is submitted to the author, the final impression, which is corrected by the reader, is termed the *press* proof.

Proof Bible, The. *See* BIBLE, SPECIALLY NAMED.

Proof prints. The first impressions of an engraving. *India proofs* are those taken off on *India paper.* Proofs before lettering are those taken off before any inscription is engraved on the plate. After the proofs the connoisseur's order of value is—(1) prints which have the letters only in outline, (2) those in which the letters are shaded with a black line, (3) those in which some slight ornament is introduced into the letters, (4) those in which the letters are filled up quite black.

Proof spirit. A term applied to spirituous liquors in which 0 495 of the *weight* and 0 5727 of the *volume* is absolute alcohol, and the specific gravity is 0 91984. When the mixture has more alcohol than water it is called *over proof*, and when less it is termed *under proof.*

Prooshan Blue. A term of great endearment, when, after the battle of Waterloo, the Prussians were immensely popular in England. Sam Weller, in *Pickwick Papers*, addresses his father as "Veil, my Prooshan Blue."

Prop, To. In horses, an Australian term to describe to come to a sudden stop. Used in application to general life in the sense of to jib, to refuse to co-operate.

Propaganda (prop a găn' da). The Congregation, or College, of the Propaganda (*Congregatio de propaganda fide*) is a committee of cardinals established in Rome by Gregory XV, in 1622, for propagating the Faith throughout the world. Hence the term is applied to any scheme, association, etc., for making proselytes or influencing public opinion in political, social, and international, as well as in religious matters.

Property Plot, in theatrical language, means a list of all the "properties" or articles which will be required in the play produced. Such as the bell when Macbeth says, "The bell invites me", the knocking apparatus for the porter ("Heard you that knocking?"); tables, chairs, banquets, tankards, etc , etc. Everything stored in a theatre for general use on the stage is a "prop," these are the manager's props, an actor's "props" are the clothing and other articles which he provides for his own use.

Prophet, The. The special title of Mohammed. According to the Koran there have been 200,000 prophets, but only six of them brought new laws or dispensations, viz. Adam, Noah, Abraham, Moses, Jesus, and Mohammed.

The Great or **Major Prophets.** Isaiah, Jeremiah, Ezekiel, and Daniel, so called because their writings are more extensive than the prophecies of the other twelve.

The **Minor** or **Lesser Prophets.** Hosea, Joel, Amos, Obadiah, Micah, Jonah, Nahum, Habakkuk, Zephaniah, Haggai, Zechariah, and Malachi, whose writings are less extensive than those of the four Great Prophets

Propositions, in logic, are of four kinds, called A, E, I, O "A" is a universal affirmative, and "E" a universal negative, "I" a particular affirmative, and "O" a particular negative
See also SYLLOGISM

Props *See* PROPERTY PLOT

Prorogue (prŏ rŏg') (Lat *pro-rogo*, to prolong) The Parliament was prorogued. Dismissed for the holidays, or suspended for a time If dismissed entirely it is said to be "dissolved"

Proscenium (prŏ sē' ni ùm). The front part of the stage, between the drop-curtain and orchestra (Gr *proskēnion*, Lat *proscēnium*)

Proscription A sort of hue and cry; so called because among the Romans the names of the persons *proscribed* were written out, and the tablets bearing their names were fixed up in the public forum, sometimes with the offer of a reward for those who should aid in bringing them before the court If the proscribed did not answer the summons, their goods were confiscated and their persons outlawed In this case the name was engraved on brass or marble, the offence stated, and the tablet placed conspicuously in the market-place

Prose means straightforward speaking or writing (Lat *oratio prosa—i e pro-versa*), in opposition to foot-bound speaking or writing, *oratio vincta* (fettered speech—*i e* poetry)
It was Monsieur Jourdain, in Molière's *Le Bourgeois Gentilhomme*, who suddenly discovered that he had been talking prose for twenty years without knowing it

Proselytes (pros e lits) From Gr *proselutos*, one who has come to a place, hence, a convert, especially (in its original application) to Judaism Among the Jews proselytes were of two kinds—viz "The proselyte of righteousness" and the "stranger that is within thy gate" (*see* HELLENES) The former submitted to circumcision and conformed to the laws of Moses, the latter went no farther than to refrain from offering sacrifice to heathen gods, and from working on the Sabbath

Proserpina or **Proserpine** (pro sěr' pi na, pros'-er pin) The Roman counterpart of the Greek goddess Persephone, queen of the infernal regions and wife of Pluto As the personification of seasonal changes she passed six months of the year on Olympus, and six in Hades, while at Olympus she was beneficent, but in Hades was stern and terrible Legend says that as she was amusing herself in the meadows of Sicily Pluto seized her and carried her off in his chariot to the infernal regions for his bride In her terror she dropped some of the lilies she had been gathering, and they turned to daffodils

O Proserpina
For the flowers now, that frighted thou let'st fall
From Dis's waggon! daffodils,
That come before the swallow dares, and take
The winds of March with beauty.
Winter's Tale, IV, 4

In later legend Proserpine was the goddess of sleep, and in the myth of *Cupid and Psyche*, by Apuleius, after Psyche had long wandered about searching for her lost Cupid, she is sent to Proserpine for "the casket of divine beauty," which she was not to open till she came into the light of day Just as she was about to step on earth Psyche thought how much more Cupid would love her if she were divinely beautiful, so she opened the casket and found it contained Sleep, which instantly filled all her limbs with drowsiness, and she slept as it were the sleep of death.

Prosperity Robinson. F J Robinson, Earl of Ripon (1782-1859), Chancellor of the Exchequer in 1823, so called by Cobbett In 1825 he boasted in the House of the prosperity of the nation, and his boast was not yet cold when a great financial crisis occurred

Prospero (pros' pe rŏ) The rightful Duke of Milan in *The Tempest*, deposed by his brother. Drifted on a desert island, he practised magic, and raised a tempest in which his brother was shipwrecked Ultimately Prospero *broke his wand*, and his daughter married the son of the King of Naples *The Tempest* was the last play that Shakespeare wrote, and it is generally thought that Prospero is an allegorical picture of the dramatist bidding farewell to his work.

Protean. *See* PROTEUS

Protectionist. One who advocates the imposition of import duties, to "protect" home produce or manufactures

Protector, The. William Marshall, Earl of Pembroke (d 1219), appointed Regent on the accession of Henry III (1216)
Humphrey, Duke of Gloucester (1391-1447), Protector of England during the minority of his nephew, Henry VI (1422-47)
Richard, Duke of Gloucester, afterwards Richard III He took Edward V into his custody on the death of Edward IV (1483), and was named Protector of the Kingdom
Edward Seymour, Duke of Somerset, Protector and Lord Treasurer in the reign of his nephew, Edward VI (1548)

The **Lord Protector of the Commonwealth.** Oliver Cromwell (1599-1658) was declared such in 1653 His son Richard succeeded as Lord Protector until the Restoration in 1660

Protestant A member of a Christian Church upholding the principles of the Reformation, or (loosely) of any Church not in communion with Rome Originally, one of the party which adhered to Luther who, in 1529, "protested" against the decree of Charles V of Germany, and appealed from the Diet of Spires to a general council

The **Protestant Pope** Clement XIV He ordered the suppression of the Jesuits (1773) and was one of the most enlightened men who ever sat in the chair of St Peter

Proteus (prŏ' tūs) In Greek legend, Neptune's herdsman, an old man and a prophet, famous for his power of assuming different shapes at will. Hence the phrase, *As many shapes as Proteus—i e* full of shifts, aliases, disguises, etc , and the adjective **protean,** readily taking on different aspects, ever-changing

Proteus lived in a vast cave, and his custom was to tell over his herds of sea-calves at noon, and then to sleep There was no way of catching him but by stealing upon him at this time and binding him, otherwise he would elude anyone by a rapid change in shape

Protevangelium (prō te văn jō′ li um) The *first* (Gr *protos*) gospel, applied to an apocryphal gospel which had been attributed to St James the Less It has been supposed by some critics that all the gospels were based upon this, although no vestige of it has been discovered. The name is also given to the curse upon the serpent in *Gen* iii, 15.—

And I will put enmity between thee and the woman, and between thy seed and her seed; it shall bruise thy head, and thou shalt bruise his heel,

which has been regarded as the earliest utterance of the gospel.

Prothalamion (prō thả lả′ mi ûn) The term coined by Spenser (from Gr. *thalamos*, a bridal chamber) as a title for his "Spousall Verse" (1596) in honour of the double marriage of Lady Elizabeth and Lady Katherine Somerset, daughters of the Earl of Worcester, to Henry Gilford and William Peter, Esquires Hence, a song sung in honour of the bride and bridegroom before the wedding

Proto-martyr. The first martyr (Gr *protos,* first) Stephen the deacon is so called (*Acts* v, vii), and St Alban is known as the proto-martyr of Britain

Protocol (prō′ tō kol) The first rough draft or original copy of a dispatch, which is to form the basis of a treaty, from Gr *proto-koleon,* a sheet glued to the front of a manuscript, or to the case containing it, and bearing an abstract of the contents and purport Also the ceremonial procedure used in affairs of diplomacy or on state occasions.

Protoplasm (prō′ tō plazm) (Gr. *proto,* first, *plasma,* thing moulded). The physical basis of life, the material composing cells, from which all living organisms are developed It is a viscid, semi-fluid, semi-transparent substance composed of a highly unstable combination of oxygen, hydrogen, carbon, and nitrogen, capable of spontaneous movement, contraction, etc It can best be seen in the simpler jellyfishes. Sarcode (Gi *sarcos,* flesh) is an earlier name of the substance

Proud, The. Otho IV, Emperor of Germany (1175, 1209-18)

Tarquin II of Rome *Superbus* (Reigned 535-10 B C , d. 496)

The proud Duke. Charles Seymour, 6th Duke of Somerset (1662-1748) He would never suffer his children to sit in his presence, and would never speak to his servants except by signs

In engineering and mechanics *proud* is a term denoting any screw or piece of metal which protrudes farther than it should

Province. From Lat. *provincia,* the name given by the Romans to a territory brought under subjugation, possibly because previously com-

quered (*pro,* before, *vincere,* to conquer). It is now applied, in the plural, to districts in a country, usually at a distance from the metropolis, whence the special meaning of *provincial* —narrow, unpolished, rude—and to the territory under the ecclesiastical control of an archbishop or metropolitan.

The Provincial of an Order is the superior of all the monastic houses of that Order in a given province

Prudhomme (proo′ dom) The French colloquialism for a man of experience and great prudence, of estimable character and practical good sense Your *Monsieur Prudhomme* is never a man of genius and originality The name arises from the character of Joseph Prudhomme in Henri Mounier's sketch thus entitled (1857)

Prunella (pru′ nel a) A dark, smooth woollen stuff of which clergymen's and barristers' gowns used to be made, probably so termed from its colour—plum, or prune It is still in use for garters and the uppers of boots.

All leather and prunella *See* LEATHER.

Prussianism. A term given to the overbearing spirit and methods characteristic of Prussians dating from the military despotism that has flourished among them since the days of Frederick the Great (1712-86) It came to full-flower after the Franco-Prussian war of 1870 when Prussia forced herself as a leader among the German states forming the new German Empire Under the last Kaiser, who was King of Prussia, the spirit of Prussianism led to World War I, and it has taken a second world war and the virtual obliteration of German civilization to break if not to destroy Prussianism.

Prussian blue. So called because it was discovered by a Prussian, viz Diesbach, a colourman of Berlin, in 1704 It was sometimes called *Berlin* blue It is hydrated ferric ferrocyanide, and *prussic acid* (hydrocyanic acid) is made from it

Pry, Paul. An idle, meddlesome fellow, who has no occupation of his own, and is always interfering with other folk's business The term comes from the hero of John Poole's comedy, *Paul Pry* (1825)

Psalmanazar, George, a classical example of the imposter A Frenchman whose real name is unknown to this day, he appeared in London in 1703 claiming to be a native of Formosa, at that time an almost unknown island In 1704 he published an account of Formosa with a grammar of the language, which was from beginning to end a fabrication of his own. The literary and critical world of London was taken in, but his imposture was soon exposed by Catholic missionaries who had laboured in Formosa, and after a time Psalmanazar publicly confessed his fraud He turned over a new leaf and applied himself to the study of Hebrew and other genuine labours, ending his days in 1763 as a man of some repute and the friend of Dr. Johnson

Psalms. Seventy-three psalms are inscribed with David's name, twelve with that of Asaph the singer, eleven go under the name of the Sons of Korah, a family of singers, one (*i.e Ps* xc) is attributed to Moses The whole compilation is divided into five books· Bk 1, from i to xli, Bk. 2, from xlii to lxxii, Bk 3, from lxxiii to lxxxix, Bk 4, from xc to cvi; Bk. 5, from cvii to cl

The *Book of Psalms*—or much of its contents—was for centuries attributed to David (hence called the *sweet psalmist* of Israel), but it is very doubtful whether he wrote any of them, and it is certain that the majority belong to a later period The tradition comes from the author of *Chronicles*, and in 2 *Sam* xxii is a psalm attributed to David that is identical with *Ps* xviii Also, the last verse of *Ps* lxxii ("the prayers of David the son of Jesse are ended") seems to suggest that he was the author up to that point

In explanation of the confusion between the R C and the Protestant psalters it should be noted that Psalms x to cxiii and cxv to cxlvi in the R.C. psalter are numbered one behind those in the A V. and Prayer Book

See GRADUAL PSALMS, PENITENTIAL PSALMS, etc

Pschent (pshent) The royal double crown of ancient Egypt, combining that of Upper Egypt—a high conical white cap terminating in a knob—with the red one of Lower Egypt, the latter being the outermost

Pseudonym. *See* NOM DE PLUME

Psyche (sīk′ ē) (Gr., breath, hence, life, or soul itself) In "the latest-born of the myths," *Cupid and Psyche,* an episode in the *Golden Ass* of Apuleius (2nd century A D.), a beautiful maiden beloved by Cupid, who visited her every night, but left her at sunrise Cupid bade her never seek to know who he was, but one night curiosity overcame her prudence, she lit the lamp to look at him, a drop of hot oil fell on his shoulder, and he awoke and fled The abandoned Psyche then wandered far and wide in search of her lover, she became the slave of Venus, who imposed on her heartless tasks and treated her most cruelly, but ultimately she was united to Cupid, and became immortal The story is told by Walter Pater in *Marius the Epicurean*

Ptolemaic System (tol e mā′ ik). The system promulgated by Ptolemy, the celebrated astronomer of Alexandria in the 2nd century A D., to account for the apparent motion of the heavenly bodies He taught that the earth is fixed in the centre of the universe, and the heavens revolve round it from east to west, carrying with them the sun, planets, and fixed stars, in their respective spheres (*q v*), which he imagined as solid coverings (like so many skins of an onion) each revolving at different velocities This theory, with slight modifications, held the field till the time of Copernicus (16th century)

Public (Lat *publicus,* earlier *poplicus* from *poplus,* later *populus,* the people) The people generally and collectively; the members generally of a state, nation, or community Also, a colloquial contraction of "public-house," frequently abbreviated still further to "pub"

The simple life I can't afford,
Besides, I do not like the grub—
I want a mash and sausage, "scored"—
Will someone take me to a pub?
G K CHESTERTON *Ballade of an Anti-Puritan*

Public-house signs. Much of a nation's history, and more of its manners and feelings, may be gleaned from its public-house signs A very large number of them are selected out of compliment to the lord of the manor, either because he is the "great man" of the neighbourhood, or because the proprietor is some servant whom "it delighted the lord to honour " When the name and titles of the lord have been exhausted, we get his cognizance or his favourite pursuit, as the *Bear and Ragged Staff,* the *Fox and Hounds* As the object of the sign is to speak to the feelings and attract, another fruitful source is either some national hero or great battle, thus we get the *Marquis of Granby* and the *Duke of Wellington,* the *Waterloo* and the *Alma* The proverbial loyalty of our nation has naturally shown itself in our tavern signs, giving us the *Victoria, Prince of Wales,* the *Albert,* the *Crown,* and so on. Literature is not well represented, though Shakespeare and Ben Jonson give their names to a good many houses, and in London there is a *Milton Arms,* a *Macaulay Arms,* a *Sir Richard Steele,* and a *Sir Walter Scott,* as well as *The Miller of Mansfield. Pindar of Wakefield, Sir John Falstaff, Robinson Crusoe,* and *Valentine and Orson. The Good Samaritan, Noah's Ark, Simon the Tanner,* and *Gospel Oak* all have a biblical flavour, and old ecclesiastical manorial rights are responsible for many tavern signs (*see The Three Kings,* below). Myth and legend are represented by houses named *The Apollo, Hercules, Phœnix, King Lud, Merlin's Cave, Man in the Moon, Punch, Robin Hood, The Moonrakers,* etc

Some signs indicate a speciality of the house, as the *Bowling Green,* the *Skittles,* some a political bias, as the *Royal Oak,* a number are reminiscent of the old trade guilds, such as the *Coopers', Bricklayers', Carpenters',* and *Haberdashers' Arms,* and some are an attempt at wit, as the *Five Alls* and *The World Turned Upside Down* The following list will serve to exemplify the subject —

The Bag 'o Nails. A corruption of the "Bacchanals "

The Barley Mow (*q v*).

The Bear. From the popular sport of bearbaiting

The Bear and Bacchus, in High Street, Warwick. A corruption of *Bear and Baculus—i e.* Bear and Ragged Staff, the badge of the Earl of Warwick

The Bell In allusion to races, a silver bell having been the winner's prize up to the reign of Charles II

The Bell Savage See LA BELLE SAUVAGE.

The Blue Boar. The cognizance of Richard III

The Boar's Head The cognizance of the Gordons, etc

The Bolt-in-Tun The punning heraldic badge of Prior *Bolton,* last of the clerical rulers of St Bartholomew's, previous to the Reformation.

The Bull The cognizance of Richard, Duke of York. The *Black Bull* is the cognizance of the house of Clare.

The Bull and Gate (q v)

The Bull's Head. The cognizance of Henry VIII

The Case is Altered See PLOWDEN.

The Castle. This, being the arms of Spain, signified that Spanish wines were to be obtained within

The Cat and Fiddle See CAT

The Cat and Wheel A corruption of "St Catherine's Wheel"; or an announcement that *cat* and balance-*wheels* are provided for the amusement of customers

The Chequers (1) in honour of the Stuarts, whose shield was "checky," like a Scotch plaid (2) In commemoration of the licence granted by the Earls of Arundel or Lords Warrenne (3) An intimation that a room is set apart for merchants and accountants, where they can be private and make up their accounts, or use their "chequers" undisturbed

The Coach and Horses A favourite sign of a posting-house or stage-coach house

The Cock and Bottle. By some said to be a corruption of the "Cork and Bottle," meaning that wine is sold there in bottles

The Cross Keys Common in the mediæval ages, and in allusion to St. Peter, or one of the bishops whose cognizance it is—probably the lord of the manor or the patron saint of the parish church The cross keys are emblems of the papacy, St. Peter, the Bishop of Gloucester, St. Servetus, St Hippolytus, St Geneviève, St Petronilla, St Osyth, St. Martha, and St Germanus.

The Devil The sign of more than one old public-house in the neighbourhood of Fleet Street. It represents St Dunstan seizing the devil by the nose *See* DEVIL

The Dog and Duck, or *The Duck in the Pond* Indicating that the sport so called could be seen there. A duck was put into water, and a dog set to hunt it, the fun was to see the duck diving and the dog following it under water

The Red Dragon The cognizance of Henry VII or the principality of Wales

The Spread Eagle The arms of Germany, to indicate that German wines could be obtained within

The Fox and Goose. To signify that there are arrangements within for playing the Royal Game of Fox and Goose

St George and the Dragon In compliment to the patron saint of England

The Globe. The royal cognizance of Portugal, intimating that Portuguese wines were stocked

The Goat and Compasses See GOAT.

The Black Goats A public-house sign, High Bridge Lincoln, formerly *The Three Goats—i e three gowts* (gutters or drains), by which the water from the Swan Pool (a large lake that formerly existed to the west of the city) was conducted into the bed of the Witham

The Golden Cross. This refers to the ensigns carried by the Crusaders

The Green Man The late gamekeeper of the lord of the manor turned publican At one time these servants were dressed in green

The Green Man and Still—i e the herbalist bringing his herbs to be distilled.

The Hare and Hounds In compliment to the sporting squire or lord of the manor

The Hole in the Wall. Probably so called because it was approached by a small passage or "hole" between houses standing in front of the tavern

The Horse and Chains A favourite sign for an inn at the foot of a hill, signifying that a chain-horse is kept

The Horse and Groom Where a stallion was kept for stud purposes

The Iron Devil Said to be a corruption of "Hirondelle" (the swallow).

The Three Kings A mediæval sign, in allusion to the three kings of Cologne the Magi *(q v)* Many public-house signs of this period had a reference to ecclesiastical matters, usually because they were church property or on church land, Such, for instance, are *The Mitre, Abbey, Priory,* and *Lamb and Flag.*

The Man with a Load of Mischief A public-house sign, Oxford Street, nearly opposite to Hanway Yard. It is said to have been painted by Hogarth, and shows a man carrying a woman and a lot of other *impedimenta* on his back

The Marquis of Granby. In compliment to John Manners (1721-70), eldest son of John, third Duke of Rutland—a bluff, brave soldier, generous, and greatly beloved by his men.

> What conquest now will Britain boast
> Or where display her banners?
> Alas! in Granby she has lost
> True courage and good Manners

The Pig and Tinder Box See PIG

The Plum and Feathers (near Stokenchurch, Oxford) A corruption of the "Plume of Feathers," meaning that of the Prince of Wales

The Queen of Bohemia In honour of James I's daughter Elizabeth, who married the King of Bohemia.

The Rose. A symbol of England, as the *Thistle* is of Scotland, and the *Shamrock* of Ireland

The Rose and Crown One of the "loyal" public-house signs.

The Rose of the Quarter Sessions A corruption of *La Rose des Quatre Saisons*

The Salutation and Cat The "Salutation" (which refers to the angel saluting the Virgin Mary) is the sign of the house, and the "Cat" is added to signify that arrangements are made for playing *cat* or tipcat

The Saracen's Head Reminiscent of the Crusades, adopted probably by some Crusader after his return home, or to excite sympathy with these quixotic expeditions

The Ship and Shovel Referring to Sir Cloudesley Shovel, a favourite admiral in Queen Anne's reign

The Seven Stars An astrological sign of the Middle Ages

The Three Suns The cognizance of Edward IV

The Sun and the Rose. The cognizance of the House of York.

The Swan with Three Necks See SWAN

The Swan and the Antelope The cognizance of Henry V

The Talbot (a hound) The arms of the Talbot family.

The Turk's Head Like the "Saracen's Head," an allusion to the Crusades

The Two Chairmen. Not an uncommon sign for small houses in districts (such as Charing Cross and Wardour Street) that were fashionable residential quarters in the 18th century, when sedan chairs were in vogue

The Unicorn The Scottish supporter in the royal arms of Great Britain

The White Hart The cognizance of Richard II, the *White Lion*, of Edward IV as Earl of March, the *White Swan*, of Henry IV and Edward III.

Publicans. The name given in the New Testament to the provincial representatives (*publicani*, servants of the state) of the *Magister* or master tax-collector who resided at Rome The taxes were farmed by a contractor called the *Manceps*, who divided the whole taxable area into convenient districts, each of which was under a *Magister*.

Pucelle, La (pü sel') Fr , "The Maid," *i e* of Orleans, Joan of Arc (1410-31) Chapelain wrote a dull heroic poem with this title, Voltaire a mock-heroic, satirical, and in parts a scurrilous one

Puck. A mischievous, tricksy sprite of popular folk-lore, also called Robin Goodfellow, originally an evil demon, but transformed and popularized in his present form by Shakespeare (*Midsummer Night's Dream*), who shows him as a merry wanderer of the night "rough, knurly limbed, faun-faced, and shock-pated, a very Shetlander among the gossamer-winged" fairies around him

Pudens (pü' denz) A soldier in the Roman army, mentioned in 2 *Tim* iv, 21, in connexion with Linus and Claudia According to tradition, Claudia, the wife of Pudens, was a British lady, Linus, otherwise called Cyllen, was her brother, and Lucius "the British king," the grandson of Linus Tradition further adds that Lucius wrote to Eleutherus, Bishop of Rome, to send missionaries to Britain to convert the people.

Pueblo (pweb' lō) The Spanish word for "people" but applied particularly to the farming, peace-loving Indians of New Mexico and Arizona, and to their commensal dwellings of adobe or stone

Puff. An onomatopœic word, suggestive of the sound made by puffing wind from the mouth. As applied to inflated or exaggerated praise, extravagantly worded advertisements. reviews, etc , it dates at least from the early 17th century, and the implication is that such commendation is really as worthless and transitory as a puff of wind

In Sheridan's *The Critic* (1779), Puff, who, he himself says, is "a practitioner in panegyric, or, to speak more plainly, a professor of the art of puffing" gives a catalogue of puffs —

Yes, sir,—puffing is of various sorts, the principal are, the puff direct, the puff preliminary, the puff collateral, the puff collusive and the puff oblique, or puff by implication These all assume, as circumstances require, the various forms of letter to the editor, occasional anecdote, impartial critique, observation from correspondent, or advertisement from the party. *The Critic*, I, ii

Puffed up. Conceited , elated with conceit or praise, filled with wind A *puff* is a tartlet with a very light or puffy crust.

That no one of you be puffed up one against another —1 *Cor* iv, 6

Puff-ball A fungus of the genus *Lycoperdon*, so called because it is ball-shaped and when it is ripe it bursts and the spores come out in a "puff" of fine powder

Puisne Judges (pü' ni) means the younger-born judges. They are the judges of the High Court of Justice other than the Lord Chancellor, the Lord Chief Justice, the Master of the Rolls, and the Lord Chief Justice of the Common Pleas. The word is the same, etymologically, as *puny* (Fr *puisné*, subsequently born, Lat *post natus*)

Puke (pūk) (U.S A.) An uncomplimentary term for a Missourian

Pukka (pūk' a) A Hindustani word that has crept into common speech meaning substantial, real, *bona fide*, conventional It has developed a somewhat derogatory implication

Pulhems. A system for assessing the physical and mental capabilities of a recruit It was introduced in the Canadian Army in 1943. The word is a mnemonic P, physical capacity, U, upper limbs, L, locomotion, H, hearing, E, eyesight, M, mental capacity, S, stability (emotional). In 1948 the system was introduced into the British armed forces, but with two E's, for the Navy and Air . Force demanded that the visual acuity of each eye be registered separately.

Pulitzer Prizes for literary work, the drama and music are awarded annually from funds left for the purpose by Joseph Pulitzer (1847-1911) a prominent and wealthy American editor and newspaper proprietor

Pull A long pull, a strong pull, and a pull all together—*i e* a steady energetic, and systematic co-operation The reference may be either to a boat, where all the oarsmen pull together with a long and strong pull at the oars, or it may be to the act of hauling with a rope, when a simultaneous strong pull is indispensable

Pull devil pull baker. Let each one do the best for himself in his own line of business, but let not one man interfere in that of another

It's all fair pulling, "pull devil, pull baker," someone has to get the worst of it Now it's us [bushrangers], now its them [the police] that gets . rubbed out —BOLDREWOOD *Robbery under Arms*, ch xxxvii.

The long pull The extra quantity of beer supplied by a publican to his customer over and above the pint or half-pint ordered and paid for Under the restrictions imposed during World War I this was abolished by order, as it is a form of "treating "

To have the pull of or over one. To have the advantage over him, to be able to dictate terms or make him do what you wish

To pull bacon To cock a snook.

To pull one's weight. To do the very best one can, exert oneself to the utmost of one's ability. The phrase comes from rowing; an oarsman who does not put all his weight into the stroke tends to become a passenger

To pull oneself together. To rouse oneself to renewed activity; to shake off depression or inertia

To pull someone's leg To delude him in a humorous way, lead him astray by chaff, exaggeration, etc

To pull the wool over someone's eyes. To deceive or hoodwink, to blind him temporarily to what is going on

To pull through. To get oneself well out of a difficulty—such as over a serious illness, through a stiff examination, etc To work in harmony with one view; to co-operate heartily

Pullman. Properly a well-fitted railway saloon or sleeping-car built at the Pullman Carriage Works, Illinois; so called from the designer, George M Pullman (1832-97) of Chicago The word is now applied to other luxurious railway saloons, and to motor-cars

Pummel. *See* POMMEL.

Pump To pump someone is to extract information out of him by artful questions, to draw from him all he knows as one draws water from a well by gradual pumping. Ben Jonson, in *A Tale of a Tub* (IV, iii) has "I'll stand aside whilst thou pump'st out of him his business"

Pumpernickel (pŭmp'ĕr nik el). The coarse rye-bread ("brown George") eaten by German peasants, especially in Westphalia. Thackeray applied the term as a satirical nickname to petty German princelings ("His Transparency the Duke of Pumpernickel") who made a great show with the court officials and etiquette, but whose revenue was almost *nil*

Pun. He who would make a pun would pick a pocket. Dr Johnson is generally credited with this silly dictum, but the correct version is—"Any man who would make such an execrable pun would not scruple to pick my pocket" the remark addressed to the critic, John Dennis (1657-1734) to Purcell. *See the Public Advertiser*, Jan 12th, 1779, and the *Gentleman's Magazine*, vol ii, p. 324, also the note to Pope's *Dunciad*, bk i, l. 63

The "execrable pun" was this Purcell rang the bell for the *drawer* or waiter, but no one answered it Purcell, tapping the table, asked Dennis "why the table was like the tavern?" Ans "Because there is no drawer in it."

Punch The name of this beverage, which was introduced into England from India in the early 17th century, has generally been held to derive from Hindustani *panch*, five, because it has five principal ingredients (viz spirit, water, spice, sugar, and some acid fruit essence) There are, however, linguistic and phonetic objections to accepting this derivation—as well as the fact that early recipes give anything from three to six principal ingredients, and there was no reason why it should have been named from five—and it is just as likely that it is merely a contraction by sailors engaged in the East Indian trade of *puncheon*, the large cask from which their grog was served

Punch, Mr. The hero of the popular puppet show, *Punch and Judy* The name comes from the Italian *Pulcinello* In the 18th century the suggestion was made that the name was from a popular and ugly low comedian named Puccio d'Aniello, but nothing definite is known

of him, and the conjecture is certainly an example of "popular etymology." Another suggestion is that the name is derived from that of Pontius Pilate in the old mystery plays

The show first appeared in England a little before the accession of Queen Anne, and the story is attributed to Silvio Fiorillo, an Italian comedian of the 17th century Punch, in a fit of jealousy, strangles his infant child, whereupon his wife, Judy, fetches a bludgeon with which she belabours him till he seizes another bludgeon, beats her to death, and flings the two bodies into the street A passing police officer enters the house, Punch flees, but is arrested by an officer of the Inquisition and shut up in prison, whence he escapes by means of a golden key The rest is an allegory, showing how the light-hearted Punch triumphs over (1) Ennui, in the shape of a dog, (2) Disease, in the disguise of a doctor, (3) Death, who is beaten to death, and (4) the Devil himself, who is out-witted.

The satirical humorous weekly paper, *Punch, or the London Charivari*, is, of course, named from "Mr Punch" It first appeared on July 17th, 1841

Pleased as Punch. Greatly delighted. Our old friend is always singing with self-satisfaction in his naughty ways, and his evident "pleasure" is contagious to the beholders

Suffolk punch. A short, thick-set cart-horse The term was formerly applied to any short fat man, and is probably the same word as above, though it may be connected with *puncheon*, the large cask.

I did hear them call their fat child Punch, which pleased me mightily, that word having become a word of common use for everything that is thick and short —*Pepys's Diary*, Apr 30th, 1669

Punctual No bigger than a point, exact to a point or moment (Lat *ad punctum*) Hence the angel, describing this earth to Adam, calls it "This spacious earth, this punctual spot"—*i.e.* a spot no bigger than a point (Milton *Paradise Lost*, viii, 23)

Punctuality is the politeness of kings (*L'exactitude est la politesse des rois*) A favourite maxim of Louis XVIII, but erroneously attributed by Samuel Smiles to Louis XIV.

Pundit (pŭn' dit) An East Indian scholar, skilled in Sanskrit, and learned in law, divinity, and science. We use the word for a learned person, also for one more stocked with book lore than deep erudition

Punic Apple (pū' nik) A pomegranate, so called because it is the pomum or "apple" belonging to the genus *Punica.*

Punica fides (pū' nik a fī' dēz) Treachery, violation of faith, the faith of the Carthaginians, Lat. *Punicus*, earlier *Pœnicus*, meaning a Phœnician, hence applied to the Carthaginians, who were of Phœnician descent The Carthaginians were accused by the Romans of breaking faith with them, a most extraordinary instance of the "pot calling the kettle black", for whatever infidelity they were guilty of, it could scarcely equal that of their accusers. *Cp* ATTIC FAITH

			Our Punic faith
Is infamous, and branded to a proverb
						ADDISON *Cato*, ii.

Pup. Slang for a *pupil*, especially an undergraduate studying with a tutor

As applied to the young of dogs, the word is an abbreviation of *puppy*, which represents Fr *poupée*, a dressed doll, a plaything

An empty-headed, impertinent young fellow is frequently called *a young puppy*, hence Douglas Jerrold's epigram—more witty than true—

Dogmatism is only puppyism come to maturity

To be sold a pup. To be swindled.

Purbeck (Dorsetshire) Noted for a marble used in ecclesiastical ornaments Chichester cathedral has a row of columns of this limestone. The columns of the Temple church, London, the tomb of Queen Eleanor, in Westminster Abbey, and the throne of the archbishop in Canterbury cathedral, are other specimens.

Pure, Simon. *See* SIMON PURE

Purgatory. The doctrine of Purgatory, according to which the souls of the departed suffer for a time till they are *purged* of their sin, is of ancient standing, and was held in a modified form by the Jews, who believed that the soul of the deceased was allowed for twelve months after death to visit its body and the places or persons it especially loved. This intermediate state they called by various names, as "the bosom of Abraham," "the garden of Eden," "upper Gehenna " The Sabbath was always a free day, and prayer was supposed to benefit those in this intermediate state

The outline of this doctrine was annexed by the early Fathers, and was considerably strengthened by certain passages in the New Testament, particularly *Rev* vi, 9-11, and 1 *Pet* iii, 18 and 19 The first decree on the subject was promulgated by the Council of Florence, in 1439, and in 1562 it was condemned by the Church of England, the XXIInd of the "Articles of Religion" stating that—

The Romish Doctrine concerning Purgatory is a fond thing vainly invented, and grounded upon no warranty of Scripture, but rather repugnant to the Word of God

Purge. A neo-euphemism in dictator countries for the elimination (usually by murder) of persons suspected of disaffection or in some other way undesirable to party leaders The most notorious of party purges was the infamous "night of the knives," on June 30th, 1934, when Roehm, a potential rival of Hitler, and some 7,000 others were murdered in cold blood within 24 hours There have been many "purges" in Bolshevist Russia, but the particulars of them have never come to the light of day

See also PRIDE'S PURGE

Puritans Seceders from the Reformed Church in the sixteenth century, so called because, wishing for a more radical purification of religion, they rejected all human traditions and interference in religious matters, acknowledging the sole authority of the "pure Word of God," without "note or comment " Their motto was "The Bible, the whole Bible, and nothing but the Bible " The English Puritans were sometimes by the Reformers called *Precisionists*, from their preciseness in matters called "indifferent " Andrew Fuller named

24*

them *Non-conformists*, because they refused to subscribe to the Act of Uniformity

The Puritan hated bearbaiting, not because it gave pain to the bear, but because it gave pleasure to the spectators Indeed he generally contrived to enjoy the double pleasure of tormenting both spectators and bear —MACAULAY *History of England*, Bk 1, ch. ii

Purler. A cropper, or heavy fall from one's horse in a steeplechase or in the hunting-field, also, a knockdown blow

Seraph's white horse cleared it, but falling with a mighty crash, gave him a purler on the opposite side —OUIDA *Under Two Flags*, ch vi

Purlieu (pĕr′lū) The outlying parts of a place, the environs, originally the borders or outskirts of a forest, especially a part which was formerly part of the forest. So called from O Fr *pouralle* a place free from the forest laws Henry II, Richard I, and John made certain lands forest lands, Henry III allowed certain portions all round to be freed from the restrictions imposed on the royal forests, and the "perambulation" by which this was effected was called *pourallee*, a going through The *lieu* (as though for "place") was an erroneous addition due to English pronunciation and spelling of the French word

In the purlieus of this forest stands
A sheepcote fenced about with olive-trees
As You Like It, iv, 3

Purple. The colour of ecclesiastical mourning and penitence (hence worn during Lent), also that of the dress of emperors, kings, and prelates, from the Lat *purpura* which was formed on Gr. *porphyra*, meaning both the shell-fish which yielded Tyrian purple (a species of *Murex*), and the purplish marble, *porphyry*. A priest is said to be raised to the purple when he is made a cardinal, though the cardinalatial colour is actually red. It is one of the tinctures (*purpure*) used in heraldry, and in engravings is shown by lines running diagonally from sinister to dexter (i e from right to left as one looks at it) *See* COLOURS

Born in the purple. Said of the child of a king or emperor (*see* PORPHYROGENITUS), hence of anyone of exalted birth or "born with a silver spoon in his mouth." The expression comes from a Byzantine custom which ordained that the empress should be brought to bed in a chamber the walls of which were lined with porphyry, or purple

Purple Heart. A U S. army medal awarded for wounds received by enemy action while on active service It consists of a silver heart bearing the effigy of George Washington, suspended from a purple ribbon with white edges

Purple patches. Highly coloured or florid passages in a literary work which is (generally speaking) otherwise undistinguished The allusion is to Horace's *De Arte Poetica*, 1, 15 —

Inceptis gravibus plerumque et magna professis,
Purpureus, late qui splendeat, unus et alter
Adsuitur pannus

(Often to weighty enterprises and such as profess great objects, one or two purple patches are sewed on to make a fine display in the distance)

Pursuivant (pĕr′swi vănt) The lowest grade of the officers of arms composing the College of Arms, or Heralds' College, the others, under the Earl Marshal, being (1) the Kings of Arms, and (2) the Heralds.

England has four Pursuivants, viz *Rouge Croix*, *Bluemantle*, *Rouge Dragon*, and *Portcullis*; Scotland has three, viz *Carrick*, *March*, and *Unicorn*, and Ireland one, *Athlone*

Pursy, Broken-winded, or in a bloated state in which the wind is short and difficult (Fr. *poussif*)

A fat and pursy man. Shakespeare has "pursy insolence," the insolence of Jesurun, "who waxed fat and kicked " In *Hamlet* we have "the fatness of these pursy times"—*i e* wanton or self-indulgent times

Puseyite (pū' zi It) A High Church follower of E B Pusey (1800-82), Professor of Hebrew at Oxford, one of the leaders of the "Oxford Movement," and a contributor to the *Tracts for the Times See* TRACTARIANS

Push. Military slang for a strong concerted forward movement, a general attack, hence, by extension, for a body of troops engaged on an offensive, a gang, crowd, "crush."

To give one the push. To give him his congé, give him the sack

To push off. To commence the game, the operations, etc A phrase from boating—one starts by pushing the boat off from the bank *Push off!* said imperatively, is equivalent to "Get you gone!" "Go to the devil!"

Puss. A conventional call-name for a cat, applied also (in the 17th century and since) to hares Its original is unknown, though it is present in many Teutonic languages The derivation from Lat. *lepus*, a hare, Frenchified into *le pus*, is of course only humorous.

Puss in Boots This nursery tale, *Le Chat Botté*, is from Straparola's *Nights* (1530), No. xi, where Constantine's cat procures his master a fine castle and the king's heiress It was translated from the Italian into French in 1585, and appeared in Perrault's *Les contes de ma Mere l'Oie* (1697), through which medium it reached England In the story the clever cat secures a fortune and a royal partner for his master, who passes off as the Marquis of Carabas, but is in reality a young miller without a penny in the world

Pussyfoot. A person with a soft, cat-like, sneaking tread

Pussyfoot Johnson was the nickname of W E Johnson (1882-1945) who gained the sobriquet from his unwavering advocacy of prohibition, and his silent, stealthy, relentless methods of enforcing it It was partly owing to his determination and pertinacity that Prohibition was introduced in U.S A in 1919

Put (pŭt) A clown, a silly shallow-pate, a butt, one easily "put upon "

Queer country puts extol Queen Bess's reign
                                    BRAMSON

Put and take. A game of chance played with a modification of the old "tee-to-tum," one side of which is marked *Put*—signifying that the player pays—and another with *Take* It was immensely popular for a few months about Christmastime, 1921

Putsch (pooch) A German word from the English *push* applied to a minor revolt or political uprising.

Pygmalion (pig mā' li on) A sculptor and king of Cyprus in Greek legend, who, though he hated women, fell in love with his own ivory statue of Aphrodite At his earnest prayer the goddess gave life to the statue and he married it

The story is told in Ovid's *Metamorphoses*, x, and appeared in English dress in John Marston's *Metamorphosis of Pygmalion's Image* (1598). Morris retold it in *The Earthly Paradise* (*August*), and W. S Gilbert adapted it in his comedy of *Pygmalion and Galatea* (1871), in which the sculptor is a married man His wife (Cynisca) was jealous of the animated statue (Galatea), which, after considerable trouble, voluntarily returned to its original state The name was used figuratively by G B. Shaw for a play produced in 1912.

Pygmy (pig' mi) The name used by Homer and other classical writers for a supposed race of dwarfs said to dwell somewhere in Ethiopia, from Gr. *pugme*, the length of the arm from elbow to knuckles Fable has it that every spring the cranes made war on them and devoured them; they used an axe to cut down corn-stalks, when Hercules went to the country they climbed up his goblet by ladders to drink from it, and while he was asleep two whole armies of them fell upon his right hand, and two upon his left and were rolled up by Hercules in his lion's skin It is easy to see how Swift has availed himself of this Grecian legend in his *Gulliver's Travels*

The term is now applied to certain dwarfish races of central Africa (whose existence was first demonstrated late in the 19th century), Malaysia, etc , also to small members of a class, as the *pygmy hippopotamus*

Pylades and Orestes (pi' lá dēz, ō res' tēz) Two friends in Homeric legend, whose names have become proverbial for friendship, like those of Damon and Pythias, David and Jonathan Orestes was the son, and Pylades the nephew, of Agamemnon, after whose murder Orestes was put in the care of Pylades' father (Strophius), and the two became fast friends. Pylades assisted Orestes in obtaining vengeance on Ægisthus and Clytemnestra, and afterwards married Electra his friend's sister.

Pylon (pi' lon) Properly a monumental gateway (Gr. *pulon*), especially of an Egyptian temple, now usually applied to the obelisks that mark out the course in an aerodrome or to the standards for electric cables

Pyramid (pir' á mid). There are some 70 pyramids still remaining in Egypt, but those specially called The Pyramids are the three larger in the group of eight known as the Pyramids of Gizeh. Of these the largest, the Great Pyramid, is the tomb of Cheops, a king of the 4th Dynasty, about 4000 B C It was 480 ft in height (now about 30 ft less), and the length of each base is 755 ft The Second Pyramid, the tomb of Chephren (also 4th Dynasty) is slightly smaller (472 ft by 700 ft), and the Third, the tomb of Menkaura, or Mycerinus (4th Dynasty, about 3630 B C), is much smaller (215 ft by 346 ft) Each contains entrances, with dipping passages leading to various sepulchral chambers

Pyramus (pir' à mùs) A Babylonian youth in classic story (*see* Ovid's *Metamorphoses*, iv), the lover of Thisbe, Thisbe was to meet him at the white mulberry-tree near the tomb of Ninus but she, scared by a lion, fled and left her veil which the lion besmeared with blood Pyramus, thinking his lady-love had been devoured, slew himself, and Thisbe coming up soon afterwards, stabbed herself also The blood of the lovers stained the white fruit of the mulberry-tree into its present colour The "tedious brief scene" and "very tragical mirth" presented by the rustics in *Midsummer Night's Dream* is a travesty of this legend

Pyrrha (pi' ra) The wife of Deucalion (*q v*) in Greek legend They were the sole survivors of the deluge sent by Zeus to destroy the whole human race, and repopulated the world by casting stones behind them which were turned into men.

> Men themselves, the which at first were framed
> Of earthly mould, and form'd of flesh and bone
> Are now transformed into hardest stone,
> Such as behind their backs (so backward bred)
> Were thrown by Pyrrha and Deucalion
> SPENSER *Fairie Queene*, V, *Introd* , 2.

Pyrrhic Dance (pi' rik) The famous war-dance of the Greeks, so called from its inventor, Pyrrichos, a Dorian It was a quick dance, performed in full armour to the flute, and its name is still used for a metrical foot of two short, "dancing" syllables The *Romaika*, still danced in Greece, is a relic of the ancient Pyrrhic dance

> Ye have the Pyrrhic dance as yet
> Where is the Pyrrhic phalanx gone?
> BYRON *The Isles of Greece*

Pyrrhic victory. A ruinous victory Pyrrhus, King of Epirus, after his victory over the Romans at Asculum (279 B C), when he lost the flower of his army, said to those sent to congratulate him, "One more such victory and Pyrrhus is undone "

Pyrrhonism. Scepticism, or philosophic doubt; so named from Pyrrho (4th century B C), the founder of the first Greek school of sceptical philosophy Pyrrho maintained that nothing was capable of proof and admitted the reality of nothing but sensations

Pythagoras (pī thag' or ăs) The Greek philosopher and mathematician of the 6th century B C (born at Samos), to whom was attributed the enunciation of the doctrines of the transmigration of souls and of the harmony of the spheres, and also the proof of the 47th proposition in the 1st book of Euclid, which is hence called the *Pythagorean proposition* He taught that the sun is a movable sphere, and that it, and the earth, and all the planets revolve round some central point which they called "the fire " He maintained that the soul has three vehicles (1) the *ethereal*, which is luminous and celestial, in which the soul resides in a state of bliss in the stars, (2) the *luminous*, which suffers the punishment of sin after death, and (3) the *terrestrial*, which is the vehicle it occupies on this earth

Pythagoras was noted for his manly beauty and long hair, and many legends are related of him, such as that he distinctly recollected previous existences of his own, having been (1) Æthalides, son of Mercury, (2) Euphorbus the

Phrygian, son of Panthous, in which form he ran Patroclus through with a lance, leaving Hector to dispatch the hateful friend of Achilles, (3) Hermotimus, the prophet of Clazomenæ, and (4) a fisherman To prove his Phrygian existence he was taken to the temple of Hera, in Argos, and asked to point out the shield of the son of Panthous, which he did without hesitation.

Rosalind alludes to this theory (*As You Like It*, iii, 2) when she says —

> I was never so be-rhymed since Pythagoras' time that I was an Irish rat, which I can hardly remember

It is also elaborated in the scene between Feste and Malvolio in *Twelfth Night*, iv, 2 —

> *Clown* What is the opinion of Pythagoras concerning wild fowl?
> *Mal* That the soul of our grandam might haply inhabit a bird
> *Clown* What thinkest thou of his opinion?
> *Mal* I think nobly of the soul, and no way approve his opinion

Other legends assert that one of his thighs was of gold, and that he showed it to Abaris, the Hyperborean priest, and exhibited it in the Olympic Games, also that Abaris gave him a dart by which he could be carried through the air and with which he expelled pestilence, lulled storms, and performed other wonderful exploits

It was also said that Pythagoras used to write on a looking-glass in blood and place it opposite the moon, when the inscription would appear reflected on the moon's disc, and that he tamed a savage Daunian bear by "stroking it gently with his hand," subdued an eagle by the same means, and held absolute dominion over beasts and birds by "the power of his voice" or "influence of his touch "

The letter of Pythagoras. The Greek upsilon, Y, so called because it was used by him as a symbol of the divergent paths of virtue and vice

The Pythagorean tables. *See* TABLE

Pythian Games (pith' i an) The games held by the Greeks at Pytho, in Phocis, subsequently called Delphi They took place every fourth year, the second of each Olympiad

Pythias. *See* DAMON

Python (pī' thon) The monster serpent hatched from the mud of Deucalion's deluge, and slain near Delphi by Apollo

Pyx (picks) A small metal vessel in which the Host is carried to sick people In pre-Reformation England it was a vessel, often in the shape of a dove, suspended above the altar, in which the sacrament was reserved Only in the churches of Amiens and Valloires is such a pyx now permitted.

Q

Q The seventeenth letter of the English alphabet, and nineteenth (*koph*) of the Phœnician and Hebrew, where, in numerical notation, it represented 90 (in late Roman, 500) In English *q* is invariably followed by *u* (except occasionally in transliteration of some Arabic words), and it never occurs at the end of a word.

Q in a corner An old children's game, perhaps the same as our "Puss in the corner"; also something not seen at first, but subsequently brought to notice. The thing to which seals are attached in legal documents is in French called the *queue*; thus we have *lettres scellées sur simple queue* or *sur double queue*, according to whether they bear one or two seals. In documents where the seal is attached to the deed itself, the corner where the seal is placed is called the *queue*, and when the document is sworn to the finger is laid on the *queue*

In a merry Q (cue) Humour, temper, thus Shakespeare says, "My cue is villainous melancholy" (*King Lear*, i, 2)

Q. The *nom de plume* of Sir Arthur Quiller-Couch (1863-1944), sometime Professor of English Literature at Cambridge, and author of novels (*e g Dead Man's Rock*, 1887) and of several anthologies of prose and verse

Old Q. William Douglas, third Earl of March, and fourth Duke of Queensberry (1724-1810), notorious for his dissolute life and escapades, especially on the turf

On the strict Q.T. With complete secrecy "Q T " stands for "quiet "

To mind one's P's and Q's. *See* P

Q E D. (Lat *quod erat demonstrandum*, which was to be demonstrated) Appended to the theorems of Euclid·—Thus have we proved the proposition stated above, as we were required to do.

Q.E F. (Lat *quod erat faciendum*, which was to be done) Appended to the problems of Euclid —Thus have we done the operation required.

Q.P. (Lat. *quantum placet*) Used in prescriptions to signify that the quantity may be as little or much as you like. Thus, in a cup of tea we might say "Milk and sugar *q p*."

Q.S (Lat. *quantum sufficit*, as much as suffices). Appended to prescriptions to denote that as much as is required may be used. Thus, after giving the drugs in minute proportions, the apothecary may be told to "mix in liquorice, *q s* "

Q V. (Lat *quantum vis*). As much as you like, or *quantum valeat*, as much as is proper.

q.v. (Lat *quod vide*) Which see.

Quack or **Quack doctor**; once called *quacksalver* A puffer of salves, an itinerant drugvendor at fairs, who mounted his tailboard and "quacked" forth the praises of his wares to the gaping rustics Hence, a charlatan
Saltimbancoes, quacksalvers, and charlatans deceive them in lower degrees —SIR THOMAS BROWNE *Pseudodoxia Epidemica*, I, iii

Quad. The university contraction for *quadrangle*, the college grounds; hence, *to be in quad* is to be confined to your college grounds The word *quad* is also applied to one of a family of quadruplets *Cp* QUOD

Quadragesima Sunday (kwod ra jes´ i ma) The first Sunday in Lent; so called because it is, in round numbers, the fortieth day before Easter.

Quadragesimals The farthings or payments formerly made in commutation of a personal visit to the mother-church on Mid-Lent Sunday, also called Whitsun farthings

Quadrant, The. The name given to the curved southern end of Regent Street, London It was designed by John Nash (1752-1835) and built between 1813 and 1820, with colonnades that were removed in 1848 The Quadrant was one of the most impressive streets in the world, but it was pulled down in an excess of iconoclasm in 1928

Quadriga (kwod´ ri ga) A two-wheeled chariot of Classic times, drawn by four horses harnessed abreast. A spirited representation of Peace riding in a quadriga, executed by Adrian Jones in 1912, was placed on the arch at the west end of Constitution Hill, in London.

Quadrilateral. The four fortresses of Peschiera and Mantua on the Mincio, with Verona and Legnago on the Adige Now demolished

The Prussian Quadrilateral. The old fortresses of Luxemburg, Coblentz, Sarrelouis, and Mayence

Quadrille (kwod ril´) An old card-game played by four persons with an ordinary pack of cards from which the eights, nines, and tens have been withdrawn. It displaced ombre (*q v*) in popular favour about 1730, and was followed by whist
The square dance of the same name was of French origin, and was introduced into England in 1813 by the Duke of Devonshire

Quadrillion. In English numeration. a million raised to the fourth power, represented by 1 followed by 24 ciphers, in American and French numeration it stands for the fifth power of a thousand, *i e* 1 followed by 15 ciphers

Quadrivium (kwod riv´ i um). The collective name given by the Schoolmen of the Middle Ages to the four "liberal arts" (Lat *quadri-*, four, *via*, way), viz . arithmetic, music, geometry, and astronomy The quadrivium was the "fourfold way" to knowledge, the *trivium* (*q v*) the "threefold way" to eloquence, both together comprehended the seven arts or sciences enumerated in the following hexameter —
Lingua, Tropus, Ratio, Numerus, Tonus, Angulus, Astra

And in the two following —
Gram loquitur, Dia vera docet, Rhet verba colorat
Mus cadit, Ar numerat, Geo ponderat, Ast colit
astra

Quadroon (kwod roon´) A person with one-fourth of black blood, the offspring of a mulatto woman by a white man The mulatto is half-blooded, one parent being white and the other black.

Quadruple. Quadruple Alliance. An international alliance for offensive or defensive purposes of four powers, especially that of Britain, France, Austria, and Holland in 1718, to prevent Spain recovering her Italian possessions, and that of Britain, France, Spain, and Portugal in 1834 as a counter-move to the "Holy Alliance" between Russia, Prussia, and Austria Another is that of 1674, when Germany, Spain, Denmark, and Holland formed an alliance against France to resist the encroachments of Louis XIV

Quadruple Treaty. An agreement signed in 1834 between Britain, France, Spain, and Portugal, whereby the succession of Isabella II to the throne of Spain was accepted despite the Salic Law (*q v*)

Quai d'Orsay (kā dôr sā). The quay in Paris running along the left bank of the Seine where are situated the departments of Foreign Affairs and other government offices The name is applied to the French Foreign Office and sometimes to the French Government as a whole

Quail The bird was formerly supposed to be of an inordinately amorous disposition, hence its name was given to a courtesan.

> Here's Agamemnon, an honest fellow enough, and one that loves quails —*Troilus and Cressida*, v, 1

Quaker. A familiar name for a member of the Society of Friends, a religious body having no definite creed and no regular ministry, founded by George Fox, 1648-50 It appears from the founder's *Journal* that they first obtained the appellation (1650) from the following circumstance —"Justice Bennet, of Derby," says Fox, "was the first to call us Quakers, because I bade him quake and tremble at the word of the Lord "

> Quakers (that, like lanterns, bear
> Their light within them) will not swear.
> BUTLER *Hudibras*, ii, 2.

The name had, however, been previously applied to a sect whose adherents shook and trembled with religious emotion

Quaker City. Philadelphia

Quaker guns Dummy guns made of wood, for drill purposes or camouflage, an allusion to the Quaker reprobation of the use of force

The Quaker Poet. Bernard Barton (1784-1849) Also the American John Greenleaf Whittier (1807-92)

Quarantine (Ital *quaranta*, forty) The period, originally forty days, that a ship suspected of being infected with some contagious disorder is obliged to lie off port Now applied to any period of segregation to prevent infection

In law the term is also applied to the forty days during which a widow who is entitled to a dower may remain in the chief mansion-house of her deceased husband

To perform quarantine is to ride off port during the time of quarantine

Quarrel (O Fr *quarel*, from late Lat *quadrellus*, diminutive of *quadrus*, a square). A short, stout, square-headed bolt or arrow used in the crossbow, also, a square or diamond-shaped pane of glass for a window

Quarrel, to engage in contention, to fall out (from O.Fr. *querele*, Lat *querela*, complaint, *queri*, to complain)

To quarrel over the bishop's cope—over something which cannot possibly do you any good, over goat's wool. A newly appointed Bishop of Bruges entered the town in his cope, which he gave to the people; and the people, to part it among themselves, tore it to shreds, each taking a piece

To quarrel with your bread and butter. To act contrary to your best interest, to snarl at that which procures your living, like a spoilt child, who shows its ill-temper by throwing its bread and butter to the ground.

Quarry. An object of chase, especially the bird flown at in hawking or the animal pursued by hounds or hunters Originally the word denoted the entrails, etc , of the deer which were placed on the animal's *skin* after it had been flayed, and given to the hounds as a reward The word is the O Fr. *curée*, skinned from *cuir* (Lat *corium*), skin

> Your castle is surprised, your wife and babes
> Savagely slaughter'd, to relate the manner,
> Were, on the quarry of these murder'd deer
> To add the death of you.
>
> *Macbeth*, iv, 2

The place where marble, stone, etc , is dug out is called a *quarry*, from O Fr *quarriere*, Lat *quadrare*, to square, because the stones were *squared* on the spot

Quart d'heure (kar děr) **Un mauvais quart d'heure** (Fr , a bad quarter of an hour), used of a short, disagreeable experience

Quarter. The fourth part of anything, as of a year or an hour, or any material thing

In weights a *quarter* is 28 lb., i e. a fourth of a hundredweight, as a measure of capacity for grain it is 8 bushels, which used to be one-fourth, but is now one-fifth, of a load. In the meat trade a *quarter* of a beast is a fourth part, which includes one of the legs. A *quarter* in the United States coinage is the fourth part of a dollar, and in an heraldic shield the *quarters* are the divisions made by central lines drawn at right angles across the shield, the 1st and 4th quarters being in the *dexter chief* and *sinister base* (i e left-hand top and right-hand bottom when looking at it), and the 2nd and 3rd in the *sinister chief* and *dexter base*

To grant quarter To spare the life of an enemy in your power The origin of the phrase is not certain, but the old suggestion that it originated from an agreement anciently made between the Dutch and the Spaniards, that the ransom of a soldier should be the quarter of his pay, is not borne out. It is more likely due to the fact that the victor would have to provide his captive with temporary quarters.

Quarters. Residence or place of abode; as **winter quarters**, the place where an army lodges during the winter months; **married quarters**, the accommodation in a barrack area allotted to regular soldiers who live with their wives and families. **Come to my quarters** is a common phrase among bachelors as an invitation to their rooms In the Southern U S A the word is used for that part of a plantation allotted to the Negroes

> There shall no leavened bread be seen with thee, neither shall there be leaven seen   in all thy quarters   *Exod* xiii, 7

A district of a town or city is often known as a *quarter*, and in this sense the French use **Quartier Latin**, in Paris, which is the district where artists live and the medical schools are situated

Quartered. *See* DRAWN AND QUARTERED.

Quarter Days. (1) New Style—Lady Day (March 25th), Midsummer Day (June 24th), Michaelmas Day (September 29th), and Christmas Day (December 25th).

(2) Old Style—Lady Day (April 6th), Old Midsummer Day (July 6th), Old Michaelmas Day (October 11th), and Old Christmas Day (January 6th)

Quarter Days in Scotland—
Candlemas Day (February 2nd), Whitsunday (May 15th), Lammas Day (August 1st), and Martinmas Day (November 11th).

Quarterdeck. The upper deck of a ship from the mainmast to the stern In men-of-war it is used by officers only. Hence, *to behave as though he were on his own quarterdeck*, to behave as though he owned the place.

Quartermaster. In the army, the officer whose duty it is to attend to the *quarters* of the soldiers He superintends the issue of all stores and equipment.

In the navy, the petty officer who, besides other duties, has charge of the steering of the ship, the signals, stowage, etc

Quarto. A size of paper made by folding the sheet twice, giving *four* leaves, or eight pages, hence, a book composed of sheets folded thus *Cp* FOLIO, OCTAVO. The word is often written "4to."

Quashee (kwosh' ē) A generic name of a Negro, from West African *Kwasi*, a name often given to a child born on a Sunday *Cp* QUASSIA

Quasi (kwā' zī) (Lat., as if) Prefixed to denote that so-and-so is not the real thing, but may be almost accepted in its place, thus a

Quasi contract is not a real contract, but something which has the force of one

Quasi historical. Apparently historical, more or less so, or pretending to be so and almost succeeding.

Quasi tenant. The tenant of a house sublet.

Quasimodo Sunday (kwä zī mō dō') The first Sunday after Easter, so called because the "Introit" of the day begins with these words *Quasi modo geniti infantes* (1 *Pet* ii, 2) Also called "Low Sunday"

Quasimodo was also the name of the hunchback in Victor Hugo's *Nôtre Dame de Paris*, 1831

Quassia (kwosh' ya) An American plant, or rather genus of plants, named after Quassi, a Negro, who, in 1730, was the first to make its medicinal properties known *See* QUASHEE

Linnæus applied this name to a tree of Surinam in honour of a negro, Quassi . who employed its bark as a remedy for fever, and enjoyed such a reputation among the natives as to be almost worshipped by some—LINDLEY and MOORE *Treatise of Botany*, Pt. ii, p 947

Que sçais-je? (kĕ sāzh). The motto adopted by Michel-Eyquem de Montaigne (1533-92), the great French essayist, as expressing the sceptical and enquiring nature of his writings

Queen. A female reigning sovereign, or the consort of a king; from A S. *cwen*, a woman (which also gives *quean*, a word still sometimes used slightingly or contemptuously of a

woman), from an ancient Aryan root that gave the Old Teutonic stem *kwen-*, Zend *genā*, Gr *guné*, Slavonic *zend*, O Ir *ben*, etc , all meaning "woman " In the 4th-century translation of the Bible by Ulfilas we meet with *gens* and *guio* ("wife" and "woman"), and in the Scandinavian languages *karl* and *kone* still mean "man" and "wife." *Cp* KING, *see* MAB

Queen Anne. Daughter of James II and Anne Hyde. She reigned over Great Britain from 1702 to 1714, and her name is still used in certain colloquial phrases

Queen Anne is dead A slighting retort made to the teller of stale news.

Queen Anne style. The style in buildings, furniture, silver-ware, etc , characteristic of her period Domestic architecture, for instance, was noted for many angles, gables, and irregularity of windows

Queen Anne's Bounty A fund created out of the firstfruits and tenths which were part of the papal exactions before the Reformation. The *firstfruits* are the whole first year's profits of a clerical living, and the *tenths* are the tenth part annually of the profits of a living Henry VIII annexed both these to the Crown, but Queen Anne formed them into a perpetual fund for the augmentation of poor livings and the building of parsonages The sum equals about £14,000 a year

Queen Anne's fan. Your thumb to your nose and your fingers spread, cocking a snook.

Queen City. Cincinnati

Queen Consort The wife of a reigning king

Queen Dick Richard Cromwell (1626-1712), son of the Protector, Oliver, was sometimes so called

In the reign of Queen Dick *See* DICK.

Queen Dowager. The widow of a deceased king

Queen Mother. The mother of a reigning sovereign

> If you hold it fit, after the play
> Let his queen mother all alone entreat him
> To show his griefs   *Hamlet*, iii, 1

Queen of the May. *See* MAY

Queen Regnant. A queen who holds the crown in her own right, in contradistinction to a *Queen Consort*

Queen's Bench, Queen's Counsel. *See* KING's.

Queen's College (Oxford), **Queens' College** (Cambridge) Note the position of the apostrophe in each case—an important matter The Oxford College was founded (1340) by Robert de Eglesfield in honour of Queen Philippa, consort of Edward III, to whom he was confessor. The Cambridge college numbers two Queens as its founders, viz Margaret of Anjou, consort of Henry VI (1448), and Elizabeth Woodville, Edward IV's consort, who refounded the college in 1465

Queen's Day November 17th, the day of the accession of Queen Elizabeth I, first publicly celebrated in 1570, and for over three centuries kept as a holiday in Government offices and at Westminster School

November 17th at Merchant Taylors' School is a holiday also, now called Sir Thomas White's Founder's Day

Queen's ware. Glazed Wedgwood earthenware of a creamy colour

Queen's weather. A fine day for a fête, so called because Queen Victoria was, for the most part, fortunate in having fine weather when she appeared in public.

The Queen of Glory. An epithet of the Virgin Mary

The Queen of Hearts Elizabeth (1596-1662), daughter of James I, the unfortunate Queen of Bohemia, so called in the Low Countries from her amiable character and engaging manners, even in her lowest estate

The Queen of Heaven The Virgin Mary In ancient times, among the Phœnicians, Astarte; Greeks, Hera, Romans, Juno, Hecate, the Egyptian Isis, etc were also so called, but as a general title it applied to Diana, or the Moon, also called *Queen of the Night*, and *Queen of the Tides* In *Jer* vii, 18, we read "The children gather wood . . and the women knead dough to make cakes to the queen of heaven," *i e* the Moon.

The Queen of Love Aphrodite, or Venus

Poor queen of love in thine own law forlorn
To love a cheek that smiles at thee in scorn!
Venus and Adonis, 251

Queen Square Hermit. Jeremy Bentham (1748-1832), who lived at No 1 Queen Square, London He was the father of the political economists called Utilitarians, whose maxim is "The greatest happiness of the greatest number"

The White Queen. Mary Queen of Scots, so called because she dressed in *white* mourning for her French husband (Francis II 1544-60).

The Queen's English. *See* ENGLISH

The Queen's Pipe. A name given in Queen Victoria's reign to a furnace at the Victoria Docks for destroying (by the Inland Revenue authorities) contraband and worthless tobacco, etc

Queenhithe (London) The hithe or strand for lading and unlading barges and lighters in the City. Called "queen" from being part of the dowry of Eleanor, Queen of Henry II

Queer. Colloquial for out of sorts, not up to the mark, also slang for drunk, and thieves' cant for anything base and worthless, especially counterfeit money

A queer cove An eccentric person, a rum customer, also *Queer card See* CARD.

In Queer Street. In financial difficulties The punning suggestion has been made that the origin of the phrase is to be found in a *query* (?) with which a tradesman might mark the name of such a one in his ledger

To queer one's pitch. To forestall him, to render his efforts nugatory by underhand means

Querno (kwĕr' nō) Camillo Querno, of Apulia, hearing that Leo X (1513-22) was a great patron of poets, went to Rome with a harp in his hand, and sang his *Alexias*, a poem containing 20,000 verses He was introduced to the Pope as a buffoon, but was promoted to the laurel

Rome in her Capitol saw Querno sit,
Thronèd on seven hills the Antichrist of wit
Dunciad, ii.

Querpo (kĕr' pō) In querpo. In one's shirtsleeves, in undress (Span *en cuerpo*, without a cloak)

Boy, my cloak and rapier; it fits not a gentleman of my rank to walk the streets in querpo —BEAUMONT AND FLETCHER *Love's Cure*, ii, 1.

Question When members of the House of Commons or other debaters call out *Question*, they mean that the person speaking is wandering away from the subject under consideration.

A leading question. *See* LEADING

An open question. A statement, proposal, doctrine, or supposed fact, respecting which private opinion is allowed In the House of Commons every member may vote as he likes, regardless of party politics, on an open question

Out of the question. Not worth discussing, not to be thought of, quite foreign to the subject

Questions and commands. An old Christmas game, in which the "commander" bids one of his subjects to answer a question which is asked If he refuses, or fails to satisfy the commander, he must pay a forfeit or have his face smutted

While other young ladies in the house are dancing, or playing at questions and commands, she [the devotee] reads aloud in her closet —*The Spectator*, No 354 (Hotspur's Letter), April 16th, 1712.

The previous question. The question whether the matter under debate shall be put to the vote or not In Parliament, and debates generally, when one party wishes that a subject should be shelved it is customary to "move the previous question", if this is carried the original discussion comes to an end, for it has been decided that the matter shall not be put to the vote.

Moving the previous question, says Erskine May—

is an ingenious method of avoiding a vote upon any question that has been proposed, but the technical phrase does little to elucidate its operation. When there is no debate, or after a debate is closed, the Speaker ordinarily puts the question as a matter of course . but by a motion for the previous question, this act may be intercepted and forbidden —*Parliamentary Practice*, p 303 (9th ed.)

A motion for "the previous question" cannot be made on an amendment, nor in a select committee, nor yet in a committee of the whole house

To beg the question. *See* BEG

To pop the question To propose or make an offer of marriage As this important demand is supposed to be unexpected, the question is said to be "popped"

Questionists. In the examinations for degrees at Cambridge it was customary, at the beginning of the January term, to hold "Acts," and the candidates for the Bachelor's degree were called "Questionists" They were examined by a moderator, and afterwards the fathers of other colleges "questioned" them for three hours in Latin, and the dismissal uttered by the Regius Professor indicated what class you would be placed in, or that respondent was plucked, in which case the words were simply *Descendus domine*

Queue (kū) French for tail (*cp* Q IN A CORNER), hence used of a pigtail, or long plait of hair, also for a line of people waiting their turn at a booking-office, theatre, shop, etc.

To queue up. A term that came into prominence during the World Wars, especially in connexion with the food shortage, when hundreds of people had to wait for hours in long lines before they could obtain their "rations" at the butcher's, grocer's, etc

Quey (quā) A female calf, a young heifer; from O Scand *kviga*, meaning the same thing

Quey calves are dear veal. An old proverb, somewhat analogous to "killing the goose which lays the golden eggs " Female calves should be kept and reared for cows

Qui vive? (kē vēv) (Fr.) Literally, *Who lives?* but used as a sentry's challenge and so equivalent to our *Who goes there?* which in French would be *Qui va là?*

To be on the qui vive On the alert; to be quick and sharp, to be on the tiptoe of expectation, like a sentinel (*See above*)

Quia Emptores (kwi' a emp tôr' ēz) A statute passed in the reign of Edward I (1290), to insure the lord paramount his fees arising from escheats, marriages, etc By it freemen were permitted to sell their lands on condition that the purchaser should hold from the chief lord, and it resulted in a great increase of landowners holding direct from the Crown. So called from its opening words.

Quibble An evasion, a juggling with words, probably a frequentative of the older *quib*, from Lat *quibus*, a word constantly occurring in legal documents and so associated with the "quirks and quillets of the law "

Quick. Living; hence animated lively, hence fast, active, brisk (A S. *cwic*, living, alive) Our expression "Look alive," means "Be brisk "

Quicksand is sand which shifts its place as if it were alive See QUICK

Quickset is living hawthorn set in a hedge, instead of dead wood, hurdles, and palings. See QUICK

Quicksilver is *argentum vivum* (living silver), silver that moves about like a living thing (A.S. *cwic seolfor*)

> Swift as quicksilver
> It courses through the natural gates
> And alleys of the body
> *Hamlet*, i, 5

The quick and dead. The living and the dead

Quickie. In film parlance, a motion picture made cheaply to catch the cheap market and make a quick return on the money invested.

Quid. Slang for a sovereign (or a pound note). It occurs in Shadwell's *Squire of Alsatia* (1688), but its origin is unknown

In *a quid of tobacco*, meaning a piece for chewing, *quid* is another form of *cud*

Quids in Extremely lucky, to have everything fall right

Quids (U.S A) A third political party (*tertium quid*) which was opposed to the administration of President Madison 1809-16

Quidlibet. *See* QUODLIBET

Quid pro quo (Lat) Tit for tat, a return given as good as that received, a Roland for an Oliver, an equivalent

Quid rides (Lat , Why are you laughing?) It is said that Lundy Foot, a Dublin tobacconist, set up his carriage, and that Curran, when asked to furnish him with a motto, suggested this. The witticism is, however, attributed also to H. Callender, who, we are assured, supplied it to one Brandon, a London tobacconist

"Rides" in English, one syllable, in Latin it is two

Quiddity. The essence of a thing or that which differentiates it from other things—"the Correggiosity of Correggio," "the Freeness of the Free." Hence used of subtle, trifling distinctions, quibbles, or captious argumentation Schoolmen say *Quid est?* (what is it?) and the reply is, the *Quid* is so and so, the *What* or the nature of the thing is as follows The latter *quid* being formed into a barbarous Latin noun becomes *Quidditas* Hence *Quid est?* (what is it?) Answer. *Talis est quidditas* (its essence is as follows)

> He knew
> Where entity and quiddity
> (The ghosts of defunct bodies) fly
> BUTLER Hudibras, i, 1

Quidnunc (Lat , What now?) One who is curious to know everything that's going on, or pretends to know it, a self-important newsmonger and gossip It is the name of the leading character in Murphy's farce *The Upholsterer*, or *What News?*

Quietism. A form of religious mysticism based on the doctrine that the essence of religion consists in the withdrawal of the soul from external objects, and in fixing it upon the contemplation of God, especially that taught by the Spanish mystic, Miguel Molinos (1640-96), who taught the direct relationship between the soul and God His followers were termed Molinists, or *Quietists. See* MOLINISM.

Quietus (late Lat *quietus est*, he is quit). The writ of discharge formerly granted to those barons and knights who personally attended the king on a foreign expedition, exempting them also from the claim of scutage or knight's fee Subsequently the term was applied to the acquittance which a sheriff receives on settling his account at the Exchequer, and, later still, to any discharge, as of an account, or even of life itself

You had the trick in audit-time to be sick till I had signed your quietus —WEBSTER. *Duchess of Malfi*, iii, 2 (1623)

> Who would fardels bear
> When he himself might his quietus make
> With a bare bodkin? *Hamlet*, iii, 1

Quill-drivers. Writing clerks

Quillet (kwil' et) An evasion This may be an abbreviation of the old word *quillity* (formed on analogy with *quiddity*) meaning a quibble, or it may be from Lat. *quidlibet, i e* "anything you choose " A fanciful suggestion is that it came to England from the French law courts, where each separate allegation in the plaintiff's charge, and every distinct plea in the defendant's answer began with *qu'il est*, whence *quillet*, to signify a false charge, or an evasive answer

Oh, some authority how to proceed,
Some tricks, some quillets, how to cheat the devil
Love's Labour Lost, iv, 3

Quinapalus (kwin ăp' a lus) A kind of "Mrs. Grundy" or "Mrs Harris" invented by Feste, the Clown in *Twelfth Night*, when he wished to give some saying the weight of authority Hence someone "dragged in" when one wishes to clench an argument by some supposed quotation

What says Quinapalus "Better a witty fool, than a foolish wit "—*Twelfth Night*, i, 5.

Quinbus Flestrin (kwin' bus fles' trin). The man-mountain So the Lilliputians called Gulliver (ch ii) Gay has an ode to this giant

Bards of old of him told,
When they said Atlas' head
Propped the skies
GAY *Lilliputian Ode*

Quincunx (kwin' kŭngks). An arrangement of five things, one in each corner and one in the middle of a square or oblong space The term is also applied to trees in an orchard so planted that those in one row face the spaces between those in the adjacent rows

Quinine. See CINCHONA

Quinquagesima Sunday (kwin kwa jes' i ma) (Lat , fiftieth) Shrove Sunday, or the first day of the week which contains Ash Wednesday It is so called because in round numbers it is the fiftieth day before Easter

Quins, The. Marie, Emilie, Yvonne, Cecile, and Annette Dionne, the famous quintuplets born May 28th, 1934, to a farmer in Callander, Ontario There are seven other children in the family Medical attention and interest was drawn to the phenomenon of their birth and successful rearing The Quins were wards of King George VI who, with the Queen, received them during the royal visit to Canada in 1939.

Quinsy (kwin' zi) This is a curious abbreviation The Latin word is *quinancia*, and the Greek *kunanché*, from *kuon anché*, dog strangulation, because persons suffering from quinsy throw open the mouth like dogs, especially mad dogs It first appeared in English (14th century) as *qwinaci* and later forms were *quynnancy* and *squinancy Squinancy-wort* is still a name given to the small woodruff (*Asperula cynanchica*), which was used as a cure for quinsy by the herbalists.

Quintain (kwin' tin). Riding at the quintain was a form of medieval knightly exercise A dummy figure—sometimes only a head—was fastened to one end of a pole swinging horizontally on an upright firmly embedded in the ground The knight, mounted or on foot, tilted at this figure, and unless he impaled it with his spear it would swing away from him and the opposite end of the pole would swing round and give him a smart blow

Quintessence The fifth essence The ancient Greeks said there are four elements or forms in which matter can exist—fire, air, water, and earth (*see* ELEMENTS), the Pythagoreans added a fifth, the fifth essence—quintessence—*ether*, more subtle and pure than fire, and possessed of an orbicular motion, which flew upwards at creation and formed the material basis of the stars. Hence the word stands for the essential principle or the most subtle extract of a body that can be procured Horace speaks of "kisses which Venus has imbued with the quintessence of her own nectar "

Swift to their several quarters hasted then
The cumbrous elements—earth, flood, fire;
But this ethereal quintessence of heaven
Flew upward . and turned to stars
Numberless as thou seest
MILTON *Paradise Lost*, iii, 716

Quintilians (kwin til' yans) Members of a 2nd-century heretical sect of Montanists, said to have been founded by one Quintilia, a prophetess They made the Eucharist of bread and cheese, and allowed women to become priests and bishops

Quintillion (kwin til' yŏn) In English, the fifth power of a million, 1 followed by 30 ciphers, in France and the United States the cube of a million, a million multiplied by a thousand four times over, 1 followed by 18 ciphers. *Cp.* BILLION

Quip Modest, The. Sir, it was done to please myself. Touchstone says (*As You Like It*, v, 4) · "If I sent a person word that his beard was not well cut, and he replied he cut it to please himself," he would answer with the quip modest, which is six removes from the lie direct; or, rather, the lie direct in the sixth degree.

Quipu (ke' poo) An ancient Peruvian device for recording events, keeping accounts, etc It consisted of a cord with knotted and coloured strings, arranged in particular designs and patterns

Quirinal (kwi' ri nal) The palace in Rome of the former kings of Italy The term was usually applied emblematically to the Italian kingdom and government as opposed to the Vatican, the seat of Papal authority and ecclesiastical government

Quirt (U S A) A riding whip with a short stock and a long lash or braided leather From the Spanish *cuerda*, cord.

Quis Latin, Who?

Quis custodiet custodes? (Lat.) [The shepherds keep watch over the sheep], but who is there to keep watch over the shepherds? Said when one is not certain of the integrity of one whom one has placed in a position of trust

Quis separabit? (Lat , Who shall separate us ?) The motto adopted by the Most Illustrious Order of St Patrick when it was founded in 1783

Quisling (kwız' lıng). Term applied to a traitor and collaborationist in time of enemy occupation. Vidkun Quisling was a Norwegian who, before the invasion of his country by the Germans in 1940, acted as their advance agent and strove for the downfall of his country He was appointed the puppet premier, but fled at the defeat of Germany and was caught and executed October 24th, 1945

Quit. (Fr. *quitter*, to leave, to depart) In U S A this word is more commonly used in the sense of to leave a job or a place

Quit rent. A rent formerly paid by a tenant whereby he was released from feudal service The term is still used of the small annual sum paid by some freeholders and copyholders in lieu of services due from them.

Quit in the sense of "acquitted" means discharged from an obligation, "acquitted."

> To John I owed great obligation;
> But John unhappily thought fit
> To publish it to all the nation—
> Now I and John are fairly quit.
> PRIOR

To be quit of. To be free from, to be rid of

Cry quits When two boys quarrel, and one has had enough, he says, 'Cry quits," meaning, "Let us leave off, and call it a drawn game " So in an unequal distribution, he who has the largest share restores a portion and ' cries quits," meaning that he has made the distribution equal. Here quit means "acquittal" or discharge.

Double or quits *See* DOUBLE.

Quixote, Don. *See* DON QUIXOTE

The Quixote of the North. Charles XII of Sweden (1682, 1697-1718), also called *The Madman*

Quixotic (kwık zot' ık) Having foolish and unpractical ideas of honour, or schemes for the general good, like Don Quixote (*q v*).

Quiz. One who banters or chaffs another The origin of the word—which appeared about 1780—is unknown, but fable accounts for it by saying that a Mr. Daly, manager of a Dublin theatre, laid a wager that he would introduce into the language within twenty-four hours a new word of no meaning Accordingly, on every wall, or all places accessible, were chalked up the four mystic letters, and all Dublin was inquiring what they meant The wager was won, and the word remains current in our language

Since World War II the word has been applied to a test, usually competitive, of general knowledge.

Quo warranto (kwō war ăn' tō) A writ against a defendant (whether an individual or a corporation) who lays claim to something he has no right to, so named because the offender is called upon to show *quo warranto* (*rem*) *usurpavit* (by what right or authority he lays claim to the matter of dispute

Quoad hoc (kwō' ăd hok) (Lat.) To this extent, with respect to this.

Quod. Slang for prison. Probably the same word as *quad* (*q.v*), which is a contraction of *quadrangle*, the enclosure in which prisoners are allowed to walk, and where whippings used to be inflicted The word was in use in the 17th century.

> Flogged and whipped in quod
> HUGHES *Tom Brown's Schooldays*.

Quodlibet (Lat , what you please) Originally a philosophical or theological question proposed for purposes of scholastic debate, hence a nice and knotty point, a subtlety. *Quidlibet* is a form of the same word

Quondam (kwon' dam) (Lat , former) We say, He is a quondam schoolfellow—former schoolfellow, my quondam friend, the quondam chancellor, etc

> My quondam barber, but "his lordship" now
> DRYDEN.

Quorum (kwôr' um) (Lat , of whom) The lowest number of members of a committee or board, etc , the presence *of whom* is necessary before business may be transacted, formerly, also, certain Justices of the Peace—hence known as Justices of the Quorum—chosen for their special ability, one or more of whom had to be on the Bench at trials before the others could act Slender calls Justice Shallow justice of the peace and quorum (*Merry Wives of Windsor*, 1, **1**)

Quos ego (kwōs eg' ō) A threat of punishment for disobedience. The words, from Virgil's *Æneid* (1, 135), were uttered by Neptune to the disobedient and rebellious winds, and are sometimes given as an example of aposiopesis, *i e* a stopping short for rhetorical effort, "Whom I—," said Neptune, the "will punish" being left to the imagination

> Neptune had but to appear and utter a *quos ego* for these windbags to collapse, and become the most subservient of salaried public servants —*Truth*, January, 1886

Quot. Quot homines, tot sententiæ (Lat) As many minds as men, there are as many opinions as there are men to hold them The phrase is from Terence's *Phormio* (II, ıv, 14)

Quot linguas calles, tot homines vales (Lat) As many languages as you know, so many separate individuals you are worth Attributed to Charles V

Quota (kwō' ta) (Lat) The allotted portion or share, the rate assigned to each Thus we say, "Every man is to pay his quota "

R

R. The eighteenth letter of the English alphabet (seventeenth of the Roman) representing the twentieth of the Phœnician and Hebrew. In the ancient Roman numeration it stood for 80 In England it was formerly used as a branding mark for rogues, particularly kidnappers

It has been called the "snarling letter" or "dog letter," because a dog in snarling utters a sound resembling r-r-r-r-r, r-r-r-r-r, etc — sometimes preceded by a g

> Irritata canis quod R R quam plurima dicat.
> *Lucilius*

In his *English Grammar made for the Benefit of all Strangers* Ben Jonson says—

R is the dog's letter, and hurreth in the sound, the tongue striking the inner palate, with a trembling about the teeth.

And see the Nurse's remark about R in *Romeo and Juliet*, ii, 4

℞ in prescriptions The ornamental part of this letter is the symbol of Jupiter (♃), under whose special protection all medicines were placed The letter itself (*Recipe*, take) and its flourish may be thus paraphrased "Under the good auspices of Jove, the patron of medicines, take the following drugs in the proportions set down." It has been suggested that the symbol is for *Responsum Raphaelis*, from the assertion of Dr Napier and other physicians of the 17th century, that the angel Raphael imparted the virtues of drugs

The R months. *See under* OYSTER

The three R's. Reading, writing, and arithmetic. The phrase is said to have been originated by Sir William Curtis (d 1829), who gave this as a toast

The House is aware that no payment is made except on the "three R's"—MR CORY, M P in House of Commons, Feb 28th, 1867

R.A.P. Rupees, annas, and pies, in India, corresponding to our £ s. d.

R.I.P. *Requiescat in pace* Latin for May he (or she) Rest in Peace, a symbol used on mourning cards, tombstones, etc

Ra (ra) The principal deity of ancient Egypt, one of the numerous forms of the sun-god, and the supposed ancestor of all the Pharaohs He was the protector of men and vanquisher of evil, Nut, the sky, was his father, and it was said of him that every night he fought with the serpent, Apepi He is usually represented as hawk-headed, and is crowned with the solar disk and uræus. *See* OSIRIS

Rabbinic (ră bin' ik) The Hebrew language as used by the rabbis in their ecclesiastical and theological writings The term is often applied to modern Hebrew Among the Jews a Rabbinist is one who follows closely the doctrines and precepts of the Talmud and the traditions of the rabbis

Rabelaisian (răb el ā' zian) Coarsely and boisterously satirical, grotesque, extravagant, and licentious in language, reminiscent in literary style of the great French satirist François Rabelais (1483-1553)

Dean Swift, Thomas Amory (d 1788, author of *John Buncle*, and Sterne have all been called "the English Rabelais"—but the title is not very fitting, indeed, the title is a contradiction in terms, Rabelais was so essentially a Frenchman of the Renaissance that it is impossible to think of an English counterpart of any period

If we are to seek for an approximation of Aristophanic humour, we shall find it perhaps in Rabelais. Rabelais exhibits a similar disregard for decency, combining the same depth of purpose and largeness of insight with the same coarse fun —J A SYMONDS *Studies of Greek Poets*

Raboin *See* TAILED MEN

Race Suicide. The extinction of a race through the undue use of contraceptives by so large a number of people that the birth rate falls below the death rate

Races. The principal horse-races in England are run at Newmarket, Doncaster, Epsom, Goodwood, and Ascot (*see* CLASSIC RACES), but there are a large number of other courses where important meetings are held, and the greatest event in the world of steeplechasing—the Grand National—is run at Aintree, near Liverpool

There are seven annual race meetings at Newmarket· (1) The Craven, (2) first spring, (3) second spring. (4) July, (5) first October, (6) second October, (7) the Houghton. .

At Doncaster races are held for two days about the middle of May, four days early in September, and two days toward the end of October.

The Epsom meeting (when the Derby, Oaks, Coronation Cup, etc , are run) is held for four days in the first week of June

Goodwood (four days) starts on the last Tuesday in July, and Ascot (four days) in the middle of June

The following are the principal English horse-races, with distances and *venue* —

Alexandra Cup (Ascot), 2 m 6 fur 75 yd.
Ascot Gold Cup, 2½ m
Ascot Gold Vase, 2 m.
Ascot Stakes, 2½ m.
The Cambridgeshire (Newmarket), 9 fur
The Cesarewitch (Newmarket), 2¼ m
Champagne Stakes (Doncaster), 6 fur. 152 yd
Champion Stakes (Newmarket), 1¼ m
Chester Cup, 2¼ m 77 yd
Chesterfield Cup (Goodwood), 1 m 2 fur.
Cheveley Park Stakes (Newmarket), 6 fur
City and Surburban Handicap (Epsom), 1¼ m
Coventry Stakes (Ascot), 5 fur
Criterion Stakes (Newmarket), 6 fur
The Derby (Epsom), 1½ m
Dewhurst Stakes (Newmarket), 7 fur.
Doncaster Cup, 2 m 2 fur.
Ebor Handicap (York), 1¾ m.
Eclipse Stakes (Sandown), 1¼ m
Goodwood Cup, 2 m. 5 fur
Goodwood Stakes, 2 m 3 fur
Grand Military Gold Cup (Sandown) 3 m 125 yd
The Grand National (Aintree), 4 m 856 yd
Great Metropolitan Handicap (Epsom), 2¼ m
Great Yorkshire Handicap (Doncaster), 1 m 6 fur. 632 yd
Jubilee Handicap (Kempton), 1½ m
July Stakes (Newmarket), 5 fur. 142 yd.
Lincolnshire Handicap (Lincoln), 1 m
Liverpool Autumn Cup 1 m 2 fur
Liverpool Summer Cup, 1 m 3 fur
Manchester Cup, 1½ m
Manchester November Handicap, 1½ m.
Middle Park Stakes (Newmarket), 6 fur
New Stakes (Ascot), 5 fur 136 yd
Northumberland Plate (Newcastle), 2 m
The Oaks (Epsom), 1½ m
The One Thousand Guineas (Newmarket), 1 m
Portland Handicap (Doncaster), 5 fur
Prince of Wales's Stakes (Newmarket), 1½ m
Royal Hunt Cup (Ascot), 7 fur 166 yd
The St Leger (Doncaster), 1¾ m 132 yd.
Stewards' Cup (Goodwood), 6 fur
The Two Thousand Guineas (Newmarket), 1 m

Many of the more important of these races will be found entered in their alphabetical places throughout this Dictionary

Rache (răch) A hound that hunts by scent (A S *raecc*, a hound, A.Nor *brache*, Ger *bracken*). They were later called "running hounds" and then simply "hounds," and were used in the Middle Ages for stag, wild boar, and buck hunting

> And first I will begin with raches and their nature, and then greyhounds and their nature, and then alaunts and their nature   and then I shall devise and tell the sicknesses of hounds and their diseases —
> EDWARD, 2ND DUKE OF YORK. *The Master of Game, Prologue* (about 1410)

Rachel (ra shel') A French actress whose real name was Elizabeth Felix (1821-58) She was the daughter of poor Jewish pedlars, but going on the stage as a girl she won a great triumph in 1843 in the name part of Racine's *Phèdre* As Adrienne Lecouvreur, in Scribe's play of that name (1849), she confirmed her position as one of the greatest tragic actresses in Europe The cosmetics bearing the name "Rachel" immortalize a Parisian beauty-specialist of the Second Empire.

Racialism. The practice of and adherence to the theory that human races have certain characteristics that unalterably mould their cultures From this arises the belief that one's own race has a right to rule less "advanced" races and is justified in asserting this right by force

Rack. A flying scud, drifting clouds (Icel *rek*, drift, *recka*, to drive)

> The cloud-capped towers, the gorgeous palaces,
> The solemn temples, the great globe itself,
> Yea, all which it inherit, shall dissolve,
> And   leave not a rack behind
> *Tempest*, IV, 1

The instrument of torture so called (connected with Ger *recken*, to strain) was a frame in which a man was fastened and his arms and legs *stretched* till the body was lifted by the tension several inches from the floor. Not infrequently the limbs were forced thereby out of their sockets Coke says that the rack was first introduced into the Tower by the Duke of Exeter, constable of the Tower, in 1447, whence it was called the "Duke of Exeter's daughter " Its use in England was abolished in 1640

Rack. The framework for putting plates and other things on, the grating for holding fodder, etc , is probably connected with this

Rack and ruin. Utter destitution Here "rack" is a variety of *wrack* and *wreck*

To lie at rack and manger. To live without thought of the morrow, like cattle or horses whose food is placed before them without themselves taking thought; hence, to live at reckless expense

> When Virtue was a country maide,
> And had no skill to set up trade,
> She came up with a carrier's jade,
> And lay at rack and manger
> *Life of Robin Goodfellow* (1628)

To rack one's brains To strain them to find out or recollect something, to puzzle about something

Rack and pinion railway. Railway designed for ascending and descending mountains It has a third rail cut with teeth over which rides a mechanism which, in the event of an accident, engages the teeth and so prevents the train from falling to the bottom.

Rack rent. The actual value or rent of a tenement, and not that modified form on which the rates and taxes are usually levied; an exorbitant rent, one which is "racked" or stretched

Racket. Noise or confusion The word is probably imitative, like *crack, bang, splash,* etc.

To stand the racket. To bear the expense, to put up with the consequences.

Racy. Having distinctive or characteristic piquancy It was first applied to wine, and comes to us from the Spanish and Portuguese *raiz* (root), meaning having a radical or distinct flavour

> Rich, racy verse, in which we see
> The soil from which they come, taste, smell, and see.
> COWLEY

The word now generally implies a hint of indecency

Racy of the soil Characteristic of the inhabitants, especially the dwellers in the country, workers on the land.

Radar Term derived from Radio-Detection-and-Ranging, primarily a means of detecting the presence of aircraft by sending out frequencies which are reflected back when they encounter a solid object Subsequently developed for use by ships navigating in fog A British invention, made by R. A W Watt, telecommunications advisor to the Air Ministry, in 1935. Britain was far ahead of the world at the start of the war, and without this invention could not have won the Battle of Britain in 1940 Two radar stations were lent to France by Britain in 1939, and a courageous Frenchman, René Varin, was dispatched from England to effect their destruction after the fall of France The United States had some experimental stations, one of which was at Pearl Harbour and plotted the incoming Japanese aircraft, though the report was unfortunately not taken seriously When in due course the Germans had developed Radar, countermeasures were developed, they took the form of bundles of tin-foil streamers dropped from bomber formations which registered on and confused the enemy's Radar screens In 1950 Radar frequencies were sent to and reflected back from the Moon

Radcliffe Library A library at Oxford, founded with a bequest of £40,000 left for the purpose by Dr John Radcliffe (1650-1714), and originally intended for a medical library Dr. Radcliffe was a prominent London physician, famous for his candour When summoned to Queen Anne he told her that there was nothing the matter with her but "vapours," and he refused to attend her on her deathbed.

Radegonde or **Radegund, St** (rǎd'e gond). Wife of Clothaire, king of the Franks (558-61)

St. Radegonde's lifted stone. A stone 60 feet in circumference, placed on five supporting stones, said by the historians of Poitou to have been so arranged in 1478, to commemorate a great fair held on the spot in the October of that year. The country people insist that Queen Radegonde brought the impost stone on her head, and the five uprights in her apron, and arranged them all as they appear to this day.

Radevore (răd′ e vôr) A kind of cloth, probably tapestry, known in the 14th century It has been suggested (Skeat) that it was named from Vaur, in Languedoc, *ras* (Eng. *rash*, a smooth—*rased*—textile fabric) *de Vor*

This woful lady ylern'd had in youthe
So that she worken and embrowden kouthe,
And weven in hire stole the radevore
As hyt of wommen had be y-woved yore
CHAUCER *Legend of Good Women*, 2351.

Radical. The term was first applied as a party name in 1818 to Henry Hunt, Major Cartwright, and others of the same clique, ultra-Liberals verging on republicanism, who wished to introduce *radical* reform, *i e.* one that would go to the root (Lat *radix, radicis*) of the matter, in the electoral system, and not merely to disfranchise and enfranchise a borough or two Bolingbroke, in his *Discourses on Parties* (1735), says, "Such a remedy might have wrought a *radical cure* of the evil that threatens our constitution " The term is not now used.

Raft (from the Middle English *raff,* abundance, plenty) is applied to express a number of persons or things

Rag. A tatter, hence a remnant (as "not a rag of decency," "not a rag of evidence"), hence a vagabond or ragamuffin.

Lash hence these overweening rags of France
Richard III, v, 3.

The word was old cant for a farthing, and was also used generally to express scarcity—or absence—of money —

Money by me? Heart and good-will you might,
But surely, master, not a rag of money
Comedy of Errors, iv, 4.

In university slang (and now in general slang) a *rag* is a boisterous jollification, in which practical jokes and horseplay have a large share To *rag* a man is to torment him in a rough and noisy fashion.

Glad rags. See GLAD.

Rag-tag and bob-tail. The rabble, the "great unwashed " The common expression in the 16th and 17th centuries was *the rag and tag*

Rag-time. Fast syncopated rhythm, usually played by coloured jazz musicians, popular in the first decade of the 20th century The name has been perpetuated in the celebrated tune *Alexander's Rag-time Band* by Irving Berlin (1912)

The Rag The Army and Navy Club. "The rag," of course, is the flag.

"By the way, come and dine to-night at the Rag," said the major.—*Truth Queer Story,* April 1st, 1886.

Rag water. Whisky (*thieves' jargon*)

To chew the rag. A slang expression for "grousing," complaining, or talking at length on one particular subject.

Ragamuffin A *muffin* is a poor thing of a creature, a "regular muff"; so that a *ragamuffin* is a sorry creature in rags

I have led my ragamuffins where they are peppered
—I *Henry IV,* v, 3

Ragged Robin. A wild flower (*Lychnis floscuculi*). The word is used by Tennyson for a pretty damsel in ragged clothes

The prince
Hath picked a ragged robin from the hedge
TENNYSON *Idylls of the King, Enid*

Ragman Roll. The set of documents recording the names of the Scottish barons who paid homage to Edward I on his progress through Scotland in 1291, now in the Public Record Office The name probably arose from the quantity of seals hanging from it, and it still survives as "rigmarole ' (*q v*).

Ragnarok (răg′ na rok). The Gotterdämmerung, or Twilight of the Gods, in the old Scandinavian mythology. The day of doom, when the present world and all its inhabitants will be annihilated. Vidar of Vali will survive the conflagration, and reconstruct an imperishable universe

And, Frithiof, mayst thou sleep away
Till Ragnarok, if such thy will.
FRITHIOF-SAGA *Frithiof's Joy*

Ragout (ra goo′) A seasoned dish; stewed meat and vegetables highly seasoned. Fr *ragoûter* (*re,* again, *goûter,* to taste) means to coax a sick person's appetite.

Rahu (ra′ hū) The demon that, according to Hindu legend, causes eclipses. He one day quaffed some of the nectar of immortality, but was discovered by the Sun and Moon, who informed against him, and Vishnu cut off his head As he had already taken some of the nectar into his mouth, the head was immortal, and he ever afterwards hunted the Sun and Moon, which he caught occasionally, causing eclipses.

Rail To sit on the rail. To hedge or to reserve one's decision A common American phrase, expressive of the same meaning as our "to sit on the fence" (*q v*)

Railroad, Railway. The former is the American form of English *railway*

To railroad (U S A) To hustle someone through (as of school) or out (as of an assembly) with unseemly haste and without reference to the proper formalities.

Railway King, The George Hudson (1800-71), chairman of the North Midland Company, and for a time the dictator of the railway speculations—known as the **Railway Mania** of 1844-45. In one day he cleared the large sum of £100,000. Sydney Smith gave him the name. His business methods, however, were of questionable honesty He was obliged to resign his many chairmanships in 1854 and to take refuge on the Continent, where he died in comparative poverty

Rain. To rain cats and dogs. In northern mythology the cat is supposed to have great influence on the weather, and English sailors still say, "The cat has a gale of wind in her tail," when she is unusually frisky. Witches that rode upon the storms were said to assume the form of cats, and the stormy north-west wind is called the *cat's-nose* in the Harz district even at the present day

The dog is a signal of *wind,* like the wolf, both of which animals were attendants of Odin, the storm god. In old German pictures the wind is figured as the "head of a dog or wolf," from which blasts issue

So cat may be taken as a symbol of the down-pouring rain, and the *dog* of the strong gusts of wind accompanying a rainstorm.

Lay by something for a rainy day. Save something against evil times.

Raining-tree or **Rain-tree** Old travellers to the Canaries frequently mentioned a linden tree from which sufficient water to supply all the men and beasts of the whole of the island of Fierro was said to fall Of course, in certain states of the weather moisture will condense and collect on the broad leaves of many trees

The *Tamia caspia* of the Eastern Peruvian Andes is known as the *rain-tree*, as also is *Pithecolobium saman*, an ornamental tropical tree, one of the mimoseæ and *Brunefelsia pubescens*, a tree whose flowers are odorous before rain

Rainbow The old fable has it that if one reaches the spot where a rainbow touches the earth and digs there one will be sure to find a pot of gold Hence visionaries, wool-gatherers, daydreamers, are sometimes called *rainbow chasers*, because of their habit of hoping for impossible things.

Rainbow Corner. In World War II Messrs. Lyons' Corner House in Shaftesbury Avenue, London, was taken over and turned into a large café and lounge for American service men under this name It became a general meeting place for Americans in London during the war The name was a sentimental reference to the earlier Rainbow Division (*q v*), plus the rainbow in the insignia of *SHAEF* (*q v*)

Rainbow Division. The most famous and finest Division of the American Army sent to Europe in World War I.

Raison d'être (rā´ zon dātr) (Fr) The reason for a thing's existence, its rational ground for being; as "Once crime were abolished there would be no *raison d'être* for the police"

Rajah (ra´ ja) Sanskrit for king, cognate with Lat *rex* The title of an Indian king or prince, given later to tribal chiefs and comparatively minor dignitaries and rulers, also to Malayan and Japanese chiefs. *Maha-rajah* means the "great-rajah"

Rake. A libertine A contraction of rakehell, used by Milton and others

> And far away amid their rakehell band,
> They speed a lady left all succourless
> > FRANCIS QUARLES

Rally is *re-alligo*, to bind together again. (French *rallier*) In Spenser it is spelt "re-allie"—

> Before they could new counsels re-allie ¬
> > *Faerie Queene.*
> Yes, we'll rally round the flag, boys,
> We'll rally once again
> > G. F ROOT *Battle-cry of Freedom*

In this sense *rally* is also the gathering together of a group or party, as **Scout Rally**, or **Nuremburg Rally** of the Nazis

A *rally* in lawn-tennis, badminton, etc, is a rapid return of strokes To rally, meaning to banter or chaff is not connected with this word, but from Fr *railler*, to deride, our *raillery* is really the same word

Ralph or **Ralpho** The squire of Hudibras (*q v*) The model was Isaac Robinson, a zealous butcher in Moorfields, always contriving some

queer art of church government He represents the Independent party, and Hudibras the Presbyterian

The name is made to rhyme with either *safe*, *Alf*, or *half*.

Ralph Roister Doister The title of the earliest English comedy, so called from the chief character Written by Nicholas Udall about 1533 for performance by the boys at Eton, where he was then headmaster

Ram. Formerly, the usual prize at wrestling matches. Thus Chaucer says of his Miller, "At wrastlynge he wolde 'bere' awey the ram" (*Canterbury Tales Prologue*, 548)

The Ram feast Formerly held on May morning at Holne, Dartmoor, when a ram was run down in the "Ploy Field" and roasted whole, with its skin and fur, close by a granite pillar At midday a scramble took place for a slice, which was supposed to bring luck to those who got it

The Ram and Teazle. A public-house sign, in compliment to the Clothiers' Company The *ram* with the golden fleece is emblematical of wool, and the *teazle* is used for raising the nap of wool spun and woven into cloth

The ram of the Zodiac. This is the famous Chrysomalion, whose golden fleece was stolen by Jason in his Argonautic expedition It was transposed to the stars, and made the first sign of the Zodiac

Rama (ra´ ma) The seventh incarnation of Vishnu (*see* AVATAR) Rama performed many wonderful exploits, such as killing giants, demons, and other monsters He won Sita to wife because he was able to bend the bow of Siva

Ramachandra. *See* AVATAR.

Ramadan (răm´ a dăn) The ninth month of the Mohammedan year, and the Mussulman's Lent or Holy Month (also transliterated Ramazan).

As the Moslem year is calculated on the system of twelve lunar months, Ramazan is liable at times to fall in the hot weather, when abstinence from drinking as well as from food is an extremely uncomfortable and inconvenient obligation What wonder, then, that the end of the fast is awaited with feverish impatience?—H M BATSON *Commentary on Fitzgerald's* '*Omar*," st xc

Rama-Yana (ra´ ma ya´ na) (*i e* the deeds of Rama) The history of Rama, the great epic poem of ancient India, ranking with the Mahabharata (*q v*), and almost with the *Iliad*. It is ascribed to the poet Valmiki, and, as now known, consists of 24,000 stanzas in seven books

Rambouillet, Hotel de (răm bwē´ yā) The house in Paris where, about 1615, the Marquise de Rambouillet, disgusted with the immoral and puerile tone of the time, founded the *salon* out of which grew the Académie française. Mme de Sévigné, Descartes, Richelieu, Bossuet, and La Rochefoucauld were among the members They had a language of their own, calling common things by uncommon names, and so on, the women were known as *Les précieuses* and the men as *Esprits doux*. Preciosity, pedantry, and affectation led to the disruption of the coterie which, after having performed a good and lasting service, was finally demolished by the satire of Molière's *Les precieuses ridicules* (1659) and *Les femmes savantes* (1672)

Rambunctious (răm bŭngk' shus). Slang term for tiresomely ferocious

Ramilie, Ramillies (răm' ı lı) A name given to certain articles of dress in commemoration of the Duke of Marlborough's victory over the French at Ramillies in 1706 The Ramillies Hat was the cocked hat worn between 1714-40, with the brim turned up in three equal-sized cocks The Ramillies wig, that lasted on until after 1760, had a long, gradually diminishing plait, called the Ramillies plait, with a large bow at the top and a smaller one at the bottom

Raminagobris (răm ın à gŏ' brıs) Rabelais (*Pantagruel* III, xxi) under this name satirizes Guillaume Cretin, a poet in the reigns of Charles VIII, Louis XII, and François I
In La Fontaine's fables the name is given to the great cat chosen as judge between the weasel and the rabbit

Rampage. On the rampage. Acting in a violently excited or angry manner The word was originally Scotch, and is probably connected with *ramp*, to storm and rage

Rampallion (răm păl' yon) A term of contempt, probably a "portmanteau word" of *ramp* and *rapscallion*, in Davenport's *A New Trick to Cheat the Devil* (1639) we have: "And bold rampallion-like, swear and drink drunk "
Away, you scullion! you rampallion! you fustilarian! I'll tickle your catastrophe.—2 *Henry IV*, ii, 1

Rampant. The heraldic term for an animal, especially a lion, shown rearing up with the fore paws in the air, strictly, a *lion rampant* should stand on the sinister hind-leg, with both fore-legs elevated, and the head in profile

Ranch (ranch) A very extensive cattle farm in North America, where large herds are maintained entirely on pasturage The word is also applied to the buildings connected with the ranch where the owner and cowboys live.

Dude ranch. A ranch run as a resort, where city-dwellers can spend their holidays attempting to be cowboys

Randan On the randan. On the spree, having a high old time in town There was a popular music-hall song in the 'nineties of last century in which the exploits of the "randy-dandy boys" out on the spree were related

Random-tandem. Three horses driven tandem fashion. *See* TANDEM

Ranee or Rani. A Hindu queen, the feminine of Rajah (q v)

Ranelagh (răn' ĕ la) An old London place of amusement on the site that now forms part of the grounds of Chelsea Hospital It was named after Richard Jones, 1st Earl of Ranelagh, who built a house and laid out gardens here in 1690. From 1742 to 1803 Ranelagh rivalled Vauxhall Gardens for concerts, masquerades, etc A notable feature was the Rotunda, built in 1742. It was not unlike the Albert Hall in design, and was 185 ft across with numerous boxes in

which refreshments were served, while the brightly lit floor formed a thronged promenade The Ranelagh Club was established in 1894 in Barns Elm Park, S W., to provide facilities for polo, tennis, golf, etc

Range (U S A). Open grazing ground in the Far West

Rangers. Picked men in the U S Army who worked with British Commandos. They were named after Rogers's Rangers, a body of colonial Indian fighters organized by Major Robert Rogers Their first appearance was on the Dieppe raid in 1942 on which a small party went as armed observers

Rank. A row, a line (especially of soldiers), also high station, dignity, eminence, as—
The rank is but the guinea's stamp,
The man's the gowd, for a' that!
BURNS *Is there for Honest Poverty?*

Rank and fashion. People of high social standing; the "Upper Ten "

Rank and file. See FILE.

Risen from the ranks. Said of a commissioned officer in the army who formerly worked his way up from private soldier—from the ranks Often called a *ranker* Hence applied to a self-made man in any walk of life

Ransom. In origin the same word as *redemption*, from Lat. *redemptionem*, through O Fr *rançon*, earlier *redempçon*

A king's ransom. A large sum of money

Rantipole (răn' tı pōl) A harum-scarum fellow, a madcap (Dut *randten*, to be in a state of idiocy, and perhaps *poll*, a head or person) Napoleon III was called *Rantipole*, for his escapades at Strasbourg and Boulogne.

Ranz des vaches (ranz dē vash) Simple melodies played by the Swiss mountaineers on their Alphorn when they drove their herds to pasture, or call them home *Des vaches* means "of the cows", the meaning of *ranz* is not so certain, but it is thought to be a dialectal variation of *ranger*, the call being made *pour ranger des vaches*, to bring the cows home

Rap. Not worth a rap. Worth nothing at all The rap was a base halfpenny, intrinsically worth about half a farthing, circulated in Ireland in 1721, because small coin was so very scarce
Many counterfeits passed about under the name of raps —SWIFT *Drapier's Letters*

Rape. One of the six divisions into which Sussex is divided, it is said that each has its own river, forest, and castle *Herepp* is Norwegian for a parish district, and *rape* in Doomsday Book is used for a district under military jurisdiction, but connexion between the two words is doubtful

Rape of the Lock. Lord Petre, in a thoughtless moment of frolic gallantry, cut off a lock of Arabella Fermor's hair, and this liberty gave rise to the bitter feud between the two families which Alexander Pope worked up into the best heroic-comic poem of the language The first sketch was published in 1712 in two cantos, and the complete work, including the most happily conceived machinery of sylphs and gnomes, in five cantos in 1714. Pope, under the name of Esdras Barnevelt,

apothecary, later pretended that the poem was a covert satire on Queen Anne and the Barrier Treaty.

> Say, what strange motive, goddess, could compel
> A well-bred lord to assault a gentle belle,
> O say, what stranger cause, yet unexplored,
> Could make a gentle belle reject a lord
> > *Introduction to the Poem.*

Raphael (răf' ăl) One of the principal angels of Jewish angelology In the book of *Tobit* we are told how he travelled with Tobias into Media and back again, instructing him on the way how to marry Sara and to drive away the wicked spirit. Milton calls him the "sociable spirit," and the "affable archangel" (*Paradise Lost*, VII, 40), and it was he who was sent by God to advertise Adam of his danger

> Raphael, the sociable spirit, hath designed
> To travel with Tobias, and secured
> His marriage with the seven-times-wedded maid
> > *Paradise Lost*, v, 221-3.

Raphael is usually distinguished in art by a pilgrim's staff, or carrying a fish, in allusion to his aiding Tobias to capture the fish which performed the miraculous cure of his father's eyesight.

Raphaelesque. In the style of the great Italian painter Raphael (1483-1520), who was specially notable for his supreme excellence in the equable development of all the essential qualities of art—composition, expression, design, and colouring

Raphael's cartoons. *See* CARTOON.

Rapparee (răp' ă rē') A wild Irish plunderer, so called from his being armed with a *rapaire*, or half-pike.

Rappee. A coarse kind of snuff, manufactured from dried tobacco by an instrument called in French a *râpe*, or rasp, so called because it is *râpé*, rasped.

Rara avis (râr' a ā' vis) (Lat , a rare bird) A phenomenon; a prodigy; a something quite out of the common course First applied by Juvenal to the black swan, which, since its discovery in Australia, is quite familiar to us, but was unknown before

> Rara avis in terris nigroque simillima cygne (a bird rarely seen on the earth, and very like a black swan) —*Juvenal*, VI, 165

Rare (U S.A.). Underdone, as of a steak; or lightly cooked, as of an egg

Rare Ben. The inscription on the tomb of Ben Jonson, the dramatist (1573-1637), in the Poets' Corner, Westminster Abbey, "O rare Ben Jonson," was, says Aubrey, "done at the charge of Jack Young (afterwards knighted), who, walking there when the grave was covering, gave the fellow eighteenpence to cut it "

Raree Show. A peep-show, a show carried about in a box. In the 17th century, when this word appears in England, most of the travelling showmen were Savoyards, and this represents their attempt at English pronunciation

Rascal. Originally a collective term for the rabble of an army, the commonalty, the mob, this word was early (14th century) adopted as a term of the chase, and for long almost exclusively denoted the lean, worthless deer of a herd In the late 16th century it was retrans-

ferred to people, and so to its present meaning, a mean rogue, a scamp, a base fellow Shakespeare says, ' Horns¹ the noblest deer hath them as huge as the rascal"; Palsgrave calls a starveling animal, like the lean kine of Pharaoh, "a rascall refus beest" (1530) The French have *racaille* (riff-raff)

> Come, you thin thing, come, you rascal —*2 Henry IV*, v, 4

Rascal counters Pitiful £ s. d , "filthy lucre " Brutus calls money paltry compared with friendship, etc.

> When Marcus Brutus grows so covetous,
> To lock such rascal counters from his friends
> Be ready, gods, with all your thunderbolts,
> Dash him to pieces
> > *Julius Cæsar*, IV, 5

Raspberry, To give a. A 20th-century slang expression, used on both sides of the Atlantic, for showing contempt of someone In action, *to give a raspberry* is to put one's tongue between the closed lips and expel air forcibly with a resulting rude noise It is otherwise known as the *Bronx cheer*

Rasselas (răs' e lăs) Prince of Abyssinia, in Dr Johnson's philosophical romance of that name (1759) He leaves a secluded "Happy Valley," shut off from all contact with the world or with evil, and his adventures in the world outside teach him that the virtuous man is not necessarily a happy one

> "Rasselas" is a mass of sense, and its moral precepts are certainly conveyed in striking and happy language The mad astronomer who imagined that he possessed the regulation of the weather and the distribution of the seasons, is an original character in romance, and the happy valley in which Rasselas resides is sketched with poetical feeling —YOUNG

Rat. The Egyptians and Phrygians deified rats. The people of Bassora and Cambay to the present time forbid their destruction. In Egypt the rat symbolized utter destruction, and also wise judgment, the latter because rats always choose the best bread

Pliny tells us (VIII, lvii) that the Romans drew presages from these animals, and to see a *white* rat foreboded good fortune The bucklers at Lanuvium being gnawed by rats presaged ill-fortune, and the battle of the Marses, fought soon after, confirmed this superstition

As wet as, or like a drowned rat. Soaking wet, looking exceedingly dejected.

I smell a rat. I perceive there is something concealed which is mischievous The allusion is to a cat *smelling* a rat, while unable to *see* it.

Irish rats rhymed to death. It was once a prevalent opinion that rats in pasturages could be extirpated by anathematizing them in rhyming verse or by metrical charms This notion is frequently alluded to by ancient authors Thus, Ben Jonson says "Rhyme them to death, as they do Irish rats" (*Poetaster*); Sir Philip Sidney says "Though I will not wish unto you   to be rimed to death, as is said to be done in Ireland" (*Defence of Poesie*), and Shakespeare makes Rosalind say: "I was never so be-rhymed since . I was an Irish rat," alluding to the Pythagorean doctrine of the transmigration of souls (*As You Like It*, III, 2).

Rats! An exclamation of incredulity, wonder, surprise, etc.

To rat. To forsake a losing side for the stronger party, as rats are said to forsake unseaworthy ships One who deserts his party, as a "blackleg" during a strike, is sometimes called a rat

> *Averting* .
> The cup of sorrow from their lips,
> And fly like rats from sinking ships.
>   SWIFT *Epistle to Mr Nugent.*

To take a rat by the tail French colloquialism (*Prendre un rat par la queue*) for to cut a purse The phrase dates back to the age of Louis XIII A cutpurse would cut the purse at the string, or else he would spill the contents

Rat, Cat, and Dog.

> The Rat, the Cat, and Lovell the Dog,
> Rule all England under the Hog

The *Rat, i e* Rat-cliff, the *Cat, i e* Cat-esby, and *Lovel the Dog*, is Francis, Viscount Lovel, the king's "spaniel. ' The *Hog* or boar was the crest of Richard III William Collingham, the author of this rhyme, was put to death for his pregnant wit.

Rat-killer. Apollo received this derogatory soubriquet from the following incident — Crinis, one of his priests, having neglected his official duties, Apollo sent against him a swarm of rats, but the priest, seeing the invaders coming, repented and obtained forgiveness of the god, who annihilated the swarms which he had sent with his far-darting arrows

Ratisbon, Interim of. *See* AUGSBURG

Rattening Destroying or taking away a workman's tools, or otherwise incapacitating him from doing work, with the object of forcing him to join a trade union or to obey its rules. The term used to be common in Yorkshire, but is not heard much nowadays

Raven. A bird of ill omen, fabled to forebode death and bring infection and bad luck generally The former notion arises from its following an army under the expectation of finding dead bodies to *raven* on, the latter notion is a mere offshoot of the former, seeing pestilence kills as fast as the sword

> The boding raven on her cottage sat,
> And with hoarse croakings warned us of our fate
>   GAY: *Pastorals The Dirge*
> Like the sad-presaging raven that tolls
> The sick man's passport in her hollow beak,
> And, in the shadow of the silent night,
> Does shake contagion from her sable wing
>   MARLOWE *Jew of Malta* (1592).

Jovianus Pontanus relates two skirmishes between ravens and kites near Beneventum, which prognosticated a great battle, and Nicetas speaks of a skirmish between crows and ravens as presaging the irruption of the Scythians into Thrace Cicero was forewarned of his death by the fluttering of ravens, and Macaulay relates the legend that a raven entered the chamber of the great orator the very day of his murder and pulled the clothes off his bed Like many other birds, ravens indicate by their cries the approach of foul weather, but "it is ful unleful to beleve that God sheweth His prevy counsayle to crowes, as Isidore sayth "

Of inspired birds ravens are accounted the most prophetical Accordingly, in the language of that district, "to have the foresight of a raven" is to this day a proverbial expression —MACAULAY *History of St Kilda,* p 174

When a flock of ravens forsakes the woods we may look for famine and mortality, because "ravens bear the characters of Saturn, the author of these calamities, and have a very early perception of the bad disposition of that planet " *See Athenian Oracle,* Supplement, p 476.

As if the great god Jupiter had nothing else to doe but to dryve about jacke-dawes and ravens —CAR-NEADES

According to Roman legend ravens were once as white as swans and not inferior in size, but one day a raven told Apollo that Coronis, a Thessalian nymph whom he passionately loved, was faithless The god shot the nymph with his dart, but, hating the tell-tale bird—

> He blacked the raven o'er,
> And bid him prate in his white plumes no more
>   ADDISON *Translation of Ovid,* Bk ii.

In Christian art the raven is an emblem of God's Providence, in allusion to the ravens which fed Elijah St Oswald holds in his hand a raven with a ring in its mouth, St Benedict has a raven at his feet, St Paul the Hermit is drawn with a raven bringing him a loaf of bread, etc

The fatal raven, consecrated to Odin, the Danish war god, was the emblem on the Danish standard, *Landeyda* (the desolation of the country), and was said to have been woven and embroidered in one noontide by the daughters of Regner Lodbrok, son of Sigurd, that dauntless warrior who chanted his deathsong (the *Krakamal*) while being stung to death in a horrible pit filled with deadly serpents. If the Danish arms were destined to defeat, the raven hung his wings, if victory was to attend them, he stood erect and soaring, as if inviting the warriors to follow

> The Danish raven, lured by annual prey
> Hung o'er the land incessant
>   THOMSON *Liberty*, Pt iv

The two ravens that sit on the shoulders of Odin are called Huginn and Muninn (*Mind and Memory*)

Ravenstone (Ger. *rabenstein*) The old stone gibbet of Germany; so called from the ravens which are wont to perch on it

> Do you think
> I'll honour you so much as save your throat
> From the Ravenstone, by choking you myself?
>   BYRON *Werner*, ii, 2

Raw. Johnny Raw. A raw recruit; a "new chum," greenhorn

To touch one on the raw. To mention something that makes a person wince, like touching a horse on a raw place in currying him.

Rawhead and Blood-Bones. A bogy at one time the terror of children

Servants awe children and keep them in subjection by telling them of Rawhead and Bloodybones —LOCKE.

Razee. An old naval term for a ship of war cut down (or *razed*) to a smaller size, as a seventy-four reduced to a frigate

Razor. To cut blocks with a razor. *See* CUT.

Razzia (răt' zi à) An incursion made by the military into an enemy's country for the purpose of carrying off cattle or slaves, or for enforcing tribute It is the French form of an Arabic word, and is usually employed in connexion with Algerian and North African affairs.

Razzle-dazzle. A boisterous spree, a jollification

On the razzle-dazzle. On the spree, on an hilarious drunken frolic

Re (rē) (Lat) Respecting; in reference to, as, "*re* Brown," in reference to the case of Brown

Reach of a river The part which lies between two points or bends, so called because it *reaches* from point to point

> When he drew near them he would turn from each,
> And loudly whistle till he passed the Reach
>   CRABBE *Borough*

Read. To read between the lines. *See* LINE.

To read oneself in. Said of a clergyman on entering upon a new incumbency, because one of his first duties is to give a public reading of the *Thirty-nine Articles* in the church to which he has just been appointed, and to make the Declaration of Assent

Reader. The designation of certain lecturers at many of the Universities, as the *Reader in Roman Law* (Durham), the *Reader in Phonetics* (London) In the Inns of Court, one who reads lectures in law In printing, one who reads and corrects proof-sheets before publication In a publisher's office, one who reads and reports on manuscripts submitted for publication

Ready. An elliptical expression for ready money Goldsmith says, *Æs in presenti perfectum format* ("Ready-money makes a man perfect"). (*Eton Latin Grammar*)

> Lord Strut was not very flush in the "ready "—DR. ARBUTHNOT

Ready-to-Halt. A pilgrim in Pt ii of Bunyan's *Pilgrim's Progress* who journeyed on crutches. He joined the party under the charge of Mr Greatheart, but "when he was sent for" he threw away his crutches, and, lo' a chariot bore him to the Celestial City

Real Presence The doctrine that Christ Himself is present in the bread and wine of the Eucharist after consecration In the Church of England "real" implies that—

> The Body of Christ is given, taken, and eaten, in the Supper, only after an heavenly and spiritual manner —(*Thirty-nine Articles*, No xxviii)

In the Roman Catholic and Lutheran Churches "real" implies that the actual Body is present—in the former case by transubstantiation, and in the latter by consubstantiation

Realism. A form of philosophy which, for example, gathered a school of eminent French writers at the end of the 19th century The leaders were Zola and Maupassant, and their aim was to describe life as it is and not as people like to think that it is or should be. The brutality and outspokenness of their writings led to an outcry; Anatole France, for example, described Zola's great novel *La Terre* as "a heap of ordure "

Ream (ultimately from Arab *rizmah*, a bundle)
A ream of paper, unless otherwise specified, contains 480 sheets, a "perfect" ream for printing papers contains 516 sheets; a ream of envelope paper contains 504 sheets, and of news, 500 sheets

An "insides" ream contains 480 sheets all "insides," i e 20 good or inside quires of 24 sheets, a "mill" ream contains 480 sheets, and consists of 18 "good" or "insides" quires of 24 sheets each, and 2 "outsides" quires of 24 sheets each

Rearmouse or Reremouse. The bat (A S *hreremus* probably the fluttering-mouse, from *hrere-an*, to move or flutter) Of course, the "bat" is not a winged mouse

Reason It stands to reason. It is logically manifest; this is the Latin *constat* (*constare*, literally, to stand together)

The Goddess of Reason. The central figure in an attempt to substitute a religion for Christianity during the French Revolution, which was known as The Feast of Reason The role was taken by various young women who, in turns, were enthroned and "worshipped" in the cathedral of Notre Dame Mlle Condeille, of the Opera, was one of the earliest of these ' goddesses" (Nov 10th, 1793), she wore a red Phrygian cap, a white frock, a blue mantle, and tricolour ribbons, her head was filleted with oak-leaves, and in her hand she carried the pike of Jupiter-Peuple Others were Mme Momoro (wife of the printer), and the actresses Mlle Maillard and Mlle Aubray The procession was attended by the municipal officers and national guards, while troops of ballet girls carried "torches of truth", and many apostate clergy stripped themselves of their canonicals, and, wearing red nightcaps, joined in this blasphemous mockery So did Julien of Toulouse, a Calvinistic minister Such Feasts of Reason were held in various towns of France for several years after

The woman's reason. "I think so just because I *do* think so" (*see* Two Gentlemen of Verona, i, 2)

> First then a woman will, or won't, depend on't;
> If she will do't, she will, and there's an end on't.
>   AARON HILL *Epilogue to "Zara "*

Rebecca's Camels Bible. *See* BIBLE, SPECIALLY NAMED.

Rebeccaites (re bek' a itz) Welsh rioters in 1843, who, led by a man in woman's clothes, went about demolishing turnpike gates The name was taken from *Gen* xxiv, 60. When Rebecca left her father's house, Laban and his family "blessed her," and said, "Let thy seed possess the gate of those that hate them."

Rebellion, The Great. In English history, the struggle between Parliament (the people) and the Crown, which began in the reign of James I, broke into Civil War in 1642, and culminated in the execution of Charles I (Jan. 29th 1649).

The revolts in favour of the Stuarts in 1715 and 1745 (*see* FIFTEEN, FORTY-FIVE) have also each been called *The Rebellion*

Rebus (rē' bus) (Lat , with things). A hieroglyphic riddle. *non verbis sed rebus*. The origin of the word has, somewhat doubtfully, been traced to the lawyers of Paris who, during the carnival, used to satirize the follies of the day in squibs called *De rebus quæ geruntur* (on the current events), and, to avoid libel actions, employed hieroglyphics either wholly or in part

In heraldry the name is given to punning devices on a coat of arms suggesting the name of the family to whom it belongs, as the broken spear on the shield of Nicholas *Breakspear* (Pope Adrian IV)

Recessional The music or words, or both accompanying the procession of clergy and choir when they retire after a service The term is often associated with Rudyard Kipling's well-known verses (1897) beginning:

> God of our fathers, known of old—
> Lord of our far-flung battle-line—
> Beneath whose awful Hand we hold
> Dominion over palm and pine—
> Lord God of Hosts, be with us yet,
> Lest we forget, lest we forget!

Rechabites (rek' a bīts) Members of a teetotal benefit society (the Independent Order of Rechabites), founded in 1835, and so named from Rechab, who enjoined his family to abstain from wine and to dwell in tents (*Jer* xxxv, 6, 7)

Recipe, Receipt. *Recipe* is Latin for take, and contracted into ℞ is used in doctors' prescriptions *See* R

Reckon. I reckon, in the sense of 'I guess" was in use in England by the early 17th century; it is now almost obsolete in Britain but is still widely used in the U S.A

Day of reckoning. Settlement day, when one has to pay up one's account or fulfil one s obligation; also used of the Day of Judgment

Dead reckoning. *See under* DEAD

Out of one's reckoning Having made a mistake—in the date, in one's expectation, etc , or an error of judgment

To reckon without one's host. *See* HOST.

Recollects. *See* FRANCISCANS

Record That which is *recorded* (originally ' got by heart"—Lat *cor, cordis*, heart), hence the modern meaning, the best performance or most striking event of its kind recorded, especially in such phrases as to beat the record, to do it in record time, etc , also the engraved disk on which music that can be audibly transmitted by means of a gramophone is recorded

Court of Record A court whose proceedings are officially recorded and can be produced as evidence.

Off the record. Originally a legal term, whereby a judge directs that improper or irrevelant evidence shall be struck off the record. This since became commonly synonymous with *in confidence, an unofficial expression of views.*

Recreant is one who yields (from O Fr *recroire*, to yield in trial by combat), alluding to the judicial combats, when the person who wished to give in cried for mercy, and was held a coward and infamous.

Rector. *See* CLERICAL TITLES

Recusants (rek' ū zants). The name given in English history to those who refused to attend services of the Church of England At different times heavy fines and even imprisonment have attached to recusancy The name was commonly used of Roman Catholics

Red. One of the primary colours (*q.v*); in heraldry said to signify magnanimity and fortitude, in ecclesiastical use worn at certain seasons, and in popular folklore the colour of magic

> Red is the colour of magic in every country, and has been so from the very earliest times The caps of fairies and musicians are well-nigh always red—YEATS *Fairy and Folk Tales of the Irish Peasantry*, p. 61

Nowadays it is more often symbolical of anarchy and revolution—"Red ruin, and the breaking up of laws" (Tennyson· *Guinevere*, 421). In the French Revolution the *Red Republicans* were those extremists who never hesitated to dye their hands in blood in order to accomplish their political object In Russia red is supposed to be the beautiful colour *Krda* is beauty, *krasne* is red This may account for its adoption by the Bolsheviki, but, in general, red is regarded as the colour of liberty See RED FLAG *below*

Red is the colour of the royal livery, and it is said that this colour—technically called "pink' (*q v*)—was adopted by huntsmen because fox-hunting was declared a royal sport by Henry II

In the old ballads *red* was frequently applied to gold ("the gude red gowd"), and this use still survives in thieves' cant, a gold watch being a *red kettle*, and the chain a *red tackle* One of the names given by the alchemists to the Philosophers' Stone (*q.v*) was *the red tincture*, because, with its help, they hoped to transmute the base metals to gold.

Red Ball Route, Express, or Highway. *See* ROUTES

Red Biddy. A noisome and highly intoxicating concoction of which cheap port is the basis, much favoured by old crones in very low-class English life

Admiral of the Red. *See* ADMIRAL.

Red Book A directory relating to the court, the nobility, and the "Upper Ten" generally. The *Royal Kalendar*, published from 1767 to 1893, was known by this name, as also Webster's *Royal Red Book*, a similar work, first issued in 1847

The name is also given to other special works covered in red, as, *e g* the old Austro-Hungarian Empire, the official parliamentary papers of which corresponded to our "Blue Books " A book which gave account of the court expenditure in France before the Revolution, and an English manuscript containing the names of those who held lands *per baroniam* in the reign of Henry II, etc.

The Red Book of Hergest. A Welsh manuscript of the 14th century, containing the *Mabinogion*, poems by Taliesin and Llywarch Hen, a history of the world from Adam to 1320, etc It is now the property of Jesus College, Oxford

The Red Book of the Exchequer. *Liber ruber Scaccarii* in the Record Office It was compiled in the reign of Henry III (1246), and contains the returns of the tenants *in capite* in 1166, who certify how many knights' fees they hold, and the names of those who hold or held them, also the only known fragment of the Pipe Roll of Henry II, copies of the important Inquisition returned into the exchequer in 13 John, and matter from the Pipe Rolls and other sources It was printed in the Rolls Series (edited by Hubert Hall) in 1896

Redbreasts The old Bow Street "runners," police officers combining the duties of informers, detectives, and general agents.

The Bow Street runners ceased out of the land soon after the introduction of the new police I remember them very well as standing about the door of the office in Bow Street They had no other uniform than a blue dress-coat, brass buttons . and a bright red cloth waistcoat The slang name for them was "Redbreasts"—DICKENS *Letters*

Red Button. In the Chinese Empire a mandarin of the first class wore one of these as a badge of honour in his cap *Cp.* PANJANDRUM

An interview was granted to the admiral [Elliot] by Kishen, the imperial commissioner, the third man in the empire, a mandarin of first class and red button — HOWITT *History of England*, p 471 (1841).

Mother Red Cap. An old nurse "at the Hungerford Stairs"

Not a red cent. No money at all, "stony-broke" An Americanism, the cent used to be copper, but is now an alloy of copper, tin, and zinc

Redcoats. British soldiers, from the colour of the uniform formerly universal in line regiments. Cromwell's New Model Army was the first to wear red coats as a uniform Each regiment was distinguished by the colour of the facings—Blue, Green, Buff, etc, and was known by that name.

Red Comyn Sir John Comyn of Badenoch, nephew of John Balliol, king of Scotland, so called from his ruddy complexion and red hair, to distinguish him from his kinsman "Black Comyn," who was swarthy and black-haired He was stabbed by Robert Bruce (1306) in the church of the Minorites at Dumfries, and afterwards dispatched by Lindesay and Kirkpatrick

The Red Crescent, Lion, Sun. The equivalent in non-Christian countries of the Red Cross (*q v*), i e the military hospital service.

Red Cross The badge adopted by all civilized nations (except those who use the *Red Crescent*, etc), in accordance with the Geneva Convention of 1864 as that of military ambulance and hospital services, hospital ships, etc It is a red Greek Cross on a white ground, and is also called the *Geneva Cross*

Hence the name of various national societies for the relief of the wounded and sick

Also, the St George's Cross (*q v*), the basis of the Union Jack, and the old national emblem of England

The Red Cross Knight in Spenser's *Faerie Queene* (Bk I) is a personification of St George, the patron saint of England He typifies Christian Holiness, and his adventures are an allegory of the Church of England The Knight is sent by the Queen to destroy a dragon which was ravaging the kingdom of Una's father. With Una he is driven into Wandering Wood, where they encounter Error, and pass the night in Hypocrisy's cell Here he is deluded by a false vision and, in consequence, abandons Una and goes with Duessa (False-faith) to the palace of Pride He is persuaded by Duessa to drink of an enchanted fountain, becomes paralysed, and is taken captive by Orgoglio, whereupon Una seeks Arthur's help, and the prince goes to the rescue He slays Orgoglio, and the Red Cross Knight is taken by Una to the house of Holiness to be healed On leaving Holiness they journey onwards, and as they draw near the end of their quest the dragon flies at the knight, who has to do battle with it for three whole days before he succeeds in slaying it The Red Cross Knight and Una are then united in marriage

The Red Feathers. *See* REGIMENTAL NICKNAMES

Red Eye (U S A) Cheap whisky.

Red Flag. The emblem of Bolshevism, Communism, and revolution generally English Communists have a "battle hymn" with this title The red flag was used during the French Revolution as the symbol of insurrection and terrorism, and in the Roman Empire it signified war and a call to arms

Red Hackle. *See* REGIMENTAL NICKNAMES

Red-handed. In the very act, as though with red blood of murder still on his hand

The Red Hand of Ulster. *See* ULSTER.

Red-haired persons have for centuries had the reputation of being deceitful and unreliable—probably owing to the tradition that Judas Iscariot (*q v*) had red hair. The fat of a dead red-haired person used to be in request as an ingredient for poisons (*see* Middleton's *The Witch*, V, ii) and Chapman says that flattery, like the plague—

> Strikes into the brain of man,
> And rageth in his entrails when he can,
> Worse than the poison of a red-hair'd man.
> *Bussy d'Ambois*, iii, ii

The old rhyme says—

> With a red man rede thy rede,
> With a brown man break thy bread,
> At a pale man draw thy knife,
> From a black man keep thy wife

See also HAIR.

The Red Hat The cardinalate.

Red Horse (U S A) A man from Kentucky

Red Herring *See* HERRING

Indian red. Red hæmatite (peroxide of iron), found abundantly in the Forest of Dean, Gloucestershire It is of a deep, laky hue, used for flesh tints Persian red, which is of a darker hue with a sparkling lustre, is imported from the island of Ormuz in the Persian Gulf.

The Romans obtained this pigment from the island of Elba.

Red Indians. The North American Indians, so called because of their copper-coloured skin, also called *Redskins* and *red men*

A red-laced jacket Old military slang for a flogging

Red-lattice phrases. Pot-house talk. A red lattice at the doors and windows was formerly the sign that an ale-house was duly licensed, see the page's quip on Bardolph in *2 Henry IV*, ii 2—"'a calls me e'en now, my lord, through a red lattice, and I could discern no part of his face from the window"

I, I, I myself sometimes leaving the fear of heaven on the left hand am fain to shuffle, to hedge and to lurch, and yet you rogue, will ensconce your rags your red-lattice phrases under the shelter of your honour —*Merry Wives of Windsor*, ii, 2

The Red Laws. The civil code of ancient Rome Juvenal says, *Per lege rubros majoram leges* (*Satires*, xiv, 193) The civil laws, being written in vermilion, were called *rubrica*, and *rubrica vetavit* means, It is forbidden by the civil laws

The prætor's laws were inscribed in *white* letters, as Quintilian informs us (xii, 3 ' *prætores edicta sua in alba proponebant*'') and imperial rescripts were written in purple

Red-letter day A lucky day, a day to be recalled with delight In almanacs, saints' days and holidays are printed in red ink, other days in black, and only the former have special services in our Prayer Book

"It's a great piece of luck, ma'am," said Mrs Belfield, "that you should happen to come here of a holiday! Why, you know, ma'am, to-day is a red-letter day—"—FANNY BURNEY *Cecilia*, X, vi

To see the red light. To be aware of approaching disaster. The phrase comes from the railway-signal, where the red light signifies danger.

Red Light District. That quarter of a large city where brothels are located, these houses being frequently indicated by a red light outside

Red man A term of the old alchemists, used in conjunction with "white woman" to express the affinity and interaction of chemicals. In the long list of terms that Surface scoffingly gives (Ben Jonson's *The Alchemist*, II, iii) "your red man and your white woman" are mentioned

The French say that a red man commands the elements, and wrecks off the coast of Brittany those whom he dooms to death The legend affirms that he appeared to Napoleon and foretold his downfall

See also RED INDIANS, *above*

To paint the town red. *See* PAINT

Red rag. Old slang for the tongue

Discovering in his mouth a tongue,
He must not his palaver balk,
So keeps it running all day long,
And fancies his red rag can talk
PETER PINDAR *Lord B and his Motions*

Also in the phrase **Like a red rag to a bull,** anything that is calculated to excite rage

Red Sea. So called by the Romans (*Mare rubrum*) and by the Greeks, as a translation of the Semitic name, the reason for which is uncertain; also formerly called the "Sedgy Sea," because of the seaweed which collects there

To see red. To give way to excessive passion or anger, to be violently moved, run amok.

Red snow. Snow reddened by the presence of a minute alga, *Protococcus nivalis*, in large numbers It is not at all uncommon in arctic and alpine regions, where its sanguine colour formerly caused it to be regarded as a portent of evil

Red tape. Official formality, or rigid adherence to rules and regulations, carried to excessive lengths, so called because lawyers and government officials tie their papers together with red tape Charles Dickens is said to have introduced the expression, but it was the scorn continually poured upon this evil of officialdom by Carlyle that brought it into popular use

Redan (re dăn′) (Fr *redent*, notched or jagged like teeth). The simplest of fieldworks, and very quickly constructed It consists of two faces at an angle formed thus ∧, the angle, or salient, being towards the enemy In the Crimean War the British failure to capture the batteries of the Redan before Sebastopol (1854-55) cost many lives and lengthened the war

Redder. One who tries to separate parties fighting, the adviser, the person who *redes* or interferes Thus the proverb, "The redder gets aye the warst lick of the fray "

Rede (A S *ræd*) Counsel, advice, also as verb

To reck one's own rede. To be governed by one's own better judgment.

Do not, as some ungracious pastors do,
Show me the steep and thorny way to heaven,
Whilst, like a puffed and reckless libertine,
Himself the primrose path of dalliance treads,
And recks not his own rede.
   Hamlet, i, 3.

Rede Lectureships Sir Robert Rede (d 1519) Lord Chief Justice of the Common Pleas, founded three public lectureships at Cambridge These were reorganized in 1858, one to be delivered by a man of eminence in science or literature

Redemptioner. An immigrant who is obliged to pay back his passage money out of his earnings after landing in the new country

Reductio ad absurdum. A proof of inference arising from the demonstration that every other hypothesis involves an absurdity. Thus, suppose I want to prove that the direct road from two given places is the shortest, I should say, ' It must either be the shortest or not the shortest If *not* the shortest, then some other road is the direct road; but there cannot be two shortest roads, therefore the direct road must be the shortest "

Reduplicated or Ricochet Words. There are probably some hundreds of these words, which usually have an intensifying force, in use in English. The following, from ancient and modern sources, will give some idea of their variety:—chit-chat, click-clack, clitter-clatter, dilly-dally, ding-dong, drip-drop, fad-lal, flim-flam, fiddle-faddle, flip-flap, flip-flop, hanky-panky, harum-scarum, helter-skelter, heyve-keyve, higgledy-piggledy, hob-nob, hodge-podge, hoity-toity, hubble-bubble, hugger-mugger, hurly-burly, mingle-mangle, mish-mash, mixy-maxy, namby-pamby, niddy-noddy, niminy-piminy, nosy-posy, pell-mell, ping-pong, pit-pat, pitter-patter, pribbles and prabbles, randem-tandem, randy-dandy, razzle-dazzle, riff-raff, roly-poly, shilly-shally, slip-slop, slish-slosh, tick-tack, tip-top, tittle-tattle, wibble-wobble, wig-wag, wiggle-waggle, wish-wash, wishy-washy.

Ree. an interjection formerly used by teamsters when they wanted the horses to go to the right "Heck!" or "Hey!" was used for the contrary direction.

> Who with a hey and ree the beasts command
> *Micro Cynicon* (1599)

> Riddle me, riddle me ree Expound my riddle rightly

Reed. A broken or bruised reed. Something not to be trusted for support, a weak adherent Egypt is called a broken reed, in which Hezekiah could not trust if the Assyrians made war on Jerusalem "which broken reed if a man leans on, it will go into his hand and pierce it" (*see* 2 *Kings* xviii, 21; *Is* xxxvi, 6).

A **reed shaken by the wind.** A person blown about by every wind of doctrine John the Baptist (said Christ) was not a "reed shaken by the wind," but from the very first had a firm belief in the Messiahship of the Son of Mary, and this conviction was not shaken by fear or favour. *See Matt* xi, 7.

Reef. He must take in a reef or so. He must reduce his expenses, he must retrench A reef is that part of a sail which is rolled and tied to reduce the area caught by the wind

Reefer. An Australian term for one searching for gold In American slang it is used for a marijuana cigarette, otherwise known as, *i e*, *tea* or *gauge*, *muggles*, *muta* In English a reefer is a short, double-breasted overcoat largely worn in the Navy

Reekie, Auld. A familiar name for Edinburgh It is said that Durham of Largo, one of the old, patriarchal lairds, was in the habit of regulating the time of evening worship by the appearance of the smoke of Edinburgh When it increased, in consequence of the good folk preparing supper, he would say, "It is time noo, bairns, to tak the buike and gang to our beds, for yonder's Auld Reekie. I see, putting on her night-cap"

Reel Right off the reel Without intermission A reel is a device for winding rope A reel of cotton is a certain quantity wound on a bobbin

> We've been travelling best part of twenty-four hours right off the reel —BOLDREWOOD *Robbery under Arms*, ch xxxi.

In the cinematograph world a *reel* is a convenient length of film for winding on one spool and showing at one performance

The Scottish dance, *reel*, is from Gaelic *rightl* or *ruithil*

Referendum. The submission of a definite political question to the whole electorate for a direct decision by the general vote. This is not done in Great Britain, but is a general rule in Switzerland After the Great War certain questions, as the apportionment of Schleswig-Holstein and other disputed areas, were submitted to a plebiscite, which is not quite the same thing as a referendum, but is the taking of a general vote as to future policy

Refresher. An extra fee paid to a barrister in long cases in addition to his retaining fee, originally to remind him of the case entrusted to his charge

Regan (rē gan) The second of King Lear's unfilial daughters, in Shakespeare's tragedy—"most barbarous, most degenerate" She was married to the Duke of Cornwall

Regatta (re gāt′ a) A boat-race, or organized series of boat-races, the name originally given to the races held between Venetian gondoliers, the Italian meaning "strife" or "contention"

Regency. There have been a number of regencies in European history, usually during the minority of a sovereign In British history the term is usually applied to the period 1811-20 when George Prince of Wales (afterwards George IV) acted as regent because of his father's insanity.

In French history the word refers to the years from 1715 to 1723 when the Duke of Orleans was regent for the minor Louis XV.

Regent's Park (London). This park, formerly called Marylebone Park, covering 472 acres, was originally attached to a palace of Queen Elizabeth I, but at the beginning of the 17th century much of the land was let on long leases, which fell in early in the 19th century It was laid out by the architect, John Nash (1752-1835) for the Prince Regent (George IV), and named in honour of him

Regicides. The name applied in English history to those men who sat in judgment on Charles I, in 1649, and especially the 58 who signed his death warrant After the Restoration, when some of the regicides were dead and others in flight, 10 were executed and 25 others imprisoned for life The bodies of Cromwell, Ireton, Bradshaw, and Pride were disinterred, and after a solemn trial for treason were dismembered and exhibited at Temple Bar and other places

Regimental and Divisional Nicknames
(In addition to the better-known ones mentioned in alphabetical order)

British Army

Assaye Regiment. The 74th Foot, so called because they first distinguished themselves in the battle of Assaye, where 2,000 British and 2,500 Sepoy troops under Wellington defeated 50,000 Mahrattas, in 1803 This regiment is now called "the 2nd Battalion of the Highland Light Infantry" The first battalion was the old No 71

Belfast Regiment, The The old 35th Foot, raised in Belfast in 1701, is now called the 1st battalion of the Royal Sussex, the 2nd battalion being the old 107th

Bloody Eleventh The Devonshire Regiment 11th Foot, raised in 1685 At the Battle of Salamanca, in the Peninsular War, the regiment fought so stubbornly that there was hardly a man among them who was not wounded, and from this exploit they got their name

Bloodsuckers The 63rd Regiment of Foot are nicknamed "the Bloodsuckers"

Brickdusts The 53rd Foot, so called from the brickdust-red colour of their facings. Also called *Five-and-thre'pennies*, a play on the number and the old rate of daily pay of the ensigns or subalterns

Now the 1st battalion of the "King's Shropshire Light Infantry" The 2nd battalion is the old 85th

Buckmaster's Light Infantry. The 3rd West India Regiment was so called from Buckmaster, the tailor, who used to issue "Light Infantry uniforms" to the officers of the corps without any authority from the Commander-in-Chief

Buffs. The Royal East Kent Regiment, the 3rd Foot They were first raised in 1572, but the Buffs actually date from 1664 when the regiment was properly constituted. They take their name from the colour of the equipment They were originally called the Holland Regiment on account of long service in that country in the 17th century

The Rothshire Buffs The old 78th, now the second battalion of the Seaforth Highlanders

The Fighting Fifth The 5th Foot, now the "Northumberland Fusiliers." This sobriquet was given to the regiment during the Peninsular War, it was also known as the "Old and Bold Fifth," and "the Duke of Wellington's Body-guard"

Heavies, The The heavy cavalry, especially the Dragoon Guards, which consists of men of greater build and height than Lancers and Hussars The term Heavies or Heavy Artillery was formerly applied to ordnance of any calibre of 6 in and over, manned by gunners of the Royal Garrison Artillery

Hindustan Regiment. The old 76th, so called because it first distinguished itself in Hindustan It is also called the *Seven and Sixpennies,* from its number Now the 2nd battalion of the West Riding, the 1st being the old No 33rd.

The Immortals In the British Army the 76th Foot were called "The Immortals," because so many were wounded, but not killed, in India (1788-1806) This regiment, with the old 33rd, now forms the two battalions of the West Riding regiment

Kirke's Lambs. The Queen's Royal West Surrey Regiment, so called from their colonel, Percy Kirke (c. 1646-91) The regiment was originally known as the Tangier Regiment, the badge of which was a Pascal Lamb, the crest of the house of Braganza, in compliment to Queen Catherine, to whom they were a guard of honour in her progress to London There was an ironical turn to the nickname as "Kirke's Lambs" were notoriously a tough lot.

Lacedæmonians, The (lăs ĕ de mō' ni anz) An old nickname of the Duke of Cornwall's Light Infantry, because in 1777 their colonel made a long harangue, under heavy fire, on Spartan discipline and the military system of the Lacedæmonians *See* RED FEATHERS

Old and Bold The old 14th Foot the Prince of Wales's Own (West Yorkshire Regiment).

Old Bold The 1st Battalion Worcestershire Regiment, the old 29th Foot

Old Bold Fifth The Northumberland Fusiliers, formerly the 5th Foot

Old Dozen. The Suffolk Regiment, formerly the 12th Foot.

Old Fogs. The 87th Foot, the Royal Irish Fusiliers, so called from the war-cry "*Fag-an-Bealach*" (Clear the way), pronounced *Faug-a-bollagh*

Orange Lilies The nickname of the old 35th Foot, now the Royal Sussex Regiment, raised at Belfast in 1701 by the Earl of Donegal A firm supporter of William III he chose orange facings for the uniform, the *lilies* represent the white plumes given in recognition of their gallantry at Quebec in 1759, when they routed the Royal Roussillon French Grenadiers

The Red Feathers The Duke of Cornwall's Light Infantry They cut to pieces General Wayne's brigade in the American War, and the Americans vowed to give them no quarter So they mounted red feathers that no others might be subjected to this threat. Later they wore red puggarees on Indian service *See* LACEDÆMONIANS

Red Hackle. The nickname of "The Black Watch," the regiment officially known as "The Royal Highlanders." They are easily recognized by the small bunch of red feathers, known as the red hackle, which they wear on their bonnets in lieu of a regimental badge.

The Saucy Greens. The 2nd Battalion Worcestershire Regiment, the old 36th Foot

The Saucy Sixth The Royal Warwickshires, formerly the 6th Foot

The Saucy Seventh The 7th (Queen's Own) Hussars

American Army

Infantry Divisions

1st· The Red One. Name given it by the Germans, who saw the red "1" on their shoulder patch According to legend, the original red "1" was improvised from the cap of an enemy soldier killed by a 1st Division doughboy in World War I when the division earned the right to proclaim itself the first American division (1918) in France, first to fire on the enemy, first to suffer casualties, first to take prisoners, first to stage a major offensive, and first to enter Germany

2nd Indian Head A long-forgotten truck driver of the division in World War I adorned the side of his vehicle with a handsome shield framing an Indian head which was adopted by the division as its shoulder insignia Hence the name "Indian Division"

3rd Marne or **Rock of the Marne** In World War I because of its impregnable stand against the Germans' last great counter-offensive The three diagonal stripes in its insignia symbolize its participation in three major battles in 1918

4th. Ivy. From its insignia. The selection of that design is one of the few known instances of authorized military frivolity "I-vy" is simply spelling out letter form the Roman numeral for "four."

5th Red Diamond From its insignia. The Red Diamond was selected at the suggestion of Major Charles A. Meals that their insignia be the "Ace of Diamonds, less the Ace" Originally there was a white "5" in the centre. This was removed when they reached France

6th· Sight Seein' Sixth. In World War I the division was in so many engagements and so many long marches that it got this name

7th: Hourglass From insignia, a red circle bearing a black hourglass which is formed by a "7" resting on an inverted "7"

8th Pathfinder From their insignia, which is a golden arrow through a figure "8" pointing the way Also called the "Golden Arrow Division"

9th: Hitler's Nemesis A newspaper at home dubbed them this

10th: Mountaineers. This division was given the task of dislodging crack German mountain troops from the heights of Mt Belvedere It was composed of famous American skiers, climbers, forest rangers, and wild life Servicemen.

24th: Victory. The Filipinos on Leyte greeted them with the "V" sign.

25th· Tropic Lightning Activated from elements of the Hawaiian Division, Regular Army troops No other division was so quickly in combat after it was formed

26th· Yankee. Originally composed of National Guard troops from the New England (Yankee) States

27th New York Division originally composed of New York State National Guard Sometimes called the "Empire Division" New York is called the Empire State

28th Keystone Troops from Pennsylvania, which is known as the "Keystone State."

29th Blue and Gray. Organized in World War I from National Guardsmen of New Jersey, Delaware, Virginia, Maryland, and the District of Columbia. Its shoulder patch of blue and grey, the colours of the rival armies in the Civil War, symbolizes unity of former embattled states They are combined in a monad, the Korean symbol for eternal life.

30th· Old Hickory. Composed after World War I from National Guardsmen of the Carolinas, Georgia, and Tennessee, Andrew Jackson's old stamping grounds He was known as "Old Hickory."

31st: Dixie. Originally composed of men of the "Deep South" or "Dixie."

32nd Red Arrow. On tactical maps the enemies' lines are indicated in red. Their patch is a reminder to those who wear it that the enemy has never stopped them. Another nickname, 'Les Terribles," was given them by an admiring French general during World War I, when they earned four battle streamers and were first to crack the Hindenberg line.

33rd: Illinois or Golden Cross The division was originally composed mostly of Illinois troops. Their shoulder patch was a yellow cross on a black circle. The cross was an old symbol for marking government property and the only paint available where they were assembling their equipment was yellow. The insignia was originally to mark equipment. It was officially known as the "Prairie Division" because its personnel came from the prairie states. It was also called the "Money Division" because of the large amount of buried treasure they unearthed.

34th Red Bull Its patch is a red bull's skull on an olla, a Mexican water bottle. Inspired by the desert country of the South-west where it trained in World War I.

35th: Santa Fe. So called because the ancestors of its personnel blazed the old Santa Fe trail. Insignia is the original marker used on the trail.

36th: Texas Personnel was from Oklahoma and Texas. The arrowhead of its insignia represented Oklahoma and the "T" was for Texas.

37th: Buckeye. Composed of Ohio troops. Ohio is known as the "Buckeye State." Insignia is that of the state flag.

38th: Cyclone Got its name in 1917 at Shelby, Mississippi, when the tent city in which it was bivouacked was levelled by winds. The division struck like a cyclone when it landed in Luzon.

40th: Sunshine From its insignia, which is symbolic of the Golden West sunshine. Troops were from California, Nevada, and Utah.

41st: Jungleers It was the first complete division to reach the South-west Pacific and has done more jungle fighting than any other American outfit.

42nd Rainbow Nickname originated from the fact that this division was composed of military groups from the district of Columbia and twenty-five states, representing several sections, nationalities, religions, and viewpoints. They blended themselves into one harmonious unit. A major in World War I, noting its various origins, said, 'This division will stretch over the land like a rainbow "

43rd: Winged Victory Received its name on Luzon. It is formed from the name of its commanding general, Maj.-Gen. Leonard F Wing, and the ultimate goal of the division.

45th: Thunderbird. Included 1,500 American Indians from twenty-eight tribes. Originally the insignia was an old Indian symbol of the swastika, but when Hitler adopted it they changed the division insignia to another traditional Indian symbol, the Thunderbird, sacred bearer of unlimited happiness.

63rd: Blood and Fire When the division was activated in June following the Casablanca Conference they adopted the conference's resolution, to make their enemies "bleed and burn in expiation of their crimes against humanity," as their symbol.

65th: Battle Axe. Its patch is a white halbert on a blue shield. The halbert, a sharp-pointed battle-axe, was a potent weapon of the 15th-century foot soldier, being suitable either for a powerful cutting smash or for a quick thrust. It is an emblem that signifies both the shock action and the speed of the modern infantry division.

66th Panther. The black panther on its shoulder patch symbolizes the attributes of a good infantryman ability to kill, to be aggressive, alert, stealthy, cunning, agile, and strong.

69th: Fighting 69th. They were given the name probably from the fact that on their first day in action they cracked the fortifications of the Siegfried Line on a front stretching more than a mile and took 200 prisoners. Before their momentum could be checked they had gone on to capture the towns of Reschil, Dickeerscheid, and Honnigen.

70th: Trailblazers Their insignia combines an axe, a snowy mountain, and a green fir tree, symbols of the pioneers who blazed the trail to Oregon and the Williamette Valley, where most of their training was accomplished.

76th Liberty Bell In World War I their original shoulder patch was a Liberty Bell. In 1919 this was officially changed to the present one a shield with a white label, an heraldic device indicating the eldest son. The 76th was the first draft division from civilian ranks. Its present nickname is 'Onaway," the alert call of the Chippewa Indians in whose hunting grounds they trained.

77th Statue of Liberty Their insignia bears the picture of the Statue of Liberty, because most of the personnel in World War I was from New York City.

78th Lightning The shoulder patch originated in World War I because the battles of that division were likened by the French to a bolt of lightning, leaving the field blood red.

79th Cross of Lorraine. Having distinguished itself at Montfaucon in Lorraine, the division selected the Cross of Lorraine, a symbol of triumph, as its insignia.

80th Blue Ridge Its insignia symbolizes the three Blue Ridge states, Pennsylvania, Virginia, and West Virginia, from which most of its World War I personnel were drawn.

81st Wild Cat. Gets its name from Wildcat Creek that flows through Fort Jackson, S C. It is generally credited as the first to wear the shoulder patch.

83rd Ohio Its insignia is the word "Ohio" in monogrammatic form. It was composed mostly of draftees from Ohio in World War I.

84th Railsplitter Primarily made up of National Guard units from Illinois, Kentucky, and Indiana, the Lincoln states. They called themselves the Lincoln Division. Their insignia is a red disc with a white axe which splits a rail. In World War II they called themselves the "Railsplitters." The Germans called them the "Hatchet-men."

85th Custer The initials on its insignia "CD" stand for Custer Division, because they were activated at Camp Custer, Michigan in World War I.

86th Blackhawk Its insignia is a black hawk with wings outspread superimposed on a red shield. On the breast of the hawk is a small red shield with black letters "B H" for its nickname. Its personnel in World War I were drawn from Illinois, Wisconsin, and Minnesota, the territory inhabited by Chief Blackhawk and his tribe. Bird symbolizes keenness, cunning, and tenacity.

87th Golden Acorn Their patch is a green field with a golden acorn which symbolizes strength.

88th Blue Devil Their patch is a blue four-leaf clover formed from two crossed Arabic numerals, "88."

89th Rolling W. The "W" on its insignia within a circle forms an "M" when it is inverted, the two letters standing for Middle West, the section of the country from which its personnel were drawn. The circle indicates speed and stability.

90th Tough 'Ombres The letter "T" of its insignia, standing for Texas, bisects the letter 'O' for Oklahoma. The men of the division say it stands for "Tough 'Ombres "

91st Powder River. The division has a war-whoop which comes from a World War I incident. When asked where they were from, they yelled, "Powder River—Let 'er buck " Powder River is in Montana, the home state of the division in World War I.

92nd: Buffalo Insignia is a black buffalo on olive drab background with black border. In the days of hostile Indians a troop of Negroes who were on border patrol killed buffaloes in the winter and used them for clothing. The Indians called them the "Black Buffaloes " The men of this Negro division in World War I were trained at Fort Huachuca in this same locality

95th Victory. Their oval blue patch bears a red numeral "9" with a white Roman numeral "V" The "V" also stands for "Victory"

96th. Deadeye Their name came from their perfect marksmanship while in training.

97th. Trident Their insignia is a trident, white on a blue field Neptune's trident represents the coastal states Maine, Vermont, and New Hampshire, from which they came There is a prong for each state The blue represents their freshwater lakes, and the white their snowy mountains

98th Iroquois Its patch consists of a shield in the shape of the great seal of the State of New York The head of the Iroquois Indian chief is in orange These were the colours of the Dutch House of Nassau, which was responsible for the settlement of New Amsterdam, later New York The five feathers worn by the Indian represent the Five Nations (Onondagas, Cayugas, Senacas, Mohawks, and Oneidas) who formed the Iroquois Confederacy The personnel of the division were from New York

99th Checkerboard. The blue and white squares resembling a checkerboard were on the coat-of-arms of William Pitt. The home station of the division was Pittsburgh

100th Century. Because of the number of the division

102nd Ozark A large golden "O" on a field of blue. Within the 'O' is the letter "Z," from which is suspended an arc This represents the word "Ozark" The personnel came from the Ozark Mountain region

103rd. Cactus A green Saguaro cactus in a blue base superimposed on a yellow disc was adopted by this Reserve division which had its headquarters in Denver, Colorado Yellow disc represents the golden sky, while the green cactus growing in the blue sage-covered earth is characteristic of the South-west

104th; Timberwolf The grey timber wolf of their patch represents the North-west, where they trained.

106th Golden Lion. Their patch represents a golden lion's face on a blue background encircled by white and red borders The blue represents the infantry, red the supporting artillery, and the lion's face strength and power.

Airborne Divisions

11th Angels. Insignia is a white numeral "11" on a red circle in a white-winged circle against a blue field The winged circle gives an appearance of an angel

13th; Blackcats. Gets its name from its flaunting of superstition Its number is "13," it was reactivated on Friday the 13th

17th: Thunderbolt. From the surprise of their attacks from the air Also called the "Golden Talon," from its shoulder patch stretching golden talons on a field of black, representing ability to seize, black suggests darkness under which many operations were carried out.

82nd: All American. In World War I the division was composed of men from every state in the union. Originally an infantry division, when it was reactivated as an airborne division it retained its insignia, adding the word "Airborne" above

101st: Screaming Eagle. Its white eagle's head with gold beak on a black shield is based on Civil War tradition The black shield recalls the "Iron Brigade," one regiment of which possessed the famous eagle "Old Abe" which went into battle with them as their screaming mascot.

Armoured Divisions

1st Old Ironsides. Once so called, but the members dropped it

2nd: Hell on Wheels. No reason found.

3rd: Spearhead. Speedy outfit which led the First Army out of Normandy and across France

B.D —25

4th Breakthrough From the big brass to the buck private the men of the division think that "4th Armoured" is sufficient, but outsiders who fought along with it gave it the name. It hammered and slammed at Nazi defences from the time of the Normandy invasion to the collapse of the Wehrmacht, and it never failed to break through

5th: Victory. Three years before it plunged into battle the division officially adopted the nickname "Victory"—V (5th) for Victory

6th: Super Sixth Chosen by themselves

7th: Lucky Seventh "7" is considered a lucky number.

8th Show Horse. Used as a training division

9th Phantom. Name given to it by the Germans.

10th Tiger Its motto is to "Terrify and Destroy."

11th Thunderbolt. Because it could strike so quickly

12th Hellcat No reason found.

13th Black Cat Tanks were offspring of caterpillar tractors called "cats" by those who operated them.

14th Liberator They freed more than 20,000 allied prisoners of war.

1st Cavalry Division: Hell for Leather No reason found, but probably came from the old saying applied to a hard rider, "Hell bent for leather"

Infantry Regiments

3rd: Old Guards This regiment is the oldest one in the Regular army. It was organized in 1784

27th: Wolfhounds. Probably took its name in the Siberian campaign in which it participated. Their mascot was a Russian wolfhound named Kolchak.

165th. Fighting Irish. No reason found

175th: Dandy Fifth No reason found.

3rd Armoured Cavalry Regiment. Brave Rifles This regiment was first organized in 1846 as a regiment of mounted riflemen In 1847 they were the first troops to enter the captured city of Mexico and raise the Stars and Stripes. General Scott addressed them "Brave Rifles! Veterans, you have been baptized in fire and blood and come out steel" This was adopted as their motto In 1861 the name of the regiment was changed to the 3rd Cavalry and is now the 3rd Armoured

7th Cavalry Regiment: Garry Owens No reason found.

Alaskan Scouts. Castner's Cutthroats No reason found

Regiomontanus (rē′ jı ŏ mon tā′ nŭs). The Latin equivalent of *Königsberger*, adopted as a patronymic by Johann Muller (1436-76), the German mathematician and astronomer, who was born at Konigsberg and became Bishop of Ratisbon

Regium donum (rē′jı um dō′ num) (Lat) An annual grant of public money to the Presbyterian, Independent, and Baptist ministers of Ireland It began in 1672, and was commuted in 1869.

Regius Professor (rē′ jus) One who holds in an English university a professorship founded by Henry VIII In the universities of Scotland they are appointed by the Crown The present stipend is about £400 or £500.

Regnal Year is the year of a sovereign's reign, accession, e g regnal year 1 of Elizabeth II dating from the accession began on February 6th, 1952 The regnal year is only used for dating Acts of Parliament

Regular (U S A) In the early 19th century this meant thorough, well founded. In the 20th century it is more usually applied to people, *e g a regular guy*, a straightforward dependable man

Regulars. All the British military forces serving in the army as a profession, as distinct from the *Auxiliary Forces*, viz the Special Reserve (which takes the place of the old Militia), and the Territorial Force (*i e* Yeomanry and the old Volunteers)

Rehabilitation is a word of wide implications, the most general of which is, perhaps, the restoration to normalcy of one who has suffered in mind or body as a result of war wounds or strain, or who has lost touch with his usual way of life for some length of time through mental or physical illness.

Rehoboam (2 *Chron* xiii, 7) A fanciful name sometimes given to a measure of claret, a double jeroboam (*q.v.*)

 1 rehoboam = 2 jeroboams or 32 pints.
 1 jeroboam = 2 tappet-hens or 16 pints
 1 tappet-hen = 2 magnums or 8 pints
 1 magnum = 2 quarts or 4 pints

Charlotte Bronte—*why* is not known—applied the name to some sort of clerical hat

He [Mr Helstone] was short of stature [and wore] a rehoboam, or shovel hat, which he did not ... remove —*Shirley*, ch 1

Reign of Terror. The period in the French Revolution from March 1793 until July 1794, when supreme power was in the hands of the Committee of Public Safety, formed by the Jacobins and dominated by Robespierre, St Just, and Couthon. In addition to supporters of the old regime, hundreds of revolutionaries themselves perished by the guillotine, drowning, or shooting, as a result of the universal atmosphere of suspicion, mistrust, hatred, and private spite.

Reilly, To lead the life of To live luxuriously From a comic song "Is That Mr Reilly," by Pat Rooney, popular in the U S A in the 1880s The song described what the hero would do if he "struck it rich "

Rein (connected with *retain*, from Lat *retinere*, to hold back). The strap attached to the bit, used in guiding horses To give the reins. To let go unrestrained; to give licence

To take the reins To assume the guidance of direction.

Reins (Lat. *renes*) The kidneys, supposed by the Hebrews and others to be the seat of knowledge, pleasure, and pain. The Psalmist says (xvi, 7), "My reins instruct me in the night season," Solomon (*Prov* xxiii, 16), "My reins shall rejoice when thy lips speak right things," and Jeremiah says (*Lam* iii, 13), God "caused his arrows to enter into my reins," *i e.* sent pain into my kidneys

Relic, Christian. The corpse of a saint or any part thereof; any part of his clothing, or anything intimately connected with him The veneration of Christian relics goes back to the 2nd century, and a vast amount of legend, exaggeration, and downright fiction has grown up around them since then Honour may be paid to those relics whose genuineness is

morally certain, but the question of their authenticity is one of fact, to be determined by the evidence, and the Church does not guarantee the genuineness of a single specific relic. Many famous relics are almost certainly spurious, but there is no need to presume deliberate fraud Many of the relics in churches in Rome and elsewhere are in themselves interesting on account of their great antiquity, even if they are not "genuine "

Relief Church. A secession from the Church of Scotland led in 1752 by Thomas Gillespie (1708-74). He offered passive obedience respecting the settlement of ministers. The "Presbytery of Relief" was constituted in 1761, in 1847 the sect was embodied in the United Presbyterian Church of Scotland.

Religious. His Most Religious Majesty. The title by which the kings of England were formerly addressed by the Pope It still survives in the Prayer Book, in the Prayer "for the High Court of Parliament under our most religious and gracious Queen at this time assembled" (which was written, probably by Laud, in 1625), and in James I's Act for a Thanksgiving on the Fifth of November occurs the expression "most great, learned, and religious king."

In the Middle Ages, and later, the Popes did not use the names of the various sovereigns. but addressed them by special appellations thus the king of France was always addressed by the Vatican as "Most Christian", the king of Austria as "Most Apostolic"; the king of Spain as "Most Catholic"; the king of Portugal as "Most Faithful", the king of England as "Most Religious "

Remember! The last injunction of Charles I, on the scaffold, to Bishop Juxon. It has been interpreted as meaning that Charles, who was at heart a Catholic, felt that his misfortunes were a divine visitation on him for retaining church property confiscated by Henry VIII, and made a vow that if God would restore him to the throne he would restore this property to the Church. He was asking the Bishop to remember this vow, and to see that his son carried it out Charles II, however, wanted all the money he could get, and the Church lands were never restored

Remigius, or Remy, St. (re mij' i us, re' mi) (438-533), bishop and confessor, is represented as carrying a vessel of holy oil, or in the act of anointing therewith Clovis, who kneels before him When Clovis presented himself for baptism, Remy said to him, "Sigambrian, henceforward burn what thou hast worshipped, and worship what thou hast burned."

Remonstrants. Another name for the Arminians (*q v.*).

Renaissance (Fr., re-birth). The term applied, broadly, to the movement and period of transition between the mediæval and modern worlds which, beginning with Petrarch and subsequent Italian humanists in the 14th century, was immensely stimulated by the fall of Constantinople (1453), resulting in the dissemination of Greek scholarship and Byzantine art, the invention of printing (about the same time), and the discovery of America (1492). In England this revival first manifested itself in the early years of the 16th century, and affected principally literature and, later, architecture

All the Renaissance principles of art tended, as I have before often explained, to the setting Beauty above Truth, and seeking for it always at the expense of Truth And the proper punishment of such pursuit —the punishment which all the laws of the universe rendered inevitable—was, that those who thus pursued beauty should wholly lose sight of beauty — RUSKIN· *Modern Painters*, IV, xvi, § 12

Renard (ren' ard). **Une queue de renard. A mockery.** At one time a common practical joke was to fasten a fox's tail behind a person against whom a laugh was designed Panurge (*q v*) never refrained from attaching a fox's tail or the ears of a leveret behind a Master of Arts or Doctor of Divinity, whenever he encountered them (*Gargantua*, ii, 16) *See also* REYNARD

    C'est une petite vipère,
    Qui n'épargnerait pas son père,
    Et qui par nature ou par art
    Sçait couper la queue au renard
    BEAUCAIRE· *L'Embarras de la Foire.*

Rendezvous. The place to which you are to repair, a meeting, a place of muster or call Also used as a verb (Fr *rendez*, betake, *vous*, yourself) In British military parlance usually contracted to R.V

His house is a grand rendezvous of the *élite* of Paris The Imperial Guard was ordered to rendezvous in the Champs de Mars

René (re' nā) **Le Bon Roi René** (1408-80) Son of Louis II, Duc d'Anjou, Comte de Provence, father of Margaret of Anjou The last minstrel monarch, just, joyous, and debonair; a friend to chase and tilt, but still more so to poetry and music. He gave in largesse to 'knights-errant and minstrels (so says Thiebault) more than he received in revenue

Studying to promote, as far as possible, the immediate mirth and good humour of his subjects   he was never mentioned by them excepting as *Le bon Roi René*, a distinction   due to him certainly by the qualities of his heart, if not by those of his head — SCOTT· *Anne of Geierstein*, ch. xxix

Reno Divorces. Reno is the largest city in the State of Nevada, where the divorce laws are easier than in most of the other States. Seven grounds for absolute divorce are recognized, and a residence of six weeks only is requisite to enable a suit to be brought

Rentier (ron' ti ā) A French term, in course of being adopted into English, describing one who does not work but derives an income from shares, land, etc

Repenter Curls The long ringlets of a lady's hair. *Repentir* is the French for a penitentiary, and *les repenties* are the girls sent there for reformation. Mary Magdalen had such long hair that she wiped off her tears therewith from the feet of Jesus Hence the association of long curls and reformed (*repenties*) prostitutes

Repertory Company. A theatrical company that produces a number of plays, operas, etc , often at successive performances, or gives, maybe, a week to each. Such companies are becoming established in many smaller towns out of reach of the big centres of population

Reply Churlish. Sir, you are no judge, your opinion has no weight with me. Or, to use Touchstone's illustration (*As You Like It*, v, 4) ' If a courtier tell me my beard is not well cut, and I disable his judgment, I give him the reply churlish, which is the fifth remove from the lie direct, or, rather, the lie direct in the fifth degree " **Reproof Valiant.** Sir, allow me to tell you that is not the truth This is Touchstone's fourth remove from the lie direct, or, rather, the lie direct in the fourth degree.

Republic of Letters, The. The world of literature, authors generally and their influence Goldsmith, in *The Citizen of the World*, No 20 (1760), says it "is a very common expression among Europeans"; it is found in Molière's *Le Mariage Force*, Sc. vi (1664)

Republican Queen. Sophia Charlotte (1668-1705), wife of Frederick I of Prussia, was so nicknamed on account of her advanced political views She was the daughter of George I of Britain, the friend of Leibniz, and a woman of remarkable culture Charlottenburg was named after her

Requests, Court of. *See* CONSCIENCE, COURT OF

Requiem (rā' kwi em) The first word of the prayer *Requiem æternam dona eis, domine, et lux perpetua luceat eis* (Eternal rest give them, O Lord, and let everlasting light shine upon them) used as the introit of a Mass for the Dead (Requiem Mass)

Reremous. *See* REARMOUSE.

Reservation (U S A) A tract of land set aside for occupation solely by Indians

Resolute. The Resolute Doctor John Baconthorp (d 1346), head of the Carmelites in England (1329-33) and commentator on Aristotle

The Most Resolute Doctor. Guillaume Durandus de St Pourçain (d. about 1333), a French Dominican philosopher, bishop of Meaux (1326), and author of *Commentaries sur Pierre Lonbard* (publ 1508).

Responsions *See* SMALLS

Restoration Term applied in British history to the recall to the throne, in 1660, of the royal family of Stuart in the person of Charles II, eldest son of Charles I, who was beheaded in 1649. After the austerity imposed on the nation by the Puritan regime of the Commonwealth, the return of the King brought about a reaction that flowered in the drama, literature, and life of the nation In France the royal house of Bourbon was restored after the fall of Napoleon in 1815 Louis XVIII was the brother of the late king Louis XVI whose son, dynastically known as Louis XVII, never came to the throne or reached manhood

Resurrection Men. Grave-robbers, body-snatchers (*q v*) The term was first applied to the infamous Burke and Hare, of Edinburgh, who in 1829 were convicted of rifling graves to sell the bodies for dissection by doctors and students at the School of Medicine. They also murdered persons to supply bodies when occasion served.

> The body-snatchers, they have come,
> And made a snatch at me,
> 'Tis very hard them kind of men
> Won't let a body be
> The cock it crows—I must be gone—
> My William, we must part,
> But I'll be yours in death although
> Sir Astley has my heart.
> HOOD *Mary's Ghost*

The reference is to Sir Astley Cooper (1768-1841), the great surgeon and lecturer on anatomy.

Retiarius (rē tĭ âr' ĭ us) (Lat.) A gladiator who made use of a net (*rete*), which he threw over his adversary

> As in the thronged amphitheatre of old
> The wary Retiarius trapped his foe
> THOMSON *Castle of Indolence,* canto ii

Retort Courteous, The. Sir, I am not of your opinion, I beg to differ from you, or, to use Touchstone's illustration (*As You Like It,* v, 4), "If I said his beard was not cut well, he was in the mind it was." The lie seven times removed, or rather, the lie direct in the seventh degree.

Retread. A U.S. and Australian term for a soldier who fought in World War I and joined up again for World War II.

Returned Letter Office *See* BLIND DEPARTMENT.

Reveille (re vāl' ĭ) (Fr. *reveiller,* to awake) The signal by bugle or beat of drum, notifying soldiers that it is time to rise, and informing the sentries that they may forbear from challenging

Revenons à nos moutons. *See* MOUTONS.

Reverend. An archbishop is *the Most Reverend* (Father in God); a bishop, *the Right Reverend,* a dean, *the Very Reverend,* an archdeacon, *the Venerable,* all the rest of the clergy, *the Reverend.*

Revised Version, The. *See* BIBLE, THE ENGLISH

Revival of Letters, The. A term applied to the Renaissance (*q.v.*) in so far as the movement reacted on literature It really commenced earlier—at the close of the Dark Ages (*q.v.*)—but it received its chief impulse from the fall of Constantinople (1453) and the consequent dispersal over Europe of Greek MSS and Greek scholars.

Revue (re vū'). A theatrical entertainment characterized by songs and music, dancing, and constant change, with a somewhat indefinite plot and (hence the name) usually allusions to current topics

> Revue amuses by fun, by satire of passing events, by gorgeous spectacle which delights the child in all of us, by song and dance, by glimpses of drama, by the agility of man and the beauty of woman, above all by the rapid alternation of these elements, its crowning virtue is variety —A. B WALKLEY. in *The Times,* Mar 22nd, 1922

Rexists. A Belgian political party formed by Leon Degrelle in 1936 advocating Fascist ideals and working hand in hand with the Nazis It was markedly collaborationist during the German occupation of Belgium and was accordingly suppressed when the country regained its liberty. The name is an adaptation of

"Christus Rex," Christ the King, the watchword of a Catholic Young People's Action Society, founded in 1925

Reynard (rā' nard) A fox Caxton's form of the name in his translation (from the Dutch) of the *Roman de Renart* (see REYNARD THE FOX, *below*). *Renart* was the Old French form, from Ger *Reginhart,* a personal name, the Dutch was *Reynaerd* or *Reynaert*

> Where prowling Reynard trod his nightly round
> BLOOMFIELD · *Farmer's Boy*

Reynard the Fox. A mediæval beast-epic, satirizing contemporary life and events, in which all the characters are animals Such anthropomorphic epics were common in mediæval France

The germ of the story is found in Æsop's fable, *The Fox and the Lion,* this was built upon by more than one writer, but the *Roman* as we now know it is by a Fleming named *Willem,* of the early 13th century, of which a new and enlarged version was written about 1380 by an unknown author, Caxton having made his translation from a late 15th-century Dutch version of this, which was probably by Herman Barkhusen

False Reynard. By this name Dryden describes the Unitarians in his *Hind and Panther*

> With greater guile
> False Reynard fed on consecrated spoil,
> The graceless beast by Athanasius first
> Was chased from Nice, then by Socinius nursed
> Pt i, 51-54

Reynard's globe of glass. Reynard, in *Reynard the Fox (see above),* said he had sent this invaluable treasure to her majesty the queen as a present, but it never came to hand, inasmuch as it had no existence except in the imagination of the fox It was supposed to reveal what was being done—no matter how far off—and also to afford information on any subject that the person consulting it wished to know Your gift was like the globe of glass of Master Reynard A great promise, but no performance

Rhadamanthus. In Greek mythology one of the three judges of hell, Minos and Æacus being the other two

Rhapsody meant originally "songs strung together" (Gr *rapto,* to sew or string together, *ode,* a song). The term was applied to portions of the *Iliad* and *Odyssey,* which bards recited, as our minstrels sang the deeds of famous heroes.

Rheims-Douai Version, The. *See* DOUAI BIBLE.

Rhetorical Question The term in Logic for a question to which no considered answer is expected or desired, the question having been asked to produce effect only An example is the once-popular 'Are we downhearted?" only asked to elicit the answer "No."

Rhino (rī' nō) Slang for money, the term was in use as early as the 17th century *See under* NOSE, *To pay through the nose*

> Some, as I know,
> Have parted with their ready rhino
> *The Seamans' Adieu* (1670)

Rhodes Scholarships. Under the will of Cecil Rhodes (1853-1902) scholarships at Oxford were endowed for foreign and overseas students By subsequent rearrangement U.S.A. sends 32 annually (4 students from each of 8 regions consisting of 6 States), India 2, 1 from each State or Province of Canada, Australia, and South Africa Scholarships are also awarded to certain schools in New Zealand, Newfoundland, Rhodesia, Jamaica, Bermuda, Malta, and East Africa 5 scholarships were allotted to Germany until 1914, and 2 for the period between the wars The scholarships are worth £400 per annum for a period of 3 years

Rhodian Bully, The. The Colossus of Rhodes (*q.v*)

> Yet fain wouldst thou the crouching world bestride,
> Just like the Rhodian bully o'er the tide
>   PETER PINDAR *The Lusiad*, canto 2

Rhodian Law, The. The earliest system of marine law known to history; compiled by the Rhodians about 900 B C

Rhopalic Verse. Verse consisting of lines in which each successive word has more syllables than the one preceding it (Gr. *rhopalon*, a club, which is much thicker at one end than at the other).

Rem	tibi	confeci	doctissime,	dulcisonorum.
Spes	deus	æternæ-est	stationis	conciliator.
Hope	ever	solaces	miserable	individuals
1	2	3	4	5

Rhyme. Neither rhyme nor reason. Fit neither for amusement nor instruction. An author took his book to Sir Thomas More, chancellor of Henry VIII, and asked his opinion Sir Thomas told the author to turn it into rhyme He did so, and submitted it again to the lord chancellor. "Ay! ay!'" said the witty satirist, "that will do, that will do 'Tis rhyme now, but before it was neither rhyme nor reason "

The lines on his pension, traditionally ascribed to Spenser, are well known '—

> I was promised on a time
> To have reason for my rhyme,
> From that time unto this season,
> I received nor rhyme nor reason.

Rhyming Slang. A kind of slang in which the word intended was replaced by one that rhymed with it, as "Charley Prescott" for *waistcoat*, "plates of meat" for *feet* When the rhyme is a compound word the rhyming part is almost invariably dropped, leaving one who does not know somewhat in the dark Thus Chivy (Chevy) Chase rhymes with "face," by dropping "chase" *chivy* remains, and becomes the accepted slang word Similarly, daisies = *boots*, thus daisy-roots will rhyme with "boots," drop the rhyme and *daisy* remains. By the same process *sky* is slang for *pocket*, the compound word which gave birth to it being ' sky-rocket '' "Christmas," a *railway guard*, as "Ask the Christmas," is, of course, from "Christmas-card", and "raspberry", *heart*, is "raspberry-tart "

> Then came a knock at the Rory o' More [door]
> Which made my raspberry beat.

Other examples are given under their proper heads.

Rhyming to death. The Irish at one time believed that their children and cattle could be "eyebitten," that is, bewitched by an evil eye, and that the "eyebitter," or witch, could "rime" them to death. *See* RATS.

Thomas the Rhymer. A border poet and seer of the close of the 13th century, also called Thomas of Erceldoune and Thomas Learmont He is the reputed author of a number of poems, including one on Tristram (which Scott believed to be genuine), and is fabled to have predicted the death of Alexander III of Scotland, the Battle of Bannockburn, the union of England and Scotland under James VI, etc He must not be confused with Thomas Rymer (d. 1713), Historiographer Royal to William III. *See* TRUE THOMAS.

Ribbon Development. Urban extension in the form of a single depth of houses along roads radiating from the town This extravagant and impractical method of development was made illegal under the Town and Country Planning Act of 1947

Ribbonism. The principles, etc, of the Ribbon Society, a secret Roman Catholic association organized in Ireland about 1808 Its two main objects were (1) to secure fixity of tenure, called the tenant-right, and (2) to deter anyone from taking land from which a tenant has been ejected The name arose from a ribbon worn as a badge in the buttonhole

Plying a person secretly with threatening letters in order to drive him out of the neighbourhood, or to compel him to do something he objects to, used to be known as the *Ribbon dodge*, because the Ribbon men sent such letters, often decorated with rude drawings of coffins, cross-bones, or daggers, to obnoxious neighbours

Ribston Pippin. So called from Ribston, in Yorkshire, where the first pippins, introduced from Normandy about 1707, were planted It is said that Sir Henry Goodriche planted three pips, two died, and from the third came all the Ribston apple-trees in England.

Rice. The custom of throwing rice after a bride comes from India, rice being, with the Hindus, an emblem of fecundity. The bridegroom throws three handfuls over the bride, and the bride does the same over the bridegroom *Cp* MARRIAGE KNOT

Rice Christians. Converts to Christianity for worldly benefits, such as a supply of rice to Indians. Profession of Christianity born of lucre, not faith

Rice-paper. *See* MISNOMERS

Richard Roe *See* DOE

Richmond Another Richmond in the field. Said when another unexpected adversary turns up. The reference is to Shakespeare's *Richard III*, v, 4, where the king, speaking of Henry of Richmond (afterwards Henry VII), says—

> I think there be six Richmonds in the field;
> Five have I slain to-day, instead of him—
> A horse! a horse! my kingdom for a horse!

Rick Mould. Fetching the rick mould is a "flat-catching" trick played during the hay-harvest The greenhorn is sent to borrow a rick-mould, with strict injunction not to drop it. Something very heavy is put in a sack and hoisted on his back; when he has carried it carefully in the hot sun to the hayfield he gets well laughed at for his pains.

Ricochet (rik' ō shā) The skipping of a flung stone over water ("ducks and drakes"), the bound of a bullet or other projectile after striking, hence, applied to anything repeated over and over again, *e g* the fabulous bird that had only one note Marshal Vauban (1633-1707) invented a *ricochet battery*, the application of which was ricochet firing

Riddle. Josephus relates how Hiram, King of Tyre, and Solomon had once a contest in riddles, when Solomon won a large sum of money, though he subsequently lost it to Abdemon, one of Hiram's subjects.

Plutarch states that Homer died of chagrin because he could not solve a certain riddle *See* SPHINX

Riddle me riddle me ree. *See* REE.

A riddle of claret. Thirteen bottles, a magnum and twelve quarts, said to be so called because in certain old golf clubs magistrates invited to the celebration dinner presented the club with this amount, sending it in a *riddle* or sieve.

Ride. To ride (U S.A) To oppress, to pick on and irritate until the person becomes exasperated

Riding the marshes. *See* BOUNDS, BEATING THE

To ride abroad with St George, but at home with St. Michael Said of a henpecked braggart St George is represented as riding on a war charger, St Michael on a dragon Abroad a man rides, like St George, on a horse which he can control and govern, but at home he has "a dragon" to manage, like St. Michael

To ride and tie. Said of a couple of travellers who have only one horse between them One rides on ahead and then ties the horse up and walks on, the other taking his turn on the horse when he has reached it.

To ride for a fall. To proceed with one's business recklessly, usually, also desperately and regardless of consequences.

To ride up Holborn Hill. *See* HOLBORN

To take for a ride. Originally this meant to pull someone's leg or make him the butt of a joke, but it has become a gangster euphemism for murder The victim is induced or forced to enter a car with one or more companions who, in the course of the ride, murder him Under the Nazi regime in Germany high officials, generals, etc (*e g* Rommel), were requested to take a car ride with one or two of Hitler's trusties and then given the alternative choice of suicide or being murdered

Rider An addition to a manuscript, such as a codicil to a will; an additional clause tacked to a bill in Parliament, *over-riding* the preceding matter when the two come into collision, hence, a corollary or obvious supplement, and, in Euclid, etc , a subsidiary problem

In American Negro parlance, a *rider* is a lover The word is found throughout Negro folk music as *easy rider.*

Ridiculous. There is but one step from the sublime to the ridiculous. In his *Age of Reason* (1794), Pt ii, *note*, Tom Paine said, "The sublime and the ridiculous are often so nearly related that it is difficult to class them separately One step above the sublime makes the ridiculous, and one step above the ridiculous makes the sublime again "

Napoleon, who was a great admirer of Tom Paine, use to say, " Du sublime au ridicule il n'y a qu'un pas "

Riding. The three administrative divisions of Yorkshire are so called because each forms the *third* part of the county, A.S. *thriding*, the initial *th-* of the old word being lost through amalgamation with the *east, west,* or *north.* The divisions of Tipperary are (and those of Lincolnshire formerly were) also called ridings Some others of the counties have special names for their parts, as the *laths* of Kent and *rapes* of Sussex.

Riaotto (ri dot' ō) (Ital) An assembly where the company is first entertained to music, and then joins in dancing The word originally meant music reduced to a full score (Lat *reductus*)

Rien de trop. *See* DE TROP

Rienzi, Cola di (rē en' zi) A patriot of Rome who incited the people to rise against the Papal and Imperial governments In May 1347, he was declared Tribune, but his power was crushed and he fled In 1354 Pope Innocent VI sent him to Rome once more as a Senator, but while attempting to quell a riot he met his death In *Rienzi* (1835) Bulwer Lytton tells the story of the Tribune

Riff-raff. The offscouring of society, perhaps the "refuse and sweepings " *Raff* in Swedish means sweepings, but the old French term *rif et raf* meant one and all, whence the phrase *Il n'a laissé ni rif ni raf* (he has left nothing behind him) Gabriel Harvey (in *Pierce's Supererogation,* 1593) speaks of "the riffe-raffe of the scribbling rascality."

Riffle (U S A.) A small rapid, a place where the current of a stream flows swiftly and the water is disturbed From this, probably, is evolved the jazz term, a *riff*, which is a short, improvised musical phrase

Rifle. The firearm gets its name from the spiral grooves (Low Ger *riffel*, Swed *refia*) in the bore, which give the bullet a rotatory motion. The verb, *to rifle*, meaning to pillage or plunder, is connected with this through the O Fr *rifler*, to graze, scratch, strip, etc.

Rift in the Lute A small defect which mars the general result

Unfaith in aught is want of faith in all
It is the little rift within the lute
That by-and-by will make the music mute,
And ever widening slowly silence all.
TENNYSON *Merlin and Vivien, Vivien's Song.*

Rig. There is more than one word composed of these three letters, but the etymology and division of them are alike uncertain In the sense of dressing it was originally applied to a ship, a ship that is thoroughly furnished with spars, gear, tackle, and so on is *well rigged,* and its ropes and stays are its *rigging.* Hence, *a good rig out,* a first-rate outfit in clothes, equipment, etc.

In the U S A before the days of motor-cars a *rig* was a carriage or private conveyance

The word also formerly was used of a strumpet, and a lewd woman was said to be *riggish* Also, a hoax or dodge, hence a swindle, and the phrase **to rig the market**, to raise or lower prices by underhand methods so that one can make a profit.

To run the rig. To have a bit of fun, or indulge in practical jokes

> He little thought when he set out
> Of running such a rig.
> COWPER· *John Gilpin.*

Rigadoon. A lively dance for two people, said to have been invented towards the close of the 17th century by a dancing-master of Marseilles named *Rigadou.*

> Isaac's Rigadoon shall live as long
> As Raphael's painting, or as Virgil's song.
> JENYNS· *Art of Dancing,* canto ii.

Right. In politics the Right is the Conservative party, because in the continental chambers the Conservatives sit on the right-hand side of the Speaker, the Liberals, Radicals, and Labour on the left.

It'll all come right in the end. The cry of the optimist when things are going wrong.

In one's right mind. Sane, in a normal state after mental excitement The phrase comes from *Mark* v, 15—

> And they . see him that was possessed with the devil, and had the legion, sitting, and clothed, and in his right mind

Miner's right. The Australian term for a licence to dig for gold—a formidable looking document, engrossed on parchment

Right as a trivet Quite right, in an excellent state The trivet was originally a three-legged stand—a tripod—and the allusion is to its always standing firmly on its three legs.

Right foot foremost. It is still considered unlucky to enter a house, or even a room, on the left foot, and in ancient Rome a boy was stationed at the door of a mansion to caution visitors not to cross the threshold with their left foot, which would have been an ill omen.

Right-hand man. An invaluable, or confidential, assistant, originally applied to the cavalryman at the right of the line, whose duties were of great responsibility.

Right Honourable. A prefix to the title of earls, viscounts, barons, and the younger sons of dukes and marquesses All privy councillors and some lord mayors, Lords Justices of Appeal, and other civic dignitaries are also *Right Honourables* The corresponding prefix for a marquess is *The Most Honourable,* and for a duke *His Grace* Younger sons of earls, and all sons of viscounts and barons are *Honourables,* as are justices of the High Court, maids of honour, and certain Colonial and other ministers Members of Parliament when in the House are usually addressed as "My honourable friend," or "the honourable member for So-and-so "

Righto! or **Right ho!** A colloquial form of cheerful assent; *right you are* is a similar exclamation.

Right of way. The legal right to make use of a certain passage whether high road, by-road, or private road Private right of way may be claimed by immemorial usage, special permission, or necessity, but a funeral *cortege* or bridal party having passed over a certain field does not give to the public the right of way, as many suppose

To do one right. To be perfectly fair to him, to do him justice

> King Charles, and who'll do him right now?
> BROWNING *Cavalier Tunes*

In Elizabethan literature the phrase is very common, and meant to answer when one's health had been drunk

> *Falstaff* [To SILENCE, *who drinks a bumper*] Why, now you have done me right.
> *2 Henry IV,* v, 3

To send one to the right about. To clear him off, send him packing

Declaration of Rights. An instrument submitted to William and Mary and accepted by them (February 13th, 1689), setting forth the fundamental principles of the constitution The chief items are The Crown cannot levy taxes without the consent of Parliament, nor keep a standing army in times of peace, the Members of Parliament are free to utter their thoughts, and a Parliament is to be convened every year, elections are to be free, trial by jury to be inviolate, the right of petition not to be interfered with, and the Sovereign should take the oath against Transubstantiation and not marry a Roman Catholic.

To put things to rights. To put every article in its proper place

Rigmarie (rig ma ′rē) An old Scottish coin of low value The word originated from one of the "billon' coins struck in the reign of Queen Mary, which bore the words *Reg Maria* as part of the legend

> Billon is mixed metal for coinage, especially silver largely alloyed with copper

Rigmarole (rig′ mā rōl). A rambling, disconnected account, an unending yarn

> You never heard such a rigmarole He said he thought he was certain he had seen somebody by the rick and it was Tom Bakewell who was the only man he knew who had a grudge against Farmer Blaize and if the object had been a little bigger he would not mind swearing to Tom and would swear to him for he was dead certain it was Tom only what he saw looked smaller and it was pitch-dark at the time etc —
> MEREDITH *Richard Feverel,* ch xi

The word is said to be a popular corruption of *Ragman Roll* (*q v*); it is recorded from the early 18th century

Rigol. A circle or diadem (Ital *rigolo,* a little wheel)

> [Sleep] That from this golden rigol hath divorced
> So many English kings
> *2 Henry IV,* iv, 4

Rig-veda. *See* VEDA.

Rile. A dialect word, common in Norfolk and other parts for stirring up water to make it muddy, hence, to excite or disturb, and hence the modern colloquial meaning, to vex, annoy, make angry It comes from O Fr *roillier,* to roll or flow (of a stream)

Rimfaxi. *See* HORSE

Rimmon. The Babylonian god who presided over storms. Milton identifies him with one of the fallen angels:

> Him followed Rimmon, whose delightful seat
> Was fair Damascus, on the fertile bank
> Of Abbana and Pharphar, lucid streams
> *Paradise Lost,* Bk 1, 467

To bow the knee to Rimmon. To palter with one's conscience; to do that which one knows to be wrong so as to save one's face The allusion is to Naaman obtaining Elisha's permission to worship the god when with his master (2 *Kings* v, 18).

Rinaldo. One of the great heroes of mediæval romance (also called Renault of Montauban, Regnault, etc), a paladin of Charlemagne, cousin of Orlando (*q v*), and one of the four sons of Aymon He was the owner of the famous horse Bayard, and is always painted with the characteristics of a borderer—valiant, ingenious, rapacious, and unscrupulous

In Tasso's *Jerusalem Delivered* Rinaldo was the Achilles of the Christian army, despising gold and power but craving renown.

In Ariosto s *Orlando Furioso* he appears as the son of the fourth Marquis d'Este, Lord of Mount Auban or Albano, eldest son of Amon or Aymon, nephew of Charlemagne He was the rival of his cousin Orlando, but Angelica detested him.

Ring. The noun (meaning a circlet) is the A S *hring,* the verb (to sound a bell, or as a bell) is from A S. *hringan,* to clash, ring, connected with Lat. *clangere,* to clang

A ring worn on the forefinger is supposed to indicate a haughty, bold, and overbearing spirit, on the long finger, prudence, dignity, and discretion, on the marriage finger, love and affection on the little finger, a masterful spirit *Cp.* WEDDING FINGER.

The wearing of a wedding-ring by married women is now universal in Christian countries but the custom varies greatly in detail It appears to have originated in the betrothal rings given as secular pledges by the Romans. Until the end of the 16th century it was the custom in England to wear the wedding-ring on the third finger of the right hand

As the forefinger was held to be symbolical of the Holy Ghost, priests used to wear their ring on this in token of their spiritual office Episcopal rings, worn by cardinals, bishops and abbots are of gold with a stone—cardinals a sapphire, bishops and abbots an amethyst—and are worn upon the third finger of the right hand The pope wears a similar ring, usually with a cameo, emerald, or ruby. A plain gold ring is put upon the third finger of the right hand of a nun on her profession.

Amongst the Romans, only senators, chief magistrates, and in later times knights, enjoyed the *jus annuli aurei,* the right to wear a ring of gold The emperors conferred this upon whom they pleased, and Justinian extended the privilege to all Roman citizens

Rings noted in Fable and History.

Agramant's ring This enchanted ring was given by Agramant to the dwarf Brunello, from whom it was stolen by Bradamant and given to Melissa It passed successively into the hands of Rogero and Angelica (who carried it in her mouth) (*Orlando Furioso,* Bk. v)

The ring of Amasis A ring with the same story as that of Polycrates *See below.*

Corcud's ring. This magic ring was composed of six metals, and ensured the wearer success in any undertaking in which he chose to embark (*Chinese Tales, Corcud and his Four Sons*)

The Doge's ring The doge of Venice, on Ascension Day, used to throw a ring into the sea from the ship *Bucentaur* (*q v*), to denote that the Adriatic was subject to the republic of Venice as a wife is subject to her husband *See* DOGE

The ring of Edward the Confessor It is said that Edward the Confessor was once asked for alms by an old man, and gave him his ring In time some English pilgrims went to the Holy Land and happened to meet the same old man, who told them he was John the Evangelist, and gave them the identical ring to take to "Saint" Edward It was preserved in Westminster Abbey

The ring of Gyges See GYGES

The ring of Innocent On May 29th, 1205, Innocent III sent John, King of England, four gold rings set with precious stones, and explained that the *rotundity* signifies *eternity*—remember we are passing through time into eternity, the *number* signifies the *four* virtues which make up constancy of mind—viz justice, fortitude, prudence, and temperance, the *material* signifies "the wisdom from on high," which is as gold purified in the fire; the *green* emerald is emblem of "faith," the *blue* sapphire of "hope," the *red* garnet of "charity," and the *bright* topaz of "good works " (Rymer *Fœdera,* vol 1, 139.)

Dame Liones' ring given by her to Sir Gareth during a tournament It ensured the wearer from losing blood when wounded

> "This ring," said Dame Liones, "increaseth my beauty That which is green it turns red, and that which is red it turns green That which is blue it turns white and that which is white it turns blue Whoever beareth this ring can never lose blood, however wounded "—*History of Prince Arthur,* i, 146

Luned's ring rendered the wearer invisible Luned or Lynet gave it to Owain, one of King Arthur's knights

> Take this ring, and put it on thy finger, with the stone inside thy hand, and close thy hand upon it As long as thou concealest the stone the stone will conceal thee —*Mabinogion (Lady of the Fountain)*

The Ring of the Nibelung See NIBELUNG

The ring of Ogier (*q v*) was given him by Morgan le Fay It removed all infirmities, and restored the aged to youth again

Otnit's ring of invisibility belonged to Otnit, King of Lombardy, and was given to him by the queen-mother when he went to gain the soldan's daughter in marriage The stone had the virtue of directing the wearer the right road to take in travelling (*The Heldenbuch*)

Polycrates' ring was flung into the sea to propitiate Nemesis, and was found again by the owner inside a fish *Cp.* KENTIGERN

Reynard's wonderful ring This ring, which existed only in the brain of Reynard, had a stone of three colours—red, white, and green. The *red* made the night as clear as the day, the *white* cured all manner of diseases, and the *green* rendered the wearer of the ring invincible (*Reynard the Fox*, ch xii)

Solomon's ring, among other wonderful things, sealed up the refractory Jinni in jars, and cast them into the Red Sea

The steel ring, made by Seidel-Beckit, enabled the wearer to read the secrets of another's heart (*Oriental Tales, The Four Talismans*).

The talking ring was given by Tartaro, the Basque Cyclops, to a girl whom he wished to marry Immediately she put it on, it kept incessantly saying, "You there, and I here.' In order to get rid of the nuisance, the girl cut off her finger and threw it and the ring into a pond

This Basque legend is given in Campbell's *Popular Tales of the West Highlands*, and in Grimm's *Tales* (*The Robber and his Sons*)

Ring of the Fisherman. A seal ring with which the pope is invested at his election, and used only for sealing papal briefs It is officially broken up at his death by the Chamberlain of the Roman Church. Its device is that of St. Peter fishing from a boat

The Ring. A phrase used in Australia in the early 19th century to describe a group of the most hard-bitten convicts at the Norfolk Island penitentiary, who exercised an evil influence over their fellows This use of the word ante-dates by some 30 years its employment in U S A

The Ring. Bookmakers or pugilists collectively, and the sports they represent, because the spectators at a prize-fight or race form a ring round the competitors Specifically, *The Ring* was the hall for prize-fights in the Blackfriars Road.

Ringleader. The moving spirit, the chief, in some enterprise, especially one of a mutinous character, from the old phrase to *lead the ring*, the *ring* being a group of associated persons

To make a ring. To combine in order to control the price of a given article. If the chief merchants of any article (say salt, flour, or sugar) combine, they can fix the selling price, and thus secure enormous profits

A swindle is also commonly found in auction rooms today, particularly at book, furniture, and art sales in the provinces The dealers present agree not to push up the prices of the goods offered, which are knocked down cheaply to one or another of the party A fresh auction is then held among the *ring* privately, whereat each dealer obtains the items he most wants at something approaching its real value, the profit thus accruing is divided among the participating members, who then get both the money and the goods. For example, books bought at one provincial sale in Great Britain in 1948 for under £20,000 were resold the same day by the ring amongst themselves for £87,000

To make rings round one. To defeat him completely in some sport or competition, etc , to outclass him easily.

To ring an anchor. To haul it up so that its ring is at the hawse-hole or cathead
25*

Ring posies or mottoes.
(1) A E I (Greek for "*Always*")
(2) For ever and for aye
(3) In thee, my choice, I do rejoice.
(4) Let love increase
(5) May God above Increase our love
(6) Not two but one Till life is gone
(7) My heart and I, Until I die.
(8) When this you see, Then think of me
(9) Love is heaven, and heaven is love.
(10) Wedlock, 'tis said, In heaven is made

Ring and the Book, The. A long poem (20,934 lines), by Robert Browning, telling twelve times over, from different points of view, the story of a *cause célèbre* of Italian history (1698) Guido Franceschini, a Florentine nobleman of shattered fortune, marries Pompilia, an heiress, to repair his state Pompilia is a supposititious child of Pietro, supplied by his wife, Violante, to prevent certain property going to an heir not his own The bride reveals to Guido this fact, and the first trial occurs to settle the said property. The count treats his bride so brutally that she quits his roof under the protection of Caponsacchi, a young priest, and takes refuge in Rome Guido follows and has them arrested; a trial ensues, a separation is permitted Pompilia is sent to a convent and Caponsacchi is suspended for three years Pompilia's health gives way, and as the birth of a child is expected, she is permitted to leave the convent and live with her putative parents She pleads for a divorce, but, pending the suit, the child is born The count, hearing thereof, murders Pietro, Violante, and Pompilia, but, being taken red-handed is executed

A ring of bells A set of bells (from three to twelve) for change ringing, tuned to the diatonic scale

It has the true ring—has intrinsic merit; bears the mark of real talent A metaphor taken from the custom of judging genuine money by its "ring" or sound.

Ring off! The expression commonly used on the telephone when one has a wrong connexion or it is desired that the conversation should cease

Ringing the changes. Properly, producing continual changes on a set of bells without repetition, *changes* being variations—according to certain rules—from the regular striking order

Figuratively the phrase has two meanings (1) to try every way of doing a thing, to "run a thing to death," work it for all it's worth, etc , as in—

I have likewise seen an Hymn in Hexameters to the Virgin *Mary* which filled a whole Book tho' it consisted but of the eight following Words.

Tot, tibi, sunt, Virgo, dotes, quot, sidera, Cœlo The Poet rung the changes upon these eight several Words and by that Means made his Verses almost as numerous as the Virtues and the Stars which they celebrated.—ADDISON *Spectator*, No. lx.

(2) to swindle one over a transaction by bamboozling him in changing money For example · A man goes to a tavern and asks for a glass of beer (8d), he lays a ten-shilling note on the bar and receives nine shillings and fourpence in change. "Oh!" says the man, "give me the note

back, I have such a lot of change " He offers ten shillings in silver as he is handed the note, but just before the barmaid takes it he puts the lot together and says, "There, let's have a quid instead of the note and silver." This is done, and, of course, the barmaid loses ten shillings by the transaction.

Riot. In Common Law there are five elements necessary to make a tumult, or disturbance of the peace, a riot, viz —

(1) A number of persons, three at least, (2) common purpose, (3) execution or conception of the common purpose, (4) an intent to help one another by force if necessary against any person who may oppose them in the execution of their common purpose, (5) force or violence not merely used in demolishing, but displayed in such a manner as to alarm at least one person of reasonable firmness and courage

If there are twelve persons or more present and they continue riotously and tumultuously together for one hour after the proclamation in the king's name ordering them to disperse has been read by a justice of the peace or other authorized person, the rioters are guilty of felony and can be punished by penal servitude for life (formerly it was a capital offence). This proclamation is popularly known as 'reading the Riot Act," for it is the opening section of the Riot Act of 1714 that is read on such occasions.

To run riot. To act without restraint or control, to act in a very disorderly way The phrase was originally used of hounds which had lost the scent.

Rip. He is a sad rip A sad rake or debauchee, seems to be a perversion of *rep*, rep-robate, as in *demirep*

Some forlorn, worn-out old rips, broken-kneed and broken-winded —DU MAURIER *Peter Ibbetson*, Pt. vi, p 376

Let her rip Let it (an engine, etc) go as fast as it can

Rip Van Winkle *See* WINKLE.

Ripon. A cathedral city in Yorkshire **True as Ripon steel** Ripon used to be famous for its steel spurs, which were the best in the world The spikes of a Ripon spur would strike through a shilling-piece without turning the point

Ripping. Excellent, tip-top

Rise. On the rise. Going up in price, becoming more valuable, especially of stocks and shares.

To get a rise Colloquial for to have an increase in salary.

To take a rise out of one. To raise a laugh at his expense, to make him a butt Hotten says this is a metaphor from fly-fishing, the fish *rise* to the fly, and are caught

Rising in the Air. *See* LEVITATION.

Risorgimento (rī sôr jĭ men' tō) The name given to the Italian movement for national freedom in the 19th century It first took active form in 1848, the year of European revolutions At that time the peninsula was divided into nine states, all—save Piedmont and the Papal States—under the direct or indirect influence of Austria Only Piedmont (the King-

dom of Sardinia) remained unmoved by this revolution, but by the genius of Cavour this kingdom obtained the moral leadership of all Italian patriots and twelve years later, under her protection, Garibaldi delivered Sicily and Naples while the Piedmontese armies came down from the north Only the city of Rome remained to the Popes and when, in 1870, Italian troops entered the city, the Kingdom of Italy under Victor Emmanuel II became a fact

Rivals. Originally "persons dwelling on opposite sides of a river" (Lat. *rivalis*, a river-man). Cælius says there was no more fruitful source of contention than river-right, both with beasts and men, not only for the benefit of its waters, but also because rivers are natural boundaries

Rivers. The following are miles in length

About 3,500, the Nile, the longest river in Africa.

About 2,400, the Volga, the longest river in Europe

About 3,200, the Yang-tze-Kiang, the longest river in Asia

About 3,900, the Lower Mississippi and the Missouri The Mississippi itself, the longest river in North America, is 2,553 miles from mouth to source

About 4,700, the Amazon, the longest river in South America and in the world

About 228, the Thames, the longest river in Great Britain

Riviera, The The name given to the Mediterranean coasts of France and Italy for a distance of about 300 miles, with its centre at Genoa From west to east the principal resorts are Hyères, Cannes, Nice, Monte Carlo, Mentone, San Remo, Bordighera, Rapallo, Savona, Spezzia.

Roach. Sound as a roach. An old saying, a translation of the French *Sain comme une gardon*

To roach is to trim a horse's mane to within an inch or so of the hide The word is also applied in this sense to a style of cutting a man's hair

Road All roads lead to Rome. All efforts of thought converge in a common centre As, from the centre of the ancient world, roads radiated to every part of the Empire, so any road, if followed to its source, must lead to the great capital city, Rome

Gentlemen of the road or knights of the road. Highwaymen

In the mountain districts of North America a highwayman used to be called a *road agent*, and the term is still applied to bandits who hold up trains, motor-cars, etc

On the road Progressing towards, as, *On the road to recovery*, said also of actors when "on tour," and of commercial travellers

Road hog. *See* HOG.

The rule of the road—

The rule of the road is a paradox quite,
 In riding or driving along,
If you go to the left you are sure to go right,
 If you go to the right you go wrong.

This is the rule in Great Britain, Austria, Hungary, Portugal, Sweden, Czechoslovakia, and Yugoslavia, also in certain cities, e g Rome In other European countries and in America traffic keeps to the right

To take to the road. To turn highwayman or become a tramp

Roadhouse. An inn, hotel, etc , by the roadside, usually at some distance outside a town, where parties can go out by car for meals, dancing, etc.

Roads or **Roadstead,** as ' Yarmouth Roads," a place where ships can safely *ride* at anchor *Road,* A S *rad,* comes from *ridan,* to ride

Roan A reddish-brown This word used to be derived from Rouen, the town, because this was an Old French spelling of it (*un cheval rouen*), but there can be no connexion, as the Italian was *rovano* or *roano,* and its etymology is unknown Rouen may have given its name to *roan,* the soft sheepskin leather.

Roan Barbary. The famous charger of Richard II, which ate from his royal hand

Oh, how it yearned my heart when I beheld
In London streets, that coronation day,
When Bolingbroke rode on roan Barbary,
That horse that thou so often hast bestrid,
That horse that I so carefully have dressed.
Richard II, v, 5.

Roar. Roarer. A broken-winded horse is so called from the noise it makes in breathing.

He drives a roaring trade. He does a great business

Roaring boys. The riotous blades of Ben Jonson's time, whose delight it was to annoy quiet folk At one time their pranks in London were carried to an alarming extent

And bid them think on Jones amidst this glee,
In hope to get such roaring boys as he
Legend of Captain Jones (1659)

Dekker and Middleton wrote a play (1611) on Moll Cutpurse (*q.v*) which they called *The Roaring Girl*

Roaring Meg. See MEG

The Roaring Forties. See FORTY.

The roaring game. So the Scots call the game of curling

Roast. To roast a person is to banter him unmercifully, also, to give him a dressing-down Shakespeare, in *Hamlet,* speaks of roasting ' in wrath and fire "

To rule the roast. To have the chief direction; to be paramount

The phrase was common in the 15th century, and it is possible that *roast* was originally *roost,* the reference being to a cock, who decides which hen is to roost nearest to him, but it is unlikely; in Thomas Heywood's *History of Women* (about 1630) we read of "her that ruled the roast in the kitchen "

John, Duke of Burgoyne, ruled the rost, and governed both King Charles . and his whole realme. —HALL. *Union* (1548)

Ah, I do domineer, and rule the roast
CHAPMAN *Gentleman Usher,* V, 1 (1606)
Geate you nowe up into your pulpittes like braggunge cocks on the rowst, flappe your winges and crowe out aloude —BP. JEWELL (*d* 1571)

Rob. To rob Peter to pay Paul. To take away from one person in order to give to another, or merely to shift a debt—to pay it off by incurring another one Fable has it that the phrase alludes to the fact that on December 17th, 1550, the abbey church of St Peter, Westminster, was/advanced to the dignity of a cathedral by letters patent; but ten years later it was joined to the diocese of London again, and many of its estates appropriated to the repairs of St Paul's Cathedral But it was a common saying long before this date, and had been used by Wyclif about 1380.—

How should God approve that you rob Peter, and give this robbery to Paul in the name of Christ?— *Select Works,* III, 174.

The hint of the President, Viglius, to the Duke of Alva when he was seeking to impose ruinous taxation in the Netherlands (1569) was that—

it was not desirable to rob St Peter's altar in order to build one to St Paul

Rob Roy (*Robert the Red*) A nickname given to Robert M'Gregor (1671-1734), a noted Scottish outlaw and freebooter, on account of his red hair He assumed the name of Campbell about 1716, and was protected by the Duke of Argyle He may be termed the Robin Hood of Scotland

Rather beneath the middle size than above it, his limbs were formed upon the very strongest model that is consistent with agility Two points in his person interfered with the rules of symmetry, his shoulders were so broad . as to give him the air of being too square in respect to his stature, and his arms, though round, sinewy, and strong, were so very long as to be rather a deformity —SCOTT: *Rob Roy,* ch. xxiii

Robert. The personal name is sometimes applied to the "man in blue," the policeman The allusion is to Sir Robert Peel—*cp* PEELER, and BOBBY

Highwaymen and bandits are called *Robert's men* from *Robin Hood*

King Robert of Sicily A metrical romance taken from the *Story of the Emperor Jovinian* in the *Gesta Romanorum,* and borrowed from the *Talmud* It finds a place in the *Arabian Nights,* the Turkish *Tutinameh,* the Sanskrit *Panchatantra,* and has been *rechauffé* by Longfellow

Robert the Devil or **Le Diable** Robert, third Duke of Normandy (1028-35), father of William the Conqueror He supported the English athelings against Canute, and made the pilgrimage to Jerusalem, many legends grew up around him, and he got his name for his daring and cruelty The Norman tradition is that his wandering ghost will not be allowed to rest till the Day of Judgment. He is also called *Robert the Magnificent.*

Meyerbeer's opera *Roberto il Diavolo* (1831) is founded on this story The duke is depicted as a libertine, and the opera shows the struggle in Robert between the virtue inherited from his mother, and the vice imparted by his father.

Robert François Damiens (1715-57), who attempted to assassinate Louis XV, was also called "Robert le Diable "

Robin. A diminutive of Robert.

Robin Goodfellow. A "drudging fiend," and merry domestic fairy, famous for mischievous pranks and practical jokes, also known as "Puck," the son of Oberon, and the fairies' jester. The story is that at night-time he will sometimes do little services for the family over which he presides The Scots call this domestic spirit a *brownie*, the Germans, *kobold* or *Knecht Ruprecht* The Scandinavians called it *Nisse God-dreng*

> Either I mistake your shape and making quite,
> Or else you are that shrewd and knavish sprite
> Called Robin Goodfellow .
> Those that Hob-goblin call you, and sweet Puck,
> You do their work, and they shall have good luck
> *Midsummer Night's Dream*, ii, 1

Robin Gray, Auld. Words by Lady Anne Lindsay, daughter of the Earl of Balcarres, and afterwards Lady Barnard, in 1772, written to an old Scotch tune called "The bridegroom grat when the sun gaed down." Auld Robin Gray was the herdsman of her father When Lady Anne had written a part, she called her younger sister for advice. She said, "I am writing a ballad of virtuous distress in humble life. I have oppressed my heroine with sundry troubles for example, I have sent her Jamie to sea, broken her father's arm, made her mother sick, given her Auld Robin Gray for a lover, and want a fifth sorrow; can you help me to one?" "Steal the cow, sister Anne," said the little Elizabeth, so the cow was stolen awa', and the song completed.

Lady Anne later wrote a sequel in which Auld Robin Gray was good enough to die, whereupon Jeannie married Jamie

Robin Hood. This traditional outlaw and hero of English ballads is mentioned by the Scottish historian Fordun, who died about 1386, and also by Langland in the *Vision of Piers Plowman*, Bk v, 402 (*q v*), but which of these is the earlier is uncertain It is doubtful whether he ever lived—the truth probably being that the stories associated with his name crystallized gradually round the personality of some popular local hero of the early 13th century—but the legends are that he was born in 1160 at Locksley, Notts, or, alternatively, that he was the outlawed Earl of Huntingdon, Robert Fitzooth, in disguise Fitz- being omitted leaves Ooth, and converting *th* into *d* it became "Ood "

Another suggestion (Ten Brink) is that in the Robin Hood legends we have a late reminder of the old Scandinavian mythology of our ancestors About the 12th century Woden was given the name "Robin" (the Fr. form of *Ruprecht*, corresponding to *Henodperaht*), and the tales of outlawry may be a later form of the legend of the Wild Huntsman, connected with Woden

According to Stow, he was an outlaw in the reign of Richard I (12th century). He entertained one hundred tall men, all good archers, with the spoil he took, but "he suffered no woman to be oppressed, violated, or otherwise molested; poore men's goods he spared, abundantlie relieving them with that which by theft he got from abbeys and houses of rich earles."

Robin Hood's companions in Sherwood Forest and Barnsdale, Yorks, were Little John, Friar Tuck, Will Scarlet, Allen-a-dale, George-a-Greene, and Maid Marion According to one tradition, Robin Hood and Little John were two heroes defeated with Simon de Montfort at the battle of Evesham, in 1265 Fuller, in his *Worthies*, considers the outlaw an historical character, but Thierry says he simply represents the remnant of the old Saxon race, which lived in perpetual defiance of the Norman oppressors from the time of Hereward

The traditions about Fulk FitzWarine, great-grandson of Warine of Metz, so greatly resemble those connected with "Robin Hood," that some suppose them to be both one. Fitz-Warine quarrelled with John, and when John was king he banished Fulk, who became a bold forester

The first published collection of ballads about the hero was the *Lytel Geste of Robin Hood*, printed by Wynkyn de Worde about 1490

The stories about him formed the basis of early dramatic representations and were later amalgamated with the morris dances (*q.v.*) and May-day revels

A Robin Hood wind. A cold thaw-wind Tradition runs that Robin Hood used to say he could bear any cold except that which a thaw-wind brought with it

Bow and arrow of Robin Hood. The traditional bow and arrow of Robin Hood are religiously preserved at Kirklees Hall, Yorkshire, the seat of Sir George Armytage, and the site of his grave is pointed out in the park.

Death of Robin Hood. He was bled to death treacherously by a nun, instigated to the foul deed by his kinsman, the prior of Kirklees, near Halifax

Epitaph of Robin Hood.

> Hear, underneath his latil stean,
> Laiz Robert earl of Huntington,
> Nea arcir ver az hie sae geud,
> An pipl kauld him Robin Heud
> Sich utlaz az he an hiz men
> VII England nivr si agen.
> *Obiit 24, Kalend Dikembris*, 1247.

Notwithstanding this epitaph other traditions assert that Robin Hood lived into the reign of Edward III, and died in 1325 One of the ballads relates how Robin Hood took service under Edward II

Many talk of Robin Hood who never shot with his bow. Many brag of deeds in which they took no part. Many talk of Robin Hood, and wish their hearers to suppose they took part in his adventures, but they never put a shaft to one of his bows, nor could they have bent it even if they had tried.

> They cry out with an open mouth, as if they outshot Robin Hood, that Plato banished them (*i e* , the Poets) out of his Commonwealth.—SIDNEY *Apologie for Poetrie*

Robin Hood and Guy of Gisborne. Robin Hood and Little John, having had a tiff, part company, when Little John falls into the hands of the sheriff of Nottingham, who binds him to a tree Meanwhile, Robin Hood meets with Guy of Gisborne, sworn to slay the "bold forrester." The two bowmen struggle together, but Guy is slain, and Robin Hood rides till he comes to the tree where Little John is bound. The Sheriff mistakes him for Guy of Gisborne, and gives him charge of the prisoner. Robin cuts the cord, hands Guy's bow to Little John, and the two soon put to flight the sheriff and his men (Percy *Reliques*.)

Robin Hood's larder. *See* OAK

To go round Robin Hood's barn. To arrive at the right conclusion by very roundabout methods

To sell Robin Hood's pennyworth is to sell things at half their value. As Robin Hood stole his wares, he sold them, under their intrinsic value, for just what he could get

Robin Redbreast. The tradition is that when our Lord was on His way to Calvary, a robin picked a thorn out of His crown, and the blood which issued from the wound falling on the bird dyed its breast with red.
Another fable is that the robin covers dead bodies with leaves, this is referred to in Webster's *White Devil*, v, 1 (1612) —

> Call for the robin-red-breast and the wren,
> Since o'er shady groves they hover,
> And with leaves and flowers do cover
> The friendless bodies of unburied men.

And in the ballad *The Babes in the Wood*—

> No burial this pretty pair
> From any man receives,
> Till Robin Redbreast piously
> Did cover them with leaves

Cp RUDDOCK

Robin Redbreasts. Bow Street runners were so called from their red waistcoats

A round robin. *See* ROUND.

Robin and Makyne. An ancient Scottish pastoral. Robin is a shepherd for whom Makyne sighs. She goes to him and tells her love, but Robin turns a deaf ear, and the damsel goes home to weep. After a time the tables are turned, and Robin goes to Makyne to plead for her heart and hand, but the damsel replies—

> The man that will not when he may
> Sall have nocht when he wald.
>
> PERCY *Reliques, etc*, series ii.

Robinson Crusoe. Defoe's novel (1719) is founded on the adventures of Alexander Selkirk (1676-1723), a buccaneer who, at his own request, was marooned, in 1704, on the uninhabited island of Juan Fernandez, off the coast of Chile. He remained there for over four years, being finally rescued by Captain Woodes Rogers in 1709
Though Robinson Crusoe's adventures are based on those of Selkirk, whom it is unlikely that Defoe ever met, the actual island he describes was not Juan Fernandez but more probably Tobago, from the mention of Trinidad in the distance, and the descriptions of tropical plants Defoe himself had never been to the West Indies.

Robot (rō'bot) An automaton with semi-human powers and intelligence. From this the term is often extended to mean a person who works automatically without employing initiative. The name comes from the mechanical creatures in Karel Capek's play *R U R* (Rossum's Universal Robots) which was successfully produced in London in 1923.

Robot Bomb, or **Pilotless Plane,** is the official name of the "Flying Bombs," "Buzz Bombs," or "Doodlebugs" launched against England by the Germans in June 1944. They were officially known in Germany as V1, or Vergeltungswaffe Ein (Reprisal Weapon No. 1)

Roc (rok) A fabulous white bird of enormous size, and such strength that it can "truss elephants in its talons," and carry them to its mountain nest, where it devours them (*Arabian Nights, The Third Calender, and Sinbad the Sailor*)

Roch, or **Roque, St.** (rosh, rok). Patron of those afflicted with the plague, because "he worked miracles on the plague-stricken, while he was himself smitten with the same judgment." He is depicted in a pilgrim's habit, lifting his dress to display a plague-spot on his thigh, which an angel is touching that he may cure it. Sometimes he is accompanied by a dog bringing bread in his mouth, in allusion to the legend that a hound brought him bread daily while he was perishing of pestilence in a forest
His feast day, August 16th, was formerly celebrated in England as a general harvest-home, and styled "the great August festival"

St. Roch et son chien. Inseparables, Darby and Joan

Roche (rōsh) **Sir Boyle Roche's bird.** Sir Boyle Roche (1743-1807) was an Irish M.P., noted for his "bulls" On one occasion in the House, quoting from Jevon's play, *The Devil of a Wife*, he said, "Mr Speaker, it is impossible I could have been in two places at once, unless I were a bird "

> You may make a remark on the ubiquitous nature of certain cards, which, like Sir Boyle Roche's bird, are in two places at once —*Drawing-room Magic*.

Rochelle Salt. A tartrate of sodium or potassium, so called because it was discovered by an apothecary of Rochelle, named Seignette, in 1672. In France it is called *sel de Seignette* or *sel des tombeaux*

Rochester, according to Bede, derives its name from "Hrof," a Saxon chieftain. (*Hrofsceaster*, Hrof's castle)

Rock. "The Rock," *par excellence*, is Gibraltar (*cp* ROCK ENGLISH, *below*) As applied to pigeons—as in Plymouth rock and blue rock—the word is short for *rock-dove* or *rock-pigeon*. "The Rock of Ages" (*see below*) is used of Jesus Christ as the unshakable and eternal foundation
In U.S.A. thieves' slang a *rock* is a diamond or other precious stone

In the sense of swinging backwards and forwards to rock is a term in jazz music meaning to work up an exciting rhythm

A house builded upon a rock. Typical of a person or a thing whose foundations are sure. The allusion is to *Matt.* vii, 24

Captain Rock. A fictitious name assumed by the leader of the Irish insurgents in 1822

On the rocks. "Stony broke," having no money, a phrase from seafaring, a ship that is on the rocks will very quickly go to pieces unless she can be got off

People of the Rock. The inhabitants of Hejaz or Arabia Petræa

Rock Day. The day after Twelfth-day, when, the Christmas holidays being over, women returned to their distaff, an old name for which was *rock*; the day is also called "St. Distaff's Day." *Cp* PLOUGH MONDAY.

Rock English. The mixed patois of Spanish and English spoken by natives at Gibraltar—Rock Lizards Similarly, Malta or Mediterranean fever, which is common at Gibraltar, is also called **Rock fever**

Rock of Ages cleft for me. It is said that this well-known hymn was written by Augustus Montague Toplady (1740-78) while seated by a great cleft rock near Cheddar, Somerset. Another story, which may belong to the realm of fable, has it that the first verse was written on the ten of diamonds in the interval between two rubbers of whist at Bath Hence a *Toplady ring* is a ring set with ten stones in the form of the pips on a ten of diamonds The phrase itself, as applied to Christ, is considerably older, and is traced to the marginal note to *Is.* xxvi, 4, where the words "everlasting strength" are stated to be, in the Hebrew, "Rock of Ages " In one of his hymns Wesley had written (1788)—

> Hell in vain against us rages,
> Can it shock
> Christ the Rock
> Of eternal Ages?
> *Praise by all to Christ is given*

Southey also has—

> These waters are the Well of Life, and lo!
> The Rock of Ages there, from whence they flow
> *Pilgrimage to Waterloo*, Pt 1, ca 111

That is the rock you'll split on. That is the danger, or the more or less hidden obstruction Another seafaring phrase, there are rocks ahead in the path of the ship, and the helmsman must exercise the greatest caution

The Ladies' Rock. A crag under the castle rock of Stirling, where ladies used to witness tournaments

Rocking Stones. *See* LOGAN STONES.

Rockefeller Foundation (rok' e fel' er) This was established by John D Rockefeller (1839-1937) in order "to promote the welfare of mankind throughout the world " From it grants have been made to educational and other societies, including the universities of Oxford, Cambridge, and London The capital is over £32,000,000 The Rockefeller Institute for Medical Research was founded in New York City in 1901. John D. Rockefeller built and endowed the buildings at a cost of £800,000

Rockefeller Center is a collection of 14 separate buildings covering almost 12 acres in New York City Radio City occupies 5 buildings in one section, and the whole Center, grouped round a 70-storey skyscraper, has a daily population of some 151,000 It was completed in 1940

Rocket, To give someone a. To reprimand severely. An expression much used by the British in World War II

Rococo (rō kō' kō) An 18th-century European decorative style, characterized by motifs taken from shells (*rocaille*) It is seen at its best in the furniture and architecture of France during the reign of Louis XV

Rod. A rod in pickle. A scolding or punishment in store Birch-rods used to be laid in brine to keep the twigs pliable

Spare the rod and spoil the child An old saying drawing attention to the folly of allowing childish faults to go unreproved, founded on *Prov* xiii, 24, "He that spareth his rod hateth his child. but he that loveth him chasteneth him betimes "

> Love is a boy, by poets styled,
> Then spare the rod, and spoil the child
> BUTLER *Hudibras*, II, 1, 842

To kiss the rod To submit to punishment or misfortune meekly and without murmuring

Rodeo (rō' de ō, or rō dā' ō) A public exhibition of horsemanship, cattle rounding-up, etc , by cowboys

Roderick or Rodrigo. A Spanish hero round whom many legends have collected He was the thirty-fourth and last of the Visigothic kings, came to the throne in 710, and was routed, and probably slain, by the Moors under Tarik in 711 Southey took him as the hero of his *Roderick, the last of the Goths* (1814), where he appears as the son of Theodofred, and grandson of King Chindasuintho Witiza, the usurper, put out the eyes of Theodofred, and murdered Favila, a younger brother of Roderick, but Roderick, having recovered his father's throne, put out the eyes of the usurper The sons of Witiza, joining with Count Julian, invited the aid of Muza ibn Nozeir, the Arab chief, who sent Tarik into Spain with a large army Roderick was routed at the battle of Guadalete, near Xeres de la Frontera (711), he himself disappeared from the battlefield, and the Spaniards transformed him into a hero who would come again to save his country. One legend relates that he was befriended by a shepherd who was rewarded with the royal chain and ring. Roderick passed the night in the cell of a hermit, who told him that by way of penance he must pass certain days in a tomb full of snakes, toads, and lizards After three days the hermit went to see him, and he was unhurt, ' because the Lord kept His anger against him " The hermit went home, passed the night in prayer, and went again to the tomb, when Rodrigo said, "They eat me now, they eat me now, I feel the adder's bite " So his sin was atoned for, and he died

Roderigo (rod e rē' gō). A Venetian gentleman in Shakespeare's *Othello* He was in love with Desdemona, and when the lady eloped with Othello, hated the "noble Moor " Iago took advantage of this temper for his own ends, told his dupe the Moor would change; therefore "put money in thy purse." The burden of his advice was always the same—"Put money in thy purse "

Rodomontade. Bluster brag, or a blustering and bragging speech, from Rodomont, the brave but braggart leader of the Saracens in Boiardo's *Orlando Innamorato*.

Rodrigo. *See* RODERICK

Roe, Richard. *See* DOE

Rogation Days. The Monday, Tuesday, and Wednesday before Ascension Day Rogation is the Latin equivalent of the Greek word "Litany," and on the three Rogation days "the Litany of the Saints" is appointed to be sung by the clergy and people in public procession ("Litany," Gr. *litaneia*, supplication "Rogation," Lat *rogatio*, same meaning)

The Rogation Days used to be called *Gang Days*, from the custom of *ganging* round the country parishes to beat the bounds (*see* BOUNDS) at this time Similarly, the weed milkwort is still called *Rogation* or *Gangflower*, from the custom of decorating the pole (carried on such occasions by the charity children) with these flowers

Roger. The cook in Chaucer's *Canterbury Tales* "He cowde roste, sethe, broille, and frie, make mortreux, and wel bake a pye," but Harry Baily, the host, said to him—

Now telle on Roger, and loke it be good,
For many a Jakk of Dover hastow sold,
That hath be twyes hoot and twyes cold
Prologue to Cook's Tale

In World War II **Roger** was a simple code word of American origin used in wireless conversations to denote "message understood." Like many war terms it passed for a time into civilian speech.

Sir Roger de Coverley. The simple, good, and altogether delightful country squire created by Steele as the chief character in the club that was supposed to write for the *Spectator* He was developed by Addison, and it is to the latter that we are indebted for this portrait of a simple English gentleman He has left his name to a popular country dance which, he tells us, was invented by his great-grandfather. Coverley is intended for Cowley, near Oxford

The Jolly Roger. The black flag with skull and cross-bones, the favourite ensign of pirates

Rogero. Ruggiero, or Rizieri (ro jẽr' ō, ruj ēr' o, ritz i ēr' i) of Risa (in *Orlando Furioso*), was brother of Marphisa, and son of Rogero and Galacella. His mother was slain by Agolant and his sons, and he was nursed by a lioness He was brought up by Atlantes, a magician, who gave him a shield of such dazzling splendour that everyone quailed who set eyes on it, but, holding it unknightly to carry a charmed shield, he threw it into a well. He deserted from the Moorish army to Charlemagne, and was baptized, and his marriage with Bradamant, Charlemagne's niece, and election to the crown of Bulgaria conclude the poem

Who more courteous than Rogero?
CERVANTES *Don Quixote*

In *Jerusalem Delivered* Rogero is brother of Bœmond, and son of Roberto Guiscardo, of the Norman race He was one of the band of adventurers in the crusading army, and was slain by Tisaphernes (Bk xx)

Rogue. One of the "canting" words used first in the 16th century to describe sturdy beggars and vagrants (perhaps from some outstanding member of the class named Roger) There is a good description of them in Harman's *Caveat for Common Cursitors vulgarly called Vagabones,* ch iv The expression *rogues and vagabonds* has since 1572 been applied in the Vagrancy Acts to all sorts of wandering, disorderly, or dissolute persons

It is Ordered and Ordained by the Lords and Commons in this present Parliament assembled and by Authority of the same, That all Stage-players and Players of Interludes and Common Plays are hereby declared to be, and are and shall be taken to be Rogues and punishable within the Statutes of the Thirty ninth year of the Reign of Queen Elizabeth and the seventh year of the Reign of King James whether they be wanderers or no —*Ordinance for Suppression of all Stage-Plays and Interludes,* Feb. 11th, 1647

Rogue in grain. *See* GRAIN.

Rogue elephant A savage and destructive elephant that lives apart from the herd, always vicious and dangerous

Rogue's badge. A race-horse or a hunter that becomes obstinate and refuses to do its work is known as a *rogue,* and the blinkers that it is made to wear are the *rogue's badge.*

Rogues' gallery. The collection of portraits of criminals kept by the police

Rogues' Latin. The same as "thieves' Latin." *See* LATIN

Rogues' March. The tune played when an undesirable soldier is drummed out of his regiment, hence, an ignominious dismissal.

Roi Panade (*King of Slops*). Louis XVIII was so nicknamed (1755, 1814-24).

Roland or (in Ital) **Orlando.** The most famous of Charlemagne's paladins, slain at the battle of Roncesvalles (778), called "The Christian Theseus" and "the Achilles of the West." He was Count of Mans and Knight of Blaives, and son of Duke Milo of Aiglant, his mother being Bertha, the sister of Charlemagne. Fable has it that he was eight feet high, and had an open countenance, which invited confidence, but inspired respect, and he is represented as brave, loyal, and simple-minded On the return of Charlemagne from Spain Roland, who commanded the rearguard, fell into the ambuscade at Roncesvalles, in the Pyrenees, and perished with all the flower of the Frankish chivalry

His achievements are recorded in the Chronicle attributed to Turpin (d 794), Archbishop of Rheims, which was not written till the 11th or 12th century, and he is the hero of the *Song of Roland* (*see* below), Boiardo's *Orlando Innamorato,* and Ariosto's *Orlando Furioso* In Pulci's *Morgante Maggiore* he is also a principal character, and converts the giant Morgante to Christianity.

In *Orlando Furioso* (i e. "Orlando mad"), although married to Aldabella he fell in love with Angelica, daughter of the infidel king of Cathay, she married Medoro, a Moor, with whom she fled to India, whereupon Orlando went mad, or rather his wits were taken from him for three months by way of punishment, and deposited in the moon. Astolpho went to the moon in Elijah's chariot, and St. John gave him an urn containing the lost wits. On reaching earth again, Astolpho first bound the madman, then, holding the urn to his nose, Orlando was cured of both his madness and his love.

A Roland for an Oliver. A blow for a blow, tit for tat. The exploits of Roland and Oliver, another of the paladins of Charlemagne, are so similar that it is difficult to keep them distinct What Roland did Oliver did, and what Oliver did Roland did At length the two met in single combat, and fought for five consecutive days on an island in the Rhine, but neither gained the least advantage Shakespeare alludes to the phrase· "England all Olivers and Rolands bred" (1 *Henry VI,* ι, 2), and Edward Hall, the historian, almost a century before Shakespeare, writes.—

But to have a Roland to resist an Oliver, he sent solempne ambassadors to the King of Englande, offeryng hym hys doughter in mariage —*Henry VI*

Childe Roland. Youngest brother of the "fair burd Helen" in the old Scottish ballad Guided by Merlin, he undertook to bring his sister from Elf-land, whither the fairies had carried her, and succeeded in his perilous exploit

Childe Roland to the dark tower came,
His word was still "Fie, foh, and fum,
I smell the blood of a Britishman "
King Lear, ιιι, 4

Browning's poem, *Child Roland to the Dark Tower Came,* is not connected in any way (except by the first line) with the old ballad

Like the blast of Roland's horn. Roland had a wonderful ivory horn, named "Olivant," that he won from the giant Jutmundus When he was set upon by the Gascons at Roncesvalles he sounded it to give Charlemagne notice of his danger At the third blast it cracked in two, but it was so loud that birds fell dead and the whole Saracen army was panic-struck Charlemagne heard the sound at St Jean Pied de Port, and rushed to the rescue, but arrived too late

Oh, for one blast of that dread horn
On Fontarabian echoes borne,
That to King Charles did come
SCOTT *Marmion,* νι, 33.

Roland's sword. Durindana, or Durandal, which was fabled to have once belonged to Hector, and which—like the horn—Roland won from the giant Jutmundus. It had in its hilt a thread from the Virgin Mary's cloak, a tooth of St Peter, one of St Denis's hairs, and a drop of St. Basil's blood. Legend relates that, to prevent Durandal falling into the hands of the Saracens, after he had received his death-wound he strove to break it on a rock, but as it was unbreakable he hurled it into a poisoned stream, where it remains for ever.

The Song (Chanson) of Roland. The 11th-century *chanson de geste* ascribed to the Norman trouvère Théroulde, or Turoldus, which tells the story of the death of Roland and all the paladins at Roncesvalles, and of Charlemagne's vengeance When Charlemagne had been six years in Spain he sent Ganelon on an embassy to Marsillus, the pagan king of Saragossa Ganelon, out of jealousy, betrayed to Marsillus the route which the Christian army designed to take on its way home. and the pagan king arrived at Roncesvalles just as Roland was conducting through the pass a rear-guard of 20,000 men, he fought till 100,000 Saracens lay slain, and only 50 of his own men survived At this juncture another army, con-

sisting of 50,000 men, poured from the mountains. Roland now blew his enchanted horn, and blew so loudly that the veins of his neck started Charlemagne heard the blast, but Ganelon persuaded him that it was only his nephew hunting the deer Roland died of his wounds.

The *Song* runs to 4,000 lines, and it was probably parts of this that—as we are told by Wace in the *Roman de Rou*—the Norman minstrel sang to encourage William's soldiers at the battle of Hastings —

Taillefer, the minstrel-knight, bestrode
A gallant steed, and swiftly rode
Before the Duke, and sang the song
Of Charlemagne, of Roland strong,
Of Oliver, and those beside
Brave knights at Roncevaux that died
Arthur S Way's rendering

To die like Roland To die of starvation or thirst One legend has it that Roland escaped the general slaughter in the defile of Roncesvalles, and died of hunger and thirst in seeking to cross the Pyrenees He was buried at Blayes, in the church of St Raymond; but his body was removed afterwards to Roncesvalles

Rolandseck Tower, opposite the Drachenfels on the Rhine, 22 miles above Cologne The legend is that when Roland went to the wars, a false report of his death was brought to his betrothed, who retired to a convent in the isle of Nonnewerth When he returned home flushed with glory, and found that his lady-love had taken the veil, he built the castle which bears his name, and overlooks the nunnery, that he might at least see his heart-treasure, lost to him for ever

Roll. The flying roll of Zechariah (v, 1-5) "Predictions of evils to come on a nation are like the flying roll of Zechariah " This roll (twenty cubits long and ten wide) was full of maledictions, threats, and calamities about to befall the Jews The parchment being unrolled fluttered in the air.

A rolling stone *See* STONE.

Rolling stock. All the wheeled equipment of a railway that is fitted to run on rails, the locomotives, passenger coaches, vans, goods trucks, etc

Roller-Coaster. An open-air railway set in pleasure grounds, etc running up and down steep inclines, an improvement on the old-fashioned switchback railway

Rolls, The. The former building in Chancery Lane where the records in the custody of the Master of the Rolls were kept; now replaced by the Public Record Office It included a court of justice and a chapel, and was originally built by Henry III as a *Domus Conversorum* (house for lay monks) for converted Jews. In the time of Edward III it was devoted to the purpose of storing records.

The Master of the Rolls. The head of the Public Record Office, an ex-officio Judge of the Court of Appeal and a member of the Judicial Committee, ranking next after the Lord Chief Justice. His jurisdiction was formerly exercised in Chancery as the deputy of the Lord Chancellor, and he also sat independently in the Rolls Chapel.

To be struck off the rolls. To be removed from the official list of qualified solicitors, and so prohibited from practising. This is done in cases of professional misconduct.

Rollrich or Rowldrich Stones (rōl' rich), near Chipping Norton (Oxfordshire). A number of large stones in a circle, which tradition says are *men* turned to stone. The highest of them is called *the King*, who "would have been king of England if he could have caught sight of Long Compton," which may be seen a few steps farther on, five other large stones are called the knights, and the rest common soldiers.

Roly-poly A crust with jam rolled up into a pudding, a little fat child. Roly is a thing rolled with the diminutive added. In some parts of Scotland the game of ninepins is called *rouly pouly*

Romaic. Modern or Romanized Greek.

Roman. Pertaining to Rome, especially ancient Rome, or to the Roman Catholic Church. As a surname or distinctive title the adjective has been applied to Giulio Pippi, *Giulio Romano* (1492-1546), the Italian artist
Adrian van Roomen (1581-1615), the famous mathematician, *Adrianus Romanus*
Stephen Picart (1631-1721), the French engraver, *le Romain*
Jean Dumont (1700-81), the French painter, *le Romain.*
Marcus Terentius Varro (116-27 B C) was called the *Most Learned of the Romans*, and Rienzi (1313-54), the Italian patriot and "last of the Tribunes," was known as *Ultimus Romanorum*, the Last of the Romans—an honorific title later applied to Horace Walpole, Charles James Fox, and others.

King of the Romans. The title usually assumed by the sovereign of the Holy Roman Empire previous to his actual coronation in the Holy City. Napoleon's son, afterwards the Duke of Reichstadt, was styled the King of Rome at his birth in 1811.

Roman architecture. A style of architecture, distinguished by its massive character and abundance of ornament, which combines the Greek orders with the use of the arch. It is largely a corruption of the Doric and Ionic.

Roman birds. Eagles; so called because the ensign of the Roman legion was an eagle

Roman figures. *See* NUMERALS.

Roman roads in Britain. *See* ERMINE, FOSSE, ICKNIELD, WATLING.
Fair weyes many on ther ben in England
But four most of all ben zunderstond
Fram the south into the north takit *Erming-ttrete*,
Fram the east into the west goeth *Ikeneld-strete*,
Fram south-est to North-west (that is sum deegrete)
Fram Dover into Chester go'th *Watling-strete*,
The forth is most of all that tills from Toteneys—
Fram the one end of Cornwall anon to Catenays
     [Caithness]—
Fram the south to North-est into Englondes end
Fosse men callith thisk voix
                              ROBERT OF GLOUCESTER
The most remarkable of the numerous Roman remains in England are probably—
The pharos, church, and trenches in Dover,

Chilham Castle, Richborough, and Reculver forts, the amphitheatres at Silchester (Berkshire), Dorchester, Nisconium (Salop), and Caerleon; Hadrian's wall (*q v.*), the wall, baths, and Newport Gate of Lincoln; the earthworks at Verulam, near St. Albans, York (Eboracum), where Severus and Constantius Chlorus died, and Constantine the Great was born; and the ancient parts of Bath.

Roman type. Ordinary type, as distinguished from italic, clarendon, gothic or "black letter," etc , so called because founded on that used in ancient Roman inscriptions and manuscripts

The Holy Roman Empire. *See* HOLY.

The Last of the Romans. *See above, also* LAST

The Roman Empire The Empire established on the ruins of the Republic by Augustus in 27 B C , and lasting till A D 395, when it was divided into the Western or Latin Empire, and the Eastern or Greek.
The Roman Empire was a power, and not a nation . The name *Roman*, in the use of Procopius, when it does not refer geographically to the elder Rome means any man, of whatever race, who is a subject of the Roman Empire or who serves in the Roman armies His nationality may not be only Greek, Macedonian, or Thracian, but Gothic, Persian, or Hunnish — FREEMAN *Historical Essays*, III, 246

The Roman Republic was established about 509 B C after the overthrow of the last of the seven kings, Tarquinius Superbus, and survived till it was superseded in 27 B C. by the Empire
For a few months in 1848-49, after the flight of Pius IX, the people of Rome declared themselves a republic under the triumvirate of Mazzini, Saffi, and Armellini. It is one of the ironies of history that this Roman Republic was destroyed by the army of Republican France

Roman de la Rose. *See* ROSE, ROMANCE OF THE

Romance. Applied in linguistics to the languages, especially Old French, sprung from the Latin spoken in the European province of the Roman Empire, hence, as a noun, the word came to mean a mediæval tale in Old French or Provençal describing, usually in mixed prose and verse, the marvellous adventures of a hero of chivalry, the transition to the modern meanings—a work of fiction in which the scenes, incidents, etc , are more or less removed from common life and are surrounded by a halo of mystery—or the atmosphere of strangeness and imaginary adventure itself—is simple.

The mediæval romances fall into three main groups or *cycles*, viz., the Arthurian, the Charlemagne cycle, and the cycle of Alexander the Great. Nearly, but not quite, all the romances are connected with one or other of these.

Romance languages. Those languages which are the immediate offspring of Latin, as the Italian, Spanish, Portuguese, and French Early French is emphatically so called, hence Bouillet says, *"Le romain était universellement parlé en Gaule au dixième siècle "*
Frankis speech is called Romance,
So say clerks and men of France.
                              ROBERT LE BRUN

Romanesque (rō mǎn esk´). A simple and severe style of European architecture which preceded the Gothic; in England it was approximately synonymous with the Norman The name comes from the fact that the style was the Christian adaptation of, or evolution from Roman architecture It has two main characteristics—the use of the rounded as opposed to the pointed arch, and great strength, used as a safety measure to overcome an ignorance of stresses which were finally mastered by Gothic architects

Romantic Revival, The. The literary movement that began in Germany in the last quarter of the 18th century having for its object a return from the Augustan or classical formalism of the time to the freer fancies and methods of romance. It was led by Schiller, Goethe, Novalis, and Tieck, spread to England, where it affected the work of Collins and Gray and received an impetus from the publication of Percy's *Reliques* and Macpherson's *Ossian*, and, immensely stimulated by the French Revolution, effected a transformation of English literature through the writings of Keats, Byron, Wordsworth, Shelley, Coleridge, Scott, etc In France its chief exponents were Chénier, Lamartine, de Musset, and Victor Hugo.

Romany. A gipsy, or the gipsy language, the speech of the Roma or Zincali. The word is from Gipsy *rom*, a man, or husband

A learned Sclavonian said of Rommany, that he found it interesting to be able to study a Hindu dialect in the heart of Europe —LELAND *English Gipsies*, ch. viii

Romany rye. One who enters into the gipsy spirit, learns their language, lives with them as one of themselves, etc *Rye* is gipsy for gentleman George Borrow's book with this title (a sequel to *Lavengro*) was published in 1857

Rome. The greatest city of the ancient world, according to legend founded (753 B C) by Romulus (*q.v.*) and named after him, but in all probability so called from Greek *rhoma* (strength), a suggestion confirmed by its other name Valentia, from *valens* (strong).

Oh, that all Rome had but one head, that I might strike it off at a blow! Caligula, the Roman emperor, is said to have uttered this sentiment

Rome penny, Rome scot. The same as Peter's penny (*q v*)

Rome's best wealth is patriotism. So said Mettius Curtius, when he jumped into the chasm which the soothsayers gave out would never close till Rome threw therein "its best wealth."

Rome was not built in a day. Achievements of great pith and moment are not accomplished without patient perseverance and a considerable interval of time It is an old saying, and is to be found in Heywood's *Collection* (1562).

'Tis ill sitting at Rome and striving with the Pope. Don't tread on a man's corns when you are living with him or are in close touch with him—especially if he's powerful

When you go to Rome, do as Rome does Conform to the manners and customs of those amongst whom you live, "Don't wear a brown hat in Friesland " St Monica and her son St Augustine said to St Ambrose. "At Rome they fast on Saturday, but not so at Milan, which practice ought to be observed?" To which St Ambrose replied, "When I am at Milan, I do as they do at Milan; but when I go to Rome, I do as Rome does!" (*Epistle* xxxvi) *Cp 2 Kings* v, 18

The saying is to be found in that great storehouse of proverbs, Porter's *Two Angry Women of Abingdon* (1599)

Romeo and Juliet (rō mē ō, joo´ li et) Shakespeare s tragedy (first published 1597) is founded on the story of the lovers of Verona as told in Arthur Brooke's poem, *The Tragicall Historye of Romeus and Juliet, containing a rare example of love constancie, with the subtill counsels and practices of an old Fryer* (1562), and a story in Painter's *Palace of Pleasure* (1576) Its earliest appearance in literature is in Masuccio's *Novelle* (Naples, 1476); next, as *La Giulietta*, by Luigi da Porta (1535), and then in Bandello's *Novella* (Lucca, 1554). It was the French translation of this latter by Pierre Belleforest that was followed by Brooke and Painter

Girolamo della Corte's *History of Verona to* 1560 places the story in 1303, when a member of the Scala family (transformed by Shakespeare to *Escalus*) was ruling in Verona, and in Dante's *Divina Commedia* (about 1300-18) the Capulets and Montagues appear among the quarrelsome inhabitants of the town.

Romulus (rom´ūlus) With his twin brother, Remus, the legendary and eponymous founder of Rome They were sons of Mars and Rhea Silvia, who, because she was a vestal virgin, was condemned to death, while the sons were exposed They were, however, suckled by a she-wolf, and eventually set about founding a city but quarrelled over the plans, and Remus was slain by his brother in anger Romulus was later taken to the heavens by his father, Mars, in a fiery chariot, and was worshipped by the Romans under the name of Quirinus

The Second Romulus. Camillus was so called because he saved Rome from the Gauls, 365 B C.

The Third Romulus. Caius Marius, who saved Rome from the Teutons and Cimbri in 101 B C.

We need no Romulus to account for Rome. We require no hypothetical person to account for a plain fact.

Roncesvalles (rons´ val) A defile in the Pyrenees, famous for the disaster which here befell the rear of Charlemagne's army, on the return march from Saragossa (778) Ganelon betrayed Roland (*q v*) to Marsillus, king of the Saracens, and an ambuscade attacking the Franks killed every man of them, including Roland, Oliver, and all the paladins See SONG OF ROLAND *under* ROLAND

Roncesvalles is said to have left its name to *rouncival* peas, a large kind of garden pea. See ROUNCIVAL In his *Glossographia* (1674) Blount has—

Rounceval Peas, a sort of great Peas, well known, and took name from Ronceval, a place at the foot of the Pyrenean Mountains from whence they first came to us

But there is no confirmation of this

Ronyon or **Runnion** (ron′ yon, rŭn′ yon) A term of contempt to a woman It is probably the French *rogneux* (scabby, mangy)

> You hag, you baggage, you polecat, you ronyon'
> out, out!—*Merry Wives of Windsor*, iv, 2
>
> "Aroint thee, witch!" the rump-fed ronyon cries.—
> *Macbeth*, i, 3.

Rood (connected with *rod*) The Cross of the Crucifixion; or a crucifix, especially the large one that was formerly set on the stone or timber rood-**screen** that divides the nave from the choir in churches This is usually richly decorated with statues and carvings of saints, emblems, etc , and frequently is surmounted by a gallery called the rood-loft.

> And then to zee the rood-loft,
> Zo bravely zet with zaints
> PERCY *Ballad of Plain Truth*, ii, 292

By the rood; by the holy rood. Old expletives used by way of asservation When the Queen asks Hamlet if he has forgotten her, he answers, "No, by the rood, not so" (iii, 4)

Rood Day, Holy Rood Day (*q v*); September 14th (the Exaltation of the Cross), or May 3rd (the Invention of the Cross).

Roodselken. An old country name for vervain, or "the herb of the cross "

> Hallowed by thou, vervain, as thou growest in the ground,
> For in the Mount of Calvary thou wast found
> Thou healedst Christ our Saviour, and staunchedst His bleeding wound;
> In the name of Father, Son and Holy Ghost, I take thee from the ground
> FOLKARD *Plant Lore*, p 47.

Rook. A cheat "To rook," to cheat, "to rook a pigeon," to fleece a greenhorn Sometimes it simply means to win from another at a game of chance or skill.

Rook, the castle in chess, is through French and Spanish from Persian *rukh*, which is said to have meant a warrior

Rookery. Any low, densely populated neighbourhood, especially one frequented by thieves and vagabonds The allusion is to the way in which rooks build their nests clustered closely together. Colonies of seals, and places where seals or seabirds collect in the breeding season are also known as "rookeries "

Room. Your room is better than your company. Your absence is more to be wished than your presence An old phrase, it occurs in Stanyhurst's *Description of Ireland* (1577), Greene's *Quip for an Upstart Courtier* (1592), etc

Roost. A strong current or furious tide betwixt island groups, especially in the Orkneys and Shetlands

To rule the roost. *See* ROAST

Root. Root and branch. The whole of it without any exceptions or omissions; "lock, stock, and barrel " The Puritans of about 1640 who wanted to extirpate the episcopacy altogether were known as "Root-and-branch men," or "Rooters," and the term has since been applied to other political factions who are anxious to "go the whole hog "

To root (U.S.A). To support a sporting team.

The root of the matter. Its true inwardness, its actual base and foundation. The phrase comes from *Job* xix, 28—

> But ye should say, Why persecute we him, seeing the root of the matter is found in me?

To take or strike root To become permanently or firmly established

Rope. A taste of the rope's end. A flogging—especially among seamen

Fought back to the ropes Fought to the bitter end A phrase from the prize-ring, the "ropes" forming the boundary of the "ring "

> It is a battle that must be fought game, and right back to the ropes.—BOLDREWOOD. *Robbery Under Arms*, ch xxxiii

Ropes of sand *See* SAND

She is on her high ropes. In a distant and haughty temper, "high and mighty " The allusion is to a rope-dancer, who looks down on the spectators

The Rope-walk Former barristers slang for an Old Bailey practice Thus, "Gone into the rope-walk" means, he has taken up practice in the Old Bailey The allusion is to the murder trials taking place there, a convicted murderer "getting the rope '

To come to the end of one's rope or tether. *See* TETHER

To fight with a rope round one's neck. To fight with a certainty of losing your life unless you conquer

> You must send in a large force, . for, as he fights with a rope round his neck, he will struggle to the last —KINGSTON· *The Three Admirals*, viii

To give one rope enough. To permit a person to continue in wrongdoing till he reaps the consequences "Give him rope enough and he'll hang himself" is a common saying of one addicted to evil courses

To know the ropes. To be up to all the tricks and dodges, to know exactly what is the proper thing to do

To rope one in. To get him to take part in some scheme, enterprise, etc. An expression from the western states of America, where horses and cattle are roped in with a lasso

You carry a rope in your pocket (Fr) Said of a person very lucky at cards, from the superstition that a bit of rope with which a man has been hanged, carried in the pocket, secures luck at cards.

Ropeable. In Australia a term now applied to a person who is in a bad temper Originally it meant cattle so wild that they could be controlled only by roping

Mistress Roper. A cant name given to the Marines by British sailors The wit lies in the awkward way that marines handle the ship's ropes

To marry Mistress Roper is to enlist in the Marines.

Ropey. A phrase widely used by the British armed forces in World War II to denote anything inferior or worn-out—synonymous, in this connexion, with "old-fashioned "

Roque, St. *See* ROCH.

Roquelaure (rōk' lōr) A cloak for men, reaching to the knees It was worn in the 18th century, and is so named from Antoine-Gaston, Duke de Roquelaure (1656-1738), a Marshal of France

"Your honour's roquelaure," replied the corporal, "has not once been had on since the night before your honour received your wound "—STERNE *Tristram Shandy, Story of Le Fevre*

Rory O'More. Slang for a *door*. *See* RHYMING SLANG

Rosabelle The favourite palfrey of Mary Queen of Scots

Rosalia, or Rosalie, St. (rō zā' li a, roz' e lē) The patron saint of Palermo, in art depicted in a cave with a cross and skull, or else in the act of receiving a rosary or chaplet of roses from the Virgin She lived in the 12th century, and is said to have been carried by angels to an inaccessible mountain, where she dwelt for many years in the cleft of a rock, a part of which she wore away with her knees in her devotions. A chapel has been built there, with a marble statue, to commemorate the event

Rosalind (roz' ā lind). The anagrammatic name under which Spenser introduces his early love, Rosa Daniel (sister of Samuel Daniel, the poet), into the *Shepherd's Calendar*, he himself figuring as "Colin Clout " She was the wife of John Florin, the lexicographer who is caricatured in *Love's Labour's Lost* as "Holofernes" (*i e* [Jo]h[an]nes Floreo)

In Shakespeare's *As You Like It* Rosalind is the daughter of the banished duke, brought up with Celia in the court of Frederick, the duke's brother, and usurper of his dominions After sundry adventures, in the course of which she disguises herself as a youth and Celia as a peasant-girl, she obtains her father's consent to marry her lover, Orlando

Rosamond, The Fair (roz' a mund) Higden, monk of Chester, writing about 1350, says· "She was the fayre daughter of Walter, Lord Clifford, concubine of Henry II, and poisoned by Queen Elianor, A D. 1177 Henry made for her a house of wonderful working, so that no man or woman might come to her This house was named Labyrinthus, and was wrought like unto a knot in a garden called a maze. But the queen came to her by a clue of thredde, and so dealt with her that she lived not long after She was buried at Godstow, in an house of nunnes, with these verses upon her tombe —

Hic jacet in tumba Rosa mundi, non Rosa munda;
Non redolet, sed olet, que redolere solet "
Here Rose the graced, not Rose the chaste, reposes,
The smell that rises is no smell of roses

This "evidence," dating nearly 200 years after the supposed event, is all the substantiation we have for the popular legend about the labyrinth; and there is none for the stories that Rosamund Clifford was the mother of William Longsword and Geoffrey, Archbishop of York A subterranean labyrinth in Blenheim Park, near Woodstock, is still pointed out as "Rosamund's Bower "

Jane Clifford was her name, as books aver
Fair Rosamund was but her *nom de guerre*
DRYDEN *Epilogue to Henry II*

Rosary (rō' zàr i) The bead-roll employed by Roman Catholics for keeping count of their repetitions of certain prayers; also, these prayers themselves The rope of beads consists of three parts, each of which symbolizes five mysteries connected with Christ or His virgin mother The word is said by some to be derived from the chaplet of beads, perfumed with roses, given by the Virgin to St Dominic. (This cannot be correct, as it was in use A D 1100) Others say the first chaplet of the kind was made of rosewood, others, again, maintain that it takes its name from the "Mystical Rose," one of the titles of the Virgin. The set is sometimes called "fifteens," from its containing 15 "doxologies," 15 "Our Fathers," and 10 times 15, or 150, "Hail Marys."

The "Devotion of the Rosary" takes different forms —(1) *the Greater Rosary*, or recitation of the whole fifteen mysteries, (2) *the Lesser Rosary*, or recitation of one of the mysteries, and (3) *the Living Rosary*, or the recitation of the fifteen mysteries by fifteen different persons in combination.

Rosciad (ros' i ād) A satire by Charles Churchill, published in 1761, it canvasses the faults and merits of the metropolitan actors.

Roscius (ros' i us) A first-rate actor, so called from Quintus Roscius (d about 62 B C), the Roman actor, unrivalled for his grace of action, melody of voice, conception of character, and delivery

What scene of death hath Roscius now to act?
3 *Henry VI*, v, 6.

Another Roscius So Camden terms Richard Burbage (d 1619).

The British Roscius Thomas Betterton (1635-1710), of whom Cibber says, "He alone was born to speak what only Shakespeare knew to write " The title was also accorded to Garrick

The Roscius of France Michel Boyron (1653-1729), generally called Baron.

The Young Roscius. William Henry West Betty (1791-1874) His first public appearance was in 1803 (as Oswyn, in *Zara*), and, after achieving astonishing success, he left the stage in 1824 It is said that in fifty-six nights he realized £34,000

Rose. Mediæval legend asserts that the first roses appeared miraculously at Bethlehem as the result of the prayers of a "fayre Mayden" who had been falsely accused and was sentenced to death by burning. As Sir John Mandeville tells the tale (*Travels*, ch. vi), after her prayer

sche entered into the Fuyer, and anon was the Fuyr quenched and oute; and the Brondes that weren brennynge, becomen red Roseres, and the Brondes that weren not kyndled, becomen white Roseres, fulle of Roses And these weren the first Roseres and Roses, both white and rede, that evere any Man saughe. And thus was this Mayden saved be the Grace of God.

The *Rose* has been an emblem of England since the time of the Wars of the Roses (*see below*), when the Lancastrians adopted a *red* rose as their badge, and the Yorkists a *white*. When the parties were united in the person of Henry VII the united Tudor rose was taken as his device.

The Red Rose of Lancaster was, says Camden, the accepted badge of Edmund Plantagenet, second son of Henry III, and of the first Duke of Lancaster, surnamed Crouch-back It was also the cognizance of John of Gaunt, second Duke of Lancaster, in virtue of his wife, who was godchild of Edmund Crouch-back, and his sole heir; and, in later times, of the Richmonds Hence the rose in the mouth of one of the foxes which figure in the sign of the Holland Arms, Kensington The daughter of the Duke of Richmond (Lady Caroline Lennox) ran away with Mr Henry Fox, after-wards Baron Holland of Foxley, the *Fox* ran off with the *Rose*.

The White Rose was not first adopted by the Yorkists during the contest for the crown, as Shakespeare says It was an hereditary cog-nizance of the House of York, and had been borne by them ever since the title was first created It was adopted by the Jacobites as an emblem of the Pretender, because his ad-herents were obliged to abet him *sub rosa* (in secret) Cecily Nevill, wife of Richard, Duke of York, and mother of Edward IV and Richard III, was known as *The White Rose of Raby*. She was a daughter of Ralph, Earl of Westmore-land, and granddaughter of John of Gaunt, and was the youngest of twenty-one children

In heraldry the Rose is also used as the mark of cadency for a seventh son

In Christian symbolism the *Rose*, as being emblematic of a paragon or one without peer, is peculiarly appropriated to the Virgin Mary, one of whose titles is "The Mystical Rose " It is also the attribute of St Dorothea, who carries roses in a basket, of St Casilda, St. Elizabeth of Portugal, and St. Rose of Viterbo, who carry roses in either their hands or caps, of St Therese of Lisieux, who scatters red roses, and of St. Rosalie, St Angelus, St Rose of Lima, St Ascylus, and St Victoria, who wear crowns of roses

In the language of flowers, different roses have a different signification For example —
The Burgundy Rose signifies simplicity and beauty
The China Rose, grace or beauty ever fresh.
The Daily Rose, a smile
The Dog Rose, pleasure mixed with pain.
A Faded Rose, beauty is fleeting
The Japan Rose, beauty your sole attraction.
The Moss Rose, voluptuous love
The Musk Rose, capricious beauty
The Provence Rose, my heart is in flames
The White Rose Bud, too young to love
The White Rose full of buds, secrecy.
A wreath of Roses, beauty and virtue re-warded.
The Yellow Rose, infidelity

Rose Alley Ambuscade, The. The attack on Dryden by masked ruffians, probably in the employ of Rochester and the Duchess of Portsmouth, on December 18th, 1679, in revenge for an anonymous *Essay on Satire* attacking the king, Rochester, and the Duchesses of Cleveland and Portsmouth, which was erroneously attributed to Dryden.

Rose Coffee-house, The. The tavern at the corner of Russell Street and Bow Street, Covent Garden, where Dryden presided over the genius of the town Formerly known as "The Red Cow," it was subsequently "Will's "

Rose of Jericho, The. The popular name of *Anastatica hierochuntina*, a small branching plant native to the sandy deserts of Arabia, Egypt, and Syria. When it is dry, if it is exposed to moisture, the branches uncurl. Also called the *rose of the Virgin*, or *Rosa Mariæ*.

Rose Noble. A gold coin worth about 6s 8d current in the 15th and 16th centuries, so called because it was stamped with a rose The value varied from time to time and place to place *Cp* NOBLE.

Rose, The Romance of the. An early French poem of over 20,000 lines, an elaborate alle-gory on the Art of Love beneath which can be seen a faithful picture of contemporary life It was begun by Guillaume de Lorris in the latter half of the 13th century, and continued by Jean de Meung in the early part of the 14th. The poet is accosted by Dame Idleness, who con-ducts him to the Palace of Pleasure, where he meets Love, accompanied by Sweet-looks, Riches, Jollity, Courtesy, Liberality, and Youth, who spend their time in dancing, sing-ing, and other amusements By this retinue the poet is conducted to a bed of roses, where he singles out one and attempts to pluck it, when an arrow from Cupid's bow stretches him fainting on the ground, and he is carried far away from the flower of his choice As soon as he recovers, he finds himself alone, and resolves to return to his rose Welcome goes with him; but Danger, Shame-face, Fear, and Slander obstruct him at every turn. Reason advises him to abandon the pursuit, but this he will not do, whereupon Pity and Liberality aid him in reaching the rose of his choice, and Venus per-mits him to touch it with his lips Meanwhile, Slander rouses up Jealousy, who seizes Wel-come, whom he casts into a strong castle, and gives the key of the castle door to an old hag Here the poet is left to mourn over his fate, and the original poem ends

In the second part—which is much the longer—the same characters appear, but the spirit of the poem is altogether different, the author being interested in life as a whole in-stead of solely in love, and directing his satire especially against women.

A 15th-century English version is often pub-lished with Chaucer's works, and it is possible that the first 1,700 lines or so are by Chaucer

Rose Sunday. The fourth Sunday in Lent, when the Pope blesses the "Golden Rose" (*q.v*).

A bed of roses *See* BED.

No rose without a thorn. There is always something to detract from pleasure—"every sweet has its sour," "there is a crook in every lot "

Sing Old Rose and burn the bellows. "Old Rose" was the title of a song now unknown, thus, Izaak Walton, in the *Compleat Angler* (1653) says, "Let's sing *Old Rose* " *Burn the bellows* may be a schoolboys' perversion of *burn libellos*. At breaking-up time the boys might say, "Let's sing *Old Rose* and burn our schoolbooks" (*libellos*) This does not accord ill with the meaning of the well-known catch—

Now we're met like jovial fellows,
Let us do as wise men tell us,
Sing *Old Rose* and burn the bellows.

Under the rose (Lat *sub rosa*). In strict confidence The origin of the phrase is wrapped in obscurity, but the story is that Cupid gave Harpocrates (the god of silence) a rose, to bribe him not to betray the amours of Venus Hence the flower became the emblem of silence, and was sculptured on the ceilings of banquet-rooms, to remind the guests that what was spoken *sub vino* was not to be uttered *sub divo* In 1526 it was placed over confessionals

The Wars of the Roses A civil contest that lasted thirty years, in which eighty princes of the blood, a large portion of the English nobility, and some 100,000 common soldiers were slain It was a struggle for the crown between the houses of York (*White rose*) and Lancaster (*Red*), York (Edward IV and V and Richard III) deriving from Edmund of Langley, Duke of York, and youngest son of Edward III, and Lancaster (Henry IV, V, and VI) from John of Gaunt, Duke of Lancaster, an elder brother of Edmund The wars started in the reign of Henry VI with a Yorkist victory at St Albans (1455) and ended with the defeat and death of the Yorkist Richard III at Bosworth (1485). His successor, Henry VII, was descended from John of Gaunt and married a descendant of Edmund of Langley, thus uniting the two houses.

Rosemary (rōz' mā ri) is *Ros-marinus* (sea-dew), and is said to be "useful in love-making." The reason is this Both Venus, the love goddess, and Rosemary or sea-dew, were offspring of the sea, and as Love is Beauty's son, Rosemary is her nearest relative

> The sea his mother Venus came on,
> And hence some reverend men approve
> Of rosemary in making love
> BUTLER   *Hudibras*, Pt ii, c 1

Rosemary, an emblem of remembrance. Thus Ophelia says, "There's rosemary, that's for remembrance." According to ancient tradition, this herb strengthens the memory As Hungary water, it was once very extensively taken to quiet the nerves It was much used in weddings, and to wear rosemary in ancient times was as significant of a wedding as to wear a white favour. When the Nurse in *Romeo and Juliet* asks, "Doth not rosemary and Romeo begin both with a [i e one] letter?" she refers to these emblematical characteristics of the herb In the language of flowers it means "Fidelity in love."

Rosemordris Circle *See* MERRY MAIDENS

Rosetta Stone, The (rō zet' a). A stone found in 1799 by M Boussard, a French officer of engineers, in an excavation made at Fort St Julien, near Rosetta, in the Nile delta It has an inscription in three different languages—the hieroglyphic, the demotic, and the Greek It was erected 195 B.C in honour of Ptolemy Epiphanes, because he remitted the dues of the sacerdotal body The great value of this stone is that it furnished the key whereby the Egyptian hieroglyphics were deciphered

Rosicrucians (roz i kroo' shåns) A secret society of mystics and alchemists that is first heard of in 1614 (when was published at Cassel the anonymous *Fama fraternitatis des löblichen Ordens des Rosenkreuzes*). But it was reputed to have been founded by a certain Christian Rosenkreutz in the second half of the 15th century Nothing is known of him or of the early history of this society, if, indeed, it ever really existed except as a kind of parody In Freemasonry there is still an order or degree named the Rosy Cross

It has been suggested that the title is neither from the founder nor from "rose cross," but from *ros crux*, dew cross Dew was considered the most powerful solvent of gold, and *cross* in alchemy is the symbol of light, because any figure of a cross contains the three letters L V X (light) "Lux" is the menstruum of the red dragon (i e corporeal light), and this gross light properly digested produces gold, and dew is the digester Hence the Rosicrucians are those who used dew for digesting lux or light, with the object of finding the philosopher's stone

> As for the Rosycross philosophers,
> Whom you will have to be but sorcerers,
> What they pretend to is no more
> Than Trismegistus did before,
> Pythagoras old Zoroaster,
> And Apollonius their master
> BUTLER   *Hudibras*, Pt. ii, 3.

Rosin Bible, The. *See* BIBLE, SPECIALLY NAMED

Rosinante. *See* ROZINANTE

Ross (Celtic) A headland; as Roslin, Culross, Rossberg, Montrose, Roxburgh, Ardrossan, etc.

Ross, from the Welsh *rhos* (a moor), found in Welsh and Cornish names. as Rossal, Rusholme, etc

The Man of Ross A name given to John Kyrle (1637-1724), a native of Whitehouse, in Gloucestershire He resided the greater part of his life in the village of Ross, Herefordshire, and was famous for his benevolence and for supplying needy parishes with churches The Kyrle Society (q v) was named in his honour.

> Who taught that heaven-directed spire to rise?
> "The Man of Ross," each lisping babe replies
> POPE *Moral Essays*.

Rosse. A famous sword which the dwarf Alberich gave to Otwit, King of Lombardy It struck so fine a cut that it left no "gap," shone like glass, and was adorned with gold

> This sword too fine I give it is all bright of hue,
> Whatever it may cleave, no gap will there ensue,
> From Alman I brought it, and Rosse is its name;
> Wherever swords are drawn, 'twill put them all to shame   *The Heldenbuch.*

Rostrum (ros' trum) A pulpit, or stand for public speakers, in Latin, the beak of a ship In Rome, the platform in the Forum from which orators addressed the public was ornamented with the *rostra*, or ship-prows, taken from the Antiates in 338 B C

Rota (rō' tá) A short-lived political club, founded in London in 1659 by James Harrington, author of *Oceana* (1656) Its objects were to introduce rotation in Government offices and voting by ballot It met at the Turk's Head, in New Palace Yard, Westminster, and did not survive the Restoration Its republican principles are outlined in *Oceana*

Rota Romana. A Roman Catholic ecclesiastical court composed of auditors under the presidency of a dean, who hear appeals and adjudicate when a conflict of rights occurs The name is said to allude to the wheel-like (Lat *rota*, wheel) plan of the room in which the court used to sit

Rotary Club. A movement among business men which takes for its motto "Service not Self" The idea originated with Paul Harris, a Chicago lawyer, in 1905 In 1911 it took root in Britain and there are now clubs in all the large towns Membership in each club is restricted to one member each of any trade, calling, or profession, lectures are delivered by experts at the weekly meetings of the clubs.

Rote. To learn by rote is to learn by means of repetition, *i e* by going over the same beaten track or *route* again and again *Rote* is really the same word as *route*

> Take hackney'd jokes from Miller got by rote
> BYRON. *English Bards, etc*

Rothschild. A family of Jewish financiers, deriving their name from the red shield by which their parent house was known in Frankfort. The family was founded by Meyer Anselm Rothschild (1743-1812) who made a fortune during the French campaigns in Germany On his death his five sons separated, extending the business throughout Europe Nathan Meyer Rothschild (1777-1836) went to London in 1805 and is reputed to have made a fortune through advance knowledge of the defeat of Napoleon at Waterloo His son Lionel (1808-79) was best known by his work for Jewish emancipation Lionel's son Nathaniel Meyer (1840-1915) was made a baron in 1885. Through the network of their continental connexions the Rothschilds have exerted great influence in many directions

Rotten Row. Said to be so called from O Fr *route le roi* or *route du roi*, because it formed part of the old royal route from the palace of the Plantagenet kings at Westminster to the royal forests Camden derives the word from *rotteran*, to muster, as the place where soldiers mustered. Another derivation is Norman *Ratten Row* (roundabout way), being the way corpses were carried to avoid the public thoroughfares. Others suggest A.S. *rot*, pleasant, cheerful, or simply *rotten*, referring to the soft material with which the road was covered

Roué (roo′ ã) The profligate Duke of Orleans, Regent of France, first used this word in its modern sense (about 1720) It was his ambition to collect round him companions as worthless as himself, and he used facetiously to boast that there was not one of them who did not deserve to be broken on the *wheel*—that being the most ordinary punishment for malefactors at the time, hence these profligates went by the name of Orleans' *roués* or wheels The most notorious *roues* were the Dukes of Richelieu, Broglie, Biron, and Brancas, together with Canillac and Nocé, in England, the Dukes of Rochester and Buckingham

Rouen (roo′ on) Aller à Rouen. To go to ruin. The French are full of these puns, and our forefathers indulged in them also, as, *You are on*

the highway to Needham (a market town in Suffolk), *i.e.* your courses will lead you to poverty.

The Bloody Feast of Rouen (1356). Charles the Dauphin gave a banquet to his private friends at Rouen, to which his brother-in-law Charles the Bad was invited While the guests were at table King John the Good entered the room with a numerous escort, exclaiming, "Traitor, thou art not worthy to sit at table with my son!" Then, turning to his guards, he added, "Take him hence! By holy Paul, I will neither eat nor drink till his head be brought me!" Then, seizing an iron mace from one of the men at arms, he struck another of the guests between the shoulders, exclaiming, "Out, proud traitor! by the soul of my father, thou shalt not live!" Four of the guests were beheaded on the spot.

Rouge (roozh) (Fr , red) Rouge Croix. One of the pursuivants of the Heralds' College (*q.v*) So called from the red cross of St. George, the patron saint of England

Rouge Dragon. The pursuivant founded by Henry VII The Red Dragon was the ensign of Cadwalader, the last Welsh king of the Britons, an ancestor of Henry VII, who employed it as the dexter supporter of his coat of arms.

Rouge et Noir (Fr , red and black). A game of chance, so called because of the red and black diamond-shaped compartments on the board. The dealer deals out to *noir* first till the sum of the pips exceeds thirty, then to *rouge* in the same manner. That packet which comes nearest to thirty-one is the winner of the stakes.

Rough. Rough-hewn. Shaped in the rough, not finished, unpolished, ill-mannered, raw, as a "rough-hewn seaman" (Bacon); a "rough-hewn discourse" (Howe).

> There's a divinity that shapes our ends,
> Rough-hew them how we will
> *Hamlet,* v, 2

Rough Music, called in Somersetshire *skimmity-riding* (*cp* SKIMMINGTON), and by the Basques *toberac* A ceremony which takes place after sunset, when the performers, to show their indignation against some man or woman who has outraged propriety, assemble before the house, and make an appalling din with bells, horns, tin pans, and other noisy instruments.

Riding rough-shod over one. Treating one without the least consideration. The shoes of a horse that is *rough-shod* has the nails projecting to prevent it slipping.

Rough and Ready. So General Zachary Taylor (1784-1850) twelfth president of the United States, was called.

There was a Colonel Rough in the battle of Waterloo, fable tells that the Duke of Wellington used to say "Rough and ready, colonel," and that the family adopted the words as their motto.

Rouncival (rown′ si val). Large; of gigantic size Certain large bones of extinct animals were at one time said to be the bones of the heroes who fell with Roland in Roncesvalles (*q v*). "Rounceval peas" are those large peas

called "marrowfats," and a very large woman
is called a *rouncival*.

> Hereof, I take it, it comes that seeing a great woman
> we say she is a *rouncival* —MANDEVILLE

Round. There is an archaic verb *to round* (A.S
runian), meaning to whisper, or to communicate confidentially. Browning uses it more than
once, *e g.*—

> First make a laughing-stock of me and mine,
> Then round us in the ears from morn to night
> (Because we show wry faces at your mirth)
> That you are robbed, starved, beaten and what not!
> *The Ring and the Book*, iv, 599.

Bunyan, in the *Pilgrim's Progress*, speaks of
"that lesson which I will round you in the ear "
Cp also—

> France . rounded in the ear with [by]   com-
> modity [self-interest] hath resolved to [on] a most
> base . . peace —*King John*, ii, l
> And ner the feend he drough as nought ne were,
> Full prively, and rouned in his eere,
> "Herké, my brother, herké, by thi faith . . "
> CHAUCER: *Canterbury Tales*, 7132

A good round sum. A large sum of money.

> Three Thousand ducats, 'tis a good round sum
> *Merchant of Venice*, i i

A round peg in a square hole. *See* PEG

A round robin. A petition or protest signed
in a circular form, so that no name heads the
list The device is French, and the term seems
to be a corruption of *rond* (round) *ruban* (a
ribbon). It was first adopted by the officers of
government as a means of making known their
grievances.

At a round pace or rate. Briskly, rapidly,
smartly

> He cried again,
> "To the wilds!'" and Enid leading down the tracks
> Round was their pace at first, but slacken'd soon
> TENNYSON *Enid and Geraint*, 28.

In round numbers. In whole numbers, without regarding the fractions Thus we say the
population of the British Isles in 1931 was
forty-nine millions, in round numbers, and
that of Greater London eight millions The
idea is that what is round is whole or perfect,
and, of course, fractions, being broken numbers, cannot belong thereto

Round dealing. Honest, straightforward dealing, without branching off into underhand
tricks, or deviating from the straight path into
the byways of finesse

> Round dealing is the honour of man's nature —
> BACON

Sellinger's Round. *See* SELLINGER.

Round-up. (Western U S A.) A corral on a
large scale Cattle were gathered together by
riding round them and driving them in Hence,
a gathering-in of scattered objects or persons,
e g. criminals.

To get round one. To take advantage of him
by cajoling or flattery, to have one's own way
through deception

To round on one. To turn on him; to turn informer against him

To walk the Round Lawyers used frequently
to give interviews to their clients in the Round
Church in the Temple, and "walking the
Round" meant loitering about the church, in
the hope of being hired for a witness.

Round Table, The. The Table fabled to have
been made by Merlin at Carduel for Uther
Pendragon Uther gave it to King Leodegraunce, of Cameliard, who gave it to King
Arthur when the latter married Guinever, his
daughter. It was circular to prevent any
jealousy on the score of precedency, it seated
150 knights and a place was left in it for the
San Graal The first reference to it is in Wace's
Roman de Brut (1155), these legendary details
are from Malory's *Morte d'Arthur*, III, i and ii

The table shown at Winchester was recognized as ancient in the time of Henry III, but
its anterior history is unknown It is of wedge-
shaped oak planks, and is 17 ft in diameter
and 2¾ in thick At the back are 12 mortice
holes in which 12 legs probably used to fit It
was for the accommodation of twelve favourite
knights Henry VIII showed it to Francis I,
telling him that it was the one used by the
British king. The Round Table was not
peculiar to the reign of King Arthur, but was
common in all the ages of chivalry Thus the
King of Ireland, father of the fair Christabelle,
says in the ballad

> Is there never a knighte of my round table
> This matter will undergo?   *Sir Cauline*

In the eighth year of Edward I, Roger de
Mortimer established a Round Table at Kenilworth for "the encouragement of military pas-
times " At this foundation 100 knights and as
many ladies were entertained at the founder's
expense About seventy years later, Edward III
erected a splendid table at Windsor It was
200 ft in diameter, and the expense of entertaining the knights thereof amounted to £100 a
week

Knights of the Round Table. According to
Malory (*Morte d'Arthur*, III, i, ii) there were
150 knights who had "sieges" at the table
King Leodegraunce brought 100 when, at the
wedding of his daughter Guinever, he gave the
table to King Arthur; Merlin filled up twenty-
eight of the vacant seats, and the king elected
Gawaine and Tor, the remaining twenty were
left for those who might prove worthy

A list of the knights and a description of
their armour is given in the *Theatre of Honour*
by Andrew Fairne (1622). According to this
list, the number was 151, but in *Lancelot of
the Lake* (vol ii, p. 81), they are said to have
amounted to 250.

These knights went forth into all countries
in quest of adventures, but their chief exploits
occurred in quest of the San Graal (*q v*) or
Holy Cup, brought to Britain by Joseph of
Arimathea.

> Sir Lancelot is meant for a model of fidelity,
> bravery, frailty in love, and repentance, Sir Galahad
> of chastity, Sir Gawain of courtesy, Sir Kay of a rude,
> boastful knight, and Sir Modred of treachery

There is still a "Knights of the Round Table"
Club, which claims to be the oldest social club
in the world, having been founded in 1721
Garrick, Dickens, Toole, Sir Henry Irving,
Tenniel, are among those who have been
members

A round table conference. A conference between political parties in which each has equal
authority, and at which it is agreed that the
questions in dispute shall be settled amicably

and with the maximum amount of "give and take" on each side

The expression came into prominence in connexion with a private conference in the house of Sir William Harcourt, January 14th, 1887, with the view of reuniting, if possible, the Liberal party, broken up by Gladstone's Irish policy.

Roundabout. A large revolving machine at fairs, circuses, etc , with wooden horses or the like, which go round and round ridden by passengers, to the strains of a mechanical brass band From this arises the device at a crossroads, whereby traffic circulates in one direction only, thus doing away with the need for holding up vehicles on one road while traffic from another crosses it

What you lose on the swings you make up on the roundabouts. *See* SWING.

Roundheads. Puritans of the Civil War period, especially Cromwell's soldiers. So called because they wore their hair short, while the Royalists wore long hair covering their shoulders

And ere their butter 'gan to coddle,
A bullet churned i' th' Roundhead's noddle

Roundle, in heraldry, is a charge of a circular form. There are a number of varieties, distinguished by their colours or tinctures, as—a *Bezant,* tincture "or", *Plate,* "argent"; *Torteau,* "gules", *Hurt,* "azure", *Ogress* or *Pellet,* "sable"; *Pomey* (because supposed to resemble an *apple,* Fr *pomme*), "vert", *Golpe,* "purpure", *Guze,* "sanguine"; *Orange,* "tenney."

Roup. the name by which an auction is called in Scotland It is a Scandinavian word, and is connected with the M.Swed *rópa,* to shout.

Rouse. A good, hearty bumper, a drinking bout. *See* CAROUSE

Rout. A common term in the 18th century for a large evening party or fashionable assemblage *Cp* DRUM, HURRICANE, etc

Routes. In N W Europe Allied routes were signposted in World War II with simple emblems instead of place names, to enable drivers to reach a destination without the use of maps The British roads, reaching from Caen to the Baltic, were easily recognizable, among them being "Hat," "Bottle," and "Diamond" These were chosen by Brig Sir Henry Floyd and Lt.-Col J. C Cockburn for an exercise in Yorkshire in which 8 Corps practised the battle they were to fight six months later south of Caen; hence when the real thing took place the same signs were used, and the routes beginning there continued across Europe The most famous American road was the Red Ball Route—a supply line for fast-moving traffic only, kept rolling 24 hours a day to maintain the impetus of Gen Patton's sensational advance across France The name came from an old American railway tradition of marking priority freight with a red ball

Routiers, or **Rutters** (roo' ti erz, rŭt'erz). Mediæval adventurers who made war a trade and let themselves out to anyone who would pay them So called because they were always on the *route* or moving from place to place

Rove. The original meaning was to shoot with arrows at marks that were selected at haphazard, the distance being unknown, with the object of practising judging distance Hence—

To shoot at rovers. To shoot at random without any distinct aim

Unbelievers are said by Clobery to "shoot at rovers"—*Divine Glimpses,* p 4 (1659).

Running at rovers. Running wild, being without restraint

Row (rou). A disturbance, noise, or tumult is late 18th-century slang, the origin of the word is unknown

"I shall now and then kick up a row in the street " —*Lolterer,* No 12

Rowdy. A ruffian brawler, a "rough," a riotous or turbulent fellow, whose delight is to make a row or disturbance Hence *rowdyism* and *rowdy-dowdy* The term was originally American (early 19th century) and denoted a wild and lawless backwoodsman

Rowan, or Mountain Ash (rou'an, rō'an) Called in Westmorland the "Wiggentree" It was greatly venerated by the Druids, and was formerly known as the "Witchen" because it was supposed to ward off witches

Their spells were vain The hags returned
To their queen in sorrowful mood,
Crying that witches have no power
Where thrives the Rowan-tree wood
Laidley Worm of Spindleston Heughs (a ballad)

Its scientific name is *Pyrus aucuparia,* and it is of the natural order Rosaceæ, while the common Ash is of the natural order Oleaceæ The Mountain Ash is *Icosandria,* but the common Ash is *Diandria,* the former is *Pentagynia,* but the latter is *Monogynia,* yet the two trees resemble each other in many respects

Rowland. *See* ROLAND

Rowley (rō'li). **Old Rowley** Charles II was so called from his favourite race-horse. A portion of the Newmarket racecourse is still called Rowley Mile, from the same horse

The Rowley Poems. *See* FORGERIES.

Roxburghe Club, The (roks'brŏ). An association of bibliophiles founded in 1812 for the purpose of printing rare works or MSS. It was named after John, Duke of Roxburghe, a celebrated collector of ancient literature (1740-1804), and remains the most distinguished gathering of bibliophiles in the world It was the forerunner of a number of similar printing clubs, as the Camden, Cheetham, Percy, Shakespeare, Surtees, and Wharton, in England, the Abbotsford, Bannatyne, Maitland, and Spalding, in Scotland, and the Celtic Society of Ireland

Roy, Le, or la Reine, s'avisera (the *king,* or *queen, will consider it*). This is the royal veto, last put in force March 11th, 1707, when Queen Anne refused her assent to a Scottish Militia Bill

During the agitation for Catholic emancipation, George III threatened a veto, but the matter was not brought to the test

Royal. A standard size of writing papers measuring 19 × 24 in In printings it is 20 × 25 in or 20 × 25½ in , hence a royal octavo book measures 10 × 6¼ in (untrimmed)

Super Royal in printing papers measures (with slight variations) 20 × 27 in., and in writing papers 19 × 27 in

Royal Academy. *See* ACADEMY

Royal American Regiment. The original name of the King's Royal Rifle Corps, which was first raised under that title in Maryland and Pennsylvania, 1755

Royal and Ancient. The name by which the game of golf has been known since early days. In 1834 the St Andrews Golf Club (founded in 1754) took the name of Royal and Ancient Golf Club, except in U S A, this club is the recognized authority on golf throughout the world, governing the game, framing rules, and settling questions and disputes

Royal Institution. An association founded in 1799 for the purpose of prosecuting scientific and literary research, to further experimental science, and give opportunities for the exchange of views and experiences Under the patronage of the sovereign, it consists of a president and a number of professors, among whom have been numbered Humphry Davy, Faraday, Tyndall, Rayleigh, Sir James Dewar.

Royal Merchants. The wealthy Venetian merchants of the 13th century, such as the Sanudos, the Justiniani, the Grimaldi, and others, who erected principalities in divers places of the Archipelago They and their descendants enjoyed almost royal rights in these districts for many centuries

> Glancing an eye of pity on his losses,
> That have of late so huddled on his back,
> Enough to press a royal merchant down
> *Merchant of Venice*, iv, 1.

Sir Thomas Gresham was called a "royal merchant", and in 1767 Fletcher's comedy, *The Beggar's Bush* (1622) was produced as an opera with the title *The Royal Merchant.*

Royal Oak. *See* OAK-APPLE DAY.

Royal Society. The premier scientific society in Britain It originated in London in 1645 when a number of learned enquirers met to discuss and experiment in various branches of science. The society was organized in 1660, meeting at Gresham College until 1710, when a move was made to Crane Court, Fleet Street In 1780 the Society moved again to Somerset House, finally settling in its present home at Burlington House in 1857. Its fellowship, the F R S, is the greatest honour in the scientific and philosophical world

Royal Titles. *See* RULERS, TITLES OF

Royston (Herts) means king's town; so called in honour of King Stephen, who erected a cross there (O.Fr *roy*, king.)

A Royston horse and Cambridge Master of Arts will give way to no one. A Cambridgeshire proverb Royston was famous for malt, which was sent to London on horseback. These heavy-laden beasts never moved out of the way. The Masters of Arts, being the great dons of Cambridge, had the wall conceded to them by the inhabitants out of courtesy.

Rozinante, Rocinante (roz i năn' ti). The wretched jade of a riding-horse belonging to Don Quixote (*q.v*). Although it was nothing

but skin and bone—and worn out at that—he regarded it as a priceless charger surpassing "the Bucephalus of Alexander and the Babieca of the Cid " The name, which is applied to similar hacks, is from Span *rocin*, a jade, the *ante* (before) implying that once upon a time, perhaps, it *had* been a horse

Rub. An impediment The expression is taken from bowls, where "rub" means that something hinders the free movement of your bowl
> Without rub or interruption.—*Swift.*
> Like a bowle that runneth in a smooth allie without anie rub —*Stanihurst*, p 10

Don't rub it in! Yes, I know I've made a fool of myself, but you needn't go on emphasizing the fact!

Rub of the green A golf term for any unsuspected misfortune to which the best played stroke may sometimes be subject.

Rubber. In whist, bridge, and some other games, a set of three games, the best two out of three, or the third game of the set. The origin of the term is uncertain, but it may be a transference from bowls, in which the collision of two balls is a *rubber*, because they rub against each other.

Those who play at bowls must look out for rubbers. There is always some risk in anything you undertake, and you've got to be prepared to meet it, you must take the rough with the smooth.

Rubberneck-wagon An excursion or sightseeing-bus in which the passengers stretch their necks to look at views or monuments.

Rubicon (roo' bi kon) **To pass the Rubicon.** To take some step from which it is not possible to recede. Thus, when the Austrians, in 1859, passed the Ticino, the act was a declaration of war against Sardinia; in 1866, when the Italians passed the Adige, it was a declaration of war against Austria; and in August 1914, when the Germans crossed the frontier into Belgium it was impossible to avoid the armed intervention of Great Britain.

The Rubicon was a small river separating ancient Italy from Cisalpine Gaul (the province allotted to Julius Cæsar) When, in 49 B C, Cæsar crossed this stream he passed beyond the limits of his own province and became an invader of Italy, thus precipitating the Civil War.

Rubric (roo' brik) (Lat *rubrica*, red ochre, or vermilion). An ordinance or law was by the Romans called a rubric, because it was written with vermilion, in contradistinction to prætorian edicts or rules of the court, which were posted on a *white* ground (*Juvenal*, xiv, 192)
> Rubrica vetavit = the law has forbidden it — (*Persius*, v, 99)

The liturgical directions, titles, etc, in a Prayer Book are known as the *Rubric* because these were (and in many cases still are) printed in red. Milton has an allusion to the custom of printing the names of certain saints (*cp* RED LETTER DAY) in red in the Prayer Book Calendar.

> No date prefix'd
> Directs me in the starry rubric set.
> *Paradise Regained*, iv, 392.

Ruby. The ancients considered the ruby to be an antidote to poison to preserve persons from plague, to banish grief, to repress the ill effects of luxuries, and to divert the mind from evil thoughts

It has always been a very valuable stone, and even to-day a fine Burma ruby will cost more than a diamond of the same size

Who can finde a virtuous woman? for her price is far above rubies —*Prov* xxxi, 10, *cp* also *Job* xxviii, 18, and *Prov* viii, 11

Marco Polo said that the king of Ceylon had the finest ruby ever seen "It is a span long, as thick as a man's arm, and without a flaw " Kublai Khan offered the value of a city for it, but the king would not part with it though all the treasures of the world were to be laid at his feet

The perfect ruby. An alchemist's term for the elixir, or philosopher's stone

He that once has the flower of the sun,
The perfect ruby, which we call elixir,
Can confer honour, love, respect, long life,
Give safety, valour, yea, and victory,
To whom he will

BEN JOHNSON *The Alchemist*, ii, 1.

Rudder Who won't be ruled by the rudder must be ruled by the rock Who won't listen to reason must bear the consequences, like a ship that runs upon a rock if it will not answer the helm

Ruddock. The redbreast, "sacred to the household gods", *see* ROBIN REDBREAST Shakespeare makes Arviragus say over Imogen—

Thou shalt not lack
The flower that's like thy face, pale primrose nor
The azured harebell . the ruddock would
With charitable bill . bring thee all these
Cymbeline, iv, 2

Rudolphine Tables, The (roo dol' fĭn) Astronomical calculations begun by Tycho Brahe, continued by Kepler, and published in 1627 They were named after Kepler's patron, Kaiser Rudolph II.

Rue (roo), called "herb of grace" (*q.v*), because it was employed for sprinkling holy water *See also* DIFFERENCE Ophelia says—

There's rue for you, and here's some for me! we may call it "herb of grace" o' Sundays —*Hamlet*, iv, 5

Ruff. An early forerunner of whist, very popular in the late 16th and early 17th centuries, later called *slamm* The act of trumping at whist, etc , especially when one cannot follow suit, is still called "the ruff."

Ruffian Hall. That part of West Smithfield, later the horse-market, where in the 16th century "tryals of skill were plaid by ordinary ruffianly people with sword and buckler" (*Blount*, p 562)

The field commonly called West-Smith field, was for many yeares called *Ruffians Hall*, by reason it was the usuall place of Frayes and common fighting, during the Time that Sword-and-Bucklers were in use — *Howes'* continuation of Stow's "Annals" (1631), p 1024.

Rufus. (*The Red*) William II of England (1056, 1087-1100)

Otho II of Germany; also called *The Bloody* (955, 973-83).

Gilbert de Clare, Earl of Gloucester, son-in-law of Edward I. (Slain 1313)

Ruggiero. *See* ROGERO.

Rule Rule of thumb *See* THUMB

Rule of the road. *See under* ROAD.

Rule the roost. *See* ROAST

Rule, or Regulus, St. A priest of Patræ in Achaia, who is said to have come to Scotland in the 4th century, bringing with him relics of St Andrew, and to have founded the town and bishopric of St Andrews The name Kilrule (*Cella Reguli*) perpetuates his memory

Rule, Britannia. Words by James Thomson (1700-48), author of *The Seasons*, music by Dr Arne (1740) It first appeared in a masque entitled *Alfred*, in which the name of David Mallett is associated with that of Thomson. There are, however, no grounds whatever for supposing that Mallet wrote a single line of the Ode In the rising of 1745 "Rule Britannia" was sung by the Jacobites with modifications appropriate to their cause

Rule nisi (nī' sī) A "rule" is an order from one of the superior courts, and a "rule nisi" (*cp* NISI) is such an order "to show cause." That is, the rule is to be held absolute *unless* the party to whom it applies can "show cause" why it should not be so

Rulers, Titles of. Titles of sovereigns and other rulers may be divided into two classes, viz (1) designations that correspond more or less to our *King* or *Emperor* (such as *Bey, Mikado, Sultan*), and (2) appellatives that were originally the proper name of some individual ruler (as *Cæsar*).

Akhoond King and high priest of the Swat (N.W Provinces, India)

Ameer, Amir. Ruler of Afghanistan, Sind, etc

Archon Chief of the nine magistrates of ancient Athens The next in rank was called *Basileus*, and the third *Polemarch* (field marshal)

Beglerbeg. See BEY

Begum A queen, princess, or lady of high rank in India

Bey—of Tunis In Imperial Turkey, a bey was usually a superior military officer, though the title was often assumed by those who held no official position

Brenn or *Brenhin* (war-chief) of the ancient Gauls A dictator appointed by the Druids in times of danger

Bretwalda (wielder of Britain). A title of some of the Anglo-Saxon kings who held supremacy over the rest; a king of the Heptarchy (*q v.*)

Cacique. See CAZIQUE

Caliph or *Calif* (successor) Successors of Mohammed in temporal and spiritual matters, after the first four successors of Mohammed the caliphate passed through various dynasties —Umayyad, Abbasid, Seljuk, Turkoman, etc In 1538 the Sultan of Turkey, Selim I, declared himself Caliph and the title rested with the sultanate until 1922 when both sultanate and caliphate were suppressed.

Caudillo (Span, "leader") The head of the Spanish State, Don Francisco Franco Bahamonde

Cazique or *Cacique*. A native prince of the ancient Peruvians, Cubans, Mexicans, etc.

Chagan The chief of the Avars

Cham See KHAN

Cral The despot of ancient Servia.

Czar See TSAR

Dey. Governor of Algiers, before it was annexed to France in 1830, also the 16th-century rulers of Tunis and Tripoli (Tuik *dāī*, uncle)

Diwan The native chief of Palanpur, India

Doge The ruler of the old Venetian Republic (697-1797); also of that of Genoa (1339-1797)

Duce (Ital., "leader") Head of the Fascist State of Italy, 1922-45, Benito Mussolini

Duke The ruler of a duchy, formerly in many European countries of sovereign rank (Lat *Dux*, a leader)

Elector A Prince of the Holy Roman Empire (of sovereign rank) entitled to take part in the election of the Emperor

Emir The independent chieftain of certain Arabian provinces, as Bokhara, Nejd, etc., also given to Arab chiefs who claim descent from Mohammed

Emperor. The paramount ruler of an empire, especially, in mediæval times, the Holy Roman Empire; from Lat *Imperator*, one who commands.

Exarch The title of a viceroy of the Byzantine Emperors, especially the *Exarch* of Ravenna, who was *de facto* governor of Italy

Fuhrer (Ger, "leader") Prime Minister and President of the Nazi German State 1934-45, Adolf Hitler

Gaekwar. Formerly the title of the monarch of the Mahrattas, now that of the native ruler of Baroda (his son being the *Gaekwad*) The word is Marathi for a cowherd

Gauleiter (Ger, "region leader") The ruler of a province under the Nazi regime, 1934-45.

Holkar The title of the Maharajah of Indore

Hospodar The title borne by the princes of Moldavia and Wallachia before the union of those countries with Rumania (Slavic, lord, master)

Imperator See EMPEROR

Inca. The title of the sovereigns of Peru up to the conquest by Pizarro (1531)

Kabaka. The native ruler of the Buganda province of the Uganda Protectorate

Kaiser The German form of Lat *Cæsar* (*see below, also* TSAR): the old title of the Emperor of the Holy Roman Empire, and of the Emperors of Germany and of Austria

Khan The chief rulers of Tartar, Mongol, and Turkish tribes, as successors of Genghis Khan (d 1227) The word means lord or prince

Khedive The title conferred in 1867 by the Sultan of Turkey on the viceroy or governor of Egypt *Cp.* VALI.

King The Anglo-Saxon *cyning*, literally "a man of good birth" (*cyn*, tribe, kin, or race, with the patronymic *-ing*)

Lama. The priest-ruler of Tibet *See* LAMA

Maharajah. (Hind, "the great king") The title of many of the native rulers of Indian States

Maharao. The title of the native rulers of Cutch, Kotah, and Sirohi, India

Maharao Rajah The native ruler of Bundi, India.

Maharawal The native rulers of Banswara, Dungarpur, Jaisalmer, and Partabgarh, India

Mikado The popular title of the hereditary ruler of Japan—officially styled "Emperor" The name (like the Turkish *Sublime Porte*) means "The August Door" *Cp* SHOGUN

Mir The native ruler of Khairpur, India

Mogul or *Great Mogul* The Emperors of Delhi, and rulers of the greater part of India from 1526 to 1857, of the Mongol line founded by Baber

Mpret The old title of the Albanian rulers (from Lat *imperator*), revived in 1913 in favour of Prince Wilham of Wied, whose Mpretship lasted only a few months.

Nawab The native rulers of Bhopal, Tonk, Jaora, and some other Indian States

Negus (properly *Negus Negust*, meaning "king of kings") The native name of the sovereign of Abyssinia—officially styled "Emperor."

Nizam The title of the native ruler of Hyderabad Deccan, since 1713.

Padishah (Pers, protecting lord) A title of the former Sultan of Turkey, the Shah of Persia, and of the former Great Moguls

Pendragon The title assumed by the ancient British overlord.

Polemarch. See ARCHON

Prince. Formerly in common use as the title of a reigning sovereign, as it still is in a few cases, such as the Prince of Monaco and Prince of Liechtenstein

Rajah Hindustani for *king* (*cp* MAHA-RAJAH). specifically the title of the native rulers of Cochin, Ratlam, Tippera, Chamba, Faridkot Mandi, Pudukota, Rajgarh, Rajpipla, Sailana, and Tehri (Garhwal). *Cp* REX.

Rex (*regem*), the Latin equivalent of our "king," connected with *regere*, to rule, and with Sanskrit *rajan* (whence RAJAH), a king

Sachem, Sagamore Chieftains of certain tribes of North American Indians

Satrap The governor of a province in ancient Persia

Shah (Pers, king). The supreme ruler of Persia and of some other Eastern countries. *Cp* PADISHAH

Sheik An Arab chief, or head man of a tribe

Shogun. The title of the virtual rulers of Japan (representing usurping families who kept the true Emperor in perpetual imprisonment) from about the close of the 12th century to the revolution of 1867-68 It means "leader of an army," and was originally the title of military governors. Also called the Tycoon

Sindhia. The special title of the Maharajah of Gwalior

Sirdar. The commander-in-chief of the Egyptian army and military governor of Egypt during the British occupation, 1882-1936

Stadtholder Originally a viceroy in a province of the Netherlands, but later the chief executive officer of the United Provinces.

Sultan (formerly also *Soldan*) The title of the rulers of certain Mohammedan States.

Tetrarch The governor of the fourth part of a province in the ancient Roman Empire

Thakur Sahib The title of the native ruler of Gondal, India

Tsar (from Lat. *Cæsar*; cp KAISER) The popular title of the former Emperors of Russia (assumed in 1547 by Ivan the Terrible), but officially his only as King of Poland and a few other parts of his Empire His wife was the *Tsarina*, his son the *Tsarevich*, and his daughter the *Tsarevna*.

Tycoon An alternative title of the Japanese Shōgun (*q v*) The word is from Chinese and means "great sovereign."

Vali The title of the governors of Egypt prior to 1867, when the style *Khedive* (*q.v*) was granted by the Sultan

Voivode, or *Vaivode* Properly (Russ) "the leader of an army," the word was for a time assumed as a title by the Princes of Moldavia and Wallachia, later called Hospodars (*q v*)

Wali A title of the native ruler, or Khan, of Kalat, India

(2) The following names have been adopted in varying degrees as royal titles among the peoples mentioned:—

Abgarus (The Grand) So the kings of Edessa were styled,

Abimelech (my father the king). The chief ruler of the ancient Philistines

Attabeg (father prince) Persia, 1118

Augustus The title of the reigning Emperor of Rome, when the heir presumptive was styled "Cæsar"

Cæsar Proper name adopted by the Roman emperors See KAISER, TSAR.

Candace Proper name adopted by the queens of Ethiopia.

Cyrus (mighty). Ancient Persia

Darius. Latin form of *Darawesh* (king). Ancient Persia

Melech (king). Ancient Semitic tribes

Pharaoh (light of the world) Ancient Egypt

Ptolemy Proper name adopted by Egypt after the death of Alexander

Sophy or *Sophi* A former title of the kings of Persia, from *Çafi-ud-din*, the founder of the ancient dynasty of the Çafi or Çafavi.

Ruminate. To think, to meditate upon some subject; properly, "to chew the cud" (Lat *rumino*, from *rumen*, the throat)

To chew the cud of sweet and bitter fancy — MILTON

On a flowery bank he chews the cud —DRYDEN.

Rump, The. The end of the backbone, with the buttocks The term was applied contemptuously to the remnant of the Long Parliament that was left after Pride's Purge (*q v*) in 1648, and lasted till it was eventually ejected by Cromwell in April, 1653, also to the later remnant of the same Parliament that was restored in May, 1659, and dissolved by Monk in the following February The ' Rump" was composed of those members who most strenuously opposed Charles I and the Restoration

The few,
Because they're wasted to the stumps,
Are represented best by rumps
BUTLER. *Hudibras*, Pt III, 2.

Rump and dozen. A rump of beef and a dozen of claret, or a rump steak and a dozen oysters A not uncommon wager among sportsmen of the late 18th and early 19th centuries.

Rumpelstilzchen (rūm pel stilts' chen) A passionate little deformed dwarf of German folktale A miller's daughter was enjoined by a king to spin straw into gold, and the dwarf did it for her, on condition that she would give him her first child The maiden married the king, and grieved so bitterly when the child was born that the dwarf promised to relent if within three days she could find out his name. Two days were spent in vain guesses, but the third day one of the queen's servants heard a strange voice singing—

Little dreams my dainty dame
Rumpelstilzchen is my name

The child was saved, and the dwarf killed himself with rage

Run. A long run, a short run. We say of a drama, "It had a long run," meaning it attracted the people to the house, and was represented over and over again for many nights The allusion is to a runner who continues his race for a long way The drama ran on night after night without change

He that runs may read. The Bible quotation in *Hab* ii, 2, is, "Write the vision, and make it plain upon tables, that he may run that readeth it " Cowper says—

But truths, on which depends our main concern ..
Shine by the side of every path we tread
With such a lustre, he that runs may read
Tirocinium

In the long run In the final result. This allusion is to race-running one may get the start for a time, but in the long run, or entire race, the result may be different The hare got the start, but in the long run the patient perseverance of the tortoise won the race.

On the run. Moving from place to place and hiding from the authorities, said specially of rebels.

To be run in To be arrested and taken to the lock-up.

To go with a run. To go swimmingly, "without a hitch " A seaman's phrase A rope goes with a run when it is let go entirely, instead of being slackened gradually.

To have the run of the house To have free access to it and liberty to partake of whatever comes to table

To run down. To cease to go or act from lack of motive force, or a clock when the spring is fully unwound.

To run a man down. To depreciate him, or to abuse him to a third party.

To run a rig See RIG.

To run amuck See AMUCK

To run into the ground To pursue too far, to exhaust a topic

To run to earth To discover in a hiding-place; to get to the bottom of a matter

To run through one's inheritance. To squander it at a rapid rate

To run riot. See RIOT

To run the show. To take charge of it, generally with ostentation, to make oneself responsible for its success

Runner-up. The competitor or team that finishes in the second place, after the winner

Runners. *See* REDBREASTS

His shoes are made of **running leather.** He is given to roving There may be a pun between *roan* and *run*

Quite out of the running. Quite out of court, not worthy of consideration, like a horse which has been scratched for some race and so is not "in the running"

Running footmen. Men servants in the early part of the 18th century, when no great house was complete without some half-dozen of them Their duty was to run beside the fat Flemish mares of the period, and advise the innkeeper of the coming guests. The pole which they carried was to help the cumbrous coach out of the numerous sloughs It is said that the notorious "Old Q" was the last to employ running footmen

Running Thursday. December 13th, 1688, two days after the flight of James II A rumour ran that the French and Irish Papists had landed; a terrible panic ensued, and the people betook themselves to the country, running for their lives

Running water. No enchantment can subsist in a living stream, if, therefore, a person can interpose a brook betwixt himself and the witches, sprites, or goblins chasing him, he is in perfect safety. Burns's tale of *Tam o' Shanter* turns upon this superstition.

Running the Hood. It is said that an old lady was passing over Haxey Hill, when the wind blew away her hood Some boys began tossing it from one to the other, and the old lady so enjoyed the fun that she bequeathed thirteen acres of land, that thirteen candidates might be induced to renew the sport on the 6th of every January

Runcible Spoon. The plate and cutlery trades have no knowledge of this utensil, which is mentioned in Edward Lear's *Owl and the Pussy Cat.*
> They dined on mince and slices of quince
> Which they ate with a runcible spoon

Some who profess to know describe it as a kind of fork having three broad prongs, one of which has a sharp cutting edge

Rune (roon). A letter or character of the earliest alphabet in use among the Gothic tribes of Northern Europe. Runes were employed for purposes of secrecy or for divination; and the word is also applied to ancient lore or poetry expressed in runes *Rune* is related to A S *rān*, secret.

There were several sorts of runes employed by the Celts, as (1) the *Evil Rune*, when evil was to be invoked; (2) the *Securable Rune*, to secure from misadventure, (3) the *Victorious Rune*, to procure victory over enemies; (4) *Medicinal Rune*, for restoring to health the indisposed, or for averting danger, etc.

Runic Staff, or **Wand.** *See* CLOG ALMANAC

Rupert. Prince Rupert's drops Bubbles made by dropping molten glass into water. Their form is that of a tadpole, and if the smallest portion of the "tail" is nipped off, the whole flies into fine dust with explosive violence

These toys were named after Prince Rupert (1619-82), grandson of James I and the leader of Royalist cavalry in the Civil Wars, who introduced them into England
> The first production of an author . is usually esteemed as a sort of Prince Rupert's drop, which is destroyed entirely if a person make on it but a single scratch —*Household Words*

Rupert of Debate. Edward Geoffrey, fourteenth Earl of Derby (1799-1869) It was when he was Mr. Stanley, and the opponent of Daniel O'Connell, that Lord Lytton so described him, in allusion to the brilliant Royalist cavalry leader, Prince Rupert
> The brilliant chief, irregularly great,
> Frank, haughty, bold—the Rupert of Debate
> *New Timon*

Ruptured Duck The nickname in World War II for the American ex-service lapel button issued to all demobilized from the forces

Ruritania (ru ri tä´ nyá) An imaginary kingdom in a pre-World-War Europe where Anthony Hope placed the adventures of his hero in the novels *The Prisoner of Zenda* (1894) and *Rupert of Hentzau* (1898) The name is frequently applied to any small state where politics and intrigues of a melodramatic importance are the natural order of the day

Rush. Friar Rush. A name given to the will-o'-the-wisp, also to a strolling demon who, it is said, once on a time got admittance into a monastery as a scullion, and played the monks divers pranks *See* FRIAR'S LANTHORN.

It's a regular rush. A barefaced swindle, an exorbitant charge Said when one is "rushed" into paying a good deal more for something than it is worth.

Not worth a rush. Worthless, not worth a straw When floors used to be strewn with rushes, distinguished guests were given clean, fresh rushes, but those of inferior grade had either the rushes which had been already used by their superiors, or none at all
> Strangers have green rushes when daily guests are not worth a rush —LYLY *Sappho and Phaon* (1584)

Rush-bearing Sunday. A Sunday, generally near the time of the festival of the saint to whom the church is dedicated, when anciently it was customary to renew the rushes with which the church floor was strewn The festival is still observed at Ambleside, Westmorland, on the last Sunday in July, the church being dedicated to St Anne, whose day is July 26th The present custom is to make the festival a flower Sunday, with rushes and flowers formed into fanciful devices The preceding Saturday is a holiday, being the day when the old rushes were removed.

Russel A common name given to a fox, from its russet colour
> Daun Russel, the fox, stert up at oones,
> And by the garget hente Chaunteclere
> And on his bak toward the wood him bere.
> CHAUCER *The Nonnes Prestes Tale.*

Russia Leather A fine leather of a smooth texture, originally produced in Russia It is the result of tanning and dyeing (usually of a red colour) by a particular process and the distinctive smell comes from the distillation of birch bark used in the manufacture

Rustam, or **Rustem**. The Persian Hercules, the son of Žal, prince of Sedjistan, famous for his victory over the white dragon Asdeev His combat for two days with Prince Isfendiar is a favourite subject with the Persian poets. Matthew Arnold's poem *Sohrab and Rustum* gives an account of Rustam fighting with and killing his son Sohrab

> Let Zâl and Rustrum bluster as they will,
> Or Hâtim call to Supper—heed not you
> FITZGERALD *Rubaiyat of Omar Khayyam*, x.

Rusty. He turns rusty. Like a rusty bolt, he sticks and will not move, he's obstinate

Rye-house Plot. A conspiracy in 1683 for the assassination of Charles II and his brother James on their way from Newmarket, hatched at the Rye House Farm, in Hertfordshire As the house in which the king was lodging accidentally caught fire, the royal party left eight days sooner than they had intended, and the plot miscarried Lord William Russell and Algernon Sidney were among those executed for complicity

Rymenhild. *See* KING HORN

Ryot. A tenant in India who pays a usufruct for his occupation. The Scripture parable of the husbandmen refers to such a tenure, the lord sent for his rent, which was not money but fruits, and the husbandmen stoned those who were sent, refusing to pay their "lord " Ryots have an hereditary and perpetual right of occupancy so long as they pay the usufruct, but if they refuse or neglect payment may be turned away.

S

S. The nineteenth letter of the English alphabet (eighteenth of the ancient Roman), representing the Phœnician and Hebrew *shin*

S in the nautical log-book signifies *smooth* (of the sea) or *snowy* (weather)

Collar of S.S or **Esses** *See* COLLAR.

'S. A euphemistic abbreviation of *God's*, formerly much in use in common oaths and expletives, as *'Sdeath* (God's death), *'Sblood*, *'Sdeins* (God's *dignes*, *i e* dignity), *'Sfoot*, etc *'Sdeins*, I know not what I should say to him, in the whole world' He values me at a crack'd three farthings, for aught I see —BEN JONSON *Every Man in his Humour*, n, 1

$. The typographical sign for the dollar. It is thought to be a variation of the 8 with which "pieces of eight" (*q v*) were stamped, and was in use in the United States before the adoption of the Federal currency in 1785. Another, perhaps fanciful, derivation is from the letters U S

S.J (*Societas Jesu*) The Society of Jesus, denoting that the priest after whose name these letters are placed is a Jesuit

S O S. The arbitrary code signal used by wireless operators on board ship to summon the assistance of any vessels within call, hence, an urgent appeal for help

The letters have been held to stand for *save our souls* or *save our ship*, but they were adopted merely for convenience, being 3 dots, 3 dashes, and 3 dots, .. — — — ..

S P Q.R. Senatus Populusque Romanus (the Roman Senate and People) Letters inscribed on the standards, etc, of ancient Rome

SS. (Ger) *Schutzstaffel*, an armed force that originated as part of Hitler's bodyguard in 1923, with the predominant SA (Sturmabteilung). In 1929 Heinrich Himmler took over the SS and defining its duties as "to find out, to fight and to destroy all open and secret enemies of the Fuhrer, the National Socialist Movement, and our racial resurrection," raised it to a position of dominating power and great numerical strength During World War II SS Divisions fought with fanatical intensity

S T.P. Sanctæ Theologiæ Professor. *Professor* is the Latin equivalent of the scholastic *Doctor*. "D D "—*i e* Doctor of Divinity—is the English equivalent of "S T P "

Sabæans, or **Sabeans** (sa bē' anz) The ancient people of Yemen, in south-western Arabia, from Arabic Saba', or Sheba, which was supposed to be the capital.

Sabaism (sāb' ā izm) The worship of the stars, or the "host of heaven" (from Heb *Caba*, host) The term is sometimes erroneously applied to the religion of the Sabians *See* SABIANISM

Sabaoth (sa bā' oth) The Bible phrase *Lord God of Sabaoth* means *Lord God of Hosts*, not *of the Sabbath*, *Sabaoth* being Hebrew for "armies" or "hosts " The epithet has been frequently misunderstood, see, for instance, the last stanza of Spenser's *Faerie Queene* (VII, viii, 2) :—

> All that moveth doth in change delight
> But thenceforth all shall rest eternally
> With Him that is the God of Sabaoth hight·
> O' that great Sabaoth God, grant me that Sabbath's
> sight!

Sabbath (sāb' âth) (Heb *shabath*, to rest) Properly, the seventh day of the week, enjoined on the ancient Hebrews by the fourth Commandment (*Exod* xx, 8-11) as a day of rest and worship, the Christian Sunday, "the Lord's Day," the first day of the week, is often, wrongly, alluded to as "the Sabbath."

A **Sabbath Day's journey** (*Exod.* xvi, 29; *Acts* i, 12), with the Jews was not to exceed the distance between the ark and the extreme end of the camp This was 2,000 cubits, somewhat short of an English mile.

> Up to the hill by Hebron, seat of giants old,
> No journey of a Sabbath Day, and loaded so
>   MILTON *Samson Agonistes.*

Days set apart as Sabbaths. *Sunday* by Christians, *Monday* by the Greeks, *Tuesday* by the Persians, *Wednesday* by the Assyrians, *Thursday* by the Egyptians, *Friday* by the Mohammedans; *Saturday* by the Jews

Witches Sabbath. *See* WITCH

Sabbathians (så bā' thi ånz) The disciples of Sabbathais Zwi, or Tsebhi of Smyrna (1626-76), perhaps the most remarkable "Messiah" of modern times. At the age of fifteen he had mastered the Talmud, and at eighteen the Cabbala When in a Turkish prison he embraced Mohammedanism, and later formed a half-Mohammedan and half-Jewish sect of Cabalists.

Sabbatical Year (sa băt' i kăl) One year in seven, when all land with the ancient Jews was to lie fallow for twelve months. This law was founded on *Exod.* xxiii, 10, etc ; *Lev* xxv, 2-7, *Deut* xv. 1-11 In certain American and other universities the custom of allowing professors every seven years one full year during which he is free to study or travel without the obligation of teaching or lecturing.

Sabean. *See* SABÆANS.

Sabellianism (sa bel' i an izm). The tenets of the *Sabellians*, an obscure sect founded in the 3rd century by Sabellius, a Libyan priest Little is known of their beliefs, but they were Unitarians and held that the Trinity merely expressed three relations or states of one and the same God. *See* PERSON (*Confounding the Persons*).

Sabines, The (săb' inz) An ancient people of central Italy, living in the Apennines N and NE of Rome, and subjugated by the Romans about 290 B C.

The Rape of the Sabine Women. The legend connected with the founding of Rome is that as Romulus had difficulty in providing his followers with wives he invited the men of the neighbouring tribes to a celebration of games In the absence of the menfolk the Roman youths raided the Sabine territory and carried off all the women they could find. The incident has frequently been treated in art, Rubens' canvas depicting the scene (now in the National Gallery, London) is one of the best known examples

Sable. The heraldic term for *black*, shown in engraving by horizontal lines crossing perpendicular ones The fur of the animal of this name is, of course, brown; but it is probable that in the 15th century, when the heraldic term was first used, the fur was dyed black, as seal fur is to-day.

Sable fur was always much sought after, and very expensive
By the Statute of Apparel (24 Henry VIII c. 13) it is ordained that none under the degree of an earl shall use sables Bishop tells us that a thousand ducats were sometimes given for a "face of sables" (*Blossoms*, 1577). Ben Jonson says, "Would you not laugh to meet a great councillor of state in a flat cap, with trunk-hose . . . and yond haberdasher in a velvet gown trimmed with sables?" (*Discoveries*)

A suit of sables. A rich courtly dress
So long? Nay, then, let the devil wear black, for
I'll have a suit of sables —*Hamlet*, iii, 2

Sabotage (săb' ŏ tazh) Wilful and malicious destruction of tools, plant, machinery, materials, etc , by discontented workmen or strikers. The term came into use after the great French railway strike in 1912, when the strikers cut the shoes (*sabots*) holding the railway lines.

Sabreur (sa brer'). Le beau sabreur, the handsome swordsman. This was the name given to Joachim Murat (1767-1815), King of Naples

and brother-in-law of Napoleon. He was in command of the cavalry in many of Napoleon's greatest battles

Sabrina (sa brī' nà) The Latin name of the river Severn, but in British legend the name of the daughter of Locrine and his concubine Estrildis Locrine's queen, Guendolen, vowed vengeance against Estrildis and her daughter, gathered an army together, and overthrew her husband Sabrina fled and jumped into the Severn, Nereus took pity on her, and made her goddess of the river, which is hence poetically called Sabrina
There is a gentle nymph not far from hence,
That with moist curb sways the smooth Severn stream,
Sabrina is her name, a virgin pure.
                                        MILTON: *Comus,* 840

Saccharissa (săk a ris' à) A name bestowed by Edmund Waller on Lady Dorothy Sidney (b 1617), eldest daughter of the Earl of Leicester, who, in 1639, married Lord Spencer of Wormleighton, afterwards Earl of Sunderland. Aubrey says that Waller was passionately in love with the lady, but the poems themselves give the impression that the affair was merely a poetical pose.

Sacco Benedetto or San Benito (săk' ŏ ben è det' ŏ, săn be nē' tŏ) (Span , the blessed sack or cloak) The yellow linen robe with two crosses on it, and painted over with flames and devils, in which persons condemned by the Spanish Inquisition were arrayed when they went to the stake *See* AUTO DA FE In the case of those who expressed repentance for their errors, the flames were directed downwards Penitents who had been taken before the Inquisition had to wear this badge for a stated period. Those worn by Jews, sorcerers, and renegades bore a St. Andrew's cross in red on back and front

Sachem (sā' chem) A chief among some of the North American Indian tribes *Sagamore* is a similar title

Sack. A bag According to tradition, it was the last word uttered before the tongues were confounded at Babel.

Sack was used of any loose upper garment hanging down the back from the shoulders, hence "sac-friars" or *fratres saccati.*

To get the sack, or **To be sacked.** To get discharged by one's employer. The phrase was current in France in the 17th century (*On luy a donné son sac*); and the probable explanation of the term is that mechanics carried their implements in a bag or sack, and when discharged received it back so that they might replace in it their tools, and seek a job elsewhere The Sultan used to put into a sack, and throw into the Bosporus, any one of his harem he wished out of the way, but there is no connexion between this and our saying

A sack race A village sport in which each runner is tied up to the neck in a sack. In some cases the candidates have to make short leaps, in other cases they are at liberty to run as well as the limits of the sack will allow them

Sack. Any dry wine, as sherry sack, Madeira sack, Canary sack, and Palm sack (From Fr. *sec,* dry)

Sackerson (săk′ er sŏn) The famous bear kept at Paris Garden (*q v*) in Shakespeare's time.

Sacrament. Originally "a military oath" (Lat. *sacramentum*) taken by the Roman soldiers not to desert their standard, turn their back on the enemy, or abandon their general We also, in the sacrament of baptism, take a military oath "to fight manfully under the banner of Christ " The early Christians used the word to signify "a sacred mystery," and hence its application to baptism, the Eucharist, marriage, confirmation, etc

The **five sacraments** are Confirmation, Penance, Orders, Matrimony, and Extreme Unction. These are not counted "Sacraments of the Gospel" See *Thirty-nine Articles*, Article xxv

The **seven sacraments** are Baptism, Confirmation, the Eucharist, Penance, Orders, Matrimony, and Extreme Unction

The **two sacraments** of the Protestant Churches are Baptism and the Lord's Supper

Sacramentarians. Those who believe that no change takes place in the eucharistic elements after consecration, but that the bread and wine are simply emblems of the body and blood of Christ The name is applied specially to a party of 16th-century German Reformers who separated from Luther

Sacred Applied to that which is consecrated (Lat *sacrare*, to consecrate), or dedicated to, or set apart for, religious use

The **Sacred Band** A body of 300 Theban "Ironsides" who fought against Sparta in the 4th century B C They specially distinguished themselves at Leuctra (371), and the Band was annihilated at Chæronea (338)

The **Sacred City.** See HOLY CITY.

The **Sacred College.** The College of Cardinals (*q v*) at Rome

The **Sacred Heart** The "Feast of the Sacred Heart of Jesus" owes its origin to a French nun of the 17th century, St Mary Margaret Alacoque, of Burgundy, who practised devotion to the Saviour's heart in consequence of a vision The devotion was sanctioned by Pope Clement XII in 1732, and extended to the whole Church by Pius IX in 1856 It is observed on the Friday after the octave of Corpus Christi

The **Sacred Isle, or Holy Island.** An epithet used of Ireland because of its many saints, and of Guernsey for its many monks The island referred [to by Moore in his *Irish Melodies* is Scattery, to which St Senanus retired, and vowed that no woman should set foot thereon

> Oh, haste and leave this sacred isle,
> Unholy bark, ere morning smile
> > *St Senanus and the Lady.*

Enhallow (from the Norse *Eyinhalga*, holy isle) is the name of a small island in the Orkney group, where cells of the Irish anchorite fathers are said still to exist.
See also HOLY ISLE.

Sacred Majesty, a title applied to the sovereigns of Great Britain in the 17th and 18th centuries

The **Sacred War.** In Greek history, one of the wars waged by the Amphictyonic League in defence of the temple and oracle of Delphi
(1) Against the Cirrhæans (594-587 B C.)
(2) For the restoration of Delphi to the Phocians, from whom it had been taken (448-447 B C.)
(3) Against Philip of Macedon (346 B C.)

The **Sacred Way.** See VIA SACRA.

The **Sacred Weed,** Vervain (*see Herba Sacra*), or—humorously—tobacco.

Sacring Bell (săk′ ring) The bell rung in R C. churches at the consecration of the Host, or at its elevation Now called **Sanctus bell,** from the words *Sanctus, sanctus, sanctus, dominus, Deus Sabaoth*, pronounced by the priest From the obsolete verb *to sacre,* to consecrate, used especially of sovereigns and bishops.

> He heard a little sacring bell ring to the elevation of a to-morrow mass —REGINALD SCOTT. *Discovery of Witchcraft* (1584)
> The sacring of the kings of France.—*Temple.*

Sacy's Bible. See BIBLES SPECIALLY NAMED.

Sad He's a sad dog. A playful way of saying a man is a debauchee.

Sad bread (Lat *panis gravis*) Heavy bread, bread that has not risen properly. Shakespeare calls it "distressful bread"—not the bread of distress, but the *panis gravis* or ill-made bread eaten by those who can't get better. In America unleavened cakes are known as *sad cakes*

Sadism (să′ dizm) The unscientific term for the obtaining of sexual satisfaction through the infliction of pain or humiliation on another person or even an animal The word is also applied to the morbid pleasure certain psychological states experience in being cruel or in watching acts of cruelty The term comes from the Marquis de Sade (1740-1814), a French writer, of notorious ill behaviour and perversion, whose novels *Justine* (1791) and *Les crimes de l'amour* (1800) exhibited this psychological state of mind

Saddle. A saddle of mutton The two loins with the connecting vertebræ.

Boot and saddle. See BOOT

Lose the horse and win the saddle *See* LOSE

Saddle-bag furniture. Chairs and so on upholstered in a cheap kind of carpeting, the design of which is based on that of the saddle-bags carried by camels in the East.

Set the saddle on the right horse Lay the blame on those who deserve it

To be in the saddle. To be in a position of authority, in office, also to be ready for work and eager to get on with it

To saddle with the responsibility. To put the responsibility on, to make responsible for

Sadducees (săd′ ū sēz) A Jewish party which existed about the time of Christ, and denied the existence of spirits and angels, and disbelieved in the resurrection of the dead, said to be so called from Sadoc or Zadok (*see* 2 *Sam* viii, 17), who is thought to have been a priest or rabbi some three centuries before the birth of

Christ. They were opposed to the Pharisees in that they did not accept the oral parts of the Law traditionally handed down from Moses, and as they did not believe in future punishments, they punished offences with the utmost severity.

Sadleirian Lectures (săd lēr′ ı ăn) Lectures on Algebra delivered in the University of Cambridge and founded in accordance with the will of Lady Sadleir (d. 1706), wife of Sir Edwin Sadleir The first lecture was delivered in Emmanuel, 1710. The lectures were discontinued in 1860 and a professorship of Pure Mathematics substituted for them.

Sadler's Wells (near Islington, London) There was a well at this place called *Holy Well*, once noted for "its extraordinary cures" The priests of Clerkenwell Priory used to boast of its virtues. At the Reformation it was stopped up, and was wholly forgotten till 1683, when a certain Sadler, in digging gravel for his garden, accidentally discovered it again. Hence the name In 1765 a builder named Rosoman converted Sadler's garden into a theatre that became famous for burlettas, musical interludes and pantomimes In 1772 the famous comedian Thomas King took over the management until he succeeded Sheridan at Drury Lane Edmund Kean, Dibdin and many other great actors appeared at Sadler's Wells, and the great clown Grimaldi made his fame there In 1844 Phelps took over the theatre and produced Shakespeare, but the boom in the West End theatres cast the Wells into the shade, though it enjoyed some popularity from 1875 until 1881 under the management of Mrs Bateman. In 1931 Lilian Baylis (d 1937), who for over thirty years had managed the Old Vic, opened Sadler's Wells for the production of ballet and opera and made it one of the leading houses in London.

Safety. Safety bicycle. *See* PENNYFARTHING

Safety matches. In 1847 Schrotter, an Austrian chemist, discovered that red phosphorus gives off no fumes, and is virtually inert, but being mixed with chlorate of potash under slight pressure it explodes with violence In 1855 Herr Bottger, of Sweden, put the one on the *box* and the other on the *match*, and later improvements have resulted in the match being tipped with a mixture of chlorate of potash, sulphide of antimony, bichromate of potassium and red lead, while on the box is a mixture of non-poisonous amorphous phosphorus and black oxide of manganese, so that the match must be rubbed on the box to bring the two together *Cp* PROMETHEANS, LUCIFERS

Saffron. He hath slept in a bed of saffron (Lat *dormivit in sacco croci*). He has a very light heart, in reference to the exhilarating effects of saffron

> With genial joy to warm his soul,
> Helen mixed saffron in the bowl

Saga (plural **Sagas**) (sa′ ga) The Teutonic and Scandinavian mythological and historical traditions, chiefly compiled in the 12th and three following centuries The most remarkable are those of *Lodbrog, Hervara, Vilkina, Voluspa, Volsunga, Blomsturvalla, Ynglinga,*

Olaf Tryggva-Sonar, with those of *Jomsvikingia* and of *Knytlinga* (which contain the legendary history of Norway and Denmark), those of *Sturlinga* and *Eryrbiggia* (which contain the legendary history of Iceland), and the collections, the *Heims-Kringla* and *New Edda*, due to Snorro-Sturleson *Cp.* EDDA.

Sagamore *See* SACHEM

Sages, The Seven. *See* WISE MEN

Sagittarius (săj ı tār′ ı us) (Lat , the archer) One of the old constellations, the ninth sign of the Zodiac, which the sun enters about November 22nd It represents the centaur Chiron, who at death was converted into the constellation

Sagittary (săj′ ı ta rı). The name given in the mediæval romances to the centaur, a mythical monster half horse and half man, whose eyes sparkled like fire and struck dead like lightning, fabled to have been introduced into the Trojan armies.

> The dreadful Sagittary
> Appals our numbers
> *Troilus and Cressida,* v, 5.

The "Sagittary" referred to in *Othello* i, 1.—
> Lead to the Sagittary the raised search,
> And there will I be with him,

was probably an inn, but may have been the Arsenal

Sahib (sab, sa′ ib) (Urdu, *friend*) A form of address used by Hindus to Europeans, about equivalent to our 'Sir" in "Yes, sir," "No, sir " Also, an Englishman or European, a woman being *Mem-sahib* The word is also used colloquially to describe a cultured, refined man

Sail. Sailing under false colours Pretending to be what you are not with the object of personal advantage. The allusion is to pirate vessels, which hoist any colours to elude detection.

To sail before the wind, close to the wind, etc *See* WIND.

To set sail. To start a voyage.

To strike sail. *See* STRIKE

You may hoist sail. Be off Maria saucily says to Viola, dressed in man's apparel—
> Will you hoist sail, sir? Here lies your way.—
> *Twelfth Night,* i, 5

Sailor King, The. William IV of England (1765, 1830-37), who entered the navy as midshipman in 1779, and was made Lord High Admiral in 1827

Saint. Individual saints who have a place in this *Dictionary of Phrase and Fable* will be found entered under their names For symbols of saints *see* SYMBOLS.

Alexander III (1159-81) was the first Pope to restrict the right of canonization (i e the making of a saint) to the Holy See, before his time it was performed by a synod of bishops and merely ratified by the Pope It was not till the 4th century that persons other than martyrs were canonized, and none was inscribed on the Roll of the Saints until 608, when Boniface IV dedicated the Pantheon to St. Mary of the Martyrs The first saint to be made direct by a Pope was St Swidborg, canonized in 752 by Stephen II at the request of Pepin St. Alban, the English protomartyr, was canonized in 749 by Hadrian I, to please the Mercian King, Offa

Popes who have been canonized. From the time of St Peter to the end of the 4th century all the Popes (with a few minor and doubtful exceptions) are popularly entitled "Saint", since then the following are the chief of those bearing the title —

Innocent I (402-17).
Leo the Great (440-61)
John I (523-26)
Gregory the Great (590-604).
Deusdedit I (615-19)
Martin I (649-54)
Leo II (682-84)
Sergius I (687-701).
Zacharias (741-52).
Paul I (757-67)
Leo III (795-816)
Paschal I (817-24).
Nicholas the Great (858-67).
Leo IX (1049-54)
Gregory VII, *Hildebrand* (1073-85).
Celestine V (1294).
Pius V (1566-72).
Among the kings and royalties so called are—

Edward the Martyr (961, 975-78)
Edward the Confessor (1004, 1042-66).
Eric IX of Sweden (? 1155-61)
Ethelred I, king of Wessex (? 866-871)
Ferdinand III of Castile and Leon (1200, 1217-52).
Irene (d. 1124), the Empress, daughter of the king of Hungary and consort of John Comnenus, Byzantine Emperor
Lawrence Justiniani, Patriarch of Venice (1390, 1451-55).
Louis IX of France (1215, 1226-70).
Margaret (d. 1093), queen of Scotland, wife of William III.
Olaus II of Norway, brother of Harald III, called "St Olaf the Double Beard" (984, 1026-30).
Stephen I of Hungary (979, 997-1038).
Theodora (d 867), Empress; consort of the Byzantine Emperor, Theophilus.
Wenceslaus (910, 928-936), king of Bohemia.
It is only rarely that persons are canonized now, Joan of Arc was canonized in 1909, in 1935 Pius XI canonized Sir Thomas More (1478-1535) and John Fisher (1459-1535), Bishop of Rochester, who had suffered for the Faith under Henry VIII.

The City of Saints. *See* CITY.

The Island of Saints. So Ireland was called in the Middle Ages.

The Latter-day Saints. The Mormons (*q v.*).

St. Befana. There is no saint of this name, which is a corruption of *Epiphany See* BEFANA.

St. Bernard Passes. Two Alpine passes into Italy, the Great St. Bernard from Switzerland, the Little St Bernard from France On the former is the famous hospice founded by St Bernard of Menthon (923-1008, canonized, 1681), served by the Augustinian Canons. From earliest times they have succoured pilgrims and others crossing the Pass, for this purpose breeding the large and handsome St. Bernard Dog, trained to track and aid travellers lost in the snow. In May, 1800, Napoleon made his famous passage of the Alps across the Great St. Bernard Pass with 30,000 men A military feat as the road did not then exist, the only track being a bridle-path.

St. Cloud. A palace where many important events in French history took place, formerly stood some mile and a half west of Paris, on the Seine It was built on the site of an older chateau in 1658 by Louis XIV, and given to his brother the Duke of Orleans. Louis XVI bought it from that family and gave it to Marie Antoinette, it was later a favourite residence of Napoleon and Napoleon III It was badly damaged during the Franco-Prussian War of 1870, and on the fall of the Empire was demolished by the Communards in 1871.

St. Cyr, or **St.-Cyr-l'Ecole.** The famous French military academy, about 14 miles south-west of Paris The building was formerly occupied by the girls' school founded by Mme de Maintenon, where Racine's *Esther* and *Athalie* were first acted. The girls' school was suppressed at the Revolution, and in 1808 Napoleon moved the military school thither from Fontainebleau The building was destroyed by the R A F in World War II.

St. Elmo, or **St. Elmo's Fire.** The corposant (Port. *corpo santo*, sacred body), or compozant, an electrical luminosity often seen on the masts and rigging of ships on dark, stormy nights. There is no saint of this name, and the suggestions are that "Elmo" is a corruption of *St. Anselm* (of Lucca), St. *Erasmus* (the patron saint of Neapolitan sailors), or of *Helena*, sister of Castor and Pollux (*q.v*), by which twin-name the St. Elmo's Fire is also known

St. Francis's Distemper. Impecuniosity; being moneyless. Those of the Order of St Francis were not allowed to carry any money about them
I saw another case of gentlemen of St Francis's distemper —RABELAIS *Pantagruel*, v, 21.

St. Germains, The Court of. The intriguing circle of exiled English nobles and others that surrounded James II after his deposition, when he had settled at the château of St Germainen-Laye (on the Seine, about 8 miles NNW. of Paris), a former residence of François I, Louis XIV, and others

St. Giles's. *See* GILES.

St. James's, The Court of. *See under* JAMES

St. John Lateran. *See* LATERAN.

St. Johnstone's Tippet. A halter, so called from Johnstone the hangman.

St. Leger Sweepstakes. A horse-race for three-year-olds, run at Doncaster early in September It was instituted in 1776 by Colonel Anthony St Leger, of Park Hill, near Doncaster, but was not called the "St. Leger" till two years afterwards

St. Martin's le Grand. The familiar name for the central offices of the General Post Office, because from 1825 its headquarters have been on and about the site of the ancient church and monastery of this name (dating from pre-Conquest times) at the south-west corner of Aldersgate Street, London.

St. Martin's Summer. See SUMMER.

St. Monday. A facetious name sometimes given to Monday because many workmen and others who like an extended "week-end" make it a holiday (*holy* day!) There is a story in the *Journal* of the Folk-lore Society recording that—

While Cromwell's army lay encamped at Perth, one of his zealous partisans, named Monday, died, and Cromwell offered a reward for the best lines on his death. A shoemaker of Perth brought the following—

Blessed be the Sabbath Day,
And cursed be worldly pelf,
Tuesday will begin the week,
Since Monday's hanged himself,

which so pleased Cromwell that he not only gave the promised reward but made also a decree that shoemakers should be allowed to make Monday a standing holiday.

St. Patrick's Purgatory. See PATRICK.

St. Petersburg. The former name of the capital of the old Russian Empire, so called in honour of Peter the Great, who founded it in 1703. Soon after the outbreak of World War I it was changed by Imperial rescript to Petrograd, this being the Russian, while the other is a German, equivalent of *Peter's Town*. In 1924 the name of the place was changed again, to Leningrad, in honour of Lenin (1870-1924) the virtual founder of the U S S.R Leningrad withstood one of the greatest sieges of World War II, from 1941 until 1944

St. Simonism. The social and political system of Count de St Simon (1760-1825), the founder of French Socialism, who proposed the institution of a European parliament to arbitrate in all matters affecting Europe, and the establishment of a social hierarchy based on capacity and labour. Fable says that he was led to his "social system" by the apparition of Charlemagne, which appeared to him one night in the Luxembourg, where he was suffering a temporary imprisonment.

St. Stephen's. The Houses of Parliament are so called, because, at one time, the Commons used to sit in St Stephen's Chapel

St. Stephen's Loaves. Stones, the allusion, of course, is to the stoning of St Stephen (*Acts* vii, 54-60).

Having said this, he took up one of St Stephen's loaves, and was going to hit him with it —RABELAIS *Pantagruel*, v, 8.

Sake. A form of the obsolete word *sac* (A.S *sacu*, a dispute or lawsuit), meaning some official right or privilege, such as that of holding a manorial court.

The common phrases *For God's sake, for conscience' sake, for goodness' sake*, etc., mean "out of consideration for" God, conscience, etc.

For old sake's sake. For the sake of old acquaintance, past times.

For one's name's sake. Out of regard for one's character or good name.

Sakes! or **Sakes alive!** Expressions of surprise, admiration, etc, commoner in the United States than in England.

Saker (sā' ker). A piece of light artillery, used, especially on board ship, in the 16th and 17th centuries. The word is borrowed from the saker hawk (falcon)

The cannon, blunderbuss, and saker,
He was the inventor of and maker
BUTLER. *Hudibras*, i, 2.

Sakuntala (sa kun' ta la). The heroine of Kalidasa's great Sanskrit drama, *Sakuntala* She was the daughter of a sage, Viswamita, and Menakâ, a water-nymph, and was brought up by a hermit. One day King Dushyanta came to the hermitage during a hunt, and persuaded her to marry him; and later, giving her a ring, returned to his throne A son was born, and Sakuntala set out with him to find his father. On the way, while bathing, she lost the ring, and the king did not recognize her owing to enchantment Subsequently it was found by a fisherman in a fish he had caught (*cp*. KENTIGERN), the king recognized his wife, she was publicly proclaimed his queen, and Bhârata, his son and heir, became the founder of the glorious race of the Bhâratas.

Sakya-Muni (sak' ya mū' ni) One of the names of Gautama Siddartha, the Buddha (*q.v*), founder of Buddhism.

Salaam (sa lam') An Oriental salutation of a ceremonious nature, often with a profound obeisance. In Arabic the word means "peace."

Salad. A pen'orth of salad oil A strapping; a castigation. It is a joke on All Fool's Day to send one to the saddler's for a "pen'orth of salad oil" The pun is between "salad oil," as above, and the French *avoir de la salade*, "to be flogged " The French *salader* and *salade* are derived from the *salle* or saddle on which schoolboys were at one time birched. A block for the purpose is still kept as a curiosity in some of our public schools.

Salad days. Days of inexperience, when persons are very green.

My salad days
When I was green in judgment
Antony and Cleopatra, i, 5.

Salamander (săl' a măn der) (Gr *salamandra*, a kind of lizard) The name is now given to a family of amphibious urodela (newts, etc), but anciently to a mythical lizard-like monster that was supposed to be able to live in fire, which, however, it quenched by the chill of its body Pliny tells us he tried the experiment once, but the creature was soon burnt to a powder (*Nat. Hist* x, 67; xxix, 4). It was adopted by Paracelsus as the name of the elemental being inhabiting fire (*gnomes* being those of the earth, *sylphs* of the air, and *undines* of the water), and was hence taken over by the Rosicrucian system, from which source Pope introduced salamanders into his *Rape of the Lock*.

When the Fair in all their Pride expire,
To their first Elements the Souls retire
The Sprites of fiery Termagants in Flame
Mount up, and take a *Salamander's* name
Rape of the Lock, i, 57.

François I of France adopted as his badge a lizard in the midst of flames, with the legend *Nutrisco et extinguo* (I nourish and extinguish) The Italian motto from which this legend was borrowed was *Nutrisco il buono e spengo il reo* (I nourish the good and extinguish the bad) Fire purifies good metal, but consumes rubbish

Falstaff calls Bardolph's nose "a burning lamp," "a salamander," and the drink that made such "a fiery meteor" he calls "fire "

I have maintained that salamander of yours with fire any time this two-and-thirty years —1 *Henry IV*, iv, 3

Salamander's wool Asbestos, a fibrous mineral, affirmed by the Tartars to be made "of the root of a tree." It is sometimes called "mountain flax," and is not combustible.

Salary. Originally "salt rations" (Lat *salarium*, *sal*, salt). The ancient Romans served out rations of salt and other necessaries to their soldiers and civil servants The rations altogether were called by the general name of *salt*, and when money was substituted for the rations the stipend went by the same name.

Sales Resistance. The negative attitude of a possible buyer which hinders or prevents the sale of a commodity.

Salic (săl' ik) Pertaining to the Salian Franks, a tribe of Franks who, in the 4th century A.D , established themselves on the banks of the Sala (now known as the Yssel), and became the ancestors of the Merovingian kings of France.
Which Salique, as I said, 'twixt Elbe and Sala, Is at this day in Germany called Meisen
Henry V, i, 2.

Salic Code. A Frankish law-book, written in Latin, extant during the Merovingian and Carolingian periods.

The Salic Law. A law derived from the Salic Code limiting succession to the throne, land, etc , to heirs male to the exclusion of females, chiefly because certain military duties were connected with the holding of lands In the early 14th century it became the fundamental law of the French monarchy, and the claim of Edward III to the French throne, based on his interpretation of the law, resulted in the Hundred Years War It was also through the operation of the Salic Law that the Crowns of Hanover and England were separated when Queen Victoria came to the throne in 1837 The revocation of the Salic Law in Spain by Ferdinand VII, in order that his daughter Isabella should succeed him on the throne, tore the country into two factions, the Isabellitas and the Carlists who fought for the claims of Ferdinand's brother Don Carlos The Carlist wars raged from 1830 to 1840 and again from 1872 to 1876.

Saliens, The. In ancient Rome, a college of twelve priests of Mars traditionally instituted by Numa The tale is that a shield (*see* ANCILE) fell from heaven, and the nymph Egeria predicted that wherever it was preserved the people would be the dominant people of the earth To prevent its being surreptitiously taken away, Numa had eleven others made exactly like it, and appointed twelve priests as guardians Every year these young patricians promenaded the city, singing and dancing, and they finished the day with a most sumptuous banquet, insomuch that *saliares cœna* became proverbial for a most sumptuous feast. The word "saliens" means dancing
Nunc est bibendum
. nunc Saliaribus
Ornare pulvinar Deorum
Tempus erat dapibus
HORACE 1 *Odes*, xxxvii, 2-4.

Salisbury Crags These rocky hills, near Arthur's Seat just outside Edinburgh, are so called from the Earl of Salisbury who accompanied Edward III on an expedition against the Scots

Sallee-man, or **Sallee rover**. A pirate-ship, so called from Sallee, a seaport on the west coast of Morocco, the inhabitants of which were formerly notorious for their piracy.

Sally Lunn. A tea-cake, so called from a woman pastrycook of that name in Bath, who used to cry them about in a basket at the close of the 18th century. Dalmer, the baker, bought her recipe, and made a song about the buns.

Salmacis (săl' ma sis) A fountain of Caria, which rendered effeminate all those who bathed therein It was in this fountain that Hermaphroditus changed his sex (Ovid: *Metamorphoses*, iv, 285, and xvi, 319)

Salmagundi (săl' ma gŭn' di) A mixture of minced veal, chicken, or turkey, anchovies or pickled herrings, and onions, all chopped together and served with lemon-juice and oil. The word appeared in the 17th century; its origin is unknown, but fable has it that it was the name of one of the ladies attached to the suite of Mary de Medicis, wife of Henri IV of France, who either invented or popularized the dish
In 1807 Washington Irving published a humorous periodical with this as the title

Salop. *See* SHROPSHIRE

Salt. Flavour, smack The salt of youth is that vigour and strong passion which then predominates.
Though we are justices, and doctors, and churchmen, Master Page, we have some salt of our youth in us —*Merry Wives of Windsor*, ii, 3

Shakespeare uses the term on several occasions for strong amorous passion Thus Iago refers to it as "hot as monkeys, salt as wolves in pride" (*Othello*, iii, 3) The Duke calls Angelo's base passion his "salt imagination," because he supposed his victim to be Isabella, and not his betrothed wife whom the Duke forced him to marry (*Measure for Measure*, v, 1)

A sailor of large experience is often called an *old salt*, the reason is obvious—he has been well *salted* by the sea

Spilling salt was held to be an unlucky omen by the Romans, and the superstition remains to this day, though, with us the evil may be averted if he who spills the salt throw a pinch of it over the *left* shoulder with the *right* hand. In Leonardo da Vinci's famous picture of the Lord's Supper, Judas Iscariot is known by the salt-cellar knocked over accidentally by his arm Salt was used in sacrifice by the Jews, as well as by the Greeks and Romans; and it is still used in baptism by Roman Catholics It was an emblem of purity and the sanctifying influence of a holy life on others Hence our Lord tells his disciples they are "the salt of the earth" (*Matt* v, 13). Spilling the salt after it was placed on the head of the victim was a bad omen, hence the superstition.

It is still not uncommon to put salt into a coffin, for it is said that Satan hates salt, because it is the symbol of incorruption and immortality, and in Scotland it was long customary to throw a handful of salt on the top of the mash when brewing, to keep the witches from it Salt really has some effect in moderating the fermentation and fining the liquor.

A covenant of salt (*Numb* xviii, 19) A covenant which could not be broken As salt was a symbol of incorruption, it, of course, symbolized perpetuity

The Lord God of Israel gave the kingdom to David . . by a covenant of salt —2 *Chron* xiii, 5.

Attic salt. See ATTIC

He won't earn salt for his porridge. He will never earn a penny.

If the salt have lost its savour, wherewith shall it be salted? (*Matt* v, 13) If men fall from grace, how shall they be restored ? The reference is to rock salt, which loses its saltness if exposed to the hot sun.

Not worth your salt. Not worth your wages The reference is to the *salary* (*q v*) composed of rations of salt and other necessaries served out by the Romans to their soldiers, etc

Put some salt on his tail Catch or apprehend him. The phrase is based on the direction given to small children to lay salt on a bird's tail if they want to catch it

The salt of the earth. Properly, the elect; the perfect, or those approaching perfection (*see Matt* v, 13).

To eat a man's salt. To partake of his hospitality. Among the Arabs to eat a man's salt was a sacred bond between the host and guest. No one who has eaten of another's salt should speak ill of him or do him an ill turn.

Why dost thou shun the salt? that sacred pledge,
Which, once partaken, blunts the sabre's edge,
Makes even contending tribes in peace unite,
And hated hosts seem brethren to the sight!
BYRON *The Corsair*, ii, iv.

To salt a mine. To introduce pieces of ore, etc., into the workings so as to delude prospective purchasers or shareholders into the idea that a worthless mine is in reality a profitable investment.

To salt an account, invoice, etc To put the extreme value upon each article, and even something more, to give it piquancy and raise its market value

To sit above the salt—in a place of distinction Formerly the family *saler* (salt cellar) was of massive silver, and placed in the middle of the table Persons of distinction sat *above* the "saler"—*i.e* between it and the head of the table; dependents and inferior guests sat below.

True to his salt. Faithful to his employers. Here *salt* means salary (*q v*)

With a grain of salt (Lat *Cum grano salis*) With great reservations or limitation, allowing it merely a *grain* of truth As salt is sparingly used in condiments, so is truth in remarks to which this phrase is applied

To row a man up Salt River (U S A) To discomfit or defeat him, especially in a political sense

Salt Hill. The mound at Eton where the Eton scholars used to collect money for the Captain at the Montem (*q v*) All the money collected was called *salt* (*cp*. SALARY)

Salt lick. A place ʃwhere salt is found naturally and in a position available to animals which resort thither to lick it from the rocks, etc

Salute, Salutation. According to tradition, on the triumphant return of Maximilian to Germany, after his second campaign, the town of Augsburg ordered 100 rounds of cannon to be discharged The officer on service, fearing to have fallen short of the number, caused an extra round to be added The town of Nuremberg ordered a like salute, and the custom became established

Salute in the British navy, between two ships of equal rank, is made by firing an equal number of guns. If the vessels are of unequal rank, the superior fires the fewer rounds

Royal salute, in the British navy, consists (1) in firing twenty-one great guns, (2) in the officers lowering their sword-points, and (3) in dipping the colours

In the Army a Royal Salute is 101 guns fired at intervals of 10 seconds

Discharging guns as a salute. To show that no fear exists, and therefore no guns will be required. This is like "burying the hatchet" (*q.v*)

Lowering swords To express a willingness to put yourself unarmed in the power of the person saluted, from a full persuasion of his friendly feeling

Presenting arms—*i e* offering to give them up, from the full persuasion of the peaceful and friendly disposition of the person so honoured.

During the British occupation of India the native rulers were all entitled by law to certain salutes, these ranged from 21 guns in the cases of the Maharajahs of Baroda, Gwalior, and Mysore, and the Nizam of Hyderabad, down to 19, 17, 15, 13, and 11 guns to rulers of lesser States

Shaking hands. A relic of the ancient custom of adversaries, in treating of a truce, taking hold of the weapon-hand to ensure against treachery.

Lady's curtsy. A relic of the ancient custom of women going on the knee to men of rank and power, originally to beg mercy, afterwards to acknowledge superiority

Taking off the hat. A relic of the ancient custom of taking off the helmet when no danger is nigh A man takes off his hat to show that he dares stand unarmed in your presence.

Salvation Army. A religious organization founded by William Booth, a Methodist minister Its origin was the East End Revival Society, which became the Christian Mission in 1865 Booth selected the name Salvation Army in 1877 and organized it on semi-military lines, himself being called ' General'' having under him "Colonels," "Adjutants," "Corporals," etc The motto adopted was "Through Blood and Fire," and the activities of the Army were turned to the relief, moral, spiritual and physical, of the poorest and least educated of the population The work has spread to every part of the world and immense good has been done by the selfless devotion of its rank and file

Salve. Latin "hail," "welcome " The word is often woven on door-mats

Salve, Regina! An antiphonal hymn to the Virgin Mary sung in Roman Catholic churches from Trinity Sunday to Advent, after lauds and compline So called from the opening words. *Salve, regina mater misericordiæ!* (Hail holy Queen, Mother of Mercy)

Sam. To stand Sam To pay the reckoning. The phrase is said to have arisen from the letters U S on the knapsacks of American soldiers. The government of "Uncle Sam" has to pay, or "stand Sam" for all, hence also the phrase *Nunky pays for all.*

Uncle Sam. The personification of the Government, or the people, of the United States—a facetious adaptation of the initials U S. (Uncle Sam) placed on government property The expression arose about 1812 and quickly became popular.

Upon my Sam (or **Sammy**)! A humorous form of asseveration, also, *'pon my sacred Sam!*

Sam Browne belt. The leather belt with straps over the shoulders and originally with a sword-frog, compulsory for officers and warrant officers in the British Army up to 1939, when it was declared optional This belt was invented by General Sir Sam Browne, V C (1824-1901) a veteran of the Indian Mutiny Its pattern has been adopted by almost every military power in the world

Samaj. *See* BRAHMO SOMAJ

Samanides (săm' a nīdz). A dynasty of ten kings in western Persia (about 872 to 1004), founded by Ismail al Samani

Samaritan. A good Samaritan. A philanthropist, one who attends upon the poor to aid them and give them relief (*Luke* x, 30-37)

Sambo. A pet name given to one of Negro race, properly applied to the male offspring of a Negro and mulatto. (Span *zambo*, bow-legged, Lat. *scambus*.)

Samian (sā' mi ăn). **The Samian letter.** The letter Y, the Letter of Pythagoras (*q.v*), employed by him as the emblem of the straight and narrow path of virtue, which is one, but, if once deviated from, the farther the lines are extended the wider becomes the breach
> When reason doubtful, like the Samian letter,
> Points him two ways, the narrower the better
> POPE *Dunciad,* IV.

The Samian Poet. Simonides the satirist, born at Samos (about 556 B C)

The Samian Sage, or **The Samian.** Pythagoras born at Samos (6th cent B.C)
> 'Tis enough,
> In this late age, adventurous to have touched
> Light on the numbers of the Samian sage
> THOMSON.

Samite (săm' īt) A rich silk fabric with a warp of six threads, generally interwoven with gold, held in high esteem in the Middle Ages. So called after the Gr. *hexamiton*, hex, six, *mitos*, a thread. *Cp* DIMITY.

Sampford Ghost, The A kind of exaggerated "Cock Lane ghost" (*q v*) or Poltergeist, which haunted Sampford Peverell, Devon, for about three years in the first decade of the 19th century. Besides the usual knockings, the inmates were beaten, in one instance a powerful "unattached arm" flung a folio Greek Testament from a bed into the middle of a room. The Rev Charles Caleb Colton (credited as the author of these freaks) offered £100 to anyone who could explain the matter except on supernatural grounds No one, however, claimed the reward Colton died 1832

Sampo *See* KALEVALA

Sampson A domine Sampson. A humble pedantic scholar, awkward, irascible, and very old-fashioned A character in Scott's *Guy Mannering*

Samson. Any man of unusual strength, so called from the ancient Hebrew hero (*Judges* xiii-xvi) The name has been specially applied to Thomas Topham (d 1753), the "British Samson," son of a London carpenter. He lifted three hogshead of water (1,836 lb) in the presence of thousands of spectators at Coldbath Fields, May 28th, 1741, and eventually committed suicide; and to Richard Joy, the "Kentish Samson," who died 1742, at the age of 67 His tombstone is in St Peter's churchyard, Isle of Thanet.

Samurai (săm' ū rī) The military class of old Japan In early feudal times the term was applied to all who bore arms (it means "guard") but eventually it corresponded roughly to the mediæval squires as distinguished from the "daimio" or nobles On the abolition of the feudal system in 1871 the samurai were forbidden to wear swords, and in 1878 the designation was changed to that of "shizoku," or gentry.

San Benito. *See* SACCO BENEDETTO

Sance-bell. Same as "Sanctus bell." *See* SACRING-BELL.

Sancho Panza (săn' chō păn zà) The squire of Don Quixote (*q v*), in Cervantes's romance, who became governor of Barataria, a short, pot-bellied rustic, full of common sense, but without a grain of "spirituality " He rode upon an ass, Dapple, and was famous for his proverbs Panza, in Spanish, means *paunch*

A Sancho Panza. A rough and ready, sharp and humorous justice of the peace. In allusion to Sancho, as judge in the isle of Barataria

Sancho Panza's wife, is called Teresa, Pt II, i, 5, Maria, Pt. II, iv, 7, Juana, Pt I, 7, and Joan, Pt I, 21

Sanchoniathon (sang ko ni' a thon) The *Fragments of Sanchoniathon* are the literary remains of a supposed ancient Phœnician philosopher (alleged to have lived before the Trojan War), which are incorporated in the Phœnician History by Philo of Byblos (1st and 2nd cents A D), which History was drawn upon by Eusebius (about 320 A D), the "Father of Church History " The name is Greek and seems to mean "the whole law of Chon ', whether this is the correct interpretation or whether Sanchoniathon is intended to be a personal name, it is probable that there was no such collection or author, and that the name was invented by Philo to give an air of authority and antiquity to his own teachings.

Sanctions. The word employed in International Law to describe the action taken by one or more states to force another state to carry out its legal or treaty obligations

Sanctum Sanctorum (săng' tum săng tôr' um) (Lat , Holy of Holies). A private room into which no one uninvited enters, properly the Holy of Holies in the Jewish Temple, a small chamber into which none but the high priest might enter, and that only on the Great Day of Atonement

Sancy Diamond, The A famous historical diamond (53½ carats) said to have belonged at one time to Charles the Bold of Burgundy, and named after the French ambassador in Constantinople, Nicholas de Harlay, Sieur de Sancy, who, about 1575, bought it for 70,000 francs. Later it was owned by Henri III and Henri IV of France, then by Queen Elizabeth I; James II carried it with him in his flight to France in 1688, when it was sold to Louis XIV for £25,000 Louis XV wore it at his coronation, but during the Revolution it was disposed of to Prince Paul Demidoff for £80,000 In 1865 the Demidoff family sold it to Sir Jamsetjee Jeejeebhoy, it was in the market again in 1889, and rumour has it that it was subsequently acquired by the Tsar of Russia Its present whereabouts is unknown

Sand. A rope of sand. Something nominally effective and strong, but in reality worthless and untrustworthy.

The sand-man is about A playful remark addressed to children who are tired and "sleepy-eyed." *Cp* DUSTMAN

The sands are running out. Time is getting short, there will be little opportunity for doing what you have to do unless you take advantage of *now* Often used in reference to one who evidently has not much longer to live. The allusion is to the hour-glass

Alas' dread lord, you see the case wherein I stand, and how little sand is left to run in my poor glass.— *Reynard the Fox,* iv

To plough or **to number the sands.** To undertake an endless or impossible task

Alas' poor duke, the task he undertakes Is numbering sands and drinking oceans dry. *Richard II,* ii, 2.

Sand-blind. Dim-sighted; not exactly blind, but with eyes of very little use *Sand-* is here a corruption of the obsolete prefix *sam-,* meaning "half " English used to have *sam-*dead, *sam-ripe,* etc , and *sam-sodden* still survives in some dialects In the *Merchant of Venice* Launcelot Gobbo connects it with *sand,* the gritty earth.

This is my true-begotten father, who, being more than sand-blind, high-gravel blind, knows me not.— *Merchant of Venice,* ii, 2.

Sandabar or **Sindibad** (sănd' a bar, sind' i bad) Names given to a mediæval collection of tales that are very much the same as those in the Greek *Syntipas the Philosopher* and the Arabic *Romance of the Seven Viziers* (known in Western Europe as *The Seven Sages (Wise Masters*), and derived from the *Fables of Bidpai (q v.).* These names do not, in all probability, stand for the author or compiler, but result from Hebrew mistransliterations of the Arabic equivalent of *Bidpai* or *Pilpay.*

Sandal. A man without sandals. A prodigal; so called by the ancient Jews, because the seller gave his sandals to the buyer as a ratification of his bargain (*Ruth* iv, 7)

He wears the sandals of Theramenes. Said of a trimmer, an opportunist Theramenes (put to death 404 B C) was one of the Athenian oligarchy, and was nicknamed *cothurnus (i e* a sandal or boot which might be worn on either foot), because no dependence could be placed on him. He blew hot and cold with the same breath.

Sandemanians or **Glassites** (sănd e măn' i anz) A religious party expelled from the Church of Scotland for maintaining that national churches, being "kingdoms of this world," are unlawful Called *Glassites* from John Glas (1695-1773), the founder (1728), and called Sandemanians from Robert Sandeman (1718-71), a disciple of his, who published a series of letters on the subject in 1755 Members are admitted by a "holy kiss," and abstain from all animal food which has not been drained of blood, they believe in the community of property, and hold weekly communions.

Sandford and Merton. The schoolboy heroes of Thomas Day's old-fashioned children's tale of this name (published in three parts, 1783-89) "Master" Tommy Merton is rich, selfish, untruthful, and generally objectionable, Harry Sandford, the farmer's son, is depicted as being the reverse in every respect

Sandwich. A piece of meat between two slices of bread, so called from the fourth Earl of Sandwich (1718-92—the noted "Jemmy Twitcher"), who passed whole days in gambling, bidding the waiter bring him for refreshment a piece of meat between two pieces of bread, which he ate without stopping from play This contrivance was not first hit upon by the earl in the reign of George III, for the Romans were very fond of "sandwiches " called by them *offula*

Sandwichman. A perambulating advertisement-displayer, with an advertisement-board before and behind.

Sang-de-bœuf (săng de berf) (Fr , bullock's blood). The deep red with which ancient Chinese porcelain is often coloured

Sang-froid (Fr., cold blood) Freedom from excitement or agitation. One does a thing "with perfect *sang-froid*" when one does it coolly and collectedly, without unnecessary display.

> cross-legg'd, with great sang-froid
> Among the scorching ruins he sat smoking
> Tobacco on a little carpet
> BYRON *Don Juan*, VIII, cxxi.

Sanger's Circus. This is one of the oldest—and at one time the best known—of the circuses on the road It was formed from nothing by "Lord" George Sanger (1827-1911) who in 1871 purchased Astley's amphitheatre and menagerie, and about the same time leased the Agricultural Hall, Islington He carried his big circus or sent subsidiary ones throughout the provinces and into Scotland, and "Sanger's Circus" became an established institution

Sangrado, Dr. (săn gra′ dō). A name often applied to an ignorant or "fossilized" medical practitioner, from the humbug in Le Sage's *Gil Blas* (1715), a tall, meagre, pale man, of very solemn appearance, who weighed every word he uttered, and gave an emphasis to his sage dicta "His reasoning was geometrical, and his opinions angular " He prescribed warm water and bleeding for every ailment, for his great theory was that "It is a gross error to suppose that blood is necessary for life "

Sangrail or **Sangreal** (săng′ grāl) The Holy Grail, *see* GRAIL Popular etymology used to explain the word as meaning the *real blood* of Christ, *sang-real*, or the wine used in the last supper; and a tradition sprang up that part of this wine-blood was preserved by Joseph of Arimathæa, in the Saint, or Holy, Grail

Sanguine (săng′ gwin) (Lat *sanguis*, *sanguinis*, blood) The term used in heraldry for the deep red or purplish colour usually known as *murrey* (from the mulberry) In engravings it is indicated by lines of vert and purpure crossed, that is, diagonals from left to right This is a word with a curious history Its actual meaning is bloody, or of the colour of blood, hence it came to be applied to one who was ruddy, whose cheeks were red with good health and well-being From this it was easy to extend the meaning to one who was full of vitality, vivacious, confident and hopeful

Sanhedrin (săn′ i drin) (Gr *syn*, together, *hedra*, a seat, *i.e* a sitting together) The supreme council of the ancient Jews, consisting of seventy priests and elders, and a president who, under the Romans, was the high priest. It took its rise soon after the exile from the municipal council of Jerusalem, and was in existence till about A D 425, when Theodosius the Younger forbade the Jews to build synagogues All questions of the "Law" were dogmatically settled by the Sanhedrin, and those who refused obedience were excommunicated

In Dryden's *Absalom and Achitophel* (*q v*), the *Sanhedrin* stands for the English Parliament

> The Sanhedrim long time as chief he ruled,
> Their reason guided, and their passion cooled.

San Marino (săn mä rē′ nō). The smallest republic in the world Surrounded by Italian territory it lies 12 m SW. of Rimini, and

26*

consists of only 38 sq miles. In 1631 the Pope formally acknowledged its independence which was recognized by Italy in 1862.

Sans. (Fr., without).

Sans Culottes (Fr , without knee-breeches) A name given during the French Revolution to the extremists of the working-classes. Hence *Sansculottism*, the principles, etc., of "red republicans."

Sans Culottides. The five complementary days added to the twelve months of the Revolutionary Calendar, each month being made to consist of thirty days The days were named in honour of the *sans culottes*, and made idle days or holidays.

Sans Gêne, Madame. The nickname of the wife of Lefebvre, Duke of Dantzic (1755-1820), one of Napoleon's marshals. She was originally a washer-woman, and followed her husband—then in the ranks—as a vivandière. She was kind and pleasant, but her rough-and-ready ways and ignorance of etiquette soon made her the butt of the court, and earned her the nickname, which means "without constraint" or "free and easy "

Sans peur et sans reproche (Fr , without fear and without reproach). Pierre du Terrail, Chevalier de Bayard (1476-1524) was called *Le chevalier sans peur et sans reproche*

Sans Souci (Fr). Free and easy, void of care It is the name given by him to the palace built by Frederick the Great near Potsdam (1747).

The Philosopher of Sans-Souci. Frederick the Great (1712, 1740-86)

Enfans Sans Souci The mediæval French Tradesmen's company of actors, as opposed to the Lawyers', the "Basochians" (*q v*). It was organized in the reign of Charles VIII, for the performance of short comedies, in which public characters and the manners of the day were turned into ridicule, *Maitre Pathelin* (*see* MOUTONS), an immense favourite with the Parisians, was one of their pieces. The manager of the "Care-for-Nothings" (*sans souci*) was called "The Prince of Fools "

Santa Casa (Ital , the holy house) The reputed house in which the Virgin Mary lived at Nazareth, miraculously translated to Dalmatia, and finally to Italy *See* LORETTO

Santa Claus A contraction of Santa Nikolaus (*i e* St Nicolas), the patron saint in Germany of children His feast-day is December 6th, and the vigil is still held in some places, but for the most part his name is now associated with Christmastide The old custom used to be for someone, on December 5th, to assume the costume of a bishop and distribute small gifts to "good children " The present custom, introduced in England from Germany about 1840, is to put toys and other little presents into a stocking late on Christmas Eve, when the children are asleep, and when they wake on Christmas morn they find in the stocking at the bedside the gift sent by Santa Claus. *See* NICHOLAS.

Santos Dumont. Alberto Santos Dumont (1873-1932) was a Brazilian balloonist who, in 1901, won the Deutsch prize for flying from St Cloud to the Eiffel Tower in a dirigible balloon of his own design and construction In 1903 he had a number of these dirigibles in his airship station at Neuilly In 1905 he began to construct heavier-than-air machines and four years later produced his "demoiselle" monoplane which proved to be the forerunner of the aeroplanes of to-day.

Sapho (săf' ŏ). Mlle de Scudéry (1607-1701), the French novelist and poet, went by this name among her own circle

Sappho (săf' ŏ). The Greek poetess of Lesbos, known as "the Tenth Muse" She lived about 600 B C , and is fabled to have thrown herself into the sea from the Leucadian promontory in consequence of her advances having been rejected by the beautiful youth Phaon

Pope used the name in his *Moral Essays* (II) for Lady Mary Wortley Montagu (*cp*. ATOSSA) *See also* SAPHO, *above*

The Sappho of Toulouse. Clémence Isaure (about 1450-1500), a wealthy lady of Toulouse, who instituted in 1490 the "Jeux Floraux," and left funds to defray their annual expenses She composed an *Ode to Spring*.

Sapphics. A four-lined verse-form of classical lyric poetry, named after the Greek poetess Sappho, who employed it, the fourth line being an Adonic There must be a cæsura at the fifth foot of each of the first three lines, which run thus —

— ᴗ | — — | — ‖ ᴗ ᴗ | — ᴗ | — ᴗ

The Adonic is—

— ᴗ ᴗ | — ᴗ *or* — —

The first and third stanzas of the famous *Ode* of Horace, *Integer vitæ* (i, 22), may be translated thus, preserving the metre —

He of sound life, who ne'er with sinners wendeth,
Needs no Moorish bow, such as malice bendeth,
Nor with poisoned darts life from harm defendeth,
    Fuscus believe me
Once I, unarmed, was in a forest roaming,
Singing love lays, when i' the secret gloaming
Rushed a huge wolf, which though in fury foaming,
    Did not aggrieve me   E C B

Probably the best example of Sapphics in English is Canning's *Needy Knife-grinder*

Saracen (săr' a sen) Ducange derives the word from *Sarah* (Abraham's wife), Hottinger from the Arabic *saraca* (to steal), Forster from *sahra* (a desert), but probably it is the Arabic *sharakyoun* or *sharkeyn* (the eastern people), as opposed to Magharibe (the western people— *i e.* of Morocco). In mediæval romance the term was applied to Moslems generally, but among the Romans it denoted any of the nomadic tribes that raided the Syrian borders of the Empire.

Saragossa (săr à gos' a) **The Maid of Saragossa.** Augustina, a young Spanish girl (d. 1857) noted for her bravery in the defence of Saragossa against the French, 1808 She was only twenty-two when, her lover being shot, she mounted the battery in his place.

Saratoga Trunk (săr à tō' gà) A huge trunk, such as used to be taken by fashionable ladies to the watering place of that name in New York State

Sarcenet. *See* SARSENET

Sarcode *See* PROTOPLASM

Sarcophagus (sar kof' a gus) (Gr *sarx*, flesh, *phagein*, to eat). A stone coffin, so called because it was made of stone which, according to Pliny, consumed the flesh in a few weeks The stone was sometimes called *lapis Assius*, because it was found at Assos of Lycia.

Sardanapalus (sar dă năp' a lus) The Greek name of Asurbanipal (mentioned in *Ezra* iv, 10, as *Asenappar*), king of Assyria in the 7th century B.C Byron, in his poetic drama of this name (1821), makes him a voluptuous tyrant whose effeminacy led Arbaces, the Mede, to conspire against him Myrra, his favourite concubine, roused him to appear at the head of his armies He won three successive battles, but was then defeated, and was induced by Myrra to place himself on a funeral pile She set fire to it, and, jumping into the flames, perished with her master

The name is applied to any luxurious, extravagant, self-willed tyrant

Sardonic Smile, Laughter. A smile of contempt; bitter, mocking laughter; so used by Homer

The Sardonic or Sardinian laugh A laugh caused, it was supposed, by a plant growing in Sardinia, of which they who ate died laughing.—TRENCH: *Words*, lecture iv, p 176.

The *Herba Sardonia* (so called from Sardis, in Asia Minor) is so arid that it produces a convulsive movement of the nerves of the face, resembling a painful grin

'Tis envy's safest, surest rule
To hide her rage in ridicule,
The vulgar eye the best beguiles
When all her snakes are decked with smiles,
Sardonic smiles by rancour raised
        SWIFT *Pheasant and Lark*.

Sardonyx (sar' don iks) A precious stone composed of white chalcedony alternating with layers of sard, which is an orange-brown variety of cornelian Pliny says it is called *sard* from Sardis, in Asia Minor, where it is found, and *onyx*, the nail, because its colour resembles that of the skin under the nail (*Nat. Hist* xxxvii, 6).

Sarsen Stones (sar' sen). The sandstone boulders of Wiltshire and Berkshire are so called The early Christian Saxons used the word *Saresyn* (*i.e* Saracen, *q v*) as a synonym of pagan or heathen, and as these stones were popularly associated with Druid worship, they were called *Saresyn* (or heathen) *stones* Robert Ricart says of Duke Rollo, "He was a Saresyn come out of Denmark into France"

Sarsenet (sar' sen et) A very fine, soft, silk material, so called from its Saracenic or Oriental origin. The word is sometimes used adjectivally of soft and gentle speech.

Sartor Resartus (sar' tor re sar' tus) (*The Tailor Patched*) A philosophical satire by Thomas Carlyle, first published in *Fraser's Magazine*, 1833-4

Diogenes Teufelsdröckh is Carlyle himself, and *Entepfuhl* is his native village of Ecclefechan.

The Rose Goddess, according to Froude, is Margaret Gordon, but Strachey says it is

Blumine, *i e* Kitty Kirkpatrick, daughter of Colonel Achilles Kirkpatrick The *Rose Garden* is Strachey's garden at Shooter's Hill, and the *Duenna* is Mrs. Strachey
The Zahdarms are Mr. and Mrs Buller, and *Toughgut* is Charles Buller
Philistine is the Rev Edward Irving.

SAS Special Air Service British volunteer troops raised in World War II to drop by parachute behind the enemy's lines in uniform (as distinct from spies or agents in civilian clothes) to damage specific targets or enemy communications in general They were evolved from the Long Range Desert Patrol (*q v*).

Sassanides (săs ăn' ı děz) A powerful Persian dynasty, ruling from about A D 225-641; so named because Ardeshir, the founder, was son of Sassan, a lineal descendant of Xerxes.

Sassenach (săs' năk) The common form of *Sassunach*, Gaelic for English or an Englishman It represents the Teutonic ethnic name, *Saxon*.

Satan (să' tăn), in Hebrew, means *adversary* or *enemy*
      To whom the Arch-enemy
   (And hence in heaven called Satan).
         MILTON *Paradise Lost*, Bk. 1, 81, 82.

In the Bible the term is usually applied to a human adversary or opposer, and only in three cases (*Zech* iii, *Job* i, 2, and 1 *Chron*. xxi, 1) does it denote an evil spirit.
The name is often used of a person of whom one is expressing abhorrence. Thus, the Clown says to Malvolio—
   Fie, thou dishonest Satan! I call thee by the most modest terms, for I am one of those gentle ones that will use the devil himself with courtesy —*Twelfth Night*, iv, 2.

The Satanic School. So Southey called Byron, Shelley, and those of their followers who set at defiance the generally received notions of religion See the Preface to his *Vision of Judgment*

Satire (săt' ir) Scaliger's derivation of this word from *satyr* is untenable. It is from *satura* (full of variety), *satura lanx*, a hotchpotch or olla podrida The term originally denoted a medley of hotchpotch in verse, now it is applied to compositions in verse or prose in which folly, vice, or individuals are held up to ridicule See Dryden's Dedication prefixed to his *Satires*

Father of satire. Archilochus of Paros, 7th century B C

Father of French satire. Mathurin Regnier (1573-1613)

Father of Roman satire. Lucilius (175-103 B C)
   Lucilius was the man who, bravely bold,
   To Roman vices did the mirror hold,
   Protected humble goodness from reproach,
   Showed worth on foot, and rascals in a coach.
         DRYDEN· *Art of Poetry*, c, ii

Saturday The seventh day of the week, called by the Anglo-Saxons Sæter-dæg, after the Latin Saturni dies, the day of Saturn *See* BLACK SATURDAY

Saturn (săt' urn) A Roman deity, identified with the Greek Kronos (*time*) (*q.v*) He devoured all his children except Jupiter (*air*), Neptune (*water*), and Pluto (*the grave*) These Time cannot consume The reign of Saturn was celebrated by the poets as a "Golden Age" According to the old alchemists and astrologers, Saturn typified lead, and was a very evil planet to be born under "The children of the sayd Saturne shall be great jangeleres and chyders . and they will never forgyve tyll they be revenged on theyr quarell " (*Compost of Ptholomeus*.)

Saturn's tree. An alchemist's name for the Tree of Diana, or Philosopher's Tree (*q v*).

Saturnalia. A time of unrestrained disorder and misrule With the Romans it was the festival of Saturn, and was celebrated the 17th, 18th, and 19th of December. During its continuance no public business could be transacted, the law courts were closed, the schools kept holiday, no war could be commenced, and no malefactor punished Under the empire the festival was extended to seven days

Saturnian. Pertaining to Saturn; with reference to the "Golden Age," to the god's sluggishness, or to the baleful influence attributed to him by the astrologers
   Then rose the seed of Chaos and of Night
   To blot out order and extinguish light
   Of dull and venal a new world to mould,
   And bring Saturnian days of lead and gold.
         POPE· *Dunciad*, iv, 13

Lead to indicate dullness, and *gold* to indicate venality

Saturnian verses A rude metre in use among the Romans before the introduction of Greek metres. Also a peculiar metre, consisting of three iambics and a syllable over, joined to three trochees, as —
   The queen was in the par-lour . .
   The maids were in the garden . . .
The Fescennine and Saturnian were the same, for as they were called Saturnian from their ancientness, when Saturn reigned in Italy, they were called Fescennine from Fescennina [*sic*] where they were first practised —DRYDEN *Dedication of Juvenal*.

Saturnine. Grave, phlegmatic, gloomy, dull and glowering Astrologers affirm that such is the disposition of those who are born under the influence of the leaden planet Saturn.

Satyr (săt' ir) One of a body of forest gods or demons who, in classical mythology, were the attendants of Bacchus Like the fauns (*q v*) they are represented as having the legs and hind-quarters of a goat, budding horns, and goat-like ears, and they were very lascivious.
Hence, the term is applied to a brutish or lustful man, and the psychological condition among males characterized by excessive venereal desire is known as *satyriasis*.

Sauce means "salted food" (Lat *salsus*), for giving a relish to meat, as pickled roots, herbs, and so on
In familiar phrase it means "cheek," impertinence, the kind of remarks one may expect from a *saucebox*—an impudent youngster.

The sauce was better than the fish. The accessories were better than the main part

To serve the same sauce. To retaliate, to give as good as you take, to serve in the same manner.

After him another came unto her, and served her with the same sauce; then a third.—LYLY *The Man in the Moon* (1609)

To sauce. To season, intermix.

Folly sauced with discretion —*Troilus and Cressida*, i, 2.

Also, to give cheek or impertinence to.

Don't sauce me in the wicious pride of your youth —DICKENS *Our Mutual Friend*, I, vii

Saucy. Cheeky, impertinent (*see* SAUCE), *also* rakish, irresistible, that care-for-nobody, jaunty, daring behaviour which has won for many of our regiments and ships the term as a compliment

How many saucy airs we meet,
From Temple Bar to Aldgate Street!
GAY· *The Barley-Mow and Dunghill.*

In Scotland the adjective is applied to one who is fastidious or dainty in eating

Saucer. Originally a dish for holding sauce, the Roman *salsarium.*

Saucer eyes Big, round, glaring eyes.

Yet when a child (bless me¹) I thought
That thou a pair of horns had'st got,
With eyes like saucers staring
PETER PINDAR *Ode to the Devil.*

Saucer oath. When a Chinese is put in the witness-box, he says "If I do not speak the truth may my soul be cracked and broken like this saucer " So saying, he dashes the saucer on the ground. The Jewish marriage custom of breaking a wineglass is of a similar character

Flying Saucers Alleged mysterious celestial phenomena resembling revolving, partially luminous discs that shoot across the sky at a high velocity and a great height No feasible explanation has been put foward for these objects, nor has any really authenticated proof been given of their existence

Saul, in Dryden's *Absalom and Achitophel*, is meant for Oliver Cromwell

They who, when Saul was dead, without a blow
Made foolish Ishbosheth [Richard Cromwell] the
crown forego   Pt, 1, 57, 58

Is Saul also among the prophets? Said (from 1 *Sam* x, 12) of one who unexpectedly bears tribute to a party or doctrine that he has hitherto vigorously assailed At the conversion of Saul, afterwards called Paul, the Jews said in substance, "Is it possible that Saul can be a convert?" (*Acts* ix, 21.)

Sauria (saw′ ri a) This is the name formerly applied to the order of reptiles which includes the lizards and snakes, but modern zoologists usually divide this order into lacertilia (lizards) and ophidia (snakes) leaving the term Sauria for certain extinct reptiles.

Sauve qui peut (sōv kē pér) (Fr , save himself who can). One of the first uses of the phrase is by Boileau (1636-1711) The phrase thus became to mean a rout. Thackeray writes of "that general *sauve qui peut* among the Tory party."

Savanna. A Spanish word, deriving from the Carib, for the natural glass land in tropical countries In Venezuela savannas are known as "llanos," as "campos" in Brazil, as "downs" in Australia, and as "park lands" in S Africa

Savannah was the first ship fitted with steam power to cross the Atlantic She was built at Savannah, Georgia. Actually the greater part of the voyage to Liverpool, which took place in 1819, was done under sail, she crossed the Atlantic in 25 days

Save. To save appearances. To do something to obviate or prevent exposure or embarrassment

To save one's bacon, skin, face. *See these words.*

Save the mark! *See* MARK.

Savoir-faire (săv′ wa făr) (Fr) Ready wit, skill in getting out of a scrape, hence *Vivre de son savoir-faire*, to live by one's wits.

Savoy, The. A precinct off the Strand, London, noted for the palace built there by Peter of Savoy, who came to England about 1245 to visit his niece Eleanor, wife of Henry III. At his death the palace became the property of the queen, who gave it to her second son, Edmund Lancaster, whence it was attached to the Duchy of Lancaster When the Black Prince brought Jean le Bon, King of France, captive to London (1356), he lodged him in the Savoy Palace, and there he died in 1364 The rebels under Wat Tyler burnt down the old palace in 1381, but it was rebuilt in 1505 by Henry VII, and converted into a hospital for the poor, under the name of St. John's Hospital, which was used by Charles II for wounded soldiers and sailors

Here, in 1552, was established the first flint-glass manufactory in England

The Chapel Royal of the Savoy (first made a Chapel Royal by George III in 1773) was built about 1510 on the ruins of John of Gaunt's earlier chapel This, largely rebuilt, is the only one of the old buildings remaining, the rest of the site being occupied by the Savoy Hotel and Savoy Theatre

In **Savoy Hill** were the first studios of the British Broadcasting Company, with the designation of 2LO It was opened in 1922 and remained headquarters after the Company had become the British Broadcasting Corporation, until 1932

Savoy Operas. The comic operas with words by W S Gilbert (1836-1911) and music by Arthur Sullivan (1842-1900), produced by R D'Oyly Carte Nearly all of them first appeared at the Savoy Theatre, which Carte built specially for these productions The players performing in the operas were known as "Savoyards" The Gilbert and Sullivan operas are the following —

Thespis, 1871, at the Royalty
Trial by Jury, 1872, at the Royalty
The Sorcerer, 1877, Opera Comique
H M S Pinafore, 1878, Opera Comique
The Pirates of Penzance, 1880, Opera Comique

Patience, 1881, Opera Comique, then trans-
ferred to the Savoy, where all the following
appeared
  Iolanthe, 1882.
  Princess Ida, 1884
  The Mikado, 1885
  Ruddigore, 1887
  The Yeomen of the Guard, 1888.
  The Gondoliers, 1889
  Utopia Limited, 1893
  The Grand Duke, 1896

Saw. In Christian art an attribute of St
Simon and St James the Less, in allusion to
the tradition of their being sawn to death in
martyrdom

Sawny or **Sandy.** A Scotchman; a contraction
of "Alexander"

Saxifrage (săks' ı frāj) A member of a genus of
small plants (*Saxifraga*) probably so called
because they grow in the clefts of rocks (Lat.
saxum, a rock, *frangere*, to break) Pliny, and
later writers following him, held that the name
was due to the supposed fact that the plant
had a medicinal value in the breaking up and
dispersal of stone in the bladder

Saxons. A Teutonic people who ravaged the
coasts of the North Sea and the English
Channel at the end of the 3rd century and settled
in districts of south-eastern England Essex,
Sussex, Middlesex, and Wessex are names that
commemorate their colonization.

Saxon Castles The principal ones remaining
in England are —
  Alnwick Castle, given to Ivo de Vesey by
the Conqueror.
  Bamborough Castle (Northumberland), the
palace of the kings of Northumberland, and
built by King Ida, who began to reign 559
  Carisbrooke Castle, enlarged by Fitz-
Osborne just after the Norman Conquest.
  Conisborough Castle (Yorks)
  Goodrich Castle (Herefordshire)
  Kenilworth Castle Kenil-worth means
"the farm of Cynehild" (a woman)
  Richmond Castle (Yorks), belonging to the
Saxon earl Edwin, given by the Conqueror to
his nephew Alan, Earl of Bretagne, a ruin for
three centuries The keep remains
  Rochester Castle, given to Odo, natural
brother of the Conqueror

Saxon Characteristics (architectural).
  (1) The quoining consists of a long stone
set at the corner, and a short one lying on it
and bonding into the wall.
  (2) The use of large heavy blocks of stone
in some parts, while the rest is built of Roman
bricks
  (3) An arch with straight sides to the upper
part instead of curves
  (4) The absence of buttresses.
  (5) The use in windows of rude balusters
  (6) A rude round staircase west of the tower,
for the purpose of access to the upper floors
  (7) Rude carvings in imitation of Roman
work (Rickman)

Saxon Shore. The coast of Norfolk, Suffolk,
Essex, Kent, Sussex, and Hampshire, where
were castles and garrisons, under the charge of

a count or military officer, called *Comes
Littoris Saxonici per Britanniam*
  Branodunum (Barncaster) was on the Norfolk
    coast
  Gariannonum (Burgh) was on the Suffolk coast
  Othona (Ithanchester) was on the Essex coast
  Regulbium (Reculver), Rutupiæ (Richborough),
    Dubris (Dover), P Lemanis (Lyme), were on
    the Kentish coast
  Anderida (Hastings or Pevensey), Portus Adurni
    (Worthing), were on the Sussex coast

Say. To take the say. To taste meat or wine
before it is presented, in order to prove that it
is not poisoned *Say* is short for *assay*, a test,
the phrase was common in the reign of Queen
Elizabeth I.

Sbirri (sbir' ē) (Ital sing *sbirro*) The Italian
police, especially the force which existed in
the Papal States. They were notorious as spies,
informers, and agents provocateurs.
  Had I been silent, not a sbirro but
  Had kept me in his eye, as meditating
  A silent, solitary, deep revenge
        BYRON *Marino Falieri*, II, ıı

Scaevola (skē' vō la) (Lat , left-handed). So
Caius Mucius, a legendary hero of ancient
Rome Purposing to kill Lars Porsena, who
was besieging Rome, he entered that king's
camp, but by mistake slew Porsena's secretary,
and was captured Taken before the king he
deliberately held his hand over the sacrificial
fire at which he was to be burnt till it was burnt
off, to show the Etruscan that he would not
shrink from torture This fortitude was so
remarkable that Porsena at once ordered his
release and made peace with the Romans.

Scales From time immemorial the scales have
been one of the principal attributes of Justice,
it being impossible to out-weigh even a little
Right with any quantity of Wrong
  .   first the right he put into one scale,
  And then the Giant strove with puissance strong
  To fill the other scale with so much wrong
  But all the wrongs that he therein could lay,
  Might not it peise
        SPENSER *Faerie Queene*, V, ıı, 46
  Call these foul offenders to their answers,
  And poise the cause in justice' equal scales,
  Whose beam stands sure, whose rightful cause pre-
  vails   *2 Henry VI*, ıı, I

  According to the Koran, at the Judgment
Day everyone will be weighed in the scales of
the archangel Gabriel The good deeds will be
put in the scale called "Light," and the evil
ones in the scale called "Darkness"; after
which they will have to cross the bridge Al
Sīrāt, not wider than the edge of a scimitar
The faithful will pass over in safety, but the
rest will fall into the dreary realms of Jehennam

To hold the scales even or true. To judge
impartially
  Kind Providence attends with gracious aid   .
  And weighs the nations in an even scale
        COWPER *Table Talk*, 251

To turn the scale Just to outweigh the other
side
  Thy presence turns the scale of doubtful fight,
  Tremendous God of battles, Lord of Hosts!
        WORDSWORTH *Ode* (1815), 112

Scallop Shell. The emblem of St. James of
Compostella (and hence of pilgrims to his

shrine), adopted, says Erasmus, because the shore of the adjacent sea abounds in them Pilgrims used them for cup, spoon, and dish On returning home, the pilgrim placed his scallop shell in his hat to command admiration, and adopted it in his coat-armour

> I will give thee a palmer's staff of ivory and a scallop-shell of beaten gold —PEELE *Old Wives' Tale* (1590).

Scalp Lock A long lock of hair allowed to grow on the scalp by the men of certain North American Indian tribes as a challenge to their scalp-hunting enemies.

Scambling Days. *See* SKIMBLE-SKAMBLE.

Scammozzi's Rule (ska mot' ziz). The jointed two-foot rule used by builders, and said to have been invented by Vincenzio Scammozzi (1552-1616), the famous Italian architect

Scamp. A deserter "from the field," *ex campo*; one who *decamps* without paying his debts

Scandal (Gr *skandalon*) means properly a pit-fall or snare laid for an enemy, hence a stumbling-block, and morally an aspersion.

In *Matt* xiii, 41-2, we are told that the angels shall gather "all things that offend . . and shall cast them into a furnace", here the Greek word is *skandalon*, and *scandals* is given as an alternative in the margin, the Revised version renders the word "all things that cause stumbling " *Cp. also* 1 *Cor* i, 23

The Hill of Scandal. So Milton calls the Mount of Olives, because King Solomon built thereon "an high place for Chemosh, the abomination of Moab . . and for Molech, the abomination of the children of Ammon" (1 *Kings* xi, 7).

> His lustful orgies he [Chemosh] enlarged
> Even to that hill of scandal by the grove
> Of Moloch homicide, lust hard by hate,
> Till good Josiah drove them thence to Hell
> *Paradise Lost*, I, 415.

Scandal broth. Tea. The reference is to the gossip held by some of the womenkind over their tea Also called "Chatter-broth."

Scandalum Magnatum (skăn' da lum măg nā' tům) (Lat , scandal of magnates) Words in derogation of the Crown, peers, judges, and other great officers of the realm, made a legal offence in the time of Richard II. What St Paul calls "speaking evil of dignities"; popularly contracted to *scanmag*

Scanderbeg (skăn' děr beg) A name given by the Turks to George Castriota (1403-68), the patriot chief of Epirus The word is a corrup-tion of *Iskander-beg*, Prince Alexander

Scanderbeg's sword must have Scanderbeg's arm. None but Ulysses can draw Ulysses' bow Mohammed I wanted to see Scanderbeg's scimitar, but when presented no one could draw it; whereupon the Turkish emperor, deeming himself imposed upon, sent it back; Scanderbeg replied he had sent his majesty his sword, not the arm that drew it

Scantling, a small quantity, is the French *echantillon*, a specimen or pattern.

> A scantling of wit —DRYDEN

Scapegoat. Part of the ancient ritual among the Hebrews for the Day of Atonement laid down by Mosaic law (*see Lev* xvi) was as follows Two goats were brought to the altar of the tabernacle and the high priest cast lots, one for the Lord and the other for Azazel (*q v*) The Lord's goat was sacrificed, the other was the *scapegoat*; and the high priest having, by confession, transferred his own sins and the sins of the people to it, it was taken to the wilderness and suffered to escape

Similar rites are not uncommon among primitive peoples The aborigines of Borneo, for instance, annually launch a small boat laden with all the sins and misfortunes of the nation, which they imagine will fall on the crew that first meets with it.

Scaphism (skā' fizm) (Gr *skaphe*, anything scooped out) A mode of torture formerly practised in Persia The victim was enclosed in the hollowed trunk of a tree, the head, hands, and legs projecting. These were anointed with honey to invite the wasps In this situation the sufferer must linger in the burning sun for several days.

Scapin (ska' pin) The knavish and intriguing valet, who makes his master his tool, in Molière's *Les Fourberies de Scapin*, 1671.

Scapular. A garment made of two strips of cloth put on over the head so that one falls in front and one behind. It is usually the width of the shoulders and reaches to the ankles; it originated in the working frock of the Benedic-tines—a sort of overall— but it is now regarded as the distinctively monastic part of many religious habits Another form of scapular is worn by lay people of various R C con-fraternities It consists of two pieces of cloth about 3 in. by 2 in , joined by strings and worn back and front next the skin

Scarab (scă' rab) An ancient gem in the form of a dung-beetle, especially *Scarabaeus sacer* It originated in pre-dynastic Egypt as an amulet, being made of polished or glazed stone, metal, or glazed faience, and was perforated lengthwise for suspension. By the XIIth Dynasty scarabs became used as seals, worn as pendants or mounted as signet rings.

Scaramouch (skăr' à mouch). The English form of Ital *Scaramuccia* (through Fr *Scaramouche*) a stock character in Old Italian farce, intro-duced into England soon after 1670. He was a braggart and fool, very valiant in words, but a poltroon, and was usually dressed in a black Spanish costume caricaturing the dons. The Neapolitan actor, Tiberio Fiurelli (1608-94), was surnamed *Scaramouch Fiurelli* He came to England in 1673, and astonished John Bull with feats of agility

> Stout Scaramoucha with rush lance rode in,
> And ran a tilt with centaur Arlequin
> DRYDEN *Epilogue to The Silent Woman*

Scarborough Warning. Blow first, warning after. In Scarborough robbers used to be dealt with in a very summary manner by a sort of Halifax gibbet-law, lynch-law, or an *à la lanterne* Another origin is given of this phrase. It is said that Thomas Stafford, in 1557, seized the castle of Scarborough, not only without warning, but even before the towns-folk knew he was afoot

This term *Scarborrow warning*, grew, some say.
  By hasty hanging for rank robbery there
Who that was met but suspect in that way,
Straight he was trust up, whatever he were.
               J HEYWOOD.

Scarlet. The colour of certain official costumes, as those of judges and cardinals, hence, sometimes applied to these dignitaries The scarlet coat worn by foxhunters is not technically *scarlet*, but *pink* (*see* PINK)

Dyeing scarlet. Heavy drinking, which in time will dye the face scarlet.

They call drinking deep, dyeing scarlet 1 *Henry IV*, ii, 4

The Scarlet Lancers. The 16th Lancers, whose tunic is red

Scarlet Letter. In the rigid Puritan regime of New England in the early days a scarlet "A," for "adulteress" used to be branded or sewn on a guilty woman's dress. The theme of Hawthorne's novel of this name (1850) is based on this custom

Scarlet Pimpernel. An elusive intriguer. The phrase comes from the nickname of the hero of several novels by Baroness Orczy In 1905 *The Scarlet Pimpernel* told the adventures of a royalist partizan in the French Revolution, who took the pimpernel as his emblem when he saved victims from the guillotine, and played other tricks on the Sansculottes.

Scarlet, Will. One of the companions of Robin Hood (*q.v.*)

The Scarlet Woman, or Scarlet Whore. The woman seen by St John in his vision "arrayed in purple and scarlet colour," sitting "upon a scarlet coloured beast, full of names of blasphemy, having seven heads and ten horns," "drunken with the blood of the saints, and with the blood of the martyrs," upon whose forehead was written "MYSTERY, BABYLON THE GREAT, THE MOTHER OF HARLOTS AND ABOMINATIONS OF THE EARTH" (*Rev* xvii, 1-6) St John was probably referring to Rome, which, at the time he was writing, was "drunken with the blood of the saints", some controversial Protestants have applied the words to the Church of Rome, and some Roman Catholics to the Protestant churches generally.

Scat Singing. A form of singing in jazz music in which meaningless syllables and sounds take the place of words, the voice being used rather as a musical instrument It was invented by the greatest of all jazz musicians, Louis Armstrong, by accident as he was making a record of Heebie Jeebies, about 1926

Scavenger's Daughter. An instrument of torture invented by Sir William Skevington, lieutenant of the Tower in the reign of Henry VIII. The machine compressed the body by bringing the head to the knees, and so forced blood out of the nose and ears

Scent. We are not yet on the right scent. We have not yet got the right clue. The allusion is to dogs following game by the scent.

Sceptic (skep' tik) literally means one who thinks for himself, and does not receive on another's testimony (from Gr. *skeptesthai*, to examine) Pyrrho founded the philosophic sect called "Sceptics," and Epictetus combated their dogmas. In theology we apply the word to those who do not accept revelation.

Sceptre (sep' ter) (Gr, a staff). The gold and jewelled wand carried by a sovereign as emblem of royalty, hence, royal authority and dignity.

This hand was made to handle nought but gold·
I cannot give due action to my words,
Except a sword, or sceptre balance it
A sceptre shall it have, have I a soul,
On which I'll toss the flower-de-luce of France
               2 *Henry VI*, v, 1.

The sceptre of the kings and emperors of Rome was of ivory, bound with gold and surmounted by a golden eagle, the British sceptre is of richly jewelled gold, and bears immediately beneath the cross and ball the great Cullinan diamond (*q.v*)

Homer says that Agamemnon's sceptre was made by Vulcan, who gave it to the son of Saturn It passed successively to Jupiter, Mercury, Pelops, Atreus, and Thyestes till it came to Agamemnon It was looked on with great reverence, and several miracles were attributed to it.

Scheherazade (she hēr' à zād). The mouthpiece of the tales related in the *Arabian Nights* (*q v*), daughter of the grand vizier of the Indies The Sultan Schahriah, having discovered the infidelity of his sultana, resolved to have a fresh wife every night and have her strangled at daybreak Scheherazade entreated to become his wife, and so amused him with tales for a thousand and one nights that he revoked his cruel decree, bestowed his affection on her, and called her "the liberator of the sex "

Schelhorn's Bible. *See* BIBLE, SPECIALLY NAMED.

Schiedam (skI dăm') Hollands gin, so called from Schiedam a town where it is principally manufactured.

Schism, The Great. The term is usually applied to the ecclesiastical dispute which rent Europe into two parties in the 14th century. Three months after the election of Urban VI, in 1378, the fifteen electing cardinals declared that the election was invalid because it had been made under fear of violence from the Roman mob Urban retorted by naming twenty-eight new cardinals, the others at once proceeded to elect a new pope, Clement VII, who went to reside at Avignon Spain, Naples, France, Provence and Scotland adhered to Clement, England, Germany, Scandinavia, Flanders and Hungary stood by Urban The Church was torn from top to bottom by the schism, both sides being in good faith and no one knowing to whom allegiance was due This confusion lasted until 1417, when Martin V was elected at the Council of Constance

Schlemihl, Peter (shlem' il). The man who sold his shadow to the devil, in Chamisso's tale so called (1814). The name is a synonym for any person who makes a desperate and silly bargain

Scholasticism. The philosophy and doctrines of the "Schoolmen" (q v) of the Middle Ages (9th to 16th cents) which were based on the logical works of Aristotle and the teachings of the Christian Fathers. It was an attempt to give a rational basis to Christianity, but the methods of the Scholastics degenerated into mere verbal subtleties, academic disputations, and quibblings, till, at the time of the Renaissance, the remnants were only fit to be swept away before the current of new learning that broke upon the world. Cp DIALECTICS

Schoolmaster. The schoolmaster is abroad. Education is spreading—and it will bear fruit Lord Brougham said, in a speech (1828) on the general diffusion of education, and of intelligence arising therefrom, "Let the soldier be abroad, if he will, he can do nothing in this age There is another personage abroad . . . the schoolmaster is abroad, and I trust to him, armed with his primer, against the soldier in full military array."

Schoolmistress, The. A quietly humorous poem in the Spenserian stanza by Shenstone (1742). The character is designed for a "portrait of Sarah Lloyd," the dame who first taught the poet himself.

Schoolmen. The Theologians of the Middle Ages, who lectured in the cloisters or cathedral schools founded by Charlemagne and his successors They followed Aristotle and the Fathers (see SCHOLASTICISM), but attempted to reduce every subject to a system They may be grouped under three periods—
First Period PLATONISTS (from 9th to 12th cents).
  Pierre Abélard (1079-1142)
  Flaccus Albinus Alcuin (735-804).
  John Scotus Erigena (d 875).
  Anselm (1030-1117) *Doctor Scholasticus.*
  Berengarius of Tours (1000-88).
  Gerbert of Aurillac (930-1003), afterwards Pope Sylvester II
  John of Salisbury (1115-80)
  Lanfranc, Archbishop of Canterbury (1005-89)
  Pierre Lombard (1100-64) *Master of the Sentences,* sometimes called the founder of school divinity.
  Roscelinus of Compiègne (about 1050-1122)
Second Period, or *Golden Age of Scholasticism* ARISTOTELIANS (13th and 14th cents)
  Alain de Lille (d. 1203) *The Universal Doctor.*
  Albertus Magnus (1206-80)
  Thomas Aquinas (1224-74). *The Angelic Doctor.*
  John Fidanza Bonaventure (1221-74) *The Seraphic Doctor*
  Alexander of Hales (d 1245) *The Irrefragable Doctor.*
  John Duns Scotus (1265-1308), *The Subtle Doctor.*
Third Period NOMINALISM REVIVED (To the 16th cent)
  Thomas de Bradwardine, Archbishop of Canterbury (d 1349), *The Profound Doctor.*
  Jean Buridan (about 1295-1360)
  William Durandus de Pourçain (d about 1333). *The Most Resolute Doctor*

  Gregory of Rimini (d. 1358) *The Authentic Doctor*
  Robert Holcot (d 1349), an English Dominican and divine.
  Raymond Lully (1234-1315) *The Illuminated Doctor.*
  William Occam (d 1349), an English Franciscan. *The Singular* or *Invincible Doctor*
  François Suarez (1548-1617), the last of the schoolmen.

Schooner (skoo' ner) In the U S A, a large glass or mug for beer Sometimes also called a "prairie schooner "

Prairie schooner was the name given to the large covered wagon in which American pioneer settlers moved west across the prairies in the mid-19th century.

Science. Literally "knowledge," the Lat *scientia* from the pres part. of *scire*, to know. The old, wide meaning of the word is shown in this from Shakespeare —
> Plutus himself,
> That knows the tinct and multiplying medicine,
> Hath not in nature's mystery more science
> Than I have in this ring   *All's Well*, v, 3.

The Dismal Science Economics, a name given to it by Carlyle.—
> The social science—not a "gay science," but a rueful—which finds the secret of this Universe in "supply and demand"   . what we might call, by way of eminence, the *dismal science* —CARLYLE *On the Nigger Question* (1849)

The Noble Science Boxing, or fencing the "noble art of self-defence "

The Seven Sciences. A mediæval term for the whole group of studies, viz Grammar, Logic, and Rhetoric (the *Trivium*), with Arithmetic, Music, Geometry, and Astronomy (the *Quadrivium*)

Science Persecuted Anaxagoras of Clazomenæ (d about 430 B C) held opinions in natural science so far in advance of his age that he was accused of impiety, thrown into prison, and condemned to death Pericles, with great difficulty, got his sentence commuted to fine and banishment
  Galileo (1564-1642) was imprisoned by the Inquisition for maintaining that the earth moved To get his liberty he abjured the heresy, but as he went his way is said, on very flimsy authority, to have whispered, "*E pur si muove*" (but nevertheless it does move).
  Roger Bacon (1214-94) was excommunicated and imprisoned for diabolical knowledge, chiefly on account of his chemical researches Dr Dee (q v) and Robert Grosseteste (d 1253), Bishop of Lincoln, were treated in much the same way Of the latter it is said that as he was accused of dealings in the black arts the Pope sent a letter to the King of England ordering that his bones should be disinterred and burnt to powder.
  Averroes, the Arabian philosopher, who flourished in the 12th century, was denounced as a heretic and degraded solely on account of his great eminence in natural philosophy and medicine
  Andrew Crosse (1784-1855), the electrician, was accused of impiety and shunned as a "profane man" who wanted to arrogate to

himself the creative power of God, because he asserted that he had seen certain animals of the genus *Acarus*, which had been developed by him out of inorganic matter.

Scio's Blind Old Bard (sī' ō). Homer Scio is the modern name of Chios, in the Ægean Sea one of the "seven cities" that claimed the honour of being his birthplace
Smyrna, Chios, Colophon, Salamis, Rhodos, Argos,
    Athenæ,
Your just right to call Homer your son you must
    settle between ye

Scire facias (sī' re fā' si as) (Lat , make him to know) A judicial writ enforcing the execution or the annulment of judgments, etc , so called from its opening words These writs were formerly the common procedure, but they are now rarely issued except for the revocation of royal charters

Sciron (sī' ron). A robber of Greek legend, slain by Theseus He infested the parts about Megara, and forced travellers over the rocks into the sea, where they were devoured by a sea monster

Scissors. The Latin *cisorium*, from *cædere*, to cut In English the word was for centuries spelt without the *c*, the *sc-* spelling appeared in the 16th century, and seems to be due to confusion with Lat *scissor*, the noun from *scindere*, to split or rend *Scythe*, formerly *sithe*, has suffered in the same way
In Johnson's Dictionary the word is entered in the singular; but the singular form has never been in common use, except in compounds such as *scissor-blade*, *scissor-tooth*, etc (*cp. billiard-ball* from *billiards*, *trouser-button* from *trousers*, etc)

Scissors and paste. Compilation, as distinguished from original literary work The allusion is obvious.

Scissors to grind. Work to do, purpose to serve *I have my own scissors to grind* is a way of saying "I've got my own work to do, or my own troubles, and can't be bothered with yours "

Scogan's Jests (skō' gan) A popular jest-book in the 16th century, said by Andrew Boorde (who published it) to be the work of one John Scogan, reputed to have been court fool to Edward IV He is referred to (anachronously) by Justice Shallow in 2 *Henry IV*, iii, 2, and must not be confused with Henry Scogan (d 1407), the poet-disciple of Chaucer to whom Ben Jonson alludes —
    Scogan? What was he?
Oh, a fine gentleman, and a master of arts
Of Henry the Fourth's times, that made disguises
For the king's sons, and writ in ballad royal
Daintily well
           The Fortunate Isles (1624)

Sconce (skons) A word with several meanings —a wall bracket for holding one or more candles or lights, the small, detached fortified earthwork or fort, the head.

Scone (skōn) A parish about 2 miles north of Perth, the site of the castle where the ancient Scottish kings were crowned It was from here that Edward I, in 1296, brought the great coronation stone on which the kings of Scot-

land used to be crowned, and which, ever since, has formed part of the Throne ("Edward the Confessor's Chair") in Westminster Abbey which British monarchs occupy at their coronation. It was stolen at Christmas, 1950, but was restored some months later and replaced in the Confessor's Chair in February, 1952.
More than one fable has attached itself to this stone The monks gave out that it was the very "pillow" on which Jacob rested his head when he had the vision of angels ascending and descending between heaven and earth (*Gen* xxviii, 11), and it was also said to be the original "Lia-faill" or "Tanist Stone" (*q v*), brought from Ireland by Fergus, son of Eric, who led the Dalriads to Argyleshire, and removed thence by King Kenneth (in the 9th cent) to Scone.

Scorched Earth. A phrase coined to describe the Chinese policy (as old as war) of retreating before the Japanese and burning the countryside as they went, in the war which began in 1937 It was a phrase much used in World War II

Score Twenty, a reckoning, to make a reckoning, so called from the custom of marking off "runs" or ' lengths," in games by the score feet.

To pay off old scores. To settle accounts; used sometimes of money debts, but usually in the sense of revenging an injury, "getting even" with one

Scorpio, Scorpion (skôr' pi ō) Scorpio is the eighth sign of the zodiac, which the sun enters about October 24th. Orion had boasted to Diana and Latona that he would kill every animal on the earth. These goddesses sent a scorpion which stung Orion to death Jupiter later raised the scorpion to heaven.
Fable has it that scorpions—like the toad—carry with them an oil which is a remedy against their stings
'Tis true, a scorpion's oil is said
To cure the wounds the venom made,
And weapons dressed with salve restore
And heal the hurts they gave before
           BUTLER *Hudibras*, iii, 2.

This oil was extracted from the flesh and given to the sufferer as a medicine, it was also supposed to be "very useful to bring away the descending stone of the kidneys" (Boyle, 1663)
Another mediæval belief was that if a scorpion were surrounded by a circle of fire it would commit suicide by stinging itself with its own tail, Byron, in the *Giaour*, extracts a simile from the legend—
The mind that broods o'er guilty woes
Is like the Scorpion girt by fire, . .
One sad and sole relief she knows,
The sting she nourish'd for her foes,
Whose venom never yet was vain
Gives but one pang, and cures all pain.

A lash or scourge of scorpions. A specially severe punishment, in allusion to the biblical passage —
My father hath chastised you with whips, but I will chastise you with scorpions.—I *Kings* xii, 11

In the Middle Ages a scourge of four or five thongs set with steel spikes and leaden weights was called a *scorpion*

Scot. Payment, reckoning The same word as *shot* (*q.v*), we still speak of *paying one's shot.*

Scot and lot. A municipal levy on all according to their ability to pay. *Scot* is the tax, and *lot* the allotment or portion allotted. *To pay scot and lot,* therefore, is to pay the general assessment and also the personal tax allotted to you.

To go scot-free. To be let off payment, to escape punishment or reprimand, etc

Scotch, Scots, Scottish. These three adjectives all mean the same thing—belonging to, native of, or characteristic of, Scotland, but their application varies, and of late years their use has become something of a shibboleth.

Scots and Scottish may be used as applicable and euphonious, Scotch describes nothing but whisky and **A Scotch breakfast,** a substantial breakfast of sundry sorts of good things to eat and drink. The Scots are famous for their breakfast-tables and teas, and no people in the world are more hospitable

Broad Scotch (Braid Scots). The vernacular of the lowlands of Scotland; very different from the enunciation of Edinburgh and from the peculiarity of the Glasgow dialect

A pound Scots was originally of the same value as an English pound, but after 1355 it gradually depreciated, until at the time of the Union of the Crowns (1603) it was but one-twelfth of the value of an English pound (1s 8d), which was divided into 20 *Scots shillings* each worth an English penny.

A Scots pint was about equivalent to three imperial pints of the present day.

The Scots Greys. The 2nd Dragoons, so called from the colour of their original facings of stone grey They have also for many years been mounted on grey horses.

See also SCOTLAND

Scotch. To make a scotch, *i e* a score or incision in, originally, but now the verb usually means to wound so that temporary disablement is caused, or to stamp out altogether. This application of the word arises from *Macbeth*, iii, 2, where Macbeth is made to say "We have scotch'd the snake, not killed it " *Macbeth* was not printed in Shakespeare's lifetime, and in the Folios the word appears as *scorch'd*; Theobald is responsible for the emendation (1726)

Out of all scotch and notch. Beyond all bounds; *scotch* was the line marked upon the ground in certain games, as Hopscotch

The word *scotch* is also applied to a wedge placed before or behind a wheel, etc , to prevent its rolling

Scotists (skō′ tists). Followers of the 13th-century scholastic philosopher, Duns Scotus, who maintained the doctrine of the Immaculate Conception in opposition to Thomas Aquinas.

Scotists and Thomists now in peace remain.
Pope Essay on Criticism

Scotland. St. Andrew is the patron saint of this country, and tradition says that his remains were brought by Regulus, a Greek monk, to the coast of Fife in 368 (*see* RULE, ST)

The old royal arms of Scotland were—Or, a lion rampant gules, armed and langued azure, within a double tressure flory-counter-flory of fleurs-de-lys of the second (this was quartered with the royal arms of the United Kingdom in 1603) *Supporters* Two unicorns argent, imperially crowned, armed, crined, and unguled or, gorged with open crowns, with chains affixed thereto, and reflexed over the back, of the last *Crest* Upon the imperial crown proper, a lion sejant affrontée gules, crowned or, holding in the dexter paw, a sword and in the sinister a sceptre, both proper. *Mottoes,* "Nemo me impune lacessit" (*q.v*), and, over the crest, "In Defence "

In Scotland now the royal arms of Great Britain are used with certain alterations, the lion supporter is replaced by another unicorn (crowned), the Scottish crest takes the place of the English, and the collar of the Thistle encircles that of the Garter.

Scotland a fief of England Edward I founded his claim to the lordship of Scotland on four grounds, viz —(1) the statement of certain ancient chroniclers that Scottish kings had occasionally paid homage to English sovereigns from time immemorial. (2) From charters of Scottish kings. as those of Edgar, those of Malcolm, William, and his son Alexander II. (3) From papal rescripts, as those of Honorius III, Gregory IX, and Clement IV (4) From a passage in *The Life and Miracles of St John of Beverley* (see Rymer's *Fœdera* I, Pt ii, p. 771), which relates how a miracle was performed in the reign of Athelstan, King of the West Saxons and Mercians, 925-940. The king was repelling a band of marauding Scots and had reached the Tyne when he found that they had retreated At midnight the spirit of St John of Beverley appeared to him and bade him cross the river at daybreak, for he "should discomfit the foe " Athelstan obeyed, and reduced the whole kingdom to subjection. On reaching Dunbar on his return march, he prayed that some sign might be vouch-safed to him to satisfy all ages that "God, by the intercession of St John, had given him the kingdom of Scotland " Then, striking the basaltic rocks with his sword, the blade sank into the solid flint "as if it had been butter," cleaving it asunder for "an ell or more," and the cleft remains to the present hour This was taken as a sign from heaven that Athelstan was rightful lord of Scotland, and if Athelstan was, argued Edward, so was he, his successor.

Scotland Yard. The headquarters of the Metropolitan Police, whence all public orders to the force proceed The original Scotland Yard, occupied by the Police from 1829-90, was a short street near Trafalgar Square, so called from a palace on the spot, given by King Edgar (about 970) to Kenneth II of Scotland when he came to London to pay homage, and subsequently used by the Scottish kings when visiting England *New Scotland Yard,* as it is officially called, is on the Thames Embankment near Westminster Bridge.

Scotus, Duns. *See* DUNCE.

Scourers. *See* SCOWERERS

Scourge. A whip or lash, commonly applied to diseases that carry off great numbers, as the scourge of influenza, the scourge of pneumonia, etc, and to persons who seem to be the instruments of divine punishment Raleigh, for instance, was called the Scourge of Spain, and Spenser, in his *Sonnet upon Scanderbeg*, calls him "The scourge of Turkes and plague of infidels."

The Scourge of God (Lat. *flagellum Dei*) Attila (d. 453), king of the Huns, so called by mediæval writers because of the widespread havoc and destruction caused by his armies

The Scourge of Homer. The carping critic, Zoilus See ZOILISM

The Scourge of Princes. Pietro Aretino (1492-1556), the Italian satirist.

Scout. This word comes from the old French *escoute*, a spy or eavesdropper, akin to the modern French *écouter*, to listen. It is now applied to a man, aeroplane, warship, etc, sent to observe the enemy's movements or obtain information of importance The word has other uses In the early days of the game the fielders at cricket were called scouts, college servants at Oxford are still known by that name, it is often used for Boy Scouts (*q.v.*).

Scowerers A set of rakes in the period about 1670 to 1720, who, with the Nickers and Mohocks, committed great annoyances in London and other large towns
> Who has not heard the Scowerers' midnight fame?
> Who has not trembled at the Mohocks' name?
> Was there a watchman took his hourly rounds,
> Safe from their blows and new-invented wounds?
> GUY *Trivia*, iii

Scrape. Bread and scrape Bread and butter, with the butter spread very thin

I've got into a bad scrape—an awkward predicament, an embarrassing difficulty We use *rub*, *squeeze*, *pinch*, to express the same idea. Thus Shakespeare says, "Ay, there's the rub"; "I am come to a pinch" (difficulty).

To scrape along. To get along in the world with difficulty, finding it hard to "make both ends meet."

To scrape an acquaintance with. To get on terms of familiarity with by currying favour and by methods of insinuation. The *Gentleman's Magazine* (N S, xxxix, 230), says that Hadrian went one day to the public baths and saw an old soldier, well known to him, scraping himself with a potsherd for want of a flesh-brush The emperor sent him a sum of money. Next day Hadrian found the bath crowded with soldiers scraping themselves with pot-sherds, and said, "Scrape on, gentlemen, but you'll not scrape acquaintance with me."

To scrape through. To pass an examination, etc., "by the skin of one's teeth," just to escape failure

Scratch. There are two colloquial "sporting" uses of this word, a horse, or other entrant in a sporting event, is said to be *scratched* when its name is withdrawn (*scratched out*) from the list of competitors, the *scratch man* in a handi-cap is he who starts from *scratch*; *i.e.* the line

marked out (originally *scratched*) to show the starting place

A scratch crew, eleven, etc. A team got together anyhow, not the regular team.

A scratch race. A race of horses, men, boys, etc, without restrictions as to age, weight, previous winnings, etc, who all start from scratch.

Old Scratch. Old Nick, the devil. From *skratta*, an old Scandinavian word for a goblin or monster (modern Icelandic *skratti*, a devil)

Scratch cradle. Another form of "cat's cradle" (*q v*).

To come up to the scratch. To be ready when wanted, to fulfil expectations In prize-fighting a line was scratched on the ground, and the toe of the fighter must come up to the scratch.

Screw. Slang for wages, salary; probably because in some industry the weekly wage was handed out in a "screw of paper"; also a slang term for a prison warder.

An old screw. A miser who has amassed wealth by "putting on the screw" (*see below*), and who keeps his money tight, doling it out only in *screws*.

He has a screw loose. He is not quite *compos mentis*, he's a little mad His mind is like a piece of machinery that needs adjusting —it won't work properly.

There's a screw loose somewhere. All is not right, there's something amiss A figurative phrase from machinery, where one screw not tightened up may be the cause of a disaster

His head is screwed on the right way. He is clear-headed and right-thinking; he knows what he's about

To put on the screw. A phrase surviving from the days when the thumb screw was used as a form of torture to extract confessions or money. To press for payment, as a screw presses by gradually increasing pressure. Hence *to apply the screw*, *to give the screw another turn*, to take steps (or additional steps) to enforce one's demands

To screw oneself up to it To force oneself to face it, etc, to get oneself into the right frame of mind for doing some unpleasant or difficult job

Screw-ball. A colloquial American term for an erratic, eccentric, or unconventional person

Screwed. Intoxicated A playful synonym of *tight*

The Screw Plot. The story is that when Queen Anne went to St Paul's in 1708 to offer thanksgiving for the victory of Oudenarde, disaffected conspirators removed certain screw-bolts from the beams of the cathedral, that the roof might fall on the queen and her suite and kill them.
> Some of your Machiavelian crew
> From heavy roof of Paul
> Most traitorously stole every screw,
> To make that fabric fall,
> And so to catch Her Majesty,
> And all her friends beguile.
> *Plot upon Plot* (about 1713).

Scribe, in the New Testament, means a doctor of the law. Thus, in *Matt* xxii, 35, we read, "Then one of them which was a *lawyer*, asked Him . . . Which is the great commandment of the law?" *Mark* (xii, 28) says, "One of the *scribes* came . . and asked Him, Which is the first commandment of all?" They were generally coupled with the Pharisees (*q v*) as being upholders of the ancient ceremonial tradition

In the Old Testament the word is used more widely. Thus Seraiah is called the *scribe* (secretary) of David (2 *Sam* viii, 17), "Shebna the scribe" (2 *Kings* xviii, 18) was secretary to Hezekiah, and Jonathan, Baruch, Gemariah, etc., who were princes, were called scribes Ezra, however, called "a ready scribe in the law of Moses," accords with the New Testament usage of the word.

Scriblerus, Martinus (mar tǐ nǔs skrǐb lěr' us) A merciless satire on the false taste in literature current in the time of Pope, for the most part written by Arbuthnot, and published in 1741. Cornelius Scriblerus, the father of Martin, was a pedant, who entertained all sorts of absurdities about the education of his son. Martin grew up a man of capacity, but though he had read everything, his judgment was vile and taste atrocious. Pope, Swift, and Arbuthnot founded a *Scriblerus Club* with the object of pillorying all literary incompetence

Scrimmage. Originally, a *skirmish*, of which word this is a variant

> Prince Ouffur at this skrymage, for all his pryde,
> Fled full and sought no guide
> > *MS Lansdowne*, 200, f 10

Scrummage was another form of *scrimmage*, as *scrum* it still survives on the Rugby football field.

Scrimshaw (skrim' shaw) The term applied to the carved or scratched work on shells, ivory, etc, often in colours. This used to be done by sailors during the long sea voyages by sail. The word is sometimes used as a verb to describe the accomplishment of some intricate job neatly.

Scriptores Decem (skrip tôr' ĕz dē' sem) A collection of ten ancient chronicles on English history, edited by Sir Roger Twysden and John Selden (1652) The ten chroniclers are Simeon of Durham, John of Hexham, Richard of Hexham, Ailred of Rieval, Ralph de Diceto (Archdeacon of London), John Brompton of Jorval, Gervase of Canterbury, Thomas Stubbs, William Thorn of Canterbury, and Henry Knighton of Leicester

A similar collection of five chronicles was published by Thomas Gale (1691) as *Scriptores Quinque.*

Scriptorium (skrip tôr' ǐ ŭm) (Lat., from *scriptus*, past part of *scribere*, to write) A writing-room, especially the chamber set apart in the mediæval monasteries for the copying of MSS., etc Sir James Murray (1837-1915) gave the name to the corrugated-iron outhouse in his garden at Mill Hill, in which he started the great *New English Dictionary.*

Scriptures, The, or **Holy Scripture** (Lat. *scriptura*, a writing). The Bible, hence applied allusively to the sacred writings of other creeds, as the Koran, *the Scripture of the Mohammedans*, the Vedas and Zendavesta, of the Hindus and Persians, etc.

Scripturists Another name for the Caraites.

Scrounge. To purloin or annex something from nowhere particular or that has no obvious owner A term much used in the army during World War I

Scruple. The name of the weight (20 grains, or $\frac{1}{24}$ oz), and the term for doubt or hesitation (as in *a scruple of conscience*), both come from Lat. *scrupulus*, meaning a sharp little pebble, such as will cause great uneasiness if it gets into one's shoe The second is the figurative use, with the name of the little weight compare that of the big one—*stone*

Scullabogue Massacre (skŭl a bōg') In the Irish rebellion of 1798 Scullabogue House, Wexford, was seized by the rebels and used for a prison Some thirty or forty prisoners confined in it were brought out and shot in cold blood, when the news of a repulse of the rebels at New Ross arrived (June 5th, 1798) The barn at the back of the house was filled with prisoners and set on fire, and Taylor, in his history, written at the time and almost on the spot, puts the number of victims at 184

Scunner. A Scottish term for a feeling of distaste amounting almost to loathing *To take a scunner at something* is to conceive a violent dislike to it

Scurry. A scratch race, or race without restrictions

Hurry-scurry. A confused bustle through lack of time, in a confused bustle A "ricochet" word

Scutage (skū' tij). In feudal times a payment in commutation of personal military service To most knights and others liable to be summoned to follow the king to war it would be more convenient to pay the tax than set out on some distant expedition, at the same time the money they paid was of use to the king to enable him to employ more reliable troops. It was levied in varying rates between 1156 and 1385.

Scuttle. To scuttle a ship is to bore a hole in it in order to make it sink. The word is from the Old French *escoutilles*, hatches, and was first applied to a hole in a roof with a door or lid, then to a hatchway in the deck of a ship with a lid, then to a hole in the bottom of a ship.

Scuttle, for coals, is the A S *scutel*, a dish; from Lat *scutella*, diminutive of *scutra*, a dish or platter In auctioneers' jargon a coal-scuttle is, quite unaccountably, called a perdonium.

To scuttle off, to make off hurriedly, was originally To scuddle off, scuddle being a frequentative of *scud*

Scylla (sil' a) In Greek legend the name (1) of a daughter of King Nisus of Megara and (2) of a sea monster
The daughter of Nisus promised to deliver Megara into the hands of her lover, Minos.

and, to effect this, cut off a golden hair on her father's head, while he was asleep. Minos despised her for this treachery, and Scylla threw herself from a rock into the sea At death she was changed into a lark, and Nisus into a hawk.

> Think of Scylla's fate
> Changed to a bird, and sent to fly in air,
> She dearly pays for Nisus' injured hair
> POPE Rape of the Lock, iii.

The sea monster dwelt on the rock Scylla, opposite Charybdis (*q v*), on the Italian side of the Straits of Messina Homer says that she had twelve feet, and six heads, each on a long neck and each armed with three rows of pointed teeth, and that she barked like a dog He makes her a daughter of Crataeis, but later accounts say that she was a nymph who, because she was beloved by Glaucus (*q v*), was changed by the jealous Circe into a hideous monster

Avoiding Scylla, he fell into Charybdis. *See* CHARYBDIS

Between Scylla and Charybdis Between two equal difficulties; between the devil and the deep sea

To fall from Scylla into Charybdis—out of the frying-pan into the fire.

Scythian (sith' i an) Pertaining to the peoples or region of Scythia, the ancient name of a great part of European and Asiatic Russia.

Scythian defiance. When Darius approached Scythia, an ambassador was sent to his tent with a bird, a frog, a mouse, and five arrows, then left without uttering a word Darius, wondering what was meant, was told by Gobrias it meant this Either fly away like a bird, hide your head in a hole like a mouse, or swim across the river, or in five days you will be laid prostrate by the Scythian arrows.

The Scythian or **Tartarian lamb.** The Russian barometz, the creeping root-stock and frond-stalks of *Cibotium barometz*, a woolly fern, which, when inverted, was supposed to have some resemblance to a lamb Mandeville in his *Travels* (ch. xxvi) gives a highly fanciful description of them.

'Sdeath, 'Sdeins. *See* 'S.

Sea Any large expanse of water, more or less enclosed, hence the expression "molten sea," meaning the great brazen vessel which stood in Solomon's temple (2 *Chron* iv, 5, and 1 *Kings* vii, 26), even the Nile, the Euphrates, and the Tigris are sometimes called seas by the prophets. The world of water is the *Ocean.*

At sea, or **all at sea.** Wide of the mark, quite wrong, like a person in the open ocean without compass or chart

Half-seas over. *See* HALF.

The four seas. The seas surrounding Great Britain, on the north, south, east, and west

The high seas. The open sea, the "main"; especially that part of the sea beyond 'the three-mile limit," which forms a free highway to all nations

The Old Man of the sea. A creature encountered by Sinbad the Sailor in his fifth voyage (*Arabian Nights*) This terrible Old Man got on Sinbad's back, and would neither dismount nor could be shaken off At last Sinbad gave him some wine, which so intoxicated him that he relaxed his grip, and Sinbad made his escape Hence the phrase is figuratively applied to bad habits, evil associates, etc , from which it is very difficult to free oneself.

The Seven Seas. *See* SEVEN

Sea Deities. In classical myth, besides the fifty Nereids (*q v*), the Oceanides (daughters of Oceanus), the Sirens (*q v*), etc , there were a number of deities presiding over, or connected with, the sea The chief of these are:—

Amphitrite, wife of Poseidon, queen goddess of the sea,

Glaucus, a fisherman of Bœotia, afterwards a marine deity.

Ino, who threw herself from a rock into the sea, and was made a sea-goddess.

Neptune, king of the ocean

Nereus and his wife *Doris* Their palace was at the bottom of the Mediterranean, his hair was sea-weed

Oceanus and his wife *Tethys* (daughter of Uranus and Ge) Oceanus was god of the *Ocean*, which formed a boundary round the world.

Portumnus (Gr ; Lat *Palemon*), the protector of harbours.

Poseidon, the Greek Neptune

Proteus, who assumed every variety of shape

Thetis, a daughter of Nereus and mother of Achilles

Triton, son of Poseidon.

Sea-girt Isle, The. England So called because, as Shakespeare has it, it is 'hedged in with the main, that water-walled bulwark" (*King John*, ii, 1)

> This precious stone set in the silver sea,
> Which serves it in the office of a wall,
> Or as a moat defensive to a house,
> Against the envy of less happier lands
> Richard II, ii, 1

Sea-green Incorruptible, The. So Carlyle called Robespierre in his *French Revolution.* He was of a sallow, unhealthy complexion

Sea Island Cotton. The cotton grown on the coast of South Carolina

Sea Lawyer. A sailor who knows all about his rights, and is always arguing, criticizing, raising objections to the orders of his superior officers, etc. In the Army such is known as a *Barrack Room Lawyer*

Sea legs. He has got his sea legs. Is able to walk on deck when the ship is rolling; able to bear the motion of the ship without sea-sickness

Sea serpent. A serpentine monster formerly supposed to inhabit the depths of the ocean As stories of the "Great Sea Serpent" are usually received with incredulity, sailors are sometimes reluctant to report its appearance, but in spite of this there have been some circumstantial accounts and very vivid

descriptions given by those who professed to have seen it Pontoppidan in his *Natural History of Norway* (1755) speaks of sea serpents 600 ft long.
See also LOCH NESS MONSTER

Seabees. U.S Naval Construction Battalions (C B s) in World War II Their alleged motto was· "The difficult we do at once. The impossible takes a little longer "

Seal. The sire is called a *bull*, his females are *cows*, the offspring are called *pups*, the breeding-place is called a *rookery*, a group of young seals a *pod*, and a colony of seals a *herd*. The immature male is called a *bachelor* A sealer is a seal-hunter, and seal-hunting is called sealing.

Sealed Orders. The term applied to orders delivered in a sealed package to naval or military commanders which they are not to read or consult before a certain time, or before reaching a certain locality, or except in certain specified conditions

Seamy Side. The "wrong" or worst side; as the "seamy side of London," "the seamy side of life." In velvet, Brussels carpets, tapestry, etc, the "wrong" side shows the seams or threads of the pattern exhibited on the right side.

Seasons, The Four. Spring, Summer, Autumn, and Winter *Spring* starts (officially) on March 21st, the Spring Equinox, when the sun enters Aries, *Summer* on June 22nd, the Summer Solstice, when the sun enters Cancer, *Autumn* on September 23rd, the Autumn Equinox, the sun entering Libra, and *Winter* on December 22nd, when the sun enters Capricornus

The ancient Greeks characterized *Spring* by Mercury, *Summer* by Apollo, *Autumn* by Bacchus, and *Winter* by Hercules.

The London Season. The part of the year when the Court and fashionable society generally is in town—May, June, and July

The silly season. *See* SILLY.

Season-ticket. A ticket giving the holder certain specified rights (in connexion with travelling, entrance to an exhibition, etc) for a certain specified period

Seat. To take a back seat. *See* BACK.

Sebastian, St. Patron saint of archers, because he was bound to a tree and shot at with arrows. As the arrows stuck in his body, thick as pins in a pincushion, he was also made patron saint of pin-makers And as he was a centurion, he is patron saint of soldiers. His feast, coupled with that of St. Fabian, is kept on January 20th

The English St. Sebastian. St. Edmund, the martyr-king of East Anglia (855-70) has been so called He gave himself up to the Danes in the hope of saving his people, but they scourged him, bound him to a tree, shot arrows at him, and finally cut off his head, which, legend relates, was guarded by a wolf till it was duly interred. The monastery and cathedral of St. Edmundsbury (Bury St Edmunds) were erected on the place of his burial. The place of his martyrdom was Hoxne, Suffolk.

Second The next after the first (Lat *secundus*)
In duelling the *second* is the representative of the principal, he carries the challenge, selects the ground, sees that the weapons are in order, and is responsible for all the arrangements.

A second of time is so called because the division of the minute into sixtieths is the *second* of the sexagesimal operations, the first being the division of the hour into minutes

To second an officer (accent on the final syllable) is, in military phraseology, to remove him temporarily from his regimental or military duties so that he may take up some other appointment.

One's second self. His *alter ego* (*q v*); one whose tastes, opinions, habits, etc, correspond so entirely with one's own that there is practically no distinction

Second Adventists. Those who believe that the Second Coming of Christ (*cp l Thess*. iv, 15) will precede the Millennium, hence sometimes also called *Premillenarians*

Second-hand. Not new or original what has already been the property of another, as, "second-hand" books, clothes, opinions, etc

Second nature. Said of a habit, way of looking at things, and so on, that has become so ingrained in one that it is next to impossible to shake it off

Second pair back The back room on the floor two flights of stairs above the ground floor, similarly the front room is called the *second pair front*.

Second sight. The power of seeing things invisible to others, the power of foreseeing future events

Second wind. *See* WIND

Secondary colours. *See under* COLOURS (*Technical Terms*)

Secret. An open secret. A piece of information generally known, but not formally announced.

Un secret de polichinelle. No secret at all. A secret known to all the world, an open secret. Polichinelle is the Punch of the old French puppet-shows, and his secrets are "stage whispers" told to all the audience

Entre nous, c'est qu'on appelle
Le secret de polichinelle.
La Mascotte, ii, 12

Secret Service. A general unofficial term applied to the organization which exists in every country, in peace or war, for the collection of information about enemies, potential enemies and disaffected persons, also for counter-espionage Such organizations have many ramifications, some quite public, others secret In Great Britain the best known is MI5, a branch of Military Intelligence in the War Office. In France such matters come under the Deuxième Bureau

Secular. From Lat *sæcularis*, pertaining to the *sæculum*, *i e*. the age of generation, hence, pertaining to this world in contradistinction to the next.

Secularism. The name given about 1851 by George Jacob Holyoake (1807-1906) to an ethical system founded on natural morality, and opposed to the tenets of revealed religion and ecclesiasticism.

Secular clergy. The Roman Catholic parish clergy who live in daily contact with the world, in contradistinction to monks, etc., who live in monasteries. Hierarchically they take precedence of regular clergy, and bishops are usually chosen from seculars

Secular games. In ancient Rome the public games lasting three days and three nights that took place only once in an age (*sæculum*), or period of 100 years

They were instituted in obedience to the Sibylline verses, with the promise that "the empire should remain in safety so long as this admonition was observed," and while the kings reigned were held in the Campus Martius, in honour of Pluto and Proserpine,

Date, quæ precamur
Tempore sacro
Quo Sibyllini monuere versus.
HORACE *Carmen Seculare*, A U.C , 737

Sedan Chair (se dăn') The covered seat so called, carried on poles by two bearers back and front, first appeared in Italy in the late 16th century, and was introduced into England by Sir S Duncombe in 1634

The name Sedan was first used in England, it was probably coined from Lat *sedere*, to sit, though it is just possible that Johnson's suggestion, viz. that it is connected with the French town, *Sedan*, has something in it

Sedan, the Man of. Napoleon III was so called, because he surrendered his sword to William, King of Prussia, after the battle of Sedan (September 2nd, 1870).

Sedulous. To play the sedulous ape to. To study the style of another, and model one's own on his as faithfully and meticulously as possible. said, usually with more or less contempt, of literary men The phrase is taken from R L Stevenson, who, in his essay, *A College Magazine* (*Memories and Portraits*), said that he had—

played the sedulous ape to Hazlitt, to Lamb, to Wordsworth, to Sir Thomas Browne, to Defoe, to Hawthorne, to Montaigne, to Baudelaire, and to Obermann . That, like it or not, is the way to learn to write.

See. The seat or throne of a bishop (Lat *sedes*, a seat). The term is applied to the place where the bishop's cathedral is located and from which he takes his title, and so is to be distinguished from *diocese*, the territory over which he has jurisdiction.

The Holy See. The Papacy, the papal jurisdiction and court.

Seel. To close the eyelids of a hawk by running a thread through them, to hoodwink. (Fr , *ciller, cil*, the eyelash)

She that so young could give out such a seeming,
To seel her father's eyes up, close as oak
Othello, III, 3

Seian Horse, The (sī' án). A possession which invariably brought ill luck with it Hence the Latin proverb *Ille homo habet equum Seianum* Cneius Seius had an Argive horse, of the breed of Diomed, of a bay colour and surpassing beauty, but it was fatal to its possessor. Seius was put to death by Mark Antony Its next owner, Cornelius Dolabella, who bought it for 100,000 sesterces, was killed in Syria during the civil wars Caius Cassius, who next took possession of it, perished after the battle of Philippi by the very sword which stabbed Cæsar Antony had the horse next, and after the battle of Actium slew himself

Like the gold of Tolosa and Hermione's necklace, the Seian or Sejan horse was a fatal possession.

Selah (sē' la) A Hebrew word occurring often in the *Psalms* (and three times in *Habakkuk* iii), indicating some musical or liturgical direction, such as a pause, a repetition, or the end of a section.

Select Man In some of the New England States a member of a board of town officers who has been deputed to be responsible for the conduct of certain branches of local administration

Selene (se lē' nē) The moon goddess of Greek mythology, daughter of Hyperion and Thea, and roughly corresponding to the Roman Diana (*q v*), the chaste huntress. Selene had fifty daughters by Endymion, and several by Zeus, one of whom was called "The Dew" Diana is represented with bow and arrow running after the stag; but Selene in a chariot drawn by two white horses, with wings on her shoulders, and a sceptre in her hand.

Selucidæ (se lū' si dē) The dynasty of Seleucus Nicator, one of *Alexander's* generals (about 358-280 B C.), who in 312 conquered Babylon and succeeded to a part of Alexander's vast empire. The monarchy consisted of Syria, a part of Asia Minor, and all the eastern provinces, and the line of the Selucids reigned till about 64 B.C

Self. Used in combination for a variety of purposes, such as (1) to express direct or indirect reflexive action, as in *self-command*, (2) action performed independently, or without external agency, as in *self-acting, self-fertilization*, (3) action or relation to the self, as in *self-conscious, self-suspicious*; (4) uniformity, naturalness, etc., as in *self-coloured, self-glazed*.

A self-made man. One who has risen from poverty and obscurity to opulence and a position of importance by his own efforts The phrase was originally American.

The Self-denying Ordinance. The bill passed by the Long Parliament in 1645 ordering that Members of either House should give up their military commands and civil appointments within forty days; the reason being the suspicion that the Civil War was being prolonged for personal ends.

Self-determination. The theory in political economy, that every nation, no matter how small or weak, has the right to decide upon its own form of government and to manage its own internal affairs The phrase acquired its present significance during the attempts to resettle Europe after World War I, but difficulties arose (as in the case of Ireland) when it was discovered that an exact and comprehensive definition of the word *Nation* could not be agreed upon.

Seljuks (sel'juks). A Perso-Turkish dynasty of eleven emperors over a large part of Asia, which lasted 138 years (1056-1194) It was founded by Togrul Beg, a descendant of Seljuk, chief of a small tribe which gained possession of Bokara

Selkirk, Alexander, was probably the original of Robinson Crusoe Born in 1676, the son of a Fifeshire shoemaker, he joined Dampier's expedition to the South Seas in 1703 and when off the island of Juan Fernandez asked to be set ashore in consequence of a quarrel with the captain He remained on the island for 52 months and was eventually picked up by Captain Woodes Rogers, whose *Cruising Voyage Round the World,* in which he tells of Selkirk, is supposed to have given Defoe the idea of Robinson Crusoe Selkirk died at sea, as mate of the *Weymouth,* in 1721.

Sell. Slang for a swindle, a hoax, a first-of-April trick; and the person hoaxed is said to be *sold*

A selling race. One in which the horses that compete are sold after the race, the sale price being determined beforehand. The winner is generally sold by auction, and the owner gets both the selling price and the stakes If at the auction a price is obtained above the ticketed price it is divided between the second best horse and the race fund. *See* HANDICAP.

Selling the pass. Betraying one's own side The phrase was originally Irish, and is applied to those who turn king's evidence, or who impeach their comrades for money The tradition is that a regiment was sent by Crotha, "lord of Atha," to hold a pass against the invading army of Trathal, "King of Cael " The pass was betrayed for money; the Firbolgs were subdued, and Trathal assumed the title of "King of Ireland."

To sell a person up. To dispose of his goods by order of the court because he cannot pay his debts, the proceeds going to his creditors

Sellinger's Round. An old country dance, very popular in Elizabethan times, in which—
the dancers take hands, go round twice and back again, then all set, turn, and repeat; then lead all forward, and back, and repeat, two singles and back, set and turn single and repeat, arms all and repeat.—
JOHN PLAYFORD *The English Dancing Master* (1651).

It is said to be so called either from Sir Thomas Sellynger, buried in St George's Chapel, Windsor, about 1470, or from Sir Anthony St. Leger, Lord Deputy of Ireland (d. 1559).

Semantics (se măn' tiks). The technical term for the study of the meanings of words rather than of their origins and derivations. As time passes the meanings and implications of words change, often imperceptibly; it is with these changes that semantics deals.

Semele (sem' e le). In Greek mythology, the daughter of Cadmus and Harmonia. By Zeus she was the mother of Dionysus, and was slain by lightning when he granted her request to appear before her as the God of Thunder.

Seminary. A college exclusively devoted to the training of candidates for the R C priesthood. The usual course is six years—two of philosophy and four of theology Seminary priests is an historical and legal term to distinguish English priests ordained abroad from those ordained in England before the accession of Queen Elizabeth I. The latter are often called Marian priests, and they were treated more leniently by the penal laws After 1585 it was high treason for a seminary priest even to be in England.

Semi-precious stones. Gems suitable for jewellery and for ornamenting other sorts of goldsmith's work; but not sufficiently beautiful, durable or rare to be ranked with such precious stones as diamonds, emeralds, rubies, and sapphires. Examples of semi-precious stones are amethysts, cairngorms, cornelian, lapis-lazuli, moonstones, and onyx

Semiramis (se mir' a mis) In the Babylonian mythology, the mother of Ninus who was King of Assyria and founded Nineveh. She waged war against the Medes and the Chaldeans (c 800 B C) After her death she became a legendary figure, identified with the Goddess Ishtar and her doves.

Semiramis of the North, The. Margaret of Denmark, Sweden, and Norway (1353-1412), and Catherine II of Russia (1729-96) have both been so called

Semitic (se mit' ic) Pertaining to the descendants of Shem (*see Gen* x), viz. the Hebrews, Arabs, Assyrians, Aramæans, etc , nowadays applied to the Jews.

The Semitic languages are the ancient Assyrian and Chaldee, Aramaic, Syriac, Arabic, Hebrew, Samaritan, Ethiopic, and old Phœnician The great characteristic of this family of languages is that the roots of words consist of three consonants

Senatus consultum (sen a' tus kon sŭl' tum). A decree of the Senate of Ancient Rome. The term was sometimes applied to a decree of any senate, especially that of the First Empire in France.

Send, To. That sends me. Amateurs of jazz use this phrase, meaning The music sends me out of myself, or into ecstasies.

Seneschal (sen' e shâl). The majordomo or steward of a great house in the Middle Ages He had full authority over the retainers and servants, supervised all ceremonial affairs, administered justice in the name of his master, and was in every way a personage of considerable importance

Se'nnight. A week; seven nights. *Fort'night,* fourteen nights These words are relics of the ancient Celtic custom of beginning the day at sunset, a custom observed by the ancient Greeks, Babylonians, Persians, Syrians, and Jews, and by the modern representatives of these people In *Gen.* i we find the evening precedes the morning, as, "The evening and the morning were the first day," etc.

Sense. Common sense. *See* COMMON

Scared out of my seven senses According to ancient teaching the soul of man, or his "inward holy body," is compounded of the seven properties which are under the influence of the seven planets Fire animates, earth gives the sense of feeling, water gives speech, air gives taste, mist gives sight, flowers give hearing, the south wind gives smelling. Hence the seven senses are animation, feeling, speech, taste, sight, hearing, and smelling (*see Ecclus* xvii, 5)

Sentences, Master of the. The Schoolman, Peter Lombard (d 1160), an Italian theologian and bishop of Paris, author of *The Four Books of Sentences* (*Sententiarum libri* iv), a compilation from the Fathers of the leading arguments pro and con, bearing on the hair-splitting theological questions of the Middle Ages

The mediæval graduates in theology, of the second order, whose duty it was to lecture on the *Sentences*, were called **Sententiatory Bachelors.**

Separation, The. The name given in the 17th century to the body of Independents and Protestant dissenters generally—called individually **Separatists** Thus the Amsterdam parson, Tribulation Wholesome, says

These chastisements are common to the saints,
And such rebukes, we of the Separation,
Must bear with willing shoulders, as the trials
Sent forth to tempt our frailties
          BEN JONSON *The Alchemist*, iii, 2

Sephardim (sef ar' dim) The Jews of Spain and Portugal, so called from *Sepharad*, a district mentioned in *Obad* 20, which was supposed by the rabbinical commentators to be intended for Spain As Jews were evidently in captivity at Sepharad at the time the passage was written this cannot possibly be the correct interpretation

Sepoy (sē' poi) The Anglicized form of Hindu and Persian *sipahi*, a soldier, from *sipah*, army, denoting a native East Indian soldier trained and disciplined in the British manner It was especially applied to such a soldier in the British Indian Army

Sept. Deriving from the O French *septe*, a variant of *secte* or sect, this term was applied especially to an Irish clan. The old Irish sept was a division of the tribe, of which it was an offshoot The freemen of the sept bore the clan name with the prefix "Ua," grandson, written in English as 'O' "

September. The seventh month from March, where the year used to commence.

The old Dutch name was *Herst-maand* (autumn-month), the old Saxon, *Gerst-monath* (barley-month), or *Hæfest-monath*, and after the introduction of Christianity *Halig-monath* (holy-month, the nativity of the Virgin Mary being on the 8th, the exaltation of the Cross on the 14th, Holy-Rood Day on the 26th and St Michael's Day on the 29th) In the French Republican calendar, it was called *Fructidor* (fruit-month, August 18th to September 21st)

September Bible. *See* BIBLE, SPECIALLY NAMED

September massacres. An indiscriminate slaughter, during the French Revolution, of loyalists confined in the Abbaye and other prisons, lasting from September 2nd to 5th, 1792 Danton gave the order after the capture of Verdun by the allied Prussian army; as many as 8,000 persons fell, among whom was the Princess de Lamballe Those who instigated or took part in the massacres were known as **Septembriseurs.**

Septentrional Signs (sep ten' tri ō nal) The first six signs of the Zodiac, because they belong to the *northern* celestial hemisphere The North was called the *septentrion* from the seven stars of the Great Bear (Lat *septem*, seven, *triones*, plough oxen). *Cp* URSA MAJOR

Septuagesima Sunday (sep tū à jes' i ma) The third Sunday before Lent, in round numbers, seventy days (Lat *septuagesima dies*) before Easter. Really only sixty-eight days before Easter

Septuagint (sep' tū à jint) A Greek version of the Old Testament and Apocrypha, so called because it was traditionally said to have been made by seventy-two Palestinian Jews in the 3rd century B C, at the command of Ptolemy Philadelphus. They worked on the island of Pharos and completed the translation in seventy-two days

This tradition applies, however, only to the Pentateuch, Greek translations of the other books were added by later writers, some, perhaps, being as late as the Christian era The name Septuagint is frequently printed LXX

Sepulchre, The Holy. The cave outside the walls of Jerusalem in which the body of Christ is believed to have lain between His burial and resurrection From at least the 4th century (*see* INVENTION OF THE CROSS, *under* CROSS) the spot has been covered by a Christian church

Knights of the Holy Sepulchre. An order of military knights founded by Godfrey of Bouillon, in 1099, to guard the Holy Sepulchre Since 1342 it has existed only as a religious body, the Latin Patriarch of Jerusalem being its Grand Master

Seraglio (sē ra' lyō) The palace of the Sultans of Turkey at Constantinople, situated on the Golden Horn, and enclosed by walls seven miles and a half in circuit The chief entrance was the Sublime Gate (*cp* SUBLIME PORTE), and the chief of the large edifices is the *Harem*, or "sacred spot," which contained numerous houses, one for each of the sultan's wives, and others for his concubines The Seraglio might be visited by strangers; not so the Harem

Seraphic (se rāf' ik) **Seraphic Blessing** The blessing written by St Francis of Assisi at the request of Brother Leo on Mt Alverna, in 1224 It is based on *Numbers* vi, 25· May the Lord bless thee and keep thee May He shew His face to thee and have mercy on thee May He turn His countenance to thee and give thee peace May the Lord bless thee, Brother Leo

The Seraphic Doctor. The scholastic philosopher, St Bonaventura (1221-74).

The Seraphic Father, or **Saint.** St Francis of Assisi (1182-1226), whence the Franciscans are sometimes called the *Seraphic Order*

The Seraphic Hymn. The Sanctus "Holy, holy, holy" (*Is* vi, 3), which was sung by the seraphim

Seraphim. The highest of the nine choirs of angels, so named from the seraphim of *Is* vi, 2 The word is probably the same as *saraph*, a serpent, from *saraph*, to burn (in allusion to its bite); and this connexion with burning suggested to early Christian interpreters that the seraphim were specially distinguished by the ardency of their zeal and love.

Seraphim is a plural form, the singular, *seraph*, was first used in English by Milton Abdiel was

> The flaming Seraph, fearless, though alone,
> Encompassed round with foes
> 					*Paradise Lost*, v, 875

Serapis (se rā′ pis) The Ptolemaic form of Apis, an Egyptian deity who, when dead, was honoured under the attributes of Osiris (*q.v*), and thus became "osirified Apis" or [O]Sorapis He was lord of the underworld, and was identified by the Greeks with Hades.

Serat, Al. *See* AL-SIRAT.

Serbonian Bog, The (sēr bō′ ni ăn) A great morass, now covered with shifting sand, between the isthmus of Suez, the Mediterranean, and the delta of the Nile, that in Strabo's time was a lake stated by him to be 200 stadia long and 50 broad, and by Pliny to be 150 miles in length. Typhon was said to dwell at the bottom of it, hence its other name, *Typhon's Breathing Hole.*

> A gulf profound as that Serbonian bog,
> Betwixt Damiata and Mount Cassius old,
> Where armies whole have sunk
> 					MILTON *Paradise Lost*, ii, 592

The term is used figuratively of a mess from which there is no way of extricating oneself.

Serendipity (se rĕn dip′ i ti) A happy coinage by Horace Walpole to denote the faculty of making lucky and unexpected "finds" by accident, In a letter to Mann (January 28th, 1754) he says that he formed it on the title of a fairy story, *The Three Princes of Serendip*, because the princes—

> were always making discoveries, by accidents and sagacity, of things they were not in quest of.

Serendip is an ancient name of Ceylon'

Serene (Lat *serenus*, clear, calm). A title formerly given to certain German princes Those who used to hold under the empire were entitled *Serene* or *Most Serene Highnesses.*

It's all serene. All right (Span *sereno*, all right—the sentinel's countersign)

The drop serene. *See* DROP

Sergeanty or **Serjeanty.** A feudal tenure, the tenant rendering some specified personal service to the king

Petit sergeanty. Holding lands of the Crown by the service of rendering annually some small implement of war, as a bow, a sword, a lance, a flag, an arrow, and the like Thus the Duke of Wellington holds Strathfieldsaye and Apsley House, London, by presenting a flag annually to the Crown on the anniversary of the battle of Waterloo, and the Duke of Marlborough pays a similar "peppercorn rent" for Blenheim Palace on the anniversary of the battle of Blenheim.

Serif and **Sanserit** (ser′ if, săn ser′ if) The former is type with the wings or finishing stroke (as T), the latter is type without the finishing strokes (as T).

Serjeants-at-Law. A superior order of barristers (*q v*) abolished in 1877 From the Low Latin *serviens ad legem*, one who serves (the king) in matters of law Serjeants Inn, formerly in Chancery Lane and later in Fleet Street, was their inn at law.

Serpent. *See also* SNAKE The serpent is symbolical of—

(1) Deity, because, says Plutarch, "it feeds upon its own body; even so all things spring from God, and will be resolved into deity again" (*De Iside et Osiride*, i, 2, p. 5, and *Philo Byblius*).

(2) Eternity, as a corollary of the former It is represented as forming a circle, holding its tail in its mouth.

(3) Renovation and the healing art It is said that when old it has the power of growing young again "like the eagle," by casting its slough, which is done by squeezing itself between two rocks It was sacred to Æsculapius (*q v.*), the Greek god of medicine, as it was supposed to have the power of discovering healing herbs Hence, two serpents appear in the badge of the Royal Army Medical Corps *See* CADUCEUS.

(4) Guardian spirit. It was thus employed by the ancient Greeks and Romans, and not unfrequently the figure of a serpent was depicted on their altars.

In the temple of Athena at Athens, a serpent, supposed to be animated by the soul of Erichthonius, was kept in a cage, and called "the Guardian Spirit of the Temple "

(5) Wisdom "Be ye therefore wise as serpents, and harmless as doves" (*Matt* x, 16).

(6) Subtlety. "Now the serpent was more subtle than any beast of the field" (*Gen* iii, 1).

It is also symbolical of the devil, as the Tempter, and in early pictures is sometimes placed under the feet of the Virgin, in allusion to the promise made to Eve after the fall (*Gen*. iii, 15).

In Christian art it is an attribute of St Cecilia, St Euphemia, St. Patrick, and many other saints, either because they trampled on Satan, or because they miraculously cleared some country of snakes

Fable has it that the cerastes hides in sand that it may bite the horse's foot and get the rider thrown In allusion to this belief, Jacob says, "Dan shall be . . an adder in the path, that biteth the horse heels, so that his rider shall fall backward" (*Gen* xlix, 17) The Bible also tells us that the serpent stops up its ears that it may not be charmed by the charmers, "charming never so wisely" (*Ps*. lviii, 4).

Another old idea about snakes was that when attacked they would swallow their young and not eject them until reaching a place of safety.

It was in the form of a serpent, says the legend, that Jupiter Ammon appeared to Olympia and became by her the father of Alexander the Great.

Pharaoh's serpent. *See* PHARAOH.

Sea serpent. *See* SEA

The serpent of old Nile. Cleopatra, so called by Antony

> He's speaking now,
> Or murmuring "Where's my serpent of old Nile?"
> For so he calls me
> *Antony and Cleopatra*, i, 5.

Their ears have been serpent-licked They have the gift of foreseeing events, the power of seeing into futurity This is a Greek superstition It is said that Cassandra and Helenus were gifted with the power of prophecy, because serpents licked their ears while sleeping in the temple of Apollo

To cherish a serpent in your bosom. To show kindness to one who proves ungrateful The Greeks say that a husbandman found a frozen serpent, which he put into his bosom The snake was revived by the warmth, and stung its benefactor. Shakespeare applies the tale to a serpent's egg

> Therefore think him as a serpent's egg
> Which, hatched, would (as his kind) grow dangerous
> *Julius Cæsar*, ii, 1

Serpentine Verses. Such as end with the same word as they begin with The following are examples —

> Crescit amor nummi, quantum ipsa pecunia crescit
> (Greater grows the love of pelf, as pelf itself grows greater)
> Ambo florentes ætatibus, Arcades ambo
> (Both in the spring of life, Arcadians both)

The allusion is to the old representations of snakes with their tails in their mouths—no beginning and no end

Serve. I'll serve him out—give him a *quid pro quo* This is the French *desservei*, to do an ill turn to one

Serves you right! You've got just what you deserved

To serve a rope To lash or whip it with thin cord to prevent it fraying

To serve a sentence. To undergo the punishment awarded

To serve a writ on To deliver into the hands of the person concerned a legal writ

To serve a mare. To place a stallion to her

To serve one's time. To hold an office or appointment for the full period allowed, to go through one's apprenticeship, also, to serve one's sentence in prison

Servus servorum (sĕr' vus sĕr vôr' um) (Lat) The slave of slaves, the drudge of a servant *Servus servorum Dei* (the servant of the servants of God) is one of the honorific epithets of the Pope, it was first adopted by Gregory the Great (590-604)

Sesame (ses' à mi) **Open, Sesame.** The "password" at which the door of the robbers' cave flew open in the tale of *The Forty Thieves* (*Arabian Nights*), hence, a key to a mystery, or anything that acts like magic in obtaining a favour, admission, recognition, etc

Sesame is an East Indian annual herb, with an oily seed which is used as a food, a laxative, etc In Egypt they eat sesame cakes, and the Jews frequently add the seed to their bread

Sesquipedalian (ses kwi pe dā' li an) is sometimes applied in heavy irony to cumbersome and pedantic words It comes from Horace's *sesquipedalia verba*, words a foot and a half long

Session, Court of. *See* COURT.

Sestina (ses tē' na) A set form of poem, usually rhymed, with six stanzas of six lines each and a final triplet The terminal words of stanzas 2 to 6 are the same as those of stanza 1 but arranged differently. Sestinas were invented by the Provençal troubadour Arnaut Daniel (13th cent); Dante, Petrarch, and others employed them in Italy, Cervantes and Camoens in the Peninsula, and an early use in English was by Drummond of Hawthornden. Swinburne's sestinas are probably the best in English.

Set. The Egyptian original of the Greek Tython (*q v*), the god of evil, brother (or son) of Osiris, and his deadly enemy. He is represented as having the body of a man and the head of some unidentified mythological beast with pointed muzzle and high square ears

Set, To. A set scene. In theatrical parlance, a scene built up by the stage carpenters, or a furnished interior, as a drawing-room, as distinguished from an ordinary or shifting scene

A set to. A boxing match, a pugilistic fight, a scolding The pugilism the combatants were by their seconds "set to the scratch" or line marked on the ground

Setting a hen Giving her a certain number of eggs to hatch The whole number for incubation is called a *setting*

Setting a saw Bending the teeth alternately to the right and left in order to make it cut.

The setting of a jewel. The frame or mount of gold or silver surrounding a jewel in a ring, brooch, etc

> This precious stone set in the silver sea ˙ ˙
> *Richard II*, ii, 1

The setting of the sun, moon, or stars. Their sinking below the horizon The saying, The sun never sets on the British dominions was used long ago of other empires Thus, in the *Pastor Fido* (1590) Guarini speaks of Philip II of Spain as—

> that proud monarch to whom, when it grows dark [elsewhere] the sun never sets

Captain John Smith in his *Advertisements for the Unexperienced* notes that—

> the brave Spanish soldiers brag The sunne never sets in the Spanish dominions, but ever shineth on one part or other we have conquered for our king

and Thomas Gage in his *Epistle* Dedicatory to his *New Survey of the West Indies* (1648) writes—

> It may be said of them [the Dutch], as of the Spaniards, that the Sun never sets upon their Dominions.

To set off to advantage. To display a thing in its best light, put the best construction on it Perhaps a phrase from the jewellers' craft

To set the Thames on fire. *See* THAMES

Setebos (set' e bos) A god or devil worshipped by the Patagonians, and introduced by

Shakespeare into his *Tempest* as the god of Sycorax, Caliban's mother

> His art is of such power,
> It would control my dam s god, Setebos
> And make a vassal of him.   *Tempest*, 1, 2

The cult of Setebos was first known in Europe through Magellan's voyage round the world, 1519-21.

Seven. A mystic or sacred number, it is composed of four and three, which, among the Pythagoreans, were, and from time immemorial have been, accounted lucky numbers Among the Babylonians, Egyptians, and other ancient peoples there were seven sacred planets, and the Hebrew verb *to swear* means literally ' to come under the influence of seven things'', thus seven ewe lambs figure in the oath between Abraham and Abimelech at Beersheba (*Gen*. xxi, 28), and Herodotus (III, viii) describes an Arabian oath in which seven stones are smeared with blood

There are seven days in creation, seven days in the week, seven graces, seven ages in the life of man, climacteric years are seven and nine with their multiples by odd numbers, and the seventh son of a seventh son was always held notable.

Among the Hebrews every seventh year was sabbatical, and seven times seven years was the jubilee. The three great Jewish feasts lasted seven days, and between the first and second were seven weeks Levitical purifications lasted seven days. The number is associated with a variety of occurrences in the Old Testament

In the Apocalypse we have seven churches of Asia, seven candlesticks, seven stars, seven trumpets, seven spirits before the throne of God, seven horns, seven vials, seven plagues, a seven-headed monster, and the Lamb with seven eyes.

The old astrologers and alchemists recognized seven planets, each having its own "heaven"—

> The bodies seven, eek, lo hem heer anoon,
> Sol gold is, and Luna silver we threpe,
> Mars yren, Mercurie quyksilver we clepe,
> Saturnus leed, and Jubitur is tyn,
> And Venus coper, by my fader kyn
> CHAUCER *Prol of the Canon's Yeoman s Tale.*

And from this very ancient belief sprang the theory that man was composed of seven substances, and has seven natures *See under* SENSE

Seven, The. Used of groups of seven people, especially (1) the "men of honest report" chosen by the Apostles to be the first Deacons (*Acts* vi, 5), viz , Stephen, Philip, Prochorus, Nicanor, Timon, Parmenas, and Nicholas, (2) the Seven Bishops (*see below*); or (3) the Seven Sages of Greece (*see* WISE MEN). *See also* SEVEN NAMES, *below*.

Seven Against Thebes, The. The seven Argive heroes (Adrastus, Polynices, Tydeus, Amphiaraus, Capaneus, Hippomedon, and Parthenopæus), who, according to Greek legend, made war on Thebes with the object of restoring Polynices (son of Œdipus), who had been expelled by his brother Eteocles All perished except Adrastus (*q v*), and the brothers slew each other in single combat The legend is the subject of one of the tragedies of Æschylus *See* NEMEAN GAMES

Seven Bishops, The. Archbishop Sancroft, and Bishops Lloyd, Turner, Ken, White, Lake, and Trelawney, who refused to read James II's Declaration of Indulgence (1688), and were in consequence sent to the Tower for non-conforming *Cp* NONJURORS

Seven Champions, The. The mediæval designation of the national patron saints of England, Scotland. Wales, Ireland, France, Spain, and Italy In 1596 Richard Johnson published a chap-book, *The Famous History of the Seven Champions of Christendom* In this he relates that *St George* of England was seven years imprisoned by the Almidor, the black king of Morocco, *St Denys* of France lived seven years in the form of a hart, *St. James* of Spain was seven years dumb out of love to a fair Jewess, *St Anthony* of Italy, with the other champions, was enchanted into a deep sleep in the Black Castle, and was released by St George's three sons, who quenched the seven lamps by water from the enchanted fountain, *St Andrew* of Scotland delivered six ladies who had lived seven years under the form of white swans; *St Patrick* of Ireland was immured in a cell where he scratched his grave with his own nails, and *St David* of Wales slept seven years in the enchanted garden of Ormandine, and was redeemed by St George

Seven Churches of Asia Those mentioned in *Rev* i, 11, viz :—

(1) Ephesus, founded by St Paul, 57, in a ruinous state in the time of Justinian

(2) Smyrna Polycarp was its first bishop

(3) Pergamos, renowned for its library

(4) Thyatira, now called Ak-hissar (the *White Castle*).

(5) Sardis, now Sart, a small village

(6) Philadelphia, now called Allah Shehr (*City of God*).

(7) Laodicea, now a deserted place called Eski-hissar (the *Old Castle*)

Seven cities warred for Homer being dead. *See* HOMER.

Seven Deadly or Capital sins. Pride, Wrath, Envy, Lust, Gluttony, Avarice, Sloth

The Island of the Seven Cities. A land of Spanish fable, where seven bishops, who quitted Spain during the dominion of the Moors, founded seven cities The legend says that many have visited the island, but no one has ever quitted it

Seven Dials (London) A column with seven dials formerly stood facing the seven streets which radiated therefrom

> Where famed St Giles's ancient limits spread
> An in-railed column rears its lofty head,
> Here to seven streets seven dials count the day,
> And from each other catch the circling ray
> GAY *Trivia*, ii

The district had at one time an unenviable reputation for squalor (*cp* GILES, ST), hence Sir W S Gilbert's—

> Hearts just as pure and fair
> May beat in Belgrave Square,
> As in the lowly air
> Of Seven Dials —*Iolanthe*.

Seven Gifts of the Spirit, The. Wisdom, Understanding, Counsel, Power or Fortitude, Knowledge, Righteousness, and Godly Fear

Seven Gods of Luck, The. In Japanese folk-lore, Benten, goddess of love, Bishamon, god of war, Daikoku, of wealth, Ebisu, of self-effacement, Fukurokujin and Jurojin, gods of longevity, and Hstei, god of generosity These are really popular conceptions of the seven Buddhist *devas* who preside over human happiness and welfare

Seven Heavens, The *See* HEAVEN.

Seven Hills. The walls of Ancient Rome, built about the 6th century B C., included the seven hills, Palatine, Capitol, Aventine, Caelian, Esquiline, Viminal and Quirinal The heart of the modern city clings to these hills, in some cases now scarcely perceptible rises in the street level.

Seven Joys, The. *See* MARY

Seven Names of God, The. The ancient Hebrews had many names for the Deity (*see under* NAME, *To take God's name in vain, and* ELOHISTIC), and the Seven over which the scribes had to exercise particular care were— El, Elohim, Adonai, YHWH (*i e* our *Jehovah*), Ehyeh-Asher-Ehyeh, Shaddai, and Zebaot In mediæval times God was sometimes called simply, *The Seven*

> Now lord, for thy naymes sevyn, that made both moyn and starnys,
> Well mo then I can neven thi will, lord, of me tharnys
> *Towneley Mysteries*, XIII, 191 (about 1460)

Seven Planets, Sacraments, The. *See these headings*

Seven Sages of Greece, The *See* WISE MEN.

Seven Sciences, The. *See* SCIENCE

Seven Seas, The. The Arctic and Antarctic, North and South Pacific, North and South Atlantic, and the Indian Oceans

Seven Sisters, The. An old name of the Pleiades, also given to a set of seven cannon, cast by one Robert Borthwick and used at Flodden (1513)

Seven Sleepers, The. Seven Christian youths of Ephesus, according to the legend, who fled in the Decian persecution (250) to a cave in Mount Celion After 230 years they awoke, but soon died, and their bodies were taken to Marseilles in a large stone coffin, still shown in Victor's church Their names are Constantine, Dionysius, John, Maximian, Malchus, Martin-ian, and Serapion. This fable took its rise from a misapprehension of the words, "They fell asleep in the Lord"—*i e* died.
The mystic number is connected with other mediæval 'Sleepers", thus, Barbarossa turns himself once every seven years, once every seven years, also, Ogier the Dane thunders on the floor with his iron mace, and it was seven years that Tannhauser and Thomas of Ercildoune spent beneath the earth in magic enthralment

Seven Sorrows. *See* MARY

Seven Stars, The. Used formerly of the planets, also of the Pleiades and the Great Bear

> *Fool:* The reason why the seven stars are no more than seven is a pretty reason
> *Lear*· Because they are not eight?
> *Fool* Yes, indeed, thou wouldst make a good fool.
> *King Lear,* I, 5

Seven Virtues. The. *See* VIRTUES

Seven Weeks War, The. The war between Austria and Prussia in 1866 (June-July), ostensibly to settle the Schleswig-Holstein question, but in fact to end the long existing rivalry between the two countries and bring Austria to her knees This was quickly done; the Austrians were decisively defeated at Sadowa (July 3rd), and her Italian allies on land at Custozza (June 24th) and at sea off Lissa (July 20th) Truce was declared on July 26th, and the Peace of Prague signed on August 23rd

Seven Wise Masters, The. A collection of Oriental tales (*see* SANDABAR) supposed to be told by his advisers to an Eastern king to show the evils of hasty punishment, with his answers to them Lucien, the son of the king (who, in some versions, is named Dolopathos), was falsely accused to him by one of his queens. By consulting the stars the prince discovered that his life was in danger, but that all would be well if he remained silent for seven days The "Wise Masters" now take up the matter, each one in turn tells the king a tale to illustrate the evils of ill-considered punish-ments, and as the tale ends the king resolves to relent, but the queen at night persuades him to carry out his sentence The seven days being passed, the prince tells a tale which embodies the whole truth, whereupon the king sentences the queen to death The tales were immensely popular, and the germs of many later stories are to be found in this collection

Seven Wonders of the World, The. *See* WONDERS

Seven Works of Mercy, The. *See* MERCY

Seven Years War, The (1756-1763) was waged by France, Austria, Russia, Sweden, Saxony, and Spain against Frederick the Great of Prussia, Great Britain, and Hanover The prime cause of the war was fear of Frederick, coupled with Maria Theresa's eagerness to regain Silesia as an Austrian possession The exhaustion of his enemies and his own superior generalship gave Frederick the victory. Britain gained most out of the war—the conquest of Bengal and the capture of Quebec and hence the whole of Canada

In the seventh heaven. *See* HEAVEN.

Seventh-day Adventists. A small sect of millenarians holding very strict sabbatarian views.

Seventh-day Baptists. Modern representa-tives of the Traskites (*q v.*), more numerous in America than in England

The seventh son of a seventh son. *See* SEVEN, *above.*

Several (late Lat *sēparāte*, from *sēparāre*, to separate) The English word used simply to denote what is severed or separate; each, as "all and several "

> Azariah was a leper, and dwelt in a several house — *2 Kings* xv, 5

And it is still used in this way, as—

> Three times slipping from the outer edge,
> I bump'd the ice into three several stars.
> TENNYSON. *The Epic,* 12.

A **several** is the old legal term for a piece of enclosed ground adjoining a common field, or an enclosed pasture as opposed to an open field or common

Severn. *See* SABRINA

Severus, St. (se vēr' ús) Patron saint of fullers, being himself of the same craft

The Wall of Severus. A stone rampart, built in 208 by the Emperor Severus, between the Tyne and the Solway It is to the north of Hadrian's wall, which was constructed in 120.

Sèvres Ware (sāvr) Porcelain of fine quality made at the French government works at Sèvres, near Paris. The factory was first established at Vincennes in 1745, in 1756 it was removed to Sèvres, and three years later was acquired by the state

Sexagesima Sunday (seks a jes' i ma) The second Sunday before Lent, so called because in round numbers it is sixty days (Lat. *sexagesima dies*) before Easter

Sextile (seks' til). The aspect of two planets when distant from each other sixty degrees or two signs. This position is marked by astrologers thus *.

> In sextile, square, and trine, and opposite
> Of noxious efficacy
> MILTON. *Paradise Lost*, x, 659.

At Eton a sixth-form boy is called a *Sextile.*

Sexton. A corruption of *sacristan*, a church official who has charge of the *sacra*, or things attached to a specific church, such as vestments, cushions, books, boxes, tools, vessels, and so on

Shaddock. A large kind of orange, now generally known as grape fruit (*citrus decumana*), so called from Captain Shaddock (early 18th century), who first transplanted one in the West Indies. It is a native of China and Japan.

Shade. Wine vaults with a lounge attached are often known as *shades*. The term originated at Brighton, where the Old Bank, in 1819, was turned into a smoking-room and bar. There was an entrance by the Pavilion *Shades*, or Arcade, and the name was soon transferred to the drinking-bar It was not inappropriate, as the room was in reality shaded by the opposite house, occupied by Mrs Fitzherbert.

To put someone in the shade To out-do him, eclipse him, to attract to yourself all the applause and encomiums he had been enjoying.

Shadow. A word with a good many figurative and applied meanings, such as, a ghost, Macbeth says to the ghost of Banquo.—

> Hence, horrible shadow' unreal mockery, hence'
> *Macbeth*, iii, 4.

An imperfect or faint representation, as "I haven't the shadow of a doubt"; a constant attendant, as in Milton's "Sin and her shadow Death" (*Paradise Lost*, ix, 12); moral darkness or gloom—"He has outsoared the shadow of our night" (Shelley, *Adonais*, xl, 1), protecting influence—

> Hither, like you ancient Tower,
> Watching o'er the River's bed,
> Fling the shadow of Thy power,
> Else we sleep among the dead
> WORDSWORTH *Hymn (Jesu! bless).*

Gone to the bad tor the shadow of an ass. "If you must quarrel, let it be for something better than the shadow of an ass" Demosthenes says a young Athenian once hired an ass to Megara The heat was so great at midday that he alighted to take shelter from the sun under the shadow of the poor beast Scarcely was he seated when the owner came up and laid claim to the shadow, saying he let the ass to the traveller, but not the ass's shadow After fighting for a time, they agreed to settle the matter in the law courts, and the suit lasted so long that both were ruined

May your shadow never grow less! May your prosperity always continue and increase. The phrase is of Eastern origin Fable has it that when those studying the black arts had made certain progress they were chased through a subterranean hall by the devil If he caught only their shadow, or part of it, they became first-rate magicians, but lost either all or part of their shadow. This would make the expression mean, May you escape wholly and entirely from the clutches of the foul fiend. A more simple explanation of the phrase is, May you never waste away but always remain healthy and robust. *See* SCHLEMIHL

To be reduced to a shadow. Of people, to become thoroughly emaciated, of things, to become an empty form from which the substance has departed

To shadow To follow about like a shadow, especially as a detective, with the object of spying out all one's doings.

Shady. A shady character. A person of very doubtful reputation, one whose character would scarcely bear investigation in the light of day

On the shady side of forty—the wrong side, meaning more than forty

SHAEF. Mnemonic of Supreme Headquarters Allied Expeditionary Forces, the supreme directive military organization, under the command of General Eisenhower, in the later stages of World War II SHAEF was disbanded in July, 1945.

Shah. The title of the king or emperor of Persia, that of his sons is *Shahzadah* It is a corruption of *padishah* (q v.).

Shake. A good shake up. Something sudden that startles one out of his lethargy and rouses him to action

A shake of the head. An indication of refusal, disapproval, annoyance, etc

I'll do it in a brace of shakes. Instantly, as soon as you can shake the dice-box twice

No great shakes. Nothing extraordinary, no such mighty bargain The reference is probably to gambling with dice

In two shakes of a lamb's tail. Instantly. American expression originating in the early 19th century

To shake hands. A very old method of salutation and farewell, when one was shaking hands one could not get at one's sword to strike a treacherous blow When Jehu asked Jehonadab if his "heart was right" with him, he said,

"If it be, give me thine hand," and Jehonadab gave him his hand (2 *Kings* x, 15). Nestor shook hands with Ulysses on his return to the Grecian camp with the stolen horses of Rhesus, Æneas, in the temple of Dido, sees his lost companions enter, and *avidi conjungere dextras ardebant* (*Æneid*, i, 514), and Horace, strolling along the Via Sacra, shook hands with an acquaintance *Arreptâque manu, "Quid agis dulcissimê rerum?"*

To shake in one's shoes. *See* SHOE

To shake one's sides. To be convulsed with laughter, *cp* Milton's "Laughter holding both his sides" (*L'Allegro*)

To shake the dust from one's feet. *See* DUST.

Come and have a shakedown at my place— a bed for the night, especially a makeshift one The allusion is to the time when men slept upon litter or clean straw.

Shakers. A sect of Second Adventists, founded in the 18th century in England by a secession from the Quakers, and transplanted in America by Ann Lee (1736-84), or "Mother Ann," as she is generally known She was an uneducated factory hand, daughter of a Manchester blacksmith
A sect of English Shakers, the "People of God," was founded in Battersea about 1864 by Mary Anne Girling (1827-86), a farmer's daughter, its chief seat was in the New Forest, and it disappeared soon after her death.

Shakespeare (1564-1616), the greatest poet and dramatist of all time and all countries William Shakespeare born at Stratford-on-Avon, the third child of John Shakespeare, an alderman and bailiff of that town (variously described as a butcher, glover, and general trader), and Mary Arden, both of yeoman stock. He received a sound education at the Stratford grammar-school, in spite of Ben Jonson's remark that he had "small Latin and less Greek." Leaving Stratford in 1585 to avoid a prosecution for poaching by Sir Thomas Lucy ("Justice Shallow"), he came to London where he acted with the Earl of Leicester's company His plays and poems were written between 1591 (*Love's Labour's Lost*) and 1611 (*The Tempest*). In the latter year he retired to Stratford, but visited London frequently, keeping up his relations with actors and poets until his death
Ben Jonson calls him "Sweet Swan of Avon," also "The applause! delight! the wonder of our stage!" and says that "He was not for an age, but for all time" (*To the Memory of Shakespeare*) Milton calls him "Dear son of Memory, great heir of fame" (*An Epitaph*), and "Sweetest Shakespeare, fancy's child" (*L'Allegro*), to Collins he was "The perfect boast of Time" (*Epistle to Sir Thos. Hanmer*), to Coleridge, "Our myriad-minded Shakespeare" (*Biog. Lit* xv); to Carlyle, "the greatest of intellects" (*Characteristics of Shakespeare*), to Christopher North, "the Poet Laureate of the Court of Faery"; to Landor, "not our poet, but the world's "
Dryden said of him—

Shakespeare's magic could not copied be,
Within that circle none durst walk but he.
Prologue to the Tempest.

And that he "was a man who of all modern and perhaps ancient poets, had the largest and most comprehensive soul " Young says— "He wrote the play the Almighty made"; (*Epistle to Lord Lansdowne*); Mallett—"Great above rule. . . Nature was his own" (*Verbal Criticism*), Dr Johnson—

Each change of many-colour'd life he drew,
Exhausted worlds, and then imagined new,
Existence saw him spurn her bounded reign,
And panting Time toiled after him in vain
Prologue, 1747

Pope—

Shakespear (whom you and every play-house bill
Style "the divine," "the matchless," what you will)
For gain, not glory, winged his roving flight,
And grew immortal in his own despite.
Imitations of Horace, Ep 1

And Matthew Arnold—

Others abide our question Thou art free
We ask and ask—Thou smilest and art still,
Out-topping knowledge—*Shakespeare*

There are thirty-seven plays credited wholly or in part to Shakespeare, and an enthusiast has discovered that they contain 106,007 lines and 814,780 words, *Hamlet* being the longest, with 3,930 lines, and the *Comedy of Errors*, with 1,777 lines the shortest The plays contain 1,277 speaking characters, of whom only 157 are females The longest part is that of Hamlet, who has 11,610 words to deliver.

Shakespeare's descendants.
Shakespeare married (1582) Anne Hathaway, of Shottery, who was eight years his senior, and died in 1623. They had one son and two daughters—Susanna (b 1583), and the twins Hamnet and Judith (1585). Hamnet died at the age of 11; Judith married Thomas Quiney, had three sons, all of whom died young and unmarried, and died in 1662 Susanna married John Hall and died in 1649, leaving only one child, Elizabeth, the last descendant of the dramatist. She married twice, but had no children, and died as Lady Bernard, wife of Sir John Bernard, of Abington Manor, Northampton, in 1670

Shakespeare; the name. There is no way of spelling the dramatist's name that is *certainly* "correct" (i e as he would himself have spelt it), because the six unquestionably genuine signatures of his that we possess (viz, three on the Will, two on the Blackfriars conveyance and mortgage, and one on his deposition in the suit brought by Stephen Bellot against Christopher Mountjoy) vary, and are very difficult to decipher The most usual modern spelling—Shakespeare—is that used throughout the First and Second Folios (1623 and 1632), and in all the Quartos with the exception of the 1598 *Love's Labour's Lost* ("Shakespere") and the first 1608, *King Lear* ("Shakspeare"), in the dedicatory epistles to *Venus and Adonis* (1593) and *Lucrece* (1594), and though on his own monument the name is given as "Shakspeare," on the tombs of his wife and daughter "Shakespeare" is the spelling. Theobald (1733) used this spelling, Rowe (1709), Pope (1725), and Hanmer (1744) all followed the Third and Fourth Folios, which spelt the name "Shakespear," Steevens and Malone (1778) preferred "Shakspeare "
The "Shakspere" spelling was used in Bell's edition of the works (1788), and in Knight's

various editions (1839), etc., but its more recent adoption in literary circles is due to Sir Frederick Madden, who advocated it on the ground that this was the spelling of the most legible of the signatures—that in the copy of Florio's *Montaigne* (1603) now in the British Museum—and to Furnivall having founded the "New *Shakspere* Society" to take the place of the defunct "*Shakespeare* Society." This signature is now, however, generally taken to be a forgery. The autograph in the Bellott-Mountjoy suit does not help matters, as it is abbreviated to "Willm Shak'p'"; and on the bond that Shakespeare took out for his marriage licence the name appears as "Shags-pere." *See* J R. Wise's *Autograph of William Shakespeare . . together with 4,000 ways of spelling the name*, published at Philadephia in 1869.

The Shakespeare of divines. Jeremy Taylor (1613-67)

The Shakespeare of eloquence. So Barnave happily characterized the Comte de Mirabeau (1749-91).

The German Shakespeare. Kotzebue (1761-1819) has been so styled.

The Spanish Shakespeare. Calderon (1600-81).

Le Shakespeare du boulevard. Guilbert de Pixerécourt.

Shakespeare-Bacon Theory. The lack of culture and education ascribed to William Shakespeare started theories of some other authorship of his works so far back as 1769, and for many years desultory attempts were made to father his plays on contemporary poets and dramatists In the 1860s Sir Robert Durning Lawrence not only ascribed Shakespeare's works to Lord Bacon but proceeded to assert that he was the real author of Montaigne's *Essais*, Marlowe's plays, Burton's *Anatomy of Melancholy* and other Elizabethan classics In 1900 a Mrs Gallup "discovered" a cipher which, applied to Shakespeare's plays, conclusively proved them to be the work of Lord Bacon This same cipher, moreover, revealed the interesting fact that Bacon had made use of Alexander Pope's translation of the *Iliad*. The extravagant and unscholarly claim of the Baconians, mostly based negatively on Shakespeare's inadequacy, have reduced the theory to little more than the hobby of a few cranks.

Shakuntala. *See* SAKUNTALA.

Shaky. Not steady, not in good health, not strictly upright; not well prepared for examination; doubtfully solvent.

Shalott, The Lady of (shá lot') A maiden of the Arthurian legends, who fell in love with Sir Lancelot of the Lake, and died because her love was not returned. Tennyson has a poem on the subject, and the story of Elaine (*q v*), "the lily maid of Astolat," is substantially the same

Shamanism (sha' má nizm) A primitive form of religion, in which those who practise it believe that the world and all events are governed by good and evil spirits who can be propitiated or bought off only through the intervention of a witch-doctor, or *Shaman* The word is Slavonic; it comes from the Samoyeds and other Siberian peoples, but is now applied to Red Indian and other primitive worship

Shamefast. Bashful, awkward through shyness, sheepish. This is the old form of *shamefaced* (which is properly an error), the *-fast* meaning "firmly fixed" or "restrained" (by shame).

Shamrock, the symbol of Ireland, because it was selected by St Patrick to illustrate to the Irish the doctrine of the Trinity According to the elder Pliny no serpent will touch this plant.

Shandean (shăn' dē án). Characteristic of Tristram Shandy or the Shandy family in Sterne's novel, *Tristram Shandy* (9 vols, 1759-67) Tristram's father, Walter Shandy, is a metaphysical Don Quixote in his way, full of superstitious and idle conceits He believes in long noses and propitious names, but his son's nose is crushed, and his name becomes *Tristram* instead of *Trismegistus*. Tristram's Uncle Toby was wounded at the siege of Namur, and is benevolent and generous, simple as a child, brave as a lion, and gallant as a courtier His modesty with Widow Wadman and his military tastes are admirable. He is said to be drawn from Sterne's father. The mother was the *beau-ideal* of nonenity; and of Tristram himself, we hear almost more before he was born than after he had burst upon an astonished world

Shanghai, To (shăng hī') An old nautical phrase meaning to drug a man insensible in order to get him on board an outward bound vessel in need of crew It would appear to have originated in the phrase "ship him to Shanghai," *i e* send him on a long voyage

Shangri La (shăng grī la') The hidden Buddhist lama paradise described in James Hilton's *Lost Horizon* (1933) In World War II the name was applied to the secret air base used by the U S.A. Air Force for the great attack on Japan

Shanks's Mare. To ride Shanks's mare is to go on foot, the *shanks* being the legs A similar phrase is "Going by the marrow-bone stage" or "by Walker's bus "

Shannon. Dipped in the Shannon. One who has been dipped in the Shannon is said to lose all bashfulness.

Shanties, Chanties. Songs sung by sailors at work, to ensure united action (Fr. *chanter*, to sing). They are in sets, each of which has a different cadence adapted to the work in hand. Thus, in sheeting topsails, weighing anchor, etc, one of the most popular of the shanty songs runs thus —

> I'm bound away, this very day,
>   I'm bound for the Rio Grande
>   Ho, you, Rio!
> Then fare you well, my bonny blue bell,
>   I'm bound for the Rio Grande.

A *shanty* is also a small wooden house, or a roughly-built hut.

Shan Van Voght. This excellent song (composed 1798) has been called the Irish *Marseillaise*. The title of it is a corruption of *An t-sean*

bhean bhocht (the poor old woman—*i e*
Ireland) The last verse is—
> Will Ireland then be free?
> Said, the Shan Van Voght [repeat]
> Yes, Ireland shall be free
> From the centre to the sea,
> Hurrah for liberty!
> Said the Shan Van Voght

Shark. A swindler, a pilferer, an extortionate
boarding-house keeper or landlord, etc , one
who snaps up things like a shark, which eats
almost anything, and seems to care little
whether its food is alive or dead, fish, flesh, or
human bodies

To shark up. To get a number of people, etc ,
together promiscuously, without consideration
of their fitness
> Now, sir, young Fortinbras .
> Hath in the skirts of Norway here and there
> Shark'd up a list of lawless resolutes,
> For food and diet, to some enterprise
> That hath a stomach in't.
> *Hamlet*, i, 1

Sharp A regular Becky Sharp. An unprincipled,
scheming young woman, who by cunning,
hypocrisy, and low smartness raises herself
from obscurity and poverty to some position
in Society, and falls therefrom in due course
after having maintained a more or less precarious foothold Of course she is good-
looking, and superficial amiability is a *sine qua
non* Becky Sharp, the original of this, is the
principal character in Thackeray's *Vanity Fair*
(1848)

Sharp practice. Underhand or dishonourable
dealing, low-down trickery intended to
advantage oneself

Sharps and flats. *See* FLAT.

Sharp's the word! Look alive, there! no
hanging about.

Sharp-set. Hungry; formerly used of hawks
when eager for their food
> If anie were so sharpe-set as to eat fried flies,
> buttered bees, stued snails, either on Fridaie or
> Sundaie, he could not be therefore indicted of haulte
> treason.—STANIHURST · *Ireland*, p 19 (1586)

Shave Just a grazing touch, *a near* or *close
shave*, a narrow escape; *to shave through an
examination*, only just to get through, narrowly
to escape being "plucked " At Oxford a pass
degree is sometimes called *a shave*

A good lather is half the shave. Your work
is half done if you've laid your plans and made
your preparations properly

To shave a customer. A draper's expression
for charging more for an article than it is
worth, because, so it is said, when the manager
sees a chance of doing this he strokes his chin
as a sign to the assistant that he may fleece
the customer all he can.

To shave an egg. To attempt to extort the
uttermost farthing, to "skin a flint "

Shaveling. Used in contempt—especially
after the Reformation—of a priest At a time
when the laity wore moustaches and beards
the clergy were not only usually clean shaven
but invariably wore large shaven tonsures.
> It maketh no matter how thou live here, so thou
> have the favour of the pope and his shavelings.—
> JOHN BRADFORD (1510-1555) a Marian martyr

B D —27

Shavian (shā′ vi ăn). After the manner of
George Bernard Shaw (1856-1950) or descriptive of his philosophy and style of humour

She. She Bible, The. *See* BIBLE, SPECIALLY
NAMED

She Stoops to Conquer. Goldsmith's comedy
(1773) owes its existence to an incident which
actually occurred to its author. When he was
sixteen years of age a wag residing at Ardagh
directed him, when passing through that
village, to Squire Fetherstone's house as the
village inn The mistake was not discovered for
some time, and then no one enjoyed it more
heartily than Oliver himself

She-wolf of France. *See* WOLF

Shear. God tempers the wind to the shorn lamb.
See GOD

Ordeal by sieve and shears. *See* SIEVE.

Shear or Shere Thursday. Maundy Thursday,
the Thursday of Holy Week, so called, it is
said, because in—
> old fadres dayes the people wolde that day shere theyr
> hedes, and clyppe theyr berdes, and poll theyr hedes,
> and so make them honest agenst Ester day.

Sheathe To sheathe the sword. To cease
hostilities, make peace In the early months of
World War I the phrase "We will not sheathe
the sword until the wrong done to Belgium has
been righted" was a common slogan

Sheba, The Queen of (shē′ bà) The queen who
visited Solomon (1 *Kings* x) is known to the
Arabs as Balkis, Queen of Saba (Koran, ch.
xxvii). Sheba was thought by the Greeks and
Romans to have been the capital of what is
now Yemen, S W Arabia, and the people
over whom the queen reigned were the
Sabæans

Shebang (she băng′) Fed up with the whole shebang. Tired of the whole concern and everything connected with it *Shebang* is American
slang for a hut or one's quarters, also for a
cart, and also, in a humorously depreciatory
way, for almost anything

Shebeen (she bēn′) A place (originally only in
Ireland) where liquor is sold without a licence,
hence applied to any low-class public house
> You've been takin' a dhrop o' the crathur' an' Danny
>   says "Troth, an' I been
> Dhrinking yer health wid Shamus O'Shea at Katty's
>   shebeen "
>   TENNYSON *To-morrow.*

Shedem *See* MAZIKEEN.

Sheep. Ram or *tup*, the sire, *ewe*, the dam,
lamb, the young till weaned, when it is called
a *tup-hogget* or *ewe-hogget*, as the case may be,
or, if the tup is castrated, a *wether-hogget*
After the removal of the *first* fleece, the tup-
hogget becomes a *shearling*, the ewe-hogget a
gimmer, and the wether-hogget a *dinmont*
After the removal of the *second* fleece, the
shearling becomes a *two-shear tup*, the gimmer
an *ewe*, and the dinmont a *wether*
After the removal of the *third* fleece, the ewe
is called a *twinter-ewe*, and when it ceases to
breed a *draft-ewe*

Sheepish. Awkward and shy; bashful
through not knowing how to deport oneself in
the circumstances

Sheep's head. A fool, a simpleton—

Gostanzo: What, sirrah, is that all?
No entertainment to the gentlewoman?
Valerio · Forsooth y'are welcome by my father's leave.
Gos. What, no more compliment? Kiss her, you sheep's head!
Lady, you'll pardon our gross bringing up?
We dwell far off from court, you may perceive.
          CHAPMAN *All Fools*, ii, 1

The Black Sheep (Kârâ-koin-loo). A tribe which established a principality in Armenia that lasted 108 years (1360-1468); so called from the device of their standard.

The White Sheep (Ak-koin-loo) A tribe which established a principality in Armenia, etc, on the ruin of the Black Sheep (1468-1508), so called from the device of their standard.

There's a black sheep in every flock. In every club or party of persons there's sure to be at least one shady character.

To cast sheep's eyes. To look askance, in a sheepish way, at a person to whom you feel lovingly inclined
But he, the beast, was casting sheep's eyes at her —
COLMAN: *Broad Grins.*

Vegetable sheep. *See* SCYTHIAN LAMB

Sheepskin (U S.A) A college diploma.

Sheer Thursday. *See* SHEAR.

Sheet. Three sheets in the wind. Very drunk; just about as drunk as one can be The *sheet* is the rope attached to the lower end of a sail, used for shortening and extending sail; if quite free, the sheet is said to be "in the wind," and the sail flaps and flutters without restraint. If all the three sails were so loosened, the ship would "reel and stagger like a drunken man."
Captain Cuttle looking, candle in hand, at Bunsby more attentively, perceived that he was three sheets in the wind, or, in plain words, drunk—DICKENS: *Dombey and Son*

That was **my sheet anchor**. My best hope, chief stay, last refuge, if that fails me, then all is indeed lost. The *sheet anchor* is the largest anchor of a ship, and in stress of weather, the sailor's chief dependence The Greeks and Romans said, "my *sacred* anchor," because the sheet anchor was always dedicated to some god.

Sheikh (shēk, shek) A title of respect among the Arabs (like the Ital *signore* Fr *sieur*, Span *señor*, etc), but properly the head of a Bedouin clan, family, or tribe, or the headman of an Arab village.

Sheikh-ul-Islam. The Grand Mufti, or supreme head of the Mohammedan hierarchy in Turkey.

Shekels (shek' elz) Colloquial for money The Hebrew shekel was a weight of about 250 grains troy, also a silver coin worth roughly 2s 6d

Shekinah (she kī' na) (Heb *shakan*, to reside). The visible glory of the Divine Presence in the shape of a cloud, which rested over the mercy-seat between the Cherubim, and in the Temple of Solomon (*see Exod* xl, 34-38). The word does not occur in the Bible, but is frequent

in the Targums, and was employed by the Jews as a periphrasis for the Divine Name

Sheldonian Theatre (shel dō' ni ân) The Senate House of Oxford, so called from Gilbert Sheldon (1598-1677), Archbishop of Canterbury, who built it

Shelf. Laid on the shelf, or shelved. Put on one side as of no further use, superannuated Said of officials and others no longer actively employed, an actor no longer assigned a part, a woman past the ordinary age of marriage, also of a pawn at the broker's, a question started and set aside, etc.

Shell (A S *scell*) The hard outside covering of nuts, eggs, molluscs, tortoises, etc , hence applied to other hollow coverings, as a light or inner coffin, and the hollow projectile filled with explosives and missiles which will explode on impact or at a set time.

Eggshells. Many persons, after eating a boiled egg, break or crush the shell This, according to Sir Thomas Browne—
is but a superstitious relict   and the intent thereof was to prevent witchcraft, for lest witches should draw or prick their names therein, and veneficiously mischief their persons, they broke the shell.—
Pseudodoxia Epidemica, V, xxii

Scallop shells were the emblem of St James the Great (*q v*), and were hence carried by pilgrims, under whose special protection they were.

Shell jacket. An undress military jacket, fatigue jacket.

Shell shock. An acute neurasthenic condition due to a shock to the system caused by the explosion of a shell or bomb at close quarters The term came into use in World War I.

Shellback. Nautical slang for an old and seasoned sailor, an "old salt."

To retire into one's shell. To become reticent and uncommunicative, to withdraw oneself from society in a forbidding way The allusion is to the tortoise, which, once it has "got into its shell," is quite unget-at-able
See also NUTSHELL.

Shelter. In World War II this word, as an abbreviation of Air Raid Shelter, was especially applied to the various excavations, buildings, or devices employed as a protection against aerial bombing Deep shelters, *e g* the London Tubes, were sufficiently far below the ground level to be immune from damage even by a direct hit Such shelters as the Anderson (half above and half below ground, and made of corrugated steel) or the Morrison (a sort of steel dining-table with room for a bed beneath) afforded exiguous protection from blast or falling masonry.

Sheol. *See* HADES

Shepherd. The Shepherd Kings. *See* HYKSOS

The Shepherd Lord Henry, tenth Lord Clifford (d. 1523), sent by his mother to be brought up by a shepherd, in order to save him from the fury of the Yorkists At the accession of Henry VII he was restored to all his rights and seigniories The story is told by

Wordsworth in *The Song for the Feast of Brougham Castle.*

The Shepherd of Banbury. The ostensible author of a Weather Guide (published 1744) He styles himself John Claridge, Shepherd, but is said to have been a Dr John Campbell

The Shepherd of the Ocean So Sir Walter Raleigh is called by Spenser —

When I asked from what place he came,
And how he hight, himselfe he did ycleape
The Shepheard of the Ocean by name,
And said he came far from the main-sea deepe
Colin Clout's Come Home Again, 64

The Shepherd of Salisbury Plain. A famous religious tract by Mrs Hannah More, first published in *The Cheap Repository* (1795), a series of moral "tales for the people." It had enormous popularity, and the story is said to be founded on the life of one David Saunders, who was noted for his homely wisdom and practical piety, whom she turns into a sort of Christian Arcadian.

The Shepherd's Sundial. The scarlet pimpernel, which opens at a little past seven in the morning and closes at a little past two When rain is at hand, or the weather is unfavourable, it does not open at all

The Shepherd's Warning

A red sky at night is the shepherd's delight,
But a red sky in the morning is the shepherd's warning

The Italian saying is *Sera rosso e bianco mattino allegra il pellegrino* (a red evening and a white morning rejoice the pilgrim)

To shepherd. To guard and guide carefully as a shepherd does his flock, in colloquial use, to follow and spy on as a detective

Sheppard, Jack (1702-24) A notorious highwayman, son of a carpenter in Smithfield, noted for his two escapes from Newgate in 1724. He was hanged at Tyburn the same year

Shere Thursday. *See* SHEAR

Sherif (she rēf') A descendant of the Prophet Mohammed, formerly applied to the governor of Mecca. The title was also adopted by the rulers of Morocco, who claimed descent from the Prophet through his grandson Hasan

Sheriff (sher' if) In mediæval and later times the sheriff (shire reeve) was an official who looked after the king's property in the various shires or counties In England and Wales each county has its sheriff, called the High Sheriff, whose duty it is to keep the peace, administer justice under the direction of the courts, execute writs by deputy, preside over parliamentary elections, etc There are sheriffs in certain cities such as Bristol, Norwich, etc , and the City of London has two.

In U S A the sheriff is the officer in a county commissioned with the enforcement of law and order

Sheriffmuir. There was mair lost at the Shirra-muir. Don't grieve for your losses, for worse have befallen others before now The battle of Sheriffmuir in 1715, between the Jacobites and Hanoverians was very bloody, both sides sustained heavy losses, and both sides claimed the victory

Sherlock Holmes The most important figure in detective fiction, the creation of Arthur Conan Doyle (1859-1930) His solutions of crimes and mysteries were related in a series of sixty stories that appeared in the *Strand Magazine* off and on between 1891 and 1927 The character was based on Dr Joseph Bell, of the Edinburgh Infirmary, whose methods of deduction suggested a system that Holmes developed into a science, his stooge Watson was a skit on Doyle himself Holmes's method is in itself simple—the observation of the minutest details and apparently insignificant circumstances, the correct interpretation and application of the information thus acquired enables him to solve the apparently unsolvable with a minimum of energy or detective apparatus

Sherrick. Yorkshire for something very small Used in Australia for a small amount of anything, particularly money

Shewbread Food for show only, and not intended to be eaten except by certain privileged persons The term is Jewish, and refers to the twelve loaves (one for each tribe, *see Exod* xxv, 30, *Lev* xxiv, 5-8) which the priest "showed" or exhibited to Jehovah, by placing them week by week on the sanctuary table. At the end of the week, the priest was allowed to take them home for his own eating, but no one else could partake of them.

Shibboleth (shib' ō leth) The password of a secret society, the secret by which those of a party know each other, also a worn-out or discredited doctrine The Ephraimites could not pronounce *sh*, so when they were fleeing from Jephthah and the Gileadites (*Judges* xii, 1-16) they were caught at the ford on the Jordan because Jephthah caused all the fugitives to say the word *Shibboleth* (meaning "a stream in flood"), which all the Ephraimites pronounced as *Sibboleth*

Shield The most famous shields in story are the *Shield of Achilles* described by Homer, of *Hercules* described by Hesiod, of *Æneas* described by Virgil, and the *Ægis* (*q v*).

Others are that of —

Agamemnon, a gorgon.

Amycos (son of Poseidon), a crayfish, symbol of prudence

Cadmus and his descendants, a dragon, to indicate their descent from the dragon's teeth

Eteocles, one of the Seven Against Thebes, a man scaling a wall

Hector, a lion

Idomeneus, a cock.

Menelaus, a serpent at his heart; alluding to the elopement of his wife with Paris

Parthenopæus, one of the Seven Against Thebes, a sphinx holding a man in its claws

Ulysses, a dolphin Whence he is sometimes called Delphinosemos

Servius says that in the siege of Troy the Greeks had, as a rule, Neptune on their bucklers, and the Trojans Minerva

It was a common custom, after a great victory, for the victorious general to hang his shield on the wall of some temple

The clang of shields. When a chief doomed a man to death, he struck his shield with the blunt end of his spear by way of notice to the royal bard to begin the death-song

> Cairbar rises in his arms,
> The clang of shields is heard.
>
> OSSIAN. Temora, 1

The Gold and Silver Shield A mediæval allegory tells how two knights coming from opposite directions stopped in sight of a shield suspended from a tree branch, one side of which was gold and the other silver, and disputed about its metal, proceeding from words to blows. Luckily a third knight came up the point was referred to him, and the disputants were informed that the shield was silver on one side and gold on the other. Hence the sayings, *The other side of the shield, It depends on which side of the shield you are looking at,* etc

The Shield of Expectation. The perfectly plain shield given to a young warrior in his maiden campaign As he achieved glory, his deeds were recorded or symbolized on it

Shi'ites (Arab *shi'ah*, a sect) Those Mohammedans who regard Ali as the first rightful Imam or Caliph (rejecting the three Sunni Caliphs), and do not consider the Sunna, or oral law of any authority, but look upon it as apocryphal. They wear *red* turbans, and are sometimes called "Red Heads" *Cp.* SUNNITES

Shillelagh (Ir) A cudgel of oak or blackthorn, so called from a village of this name in County Wicklow

Shilling (A S *scilling*, which is connected either with O Teut *skel-*, to resound or ring, or *skil-*, to divide) The coin was originally made with a deeply indented cross, and could easily be divided into halves or quarters

Shilling shocker. *See* PENNY DREADFUL.

To be cut off with a shilling *See* CUT

To take the Queen's (or King's) shilling. To enlist, in allusion to the former practice of giving each recruit a shilling when he was sworn in.

Shilly Shally. To hesitate, act in an undecided, irresolute way, a corruption of "Will I, shall I," or "Shall I, shall I?"

> There's no delay, they ne'er stand shall I, shall I,
> Hermogenes with Dalhla doth dally
>
> *Taylor's Workes*, III, 3 (1630).

Shindig (shin' dig). A slang term for a dance, a noisy celebration party, etc

Shindy. A row, a disturbance To *kick up a shindy,* to make a row The word is probably connected with *shinty* or *shinny,* a primitive kind of hockey played in the north

Shine. To take the shine out of one. To humiliate him, "take him down a peg or two", to outshine him

Shiner. A black eye

Shin Plaster. An old American and also Australian phrase still occasionally used for paper tokens issued by rural stores as small change It is said that some storekeepers baked them to make them brittle so that they would powder to nothing in the recipient's pocket.

Shintoism, the national religion of Japan. Worship takes the form of offerings and prayers for temporal blessings, litanies read by priests, reverence for ancestors and an unquestioning loyalty to the State The chief of numerous deities is Ameratasu, the sun goddess from whom the emperors claim descent.

Ship. In the printing-house the body of compositors engaged for the time being on one definite piece of work is known as a *ship*, this is said to be short for *companionship*, but it is worth noting that many printing-house terms (*cp* CHAPEL, FRIAR, MONK) have an ecclesiastical origin, and *ship* was an old name for the nave of a church

Losing a ship for a ha'porth o' tar. Suffering a great loss out of stinginess By mean savings, or from want of some necessary outlay, to lose the entire article For example, to save the expense of a nail and lose the horseshoe as the first result, then to lame the horse, and finally perhaps kill it

Ship-money A tax formerly levied in time of war on ports and seaboard counties for the maintenance of the Navy It was through Charles I levying this tax in 1634-7 without the consent of Parliament, and extending it to the inland counties illegally, that the Puritan party, led by Hampden, refused to pay and thus began the struggle which culminated in the Civil War.

Shipshape. As methodically arranged as things in a ship, in good order When a vessel is sent out temporarily rigged, it is termed "jury-rigged," and when the jury rigging has been duly changed for ship rigging, the vessel is "shipshape," *i e* in due or regular order

Ship's husband The agent on land who represents the owners and attends to the repairs, provisioning and other necessaries and expenses of the ship.

Ships of the line Men-of-war large enough to have a place in a line of battle

The ship of the desert. The camel

To take shipping. To set out on a voyage, to embark on board ship

When my ship comes home When my fortune is made The allusion is to the argosies returning from foreign parts laden with rich freights, and so enriching the merchants who sent them forth

Shipton, Mother This so-called prophetess is first heard of in a tract of 1641, in which she is said to have lived in the reign of Henry VIII, and to have foretold the death of Wolsey, Cromwell, Lord Percy, etc In 1677 the pamphleteering publisher, Richard Head, brought out a *Life and Death of Mother Shipton*, and in 1862 Charles Hindley brought out a new edition in which she was credited with having predicted steam-engines, the telegraph, and other modern inventions, as well as the end of the world in 1881

Shire When the Saxon kings created an earl, they gave him a *shire* (A S *scir*) or division of land to govern *Scir* meant originally employment or government, and is connected with *scirian*, to appoint, allot At the Norman

Conquest *count* superseded the title *earl*, and the shire or earldom was called a *county* Even to the present hour we call the wife of an earl a countess

Knight of the Shire. *See* KNIGHT

The shires. The English counties whose names terminate in -*shire*, but, in a narrower sense, the Midland counties noted for fox-hunting, especially Leicestershire, Northamptonshire, and Rutland.

Shire horse. The old breed of large, heavily built English cart-horse, originally raised in the Midland shires The term is applied to any draught horse of a certain character which can show a registered pedigree The sire and dam, with a minute description of the horse itself, its age, marks and so on, must be shown in order to prove the claim of a "shire horse"

Clydesdale horses are Scotch draught horses, not equal to shire horses in size, but of great endurance

Shirt. A boiled shirt. An Americanism for a stiff white shirt, as opposed to an unstarched coloured one

Close sits my shirt, but closer my skin. My property is dear to me, but dearer my life; my belongings sit close to my heart, but *Ego proximus mihi*

Not a shirt to one's name. Nothing at all; penniless and propertyless

The shirt of Nessus *See* NESSUS

To get one's shirt out To lose one's temper, to get in a rage A variant is *to get one's rag out*

Shirty. Bad-tempered; very cross and offended, in the state one is when somebody has 'got your shirt out'

To give the shirt off one's back All one has.

To put one's shirt on a horse To back it with all the money one possesses

Shirts as party emblems. The custom of wearing coloured shirts as a political gesture originated in the Garibaldi Italian campaign of 1848-49 While in S America, fighting for the Uruguayan Republic, Garibaldi and his men were issued with red shirts bought as a job lot by the government from a mercantile house in Montevideo On their arrival in Europe the Italian patriots accompanying Garibaldi still wore these shirts, which became an emblem of hope and patriotism that reached its culmination when Garibaldi led his red-shirted Thousand to the conquest of Sicily and South Italy in 1860. Mussolini adopted the Black Shirt as the emblem of Fascism in the 1920s, Hitler clothed his henchmen in Brown Shirts, other colours have been chosen by ardent though less eminent imitators.

Shiva. *See* SIVA

Shivering Mountain. Mam Tor, a hill on the Peak of Derbyshire, so called from the waste of its mass by "shivering"—that is, breaking away in "shivers" or small pieces This has been going on for ages, as the hill consists of alternate layers of shale and gritstone The former,

being soft, is easily reduced to powder, and, as it crumbles small "shivers" of the gritstone break away from want of support

Shmoo (U S A.) A small being, the characteristics of which are that it can at will become whatever you wish It was invented by Al Capp (inventor of Little Abner) in 1948 and became a craze in strip form, books, boy's balloons, and other representations. It also became a nation-wide cause of dissension, some seeing behind the idea a subtle political attack on the Capitalist system.

Shoat (U S A) A half-grown pig, hence an uncomplimentary term for a person of no account.

Shoddy. Worthless stuff masquerading as something that is really good, from the cheap cloth called *shoddy* which is made up out of cloth from old garments torn to pieces and shredded, mixed with new wool

Shoddy characters. Persons of tarnished reputation, like cloth made of shoddy or refuse wool.

Shoe. It was at one time thought unlucky to put on the left shoe before the right, or to put either shoe on the wrong foot It is said that Augustus Cæsar was nearly assassinated by a mutiny one day when he put on his left shoe first.

One of the sayings of Pythagoras was "When stretching forth your feet to have your sandals put on, first extend your right foot, but when about to step into a bath, let your left foot enter first." Iamblichus says the hidden meaning is that worthy actions should be done heartily, but base ones should be avoided (*Protreptics*, symbol XII)

It has long been a custom to throw an old shoe, or several shoes, at the bride and bridegroom when they quit the bride's home, after the wedding breakfast, or when they go to church to get married.

> Now, for goode luck caste an old shoe after me —
> HAYWOOD (1693-1756)
> Ay, with all my heart, there's an old shoe after you.
> —*The Parson's Wedding (Dodsley*, vol IX, p 499)

In Anglo-Saxon marriages the father delivered the bride's shoe to the bridegroom, who touched her with it on the head to show his authority, and it is said that in Turkey the bridegroom is chased by the guests, who either administer blows by way of adieux, or pelt him with slippers.

Some think this shoe-throwing represents an assault and refers to the notion that the bridegroom carried off the bride with force and violence Others look upon it as a relic of the ancient law of exchange, implying that the parents of the bride give up henceforth all right of dominion to their daughter. Luther told the bridegroom at a wedding that he had placed the husband's shoe on the head of the bed so that he should take to himself the mastery and governing of his wife.

Loosing the shoe (*cp Josh* v, 15) is a mark of respect in the East to the present hour The Mussulman leaves his slippers at the door of the mosque, and when making a visit of ceremony to a European visitor, at the tent entrance.

In *Deut* xxv, 5-10 we read that the widow

refused by the surviving brother, asserted her independence by "loosing his shoe", and in the story of Ruth we are told "that it was the custom" in exchange to deliver a shoe in token of renunciation When Boaz, therefore, became possessed of his lot, the kinsman's kinsman indicated his assent by giving Boaz his shoe. "A man without sandals" was a proverbial expression among the Jews for a prodigal, from the custom of giving one's sandals in confirmation of a bargain.

Another man's shoes "To stand in another man's shoes" is to occupy the place of another Among the ancient Northmen, when a man adopted a son, the person adopted put on the shoes of the adopter.
In *Reynard the Fox* (q v) Reynard, having turned the tables on Sir Bruin the Bear, asked the queen to let him have the shoes of the disgraced minister, so Bruin's shoes were torn off and put upon the new favourite

Another pair of shoes. A different thing altogether, quite another matter.

A shoe too large trips one up. A Latin proverb, *Calceus major subvertit* An empire too large falls to pieces, a business too large comes to grief; an ambition too large fails altogether.

No one knows where the shoe pinches like the wearer This was said by a Roman sage who was blamed for divorcing his wife, with whom he seemed to live happily
> For, God it wot, he sat ful still and song,
> When that his scho ful bitterly him wrong
>   CHAUCER *Canterbury Tales*, 6,074.

The *fons et origo* of some trouble is called "the place where the shoe pinches"

Over Edom will I cast my shoe (*Ps* lx, 8, cviii, 9). Will I march and triumph.

Over shoes, over boots. In for a penny, in for a pound.
> Where true courage roots,
> The proverb says, "once over shoes, o'er boots"
>   *Taylor's Workes*, ii, 145 (1690)

To die in one's shoes. To die a violent death, especially one on the scaffold
> And there is M'Fuze, and Lieutenant Tregooze,
> And there is Sir Carnaby Jenks, of the Blues
> All come to see a man die in his shoes
>   *Ingoldsby Legends* *The Execution*

To shake in one's shoes. To be in a state of nervous terror

To shoe a goose To engage in a silly and fruitless task.

To shoe the anchor. To cover the flukes of an anchor with a broad triangular piece of plank, in order that the anchor may have a stronger hold in soft ground

To shoe the cobbler. To give a quick peculiar movement with the front foot in sliding

To shoe the wild colt To exact a fine called "footing" from a newcomer, who is called the "colt." Colt is a common synonym for a greenhorn, or a youth not broken in Thus Shakespeare says—"Ay, that's a colt indeed, for he doth nothing but talk of his horse" (*Merchant of Venice*, i, 2)

Waiting for dead men's shoes. Looking out for legacies, looking to stand in the place of some moneyed man when he is dead and buried

Whose shoes I am not worthy to bear (*Matt* iii, 11) This means, "I am not worthy to be his humblest slave" It was the business of a slave recently purchased to loose and carry his master's sandals When the Emperor Wladimir proposed marriage to the daughter of Reginald, she rejected him, saying, "I will not take off my shoe to the son of a slave"

Shoemakers. The patron saints of shoemakers are St Crispin and his brother Crispian, who supported themselves by making shoes while they preached to the people of Gaul and Britain. In compliment to these saints the trade of shoemaking is called "the gentle craft"

Shofar (shō'far) A Hebrew trumpet still used in the modern synagogue It is made of the horn of a ram or any ceremonially clean animal, and produces only the natural series of harmonics from its fundamental note.

Shogun (shō'gun) The title of the actual ruler of Japan from the 12th century to the modernization of the country in 1868. The Shoguns were hereditary commanders-in-chief (the word means "army leader"), and took the place of the Mikados, whom they kept in a state of perpetual imprisonment. Also called the *Tycoon* (q v)

Shoot. See also SHOT.

Shooting-iron Slang (originally American) for a firearm, especially a revolver

Shooting stars Incandescent meteors shooting across the sky, formerly, like comets, fabled to presage disaster—
> A little ere the mightiest Julius fell,
> The graves stood tenantless, and the sheeted dead
> Did squeak and gibber in the Roman streets
> As stars with trains of fire and dews of blood,
> Disasters in the sun.   *Hamlet*, i, 1

They were called in ancient legends the "fiery tears of St Lawrence," because one of the periodic swarms of these meteors is between August 9th and 14th, about the time of St. Lawrence's festival, which is on the 10th. Other periods are from November 12th to 14th, and from December 6th to 12th.
Shooting stars are said by the Arabs to be firebrands hurled by the angels against the inquisitive genii, who are for ever clambering up on the constellations to peep into heaven.

To go the whole shoot. To do all there is to do, go the whole hog, run through the gamut.

To shoot a line. To boast

To shoot one's linen. To display an unnecessary amount of shirt-cuff to show off

To shoot the moon. To remove one's household goods by night to avoid distraint, to "do a moonlight flit."

To shoot the sun. A sailor's expression for taking the sun's meridional altitude, which is done by aiming at the reflected sun through the telescope of the sextant

Shoot! Go ahead, say what you have to say Let's have it! In motion pictures it is the word used in the studios for the cameras to begin turning when all is ready.

Shop. The Shop, in military slang, is the Royal Military Academy, Woolwich, on the Stock Exchange it is the South African gold market

All over the shop Scattered in every direction, all over the place, or pursuing an erratic course

To shop a person To put him in prison, or to inform against him so that he is arrested, similarly, a billiard player will speak of "shopping the white," i e putting his opponent's ball down in the pocket

To shut up shop. To retire from business, withdraw from participation in the undertaking, etc.

To talk shop. To talk about one's affairs or business, to draw allusions from one's business, as when Ollapod, the apothecary in Colman's *Poor Gentleman*, talks of a uniform with rhubarb-coloured facings

You've come to the wrong shop I can't help you, I can't give you the information, and so on, you require

Shopkeepers. A nation of shopkeepers. This phrase, applied to Englishmen by Napoleon in contempt, comes from Adam Smith's *Wealth of Nations* (iv, 7), a book well known to the Emperor He says—
To found a great empire for the sole purpose of raising up a people of customers, may at first sight appear a project fit only for a nation of shopkeepers.

Ten years earlier, in 1766, J Tucker had written in the third of his *Four Tracts* —
A Shop-keeper will never get the more Custom by beating his Customers; and what is true of a Shop-keeper, is true of a Shop-keeping Nation

Shoreditch, according to tradition, is so called from Jane Shore, the mistress of Edward IV, who, it is said, died there in a ditch This tale comes from a ballad in Pepys' collection—
I could not get one bit of bread
Whereby my hunger might be fed   .
So, weary of my life, at length
I yielded up my vital strength
Within a ditch   which since that day
Is Shoreditch called, as writers say—

But the truth is, it appears in the Index to Kemble's *Codex Diplomaticus* as *Sordic*, in the 14th century as *Soerditch*, and Stow says that in the 12th century it was called *Soersditch* It is probable that it is from a former Anglo-Saxon proprietor, *Soer*
Jane Shore is supposed to have died about 1527, but the date and place are alike unknown

The Duke of Shoreditch. The most successful of the London archers received this playful title
Good king, make not good Lord of Lincoln Duke of Shoreditch!—*The Poore Man's Peticion to the Kinge* (1603)

Shorne, John. A rector of North Marston, Buckinghamshire, at the close of the 13th century He is said to have blessed a well, which became the resort of multitudes and brought in a yearly revenue of some £500, and

to have conjured the devil into a boot. After his death he was prayed to by sufferers from ague
Maister John Shorne, that blessed man borne,
    For the ague to him we apply,
Which juggleth with a bote; I beschrewe his herte rote
    That will trust him, and it be I.
                    Fantassie of Idolatrie

Short. A drop of something short. A tot of whisky, gin, or other spirit, as opposed to a glass of beer

Cut it short! Don't be so prolix, come to the point; "cut the cackle and come to the 'osses " Said to a speaker who goes round and round his subject

My name is Short. I'm in a hurry and cannot wait
Well, but let us hear the wishes (said the old man); my name is short, and I cannot stay much longer —
W. YEATS *Fairy Tales of the Irish Peasantry*, p 240

Short commons. *See* COMMONS

Short thigh. *See* CURTHOSE

The short cut is often the longest way round. It does not always pay to avoid taking a little trouble, e g there is no short cut to knowledge Bacon has the same idea—
It is in life, as it is in ways, the shortest way is commonly the foulest, and surely the faire way is not much about —*Advancement of Learning*, 66, ii

To break off short. Abruptly, without warning, but completely

To sell short. A Stock Exchange phrase meaning to sell stock that one does not at the moment possess on the chance that before the date of delivery the price will have fallen, the same as "selling for a fall," or "selling a bear "

To make short work of it To dispose of it quickly, to deal summarily with it

To win by a short head. Only just to outdistance one's competitors, to win with practically nothing to spare The phrase is from horse-racing

Shorter Catechism The name given to a confession of faith which sets forth the Presbyterian doctrines of the Church of Scotland Drawn up in 1647 it was called the "shorter" to distinguish it from the larger catechism which was too complicated and difficult for ordinary instruction.

Shorthand. The earliest shorthand was invented in Rome by M Tullius Tiro (63 B C) who used it to take down Cicero's speeches Various systems were in use during the Middle Ages, but in *The Arte of Stenographie*, 1602, John Willis devised a system based on sound rather than on spelling. This was improved on by Thomas Shelton (1630) in a system later employed by Samuel Pepys in setting down his diary. In 1786 Samuel Taylor published an essay attempting to set up a standard phonetic system which was, in 1840, improved and modified by Isaac Pitman This is one of the two systems now in general use, the other being devised (1888) on a monoslope basis by John Robert Gregg Gregg's shorthand is in general use in U S A whereas Pitman's is the more popular in Great Britain.

Shot. A fool's bolt is soon shot. *See* BOLT

Big shot. An important person 20th-century development of the 19th-century "great gun" or "big bug."

Down with your shot. Your reckoning or quota, your money *See* SCOT

> As the fund of our pleasure, let us each pay his shot.
> BEN JONSON

He shot wide of the mark. He was altogether in error The allusion is to shooting at the mark or bull's-eye of a target.

I haven't a shot in the locker. Not a penny to bless myself with, my last resources are used up A phrase from the days of the old men-of-war, when the ammunition was kept in lockers

Like a shot With great rapidity, or, without hesitation, most willingly.

Shotten Herring A lean, spiritless creature, a Jack-o'-Lent, like a herring that has *shot*, or ejected, its spawn. Herrings gutted and dried are so called also

> Though they like shotten-herrings are to see,
> Yet such tall souldiers of their teeth they be,
> That two of them, like greedy cormorants,
> Devour more then sixe honest Protestants
> *Taylor's Workes*, iii, 5

Shoulder. Showing the cold shoulder. Receiving without cordiality someone who was once on better terms with you *See* COLD

Straight from the shoulder. With full force A boxing term

The government shall be upon his shoulder (*Is.* ix, 6). The allusion is to the key slung on the shoulder of Jewish stewards on public occasions, and as a key is emblematic of government and power, the metaphor is very striking

Soft shoulders. A warning sign on roads in the U S A, drawing driver's attention to the fact that the clay edges of the road outside the macadam are unsafe.

Shouting, All over but the Success is so certain that only the applause is lacking The phrase perhaps originated in a hotly contested election.

Shovel Board. A game in which three counters, or coins, were shoved or slid over a smooth board, very popular in the sixteenth and seventeenth centuries The "two Edward shovelboards" mentioned by Slender in the *Merry Wives of Windsor* (i, 1), were the broad shillings of Edward VI used in playing the game

Show. Australian, a gold mine. "Give him a show," give him a chance, i.e. originally let him stake out his own claim

Shrapnel. A type of shell containing a number of bullets which are released and travel forwards with a high velocity when the shell is shattered by the bursting charge It was invented in 1784 by Col Henry Shrapnel (1761-1842) and was adopted in 1803 by the British army In World War II this type of projectile was not used, but the term was loosely applied to all high-explosive fragments

Shrew-mouse. A small insectivorous mammal, resembling a mouse, formerly supposed to have the power of poisoning cattle and young children by running over them To provide a remedy our forefathers used to plug the creature into a hole made in an ash-tree, then any branch from it would cure the mischief done.

Shrift. The shriving of a person; i e his confession to a priest, and the penance and absolution arising therefrom.

To give short shrift to. To make short work of *Short shrift* was the few minutes in which a criminal about to be executed was allowed to make his confession.

Shrimp. A child, a puny little fellow, in the same ratio to a man as a shrimp to a lobster *Fry*, and *small fry*, are also used for children

> It cannot be this weak and writhled shrimp
> Would strike such terror to his enemies.
> 1 *Henry VI*, ii, 3

Shrivatsa. *See* VISHNU

Shroff. An Oriental term, in India applied to a money-changer or banker, in China to an expert who tests gold and silver coins for their genuineness

Shropshire. The "shire of shrubs." The Anglo-Saxon name of Shrewsbury was *scrobbes byrg*, the burgh among the shrubs. The Normans could not pronounce *sc-*; so the A S name became *Salopesbury*, and for the name of the county the *-bury* (=town) was dropped, giving *Salop*, a name still used as an alternative for Shropshire, whence *Salopian*, a native of the county

Shrovetide. The three days just before the opening of Lent, when people went to confession and afterwards indulged in all sorts of sports and merry-making

Shrove Tuesday. The day before Ash Wednesday, "Pancake day" It used to be the great "Derby Day" of cock-fighting in England.

> Or martyr beat, like Shrovetide cocks, with bats
> PETER PINDAR *Subjects for Painters*

Shun-pike (U S A) A side-road is so called because it is used to avoid the pike, or turnpike, where toll had to be paid

Shut Up. Hold your tongue Shut up your mouth

Shy To have a shy at anything. To fling at it, to try and shoot it

Shylock, A (shĭ' lok) A grasping, stonyhearted moneylender, in allusion to the Jew in Shakespeare's *Merchant of Venice*

> A stony adversary, an inhuman wretch
> Uncapable of pity, void and empty
> From any dram of mercy   iv, 1

Shyster. A mean, tricky sort of person, originally American slang for a low-class lawyer hanging about the courts on the off-chance of exploiting petty criminals

Si (sē), the seventh note in music, was not introduced till the 17th century. Guido d'Arezzo's original scale consisted of only six notes *See* ARETINIAN SYLLABLES

Si Quis (sī kwīs) (Lat , if anyone) A notice
to all whom it may concern, given in the
parish church before ordination, that a
resident means to offer himself as a candidate
for holy orders, and *if anyone* knows any just
cause or impediment thereto, he is to declare
the same to the bishop

Siamese Twins (sī' a mēz) Yoke-fellows, inseparables, so called from the original pair,
Eng and Chang, who were born of Chinese
parents about 1814 and discovered at Mekong,
Siam, in 1829, and were subsequently exhibited
as freaks Their bodies were united by a band
of flesh, stretching from breast-bone to breast-
bone They married two sisters, had offspring,
and died within three hours of each other on
January 17th, 1874.

Other so-called Siamese twins were Barnum's
"Orissa twins," born at Orissa, Bengal, and
joined by a band of cartilage at the waist
only, "Millie-Christine," two joined South
Carolina negresses who appeared all over the
world as the "Two-headed Nightingale", and
Josepha and Roza Blazek, natives of Bohemia,
who were joined by a cartilaginous ligament
above the waist They died practically simultaneously in Chicago (1922), Josepha leaving
a son aged 12.

Sibyl (sib' il) A prophetess of classical legend,
who was supposed to prophesy under the
inspiration of a deity, the name is now applied
to any prophetess or woman fortune-teller
There were a number of sibyls, and they had
their seats in widely separate parts of the
world—Greece, Italy, Babylonia, Egypt, etc.

Plato mentions only one, viz., the *Erythræan*
—identified with Amalthea, the *Cumæan Sibyl*,
who was consulted by Æneas before his
descent into Hades and who sold the Sibylline
books (*q v.*) to Tarquin, Martian Capella
speaks of two, the *Erythræan* and the *Phrygian*,
Ælian of four, the *Erythræan*, *Samian*,
Egyptian, and *Sardian*, Varro tells us there were
ten, viz the *Cumæan*, the *Delphic*, *Egyptian*,
Erythræan, *Hellespontine*, *Libyan*, *Persian*,
Phrygian, *Samian* and *Tiburtine*
How know we but that she may be an eleventh
Sibyl or a second Cassandra?—RABELAIS *Gargantua
and Pantagruel*, III, 16

The mediæval monks "adopted" the sibyls
—as they did so much of pagan myth; they
made them twelve, and gave to each a separate
prophecy and distinct emblem —
(1) The *Libyan* "The day shall come when
men shall see the King of all living things"
Emblem, a lighted taper
(2) The *Samian* "The Rich One shall be
born of a pure virgin" *Emblem*, a rose
(3) The *Cuman* "Jesus Christ shall come
from heaven, and live and reign in poverty
on earth" *Emblem*, a crown
(4) The *Cumæan* "God shall be born of a
pure virgin, and hold converse with sinners"
Emblem, a cradle
(5) The *Erythræan*. "Jesus Christ, Son of
God, the Saviour" *Emblem*, a horn
(6) The *Persian* "Satan shall be overcome
by a true prophet." *Emblem*, a dragon under
the sibyl's feet, and a lantern.
(7) The *Tiburtine* "The Highest shall
27*

descend from heaven, and a virgin be shown
in the valleys of the deserts" *Emblem*, a dove.
(8) The *Delphic* "The Prophet born of the
virgin shall be crowned with thorns" *Emblem*,
a crown of thorns.
(9) The *Phrygian* "Our Lord shall rise
again" *Emblem*, a banner and a cross
(10) The *European* "A virgin and her Son
shall flee into Egypt" *Emblem*, a sword
(11) The *Agrippine*. "Jesus Christ shall be
outraged and scourged" *Emblem*, a whip
(12) The *Hellespontic* "Jesus Christ shall
suffer shame upon the cross" *Emblem*, a T
cross.

Sibylline Books, The A collection of oracles
of mysterious origin, preserved in ancient
Rome, and consulted by the Senate in times of
emergency or disaster. According to Livy
there were originally nine: these were offered
in sale by Amalthea, the Sibyl of Cumæ, in
Æolia, to Tarquin, the offer was rejected, and
she burnt three of them After twelve months
she offered the remaining six at the same price.
Again being refused, she burnt three more,
and after a similar interval asked the same
price for the three left The sum demanded
was now given, and Amalthæa never appeared
again

The three books were preserved in a stone
chest underground in the temple of Jupiter
Capitolinus, and committed to the charge of
custodians chosen in the same manner as the
high priests. The number of custodians was
at first two, then ten, and ultimately fifteen.
Augustus had some 2,000 of the verses
destroyed as spurious, and placed the rest in
two gilt cases, under the base of the statue of
Apollo, in the temple on the Palatine Hill, but
the whole perished when the city was burnt in
the reign of Nero

A Greek collection in eight books of poetical
utterances relating to Jesus Christ, compiled
in the 2nd century, is entitled *Oracula Sibylina*,
or the *Sibylline Books*.

Sic (sik) (Lat., thus, so). A word used by
reviewers, quoters, etc , after a doubtful
word or phrase, or a misspelling, to indicate
that it is here printed exactly as in the original
and to call attention to the fact that it is wrong
in some way

Sicilies, The Two. The old name for the Spanish
and Bourbon kingdom of Naples, united to
the kingdom of Italy in 1860. It consisted of
the island of Sicily, and, on the mainland of
the peninsula, the provinces of Abruzzi and
Molise, Apulia, Campania, Basilicata, and
Calabria. The origin of this ambiguous name
is not now known.

Sicilian Vespers. The massacre of the French
in Sicily, which began at the hour of vespers on
Easter Monday in 1282 The term is used
proverbially of any treacherous and bloody
attack

Sick Man, The. So Nicholas of Russia (in
1844) called the Ottoman Empire, which had
been declining ever since 1586.
I repeat to you that the sick man is dying, and we
must never allow such an event to take us by surprise.
—*Annual Register*, 1853

Don John, Governor-General of the Netherlands, writing in 1579 to Philip II of Spain, calls the Prince of Orange *the sick man*, because he was in the way, and he wanted him "finished."

"Money" (he says in his letter) "is the gruel with which we must cure this sick man [for spies and assassins are expensive drugs]"—MOTLEY. *Dutch Republic*, Bk. v, 2

Side. On the side of the angels. The famous phrase with which Disraeli thought he had settled the questions raised by Darwin's theory of the origin of species It occurred in his speech at the Oxford Diocesan Conference in 1864—

The question is this Is man an ape or an angel? I, my lord, am on the side of the angels

It was the same statesman who said in the House of Commons (May 14th, 1866), "Ignorance never settles a question"

Putting on side. Giving oneself airs; being bumptious *To put on side* in billiards is to give your ball a twist or spin with the cue as you strike it.

To side-track. Originally an American railroad term; hence, to get rid of, shelve, put on one side indefinitely.

Sideburns (U S.A.). Short side-whiskers worn with a smooth chin. Originally called Burnsides from the Federal general A E Burnside (1824-1881) who wore such whiskers and whose face was familiar to many Americans.

Sidney, Sir Philip (1554-86), often taken as the type of the magnanimous and perfect soldier and statesman—the Happy Warrior After he had received his death wound at the battle of Zutphen a soldier brought him some water, but as he was about to drink he observed a wounded man eye the draught with longing looks Sir Philip gave up the water to him, saying, "Poor fellow, thy necessity is greater than mine" Spenser laments him in his *Astrophel* (*q v*), and largely modelled the Prince Arthur of the *Faerie Queene* on him

Sidney's sister, Pembroke's mother. Mary Herbert (*née* Sidney), Countess of Pembroke, poetess, etc (died 1621). The line is from her *Epitaph*, which has been claimed both for Ben Jonson and for William Browne.

Sidney Sussex College. Cambridge, founded by Lady Frances Sidney, Countess of Sussex, in 1598.

Sidrac (sid' răk). An old French romance which tells how Sidrac converted to Christianity Boccus, an idolatrous king and magician of India Sidrac lived only 847 years after Noah, and became possessed of Noah's wonderful book on astronomy and the natural sciences. This passed through various hands, including those of a pious Chaldean, and Naaman the Syrian, until, as legend relates, Roger of Palermo translated it at Toledo into Spanish The work is more a romance of Arabian philosophy than of chivalry. In Henry VI's reign an English metrical version was made by Hugh Campeden, and this was printed in 1510 as *The Historye of King Boccus and Sydracke.*

Siege Perilous. In the cycle of Arthurian romances a seat at the Round Table which was kept vacant for him who should accomplish the quest of the Holy Grail For any less a person to sit in it was fatal. As the crown of his achievement Sir Galahad took his seat in the Siege Perilous.

Siegfried (sēg' frēd) Hero of the first part of the *Nibelungenlied* He was the youngest son of Siegmund and Sieglind, king and queen of the Netherlands. He married Kriemhild, Princess of Burgundy, and sister of Gunther Gunther craved his assistance in carrying off Brunhild from Issland, and Siegfried succeeded by taking away her talisman by main force This excited the jealousy of Gunther, who induced Hagen, the Dane, to murder Siegfried. Hagen struck him with a spear in the only vulnerable part (between the shoulder-blades), while he stooped to quench his thirst at a fountain

Siegfried's cloak of invisibility, called "tarnkappe" (*tarnen*, to conceal, *kappe*, a cloak) It not only made the wearer invisible, but also gave him the strength of twelve men

Siegfried Line. The defences built by the Germans on their Western frontier before and after 1939 as a reply to France's Maginot Line The British song, popular in 1939, entitled "We'll hang out the washing on the Siegfried Line" was held in derision after Dunkirk in 1940, but when the Canadian troops penetrated the Line in 1945 they hung up a number of sheets and erected a large notice bearing the simple words "The Washing"

Sierra (sē ĕr' a) (Span, a saw) A mountain whose top is indented like a saw, a range of mountains whose tops form a saw-like appearance, a line of craggy rocks; as *Sierra Morena* (where many of the incidents in *Don Quixote* are laid), *Sierra Nevada* (the snowy range) *Sierra Leone* (in West Africa, where lions abound), etc.

Siesta (sē es' ta) Spanish for "the sixth hour" —*i.e.* noon (Lat *sexta hora*) It is applied to the short sleep taken in Spain during the midday heat

Sieve and Shears. The oracle of sieve and shears. This method of divination is mentioned by Theocritus The *modus operandi* was as follows:—The points of the shears were stuck in the rim of a sieve, and two persons supported them with their finger-tips Then a verse of the Bible was read aloud, and St Peter and St. Paul were asked if it was A, B, or C (naming the persons suspected) When the right person was named, the sieve would suddenly turn round

Searching for things lost with a sieve and shears.— BEN JONSON· *Alchemist,* i, 1

Sight, for "multitude," though now regarded as a colloquialism or as slang, is good old English, and was formerly in literary use, the earlier significance being "a show or display of something" Thus, Juliana Berners, lady prioress in the 15th century of Sopwell nunnery, speaks of a *bombynable syght of monkes* (a large number of friars), and in one of the *Paston Letters* (May 25th, 1449) we read—

ye sawe never suche a syght of schyppys take in to Englond thys c [hundred] wynter

A sight for sore eyes. Something that it is very pleasurable to see or witness, especially something unexpected

Second sight *See* SECOND

Though lost to sight, to memory dear. This occurs in a song by Geo Linley (*c* 1835), but it is found as an "axiom" in the *Monthly Magazine*, Jan., 1827, and is probably of much earlier date Horace F. Cutter (*pseudonym* Ruthven Jenkyns) uses the expression in the *Greenwich Magazine for Mariners*, 1707, but this date is fictitious

To do a thing on sight. At once, without any hesitation

Sign Royal Sign Manual. A stamp reproducing the royal signature, used when the sovereign is too ill to sign documents

To sign off. In the 19th century this denoted leaving one religious denomination in a formal manner for another. In the 20th century it was for long used in radio as synonymous with the termination of a performance by a regular broadcaster known to the public, hence

Signature tune. A musical theme played regularly as a means of identification when introducing a well-known artist, dance band, etc.

Significavit (sig ni fi cā′ vit) A writ of Chancery given by the ordinary to keep an excommunicate in prison till he submitted to the authority of the Church The writ, which is now obsolete, used to begin with *Significavit nobis venerabilis pater*, etc Chaucer says of his Sompnour—

And also ware him of a significavit
Canterbury Tales (*Prologue*), 664

Sigurd (sig′ ĕrd). The Siegfried (*q v.*) of the *Volsunga Saga*, the Scandinavian version of the *Niebelungenlied* (*q v*) He falls in love with Brynhild, but, under the influence of a love-potion, marries Gudrun, a union which brings about a volume of mischief

Sikes, Bill. The type of a ruffianly house-breaker, from the fellow of that name in Dickens's *Oliver Twist* The only rudiment of a redeeming feature he possessed was a kind of affection for his dog

Sikh (sik) (Hindu *sikh*, disciple) The Sikhs were originally a monotheistic body founded in the Punjab by Nanak (1469-1539). They soon became a military community, and in 1764 formally assumed national independence In 1809 their ruler, Rangit Singh made a treaty with Britain, but the anarchy following upon his death led to the Sikh Wars of 1845-46 and 1848-49 During the Mutiny they remained loyal to Britain

Silbury, near Marlborough A prehistoric artificial mound, 130 feet high, and covering seven acres of ground, said to be the largest in Europe, and to have been erected by the Celts about 1600 B C. Some say it is where "King Sel" was buried, others, that it is a corruption of *Solis-bury* (mound of the sun), others, that it is Sel-barrow (great tumulus), in honour of some ancient prince of Britain.

Silence. Silence gives consent. A saying (common to many languages) founded on the old Latin law maxim—*Qui tacet consentire videtur* (who is silent is held to consent)

But that you shall not say I yield, being silent,
I would not speak ● *Cymbeline*, ii, 3.

Silence is golden. *See under* SPEECH

The rest is silence The last words of the dying Hamlet (*Hamlet*, v, 2)

Towers of Silence. The small towers on which the Parsees and Zoroastrians place their dead to be consumed by birds of prey. The bones are picked clean in the course of a day, and are then thrown into a receptacle and covered with charcoal

Parsees do not burn or bury their dead, because they consider a corpse impure, and they will not defile any of the elements. They carry it on a bier to the tower At the entrance they look their last on the body, and the corpse-bearers carry it within the precincts and lay it down to be devoured by vultures which are constantly on the watch

Two-minute Silence. A cessation of traffic and all other activities for two minutes at 11 a m. on November 11th, to commemorate those who died in World War I It was first observed in 1919 and discontinued in 1947 when the day was named Remembrance Day in memory of the fallen in both World Wars, and observed on the Sunday preceding November 11th.

Silent, The. William I, Prince of Orange (1533-84), so called because when (1559) Henri II of France, thinking that he would be a ready accomplice, revealed to him the plans for a general massacre of Protestants in the Netherlands—

the Prince, although horror-struck and indignant at the royal revelations, held his peace, and kept his countenance . without revealing to the monarch, by word or look, the enormous blunder which he had committed —MOTLEY *Dutch Republic*, II, 1

Silenus (sī lē′ nŭs). The drunken companion and nurse of Dionysus (Bacchus) in Greek mythology, fond of music, and a prophet, but incurably lazy, wanton, and given to debauch. He is described as a jovial old man, with bald head, pug nose, and face like Bardolph's.

Within his car, aloft, young Bacchus stood,
Trifling his ivy-dart, in dancing mood,
With sidelong laughing, .
And near him rode Silenus on his ass,
Pelted with flowers as he on did pass
Tipsily quaffing KEATS *Endymion*, iv, 209

Silhouette (sil oo et′) A black profile, so called from Etienne de Silhouette (1709-67), Contrôleur des Finances, 1759, who made great savings in the public expenditure of France. Some say the black portraits were named after him in allusion to the sacrifices he demanded from the nobles—*silhouette* being the popular term for a figure reduced to its simplest form, others assert that he devised this way of taking likenesses to save expense

Silk. To take silk. Said of a barrister who has been appointed a Queen's Counsel (Q C), because he then exchanges his stuff gown for a silk one.

You cannot make a silk purse of a sow's ear. You cannot make something good of what is by its nature bad or inferior in quality "You cannot make a horn of a pig's tail."

Silly is the German *selig* (blessed) and used to mean in English "happy through being innocent"; whence the infant Jesus was termed "the harmless silly babe," and sheep were called "silly" As the "innocent" are easily taken in by worldly cunning, the word came to signify "gullible," "foolish."

Silly-how. An old name—still used in Scotland—for a child's caul It is a rough translation of the German term *glückshaube*, lucky cap. The caul has always been supposed to bring luck to its original possessor.

The silly season. An obsolescent journalistic expression for the part of the year when Parliament and the Law Courts are not sitting (about August and September), when, through lack of news, the papers had to fill their columns with trivial items—such as news of giant gooseberries and sea serpents—and long correspondence on subjects of evanescent (if any) interest

Silurian. Of or pertaining to the ancient Silures or the district they inhabited, viz. Hereford, Monmouth, Radnor, Brecon, and Glamorgan The "sparkling wines of the Silurian vats" are cider and perry

From Silurian vats, high-sparkling wines
Foam in transparent floods
THOMSON: *Autumn*

Silurian rocks. A name given by Sir R. Murchison to what miners call *gray-wacke*, and Werner termed *transition rocks* Sir Roderick thus named them (1835) because it was in the region of the ancient Silures that he first investigated their structure.

Silurist, The. A surname adopted by the mystical poet Henry Vaughan (1621-95), who was born and died in Brecknockshire.

Silver. In England *standard silver* (*i.e.* that used for the coinage) formerly consisted of thirty-seven fortieths of fine silver and three fortieths of alloy (fineness, 925); but by an Act passed in 1920 the proportions, for reasons of economy, were changed to one half silver and one half alloy (fineness, 500). The Coinage Act of 1946 permitted copper-nickel coins, with no silver whatever, to replace the former silver coins.

Silver is not legal tender for sums over £2

Silver articles are marked with five marks (*see* HALL MARK): the maker's private mark, the standard or assay mark, the hall mark, the duty mark, and the date mark The standard mark states the proportion of silver, to which figure is added a *lion passant* for England, a *harp* crowned for Ireland, a *thistle* for Edinburgh, and a *lion rampant* for Glasgow.

Among the ancient alchemists *silver* represented the Moon, or Diana; in heraldry it is known by its French name, *Argent* (which also gives its chemical symbol, "Ag"), and is indicated in engravings by the silver (argent) portion being left blank

A silver lining The prospect of better days, the promise of happier times The saying, **Every cloud has a silver lining**, is an old one, thus in Milton's *Comus*, the Lady lost in the wood resolves to hope on, and sees a "sable cloud turn forth its silver lining to the night "

Born with a silver spoon in one's mouth. *See* BORN.

Silver of Guthrum. *See* GUTHRUM.

Silver Star. A U S A military medal awarded to an officer or man who has been cited for gallantry in action of a less conspicuous nature than would warrant a citation for the Medal of Honor or the Distinguished Service Cross. It consists of a bronze star bearing a small silver star in its centre.

Silver-tongued. An epithet bestowed on many persons famed for eloquence, especially William Bates, the Puritan divine (1625-99); Anthony Hammond, the poet (1668-1738); Henry Smith, preacher (1550-1600); and Joshua Sylvester (1563-1618), translator of Du Bartas.

Silver Wedding. The twenty-fifth anniversary, when presents of silver plate (in Germany a silver wreath) are given to the happy pair

Speech is silver. *See* SPEECH

The Silver Age. The second of the Ages of the World (*q v*), according to Hesiod and the Greek and Roman poets, fabled as a period that was voluptuous and godless, and much inferior in simplicity and true happiness to the Golden Age.

The silver cooper. A kidnapper. "To play the silver cooper," to kidnap A cooper is one who *coops up* another.

The Silver-Fork School. A name given in amused contempt (about 1830) to the novelists who were sticklers for the etiquette and graces of the Upper Ten and showed great respect for the affectations of gentility Theodore Hook, Lady Blessington, and Bulwer Lytton might be taken as representatives of it

The Silver Streak The English Channel.

Thirty pieces of silver. The sum of money that Judas Iscariot received from the chief priest for the betrayal of his Master (*Matt* XXVI, 15); hence used proverbially of a bribe or ' blood-money "

With silver weapons you may conquer the world. The Delphic oracle to Philip of Macedon, when he went to consult it Philip, acting on this advice, sat down before a fortress which his staff pronounced to be impregnable "You shall see," said the king, "how an ass laden with silver will find an entrance "

Simeon, St. (sim' ē on), is usually depicted as bearing in his arms the infant Jesus, or receiving Him in the Temple His feast-day is February 18th.

St. Simeon Stylites. *See* STYLITES

Similia similibus curantur (sim il' iä si mil' i büs kū răn' ter) (Lat) Like cures like, or, as we say, "Take a hair of the dog that bit you "

Simkin. Anglo-Indian for champagne—of which word it is an Urdu mispronunciation.

Simnel Cakes. Rich cakes formerly eaten (especially in Lancashire) on Mid-Lent Sunday ("Mothering Sunday '), Easter, and Christmas Day. They were ornamented with scallops, and were eaten at Mid-Lent in commemoration of the banquet given by Joseph to his brethren, which forms the first lesson of Mid-Lent Sunday, and the feeding of five thousand, which forms the Gospel of the day

The word *simnel* is through O Fr from late Lat. *siminellus*, fine bread, Lat. *simila*, the finest wheat flour.

Simon, St. (Zelotes), is represented with a saw in his hand, in allusion to the instrument of his martyrdom He sometimes bears fish in the other hand, in allusion to his occupation as a fishmonger His feast day is October 28th

Simon Magus. Isidore tells us that Simon Magus died in the reign of Nero, and adds that he had proposed a dispute with Peter and Paul, and had promised to fly up to heaven He succeeded in rising high into the air, but at the prayers of the two apostles he was cast down to earth by the evil spirits who had enabled him to rise.

Milman, in his *History of Christianity* (ii, p 51) tells another story. He says that Simon offered to be buried alive, and declared that he would reappear on the third day. He was actually buried in a deep trench, "but to this day," says Hippolytus, "his disciples have failed to witness his resurrection."

His followers were known as Simonians, and the sin of which he was guilty, viz the trafficking in sacred things, the buying and selling of ecclesiastical offices (*see Acts* viii, 18) is still called *simony*.

Simon Pure. The real man, the authentic article, etc In Mrs Centlivre's *Bold Stroke for a Wife*, a Colonel Feignwell passes himself off for Simon Pure, a Quaker, and wins the heart of Miss Lovely. No sooner does he get the assent of her guardian, than the Quaker turns up, and proves, beyond a doubt, he is the "real Simon Pure "

Simple Simon A simpleton, a gullible booby, from the character in the well-known anonymous nursery tale, who "met a pie-man "

Simple, The. Charles III of France (879, 893-929)

The simple life. A mode of living in which the object is to eliminate as far as possible all luxuries and extraneous aids to happiness, etc, returning to the simplicity of life as imagined by the pastoral poets.

Simplicity is *sine plica*, without a fold; as duplicity is *duplex plica*, a double fold. Conduct ' without a fold" is *straightforward, simple*

The flat simplicity of that reply was admirable.—VANBRUGH *The Provoked Husband*, i

Disraeli spoke in the House of Commons (February 19th, 1850) of "The sweet simplicity of the Three per Cents," plagiarizing Lord Stowell, who had earlier spoken of their "elegant simplicity" (*see* Campbell's *Lives of the Chancellors*, vol. x)

Simplon Pass, over the Alps leads from Brieg in Canton Vaud to Domodossola in Piedmont at an altitude of 6,582 feet The Simplon Road was begun by Napoleon in 1800 to shorten the advance into Italy The railway tunnel through the mountain is one of the longest in the world, being over twelve miles long, it was opened in 1906, operations having been begun at either end and meeting midway beneath the mountain with only a few inches discrepancy A second tunnel was opened in 1921

Sin, according to Milton, is twin-keeper with Death of the gates of Hell She sprang full-grown from the head of Satan

> Woman to the waist, and fair,
> But ending foul in many a scaly fold
> Voluminous and vast, a serpent armed
> With mortal sting   *Paradise Lost*, ii, 650-653

Original sin. That corruption which is born with us, and is the inheritance of all the off-spring of Adam Theology teaches that as Adam was founder of his race, when Adam fell the taint and penalty of his disobedience passed to all his posterity.

Sin-eaters. Persons hired at funerals in ancient times, to eat beside the corpse and so take upon themselves the sins of the deceased, that the soul might be delivered from purgatory.

Notice was given to an old sire before the door of the house, when some of the family came out and furnished him a cricket [low stool], on which he sat down facing the door, then they gave him a groat which he put in his pocket, a crust of bread which he ate, and a bowl of ale which he drank off at a draught. After this he got up from the cricket and pronounced the ease and rest of the soul departed, for which he would pawn his own soul —*Bagford's letter on Leland's Collectanea*, i, 76.

The Man of Sin. (2 *Thess* ii, 3). Generally held to signify the Antichrist (*q v*), but applied by the old Puritans to the Pope of Rome, by the Fifth Monarchy men to Cromwell, and by many modern theologians to that "wicked one" (identical with the "last horn" of *Dan* vii) who is immediately to precede the Second Advent

The seven deadly sins. Pride, Wrath, Envy, Lust, Gluttony, Avarice, and Sloth

To earn the wages of sin. To be hanged, or condemned to death

The wages of sin is death —*Rom* vi, 23.

To sin one's mercies To be ungrateful for the gifts of Providence

Sinbad the Sailor (sin' băd) The hero of a story of this name in the *Arabian Nights Entertainments* A wealthy citizen of Bagdad, he was called "The Sailor" because of his seven voyages in which, among other high adventures, he discovered the Roc's egg and the Valley of Diamonds, and killed the Old Man of the Sea who had got on his back and would not be dismounted

Sine (Lat) Without.

Sine die (Lat.). No time being fixed; indefinitely in regard to time When a proposal is deferred *sine die*, it is deferred without fixing a day for its reconsideration, which is virtually "for ever."

Sine qua non (Lat) An indispensable condition Lat *Sine qua non potest esse* or *fieri* (that without which [the thing] cannot be, or be done)

Sinecure (Lat *sine cura*, without cure, or care) An enjoyment of the money attached to a benefice without having the trouble of the "cure", applied to any office to which a salary is attached without any duties to perform.

Sinews of War. Essential funds for the prosecution of a war. Troops have to be paid and fed and the materials of war are costly

The English phrase comes from Cicero's *Nervos belli pecuniam* (*Phil* V, 11, 5), money makes the sinews of war Rabelais (I, xlvi) uses the same idiom—*Les nerfs des batailles sont les pecunes*

> Victuals and ammunition,
> And money too, the sinews of the war,
> Are stored up in the magazine
> BEAUMONT AND FLETCHER *Fair Maid of the Inn*, i, 1

Sing. Singing bread (Fr *pain à chanter*) An old term for the wafer used in celebration of the Mass, because singing was in progress during its consecration The Reformers directed that the sacramental bread should be similar in fineness and fashion to the round bread and water *singing-cakes* used in private Masses.

Swans sing before they die. *See* SWAN.

To make one sing another tune. To make him change his behaviour altogether, make him recant what he has said

To sing in tribulation. Old slang for to confess when put to the torture One who did this was termed in jail slang a "canary bird"

> "This man, sir, is condemned to the galleys for being a canary-bird" "A canary-bird" exclaimed the knight "Yes, sir," added the arch-thief, "I mean that he is very famous for his singing" "What!" said Don Quixote, "are people to be sent to the galleys for singing?" "Marry, that they are," answered the slave "for there is nothing more dangerous than singing in tribulation"—CERVANTES *Don Quixote*, iii, 8

To sing out To cry or squeal from chastisement, formerly said also of a prisoner who turned informer against his comrades *See above*

To sing small. To cease boasting and assume a lower tone

Single-speech Hamilton William Gerard Hamilton (1729-96), who was Chancellor of the Exchequer in Ireland, 1763-84 So called from his maiden speech in Parliament (1755), a masterly torrent of eloquence which astounded everyone

Single Tax. The doctrine that land rent alone should be subject to taxation, propounded by Henry George in *Progress and Poverty* (1879)

Sinis (sī′ nis) A Corinthian robber of Greek legend, known as *the Pinebender*, because he used to fasten his victims to two pine-trees bent towards the earth, and then leave them to be rent asunder when the trees were released He was captured by Theseus and put to death in this same way.

Sinister (sin′ is ter) (Lat, on the left hand) Foreboding of ill, ill-omened According to augury, birds, etc, appearing on the left-hand side forbode ill-luck, but on the right-hand side, good luck Plutarch, following Plato and Aristotle, gives as the reason that the west (or left side of the augur) was towards the setting or departing sun.

Corva sinistra (a crow on the left-hand) is a sign of ill-luck which belongs to English

superstitions as much as to the ancient Roman or Etruscan (Virgil. *Eclogues*, i, 18.)

> That raven on yon left-hand oak
> (Curse on his ill-betiding croak)
> Bodes me no good   GAY *Fable*, xxxvii

Bar sinister. *See* BAR.

Sinn Fein (shin fān) Irish for "Ourselves alone" This was the Nationalist movement that finally brought about the establishment of the Irish Free State in 1921. The rebellion of 1916 was its first overt act of great importance, in the following year Eamonn de Valera was elected president of the movement and the new republican policy was inaugurated In December, 1918, Sinn Fein candidates were elected for 73 out of 105 Irish seats in Parliament and these constituted themselves as Dail Eireann The Irish republican army was organized and carried on a violent guerrilla warfare against the military and the police In December, 1921, negotiations were opened between the Sinn Fein leaders and the British government, and the Treaty of independence of Eire was signed

Sinon (sī′ non) The Greek who induced the Trojans to receive the wooden horse (Virgil: *Æneid*, ii, 102, etc). Anyone deceiving to betray is called "a Sinon"

Sioux (soo) A North American Indian tribe who call themselves Dakotas, Sioux being the termination of the French form of their Ojibwa name meaning "enemies" The name is used for the Siouan family generally, comprising many tribes in the Mississippi and Missouri basins

Sir. Lat *senex*, Span *señor*, Ital *signor*, Fr *sieur*, *sire*

As a title of honour prefixed to the Christian name of baronets and knights, *Sir* is of great antiquity, and the clergy had at one time *Sir* prefixed to their name This is merely a translation of the university word *dominus* given to graduates, as "*Dominus* Hugh Evans," etc. Spenser uses the title as a substantive, meaning a parson—

> But this, good Sir, did follow the plaine word — *Mother Hubberd's Tale*, 390.

Sirat, Al. *See* AL-SIRAT

Sirdar (ser′ dar) A native noble in India. Also the former official title of the British commander-in-chief of the Egyptian army

Siren (sī′ ren) One of the mythical monsters, half woman and half bird, said by Greek poets (*see Odyssey*, xii) to entice seamen by the sweetness of their song to such a degree that the listeners forgot everything and died of hunger (Gr *sirenes*, entanglers), hence applied to any dangerous, alluring woman.

In Homeric mythology there were but two sirens, later writers name three, viz Parthenope, Ligea, and Leucosia; and the number was still further augmented by later writers

Ulysses escaped their blandishments by filling his companions' ears with wax and lashing himself to the mast of his ship

> What Song the Syrens sang, or what name Achilles assumed when he hid himself among women, though puzzling questions are not beyond all conjecture —SIR THOS BROWNE *Urn Burial*, v

Plato says there were three kinds of sirens—the *celestial*, the *generative*, and the *cathartic* The first were under the government of Jupiter, the second under that of Neptune, and the third of Pluto When the soul is in heaven the sirens seek, by harmonic motion, to unite it to the divine life of the celestial host, and when in Hades, to conform them to the infernal regimen, but on earth they produce generation, of which the sea is emblematic. (Proclus *On the Theology of Plato*, Bk vi.)

In more recent times the word has been applied to the loud mechanical whistle sounded at a factory, etc., to indicate that work is to be started or finished for the day. Sirens with two or more recognizable notes were employed in World War II to give warning of the approach or departure of hostile aircraft

Siren suit. A one-piece garment, on the lines of a boiler suit, sometimes worn in London during the bombing raids of World War II It is so named from its being slipped on over the night clothes at the first moan of the siren

Sirius (sir' i us). The Dog-star; so called by the Greeks from the adjective *seirios*, hot and scorching The Romans called it *canicula*, whence our Canicular days (*q.v*), and the Egyptians *sept*, which gave the Greek alternative *sothis* *See* SOTHIC YEAR

Sirloin. Properly *surloin*, from Fr *sur-longe*, above the loin. The mistaken spelling *sir-* has given rise to a number of stories of the joint having been "knighted" because of its estimable qualities Fuller tells us that Henry VIII did so—

Dining with the Abbot of Reading, he [Henry VIII] ate so heartily of a loin of beef that the abbot said he would give 1,000 marks for such a stomach "Done!" said the king, and kept the abbot a prisoner in the Tower, won his 1,000 marks, and knighted the beef.— *Church History*, vi, **2**, p 299 (1655)

Another tradition fathers the joke on James I —

"I vow, 'tis a noble sirloin!"
"Ay, here's cut and come again "
"But pray, why is it called a sirloin?"
"Why you must know that our King James I, who loved good eating, being invited to dinner by one of his nobles, and seeing a large loin of beef at his table, he drew out his sword, and in a frolic knighted it Few people know the secret of this "
JONATHAN SWIFT *Polite Conversation* ii

And yet another on Charles II

In any case the joke is an old one, in Taylor the Water Poet's, *Great Eater of Kent* (1680) we read of one who—

should presently enter combate with a worthy knight, called Sir Loyne ot Beefe, and overthrow him

Sirocco (si rok' ō) A wind from northern Africa that blows over Italy, Sicily, etc, producing extreme languor and mental debility.

Sise Lane. *See* TOOLEY STREET

Sistine (sis' tin, sis' tĕn). **The Sistine Chapel.** The private chapel of the Pope in the Vatican, so called because built by Pope Sixtus IV (1471-84) It is decorated with the frescoes of Michelangelo and others

Sistine Madonna, The, or the **Madonna di San Sisto.** The Madonna painted by Raphael (about 1518) for the church of St. Sixtus (San Sisto) at Piacenza; St Sixtus is shown kneeling at the right of the Virgin The picture was in the Royal Gallery, Dresden, but after World War II passed into Russian hands.

Sisyphus (sis' i fus) A legendary king of Corinth, crafty and avaricious, said to be the son of Æolus, or—according to later legend, which also makes him the father of Ulysses—of Autolycus His task in the world of shades is to roll a huge stone up a hill till it reaches the top, as the stone constantly rolls back his work is incessant, hence "a labour of Sisyphus" or "Sisyphean toil" is an endless, heart-breaking job

Sit. To make one sit up. To astonish or disconcert him considerably, to stir him up to action

To sit on or **upon.** To snub, squash, smother, put in his place

Sit on has other meanings also; thus *to sit on a corpse* is to hold a coroner's inquest on it, *to sit on the bench* is to occupy a seat as a judge or magistrate

To sit on the fence *See* FENCE

To sit tight. To keep your own counsel; to remain in or as in hiding The phrase is from poker, where, if a player does not want to continue betting and at the same time does not wish to throw in his cards, he "sits tight "

To sit under. A colloquialism for attending the ministrations of the clergyman named The phrase was common three hundred years ago, and is still in use

There would then also appear in pulpits other visages, other gestures, and stuff otherwise wrought than what we now sit under, oft-times to as great a trial of our patience as any other than they preach to us —MILTON *Of Education* (1644)

Sit-down strike. A strike in which the workers remain at their factory, etc, but refuse to work themselves or allow others to do so

Sitting Bull. A famous warrior chief of the Sioux Indians, born on Grand River, South Dakota, in 1834 He commanded the Indians who defeated General Custer at Little Big Horn, 1876, but was killed on December 5th, 1890 while resisting arrest at Fort Yates, N Dakota, during the Sioux rebellion of that year.

Siva or **Shiva** (sē' va, shē' va) The third person of the Hindu Trinity, or *Trimurti*, representing the destructive principle in life and also, as in Hindu philosophy restoration is involved in destruction, the reproductive or renovating power. He is a great worker of miracles through meditation and penance, and hence is a favourite deity with the ascetics He is a god of the fine arts, and of dancing, and Siva, one only of his very many names, means "the Blessed One "

Six. At sixes and sevens. Higgledy-piggledy, in a state of confusion, or of persons, unable to come to an agreement. The phrase comes from dicing.

> The goddess would no longer wait;
> But rising from her chair of state,
> Left all below at six and seven,
> Harness'd her doves, and flew to heaven
> SWIFT *Cadenus and Vanessa (closing lines).*

A six-hooped pot. A two-quart pot Quart pots were bound with three hoops, and when three men joined in drinking each man drank his hoop Mine host of the Black Bear (*Kenilworth*, ch iii), calls Tressalian "a six-hooped pot of a traveller," meaning a first-class guest, because he paid freely, and made no complaints.

Six Principle Baptists. A sect of Arminian Baptists, founded about 1639, who based their creed on the six principles enunciated in *Heb.* vi, viz, repentance, faith, baptism, the laying on of hands, resurrection of the dead, and eternal life

Six of one and half a dozen of the other. There is nothing to choose between them, they are both in the wrong—*Arcades ambo.*

The Six Articles An Act of Parliament passed in 1539 (repealed 1547) enjoining belief in (1) the real presence of Christ in the Eucharist; (2) the sufficiency of communion in one kind, (3) the celibacy of the priests; (4) the obligation of vows of chastity (5) the expediency of private masses; and (6) the necessity of auricular confession, and decreeing death on those who denied the doctrine of Transubstantiation It was also known as *The Bloody Bill,* and the *Six Stringed Whip.*

The Six Clerks Office. An old name for the Court of Chancery because there were six highly paid clerks connected with it

The six-foot way. The strip of ground between two parallel sets of railway lines

The Six Nations. The confederacy of North American Indian tribes consisting of the Five Nations (*q v*) and the Tuscaroras (formerly of North Carolina but now of New York and Ontario) who joined about 1715.

The Six Points of Ritualism. Altar lights, eucharistic vestments, the eastward position, wafer bread, the mixed chalice, and incense. These were sanctioned in the Church of England in the time of Edward VI, and, it is held by many, were never forbidden by competent authority.

The Six Stringed Whip. The Six Articles (*see above*).

Sixteen-string Jack John Rann a highwayman (hanged 1774), noted for his foppery. He wore sixteen tags. eight at each knee

> Dr Johnson said that Gray's poetry towered above the ordinary run of verse as Sixteen-string Jack above the ordinary foot-pad —BOSWELL *Life of Johnson*

Sizar (sī' zar) An undergraduate of Cambridge, or of Trinity College, Dublin, who receives a grant from his college to assist in paying his expenses Formerly sizars were expected to undertake certain menial duties now performed by college servants, and the name is taken to show that one so assisted received his *sizes* or *sizings* free

Sizings. The allowance of food provided by the college for undergraduates at a meal, a pound loaf, two inches of butter, and a pot of milk used to be the "sizings" for breakfast, meat was provided for dinner, but any extras had to be *sized* for The word is a contraction of *assize*, a statute to regulate the size or weight of articles sold

> A size is a portion of bread or drinke, it is a farthing which schollers in Cambridge have at the buttery It is noted with the letter S —MINSHIEU *Ductor* (1617)

Skains-mate.

> Scurvy knave!   I am none of his skains-mates
> —*Romeo and Juliet*, ii, 4

The meaning of the word is uncertain, but *skene* or *skean* is the long dagger formerly carried by the Irish and Scots (Gael *scian*, *sgian*), so it may mean a dagger-comrade or fellow-cut-throat

Swift, describing an Irish feast (1720), says, "A cubit at least the length of their skains," and Greene, in his *Quip for an Upstart Courtier* (1592), speaks of "an ill-favoured knave, who wore by his side a skane, like a brewer's bung-knife."

Skanda. *See* KARTTIKEYA

Skedaddle. To run away hastily, make off in a hurry, to be scattered in rout The Scots apply the word to the milk spilt over the pail in carrying it During the American Civil War the word came into prominence with its present meaning

Skeleton. The family skeleton, or the skeleton in the cupboard. Some domestic secret that the whole family conspires to keep to itself, every family is said to have at least one

The story is that someone without a single care or trouble in the world had to be found After long and unsuccessful search a lady was discovered whom all thought would "fill the bill", but to the great surprise of the inquirers, after she had satisfied them on all points and the quest seemed to be achieved, she took them upstairs and there opened a closet which contained a human skeleton "I try," said she, "to keep my trouble to myself, but every night my husband compels me to kiss that skeleton" She then explained that the skeleton was once her husband's rival, killed in a duel.

The skeleton at the feast The thing or person that acts as a reminder that there are troubles as well as pleasures in life Plutarch says in his *Moralia* that the Egyptians always had a skeleton placed in a prominent position at their banquets

Skevington's Daughter. *See* SCAVENGER'S.

Skiddaw (skid' aw) **Whenever Skiddaw hath a cap, Scruffell wots full well of that** (Fuller *Worthies*). When my neighbour's house is on fire mine is threatened, when you are in misfortune I also am a sufferer, when you mourn I have cause also to lament Skiddaw and Scruffell, or Scawfell, are neighbouring hills in Cumberland When Skiddaw is capped with clouds, it will be sure to rain ere long at Scawfell.

Skid Row (U S A.) A district populated by vicious characters or down-and-outs, i e those who have skidded from the path of virtue.

Skill. It skills not. It makes no difference; it doesn't matter one way or the other. The phrase was once very common, but is now looked upon as an archaism

> Whether he [Callimachus] be now lyving I know not but whether he be or no, it skilleth not —LYLY *Euphues and his England* (1580)

Similarly, **What skills talking?** What is the use of talking?

Skimble-skamble. Rambling worthless "Skamble" is merely a variety of *scramble*, hence "scambling days," those days in Lent when no regular meals are provided, but each person "scrambles" or shifts for himself "Skimble" is added to give force

> And such a deal of skimble-skamble stuff
> As put me from my faith
> 1 *Henry IV*, iii, 1.

> With such scamble-scemble, spitter-spatter,
> As puts me cleane beside the money-matter.
> TAYLOR, *The Water Poet*, ii, 39 (1630).

Skimmington. It was an old custom in rural England and Scotland to make an example of nagging wives and unfaithful husbands by forming a ludicrous procession through the village for the purpose of ridiculing the offender In cases of hen-pecking Grose tells us that the man rode behind the woman, with his face to the horse's tail The man held a distaff, and the woman beat him about the jowls with a ladle As the procession passed a house where the woman was paramount, each gave the threshold a sweep This performance was called *riding Skimmington* (also *riding the stang*—see STANG), and the husband or wife was, for the time, known as *Skimmington* The origin of the name is uncertain, but in an illustration of the procession of 1639 the woman is shown belabouring her husband with a *skimming*-ladle

The custom was not peculiar to Britain, it prevailed in Scandinavia, Spain, and elsewhere The procession is described at length in *Hudibras*, II, ii.

Skin By the skin of one's teeth. Only just, by a mere hair's breadth The phrase comes from the book of *Job* (xix, 20) —

> My bone cleaveth to my skin and to my flesh, and I am escaped with the skin of my teeth

Coverdale's rendering of the passage is—

> My bone hangeth to my skynne, and the flesh is awaye only there is left me the skynne aboute my teth

To save one's skin. To get off with one's life

To sell the skin before you have caught the bear. To count your chickens before they are hatched Shakespeare alludes to a similar practice —

> The man that once did sell the lion's skin
> While the beast lived, was killed with hunting him.
> *Henry V*, iv, 3.

To skin a flint To be very exacting in making a bargain The French say, *Tondre sur un œuf* The Latin *lana caprina* (goat's wool), means something as worthless as the skin of a flint or fleece of an eggshell. Hence a **skinflint**, a pinch-farthing, a niggard

Skinners. A predatory band in the American Revolutionary War which roamed over Westchester County, New York, robbing and fleecing those who refused to take the oath of fidelity to the Republic

Skirt. To sit upon one's skirt. To insult, or seek occasion of quarrel. Tarlton, the clown, told his audience the reason why he wore a jacket was that "no one might sit upon his skirt" Sitting on one's skirt is, like stamping on one's coat in Ireland, a fruitful source of quarrels, often provoked.

> Crosse me not, Liza, nether be so perte,
> For if thou dost, I'll sit upon thy skirte
> *The Abortive of an Idle Houre* (1620)

In English slang a skirt is a girl.

Skull Skull and crossbones. An emblem of mortality, specifically, the pirate's flag. The "crossbones" are two human thigh-bones laid across one another

Sky. Rhyming slang for pocket, the missing word being *rocket* See RHYMING SLANG.

If the sky falls we shall catch larks. A bantering reply to those who suggest some very improbable or wild scheme

Lauded to the skies. Extravagantly praised, praised to the heights

Sky-raker. A nautical term for any topsail, strictly speaking, a sail above the fore-royal, the main-royal, or the mizzen-royal.

Skyscraper. A very tall building, especially one in New York or some other American city Some of them run to a hundred floors, and more Also applied by sailors to a *sky-raker*.

To skylark about. To amuse oneself in a frolicsome way, jump around and be merry, indulge in mild horseplay The phrase was originally nautical and referred to the sports of the boys among the rigging after work was done

Slam. A term in card-playing denoting winning all the tricks in a deal In Bridge this is called *Grand slam*, and winning all but one, *Little slam* Cp RUFF

Slander Literally, a stumbling-block (*cp* SCANDAL), or something which trips a person up (Gr. *skandalon*, through Fr *esclandre*)

Slang. As denoting language or jargon of a low or colloquial type the word first appeared in the 18th century, its origin is not known, but it is probably connected with *slung* (*cp*. *mud-slinging*, for hurling abuse at one) Slang is of various sorts, fashionable, professional, schoolboy, sporting, etc Some of it is introduced into the language from below, *i e* from the ranks of thieves, rogues, and vagabonds It usually has an element of humour about it, through exaggeration or absurd juxtaposition Slang is always invented by individuals and adopted later by the public When the adoption becomes so general and so approved that the expression in question is accepted as standard English, it ceases to be slang
See also BACK-SLANG, RHYMING SLANG

To slang a person. To abuse him, give him a piece of your mind

Slap-bang. At once, without hesitation—done with a slap and a bang The term was formerly applied to cheap eating-houses, where one slapped one's money down as the food was banged on the table

They lived in the same street, walked to town every morning at the same hour, dined at the same slap-bang every day —DICKENS *Sketches by Boz*, III, 36

Slap-dash. In an off-hand manner done hurriedly as with a slap and a dash Rooms used to be decorated by slapping and dashing the walls so as to imitate paper, and at one time slap-dash walls were very common.

Slap-up. First-rate, grand, stylish.

[The] more slap-up still have the shields painted on the panels with the coronet over.—THACKERAY

Slapstick. Literally the two or more laths bound together at one end with which harlequins, clowns, etc., strike other performers with a resounding slap or crack; but more often applied to any broad comedy with knock-about action and horseplay

Slate. Slate club. A sick benefit club for working-men. Originally the names of the members and the money paid in were entered on a folding slate.

To have a slate or tile loose. *See* TILE.

To slate one. To reprove, abuse, or criticize him savagely. It is not known how the term arose, but perhaps it is because at school the names of bad boys were chalked up on the slate as an exposure

The journalists there lead each other a dance If one man 'slates" another for what he has done, It is pistols for two, and then coffin for one *Punch (The Pugnacious Penmen),* 1885

To start with a clean slate. To be given another chance, one's past misdeeds having been forgiven and expunged, as writing is sponged from a slate

Slav. This is an example of the strange changes which come over some words. The *Slavi* were a tribe which once dwelt on the banks of the Dnieper, and were so called from *slav* (noble, illustrious), but as, in the later stages of the Roman Empire, vast multitudes of them were spread over Europe as captives, the word acquired its present meaning.

Similarly, *Goths* means the good or godlike men, but since the invasion of the Goths the word has become synonymous with barbarous, bad, ungodlike

In World War II a slave was a vehicle with electrical equipment designed to serve tanks—*i.e.* charge their batteries, and start them in the morning

Sleave. The ravelled sleave of care (*Macbeth* ii, 2) The sleave is the knotted or entangled part of thread or silk, the raw, unwrought floss silk, hence, any tangle Churton Collins (in *Studies in Shakespeare*) speaks of smoothing "the tangled sleave of Shakespearean expression "

Sledge-hammer. A sledge-hammer argument. A clincher, an argument which annihilates opposition at a blow. The sledge-hammer (A S *slecge*) is the largest hammer used by smiths, and is wielded by both hands

Sleep. To sleep away. To pass away in sleep, to consume in sleeping; as, "to sleep one's life away "

To sleep like a top. Excellently, go the night through without waking or discomfort When peg-tops are at the acme of their gyration they become so steady and quiet that they do not seem to move, in this state they are said to "sleep " Congreve plays on the two meanings —

Hang him, no, he a dragon! If he be, 'tis a very peaceful one I can ensure his anger dormant, or should he seem to rouse, 'tis but well lashing him and he will sleep like a top —*Old Bachelor*, i, 5

To sleep off. To get rid of by sleep.

To sleep on a matter. To let a decision on it stand over till to-morrow

Sleeper, The. Epimenides, the Greek poet, is said to have fallen asleep in a cave when a boy, and not to have waked for fifty-seven years, when he found himself possessed of all wisdom

In mediæval legend stories of those who have gone to sleep and have been—or are to be—awakened after many years are very numerous Such legends hang round the names of King Arthur, Charlemagne, and Barbarossa *Cp* also the stories of the Seven Sleepers of Ephesus, Tannhauser, Ogier the Dane, Kilmeny, and Rip van Winkle

Sleeper Awakened, The. *See* SLY, CHRISTOPHER.

Sleepers. In Britain, the timber or steel supports for the chairs which carry the rails on a railway line (from the Norwegian *sleip*, a roller or timber laid along a road) In U S A these supports are called *ties* A *sleeper*, in U S A means a railway sleeping-car.

Sleeping Beauty, The This charming nursery tale comes from the French *La Belle au Bois Dormant*, by Charles Perrault (1628-1703). (*Contes de ma mère l'Oye*, 1697) The Princess is shut up by enchantment in a castle, where she sleeps a hundred years, during which time an impenetrable wood springs up around Ultimately she is disenchanted by the kiss of a young Prince, who marries her

Sleeping partner. A partner in a business who takes no active share in running it beyond supplying capital.

Sleeping sickness. A West African disease caused by a parasite, *Trypanosoma Gambiense*, characterized by fever and great sleepiness, and usually terminating fatally The disease known in England, which shows similar symptoms is usually called *Sleeping illness* or *Sleepy sickness* as a means of distinction, its scientific name is *Encephalitis lethargica*

Sleepy. Pears are said to be "sleepy" when they are beginning to rot, and cream when, in the course of its making, the whole assumes a frothy appearance.

Sleepy hollow. Any village far removed from the active concerns of the outside world The name given in Washington Irving's *Sketch Book* to a quiet old-world village on the Hudson

Sleepy sickness *See* SLEEPING SICKNESS, *above*

Sleeve. To hang on one's sleeve. To listen devoutly to what one says to surrender your freedom of thought and action to the judgment of another

To have up one's sleeve. To hold in reserve, to have it ready to bring out in a case of emergency The allusion is to conjurers, who frequently conceal in the sleeve the means by which they do the trick

To laugh in one's sleeve. To ridicule a person not openly but in secret At one time it was quite possible to conceal a laugh by hiding one's face in the large sleeves worn by men The French say, *rire sous cape.*

To pin to one's sleeve, as, "I shan't pin my faith to your sleeve," meaning, "I shall not slavishly believe or follow you " The allusion is to the practice of knights, in days of chivalry, pinning to their sleeve some token given them by their lady-love This token was a pledge that he would do or die

To wear one's heart on one's sleeve, to expose all one's feelings to the eyes of the world Iago wears his heart on his sleeve, displaying a feigned devotion to his master (*Othello*, i, 1).

Sleeveless. In the 16th century *sleeveless* was very commonly applied to *errand, answer, message,* etc , signifying that it was fruitless or futile, an errand, etc , that has no result In *Eikonoclastes* Milton speaks of sleeveless reason, meaning reasoning that leads nowhere and proves nothing, and *a sleeveless message* was used of a kind of April fool trick—the messenger being dispatched merely so as to get rid of him for a time

> If all these faile, a beggar-woman may
> A sweet love-letter to her hands convey,
> Or a neat laundresse or a hearb-wife can
> Carry a sleeveless message now and than
> 					*Taylor's Workes*, ii, 111 (1630)

Sleuth-hound. A blood-hound which follows the *sleuth* (old Norse *sloth,* our more modern *slot*) or track of an animal Hence used, especially in America, of a detective.

> There is a law also among the Borderers in time of peace, that whoso denieth entrance or sute of a sleuth-hound in pursuit made after fellons and stolen goods, shall be holden as accessarie unto the theft — HOLINSHED *Description of Scotland*, p 14

Slewed. Intoxicated When a vessel changes her tack she staggers and gradually heels over A drunken man moves like a ship changing her angle of sailing

Slick. Adroit, dextrous, smart, the word is a variant of *sleek.*

Sliding Scale. A scale of duties, prices, payment, etc , which slides up and down as the article to which it refers becomes dearer or cheaper, or by which such payments accommodate themselves to the fluctuations in other conditions previously named

Slip Many a slip 'twixt the cup and the lip Everything is uncertain till you possess it *Cp* ANCÆUS

Multa cadunt inter calicem supremaque labra — HORACE

To give one the slip. To steal off unperceived, to elude pursuit A sea phrase, a cable and

buoy are fastened to the anchor-chain, which is let slip though the hawse-pipe, Done to save time in weighing anchor. The metaphor probably came originally from the action of "slipping" a hound, *i e* allowing it to run free by slipping the lead from its collar In coursing the official who releases the greyhounds is still called the *slipper*

Sloane MSS. 3,560 MSS. collected by Sir Hans Sloane (1660-1753), and left to the nation, together with his library (50,000 vols) and other collections on condition that his heirs received £20,000 which was far less than their value These collections were bought and housed in Montague House, and formed the nucleus of the British Museum

Slogan (slō' gan) The war-cry of the old Highland clans (Gael *sluagh,* host, *ghairm,* outcry) Hence, any warcry; and, in later use, a political party cry, an advertising catch-phrase, etc *Cp* SLUGHORN

Slop, Dr. The nickname given by Wm. Hone to Sir John Stoddart (1773-1856), a choleric lawyer and journalist who assailed Napoleon most virulently in *The Times* (1812-16) The allusion was to Dr Slop the ignorant man-midwife in Sterne's *Tristram Shandy*

Slope. To decamp, to run away The term came from the United States, and may be a contraction of *let's lope, lope* being a dialect variation of *loup* (leap), to run or jump away

The slippery slope. The broad and easy way "that leadeth to destruction " *Facilis descensus Averno. See* AVERNUS

Slops. Police, originally "ecilop " *See* BACK-SLANG

> I dragged you in here and saved you,
> 		And sent out a gal for the slops,
> Ha' they're acomin', sir' Listen!
> 	The noise and the shoutin' stops
> SIMS *Ballads of Babylon (The Matron's Story).*

Slough of Despond. A period of, or fit of, great depression In Bunyan's *Pilgrim's Progress,* Pt i, it is a deep bog which Christian has to cross in order to get to the Wicket Gate Help comes to his aid, but Neighbour Pliable turns back

Slow. Slow burn. A comedy routine invented by the Hollywood comedian Edgar Kennedy It consists in struggling to preserve one's patience by passing the hands slowly over the face, but finally losing control and degenerating into hysteria Kennedy's enormous success in exploiting this trick is undoubtedly due to the fact that it expresses to perfection the helpless exasperation of the little man in a bureaucratic and machine-ridden existence

Slow-coach. A dawdle As a slow coach in the old coaching-days got on slowly, so one that gets on slowly is a slow coach

Slow-worm. *See* MISNOMERS

Slubberdegullion (slŭb er de gŭl' yon) A nasty, paltry fellow To *slubber* is to do things by halves, to perform a work carelessly, *degullion* is a fanciful addition (as in *rapscallion*)

> Quoth she, "Although thou hast deserved,
> 	Base slubber-degullion, to be served
> As thou didst vow to deal with me
> 					BUTLER *Hudibras*, i, 3.

Slug (U.S.A.) A $50 gold piece.

Slugabed. A late riser. *To slug* used to be quite good English for to be thoroughly lazy Sylvester has—

> The Soldier, slugging long at home in Peace,
> His wonted courage quickly doth decrease
> *Du Bartas*, I, vii, 340 (1591)

Slug-horn A battle-trumpet; the word being the result of an erroneous reading by Chatterton of the Gaelic *slogan* He thought the word sounded rather well, and, as he did not know what it meant, gave it a meaning that suited him —

> Some caught a slughorne and an onsett wounde.—
> *The Battle of Hastings*, ii, 99

Browning adopted it in the last line but one of his *Childe Rolande to the Dark Tower Came*, and thus this "ghost-word" (*q v*) got a footing in the language

Sly, Christopher. A keeper of bears and a tinker, son of a pedlar, and a sad, drunken sot in the Induction of the *Taming of the Shrew* Shakespeare mentions him as a well-known character of Wincot, a hamlet near Stratford-on-Avon, and it is more than probable that in him we have an actual portrait of a contemporary.

Sly is found dead drunk by a lord, who commands his servants to put him to bed, and on his waking to attend upon him like a lord and bamboozle him into the belief that he is a great man. the play is performed for his delectation. The same trick was played by the Caliph Haroun al-Raschid on Abou Hassan, the rich merchant, in *The Sleeper Awakened* (*Arabian Nights*), and by Philippe the Good, Duke of Burgundy, on his marriage with Eleanor, as given in Burton's *Anatomy of Melancholy* (Pt. ii, sec 2, num 4).

Sly-boots. One who appears to be a dolt, but who is really wide awake, a cunning dolt.

> The frog called the lazy one several times, but in vain, there was no such thing as stirring him, though the sly-boots heard well enough all the while -
> *Adventures of Abdalla*, p 32 (1729)

You're a sly dog. A playful way of saying, You pretend to be disinterested, but I can read between the lines

Small. A small and early. An evening party on a modest scale, with not a lot of guests, and not late hours.

Small-back. Death So called because he is usually drawn as a skeleton

Small beer. Properly, beer of only slight alcoholic strength; hence, trivialities, persons or things of small consequence

> *Iago* She was a wight, if ever such wight were,—
> *Des* To do what?
> *Iago* To suckle fools and chronicle small beer
> *Des* O most lame and impotent conclusion'
> *Othello*, ii, 1

Hence, *he does not think small beer of himself*, he has a very good opinion of himself

> To express her self-esteem [it might be said] that she did not think small beer of herself —DE QUINCEY *Historical Essays*

Small clothes An obsolete term for breeches

Small-endians. See LITTLE-ENDIANS.

Small fry. A humorous way of referring to a number of young children, from the numerous fry or young of fish and other creatures

Small holding A small plot of land (but larger than an allotment) let by a local or county council to a tenant for agricultural purposes The Act of 1892 lays down that a small holding shall be not less than one acre nor more than fifty, and should not exceed £50 in annual value

Small talk. Chit-chat, trivial gossip.

The small hours. The hours from 1 A M to 4 or 5 A.M , when you are still in the small, or low, numbers

The small of the back. The slenderer, narrower part, just above the buttocks

To feel small. To feel humiliated, "taken down a peg or two "

To live in a small way. Keep a modest, unpretentious household, make both ends meet, but with little to spare and no ostentation,

To sing small. To adopt a humble tone, to withdraw some sturdy assertion and apologize for having made it

Smalls The undergraduates' name at Oxford for Responsions, i e. the first of the three examinations for the B A degree, about corresponding to the Cambridge Little-go

Smart Money. Money paid by a person to obtain exemption from some disagreeable office or duty, or given to soldiers or sailors for injuries received in the service, in law it means a heavy fine It either makes the person "smart," i e suffer, or else the person who receives it is paid for smarting.

Smear A figurative sense of this word is to besmirch a reputation, to hint unpleasant things without specifying or doing more than suggest something derogatory.

Smectymnuus (smek tim' nŭs) The name under which was published (1641) an anti-episcopalian tract in answer to Bishop Hall's *Divine Right of Episcopacy*. The name is a sort of acrostic, composed of the initials of the authors, viz —

> *Stephen Marshal, Edward Calamy, Thomas Young, Matthew Newcomen,* and *William Spurstow*

Milton published his *Apology for Smectymnuus*, another reply to Hall, in 1642

Also contracted to smec.

> The handkerchief about the neck,
> Canonical cravat of Smec
> BUTLER *Hudibras*, Pt i, 5

Smelfungus. See MUNDUNGUS

Smell, To. Often used figuratively for to suspect, to discern intuitively, as in *I smell a rat* (see RAT), *to smell treason*, to discern indications of treason, etc

Shakespeare has, "Do you smell a fault?" (*Lear*, i, 1); and Iago says to Othello, "One may smell in this a will most rank " St Jerome says that St. Hilarion had the gift of knowing what sins or vices anyone was inclined to by simply smelling either the person or his garments, and by the same faculty could discern good feelings and virtuous propensities

It smells of the lamp. See LAMP

Smiler. Another name for shandy-gaff—a mixture of ale and lemonade or ginger-beer.

Smith of Nottingham. Applied to conceited persons who imagine that no one is able to compete with themselves Ray, in his *Collection of Proverbs*, has the following couplet.—

> The little Smith of Nottingham
> Who doth the work that no man can

Smith's Prize-man One who has obtained the prize (£25), founded at Cambridge by Robert Smith, D D (1689-1768) (Master of Trinity, 1742-68), for proficiency in mathematics and natural philosophy. There are annually two prizes, awarded to two commencing Bachelors of Arts.

Smithfield. The smooth field (A S. *smethe*, smooth), called in Latin *Campus Planus*, and described by Fitz-Stephen in the 12th century as a "plain field where every Friday there is a celebrated rendezvous of fine horses brought thither to be sold." Bartholomew Fair was held here till 1855, at which date also the cattle-market was removed to Copenhagen Fields, Islington

Smoke To detect, or rather to get a scent of, some plot or scheme. The allusion may be to the detection of the enemy by smoke seen to issue from their place of concealment.

Cape smoke. A cheap and villainous kind of whisky sold in South Africa

No smoke without fire Every slander has some foundation. The reverse proverb, "No fire without smoke," means no good without some drawback.

Smoke-farthings, smoke-silver. An offering formerly given to the priest at Whitsuntide, according to the number of chimneys in his parish

> The Bishop of Elie hath out of everie parish in Cambridgeshire a certain tribute called . *smoke-farthings*, which the churchwardens do levie according to the number of   chimneys that be in a parish —*MSS Baker*, xxxix, 326

To end in smoke To come to no practical result The allusion is to kindling, which smokes, but will not light a fire

To smoke the pipe of peace. *See* CALUMET.

Snack (a variant of *snatch*)

To go snacks. To share and share alike.

To take a snack. To take a morsel.

Snag To come up against a snag. To encounter some obstacle in your progress The phrase is from the American lumber camps, a *snag* being a tree-trunk lodged in the bottom of the river and reaching the surface, or near it.

Snake. Rhyming-slang (*q v*) for a looking-glass, the missing portion being "in the grass " It was an old idea that snakes in casting their sloughs annually gained new vigour and fresh strength; hence Shakespeare's allusion—

> When the mind is quicken'd, out of doubt,
> The organs, though defunct and dead before,
> Break up their drowsy grave, and newly move
> With casted slough and fresh legerity
>   *Henry V*, ii, 1.

And another notion was that one could regain one's youth by feeding on snakes.

> You have eat a snake
> And are grown young, gamesome and rampant
> BEAUMONT AND FLETCHER *Elder Brother*, iv, 4.

A snake in the grass. A hidden or hypocritical enemy, a disguised danger. The phrase is from Virgil (*Ecl* iii, 93) *Latet anguis in herba*, a snake is lurking in the grass

Great snakes! An exclamation of surprise

To see snakes, to have snakes in one's boots, etc To suffer from delirium tremens This is one of the delusions common to those so afflicted.

Snake-eyes. A double one, in throwing dice (U.S A)

Snake stones. The fossils called Ammonites (*q v*)

Snap. Not worth a snap of the fingers Utterly worthless and negligible.

Snapdragon. The same as *"flapdragon"* (*q v.*); also, a plant of the genus *Antirrhinum* with a flower opening like a dragon's mouth

Snapshot. Formerly applied to a shot fired without taking aim, but now almost exclusively to an instantaneous photograph Hence *to snapshot a person*, to take an instantaneous photograph of him.

Snap vote. A vote taken unexpectedly, especially in Parliament The result of a "snap vote" has, before now, been the overthrow of the ministry.

To snap one's nose off. *See* NOSE.

Snark. The imaginary animal invented by Lewis Carroll as the subject of his mock heroic poem, *The Hunting of the Snark* (1876). It was most elusive and gave endless trouble, and when eventually the hunters thought they had tracked it down their quarry proved to be but a Boojum The name (a "portmanteau word" of *snake* and *shark*) has hence sometimes been given to the quests of dreamers and visionaries.

It was one of Rossetti's delusions that in *The Hunting of the Snark* Lewis Carroll was caricaturing him

Snarling Letter (Lat. *litera canina*). The letter *r See* R.

Sneck Posset. To give one a sneck posset is to give him a cold reception, to slam the door in his face (Cumberland and Westmorland) The "sneck" is the latch of a door, and to "sneck the door in one's face" is to shut a person out.

Sneeze. St. Gregory has been credited with originating the custom of saying "God bless you" after sneezing, the story being that he enjoined its use during a pestilence in which sneezing was a mortal symptom. Aristotle, however, mentions a similar custom among the Greeks, and Thucydides tells us that sneezing was a crisis symptom of the great Athenian plague

The Romans followed the same custom, their usual exclamation being *Absit omen !* The Parsees hold that sneezing indicates that evil spirits are abroad, and we find similar beliefs in India, Africa, ancient and modern Persia, among the North American Indian tribes, etc

> We are told that when the Spaniards arrived in Florida the Cazique sneezed, and all the court lifted up their hands and implored the sun to avert the evil omen

It is not to be sneezed at—not to be despised.

Snickersnee A large clasp-knife, or combat with clasp-knives The word is a corruption of the old *snick and snee* or *snick or snee*, cut and thrust, from the Dutch.

Snide. A slang term for counterfeit, bogus. In the U S A mean, contemptible

Snidesman. An utterer of false coin.

Snob. A vulgar person who apes the ways of, and truckles to those in a higher social position than himself

Thackeray calls George IV a snob, because he assumed to be "the first gentleman in Europe," but had not the genuine stamp of a gentleman's mind.

The word actually means a journeyman cobbler or a shoemaker's apprentice, at Cambridge it denotes a townsman as opposed to a gownsman

Snood. The lassie lost her silken snood. The snood was a ribbon with which a Scots lass braided her hair, and was the emblem of her maiden character When she married she changed the snood for the curch or coif, but if she lost the name of virgin before she obtained that of wife, she "lost her silken snood," and was not privileged to assume the curch.

In more recent times the word has been applied to the net in which women confine their hair

Snooks An exclamation of incredulity or derision To cock or pull a snook, to make a gesture of contempt by putting the thumb to the nose and spreading the fingers.

Snotty. Sailors' slang for a midshipman.

Snow King, The. So the Austrians called Gustavus Adolphus of Sweden (1594, 1611-1632), because, said they, he "was kept together by the cold, but would melt and disappear as he approached a warmer soil."

Snuff. To be snuffed out—put down, eclipsed; killed To **snuff it** is a euphemism for to die The allusion is to a candle snuffed with snuffers

'Tis strange the mind, that very fiery particle,
Should let itself be snuffed out by an article
BYRON. *Don Juan*, xi, 60.

Took it in snuff—in anger, in huff
You'll mar the light by taking it in snuff.
Love's Labour's Lost, v, 2
Who .. when it next came there, took it in snuff
—1 *Henry IV*, i, 3.

Up to snuff. Wide awake, knowing, sharp, not easily taken in or imposed upon.

Soap, or **Soft Soap.** Flattery especially of an oily, unctuous kind.

How are you off for soap? A common street-saying of the mid-19th century, of indeterminate meaning It may mean "What are you good for?" in the way of cash, or anything else, and it was often just a general piece of cheek *Cp* "What! No soap?" in Foote's nonsense passage (*see* PANJANDRUM)

In soaped-pig fashion. Vague, a method of speaking or writing which always leaves a way of escape The allusion is to the custom at fairs, etc., of soaping the tail of a pig before turning it out to be caught by the tail.

He is vague as may be; writing in what is called the "soaped-pig" fashion —CARLYLE *The Diamond Necklace*, ch iv

Soap-lock (U S A) A fashion in men's hairdressing *c* 1840 when the hair was parted and came down long on either side Also a rowdy, who did his hair in this way.

Soapy Sam. Samuel Wilberforce (1805-1873), Bishop of Oxford, and afterwards of Winchester, so called because of his persuasive and unctuous way of speaking It is somewhat remarkable that the floral decorations above the stall of the bishop and of the principal of Cuddesdon, were S. O A. P , the initials of Sam Oxon and Alfred Port

Someone asking the bishop why he was so called, received the answer, ' Because I am often in hot water and always come out with clean hands."

Sob Stuff. A phrase describing newspaper, film, or other stories of a highly sentimental kind.

Sob Sister. A woman reporter.

Sobersides. A grave, steady-going, serious-minded person, called by some "a stick-in-the-mud", generally **Old Sobersides.**

Social. Pertaining to society, the community as a whole, or to the intercourse and mutual relationships of mankind at large

The social evil, or **plague.** Euphemisms for prostitution and venereal diseases

Society The upper ten thousand, or "the upper ten " When persons are in "society," they are on the visiting lists of the fashionable social leaders

Society of Friends *See* QUAKERS

Society verse. *See* VERS DE SOCIÉTÉ

Socinianism (so sin' yan izm) A form of Unitarianism which, on the one hand, does not altogether deny the supernatural character of Christ, but, on the other, goes farther than Arianism, which, while upholding His divinity, denies that He is coequal with the Father So called from the Italian theologian, Faustus Socinus (1539-1604), who, with his brother, Lælius (1525-62), propagated this doctrine

Sock. The light shoe worn by the comic actors of Greece and Rome (Lat. *soccus*), hence applied to comedy itself
Then to the well-trod stage anon,
If Jonson's learned sock be on
MILTON *L'Allegro*

The difference between the sock of comedy and the buskin (*q v*) of tragedy was that the sock reached only to the ankle, but the buskin extended to the knee

Socrates (sok' ra tēz) The great Greek philosopher, born and died at Athens (about 470-399 B C) He used to call himself "the midwife of men's thoughts"; and out of his intellectual school sprang those of Plato and the Dialectic system, Euclid and the Megaric, Aristippus and the Cyrenaic, Antisthenes and the Cynic Cicero said of him that "he brought down philosophy from the heavens to earth"; and he was certainly the first to teach that "the proper study of mankind is man " He was condemned to death for the corruption of youth by introducing new gods (thus being guilty of impiety) and drank hemlock in prison, surrounded by his disciples

Socratic irony. Leading on your opponent in an argument by simulating ignorance, so that he "ties himself in knots" and eventually falls an easy prey—a form of procedure used with great effect by Socrates.

The Socratic method. The method of conducting an argument, imparting information, etc , by means of question and answer

Soda-jerker. An attendant at an ice-cream soda fountain in the U S A

Sodom. Apples of Sodom. See APPLE.

Soft, or softy. A mentally retarded or undeveloped person, one whose brain shows signs of softening

A soft fire makes sweet malt. Too much hurry or precipitation spoils work, just as too fierce a fire would burn the malt and destroy its sweetness "Soft and fair goes far," "the more haste the less speed" are sayings of similar meaning

Soft sawder Flattery, adulation Soft solder (pronounced *sawder*) is a composition of tin and lead, used for soldering zinc, lead, and tin; hard solder for brass, etc.

Soft soap. See SOAP.

Soft words butter no parsnips. See BUTTER

Soho! (sō hō') An exclamation used by huntsmen, especially in hare-coursing when a hare has been started. It is a very old call dating from at least the 13th century, and corresponds to the "Tally-ho!" of fox-hunters when the fox breaks cover.

Soho, the district in London, is so called from a mansion which stood there in the time of Charles II, belonging to the Duke of Monmouth.

Sol-disant (swa dē' zon) (Fr) Self-styled, would-be

Soil. A son of the soil. One native to that particular place, whose family has been settled there for generations, especially if engaged in agriculture

To take soil. A hunting term, signifying that the deer has taken to the water. *Soil* here is the Fr *souille*, mire in which a wild boar wallows

Fida went downe the dale to seeke the hinde,
And founde her taking soyle within a flood
BROWNE *Britannia's Pastorals*, 1, 84

Sol. The Roman sun god, hence used for the sun itself.

Sol through white curtains shot a timorous ray,
And oped those eyes that must eclipse the day
POPE *Rape of the Lock*, 1, 13

The name was given by the old alchemists to gold, and in heraldry it represents *or* (gold)
In music *sol* is the name of the fifth note of the diatonic scale (*see* DOH).

Solano (so la' nō) Ask no favour during the Solano. A popular Spanish proverb, meaning —Ask no favour during a time of trouble or adversity The *solano* (*solanus*, sun, *see* SOL) of

Spain is a south-east wind, extremely hot, and loaded with fine dust; it produces giddiness and irritation.

Sold down the river (U S.A) Deceived or demoted From the practice of selling slaves in the upper Southern States to the cotton and sugar plantation owners farther South, and so breaking up families and causing distress

Soldan or Sowdan. A corruption of sultan, meaning in mediæval romance the Saracen king, but, with the usual inaccuracy of these writers, we have the Soldan of Egypt, the Soudan of Persia, the Sowdan of Babylon, etc , all represented as accompanied by grim Saracens to torment Christians

In Spenser's *Faerie Queene* (V, vii) the Soldan typifies Philip II of Spain who used all his power to bribe and seduce the subjects of Elizabeth I, here figuring as Queen Mercilla.

Soldier originally meant a hireling or mercenary; one paid a *solidus*, or wage, for military service; but hireling and soldier convey now very different ideas.

Soldier's battles. Engagements which are more of the nature of hand to hand encounters than regular pitched battles, those that have to be fought by the soldiers themselves, their leaders not having been able to take up strategical positions. The principal "Soldiers' Battles" of English history are Malplaquet, 1709, and Inkermann, 1854.

Soldiers of fortune. Men who live by their wits, *chevaliers de l'industrie*. Referring to those men in mediæval times who let themselves for hire into any army.

To come the old soldier over one. To dictate peremptorily and profess superiority of knowledge and experience; also to impose on one

But you needn't try to come the old soldier over me. I'm not quite such a fool as that —HUGHES *Tom Brown at Oxford*, II, xvii

Solecism (sō' lĕ sizm). A deviation from correct idiom or grammar, from the Greek *soloikos*, speaking incorrectly, so named from Soloi, a town in Cilicia, the Attic colonists of which spoke a debased form of Greek

The word is also applied to any impropriety or breach of good manners.

Solemn. The Solemn League and Covenant. A league entered into by the General Assembly of the Church of Scotland, the Westminster Assembly of English Divines, and the English Parliament in 1643, for the establishment of Presbyterianism and suppression of Roman Catholicism in both countries. Charles II swore to the Scots that he would abide by it and therefore they crowned him in 1651 at Dunbar, but at the Restoration he not only rejected the Covenant, but had it burnt by the common hangman

Sol-fa. See TONIC SOL-FA.

Solicitor. See ATTORNEY.

Solid. In the 18th century this denoted a man of property and position, hence later it became synonymous with honest, genuine, in the 20th century it has kept the same meaning but only in U S A. slang—a fine jazz tune, for instance, being a *solid sender.*

Solid Doctor, The. Richard Middleton, (fl 1280), a Franciscan Schoolman, author of works on theology and canon law.

Solipsism (sō lip' sizm) (Lat. *solus*, alone, *ipse*, self) Absolute egoism; the metaphysical theory that the only knowledge possible is that of oneself.

Solomon. King of Israel (d about 930 B.C.). He was specially noted for his wisdom, hence his name has been used for wise men generally

The English Solomon. James I (1603-25), whom Sully called "the wisest fool in Christendom"

The Solomon of France. Charles V (1364-80) *le Sage*

Solomon's Carpet. *See* CARPET, THE MAGIC

Solomon's Ring Rabbinical fable has it that Solomon wore a ring with a gem that told him all he desired to know.

Solomon's Seal. *Polygonatum multiflorum*, a plant with drooping white flowers. As the stems decay the root-stalk becomes marked with scars that have some resemblance to seals, this, according to some, accounts for the name, but another explanation offered is that the root has medicinal value in *sealing* up and closing green wounds

Solon (sō' lon) A wiseacre or sage, from the great lawgiver of ancient Athens (d. about 560 B C) one of the Seven Sages of Greece.

The Solon of Parnassus So Voltaire called Boileau (1636-1711), in allusion to his *Art of Poetry.*

Solstice (sol' stis) The summer solstice is June 21st; the winter solstice is December 22nd, so called because on or about these dates the sun reaches its extreme northern and southern points in the ecliptic and appears to stand still (Lat *sol*, sun, *sistit*, stands) before it turns back on its apparent course

Solyman (sol' i màn) King of the Turks (in *Jerusalem Delivered*), whose capital was Nice. Being driven from his kingdom, he fled to Egypt, and was there appointed leader of the Arabs (Bk ix)

Soma (sō' ma) An intoxicating drink anciently made, with mystic rites and incantations, from the juice of some Indian plant by the priests, and drunk by the Brahmins as well as offered as libations to their gods It was fabled to have been brought from heaven by a falcon, or by the daughters of the Sun, and it was itself personified as a god, and represented the moon The plant was probably a species of *Asclepias*

To drink the Soma. To become immortal, or as a god

Some. Used—originally in America—with a certain emphasis as an adjective-adverb of all work, denoting some special excellence or high degree "This is *some* book," for instance, means that it is a book that particularly fascinates, appeals to, or "intrigues" the speaker, "*some* golfer," a super-excellent golfer, "going *some*," going the pace.

Some pumpkins (U S A.) Substantial, important; the opposite of "small potatoes "

Somerset House occupies the site in the Strand, London, of a princely mansion built by Somerset the Protector, brother of Lady Jane Seymour, and uncle of Edward VI At the death of Somerset on the scaffold it became the property of the Crown, and in the reign of James I was called Denmark House in honour of Anne of Denmark, his queen Old Somerset House was pulled down in the 18th century, and the present structure was erected by Sir William Chambers in 1776 as government offices for the Board of Inland Revenue, Registrar General, Wills and Probates, etc.

Somoreen. *See* ZAMORIN.

Song. An old song. A mere trifle, something hardly worth reckoning, as "It went for an old song," it was sold for practically nothing

Don't make such a song about it! Be more reasonable in your complaints, don't make such a fuss about it

The Songs of Degrees. Another name for the Gradual Psalms (*q v.*)

The Song of Roland. *See under* ROLAND.

The Song of Songs. The *Canticles*, or the *Song of Solomon*, in the Old Testament

Sonnet. Prince of the sonnet. Joachim du Bellay, a French sonneteer (1526-60), but Petrarch (1304-74) better deserves the title.

Sooner. Slang for a sponger, one who lives on his wits and will do anything *sooner* than work for his living

In America the term is applied to settlers in the western districts who peg out their claims in the territory before the time appointed by the Government

Sooterkin. A kind of after-birth fabled to be produced by Dutch women through sitting over their stoves, hence an abortive proposal or scheme, and, as applied to literature, an imperfect or a supplementary work

> For knaves and fools being near of kin
> As Dutch boors are t'a sooterkin,
> Both parties join'd to do their best
> To damn the public interest
> BUTLER *Hudibras*, III, ii, 145

Sop. A sop in the pan. A tit-bit, dainty morsel, a piece of bread soaked in the dripping of meat caught in a dripping-pan, a bribe (*see below*)

To give a sop to Cerberus. To give a bribe, to quiet a troublesome customer, Cerberus is Pluto's three-headed dog, stationed at the gates of the infernal regions When persons died the Greeks and Romans used to put a cake in their hands as a sop to Cerberus, to allow them to pass without molestation

Soph. A student at Cambridge is a Freshman for the first term, a Junior Soph for the second year, and a Senior Soph for the third year The word Soph is a contraction of "sophister," which is the Greek and Latin *sophistes* (a sophist). In former times these students had to maintain a given question in the schools by opposing the orthodox view of it. These opponencies are now limited to Law and Divinity degrees.

In American Universities *Soph* is an abbreviation of **Sophomore,** a term applied to students in their second year.

Sophia, Santa (so fī′ a) The great metropolitan cathedral of the Orthodox Greek Church at Istanbul It was built by Justinian (532-7), but since the capture of the city by the Turks (1453) has been used as a mosque It was not dedicated to a saint named Sophia, but to the "Logos," or Second Person of the Trinity, called *Hagia Sophia* (Sacred Wisdom).

Sophist, Sophistry, Sophism, Sophisticator, etc. These words have quite run from their legitimate meaning Before the time of Pythagoras (586-506 B C) the sages of Greece were called *sophists* (wise men) Pythagoras out of modesty called himself a *philosopher* (a wisdom-lover) A century later Protagoras of Abdera resumed the title, and a set of quibblers appeared in Athens who professed to answer any question on any subject, and took up the title discarded by the Wise Samian From this movement *sophos* and all its family of words were applied to "wisdom falsely so called," and *philo-sophos* to the "modest search after truth "

Sophy, The. An old title of the rulers of Persia, first given to Sheik Juneyd u Dien, founder of the Safi dynasty (about 1500-1736).

Soppy. Mawkish (of people) ultra-sentimental (of stories etc.) *A soppy boy* is one who is "tied to his mother's apron-strings "

Sorbonne. The institution of theology, science, and literature in Paris founded by Robert de Sorbon, Canon of Cambrai, in 1252 In 1808 the buildings erected by Richelieu in the 17th century, were given to the University, and a great scheme of reconstruction was carried out in 1885 Since 1896 the Sorbonne has been the University of Paris

Sordello (sôr del′ ō) A Provençal troubadour (d. about 1255), mentioned a number of times by Dante in the *Purgatorio*, now remembered because of Browning's very obscure poem of this name (1840) It details, in a setting which shows the restless condition of northern Italy in the early 13th century, the conflict of a poet about the best way of making his influence felt, whether personally or by the power of song Browning said of it —

> The historical decoration was purposely of no more importance than a background requires, and my stress lay on the incidents in the development of a soul, little else is worth study I, at least, always thought so

Tennyson's reference to *Sordello* is well known He said he had done his best with it, but there were only two lines he understood—the first and the last—and they were both untrue. These are —

> Who will, may hear Sordello's story told
> Who would has heard Sordello's story told

Sorites (sôr′ ītz) A "heaped-up" (Gr *soros* a heap) or cumulative syllogism, the predicate of one forming the subject of that which follows, the subject of the first being ultimately

united with the predicate of the last. The following will serve as an example —

> All men who believe shall be saved
> All who are saved must be free from sin
> All who are free from sin are innocent in the sight of God
> All who are innocent in the sight of God are meet for heaven
> All who are meet for heaven will be admitted into heaven
> Therefore all who believe will be admitted into heaven.

The famous Sorites of Themistocles was That his infant son commanded the whole world, proved thus —

> My infant son rules his mother
> His mother rules me
> I rule the Athenians
> The Athenians rule the Greeks
> The Greeks rule Europe
> And Europe rules the world.

Sorrow. The Seven Sorrows of the Virgin. *See* MARY

Sort Out of sorts. Not in good health and spirits The French *être dérangé* explains the metaphor If cards are *out of sorts* they are *deranged*, and if a person is *out of sorts* the health or spirits are out of order

In printers' language *sorts* is applied to particular pieces of type considered as part of the fount, and a printer is *out of sorts* when he has run short of some particular letters, figures, stops, etc.

To run upon sorts. In printing, said of work which requires an unusual number of certain letters, etc ; as an index, which requires a disproportionate number of capitals.

Sortes (sôr′ tēz) (Lat *sors*, *sortis*, chance, lot) A species of divination performed by selecting passages from a book haphazard Virgil's *Æneid* was anciently the favourite work for the purpose (*Sortes Virgilianæ*), but the Bible (*Sortes Biblicæ*) has also been in common use.

The method is to open the book at random, and the passage you touch by chance with your finger is the oracular response Severus consulted Virgil, and read these words "Forget not thou, O Roman, to rule the people with royal sway " Gordianus, who reigned only a few days, hit upon this verse "Fate only showed him on the earth, but suffered him not to tarry", and Dr Wellwood gives an instance respecting King Charles I and Lord Falkland. Falkland, to amuse the king, suggested this kind of augury, and the king hit upon iv, 615-620, the gist of which is that "evil wars would break out, and the king lose his life " Falkland, to laugh the matter off said he would show his Majesty how ridiculously the "lot" would foretell the next fate, and he lighted on xi, 152-181, the lament of Evander for the untimely death of his son Pallas King Charles soon after mourned over his noble friend who was slain at Newbury (1643)

In Rabelais (III, x) Panurge consults the *Sortes Virgilianæ et Homericæ* on the burning question, whether or not he should marry In Cornelius Agrippa's *De Vanitate Scientiarum*, c iv, there is a passage violently reprobating the *Sortes*.

S O S. *See under* S.

Sotadic Verse. *See* PALINDROME.

Soter (sō′ tēr) Ptolemy I of Egypt (d 283 B.C.) was given this surname, meaning *the Preserver* by the Rhodians because he compelled Demetrius to raise the siege of Rhodes (304 B C).

Sothic Period, Year. The Persian year consists of 365 days, so that a day is lost in four years, amounting in the course of 1,460 years to a year This period of 1,460 years is called a *sothic period* (Gr. *sothis,* the dog-star, at whose rising it commences), and the reclaimed year made up of the bits is called a *sothic year See* CANICULAR PERIOD.

Soul. Among the ancient Greeks the *soul* was the seat of the passions and desires, which animals have in common with man, and the *spirit* the highest and distinctive part of man In 1 *Thess* Paul says; "I pray God your whole spirit, soul, and body be preserved blameless unto the coming of our Lord Jesus Christ." *See also Heb* iv, 12, 1 *Cor.* ii, 14 and 15, xv, 45, 46.

Heraclitus held the soul to be a spark of the stellar essence, *scintilla stellaris essentiæ* (Macrobius *Somnium Scipionis,* i, 14)

> Vital spark of heavenly flame!
> Quit, oh quit this mortal frame
> POPE. *The Dying Christian to his Soul*

Both the Greeks and Romans seemed to think that the soul made its escape with life out of the death-wound

The Moslems say that the souls of the faithful assume the forms of snow-white birds, and nestle under the throne of Allah until the resurrection, and hold that it is necessary, when a man is bow-strung, to relax the rope a little before death occurs to let the soul escape

In Egyptian hieroglyphics the soul is represented by several emblems, as a basket of fire, a heron, a hawk with a human face, and a ram.

All Souls' Day. November 2nd, the day following All Saints' Day, set apart by the Roman Catholic Church for a solemn service for the repose of the departed In England it was formerly observed by ringing the *soul bell* (or passing-bell), by making and distributing *soul cakes,* blessing beans, etc.

Soul cakes Cakes formerly given in Staffordshire, Cheshire, and elsewhere on All Souls' Day, to the poor who go *a-souling, i.e* begging for soul cakes The words used were—

> Soul, soul, for soul-cake
> Pray you, good mistress, a soul cake

Sourdough (sour′ dō) A miner, especially a prospector, in Alaska or Canada, an old-timer

Sour Grapes *See* GRAPES

South-Sea Scheme or **Bubble.** A stock-jobbing scheme devised by Sir John Blunt, a lawyer, in 1710, and floated by the Earl of Oxford in the following year The object of the company was to buy up the National Debt, and to be allowed the sole privilege of trading in the South Seas Spain refused to give trading facilities, so the money was used in other speculative ventures and, by careful "rigging" of the market, £100 shares were run up to over ten times that sum. The bubble burst in 1720 and ruined thousands. The term is applied to any hollow scheme which has a splendid promise, but whose collapse will be sudden and ruinous. *Cp.* MISSISSIPPI BUBBLE.

Southcottians. The followers of Joanna Southcott (1750-1814), a domestic servant who became a religious fanatic and gave herself out as the

> "woman clothed with the sun, and the moon under her feet, and upon her head a crown of twelve stars "
> —(*Rev* xii, 1).

Although 64 years old she was to be delivered of a son, the Shiloh of *Gen* xlix, 10—

> The sceptre shall not depart from Judah, nor a lawgiver from between his feet, until Shiloh come, and unto him shall the gathering of the people be

October 19th, 1814, was the date fixed for the birth, but no birth took place, and the expectant mother died of brain fever ten days later She left a locked wooden box that was not to be opened until the time of a national crisis, and then only in the presence of all the bishops in England Various attempts were made to persuade the episcopate to assemble for this purpose, during the Crimean War and again in World War I At last it was opened in 1928 in the presence of one reluctant prelate, and found to contain some odds and ends including a horse pistol and a few unimportant papers Among her 60 publications was *The Book of Wonders* (1813-14) containing her prophecies The sect she founded still exists

South Paw (U S A) In baseball, a left-handed pitcher or any left-handed player in games generally A boxer who puts up his guard with his right forward

Sovereign. A strangely misspelled word (from Lat *superanus,* supreme), the last syllable being assimilated to *reign* French *souverain* is nearer the Latin, Ital, *sovrano,* Span *soberano*

A gold coin of this name, value 22s 6d , was issued by Henry VIII, and so called because he was represented on it in royal robes, but the modern sovereign of 20s value was not issued till 1817 Just a hundred years later, during World War I, its issue was suspended in Britain and its place taken by paper Treasury Notes

Sow (sou) **A pig of** my own sow. Said of that which is the result of one's own action

A still sow. A cunning and selfish man, one wise in his own interest, one who avoids talking at meals that he may enjoy his food the better So called from the old proverb, "The still sow eats the wash" or "draff "

> We do not act that often jest and laugh,
> 'Tis old, but true, "Still swine eat all the draugh "
> *Merry Wives of Windsor,* iv, 2.

As drunk as David's sow. Very drunk indeed.

To get the wrong sow by the ear. To capture the wrong individual, to take the wrong end of the stick, hit upon the wrong thing.

To send a sow to Minerva To teach your grandmother how to suck eggs, to instruct one more learned in the subject than yourself From the old Latin proverb, *Sus Minervam docet* (a pig teaching Minerva), which meant the same thing.

You cannot make a silk purse out of a sow's ear. *See* SILK

See also PIG-IRON.

Spade. The spade of playing cards is so called from Span *espada*, a sword, the suit in Spanish packs being marked with short swords, in French and British cards the mark—largely through the similarity in name—has been altered to something like the blade of a sharp-pointed spade.

Spade guinea. An English gold coin value 21s, minted 1787-99, so called because it bears a shield like the "spade" on playing cards on the reverse The legend is M B F. et H Rex F. D. B L D S R I A. T et E.— Magnæ Britanniæ, Franciæ, et Hiberniæ Rex, Fidei Defensor; Brunsvicensis, Lunenburgensis Dux, Sacri Romani Imperii Archi Thesaurarius et Elector

To call a spade a spade. To be straightforward, outspoken, and blunt, even to the point of rudeness, to call things by their proper names without any beating about the bush

I have learned to call wickedness by its own terms a fig a fig, and a spade a spade —JOHN KNOX

This is a translation of Erasmus's rendering of the old Latin proverb—*ficus ficus, ligonem ligonem vocat*

Spagyric (spà jir' ik) Pertaining to alchemy, the term seems to have been invented by Paracelsus. Alchemy is "the spagyric art," and an alchemist a "spagyrist"

Spagyric food. Cagliostro's name for the elixir of immortal youth

Spain. *See* HISPANIA

Castles in Spain. *See* CASTLE.

Patron saint of Spain. St James the Greater, who is said to have preached the Gospel in Spain, where his relics are preserved at Compostella.

Spanish fly. The cantharis, a coleopterous insect used in medicine Cantharides are dried and used externally as a blister and internally as a stimulant to the genito-urinary organs, they were formerly considered to act as an aphrodisiac

Spanish moss. A plant of the family Bromeliaceæ which hangs in long grey festoons from the branches of trees, especially the live oak, in tropical and sub-tropical American forests.

Spanish worm. An old name for a nail concealed in a piece of wood, against which a carpenter jars his saw or chisel

The Spanish Main. Properly, the northern coast of South America, going westward from the mouth of the Orinoco to the Isthmus of Panama, or a bit farther, the *main*-land bordering the Caribbean Sea, called by the Spanish conquerors *Tierra Firme*. The term is often applied, however, to the curving chain of islands forming the northern and eastern boundaries of the Caribbean Sea, beginning from Mosquito, near the isthmus, and including Jamaica, St Domingo, the Leeward Islands, and the Windward Islands, to the coast of Venezuela in South America.

To walk Spanish. To walk on tiptoe, being lifted and pushed by a more powerful person From the behaviour of the pirates of the Spanish Main towards their captives

Span New. *See* SPICK

Spaniel. The Spanish dog, from *español*, through the French

Spanker. Used of a fast horse, also—colloquially—of something or someone that is an exceptionally fine specimen, a "stunner"

In nautical language the *spanker* is the fore-and-aft sail set upon the mizen-mast of a three-masted vessel, and the jigger-mast of a four-masted vessel. There is no spanker in a one- or two-masted vessel of any rig.

Spare the rod, etc. *See* ROD

Spartacists. An extreme Socialist group in Germany that flourished between 1916 and 1919. It was founded by Karl Liebknecht who, with Rosa Luxemburg led an attempted revolution in January of the latter year, in the suppression of which they were both killed The movement was finally crushed by Ebert's government in the April. The original Spartacus was a Thracian who commanded a band of insurgents in the third Servile war of Rome, 71 B C

Spartan. The inhabitants of ancient Sparta, one of the leading city-states of Greece, were noted for their frugality, courage, and stern discipline, hence, one who can bear pain unflinchingly is termed "a Spartan," a very frugal diet is "Spartan fare," etc. It was a Spartan mother who, on handing her son the shield he was to carry into battle, said that he must come back either with it or on it.

Spartan dog. A blood-hound, a blood-thirsty man

O Spartan dog
More fell than anguish, hunger or the sea
Othello, v, 2.

Spasmodic School. The. A name applied by Professor Aytoun to certain authors of the 19th century, whose writings were distinguished by forced conceits and unnatural style The most noted are Bailey (author of *Festus*), Gerald Massey, Alexander Smith, and Sydney Dobell

Spats. Short cloth or leather gaiters The word comes from

Spatterdashes Long gaiters, usually of cloth, worn to protect the stockings or trousers from mud In military uniform they are generally waterproof and button or lace to some inches above the ankle

Speak-easy. A place where alcoholic liquors are sold without a licence, or in some illegal way.

Speaker. The title of the presiding officer and official spokesman of the British House of Commons, the United States House of

Representatives, and of some other legislative assemblies.

The Speaker of the House of Commons has autocratic and almost absolute power in the control of debates and internal arrangements of the House, etc , he is elected by the members irrespective of party, and ceases to be a "party man," having no vote—except in cases of a tie, when he can give a casting vote He holds office for the duration of that Parliament, but by custom (not law) is re-appointed unless he wishes to resign (in which case he goes to the House of Lords).

The Lord Chancellor is *ex officio* Speaker of the House of Lords

To catch the Speaker's eye. The rule in the House of Commons is that the member whose rising to address the House is first observed by the Speaker is allowed precedence.

Speaking. A speaking likeness. A very good and lifelike portrait; one that makes you imagine that the subject is just going to speak to you

Speaking heads. Fables and romance tell of a good many artificial heads that could speak (*cp* BRAZEN HEAD), among the best known are:—

The statue of Memnon, in Egypt, which uttered musical sounds when the morning sun darted on it

That of Orpheus, at Lesbos, which is said to have predicted the bloody death that terminated the expedition of Cyrus the Great into Scythia

The head of Minos, fabled to have been brought by Odin to Scandinavia, and to have uttered responses.

The Brazen Head (*q v.*) of Roger Bacon, and that of Gerbert, afterwards Pope Sylvester II (10th cent)

An earthen head made by Albertus Magnus in the 13th century, which both spoke and moved Thomas Aquinas broke it, whereupon the mechanist exclaimed; "There goes the labour of thirty years!"

Alexander's statue of Esculapius, it was supposed to speak, but Lucian says the sounds were uttered by a concealed man, and conveyed by tubes to the statue

The "ear of Dionysius" communicated to Dionysius, Tyrant of Syracuse, whatever was uttered by suspected subjects shut up in a state prison This "ear" was a large black opening in a rock, about 50 ft high, and the sound was communicated by a series of channels not unlike those of the human ear

They are not on speaking terms. Said of friends who have fallen out

Spear If a knight kept the point of his spear forward when he entered a strange land, it was a declaration of war; if he carried it on his shoulder with the point behind him, it was a taken of friendship In Ossian (*Temora*, i) Cairbar asks if Fingal comes in peace, to which Mor-annal replies "In peace he comes not, king of Erin, I have seen his forward spear "

The spear of Achilles. *See* ACHILLES' SPEAR, ACHILLEA.

The spear of Ithuriel. *See* ITHURIEL

The spear-side. The male line of descent, called by the Anglo-Saxons *spere-healfe Cp* SPINDLE-SIDE

To break a spear To fight a tournament

To pass under the spear To be sold by auction, sold "under the hammer " Writing to Pepys (Aug. 12th, 1689) Evelyn speaks of "the noblest library that ever passed under the speare " The phrase is from the Latin *sub hasta vendere*

Special Pleading. Quibbling, making your own argument good by forcing certain words or phrases from their obvious and ordinary meaning A pleading in law means a written statement of a cause *pro* and *con*, and "special pleaders" are persons who have been called to the bar, but do not speak as advocates They advise on evidence, draw up affidavits, state the merits and demerits of a cause, and so on After a time most special pleaders go to the bar, and many get advanced to the bench

Specie, Species, means literally "what is visible" (Lat *species,* appearance) As things are distinguished by their visible forms, it has come to mean *kind* or *class* As drugs and condiments at one time formed the most important articles of merchandise, they were called *species*—still retained in the French *épices,* and English *spices* Again, as bank-notes represent money, money itself is called *specie,* the thing represented

Spectacles. In cricket, when a player scores a "duck's egg" (*i e* nothing at all) in each of his two innings of one match, he is said to make "a pair of spectacles "

Spectre of the Brocken. An optical illusion, first observed on the Brocken (the highest peak of the Hartz range in Saxony), in which shadows of the spectators, greatly magnified, are projected on the mists about the summit of the mountain opposite In one of De Quincey's opium-dreams there is a powerful description of the Brocken spectre

Spectrum, Spectra, Spectre (Lat *specto,* I behold) In optics a *spectrum* is the image of a sunbeam beheld on a screen, after refraction by one or more prisms *Spectra* are the images of objects left on the eye after the objects themselves are removed from sight A *spectre* is the apparition of a person no longer living or not bodily present

Speculate (spek' ū lāt) means to look out of a watch-tower, to spy about (Lat *speculari*) Metaphorically, to look at a subject with the mind's eye, to spy into it; in *commerce,* to purchase articles or shares which you expect will prove profitable

Specularis lapis, what we should now call window-glass, was some transparent stone or mineral, such as mica

Speculum Humanæ Salvationis (*The Mirror of Human Salvation*). A kind of extended *Biblia Pauperum* (*q v*) telling pictorially the Bible story from the fall of Lucifer to the Redemption of Man, with explanations of each picture in Latin rhymes MS copies of the 12th century are known, but its chief interest is that it was one of the earliest of printed books, having been printed about 1467

Speech. Parts of speech. *See* PART Speech is silver (or silvern), silence is golden. An old proverb, said to be of oriental origin, pointing to the advantage of keeping one's own counsel The Hebrew equivalent is "If a word be worth one shekel, silence is worth two "

Speech was given to man to disguise his thoughts. This epigram was attributed to Talleyrand by Barrère in his *Memoirs*, but though Talleyrand no doubt used it he was not its author Voltaire, in his XIVth Dialogue (*Le Chapon et la Poularde*), had said—

Men use thought only as authority for their injustice, and employ speech only to conceal their thoughts

Goldsmith, in *The Bee*, III (1759), has—

The true use of speech is not so much to express our wants as to conceal them.

And Robert South (1634-1716) preaching on April 30th, 1676, said in his sermon—

Speech was given to the ordinary sort of men, whereby to communicate their mind, but to wise men, whereby to conceal it

Spell. A turn of work done by a man or group of men in relief of another man or group; hence, the period of one's turn of work The word was formerly applied to the gang itself, and is probably the A S. *spala*, a substitute. *Spell*, in the sense of saying or writing the letters forming a word, is often used with the meaning to hint very broadly, especially of children

A pretty good spell A long bout or pull, as a "spell at the capstan," etc.

Spell ho! An exclamation to signify that the allotted time has expired, and men are to be relieved by another set

To spell is to relieve another at his work.

Spellbinders. Orators who hold their audience *spellbound*, that is, fascinated, charmed, as though bound by a spell or magic incantation.

Potent was the spell that bound thee
Not unwilling to obey
WORDSWORTH. *Poems of the Imagination*, xxxv

The word came into use in America in the presidential election of 1888, and has been used of British political orators of persuasive eloquence

Spencean Philanthropists Disciples of Thomas Spence (1750-1814) who, in 1775, devised a system of land nationalization The inhabitants of each parish would form a corporation and appoint local officials to collect rents, deduct expenses, and divide what was left among the parishioners No tax or toll would be required beyond the rent A day of rest would be allowed every five days 'Whether the title of King, President, Consul or the like is assumed by the head of the country is quite indifferent to me " A number of hot-headed and woolly-minded persons thought that this plan heralded the Millennium and in 1816 "The Society of Spencean Philanthropists" was founded That year they arranged the Spa Fields Meeting, Bermondsey, which ended in a riot The Cato Street Conspirators and other dangerous demagogues were disciples of Spence.

Spencer. Now applied to a close-fitting bodice worn by women, but formerly the name of an outer coat without skirts worn by men; so named from the second Earl Spencer (1758-1834.)

Spencerian Handwriting is the name given to a style of calligraphy introduced by Platt Rogers Spencer (1800-61), an American calligrapher Written with a fine pen, with the down-strokes tapering from top to bottom and large loops, the writing has a forward slope and marked terminal flourishes. Spencer taught this style in many parts of U S A and it is said to have had a marked influence on American calligraphy.

Spenserian Metre. The metre devised by Spenser (1592), founded on the Italian *ottava rima*, for his *Faerie Queene* It is a stanza of nine iambic lines, all of ten syllables except the last, which is an Alexandrine. Only three different rhymes are admitted into a stanza, and these are disposed: a b a b b c b c c

The stanza was used by Thomson (*Castle of Indolence*), Shenstone (*Schoolmistress*), Byron (*Childe Harold*), etc

Spheres. In the Ptolemaic system of astronomy (*q v*) the earth, as the centre of the universe, was supposed to be surrounded by nine spheres of invisible space, the first seven carrying the "planets" as then known, viz, (1) Diana or the Moon, (2) Mercury, (3) Venus, (4) Apollo or the Sun, (5) Mars, (6) Jupiter, and (7) Saturn, the eighth, the Starry Sphere, carrying the fixed stars, and the ninth, the Crystalline Sphere, added by Hipparchus in the 2nd century B C. to account for the precession of the equinoxes. Finally, in the Middle Ages, was added a tenth sphere, the *Primum mobile* (*q v*), a solid barrier which enclosed the universe and shut it off from Nothingness and the Empyrean These last two spheres carried neither star nor planet

They pass the planets seven, and pass the fixed [starry sphere],
And that crystalline sphere   and that First-Moved   MILTON *Paradise Lost*, III, 482,

The music, or harmony, of the spheres Pythagoras, having ascertained that the pitch of notes depends on the rapidity of vibrations, and also that the planets move at different rates of motion, concluded that the planets must make sounds in their motion according to their different rates; and that, as all things in nature are harmoniously made, the different sounds must harmonize, whence the old theory of the "harmony of the spheres " Kepler has a treatise on the subject

There's not the smallest orb which thou behold'st
But in his motion like an angel sings,
Still quiring to the young-eyed cherubims.
Merchant of Venice, v, 1.

Plato says that a siren sits on each planet, who carols a most sweet song, agreeing to the motion of her own particular planet, but harmonizing with all the others Hence Milton speaks of the "celestial syrens' harmony that sit upon the nine enfolded spheres." (*Arcades*)

Sphinx (sfingks) A monster of ancient mythology, in Greece represented as having the head of a woman, the body of a lion, and winged, in Egypt as a wingless lion with the head and breast of a man

The Grecian Sphinx was generally said to be the daughter of Typhon and Chimæra; she infested Thebes, setting the inhabitants a riddle and devouring all those who could not solve it The riddle was—

What goes on four feet, on two feet, and three,
But the more feet it goes on the weaker it be?

and it was at length solved by Œdipus (q v) with the answer that it was a man, who as an infant crawls upon all-fours, in manhood goes erect on his two feet, and in old age supports his tottering legs with a staff On hearing this correct answer the Sphinx slew herself, and Thebes was delivered

The Egyptian sphinx is a typification of Ra, the sun god. The colossal statue of the reclining monster was old in the days of Cheops, when the Great Pyramid, near which it lies, was built. It is hewn out of the solid rock, its length is 140 ft., and its head 30 ft from crown to chin.

Spick and Span New. Quite and entirely new A *spic* is a spike or nail, and a *span* is a chip So that a spick and span new ship is one in which every nail and chip is new According to Dr Johnson, who, in recording the term says it is one which he "should not have expected to have found authorized by a polite writer," *span new* is from A S *spannan*, to stretch, and was originally used of cloth newly extended or dressed at the cloth-maker's, and *spick and span* is newly extended on the spikes or tenters He gives quotations from Samuel Butler, Bishop Burnet, and Dean Swift, but cannot help adding "it is however a low word "

Spider. There are many old wives' fables about spiders, the most widespread being that they are venomous. Shakespeare alludes to this more than once—

Let thy spiders, that suck up thy venom,
And heavy-gaited toads lie in their way.
                    Richard II, iii, 2

There may be in the cup
A spider steep'd, and one may drink, depart,
And yet partake no venom *Winter's Tale*, ii, 1.

and in the examination into the murder of Sir Thomas Overbury, one of the witnesses deposed "that the countess wished him to get the strongest poison that he could . . ." Accordingly he brought seven great spiders.

Other tales were that spiders would never spin a web on a cedar roof, and that fever could be cured by wearing a spider in a nutshell round the neck

Spiders were credited with other medicinal virtues A common cure for jaundice in country parts of England was to swallow a large live house-spider rolled up in butter, while in the south of Ireland a similar remedy was given for ague

Yet another story was that spiders spin only on dark days—

The subtle spider never spins
But on dark days, his slimy gins.
        S BUTLER *On a Nonconformist*, iv

Bruce and the spider. In 1305 Robert Bruce was crowned at Scone king of Scotland, but, being attacked by the English, retreated to Ireland, and all supposed him to be dead. While lying *perdu* in the little island of Rathlin he one day noticed a spider try six times to

fix its web on a beam in the ceiling "Now shall this spider (said Bruce) teach me what I am to do, for I also have failed six times " The spider made a seventh effort and succeeded, whereupon Bruce left the island (1307), collected 300 followers, landed at Carrick, and at midnight surprised the English garrison in Turnberry Castle, he next overthrew the Earl of Gloucester, and in two years made himself master of well-nigh all Scotland, which Edward III declared in 1328 to be an independent kingdom.

Frederick the Great and the spider. While Frederick II was at Sans Souci, he one day went into his ante-room, as usual, to drink a cup of chocolate, but set his cup down to fetch his handkerchief from his bedroom On his return he found a great spider had fallen from the ceiling into his cup. He called for fresh chocolate, and next moment heard the report of a pistol The cook had been suborned to poison the chocolate, and, supposing his treachery had been found out, shot himself On the ceiling of the room in Sans Souci a spider has been painted (according to tradition) in remembrance of this story.

Mohammed and the spider. When Mohammed fled from Mecca he hid in a certain cave, with the Koreishites close upon him Suddenly an acacia in full leaf sprang up at the mouth of the cave, a wood-pigeon had its nest in the branches, and a spider had woven its net between the tree and the cave When the Koreishites saw this, they felt persuaded that no one could have entered recently, and went on

Spigot. Spare at the spigot and spill at the bung To be parsimonious in trifles and wasteful in great matters, like a man who stops his beer-tub at the vent-hole and leaves it running at the bung-hole.

Spike. Slang for the workhouse, to go on the spike is to become a workhouse inmate

To get the spike. To get the needle. *See* NEEDLE.

To spike one's guns for him To render his plans abortive, frustrate the scheme he has been laying, "draw his teeth." The allusion is to the old way of making a gun useless by driving a spike into the touch-hole

To spike a drink. To add strong spirits to increase the alcoholic content.

Spill the Beans, To To reveal a secret prematurely, to let the cat out of the bag, to upset the applecart.

Spilt milk. *See* CRY

Spindle-side. The female line of descent (*cp.* SPEAR-SIDE). The spindle was the pin on which the thread was wound from the spinning-wheel

Spinster. An unmarried woman The fleece which was brought home by the Anglo-Saxons in summer, was spun and woven into clothing by the female part of each family during the winter. King Edward the Elder commanded his daughters to be instructed in the use of the distaff Alfred the Great, in his will, calls the female part of his family the *spindle side*; and it was a regularly received axiom with our forefathers, that no young woman was fit to be a wife till she had spun for herself a set of body, table, and bed linen. Hence the maiden was termed a spinner or spinster

It is said that the heraldic *lozenge*, in which the armorial bearings of a woman are depicted instead of, in the case of a man, on a *shield*, originally represented a spindle Among the Romans the bride carried a distaff, and Homer tells us that Kryseis was to spin and share the king's bed

Spirit. Properly, the breath of life, from Lat *spiritus* (*spirare*, to breathe, blow) —

And the Lord God formed man of the dust of the ground, and breathed into his nostrils the breath of life, and man became a living soul —*Gen* ii, 7.

Hence, life or the life principle, the soul, a disembodied soul (a ghost or apparition), or an immaterial being that never was supposed to have had a body (sprite), as a gnome, elf, or fairy; also, the temper or disposition of mind as animated by the breath of life, as *in good spirits*, *high-spirited*, *a man of spirit*.

The mediæval physiological notion (adopted from Galen) was that spirit existed in the body in three kinds, viz , (1) the *Natural spirit*, the principle of the "natural functions"— growth, nutrition, and generation, said to be a vapour rising from the blood and having its seat in the liver, (2) the *Vital spirit*, which arose in the heart by mixture of the air breathed in with the natural spirit and supplied the body with heat and life. and (3) the *Animal spirit*, which was responsible for the power of motion and sensation, and for the rational principle generally, this was a modification of the vital spirit, effected in the brain

Spirit also came to mean any volatile or airy agent of essence; and hence, through the old alchemists, is still used of solutions in alcohol of a volatile principle and of any strong distilled alcoholic liquor The alchemists named four substances only as "spirits," viz , mercury, arsenic, sal ammoniac, and sulphur.—

The first spirit quyksilver called is
The secound orpiment, the thrid I wis
Sal armoniac, and the ferth bremstoon.
CHAUCER *Canon's Yeoman's Prologue.*

The **Elemental spirits** of Paracelsus and the Rosicrucians, *i e* those which presided over the four elements, were—the *Salamanders* (of fire), *Gnomes* (earth), *Sylphs* (air), and *Undines* (water)

To spirit away. To kidnap, abduct, to make away with speedily and secretly. The phrase first came into use in the 17th century, in connexion with kidnapping youths and transporting them to the West Indian plantations

Spiritualism. The belief that communication between the living and the spirits of the departed can and does take place, usually through the agency of a specially qualified person (a medium) and often by means of rapping, table-turning, or automatic writing, the system, doctrines, practice, etc , arising from this belief. Hence **Spiritualist**, one who maintains or practises this belief

In Philosophy Spiritualism—the antithesis of materialism—is the doctrine that the spirit exists as distinct from matter, or as the only reality.

Spit Spitting for luck. Spitting was a charm against enchantment among the ancient Greeks and Romans. Pliny says it averted witchcraft, and availed in giving an enemy a shrewder blow.

Thrice on my breast I spit to guard me safe
From fascinating charms. *Theocritus.*

Countrymen spit for luck on a piece of money given to them; boxers spit on their hands, and costermongers on the first money they take in the day for the same reason

Spital or **Spittle.** A hospital.

A spittle or hospitall for poore folks diseased, a spittle hospitall, or lazarhouse for lepers.—BARET *Alveaire* (1580).

Hence **Spitalfields**, the site in London where, in 1197, a spital or almshouse was built in the fields by Walter Brune and his wife Rosia.

Spittle Sermons. Sermons preached formerly on Easter Monday and Tuesday at St Mary Spital, Spitalfields, in a pulpit erected expressly for the purpose Subsequently they were given at St Bride's, and later at Christchurch, Newgate Street Ben Jonson alludes to them in his *Underwoods*, lx.

Spitfire. An irascible person, whose angry words are like fire spit from the mouth of a fire-eater.

Spiv. A word that came into general usage during World War II It is applied to a flashy fellow who lives by his wits without working, and, if possible, without committing actual crime The word was sometimes used by race-course gangs in the 1890s, it comes from the slang "spiff," meaning smart and is still used in the word "spiffing."

Splay is a contraction of *display* (to unfold; Lat *dis-plico*). A *splay window* is one in a V-shape, the external opening being very wide, to admit as much light as possible, but the inner opening being very small A *splay-foot* is a foot displayed or turned outward. A *splay-mouth* is a wide mouth, like that of a clown.

Spleen. The soft vascular organ placed to the left of the stomach and acting on the blood, was once believed to be the seat of melancholy and ill-humour. The fern *spleenwort* was supposed to remove splenic disorders.

Splice. To marry Very strangely, "splice" means to *split* or *divide* (Ger *spleissen*, to split) The way it came to signify *unite* is this· Ropes' ends are first untwisted or split before the strands are interwoven. Joining two ropes together by interweaving their strands is "splicing" them Splicing wood is joining two boards together, the term being borrowed from the sailor

To splice the main brace. *See* MAIN BRACE

Split. To give away one's accomplices, betray secrets, "peach "

To split hairs. *See* HAIR

To split with laughter. To laugh uproariously or unrestrainedly, to "split one's sides."

To split the infinitive. To interpose some word between *to* and the verb, as "to thoroughly understand the subject." This construction is branded as a solecism by pedants, but it is as old as the English language, and there are few of our best writers who have not employed it.

Without permitting himself *to* actually mention the name.—MATTHEW ARNOLD *On Translating Homer,* iii

It becomes a truth again, after all, as he happens to newly consider it —BROWNING *A Soul's Tragedy*

Implore them to partially enlighten her —GEO. MEREDITH *The Egoist.*

Spoils System. The practice in the United States by which the victorious party in an election rewards its supporters by appointments to public office Adopted and approved by Andrew Jackson at his election as President in 1829 "To the victors belong the spoils"

Spoke. To put a spoke in one's wheel. To interfere with his projects and frustrate them; to thwart him When solid wheels were used, the driver was provided with a pin or spoke, which he thrust into one of the three holes made to receive it, to skid the cart when it went down-hill.

Sponge. To throw up the sponge. Give up, confess oneself beaten The metaphor is from boxing matches, for when a second tossed a sponge into the air it was a sign that his man was beaten

To sponge on a man. To live on him like a parasite, sucking up all he has as a dry sponge will suck up water

A sponger is a mean parasite who is always accepting the hospitality of those who will give it and never make any adequate return

Sponging House. A house where persons arrested for debt were kept for twenty-four hours, before being sent to prison They were generally kept by a bailiff, and the person lodged was "sponged" of all his money before leaving.

Sponsored Programme. A wireless programme which is sponsored, i e chosen and paid for, by a commercial company, which utilizes a few moments at the beginning and the end of the programme for advertising its own product

Spoon A simpleton, a shallow prating duffer used to be called a *spoon*, and hence the name came to be applied to one who indulged in foolish, sentimental love-making, and such a one is said to be *spoony*, and to be *spoons on* the girl

In nautical phrase *to spoon* is to scud before the wind; and in sculling to dip the sculls so lightly in the water as to do little more than skim the surface.

Apostle spoons. *See* APOSTLE.

He hath need of a long spoon that eateth with the devil. You will want all your wits about you if you ally yourself with evil Shakespeare alludes to this proverb in the *Comedy of Errors,* iv, 3, and again in the *Tempest,* ii, 2, where Stephano says. "Mercy! mercy! this

is a devil . I will leave him, I have no long spoon."

> Therefor behoveth hire a ful long spoon
> That schal ete with a feend
>   CHAUCER *Squire's Tale*, 594

To be born with a silver spoon in one's mouth. *See* BORN.

Spoonerism. A ludicrous form of metathesis (*q v*) that consists of transposing the initial sounds of words so as to form some laughable combination, so called from the Rev W A Spooner (1844-1930), Warden of New College, Oxford. Some of the best attributed to him are—"We all know what it is to have a half warmed fish within us" (for "half-formed wish"); "Yes indeed, the Lord is a shoving leopard", and "Kinkering Kongs their titles take." Sometimes the term is applied to the accidental transposition of whole words, as when the tea-shop waitress was asked for "a glass bun and a bath of milk."

Sport. To sport one's oak *See* OAK

The figurative meaning of *to sport* is to exhibit in public in a somewhat ostentatious way, a young man for instance, may *sport* a highly coloured pair of socks, a new fashion in hats, or a monocle

Sporting Seasons in England. The lawful season for venery, which began at Midsummer and lasted to Holy Rood Day, used to be called *the Time of Grace* The fox and wolf might be hunted from the Nativity to the Annunciation, the roebuck from Easter to Michaelmas, the roe from Michaelmas to Candlemas, the hare from Michaelmas to Midsummer, and the boar from the Nativity to the Purification

The times are as follows: those marked thus (*) are fixed by Act of Parliament

Black Game, * from August 20th to December 10th, but in Somerset, Devon, and New Forest, from September 1st to December 10th
Blackcock, August 20th to December 10th
Buck hunting, August 20th to September 17th.
Bustard, * September 1st to March 1st
Red Deer hunted, August 20th, to September 30th.
Eels, (about) April 20th to October 28th
Fox hunting, (about) October to Lady Day
Fox Cubs, August 1st to the first Monday in November
Grouse shooting,* August 12th to December 10th.
Hares, March 12th to August 12th
Hind, hunted in October and again between April 10th and May 20th
Oyster season, August 5th to May
Partridge shooting,* September 1st to February 1st
Pheasant shooting,* October 1st to February 1st
Ptarmigan, August 12th to December 10th
Quail, August 12th to January 10th
Rabbits, between October and March Rabbits, as vermin, are shot at any time
Salmon, * February 1st to September 1st
Salmon, rod fishing,* November 1st to September 1st
Trout fishing, May 1st to September 10th
Trout, in the Thames, April 1st to September 10th
Woodcock, (about) November to January

For Ireland and Scotland there are special game-laws

N.B.—Game in *England* hare, pheasant, partridge, grouse, and moor-fowl, in *Scotland,* same as England, with the addition of ptarmigan, in *Ireland,* same as England, with the addition of deer, black-game, landrail, quail, and bustard

Spot **On the spot.** At once; without having time to move away or do anything else, as— "He answered on the spot," immediately, without hesitation A further colloquial meaning of *on the spot* is, in danger of death, in an embarrassing situation.

To knock spots off one. To excel him completely in something; originally an Americanism

Spotting. The practice in the New Zealand settling days of buying up the land round all available creeks and streams, so that the adjoining territory would have no access to water and hence would find no buyer

Spouse means one who has promised (Lat. *sponsus*, past part of *spondere* to promise). In ancient Rome the friends of the parties about to be married met at the house of the woman's father to settle the marriage contract This contract was called *sponsalia* (espousal), the man, *sponsus*, and the woman, *sponsa*.

The spouse of Jesus. St Teresa of Avila (1515-82) was given this title by some of her contemporaries

All thy good works . shall
Weave a constellation
Of Crowns, with which the King thy spouse
Shall build up thy triumphant brows
CRASHAW *Hymn to St Theresa* (1652).

Spout. To utter in a bombastic, declamatory manner; to declaim

Up the spout. At the pawnbroker's In allusion to the "spout" up which brokers send the articles ticketed. When redeemed they return down the spout—*i e.* from the storeroom to the shop

Sprat. **To throw a sprat to catch a mackerel** To give a small thing in the hope of getting something much more valuable

Spread-eagle. The "eagle displayed" of heraldry, *i e.* an eagle with legs and wings extended, the wings being elevated. It is the device of the United States

In the navy a man was said to be **spread-eagled** when he was lashed to the rigging for flogging, with outstretched arms and legs

Spread-eaglism in a United States citizen is very much the counterpart of the more aggressive and bombastic forms of Jingoism (*q v*) in the Briton

Spread-eagle oratory. "A compound of exaggeration, effrontery, bombast, and extravagance, mixed with metaphors, platitudes, threats and irreverent appeals flung at the Almighty " (*North American Review*, November, 1858)

Springers. The Wiltshire Regiment, raised in 1758, and so nicknamed from its speed of movement during the American War of Independence

Spring Tide. The tide that springs or leaps or swells up These full tides occur a day or two after the new and full moon, when the attraction of both sun and moon act in a direct line.

Spruce. Smart, dandified. The word is from the old Fr *Pruce* (Ger. *Preussen*), Prussia, and

was originally (16th cent) applied to Prussian leather of which particularly neat and smart-looking jerkins were made

And after them, came, syr Edward Haward, then admyral, and with him sir Thomas Parre, in doblettes of Crimosin velvet, voyded lowe on the backe, and before to the cannell bone, laced on the breastes with chaynes of silver, and over that shorte clokes of Crimosyn satyne, and on their heades hattes after dauncers fashion, with fesauntes fethers in them, They were appareyled after the fashion of Prusia or Spruce.—*Hall's Chronicle Henry VIII*, year 1 (1542)

Spruce beer is made from the leaves of the *spruce fir*, this being a translation of the German name of the tree, *Sprossen-fichte*, literally "sprouts-fir "

Spunging House *See* SPONGING.

Spur. **On the spur of the moment** Instantly; without stopping to take thought

Spur money. A small fine formerly imposed on those who entered a church wearing spurs, because of the interruption caused to divine service by their ringing It was collected by the choir-boys or the beadles

The Battle of Spurs. A name given to the battles of Guinegate (1513) and Courtrai (1302), The former, between Henry VIII and the Duc de Longueville, was so called because the French used their spurs in flight more than their swords in fight, and the battle of Courtrai because the victorious Flemings gathered from the field more than 700 gilt spurs, worn by French nobles slain in the fight.

To dish up the spurs. In Scotland, during the times of the Border feuds, when any of the great families had come to the end of their provisions the lady of the house sent up a pair of spurs for the last course, to intimate that it was time to put spurs to the horses and make a raid upon England for more cattle

To ride whip (or switch) and spur. To ride with all possible speed to trample down obstacles ruthlessly.

To win his spurs To gain the rank of knighthood When a man was knighted, the person who dubbed him presented him with a pair of gilt spurs

Spy Wednesday. A name given in Ireland to the Wednesday before Good Friday, when Judas bargained to become the spy of the Jewish Sanhedrin (*Matt* xxvi, 3-5, 14-16).

Squab. Short and fat, plump, a person, cushion, etc , like this (a fat woman is *squabba* in Swedish) A young pigeon—especially an unfledged one—is called a *squab*, and a pie of mutton, apples, and onions is called a squab pie in some parts of the country

Cornwall squab-pie, and Devon white-pot brings,
And Leicester beans and bacon, fit for kings
KING *Art of Cookery*

Poet Squab. So Rochester called Dryden, who was very corpulent

Squad, Squadron. *See* AWKWARD SQUAD.

Squalls. **Look out for squalls** Expect to meet with difficulties. A nautical term, a squall being a succession of sudden and violent gusts of wind (Icel. *skvata*)

D D —28

Square. On the square. Straight and above board, honest Also said of a Freemason, with allusion to the Masonic emblem of a square and compasses

To square a person To bribe him, or to pay him for some extra trouble he has taken.

To square the circle To attempt an impossibility The allusion is to the impossibility of exactly determining the precise ratio between the diameter and the circumference of a circle, and thus constructing a circle of the same area as a given square. Popularly it is 3 14159 . . the next decimals would be 26537, but the numbers would go on *ad infinitum*.

To square up to a person. To put oneself in a fighting attitude.

> Are you such fools
> To square for this?
> *Titus Andronicus*, ii, 1.

Squatter. Used first in the U.S.A of a person settling on land without a legal title Thence went to Australia in the early 19th century to describe ex-convicts who established themselves on unoccupied land and stole cattle from their more honest neighbours to enrich themselves.

> A squatter . . is the horror of all his honest neighbours.—CHARLES DARWIN *Voyage of the Beagle.*

Squeers. *See* DOTHEBOYS HALL

Squib. A political joke, printed and circulated especially at election times against a candidate, with intent to bring him into ridicule, and to influence votes

> Allowing that the play succeeds, there are a hundred squibs flying all abroad to show that it should not have succeeded.—GOLDSMITH *Polite Learning*

Squinancy. *See* QUINSY.

Squintum, Doctor. George Whitefield (1714-70), so called by Foote in his farce *The Minor*

Theodore Hook applied the sobriquet to Edward Irving the preacher (1792-1834), who had an obliquity of the eyes

Squire. In mediæval times a youth of gentle birth attendant on a knight (*see* ESQUIRE); now a landed proprietor, the chief country gentleman of a place

Squire of dames. Any cavalier who is devoted to ladies Spenser, in his *Faerie Queene*, introduces the "squire," and records his adventures

Stabat Mater (sta' băt ma' ter (Lat, The Mother was standing) The Latin hymn reciting the Seven Sorrows of the Virgin at the Cross, so called from its opening words, forming part of the service during Passion week, in the Roman Catholic Church It was composed by the Franciscan Jacopone da Todi (1220-1306), and has been set to music by Pergolese, Rossini, Haydn, etc.

Stable. Locking the stable door after the horse is stolen. Taking precautions after the mischief is done.

Staff. I keep the staff in my own hand I keep possession, I retain the right The staff was the ancient sceptre, and therefore, figuratively, it means power, authority, dignity, etc.

> Give up your staff, sir, and the king his realm
> 2 *Henry VI*, ii, 3.

The staff of life. Bread, which is the *support* of life

"Bread," says he, "dear brothers, is the staff of life ' —SWIFT *Tale of a Tub*, iv

Shakespeare says, "The boy was the very staff of my age." The allusion is to a staff which supports the feeble in walking

To put down one's staff in a place. To abide for a while, to set down one's staff, as a traveller at an inn The phrase was first used by Thomas Adams (fl 1612-53) "the prose Shakespeare of Puritan theologians "

To strike staff. To lodge for the time being

Stafford. He has had a treat in Stafford Court. He has been thoroughly cudgelled, a pun on the word *staff*, a stick. The French have a similar phrase. *Il a été au festin de Martin Baston* (he has been to Jack Drum's entertainment)

Similarly, Stafford law is club law—a good beating

Stag. The reason why a stag symbolizes Christ is from the ancient idea that by its breath it draws serpents from their holes, and then tramples them to death (Pliny *Natural History*, viii, 50.)

Stag in Christian art. The attribute of St Julian Hospitaller, St Felix of Valois, and St Aidan. When it has a crucifix between its horns it alludes to the legend of St. Hubert When luminous it belongs to St Eustachius.

Stag Line. At American dances, a number of extra men guests who stand at the edge of the dance-floor, without partners, but having the privilege of breaking in on any dancing couple and claiming the girl as a partner.

Stag party. A gathering of men only.

Stags. In Stock Exchange phraseology, are persons who apply for new shares, etc., on allotment, not because they wish to hold the shares, but because they hope to sell the allotment at a premium.

Stagirite or **Stagyrite** (stăj' ı rīt) Aristotle, who was born at Stagira, in Macedon (4th cent B C).

> In one rich soul
> Plato, the Stagyrite, and Tully joined
> THOMSON *Summer*, 1541
> And rules as strict his laboured work confine
> As if the Stagirite o'erlooked each line
> POPE *Essay on Criticism*

Stakhanovism (stăk ăn 'ŏ vizm). Alexei Stakhanov, a Donetz coal miner, discovered in the 1930s that by concentrating on one aspect of his job and rationalizing the distribution of his work he could increase his daily output of coal by a substantial quantity. This aroused enthusiastic emulation among the younger and more skilled workers of his own and other trades, and was raised into a serious cult by the government.

Stalemate. To stalemate a person. To bring him to a standstill, render his projects worthless or abortive. The phrase is from chess, *stalemate* being the position in which the king is the only movable piece and he, though not in check, cannot move without becoming so *Stale* in this word is probably from O.Fr. *estal* (our *stall*), a fixed position.

Stalingrad (sta′lin grad), formerly Tsaritsyn, an important railway centre and manufacturing town on the Volga, in the S E. Soviet Union. In 1917 Stalin defended Tsaritsyn against the White Army and its name was changed to commemorate the incident In World War II Stalingrad was attacked by the Germans in their Caucasus drive in August 1942, but the Russians made a gallant defence that ended (Feb , 1943) in the capitulation of the Germans under Field-Marshal Paulus From that time onward the Nazi offensive in Russia was turned into a retreat and eventually a rout

Stalking-horse. A mask to conceal some design, a person put forward to mislead, a sham Sportsmen often used to conceal themselves behind horses, and go on stalking step by step till they got within shot of the game
 He uses his folly like a stalking-horse, and under the presentation of that he shoots his wit —*As You Like It*, v, 4

Stammerer, The. Louis II of France, *le Bégue* (846 877-9)
 Michael II, Emperor of the East (820-829)
 Notker of St Gall (830-912)

Stamp. 'Tis of the right stamp.—has the stamp of genuine merit. A metaphor taken from current coin, which is stamped with a recognized stamp and superscription
 I weigh the man, not his title, 'tis not the king's stamp can make the metal heavier or better — WYCHERLEY *The Plain Dealer*, i, 1 (1677).
 The rank is but the guinea stamp;
 The man's the gowd for a' that'
   BURNS *Is There, for Honest Poverty?*

Stand. To be at a stand. To be in doubt as to further progress, perplexed at what to do next

 To let a thing stand over. To defer consideration of it to a more favourable opportunity.

 To stand by. To be ready to give assistance in case of need A *stand-by* is a person or thing on which one can confidently rely

 To stand for a child. To be sponsor for it, to stand in its place and answer for it

 To stand in with. To go shares, also, to have an understanding or community of interests with

 To stand it out—persist in what one says. A translation of "persist" (Lat. *per-sisto* or *per-sto*)

 To stand off and on. A nautical phrase for tacking in and out along the shore

 To stand Sam, stand to reason, stand treat, etc. *See these words*

 To stand to one's guns. To persist in a statement, not to give way A military phrase.

 To stand up for. Support, take his (or its) part

 To stand up for one's privilege or **on punctilios** Quietly to insist on one's position, etc , being recognized; this is the Latin *insisto*.

Stand-in In motion-picture parlance a substitute for a film star who takes his or her place during the preparations for lighting, etc , performs any really dangerous stunts the part demands, and in general relieves the star of all but the glamorous, romantic, or publicity-value work of the part.

Standing orders. Rules or instructions constantly in force, especially those by-laws of the Houses of Parliament for the conduct of proceedings which stand in force till they are rescinded or suspended. Their suspension is generally caused by a desire to hurry through a Bill with unusual expedition

The Standing Fishes Bible. *See* BIBLE, SPECIALLY NAMED

Stand-offish Unsociable, rather contemptuously reserved.

Standard. A banner as the distinctive emblem of a Royal House, an army, or a nation, etc. The word first came into use in England in connexion with the Battle of the Standard (*see below*), in telling of which Richard of Hexham (about 1139) says that the standard (a ship's mast with flags at the top) was so called because "it was there that valour took its *stand* to conquer or die " The word is, however, from Lat *extendëre*, to stretch out, through O Fr *estandard*.
 Standards were formerly borne by others than royalties and nations, and varied in size according to the rank of the bearer. Thus that of an *emperor* was 11 yards in length, of a *king*, 9 yards, of a *prince*, 7 yards, of a *marquis*, 6½ yards, of an *earl*, 6 yards, of a *viscount* or *baron*, 5 yards, of a *knight-banneret*, 4½ yards; of a *baronet*, 4 yards. They generally contained the arms of the bearer, his cognizance and crest, his motto or war-cry, and were fringed with his livery.

 Standard is also applied to a measure of extent, weight, value, etc , which is established by law or custom as an example or criterion for others, and, in figurative use from this, to any criterion or principle, as "The standard of political rectitude " The weights and measures were formerly known as "the king's standard," as being official and recognized by royal authority
 In uses such as an **electric-light standard** (the lamp-post), **standard rose** (i e one that stands on its own stem and is not trained to a wall or espalier), etc , the word is the result of confusion with *stand*

 The Battle of the Standard, between the English and the Scots, at Cuton Moor, near Northallerton, in 1138 Here David I, fighting on behalf of Matilda, was defeated by King Stephen's army under Raoul, Bishop of Durham, and Thurstan, Archbishop of York It received its name from a ship's mast erected on a wagon, and placed in the centre of the English army, the mast displayed the banner of St Peter of York, St John of Beverley, and St Wilfred of Ripon On the top was a little casket containing the consecrated Host

 The gold standard A monetary standard based only on the value of gold

 The standard of living. A conventional term to express the supposed degree of comfort or luxury usually enjoyed by a man, a family, or a nation this may be *high* or *low* according to circumstances

Stang. To ride the stang. At one time a man who ill-treated his wife was made to sit on a *stang* (A S *stæng*, a pole) ho.sted on men's shoulders On this uneasy conveyance the "stanger" was carried in procession amidst the hootings and jeerings of his neighbours *Cp* SKIMMINGTON

Stanhope (stăn' óp) The **Stanhope lens,** a cylindrical lens with spherical ends of different radii, and the **Stanhope press,** the first iron printing press to be used (1798), are so called from the inventor, Charles, 3rd Earl of Stanhope (1753-1816)

The light open-seated carriage, with two or four wheels, called a **Stanhope,** gets its name from Fitzroy Stanhope (1787-1864), for whom the first of these conveyances was made

Stannaries, The. The tin-mining districts of Cornwall and Devon (Lat *stannum,* tin), which, from the earliest times to 1752 had their own parliament, consisting of twenty-four *stannators,* convened by the Lord Warden to the Duke of Cornwall Until 1896 the administration of justice among the miners and others of these districts was in the hands of *Stannary Courts,* but at this date the business was transferred by Act of Parliament to the ordinary County Court.

Star. Figuratively applied to a specially prominent film or other actor, of either sex, etc , hence **star part,** the part taken by a leading actor, **star turn,** etc

In ecclesiastical art a number of saints may be recognized by the star depicted with them, thus, St Bruno bears one on his breast, St Dominic, St Humbert, St Peter of Alcantara, one over their head, or on their forehead, etc

A star of some form constitutes part of the insignia of every order of knighthood, the Star and Garter, a common inn sign, being in reference to the Most Noble Order of the Garter

The stars were said by the old astrologers to have almost omnipotent influence on the lives and destinies of man (*cp Judges* v, 20—"The stars in their courses fought against Sisera"), and to this old belief is due a number of phrases still common, as—**Bless my stars! You may thank your lucky stars, star-crossed** (not favoured by the stars, unfortunate), **to be born under an evil star,** etc

She made it plain, that Human Passion
Was order'd by Predestination,
That, if weak women went astray,
Their Stars were more in Fault than They.
PRIOR. *Hans Carvel*

His star is in the ascendant He is in luck's way, said of a person to whom some good fortune has fallen and who is very prosperous According to astrology, those leading stars which are above the horizon at a person's birth influence his life and fortune, when those stars are in the ascendant, he is strong, healthy, and lucky, but when they are in the descendant below the horizon, his stars do not shine on him, he is in the shade and subject to ill-fortune *Cp* HOUSES, ASTROLOGICAL

I'll make you see stars! "I'll put you through it"; literally, will give you such a blow in the eye with my fist that, when you are struck, you'll experience the optical illusion of seeing

brilliant streaks, radiating and darting in all directions.

Star Chamber. A court of civil and criminal jurisdiction at Westminster, abolished in 1641, and notorious for its arbitrary proceedings, its chief activity being the punishment of such offences as the law had made no provision for

So called either because the ceiling or roof was decorated with gilt stars, or because it was the chamber where the "starrs" or Jewish documents were kept

It is well known that, before the banishment of the Jews by Edward I, their contracts and obligations were denominated   starra or stars .   The room in the exchequer where the chests   were kept was   the star-chamber —BLACKSTONE. *Commentaries,* vol ii, bk iv, p 266

Star of Bethlehem. A bulbous plant of the lily family (*Ornithogallum umbellatum*), with star-shaped white flowers The French peasants call it *La dame d'onze heures,* because it opens at eleven o'clock.

Star of David. A large yellow cloth star which Jews and persons of Jewish descent were forced to wear on their clothes under the Nazi and Fascist regimes To express his disapproval of this racial indignity King Christian X of Denmark himself wore a Star of David during the German occupation of his country

Star of India. A British order of knighthood, *The Most Exalted Order of the Star of India,* instituted in 1861 by Queen Victoria as a reward for services in and for India and a means of recognizing the loyalty of native rulers. Its motto is "Heaven's Light our Guide "

Stars and Bars. The flag of the eleven Confederate States of America who broke away from the Union in 1860. It consisted of two broad horizontal red bars with a narrow white bar between them, in the top left corner a blue union bearing eleven white stars arranged in a circle

Stars and Stripes or the **Star-spangled Banner,** the flag of the United States of North America The *stripes* are emblematic of the original thirteen States, and the *stars*—of which there are now forty-eight—of the States that now constitute the Union

The first flag of the United States, raised by Washington June 2, 1776, consisted of thirteen stripes, alternately red and white, with a blue canton emblazoned with the crosses of St George and St. Andrew

In 1777 Congress ordered that the canton should have thirteen white stars in a blue field

In 1794 (after the admission of Vermont and Kentucky) the stripes and stars were each increased to fifteen.

In 1818 it was decided that the original thirteen stripes should be restored, and stars added to signify the States in the union

The flag preceding 1776 represented a coiled rattlesnake with thirteen rattles, and the motto *Don't tread on me* This was an imitation of the Scotch thistle and the motto *Nemo me impune lacessit*

Oh' say, does that star-spangled banner yet wave
O'er the land of the free and the home of the brave?
F S KEY

Starboard and Larboard. Star- is the Anglo-Saxon *steor,* rudder, *bord,* side, meaning the right side of a ship (looking forwards) Larboard, for the left-hand side, is now obsolete, and "port" is used instead The word was earlier *leereboard* (A.S *lære*, empty) that side being clear as the steersman stood on the star (*steer*) board

Starvation Dundas. Henry Dundas, Horace Lord Melville (1740-1811) was so called by Walpole, because when the Opposition denounced the Bill for restraining trade and commerce with the New England colonies (1775) on the ground that it would cause a famine in which the innocent would suffer with the guilty, he said that he was "afraid" the Bill would not have this effect The word "starvation" was first used by Dundas

Starved With Cold. Half dead with cold (A.S. *steorfan*, to die).

States, The A common term for the United States of America

States General. The supreme legislative assembly of France before the Revolution of 1789 It was only summoned as a last resort, prior to 1789 not having been called since 1614 It consisted of the three Estates of the realm, nobles, clergy, and the Third Estate (*Tiers etat*) or commoners The name is still applied to the parliament of the kingdom of the Netherlands

Station. This word with the meaning of a place where people assemble for a specific duty or purpose has many applications, *e g* a railway station (U S.A depot), a police station, lifeboat station, etc In Australia it was used as early as 1830 in the sense of a cattle farm or ranch Thus, **station black**, an aboriginal; **station super**, a manager, **station mark**, a brand, **station jack**, a sort of meat pudding.

The Stations of the Cross, known as the *via Calvaria* or *via Crucis*. Each station represents, by fresco, picture, or otherwise, some incident in the passage of Christ from the judgment hall to Calvary, and at each prayers are offered up in memory of the event represented They are as follows —
(1) The condemnation to death
(2) Christ is made to bear His cross
(3) His first fall under the cross
(4) The meeting with the Virgin
(5) Simon the Cyrenean helps to carry the cross
(6) Veronica wipes the sacred face
(7) The second fall
(8) Christ speaks to the daughters of Jerusalem
(9) The third fall
(10) Christ is stripped of His garments
(11) The nailing to the cross
(12) The giving up of the Spirit
(13) Christ is taken down from the cross.
(14) The deposition in the sepulchre

Stator (stā' tôr) (Lat , the stopper or arrester) When the Romans fled from the Sabines, they stopped at a certain place and made terms with the victors On this spot they afterwards built a temple to Jupiter and called it the temple of Jupiter Stator or Jupiter who caused them to stop in their flight
> Here, Stator Jove and Phœbus, god of verse
> The votive tablet I suspend   PRIOR

Statute (Lat *statutum*, from *statuere*, to cause to stand, the same word, etymologically, as *statue*) A law enacted by a legislative body, an Act of Parliament, also laws enacted by the king and council before there were any regular parliaments Hence, a *statute mile*, a *statute ton*, etc , is the measure as by law established and not according to local custom

On the statute book. Included among the laws of the nation the *statute book* is the whole body of the laws

Statute fair. A mop fair *See* MOP.

Steaks, Sublime Society of the. *See* BEEFSTEAK CLUB, THE

Steal. One man may steal a horse, but another must not look over the hedge. *See* HORSE.

To steal a march on one. To obtain an advantage by stealth, as when an army appears unexpectedly before an enemy

Stolen sweets are always sweeter. Things procured by stealth, and game illicitly taken, have the charm of illegality to make them the more palatable Solomon says, "Stolen waters are sweet. and bread eaten in secret is pleasant" (*Prov.* IX, 17)
> From busie cooks we love to steal a bit
> Behind their backs and that in corners eat,
> Nor need we here the reason why entreat,
> All know the proverb, "Stolen bread is sweet."
>   *History of Joseph*, n d

In one of the songs in Act III, sc IV, of Randolph's *Amyntas* (1638) are the lines —
> Furto cuncta magis bella,
> Furto dulcior Puella,
> Furto omnia decora,
> Furto poma dulciora,

which were translated by Leigh Hunt as:—
> Stolen sweets are always sweeter,
> Stolen kisses much completer,
> Stolen looks are nice in chapels,
> Stolen, stolen, be your apples.

Steelyard. A place (formerly a *yard* or enclosure) on the Thames just above London Bridge, where the Hanse merchants had their depot The name is a mistranslation of Ger. *staalhof*, sample yard, *staal* meaning both *sample* and *steel*

Steelyard, the weighing machine with unequal arms, in which the article to be weighed is hung from the shorter arm and a weight moved along the other till they balance, is named from the metal and the measure (A S. *gyrd*, *gerd*, a stick).

Steene. A nickname given by James I to the handsome George Villiers, Duke of Buckingham The allusion is to *Acts* VI, 15, where those who looked on Stephen the martyr "saw his face as it had been the face of an angel."

Steeplechase A horse-race across fields, hedges, ditches, and other obstacles The term arose in the late 18th century from a party of foxhunters agreeing, on their return from an unsuccessful chase, to race in a direct line to the village church, the steeple of which was in sight, regardless of anything that happened to lie in the way

For the principal English steeplechases, *see* RACES

Steeple house. The old Puritan epithet for a church

Stentor (sten' tôr) **The voice of a Stentor** A very loud voice Stentor was a Greek herald in the Trojan war According to Homer (*Iliad*

v. 783), his voice was as loud as that of fifty men combined, hence **stentorian,** loud voiced.

Step-. A prefix used before *father, mother, brother, sister, son, daughter,* etc , to indicate that the person spoken of is a relative only by the marriage of a parent, and not by blood (A.S *stéop,* connected with *astieped,* bereaved) Thus, a man who marries a widow with children becomes *stepfather* to those children, and if he has children by her these and those of the widow's earlier marriage are *stepbrothers* or *stepsisters* The latter are also called *half-brothers* and *half-sisters,* but some make a distinction between the terms, *half-brother* being kept for what we have already defined as a *stepbrother,* this latter term being applied only between the children of former marriages when both parents have been previously married.

I feel like a stepchild Said by one who is being left out of the fun or getting none of the titbits. Step-children are proverbially treated by the step-parent with somewhat less consideration than the others

Stephen, St. The first Christian martyr—the "protomartyr " He was accused of blasphemy and stoned to death (*Acts* vii, 58) He is commemorated on December 26th, the name means "wreath" or "crown" (Gr *stephanos*)

Fed with St. Stephen's bread Stoned

The Crown of St. Stephen. The crown of Hungary, this St Stephen being the first king of Hungary (1000-38) He was a pagan, born at Gran about 969, and was converted to Christianity about 995 During his reign the faith became firmly established in his kingdom He was canonized by Benedict IX shortly after his death, and is commemorated on September 2nd

If Hungarian independence should be secured through the help of Prince Napoleon, the Prince himself should receive the crown of St Stephen — Kossuth *Memoirs of my Exile* (1880)

Sterling, when applied to coins and metal, denotes that they are of standard value (92 5 parts of silver to 7 5 of copper or other metal), genuine, hence applied figuratively to anything of sound, intrinsic worth, as *A man of sterling qualities.* The word—first met with about the early 12th century—has been held to be a corruption of *Easterlings,* the Hanse merchants trading with England, but this is unlikely, and the suggestions are that it is either *steorling,* the coin with a star, some of the early Norman coins having a small star on them, or the bird *starling,* some of Edward the Confessor's coins bearing four martlets.

Stern. To sit at the stern, At the stern of public affairs. Having the management of public affairs The stern is the *steorne,* or steering-place, hence the helm

Sit at chiefest stern of public weal
1 Henry VI, i, 1

Sternhold and Hopkins. The old metrical version of the Psalms that used to be bound up with the Book of Common Prayer and sung in churches. They were mainly the work of Thomas Sternhold (d. 1549) and John Hopkins (d 1570) The completed version appeared in 1562.

Mistaken choirs refuse the solemn strain
Of ancient Sternhold —Crabbe *Borough*

Stet (Lat , let it stand) An author's or editor's direction to the printer to cancel a correction previously made in a MS , proof, etc

Stew. In a stew. In a fix, a flurry; in a state of mental agitation.

Irish stew A dish made by stewing together meat, onions, and potatoes Called "Irish" from the predominance of potatoes.

To stew in one's own juice. To suffer the natural consequences of one's actions, to reap as you have sown. Chaucer has —

In his own gress I made him frie,
For anger and for verry jalousie
Wife of Bath's Tale (Prologue)

The Russian ambassador, when Louis Philippe fortified Paris, remarked, if ever again Paris is in insurrection, it "can be made to stew in its own gravy (jus)", and Bismarck, at the siege of Paris, in 1871, said, the Germans intend to leave the city "to seethe in its own milk "

Stick. An old stick-in-the-mud. A dull, unprogressive old fogy

It sticks out a mile! Said to one who is trying to conceal some very obvious fault, disability, undesirable characteristic, etc., concerning that, as, "Anyone can see he's a welsher—it sticks out a mile ! "

Over the sticks. Over the hurdles hence, a hurdle-race, or steeplechase

The policy of the big stick. Threats, with some show of warlike attitude to back them up, and the same as "rattling the sword in the scabbard " The phrase was a favourite one with President Theodore Roosevelt

The sticking-place The point at which a screw becomes tight, hence, the point aimed at Shakespeare's use of the word is probably an allusion from the peg of a musical instrument, which is not much use unless it is actually at the "sticking-place "

We fail!
But screw your courage to the sticking-place,
And we'll not fail   *Macbeth,* i, 7

The wrong end of the stick. Not the true facts, a distorted version *To have got hold of the wrong end of the stick* is to have misunderstood the story.

To cut one's stick. *See* Cut.

To stick at nothing To be heedless of all obstacles in accomplishing one's desire, to be utterly unscrupulous

To stick it up. Old slang for leaving one's "score" at the tavern to be paid later, a note of it was stuck, or chalked up, at the back of the door.

To stick up. Australian for to waylay and rob a coach, etc , also in common use for raiding a bank and so on in daylight, the raiders closing the doors and covering all present with revolvers telling them to "stick 'em up," or hold up their hands above their heads.

Stuck up. Said of pretentious people who give themselves airs, nobodies who assume to be somebodies The allusion is to the peacock, which sucks up its train to add to its "importance" and "awe down" antagonists.

To stare like a stuck pig. *See* PIG

Stickit. A Scotticism for "stuck (*stick-ed*) half-way," as a stickit job, one that is unfinished or unsatisfactory, hence, applied to persons who have given up their work through lack of means or capacity or some other reason, as a *stickit minister*, one who has failed to get a pastoral charge, or to obtain preferment.

Stickler. A stickler over trifles One particular about things of no moment *Sticklers* were the umpires in tournaments, or seconds in single combats, very punctilious about the minutest points of etiquette The word is connected with A S *stihtan*, to arrange, regulate

Stiff Slang for a corpse, also for a horse that is sure to lose in a race, also (with reference to the stiff interest exacted by moneylenders) an I O U, a bill of acceptance
His "stiff" was floating about in too many directions, at too many high figures —OUIDA *Under Two Flags*, ch. vii

Stigmata (stig' må ta) Marks developed on the body of certain persons, which correspond to some or all of the wounds received by our Saviour in His trial and crucifixion. It is a well-known psychological phenomenon and has been demonstrated in many modern instances From Gr *stigma*, the brand with which slaves and criminals in ancient Greece and Rome were marked, hence our verb stigmatize, to mark as with a brand of disgrace.
Among those who are said to have been marked with the stigmata are—
(1) MEN. St. Paul, who said "I bear in my body the marks of the Lord Jesus" (*Gal* vi, 17), Angelo del Paz (all the marks), Benedict of Reggio (the crown of thorns), 1602, Carlo di Saeta (the lance-wound), Francis of Assisi (all the marks), September 15th, 1224, and Nicholas of Ravenna
(2) WOMEN Bianca de Gazeran, Catharine of Siena, Catharine di Raconisco (the crown of thorns), 1583, Cecilia di Nobili of Nocera 1655, Clara di Pugny (mark of the spear), 1514, "Estatica" of Caldaro (all the marks), 1842, Gabriella da Piezolo of Aquila (the spear-mark), 1472, Hieronyma Carvaglio (the spear-mark, which bled every Friday), Joanna Maria of the Cross, Maria Razzi of Chio (marks of the thorny crown), Maria Villani (ditto); Mary Magdalen di Pazzi; Mechtildis von Stanz, Ursula of Valencia, Veronica Giuliani (all the marks) 1694, Vincenza Ferreri of Valencia, Anna Emmerich, of Dulmen, Westphalia (d 1824), Maria von Morl (in 1839), Louise Lateau (1860), and Anne Girling, the foundress of the English "Shakers" (*q v*) Theresa Neumann, of Kennersreuth, Germany, (b 1898) received her first stigmata on the tops of her hands and feet, on Good Friday, 1926 In subsequent years more marks appeared, on her side, shoulders, and brow Stigmata, as studied in her case, never heal and never suppurate

Stilo Novo (stī' lō nō' vō) (Lat., in the new style). Newfangled notions. When the calendar was reformed by Gregory XIII (1582), letters used to be dated *stilo novo*, which grew in time to be a cant phrase for any innovation
And so I leave you to your *stilo novo*.
BEAUMONT AND FLETCHER *Woman's Prize*, iv, 4.

Stir Up Sunday. The last Sunday in Trinity. So called from the first two words of the collect "Stir up, we beseech Thee, O Lord, the wills of Thy faithful people . . ". It was an old custom to stir the Christmas plum pudding on this day, hence the old schoolboy rhyme beginning, "Stir up, we beseech thee, the pudding in the pot "

Stirrup. Literally, a rope to climb by (A S. *stirrap*, from *stigan*, to climb, and *rāp*, a rope)

Stirrup cup A "parting cup," given, especially in the Highlands, to guests on leaving when their feet are in the stirrups. *Cp*. DOCH-AN-DOROCH
Lord Marmion's bugles blew to horse,
Then came the stirrup-cup in course,
Between the baron and his host
No point of courtesy was lost
SCOTT. *Marmion*, i, 21
Among the ancient Romans a "parting cup" was drunk in honour of Mercury to insure sound sleep. *See* Ovid, *Fasti*, ii, 635

Stirrup oil. A beating, a variety of "strap oil" (*q v*.).

Stiver (stī' vêr). Not a stiver. Not a penny, not a cent The stiver (*stuiver*) was a Dutch coin, equal to about a penny
Set him free,
And you shall have your money to a stiver
And present payment
FLETCHER *Beggars' Bush*, i, 3.

Stock. Originally, a tree-trunk, or stem (connected with *stick*), hence, in figurative uses, something fixed, also something regarded as the origin of families, groups, etc , as He comes of a good stock, from a good stem, of good line of descent, Languages of Indo-Germanic stock, etc To worship stocks and stones is to worship idols, *stock* here being taken as a type of a motionless, fixed thing, like a tree-stump The village *stocks*, in which petty offenders were confined by the wrists and ankles, are so called from the stakes or posts at the side In its financial meaning *stock* in the sense of a fund or capital derives from that part of the old wooden tally which the creditor took with him as evidence of the king's debt, the other portion, known as the counterstock remaining in the Exchequer The word was applied to the money which this tally represented, *i e* money lent to the government

It is on the stocks It is in hand, but not yet finished The stocks is the frame in which a ship is placed while building and so long as it is in hand it is said to be or to lie on the stocks.

Live stock. The cattle, sheep, pigs, horses, etc , belonging to a farmer, that part of his "stock in trade" which is alive. In slang use, lice or other parasitical vermin.

Lock, stock, and barrel. *See* LOCK.

Stock-broker, stock-jobber. The *broker* is engaged in the purchase of stocks and shares for clients on commission, the *jobber* speculates in stocks and shares so as to profit by market fluctuations, and acts as an intermediary between buying and selling brokers The jobber must be a member of a Stock Exchange, but a broker need not necessarily be, if he is not he is known as an "outside broker" or a "kerbstone operator " *Cp* BUCKET-SHOP.

Stock in trade. The fixed capital of a business, the goods, tools, and other requisites of a trade or profession.

Stock-rider. The Australian term for one in charge of cattle, *i e* stock He uses a *stock-whip*, and herds his beasts in a *stock-yard*.

To take stock To ascertain how one's business stands by taking an inventory of all goods and so on in hand, balancing one's books, etc , hence, to survey one's position and prospects.

Stockdove. The wild pigeon, so called because it nests in the stocks of hollow trees.

Stockfish Dried cod, cured without salt. In Shakespeare's day the word was often used as a contemptuous epithet of abuse, thus Falstaff shouts at Prince Henry—

Away, you starveling, you elf-skin, you dried neat's tongue, bull's pizzle, you stock-fish'—I *Henry IV*, ii, 4

I will beat thee like a stock-fish Moffat and Bennet, in their *Health's Improvement* (p 262), inform us that dried cod, till it is beaten, is called *buckhorn*, because it is so tough, but after it has been beaten on the stock, it is termed stockfish.

Peace' thou wilt be beaten like a stockfish else — JONSON· *Every Man in his Humour*, iii, 2

Stocking Used of one's savings or "nest-egg," because formerly money used to be hoarded up in an old stocking, which was frequently hung up the chimney for safety

Blue stocking. *See under* BLUE.

Stockwell Ghost. A supposed ghost that created a great sensation in Stockwell, London, in 1772. The author of the strange noises was Anne Robinson, a servant *Cp* COCK LANE.

Stoga, Stogy (U S A). An abbreviation of Conestoga Applied to farmers' rough shoes, and to common cigars

Stoic (stō′ ik) A school of Greek philosophers (founded by Zeno, about 308 B C) who held that virtue was the highest good, and that the passions and appetites should be rigidly subdued It was so called because Zeno gave his lectures in the *Stoa Poikile*, the Painted Porch (*see* PORCH) of Athens.

Epictetus was the founder of the New Stoic school (1st cent A D).

The ancient Stoics in their porch
With fierce dispute maintained their church,
Beat out their brains in fight and study
To prove that virtue is a body,
That *bonum* is an animal,
Made good with stout polemic bawl.
BUTLER *Hudibras*, ii, 2

Stole (Lat *stola*) An ecclesiastical vestment, also called the Orarium. Deacons wear the stole over the left shoulder, and loop the two parts together, that they may both hang on the right side. Priests wear it over both shoulders and hanging loose in front.

Stole, Groom of the. Formerly, the first lord of the bedchamber, a high officer of the Royal Household ranking next after the vice-chamberlain. The office was allowed to lapse on the accession of Queen Victoria, in the reign of Queen Anne it was held by a woman

Stole, here, is not connected with Lat. *stola*, a robe, but refers to the king's *stool*, or privy As late as the 16th century, when the king made a royal progress his close-stool formed part of the baggage and was in charge of a special officer or groom.

Stolen Things. *See under* STEAL.

Stomach. Used figuratively of inclination, appetite, etc
He who hath no stomach for this fight —SHAKE-SPEARE *Henry V*, iv, 3
Wolsey was a man of an unbounded stomach — *Henry VIII*, iv, 2
Let me praise you while I have the stomach.— *Merchant of Venice*, iii, 5

To stomach an insult. To swallow it and not resent it
If you must believe, stomach not all —SHAKE-SPEARE: *Antony and Cleopatra*, iii, 4.

Stone. Used in a figurative sense in many ways when some characteristic of a stone is to be pointed out, as, *stone blind, stone cold, stone dead, stone still*, etc , as blind, cold, dead, or still as a stone
I will not struggle, I will stand stone still.
King John, iv, 1.

In all ages stones, especially those of meteoric origin or those fabled to have "fallen from heaven," have been set up and worshipped by primitive peoples, and the great stone circles of Stonehenge, Avebury, the Orkneys, Carnac, etc , are relics of religious rites Anaxagoras mentions a stone that fell from Jupiter in Thrace, a description of which is given by Pliny. The Ephesians asserted that their image of Diana came from Jupiter. The stone at Emessa, in Syria, worshipped as a symbol of the sun, was a similar meteorite. At Abydos and Potidæa similar stones were preserved At Corinth was one venerated as Zeus At Cyprus was one dedicated to Venus, a description of which is given by Tacitus and Maximus Tyrus Herodian describes one in Syria, and the famous "black stone" (*see* HAJAR AL-ASWAD), set in the Kaaba of the Moslems, is a similar meteorite
After the Moslem pilgrim has made his seven processions round the Kaaba, he repairs to Mount Arafat, and before sunrise enters the valley of Mena, where he throws seven stones at each of three pillars, in imitation of Abraham and Adam, who thus drove away the devil when he disturbed their devotions

A rolling stone gathers no moss One who is always "chopping and changing" and won't settle down will never become wealthy. So says the proverb (which is common to many languages), but it is not always borne out by facts—and its reverse does not hold true.

Tusser, in his *Five Hundred Points of Good Husbandrie* (1573) has—

The stone that is rolling can gather no moss,
For master and servant oft changing is loss.

Hag-stones. Flints naturally perforated, used in country places as charms against witches, the evil eye, etc They are hung on the key of an outer door, round the neck for luck, on the bed-post to prevent nightmare, on a horse's collar to ward off disease, etc

Stone soup or St Bernard's soup. The story goes that a beggar asked alms at a lordly mansion, but was told by the servants they had nothing to give him "Sorry for it," said the man, "but will you let me boil a little water to make some soup of this stone?" This was so novel a proceeding, that the curiosity of the servants was aroused, and the man was readily furnished with saucepan, water, and a spoon In he popped the stone, and begged for a little salt and pepper for flavouring Stirring the water and tasting it, he said it would be the better for any fragments of meat and vegetables they might happen to have These were supplied, and ultimately he asked for a little ketchup or other sauce. When ready the servants tasted it, and declared that "stone soup" was excellent

This story, which was a great favourite in the 16th and 17th centuries, was told with many variations, horseshoes, nails, rams-horns, etc., taking the place of the stone as narrated above.

Stone of stumbling. An obstacle, stumbling-block, or an occasion for being hindered The phrase is from *Isa* viii, 14 —

He shall be . for a stone of stumbling and for a rock of offence to both the houses of Israel

The Standing Stones of Stennis, in the Ork-neys, resemble Stonehenge, but are unlikely to have been Druidical. The custom of constructing these circles was prevalent in Scandinavia as well as in Gaul and Britain, and as common to the mythology of Odin as to Druidism They were places of public assembly, and in the *Eyrbiggia Saga* is described the manner of setting apart the Helga Felt (Holy Rocks) by the pontiff Thorolf for solemn meetings.

The Stone Age. The period when stone implements were used by primitive man It preceded the Bronze Age, and some peoples, such as certain tribes in Papua, have not yet emerged from it *See* PALÆOLITHIC.

The stone jacket or jug. Slang for prison. *See* JUG

To cast the first stone. To take the lead in criticizing, fault-finding, quarrelling, etc. The phrase is from *John* viii, 7 —

He that is without sin among you, let him first cast a stone at her

To kill two birds with one stone. *See* BIRD.

To leave no stone unturned To spare no trouble, time, expense, etc , in endeavouring to accomplish your aim After the defeat of Mardonius at Platæa (477 B C), a report was current that the Persian general had left great treasures in his tent Polycrates the Theban sought long but found them not. The Oracle of

Delphi, being consulted, told him "to leave no stone unturned," and the treasures were discovered

You have stones in your mouth. Said to a person who stutters or speaks very indistinctly Demosthenes cured himself of stuttering by putting pebbles in his mouth and declaiming on the seashore

The orator who once
Did fill his mouth with pebble stones
When he harangued —BUTLER *Hudibras*, i, 1.

See also ÆTITES, PHILOSOPHERS' STONE, PRECIOUS STONES, TOUCHSTONE, etc

Stonebrash A name given in Wiltshire to the subsoil of the north-western border, which consists of a reddish calcareous loam, mingled with flat stones; a soil made of small stones or broken rock.

Stony Arabia. A mistranslation of *Arabia Petræa*, where Petræa is supposed to be an adjective formed from the Greek *petros* (a stone) The name is really taken from the city of Petra, the capital of the Nabathæans. *Cp* YEMEN

Stonehenge. The great prehistoric (Neolithic or early Bronze Age) monument on Salisbury Plain, originally consisting of two concentric circles of upright stones, enclosing two rows of smaller stones, and a central block of blue marble (18 ft by 4 ft.), known as the Altar Stone The Friar's Heel (*q.v.*) stands outside the circle to the NE Many theories as to its original purpose and original builders have been propounded. It was probably used (if not built) by the Druids, and from its plotting, which had an astronomical basis, it is thought to have been the temple of a sun god and to have been built about 1680 B C.

The *-henge* of the name seems to refer to something hanging (A S *hengen*) in, or supported in, the air, viz , the huge transverse stones, but Geoffrey of Monmouth connects it with Hengist, and says that Stonehenge was erected by Merlin to perpetuate the treachery of Hengist in falling upon Vortigern and putting him and his 400 attendants to the sword Aurelius Ambrosius asked Merlin to devise a memento of this event, whereupon the magi-cian transplanted from Ireland the "Giant s Dance" stones which had been brought thither from Africa by a race of giants and all of which possessed magic properties

Stonewall, To. A cricketer's term for adopting purely defensive measures when at the wicket, blocking every ball and not attempting to score It was originally Australian political slang and was used of obstructing business

Stonewall Jackson. Thomas J Jackson (1824-63), one of the Confederate generals in the American Civil War; so called because at the Battle of Bull Run (1861) General Bee, of South Carolina, observing his men to waver, exclaimed, "Look at Jackson's men; they stand like a stone wall!"

Stooge (stooj) The second partner in a comic music-hall act whose role is to be stupid, ask questions, and make the comedian say every-thing twice and very distinctly so that the jokes get over to the audience. Hence the term has

28*

passed into common parlance for a confederate or a decoy.

Stool Pigeon A police spy or informer, also a person employed by gamblers, etc, as a decoy or secret confederate.

Stool of Repentance. The cutty stool, a low stool placed in front of the pulpit in Scottish churches, on which persons who had incurred ecclesiastical censure were placed during divine service When the service was over the penitent had to stand on the stool and receive the minister's rebuke.

Store. Store cattle. Beasts kept on a farm for breeding purposes, or thin cattle bought for fattening.

Store is no sore. Things stored up for future use are no evil *Sore* means grief as well as wound, our *sorrow*

To set store by. To value highly.

Stork. According to the Swedish legend, the stork received its name from flying round the cross of the crucified Redeemer, crying *Styrka ! styrka !* (Strengthen ! strengthen !). Many fables and legends have grown up around this bird. Lyly refers to it more than once in his *Euphues* (1850), as—

Ladies use their lovers as the stork doth her young ones who pecketh them till they bleed with her bill, and then healeth them with her tongue

And again—

Constancy is like unto the stork, who wheresoever she fly cometh into no nest but her own

And—

It fareth with me . as with the stork, who, when she is least able carrieth the greatest burden

Dutch and German mothers tell their children that babies are brought by storks, and another common belief was that the stork, like the secretary bird, will kill snakes "on sight",

'Twill profit when the stork, sworn foe of snakes, Returns, to show compassion to thy plants
PHILIPS *Cyder,* Bk. 1

King Stork. A tyrant that devours his subjects, and makes them submissive with fear and trembling. The allusion is to the fable of *The Frogs desiring a King. See* LOG.

Storks' law or **Lex ciconaria** A Roman law which obliged children to maintain their necessitous parents in old age, "in imitation of the stork " Also called "Antipelargia "

Storm (Austr) Young grass which has grown after a rainfall in dry areas. Travelling from storm to storm is to *storm along*

A brain-storm. A sudden and violent upheaval in the brain, causing temporary loss of control, or even madness *Nerve-storm* is used in much the same way of the nerves

A storm in a teacup. A mighty to-do about a trifle; making a great fuss about nothing

Storm and stress. *See* STURM UND DRANG

The Cape of Storms. So Bartholomew Diaz named the south cape of Africa in 1486, but John II of Portugal (d 1495) changed it to the *Cape of Good Hope*

To take by storm. To seize by a sudden and irresistible attack, a military term used figuratively, as of one who becomes suddenly famous or popular; an actor, suddenly springing to fame, "takes the town by storm "

Stormy Petrel. *See* PETREL

Stornello Verses (stôr nel' ō) are those in which certain words are harped on and turned about and about They are common among the Tuscan peasants The word is from *tornare* (to return)
I'll tell him the *white*, and the *green*, and the *red*, Mean our country has flung the vile yoke from her head,
I'll tell him the *green*, and the *red*, and the *white*, Would look well by his side as a sword-knot so bright,
I'll tell him the *red*, and the *white*, and the *green*, Is the prize that we play for, a prize we will win.
Notes and Queries.

Storthing (stôr' ting) The Norwegian Parliament, elected every three years (*stor*, great, *thing*, assembly).

Stoush (stoush). Australian, a brawl. World War I was known by Australian troops as the *Big Stoush* Probably from English *stashie* an uproar.

Stovepipe Hat. An old-fashioned tall silk hat, a chimney-pot hat (*q v*)
High collars, tight coats, and tight sleeves were worn at home and abroad, and, as though that were not enough, a stovepipe hat —*Illustrated Sporting and Dramatic News,* Sept 1891

Strad. A colloquial name for a violin made by the famous maker Antonio Stradivarius (1644-1737) of Cremona His best period was about 1700 to 1725; he sold his violins for about £4 each, they have since realized as much as £3,000, and one of his 'cellos £4,000.

Strafe (straf) (Ger *strafen*, to punish) A word borrowed in good-humoured contempt from the Germans during World War I One of their favourite slogans was *Gott strafe England !* The word was applied to any sharp and sudden bombardment

Strain. The quality of mercy is not strained (*Merchant of Venice,* iv, 1)—constrained or forced, but cometh down freely as the rain, which is God's gift.

To strain a point. To go beyond one's usual, or the proper, limits, to give way a bit more than one has any right to.

To strain at a gnat and swallow a camel. To make much fuss about little peccadilloes, but commit offences of real magnitude The proverb comes from *Matt* xxiii, 24, which in Tyndale's, Coverdale's, and other early versions reads *to strain out,* etc , meaning to filter out a gnat before drinking the wine The Revised Version also adopts this form, but the Authorized Version's rendering (*to strain at*) was in use well before the date of its issue (1611), so the *at* is not—as has been sometimes stated—a misprint or mistake for *out.* Greene in his *Mamillia* (1583) speaks of "straining at a gnat and letting pass an elephant "

To strain courtesy. To stand upon ceremony. Here, *strain* is *to stretch,* as parchment is strained on a drum-head

Strand, The. One of the most famous of London thoroughfares, leading from the City of London to that of Westminster, along the Riverside, whence its name It was little more than a country road until 1532 when it was paved Nobles and no fewer than nine bishops had their inns or houses in the Strand, and no street in the metropolis has more historical or social associations, though within the last fifty years it has been widened and altered beyond recognition

Stranger. Originally, a foreigner, from O Fr *estrangier* (Mod Fr *étranger*), which is the Latin *extraneus*, one without (*extra*, without)

It is said that Busiris, King of Egypt, sacrificed to his gods all strangers who set foot on his territories Diomed (*q v.*) gave strangers to his horses for food

Floating tea-leaves in one's cup, charred pieces of wick that make the candle gutter, little bits of soot hanging from the bars of the grate, etc , are called "strangers," because they are supposed to foretell the coming of visitors

I spy strangers! The recognized form of words by which a member of Parliament conveys to the Speaker the information that there is an unauthorized person in the House

The little stranger. A new-born infant

The stranger that is within thy gates. *See* PROSELYTES.

Strap. A taste of the strap, or a **strapping** is a flogging, properly with a leather strap

A strapping young fellow. A big, sturdy chap, a robust, vigorous young woman is similarly termed *a strapper.*

Straphanger. One who cannot get a seat in a train, omnibus, etc , and so has to do his journey standing on the floor and clinging to a strap suspended from the roof for the purpose

Strap oil. Slang for a thrashing *See above.*

Strappado (strå pä´ dō) (Ital *strappare*, to pull) A mode of torture formerly practised for extracting confessions, retractations, etc. The hands were tied behind the back, and the victim was pulled up to a beam by a rope tied to them and then let down suddenly, by this means a limb was not infrequently dislocated.

Were I at the strappado or the rack, I'd give no man a reason on compulsion —1 *Henry IV*, ii, 4.

Strassburg Goose A goose fattened, crammed, and confined in order to enlarge its liver from which is made true paté de foie gras

Straw. As used in phrases *straw* is generally typical of that which is worthless, as **Not worth a straw**, quite valueless, not worth a rap, a fig, etc , to care not a **straw**, not to care at all

A man of straw. A man without means, with no more substance than a straw doll also, an imaginary or fictitious person put forward for some reason.

A straw shows which way the wind blows. Mere trifles often indicate the coming of momentous events They are shadows cast before coming events

I have a straw to break with you. I have something to quarrel with you about, or am displeased with you; I have a reproof to give you In feudal times possession of a fief was conveyed by giving a straw to the new tenant. If the tenant misconducted himself, the lord dispossessed him by going to the threshold of his door and breaking a straw, saying as he did so, "As I break this straw, so break I the contract made between us " In allusion to this custom, it is said in *Reynard the Fox*—

The kynge toke up a straw fro the ground and pardoned and forgaf the foxe alle the mysdedes and trespaces of his fader and of hym also.—Ch xvii

on condition that the Fox showed King Lion where the treasures were hid

In the straw. Applied to women in childbirth The allusion is to the straw with which beds were at one time usually stuffed, and not to the litter laid before a house to break the noise of wheels passing by.

The last straw. "'Tis the last straw that breaks the camel's back " There is an ultimate point of endurance beyond which calamity breaks a man down

To catch at a straw. A forlorn hope A drowning man will catch at a straw

To make bricks without straw. To attempt to do something without the proper and necessary materials The allusion is to the exaction of the Egyptian taskmasters mentioned in *Exod.* v 6-14

To pick straws To show fatigue or weariness, as birds pick up straws to make their nests (or bed)

Their eyelids did not once pick straws,
And wink, and sink away,
No, no, they were as brisk as bees,
And loving things did say
, PETER PINDAR *Orson and Ellen*, canto v

To stumble at a straw. To be pulled up short by a trifle

To throw straws against the wind To contend uselessly and feebly against what is irresistible; to sweep back the Atlantic with a besom

Strawberry. So called from *straw*, probably because the achenes with which the surface is dotted somewhat resemble finely chopped straw

We may say of angling as Dr Boteler said of strawberries, "Doubtless God could have made a better berry, but doubtless God never did "—IZAAK WALTON *Compleat Angler*, ch v

Strawberry mark. A birthmark something like a strawberry. In Morton's *Box and Cox* the two heroes eventually recognize each other as long-lost brothers through one of them having a strawberry-mark on his left arm

Strawberry preachers. So Latimer called the non-resident country clergy, because they "come but once a yeare and tarie not long" (*Sermon on the Plough*, 1549)

The strawberry leaves. A dukedom, the honour, rank, etc , of a duke The ducal coronet is ornamented with eight strawberry leaves

Street Arab. *See* BEDOUIN

Strenia (strē' nı a) The goddess who presided over the New Year festivities in ancient Rome Tatius, the legendary Sabine king, entered Rome on New Year's Day, and received from some augurs palms cut from the sacred grove, dedicated to her After his seizure of the city, he ordained that January 1st should be celebrated by gifts to be called *strenæ*, consisting of figs, dates, and honey The French *etrenne*, a New Year's gift, is from this goddess

Strephon (stref' ón). A stock name for a rustic lover, from the languishing lover of that name in Sidney's *Arcadia.*

Strike. A cessation of work by a body of employees with the object of inducing the employers to grant some demand, such as one for higher wages, shorter hours, better working conditions, etc , or sometimes for no direct reason, but out of sympathy for other workers or for the furtherance of some political object A lightning strike is one of which no notice has been given, and the converse of a strike, *i e* the refusal of the masters to allow the men to work until certain conditions are agreed upon or rules complied with, is termed a *lock-out*

The word first appears in this sense in 1768, and seems to have had a nautical origin, sailors who refused to go to sea because of some grievance *struck* (lowered) the yards of their ship

Strike-breaker. A "blackleg," a worker induced by the employer to carry on when the rest of the men have struck

Strike is the name of an old grain measure, still unofficially used in some parts of England, and varying locally from half a bushel to four bushels Probably so called because when filled the top of the measure was "struck off" and so levelled instead of being left heaped up

It strikes me that . . . It occurs to me that . , it comes into my mind that .

Strike-a-light. The flint formerly used with tinder-boxes for striking fire, also, the shaped piece of metal used to strike the flint

The collar of the Order of the Golden Fleece is composed of linked pieces of metal of this shape, and so is sometimes called the "collar of strike-a-lights "

Strike, but hear me! (Lat *verbeı a, sed audı*) Carry out your threats—if you must—but at least hear what I have to say The phrase comes from Plutarch's life of Themistocles. He strongly opposed the proposal of Eurybiades to quit the bay of Salamis The hot-headed Spartan insultingly remarked that 'those who in the public games rise up before the proper signal are scourged." "True," said Themistocles, ' but those who lag behind win no laurels " On this, Eurybiades lifted up his staff to strike him, when Themistocles earnestly but proudly exclaimed, "Strike, but hear me!"

Bacon (*Advancement of Learning*, ıı) calls this "that ancient and patient request."

Strike me dead! blind! etc Vulgar expletives, or exclamations of surprise, dismay, wonder, and so on Strike-me-dead is also sailor's slang for thin, wishy-washy beer.

Strike while the iron is hot. Act while the impulse is still fervent, *or* do what you do at the right time The metaphor is taken from the blacksmith's forge; a horse-shoe must be struck while the iron is red-hot or it cannot be moulded into shape Similar proverbs are· "Make hay while the sun shines," "Take time by the forelock "

To be struck all of a heap. *See* HEAP.

To be struck on a person A colloquialism for to be much interested in him (or her), or to have fallen in love with the person named

To strike an attitude. To pose, to assume an exaggerated or theatrical attitude

To strike a balance. *See* BALANCE.

To strike a bargain (Lat *fœdus ferıre*) To determine or settle it The allusion is to the ancient custom of making a sacrifice in concluding an agreement. After calling the gods to witness, they struck—*ı e* slew—the victim which was offered in sacrifice *Cp* To STRIKE HANDS *below.*

To strike at the foundations. To attempt to undermine the whole thing, to overthrow it utterly

To strike camp. To lower the tents and move off, hence, to abandon one's position A military phrase, adopted from the nautical phrase ' to strike colours." *See* FLAG

To strike hands upon a bargain. To confirm it by shaking or striking hands, to ratify it *Cp.* To STRIKE A BARGAIN *above*

To strike lucky. To have an unexpected piece of good fortune, a phrase from the miner's camps To strike oil (*see* OIL) means much the same thing, and has a similar origin

To strike one's colours, or flag. *See* FLAG.

To strike out in another direction. To open up a new way for oneself, to start a new method, a fresh business

To strike sail. To acknowledge oneself beaten, to eat humble pie A nautical expression. When a ship in fight or on meeting another ship, let down her topsails at least half-mast high, she was said to *strike*, meaning that she submitted or paid respect to the other.

> Now Margaret
> Must strike her sail, and learn awhile to serve
> When kings command
> *3 Henry VI*, iii, 3

To strike up. To begin, start operations. as *to strike up an acquaintance*, to set it going Originally of an orchestra or company of singers, who "struck up" the music

Willing to wound, and yet afraid to strike. Said of one who dare not do the injury or take the revenge that he wishes. The "tag" is from Pope's *Epistle to Dr Arbuthnot* (1735)

String. Always harping on one string. Always talking on one subject, always repeating the same thing. The allusion is to the ancient harpers

To have two strings to one's bow. *See* Bow.

Strip. To tear a strip off a person. To give him a severe reprimand

Strip-tease. A theatrical or cabaret performance in which an actress slowly and provocatively undresses herself

Stroke. The oarsman who sits on the bench next the coxswain, and sets the time of the stroke for the rest

To stroke one the wrong way. To vex him, ruffle his temper

Strong. A strong verb is one that forms inflexions by internal vowel-change (such as *bind, bound, speak, spoke*); weak verbs add a syllable, or letter (as *love, loved, refund, refunded*)

Going strong. Prospering, getting on famously, in excellent state of health.

To come it strong *See* COME.

Strontium (stron' shŭm) This element, a yellowish metal resembling calcium, receives its name from Strontian, in Argyllshire, where it was discovered in 1792 by Thomas Charles Hope (1766-1844)

Struldbrugs (strŭld' brŭgz) Wretched inhabitants of Luggnagg (in Swift's *Gulliver's Travels*), who had the privilege of immortality without having eternal vigour, strength, and intellect

Stubble Geese The geese turned into the stubble-fields to pick up the corn left after harvest

Stuck up *See* STICK

Stuff Gown. A barrister (*q v*) who has not yet 'taken silk," *i e* become a Q C *See* SILK

Stuka (stū' kå) A German dive-bombing aeroplane in World War II, from *Stutzkampfbomber*

Stumer (stū' mer) A swindle, or a swindler, a forged banknote or "dud" cheque a fictitious bet recorded by the bookmakers, and published in the papers, to deceive the public by running up the odds on a horse which is not expected to win

Stump A stump orator. A ranting, bombastic speaker, who harangues all who will listen to him from some point of vantage in the open air, such as the stump of a tree, a "tub-thumper," mob orator. Hence such phrases as *to stump the country, to take to the stump,* to go from town to town making inflammatory speeches

Stumped out. Outwitted, put down A term borrowed from cricket

To stir one's stumps. To get on faster, to set upon something expeditiously
> This makes him stirre his stumps
> *The Two Lancashire Lovers* (1640)

The stumps are the legs, or wooden legs fastened to stumps of mutilated limbs
> For Witherington needs must I wayle,
> As one in doleful dumpes,
> For when his leggs were smitten off,
> He fought upon his stumpes
> *Ballad of Chevy Chase.*

To stump up To pay one's reckoning, pay what is due. Ready money is called *stumpy* or *stumps* An Americanism, meaning money paid down on the spot—*i e* on the stump of a tree *Cp* NAIL, ON THE.

Stunt A feat, performance, especially one of a startling or sensational nature Hence, *to stunt*, to do something surprising or hazardous, an aerobatic turn or trick; a newspaper stunt, a movement, party cry, sensation, etc, worked by a newspaper and boomed by publicity men

The word was originally American college slang for some exceptional athletic feat

Stupor Mundi So the Emperor Frederick II (1194-1250) was called, as being the greatest sovereign, soldier, and patron of artists and scholars during the 13th century

Sturm und Drang (stoorm und drang) (Ger, storm and stress) The name given to the intellectual awakening of Germany towards the close of the 18th century It had a considerable effect on our own Romantic Movement, and was so called from a drama of that name by Friedrich Maximilian von Klinger (1752-1831). Goethe and Schiller contributed to the movement.

Sty, an inflamed pimple on the eyelid, is shortened from the earlier *styany* (taken as meaning *sty-on-eye*), which is from A S *stigend,* something that rises (*stīgan,* to rise)

Stygian (stĭ' ji an) Infernal, gloomy; pertaining to the river Styx (*q v*).
> At that so sudden blaze the Stygian throng
> Bent their aspect —MILTON *Paradise Lost,* x, 453

Style is from the Latin *stylus* (a metal pencil for writing on waxen tablets, etc). The characteristic of a person's writing is called his style Metaphorically it is applied to composition and speech Good writing is *stylish,* and, by extension, smartness of dress and deportment is so called
> Style is the dress of thought, and a well-dressed thought like a well-dressed man, appears to great advantage —CHESTERFIELD *Letter* ccxl

The style is the man. A mistranslation of "Le style, c'est de l'homme même" from the discourse of Buffon (1707-88) on his reception into the French Academy

New style, Old style. *See* CALENDAR.

To do a thing in style. To do it splendidly, regardless of expense

Styles. Tom Styles or John a Styles, connected with *John-a-Nokes* (*q v*) an imaginary plaintiff or defendant in a law suit or an ancient order of ejectment, like "John Doe" and "Richard Roe '"
> And, like blind Fortune, with a sleight
> Convey men's interest and right
> From Stiles's pocket into Nokes's
> BUTLER *Hudibras,* iii, 3

Stylites or **Pillar Saints** (stī lī' tēz) A class of early and mediæval ascetics, chiefly of Syria, who took up their abode on the tops of pillars, from which they never descended The most celebrated are Simeon Stylites, of Syria, and Daniel the Stylite of Constantinople Simeon (390-459) spent forty years on different pillars, each loftier and narrower than the preceding, the last being 66 feet high. Daniel (d. 494) lived thirty-three years on a pillar, and was not infrequently nearly blown from it by the storms from Thrace This form of asceticism was in vogue as late as the 16th century.

Styx (stiks) The river of Hate (Gr *stugein*, to hate)—called by Milton ' abhorred Styx, the flood of burning hate" (*Paradise Lost*, ii, 577)—that, according to classical mythology, flowed nine times round the infernal regions
The fables about the Styx are of Egyptian origin, and we are told that Isis collected the various parts of Osiris (murdered by Typhon) and buried them in secrecy on the banks of the Styx Charon (*q v.*), as Diodorus informs us, is an Egyptian word for a ' ferryman '' If the gods swore by the Styx, they dared not break their oath
> By the black infernal Styx I swear
> (That dreadful oath which binds the Thunderer)
> 'Tis fixed! POPE *Thebais of Statius*, 1

Suaviter (swä' vi ter). *Suaviter in modo, fortiter in re* (Lat.), gentle in manner, resolute in action Said of one who does what is to be done with unflinching firmness, but in the most inoffensive manner possible

Sub hasta (sŭb hăs' ta) (Lat). By auction When an auction took place among the Romans, it was customary to stick a spear in the ground to give notice of it to the public, literally, under the spear *Cp* SPEAR.

Sub Jove (Lat) Under Jove, in the open air Jupiter is the god of the upper regions of the air, as Juno is of the lower regions, Neptune of the waters of the sea, Vesta of the earth, Ceres of the surface soil, and Hades of the invisible or under-world

Sub judice. Under judicial consideration, not yet decided or awarded in a court of law

Sub rosa. *See* ROSE.

Subject and Object. In metaphysics the *Subject* is the ego, the mind, the conscious self, the substance or substratum to which attributes must be referred, the *Object* is an external as distinct from the ego, a thing or idea brought before the consciousness Hence *subjective criticism, art*, etc , is that which proceeds from the individual mind and is consequently individualistic, fanciful, imaginative, while *objective criticism* is that which is based on knowledge of the externals.

Subject-object. The immediate object of thought as distinguished from the material thing of which one is thinking
The thought is necessarily and universally subject-object Matter is necessarily, and to us universally, object-subject —LEWES *History of Philosophy*, II 485

Sublapsarian (or **Infralapsarian**) (sŭb lăp sâr' i an) A Calvinist who maintains that God devised His scheme of redemption *after* he had permitted the "lapse" or fall of Adam, when He elected some to salvation and left others to run their course The *supra*-lapsarian maintains that all this was ordained by God from the foundation of the world, and therefore *before* the "lapse" or fall of Adam

Sublime. From Lat *sub*, up to, *limen*, the lintel, hence, lofty, elevated in thought or tone.

From the sublime to the ridiculous is only one step. A favourite saying of Napoleon's, *Du sublime au ridicule il n'y a qu'un pas*, probably taken from Tom Paine, who has—
> The sublime and the ridiculous are so often so nearly related that it is difficult to class them separately One step above the sublime makes the ridiculous, and one step above the ridiculous makes the sublime again —*Age of Reason* Pt ii (*note*)

The Sublime Porte. *See* PORTE.

The Sublime Society of Steaks. *See* BEEF-STEAK CLUB.

Submerged or **Submerged Tenth, The** The proletariat, sunk or submerged in poverty
All but the 'submerged" were bent upon merry-making —*Society*, Nov 12th, 1892, p 1273

Subpœna (sŭb pē' na) (Lat , under penalty) is a writ commanding a man to appear in court usually unwillingly to bear witness or give evidence on a certain trial named It is so called because the party summoned is bound to appear *sub pœna centum librorum* (under a penalty of £100) We have the verb *to sub-pœna*.

Subsidy (Lat *sub-sedere*, to sit down) The *subsidii* of the Roman army were the troops held in reserve, the auxiliaries, supports, hence the word came to be applied to a support generally, and (in English) specially to financial support granted by Parliament to the king It now usually means a contribution granted by the state in aid of some commercial venture of public importance.

Subsidiary, auxiliary, supplemental, is, of course, from the same word.

Subtle Doctor, The (*Doctor Subtilis*). The Scottish schoolman and Franciscan friar, Duns Scotus (about 1265-1308)

Succotash (U S A) A dish of Indian corn and beans boiled together Originally an Indian dish

Succoth The Jewish name for the Feast of Tabernacles (Heb *sukkoth*, booths) *See* TABERNACLE

Suck, or **Suck-in** A swindle, hoax, deception, a fiasco

Sucking is used (after *sucking-pig*) of a youth who is training for something, as, *a sucking lawyer*, an articled clerk, *a sucking curate*, a student at a theological college who is trying his hand at parochial work

To suck the monkey. *See* MONKEY

To teach one's grandmother to suck eggs. *See* EGGS

Sudetenland (soo dā' tĕn land) A mountainous region on the old Czech-German frontier, inhabited principally by Germans though the territory was—and is—actually in Czecho-slovakia The annexation of this land was claimed by the German Nazis and a European war was only averted or postponed in 1938 by its cession to Germany at the expense of Czechoslovakia Sudetenland was restored to the latter country in 1945.

Suède (swād) Undressed kid-skin; so called because the gloves made of this originally came from Sweden (Fr *gants de Suede*)

Suffering. The Meeting for Sufferings. The standing representative Committee of the Yearly Meeting of the Society of Friends (Quakers), which deals with questions affecting the Society, so called because when originally appointed in the 17th century its chief function was to relieve the sufferings caused to Quakers by distraint for tithes, persecution, etc

Suffragan (sŭf' ra găn) An auxiliary bishop, one who has not a see of his own but is appointed to assist a bishop in a portion of his see In relation to a metropolitan or archbishop all bishops are suffragans, and they were so called because they could be summoned to a synod to give their *suffrage*

Suffrage. One's vote, approval, consent, or, one's right to vote, especially at parliamentary and municipal elections. The word is from Lat. *suffrago*, the hough or ankle-bone of a horse, which was used by the Romans for balloting with, whence the voting table came to be called *suffragium*

Hence **Suffragette,** a woman (usually more or less "militant") who in the ten years or so preceding World War I "agitated" for the parliamentary vote The Suffragettes' campaigns of disturbance, violence, assault, wanton destruction of public property, arson, and attempted terrorism (for which many women were imprisoned and went on "hunger-strike") reached alarming proportions; but it stopped dead on the outbreak of War, and in 1918 women of 30 were not only enfranchised but made eligible for seats in Parliament In 1928 enfranchisement was made on the same terms as for men

The 19th Amendment of the Constitution of the United States of America enacted Woman Suffrage in August, 1920

Sui generis (sū' ĭ jen' er is) (Lat , of its own kind) Having a distinct character of its own, unlike anything else

Sui juris (Lat) Of one's own right, the state of being able to exercise one's legal rights—*i e* freedom from legal disability

Suicides were formerly buried ignominiously on the high-road, with a stake thrust through their body, and without Christian rites (Lat. *sui,* of oneself *-cidium,* from *cædere,* to kill)

> They buried Ben at four cross roads,
> With a stake in his inside
>   HOOD *Faithless Nelly Gray*

Suit. A suit of dittoes *See* DITTO

To follow suit. To follow the leader, to do as those do who are taken as your exemplars. The term is from games of cards

Sultan (Arab , king, *cp* SOLDAN) The chief ruler of Turkey, and of some other Mohammedan countries, as Oman, Zanzibar, and—since 1914 (*cp* KHEDIVE)—Egypt

The wife (or sometimes the mother, sister, or concubine) of the Sultan is the Sultana, a name also given to a small, seedless raisin grown near Smyrna and to the purple gallinule

(*Porphyrio cæruleus*), a beautiful bird allied to the moorhen

> Some purple-wing'd Sultana sitting
>   Upon a column, motionless
> And glittering, like an idol-bird.
>   MOORE *Paradise and the Peri*

Summer. The second or autumnal summer, said to last thirty days, begins shortly before the sun enters Scorpio (Oct 23rd). It is variously called—

St. Martin's summer, a late spell of fine weather. St Martin's Day is Nov 11th

> Expect St Martin's summer, halcyon days
>   1 *Henry VI,* i, 2

All Saints' or **All Hallows' summer** (All Saints' is Nov 1st)

> Farewell, All Hallowen summer —1 *Henry IV,* i, 2.

St Luke's little summer (St Luke's day is Oct 18th), and—especially in the United States—the Indian summer.

Summer Time. *See* TIME

Summum bonum (sŭm' ŭm bŏ' nŭm) (Lat., the highest good) The chief excellence, the highest attainable good

Socrates said knowledge is virtue, and ignorance is vice

Aristotle said that happiness is the greatest good

Bernard de Mandeville and *Helvetius* contended that self-interest is the perfection of the ethical end

Bentham and *Mill* were for the greatest happiness of the greatest number

Herbert Spencer placed it in those actions which best tend to the survival of the individual and the race, and

Robert Browning (see his poem of this name) "in the kiss of one girl "

Sumptuary Laws Laws to limit the expenses of food and dress, or any luxury. The Romans had their *leges sumptuariæ,* and they have been enacted in many states at various times. Those of England were all repealed by 1 James I c 25, but during the two World Wars, with the rationing of food, coals, etc, and the compulsory lowering of the strength of beer and whisky we had a temporary return to sumptuary legislation

Sun The source of light and heat, and consequently of life, to the whole world, hence, regarded as a deity and worshipped as such by all primitive peoples and having a leading place in all mythologies *Shamash* was the principal sun god of the Assyrians, *Merodach* of the Chaldees, *Ormuzd* of the Persians, *Ra* of the Egyptians, *Tezcatlipoca* of the Mexicans, and *Helios* (known to the Romans as *Sol*) of the Greeks Helios drove his chariot daily across the heavens, rising from the sea at dawn and sinking into it in the west at sunset, the names of his snow-white, fire-breathing coursers are given as Brontē (*thunder*), Eoos (*day-break*), Ethiops (*flashing*), Ethon (*fiery*), Erythreos (*red-producer*), Philogea (*earth-loving*), and Pyrois (*fiery*)

The Scandinavian sun god, *Sunna,* who was in constant dread of being devoured by the wolf Fenris (a symbol of eclipses), was similarly borne through the sky by the horses Arvakur, Aslo, and Alsvidur

Apollo was also a sun god of the Greeks, but he was the personification not of the sun itself but of its all-pervading light and life-giving qualities.

A place in the sun. A favourable position that allows room for development, a share in what one has a natural right to. The phrase was popularized by William II of Germany during the crisis of 1911. In his speech at Hamburg (Aug. 27th) he spoke of the German nation taking steps that would make them—sure that no one can dispute with us the place in the sun that is our due

It had been used by Pascal some two hundred years before

Heaven cannot support two suns, nor earth two masters. So said Alexander the Great when Darius (before the battle of Arbela) sent to offer terms of peace. *Cp* Shakespeare.—

> Two stars keep not their motion in one sphere,
> Nor can one England brook a double reign,
> Of Harry Percy and the Prince of Wales
>   1 *Henry IV*, v, 4

More worship the rising than the setting sun More persons pay honour to ascendant than to fallen greatness. The saying is attributed to Pompey.

> I should fear those that dance before me now
> Would one day stamp upon me, it has been done,
> Men shut their doors against a setting sun
>   *Timon of Athens*, i, 2

Out of God's blessing into the warm sun. One of Ray's proverbs, meaning from good to less good. When the king says to Hamlet "How is it that the clouds still hang on you?" the prince answers, "No, my lord, I am too much i' the sun," meaning, "I have lost God's blessing, for too much of the sun"—*i e* this far inferior state

> Thou out of heaven's benediction comest
> To the warm sun
>   *King Lear*, ii, 2

The City of the Sun. *See* CITY

The empire on which the sun never sets. *See* SET. (*The setting of the sun*).

The Southern Gate of the Sun. The sign Capricornus or winter solstice. So called because it is the most southern limit of the sun's course in the ecliptic

The sun of Austerlitz. When Napoleon fought the Russians and Austrians at Austerlitz (Dec 2nd, 1805), a brilliant sun suddenly burst through and scattered the mists, thus enabling him to gain an overwhelming victory. Napoleon ever after looked upon this as a special omen from heaven

The Sun of Righteousness Jesus Christ (*Mal.* iv, 2)

To have been out in the sun, or to have the sun in one's eyes. To be slightly inebriated

To make hay while the sun shines *See* HAY.

Sundowner Australian for a tramp who times his arrival at the houses of the hospitable at sundown, so as to get a night's lodging

Sunday (A S *sunnendæg*) The first day of the week, so called because anciently dedicated to the sun, as Monday was to the moon (*see* WEEK, DAYS OF THE) *See also* SABBATH.

Not in a month of Sundays. Not in a very long time.

One's Sunday best, or Sunday-go-to-meeting togs. One's best clothes, kept for wearing on Sundays

Sunday saint. One who observes the ordinances of religion, and goes to church on a Sunday, but is worldly, grasping, "indifferent honest," the following six days

When three Sundays come together. Never.

Sundew, the *Drosera*, which is from the Greek *drosos*, dew. So called from the dew-like drops which rest on the hairy fringes of the leaves

Sunflower. What we know as the sunflower is the *Helianthus*, so called, not because it follows the sun, but because it resembles a conventional drawing of the sun. A bed of these flowers will turn in every direction, regardless of the sun. The *Turnsole* (*Heliotropium*), belonging to quite another order of plants, is the flower that turns to the sun

> The sunflower turns on the god, when he sets
> The same look which she turned when he rose.
> T MOORE (*Believe me if all those endearing young charms*)

The Sunflower State (U S.A). Kansas

Sunna (sŭn' ä) (Arab , custom, divine law) Properly, the sayings and example of Mohammed and his immediate followers in so far as they conform to the Koran, hence applied to the collections of legal and moral traditions attributed to the Prophet, supplementary to the Koran as the Hebrew Mishna is to the Pentateuch.

Sunnites. The orthodox and conservative body of Moslems, who consider the Sunna as authentic as the Koran itself and acknowledge the first four caliphs to be the rightful successors of Mohammed. They form by far the largest section of Mohammedans, and are divided into four sects, viz , Hanbalites, Hanafites, Malikites, and Shafiites (*cp.* SHIITES).

Suo marte (sū' ŏ mar' te) (Lat). By one's own strength or personal exertions

Super (sū' per) In theatrical parlance, "supers" are supernumeraries, or persons employed to make up crowds, processions, dancing or singing choirs, messengers, etc , where little or no speaking is needed

Supercilious. Having an elevated eyebrow (Lat *super*, over, *cilium*, eyebrow), hence contemptuous, haughty.

Supererogation. Works of supererogation. The term used by theologians for good works which are performed but are not actually enjoined on Christians (Lat. *super*, over, above, *erogare*, to pay out) In common use as a phrase

Superman. A hypothetical superior human being of high intellectual and moral attainments, fancied as evolved from the normally existing type. The term (*übermensch*) was invented by the German philosopher Nietzsche

(d 1900), and popularized in England by G B Shaw's play, *Man and Superman* (1903)
The wide popularity of the term gave rise to many compounds, such as *superwoman*, *super-critic*, *super-tramp*, *super-Dreadnought*, and *super-tax*

Supernaculum. The very best wine. The word is Low Latin for "upon the nail" (*super unguem*), meaning that the wine is so good the drinker leaves only enough in his glass to make a bead on his nail The French say of first-class wine, "It is fit to make a ruby on the nail" (*faire rubis sur l'ongle*) Nashe says that after a man had drunk his glass, it was usual, in the North, to turn the cup upside down, and let a drop fall upon the thumb-nail If the drop rolled off, the drinker was obliged to fill and drink again (*Pierce Pennilesse*, 1592). Bishop Hall alludes to the same custom·
"The Duke Tenterbelly exclaims .. 'Let never this goodly-formed goblet of wine go jovially through me,' and then he set it to his mouth, stole it off every drop, save a little remainder, which he was by custom to set upon his thumb-nail and lick off "

> 'Tis here! the supernaculum! twenty years
> Of age, if 'tis a day —BYRON *Werner*, 1, 1

Hence, *to drink supernaculum* is to leave no heel-taps, to leave just enough not to roll off one's thumb-nail if poured upon it

Supply. One who acts as a substitute, temporarily taking the place of another, used principally of clergymen, school teachers, and domestic servants
In Parliamentary language **supplies** is used of money granted for the purposes of government which is not provided by the revenue. In Britain all money bills, *i e* those authorizing expenditure, must originate in the House of Commons and must be based on resolutions passed by a *Committee of Supply*

The law of supply and demand. The economic statement that the competition of buyers and sellers tends to make such changes in price that the demand for any article in a given market will become equal to the supply In other words, if the demand exceeds the supply the price rises, operating so as to reduce the demand and so enable the supply to meet it, and *vice versa*

Supralapsarian. *See* SUBLAPSARIAN

Surgeon. A contraction of the earlier *chirurgeon*, from Gr *cheir*, hand, *egein*, to work—one who works with his hands, or works by manual operations instead of through the agency of physic (as does the *physician*) The word is, etymologically, identical with *manufacturer* (Lat *manus*, hand, *facere*, to work).

Surloin. *See* SIRLOIN

Surname The name added to, or given over and above, the Christian or personal name (O Fr *sur-*, from Lat *super-*, over, above) English surnames (of which it is said, there are some 30,000) came into use in the latter part of the 10th century, but were not widely used till much later, In origin they are for the most part appellations denoting a trade or occupation, the place of residence, or some peculiar characteristic.

Surplice. Over the *pelisse* or fur robe (Lat *super-pellicium*, from *pellis*, skin) The clerical robe worn over the bachelor's ordinary dress, which was anciently made of sheepskin.

Surrealism. A school of art beginning in 1924 which regarded the subconscious as the essential source of art drawing inspiration from "all that is contrary to the general appearance of reality " It falls into two groups "hand painted dream photographs" (Dali), and an endeavour to achieve complete spontaneity of technique as well as subject matter by use of contrast Chief exponents Picasso, Max Ernst, Arp, Man Ray, Miró and Salvador Dali. The literary exponent was André Breton

Susanna and the Elders A favourite subject among Renaissance and later artists. The *Story of Susanna*, one of the books of the Old Testament Apocrypha, tells how Susanna was accused of adultery by certain Jewish elders who had unsuccessfully attempted her chastity how her innocence was proved by Daniel, and the Elders put to death

Sutor. *Ne sutor*, etc. *See* COBBLER.

Sutras (sū´ tras). Ancient Hindu aphoristic manuals giving the rules of systems of philosophy, grammar, etc , and directions concerning religious ritual and ceremonial customs They form a link between the Vedic and later Sanskrit literature, and are so called from Sansk *sutra*, a thread, the aphorisms being, as it were, threaded together

Suttee (sŭt´ ē) The Hindu custom of burning the widow on the funeral pyre of her deceased husband, also, the widow so put to death (from Sansk *sati*, a virtuous wife) In theory the practice, which lasted for some 2,000 years, was optional, but public opinion and the very severe form of ostracism the defaulting widow had to endure gave her practically no option Women with child and mothers of children not yet of age could not perform suttee The practice was declared illegal in British India in 1829, but even now it is probably not completely stamped out.

Swaddlers. An early nickname for Wesleyan Methodists, applied later (by Roman Catholics) to Dissenters and Protestants generally. Cardinal Cullen, in 1869, gave notice that he would deprive of the sacraments all parents who sent their children to mixed Model schools, where they were associated with "Presbyterians, Socinians, Arians, and Swaddlers"(*Times*, September 4th, 1869)
There is more than one explanation of the origin of the term Southey's (*Life of Wesley*, ii, 153) is as follows —
It happened that Cennick, preaching on Christmas Day, took for his text these words from St. Luke's Gospel "And this shall be a sign unto you, ye shall find the babe wrapped in swaddling clothes lying in a manger " A Catholic who was present, and to whom the language of Scripture was a novelty, thought this so ridiculous that he called the preacher a swaddler in derision, and this unmeaning word became a nickname for "Protestant," and had all the effect of the most opprobrious appellation.

Swag (connected with Norwegian *svagga*, to sway from side to side) One's goods carried in a pack or bundle, hence, the booty obtained by a burglary—which is often carried away in a sack. To get away with the swag is used figuratively of profiting by one's cleverness or sharp practice.

Swagman. The Australian term for a man who carries his *swag* about with him while on the search for work.

Swag-shop. A place kept by a "fence," where thieves can dispose of their "swag"; also, a low-class shop where cheap and trashy articles are sold.

Swagger (frequentative of SWAG) To strut about with a superior or defiant air; to bluster, make oneself out a very important person; hence, ostentatiously smart or "swell", as *a swagger dinner, a swagger car*, etc

Swagger-stick. The small cane a soldier was formerly obliged to carry when walking out

Swainmote. *See* SWANIMOTE.

Swallow. According to Scandinavian tradition, this bird hovered over the cross of our Lord, crying "*Svala! svala!*" (Console! console!) whence it was called *svalow* (the bird of consolation)

Ælian says that the swallow was sacred to the Penates or household gods, and therefore to injure one would be to bring wrath upon your own house. It is still considered a sign of good luck if a swallow or martin builds under the eaves of one's house

Perhaps you failed in your foreseeing skill,
For swallows are unlucky birds to kill
DRYDEN *Hind and Panther*, Pt III

Longfellow refers to another old fable regarding this bird:—
Seeking with eager eyes that wondrous stone which the swallow
Brings from the shore of the sea to restore the sight of its fledglings
Evangeline, Pt I

One swallow does not make a summer. You are not to suppose summer has come to stay just because you have seen a swallow; nor that the troubles of life are over because you have surmounted one difficulty. The Greek proverb, "One swallow does not make a spring" is to be found in Aristotle's *Nicomachæan Ethics* (I, vii, 16).

Swan. The fable that the swan sings beautifully just before it dies is very ancient, though baseless Swans do not "sing" at all, in the ordinary sense of the term, and the only one for which song of any kind can be claimed is the Whistling Swan (*Cygnus musicus*) of Iceland, of which it is reported—
during the long dark nights their wild song is often heard resembling the tones of a violin, though somewhat higher and remarkably pleasant —NICOL *Account of Iceland.*

The superstition was credited by Plato, Aristotle, Euripides, Cicero, Seneca, Martial, etc, and doubted by Pliny and Ælian

Shakespeare refers to it more than once. Emilia, just before she dies says—
I will play the swan,
And die in music		*Othello*, v, 2.

In the *Merchant of Venice*, (iii, 2) Portia says—
He makes a swan-like end,
Fading in music.

And Lucrece (*Rape of Lucrece*, 1, 1611)—
And now this pale swan in her watery nest
Begins the sad dirge of her certain ending

Spenser speaks of the swan as though it sang quite regardless of death—
He, were he not with love so ill bedight,
Would mount as high and sing as soote [sweetly] as Swanne *Shepheardes Calender* October, 89

And Coleridge, referring to poetasters of the time, gives the old superstition an epigrammatic turn—
Swans sing before they die, 'twere no bad thing
Did certain persons die before they sing.

One Greek legend has it that the soul of Apollo, the god of music, passed into a swan, and in the *Phædo* Plato makes Socrates say that at their death swans sing—
not out of sorrow or distress, but because they are inspired of Apollo, and they sing as foreknowing the good things their god hath in store for them

This idea made the Pythagorean fable that the souls of all good poets passed into swans hence, the *Swan of Mantua*, etc (*see below*)

The male swan is called a *cob*, the female a *pen*, a young swan a *cygnet*

See also FIONNUALA, LEDA; LOHENGRIN.

To swan. A word of doubtful origin much used in N W Europe in World War II. It denoted taking a vehicle off for a drive for one's own amusement when off duty. It came to be applied to any apparently aimless movements, *e g* one who drove his tank about without apparent purpose might be described as "swanning about the battlefield"

The Swan of Avon Shakespeare, so called by Ben Jonson in allusion to his birthplace, Stratford-on-Avon *Swan*, as applied to poets (because Apollo was fabled to have been changed into a swan), is of very old standing; thus, Virgil was known as *the Mantuan Swan*, Homer *the Swan of Meander*, etc.; and Anna Seward (1747-1809) was named *the Swan of Lichfield*

The Swan of Usk. So Henry Vaughan, the Silurist (1622-95) was called, having given one of his volumes of verse this name—*Olor Iscanus.*

A black swan. A curiosity, a *rara avis* (q v)

All your swans are geese All your fine promises or expectations have proved fallacious "Hope told a flattering tale " The converse, All your geese are swans, means all your children are paragons, and whatever you do is in your own eyes superlative work

Leda and the swan. *See* LEDA.

Swan-maidens. Fairies of northern folklore who can become maidens or swans at will by means of the *swan shift*, a magic garment of swan's feathers Many stories are told of how the swan shift was stolen, and the fairy was obliged to remain thrall to the thief until rescued by a knight

Swan song. The song fabled to be sung by swans at the point of death (*see above*), hence, the last work of a poet, composer, etc.

Swan-upping A taking up of swans and placing the marks of ownership on their beaks The term is specially applied to annual expeditions for this purpose up the Thames, when the marks of the owners (viz. the Crown and the Dyers' and Vintners' Companies) are made. The royal swans are marked with five nicks—two lengthwise, and three across the bill—and the Companies' swans with two nicks Also called *Swan-hopping*

The Swan with Two Necks The emblem of the Vintners' Company, and an old tavern sign *Necks* is a corruption of *Nicks*

The Knight of the Swan. Lohengrin (*q v*).

The Order of the Swan. An order of knighthood instituted by Frederick II of Brandenburg in 1440 (and shortly after in Cleves) in honour of the Lohengrin legend It died out in the 16th century, but it is still commemorated in our *White Swan* public-house sign, which was first used in honour of Anne of Cleves, one of the wives of Henry VIII The badge was a silver swan surmounted by an image of the Virgin

Swanhild (swän' hild) An old Norse legendary heroine, daughter of Sigurd and Gudrun She was falsely accused of adultery with the son of the king who was wooing her, and the king had him hanged and her trampled to death by horses

Swanimote (swän' i mōt) A court held thrice a year before forest verderers by the steward of the court So called from A S. *swangemot*, a meeting of swineherds, because, under the *Charta de Foresta* (1217), it was a meeting of the keepers of the royal forests to arrange for the depasturing of pigs in autumn, the clearance of cattle during the deer's fawning season, etc.

Swank. To behave in an ostentatious manner, to show off and "cut a dash" to impress the observers with one's cleverness, smartness, or rank, etc It is an old dialect word adopted as modern slang.

Swap. To exchange.

To swap horses in midstream. To change leaders at the height of a crisis Abraham Lincoln, in an address, June 9th, 1864, referring to the fact that his fellow Republicans, though many were dissatisfied with his conduct of the Civil War, had renominated him for President, said that the Convention had concluded "that it is best not to swap horses while crossing the river "

Swashbuckler. A ruffian, a swaggerer "From swashing," says Fuller (*Worthies*, 1662), "and making a noise on the buckler " The swordplayers used to "swash" or tap their shield, as fencers tap their foot upon the ground when they attack. *Cp* SWINGE-BUCKLER

A brave, a swashbuckler, one that for money and good cheere will follow any man to defend him, but if any danger come, he runs away the first, and leaves him in the lurch —FLORIO: *Worlde of Wordes* (1598)

Swastika. The gammadion, or fylfot (*q.v*), an elaborated cross-shaped design used as a charm to ward off evil and bring good luck, the emblem of Nazi Germany, personally chosen as such by Adolf Hitler The word is Sanskrit, from *svasti*, good fortune.

Swear, To Originally used only of solemnly affirming, by the invocation of God or some sacred person or object as witness to the pledge, to take an oath Swearing came later to mean using bad language by way of expletives, intensives, and in moments of sudden anger through the sacred expressions being used in a profane way in lightly and irreverently taking oaths

The modern practice of swearing, in either its flippant or vituperative shape is derived from the break-up of the process once devised as a protection of truthfulness and fair dealing . . It must be remembered that the subject of vituperative swearing is interwoven with that of legal and religious ordinances —SHARMAN *A Cursory History of Swearing*, ch ii (1884)

To swear black is white. To swear to any falsehood

To swear like a trooper To indulge in very strong blasphemy or profanity —" 'Our armies swore terribly in Flanders,' cried my Uncle Toby" (Sterne. *Tristram Shandy*, II, xi).

Sweat. To sweat a person is to exact the largest possible amount of labour from him at the lowest possible pay, to keep him working at starvation wages The term is also used of bleeding, or fleecing, a man; and of rubbing down coins so that one can obtain and use the gold or silver taken from them.

Sweat-box (U S A) A form of punishment of long standing which consists of imprisoning a man in a box no bigger than himself often in the sun, so that he becomes exhausted by the terrific temperature Hence, **to sweat it out of him** is to extort a confession or agreement by such use of threats and violence as may be necessary until the victim breaks under the ordeal.

Sweating sickness. A form of malaria epidemic, which appeared in England about a century and a half after the *Black Death* (1485) It broke out amongst the soldiers of Richmond's army as a violent inflammatory fever, without boils or ulcers, after the battle of Bosworth, and lasted five weeks Between 1485 and 1529 there were five outbreaks, the first four being confined to England and France, the fifth spreading over Germany, Turkey, and Austria.

Swedenborgians (swē' den bôr' ji ánz). Followers of Emanuel Swedenborg (1688-1772), called by themselves "the New Jerusalem Church" (*Rev* xxi, 2). Their views of salvation, inspiration of Scripture, and a future state, differ widely from those of other Christians, and they believe the Trinity to be centred in the person of Jesus Christ (*Col.* ii, 9).

Sweep. To sweep the threshold. To announce to all the world that the woman of the house is paramount When the procession called "Skimmington" (*q v*) passed a house where the woman "wore the breeches" everyone gave the threshold a sweep with a broom or bunch of twigs.

Sweepstakes. A race in which stakes are made by the owners of horses engaged, to be awarded to the winner or other horse in the race Entrance money has to be paid to the race fund. If the horse runs, the full stake must be paid, but if it is withdrawn, a forfeit only is imposed

Also a gambling arrangement in which a number of persons stake money on some event (usually a horse-race), each of whom draws a lot for every share bought, the total sum deposited being divided among the drawers of winners (or sometimes of starters). Some "sweeps" have very valuable prizes, as the "Calcutta Sweep" on the Derby (organized by the Calcutta Club), the first prize of which comes to over £100,000

Sweet. The **sweet singer of Israel** King David (about 1074-1001 B.C).

To be sweet on To be enamoured of, in love with

To have a sweet tooth. To be very fond of dainties and sweet things generally.

Sweetness and light. A favourite phrase with Matthew Arnold "Culture," he said, "is the passion for sweetness and light, and (what is more) the passion for making them prevail" (*Preface* to *Literature and Dogma*) The phrase was used by Swift (*Battle of the Books*, 1697) in an imaginary fable by Æsop as to the merits of the bee (the ancients) and the spider (the moderns). It concludes —

The difference is that instead of dirt and poison, we have rather chosen to fill our hives with honey and wax, thus furnishing mankind with the two noblest of things, which are *sweetness* and *light*

Swell. A person showily dressed, one who puffs himself out beyond his proper dimensions, like the frog in the fable, hence, a fashionable person, one of high standing or importance In American usage as an adjective, fine, stylish, first rate, just right

Swell mob. The better-dressed thieves and pickpockets.

Swelled head. An exaggerated sense of one's own dignity, usefulness, importance, etc.

Swim In the swim. In a favourable position in society of any kind, a racing-man who is "in the swim" is one who mixes with the class from which he can get the best "tips"; and similarly with a diplomatist, a stockbroker, or a society lady It is an angler's phrase A lot of fish gathered together is called a *swim*, and when an angler can pitch his hook in such a place he is said to be "in a good swim"

Sink or swim. No matter what happens. Convicted witches were thrown into the water to "sink or swim", if they sank they were drowned, if they swam it was clear proof they were in league with the Evil One, so it did not much matter, one way or the other

To swim with the stream. To allow one's actions and principles to be guided solely by the force of public opinion

Swindle. To cheat, defraud, gain a mean advantage by trickery The verb is formed from the noun *swindler*, which was introduced into England by German Jews about 1760, from Ger *schwindler*, a cheating company promoter (from *schwindeln*, to act heedlessly or extravagantly).

Swing. Captain Swing. The name assumed by certain persons who, about 1830, sent threatening letters to farmers who employed mechanical

means, such as threshing machines, to save labour "Captain Swing" was an entirely imaginary person but three so-called *Lives* of him appeared in 1830 and 1831

The neighbours thought all was not right,
Scarcely one with him ventured to parley,
And Captain Swing came in the night,
And burnt all his beans and his barley
BARHAM *Babes in the Wood* (*Ingoldsby Legends*)

A type of jazz with a catchy rhythm. The word originated in Negro parlance to describe really moving music well played, but later (1930s) came to denote a debased type of popular dance music which the uninformed imagined had some connection with jazz.

I don't care if I swing for him! A remark of one very revengefully inclined, implying that the speaker will even go to the length of murdering the enemy, and getting hanged in consequence

In full swing. Going splendidly; everything prosperous and in perfect order.

It went with a swing. Said of a ceremony, function, entertainment, etc, that passed off without a hitch and was a great success.

What you lose on the swings you get back on the roundabouts A rough way of stating the law of averages, if you have bad luck on one day you have good on another, if one venture results in loss try a fresh one—it may succeed

Swinge-buckler. A roisterer, a rake who went a bit further than a swashbuckler (*q v.*), in that he *swinged* (beat) his man, as well as *swashed* his buckler The continuation of Stow's *Annals* tells us that in Elizabeth's time the "blades" of London used to assemble in West Smithfield with sword and buckler for mock fights, called "bragging" fights They swashed and swinged their bucklers with much show of fury, "but seldome was any man hurt "

There was I, and little John Doit of Staffordshire, and black George Barnes, and Francis Pickbone, and Will Squele, a Cotswold man, you had not four such swinge-bucklers in all the Inns-of-court, and, I may say to you, we knew where the bona-robas were —2 *Henry VI*, iii, 2.

Swiss. The nickname of a Swiss is "Colin Tampon "

No money—no Swiss—*i e* no assistance The Swiss were for centuries the mercenaries of Europe—willing to serve anyone for pay—and were usually called in England *Switzers*, as in Shakespeare's "Where are my Switzers? Let them guard the door" (*Hamlet* iv, 5) In France an hotel-porter—also the beadle of a church—is called *un suisse*

Swithin, St. If it rains on St. Swithin's day (July 15th), **there will be rain for forty days.**

St Swithin's day, gif ye do rain, for forty days it will remain,

St Swithin's day, an ye be fair, for forty days 'twill rain nae mair

The legend is that St Swithin, Bishop of Winchester, who died 862, desired to be buried in the church-*yard* of the minster, that the "sweet rain of heaven might fall upon his grave " At canonization the monks thought to honour the saint by removing his body into the choir, and fixed July 15th for the ceremony, but it rained day after day for forty days, so that the monks saw the saint was averse to their project, and wisely abandoned it.

The St. Swithin of France is St Gervais (q v , and see MÉDARD) The rainy saint in Flanders is St Godelìève, in Germany, the Seven Sleepers

Switzers. See SWISS

Swollen Head. See SWELLED HEAD.

Sword. At sword's point In deadly hostility, ready to fight each other with swords

Fire and sword. Rapine and destruction perpetrated by an invading army.

Poke not fire with a sword. This was a precept of Pythagoras, meaning add not fuel to fire, or do not irritate an angry man by sharp words which will only increase his rage. (*See* Iamblichus *Protreptics*, symbol IX)

Sword and buckler. An old epithet for brag and bluster, as *a sword and buckler voice, sword and buckler men*, etc Hotspur says of the future Henry V—

And that same sword and buckler Prince of Wales,
.
I'd have him poisoned with a pot of ale.
                              1 *Henry IV*, I, 3.

Sword and Cloak Plays. *See* CLOAK AND SWORD

Sword dance. A Scottish dance performed over two swords laid crosswise on the floor, or sometimes danced among swords placed point downwards in the ground: also a dance in which the men brandish swords and clash them together, the women passing under them when crossed.

Sword dollar. A Scottish silver coin of James VI, marked with a sword on the reverse It was worth 30s Scots (=2s 6d in English contemporary money)

The sword of Damocles *See* DAMOCLES

The Sword of God. Khaled Ibn al Waled (d. 642), the Mohammedan conqueror of Syria, was so called for his prowess at the battle of Muta

The Sword of Rome. Marcellus, who opposed Hannibal (216-14 B C)

The Sword of the Spirit. The Word of God (*Eph* VI, 17)

To put to the sword. To slay

Your tongue is a double-edged sword. Whatever you say wounds, your argument cuts both ways. The allusion is to the double-edged sword out of the mouth of the Son of Man—one edge to condemn, and the other to save (*Rev* I, 16)

Yours is a Delphic sword—it cuts both ways Erasmus says a Delphic sword is that which accommodates itself to the *pro* or *con* of a subject The reference is to the double meanings of the Delphic oracles.

Some famous swords. In the days of chivalry a knight's horse and sword were his most treasured and carefully kept possessions, and his sword—equally with his horse—had its own name. The old romances, especially those of the Charlemagne and Arthurian cycles, are full of these names, we give below a list of the more noteworthy, and further particulars of these and others will be found throughout this Dictionary

Angurvadal (stream of anguish), Frithiof's sword
Arondight, the sword of Launcelot of the Lake.
Azoth, the sword of Paracelsus (Browning's *Paracelsus*, Bk v)
Balisarda, Rogero's sword, made by a sorceress
Balmung, one of the swords of Siegfried, made by Wieland
Caliburn, another name of *Excalibur* (q v.) .
Chrysaor (sword, as good as gold), Artegal's sword (Spenser's *Faerie Queene*).
Colada, the Cid's sword
Corrougue, Otuel's sword
Courtain (the short sword), one of the swords of Ogier the Dane. *Sauvagine* was the other, and they both took Munifican three years to make
Curtana, the blunted sword of Edward the Confessor.
Durandan, Durandal, or Durandana (the inflexible), Orlando's sword
Excalibur, the sword of King Arthur (*Ex cal[ce]-liber[are]*, to liberate from the stone)
Flamberge or *Floberge* (the flame-cutter), the name of one of Charlemagne's swords, and also that of Rinaldo's and Maugis or Maligigi's
Frusberta, Rinaldo's sword
Glorious, Oliver's sword, which hacked to pieces the nine swords made by Ansias, Galas, and Munifican
Gram (grief), one of the swords of Siegfried.
Grey-steel, the sword of Koll the Thrall
Haute-claire (very bright), both Closamont's and Oliver's swords were so called.
Joyeuse (joyous), one of Charlemagne's swords it took Galas three years to make
Merveilleuse (the marvellous), Doolin's sword.
Mimung, the sword that Wittich lent Siegfried
Morglay (big glaive), Sir Bevis's sword.
Nagelring (nail-ring), Dietrich's sword
Philippan The sword of Antony, one of the triumvirs
Quern-biter (a foot-breadth), both Haco I, and Thoralf Skolimson had a sword so called
Sanglamore (the big bloody glaive), Braggadochio's sword (Spenser's *Faerie Queene*)
Sauvagine (the relentless) *see* COURTAIN *above.*

Sybarite (sĭ' bàr ĭt). A self-indulgent person, a wanton The inhabitants of Sybaris, in South Italy, were proverbial for their luxurious living and self-indulgence A tale is told by Seneca of a Sybarite who complained that he could not rest comfortably at night, and being asked why, replied, "He found a rose-leaf doubled under him, and it hurt him."

Fable has it that the Sybarites taught their horses to dance to the pipe When the Crotians marched against Sybaris they played on their pipes, whereupon all the Sybarite horses began to dance, disorder soon prevailed in the ranks, and the victory was quick and easy.

Sycamore and Sycomore (sĭk' à môr) The *Sycamore* is the common plane-tree of the maple family (*Acer pseudo-platānus*, or greater maple), the *sycomore* is the Egyptian fig-tree, and is the tree into which Zacchæus climbed (*Luke* xix, 4) to see Christ pass Coverdale's. the Geneva, and other early English Bibles, call it the "wyld figge tre." Both words are from Gr. *sukon*, fig, and *moron*, mulberry.

Sycophant (sĭk' ŏ fănt) A sponger, parasite, or servile flatterer, the Greek *sukophantes* (*sukon*, fig, *phainein*, to show), which is said to have meant an informer against persons who exported figs or robbed the sacred fig-trees There is no corroboration of this, but the widely accepted story is that the Athenians passed a law forbidding the exportation of figs, and there were always found mean fellows who, for their own private ends, impeached those who violated it; hence *sycophantes* came to signify first a government toady, and then a toady generally.

Sycorax (sī' ko răks) A witch, mother of Caliban, in Shakespeare's *Tempest*.

Syllogism (sil' ō jizm) A form of argument consisting of three propositions, a *major premise* or general statement, a *minor premise* or instance, and the *conclusion*, which is deduced from these

The five hexameter verses which contain the symbolic names of all the different syllogistic figures are as follow.—

Barbara, Celarent, Darii, Ferioque, *prioris.*
Cesare, Camestres, Festino, Baroko, *secundæ.*
Tertia, Darapti, Disamis, Datisi, Felapton,
Bokardo, Ferison, *habet Quarta insuper addit*
Bramantip, Camenes, Dimaris, Fesapo, Fresison.

The significance of these words lies in their vowels:

A universal affirmative
E universal negative
I particular affirmative.
O particular negative.

Taking the first line as the standard, the initials of all the words below it show to which standard the syllogism is to be reduced, thus, Baroko is to be reduced to "Barbara," Cesare to "Celarent," and so on.

Sylph (silf) An elemental spirit of air; so named in the Middle Ages by the Rosicrucians and Cabalists, from the Greek *silphe*, some kind of beetle, or a grub that turns into a butterfly. *Cp* SALAMANDER

Any mortal who has preserved inviolate chastity might enjoy intimate familiarity with these gentle spirits, and deceased coquettes were said to become sylphs, "and sport and flutter in the fields of air"

Whoever, fair and chaste,
Rejects mankind, is by some sylph embraced
POPE: *Rape of the Lock*, 1

Symbolists. A group of French writers who, towards the end of the 19th century revolted against Naturalism and Parnassianism Their aim was to suggest rather than to depict or transcribe, and their watchword was Verlaine's "Pas de couleur, rien que la nuance" Their precursors were Baudelaire, Banville, G de Nerval and Villiers de l'Isle Adam Chief Symbolists in verse, Verlaine, Rimbaud, Mallarme, in prose, Huysmans.

Symbols of Saints.

SAINTS		SYMBOLS
Agatha	..	. With her severed breasts pierced by a sword or on a dish, also with a book in one hand, and a palm or pair of pincers in the other
Agnes	..	.. With a lamb or a guardian angel at her side; sometimes standing on a flaming pyre with a sword in her hand
Alban	..	.. As a Roman soldier, bearing a sword, and the palm or cross
Ambrose		With a beehive
Anastasius		With a hatchet, or carrying his cowled head on a plate
Andrew		A saltire cross.
Andrew Corsini		Between a wolf and a lamb (in allusion to his unregenerate youth and saintly old age)
Anne	..	. A book in her hand
Antony	..	.. A tau cross, with a bell at the end, and a pig by his side, or with the bell tied to the neck of the pig
Antony of Padua	..	Carrying the infant Jesus in his arms, or with a mule kneeling at his side.
Apollinaris	..	. A bishop, bearing a sword or club, and having a raven at his side
Appollonia	..	.. A tooth and palm branch, or a tooth grasped in a pair of forceps, She is applied to by those who suffer from tooth-ache
Arcadius	..	. A torso (he was dismembered joint by joint, and limb by limb)
Augustine (of Hippo)		Holding a burning heart
Barbara	.	. With a three-windowed tower and carrying a chalice with the Host above it.
Barbatus	..	.. A hatchet in his hand and a golden snake under his foot
Barnabas	..	.. Carrying the Gospel in one hand, and a pilgrim's staff or a stone in the other
Bartholomew		.. With a butcher's flaying knife (the instrument of his martyrdom), or a human skin with the face showing
Benedict	..	. Usually with his Rule in his hand and its first words (*Ausculta, O fili*) issuing on a scroll from his mouth, sometimes with his finger to his lip (enjoining silence), and with a scourge or rose-bush at his side and a broken goblet in his hand
Bernard	.	With a hive of bees
Bernard of Menthon		Bearing a blazing heart
Bernardine of Siena		As a Minorite, with the "I H S" surrounded by rays on his breast, and at his side three mitres, in allusion to his frequent refusals of a bishopric
Blaise	..	. Iron combs, with which his body was torn to pieces
Bridget (of Sweden)		A crozier and book
Bruno (founder of the Carthusians)		Contemplating a crucifix with "O Bonitas" issuing on a scroll from his mouth, and sometimes carrying an olive-branch
Catherine	.	An inverted sword, or large wheel
Catherine of Siena		With a crown of thorns, receiving a ring from Christ, or exchanging hearts with Him
Cecilia	.	. Playing on a harp or organ
Christopher	.	A gigantic figure carrying Christ over a river
Clement	..	A papal crown, or an anchor He was drowned with an anchor tied round his neck
Cloud	..	With nails (he is the patron saint of nail-makers).
Crispin and Crispian		With shoemaker's tools, or with millstones round their necks
Cuthbert	..	St Osbald's head in his hand
David	.	A leek, in commemoration of his victory over the Saxons
Denys	.	Holding his mitred head in his hand
Dominic	.	. With a star on his brow

Dorothy	Carrying a basket of fruit
Edward the Confessor	Crowned with a nimbus, and holding a sceptre.
Elizabeth . .	St John and the lamb at her feet
Eloy (or Eligius) .	Dressed as a farrier and holding a horse's leg (alluding to the legend that once when shoeing a restive horse he detached the leg, shod it, and then replaced it)
Eustace . .	With a stag bearing a crucifix between its horns.
Faith . .	A gridiron
Felix .	An anchor
Francis of Assisi .	Wearing the habit of his Order, bearded, and showing the stigmata in his hands
Francis of Paula .	Standing on his cloak, and with "Caritas" written across his breast, sometimes also with an ass beside a forge
Frideswide .	Beside a fountain, bearing a pastoral staff, and with an ox at her feet
Gall .	With a bear at his feet
Genevieve . .	With the keys of Paris at her girdle, sometimes carrying a candle which an angel is relighting just after the devil has blown it out
George . .	Mounted on horseback, and transfixing a dragon.
Gerasimus	With a tame lion
Germanus .	With an ass at his feet
Gertrude .	A pastoral staff with a mouse running up it
Giles .	A hind, with its head in the saint's lap
Gregory the Great	In papal robes, with a dove, and a roll of music in his hand
Guido, or Guy .	As a pilgrim, with a horse and ox at his feet, two palms in his hand, and a harrow at his side
Hedwige . .	Crowned and veiled, barefooted, with her shoes in her hand
Hubert . .	In bishop's robes, with a stag bearing the crucifix between its horns
Hugh . .	As a bishop, holding a ciborium above which is a Host with a child in the midst of the wafer; also, a swan at his own feet
Humbert . .	With a cross marked on his head, and a docile bear at his side
Ignatius . .	The monogram "I H S" on the breast or in the sky, circled with a glory
Isidore . .	With a pen and a hive of bees
James the Greater	A pilgrim's staff, or a scallop shell
James the Less	A fuller's club; he was killed by Simon the fuller
Jerome . .	Studying a large volume wearing the red hat of a cardinal (though he was never a cardinal), and with a lion crouching at his feet
Joan of Arc	In armour, with a long pennant painted with a picture of Christ holding a globe in one hand and the other raised in benediction, the words "Jhesus—Maria" above, and the background powdered with the royal lilies in gold
John the Baptist	A camel-hair garment, small rude cross, and a lamb at his feet
John the Evangelist .	A chalice, out of which a dragon or serpent is issuing, and an open book, or a young man with an eagle in the background
Jude . . .	With a club, a cross, or a carpenter's square
Kentigern (or Mungo)	With his episcopal cross in one hand, and in the other a salmon and a ring
Lawrence	A book and gridiron
Leger (or Leodegar)	With gimlets in his eyes, or holding them with pincers
Loius . .	A king kneeling, with the arms of France at his feet, a bishop blessing him, and a dove descending on his head.
Loy (see ELOY)	
Lucy . . .	With a short staff in her hand, and the devil behind her; or with eyes in a dish, and rays of light coming from a gash in her throat
Luke .	.. Sitting at a reading-desk, beneath which appears an ox's head, or painting the Virgin or a Bambino.
Marcellus .	As a bishop, leading a dragon through the streets of Paris by his stole.
Margaret	Treading on a dragon, or piercing it with the cross.
Margaret of Cortona	Gazing at a skull, or a corpse, with a dog at her side.
Mark . .	A man seated writing, with a lion couchant at his feet.
Martin .	On horseback, dividing his cloak with a beggar behind him on foot.
Mary Magdalen	A box of ointment.
Mary of Egypt .	Carrying three loaves, and dressed as a hermit with very long hair.
Mary the Virgin	Carrying the child Jesus, a lily is somewhere displayed
Matthew . .	With a halberd, with which Nadabar killed him, or with the Gospel, and a purse or money-box As an evangelist, he holds a pen, with which he is writing on a scroll His most ancient symbol is a man's face
Maurus . .	.. With weights and measures (St Benedict appointed him to decide on the allowance of bread, etc , for his monks)
Michael . .	.. In armour, with a cross, or else holding scales, in which he is weighing souls.
Neot . .	.. Ploughing with deer instead of oxen
Nicholas . .	. With three golden balls or purses, or with a tub with naked infants in it He is patron saint of children
Nicholas of Tolentino	With a star over his head, a lily in his hand, and Purgatory yawning at his feet
Osyth .	Carrying her head in her hands.
Pancras . .	A youth with a sword in one hand and a palm in the other
Patrick .	A shamrock leaf (which he showed to the Irish heathen as a symbol of the Trinity)
Paul .	A sword and a book. Dressed as a Roman
Peter	Keys and a triple cross, or a fish, or a cock
Peter Gonzales .	In Dominican habit, and holding a blue candle.
Peter Martyr	With a hatchet sticking in a cleft in his head

Philip	.. ..	A pastoral staff, surmounted with a cross, or carrying a basket containing loaves and fishes (*John* vi, 5-7)
Praxedis	.. .	With a basin in one hand and palms in the other
Roche	.. .	A wallet, and a dog with a loaf in its mouth sitting by He shows a boil in his thigh
Sebastian	.. ..	Bound to a tree, his arms tied behind him, and his body transfixed with arrows
Simeon	.	An aged man, with a cross
Simon Zelotes		A saw, because he was sawn asunder
Stephen	.. .	A book and a stone in his hand
Theodora	.. .	The devil holding her hand and tempting her
Theodore	.. .	Armed with a halberd in his hand, and with a sabre by his side
Theresa	..	With a flaming arrow piercing her heart
Thomas	.. ..	With a builder's rule, or a stone in his hand, or holding the lance with which he was slain at Meliapour
Ulric	.. ..	With an angel bestowing on him a cross
Ursula	.. ..	A book and arrows She was shot through with arrows by the Prince of the Huns
Verena	.. .	A comb
Veronica	.. .	The sacred veil, which retained the impression of our Lord's face after she had wiped the sweat from his brow when on the way to Calvary
Walburga	.	With a flask of oil

(*See* APOSTLES, EVANGELISTS, etc)

Symbols of other sacred characters.

Abraham	..	An old man grasping a knife, ready to strike his son Isaac, who is bound on an altar An angel arrests his hand, and a ram is caught in the thicket
David	.. ..	Kneeling, above is an angel with a sword Sometimes he is represented playing a harp
Esau	.. .	With bow and arrows, going to meet Jacob
Gabriel	. ..	A flower-pot full of lilies between him and the Virgin.
Job	.. ..	Sitting naked on the ground, with three friends talking to him
Judas Iscariot	.	With a money bag In the last supper he has knocked over the salt with his right elbow
Judith	.. .	With Holofernes' head in one hand, and a sabre in the other
Noah	.. .	Looking out of the ark window at a dove, which is flying to the ark, olive branch in its beak
King Saul	.	Arrayed in a rich tunic and crowned A harp is placed behind him.
Solomon	.	In royal robes, standing under an arch

Symplegades, The. *See* CYANEAN ROCKS

Symposium (sĭm pō' zĭ um) Properly, a drinking together (Gr *syn*, together, *posis*, drink), hence, a convivial meeting for social and intellectual entertainment, hence, a discussion upon a subject, and the collected opinions of different authorities printed and published in a review, etc

The Symposium is the title given to a dialogue by Plato, and another by Xenophon, in which the conversation of Socrates and others is recorded

Syndicalism. The doctrine in economics that all the workers in any industry should have a share in the control and in the profits arising from it, and that to compass this end the workers in the different trades should federate and enforce their demands by sympathetic strikes The word was first used about 1907, and was coined from the French *chambre syndicale* (*syndic*, a delegate), a trade union

Synecdoche (sĭ nek' dō ke) The figure of speech which consists of putting a part for the whole, the whole for the part, a more comprehensive for a less comprehensive term, or *vice versa* Thus, *a hundred bayonets* (for a hundred soldiers), *the town was starving* (for *the people in the town*).

Now will I remember you farther of that manner of speech which the Greekes call *Synecdoche*, and we the figure of *quick conceite* . as when one would tell me how the French king was overthrown at Saint Quintans, I am enforced to think that it was not the king himselfe in person, but the Constable of Fraunce with the French kings power —PUTTENHAM *Arte of English Poesie*, Bk III (1589)

Synoptic Gospels, The. Those of Matthew, Mark, and Luke, so called because, taken together and apart from that of John, they form a *synopsis* (Gr., a seeing together), i e a general view or conspectus, of the life and sayings of Christ

Hence, the *Synoptic Problem*, the questions as to the origin and relationship of these three, *Mark* is generally supposed to be a source of *Matthew* and *Luke*, and *Luke* to have borrowed from *Matthew*

Syntax, Doctor (sĭn' tăks) The pious, henpecked clergyman, very simple-minded but of excellent taste and scholarship, created by William Combe (1741-1823) to accompany a series of coloured comic illustrations by Rowlandson His adventures are told in eight-syllabled verse in the *Three Tours of Dr. Syntax* (1812, 1820, and 1821)

Syrinx (sĭ' rĭngks). An Arcadian nymph of Greek legend On being pursued by Pan she took refuge in the river Ladon, and prayed to be changed into a reed, the prayer was granted, and of the reed Pan made his pipes Hence the name is given to the *Pan-pipe*, or reed mouth-organ, and also to the vocal organ of birds.

T

T The twentieth letter of the alphabet, representing Semitic *taw* and Greek *tau*, which meant "a mark" Our T is a modification of the earlier form, X. *See also* TAU

It fits to a T. Exactly The allusion is to work that mechanics square with a *T-square*, a ruler with a cross-piece at one end, especially useful in making right angles, and in obtaining perpendiculars and parallel lines

Marked with a T. Notified as a felon Persons convicted of felony, and admitted to the benefit of clergy, were branded on the thumb with the letter T (*thief*) The law authorizing this was abolished in 1827.

Taal (tal) The dialect of Dutch spoken in South Africa. It originated in the colloquial North Dutch of the 17th century but early underwent great changes. It is now frequently called Afrikaans

Tabard (tăb' ard) A jacket with short pointed sleeves, whole before, open on both sides, with a square collar, winged at the shoulder like a cape, and worn by military nobles over their armour It was generally emblazoned with heraldic devices. Heralds still wear tabards.

The Tabard Inn The inn whence pilgrims from London used to set out on their journey to Canterbury, it was on the London estate of the abbots of Hyde, and lay in the Southwark (now Borough) High Street, a little to the south of London Bridge It and its host, Harry Baily, are immortalized in Chaucer's *Canterbury Tales*

Tabardar A scholar on the foundation of Queen's College, Oxford, so called because they wore gowns with tabard sleeves—that is, loose sleeves, terminating a little below the elbow in a point

Tabby. Originally the name (from Arabic) of a silk material with a "watered" surface, giving an effect of wavy lines, applied to the brownish cat with dark stripes, because its markings resembled this material.

> Demurest of the tabby kind,
> The pensive Selima reclined
>   GRAY *On the Death of a Favourite Cat*

Tabernacles, Feast of A Jewish festival lasting eight days and beginning on the 15th Tisri (towards the end of September) Kept in remembrance of the sojourn in the wilderness, it was also the Feast of Ingathering It was formerly a time of great rejoicing

Table. Apelles' table. A pictured board (Lat *tabula*) or table, representing the excellency of sobriety on one side and the deformity of intemperance on the other

Table d'hôte (Fr , the host's table) The "ordinary" at an hotel or restaurant, the meal for which one pays a fixed price whether one partakes of all the courses provided or not In the Middle Ages, and even down to the reign of Louis XIV, the landlord's or host's table was the only public dining-place known in Germany and France

Table money or charge. A charge additional to that of the meal made at restaurants, etc , towards the cost of attendance, or a small fee charged to players at Bridge clubs, also , in the Army, Navy, and Diplomatic Service, an allowance made to assist in meeting the expense of official entertaining.

Table-talk. Small talk, chit-chat, familiar conversation

Table-turning. The turning of tables without the application of mechanical force, which in the early days of spiritualism was commonly

practised at séances, and sank to the level of a parlour trick. It was said by some to be the work of departed spirits, and by others to be due to a force akin to mesmerism.

Table of Pythagoras. The common multiplication table, carried up to ten The table is parcelled off into a hundred little squares or cells The name first appears in a corrupt text of Boethius, who was really referring to the abacus (*q v*)

Tables of Cebes. Cebes was a Theban philosopher, a disciple of Socrates, and one of the interlocutors of Plato's *Phædo* His *Tables* or *Tableau* supposes him to be placed before a tableau or panorama representing the life of man, which the philosopher describes with great accuracy of judgment and splendour of sentiment. It is sometimes appended to the works of Epictetus

The Round Table, or Table Round. *See* ROUND

The Tables of Toledo *See* TABULÆ TOLETANÆ

The Twelve Tables. The tables of the Roman laws engraved on brass, brought from Athens to Rome by the decemvirs

To lay on the table. The parliamentary phrase for postponing consideration of a motion, proposal, bill, etc , indefinitely. Hence, *to table a matter* is to defer it *sine die*

To turn the tables. To reverse the conditions or relations, as, for instance, to rebut a charge by bringing forth a counter-charge. The phrase comes from the old custom of reversing the *table* or board, in games such as chess and draughts, so that the opponent's relative position is altogether changed

Tableaux vivants (Fr , living pictures) Representations of statuary groups by living persons; said to have been invented by Madame de Genlis (1746-1830) while she had charge of the children of the Duc d'Orleans

Taboo, tabu (Maori *tapu*) A custom among the South Sea Islanders of prohibiting the use of certain persons, places, animals, things, etc , or the utterances of certain names and words, it signifies that which is banned, interdicted, or "devoted" in a religious sense. Thus, a temple is *taboo*, and so is he who violates a temple, Not only so, but everyone and everything connected with what is taboo becomes taboo also, Captain Cook was *taboo* because some of his sailors took wood from a Hawaiian temple to supply themselves with fuel, and being "devoted," he was slain The whole subject of taboo is a highly complicated and technical department of sociology

With us, a person who is ostracized, or an action, custom etc , that is altogether forbidden by Society, is said to be taboo, or tabooed

> Women, up till this
> Cramped under worse than South-sea-isle taboo,
> Dwarfs of the gynæceum, fail
>   TENNYSON *Princess*, iii, 278

Tabouret (tăb' oo ret) (Fr) A low stool without back or arms In the ancient French court certain ladies had the *droit de tabouret* (right of sitting on a tabouret in the presence of the queen). At first it was limited to princesses, but subsequently it was extended to all the chief ladies of the queen's household, and later still the wives of ambassadors, dukes, lord chancellors, and keepers of the seals, enjoyed the privilege Gentlemen similarly privileged had the *droit de fauteuil*

Tabula rasa (tăb′ û la rä′ zà) (Lat , a scraped tablet) A clean slate—literally and figuratively —on which anything can be written Thus, we say that the mind of a person who has been badly taught must become a *tabula rasa* before he can learn anything properly

Tabulæ Toletanæ (tăb′ û lē tol e tā′ nē) The astronomical tables composed by order of Alphonso X of Castile, hence they are also known as the Alphonsine Tables They were produced in 1252, being compiled by 50 astronomers working at Toledo and basing their calculations on that point.

His Tables Tolletanes forth he brought,
Ful wel corrected ne ther lakked nought
CHAUCER. *Franklin's Tale*, 545.

Tace Latin for candle. Silence is most discreet *Tace* is Latin for "be silent," and candle is symbolical of *light*. The phrase means "keep it dark," do not throw light upon it Fielding, in *Amelia* (ch x), says, "*Tace*, madam, is Latin for candle" There is an historical allusion worth remembering It was customary at one time to express disapprobation of a play or actor by throwing a candle on the stage, and when this was done the curtain was immediately drawn down W C Oulton's *History of the Theatres of London* (1796) gives us an instance of this which occurred January 25th, 1772, at Covent Garden Theatre, when the piece before the public was *An Hour Before Marriage* Someone threw a candle on the stage, and the curtain was dropped at once

There are some auld stories that cannot be ripped up again with entire safety to all concerned *Tace* is Latin for candle —SCOTT *Redgauntlet*, ch xi
Mum William mum *Tace* is Latin for candle — W B YEATS *Fairy Tales of the Irish Peasantry*, p 205

We have several of these phrases, *see* BRANDY IS LATIN FOR GOOSE

Tack The use of this word by sailors as meaning food is of unknown origin **Hard Tack** is a large, coarse, hard biscuit baked with salt and at one time a staple of diet in the foc'sle mess **Soft tack** is good, easily masticated food such as was served at the captain's table

Tacky (U.S A) Small pony—a derogatory term

Tactics, in the science of war is the art of manœuvring bodies of men, ships etc , in contact with the enemy, strategy is the art of manœuvring before contact, so that when contact is made it will be to the enemy's disadvantage

Tages (tā′ jēz) In Etruscan mythology a mysterious boy with the wisdom of an old man who was ploughed up, or who sprang from, the ground at Tarquinii He is said to have been the grandson of Jupiter and to have instructed the Etruscans in the arts of augury The latter wrote down his teaching in twelve

books, which were known as "the books of Tages," or "the Acherontian books "

Tae-pings. Chinese rebels of about 1850 to 1864. The word means *Universal Peace*, and arose thus, Hung Hsiu-ch'uan, a man of humble birth, and an unsuccessful candidate for a government office, was converted to Christianity and gave out that he was the chosen instrument in God's hands to uproot idolatry and establish the dynasty of Universal Peace He soon collected a numerous following, and in 1853 seized the city of Nanking. In 1864 Major Gordon ("Chinese Gordon") overthrew Hung's army, and the insurrection was put down, after the loss of over a million lives and incalculable property

Taffeta or **Taffety** (tăf′ e tå, tăf′ e ti) A material made of silk, at one time it was watered, hence Taylor says, "No taffaty more changeable than they " The word is from the Persian *taftan*, to twist or cure

The fabric has often changed its character At one time it was silk and linen, at another silk and wool In the eighteenth century it was lustrous silk, sometimes striped with gold.

Taffeta phrases. Smooth sleek phrases, euphemisms We also use the words *fustian, stuff, silken, shoddy, buckram, velvet,* etc , to qualify phrases and literary compositions spoken or written

Taffata phrases, silken terms precise,
Three-piled hyperboless
Love' Labour's Lost, v, 2

Taffy. A Welshman So called from *David*, a very common name in Wales. Familiarly *Davy*, it becomes in Welsh *Taffid, Taffy*

Tag, is the usual American name for the British children's game of "He "

Tag, rag and bobtail. *See* RAG, TAG AND BOBTAIL

Tail. According to an old fable lions wipe out their footsteps with their tail, that they may not be tracked

To tail is to follow a suspected person, keep him under observation, and prevent his escaping

Out of the tail of one's eye With a sidelong glance, just to see a thing "out of the corner of your eye "

To put salt on the tail. *See* SALT.

To turn tail. To turn one's back and run away

Twisting the lion's tail. Seeing how far the "Britishers" will bear provocation. "To give the lion s tail another twist" is to tax the British forbearance a little further. The nation will put up with a deal rather than resort to the arbitration of arms

With his tail between his legs Very dejected, quite downcast The allusion is to dogs

Tailed men. There are no such beings as tailed men, but until the mid-19th century reports every now and then cropped up of tribes with tails having been discovered in Central Africa, New Guinea, or other little-known parts

In the early Middle Ages it was widely believed on the Continent, especially in France, that all Englishmen had tails, and it was for long a saying that the men of Kent (the part nearest to France) were born with tails, as a punishment for the murder of Thomas a Becket

> For Becket's sake, Kent always shall have tails
> *Andrew Marvell*

A *Warwickshire* Man will be known by his Grinn, as Roman-Catholicks imagine a *Kentish* Man by his Tail —ADDISON *Spectator*, 173.

One account fastens the legend on the town of Strood —

> As Becket, that good saint, sublimely rode,
> Thoughtless of insult, through the town of Strode,
> What did the mob? Attacked his horse's rump
> And cut the tail, so flowing, to the stump
> What does the saint? Quoth he, "For this vile trick
> The town of Strode shall heartily be sick"
> And lo! by power divine, a curse prevails—
> The babes of Strode are born with horse's tails
> PETER PINDAR *Epistle to the Pope*

But in Ray's time (early 17th cent.) St Augustine was generally credited with the miracle He, it was said, was preaching to some pagan villagers when they, to make fun of him, fastened fish-tails to their posteriors, whereupon Augustine ordained that all the next generation should be born with tails, and it was so. This, moreover, was said to have taken place in Cerne, Dorsetshire, and not in Kent at all

In the Middle Ages it was also popularly held that Jews were born with tails, this arose from a confusion of the word *rabbi* with *rabom* or *rabumo*, the devil, from Span *rabo*, a tail

Tail-end Charlie. An R A F phrase in World War II for the last aircraft of a group on a mission—usually far behind the others and the recipient of spiteful attention from the enemy

Taillefer (tī á fâr) A minstrel and warrior who accompanied William of Normandy to England in 1066 He went before the Norman army, singing of Charlemagne, Roland, and those who died at Roncesvalles He obtained permission to strike the first blow in the Battle of Hastings, where he was killed.

Tailor Nine tailors make a man. An old expression of contempt at the expense of tailors signifying that a tailor is so much more feeble than anyone else that it would take nine of them to make a man of average stature and strength As a fact, the occupation of a tailor, and the cramped position in which he works are not conducive to good physique, but it has been suggested that *tailor* is probably a facetious transformation of *teller*, a *teller* being a stroke on the bell at a funeral, three being given for a child, six for a woman, and *nine* for a *man*

The number mentioned is sometimes only three —

> Some foolish knave, I thinke, at first began
> The slander that three taylers are one man
> TAYLOR *Workes*, iii, 73 (1630).

The three tailors of Tooley Street. Canning says that three tailors of Tooley Street, Southwark, addressed a petition of grievances to the House of Commons, beginning—"We,

the people of England" Hence the phrase is used of any pettifogging coterie that fancies it represents the nation

Taiping. *See* TAEPING.

Taj Mahal (taj ma hal') A mausoleum near Agra, built in 1650 by the great Mogul emperor Shah Jehan in memory of his favourite wife, Mumtaz Mahal The name comes from one of her titles—Taj Mahal, Crown of the Palace Designed by Ustad Isa, a Turk or Persian, this white marble building is the supreme achievement of the Mogul style

Take. To be taken aback. To be quite surprised for the moment, flabbergasted From a nautical term, used when a ship's sails are so caught by the wind that they are forced back against the mast and thus impede any way the ship may have on her

To have a taking way with one. To be of an ingratiating disposition, able to make oneself liked at once, *fetching way, winning way,* mean the same thing

To take after. To have a strong resemblance to, physically, mentally, etc "Doesn't little Johnny take after his father?" "Most of Lawrence's paintings seem to take after Romney"

To take back one's words. To withdraw them, to recant

To take down a peg. *See* PEG

To take in. To deceive, gull Hence, *a regular take-in,* a hoax, swindle.

To take into one's head. To conceive the notion that . , to resolve to do so and so.

To take it out of someone. To exact satisfaction, to get one's own back, or, of oneself, to become thoroughly exhausted, as "Working after midnight does take it out of me"

To take it upon oneself. To make oneself responsible (perhaps unwarrantably) to assume control

To take off. To mimic or ridicule, also to start, especially of an aeroplane or of one in an athletic contest, as jumping or racing.

To take on. To be upset or considerably affected In the U S A , to assume, or adopt

To take over. To assume the management, control, or ownership.

To take up. To take into custody, arrest, also used of patronizing people and getting them introductions into good society, etc

> "Yes, Lady Rockminster has took us up," said Lady Clavering
> "Taken us up, Mamma," cried Blanche, in a shrill voice
> "Well, taken us up, then," said my lady, "it's very kind of her, and I dare say we shall like it when we git used to it, only at first one don't fancy being took—well, taken up, at all"—THACKERAY *Pendennis*, ch. xxxvii

Tale. A tally; a reckoning In *Exod* v, 8, we have *tale of bricks* A measure by number, as of a shepherd counting his sheep —

> And every shepherd tells his tale
> Under the hawthorn in the dale
> MILTON *L'Allegro*, 67

An old wife's tale. Any marvellous legendary story The phrase was used by George Peele as the title of a play (1595), and by Arnold Bennett as that of a novel (1908).

A tale of a tub. *See* TUB.

To tell tales out of school. To utter abroad affairs not meant for the public ear

Talent. Ability, aptitude, a "gift" for something or other The word is borrowed from the parable in *Matt* xxv, 14-30, and was originally the name of a weight and piece of money in Assyria, Greece, Rome, etc (Gr *talanton*, a balance) The value varied, the later Attic talent weighing about 57 lb troy, and being worth about £250

The Ministry of All the Talents The name ironically given to Grenville's coalition of 1806 It included Fox, Erskine, Fitzwilliam, Ellenborough, and Sidmouth. The term has also been applied—ironically—to later coalitions

Tales (tā' lēz) Persons in the court from whom selection is made to supply the place of jurors who have been empanelled, but are not in attendance. It is the first word of the Latin sentence providing for this contingency— *Tales de circumstantibus*, *i e* "from such (persons) as are standing about "
    To serve for jurymen or tales
                BUTLER *Hudibras*, Pt iii, 8

To pray a tales. To pray that the number of jurymen may be completed
    In the celebrated action Bardell *v* Pickwick—
It was discovered that only ten special jurymen were present Upon this, Mr Serjeant Buzfuz prayed a *tales*, the gentleman in black then proceeded to press into the special jury, two of the common jurymen, and a greengrocer and a chemist were caught directly —DICKENS *Pickwick Papers* ch xxxiv

Those who supplement the jury are called *talesmen*, and their names are set down in the *talesbook.*

Taliesin (tăl ı ēs' ın, tăl' ı sın) An ancient Welsh bard of whom very little is known He is placed in the 6th century, is said to have been a schoolfellow of Gildas, and to have been buried at Aberystwyth The so-called *Book of Taliesin* (given in the *Mabinogion*) is not earlier than the 13th century
    Taliesin is said to have prophesied that his nation would once again rule over England— a prophecy which was verified by the accession of Henry VII, son of Owen Tudor Hence Gray's allusion to him—
  What strings symphonious tremble in the air,
  What strains of vocal transport round her play!
  Hear from the grave great Taliessin, hear,
  They breathe a soul to animate the clay
                   The Bard

Talisman. A charm or magical figure or word, such as the Abraxas (*q v*), which is cut on metal or stone, under the influence of certain planets, it is supposed to be sympathetic, and to receive an influence from the planets which it communicates to the wearer
    In Arabia a talisman consisting of a piece of paper, on which are written the names of the Seven Sleepers and their dog, to protect a house from ghosts and demons, is still used, and in order to free any place of vermin a talisman consisting of the figure of the obnoxi-

ous animal is made in wax or consecrate metal, in a planetary hour.
  He swore that you had robbed his house,
  And stole his talismanic louse
            BUTLER *Hudibras*, pt iii, 1

The word is the Arabic *tilasman* from la Greek *telesma*, mystery.

Tall anciently meant comely, fine, handsome hence brave and valiant, and such phrases a *a tall and proper man, a tall ship* (*i e* one stron and well found in every respect) were use without any special reference to height
  You were good soldiers, and tall fellows —SHAKI
SPEARE *Merry Wives of Windsor*, ii, 2
  The undaunted resolution and stubborn ferocity c
Gwenwyn   had long made him beloved among th
"Tall Men" or champions of Wales —SCOTT *Th Betrothed*, ch i
Beyond the extreme sea-wall, and between the remot
    sea-gates,
Waste water washes, and tall ships founder, and dee;
    death waits   SWINBURNE *Hymn to Proserpine.*

A tall tale. An incredible story.

Tally. To correspond The tally used in the Exchequer was a rod of wood, marked on one face with notches (Fr *taille*, a notch or in cision) corresponding to the sum for which it was an acknowledgment Two other sides contained the date, the name of the payer, and so on The rod was then cleft in such a manner that each half contained one written side and half of every notch One part was kept in the Exchequer, and the other was circulated When payment was required the two parts were compared, and if they "tallied," or made a tally, all was right, if not, there was some fraud, and payment was refused
    The last tally was issued in 1826 In 1834 orders were issued for their destruction Two cartloads of them were lighted as a bonfire, and the conflagration set on fire the Houses of Parliament, which, with their offices and part of the Palace of Westminster, were burnt to the ground

Tallyman. A travelling hawker who calls at private houses to sell wares on the *tally system*—that is, part payment on account, and other parts when the man calls again, so called because he keeps a *tally* or score of his transactions

To live tally, or make a tally bargain. Said of a couple who live together as man and wife without being married—presumably because they do so as their tastes *tally*, and not from any reason of compulsion.

Tally-ho! The cry of fox-hunters on catching sight of the fox. It is the English form of the old French *taiant*, which was similarly used in deer-hunting, and also as a cry to the hounds when their share of the disembowelled stag was thrown to them

Talmud, The (tăl' mŭd) (Heb , instruction) The body of Jewish civil and religious law not contained in, but largely derived from, the Pentateuch The name was originally applied only to the Gemara (*q v*), but it now usually includes also the Mishna (*q v*).
    When the *Talmud* is spoken of without any qualification the reference is to the *Babylonian Talmud*, one of the two recensions of the

Gemara, the other being the *Palestinian Talmud*, which is of only about a fourth the volume of the *Babylonian*, and is considered by Jews of less authority The *Babylonian* codification dates from the 5th or 6th century, the *Palestinian* (or *Jerusalem*) from about a century earlier.

Talus (tā′lus) In Greek mythology, a man of brass, made by Hephæstus (Vulcan), the guardian of Crete Whenever he caught a stranger on the island he made himself red-hot and embraced him to death

He is introduced by Spenser into the *Faerie Queene* (Bk. v) as the "yron man" attendant upon Sir Artegal, and representing executive power—"swift as a swallow, and as lion strong "

Tamasha (tà ma′ sha). A Hindustani word meaning a spectacle, an entertainment on a lavish scale, a show worth seeing

Tamburlaine, Tamerlane (tăm′ bĕr lān, tăm′ ĕr lăn) Names under which the Tartar conqueror Timur, or Timur-leng, *i e* "Timur the Lame" (1333-1405), is immortalized in Elizabethan drama He had his capital at Samarkand, was ruler of vast territories in central Asia and a great part of India, and died while preparing to invade China. *Tamburlaine the Great* (acted in 1587), a blank verse tragedy, was Marlowe's first play. In Rowe's play, *Tamerlane* (1702), the warrior appears as a calm, philosophic prince—out of compliment to William III

Taming of the Shrew, The. Shakespeare's play (first printed in the 1623 Folio) was a re-writing of an anonymous comedy—*The Taming of A Shrew*—printed in 1594, its theme, a recipe for the management of wives, was very popular with contemporary audiences *See* SLY

Tammany Hall (tăm′ á ni) The headquarters (in 14th Street, New York) of the controlling organization of the Democratic Party in New York City and State, hence, the Party itself, and, as this has been so frequently prosecuted and exposed for bribery and corruption, used figuratively for wholesale and systematic political or municipal malpractice

Tammany was the name of a 17th-century Delaware chief, and the patriotic, anti-British leagues of pre-Revolutionary days adopted the name "St Tammany" to ridicule the titles of loyalist organizations—Societies of St George, St Andrew, and so on. After the Revolution these leagues became anti-aristocratic clubs, but all soon died a natural death except "Tammany Society, No. 1," which was that of New York This flourished, and was converted into a political machine by Aaron Burr in his conflict with Alexander Hamilton (about 1798), and in 1800 played a prominent part in the election of Jefferson to the Presidency

Tammuz. *See* THAMMUZ.

Tam-o'-Shanter. The hero of Burns's poem of that name, the soft cloth headdress is so called from him

Remember Tam-o'-Shanter's mare. You may pay too dear for your whistle, as Meg lost her tail, pulled off by Nannie of the "Cutty-sark," in Burns's poem

> Think, ye may buy the joys owre dear—
> Remember Tam-o'-Shanter's mare
>   BURNS *Tam-o'-Shanter*

Tanagra (tăn′ a gra). The general name given to terracotta figurines of dancing girls, etc. Mostly of the 4th and 3rd centuries B C, they were originally used as household gods or as ornaments, and buried in Greek tombs in Asia Minor, Greece, Sicily, and S Italy A great number of examples were found in 1870-72 in Tanagra, an ancient town of Bœotia

Tancred (d 1112) One of the chief heroes of the First Crusade, and a leading character in Tasso's *Jerusalem Delivered* He was the son of Eudes (Otho) and Emma (sister of Robert Guiscard), Bœmond or Bohemond was his cousin In the epic he was the greatest of all the Christian warriors except Rinaldo

Disraeli's novel, *Tancred* (1846), is a fantastic romance, telling how an early-19th-century heir to a dukedom goes on a "New Crusade" to the Holy Land

Tandem. A pair of horses harnessed one behind the other, hence applied to a bicycle ridden by two persons in this position. The word is a punning use of the Latin *tandem*, at length, *i e* of time, the horses being "lengthways" instead of side by side.

Tangie. A water sprite of the Orkneys; from Dan *tang*, sea-weed, with which it is covered. It is fabled to appear sometimes in human form, and sometimes as a little apple-green horse.

Tangram. A Chinese puzzle consisting of a square cut into seven pieces—a square, a rhomboid, and five triangles, which can be fitted together to form a number of shapes and figures

Tanist (Gael *tanaiste*). The elected heir presumptive to an ancient Irish chieftain, chosen generally from among the chief's relations Hence, tanistry, the ancient Irish tenure of lands and chieftainship.

Tanist stone. The monolith erected by the ancient Gaelic kings at their coronation; especially that called *Liafail*, which, according to tradition, is identical with the famous stone of Scone (*q v*), now forming part of the Coronation Chair in Westminster Abbey. It is said to have been set up at Icolmkil for the coronation of Fergus I of Scotland, a contemporary of Alexander the Great (about 300 B C), and son of Ferchard, King of Ireland

Tank. The heavily armoured military motor fort, running on "caterpillar" wheels, enclosed, and with room in the interior for quick-firing guns and several men, was so called by the War Office before it made its first appearance to prevent information as to its real nature leaking out to the enemy Telegrams, etc, with inquiries about *tanks* would cause no suspicion if they fell into enemy hands Tanks were invented during World War I, and were first used in the British attack on the German lines at Flers, September 15th, 1916.

Tanner Slang for a sixpenny piece The term has been in use for over a hundred years.

Tannhäuser (tăn' hoi zer) A lyrical poet, or *minnesinger*, of Germany, who flourished in the second half of the 13th century He led a wandering life, and is said even to have visited the Far East, this fact, together with his *Buszlied* (song of repentance), and the general character of his poems, probably gave rise to the legend about him—which first appeared in a 16th-century German ballad. This relates how he spends a voluptuous year with Venus, in the Venusberg, a magic land reached through a subterranean cave, at last he obtains leave to visit the upper world, and goes to Pope Urban for absolution "No," said His Holiness, "you can no more hope for mercy than this dry staff can be expected to bud again" Tannhauser departs in despair, but on the third day the papal staff bursts into blossom; the Pope sends in every direction for Tannhauser, but the knight is nowhere to be found, for, mercy having been refused, he has returned to end his days in the arms of Venus

Tansy. A yellow-flowered perennial herb, so called from Gr *athanasia*, immortality, because it is a sort of everlasting flower

Tantalus (tăn' tà lus) In Greek mythology, the son of Zeus and Pluto (daughter of Himantes) He was a Lydian king, highly honoured and prosperous; but, because he divulged to mortals the secrets of the gods, he was plunged up to the chin in a river of Hades, a tree hung with clusters of fruit being just above his head As every time he tried to drink, the waters receded from him, and as the fruit was just out of reach, he suffered agony from thirst, hunger, and unfulfilled anticipation

Hence our verb, *to tantalize*, to excite a hope and disappoint it, and hence the name *tantalus* applied to a lock-up spirit chest in which the bottles are visible but un-get-at-able without the key

Tantivy Men (tăn tiv' i). The High Churchmen and Tories of the post-Restoration period, so called because about 1680 they were caricatured as being mounted on the Church of England, "riding tantivy" to Rome *To ride tantivy* (a hunting term) is to ride at a rapid gallop

Tantony Pig. The smallest pig of a litter, which, according to the old proverb, will follow its owner anywhere. So called in honour of St Anthony, who was the patron saint of swineherds and is frequently represented with a little pig at his side.

Tantony is also applied to a small church bell—or to any hand-bell—for there is usually a bell round the neck of St Anthony's pig or attached to the Tau-cross he carries *See* ANTHONY, ST

Tantras, The (tăn' tras) Sanskrit religious writings, forming the Bible of the Shaktas, a Hindu religion the adherents of which worship the divine power in its female aspect

The Tantras consist of magical formulas for the most part in the form of dialogues between Shiva and his wife, and treat of the creation and ultimate destruction of the world,

divine worship, the attainment of superhuman power, and final union with the Supreme Spirit They are of comparatively recent date (6th or 7th cent A D)

Tantra is Sanskrit for thread, or warp, and hence is used of groundwork, order, or doctrine of religion

Taoism (tä' ō izm) One of the three great religious systems of China (Confucianism and Buddhism being the others), founded by the philosopher Lao-tsze (about 604–523 B C), and based on the *Tao-teh-king* (Book of Reason and Virtue), reputed to be by him.

Tap Dance. A quick-time dance in which the rhythm is beaten out on the floor with the dancer's toe or heel, or both alternately On the stage shoes with a double sole are worn in order that the tap will be more readily audible

Tap-up Sunday. An old local name for the Sunday preceding October 2nd, when a fair was held on St. Catherine's Hill, near Guildford So called because any person, with or without a licence, might open a "tap," or sell beer on the hill for that one day.

Tapis (tăp' ē) **On the tapis** On the carpet, under consideration, now being ventilated An English-French phrase, referring to the *tapis* or cloth with which the table of the council chamber is covered, and on which are laid the motions before the House

My business comes now upon the tap,s —
FARQUHAR *The Beaux Stratagem*, iii, 3

Tapley, Mark Martin's servant and companion in Dickens's *Martin Chuzzlewit*, often taken as the type of one who is jolly under all circumstances, never downhearted, and invariably cheerful.

Tappit-hen. A Scots term, properly for a hen with a crest on its head, but generally used for a large beer or wine measure Readers of *Waverley* will remember (in ch xi) the Baron Bradwardine's tappit-hen of claret "containing at least three English quarts "
Weel she lo'ed a Hawick gill
And leugh to see a tappit-hen

To have a tappit-hen under the belt is to have swallowed three quarts *Cp* HEN AND CHICKENS, JEROBOAM

Tar. Jack Tar. A sailor, probably an abbreviation of *tarpaulin*, of which sailors' caps and overalls are made Tarpaulins are tarred cloths, and are commonly used on board ship to keep articles from the sea-spray, etc

To beat the tar out of. To belabour, or beat without mercy The phrase possibly originated in the attempt to free a sheep's wool from the tar applied to heal any cuts received during shearing

Tar-heel, the colloquial name for a native of North Carolina, that State is known as the Tar-heel State

All tarred with the same brush All alike to blame, all sheep of the same flock The allusion is to the custom of distinguishing the sheep of any given flock by a common mark with a brush dipped in tar

Tarred and feathered. Stripped to the skin, daubed with tar, and then rolled in feathers so that the feathers adhere, a common popular punishment in primitive communities, and still occasionally resorted to

The first record of this punishment is in 1189 (1 *Rich* 1) A statute was made that any robber voyaging with the crusaders "shall be first shaved, then boiling pitch shall be poured upon his head, and a cushion of feathers shook over it " The wretch was then to be put on shore at the very first place the ship came to (Rymer· *Fœdera*, i, 65)

Tarantella (tăr ĕn tel' a) A very quick Neapolitan dance (or its music) for one couple, said to have been based on the gyrations practised by those whom the tarantula had poisoned

Tarantula (ta răn' tū lä) A large and hairy venomous spider (so called from *Taranto*, Lat. *Tarentum*, a town in Apulia, Italy, where they abound), whose bite was formerly supposed to be the cause of the dancing mania hence known as *tarantism* This was an hysterical disease, common, epidemically, in southern Europe from the 15th to the 17th centuries

At the close of the fifteenth century we find that Tarantism has spread beyond the boundaries of Apulia, and that the fear of being bitten by venomous spiders had increased Nothing short of death itself was expected from the wound which these insects inflicted, and if those who were bitten escaped with their lives, they were said to be seen pining away in a desponding state of lassitude —HECKER *Epidemics of the Middle Ages* (1859)

Targums. The name given to the various Aramaic (Chaldean) translations and interpretations of the Old Testament They were transmitted orally from the period soon after the Captivity, and were not written down until about the close of the 1st century A.D.

Tariff. A table of duties or customs, payable on the importation or exportation of goods, hence, a table of charges generally, as of those at an hotel or restaurant The word is the Arabic *tarif*, information, which was adopted in Old French as *tariffe*, for arithmetic.

Tariff reform A political movement in Great Britain, inaugurated in 1903 by Joseph Chamberlain (1836-1914), for the extension of the tariff on imports, principally with the object of preventing "dumping" (i e the disposal in our own country of surplus or unsaleable goods manufactured abroad at such a price that the home markets are cut out), and for the protection of home industries

Tarot Cards (tă' rot) Italian playing-cards, first used in the 14th century and still occasionally employed for fortune-telling A pack contains 78 cards, 4 suits of numeral cards with four coat-cards, i e king, queen, chevalier, and valet, and in addition to the four suits 22 *atutti* cards, or trumps, known as *tarots*

Tarpaulin. *See* TAR

Tarpeian Rock (tär pē' ăn) An ancient rock or peak (now no longer in existence) of the Capitoline Hill, Rome, so called from Tarpeia, a vestal virgin, the daughter of Spurius Tarpeius, governor of the citadel, who, according to the legend, agreed to open the gates to the Sabines if they would give her "what they wore on their arms" (meaning their bracelets). The Sabines, "keeping their promise to the ear," crushed her to death with their shields, and her body was hurled from the Tarpeian Rock Subsequently, traitors were cast down this rock and so killed.

Bear him to the rock Tarpeian, and from thence Into destruction cast him
Coriolanus, iii, 1

Tarquin (tar' kwin). The family name of a legendary line of early Roman kings, Tarquinius Priscus, the fifth king of Rome, is dated 617-578 B C. His son, Tarquinius Superbus, was the seventh (and last) king of Rome, and it was his son, Tarquinius Sextus, who committed the rape on Lucretia, in revenge for which the Tarquins were expelled from Rome and a Republic established.

Tarquin is also the name of a "recreant knight" figuring in the Arthurian cycle.

Tart. As applied to a harlot or girl of loose sexual morals this word dates back to Victorian times and in all probability is a contraction of "sweetheart "

Tartan Plaid A plaid of a *tartan*, or chequered, pattern A *plaid* is some twelve yards of narrow cloth wrapped round the waist, or over the chest and one shoulder, and reaching to the knees It may be chequered or not, but the English use of the word in such a compound as *Scotch plaids*, meaning chequered cloth, is a blunder for *Scotch tartans* The *tartan* is the chequered pattern, every clan having its own tartan. Though the thing is now typically Scottish, the word is from *Tartar* (Lat. *Tartenus*).

Tartar or Tatar. The name employed in China and in mediæval Europe for the tribes of Central Asian nomads Under Jenghiz Khan and his successors they established the kingdom of Tartary, and from 1238 to 1462 dominated Eastern Europe The Tatar Republic is an autonomous republic of the U.S.S.R., with its capital in Kazan

To catch a Tartar. *See* CATCH

Tartarian Lamb. *See* SCYTHIAN

Tartarus. The infernal regions of classical mythology; used as equivalent to Hades (*q v*) by later writers, but by Homer placed as far beneath Hades as Hades is beneath the earth. It was here that Zeus confined the Titans. *Cp.* HELL

Tartuffe (tar tuf') The principal character of Molière's comedy so titled, [a pedantic, obscene, and hypocritical poltroon, said to be drawn from the Abbé de Roquette, a parasite of the Prince de Condé The name is from the Italian *tartuffoli* (truffles), and was suggested to Molière on seeing the sudden animation which lighted up the faces of certain monks when they heard that a seller of truffles awaited their orders

Tassel-gentle. The male goshawk trained for falconry, *tassel* being a corruption of *tiercel*, a male hawk, which is a third (*tierce*) less in size than the female, and called *gentle* because of its tractable disposition.

Shakespeare uses the term figuratively for a sweetheart.—

O for a falconer's voice
To lure this tassel-gentle back again'
Romeo and Juliet, ii, 2.

Tattoo. The beat of drum at night to recall soldiers to barracks is so called from Dutch *taptoe*, closed or put to In the mid-17th century, when the word came into use, it was written *tap-too, tapp-too*, etc

The other **tattoo**, to mark the skin by rubbing indelible pigments into small punctures, is one of our very few words from Polynesian It is Tahitian (*tatau*, mark), and was introduced by Captain Cook (1769)

The devil's tattoo. *See* DEVIL

Torchlight tattoo. A military entertainment, carried out at night in the open air with illuminations, evolutions, and a lot of music

Tau. The letter T in Greek and the Semitic languages Anciently it was the last letter of the Greek alphabet (as it still is of the Hebrew), and in Middle English literature the phrase *Alpha* to *Omega* was not infrequently rendered *Alpha to Tau.*

Tau cross. A T-shaped cross, especially St Anthony's cross.

Tauchnitz (*touch'* nits) The famous library of British and American books in English, bound in paper for circulation on the Continent of Europe, was founded by the Freiherr Christian Bernhard Tauchnitz (1816-95) in 1841, in Leipzig He came of a family which had been in the publishing business for several generations

Taurus (taw' rùs) (Lat , the bull). The second zodiacal constellation, and the second sign of the Zodiac, which the sun enters about April 21st

> As bees
> In spring-time, when the sun with Taurus rides,
> Put forth their populous youth about the hive
> In clusters —MILTON *Paradise Lost*, I, 768

Taverner's Bible. *See* BIBLE, THE ENGLISH.

Tawdry. A corruption of *St Audrey* (*Audrey* itself being a corruption of *Etheldrida*) At the annual fair of St Audrey, in the isle of Ely, cheap jewellery, and showy lace called *St. Audrey's lace* was sold, hence *tawdry*, which is applied to anything gaudy, in bad taste, and of little value *Cp* TANTONY

> Come, you promised me a tawdry lace and a pair of sweet gloves —*Winter's Tale*, iv, 4

Taxi, short for **taximeter,** is the accepted term for a motor cab In France the taximeter for registering distances and fares was employed on horse-drawn cabs or *fiacres* long before motor cabs were put on the road In Britain the taximeter became common only with the appearance of motor cabs, and the term accordingly became associated with them An aeroplane is said to taxi when it moves along the ground under its own power

Taylor's Institute. The University Museum at Oxford So called from Sir Robert Taylor (1714-88), who made large bequests towards its erection.

Te Deum, The (tē dē' um) This liturgical hymn, so called from the opening words of the Latin original, *Te Deum laudamus* ("Thee, God, we praise") was formerly ascribed to St Ambrose, but is probably of later date The story was that St. Ambrose improvised it while baptizing St. Augustine (386) In allusion to this tradition, it is sometimes called "the

Ambrosian Hymn," and in some of our early psalters it is entitled "Canticum Ambrosii et Augustini "

Te Igitur. One of the service-books of the Roman Catholic Church, so called from the first words of the canon of the Mass, *Te igitur* ("Thee, therefore ') *clementissime Pater*

Oaths upon the Te Igitur. Oaths sworn on this service-book, which were regarded as especially sacred

Tea. A nice old cup of tea. An ironical slang expression, which is applied to awkward occurrences, unpleasant situations, or muddles

A tea-fight. A tea-party, especially a church or chapel gathering at which tea and buns, etc , are provided.

Tea-kettle broth. "Poor man's soup," consisting of hot water, bread, and a small lump of butter, with pepper and salt, the French *soup maigre.*

Not my cup of tea Not at all in my line, not what I want or am suited for

Teapoy (tē' poi) A small, three- or four-legged occasional table Though largely used for standing a teatray upon, the teapoy has really nothing to do with tea, the name coming from the Hindustani *teen*, three and the Persian *pae*, a foot.

Teague. A contemptuous name for an Irishman (from the Irish personal name), rarely used nowadays but common in the 17th and 18th centuries

> Was't Carwell, brother James, or Teague,
> That made thee break the Triple League?
> ROCHESTER · *History of Insipids*

Tear (târ). **To tear Christ's body.** To use imprecations The common oaths of mediæval times were by different parts of the Lord's body; hence the preachers used to talk of "tearing God's body by imprecations "

> Hir othes been so grete and so dampnable
> That it is grisly for to heere hem swere;
> Our blissed Lordes body thay to-tere
> CHAUCER · *Pardoner's Tale*, 144

Tear (tēr) **Tear-shell.** A projectile which, on bursting, liberates gases which irritate the lachrymatory glands of all within range, causing the eyes to water and rendering them temporarily useless Also called a "lachrymatory shell."

Tears of Eos. The dewdrops of the morning were so called by the Greeks Eos was the mother of Memnon (*q v.*), and wept for him every morning

St. Lawrence's tears. *See* LAWRENCE.

The Vale of Tears. This world (*cp*. BACA)

Tec, or **'Tec.** Slang for a detective

Teeth *See* TOOTH.

Teetotal. A word expressive of total abstinence from alcoholic liquors as beverages, coined about 1833 by Dick Turner, an artisan at Preston, Lancashire

> Turner's tombstone contains the inscription "Beneath this stone are deposited the remains of Richard Turner, author of the word *Teetotal* as applied to abstinence from all intoxicating liquors, who departed this life on the 27th day of October, 1846, aged 56 years "

Teetotum. A top for spinning with the fingers, having usually four or six flat sides each of which is marked with a letter, figure, or other symbol The top is spun, and the players follow the direction indicated by the side that is uppermost when it comes to rest The modern "Put and Take" (*q v*) is an adaptation of the teetotum, the early forms of which had four sides, marked "T" (Lat *totum*, all, meaning take all the stakes), "P" (Lat *pone*, put, *i e* put down, or pay in), "N" (*nihil*, nothing), and "H" (half), or sometimes "A" (*aufer*, take away).

Teian Muse, The (tī' an) Anacreon (about B C 563-478), who was born at Teos, Asia Minor

> The Scian and the Teian muse,
> The hero's heart, the lover's lute,
> Have found the fame your shores refuse
> BYRON *The Isles of Greece*

Telamones (tĕl a mō' nēz) Large, sculptured male figures (*cp* ATLANTES, CARYATIDES) serving as architectural columns or pilasters So called from the Greek legendary hero Telamon (father of Ajax) who took part in the Calydonian hunt and the expedition of the Argonauts

Telemachus (te lem' à kus) The only son of Ulysses and Penelope After the fall of Troy he went, attended by Athene in the guise of Mentor, in quest of his father He ultimately found him, and the two returned to Ithaca and slew Penelope's suitors

Telemark (tel' e mark). The name of a swing or turn in ski-ing Telemark is the district in Norway where ski-ing began as a sport, about 1860

Telepathy (tĕ lep' à thi) The word invented in 1882 by F. W H Myers to describe "the communication of impressions of any kind from one mind to another independently of the recognized channels of sense." The term "thought-transference" is often used for this phenomenon and more nearly expresses its implications, for it indicates the communication of thought from one person to another without the medium of speech

Telephus *See* ACHILLEA

Tell, William The legendary national hero of Switzerland, whose deeds are based on a Teutonic myth of widespread occurrence in northern Europe.

Fable has it that Tell was the champion of the Swiss in the War of Independence against the Emperor Albert I (slain 1308) Tell refused to salute the cap of Gessler, the imperial governor, and for this act of independence was sentenced to shoot with his bow and arrow an apple from the head of his own son He succeeded in this dangerous trial, but in his agitation dropped an arrow from his robe The governor insolently demanded what the second arrow was for, and Tell fearlessly replied, "To shoot you with, had I failed in the task imposed upon me" Gessler now ordered him to be carried in chains across the lake, and cast into Küssnacht castle, a prey "to the reptiles that lodged there" He was, however, rescued by the peasantry, and, having shot Gessler, freed his country from the Austrian yoke

B D —29

The earliest form of the legend is found in the old Norse *Vilkina Saga* (based on Teutonic sources)

Saxo Grammaticus tells nearly the same story respecting Toki, who killed Harald, and similar tales are told of Adam Bell, Clym of the Clough, William of Cloudeslic and Henry IV, Olaf and Eindridi, etc

Kissling's monument at Altorf (1892), has four reliefs on the pedestal (1) Tell shooting the apple, (2) Tell's leap from the boat, (3) Gessler's death, and (4) Tell's death at Schachenbach

Teller. Anciently, one who kept the tallies (Anglo-Fr *talier*) and counted the money; now, a bank-clerk who receives and pays out money at the counter

Up to 1834 there were four officers of the Exchequer known as *Tellers of the Exchequer,* whose duty was to receive and pay out moneys. *See* TALLY

> When shall our prayers end?
> I tell thee (priest) .
> When proud surveyors take no parting pence,
> When Silver sticks not on the Teller's fingers,
> And when receivers pay as they receive
> GASCOIGNE *The Steel Glass* (1576)

Temora (tem' ôr à) One of the principal poems of Ossian (*q v*), in eight books, so called from the royal residence of the kings of Connaught

Templars or **Knights Templar.** Nine French knights bound themselves, at the beginning of the 12th century, to protect pilgrims on their way to the Holy Land, and received the name of *Templars,* because their arms were kept in a building given to them for the purpose by the abbot of the convent on the site of the old Temple of Solomon, at Jerusalem They used to call themselves the "Poor Soldiers of the Holy City "

Their habit was a long white mantle, to which subsequently was added a red cross on the left shoulder Their war-cry was *Bauseant* (an old French name for a black and white horse), from their banner, which was striped black and white, and charged with a red cross Their seal showed two knights riding on one horse, the story being that the first Master was so poor that he had to share a horse with one of his followers

The Order afterwards became very wealthy and corrupt, and so powerful that its suppression (effected in 1312) was necessary for the peace of Europe

In England the Order had its first house (built about 1121) near Holborn Bars, London, but a site between Fleet Street and the Thames was given to them by 1162, and here they were settled till Edward II suppressed the English branch and confiscated its possessions The lands and buildings went to the Knights Hospitallers who, in the reign of Edward III, granted them to the "students of the Common laws of England" (Stow)

In Paris the stronghold of the Knights Templar was taken over in 1313 by the Knights of St. John The old tower later became a prison where, in 1792, the royal family of France was incarcerated Louis XVI, Marie Antoinette, and Princess Elizabeth went thence to the guillotine, and the Dauphin

(Louis XVII) probably died within its walls The tower was demolished by Napoleon in the early years of the Empire

Temple, The. The site between Fleet Street and the Thames formerly occupied by the buildings of the Knights Templar (*see* TEMPLARS *above*), of which the Temple Church (dating from 1185) is the only portion now remaining though it was badly damaged in the air raids on London in 1940

Since 1346 the Temple has been in the possession of doctors and students of the law, who, since 1609, have formed the two Inns of Court (*q v*) known as the *Inner* and *Middle Temples* The badge of the former is the Winged Horse (*Pegasus*), that of the latter the Lamb (*Agnus Dei*)

The Inner Temple Hall is modern (1870), but that of the Middle Temple was one of the finest Elizabethan halls in existence It was built in 1572, and Shakespeare's play of *Twelfth Night* was probably performed here in 1602. Both were destroyed in air raids, but have since been rebuilt

Temple Bar. The old Fleet Street gateway into the City, formerly situated close to the entrance into the Temple, on the spot now marked by the monument known as the "Griffin " It was built by Wren in 1670, and was removed and re-erected in private grounds at Theobalds Park, Cheshunt, Herts, in 1878 It was long used for the exhibition of the heads of traitors and conspirators, and was hence sometimes called "the City Golgotha."

Temple. The name of the place of worship is the Lat *templum*, from Gr *temenos*, a sacred enclosure, i e a space *cut off* from its surroundings (Gr *temnein*, to cut) The Lat. *templum* originally denoted the space marked out by the augurs (*q v*) within which the sign was to occur

The *temples* of the forehead represent Lat. *tempora* (pl of *tempus*, time), the fatal spot, the temples

Temple of Solomon, The The central place of Jewish worship, erected by Solomon and his Tyrian workmen (probably on Phœnician models) on Mount Moriah, Jerusalem, about 1006 B C It was destroyed at the siege of Jerusalem by Nebuchadnezzar (588 B C), and some 70 years later the Temple of Zerubbabel was completed on its site In 20 B C Herod the Great began the building of the last Temple —that of the New Testament—which was utterly destroyed during the siege of Jerusalem by Vespasian and Titus in A D. 70 For many centuries the site has been covered by the Moslem mosque of Haram esh Sherif

The chief emblems of the Jewish Temple were —

The *golden candlestick.*
The *shewbread* The twelve loaves representing the twelve tribes of Israel
The *incense* of sweet spices, Prayer, which rises to heaven as incense.
The *Holy of Holies* The nation of the Jews as God's peculiar people

See Exod xxv, 30-32, *Rev.* 1, 12-20, *and see also* JACHIN AND BOAZ

Tempora mutantur (Lat , the times are changed) The tag is founded on *Omnia mutantur, nos et*

mutamur in illis (all things are changed, and we with them), a saying of Nicholas Borbonius, a Latin poet of the 16th century Lothair, Emperor of the Holy Roman Empire, had, it is stated, already said, *Tempora mutantur, nos et mutamur in illis.*

Ten. Ten to one Expressive of a very strong probability, as, "It's ten to one that it will rain to-night," i e. it's extremely likely to, *a ten to one chance*, one in which it is very much more likely that you will win than lose

The Council of Ten. A secret tribunal exercising unlimited powers in the old Venetian republic Instituted in 1310 with ten members, it was later enlarged to 17, and continued in active existence till the fall of the republic in 1797

The Ten Commandments. A humorous expression for the ten fingers, especially when used by an angry woman for scratching her opponent's face
> Could I come near your beauty with my nails,
> I'd set my ten commandments in your face
> 2 *Henry VI*, 1, 3

The Upper Ten. The aristocracy, the cream of society Short for *the upper ten thousand* The term was first used by N P Willis, (1806-67) a spirited American journalist, in speaking of the fashionables of New York.

Ten-cent Jimmy. James Buchanan (1791-1868), 15th President of the U S A (1857-61) was so nicknamed on account of his advocacy of low tariffs and low wages

Tenner. A ten-pound note, as *fiver* is a five-pound note

Tenpenny nails. Large-sized nails, originally so called because they were sold at 10d a hundred. Smaller nails used to be known as *eightpenny, sixpenny, fourpenny nails.*

The submerged tenth (sometimes called *the Tenth Legion*) *See* SUBMERGED

The Tenth Muse. A name given originally to Sappho (*q v*) there being *nine* true Muses (*see* MUSE), and afterwards applied to various literary women, as Mme de la Garde Deshoulières (1638-94), Mlle de Scudéry (1607-1701), Queen Christina of Sweden (1626-89), and the English novelist and essay-writer, Hannah More (1745-1833)

The tenth wave *See* WAVE

Tenant. One who holds property—land, house, etc —anciently by any kind of title, in modern use from the owner or landlord for payment; the French *tenant*, holding (*tenir*, to hold, Lat. *tenere*) Theoretically, all land in the United Kingdom belongs to the Crown, and all landholders are therefore tenants

Tenant at will. One who can at any moment be dispossessed of his tenancy at the will of the landlord or lessor

Tenant by frank-marriage. One holding lands or tenements by virtue of a gift thereof made to him upon his marriage.

Tenant in chief. One who holds from the king direct

Tenant-right. The right of an out-going tenant to claim from an incoming tenant compensation for the improvements he has made on the farm, etc , during his tenancy In Elizabethan times the term denoted the right that certain tenants possessed of passing on the tenancy, at decease, to the eldest surviving issue, and it is now sometimes applied to the right of a well-behaved tenant to compensation if deprived of his tenancy

Tender *See* LEGAL TENDER

Tenderfoot (pl -foots or feet) A novice, an inexperienced person, a term originally applied to a soft, unacclimatized newcomer to the ranches or mines of the Western States of U.S A

Tenderloin is the tender portion of meat lying under the short ribs of beef and pork, also a cut of beef between the sirloin and ribs. The word is also used as the name of the district in American cities where vice and police corruption are at their worst, the name thus arising from such a place being the "best cut" for political graft

Tendon of Achilles. *See* ACHILLES

Tennis. The real game of tennis (from which lawn tennis takes its name) is played with a ball and rackets by two or four persons on a walled court divided across the middle by a net. The court—96 ft by 32 ft —is surrounded by a wall from which a sloping roof, called the penthouse, extends on three sides to an inner wall, 7 ft high The server hits a ball with his racket so that it strikes the penthouse or the wall above it and rebounds into the court of his opponent's side of the net The game is extremely complicated, strokes being won or lost according to how they strike or fail to strike the walls or penthouse The old scoring of 15, 30, etc , with deuce and advantage have been adopted into lawn tennis

Tennis is of great age The king of France sent Henry V a box of tennis balls, all modern courts are modelled on that in which Henry VIII played at Hampton Court Lawn tennis first became popular in the late 1870s

Tenson. A contention in verse between rival troubadours; a metrical dialogue consisting of smart repartees, usually on women and love A sub-division of the troubadours' love lyrics also had the same name

Tenterden. Tenterden steeple was the cause of Goodwin Sands. A satirical remark made when some ridiculous reason is given for a thing. The story, according to one of Latimer's sermons, is that a Mr. Moore, being sent into Kent to ascertain the cause of the Goodwin Sands, called together the oldest inhabitants to ask their opinion. A very old man said, "I believe Tenterden steeple is the cause," and went on to explain that in his early days there was no Tenterden steeple, and there were no complaints about the sands This reason seemed ridiculous enough, but the fact seems to be that the Bishops of Rochester applied to the building of Tenterden steeple moneys raised in the county for the purpose of keeping Sandwich haven clear, so that when they found the harbour was getting blocked up

there was no money for taking the necessary steps *Cp* GOODWIN SANDS

Tenterhooks. I am on tenterhooks, or on tenterhooks of great expectation. My curiosity is on the full stretch, I am most curious or anxious to hear the issue Cloth, after being woven, is stretched or "tentered" on hooks passed through the selvedges (Lat *tentus,* stretched, hence "tent," canvas stretched)

Teraphim (ter' a fim) The idols or images of the ancient Hebrews and other Semitic peoples, worshipped by them as household gods or individual protecting deities, it was her father Laban's teraphim that Rachel stole and hid in the camel's saddle in *Gen* xxxi, 17-35

Term. In schools and the universities, the period during which instruction is given, in the law courts, the period during which the courts are in session

At Oxford and Cambridge there are three terms in a year; at the latter, Lent, Easter, and Michaelmas, and at Oxford, viz , Hilary, Trinity, and Michaelmas

LENT and HILARY—

Cambridge, begins January 13th, and ends on the Friday before Palm Sunday
Oxford, begins January 14th, and ends on the Saturday before Palm Sunday.

EASTER and TRINITY—

Cambridge, begins on the Friday of Easter-week, and ends Friday nearest June 20th
Oxford, begins on the Wednesday of Easter week, and ends Friday before Whit Sunday. The continuation, called "Trinity term," runs on till the second Saturday of July.

MICHAELMAS—

Cambridge, begins October 1st, and ends December 16th
Oxford, begins October 10th, and ends December 17th

The lawyers' terms, called, since 1873, law sessions, are.—

Michaelmas Sessions begin October 12th, and end December 21st
Hilary Sessions begin January 11th, and end the Wednesday before Easter
Easter Sessions begin the Tuesday after Easter week, and end the Friday before Whit Sunday
Trinity Sessions begin the Tuesday after Trinity Sunday and end August 8th

These are of Norman origin, and the Long Vacation was intended to coincide with the time of vintage

To bring to terms To force a person to accept one's conditions

To come to terms. To make an agreement with; decide the terms of a bargain

Termagant. The name given by the Crusaders and in mediæval romances, to an idol or deity that the Saracens were popularly supposed to worship. He was introduced into the morality plays as a most violent and turbulent person in long, flowing Eastern robes, a dress that led to his acceptance as a woman, whence the name came to be applied to a shrewish violently abusive virago

In the Romances his name was usually joined with that of Mohammed, and the *-magaunt* of *Termagaunt* may represent

Mahound, but as an early version of the name was *Tervagant* it has been suggested that perhaps the word is the Latin *ter vagantem*, the thrice wandering, with reference to Selene, or the Moon

> Twas time to counterfeit, or that hot termagant Scot [Douglas] had paid me scot and lot too —1 *Henry IV*, v, 4

Outdoing Termagant (*Hamlet*, iii, 2) In old drama the degree of rant was the measure of villainy. Termagant and Herod, being considered the *beau-ideal* of all that is bad, were represented as settling everything by club law, and bawling so as to split the ears of the groundlings *Cp* HEROD

That beats Termagant. Your ranting, raging pomposity, or exaggeration, surpasses that of Termagant of the old moralities

Terpsichore (těrp sik' ôr ı). One of the nine Muses (*q v*) of ancient Greece, the Muse of dancing and the dramatic chorus, and later of lyric poetry She is usually represented seated, and holding a lyre Hence, *Terpsichorean*, pertaining to dancing.

Terra firma. Dry land, in opposition to water; the continents as distinguished from islands. The Venetians so called the mainland of Italy under their sway, and the continental parts of America belonging to Spain were called by the same term

Terracotta. Unglazed earthenware of fine fired clay, either red or yellow The ancient Greeks employed terracotta extensively in architecture and statuary In the 14th century terracotta revived and was made much use of in the Renaissance age In the later years of the 19th century the material was favoured for facing and decorating important buildings, *e g.* the Natural History Museum, S Kensington (1873-80).

Terrapin War (ter' a pin) (U S A.) The name for the war with Britain in 1812, so called because, through the blockade of foreign vessels and trade, the U S A. was shut up in its shell like a terrapin

Terrible, The. Ivan IV (or II) of Russia (1529, 1533-84)

Terrier. A dog that "takes the earth," or unearths his prey (Fr , from Lat *terra*, earth), also formerly applied to the burrows of foxes, badgers, rabbits, and so on
Also slang for a member of the Territorial Army
A land-roll or description of estates is called a *terrier* from Fr *papier terrier*, a register of land.

Territorial Army. The British home defence force which, in 1908, superseded the old Militia, Yeomanry, and Volunteers, on a territorial basis
The infantry regiments of the line have been known as the *Territorial regiments* since 1881, when, following a new scheme of organization, each became associated in name, depot, etc , with some particular county or district

Terror, The, or the Reign of Terror. The period in the French Revolution between the fall of the Girondists and the overthrow of Robespierre It lasted 420 days, from May 31st, 1793, to July 27th, 1794 Also applied to similar cataclysms in the history of other nations, as the Russian Revolution (the *Red Terror*, March-Sept., 1917)

Terry Alts. Insurgents of Clare, who appeared after the Union (1798) and committed numerous outrages These rebels were similar to "the Thrashers" of Connaught, "the Carders," and the followers of "Captain Rock" in 1822

Ter-Sanctus. *See* TRISAGION.

Tertium quid A third party which shall be nameless, a third thing resulting from the combination of two things, but different from both Fable has it that the expression originated with Pythagoras, who, defining bipeds, said :—

> Sunt *bipes* homo, et avis, et tertium quid
> A man is a bipod, so is a bird, and a third thing (which shall be nameless).

Iamblichus says this third thing was Pythagoras himself
In chemistry, when two substances chemically unite, the new substance is called a *tertium quid*, as a neutral salt produced by the mixture of an acid and alkali

Terza Rima. An Italian verse-form in triplets, the second line rhyming with the first and third of the succeeding triplet. In the first triplet lines 1 and 3 rhyme, and in the last there is an extra line, rhyming with its second
Dante's *Divine Comedy* is in this metre, it was introduced into England by Sir Thomas Wyatt in the 16th century, and was largely employed by Shelley, as also by Byron in *The Prophecy of Dante.*

Test Act An Act of Parliament directed against Roman Catholics and Nonconformists, especially that of 1673, which decreed that all holders of public offices must take the Oaths of Allegiance and Supremacy, receive the Church of England sacrament, renounce the doctrine of Transubstantiation, etc. It was repealed in 1828
Hence, *to take the test*, to comply with the requirements of the Test Act

Test Match. In cricket, one of the matches played in a series between two national teams
England v. Australia First played, 1876. England has won (1951) 56 matches, Australia 68 matches, and 34 matches have been drawn.
England v South Africa First played, 1888. England 37 matches, South Africa 13, and 29 drawn
England v West Indies First played, 1928 England 9 matches, West Indies 8, and 8 drawn
England v New Zealand First played, 1929 England 3 matches, New Zealand 0, and 14 drawn
England v India First played, 1932 England 6 matches, and 4 drawn

Tester. A sixpenny piece, so-called from the *teston* of Henry VII, a coin which got its name from Ital *testa*, head, because it was stamped on one side with the *head* of the reigning sovereign Similarly, the head canopy of a bed is called its *tester*

> Hold, there's a tester for thee —2 *Henry IV*, iii, 2

Testers are gone to Oxford, to study at **Brazenose.** When Henry VIII debased the silver testers, the alloy broke out in red pimples through the silver, giving the royal likeness in the coin a blotchy appearance, hence the punning proverb

Testudo. *See* TORTOISE

Tête-à-tête (Fr , head to head) A confidential conversation, a heart to heart talk

Tête du pont. The barbican or watch-tower placed on the head of a drawbridge

Tether. He has come to **the end of his tether** He has outrun his fortune, he has exhausted all his resources The reference is to an animal tied to a rope (he can graze only so far as his tether can be carried out), or to a cable run out to the "bitter end" (*q v*)
Horace calls the end of life *ultima linea rerum,* the end of the goal, referring to the white chalk mark at the end of a racecourse

Tethys A sea goddess of the ancient Greeks, wife of Oceanus, hence, the sea itself

Tetragrammaton. A word of four letters, especially the name of the Deity, JHVR (*see* JEHOVAH), which the ancient Jews never pronounced The word means "I am," or "I exist" (*Exod.* iii, 14), but Rabbi Bechai says the letters include the three times—past, present, and future
Pythagoras called Deity a Tetrad or Tetractys, meaning the "four sacred letters," and it is curious that in so many languages the name of the Supreme Being should be composed of four letters; thus there are the Greek *Zeus* and θεος, in Latin *Jove* and *Deus*; Fr. *Dieu,* Dutch *Godt,* Ger. *Gott,* Dan *Godh,* Swed *Goth,* Arab. *Alla,* Sansk *Deva,* Span *Dios,* Scand *Odin,* and our *Lord*
> Such was the sacred Tetragrammaton.
> Things worthy silence must not be revealed
>   DRYDEN *Britannia Rediviva*

Tetrarch (tet′rark). Originally meaning the ruler of one of four parts of a region (Gr *tettares,* four, *archein,* to rule) under the Roman empire the term came to be applied to minor rulers, especially to the princes of Syria subject to the Roman Emperor In World War II the name of a very light British Airborne tank which was landed by glider

Teucer. In the *Iliad,* the son of Telamon, and step-brother of Ajax, he went with the allied Greeks to the siege of Troy, and on his return was banished by his father for not avenging on Ulysses the death of his brother

Teutons. The Germans, and Germanic peoples, from the Latin name, *Teutones,* for an ancient northern tribe, their own name for themselves being *Thiudans,* i e kings or lords *Cp* A S *theoden,* a king Our *Dutch* and the German *Deutsch* are variations of the same word, originally written *Theodisk*

Teutonic Cross. A cross potent, the badge of the order of Teutonic Knights *See* POTENT

Teutonic Knights. An order which arose at the time of the Crusades Originally only Germans of noble birth were admitted to the order Abolished by Napoleon in 1809, it was revived again in Austria in 1840.

Texarkana (teks ar kǎn′ à) A community formed of two cities, one in Texas and one in Arkansas, the States' boundary line running through the centre of the place The cities have separate municipal governments, but they are socially and commercially one, much as its various boroughs are part of London.

Texas Rangers. A constabulary force enlisted in Texas in 1835 to control the lawlessness of cattle-thieves and other outlaws, and the hostile Indians The Rangers' headquarters were at the fort now grown into the town of Ranger Their resourcefulness and toughness have surrounded their name with a sort of legendary splendour in the annals of the Wild West.

Th (θ, *theta*) The sign given in the verdict of the Areopagus of condemnation to death (*thanatos*).

Thaïs (thā′ is) The Athenian courtesan who, it is said, induced Alexander the Great, when excited with wine, to set fire to the palace of the Persian kings at Persepolis
> The king seized a flambeau with zeal to destroy,
> Thaïs led the way to light him to his prey,
> And, like another Helen, fired another Troy
>   DRYDEN *Alexander's Feast*

This is also the title of an historico-political novel (1890) by Anatole France

Thales. *See* SEVEN SAGES

Thalestris (thà les′ tris) A queen of the Amazons, who went with 300 women to meet Alexander the Great, under the hope of raising a race of Alexanders.

Thalia (thà li′ a) One of the Muses (*q v*), generally regarded as the patroness of comedy She was supposed by some, also, to preside over husbandry and planting, and is represented holding a comic mask and a shepherd's crook.

Thames (temz) The Latin *Thamesis* (the broad Isis, where *isis* is a mere variation of *esk, ouse, uisg,* etc , meaning water) It rises near Cirencester as the *Isis,* a name which has been applied to it as far as its junction with the *Thame,* near Dorchester
> Around his throne the sea-born brothers stood,
> Who swell with tributary urns his flood —
> First the famed authors of his ancient name
> The winding Isis and the fruitful Thame!
>   POPE: *Windsor Forest*

He'll never set the Thames on fire. He'll never make any figure in the world, never do anything wonderful and print his footsteps on the sands of time. The popular explanation is that the word *Thames* is a pun on the word *temse,* a corn-sieve, and that the parallel French locution *He will never set the Seine on fire* is a pun on *seine,* a drag-net, but these solutions are not tenable There is a Latin saw, *Tiberim accendere nequaquam potest,* which is probably the *fons et origo* of other parallel sayings; and the Germans had *Den Rhein anzunden* (to set the Rhine on fire) as early as 1630

Thammuz (thăm′ ūz). A Sumerian, Babylonian and Assyrian god who died every year and rose again in the spring He is identified with the Babylonian Marduk and the Greek Adonis.

In *Ezek* viii, 14, reference is made to the heathen "women weeping for Tammuz "

> Thammuz came next behind,
> Whose annual wound on Lebanon allured
> The Syrian damsels to lament his fate
> In amorous ditties all a summer's day,
> While smooth Adonis from his native rock
> Ran purple to the sea, supposed with blood
> Of Thammuz yearly wounded
>   MILTON. *Paradise Lost*, iii, 446.

Thamyris (thăm' i ris) A Thracian bard mentioned by Homer (*Iliad*, ii, 595) He challenged the Muses to a trial of skill, and, being overcome in the contest, was deprived by them of his sight and power of song He is represented with a broken lyre in his hand

> Blind Thamyris and blind Mæonides [Homer]
> And Tiresias and Phineus, prophets old,
>   MILTON *Paradise Lost*, iii, 35

Thane. The name given in Anglo-Saxon England to a class of soldiers and landholders ranking between the earl and the churl. The rank of thane could be attained by a man of lower degree. After the Norman Conquest the word disappeared in England, giving place to *knight*. In Scotland a thane ranked with an earl's son, holding his land direct from the king, the title was given also to the chief of a clan who became one of the king's barons

Thanksgiving Day. An annual holiday in U S A usually held on the last Thursday in November and observed as an acknowledgement of the divine favours received during the year It was first celebrated by the Plymouth Colony in 1621 After the Revolution it became general throughout the Republic, and since 1863 its observance has been annually recommended by the President.

That. Seven "thats" may follow each other, and make sense

> For be it known that we may safely write
> Or say that "that *that*" that that man wrote was right,
> Nay, e'en that that *that*, that "that THAT" has followed,
> Through six repeats the grammar's rule has hallowed,
> And that that *that* that *that* "that THAT" began
> Repeated seven times is right, deny't who can.

My lords, with humble submission *that* that I say is this, That that that "that that" that that gentleman has advanced is not *that* that he should have proved to your lordships —*Spectator*, No 86

Another *that* catch is to make sense of the following by supplying the missing punctuation —

> that that is is that that is not is not is that it it is

And that's that! A colloquial way of emphatically and triumphantly making one's point, closing the argument, and so on

Thaumaturgus (thaw ma těr' gus) (Gr., a conjuror, or wonder-worker) A miracle-worker, applied to saints and others who are reputed to have performed miracles, especially.—

Apollonius of Tyana, Cappadocia (A D 3-98)
St. Bernard of Clairvaux, "the Thaumaturgus of the West" (1091-1153).
St Filumena (*q.v*)
St Francis of Assisi, founder of the Franciscan order (1182-1226).
Gregory, Bishop of Neo-Cæsarea, in Cappadocia, called emphatically "Thaumaturgus," from the numerous miracles he is reported to have performed (died about 270)
Plotinus (died about 270), and several other Neoplatonists

Simon Magus, of Samaria, called "the Great Power of God" (*Acts* viii, 10)
St Vincent de Paul, founder of the "Sisters of Charity" (1576-1660)

Thé dansant An afternoon tea party, with dancing

Theagenes and Chariclea (thē āj' ė něz, chăr i klē' a) The hero and heroine of an erotic romance in Greek by Heliodorus, Bishop of Trikka (4th century)

Thebes, called *The Hundred-Gated*, was not Thebes of Bœotia, but the chief town of the Thebaid, on the Nile in Upper Egypt, said to have extended over twenty-three miles of land Homer says out of each gate the Thebans could send forth 200 war-chariots

> The world's great empress on the Egyptian plain,
> That spreads her conquests o'er a thousand states,
> And pours her heroes through a hundred gates,
> Two hundred horsemen and two hundred cars
> From each wide portal issuing to the wars
>   POPE· *Iliad*, i.

It is here that the vocal statue of Memnon stood, and here too are the tombs of the kings, including the tomb of Tutankhamun (reigned 1360-1350 B C) which was discovered in 1932, with its wealth and equipment almost intact The temple of Karnak, and large numbers of sculptures, sphinxes, etc , are to be seen in the village of Luxor, which now marks the site

The Seven against Thebes. An expedition in Greek legend fabled to have taken place against Thebes of Bœotia before the Trojan War The Seven were the Argive chiefs Adrastus, Polynices, Tydeus, Amphiaraus, Hippomedon, Capaneus, and Parthenopæus.

When Œdipus abdicated his two sons agreed to reign alternate years, but at the expiration of the first year, the elder, Eteocles, refused to give up the throne, whereupon Polynices, the younger brother, induced the six chiefs to espouse his cause The allied army laid siege to Thebes, but without success, and all the heroes perished except Adrastus. Subsequently, seven sons of the chiefs resolved to avenge their fathers' deaths, marched against the city, took it, and placed Terpander, one of their number, on the throne These are known as the *Epigoni* (Gr , descendants) The Greek tragic poets Æschylus and Euripides dramatized the legend.

Theban Bard or Eagle, The. Pindar, born at Thebes (about 520-435 B C)

Theban Legion, The. Another name for the "Thundering Legion" (*q.v*), which was raised in the Thebaid of Egypt, composed of Christian soldiers, and led by St Maurice.

Thecla, St. (thek' là) The first woman martyr, as St Stephen is the protomartyr. All that is known of her is from the *Acts of Paul and Thecla*, pronounced apocryphal by Pope Gelasius. According to the legend she was born of a noble family in Iconium, and was converted by the preaching of St Paul Her feast day is 23rd September

Theist, Deist, Atheist, Agnostic. A *theist* believes there is a God who made and governs all creation, but does not believe in the doctrine of the Trinity, nor in a divine revelation

A *deist* believes there is a God who created all things, but does not believe in His superintendence and government. He thinks the Creator implanted in all things certain immutable laws, called the *Laws of Nature*, which act *per se*, as a watch acts without the supervision of its maker Like the theist, he does not believe in the doctrine of the Trinity, nor in a divine revelation.

The *atheist* disbelieves even the existence of a God He thinks matter is eternal, and what we call "creation" is the result of natural laws

The *agnostic* believes only what is knowable He rejects revelation and the doctrine of the Trinity as "past human understanding." He is neither theist deist, nor atheist, as all these subscribe to doctrines that are incapable of scientific proof

Thellusson Act (thel' u son) The 39th and 40th George III, cap 98 An Act (1800) to prevent testators from leaving their property to accumulate for more than twenty-one years It was passed in reference to the will of Peter Thellusson, a London banker who died in 1797 and left £600,000 and £4,500 a year to accumulate for the benefit of his eldest greatgrandson after the death of all his sons and grandsons The last grandson died in 1856, and the expense of the legal actions that followed swallowed up all the accumulated interest, so that Thellusson's eldest son's eldest grandson received barely the amount of the original legacy.

Theodomas (thē od' ō màs) A famous trumpeter at the siege of Thebes

> At every court ther cam loud menstralcye
> That never tromped Joab for to heere,
> Ne he Theodomas yit half so cleere
> At Thebes, when the cite was in doute
> CHAUCER *Canterbury Tales*, 9,592

Theodoric (thē od' ō rik). A king of the East Goths (d. 526), who became celebrated in German legend as Dietrich of Bern (*q v*), and also has a place in the Norse romances and the *Nibelungen Saga* He invaded Italy about 490, and three years later slew Odoacer and became sole ruler.

Theodosian Table. *See* ITINERARY.

Theon (thē' on) A satirical poet of ancient Rome, noted for his mordant writings, Hence, *Theon's tooth*, the bite of an ill-natured or carping critic

Dente Theonino circumrodi (Horace *Ep.* 1, 18, 82) to be nastily aspersed

Theophany *See* TIFFANY

Theorbo (thē ôi' bō). A large bass lute with a double neck, having two sets of tuning pegs The lower set is applied to the strings over the fretted finger-board, tuned in 4ths, with a 3rd in the middle, the upper pegs hold the bass strings, tuned in 2nds and played as open notes.

Theosophy (Gr the wisdom of God) The name adopted by the Theosophical Society (founded in 1875 by Mme Blavatsky, Mrs Besant, Col Olcott, and others) to define their religious or philosophical system, which aims at the knowledge of God by means of intuition and contemplative illumination, or by direct communion *Esoteric Buddhism* is another name for it, and its adherents claim that the doctrines of the great world religions are merely the exoteric expressions of their own esoteric traditions.

The Theosophist is a man who, whatever be his race, creed, or condition, aspires to reach this height of wisdom and beatitude by self-development — OLCOTT *Theosophy*, p 144 (1885)

The name was formerly applied to the philosophical system of Boehme (d 1624)

Theot, Catharine (tā' ō) (1725-94) A visionary born at Avranches, who gave herself out to be (like Joanna Southcott) the mother of God, and changed her name *Theot* into *Theos* (God) She preached in Paris in 1794, at the very time that the worship of the Supreme Being was instituted, and declared that Robespierre was the forerunner of the Word. The *Comité de la Sureté Generale* had her arrested, and she was guillotined Catharine Theot was called by Dom Gerle *la mère de dieu*, and she named Maximilien Robespierre "her wellbeloved son and chief prophet."

Theramanes. *See* SANDAL

Therapeutæ (thĕr a pū' tē) (Gr., servants, ministers) A sect of Jewish mystics described in Philo's *De Vita Contemplativa*. They were a branch of the Essenes (*q v*) and were settled in Egypt in the 1st century A D

Therm. In physics the name given to the British thermal unit of heat (B Th U.) which is the amount of heat required to raise 1 lb of water at its maximum density through 1° F. The calorie is the corresponding metric unit of heat; a therm equals nearly 252 calories The gas therm, by which gas is charged to consumers, is equal to 100,000 B.Th U *Therm* is a small gnome-like figure resembling a flame who was introduced to advertise gas in Britain in the 1930s

Thermidor (thĕr' mi dôr) The eleventh month of the French Republican calendar, containing thirty days from July 19th So named from Gr *therme* heat, *doron* a gift.

Thermidorians. The French Revolutionists who took part in the *coup d'état* which effected the fall of Robespierre, on Thermidor 9th of the second Republican year (July 27th, 1794), thus bringing the Reign of Terror (*q v*) to a close

Thermopylæ (thĕr mop' i li). In ancient geography the pass from Thessaly to Locris, being the only passage for an army from northern to southern Greece In 480 B C. it was heroically defended against the invading Persians under Xerxes by some 300 men under Leonidas, King of Sparta. As the result of treachery the Persians got to the rear of the Greeks, who were all slain

Thersites (thĕr sī' tēz). A deformed, scurrilous officer in the Greek army at the siege of Troy He was always railing at the chiefs, hence the name is applied to any dastardly, malevolent, impudent railer against the powers that be Achilles felled him to the earth with his fist and killed him

In *Troilus and Cressida* he is "A slave whose gall coins slanders like a mint."

Theseus (thē' sūs). The chief hero of Attica in ancient Greek legend, son of Ægeus, and the centre of innumerable exploits. Among his deeds are the capture of the Marathonian bull, the slaying of the Minotaur (*q v*), his war against the Amazons, the Calydonian hunt, and his desertion of Ariadne in Naxos He was foully murdered by Lycomedes in Scyios. *See* SINIS.

Theseus is also the name of the Duke of Athens in Chaucer's *Knight's Tale* He married Hippolita, and as he returned home with his bride, and Emily her sister, was accosted by a crowd of female suppliants who complained of Creon, king of Thebes The duke forthwith set out for Thebes, slew Creon, and took the city by assault Many captives fell into his hands, amongst whom were the two knights, Palamon and Arcite (*q v*)

Shakespeare gives the same name to the Duke of Athens in *Midsummer Night's Dream*

Thespians (thes' pi anz) Actors; so called from Thespis, an Attic poet of the 6th century B.C., reputed to be the father of Greek tragedy.

> Thespis, the first professor of our art,
> At country wakes sang ballads from a cart
>   DRYDEN *Prologue to Sophonisba*

Thestylis (thes' ti lis) A stock poetic name for a rustic maiden, from a young female slave of that name in the *Idylls* of Theocritus

> And then in haste her bower she leaves,
> With Thestylis to bind the sheaves
>   MILTON *L'Allegro*

Thetis (thē' tis) The chief of the Nereids (*q v*) of Greek legend By Peleus she was the mother of Achilles

Thetis's hair-stone A fancy-name given to pieces of rock-crystal enclosing hair-like filaments

Thick. It's a bit thick! A colloquial expression used to express annoyance, as *when one has had a stroke of bad luck, when things have not come up to expectation, when one has been charged more than—or received less than—one thinks fair, etc*

Those two are very thick. They are very good friends, on excellent terms with one another **As thick as thieves** is a similar saying.

Through thick and thin. Through evil and through good report, under any conditions, undauntedly

> A griesly foster forth did rush ,
> Through thick and thin, both over bank and bush
> In hope her to attain by hook or crook
>   SPENSER *Faerie Queene*, III, i, 17.

Thick and thin blocks are pulley-blocks with two sheaves of different thickness, to accommodate different sizes of ropes.

Thick-skinned. Not sensitive, not irritated by rebukes and slanders **Thin-skinned**, on the contrary, means impatient of reproof or censure, having skin so thin that it is an annoyance to be touched

Thick 'un. Slang for a sovereign

Thief, The Penitent *See* DYSMAS

Thieves' Latin Slang, gibberish.

Thimble. From A S *thymel*, a thumb-stall, so called because it was originally worn on the thumb, as sailors still wear their thimbles

Just a thimbleful, A very little drop—usually of spirits *Thimble* is sometimes used in place of *thimbleful* —

> 'Tis true to her cottage still they came
> And never swallow'd a thimble the less
> Of something the Reader is left to guess
>   HOOD *A Tale of a Trumpet*

Thimble-rigging A form of cheating, carried on with three thimbles and a pea, principally on or about race courses. A pea is put on a table, and the manipulator places three thimbles over it in succession, and then, setting them on the table, asks you to say under which thimble the pea is. You are sure to guess wrong

The term *thimble-rigging* is used allusively of any kind of mean cheating or jiggery-pokery

Thin. It's a lot too thin! Said of an excuse, explanation, story, etc , that sounds plausible but is quite unacceptable The idea is that it is so thin as to be transparent—it is easily seen through.

The thin red line. *See* LINE

Thin-skinned. *See* THICK-SKINNED.

Thing. The Old Norse word for the assembly of the people, the legislature, "parliament," court of law, etc It is etymologically the same word as our *thing* (an object), the original meaning of which was a discussion (from *thingian*, to discuss), hence a cause, an object

The great national diet of Norway is still called a *stor-thing* (great legislative assembly), and the two chambers which form it are the *lag-thing* (law assembly) and the *odels-thing* (free-holders' assembly)

A poor thing A person (or, sometimes, an inanimate object) that is regarded with pity or disparagement Touchstone's remark about Audrey—"An ill-favoured thing, sir, but mine own" (*As You Like It*, v, 4)—is frequently misquoted, "A poor thing, but mine own " when employed in half ironical disparagement of one's own work

Old thing A familiar mode of address between friends

One's things. One's minor belongings, especially clothes, or personal luggage

The thing. The proper thing to do, as, "It's not the thing to play leap-frog down Bond Street in a top-hat and spats "

The very thing Just what I was wanting, just what will meet the case

You can have too much of a good thing "Enough is as good as a feast "

> People may have too much of a good thing—
> Full as an egg of wisdom thus I sing
>   PETER PINDAR *The Gentleman and his Wife*

Third. *See under* THREE

Thirteen. It is said that the origin of sitting down thirteen at table being deemed unlucky is because, at a banquet in Valhalla, Loki once intruded, making thirteen guests, and Balder was slain

In Christian countries the superstition was confirmed by the Last Supper of Christ and His twelve apostles, but the superstition itself is much anterior to Christianity.

The Italians never use the number in their lotteries, and in Paris no house bears it, and persons, called *Quartorziemes*, are available to make a fourteenth at dinner parties Sailors strongly object to leaving port on the 13th of the month—especially if it happens to be a Friday—and they always start on their thirteenth voyage with apprehension.

Thirteenpence-halfpenny. A hangman So called because thirteenpence-halfpenny was at one time his wages for hanging a man

Thirty. A man at thirty must be either a fool or a physician. A saying attributed by Tacitus (*Annals*, VI, xlvi) to the Emperor Tiberius, who died at the age of 77 in A D 37 (Plutarch gives the story, but changes the age to *sixty*) The idea seems to be that if a man has not learned to look after his health by the time he is thirty he must be a fool

The Thirty Tyrants. *See* TYRANT.

Thirty Years War. A series of wars between the Catholics and Protestants of Germany in the 17th century, in which France, Sweden, and other peoples participated from time to time It began in Bohemia in 1618, and ended in 1648 with the Peace of Westphalia

Thirty-six Line Bible, The. *See* BIBLE, SPECIALLY NAMED.

Thirty-nine Articles, The. The articles of faith of the Church of England, the acceptance of which is obligatory on its clergy They were originally issued in 1551 as forty-two, but in 1563 were modified and reduced to their present number They received parliamentary authority in 1571

Thisbe. *See* PYRAMUS.

Thistle. The heraldic emblem of Scotland, said to have been adopted at least as early as the 8th century in commemoration of an unsuccessful night attack by the Danes on Stirling Castle Their presence was unsuspected, and was revealed through the barefooted scouts treading on thistles and suddenly crying out, the alarm was given, the Scots fell upon the party and defeated them with terrible slaughter

With the thistle was adopted the motto *Nemo me impune lacessit*, "Nobody touches (or provokes) me with impunity"

The Most Ancient and Most Noble Order of the Thistle The Scottish order of Knighthood (ranking only second to the Garter in the list of British Orders), traditionally said to have been founded in 787 by Achaius king of the Scots, who, with Hungus, king of the Picts, was fighting an English king, in commemoration of a bright cross they saw in the heavens the night before the battle It is said to have been refounded in 1540 by James V, and was certainly restored in 1687 by James VII and II, only to collapse in the Revolution of the following year, to be finally re-established by Queen Anne in 1703 Membership is confined to 16 Knights (beside Royalty), a Chancellor,
29*

Dean, Secretary, the Lyon King-of-Arms, and the Gentleman Usher of the Green Rod Its insignia comprise the Badge (an elongated eight-pointed star with a figure of St Andrew and his cross), Star, Collar of golden thistles and sprigs of rue, Mantle, and dark green Ribbon

Thistles, especially "Our Lady's Thistle," are said to be a cure for stitch in the side. According to the doctrine of signatures Nature has labelled every plant, and the prickles of the thistle tell us the plant is efficacious for *pricles* or the stitch The species called *Silybum Marianum*, we are told, owes the white markings on its leaves to milk from Our Lady's breast, some of which fell thereon and left a white mark behind

Thomas St. Thomas. The Apostle who doubted (*John* xxi, 25), hence the phrase, *a doubting Thomas* applied to a sceptic

The story told of him in the Apocryphal *Acts of St Thomas* is that he was deputed to go as a missionary to India, and, on refusing, Christ appeared and sold him as a slave to an Indian prince who was visiting Jerusalem He was taken to India, where he baptized the prince and many others, and was finally martyred at Meliapore

Another legend has it that Gondoforus, king of the Indies, gave him a large sum of money to build a palace St. Thomas spent it on the poor, "thus erecting a superb palace in heaven " On account of this he is the patron saint of masons and architects, and his symbol is a builder's square

Another legend relates that he once saw a huge beam of timber floating on the sea near the coast, and the king unsuccessfully endeavouring, with men and elephants, to haul it ashore St Thomas desired leave to use it in building a church, and, his request being granted, he dragged it easily ashore with a piece of packthread.

His feast day is December 21st

Christians of St. Thomas. There are said to have been in the southern parts of Malabar some 200,000 persons who called themselves "Christians of St Thomas" when Vasco da Gama reached India in 1498 They had been 1,300 years under the jurisdiction of the patriarch of Babylon, who appointed their *Materene* (archbishop) In 1625 a stone was found near Siganfu with a cross on it, and containing a list of the *Materenes* of India and China

Thomas the Rhymer. *See* RHYMER.

Thomasing Collecting small sums of money or obtaining drink from employers on St Thomas's Day, a custom that still exists in some districts In London on December 21st every one of the Common Council has to be either elected or re-elected

Thomists. Followers of St Thomas Aquinas (d 1274)—styled ' Doctor Angelicus" and, by Pius V, "the Fifth Doctor of the Church" —and opponents of the *Scotists*, or followers of Duns Scotus

Scotists and Thomists now in peace remain
POPE *Essay on Criticism*, 444

Thone or **Thonis** In Greek mythology the governor of a province of Egypt to which, it is said by post-Homeric poets, Paris took Helen, who was given by Polydamnia, wife to Thone, the drug *nepenthes*, to make her forget her sorrows

Not that nepenthes which the wife of Thone
In Egypt gave to love-lorn Helena,
Is of such power to stir up joy as this
        MILTON, *Comus*, 695-697.

Thopas, Rime of Sir (thō' păs) A burlesque on contemporary metrical romances, told as Chaucer's own tale in the *Canterbury Tales*

Thor (thôr) Son of Woden, god of war, and the second god in the pantheon of the ancient Scandinavians—their Vulcan, and god of thunder He had three principal possessions, a Hammer (*Mjolnir*), typifying thunder and lightning, and having the virtue of returning to him after it was thrown, a Belt (*Meginjardir*) which doubled his power, and Iron Gloves to aid him in throwing his hammer

He was god of the household, and of peasants, and was married to Sip, a typical peasant woman. His name is still perpetuated in our *Thursday*, and in a number of place-names, as *Thorsby* (Cumberland), *Torthorwald* (Dumfries), and *Thurso* (Caithness)

Thorn. A thorn in the flesh. A source of constant irritation, annoyance, or affliction, said of objectionable and parasitical conditions, of a "skeleton in the cupboard," etc There was a sect of the Pharisees (*q v*) which used to insert thorns in the borders of their gaberdines to prick their legs in walking and make them bleed The phrase is taken from St. Paul's reference to some physical complaint or misfortune, 2 *Cor.* xii, 7

On thorns. In a state of painful anxiety and suspense; fearful that something is going wrong (*cp* TENTERHOOKS)

The Crown of Thorns. That with which our Saviour was crowned in mockery (*Matt* xxvii, 29), hence sometimes used of a very special affliction with which one is unjustly burdened Calvin (*Admonitio de Reliquiis*) gives a long list of places claiming to possess one or more of the thorns which composed the Saviour's crown. To his list may be added Glastonbury Abbey, where was also the spear of Longius or Longinus.

The Glastonbury Thorn. *See* GLASTONBURY

Thorough. The name given by the Earl of Strafford (executed 1641) to his uncompromising absolutist policy in favour of Charles I and against Parliament, especially to his harsh Irish policy, which he was determined to carry through regardless of all opposition and of all suffering.

Thoroughbred. Of pure or unmixed breed, especially said of horses and cattle A thoroughbred is a race horse of English breed remotely derived by crossing with Arab and other strains

Thoth. The Hermes of Egyptian mythology. He is represented with the head of an ibis on a human body He is the inventor of the arts and sciences, music and astronomy, speech and letters The name means "Logos" or "the Word."

Thousand He's one in a thousand Said of a man who is specially distinguished by his excellent qualities, similarly, *a wife in a thousand*, a perfect wife, or one that exactly suits the speaker's ideas of what a wife should be

Thousand is frequently used of large indefinite numbers as in Byron's

A small drop of ink,
Falling like dew, upon a thought, produces
That which makes thousands, perhaps millions, think
        Don Juan, III, lxxxviii

Thread. The thread of destiny. That on which destiny depends According to Greek mythology, Clotho, one of the Fates (*q v*), spun from her distaff the destiny of man, and as she span her sister Lachesis worked out the events which were in store, and Atropos cut the thread at the point when death was to occur

The Triple Thread. Brahminism. The ancient Brahmins wore a symbol of three threads, reaching from the right shoulder to the left Faria says that their religion sprang from fishermen, who left the charge of the temples to their successors on the condition of their wearing some threads of their nets in remembrance of their vocation; but Osorius maintains that the triple thread symbolizes the Trinity

Threadneedle Street. The street in the City of London leading from Bishopsgate to the Bank of England The name first appears—as *Three needle Street*—in 1598, and previously it seems to have been called *Broad Street*, as forming part of the present *Old Broad Street* The name may have arisen from the sign of an inn, *The Three Needles* (though none of that name is recorded in the neighbourhood), or from some connexion with the Needlemakers' Company, whose arms are "three needles in fesse argent "

The Old Lady of Threadneedle Street. The Bank of England which stands in this street The term dates from the late 18th century, and there is a caricature by Gilray, dated May 22, 1797, entitled *The Old Lady in Threadneedle Street in Danger*, which refers to the temporary stopping of cash payments, February 26, 1797, and to the issue of one pound banknotes on March 4 the same year.

The directors of the Bank of England were called Old Ladies of Threadneedle Street by William Cobbett, because, like Mrs Partington, they tried with their broom to sweep back the Atlantic waves of national progress

Three Pythagoras calls three the perfect number, expressive of "beginning, middle, and end," wherefore he makes it a symbol of Deity.

A Trinity is by no means confined to the Christian creed The Brahmins represent their god with three heads, the world was supposed by the ancients to be under the rule of three gods, viz Jupiter (heaven), Neptune (sea), and Pluto (Hades) Jove is represented with three-forked lightning, Neptune with a trident, and Pluto with a three-headed dog The Fates are three, the Furies three, the Graces three, the Harpies three, the Sibylline books three times three (of which only three survived), the fountain from which Hylas drew water was presided over by three nymphs; the Muses were three times three; the pythoness sat on a three-legged stool, or tripod, and in Scandinavian mythology we hear ot "the Mysterious Three," viz "Har" (the Mighty), the "Like-Mighty," and the "Third Person," who sat on three thrones above the rainbow

Man is threefold (body, soul, and spirit), the world is threefold (earth, sea, and air), the enemies of man are threefold (the world, the flesh, and the devil), the Christian graces are threefold (Faith, Hope, and Charity), the kingdoms of Nature are threefold (mineral, vegetable, and animal), the cardinal colours are three in number (red, yellow, and blue), etc *Cp* NINE, which is three times three

Three acres and a cow. A phrase which came into use after the formation by the Dukes of Argyll and Westminster of the National Land Company, in 1885. The object of this concern was to acquire large tracts of land and let it out for farming in small portions

Three Choirs Festival. Musical festival for the performance of sacred music given since 1724 by the choirs of the cathedrals of Gloucester, Worcester, and Hereford

A three-cornered fight. A parliamentary (or other) contest in which there are three competitors.

A three-decker. Properly, a sailing ship having three decks, a warship carrying guns on three decks, but applied to other triplicates, such as the old-fashioned pulpit, reading-desk, and clerk's desk arranged one above the other, and to the three-volume novel—the usual way of publishing fiction in most of the 19th century up to about 1895

In the midst of the church stands the offensive structure of pulpit, reading-desk, and clerk's desk, in fact, a regular old three-decker in full sail westward — *The Christian Remembrancer,* July, 1852, p 92

The Three Estates of the Realm. *See* ESTATES

Three Kings' Day. Epiphany or Twelfth Day, designed to commemorate the visit of the "three kings" or Wise Men of the East to the infant Jesus. *See* MAGI.

The three-legged mare. An obsolete slang term for the gallows, which at Tyburn was a triple erection in triangular plan.

Three Mile Limit. In International Law the limit of waters around its coast under the jurisdiction of a sovereign state.

Three Musketeers. Athos, Porthos, and Aramis, the three heroes of Dumas's novels *The Three Musketeers,* 1844, *Twenty Years Afterwards,* 1845; and *Vicomte de Bragelonne,* 1848-50. The Musketeers were a mounted guard of gentlemen in the service of the kings of France from 1661 until the Revolution, 1791. They formed two companies, called the Grey and the Black from the colour of their horses The uniform was scarlet, hence their quarters were known as La Maison Rouge In peacetime the Musketeers formed the king's bodyguard, but in war they fought on foot or on horseback with the army Their ranks included many Scots, either Jacobite exiles or mere soldiers of fortune

The Three R.'s. *See* R.

Three sheets in the wind *See* SHEET.

Three-tailed bashaw. *See* BASHAW

The three tailors of Tooley Street. *See* TAILOR

The three tongues Those in which the inscription on the Cross were written, viz Hebrew, Greek, and Latin In the Middle Ages it was considered that a thorough knowledge of these was necessary before one could begin to understand theology

Rule of Three. The rule of simple proportion, by which, given the relationship of two entities, the proportional relationship of a third can be ascertained.

The Battle of the Three Emperors The Battle of Austerlitz (December 2nd, 1805), when Napoleon inflicted a heavy defeat on the Russians and Austrians The Emperors of the three Empires were all present in person.

To give one three times three. To give him a rousing ovation, cheer after cheer

We three "Did you never see the picture of *We Three?*" asks Sir Andrew Aguecheek (*Twelfth Night,* ii, 3)—not meaning himself, Sir Toby Belch, and the clown, but referring to a public-house sign of *Two Loggerheads,* with the inscription, "We three loggerheads be," the third being the spectator.

"When shall we three meet again?"—the title of a picture of *two* asses—is a similar "joke"

Threescore years and ten. A ripe old age—not necessarily (in allusive use) exactly 70 years The reference is to *Ps* xc, 10 —

The days of our years are threescore years and ten, and if by reason of strength they be fourscore years yet is their strength labour and sorrow, for it is soon cut off, and we fly away

Third Degree. The highest degree, that of Master Mason, in British Freemasonry In U S A. the term is applied to the use of exhaustive questioning and cross questioning by the police in the endeavour to extort a confession or compromising information from a criminal, accomplice, or witness

Third Estate The Commons, as the third estate of the realm coming after the Sovereign and the Peers. The term is a translation of the French *Tiers Etat,* being the third and lower body of representatives in the States General (*q v*)

Throat. Clergyman's throat Chronic inflammation of the pharynx, to which clergymen and others who habitually overstrain the vocal organs are specially liable

To cut one's own throat. Figuratively, to adopt a policy, or take action that ruins one's own chances, plans, etc Similarly, *to cut one another's throat* is to ruin one another by excessive competition

To jump down a person's throat. To interrupt and affront him, suddenly, sharply, and decisively

To lie in one's throat To lie most outrageously, well knowing that you are lying, and meaning to do so

Throgmorton Street. The financial world at large, or the Stock Exchange, which is situated in this narrow London street. So named from Sir Nicholas Throckmorton (1515-71), head of the ancient Warwickshire family, and ambassador to France in the reign of Elizabeth I

Throne, The. A comprehensive name for the office of King, e.g He ascended the throne

Thrones, principalities and powers, in the teachings of Fathers of the Church, are three choirs of the celestial hierarchy, or the assemblage of beneficent supernatural beings

Through-stone A flat gravestone, a stone coffin or sarcophagus, also a bond stone which extends over the entire thickness of a wall

Throw. To throw away one's money. To spend it carelessly, recklessly, extravagantly.

To throw back. To revert to ancestral traits, hence, *a throw-back* is one (human or animal) who does this

To throw oneself on someone To commit oneself to his protection, favour, mercy, etc

To throw the helve after the hatchet. *See* HELVE.

To throw in one's hand. To abandon one's projects A metaphor from card-playing

Thrums. The fringe of warp threads left when the web has been cut off, weavers' ends and fag-ends of carpet, used for common rugs

Thread and thrum Everything, good and bad together

Come, sisters, come, cut thread and thrum,
Quail, crush, conclude, and quell!
Midsummer Night's Dream, v, 1

The town immortalized by Sir James Barrie in *A Window in Thrums* (1889) is Kirriemuir, Forfarshire, his birthplace

Thug A member of a religious body of northern India, worshippers of Kali (*q v*), who could be propitiated only by human victims who had been strangled. Hence, the Thugs became a professional fraternity of stranglers, and supported themselves by the plunder obtained from those they strangled Their native name is *P'hansigars* (stranglers), that of *Thug* (i e cheat) was given them in 1810 Their methods were rigorously suppressed under British rule, and were practically extinct by 1840 In common parlance the word is used for a violent "tough."

Thuggee. The system of secret assassination preached by Thugs, the practice of Thugs

Thule. The name given by the ancients to an island, or point of land, six days' sail north of Britain, and considered by them to be the extreme northern limit of the world The name is first found in the account by Polybius (about 150 B C) of the voyage made by Pytheas in the late 4th century B C. Pliny says, "It is an island in the Northern Ocean discovered by Pytheas, after sailing six days from the Orcades," Others, like Camden, consider it to be Shetland, in which opinion they agree with Marinus, and the descriptions of Ptolemy and Tacitus, and still others that it was some part of the coast of Norway The etymology of the name is unknown

Ultima Thule. The end of the world, the last extremity

Tibi serviat Ultima Thule.
VIRGIL *Georgics*, i, 30

Thumb. In the ancient Roman combats, when a gladiator was vanquished it rested with the spectators to decide whether he should be slain or not If they wished him to live, they *shut up* their thumbs in their fists (*pollice compresso favor judicabatur*); if to be slain, they *turned out* their thumbs See Pliny, xxviii, 2, Juvenal, iii, 36, Horace I *Epist* xviii, 66

Influenced by the rabble's bloody will,
With thumbs bent back, they popularly kill
DRYDEN *Third Satire*

Our popular saying, **Thumbs up!** expressive of pleasure or approval, is probably a perversion of this custom

Every honest miller has a thumb of gold. Even an honest miller grows rich with what he filches, for he simply can't help *some* of the flour that ought to go into the loaf sticking to his thumb! Chaucer says of his miller—

Wel koude he stelen corn and tollen thries,
And yet he hadded a thombe of gold, pardee
Canterbury Tales Prologue, 562

Rule of thumb A rough, guesswork measure, practice or experience, as distinguished from theory. In some places the heat required in brewing is determined by dipping the thumb into the vat.

The pricking of one's thumb In popular superstition, a portent of evil The Second Witch in *Macbeth* (iv, 1) says —

By the pricking of my thumbs,
Something wicked this way comes

And Macbeth enters

Another proverb says, My little finger told me that. When your *ears tingle* it is to indicate that someone is speaking about you; when a sudden fit of *shivering* occurs, it is because someone is treading on the place which is to form your grave, when the *eye itches*, it indicates the visit of a friend, when the *palm itches* it shows that a present will shortly be received, and when the *bones ache* a storm is prognosticated Sudden pains and prickings are the warnings of evil on the road, sudden glows and pleasurable sensations are the couriers to tell us of joy close at hand

In ancient Rome the augurs took special notice of the palpitation of the heart, the flickering of the eye, and the pricking of the thumb In regard to the last, if the pricking was on the left hand it was considered a very bad sign, indicating mischief at hand.

Thumb index. Grooves cut in the pages of a book showing initial letters or other particulars to enable the reader to find a reference easily

Thumb-nail. Used attributively of various things, especially sketches, portraits, and so on, that are on a very small scale

To thumb a ride. To ask for a lift in a motor car by holding out the hand with the thumb pointing in the direction in which one wants to go

To bite one's thumb at one To insult him Formerly a way of expressing defiance and contempt was by snapping the finger or putting the thumb in the mouth. Both these acts are termed a *fico*, whence "I don't care a fig for you" (*see* FIG) Dekker, describing St Paul's Walk, speaks of the biting of thumbs to beget quarrels, and biting one's glove (*see* GLOVE) was a similar token

> I see Contempt marching forth, giving mee the fico with his thombe in his mouth —*Wits Miserie* (1596)
> I will bite my thumb at them, which is a disgrace to them, if they bear it —*Romeo and Juliet*, i, 1

Tom Thumb. *See* TOM

Under one's thumb. Under the influence or power of the person named

Thumbikins, Thumbscrew An instrument of torture used largely by the Inquisition, whereby the thumbs are compressed between two bars of iron, by means of a screw William Carstairs (1649-1715) was the last person put to the torture in Britain, as the Law of England would not permit torture, he was sent by the Privy Council for examination in Edinburgh, to elicit the names of the accomplices in the Rye House Plot (*q v.*)

Thunder Used figuratively of any loud noise, also of vehement denunciations or threats, as, the thunders of the Vatican, meaning the anathemas and denunciations of the Pope.

Jupiter was the god of thunder in the Roman mythology, hence Dryden's allusion to the inactivity of Louis XIV —

> And threatening France, placed like a painted Jove,
> Kept idle thunder in his lifted hand
> *Annus Mirabilis*, xxxix.

Sons of thunder *See* BOANERGES

To steal one's thunder To forestall him, or to adopt his own special methods as one's own. The phrase comes from the anecdote of John Dennis (1657-1734) the critic and playwright who invented an effective device for producing stage thunder, for his play *Applus and Virginia* The play was a failure and was withdrawn, but shortly afterwards Dennis heard his thunder used in a performance of *Macbeth.* "My God," he exclaimed, "The villains will play my thunder but not my plays!"

Thunderbolt. A missile or mass of heated matter that was formerly supposed on occasion to be discharged from thunder-clouds during a storm; used figuratively of an irresistible blow, a sudden and overwhelming shock (*cp.* BOLT FROM THE BLUE)

> Be ready, gods, with all your thunderbolts,
> Dash him to pieces!
> *Julius Cæsar*, iv, 3.

Jupiter was depicted by the ancients as a man seated on a throne, holding a sceptre in his left hand and thunderbolts in his right

The Thunderbolt of Italy. Gaston de Foix, Duc de Nemours (1489-1512), nephew of Louis XII, was so called because of his brilliant campaign in Italy (1512).

Thunderday. *See* THURSDAY.

Thunderer, The. A name facetiously applied to *The Times* newspaper in the mid-19th century, in allusion to an article by the assistant editor, Edward Sterling (d 1847), beginning:—

> We thundered forth the other day an article on the subject of social and political reform —*The Times*

Thundering Legion, The (*Legio fulminans*). The XIIth Legion of the Roman army, probably so called because its ensign was a representation of Jupiter Tonans

The name dates from much earlier times than those of Marcus Aurelius, but fable relates that it arose because in this Emperor's expedition against the Sarmatæ, Marcomanni, etc , the XIIth Legion—stated for the purpose of the legend to have consisted of Christians—saved the whole army during a terrible drought by praying for rain A terrible thunderstorm burst, and not only furnished a plentiful supply of water, but dispersed the enemy with lightning and thunderbolts

> What wonders, yea, what apparent miracles did the prayers of former Christians procure! hence the Christian soldiers in their Army was called the Thundering Legion, they could do more by their prayers than the rest by their arms —BAXTER *Saints' Everlasting Rest*, II, vi, 6

The fable was long believed, but is none the less fictitious

Thursday. The day of the god Thor (*q v*), called by the French *jeudi*, that is, Jove's day Both Jove and Thor were gods of thunder, and formerly Thursday was sometimes called *Thunderday See also* BLACK, HOLY, MAUNDY THURSDAY

When three Thursdays come together One of many circumlocutions for *Never.*

Thyrsus. The staff carried by Dionysus and his followers *See* TORSO

Tiara (tē a′ rà) Anciently the name of the head-dress of the Persian kings, now applied to a coronet-like ornament, and especially to the triple crown of the Pope This typifies the temporal claims of the papacy, and is composed of gold cloth encircled by three crowns and surmounted by a golden globe and cross.

Tradition has it that for the first five centuries the bishops of Rome wore a simple mitre like other bishops, and that Hormisdas (514-23) placed on his bonnet the crown sent him by Clovis Boniface VIII (1294-1303) added a second crown during his struggles with Philip the Fair; and John XXII (1410-17) assumed the third

There are other accounts of the original adoption of the crowns, and of their meanings; some say that the second was added in 1335 by Benedict XII, to indicate the prerogatives of spiritual and temporal power combined in the papacy, and that the third is indicative of the Trinity, and Pius IX, in 1871, spoke of it as —

> The symbol of my threefold dignity, in heaven, upon earth, and in purgatory.

Still another suggestion is that as the Pope claims to be (1) Head of the Catholic or Universal Church; (2) Sole Arbiter of its Rights, and (3) Sovereign Father of all the kings of the earth, he wears one crown as High Priest, one as Emperor, and one as King

The papal tiara is very richly ornamented, and contains 146 jewels of all colours, 11 brilliants, and 540 pearls

Tib. The ace of trumps in the game of Gleek. Tom is the knave.

> That gamester needs must overcome,
> That can play both Tib and Tom.
> RANDOLPH *Hermaphrodite*

St. Tib's Eve. Never A corruption of St Ubes There is no such saint in the calendar as St Ubes, and therefore her eve falls on the "Greek Calends" (*q v.*), neither before Christmas Day nor after it

Tichborne Case. The most celebrated impersonation case in English law In March, 1853, Roger Charles Tichborne, heir to an ancient Hampshire baronetcy, sailed for Valparaiso, and after travelling a while in S. America embarked on April 20th, 1854, in a sailingship named the *Bella*, bound for Jamaica The ship went down, and nothing more was heard or seen of Roger Tichborne. In October, 1865, "R C Tichborne" turned up at Wagga Wagga, in Australia, in the person of a man locally known as Tom Castro On Christmas Day, 1866, he landed in England as a claimant to the Tichborne baronetcy, asserting that he was the lost Roger Lady Tichborne, the real Roger's mother, professed to recognize him, but the family could not be deceived The case came into the Courts where the fellow's claims were proved to be false and he himself identified as Arthur Orton, the son of a Wapping butcher A further trial for perjury ended in his being sentenced to 14 years penal servitude

The Tichborne Case has been acknowledged as the greatest *cause célèbre* of English law, public feeling ran high, and a by-election was said to have been lost because the candidate expressed his doubts as to the claimant's genuineness.

Tick. To go on tick. To owe for what one buys. In the 17th century *ticket* was the ordinary term for the written acknowledgment of a debt, and one living on credit was said to be *living on ticket*, or *tick*

> If a servant usually buy for the master upon tick, and the servant buy some things without the master's order . the master is liable.—*Chief Justice Holt (Blackstone, ch. xv, p 468)*

Tick-tack. The system of signals by which bookmakers' scouts inform their principals of the odds being offered by other bookmakers on a race course

Ticket (U.S.A). The list of nominees for office "I intend to vote the straight Republican ticket "

As a seafaring term to get one's ticket is to qualify for promotion

That's the ticket or That's the ticket for soup. That's the right thing. The ticket to be shown in order to obtain something

Ticket of leave. A warrant given to convicts to have their liberty on condition of good behaviour, hence, *Ticket-of-leave man*, a convict freed from prison but obliged to report himself to the police from time to time until his sentence was completed The system is now discontinued

To work one's ticket. An army expression meaning to get one's discharge before the contract of service has expired

Tide. Used figuratively of a tendency, a current or flow of events, etc , as in *a tide of feeling*, and in Shakespeare's—

> There is a tide in the affairs of men,
> Which, taken at the flood, leads on to fortune
> *Julius Cæsar*, IV, 3

Lose not a tide. Waste no time, set off at once on the business

Tide-waiters Custom-house officers who board ships entering ports and see that the customs regulations are carried out The term has been figuratively applied to those who vote against their opinions.

To tide over a difficulty, hard times, etc Just to surmount the difficulty, just to come through the hard times, by force of circumstances and a little luck, rather than by one's own endeavours

Tidy means in *tide*, in season, in time We retain the word in eventide, springtide, and so on Tusser has the phrase, 'If the weather be fair and tidy," meaning seasonable Things done punctually and in their proper season are sure to be done orderly, and what is orderly done is neat and well arranged Hence we get the notion of methodical, neat, well arranged, associated with tidy

The word is also used in the sense of a thing being worth consideration **A tidy penny,** quite a good sum; **a tidy fortune,** an inheritance worth having.

Tied House. A retail business, especially a public-house, that is obliged by a contract to obtain its supplies from some particular firm.

> There are tied houses in the drapery, grocery, dairy, boot and shoe, hardware, liquor, and book trades — *Liberty Review*, 14th April, 1894

Tiercel. See TASSEL-GENTLE.

Tiffany. A kind of thin silk-like gauze The word is a corruption of *Theophany* (Gr *theos*, god, *ephainein*, to show), the manifestation of God to man, the Epiphany, and the material was so called because it used to be worn at the Twelfth Night (Epiphany) revels

Tiffin. An old Northern English dialect word for a small draught of liquor, it was introduced into India, where it acquired its modern meaning of a lunch, or light meal between breakfast and dinner.

Tiger. The nickname of the French statesman Georges Clemenceau (1841-1929).

A liveried servant who rides out with his master used to be called a *tiger*, also a boy in buttons, a page, but the expression is now obsolete The same name is given in America to a final yell in a round of cheering

Tight. Intoxicated

Blow me tight! An old expression of surprise, wonder, incredulity, etc

> If there's a soul will give me food or find me in employ,
> By day or night, then blow me tight! (he was a vulgar boy)
> BARHAM *Misadventures at Margate (Ingoldsby Legends)*

Tike A provincial word (from Old Norse) for a dog or cur, hence used of a low fellow, as in the contemptuous insult, *You dirty tike.*

A Yorkshire tike. A rustic of that county

Tilbury. A two-wheeled horse carriage without a top or cover It was named after its designer, a London coach-maker of the early 19th century.

Tilde The sign ~ placed over the letter *n* in Spanish words when this is to be pronounced like our *ni* in *bunion*, e g *cañon* (canyon). It is a relic of the small *n* placed over a word in Latin MSS. to indicate a contraction, and the name is a variant of Span *titulo*, title

The tilde is also occasionally placed over an *l* to indicate the sound in *million*, and in Portuguese (called *til*) over the first vowel of a diphthong to indicate that the diphthong is to have a nasal pronunciation. In Portuguese, too, our *ni* of *bunion* is represented by *nh*, not by *ñ*

Tile. Old slang for a hat, this being to the head what the tiles are to a house.

He has a tile loose. He is not quite *compos mentis*, not all there.

In Freemasonry, **to tile a lodge** means to close and guard the doors to prevent anyone uninitiated from entering, the officer who does this being called the *Tiler*, sometimes spelled *tyler*

Timber (U S A). To take the tall timber; to depart or escape suddenly and unceremoniously

Time. Summer time. The legal, as apart from Greenwich time during a certain portion of the year in Great Britain and some other countries. In the spring of 1916 the Summer Time Act was passed ordaining that—

During the prescribed period in each year during which this Act is in force the time for general purposes in Great Britain shall be one hour in advance of Greenwich Mean Time

The scheme had been proposed in 1906 by William Willett, a Chelsea builder

Until 1939 the prescribed period was "from two o'clock in the morning following the third Saturday in April . . until two o'clock in the morning next following the first Saturday in October "

During World War II the dates were varied, and the actual period of Summer Time has since 1939 been annually prescribed by Order in Council

Between the years 1941 and 1945 Double Summer Time was introduced, this enforcing the addition of an hour to the Summer Time, thus making legal time two hours ahead of Greenwich time.

Take time by the forelock Seize the present moment, *Carpe diem*. Time called by Shakespeare "that bald sexton" (*King John* iii, 1), is represented with a lock of hair on his forehead but none on the rest of his head, to signify that time past cannot be used, but time present may be seized by the forelock The saying is attributed to Pittacus of Mitylene, one of the Seven Sages of Greece.

Time and tide wait for no man. One of many sayings pointing the folly of procrastination. It appears in Ray's *Scottish Proverbs* as "Time bides na man."

> For the next inn he spurs amain,
> In haste alights, and scuds away—
> But time and tide for no man stay
> SOMERVILE *The Sweet-scented Miser*

Time-expired. Applied to soldiers whose term of service is completed. Also used of convicts who have served their sentences.

Time-honoured Lancaster. Old John of Gaunt, Duke of Lancaster (about 1340-99), so called by Shakespeare (*Richard II*, 1, 1) because his memory had been honoured by Time His father was Edward III, his son Henry IV, his nephew Richard II, and through his great granddaughter, Margaret Beaufort, he is the ancestor of all our sovereigns from Henry VII, Margaret's son. Shakespeare calls him "old", he was only fifty-nine at his death.

Time is, Time was, Time's past. *See* BRAZEN HEAD

Time of Grace. *See* SPORTING SEASONS.

Time lag, term given to the pause that elapses between a cause and its effect

Time signal. A visual or wireless signal indicating exact noon or some other recognized hour

Time zone One of the 24 longitudinal divisions of the globe, corresponding mostly with meridians of 15° from the meridian of Greenwich These divisions or zones are successively of one hour of time interval.

To have had one's time. A British soldiers' expression in World War II for being ripe for death, to expect imminent disaster

To know the time o' day. To be smart, wide awake

Timeo Danaos *See* GREEK GIFT.

Timoleon (tī mō' lē ón) The Greek general and statesman (d about 336 B C) who so hated tyranny that he voted for the death of his own brother Timophanes when he attempted to make himself absolute in Corinth.

> The fair Corinthian boast
> Timoleon, happy temper, mild and firm,
> Who wept the brother while the tyrant bled
> THOMSON. *Winter*

Timon of Athens (tī' mon) An Athenian misanthrope of the late 5th century B C, and the principal figure in Shakespeare's play so called The play, was acted about 1607 and printed in 1623.

Macaulay uses the expression to "out-Timon Timon"—*i.e* to be more misanthropical than even Timon.

Timur. *See* TAMBURLAINE

Tin. Money A depreciating synonym for silver, called by alchemists "Jupiter "

Tin fish Naval slang for a torpedo

Tin hat. A soldiers' name for a metal shrapnel helmet. To put the tin hat on it, to bring something to an abrupt and conclusive end

Tin-pan Alley. The district of New York City where popular music is published. The phrase is often used generically of the composers of this type of music.

Tintype. A positive photograph taken on a sensitized sheet of enamelled tin Tintypes were cheap and very popular at fairs, amusement parks, etc.

Tincture. The heraldic term for a colour as opposed to a metal or fur

Tine-man, The. Archibald Douglas, 4th Earl of Douglas, who died 1424

In old Scottish a *tiner* was a *loser*, and Douglas was said to have lost every battle or skirmish he ever took part in.

Tinker's damn Not worth a tinker's damn. Absolutely worthless It has been suggested that the term originated in the old-time tinker's custom of blocking up the hole in the article he was mending with a pellet of bread, thus making a dam which would prevent the solder from running through This pellet was, of course, thrown away as useless when the job was finished

Tintagel (tin täj′ el). The castle on the north coast of Cornwall where, according to tradition, Uther died and King Arthur was born Its ruins still exist, on a rocky headland jutting into the sea

Tip. A small present of money, such as that given to a waiter, porter, or schoolboy; from the cant verb (common in the 16th and 17th centuries) *to tip*, meaning to hand over, which also gives rise to the other signification of the verb, viz, private warning, such secret information as may guide the person *tipped* to make successful bets or gain some other advantage A *straight tip* comes straight or direct from the owner or trainer of a horse, or from one in a position to know

Tip and Run Raid A phrase used in World War II when hostile aircraft flew in across the sea, hurriedly—and often indiscriminately—dropped their bombs, and immediately sped homewards So called from the light-hearted form of holiday cricket in which the batsman is forced to run every time he touches the ball.

Tip off. To warn or give a hint, especially timely warning of a police raid

Tip-top First rate, capital, splendid

To have a thing on the tip of one's tongue. To have it so pat that it comes without thought, also, to have it on the verge of one's memory, but not quite perfectly remembered

To tip one the wink. To make a signal to another by a wink

Tiphany. The name given in the old romances to the mother of the Magi It is a corruption of *Epiphany. See* TIFFANY

Tiphys The pilot of the Argonauts (*q v*), hence a generic name for pilots

"Tipperary." This song, that will be forever associated with World War I, was composed by Jack Judge (d 1938), of Oldbury, Birmingham. The words were by Harry J Williams, of Temple Balsall, Warwickshire, and the first line of the song is engraved on his tombstone "Tipperary" was composed in 1912 and was already popular on the music-hall stage by 1914 It was sung by troops embarking for France, by men "going over the top," by WAACS and WRENS The refrain was —

Goodbye Piccadilly, farewell Leicester Square
It's a long, long way to Tipperary
My heart's right there

Tipperary Rifle A shillelagh or stick made of blackthorn

Tippling House. A contemptuous name for a tavern or public-house A *tippler* was formerly a tavern-keeper or tapster, and the tavern was called a *tippling house* At Boston, Lincolnshire, in 1577, five persons were appointed "tipplers of Lincoln beer," and no "other tippler [might] draw or sell beer . . " under penalties.

Tipstaff. A constable, bailiff, or sheriff's officer, so called because he carried a staff tipped with a bull's horn or with metal. In the documents of Edward III allusion is often made to his staff

Tirant lo Blanch. A romance of chivalry by Johannot Martorell and Johan de Galba, written in Catalan and published at Valencia in 1490 A favourite book of Cervantes, and one which figures in Don Quixote's library.

Tiresias (tī rē′ si às) A Theban of Greek legend, who by accident saw Athene bathing, and was therefore struck with blindness by her splashing water in his face. She afterwards repented, and, as she could not restore his sight, conferred on him the power of sooth-saying and of understanding the language of birds, and gave him a staff with which he could walk as safely as if he had his sight He found death at last by drinking from the well of Tilphosa

Tirl. A Scottish variant of *twirl.*

He tirled at the pin. He twiddled or rattled with the latch before opening the door The pin was not only the latch of chamber doors and cottages, but the "rasp" of castles used instead of the modern knocker It was attached to a ring, which produced a grating sound to give notice to the warder

Sae licht he jumped up the stair,
And tirled at the pin;
And wha sae ready as hersel'
To let the laddie in
Charlie is my Darling

Tironian (ti rō′ ni ân) Pertaining to a system of shorthand said to have been invented by Tiro, the freedman and amanuensis of Cicero. Our "&" (*see* AMPERSAND) is still sometimes called the *Tironian sign*, for it represents the contraction of Lat *et* introduced by Tiro

With regard to this Maunde Thompson (*Handbook to Greek and Latin Palæography*, p 84) says, "Suetonius has it that 'Vulgares notas *Ennius* primus mille et centum invenit'," and adds that more generally the name of Cicero's freedman, Tiro, is associated with the invention, the signs being commonly named "notæ Tironianæ " *See also* SHORTHAND

Tirynthian (ti rin′ thi àn). Hercules is called by Spenser the *Tirynthian Swain* (*Faerie Queene*, VI, xii, 35), and the *Tirynthian Groom* (*Epithalamium*, 329), because he generally resided at Tiryns, an ancient city of Argolis in Greece, famous for its Cyclopean architecture, which is mentioned by Homer, and the ruins of which are still magnificent

Tit for Tat. Retaliation; probably representing *tip for tap*, i e blow for blow J. Bellenden Ker says this is the Dutch *dit vor dat* (this for that), Lat *quid pro quo* Heywood uses the phrase *tit for tat*, perhaps the French *tant pour tant*.

Titan (tī′ tan) Primordial being of Greek mythology, of enormous size and strength, and typical of lawlessness and the power of force. There were twelve, six male (Oceanus, Cœus, Crius, Hyperion, Japetus, and Cronus) and six female (Theia, Rhea, Themis, Mnemosyne, Phœbe, and Tethys), children of Uranus and Ge (Heaven and Earth) Legends vary, but one states that Cronus swallowed the rest of them, and that when liberated by Zeus (son of Cronus), they dethroned and emasculated their father, Uranus, whereupon they made war on Zeus, who, after defeating them, imprisoned them all—Oceanus alone excepted—in Tartarus

By Virgil and Ovid the Sun was sometimes surnamed *Titan*, hence Shakespeare's —

And flecked Darkness like a drunkard reels
From forth Day's path and Titan's fiery wheels
Romeo and Juliet, ii, 3.

Titania (tī tan′ yā) Wife of Oberon (*q v*), and Queen of the Fairies in *A Midsummer Night's Dream* Shakespeare was, apparently, the first to use this name

Titanic. A White Star liner, at the time of her launching the biggest vessel in the world and reputed unsinkable While on her maiden voyage from Southampton to New York she collided, it is believed, with a submerged iceberg and in less than three hours went to the bottom, at 2 20 a m, April 15th, 1912. The *Carpathia* picked up about 700 survivors, but over 1,500 lives were lost.

Tithonus (tī thō′ nūs) A beautiful Trojan of Greek legend, brother to Laomedon, and beloved by Eos (Aurora) At his prayer the goddess granted him immortality, but as he had forgotten to ask for youth and vigour he grew old, and life became insupportable He now prayed Eos to remove him from the world, this, however, she could not do, but she changed him into a grasshopper

Titi, Prince (tē′ tē). The nickname of Frederick, Prince of Wales, eldest son of George II In constant opposition to his father, in 1735 he wrote an *Histoire du Prince Titi* which contained gross and unmanly caricatures of his father and mother Two English translations of this offensive work appeared in 1736

Titles of Kings. *See* RULERS, RELIGIOUS

Title-role, in a play, opera or film, is the part or role from which the title is taken, *e g* Carmen, Hamlet, Aïda

Titmouse. *See* MISNOMERS

Titular Bishops. The Roman Catholic dignitaries formerly known as bishops *in partibus. See* IN PARTIBUS

Titus (tī′ tūs) An alternative name of the Penitent Thief *See* DYSMAS

The Arch of Titus. The arch built in Rome in commemoration of the capture of Jerusalem by Titus and Vespasian (A.D. 70) shortly after that event It is richly sculptured, and the trophies taken at the destruction of the temple are shown in relief

Tityrus (tit′ ı rus) A poetical surname for a shepherd, from its use in Greek idylls and Virgil's first *Eclogue* In the *Shepheardes Calendar* (*Feb*, *June*, and *Dec*) Spenser calls Chaucer by this name.

Heroes and their feats
Fatigue me, never weary of the pipe
Of Tityrus, assembling as he sang
The rustic throng beneath his favourite beech
COWPER *The Winter Evening*, 750.

Tityre Tus. Dissolute young scapegraces of the late 17th century (*cp* MOHOCKS) whose delight was to annoy the watchmen, upset sedans, wrench knockers off doors, and insult pretty women The name comes from the first line of Virgil's first Eclogue *Tityre, tu patulæ recubans sub tegmine fagi*, because the Tityre Tus loved to lurk in the dark night looking for mischief

Tityus (tit′ ı ūs) A gigantic son of Zeus and Ge in Greek mythology whose body covered nine acres of land He tried to defile Latona, but Apollo cast him into Tartarus, where a vulture fed on his liver, which grew again as fast as it was devoured (*Cp* PROMETHEUS) He was the father of Europa.

Tiu Son of Woden (Scandinavian mythology), and a younger brother of Thor The wolf Fenrir bit off his hand

Tizzy. A sixpenny-piece, a variant of *tester* (*q v*).

Tmesis (tme′ sis) The grammatical term for the separation of the parts of a compound word by inserting between them other words, or the re-arrangement in this manner of the words of a phrase, *e g*. "A large meal and rich," instead of a large, rich meal "The greatness of his power to usward" (*Eph* i, 19) instead of The greatness of his power toward us

To-do. Here's a pretty to-do. Disturbance

To-remain Bible. *See* BIBLE, SPECIALLY NAMED.

Toads The device of Clovis was three toads (or *botes*, as they were called in O Fr), legend relates that after his conversion and baptism the Arians assembled a large army under King Candat against him While on his way to meet the heretics Clovis saw in the heavens his device miraculously changed into three lilies *or* on a banner *azure* He instantly had such a banner made, and called it his *oriflamme*, and even before his army came in sight of King Candat the host of the heretic lay dead, slain, like the army of Sennacherib, by a blast from the God of Battles (Raoul de Presles *Grans Croniques de France*)

The toad, ugly and venomous, wears yet a precious jewel in its head Fenton says "There is to be found in the heads of old and great toads a stone they call borax or stelon, which, being used as rings, give forewarning against venom" (1569) These stones always bear a figure resembling a toad on their surface

Lupton says "A toad-stone, called *crepuudia*, touching any part envenomed by the bite of a rat, wasp, spider, or other venomous beast, ceases the pain and swelling thereof" In the Londesborough Collection is a silver ring of the 15th century, in which one of these toad-stones is set The stone was supposed to sweat and change colour when poison was in its proximity Technically called the *Batrachyte* or *Batrachos*, an antidote to all sorts of poison.

Toads unknown in Ireland. It is said that St Patrick cleared the island of all vermin by his malediction

Toad-eater or Toady. A cringing, obsequious parasite The old mountebanks used to take around with them a boy who ate—or pretended to eat—toads which at that time were supposed to be poisonous This gave his master an opportunity to exhibit his skill in expelling poison

> Be the most scorn'd Jack-pudding of the pack,
> And turn toad-eater to some foreign quack
> TOM BROWNE (*Works*, I, 71)

Toad-in-the-hole. A piece of beef, sausage, chop, etc, baked in batter

Toast The person, cause, object, etc, to which guests are invited to drink in compliment, as well as the drink itself. The word is taken from the piece of toast which used at one time to be put into the tankard, and which still floats in the loving-cups at the Universities

The story goes that in the reign of Charles II a certain beau pledged a noted beauty in a glass of water taken from her bath, whereupon another roysterer cried out he would have nothing to do with the liquor, but would have the toast—*i e* the lady herself (*Rambler*, No 24)

> Let the toast pass, drink to the lass —SHERIDAN·
> *School for Scandal.*
> Say, why are beauties praised and honoured most,
> The wise man's passion and the vain man's toast
> POPE *Rape of the Lock*, canto i

Toaster, Toasting-iron. *See* CHEESE-TOASTER

Toast-master. The official who announces the after-dinner speakers at a formal banquet He must be a man of stentorian voice and enjoy a nice knowledge of precedence.

Tobit The principal character of the Book of Tobit, a romance included in the Old Testament Apocrypha While sleeping outside the wall of his courtyard he was blinded by sparrows "muting warm dung into his eyes." His son Tobias was attacked on the Tigris by a fish, which leapt out of the water and which he caught at the bidding of the angel Raphael, his mentor. Tobit was cured of his blindness by applying to his eyes the gall of this fish

Toboso (tȯ bȯ' zȯ) The village home of Don Quixote's lady-love, whom he renamed Dulcinea (*q v*) It is a few miles east of Ciudad Real.

Toby. The dog in the puppet-show of Punch and Judy (*q v*) He wears a frill garnished with bells, to frighten away the devil from his master

My Uncle Toby. Captain Shandy, the uncle of Tristram Shandy in Sterne's novel of that name. He is the embodiment of the wisdom of love, as his brother is that of the love of wisdom.

The high toby, the high road, the low toby, the by-road A highwayman is a "high tobyman"; a mere footpad is a "low tobyman" This is probably from the Shelta (*i e* tinkers' jargon) word for road, *tobar*

Toby jug. A small jug in the form of a squat old man in 18th-century dress, wearing a three-cornered hat, one corner of which forms the lip. The name comes from a poem (1761) about one "Toby Philpot," adapted from the Latin by Francis Fawkes, and the design of the jug from a print sold by Carrington Bowles, a London print-seller, to Ralph Wood, the potter, who turned out a great number of Toby Jugs

Toc H. The morse pronunciation of the letters T H., the initials of Talbot House The term was used in World War I, when the first Talbot House was founded, in December 1915, at Poperinghe, in memory of Gilbert Talbot, son of the Bishop of Winchester, who had been killed at Hooge in the preceding July The Rev. P B. Clayton, M C made it a famous rest and recreation centre In 1920 he founded a similar centre in London, also known as Toc H, which developed into an interdenominational association for Christian social service

Tocsin (tok' sin) An alarm signal given by the ringing of church bells As *tocksaine* it is an old English word coming through the French *toquesin*, from *toquer*, to touch, and *senh*, Provençal for a bell

Toddy. Properly the juice obtained by tapping certain palms, fermented so as to become intoxicating (Hindu *tadi*, from *tar*, a palm) It is also applied to a beverage compounded of spirits, hot water, and sugar, a kind of punch

Tofana (to fa' nä) An old woman of Naples (d. 1730) immortalized by her invention of a tasteless and colourless poison, called by her the *Manna of St. Nicola of Bari*, but better known as *Aqua Tofana*. Above 600 persons fell victims to this insidious drug

Toga (tō' gä) The usual outer dress of a Roman citizen when appearing in public, the Romans were hence the *Gens togata* (*q v*), the "togaed people"

The toga consisted of a single piece of undyed woollen cloth, cut almost in a semi-circle and worn in a flowing fashion round the shoulders and body

Toga picta. The toga embroidered with golden stars that was worn by the emperor on special occasions, by a victorious general at his "triumph," etc

Toga prætexta The toga with a purple border that was worn by children, by those engaged in sacred rites, magistrates, etc

Toga virilis. The toga worn by men (*virilis*, manly), assumed by boys when 15.

Toggle (U S A) A verb meaning to fasten together with bits of rope The word is a seaman's word of the 17th century, a toggle being a wooden pin passed through the eye or loop of a rope, or through a link of a chain In World War II a toggle rope was a length of stout cord with a small bar of wood spliced into it at one end and a loop at the other, it was used for a variety of purposes and was carried by British Commandos

Togs Slang for clothes, hence *togged out in his best*, dressed in his best clothes, *toggery*, finery The word may be connected with *toga* (*see above*).

Token Payment. A small payment made as a formal and binding acknowledgement of indebtedness The word "token" is often used to describe some action or phrase used in lieu of—but acknowledging—a greater obligation

Tokyo Rose. The name given by U S service men to a woman broadcaster of propaganda from Japan during World War II Several U S A -born Japanese (Nisei) girls were identified as taking part in these broadcasts, notably Iva Togori, of California, and Ruth Hayakawa

Toledo (tò lē' dō) A sword made at Toledo in Spain. which place, long before and after the Middle Ages, was specially famous for them
I give him three years and a day to match my Toledo
And then we'll fight like dragons.
　　　　MASSINGER *The Maid of Honour*, ii, 2

Tollbooth (tōl' booth) Originally a booth or stall where taxes were collected
And whanne Jesus passide fro thennis, he saw a man, Matheu bi name, sittingge in a tolbothe —
WYCLIF, *Matt* ix, 9

In Scotland the term was applied to the town gaol, from the custom of confining offenders against the laws of a fair or market in the booth where market dues were collected

Tolosa (to lō' sà) **He has got the gold of Tolosa.** His ill-gotten wealth will do him no good.
See under GOLD

Tom, Tommy. Short for *Thomas*. used of the male of certain animals (especially the cat), and generically—like *Jack* (*q v*)—for a man. It is also a generic name for a little boy. When contrasted, *Jack* is usually the sharp, shrewd, active fellow, and *Tom* the honest dullard No one would think of calling the thick-headed male cat a *Jack*, nor the pert, dexterous, thieving daw a *Tom* The former is almost instinctively called a *Tom-cat*, and the latter a *Jack-daw*
　　The man that hails you Tom or Jack,
　　And proves by thumps upon your back
　　How he esteems your merit,
　　Is such a friend, that one had need
　　Be very much his friend indeed
　　To pardon or to bear it
　　　　COWPER *Friendship*.

Great Tom of Lincoln. A bell at Lincoln Cathedral weighing 5 tons 8 cwt.

Great Tom of Oxford. A bell in Tom Gate Tower (*see* TOM GATE) at Oxford, tolled every night. It weighs 7 tons 12 cwt

Long Tom. A familiar name for any gun of great length; especially the naval 4 7s used on land in the Boer War

Old Tom. A specially potent gin. The story goes that a Thomas Norris, employed in Messrs Hodges' distillery, opened a gin palace in Great Russell Street, Covent Garden, in the late 18th century, and called the gin concocted by Thomas Chamberlain, one of the firm of Hodges, "Old Tom," in compliment to his former master

Tom and Jerry. Types of the roystering young man about town, from Pierce Egan's *Life in London, or, The Day and Night Scenes of Jerry Hawthorn, Esq , and his Elegant Friend Corinthian Tom* (1821) *Cp* JERRYSHOP

Tomboy. A romping girl The word was formerly used of a loose or immodest woman, whence the slang, *Tom*, applied to a prostitute
　　　　　　　　A lady
　　So fair　　to be partner'd
　　With tomboys
　　　　　　　　Cymbeline, i, 6

Tom Collins A long drink of gin, lemon or lime, and some sparkling aerated water—in England bitter beer Many localities claim the original Tom Collins; whoever he was or wherever he lived he deserves well of posterity

Tom, Dick, and Harry. A Victorian term for "the man in the street," more particularly persons of no note, persons unworthy notice "Brown, Jones, and Robinson" are far other men, they are the vulgar rich, who give themselves airs, especially abroad, and look with scorn on all foreign manners and customs which differ from their own

Tom Fool. A clumsy, witless fool, fond of stupid practical jokes; hence, *tomfoolery*.

Tom Gate, The. The great gate of Christ Church, Oxford, begun by Wolsey and completed (1682) by Wren In its tower is "Great Tom" (*see above*)

Tom Quad. The great quadrangle of Christ Church, Oxford

Tom Long. Any lazy, dilatory man *To be kept waiting for Tom Long* is to be kept hanging about for a wearisome time.

Tom Noddy. A puffing, fuming, stupid creature.

Tom o' Bedlam. A mendicant who levies charity on the plea of insanity In the 16th and 17th centuries applications for admission to Bedlam (*q.v*) became so numerous that many inmates were dismissed half cured These "ticket-of-leave men" wandered about chanting mad songs, and dressed in fantastic dresses, to excite pity Posing as these harmless "innocents," a set of sturdy rogues appeared, called *Abram men* (*q v*), who shammed lunacy, and committed great depredations
　　With a sigh like Tom o' Bedlam
　　　　SHAKESPEARE *King Lear*, i, 2

Tom Thumb. Any dwarfish or insignificant person is so called; from the pigmy hero of the old nursery tale, popular in the 16th century. *The History of Tom Thumb* was published by R. Johnson in 1621, and there is a similar tale by Perrault (*Le Petit Poucet*), in 1630
The American dwarf Charles Sherwood Stratton (1838-83) was popularly called "General Tom Thumb" (*see* DWARFS); and Fielding wrote a burlesque (acted 1730) entitled *Tom Thumb the Great See also* BOAST OF ENGLAND

Tom Tiddler's ground. A place where it is easy to pick up a fortune or make a place in the world for oneself. from the old children's game in which a base-keeper, who is called

Tom Tiddler, tries to keep the other children who sing —

> Here we are on Tom Tiddler's ground
> Picking up gold and silver

from crossing the boundary into his base

Tom Tiller. A hen-pecked husband

Tom's A noted coffee-house of the late 18th century, that was in existence in Russell Street, Covent Garden, as late as 1865 It was owned by and named after Thomas West, and here in 1764 was founded *Tom's Club*, which included all the literary and social notabilities of the time.

Tommy, or **Tommy Atkins.** A British private soldier, as a Jack Tar is a British sailor At one time all recruits were served out with manuals in which were to be entered the name, age, date of enlistment, length of service, wounds, medals, and so on of the holder With each book was sent a specimen form showing how the one in the manual should be filled in, and the hypothetical name selected was Thomas Atkins

Tommy bar. This is a small bar of rounded metal used for inserting into and turning box-spanners and similar tools

Tommy-cooker. A small individual stove using solid fuel, invented in the time of World War I and issued to Allied troops in World War II It was also the name given by the Germans to the Sherman Tank, which caught fire very easily when hit

Tommy Dodd The "odd" man who, in tossing up, either wins or loses according to agreement with his confederate

To go Tommy Dodd for drinks etc, is to toss "odd man out," the odd man dropping out until there are only two left, who toss for who pays

Tommy gun. A Thompson short-barrelled, sub-machine gun

Tommy rot. Utter nonsense, rubbish, a cock-and-bull story (*q v.*)

Tommy shop A shop where vouchers, given by an employer in lieu of money, can be exchanged for goods, commonly run by large employers of labour before the truck system was made illegal.

Tomahawk (tom' a hawk) The war axe of the N. American Indians, pre-historically made of stone or deer-horn but after the coming of the white man of iron or steel with a wooden handle Sometimes the blunt end of the head was hollowed into a pipe-bowl, the handle being bored to form a stem It was the custom of the Indians to bury the tomahawk when making peace, and dig it up again on the outbreak of war—hence the phrase *To bury the hatchet*

Tombland Fair See MAUNDY THURSDAY

To-morrow To-morrow come never Never at all—when two Sundays, or three Thursdays, meet

To-morrow never comes. Because, when it *does* come it ceases to be *to-morrow* and becomes *to-day*, a reproof to those who defer till to-morrow what should be done to-day.

A similar—though more caustic—saying is —

> Treason doth never prosper, what's the reason?
> For if it prosper, none dare call it treason
> SIR JOHN HARRINGTON (d 1612)

Tone Poem, or **Symphonic Poem,** is a form of orchestral work which is intended to describe some literary or other subject As with other programme music it requires an accompanying explanatory description The term Symphonic Poem was first used by Liszt, who wrote thirteen works of this description

Tong A Chinese association or political party In U S A the tongs are frequently looked upon by the police with suspicion, the rigid exclusiveness of the society and the secrecy attending its meetings being suggestive of subversive intentions

Tongue. A lick with the rough side of the tongue A severe reprimand, a good slating

The gift of tongues Command of foreign languages, also the power claimed by the Early Church and by some later mystics (as the Irvingites) of conversing and understanding unknown tongues (from the miracle at Pentecost—*Acts* ii, 4)

The three tongues. See THREE.

The tongue of the trump. The spokesman or leader of a party

> The tongue of the trump to them a'
> BURNS *The Election Ballads*, III.

To give someone the length of one's tongue. To talk to him "like a Dutch uncle", to tell him in unmeasured language what you really think of him

To give tongue. Properly used of a dog barking when on the scent, hence sometimes applied to people Thus Polonius says to his son —

> Give thy thoughts no tongue,
> Nor any unproportioned thought his act
> *Hamlet*, i, 3

To hold one's tongue. To keep silent when one might speak, to keep a secret

To lose one's tongue. To become tongue-tied or speechless through shyness, fear, etc

To speak with one's tongue in one's cheek. Insincerely, saying one thing and meaning another

Tongue-tied. Speechless, usually through bashfulness or modesty, also (literally) having an impediment of the speech through shortness of the frænum

Tonic Sol-fa A system of musical notation in which diatonic scales are written always in one way (the keynote being indicated), the tones being represented by syllables or initials, and time and accents by dashes and colons. *Tonic* is a musical term denoting pertaining to or founded on the keynote, *sol* and *fa* are two of the Aretinian Syllables (*q v*). *See also* DOH, GAMUT

Tonquin Bean. *See* MISNOMERS

Tonsure. The sacerdotal custom among priests of "being tonsured," *i e* having the head, or part of it, shaved (Lat *tonsura*, a shearing), dates from the 5th or 6th centuries, and symbolizes Christ's crown of thorns That of the secular clergy is a round space about the size of a half-crown at the crown of the head In Britain, U S A and other countries where it would not be in accordance with the customs of the people the tonsure is not retained after ordination Among regulars there is a great variety of tonsure, Carthusians and Camaldolese shave the whole head except for a horizontal strip (*corona*) about half an inch wide, Friars Minor, Cistercians, and Benedictines have a wider *corona*, Dominicans shave the whole crown above the top of the ears, these are all called the great tonsure The tonsure of Eastern monks is a cruciform cutting of part of the hair The Celtic tonsure was made by cutting off all the hair in front of a line drawn over the head from ear to ear

Tontine (ton' tēn). A form of annuity shared by several subscribers, in which the shares of those who die are added to the holdings of the survivors till the last survivor inherits all So named from Lorenzo Tonti, a Neapolitan banker, who introduced the system into France in 1653 In 1765 the House of Commons raised £300,000 by way of tontine annuities at 3 per cent., and so late as 1871 the *Daily News* announced a proposed tontine to raise £650,000 to purchase the Alexandra Palace and 100 acres of land

Tool To tool a coach To drive one; generally applied to a gentleman driver who undertook stage-coach driving for his own amusement

Tooley Street. A corruption of St Olaf—*i e.* 'T-olaf, Tolay, Tooley. Similarly, Sise Lane is St. Osyth's Lane

The three tailors of Tooley Street. *See* TAILOR

Toom Tabard (Scot , empty jacket). A nickname given to John Baliol (1249-1315), because of his poor spirit, and sleeveless appointment to the throne of Scotland The honour was an "empty jacket," which he enjoyed only from 1292 to 1296 He died in Normandy.

Tooth, Teeth. Golden tooth. *See* GOLDEN

Tooth and egg. An obsolete corruption of *tutenag* (from Arab. *tuttya*), an alloy rich in zinc, coming from China and the East Indies and largely used for lining tea-chests.

With tooth and nail In right good earnest, with one's utmost power, as though biting and scratching

By the skin of one's teeth. *See* SKIN

From the teeth outwards. Merely talk; without real significance

He has cut his eye-teeth. He is "wide awake," quite sophisticated, he has "his weather-eye open." The eye-teeth (*i.e.* the upper canines) are cut late —

	Months		
First set	5 to 8,	the four central incisors
	7 „ 10 „	lateral incisors
	12 „ 16 „	anterior molars.
	14 „ 20 „	eye-teeth
	Years		
Second set—	5 to 6,	the anterior molars
	7 „ 8 „	incisors
	9 „ 10 „	bicuspids
	11 „ 12 „	eye-teeth

See also EYE-TEETH.

His teeth are drawn. His power of doing mischief is taken from him. The phrase comes from the fable of the lion in love, who consented to have his teeth drawn and claws cut, in order that a fair damsel might marry him When this was done the girl's father fell on the lion and slew him

In spite of his teeth. In opposition to his settled purpose or resolution, even though he snarl and show his teeth like an angry dog Holinshed tells us of a Bristol Jew, who suffered a tooth to be drawn daily for seven days before he would submit to the extortion of King John

> In despite of the teeth of all the rhyme and reason
> —*Merry Wives*, v, 4

In the teeth of the wind. With the wind dead against one, blowing in or against the teeth

> To strive with all the tempest in my teeth
> POPE *Epistles of Horace*, II, ii

To cast into one's teeth. To utter reproaches

> All his faults observed,
> Set in a note-book, learned, and conned by rote,
> To cast into my teeth
> *Julius Cæsar*, IV, 3

To set one's teeth on edge *See* EDGE.

Top. *See also* MIZENTOP

Over the top. One is said *to go over the top* when he takes the final plunge A phrase from the trench warfare of World War I when, at zero hour, troops climbed over the parapet of the front-line trenches to advance across No-man's-land to attack the enemy front line .

The Big Top is the big circus tent in which the main performance takes place

Top dog, the one who by skill, personality or violence obtains the mastery, as the dog who is on top of his adversary in a fight

To blow one's top. To go mad, to lose all control of oneself

The top o' the morning to ye! A cheery greeting on a fine day, especially in Ireland It is about the same as "The best of everything to you!"

Top-heavy. Liable to tip over because the centre of gravity is too high, intoxicated

Top sawyer. A first-rate fellow, a distinguished man Literally, the sawyer who works the upper handle in a saw-pit, hence one who holds a superior position

To sleep like a top. *See* SLEEP

Topham. Take him, Topham. Catch him if you can, lay hold of him, tipstaff Topham was the Black Rod of the House of Commons in the reign of Charles II, very active in apprehending suspects during the supposed conspiracy revealed by Titus Oates 'Take him, Topham," became a proverbial saying of the time.

Tophet (tō' fet). A valley to the south of Jerusalem, at the south-east of Gehenna (*q v*), where children were made to "pass through the fire to Moloch " Josiah threw dead bodies, ordure, and other unclean things there, to prevent all further application of the place to religious use (2 *Kings* xxiii, 10), and here Sennacherib's army was destroyed (*Is.* xxx,

31-33) A perpetual fire was kept burning in it to consume the dead bodies, bones, filth, etc., deposited there, and hence it was taken as symbolical of Sheol or Hell The name is Hebrew, and may mean "a place to be spat upon"

Toplady Ring *See* ROCK OF AGES.

Topsy. The little slave girl in Harriet Beecher Stowe's *Uncle Tom's Cabin* (1852), chiefly remembered because when asked by "Aunt Ophelia" about her parents she maintained that she had had neither father nor mother, her solution of her existence being "I 'spects I growed"

Topsy-turvy. Upside down, probably *top*, with *so* and obsolete *terve*, connected with A S *tearflian*. to turn or roll over Shakespeare says, "Turn it topsy-turvy down" (1 *Henry IV*, IV, 1) *Cp* HALF-SEAS OVER

Torah (tôr'a). The Hebrew term for the Pentateuch or Five Books of Moses The word is also used collectively for the entire Scriptures and the corpus of Jewish religious literature

Torch (U S A.) To carry the torch for someone means to admire or love that person—the torch being the torch of love

Toreador (tor'e a dôr) A popular misnomer for *torero*, a Spanish bull-fighter.

Torpids. The name given to the Lent boat races at Oxford, between the second crews of colleges A second-class racing boat is a torpid

Torricelli An Italian mathematician (1608-47), noted for his explanation of the rise of mercury in a common barometer Galileo explained the phenomenon by the *ipse dixit* of "Nature abhors a vacuum"
Hence *Torricellian tube*, the barometer, and *Torricellian vacuum*, the vacuum above the mercury in this.

Torso. A statue which has lost its head and limbs The word is Ital for a stump or stalk, from Lat *thyrsus*, the attribute of Bacchus, consisting of a spear-shaft wreathed with ivy or vine branches and tipped with a fir-cone
The *Torso Belvedere*, the famous torso of Hercules, in the Vatican, was discovered in the fifteenth century It is said that Michael Angelo greatly admired it

Tortoise. The name is given to the ancient Roman *testudo*, i.e the screen formed by the overlapping shields held above their heads by soldiers when attacking a fort The animal is frequently taken as the type of plodding perseverance—"slow but sure"
The tortoise which, according to Hindu myth, supports Maha-pudma, the elephant which, in its turn, supports the world, is Chukwa

Achilles and the tortoise. *See* ACHILLES.

Like the hare and the tortoise *See* HARE.

Tory (tôr'i) The name given in the 17th century to the Irish who were turned out of their holdings by English settlers, and so took to the hills and bogs and developed into brigands and outlaws (from *toraidhe*, a pursued person) During the Revolution it was applied to the Catholics fighting for James II, hence to those in England who refused to concur in

excluding James from the throne. Until the accession of George III the party had a Stuart bias, but it then decided vigorously to uphold the Crown, the Church as by law established, and all constituted authority As the name of the political and parliamentary party it was gradually superseded after 1830 by "Conservative" (*q v*), but it has been retained to denote the principles and policy of the party. *Cp* DIE-HARDS, LIBERAL, UNIONIST.

Totalizator (tō tǎl i zā' tôr). A machine used for betting on horse races and other sporting events Known in France as the Pari Mutuel, its use was legalized in Britain in 1928, when a number were installed on the principal racecourses Worked by electricity the totalizator automatically records the number of bets on a given horse, etc., and registers the amount of money due to the successful backers.

Totalitarian (tō tǎl i târ' i an) An ugly neologism invented to describe an ugly thing—a form of government that neither tolerates nor recognizes any persons or parties holding views differing from its own.

Totem (tō' tem) A North American Indian (Algonkin) word for some natural object, usually an animal, taken as the emblem of a person or clan on account of a supposed relationship. Totemism, which is common among primitive peoples, has a distinct value in preventing intermarriage among near relations, for if persons bearing the same totem (as, for instance, in the case of brothers and sisters) intermarry the punishment is death Another custom is that one is not allowed to kill or eat the animal borne as one's totem.
This very extraordinary institution, whatever its origin, cannot have arisen except among men capable of conceiving kinship and all human relationships as existing between themselves and all animate and inanimate things It is the rule and not the exception that all savage societies are founded upon this belief
—ANDREW LANG *Myth, Ritual, and Religion*

Totem pole The post standing before a dwelling on which grotesque and, frequently, brilliantly coloured representations of the totem were carved or hung It is often of great size, and sometimes so broad at the base that an archway is cut through it

Touch and Go. A very narrow escape, a metaphor derived, perhaps, from driving when the wheel of one vehicle touches that of another passing vehicle without doing mischief It was a *touch*, but neither vehicle was stopped, each could *go* on

Touch down In Rugby and American football, to score by touching the ball on the ground within a certain defined area behind the opponent's goal posts

Touchy Apt to take offence on slight provocation *Ne touchez pas*, *Noli me tangere*, one not to be touched

Touchstone. A dark flinty schist, jasper, or basanite (the *Lapis Lydius* of the ancients), so called because gold is tried by it A series of needles are formed (1) of pure gold, (2) of 23 gold and 1 copper, (3) of 22 gold and 2 copper, and so on The assayer selects one of these and rubs it on the touchstone, when it leaves a mark that is reddish in proportion to the quantity of alloy, the article to be tested is then similarly "touched" and the marks compared Hence the word is often used of any criterion or standard

Fable has it that Battus saw Mercury steal Apollo's oxen, and Mercury gave him a cow to secure his silence, but, being distrustful of the man, changed himself into a peasant, and offered him a cow and an ox if he would tell him where he got the cow Battus, caught in the trap, told the secret, and Mercury changed him into a touchstone (Ovid. *Metamorphoses*, 11)

Men have a touchstone whereby to try gold, but gold is the touchstone whereby to try men —FULLER *Holy and Profane State (The Good Judge).*

Touchstone. A clown whose mouth is filled with quips and cranks and witty repartees, in Shakespeare's *As You Like It*. The original actor of the part was Tarlton

Tour The Grand Tour. In the 17th, 18th, and early 19th centuries it was the custom for families of rank and substance to finish their sons' education by sending them, under the guardianship of a tutor, on a tour through France, Switzerland, Italy, and home through western Germany This was known as the Grand Tour and sometimes a couple of years were devoted to it. The young men were supposed to study the history, language, etc , of each country they visited

Tour de force (Fr) A feat of strength or skill

Tournament (O.Fr *tornelement*, from Lat *tornare*, to turn) A tilt of knights, the chief art of the game being so to manœuvre or *turn* your horse as to avoid the adversary's blow

The Tournament of Tottenham. A comic romance, given in Percy's *Reliques* A number of clowns are introduced, practising warlike games, and making vows like knights of high degree They ride tilt on cart-horses, fight with ploughshares and flails, and wear for armour wooden bowls and saucepan-lids.

The Eglinton Tournament. At Eglinton Castle, Ayrshire, an attempt was made to revive the mediæval tournament, on August 28th, 1839. The lists were richly decorated, the ladies wore 14th and 15th century costumes, and young society men practised how to ride a charger in full armour and wielding a tilting-lance The Marquess of Londonderry was King of the Tournament, Lady Seymour, later Duchess of Somerset, was Queen of Love and Beauty Fifteen knights took part; but the affair was entirely ruined by the heavy rain that fell without ceasing throughout the day

Tours (toor) Geoffrey of Monmouth says, "In the party of Brutus was one Turones, his nephew, inferior to none in courage and strength, from whom Tours derived its name, being the place of his sepulture " This fable is wholly worthless historically Tours is the city of the Turones, a people of Gallia Lugdunensis.

Tout ensemble (too ton sombl) (Fr) The whole massed together, the general effect.

Tow. To take in tow. Take under guidance A man who takes a lad in tow acts as his guide

and director To tow a ship or barge is to guide and draw it along by tow-lines
Too proud for bards to take in tow my name
PETER PINDAR *Future Laureate*, Pt ii.

Tower. Tower Liberty The Tower of London, with the fortifications and Tower Hill. This formed part of the ancient demesne of the Crown, with jurisdiction and privileges distinct from and independent of the City *Cp. Liberty of the Fleet, under* LIBERTY.

Tower of London. The architect was Gundulphus, Bishop of Rochester, who also built or restored Rochester keep, in the time of William I Tradition has it that the White Tower, the central and oldest portion, is on the site of a fort erected by Julius Cæsar to awe the ancient inhabitants, hence Gray's well-known allusion in *The Bard* '—
Ye Towers of Julius, London's lasting shame,
With many a foul and midnight murther fed

In the precincts of the Tower lie buried Anne Boleyn and her brother, Catherine Howard and Lady Rochford her associate, the venerable Lady Salisbury, and Cromwell the minister of Henry VIII, the two Seymours, the admiral and the protector of Edward VI, the Duke of Norfolk and Earl of Sussex (Elizabeth I's reign); the Duke of Monmouth, son of Charles II, the Earls of Balmerino and Kilmarnock, and Lord Lovat; Bishop Fisher and his illustrious friend Sir Thomas More The bones of the "little Princes," Edward V and his brother the Duke of York, murdered there by order of Richard III in 1483, were discovered in 1674 and removed to Westminster Abbey

Towers of Silence. See SILENCE

Town. A S. *tun*, a plot of ground fenced round or enclosed by a hedge (connected with Ger *zaun*, a hedge), a single dwelling, a number of dwelling-houses forming a village or burgh

A man about town. *See* MAN

A woman of the town. A prostitute

The little stranger has come to town. The expected child is born.

Town and Gown. The two sections of a university town; composed of those who are not attached to the university and those who are, hence, *a town and gown row*, a collision, often leading to a fight, between the students and non-gownsmen *Cp* PHILISTINES

Town bull. A bull kept by the parish, in country places, for breeding purposes.
And so, brother *Toby*, this poor Bull of mine . might have been driven into Doctors' Commons and lost his character—which to a Town Bull, brother *Toby*, is the very same thing as his life —STERNE *Tristram Shandy*, IX, xxiii

Town crier. A municipal official who goes about the streets, usually in a robe, ringing a bell and crying, *Oyez! Oyez!* (*q v.*) to attract attention to his proclamations of notices, coming events, lost property, etc.

Town house One's residence in town as apart from that in the country

Town is empty The season (*q.v.*) is over. society has left town for the country The few millions who live there and work do not count

Town planning. The regulating of the ground plan or extension of a town with a view to securing the greatest advantages from the point of view of health, public amenities, convenience in transport, etc The Town Planning Act was passed in 1909—and various amending and other Acts came into force in subsequent years In 1943 a Ministry of Town and Country Planning was constituted, with wide powers to originate and control development

Going to town. Full of life and high spirits. An American expression, probably originating among backwoodsmen

Toyshop of Europe, The. So Burke called Birmingham Here the word "toy" does not refer to playthings for children, but to trinkets, knick-knacks, and similar articles.

Tracts for the Times. A series of papers on theological and liturgical subjects, published at Oxford (hence sometimes called *The Oxford Tracts*) between 1833 and 1841. They were started by the Rev J H Newman (afterwards Cardinal Newman) with the object of arresting "the advance of Liberalism in religious thought," and reviving "the true conception of the relation of the Church of England to the Catholic Church at large" The authors, who used the first seven letters as signatures to their contributions, were —

A —John Keble, M A , author of the *Christian Year* fellow of Oriel, and Professor of Poetry at Oxford

B.—Isaac Williams, Fellow of Trinity, author of *The Cathedral, and other Poems*

C.—E B Pusey, D D , Regius Professor of Hebrew, and Canon of Christ Church

D —John Henry Newman, D.D , Fellow of Oriel.

E.—Thomas Keble

F —Sir John Provost, Bart.

G —R F Wilson, of Oriel.

The series came to an end (at the request of the Bishop of Oxford) with Newman's *Tract No xc*, "On Certain Passages in the XXXIX Articles", and later many of the Tractarians entered the Roman Catholic Church.

Tracy All the Tracys have the wind in their faces. Those who do wrong will always meet with punishment William de Traci was the most active of the four knights who slew Thomas à Becket, and for this misdeed all who bore the name were saddled by the Church with this ban —

Wherever by sea or land they go
For ever the wind in their face shall blow.

Fuller, with his usual *naïveté*, says, "So much the better in hot weather, as it will save the need of a fan

Trade. Free Trade. *See* FREE

The balance of trade *See* BALANCE

The Board of Trade. A Government department—officially a Committee of the Privy Council—dealing with commercial and industrial affairs, such as bankruptcy, company matters, railways, weights and measures, harbours, patents, trade and merchandise marks, etc. Originally established by Oliver Cromwell, it has grown in scope of its duties and power

The trade Usually the liquor trade, more particularly those engaged in the brewing and distilling industries, but applied also to the general body of persons engaged in the particular trade that is being spoken of.

To blow trade *See* TRADE WINDS, *below*

To trade something off To barter or exchange it, to sell it as a "job lot "

To trade upon To make use of so as to obtain some advantage The phrase is usually employed to describe the unscrupulous use of private knowledge or even of a personal affliction to arouse sympathy

Trade board. An official council set up to regulate the conditions of labour in certain trades that otherwise might be "sweated "

Trade dollar. A United States silver dollar formerly coined specially for Oriental trade. It weighed 420 gr , instead of the 412 5 gr of the ordinary dollar, and has not been coined since 1887

Trade follows the flag. Wherever the flag flies trade with the mother country springs up and prospers

Trade-last (U S A) A compliment offered in exchange for another "I have a trade-last for you," means, "I have heard something flattering about you which I will tell you after you have told me a flattering remark you have heard about me " The phrase is common among juveniles and adolescents.

Trade mark. The name or distinctive device for an article made for sale, indicating that it was produced by the holder of this device In most countries trade marks are protected by law, it being a misdemeanour to forge or counterfeit such a mark In Britain and U S A a trade mark must be registered with the Government in order to secure full protection

Trade Union An association of employees in a trade or industry, formed for the promotion and protection of their common interests in regard to conditions of labour, wages, etc , and often for providing its members with payments during temporary unemployment, sickness, or strikes, and pensions in old age.

The earliest forerunner of the modern trade union was probably the combination of London cordwainers against their overseers in 1387, but until the passing of the first Trade Union Act (1871), all trade unions were, in so far as their objects could be held to be "in restraint of trade," illegal associations

As early as the time of Henry V it was decided that a contract imposing a general restraint upon trade was void, and agreements between workmen not to take work except upon certain terms are at common law bad, and consequently any association which exists to promote such agreements or to enforce such terms is illegal   By the Trade Union Act, 1871, it was declared that a Trade Union merely because its objects were in restraint of trade should not be held to be unlawful, and its agreements were made binding, so that they would be recognised in law — *The Labour Year Book*, 1916 (p 174)

The modern trade union, and the name, came into being about 1830

Trade winds. Winds that *blow trade*, i e. regularly in one track or direction (Low Ger *trade*, track) In the northern hemisphere they blow from the *north-east*, and in the southern hemisphere from the *south-east*, about thirty degrees each side of the equator In some places they blow six months in one direction, and six in the opposite The term is sometimes applied to the Indian monsoons

Tragedy. Literally, a goat-song (Gr. *tragos*, goat, *ode*, song), though why so called is not clear Horace (*Ars Poetica*, 220) says, because the winner at choral competitions received a goat as a prize, but the explanation has no authority.

It was Aristotle (in his *Poetics*) who said that tragedy should move one "by pity and terror" —

> The plot ought to be so constructed that, even without the aid of the eye, he who hears the tale told will thrill with horror and melt to pity at what takes place —ARISTOTLE *Poetics*, XIX (*Butcher*)

The Father of Tragedy. A title given to Æschylus (d 456 B C), author of the Orestean trilogy and many other tragedies, and to Thespis *See* THESPIANS

Traitor's Gate, The The gloomy water-passage leading from the Tower of London to the Thames, by which persons accused of treason entered their prison An old proverb says :—

> A loyal heart may be landed at the Traitors' Gate

Trajan (trā' jàn) **Trajan's Arch.** There are two arches known by this name, commemorating the triumphs of Trajan One, the finest ancient arch in existence, was erected in A D. 114 over the Appian Way at Benevento, and the other in 112 at Ancona. Both are of white marble

Trajan's Column. The great monument in Rome (dedicated A D 114) commemorating Trajan's victories. It is a Roman Doric column of marble, 127½ ft high, covered with reliefs representing over 2,000 persons, besides many animals It formed the model for the column in the Place Vendôme, Paris, and is now surmounted by a statue of St Peter

Trajan's Wall. A line of fortifications stretching across the Dobrudja from Czernavoda to the Black Sea

Tram. The old "popular" derivation of this word from the name of Benjamin Outram, who ran vehicles on stone rails at Little Eaton, Derbyshire, in 1800, is discredited The word is connected with Low Ger *traam*, a baulk or beam, and was applied as early as the 16th century to trucks used in coal mines, and run on long wooden beams as rails.

> Trams are a kind of sledge on which coals are brought from the place where they are hewn to the shaft A tram has four wheels, but a sledge is without wheels —BRAND *History of Newcastle-upon-Tyne*, vol II, p 681 (1789)

Tramontane (tra' mon' tān). The north wind, so called by Italians because to them it comes from over the mountains (Lat *trans*, across, *montem*, mountain) The Italians also apply the term to peoples, etc , north of the Alps French lawyers, on the other hand, apply the word to Italian canonists, whom they consider too Romanistic

Transept An architectural term (from the Lat. *trans*, across, *septum*, enclosure) for the transverse portion of any building lying across the main body of that building The transept became common in ecclesiastical architecture in the Middle Ages and almost universal in the Gothic period The cross is often surmounted by a tower, spire or dome. In a basilica church the transept is the transverse portion in front of the choir.

Translator-General So Fuller, in his *Worthies* (1662), calls Philemon Holland (1552-1637), who translated works by Pliny, Livy, Plutarch, and a large number of other Greek and Latin classics

Transportation of Convicts A system of punishment by which criminals are removed to some penal settlement outside their own country for a period of years or for life Until the War of Independence convicts were shipped from Britain to certain districts of her American colonies, in January, 1788, the first batch of convicts were landed at Botany Bay, New South Wales The system worked well, and successive fleets took convicted felons to Australia until 1840 when the reception area was confined to Tasmania Transportation was abolished in British law in 1853, though it still exists in France, where the penal settlements at Cayenne are in full use

Trap Slang for a policeman, also for the mouth. **Shut your trap,** be quiet

Traps. Luggage, one's personal belongings, and so on (as in *Leave your traps at the station*), are called *traps* as short for *trappings*, bits of additional finery and decoration, properly ornamental harness or caparison for a horse The word is also used for the row of pens from which the dogs are simultaneously released in greyhound racing

Trappists A religious order, so called from La Trappe, an abbey founded at Soligny la Trappe (Orne, France) in 1140, by Rotron, Count de Perche It is a branch of the Cistercian order, and is noted for the extreme austerity of its rules which include perpetual silence except in cases of strict necessity

Traskites A sect of Puritan Sabbatarians founded by John Trask, a Somerset man, about 1620. They believed that the law as laid down for the ancient Hebrews was to be taken literally and applied to themselves and all men Trask was brought before the Star Chamber and pilloried. He is said to have recanted later and to have become an Antinomian, and his followers became absorbed by the Seventh-day Baptists (*q v*)

Travellers' Tales Tall yarns; exaggerated stories of wonderful adventures and sights Telling such tales used to be called *tipping one the traveller.*

Travelogue (trăv è log') A lecture or running commentary delivered to accompany a moving picture of travel

Travertine (trăv ĕi tin) A limestone formed by the deposit of springs and rivers, of a browny-grey appearance and peculiarly suitable for building purposes The stone has been extensively used in the building of Rome in all periods, it takes its name, indeed, from the Late Latin Tiburtino, or Tibur, now known as Tivoli, near Rome

Tre, Pol, Pen. Very common prefixes for personal and place names in Cornwall—

By their Tre, their Pol, and Pen,
Ye shall know the Cornish men.

The extreme east of Cornwall is noted for *Tre* (old Cornish, or Welsh, for house), the extreme west for *Pol* (=pool), the centre for *Pen* (=height, peak).

On December 19th, 1891, the following residents are mentioned by the *Launceston Weekly News* as attending the funeral of a gentleman who lived at Tre-hummer House, Tresmere —Residents from Trevell, Tresmarrow, Treglith, Trebarrow, Treludick, etc., with Treleaven the Mayor of Launceston

Treacle properly means an antidote against the bite of wild beasts (Gr *theriake*, from *ther* a wild beast) The ancients gave the name to several sorts of antidotes, but ultimately it was applied chiefly to Venice treacle (*theriaca androchi*), a compound of some sixty-four drugs in honey

Sir Thomas More speaks of "a most strong treacle [*i.e.* antidote] against these venomous heresies", and in the *Treacle Bible, see* BIBLE, SPECIALLY NAMED, *balm* (*Jer* viii, 22) is translated *treacle*—"Is there no tryacle in Gilead? Is there no phisitian there?"

Treadmill. A wheel turned by the weight of a person or persons treading on steps fixed to the periphery It was formerly used in prisons as a means of discipline or as a part of hard labour, the power being sometimes employed for turning machinery or grinding corn

Treason. Betrayal of a trust or of a person **High Treason** is an act of treachery against the Sovereign or the State, a violation of one's allegiance, petty treason is the same against a subject, as the murder of a master by his servant

Treasure. These are my treasures, meaning the sick and poor. So said St Lawrence (*q v*) when the Roman prætor commanded him to deliver up his treasures

One day a lady from Campania called upon Cornelia, the mother of the Gracchi, and after showing her jewels, requested in return to see those belonging to the famous mother-in-law of Africanus. Cornelia sent for her two sons, and said to the visitor, "These are my jewels, in which alone I delight."

Treasure Trove. The term applied to coins and other valuables of gold or silver found in the ground or some other hiding-place, whose owner is unknown In the legal sense these objects must have been originally placed there with the purpose of concealment, gold ornaments, etc, found in tombs or tumuli where they were deliberately placed with no intention of concealment are not treasure trove Treasure trove belongs to the Crown, but in practice the finder is usually given the market value of the objects found

Treasury. Treasury Bills are a form of British government security issued in multiples of £1,000 and repayable in 3, 6, 9 or 12 months.

Treasury Bonds are for money borrowed for a number of years

Treasury Notes were issued by the Treasury from 1914 to 1928 for £1 and 10s Their place was then taken by notes issued by the Bank of England

Treasury of the Church, or **Treasury of Merits.** The theological term for the superabundant store of merits and satisfactions of Christ which were beyond the needs of the salvation of the human race To these are added the excess of merits and satisfactions of the B V.M. and the saints It is by drawing on this treasury that the Pope grants indulgences.

Treat. To stand treat. To pay the expenses of some entertainment, especially to pay for drinks consumed by others.

Tree. For particulars of some famous and patriarchal trees *see under* OAK *and* YEW

In the Natural History Museum, South Kensington, is the section of a *Sequoia gigantea* with 1,335 rings, representing that number of years There are, however, yet older trees still in full life in the forests of America

The eight olive-trees on the Mount of Olives are said to have been flourishing when the Turks took Jerusalem in 1187, and there is a lime-tree in the Grisons which is supposed to be over 660 years old.

The spruce will reach the age of 1,200 years Trees burst into leaf—

	earliest		latest	
Ash	May 13th,	„	June	14th
Beech	April 19th,	„	May	7th.
Damson	March 28th,	„	May	13th
Horse-chestnut	March 17th,	„	April	19th.
Larch	March 21st,	„	April	14th.
Lime	April 6th,	„	May	2nd.
Mulberry	May 12th,	„	June	23rd
Oak	April 10th,	„	May	26th
Poplar	March 6th,	„	April	19th.
Spanish chesnut	April 20th,	„	May	20th
Sycamore	March 28th,	„	April	23rd.

The cross on which Our Lord was crucified is frequently spoken of in hymns and poetry as *the tree See Acts* v, 30 —" . Jesus, whom ye slew and hanged on a tree", 1 *Pet* ii, 24 — "Who his own self bare our sins in his own body on the tree "

The gallows is also called *the tree*, **Tyburn tree,** the fatal tree, etc

A tree must be bent while it is young You can't teach an old dog tricks. The Scots say, "Thraw the wand while it is green "

At the top of the tree. At the highest position attainable in one's profession, calling, etc

The tree is known by its fruit. One is judged by what one does, not by what one says The saying is from *Matt.* xii, 33

The tree of Buddha, or **of Wisdom.** The bo-tree (*q v*)

The tree of Diana. *See* PHILOSOPHER'S TREE, THE

The Tree of Liberty. A post or tree set up by the people, hung with flags and devices, and crowned with a cap of liberty In the United States poplars and other trees were planted during the War of Independence, "as symbols of growing freedom " The Jacobins in Paris planted their first trees of liberty in

1790, and used to decorate them with tri-coloured ribbons, circles to indicate unity, triangles to signify equality, and Caps of Liberty. Trees of liberty were also planted by the Italians in the revolutions of 1848

The Tree of the Universe. Yggdrasil (*q v*)

The treeness of the tree. The essential qualities that compose a tree, in the absence of which a tree would cease to be a tree Hence, the absolute essentials of anything. The phrase is evidently modelled on Sterne's "Corregiosity of Corregio" (*Tristram Shandy* III, xii)

Up a tree. In a difficulty, in a mess, non-plussed An American phrase, from 'coon hunting. As soon as the 'coon is driven up a tree he is helpless
    It is said that Spurgeon used to practise his students in extempore preaching, and that one of his young men, on reaching the desk and opening the note containing his text, read the single word "Zacchæus " He thought a minute or two, and then delivered himself thus —

Zacchæus was a little man, so am I, Zacchæus was up a tree, so am I, Zacchæus made haste and came down, and so do I

You cannot judge of a tree by its bark. Don't go by appearances; an old proverb.

Tregeagle (treg ēgl) A fabulous giant of Dosmary Pool, Bodmin Downs (Cornwall), whose allotted task is to bale out the water with a limpet-shell. When the wintry blast howls over the downs, the people say it is the giant roaring

Trench Fever. A remittent or relapsing fever affecting men living in trenches, dug-outs, etc , and transmitted by the excrement of lice It first appeared in World War I, in the static warfare on the western front.

Trencher. A good trencher-man. A good eater. The trencher is the platter on which food is cut (Fr. *trancher*, to cut), by a figure of speech applied to food itself

He that waits for another's trencher eats many a late dinner. He who is dependent on others must wait, and wait, and wait, happy if after waiting he gets anything at all

Trencher cap. The mortar-board (*q.v*) worn at college, so called from the *trenchered* or split boards which form the top.

Trencher friends. Persons who cultivate the friendship of others for the sake of sitting at their board, and the good things they can get.

Trencher knight A table knight, a suitor from cupboard love

Trenchmore. A popular dance in the 16th and 17th centuries
Like one dancing the trenchmore he stamped up and downe the yard, holding his hips in his hands — T DELONEY *The Gentle Craft*, 1597.

Tressure. A border within an heraldic shield and surrounding the bearings The origin of the "double tressure flory-counterflory gules" in the royal arms of Scotland is traced by old heralds to the 9th century. They assert that Charlemagne granted it to King Achaius of Scotland in token of alliance, and as an assurance that "the lilies of France should be a defence to the lion of Scotland "

Treves (trēvz, trāv). The Holy Coat of Treves A relic preserved in the cathedral of Treves It is one of several said to be the seamless coat of our Saviour, which the soldiers would not rend, and therefore cast lots for (*John* xix, 23, 25), which, according to tradition, was found and preserved by the Empress Helena in the 4th century Its written history goes back only to the 12th century, whereas the Holy Coat of Argenteuil, with similar claims, is traced to Charlemagne There is little to choose between the two traditions

Tria Juncta in Uno (Lat , three combined in one) The motto of the Order of the Bath. It refers to the three classes of which the order consists, viz. Knights Grand Cross, Knights Commanders, and Companions.

Triads. Three subjects more or less connected treated as a group, as *the Creation. Redemption, and Resurrection, Brahma, Vishnu, and Siva, Alexander the Great, Julius Cæsar, and Napoleon, Law, Physic, and Divinity*
    The Welsh *Triads* are collections of historic facts, mythological traditions, moral maxims, or rules of poetry disposed in groups of three for mnemonic purposes

Trials at Bar. *See* BAR

Tribune (trib' ūn) A chief magistrate, and very powerful official among the ancient Romans During the revolt of the plebs in 494 B.C. they appointed two tribunes as protectors against the patricians' oppression, later the number was increased to ten and their office put on a proper footing. They were personally inviolable, and could separately veto measures and proceedings
    As a military title *tribune* denoted the commander of a cohort.

A tribune of the people. A democratic leader

The Last of the Tribunes. Cola di Rienzi (1313-54)

Trice. In a trice. In an instant, in a twinkling.
To tell you what conceyte
I had then in a tryce,
The matter were too nyse
SKELTON *Phyllyp Sparowe* (c 1505)

Trice is probably the same word as *trice*, to haul, to tie up, the idea being "at a single tug."
    The older form was At a trice.
At door where this trull was,
I was at a tryce.
JOHN T HEYWOOD *Play of Love*, 1534

Trick. Besides its usual significance of a sly or mean deception, a clever device, a dodge, etc., this word denominates the cards played and won in a round; also a spell of duty as at a ship's wheel

Tricolour. A flag of three broad strips of different colours, especially the national standard of France, blue, white, and red. The first flag of the Republicans was *green*. The tricolour was adopted July 11, 1789, when the people were disgusted with the king for dismissing Necker, the popular tale is that the insurgents had adopted for their flag the two colours, *red and blue* (the colours of the city of Paris) but that Lafayette persuaded them to add the Bourbon *white*, to show that they bore no hostility to the king

Other tricolours are the flags of —

Belgium, black, yellow, red, divided vertically.
Bulgaria, white, green, red, horizontally.
Eire, green, white, yellow, vertically
Holland, red, white, blue, horizontally.
Italy, green, white, red; vertically
Persia, green, white, red, horizontally
Romania, blue, yellow, red, vertically.
Serbia, red, blue, white; horizontally.
Bolivia, red, yellow, green, horizontally.
Mexico, green, white, red, vertically
Venezuela, yellow, blue, red, horizontally
Yugoslavia, blue, white, red, horizontally.

Tricoteuses (trē kot ĕrz') Parisian women who, during the French Revolution, used to attend the meetings of the Convention and, while they went on with their *tricotant* (knitting), encouraged the leaders in their bloodthirsty excesses. They gained for themselves the additional title, *Furies of the Guillotine*

Trident. In Greek mythology the three-pronged spear which Poseidon (Roman Neptune) god of the sea, bore as the symbol of his sovereignty It has come to be regarded as the emblem of sea power and as such is borne by Britannia In gladiatorial combats in Rome the trident was used by the retiarii, whose skill lay in entangling their opponents in nets, and then despatching them with tridents

Trigon (trī' gon) The junction of three signs. The zodiac is partitioned into four trigons, named respectively after the four elements; the *watery* trigon includes Cancer, Scorpio, and Pisces, the *fiery*, Aries, Leo, and Sagittarius; the *earthy*, Taurus, Virgo, and Capricornus, and the *airy*, Gemini, Libra, and Aquarius

Trilogy (tril' ŏ ji) A group of three tragedies Everyone in Greece who took part in the poetic contest had to produce a trilogy and a satyric drama. There is only one complete specimen extant, viz. that embracing the *Agamemnon*, the *Choephorae*, and the *Eumenides*, by Æschylus

Trim, Corporal. The old soldier-orderly of "my Uncle Toby" in Sterne's *Tristram Shandy*, a faithful, simple-minded friend who enters into his whims, especially the absorbing hobby of reproducing in miniature the campaign in Flanders when they both served under the Duke of Marlborough.

Trimalchio (tri mǎl' ki ŏ). The vulgar and ostentatious multi-millionaire of Petronius Arbiter's *Satyricon* (1st cent A D); the subject of allusion on account of the colossal and extravagant banquet that he gave

Trimmer. One who runs with the hare and hunts with the hounds George Savile, Marquis of Halifax, adopted the term in the reign of Charles II to signify that he was neither an extreme Whig nor an extreme Tory.

Trine. In astrology, a planet distant from another one-third of the circle is said to be in trine, one-fourth, it is in square, one-sixth or two signs, it is in sextile, but when one-half distant, it is said to be "opposite "

In sextile, square, and trine, and opposite
Of noxious efficacy
                    MILTON *Paradise Lost*, x, 659

Planets distant from each other six signs or half a circle have opposite influences, and are therefore opposed to each other

Trinity. The three Persons in one God—God the Father, God the Son, and God the Holy Ghost

And in this Trinity none is afore or after other, none is greater, or less than another, but the whole three Persons are co-eternal together and co-equal — *The Athanasian Creed*

Cp PERSONS (*Confounding the Persons*)

Tertullian (about 160-240) introduced the word into Christian theology, Almost every mythology has a threefold deity *See* THREE

Trinity House. The association, incorporated by Royal Charter and Acts of Parliament, and, for many purposes, forming a branch of the Board of Trade, constituting the chief pilotage authority of the United Kingdom and being responsible for lighthouses and seamarks in home waters. properly called The Corporation of Trinity House, from its headquarters on Tower Hill London

It was granted its first charter by Henry VIII in 1514, and now consists of a Master, ten Acting Elder Brethren, and a number of Honorary Elder Brethren, among whom are usually the King and other members of the Royal Family, Cabinet Ministers, etc. The Acting Elder Brethren (one a retired naval officer, and nine retired mercantile marine commanders) sit with the judges of the Admiralty Division as nautical assessors in marine causes

Trinity Sunday The Sunday next after Whit Sunday It has been observed in honour of the Trinity from very early times, but was first enjoined as a festival by the Synod of Arles in 1260 The Epistle and Gospel used in the Church of England on this day are the same as those in the Lectionary of St Jerome, and the Collect comes from the Sacramentary of St. Gregory

Trinity Term The period of law sittings in England from the first Tuesday after Trinity Sunday to the end of July.

Trinobantes (trin ŏ bǎn' tēz). Inhabitants of Middlesex and Essex, referred to in Cæsar's *Gallic Wars* This word, converted into *Trinovantes*, gave rise to the myth that the people referred to came from Troy *See* TROYNOVANT

Tripe. Journalists' slang for very second-rate "copy" whose only use is as "fill-ups " *Cp* BILGE-WATER

Tripehound. In Australian slang a dog on a sheep station The term has spread to England as a term of opprobrium

Tripitaka (trip it' a ka) (Pali *tipitaka*, the three baskets) The three classes into which the sacred writings of the Buddhists are divided— viz the *Sutrapitaka* (Basket of Aphorisms or

Discourses) or *Sutras*, the *Vinayapitaka* (Basket of Disciplinary Directions), and *Abidhammapitaka* (Basket of Metaphysics)

Triple Alliance. A treaty entered into by England, Sweden, and Holland against Louis XIV in 1668 It ended in the treaty of Aix-la-Chapelle

A treaty between England, France, and Holland against Spain in 1717 In the following year it was joined by Austria, and became a Quadruple Alliance

The alliance between Germany, Austria and Italy, signed in 1882 It was renewed several times but finally broken in 1914 when Italy refused to join in the war against Britain and France

The **Triple Entente** is the name given to various agreements or understandings made in the 20th century between Britain, France and Tsarist Russia

Tripos (tri' pos) (Gr. *treis*, three, *pous*, foot) A Cambridge term, meaning the *three* honour classes in which the best men are grouped at the final examination, whether of Mathematics, Law, Theology, or Natural Science, etc The word is often emphatically applied to the voluntary classical examination So called because the champion in the old university disputations held during the admission of graduates to their degrees used to sit on a *three-legged* stool.

Triptolemus (trip tol' ē mŭs) A Greek hero and demi-god, worshipped chiefly at Eleusis as the giver to man of grain and the first instructor in agriculture

Triptych (trip' tik) In ecclesiastical painting a set of three upright panels joined together by hinges, each panel being painted with a separate subject The wings were frequently painted on both sides so that when folded a fresh picture was presented The Van Eycks and most of the great religious painters of the early Renaissance used the triptych, but it fell into disuse in the 16th century

Trisagion (tris ăg' i on) (Gr , thrice holy) A hymn in the liturgies of the Greek and Eastern Churches in which (after *Is* vi, 3) a threefold invocation to the Deity is the burden —"Holy God, Holy and Mighty, Holy and Immortal, have mercy upon us"

The name is sometimes applied to Bishop Heber's hymn for Trinity Sunday—

Holy, Holy, Holy! Lord God Almighty!
Early in the morning our song shall rise to Thee—
which is more properly called the *Ter-Sanctus*

Triskelion (tri skel' i on) (Gr , three-legged) The emblem of the Isle of Man, and of Sicily; three human legs, bent at the knee, and joined at the thigh

Trismegistus (tris me jis' tus) (Gr , thrice great). A name given to Hermes (*q v*), the Egyptian philosopher, or Thoth, councillor of Osiris, to whom is attributed a host of inventions—amongst others the art of writing in hieroglyphics, the first code of Egyptian laws, harmony, astrology, the lute and lyre, magic, and all mysterious sciences

Tristram, Sir (Tristrem, **Tristan,** or **Tristam**). A hero of mediæval romance whose exploits,

though originally unconnected with it, became attached to the Arthurian cycle, he himself being named as one of the Knights of the Round Table There are many versions of his story, which is, roughly, that he was cured of a wound by Iseult, or Ysolde, daughter of the king of Ireland, and on his return to Cornwall told his uncle, King Mark, of the beautiful princess Mark sent him to solicit her hand in marriage, and was accepted Tristram escorted her to England, but on the way they both unknowingly partook of a magic potion and became irretrievably enamoured of each other Iseult married the king, and on Mark's discovering their liaison Tristram fled to Brittany and married Iseult, daughter of the Duke of Brittany. Wounded by a poisoned weapon, he sent for Iseult of Ireland to come and heal him The vessel in which she was to come had orders to hoist a white sail if she was on board, otherwise a black sail Tristram's wife, seeing the vessel approach, told her husband, from jealousy, that it bore a black sail In despair, Tristram died, Iseult of Ireland, arriving too late, killed herself

The name was originally *Drystan*, from the Pictish name *Drostan*, and the initial was changed to *T* apparently to connect it with Lat *tristis*, sad

Triton. Son of Poseidon and Amphitrite, represented as a fish with a human head. It is this sea god that makes the roaring of the ocean by blowing through his shell

A Triton among the minnows. A great man amid a host of inferiors

Triumph. A word formed from Gr *thriambos*, the Dionysiac hymn, *Triumphe* being an exclamation used in the solemn processions of the Arval Brothers.

Some have assigned the origin of . triumphal processions to the mythic pomps of Dionysus, after his conquests in the East, the very word *triumph* being the Dionysiac hymn —PATER. *Marius the Epicurean*, ch xii

The old Roman *triumphus* was the solemn and magnificent entrance of a general into Rome after having obtained a great or decisive victory Cp OVATION

Triumvir (tri üm' vĕr). In ancient Rome a member of a commission of three charged with some special duty, such as repairing tombs, coining money, or even founding colonies The most famous triumvirate was that of Octavian, Antony, and Lepidus, 43 B C, which was known as the Second Triumvirate to distinguish it from the private combination of Cæsar, Pompey, and Crassus in 60 B C., popularly known as the First Triumvirate

Trivet. Right as a trivet. See RIGHT.

Trivia. Gray's name for his invented goddess of streets and ways. His burlesque in three books so entitled (1716) is a mine of information on the outdoor life of Queen Anne's time

Thou, Trivia, aid my song
Through spacious streets conduct thy bard along ..
To pave thy realm, and smooth the broken ways,
Earth from her womb a flinty tribute pays
GAY *Trivia*, Bk 1.

Trivia is also the plural of *trivium*

Trivium. The three roads (Lat *tres*, three, *via*, a road) to learning in the Middle Ages, *i.e* Grammar, Rhetoric, and Logic, forming the lower division of the seven liberal arts (*see* QUADRIVIUM)

Trochilus. A small Egyptian bird said by the ancients to enter with impunity the mouth of the crocodile and to pick its teeth, especially of a leech which greatly tormented the creature It is now known as the Crocodile-bird, *Pluvianus aegyptus*, a species of plover which not only picks the crocodile's teeth but by its cry gives warning of an approaching foe

Troglodytes. A people of Ethiopia, south-east of Egypt, so called from Gr *trogle*, cave, *duein*, to go into, because they lived in cave dwellings, remains of which are still to be seen along the banks of the Nile. Hence applied to other cave-dwellers, and, figuratively to those who live in seclusion. There were troglodytes of Syria and Arabia also, according to Strabo, and Pliny (v, 8) asserts that they fed on serpents

Troilus. The prince of chivalry, one of the sons of Priam, killed by Achilles in the siege of Troy (Homer's *Iliad*)
The loves of Troilus and Cressida, celebrated by Shakespeare and Chaucer, form no part of the old classic tale The story appears for the first time in the *Roman de Troie* by the 12th-century *trouvère*, Benoit de Ste More Guido delle Colonne included it in his *Historia Tiojana* (about 1290), it thence passed to Boccaccio, whose *Il Filostrato* (1344)—where Pandarus first appears—was the basis of Chaucer's *Troilus and Criseyde.*

As true as Troilus. Troilus is meant by Shakespeare to be the type of constancy, and Cressida the type of female inconstancy
      After all comparisons of truth   .
"As true as Troilus ' shall crown up the verse,
And sanctify the numbers
                    Troilus and Cressida, iii, 2

Trojan. He is a regular Trojan. A fine fellow, with courage and spirit, who works very hard, usually at an uncongenial task, indeed, doing more than could be expected of him The Trojans in Homer's *Iliad* and Virgil's *Æneid* are described as truthful, brave, patriotic, and confiding.
      There they say right, and like true Trojans
                    BUTLER *Hudibras*, i, 1

Trojan War. The legendary war sung by Homer in the *Iliad* (*q.v*) as having been waged for ten years by the confederated Greeks against the men of Troy and their allies, in consequence of Paris, son of Priam, the Trojan king, having carried off Helen, wife of Menelaus, king of Lacedemon (or of Sparta). The last year of the siege is the subject of the *Iliad*; the burning of Troy and the flight of Æneas is told by Virgil in his *Æneid*
There is no doubt whatever that the story of the siege of Troy has some historical basis, but when it took place is purely a matter of conjecture Many dates, ranging from the 11th to the 14th centuries B C have been assigned to it

Trolls Dwarfs of Northern mythology, living in hills, underground in caverns or beneath; they are represented as stumpy, misshapen, and humpbacked, inclined to thieving, and fond of carrying off human children and substituting their own. These hill people, as they are called, are especially averse to noise, from a recollection of the time when Thor used to be for ever flinging his hammer after them

Troll-madam, or Troll-my-dames. A popular indoor game in the 16th and 17th centuries (also known as *trunks*, *pigeon-holes*, or *nine-holes*), borrowed from the French and called by them *trou* (hole) *madame* It resembled bagatelle, and was played on a board having at one end a number of arches, like pigeon-holes, into which balls were rolled. Shakespeare has a reference to it in *A Winter's Tale* (iv, 2)

Trooping. The trooping season. The season when the annual reliefs of the British forces in India were made, usually beginning in late February or March

Trooping the colour. A military ceremonial parade in which the regimental flag, the *colour*, is carried between files of troops and received by the sovereign or a representative
The ceremony dates from the 18th century (probably from Marlborough's time), and was originally a guard-mounting ceremony, the battalion finding the guards for the day "trooping" the colour to be carried on king's guard.
Many years ago it became the custom to find the public guards on the King's birthday from the flank companies (picked companies) of the whole Brigade, instead of from one battalion, and it is from this custom that the ceremony of Trooping the Colour on his Majesty's birthday by detachments of the flank companies of all the battalions in London originates The Field-Officer-in-Brigade-Waiting always commands the troops on this parade, irrespective of the regiment to which he belongs —*The Times*, 3 June, 1922

Trophonius (trŏ fŏ' ni us) An architect, celebrated in Greek legend as the builder of the temple of Apollo at Delphi After his death he was deified, and had an oracle in a cave near Lebadeia, Bœotia, which was so awe-inspiring that those who entered and consulted the oracle never smiled again. Hence a melancholy or habitually terrified man was said to have *visited the cave of Trophonius*.

Trophy Originally the arms of a vanquished foe, collected and set up by the victors on the field of battle The captured standards were hung from the branches of an oak tree, a portion of the booty being laid at the foot of the tree and dedicated to the tutelary deity. The Romans frequently bore their trophies to Rome, under the Empire the triumphs of the victorious generals were also celebrated with arches and columns

Troubadours. Minstrels of the south of France in the 11th, 12th, and 13th centuries, so called from the Provençal verb *trobar*, to find or invent (*cp* "poet," which means "a maker ") They wrote in the *langue d'oc*, or Provençal, principally on love and chivalry Cp. TROU-VÈRES.

Trouvères (troo' vâr) The troubadours of the north of France, in the 12th, 13th, and 14th centuries So called from Fr *trouver*, to find or invent (*cp* TROUBADOURS) They wrote in the *langue d'oil* or *langue d'oui*, chiefly on amatory subjects

Trows, or **Drows** Dwarfs of Orkney and Shetland mythology, similar to the Scandinavian Trolls There are land-trows and sea-trows "Trow tak' thee" is a phrase still used by the island women when angry with their children

Troy. The Siege of Troy. See ILIAD, HELEN, TROJAN WAR, etc

Troy Town. A Cornish expression for a labyrinth of streets, a regular maze In several novels "Q" (Sir A. Quiller Couch) used the name as a disguise for Fowey *Troy* was formerly used figuratively of any scene of disorder or confusion, a room with its disorder or confusion, a room with its furniture all higgledy-piggledy, for instance, would be called a *Troy fair*

Troy weight. The system of weights used in weighing precious metals and gems, the pound of 12 ounces weighing 5760 grains as compared with the pound avoirdupois which weighs 7000 grains and is divided into 16 ounces (*cp* AVOIRDUPOIS) Why so called is not certainly known, but probably it was the system used at the great fairs at Troyes, in France. l lb troy= 0 822861 lb av , rather over four-fifths

Troynovant The name given by the early chroniclers to London, anciently the city of the Trinobantes (*q v*); a corruption of *Trinovant.* As *Troynovant* was assumed to mean *The New Troy*, the name gave rise to the tradition that Brute, a Trojan refugee (from whom they derived the name *Britain*) came to England and founded London

For noble Britons sprong from Trojans bold,
And Troy-novant was built of old Troyes ashes cold
					SPENSER *Faerie Queene*, iii, 9.

Truce of God. In 1041 the Church attempted to limit private war, and decreed that there should be no hostilities between Lent and Advent or from the Thursday to the next Monday at the time of great festivals This *Truce of God* was confirmed by the Lateran Council in 1179, and was agreed to by England, France, Italy, and other countries, but little attention was ever paid to it

Truck System, The. The paying of employees otherwise than in current coin, or making it a condition that they shall buy food or other articles from some particular shop In Britain this was made illegal by Acts passed in 1831, 1887, and 1896

True A true bill. See BILL

True blue See BLUE

True-lovers' knot. A complicated double knot with two interlacing bows on each side and two ends, used as a symbol of love

Three times a true-love's knot I tie secure,
Firm be the knot, firm may his love endure
					Gay's Pastorals The Spell

True Thomas Thomas the Rhymer See RHYMER

Truepenny Hamlet says to the Ghost, "Art thou there, Truepenny?" Then to his comrades,

"You hear this fellow in the cellarage" (i, 5) And again, "Well said, old mole, canst work?" The reference is to the sterling worth of his father—he was as honest and *true* as a genuine coin

Trump This word in such phrases as *a trumped up affair, trumpery*, etc, is the same word as *trumpet*, from Fr *trompe*, a trumpet, whence *tromper* which, originally meaning "to play on a trumpet,' came to mean to beguile, deceive, impose upon

Trump in cards is from Fr *triomphe* (triumph), the name of an old variant of écarté

The last trump. The final end of all things earthly, the Day of Judgment

We shall not all sleep, but we shall all be changed, in a moment, in the twinkling of an eye, at the last trump—1 *Cor* xv, 51, 52

To play one's last trump. To be reduced to one's last expedient, a phrase from card-playing

To turn up trumps. Unexpectedly to prove very friendly and helpful

Trumpet. See TRUMP *above*

The Feast of Trumpets A Jewish festival, held on the first two days of Tisri (about mid Sept to mid Oct), the beginning of the ecclesiastical year, at which the blowing of trumpets formed a prominent part of the ritual See *Num* XXIX, 1

To blow one's own trumpet. To publish one's own praises, good deeds, etc The allusion is to heralds, who used to announce with a flourish of trumpets the knights who entered a list Similarly, *your trumpeter is dead* means that you are obliged to sound your own praises because no one will do it for you.

Trunk. In its sense of denominating the main body as opposed to the roots and branches, the word is used to describe the main lines of railway, postal, telephone systems, from which branch lines radiate A **trunk call** is a telephone call on a trunk line from one town to another **Trunk road** is a main highway between two principal towns **Trunk hose** were a style of breeches worn in the 16th and 17th centuries, reaching from the waist to the middle of the thigh **Trunk drawers**, or **trunks** are pants reaching only to the knee

Trust A combination of a number of companies or businesses doing similar trade, for the purpose of defeating competition or creating a monopoly, under one general control So called because each member is on trust not to under-sell the others, but to remain faithful to the terms agreed on

Trusty. In American penology a well-behaved, long-term prisoner who is allowed to help the warders in some of their duties and is granted certain privileges not allowed to other convicts

Truth Pilate said, *"What is truth?"* (*John* xviii, 38) This was the great question of the Platonists Plato said we could know truth if we could sublimate our minds to their original purity. Arcesilaus said that man's understanding is not capable of knowing what truth is Carneades maintained that not only our understanding could not comprehend it, but even our senses are wholly inadequate to help us in the investigation. Gorgias the Sophist said, "What is right but what we prove to be right? and what is truth but what we believe to be truth?"

Pilate asked *Quid est veritas* ? And then some other matter took him in the head, and so up he rose and went his way before he had his answer He deserved never to find what truth was —BP ANDREWS *Sermon on the Resurrection* (1613)

Truth lies at the bottom of a well. This expression has been attributed to Heraclitus. Cleanthes, Democritus the Derider, and others

Naturam accusa, quæ in profundo veritatem (ut ait Democritus) penitus abstrusent —CICERO *Academics*, i, 10

Truth drug. Alkaloid scopolamin. An American doctor, R E House, used this drug to induce a state of lethargic intoxication in which the patient lost many of his defences and spoke the truth concerning matters about which he would normally have lied or prevaricated. The value of this and other truth drugs in penology has by no means been established

Trygon (tri' gon). The sting-ray, a fish with a sharp spine in its tail It is said that Telegonus, son of Ulysses by Circe, coming to Ithaca to see his father, was denied admission by the servants, whereupon a quarrel ensued, and his father, coming out to see what was the matter, was accidentally struck with his son's arrow, pointed with a trygon's spine, and died

Tu autem (tū aw' tem) (Lat , But thou). A hint to leave off, "hurry up and come to the last clause " In the long Latin grace at St John's College, Cambridge, the last clause used to be *Tu autem miserere mei, Domine Amen*, and it was not unusual, when a scholar read slowly, for the senior Fellow to whisper *Tu autem—i e.* Skip all the rest and give us only the last sentence.

Tu quoque (Lat , You too) A retort implying that the one addressed is in the same case as the speaker—no better and no worse

The tu quoque style of argument Personal invective, the argument of personal application, *argumentum ad hominem*

Tuatha De Danann (twa' thə de dăn' an) A legendary race of super-human heroes which invaded Ireland, overthrow the Firbolgs and Fomors, and were themselves overthrown by the Milesians, who later worshipped them as gods.

Tub Tubs, in rowing slang, are gig pairs of college boat clubs, who practise for the term's races They are pulled on one side when a pair-oar boat in uniform makes its appearance

Tubbing is taking out pairs under the supervision of a coach to train men for taking part in the races.

A tale of a tub. A cock-and-bull story, a rigmarole, a nonsensical romance.

There is a comedy of this name by Ben Jonson (produced 1633), and a prose satire by Swift (1704) which portrays allegorically

the failings of the English, Roman, and Presbyterian Churches

A tub of naked children. Emblematical in religious paintings of St. Nicholas (*q v*), in allusion to the two boys murdered and placed in a pickling tub by a landlord, but raised to life again by this saint

To throw a tub to the whale. To create a diversion in order to avoid a real danger; to bamboozle or mislead an enemy In whaling, according to Swift, when a ship was threatened by a school of whales, it was usual to throw a tub into the sea to divert their attention

Tub-thumper. A blustering, ranting public speaker, a "stump-orator " In allusion to the upturned tub frequently used as a rostrum at open-air meetings

Tuck. This word, in the sense of eatables is a mid-18th-century slang word, especially among schoolboys whose "tuck-box," brought from home at the beginning of term, contained sweets, jams, etc , to supplement school fare From this came the phrase To tuck in, meaning to eat heartily and with relish. In Australia the word became tucker, meaning any kind of food, but particularly that carried on long journeys, etc

To tuck one up. To finish him, do for him. The allusion is probably to tucking children up in bed for the night—they are finished with till next morning, but there may be some reference to the long narrow duellist's rapier formerly called a *tuck* (Fr *étoc*, stock)

Tuck, Friar. See FRIAR TUCK

Tucker The ornamental frill of lace or muslin worn by women in the 17th and 18th centuries round the top of their dresses to cover the neck and shoulders Hence, *with clean bib and tucker*, nicely dressed, looking fresh and spruce *See also* TUCK

Tuckahoe (tŭk' a hō) (U S.A) An inhabitant of that part of the State of Virginia that lies east of the Blue Ridge Mountains

Tudor (tū' dor) The general descriptive term given to the architecture, etc., characteristic of the late 15th and the whole of the 16th centuries, when the Tudor sovereigns Henry VII, Henry VIII, Edward VI, Mary I, and Elizabeth I reigned in England Tudor architecture is of the late style of Gothic, with wide, broad-pointed windows and doorways

Tuffet. A dialect variant of *tuft* which was formerly used of a small grassy mound or hillock

Little Miss Muffet
Sat on a tuffet
Eating her curds and whey
Nursery Rhyme

Tuft The name formerly given at Oxford University to a peer's son or a fellow commoner because he wore a gold tassel or tuft on his college cap This practice was discontinued in 1870, but it survives in

Tuft-hunter; one who tries to curry favour with the wealthy and great for the sake of feeding on the crumbs which fall from the rich man's table.

Tug. A name by which Collegers are known at Eton, from the *tog* (*i e toga*) worn by them to distinguish them from the rest of the school

Tug of war. A rural sport in which a number of men, divided into two bands, lay hold of a strong rope and pull against each other till one side has tugged the other over the dividing line

When Greek meets Greek then is the tug of war *See* GREEK

Tuileries (twē' lē rē) A former palace in Paris, so named from the tile-yards (*tuileries*) once on the site It stood between the Louvre and the Place de la Concorde The palace was designed by Philibert de l'Orme for Catherine de' Medici, 1564, and long served as a residence for the sovereigns of France In 1871 it was burned down by the Communards, but the gardens remain as a pleasant public open space

Tulchan Bishops Certain Scotch bishops appointed by the Regent Morton, in 1572, with the distinct understanding that they were to hand over a fixed portion of the revenue to the patron A *tulchan* is a stuffed calf-skin, placed under a cow that withholds her milk The cow, thinking the "tulcan" to be her calf, readily yields her milk to the milk-pail, the bishop was to have the empty title, and the Regent was to get the "milk "

Tulip Mania. A reckless mania for the purchase of tulip-bulbs that arose in Holland in the 17th century and was at its greatest height about 1634-1637 A root of the species called *Viceroy* sold for £250, *Semper Augustus*, more than double that sum The mania spread all over Europe, and became a mere stock-jobbing speculation.

To number the streaks of the tulip. To devote too much attention to minute details—characteristic in the view of 18th-century critics, of a bad poet The phrase comes from Imlac's dissertation on poetry (*Rasselas*, Ch. x) where the principle is laid down that a poet must examine not the individual but the species, and concern himself with the general rather than the particular.

Tumbledown Dick Anything that will not stand firmly "Dick" is Richard Cromwell (1626-1712), the Protector's son, who was but a tottering wall at best

Tumbler. A word with several meanings, all deriving from the verb "to tumble " Drinking tumblers are stemless glasses, now made with a flat bottom but originally with a rounded bottom that made the glass tumble over if set down on a table; hence requiring that it should be held until emptied The performing tumbler was an acrobat whose turn consisted in somersaults, etc , and thus a tumbler pigeon was one who performed such tricks in the air The tumbler of a lock is a pivoted piece that has to be raised by the key for opening, and tumbles back into place when released, thus preventing the bolt from being drawn

B D —30

Tune. The tune the old cow died of. Advice instead of relief, remonstrance instead of help
The reference is to the song—
There was an old man, and he had an old cow,
   But he had no fodder to give her,
So he took up his fiddle and played her the tune;
   "Consider, good cow, consider,
This isn't the time for the grass to grow,
   Consider, good cow, consider "

To change one's tune, or sing another tune. *See* SING.

To the tune of. To the amount of, as, "I had to pay up to the tune of ±500 "

Tuneful Nine, The. The nine Muses (*q v*)
When thy young Muse invok'd the tuneful Nine,
To say how LOUIS did not pass the RHINE,
What Work had We with WAGENINGHEN, ARNHEIM,
Places that could not be reduced to Rhime?
   PRIOR *Letter to Boileau Despreaux* (1704)

Tunkers or **Dunkers** (Ger , Dippers). A religious sect akin to the Baptists, founded in Germany in 1708 by Alexander Mack. In 1719 a party of them emigrated to Pennsylvania, and the sect has spread considerably in the Western States They follow Bible teaching as closely as possible and adhere to the simplicity of the primitive Church

Turban. The head-dress of many Mohammedan races, consisting of a scarf of cotton or silk wound round the head the manner of arranging the folds varying according to rank and country The tarbush or fez is used as the foundation for a turban, and often as a headdress in itself, though in Turkey this was prohibited by law in 1925, when it was decreed that all Turks should wear European hats.

Turf, The The racecourse, the profession of horse-racing, which is done on turf or grass A *turfite* is one who lives by the turf, either by running horses or betting.

Turk. Applied to barbarous, savage, cruel men, because these qualities have been for centuries attributed to Turks, also to mischievous and unruly children, as *You little Turk !*

The Young Turks The reforming party in the Ottoman Empire who, in the early part of the present century, introduced the methods of modern Europe into the government Through many stormy scenes and much involved politics the party steered its country through World War I, and, dragged in divergent directions by the conflicting interests and policies of the European powers, survived in spite of all, to get rid (1922) of the decadent sultans of the House of Othman and declare Turkey a republic

Turk Gregory. Falstaff's *ne plus ultra* of military valour—a humorous combination of the Sultan with Gregory VII (Hildebrand), probably the strongest of all the Popes
Turk Gregory never did such deeds in arms as I have done this day —1 *Henry IV*, v, 3

Turkey To talk turkey. (U S A) To talk seriously

Turkey rhubarb *See* MISNOMERS

Turn. Done to a turn. Cooked exactly right; another turn on the gridiron would be one too much.

He felt that the hour for the up-turning of his glass was at hand He knew that the sand of life was nearly run out, and that death was about to turn his hour-glass upside down.

One good turn deserves another. A benefit received ought to be repaid

To serve its turn. To be appropriate—the right thing in the right place, often said of something that only barely meets its requirements

To turn down To reject; a candidate at an examination, election, etc , who does not meet with success is said to be *turned down*

In Eastern countries a glass is turned down at convivial gatherings as a memento of a recently departed companion —

And when thyself with shining feet shalt pass
Among the guests star-scattered on the grass
And in thy joyous errand reach the spot
Where I made one—turn down an empty glass'
         FITZGERALD'S *Omar Khayyam*

To turn the tables. *See* TABLE.

To turn turtle To turn completely over, upside down, topsy-turvy Usually said of boats, from the fact that a turtle, when turned on its back, is quite helpless

To turn up. To arrive, often unexpectedly, to appear

A turn-up for the book A bit of good luck, unexpected good fortune

Waiting for something to turn up. Expectant that the luck will change, that good fortune will arrive without much effort on one's own part Mr Micawber's philosophy of life, in *David Copperfield*

Turncoat. A renegade, one who deserts his principles or party.

Fable has it that a certain Duke of Saxony, whose dominions were bounded in part by France, hit upon the device of a coat *blue* one side, and *white* the other. When he wished to be thought in the French interest he wore the white outside, otherwise the blue Whence a Saxon was nicknamed *Emmanuel Turncoat*

Turnspit One who has all the work but none of the profit, he turns the spit but eats not of the roast. The allusion is to the *turnspit*, a small dog which was used to turn the roasting-spit by means of a kind of tread-wheel. Topsell says, "They go into a wheel, which they turn round about with the weight of their bodies, so diligently . that no drudge . can do the feate more cunningly" (1607)

Turnip. Common slang for a large, old-fashioned silver watch.

Turpin. A contemporary of Charlemagne, Archbishop of Rheims from 753 to 794, on whom has been fathered a French chronicle history, written in Latin in the first half of the 11th century The probable author was a canon of Barcelona. It relates the expedition of Charlemagne to Spain in 777, and his return to France after subduing Navarre and Aragon

Turret. A small tower, used for decorative purpose, on a building In a battleship the turret is a circular armoured structure on the deck in which the heavy guns are mounted By hydraulic or electrical power the turret can be moved round as required Its understructure goes to the bottom of the ship where are the magazines In a tank it is a similar rotating structure, mounted on the hull, containing the main armament and periscope through which the commander may see when all the hatches are shut down

Tut A word used in Lincolnshire for a phantom, as the *Spittal Hill Tut Tom Tut will get you* is a threat to frighten children *Tut-gotten* is panic-struck

Tutankhamun (too tăn kă moon') A Pharaoh who lived in the middle of the 14th century B C. In the winter of 1922/23 an expedition led by Howard Carter uncovered the burial place in the Valley of the Tombs of the Kings, in the face of the Nile cliffs Unique treasure of mortuary furniture was found, most of which is now in the Cairo Museum The mummy in its gorgeous coffin showed that the Pharaoh was little more than eighteen years old at the time of his death.

Tutenag. *See* TOOTH (*Tooth and egg*).

Tutivillus (tū ti vil' ŭs) The demon of mediæval legend who collects all the words skipped over or mutilated by priests in the celebration of the Mass These literary scraps or shreds he deposits in that pit which is said to be paved with "good intentions" never brought to effect

Tutor. A private teacher, in English universities a Fellow or other college official He has the direction of the studies of a certain number of undergraduates who are placed under his care for the time they are up at the university. In Law a tutor is the guardian of a minor

Tweed. The origin of this name of a woollen cloth used for garments is to be found in a blunder. It should have been *tweal*, the Scots form of *twill*, but when the Scotch manufacturer sent a consignment to James Locke, of London, in 1826, the name was badly written and misread, and as the cloth was made on the banks of the Tweed, *tweed* was accordingly adopted *Twill*, like *dimity* (*q.v.*), means " two-threaded "

Tweedledum and Tweedledee. Names invented by John Byrom (1692-1763) to satirize two quarrelling schools of musicians between whom the real difference was negligible. Hence used of people whose persons or opinions—are "as like as two peas."

Some say compared to Bononcini
That mynheer Handel's but a ninny;
Others aver that he to Handel
Is scarcely fit to hold a candle
Strange all this difference should be
'Twixt Tweedledum and Tweedledee
         J BYROM

The Duke of Marlborough and most of the nobility took the side of G B Bononcini (d. about 1752), but the Prince of Wales, with Pope and Arbuthnot, was for Handel *Cp.* GLUCKISTS

Twelve, Twelfth. Each English archer carries twelve Scotsmen under his girdle This was a common saying at one time, because the English were unerring archers, and each carried twelve arrows in his belt

Twelve-note music. A modern system of musical composition in which the twelve notes of the chromatic scale have each exactly the same importance, not being centred round any one tone By a selected order of tones these are unified for any given composition

The **twelve tables** The earliest code of Roman law, compiled by the Decemviri, and engraved on twelve bronze tablets (Livy, iii, 57, Diodorus, xii, 56)

Twelfth, The The 12th of August, "St Grouse's Day", the first day of grouse-shooting

Twelfth man, The The reserve chosen for a cricket team of eleven, hence, anyone who just misses distinction.

Twelfth Night January 5th, the eve of Twelfth Day, or the Feast of the Epiphany, twelve days after Christmas, Jan 6th Formerly this was a time of great merrymaking, and the games that took place were, with little doubt, a survival of the old Roman *Saturnalia*, which was held at the same season By the Julian calendar Twelfth Day is Old Christmas Day

Shakespeare's play of this name (produced in 1602) was so called because it was written for acting at the Twelfth Night festivities, the groundwork of the plot was ultimately drawn—through various sources—from the Italian of Bandello

Twerp A slang term of a mildly derogatory implication descriptive of a stupid and contemptible fellow

Twickenham. The Bard of Twickenham. Alexander Pope (1688-1744), who lived there for thirty years

Twig I twig you. I catch your meaning, I understand (Irish *twigim*, I understand)

Twilight Sleep A state of semi-consciousness produced by injection of scopolamine and morphia in which a woman can undergo childbirth with comparatively little pain

Twins, The. A constellation and sign of the zodiac (May 21st to June 21st), representing Castor and Pollux (*q.v.*), the "great twin brethren" of classical mythology

Twist. Like Oliver Twist, asking for more. Oliver Twist, the workhouse-boy hero of Dickens's novel of that name (1838), astonished the workhouse-master and caused general consternation by once actually asking for more gruel.

To **twist it on one** Slang for to swindle one or to bamboozle him to one's own advantage Also (with allusion to giving the screw another twist), to extract from a person all one can—and a bit over

Twitcher, Jemmy. A cunning, treacherous highwayman in Gay's *Beggar's Opera* The name was given about 1765, in a poem by Gray, to John, Lord Sandwich (1718-92), noted for his *liaison* with Miss Ray, who was shot

by the Rev "Captain" Hackman out of jealousy
See Jemmy Twitcher shambles—stop, stop thief!

Two. The evil principle of Pythagoras. Accordingly the second day of the second month of the year was sacred to Pluto, and was esteemed unlucky

The **two eyes of Greece** Athens and Sparta

To **have two strings to one's bow.** See BOW.

Two heads are better than one. Outside advice is often very useful To the saying are sometimes added the words—*or why do folks marry?*

Two is company, three is none. An old saying, much used by lovers, it is given in Heywood's collection of proverbs (1546)

Two may keep counsel—if one of them's dead. A caustic saying expressive of the great difficulty of being *certain* that a secret is not told once it is imparted to someone else Shakespeare has—

> Two may keep counsel when the third's away
> *Titus Andronicus*, iv, 2

And in *The Testament of Love*, formerly attributed to Chaucer, is—

> For thre may kepe a counsel, if twain be awaie

Two of a trade did never agree. A very old proverb (it occurs in Hesiod's *Works and Days*), but one that is by no means of universal application.

> In every age and clime we see
> Two of a trade can ne'er agree
> GAY *Fables*, I, xxi

When two Fridays come together. One of a large number of circumlocutions for *Never!*

Two Gentlemen of Verona, The. Shakespeare's comedy (written certainly before 1598, but not printed till the Folio of 1623) is principally indebted for the story to the pastoral romance of *Diana*, by George of Montemayor, a Spaniard, a translation of which by Bartholomew Yonge was in existence in 1582, but not printed till 1598 Other Italian stories, and perhaps Sidney's *Arcadia*, were drawn upon, and the love adventure of Julia resembles that of Viola in *Twelfth Night*

Twopenny. Often used slightingly of things of very little value

Tuck in your twopenny! The schoolboy's warning to the boy over whose back the leap is to be made in leap-frog

Twopenny damn *See* DAMN.

The Twopenny Tube. The Central London Railway was so called, because for some years after its opening (1900) the fare between any two stations was 2d.

Tybalt (tib' alt) Formerly a name commonly given to cats (*cp.* TIBERT, in *Reynard the Fox*), hence the allusions to cats in connexion with Tybalt, one of the Capulet family in Shakespeare's *Romeo and Juliet* Mercutio says, "Tybalt, you rat-catcher, will you walk?" (iii, 1), and again, when Tybalt asks, "What wouldst thou have with me?" Mercutio answers, "Good king of cats! nothing but one of your nine lives" (iii, 1).

Tyburn (ti' bern) A former tributary of the Thames rising at Hampstead, which gave its name to the district where now stands the Marble Arch, and where public executions formerly took place Hence **Tyburn tree,** the gallows, **to take a ride to Tyburn,** to go to one's hanging, **Lord of the Manor of Tyburn,** the common hangman, etc

The site of the gallows is marked by three brass triangles let into the road pavement at the junction of Edgeware Road and Bayswater Road The last criminal to be hanged there, in 1783, was one Ryland, a forger, after that date executions were carried out at Newgate, until that prison was demolished

Tyburn Ticket A certificate which, under a statute of William III, was granted to prosecutors who had secured a capital conviction against a criminal, exempting them from all parish and ward offices within the parish in which the felony had been committed This, with the privilege it conferred, might be sold once, and once only, and the *Stamford Mercury* for March 27th, 1818, announced the sale of one for £280 The Act was repealed by 58 Geo III, c 70

Tyburnia. The Portman and Grosvenor Squares district of London, described by Thackeray as "the elegant, the prosperous, the polite Tyburnia, the most respectable district of the habitable globe."

Tycoon (ti koon') A title of the Shogun (*q.v.*), applied in the U S.A to an industrial magnate

Tyke. *See* TIKE.

Tyler's Insurrection An armed rebellion of peasants in southern England in 1381, led by Wat Tyler (an Essex man), in consequence of discontent aroused by the Statute of Labourers, and the heavy taxation, especially a poll-tax of three groats to defray the expenses of a war with France Wat Tyler was slain by Sir William Walworth, the Lord Mayor, at Smithfield, the revolt was crushed, and many of the rebels executed.

Tylwyth Teg (til' with teg) (Welsh, the Fair family). A sort of kobold family of Welsh folklore, but not of diminutive size They lived in a lake near Brecknock.

Tyndale's Bible. *See* BIBLE, THE ENGLISH

Type. Before the introduction of the point system the principal sizes of printing type were —

Great primer (pron prim' er), a large, 18-pt. type, 4¼ lines to the inch.

Long primer, 10 pt , 7½ lines to the inch. These were so called from being used for the printing of primers, or prayer-books

Pica 12 pt , 6 lines to the inch

Brevier, 8 pt , 9½ lines to the inch. Many breviaries were printed in this

Minion, 7 pt , 10 lines to the inch

A fount of type. *See* LETTER.

In an ordinary fount the proportion of the various letters is usually as follows.—

a	8,500	h	6,400	o	8,000	v	1,200
b	1,600	i	8,000	p	1,700	w	2,000
c	3,000	j	400	q	500	x	400
d	4,400	k	800	r	6,200	y	2,000
e	12,000	l	4,000	s	8,000	z	200
f	2,500	m	3,000	t	9,000	, 4,500 , 800
g	1,700	n	8,000	u	3,400	2,000 . 600

Typographical Signs. ´ An acute accent In Greek it indicates a rise in the voice, in French vowel quality, in Spanish stress; in Bohemian and Hungarian a long vowel

` A grave accent In Greek indicating a fall of the voice, in French vowel quality, or sometimes a differentiation (as in *la, là*), and in English that the accented syllable is to be pronounced (as in *blessèd*)

^ A circumflex, in French usually indicating that an *s* has been dropped (as *être* for older *estre*), and that the marked vowel is long

¸ under the letter *c* in French, is called a *cedilla,* and indicated that the *c* (*ç*) is to be pronounced as *s* It represents the Greek *zeta* (z), which formerly followed the *c* to indicate an *s* sound.

·· over the second of two vowels, as in *reestablish,* denotes that each vowel is to be sounded and is called the *diæresis,* in French, *trema* In German it is the *umlaut* or *zweipunct* (*two dots*), and denotes a change in the vowel sound, a following vowel (usually *e*) having been dropped.

° over a vowel, is the Scandinavian form of the *umlaut* or *zweipunct* (*see above*).

˜ The *tilde* (*q v*), used in Spanish, over the *n* (as *Oñoro*) to show that it is pronounced *ny*

& And, the Tironian Sign, or Ampersand (*qq v.*).

? The note of interrogation, or query mark; said to have been formed from the first and last letters of Lat *Quæstio* (question), which were contracted to $\overset{Q}{_o}$

! The note of exclamation; representing the Latin *Io* (joy), written vertically $\overset{I}{_o}$.

' The apostrophe, indicating that a letter (or figure has been omitted, as *don't, I'm, the rebellion of '98* (for 1798), also marking the possessive case (*John's book*).

*, †, ‡ The asterisk, dagger (or obelisk), and double dagger, used as reference marks, etc Another reference mark is

⁎ or *⁎* The asterism

§ The section mark, said to represent the old long initial *s's* (*ff*) of Lat *signum sectionis* sign of a section

☞ An index-hand, called by printers a "fist," to draw attention to a statement

¶ A blind P (a modification of the initial letter of *paragraph*), marks a new paragraph

( ) Called parentheses, and

[ ] Called brackets, separate some explanatory or collateral matter from the real sequence

Typhœus, (ti fē' ús) A giant of Greek mythology, with a hundred heads, fearful eyes, and a terrible voice He was the father of the Harpies. Zeus killed him with a thunderbolt, and he lies buried under Mount Etna

Typhon (ti' fon) Son of Typhœus. He was so tall that he touched the skies with his head. His offspring were Gorgon, Geryon, Cerberus, and the hydra of Lerne Like his father, he lies buried under Etna. *See also* SET.

Tyrant In ancient Greece the *tyrant* was merely the absolute ruler, the *despot,* of a state, and at first the word had no implication of cruelty or what we call *tyranny* Many of the Greek tyrants were pattern rulers, as Pisistratus and Pericles, of Athens. Periander, of Corinth; Dionysius the Younger, Gelon, and his brother Hiero of Syracuse, Phidion, of Argos, Polycrates, of Samos etc The word (*turannos*) soon, however, obtained much the same meaning as it has with us

A tyrant's vein. A ranting, bullying manner In the old moralities the tyrants were made to rant, and the loudness of their rant was proportionate to the villainy of their dispositions

The Thirty Tyrants The thirty magistrates appointed by Sparta over Athens, at the termination of the Peloponnesian war This "reign of terror," after one year's continuance, was overthrown by Thrasybulos (403 B C)
In the Roman empire those military usurpers who endeavoured, in the reigns of Valerian and Gallienus (253-268), to make themselves independent princes, are also called *the Thirty Tyrants* The number must be taken with great latitude, as only nineteen are given, and their resemblance to those of Athens is extremely fanciful.

The Tyrant of the Chersonese Miltiades was so called, and yet was he, as Byron says (in *The Isles of Greece*), "Freedom's best and bravest friend."

Tyrian Purple. This dye of ancient fame was, properly speaking, a crimson, produced from an animal juice found in the shell-fish *Murex*

Tyrtæus (tĕr tē' ŭs) A lame schoolmaster and elegiac poet of Athens who is said to have so inspired the Spartans by his songs that they defeated the Messenians (7th cent. B C) The name has hence been given to many martial poets who have urged on their countrymen to deeds of arms and victory.

U

U. The twenty-first letter of the English alphabet, in form a modification of V with which for many centuries it was interchangeable Words beginning with U and V were (like those in I and J) not separated in English dictionaries till about 1800, and in 16th- and early-17th-century books spellings such as *vpon* and *haue* are the rule rather than the exception The following from the title-page of *Polymanteia* (Anon , 1595) is a good example of the confusion.—

Polimanteia, or, The meanes to ivdge of the fall of a Commonwealth, against the friuoulous and foolish coniectures of this age. Whereunto is added, a Letter . perswading them to a constant vnitie . for the defence of our . . . natiue country .
—*Printed by John Legate, Printer to the Vniversitie of Cambridge, 1595*

U-boat. A German submarine; the term is adapted from the German *Unterseeboot* (under-water vessel)

Udal Tenure. The same as "allodial tenure," the opposite of "feudal tenure," which was the holding of a tenement under a feudal lord Udal tenure is a sort of freehold, held by the right of long possession, and is obsolete,

except in the Orkneys and Shetlands The more correct spelling is *odal* (Icel *othal*)

Ugly Duckling. An unpromising child who develops into a beautiful and admired grown-up, from this the term is extended to anything of an unprepossessing nature that may change with time into its very reverse The phrase is taken from Hans Andersen's story of the ugly duckling that pioved to be a cygnet and to its foster-mother's surprise, grew up into a lovely swan

Ugolino (oo gō lē' nō). A Ghibelline (Ugolino della Gherardesca, Count of Pisa) who, about 1270, deserted his party and, with the hope of usurping supreme power in Pisa, formed an alliance with Giovanni Visconti, the head of the Guelphs The plot failed, Giovanni died, and Ugolino joined the Florentines and forced the Pisans to restore his territories. In 1284 Genoa made war against Pisa, and the Count again treacherously deserted the Pisans, causing their total overthrow. At length a conspiracy was formed against him, and in 1288 he was cast with his two sons and two grandsons into the tower of Gualandi, where they were all starved to death Dante, in his *Inferno*, has given the sad tale undying publicity

Uhlans (oo' lānz). The former Prussian light cavalry, chiefly employed in reconnoitring, skirmishing, and outpost duty

Uitlander (oit' lan der). A S African term for a foreigner—an out-lander It is particularly applied to white inhabitants of other than Boer nationality, and was a term that aroused violent political feeling at the period of the Anglo-Boer War

Ukase (ū kāz) In the Russian Empire, an edict either proceeding from the senate or direct from the emperor Hence, a rigid order or official decree of any kind

Ukelele (ū ke lā' le) A small 4-stringed instrument shaped like a guitar and used in the South Seas as the "small brother" of the Hawaiian guitar. It enjoyed a vogue in the U S.A and Britain in the 1920s

Ulema (ū lē' mä). The learned classes in Mohammedan countries, interpreters of the Koran and the law, from whose numbers are chosen the mollahs, imaums, muftis, cadis, etc (ministers of religion, doctors of law, and administrators of justice) *Ulema* is the plural of *ulim*, a wise man The body is under the presidency of the Sheikh-ul-Islam.

Ullage (ŭl' āj) The difference between the amount of liquid a vessel can contain and what it actually does contain. The term is applied particularly to a bottle of wine of which part of the contents have evaporated on account of the cork being old or faulty

Ullin. Fingal's aged bard (*Ossian*)

Ulster. The northernmost province of Ireland, which was forfeited to the Crown in James I's reign in consequence of the rebellions of Tyrconnel and Tyrone, and colonized (1609-12) by English and Scottish settlers, who were forbidden to sell land to any Irishman Since then the Ulstermen (*cp* ORANGEMEN) have been intensely British and anti-Irish in sentiment and action, and have refused to form part of or have any share in the independent state of Eire

The long loose overcoat known as an *ulster* is so called because originally made of Ulster frieze.

The Red, or Bloody, Hand of Ulster. The badge of Ulster, a sinister hand, erect, open, and couped at the wrist, gules; also carried as a charge on the coat of arms of baronets of England, Great Britain, and the United Kingdom, in commemoration of the fact that this order was created by James I (1611) with the ostensible object of raising funds for the settlement of Ulster. *See* BARONET

Legend has it that in an ancient expedition to Ireland, it was given out that whoever first touched the shore should possess the territory which he touched, O'Neill, seeing another boat likely to outstrip his own, cut off his left hand and threw it on the coast From this O'Neill the princes of Ulster were descended, and the motto of the O'Neills is to this day *Lamh dearg Eirin*, "red hand of Erin"

Ulster King-of-Arms. Chief heraldic officer of Ireland, and Registrar to the Order of St. Patrick Created by Edward VI in 1552

Ultima Thule. *See* THULE

Ultimus Romanorum (ŭl' tĭ mŭs rō ma nôr' ŭm) (Lat) The Last of the Romans *See* LAST

Ultor (ŭl' tôr) (Lat, the Avenger) A title given to Mars (*q v*) when, after defeating the murderers of Julius Cæsar, Augustus built a temple to him in the Forum at Rome

Ultra vires (ŭl' tra vī' rēz) (Law Lat *ultra*, beyond, *vires*, pl of *vis*, strength) In excess of the power possessed, transcending authority If the Bank of England were to set up a mint on its premises, it would be acting *ultra vires*.

Ultramontane Party The extreme party in the Church of Rome. *Ultramontane* opinions or tendencies are those which favour the high "Catholic" party *Ultramontane* (beyond the mountains, *i e* the Alps) means Italy or the old Papal States The term was first used by the French, to distinguish those who look upon the Pope as the fountain of all power in the Church, in contradistinction to the Gallican school, which maintained the right of self-government by national churches. *Cp.* TRAMONTANE

Ulysses, or Odysseus (ŭ lis' ēz, o dis' ŭs) ("the hater'). A mythical king of Ithaca, a small rocky island of Greece, one of the leading chieftains of the Greeks in Homer's *Iliad*, and the hero of his *Odyssey* (*q.v*), represented by Homer as wise, eloquent, and full of artifices

According to Virgil it was he who suggested the device of the wooden horse through which Troy was ultimately taken

Ulysses' bow. Only Ulysses could draw his own bow, and he could shoot an arrow through twelve rings. By this sign Penelope recognized her husband after an absence of twenty years

The bow was prophetic It belonged at one time to Eurytus of Œchalia.

Umble Pie. A pie made of umbles—*i e.* the liver, kidneys, etc, of a deer Such offal was the perquisite of the keeper, and umble pie was a dish for servants and inferiors.

The keeper hath the skin, head, umbles, chine, and shoulders —HOLINSHED *Chronicle*, i, 204

This is the origin of our phrase usually rendered "to eat *humble* pie"

Umbrage (Lat *umbra*, shade) To take umbrage. Originally to feel overshadowed, slighted and hence to take offence

Umbrella. Used in China in the 11th century B C, in ancient Babylon and Egypt, and known in England in Anglo-Saxon times, though not commonly in use till the early 18th century, and, apparently, not introduced into Scotland till 1780 Umbrellas are mentioned by Drayton in his *Muses Elizium* (1630)—

And like umbrellas, with their feathers,
Shield you in all sorts of weathers

And Quarles in his *Emblems* (1635) uses the word to signify the Deity hidden in the manhood of Christ—"Nature is made th' umbrella of the Deity" (iv, 14) Another mention is in Swift's *City Shower* (1710), in Gay's *Trivia* (1711), and *The Tatler*, in No. 238 (Oct. 17th 1710), says:

The young gentlemen belonging to the Custom House .. borrowed the umbrella from Wilk's coffee-house

Jonas Hanway (1712-86), the Persian traveller, seems to have popularized umbrellas, for his use of one in London to keep off the rain created a disturbance among the chairmen and public coachmen, showing that they were not commonly used in the streets at the time

Under the umbrella of So-and-so Under his dominion, regimen, influence The allusion is to the umbrella which, as an emblem of sovereignty, is carried over certain African potentates as the Sultan of Morocco. In *Travels of Ali Bey* (*Penny Magazine*, Dec, 1835), we are told, "The retinue of the sultan was composed of a troop of from fifteen to twenty men on horseback About 100 steps behind them came the sultan, mounted on a mule, with an officer bearing his umbrella, who rode beside him on a mule . . . Nobody but the sultan himself [not even] his sons and brothers, dares to make use of it"

In 1874 the sacred umbrella of Koffee, King of the Ashantis, was captured. It was placed in the South Kensington Museum

In World War II the term *umbrella* was used to denote the air-cover over land or sea operations

Umlaut (um' lout) The change or modification of sound characteristic of certain Germanic languages occasioned when a vowel is influenced by a following vowel. The second or modifying vowel can appear, or it can be replaced by a diaeresis, itself called an umlaut, as Goethe, Göthe Duerer, Durer.

U N The United Nations This is the official designation, since the San Francisco meeting of June, 1945, of what had hitherto been known as U N O, the United Nations Organization The preamble of its charter opens —"We, the peoples of the United Nations, determined to save succeeding

generations from the scourge of war .. and to reaffirm faith in fundamental human rights, in dignity and worth of the human person, in the equal rights of men and women and of nations large and small . have resolved to combine our efforts to accomplish these aims "
U N. formally came into existence October 24th 1945 with its seat in U S A , temporarily at Lake Success, Long Island Fifty-eight States were signatories to the Charter.

Una (ū' nȧ) The heroine of the first book of Spenser's *Faerie Queene*, typifying Truth (*Una*, the One)

Unam Sanctam (ū' năm săngkt' ăm) (Lat , one Holy, i e. Church) A bull issued in 1302 by Boniface VIII during his quarrel with Philip IV of France, declaring that temporal power is inferior to spiritual, and that the Pope is a Sovereign over Sovereigns So called—as is usual in bulls—from its opening words.

Unaneled Unanointed, without having had extreme unction (*A S ele*, oil, Lat *oleum*)
Unhouseled, disappointed, unaneled
Hamlet, i, 5.

Unhouseled is without having had the Eucharist, especially in the hour of death (A S *husel*, sacrifice, Eucharist)

Uncials (ŭn' si ȧlz). A kind of majuscule script used in MSS. dating from about the 1st century B C to the 9th century A D , so called because they are about an inch (Lat *uncia*) in height

Uncle. Slang for a pawnbroker, in use as early as 1756. Its origin is unknown An article that has *gone to my uncle's*, is pawned.

Don't come the uncle over me In Latin, *Ne sis patruus mihi* (Horace 2 *Sat* iii, 88)— i e do not overdo your privilege of reproving or castigating me. The Latin notion of a *patruus* or uncle left guardian was that of a severe castigator and reprover Similarly, their idea of a stepmother was a woman of stern, unsympathetic nature, who was unjust to her stepchildren, and was generally disliked.

Uncle George King George III

Uncle Joe. A humorous nickname for Joseph Stalin, President of the U S S R

Uncle Remus (rē' mŭs) The old plantation Negro whose quaint and proverbial wisdom, and stories of Brer Rabbit and Brer Fox were related by Joel Chandler Harris (1848-1908) in *Uncle Remus, his Songs and Sayings* (1880), and *Nights with Uncle Remus* (1883)

Uncle Sam. *See* SAM

Uncle Tom's Cabin. A story by Harriet Beecher Stowe (1811-96) that appeared in 1852 It tells of the sale of a pious and faithful old Negro slave to a bad owner By its emphasis on the worst sides of negro slavery the book helped in no small degree to arouse the American nation to an understanding of the iniquities of the system. The original of Uncle Tom was a slave subsequently ordained as the Rev J Henson He came to London in 1876 and was presented to Queen Victoria

Welsh Uncle. The husband of a parent s cousin, sometimes a parent's first cousin

Unco. A Scottish variant of *uncouth* (unknown; hence, strange, extraordinary) It has two meanings. As an *adjective* it means unknown, strange, unusual. but as an *adverb* it means very—as unco good, unco glad, etc The "unco guid" are the pinchbeck saints, too good by half

Unconscious, The. In psychology the mental processes which the individual cannot bring into consciousness—they are, indeed, often unknown to him

Uncumber, St., formerly called St Wilgefortis, a very mythical saint "Women changed her name" (says Sir Thomas More) "because they reken that for a pecke of oats she will not faile to *uncumber* them of their husbondys." The tradition says that she was one of seven beautiful daughters born at a birth to a queen of Portugal, wishing to lead a single life she prayed that she might have a beard. The prayer was granted; and she was no more cumbered with lovers, but one of them, a prince of Sicily, was so enraged that he had her crucified
If a wife were weary of a husband, she offered oats at Poules . to St Uncumber —MICHAEL WOODE (1554)

Undecimilla *See* URSULA.

Under-. Under-cover. Working out of sight. An under-cover agent is one who pursues his enquiries or work unknown to any but his employer.

Underground. A political or military movement carried on in secret against an oppressor government or an occupying enemy administration During World War II there were many effectively organized underground movements in all countries occupied by German forces

Underground Railroad The route by which runaway slaves were secretly transported through the Northern States to Canada and freedom.

Undertaker. The application of this word to one who carries out funerals—in U S A termed a mortician—dates from the 17th century, though its origin is unknown

Underwriter. One who engages to buy at a certain prearranged price all the stock in a new company, of a new issue, etc , that is not taken up by the public An underwriter at Lloyd's is one who insures a ship or its merchandise and undertakes other insurance to a stated amount So called because he writes his name under the policy.

Undine (ŭn dēn') One of the elemental spirits of Paracelsus (*cp,* SYLPH), the spirit of the waters She was created without a soul, but had this privilege, that by marrying a mortal and bearing him a child she obtained a soul, and with it all the pains and penalties of the human race. She is the subject of a tale (*Undine*, 1811) by de la Motte Fouqué (1777-1843)

Unearned Increment. The increase in the value of land which results from the building of roads or railways, from the growth of population, or from the working of mines beneath the surface

UNESCO. The United Nations Educational, Scientific, and Cultural Organization Founded in 1945 as a specialized agency of the United Nations, "the purpose of the Organization is to contribute to peace and security by promoting collaboration among the nations through education, science, and culture."

Unfinished Symphony. Schubert's Symphony in B minor, of which only two movements were completed Other work or disinclination caused the composer to leave unfinished the four movements he had originally designed.

Unfrock. In ecclesiastical parlance, to deprive a priest of his clerical robes and reduce him to lay estate It is rarely done—so rarely in the R C Church that the last case of a solemn unfrocking was in Poland, in 1853, when a priest was publicly degraded before execution for a murder After his death it was discovered that he had suffered innocently on behalf of another, of whose guilt he knew only under the seal of confession

Unguem (ŭn′ gwem) Ad unguem. To the minutest point To finish a statue ad unguem is to finish it so smoothly and perfectly that when the nail is run over the surface it can detect no imperfection See FINGER (to have it at one's fingers' ends)

Unhinged. I am quite unhinged. My nerves are shaken, my equilibrium of mind is disturbed; I am like a door which has lost one of its hinges.

Unhouseled. See UNANELED

Unicorn (ū′ ni kŏrn) (Lat. unum cornu, one horn). A mythical and heraldic animal, represented by mediæval writers as having the legs of a buck, the tail of a lion, the head and body of a horse, and a single horn, white at the base, black in the middle, and red at the tip, in the middle of its forehead The body is white, the head red, and eyes blue The oldest author that describes it is Ctesias (400 B C), the mediæval notions concerning it are well summarized in the following extract

The unicorn has but one horn in the middle of its forehead It is the only animal that ventures to attack the elephant, and so sharp is the nail of its foot, that with one blow it can rip the belly of that beast. Hunters can catch the unicorn only by placing a young virgin in his haunts No sooner does he see the damsel, than he runs towards her, and lies down at her feet, and so suffers himself to be captured by the hunters The unicorn represents Jesus Christ, who took on Him our nature in the virgin's womb, was betrayed by the Jews, and delivered into the hands of Pontius Pilate Its one horn signifies the Gospel of Truth —Le Bestiaire Divin de Guillaume, Clerc de Normandie (13th century)

Another popular belief was that the unicorn by dipping its horn into a liquid could detect whether or not it contained poison In the designs for gold and silver plate made for the Emperor Rudolph II by Ottavio Strada is a cup on which a unicorn stands as if to assay the liquid.

The supporters of the old royal arms of Scotland are two Unicorns, when James VI of Scotland came to reign over England (1603) he brought one of the Unicorns with him, and with it supplanted the Red Dragon which, as representing Wales, was one of the supporters of the English shield, the other being the Lion

The animosity which existed between the lion and the unicorn referred to by Spenser in his Faerie Queene (II, v)—

Like as a lyon, whose imperiall powre
A prowd rebellious unicorn delyes—

is allegorical of that which once existed between England and Scotland

Driving unicorn. Two wheelers and one leader. The leader is the one horn.

Unigenitus (ū ni jen′ i tus) (Lat, the Only-Begotten) A Papal bull, so called from its opening sentence Unigenitus Dei Filius, issued in 1713 by Clement XI in condemnation of Quesnel's Reflexions Morales which favoured Jansenism. It was a damnatio in globo —i e a condemnation of the whole book without exception It was confirmed in 1725, but in 1730 was condemned by the civil authorities of Paris and the controversy died out

Unilateral. One-sided In a political sense this term implies action by one party to a treaty or agreement without the consent of the other party or parties involved

Union The Union. A short term for the United States of America, and (in England) a once familiar euphemism for the workhouse

The Act of Union. Specifically, the Act of 1706 declaring that on and after May 1st, 1707, England and Scotland should have a united Parliament The two countries had been united under one sovereign since 1603.

The term is also applied to the Act of 1536 incorporating Wales with England, and to that of 1800, which united the kingdoms of Great Britain and Ireland on and after January 1st, 1801

Union of South Africa. The self-governing former colonies of Cape of Good Hope, Natal, the Transvaal, Orange River Colony, united in a legislature in 1910, with its capital at Pretoria and the seat of government at Capetown

The Union Rose. The combined emblematic rose of the Houses of York and Lancaster, the petals of which are white and red; white representing York, and red representing Lancaster See under ROSE

Union is strength. The wise saw of Periander, "tyrant" of Corinth (665-585 B C)

Union Jack The national banner of Great Britain and Ireland. It consists of three united crosses—that of St. George for England, the saltire of St Andrew for Scotland (added by James I), and the cross of St Patrick for Ireland (added at the Union in 1801).

The white edging of St George's cross shows the white field. In the saltire the cross is reversed on each side, showing that the other half of the cross is covered over. The broad white band is the St Andrew's cross and should be uppermost at the top left-hand corner of the flag The narrow white edge is the white field of St Patrick's cross

The Union Jack is technically described thus:—

The Union Flag shall be azure, the Crosses saltire of St Andrew and St Patrick quarterly per saltire, counter-changed, argent and gules, the latter fimbriated of the second, surmounted by the Cross of St. George of the third, fimbriated as the saltire —By order of the Council

For the word "Jack," see JACK.

Unionists The Liberal and Radical party opposed to Home Rule in Ireland which was formed in 1886, and in 1895 joined the Conservative government, so named by Lord Randolph Churchill After the formation of the Coalition Ministry in 1915 and, still more, after the granting of Home Rule to Ireland (1914 and 1920), the name tended to become obsolete though the party has never been formally dissolved.

Unitarians. Christians who deny the doctrine of the Trinity, maintaining that God exists in one Person only. Many of the early heretical sects were unitarian in belief though not in name; and at the time of the Reformation Servetus, Hetzer (*Switzerland*), Palæologus, Sega (*Italy*), Flekwyk (*Holland*), the "Holy Maid of Kent" (*England*), Aikenhead (*Scotland*), Catherine Vogel (*Poland*), Dolet (*France*), and hundreds of others were put to death for holding this opinion.

The modern Unitarians in England ascribe their foundation to John Biddle (1615-62), and among the famous men who have belonged to the body are Dr Samuel Clarke, Joseph Priestley, Dr. Lardner, James Martineau, Sir Edward Bowring, and Joseph Chamberlain.

United Kingdom. The name adopted on January 1st, 1801, when Great Britain and Ireland were united.

United States. The forty-eight States, and one Federal District, composing the Federal Republic. Thirteen of these are original States, and seven were admitted without previous organization as Territories

The nickname of a United States man is a *Yank*, or *Yankee* (*q v*), of the people in the aggregate *Brother Jonathan* (*q v*), and of the Government *Uncle Sam See* SAM

Most of the States have an official abbreviation and a familiar nickname, as the Cotton State for Alabama, the Apache State, Arizona, etc The following is a list of the States with their abbreviations and nicknames —

Alabama (Ala), Cotton
Arizona (Ariz), Apache
Arkansas (Ark), Wonder
California (Cal), Golden
Colorado (Colo), Centennial.
Connecticut (Conn), Nutmeg.
Delaware (Del), Diamond
Florida (Fla), Peninsular
Georgia (Ga.), Goober, i.e peanut.
Idaho, Gem
Illinois (Ill), Prairie
Indiana (Ind), Hoosier
Iowa, Hawkeye
Kansas (Kan), Sunflower
Kentucky (Ky), Blue Grass.
Louisiana (La), Pelican
Maine (Me), Pine Tree
Maryland (Md.), Old Line
Massachusetts (Mass), Bay
Michigan (Mich), Wolverine.
Minnesota (Minn), Gopher
Mississippi (Mis), Magnolia.
Missouri (Mo), Show-Me
Montana (Mont), Bonanza
Nebraska (Neb), Golden rod
Nevada (Nev), Sagebrush
New Hampshire (N H), Granite
New Jersey (N.J), Garden
New Mexico (N Mex), Sunshine
New York (N Y), Empire
North Carolina (N C), Tar Heel
North Dakota (N Dak), Flickertail.

30*

Ohio, Buckeye
Oklahoma (Okla), Sooner
Oregon (Oreg), Beaver
Pennsylvania (Pa), Keystone
Rhode Island, (R I), Gun Flint
South Carolina (S C), Palmetto.
South Dakota (S Dak), Coyote.
Tennessee (Ten), Volunteer
Texas (Tex), Lone Star
Utah, Mormon
Vermont (Vt), Green Mountain
Virginia (Va), The Old Dominion.
Washington (Wash), Evergreen
West Virginia (W Va), Panhandle.
Wisconsin (Wis), Badger
Wyoming (Wyo), Equality
Dist of Columbia (D C)

Unities, The Dramatic *See* DRAMATIC

Universal Doctor. Alain de Lille (1114-1203)

University First applied to collegiate societies of learning in the 12th century, because the *universitas literarum* (entire range of literature) was taught in them—*i e* arts, theology, law, and physics, still called the "learned" sciences Greek, Latin, grammar, rhetoric, and poetry are called *humanity studies*, or *humaniores literæ*, meaning "lay" studies in contradistinction to divinity, which is the study of *divine* things.

The University Tests Act. An Act passed in 1871 abolishing in the Universities of Oxford, Cambridge, and Durham subscriptions to the XXXIX Articles, all declarations and oaths concerning religious belief, and all compulsory attendance at public worship.

Unknown. The Great Unknown. Sir Walter Scott So called (first by his publisher, James Ballantyne) because the *Waverley Novels* were published anonymously

Unknown Warrior. The body of an unknown, and now unidentifiable, British soldier brought home from one of the battlefields of World War I and "buried among the kings" in Westminster Abbey. Several bodies of unknown soldiers were disinterred at random from battlefields of the Western Front, choice among these was again made at random, and one body was brought back to London to represent in splendid anonymity the 800,000 British warriors who fell in battle. On November 11th, 1920, the body was placed in the nave of the Abbey. Similar tombs are in the National Cemetery at Arlington, Virginia, beneath the Arc de Triomphe in Paris, and in the Unter den Linden, Berlin

Unlearned Parliament, The. Henry IV's Parliament, which met at Coventry in 1404; so called by Sir Edward Coke because it contained no lawyers, hence also sometimes spoken of as the *Lawless Parliament*

Unmentionables. One of the 19th-century prudish euphemisms for breeches, pantaloons, or trousers

Corinthians and exquisites from Bond Street, sporting an eye-glass, . waiting-men in laced coats and plush unmentionables of yellow, green, blue, red, and all the primary colours —REV N S WHEATON *Journal* (1830)

Unmerciful Parliament The. Another name for the Wonderful Parliament (*q v.*).

U.N R R.A. United Nations Relief and Rehabilitation Administration An agency set up in U.S A. in November, 1943, to help victims of World War II in liberated areas Food, clothing, medicines, fuel, fertilizers, seeds, etc , were distributed by trained personnel and the administration also saw to the repatriation of millions of displaced persons Its work having been largely completed by June, 1947, the Administration came to an end, passing over certain of its obligations to I R O , (International Refugee Organization) of United Nations

Unready, The Ethelred II, King of England 978-1016 So called because he was *redeless*, or deficient in counsel

Unrighteous Bible, The *See* BIBLE, SPECIALLY NAMED.

Untouchables. The lowest caste in India, whose touch was believed to sully a high-caste Hindu In 1948 such caste distinction was abolished, largely through influence of the teaching of Mahatma Gandhi

Unwritten Law. Uncodified and unjudicial law which rests for its authority on the supposed right of the individual to take into his own hands the avenging of personal wrongs—especially sexual offences against his womenkind.

Up. The House is up The business of the day is ended, and members of Parliament may go home

    A. B is up. A B is actually making a speech in Parliament

    "Up Guards, and at them!" In his *Fifteen Decisive Battles*, Creasy states that the Duke of Wellington gave this order in the final charge at the battle of Waterloo It is impossible to say on what he based this odd statement, it was not the Guards, but the 52nd Light Infantry which broke the column of the French Imperial Guard in the final charge

    Up country. Remote from the coast, in the interior. The term, which is common in America and Australia, is sometimes used in the derogatory sense of unsophisticated, or rustic

    Up stage. As a technical theatrical direction this means at the back of the stage, which in many theatres slopes down slightly to the footlights Colloquially the phrase *up-stage* means aloof, putting on airs of consequence or superiority.

    Up State. In the U S A the part of a State furthest north or distant from the coast, the term is used more particularly of the northern parts of New York State.

Upper Ten, The. *See* TEN

Upanishads (ū pän' ı shädz) The oldest speculative literature of the Hindus, a collection of treatises on the nature of man and the universe, forming part of the Vedic writings, the earliest dating from about the 6th century B C The name is Sanskrit, and means "a sitting down (at another's feet)," hence "a confidential talk," "esoteric doctrine "

Upas Tree (ū' päs) The Javanese tree, *Antiaris toxicaria*, the milky juice of which contains a virulent poison and is used for tipping arrows

Fable has it that a putrid steam rises from it, and that whatever the vapour touches dies Foersch, a Dutch physician, wrote in 1783, "Not a tree, nor blade of grass is to be found in the valley or surrounding mountains Not a beast or bird, reptile or living thing, lives in the vicinity." He adds that on "one occasion 1,600 refugees encamped within fourteen miles of it, and all but 300 died within two months " This "traveller's tale" has given rise to the figurative use of *upas* for a corrupting or pernicious influence

Upsee Used in combination with *Dutch, Freeze, English,* as jesting terms for drunk or tippling *Upsee Dutch* is "in the manner of the Dutch," *upsee Freeze,* in the manner of a Frisian, etc.

    Teach me how to take the German upsy freeze, the Danish rouser, the Switzer's stoop of Rhenish —
    DEKKER *Gull's Hornbook* (1609)
        I do not like the dulness of your eye,
        It hath a heavy cast, 'tis upsee-Dutch,
        And says you are a lumpish whoremaster
        BEN JONSON *The Alchemist*, IV, 4
    Yet whoop, Barnaby! off with thy liquor,
    Drink upsees out, and a fig for the vicar
        SCOTT *Lady of the Lake*, VI, 5

Upset Price. The price at which goods sold by auction are first offered for competition If no advance is made they fall to the person who made the upset price *Reserved bid* is virtually the same thing

Urania (ū rä' nı a). The Muse of Astronomy in Greek mythology, usually represented pointing at a celestial globe with a staff. Milton (*Paradise Lost*, VII, 1-20) makes her the spirit of the loftiest poetry, and calls her "heavenly born" (the name means "the heavenly one") and sister of Wisdom

        Where was lorn Urania
    When Adonais died? With veiled eyes,
    'Mid listening Echoes, in her Paradise
    She sate   SHELLEY *Adonais*, II.

Uranus (ū' rä nus) In Greek mythology the personification of Heaven, son and husband of Ge (the earth), and father of the Titans, the Cyclops, the Furies, etc. He hated his children and confined them in Tartarus; but they broke out (*see* TITANS) and his son Kronos dethroned him

    The planet Uranus was discovered in 1781 by Herschell, and named by him *Georgium Sidus* in honour of George III Its four satellites are named *Ariel, Umbriel, Titania,* and *Oberon.*

Urbanists. *See* FRANCISCANS

Urbi et Orbi (er' bi et ôr' bi) (Lat , To the city [Rome] and the world) A phrase applied to the solemn blessing publicly given by the pope from the balcony of St Peter's on special occasions, such as his election The custom fell into abeyance after 1870 but at his election on February 22nd, 1922, Pope Pius XI gave the blessing Urbi et Orbi from the façade of St. Peter's

Urdu (ēr' dū) One of the most important dialects of India, spoken by the Mohammedans, so named from Hindu *urdu-zaban,* the language of the camp

Ur-Hamlet. *See* HAMLET

Uriah (ū rī' ȧ). Letter of Uriah. A treacherous letter, importing friendship but in reality a death warrant (See II Sam. xi, 15)

Uriel (ū' ri ěl). One of the seven archangels of rabbinical angelology, sent by God to answer the questions of Esdras (2 Esdras, iv) In Milton's Paradise Lost (iii, 690) he is the "Regent of the Sun," and "sharpest-sighted spirit of all in heaven "

Urim and Thummim (ū' rim, thŭm' im). Two objects of uncertain form and material used in the early forms of ancient Hebrew worship, probably in connexion with divination and obtaining oracular answers from Jehovah They are mentioned in Ex. xxviii, 30, 1 Sam xxviii, 6, Deut xxxiii, 8, Ezra ii, 63, etc., but fell out of use in post-exilic times, evidently through the Jews developing a higher conception of the Deity.

Ursa Major. The Great Bear, or Charles's Wain (q.v.), the most conspicuous of the northern constellations
    The legend is that Calisto, daughter of Lycaon, was violated by Jupiter Juno changed her into a bear, and Jupiter placed her among the stars that she might be more under his protection Homer calls it Arktos, the Bear, and Hamaxa, the Wagon The Romans called it Ursa, the Bear, and Septemtriones, the Seven Ploughing Oxen; whence Septentrionalis came to signify the north
    Boswell's father used to call Dr Johnson Ursa Major

Ursa Minor The Little Bear, the northern constellation known also as Cynosura, or "Dog's tail," from its circular sweep The Pole Star is a in the tail. See CYNOSURE.

Ursula, St Ursula was a Cornish princess and, as the story says, was going to France with eleven thousand companions when the galley was driven by adverse winds to Cologne, where they were all massacred by the Huns Nothing at all is known of these maidens beyond the fact that they were martyrs at Cologne before the 4th century Their number, "eleven thousand" is purely fabulous, early mediæval calendars vary between five and eleven—units, not thousands The Roman Martyrology has on October 21st, "At Cologne, the birthday of SS Ursula and her companions," etc

Ursulines. An order of nuns founded by St Angela Merici of Brescia about 1537, so called from their patron saint, St Ursula The chief work of the order is the education of girls

Useless Parliament, The. The Parliament convened by Charles I, on June 18th, 1625, adjourned to Oxford, August 1st, and dissolved August 12th, having done nothing but offend the king.

Usher. From Fr huissier, a door-keeper.

    Gentleman Usher of the Black Rod See BLACK ROD

    Usher of the Green Rod. An officer in attendance on the Knights of the Thistle at their chapters

Usquebaugh. Whisky (Ir uisgebeatha, water of life) Similar to the Latin aqua vitæ, and the French eau de vie

U.S.S.R. The initials of Union of Soviet Socialist Republics, in Russian S.S.S.R. (Soyuz Sovetskikh Sotsialisticheskikh Respublik), the government of Russia and Russian Asia that came into being after the revolution of 1917

Uther (ū' ther) A legendary king, or pendragon (q v) of the Britons, by an adulterous amour with Igerna (wife of Gorlois, Duke of Cornwall) he became the father of Arthur, who succeeded him

Uti possidetis (ū' tǐ pos i dē' tis) (Lat , as you at present possess them) The principle in international law that the belligerents are to retain possession of all the places taken by them before the treaty commenced

Uticensis (ū ti sen' sis). Cato the Younger was so called from Utica, the place of his death.

Utility The name given during and after World War II to articles of wear, etc , the quality of which was sponsored by the Government Utility goods were sold to the public at officially controlled prices

Utilitarianism. The ethical doctrine that actions are right in proportion to their usefulness or as they tend to promote happiness; the doctrine that the end and criterion of public action is "the greatest happiness of the greatest number "
    John Stuart Mill coined the word; but Jeremy Bentham, the official founder of the school, employed the word "Utility" to signify the doctrine which makes "the happiness of man" the one and only measure of right and wrong

Utopia. Nowhere (Gr ou, not, topos, a place). The name given by Sir Thomas More to the imaginary island in his political romance of the same name (1516), where everything is perfect—the laws, the morals, the politics, etc , and in which the evils of existing laws, etc , are shown by contrast. See COMMONWEALTHS, IDEAL
    This island has given us the adjective Utopian, applied to any highly desirable but impracticable scheme
    Rabelais (in Bk II, ch xxiv) sends Pantagruel and his companions to Utopia, where they find the citizens of its capital, Amaurot, most hospitable

Utraquists (Lat, utraque specie, in both kinds) Another name for the Calixtines (q v), so called because they insisted that both the elements should be administered to all communicants in the Eucharist

Utter and Inner Barristers. An utter or outer barrister means (in some cases at least) a full-fledged barrister, one licensed to practise An inner barrister means a student

Uzziel. One of the principal angels of rabbinical angelology, the name meaning "Strength of God " He was next in command to Gabriel, and in Milton's Paradise Lost (iv, 782) is commanded by Gabriel to "coast the south with strictest watch."

V

V. The twenty-second letter of the alphabet, formerly sharing its form with U (*q v*)

In the Roman notation it stands for 5, and represents ideographically the four fingers and thumb with the latter extended

V-for Victory. On January 14th, 1941, M Victor de Lavaleye, a member of the exiled Belgian government in London, proposed in a broadcast to Belgium that the letter V should be used as a simple substitute for the letters R A F. which were being chalked up on walls, etc , in Belgium V had the advantage of standing for the word *Victory* in all Western European languages The plan was immediately adopted and it soon became the most ambitious propaganda campaign of World War II The Morse Code V (ᐧ ᐧ ᐧ —) was featured in every B B.C broadcast to Europe, this was followed by the use of the opening bar of Beethoven's 5th Symphony which has the same rhythm. "Colonel Britton" (Douglas E Ritchie, director of the B B C European news service) was responsible for this extensive and most powerful diffusion of the V-sign propaganda, which stiffened resistance and gave hope to the many thousands in bondage to the Germans Winston Churchill popularized the sign of two up-raised fingers outspread in the form of a V.

V-1. Jet-propelled robot plane bomb sent against Britain by the Germans, June-August, 1944, subsequently sent by them against Antwerp. V = *Vergeltungswaffe* (Revenge weapon).

V-2. Jet-propelled rocket bomb, projected against England by the Germans in autumn, 1944.

V D. M I. Æ Lat *Verbum Dei manet in æternum*, *i e.* the word of God endureth for ever The inscription on the liveries of the servants of the Duke of Saxony and Landgrave of Hesse, the Lutheran princes, at the Diet of Spires in 1526

V.E. Day. The end of hostilities in Europe after World War II, May 9th, 1945.

V.J. Day. The end of hostilities in the Far East, August 15th, 1945

V-Mail (World War II) Reduced photostats of letters to and from soldiers overseas and their families, to save shipping space.

Vacuum (Lat *vacare*, to be empty) A space from which air has been expelled Descartes remarked, "If a vacuum could be effected in a vessel, the sides would be pressed into contact "

Nature abhors a vacuum Galileo's way of accounting for the rise of water in pumps *See* TORRICELLI

Vade mecum (vā' de mē' kŭm) (Lat , go-with-me) A pocket-book, memorandum-book, pocket cyclopædia, lady's pocket companion, or anything else which contains many things of daily use in a small compass

Væ Victis' (vē vīk' tis) (Lat.) Woe to the vanquished! So much the worse for the conquered! This was the exclamation of Brennus, the Gaulish chief, on throwing his sword into the balance as a make-weight, when determining the price of peace with Rome (390 B C)

Vagabond. An idle, disreputable person who wanders about from place to place without any settled home (late Lat *vagabundas*, from *vagari*, to wander) Under the Vagrancy Act (1824) the term is applied to such as sleep out without visible means of subsistence *Cp* ROGUE

Vail. To lower, to cast down. From Fr. *avaler*, to descend.

> The time is come
> That France must vail her lofty plumed crest
> 1 *Henry VI*, v, 3

Vails, an obsolete term for a tip given to servants by visitors or for a bribe, is from Fr *valoir*, Lat. *valere*, to be worth.

> 2 *Fish* Ay, but hark you, my friend, 'twas we that made up this garment through the rough seams of the water, there are certain condolements, certain vails I hope, sir, if you thrive, you'll remember from whence you had it
> *Per* , Believe it, I will —*Pericles*, ii, 1

Vale! Farewell! 2nd pers sing. imp of Lat *valere*, to be worth, or to fare well

> I thought once againe heare to have made an ende, with a heartie *Vale* of the best fashion —SPENSER· *Letter to Gabriel Harvey* (1580)

Ave atque vale! Hail and farewell, the words of Catullus at his brother's tomb.

Valentine. Valentine, St. A priest of Rome who was imprisoned for succouring persecuted Christians He became a convert himself, and although he restored the sight of his gaoler's blind daughter he was martyred by being clubbed to death (February 14th, 269)

St. Valentine's Day. February 14th, the day when, according to ancient tradition, the birds choose their mates for the year Chaucer refers to this (*Parliament of Foules*, 309), as also does Shakespeare —

> Good morrow, friends' St Valentine is past,
> Begin these wood-birds but to couple now?
> *Midsummer Night's Dream*, iv, 1.

It was an old custom in England to draw lots for lovers on this day, the person drawn being the drawer's *valentine*, and given a present, sometimes of an expensive kind, but oftener of a pair of gloves The valentine is now frequently represented by a greeting card of a sentimental, humorous, or merely vulgar character

> If I stood affected that way [*i e* , to marriage] I would choose my wife as men do Valentines—blindfold, or draw cuts for them, for so I shall not be deceived in the choosing —CHAPMAN *Monsieur d'Olive*, I (1605)

The custom is said to have had its origin in a pagan practice connected with the worship of Juno on or about this day

Valentine and Orson. An old French romance, connected with the Alexander cycle.

The heroes—from whom it is named—were the twin sons of Bellisant, sister of King Pepin and Alexander, and were born in a forest near Orleans Orson (*q.v*) was carried off by a bear, and became a wild man While the mother was searching for him Valentine was carried off by his uncle, the king Each had many adventures, but all ended happily, and Valentine married Clerimond, sister of the Green Knight, while Orson married a daughter of the Duke of Aquitaine

Valhalla In Scandinavian mythology, the hall in the celestial regions whither the souls of heroes slain in battle were borne by the Valkyries, to spend eternity in joy and feasting (*valr*, the slain, and *hall*)

Hence the name is applied to buildings, such as Westminster Abbey, used as the last resting-place of a nation's great men

Valkyries, The (văl kir' iz, văl kir' iz, văl' ki riz) (Old Norse, The Choosers of the Slain) The twelve nymphs of Valhalla, who, mounted on swift horses, and holding drawn swords, rushed into the *mêlée* of battle and selected those destined to death These heroes they conducted to Valhalla, where they waited upon them and served them with mead and ale in the skulls of the vanquished The chief were Mista, Sangrida, and Hilda

Vallary Crown The same as a *mural crown* (*see under* CROWN)

Valley Forge. A village in south Pennsylvania where George Washington set up the winter quarters of his army, amid great privations, in the campaign of 1777-78

Vallombrosa (văl om brō' zà) Milton says, "Thick as autumnal leaves that strew the brooks in Vallombrosa" (*Paradise Lost*, i, 302) The name, meaning Shady Valley, comes from the great woods of fir, chestnut, and beech that have long made Vallombrosa one of the most popular summer resorts in N Italy. Nearby are La Verna and other places associated with St Francis.

Vamana. *See* AVATAR

Vamoose (và moos') A slang word (deriving from the Spanish *vamos*, let us go) meaning to decamp, to make off hurriedly

Vamp To vamp up an old story, to refurbish it, *to vamp an accompaniment to a song*, to improvise as one goes along

To vamp is properly to put new uppers to old boots, and *vamps* were short hose covering the feet and ankles (Fr *avant-pied*, the forepart of the foot).

Another verb **To vamp** (derived from *Vampire* (*q v*) means to flirt outrageously or allure with the intent of gaining some personal end

Vampire A fabulous being, supposed to be the ghost of a heretic, excommunicated person, or criminal, that returns to the world at night in the guise of a monstrous bat and sucks the blood of sleeping persons who, usually, become vampires themselves

But first on earth, as vampire sent,
Thy corse shall from the tomb be rent,
Then ghastly haunt thy native place
And suck the blood of all thy race
BYRON *The Giaour*

The word is applied to one who preys upon his fellows—a "blood-sucker."

One of the classics of English horror-romances, *Dracula* (1897) by Bram Stoker was centred on vampires.

Vandals. A Teutonic race from the Baltic (allied to the *Wends*, i e *Wanderers*), which in the 5th century A D ravaged Gaul and, under Genseric, captured Rome and despoiled it of its treasures of art, literature, and civilization generally

The name is hence applied to those who wilfully or ignorantly destroy works of art, etc

Vandyke (văn dīk') To scallop an edge after the fashion of the collars painted by Van Dyck in the reign of Charles I The scalloped edges are said to be *vandyked*

Vandyke beard. A pointed beard such as those frequently shown in Van Dyck's portraits, especially of Charles I

Vanessa (và nes' a) Dean Swift's name for his friend and correspondent, Esther Vanhomrigh, made by compounding *Van*, the first syllable of her surname, with *Essa*, the pet form of Esther Swift called himself *Cadenus*, an anagram on *Decanus* (Lat for *Dean*).

Vanguard. *See* AVANT-GARDE

Vanity Fair. In Bunyan's *Pilgrim's Progress*, a fair established by Beelzebub, Apollyon, and Legion, in the town of Vanity, and lasting all the year round Here were sold houses, lands, trades, places, honours, preferments, titles, countries, kingdoms, lusts, pleasures, and delights of all sorts

Thackeray adopted the name for the title of his novel (1847) satirizing the weaknesses and follies of human nature

Vantage Loaf The thirteenth loaf of a baker's dozen

Varaha. *See* AVATAR.

'Varsity. A shortened form of *university*, but, in England, properly used only of Oxford or Cambridge

Varuna. The Hindu Neptune He is represented as an old man rising on a sea monster, with a club in one hand and a rope in the other In the Vedic hymns he is the night sky, and Mitra the day sky Varuna is said to set free the "waters of the clouds"

Vassal (văs' àl) A man in the feudal system who held his land with the obligation of rendering military service to his superior hence the term was extended to include a servant or even a slave

Vathek (văth' ek) The hero of Beckford's oriental romance of the same name (1784) The ninth caliph of the Abbasside dynasty, he is a haughty, effeminate monarch, induced by a malignant genius to commit all sorts of crimes He abjures his faith, and offers allegiance to Eblis, under the hope of obtaining the throne of the pre-Adamite sultans This he gained, only to find that it was a place of torture and that he was doomed to remain in it for ever

Vatican (văt' i kàn) The palace of the Pope, so called because it stands on the *Vaticanus Mons* (Vatican Hill) of ancient Rome, which got its name through being the headquarters of the *vaticinatores*, or soothsayers

The City of the Vatican is the area of Rome recognized by the Treaty of the Lateran (1929) as constituting the territorial extent of the temporal power of the Holy See Strictly speaking, the Vatican consists of the Papal palace, the court and garden of Belvidere, the library, and the museum, the Piazza of St Peter, and contiguous buildings, in all an area of just under a square mile Its population is about 500, of whom a number are clerics, and all male adults are in some way engaged in the immediate service of the Church Under the pope it is governed by a layman.

The Council of the Vatican The twenty-first Œcumenical Council (*q v*), opened at the Vatican in 1870 under Pius IX and not yet officially concluded

The Thunders of the Vatican *See* THUNDER.

Vaudeville (vōd' vil) A corruption of *Val de Vire*, or in O Fr *Vau de Vire*, the native valley of Oliver Basselin, a Norman poet (d 1418), author of convivial songs, which he called after the name of his birthplace It is now applied to a variety entertainment

Vaudois. *See* WALDENSIANS (*cp* VOODOO)

Vauxhall (vawks' awl) A part of Lambeth, London, so called from *Falkes* (or *Fulkes*) de Breauté, who was lord of the manor in the early 13th century.

Vauxhall Gardens A very popular pleasure resort for Londoners, from 1661, when it was opened, till 1859 Pepys, who calls it Fox Hall, says the entertainments there are "mighty diverting", and for the next two centuries its attractions and diversions furnished many writers and artists with incidents and scenes for their works

Vedas or **Vedams.** The four sacred books of the Brahmans, comprising (1) the *Rig* or *Rish Veda*, (2) *Yajur Veda*, (3) the *Sama Veda*, and (4) the *Atharva Veda*. The first consists of prayers and hymns in verse, the second of prayers in prose, the third of prayers for chanting, and the fourth of formulas for consecration, imprecation, expiation, etc. The word *Veda* means knowledge

Vegetarianism. A movement which aims at making vegetable foods the sole diet of human beings It began about 1850, although it had had many isolated adherents or sects throughout the preceding centuries Strict vegetarians (sometimes called Vegas) abstain from all food which comes from animals, such as milk, eggs, butter, cheese etc Akin to vegetarians are fruitarians who maintain life solely on fruit.

Vehmgerichte (vām' ge rich te) Courts of justice, or tribunals, held in Germany (especially Westphalia) from about the 12th to the 16th centuries, for the preservation of public peace, suppression of crime, and maintenance of the Catholic religion. In all serious cases, such as heresy, witchcraft, or murder, the sentence was death, and the proceedings were conducted in absolute secrecy; the judges were

enveloped in profound mystery, they had their secret spies through all Germany, their judgments were certain, but no one could discover the executioner.

Velocipede (ve los' i pēd) An early form of bicycle, introduced about 1819 It consisted of two wheels connected by a bar on which was the rider's seat Thus placed, with his feet touching the ground, he propelled himself along by the alternate thrust of each foot upon the ground A later development was the introduction of treadles operating directly on cranks on the axle of the front wheel

Velvet. On velvet On a sure thing, certain of success One who makes a bet that he is bound to win is said to be "on velvet "

To prophesy upon velvet To prophesy what is already a known fact

Vendée, War of La (la von' dā) The rising of royalists against the French Republic in 1793-5 in La Vendée, a Department of western France, and Brittany It was followed by the War of the Chouans (*see* CHOUAN), which was finally suppressed by Napoleon in 1800

Vendémiaire (von dā mē ār) The first month in the French Republican calendar, from September 22nd to October 21st. The word means "Vintage "

Vendetta (ven det' à) (Lat *vindicta*, revenge) The blood-feud, or duty of the nearest kin of a murdered man to kill the murderer. It prevailed in Corsica, Sicily, Sardinia, and Calabria, and in principle is not yet extinct.

Vendue (U S A). A word of obvious French origin meaning an auction sale, used from about the mid-18th century to the mid-19th century

Venerable (Lat *venerabilis*, worthy of honour) The title applied to archdeacons in formally addressing them ("The Venerable the Archdeacon of Barset," or "The Venerable Archdeacon Brown"), and also, in the Roman Catholic Church, the title of one who has attained the first of the three degrees of canonization

It specially belongs to Bede—the Venerable Bede—the monk of Jarrow, an English ecclesiastical historian (d 735), and to William of Champeaux (d. 1121), the French scholastic philosopher and opponent of Abelard.

Veneralia *See* VENUS (*Venus Verticordia*)

Veni, Creator Spiritus (vā nē krā a tôr spē' ri tus) (Lat , "Come Creator Spirit") A hymn of the Roman Breviary ascribed to both Charlemagne and Pope Gregory I. It is, however, probably the work of Rabanus Maurus, in the early 9th century It is sung at Vespers and Terce during Pentecost and on numerous occasions such as the consecration of a bishop, dedication of a church, etc

Veni, Sancte Spiritus (Lat , "Come, Holy Spirit"). A mediæval Latin hymn, used as a sequence at Pentecost in the Roman Church

Veni, vidi, vici (Lat "I came, I saw, I conquered") According to Plutarch it was thus that Julius Cæsar announced to his friend Amintius his victory at Zela (47 B C.), in Asia

Minor, over Pharnaces, son of Mithridates, who had rendered aid to Pompey.

Suetonius, however, says that the words were displayed before his title after his victories in Pontus, and does not ascribe them to Cæsar himself

They are often used as an example of laconism, extreme concision

Venial Sin. One that may be pardoned, one that does not forfeit grace In the Catholic Church sins are of two sorts, *mortal* and *venial* (Lat *venia*, grace, pardon) *See Matt* xii, 31

Venice Glass. The drinking-glasses of the Middle Ages, made at Venice, were said to break into shivers if poison were put into them

Doge: 'Tis said that our Venetian crystal has
Such pure antipathy to poison, as
To burst, if aught of venom touches it.
BYRON. *The Two Foscari,* v, 1

Venice glass, from its excellency, became a synonym for *perfection*

Venire facias A writ directing the sheriff to assemble a jury. So called from its opening Latin words—"Cause to come"

Venison Anything taken in hunting or by the chase. Hence Jacob bids Esau to go and get *venison* such as he loved (*Gen.* xxvii, 3), meaning the wild kid The word is the Latin *venatio*, hunting, but is now restricted to the flesh of deer

Venner's Plot. A plot made by the Fifth Monarchy Men under Thomas Venner to seize Whitehall in 1661 during the absence of Charles II The plot failed, and Venner and many of his followers were put to death.

Venom. The venom *is* in the *tail*. The real difficulty is the conclusion The allusion is to the scorpion, which has a sting in its tail.

Ventose (von' tōz) (Fr., windy) The sixth month of the French Revolutionary calendar. February 19th to March 20th

Ventre-saint-Gris (vontr sǎng grē) The usual oath of Henri IV of France, *Gris* being a euphemism for *Christ*, and *ventre*, stomach. Oaths not infrequently took this form of blasphemy—*God's nails, God's teeth*, etc., were common in England

A similar oath is *Par le ventre de Dieu* Rabelais has *Par \ainct Gris*, and the suggestion has been made that the allusion was to Francis of Assisi, who was *ceint* (girdled) and clad in *gris* (grey).

Ventriloquism. The trick of producing vocal sounds so that they appear to come, not from the person producing them, but from some other quarter. So called from Lat *venter*, belly, *loqui*, to speak (speaking from the belly), with the erroneous notion that the voice of the *ventriloquist* proceeded from his stomach

Venus (vē' nus). The Roman goddess of beauty and sensual love, identified with the Aphrodite (*q v*) of the Greeks She is said in some accounts to have sprung from the foam of the sea, but in others to have been the daughter of Jupiter and Dione Vulcan was her husband, but she had amours with Mars and many other gods and demi-gods; by Mercury she was the mother of Cupid, and by the hero Anchises

the mother of Æneas, through whom she was regarded by the Romans as the foundress of their race. Her chief festival was April 1st (*see* VENUS VERTICORDIA, *below*)

Her name is given to the second planet from the sun, and in astrology "signifiethe white men or browne . joyfull, laughter, liberall, pleasers, dauncers, entertayners of women, players, perfumers, musitions, messengers of love"

Venus loveth ryot and dispense
CHAUCER *Wife of Bath's Prol* , 700

By the alchemists *copper* was designated *Venus*, probably because mirrors were anciently made of copper A mirror is still the astronomical symbol of the planet Venus.

The best cast at dice (three sixes) used to be called *Venus*, and the worst (three aces) *Canis* (dog), hence the phrase, "My Venus has turned out a whelp," equivalent to "all my swans are geese"

Venus Anadyomene Venus rising from the sea, accompanied by dolphins The name is given to the famous lost painting by Apelles, and to that by Botticelli in the Accademia delle Belle Arti at Florence

Venus Callipyge (Gr , with the beautiful buttocks) The name given to a late Greek statue in the Museo Nazionale at Naples There is no real ground for connecting the statue with Venus

Venus de Medici. A famous statue, since 1860 in the Uffizzi Gallery, Florence, ranking as a canon of female beauty It is supposed to date from the time of Augustus, and was dug up in the 17th century in the villa of Hadrian, near Tivoli, in eleven pieces It was kept in the Medici Palace at Rome till its removal to Florence by Cosimo III

Venus Genetrix (Lat , she that produces). Venus worshipped as a symbol of marriage and motherhood There are several statues of this name, she being represented as carrying light drapery and holding an apple—the emblem of fecundity

Venus of Cnidus. The nude statue of Praxiteles, purchased by the ancient Cnidians, who refused to part with it, although Nicomedes, king of Bithynia, offered to pay off their national debt as its price It was subsequently removed to Constantinople, and perished in the great fire during the reign of Justinian (A D 532), but an ancient reproduction is in the Vatican

Venus of Milo, or Melos. This statue, with three of Hermes, was discovered in 1820 by Admiral Dumont in Milo or Melos, one of the Greek islands It dates from about 400 B C., and is probably the finest single work of ancient art extant It now stands in the Louvre

Venus Verticordia A temple was founded at Rome on April 1st, 114 B C, to Venus Verticordia as expiation for the loss of their virginity by three of the Vestal Virgins. April 1st thus became the *Veneralia*, or chief festival of Venus

Venus Victrix. Venus, as goddess of victory, represented on numerous Roman coins

Venus's hair-stone, or pencil Rock-crystal or quartz penetrated by acicular crystals of rutile which show through as hair-like filaments.

Venusberg The Horselberg, or mountain of delight and love, situated between Eisenach and Gotha, in the caverns of which, according to mediæval German legend, the Lady Venus held her court. Human beings were occasionally permitted to visit her, as Heinrich von Limburg did, and the noble Tannhauser (*q v*), but as such persons ran the risk of eternal perdition, Eckhardt the Faithful, who sat before the gate, failed not to warn them against entering

Vera causa (vē′ ra kaw′ za) (Lat , a true cause) A cause in harmony with other causes already known A fairy godmother may be assigned in story as the cause of certain marvellous effects, but is not a *vera causa* The revolution of the earth round the sun may be assigned as the cause of the four seasons, and is a *vera causa*

Verb. sap. (Lat *verbum sapienti*, a word to the wise). A hint is sufficient to any wise man

Verb. sat. (Lat *verbum satienti*, a word is enough) Similar to the above A word to the wise is enough.

Verbatim et literatim (Lat) Accurately rendered, "word for word and letter for letter "

Verdant Green. An excessively "green" or unsophisticated young man The character was epitomized in the book of this name (1860) by "Cuthbert Bede" (Rev Edward Bradley) Verdant's adventures at Oxford, whither he goes as a very green young undergraduate, the victim of endless practical jokes and impostures, make an entertaining and enlightening commentary on life at the University in the 1850s

Verderer. In English forest law an official of the Crown having jurisdiction in the Royal Forests, with especial charge of the trees and undergrowth

Vere adeptus (Lat , one who has truly attained) One admitted to the fraternity of the Rosicrucians

> In Rosycrucian lore as learned
> As he the Vere-adeptus earned
>   BUTLER *Hudibras*

Verger. The beadle in a church who carries the rod or staff, which was formerly called the *verge* (Lat *virga*, a rod).

Vergil. *See* VIRGIL.

Veronica, St. (ve ron′ i kà). A late mediæval legend says that a maiden handed her handkerchief to our Lord on His way to Calvary He wiped the sweat from His brow, returned the handkerchief to the owner, and went on The handkerchief was found to bear a perfect likeness of the Saviour, and was called *Vera-Icon* (true likeness), the maiden became *St Veronica* It is one of the relics preserved in St Peter's, Rome In Spanish bull-fighting the most classic movement with the cape is called the Veronica, the cape being swung so slowly before the face of the charging bull that it resembles St Veronica's wiping of the Holy Face.

Vers de société (Fr , Society verse) Light poetry of a witty or fanciful kind, generally with a slight vein of social satire running through it.

Versailles (vâr sī′) The great palace built by Louis XIV in the town of that name to the NNW of Paris The palace had been actually begun by Louis XIII, but the great enlargement was started in 1661 that made of Versailles the greatest palace in Europe The splendours of the palace and grounds and the part it has played in French history make brief description impossible Some of the royal and other apartments are kept in their original condition, but much of the palace is used as a national museum of French history The first constitution of Germany was signed in the famous Galerie des Glaces in 1871, when the Prussians were in occupation And in the same hall was also drawn up **The Treaty of Versailles,** the treaty made after World War I between the Allied states, 26 in number, on the one part, and Germany on the other Its articles included the formation of the League of Nations, the cession of Alsace and Lorraine to France, of Posen and West Prussia to Poland, the prohibition of Germany possessing submarines, a military, naval, or air force beyond certain limits, and the occupation of the country for a certain period by Allied troops As time went on most of these conditions were evaded, but the injustice of the Treaty of Versailles formed a never-failing subject for Adolf Hitler's fury and invective The Treaty was signed on June 28th, 1919 and ratified on January 10th, 1920. China declined to sign, and the U.S A senate rejected it.

Versi Berneschi. *See* BERNESQUE

Vert (vērt) The heraldic (from French) term for *green*, said to signify love, joy, and abundance, in engravings it is indicated by lines running diagonally across the shield from right to left

Vertumnus (vēr tŭm′ nus) The ancient Roman god of the seasons, and the deity presiding over gardens and orchards He was the husband of Pomona. August 12th was his festival

Vervain (vēr′ vān) Called "holy herb," from its use in ancient sacred rites Also called "pigeons' grass," "Juno's tears," and "simpler's joy " Supposed to cure scrofula, the bite of rabid animals, to arrest the diffusion of poison, to avert antipathies, to conciliate friendships, and to be a pledge of mutual good faith, hence it was anciently worn by heralds and ambassadors

Verbena is its botanical name

Vesica Piscis (ves′ i ka pis′ is) (Lat., fishbladder) The ovoidal frame or glory which, in the 12th century, was much used, especially in painted windows, to surround pictures of the Virgin Mary and of our Lord It is meant to represent a fish, from the anagram ICHTHUS (*q v*)

Vespers The sixth of the seven canonical hours in the Greek and Roman Churches; sometimes also used of the Evening Service in the English Church From Lat *vesperus*, the evening, cognate with *Hesperus* (*q v*), Gr *Hesperos*, the evening star

The Fatal Vespers. October 26th, 1623 A congregation of some 300 had assembled in a small gallery over the gateway of the French ambassador, in Blackfriars, to hear Father Drury, a Jesuit, preach The gallery gave way, and Drury with another priest and about 100 of the congregation were killed This accident was attributed to God's judgment against the Jesuits.

The Sicilian Vespers. *See* SICILIAN

Vesta. The virgin goddess of the hearth in Roman mythology, corresponding to the Greek *Hestia*, one of the twelve great Olympians. She was custodian of the sacred fire brought by Æneas from Troy, which was never permitted to go out lest a national calamity should follow

Wax matches are named from her

Vestals The six spotless virgins who tended the sacred fire brought by Æneas from Troy and preserved by the state in a sanctuary in the Forum at Rome They were subjected to very severe discipline, and in the event of losing their virginity were buried alive

Other duties of the Vestal Virgins were to prepare from the first fruits of the May harvest the sacrificial meal for the Lupercalia, the Vestalia, and the Ides of September

The word *vestal* has been figuratively applied to any woman of spotless chastity Thus, Shakespeare calls Elizabeth I—

A fair vestal, throned by the west
Midsummer Night's Dream, ii, 1

See also VENUS VERTICORDIA.

Veteran. Whereas in Britain this word is applied only to soldiers, etc, who have had long service under arms, in the U S A one who has had any service or experience in some field of warfare, however brief or casual, is termed a veteran

Veto (vē' tō) (Lat., I forbid) Louis XVI and Marie Antoinette were called *Monsieur* and *Madame Veto* by the Republicans, because the Constituent Assembly (1791) allowed the king to have the power of putting his veto upon any decree submitted to him and he abused it

The power exercised by the head of a state to annul or negative a law or ordinance passed by a lower body, in brief, the right to say "No"

Vexillum (veks il' ûm) (Lat, a standard). The standard borne by troops of the Roman army In particular it was the red flag flown on the general's tent as a signal for marching or for battle

Via. A way (Lat *via*) Our use of the word, as in *I'll go via Chester*, i e "by way of Chester," is *via*, the ablative of *via*.

Via Appia. The Appian Way (*q v*)

Via Dolorosa The way our Lord went from the Mount of Olives to Golgotha, about a mile in length

Via Lactea. The Milky Way (*q v*)

Via Sacra, the street in ancient Rome where Romulus and Tatius (the Sabine) swore mutual alliance It does not mean the "holy street," but the "street of the oath "

Vial. Vials of wrath. Vengeance, the execution of wrath on the wicked The allusion is to the seven angels who pour out upon the earth their vials full of wrath (*Rev.* xvi)

Viaticum (Lat) The Eucharist administered to the dying The word means "provision for a journey" and its application is obvious

Vicar. A parish priest who receives a stipend, the tithes belonging to a chapter, religious house, layman, etc (*cp* CLERICAL TITLES). At the Reformation the rectorial offices and tithes of many parishes hitherto administered by the religious orders, were granted to laymen, colleges, etc, who were under obligation of appointing vicars to perform the sacred offices

Lay vicar. A cathedral officer who sings those portions of the liturgy not reserved for the clergy Formerly called a *clerk vicar*

Vicar apostolic In the Roman Catholic Church, a titular bishop appointed to a place where no episcopate has been established, or where the succession has been interrupted. From 1623 until 1850 the Roman Catholic Church in England was governed by vicars apostolic The term formerly denoted a bishop to whom the Pope delegated some part of his jurisdiction

Vicar choral. One of the minor clergy, or a layman, attached to a cathedral for singing certain portions of the service

Vicar forane. A priest appointed by a Roman Catholic bishop to exercise limited (usually disciplinary) jurisdiction in a particular part of his diocese

Vicar-General An ecclesiastical functionary assisting a bishop or archbishop in his visitations, etc.

The Vicar of Bray A semi-legendary vicar of Bray, Berkshire, who, between 1520 and 1560, was twice a Papist and twice a Protestant in successive reigns. His name has been given as Symonds, Alleyne, and Pendelton, and his date transferred to the time of Charles II Historically nothing is known of him, the well-known song is said to have been written in Restoration times by an officer in Colonel Fuller's regiment

Brome says of Simon Alleyn that he "lived in the reigns of Henry VIII, Edward VI, Mary, and Elizabeth In the first two reigns he was Protestant, in Mary's reign he turned Papist, and in the next reign recanted—being resolved, whoever was king, to die Vicar of Bray "

The Vicar of Christ. A title given to the Pope, in allusion to his claim to be the representative of Christ on earth

The Vicar of Hell A name playfully given by Henry VIII to John Skelton, his "poet laureate," perhaps because Skelton was rector of Diss, in Norfolk, the pun being on Dis (*q v*) Milton refers to the story in his *Areopagitica* —

I name not him for posterity's sake, whom Henry the Eighth named in merriment his vicar of hell

Vice. The buffoon in the old English moralities He wore a cap with ass's ears, and was generally named after some particular vice, as Gluttony, Pride, etc.

Vice versa (vī' sɪ vēr' sa) (Lat , *vicis*, change, *versa*, turned) The reverse, the terms of the case being reversed

Vicegerent (vīs jer' ent) An official deputed by the head of the state to exercise that ruler's powers and authority The word is often confused with a vice-regent, who is, as the term implies, a deputy regent, or one who acts for a regent when he is unable by illness or from some other cause to exercise his powers

Vichy (vish' ɪ) A little town in the Department of Allier, in central France, formerly fashionable on account of its thermal and medicinal springs The name of Vichy will, however, be remembered in future as the seat of government set up by Marshal Petain after the fall of France, in June, 1940 By the armistice of July 10th France was divided into two zones, one occupied by the Germans, the other unoccupied and a totalitarian state under the rule of Pétain On the landing of the Allies in North Africa in the autumn of 1942 the Germans declared the whole country to be in danger of invasion and seized the excuse to occupy the *soi-disant* independent zone of France

Vicious Circle. A chain of circumstances, in which the solving of a problem creates a new problem which makes the original problem more difficult of solution

In logic, the fallacy of proving one statement by another which itself rests on the first for proof

Victoria Cross. A decoration for "conspicuous bravery or devotion to the country in the presence of the enemy." The decoration was instituted by Queen Victoria in 1856, the design being a Maltese cross of bronze, with a scroll underneath bearing the words "For Valour." It is worn on the left breast, suspended by a red ribbon and takes precedence of all other decorations Until 1942 the crosses were made from the metal of guns captured by the British at Sevastopol Well over a thousand Crosses have been awarded Only three men have won a bar to the V C

Victory Medal. A bronze medal with a double rainbow ribbon, awarded to Allied soldiers who served in a field of war in World War I

Victrola (U S.A.) Although the trade name of a certain make of phonograph (gramophone) the word is frequently used for any type of that instrument.

View Holloa. The shout of huntsmen when a fox breaks cover = "Gone away!" *Cp* SOHO, TALLY-HO

Vigilance Committee. A privately formed body of citizens taking upon themselves to assist in the maintenance of law and order in their town The Southern States citizens sometimes form themselves into Vigilance Committees for the purpose of intimidating Negroes During the Civil War (1861-65) they also strove to suppress the activities of loyalists to the Northern cause Members of these committees are called *Vigilantes*

Vignette (vɪ nyet) An engraving, especially on the title-page of a book, that is not enclosed within a border, properly, a likeness having a border of vine-leaves round it (Fr., little vine, tendril)

Viking (vīk' ɪng. vī' kɪng) A Norse pirate of about the 8th to 10th centuries A D , probably so called from Icel. *vig* war, cognate with Lat *vincere*, to conquer The word is not connected with *king*. There were *sea-kings*, sometimes, but erroneously, called "vikings," connected with royal blood, and having small dominions on the coast, who were often *vikingr* or vikings, but the reverse is not true that every *viking* or pirate was a sea-king.

Villain means simply one attached to a villa or farm (late Lat *villanus*, a farm-servant, from *villa*, a farm) In feudal times the lord was the great landowner, and under him were a host of tenants called *villains* (sometimes spelt *villein*, to differentiate this from the modern meaning) The highest class of villains were called *regardant*, and were annexed to the manor; then came the *Colibertı* or *Bures*, who were privileged vassals, then the *Bordarıı* or cottagers (A S *bord*, a cottage), who rendered certain menial offices to their lord for rent, then the *Coscets, Cottarıı*, and *Cotmannı*, who paid partly in produce and partly in menial service, and, lastly, the *villains in gross*, who were annexed to the person of the lord, and might be sold or transferred as chattels The notion of wickedness and worthlessness associated with the word is simply the effect of aristocratic pride and exclusiveness

I am no villain; I am the youngest son of Sir Rowland de Boys, he was my father, and he is thrice a villain that says such a father begot villains.—*As You Like It*, ɪ, ɪ

Vim. Slang for energy, force, "go." The accusative of Lat *vis*, strength

Vin. (Fr , wine)

Vin de Goutte. The last pressing of grapes, yielding an inferior wine

Vin de Paille. A sweet wine from the Jura, made from grapes dried on straw before pressing

Vin Gris. A cheap wine made in eastern France by mixing red and white grapes.

Vin ordinaire. A cheap wine served in restaurants when no style or mark is asked for

Vin Rosé. Pink wine made in France by one of three methods, by mixing red and white grapes, by colouring white wine with cochineal, or from black grapes the skins of which are not left to ferment in the wine.

Vintage. Gathering of grapes The year in which a certain wine was made. Since good vintages are more generally remembered, "a vintage year" has become a phrase descriptive of a year notable in any walk of life

Vinaigret (vin ā gret'). A small bottle, usually delicately ornamented, containing aromatic vinegar, smelling salts, etc., in use among women when fainting was a more common expression of emotion

Vinayapitaka *See* TRIPITAKA.

Vincent, St A deacon of Saragossa, martyred in the Dacian persecution, 304, and commemorated on January 22nd He is a patron saint of drunkards, for no apparent reason, an old rhyme says —

> If on St Vincent's Day the sky is clear
> More wine than water will crown the year

Vincentian. A Lazarist (*q v*), a member of the order of Lazarites, founded by St Vincent de Paul in the 17th century

Vine. The Rabbis say that the fiend buried a lion, a lamb and a hog at the foot of the first vine planted by Noah, and that hence men receive from wine ferocity, mildness, or wallowing in the mire

Vinegar. Livy tells us that when Hannibal led his army over the Alps to enter Rome he used vinegar to dissolve the snow, and make the march less slippery Nepos has left a short memoir of Hannibal, but says nothing about the vinegar. (Livy, 59 B C to A D 17; Nepos about the same time; Hannibal, 247-183 B C)

The Vinegar Bible. *See* BIBLE SPECIALLY NAMED

Vinegar Joe. World War II nickname of General Joseph W Stilwell, U.S Commander of troops in China

Vineyard Controversy A paper war provoked by Daines Barrington (1727-1800), a well-known lawyer, naturalist, and antiquary, who entered the lists to overthrow all chroniclers and antiquaries from William of Malmesbury to Samuel Pegge, respecting the vineyards of Domesday Book He maintained that the vines were currants, and the vineyards currant gardens

Vinland. The name given in the old Norse Sagas to a portion of the coast of North America discovered by wanderers from Denmark or Iceland about the opening of the 11th century There have been many conjectures as to the locality, but scholars incline to the opinion that it was in or near Mount Hope Bay, Rhode Island, and got its old name because of grape-vines found growing there

Vino (vī′ nō) **In vino veritas** (Lat) In wine is truth, meaning when persons are more or less intoxicated they utter many things they would at other times conceal or disguise

Vintage. *See* VIN.

Vintry Ward (London) So called from the site occupied by the Vintners or wine-merchants from Bordeaux, who anciently settled on this part of the Thames bank They landed their wines here, and, till the 28th Edw I, were obliged to sell what they landed within forty days.

Vinum Theologicum (vī′ num thē ō loj′ i kum). An old term for the best wine obtainable Holinshed (i, 282) says it was so called because religious men would be sure "neither to drinke nor be served of the worst, or such as was anie waies vined by the vintner, naie, the merchant would have thought that his soule would have gone streightwaie to the devil if he would have served them with other than the best "

Violet. A flower, nowadays usually taken as the type of modesty, but fabled by the ancients to have sprung from the blood of the boaster Ajax

The colour indicates the *love of truth* and the *truth of love* For ecclesiastical and symbolical uses, *see* COLOURS.

In "flower language" the violet is emblematical of *innocence*, and Ophelia says in *Hamlet* that the King, the Queen, and even Hamlet himself, now he has killed Polonius, are unworthy of this symbol

Corporal Violet. Napoleon Bonaparte, because when banished to Elba he told his friends he would return with the violets "Corporal Violet" became a favourite toast of his partisans, and when he reached Fréjus a gang of women assembled with violets, which were freely sold The shibboleth was, "Do you like violets?" If the answer given was "*Oui*," the person was known not to be a confederate; but if the answer was "*Eh bien*," the respondent was recognized as an adherent

The Violet-crowned City. *See* CITY

The violet on the tyrant's grave (Tennyson, *Aylmer's Field*) The reference is to Nero It is said that some unknown hand went by night and strewed violets over his grave We are told that at his death his statues were "crowned with garlands of flowers."

Violin *See* AMATI, CREMONA, STRAD, FIDDLE.

V.I.P Very Important Person, a phrase originated in World War II to indicate one whose importance was considered such as to entitle him to preferential treatment in travelling, etc

Viper (U S.A) A slang term for a smoker of marijuana

Viper and File The biter bit Æsop says a viper found a file, and tried to bite it, under the supposition that it was good food; but the file said that its province was to bite others, and not to be bitten

Virago (vi ra′ gō) Literally a man-like woman, but a term usually employed to designate a turbulent or scolding shrew

Viraj *See* MENU

Virgate. An early English measure of land; equal, sometimes to a quarter of a hide (i e. about 30 acres), and sometimes to a quarter of an acre. So called from Lat. *virga*, a measuring rod

Virgil (vėr′ jil) The greatest poet of ancient Rome, Publius Virgilius Maro (70-19 B C), born near Mantua (hence called *The Mantuan Swan*), a master of epic, didactic, and idyllic poetry His chief works are the *Æneid*, the *Eclogues* or *Bucolics*, and the *Georgics* From the *Æneid* grammarians illustrated their rules and rhetoricians selected the subjects of their declamations, and even Christians looked on the poet as half inspired, hence the use of his poems in divination *See* SORTES.

In the Middle Ages Virgil came to be represented as a magician and enchanter, and it is this traditional character that furnishes Dante with his conception of making Virgil, as the personification of human wisdom, his guide through the infernal regions

Virgil was wise, and as craft was considered a part of wisdom, especially over-reaching the spirits of evil, so he is represented by mediæval writers as outwitting the demon On one occasion, the legend says, he saw an imp in a hole on a mountain and the imp promised to teach the poet the black art if he released him Virgil did so, and after learning all the imp could teach him, expressed amazement that one of such imposing stature could be squeezed into so small a rift The imp said, "Oh, that is not wonderful," and crept into the hole to show Virgil how it was done, whereupon Virgil closed up the hole and kept the imp there This tale is almost identical with that of the *Fisherman and the Genie* in the *Arabian Nights*, indeed, most of the mediæval stories that have crystallized round the name of the great Roman poet (*see*, for instance, those in the *Gesta Romanorum*) have a strong Oriental colouring

The Christian Virgil. Marco Girolamo Vida (d. 1566), an Italian Latin poet, author of *Christias* in six books (1535), an imitation of the *Æneid*

The Virgil and Horace of the Christians. So Bentley calls Aurelius Clemens Prudentius (fl about A D 400) He was a native of Spain, and the author of several Latin hymns and religious poems

Virgin One of the ancient constellations (*Virgo*), and a sign of the Zodiac (Aug 23rd to Sept 23rd) The constellation is the metamorphosis of Astræa (*q v*), goddess of justice, who was the last of the deities to quit our earth *See* ICARIUS

The word *virgin* is used as a prefix denoting that the article has never been used, tried, or brought into cultivation, as *paper of virgin whiteness*, paper that is unwritten, or unprinted upon, a *virgin fortress*, one that has never been captured; a *virgin forest*, one that man has never attempted to tame or make use of

Virgin Birth. In theology the doctrine—in the R C Church the dogma—that the miraculous birth of Christ did not impair the virginity of His mother, our Lady, and that she remained a virgin to the day of her death

The Virgin Mary's Bodyguard. The name given to the old Scottish guard in France, organized in 1448 by Charles VII, because—it is said—Louis XI nominated the Blessed Virgin their colonel, also to the 7th Dragoon Guards, because in the time of George II they served under Maria Theresa of Austria.

The Virgin Queen. Elizabeth I, also called (by Shakespeare) "the fair Vestal"

Virginal A musical instrument of the 16th and 17th centuries, also called *a pair of virginals*. It has been suggested that it was so called because it was used in convents to lead the *virginals* or hymns to the Virgin, but it is more probable that it was simply because it was adapted to the use of young girls. It was a quilled keyboard instrument of two or three octaves

Virginia. The State of Virginia is the first of the original American colonies, having been founded by Sir Walter Raleigh in 1584 and named after Elizabeth I of England, the Virgin Queen His colony was probably planted on Roanoke Island and was in what is now North Carolina, but for many years the whole seaboard from Florida to Newfoundland was known as Virginia

Virginia fence. An irregular fence made of roughly laid logs. Benjamin Franklin describes a drunkard's uncertain progression as resembling a Virginia fence.

Virgo. *See* VIRGIN

Virtues, The Seven Faith, Hope, Charity, Prudence, Justice, Fortitude, and Temperance The first three are called the *supernatural, theological*, or *Christian* virtues, the remaining four are Plato's *Cardinal* virtues *Cp* SEVEN DEADLY SINS

Virtuoso (vĕr tū ō' zō) An Italian word meaning skilled It is now applied almost exclusively to a musical artist who has achieved an eminent mastery over the instrument upon which he performs

Vis inertiæ (vis in ĕr' shē) (Lat , the power of inactivity) It is a common mistake to imagine that inertia means absence of motion, inertia is that property of matter which makes it resist any change Thus it is hard to set in motion what is still, or to stop what is in motion Figuratively, it applies to that unwillingness of change which makes men "rather bear the ills they have than fly to others they know not of."

Visa (vē' za) The official endorsement made on a passport by the embassy or consulate of the country to which the traveller intends to go Without such visa he would not be allowed entry

Viscount (vī' kount) A peer ranking next below an Earl and above a Baron In 1440 the title became a degree of honour and was made hereditary, the first Viscount being John, Lord Beaumont The coronet of a Viscount bears 16 silver balls, and he is styled by the Sovereign "Our right trusty and well-beloved Cousin."

Vishnu (vish' nū) The Preserver, the second member of the Hindu trinity, though worshipped by many Hindus as the supreme deity He has had 9 incarnations, or *Avatars* (*q v*), and there is one—Kalki—still to come, during which Vishnu will at the end of four ages destroy sin, the sinful, and all the enemies of the world He is usually represented as four-armed and carrying a club, a shell, a discus, and a lotus, a bow and sword are slung at his side, and on his breast is a peculiar mark called the *Shrivatta* He has millions of worshippers, especially under his Avatars as Rama and Krishna

Vision of Piers Plowman, The. A long allegorical poem in Middle English alliterative verse, written between 1362 and 1400 by probably as many as four or five different authors On internal evidence the first part has for long been ascribed to William Langland or Langley, who came from Shropshire and settled in London

The title should really be "The Vision concerning Piers the Plowman," for in the earlier part Piers typifies the simple, pious, English labourer, and in the later Christ Himself. The poet supposes himself falling asleep on the Malvern Hills, and in his dream sees various visions of an allegorical character, bearing on the vices of the times The whole poem consists of nearly 15,000 verses, and is divided into twenty parts, each part being called a *passus*.

As a whole the picture is confused and depressing, but in detail it is often very powerful, e g the description of the crowded scene in the first prologue, the figures of Holy Church, Lady Meed, the Seven Deadly Sins, Piers himself, the Rat Parl ament, etc. It lacks Chaucer's humorous and cultured touch, but atones by its earnestness and sympathy.—E W EDMUNDS: *Hist Summary of Eng Lit*, II, D, iii,

Visitation. In common parlance this means an unwanted—and usually protracted—visit from an unwelcome person As an ecclesiastical term it is applied to the official visit a bishop pays to every parish in his diocese. **A herald's visitation** was the tour a herald made among country towns and seats to ascertain and record the genealogies and right to bear coat armour of the nobility and gentry of England This was primarily done for the purposes of taxation.

The **Visitation** is the term applied in theology to Our Lady's visit to St Elizabeth before the birth of John *Luke* i, 40 et seq It is celebrated on 2 July.

Visual Aids. Instructive diagrams, pictures, pictorial maps, etc., hung on schoolroom walls to familiarize the scholars with the information contained on them.

Vitex (vī′ teks) The Latin name of the *Agnus Castus*, or *chaste-tree* In the language of flowers it means "insensibility to love" Dioscorides, Pliny, and Galen mention the plant as a mild anaphrodisiac and say that the Athenian ladies used to strew their couches with the leaves of *vitex* as a palladium of chastity *Vitex*, from *vieo*, to bind with twigs; so called from the flexible nature of the twigs

Vitus, St. (vī′ tus) A Sicilian youth who was martyred with Modestus, his tutor, and Crescentia, his nurse, during the Diocletian persecution, 303. All three are commemorated on June 15th

St Vitus's dance In Germany it was believed in the 16th century that good health for a year could be secured by anyone who danced before a statue of St. Vitus on his feast day, this dancing developed almost into a mania, and came to be confused with chorea, which was subsequently known as *St Vitus's dance*, the saint being invoked against it.

Viva! (vī′ vä, vē′ vä). An exclamation of applause or joy, Italian, meaning (long) live

Viva voce (Latin, with the living voice) Orally, by word of mouth. A *viva voce* examination is one in which the respondent answers by word of mouth

Vivat regina (rex)′ (Lat) Long live the Queen (King)′ At the coronation of British Sovereigns the boys of Westminster School have the privilege of acclaiming the King or Queen with shouts of "Vivat Rex (or Regina) "

Vivandière (vē von dē âr′) A woman officially attached to a French regiment for the purpose of selling liquor to the troops.

Vivien (viv′ yen). An enchantress of the Arthurian romances, called also *Nimue* and, because she lived in a palace in the middle of a magic lake, *The Lady of the Lake*. It was here that she brought up Launcelot, hence called *Launcelot of the Lake*

Vixen (A S *fyxen*) A female fox Metaphorically, a shrewish woman, one of villainous and ungovernable temper

Vixere fortes ante Agamemnona. *See* AGAMEMNON

Viz. A contraction of Lat *videlicet*, meaning *namely*, *to wit* The z represents 3, a common mark of contraction in the Middle Ages; as hab3—*habet*, omnib3—*omnibus*

Vizier (vi zēr′). An Oriental title held by the minister of the Abbaside monarchs In prerevolution Turkey the head of each department of the council was styled Vizier The title was also held by the chief officer of the Mogul emperors

Vodka. A Russian spirituous liquor distilled from rye, barley, oats, potatoes, or maize It contains up to 95 per cent of alcohol, although for consumption this percentage is diluted down to about 50 per cent It is thus one of the strongest spirituous beverages drunk.

Vogue (vōg) A French word "In vogue" means in repute, in the fashion. The verb *voguer* means to sail or move forwards Hence the idea of sailing with the tide

Vogue la galère (Fr , lit , row the galley). Let the world go how it will, let us keep on, whatever happens, *arrive qui pourra*

Volapük (vol′ a puk) An artificial language invented in 1880 by Fr F Schleyer, an Austrian priest. It was supposed to be based on European languages, 40 per cent being English, but the words were so distorted and twisted by terminations and modifications that no original was recognizable For example, the name itself was said to be English —*Vol*, "English" *world*, *pük*, "English" *speech*.

Vole (Fr *voler*, to fly) He has gone the vole. He has been everything by turns *Vole* is a deal at cards that draws the whole tricks To vole is to win all the tricks.

Volstead Act A J Volstead (1860-1946) was one of the active Congressmen who secured the passing of the 18th Amendment to the Constitution of the U S A prohibiting the sale of intoxicating liquors On October 18th, 1919, he secured the passing of an Act of which he was the author to define the quantity of alcohol which made a particular liquor intoxicating This, together with the Amendment (which had passed over the veto of President Wilson) was repealed on December 5th, 1933.

Voltaic Battery An apparatus for accumulating electricity So called from the Italian physicist, Alessandro Volta (1745-1827), who first contrived it.

Voltaire. The assumed name of François Marie Arouet (1694-1778), the great French philosopher, poet, dramatist, and author He began to use the name on issuing from imprisonment in the Bastille, in 1718 *Voltaire* is an anagram of Arouet L I (*le jeune*).

Volume. The *word* shows the ancestry of the *thing*; for it comes from Lat *volvere*, to roll, and anciently books were written on sheets fastened together lengthwise and *rolled* on a pin or roller

Volund. *See* WAYLAND

Voodoo, or **Voodooism.** A system of magic and witchcraft which includes snake-worship and, in its extreme forms, human sacrifices and cannibalism It is said to be a relic of African barbarism and is still practised in Haiti and other parts of the West Indies and Southern American States

The name is thought to have been first given to it by missionaries from Fr *Vaudois*, a Waldensian, as these were accused of sorcery, but Sir Richard Burton derived it from *vodun*, a dialect form of Ashanti *obosum*, a fetish or tutelary spirit.

Vorticism (vôr' ti sizm) The name adopted in the early 20th century to describe an artistic movement on Futurist lines, and, like Futurism, including literature It insisted on the imaginative reconstruction of nature in formal designs, regarding the question of representation as irrelevant. Vorticist designs are in straight lines and angular patterns

Votive Offerings *See* ANATHEMA.

Voyageur (vwa ya zhĕr') A French Canadian or half-breed hired as a guide to the remoter stations of a fur or trading company on account of his skill as a boatman, tracker, and woodsman

Vox. Vox et præterea nihil (Lat , a voice, and nothing more) Empty words—"full of sound and fury, signifying nothing", a threat not followed out. When the Lacedemonian plucked the nightingale, on seeing so little substance he exclaimed, *Vox tu es, et nihil præterea* (Plutarch *Apophthegmata Laconica*)

Vox populi vox Dei (Lat , the voice of the people is the voice of God) This does not mean that the voice of the many is wise and good, but only that it is irresistible After Edward II had been dethroned by the people in favour of his son (Edward III), Simon Mepham, Archbishop of Canterbury, preached from these words as his text

Vulcan. A son of Jupiter and Juno, and god of fire, and the working of metals, and patron of handicraftsmen in mythology, identified with the Gr Hephæstus, and called also Mulciber, *i e* the softener.

His workshop was on Mount Etna, where the Cyclops assisted him in forging thunderbolts for Jove It is said that he took the part of Juno against Jupiter, and Jupiter hurled him out of heaven He was nine days in falling, and at last was picked up, half dead and with one leg broken, by the fishermen of the island of Lemnos It was he who, with the stroke of an axe, delivered Minerva from the head of Jupiter, and he was the author of Pandora, and the golden dogs of Alcinous, as he had the power of conferring life upon his creations Venus was his wife, and in consequence of her amour with Mars he came to be regarded as the special patron of cuckolds

Vulcanist. One who supports the Vulcanian or Plutonian theory, which ascribes the changes on the earth's surface to the agency of fire These theorists say the earth was once in a state of igneous fusion, and that the crust has gradually cooled down to its present temperature *Cp* NEPTUNIAN

Vulgate, The. The Latin translation of the Bible, made about 385-405 by St Jerome (*q v*), still used, with some modifications, as the authorized version by Roman Catholics In 1907 Pope Pius X entrusted to the Benedictines the revision of the Vulgate, and by 1949 the first eight books of the Old Testament had been issued by them

VXL. A punning monogram on lockets, etc , standing for U XL (you excel). U and V were formerly interchangeable

W

W. The twenty-third letter of the English alphabet The form is simply a ligature of two V's (VV); hence the name, for V was formerly the symbol of U (*q v*) as well as of V

Waac. The familiar name of a member of the *Women's Army Auxiliary Corps*, a body of women raised for non-combatant army service in World War I In World War II they were termed A T S (later R A T S) (Royal) Auxiliary Territorial Services

W.A.C (U S A) In World War II the Women's Army Corps, equivalent to the British R A T S

Wad. A roll of paper money, and hence money itself

Wade General Wade. The old rhyme—
Had you seen but these roads before they were made,
You would hold up your hands and bless General Wade

refers to Field-Marshal George Wade (1673-1748), famous for military highways in the Highlands, which proceed in a straight line up and down hill like a Roman road, and were made about 1726-33.

Wade's boat
They can so moché craft of Wadés boot,
So moché broken harm whan that hem list,
That with hem schuld I never lyv in rest
CHAUCER *Merchant's Tale*, 180

Wade was a hero of mediæval romance, whose adventures were a favourite theme in the 16th century His famous boat was named *Guingelot*

Wadham College (Oxford) was founded in 1613 by a bequest from Nicholas Wadham (1532-1609)

Wafer Ecclesiastically a thin disk of unleavened bread used in the Eucharist

Before the device of gummed envelope flaps was introduced, thin round disks of dried paste or gelatine were inserted between the flap and the envelope—or, earlier still, between the outer sides of the folded letter—and having been moistened and pressed with a seal served the same purpose of keeping the paper closed

Wag. Meaning a humorous person this word comes from the Old English *wagge*, probably from the facetious use of *waghalter*, a merry rogue

A wag is the last order even of pretenders to wit and good-humour. He laughs not because it is ridiculous but because he is under a necessity of laughing — STEELE *Tatler* No 184

Wager Anything staked or hazarded on the event of a contest, etc Connected with *gage* and *wage* (low Lat *wadiare*, to pledge)

Wager of battle. The decision of a contested claim by single combat—a common and legal method in Anglo-Saxon and early Norman times It had legal status in England until abolished by Act of Parliament in 1818

Wagga Blanket. A sort of sleeping-bag made of two corn sacks cut open and stitched together The name is taken from the town of Wagga Wagga. N S W

Waggoner An old sailors' name for a book of sea-charts, Dalrymple's Charts being known as the *English Waggoner* A corruption of Lukas *Waganaar*, a Dutch geographer whose charts were in use for long after their first appearance in the 16th century

Wagoner *See* BOÖTES

Wahabites (wa ha' bīts). A Mohammedan sect, whose object is to bring back the doctrines and observances of Islam to the literal precepts of the Koran, so called from the founder, Ibn-abd-ul-Wahab (d. 1787).

Wailing Wall of the Jews An enclosure in Jerusalem containing a wall said to be built of stones from Solomon's Temple Traditionally the Jews gather there every Friday for prayers and lamentations for the Dispersion and lost glories of Israel

Wait. Wait and see This was one of the most widely used and frequently caricatured political phrases of modern times. It was first used by H. H Asquith (Earl of Oxford & Asquith) as his answer to a question in the House of Commons, April 4th, 1910 No exception was taken to the answer at the moment, but when Asquith took to repeating it whenever posed with an awkward question, Members took it up and a time came when it was chanted by the whole Opposition when any question was put to him It soon took on as a catchword with the public, and remained for many years

Lords in Waiting, Gentlemen in Waiting, Grooms in Waiting, etc., are functionaries in the Royal Household for personal attendance upon the sovereign

Ladies in waiting (in the Queen's Household) are officially styled *Ladies of the Bedchamber*, *Bedchamber Women*, and *Maids of Honour*.

Waits. Street musicians, who serenade the principal inhabitants at Christmas-time, especi-

ally on Christmas Eve From Rymer's *Fœdera* we learn it was the duty of musical watchmen "to pipe the watch" nightly in the kings court four times from Michaelmas to Shrove Thursday, and three times in the summer, and they had also to make "the bon gate" at every door, to secure them against "pyckeres and pillers " They form a distinct class from both the watch and the minstrels Oboes were at one time called "waits "

Wake. The feast of the dedication of a church, which was formerly kept by watching all night, also the merrymaking held in connexion with this, hence merrymaking generally.

In Ireland the term denotes the watching of a dead body before the funeral by the friends and neighbours of the deceased, in which the lamentations were often followed by an orgy

Waking a witch If a witch were obdurate, the most effectual way of obtaining a confession was by what was termed *waking* her An iron bridle or hoop was bound across her face with prongs thrust into her mouth, this was fastened to the wall by a chain in such a manner that the victim was unable to lie down; and men were constantly by to keep her awake, sometimes for several days

Wake-robin. In England an arum, usually the cuckoo-pint. In the U S A a trillium, or jack-in-the-pulpit.

Walcheren Expedition, The (wol' sher ĕn) A disastrous undertaking during the French wars (1809) which, largely owing to the dilatoriness of the leaders, and to an outbreak of fever during which 7,000 British soldiers died, effected nothing, except the capture of Flushing Lord Chatham and Sir Richard Strachan had been sent to the island of Walcheren to destroy the French fleet in the Scheldt and take Antwerp The incident is commemorated in the following contemporary epigram —

> Lord Chatham, with his sword undrawn
> Is waiting for Sir Richard Strachan,
> Sir Richard, longing to be at 'em,
> Is waiting for the Earl of Chatham.

Waldensians or **Waldenses** (wol den' zianz, wol den' zēz) (also called the *Vaudois*) Followers of Peter Waldo of Lyons, who began a reform movement in the Church about 1170 They threw off the authority of the Pope, bishops, and all clergy, appointed lay-preachers (women among them), rejected infant baptism and many other rites, and made themselves so obnoxious to the ecclesiastical powers that they met with considerable persecution celebrated in one of Milton's sonnets This they survived, and their descendants in doctrine still exist, principally in the Alpine valleys of Dauphiné, and Piedmont.

Wales. The older form is *Wealthas* (plural of *Wealh*) an Anglo-Saxon word denoting foreigners, and applied by them to the ancient Britons, hence, also, *Corn-wall*, the horn occupied by the same "refugees " The Welsh proper are *Cimbri*, and call their country *Cymru*, those driven thither by the Teutonic invaders were refugees or strangers. *Cp* WALNUT

The Prince of Wales. The popular story is that the title arose thus When Edward I subdued Wales, he promised the Welsh, if they would lay down their arms, that he would give them a native prince who could not speak a word of English. His queen (Eleanor) having given birth to a son in Wales, the new-born child was entitled Edward, Prince of Wales, and ever since then the eldest son of the British sovereign has retained the title

The facts, however, are that Edward I obtained the submission of the Welsh in 1276, his eldest son, afterwards Edward II, was born at Carnarvon in 1284, and it was not till 1301 that he was created Prince of Wales

The male heir apparent to the throne is born *Duke of Cornwall*, but is not *Prince of Wales* until this title is conferred upon him, which it usually is At death, or succession to the Throne, it lapses to the Crown and can only be renewed at the Sovereign's pleasure Thus, when Edward VII became King his son did not immediately become Prince of Wales, the title was conferred on him eight months later

The Prince of Wales's feathers. The tradition is that the Black Prince, having slain John of Luxemburg, King of Bohemia, in the Battle of Cressy, assumed his crest and motto The crest consisted of three ostrich feathers, and the motto was *Ich dien* (I serve) Much controversy has arisen on the question, the crest, for instance, has been stated to be a rebus of Queen Philippa's hereditary title— viz Countess of *Ostre-vant* (ostrich-feather), and the motto a corruption of Welsh *Eich dyn,* behold the man *See* ICH DIEN

It should be noted that *Prince of Wales's feathers* is technically a misnomer, for the plume does not belong to him *as* Prince of Wales, but is the badge of the Heir Apparent, whether he holds that title or not.

Walhalla. *See* VALHALLA

Walk This is a remarkable word. It comes from the A S *wealcan,* to roll; whence we get *wealcere,* a fuller of cloth In Percy's *Reliques* we read —

> She cursed the weaver and the walker,
> The cloth that they had wrought

A walk-over. A very easy victory, as in a running match when one's rivals could be beaten by walking.

To make a man walk Spanish. To give him the sack, to give him his discharge

To walk into To thrash, also, to partake heartily of, as "to walk into an apple tart "

To walk off with To steal and decamp with

To walk out with To court, as a preliminary to marriage

In America a strike is called a *walk out*

To walk the chalk. An ordeal used at police stations, in barracks, on board ship, etc , as a test of sobriety. Two parallel lines are chalked on the floor and the delinquent must walk between them without stepping on either.

To walk the hospitals. To attend the hospitals as a medical student

To walk the plank. *See* PLANK

To walk through one's part. To repeat one's part at rehearsal verbally, but without dressing for it or acting it, to do anything appointed you in a listless, indifferent manner

Walking-out dress. Uniform, smarter than that used on duty, which British soldiers assume when leaving barracks in their free time

A walking-on part A part in a play in which the actor has only to walk about on the stage, sometimes with a word or two to say.

Walk not in the public ways The fifth symbol of the *Protreptics* of Iamblichus, meaning follow not the multitude in their evil ways, or, wide is the path of sin and narrow the path of virtue, few being those who find it.

Broad is the way that leadeth to destruction — *Matt* vii, 13

Hookey Walker! An early Victorian derisive exclamation meaning *Nonsense' Incredible'* used when hearing a "tall story" or some statement that cannot be trusted Many ingenious and patently inaccurate stories have been advanced to explain this phrase, its origin is unknown

To go by Walker's bus. To walk Similar expressions are, "To go by the Marrowbone stage," "To ride Shanks's pony "

Walkie-Talkie. (World War II) American small portable short-range wireless (containing receiver and transmitter) for use by infantry. Its equivalent has been adopted elsewhere by police, etc.

Walking Stewart. The nickname of John Stewart (1749-1822) The son of a London linen-draper, he secured a post in the East India Company and went to Madras After serious quarrels with his superiors he resigned and started out on his travels During the following years he went on foot through Hindustan, Persia, Nubia, Abyssinia, across the Arabian Desert, through Europe from Constantinople to England, passing through most of the Continental countries. In 1791 he crossed to America and walked through what was then known of Canada and the United States De Quincey says of him.—

A most interesting man   contemplative and crazy . yet sublime and divinely benignant in his visionariness This man as a pedestrian traveller had seen more of the earth's surface than any man before or since

Wall. To give the wall. To allow another, as a matter of courtesy, to pass by on the pavement at the side farthest from the gutter, hence, to be courteous. At one time pedestrians *gave the wall* to persons of a higher rank than themselves

Nathaniel Bailey's explanation of this phrase (1721) is worth perpetuating He says it is—

a compliment paid to the female sex, or those to whom one would show respect, by letting them go nearest the wall or houses, upon a supposition of its being the cleanest This custom is chiefly peculiar to England, for in most parts abroad they will give them the right hand, though at the same time they trust them into the kennel

To go to the wall To be put on one side; to be shelved This is in allusion to another phrase, *Laid by the wall*—*i e* dead but not buried, put out of the way

To hang by the wall To hang up neglected, not to be made use of (*Cymbeline*, iii, 4)

To take the wall To take the place of honour

I will take the wall of any man or maid of Montague's —*Romeo and Juliet*, i, 1

Walls have ears. Things uttered in secret get rumoured abroad, there are listeners everywhere, and you'd better be careful Certain rooms in the Louvre were said to be so constructed in the time of Catherine de' Medicis, that what was said in one room could be distinctly heard in another It was by this contrivance that the suspicious queen became acquainted with state secrets and plots The tubes of communication were called the *auriculaires* Cp DIONYSIUS'S EAR *under* EAR.

Wall Street. The thoroughfare in New York City which contains the Stock Exchange The name is hence used as a synonym for the American stock market.

The Roman Wall, from the Tyne to Bowness, on the Solway Firth, a distance of 80 miles Called—

The Roman Wall, because it was the work of the Romans.
Agricola's Wall, because Agricola made the south bank and ditch
Hadrian's Wall, because Hadrian added another vallum and mound parallel to Agricola's
The Wall of Severus, because Severus followed in the same line with a stone wall, having castles and turrets
The Picts' Wall, because its object was to prevent the incursions of the Picts

The Wall of Antoninus, now called *Graeme's Dyke*, from Dunglass Castle on the Clyde to Blackness Castle on the Forth, was made by Lollius Urbicus, legate of Antoninus Pius A D 140 It was a turf wall

Wall-eyed. The M E *wald-eyed*, a corruption of Icel *vald eygthr*, having a beam in the eye (*vagl* beam) Persons are wall-eyed when the white is unusually large, and the sight defective, due to opacity of the cornea, or when they have a divergent squint Shakespeare has *wall-eyed wrath or staring rage* (*King John*, iv, 3).

Wallaby. A small Australian kangaroo.

On the wallaby, or on the wallaby track. On the tramp—usually because out of work.

Wallace, Sir William (c. 1270-1305) One of the great national leaders of the Scots He was the son of Sir William Wallace, of Elderslie, Renfrewshire He totally defeated an English army of 50,000 men at Stirling, Sept 11th, 1297, thus driving the English from Scotland Edward I, however pursued Wallace as far as Falkirk where, on July 22nd, 1298, he routed the Scots army The beaten leader fled and little more is known of him until his betrayal to the English, near Glasgow, by Sir John Menteith, August 5th, 1305 Condemned as a traitor and rebel, Wallace was executed in London, August 22nd, 1305, his quarters being hung on gibbets at Newcastle-on-Tyne, Berwick, Stirling, and Perth

Wallace's Larder. *See* LARDER

Wallah (wol' a) Anglo-Indian for one who does something, as *Competition wallah*, the old nickname for a successful competitor in the Indian Civil Service exams, *bathroom wallah*, the man who looks after the bathrooms in an hotel, etc.

Wallflower. So called because it grows on old walls and ruined buildings It is a native plant Similarly, *wall cress, wall creeper*, etc, are plants which grow on dry, stony places, or on walls *Wall fruit* is fruit trained against a wall Cp WALNUT

Herrick has a pretty fancy on the origin of this flower. A fair damsel was long kept away from her lover, but at last.

Up she got upon a wall
'Tempting down to slide withal;
But the silken twist untied,
So she fell, and, bruised, she died
Love, in pity of the deed,
And her loving luckless speed,
Turned her to this plant we call
Now the "Flower of the wall"

Girls who sit out against the wall, not having partners during a dance, are called "wallflowers"

Walloon (wà loon') A people of mixed Italic, Teutonic, and Celtic stock descended from the Belgæ of ancient Gaul. They occupied the low track along the frontiers of the German-speaking territory, as Artois, Hainault, Namur, Liege, Luxemburg, with parts of Flanders and Brabant.

Wallop (wol' ŏp) To thrash; properly, to boil with a noisy bubbling sound The word is the same as *gallop* It is also a slang term for ale

Walnut The foreign nut; called in M E *wal-note*, from A S *wealh*, foreign It came from Persia, and was so called to distinguish it from nuts native to Europe, as hazel, filbert, chestnut.

Some difficulty there is in cracking the name thereof Why walnuts, having no affinity to a wall, should be so called The truth is *gual* or *wall* in the old Dutch signifieth "strange" or "exotic" (whence *Welsh* foreigners); these nuts being no natives of England or Europe—FULLER *Worthies of England*

It is said that the walnut tree thrives best if the nuts are beaten off with sticks, and not gathered Hence Fuller says, "Who, like a nut tree, must be manured by beating, or else would not bear fruit" (Bk ii, ch. 11). The saying is well known that—

A woman, a dog, and a walnut tree,
The more you beat them the better they be

Walpurgis Night (wol pĕr' gis). The eve of May Day, when the witch-world was supposed to hold high revelry under its chief on certain high places, particularly the Brocken, in Germany
Walpurgis was an English nun concerned in the introduction of Christianity into Germany She died Feb 25th, 779

Walstan, St The patron saint in England of husbandmen He was a rich Briton who gave up all his wealth, and supported himself by husbandry He died mowing in 1016, and is usually depicted with a scythe in his hand, and cattle in the background

Waltham Blacks. *See* BLACK ACT

Waltzing Matilda. A song sung by the Australian forces in the Middle East in World War II, and sharing with *Lili Marlene* (*q v*) pride of place as the best soldiers' song of the period. The phrase was originally "Walking Matilda," and as such is found in Australia in the late 19th century, it means carrying one's bag or roll, as a tramp does. The reason for a tramp's roll being called a "Matilda" is obscure, "to waltz" meaning to carry is American slang, and is found in Mark Twain's *Huckleberry Finn*, 1884

Once a jolly swagman camped by a billabong
Under the shade of a coolibah tree,
And he sang as he watched and waited till his billy
    boiled
"You'll come a waltzing Matilda with me "

Wampum (wom' pŭm) Shell beads strung for ornament, currency, and tribal records by some North American Indian peoples They are made of the perforated central columns of several kinds of marine shells The name comes from the Algonquin *wompi*, white

Wand. The long, slender rod used by magicians and conjurers; also by certain court functionaries as a staff of office, and by musical conductors as a baton

Wandering Jew, The. The central figure of a very widespread mediæval legend which tells how a Jew who refused to allow Christ to rest at his door while He was bearing his cross to Calvary, was condemned to wander over the face of the earth till the end of the world The usual form of the legend says that he was Ahasuerus, a cobbler The craftsman pushed Him away, saying, "Get off! Away with you, away!" Our Lord replied, "Truly I go away, and that quickly, but tarry thou till I come "

Another tradition has it that the Wandering Jew was Kartaphilos, the door-keeper of the judgment hall in the service of Pontius Pilate He struck our Lord as he led Him forth, saying, "Go on faster, Jesus", whereupon the Man of Sorrows replied, "I am going, but thou shalt tarry till I come again" (*Chronicle of St Albans Abbey*, 1228)

The same *Chronicle*, continued by Matthew Paris, tells us that Kartaphilos was baptized by Ananias, and received the name of Joseph At the end of every hundred years he falls into a trance, and wakes up a young man about thirty

In German legend he is associated with John Buttadæus, seen at Antwerp in the 13th century, again in the 15th, and a third time in the 16th His last appearance was in 1774 at Brussels In the French version he is named Isaac Laquedem, or Lakedion, another story has it that he was Salathiel ben Sadi, who appeared and disappeared towards the close of the 16th century, at Venice, in so sudden a manner as to attract the notice of all Europe, and another connects him with the Wild Huntsman (*q.v.*)

Wanderjahre (van' der ya' rě) In Germany, the year of travel a journeyman used to make before settling down to work This gave him an idea of how tradesmen of his own craft in other places worked

Wangle To achieve some object by sly, roundabout, or underhand methods, to cook accounts (for instance), to manipulate The word came into wide use during World War I,

but it was well-known slang among printers from very early times

Wanion. With a wanion. An old imprecation, the word is pres part of *wanion*, to wane, and meant misfortune, ill-luck

Look how thou stirrest now! come away, or I'll
fetch thee with a wannion —*Pericles*, ii, 1

Wantley, The Dragon of An old story, preserved in Percy's *Reliques*, tells of this monster, which was slain by More, of More Hall He procured a suit of armour studded with spikes, and kicked the Dragon in the mouth, where alone it was vulnerable Percy says the Dragon was an overgrown, rascally attorney, who cheated some children of their estate, and was made to disgorge by one named More, who went against him, "armed with the spikes of the law," after which the attorney died of vexation Wantley is Wharncliffe in Yorkshire

Wapentake (wop' en täk) A division of Yorkshire and certain East Anglian counties, similar to that better known as a *hundred* The word means "touch-arms" (A S *wæpengetæcke*, from Icel *vapn*, weapon, *taka*, to touch or take), it being the custom of each vassal, when he attended the assemblies of the district, "to touch the spear of his over-lord in token of homage "

Wapinshaw (wop' in shaw) The Scottish name for a meeting for rifle-shooting, curling, or similar sport Formerly, the periodical review of clansmen under arms, a *weapon-show*

War A holy war War undertaken from religious motives, such as the Crusades, or in defence of a religion

On the war-path. Looking for one's adversary with every intention of catching him, thoroughly roused or incensed

War game. A military training exercise consisting of a game played with maps, etc for developing skill in manœuvring troops and designing both strategy and tactics

War head The explosive head of a torpedo or bomb

War-horse. Used figuratively of a veteran who is overflowing with warlike memories, a "fire-eater "

War paint. The paint applied to their faces by Red Indians and other peoples to make their appearance terrifying before going out on the warpath *Putting on one's war paint* is a phrase applied figuratively to getting ready to enter energetically into a dispute or to putting on lipstick, powder, etc., in order to overcome one's rivals.

Ward A district under the charge of a *warden*. The word is applied to the subdivisions of Cumberland, Westmorland, and Durham, which, being contiguous to Scotland, were placed under the charge of lord wardens of the marches whose duty it was to protect these counties from inroads See HUNDRED.

The word has other applications —The administrative division of a town or city, a large room or division of a hospital; each of the separate divisions of a prison (under a *warder*), a minor placed under the care of a guardian, a part of a lock or of a key.

Ward Room. In British warships a mess shared by the Commander—unless he is in command of the vessel, when he messes alone —and all other officers down to and including lieutenants Junior officers mess in the gun room

Warden Pie Pie made of the Warden pear Warden pears are said to be so called from Warden, in Bedfordshire, but it is quite likely that the word is merely O Fr *wardant*, keeping, because they are good keeping pears.

> Myself with denial I mortify
> With a dainty bit of a Warden-pie
> *The Friar of Orders Grey*

Wardour Street English The affected use of archaic words and phrases The term was first applied by William Morris, in 1888, to a translation of the *Odyssey*, couched in language which reminded him of the pseudo-antique furniture that in those days was sold in Wardour Street, London

Warlock An evil spirit, a wizard A.S *war-loga*, a traitor, one who breaks his word

Warm Used in slang with much the same force as *hot* (*q v.*), as a *warm member*, said of a man who "goes the pace," of a sharper, or of one who is particularly notable in connexion with whatever happens to be the subject of discussion *Warm thanks*, are hearty thanks, *he's in a warm corner* means he's in an awkward position.

A house-warming. An entertainment given by new occupiers of a house, a first welcoming of friends to a fresh residence.

Warming-pan. One who holds a place temporarily for another, used specially of a clergyman who officiates while the actual holder of the living is qualifying In public schools it used to be the custom to make a fag warm his "superior's" bed by lying in it till the proper occupant was ready to turn him out

Jacobites used to be nicknamed *Warming-pans*, because of the widely believed story that the "Old Pretender" was a child who was introduced into the lying-in-chamber of Mary of Modena, queen of James II, in a warming-pan, her own child having been still-born

Warp The threads running the long way of a woven fabric, crossed by the *woof*, i e those running from selvedge to selvedge. *Warp* (A S *wearp*) is connected with Icel *varpa*, to throw, *woof* with A S *wef*, web

> Weave the warp and weave the woof,
> The winding-sheet of Edward's race,
> Give ample room and verge enough
> The characters of hell to trace
> GRAY *The Bard*

To warp is a nautical term, meaning to shift the position of a vessel, which is done by means of a rope called a *warp* Kedging is when the warp is bent to a kedge, which is let go, and the vessel is hove ahead by the capstan

In Lancashire, *warping* means laying eggs; and boys, on finding a bird's nest, will ask— 'And how many eggs has she warped ?''

Warrant Officer. In the British navy this is a rank between a commissioned officer and petty officers and men Warrant officers are promoted from the lower deck

In the Army and Air Force warrant officer is a rank between that of commissioned officer and non-commissioned officer

Warrior Queen, The. Boadicea, Queen of the Iceni, an ancient tribe of Eastern Britain subjugated by the Romans in A D 62

> When the British warrior queen,
> Bleeding from the Roman rods,
> Sought, with an indignant mien,
> Counsel of her country's gods
> COWPER *Boadicea*

The Iceni were the faithful allies of Rome, but, on the death of Prasutagus, king of that tribe, the Roman procurator took possession of his kingdom, and when his widow Boadicea complained, the procurator had her beaten with rods like a slave

Wash It will all come out in the wash. Everything will turn out all right in the end The phrase is Spanish, and occurs in *Don Quixote*

Quite washed out. Thoroughly exhausted, done up, with no strength or spirit left

That story won't wash! It won't do at all, you'll have to think of something better than *that*! Said of an excuse or explanation that is palpably false, far-fetched, or exaggerated.

To wash a brick To engage in an utterly unprofitable enterprise, to do useless work An old Latin proverbial expression (*laterem lavem*, Terence's *Phormio*, I, iv, 9)

To wash one's dirty linen in public To expose the family skeletons to the public gaze, openly to discuss private affairs that are more or less discreditable

Wash-out. A phrase made popular in World War I meaning a failure or fiasco As an imperative verb it means, cancel, disregard— "Wash out that instruction," disregard that order, consider it as never having been given It is really old Naval slang, dating from the times when signal messages were taken down on a slate which was washed clean when the message had been transmitted to the proper quarters

To wash one's hands of. *See* HAND.

Wassail A carouse, drinking bout, or other festive occasion

> The king doth wake to-night and takes his rouse,
> Keeps wassail *Hamlet*, i, 4

Formerly a salutation used specially at the New Year over the spiced ale cup, hence called the "wassail bowl" (A S *Wæs hæl*, be whole, be well)

An old story has it that when Vortigern was invited to dine at the house of Hengist, Rowena, the daughter, of the host, brought a cup of wine which she presented to their royal guest, saying, "*Wæs hæl*, *hlaford cyning*' (Your health, lord king). Robert de Brunne (late 13th cent) refers to this custom :—

> This is ther custom and hev gest
> When they are at the ale or fest
> Ilk man that levis gware him drink
> Salle say "Wasseille" to him drink,
> He that biddis sall say "Wassaile,"
> The tother salle say again "Drinkaille "
> That says "Wasseille" drinks of the cup
> Kiss and his felaw he gives it up

Hence *wassailers*, those who join a wassail, revellers, drunkards.

> I should be loath
> To meet the rudeness and swilled insolence
> Of such late wassailers   MILTON *Comus*

Waster, wastrel A good-for-nothing fellow; a prodigal, spendthrift

Wat. An old name for a hare, short for *Walter* Cp *Tom* for a cat, *Neddy* for a donkey, *Jenny* wren, etc

> By this, poor Wat, far off upon a hill,
> Stands on his hinder legs, with listening ear
> *Venus and Adonis*

Watch. In nautical usage, the time during which each division of a ship's crew is alternately on duty (four hours except during the *dog-watches* of two hours by which the change from night to day duty is arranged), also, either half (*starboard* or *port watch* from the position of the sailors' bunks in the forecastle) into which the officers and crew are divided, taking duty alternately.

12 to 4 p m.	Afternoon watch
4 to 6 „	First dog-watch
6 to 8 „	Second dog-watch
8 to 12 ,	First night watch.
12 to 4 a m	Middle watch
4 to 8 „	Morning watch
8 to 12 „	Forenoon watch

The Black Watch. *See* BLACK.

The Watch on the Rhine. A national song of the old German Empire, sharing the place of honour with *Deutschland uber Alles* (Germany over all)

Watch and ward Continuous vigilance, guard by night (*watch*) and by day (*ward*) In feudal times service "by watch and ward" was due by certain tenants in towns; later the term was applied to the constabulary

Watch Night. December 31st, to see the Old Year out and the New Year in by a religious service John Wesley grafted it on the religious system, and it has been adopted by many Christian communities

Watchful Waiting. A phrase used by President Wilson in 1915 to describe the policy of the U.S A towards Mexico, whose attitude was extremely unfriendly and provocative

Watchword. A word given to sentries as a signal that one has the right of admission, a password, hence, a motto, word, or phrase symbolizing or epitomizing the principles of a party, etc

Water. Blood thicker than water. *See* BLOOD

Court holy water Fair but empty words In French, *eau benite de cour*

I am for all waters (*Twelfth Night*, IV, 2) I am a Jack of all trades, can turn my hand to anything, a good all-round man Like a fish which can live in salt or fresh water.

In deep water. In difficulties, in great perplexity, similarly, *in smooth water* means all is plain sailing, one's troubles and anxieties are things of the past

In low water. Hard up, in a state of financial (or other) depression

It makes my mouth water. It is very alluring, it makes me long for it Saliva is excited in the mouth by strong desire

More water glideth by the mill than wots the miller of (*Titus Andronicus*, II, 1) The Scots say, "Mickle water goes by the miller when he sleeps " *See* MILLER.

Of the first water. Of the highest type, very excellent. *See* DIAMOND

Smooth, or still, waters run deep. Deep thinkers are persons of few words, he (or she) thinks a good deal more than is suspected, silent conspirators are the most dangerous, barking dogs do not bite A calm exterior is far more to be feared than a tongue-doughty Bobadil

> Smooth runs the water where the brook is deep,
> And in his simple show he harbours treason
> The fox barks not when he would steal the lamb
> No, no, my sovereign, Gloucester is a man
> Unsounded yet, and full of deep deceit
> *2 Henry VI*, III, 1

That won't hold water. That is not correct, it is not tenable It is a vessel which leaks.

The Father of Waters. The Mississippi, the chief river of North America The Missouri is its child The Irrawaddy is so called also

The water of jealousy If a woman was known to have committed adultery she was to be stoned to death, according to the Mosaic law (*Deut* xxii, 22) If, however, the husband had no proof, but only suspected his wife of infidelity, he might take her before the Sanhedrin to be examined, and if she denied it, she was given the "water of jealousy" to drink (*Numb* v, 11-29) In this water some of the dust of the sanctuary was mixed, and the priest said to the woman, "If thou hast gone aside may Jehovah make this water bitter to thee, and bring on thee all the curses written in this law." He then wrote on a roll the curses, sprinkled the writing with the water, gave it to the woman, and then handed to her the "water of jealousy" to drink

To back water To row backwards in order to reverse the forward motion of a boat in rowing, hence, to go easy, to retrace one's steps, to retract

To carry water to the river. To carry coals to Newcastle

To fish in troubled waters. To seek to turn a state of disturbance to one's own advantage, to "profiteer" during a time of war, to seize power during a revolution, and so on

To get into hot water. *See* HOT

To keep one's head above water. *See* HEAD

To throw cold water on a scheme To discourage the proposal; to speak of it slightingly

To turn on the waterworks. To cry, blubber

To water stock. To add extra shares Suppose a "trust" (*q.v*) consists of 1,000 shares of £50 each, and the profit available for dividend is 40 per cent , the managers "water the stock," that is, add another 1,000 fully paid-up shares to the original 1,000 There are now 2,000 shares, and the dividend, instead of £40 per cent , is reduced to £20, but the shares are more easily sold, and the shareholders are increased in number.

Water-gall. The dark rim round the eyes after much weeping A peculiar appearance in a rainbow which indicates more rain at hand

And round about her tear-distained eye
Blue circles streamed, like rainbows in the sky;
These watergalls foretell new storms
Rape of Lucrece

Waterman A boatman, especially one who rows a boat or skiff as a means of transport The Thames watermen were a feature of old London, when much passenger traffic was carried by water from Westminster as far down as Greenwich

Hackney-coach stands and cab ranks were each supplied with a licensed waterman whose duty it was to water the cab-horses and see that the drivers accepted fares in rotation

Watermark. A design impressed into paper while in course of manufacture. Watermarks were employed as early as 1282, and served to identify the product of each paper mill, the designs chosen (many of them extremely complicated) frequently also expressing emblematically the tenets of the manufacturers The art of papermaking was almost entirely in the hands of the Huguenots and previous Protestants (Albigenses, Waldenses, Cathari, etc), and the *Bull's head*, for instance, was an emblem of the Albigenses

The watermark has in many cases been the origin of paper-trade terminology, thus the mark of the *cap and bells* gave us *Foolscap*, the *Post-horn*, *Post*, the *Pot*, *Pott*, and so on—all sizes of paper

Water Poet. John Taylor (1580-1654), the humorous and sometimes scurrilous Thames waterman who confessed he never learnt a word of grammar, and yet wrote fourscore books and verse pamphlets In his closing days he opened an ale-house in Long Acre.

Taylor, their better Charon, lends an oar,
Once swan of Thames, though now he sings no more *Dunciad*, iii

Water-sky. The term used by Arctic navigators to denote a dark or brown sky, indicating an open sea An *ice-sky* is a white one, or a sky tinted with orange or rose-colour, indicative of a frozen sea (*cp.* ICE-BLINK)

Waterloo He met his Waterloo He had a final and crushing defeat, in allusion, of course, to the decisive defeat inflicted on Napoleon by Wellington at Waterloo in 1815.

The Waterloo Cup. The "Derby" of the coursing fraternity, the great dog-race held annually at Altcar during three days in February

It was founded in 1836 by a man named Lynn, the sporting owner of the Waterloo Hotel in Liverpool (whence its name) Lynn was also the founder of the Grand National, run at Aintree

Watling Street. The great Roman road extending east and west across Britain Beginning at Dover, it ran through Canterbury to London, thence through St Albans, Dunstable, along the boundary of Leicester and Warwick

to Wroxeter on the Severn, and so to Chester and Cardigan. *Watling* is said to be a corruption of *Vitellina strata*, the paved road of Vitellius, called by the Britons Guetalin.

Watson. *See* SHERLOCK HOLMES

Wattle. Australian settlers built wattle-and-daub huts after the English manner from twigs of the abundant acacia trees, which hence became known as Wattles *Wattle Day* is a national festival in Australia, held on August 1st, or September 1st according to the peak of the flowering of the wattle in each State

Wave. The tenth wave. A notion prevails that the waves keep increasing in regular series till the maximum arrives and then the series begins again No doubt when two waves coalesce they form a large one, but this does not occur at fixed intervals

The most common theory is that the *tenth* wave is the largest, but Tennyson says the *ninth*.

And then the two
Dropt to the cove, and watch'd the great sea fall,
Wave after wave, each mightier than the last,
Till last, a ninth one, gathering half the deep
And full of voices, slowly rose and plunged
Roaring, and all the wave was in a flame
The Holy Grail

Wavy Navy. The Naval slang name for the Royal Naval Volunteer Reserve (R N V.R.), the officers of which, in war-time, have the gold braid on their sleeves in wavy lines instead of straight

Waverley Novels. The novels of Sir Walter Scott (1771-1832) which took their name from the first of the series They were published anonymously "By the Author of Waverley" until 1827, when the author disclosed his identity as "The Great Unknown" at a public dinner at Edinburgh

Waverley, 1814, *Guy Mannering*, 1815 *The Antiquary, Old Mortality, Black Dwarf*, 1816, *Rob Roy, Heart of Midlothian*, 1818, *Bride of Lammermoor, Legend of Montrose*, 1819, *Ivanhoe, Monastery, Abbot*, 1820, *Kenilworth*, 1821, *The Pirate, Fortunes of Nigel*, 1822; *Peveril of the Peak, Quentin Durward*, 1823; *St. Ronan's Well, Redgauntlet*, 1824, *The Betrothed, Talisman*, 1825, *Woodstock*, 1826, *Two Drovers, Highland Widow, Surgeon's Daughter*, 1827, *Fair Maid of Perth*, 1828, *Anne of Geierstein*, 1829, *Count Robert of Paris*, 1831; *Castle Dangerous*, 1832

Wax Slang for temper, anger, *he's in an awful wax*, he's in a regular rage Hence waxy, irritated, vexed, angry

A man of wax. A model man, like one fashioned in wax Horace speaks of the "waxen arms of Telephus," meaning model arms, or of perfect shape and colour, and the nurse says of Romeo, "Why, he's a man of wax (i, 3), which she explains by saying, "Nay, he's a flower, i' faith a very flower "

A nose of wax Mutable and accommodating (faith) A waxen nose may be twisted any way.

Way The way of all flesh. Death

The way of the Cross *See* STATIONS OF THE CROSS

Under way Said of a ship in motion, it is a mistake to take this as "under *weigh*," and connect it with weighing the anchor

Wayleave. Right of way through private property for the laying of water-pipes, making of sewers, carrying of telephone wires, etc

Ways and Means A parliamentary term, meaning the method of raising the supply of money for the current requirements of the state.

Wayland A wonderful and invisible smith of English legend, the English form of Scandinavian Volund, a supernatural smith and King of the Elves, a kind of Vulcan He was bound apprentice to Mimi the smith. King Nidung cut the sinews of his feet, and cast him into prison, but he escaped in a feather boat He and Amilias had a contest of skill in their handicraft Wayland's sword, Balmung, cleft his rival down to the thighs, but it was so sharp that Amilias was not aware of the cut till he attempted to stir, when he divided into two pieces Tradition has placed his forge near Lambourn, Berks (since called *Wayland Smith's Cave*), where it was said that if a traveller tied up his horse there, left sixpence for a fee, and retired from sight, he would find the horse shod on his return

Wayzgoose An annual dinner, picnic, or "beanfeast" given to, or held by, those employed in a printing-house *Wayz* is an obsolete word for stubble, and a *wayzgoose* a "stubble goose," properly the crowning dish of the entertainment *See* BEANFEAST, ST MARTIN'S GOOSE

We. Used of himself by a Sovereign, as representing his subjects, by the editor of a newspaper, as the public representative of a certain body of opinion, and by a writer of an unsigned article, as representing the journal for which he is writing

Coke, in the *Institutes*, says the first king that wrote *we* in his grants was King John. All the kings before him wrote *ego* (I) This is not correct, as Richard *Lion-heart* adopted the royal "We " *See* Rymer's *Fœdera*.

"We are not amused!" A reproof attributed to Queen Victoria and frequently used as an ironical rebuke There is no authority whatever for supposing that the Queen made this remark. There is no record of her ever having used the royal "we" in other than official proclamations, nor is the spirit of the words in keeping with Queen Victoria's character.

Weal A prosperous or sound state of affairs, the A S. *wela*, cognate with *well* Hence, the *common weal*, or the *public weal*, the welfare or prosperity of the community at large

Weapon Salve. A salve said to cure wounds by sympathy, applied not to the wound, but to the instrument which gave the wound The direction "Bind the wound and grease the nail" is still common Sir Kenelm Digby says the salve is sympathetic, and quotes several instances to prove that "as the sword is treated the wound inflicted by it feels. Thus, if the instrument is kept wet, the wound will feel cool, if held to the fire, it will feel hot", etc.

Weapon-schaw. *See* WAPINSHAW.

"Wearing of the Green, The." An immensely popular Irish revolutionary song, written about 1798, and known in Irish as "Shan Van Voght."

Weasel. Weasels suck eggs, hence Shakespeare:—

> The weazel Scot
> Comes sneaking, and so sucks the princely egg
> *Henry V*, i, 2

> I can suck melancholy out of a song, as a weazel sucks eggs —*As You Like It*, ii, 5

To catch a weasel asleep To expect to find a very vigilant person off his guard, to suppose that one who has his weather-eye open cannot see what is passing before him The vigilant habits of these animals explain the allusion

Pop Goes the Weasel The title of this song is said to refer the habit of London hatters of "popping," or pawning, their "weasels," or accessories, on Saturday nights, to buy liquor

(World War II.) A weasel is a jeep fitted with wide tracks instead of wheels, for carrying stores and personnel over deep mud The load was reduced to 1½ lb per square inch, a remarkable achievement.

Weather. A weather breeder. A day of unusual fineness coming suddenly after a series of damp dull ones, especially at the time of the year when such a genial day is not looked for Such a day is generally followed by foul weather.

Fair-weather friends Those that stick to you so long as all is going well, but desert you as soon as storms gather round your head and you look as though you might "go under"

I have my weather-eye open. I have my wits about me, I know what I am after. The weather-eye is towards the wind to forecast the weather

The peasant's weather-glass. A local name for the scarlet pimpernel, which closes its petals at the approach of rain It is also called *the poor man's warning*.

> Closed is the pink-eyed pimpernel
> 'Twill surely rain, I see with sorrow,
> Our jaunt must be put off to-morrow
> *Dr Jenner*

To get the weather-gage of a person. To get the advantage over him A ship is said to have the weather-gage of another when it has got to the windward thereof.

> Were the line
> Of Rokeby once combined with mine,
> I gain the weather-gage of fate
> *Scott Rokeby.*

To keep the weather of. To get round, or get the better of. A phrase from the seaman's vocabulary.

> Mine honour keeps the weather of my fate
> Life every man holds dear but the dear man
> Holds honour far more precious dear than life
> *Troilus and Cressida*, v, 3

To make fair weather. To flatter, conciliate, make the best of things

> But I must make fair weather yet awhile,
> Till Henry be more weak, and I more strong
> *2 Henry VI*, v, 1

Weathercock. By a Papal enactment made in the middle of the 9th century, the figure of a cock was set up on every church steeple as the emblem of St Peter The emblem is in allusion to his denial of our Lord thrice before the cock crew twice On the second crowing of the cock the warning of his Master flashed across his memory, and the repentent apostle "went out and wept bitterly "

A person who is always changing his mind is, figuratively, a *weathercock*.

> Ther is no feith that may your herte embrace,
> But, as a wedercock, that turneth his face
> With every wind, so fare.
> CHAUCER (?) *Balade Against Women Unconstant*

Web. *See* WARP

The web of life. The destiny of an individual from the cradle to the grave The allusion is to the three Fates who, according to Roman mythology spin the thread of life, the pattern being the events which are to occur.

Web and pin. An old name for cataract, or a disease of the eye caused by some excrescence on the ball

> This is the foul fiend Flibbertigibbet . . he gives the web and pin, squints the eye, and makes the harelip —*King Lear*, iii, 4

Wed, Wedding. Wed is Anglo-Saxon, and means a *pledge* The ring is the pledge given by the man to avouch that he will perform his part of the contract

Wedding Anniversaries. Fanciful names have been given to many wedding anniversaries, the popular idea being that they designate the nature of the gifts suitable for the occasion The following list is fairly complete, and of these very few except the twenty-fifth and fiftieth are ever noticed

First	Cotton Wedding
Second	Paper Wedding
Third	Leather Wedding
Fifth	Wooden Wedding
Seventh	Woollen Wedding
Tenth	Tin Wedding
Twelfth	Silk and Fine Linen Wedding
Fifteenth	Crystal Wedding
Twentieth	China Wedding
Twenty-fifth	Silver Wedding
Thirtieth	Pearl Wedding
Fortieth	Ruby Wedding
Fiftieth	Golden Wedding
Seventy-fifth	Diamond Wedding

The sixtieth anniversary is often reckoned the "Diamond Wedding" in place of the seventy-fifth, as the sixtieth year of Queen Victoria's reign was her "Diamond Jubilee "

Wedding Finger. The fourth finger of the left hand Macrobius says the thumb is too busy to be set apart, the forefinger and little finger are only half protected, the middle finger is called *medicus*, and is too opprobious for the purpose of honour, so the only finger left is the *pronubus*.

Aulus Gellius tells us that Appianus asserts in his Egyptian books that a very delicate nerve runs from the fourth finger of the left hand to the heart, on which account this finger is used for the marriage ring

> The finger on which this ring [the wedding-ring] is to be worn is the fourth finger of the left hand, next unto the little finger, because by the received opinion of the learned in ripping up and anatomising men's bodies, there is a vein of blood, called *vena amoris*, which passeth from that finger to the heart —HENRY SWINBURNE: *Treaties of Spousals* (1680).

In the Roman Catholic Church, the thumb and first two fingers represent the Trinity, thus the bridegroom says, "In the name of the Father," and touches the thumb, "in the name of the Son," and touches the first finger, and "in the name of the Holy Ghost" he touches the long or second finger, with the word "Amen" he then puts it on the third finger and leaves it there In some countries the wedding-ring is worn on the right hand, this was the custom generally in England until the end of the 16th century, and among Roman Catholics until much later.

In the Hereford, York, and Salisbury missals, the ring is directed to be put first on the thumb, then on the first finger, then on the long finger, and lastly on the ring-finger, *qua in illo digito est quædam vena procedens usque ad cor*

Wedlock This word comes from Old English *wed*, a pledge, and *lac*, a promise, the whole meaning the marriage vow It does not, therefore, imply the unopenable lock of marriage, as has sometimes been supposed.

Wednesday Woden-es or Odin-es Day, called by the French "Mercredi" (Mercury's Day) The Persians regard it as a "red-letter day," because the moon was created on the fourth day (*Gen.* i, 14-19)

Weeds. The mourning worn by a widow, from A S. *wæde*, a garment Spenser speaks of—

> A goodly lady clad in hunter's weed
> *Faerie Queene*, II, iii, 21

Shakespeare has—

> And there the snake throws her enamell'd skin,
> Weed wide enough to wrap a fairy in
> *Midsummer Night's Dream*, ii, 1

And in *Timon of Athens* (i, 1) we get the modern meaning—

> Hail, Rome, victorious in thy mourning weeds!

Week, Days of the. It is curious that while we owe the names of all the *months* to Rome, those of the *days* are Anglo-Saxon

Sunday (A S *Sunnandæg*) day of the sun
Monday (A S *Monandæg*), day of the moon
Tuesday (A S *Tiwesdæg*), from Tiw, the god of war.
Wednesday (A S *Wodnesdæg*), from Odin the god of storms
Thursday (A S *Thuresdæg*), day of Thor, the god of thunder
Friday (A S *Frigedæg*), day of Freya, goddess of marriage
Saturday (A S *Saterdæg* Lat *Dies Saturnus*), day of Saturn, the god of time

A week of Sundays A long time, an indefinite period

Weep. Weeper. In the old-fashioned, formal style of funerals—only abandoned with the opening of this century—undertakers' attendants (called mutes) and the principal male mourners wore long streamers of black material hanging from the hatband These were commonly known as weepers In humorous allusion to these the long side whiskers in fashion in the 1860s were called Piccadilly Weepers

Weeping A notion long prevailed in this country that it augured ill for future married happiness if the bride did not weep profusely at the wedding.

As no witch could shed more than three tears, and those from her left eye only, a copious flow of tears gave assurance to the husband that the lady had not "plighted her troth" to Satan, and was no witch

The **Weeping Philosopher** Heraclitus (d about 475 B C), so called because he grieved at the folly of man.

The **Weeping Saint** St Swithin (*q v*), because of the tradition of forty days' rain if it rains on July 15th.

To go by Weeping Cross. To suffer and repent of one's misdeeds. There are said to have been crosses called thus at Oxford, Shrewsbury, and Stafford

The tyme will come when comming home by weeping crosse, thou shalt confesse, that it is better to be at home in the cave of an Hermit than abroad in the court of an Emperor —LYLY: *Euphues and his England* (1580)

Weigh (A S *wegan*, to carry) To weigh anchor. To raise the anchor preparatory to sailing

Under weigh. A solecism for *under way See* WAY.

Weighed in the balance and found wanting Tested, and proved to be at fault, or a failure The phrase is from Daniel's interpretation of the vision of Belshazzar (*Dan* v, 27)

A dead weight. *See* DEAD

A weight-for-age race A sort of handicap (*q v*), in which the weights carried are apportioned according to certain conditions. Horses of the same age carry similar weights, *cæteris paribus*

Welch. An old spelling of *Welsh*, still retained in the name of the *Welch Regiment*

Welfare Work. The organized work undertaken by carefully trained personnel to promote the well-being of factory workers, the employees of large businesses, etc It is extended to many activities such as hospital almoners, police-court missionaries, and so forth, as well as to many tasks that have hitherto been left to the exertions of charity

Well. Well-beloved. Charles VI of France, *le Bien-aimé* (1368, 1380-1422), also applied to Louis XV

Well-founded Doctor. Ægidius de Columna (d 1316)

Welland Canal. A Canadian waterway, named from the Welland River, running from Port Dalhousie on Lake Ontario to Port Colborne, on Lake Erie, a length of 27 miles It contains eight locks and enables vessels of not more than 325 feet in length to pass from lake to lake

Wellington The Duke of Wellington (1769-1852) left his name to two kinds of boot, a tree (of the sequoia family—the *Wellingtonia*), and as a term in cards Men's riding-boots are called Wellingtons, with the front coming over the knee, and a shorter top-boot coming to just below the knee and often made of rubber Half-Wellingtons are shorter boots of which the foot is made of patent leather, and the top part (of inferior and softer material) extends halfway up the calf inside the tight

trousers of British army mess dress In "Nap" a call of *Wellington* doubles *Napoleon*—i e the caller has to take all five tricks and wins (or loses) double stakes

Welsh. Pertaining to Wales (*q v*), i e the country of foreigners (A S *wælse*, foreign) *Welsch* is German for *foreign*, and the Germans call Italy *Welschland Taffy* is the generic name for a Welshman, from *David*, the patron saint

Welsh harp. The musical instrument of the ancient Welsh bards, a large harp with three rows of strings, two tuned diatonically in unison, the third supplying the chromatic sharps and flats

Welsh Main. In cock-fighting, another term for a battle royal (*q.v.*)

Welsh mortgage. A pledge of land in which no day is fixed for redemption

Welsh rabbit. Cheese melted and spread over buttered toast *Rabbit* is not a corruption of *rare-bit*, the term is on a par with "mock-turtle," "Bombay duck," etc.

Welsher. A race-course pest who sets up as a bookmaker, and, when he sees the "book" is against him, makes off without paying out Also applied to a punter who absconds without paying his losses Hence, *to welsh*, to do this The term is modern (though the practice is as old as horse-racing), and its origin is unknown

Welter-weight A boxer between light and middle weight, about 147 lb In racing the term is applied to any extra heavy weight

Welt-politik (velt pol' i tik) The German phrase (world politics) for the policy a nation pursues in its relations with the world at large

Wen. The Great Wen So William Cobbett (1762-1835) in his *Rural Rides* called London, meaning that it was an abnormal growth, a blotch on the land

Wends. Slavic people inhabiting Saxony, Prussia, and Eastern Germany generally The word is probably connected with *wander*

Werewolf *See* WERWOLF

Wergild (wēr' gild) The "blood-money" (*wer*, man, *gild*, payment) paid in Anglo-Saxon times by the kindred of the slayer to the kindred of the slain to avoid a blood-feud in cases of murder or manslaughter There was a fixed scale —1,200 shillings (about £24) for a freeman, 200 shillings for a villain, and 40 pence for a serf.

Werther (wēr' ter) The sentimental hero of Goethe's romance, *The Sorrows of Werther* (1774), who was so overcome by his unrequited love for Lotte that he took his life. As Thackeray travestied the story—

Charlotte, having seen his body
Borne before her on a shutter,
Like a well-conducted person,
Went on cutting bread and butter

Werwolf (wēr' wulf) A "man-wolf" (A. S. *wer*, man), i.e a man who, according to mediæval belief, was turned—or could at will turn himself—into a wolf (the *loup-garou* of

France). It had the appetite of a wolf, and roamed about at night devouring infants and sometimes exhuming corpses Its skin was proof against shot or steel, unless the weapon had been blessed in a chapel dedicated to St. Hubert

This belief was once common to almost all Europe, and still lingers in Brittany, Limousin, Auvergne, Servia, Wallachia, and White Russia, while in the 15th century a council of theologians, convoked by the Emperor Sigismund, decided that the werwulf was a reality

The study of lycanthropy, *i e* of wolf-men, is, indeed, an important branch of the science of comparative religion At one time or another the belief in animal-men has been prevalent in every part of the world, tigers, leopards, hyenas and other ferocious animals being thus associated with the magic

Ovid tells the story of Lycaon, King of Arcadia, turned into a wolf because he tested the divinity of Jupiter by serving up to him a "hash of human flesh", Herodotus describes the Neuri as having the power of assuming once a year the shape of wolves; Pliny relates that one of the family of Antæus was chosen annually, by lot, to be transformed into a wolf, in which shape he continued for nine years, and St. Patrick, we are told, converted Vereticus, King of Wales, into a wolf

Werewolves. (World War II) Term coined by the Germans for the fanatical saboteurs who, they said, were going to carry on harassing tactics against the Allies after the defeat of Germany in the field.

Wesleyan. A member of the Nonconformist church founded by John Wesley (1703-91) about 1739.

Wessex The ancient kingdom of the West Saxons; it included Hants, Dorset, Wilts, Somerset, Surrey, Gloucestershire, and Bucks

The Novelist of Wessex. Thomas Hardy (1840-1928), the scenes of whose novels are laid in this country.

West. The West End. The fashionable quarter of London, lying between Charing Cross and the western boundary of Hyde Park Hence *West-end style,* ultra-fashionable

To go west. Of persons, to die, of things, to be lost, rendered useless, never obtained, as *My chance of promotion has gone west*

The phrase came into very wide use during World War I, but it is older than that, and originated in the United States, the reference being to the setting sun, which "goes west," and then expires. The idea is very old, it occurs in a Greek proverb, and *cp.* Tennyson's—

My purpose holds
To sail beyond the sunset, and the paths
Of all the western stars, until I die   *Ulysses.*

West, Mae *See* MAE WEST

The Western Church. The Roman Catholic Church, which, after the Great Schism in the 9th century, acknowledged the headship of the Pope

The Western Empire The western division of the Roman Empire having Rome as

B D.—31

capital, after the division into an Eastern and Western Empire by Theodosius in 395.

Wet. Slang for a drink; hence, **to have a wet,** to have a drink, and **to wet one's whistle,** meaning the same thing. This last is a very old phrase, Chaucer has "So was her joly whistle wel y-wet" (*Reeve's Tale,* 235), and in No xiii of the *Towneley Plays* (about 1388) is

Had she oones wett hyr Whystyll she could syng full clere
Hyr pater noster

A wet blanket. *See* BLANKET

Wetback. An illegal immigrant to U S.A from Mexico. The term originates in the fact that such interlopers usually had to swim the Rio Grande

Wet bob At Eton a wet bob is a boy who goes in for boating, a dry bob one who chooses cricket

Wet nurse. A woman employed to suckle children not her own

W H. Mr. When Shakespeare's *Sonnets* appeared in 1609 they were dedicated to a Mr W H, called their "onlie begetter" The identity of this friend of Shakespeare's has puzzled critics and biographers ever since, and is still unknown Numerous names have been suggested, among them William Herbert, 3rd Earl of Pembroke, one of the dedicatees of the First Folio Shakespeare, and Henry Wriothesley, 3rd Earl of Southampton, to whom *Venus and Adonis* and *Lucrece* were dedicated Other enquirers have preferred to postulate, from the internal evidence of the sonnets, the existence of an otherwise unknown William Hughes

Whale. Very like a whale. Very much like a cock-and-bull story Hamlet chaffs Polonius by comparing a cloud to a camel, and then to a weasel, and when the courtier assents Hamlet adds, "Or like a whale", to which Polonius answers, "Very like a whale" (Act iii, 2)

In American slang, something very fine or big, *e g* **a whale of a lot,** a great amount.

Whalebone. *See* MISNOMERS

White as whalebone. An old simile, whalebone is far from white Our forefathers seemed to confuse the walrus with the whale, and "white as whalebone" is really a blunder for "white as walrus-ivory"

What we Gave we Have. The epitaph on "the Good Earl of Courtenay" (*see* Gibbon's *Decline and Fall,* vol vi, Ch 61) —

What wee gave, wee have,
What wee spent, wee had,
What wee left, wee lost

is a free rendering of Martial's—

Extra fortunam est quidquid donatur amicis
Quas dederis, solas semper habebis opes.

There are similar epitaphs in many churches, one in St George's, Doncaster, runs thus —

How now, who is here?
I, Robin of Doncastere
And Margaret, my feere
That I spent, that I had,
That I gave, that I have,
That I left, that I lost.

He knows what's what 'He is a shrewd fellow not to be imposed on One of the senseless questions of logic was *Quid est quid?*
He knew what's what, and that's as high
As metaphysic wit can fly
         BUTLER· *Hudibras*, Pt 1, canto 1.

What-not In Victorian drawing-room furniture a small stand with shelves for bibelots and knick-knacks of all sorts Colloquially the phrase has come to be synonymous with "and so forth"—*e g.* "Photos, sketches and what-not."

Whatever are you at? So Dr W. G. Grace is reported to have called out when, in 1896, Ernest Jones, the Australian fast bowler, bowled through W. G's beard

Wheatear. The stonechat, a bird with a white tail The name has no connexion with either *wheat* or *ear*, but it is the A S *hwit*, white, *ears*—still in vulgar use as *arse*—the buttocks or rump. The French name of the bird, *culblanc*, signifies exactly the same thing.

Wheel. The invention of the wheel dates from late prehistoric times, its origin having been probably in Eastern Europe or Asia Minor It was not known to the peoples of the Far East until much later, for the Asiatic emigrants to North America and the ancient civilizations of Central America knew nothing of this invention upon which the world's progress has so largely advanced Emblematical of St Catharine (*q v*)

St Donatus bears a wheel set round with lights

St Euphemia and St Willigis both carry wheels.

St. Quintin is sometimes represented with a broken wheel at his feet

Broken on the wheel. *See* BREAK

The wheel is come to full circle Just retribution has followed The line is from Shakespeare's *King Lear*, v, 3

The wheel of Fortune Fortuna, the goddess, is represented on ancient monuments with a wheel in her hand, emblematical of her inconstancy
Though Fortune's malice overthrow my state,
My mind exceeds the compass of her wheel
         SHAKESPEARE 3 *Henry VI*, IV, 3

To put a spoke in one's wheel *See* SPOKE

Wherewithal. In older writings this is a form of *wherewith* as in
Wherewithal shall a young man cleanse his way —
Ps CXIX, 9

Colloquially it is now used as a noun, with the connotation of *money*

Whetstone *See* ACCIUS NÆVIUS

Lying for the whetstone Said of a person who is grossly exaggerating or falsifying a statement One of the Whitsun amusements of our forefathers was the lie-wage or lie-match, he who could tell the greatest lie was rewarded with a whetstone to sharpen his wit The nature of these contests may be illustrated by the following one of the combatants declared he could see a fly on the top of a church steeple,

the other replied, "Oh, yes, I saw him wink his eye "

The Whetstone of Witte A famous treatise on algebra (1556) by Robert Recorde The old name for algebra was the "Cossic Art," and *Cos ingenii* rendered into English is "the Whetstone of Wit " In Scott's *Fortunes of Nigel* the maid told the belated traveller that her master had "no other books but her young mistress's Bible and her master's *Whetstone of Witte*, by Robert Recorde "

Whig. The political party opposed to the Tories (*q v*), roughly speaking, the party in favour of gradual change towards more democratic government.
The name came into use in the later 17th century, and was supplanted by "Liberal" (*q v*) in the early 19th It is from obsolete *whiggamore*, a nickname for certain Scots who came to buy corn at Leith, from *whiggam*, an old Scottish equivalent to our *Gee up!* addressed to horses, and was originally applied to the Covenanters

The south-west counties of Scotland have seldom corn enough to serve them all the year round, and, the northern parts producing more than they used, those in the west went in summer to buy at Leith the stores that came from the north From the word *whiggam*, used in driving their horses, all that drove were called the *whiggamors*, contracted into *whigs* Now, in the year before the news came down of Duke Hamilton's defeat, the ministers animated their people to rise and march to Edinburgh, and they came up, marching at the head of their parishes with an unheard-of fury, praying and preaching all the way as they came The Marquis of Argyle and his party came and headed them, they being about 6,000 This was called the "Whiggamors' Inroad", and ever after that, all who opposed the court came in contempt to be called *whigs* From Scotland the word was brought into England, where it is now one of our unhappy terms of disunion —BISHOP BURNET *Own Times* (1723).

The Whig Party in the U S A was active from about 1824 to 1854 under the leadership of Henry Clay and Daniel Webster

The Whig Bible. *See* BIBLE, SPECIALLY NAMED.

Whip. A member of Parliament appointed unofficially, and without salary (as such), whose duty is to see that the members of his party vote at important divisions, and to discipline them if they do not attend, or vote against the party The Whips give notice to members that a motion is expected when their individual vote may be desirable The circular, or *whip*, runs "A motion is expected when your vote is 'earnestly' required " If the word "earnestly" has only one red-ink dash under it the receiver is *expected* to come, if it has two dashes it means that he *ought* to come, if it has three dashes, or is a "three-line whip," it means that he *must* come, if four dashes it means "stay away at your peril." These notices are technically called *Red whips* (*Annual Register*, 1877, p 86)

A whip-round. An impromptu collection for some benevolent object

The whip with six strings. *See under* SIX.

Whip-dog Day. October 18th, St Luke's Day Brand tells us (*Popular Antiquities*, II, 273) that it is so called because a priest about to celebrate mass on St Luke's Day happened to drop the pyx, which was snatched up by a dog

Whipper-snapper. An inexperienced—and often cheeky—young man The word probably derives from *whip snapper*, one who has nothing to do but crack a whip.

Whipping Boy. A boy kept to be whipped when a prince deserved chastisement Mungo Murray stood for Charles I, Barnaby Fitzpatrick for Edward VI (Fuller: *Church History*, ii, 342) When Henry IV of France abjured Protestantism and was received into the Catholic Church in 1595, two ambassadors (D'Ossat and Du Perron, afterwards cardinals) were sent to Rome and knelt in the portico of St Peter, singing the *Miserere* At each verse a blow with a switch was given on their shoulders.

Whisky. *See* USQUEBAUGH The light one-horse gig of this name from *whisk*, to flourish a thing about with a quick movement.

Whisky Insurrection. A riotous outbreak in Western Pennsylvania, in 1794, in protest against the excise laws on spirits In the country districts many small stills were worked by private persons, and when the excise officers attempted to deal with these, they were repulsed with violence and organized resistance. President Washington sent the militia to repress this outbreak and enforce the law, and the insurrection was put down without bloodshed

Whisper. Pig's whisper. *See* PIG

To give the whisper To give the tip, the warning; to pass some bit of secret information.

Whist. The card game originated in England (16th cent) and was first called *Triumph* (whence *trump*), then *Ruff* or *Honours*, and then, early in the 17th century, *Whisk*, in allusion to the sweeping up of the cards *Whist*, the later name, appears in Butler's *Hudibras* (1663), and was adopted through confusion with *Whist!* meaning Hush! Silence!

Let nice Piquette the boast of France remain,
And studious Ombre be the pride of Spain!
Invention's praise shall England yield to none,
While she can call delightful Whist her own
ALEXANDER THOMSON *Whist* (2nd edn., 1792)

Whistle. To whistle down the wind To defame a person The cognate phrase "blown upon" is more familiar. The idea is to whistle down the wind that the reputation of the person may be blown upon.

To whistle for it. It was an old superstition among sailors that when a ship was becalmed a wind could be raised by whistling By a perversion of sense the phrase "You can whistle for it" now means "You won't get it."

Worth the whistle Worth calling, worth inviting, worth notice The dog is worth the pains of whistling for Thus Heywood, in one of his dialogues consisting entirely of proverbs, says, "It is a poor dog that is not worth the whistling " Goneril says to Albany—

I have been worth the whistle.
King Lear, iv, 2

You paid too dearly for your whistle. You paid dearly for something you fancied, but found that it did not answer your expectation. The allusion is to a story told by Dr Franklin of his nephew, who set his mind on a common whistle, which he bought of a boy for four times its value.

To wet one's whistle. To drink.

Whit Sunday. White Sunday The seventh Sunday after Easter, to commemorate the descent of the Holy Ghost on the day of Pentecost, In the primitive Church the newly baptized wore *white* from Easter to Pentecost, and were called *albati* (white-robed) The last of the Sundays, which was also the chief festival, was called emphatically *Dominica in Albis* (Sunday in White)

As an old play on the name it was called *Wit* or *Wisdom* Sunday, the day when the Apostles were filled with wisdom by the Holy Ghost

This day Whit-sonday is cald,
For wisdom and wit sevene fald,
Was zonen to the Apostles as this day.
Cambr Univer MSS , Dd 1, p 234

We ought to kepe this our Wytsonday bicause the law of God was then of the Holy Wyght or Ghost deliured gostly vnto vs —*Taverner* (1540)

This day is called Wytsonday because the Holy Ghost brought wytte and wysdom into Christis disciples   and filled them full of ghostly wytte —*In die Pentecostis* (printed by Wynkyn de Worde).

Whitsun farthings. *See* QUADRAGESIMALS

White denotes purity, simplicity, and candour, innocence, truth, and hope *See* COLOURS, SYMBOLISM OF

The ancient Druids, and indeed the priests generally of antiquity, used to wear white vestments The magi also wore white robes

The head of Osiris, in Egypt, was adorned with a white tiara, all his ornaments were white; and his priests were clad in white

The priests of Jupiter, and the Flamen Dialis of Rome, were clothed in white, and wore white hats The victims offered to Jupiter were white The Roman festivals were marked with white chalk, and at the death of a Cæsar the national mourning was white; white horses were sacrificed to the sun, white oxen were selected for sacrifice by the Druids, and white elephants are held sacred in Siam.

The Persians affirm that the divinities are habited in white

Whitebait Dinner. A dinner of Cabinet Ministers and prominent politicians that, until the early 1890s, was held at Blackwall or Greenwich toward the close of the parliamentary session. The time of meeting was Trinity Monday, or as near Trinity Monday as circumstances would allow

Yesterday the Cabinet Ministers went down the River in the Ordnance barge to Lovegrove's "West India Dock Tavern," Blackwall, to partake of their annual fish dinner Covers were laid for thirty-five gentlemen —*The Times*, Sept 10, 1835

To hit the white To be quite right, make a good shot. The phrase is from the old days of archery, the *white* being the inner circle of the target—the bull's eye

The white bird. Conscience, or the soul of man The Mohammedans have preserved the old Roman idea in the doctrine that the souls of the just lie under the throne of God, like white birds, till the resurrection morn *Cp* DOVE

Whiteboys. A secret agrarian association organized in Ireland about the year 1760 So called because they wore white shirts in their nightly expeditions. In 1787 a new association appeared, the members of which called themselves "Right-boys" The White-boys were originally called Levellers (*q v*), from their throwing down fences and levelling enclosures

The White Brethren. A sect of Catholic reformers that appeared early in the 15th century Mosheim says (Bk ii, p 2, ch. v) a certain priest came from the Alps with an immense concourse of followers, all dressed in white linen. They marched through several provinces, following a cross borne by their leader Boniface X ordered their leader to be burnt, and the multitude dispersed

The White Cockade. The badge worn by the followers of Charles Edward, the Young Pretender

White collar worker. The professional or clerical worker whose calling demands a certain nicety of attire.

The White Company. A band of French cut-throats organized by Bertrand du Guesclin in 1366, and led against Pedro the Cruel, so called because they wore a white cross on the shoulder The name had previously (13th cent) been given to a gang of assassins led by Folquet, the villainous Bishop of Toulouse, who massacred all suspected of heresy.

White elephant. *See* ELEPHANT

White-face. A nickname for a man from Hereford, from the white faces of Hereford-shire cattle

To show the white feather. To show coward-ice, a phrase from the cockpit when a game-cock is getting the worst of the fight and wants to stop, he makes the fact known by lifting his hackle—a long narrow feather on the neck The under rim of the hackle is edged with white feathers

White flag An all-white flag is universally used as the signal of surrender or of desiring to parley A messenger bearing a white flag is by international decency immune from harm

White Friars The Carmelites (*q v*), so called because of the white mantle they wear over a brown habit One of their houses, founded in London on the south side of Fleet Street in 1241, gives the name to that district, and was for many centuries a sanctuary

White harvest. A late harvest, when the ground is white of a morning, with hoar frost

The White Horse. The standard of the ancient Saxons, hence the emblem of Kent A galloping white horse is the device of the House of Hanover, and it is from this that

many public houses bear the sign of "The White Horse"

On Uffington Hill, Berks, there is formed in the chalk an enormous white horse, supposed to have been cut there after the battle in which Ethelred and Alfred defeated the Danes (871) This rude design is about 374 ft. long, and 1,000 ft above the sea-level It may be seen twelve or fifteen miles off, and gives its name to the *Vale of White Horse*, west of Abingdon

An annual ceremony was once held, called "Scouring the White Horse."

Foam-crested waves are popularly called *White horses*

> Now the great winds shoreward blow,
> Now the salt tides seaward flow,
> Now the wild white horses play,
> Champ and chafe and toss in the spray
> MATTHEW ARNOLD: *The Forsaken Merman*

White House. The presidential mansion in Washington, D C It is a building of freestone, painted white. The cornerstone was laid by Washington, and the house was remodelled in 1902 Figuratively, it means the Presidency of the U.S A

White Lady. A sort of ghostly spirit in many countries, the appearance of which generally forebodes death in the house. It is a relic of Teutonic mythology, representing Holda, or Berchta, the goddess who received the souls of maidens and young children

German legend says that when the castle of Neuhaus, Bohemia, was being built a white lady appeared to the workmen and promised them a sweet soup and carp on the completion of the castle In remembrance thereof, these dainties were for long given to the poor of Bohemia on Maundy Thursday She is also said to have been heard to speak on two occasions, once in December, 1628, when she said, "I wait for judgment" and once at Neuhaus, when she said to the princes, " 'Tis ten o'clock "

The first recorded instance of this apparition was in the 16th century, and the name given to the lady is Bertha von Rosenberg. She last appeared, it is said, in 1879, just prior to the death of Prince Waldemar She carries a bunch of keys at her side, and is always dressed in white

In Normandy the White Ladies lurk in ravines, fords, bridges, and other narrow passes, and ask the passenger to dance If they receive a courteous answer, well, but if a refusal, they seize the churl and fling him into a ditch, where thorns and briers may serve to teach him gentleness of manners.

The most famous of these ladies is *La Dame d'Aprigny*, who used to occupy the site of the present Rue St Quentin, at Bayeux, and *La Dame Abonde*

> One kind of these the Italians *Fata* name;
> The French call *Fée*, we *Sybils*, and the same
> Others *White Dames*, and those that them have seen,
> *Night Ladies* some, of which Habundia's queen
> *Hierarchie*, viii, p 507

White League A name of the Ku Klux Klan (*q v*)

A white lie. An excusable or pardonable untruth

White-livered. Mean or cowardly. It was an old notion that the livers of cowards were bloodless

> How many cowards, whose hearts are all as false
> As stairs of sand, wear yet upon their chins
> The beards of Hercules and frowning Mars,
> Who, inward search'd, have livers white as milk!
> *Merchant of Venice*, iii, 2

A white man A thoroughly straightforward and honourable man.

White magic. Sorcery in which the devil was not invoked and played no part, opposed to black magic (*q v*)

White Man's Burden The duty supposed to be thrust on the white races, especially the British, to educate and govern the untutored coloured races for their own welfare The phrase arose during the imperial fervour of the later 19th century.—

> Take up the White Man's Burden—
> Send forth the best you breed
> Go bind your sons to exile
> To serve the captives' need
> KIPLING.

White Man's Grave. The unhealthy areas of equatorial West Africa, especially Sierra Leone

The White Merle. A white fairy bird of old Basque folklore, whose singing would restore sight to the blind.

A white night. A sleepless night, the French have the phrase *Passer une nuit blanche.*

White Paper A publication issued by the British government giving information on matters of interest, reports of committees, etc., and on sale to the public Since 1919 Government papers have been marked "Cmd.", command

White rent. Rent payable in silver money. An annual duty of eightpence payable by every tin-miner in Devon and Cornwall to the Duke of Cornwall as lord of the soil.

The White Rose. The House of York, whose emblem it was (*see under* ROSE)

White Rose League. A society adhering in theory to the claims of the House of Stuart to the throne of Great Britain It is of a purely sentimental and historical nature, harbouring no disloyalty to the Crown

White Satin An old nickname for gin

White Slave A woman who is sold or forced into prostitution The problem of White Slave Traffic, especially to South America, was taken up vigorously by the League of Nations, and in some measure the evil was mitigated through its exertions.

A white squall. One which produces no diminution of light, in contradistinction to a *black* squall, in which the clouds are black and heavy.

Days marked with a white stone. Days to be remembered with gratification. The Romans used a white stone or piece of chalk to mark their lucky days on the calendar. Days that were unlucky they marked with charcoal (*cp* RED-LETTER DAY)

White tincture. The alchemist's name for a preparation that should convert any base metal into silver. It was also called the Stone

31*

of the Second Order, the Little Elixir, and the Little Magisterium (*cp.* RED TINCTURE)

The White Tsar. An epithet of the former Tsars of Russia, as Tsars of Muscovy, the King of Muscovy was called the White King from the robes which he wore. The King of Poland was called the Black King

Whitewash. Excuses made in palliation of bad conduct, a false colouring given to a person's character or memory to counteract disreputable allegations
The term is also applied to the clearance by a bankrupt of his debts, not by paying them, but by judicial process.

White wine. Any wine of a light colour, not red, as champagne, hock, sauterne, moselle, etc

White witch One who practised white magic (*q v*) only.

Whitechapel. A quarter in the East End of London A *Whitechapel cart* is a light, two-wheeled spring cart, as used by small tradesmen for delivering goods.

Whittington, Dick. Sir Richard Whittington, "thrice Lord Mayor of London," about whom the well-known nursery story is told, was born about 1358, the son of Sir William de Whityngdon, lord of the manor of Pauntley, Gloucester Being a younger son and unprovided for, he walked to London, was trained by a relative as a merchant, married his master's daughter and so prospered that he was able to lend Henry IV £1,000—equal to over £30,000 in present money
He was Lord Mayor of London in 1397, 1406, and 1419, besides being once named by Richard II to succeed a mayor who had died in office He died in 1423
The legend that Whittington made his wealth largely through the agency of a cat seems to be founded on a confusion between Fr *achat* and Eng *a cat*. In the 14th and early 15th centuries trading, or buying and selling at a profit, was known among the educated classes as *achat* (French for "purchase"), which was written—and probably pronounced —*acat* (see Riley's *Introduction* to the *Liber Albus*)
Another suggestion is that it arose through confusion with the *cat*, a ship on the Norwegian model, having a narrow stern, projecting quarters, and deep waist, and used in the coal trade According to tradition, Sir Richard made his money by trading in coals, which he conveyed in his "cat" from Newcastle to London. The black faces of his coalheavers gave rise to the tale about the Moors But there are Eastern tales of the same kind, and it is probably one of these that became attached to the popular Lord Mayor.

Who dun it. (U S A slang) A crude detective story.

Whoopee (woo pē') (Slang) Uproariousness, noisy merriment As an exclamation it is one of excited pleasure

Wicked. Connected with A S *wicca*, a wizard

The Wicked Bible *See* BIBLE, SPECIALLY NAMED

The **Wicked Prayer Book.** Printed 1686, octavo. In the Epistle for the Fourteenth Sunday after Trinity the following passage occurs.—

> Now the works of the flesh are manifest, which are these, adultery, fornication, uncleanliness, idolatry they who do these things shall inherit the kingdom of God

("Shall inherit" should be "shall *not* inherit.")

Wide. Slang for cunning, artful, or for one who is very wideawake.

Wideawake. Certain felt hats were so called by a pun, because they never had a *nap*. The term is now applied to any felt hat with a very wide brim

Wide Boy. The predecessor of the Spiv (*q v*), active in the years 1920-40

Widow, The. Old slang for the gallows Also Victorian slang for champagne, from the well-known brand Veuve Cliquot

Widow bench. An obsolete law term for the share of her husband's estate allowed to a widow over and above her jointure

The widow's cruse. A small supply of anything which, by good management, is made to go a long way and to be apparently inexhaustible In allusion to the miracle of the cruse of oil in 2 *Kings* iv.

Widow's man. Old naval slang for a non-existent seaman whose name was borne on the ship's book, his pay, prize-money, etc , going to Greenwich Hospital or to a fund for widows

Widow's weeds. *See* WEEDS

The Widow at Windsor. The name applied to Queen Victoria by Rudyard Kipling in his Barrack Room Ballad of that name

Wieland (vē′ länt). Another form of *Volund* (*see* WAYLAND), the wonder-working smith of Norse mythology

Wife. A S *wif*, a woman The ultimate root of the word is obscure, but it is "certainly not allied to *weave* (A S *weafn*), as the fable runs" (Skeat)
The old meaning, *a woman*, still appears in such combinations as *fish-wife, housewife*, etc , and in the phrase *an old wife's tale* (*see* 1 *Tim* iv, 7) for an incoherent and unconvincing story.

The Wife-hater Bible. *See* BIBLE, SPECIALLY NAMED.

Wig. A shortened form of *periwig* (earlier, *perwig*), from Fr *peruke*. In the middle of the 18th century we meet with thirty or forty different names for wigs· as the artichoke, bag, barrister's, bishop's, brush, bush (buzz), buckle, busby, chain, chancellor's, corded, wolf's paw, Count Saxe's mode, the crutch, the cut bob, the detached buckle, the Dalma-hoy (a bob wig worn by tradesmen), the drop, the Dutch, the full, the half natural, the Jan-senist bob, the judge's, the ladder, the long bob, the Louis, the pigeon's wing, the rhin-oceros, the rose, the scratch, the she-dragon, the small back, the spinach seed, the staircase, the Welsh, the wild boar's back.

A bigwig. A magnate, in allusion to the large wigs that in the 17th and 18th centuries encumbered the head and shoulders of the aristocracy of England and France. They are still worn by the Lord Chancellor, judges, and barristers; bishops used to wear them in the House of Lords till 1880.

Dash my wig! A mild imprecation, formerly very common.

> Fleas are not lobsters, dash my wig
> BUTLER *Hudibras.*

Scratch wig. A small one just large enough to cover the bald patch, as opposed to the full-bottomed wig

Wigs on the green. A serious disagreement likely to lead to a scrimmage, a rumpus.

Wigging. A scolding, a reprimand, This word may be connected with *wig*, but it is not certain.

Wiggen tree. *See* ROWAN.

Wight (wit) An Old English word meaning a person, a human being It chiefly survives in the phrase "a luckless wight," a man for whom everything goes wrong

Wigwam (wig′ wom). An American Indian term for a house or tent

Wild. Wildcat. An American phrase for any unauthorized activity, as *Wildcat Strike*, an unofficial strike, *wildcat cartridges*, shot-gun cartridges made privately by gunsmiths or amateurs, not the standard product of a commercial firm

A wild-cat scheme. A rash and hazardous financial venture, a speculation in which one would have about as much chance of making a profit as of catching a wild-cat in the woods

Wild fire. A very old English description of a composition of inflammable materials that catch fire quickly. It is now used figuratively in the phrase To catch like wildfire, to take on with the public instantaneously

The wild huntsman. A spectral hunter of mediæval legend who, with a pack of spectral dogs, frequents certain forests and occasionally appears to mortals. One account has it that he was a Jew who would not suffer Jesus to drink out of a horse-trough, but pointed to some water in a hoof-print as good enough for "such an enemy of Moses "
The Germans locate him in the Black Forest, the French in the Forest of Fontaine-bleau—and confuse him with St. Hubert, and in England he became Herne the Hunter (*q v*), once a keeper in Windsor Forest, who "walks" in winter time, about midnight, and blasts trees and cattle He wears horns, and rattles a chain in a "most hideous manner" (*Merry Wives of Windsor*, iv, 4)

To lead one a wild-goose chase. To beguile one with false hopes, or put one on an impracticable pursuit, or after something that is not worth the chase. A wildgoose is very hard to catch, and very little use when caught

To sow one's wild oats. *See* OAT

Wild men. A term often applied, in politics, to intransigents, the extremists of either party who will not accommodate their views and actions to changing conditions or public opinion

Women who took an active part in the movement for obtaining votes and political recognition were sometimes called *wild women*.

Wild West. The western frontier of the U.S A before a stable government was in being The phrase really refers to the days of the mid-19th century before the whole continent was known and developed, and the ever-shifting frontiers of civilization in the west were the resort of desperadoes, cattle-thieves, etc The term is often applied to stories of adventure dealing with that period and those localities.

Wilderness To go into the wilderness. A figurative description of being deprived of political office through a change of government.

Wilfrid, St. A noble of Northumbria, who became Abbot of Ripon in 661, and in 705 Bishop of Hexham It was he who at the Synod of Whitby (664) succeeded in substituting the Roman uses and their observance of Easter in England for the Celtic. For many centuries his banner was carried to the wars.

St. Wilfrid's Needle. A narrow passage in the crypt of Ripon cathedral, built by Odo, Archbishop of Canterbury, and said to have been used to test a woman's chastity, as none but a virgin was able to squeeze through.

Wilgefortis, St. *See* UNCUMBER.

Wilhelmstrasse (vil' helm stra se) A street in Berlin where the principal government offices, including the Foreign Office, were situated. The term is usually applied to the German Foreign Office and its policy. In the Allied bombing of Berlin in World War II most of the street was levelled with the ground.

Will-o'-the-wisp. *See* FRIAR'S LANTHORN; IGNIS FATUUS.

William. One of the most popular of Christian names, Fr. *Guillaume*, Ger *Wilhelm*, it means *a protector*, literally, *a resolute helmet*—Ger *wille helm*

The **william pear.** Properly the **William's pear**, or Bon Chretien is so called from the name of its introducer into England For a like reason it is known in the U S A as the Bartlett Pear Sweet william is an old English name for an English flower, *Dianthus barbatus*, a member of the pink family.

William of Cloudeslie. A noted outlaw and famous archer of the "north countrie " *See* CLYM OF THE CLOUGH

William of Wykeham. *See* WYKEHAMIST

William the Silent. *See* SILENT

Of the many saints of this name the following are perhaps the most noteworthy —

St. William of Aquitaine. A soldier of Charlemagne's, who helped to chase the Saracens from Languedoc In 808 he renounced the world, and died 812. He is usually represented as a mailed soldier

St. William of Maleval A French nobleman who went as pilgrim to Jerusalem, and on his return retired to the desert of Maleval, where he died in 1157 The *Guillemites* a branch of the Benedictine order, was founded by Albert, one of his disciples, and named in his honour He is depicted in a Benedictine's habit, with armour lying beside him

St. William of Montpelier is represented with a lily growing from his mouth, with the words *Ave Maria* in gold letters on the flower.

St. William of Monte Virgine (d 1142) is shown with a wolf by his side

St. William of Norwich was the child said to have been crucified by the Jews in 1137 He is represented crowned with thorns, or crucified, or holding a hammer and nails in his hands, or wounded in his side with a knife (*see* Drayton's *Polyolbion*, song xxiv).

In Percy's *Reliques* (Bk. i, 3) there is a tale of a lad named Hew, son of Lady Helen, of Merryland town (Milan), who was allured by a Jew's daughter with an apple She stuck him with a penknife, rolled him in lead, and cast him into a well Lady Helen went in search of her boy, and the child's ghost cried out from the bottom of the well—

> The lead is wondrous heavy, mither,
> The well is wondrous deip,
> A keen penknife sticks in my heirt, mither,
> A word I dauna speik.

St. William of York (d. 1154) was a nephew of King Stephen, and became Archbishop of York in 1140 He was canonized by Honorius III about 1220 on account of the many miracles reported to have been performed at his tomb.

Willie-Wastle. This child's game is said to be named from William Wastle, governor of Hume Castle, Haddington When Cromwell, so the story goes, sent a summons to him to surrender, he replied—

> Here I, Willie Wastle,
> Stand firm in my castle,
> And all the dogs in the town
> Shan't pull Willie Wastle down.

Willis's Rooms. *See* ALMACK'S.

Willow. To handle the willow. To be a cricket-player. Cricket-bats are made of willow, hence the game is sometimes called *King Willow* (*see* the Harrow school song of this name)

To wear the willow. To go into mourning, especially for a sweetheart or bride. The willow, especially the weeping willow, has from time immemorial been associated with sorrow and taken as an emblem of desolation or desertion. Fuller says, "The willow is a sad tree, whereof such as have lost their love make their mourning garlands," and the psalmist tells us that the Jews in captivity hung their harps upon the willows in sign of mourning (cxxxvii)

Desdemona says in *Othello* (iv, 3):—

> My mother had a maid call'd Barbara,
> She was in love, and he she lov'd prov'd mad
> And did forsake her; she had a song of "willow",
> An old thing 'twas, but it expressed her fortune,
> And she died singing it.

And then comes the song—
The poor soul sat sighing by a sycamore tree,
Sing all a green willow,
Her hand on her bosom, her head on her knee,
Sing willow, willow, willow,
The fresh streams ran by her, and murmur'd her
    moans,
Sing willow, willow, willow'
Her salt tears fell from her, and soften'd the stones,
Sing willow, willow, willow.

The **Willow Pattern** A favourite design for blue china plates, imitating (but not copying) the Chinese style of porcelain decoration It was introduced into England by Thomas Turner of Caughley about 1780, when the craze for things Chinese was at its height

To the right is a mandarin's country seat, two stories high to show the rank and wealth of the possessor, in the foreground a pavilion, in the background an orange-tree, and to the right of the pavilion a peach-tree in full bearing The estate is enclosed by a wooden fence, and a river crossed by a bridge, at one end of which is the famous willow-tree and at the outer the gardener's humble cottage At the top of the pattern (left-hand side) is an island The three figures on the bridge are the mandarin and the lovers, the latter also being shown in a boat on the river.

The willow pattern does not illustrate any Chinese story or legend, and is not Chinese in origin

Will's and Button's Coffee-houses. These once famous resorts of the London wits were both situated in Russell Street, Covent Garden. Will's, at the corner of Bow Street, took its name from Will Urwin, who was already the proprietor in 1660, for Pepys says (October 2nd, 1660) "At Will's I met Mr Spicer and with him to the abbey " "It was Dryden," says Pope, "who made Will's Coffee House the great resort of wits of his time " According to Dr Johnson, Dryden had a particular chair to himself which was set by the fire in winter and was carried out for him to the balcony in the summer

When a mere child Pope was taken to Will's to see the great man, and in after years was himself the centre of a circle of wits there

On the opposite side of Russell Street was Button's Coffee-house, established in 1712 by Daniel Button, a former servant of Joseph Addison There Addison held his literary court, attended by Steele Budgell, Ambrose Philips, Carey, and Davenant.

Further along Russell Street was Tom's, a coffee-house established in 1700 by Thomas West, and in the early years of George III patronized by Garrick, Foote, Dr. Johnson, Goldsmith, and others

Willy-nilly. *Nolens volens*, willing or not Will-he, nill-he, *nill* being *n'* (negative), *will*, just as Lat *nolens* is *n'-volens*

Willy-willy. The Australian aboriginal term for the sudden whirlwinds which are common on the north-west coast They can be seen approaching in a high circular column of leaves and dust from a great distance

Wimbledon A suburb of London, and home of the All England Croquet Club In the middle of the 1870s the Club, being in low water, added "Lawn Tennis" to its title, this being then a new game increasing in popularity. On the Club's courts the first lawn tennis

Championship in the world was held in 1877 The annual tournament run by the All England Club at Wimbledon still ranks as the premier championship

Win, To. A slang term of World War II, meaning to acquire by deceit or theft, an aggravated "scrounge "

Winchester. Identified by Malory and other old writers with the *Camelot* (*q v*) of Arthurian romance.

Wind According to classical mythology, the north, south, east, and west winds (*Boreas*, *Notus*, *Eurus*, and *Zephyrus*) were under the rule of Æolus, who kept them confined in a cave on Mount Hæmus, Thrace Other strong winds of a more destructive nature were the brood of Typhœus

The story says that Æolus gave Ulysses a bag, tied with a silver string, in which were all the hurtful and unfavourable winds, so that he might arrive home without being delayed by tempests. His crew, however, opened the bag in the belief that it contained treasure, the winds escaped, and a terrible storm at once arose, driving the vessel out of its course and back to the island it had left

Latin names for other winds are north-east, *Argestes*, north-west, *Corus*; south-east, *Volturnus*, south-west, *Afer ventus*, *Africus*, *Africanus*, or *Libs*. The *Thrascias* is a north wind, but not due north *Aquilo* is another name for the north wind, as *Auster* is of the south and *Favonius* of the west

Boreas and Cæcias, and Argestes loud,
And Thrascias rend the woods, and seas upturn,
Notus and Afer, black with thunderous clouds,
From Serraliona Thwart of these, as fierce,
Forth rush   . Eurus and Zephyr . . . .
Sirocco and Libecchio [Libycus]
                    MILTON *Paradise Lost*, x, 699-706.

For some specially named winds *see* ETESIAN, HARMATTAN, KAMSIN, MISTRAL, MONSOON, PAMPERO, SIROCCO, SOLANO, TRADE WINDS, etc.

A wind egg. An egg without a shell, or an unfertilized one, from the old superstition that the hen that lays it was impregnated, like the "Thracian mares," by the wind.

In the wind's eye. *See* EYE

Second wind. Soon after the start in running, unless the runner is very fit he gets out of breath; but, as the body becomes heated, breathing becomes more easy, and endures till fatigue produces exhaustion; this is called the *second wind*

There's something in the wind. There are signs that something is going to happen, some hitherto unanticipated development is about to take place

Three sheets in the wind. *See* SHEET.

'Tis an ill wind that blows nobody any good. Someone profits by every loss; someone is benefited by every misfortune

Except wind stands as never it stood,
It is an ill-wind turns none to good
TUSSER *Five Hundred Points of Good Husbandry*, xiii.

To get the wind up. To become thoroughly alarmed and, in consequence nervous, over-anxious, funky A suggested origin of this phrase dates it from the early days of flying when pilots had to stretch their legs out in mid-air to reach the rudder bar In any sudden fall of the plane in an air pocket the wind would rush up and give the learner a fright.

To know which way the wind blows. To be aware of the true state of affairs.

To raise the wind To obtain ready money by hook or by crook

To sail before the wind To prosper, to go on swimmingly, to meet with great success, to go as smoothly and rapidly as a ship before the wind

To sail close to the wind. In nautical use, to keep the vessel's head as near the quarter from which the wind is blowing as possible while keeping the sails filled, figuratively, to go to the very verge of what decency or propriety allow, to act so as just to escape the letter of the law

To take or have the wind To get or keep the upper hand Bacon uses the phrase *To have the wind of a ship* is to be to the windward of it

To take the wind out of one's sails To forestall him, "steal his thunder" (*see* THUNDER), frustrate him by utilizing his own material or methods Literally, it is to sail to the windward of a ship and so rob its sails of the wind.

Windbag. A long-winded, bombastic speaker, who uses inflated phrases and promises far more than he can perform.

Windfall. An unexpected piece of good luck, especially an unexpected legacy; something worth having that comes to one without any personal exertion—like fruit which has fallen from the tree and so does not have to be picked

Windjammer A sailing ship, or one of its crew. The term is a modern one, born since steam superseded sail.

Windy City. Chicago

Windmill. To fight with windmills. To face imaginary adversaries, combat chimeras The allusion is to the adventure of Don Quixote who, when riding through the plains of Montiel, approached thirty or forty windmills, which he declared to Sancho Panza "were giants, two leagues in length or more " Striking his spurs into Rosinante, with his lance in rest, he drove at one of the "monsters dreadful as Typhœus" the lance lodged in the sail, and the latter lifted both man and beast into the air. When the valiant knight and his steed fell they were both much injured, and Don Quixote declared that the enchanter Freston, "who carried off his library with all the books therein," had changed the giants into windmills "out of malice" (Bk. 1, ch. viii).

To have windmills in your head. To be full of fancies, to have "bees in your bonnet" (*q v*). Sancho Panza says—

Did I not tell your worship they were windmills? and who could have thought otherwise, except such as had windmills in their head?—CERVANTES *Don Quixote* Bk 1, ch viii

Window. Window dressing. Properly, the display of goods in a shop window for the purpose of attracting customers Figuratively, the phrase is applied to the specious display of whatever is attractive in a project, plan, or the like

All his goods in the window, is of much the same origin and meaning, implying that a man is displaying all his advantages with nothing substantial behind them, so to speak, in stock

Windsor. The House of Windsor. The official title of the reigning dynasty of Great Britain and the British Dominions beyond the Seas since July 17th, 1917, when King George V signed a proclamation adopting this style for the Royal Family and declared that—

all the descendants in the male line of Queen Victoria who are subjects of these realms, other than female descendants who may marry or may have married, shall bear the name of Windsor

From the time of George I to the death of Queen Victoria the dynasty was known as the *House of Hanover*; from the accession of Edward VII to the date of this proclamation it was the *House of Saxe-Coburg*, so named from Edward VII's father, Albert, Duke of Saxony, Prince of Coburg and Gotha

After his abdication, December 11th, 1936, King Edward VIII was created Duke of Windsor

The Knights of Windsor. *See under* KNIGHT

Windsor Herald. One of the six Heralds attached to the College of Arms (*see* HERALD)

Widow of Windsor. *See* WIDOW.

Wine. At the universities *a wine* is a convivial gathering at which wine, as a rule, is drunk

Wine of ape (Chaucer). "I trow that ye have drunken win of ape"—*i e* wine to make you drunk, in French, *vin de singe* There is a Talmud parable which says that Satan came one day to drink with Noah, and slew a lamb, a lion, a pig, and an ape, to teach Noah that man before wine is in him is a *lamb*, when he drinks moderately he is a *lion*, when like a sot he is a *swine*, but after that any further excess makes him an *ape* that senselessly chatters and jabbers

See also VIN

Wing. This word, naturally applied to the ailerons of an aeroplane, is used as a collective term in the R A F for a group of three squadrons, under a Wing-Commander, ranking with a Commander in the Navy and a Lieut.-Colonel in the Army

Don't try to fly without wings. Attempt nothing you are not fit for A Latin saying, Plautus has (*Pœnulus* IV, ii, 47) *Sine pennis volare haud facile est*, It is by no means easy to fly without wings

On the wing About to leave Young (*Night Thoughts*, vii) speaks of "restless Hope, for ever on the wing "

The wings of Azrael. *See* AZRAEL

To clip one's wings. To take down one's conceit; to hamper one's freedom of action

To lend wings. To spur one's speed.

To take one under your wing To patronize and protect The allusion is to a hen gathering her chicks under her wing

To take wing. To fly away, to depart without warning

> Oh, God! it is a fearful thing
> To see the human soul take wing
> BYRON. *Prisoner of Chillon*

Winifred, St. Patron saint of virgins, because she was beheaded by Prince Caradoc for refusing to marry him She was Welsh by birth, and the legend says that where her head fell on the ground sprang up the famous healing well of St Winifred in Flintshire She is usually drawn like St Denis, carrying her head in her hand Holywell is St Winifred's Well, celebrated for its "miraculous" virtues

Wink A nod is as good as a wink to a blind horse. *See* NOD

Forty winks. A short nap, a doze

Like winking. Old slang for very quickly, as in "to give an answer like winking"

To tip one the wink. To give him a hint privately, to "put him wise"

To wink at. To connive at, or to affect not to notice

> He knows not how to wink at human frailty
> Or pardon weakness that he never felt
> ADDISON *Cato*, v, 4.

Winkle, Rip van. The creation of Washington Irving, hero of one of the stories in the *Sketch Book* (1819) which tells how he, a Dutch colonist of New York in pre-Revolutionary days, met with a strange man in a ravine of the Catskill Mountains. Rip helps him to carry a keg, and when they reach the destination sees a number of odd creatures playing nine-pins, but no one utters a word Master Winkle seizes the first opportunity to take a sip at the keg, falls into a stupor, and sleeps for twenty years On waking, he finds that he is a tottering old man, his wife is dead and buried, his daughter is married, his native village has been remodelled, and America has become independent

Winter. Winter's King and Queen. Ferdinand V, Elector Palatine, and his wife Elizabeth, who reigned in Bohemia from August, 1619 to November, 1620 Elizabeth was a daughter of Charles I of England, and her beauty inspired one of the finest lyrics of the century —Sir Henry Wotton's "You meaner beauties of the night."

Winter's Tale, The. One of the last of Shakespeare's plays, acted in 1611 but not printed till 1623 (first Folio) It is founded on Greene's *Pandosto, The Triumph of Time* (1588), which was written round an actual incident that occurred in the Bohemian and Polish courts in the late 14th century.
In the play Polixenes, King of Bohemia, is invited to Sicily by King Leontes, and unwittingly excites the jealousy of his friend because he prolongs his stay at the entreaty of Queen Hermione Leontes orders Camillo to poison the royal guest, but, instead of doing so, Camillo flees with him to Bohemia In time Florizel, the son and heir of Polixenes, falls in love with Perdita, the lost daughter of Leontes Polixenes forbids the match, and the young lovers, under the charge of Camillo, flee to Sicily Polixenes follows the fugitives,

the mystery of Perdita is cleared up, the lovers are married, and the two kings resume their friendship
In Greene's romance Polixenes is *Pandosto*, Hermione *Bellaria*, Leontes *Egistus*, and Florizel and Perdita *Dorastus* and *Fawnia*

Wipe. Old slang for a pocket-handkerchief

To wipe one's nose. To affront him, to give him a blow on the nose Similarly, *to wipe a person's eye*, to steal a march on him, to *fetch one a wipe over the knuckles*, to give him a good rap

Wiped out. Destroyed, annihilated, quite obliterated

Wire. Used as a verb, meaning *to telegraph to*. "Wire me without delay," telegraph to me at once

Wireless Applied to telegraphic and telephonic communications sent through space instead of along a wire A more colloquial term is "radio."

To pull the wires. To control events, politics, etc , clandestinely from behind the scenes, as the unseen operator manipulates the marionettes in a puppet-show

Wisdom Wisdom of Solomon. A book of the Old Testament Apocrypha, written by an Alexandrian Jew, probably between A.D. 1 and A D 40, to counteract the scepticism and Epicureanism presented in the Apocryphal book of Ecclesiasticus.

Wisdom tooth The popular name for the third molar in each jaw Wisdom teeth appear between the ages of 17 and 25.

Cut your wisdom teeth When persons say or do silly things, the remark is made to them that "they have not yet cut their wisdom teeth," or reached years of discretion

The wisdom of many and the wit of one. Lord John Russell's definition of a proverb

Wise. To put one wise. An Americanism, meaning to acquaint him with the facts, with the true position of affairs; to give him the necessary information

Wisecrack. (Slang) A facetious or witty remark

Wisest Fool in Christendom. James I of England (1566-1625)
The following have been surnamed The Wise.—

ALBERT II, Duke of Austria, called *The Lame and Wise* (1289, 1330-58)
ALFONSO X (or IX) of Leon, and IV of Castile, called *The Wise* and *The Astronomer.* (1203, 1252-85)
CHARLES V of France, called *Le Sage*. (1337, regent 1358-60, king 1364-80)
FREDERICK II, Elector of Saxony (1482, 1544-56)
JOHN V of Brittany, called *The Good and Wise* (1389, 1399-1442)

Wise Men of Greece, The, also known as *The Seven Sages*
Solon of Athens (about 638-559 B C) whose motto was, "Know thyself "

Chilo of Sparta (d 597 B.C.)—"Consider the end." *See* DE MORTUIS.

Thales of Miletus (d. 548 B.C.)—"Who hateth suretyship is sure"

Bias of Priene (fl. 6th cent. B.C.)—"Most men are bad."

Cleobulus of Lindos (d 564 B.C.)—"The golden mean," or "Avoid extremes"

Pittacus of Mitylene (d 570 B.C.)—"Seize Time by the forelock"

Periander of Corinth (d 585 B.C.)—"Nothing is impossible to industry"

The Wise Men of the East. *See* MAGI.

Wisest Man of Greece, The. So the Delphic oracle pronounced Socrates to be, and Socrates modestly made answer, "'Tis because I alone of all the Greeks know that I know nothing"

Wiseacre (Ger *weissager*, a soothsayer or prophet) This word, like the Greek "sophism," has quite lost its original meaning, and is applied to dunces, wise only in their own conceit.

There is a story told that Ben Jonson, at the Devil, in Fleet Street, said to a country gentleman who boasted of his estates, "What care we for your dirt and clods? Where you have an acre of land, I have ten acres of wit" The landed gentleman retorted by calling Ben "Good Mr. Wiseacre" The story may pass for what it is worth.

Wish. The wish is father to the thought. We are always ready to believe what we most want to believe When the Prince says to his dying father "I never thought to hear you speak again," Henry IV replies—

Thy wish was father, Harry, to that thought·
I stay too long for thee, I weary thee
                              2 Henry IV, IV, 4

To wish one farther. To prefer his room to his company; to wish him gone

Wishing bone. *See* MERRYTHOUGHT.

Wishing cap. Fortunatus (*q v.*) had an inexhaustible purse and a wishing cap, but these gifts proved the ruin of himself and his sons. The object of the tale is to show the vanity of human prosperity

Wishful thinking A popular psychoanalytical term that has gained general acceptance as describing the unconscious expression of one's desire in accordance with one's opinion; the thinking a thing to be true because one wants it to be so

Wit. Understanding, intelligence (A S *witt*, knowledge), hence, the power of perceiving analogies and other relations between apparently incongruous ideas or of forming unexpected, striking, or ludicrous combinations of them, and so, a person distinguished for this power, a witty person

At one's wits' end. Quite at a loss as to what to say or what to do next, "flummoxed"

Great wits jump Great minds think alike, tally Shakespeare says, "It jumps with my humour" (1 *Henry IV*, IV, 2)

The five wits *See* FIVE

To have one's wits about one. To be wide awake, observant of all that is going on and prepared to take advantage of any opportunity that offers.

To wit. Namely, that is to say

Witch. (A.S. *wiccian*, to practise sorcery.)

Innocent VIII issued the celebrated bull *Summis Desiderantes* in 1484, directing inquisitors and others to put to death all practisers of witchcraft and other diabolical arts, and it has been computed that as many as nine millions of persons have suffered death for witchcraft since that date

By drawing the blood of a witch you deprive her of her power of sorcery Glanvil says that when Jane Brooks, the demon of Tedworth, bewitched a boy, his father scratched her face and drew blood, whereupon the boy instantly exclaimed that he was well

Blood will I draw on thee, thou art a witch.
                              1 *Henry VI*, 1, 5.

John Fian, a schoolmaster at Saltpans, near Edinburgh, was tortured and then burnt at the stake on the Castle Hill of Edinburgh in 1591, because he refused to acknowledge that he had raised a storm at sea, to wreck James VI on his voyage to Denmark to visit his future queen.

Matthew Hopkins, the notorious "witchfinder," who, in the middle of the 17th century, travelled through the Eastern Counties to hunt out witches, is said to have hanged sixty in one year in Essex alone At last he himself was tested by his own rule; when cast into a river he floated, and so was declared to be a wizard, and was put to death.

It is said that in England between three and four thousand persons suffered death for witchcraft between 1643 and 1661, and as late as 1705 two women were executed at Northampton

Witch hazel. A North American shrub (*Hamamelis virginiana*) having several large branches It is so called because its twigs are used as divining rods

Witches Sabbath. The muster at nighttime of witches (called a "coven") and demons to concoct mischief. The witch first anointed her feet and shoulders with the fat of a murdered babe, then mounting a broomstick, distaff, or rake, made her exit by the chimney, and rode through the air to the place of rendezvous The assembled witches feasted together, and concluded with a dance, in which they all turned their backs to each other.

Witchen. *See* ROWAN.

Witenagemot (wĭt' e ne gĕ mŏt) The Anglo-Saxon parliament *Witan* is A S for *wise men* (connected with *witt*, knowledge); *gemote* is *ge-*, together, *moot*, meet, hence "an assembly of wise men"

The famous assembly of our forefathers was called by various names [as] *Mycel Gemot* (or great meeting), the Witenagemot (or meeting of the wise), and sometimes the Mycel Getheaht (or great thought) — FREEMAN· *The Norman Conquest*, 1, 3

Withers A horse's *withers* are the muscles uniting the neck and shoulders, or the ridge between the shoulder-blades, so called from A S *wither*, against, because this part is *against* the collar or load. Hamlet says (iii, 2):—

> Let the galled jade wince, our withers are unwrung

That is, let those wince who are galled, as for myself, my withers are not wrung The skin of this part is often galled by the pommel of an ill-fitting saddle, and then the irritation of the saddle makes the horse wince In 1 *Henry IV*, ii, 1, one of the carriers gives direction to the ostler to ease the saddle of his horse, Cut. "I prythee, Tom, beat Cut's saddle . the poor jade is wrung on the withers," that is, the muscles are wrung, and the skin galled by the saddle

Withershins. An Anglo-Saxon word, still in use in Scotland and in north-country dialects, denoting a movement in a contrary direction to that of the sun—as of a clock whose hands are going backwards (Icel *vithr.* against, *sinni*, movement). Hence, contrariwise, topsy-turvy

The opposite of *withershins* is *deiseal*, a Gaelic word meaning "righthandwise "

Wittelsbach, House of. The former reigning dynasty in Bavaria

Wivern (wī' vern). A fabulous creature of heraldry consisting of a winged dragon ending in a barbed, serpent's tail

Wizard of Oz. The central figure in a very popular children's book *The Wonderful Wizard of Oz*, (1900) by Lyman Frank Baum (1856-1919), a well-known American journalist The musical comedy of the same name (1901) was a great success, which was carried on to the film of some years later.

> We're off to see the Wizard
> The Wonderful Wizard of Oz
> We hear he's a whiz of a Wizard,
> If ever a Wiz there was

Woden (wō' den) The Anglo-Saxon form of *Odin* (*q.v*), the name of the supreme god of the later Scandinavian pantheon, he having supplanted Thor Woden was the god of agriculture, and on this account Wednesday (Woden's Day) was considered to be specially favourable for sowing

Woe. Wo, or **Woe worth the day!** Cursed be the day! Evil betide it!

> Thus saith the Lord God Howl ye, woe worth the day!—*Ezek.* xxx, 2

Worth here is A S *weothan*, to become

Woebegone. Overwhelmed by woe, especially applied to the appearance—*A woebegone countenance* At first sight it would seem that the words imply the reverse of this, but *begone* is the p p. of the old English verb *began*, to surround It thus means "surrounded with woe" rather than "woe go away, be gone "

The Knight of the Woeful Countenance. The title given by Sancho Panza to Don Quixote (Bk iii, ch. v).

Wolf. The tradition that wolves were extirpated from Great Britain in the reign of Edgar (959-975) is based upon the words of William of Malmesbury, who says (Bk. ii, ch viii) that the tribute paid by the King of Wales, consisting of 300 wolves, ceased after the third year, because he could find no more; but in 1076 we find that Robert de Umfraville, knight, held his lordship of Riddlesdale in Northumberland by service of defending that part of the kingdom from "wolves " In 1369 Thomas Engarne held lands in Pitchley, Northamptonshire, by service of finding dogs at his own cost for the destruction of "wolves" and foxes, and even as late as 1433 Sir Robert Plumpton held one bovate of land in the county of Notts by service of "frighting the wolves" in Sherwood Forest

Wolf has been applied as an epithet to many persons of savage and inhuman disposition, especially to Isabella, the *She-wolf of France*, the queen of Edward II According to tradition, she murdered her royal husband by thrusting a hot iron into his bowels

> She-wolf of France, with unrelenting fangs,
> That tear'st the bowels of thy mangled mate
> GRAY *The Bard*

Dryden gave the name to the Presbytery in his *Hind and Panther*

> Unkennelled range in thy Polonian plains,
> A fiercer foe the insatiate Wolf remains

In music a discordant sound (occasioned by a faulty interval) in certain chords of the organ and stringed instruments such as the piano, violin, harp, etc , is called a *wolf*

> Nature hath implanted so inveterate a hatred atweene the wolfe and the sheepe, that, being dead, yet in the operation of Nature appeareth there a sufficient trial of their discording nature; so that the enmity betweene them seemeth not to dye with their bodies, for if there be put upon a harpe . strings made of the intralles of a sheepe, and amongst them . one made of the intralles of a wolfe the musician . . . cannot reconcile them to a unity and concord of sounds, so discording is that string of the wolfe —FERNE *Blazon of Gentrie* (1586)

The squeak made in *reed* instruments by unskilled players is termed a "goose "

Wolf call (U.S.A.). An admiring exclamation, usually whistled, at sight of a girl

Wolf Cub. A Boy Scout of the most junior rank, aged from eight to eleven years.

A wolf pack, in World War II was a group of German submarines working as a unit in an attack on a merchant or other ship

Between dog and wolf. Neither daylight nor dark, the blind man's holiday Generally applied to the evening dusk In Latin, *Inter canem et lupum*, in French, *Entre chien et loup*

Dark as a wolf's mouth. Pitch dark.

He has seen a wolf. Something or other has frightened him, formerly said of a person who had lost his voice Our forefathers believed that if a man saw a wolf before the wolf saw him, he became dumb, at least for a time

To see a wolf is also a good sign, inasmuch as the wolf was dedicated to Odin, the giver of victory

A wolf in sheep's clothing An enemy posing as a friend. The phrase is taken from the well-known fable of Æsop

He put his head into the wolf's mouth. He exposed himself to needless danger. The allusion is to Æsop's fable of the crane that put its head into a wolf's (or fox's) mouth in order to extract a bone.

Holding a wolf by the ears. An old Greek saying, Augustus used it of his situation in Rome, meaning it was equally dangerous to keep hold or to let go

He that goes to law (as the proverb is) holds a wolf by the ears —BURTON *Anatomy of Melancholy* (*Democritus to the Reader*)

To cry "Wolf!" To give a false alarm. The allusion is to the well-known fable of the shepherd lad who so often cried "Wolf!" merely to make fun of the neighbours, that when at last the wolf came no one would believe him

To keep the wolf from the door. To ward off starvation We say of a ravenous person "He has a wolf in his stomach," and one who eats voraciously is said *to wolf* his food French *manger comme un loup* is to eat voraciously

Wake not a sleeping wolf! (2 *Henry IV*, i, 2) A variant of "Let sleeping dogs lie!"—let well alone.

Wolf's-bane. A species of aconite, *Aconitum lycoctonum* The name is said to have arisen through a curious double etymological confusion *Bane* is a common term for poisonous plants, and by some early botanist it was translated into Gr. *kuamos*, which means *bean*. The plant has a pale yellow flower, and was so called the *white-bane* to distinguish it from the *blue* aconite. The Greek for white is *leukos*, hence *leukos-kuamos*, but *lukos* is the Greek for wolf, and by a blunder *leukos-kuamos* (white-bean) got muddled into *lukos-kuamos* (wolf-bean) Botanists, seeing the absurdity of calling aconite a *bean*, restored the original word *bane* but retained the corrupt word *lukos* (a wolf), and hence we get the name wolf's-bane for white aconite

Another, more plausible, explanation would probably be that the plant is so called because meat saturated with its juice was supposed to be a wolf-poison

Wolfe's Own. The 1st Battalion, the Loyal Regiment, so called for their distinguished service under Wolfe, at Louisburg (1758) and Quebec (1759).

Woman's Suffrage *See* SUFFRAGE.

Womble Cropped. An American word in use about 1800, denoting a feeling of uneasiness about anything.

Wonder. A nine days' wonder. Something that causes a sensational astonishment for a few days, and is then placed in the limbo of "things forgot " Three days' amazement, three days' discussion of details, and three days of subsidence

For whan men han wel cried, than let hem roune! For wonder last but nine night nevere in toune! CHAUCER *Troilus and Criseyde*, iv 587

The Seven Wonders of the World.
The Pyramids of Egypt
The Hanging Gardens of Babylon.
The Tomb of Mausolus
The Temple of Diana at Ephesus
The Colossus of Rhodes
The Statue of Jupiter, by Phidias
The Pharos of Alexandria

A later list gives :—
The Coliseum of Rome.
The Catacombs of Alexandria.
The Great Wall of China
Stonehenge
The Leaning Tower of Pisa
The Porcelain Tower of Nankin.
The Mosque of St Sophia at Constantinople.

The Wonder of the World. The title given to Otto III, Emperor of the Holy Roman Empire, 983-1002, on account of his brilliant intellectual endowments The Emperor Frederick II (1215-50) was also so called.

The Wonderful, or Wondermaking, Parliament. The same as "The Unmerciful Parliament", convened in the reign of Richard II (February 3rd, 1388). By playing into the hands of the Duke of Gloucester it checkmated the king

Wonder-worker. St. Gregory, Bishop of Neo-Cæsarea, in Pontus, and one of the Fathers of the Eastern Church (d. 270). So called because he "recalled devils, stayed a river, changed a lake into solid earth, and did many other wonderful things." *See* THAUMATURGUS.

Wonkey (wong' ki). A modern slang word meaning unsound or unsteady It comes from the Old English *wancol*, of precisely the same meaning.

Wood, Wooden. Drawn from the wood. Taken direct from the cask to the tankard or glass Said of beer, wines, and spirits

Don't cry (or halloo) till you are out of the wood. Do not rejoice for having escaped danger till the danger has passed away. "Call no man happy till he is dead", "there's many a slip 'twixt the cup and the lip "

One can't see the wood for the trees. There is such a mass of detail that it is almost impossible to arrive at a true estimate of the thing as a whole.

Woodbine. A name given in different localities to many plants that bind or wind themselves around trees, especially the honeysuckle and the convolvulus In the first quotation below probably the former is intended; in the second the latter.

Where the bee
Strays diligent, and with extracted balm
Of fragrant woodbine loads his little thigh
PHILLIPS

Shakespeare says—
So doth the woodbine, the sweet honeysuckle
Gently entwist *Midsummer Night's Dream*, iv, 1.

Woodchuck. A marmot (*Arctomys monax*) of North America, also called the *ground-hog*. Its name is a corruption of its North American Indian name, *wejack*, and has given rise to the punning conundrum—

How much wood would a woodchuck chuck, if a woodchuck could chuck wood?

Woodcock Old slang for a simpleton, from the supposition that woodcocks are without brains Polonius tells his daughter that protestations of love are "springes to catch woodcocks" (*Hamlet*, i, 3)

Wooden. Used of one who is awkward and ungainly, or of a spiritless, emotionless person

The wooden horse. An enchanted horse of the old romance that could be directed by a peg turned by the rider and could fly through the air. Cambuscan (*q.v*) had such a horse, but his was of brass

This very day may be seen in the king's armoury the identical peg with which Peter of Provence turned his Wooden Horse, which carried him through the air It is rather bigger than the pole of a coach, and stands near Babieca's saddle —*Don Quixote,* pt 1, bk IV, 19

The wooden horse of Troy. Virgil tells us that Ulysses had a monster wooden horse made after the death of Hector, and gave out that it was an offering to the gods to secure a prosperous voyage back to Greece The Trojans dragged the horse within their city, but it was full of Grecian soldiers, who at night stole out of their place of concealment, slew the Trojan guards, opened the city gates, and set fire to Troy. Menelaus was one of the Greeks shut up in it. It was made by Epeios.

The wooden mare. "The mare foaled of an acorn." An instrument of torture to enforce military discipline, used in the reign of Charles II and long after The horse was made of oak, the back was a sharp ridge, supported on four tall legs The victim was seated on the ridge, with a firelock fastened to each foot and kept in this painful position for the term of the sentence.

Wooden nutmegs. Connecticut was in the early 19th century referred to derisively as the land of wooden nutmegs because certain dishonest merchants from the State were said to have exported nutmegs made of wood and other worthless goods

The wooden wedge. Last in the classical tripos When, in 1824, the classical tripos was instituted at Cambridge, it was debated by what name to call the last on the list It so happened that the last on the list was Wedgewood, and the name was adopted for this slightly modified form.

Wooden walls Ships of war Before the advent of ironclads England's defence literally was "wooden walls "

When the Greeks sent to Delphi to ask how they were to defend themselves against Xerxes, who had invaded their country, the evasive answer given was to this effect.

Pallas hath urged, and Zeus, the sire of all,
Hath safety promised in a wooden wall,
Seed-time and harvest, weeping sires shall tell
How thousands fought at Salamis and fell.

Wood's Halfpence. The copper coinage for which William Wood, a copper-founder of Wolverhampton, obtained from the Government the valuable privilege of supplying to Ireland, in 1722 The outcry against this was so great (*see* DRAPIER'S LETTERS) that the patent was revoked in 1725

Woof. *See* WARP

Wookey Hole. A noted cavern near Wells in Somerset which has given birth to as many weird stories as the Sibyls' Cave in Italy *Wicked as the Witch of Wookey* is an old local simile, and we read in Percy's *Reliques* that the witch was metamorphosed into stone by a "lerned wight" from Gaston, but left her curse behind, so that the fair damsels of Wookey rarely find "a gallant "

Wool. Great cry and little wool. *See* CRY.

Dyed in the wool. Cloth which is wool-dyed (not piece-dyed) is true throughout and will wash Hence the phrase is used to describe anything or person absolutely genuine

No wool is so white that a dyer cannot blacken it. No one is so free from faults that slander can find nothing to say against him; no book is so perfect as to be free from adverse criticism.

Your wits are gone wool-gathering You are absent-minded; you're not thinking of the matter in hand. As children sent to gather wool from hedges wander hither and thither apparently aimlessly, so absent-minded persons can hold their minds to nothing, but wander in their thoughts from point to point.

Woollen. In 1666 an Act of Parliament was passed for "burying in woollen only," which was intended for "the encouragement of the woollen manufactures of the kingdom, and prevention of the exportation of money for the buying and importing of linen " The Act was repealed in 1814, but long before then it had fallen into abeyance

"Odious! in woollen! 'twould a saint provoke!"
(Were the last words that poor Narcissa spoke)
"No! let a charming chintz and Brussels lace
Wrap my cold limbs, and shade my lifeless face.
One would not, sure, be frightful when one's dead,
And—Betty—give the cheeks a little red."
POPE *Moral Essays, Ep.* i.

Woolsack, The. The official seat of the Lord Chancellor when presiding over the House of Lords It is a large, square bag of wool—somewhat resembling an ottoman—covered with red material and having neither sides nor back There were originally four such woolsacks in the Lords' chamber, on which sat the Judges, the Barons of the Exchequer, the Serjeants-at-Law, and the Masters in Chancery. None of these officials had any voice in the proceedings of the House, and their woolsacks were not, technically, within its precincts This still applies to the Lord Chancellor's woolsack, as by standing orders when he wishes to address the House he is "to go to his own place as a peer." The term Woolsack is often applied to the office of Lord Chancellor

Word. A man of his word. One whose word may be depended on; trustworthy; he is "as good as his word," and "his word is as good as his bond "

A word to the wise! Said when giving advice as a hint that it would be well for the recipient to follow it The Latin *Verbum satis sapienti,* a word is enough to the wise

By word of mouth. Orally As "he took it down by word of mouth" (as it was spoken by the speaker)

I take you at your word. I will act in reliance upon what you tell me.

Many words will not fill a bushel. Mere promises will not help the needy If we say to a beggar, "Be thou filled," is he filled?

Pray, make no words about it. Don't mention it, make no fuss about it

Put in a good word for me, please! Do your best to get me some privilege or favour; put my claims, my deeds, etc, in the best light possible

Soft words butter no parsnips. *See* BUTTER

The Word. The Scriptures; Christ as the Logos (*see John* 1, 1)

The object of words is to conceal thoughts. *See* SPEECH.

To give, or pass one's word. To give a definite undertaking, make a binding promise

To have words with one. To quarrel; to have an angry discussion *To have a word with one.* is to have a brief conversation with him

Upon my word. Assuredly, by my troth.

Upon my word and honour! A strong affirmation of the speaker as to the truth of what he has asserted

World. A man or woman of the world. One who is acquainted with the ways of public and social life, not quite the same as a *worldly* man or woman, which expression would denote one that cares *only* for the things of this world

In Shakespeare's time a *woman of the world* was merely a married woman:—

Touchstone To-morrow will we be married
Audrey I do desire it with all my heart, and I hope it is no dishonest desire to be a woman of the world —
As You Like It, v, 3

Everyone goes to the world but I, and I may sit in a corner and cry heigho! for a husband —*Much Ado About Nothing*, ii, 1

All the world and his wife. Everyone without exception

The world, the flesh, and the devil. "The world," *i e* the things of this world, in contra-distinction to religious matters, "the flesh," i e. love of pleasure and sensual enjoyments, "the devil," *i e* all temptations to evil of every kind, as theft, murder, lying, blasphemy, and so on

From all the deceits of the world, the flesh, and the devil, Good Lord, deliver us —*The Litany* (*Book of Common Prayer*)

World Court. The Permanent Court of International Justice, set up at The Hague under the Covenant of the League of Nations in September, 1921, and confirmed by the Charter of the United Nations in November, 1946 It has 15 judges elected by the Powers and it considers and passes judgment (from which appeal may be made to the Security Council) on all international disputes which may involve recourse to arms

The World Turned Upside Down An inn-sign alluding to Captain Cook's discovery of Australia, where the inhabitants were thought of as hanging down into space

World Wars The name given generally—and throughout this book—to the two great wars of 1914-18 and 1939-45 in which most civilized nations of the world were participants

World War II abbreviations. World War II was made a nightmare for those taking part by the habit of contracting all official names into initials which formed words easily remembered but seldom understood Among the most frequently used were —

AAF	American Air Force
ABCA	Army Bureau of Current Affairs (British)
AIF	Australian Imperial Forces
AMGOT	Allied Military Government of Occupied Territory
ARP·	Air Raid Precautions (British)
ATC	Air Transport Command, earlier Ferry Command. Main function was flying planes from U S A to Britain
ATS	Auxiliary Territorial Service, women in military service (British)
BAR	Browning automatic rifle (U S A.)
BAOR	British Army of the Rhine
CARE.	Cooperative for American Remittances to Europe A non-profit making organization for sending food parcels to Europe, continued after the war
COSSAC·	Chief of Staff to the Supreme Allied Commander, the word Cossac became the code word for the Allied headquarters in London
DP	Displaced Person. Term applied to foreign forced labour and other refugees liberated by the Allied armies in Europe Sarcastically referred to as "Displeased Persons" by the harassed troops who had to cope with the innumerable problems these thousands of broken lives presented
DZ	Dropping Zone The target area in which paratroops intended to land
ETA·	Estimated Time of Arrival
ETO	European Theatre of Operations
ETOUSA:	European Theatre of Operations United States Army
FFI.	French Forces of the Interior.
GI.	Government issue From equipment its use extended to American enlisted men
LDV	Local Defence Volunteers (British) Later Home Guard
LCI·	Landing Craft, Infantry.
LST·	Landing Ship, Tank
LZ,	Landing Zone The target area in which gliders intend to land.
MTOUSA	Mediterranean Theatre of Operations United States Army
NATOUSA	North African Theatre of Operations United States Army
OCS,	Officer Candidate School (U.S A)
OCTU	Officer Cadet Training Unit (British)
OSS	Office of Strategic Services (U S A) Organization for the gathering of strategic information and the execution of special missions in enemy territory
OWI	Office of War Information (U S A)
PIAT	Projectile Infantry Anti-Tank (British) A tank-destroying weapon operated on the same principle as the American bazooka and German Panzerfaust
SAAFA	Soldiers', Army and Air Force Families Association (British) An organization to help deal with domestic problems of men absent in the forces
SHAEF	Supreme Headquarters Allied Expeditionary Forces
VIP	Very Important Person, requiring special accommodation or transport
WAAC	Women's Army Auxiliary Corps (U S A) Similar to British ATS
WAAF	Women's Auxiliary Air Force
WRNS	Women's Royal Naval Service, Wrens
WVS	Women's Voluntary Services (British), started 1938

Worm The word was formerly used of dragons and great serpents, especially those of Teutonic and old Norse legend, it is now figuratively applied to miserable, grovelling creatures; also to the ligament under a dog's tongue

Idle worms It was once supposed that little worms were bred in the fingers of idle servants To this Shakespeare alludes—

A round little worm
Pricked from the lazy finger of a maid
Romeo and Juliet, 1, 4

To be food for worms. To be dead

Your worm is your only emperor for diet, we fat all creatures else, to fat us, and we fat ourselves for maggots —*Hamlet*, iv, 3

To have a worm in one's tongue. To be cantankerous; to snarl and bite like a mad dog

There is one easy artifice
That seldom has been known to miss—
To snarl at all things right or wrong,
Like a mad dog that has a worm in's tongue
BUTLER *Upon Modern Critics*

To satisfy the worm. To appease one's hunger

To worm out information. To elicit information indirectly and piecemeal.

To worm oneself into another's favour. To insinuate oneself into the good graces of another person

Wormwood. The common name for the aromatic herbs of the genus *Artemisia*, especially *A. absinthium*, from which absinthe and vermouth are concocted The name, which is of very great antiquity, almost certainly comes from the ancient legend that this plant sprang up in the track of the serpent as it writhed along the ground when driven out of Paradise

Worship. Literally "worth-ship," honour, dignity, reverence, in its highest and now usual sense the respect and reverence man pays to God In R C theology there are three kinds of worship—*latria*, the worship due to God alone, *hyperdulia*, the lesser worship paid to the B.V M , and *dulia*, the respect paid to the saints.

At one time the word carried a sense of personal respect "Thou shalt have *worship* in the presence of them that sit at meat with thee" (*Luke* xiv, 10) means "Thou shalt have *worth-ship*—value or appreciation " In the marriage service the man says to the woman, "With my body I thee worship, and with all my worldly goods I thee endow"—that is, I confer on you my rank and dignities, and endow you with my wealth, the worthship attached to my person I share with you, and the wealth which is mine is thine also.

Magistrate and mayors are addressed as *Your Worship*, and in writing a mayor is *The Worshipful Mayor, Mr A.*

Worst. If the worst comes to the worst. Even if the very worst occurs.

To get the worst of it. To come off second best, to be defeated, worsted

Worsted (wer' sted). Yarn or thread made of wool, so called from Worsted, a village near Norwich, once the centre of an extensive woollen-weaving industry. The name occurs as early as the 13th century.

Worthies, the Nine. Nine heroes—three from the Bible, three from the classics, and three from romance—who were frequently bracketed together, as in the burlesque Pageant of the Nine Worthies in Shakespeare's *Love's Labour's Lost.* They are—Joshua, David, and Judas Maccabæus; Hector, Alexander, and Julius Cæsar, Arthur, Charlemagne, and Godfrey of Bouillon

Nine worthies were they called, of different rites—
Three Jews, three pagans, and three Christian knights
DRYDEN *The Flower and the Leaf*

The Nine Worthies of London A kind of chronicle-history in mixed verse and prose of nine prominent citizens of London, published in 1592 by Richard Johnson, author also of *The Seven Champions of Christendom.* His "Worthies" are—

Sir William Walworth, who stabbed Wat Tyler, the rebel, and was twice Lord Mayor (1374, 1380)

Sir Henry Pritchard, who (in 1356) feasted Edward III (with 5,000 followers), Edward the Black Prince, John, King of Austria, the King of Cyprus, and David, King of Scotland

Sir William Sevenoke, who fought with the Dauphin of France, built twenty almshouses and a free school (1418)

Sir Thomas White, merchant tailor, who, in 1553, kept the citizens loyal to Queen Mary during Wyatt's rebellion

Sir John Bonham, entrusted with a valuable cargo for the Danish market, and made commander of the army raised to stop the progress of the great Solyman

Christopher Croker Famous at the siege of Bordeaux, and companion of the Black Prince when he helped Don Pedro to the throne of Castile

Sir John Hawkwood One of the Black Prince's knights, and immortalized in Italian history as Giovanni Acuti Cavaliero.

Sir Hugh Caverley Famous for ridding Poland of a monstrous bear

Sir Henry Maleverer, generally called Henry of Cornhill, who lived in the reign of Henry IV He was a crusader, and became the guardian of "Jacob's well "

Wouldn't it! (Austr.) This was a very generally used phrase, being short for "Wouldn't it suit you!" It could be used as a sarcastic reply to any statement

Wound. Bind the wound, and grease the weapon. A Rosicrucian maxim. *See* WEAPON-SALVE

Wove. Applied to papers made on an ordinary dandy roll or mould in which the wires are woven Used in contradistinction to *laid* (*q v*)

Wowser (wou' zer) An Australian term dating from about 1900, meaning a narrow-minded bigot who criticizes and seeks to interfere with civil liberties and the amusements of the people—a splendid Australian word which has not taken root elsewhere.

Wraf. A member of the Women's Royal Air Force, formerly called a Waaf (Women's Auxiliary Air Force)

Wraith (rāth) The phantom or spectral appearance of a still living person, usually taken as a warning that that person is very shortly going to die It appears to persons at a distance, and forewarns them of the event.

Wrangler. The Cambridge term for one who has obtained a place in the highest class of the mathematical tripos The first man used to be termed the *Senior Wrangler*, and the rest were arranged according to respective merit, but since 1909 this arrangement has been dropped and no one now can claim the title of *Senior Wrangler*

In the Middle Ages college exercises were called *disputations*, and those who performed them *disputants*, because the main part consisted in pitting two men against one another, one to argue *pro* and the other *con*. In the law and theological "schools" this is still done for the bachelor's and doctor's degrees

In the Western U.S A a wrangler is a herdsman.

Wren A member of the *W*omen's *R*oyal *N*aval Service.

Wrenning Day. St Stephen's Day (Dec 26th) used to be so called, because it was a custom among villagers to stone a wren to death on that day in commemoration of the saint's martyrdom

Wright of Norwich. Do you know Dr. Wright of Norwich. A reproof given to a person who stops the decanter at dinner. Dr Wright, of Norwich, was a great dinner-out and excellent talker When a person stops the bottle and is asked this question, it is as much as to say, Dr Wright had the privilege of doing so because he entertained the table with his conversation, but you are no Dr. Wright, except in stopping the circulation of the wine

A similar reproof is given in the combination room of our universities in this way: The bottle-stopper is asked if he knows A or B (*any name*), and after several queries as to who A or B is, the questioner says, "He was hanged," and being asked what for, replies, "For stopping the bottle."

Wrinkle. Familiar slang for a useful bit of information, a "tip" or a dodge For instance, if a man were going abroad for the first time he might go to a friend who was a frequent visitor *to get a wrinkle or two, i e* learn about the things to see, the way of living there, how to get through the Customs, etc

Write. A S *writan*, connected with Icel *rita*, to tear, to cut, scratch out, etc

To write down, besides meaning to commit to writing, means to criticize unfavourably, to depreciate Contrariwise, **to write up** is to puff, to bring into public notice or estimation by favourable criticisms or accounts.

To write off a debt. To cancel it

To write oneself out To exhaust one's powers of literary production

Writer. The Scottish term for a solicitor or attorney, in full a **Writer to the Signet,** the Signet being the smaller seal of the Sovereign.

In the navy a *writer* is a paymaster's non-commissioned assistant, a clerk to a paymaster, either afloat or ashore

Wrong. The king can do no wrong. A legal maxim enshrining two truths, firstly, that as the monarch is—in theory—the creator of all law he cannot be subject to it, and, secondly, that the Sovereign, *as* Sovereign, does nothing except on the advice and with the consent of his ministers.

Wrong 'un. A swindler, a cheat, a palpably dishonest person, applied also to false coin and many things that are not what they purport to be, also to a horse which has run at any flat-race meeting not recognized by the Jockey Club, and so is boycotted by the Club

In cricket, the word **wrong** is applied to a ball which breaks the opposite way from what the batsman has every reason to expect from his observation of the bowler's grip of the ball and manner of delivery, it is also called a "Chinaman"

Wroth Money or Wroth Silver. Money paid to the lord in lieu of castle guard for military service, a tribute paid for killing accidentally some person of note, a tribute paid in acknowledgement of the tenancy of unenclosed land Dugdale, in his *History of Warwickshire*, says —

There is a certain rent due unto the lord of this Hundred (*i e.* of Knightlow, the property of the Duke of Buccleuch) called wroth money, or warth-money, or swarff-penny

The rent must be paid on Martinmas Day (Nov 11th), in the morning at Knightlow Cross, before sunrise The party paying it must go thrice about the cross and say, "The wrath-money," and then lay it (varying from 1d to 2s 3d) in a hole in the said cross before good witnesses, or forfeit a white bull with red nose and ears The amount thus collected reached in 1892 to about 9s, and all who complied with the custom were entertained at a substantial breakfast at the Duke's expense, and were toasted in a glass of rum and milk

Wulstan, St A Saxon Bishop of Worcester, who received his see from Edward the Confessor, and died in 1075. He fought against William the Conqueror, and when ordered to resign his see, planted his crozier in the shrine of the Confessor, declaring if any of his accusers could draw it out he would resign, as no one could do so but St. Wulstan himself, his innocence was admitted.

Wuyck's Bible. *See* BIBLE.

Wych Hazel. *See* WITCH HAZEL

Wyclif's Bible *See* BIBLE, THE ENGLISH.

Wycliffite (wik' lif īt). A Lollard (*q v*), a follower of John Wyclif (*c* 1320-84), the religious reformer, called "The Morning Star of the Reformation." He denied transubstantiation, condemned monasticism, and taught that all ecclesiastical and secular authority is derived from God and is forfeited by one who is living in mortal sin

Wykehamist (wik' ăm ist). A member of Winchester College, past or present, which was founded in 1378 by William of Wykeham (1324-1404), Bishop of Winchester and Lord High Chancellor. Wykeham is a small place in Hampshire

X

X. The twenty-fourth letter of the alphabet, representing the fourteenth letter of the Greek alphabet (*ksi*), and denoting in Roman numeration 10, or, on its side (✕) 1,000, and with a dash over it (X̄) 10,000

In algebra and mathematics generally *x* denotes an unknown quantity The reason of this is that algebra came into use in Europe from Arabia, and that Arabic *shei*, a thing, a something (*cp cosa* under Coss, Rule of) was used in the Middle Ages to designate the mathematically "unknown," and that this was transcribed as *xei*

X on beer casks formerly indicated beer which had paid the old 10s. duty, and hence it came to mean beer of a given quality. Two or three crosses are mere trade-marks, intended to convey the impression that the beer so marked was twice or thrice as strong as that which paid this duty

Xanthian Marbles, The (zăn' thi an) A collection of ancient sculptures and friezes discovered by Sir Charles Fellows in 1838 at Xanthus, a Greek city of Lycia, Asia Minor, and now in the British Museum.

Xanthippe or Xantippe (zăn tip' i) Wife of the philosopher Socrates. Her bad temper shown towards her husband has rendered her name proverbial for a conjugal scold.

Be she as foul as was Florentius' love,
As old as Sibyl, and as curst and shrewd
As Socrates' Xanthippe, or a worse,
She moves me not.
Taming of the Shrew, i, 2.

Xanthus (zăn' thŭs) (Gr, reddish yellow) Achilles' wonderful horse, brother of Balios, Achilles' other horse, and offspring of Zephyrus and the harpy, Podarge Being chid by his master for leaving Patroclus on the field of battle, Xanthus turned his head reproachfully, and told Achilles that he also would soon be numbered with the dead, not from any fault of his horse, but by the decree of inexorable destiny (*Iliad*, xix) (*Cp. Numb.* xxii, 28-30)

Xanthus is also the ancient name of the Scamander and of a city on its banks Elian and Pliny say that Homer called the Scamander "Xanthos" or the "Gold-red river," because it coloured with such a tinge the fleeces of sheep washed in its waters Others maintain that it was so called because a Greek hero of this name defeated a body of Trojans on its banks, and pushed half of them into the stream.

Xaverian Brothers, The (zăv ēr' i ăn) A Roman Catholic congregation founded in Holland in 1846, and so named from St Francis Xavier (1506-52), one of the earliest of the Jesuits and the great missionary to India and the Far East It is concerned chiefly with the education of youth, and has branches in England and the United States ,

Xenocratic (zen ŏ krăt' ik). Pertaining to the doctrine of Xenocrates (396-314 B C), a disciple of Plato, noted for his continence and contempt of wealth. He combined Pythagoreanism with Platonism.

Warmed by such youthful beauty, the severe
Xenocrates would not have more been chaste
Orlando Furioso, xi, 8

Xerxes (zerks' ēz). A Greek way of writing the Persian *Ksathra* or *Kshatra* Xerxes I, the great Xerxes, is identical with the Ahasuerus of the Bible

When Xerxes invaded Greece he constructed a pontoon bridge across the Dardanelles, which was swept away by the force of the waves; this so enraged the Persian despot that he "inflicted three hundred lashes on the rebellious sea, and cast chains of iron across it " This story is a Greek myth, founded on the peculiar construction of Xerxes' second bridge, which consisted of three hundred boats, lashed by iron chains to two ships serving as supporters.

Another story told of him is that when he reviewed his enormous army before starting for Greece, he wept at the thought of slaughter about to take place. "Of all this multitude, who shall say how many will return?" Similarly, it is said that Charlemagne viewed the fleet of the Norsemen in the Mediterranean with tears in his eyes, and remarked, "There was reason for these Xerxes' tears."

Ximena (zim ē' nä) The Cid's bride.

Xiphias (zif' i ås) (Gr. *xiphios*, a sword) The name used in mediæval times for a sword-shaped comet, also for the southern constellation now called *Dorado*; and a poetical name given to the swordfish (genus *Xiphias*).

Strong is the horse upon his speed;
Strong in pursuit the rapid glede,
Which makes at once his game:
Strong the tall ostrich on the ground;
Strong through the turbulent profound
Shoots Xiphias to his aim
Chris Smart *Song to David*

X.Y.Z. Correspondence. In 1797 the President of the U S A , John Adams, sent his agents Pinckney, Marshall, and Gerry to France to negotiate a treaty for the regulation of certain maritime matters. From Paris they reported that three French agents had intercepted them and demanded a large sum of money before the Directory would receive any American diplomats, alternatively a loan would have to be granted by U S.A to France. The Americans refused to negotiate on these terms, and the whole correspondence with the three French agents, whom they designated as X Y. and Z., was published in Washington.

Y

Y. The twenty-fifth letter of the alphabet, is a differentiation of the Greek y (*see* Samian Letter) added by the Greeks to the Phœnician alphabet

In Algebra it denotes the second unknown quantity (*cp.* X), and in the Middle Ages it was used in Roman numeration for 150. *See also* Ye.

Yahoo (ya' hoo) Swift's name, in *Gulliver's Travels*, for brutes with human forms and vicious propensities They are subject to the *Houyhnhnms*, the horses with human reason. Hence applied to coarse, brutish, or degraded persons.

Yahweh. *See* JEHOVAH

Yama (ya' ma). The god of the dead in Hindu mythology, the Hindu Pluto. The story is that he was the first mortal to die and so was made a god.

Yank. To yank, to pull with a jerk. A word of uncertain origin

Yankee (yăng' ki). Properly a New Englander or one of New England stock; but extended to mean, first, an inhabitant of the Northern as apart from the Southern United States, and later to comprise all United States citizens
It is generally taken to be a North American Indian corruption of *English* (or of Fr *Anglais*) The story is that in 1713 one Jonathan Hastings, a farmer of Cambridge, Massachusetts, used the word as a puffing epithet, meaning genuine, what cannot be surpassed, etc ; as, a "Yankee horse," "Yankee cider," and so on The students at Harvard, catching up the term, called Hastings, "Yankee Jonathan " It soon spread, and became the jocose pet name of the New Englander.

Yankee Doodle The quasi national air of the United States, the doggerel words of which are said to have been written by Dr Shuckburgh, a surgeon in Lord Amherst's army during the French and Indian war of 1755.
The origin of the tune is disputed: some say that it comes from a mediæval church service, others that it was composed in England in Cromwell's time, others that it was played by the Hessian troops during the American Revolution and adopted by the revolutionaries in mockery A Dutch origin has also been suggested

Yarborough. A hand at bridge in which there is no card higher than a nine So called because the second Lord Yarborough (early 19th cent) used to lay 1,000 to 1 against such an occurrence in any named hand The actual mathematical odds are 1,827 to 1 against

Yashmak (yăsh' măk) The veil worn by Moslem women It consists of a white or a black veil, either covering the whole face or hanging from immediately below the eyes

Yclept (i klept'). An old English word meaning called, named, styled It is now only used in a sort of arch facetiousness that Fowler calls "Worn-out Humour."

Ye. An archaic way of writing *the*, the *y* representing A.S 3 *(ge)* which in Middle English became confused with þ, the character representing our *th* as in *then* It never was pronounced other than *the*.

Year (connected with Gr *horos*, a season, and Lat. *hora*, an hour). The period of time occupied by the revolution of the earth round the sun.
The Astronomical, Equinoctial, Natural, Solar, or Tropical year, is the time taken by the sun in returning to the same equinox, in mean length, 365 days 5 hours 48 min. and
46 sec

The Astral or Sidereal year is the time in which the sun apparently returns to the same place in relation to the fixed stars. 365 days 6 hours 9 min and 9 sec
The Platonic, Great, or Perfect year *(Annus magnus)*, was estimated by early Greek and Hindu astronomers at about 26,000 years, at the end of which all the heavenly bodies were imagined to return to the same places as they occupied at the Creation
The Chaldean astronomers observed that the fixed stars shift their places at about the rate of a degree in seventy-two years, according to which calculation they will perform one revolution in 25,920 years, at the end of which time they will return to their "as you were." The Egyptians made it 30,000 years, and the Arabians 49,000.

For a year and a day. In law many acts are determined by this period of time—*e g* if a person wounded does not die within a year and a day, the offender is not guilty of murder, if an owner does not claim an estray within the same length of time, it belongs to the lord of the manor; a year and a day is given to prosecute appeals, etc.

Year of Grace. A year of the Christian era.

Year in year out. All the year round, without cessation.

Yellow (A.S *geolo*, connected with Gr. *chloros*, green, and with *gall*, the yellowish fluid secreted by the bile). Indicating in symbolism jealousy, inconstancy, and adultery. In France the doors of traitors used to be daubed with yellow. In some countries the law ordained that Jews must be clothed in yellow, because they betrayed our Lord, hence Judas, in mediæval pictures, is arrayed in yellow In Spain at an *auto-de-fé* the victims were robed in yellow, to denote heresy and treason
In heraldry and in ecclesiastical symbolism yellow is frequently used in place of gold.
As a slang or colloquial term yellow is applied to a coward.

Yellow-back A cheap novel, particularly one of the sensational kind So called because of the yellow board bindings so well known on railway bookstalls up to about the early 'nineties of last century

Yellow-bellies. Slang for inhabitants of the fenlands of East Anglia and Lincolnshire; the allusion being to frogs The Mexicans are also so called

Yellow Books. Official documents, Government reports, etc , in France, corresponding to British "Blue Books" *(q.v)*, so called from the colour of their covers

Yellow boy. Slang for a golden sovereign, once fairly common in Great Britain
John did not starve the cause· there wanted not yellow-boys to fee counsel —ARBUTHNOT *John Bull* (1712).

Yellow-hammer. A bunting with yellowish head, neck, and breast (A S *amore*, Ger *ammer*, a bunting). The tradition is that the bird fluttered about the Cross, and got stained with the Blood in its plumage, and by way of punishment its eggs were doomed ever after to bear marks of blood Because the bird was "cursed," boys were taught that it was right and proper to destroy its eggs

Yellow Jack. The yellow fever; also the flag displayed from lazarettos, naval hospitals, and vessels in quarantine

Yellow Peril, The. A scare, originally raised in Germany in the late 'nineties of last century, that the yellow races of China and Japan would in a very few years have increased in population to such an extent that incursions upon the territories occupied by the white races—followed by massacres and every conceivable horror—were inevitable

Yellow Press, The Sensational and jingoist newspapers or journalism The name arose in the United States about 1898 in consequence of scaring articles on the "Yellow Peril"

Yemen (ye' men) The south-west corner of the Arabian peninsula, called by the ancients Arabia Felix. *Felix* is a mistranslation by Ptolemy of *Yemen*, which means to the "right"—*i e* of Mecca

Yeoman. Anciently, a forty-shilling freeholder, and as such qualified to vote and serve on juries, but not qualified to rank as one of the gentry In more modern times it meant a farmer who cultivated his own freehold. Later still, an upper farmer, tenant, or otherwise, is often called a yeoman

Yeoman's service. Hard work, effectual service, excellent service whether in a good or bad cause The reference is to the yeomen of the Free Companies

Hamlet says—
> I once did hold it, as our statists do,
> A baseness to write fair, and labour'd much
> How to forget that learning, but, sir, now
> It did me yeoman's service
> *Hamlet*, v, 2.

Yeomen of the Guard The beefeaters (*q v*)

Yes-man. An expressive colloquialism for one who expresses agreement with his superior in everything, whatever his private opinion may be

Yeth-hounds. Dogs without heads, of west country folklore, said to be the spirits of unbaptized children, which ramble among the woods at night, making wailing noises

Yew. The yew is a British tree, and is commonly planted in churchyards because, as it is an evergreen, it is a symbol of immortality It was planted by the Druids near their temples.

Some famous yews—
Of *Braburn,* in Kent, according to De Candolle, is 3,000 years old
The *Scotch yew at Fortingal,* in Perthshire, is between 2,500 and 3,000 years.
Of *Darley churchyard,* Derbyshire, about 2,050 years.
Of *Crowhurst,* Surrey, about 1,400
The three at *Fountains Abbey,* in Yorkshire, at least 1,200 years Beneath these trees the founders of the abbey held their council in 1132
The yew grove of *Norbury Park,* Surrey, was standing in the time of the Druids.

The yew trees at *Kingsley Bottom,* near Chichester, were standing when the sea-kings landed on the Sussex coast.
The yew tree of *Harlington churchyard,* Middlesex, is above 850 years old
That at *Ankerwyke House,* near Staines, was noted when Magna Charta was signed in 1215, and it was the trysting tree for Henry VIII and Anne Boleyn.

Yggdrasil (ig' drå sil). The world tree of Scandinavian mythology that, with its roots and branches, binds together heaven, earth, and hell. It is an ash, and at the root is a fountain of wonderful virtues, In the tree, which drops honey, sit an eagle, a squirrel, and four stags.
The tree is a late addition to Scandinavian myth, and the name was probably originally that of one of the winds (*Yggr,* a name of Odin, and *dressill,* a horse)

Yiddish. A Middle German dialect developed under Hebrew and Slavic influence, written in Hebrew characters, and used as a language by German and other Jews (Ger *judisch,* Jewish).

Ymir (im' ir) The primeval being of Scandinavian mythology, the giant from whose body the world was created He was nourished by the four milky streams which flowed from the cow Audhumla

Yodel (yō' del). To sing with frequent alternations between the ordinary voice and falsetto It is really peculiar to Switzerland and is a development of the Ranz des Vaches, or cowherd's call when driving the cattle to the mountain pastures with the coming of spring Like the cowhorn, the yodel has a restricted scale of natural harmonics

Yoga (yō' gä) A practice of Hindu philosophy seeking to unite the human soul with the Universal Spirit by concentrating the mind on some eternal truth and withdrawing the physical senses from external objects Adepts in yoga are able to hold their breath for protracted periods and do other things in apparent contravention of natural requirements

Yoke. To pass under the yoke. To make a humiliating submission, to suffer the disgrace of a vanquished army The Romans made a yoke of three spears—two upright and one resting on them. When an army was vanquished, the soldiers had to lay down their arms and pass under this archway of spears

Yom Kippur (yom ki pēr') The Jewish Day of Atonement, on the 10th day of the first month, Tishri It is observed by a strict fast and ceremonies of supplication mostly dating from the 3rd century B C.

Yorick (yor' ik). The King of Denmark's deceased jester, "a fellow of infinite jest and most excellent fancy," whose skull is apostrophized by Hamlet (Act v, 1). In *Tristram Shandy* Sterne introduces a clergyman of that name, meant for himself.

York. The Anglo-Saxon *Eure-wic* (pron. *Yorric*), the town on the Eure, now called the Ouse The Romans Latinized the word *Eure* or *Evre* into "Evora" or "Ebora," and *wic* into "vicum"; whence Ebora-vicum, contracted into *Eboracum.*

Yorkshire I'se Yorkshire, too. I am as deep as you are, and am not to be bamboozled The north countrymen are proverbially "long-headed and cannie "

The Yorkshireman's toast. "Here's tiv us, all on us, may we never want nowt, noan on us, nor me nawther "

Yorker. A cricketing term for a ball bowled so as to pitch three or four feet from the wicket, immediately in front of the bat Probably so called because first effectively used by a Yorkshire bowler.

Yorkist. A partisan of the White Rose in the Wars of the Roses *See* ROSE

Young. Used as an epithet in the names of political parties who strive to sweep away abuses and introduce reforms.

Young Buffs The East Surrey Regiment, the 31st Foot, raised as Marines in 1702 Their name was coined at the Battle of Dettingen, 1743 George II, observing that their 1st Battalion was fighting well, cried, "Well done, the Buffs!"'—thinking them to be the West Surreys His mistake was pointed out to him and he was told they were a younger regiment than the Buffs, whereupon he cried, "Well done, the Young Buffs!"

Young Germany. A school headed by Heine in the mid-19th century, whose aim was to liberate politics, religion, and manners from the old conventional trammels

Young Ireland. The Irish politicians and agitators (at first led by O'Connell) who effected the rising of 1848

Young Italy (Giovine Italia) A league of Italian refugees, who associated themselves with the French republican party, called the *Charbonnerie Démocratique* It was organized at Marseilles by Mazzini about 1834, and its chief object was to diffuse republican principles

Yours truly. This conventional ending to letters is sometimes used vulgarly to indicate the speaker—"There were X, Y., and Yours truly "

Ysolde (Yseult, Isolde, etc). The name of two heroines of Arthurian romance, the more important *Ysolde the Fair,* King Mark's wife, being the lover of Tristram (*q.v*), the other, *Ysolde of the White Hands,* or *Ysolde of Brittany,* being his wife, with whom he made a "Maiden Marriage" after he had been discovered by King Mark and had been obliged to flee

It was through the treachery of Ysolde of the White Hands that Sir Tristram died, and that Ysolde the Fair died in consequence The story has it that King Mark buried the two in one grave, and planted over it a rose-bush and vine, which so intermingled their branches as they grew up that no man could separate them

Yuga One of the four ages of the world into which, according to Hindu cosmogony, mundane time is divided

Yule, Yuletide. Christmas time A S *geola,* from Icel *jol* (with which possibly our *jolly* is connected), the name of a heathen festival at the winter solstice

Yule log. A great log of wood laid in ancient times across the hearth-fire on Christmas Eve. This was done with certain ceremonies and much merrymaking

Yves or **Yvo, St.** (ēv, ē' vō) Patron saint of lawyers, being himself a lawyer He was an ecclesiastical judge at Rennes, was ordained priest in 1285, died in 1303, and was canonized in 1347 As he used his knowledge of the law in defending the oppressed, he is still called in Brittany (where his festival is kept on May 19th) "the poor man's advocate "

> Advocatus, sed non latro,
> Res miranda populo —*Hymn to St Yves*

Yvetot (ēv' tō) **The King of Yvetot.** A man of mighty pretensions but little merit Yvetot is a town in Normandy and the "king" was the lord of the town

The tradition is that Clotaire, son of Clovis, having slain Gaulthier, lord of Yvetot, before the high altar of Soissons, made atonement by conferring the title of *king* on the heirs of the murdered man

Z

Z. The last letter of the alphabet, called *zed* in England, but in America *zee* Its older English name was *izzard*

In mathematics it denotes the third unknown quantity (*see* X), and in mediæval times it was used as a Roman numeral for 2,000

Zadig. Possibly the best of Voltaire's short novels, published in 1748 Zadig was a Babylonian philosopher whose determination to lead a life of virtue and wisdom was rewarded by a series of ever-worsening calamities

Zadikim. *See* CHASIDIM.

Zadkiel (zăd' kēl) In Rabbinical angelology, the angel of the planet Jupiter The name was adopted as a pseudonym by the astrologer Richard James Morrison (1795-1874), a naval lieutenant, author of the *Prophetic Almanac,* commonly called **Zadkiel's Almanac.**

Zadoc (zăd' ok), in Dryden's satire of *Absalom and Achitophel,* is designed for Sancroft, Archbishop of Canterbury.

> Zadoc the priest, whom (shunning power and place)
> His lowly mind advanced to David's [Charles II] grace,
> Pt i, lines 801-2

Zamorin (zăm' or in) The title of the native ruler of Calicut and the surrounding country

Zany (zā' ni) The buffoon who mimicked the clown in the Commedia dell'Arte; hence a simpleton, one who "acts the goat " The name is the Italian *zanni,* a buffoon, fem of *Giovanni* (i e. John), our *Jane*

> For indeed,
> He's like the zani to a tumbler
> That tries tricks after him to make men laugh.
> B JONSON *Every Man out of his Humour,* iv, 2

Zeitgeist (zit' gist) (Ger *zeit,* time, *geist,* spirit) The spirit of the time, the moral or intellectual tendency characteristic of the period

Zemindar (zem' ın dar) An Indıan landowner holding direct from the Government and paying a fixed rent based on the revenue from his land

Zemire. *See* AZOR'S MIRROR, BEAUTY AND THE BEAST.

Zemstvo (zemst' vō) The elected local district and provincial administrative assembly ın Russıa under the old Empire Theoretically it had large powers and was democratic; but it was always under the thumb of the great landowners, and all its decrees were subject to the approval of the Governor.

Zem Zem. The sacred well near the Kaaba at Mecca According to Arab tradition, this ıs the very well that was shown to Hagar when Ishmael was perishing of thirst.

Zenana (ze na' na) The Hındu harem or apartment where the women of the family are kept secluded

Zend-Avesta. The sacred writings of Zoroaster (or Zarathustra) that formed the basıs of the religion that prevailed ın Persıa from the 6th century B C to the 7th century A D. *Avesta* means the text, and *Zend* its interpretation into a more modern and intelligible language, hence the latter name has been given to the ancient Iranıan language ın which the *Zend-Avesta* ıs written.

Zenith, Nadir (zen' ıth, nād' ır) (Arabıc). *Zenith* ıs the point of the heavens immediately over the head of the spectator *Nadir* ıs the opposite point, immediately beneath the spectator's feet Hence, to go from the zenith of prosperity to the nadir ıs to fall from the height of fortune to the depths of poverty

Zephyr (zef' ır) The west wınd ın classical mythology, son of Æolus and Aurora, and lover of Flora, hence, any soft, gentle wınd

Faır laughs the Morn and soft the Zephyr blows
While proudly riding o'er the azure realm
In gallant trım the gilded vessel goes,
Youth on the prow, and Pleasure at the helm
GRAY *The Bard*

Zero (zē' rō) (Arabıc, a cipher) The figure 0, nothing; especially the point on a scale (such as that of a thermometer) from which positive and negative quantities are measured, on the Centigrade and Reaumur thermometers fixed at the freezing-point of water, on the Fahrenheit 32° below this

Absolute zero ıs the point at which it would be impossible for a body to get any colder, ı e that at which it ıs totally devoid of heat (estimated at about – 273° C).

Zero hour. A military term (first used ın World War I) for the exact time at which an attack etc , ıs to be begun From this are timed the consequent operations, e g zero + 3 means 3 minutes after zero hour. Succeeded ın World War II by H-hour

Zero point. In *Time*, 12 o'clock, midday, the time at which 24-hour clocks begin the day

Zeugma (zūg' mà). A grammatical and logic term for a phrase ın which one word modıfıes or governs two or more not connected ın meaning A well-known example ıs, "Mıss

Bolo went straight home ın a flood of tears and a sedan chaır "—*Pickwick Papers*, xxxv

Zeus (zūs) The Grecian Jupiter (*q v*) The word means the "lıvıng one" (Sanskrıt, *Djaus*, heaven)

Zimrı (zım' rı) The name given by Dryden ın *Absalom and Achitophel* (*q v*) to George Villiers, 2nd Duke of Buckingham (1628-87), ın allusion to the King of Israel who "slew his master" and was himself overthrown (1 *Kings* xvı)

Some of the chiefs were princes ın the land,
In the first rank of these did Zımrı stand,
A man so various that he seemed to be
Not one, but all mankind's epitome
Stıff ın opinions, always ın the wrong,
Was everything by starts, and nothing long
Pt, i, 543-548

Zincali or **Zingari** (zing' ka lı) Gipsies, so called ın Spaın from *Sinte* or *Sind* (India) and *calo* (black), on the supposition that they came from India which no doubt ıs true The Persian *Zangi* means an Ethiopian or Egyptian

I **Zingarı** (I Z.) An exclusive nomadic cricket club, founded ın 1845 by William Bolland. The club has no ground of its own

Zion (Heb *Tsiyon*, a hill) Daughter of Zion. Jerusalem or its people The city of Davıd stood on Mount Zıon
In *Pilgrim's Progress* Bunyan calls the Celestial City (ı e Heaven) *Mount Zion*.

Zodiac (Gr. *zodiakos*, pertaining to animals, from *zōon*, an animal) The imaginary belt or zone ın the heavens, extending about eight degrees each side of the ecliptic, which the sun traverses every year

Signs of the Zodiac. The zodiac was divided by the ancients into twelve equal parts, proceeding from west to east, each part of thirty degrees, and distinguished by a sign, these originally corresponded to the zodiacal constellations bearing the same names, but now, through the precession of the equinoxes, they coincide with the constellations bearing the names next ın order
Beginning with Aries, we have first six on the north side and six on the south side of the equator, beginning with Capricornus, we have six *ascending* and then six *descending* signs—ı e. six which ascend higher and higher towards the north, and six which descend lower and lower towards the south The six northern signs are *Aries* (the ram), *Taurus* (the bull), *Gemini* (the twins), spring signs, *Cancer* (the crab), *Leo* (the lion), *Virgo* (the virgin), summer signs. The six southern are *Libra* (the balance), *Scorpio* (the scorpion), *Sagittarius* (the archer), autumn signs, *Capricornus* (the goat), *Aquarius* (the water-bearer), and *Pisces* (the fishes), winter signs

Our vernal signs the RAM begins,
Then comes the BULL ın May the TWINS,
The CRAB ın June, next LEO shines,
And VIRGO ends the northern signs.

The BALANCE brings autumnal fruits,
The SCORPION stings, the ARCHER shoots;
December's GOAT brings wintry blast,
AQUARIUS rain, the FISH come last —*E.C.B*

Zoïlus A Greek rhetorician of the 4th century B C, a literary Thersites, shrewd, witty, and spiteful, nicknamed *Homeromastix* (Homer's scourge), because he mercilessly assailed the epics of Homer, and called the companions of Ulysses in the island of Circe "weeping porkers" ("*choiridia klaionta*") He also flew at Plato, Isocrates, and other high game

Zollverein The customs union that existed from about 1820 between the States of the former German Empire for the purpose of establishing a uniform tariff of duties and maintaining Free Trade among themselves

Zombie (zom' bi) The python god of certain West African tribes Its worship was carried to the West Indies with the slave trade, and still somewhat covertly flourishes in Voodoo ceremonies in Haiti and some of the Southern States of the U S A The word *zombie* is commonly applied to an alleged dead body brought by Voodoo magic to life in a more or less cataleptic or automaton state

Zoom To fly an aeroplane sharply upward for a short distance at a great speed in order to regain altitude or clear an obstacle, etc.

Zoot-suit (U S A) An exaggerated style of clothing adopted in the late 1930s by *hepcats* (*q v.*) and followers of fashionable swing music. It usually consisted of baggy trousers caught in at the bottom, a long coat resembling a frock coat, a broad-brimmed hat, and a flowing tie, all in vivid colours An essential article of equipment was a vast key-chain

Zounds! A minced oath; euphemistic for *God's wounds*

Zuchetto (zu ket' ō) The small skull-cap worn by Roman Catholic clergy, white for the pope, red for a cardinal, purple for a bishop, and black for others

Zuleika The name traditionally ascribed to the wife of Joseph, and a very common name in Persian poetry

Zurich Bible, The. *See* BIBLE, SPECIALLY NAMED

Zwichau Prophets, The. *See* ABECEDARIAN

A.M.D.G.